5th Edition

UNUSUAL WORLD COINS

COMPANION VOLUME TO STANDARD CATALOG OF® WORLD COINS

Colin R. Bruce II
Senior Editor

Thomas Michael
Market Analyst

George Cuhaj
Editor

Merna Dudley
Cordination Editor

Deborah McCue
Database Specialist

Randy Thern
Numismatic Cataloging Supervisor

Special Contributors
Serge Huard, Peter Jackson, Bernard von Nothaus

Bullion Value (BV) Market Valuations

Valuations for all platinum, gold, palladium and silver coins of the more common, basically bullion types, or those possessing only modest numismatic premiums are presented in this edition based on the market levels of:

$1,200-$1,350 per ounce for **platinum**
$650-$675 per ounce for **gold**
$330-$345 per ounce for **palladium**
$12.50-$13.75 per ounce for **silver**

Published by

700 East State Street • Iola, WI 54990-0001
715-445-2214 • 888-457-2873
www.krausebooks.com

Our toll-free number to place an order or obtain
a free catalog is (800) 258-0929.

Library of Congress Control Number: 2007924549

ISBN-13: 978-089689576-8

ISBN-10: 0-89689-576-9

Designed by Stacy Bloch

Edited by Randy Thern

Printed in United States of America

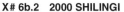

X# 6b.2 2000 SHILINGI
20.0000 g., Gilt Alloy, 38 mm. **Subject:** 35th Anniv. Independence / Olympics Centenary / XXVI Olympics - Atlanta **Obv:** Large arms, squared panels behind **Rev:** Male sprinter facing, running **Edge:** Plain **Note:** Error, denomination "SHILLINGI".

Date	Mintage	F	VF	XF	Unc	BU
1996 Proof	25	Value: 50.00				

X# 6c.1 2000 SHILINGI
23.0000 g., Tri-Metallic Silvered and gilt Brass, 38 mm. **Subject:** 35th Anniv. Independence / Olympics Centenary / XXVI Olympics - Atlanta **Obv:** Large arms, squared panels behind **Rev:** Male sprinter facing, running **Edge:** Reeded **Note:** Error, denomination "SHILLINGI".

Date	Mintage	F	VF	XF	Unc	BU
1996 Proof	25	Value: 75.00				

X# 6c.2 2000 SHILINGI
23.0000 g., Tri-Metallic Silvered and gilt Brass, 38 mm. **Subject:** 35th Anniv. Independence / Olympics Centenary / XXVI Olympics - Atlanta **Obv:** Large arms, squared panels behind **Rev:** Male sprinter facing, running **Edge:** Plain **Note:** Error, denomination "SHILLINGI".

Date	Mintage	F	VF	XF	Unc	BU
1996 Proof	25	Value: 75.00				

X# 6d.1 2000 SHILINGI
6.0000 g., Aluminum, 38 mm. **Subject:** 35th Anniv. Independence / Olympics Centenary / XXVI Olympics - Atlanta **Obv:** Large arms, squared panels behind **Rev:** Male sprinter facing, running **Edge:** Reeded **Note:** Error, denomination "SHILLINGI".

Date	Mintage	F	VF	XF	Unc	BU
1996 Proof	25	Value: 50.00				

X# 6d.2 2000 SHILINGI
6.0000 g., Aluminum, 38 mm. **Subject:** 35th Anniv. Independence / Olympics Centenary / XXVI Olympics - Atlanta **Obv:** Large arms, squared panels behind **Rev:** Male sprinter facing, running **Edge:** Plain **Note:** Error, denomination "SHILLINGI".

Date	Mintage	F	VF	XF	Unc	BU
1996 Proof	25	Value: 50.00				

X# 6e.1 2000 SHILINGI
23.0000 g., Copper, 38 mm. **Subject:** 35th Anniv. Independence / Olympics Centenary / XXVI Olympics - Atlanta **Obv:** Large arms, squared panels behind **Rev:** Male sprinter facing, running **Edge:** Reeded **Note:** Error, denomination "SHILLINGI".

Date	Mintage	F	VF	XF	Unc	BU
1996 Proof	25	Value: 50.00				

X# 6e.2 2000 SHILINGI
6.0000 g., Copper, 38 mm. **Subject:** 35th Anniv. Independence / Olympics Centenary / XXVI Olympics - Atlanta **Obv:** Large arms, squared panels behind **Rev:** Male sprinter facing, running **Edge:** Reeded **Note:** Error, denomination "SHILLINGI".

Date	Mintage	F	VF	XF	Unc	BU
1996 Proof	25	Value: 50.00				

X# 6f.1 2000 SHILINGI
20.0000 g., Copper-Nickel, 38 mm. **Subject:** 35th Anniv. Independence / Olympics Centenary / XXVI Olympics - Atlanta **Obv:** Large arms, squared panels behind **Rev:** Male sprinter facing, running **Edge:** Reeded **Note:** Error, denomination "SHILLINGI".

Date	Mintage	F	VF	XF	Unc	BU
1996 Proof	25	Value: 50.00				

X# 6f.2 2000 SHILINGI
Copper-Nickel, 38 mm. **Subject:** 35th Anniv. Independence / Olympics Centenary / XXVI Olympics - Atlanta **Obv:** Large arms, squared panels behind **Rev:** Male sprinter facing, running **Edge:** Plain **Note:** Error, denomination "SHILLINGI".

Date	Mintage	F	VF	XF	Unc	BU
1996 Proof	25	Value: 50.00				

X# 7 2000 SHILINGI
8.0000 g., 0.7500 Gold 0.1929 oz. AGW, 22.1 mm. **Subject:** 35th Anniv. Independence / Olympics Centenary / XXVI Olympics - Atlanta **Obv:** Large arms, squared panels behind **Rev:** Two males boxing **Edge:** Reeded **Note:** Error, denomination "SHILLINGI".

Date	Mintage	F	VF	XF	Unc	BU
1996 Proof	24	Value: 400				

X# 8.1 2000 SHILINGI
24.0000 g., 0.9250 Silver 0.7137 oz. ASW, 38 mm. **Subject:** 35th Anniv. Independence / Olympics Centenary / XXVI Olympics - Atlanta **Obv:** Small arms **Rev:** Two males boxing **Edge:** Reeded **Note:** Corrected denomination.

Date	Mintage	F	VF	XF	Unc	BU
1996 Proof	100	Value: 50.00				

X# 8.2 2000 SHILINGI
24.0000 g., 0.9250 Silver 0.7137 oz. ASW, 38 mm. **Subject:** 35th Anniv. Independence / Olympics Centenary / XXVI Olympics - Atlanta **Obv:** Small arms **Rev:** Two males boxing **Edge:** Plain **Note:** Corrected denomination.

Date	Mintage	F	VF	XF	Unc	BU
1996 Proof	100	Value: 50.00				

X# 8a.1 2000 SHILINGI
23.0000 g., Brass, 38 mm. **Subject:** 35th Anniv. Independence / Olympics Centenary / XXVI Olympics - Atlanta **Obv:** Small arms **Rev:** Two males boxing **Edge:** Reeded **Note:** Corrected denomination.

Date	Mintage	F	VF	XF	Unc	BU
1996 Proof	100	Value: 30.00				

X# 8a.2 2000 SHILINGI
23.0000 g., Brass, 38 mm. **Subject:** 35th Anniv. Independence / Olympics Centenary / XXVI Olympics - Atlanta **Obv:** Small arms **Rev:** Two males boxing **Edge:** Plain **Note:** Corrected denomination.

Date	Mintage	F	VF	XF	Unc	BU
1996 Proof	100	Value: 30.00				

X# 8b.1 2000 SHILINGI
20.0000 g., Gilt Alloy, 38 mm. **Subject:** 35th Anniv. Independence / Olympics Centenary / XXVI Olympics - Atlanta **Obv:** Small arms **Rev:** Two males boxing **Edge:** Reeded **Note:** Corrected denomination.

Date	Mintage	F	VF	XF	Unc	BU
1996 Proof	100	Value: 30.00				

X# 8b.2 2000 SHILINGI
20.0000 g., Gilt Alloy, 38 mm. **Subject:** 35th Anniv. Independence / Olympics Centenary / XXVI Olympics - Atlanta **Obv:** Small arms **Rev:** Two males boxing **Edge:** Plain **Note:** Corrected denomination.

Date	Mintage	F	VF	XF	Unc	BU
1996 Proof	100	Value: 30.00				

X# 8c.1 2000 SHILINGI
23.0000 g., Tri-Metallic Silvered and gilt Brass, 38 mm. **Subject:** 35th Anniv. Independence / Olympics Centenary / XXVI Olympics - Atlanta **Obv:** Small arms **Rev:** Two males boxing **Edge:** Reeded **Note:** Corrected denomination.

Date	Mintage	F	VF	XF	Unc	BU
1996 Proof	100	Value: 50.00				

X# 8c.2 2000 SHILINGI
23.0000 g., Tri-Metallic Silvered and gilt Brass, 38 mm. **Subject:** 35th Anniv. Independence / Olympics Centenary / XXVI Olympics - Atlanta **Obv:** Small arms **Rev:** Two males boxing **Edge:** Plain **Note:** Corrected denomination.

Date	Mintage	F	VF	XF	Unc	BU
1996 Proof	100	Value: 50.00				

X# 8d.1 2000 SHILINGI
6.0000 g., Aluminum, 38 mm. **Subject:** 35th Anniv. Independence / Olympics Centenary / XXVI Olympics - Atlanta **Obv:** Small arms **Rev:** Two males boxing **Edge:** Reeded **Note:** Corrected denomination.

Date	Mintage	F	VF	XF	Unc	BU
1996 Proof	100	Value: 30.00				

X# 8d.2 2000 SHILINGI
6.0000 g., Aluminum, 38 mm. **Subject:** 35th Anniv. Independence / Olympics Centenary / XXVI Olympics - Atlanta **Obv:** Small arms **Rev:** Two males boxing **Edge:** Plain **Note:** Corrected denomination.

Date	Mintage	F	VF	XF	Unc	BU
1996 Proof	100	Value: 30.00				

X# 8e.1 2000 SHILINGI
23.0000 g., Copper, 38 mm. **Subject:** 35th Anniv. Independence / Olympics Centenary / XXVI Olympics - Atlanta **Obv:** Small arms **Rev:** Two males boxing **Edge:** Reeded **Note:** Corrected denomination.

Date	Mintage	F	VF	XF	Unc	BU
1996 Proof	100	Value: 30.00				

X# 8e.2 2000 SHILINGI
23.0000 g., Copper, 38 mm. **Subject:** 35th Anniv. Independence / Olympics Centenary / XXVI Olympics - Atlanta **Obv:** Small arms **Rev:** Two males boxing **Edge:** Plain **Note:** Corrected denomination.

Date	Mintage	F	VF	XF	Unc	BU
1996 Proof	100	Value: 30.00				

X# 8f.1 2000 SHILINGI
20.0000 g., Copper-Nickel, 38 mm. **Subject:** 35th Anniv. Independence / Olympics Centenary / XXVI Olympics - Atlanta **Obv:** Small arms **Rev:** Two males boxing **Edge:** Reeded **Note:** Corrected denomination.

Date	Mintage	F	VF	XF	Unc	BU
1996 Proof	100	Value: 30.00				

X# 8f.2 2000 SHILINGI
20.0000 g., Copper-Nickel, 38 mm. **Subject:** 35th Anniv. Independence / Olympics Centenary / XXVI Olympics - Atlanta **Obv:** Small arms **Rev:** Two males boxing **Edge:** Plain **Note:** Corrected denomination.

Date	Mintage	F	VF	XF	Unc	BU
1996 Proof	100	Value: 30.00				

X# 9.1 2000 SHILINGI
24.0000 g., 0.9250 Silver 0.7137 oz. ASW, 38 mm. **Subject:** 35th Anniv. Independence / Olympics Centenary / XXVI Olympics - Atlanta **Obv:** Small arms **Rev:** Male discus thrower **Edge:** Reeded **Note:** Corrected denomination.

Date	Mintage	F	VF	XF	Unc	BU
1996 Proof	100	Value: 50.00				

X# 9.2 2000 SHILINGI
24.0000 g., 0.9250 Silver 0.7137 oz. ASW, 38 mm. **Subject:** 35th Anniv. Independence / Olympics Centenary / XXVI Olympics - Atlanta **Obv:** Small arms **Rev:** Male discus thrower **Edge:** Plain **Note:** Corrected denomination.

Date	Mintage	F	VF	XF	Unc	BU
1996 Proof	100	Value: 50.00				

X# 9a.1 2000 SHILINGI
23.0000 g., Brass, 38 mm. **Subject:** 35th Anniv. Independence / Olympics Centenary / XXVI Olympics - Atlanta **Obv:** Small arms **Rev:** Male discus thrower **Edge:** Reeded **Note:** Corrected denomination.

Date	Mintage	F	VF	XF	Unc	BU
1996 Proof	100	Value: 30.00				

X# 9a.2 2000 SHILINGI
23.0000 g., Brass, 38 mm. **Subject:** 35th Anniv. Independence / Olympics Centenary / XXVI Olympics - Atlanta **Obv:** Small arms **Rev:** Male discus thrower **Edge:** Reeded **Note:** Corrected denomination.

Date	Mintage	F	VF	XF	Unc	BU
1996 Proof	100	Value: 30.00				

X# 9b.1 2000 SHILINGI
20.0000 g., Gilt Alloy, 38 mm. **Subject:** 35th Anniv. Independence / Olympics Centenary / XXVI Olympics - Atlanta **Obv:** Small arms **Rev:** Male discus thrower **Edge:** Reeded **Note:** Corrected denomination.

Date	Mintage	F	VF	XF	Unc	BU
1996 Proof	100	Value: 30.00				

X# 9b.2 2000 SHILINGI
20.0000 g., Gilt Alloy, 38 mm. **Subject:** 35th Anniv. Independence / Olympics Centenary / XXVI Olympics - Atlanta **Obv:** Small arms **Rev:** Male discus thrower **Edge:** Plain **Note:** Corrected denomination.

Date	Mintage	F	VF	XF	Unc	BU
1996 Proof	100	Value: 30.00				

X# 9c.1 2000 SHILINGI
23.0000 g., Tri-Metallic Silvered and gilt Brass, 38 mm. **Subject:** 35th Anniv. Independence / Olympics Centenary / XXVI Olympics - Atlanta **Obv:** Small arms **Rev:** Male discus thrower **Edge:** Reeded **Note:** Corrected denomination.

Date	Mintage	F	VF	XF	Unc	BU
1996 Proof	25	Value: 50.00				

X# 9c.2 2000 SHILINGI
Tri-Metallic Silvered and gilt Brass, 38 mm. **Subject:** 35th Anniv. Independence / Olympics Centenary / XXVI Olympics - Atlanta **Obv:** Small arms **Rev:** Male discus thrower **Edge:** Plain **Note:** Corrected denomination.

Date	Mintage	F	VF	XF	Unc	BU
1996 Proof	25	Value: 50.00				

X# 9d.1 2000 SHILINGI
6.0000 g., Aluminum, 38 mm. **Subject:** 35th Anniv. Independence / Olympics Centenary / XXVI Olympics - Atlanta **Obv:** Small arms **Rev:** Male discus thrower **Edge:** Reeded **Note:** Corrected denomination.

Date	Mintage	F	VF	XF	Unc	BU
1996 Proof	100	Value: 30.00				

X# 9d.2 2000 SHILINGI
6.0000 g., Aluminum, 38 mm. **Subject:** 35th Anniv. Independence / Olympics Centenary / XXVI Olympics - Atlanta **Obv:** Small arms **Rev:** Male discus thrower **Edge:** Plain **Note:** Corrected denomination.

Date	Mintage	F	VF	XF	Unc	BU
1996 Proof	100	Value: 30.00				

X# 9e.1 2000 SHILINGI
23.0000 g., Copper, 38 mm. **Subject:** 35th Anniv. Independence / Olympics Centenary / XXVI Olympics - Atlanta **Obv:** Small arms **Rev:** Male discus thrower **Edge:** Reeded **Note:** Corrected denomination.

Date	Mintage	F	VF	XF	Unc	BU
1996 Proof	100	Value: 30.00				

X# 9e.2 2000 SHILINGI
23.0000 g., Copper, 38 mm. **Subject:** 35th Anniv. Independence / Olympics Centenary / XXVI Olympics - Atlanta **Obv:** Small arms **Rev:** Male discus thrower **Edge:** Plain **Note:** Corrected denomination.

Date	Mintage	F	VF	XF	Unc	BU
1996 Proof	100	Value: 30.00				

X# 9f.1 2000 SHILINGI
20.0000 g., Copper-Nickel, 38 mm. **Subject:** 35th Anniv. Independence / Olympics Centenary / XXVI Olympics - Atlanta **Obv:** Small arms **Rev:** Male discus thrower **Edge:** Reeded **Note:** Corrected denomination.

Date	Mintage	F	VF	XF	Unc	BU
1996 Proof	100	Value: 30.00				

X# 9f.2 2000 SHILINGI
20.0000 g., Copper-Nickel, 38 mm. **Subject:** 35th Anniv. Independence / Olympics Centenary / XXVI Olympics - Atlanta **Obv:** Small arms **Rev:** Male discus thrower **Edge:** Plain **Note:** Corrected denomination.

Date	Mintage	F	VF	XF	Unc	BU
1996 Proof	100	Value: 30.00				

X# 10.1 2000 SHILINGI
24.0000 g., 0.9250 Silver 0.7137 oz. ASW, 38 mm. **Subject:** 35th Anniv. Independence / Olympics Centenary / XXVI Olympics - Atlanta **Obv:** Small arms **Rev:** Female hurdler right **Edge:** Reeded **Note:** Corrected denomination.

Date	Mintage	F	VF	XF	Unc	BU
1996 Proof	100	Value: 50.00				

X# 10.2 2000 SHILINGI
24.0000 g., 0.9250 Silver 0.7137 oz. ASW, 38 mm. **Subject:** 35th Anniv. Independence / Olympics Centenary / XXVI Olympics - Atlanta **Obv:** Small arms **Rev:** Female hurdler right **Edge:** Plain **Note:** Corrected denomination.

Date	Mintage	F	VF	XF	Unc	BU
1996 Proof	100	Value: 50.00				

X# 10a.1 2000 SHILINGI
23.0000 g., Brass, 38 mm. **Subject:** 35th Anniv. Independence / Olympics Centenary / XXVI Olympics - Atlanta **Obv:** Small arms **Rev:** Female hurdler right **Edge:** Reeded **Note:** Corrected denomination.

Date	Mintage	F	VF	XF	Unc	BU
1996 Proof	100	Value: 30.00				

X# 10a.2 2000 SHILINGI
23.0000 g., Brass, 38 mm. **Subject:** 35th Anniv. Independence / Olympics Centenary / XXVI Olympics - Atlanta **Obv:** Small arms **Rev:** Female hurdler right **Edge:** Plain **Note:** Corrected denomination.

Date	Mintage	F	VF	XF	Unc	BU
1996 Proof	100	Value: 30.00				

X# 10b.1 2000 SHILINGI
20.0000 g., Gilt Alloy, 38 mm. **Subject:** 35th Anniv. Independence / Olympics Centenary / XXVI Olympics - Atlanta **Obv:** Small arms **Rev:** Female hurdler right **Edge:** Reeded **Note:** Corrected denomination.

Date	Mintage	F	VF	XF	Unc	BU
1996 Proof	100	Value: 30.00				

X# 10b.2 2000 SHILINGI
20.0000 g., Gilt Alloy, 38 mm. **Subject:** 35th Anniv. Independence / Olympics Centenary / XXVI Olympics - Atlanta **Obv:** Small arms **Rev:** Female hurdler right **Edge:** Plain **Note:** Corrected denomination.

Date	Mintage	F	VF	XF	Unc	BU
1996 Proof	100	Value: 30.00				

X# 10c.1 2000 SHILINGI
23.0000 g., Tri-Metallic Silvered and gilt Brass, 38 mm. **Subject:** 35th Anniv. Independence / Olympics Centenary / XXVI Olympics - Atlanta **Obv:** Small arms **Rev:** Female hurdler right **Edge:** Reeded **Note:** Corrected denomination.

Date	Mintage	F	VF	XF	Unc	BU
1996 Proof	25	Value: 50.00				

X# 10c.2 2000 SHILINGI
23.0000 g., Tri-Metallic Silvered and gilt Brass, 38 mm. **Subject:** 35th Anniv. Independence / Olympics Centenary / XXVI Olympics - Atlanta **Obv:** Small arms **Rev:** Female hurdler right **Edge:** Plain **Note:** Corrected denomination.

Date	Mintage	F	VF	XF	Unc	BU
1996 Proof	25	Value: 50.00				

X# 10d.1 2000 SHILINGI
6.0000 g., Aluminum, 38 mm. **Subject:** 35th Anniv. Independence / Olympics Centenary / XXVI Olympics - Atlanta **Obv:** Small arms **Rev:** Female hurdler right **Edge:** Reeded **Note:** Corrected denomination.

Date	Mintage	F	VF	XF	Unc	BU
1996 Proof	100	Value: 30.00				

X# 10d.2 2000 SHILINGI
6.0000 g., Aluminum, 38 mm. **Subject:** 35th Anniv. Independence / Olympics Centenary / XXVI Olympics - Atlanta **Obv:** Small arms **Rev:** Female hurdler right **Edge:** Plain **Note:** Corrected denomination.

Date	Mintage	F	VF	XF	Unc	BU
1996 Proof	100	Value: 30.00				

X# 10e.1 2000 SHILINGI
23.0000 g., Copper, 38 mm. **Subject:** 35th Anniv. Independence / Olympics Centenary / XXVI Olympics - Atlanta **Obv:** Small arms **Rev:** Female hurdler right **Edge:** Reeded **Note:** Corrected denomination.

Date	Mintage	F	VF	XF	Unc	BU
1996 Proof	100	Value: 30.00				

X# 10e.2 2000 SHILINGI
23.0000 g., Copper, 38 mm. **Subject:** 35th Anniv. Independence / Olympics Centenary / XXVI Olympics - Atlanta **Obv:** Small arms **Rev:** Female hurdler right **Edge:** Plain **Note:** Corrected denomination.

Date	Mintage	F	VF	XF	Unc	BU
1996 Proof	100	Value: 30.00				

X# 10f.1 2000 SHILINGI
20.0000 g., Copper-Nickel, 38 mm. **Subject:** 35th Anniv. Independence / Olympics Centenary / XXVI Olympics - Atlanta **Obv:** Small arms **Rev:** Female hurdler right **Edge:** Reeded **Note:** Corrected denomination.

Date	Mintage	F	VF	XF	Unc	BU
1996 Proof	100	Value: 30.00				

X# 10f.2 2000 SHILINGI
20.0000 g., Copper-Nickel, 38 mm. **Subject:** 35th Anniv. Independence / Olympics Centenary / XXVI Olympics - Atlanta **Obv:** Small arms **Rev:** Female hurdler right **Edge:** Plain **Note:** Corrected denomination.

Date	Mintage	F	VF	XF	Unc	BU
1996 Proof	100	Value: 30.00				

X# 11.1 2000 SHILINGI
24.0000 g., 0.9250 Silver 0.7137 oz. ASW, 38 mm. **Subject:** 35th Anniv. Independence / Olympics

Centenary / XXVI Olympics - Atlanta **Obv:** Small arms **Rev:** Male decathlon runner 3/4 right **Edge:** Reeded **Note:** Corrected denomination.

Date	Mintage	F	VF	XF	Unc	BU
1996 Proof	100	Value: 50.00				

X# 11.2 2000 SHILINGI
24.0000 g., 0.9250 Silver 0.7137 oz. ASW, 38 mm. **Subject:** 35th Anniv. Independence / Olympics Centenary / XXVI Olympics - Atlanta **Obv:** Small arms **Rev:** Male decathlon runner 3/4 right **Edge:** Plain **Note:** Corrected denomination.

Date	Mintage	F	VF	XF	Unc	BU
1996 Proof	100	Value: 50.00				

X# 11a.1 2000 SHILINGI
23.0000 g., Brass, 38 mm. **Subject:** 35th Anniv. Independence / Olympics Centenary / XXVI Olympics - Atlanta **Obv:** Small arms **Rev:** Male decathlon runner 3/4 right **Edge:** Reeded **Note:** Corrected denomination.

Date	Mintage	F	VF	XF	Unc	BU
1996 Proof	100	Value: 30.00				

X# 11a.2 2000 SHILINGI
23.0000 g., Brass, 38 mm. **Subject:** 35th Anniv. Independence / Olympics Centenary / XXVI Olympics - Atlanta **Obv:** Small arms **Rev:** Male decathlon runner 3/4 right **Edge:** Plain **Note:** Corrected denomination.

Date	Mintage	F	VF	XF	Unc	BU
1996 Proof	100	Value: 30.00				

X# 11b.1 2000 SHILINGI
20.0000 g., Gilt Alloy, 38 mm. **Subject:** 35th Anniv. Independence / Olympics Centenary / XXVI Olympics - Atlanta **Obv:** Small arms **Rev:** Male decathlon runner 3/4 right **Edge:** Reeded **Note:** Corrected denomination.

Date	Mintage	F	VF	XF	Unc	BU
1996 Proof	—	Value: 30.00				

X# 11b.2 2000 SHILINGI
20.0000 g., Gilt Alloy, 38 mm. **Subject:** 35th Anniv. Independence / Olympics Centenary / XXVI Olympics - Atlanta **Obv:** Small arms **Rev:** Male decathlon runner 3/4 right **Edge:** Plain **Note:** Corrected denomination.

Date	Mintage	F	VF	XF	Unc	BU
1996 Proof	—	Value: 30.00				

X# 11c.1 2000 SHILINGI
23.0000 g., Tri-Metallic Silvered and gilt Brass, 38 mm. **Subject:** 35th Anniv. Independence / Olympics Centenary / XXVI Olympics - Atlanta **Obv:** Small arms **Rev:** Male decathlon runner 3/4 right **Edge:** Reeded **Note:** Corrected denomination.

Date	Mintage	F	VF	XF	Unc	BU
1996 Proof	25	Value: 50.00				

X# 11c.2 2000 SHILINGI
23.0000 g., Tri-Metallic Silvered and gilt Brass, 38 mm. **Subject:** 35th Anniv. Independence / Olympics Centenary / XXVI Olympics - Atlanta **Obv:** Small arms **Rev:** Male decathlon runner 3/4 right **Edge:** Plain **Note:** Corrected denomination.

Date	Mintage	F	VF	XF	Unc	BU
1996 Proof	25	Value: 50.00				

X# 11d.1 2000 SHILINGI
6.0000 g., Aluminum, 38 mm. **Subject:** 35th Anniv. Independence / Olympics Centenary / XXVI Olympics - Atlanta **Obv:** Small arms **Rev:** Male decathlon runner 3/4 right **Edge:** Reeded **Note:** Corrected denomination.

Date	Mintage	F	VF	XF	Unc	BU
1996 Proof	100	Value: 30.00				

X# 11d.2 2000 SHILINGI
6.0000 g., Aluminum, 38 mm. **Subject:** 35th Anniv. Independence / Olympics Centenary / XXVI Olympics - Atlanta **Obv:** Small arms **Rev:** Male decathlon runner 3/4 right **Edge:** Plain **Note:** Corrected denomination.

Date	Mintage	F	VF	XF	Unc	BU
1996 Proof	100	Value: 30.00				

X# 11e.1 2000 SHILINGI
23.0000 g., Copper, 38 mm. **Subject:** 35th Anniv. Independence / Olympics Centenary / XXVI Olympics - Atlanta **Obv:** Small arms **Rev:** Male decathlon runner 3/4 right **Edge:** Reeded **Note:** Corrected denomination.

Date	Mintage	F	VF	XF	Unc	BU
1996 Proof	100	Value: 30.00				

X# 11e.2 2000 SHILINGI
23.0000 g., Copper, 38 mm. **Subject:** 35th Anniv. Independence / Olympics Centenary / XXVI Olympics - Atlanta **Obv:** Small arms **Rev:** Male decathlon runner 3/4 right **Edge:** Plain **Note:** Corrected denomination.

Date	Mintage	F	VF	XF	Unc	BU
1996 Proof	100	Value: 30.00				

X# 11f.1 2000 SHILINGI
20.0000 g., Copper-Nickel, 38 mm. **Subject:** 35th Anniv. Independence / Olympics Centenary / XXVI Olympics - Atlanta **Obv:** Small arms **Rev:** Male decathlon runner 3/4 right **Edge:** Reeded **Note:** Corrected denomination.

Date	Mintage	F	VF	XF	Unc	BU
1996 Proof	100	Value: 30.00				

X# 11f.2 2000 SHILINGI
20.0000 g., Copper-Nickel, 38 mm. **Subject:** 35th Anniv. Independence / Olympics Centenary / XXVI Olympics - Atlanta **Obv:** Small arms **Rev:** Male decathlon runner 3/4 right **Edge:** Plain **Note:** Corrected denomination.

Date	Mintage	F	VF	XF	Unc	BU
1996 Proof	100	Value: 30.00				

X# 12.1 2000 SHILINGI
24.0000 g., 0.9250 Silver 0.7137 oz. ASW, 38 mm. **Subject:** 35th Anniv. Independence / Olympics Centenary / XXVI Olympics - Atlanta **Obv:** Small arms **Rev:** Male judo wrestler facing, lunging **Edge:** Reeded **Note:** Corrected denomination.

Date	Mintage	F	VF	XF	Unc	BU
1996 Proof	100	Value: 50.00				

X# 12.2 2000 SHILINGI
24.0000 g., 0.9250 Silver 0.7137 oz. ASW, 38 mm. **Subject:** 35th Anniv. Independence / Olympics Centenary / XXVI Olympics - Atlanta **Obv:** Small arms **Rev:** Male judo wrestler facing, lunging **Edge:** Plain **Note:** Corrected denomination.

Date	Mintage	F	VF	XF	Unc	BU
1996 Proof	100	Value: 50.00				

X# 12a.1 2000 SHILINGI
23.0000 g., Brass, 38 mm. **Subject:** 35th Anniv. Independence / Olympics Centenary / XXVI Olympics - Atlanta **Obv:** Small arms **Rev:** Male judo wrestler facing, lunging **Edge:** Reeded **Note:** Corrected denomination.

Date	Mintage	F	VF	XF	Unc	BU
1996 Proof	100	Value: 30.00				

X# 12a.2 2000 SHILINGI
23.0000 g., Brass, 38 mm. **Subject:** 35th Anniv. Independence / Olympics Centenary / XXVI Olympics - Atlanta **Obv:** Small arms **Rev:** Male judo wrestler facing, lunging **Edge:** Plain **Note:** Corrected denomination.

Date	Mintage	F	VF	XF	Unc	BU
1996 Proof	100	Value: 30.00				

X# 12b.1 2000 SHILINGI
20.0000 g., Gilt Alloy, 38 mm. **Subject:** 35th Anniv. Independence / Olympics Centenary / XXVI Olympics - Atlanta **Obv:** Small arms **Rev:** Male judo wrestler facing, lunging **Edge:** Reeded **Note:** Corrected denomination.

Date	Mintage	F	VF	XF	Unc	BU
1996 Proof	100	Value: 30.00				

X# 12b.2 2000 SHILINGI
20.0000 g., Gilt Alloy, 38 mm. **Subject:** 35th Anniv. Independence / Olympics Centenary / XXVI Olympics - Atlanta **Obv:** Small arms **Rev:** Male judo wrestler facing, lunging **Edge:** Plain **Note:** Corrected denomination.

Date	Mintage	F	VF	XF	Unc	BU
1996 Proof	100	Value: 30.00				

X# 12c.1 2000 SHILINGI
23.0000 g., Tri-Metallic Silvered and gilt Brass, 38 mm. **Subject:** 35th Anniv. Independence / Olympics Centenary / XXVI Olympics - Atlanta **Obv:** Small arms **Rev:** Male judo wrestler facing, lunging **Edge:** Reeded **Note:** Corrected denomination.

Date	Mintage	F	VF	XF	Unc	BU
1996 Proof	100	Value: 50.00				

X# 12c.2 2000 SHILINGI
23.0000 g., Tri-Metallic Silvered and gilt Brass, 38 mm. **Subject:** 35th Anniv. Independence / Olympics Centenary / XXVI Olympics - Atlanta **Obv:** Small arms **Rev:** Male judo wrestler facing, lunging **Edge:** Plain **Note:** Corrected denomination.

Date	Mintage	F	VF	XF	Unc	BU
1996 Proof	100	Value: 50.00				

X# 12d.1 2000 SHILINGI
6.0000 g., Aluminum, 38 mm. **Subject:** 35th Anniv. Independence / Olympics Centenary / XXVI Olympics - Atlanta **Obv:** Small arms **Rev:** Male judo wrestler facing, lunging **Edge:** Reeded **Note:** Corrected denomination.

Date	Mintage	F	VF	XF	Unc	BU
1996 Proof	100	Value: 30.00				

X# 12d.2 2000 SHILINGI
6.0000 g., Aluminum, 38 mm. **Subject:** 35th Anniv. Independence / Olympics Centenary / XXVI Olympics - Atlanta **Obv:** Small arms **Rev:** Male judo wrestler facing, lunging **Edge:** Plain **Note:** Corrected denomination.

Date	Mintage	F	VF	XF	Unc	BU
1996 Proof	100	Value: 30.00				

X# 12e.1 2000 SHILINGI
23.0000 g., Copper, 38 mm. **Subject:** 35th Anniv. Independence / Olympics Centenary / XXVI Olympics - Atlanta **Obv:** Small arms **Rev:** Male judo wrestler facing, lunging **Edge:** Reeded **Note:** Corrected denomination.

Date	Mintage	F	VF	XF	Unc	BU
1996 Proof	100	Value: 30.00				

X# 12e.2 2000 SHILINGI
23.0000 g., Copper, 38 mm. **Subject:** 35th Anniv. Independence / Olympics Centenary / XXVI Olympics - Atlanta **Obv:** Small arms **Rev:** Male judo wrestler facing, lunging **Edge:** Plain **Note:** Corrected denomination.

Date	Mintage	F	VF	XF	Unc	BU
1996 Proof	100	Value: 30.00				

X# 12f.1 2000 SHILINGI
20.0000 g., Copper-Nickel, 38 mm. **Subject:** 35th Anniv. Independence / Olympics Centenary / XXVI Olympics - Atlanta **Obv:** Small arms **Rev:** Male judo wrestler facing, lunging **Edge:** Reeded **Note:** Corrected denomination.

Date	Mintage	F	VF	XF	Unc	BU
1996 Proof	100	Value: 30.00				

X# 12f.2 2000 SHILINGI
20.0000 g., Copper-Nickel, 38 mm. **Subject:** 35th Anniv. Independence / Olympics Centenary / XXVI Olympics - Atlanta **Obv:** Small arms **Rev:** Male judo wrestler facing, lunging **Edge:** Plain **Note:** Corrected denomination.

Date	Mintage	F	VF	XF	Unc	BU
1996 Proof	100	Value: 30.00				

X# 13.1 2000 SHILINGI
24.0000 g., 0.9250 Silver 0.7137 oz. ASW, 38 mm. **Subject:** 35th Anniv. Independence / Olympics Centenary / XXVI Olympics - Atlanta **Obv:** Small arms **Rev:** Male sprinter facing, running **Edge:** Reeded **Note:** Corrected denomination.

Date	Mintage	F	VF	XF	Unc	BU
1996 Proof	100	Value: 50.00				

X# 13.2 2000 SHILINGI
24.0000 g., 0.9250 Silver 0.7137 oz. ASW, 38 mm. **Subject:** 35th Anniv. Independence / Olympics Centenary / XXVI Olympics - Atlanta **Obv:** Small arms **Rev:** Male sprinter facing, running **Edge:** Plain **Note:** Corrected denomination.

Date	Mintage	F	VF	XF	Unc	BU
1996 Proof	100	Value: 50.00				

X# 13a.1 2000 SHILINGI
23.0000 g., Brass, 38 mm. **Subject:** 35th Anniv. Independence / Olympics Centenary / XXVI Olympics - Atlanta **Obv:** Small arms **Rev:** Male sprinter facing, running **Edge:** Reeded **Note:** Corrected denomination.

Date	Mintage	F	VF	XF	Unc	BU
1996 Proof	100	Value: 30.00				

X# 13a.2 2000 SHILINGI
23.0000 g., Brass, 38 mm. **Subject:** 35th Anniv. Independence / Olympics Centenary / XXVI Olympics - Atlanta **Obv:** Small arms **Rev:** Male sprinter facing, running **Edge:** Plain **Note:** Corrected denomination.

Date	Mintage	F	VF	XF	Unc	BU
1996 Proof	100	Value: 30.00				

X# 13b.1 2000 SHILINGI
20.0000 g., Gilt Alloy, 38 mm. **Subject:** 35th Anniv. Independence / Olympics Centenary / XXVI Olympics - Atlanta **Obv:** Small arms **Rev:** Male sprinter facing, running **Edge:** Reeded **Note:** Corrected denomination.

Date	Mintage	F	VF	XF	Unc	BU
1996 Proof	100	Value: 30.00				

X# 13b.2 2000 SHILINGI
20.0000 g., Gilt Alloy, 38 mm. **Subject:** 35th Anniv. Independence / Olympics Centenary / XXVI Olympics - Atlanta **Obv:** Small arms **Rev:** Male sprinter facing, running **Edge:** Plain **Note:** Corrected denomination.

Date	Mintage	F	VF	XF	Unc	BU
1996 Proof	100	Value: 30.00				

X# 13c.1 2000 SHILINGI
23.0000 g., Tri-Metallic Silvered and gilt Brass, 38 mm. **Subject:** 35th Anniv. Independence / Olympics Centenary / XXVI Olympics - Atlanta **Obv:** Small arms **Rev:** Male sprinter facing, running **Edge:** Reeded **Note:** Corrected denomination.

Date	Mintage	F	VF	XF	Unc	BU
1996 Proof	25	Value: 50.00				

X# 13c.2 2000 SHILINGI
23.0000 g., Tri-Metallic Silvered and gilt Brass, 38 mm. **Subject:** 35th Anniv. Independence / Olympics Centenary / XXVI Olympics - Atlanta **Obv:** Small arms **Rev:** Male sprinter facing, running **Edge:** Plain **Note:** Corrected denomination.

Date	Mintage	F	VF	XF	Unc	BU
1996 Proof	25	Value: 50.00				

X# 13d.1 2000 SHILINGI
6.0000 g., Aluminum, 38 mm. **Subject:** 35th Anniv. Independence / Olympics Centenary / XXVI Olympics - Atlanta **Obv:** Small arms **Rev:** Male sprinter facing, running **Edge:** Reeded **Note:** Corrected denomination.

Date	Mintage	F	VF	XF	Unc	BU
1996 Proof	100	Value: 30.00				

X# 13d.2 2000 SHILINGI
6.0000 g., Aluminum, 38 mm. **Subject:** 35th Anniv. Independence / Olympics Centenary / XXVI Olympics - Atlanta **Obv:** Small arms **Rev:** Male sprinter facing, running **Edge:** Plain **Note:** Corrected denomination.

Date	Mintage	F	VF	XF	Unc	BU
1996 Proof	100	Value: 30.00				

X# 13e.1 2000 SHILINGI
23.0000 g., Copper, 38 mm. **Subject:** 35th Anniv. Independence / Olympics Centenary / XXVI Olympics - Atlanta **Obv:** Small arms **Rev:** Male sprinter facing, running **Edge:** Reeded **Note:** Corrected denomination.

Date	Mintage	F	VF	XF	Unc	BU
1996 Proof	100	Value: 30.00				

X# 13e.2 2000 SHILINGI
23.0000 g., Copper, 38 mm. **Subject:** 35th Anniv. Independence / Olympics Centenary / XXVI Olympics - Atlanta **Obv:** Small arms **Rev:** Male sprinter facing, running **Edge:** Plain **Note:** Corrected denomination.

Date	Mintage	F	VF	XF	Unc	BU
1996 Proof	100	Value: 30.00				

X# 13f.1 2000 SHILINGI
20.0000 g., Copper-Nickel, 38 mm. **Subject:** 35th Anniv. Independence / Olympics Centenary / XXVI Olympics - Atlanta **Obv:** Small arms **Rev:** Male sprinter facing, running **Edge:** Reeded **Note:** Corrected denomination.

Date	Mintage	F	VF	XF	Unc	BU
1996 Proof	100	Value: 30.00				

X# 13f.2 2000 SHILINGI
20.0000 g., Copper-Nickel, 38 mm. **Subject:** 35th Anniv. Independence / Olympics Centenary / XXVI Olympics - Atlanta **Obv:** Small arms **Rev:** Male sprinter facing, running **Edge:** Plain **Note:** Corrected denomination.

Date	Mintage	F	VF	XF	Unc	BU
1996 Proof	100	Value: 30.00				

PIEFORTS

X#	Date	Mintage	Identification	Mkt Val
P1	1996	—	2000 Shilingi. 0.9250 Silver. 48.0000 g. X1.1.	120
P2	1996	—	2000 Shilingi. 0.9250 Silver. 48.0000 g. X1.2.	120
P3	1996	—	2000 Shilingi. 0.9250 Silver. 48.0000 g. X2.1.	120
P4	1996	—	2000 Shilingi. 0.9250 Silver. 48.0000 g. X2.2.	120
P5	1996	—	2000 Shilingi. 0.9250 Silver. 48.0000 g. X3.1.	120
P6	1996	—	2000 Shilingi. 0.9250 Silver. 48.0000 g. X3.2.	120
P7	1996	—	2000 Shilingi. 0.9250 Silver. 48.0000 g. X4.1.	120
P8	1996	—	2000 Shilingi. 0.9250 Silver. 48.0000 g. X4.2.	120
P9	1996	—	2000 Shilingi. 0.9250 Silver. 48.0000 g. X5.1.	120
P10	1996	—	2000 Shilingi. 0.9250 Silver. 48.0000 g. X5.2.	120
P11	1996	—	2000 Shilingi. 0.9250 Silver. 48.0000 g. X6.1.	120
P12	1996	—	2000 Shilingi. 0.9250 Silver. 48.0000 g. X6.2.	120
P13	1996	—	2000 Shilingi. 0.9250 Silver. 48.0000 g. X8.1.	75.00
P14	1996	—	2000 Shilingi. 0.9250 Silver. 48.0000 g. X8.2.	75.00
P15	1996	—	2000 Shilingi. 0.9250 Silver. 48.0000 g. X9.1.	75.00
P16	1996	—	2000 Shilingi. 0.9250 Silver. 48.0000 g. X9.2.	75.00
P17	1996	—	2000 Shilingi. 0.9250 Silver. 48.0000 g. X10.1.	75.0
P18	1996	—	2000 Shilingi. 0.9250 Silver. 48.0000 g. X10.2.	75.0
P19	1996	—	2000 Shilingi. 0.9250 Silver. 48.0000 g. X11.1.	75.0
P20	1996	—	2000 Shilingi. 0.9250 Silver. 48.0000 g. X11.2.	75.0
P21	1996	—	2000 Shilingi. 0.9250 Silver. 48.0000 g. X12.1.	75.0
P22	1996	—	2000 Shilingi. 0.9250 Silver. 48.0000 g. X12.2.	75.0
P23	1996	—	2000 Shilingi. 0.9250 Silver. 48.0000 g. X13.1.	75.0
P24	1996	—	2000 Shilingi. 0.9250 Silver. 48.0000 g. X13.2.	75.0

TARIM

KINGDOM

MEDALLIC COINAGE

Bernard M. O'Hea Issues

X# 1 DINAR
Aluminum, 23 mm. **Obv. Legend:** "There is no God but Allah/Mohammed is God's Prophet **Rev. Legend:** Value in sprays

Date	Mintage	F	VF	XF	Unc	BU
AH1352	—	—	—	4.00	8.00	-

X# 1a DINAR
Aluminum-Bronze, 23 mm. **Obv. Legend:** "There is no God but Allah/Mohammed is God's Prophet" **Rev:** Value in sprays

Date	Mintage	F	VF	XF	Unc	BU
AH1352	—	—	—	4.00	8.00	-

X# 1b DINAR
Bronze, 23 mm. **Obv. Legend:** "There is no God but Allah/Mohammed is God's Prophet **Rev:** Value in sprays

Date	Mintage	F	VF	XF	Unc	BU
AH1352	—	—	—	4.00	8.00	-

X# 1c DINAR
Copper-Nickel, 23 mm. **Obv. Legend:** "There is no God but Allah/Mohammed is God's Prophet" **Rev:** Value in sprays

Date	Mintage	F	VF	XF	Unc	BU
AH1352	—	—	—	4.00	8.00	-

X# 1d DINAR
Silver, 23 mm. **Obv. Legend:** "There is no God but Allah/Mohammed is God's Prophet" **Rev:** Value in sprays

Date	Mintage	F	VF	XF	Unc	BU
AH1352 Proof	—	Value: 25.00				

X# 1e DINAR
Gold, 23 mm. **Obv. Legend:** "There is no God but Allah/Mohammed is God's Prophet" **Rev:** Value in sprays

Date	Mintage	F	VF	XF	Unc	BU
AH1352 Proof	—	Value: 200				

X# 1f DINAR
Platinum APW, 23 mm. **Obv. Legend:** "There is no God but Allah/Mohammed is God's Prophet" **Rev:** Value in sprays

Date	Mintage	F	VF	XF	Unc	BU
AH1352 Proof	3	Value: 350				

X# 2 DINAR
Silver, 38 mm. **Obv. Legend:** "There is no God but Allah/Mohammed is God's Prophet" **Rev:** Value in sprays

Date	Mintage	F	VF	XF	Unc	BU
AH1352 Proof	—	Value: 125				

 # 2a DINAR
ver, 38 mm. **Obv. Legend:** "There is no God but ah/Mohammed is God's Prophet" **Rev:** Value in rays **Note:** Countermarked: A.

e	Mintage	F	VF	XF	Unc	BU
1352 Proof	—	Value: 110				

 # 2b DINAR
uminum-Bronze, 38 mm. **Obv. Legend:** "There is no od but Allah/Mohammed is God's Prophet" **Rev:** Value sprays

e	Mintage	F	VF	XF	Unc	BU
1352 Proof	—	Value: 20.00				

 # 2c DINAR
onze, 38 mm. **Obv. Legend:** "There is no God but ah/Mohammed is God's Prophet" **Rev:** Value in rays **Note:** Countermarked: BRONZE.

e	Mintage	F	VF	XF	Unc	BU
1352 Proof	—	Value: 20.00				

 # 2d DINAR
ld, 38 mm. **Obv. Legend:** "There is no God but ah/Mohammed is God's Prophet" **Rev:** Value in sprays

e	Mintage	F	VF	XF	Unc	BU
1352 Proof	10	Value: 650				

 # 2e DINAR
atinum APW, 38 mm. **Obv. Legend:** "There is no od but Allah/Mohammed is God's Prophet" **Rev:** Value sprays

e	Mintage	F	VF	XF	Unc	BU
1352 Proof	3	Value: 1,000				

TENDER ISLAND

IMAGINARY STATE

FANTASY COINAGE

 # 1 LINDEN DOLLAR
)000 g., Copper-Nickel-Zinc, 25 mm. **Issuer:** David n Gent **Subject:** Second Life Friendship **Obv:** Arms **v. Legend:** TENDER ISLAND **Rev:** Value "L$1" on and outline, "Second Life Grid" **Rev. Legend:** X, Y 58, 1160 **Edge:** Plain

e	Mintage	F	VF	XF	Unc	BU
07	25	—	—	—	—	—

 # 1a LINDEN DOLLAR
5000 g., 0.9990 Silver 0.2409 oz. ASW, 25 mm. **Issuer:** vid van Gent **Subject:** Second Life Friendship **Obv:** ms **Rev:** Value "L$1" on island outline, Second Life Grid **v. Legend:** X, Y 1058, 1160 **Edge:** Plain

e	Mintage	F	VF	XF	Unc	BU
07 Proof	50	—	—	—	25.00	—

THAILAND

KINGDOM OF SIAM

until 1939

BULLET COINAGE

Silver Pot Duang

C# 120 1/128 BAHT
0.1200 g., Silver **Ruler:** Rama IV

Date	Mintage	VG	F	VF	XF	Unc
ND P'ra Tao	—	—	—	—	—	—

Note: Confirmed as an unofficial hill tribe piece only; This weight never issued as an official coin

C# 127 BAHT
Silver **Ruler:** Rama IV **Note:** Observed weight range 14.86-15.43 grams.

Date	Mintage	VG	F	VF	XF	Unc
P"ra Tao	—	—	—	—	—	—

Note: Confirmed only as a fantasy piece

C# 32 4-1/2 BAHT
Silver **Ruler:** Rama III

Date	Mintage	VG	F	VF	XF	Unc
ND Krut Sio	—	—	—	—	—	—

Note: Confirmed only as a fantasy piece

C# 33 8 BAHT
123.2000 g., Silver **Ruler:** Rama III

Date	Mintage	VG	F	VF	XF	Unc
ND Krut Sio	—	—	—	—	—	—

Note: Confirmed only as a fantasy piece

FANTASY COINAGE

X# 8 1/16 FUANG (1 Solot)
Copper **Note:** Believed to be a modern concoction.

Date	Mintage	F	VF	XF	Unc	BU
ND	—	—	—	—	—	—

X# 9 2 ATT
Copper **Note:** Believed to be a modern concoction.

Date	Mintage	F	VF	XF	Unc	BU
RS112(1893)	—	—	—	—	—	—

PRESENTATION COINAGE

Bannakin (Royal Gift) Coins

X# 11 FUANG (1/8 Baht)
2.0000 g., Silver **Ruler:** Rama IV **Obv:** Larger crown **Edge:** Plain **Note:** Similar to 1/8 Baht, Y#8. Prev. KM#11.

Date	Mintage	F	VF	XF	Unc	BU
ND(1857-58)	—	—	1,000	2,000	3,000	—

X# 12 SALU'NG (1/4 Baht)
3.9000 g., Silver **Ruler:** Rama IV **Edge:** Plain **Note:** Prev. KM#12.

Date	Mintage	F	VF	XF	Unc	BU
ND(1857-58)	—	—	3,000	4,000	6,000	—

X# 13 1/2 BAHT
Silver **Ruler:** Rama IV **Edge:** Plain **Note:** Prev. KM#13.

Date	Mintage	F	VF	XF	Unc	BU
ND(1857-58) Rare	—	—	—	—	—	—

Note: The total mintage for KM#11-13 equalled 840 Baht

X# 14 BAHT
15.5000 g., Silver **Ruler:** Rama IV **Edge:** Milled **Note:** Prev. KM#14.

Date	Mintage	F	VF	XF	Unc	BU
ND(1857-58)	2,400	—	4,000	5,000	6,000	—
ND(c.1868) Rare	—	—	—	—	—	—

Note: Spink-Taisei Auction #4, Feb. 1988, realized $20,125

X# 10 2-1/2 BAHT
2.1500 g., Gold **Ruler:** Rama IV **Note:** Prev. KM#10.

Date	Mintage	F	VF	XF	Unc	BU
ND(1857-58) Rare	—	—	—	—	—	—

TRADE COINAGE

Yong Kim Hong Assay House - Bangkok

X# 37 BAHT
15.4500 g., 0.9000 Silver 0.4470 oz. ASW
Countermark: "Yong Kim" in Chinese or Thai
Note: Countermarked on Thailand Baht, Y#11.

Date	Mintage	VG	F	VF	XF	Unc
ND(1860)	—	15.00	25.00	40.00	140	—

X# 38 BAHT

Silver **Countermark:** "Yong Kim" in Chinese or Thai **Note:** Countermarked on Thailand Baht, Y#31.

Date	Mintage	VG	F	VF	XF	Unc
ND(1869)	—	15.00	25.00	40.00	135	—

X# 1 DOLLAR

0.9000 Silver **Countermark:** "Yong Kim" in Chinese or Thai **Note:** Countermarked on British Trade Dollar, KM#T5.

Date	Mintage	VG	F	VF	XF	Unc
1895-1935	—	12.00	20.00	30.00	50.00	—

X# 2 DOLLAR

0.9000 Silver **Countermark:** "Yong Kim" in Chinese or Thai **Note:** Countermarked on Straits Settlements Dollar, KM#25.

Date	Mintage	VG	F	VF	XF	Unc
1903-04B	—	15.00	25.00	35.00	65.00	—

X# 5 DOLLAR

0.9000 Silver **Countermark:** "Yong Kim" in Chinese or Thai **Note:** Countermarked on Straits Settlements Dollar, KM#26.

Date	Mintage	VG	F	VF	XF	Unc
1907-09	—	12.00	20.00	30.00	60.00	—

X# 49 DOLLAR

0.9000 Silver **Countermark:** "Yong Kim" in Chinese or Thai **Note:** Countermarked on China Szechuan Dollar, Y#243.1.

Date	Mintage	VG	F	VF	XF	Unc
ND(1909-11)	—	15.00	25.00	45.00	90.00	—

X# 46 DOLLAR

0.9000 Silver **Countermark:** "Yong Kim" in Chinese or Thai **Note:** Countermarked on China Yunnan Dollar, Y#258.

Date	Mintage	VG	F	VF	XF	Unc
ND(1911-15)	—	15.00	25.00	35.00	50.00	—

X# 15 DOLLAR

26.4000 g., 0.8900 Silver 0.7554 oz. ASW **Countermark:** "Yong Kim" in Chinese or Thai **Note:** Countermarked on China Dollar, Y#329.

Date	Mintage	VG	F	VF	XF	Unc
Yr. 3 (1914)	—	12.50	17.50	25.00	32.50	—

X# 16 DOLLAR

27.0000 g., 0.8900 Silver 0.7726 oz. ASW **Countermark:** "Yong Kim" in Chinese or Thai **Note:** Countermarked on China Dollar, Y#318a.1.

Date	Mintage	VG	F	VF	XF
ND(1927)	—	12.50	17.50	24.00	30.00

X# 18 DOLLAR

25.6000 g., Silver **Countermark:** "Yong Kim" in Chinese or Thai **Note:** Countermarked on China Yunnan Dollar, Y#156.

Date	Mintage	VG	F	VF	XF
Yr. 1	—	15.00	22.50	35.00	70.00

X# 17 DOLLAR

26.7000 g., 0.8800 Silver 0.7554 oz. ASW **Countermark:** "Yong Kim" in Chinese or Thai **Note:** Countermarked on China Dollar, Y#345.

Date	Mintage	VG	F	VF	XF
Yr. 22	—	13.50	22.50	30.00	45.00
Yr. 23	—	12.50	20.00	27.50	32.50

X# 47 DOLLAR

0.9000 Silver **Countermark:** "Yong Kim" in Chines or Thai **Note:** Countermarked on China Chihli Dollar KM#73.2.

Date	Mintage	VG	F	VF	XF
Yr. 33, 34	—	16.00	25.00	40.00	60.00

X# 3 8 REALES

0.8960 Silver **Countermark:** "Yong Kim" in Chinese or Thai **Note:** Countermarked on Mexico City 8 Reales, KM#109

Date	Mintage	VG	F	VF	XF	Unc
1791-1808	—	35.00	65.00	100	150	—

X# 42 8 REALES

0.8960 Silver **Countermark:** "Yong Kim" in Chinese or Thai **Note:** Countermarked on Bolivia Potosi 8 Reales, KM#84.

Date	Mintage	VG	F	VF	XF	Unc
1808-25	—	37.50	55.00	90.00	165	—

X# 32 8 REALES

27.0674 g., 0.8960 Silver 0.7797 oz. ASW **Countermark:** "Yong Kim" in Chinese or Thai **Note:** Countermarked on Peru Lima Mint 8 Reales, KM#117.1.

Date	Mintage	VG	F	VF	XF	Unc
1811-24	—	35.00	60.00	90.00	110	—

Note: Values are for common dates

X# 6 8 REALES

0.8960 Silver **Countermark:** "Yong Kim" in Chinese or Thai **Note:** Countermarked on Mexico City 8 Reales, KM#111

Date	Mintage	VG	F	VF	XF	Unc
1811-21	—	30.00	45.00	75.00	125	—

X# 26 8 REALES

27.0700 g., 0.9030 Silver 0.7859 oz. ASW
Countermark: "Yong Kim" in Chinese or Thai
Note: Countermarked on Mexico Zacatecas Mint 8 Reales, KM#111.5.

Date	Mintage	VG	F	VF	XF	Unc
1813-22	—	40.00	50.00	65.00	120	—

Note: Values are for common dates

X# 33 8 REALES

27.0700 g., 0.9030 Silver 0.7859 oz. ASW
Countermark: "Yong Kim" in Chinese or Thai
Note: Countermarked on Peru Cuzco Mint 8 Reales, KM#142.4.

Date	Mintage	VG	F	VF	XF	Unc
1830-34	—	22.00	30.00	50.00	100	—

Note: Values are for common dates

X# 34 8 REALES

27.0700 g., 0.9030 Silver 0.7859 oz. ASW
Countermark: "Yong Kim" in Chinese or Thai
Note: Countermarked on Peru Lima Mint 8 Reales, KM#142.10.

Date	Mintage	VG	F	VF	XF	Unc
1841-52	—	20.00	35.00	65.00	160	—

Note: Values are for common dates

X# 44 8 SOLES

0.9030 Silver **Countermark:** "Yong Kim" in Chinese or Thai **Note:** Countermarked on Boliva Potosi 8 Soles, KM#109.

Date	Mintage	VG	F	VF	XF	Unc
1827-40	—	25.00	35.00	60.00	90.00	—

Note: Valuess for common dates

X# 4 8 SOLES

0.9030 Silver **Countermark:** "Yong Kim" in Chinese or Thai **Note:** Countermarked on Bolivia Potosi 8 Soles, KM#109.

Date	Mintage	VG	F	VF	XF	Unc
1848-51	—	40.00	70.00	120	175	—

X# 20 PIASTRE
27.0000 g., 0.9000 Silver 0.7812 oz. ASW
Countermark: "Yong Kim" in Chinese or Thai **Note:** Countermarked on French Indochina Piastre, KM#5a.1.

Date	Mintage	VG	F	VF	XF	Unc
1895-1928	—	15.00	20.00	27.50	35.00	—

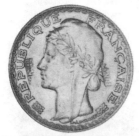

X# 21 PIASTRE
20.0000 g., 0.9000 Silver 0.5787 oz. ASW
Countermark: "Yong Kim" in Chinese or Thai **Note:** Countermarked on French Indochina Piastre, KM#19.

Date	Mintage	VG	F	VF	XF	Unc
1931(a)	—	12.50	20.00	35.00	65.00	—

X# 24 YEN
Silver **Countermark:** "Yong Kim" in Chinese or Thai **Note:** Countermarked on Japan Yen, Y#A25.3.

Date	Mintage	VG	F	VF	XF	Unc
ND	—	13.50	22.50	40.00	60.00	—

Note: Values are for common dates

X# 27 PESO
27.0730 g., 0.9030 Silver 0.7860 oz. ASW
Countermark: "Yong Kim" in Chinese or Thai
Note: Countermarked on Mexico Culiacan Mint Peso, KM#409.

Date	Mintage	VG	F	VF	XF	Unc
1898-1905	—	13.50	20.00	30.00	65.00	—

Note: Values are for common dates

X# 30 2-1/2 GULDEN
25.0000 g., 0.7200 Silver 0.5787 oz. ASW
Countermark: "Yong Kim" in Chinese or Thai
Note: Countermarked on Netherlands 2-1/2 Gulden, KM#165.

Date	Mintage	VG	F	VF	XF	Unc
1929-40	—	10.00	18.00	25.00	30.00	—

Note: Values are for common dates

X# 40 5 BOLIVARES
25.0000 g., 0.9000 Silver 0.7234 oz. ASW
Countermark: "Yong Kim" in Chinese or Thai
Note: Countermarked on Venezuela 5 Bolivares, Y#24.2.

Date	Mintage	VG	F	VF	XF	Unc
1900-36	—	12.50	16.50	27.50	40.00	—

Note: Values are for common dates

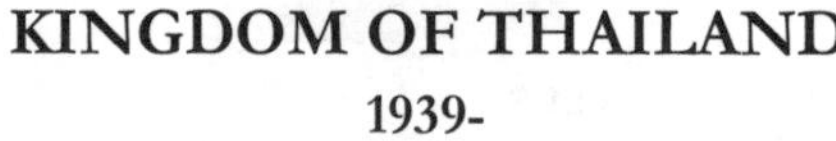

KINGDOM OF THAILAND

1939-

DECIMAL COINAGE

25 Satang = 1 Salung; 100 Satang = 1 Baht

Y# 400 10 BAHT
8.5500 g., Bi-Metallic Brass center in Copper-Nickel ring, 26 mm. **Ruler:** Bhumipol Adulyadej (Rama IX)
Obv: Head left **Rev:** APEC logo **Edge:** Segmented reeding

Date	Mintage	F	VF	XF	Unc	BU
BE2546-2003	—	—	—	—	3.00	—

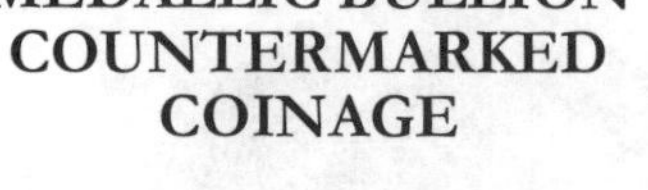

MEDALLIC BULLION COUNTERMARKED COINAGE

X# MB1 8 REALES (5 Ounces)
155.5150 g., 0.9990 Silver 4.9947 oz. ASW **Series:** King Rama IX 60th Birthday **Countermark:** "1987 Visit Thailand Year" and "Treasury Department" **Note:** Countermarked on Mexico X#MB2.1.

Date	Mintage	F	VF	XF	Unc	BU
1987 Proof	192	Value: 275				

TIBET

CHINESE AUTHORITY

MEDALLIC COINAGE

Australian Mint Issues

Authorized by the Dalai Lama in exile and produced by the Royal Australian Mint in May, 1978.

X# 1 5 SHO
Copper, 29.50 mm. **Obv:** Lion standing left, mountain behind **Edge:** Reeded

Date	Mintage	F	VF	XF	Unc	BU
Yr.16-21 (1947) Proof	2,000	Value: 20.00				

X# 2 5 SHO
0.9250 g., Silver, 29.50 mm. **Obv:** Lion standing left, mountain behind **Edge:** Reeded

Date	Mintage	F	VF	XF	Unc	BU
Yr.16-21 (1947) Proof	1,000	Value: 50.00				

X# 3 5 SHO
13.0400 g., 0.5000 Gold 0.2096 oz. AGW, 29.50 mm. **Obv:** Lion standing left, mountain behind **Edge:** Reeded

Date	Mintage	F	VF	XF	Unc	BU
Yr.16-21 (1947) Proof	250	Value: 325				

X# 4 10 SRANG
Copper Nickel, 32.20 mm. **Obv:** Lion standing left, mountain behind **Edge:** Reeded

Date	Mintage	F	VF	XF	Unc	BU
Yr. 16-24 (1950) Proof	5,000	Value: 25.00				

X# 5 10 SRANG
0.9250 Silver, 32.20 mm. **Obv:** Lion standing left, mountain behind **Edge:** Reeded

Date	Mintage	F	VF	XF	Unc	BU
Yr. 16-24 (1950) Proof	2,000	Value: 75.00				

X# 6 10 SRANG
0.5000 Gold, 32.20 mm. **Obv:** Lion standing left, mountain behind **Edge:** Reeded

Date	Mintage	F	VF	XF	Unc	BU
Yr. 16-24 (1950) Proof	500	Value: 450				

Franklin Mint Issues

X# 7 CROWN
Franklinium **Subject:** Liberty Commemorative

Date	Mintage	F	VF	XF	Unc	BU
ND Prooflike	600	—	—	—	25.00	—
ND Proof	600	Value: 35.00				

X# 9 CROWN
0.9990 Silver **Subject:** Liberty Commemorative

Date	Mintage	F	VF	XF	Unc	BU
ND Proof	100	Value: 125				

X# 10 CROWN
0.7500 Gold **Subject:** Liberty Commemorative

Date	Mintage	F	VF	XF	Unc	BU
ND Proof	1	—	—	—	—	—

KINGDOM

TRADE COINAGE

X# T1 TAEL / (LIANG)
21.3200 g., Silver, 39 mm. **Series:** Furnace Start Up **Obv. Inscription:** Kuang-hsü Yüan-pao - Kuan-chü Lu-chu **Rev. Inscription:** "Hsi-tsang Yi-liang (Tibet 1 Liang) **Edge:** Reeded **Note:** A modern concoction.

Date	Mintage	F	VF	XF	Unc	BU
ND(1875-1908)	—	—	11.50	18.50	—	—

PATTERNS

Including off metal strikes

X#	Date	Mintage	Identification	Issue Price	Mkt Val
Pn1	ND(1875-1908)	—	Tael / (Liang). Silver. 40.1500 g. 50.3 mm. X#T1. Modern concoction.	—	25.00

TONGA

KINGDOM

MEDALLIC COINAGE

X# M1 5 PA'ANGA
Copper-Nickel **Subject:** International Games - Judo

Date	Mintage	F	VF	XF	Unc	BU
1984 Proof	—	Value: 16.50				

X# M2 5 PA'ANGA
Copper-Nickel **Subject:** International Games - Relay **Obv:** King's portrait **Rev:** Relay runners

Date	Mintage	F	VF	XF	Unc	BU
1984 Proof	—	Value: 16.50				

TORGU

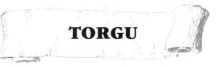

KINGDOM

TOKEN COINAGE

X# Tn1 1/2 LITRE
12.0000 g., Aluminum-Bronze, 32 mm. **Ruler:** Kirill I **Obv:** Head left **Rev:** Crowned arms **Rev. Legend:**

TORGU KUNINGRIIK **Note:** Pegged to 1/2 Litre of Estonian White Vodka

Date	Mintage	F	VF	XF	Unc	BU
1993	2,000	—	—	—	27.50	—

X# Tn2 1/2 LITRE
13.0000 g., Copper-Nickel, 32 mm. **Ruler:** Kirill I **Subject:** Fifth Anniversary of Reign **Obv:** Head left, "V" below at right **Rev:** Crowned arms **Rev. Legend:** TORGU KUNINGRIIK **Note:** Pegged to 1/2 Litre of Estonian White Vodka.

Date	Mintage	F	VF	XF	Unc	BU
1998	500	—	—	—	32.50	—

X# Tn3 1/2 LITRE
13.0000 g., Copper-Nickel, 32 mm. **Ruler:** Kirill I **Subject:** 10th Anniversary of Reign **Obv:** Head left, "X" below at right **Rev:** Crowned arms **Rev. Legend:** TORGU KUNINGRIIK **Note:** Pegged to 1/2 Litre of Estonian White Vodka.

Date	Mintage	F	VF	XF	Unc	BU
2002	250	—	—	—	55.00	—

X# Tn4 1/2 LITRE
13.0000 g., Goldine, 32 mm. **Ruler:** Kirill I **Subject:** 50th Birthday of King Kirill I **Obv:** Head left, date 25.08.2002 below, L at right **Rev:** Crowned arms **Rev. Legend:** TORGU KUNINGRIIK **Note:** Pegged to 1/2 Litre of Estonian White Vodka

Date	Mintage	F	VF	XF	Unc	BU
2002	75	—	—	—	115	—

TRANSYLVANIA

AUSTRIAN RULE

TRADE COINAGE

X# 5 1/2 RIJKSDAALDER
Silver, 35 mm. **Ruler:** Gabriel Bethlem **Obv:** Bust right, sword upright, holding shield **Obv. Legend:** MO • ARG • PRO-CONFOE • BELG • TRANS **Rev:** Crowned shield with Netherlands rampant lion left **Rev. Legend:** * CONCORDIA • RES • PARVAE CRESCVNT **Edge:** Plain **Note:** Imitation of Dutch issue.

Date	Mintage	Good	VG	F	VF	XF
1619	—	15.00	30.00	60.00	100	175

PRINCIPALITY

TRADE COINAGE

X# 1 DUCAT
3.5000 g., 0.9860 Gold 0.1109 oz. AGW
Ruler: Andreas Miser **Obv:** Bust of Andreas Miser 3/4-right wearing Cardinal's cap **Obv. Legend:** ANDREAS • MISER • DIV • CARDIN • TR • MOL • ET • VAL ★ **Rev:** Hat over Bathori arms **Rev. Legend:** PRINC • EPISC • VARMIENS • SIC • COM • **Note:** Resch #8.

Date	Mintage	F	VF	XF	Unc	BU
1599NB	—	—	—	—	—	—

X# 15 DUCAT
3.5000 g., 0.9860 Gold 0.1109 oz. AGW
Shape: 8-pointed star **Note:** Prev. KM#475.

Date	Mintage	VG	F	VF	XF	Unc
1678 Rare	—	—	—	—	—	—

Note: 19th Century Novodel

X# 10 2 DUCAT
7.0000 g., 0.9860 Gold 0.2219 oz. AGW **Note:** Half-moon planchet. Prev. KM#398.

Date	Mintage	VG	F	VF	XF	Unc
1668 AF Rare	—	—	—	—	—	—

Note: 19th Century Novodel

X# 11 4-1/2 DUCAT
15.7500 g., 0.9860 Gold 0.4993 oz. AGW
Subject: Michael Apafi **Shape:** 8-pointed star **Note:** Struck from 1 Ducat dies. Prev. KM#401.

Date	Mintage	VG	F	VF	XF	Un
1668 AF Rare	—	—	—	—	—	—

X# 26 10 DUCAT
35.1000 g., 0.9860 Gold 1.1126 oz. AGW
Subject: Leopold I **Shape:** 6-pointed star **Note:** Struck with 1 Ducat dies. Prev. KM#513.

Date	Mintage	VG	F	VF	XF	Un
1694CV Rare	—	—	—	—	—	—

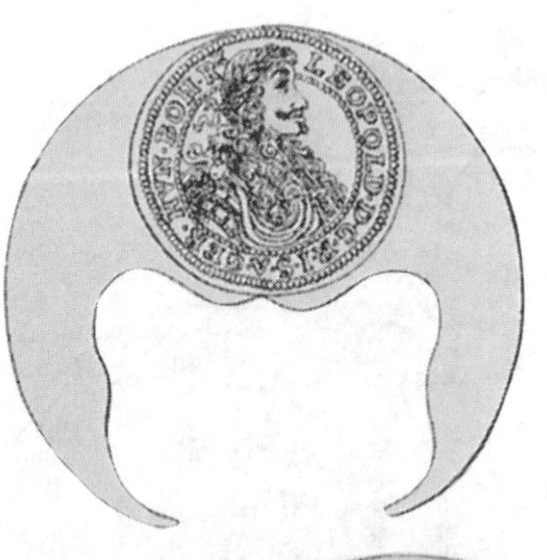
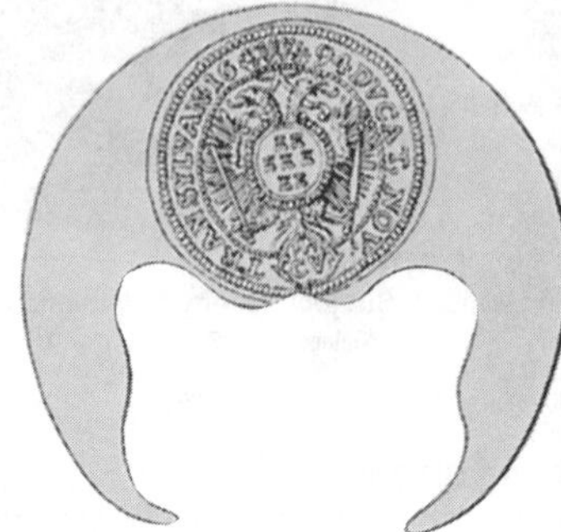

X# 25 10 DUCAT
35.1000 g., 0.9860 Gold 1.1126 oz. AGW **Shape:** Crescent **Note:** Struck with 1 Ducat dies. Prev. KM#25

Date	Mintage	VG	F	VF	XF	Un
1694CV Rare	—	—	—	—	—	—

X# 20 25 DUCAT

…5000 g., 0.9860 Gold 2.7737 oz. AGW
…bject: Michael Apafi **Shape:** Hexagon **Note:** Klippe. …stration reduced - actual size 95 x 73mm. Struck from … Ducat (Thaler) dies. Prev. KM#495.

…e	Mintage	VG	F	VF	XF	Unc
…7 Rare	—	—	—	—	—	—

X# 16 100 DUCAT

…0.0000 g., 0.9860 Gold 11.094 oz. AGW, 115 mm.
Note: Illustration reduced. Struck with 1 Ducat die (10) and 10 ducat (Thaler) die (1). Prev. KM#460.

Date	Mintage	VG	F	VF	XF	Unc
1674 Rare	—	—	—	—	—	—

X# 17 100 DUCAT

350.0000 g., 0.9860 Gold 11.094 oz. AGW, 102 mm.
Note: Illustration reduced. Struck with 1 Ducat die (9) and 10 ducat (Thaler) die (1). Prev. KM#464.

Date	Mintage	VG	F	VF	XF	Unc
1675AF Rare	—	—	—	—	—	—

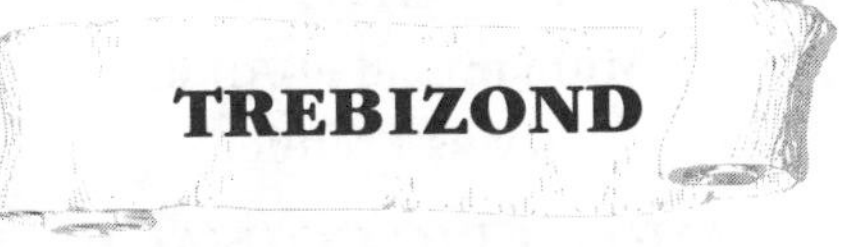

TREBIZOND

EMPIRE

FANTASY COINAGE

X# 1 10 CENTIMES

Copper

Date	Mintage	F	VF	XF	Unc	BU
1955 Proof	100	Value: 45.00				

X# 2 5 FRANCS

25.0000 g., 0.9000 Silver 0.7234 oz. ASW
Subject: Michael III

Date	Mintage	F	VF	XF	Unc	BU
1955 Proof	100	Value: 95.00				

X# 4 5 FRANCS

28.2700 g., 0.9000 Gold 0.8180 oz. AGW **Obv:** 8-pointed star at left under truncation **Rev:** *900* and hallmark *43HI</> at bottom*

Date	Mintage	F	VF	XF	Unc	BU
1955 Matte	—	—	—	—	750	—

X# 3 20 FRANCS

6.4500 g., 0.9000 Gold 0.1866 oz. AGW
Subject: Michael III

Date	Mintage	F	VF	XF	Unc	BU
1955 Proof	100	Value: 325				

PROOF SETS

X#	Date	Mintage	Identification	Issue Price	Mkt Val
XPS1	1955 (3)	100	X1-X3 w/medal	—	425

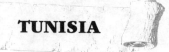

TUNISIA

FRENCH PROTECTORATE

MEDALLIC COINAGE

X# 1 10 FRANCS
10.0000 g., 0.6800 Silver 0.2186 oz. ASW
Ruler: Muhammad al-Amin Bey "Struck in his name"
Obv. Legend: MUHAMMAD AL-AMIN BEY
Note: Previous KM#M4.

Date	Mintage	F	VF	XF	Unc	BU
AH1365//1945(a)	2,606	—	—	75.00	125	—
AH1366//1946(a)	1,103	—	—	75.00	125	—
AH1367//1947(a)	1,103	—	—	75.00	125	—
AH1368//1948(a)	1,103	—	—	75.00	125	—
AH1369//1949(a)	1,103	—	—	75.00	125	—
AH1370//1950(a)	1,103	—	—	75.00	125	—
AH1371//1951(a)	1,703	—	—	75.00	125	—
AH1372//1952(a)	1,703	—	—	75.00	125	—
AH1373//1953(a)	1,703	—	—	75.00	125	—
AH1374//1954(a)	1,703	—	—	75.00	125	—
AH1375//1955(a)	1,703	—	—	75.00	125	—

X# 2 20 FRANCS
20.0000 g., 0.6800 Silver 0.4372 oz. ASW
Ruler: Muhammad al-Amin Bey "Struck in his name"
Obv. Legend: MUHAMMAD AL-AMIN BEY
Note: Previous KM#M5.

Date	Mintage	F	VF	XF	Unc	BU
AH1365//1945(a)	156	—	—	200	400	—
AH1366//1946(a)	53	—	—	200	450	—
AH1367//1947(a)	53	—	—	200	450	—
AH1368//1948(a)	53	—	—	200	450	—
AH1369//1949(a)	53	—	—	200	450	—
AH1370//1950(a)	53	—	—	200	450	—
AH1371//1951(a)	303	—	—	200	400	—
AH1372//1952(a)	303	—	—	200	400	—
AH1373//1953(a)	303	—	—	200	400	—
AH1374//1954(a)	303	—	—	200	400	—
AH1375//1955(a)	303	—	—	200	400	—

X# 3 100 FRANCS
6.5500 g., 0.9000 Gold 0.1895 oz. AGW **Ruler:** Ahmad Pasha Bey "Struck in his name" **Obv. Legend:** AHMED BEY **Edge:** Lettered **Note:** Previous KM#M1.1.

Date	Mintage	F	VF	XF	Unc	BU
AH1357//1938(a)	66	—	—	475	650	—
AH1358//1939(a)	33	—	—	575	750	—
AH1359//1940(a)	33	—	—	575	750	—

X# 4 100 FRANCS
6.5500 g., 0.9000 Gold 0.1895 oz. AGW **Ruler:** Ahmad Pasha Bey "Struck in his name" **Obv. Legend:** AHMED BEY **Edge:** Milled **Note:** Previous KM#M1.2.

Date	Mintage	F	VF	XF	Unc	BU
AH1360//1941(a)	33	—	—	575	750	—
AH1361//1942(a)	33	—	—	575	750	—

X# 5 100 FRANCS
6.5500 g., 0.9000 Gold 0.1895 oz. AGW
Ruler: Muhammad al-Munsif Bey "Struck in his name"
Obv. Legend: MUHAMMAD AL-MUNSIF BEY
Note: Previous KM#M2.

Date	Mintage	F	VF	XF	Unc	BU
AH1362//1943(a)	33	—	—	750	1,100	—

X# 6 100 FRANCS
6.5500 g., 0.9000 Gold 0.1895 oz. AGW
Ruler: Muhammad al-Amin Bey "Struck in his name"
Obv. Legend: MUHAMMAD AL-AMIN BEY
Note: Previous KM#M3.

Date	Mintage	F	VF	XF	Unc	BU
AH1363//1943(a)	66	—	—	425	600	—
AH1364//1944(a)	68	—	—	475	650	—
AH1365//1945(a)	33	—	—	575	750	—
AH1366//1946(a)	33	—	—	575	750	—
AH1367//1947(a)	33	—	—	575	750	—
AH1368//1948(a)	33	—	—	575	750	—
AH1369//1949(a)	33	—	—	575	750	—
AH1370//1950(a)	33	—	—	575	750	—
AH1371//1951(a)	63	—	—	475	650	—
AH1372//1952(a)	63	—	—	475	650	—
AH1373//1953(a)	63	—	—	475	650	—
AH1374//1954(a)	63	—	—	475	650	—
AH1375//1955(a)	63	—	—	475	650	—

KINGDOM

Muhammad al-Amin Bey as Premier

MEDALLIC COINAGE

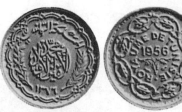

X# 7 10 FRANCS
10.0000 g., 0.6800 Silver 0.2186 oz. ASW
Obv. Legend: MUHAMMAD AL-AMIN, PREMIER
Note: Previous KM#M6.

Date	Mintage	F	VF	XF	Unc	BU
AH1376/1956(a)	1,703	—	—	150	275	—

X# 8 20 FRANCS
20.0000 g., 0.6800 Silver 0.4372 oz. ASW
Obv. Legend: MUHAMMAD AL-AMIN, PREMIER
Note: Previous KM#M7.

Date	Mintage	F	VF	XF	Unc
AH1376/1956(a)	303	—	—	250	450

X# 9 100 FRANCS
6.5500 g., 0.9000 Gold 0.1895 oz. AGW **Obv. Lege** MUHAMMAD AL-AMIN, PREMIER **Note:** Prev. KM#

Date	Mintage	F	VF	XF	Unc
AH1376/1956(a)	63	—	—	600	1,000

TURKEY

EMPIRE

MEDALLIC COINAGE

X# M10 2 RUMI ALTIN
3.4700 g., Gold, 31.82 mm. **Series:** Jewelry
Obv: Toughra at center within legend **Rev:** Regnal ye and mintname at center within legend

Date	Mintage	VG	F	VF	XF
8602//AH1223/11	—	—	—	—	75.00

SULTANATE

BULLION COINAGE

Issued by the Istanbul Mint

X# 15 NON-DENOMINATED
231.1000 g., 0.9990 Silver 7.4223 oz. ASW
Note: Illustration reduced.

Date	Mintage	F	VF	XF	Unc
ND	—	150	200	—	—

X# 10 20 KURUSH
22.0600 g., Copper **Issuer:** Von Mandslay Son & Field, Lamberth **Obv:** Ornate design **Rev:** Mint, date
Note: Manufacturer's salesman's sample.

Date	Mintage	F	VF	XF	Unc	BU
AH1255 (1839)	—	—	—	—	—	—

REPUBLIC

FANTASY EURO PATTERNS

INA Issue

X# Pn1 EURO CENT
Copper Plated Steel, 16.8 mm. **Issuer:** INA **Obv:** Yacht near Kiz Kalesi fortress **Rev:** Turkish flag **Edge:** Plain

Date	Mintage	F	VF	XF	Unc	BU
2004	27,500	—	—	—	—	1.50
2004 Proof	—	Value: 2.50				

X# Pn2 2 EURO CENT
Copper Plated Steel, 18.5 mm. **Issuer:** INA **Obv:** Yacht near Kiz Kalesi fortress **Rev:** Turkish flag **Edge:** Plain

Date	Mintage	F	VF	XF	Unc	BU
2004	27,500	—	—	—	—	2.00
2004 Proof	—	Value: 3.00				

X# Pn3 5 EURO CENT
Copper Plated Steel, 20.7 mm. **Issuer:** INA **Obv:** Yacht near Kiz Kalesi fortress **Rev:** Turkish flag **Edge:** Plain

Date	Mintage	F	VF	XF	Unc	BU
2004	27,500	—	—	—	—	2.50
2004 Proof	—	Value: 3.50				

X# Pn4 10 EURO CENT
Goldine, 19.3 mm. **Issuer:** INA **Obv:** St. Sophia Church **Rev:** Turkish flag **Edge:** Plain

Date	Mintage	F	VF	XF	Unc	BU
2004	27,500	—	—	—	—	3.00
2004 Proof	—	Value: 4.00				

X# Pn5 20 EURO CENT
Goldine, 22 mm. **Issuer:** INA **Obv:** St. Sophia Church **Rev:** Turkish flag **Edge:** Plain

Date	Mintage	F	VF	XF	Unc	BU
2004	27,500	—	—	—	—	3.50
2004 Proof	—	Value: 5.00				

X# Pn6 50 EURO CENT
Goldine, 24.3 mm. **Issuer:** INA **Obv:** St. Sophia Church **Rev:** Turkish flag **Edge:** Plain

Date	Mintage	F	VF	XF	Unc	BU
2004	27,500	—	—	—	—	4.00
2004 Proof	—	Value: 6.00				

X# Pn7 EURO
Bi-Metallic, 22.8 mm. **Issuer:** INA **Obv:** Bust of Suleiman 3/4 left **Rev:** Sailing ship "Fethiye" **Edge:** Plain

Date	Mintage	F	VF	XF	Unc	BU
2004	27,500	—	—	—	—	6.00
2004 Proof	—	Value: 8.00				

X# Pn8 2 EURO
Bi-Metallic, 25.7 mm. **Issuer:** INA **Obv:** Bust of Kemal Ataturk 3/4 right **Rev:** Sailing ship "Fethiye" **Edge:** Plain

Date	Mintage	F	VF	XF	Unc	BU
2004	27,500	—	—	—	—	8.00
2004 Proof	—	Value: 10.00				

X# Pn9 5 EURO
Goldine **Issuer:** INA **Obv:** Bust of Kemal Ataturk 3/4 right **Edge:** Plain

Date	Mintage	F	VF	XF	Unc	BU
2004 Proof	—	Value: 12.50				

MDS (Germany) Issue

X# Pn10 3 EURO
Bi-Metallic, 35 mm. **Issuer:** MDS (Germany) **Obv:** Map of Europe, large value "3" **Rev:** Bust of Atatürk facing 3/4 left **Rev. Legend:** MUSTAFA KEMAL ATATÜRK

Date	Mintage	F	VF	XF	Unc	BU
2004	—	—	—	—	—	10.00

X# Pn11 3 EURO
Bi-Metallic, 35 mm. **Issuer:** MDS (Germany) **Obv:** Map of Europe, large value "3" **Rev:** Great Mosque, Istanbul **Rev. Legend:** SULTAN AHMET CAMII

Date	Mintage	F	VF	XF	Unc	BU
2004	—	—	—	—	—	—

X# Pn12 3 EURO
Bi-Metallic, 35 mm. **Issuer:** MDS (Germany) **Obv:** Map of Europe, large value "3" **Rev:** Male chef carving gyro meat **Rev. Legend:** YASASIN DÖNER

Date	Mintage	F	VF	XF	Unc	BU
2004	—	—	—	—	—	10.00

MINT SETS

X#	Date	Mintage	Identification	Issue Price	Mkt Val
XMS1	2004 (8)	27,500	X#Pn1-Pn8	—	30.00

PROOF SETS

X#	Date	Mintage	Identification	Issue Price	Mkt Val
XPS1	2004 (9)	—	X#Pn1-Pn9	—	50.00

UGANDA

REPUBLIC

MEDALLIC COINAGE

KM# M1 POUND
7.9800 g., 0.9170 Gold 0.2353 oz. AGW, 22 mm. **Subject:** OAU **Obv:** Idi Amin right **Rev:** Ugandan arms **Edge:** Reeded

Date	Mintage	F	VF	XF	Unc	BU
1975	2,000	—	—	—	350	—
1975 Proof	200	Value: 750				

UKRAINE

REPUBLIC

MEDALLIC COINAGE

X# 21 20 HRIVNA
Silver, 40 mm. **Series:** Secretaries - General **Subject:** 60th Anniversary of United Nations **Obv:** Seal of United Nations, flag at left, Ukraine arms at right **Rev:** Bust of Trygve Lie facing **Rev. Legend:** NATIONS UNITED FOR PEACE **Edge:** Reeded

Date	Mintage	F	VF	XF	Unc	BU
2005 Proof	—	Value: 60.00				

X# 21a 20 HRIVNA
Silver Gilt, 40 mm. **Series:** Secretaries - General **Subject:** 60th Anniversary of United Nations **Obv:** Seal of United Nations, flag at left, Ukraine arms at right **Rev:** Bust of Trygve Lie facing **Rev. Legend:** NATIONS UNITED FOR PEACE **Edge:** Reeded

Date	Mintage	F	VF	XF	Unc	BU
2005 Proof	—	Value: 50.00				

X# 22 20 HRIVNA
Silver, 40 mm. **Series:** Secretaries - General **Subject:** 60th Anniversary of United Nations **Obv:** Seal of United Nations, flag at left, Ukraine arms at right **Rev:** Bust of Dag Hammarskjold facing **Rev. Legend:** NATIONS UNITED FOR PEACE **Edge:** Reeded

Date	Mintage	F	VF	XF	Unc	BU
2005 Proof	—	Value: 60.00				

X# 22a 20 HRIVNA
Silver Gilt, 40 mm. **Series:** Secretaries - General **Subject:** 60th Anniversary of United Nations **Obv:** Seal of United Nations, flag at left, Ukraine arms at right **Rev:** Bust of Dag Hammarskjold facing **Rev. Legend:** NATIONS UNITED FOR PEACE **Edge:** Reeded

Date	Mintage	F	VF	XF	Unc	BU
2005 Proof	—	Value: 50.00				

X# 23 20 HRIVNA
Silver, 40 mm. **Series:** Secretaries - General **Subject:** 60th Anniversary of United Nations **Obv:** Seal of United Nations, flag at left, Ukraine arms at right **Rev:** Bust of U Thant facing **Rev. Legend:** NATIONS UNITED FOR PEACE **Edge:** Reeded

Date	Mintage	F	VF	XF	Unc	BU
2005 Proof	—	Value: 60.00				

X# 23a 20 HRIVNA
Silver Gilt, 40 mm. **Series:** Secretaries - General **Subject:** 60th Anniversary of United Nations **Obv:** Seal of United Nations, flag at left, Ukraine arms at right **Rev:** Bust of U Thant facing **Rev. Legend:** NATIONS UNITED FOR PEACE **Edge:** Reeded

Date	Mintage	F	VF	XF	Unc	BU
2005 Proof	—	Value: 50.00				

X# 24 20 HRIVNA
Silver, 40 mm. **Series:** Secretaries - General **Subject:** 60th Anniversary of United Nations **Obv:** Seal of United Nations, flag at left, Ukraine arms at right **Rev:** Bust of Kurt Waldheim facing **Rev. Legend:** NATIONS UNITED FOR PEACE **Edge:** Reeded

Date	Mintage	F	VF	XF	Unc	BU
2005 Proof	—	Value: 60.00				

X# 24a 20 HRIVNA
Silver Gilt, 40 mm. **Series:** Secretaries - General **Subject:** 60th Anniversary of United Nations **Obv:** Seal of United Nations, flag at left, Ukraine arms at right **Rev:** Bust of Kurt Waldheim facing **Rev. Legend:** NATIONS UNITED FOR PEACE **Edge:** Reeded

Date	Mintage	F	VF	XF	Unc	BU
2005 Proof	—	Value: 50.00				

X# 25 20 HRIVNA
Silver, 40 mm. **Series:** Secretaries - General **Subject:** 60th Anniversary of United Nations **Obv:** Seal of United Nations, flag at left, Ukraine arms at right **Rev:** Bust of Javier de Perez de Cuellar facing **Rev. Legend:** NATIONS UNITED FOR PEACE **Edge:** Reeded

Date	Mintage	F	VF	XF	Unc	BU
2005 Proof	—	Value: 60.00				

X# 25a 20 HRIVNA
Silver Gilt, 40 mm. **Series:** Secretaries - General **Subject:** 60th Anniversary of United Nations **Obv:** Seal of United Nations, flag at left, Ukraine arms at right **Rev:** Bust of Javier de Perez de Cuellar facing **Rev. Legend:** NATIONS UNITED FOR PEACE **Edge:** Reeded

Date	Mintage	F	VF	XF	Unc	BU
2005 Proof	—	Value: 50.00				

X# 26 20 HRIVNA
Silver, 40 mm. **Subject:** 60th Anniversary of United Nations **Obv:** Seal of United Nations, flag at left, Ukraine arms at right **Rev:** Bust of Boutros Boutros-Ghali facing **Rev. Legend:** NATIONS UNITED FOR PEACE **Edge:** Reeded

Date	Mintage	F	VF	XF	Unc	BU
2005 Proof	—	Value: 60.00				

X# 26a 20 HRIVNA
Silver Gilt, 40 mm. **Subject:** 60th Anniversary of United Nations **Obv:** Seal of United Nations, flag at left, Ukraine arms at right **Rev:** Bust of Boutros Boutros-Ghali facing **Rev. Legend:** NATIONS UNITED FOR PEACE **Edge:** Reeded

Date	Mintage	F	VF	XF	Unc	BU
2005 Proof	—	Value: 50.00				

X# 11 100 HRYVEN
62.1400 g., 0.9990 Silver 1.9958 oz. ASW, 38.5 mm. **Subject:** 100th Anniversary of Birth **Obv:** Arms **Rev:** Male bust facing **Edge:** Reeded

Date	Mintage	F	VF	XF	Unc	BU
1991 Proof	—	Value: 45.00				

FANTASY EURO PATTERNS

X# Pn1 EURO CENT
Copper Plated Steel **Edge:** Plain

Date	Mintage	F	VF	XF	Unc	BU
2004	7,000	—	—	—	—	1.50

X# Pn2 2 EURO CENT
Copper Plated Steel **Edge:** Plain

Date	Mintage	F	VF	XF	Unc	BU
2004	7,000	—	—	—	—	2.00

X# Pn3 5 EURO CENT
Copper Plated Steel **Edge:** Plain

Date	Mintage	F	VF	XF	Unc	BU
2004	7,000	—	—	—	—	2.50

X# Pn4 10 EURO CENT
Goldine **Edge:** Plain

Date	Mintage	F	VF	XF	Unc	BU
2004	7,000	—	—	—	—	3.00

X# Pn5 20 EURO CENT
Goldine **Edge:** Plain

Date	Mintage	F	VF	XF	Unc	BU
2004	7,000	—	—	—	—	3.50

X# Pn6 50 EURO CENT
Goldine **Edge:** Plain

Date	Mintage	F	VF	XF	Unc	BU
2004	7,000	—	—	—	—	4.50

X# Pn7 EURO
Bi-Metallic **Obv:** Head facing 3/4 right **Rev:** Leaf design, large value "1" **Edge:** Plain

Date	Mintage	F	VF	XF	Unc	BU
2004	7,000	—	—	—	—	6.50

X# Pn8 2 EURO
Bi-Metallic **Obv:** Head facing 3/4 right **Rev:** Leaf design, large value "2" **Edge:** Plain

Date	Mintage	F	VF	XF	Unc	BU
2004	7,000	—	—	—	—	9.00

MINT SETS

X#	Date	Mintage	Identification	Issue Price	Mkt Val
XMS1	2004 (8)	7,000	X#Pn1-Pn8	—	35.00

PROOF SETS

X#	Date	Mintage	Identification	Issue Price	Mkt Val
XPS1	2005 (6)	—	X#21-26	250	250
XPS2	2005 (6)	—	X#21a-26a	300	300

UNION OF NORTH AMERICA

UNION

FANTASY PATTERNS

X# P10 1 AMERO
0.9990 Copper, 25 mm. **Obv:** Female seated **Obv. Designer:** Daniel Carrr **Rev:** Eagle **Rev. Legend:** UNION OF NORTH AMERICA **Rev. Designer:** Daniel Carr

Date	Mintage	F	VF	XF	Unc	BU
2007 D Satin	—	—	—	—	5.00	—
2007 Prooflike	—	—	—	—	6.00	—

X# P12 2 AMEROS
0.9990 Copper, 27 mm. **Obv:** Female seated **Rev:** Eagle **Rev. Legend:** UNION OF NORTH AMERICA

Date	Mintage	F	VF	XF	Unc	BU
2007 D Satin	—	—	—	—	6.00	—
2007 D Prooflike	—	—	—	—	7.00	—

X# P14 5 AMEROS
0.9990 Copper, 30 mm. **Obv:** Female seated **Rev:** Eagle **Rev. Legend:** UNION OF NORTH AMERICA

Date	Mintage	F	VF	XF	Unc	BU
2007I D Satin	—	—	—	—	7.00	—
2007 D Prooflike	—	—	—	—	8.00	—

X# P16 10 AMEROS
0.9990 Copper, 34 mm. **Obv:** Female seated **Rev:** Eagle **Rev. Legend:** UNION OF NORTH AMERICA

Date	Mintage	F	VF	XF	Unc	BU
2007 D Satin	—	—	—	—	8.00	—
2007 D Prooflike	—	—	—	—	9.00	—

 # P18 20 AMEROS
)990 Copper, 39 mm. **Obv:** Female seated right
:ing left, holding torch and spear, gear in background
v: Eagle holding lightning and olive branch, globe
low **Rev. Legend:** UNION OF NORTH AMERICA

te	Mintage	F	VF	XF	Unc	BU
)7 D Prooflike	—	—	—	—	10.00	—

 # P20 25 AMEROS
7857 g., 0.9990 Silver 0.2501 oz. ASW, 25 mm.
)v: Female seated right, facing left, holding globe and
ear, sun rays in background **Rev:** Eagle holding
'htning and olive branch, globe below **Rev. Legend:**
NION OF NORTH AMERICA

te	Mintage	F	VF	XF	Unc	BU
)7 D Satin	—	—	—	—	10.00	—
)7 D Prooflike	—	—	—	—	12.00	—

 # P22 50 AMEROS
.5520 g., 0.9990 Silver 0.4995 oz. ASW, 30 mm.
)v: Female seated **Rev:** Eagle

te	Mintage	F	VF	XF	Unc	BU
)7 D Satin	—	—	—	—	15.00	—
)7 D Prooflike	—	—	—	—	18.00	—

 # P24 100 AMEROS
.1050 g., 0.9990 Silver 0.9990 oz. ASW, 39 mm.
bv: Female seated **Rev:** Eagle

te	Mintage	F	VF	XF	Unc	BU
)7 D Prooflike	—	—	—	—	35.00	—

X# P26 100 AMEROS
31.1050 g., 0.9990 Silver 0.9990 oz. ASW **Obv:** Pocahontas facing **Obv. Legend:** JAMESTOWN 1607 / 2007 **Rev:** Eagle holding lightning and olive branch, globe below

Date	Mintage	F	VF	XF	Unc	BU
2007 D Satin	—	—	—	—	35.00	—
2007 Proof	—	—	—	—	40.00	—

X# P28 500 AMEROS
15.5520 g., 0.9990 Gold 0.4995 oz. AGW, 27 mm. **Obv:** Female seated **Rev:** Eagle

Date	Mintage	F	VF	XF	Unc	BU
2007 D Satin	—	—	—	—	—	475
2007 D Prooflike	—	—	—	—	—	525

X# P30 1000 AMEROS
31.1050 g., 0.9990 Gold 0.9990 oz. AGW, 34 mm. **Obv:** Female seated **Rev:** Eagle

Date	Mintage	F	VF	XF	Unc	BU
2007 D Satin	—	—	—	—	—	875
2007 D Prooflike	—	—	—	—	—	950

UNITED ARAB EMIRATES

UNITED EMIRATES

STANDARD COINAGE

X# M3 1000 DIRHAMS
39.9400 g., 0.9170 Gold 1.1775 oz. AGW, 40 mm. **Subject:** 25th Anniversary of the UAE - National Day Issue **Obv:** Bust of Shaikh Zayed half right **Rev:** Heraldic eagle **Note:** Similar to 50 Dirhams, KM#21. Prev. KM#29.

Date	Mintage	F	VF	XF	Unc	BU
1996 Proof	4,000	Value: 750				

X# M4 1000 DIRHAMS
39.9400 g., 0.9170 Gold 1.1775 oz. AGW, 40 mm. **Subject:** 30th Anniversary - Reign of Shaikh Zayed **Obv:** Bust of Shaikh Zayed half right **Rev:** Circular design of Arabic lettering **Note:** Similar to 50 Dirhams, KM#22. Prev. KM#30.

Date	Mintage	F	VF	XF	Unc	BU
1996 Proof	4,000	Value: 750				

MEDALLIC COINAGE

X# M5 500 DIRHAMS
20.0000 g., 0.9170 Gold 0.5896 oz. AGW, 28 mm. **Subject:** 1998 Humanitarian Personality - Sheikha Mubarak **Obv:** Bust of Shaikh Zayed half right **Rev:** Toughra

Date	Mintage	F	VF	XF	Unc	BU
ND(1999) Proof	1,000	—	—	—	—	—

X# M6 500 DIRHAMS
20.0000 g., 0.9170 Gold 0.5896 oz. AGW, 28 mm. **Subject:** 35th Anniversary of National Bank of Abn Dhabi (NBAD)

Date	Mintage	F	VF	XF	Unc	BU
ND(2003) Proof	—	—	—	—	—	—

X# M7 1000 DIRHAMS
40.0000 g., 0.9170 Gold 1.1792 oz. AGW, 40 mm. **Subject:** 1998 Humanitarian Personality - Fatima Bint Mubarak **Obv:** Bust of Shaikh Zayed half right **Rev:** Toughra

Date	Mintage	F	VF	XF	Unc	BU
ND(1999) Proof	1,000	—	—	—	—	—

X# M8 1000 DIRHAMS
40.0000 g., 0.9160 Gold 1.1780 oz. AGW, 40 mm. **Subject:** Islamic Personality of the Year - Sheikh Zayed Bin Sultan Al-Nahyan **Obv:** Bust of Shaikh Zayed half right

Date	Mintage	F	VF	XF	Unc	BU
ND(2000) Proof	2,000	—	—	—	—	—

X# M9 1000 DIRHAMS
40.0000 g., 0.9160 Gold 1.1780 oz. AGW, 40 mm. **Subject:** 30th Anniversary of Central Bank of the UAE **Obv:** Bust of Sheikh Zayed bin Sultan Al-Nahyan half right **Rev:** Bust of Sheikh Maktoum bin Rashid Al-Maktoum half right

Date	Mintage	F	VF	XF	Unc	BU
ND(2003) Proof	2,000	—	—	—	—	—

X# M10 1000 DIRHAMS
40.0000 g., 0.9160 Gold 1.1780 oz. AGW, 40 mm. **Subject:** 58th Annual Meetings of the World Bank Group and Int'l Monetary Fund (Dubai 2003) **Obv:** Multicolor dots at center **Rev:** Bust of Shaikh Zayed half right

Date	Mintage	F	VF	XF	Unc	BU
ND(2003) Proof	4,000	—	—	—	—	—

X# M11 1000 DIRHAMS
40.0000 g., 0.9170 Gold 1.1792 oz. AGW, 40 mm. **Subject:** 35th Anniversary of the National Bank of Abn Dhabi (NBAD)

Date	Mintage	F	VF	XF	Unc	BU
ND(2003) Proof	—	—	—	—	—	—

X# M12 1000 DIRHAMS
40.0000 g., 0.9170 Gold 1.1792 oz. AGW, 40 mm. **Subject:** 40th Anniversary of First Oil Export from Abu Dhabi Oil Fields **Obv:** Bust of Sheikh Zayed bin Sultan Al Nahyan half right **Rev:** Logo of Oil derrick

Date	Mintage	F	VF	XF	Unc	BU
ND(2004) Proof	—	—	—	—	—	—

X# M1 5000 DIRHAMS
200.0000 g., 0.9167 Gold 5.8943 oz. AGW, 65 mm. **Subject:** 25th Anniversary of the UAE - National Day Issue **Obv:** Bust of Shaikh Zayed half right **Rev:** Heraldic eagle **Note:** Similar to 50 Dirhams, KM#21. Prev. KM#M1.

Date	Mintage	F	VF	XF	Unc	BU
1996 Proof; Rare	1,000	—	—	—	—	—

X# M2 5000 DIRHAMS
200.0000 g., 0.9167 Gold 5.8943 oz. AGW, 65 mm.
Subject: 30th Anniversary - Reign of Shaikh Zayed
Obv: Bust of Shaikh Zayed half right **Rev:** Circular design of Arabic lettering **Note:** Similar to 50 Dirhams, KM#22. Prev. KM#M2.

Date	Mintage	F	VF	XF	Unc	BU
1996 Proof; Rare	1,000	—	—	—	—	—

UNITED FEDERATION OF KORONIS

FEDERATION

MEDALLIC COINAGE

X# M4 KAO
Gilt And Multicolored Litho Flan, 50 mm.
Obv: Helmeted and supported arms **Obv. Legend:** United Federation of Koronis **Rev:** Similar to obverse

Date	Mintage	VG	F	VF	XF	Unc
2006	50	—	—	—	—	15.00

X# M1 5 KAO
Silvered And Multicolored Litho Flan, 25 mm.
Obv: Helmeted and supported arms **Obv. Legend:** United Federation of Koronis

Date	Mintage	VG	F	VF	XF	Unc
2006	50	—	—	—	—	5.00

X# M2 10 KAO
Silvered And Multicolored Litho Flan, 50 mm. **Obv:** Helmeted and supported arms **Obv. Legend:** United Federation of Koronis

Date	Mintage	VG	F	VF	XF	Unc
2006	50	—	—	—	—	8.00

X# M3 25 KAO
Gilt And Multicolored Litho Flan, 25 mm.
Obv: Helmeted and supported arms **Obv. Legend:** United Federation of Koronis **Rev:** Similar to obverse

Date	Mintage	VG	F	VF	XF	Unc
2006	50	—	—	—	—	12.00

UNITED KINGDOM

KINGDOM

FANTASY EURO PATTERNS 2006 INA ISSUE

X# Pn19 EURO CENT
Copper, 16.8 mm. **Ruler:** Elizabeth II **Issuer:** INA
Obv: Tiara bust right **Obv. Legend:** UNITED KINGDOM
Rev: Scales at right **Edge:** Plain

Date	Mintage	F	VF	XF	Unc	BU
2006 Proof	—	Value: 3.00				

X# Pn20 2 EURO CENT
Copper, 18.5 mm. **Ruler:** Elizabeth II **Issuer:** INA
Obv: Tiara bust right **Obv. Legend:** UNITED KINGDOM
Rev: Scales at right **Edge:** Plain

Date	Mintage	F	VF	XF	Unc	BU
2006 Proof	—	Value: 3.50				

X# Pn21 5 EURO CENT
Copper, 20.7 mm. **Ruler:** Elizabeth II **Issuer:** INA
Obv: Tiara bust right **Obv. Legend:** UNITED KINGDOM
Rev: Scales at right **Edge:** Plain

Date	Mintage	F	VF	XF	Unc	BU
2006 Proof	—	Value: 4.50				

X# Pn22 10 EURO CENT
Goldine, 19.3 mm. **Ruler:** Elizabeth II **Issuer:** INA
Obv: Tiara bust right **Obv. Legend:** UNITED KINGDOM
Rev: Dove superimposed on globe at left **Edge:** Plain

Date	Mintage	F	VF	XF	Unc	BU
2006 Proof	—	Value: 5.50				

X# Pn23 20 EURO CENT
Goldine, 22 mm. **Ruler:** Elizabeth II **Issuer:** INA
Obv: Tiara bust right **Obv. Legend:** UNITED KINGDOM
Rev: Dove superimposed on globe at left **Edge:** Plain

Date	Mintage	F	VF	XF	Unc	BU
2006 Proof	—	Value: 6.50				

X# Pn24 50 EURO CENT
Goldine, 24.3 mm. **Ruler:** Elizabeth II **Issuer:** INA
Obv: Tiara bust right **Obv. Legend:** UNITED KINGDOM
Rev: Dove superimposed on globe at left **Edge:** Plain

Date	Mintage	F	VF	XF	Unc	BU
2006 Proof	—	Value: 7.50				

X# Pn25 EURO
Bi-Metallic Goldine ring, copper-nickel center, 22.8 m
Ruler: Elizabeth II **Issuer:** INA **Obv:** Tiara bust righ
Obv. Legend: UNITED KINGDOM **Rev:** Globe at ri
Edge: Plain

Date	Mintage	F	VF	XF	Unc
2006 Proof	—	Value: 11.50			

X# Pn26 2 EURO
Bi-Metallic Goldine ring, copper-nickel center, 25.7 m
Ruler: Elizabeth II **Issuer:** INA **Obv:** Tiara bust righ
Obv. Legend: UNITED KINGDOM **Rev:** Globe at ri
Edge: Plain

Date	Mintage	F	VF	XF	Unc
2006 Proof	—	Value: 14.00			

X# Pn27 5 EURO
Goldine, 36 mm. **Ruler:** Elizabeth II **Issuer:** INA
Obv: Tiara bust right **Obv. Legend:** UNITED KINGDC
Rev: Stars in border around map of Europe **Edge:** Pl

Date	Mintage	F	VF	XF	Unc
2006 Proof	—	Value: 20.00			

MEDALLIC COINAGE

Ecu Series

X# M20 SILVER ECU
25.0000 g., 0.9600 Silver 0.7716 oz. ASW, 37.9 mm.
Ruler: Elizabeth II **Obv:** Neptune and Europa behind E
Nations globe **Rev:** Ship on Thames River approachi
Tower Bridge **Edge:** Reeded **Note:** Prev. X#20.

Date	Mintage	F	VF	XF	Unc
1993 Proof	—	Value: 35.00			

X# M11 1/10 ECU
Bronze, 18 mm. **Ruler:** Elizabeth II **Obv:** Neptune a
Europa behind Ecu Nations globe **Obv. Legend:** • EUROPE ★ EUROPA • UNITED KINGDOM
Rev: Mayflower ship **Edge:** Plain

Date	Mintage	F	VF	XF	Unc
1992	—	—	—	—	—

X# M12 1/4 ECU

Bronze, 26 mm. **Ruler:** Elizabeth II **Obv:** Neptune and Europa behind Ecu Nations globe **Obv. Legend:** • EUROPE ★ EUROPA • UNITED KINGDOM **Rev:** British Parliament Building **Edge:** Plain

Date	Mintage	F	VF	XF	Unc	BU
1992	—	—	—	—	—	—

X# M13 1/2 ECU

Copper-Nickel, 19.5 mm. **Ruler:** Elizabeth II **Obv:** Neptune and Europa behind Ecu Nations globe **Obv. Legend:** • EUROPE ★ EUROPA • UNITED KINGDOM **Rev:** British lion walking left **Edge:** Plain

Date	Mintage	F	VF	XF	Unc	BU
1992	—	—	—	—	—	—

X# M14 ECU

Copper-Nickel, 23 mm. **Ruler:** Elizabeth II **Obv:** Neptune and Europa behind Ecu Nations globe **Obv. Legend:** • EUROPE ★ EUROPA • UNITED KINGDOM **Rev:** Bust of helmeted Britannia facing 3/4 right **Edge:** Plain

Date	Mintage	F	VF	XF	Unc	BU
1992	—	—	—	—	—	—

X# M21 ECU

4.2800 g., 0.7500 Gold 0.1032 oz. AGW, 19.1 mm. **Ruler:** Elizabeth II **Obv:** Neptune and Europa behind Ecu Nations globe **Rev:** Ship on Thames River approaching Tower Bridg **Edge:** Reeded **Note:** Prev. X#21.

Date	Mintage	F	VF	XF	Unc	BU
1993 Proof	2,500	Value: 125				

X# M22 ECU

5.6400 g., 0.7500 Gold 0.1360 oz. AGW, 22.3 mm. **Ruler:** Elizabeth II **Obv:** Neptune and Europa behind Ecu Nations globe **Rev:** Ship on Thames River approaching Tower Bridge **Edge:** Reeded **Note:** Prev. X#22.

Date	Mintage	F	VF	XF	Unc	BU
1993 Proof	—	Value: 145				

X# M15 2 ECU

Copper-Nickel, 29.5 mm. **Ruler:** Elizabeth II **Obv:** Neptune and Europa behind Ecu Nations globe **Obv. Legend:** • EUROPE ★ EUROPA • UNITED KINGDOM **Rev:** Britannia standing right holding trident and shield, sailing ship in background **Edge:** Plain

Date	Mintage	F	VF	XF	Unc	BU
1992	—	—	—	—	—	—

X# M16 5 ECU

Copper-Nickel, 38.1 mm. **Ruler:** Elizabeth II **Obv:** Neptune and Europa behind Ecu Nations globe **Obv. Legend:** • EUROPE ★ EUROPA • UNITED KINGDOM **Rev:** Three Graces standing **Edge:** Plain

Date	Mintage	F	VF	XF	Unc	BU
1992	—	—	—	—	—	—

X# M17 10 ECU

Gilt Copper-Nickel, 31.1 mm. **Ruler:** Elizabeth II **Obv:** Neptune and Europa behind Ecu Nations globe **Obv. Legend:** • EUROPE ★ EUROPA • UNITED KINGDOM **Rev:** St. George horseback slaying dragon **Edge:** Plain

Date	Mintage	F	VF	XF	Unc	BU
1992	—	—	—	—	—	—

X# M18 25 ECU

Bi-Metallic Copper-Nickel and Bronze, 38.1 mm. **Ruler:** Elizabeth II **Obv:** Neptune and Europa behind Ecu Nations globe **Obv. Legend:** • EUROPE ★ EUROPA • UNITED KINGDOM **Rev:** Three Graces standing **Edge:** Reeded

Date	Mintage	F	VF	XF	Unc	BU
1992	—	—	—	—	—	—

X# M18a 25 ECU

23.0000 g., 0.9250 Silver 0.6840 oz. ASW, 38.1 mm. **Ruler:** Elizabeth II **Obv:** Neptune and Europa behind Ecu Nations globe **Obv. Legend:** • EUROPE ★ EUROPA • UNITED KINGDOM **Rev:** Three Graces standing **Edge:** Reeded

Date	Mintage	F	VF	XF	Unc	BU
1992 Proof	25,000	—	—	—	—	—

X# M19 200 ECU

0.7500 Gold, 22 mm. **Ruler:** Elizabeth II **Obv:** Neptune and Europa behind Ecu Nations globe **Obv. Legend:** • EUROPE ★ EUROPA • UNITED KINGDOM **Rev:** Bust of helmeted Britannia facing 3/4 right **Edge:** Reeded

Date	Mintage	F	VF	XF	Unc	BU
1992	—	—	—	—	—	—

FANTASY EURO PATTERNS

2002 INA Issue

X# Pn1 EURO CENT

Copper Plated Steel, 16.8 mm. **Ruler:** Elizabeth II **Issuer:** INA **Obv:** Tiara bust right **Obv. Legend:** UNITED KINGDOM **Rev:** Scales at right **Edge:** Plain

Date	Mintage	F	VF	XF	Unc	BU
2002	20,000	—	—	—	—	2.50
2002 Proof	20,000	Value: 3.00				

X# Pn1a EURO CENT

Silver, 16.8 mm. **Ruler:** Elizabeth II **Issuer:** INA **Obv:** Tiara bust right **Obv. Legend:** UNITED KINGDOM **Rev:** Scales at right **Edge:** Plain

Date	Mintage	F	VF	XF	Unc	BU
2002 Proof	2,500	Value: 6.00				

X# Pn2 2 EURO CENT

Copper Plated Steel, 18.5 mm. **Ruler:** Elizabeth II **Issuer:** INA **Obv:** Tiara bust right **Obv. Legend:** UNITED KINGDOM **Rev:** Scale at right **Edge:** Plain

Date	Mintage	F	VF	XF	Unc	BU
2002	20,000	—	—	—	—	3.00
2002 Proof	20,000	Value: 3.50				

X# Pn2a 2 EURO CENT

Silver, 18.5 mm. **Ruler:** Elizabeth II **Issuer:** INA **Obv:** Tiara bust right **Obv. Legend:** UNITED KINGDOM **Rev:** Scale at right **Edge:** Plain

Date	Mintage	F	VF	XF	Unc	BU
2002 Proof	2,500	Value: 7.00				

X# Pn3 5 EURO CENT

Copper Plated Steel, 20.7 mm. **Ruler:** Elizabeth II **Issuer:** INA **Obv:** Tiara bust right **Obv. Legend:** UNITED KINGDOM **Rev:** Scale at right **Edge:** Plain

Date	Mintage	F	VF	XF	Unc	BU
2002	20,000	—	—	—	—	3.50
2002 Proof	20,000	Value: 4.50				

X# Pn3a 5 EURO CENT

Silver, 20.7 mm. **Ruler:** Elizabeth II **Issuer:** INA **Obv:** Tiara bust right **Obv. Legend:** UNITED KINGDOM **Rev:** Scale at right **Edge:** Plain

Date	Mintage	F	VF	XF	Unc	BU
2002 Proof	2,500	Value: 8.50				

X# Pn4 10 EURO CENT

Goldine, 19.3 mm. **Ruler:** Elizabeth II **Issuer:** INA **Obv:** Tiara bust right **Obv. Legend:** UNITED KINGDOM **Rev:** Dove in flight **Edge:** Plain

Date	Mintage	F	VF	XF	Unc	BU
2002	20,000	—	—	—	—	4.00

X# Pn4a 10 EURO CENT
Silver, 19.3 mm. **Ruler:** Elizabeth II **Issuer:** INA **Obv:** Tiara bust right **Obv. Legend:** UNITED KINGDOM **Rev:** Dove in flight **Edge:** Plain

Date	Mintage	F	VF	XF	Unc	BU
2002 Proof	2,500	Value: 10.00				

X# Pn5 20 EURO CENT
Goldine, 22 mm. **Ruler:** Elizabeth II **Issuer:** INA **Obv:** Tiara bust right **Obv. Legend:** UNITED KINGDOM **Rev:** Dove in flight **Edge:** Plain

Date	Mintage	F	VF	XF	Unc	BU
2002	20,000	—	—	—	—	5.00
2002 Proof	20,000	Value: 6.50				

X# Pn5a 20 EURO CENT
Silver, 22 mm. **Ruler:** Elizabeth II **Issuer:** INA **Obv:** Tiara bust right **Obv. Legend:** UNITED KINGDOM **Rev:** Dove in flight **Edge:** Plain

Date	Mintage	F	VF	XF	Unc	BU
2002 Proof	2,500	Value: 12.50				

X# Pn6 50 EURO CENT
Goldine, 24.3 mm. **Ruler:** Elizabeth II **Issuer:** INA **Obv:** Tiara bust right **Obv. Legend:** UNITED KINGDOM **Rev:** Dove in flight **Edge:** Plain

Date	Mintage	F	VF	XF	Unc	BU
2002	20,000	—	—	—	—	6.00
2002 Proof	20,000	Value: 7.50				

X# Pn6a 50 EURO CENT
Silver, 24.3 mm. **Ruler:** Elizabeth II **Issuer:** INA **Obv:** Tiara bust right **Obv. Legend:** UNITED KINGDOM **Rev:** Dove in flight **Edge:** Plain

Date	Mintage	F	VF	XF	Unc	BU
2002 Proof	2,500	Value: 15.00				

X# Pn7 EURO
Bi-Metallic, 22.8 mm. **Ruler:** Elizabeth II **Issuer:** INA **Obv:** Tiara bust right **Obv. Legend:** UNITED KINGDOM **Rev:** Medieval sailing ship **Edge:** Plain

Date	Mintage	F	VF	XF	Unc	BU
2002	20,000	—	—	—	—	8.00
2002 Proof	20,000	Value: 11.50				

X# Pn7a EURO
Bi-Metallic Goldine center in Silver ring, 22.8 mm. **Ruler:** Elizabeth II **Issuer:** INA **Obv:** Tiara bust right **Obv. Legend:** UNITED KINGDOM **Rev:** Medieval sailing ship **Edge:** Plain

Date	Mintage	F	VF	XF	Unc	BU
2002 Proof	2,500	Value: 22.50				

X# Pn8 2 EURO
Bi-Metallic, 25.7 mm. **Ruler:** Elizabeth II **Issuer:** INA **Obv:** Tiara bust right **Obv. Legend:** UNITED KINGDOM **Rev:** Medieval sailing ship **Edge:** Plain

Date	Mintage	F	VF	XF	Unc	BU
2002	20,000	—	—	—	—	10.00
2002 Proof	20,000	Value: 14.00				

X# Pn8a 2 EURO
Bi-Metallic Goldine center in Silver ring, 25.7 mm. **Ruler:** Elizabeth II **Issuer:** INA **Obv:** Tiara bust right **Obv. Legend:** UNITED KINGDOM **Rev:** Medieval sailing ship **Edge:** Plain

Date	Mintage	F	VF	XF	Unc	BU
2002 Proof	2,500	Value: 28.50				

X# Pn9 5 EURO
Goldine, 36 mm. **Ruler:** Elizabeth II **Issuer:** INA **Obv:** Tiara bust right **Obv. Legend:** UNITED KINGDOM **Rev:** Britannia standing, trident, globe and shield, sailing ship at right **Edge:** Plain

Date	Mintage	F	VF	XF	Unc	BU
2002 Proof	20,000	Value: 20.00				

X# Pn9a 5 EURO
Silver, 36 mm. **Ruler:** Elizabeth II **Issuer:** INA **Obv:** Tiara bust right **Obv. Legend:** UNITED KINGDOM **Rev:** Britannia standing, trident, globe and shield, sailing ship at right **Edge:** Plain

Date	Mintage	F	VF	XF	Unc	BU
2002 Proof	2,500	Value: 40.00				

2003 INA Issue

X# Pn10 EURO CENT
Copper Plated Steel, 16.8 mm. **Ruler:** Elizabeth II **Issuer:** INA **Obv:** Elizabeth II on throne facing **Obv. Legend:** UNITED KINGDOM **Rev:** Scale at right **Edge:** Plain

Date	Mintage	F	VF	XF	Unc	BU
2003	24,000	—	—	—	—	2.00
2003 Proof	16,000	Value: 2.50				

X# Pn10a EURO CENT
Silver, 16.8 mm. **Ruler:** Elizabeth II **Issuer:** INA **Obv:** Elizabeth II on throne facing **Obv. Legend:** UNITED KINGDOM **Rev:** Scale at right **Edge:** Plain

Date	Mintage	F	VF	XF	Unc	BU
2003 Proof	1,250	Value: 6.00				

X# Pn11 2 EURO CENT
Copper Plated Steel, 18.5 mm. **Ruler:** Elizabeth II **Issuer:** INA **Obv:** Elizabeth II on throne facing **Obv. Legend:** UNITED KINGDOM **Rev:** Scale at right **Edge:** Plain

Date	Mintage	F	VF	XF	Unc	BU
2003	24,000	—	—	—	—	2.50
2003 Proof	16,000	Value: 3.00				

X# Pn11a 2 EURO CENT
Silver, 18.5 mm. **Ruler:** Elizabeth II **Issuer:** INA **Obv:** Elizabeth II on throne facing **Obv. Legend:** UNITED KINGDOM **Rev:** Scale at right **Edge:** Plain

Date	Mintage	F	VF	XF	Unc	BU
2003 Proof	1,250	Value: 7.00				

X# Pn12 5 EURO CENT
Copper Plated Steel, 20.7 mm. **Ruler:** Elizabeth II **Issuer:** INA **Obv:** Elizabeth II on throne facing **Obv. Legend:** UNITED KINGDOM **Rev:** Scale at right **Edge:** Plain

Date	Mintage	F	VF	XF	Unc	BU
2003	24,000	—	—	—	—	3.00
2003 Proof	16,000	Value: 4.50				

X# Pn12a 5 EURO CENT
Silver, 20.7 mm. **Ruler:** Elizabeth II **Issuer:** INA **Obv:** Elizabeth II on throne facing **Obv. Legend:** UNITED KINGDOM **Rev:** Scale at right **Edge:** Plain

Date	Mintage	F	VF	XF	Unc	BU
2003 Proof	1,250	Value: 8.50				

X# Pn13 10 EURO CENT
Goldine, 19.3 mm. **Ruler:** Elizabeth II **Issuer:** INA **Obv:** Elizabeth II horseback left **Obv. Legend:** UNITED KINGDOM **Rev:** Dove, value in wreath of hands **Edge:** Plain

Date	Mintage	F	VF	XF	Unc	BU
2003	24,000	—	—	—	—	3.50
2003 Proof	16,000	Value: 4.00				

X# Pn13a 10 EURO CENT
Silver, 19.3 mm. **Ruler:** Elizabeth II **Issuer:** INA **Obv:** Elizabeth II horseback left **Obv. Legend:** UNITED KINGDOM **Rev:** Dove, value in wreath of hands **Edge:** Plain

Date	Mintage	F	VF	XF	Unc	BU
2003 Proof	1,250	Value: 10.00				

X# Pn14 20 EURO CENT
Goldine, 22 mm. **Ruler:** Elizabeth II **Issuer:** INA **Obv:** Elizabeth II horseback left **Obv. Legend:** UNITED KINGDOM **Rev:** Dove, value in wreath of hands **Edge:** Plain

Date	Mintage	F	VF	XF	Unc	BU
2003	24,000	—	—	—	—	4.0
2003 Proof	16,000	Value: 5.00				

X# Pn14a 20 EURO CENT
Silver, 22 mm. **Ruler:** Elizabeth II **Issuer:** INA **Obv:** Elizabeth II horseback left **Obv. Legend:** UNITED KINGDOM **Rev:** Dove, value in wreath of hands **Edge:** Plain

Date	Mintage	F	VF	XF	Unc	BU
2003 Proof	1,250	Value: 12.50				

X# Pn15 50 EURO CENT
Goldine, 24.3 mm. **Ruler:** Elizabeth II **Issuer:** INA **Obv:** Elizabeth II horseback left **Obv. Legend:** UNITED KINGDOM **Rev:** Dove, value in wreath of hands **Edge:** Plain

Date	Mintage	F	VF	XF	Unc	BU
2003	24,000	—	—	—	—	5.0
2003 Proof	16,000	Value: 6.00				

X# Pn15a 50 EURO CENT
Silver, 24.3 mm. **Ruler:** Elizabeth II **Issuer:** INA **Obv:** Elizabeth II horseback left **Obv. Legend:** UNITED KINGDOM **Rev:** Dove, value in wreath of hands **Edge:** Plain

Date	Mintage	F	VF	XF	Unc	BU
2003 Proof	1,250	Value: 15.00				

X# Pn16 EURO
Bi-Metallic Copper-Nickel center in Goldine ring, 22.8 mm. **Ruler:** Elizabeth II **Issuer:** INA **Obv:** Elizabeth II on throne facing **Obv. Legend:** UNITED KINGDOM **Rev:** Sailing ship "Golden Hind" at right **Edge:** Plain

Date	Mintage	F	VF	XF	Unc	BU
2003	20,000	—	—	—	—	6.5
2003 Proof	20,000	Value: 8.00				

X# Pn16a EURO
Bi-Metallic Silver center in Goldine ring, 22.8 mm. **Ruler:** Elizabeth II **Issuer:** INA **Obv:** Elizabeth II on throne facing **Obv. Legend:** UNITED KINGDOM **Rev:** Sailing ship "Golden Hind" at right **Edge:** Plain

Date	Mintage	F	VF	XF	Unc	BU
2003 Proof	1,250	Value: 22.50				

X# Pn17 2 EURO
Bi-Metallic Goldine center in Copper-Nickel ring, 25.7 mm. **Ruler:** Elizabeth II **Issuer:** INA **Obv:** Elizabeth II on throne facing **Obv. Legend:** UNITED KINGDOM **Rev:** Sailing ship "Golden Hind" at right **Edge:** Plain

Date	Mintage	F	VF	XF	Unc	BU
2003	24,000	—	—	—	—	8.5
2003 Proof	16,000	Value: 10.00				

X# Pn17a 2 EURO
Bi-Metallic Goldine center in Silver ring, 25.7 mm. **Ruler:** Elizabeth II **Issuer:** INA **Obv:** Elizabeth II on throne facing **Obv. Legend:** UNITED KINGDOM **Rev:** Sailing ship "Golden Hind" at right **Edge:** Plain

Date	Mintage	F	VF	XF	Unc	BU
2003 Proof	1,250	Value: 28.50				

X# Pn18 5 EURO
Goldine Gilt, 36 mm. **Ruler:** Elizabeth II **Issuer:** INA **Obv:** Elizabeth II on throne facing **Obv. Legend:** UNITED KINGDOM **Rev:** Three Graces standing representing the Unification of English and Scottish thrones in 1603, sailing ship at right **Edge:** Plain

Date	Mintage	F	VF	XF	Unc	BU
2003 Proof	16,000	Value: 12.50				

X# Pn18a 5 EURO
Silver, 36 mm. **Ruler:** Elizabeth II **Issuer:** INA
Obv: Elizabeth II on throne facing **Obv. Legend:** UNITED KINGDOM **Rev:** Three Graces standing representing the Unification of English and Scottish thrones in 1603, sailing ship at right **Edge:** Plain

Date	Mintage	F	VF	XF	Unc	BU
2003 Proof	1,250	Value: 40.00				

PIEFORTS

X#	Date	Mintage	Identification	Mkt Val
P91	1992	5,000	25 Ecu. 0.9250 Silver. 46.0000 g. X#M18a.	—
P101	2002	5,000	5 Euro. 0.9250 Silver. 34.5000 g. X#Pn9a.	60.00
P102	2003	1,250	5 Euro. 0.9250 Silver. 34.5000 g. X#Pn18a.	65.00

MINT SETS

X#	Date	Mintage	Identification	Issue Price	Mkt Val
XMS1	2002 (8)	20,000	X#Pn1-Pn8	—	40.00
XMS2	2003 (8)	24,000	X#Pn10-Pn17	—	35.00

PROOF SETS

X#	Date	Mintage	Identification	Issue Price	Mkt Val
XPS1	2002 (9)	20,000	X#Pn1-Pn9	—	75.00
XPS2	2002 (9)	2,500	X#Pn1a-Pn9a	—	150
XPS3	2003 (9)	16,000	X#Pn10-Pn18	—	50.00
XPS4	2003 (9)	1,250	X#Pn10a-Pn18a	—	150

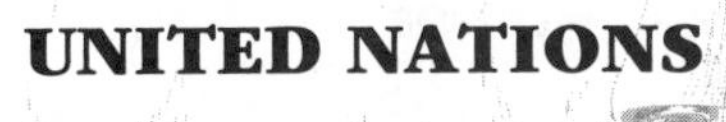

MULTI-NATIONAL BODY

ESSAIS

X# 1 DUCATON
Silver, 37.40 mm. **Obv:** Five flags **Obv. Legend:** MONETARY UNITY / WORLD PEACE **Rev:** Five figures **Rev. Legend:** FREEDOM - RELIGION • FEAR • SPEECH • WANT • **Edge:** Plain

Date	Mintage	F	VF	XF	Unc	BU
1946	1,000	—	—	50.00	100	—

X# 1a DUCATON
Bronze, 37.40 mm. **Obv:** Five flags **Obv. Legend:** MONETARY UNITY / WORLD PEACE **Rev:** Five figures **Rev. Legend:** FREEDOM - RELIGION • FEAR • SPEECH • WANT • **Edge:** Plain **Note:** Prev. X#2.

Date	Mintage	F	VF	XF	Unc	BU
1946	1,000	—	—	25.00	35.00	—

X# 1b DUCATON
31.3500 g., Gold, 37.40 mm. **Obv:** Five flags **Obv. Legend:** MONETARY UNITY / WORLD PEACE **Rev:** Five figures **Rev. Legend:** FREEDOM - RELIGION • FEAR • SPEECH • WANT • **Edge:** Plain **Note:** Prev. X#3.

Date	Mintage	F	VF	XF	Unc	BU
1946	313	—	—	700	950	—

X# 1c DUCATON
Gilt Bronze, 37.40 mm. **Obv:** Five flags **Obv. Legend:** MONETARY UNITY / WORLD PEACE **Rev:** Five figures **Rev. Legend:** FREEDOM - RELIGION • FEAR • SPEECH • WANT • **Edge:** Plain

Date	Mintage	F	VF	XF	Unc	BU
1946	—	—	—	35.00	50.00	—

PIEFORTS

X#	Date	Mintage	Identification	Mkt Val
P1	1946	—	Ducaton. Gold. X#1b. 4.00 oz.	—
P2	1946	—	Ducaton. Gold. X#1b. 6.00 oz.	—

UNITED STATES

REPUBLIC

MEDALLIC COINAGE

X# 195 5 CENTS
5.2800 g., 0.9250 Silver 0.1570 oz. ASW, 21.4 mm. **Issuer:** International Currency Bureau **Obv:** Bust of Thomas Jefferson left **Obv. Legend:** LIBERTY - IN GOD WE TRUST **Rev:** Monticello **Rev. Inscription:** E PLURIBUS UNUM

Date	Mintage	F	VF	XF	Unc	BU
1938 Proof	—	Value: 100				

X# 195a 5 CENTS
Nickel, 21.4 mm. **Issuer:** International Currency Bureau **Obv:** Bust of Thomas Jefferson left **Obv. Legend:** LIBERTY - IN GOD WE TRUST **Rev:** Monticello **Rev. Inscription:** E PLURIBUS UNUM

Date	Mintage	F	VF	XF	Unc	BU
1938	70	—	—	—	—	120
1938 Proof	70	Value: 150				

X# M40 DIME
3.1400 g., 0.9990 Silver 0.1008 oz. ASW, 17.7 mm. **Obv:** Head of President Reagan left **Obv. Legend:** LIBERTY **Rev:** Torch between branches **Rev. Legend:** UNITED STATES OF AMERICA **Rev. Inscription:** EPLU - RIB - US - U - NUM **Edge:** Reeded

Date	Mintage	F	VF	XF	Unc	BU
2006 Proof	47,500	Value: 10.00				

X# M40a DIME
3.1400 g., 0.9990 Silver Gilt 0.1008 oz. ASW, 17.7 mm. **Obv:** Head of President Reagan left **Obv. Legend:** LIBERTY **Rev:** Torch between branches **Rev. Legend:** UNITED STATES OF AMERICA **Rev. Inscription:** EPLU - RIB - US - U - NUM **Edge:** Reeded

Date	Mintage	F	VF	XF	Unc	BU
2006 Proof	—	Value: 15.00				

SILVER BULLION TRADE UNIT

Argentum Universal Issues

Source unknown.

X# 1 1/5 TALENT
Silver

Date	Mintage	F	VF	XF	Unc	BU
1896 Rare	—	—	—	—	—	—

X# 2 TALENT
Silver

Date	Mintage	F	VF	XF	Unc	BU
1896	—	—	—	—	—	—

Note: Reported, not confirmed

Wade-Ventures Issues

X# 4 MUNDINERO
32.5560 g., 0.9990 Silver 1.0456 oz. ASW, 38.60 mm. **Obv:** Shield in sprays **Rev:** Eliptical globe in circular frame **Note:** Issued by Wade-Ventures.

Date	Mintage	F	VF	XF	Unc	BU
1973	—	—	—	15.00	20.00	35.00

X# 5 2 MUNDINEROS
62.2683 g., 0.9990 Silver 1.9999 oz. ASW, 38.6 mm. **Issuer:** Wade-Ventures **Obv:** Shield in sprays **Rev:** Eliptical globe in circular frame **Edge:** Reeded

Date	Mintage	F	VF	XF	Unc	BU
1973	—	—	—	30.00	45.00	65.00

X# 6 3 MUNDINEROS
93.4024 g., 0.9990 Silver 2.9998 oz. ASW, 38.6 mm.
Issuer: Wade-Ventures **Obv:** Shield in sprays
Rev: Eliptical globe in circular frame **Edge:** Reeded

Date	Mintage	F	VF	XF	Unc	BU
1973	—	—	—	40.00	55.00	85.00

MILLED COINAGE

X# 295 20 DOLLARS
7.2400 g., 0.5833 Gold 0.1358 oz. AGW, 32 mm.
Obv: Eagle arms **Obv. Legend:** AMERICAN - DOUBLE EAGLE **Rev:** Eagle alighting **Rev. Legend:** LIBERTY
Edge: Reeded

Date	Mintage	F	VF	XF	Unc	BU
1985 Proof	—	Value: 100				

MEDALLIC COINAGE

Square Deal Productions Issues

X# 301 QUARTER
8.5600 g., Copper-Nickel-Zinc **Obv:** Stylized bust of George Washington left **Obv. Designer:** Andor Orand **Rev:** Eagle with wings spread facing left **Edge:** Reeded **Shape:** Square 22.40 x 22.40 mm

Date	Mintage	F	VF	XF	Unc	BU
1984 Proof	330	Value: 50.00				

X# 301a QUARTER
7.7758 g., 0.9990 Silver 0.2497 oz. ASW **Obv:** Stylized bust of George Washington left **Obv. Designer:** Andor Orand **Rev:** Eagle with wings spread facing left
Edge: Reeded **Shape:** Square 22.40 x 22.40 mm
Note: This was the first successful attempt of creating a square coin with reeded edge intended for the artist's community.

Date	Mintage	F	VF	XF	Unc	BU
1984 Proof	1,310	Value: 200				

X# 301b QUARTER
15.5515 g., 0.9990 Silver 0.4995 oz. ASW
Obv: Stylized bust of George Washington left **Obv. Designer:** Andor Orand **Rev:** Eagle with wings spread facing left **Edge:** Reeded **Shape:** Square 26 x 26 mm

Date	Mintage	F	VF	XF	Unc	BU
1984 Proof	602	Value: 300				

X# 301c QUARTER
Bronze **Obv:** Stylized bust of George Washington left **Obv. Designer:** Andor Orand **Rev:** Eagle with wings spread facing left **Edge:** Reeded **Shape:** Square 22.40 x 22.40 mm

Date	Mintage	F	VF	XF	Unc	BU
1984 Proof	15	—	—	—	—	—

X# 301d QUARTER
10.3676 g., 0.9167 Gold 0.3055 oz. AGW **Obv:** Disfigured bust of George Washington left **Obv. Designer:** Andor Orand **Rev:** Eagle with wings spread facing left
Edge: Reeded **Shape:** Square 22.40 x 22.40 mm

Date	Mintage	F	VF	XF	Unc	BU
1984 Proof	12	—	—	—	—	—

X# 301e QUARTER
Brass **Obv:** Stylized bust of George Washington left **Obv. Designer:** Andor Orand **Rev:** Eagle with wings spread facing left **Edge:** Reeded **Shape:** Square 22.50 x 22.50 mm

Date	Mintage	F	VF	XF	Unc	BU
1984 Proof	—	—	—	—	—	—

GALLERY MINT MUSEUM

Federal Coinage

X# 501 HALF CENT
6.7400 g., Copper, 22 mm.

Date	Mintage	F	VF	XF	Unc	BU
1793	4,118	—	—	—	—	8.00
1793 Proof	1,000	Value: 17.00				

X# 510 HALF CENT
Copper

Date	Mintage	F	VF	XF	Unc	BU
1794	—	—	—	—	—	—
1794 Proof	940	—	—	—	—	—

X# 525 HALF CENT
Copper **Subject:** Liberty Head with Pole

Date	Mintage	F	VF	XF	Unc	BU
1796	—	—	—	—	—	—

X# 526 HALF CENT
Copper **Subject:** Liberty Head without Pole

Date	Mintage	F	VF	XF	Unc	BU
1796	—	—	—	—	—	—

X# 503 CENT
13.4800 g., Copper, 29 mm. **Note:** Liberty Cap, Type I. Large Head.

Date	Mintage	F	VF	XF	Unc	BU
1793	5,169	—	—	—	—	8.00
1793 Proof	1,200	Value: 17.00				

X# 502 CENT
Copper **Note:** Wreath reverse.

Date	Mintage	F	VF	XF	Unc	BU
1793	6,000	—	—	—	—	8.00
1793 Proof	500	Value: 17.00				

X# 504 CENT
Copper **Note:** Liberty Cap, Type II. Small head.

Date	Mintage	F	VF	XF	Unc	BU
1793	4,687	—	—	—	—	12.00

X# 511 CENT
Copper

Date	Mintage	F	VF	XF	Unc	BU
1794	—	—	—	—	—	—
1794 Proof	940	—	—	—	—	—

X# 527 CENT
Copper **Subject:** Liberty Cap

Date	Mintage	F	VF	XF	Unc	BU
1796	—	—	—	—	—	—

X# 528 CENT
Copper **Subject:** Draped Bust

Date	Mintage	F	VF	XF	Unc	BU
1796	—	—	—	—	—	—

X# 545 CENT
Copper

Date	Mintage	F	VF	XF	Unc	BU
1799	—	—	—	—	—	—

X# M5 CENT
Copper **Note:** Struck for Philadelphia ANA Convention first steam press restoration

Date	Mintage	F	VF	XF	Unc	BU
1836	—	—	—	—	—	—
1836	—	—	—	—	—	—

X# 512 HALF DIME
Silver

Date	Mintage	F	VF	XF	Unc	BU
1794	—	—	—	—	—	—
1794 Proof	940	—	—	—	—	—

X# 529 HALF DIME
Silver

Date	Mintage	F	VF	XF	Unc	BU
1796	—	—	—	—	—	—

X# 530 DIME
Silver

Date	Mintage	F	VF	XF	Unc	BU
1796	—	—	—	—	—	—

X# 531 QUARTER
Silver

Date	Mintage	F	VF	XF	Unc	BU
1796	—	—	—	—	—	—

X# 513 HALF DOLLAR
Silver

Date	Mintage	F	VF	XF	Unc	BU
1794	—	—	—	—	—	—
1794 Proof	490	—	—	—	—	—

X# 532 HALF DOLLAR
Silver **Subject:** 15 Star obverse

Date	Mintage	F	VF	XF	Unc	BU
1796	—	—	—	—	—	—

X# 533 HALF DOLLAR
Silver **Subject:** 16 Star obverse

Date	Mintage	F	VF	XF	Unc	BU
1796	—	—	—	—	—	—

X# 514 DOLLAR
Silver

Date	Mintage	F	VF	XF	Unc	BU
1794	—	—	—	—	—	—
1794 Proof	490	—	—	—	—	—

X# 534 DOLLAR
Silver

Date	Mintage	F	VF	XF	Unc	BU
1796	—	—	—	—	—	—

X# 515 DOLLAR
31.1000 g., 0.9990 Silver 0.9988 oz. ASW
Subject: 200th Anniversary of the Dollar Coinage

Date	Mintage	F	VF	XF	Unc	BU
17/996	1,758	—	—	—	—	50.00

X# 550 DOLLAR
Silver

Date	Mintage	F	VF	XF	Unc	BU
1804	—	—	—	—	—	—
1804 Proof	—	—	—	—	—	—

535 $2.50 (Quarter Eagle)

old **Note:** No stars on obverse.

te	Mintage	F	VF	XF	Unc	BU
96	—	—	—	—	—	—

536 $2.50 (Quarter Eagle)

old **Note:** Stars on obverse.

te	Mintage	F	VF	XF	Unc	BU
96	—	—	—	—	—	—

520 $5 (Half Eagle)

7500 g., 0.9167 Gold 0.2579 oz. AGW

te	Mintage	F	VF	XF	Unc	BU
95	564	—	—	—	—	175
95 Proof	200	Value: 215				

537 $5 (Half Eagle)

old

te	Mintage	F	VF	XF	Unc	BU
96	—	—	—	—	—	—

538 $10 (Eagle)

old

te	Mintage	F	VF	XF	Unc	BU
96	—	—	—	—	—	—

580 CONCEPT

oldine **Obv:** Liberty Head **Rev:** Eagle

te	Mintage	F	VF	XF	Unc	BU
95	1,371	—	—	—	—	7.50

581 CONCEPT

rass **Obv:** Statue of Liberty **Rev:** Eagle and sunrise

te	Mintage	F	VF	XF	Unc	BU
00	2,500	—	—	—	—	7.50

582 CONCEPT

rass **Obv:** Liberty head **Rev:** Eagle

ate	Mintage	F	VF	XF	Unc	BU
00	2,500	—	—	—	—	25.00

Federal Coinage Patterns

Pn5 CENT

opper **Subject:** Birch Cent

ate	Mintage	F	VF	XF	Unc	BU
792	—	—	—	—	—	—

Pn6 CENT

opper Silver center

ate	Mintage	F	VF	XF	Unc	BU
792	—	—	—	—	—	—

Pn7 HALF DISME

ilver

ate	Mintage	F	VF	XF	Unc	BU
792	—	—	—	—	—	—

Pn7a HALF DISME

opper

ate	Mintage	F	VF	XF	Unc	BU
792	—	—	—	—	—	—

Pn8 DISME

ilver

ate	Mintage	F	VF	XF	Unc	BU
792	—	—	—	—	—	—

Pn8a DISME

opper

ate	Mintage	F	VF	XF	Unc	BU
792	—	—	—	—	—	—

Pn9 QUARTER

ilver

ate	Mintage	F	VF	XF	Unc	BU
792	—	—	—	—	—	—

Pn9a QUARTER

ewter

ate	Mintage	F	VF	XF	Unc	BU
792	—	—	—	—	—	—

FANTASY COINAGE

Shire Post Mint Issues

X# 401 DOLLAR

31.3400 g., 0.9990 Silver 1.0066 oz. ASW, 38.29 mm. **Obv. Inscription:** YOCUM / DOLLAR **Rev. Inscription:** $ / DOLLAR / $ **Edge:** Plain

Date	Mintage	F	VF	XF	Unc	BU
ND(2006)	—	—	—	—	50.00	—

X# 402 DOLLAR

, 31.51 mm. **Obv:** Owl facing perched on branch, 1839 below **Obv. Legend:** JACOB - SPRINKLE **Rev:** Stylized 6-pointed design **Edge:** Plain

Date	Mintage	F	VF	XF	Unc	BU
ND(2006)	—	—	—	—	—	50.00

SILVER BULLION TRADE UNIT

X# 123 100 DOLLARS (20 OUNCE)

62.2000 g., 0.9990 Silver 1.9977 oz. ASW, 48 mm. **Issuer:** Crabtree Mint **Obv:** Scale, 13 grain stalk at left and right, "APM" monogram below **Obv. Legend:** TWO TROY OUNCES **Rev. Inscription:** CRAB (tree) REE / MINT / PARADISE, CALIF. **Edge:** Reeded **Note:** Medal alignment.

Date	Mintage	F	VF	XF	Unc	BU
ND(1980s) Proof	—	Value: 40.00				

X# 124 1/2 OUNCE

15.5500 g., 0.9990 Silver 0.4994 oz. ASW, 31.5 mm. **Obv:** Scale, 7 grain stalk at left and right **Obv. Legend:** ONE HALF TROY OUNCE **Rev:** Elk head in front of clock face **Rev. Legend:** B • P • - • O • E • **Edge:** Reeded **Note:** Medal alignment.

Date	Mintage	F	VF	XF	Unc	BU
ND(1980s) Proof	—	Value: 8.00				

X# 125 1/2 OUNCE

15.5500 g., 0.9990 Silver 0.4994 oz. ASW, 33 mm. **Obv:** Eagle left alighting **Obv. Legend:** ★ 1/2 TROY OUNCE ★ **Rev:** Liberty walking facing **Rev. Legend:** LIBERTY **Edge:** Reeded **Note:** Coin alignment.

Date	Mintage	F	VF	XF	Unc	BU
1984 Proof	—	Value: 8.00				

X# 101 OUNCE

31.1000 g., 0.9990 Silver 0.9988 oz. ASW, 40 mm. **Obv:** Scale **Obv. Legend:** ONE TROY OUNCE **Rev:** Eight stars above eagle alighting with flag, thin leafed sprays below **Edge:** Reeded **Note:** Medal alignment.

Date	Mintage	F	VF	XF	Unc	BU
ND(1980s)	—	—	—	—	12.50	—

X# 102 OUNCE

31.1000 g., 0.9990 Silver 0.9988 oz. ASW, 40 mm. **Obv:** Scale, thin grain stalks at left and right **Obv. Legend:** ONE TROY OUNCE **Rev:** Eight stars above eagle alighting with flag, thick leafed sprays below **Edge:** Reeded **Note:** Medal alignment.

Date	Mintage	F	VF	XF	Unc	BU
ND(1980s)	—	—	—	—	12.50	—

X# 103 OUNCE

31.1000 g., 0.9990 Silver 0.9988 oz. ASW, 40 mm. **Obv:** Scale, thick grain stalks at left and right **Obv. Legend:** ONE TROY OUNCE **Rev:** Eight starrs above eagle alighting with flag, thick leafed sprays below **Edge:** Reeded **Note:** Medal alignment.

Date	Mintage	F	VF	XF	Unc	BU
ND(1980s)	—	—	—	—	12.50	—

X# 104 OUNCE

31.1000 g., 0.9990 Silver 0.9988 oz. ASW, 40 mm. **Obv:** Scale, thin grain stalks at left and right **Obv. Legend:** ONE TROUNCE **Rev:** Divided in two 1/4 ounce and one 1/2 ounce **Edge:** Reeded **Note:** Medal alignment.

Date	Mintage	F	VF	XF	Unc	BU
ND(1980s) Proof	—	Value: 12.50				

X# 105 OUNCE

31.1000 g., 0.9990 Silver 0.9988 oz. ASW, 40 mm. **Obv:** Scale **Obv. Legend:** ONE TROY OUNCE **Rev. Inscription:** Ohio - Sealy **Edge:** Reeded **Note:** Medal alignment.

Date	Mintage	F	VF	XF	Unc	BU
ND(1980s) Proof	—	Value: 12.50				

X# 108 OUNCE

31.1000 g., 0.9990 Silver 0.9988 oz. ASW, 40 mm. **Obv:** Scale, 11 grain stalk at left and right, small "APM" monogram below **Obv. Legend:** ONE TROY OUNCE **Rev:** Eight stars above eagle alighting with flag, sprays below **Edge:** Reeded **Note:** Medal alignment.

Date	Mintage	F	VF	XF	Unc	BU
ND(1980s) Proof	—	Value: 12.50				

X# 110 OUNCE

31.1000 g., 0.9990 Silver 0.9988 oz. ASW, 40 mm. **Obv:** Scale, 11 grain stalk at left and right, very small "APM" monogram below **Obv. Legend:** ONE TROY OUNCE **Rev:** Liberty standing **Rev. Legend:** LIBERTY **Rev. Designer:** Saint Gaudens copy **Edge:** Reeded **Note:** Medal alignment.

Date	Mintage	F	VF	XF	Unc	BU
ND(1980) Proof	—	Value: 12.50				

X# 111 OUNCE

31.1000 g., 0.9990 Silver 0.9988 oz. ASW, 40 mm. **Obv:** Scale, 11 grain stalk at left and right **Obv. Legend:** ONE TROY OUNCE **Rev:** Eight stars above eagle alighting with flag, sprays below **Edge:** Reeded **Note:** Medal alignment.

Date	Mintage	F	VF	XF	Unc	BU
ND(1980s)	—	—	—	—	12.50	—

X# 113 OUNCE

31.1000 g., 0.9990 Silver 0.9988 oz. ASW, 40 mm. **Obv:** Scale, 13 grain stalk at left, 11 grain stalk at right **Obv. Legend:** ONE TROY OUNCE **Rev:** Stars and rays above eagle with wings outspread, olive branch and arrows in talons **Edge:** Reeded **Note:** Medal alignment.

Date	Mintage	F	VF	XF	Unc	BU
ND(1980s) Proof	—	Value: 12.50				

X# 115 OUNCE

31.1000 g., 0.9990 Silver 0.9988 oz. ASW, 40 mm. **Obv:** Scale **Obv. Legend:** ★ ONE TROY OUNCE ★ **Rev:** Emblem in sprays **Rev. Legend:** • Valley Bank • Valued Customer **Edge:** Reeded **Note:** Medal alignment.

Date	Mintage	F	VF	XF	Unc	BU
ND(1980s) Proof	—	Value: 12.50				

X# 117 OUNCE

31.1000 g., 0.9990 Silver 0.9988 oz. ASW, 40 mm. **Obv:** Scale, 11 grain stalk at left and right **Rev:** Roses **Rev. Legend:** Portland, Ore. **Rev. Inscription:** City of Roses **Edge:** Reeded **Note:** Coin alignment.

Date	Mintage	F	VF	XF	Unc	BU
ND(1980s)	—	—	—	—	12.50	—

X# 118 OUNCE

31.1000 g., 0.9990 Silver 0.9988 oz. ASW, 38 mm. **Obv:** Scale, 11 grain stalk at left and right **Obv. Legend:** ONE TROY OUNCE **Rev:** Liberty head left, stars in border **Rev. Legend:** E • PLURIBUS • UNUM **Rev. Designer:** Morgan copy **Edge:** Reeded **Note:** Coin alignment.

Date	Mintage	F	VF	XF	Unc	BU
ND(1980s)	—	—	—	—	12.50	—

X# 119 OUNCE

31.1000 g., 0.9990 Silver 0.9988 oz. ASW, 38 mm. **Obv:** Scale, 11 grain stalk at left and right **Obv. Legend:** ONE TROY OUNCE **Rev:** Liberty head left, stars in border **Rev. Legend:** E • PLURIBUS • UNUM **Edge:** Reeded **Note:** Coin alignment.

Date	Mintage	F	VF	XF	Unc	BU
ND(1980s) Proof	—	Value: 12.50				

X# 120 OUNCE

31.1000 g., 0.9990 Silver 0.9988 oz. ASW, 38 mm. **Obv:** Scale, 11 grain stalk at left and right **Obv. Legend:** ONE TROY OUNCE **Rev:** Guard's tower, bust of p.o.w. right, sprays below **Rev. Legend:** ★ POW ★ MIA ★ YOU ARE NOT FORGOTTEN **Edge:** Reeded **Note:** Coin alignment.

Date	Mintage	F	VF	XF	Unc	BU
ND(1980s) Proof	—	Value: 12.50				

X# 122 OUNCE

31.1000 g., 0.9990 Silver 0.9988 oz. ASW, 39 mm. **Obv:** Scale, outlined grain stalk at left and right **Obv. Legend:** ONE TROY OUNCE **Rev:** Eagle walking left, olive branches, arrows below **Rev. Legend:** UNITED STATES OF AMERICA **Edge:** Partially reeded **Note:** Medal alignment.

Date	Mintage	F	VF	XF	Unc	BU
ND(1980s)NWTM Proof	—	Value: 12.50				

X# 131 OUNCE

31.1000 g., 0.9990 Silver 0.9988 oz. ASW, 39 mm. **Issuer:** A. S. & M. Co. **Obv:** Small Liberty ball **Obv. Legend:** ONE TROY OUNCE **Rev:** Eagle in flight right, olive branches and arrows in talons, stars in border **Rev. Legend:** AMERICAN / EAGLE **Note:** Coin alignment.

Date	Mintage	F	VF	XF	Unc	BU
ND(1980s)	—	—	—	—	12.50	—

X# 132 OUNCE

31.1000 g., 0.9990 Silver 0.9988 oz. ASW **Issuer:** A. S. & M. Co. **Obv:** Large Liberty bell **Obv. Legend:** ONE TROY OUNCE **Rev:** Eagle in flight, olive branch and arrows in talons **Rev. Legend:** AMERICAN / EAGLE - ONE TROY OUNCE - .999 FINE SILVER **Edge:** Reeded

Date	Mintage	F	VF	XF	Unc	BU
ND(1980s)	—	—	—	—	12.50	—

X# 133 OUNCE

31.1030 g., 0.9990 Silver 0.9989 oz. ASW, 38 mm. **Obv:** Large "$" **Obv. Legend:** ★ ONE SILVER TRADE UNIT ★ FINE SILVER **Rev:** Liberty head left, stars in borders **Rev. Legend:** E • PLURIBUS • UNUM **Rev. Designer:** Morgan copy **Edge:** Reeded **Note:** Coin alignment.

Date	Mintage	F	VF	XF	Unc	BU
ND(1980s) Prooflike	—	—	—	—	12.50	—

X# 134 OUNCE

31.1030 g., 0.9990 Silver 0.9989 oz. ASW, 39 mm. **Obv:** Large "$" **Obv. Legend:** ONE SILVER TRADE UNIT - FINE SILVER **Rev:** Liberty head left, stars in border **Rev. Designer:** De Francisci copy **Edge:** Reeded **Note:** Coin alignment.

Date	Mintage	F	VF	XF	Unc
ND(1980s)	—	—	—	—	12.50

X# 135 OUNCE

31.1000 g., 0.9990 Silver 0.9988 oz. ASW, 39.5 mm. **Obv:** Christ on cross **Obv. Legend:** SILVER TRADE UNIT **Rev:** Half-length figure of Pope John Paul 3/4 le **Rev. Legend:** FATHER FORGIVE THEM... **Edge:** Reeded **Note:** Medal alignment.

Date	Mintage	F	VF	XF	Unc
ND(1980s) Proof	—	Value: 12.50			

X# 137 OUNCE

31.1030 g., 0.9990 Silver 0.9989 oz. ASW, 39 mm. **Obv:** Music sheet on record **Obv. Legend:** SILVER

TRADE UNIT **Rev:** Full-length figure a bust of Elvis Presley **Edge:** Reeded **Note:** Medal alignment.

Date	Mintage	F	VF	XF	Unc	BU
ND(1980s) Proof	—	Value: 12.50				

X# 138 OUNCE

31.1030 g., 0.9990 Silver 0.9989 oz. ASW, 39 mm. **Obv:** Guitar on music sheets "Peace" **Obv. Legend:** SILVER TRADE UNIT **Rev:** Head of John Lennon 3/4 left, small head of Yoko Ono right **Edge:** Reeded **Note:** Medal alignment.

Date	Mintage	F	VF	XF	Unc	BU
ND(1980s) Proof	—	Value: 12.50				

X# 139 OUNCE

31.1030 g., 0.9990 Silver 0.9989 oz. ASW, 51x29 mm. **Obv:** Banner **Obv. Legend:** ONE TROY OUNCE / SILVER TRADE UNIT **Rev:** Eagle alighting with flag, sprays below, stars in upper borders **Shape:** Rectangular

Date	Mintage	F	VF	XF	Unc	BU
ND(1980s) Proof	—	Value: 13.50				

X# 141 OUNCE

31.1000 g., 0.9990 Silver 0.9988 oz. ASW, 37 mm. **Obv:** Scale, 11 grain stalk at left and right **Obv. Legend:** ONE TROY OUNCE **Rev:** Pelican on piling **Rev. Legend:** FLORIDA - SUNSHINE STATE **Edge:** Reeded **Note:** Coin alignment.

Date	Mintage	F	VF	XF	Unc	BU
ND(1980s) Proof	—	Value: 14.00				

X# 142 OUNCE

31.1000 g., 0.9990 Silver 0.9988 oz. ASW, 38.5 mm. **Obv:** Scale, 11 grain stalk at left and right **Obv. Legend:** ONE TROY OUNCE **Rev:** Stars around border **Rev. Inscription:** PRESTIGE / PREMIUMS **Edge:** Reeded **Note:** Medal alignment.

Date	Mintage	F	VF	XF	Unc	BU
ND(1980s) Prooflike	—	—	—	—	12.50	—

X# 126 OUNCE

0.9990 Silver, 39 mm. **Obv:** Eagle alighting with flag **Obv. Legend:** ONE TROY OUNCE **Rev. Legend:** MINTED FROM U.S. STRATEGIC STOCKPILE SILVER **Rev. Inscription:** U.S. ASSAY / OFFICE / SAN FRANCISCO **Edge:** Reeded **Note:** Medal alignment.

Date	Mintage	F	VF	XF	Unc	BU
1981 Proof	—	Value: 15.00				

X# 127 OUNCE

31.1000 g., 0.9990 Silver 0.9988 oz. ASW, 39 mm. **Obv:** Eagle alighting with flag, 11 grain stalk at left and right **Obv. Legend:** ONE TROY OUNCE **Rev. Legend:** MINTED FROM U.S. STRATEGIC STOCKPILE SILVER **Rev. Inscription:** U.S. ASSAY / OFFICE / SAN FRANCISCO **Edge:** Reeded **Note:** Coin alignment.

Date	Mintage	F	VF	XF	Unc	BU
1981	—	—	—	—	15.00	—

X# 128 OUNCE

31.1000 g., 0.9990 Silver 0.9988 oz. ASW, 39 mm. **Obv:** Eagle alighting, flag behind, 11 grain stalk at left and right **Obv. Legend:** ONE TROY OUNCE **Rev. Legend:** MINTED FROM U.S. STRATEGIC STOCKPILE SILVER **Rev. Inscription:** U.S. ASSAY / OFFICE / SAN FRANCISCO **Edge:** Reeded **Note:** Medal alignment.

Date	Mintage	F	VF	XF	Unc	BU
1981 Proof	—	Value: 15.00				

X# 136 OUNCE

31.1030 g., 0.9990 Silver 0.9989 oz. ASW, 39 mm. **Obv:** Scroll in sprays **Obv. Legend:** SILVER TRADE UNIT **Rev. Inscription:** The / Ruff / Times / National / Convention / '81 **Edge:** Reeded **Note:** Coin alignment.

Date	Mintage	F	VF	XF	Unc	BU
(19)81 Proof	—	Value: 15.00				

X# 140 OUNCE

31.1000 g., 0.9990 Silver 0.9988 oz. ASW, 37.5 mm. **Obv:** Eagle alighting, flag above, 11 grain stalk at left and right **Obv. Legend:** ONE TROY OUNCE **Rev. Legend:** MINTED FROM U.S. STRATEGIC STOCKPILE SILVER **Rev. Inscription:** U.S. ASSAY / OFFICE / SAN FRANCISCO **Edge:** Reeded **Note:** Coin alignment.

Date	Mintage	F	VF	XF	Unc	BU
1981	—	—	—	—	15.00	—

X# 112 OUNCE

31.1000 g., 0.9990 Silver 0.9988 oz. ASW, 40 mm. **Obv:** Scale, thick 11 grain stalk at left and right **Obv. Legend:** ONE TROY OUNCE **Rev:** Liberty head left **Rev. Designer:** Morgan copy **Edge:** Reeded **Note:** Medal alignment.

Date	Mintage	F	VF	XF	Unc	BU
1982 Proof	—	Value: 12.50				

X# 143 OUNCE

31.1000 g., 0.9990 Silver 0.9988 oz. ASW, 149x29 mm. **Obv:** Banner **Obv. Inscription:** ONE TROY OUNCE / SILVER TRADE UNIT **Rev:** Saint Nicholas head, sprays below **Rev. Inscription:** Merry Christmas **Shape:** Rectangular **Note:** Illustration reduced.

Date	Mintage	F	VF	XF	Unc	BU
1982 Proof	—	Value: 12.50				

X# 107 OUNCE

31.1000 g., 0.9990 Silver 0.9988 oz. ASW, 40 mm. **Obv:** Scale, thin grain stalk at left and right, medium "APM" monogram below **Rev:** Liberty head left **Rev. Designer:** Morgan copy **Edge:** Reeded **Note:** Medal alignment.

Date	Mintage	F	VF	XF	Unc	BU
1983 Proof	—	Value: 12.50				

X# 109 OUNCE

31.1000 g., 0.9990 Silver 0.9988 oz. ASW, 40 mm. **Obv:** Scale, 9 grain stalk at left and right, small "APM" monogram below **Rev:** Liberty head left **Rev. Designer:** Morgan copy **Edge:** Reeded **Note:** Medal alignment.

Date	Mintage	F	VF	XF	Unc	BU
1983 Proof	—	Value: 12.50				

X# 116 OUNCE

31.1000 g., 0.9990 Silver 0.9988 oz. ASW, 40 mm. **Obv:** Scale, 11 grain stalk at left and right **Obv. Legend:** ONE TROY OUNCE **Rev:** Liberty head left, stars in border **Rev. Legend:** E • PLURIBUS • UNUM **Rev. Designer:** Morgan copy **Edge:** Reeded **Note:** Medal alignment.

Date	Mintage	F	VF	XF	Unc	BU
1983 Proof	—	Value: 12.50				

X# 106 OUNCE

31.1000 g., 0.9990 Silver 0.9988 oz. ASW **Obv:** Scale, grain stalk at left and right, large "APM" monogram below **Obv. Legend:** ONE TROY OUNCE **Rev:** Greek temple facade **Rev. Legend:** ACADEMY CORPORATION **Edge:** Reeded **Note:** Medal alignment.

Date	Mintage	F	VF	XF	Unc	BU
1986 Proof	—	Value: 12.50				

X# 129 OUNCE

31.1000 g., 0.9990 Silver 0.9988 oz. ASW, 39.5 mm. **Obv:** Eagle, wings spread, olive branch and arrows in talons **Obv. Legend:** ...ONE TROY OUNCE... **Rev:** Liberty head left, stars in border **Rev. Legend:** E • PLURIBUS • UNUM **Edge:** Reeded **Note:** Coin alignment.

Date	Mintage	F	VF	XF	Unc	BU
1986	—	—	—	—	12.50	—

X# 130 OUNCE

31.1030 g., 0.9990 Silver 0.9989 oz. ASW, 40 mm. **Obv:** Eagle perched right **Obv. Legend:** SILVER TRADE UNIT **Rev:** Liberty head left **Edge:** Reeded **Note:** Medal alignment.

Date	Mintage	F	VF	XF	Unc	BU
1986	—	—	—	—	12.50	—

X# 121 OUNCE

31.1000 g., 0.9990 Silver 0.9988 oz. ASW, 39 mm. **Obv:** Scale, outlined grain stalks at left and right **Obv. Legend:** ONE TROY OUNCE **Rev:** Aerial view of Northwest Territory **Edge:** Reeded **Note:** Coin alignment

Date	Mintage	F	VF	XF	Unc	BU
1987 Proof	—	Value: 12.50				

X# 114 OUNCE

31.1000 g., 0.9990 Silver 0.9988 oz. ASW, 39 mm. **Obv:** Scale **Obv. Legend:** ★ ONE TROY OUNCE ★ **Rev:** Star **Rev. Inscription:** Silver / City / LAS VEGAS CASINO **Edge:** Reeded **Note:** Medal alignment.

Date	Mintage	F	VF	XF	Unc	BU
1988 Proof	—	Value: 12.50				

COPPER CURRENCY COINAGE

Liberty Dollar Org. Issues

X# 252 DOLLAR

28.3500 g., 0.9900 Copper 0.9023 oz., 39.0 mm. **Obv:** Head of Ron Paul 3/4 left **Obv. Legend:** GOLD STANDARD IN LEADERSHIP **Obv. Inscription:** TRUST IN / GOD - RON PAUL / FOR PRESIDENT / 2008 **Rev:** Torch **Rev. Legend:** VOTE FOR TRUTH

Date	Mintage	F	VF	XF	Unc	BU
2007	—	—	—	—	1.00	—

X# 251 LIBERTY DOLLAR

28.3300 g., Copper, 38.97 mm. **Obv:** Liberty head left **Obv. Legend:** LIBERTY **Obv. Inscription:** TRUST IN / GOD **Rev:** Torch at center **Rev. Inscription:** LIBERTY / DOLLAR at left **Edge:** Reeded

Date	Mintage	F	VF	XF	Unc	BU
2007	60,000	—	—	—	1.25	—

SILVER CURRENCY COINAGE

NORFED Distribution Issues

X# 217.1 LIBERTY DOLLAR
1.6000 g., 0.9990 Silver 0.0514 oz. ASW, 16.7 mm. **Obv:** Liberty head left **Obv. Legend:** LIBERTY **Obv. Inscription:** TRUST IN GOD / USA **Rev:** Torch, round top "3" **Rev. Legend:** LIBERTY DOLLAR **Edge:** Reeded

Date	Mintage	F	VF	XF	Unc	BU
2003 Proof	—	Value: 5.00				

X# 217.2 LIBERTY DOLLAR
1.6000 g., 0.9990 Silver 0.0514 oz. ASW, 16.7 mm. **Obv:** Liberty head left **Obv. Legend:** LIBERTY **Obv. Inscription:** TRUST IN GOD / USA **Rev:** Torch, flat top "3" **Edge:** Reeded

Date	Mintage	F	VF	XF	Unc	BU
2003 Proof	—	Value: 5.00				

X# 207 LIBERTY DOLLAR
1.5800 g., 0.9990 Silver 0.0507 oz. ASW, 16.78 mm. **Subject:** 5th Anniversary **Obv:** Liberty head left **Obv. Legend:** LIBERTY **Obv. Inscription:** TRUST IN GOD / USA **Rev:** Torch at center **Rev. Legend:** LIBERTY DOLLAR **Edge:** Reeded

Date	Mintage	F	VF	XF	Unc	BU
2003 Proof	50,000	Value: 10.00				

X# 218 2 LIBERTY DOLLARS
1.6000 g., 0.9990 Silver 0.0514 oz. ASW, 16.7 mm. **Obv:** Liberty head left **Obv. Legend:** LIBERTY **Obv. Inscription:** TRUST IN GOD / USA **Rev:** Torch **Rev. Legend:** LIBERTY DOLLARS **Edge:** Reeded **Note:** Error with "TWO".

Date	Mintage	F	VF	XF	Unc	BU
2005 Proof	—	Value: 15.00				

X# 208 5 LIBERTY DOLLARS
15.5359 g., 0.9990 Silver 0.4990 oz. ASW, 32.42 mm. **Subject:** 5th Anniversary **Obv:** Liberty head left **Obv. Legend:** LIBERTY **Obv. Inscription:** TRUST IN GOD / USA **Rev:** Torch at center **Rev. Inscription:** LIBERTY DOLLAR **Edge:** Reeded

Date	Mintage	F	VF	XF	Unc	BU
2003 Proof	25,000	Value: 15.00				

X# 201 10 LIBERTY DOLLARS
31.2000 g., 0.9990 Silver 1.0021 oz. ASW, 38.82 mm. **Obv:** Liberty head left **Obv. Legend:** LIBERTY **Obv. Inscription:** USA **Rev:** Temple at center **Rev. Legend:** NATIONAL ORGANIZATION FOR THE REPEAL OF THE FEDERAL RESERVE ACT / ★ NORFED ★ / THE SHELTER SYSTEM **Edge:** Reeded **Note:** Type I.

Date	Mintage	F	VF	XF	Unc	BU
1998 Proof	—	Value: 200				

X# 202 10 LIBERTY DOLLARS
31.2000 g., 0.9990 Silver 1.0021 oz. ASW, 38.82 mm. **Obv:** Liberty head left **Obv. Legend:** LIBERTY **Obv. Inscription:** USA **Rev:** Torch at center **Rev. Legend:** FOR THE REPEAL OF ...... **Rev. Inscription:** AMERICAN / LIBERTY / DOLLAR ® **Edge:** Reeded **Note:** Type II.

Date	Mintage	F	VF	XF	Unc	BU
1998//1999 Proof	—	Value: 250				

X# 203 10 LIBERTY DOLLARS
31.2000 g., 0.9990 Silver 1.0021 oz. ASW, 38.82 mm. **Obv:** Liberty head left **Obv. Legend:** LIBERTY **Obv. Inscription:** TRUST IN GOD / USA **Rev:** Torch at center **Rev. Legend:** FOR THE REPEAL OF... **Rev. Inscription:** AMERICAN / LIBERTY / DOLLAR ® **Edge:** Reeded **Note:** Type III.

Date	Mintage	F	VF	XF	Unc	BU
1999 Proof	—	Value: 55.00				

X# 204 10 LIBERTY DOLLARS
31.2000 g., 0.9990 Silver 1.0021 oz. ASW, 38.82 mm. **Obv:** Liberty head left **Obv. Legend:** LIBERTY **Obv. Inscription:** USA **Rev:** Torch at center **Rev. Legend:** AMERICAN LIBERTY CURRENCY **Rev. Inscription:** AMERICAN / LIBERTY / DOLLAR ® **Edge:** Reeded **Note:** Type IV.

Date	Mintage	F	VF	XF	Unc	BU
2000 Proof	Est. 3,000	Value: 85.00				

X# 205 10 LIBERTY DOLLARS
31.2000 g., 0.9990 Silver 1.0021 oz. ASW, 38.82 mm. **Obv:** Liberty head left **Obv. Legend:** LIBERTY **Obv. Inscription:** TRUST IN GOD / USA **Rev:** Torch at center **Rev. Legend:** AMERICAN LIBERTY CURRENCY **Edge:** Reeded **Note:** Type V.

Date	Mintage	F	VF	XF	Unc	BU
2000 Proof	—	Value: 100				

X# 206 10 LIBERTY DOLLARS
31.2000 g., 0.9990 Silver 1.0021 oz. ASW, 38.82 mm. **Obv:** Liberty head left **Obv. Legend:** LIBERTY **Obv. Inscription:** TRUST IN GOD / USA **Rev:** Torch

at center **Rev. Legend:** AMERICAN LIBERTY CURRENCY **Rev. Inscription:** LIBERTY DOLLAR ® **Edge:** Reeded **Note:** Type VI.

Date	Mintage	F	VF	XF	Unc	BU
2000 Proof	—	Value: 30.00				

X# 211 10 LIBERTY DOLLARS

31.2000 g., 0.9990 Silver 1.0021 oz. ASW **Subject:** Pennsylvania Freedom Conference **Countermark:** PFC **Edge:** Reeded **Note:** Hallmarked "PFC" on 10 Dollars, X#209. Estimated mintage.

Date	Mintage	F	VF	XF	Unc	BU
2003 Proof	150	Value: 100				
Note: Estimated mintage						

X# 209.1 10 LIBERTY DOLLARS

31.2000 g., 0.9990 Silver 1.0021 oz. ASW, 38.82 mm. **Subject:** 5th Anniversary **Obv:** Liberty head left **Obv. Legend:** LIBERTY with small "E" **Obv. Inscription:** TRUST IN GOD / USA **Rev:** Torch at center **Rev. Legend:** AMERICAN LIBERTY CURRENCY **Rev. Inscription:** LIBERTY DOLLAR ® 1998 to/2003 **Edge:** Reeded **Note:** Type VII. Two minor obverse varieties exist with a wide rim.

Date	Mintage	F	VF	XF	Unc	BU
2003 Proof	—	Value: 15.00				

X# 209.2 10 LIBERTY DOLLARS

31.2000 g., 0.9990 Silver 1.0021 oz. ASW, 38.82 mm. **Obv:** Liberty head left **Obv. Legend:** LIBERTY with large "E" **Obv. Inscription:** TRUST IN GOD / USA **Rev:** Torch at center **Rev. Legend:** AMERICAN LIBERTY CURRENCY **Rev. Inscription:** LIBERTY DOLLAR® 1998 to/2003 **Edge:** Reeded **Note:** Type VII.

Date	Mintage	F	VF	XF	Unc	BU
2003 Proof	—	Value: 30.00				

X# 210 50 LIBERTY DOLLARS

155.8500 g., 0.9990 Silver 5.0055 oz. ASW, 63.90 mm. **Subject:** 5th Anniversary **Obv:** Liberty head left **Obv. Legend:** LIBERTY **Obv. Inscription:** TRUST IN GOD / USA **Rev:** Torch at center **Rev. Legend:** AMERICAN LIBERTY DOLLAR **Rev. Inscription:** 1998 to/2003 **Edge:** Reeded **Note:** Microprinting around obverse rim. Illustration reduced.

Date	Mintage	F	VF	XF	Unc	BU
2003 Proof	5,000	Value: 70.00				

Liberty Dollar Org. Issues

X# 224 5 LIBERTY DOLLARS

7.8200 g., 0.9990 Silver 0.2512 oz. ASW, 27 mm. **Obv:** Liberty head left **Obv. Legend:** LIBERTY **Obv. Inscription:** TRUST IN/GOD-USA **Rev:** Truncated torch at center **Rev. Inscription:** "LIBERTY DOLLAR" **Edge:** Reeded

Date	Mintage	F	VF	XF	Unc	BU
2006 Proof	—	Value: 6.00				

X# 213 10 LIBERTY DOLLARS

31.2200 g., 0.9990 Silver 1.0027 oz. ASW, 38.95 mm. **Obv:** Liberty head left **Obv. Legend:** LIBERTY

Obv. Inscription: USA, TRUST IN GOD **Rev:** Torch **Rev. Legend:** LIBERTY DOLLAR.ORG **Rev. Inscription:** LIBERTY DOLLAR ® **Edge:** Reede **Note:** Type VIII.

Date	Mintage	F	VF	XF	Unc	B
2005 Proof	—	Value: 10.00				

X# 214 10 LIBERTY DOLLARS

15.5500 g., 0.9990 Silver 0.4994 oz. ASW, 32.5 mm. **Obv:** Liberty head left **Obv. Legend:** LIBERTY **Obv. Inscription:** USA, TRUST IN GOD **Rev:** Torch **Rev. Legend:** LIBERTY / DOLLAR ® **Edge:** Reeded

Date	Mintage	F	VF	XF	Unc	B
2005 Proof	—	Value: 10.00				

X# 221.2 10 LIBERTY DOLLARS

31.2000 g., 0.9990 Silver 1.0021 oz. ASW, 39 mm. **Obv:** Liberty head left **Obv. Legend:** LIBERTY **Obv. Inscription:** TRUST IN GOD / USA **Rev:** Torch, with handstamped serial number **Rev. Legend:** PUERTO RICO **Rev. Inscription:** *LIBERTY DOLLAR* **Edge:** Reeded **Note:** 25 states and Puerto Rico, plus Marco Island were minted, numbered and hallmarked with the shape and initials of each.

Date	Mintage	F	VF	XF	Unc	BU
2006 Proof	—	—	—	—	—	—

X# 221.1 10 LIBERTY DOLLARS

31.2000 g., 0.9990 Silver 1.0021 oz. ASW, 39 mm. **Obv:** Liberty head left **Obv. Legend:** LIBERTY **Obv. Inscription:** TRUST IN GOD / USA **Rev:** Torch,

thout serial number **Rev. Legend:** PUERTO RICO **ev. Inscription:** *LIBERTY DOLLAR* **Edge:** Reeded **ote:** Type X.

te	Mintage	F	VF	XF	Unc	BU
06 Proof	—	—	—	—	—	—

 # 212 20 LIBERTY DOLLARS
.1400 g., 0.9990 Silver 1.0000 oz. ASW, 38.9 mm. **bv:** Liberty head left **Obv. Legend:** LIBERTY **bv. Inscription:** USA **Rev:** Torch **Rev. Inscription:** BERTY DOLLAR ® **Edge:** Reeded

te	Mintage	F	VF	XF	Unc	BU
04 Proof	—	Value: 20.00				
05 Proof	—	Value: 20.00				

 # 219 20 LIBERTY DOLLARS
1.2200 g., 0.9990 Silver 1.0027 oz. ASW **Obv:** Liberty ead left **Obv. Legend:** LIBERTY **Obv. Inscription:** RUST IN GOD / USA **Rev:** Torch **Rev. Inscription:** *IBERTY DOLLAR* **Edge:** Reeded

te	Mintage	F	VF	XF	Unc	BU
05 Proof	—	Value: 25.00				

 # 225 20 LIBERTY DOLLARS
1.2200 g., 0.9990 Silver 1.0027 oz. ASW, 38.95 mm. **bv:** Liberty head left **Obv. Legend:** LIBERTY **bv. Inscription:** TRUST IN GOD / USA **Rev:** Torch **ev. Legend:** ALABAMA **Rev. Inscription:** *Liberty / ollar* **Edge:** Reeded **Note:** May exist with hallmark or ith hallmark and serial number.

te	Mintage	F	VF	XF	Unc	BU
06 Proof	—	Value: 20.00				

 # 226 20 LIBERTY DOLLARS
1.2200 g., 0.9990 Silver 1.0027 oz. ASW, 38.95 mm. **bv:** Liberty head left **Obv. Legend:** LIBERTY **bv. Inscription:** TRUST IN GOD / USA **Rev:** Torch **ev. Legend:** ALASKA **Rev. Inscription:** *Liberty / ollar* at left. **Edge:** Reeded **Note:** May exist with allmark or with hallmark and serial number.

te	Mintage	F	VF	XF	Unc	BU
06 Proof	—	Value: 20.00				

 # 227 20 LIBERTY DOLLARS
1.2200 g., 0.9990 Silver 1.0027 oz. ASW, 38.95 mm. **bv:** Liberty head left **Obv. Legend:** LIBERTY

Obv. Inscription: TRUST IN GOD / USA **Rev:** Torch **Rev. Legend:** CALIFORNIA **Rev. Inscription:** *Liberty / Dollar* at left **Edge:** Reeded **Note:** May exist with hallmark or with hallmark and serial number.

Date	Mintage	F	VF	XF	Unc	BU
2006 Proof	—	Value: 20.00				

X# 223 20 LIBERTY DOLLARS
31.2200 g., 0.9990 Silver 1.0027 oz. ASW, 38.95 mm. **Obv:** Liberty head left **Obv. Legend:** LIBERTY **Obv. Inscription:** TRUST IN GOD / USA **Rev:** Torch **Rev. Legend:** COLORADO **Rev. Inscription:** *Liberty / Dollar* at left **Edge:** Reeded **Note:** May exist with hallmark or with hallmark and serial number.

Date	Mintage	F	VF	XF	Unc	BU
2006 Proof	—	Value: 20.00				

X# 228 20 LIBERTY DOLLARS
31.2200 g., 0.9990 Silver 1.0027 oz. ASW, 38.95 mm. **Obv:** Liberty head left **Obv. Legend:** LIBERTY **Obv. Inscription:** TRUST IN GOD / USA **Rev:** Torch **Rev. Legend:** FLORIDA **Rev. Inscription:** *Liberty / Dollar* at left **Edge:** Reeded **Note:** May exist with hallmark or with hallmark and serial number.

Date	Mintage	F	VF	XF	Unc	BU
2006 Proof	—	Value: 20.00				

X# 229 20 LIBERTY DOLLARS
31.2200 g., 0.9990 Silver 1.0027 oz. ASW, 38.95 mm. **Obv:** Liberty head left **Obv. Legend:** LIBERTY **Obv. Inscription:** TRUST IN GOD / USA **Rev:** Torch **Rev. Legend:** GEORGIA **Rev. Inscription:** *Liberty / Dollar* at left **Edge:** Reeded **Note:** May exist with hallmark or with hallmark and serial number.

Date	Mintage	F	VF	XF	Unc	BU
2006 Proof	—	Value: 20.00				

X# 230 20 LIBERTY DOLLARS
31.2200 g., 0.9990 Silver 1.0027 oz. ASW, 38.95 mm. **Obv:** Liberty head left **Obv. Legend:** LIBERTY **Obv. Inscription:** TRUST IN GOD / USA **Rev:** Torch **Rev. Legend:** IDAHO **Rev. Inscription:** *Liberty / Dollar* at left **Edge:** Reeded **Note:** May exist with hallmark or with hallmark and serial number.

Date	Mintage	F	VF	XF	Unc	BU
2006 Proof	—	Value: 20.00				

X# 231 20 LIBERTY DOLLARS
31.2200 g., 0.9990 Silver 1.0027 oz. ASW, 38.95 mm. **Obv:** Liberty head left **Obv. Legend:** LIBERTY **Obv. Inscription:** TRUST IN GOD / USA **Rev:** Torch **Rev. Legend:** ILLINOIS **Rev. Inscription:** *Liberty / Dollar* at left **Edge:** Reeded **Note:** May exist with hallmark or with hallmark and serial number.

Date	Mintage	F	VF	XF	Unc	BU
2006 Proof	—	Value: 20.00				

X# 232 20 LIBERTY DOLLARS
31.2200 g., 0.9990 Silver 1.0027 oz. ASW, 38.95 mm. **Obv:** Liberty head left **Obv. Legend:** LIBERTY **Obv. Inscription:** TRUST IN GOD / USA **Rev:** Torch **Rev. Legend:** INDIANA **Rev. Inscription:** *Liberty / Dollar at left* **Edge:** Reeded **Note:** May exist with hallmark or with hallmark and serial number.

Date	Mintage	F	VF	XF	Unc	BU
2006 Proof	—	Value: 20.00				

X# 233 20 LIBERTY DOLLARS
31.2200 g., 0.9990 Silver 1.0027 oz. ASW, 38.95 mm. **Obv:** Liberty head left **Obv. Legend:** LIBERTY **Obv. Inscription:** TRUST IN GOD / USA **Rev:** Torch **Rev. Legend:** MAINE **Rev. Inscription:** *Liberty / Dollar* at left **Edge:** Reeded **Note:** May exist with hallmark or with hallmark and serial number.

Date	Mintage	F	VF	XF	Unc	BU
2006 Proof	—	Value: 25.00				

X# 234 20 LIBERTY DOLLARS
31.2200 g., 0.9990 Silver 1.0027 oz. ASW, 38.95 mm. **Obv:** Liberty head left **Obv. Legend:** LIBERTY **Obv. Inscription:** TRUST IN GOD / USA **Rev:** Torch

Rev. Legend: MASSACHUSSETTS **Rev. Inscription:** *Liberty / Dollar* at left **Edge:** Reeded **Note:** May exist with hallmark or with hallmark and serial number.

Date	Mintage	F	VF	XF	Unc	BU
2006 Proof	—	Value: 20.00				

X# 220 20 LIBERTY DOLLARS
31.2200 g., Silver, 38.95 mm. **Obv:** Liberty head left **Obv. Legend:** LIBERTY **Obv. Inscription:** TRUST IN GOD / USA **Rev:** Torch **Rev. Legend:** MICHIGAN **Rev. Inscription:** *Liberty / Dollar* at left **Edge:** Reeded **Note:** May exist with hallmark or with hallmark and serial number.

Date	Mintage	F	VF	XF	Unc	BU
2006 Proof	—	Value: 20.00				

X# 235 20 LIBERTY DOLLARS
31.2200 g., 0.9990 Silver 1.0027 oz. ASW, 38.95 mm. **Obv:** Liberty head left **Obv. Legend:** LIBERTY **Obv. Inscription:** TRUST IN GOD / USA **Rev:** Torch **Rev. Legend:** MISSISSIPPI **Rev. Inscription:** *Liberty / Dollar* **Edge:** Reeded **Note:** May exist with hallmark or with hallmark and serial number.

Date	Mintage	F	VF	XF	Unc	BU
2006 Proof	—	Value: 25.00				

X# 236 20 LIBERTY DOLLARS
31.2200 g., 0.9990 Silver 1.0027 oz. ASW, 38.95 mm. **Obv:** Liberty head left **Obv. Legend:** LIBERTY **Obv. Inscription:** TRUST IN GOD / USA **Rev:** Torch **Rev. Legend:** MISSOURI **Rev. Inscription:** *Liberty / Dollar* **Edge:** Reeded **Note:** May exist with hallmark or with hallmark and serial number.

Date	Mintage	F	VF	XF	Unc	BU
2006 Proof	—	Value: 20.00				

X# 237 20 LIBERTY DOLLARS
31.2200 g., 0.9990 Silver 1.0027 oz. ASW, 38.95 mm. **Obv:** Liberty head left **Obv. Legend:** LIBERTY **Obv. Inscription:** TRUST IN GOD / USA **Rev:** Torch **Rev. Legend:** MONTANA **Rev. Inscription:** *Liberty / Dollar* at left **Edge:** Reeded **Note:** May exist with hallmark or with hallmark and serial number.

Date	Mintage	F	VF	XF	Unc	BU
2006 Proof	—	Value: 20.00				

X# 238 20 LIBERTY DOLLARS
31.2200 g., 0.9990 Silver 1.0027 oz. ASW, 38.95 mm. **Obv:** Liberty head left **Obv. Legend:** LIBERTY **Obv. Inscription:** TRUST IN GOD / USA **Rev:** Torch **Rev. Legend:** NEW HAMPSHIRE **Rev. Inscription:** *Liberty / Dollar* at left **Edge:** Reeded **Note:** May exist with hallmark or with hallmark and serial number.

Date	Mintage	F	VF	XF	Unc	BU
2006 Proof	—	Value: 20.00				

X# 239 20 LIBERTY DOLLARS
31.2200 g., 0.9990 Silver 1.0027 oz. ASW, 38.95 mm. **Obv:** Liberty head left **Obv. Legend:** LIBERTY **Obv. Inscription:** TRUST IN GOD / USA **Rev:** Torch **Rev. Legend:** NEW MEXICO **Rev. Inscription:** *Liberty / Dollar* at left **Edge:** Reeded **Note:** May exist with hallmark or with hallmark and serial number.

Date	Mintage	F	VF	XF	Unc	BU
2006 Proof	—	Value: 20.00				

X# 221 20 LIBERTY DOLLARS
31.2200 g., 0.9990 Silver 1.0027 oz. ASW, 38.95 mm. **Obv:** Liberty head left **Obv. Legend:** LIBERTY **Obv. Inscription:** TRUST IN GOD / USA **Rev:** Torch **Rev. Legend:** NEW YORK **Rev. Inscription:** *Liberty / Dollar* at left **Edge:** Reeded **Note:** May exist with hallmark or with hallmark and serial number.

Date	Mintage	F	VF	XF	Unc	BU
2006 Proof	—	Value: 20.00				

X# 240 20 LIBERTY DOLLARS
31.2200 g., 0.9990 Silver 1.0027 oz. ASW, 38.95 mm. **Obv:** Liberty head left **Obv. Legend:** LIBERTY **Obv. Inscription:** TRUST IN GOD / USA **Rev:** Torch **Rev. Legend:** NORTH CAROLINA **Rev. Inscription:** *Liberty / Dollar* at left **Edge:** Reeded **Note:** May exist with hallmark or with hallmark and serial number.

Date	Mintage	F	VF	XF	Unc	BU
2006 Proof	—	Value: 20.00				

X# 241 20 LIBERTY DOLLARS
31.2200 g., 0.9990 Silver 1.0027 oz. ASW, 38.95 mm. **Obv:** Liberty head left **Obv. Legend:** LIBERTY **Obv. Inscription:** TRUST IN GOD / USA **Rev:** Torch **Rev. Legend:** NORTH DAKOTA **Rev. Inscription:** *Liberty / Dollar* at left **Edge:** Reeded **Note:** May exist with hallmark or with hallmark and serial number.

Date	Mintage	F	VF	XF	Unc	BU
2006 Proof	—	Value: 20.00				

X# 242 20 LIBERTY DOLLARS
31.2200 g., 0.9990 Silver 1.0027 oz. ASW, 38.95 mm **Obv:** Liberty head left **Obv. Legend:** LIBERTY **Obv. Inscription:** TRUST IN GOD / USA **Rev:** Torc **Rev. Legend:** OREGON **Rev. Inscription:** *Liberty / Dollar* at left **Edge:** Reeded **Note:** May exist with hallmark or with hallmark and serial number.

Date	Mintage	F	VF	XF	Unc
2006 Proof	—	Value: 25.00			

X# 243 20 LIBERTY DOLLARS
31.2200 g., 0.9990 Silver 1.0027 oz. ASW, 38.95 mm **Obv:** Libert head left **Obv. Legend:** LIBERTY **Obv. Inscription:** TRUST IN GOD / USA **Rev:** Torc **Rev. Legend:** PENNSYLVANIA **Rev. Inscription:** *Liberty / Dollar* at left **Edge:** Reeded **Note:** May exis with hallmark or with hallmark and serial number.

Date	Mintage	F	VF	XF	Unc
2006 Proof	—	Value: 20.00			

X# 222 20 LIBERTY DOLLARS
31.2200 g., 0.9990 Silver 1.0027 oz. ASW, 38.95 mm **Obv:** Liberty head left **Obv. Legend:** LIBERTY **Obv. Inscription:** TRUST IN GOD / USA **Rev:** Torc **Rev. Legend:** TEXAS **Rev. Inscription:** *Liberty / Doll* at left **Edge:** Reeded **Note:** May exist with hallmark o with hallmark and serial number.

Date	Mintage	F	VF	XF	Unc
2006 Proof	—	Value: 20.00			

X# 244 20 LIBERTY DOLLARS
31.2200 g., 0.9990 Silver 1.0027 oz. ASW, 38.95 mm **Obv:** Liberty head left **Obv. Legend:** LIBERTY **Obv. Inscription:** TRUST IN GOD / USA **Rev:** Torc **Rev. Legend:** VIRGINIA **Edge:** Reeded **Note:** May exist with hallmark or with hallmark and serial numbe

Date	Mintage	F	VF	XF	Unc
2006 Proof	—	Value: 20.00			

X# 245 20 LIBERTY DOLLARS
31.2200 g., 0.9990 Silver 1.0027 oz. ASW, 38.95 mm. **Obv:** Liberty head left **Obv. Legend:** LIBERTY **Obv. Inscription:** TRUST IN GOD / USA **Rev:** Torch **Rev. Legend:** WASHINGTON **Rev. Inscription:** *Liberty / Dollar* at left **Edge:** Reeded **Note:** May exist with hallmark or with hallmark and serial number.

Date	Mintage	F	VF	XF	Unc	BU
2006 Proof	—	Value: 20.00				

X# 246 20 LIBERTY DOLLARS
, 38.95 mm. **Obv:** Liberty head left **Obv. Legend:** LIBERTY **Obv. Inscription:** TRUST IN GOD / USA **Rev:** Torch **Rev. Legend:** MARCO ISLAND **Rev. Inscription:** *Liberty / Dollar* at left **Edge:** Reeded **Note:** Located off the Florida coast.

Date	Mintage	F	VF	XF	Unc	BU
2006 Proof	—	Value: 20.00				

X# 247 20 LIBERTY DOLLARS
31.2200 g., 0.9990 Silver 1.0027 oz. ASW, 38.95 mm. **Obv:** Liberty head left **Obv. Legend:** LIBERTY **Obv. Inscription:** TRUST IN GOD / USA **Rev:** Torch **Rev. Inscription:** *Liberty / Dollar* **Edge:** Reeded

Date	Mintage	F	VF	XF	Unc	BU
2006 Proof	—	Value: 20.00				

X# 253 20 LIBERTY DOLLARS
31.2200 g., 0.9990 Silver 1.0027 oz. ASW, 38.95 mm. **Obv:** Head of Ron Paul 3/4 left **Obv. Legend:** GOLD STANDARD IN LEADERSHIP **Obv. Inscription:** TRUST IN /GOD - RON PAUL / FOR PRESIDENT / 2008 **Rev:** Torch **Rev. Legend:** VOTE FOR TRUTH **Rev. Inscription:** *Liberty / Dollar* at left **Edge:** Reeded

Date	Mintage	F	VF	XF	Unc	BU
ND(2007) Proof	—	Value: 20.00				

X# 256 20 LIBERTY DOLLARS
31.1900 g., 0.9990 Silver 1.0017 oz. ASW, 38.98 mm. **Obv:** Liberty head left **Obv. Legend:** LIBERTY **Obv. Inscription:** TRUST IN GOD / USA **Rev:** Torch **Rev. Legend:** MILWAUKEE • ANA **Rev. Inscription:** *Liberty /Dollar* at left **Edge:** Reeded **Note:** Hallmarked on reverse.

Date	Mintage	F	VF	XF	Unc	BU
2007 Proof	500	Value: 27.50				

X# 257 20 LIBERTY DOLLARS
31.2200 g., 0.9990 Silver 1.0027 oz. ASW, 38.95 mm. **Obv:** Liberty head left **Obv. Legend:** LIBERTY **Obv. Inscription:** TRUST IN / GOD **Rev:** Bear walking left **Rev. Legend:** LIBERTY DOLLAR **Rev. Inscription:** CALIFORNIA **Edge:** Reeded

Date	Mintage	F	VF	XF	Unc	BU
2007 Proof	—	Value: 20.00				

X# 258 20 LIBERTY DOLLARS
31.2200 g., 0.9990 Silver 1.0027 oz. ASW, 38.95 mm. **Obv:** Liberty head left **Obv. Legend:** LIBERTY **Obv. Inscription:** TRUST IN / GOD **Rev:** Supported arms **Rev. Legend:** LIBERTY DOLLAR **Rev. Inscription:** CHAMBERSBURG **Edge:** Reeded

Date	Mintage	F	VF	XF	Unc	BU
2007 Proof	—	Value: 20.00				

X# 250 100 LIBERTY DOLLARS
155.7300 g., 0.9990 Silver 5.0016 oz. ASW, 63.80 mm. **Obv:** Liberty head left **Obv. Legend:** LIBERTY **Obv. Inscription:** TRUST IN / GOD - USA **Rev:** Torch at center **Rev. Legend:** INFLATION PROOF CURRENCY **Rev. Inscription:** LIBERTY / DOLLAR at left, 1998 / 2006 at right **Edge:** Reeded

Date	Mintage	F	VF	XF	Unc	BU
2006 Proof	—	Value: 500				

X# 223.1 1000 LIBERTY DOLLARS
31.1200 g., 0.9990 Gold 0.9995 oz. AGW, 32.45 mm. **Obv:** Liberty head left **Obv. Legend:** LIBERTY **Obv. Inscription:** TRUST IN GOD / USA **Rev:** Torch, with handstamped serial number **Rev. Legend:** LIBERTY DOLLAR **Edge:** Reeded

Date	Mintage	F	VF	XF	Unc	BU
2006 Proof	—	—	—	—	—	—

X# 223.2 1000 LIBERTY DOLLARS
31.1200 g., 0.9990 Gold 0.9995 oz. AGW, 32.45 mm. **Obv:** Liberty head left **Obv. Legend:** LIBERTY **Obv. Inscription:** TRUST IN GOD / USA **Rev:** Torch, without serial number **Rev. Legend:** LIBERTY DOLLAR **Edge:** Reeded

Date	Mintage	F	VF	XF	Unc	BU
2006 Proof	—	Value: 750				

GOLD CURRENCY COINAGE

NORFED Distribution Issues

X# 215 500 LIBERTY DOLLARS
31.1061 g., 0.9999 Gold 0.9999 oz. AGW, 32 mm. **Obv:** Liberty head left **Obv. Legend:** LIBERTY **Obv. Inscription:** TRUST IN GOD **Rev:** Torch **Rev. Legend:** AMERICAN LIBERTY CURRENCY

Date	Mintage	F	VF	XF	Unc	BU
2000 Proof	—	Value: 750				

Liberty Dollar Org.

X# 254 1000 LIBERTY DOLLARS
31.1030 g., 0.9999 Gold 0.9998 oz. AGW, 32 mm. **Obv:** Head of Ron Paul left **Obv. Legend:** GOLD STANDARD IN LEADERSHIP **Obv. Inscription:** TRUST IN / GOD - RON PAUL / FOR PRESIDENT / 2008 **Rev:** Torch at center **Rev. Legend:** LIBERTY DOLLAR **Edge:** Reeded **Note:** Handstamped serial number on reverse.

Date	Mintage	F	VF	XF	Unc	BU
2007 Proof	—	Value: 1,000				

DANIEL CARR PROTOTYPE STATE QUARTER

X# 308a CARRTER DOLLAR
Copper Nickel **Subject:** Maine **Obv:** Bust 3/4 left of Carr wearing glasses **Obv. Legend:** ALTERED STATES OF AMERICA / CARRter DOLLAR **Rev:** Pemaquid Point lighthouse **Rev. Legend:** MAINE / 1820 / 2003

Date	Mintage	F	VF	XF	Unc	BU
2003	284	—	—	—	—	10.00

X# 308b CARRTER DOLLAR
Yellow Brass **Subject:** Maine **Obv:** Bust 3/4 left of Carr wearing glasses **Obv. Legend:** ALTERED STATES OF AMERICA / CARRter DOLLAR **Rev:** Pemaquid Point lighthouse **Rev. Legend:** MAINE / 1820 / 2003

Date	Mintage	F	VF	XF	Unc	BU
2003	82	—	—	—	—	20.00

X# 308c CARRTER DOLLAR
7.7857 g., 0.9990 Silver 0.2501 oz. ASW
Subject: Maine **Obv:** Bust 3/4 left of Carr wearing glasses **Obv. Legend:** ALTERED STATES OF AMERICA / CARRter DOLLAR **Rev:** Pemaquid Point lighthouse **Rev. Legend:** MAINE / 1820 / 2003

Date	Mintage	F	VF	XF	Unc	BU
2003	20	—	—	—	—	—

X# 302a CARRTER DOLLAR
Copper Nickel **Subject:** Colorado 10th Mountain Division **Obv:** Bust 3/4 left of Carr wearing glasses **Obv. Legend:** ALTEREED STATES OF AMERICA / CARRter DOLLAR **Rev:** Skier **Rev. Legend:** COLORADO / 1876 / 10TH MOUNTAIN / DIVISION / 2006

Date	Mintage	F	VF	XF	Unc	BU
2006	140	—	—	—	—	20.00

X# 302b CARRTER DOLLAR
Yellow Brass **Subject:** Colorado 10th Mountain Division **Obv:** Bust 3/4 left of Carr wearing glasses **Obv. Legend:** ALTERED STATES OF AMERICA / CARRter DOLLAR **Rev:** Skier **Rev. Legend:** COLORADO / 10TH MOUNTAIN / DIVISION / 2006

Date	Mintage	F	VF	XF	Unc	BU
2006	83	—	—	—	—	20.00

X# 302c CARRTER DOLLAR
7.7857 g., 0.9990 Silver 0.2501 oz. ASW **Subject:** Colorado 10th Mountain Division **Obv:** Bust 3/4 left of Carr wearing glasses **Obv. Legend:** ALTERED STATES OF AMERICA / CARRter DOLLAR **Rev:** Skier **Rev. Legend:** COLORADO / 10TH MOUNTAIN / DIVISION / 2006

Date	Mintage	F	VF	XF	Unc	BU
2006	15	—	—	—	—	60.00

X# 303a CARRTER DOLLAR
Copper Nickel **Subject:** Colorado - Pikes Peak **Obv:** Bust 3/4 left of Carr wearing glasses **Obv. Legend:** ALTERED STATES OF AMERICA / CARRter DOLLAR **Rev:** Pikes Peak **Rev. Legend:** COLORADO / 1876 / 2006

Date	Mintage	F	VF	XF	Unc	BU
2006	144	—	—	—	—	10.00

X# 303b CARRTER DOLLAR
Yellow Brass **Subject:** Colorado / Pikes Peak **Obv:** Bust 3/4 left of Carr wearing glasses **Obv. Legend:** ALTERED STATES OF AMERICA / CARRter DOLLAR **Rev:** Pikes Peak **Rev. Legend:** COLORADO / 1876 / 2006

Date	Mintage	F	VF	XF	Unc	BU
2006	82	—	—	—	—	20.00

X# 303c CARRTER DOLLAR
7.7857 g., 0.9990 Silver 0.2501 oz. ASW
Subject: Colorado / Pikes Peak **Obv:** Bust 3/4 left of Carr wearing glasses **Obv. Legend:** ALTERED STATES OF AMERICA / CARRter DOLLAR **Rev:** Pikes Peak **Rev. Legend:** COLORADO / 1876 / 2006

Date	Mintage	F	VF	XF	Unc	BU
2006	10	—	—	—	—	—

X# 304a CARRTER DOLLAR
Copper Nickel **Subject:** Colorado - Mesa Verde **Obv:** Bust 3/4 left of Carr wearing glasses **Obv. Legend:** ALTERED STATES OF AMERICA / CARRter DOLLAR **Rev:** Mesa Verde cliff dwellings **Rev. Legend:** COLORADO / 1876 / MESA VERDE / 2006

Date	Mintage	F	VF	XF	Unc	BU
2006	142	—	—	—	—	10.00

X# 304b CARRTER DOLLAR
Yellow Brass **Subject:** Colorado - Mesa Verde **Obv:** Bust 3/4 left of Carr wearing glasses **Obv. Legend:** ALTERED STATES OF AMERICA / CARRter DOLLAR **Rev:** Mesa Verde cliff dwellings **Rev. Legend:** COLORADO / 1876 / MESA VERDE / 2006

Date	Mintage	F	VF	XF	Unc	BU
2006	61	—	—	—	—	20.00

X# 304c CARRTER DOLLAR
7.7857 g., 0.9990 Silver 0.2501 oz. ASW
Subject: Colorado / Mesa Verde **Obv:** Bust 3/4 left of Carr wearing glasses **Obv. Legend:** ALTERED STATES OF AMERICA / CARRter DOLLAR **Rev:** Mesa Verde cliff dwellings **Rev. Legend:** COLORADO / 1876 / MESA VERDE / 2006

Date	Mintage	F	VF	XF	Unc	BU
2006	10	—	—	—	—	—

X# 305a CARRTER DOLLAR
Copper Nickel **Subject:** Colorado 3D map **Obv:** Bust 3/4 left of Carr wearing glasses **Obv. Legend:** ALTERED STATES OF AMERICA / CARRter DOLLAR **Rev:** 3D map of Colorado **Rev. Legend:** COLORADO / 1876 / PLATEAU, MOUNTAIN & PLAIN / 2006

Date	Mintage	F	VF	XF	Unc	BU
2006	142	—	—	—	—	10.00

X# 305b CARRTER DOLLAR
Yellow Brass **Subject:** Colorado - 3D map **Obv:** Bust 3/4 left of Carr wearing glasses **Obv. Legend:** ALTERED STATES OF AMERICA / CARRter DOLLAR **Rev:** 3D map of Colorado **Rev. Legend:** COLORADO / 1876 / PLATEAU, MOUNTAIN & PLAIN / 2006

Date	Mintage	F	VF	XF	Unc	BU
2006	62	—	—	—	—	20.00

X# 305c CARRTER DOLLAR
7.7857 g., 0.9990 Silver 0.2501 oz. ASW
Subject: Colorado 3D map **Obv:** Bust 3/4 left of Carr wearing glasses **Obv. Legend:** ALTERED STATES OF AMERICA / CARRter DOLLAR **Rev:** 3D map of Colorado **Rev. Legend:** COLORADO / 1876 / PLATEAU, MOUNTAIN & PLAIN / 2006

Date	Mintage	F	VF	XF	Unc	BU
2006	10	—	—	—	—	—

X# 306a CARRTER DOLLAR
Copper Nickel **Subject:** Nevada **Obv:** Bust 3/4 left of Carr wearing glasses **Obv. Legend:** ALTERED STATES OF AMERICA / CARRter DOLLAR **Rev:** Steam engine and Nevada state map **Rev. Legend:** NEVADA / 1864 / THE SILVER STATE / 2006

Date	Mintage	F	VF	XF	Unc	BU
2006	262	—	—	—	—	10.00

X# 306b CARRTER DOLLAR
Yellow Brass **Subject:** Nevada **Obv:** Bust 3/4 left of Carr wearing glasses **Obv. Legend:** ALTERED STATES OF AMERICA / CARRter DOLLAR **Rev:** Steam engine and Nevada state map **Rev. Legend:** NEVADA / 1864 / THE SILVER STATE / 2006

Date	Mintage	F	VF	XF	Unc	BU
2006	86	—	—	—	—	20.00

X# 306c CARRTER DOLLAR
7.7857 g., 0.9990 Silver 0.2501 oz. ASW **Subject:** Nevada **Obv:** Bust 3/4 left of Carr wearing glasses **Obv. Legend:** ALTERED STATES OF AMERICA / CARRter DOLLAR **Rev:** Steam engine and Nevada state map **Rev. Legend:** NEVADA / 1864 / THE SILVER STATE / 2006

Date	Mintage	F	VF	XF	Unc	BU
2006	15	—	—	—	—	75.00

DANIEL CARR PARODY STATE QUARTER

X# 307a CARRTER DOLLAR
Yellow Brass **Obv:** Bust 3/4 left of Carr wearing glasses, satin finish **Obv. Legend:** ALTERED STATES OF AMERICA / CARRter DOLLAR **Rev:** Bust 3/4 left of Carr wearing glasses, proof finish **Rev. Legend:** ALTERED STATES OF AMERICA / CARRter DOLLAR

Date	Mintage	F	VF	XF	Unc	BU
ND	36	—	—	—	—	10.00

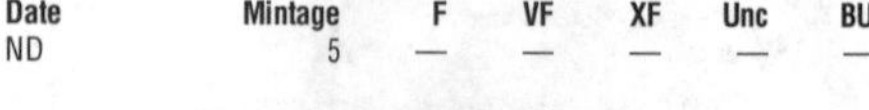

X# 307b CARRTER DOLLAR
7.7857 g., 0.9990 Silver 0.2501 oz. ASW **Obv:** Bust 3/4 left of Carr wearing glasses, satin finish **Obv. Legend:** ALTERED STATES OF AMERICA / CARRter DOLLAR **Rev:** Bust 3/4 left of Carr wearing glasses, proof finish **Rev. Legend:** ALTERED STATES OF AMERICA / CARRter DOLLAR

Date	Mintage	F	VF	XF	Unc	BU
ND	5	—	—	—	—	—

X# 310a CARRTER DOLLAR
Copper Nickel **Subject:** New Jersey **Obv:** Bust 3/4 left of Carr wearing glasses **Obv. Legend:** ALTERED STATES OF AMERICA / CARRter DOLLAR **Rev:** Car at Turnpike toll booth

Date	Mintage	F	VF	XF	Unc	BU
1999	—	—	—	—	—	7.00

X# 310b CARRTER DOLLAR

Yellow Brass **Subject:** New Jersey **Obv:** Bust 3/4 left of Carr wearing glasses **Obv. Legend:** ALTERED STATES OF AMERICA / CARRter DOLLAR **Rev:** Car at Turnpike toll booth

Date	Mintage	F	VF	XF	Unc	BU
1999	63	—	—	—	—	15.00

X# 310c CARRTER DOLLAR

7.7857 g., 0.9990 Silver 0.2501 oz. ASW **Subject:** New Jersey **Obv:** Bust 3/4 left of Carr wearing glasses **Obv. Legend:** ALTERED STATES OF AMERICA / CARRter DOLLAR **Rev:** Car at Turnpike toll booth

Date	Mintage	F	VF	XF	Unc	BU
1999	11	—	—	—	—	—

X# 313b CARRTER DOLLAR

Yellow Brass **Subject:** Rhode Island **Obv:** Bust 3/4 left of Carr wearing glasses **Obv. Legend:** ALTERED STATES OF AMERICA / CARRter DOLLAR **Rev:** Small State in ocean

Date	Mintage	F	VF	XF	Unc	BU
1999	63	—	—	—	—	15.00

X# 311c CARRTER DOLLAR

7.7857 g., 0.9990 Silver 0.2501 oz. ASW **Subject:** Virginia **Obv:** Bust 3/4 left of Carr wearing glasses **Obv. Legend:** ALTERED STATES OF AMERICA / CARRter DOLLAR **Rev:** Map of WVA and VA

Date	Mintage	F	VF	XF	Unc	BU
2000	10	—	—	—	—	—

X# 311a CARRTER DOLLAR

Copper Nickel **Subject:** Virginia **Obv:** Bust 3/4 left of Carr wearing glasses **Obv. Legend:** ALTERED STATES OF AMERICA / CARRter DOLLAR **Rev:** Map of WVA and VA

Date	Mintage	F	VF	XF	Unc	BU
2000	—	—	—	—	—	7.00

X# 311b CARRTER DOLLAR

Yellow Brass **Subject:** Virginia **Obv:** Bust 3/4 left of Carr wearing glasses **Obv. Legend:** ALTERED STATES OF AMERICA / CARRter DOLLAR **Rev:** Map of WVA and VA

Date	Mintage	F	VF	XF	Unc	BU
2000	60	—	—	—	—	15.00

X# 312a CARRTER DOLLAR

Copper Nickel **Subject:** New York **Obv:** Bust 3/4 left of Carr wearing glasses **Obv. Legend:** ALTERED STATES OF AMERICA / CARRter DOLLAR **Rev:** Statue of Liberty and buildings

Date	Mintage	F	VF	XF	Unc	BU
2001	—	—	—	—	—	7.00

X# 312b CARRTER DOLLAR

Yellow Brass **Subject:** New York **Obv:** Bust 3/4 left of Carr wearing glasses **Obv. Legend:** ALTERED STATES OF AMERICA / CARRter DOLLAR **Rev:** Statue of Liberty and buildings

Date	Mintage	F	VF	XF	Unc	BU
2001	80	—	—	—	—	15.00

X# 312c CARRTER DOLLAR

7.7857 g., 0.9990 Silver 0.2501 oz. ASW **Subject:** New York **Obv:** Bust 3/4 left of Carr wearing glasses **Obv. Legend:** ALTERED STATES OF AMERICA / CARRter DOLLAR **Rev:** Statue of Liberty and buildings

Date	Mintage	F	VF	XF	Unc	BU
2001	15	—	—	—	—	—

X# 313a CARRTER DOLLAR

Copper Nickel **Subject:** Rhode Island **Obv:** Bust 3/4 left of Carr wearing glasses **Obv. Legend:** ALTERED STATES OF AMERICA / CARRter DOLLAR **Rev:** Small State in ocean

Date	Mintage	F	VF	XF	Unc	BU
2001	—	—	—	—	—	7.00

X# 313c CARRTER DOLLAR

7.7857 g., 0.9990 Silver 0.2501 oz. ASW **Subject:** Rhode Island **Obv:** Bust 3/4 left of Carr wearing glasses **Obv. Legend:** ALTERED STATES OF AMERICA / CARRter DOLLAR **Rev:** Small State in ocean

Date	Mintage	F	VF	XF	Unc	BU
2001	10	—	—	—	—	—

X# 314a CARRTER DOLLAR

Copper Nickel **Subject:** Indiana **Obv:** Bust 3/4 left of Carr wearing glasses **Obv. Legend:** ALTERED STATES OF AMERICA / CARRter DOLLAR **Rev:** Indiana map and death spiral

Date	Mintage	F	VF	XF	Unc	BU
2002	—	—	—	—	—	7.00

X# 314b CARRTER DOLLAR

Yellow Brass **Subject:** Indiana **Obv:** Bust 3/4 left of Carr wearing glasses **Obv. Legend:** ALTERED STATES OF AMERICA / CARRter DOLLAR **Rev:** Indiana map and death spiral

Date	Mintage	F	VF	XF	Unc	BU
2002	63	—	—	—	—	15.00

X# 314c CARRTER DOLLAR

7.7857 g., 0.9990 Silver 0.2501 oz. ASW **Subject:** Indiana **Obv:** Bust 3/4 left of Carr wearing glasses **Obv. Legend:** ALTERED STATES OF AMERICA / CARRter DOLLAR **Rev:** Indiana map and death spiral

Date	Mintage	F	VF	XF	Unc	BU
2002	10	—	—	—	—	—

X# 315a CARRTER DOLLAR

Copper Nickel **Subject:** Maine **Obv:** Bust 3/4 left of Carr wearing glasses **Obv. Legend:** ALTERED STATES OF AMERICA / CARRter DOLLAR **Rev:** Large lobster monster

Date	Mintage	F	VF	XF	Unc	BU
2003	—	—	—	—	—	7.00

X# 315b CARRTER DOLLAR

Yellow Brass **Subject:** Maine **Obv:** Bust 3/4 left of Carr wearing glasses **Obv. Legend:** ALTERED STATES OF AMERICA / CARRter DOLLAR **Rev:** Large lobster monster

Date	Mintage	F	VF	XF	Unc	BU
2003	61	—	—	—	—	15.00

X# 315c CARRTER DOLLAR

7.7857 g., 0.9990 Silver 0.2501 oz. ASW **Subject:** Maine **Obv:** Bust 3/4 left of Carr wearing glasses **Obv. Legend:** ALTERED STATES OF AMERICA / CARRter DOLLAR **Rev:** Large lobster monster

Date	Mintage	F	VF	XF	Unc	BU
2003	10	—	—	—	—	—

X# 316a CARRTER DOLLAR

Copper Nickel **Subject:** Florida **Obv:** Bust 3/4 left of Carr wearing glasses **Obv. Legend:** ALTERED STATES OF AMERICA / CARRter DOLLAR **Rev:** Hanging chad and State map

Date	Mintage	F	VF	XF	Unc	BU
2004	—	—	—	—	—	7.00

X# 316b CARRTER DOLLAR

Yellow Brass **Subject:** Florida **Obv:** Bust 3/4 left of Carr wearing glasses **Obv. Legend:** ALTERED STATES OF AMERICA / CARRter DOLLAR **Rev:** Hanging chad and State map

Date	Mintage	F	VF	XF	Unc	BU
2004	61	—	—	—	—	15.00

X# 316c CARRTER DOLLAR

7.7857 g., 0.9990 Silver 0.2501 oz. ASW **Subject:** Florida **Obv:** Bust 3/4 left of Carr wearing glasses **Obv. Legend:** ALTERED STATES OF AMERICA / CARRter DOLLAR **Rev:** Hanging chad and State map

Date	Mintage	F	VF	XF	Unc	BU
2004	10	—	—	—	—	—

X# 317a CARRTER DOLLAR

Copper Nickel **Subject:** Texas **Obv:** Bust 3/4 left of Carr wearing glasses **Obv. Legend:** ALTERED STATES OF AMERICA / CARRter DOLLAR **Rev:** Texas within Alaska map

Date	Mintage	F	VF	XF	Unc	BU
2004	—	—	—	—	—	7.00

X# 317b CARRTER DOLLAR

Yellow Brass **Subject:** Texas **Obv:** Bust 3/4 left of Carr wearing glasses **Obv. Legend:** ALTERED STATES OF AMERICA / CARRter DOLLAR **Rev:** Texas within Alaska map

Date	Mintage	F	VF	XF	Unc	BU
2004	60	—	—	—	—	15.00

X# 317c CARRTER DOLLAR

7.7857 g., 0.9990 Silver 0.2501 oz. ASW **Subject:** Texas **Obv:** Bust 3/4 left of Carr wearing glasses **Obv. Legend:** ALTERED STATES OF AMERICA / CARRter DOLLAR **Rev:** Texas within Alaska map

Date	Mintage	F	VF	XF	Unc	BU
2004	10	—	—	—	—	—

X# 318a CARRTER DOLLAR

Copper Nickel **Subject:** Kalifornia **Obv:** Bust 3/4 left of Carr wearing glasses **Obv. Legend:** ALTERED STATES OF AMERICA / CARRter DOLLAR **Rev:** Map of California after earthquake

Date	Mintage	F	VF	XF	Unc	BU
2005	—	—	—	—	—	7.00

X# 318b CARRTER DOLLAR

Yellow Brass **Subject:** Kalifornia **Obv:** Bust 3/4 left of Carr wearing glasses **Obv. Legend:** ALTERED STATES OF AMERICA / CARRter DOLLAR **Rev:** Map of California after earthquake

Date	Mintage	F	VF	XF	Unc	BU
2005	82	—	—	—	—	15.00

X# 318c CARRTER DOLLAR

7.7859 g., 0.9990 Silver 0.2501 oz. ASW **Subject:** Kalifornia **Obv:** Bust 3/4 left of Carr in glasses **Obv. Legend:** ALTERED STATES OF AMERICA / CARRter DOLLAR **Rev:** Map of California after earthquake

Date	Mintage	F	VF	XF	Unc	BU
2005	12	—	—	—	—	—

X# 319a CARRTER DOLLAR

Copper Nickel **Subject:** Oregon **Obv:** Bust 3/4 left of Carr wearing glasses **Obv. Legend:** ALTERED STATES OF AMERICA / CARRter DOLLAR **Rev:** Recycle logos flank legend

Date	Mintage	F	VF	XF	Unc	BU
2005	—	—	—	—	—	7.00

X# 319b CARRTER DOLLAR

Yellow Brass **Subject:** Oregon **Obv:** Bust 3/4 left of Carr wearing glasses **Obv. Legend:** ALTERED STATES OF AMERICA / CARRter DOLLAR **Rev:** Recycle logos flank legend

Date	Mintage	F	VF	XF	Unc	BU
2005	62	—	—	—	—	—

X# 319c CARRTER DOLLAR

7.7859 g., 0.9990 Silver 0.2501 oz. ASW **Subject:** Oregon **Obv:** Bust 3/4 left of Carr wearing glasses **Obv. Legend:** ALTERED STATES OF AMERICA / CARRter DOLLAR **Rev:** Recycle logos flank legend

Date	Mintage	F	VF	XF	Unc	BU
2005	70	—	—	—	—	—

X# 320a CARRTER DOLLAR

Copper Nickel **Subject:** Colorado **Obv:** Bust 3/4 left of Carr wearing glasses **Obv. Legend:** ALTERED STATES OF AMERICA / CARRter DOLLAR **Rev:** Overturned SUV on snowy road

Date	Mintage	F	VF	XF	Unc	BU
2006	—	—	—	—	—	7.00

X# 320b CARRTER DOLLAR

Yellow Brass **Subject:** Colorado **Obv:** Bust 3/4 left of Carr wearing glasses **Obv. Legend:** ALTERED STATES OF AMERICA / CARRter DOLLAR **Rev:** Overturned SUV on snowy road

Date	Mintage	F	VF	XF	Unc	BU
2006	82	—	—	—	—	15.00

X# 320c CARRTER DOLLAR

7.7857 g., 0.9990 Silver 0.2501 oz. ASW **Subject:** Colorado **Obv:** Bust 3/4 left of Carr wearing glasses **Obv. Legend:** ALTERED STATES OF AMERICA / CARRter DOLLAR **Rev:** Overturned SUV on snowy road

Date	Mintage	F	VF	XF	Unc	BU
2006	10	—	—	—	—	—

X# 321a CARRTER DOLLAR

Copper Nickel **Subject:** South Dakota **Obv:** Bust 3/4 left of Carr wearing glasses **Obv. Legend:** ALTERED STATES OF AMERICA / CARRter DOLLAR **Rev:** Map of South Dakota and DMZ area

Date	Mintage	F	VF	XF	Unc	BU
2006	—	—	—	—	—	7.00

X# 321b CARRTER DOLLAR

Yellow Brass **Subject:** South Dakota **Obv:** Bust 3/4 left of Carr wearing glasses **Obv. Legend:** ALTERED STATES OF AMERICA / CARRter DOLLAR **Rev:** Map of South Dakota and DMZ area

Date	Mintage	F	VF	XF	Unc	BU
2006	62	—	—	—	—	15.00

X# 321c CARRTER DOLLAR

7.7857 g., 0.9990 Silver 0.2501 oz. ASW **Subject:** South Dakota **Obv:** Bust 3/4 left of Carr wearing glasses **Obv. Legend:** ALTERED STATES OF AMERICA / CARRter DOLLAR **Rev:** Map of South Dakota and DMZ area

Date	Mintage	F	VF	XF	Unc	BU
2006	10	—	—	—	—	—

X# 322a CARRTER DOLLAR

Copper Nickel **Subject:** Wyoming **Obv:** Bust 3/4 left of Carr wearing glasses **Obv. Legend:** ALTERED STATES OF AMERICA / CARRter DOLLAR **Rev:** Blank State map

Date	Mintage	F	VF	XF	Unc	BU
2007	—	—	—	—	—	7.00

X# 322b CARRTER DOLLAR

Yellow Brass **Subject:** Wyoming **Obv:** Bust 3/4 left of Carr wearing glasses **Obv. Legend:** ALTERED STATES OF AMERICA / CARRter DOLLAR **Rev:** Blank State map

Date	Mintage	F	VF	XF	Unc	BU
2007	63	—	—	—	—	15.00

X# 322c CARRTER DOLLAR

7.7857 g., 0.9990 Silver 0.2501 oz. ASW **Subject:** Wyoming **Obv:** Bust 3/4 left of Carr wearing glasses **Obv. Legend:** ALTERED STATES OF AMERICA / CARRter DOLLAR **Rev:** Blank State map

Date	Mintage	F	VF	XF	Unc	BU
2007	10	—	—	—	—	—

X# 323a CARRTER DOLLAR

Copper Nickel **Subject:** Nuke Mexico **Obv:** Bust 3/4 left of Carr wearing glasses **Obv. Legend:** ALTERED STATES OF AMERICA / CARRter DOLLAR **Rev:** Mushroom cloud and State map

Date	Mintage	F	VF	XF	Unc	BU
2008	—	—	—	—	—	7.00

X# 323b CARRTER DOLLAR

Yellow Brass **Subject:** Nuke Mexico **Obv:** Bust 3/4 left of Carr wearing glasses **Obv. Legend:** ALTERED STATES OF AMERICA / CARRter DOLLAR **Rev:** Mushroom cloud and State map

Date	Mintage	F	VF	XF	Unc	BU
2008	82	—	—	—	—	15.00

X# 323c CARRTER DOLLAR

7.7857 g., 0.9990 Silver 0.2501 oz. ASW **Subject:** Nuke Mexico **Obv:** Bust 3/4 left of Carr wearing glasses **Obv. Legend:** ALTERED STATES OF AMERICA / CARRter DOLLAR **Rev:** Mushroom cloud and State map

Date	Mintage	F	VF	XF	Unc	BU
2008	10	—	—	—	—	—

DANIEL CARR PROTOTYPE DOLLARS

X# 366a 01

Brass, 27 mm. **Obv:** Pilot Bessie Coleman **Obv. Legend:** LIBERTY **Rev:** Eagle in flight over sun **Rev. Legend:** USA / O1

Date	Mintage	F	VF	XF	Unc	BU
2001 Prooflike	650	—	—	—	—	20.00
2001 Satin	100	—	—	—	—	25.00

X# 366b 01

15.5520 g., 0.9990 Silver 0.4995 oz. ASW, 27 mm. **Obv:** Pilot Bessie Coleman **Obv. Legend:** LIBERTY **Rev:** Eagle in flight over sun **Rev. Legend:** USA / O1 **Edge Lettering:** .999 fine silver

Date	Mintage	F	VF	XF	Unc	BU
2001 Prooflike	100	—	—	—	—	40.00
2001 Satin	25	—	—	—	—	75.00

X# 369a 1000000

Brass, 27 mm. **Obv:** Sacagawea facing **Rev:** Eagle in flight over sun, globe and moon **Rev. Legend:** UNITED STATES OF AMERICA / E PLURIBUS UNUM / PEACE

Date	Mintage	F	VF	XF	Unc	BU
2003 Prooflike	450	—	—	—	—	30.00
2003 Satin	100	—	—	—	—	35.00

X# 369b 1000000

15.5520 g., 0.9990 Silver 0.4995 oz. ASW, 27 mm. **Obv:** Sacagawea facing **Rev:** Eagle in flight over sun, globe and moon **Rev. Legend:** UNITED STATES OF AMERICA / E PLURIBUS UNUM / PEACE **Edge Lettering:** .999 fine silver

Date	Mintage	F	VF	XF	Unc	BU
2003 Prooflike	50	—	—	—	—	80.00
2003 Satin	25	—	—	—	—	90.00

:# 370a 1000000

rass, 27 mm. **Obv:** Sacagawea facing **Rev:** Eagle in ght over sun, globe and moon **Rev. Legend:** UNITED TATES OF AMERICA / E PLURIBUS UNUM

ate	Mintage	F	VF	XF	Unc	BU
)03 Prooflike	450	—	—	—	—	30.00
)03 Satin	100	—	—	—	—	35.00

:# 370b 1000000

5.5520 g., 0.9990 Silver 0.4995 oz. ASW, 27 mm. **)bv:** Sacagawea facing **Rev:** Eagle in flight over sun, lobe and moon **Rev. Legend:** UNITED STATES OF MERICA / E PLURIBUS UNUM

ate	Mintage	F	VF	XF	Unc	BU
003 Prooflike	50	—	—	—	—	80.00
)03 Satin	25	—	—	—	—	95.00

X# 367a NON DOLLAR

3rass, 27 mm. **Obv:** Pilot Bessie Coleman **)bv. Legend:** LIBERTY **Rev:** Eagle in flight over sun **Rev. Legend:** UNITED STATES OF AMERICA / E PLURIBUS UNUM / PEACE

ate	Mintage	F	VF	XF	Unc	BU
'001 Prooflike	450	—	—	—	—	25.00
'001 Satin	100	—	—	—	—	30.00

X# 367b NON DOLLAR

15.5520 g., 0.9990 Silver 0.4995 oz. ASW, 27 mm. **Obv:** Pilot Bessie Coleman **Obv. Legend:** LIBERTY **Rev:** Eagle in flight over sun **Rev. Legend:** UNITED STATES OF AMERICA / E PLURIBUS UNUM / PEACE **Edge Lettering:** .999 fine silver

Date	Mintage	F	VF	XF	Unc	BU
2001 Prooflike	50	—	—	—	—	65.00
2001 Satin	25	—	—	—	—	70.00

X# 368a NON DOLLAR

Brass, 27 mm. **Obv:** Pilot Bessie Coleman **Obv. Legend:** LIBERTY **Rev:** Eagle in flight over sun **Rev. Legend:** UNITED STATES OF AMERICA / E PLURIBUS UNUM

Date	Mintage	F	VF	XF	Unc	BU
2001 Prooflike	450	—	—	—	—	25.00
2001 Satin	100	—	—	—	—	30.00

X# 368b NON DOLLAR

15.5520 g., 0.9990 Silver 0.4995 oz. ASW, 27 mm. **Obv:** Pilot Bessie Coleman **Obv. Legend:** LIBERTY **Rev:** Eagle in flight over sun **Rev. Legend:** UNITED STATES OF AMERICA / E PLURIBUS UNUM **Edge Lettering:** .999 fine silver

Date	Mintage	F	VF	XF	Unc	BU
2001 Prooflike	50	—	—	—	—	65.00
2001 Satin	25	—	—	—	—	70.00

X# 371a NON DOLLAR

Brass, 27 mm. **Obv:** Sacagawea facing **Rev:** Eagle in flight over sun **Rev. Legend:** UNITED STATES OF AMERICA / E PLURIBUS UNUM / PEACE

Date	Mintage	F	VF	XF	Unc	BU
2003 Prooflike	450	—	—	—	—	30.00
2003 Satin	100	—	—	—	—	35.00

X# 371b NON DOLLAR

15.5520 g., 0.9990 Silver 0.4995 oz. ASW, 27 mm. **Obv:** Sacagawea facing **Rev:** Eagle in flight over sun **Rev. Legend:** UNITED STATES OF AMERICA / E PLURIBUS UNUM / PEACE **Edge Lettering:** .999 fine silver

Date	Mintage	F	VF	XF	Unc	BU
2003 Prooflike	50	—	—	—	—	85.00
2003 Satin	25	—	—	—	—	95.00

X# 372a NON DOLLAR

Brass, 27 mm. **Obv:** Sacagawea facing **Rev:** Eagle in flight over sun **Rev. Legend:** UNITED STATES OF AMERICA / E PLURIBUS UNUM

Date	Mintage	F	VF	XF	Unc	BU
2003 Prooflike	450	—	—	—	—	30.00
2003 Satin	100	—	—	—	—	35.00

X# 372b NON DOLLAR

15.5520 g., 0.9990 Silver 0.4995 oz. ASW, 27 mm. **Obv:** Sacagawea facing **Rev:** Eagle in flight over sun **Rev. Legend:** UNITED STATES OF AMERICA / E PLURIBUS UNUM **Edge Lettering:** .999 fine silver

Date	Mintage	F	VF	XF	Unc	BU
2003 Prooflike	50	—	—	—	—	85.00
2003 Satin	25	—	—	—	—	95.00

X# 365 ONE ROLLER

8.1000 g., Brass, 27 mm. **Obv:** Astronaut holding American flag on moon **Obv. Legend:** UNITED STATES OF AMERICA / 2001 **Rev:** Eagle in flight over sun **Rev. Legend:** LIBERTY / ONE ROLLER

Date	Mintage	F	VF	XF	Unc	BU
2001 Prooflike	900	—	—	—	—	20.00

X# 365a ONE ROLLER

12.6000 g., Brass, 27 mm. **Obv:** Astronaut holding American flag on moon **Obv. Legend:** UNITED STATES OF AMERICA / 2001 **Rev:** Eagle in flight over sun **Rev. Legend:** LIBERTY / ONE ROLLER

Date	Mintage	F	VF	XF	Unc	BU
2001 Prooflike	50	—	—	—	—	—
2001 Satin	100	—	—	—	—	30.00

X# 365b ONE ROLLER

7.7857 g., 0.9990 Silver 0.2501 oz. ASW, 27 mm. **Obv:** Astronaut holding American flag on moon **Obv. Legend:** UNITED STATES OF AMERICA / 2001 **Rev:** Eagle in flight over sun **Rev. Legend:** LIBERTY / ONE ROLLER **Edge Lettering:** .999 fine silver

Date	Mintage	F	VF	XF	Unc	BU
2001 Prooflike	9	—	—	—	—	—

Note: Error in planchet size.

X# 365c ONE ROLLER

15.5520 g., 0.9990 Silver 0.4995 oz. ASW, 27 mm. **Obv:** Astronaut holding American flag on moon **Obv. Legend:** UNITED STATES OF AMERICA / 2001 **Rev:** Eagle in flight over sun **Rev. Legend:** LIBERTY / ONE ROLLER **Edge Lettering:** .999 fine silver

Date	Mintage	F	VF	XF	Unc	BU
2001 Prooflike	100	—	—	—	—	50.00
2001 Satin	25	—	—	—	—	100

X# 373a S1

Brass, 27 mm. **Obv:** Daniel Carr 3/4 portrait left wearing glasses **Rev:** Statue of Liberty **Rev. Legend:** UNITED STATES OF AMERICA

Date	Mintage	F	VF	XF	Unc	BU
2007 Prooflike	10	—	—	—	—	—
2007 Satin	5	—	—	—	—	—

X# 373b S1

15.5520 g., 0.9990 Silver 0.4995 oz. ASW, 27 mm. **Obv:** Daniel Carr 3/4 portrait left wearing glasses **Obv. Legend:** DANIEL CARR 45TH PRESIDENT 2017 - 2021 **Rev:** Statue of Liberty **Rev. Legend:** UNITED STATES OF AMERICA **Edge Lettering:** .999 fine silver

Date	Mintage	F	VF	XF	Unc	BU
2007 Prooflike	20	—	—	—	—	35.00
2007 Satin	250	—	—	—	—	7.00

X# 375a S1

Brass **Obv:** George Washington bust 3/4 left **Rev:** Eagle head in shield

Date	Mintage	F	VF	XF	Unc	BU
2007 Prooflike	250	—	—	—	—	25.00
2007 Satin	2,765	—	—	—	—	6.00

X# 375b S1

15.5520 g., 0.9990 Silver 0.4995 oz. ASW **Obv:** George Washington bust 3/4 left **Rev:** Eagle head in shield **Edge Lettering:** .999 fine silver

Date	Mintage	F	VF	XF	Unc	BU
2007 Prooflike	40	—	—	—	—	60.00
2007 Satin	40	—	—	—	—	50.00

X# 376a S1

Brass, 27 mm. **Obv:** George Washington bust 3/4 left **Rev:** Statue of Liberty

Date	Mintage	F	VF	XF	Unc	BU
2007 Prooflike	85	—	—	—	—	35.00
2007 Satin	10,041	—	—	—	—	5.00

X# 376b S1

15.5520 g., 0.9990 Silver 0.4995 oz. ASW, 27 mm. **Obv:** George Washington bust 3/4 left **Rev:** Statue of Liberty **Edge Lettering:** .999 fine silver or .999 Ag.

Date	Mintage	F	VF	XF	Unc	BU
2007 Prooflike	30	—	—	—	—	75.00
2007 Satin	11	—	—	—	—	95.00

X# 377a S1

Brass, 27 mm. **Obv:** John Adams bust 3/4 right **Obv. Legend:** JOHN ADAMS / 1797 / 1801 **Rev:** Eagle head in shield **Rev. Legend:** UNITED STATES OF AMERICA / 2007 / S1

Date	Mintage	F	VF	XF	Unc	BU
2007 Prooflike	250	—	—	—	—	20.00
2007 Satin	2,760	—	—	—	—	5.00

X# 377b S1

15.5520 g., 0.9990 Silver 0.4995 oz. ASW, 27 mm. **Obv:** John Adams bust 3/4 right **Obv. Legend:** JOHN ADAMS / 1797 / 1801 **Rev:** Eagle head in shield **Rev. Legend:** UNITED STATES OF AMERICA / 2007 / S1

Date	Mintage	F	VF	XF	Unc	BU
2007 Prooflike	40	—	—	—	—	55.00
2007 Satin	40	—	—	—	—	45.00

X# 378a S1

Brass, 27 mm. **Obv:** John Adams bust 3/4 right **Obv. Legend:** JOHN ADAMS / 1797 / 1801 **Rev:** Statue of Liberty **Rev. Legend:** UNITED STATES OF AMERICA / 2007 / S1

Date	Mintage	F	VF	XF	Unc	BU
2007 Prooflike	55	—	—	—	—	35.00
2007 Satin	10,017	—	—	—	—	4.00

X# 378b S1

15.5520 g., 0.9990 Silver 0.4995 oz. ASW **Obv:** John Adams bust 3/4 right **Obv. Legend:** JOHN ADAMS / 1797 / 1801 **Rev:** Statue of Liberty **Rev. Legend:** UNITED STATES OF AMERICA / 2007 / S1

Date	Mintage	F	VF	XF	Unc	BU
2007 Prooflike	20	—	—	—	—	75.00
2007 Satin	11	—	—	—	—	80.00

X# 379a S1

Brass, 27 mm. **Obv:** Thomas Jefferson bust 3/4 facing right **Obv. Legend:** THOMAS JEFFERSON / 1801 / 1809 **Rev:** Eagle head in shield **Rev. Legend:** UNITED STATES OF AMERICA / 2007 / S1

Date	Mintage	F	VF	XF	Unc	BU
2007 Prooflike	250	—	—	—	—	20.00
2007 Satin	2,765	—	—	—	—	6.00

X# 379b S1

15.5520 g., 0.9990 Silver 0.4995 oz. ASW, 27 mm. **Obv:** Thomas Jefferson bust 3/4 facing right **Obv. Legend:** THOMAS JEFFERSON / 1801 / 1809 **Rev:** Eagle head in shield **Rev. Legend:** UNITED STATES OF AMERICA / 2007 / S1

Date	Mintage	F	VF	XF	Unc	BU
2007 Prooflike	40	—	—	—	—	60.00
2007 Satin	40	—	—	—	—	55.00

X# 380a S1

Brass, 27 mm. **Obv:** Thomas Jefferson bust 3/4 facing right **Obv. Legend:** THOMAS JEFFERSON / 1801 / 1809 **Rev:** Statue of Liberty **Rev. Legend:** UNITED STATES OF AMERICA / 2007 / S1

Date	Mintage	F	VF	XF	Unc	BU
2007 Prooflike	55	—	—	—	—	35.00
2007 Satin	10,019	—	—	—	—	5.00

X# 380b S1

15.5520 g., 0.9990 Silver 0.4995 oz. ASW, 27 mm. **Obv:** Thomas Jefferson bust 3/4 facing right **Obv. Legend:** THOMAS JEFFERSON / 1801 / 1809 **Rev:** Statue of Liberty **Rev. Legend:** UNITED STATES OF AMERICA / 2007 / S1

Date	Mintage	F	VF	XF	Unc	BU
2007 Prooflike	20	—	—	—	—	85.00
2007 Satin	11	—	—	—	—	95.00

X# 381a S1

Brass **Obv:** James Madison bust 3/4 facing left **Obv. Legend:** JAMES MADISON / 1809 / 1817 **Rev:** Eagle head in shield **Rev. Legend:** UNITED STATES OF AMERICA / 2007 / S1

Date	Mintage	F	VF	XF	Unc	BU
2007 Prooflike	255	—	—	—	—	20.00
2007 Satin	2,760	—	—	—	—	5.00

X# 381b S1

15.5520 g., 0.9990 Silver 0.4995 oz. ASW **Obv:** James Madison bust 3/4 facing left **Obv. Legend:** JAMES MADISON / 1809 / 1817 **Rev:** Eagle head in shield **Rev. Legend:** UNITED STATES OF AMERICA / 2007 / S1 **Edge Lettering:** .999 fine silver

Date	Mintage	F	VF	XF	Unc	BU
2007 Prooflike	40	—	—	—	—	55.00
2007 Satin	40	—	—	—	—	45.00

X# 382a S1

Brass **Obv:** James Madison bust 3/4 facing left **Obv. Legend:** JAMES MADISON / 1809 / 1817 **Rev:** Statue of Liberty **Rev. Legend:** UNITED STATES OF AMERICA / 2007 / S1

Date	Mintage	F	VF	XF	Unc	BU
2007 Prooflike	55	—	—	—	—	35.00
2007 Satin	10,016	—	—	—	—	4.00

X# 382b S1

15.5520 g., 0.9990 Silver 0.4995 oz. ASW **Obv:** Jame Madison bust 3/4 facing left **Obv. Legend:** JAMES MADISON / 1809 / 1817 **Rev:** Statue of Liberty **Rev. Legend:** UNITED STATES OF AMERICA / 200 / S1 **Edge Lettering:** .999 fine silver

Date	Mintage	F	VF	XF	Unc	B
2007 Prooflike	20	—	—	—	—	75.
2007 Satin	12	—	—	—	—	80.

X# 374 TWO ROLLERS

Bi-Metallic **Ring Composition:** Brass **Center Weight** 7.7857 g. **Center Composition:** 0.9990 Silver 0.2501 oz. ASW , 30 mm. **Obv:** Astronaut holding fla on moon **Obv. Legend:** UNITED STATES OF AMERICA / 2009 **Rev:** Eagle in flight over sun **Rev. Legend:** LIBERTY / TWO ROLLERS

Date	Mintage	F	VF	XF	Unc	B
2009 Prooflike	250	—	—	—	—	40.0
2009 Satin	100	—	—	—	—	50.0

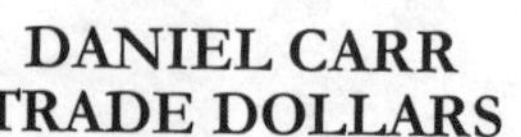

DANIEL CARR TRADE DOLLARS

X# 399 20 DOLLARS

31.1050 g., 0.9990 Silver 0.9990 oz. ASW, 39 mm. **Obv:** Liberty seated right holdign spear and torch, globe, gear, stars and rays in background **Rev:** Eagle holding lightning and olive branch **Rev. Legend:** UNITED STATES OF AMERICA / 20 TRADE DOLLARS **Edge:** Reeded

Date	Mintage	F	VF	XF	Unc	BU
2007 D	—	—	—	—	35.00	—

PATTERNS

INA Issues

X#	Date	Mintage	Identification	Mkt Va
Pn1	1795 (2006)	—	Dollar. Copper-Nickel-Zinc. Plain edge.	—

X#	Date	Mintage	Identification	Mkt Val
Pn2	1795 (2006)	—	Dollar. Copper. Plain edge.	—
Pn3	1795 (2006)	—	Dollar. Goldine. Plain edge.	—

X#	Date	Mintage	Identification	Mkt Val
Pn4	1836 (2006)	—	Dollar. Copper-Nickel-Zinc. Gobrecht, plain edge.	—
Pn10	1836 (2006)	—	Dollar. Copper. Gobrecht, Plain edge.	—
Pn11	1836 (2006)	—	Dollar. Goldine. Gobrecht, plain edge.	—

X#	Date	Mintage	Identification	Mkt Val
Pn12	1863 (2006)	—	Dollar. Copper-Nickel-Zinc. Plain edge.	—
Pn13	1863 (2006)	—	Dollar. Copper. Plain edge.	—
Pn14	1863 (2006)	—	Dollar. Goldine. Plain edge.	—

X#	Date	Mintage	Identification	Mkt Val
Pn15	1871 (2006)	—	Dollar. Copper-Nickel-Zinc. Longacre, plain edge.	—
Pn16	1871 (2006)	—	Dollar. Copper. Longacre, plain edge.	—
Pn17	1871 (2006)	—	Dollar. Goldine. Longacre, plain edge.	—

X#	Date	Mintage	Identification	Mkt Val
Pn18	1879 (2006)	—	Dollar. Copper-Nickel-Zinc. Morgan's "Schoolgirl", plain edge.	—
Pn19	1879 (2006)	—	Dollar. Copper. Morgan's "Schoolgirl", plain edge.	—
Pn20	1879 (2006)	—	Dollar. Goldine. Morgan's "Schoolgirl", plain edge.	—

X#	Date	Mintage	Identification	Mkt Val
Pn21	1879 (2006)	—	Dollar. Copper-Nickel-Zinc. Morgan/Barber, plain edge	—
Pn22	1879 (2006)	—	Dollar. Copper. Morgan/Barber, plain edge	—
Pn23	1879 (2006)	—	Dollar. Goldine. Morgan/Barber, plain edge	—

PIEFORTS

NORFED Distribution Issues

X#	Date	Mintage	Identification	Mkt Val
P1	2004	—	20 Liberty Dollars. Silver. 62.3000 g. Serial number on rim.	75.00
P2	2004	4,000	20 Liberty Dollars. Silver. 62.7300 g. "UNCIRCULATED" edge.	60.00

TRIAL STRIKES

NORFED Distribution Issues

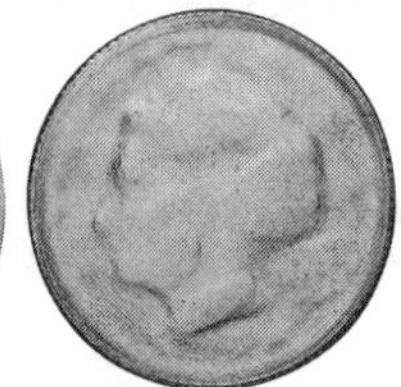

X#	Date	Mintage	Identification	Mkt Val
TS1	2006	—	5 Liberty Dollars. Silver. 7.7800 g. 17.1 mm. Obverse X#224.	—
TS2	2006	—	5 Liberty Dollars. Silver. 7.7800 g. 17.1 mm. Reverse X#224.	—

PROOF SETS

X#	Date	Mintage	Identification	Issue Price	Mkt Val
XPS1	2003 (3)	—	X#207, 208, 209.2	44.00	28.75
XPS2	1795 (2006) (3)	—	XPn1-XPn3	—	—
XPS3	1836 (2006)	—	XPn4, 10-11	—	—
XPS4	1863 (2006) (3)	—	XPn12-14	—	—
XPS5	1871 (2006) (3)	—	XPn15-17	—	—
XPS6	1879 (2006) (3)	—	XPn18-20	—	—
XPS7	1879 (2006) (3)	—	XPn21-23	—	—

ALASKA

TERRITORY

TOKEN COINAGE

X# Tn2 1/4 PENNY WEIGHT

0.4430 g., Gold, 9.5 mm. **Issuer:** A.Y.P.E. **Obv:** Miner standing facing with pick axe **Obv. Legend:** ALASKA GOLD **Rev:** Shield in sprays

Date	Mintage	F	VF	XF	Unc	BU
1909	—	—	—	—	150	200

X# Tn3 1/2 PENNY WEIGHT

0.8860 g., Gold, 11.8 mm. **Issuer:** A.Y.P.E. **Obv:** Miner standing facing with pick axe **Obv. Legend:** ALASKA GOLD **Rev:** Shield in sprays

Date	Mintage	F	VF	XF	Unc	BU
1909	—	—	—	—	175	225

X# Tn4 PENNY WEIGHT

Gold, 14 mm. **Issuer:** A.Y.P.E. **Obv:** Miner standing facing with pick axe **Obv. Legend:** ALASKA GOLD **Rev:** Shield in sprays

Date	Mintage	F	VF	XF	Unc	BU
1909	—	—	—	—	200	250

X# Tn5 2 TOO WAH
Gold, 14.5 mm. **Obv:** Bust of Eskimo facing **Obv. Legend:** ALASKAN GOLD **Rev:** Value above dogsled

Date	Mintage	F	VF	XF	Unc	BU
1862 (1910)	—	—	—	—	400	—
1862(1910) Restrike	—	—	—	70.00	100	—

X# Tn8 1/4 DOLLAR
Brass **Obv:** Indian head right **Rev:** Value, legend in sprays **Rev. Legend:** ALASKA GOLD **Shape:** Octagonal

Date	Mintage	F	VF	XF	Unc	BU
1897	—	—	—	—	—	—

X# Tn20 1/4 DOLLAR
Gold **Obv:** Indian head left **Rev:** Value, legend in sprays **Rev. Legend:** ALASKA GOLD

Date	Mintage	F	VF	XF	Unc	BU
1902	—	—	—	—	—	—

X# Tn21 1/4 DOLLAR
Gold **Obv:** Parka head right **Rev:** Rising sun, value in sprays **Rev. Legend:** ALASKA GOLD **Note:** Varietes exist.

Date	Mintage	F	VF	XF	Unc	BU
1911	—	—	—	—	—	—

X# Tn15 1/2 DOLLAR
Brass **Obv:** Indian head right **Rev:** Value, legend in sprays **Rev. Legend:** ALASKA GOLD **Shape:** Octagonal

Date	Mintage	F	VF	XF	Unc	BU
1900	—	—	—	—	—	—

X# Tn22 1/2 DOLLAR
Gold **Obv:** Parka head right **Rev:** Rising sun, value in sprays **Rev. Legend:** ALASKA GLD **Note:** Varieties exist.

Date	Mintage	F	VF	XF	Unc	BU
1911	—	—	—	—	—	—

X# Tn9 DOLLAR
Brass **Obv:** Indian head right **Rev:** Value, legend in sprays **Rev. Legend:** ALASKA GOLD

Date	Mintage	F	VF	XF	Unc	BU
1897	—	—	—	—	—	—

X# Tn10 DOLLAR
Gold **Obv:** Indian head left **Rev:** Sunrise, value in sprays **Rev. Legend:** ALASKA GOLD

Date	Mintage	F	VF	XF	Unc	BU
1897	—	—	—	—	—	—

X# Tn23 DOLLAR
Gold **Obv:** Parka head right **Rev:** Rising sun, value in sprays **Rev. Legend:** ALASKA GOLD **Note:** Varieties exist.

Date	Mintage	F	VF	XF	Unc	BU
1911	—	—	—	—	—	—

X# Tn12 1/4 PINCH
Gold **Obv:** Indian head left **Rev:** Value, legend in sprays **Rev. Legend:** ALASKA GOLD

Date	Mintage	F	VF	XF	Unc	BU
1899	—	—	—	—	—	—

X# Tn16 1/4 PINCH
Gold **Obv:** Indian head right **Rev:** Value, legend in sprays **Rev. Legend:** ALASKA GOLD

Date	Mintage	F	VF	XF	Unc	BU
1901	—	—	—	—	—	—

X# Tn17 1/4 PINCH
Gold **Obv:** Indian head left **Rev:** Value, legend in sprays **Rev. Legend:** ALASKA GOLD

Date	Mintage	F	VF	XF	Unc	BU
1901	—	—	—	—	—	—

X# Tn18 1/4 PINCH
Gold **Obv:** Indian head right **Rev:** Value in sprays **Rev. Legend:** ALASKA GOLD **Shape:** Octagonal

Date	Mintage	F	VF	XF	Unc	BU
1902	—	—	—	—	—	—

X# Tn19 1/4 PINCH
Gold **Obv:** Indian head left **Rev:** Value, legend in sprays **Rev. Legend:** ALASKA GOLD **Shape:** Octagonal

Date	Mintage	F	VF	XF	Unc	BU
1902	—	—	—	—	—	—

X# Tn11 1/2 PINCH
Gold **Issuer:** M.E. Hart **Obv:** Indian head right **Rev:** Value, legend in sprays **Rev. Legend:** ALASKA GOLD

Date	Mintage	F	VF	XF	Unc	BU
1899	—	—	—	—	—	—

X# Tn13 1/2 PINCH
Gold **Obv:** Indian head left **Rev:** Value, legend in sprays **Rev. Legend:** ALASKA GOLD **Shape:** Octagonal

Date	Mintage	F	VF	XF	Unc	BU
1900	—	—	—	—	—	—

X# Tn14 1/2 PINCH
Gold **Obv:** Indian head right **Rev:** Value, legend in sprays **Rev. Legend:** ALASKA GOLD **Shape:** Octagonal

Date	Mintage	F	VF	XF	Unc	BU
1900	—	—	—	—	—	—

X# Tn1 PINCH
Gold, 12 mm. **Obv:** Indian head right **Obv. Legend:** ALASKA GOLD **Rev:** Value, legend in sprays

Date	Mintage	F	VF	XF	Unc	BU
1897	—	—	—	—	350	450
1897 Restrike	—	—	—	—	35.00	—

Note: Restrikes are normally fairly tarnished

X# Tn6 PINCH
Gold **Obv:** Indian head right **Rev:** Value, legend in sprays **Rev. Legend:** ALASKA GOLD **Shape:** Octagonal

Date	Mintage	F	VF	XF	Unc	BU
1898	—	—	—	—	—	—

ARIZONA

TERRITORY

TOKEN COINAGE

X# Tn1 DOLLAR
0.4167 Gold **Ruler:** (no rulers) **Issuer:** M.E. Hart **Obv:** Indian head left **Rev:** Value, legend in wreath **Rev. Legend:** ARIZONA GOLD

Date	Mintage	F	VF	XF	Unc	BU
1849 Rare	—	—	—	—	—	—

CALIFORNIA

REPUBLIC

PATTERNS

X# Pn1 100 RAMBO TRADE UNITS
Aluminum, 39 mm. **Countermark:** "COPY" **Obv:** Eagle with wings outspread **Rev:** Bust of Sylvester Stallone as "Rambo" **Note:** 100 RAMBO ® TRADE UNITS.

Date	Mintage	F	VF	XF	Unc	BU
ND(1985)	—	—	—	3.00	6.00	8.00

STATE

TOKEN COINAGE

X# Tn3 1/4 DOLLAR
Gold **Issuer:** M.E. Hart **Obv:** Indian head left **Rev. Legend:** CALIFORNIA GOLD

Date	Mintage	F	VF	XF	Unc	BU
1860	—	—	—	—	—	—

X# Tn6 1/4 DOLLAR
Gold **Issuer:** M.E. Hart **Obv:** Indian head left **Rev. Legend:** CALIFORNIA GOLD **Shape:** Octagonal

Date	Mintage	F	VF	XF	Unc	BU
1902	—	—	—	—	—	—

X# Tn7 1/4 DOLLAR
Gold **Issuer:** M.E. Hart **Obv:** Liberty head left **Rev. Legend:** CALIFORNIA GOLD

Date	Mintage	F	VF	XF	Unc	BU
1915	—	—	—	—	—	—

X# Tn10 1/4 DOLLAR
Gold **Issuer:** M.E. Hart **Obv:** Liberty head left **Rev:** Value over bear walking right **Rev. Legend:** CALIFORNIA GOLD **Shape:** Octagonal

Date	Mintage	F	VF	XF	Unc	BU
1915	—	—	—	—	—	—

X# Tn1 1/2 DOLLAR
Gold **Issuer:** M.E. Hart **Obv:** Indian head left **Rev. Legend:** CALIFORNIA GOLD

Date	Mintage	F	VF	XF	Unc	BU
1849	—	—	—	—	—	—

X# Tn5 1/2 DOLLAR
Gold **Issuer:** M.E. Hart **Rev:** Value over bear walking right **Rev. Legend:** CALIFORNIA GOLD

Date	Mintage	F	VF	XF	Unc	BU
1900	—	—	—	—	—	—

X# Tn8 1/2 DOLLAR
Gold **Issuer:** M.E. Hart **Obv:** Liberty head left **Rev. Legend:** CALIFORNIA GOLD

Date	Mintage	F	VF	XF	Unc	BU
1915	—	—	—	—	—	—

X# Tn11 1/2 DOLLAR
Gold **Issuer:** M.E. Hart **Obv:** Liberty head left **Rev. Legend:** CALIFORNIA GOLD **Shape:** Octagonal

Date	Mintage	F	VF	XF	Unc	BU
1915	—	—	—	—	—	—

X# Tn2 DOLLAR
Gold **Issuer:** M.E. Hart **Obv:** Indian head left **Rev. Legend:** CALIFORNIA GOLD

Date	Mintage	F	VF	XF	Unc	BU
1849	—	—	—	—	—	—

X# Tn4 DOLLAR
Gold **Issuer:** M.E. Hart **Obv:** Indian head right **Rev. Legend:** CALIFORNIA GOLD **Shape:** Octagonal

Date	Mintage	F	VF	XF	Unc	BU
1898	—	—	—	—	—	—

X# Tn9 DOLLAR
Gold **Issuer:** M.E. Hart **Obv:** Liberty head left **Rev. Legend:** CALIFORNIA GOLD

Date	Mintage	F	VF	XF	Unc	BU
1915	—	—	—	—	—	—

X# Tn12 DOLLAR
Gold **Issuer:** M.E. Hart **Obv:** Liberty head left **Rev. Legend:** CALIFORNIA GOLD **Shape:** Octagonal

Date	Mintage	F	VF	XF	Unc	BU
1915	—	—	—	—	—	—

FANTASY COINAGE

X# 1 UNIVERSARO
31.1030 g., 0.9990 Silver 0.9989 oz. ASW
Subject: World Trade **Note:** Their mint report states over 2,000,000 pieces struck.

Date	Mintage	F	VF	XF	Unc	BU
1972	—	—	—	8.00	10.00	—
1973	—	—	—	8.00	10.00	—
1974	—	—	—	8.00	10.00	—
1975	—	—	—	8.00	10.00	—

CONFEDERATE STATES OF AMERICA

SECESSIONIST STATES

(1861 - 1865)

CAPTAIN J.W. HASELTINE RESTRIKE ISSUE

The restrikes listed below were produced by Captain J.W. Haseltine, a Philadelphia coin dealer in 1874. The dies were originally engraved by Robert Lovett, Jr. in Philadelphia for the Confederacy. Only 12 pieces were struck in Copper-Nickel and as hostilities broke out between the North and the South, Lovett stored the dies and the original cents.

(In 1961 Robert Bashlow, a New York coin dealer, obtained the defaced cent dies. He ordered a set of transfer dies prepared from August Frank Co. of Phildelphia, Pennsylvania and using a wide variety of metals and even including red fibre he had over 25,000 examples struck as follows: Bronze (20,000); Silver or Goldine (5,000 each); Copper-Nickel-Zinc, Aluminum, Lead, Tin, Zinc or red fibre (50 pieces each); Gold or Platinum (3 pieces each). Uniface impressions in gold or silver have been noted.)

X# 1 CENT
Copper

Date	Mintage	F	VF	XF	Unc	BU
1861 (1874) Proof	55	Value: 5,000				

X# 1a CENT
Silver

Date	Mintage	F	VF	XF	Unc	BU
1861 (1874) Proof	12	Value: 7,500				

X# 1b CENT
Gold

Date	Mintage	F	VF	XF	Unc	BU
1861 (1874) Proof	7	Value: 33,000				

J.W. SCOTT RESTRIKE ISSUE

Restruck counterstamped 1861-O half dollar. Liberty's appearance is slightly flattened. Both known examples grade AM-55 on the confederate side.

After producing two pieces in 1879 the legend around the eagle was still visible and J. W. Scott decided to shave the eagle effigy of the following 500 pieces producing a more realistic version of a restrike. The original four pieces struck at the New Orleans mint using the 1861-O half dollar Liberty Seated die mated with the new Confederate Arms die were all struck in proof. It has been noted that the original proof Liberty Seated die used had a crack protruding from the center of her nose to the edge. A few similar circulation strikes used in the later ""shaved flan"" process also bare this flaw and are considered much scarcer.

X# 2 1/2 DOLLAR
12.4400 g., 0.9000 Silver 0.3599 oz. ASW

Date	Mintage	F	VF	XF	Unc	BU
1861O	2	—	—	6,000	8,000	—

X# 2a.1 1/2 DOLLAR
0.9000 Silver **Note:** Weight varies: 11.99-12.18 grams. These were struck on a shaved flan reverse.

Date	Mintage	F	VF	XF	Unc	BU
1861O	500	—	—	3,500	5,000	—

X# 2a.2 1/2 DOLLAR
0.9000 Silver **Note:** Weight varies: 11.99-12.18 grams.

Date	Mintage	F	VF	XF	Unc	BU
1861O	Inc. above	—	—	—	7,500	—

J.W. SCOTT MEDALLIC ISSUE

X# M2 1/2 DOLLAR
White Metal **Note:** Struck for J. W. Scott of New York City, as a companion offering to his silver half dollars.

Date	Mintage	F	VF	XF	Unc	BU
ND(1879)	500	—	—	300	450	—

CONFEDERATE CENTENNIAL MEDALLIC ISSUE

Struck for the Centennial by the Coin-of-the-Month Club, Sioux Falls, South Dakota.

X# M1 1/2 DOLLAR
0.9250 Silver

Date	Mintage	F	VF	XF	Unc	BU
ND(1961) Proof	—	Value: 20.00				

X# M1a 1/2 DOLLAR
Copper-Nickel-Zinc

Date	Mintage	F	VF	XF	Unc	BU
ND(1961) Proof	—	Value: 5.00				

X# M1c 1/2 DOLLAR
Copper-Nickel-Zinc Oxidized

Date	Mintage	F	VF	XF	Unc	BU
ND(1961) Proof	—	Value: 5.00				

X# M1d 1/2 DOLLAR
Bronze Golden

Date	Mintage	F	VF	XF	Unc	BU
ND(1961) Proof	—	Value: 5.00				

X# M1b 1/2 DOLLAR
Bronze Oxidized

Date	Mintage	F	VF	XF	Unc	BU
ND(1961) Proof	—	Value: 5.00				

X# M1e 1/2 DOLLAR
Bronze Gilt

Date	Mintage	F	VF	XF	Unc	BU
ND(1961) Proof	—	Value: 5.00				

MEDALLIC COINAGE

X# M21 DOLLAR
31.1300 g., 0.9990 Silver 0.9998 oz. ASW, 38 mm.
Series: Rebels of Liberty **Obv:** Bust of President Jefferson Davis facing 3/4 right **Obv. Legend:** IN GOD WE TRUST **Rev:** Confederate battle flag **Edge:** Reeded

Date	Mintage	F	VF	XF	Unc	BU
ND(2004) Proof	—	Value: 40.00				

X# M22 DOLLAR

31.1300 g., 0.9990 Silver 0.9998 oz. ASW, 38 mm. **Series:** Rebels of Liberty **Obv:** Bust of General Jeb Stuart facing slightly left **Obv. Legend:** IN GOD WE TRUST **Rev:** Confederate battle flag **Edge:** Reeded

Date	Mintage	F	VF	XF	Unc	BU
ND(2004) Proof	1,000	Value: 40.00				

X# M25 DOLLAR

31.1300 g., 0.9990 Silver 0.9998 oz. ASW, 38 mm. **Series:** Rebels of Liberty **Obv:** Bust of General Patrick Cleburne facing slightly right **Obv. Legend:** IN GOD WE TRUST **Rev:** Confederate battle flag **Edge:** Reeded

Date	Mintage	F	VF	XF	Unc	BU
ND(2004) Proof	1,000	Value: 40.00				

X# M28 DOLLAR

31.1300 g., 0.9990 Silver 0.9998 oz. ASW, 38 mm. **Series:** Rebels of Liberty **Obv:** Bust of General John Bell Hood facing slightly right **Obv. Legend:** IN GOD WE TRUST **Rev:** Confederate battle flag **Edge:** Reeded

Date	Mintage	F	VF	XF	Unc	BU
ND(2004) Proof	1,000	Value: 40.00				

X# M23 DOLLAR

31.1300 g., 0.9990 Silver 0.9998 oz. ASW, 38 mm. **Series:** Rebels of Liberty **Obv:** Bust of General William Barksdale facing 3/4 left **Obv. Legend:** IN GOD WE TRUST **Rev:** Confederate battle flag **Edge:** Reeded

Date	Mintage	F	VF	XF	Unc	BU
ND(2004) Proof	1,000	Value: 40.00				

X# M26 DOLLAR

31.1300 g., 0.9990 Silver 0.9998 oz. ASW, 38 mm. **Series:** Rebels of Liberty **Obv:** Bust of General Nathan Bedford Forest facing **Obv. Legend:** IN GOD WE TRUST **Rev:** Confederate battle flag **Edge:** Reeded

Date	Mintage	F	VF	XF	Unc	BU
ND(2004) Proof	1,000	Value: 40.00				

X# M29 DOLLAR

31.1300 g., 0.9990 Silver 0.9998 oz. ASW, 38 mm. **Series:** Rebels of Liberty **Obv:** Bust of General Stonewall Jackson facing slightly left **Obv. Legend:** IN GOD WE TRUST **Rev:** Confederate battle flag **Edge:** Reeded

Date	Mintage	F	VF	XF	Unc	BU
ND(2004) Proof	1,000	Value: 40.00				

X# M24 DOLLAR

31.1300 g., 0.9990 Silver 0.9998 oz. ASW, 38 mm. **Series:** Rebels of Liberty **Obv:** Bust of General P.G.T. Beauregard facing 3/4 left **Obv. Legend:** IN GOD WE TRUST **Rev:** Confederate battle flag **Edge:** Reeded

Date	Mintage	F	VF	XF	Unc	BU
ND(2004) Proof	1,000	Value: 40.00				

X# M27 DOLLAR

31.1300 g., 0.9990 Silver 0.9998 oz. ASW, 38 mm. **Series:** Rebels of Liberty **Obv:** Bust of General A.P. Hill facing 3/4 right **Obv. Legend:** IN GOD WE TRUST **Rev:** Confederate battle flag **Edge:** Reeded

Date	Mintage	F	VF	XF	Unc	BU
ND(2004) Proof	1,000	Value: 40.00				

X# M30 DOLLAR

31.1300 g., 0.9990 Silver 0.9998 oz. ASW, 38 mm. **Series:** Rebels of Liberty **Obv:** Bust of General Robert E. Lee facing 3/4 left **Obv. Legend:** IN GOD WE TRUST **Rev:** Confederate battle flag **Edge:** Reeded

Date	Mintage	F	VF	XF	Unc	BU
ND(2004) Proof	1,000	Value: 40.00				

X# M31 DOLLAR

31.1300 g., 0.9990 Silver 0.9998 oz. ASW, 38 mm. **Series:** Rebels of Liberty **Obv:** Bust of General James Longstreet facing slightly right **Obv. Legend:** IN GOD WE TRUST **Rev:** Confederate battle flag **Edge:** Reeded

Date	Mintage	F	VF	XF	Unc	BU
ND(2004) Proof	—	Value: 40.00				

X# M32 DOLLAR

31.1300 g., 0.9990 Silver 0.9998 oz. ASW **Series:** Rebels of Liberty **Obv:** Bust of General John Hunt Morgan facing 3/4 right **Obv. Legend:** IN GOD WE TRUST **Rev:** Confederate battle flag **Edge:** Reeded

Date	Mintage	F	VF	XF	Unc	BU
ND(2004) Proof	1,000	Value: 40.00				

X# M33 DOLLAR

3.1400 g., 0.9990 Silver 0.1008 oz. ASW, 38 mm. **Series:** Rebels of Liberty **Obv:** Bust of General Pickett facing slightly right **Obv. Legend:** IN GOD WE TRUST **Rev:** Confederate battle flag

Date	Mintage	F	VF	XF	Unc	BU
ND(2004) Proof	1,000	Value: 40.00				

X# M35 DOLLAR

31.1300 g., 0.9990 Silver Multi-colored flags 0.9998 oz. ASW, 38 mm. **Issuer:** Richard Liptock, Tennessee **Series:** Reflections of CSA **Obv:** Confederate flag "Stars and Bars" **Obv. Legend:** IN GOD WE TRUST **Rev:** Confederate battle flag **Edge:** Reeded

Date	Mintage	F	VF	XF	Unc	BU
ND(2004) Proof	—	—	—	—	—	—

X# M36 DOLLAR

31.1300 g., 0.9990 Silver 0.9998 oz. ASW, 38 mm. **Issuer:** Richard Liptock, Tennessee **Series:** Reflections of CSA **Obv:** General N.B. Forrest horseback right **Obv. Legend:** IN GOD WE TRUST **Rev:** Confederate battle flag **Edge:** Reeded

Date	Mintage	F	VF	XF	Unc	BU
ND(2004) Proof	—	Value: 40.00				

X# M37 DOLLAR

31.1300 g., 0.9990 Silver 0.9998 oz. ASW, 38 mm. **Issuer:** Richard Liptock, Tennessee **Series:** Reflections of CSA **Obv:** Bust of Admiral Raphael Semmes facing, slightly left **Obv. Legend:** IN GOD WE TRUST **Rev:** Confederate battle flag above warship CSS Alabama **Edge:** Reeded

Date	Mintage	F	VF	XF	Unc	BU
ND(2004) Proof	—	Value: 40.00				

X# M21b DOLLAR

38.8788 g., 0.9990 Gold 1.2487 oz. AGW, 38 mm. **Series:** Rebels of Liberty **Obv:** Bust of President Jefferson Davis facing 3/4 right **Obv. Legend:** IN GOD WE TRUST **Rev:** Confederate battle flag **Edge:** Reeded

Date	Mintage	F	VF	XF	Unc	BU
ND(2004) Proof	—	Value: 900				

PROOF SETS

X#	Date	Mintage	Identification	Issue Price	Mkt Val
XPS1	ND(2004) (13)	—	XM21-33	600	600

HAWAII

STATE

SILVER CURRENCY COINAGE - LIBERTY SERVICES ISSUES

X# 21 20 LIBERTY DOLLARS

31.1500 g., 0.9990 Silver 1.0005 oz. ASW, 38.9 mm. **Obv:** Crowned arms, island group at upper right **Obv. Legend:** HAWAII DALA **Obv. Inscription:** "Liberty Dollar" **Rev:** Kamehamela the Great standing facing 3/4 right with spear **Rev. Inscription:** KING / KAMEHAMEHA - HAWAII **Edge:** Reeded

Date	Mintage	F	VF	XF	Unc	BU
2007 RHM Proof	—	Value: 25.00				

X# 22 20 LIBERTY DOLLARS

31.1500 g., 0.9990 Silver 1.0005 oz. ASW, 38.9 mm. **Obv:** Crowned arms, island group at upper right **Obv. Legend:** HAWAII DALA **Obv. Inscription:** "Liberty Dollar" **Rev:** Bust of Liliuokalani left **Rev. Legend:** LILIUOKALANI QUEEN OF HAWAII **Edge:** Reeded

Date	Mintage	F	VF	XF	Unc	BU
2007 RHM Proof	—	Value: 25.00				

X# 23 20 LIBERTY DOLLARS

31.1500 g., 0.9990 Silver 1.0005 oz. ASW, 38.9 mm. **Subject:** 2000th Annivewrsary Discovery of Hawaii **Obv:** Crowned arms, island group at upper right **Obv. Legend:** HAWAII DALA **Obv. Inscription:** "Liberty Dollar" **Rev:** Two portraits, male and female **Rev. Legend:** HO' OMANA'O - HAWAII / 2000TH ANNIVERSARY **Edge:** Reeded

Date	Mintage	F	VF	XF	Unc	BU
2007 RHM Proof	—	Value: 25.00				

X# 24 20 LIBERTY DOLLARS

31.1500 g., 0.9990 Silver 1.0005 oz. ASW, 38.9 mm. **Obv:** Crowned arms, island group at upper right **Obv. Legend:** HAWAII DALA **Obv. Inscription:** "Liberty Dollar" **Rev:** Head of Victoria right **Rev. Legend:** PRINCESS VICTORIA • KAIULANI • HEIR APPARENT 1891 **Edge:** Reeded

Date	Mintage	F	VF	XF	Unc	BU
2007 RHM Proof	—	Value: 25.00				

X# 25 20 LIBERTY DOLLARS

31.1500 g., 0.9990 Silver 1.0005 oz. ASW, 38.9 mm. **Subject:** 200th Anniversary of Uniting the Islands **Obv:** Crowned arms, island group at upper right **Obv. Legend:** HAWAII DALA **Obv. Inscription:** "Liberty Dollar" **Rev:** Bust of Kamchameha right with spear **Rev. Legend:** 200 LA HO'OMANA'O / KING KAMEHAME HA I **Edge:** Reeded

Date	Mintage	F	VF	XF	Unc	BU
2007 RHM Proof	—	Value: 25.00				

X# 26 20 LIBERTY DOLLARS

31.1500 g., 0.9990 Silver 1.0005 oz. ASW, 38.9 mm. **Obv:** Crowned arms, island group at upper right **Obv. Legend:** HAWAII DALA **Obv. Inscription:** "Liberty Dollar" **Rev:** Head of Kalakaua **Rev. Legend:** KALAKAUA I KING OF HAWAII **Edge:** Reeded

Date	Mintage	F	VF	XF	Unc	BU
2007 RHM Proof	—	Value: 25.00				

IDAHO

STATE

TOKEN COINAGE

X# Tn1 1/4 DOLLAR

0.4167 Gold **Issuer:** M.E. Hart **Obv:** Indian head left **Obv. Legend:** IDAHO GOLD **Rev:** Mountain scene **Rev. Legend:** ESTO PERPETUA

Date	Mintage	F	VF	XF	Unc	BU
1914	—	—	—	—	—	—

X# Tn2 1/2 DOLLAR

0.4167 Gold **Obv:** Indian head left **Obv. Legend:** IDAHO GOLD **Rev:** Mountain scene **Rev. Legend:** ESTO PERPETUA

Date	Mintage	F	VF	XF	Unc	BU
1914	—	—	—	—	—	—

X# Tn3 DOLLAR

Gold **Issuer:** M.E. Hart **Obv:** Indian head left **Obv. Legend:** IDAHO GOLD **Rev:** Mountain scene **Rev. Legend:** ESTO PERPETUA

Date	Mintage	F	VF	XF	Unc	BU
1914	—	—	—	—	—	—

STATE

Coeur D'Alene Mines

MEDALLIC SILVER BULLION

X# MB5 SILVER FREEDOM

31.1341 g., 0.9990 Silver 0.9999 oz. ASW, 38.7 mm. **Obv:** Eagle in flight, mountain range **Rev:** Male lion walking right **Edge:** Reeded

Date	Mintage	F	VF	XF	Unc	BU
1985 Proof	—	Value: 15.00				

ILLINOIS

NATION OF CELESTIA

CELESTIAL SPACE COINAGE

Chartered on December 20, 1948 by James T. Mangan, the Prime Minister, Evergreen Park, Illinois, U.S.A.

X# 1 JOULE
4.1500 g., 0.9250 Silver 0.1234 oz. ASW **Obv:** Head of Princess Ruth Marie Mangan left

Date	Mintage	F	VF	XF	Unc	BU
1961	—	—	—	—	50.00	75.00

X# 2 CELESTON
2.2000 g., 0.9000 Gold 0.0637 oz. AGW, 13.9 mm. **Obv:** Head of Princess Ruth Marie Mangan left

Date	Mintage	F	VF	XF	Unc	BU
1959	—	—	—	—	175	—
1959 Proof	—	Value: 200				
1960	—	—	—	—	175	—
1960 Proof	—	Value: 200				
1961 Proof	—	Value: 200				

X# 3 CELESTON
2.2000 g., 0.9000 Gold 0.0637 oz. AGW **Subject:** Princess Ruth Marie Mangan **Obv:** Small "R"

Date	Mintage	F	VF	XF	Unc	BU
1959 Proof	—	Value: 200				

PATTERNS

X# Pn1 CELESTON
1.1000 g., Copper, 14 mm.

Date	Mintage	F	VF	XF	Unc	BU
1959	—	Value: 250				

Note: Weak strikes are known.

X# Pn2 CELESTON
1.1000 g., Copper, 14 mm.

Date	Mintage	F	VF	XF	Unc	BU
1960	—	Value: 250				

LOUISIANA

STATE

TOKEN COINAGE

X# Tn1 1/4 DOLLAR
Gold, 9.6 mm. **Subject:** Louisiana Purchase Exposition **Obv. Legend:** LOUISIANA GOLD **Rev:** Fleur de lis with "L P E" on petals

Date	Mintage	F	VF	XF	Unc	BU
1904	—	—	—	—	100	125

Note: Two varieties exist

X# Tn2 1/2 DOLLAR
Gold, 11.2 mm. **Subject:** Louisiana Purchase Exposition **Obv. Legend:** LOUISIANA GOLD **Rev:** Fleur de lis with "L P E" on petals

Date	Mintage	F	VF	XF	Unc	BU
1904	—	—	—	—	125	150

TERRITORY

COUNTERMARKED COINAGE

Spurious countermarks produced ca.1950

X# 2 4 BITS
0.9000 Silver **Countermark:** "LOUISIANA" and "4 BITS" **Note:** Countermark on Kingdom of Napoleon 2 Lire, KM#9.

CM Date	Host Date	Good	VG	F	VF	XF
ND	1807-13	35.00	55.00	85.00	—	—

X# 4 8 BITS
0.9170 Silver **Countermark:** "LOUISIANA" and "8 BITS" **Note:** Countermark on French Ecus, KM#512.13.

CM Date	Host Date	Good	VG	F	VF	XF
ND	1758M	50.00	85.00	125	—	—

X# 5 8 BITS
0.9000 Silver **Countermark:** "LOUISIANA" and "8 BITS" **Note:** Countermark on various French 5 Francs

CM Date	Host Date	Good	VG	F	VF	XF
ND	1807-13	35.00	50.00	75.00	—	—

MARYLAND

STATE

FANTASY COINAGE

X# 1 DAALDER
Copper-Nickel, 29.5 mm. **Ruler:** no Ruler Name **Subject:** 1993 National Convention **Obv:** Mintmaster's signature and date **Obv. Legend:** •THE DUTCH MINT•A.N.A. CONVENTION•BALTIMORE, MD• **Rev:** Sailing ship with denomination, English legend flanked by mintmaster's insignia "bow & arrow" **Rev. Legend:** HALVE MAEN • HALF MOON **Edge:** Plain

Date	Mintage	F	VF	XF	Unc	BU
1993	—	—	—	—	5.00	—

MICHIGAN/UPPER PENINSULA

STATE

MEDALLIC COINAGE

X# 5 DOLLAR
11.0000 g., Brass, 31.9 mm. **Obv:** Bald Eagle with wings spread left standing on flag **Obv. Legend:** UNITED STATES OF AMERICA **Rev:** Outlined map of the Upper Peninsula **Rev. Legend:** UPPER PENINSULA **Edge:** Reeded

Date	Mintage	VG	F	VF	XF	Unc
ND	—	—	—	—	2.00	4.00

MONTANA

STATE

TOKEN COINAGE

 # Tn1 1/4 DOLLAR
.4167 Gold **Issuer:** M.E. Hart **Obv:** Indian head left **bv. Legend:** MONTANA GOLD **Rev:** Mountain scene **ev. Legend:** ORO Y PLATA

ate	Mintage	F	VF	XF	Unc	BU
914	—	—	—	—	—	—

 # Tn2 1/2 DOLLAR
.4167 Gold **Issuer:** M.E. Hart **Obv:** Indian head left **bv. Legend:** MONTANA GOLD **Rev:** Mountain scene **ev. Legend:** ORO Y PLATA

ate	Mintage	F	VF	XF	Unc	BU
914	—	—	—	—	—	—

 # Tn3 DOLLAR
.4167 Gold **Issuer:** M.E. Hart **Obv:** Indian head left **bv. Legend:** MONTANA GLD **Rev:** Mountain scene **ev. Legend:** ORO Y PLATA

ate	Mintage	F	VF	XF	Unc	BU
914	—	—	—	—	—	—

BULLION COINAGE

 # 5 OUNCE
.0010 g., 0.9990 Silver 0.0321 oz. ASW, 39 mm. **Issuer:** ontana Silver Association **Obv:** Shield with mining tools, tream **Rev:** Refinery **Rev. Inscription:** SILVER THE EY / - TO - / • PROSPERITY • **Note:** HK#820.

ate	Mintage	F	VF	XF	Unc	BU
933	—	35.00	60.00	100	175	—

NEW HAMPSHIRE

INTERNATIONAL FOUNDATION FOR INDEPENDENCE

FANTASY COINAGE

 # 1 1/2 GLOBE
5.5515 g., 0.9990 Silver 0.4995 oz. ASW

ate	Mintage	F	VF	XF	Unc	BU
973 Proof	2,000	Value: 20.00				

X# 2 GLOBE
31.1030 g., 0.9990 Silver 0.9989 oz. ASW **Note:** 1/4, 1/2 and 1 oz. pieces struck in gold have been reported but not confirmed.

Date	Mintage	F	VF	XF	Unc	BU
1973 Proof	2,000	Value: 35.00				
1974 Reported, not confirmed	—	—	—	—	—	—

NEW YORK

HUDSON FULTON CELEBRATION

FANTASY COINAGE

Thomas Elder Issues

Issued by Thomas L. Elder, New York coin dealer commemorating the 300th Anniversary of the Discovery of the Hudson River and Centenary of Successful Steamboat Navigation.

X# 1 DAALDER
Silver **Subject:** Hudson - Fulton Celebration 1909 New York City **Obv:** Bust 3/4 right **Obv. Legend:** HENDRIK HUDSON **Rev:** Sailing ship **Rev. Legend:** NIEUW • AMSTERDAM

Date	Mintage	F	VF	XF	Unc	BU
MCMIX	75	—	—	125	200	—

X# 1a DAALDER
Aluminum **Subject:** Hudson - Fulton Celebration 1909 New York City **Obv:** Bust 3/4 right **Obv. Legend:** HENDRIK HUDSON **Rev:** Sailing ship **Rev. Legend:** NIEUW • AMSTERDAM

Date	Mintage	F	VF	XF	Unc	BU
MCMIX	Est. 200	—	—	35.00	50.00	—

X# 1b DAALDER
Bronze **Subject:** Hudson - Fulton Celebration 1909 New York City **Obv:** Bust 3/4 right **Obv. Legend:** HENDRIK HUDSON **Rev:** Sailing ship **Rev. Designer:** NIEUW • AMSTERDAM **Edge:** Plain

Date	Mintage	F	VF	XF	Unc	BU
MCMIX	—	—	—	120	200	—

X# 2 DAALDER
Gold, 15 mm. **Note:** Reduced size, similar to X#1.

Date	Mintage	F	VF	XF	Unc	BU
MCMIX	Est. 50	—	—	200	275	—

X# 2a DAALDER
Silver, 15 mm.

Date	Mintage	F	VF	XF	Unc	BU
MCMIX	Est. 50	—	—	100	175	—

X# 2b DAALDER
Bronze, 15 mm.

Date	Mintage	F	VF	XF	Unc	BU
MCMIX	Est. 50	—	—	70.00	100	—

X# 2c DAALDER
Brass, 15 mm.

Date	Mintage	F	VF	XF	Unc	BU
MCMIX	—	—	—	70.00	100	—

X# 2d DAALDER
Aluminum, 15 mm.

Date	Mintage	F	VF	XF	Unc	BU
MCMIX	—	—	—	20.00	30.00	—

X# Tn3 DAALDER
Gold, 14.7 mm. **Subject:** Hudson-Fulton **Obv:** Bust of Robert Fulton 3/4 right **Rev:** Sailing-steam powered ship "The Clermont" **Rev. Legend:** NEW YORK TO ALBANY - ONE TRIP

Date	Mintage	F	VF	XF	Unc	BU
ND(1909)	Est. 75	—	—	200	275	—

X# Tn3a DAALDER
Silver, 14.7 mm. **Subject:** Hudson-Fulton **Obv:** Bust of Robert Fulton 3/4 right **Rev:** Sailing-steam powered ship "The Clermont" **Rev. Legend:** NEW YORK TO ALBANY - ONE TRIP

Date	Mintage	F	VF	XF	Unc	BU
ND(1909)	Est. 50	—	—	125	175	—

X# Tn3b DAALDER
Bronze, 14.7 mm. **Subject:** Hudson-Fulton **Obv:** Bust of Robert Fulton 3/4 right **Rev:** Sailing-steam powered ship "The Clermont" **Rev. Legend:** NEW YORK TO ALBANY - ONE TRIP

Date	Mintage	F	VF	XF	Unc	BU
ND(1909)	Est. 50	—	—	70.00	100	—

X# Tn3c DAALDER
Bronze Gilt, 14.7 mm. **Subject:** Hudson-Fulton **Obv:** Bust of Robert Fulton 3/4 right **Rev:** Sailing-steam powered ship "The Clermont" **Rev. Legend:** NEW YORK TO ALBANY - ONE TRIP

Date	Mintage	F	VF	XF	Unc	BU
ND(1909)	Est. 25	—	—	125	175	—

New Netherlands Museum Issue

X# 5 DAALDER
25.0000 g., Silver, 37.9 mm. **Issuer:** New Netherlands Museum **Obv:** Bust of Henry Hudson 3/4 right **Rev:** Sailing ship "Half Moon"

Date	Mintage	F	VF	XF	Unc	BU
ND(1999)	—	—	—	—	12.50	—

PRIVATE

GOLD STANDARD CORPORATION

X# 10 1/20 GOLD STANDARD UNIT
1.7800 g., 0.9990 Gold 0.0572 oz. AGW **Obv:** Nicholas Deak bust facing **Obv. Legend:** INTERNATIONAL-IZATION OF SOUND MONEY NICHOLAS L. DEAK **Rev:** Large value G.05 **Rev. Legend:** FOR INTEGRITY THERE IS NO SUBSTITUTE **Note:** Struck at the Roger Williams Mint

Date	Mintage	F	VF	XF	Unc	BU
1980	11,042	—	—	—	—	55.00
1981	1,423	—	—	—	—	47.50
1982	470	—	—	—	—	50.00
1983	235	—	—	—	—	55.00
1984	110	—	—	—	—	60.00
1985	60	—	—	—	—	65.00

X# 11 1/10 GOLD STANDARD UNIT
3.5400 g., 0.9990 Gold 0.1137 oz. AGW **Obv:** Adam Smith head facing **Obv. Inscription:** TRUST IN GOD / ADAM / SMITH **Rev:** Large value **Rev. Legend:** FOR INTEGRITY THERE IS NO SUBSTITUTE **Note:** Struck at the Roger Williams Mint

Date	Mintage	F	VF	XF	Unc	BU
1979	17,525	—	—	—	—	85.00
1980	3,547	—	—	—	—	80.00
1981	1,723	—	—	—	—	85.00
1982	420	—	—	—	—	90.00
1983	205	—	—	—	—	95.00
1984	95	—	—	—	—	110
1985	63	—	—	—	—	120

X# 11a 1/10 GOLD STANDARD UNIT
0.9990 Platinum APW **Obv:** Adam Smith head facing

Date	Mintage	F	VF	XF	Unc	BU
1983	95	—	—	—BV+20%		—
1984	65	—	—	—BV+25%		—
1985	—	—	—	—BV+30%		—

X# 12 1/4 GOLD STANDARD UNIT
8.5000 g., 0.9990 Gold 0.2730 oz. AGW **Obv:** Henry Hazlitt head left **Obv. Legend:** FREE CHOICE OF CURRENCIES / HENRY HAZLITT **Rev:** Large value **Rev. Legend:** FOR INTEGRITY THERE IS NO SUBSTITUTE **Note:** Struck at the American Pacific Mint

Date	Mintage	F	VF	XF	Unc	BU
1979	3,180	—	—	—	185	—
1980	574	—	—	—	200	—
1981	327	—	—	—	200	—
1982	175	—	—	—	220	—
1983	160	—	—	—	220	—
1984	87	—	—	—	250	—
1985	45	—	—	—	275	—

X# 6 1/4 GOLD STANDARD UNIT
8.5000 g., 0.9990 Silver 0.2730 oz. ASW **Obv:** Henry Hazlitt head left **Obv. Legend:** FREE CHOICE OF CURRENCIES / HENRY HAZLITT **Rev:** Large value **Rev. Legend:** FOR INTEGRITY THERE IS NO SUBSTITUTE **Note:** Struck at the Rodger Williams Mint

Date	Mintage	F	VF	XF	Unc	BU
1982	—	—	—	—	—	—

X# 12b 1/4 GOLD STANDARD UNIT
0.9990 Platinum APW **Obv:** Henry Hazlitt head left

Date	Mintage	F	VF	XF	Unc	BU
1983	95	—	—	—	—	—
1984	65	—	—	—	—	—
1985	—	—	—	—	—	—

X# 13 1/2 GOLD STANDARD UNIT
17.1000 g., 0.9990 Gold 0.5492 oz. AGW **Obv:** Friedrich A. Hayek head 3/4 right **Obv. Legend:** DENATIONALIZATION OF MONEY / FRIEDRICH A. HAYEK **Rev:** Large value **Rev. Legend:** FOR INTEGRITY THERE IS NO SUBSTITUTE **Note:** Struck at the American Pacific Mint

Date	Mintage	F	VF	XF	Unc	BU
1979	2,833	—	—	—	—	350
1980	419	—	—	—	—	375
1981	361	—	—	—	—	375
1982	135	—	—	—	—	400
1983	159	—	—	—	—	400
1984	77	—	—	—	—	425
1985	32	—	—	—	—	450

X# 13a 1/2 GOLD STANDARD UNIT
0.9990 Silver **Obv:** Friedrich A. Hayek head 3/4 left.

Date	Mintage	F	VF	XF	Unc	BU
1981	600	—	—	—	30.00	—
1982	150	—	—	—	35.00	—
1983	165	—	—	—	35.00	—
1984	97	—	—	—	40.00	—
1985	Est. 54	—	—	—	45.00	—

X# 13b 1/2 GOLD STANDARD UNIT
0.9990 Platinum APW **Obv:** Friedrich A. Hayek head 3/4 right.

Date	Mintage	F	VF	XF	Unc	BU
1983	75	—	—	—	—	—
1984	46	—	—	—	—	—
1985	—	—	—	—	—	—

X# 14 GOLD STANDARD UNIT
Gold **Obv:** Edward C. Harwood head left **Obv. Legend** SOUND COMMERCIAL BANKING / EDWARD C. HARWOOD **Rev:** Large value **Rev. Legend:** FOR INTEGRITY THERE IS NO SUBSTITUTE **Note:** Struck at the Roger Williams Mint

Date	Mintage	F	VF	XF	Unc	BU
1980	825	—	—	—	—	80
1981	506	—	—	—	—	82
1982	134	—	—	—	—	87
1983	165	—	—	—	—	87
1984	86	—	—	—	—	90
1985	38	—	—	—	—	95

X# 14a GOLD STANDARD UNIT
0.9990 Silver **Obv:** Edward C. Harwood head left.

Date	Mintage	F	VF	XF	Unc	BU
1980	3,117	—	—	—	—	45.0
1981	2,318	—	—	—	—	45.0
1982	213	—	—	—	—	55.0
1983	185	—	—	—	—	55.0
1984	112	—	—	—	—	60.0
1985	Est. 70	—	—	—	—	65.

X# 14b GOLD STANDARD UNIT
0.9990 Platinum APW **Obv:** Edward C. Harwood head left.

Date	Mintage	F	VF	XF	Unc	BU
1981	376	—	—	—	—	-
1982	72	—	—	—	—	-
1983	75	—	—	—	—	-
1984	44	—	—	—	—	-
1985	—	—	—	—	—	-

X# 12a GOLD STANDARD UNIT
0.9990 Silver **Obv:** Henry Hazlitt head left.

Date	Mintage	F	VF	XF	Unc	BU
1981	336	—	—	—	16.50	-
1982	200	—	—	—	17.50	-
1983	165	—	—	—	18.50	-
1984	96	—	—	—	20.00	-
1985	54	—	—	—	22.50	-

X# 15 GOLD STANDARD UNIT
34.2200 g., Silver **Obv:** Edward C. Harwood head left **Obv. Legend:** SOUND COMMERCIAL BANKING / EDWARD C. HARWOOD **Rev:** Large value **Rev. Legend:** FOR INTEGRITY THERE IS NO SUBSTITUTE **Note:** Struck at the American Pacific Mint

Date	Mintage	F	VF	XF	Unc	BU
1984 Proof	—	Value: 60.00				

STATE

MILLED COINAGE

X# 7 10 DOLLARS
0.9250 Silver, 32.1 mm. **Obv:** Bust of Nicholas L. Deak left **Rev:** Lizard standing on tree branch **Note:** Serial numbered on reverse.

Date	Mintage	F	VF	XF	Unc	BU
1978 Proof	—	Value: 17.50				

OREGON

STATE

TOKEN COINAGE

X# Tn1 1/4 DOLLAR

Gold, 9.5 mm. **Subject:** L. & C. Expo **Obv:** Grape branches, value **Obv. Legend:** OREGON GOLD **Rev:** Mt. Hood

Date	Mintage	F	VF	XF	Unc	BU
1905	—	—	—	—	125	200

X# Tn3 1/4 DOLLAR

Gold

Date	Mintage	F	VF	XF	Unc	BU
1914	—	—	—	—	—	—

X# Tn2 1/2 DOLLAR

Gold, 11.2 mm. **Subject:** L. & C. Expo **Obv:** Grape branches, value **Obv. Legend:** OREGON GOLD **Rev:** Mt. Hood

Date	Mintage	F	VF	XF	Unc	BU
1905	—	—	—	—	145	225

X# Tn4 1/2 DOLLAR

Gold

Date	Mintage	F	VF	XF	Unc	BU
1914	—	—	—	—	—	—

X# Tn5 DOLLAR

Gold

Date	Mintage	F	VF	XF	Unc	BU
1914	—	—	—	—	—	—

TEXAS

REPUBLIC

COUNTERMARKED COINAGE

Spurious countermarks produced ca.1950

X# 25 DOLLAR

Silver **Subject:** Alamo Commemorative

CM Date	Host Date	Good	VG	F	VF	XF
	1836	—	—	—	75.00	145

X# 3 2 BITS

0.9030 g., Silver **Countermark:** "TEXAS" and "2 BITS" **Note:** Countermarks on Mexico City Mint 2 Reales, KM#88.2.

CM Date	Host Date	Good	VG	F	VF	XF
ND	1781FF	25.00	40.00	60.00	—	—

X# 1.2 2 BITS

0.9030 g., Silver **Countermark:** "TEXAS" and "2 BITS" **Note:** Countermarks on Mexico City Mint 2 Reales, KM#93.

CM Date	Host Date	Good	VG	F	VF	XF
ND	1818JJ	25.00	40.00	60.00	—	—

X# 1.1 2 BITS

0.9030 g., Silver **Countermark:** "TEXAS" and "2 BITS" **Note:** Countermarks on Lima Mint 2 Reales, KM#115.1.

CM Date	Host Date	Good	VG	F	VF	XF
ND	1818JP	25.00	40.00	60.00	—	—

X# 9 4 BITS

0.8920 g., Silver **Countermark:** "TEXAS" and "4 BITS" **Note:** Countermarks on United States "Flowing Hair" 1/2 Dollar, KM#16.

CM Date	Host Date	Good	VG	F	VF	XF
ND	1794-95	500	600	—	—	—

X# 8 4 BITS

0.9030 g., Silver **Countermark:** "TEXAS" and "4 BITS" **Note:** Countermarks on Spanish 10 Reales de Vellon, KM#138.1.

CM Date	Host Date	Good	VG	F	VF	XF
ND	1821BO	25.00	40.00	60.00	—	—

X# 10 4 BITS

0.6670 g., Silver **Countermark:** TEXAS, 4 BITS **Note:** Countermarks on Cuzco Mint 4 Reales, KM#151.1.

CM Date	Host Date	Good	VG	F	VF	XF
ND(1835)	ND(1778-1798)	35.00	55.00	85.00	—	—

X# 5 4 BITS

0.9030 g., Silver **Countermark:** "TEXAS" and "4 BITS" **Note:** Countermarks on Guadalajara Mint 4 Reales, KM#375.2.

CM Date	Host Date	Good	VG	F	VF	XF
ND	1845JG	35.00	55.00	85.00	—	—

X# 15 8 BITS

Silver **Countermark:** TEXAS, 8 BITS **Note:** Countermarks on Potosi Mint 8 Reales, KM#54.

CM Date	Host Date	Good	VG	F	VF	XF
ND	1778	40.00	70.00	120	—	—

X# 16 8 BITS

Silver **Countermark:** "TEXAS" and "8 BITS" **Note:** Countermarks on Mexico City Mint 8 Reales, KM#109.

CM Date	Host Date	Good	VG	F	VF	XF
ND	1794FM	40.00	70.00	120	—	—
ND	1796FM	40.00	70.00	120	—	—

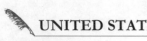

X# 18 8 BITS

0.8920 g., Silver **Countermark:** "TEXAS" and "8 BITS" **Note:** Countermarks on United States "Flowing Hair" Dollar, KM#17.

CM Date	Host Date	Good	VG	F	VF	XF
ND	1795	850	1,000	—	—	—

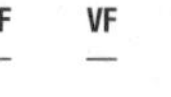

X# 11 8 BITS

0.9030 g., Silver **Countermark:** "TEXAS" and "8 BITS" **Note:** Countermarks with 5-pointed star on Mexico City Mint 8 Reales, KM#377.10.

CM Date	Host Date	Good	VG	F	VF	XF
ND	1834ML	65.00	100	150	—	—

X# 14 8 BITS

Silver **Countermark:** "TEXAS" and "8 BITS" **Note:** Countermarks on Spanish Colonial "cob" 8 Reales.

CM Date	Host Date	Good	VG	F	VF	XF
ND	ND	65.00	100	150	—	—

FANTASY COINAGE

X# 41 GERAH-1/20 TEXAS SHEKEL

0.9990 g., Silver **Obv:** Star in wreath **Obv. Legend:** REPUBLIC OF TEXAS - THE GREAT NATION **Rev:** Star with T • E • X • A • S in angles

Date	Mintage	F	VF	XF	Unc	BU
ND	—	—	—	—	—	—

STATE

MEDALLIC COINAGE

Texas Mint & Mercantile Issue

X# 35 10 CENTS

6.7000 g., 0.9990 Silver 0.2152 oz. ASW, 21.8 mm. **Obv:** Large star, value at center, small heart below **Rev:** Dragonfly **Edge:** Plain **Note:** Coin alignment.

Date	Mintage	F	VF	XF	Unc	BU
ND(2004) Proof	—	Value: 17.50				

X# 37 10 CENTS

6.3500 g., 0.9990 Silver 0.2039 oz. ASW, 22 mm. **Obv:** Large star, value at center, small heart below **Obv. Legend:** THE LONE STAR STATE - TEXAS **Rev:** Horned toad left **Edge:** Plain **Note:** Coin alignment.

Date	Mintage	F	VF	XF	Unc	BU
ND(2005) Proof	—	Value: 17.50				

X# 31 DOLLAR

31.2000 g., 0.9990 Silver 1.0021 oz. ASW, 39.15 mm. **Obv:** Star in sprays, heart below **Obv. Legend:** TEXAS ONE DOLLAR **Rev:** Stars in border around Longhorn skull, outline of Texas **Edge:** Reeded **Note:** Coin alignment.

Date	Mintage	F	VF	XF	Unc	BU
2000 Proof	—	Value: 27.50				

X# 31a DOLLAR

31.1030 g., 0.9990 Gold 0.9989 oz. AGW, 39.15 mm. **Obv:** Star in sprays, heart below **Rev:** Stars in border around Longhorn skull, outline of Texas **Edge:** Reeded **Note:** Coin alignment.

Date	Mintage	F	VF	XF	Unc	BU
2000 Proof	Est. 250	Value: 500				

X# 32 DOLLAR

31.5200 g., 0.9990 Silver 1.0123 oz. ASW, 39.15 mm. **Obv:** Radiant star, rope border **Obv. Legend:** STATE OF TEXAS **Rev:** Steer skull, rope border, desert landscape **Edge:** Reeded **Note:** Coin alignment.

Date	Mintage	F	VF	XF	Unc	BU
2001 Proof	—	Value: 27.50				

X# 33 DOLLAR

31.0500 g., 0.9990 Silver 0.9972 oz. ASW, 39.15 mm. **Obv:** Large star, small heart in center, rope border **Rev:** Ranch hand horseback right **Edge:** Reeded **Note:** Coin alignment.

Date	Mintage	F	VF	XF	Unc	BU
2002 Proof	—	Value: 27.50				

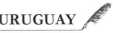

X# 34 DOLLAR
31.1100 g., 0.9990 Silver 0.9992 oz. ASW, 39.15 mm. **Obv:** Large star, small outline of Texas at center **Rev:** Mustang horse head left **Edge:** Reeded **Note:** Coin alignment.

Date	Mintage	F	VF	XF	Unc	BU
2003 Proof	—	Value: 27.50				

X# 36 DOLLAR
31.4000 g., 0.9990 Silver 1.0085 oz. ASW, 39.20 mm. **Obv:** Large star with small hearts in angles **Rev:** Bust of cowgirl facing wearing 10 gallon hat, stars in border **Edge:** Reeded **Note:** Coin alignment.

Date	Mintage	F	VF	XF	Unc	BU
2004 Proof	—	Value: 27.50				

X# 38 DOLLAR
31.1000 g., 0.9990 Silver 0.9988 oz. ASW, 39.20 mm. **Obv:** Large star, longhorned steer head at center **Rev:** Bronc buster **Edge:** Reeded **Note:** Coin alignment.

Date	Mintage	F	VF	XF	Unc	BU
2005 Proof	—	Value: 27.50				

WASHINGTON

TERRITORY

TOKEN COINAGE

X# Tn1 1/4 DOLLAR
0.9990 Gold **Obv:** Indian head left **Rev. Legend:** LIBERTY, WASH

Date	Mintage	F	VF	XF	Unc	BU
1871	—	—	—	—	—	—

X# Tn3 1/4 DOLLAR
0.4167 Gold **Issuer:** M.E. Hart **Obv:** Indian head left **Obv. Legend:** WASHINGTON GOLD **Rev:** USA Shield in sprays

Date	Mintage	F	VF	XF	Unc	BU
1914	—	—	—	—	—	—

X# Tn4 1/2 DOLLAR
0.4167 Gold **Issuer:** M.E. Hart **Obv:** Indian head left **Obv. Legend:** WASHINGTON GOLD **Rev:** USA shield in sprays

Date	Mintage	F	VF	XF	Unc	BU
1914	—	—	—	—	—	—

X# Tn5 DOLLAR
0.4167 Gold **Issuer:** M.E. Hart **Obv:** Indian head left **Obv. Legend:** WASHINGTON GOLD **Rev:** USA shield in sprays

Date	Mintage	F	VF	XF	Unc	BU
1914	—	—	—	—	—	—

UNITED TRANSNATIONAL REPUBLICS

UNION

COUNTERSTAMPED COINAGE

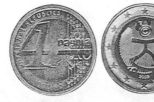

X# 1.1 4 PAYOLA
7.5000 g., Bi-Metallic, 23.3 mm. **Subject:** International Biennial of Young Art, Turin, Italy **Counterstamp:** Stylized youth // value **Edge:** Alternate reeding **Note:** Counterstamped on Germany 1 Euro, KM#213.

CS Date	Host Date	Mintage	F	VF	XF	Unc
ND	2002	—	—	—	—	—

X# 1.2 4 PAYOLA
7.5000 g., Bi-Metallic, 23.3 mm. **Subject:** International Biennial of Young Art, Turin, Italy **Counterstamp:** Stylized youth // value **Edge:** Alternate reeding **Note:** Counter-stamped on Italy 1 Euro, KM#216. Mintage Inc. X#1.1.

CS Date	Host Date	Mintage	VF	XF	Unc	BU
ND	2002	—	—	—	—	—

MEDALLIC COINAGE

X# 2 10 PAYOLA
Copper-Nickel, 30 mm. **Issuer:** Central Bank **Subject:** International Biennial of Young Art, Turin, Italy **Obv:** Large value "10" **Rev:** Stylized youth in molecule design **Edge:** Reeded

Date	Mintage	F	VF	XF	Unc	BU
2002	2,500	—	—	—	20.00	—

X# 2a 10 PAYOLA
0.9990 Silver, 30 mm. **Issuer:** Central Bank **Subject:** International Biennial of Young Art, Turin, Italy **Obv:** Large value "10" **Rev:** Stylized youth in molecule design **Edge:** Reeded

Date	Mintage	F	VF	XF	Unc	BU
2002	50	—	—	—	75.00	—

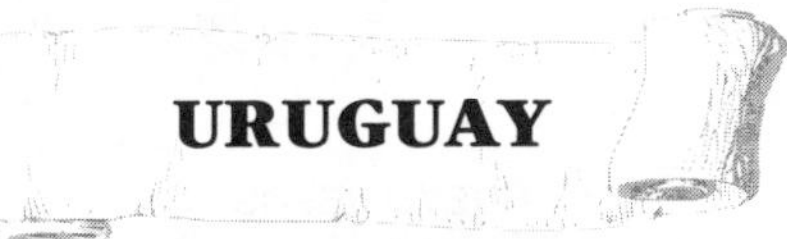

URUGUAY

REPUBLIC

MEDALLIC COINAGE

X# 1 2000 NUEVO PESOS
65.0000 g., 0.9000 Silver 1.8807 oz. ASW, 50.50 mm. **Subject:** Proposed Spanish Royal Visit **Obv:** Busts of Juan Carlos I and Sofia left **Obv. Legend:** VISITA DE LOS REYES DE ESPÁNA A LA RO DEL URUGUAY **Rev:** Arms of Uruguay and Spain **Edge:** Reeded **Note:** Prev. KM#M1 and KM#118.

Date	Mintage	F	VF	XF	Unc	BU
1983 Proof	20,000	Value: 65.00				

X# 1a 2000 NUEVO PESOS
0.9000 Gold, 50.50 mm. **Subject:** Proposed Spanish Royal Visit **Obv:** Busts of Juan Carlos I and Sofia left **Obv. Legend:** VISITA DE LOS REYES DE ESPÁNA A LA RO DEL URUGUAY **Rev:** Arms of Uruguay and Spain **Note:** Prev. KM#M1a.

Date	Mintage	F	VF	XF	Unc	BU
1983 Proof	—	Value: 1,400				

X# 1b 2000 NUEVO PESOS
Copper, 50.50 mm. **Subject:** Proposed Spanish Royal Visit **Obv:** Busts of Juan Carlos I and Sofia left **Obv. Legend:** VISITA DE LOS REYES DE ESPÁNA A LA RO DEL URUGUAY **Rev:** Arms of Uruguay and Spain **Edge:** Reeded

Date	Mintage	F	VF	XF	Unc	BU
1983 Proof	200	Value: 30.00				

X# 2 20000 NUEVO PESOS
20.0000 g., 0.9000 Gold 0.5787 oz. AGW, 33.15 mm. **Subject:** Proposed Spanish Royal Visit **Obv:** Busts of Juan Carlos I and Sofia left **Obv. Legend:** VISITA DE LOS REYES DE ESPAÑA A LA RO DEL URUGUAY **Rev:** Arms of Uruguay and Spain **Edge:** Reeded

Date	Mintage	F	VF	XF	Unc	BU
1983 Proof	1,500	Value: 375				

X# 2a 20000 NUEVO PESOS
20.0000 g., 0.9000 Silver 0.5787 oz. ASW, 33.15 mm. **Subject:** Proposed Spanish Royal Visit **Obv:** Busts of Juan Carlos I and Sofia left **Obv. Legend:** VISITA DE LOS REYES DE ESPAÑA A LA RO DEL URUGUAY **Rev:** Arms of Uruguay and Spain **Edge:** Reeded **Note:** Prev. KM#M3.

Date	Mintage	F	VF	XF	Unc	BU
1983 Proof	100	Value: 75.00				

TRIAL STRIKES

X#	Date	Mintage	Identification	Mkt Val
TS1	1953	—	Peso. Silver. 30.4600 g. 38.9 mm. Plain edge.	35.00
TS2	1953	—	Peso. Aluminum-Bronze. 38.9 mm. Prev. KM#PnA51.	—

X#	Date	Mintage	Identification	Mkt Val
TS3	1953	—	Peso. Copper-Nickel. 38.1 mm. Plain edge.	—
TS4	1953	—	Peso. Bronze. 38.1 mm. Plain edge.	—

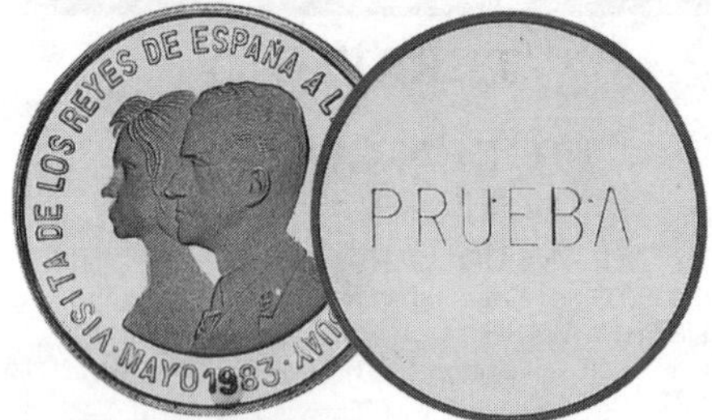

X#	Date	Mintage	Identification	Mkt Val
TS9	1983	—	20000 Nuevo Pesos. Silver. 19.6600 g. X#M2, PRUEBA. Reeded edge. Prev. KM#TS5.	125

X#	Date	Mintage	Identification	Mkt Val
TS10	1983	—	20000 Nuevo Pesos. Silver. #XM2, PREUBA. Reeded edge. Prev. KM#TS6.	125
TS11	1983	—	20000 Nuevo Pesos. Copper. X#M2, PREUBA. Reeded edge. Prev. KM#TS7.	80.00
TS12	1983	—	20000 Nuevo Pesos. Copper. X#M2, PREUBA. Reeded edge. Prev. KM#TS8.	80.00

X#	Date	Mintage	Identification	Mkt Val
TS5	1983	10	2000 Nuevo Pesos. Silver. X#M1, PRUEBA. Reeded edge. Prev. KM#TS1.	150

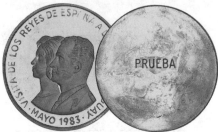

X#	Date	Mintage	Identification	Mkt Val
TS6	1983	—	2000 Nuevo Pesos. Silver. X#M1, PREUBA. Reeded edge. Prev. KM#TS2.	150
TS7	1983	—	2000 Nuevo Pesos. Copper. X#M1b, PREUBA. Plain edge. Prev. KM#TS3.	100
TS8	1983	—	2000 Nuevo Pesos. Copper. X#M1b, PREUBA. Plain edge. Prev. KM#TS4.	100

PIEFORTS

Double Thickness

X#	Date	Mintage	Identification	Mkt Val
P1	1983	10	2000 Nuevo Pesos. Silver. 64.5700 g. Reeded edge. X#M1. Prev. KM#P2.	300
P2	1983	10	2000 Nuevo Pesos. Copper. Plain edge. X#M1b. Prev. KM#P3.	145
P3	1983	—	20000 Nuevo Pesos. Gold. X#M1. Prev. KM#PA4.	950
P4	1983	10	20000 Nuevo Pesos. Silver. 39.7000 g. X#M2a. Prev. KM#P4.	165
P5	1983	—	20000 Nuevo Pesos. Copper. Plain edge. X#M2. Prev. KM#P5.	90.00

UTOPIA - A WORLD UNITED

UNITED NATIONS ADMINISTRATION

FANTASY COINAGE

Struck by the Medallic Art Co., New York

X# 1 DOLLAR
0.9000 Silver **Obv:** Dragon and eagle **Rev:** United Nations arms **Rev. Legend:** NVMMVS ARGENTEVS **Note:** Prev. KY#16.

Date	Mintage	F	VF	XF	Unc	B
1948	25	—	—	175	275	–

X# 1a DOLLAR
Lead **Obv:** Dragon and eagle **Rev:** United Nations arms **Note:** Prev. KY#16a.

Date	Mintage	F	VF	XF	Unc	B
1948	2	—	—	—	—	–

X# 1b DOLLAR
Gold **Obv:** Dragon and eagle **Rev:** United Nations arms **Note:** Prev. KY#16b.

Date	Mintage	F	VF	XF	Unc	B
1948	6	—	—	—	—	–

X# 2 1-1/4 OUNCES
0.7500 Gold **Obv:** Dragon and eagle **Rev:** United Nations arms **Rev. Legend:** NVMMVS AVREVS **Note:** Prev. KY#16c.

Date	Mintage	F	VF	XF	Unc	B
1948	—	—	—	—	550	70

X# 3 2-1/2 OUNCES
0.7500 Gold **Obv:** Dragon and eagle **Rev:** United Nations arms **Note:** Prev. KY#16d.

Date	Mintage	F	VF	XF	Unc	B
1948	—	—	—	—	1,000	1,25

X# 4 3-3/4 OUNCES
0.7500 Gold **Obv:** Dragon and eagle **Rev:** United Nations arms **Note:** Prev. KY#16e.

Date	Mintage	F	VF	XF	Unc	B
1948	—	—	—	—	1,400	1,65

VANUATU

REPUBLIC

MEDALLIC BULLION COINAGE

Na-Griamel Federation Bank

 # MB1 OUNCE
.1030 g., 0.9990 Silver 0.9989 oz. ASW
bv: President Moly **Rev:** Arms

te	Mintage	F	VF	XF	Unc	BU
76 Proof	—	Value: 60.00				

VATICAN CITY

CITY STATE

STANDARD COINAGE

100 Centesimi = 1 Lira

 # 1 50 LIRE
2.7000 g., Copper-Nickel Actual Coin Encased in Gold ated Copper-Nickel ring, 32 mm. **Ruler:** Benedict XVI **ubject:** John Paul II Memorial Encasement **bv. Legend:** "JOHN PAUL II 1920-2005" **ev. Legend:** "THE POPE OF THE PEOPLE" :LECTED POPE 1978" **Edge:** Plain

ate	Mintage	F	VF	XF	Unc	BU
)(2005)R	—	—	—	—	5.00	—

EURO COINAGE

Benedict XVI

 # 379 20 EURO CENT
.7200 g., Brass, 22.23 mm. **Ruler:** Benedict XVI **bv:** Pope's bust facing 3/4 right **Obv. Legend:** CITTA' EL VATICANO **Rev:** Map and value **Edge:** Plain with even indents

ate	Mintage	F	VF	XF	Unc	BU
)06R	85,000	—	—	—	40.00	50.00
)06R Proof	16,000	Value: 90.00				
)07R	—	—	—	—	—	—
)07R Proof	16,000	—	—	—	—	—

FANTASY EURO PATTERNS

I.M. International Issue

 # Pn11 50 EURO CENT
rass, 25 mm. **Ruler:** John Paul II **Obv:** Bust right **bv. Legend:** JOANNES PAVLVS II PONT MAX **ev:** Euro map and stars design

ate	Mintage	F	VF	XF	Unc	BU
)00	5,000	—	—	—	18.00	22.00

2002 Issue

X# Pn1 EURO CENT
Copper Plated Steel, 16.8 mm. **Ruler:** John Paul II **Obv:** Bust right **Obv. Legend:** IOANNES PAVLVS II - PONTIFEX MAXIMUS **Rev:** Dove in flight at right **Edge:** Plain

Date	Mintage	F	VF	XF	Unc	BU
2002	10,000	—	—	—	—	2.50
2002 Proof	2,500	Value: 3.00				

X# Pn1a EURO CENT
Silver, 16.8 mm. **Ruler:** John Paul II **Obv:** Bust right **Obv. Legend:** IOANNES PAVLVS II - PONTIFEX MAXIMUS **Rev:** Dove in flight at right **Edge:** Plain

Date	Mintage	F	VF	XF	Unc	BU
2002 Proof	500	Value: 6.00				

X# Pn2 2 EURO CENT
Copper Plated Steel, 18.5 mm. **Ruler:** John Paul II **Obv:** Bust right **Obv. Legend:** IOANNES PAVLVS II - PONTIFEX MAXIMUS **Rev:** Dove in flight at right **Edge:** Plain

Date	Mintage	F	VF	XF	Unc	BU
2002	10,000	—	—	—	—	3.00
2002 Proof	2,500	Value: 3.50				

X# Pn2a 2 EURO CENT
Silver, 18.5 mm. **Ruler:** John Paul II **Obv:** Bust right **Obv. Legend:** IOANNES PAVLVS II - PONTIFEX MAXIMUS **Rev:** Dove in flight at right **Edge:** Plain

Date	Mintage	F	VF	XF	Unc	BU
2002 Proof	500	Value: 7.00				

X# Pn3 5 EURO CENT
Copper Plated Steel, 20.7 mm. **Ruler:** John Paul II **Obv:** Bust right **Obv. Legend:** IOANNES PAVLVS II - PONTIFEX MAXIMUS **Rev:** Dove in flight at right **Edge:** Plain

Date	Mintage	F	VF	XF	Unc	BU
2002	10,000	—	—	—	—	3.50
2002 Proof	2,500	Value: 4.50				

X# Pn3a 5 EURO CENT
Silver, 20.7 mm. **Ruler:** John Paul II **Obv:** Bust right **Obv. Legend:** IOANNES PAVLVS II - PONTIFEX MAXIMUS **Rev:** Dove in flight at right

Date	Mintage	F	VF	XF	Unc	BU
2002 Proof	500	Value: 8.50				

X# Pn4 10 EURO CENT
Goldine, 19.3 mm. **Ruler:** John Paul II **Obv:** Bust right **Obv. Legend:** IOANNES PAVLVS II - PONTIFEX MAXIMUS **Rev:** St. George horseback right at left **Edge:** Plain

Date	Mintage	F	VF	XF	Unc	BU
2002	10,000	—	—	—	—	4.00
2002 Proof	2,500	Value: 5.50				

X# Pn4a 10 EURO CENT
Silver, 19.3 mm. **Ruler:** John Paul II **Obv:** Bust right **Obv. Legend:** IOANNES PAVLVS II - PONTIFEX MAXIMUS **Rev:** St. George horseback right at left **Edge:** Plain

Date	Mintage	F	VF	XF	Unc	BU
2002 Proof	500	Value: 10.00				

X# Pn5 20 EURO CENT
Goldine, 22 mm. **Ruler:** John Paul II **Obv:** Bust right **Obv. Legend:** IOANNES PAVLVS II - PONTIFEX MAXIMUS **Rev:** St. George horseback right at left **Edge:** Plain

Date	Mintage	F	VF	XF	Unc	BU
2002	10,000	—	—	—	—	5.00
2002 Proof	2,500	Value: 6.50				

X# Pn5a 20 EURO CENT
Silver, 22 mm. **Ruler:** John Paul II **Obv:** Bust right **Obv. Legend:** IOANNES PAVLVS II - PONTIFEX MAXIMUS **Rev:** St. George horseback right at left **Edge:** Plain

Date	Mintage	F	VF	XF	Unc	BU
2002 Proof	500	Value: 12.50				

X# Pn6 50 EURO CENT
Goldine, 24.3 mm. **Ruler:** John Paul II **Obv:** Bust right **Obv. Legend:** IOANNES PAVLVS II - PONTIFEX MAXIMUS **Rev:** St. George horseback right at left **Edge:** Plain

Date	Mintage	F	VF	XF	Unc	BU
2002	10,000	—	—	—	—	6.00
2002 Proof	2,500	Value: 7.50				

X# Pn6a 50 EURO CENT
Silver, 24.3 mm. **Ruler:** John Paul II **Obv:** Bust right **Obv. Legend:** IOANNES PAVLVS II - PONTIFEX MAXIMUS **Rev:** St. George horseback right at left **Edge:** Plain

Date	Mintage	F	VF	XF	Unc	BU
2002 Proof	500	Value: 15.00				

X# Pn8 2 EURO
Bi-Metallic Goldine center in Copper-Nickel ring, 25.7 mm. **Ruler:** John Paul II **Obv:** Bust right **Obv. Legend:** IOANNES PAVLVS II - PONTIFEX MAXIMUS **Rev:** Archways at right **Edge:** Plain

Date	Mintage	F	VF	XF	Unc	BU
2002	10,000	—	—	—	—	10.00
2002 Proof	2,500	Value: 14.00				

X# Pn8a 2 EURO
Bi-Metallic Brass center in Silver ring, 25.7 mm. **Ruler:** John Paul II **Obv:** Bust right **Obv. Legend:** IOANNES PAVLVS II - PONTIFEX MAXIMUS **Rev:** Archways at right **Edge:** Plain

Date	Mintage	F	VF	XF	Unc	BU
2002 Proof	500	Value: 28.50				

X# Pn9 5 EURO
Goldine, 36 mm. **Ruler:** John Paul II **Edge:** Plain

Date	Mintage	F	VF	XF	Unc	BU
2002 Proof	2,500	Value: 20.00				

X# Pn9a 5 EURO
Silver, 36 mm. **Ruler:** John Paul II **Edge:** Plain

Date	Mintage	F	VF	XF	Unc	BU
2002 Proof	500	Value: 40.00				

2004 Issue

X# Pn21 EURO CENT
Copper Plated Steel **Ruler:** John Paul II **Obv:** Head right **Edge:** Plain

Date	Mintage	F	VF	XF	Unc	BU
XXVI (2004)	7,500	—	—	—	—	2.50

X# Pn22 2 EURO CENT
Copper Plated Steel **Ruler:** John Paul II **Obv:** Head right **Edge:** Plain

Date	Mintage	F	VF	XF	Unc	BU
XXVI (2004)	7,500	—	—	—	—	3.00

X# Pn23 5 EURO CENT
Copper Plated Steel **Ruler:** John Paul II **Obv:** Head right **Edge:** Plain

Date	Mintage	F	VF	XF	Unc	BU
XXVI (2004)	7,500	—	—	—	—	3.50

X# Pn24 10 EURO CENT
Goldine **Ruler:** John Paul II **Obv:** Head right **Edge:** Plain

Date	Mintage	F	VF	XF	Unc	BU
XXVI (2004)	7,500	—	—	—	—	4.00

X# Pn25 20 EURO CENT
Goldine **Ruler:** John Paul II **Obv:** Head right **Edge:** Plain

Date	Mintage	F	VF	XF	Unc	BU
XXVI (2004)	7,500	—	—	—	—	5.00

X# Pn26 50 EURO CENT
Goldine **Ruler:** John Paul II **Obv:** Head right **Edge:** Plain

Date	Mintage	F	VF	XF	Unc	BU
XXVI (2004)	7,500	—	—	—	—	6.00

X# Pn27 EURO
Goldine **Ruler:** John Paul II **Obv:** Head right

Date	Mintage	F	VF	XF	Unc	BU
XXVI (2004)	7,500	—	—	—	—	8.00

X# Pn28 2 EURO

Bi-Metallic **Ruler:** John Paul II **Obv:** Head right **Edge:** Plain

Date	Mintage	F	VF	XF	Unc	BU
XXVI (2004)	7,500	—	—	—	—	10.00

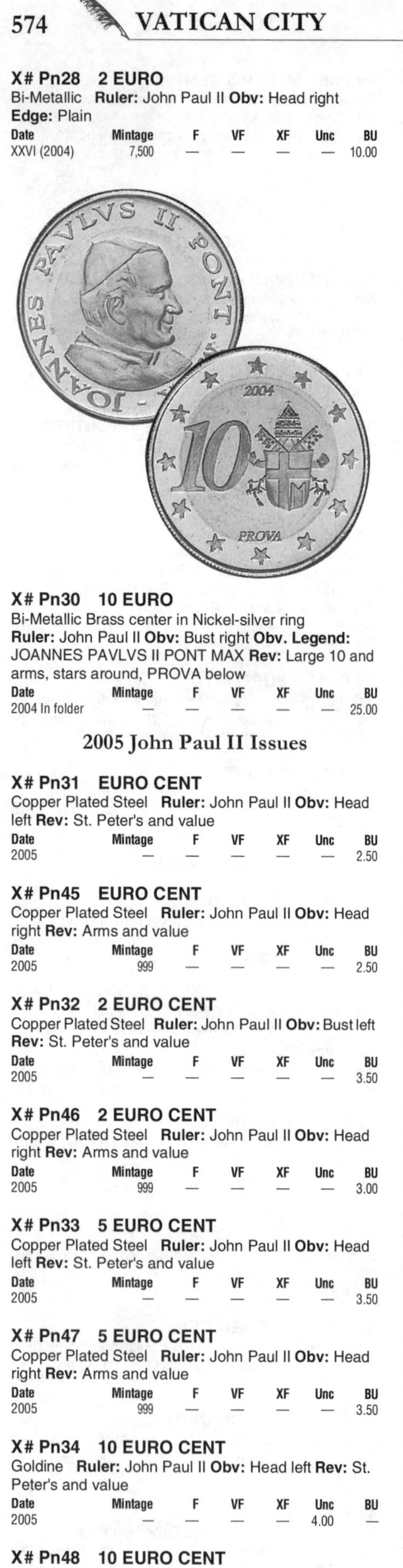

X# Pn30 10 EURO

Bi-Metallic Brass center in Nickel-silver ring **Ruler:** John Paul II **Obv:** Bust right **Obv. Legend:** JOANNES PAVLVS II PONT MAX **Rev:** Large 10 and arms, stars around, PROVA below

Date	Mintage	F	VF	XF	Unc	BU
2004 In folder	—	—	—	—	—	25.00

2005 John Paul II Issues

X# Pn31 EURO CENT

Copper Plated Steel **Ruler:** John Paul II **Obv:** Head left **Rev:** St. Peter's and value

Date	Mintage	F	VF	XF	Unc	BU
2005	—	—	—	—	—	2.50

X# Pn45 EURO CENT

Copper Plated Steel **Ruler:** John Paul II **Obv:** Head right **Rev:** Arms and value

Date	Mintage	F	VF	XF	Unc	BU
2005	999	—	—	—	—	2.50

X# Pn32 2 EURO CENT

Copper Plated Steel **Ruler:** John Paul II **Obv:** Bust left **Rev:** St. Peter's and value

Date	Mintage	F	VF	XF	Unc	BU
2005	—	—	—	—	—	3.50

X# Pn46 2 EURO CENT

Copper Plated Steel **Ruler:** John Paul II **Obv:** Head right **Rev:** Arms and value

Date	Mintage	F	VF	XF	Unc	BU
2005	999	—	—	—	—	3.00

X# Pn33 5 EURO CENT

Copper Plated Steel **Ruler:** John Paul II **Obv:** Head left **Rev:** St. Peter's and value

Date	Mintage	F	VF	XF	Unc	BU
2005	—	—	—	—	—	3.50

X# Pn47 5 EURO CENT

Copper Plated Steel **Ruler:** John Paul II **Obv:** Head right **Rev:** Arms and value

Date	Mintage	F	VF	XF	Unc	BU
2005	999	—	—	—	—	3.50

X# Pn34 10 EURO CENT

Goldine **Ruler:** John Paul II **Obv:** Head left **Rev:** St. Peter's and value

Date	Mintage	F	VF	XF	Unc	BU
2005	—	—	—	—	4.00	—

X# Pn48 10 EURO CENT

Goldine **Ruler:** John Paul II **Obv:** Head right **Rev:** Arms and value

Date	Mintage	F	VF	XF	Unc	BU
2005	999	—	—	—	—	4.00

X# Pn35 20 EURO CENT

Goldine **Ruler:** John Paul II **Subject:** Bust left **Rev:** St. Peter's and value

Date	Mintage	F	VF	XF	Unc	BU
2005	—	—	—	—	—	5.00

X# Pn49 20 EURO CENT

Goldine **Ruler:** John Paul II **Obv:** Head right **Rev:** Arms and value

Date	Mintage	F	VF	XF	Unc	BU
2005	999	—	—	—	—	5.00

X# Pn36 50 EURO CENT

Goldine **Ruler:** John Paul II **Obv:** Head left **Rev:** St. Peter's and value

Date	Mintage	F	VF	XF	Unc	BU
2005	—	—	—	—	—	6.00

X# Pn50 50 EURO CENT

Goldine **Ruler:** John Paul II **Obv:** Head right **Rev:** Arms and value

Date	Mintage	F	VF	XF	Unc	BU
2005	999	—	—	—	—	6.00

X# Pn37 EURO

Bi-Metallic **Ruler:** John Paul II **Obv:** Head left **Rev:** St. Peter's and value

Date	Mintage	F	VF	XF	Unc	BU
2005	—	—	—	—	—	8.00

X# Pn51 EURO

Bi-Metallic **Ruler:** John Paul II **Obv:** Head right **Rev:** Arms and value

Date	Mintage	F	VF	XF	Unc	BU
2005	999	—	—	—	—	8.00

X# Pn38 2 EURO

Bi-Metallic **Ruler:** John Paul II **Obv:** Head left **Rev:** St. Peter's and value

Date	Mintage	F	VF	XF	Unc	BU
2005	—	—	—	—	—	10.00

X# Pn52 2 EURO

Bi-Metallic **Ruler:** John Paul II **Obv:** Head right **Rev:** Arms and value

Date	Mintage	F	VF	XF	Unc	BU
2005	999	—	—	—	—	10.00

X# Pn39 5 EURO

Bi-Metallic **Ruler:** John Paul II **Obv:** Head left **Rev:** St. Peter's and value

Date	Mintage	F	VF	XF	Unc	BU
2005 Proof	—	Value: 20.00				

2005 Sede Vacante Issue

X# Pn55 EURO CENT

Copper Plated Steel **Ruler:** Sede Vacante **Obv:** Canopy above crossed keys **Rev:** Dove

Date	Mintage	F	VF	XF	Unc	BU
2005	5,000	—	—	—	—	2.50

X# Pn56 2 EURO CENT

Copper Plated Steel **Ruler:** Sede Vacante **Obv:** Canopy above crossed keys **Rev:** Dove

Date	Mintage	F	VF	XF	Unc	BU
2005	5,000	—	—	—	—	3.00
2005 Proof	2,000	Value: 3.50				

X# Pn57 5 EURO CENT

Chrome Plated Steel **Ruler:** Sede Vacante **Obv:** Canopy above crossed keys **Rev:** Dove

Date	Mintage	F	VF	XF	Unc	BU
2005	5,000	—	—	—	—	3.50
2005 Proof	2,000	Value: 4.50				

X# Pn58 10 EURO CENT

Goldine **Ruler:** Sede Vacante **Obv:** Canopy above crossed keys **Rev:** Dove

Date	Mintage	F	VF	XF	Unc	BU
2005	5,000	—	—	—	—	4.00
2005	2,000	Value: 10.00				

X# Pn59 20 EURO CENT

Goldine **Ruler:** Sede Vacante **Obv:** Canopy above crossed keys **Rev:** Dove

Date	Mintage	F	VF	XF	Unc	
2005	5,000	—	—	—	—	5
2005 Proof	2,000	Value: 7.50				

X# Pn60 50 EURO CENT

Goldine **Ruler:** Sede Vacante **Obv:** Canopy above crossed keys **Rev:** Dove

Date	Mintage	F	VF	XF	Unc	
2005	5,000	—	—	—	—	6
2005 Proof	2,000	Value: 15.00				

X# Pn61 EURO

Bi-Metallic **Ruler:** Sede Vacante **Obv:** Canopy abov crossed keys **Rev:** Dove

Date	Mintage	F	VF	XF	Unc	
2005	5,000	—	—	—	—	8
2005 Proof	2,000	Value: 8.00				

X# Pn62 2 EURO

Bi-Metallic **Ruler:** Sede Vacante **Obv:** Canopy abov crossed keys **Rev:** Dove

Date	Mintage	F	VF	XF	Unc	
2005	5,000	—	—	—	—	10
2005 Proof	2,000	Value: 28.50				

X# Pn63 5 EURO

Goldine **Ruler:** Sede Vacante **Obv:** Canopy above crossed keys **Rev:** Dove

Date	Mintage	F	VF	XF	Unc
2005 Proof	2,000	Value: 20.00			

2005 Benedict XVI Issues

X# Pn65 EURO CENT

Copper Plated Steel **Ruler:** Benedict XVI **Obv:** Bus 3/4 left in cassock **Rev:** Tiara above crossed keys

Date	Mintage	F	VF	XF	Unc	
2005	—	—	—	—	—	2.

X# Pn75 EURO CENT

Copper Plated Steel **Ruler:** Benedict XVI **Obv:** Bus 3/4 left in vestments **Rev:** Balance scale and value

Date	Mintage	F	VF	XF	Unc	
2005	3,000	—	—	—	—	2.
2005 Proof	2,000	Value: 3.50				

X# Pn85 EURO CENT

Copper Plated Steel **Ruler:** Benedict XVI **Obv:** Bust rig

Date	Mintage	F	VF	XF	Unc	
2005	—	—	—	—	—	2.

X# Pn66 2 EURO CENT

Copper Plated Steel **Ruler:** Benedict XVI **Obv:** Bus 3/4 left in cassock **Rev:** Tiara above crossed keys

Date	Mintage	F	VF	XF	Unc	
2005	—	—	—	—	—	3.

X# Pn76 2 EURO CENT

Copper Plated Steel **Ruler:** Benedict XVI **Obv:** Bus 3/4 left in vestments **Rev:** Balance scale and value

Date	Mintage	F	VF	XF	Unc	
2005	3,000	—	—	—	—	3.
2005 Proof	—	Value: 4.00				

X# Pn86 2 EURO CENT

Copper Plated Steel **Ruler:** Benedict XVI **Obv:** Bust rig

Date	Mintage	F	VF	XF	Unc	
2005	—	—	—	—	—	3.

X# Pn67 5 EURO CENT

Copper Plated Steel **Ruler:** Benedict XVI **Obv:** Bus 3/4 left in cassock **Rev:** Tiara above crossed keys

Date	Mintage	F	VF	XF	Unc	
2005	—	—	—	—	—	3.

X# Pn77 5 EURO CENT

Copper Plated Steel **Ruler:** Benedict XVI **Obv:** Bus 3/4 left in vestments **Rev:** Balance scale and value

Date	Mintage	F	VF	XF	Unc	
2005	3,000	—	—	—	—	3.
2005 Proof	2,000	Value: 4.50				

X# Pn87 5 EURO CENT

Copper Plated Steel **Ruler:** Benedict XVI **Obv:** Bust right

Date	Mintage	F	VF	XF	Unc	BU
2005	—	—	—	—	—	3.50

X# Pn68 10 EURO CENT

Goldine **Ruler:** Benedict XVI **Obv:** Bust 3/4 left in cassock **Rev:** Tiara above crossed keys

Date	Mintage	F	VF	XF	Unc	BU
2005	—	—	—	—	—	4.00

X# Pn78 10 EURO CENT

Goldine **Ruler:** Benedict XVI **Obv:** Bust 3/4 left in vestments **Rev:** Value and dove in circle

Date	Mintage	F	VF	XF	Unc	BU
2005	3,000	—	—	—	—	4.50
2005 Proof	2,000	Value: 5.00				

X# Pn88 10 EURO CENT

Goldine **Ruler:** Benedict XVI **Obv:** Bust right

Date	Mintage	F	VF	XF	Unc	BU
2005	—	—	—	—	—	4.00

X# Pn69 20 EURO CENT

Goldine **Ruler:** Benedict XVI **Obv:** Bust 3/4 left in cassock **Rev:** Tiara above crossed keys

Date	Mintage	F	VF	XF	Unc	BU
2005	—	—	—	—	—	5.00

X# Pn79 20 EURO CENT

Bi-Metallic **Ruler:** Benedict XVI **Obv:** Bust 3/4 left in vestments **Rev:** Value and dove in circle

Date	Mintage	F	VF	XF	Unc	BU
2005	3,000	—	—	—	5.00	—
2005 Proof	2,000	Value: 6.00				

X# Pn89 20 EURO CENT

Goldine **Ruler:** Benedict XVI **Obv:** Bust right

Date	Mintage	F	VF	XF	Unc	BU
2005	—	—	—	—	—	4.50

X# Pn70 50 EURO CENT

Goldine **Ruler:** Benedict XVI **Obv:** Bust 3/4 left in cassock **Rev:** Tiara above crossed keys

Date	Mintage	F	VF	XF	Unc	BU
2005	—	—	—	—	—	4.50

X# Pn80 50 EURO CENT

Bi-Metallic **Ruler:** Benedict XVI **Obv:** Bust 3/4 left in vestments **Rev:** Value and dove in circle

Date	Mintage	F	VF	XF	Unc	BU
2005	3,000	—	—	—	—	6.00
2005 Proof	2,000	Value: 9.00				

X# Pn90 50 EURO CENT

Goldine **Ruler:** Benedict XVI **Obv:** Bust right

Date	Mintage	F	VF	XF	Unc	BU
2005	—	—	—	—	—	5.00

X# Pn71 EURO

Bi-Metallic **Ruler:** Benedict XVI **Obv:** Bust 3/4 left in cassock **Rev:** Tiara above crossed keys

Date	Mintage	F	VF	XF	Unc	BU
2005	—	—	—	—	—	8.00

X# Pn81 EURO

Bi-Metallic **Ruler:** Benedict XVI **Obv:** Bust 3/4 left in vestments **Rev:** Value and dove in circle

Date	Mintage	F	VF	XF	Unc	BU
2005	3,000	—	—	—	—	8.00
2005 Proof	2,000	Value: 9.00				

X# Pn91 EURO

Bi-Metallic **Ruler:** Benedict XVI **Obv:** Bust right

Date	Mintage	F	VF	XF	Unc	BU
2005	—	—	—	—	—	7.50

X# Pn72 2 EURO

Goldine **Ruler:** Benedict XVI **Obv:** Bust 3/4 left in cassock **Rev:** Tiara above crossed keys

Date	Mintage	F	VF	XF	Unc	BU
2005	—	—	—	—	—	9.00

X# Pn82 2 EURO

Bi-Metallic **Ruler:** Benedict XVI **Obv:** Bust 3/4 left in vestments **Rev:** Value and dove in circle

Date	Mintage	F	VF	XF	Unc	BU
2005	3,000	—	—	—	—	9.00
2005 Proof	2,000	Value: 10.00				

X# Pn92 2 EURO

Goldine **Ruler:** Benedict XVI **Obv:** Bust right

Date	Mintage	F	VF	XF	Unc	BU
2005	—	—	—	—	—	8.00

X# Pn95 2 EURO

Bi-Metallic **Ruler:** Benedict XVI **Subject:** World Youth Day **Obv:** Bust right **Rev:** Cologne Cathedral, crossed keys behind

Date	Mintage	F	VF	XF	Unc	BU
2005	3,000	—	—	—	—	10.00

X# Pn83 5 EURO

Goldine **Ruler:** Benedict XVI **Obv:** Bust 3/4 left in vestments **Rev:** Value and dove in circle

Date	Mintage	F	VF	XF	Unc	BU
2005 Proof	2,000	Value: 15.00				

PIEFORTS

X#	Date	Mintage	Identification	Mkt Val
P1	2002	500	5 Euro. Silver. X#Pn9.	85.00

MINT SETS

X#	Date	Mintage	Identification	Issue Price	Mkt Val
XMS1	2002 (8)	2,500	X#Pn1-Pn8 with serial #	—	50.00
XMS3	XXVI (2004) (8)	7,500	X#Pn21-Pn28	—	40.00
XMS4	2005 (8)	—	X#Pn31-X#Pn38	—	25.00
XMS5	2005 (8)	999	X#Pn45-X#Pn52	—	25.00
XMS6	2005 (8)	5,000	X#Pn55-X#Pn62	—	35.00
XMS7	2005 (8)	—	X#Pn65-X#Pn72	—	25.00
XMS8	2005 (8)	—	X#Pn85-X#Pn92	—	25.00
XMS9	2005 (8)	3,000	X#Pn75-X#Pn82	—	25.00

PROOF SETS

X#	Date	Mintage	Identification	Issue Price	Mkt Val
XPS1	2002 (9)	2,500	X#Pn1-Pn9	—	75.00
XPS2	2002 (9)	500	X#Pn1a-Pn9a	—	150
XPS3	2005 (9)	—	X#Pn31-X#Pn39	—	35.00
XPS4	2005 (9)	2,000	X#Pn55-X#Pn63	—	40.00
XPS5	2005 (9)	2,000	X#Pn75-X#Pn83	—	40.00

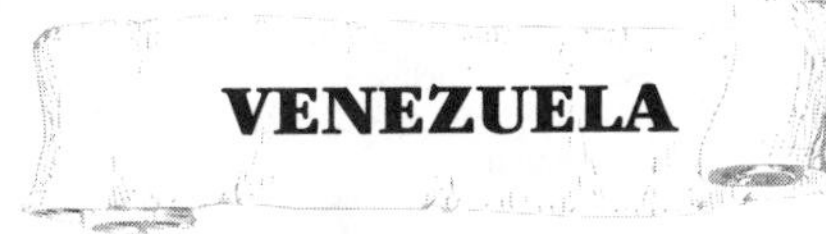

VENEZUELA

REPUBLIC

MEDALLIC COINAGE

X# 11 1300 BOLIVARES

39.8700 g., 0.9990 Silver 1.2805 oz. ASW, 40.5 mm. **Subject:** Centenary of Zulia University **Obv:** University Centenial logo **Rev:** Facing busts of Rectors Dr. F. Ochoa (1891) and Dr. J. E. Lossada (1946)

Date	Mintage	F	VF	XF	Unc	BU
ND(1991) Proof	1,500	Value: 45.00				

Inter-Change Bank Suiza - Chiefs Series

X# MB121 5 BOLIVARES

0.9000 Gold, 13.9 mm. **Series:** 16th Century Chiefs **Obv:** Crossed arrows **Obv. Legend:** CACIQUES DE VENEZUELA **Rev:** Head facing slightly left **Rev. Legend:** CACIQUES DE VENEZUELA - GUAICAIPURO **Edge:** Reeded **Note:** Weight varies: 1.43-1.52 grams.

Date	Mintage	F	VF	XF	Unc	BU
ND(1962?)	—	—	—	BV	45.00	—

X# MB122 5 BOLIVARES

0.9000 Gold, 13.9 mm. **Series:** 16th Century Chiefs **Obv:** Crossed arrows **Obv. Legend:** CACIQUES DE VENEZUELA **Rev:** Head facing **Rev. Legend:** CACIQUES DE VENEZUELA - TIUNA **Edge:** Reeded **Note:** Weight varies: 1.43-1.52 grams.

Date	Mintage	F	VF	XF	Unc	BU
ND(1962?)	—	—	—	BV	45.00	—

X# MB123 5 BOLIVARES

0.9000 Gold, 13.9 mm. **Series:** 16th Century Chiefs **Obv:** Crossed arrows **Obv. Legend:** CACIQUES DE VENEZUELA **Rev:** Head facing almost right **Rev. Legend:** CACIQUES DE VENEZUELA - CHACAO **Edge:** Reeded **Note:** Weight varies: 1.43-1.52 grams.

Date	Mintage	F	VF	XF	Unc	BU
ND(1962?)	—	—	—	BV	45.00	—

X# MB124 5 BOLIVARES

0.9000 Gold, 13.9 mm. **Series:** 16th Century Chiefs **Obv:** Crossed arrows **Obv. Legend:** CACIQUES DE VENEZUELA **Rev:** Head facing 3/4 right **Rev. Legend:** CACIQUES DE VENEZUELA - MARA **Edge:** Reeded **Note:** Weight varies: 1.43-1.52 grams.

Date	Mintage	F	VF	XF	Unc	BU
ND(1962?)	—	—	—	BV	45.00	—

X# MB125 5 BOLIVARES

0.9000 Gold, 13.9 mm. **Series:** 16th Century Chiefs **Obv:** Crossed arrows **Obv. Legend:** CACIQUES DE VENEZUELA **Rev:** Head facing slightly right **Rev. Legend:** CACIQUES DE VENEZUELA - NAIGUATÁ **Edge:** Reeded **Note:** Weight varies: 1.43-1.52 grams.

Date	Mintage	F	VF	XF	Unc	BU
ND(1962?)	—	—	—	BV	45.00	—

X# MB126 5 BOLIVARES

0.9000 Gold, 13.9 mm. **Series:** 16th Century Chiefs **Obv:** Crossed arms **Obv. Legend:** CACIQUES DE VENEZUELA **Rev:** Head left **Rev. Legend:** CACIQUES DE VENEZUELA - SOROCAIMA **Edge:** Reeded **Note:** Weight varies: 1.43-1.52 grams.

Date	Mintage	F	VF	XF	Unc	BU
ND(1962?)	—	—	—	BV	45.00	—

X# MB127 5 BOLIVARES

0.9000 Gold, 13.9 mm. **Series:** 16th Century Chiefs **Obv:** Crossed arms **Obv. Legend:** CACIQUES DE VENEZUELA **Rev:** Head facing slightly right **Rev. Legend:** CACIQUES DE VENEZUELA - PARAMACAY **Edge:** Reeded **Note:** Weight varies: 1.43-1.52 grams.

Date	Mintage	F	VF	XF	Unc	BU
ND(1962?)	—	—	—	BV	45.00	—

X# MB128 5 BOLIVARES

0.9000 Gold, 13.9 mm. **Series:** 16th Century Chiefs **Obv:** Crossed arrows **Obv. Legend:** CACIQUES DE VENEZUELA **Rev:** Head facing **Rev. Legend:** CACIQUES DE VENEZUELA - TAMANACO **Edge:** Reeded **Note:** Weight varies: 1.43-1.52 grams.

Date	Mintage	F	VF	XF	Unc	BU
ND(1962?)	—	—	—	BV	45.00	—

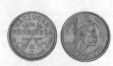

X# MB129 5 BOLIVARES
0.9000 Gold, 13.9 mm. **Series:** 16th Century Chiefs **Obv:** Crossed arrows **Obv. Legend:** CACIQUES DE VENEZUELA **Rev:** Head right **Rev. Legend:** CACIQUES DE VENEZUELA - GUAICAMACUTO **Edge:** Reeded **Note:** Weight varies: 1.43-1.52 grams.

Date	Mintage	F	VF	XF	Unc	BU
ND(1962?)	—	—	—	BV	45.00	—

X# MB130 5 BOLIVARES
0.9000 Gold, 13.9 mm. **Series:** 16th Century Chiefs **Obv:** Crossed arms **Obv. Legend:** CACIQUES DE VENEZUELA **Rev:** Head facing slightly left **Rev. Legend:** CACIQUES DE VENEZUELA - ARICHUNA **Edge:** Reeded **Note:** Weight varies: 1.43-1.52 grams.

Date	Mintage	F	VF	XF	Unc	BU
ND(1962?)	—	—	—	BV	45.00	—

X# MB131 5 BOLIVARES
0.9000 Gold, 13.9 mm. **Series:** 16th Century Chiefs **Obv:** Crossed arms **Obv. Legend:** CACIQUES DE VENEZUELA **Rev:** Head 3/4 left **Rev. Legend:** CACIQUES DE VENEZUELA - MURACHI **Edge:** Reeded **Note:** Weight varies: 1.43-1.52 grams.

Date	Mintage	F	VF	XF	Unc	BU
ND(1962?)	—	—	—	BV	45.00	—

X# MB132 5 BOLIVARES
0.9000 Gold, 13.9 mm. **Series:** 16th Century Chiefs **Obv:** Crossed arrows **Obv. Legend:** CACIQUES DE VENEZUELA **Rev:** Head left **Rev. Legend:** CACIQUES DE VENEZUELA - TEREPAIMA **Edge:** Reeded **Note:** Weight varies: 1.43-1.52 grams.

Date	Mintage	F	VF	XF	Unc	BU
ND(1962?)	—	—	—	BV	45.00	—

X# MB133 5 BOLIVARES
0.9000 Gold, 13.9 mm. **Series:** 16th Century Chiefs **Obv:** Crossed arrows **Obv. Legend:** CACIQUES DE VENEZUELA **Rev:** Head slightly left **Rev. Legend:** CACIQUES DE VENEZUELA - PARAMACONI **Edge:** Reeded **Note:** Weight varies: 1.43-1.52 grams.

Date	Mintage	F	VF	XF	Unc	BU
ND(1962?)	—	—	—	BV	45.00	—

X# MB134 5 BOLIVARES
0.9000 Gold, 13.9 mm. **Series:** 16th Century Chiefs **Obv:** Crossed arrows **Obv. Legend:** CACIQUES DE VENEZUELA **Rev:** Head facing **Rev. Legend:** CACIQUES DE VENEZUELA - MANAURE **Edge:** Reeded **Note:** Weight varies: 1.43-1.52 grams.

Date	Mintage	F	VF	XF	Unc	BU
ND(1962?)	—	—	—	BV	45.00	—

X# MB135 5 BOLIVARES
0.9000 Gold, 13.9 mm. **Series:** 16th Century Chiefs **Obv:** Crossed arrows **Obv. Legend:** CACIQUES DE VENEZUELA **Rev:** Two heads jugate almost right **Rev. Legend:** CACIQUES DE VENEZUELA - CHICURAMAY **Edge:** Reeded **Note:** Weight varies: 1.43-1.52 grams.

Date	Mintage	F	VF	XF	Unc	BU
ND(1962?)	—	—	—	BV	45.00	—

X# MB136 5 BOLIVARES
0.9000 Gold, 13.9 mm. **Series:** 16th Century Chiefs **Obv:** Crossed arrows **Obv. Legend:** CACIQUES DE VENEZUELA **Rev:** Head 3/4 right **Rev. Legend:** CACIQUES DE VENEZUELA - YORACUY **Edge:** Reeded **Note:** Weight varies: 1.43-1.52 grams.

Date	Mintage	F	VF	XF	Unc	BU
ND(1962?)	—	—	—	BV	45.00	—

X# MB137 5 BOLIVARES
0.9000 Gold, 13.9 mm. **Series:** 16th Century Chiefs **Obv:** Crossed arrows **Obv. Legend:** CACIQUES DE VENEZUELA **Rev:** Head facing **Rev. Legend:** CACIQUES DE VENEZUELA - URIMARE **Edge:** Reeded **Note:** Weight varies: 1.43-1.52 grams.

Date	Mintage	F	VF	XF	Unc	BU
ND(1962?)	—	—	—	BV	45.00	—

X# MB138 5 BOLIVARES
0.9000 Gold, 13.9 mm. **Series:** 16th Century Chiefs **Obv:** Crossed arms **Obv. Legend:** CACIQUES DE VENEZUELA **Rev:** Two heads jugate left **Rev. Legend:** CACIQUES DE VENEZUELA - YORACO **Edge:** Reeded **Note:** Weight varies: 1.43-1.52 grams.

Date	Mintage	F	VF	XF	Unc	BU
ND(1962?)	—	—	—	BV	45.00	—

X# MB139 10 BOLIVARES
0.9000 Gold, 19 mm. **Series:** 16th Century Chiefs **Obv:** Crossed arrows **Obv. Legend:** CACIQUES DE VENEZUELA **Rev:** Head facing slightly left **Rev. Legend:** CACIQUES DE VENEZUELA - GUAICAIPURO **Edge:** Reeded

Date	Mintage	F	VF	XF	Unc	BU
ND(1962?)	—	—	—	BV	75.00	—

X# MB140 10 BOLIVARES
0.9000 Gold, 19 mm. **Series:** 16th Century Chiefs **Obv:** Crossed arrows **Obv. Legend:** CACIQUES DE VENEZUELA **Rev:** Head facing **Rev. Legend:** CACIQUES DE VENEZUELA - TIUNA **Edge:** Reeded

Date	Mintage	F	VF	XF	Unc	BU
ND(1962?)	—	—	—	BV	75.00	—

X# MB141 10 BOLIVARES
0.9000 Gold, 19 mm. **Series:** 16th Century Chiefs **Obv:** Crossed arrows **Obv. Legend:** CACIQUES DE VENEZUELA **Rev:** Head facing almost right **Rev. Legend:** CACIQUES DE VENEZUELA - CHACAO **Edge:** Reeded

Date	Mintage	F	VF	XF	Unc	BU
ND(1962?)	—	—	—	BV	75.00	—

X# MB142 10 BOLIVARES
0.9000 Gold, 19 mm. **Series:** 16th Century Chiefs **Obv:** Crossed arrows **Obv. Legend:** CACIQUES DE VENEZUELA **Rev:** Head facing 3/4 right **Rev. Legend:** CACIQUES DE VENEZUELA - MARA **Edge:** Reeded

Date	Mintage	F	VF	XF	Unc	BU
ND(1962?)	—	—	—	BV	75.00	—

X# MB143 10 BOLIVARES
0.9000 Gold, 19 mm. **Series:** 16th Century Chiefs **Obv:** Crossed arrows **Obv. Legend:** CACIQUES DE VENEZUELA **Rev:** Head facing slightly right **Rev. Legend:** CACIQUES DE VENEZUELA - NAIGUATÁ **Edge:** Reeded

Date	Mintage	F	VF	XF	Unc	BU
ND(1962?)	—	—	—	BV	75.00	—

X# MB144 10 BOLIVARES
0.9000 Gold, 19 mm. **Series:** 16th Century Chiefs **Obv:** Crossed arrows **Obv. Legend:** CACIQUES DE VENEZUELA **Rev:** Head left **Rev. Legend:** CACIQUES DE VENEZUELA - SOROCAIMA **Edge:** Reeded

Date	Mintage	F	VF	XF	Unc	BU
ND(1962?)	—	—	—	BV	75.00	—

X# MB145 10 BOLIVARES
0.9000 Gold, 19 mm. **Series:** 16th Century Chiefs **Obv:** Crossed arrows **Obv. Legend:** CACIQUES DE VENEZUELA **Rev:** Head left **Rev. Legend:** CACIQUES DE VENEZUELA - SOROCAIMA **Edge:** Reeded

Date	Mintage	F	VF	XF	Unc	BU
ND(1962?)	—	—	—	BV	75.00	—

X# MB146 10 BOLIVARES
0.9000 Gold, 19 mm. **Series:** 16th Century Chiefs **Obv:** Crossed arrows **Obv. Legend:** CACIQUES DE VENEZUELA **Rev:** Head facing **Rev. Legend:** CACIQUES DE VENEZUELA - TAMANACO **Edge:** Reeded

Date	Mintage	F	VF	XF	Unc	BU
ND(1962?)	—	—	—	BV	75.00	—

X# MB147 10 BOLIVARES
0.9000 Gold, 19 mm. **Series:** 16th Century Chiefs **Obv:** Crossed arrows **Obv. Legend:** CACIQUES DE VENEZUELA **Rev:** Head right **Rev. Legend:** CACIQUES DE VENEZUELA - GUIACAMACUTO **Edge:** Reeded

Date	Mintage	F	VF	XF	Unc	BU
ND(1962?)	—	—	—	BV	75.00	—

X# MB148 10 BOLIVARES
0.9000 Gold, 19 mm. **Series:** 16th Century Chiefs **Obv:** Crossed arrows **Obv. Legend:** CACIQUES DE VENEZUELA **Rev:** Head facing slightly left **Rev. Legend:** CACIQUES DE VENEZUELA - ARICHUNA **Edge:** Reeded

Date	Mintage	F	VF	XF	Unc	BU
ND(1962?)	—	—	—	BV	75.00	—

X# MB149 10 BOLIVARES
0.9000 Gold, 19 mm. **Series:** 16th Century Chiefs **Obv:** Crossed arrows **Obv. Legend:** CACIQUES DE VENEZUELA **Rev:** Head 3/4 left **Rev. Legend:** CACIQUES DE VENEZUELA - MURACHI **Edge:** Reeded

Date	Mintage	F	VF	XF	Unc	BU
ND(1962?)	—	—	—	BV	75.00	—

X# MB150 10 BOLIVARES
0.9000 Gold, 19 mm. **Series:** 16th Century Chiefs **Obv:** Crossed arrows **Obv. Legend:** CACIQUES DE VENEZUELA **Rev:** Head left **Rev. Legend:** CACIQUES DE VENEZUELA - TEREPAIMA **Edge:** Reeded

Date	Mintage	F	VF	XF	Unc	BU
ND(1962?)	—	—	—	BV	75.00	—

X# MB151 10 BOLIVARES
0.9000 Gold, 19 mm. **Series:** 16th Century Chiefs **Obv:** Crossed arrows **Obv. Legend:** CACIQUES DE VENEZUELA **Rev:** Head slightly left **Rev. Legend:** CACIQUES DE VENEZUELA - PARAMACONI **Edge:** Reeded

Date	Mintage	F	VF	XF	Unc	BU
ND(1962?)	—	—	—	BV	75.00	—

X# MB152 10 BOLIVARES
0.9000 Gold, 19 mm. **Series:** 16th Century Chiefs **Obv:** Crossed arrows **Obv. Legend:** CACIQUES DE VENEZUELA **Rev:** Head facing **Rev. Legend:** CACIQUES DE VENEZUELA - MANAURE **Edge:** Reeded

Date	Mintage	F	VF	XF	Unc	BU
ND(1962?)	—	—	—	BV	75.00	—

X# MB153 10 BOLIVARES
0.9000 Gold, 19 mm. **Series:** 16th Century Chiefs **Obv:** Crossed arrows **Obv. Legend:** CACIQUES DE VENEZUELA **Rev:** Two heads jugate almost right **Rev. Legend:** CACIQUES DE VENEZUELA - CHICURAMAY **Edge:** Reeded

Date	Mintage	F	VF	XF	Unc	BU
ND(1962?)	—	—	—	BV	75.00	—

X# MB154 10 BOLIVARES
0.9000 Gold, 19 mm. **Series:** 16th Century Chiefs **Obv:** Crossed arrows **Obv. Legend:** CACIQUES DE VENEZUELA **Rev:** Head 3/4 right **Rev. Legend:** CACIQUES DE VENEZUELA - YORACUY **Edge:** Reeded

Date	Mintage	F	VF	XF	Unc	BU
ND(1962?)	—	—	—	BV	75.00	—

X# MB155 10 BOLIVARES
0.9000 Gold, 19 mm. **Series:** 16th Century Chiefs **Obv:** Crossed arrows **Obv. Legend:** CACIQUES DE VENEZUELA **Rev:** Head facing **Rev. Legend:** CACIQUES DE VENEZUELA - URIMARE **Edge:** Reeded

Date	Mintage	F	VF	XF	Unc	BU
ND(1962?)	—	—	—	BV	75.00	—

X# MB156 10 BOLIVARES
0.9000 Gold, 19 mm. **Series:** 16th Century Chiefs **Obv:** Crossed arrows **Obv. Legend:** CACIQUES DE VENEZUELA **Rev:** Two heads jugate left **Rev. Legend:** CACIQUES DE VENEZUELA - YORACO **Edge:** Reeded

Date	Mintage	F	VF	XF	Unc	BU
ND(1962?)	—	—	—	BV	75.00	—

X# MB85 20 BOLIVARES

6.6667 g., 0.9000 Gold 0.1929 oz. AGW, 21.2 mm. **Series:** 16th Century Indian Chiefs **Obv:** Hand holding bunch of arrows **Obv. Legend:** CACIQUES DE VENEZUELA **Rev:** Head facing slightly left **Rev. Legend:** CACIQUES DE VENEZUELA - GUAICAIPURO **Edge:** Reeded **Note:** Weight varies: 5.95-6.00 grams.

Date	Mintage	F	VF	XF	Unc	BU
1957	—	—	—	BV	145	—

X# MB86 20 BOLIVARES

6.6667 g., 0.9000 Gold 0.1929 oz. AGW, 21.2 mm. **Series:** 16th Century Indian Chiefs **Obv:** Hand holding bunch of arrows **Obv. Legend:** CACIQUES DE VENEZUELA **Rev:** Head facing **Rev. Legend:** CACIQUES DE VENEZUELA - TIUNA **Edge:** Reeded **Note:** Weight varies: 5.95-6.00 grams.

Date	Mintage	F	VF	XF	Unc	BU
1957	—	—	—	BV	145	—

X# MB87 20 BOLIVARES

6.6667 g., 0.9000 Gold 0.1929 oz. AGW, 21.2 mm. **Series:** 16th Century Indian Chiefs **Obv:** Hand holding bunch of arrows **Obv. Legend:** CACIQUES DE VENEZUELA **Rev:** Head facing almost right **Rev. Legend:** CACIQUES DE VENEZUELA - CHACAO **Edge:** Reeded **Note:** Weight varies: 5.95-6.00 grams.

Date	Mintage	F	VF	XF	Unc	BU
1957	—	—	—	BV	145	—

X# MB88 20 BOLIVARES

6.6667 g., 0.9000 Gold 0.1929 oz. AGW, 21.2 mm. **Series:** 16th Century Indian Chiefs **Obv:** Hand holding bunch of arrows **Obv. Legend:** CACIQUES DE VENEZUELA **Rev:** Head facing 3/4 right **Rev. Legend:** CACIQUES DE VENEZUELA - MARA **Edge:** Reeded **Note:** Weight varies: 5.95-6.00 grams.

Date	Mintage	F	VF	XF	Unc	BU
1957	—	—	—	BV	145	—

X# MB89 20 BOLIVARES

6.6667 g., 0.9000 Gold 0.1929 oz. AGW, 21.2 mm. **Series:** 16th Century Indian Chiefs **Obv:** Hand holding bunch of arrows **Obv. Legend:** CACIQUES DE VENEZUELA **Rev:** Head facing slightly right **Rev. Legend:** CACIQUES DE VENEZUELA - NAIGUATÁ **Edge:** Reeded **Note:** Weight varies: 5.95-6.00 grams.

Date	Mintage	F	VF	XF	Unc	BU
1957	—	—	—	BV	145	—

X# MB90 20 BOLIVARES

6.6667 g., 0.9000 Gold 0.1929 oz. AGW, 21.2 mm. **Series:** 16th Century Indian Chiefs **Obv:** Hand holding bunch of arrows **Obv. Legend:** CACIQUES DE VENEZUELA **Rev:** Head left **Rev. Legend:** CACIQUES DE VENEZUELA - SOROCAIMA **Edge:** Reeded **Note:** Weight varies: 5.95-6.00 grams.

Date	Mintage	F	VF	XF	Unc	BU
1957	—	—	—	BV	145	—

X# MB91 20 BOLIVARES

6.6667 g., 0.9000 Gold 0.1929 oz. AGW, 21.2 mm. **Series:** 16th Century Indian Chiefs **Obv:** Hand holding bunch of arrows **Obv. Legend:** CACIQUES DE VENEZUELA **Rev:** Head facing slightly right **Rev. Legend:** CACIQUES DE VENEZUELA - PARAMACAY **Edge:** Reeded **Note:** Weight varies: 5.95-6.00 grams.

Date	Mintage	F	VF	XF	Unc	BU
1957	—	—	—	BV	145	—

X# MB92 20 BOLIVARES

6.6667 g., 0.9000 Gold 0.1929 oz. AGW, 21.2 mm. **Series:** 16th Century Indian Chiefs **Obv:** Hand holding bunch of arrows **Obv. Legend:** CACIQUES DE VENEZUELA **Rev:** Head facing **Rev. Legend:** CACIQUES DE VENEZUELA - TAMANACO **Edge:** Reeded **Note:** Weight varies: 5.95-6.00 grams.

Date	Mintage	F	VF	XF	Unc	BU
1957	—	—	—	BV	145	—

X# MB93 20 BOLIVARES

6.6667 g., 0.9000 Gold 0.1929 oz. AGW, 21.2 mm. **Series:** 16th Century Indian Chiefs **Obv:** Hand holding bunch of arrows **Obv. Legend:** CACIQUES DE VENEZUELA **Rev:** Head right **Rev. Legend:** CACIQUES DE VENEZUELA - GUAICAMACUTO **Edge:** Reeded **Note:** Weight varies: 5.95-6.00 grams.

Date	Mintage	F	VF	XF	Unc	BU
1957	—	—	—	BV	145	—

X# MB94 20 BOLIVARES

6.6667 g., 0.9000 Gold 0.1929 oz. AGW, 21.2 mm. **Series:** 16th Century Indian Chiefs **Obv:** Hand holding bunch of arrows **Obv. Legend:** CACIQUES DE VENEZUELA **Rev:** Head facing slightly left **Rev. Legend:** CACIQUES DE VENEZUELA - ARICHUNA **Edge:** Reeded **Note:** Weight varies: 5.95-6.00 grams.

Date	Mintage	F	VF	XF	Unc	BU
1957	—	—	—	BV	145	—

X# MB95 20 BOLIVARES

6.6667 g., 0.9000 Gold 0.1929 oz. AGW, 21.2 mm. **Series:** 16th Century Indian Chiefs **Obv:** Hand holding bunch of arrows **Obv. Legend:** CACIQUES DE VENEZUELA **Rev:** Head 3/4 left **Rev. Legend:** CACIQUES DE VENEZUELA - MURACHI **Edge:** Reeded **Note:** Weight varies: 5.95-6.00 grams.

Date	Mintage	F	VF	XF	Unc	BU
1957	—	—	—	BV	145	—

X# MB96 20 BOLIVARES

6.6667 g., 0.9000 Gold 0.1929 oz. AGW **Series:** 16th Century Indian Chiefs **Obv:** Hand holding bunch of arrows **Obv. Legend:** CACIQUES DE VENEZUELA **Rev:** Head left **Rev. Legend:** CACIQUES DE VENEZUELA - TEREPAIMA **Edge:** Reeded **Note:** Weight varies: 5.95-6.00 grams.

Date	Mintage	F	VF	XF	Unc	BU
1957	—	—	—	BV	145	—

X# MB97 20 BOLIVARES

6.6667 g., 0.9000 Gold 0.1929 oz. AGW, 21.2 mm. **Series:** 16th Century Indian Chiefs **Obv:** Hand holding bunch of arrows **Obv. Legend:** CACIQUES DE VENEZUELA **Rev:** Head slightly left **Rev. Legend:** CACIQUES DE VENEZUELA - RARAMACONI **Edge:** Reeded **Note:** Weight varies: 5.95-6.00 grams.

Date	Mintage	F	VF	XF	Unc	BU
1957	—	—	—	BV	145	—

X# MB98 20 BOLIVARES

6.6667 g., 0.9000 Gold 0.1929 oz. AGW **Series:** 16th Century Indian Chiefs **Obv:** Hand holding bunch of arrows **Obv. Legend:** CACIQUES DE VENEZUELA **Rev:** Head facing **Rev. Legend:** CACIQUES DE VENEZUELA - MANAURE **Edge:** Reeded **Note:** Weight varies: 5.95-6.00 grams.

Date	Mintage	F	VF	XF	Unc	BU
1957	—	—	—	BV	145	—

X# MB99 20 BOLIVARES

6.6667 g., 0.9000 Gold 0.1929 oz. AGW **Series:** 16th Century Indian Chiefs **Obv:** Hand holding bunch of arrows **Obv. Legend:** CACIQUES DE VENEZUELA **Rev:** Two heads jugate almost right **Rev. Legend:** CACIQUES DE VENEZUELA - CHICURAMAY **Edge:** Reeded **Note:** Weight varies: 5.95-6.00 grams.

Date	Mintage	F	VF	XF	Unc	BU
1957	—	—	—	BV	145	—

X# MB100 20 BOLIVARES

6.6667 g., 0.9000 Gold 0.1929 oz. AGW, 21.2 mm. **Series:** 16th Century Indian Chiefs **Obv:** Hand holding bunch of arrows **Obv. Legend:** CACIQUES DE VENEZUELA **Rev:** Head 3/4 right **Rev. Legend:** CACIQUES DE VENEZUELA - YORACUY **Edge:** Reeded **Note:** Weight varies: 5.95-6.00 grams.

Date	Mintage	F	VF	XF	Unc	BU
1957	—	—	—	BV	145	—

X# MB101 20 BOLIVARES

6.6667 g., 0.9000 Gold 0.1929 oz. AGW, 21.2 mm. **Series:** 16th Century Indian Chiefs **Obv:** Hand holding bunch of arrows **Obv. Legend:** CACIQUES DE VENEZUELA **Rev:** Head facing **Rev. Legend:** CACIQUES DE VENEZUELA - URIMARE **Edge:** Reeded **Note:** Weight varies: 5.95-6.00 grams.

Date	Mintage	F	VF	XF	Unc	BU
1957	—	—	—	BV	145	—

X# MB102 20 BOLIVARES

6.6667 g., 0.9000 Gold 0.1929 oz. AGW, 21.2 mm. **Series:** 16th Century Indian Chiefs **Obv:** Hand holding bunch of arrows **Obv. Legend:** CACIQUES DE VENEZUELA **Rev:** Two heads jugate left **Rev. Legend:** CACIQUES DE VENEZUELA - YORACO **Edge:** Reeded **Note:** Weight varies: 5.95-6.00 grams.

Date	Mintage	F	VF	XF	Unc	BU
1957	—	—	—	BV	145	—

X# MB67 60 BOLIVARES

22.2000 g., 0.9000 Gold 0.6423 oz. AGW, 30.1 mm. **Series:** 16th Century Indian Chiefs **Obv:** Hand holding bunch of arrows **Obv. Legend:** CACIQUES DE VENEZUELA **Rev:** Head facing slightly left **Rev. Legend:** CACIQUES DE VENEZUELA - GUAICAIPURO **Edge:** Reeded

Date	Mintage	F	VF	XF	Unc	BU
1955	—	—	—	BV	475	—

X# MB68 60 BOLIVARES

22.2000 g., 0.9000 Gold 0.6423 oz. AGW, 30.1 mm. **Series:** 16th Century Indian Chiefs **Subject:** Hand holding bunch of arrows **Obv. Legend:** CACIQUES DE VENEZUELA **Rev:** Head facing **Rev. Legend:** CACIQUES DE VENEZUELA - TIUNA **Edge:** Reeded

Date	Mintage	F	VF	XF	Unc	BU
1955	—	—	—	BV	475	—

X# MB69 60 BOLIVARES

22.2000 g., 0.9000 Gold 0.6423 oz. AGW, 30.1 mm. **Series:** 16th Century Indian chiefs **Obv:** Hand holding bunch of arrows **Obv. Legend:** CACIQUES DE VENEZUELA **Rev:** Head facing almost right **Rev. Legend:** CACIQUES DE VENEZUELA - CHACAO **Edge:** Reeded

Date	Mintage	F	VF	XF	Unc	BU
1955	—	—	—	BV	475	—

X# MB70 60 BOLIVARES

22.2000 g., 0.9000 Gold 0.6423 oz. AGW, 30.1 mm. **Series:** 16th Century Indian Chiefs **Obv:** Hand holding bunch of arrows **Obv. Legend:** CACIQUES DE VENEZUELA **Rev:** Head facing 3/4 right **Rev. Legend:** CACIQUES DE VENEZUELA - MARA **Edge:** Reeded

Date	Mintage	F	VF	XF	Unc	BU
1955	—	—	—	BV	475	—

X# MB71 60 BOLIVARES

22.2000 g., 0.9000 Gold 0.6423 oz. AGW, 30.1 mm. **Series:** 16th Century Indian Chiefs **Obv:** Hand holding bunch of arrows **Obv. Legend:** CACIQUES DE VENEZUELA **Rev:** Head facing slightly right **Rev. Legend:** CACIQUES DE VENEZUELA - NAIGUATÁ **Edge:** Reeded

Date	Mintage	F	VF	XF	Unc	BU
1955	—	—	—	BV	475	—

X# MB72 60 BOLIVARES

22.2000 g., 0.9000 Gold 0.6423 oz. AGW, 30.1 mm. **Series:** 16th Century Indian Chiefs **Obv:** Hand holding bunch of arrows **Obv. Legend:** CACIQUES DE VENEZUELA **Rev:** Head left **Rev. Legend:** CACIQUES DE VENEZUELA - SOROCAIMA **Edge:** Reeded

Date	Mintage	F	VF	XF	Unc	BU
1955	—	—	—	BV	475	—

X# MB73 60 BOLIVARES
22.2000 g., 0.9000 Gold 0.6423 oz. AGW, 30.1 mm.
Series: 16th Century Indian Chiefs **Obv:** Hand holding bunch of arrows **Obv. Legend:** CACIQUES DE VENEZUELA **Rev:** Head facing slightly right **Rev. Legend:** CACIQUES DE VENEZUELA - PARAMACAY **Edge:** Reeded

Date	Mintage	F	VF	XF	Unc	BU
1955	—	—	—	BV	475	—

X# MB74 60 BOLIVARES
22.2000 g., 0.9000 Gold 0.6423 oz. AGW, 30.1 mm.
Series: 16th Century Indian Chiefs **Obv:** Hand holding bunch of arrows **Obv. Legend:** CACIQUES DE VENEZUELA **Rev:** Head facing **Rev. Legend:** CACIQUES DE VENEZUELA - TAMANACO **Edge:** Reeded

Date	Mintage	F	VF	XF	Unc	BU
1955	—	—	—	BV	475	—

X# MB75 60 BOLIVARES
22.2000 g., 0.9000 Gold 0.6423 oz. AGW, 30.1 mm.
Series: 16th Century Indian Chiefs **Obv:** Hand holding bunch of arrows **Obv. Legend:** CACIQUES DE VENEZUELA **Rev:** Head right **Rev. Legend:** CACIQUES DE VENEZUELA - GUAICAMACUTO **Edge:** Reeded

Date	Mintage	F	VF	XF	Unc	BU
1955	—	—	—	BV	475	—

X# MB76 60 BOLIVARES
22.2000 g., 0.9000 Gold 0.6423 oz. AGW, 30.1 mm.
Series: 16th Century Indian Chiefs **Obv:** Hand holding bunch of arrows **Obv. Legend:** CACIQUES DE VENEZUELA **Rev:** Head facing slightly left **Rev. Legend:** CACIQUES DE VENEZUELA - ARICHUNA **Edge:** Reeded

Date	Mintage	F	VF	XF	Unc	BU
1955	—	—	—	BV	475	—

X# MB77 60 BOLIVARES
22.2000 g., 0.9000 Gold 0.6423 oz. AGW, 30.1 mm.
Series: 16th Century Indian Chiefs **Obv:** Hand holding bunch of arrows **Obv. Legend:** CACIQUES DE VENEZUELA **Rev:** Head 3/4 left **Rev. Legend:** CACIQUES DE VENEZUELA - MURACHI **Edge:** Reeded

Date	Mintage	F	VF	XF	Unc	BU
1955	—	—	—	BV	475	—

X# MB78 60 BOLIVARES
22.2000 g., 0.9000 Gold 0.6423 oz. AGW, 30.1 mm.
Series: 16th Century Indian Chiefs **Obv:** Hand holding bunch of arrows **Obv. Legend:** CACIQUES DE VENEZUELA **Rev:** Head left **Rev. Legend:** CACIQUES DE VENEZUELA - TEREPAIMA **Edge:** Reeded

Date	Mintage	F	VF	XF	Unc	BU
1955	—	—	—	BV	475	—

X# MB79 60 BOLIVARES
22.2000 g., 0.9000 Gold 0.6423 oz. AGW, 30.1 mm.
Series: 16th Century Indian Chiefs **Obv:** Hand holding bunch of arrows **Obv. Legend:** CACIQUES DE VENEZUELA **Rev:** Head slightly left **Rev. Legend:** CACIQUES DE VENEZUELA - PARAMACONI **Edge:** Reeded

Date	Mintage	F	VF	XF	Unc	BU
1955	—	—	—	BV	475	—

X# MB80 60 BOLIVARES
22.2000 g., 0.9000 Gold 0.6423 oz. AGW, 30.1 mm.
Series: 16th Century Indian Chiefs **Obv:** Hand holding bunch of arrows **Obv. Legend:** CACIQUES DE VENEZUELA **Rev:** Head facing **Rev. Legend:** CACIQUES DE VENEZUELA - MANAURE **Edge:** Reeded

Date	Mintage	F	VF	XF	Unc	BU
1955	—	—	—	BV	475	—

X# MB81 60 BOLIVARES
22.2000 g., 0.9000 Gold 0.6423 oz. AGW, 30.1 mm.
Series: 16th Century Indian Chiefs **Obv:** Hand holding bunch of arrows **Obv. Legend:** CACIQUES DE VENEZUELA **Rev:** Two heads jugate almost right **Rev. Legend:** CACIQUES DE VENEZUELA - CHICURAMAY **Edge:** Reeded

Date	Mintage	F	VF	XF	Unc	BU
1955	—	—	—	BV	475	—

X# MB82 60 BOLIVARES
22.2000 g., 0.9000 Gold 0.6423 oz. AGW, 30.1 mm.
Series: 16th Century Indian Chiefs **Obv:** Hand holding bunch of arrows **Obv. Legend:** CACIQUES DE VENEZUELA **Rev:** Head 3/4 right **Rev. Legend:** CACIQUES DE VENEZUELA - YARACUY **Edge:** Reeded

Date	Mintage	F	VF	XF	Unc	BU
1955	—	—	—	BV	475	—

X# MB83 60 BOLIVARES
22.2000 g., 0.9000 Gold 0.6423 oz. AGW, 30.1 mm.
Series: 16th Century Indian Chiefs **Obv:** Hand holding bunch of arrows **Obv. Legend:** CACIQUES DE VENEZUELA **Rev:** Head facing **Rev. Legend:** CACIQUES DE VENEZUELA - URIMARE **Edge:** Reeded

Date	Mintage	F	VF	XF	Unc	BU
1955	—	—	—	BV	475	—

X# MB84 60 BOLIVARES
22.2000 g., 0.9000 Gold 0.6423 oz. AGW, 30.1 mm.
Series: 16th Century Indian Chiefs **Obv:** Hand holding bunch of arrows **Obv. Legend:** CACIQUES DE VENEZUELA **Rev:** Two heads jugate left **Rev. Legend:** CACIQUES DE VENEZUELA - YORACO **Edge:** Reeded

Date	Mintage	F	VF	XF	Unc	BU
1955	—	—	—	BV	475	—

X# MB103 60 BOLIVARES
20.0000 g., 0.9000 Gold 0.5787 oz. AGW, 37.10 mm.
Series: 16th Century Chiefs, 1955-1960 **Obv:** Condor **Obv. Legend:** CACIQUES DE VENEZUELA **Rev:** Head facing slightly left **Rev. Legend:** CACIQUES DE VENEZUELA - GUAICAIPURO **Edge:** Reeded

Date	Mintage	F	VF	XF	Unc	BU
ND(1961)	—	—	—	BV	425	—

X# MB104 60 BOLIVARES
20.0000 g., 0.9000 Gold 0.5787 oz. AGW, 37.10 mm.
Series: 16th Century Chiefs, 1955-1960 **Obv:** Condor **Obv. Legend:** CACIQUES DE VENEZUELA **Rev:** Head facing **Rev. Legend:** CACIQUES DE VENEZUELA - TIUNA **Edge:** Reeded

Date	Mintage	F	VF	XF	Unc	BU
ND(1961)	—	—	—	BV	425	—

X# MB105 60 BOLIVARES
20.0000 g., 0.9000 Gold 0.5787 oz. AGW, 37.10 mm.
Series: 16th Century Chiefs, 1955-1960 **Obv:** Condor **Obv. Legend:** CACIQUES DE VENEZUELA **Rev:** Head facing almost righ **Rev. Legend:** CACIQUES DE VENEZUELA - CHACAO **Edge:** Reeded

Date	Mintage	F	VF	XF	Unc	BU
ND(1961)	—	—	—	BV	425	—

X# MB106 60 BOLIVARES
20.0000 g., 0.9000 Gold 0.5787 oz. AGW, 37.10 mm.
Series: 16th Century Chiefs, 1955-1960 **Obv:** Condor **Obv. Legend:** CACIQUES DE VENEZUELA **Rev:** Head facing 3/4 right **Rev. Legend:** CACIQUES DE VENEZUELA - MARA **Edge:** Reeded

Date	Mintage	F	VF	XF	Unc	BU
ND(1961)	—	—	—	BV	425	—

X# MB107 60 BOLIVARES
20.0000 g., 0.9000 Gold 0.5787 oz. AGW, 37.10 mm.
Series: 16th Century Chiefs, 1955-1960 **Obv:** Condor **Obv. Legend:** CACIQUES DE VENEZUELA **Rev:** Head facing slightly right **Rev. Legend:** CACIQUES DE VENEZUELA - NAIGUATÁ **Edge:** Reeded

Date	Mintage	F	VF	XF	Unc	BU
ND(1961)	—	—	—	BV	425	—

X# MB109 60 BOLIVARES
20.0000 g., 0.9000 Gold 0.5787 oz. AGW, 37.10 mm.
Series: 16th Century Chiefs, 1955-1960 **Obv:** Condor **Obv. Legend:** CACIQUES DE VENEZUELA **Rev:** Head left **Rev. Legend:** CACIQUES DE VENEZUELA - SOROCAIMA **Edge:** Reeded

Date	Mintage	F	VF	XF	Unc	BU
ND(1961)	—	—	—	BV	425	—

X# MB110 60 BOLIVARES
20.0000 g., 0.9000 Gold 0.5787 oz. AGW, 37.10 mm.
Series: 16th Century Chiefs, 1955-1960 **Obv:** Condor **Obv. Legend:** CACIQUES DE VENEZUELA **Rev:** Head facing slightly right **Rev. Legend:** CACIQUES DE VENEZUELA - PARAMACAY **Edge:** Reeded

Date	Mintage	F	VF	XF	Unc	BU
ND(1961)	—	—	—	BV	425	—

X# MB111 60 BOLIVARES
20.0000 g., 0.9000 Gold 0.5787 oz. AGW, 37.10 mm.
Series: 16th Century Chiefs, 1955-1960 **Obv:** Condor **Obv. Legend:** CACIQUES DE VENEZUELA **Rev:** Head facing **Rev. Legend:** CACIQUES DE VENEZUELA - TAMANACO **Edge:** Reeded

Date	Mintage	F	VF	XF	Unc	BU
ND(1961)	—	—	—	BV	425	—

X# MB112 60 BOLIVARES
20.0000 g., 0.9000 Gold 0.5787 oz. AGW, 37.10 mm.
Series: 16th Century Chiefs, 1955-1960 **Obv:** Condor **Obv. Legend:** CACIQUES DE VENEZUELA **Rev:** Head right **Rev. Legend:** CACIQUES DE VENEZUELA - GUAICAMACUTO **Edge:** Reeded

Date	Mintage	F	VF	XF	Unc	BU
ND(1961)	—	—	—	BV	425	—

X# MB113 60 BOLIVARES
20.0000 g., 0.9000 Gold 0.5787 oz. AGW, 37.10 mm.
Series: 16th Century Chiefs, 1955-1960 **Obv:** Condor **Obv. Legend:** CACIQUES DE VENEZUELA **Rev:** Head facing slightly left **Rev. Legend:** CACIQUES DE VENEZUELA - ARICHUNA **Edge:** Reeded **Note:** Prev. XMB74.

Date	Mintage	F	VF	XF	Unc	BU
ND(1961)	—	—	—	BV	425	—

X# MB114 60 BOLIVARES
20.0000 g., 0.9000 Gold 0.5787 oz. AGW, 37.10 mm.
Series: 16th Century Chiefs, 1955-1960 **Obv:** Condor **Obv. Legend:** CACIQUES DE VENEZUELA **Rev:** Head 3/4 left **Rev. Legend:** CACIQUES DE VENEZUELA - MURACHI **Edge:** Reeded

Date	Mintage	F	VF	XF	Unc	BU
ND(1961)	—	—	—	BV	425	—

 # MB115 60 BOLIVARES

.0000 g., 0.9000 Gold 0.5787 oz. AGW, 37.10 mm. ries: 16th Century Chiefs, 1955-1960 **Obv:** Condor v. **Legend:** CACIQUES DE VENEZUELA v: Head left **Rev. Legend:** CACIQUES DE :NEZUELA - TEREPAIMA **Edge:** Reeded

e	Mintage	F	VF	XF	Unc	BU
(1961)	—	—	—	BV	425	—

 # MB116 60 BOLIVARES

.0000 g., 0.9000 Gold 0.5787 oz. AGW, 37.10 mm. ries: 16th Century Chiefs, 1955-1960 **Obv:** Condor bv. **Legend:** CACIQUES DE VENEZUELA v: Head slightly left **Rev. Legend:** CACIQUES DE :NEZUELA - PARAMACONI **Edge:** Reeded

e	Mintage	F	VF	XF	Unc	BU
(1961)	—	—	—	BV	425	—

 # MB117 60 BOLIVARES

.0000 g., 0.9000 Gold 0.5787 oz. AGW, 37.10 mm. ries: 16th Century Chiefs, 1955-1960 **Obv:** Condor bv. **Legend:** CACIQUES DE VENEZUELA ev: Head facing **Rev. Legend:** CACIQUES DE :NEZUELA - MANAURE **Edge:** Reeded

e	Mintage	F	VF	XF	Unc	BU
(1961)	—	—	—	BV	425	—

 # MB118 60 BOLIVARES

).0000 g., 0.9000 Gold 0.5787 oz. AGW, 37.10 mm. eries: 16th Century Chiefs, 1955-1960 **Obv:** Condor bv. **Legend:** CACIQUES DE VENEZUELA **Rev:** Two eads jugate almost right **Rev. Legend:** CACIQUES E VENEZUELA - CHICURAMAY **Edge:** Reeded

te	Mintage	F	VF	XF	Unc	BU
)(1961)	—	—	—	BV	425	—

:# MB119 60 BOLIVARES

0.0000 g., 0.9000 Gold 0.5787 oz. AGW, 37.10 mm. eries: 16th Century Chiefs, 1955-1960 **Obv:** Condor bv. **Legend:** CACIQUES DE VENEZUELA ev: Head 3/4 right **Rev. Legend:** CACIQUES DE ENEZUELA - YARACUY **Edge:** Reeded

ate	Mintage	F	VF	XF	Unc	BU
D(1961)	—	—	—	BV	425	—

:# MB120 60 BOLIVARES

0.0000 g., 0.9000 Gold 0.5787 oz. AGW, 37.10 mm. eries: 16th Century Chiefs, 1955-1960 **Obv:** Condor)bv. **Legend:** CACIQUES DE VENEZUELA **Rev:** Two eads jugate left **Rev. Legend:** CACIQUES DE 'ENEZUELA - YORACO **Edge:** Reeded

ate	Mintage	F	VF	XF	Unc	BU
D(1961)	—	—	—	BV	425	—

REPUBLIC OF VENEZUELA

MEDALLIC COINAGE

Banco Italo - Venezolana - Personalities of World War II Series

Struck by the Karlsruhe Mint, Baden, Germany

X# MB1 20 BOLIVARES

6.0000 g., 0.9000 Gold 0.1736 oz. AGW **Rev:** Bust of Mackenzie King of Canada

Date	Mintage	F	VF	XF	Unc	BU
1957	—	—	—	120	135	150

X# MB2 20 BOLIVARES

6.0000 g., 0.9000 Gold 0.1736 oz. AGW **Rev:** Bust of Chiang Kai-shek of China

Date	Mintage	F	VF	XF	Unc	BU
1957	—	—	—	120	135	150

X# MB3 20 BOLIVARES

6.0000 g., 0.9000 Gold 0.1736 oz. AGW **Rev:** Bust of Mannerheim of Finland

Date	Mintage	F	VF	XF	Unc	BU
1957	—	—	—	120	135	150

X# MB4 20 BOLIVARES

6.0000 g., 0.9000 Gold 0.1736 oz. AGW **Rev:** Bust of Charles de Gaulle of France

Date	Mintage	F	VF	XF	Unc	BU
1957	—	—	—	120	135	150

X# MB5 20 BOLIVARES

6.0000 g., 0.9000 Gold 0.1736 oz. AGW **Rev:** Bust of Marshal Petain of France

Date	Mintage	F	VF	XF	Unc	BU
1957	—	—	—	120	135	150

X# MB6 20 BOLIVARES

6.0000 g., 0.9000 Gold 0.1736 oz. AGW **Rev:** Bust of Adolf Hitler of Germany

Date	Mintage	F	VF	XF	Unc	BU
1957	—	—	—	120	135	150

X# MB7 20 BOLIVARES

6.0000 g., 0.9000 Gold 0.1736 oz. AGW **Rev:** Bust of Erwin Rommel of Germany

Date	Mintage	F	VF	XF	Unc	BU
1957	—	—	—	120	135	150

X# MB8 20 BOLIVARES

6.0000 g., 0.9000 Gold 0.1736 oz. AGW **Rev:** Bust of Winston Churchill of Great Britain

Date	Mintage	F	VF	XF	Unc	BU
1957	—	—	—	120	135	150

X# MB9 20 BOLIVARES

6.0000 g., 0.9000 Gold 0.1736 oz. AGW **Rev:** Bust of Bernard Montgomery of Great Britain

Date	Mintage	F	VF	XF	Unc	BU
1957	—	—	—	120	135	150

X# MB10 20 BOLIVARES

6.0000 g., 0.9000 Gold 0.1736 oz. AGW **Rev:** Bust of Benito Mussolini of Italy

Date	Mintage	F	VF	XF	Unc	BU
1957	—	—	—	120	135	150

X# MB11 20 BOLIVARES

6.0000 g., 0.9000 Gold 0.1736 oz. AGW **Rev:** Bust of Vittorio Emanuel III of Italy

Date	Mintage	F	VF	XF	Unc	BU
1957	—	—	—	120	135	150

X# MB12 20 BOLIVARES

6.0000 g., 0.9000 Gold 0.1736 oz. AGW **Rev:** Bust of Tojo of Japan

Date	Mintage	F	VF	XF	Unc	BU
1957	—	—	—	120	135	150

X# MB13 20 BOLIVARES

6.0000 g., 0.9000 Gold 0.1736 oz. AGW **Rev:** Bust of Dwight D. Eisenhower of U.S.A.

Date	Mintage	F	VF	XF	Unc	BU
1957	—	—	—	120	135	150

X# MB14 20 BOLIVARES

6.0000 g., 0.9000 Gold 0.1736 oz. AGW **Rev:** Bust of Douglas MacArthur of U.S.A.

Date	Mintage	F	VF	XF	Unc	BU
1957	—	—	—	120	135	150

X# MB16 20 BOLIVARES

6.0000 g., 0.9000 Gold 0.1736 oz. AGW **Rev:** Bust of Harry S. Truman of U.S.A.

Date	Mintage	F	VF	XF	Unc	BU
1957	—	—	—	120	135	150

X# MB17 20 BOLIVARES

6.0000 g., 0.9000 Gold 0.1736 oz. AGW **Rev:** Bust of Joseph Stalin of U.S.S.R.

Date	Mintage	F	VF	XF	Unc	BU
1957	—	—	—	120	135	150

X# MB18 20 BOLIVARES

6.0000 g., 0.9000 Gold 0.1736 oz. AGW **Rev:** Bust of Marshall Tito of Yugoslavia

Date	Mintage	F	VF	XF	Unc	BU
1957	—	—	—	120	135	150

X# MB19 60 BOLIVARES

22.2000 g., 0.9000 Gold 0.6423 oz. AGW **Rev:** Bust of Mackenzie King of Canada

Date	Mintage	F	VF	XF	Unc	BU
1957	—	—	—	435	450	475

X# MB20 60 BOLIVARES

22.2000 g., 0.9000 Gold 0.6423 oz. AGW **Rev:** Bust of Chiang Kai-shek of China

Date	Mintage	F	VF	XF	Unc	BU
1957	—	—	—	435	450	475

X# MB21 60 BOLIVARES

22.2000 g., 0.9000 Gold 0.6423 oz. AGW **Rev:** Bust of Mannerheim of Finland

Date	Mintage	F	VF	XF	Unc	BU
1957	—	—	—	435	450	475

X# MB22 60 BOLIVARES

22.2000 g., 0.9000 Gold 0.6423 oz. AGW **Rev:** Bust of Charles de Gaulle of France

Date	Mintage	F	VF	XF	Unc	BU
1957	—	—	—	435	450	475

X# MB23 60 BOLIVARES

22.2000 g., 0.9000 Gold 0.6423 oz. AGW **Rev:** Bust of Marshal Petain of France

Date	Mintage	F	VF	XF	Unc	BU
1957	—	—	—	435	450	475

X# MB24 60 BOLIVARES

22.2000 g., 0.9000 Gold 0.6423 oz. AGW **Rev:** Bust of Adolf Hitler of Germany

Date	Mintage	F	VF	XF	Unc	BU
1957	—	—	—	435	450	475

X# MB25 60 BOLIVARES

22.2000 g., 0.9000 Gold 0.6423 oz. AGW **Rev:** Bust of Erwin Rommel of Germany

Date	Mintage	F	VF	XF	Unc	BU
1957	—	—	—	435	450	475

X# MB26 60 BOLIVARES

22.2000 g., 0.9000 Gold 0.6423 oz. AGW **Rev:** Bust of Winston Churchilll of Great Britain

Date	Mintage	F	VF	XF	Unc	BU
1957	—	—	—	435	450	475

X# MB27 60 BOLIVARES

22.2000 g., 0.9000 Gold 0.6423 oz. AGW **Rev:** Bust of Bernard Montgomery of Great Britain

Date	Mintage	F	VF	XF	Unc	BU
1957	—	—	—	435	450	475

X# MB28 60 BOLIVARES

22.2000 g., 0.9000 Gold 0.6423 oz. AGW **Rev:** Bust of Benito Mussolini of Italy

Date	Mintage	F	VF	XF	Unc	BU
1957	—	—	—	435	450	475

X# MB29 60 BOLIVARES

22.2000 g., 0.9000 Gold 0.6423 oz. AGW **Rev:** Bust of Vittorio Emanuel III of Italy

Date	Mintage	F	VF	XF	Unc	BU
1957	—	—	—	435	450	475

X# MB30 60 BOLIVARES

22.2000 g., 0.9000 Gold 0.6423 oz. AGW **Rev:** Bust of Tojo of Japan

Date	Mintage	F	VF	XF	Unc	BU
1957	—	—	—	435	450	475

X# MB31 60 BOLIVARES

22.2000 g., 0.9000 Gold 0.6423 oz. AGW **Rev:** Bust of Dwight D. Eisenhower of U.S.A.

Date	Mintage	F	VF	XF	Unc	BU
1957	—	—	—	435	450	475

X# MB32 60 BOLIVARES

22.2000 g., 0.9000 Gold 0.6423 oz. AGW **Rev:** Bu of Douglas MacArthur of U.S.A.

Date	Mintage	F	VF	XF	Unc
1957	—	—	—	435	450

X# MB33 60 BOLIVARES

22.2000 g., 0.9000 Gold 0.6423 oz. AGW **Rev:** Bu of Franklin D. Roosevelt of U.S.A.

Date	Mintage	F	VF	XF	Unc
1957	—	—	—	435	450

X# MB34 60 BOLIVARES

22.2000 g., 0.9000 Gold 0.6423 oz. AGW **Rev:** Bu of Harry S. Truman of U.S.A.

Date	Mintage	F	VF	XF	Unc
1957	—	—	—	435	450

X# MB35 60 BOLIVARES

22.2000 g., 0.9000 Gold 0.6423 oz. AGW **Rev:** Bu of Joseph Stalin of U.S.S.R.

Date	Mintage	F	VF	XF	Unc
1957	—	—	—	435	450

X# MB36 60 BOLIVARES

22.2000 g., 0.9000 Gold 0.6423 oz. AGW **Rev:** Bu of Marshall Tito of Yugoslavia

Date	Mintage	F	VF	XF	Unc
1957	—	—	—	435	450

X# MB60 160 BOLIVARES

50.0000 g., 0.9000 Gold 1.4467 oz. AGW **Rev:** Bu of Adolf Hitler of Germany

Date	Mintage	F	VF	XF	Unc
1959 Proof	—	Value: 1,150			

PRIVATE PATTERNS

Karl Goetz Issues

Struck at later dates using original or imit tion dies. Additional mulings with Goetz Ge man patterns exist, but are most likely moder restrikes or reproductions

X# Pn1 5 BOLIVARES

25.0000 g., 0.9000 Silver 0.7234 oz. ASW **Rev:** Bus of General Juan Gomez

Date	Mintage	F	VF	XF	Unc
1930	—	—	—	65.00	120

X# Pn2 5 BOLIVARES

Nickel **Rev:** Bust of General Juan Gomez

Date	Mintage	F	VF	XF	Unc
1930	—	—	—	45.00	90.00

X# Pn3 5 BOLIVARES

Copper **Rev:** Bust of General Juan Gomez

Date	Mintage	F	VF	XF	Unc
1930	—	—	—	45.00	90.00

X# Pn4 5 BOLIVARES

Gilt Copper **Rev:** Bust of General Juan Gomez

Date	Mintage	F	VF	XF	Unc
1930	—	—	—	45.00	90.00

X# Pn5 5 BOLIVARES
Aluminum-Bronze **Rev:** Bust of General Juan Gomez

Date	Mintage	F	VF	XF	Unc	BU
1930	—	—	—	45.00	90.00	—

X# Pn6 5 BOLIVARES
33.9400 g., Gold **Rev:** Bust of General Juan Gomez

Date	Mintage	F	VF	XF	Unc	BU
1930	—	—	—	750	1,000	—

X# Pn7 5 BOLIVARES
Platinum APW **Rev:** Bust of General Juan Gomez **Note:** Prepared by Karl Goetz. Weight varies: 36.15-40.90 grams.

Date	Mintage	F	VF	XF	Unc	BU
1930	4	—	—	1,250	1,650	—

TRIAL STRIKES

X#	Date	Mintage	Identification	Mkt Val
TS1	1930	—	5 Bolivares. Nickel. Obv.	50.00
TS2	1930	—	5 Bolivares. Nickel. Rev.	50.00
TS3	1930	—	5 Bolivares. Copper. Obv.	50.00
TS4	1930	—	5 Bolivares. Copper. Rev.	50.00
TS5	1930	—	5 Bolivares. Aluminum-Bronze. Obv.	45.00
TS6	1930	—	5 Bolivares. Aluminum-Bronze. Rev.	45.00
TS7	1930	—	5 Bolivares. Aluminum. Obv.	45.00
TS8	1930	—	5 Bolivares. Aluminum. Rev.	—

VIET NAM

REPUBLIC

BULLION COINAGE

Kim-Thanh Issues

X# B1 14 GRAMS
Gold, 36x96 mm. **Obv:** Ornate "TT" in circle in four corners **Obv. Inscription:** KIM-THANH / SAIGON - HONG KONG / HANOI - PNOMPENH **Shape:** Rectangular **Note:** Weight and actual size varies.

Date	Mintage	Good	VG	F	VF	XF
ND(1960)	—	—	—	—	—	—

Note: These were usually issued in total weight of 1 Tael (37.5 grams) composed of two complete wafers and a clipped partial piece in a special paper wrapper

The Lion Issues

X# B3 14 GRAMS
1.0000 Gold, 46x101 mm. **Obv:** Lion standing facing **Obv. Inscription:** PURE GOLD / GUARANTEED - THE LION / TRADE MARK **Note:** Weight and actual size varies.

Date	Mintage	Good	VG	F	VF	XF
ND(1960)	—	—	—	—	—	—

Note: These were usually issued in total weight of 1 Tael (37.5 grams) composed of two complete wafers and a clipped partial piece in a special paper wrapper

X# B4 14 GRAMS
1.0000 Gold **Countermark:** "QUANGTHAI" **Obv:** Lion standing facing, trademark above, below fineness in sprays **Obv. Inscription:** PURE GOLD / GUARANTEED - THE LION / TRADE MARK
Note: Weight and actual size varies.

Date	Mintage	Good	VG	F	VF	XF
ND(1960)	—	—	—	—	—	—

Note: These were usually issued in total of 1 Tael (37.5 grams) composed of two complete wafers and a clipped partial piece in a special paper wrapper

MEDALLIC BULLION

Agribank AJC issues

X# MB6 2 CHI
7.5000 g., 0.9990 Gold 0.2409 oz. AGW, 22.13 mm. **Obv:** Country outline **Obv. Legend:** NUOC CONG HOA XA HOI CHU NGHIA VIET NAM **Obv. Inscription:** 60 / nam (years) **Rev:** Bank logo **Rev. Legend:** * NGAN HANG NONG NGHIEP PTNT VIET NAM * AGRIBANK - AJC **Edge:** Plain

Date	Mintage	F	VF	XF	Unc	BU
ND(2005) Prooflike	—	—	—	—	175	—

X# MB8 LUONG
37.5000 g., 0.9999 Gold 1.2055 oz. AGW, 35.97 mm. **Obv:** Country outline **Obv. Legend:** NUOC CONG HOA XA HOI CHU NGHIA VIET NAM **Obv. Inscription:** 60 / nam (years) **Rev:** Bank logo **Rev. Legend:** * NGAN HANG NONG NGHIEP PTNT VIET NAM * AGRIBANK **Edge:** Plain

Date	Mintage	F	VF	XF	Unc	BU
ND(2005)	—	—	—	BV	850	—

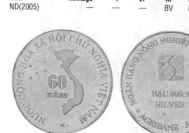

X# MB2 9 GRAMS
9.2500 g., 0.9999 Silver 0.2974 oz. ASW, 28.06 mm. **Obv:** Country outline **Obv. Legend:** NUOC CONG HOA XA HOI CHU NGHIA VIET NAM **Obv. Inscription:** 60 / nam (years) **Rev:** Bank logo **Rev. Legend:** * NGAN HANG NONG NGHIEP PTNT VIET NAM * AGRIBANK - AJC **Edge:** Plain

Date	Mintage	F	VF	XF	Unc	BU
ND(2005)	—	—	—	BV	6.50	—

X# MB3 19 GRAMS
19.6500 g., 0.9999 Silver 0.6317 oz. ASW, 35.93 mm. **Obv:** Country outline **Obv. Legend:** NUOC CONG HOA XA HOI CHU NGHIA VIET NAM **Obv. Inscription:** 60 / nam (years) **Rev:** Bank logo **Rev. Legend:** * NHAN HANG NONG NGHIEP PTNT VIET NAM * AGRIBANK - AJC **Edge:** Plain

Date	Mintage	F	VF	XF	Unc	BU
ND(2005)	—	—	—	BV	13.50	—

SOUTH DAI VIET

CAST COINAGE

X# 21 15 VAN
Cast Copper, 35 mm. **Obv. Inscription:** Ham Nghi Trung Bao **Rev:** Plain

Date	Mintage	Good	VG	F	VF	XF
ND(1884-85)	—	3.50	7.50	12.50	20.00	—

X# 22 30 VAN
Cast Copper, 35.1 mm. **Ruler:** Ham Nghi **Obv. Inscription:** Ham Nghi ... Bao **Rev:** Value

Date	Mintage	Good	VG	F	VF	XF
ND(1884-85)	—	3.50	7.50	12.50	20.00	—

GOLD MILLED COINAGE

X# 13 7 TIEN
Gold **Ruler:** Tu Duc **Obv:** Large characters **Rev:** Large, thick facing dragons **Note:** Schroeder #402.2. Weight varies: 26.45-27.00 grams. Prev. KM#552.

Date	Mintage	VG	F	VF	XF	Unc
ND(1848-83)	—	1,250	2,500	4,000	6,000	—

Note: A French copy

FRENCH PROTECTORATE OF ANNAM

CAST COINAGE

X# 31 15 VAN
9.2200 g., Cast Copper, 33.1 mm. **Obv. Inscription:** Thanh Dinh Trung Bao **Rev:** Plain

Date	Mintage	F	VF	XF	Unc	BU
ND(1916-25)	—	7.50	12.50	—	—	—

MEDALLIC COINAGE

Bao Chien Issues

The Bao Chien issues are normally encountered with small holes used for attaching silk thread tassles as these were given as awards of various services. Unholed examples command a moderate premium.

X# M4 2 TIEN
Silver **Ruler:** Khai Dinh **Obv. Inscription:** Khai Dinh Thong Bao **Rev:** Legend between sun, moon and clouds **Rev. Inscription:** Nhi Nghi **Note:** Prev. KM#M4. Weight varies: 7.30-7.60 grams.

Date	Mintage	F	VF	XF	Unc	BU
ND(1916-25)	—	60.00	100	175	300	—

X# M3.3 2 TIEN
Silver **Ruler:** Bao Dai **Obv:** Flaming pearl at center **Obv. Inscription:** Bao Dai Bao Chien **Rev:** Clouds deviating in style **Rev. Inscription:** Nhi Nghi

Date	Mintage	F	VF	XF	Unc	BU
ND(1926-45)	—	60.00	100	175	300	—

 # M3.4 2 TIEN

ilver **Ruler:** Bao Dai **Obv:** Large flaming pearl at enter **Obv. Inscription:** Bao Dai Bao Chien **Rev:** louds deviating in style **Rev. Inscription:** Nhi Nghi

ate	Mintage	F	VF	XF	Unc	BU
)(1926-45)	—	60.00	100	175	300	—

‹# M3.1 2 TIEN

ilver **Ruler:** Bao Dai **Obv. Inscription:** Bao Dai Bao Chien **Rev:** Legend between sun, moon and clouds **Rev. Inscription:** Nhi Nghi **Note:** Prev. KM#M3.1.

ate	Mintage	F	VF	XF	Unc	BU
D(1926-45)	—	60.00	100	175	300	—

‹# M3.2 2 TIEN

ilver **Ruler:** Bao Dai **Obv:** Without flaming pearl at center **Obv. Inscription:** Bao Dai Bao Chien **Rev:** Legend between sun, moon and clouds **Rev. Inscription:** Nhi Nghi **Note:** Prev. KM#M3.2.

ate	Mintage	F	VF	XF	Unc	BU
D(1926-45)	—	60.00	100	175	300	—

X# M8 4 TIEN

Silver **Ruler:** Bao Dai **Obv:** Flaming pearl at center **Obv. Inscription:** Bao Dai Bao Chien **Rev:** Dragon left facing right

Date	Mintage	F	VF	XF	Unc	BU
ND(1926-45)	—	75.00	125	200	350	—

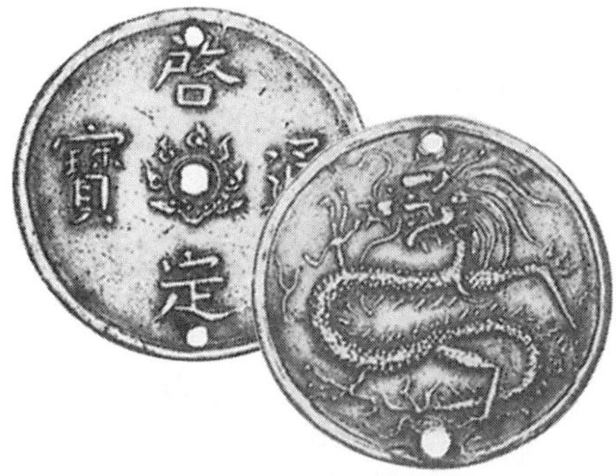

X# M5.1 5 TIEN

18.3500 g., Silver **Ruler:** Khai Dinh **Obv. Inscription:** Khai Dinh Thong Bao **Rev:** Thin dragon **Note:** Prev. KM#M5.1.

Date	Mintage	F	VF	XF	Unc	BU
ND(1916-25)	—	90.00	150	250	400	—

X# M5.2 5 TIEN

18.3500 g., Silver **Ruler:** Khai Dinh **Obv. Inscription:** Khai Dinh Thong Bob **Rev:** Fat dragon **Note:** Prev. KM#M5.2.

Date	Mintage	F	VF	XF	Unc	BU
5 (1920)	—	90.00	150	250	400	—

X# M1.2 7 TIEN

Silver **Ruler:** Khai Dinh **Obv:** Flaming pearl at center **Obv. Inscription:** Khai Dinh Bao Chien **Rev:** Artistic dragon left

Date	Mintage	F	VF	XF	Unc	BU
ND(1916-25)	—	125	200	350	600	—

X# M1.1 7 TIEN

Silver **Ruler:** Khai Dinh **Obv. Inscription:** Khai Dinh Bao Chien **Rev:** Stylized dragon with short tail **Note:** Prev. KM#M1.1. Weight varies: 26.30-26.94 grams. The X#M1.1 medallic pieces have been found struck over earlier Minh Mang 7 Tien pieces.

Date	Mintage	F	VF	XF	Unc	BU
ND(1916-25)	—	125	200	350	550	—

X# M6 7 TIEN

Silver **Ruler:** Khai Dinh **Obv. Inscription:** Khai Dinh Bao Chien **Rev:** Classic stylized dragon **Note:** Prev. X#M1.2. Weight varies: 26.30-26.94 grams.

Date	Mintage	F	VF	XF	Unc	BU
ND(1916-25)	—	—	200	350	500	—

X# M7 7 TIEN

Silver 26.30-26.94 g **Ruler:** Khai Dinh **Obv. Inscription:** Khai Dinh Bao Chien **Rev:** Large stylized dragon **Note:** Prev. X#M1.3. Illustration reduced.

Date	Mintage	F	VF	XF	Unc	BU
ND	—	110	180	300	500	—

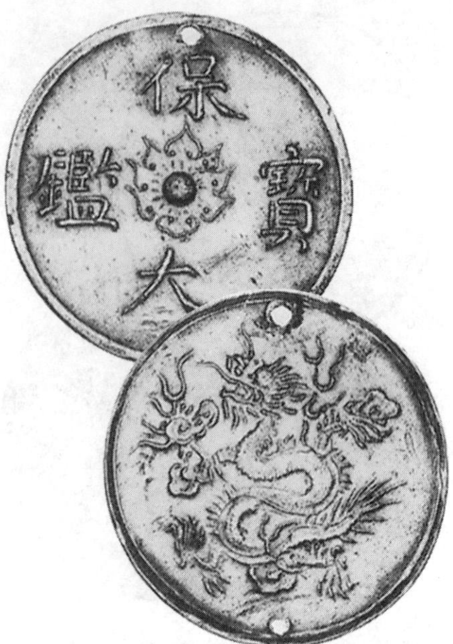

X# M2 7 TIEN
Silver **Ruler:** Bao Dai **Obv. Inscription:** Bao Dai Bao Chien **Note:** Prev. KM#M2.

Date	Mintage	F	VF	XF	Unc	BU
ND(1926-45)	—	—	180	300	500	—

VINLAND

KINGDOM

FANTASY COINAGE

Issued by the Shire Post Mint.

X# 1 PENNY
3.1000 g., Copper **Ruler:** Leif Eiricsson **Obv:** Bust helmeted left **Obv. Legend:** LEIF EIRICSSON **Rev:** Short cross, pellet in each angle **Rev. Legend:** VINLAND MONETA (hammer)

Date	Mintage	F	VF	XF	Unc	BU
ND	1,000	—	—	2.00	—	—

X# 5 PENNY
2.4000 g., 0.9000 Silver 0.0694 oz. ASW **Ruler:** Leif Eiricsson **Obv:** Bust helmeted left **Obv. Legend:** LEIF EIRICSSON **Rev:** Short cross, pellet in each angle **Rev. Legend:** VINLAND MONETA (hammer)

Date	Mintage	F	VF	XF	Unc	BU
ND	500	—	—	10.00	—	—

WESTANTARCTICA TERRITORIES

BALLENY ISLANDS

GRAND DUCHY

MILLED COINAGE

X# 1 DOLLAR
10.0000 g., Bronze, 25.7 mm. **Ruler:** Grand Duke Travis I **Obv:** Arms **Obv. Legend:** GOVERNMENT OF THE BALLENY ISLANDS **Rev:** Map of islands **Rev. Legend:** BALLENY ISLANDS - WESTANTARCTICA TERRITORIES **Edge:** Plain **Note:** Prev. X#E1.

Date	Mintage	F	VF	XF	Unc	BU
2005 Proof	150	Value: 15.00				

X# 1a DOLLAR
Silver, 25.7 mm. **Ruler:** Grand Duke Travis I **Obv:** Arms **Obv. Legend:** GOVERNMENT OF THE BALLENY ISLANDS **Rev:** Map of islands **Rev. Legend:** BALLENY ISLANDS - WESTANTARCTICA **Edge:** Plain **Note:** Prev. X#E1a.

Date	Mintage	F	VF	XF	Unc	BU
2005 Proof	20	Value: 35.00				

ESSAIS

X#	Date	Mintage	Identification	Issue Price	Mkt Val
E1	2005	—	Dollar. Bronze. Prev. X#Pn1.	16.00	16.00
E2	2005	—	Dollar. Silver. Prev. X#Pn2.	16.00	16.00

WESTEROS

KINGDOM

STANDARD COINAGE

Shire Post Mint Issue

X# 3 PENNY
3.1000 g., Bronze **Ruler:** King Torrhen Stark **Obv:** Crowned bust flanked by sceptres **Obv. Legend:** TORRHEN • STARK • **Rev:** Head of Dire Wolf **Rev. Legend:** WINTERFELL •

Date	Mintage	F	VF	XF	Unc	BU
ND	250	—	—	—	3.00	—

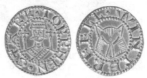

X# 7 STAG
2.4000 g., 0.9000 Silver 0.0694 oz. ASW **Ruler:** King Torrhen Stark **Obv:** Crowned bust facing holding sceptres **Obv. Legend:** TORRHEN • STARK • **Rev:** Head facing of Dire Wolf **Rev. Legend:** WINTERFELL •

Date	Mintage	F	VF	XF	Unc	BU
ND	100	—	—	—	10.00	—

X# 8 STAG
2.4000 g., 0.9000 Silver 0.0694 oz. ASW **Ruler:** King Aerys II **Obv:** Crowned half-length figure facing holding sceptre and gl. cr. **Obv. Legend:** AERYS II TARGARYEN **Rev:** Stag standing right **Rev. Legend:** WESTROS / OT

Date	Mintage	F	VF	XF	Unc	BU
ND	100	—	—	—	10.00	

X# 9 STAG
2.4000 g., 0.9000 Silver 0.0694 oz. ASW **Ruler:** King Aegon Targaryen **Obv:** Crowned Triyne (Facing male head with two profile female heads) **Obv. Legend:** AEGON / TARGARYEN **Rev:** Stag standing left **Rev. Legend:** DRAGONSTONE

Date	Mintage	F	VF	XF	Unc	BU
ND	200	—	—	—	12.00	

X# 4 STAR
17.0000 g., Copper **Ruler:** Robert Baratheon **Obv:** Head left within vertical oval **Obv. Legend:** ROBERT BARATHEON **Rev:** Seven-pointed star **Rev. Legend:** OLDTOWN • WESTEROS •

Date	Mintage	F	VF	XF	Unc	BU
ND	460	—	—	—	10.00	

X# 15 PUL
1.5000 g., Copper **Ruler:** Khal Drogo **Obv:** Horseman right **Rev. Inscription:** KHAL / DROGO / DOTHAR / AKI **Note:** Wire money, one, two or ten impressions connected.

Date	Mintage	F	VF	XF	Unc	BU
ND	41	—	—	—	2.00	

X# 16 DENGA
1.7000 g., 0.9250 Silver 0.0506 oz. ASW **Ruler:** Khal Drogo **Obv:** Horseman right **Rev. Inscription:** KHAL / DROGO / DOTHR / AKI **Note:** Wire money, one, two or ten impressions connected

Date	Mintage	F	VF	XF	Unc	BU
ND	72	—	—	—	—	8.0

TOKEN COINAGE

Shire Post Mint Issue

 # Tn1 ONE
4000 g., 0.9000 Silver 0.0694 oz. ASW **Ruler:** King rys II **Obv:** Peach **Obv. Legend:** THE PEACH ONEY SEPT **Rev:** Large ONE within rays **te:** Brothel token

e	Mintage	F	VF	XF	Unc	BU
	100	—	—	—	10.00	—

TRIAL STRIKE

 # Ts1 STAR
uminum **Ruler:** King Aerys II **Obv:** Head left within rtical oval **Rev:** Seven-pointed star **Note:** Oversize n. X #4.

te	Mintage	F	VF	XF	Unc	BU
	—	—	—	—	—	—

WIKINGLAND

FANTASY REPUBLIC

STANDARD COINAGE

 # 13 10 MARK
ckel-Brass, 38.5 mm. **Ruler:** Reinhold I **Obv:** Vertical les at left, large "R1" above value at right **bv. Inscription:** Reinhold 1 / fürstentum / Wikingland **ev:** Cross on stave **Rev. Inscription:** Date 2244

te	Mintage	F	VF	XF	Unc	BU
) Prooflike	—	—	—	—	20.00	—

X# 1 10 MARK
Copper-Nickel-Zinc, 38.5 mm. **Ruler:** Reinhold I **Obv:** Vertical titles at left, large "R1" above value at right **Obv. Inscription:** Reinhold 1 / fürstentum / Wikingland **Rev:** Viking ship, outline of eastern Canada and United States, Southern Greenland

Date	Mintage	F	VF	XF	Unc	BU
1985	500	—	—	—	20.00	—

X# 9 10 MARK
Nickel-Brass, 38.5 mm. **Ruler:** Reinhold I **Obv:** Vertical titles at left, large "R1" above value at right **Obv. Inscription:** Reinhold 1 / fürstentum / Wikingland **Rev:** Viking anchor

Date	Mintage	F	VF	XF	Unc	BU
1993 Prooflike	—	—	—	—	20.00	—

PIEFORTS

X#	Date	Mintage	Identification	Mkt Val
P1	ND	24	10 Mark. Copper. X13.	40.00

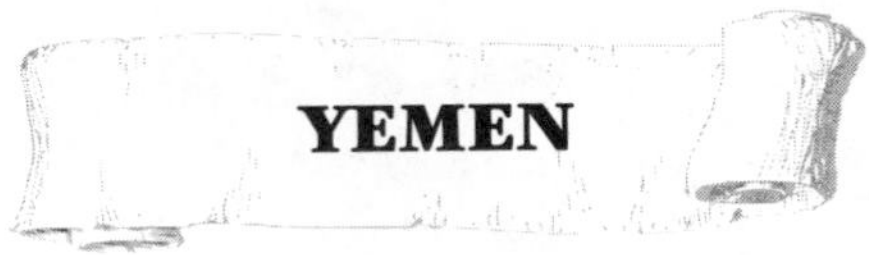

YEMEN

KINGDOM

CUT & COUNTERMARKED COINAGE

X# 1 1/2 AHMADI RIYAL
0.8330 Silver **Countermark:** No Value **Note:** Countermarked: Arabic on outer ring of Austria Maria Theresa Thaler. The center was used to strike 1/2 Amadi Riyals dated AH1367-73.

Date	Mintage	F	VF	XF	Unc	BU
ND1780	—	—	175	250	400	—

X# 2 AHMADI RIYAL
28.0668 g., 0.8330 Silver 0.7516 oz. ASW **Counterstamp:** 1/16 Ahmadi Riyal **Note:** Counterstamped on Austria Maria Theresa Thaler, KM#T1.

Date	Mintage	Good	VG	F	VF	XF
AH1780	—	100	150	225	350	—

X# 3 AHMADI RIYAL
28.0668 g., 0.8330 Silver 0.7516 oz. ASW **Counterstamp:** 1/16 Ahmadi Riyal **Note:** Counterstamped on Eritrea Tallero, KM#5.

Date	Mintage	Good	VG	F	VF	XF
1981	—	250	350	550	750	—

ROYALIST GOVERNMENT

In Exile

FANTASY COINAGE

X# A1 RIAL
24.9200 g., 0.7200 Silver 0.5768 oz. ASW **Ruler:** Imam Badr **Subject:** Sir Winston Churchill Memorial **Obv:** Ornate crowned and flag draped arms **Rev:** Facing bust of Churchill

Date	Mintage	F	VF	XF	Unc	BU
AH1385//1965	6,000	—	—	15.00	30.00	60.00

YUGOSLAVIA

EUROPEAN COMMUNITY

Established in July 1991

ECU COINAGE

X# 1 25 ECU
25.0000 g., 0.9990 Silver 0.8029 oz. ASW, 40 mm. **Obv:** Outlined map of Yugoslavia **Rev:** 12 stars in outer circle, value and date in center **Edge:** Reeded

Date	Mintage	F	VF	XF	Unc	BU
1992	7,500	—	—	—	70.00	—
1992 Proof	2,500	Value: 100				

ROYAL GOVERNMENT

Peter II (In Exile)

ESSAIS

Franklin Mint, U.S.A. Issues

X# E1 CROWN
Franklinium **Ruler:** Petar II **Obv:** Head right **Obv. Legend:** ПЕТАР II КРАЉ ЈУГОСЛАВИЈЕ • PETAR II KRALJ JUGOSLAVIJE **Rev:** Crowned and mantled arms

Date	Mintage	F	VF	XF	Unc	BU
1967 Prooflike	1,002	—	—	—	—	75.00

X# E2 CROWN

0.9170 Silver **Ruler:** Petar II **Obv:** Head right **Obv. Legend:** ПЕТАР II КРАЉ ЈУГОСЛАВИЈЕ • PETAR II KRALJ JUGOSLAVIJE **Rev:** Crowned and mantled arms

Date	Mintage	F	VF	XF	Unc	BU
1967 Proof	738	Value: 125				

X# E3 CROWN

0.9990 Silver **Ruler:** Petar II **Obv:** Head right **Obv. Legend:** ПЕТАР II КРАЉ ЈУГОСЛАВИЈЕ • PETAR II KRALJ JUGOSLAVIJE **Rev:** Crowned and mantled arms

Date	Mintage	F	VF	XF	Unc	BU
1967 Proof	803	Value: 125				

X# E4 CROWN

0.7500 Gold **Ruler:** Petar II **Obv:** Head right **Obv. Legend:** ПЕТАР II КРАЉ ЈУГОСЛАВИЈЕ • PETAR II KRALJ JUGOSLAVIJE **Rev:** Crowned and mantled arms

Date	Mintage	F	VF	XF	Unc	BU
1967 Proof; Unique	—	—	—	—	—	—

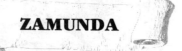

ZAMUNDA

KINGDOM

FANTASY COINAGE

X# 1 5 POUNDS

Copper-Nickel **Obv:** Bust of Prince Akeem left **Rev:** Arms **Note:** A 100 £ note of the Bank of Zamunda was also produced for use in the film.

Date	Mintage	F	VF	XF	Unc	BU
1988	—	—	—	20.00	25.00	35.00

X# 1a 5 POUNDS

Brass plated Copper-Nickel **Obv:** Bust of Prince Akeem left **Rev:** Arms

Date	Mintage	F	VF	XF	Unc	BU
1988	—	—	—	12.50	17.50	25.00

X# 1b 5 POUNDS

Gold Plated Copper-Nickel **Obv:** Bust of Prince Akeem left **Rev:** Arms **Note:** Reportedly used in the movie.

Date	Mintage	F	VF	XF	Unc	BU
1988	—	—	—	—	—	—

X# 1c 5 POUNDS

Gold **Obv:** Bust of Prince Akeem left **Rev:** Arms **Note:** Reportedly struck as a presentation gift for Eddie Murphy.

Date	Mintage	F	VF	XF	Unc	BU
1988 Reported, not confirmed	—	—	—	—	—	—

Greetings from the Editors

Welcome to this 5th edition of Unusual World Coins. A coin collector might ask, "What exactly is an Unusual World Coin and what isn't?" Coins are items issued by legitimate governments and accepted by merchants, the people and other goverments in payment of debts – namely legal tender. They accommodate commerce and wages.

Items were sometimes made to a coin standard. The Venetians started making New Year's coin-like medallions called "Oselles" struck in silver and gold. In the South American Spanish Colonies, cites often issued proclimate medals, to a coin standard. In the 19th century certain European mints, such as those in the Netherlands, struck numerous special silver and gold off metal strikes of various circulating coins primarily for collectors.

As we passed the mid-20th century mark, private mints began competing with the traditional "national" mints for contracts from various nations. In addition to striking circulating coins, they also struck proof versions. The NCLT (Non-circulating Legal Tender) boom began, primarily in silver and gold commemorative issues. The traditional mints were not to be left behind and their focus increased on the production of commemoratives.

During the last two centuries, there were all sorts of unusual "coin-like" emissions. Some were salesman's samples while others were privately struck patterns that would hopefully be adopted as traditional designs for general circulation.

Along the path, we started to record issues of governments in exile. Later we have wannabe micro nations, duchies, and outright fantasy lands with their subsequent issues, which are popping up like spring flowers in a pasture.

Fantasy "coins" are nothing new to numismatics. The Chinese have been producing them for well over a century and are still doing it today. As the Ecu became a standard accounting term of value, we started seeing Ecu coinage – some being legal tender, but most are not and the Ecu was eventually replaced by the Euro.

The latest innovation, which is actually very popular in Europe, is the striking of "probe" – Euro issues for non-Euro nations including some regional areas. They are very attractive 8 or 9 piece sets in informative folders.

Summing it up, we have done the best we could to capture as many types of the "unusual" for this edition. As always, we look forward to your comments, critiques or assistance in corrections or additions to this, our 5th edition of *Unusual World Coins*.

Now, visit the Standard Catalog series on-line at www.numismater.com.

Your Editors,
Colin R. Bruce, II; George S. Cuhaj, Tom Michael

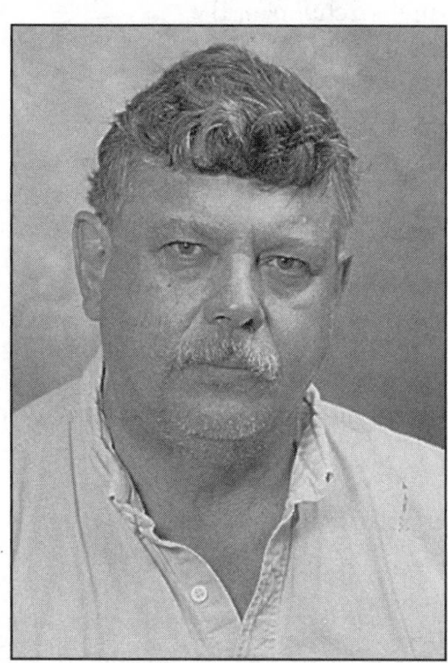

Acknowledgments

Many individuals have contributed countless additions and alterations, which have been incorporated into previous and now this expanded fifth edition. While all may not be acknowledged, special appreciation is extended to the following who have exhibited exceptional enthusiasm during the production of this volume.

Dr. Lawrence A. Adams
Esko Ahlroth
Stephen Album
David T. Alexander
Jim Anderson
John, Grand Duke of Avram
Albert Beck
Richard Benson
Peter N. Berger
Allen G. Berman
Christopher J. Budesa
Daniel Carr
Mark Wm Clark
Scott E. Cordry
George Cruickshank
Raymond E. Czahor
Howard A. Daniel III
Jorge Fernández Videl
Greg Franck-Weiby
Eugene Freeman
Walter Giuliani
Ron Goodger
Ron Guth
Edmond Hakimian
Flemming Lyngbeck Hansen
David Harrison
Serge Huard
Louis Hudson
Peter Jackson
Hector Carlos Janson
Tolling Jennings
Børge R. Juul
Craig Keplinger
Samson Kin Chiu Lai
Joseph E. Lang
Alex Lazarovici
Mike Locke
Richard Lobel
Ma Tak Wo
Enrico Manara
Ranko Mandic
Greg MacLean
Tom Maringer
Franck Medina
Juozas Minikevicius
Robert Mish
Paul Montz
Edward Moschetti
Bernard von NotHaus
Joseph Paonessa
Walter Patrick
Oded Paz
Juan Peña
Jens Pilegaard
Richard Ponterio
Kent Ponterio
Martin Purdy
Frank Putrow
Tony Raymond
William M. Rosenblum
Remy Said
Leon A. Saryan, Phd
Erwin Schaffer
Gerhard Schön
Dr. Wolfgang Schüster
Alexander Shapiro
Chaim D. Shiboleth
Jorgen Sømod
Robert Steinberg
M. Louis Teller
David van Geat
Jorge Vidal
Stephen Vogelsang
Dusan Vrabel
Paul Welz
Stewart Westdal
Isaac Zadeh
Joseph Zaffern
Fred Zinkann

AUCTION HOUSES AND DISTRIBUTORS

Bruun Rasmussen
Dix-Noonan-Webb
Jean Elsen, S.A.
Frankfurter Münzhandlung, GmbH
Gorny & Mosch - Giessner Münzhandlung
Heritage World Coin Auctions
Hess-Divo Ltd.
Gerhard Hirsch
Thomas Høiland Møntauktion
Fritz Rudolf Künker
Münzenhandlung Harald Möller, GmbH
Münz Zentrum
Noble Numismatics, Pty. Ltd.
Ponterio & Associates
Laurens Schulman, BV
Stack's - Coin Galleries
UBS, AG
World Wide Coins of California

SOCIETIES, INSTITUTIONS AND INTERNATIONAL MINTS

American Numismatic Association
American Numismatic Society
British Museum
Europ Mint
International Numismatic Agency, Ltd.
Numismatics International
Russian Numismatic Society
Singapore Mint
Smithsonian Institution
Turino IM Mint
Unrecognised States Numismatic Society

A special thanks to these members of the KP Book database publishing team:

Stacy Bloch

Clifford Mishler

The purpose of *Unusual World Coins* is to chronicle the sometimes confusing, often deceptive realm of numismatic emissions, primarily created with the commercial marketplace in mind, which purport to represent sovereign governmental entities. As the *Standard Catalog of World Coins* mission is focused on the circulating and non-circulating legal tender coins of national governments, such issues included here are generally exempted from coverage in *SCWC*. While some early issues in the *Unusual World Coins* realm were documented by Richard D. Kenney in his study *Unofficial Coins of the World* (as published in the Numismatist 1962-64), the number of offerings appearing in the marketplace multiplied exponentially from decade to decade since the 1960s into these early years of the 21st century. The purpose of *Unusual World Coins* is to provide order to this universe as it relates, compares and contrasts to the *SCWC* realm.

Clifford Mishler
Past President Krause Publications

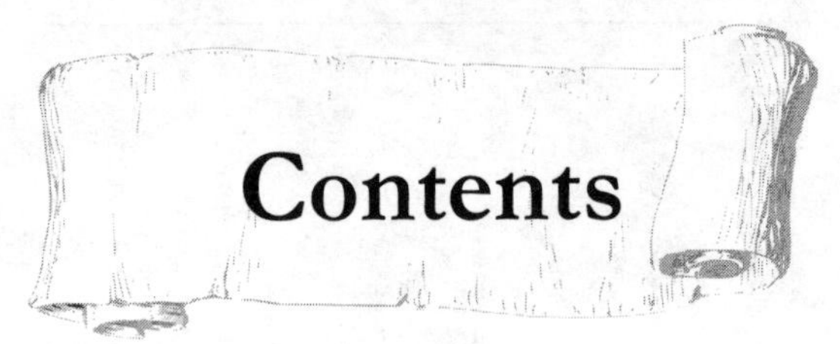

Contents

Introduction III
Acknowledgement IV
Dedication V
Country Index VIII
Denomination Index XIV
Hejira Date Chart XXVI
How To Use This Catalog XVII
Standard International Numeral Systems XXVIII
Silver Bullion Chart XXX
Gold Bullion Chart XXXII
Foreign Exchange XXIX

Advertising Index

Ponterio VII
Daniel Carr IX
Money Art XI
Numismaster XIII
Unrecognized States Numismatic Society XI
Chicago Paper Money Expo (CPMX) XXVII
Chicago International Coin Fair (CICF) XXV
Krause Publications - Books XXXVI

krause publications
2004
20 YEAR
CUSTOMER SERVICE AWARD

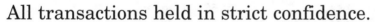

Country Index

Afghanistan....1
Aland islands....1
Alaska....562
Albania....1
Alderney....1
Algeria....2
Alghero....314
Andaman Islands....2
Andean Group....2
Andorra....2
Angband....371
Anguilla....5
Anticosti Island....54
Antioquia....109
Aquitaine....169
Araucania-Patagonia....6
Argentina....9
Arizona....562
Armenia....10
Aruba....11
Asiago....314
Atlantis....12
Atlantium....13
Augsburg....174
Australia....13
Australia-Victoria....18
Austria....20
Austria-Grinzing District....24
Austrian Netherlands....25
Austrian States-Salzburg....25
Avram....25
Awadh....286
Azerbaijan....26
Azores....26
Baden....174
Bahawalpur....286
Bahrain....27
Balearic Islands....27
Balleny Islands....584
Barbe Island....27
Baroda....287
Bavaria....174
Belarus....27
Belgium....28
Belgium Moresney....29
Bermania....30
Bermuda....30
Bern....511
Bhadranath....287
Bhutan....31
Bikanir....287
Bohemia....31
Bolivar....109
Bologna....308
Bolivia....31
Bophuthatswana....32
Bouillon....169
Boyaca....110
Brazil....32
Bremen....175
British columbia....52
British East Africa....40
British Honduras....40
British North Borneo....41
British West Africa....41
Buck Island....41
Bulgaria....42
Burkina Faso....44
Burma....44
Burundi....45
Cabinda....46
California....562
Cambodia....47
Camelot....49
Campilioni....511
Canada....49
Canada-Doninion....54
Canary Islands....55
Cape of Good Hope....55
Cape Verde....56
Cartago....56
catalonia....502
Cauca....110
Ceara....37
Central America....56
Central American States....56
Central American Union....57
Ceylon....57
Chechnya....443
Cherokee Nation....58
Chile....58
China....60
China, Japanese Puppet States....83
Chincha Islands....425
Christiania....104
Cocos (Keeling) Islands....108
Colombia....109
Conch Republic....110
Confederate States of America....563
Cooch Behar....287
Copiapo....59
Corvey....176
Corsica Island....110
Costa Rica....110
Creek Nation....111
Crete....113
Croatia....113
Cuba....114
Cundinamarca....110
Cyprus....120
Czech Republic....123
Czechoslovakia....125
Dale Town....371
Damanhur....128
Danish West Indies....129
Danzig....429
Datia....288
Denmark....132
Dhar....288
Dominica....135
Dominican Republic....135
Durango....370
East Caribbean States....136
Ecuador....137
Egypt....137
El Salvador....138
Enderbyland....139
England....225
Equatorial Guinea....139
Eregion....371
Esperanto....142
Estonia....142
Ethiopia....144
Europa....146
Eutopia....157
Faeroe Islands....157
Falkland Islands....157
Far Haraud....372
Faridkot....288
Finland....158
Flanders....504
Foutah Djalon....237
France....160
Frankfurt Am Main....176
Freedonia....170
French Antilles....170
French Guiana....170
French Polynesia....171
French Somaliland....172
French Southern & Antarctic Territories....172
Friesland....402
Friuli-Venezia....173
Fujairah....173
Fukien Province....81
Gabriola Island....52
Gaeta....308
Gardiner's Island....405
Geneva....511
Georgia....173
German States....174
Germany....183
Germany, Third Reich....200
Germany, Weimar Republic....200
Germany-Empire....207
Germany-Federal Republic....183
Ghana....208
Gibraltar....211

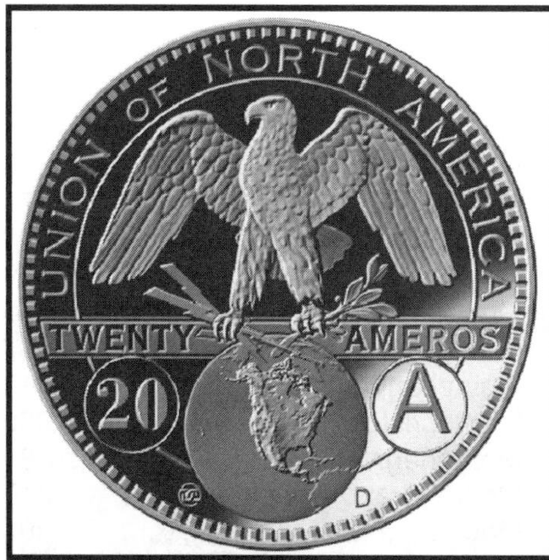
UNION OF NORTH AMERICA
TWENTY
AMEROS
20
A
D

FORT COLLINS COIN CLUB
COLORADO
1955
HORSETOOTH ROCK
2005
LARIMER COUNTY
50TH ANNIVERSARY

UNITED STATES MINT
DENVER
COLORADO
$
20
1 TROY OZ. .999 SILVER
1906 - CENTENNIAL - 2006

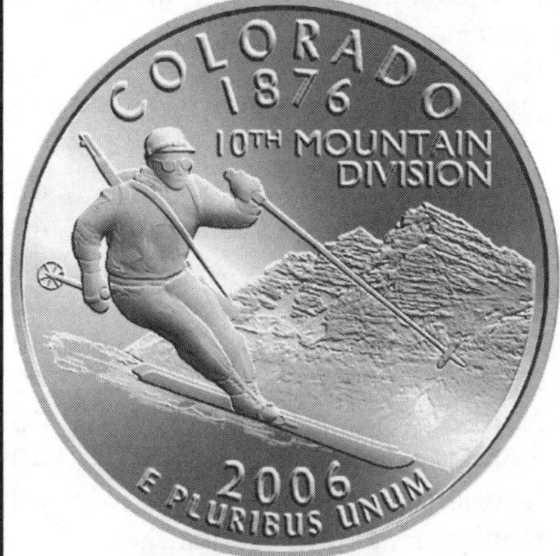
COLORADO
1876
10TH MOUNTAIN
DIVISION
2006
E PLURIBUS UNUM

"He tames the
thundering bolt of
love and annihilates
time and space"
NIKOLA TESLA

GEORGE WASHINGTON
1789
1797
1
DC

UNITED STATES of AMERICA
E PLURIBUS UNUM
DC
NON
DOLLAR

Country Index cont...

Gold Coast....212
Gondor....372
Gough Island....213
Grande Terre....233
Graubunden....511
Great Britain....213
Greece....226
Greenland....229
Grenada....230
Griquatown....230
Guadeloupe....231
Guam....233
Guatemala....234
Guernsey....236
Guinea....237
Guinea-Bissau....238
Haiti....238
Hamburg....176
Hannover....176
Hawaii....239, 565
Hejaz....254
Hesse-Darmstadt....176
Honduras....256
Hong Kong....256
Hungary....259
Hutt River Province....264
Iceland....284
Ico....38
Idaho....565
Ile Crescent....171
Ile De Amsterdam & St. Paul....172
Illinois....566
India-Princely States....286
India-British....290
India-Independent Kingdoms....285
India-Republic....295
Indonesia....297
Ionian Islands....297
Iran....297
Iraq....301
Ireland....301
Ireland Republic....303
Isenburg....177
Isle Desirade....233
Isle of Man....305
Isle of Wight....306
Isle of Heliopolis....256
Isola D'elba....314
Israel....307
Italian States....307
Italy....310
Izan Gaarda....372
Jalisco....371
Japan....317
Jersey....318
Jind....288
Jubbal....288
Juliana....38
Kamberra Island....320
Kansu Province....82
Karauli....288
Kayless....321
Kerguelen Islands....321
Kirin Province....82
Kishangarh....288
Kelantan....339
Kosovo....322
Kurdistan....322
Kutch....285
Kuwait....323
Laino D'intelvi....314
Lapland....324
Lasqueti Island....53
Latvia....325
League of Nations....327
Les Saintes....233
Lesotho....327
Liberia....327
Libya....329
Liechtenstein....329
Liege....331
Lithuania....331
Louisiana....566
Lundy....332
Luxembourg....333
Macao....336
Macedonia....336
Madagascar....337
Madeira Islands....338
Magdalena....110
Malaya....339
Maldive Islands....339
Malta....340
Manchoukuo....83
Manchukuo....357
Mansfeld-Eisleben....177
Maratha Confederacy....286
Martinique....357
Maryland....566
Mauritania....358
Mauritius....358
Mayotte....359
McMurdo....438
Mecklenburg-Strelite....177
Mexico....359
Mexico-Revolutionary....370
Michigan....566
Middle Earth....371
Miglianico....314
Milan....307
Min-che-kan Soviet....90
Minerva....378
Moldova....378
Molossia....378
Mombasa....378
Monaco....379
Mongolia....380
Montana....567
Montecantini....315
Montecristo....380
Montenegro....381
Montesilvano Commune....315
Moon....381
Mordaur....373
Morocco....381
Mozambique....381
Mouria....373
Munster....178
Namibia....382
Napoli....315
Nassau....178
Nejd....382
Nepal....384
Netherlands....384
Netherlands Antilles....402
Netherlands East Indies....403
New Caledonia....403
New France....403
New Guinea....405
New Hampshire....567
New Hebrides....405
New Island....405
New York....405, 567
New Zealand....406
Newfoundland....408
Nicaragua....408
Nichtsburg-Zilchstadt....408
Nigerian Scams....409
Nightingale Island....409
Nord....409
North Mexico....409
Northern Ireland....304
Northern Mariana Islands....409
Norway....410
Nurnberg....178
Obock....172
Occussi-Ambeno....412
Oman....413
Orange Free State....491
Order of Malta....342
Oregon....568
Ortiesi St. Ulrich....315
Osnabruck....179
Outer Baldonia....413
Paderborn....179
Pakistan....413
Palenstine....413

Country Index cont...

Panama 414
Papel States 307
Paradise 416
Paraguay 416
Pemba 417
Peoples Republic of China 85
Peru 417
Philippines 425
Pirantini, Republic of 39
Poarch Band 111
Poland 426
Pomerania 179
Portugal 429
Prussia 180
Puerto Rico 431
Purple Shaftieuland 431
Quebec 54
Ragazzi 432
Rajkot 289
Rapa Nui - Isla De Pascua - Easter Island 432
Ratlam 289
Republic of China 91
Reunion 433
Rewa 289
Rimini 315
Rio Grande 433
Rohaun 373
Roman Republic 309
Romania 433
Ross Island 438
Russia (Kaliningrad) 441
Russian Caucasia 443
Saint Barthelemy 443
Saint Croix 444
Saint Helena 444
Saint Hildegard 445
Saint Lucia 447
Saint Martin 403
Saint Pierre & Miquelon 447
Saint Thomas & Prince Island 448
Salta 10
San Marino 448
San Raffaele Cimena Commune 315
San Remo 315
San Serriffe 448
Santander 110
Sark Island 448
Sassello Commune 316
Saudi Arabia 449
Saxe-Meiningen 181
Saxe-Saalfeld 181
Saxony 181
Scotland 449
Sealand 451
Seborga 453
Serbia 453
Serbia and Bosnia 454
Settimo Torinese City 316
Sharjah 454
Shawnee Tribal Nation 454
Shetland Islands 456
Shire 374
Siberia 457
Sierra Leone 458
Sikh Empire 286
Singapore 473
Sinkiang Province 82
Sirmione 317
Slovakia 480
Slovenia 481
Solomon Islands 483
Somalia 483
Somaliland 488
Somers Islands 31
Sorrento 317
South Africa 488
Southern Africa 492
Southern Rhodesia 493
Spain 494
Spanish Colonial 503
Spanish Netherlands 503
Spitzbergen 504
Sri Lanka 505
Straits Settlements 505
Sweden 505
Swiss Cantons 511
Switzerland 512
Syria 523
Taiwan 104
Tajikistan 523
Tanzaniz 523
Taormina 317
Tarapaca 60
Tarim 530
Tender Island 531
Texas 568
Thailand 531
Tibet 534
Tierra Del Fuego 10
Tolima 10
Tonga 535
Torgu 535
Transylvania 536
Travancore 289
Trebizond 537
Tripura 286
Tunisia 538
Turkey 538
Uganda 539
Ukraine 539
Union of North America 540
United Arab Emirates 541
United Federation of Koronis 542
United Kingdom 542
United Nations 545
United States 545
United Transnational Republics 571
Uruguay 571
Utopia 157
Utopia-A World United 572
Vancouver Island 53
Vanuatu 573
Vatican City 573
Venezuela 575
Venice 310
Viet Nam 581
Vinland 584
Wales 225
Wallenstein 127
Washington 571
Westantarctica 584
Westeros 584
Wikingland 585
Wolgast 181
Wurttemberg 182
Wurzburg 182
Yemen 585
Yugoslavia 585
Yunnan Province 83
Zamunda 586
Zante 297
Zeeland 402
Zurich 512

Denomination Index

AFRO - Southern Africa
ANNA - India-British
ASPRA - Ionian Islands
ATT - Thailand
AXE - Middle Earth
BAHT - Thailand
BAIOCCHI - Italian States
BALBOA - Panama
BIPKWELE - Equatorial Guinea
BIRR - Ethiopia
BIT - Guadeloupe
United States
BITS - United States
BOLIVAR - Venezuela
BOLIVARES - Venezuela
BOLIVIANO - Bolivia
BRACTEATE - Hungary
BUCK - Buck Island
CALI - Damanhur
CASH - China
China, Republic Of
CELESTON - United States
CENT - China
China, Republic Of
Cocos (Keeling) Islands
Danish West Indies
Dominica
East Caribbean States
Great Britain
Hutt River Province
Liberia
Netherlands
Paraguay
Sealand
Straits Settlements
United States
CENTAVO - Argentina
Central American Union
Chile
Colombia
Cuba
New France
Peru
Philippines
CENTESIMI - Seborga
CENTIME - Belgium
Cambodia
Danish West Indies
France
French Guiana
Madagascar
New Caledonia
New France
Trebizond
CENTIMO - Andorra
Puerto Rico
Spain
CENTUM - Great Britain
CEROS - Iceland
Liechtenstein
Switzerland
CHIEN - Manchukuo
ÇOLES - Heliopolis, Isle Of
COPPERS - China, Republic Of
CORONAS - San Serriffe
CREDITI - Damanhur
CREDITO - Damanhur
CROWN - Australia
Bermuda
British East Africa
British North Borneo
British West Africa
Burma
Canada
Ceylon
Cyprus
Danish West Indies
Ethiopia
Falkland Islands
Ghana
Gibraltar
Gold Coast
Great Britain
Haiti
Hawaii
Hong Kong
India-British
Ireland
Isle Of Man
Mauritius
Middle Earth
New Guinea
New Zealand
Newfoundland
Palestine
Scotland
Sierra Leone
South Africa
Southern Rhodesia
Straits Settlements
Tibet
Yugoslavia
DAALDER - Netherlands
United States
DALA - Hawaii
DALER - Aland Islands
Norway
DECA - Atlantis
DENAR - Bermania
Hungary
DENARI - Bermania
DENARII - Liege
DENGA - Westeros
DENIER - France
Guadeloupe
Hungary
DENOMINATION - Sark Island
DINAR - Bahrain
Fujairah, Al
Iraq
Kurdistan
Kuwait
Saudi Arabia
Tarim
DINARA - Serbia And Bosnia
DINDERO - Spanish Colonial
DINER - Andorra
DIRHAM - Morocco
Saudi Arabia
United Arab Emirates
DOBRA - Saint Thomas & Prince Island
DOLLAR - Anguilla
Australia
Canada
China
China, Republic Of
Cocos (Keeling) Islands
Creek Nation
Danish West Indies
Eutopia
Freedonia
Great Britain
Grenada
Guam
Hawaii
Hong Kong
Hutt River Province
Liberia
Madagascar
Namibia
New Zealand
Northern Mariana Islands
Occussi - Ambeno
Philippines
Ross Island
Saint Croix
Sealand
Shawnee Tribal Nation
Solomon Islands
Somalia
Somaliland
Straits Settlements
Thailand
United States
Utopia - A World United
Westantarctica Territories
DOLLARS - Atlantis
China, People'S Republic
Minerva
DOLYA - Russia
DRAM - Armenia
Middle Earth
DUCAL - Avram
DUCALS - Avram
DUCAT - Austria
Austrian States
Czech Republic
Czechoslovakia
Estonia
German States
Germany - Federal Republic
Germany, Weimar Republic
Greece
Hungary
Italian States
Netherlands
Netherlands East Indies
Poland
Russia
Sweden
Swiss Cantons
Transylvania
DUCATEN - Europa
German States
DUCATONUnited Nations
DUCATSGermany - Federal Republic
DUKATBulgaria
Czechoslovakia
DUKATENCzechoslovakia
Europa
DUPEE - Paradise
EAGLE - Cherokee Nation
ECU - Albania
Austria
Belgium
British Honduras
Bulgaria
Czechoslovakia
Danish West Indies
Denmark
Europa
Finland
France
Great Britain
Greece
Greenland
Guadeloupe
Guernsey
Hungary
Iceland
Ireland Republic
Ireland-Northern
Isle Of Wight
Italy
Latvia
Liechtenstein
Luxembourg
Madeira Islands
Monaco
Netherlands
New France
Norway
Poland
Portugal
Russia
Scotland
Spain
Sweden
Switzerland
United Kingdom
Yugoslavia
ESCUDO - Bolivia
EURO - Albania
Alderney
Andorra
Armenia
Aruba
Austria
Balearic Islands
Belarus
Bulgaria
Canary Islands
Cape Verde
Cartago
Corsica Island
Crete
Croatia
Cyprus
Czech Republic
Denmark
Estonia
Faeroe Islands
Finland
France
French Antilles
French Guiana
French Southern & Antarctic Territories
Georgia
Gibraltar
Great Britain
Greece
Greenland
Guadeloupe
Guernsey
Hungary
Ireland Republic
Isle Of Man
Isle Of Wight

Israel
Italy
Jersey
Kosovo
Lapland
Latvia
Liechtenstein
Lithuania
Macedonia
Madeira Islands
Malta
Martinique
Mayotte
Moldova
Monaco
Mongolia
Montenegro
Netherlands
Netherlands Antilles
Norway
Poland
Portugal
Reunion
Romania
Russia
Russian Caucasia
Saint Barthelemy
Saint Helena
Saint Pierre & Miquelon
San Marino
Serbia
Siberia
Slovakia
Slovenia
Spain
Sweden
Turkey
Ukraine
United Kingdom
Vatican City
EUROP - Albania
Bulgaria
Iceland
Liechtenstein
Norway
Romania
Serbia
Switzerland
EUROPA - Europa
EUROPINOS - Europa
EYE - Middle Earth
FARTHING - Great Britain
Middle Earth
FED - Christiania
FIL - Fujairah, Al
Iraq
FINDIK - Egypt
FLEUR D'ARGENT - Saint Hildegard
FLORIN - Australia
Austria
Europa
Great Britain
Ireland
Saint Hildegard
FOAL - Middle Earth
FOLLIS - Saint Hildegard
FORINT - Croatia
Hungary
FRANC - Belgium
Belgium Moresnet
Burundi
Cambodia
Danish West Indies
France
French Guiana
Guadeloupe
Guinea
Kerguelen Islands
League Of Nations
Luxembourg
Madagascar
Monaco
New Caledonia
New Hebrides
Switzerland
Trebizond
Tunisia
FRANCS - Saint Barthelemy
FRANKEN - Liechtenstein
FUANG - Thailand
FURLANS - Friuli-Venezia Giulia
GALLEON - Great Britain
GASCON - France
GERAH - United States
GHIRSH - Saudi Arabia
GLOBE - United States
GOLD STANDARD UNIT - United States
GOLDGULDEN - German States
Hungary
GRAM - Hawaii
GRAMMES - India-British
India-Republic
GRAMO - Argentina
Bolivia
GRAMOS - Bolivia
GRAMS - China, People'S Republic
Hawaii
Singapore
Sri Lanka
GRANI - Malta, Order Of
GRIVENNIK - Russia
GRIVNA - Russia
GROATS - Great Britain
GROSCHEN - Hungary
GROSZ - Poland
GROSZE - Poland
GROSZY - Poland
GUARANI - Paraguay
GUINEA - India-British
Saudi Arabia
Scotland
GULDENAustria
German States
Latvia
GULDINERAustria
HALF-AS Camelot
HANDMiddle Earth
HELLERGerman States
HLOKARPENIMiddle Earth
HLOKARTHARANTIINMiddle Earth
HRIVNAUkraine
HRYVENUkraine
JAGOTHALERGerman States
JEDIDEgypt
JOULEUnited States
K'HLUK Kayless
KIROBOMadagascar
KLUMPChristiania
KNUTGreat Britain
KOPEKSpitzbergen
KORIIndia - Independent Kingdoms
KORONAHungary
KRANIran
KRANSIran
KREUZERAustria
German States
KRONE - Austria
KRONER - Denmark
Shetland Islands
KRONUR - Iceland
KROONI - Estonia
Mombasa
South Africa
KUNA - Croatia
KYAT - Burma
KYATS - Burma
LADY - Middle Earth
LEAF - Middle Earth
LEGA - Nord
LEI - Romania
LEMPIRAS - Honduras
LEONE - Belgium
LIBERTY DOLLARS - United States
LIP - Slovenia
LIPA - Slovenia
LIPE - Slovenia
LIRA - Malta, Order Of
LIRAS - Malta, Order Of
LIRE - Italian States
Italy
LITRE - Torgu
LIVRE - Guadeloupe
LøN - Christiania
LOUIS D'OR - New France
LOWE - Bophuthatswana
LUIGINO - Seborga
MACE - China
China, Republic Of
MALOTI - Lesotho
MARAVEDI - Danish West Indies
MARENGO - Italy
MARK - German States
Germany - Federal Republic
Germany, Weimar Republic
Germany-Empire
Namibia
Norway
Poland
Sweden
Wikingland
MARKA - Russia (Kaliningrad)
MATADES - Mozambique
MATHOM - Middle Earth
MERITI - Ragazzi
MERITO - Ragazzi
MIDEN - Nichtsburg - Zilchstadt
MILLE - Great Britain
MOHURIndia - Independent Kingdoms
India - Princely States
India-British
MONJapan
MUBurma
MUMAKMiddle Earth
MUMAKILMiddle Earth
MUNDINEROUnited States
MUNDINEROSUnited States
NGULTRUMBhutan
NKWEBophuthatswana
NON-DENOMINATED Christiania
Guadeloupe
Hong Kong
India - Princely States
Iran
Japan
Libya
Mexico
Morocco
Nepal
New York
Turkey
NUDGE - Purple Shaftieuland
NUMISMA - Kamberra Island
OBOL - Hungary
OBOLES - France
OCTORINO - Great Britain
OLIOPHAUNT - Middle Earth
ONE - Middle Earth
Westeros
ONZA - Armenia
Chile
Cuba
Mexico
ONZAS - Mexico
OUGUIYA - Mauritania
OUNCE - Argentina
Australia
Brazil
Burkina Faso
Canada
China, People'S Republic
China, Republic Of
Conch Republic
Dominican Republic
Egypt
Great Britain
Guatemala
Hawaii
Hong Kong
Latvia
Macao
Namibia
New Zealand
Russia
Singapore
South Africa
Spain
Switzerland
United States
Vanuatu
OUNCES - Australia
Brazil
Canada
Hawaii
Hong Kong
Utopia - A World United
PA'ANGA - Tonga
PAGODA - India - Princely States
PAHLAVI - Iran
PAISA - India - Independent Kingdoms
India - Princely States
PATACON - Argentina
PATAGON - Belgium
PAYOLA - United Transnational Republics
PENCE - Australia
Bermuda
Danish West Indies
Great Britain
Griquatown
Ireland
Isle Of Man
Middle Earth
South Africa
PENGO - Hungary
PENNIA - Finland
PENNY - Cape Of Good Hope
Danish West Indies
Great Britain
Griquatown
Middle Earth
New Zealand
Saint Hildegard
South Africa
United States
Vinland
Westeros
PESETA - Philippines
Spain
PESETAS - Spain
PESO - Andean Group
Araucania - Patagonia

Brazil
Central America
Central American States
Chile
Cuba
Dominican Republic
El Salvador
Guinea-Bissau
Mexico
Mexico-Revolutionary
New France
Uruguay
PESOS - Araucania - Patagonia
Cuba
PFENNIG - Germany - Federal Republic
Germany, Weimar Republic
Germany-Empire
PIASTER - Greenland
PIASTRE - Cambodia
Cyprus
Hejaz
Nejd
PIASTRES - Cyprus
Egypt
PIECES OF SEVEN - Middle Earth
PINCH - United States
POILS - Barbe Island
POLTINA - Russia
POND - South Africa
POUND - Cyprus
Ghana
Great Britain
Syria
Zamunda
PUELAHawaii
PUFFINLundy
PULWesteros
QUADRUBLEAlgeria
QUETZALGuatemala
QUETZALESGuatemala
RANDNamibia
REAL - Bolivia
El Salvador
Guatemala
Spanish Colonial
REALE - Danish West Indies
REALESArgentina
Brazil
British Honduras
Burma
Costa Rica
Danish West Indies
Ecuador
Egypt
El Salvador
Guatemala
Mexico
Paraguay
Peru
Spain
Spanish Colonial
Thailand
REALS - Brazil
REAUX - Philippines
REICHSMARK - Germany - Federal Republic
Germany, Third Reich
REIS - Brazil
Danish West Indies
RIAL - Yemen Mutawakkilite
RIKSDALER - Norway
RIXDOLLAR - Ceylon
RIYAL - Yemen Mutawakkilite
ROGER - New Island
RONDS - Switzerland
ROUBLE - Russia
Spitzbergen
Tajikistan
RUBLE - Armenia
Russia
RUBLES - Armenia
Azerbaijan
RUFIYAA - Maldive Islands
RUPAYA - India-British
RUPEE - Andaman Islands
Burma
China
Djibouti
India - Independent Kingdoms
India - Princely States
India-British
India-Republic
Pemba
Sharjah
RUPIAIndonesia
RYALHejaz
Oman
SANTIMBulgaria
SCHILLINGAustria
SCUDIMalta, Order Of
SCUDOItalian States
Malta, Order Of
Switzerland
SHAFTPurple Shaftieuland
SHEKELSIsrael
SHILINGITanzania
SHILLINGAustralia
Danish West Indies
Great Britain
Ireland
Isle Of Man
Jersey
Middle Earth
Saint Barthelemy
Somaliland
South Africa
Southern Rhodesia
SHO - China
Tibet
SICKLE - Great Britain
SIKA - Ghana
SILBERTALER - Switzerland
SILGOLD - Macao
SILIQUA - Camelot
SILVER FREEDOM - United States
SINGOLD - Singapore
SKALOJ - Atlantis
SOBERANO - Araucania - Patagonia
SOL - Bolivia
Brazil
France
Guadeloupe
New France
SOLE - Peru
SOLIDI - Atlantium
SOLIDUS - Camelot
SOM - Russian Caucasia
SOU - Guadeloupe
SOUVERAIN - Belgium
SOVEREIGN - Australia
Bermuda
British East Africa
British North Borneo
Burma
Canada
Ceylon
China, People'S Republic
Cyprus
Enderbyland
Falkland Islands
Gibraltar
Gold Coast
Great Britain
Hong Kong
Hutt River Province
India-British
Isle Of Man
Mauritius
Morocco
New Guinea
New Zealand
Newfoundland
Palestine
Sierra Leone
South Africa
Southern Rhodesia
Straits Settlements
SOVRANO - Malta, Order Of
SPESMILO - Esperanto
SPESMILOJ - Esperanto
SRANG - Tibet
STAG - Westeros
STAR - Westeros
STELO - Esperanto
STELOJ - Esperanto
SYLI - Guinea
TAEL - Burma
Canada
China
China, People'S Republic
China, Republic Of
Hong Kong
Netherlands East Indies
Tibet
TAELS - China
China, People'S Republic
TALARI - Ethiopia
TALENT - United States
TALER - Liechtenstein
TANGA - China
TARI - Malta, Order Of
TEST - Cambodia
TESTOON - Great Britain
Scotland
THALER - Austria
Djibouti
Europa
German States
Germany - Federal Republic
Hejaz
Hungary
Pemba
Poland
Portugal
Switzerland
THARANTIIN - Middle Earth
THARNI - Middle Earth
TICAL - Burma
Cambodia
TIEN - Viet Nam
TOLA - India-British
India-Republic
Nepal
Pakistan
TOLAS - India-British
India-Republic
TOMAN - Iran
Russian Caucasia
TOO WAH - United States
TRADE UNITS - United States
TREMISSIS - Saint Hildegard
TUGRIK - Mongolia
TUNAR - Outer Baldonia
TWIST - Purple Shaftieuland
UNCIA - Hungary
UNIVERSARO - United States
UNZE - Switzerland
UNZEN - Austria
Namibia
Switzerland
VAN - Viet Nam
VINAR - Slovenia
WEN - China
YEN - Japan
YUAN - China, Republic Of
ZECCHINI - Italian States
ZECCHINO - Italian States
Malta, Order Of
ZLOTYCH - Poland
ZOLOTNIK - Russia

How To Use This Catalog

This catalog series is designed to serve the needs of both the novice and advanced collectors. It provides a comprehensive guide to over 200 years of unusual world coinage. It is generally arranged alphabetically, under issuing country, as named on the coin. In just a few instances, where that name is a province, than those issues are listed under the main country, and then the individual provinces. The following explanations summarize the general practices used in preparing this catalog's listings. However, because of specialized requirements, which may vary by country and era, these must not be considered ironclad. Where these standards have been set aside, appropriate notations of the variations are incorporated in that particular listing.

ARRANGEMENT

Countries are arranged alphabetically. Political changes within a country are arranged chronologically. In countries where Rulers are the single most significant political entity a chronological arrangement by Ruler has been employed. Distinctive sub-geographic regions are listed alphabetically following the countries main listings. A few exceptions to these rules may exist. Please refer to the Country Index found elsewhere in this catalog.

Diverse coinage types relating to fabrication methods, revaluations, denomination systems, non-circulating categories such as patterns, pieforts and sets have been identified, separated and arranged in logical fashion. Chronological arrangement is employed for most circulating coinage, i.e., Monetary reforms will flow in order of their institution. Non-circulating types such as Essais, Pieforts, Patterns, Trial Strikes, Mint and Proof sets will follow the main listings, as will Medallic coinage and Token coinage.

Within a coinage type coins will be listed by denomination, from smallest to largest. Numbered types within a denomination will be ordered by their first date of issue.

IDENTIFICATION

The most important step in the identification of a coin is the determination of the nation of origin. This is generally easily accomplished where English-speaking lands are concerned, however, use of the country index is sometimes required. The coins of Great Britain provide an interesting challenge. For hundreds of years the only indication of the country of origin was in the abbreviated Latin legends. In recent times there have been occasions when there has been no indication of origin. Only through the familiarity of the monarchical portraits, symbols and legends or indication of currency system are they identifiable.

The coins of many countries beyond the English-language realm, such as those of French, Italian or Spanish heritage, are also quite easy to identify through reference to their legends, which appear in the national languages based on Western alphabets. In many instances the name is spelled exactly the same in English as in the national language, such as France; while in other cases it varies only slightly, like Italia for Italy, Belgique or Belgie for Belgium, Brasil for Brazil and Danmark for Denmark.

This is not always the case, however, as in Norge for Norway, Espana for Spain, Sverige for Sweden and Helvetia for Switzerland. Some other examples include:

DEUTSCHES REICH - Germany 1873-1945

BUNDESREPUBLIC DEUTSCHLAND - Federal Republic of Germany.

DEUTSCHE DEMOKRATISCHE REPUBLIK - German Democratic Republic.

EMPIRE CHERIFIEN MAROC - Morocco.

ESTADOS UNIDOS MEXICANOS - United Mexican States (Mexico).

ETAT DU GRAND LIBAN - State of Great Lebanon (Lebanon).

Thus it can be seen there are instances in which a little schooling in the rudiments of foreign languages can be most helpful. In general, colonial possessions of countries using the Western alphabet are similarly identifiable as they often carry portraits of their current rulers, the familiar lettering, sometimes in combination with a companion designation in the local language.

Collectors have the greatest difficulty with coins that do not bear legends or dates in the Western systems. These include coins bearing Cyrillic lettering, attributable to Bulgaria, Russia, the Slavic states and Mongolia, the Greek script peculiar to Greece, Crete and the Ionian Islands; The Amharic characters of Ethiopia, or Hebrew in the case of Israel. Dragons and sunbursts along with the distinctive word characters attribute a coin to the Oriental countries of China, Japan, Korea, Tibet, Viet Nam and their component parts.

The most difficult coins to identify are those bearing only Persian or Arabic script and its derivatives, found on the issues of nations stretching in a wide swath across North Africa and East Asia, from Morocco to Indonesia, and the Indian subcontinent coinages which surely are more confusing in their vast array of Nagari, Sanskrit, Ahom, Assamese and other local dialects found on the local issues of the Indian Princely States. Although the task of identification on the more modern issues of these lands is often eased by the added presence of Western alphabet legends, a feature sometimes adopted as early as the late 19th Century, for the earlier pieces it is often necessary for the uninitiated to laboriously seek and find.

Except for the cruder issues, however, it will be found that certain characteristics and symbols featured in addition to the predominant legends are typical on coins from a given country or group of countries. The toughra monogram, for instance, occurs on some of the coins of Afghanistan, Egypt, the Sudan, Pakistan, Turkey and other areas of the late Ottoman Empire. A predominant design feature on the coins of Nepal is the trident; while neighboring Tibet features a lotus blossom or lion on many of their issues.

Coins from some fantasy lands often carry unique languages. The fantasy relms of Middle Earth, for example, use elvish and other languages unique to those places as created by J.R.R. Tolkein.

We also suggest reference to the Index of Coin Denominations presented here and also the comprehensive Country Index, where the inscription will be found listed just as it appears on the coin for nations using the Western alphabet.

DATING

Coin dating is the final basic attribution consideration. Here, the problem can be more difficult because the reading of a coin date is subject not only to the vagaries of numeric styling, but to calendar variations caused by the observance of various religious eras or regal periods from country to country, or even within a country. Here again with the exception of the sphere from North Africa through the Orient, it will be found that most countries rely on Western date numerals and Christian (AD) era reckoning, although in a few instances, coin dating has been tied to the year of a reign or government. The Vatican, for example dates its coinage according to the year of reign of the current pope, in addition to the Christian-era date.

Countries in the Arabic sphere generally date their coins to the Muslim era (AH), which commenced on July 16, 622 AD (Julian calendar), when the prophet Mohammed fled from Mecca to Medina. As their calendar is reckoned by the lunar year of 354 days, which is about three percent (precisely 2.98%) shorter than the Christian year, a formula is required to convert AH dating to its Western equivalent. To convert an AH date to the approximate AD date, subtract three percent of the AH date (round to the closest whole number) from the AH date and add 622. A chart converting all AH years from 1010 (July 2, 1601) to 1421 (May 25, 2028) is presented as the Heijra Chart on page 35.

The Muslim calendar is not always based on the lunar year (AH), however, causing some confusion, particularly in Afghanistan and Iran, where a calendar based on the solar year (SH) was introduced around 1920. These dates can be converted to AD by simply adding 621. In 1976 the government of Iran implemented a new solar calendar based on the foundation of the Iranian monarchy in 559 BC. The first year observed on the new calendar was 2535 (MS), which commenced March 20, 1976. A reversion to the traditional SH dating standard occurred a few years later.

Several different eras of reckoning, including Christian and Muslim (AH), have been used to date coins of the Indian subcontinent. The two basic systems are the Vikrama Samvat (VS), which dates from Oct. 18, 58 BC, and the Saka era, the origin of which is reckoned from March 3, 78 AD. Dating according to both eras appears on various coins of the area.

Coins of Thailand (Siam) are found dated by three different eras. The most predominant is the Buddhist era (BE), which originated in 543 BC. Next is the Bangkok or Ratanakosindsok (RS) era, dating from 1781 AD; followed by the Chula-Sakarat (CS) era, dating from 638 AD. The latter era originated in Burma and is used on that country's coins.

Other calendars include that of the Ethiopian era (EE), which commenced seven years, eight months after AD dating; and that of the Jewish people, which commenced on Oct. 7, 3761 BC. Korea claims a legendary dating from 2333 BC, which is acknowledged in some of its coin dating. Some coin issues of the Indonesian area carry dates determined by the Javanese Aji Saka era (AS), a calendar of 354 days (100 Javanese years equal 97 Christian or Gregorian calendar years), which can be matched to AD dating by comparing it to AH dating.

The following table indicates the year dating for the various eras, which correspond to 2005 in Christian calendar reckoning, but it must be remembered that there are overlaps between the eras in some instances.

Christian era (AD)	-2007
Muslim era (AH)	-AH1428
Solar year (SH)	-SH1385
Monarchic Solar era (MS)	-MS25664
Vikrama Samvat (VS)	-VS2064
Saka era (SE)	-SE1929
Buddhist era (BE)	-BE2550
Bangkok era (RS)	-RS226
Chula-Sakarat era (CS)	-CS1369
Ethiopian era (EE)	-EE2001
Korean era	-4340
Javanese Aji Saka era (AS)	-AS1940
Fasli era (FE)	-FE1417
Jewish era (JE)	-JE5767

Coins of Asian origin - principally Japan, Korea, China, Turkestan and Tibet and some modern gold issues of Turkey - are generally dated to the year of the government, dynasty, reign or cyclic eras, with the dates indicated in Asian characters which usually read from right to left. In recent years, however, some dating has been according to the Christian calendar and in Western numerals. In Japan, Asian character dating was reversed to read from left to right in Showa year 23 (1948 AD).

More detailed guides to less prevalent coin dating systems, which are strictly local in nature, are presented with the appropriate listings.

Some coins carry dates according to both locally observed and Christian eras. This is particularly true in the Arabic world, where the Hejira date may be indicated in Arabic numerals and the Christian date in Western numerals, or both dates in either form.

The date actually carried on a given coin is generally cataloged here in the first column (Date) to the right of the catalog number. If this date is by a non-Christian dating system, such as 'AH'(Muslim), the Christian equivalent date will appear in parentheses(), for example AH1336(1917). Dates listed alone in the date column which do not actually appear on a given coin, or dates which are known, but do not appear on the coin, are generally enclosed by parentheses with 'ND' at the left, for example ND(1926).

Timing differentials between some era of reckoning, particularly the 354-day Mohammedan and 365-day Christian years, cause situations whereby coins which carry dates for both eras exist bearing two year dates from one calendar combined with a single date from another.

Countermarked Coinage is presented with both 'Countermark Date' and 'Host Coin' date for each type. Actual date representation follows the rules outlined above.

NUMBERING SYSTEM

Items listed in this catalog mostly carry an X# prefix. In addition, some still carry KM# prefixes. These generally have been previously listed in the Standard Catalog series of books. When number prefixes have changed, the previous number is incorporated in the listing as a cross reference. Some Chinese coins include references to E. Kann's (K#) Illustrated Catalog of Chinese Coins and T.K. Hsu's (Su) work of similar title.

The use of additional prefix letters in the catalog number often describe the coinage types: M for Medallic (items struck to a standard denomination size and weight, but lacking denomination in the design), MB for Medallic Bullion (struck to a bullion weight standard of 1/10, 1/4, 1/2, or Ounce and its multiples), P for Piefort (a double weight coin) or Pn for Pattern. These designations have previously been used in the Standard Catalog series and have been continued here.

DENOMINATIONS

The second basic consideration to be met in the attribution of a coin is the determination of denomination. Since denominations are usually expressed in numeric, rather than word form on a coin, this is usually quite easily accomplished on coins from nations, which use Western numerals, except in those instances where issues are devoid of any mention of face value, and denomination must be attributed by size, metallic composition or weight. Coins listed in this volume are generally illustrated in actual size. Where size is critical to proper attribution, the coin's millimeter size is indicated.

The sphere of countries stretching from North Africa through the Orient, on which numeric symbols generally unfamiliar to Westerners are employed, often provide the collector with a much greater challenge. This is particularly true on nearly all pre-20th Century issues. On some of the more modern issues and increasingly so as the years progress, Western-style numerals usually presented in combination with the local numeric system are becoming more commonplace on these coins.

Determination of a coin's currency system can also be valuable in attributing the issue to its country of origin. A comprehensive alphabetical index of currency names, applicable to the countries as cataloged in this volume, with all individual nations of use for each, is presented in this section.

The included table of Standard International Numeral Systems presents charts of the basic numeric designations found on coins of non-Western origin. Although denomination numerals are generally prominently displayed on coins, it must be remembered that these are general representations of characters, which individual coin engravers may have rendered in widely varying styles. Where numeric or script denominations designation forms peculiar to a given coin or country apply, such as the script used on some Persian (Iranian) issues. They are so indicated or illustrated in conjunction with the appropriate listings.

MINTAGES

Quantities minted of each date are indicated where that information is available. For combined mintage figures the abbreviation "Inc. Above" means Included Above, while "Inc. Below" means Included Below. "Est." beside a mintage figure indicates the number given is an estimate or mintage limit.

MINT AND PRIVY MARKS

The presence of distinctive, but frequently inconspicuously placed, mintmarks indicates the mint of issue for many of the coins listed in this catalog. An appropriate designation in the date listings notes the presence, if any, of a mint mark on a particular coin type by incorporating the letter or letters of the mint mark adjoining the date, i.e., 1950D or 1927R.

The presence of mint and/or mintmaster's privy marks on a coin in non-letter form is indicated by incorporating the mint letter in lower case within parentheses adjoining the date; i.e. 1927(a). The corresponding mark is illustrated or identified in the introduction of the country.

In countries such as France and Mexico, where many mints may be producing like coinage in the same denomination during the same time period, divisions by mint have been employed. In these cases the mint mark may appear next to the individual date listings and/or the mint name or mint mark may be listed in the Note field of the type description.

Where listings incorporate mintmaster initials, they are always presented in capital letters separated from the date by one character space; i.e., 1850 MF. The different mintmark and mintmaster letters found on the coins of any country, state or city of issue are always shown at the beginning of listings.

METALS

Each numbered type listing will contain a description of the coins metallic content. The traditional coinage metals and their symbolic chemical abbreviations sometimes used in this catalog are:

Platinum - (PT)	Copper - (Cu)
Gold - (Au)	Brass -
Silver - (Ag)	Copper-nickel- (CN)
Billion -	Lead - (Pb)
Nickel - (Ni)	Steel -
Zinc - (Zn)	Tin - (Sn)
Bronze - (Ae)	Aluminum - (Al)

During the 18th and 19th centuries, most of the world's coins were struck of copper or bronze, silver and gold. Commencing in the early years of the 20th century, however, numerous new coinage metals, primarily non-precious metal alloys, were introduced. Gold has not been widely used for circulation coinages since World War I, although silver remained a popular coinage metal in most parts of the world until after World War II. With the disappearance of silver for circulation coinage, numerous additional compositions were introduced to coinage applications.

Most recent is the development of clad or plated planchets in order to maintain circulation life and extend the life of a set of production dies as used in the production of the copper-nickel clad copper 50 centesimos of Panama or in the latter case to reduce production costs of the planchets and yet provide a coin quite similar in appearance to its predecessor as in the case of the copper plated zinc core United States 1983 cent.

Modern commemorative coins have employed still more unusual methods such as bimetallic coins, color applications and precious metal or gem inlays.

OFF-METAL STRIKES

Off-metal strikes previously designated by "(OMS)" which also included the wide range of error coinage struck in other than their officially authorized compositions have been incorporated into Pattern listings along with special issues, which were struck for presentation or other reasons.

Collectors of Germanic coinage may be familiar with the term "Abschlag" which quickly identifies similar types of coinage.

PRECIOUS METAL WEIGHTS

Listings of weight, fineness and actual silver (ASW), gold (AGW), platinum or palladium (APW) content of most machine-struck silver, gold, platinum and palladium coins are provided in this edition. This information will be found incorporated in each separate type listing, along with other data related to the coin.

The ASW, AGW and APW figures were determined by multiplying the gross weight of a given coin by its known or tested fineness and converting the resulting gram or grain weight to troy ounces, rounded to the nearest ten-thousandth of an ounce. A silver coin with a 24.25-gram weight and .875 fineness for example, would have a fine weight of approximately 21.2188 grams, or a .6822 ASW, a factor that can be used to accurately determine the intrinsic value for multiple examples.

The ASW, AGW or APW figure can be multiplied by the spot price of each precious metal to determine the current intrinsic value of any coin accompanied by these designations.

Coin weights are indicated in grams (abbreviated "g") along with fineness where the information is of value in differentiating between types. These weights are based on 31.103 grams per troy (scientific) ounce, as opposed to the avoirdupois (commercial) standard of 28.35 grams. Actual coin weights are generally shown in hundredths or thousands of a gram; i.e., 0.500 SILVER 2.9200g.

WEIGHTS AND FINENESSES

As the silver and gold bullion markets have advanced and declined sharply in recent years, the fineness and total precious metal content of coins has become especially significant where bullion coins - issues which trade on the basis of their intrinsic metallic content rather than numismatic value - are concerned. In many instances, such issues have become worth more in bullion form than their nominal collector values or denominations indicate.

Establishing the weight of a coin can also be valuable for determining its denomination. Actual weight is also necessary to ascertain the specific gravity of the coin's metallic content, an important factor in determining authenticity.

TROY WEIGHT STANDARDS

24 Grains = 1 Pennyweight
480 Grains = 1 Ounce
31.103 Grams = 1 Ounce

UNIFORM WEIGHTS

15.432 Grains = 1 Gram
0.0648 Gram = 1 Grain

AVOIRDUPOIS STANDARDS

27-11/32 Grains = 11 Dram
437-1/2 Grains = 1 Ounce
28.350 Grams = 1 Ounce

BULLION VALUE CHARTS

Universal silver, gold, and platinum bullion value charts are provided for use in combination with the ASW, AGW and APW factors to determine approximate intrinsic values of listed coins. By adding the component weights as shown in troy ounces on each chart, the approximate intrinsic value of any silver, gold or platinum coin's precious metal content can be determined.

Again referring to the examples presented in the above section, the intrinsic value of a silver coin with a .6822 ASW would be indicated as $4.43 + based on the application of the silver bullion chart. This result is obtained by moving across the top to the $6.50 column, then moving down to the line indicated .680 in the far left hand corner which reveals a bullion value of $4.420. To determine the value of the remaining .0022 of ASW, return up the same column to the .002 line, the closest factor available, where a $ .0130 value is indicted. The two factors total $4.433, which would be slightly less than actual value.

The silver bullion chart provides silver values in thousandths from .001 to .009 troy ounce, and in hundredths from .01 to 1.00 in 50¢ value increments from $3.00 to $10.50. If the market value of silver exceeds $10.50, doubling the increments presented will provide valuations in $1 steps from $6.00 to $21.00.

The gold/platinum bullion chart is similarly arranged in $10 increments from $350 to $490, and by doubling the increments presented, $20 steps from $700 to $980 can be determined.

Valuations for most of the silver, gold, platinum and palladium coins listed in this edition are based on assumed market values of $6.85 per troy ounce for silver, $430 for gold, $860 for platinum, and $185 for palladium. To arrive at accurate current market indications for these issues, increase or decrease the valuations appropriately based on any variations in these indicated levels.

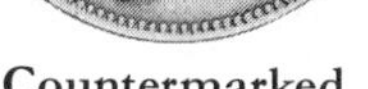
Countermarked

Counterstamped

COUNTERMARKS/COUNTERSTAMPS

There is some confusion among collectors over the terms "countermark" and "counterstamp" when applied to a coin bearing an additional mark or change of design and/or denomination.

To clarify, a countermark might be considered similar to the "hall mark" applied to a piece of silverware, by which a silversmith assured the quality of the piece. In the same way, a countermark assures the quality of the coin on which it is placed, as, for example, when the royal crown of England was countermarked (punched into) on segmented Spanish reales, allowing them to circulate in commerce in the British West Indies. An additional countermark indicating the new denomination may also be encountered on these coins.

Countermarks are generally applied singularly and in most cases indiscriminately on either side of the "host" coin.

Counterstamped coins are more extensively altered. The counterstamping is done with a set of dies, rather than a hand punch. The coin being counterstamped is placed between the new dies and struck as if it were a blank planchet as found with the Manila 8 reales issue of the Philippines. A more unusual application where the counterstamp dies were smaller than the host coin in the revalidated 50 centimos and 1 colon of Costa Rica issued in 1923.

PHOTOGRAPHS

To assist the reader in coin identification, every effort has been made to present actual size photographs. Obverse and reverse are

Coin Alignment

Medal Alignment

COIN vs MEDAL ALIGNMENT

Some coins are struck with obverse and reverse aligned at a rotation of 180 degrees from each other. When a coin is held for vertical viewing with the obverse design aligned upright and the index finger and thumb at the top and bottom, upon rotation from left to right for viewing the reverse, the latter will be upside down. Such alignment is called "coin rotation." Other coins are struck with the obverse and reverse designs mated on an alignment of zero or 360 degrees. If such an example is held and rotated as described, the reverse will appear upright. This is the alignment, which is generally observed in the striking of medals, and for that reason coins produced in this manner are considered struck in "medal rotation". In some instances, often through error, certain coin issues have been struck to both alignment standards, creating interesting collectible varieties, which will be found noted in some listings. In addition, some countries are now producing coins with other designated overse to reverse alignments which are considered standard for tis type.

illustrated, except when a change in design is restricted to one side, and the coin has a diameter of 39mm or larger, in which case only the side required for identification of the type is generally illustrated. All coins up to 57mm are illustrated actual size, to the nearest 1/2mm up to 25mm, and to the nearest 1mm thereafter. Coins larger than 57mm diameter are illustrated in reduced size, with the actual size noted in the descriptive text block. Where slight change in size is important to coin type identification, actual millimeter measurements are stated.

VALUATIONS

Values quoted in this catalog represent the current market and are compiled from recommendations provided and verified through various source documents and specialized consultants. It should be stressed, however, that this book is intended to serve only as an aid for evaluating coins, actual market conditions are constantly changing and additional influences, such as particularly strong local demand for certain coin series, fluctuation of international exchange rates and worldwide collection patterns must also be considered. Publication of this catalog is not intended as a solicitation by the publisher, editors or contributors to buy or sell the coins listed at the prices indicated.

All valuations are stated in U.S. dollars, based on careful assessment of the varied international collector market. Valuations for coins priced below $100.00 are generally stated in full amounts - i.e. 37.50 or 95.00 - while valuations at or above that figure are rounded off in even dollars - i.e. $125.00 is expressed 125. A comma is added to indicate thousands of dollars in value.

For the convenience of overseas collectors and for U.S. collectors doing business with overseas dealers, the base exchange rate for the national currencies of approximately 180 countries are presented in the Foreign Exchange Table.

It should be noted that when particularly select uncirculated or proof-like examples of uncirculated coins become available they can be expected to command proportionately high premiums. Such examples in reference to choice Germanic Thalers are referred to as "erst schlage" or first strikes.

TOKEN COINAGE

At times local economic conditions have forced regular coinage from circulation or found mints unable to cope with the demand for coinage, giving rise to privately issued token coinage substitutes. British tokens of the late 1700s and early 1880s, and the German and French and French Colonial emergency emissions of the World War I era are examples of such tokens being freely accepted in monetary transactions over wide areas. Tokens were likewise introduced to satisfy specific restricted needs, such as the leper colony issues of Brazil, Colombia and the Philippines.

This catalog includes introductory or detailed listings with "Tn" prefixes of many token coinage issues, particularly those which enjoyed wide circulation and where the series was limited in diversity. More complex series, and those more restricted in scope of circulation are generally not listed, although a representative sample may be illustrated and a specialty reference provided.

MEDALLIC ISSUES

Medallic issues are segregated following the regular issue listings. Grouped there are coin-type issues, which can generally be identified as commemoratives produced to the country's established coinage standards but without the usual indicator of denomination. These pieces may or may not feature designs adapted from the country's regular issue or commemorative coinage, and may or may not have been issued in conjunction with related coinage issues.

RESTRIKES, COUNTERFEITS

Deceptive restrike and counterfeit (both contemporary and modern) examples exist of some coin issues. Where possible, the existence of restrikes is noted. Warnings are also incorporated in instances where particularly deceptive counterfeits are known to exist. Collectors who are uncertain about the authenticity of a coin held in their collection, or being offered for sale, should take the precaution of having the coin authenticated by a third-party grading service.

NON-CIRCULATING LEGAL TENDER COINS

Coins of non-circulating legal tender (NCLT) origin are individually listed and integrated by denomination into the regular listings for each country. These coins fall outside the customary definitions of coin-of-the-realm issues, but where created and sold by, or under authorization of, agencies of sovereign governments expressly for collectors. These are primarily individual coins and sets of a commemorative nature, marketed at prices substantially in excess of face value, and usually do not have counterparts released for circulation.

EDGE VARIETIES

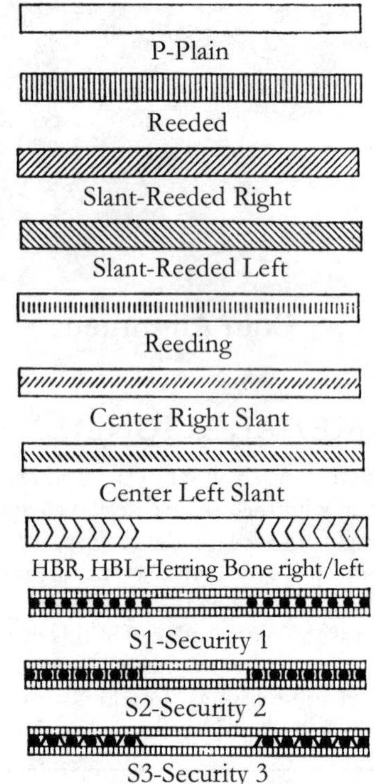

SETS

Listings in this catalog for specimen, proof and mint sets are for official, government-produced sets. In many instances privately packaged sets also exist.

Mint Sets/Fleur de Coin Sets: Specially prepared by worldwide mints to provide banks, collectors and government dignitaries with examples of current coinage. Usually subjected to rigorous inspection to insure that top quality specimens of selected business strikes are provided.

The Paris Mint introduced polyvinyl plastic cases packed within a cardboard box for homeland and colonial Fleur de Coin sets of the 1960s. British colonial sets were issued in velvet-lined metal cases similar to those used for proof sets. For its client nations, the Franklin Mint introduced a sealed composition of cardboard and specially molded hard clear plastic protective container inserted in a soft plastic wallet. Recent discovery that soft polyvinyl packaging has proved hazardous to coins has resulted in a change to the use of hard, inert plastics for virtually all mint sets.

Some of the highest quality mint sets ever produced were those struck by the Franklin Mint during 1972-74. In many cases matte finish dies were used to strike a polished proof planchet. Later on, from 1975, sets contained highly polished, glassy-looking coins (similar to those struck by the Bombay Mint) for collectors over a period of 12 years.

Specimen Sets: Forerunners of today's proof sets. In most cases the coins were specially struck, perhaps even double struck, to produce a very soft or matte finish on the effigies and fields, along with high, sharp, "wire" rims. The finish is rather dull to the naked eye.

The original purpose of these sets was to provide VIPs, monarchs and mintmasters around the world with samples of the highest quality workmanship of a particular mint. These were usually housed in elaborate velvet-lined leather and metal cases.

Proof Sets: This is undoubtedly among the most misused terms in the hobby, not only by collectors and dealers, but also by many of the world mints.

A true proof set must be at least double-struck on specially prepared polished planchets and struck using dies (often themselves polished) of the highest quality.

Modern-day proof quality consists of frosted effigies surrounded by absolute mirror-like fields.

Listings for proof sets in this catalog are for officially issued proof sets so designated by the issuing authority, and may or may not possess what are considered modern proof quality standards.

It is necessary for collectors to acquire the knowledge to allow them to differentiate true proof sets from would-be proof sets and proof-like sets which may be encountered.

CONDITIONS/GRADING

Wherever possible, coin valuations are given in four or five grades of preservation. For modern commemoratives, which do not circulate, only uncirculated values are usually sufficient. Proof issues are indicated by the word "Proof" next to the date, with valuation proceeded by the word "value" following the mintage. For very recent circulating coins and coins of limited value, one, two or three grade values are presented.

There are almost no grading guides for world coins. What follows is an attempt to help bridge that gap until a detailed, illustrated guide becomes available.

In grading world coins, there are two elements to look for: 1) Overall wear, and 2) loss of design details, such as strands of hair, feathers on eagles, designs on coats of arms, etc.

The age, rarity or type of a coin should not be a consideration in grading.

Grade each coin by the weaker of the two sides. This method appears to give results most nearly consistent with conservative American Numismatic Association standards for U.S. coins. Split grades, i.e., F/VF for obverse and reverse, respectively, are normally no more than one grade apart. If the two sides are more than one grade apart, the series of coins probably wears differently on each side and should then be graded by the weaker side alone.

Grade by the amount of overall wear and loss of design detail evident on each side of the coin. On coins with a moderately small design element, which is prone to early wear, grade by that design alone. For example, the 5-ore (KM#554) of Sweden has a crown above the monogram on which the beads on the arches show wear most clearly. So, grade by the crown alone.

For **Brilliant Uncirculated** (BU) grades there will be no visible signs of wear or handling, even under a 30-power microscope. Full mint luster will be present. Ideally no bags marks will be evident.

For **Uncirculated** (Unc.) grades there will be no visible signs of wear or handling, even under a 30-power microscope. Bag marks may be present.

For **Almost Uncirculated** (AU), all detail will be visible. There will be wear only on the highest point of the coin. There will often be half or more of the original mint luster present.

On the **Extremely Fine** (XF or EF) coin, there will be about 95% of the original detail visible. Or, on a coin with a design with no inner detail to wear down, there will be a light wear over nearly all the coin. If a small design is used as the grading area, about 90% of the original detail will be visible. This latter rule stems from the logic that a smaller amount of detail needs to be present because a small area is being used to grade the whole coin.

The **Very Fine** (VF) coin will have about 75% of the original detail visible. Or, on a coin with no inner detail, there will be moderate wear over the entire coin. Corners of letters and numbers may be weak. A small grading area will have about 66% of the original detail.

For **Fine** (F), there will be about 50% of the original detail visible. Or, on a coin with no inner detail, there will be fairly heavy wear over all of the coin. Sides of letters will be weak. A typically uncleaned coin will often appear as dirty or dull. A small grading area will have just under 50% of the original detail.

On the **Very Good** (VG) coin, there will be about 25% of the original detail visible. There will be heavy wear on all of the coin.

The **Good** (G) coin's design will be clearly outlined but with substantial wear. Some of the larger detail may be visible. The rim may have a few weak spots of wear.

On the **About Good** (AG) coin, there will typically be only a silhouette of a large design. The rim will be worn down into the letters if any.

Strong or weak strikes, partially weak strikes, damage, corrosion, attractive or unattractive toning, dipping or cleaning should be described along with the above grades. These factors affect the quality of the coin just as do wear and loss of detail, but are easier to describe.

In the case of countermarked/counterstamped coins, the condition of the host coin will have a bearing on the end valuation. The important factor in determining the grade is the condition, clarity and completeness of the countermark itself. This is in reference to countermarks/counterstamps having raised design while being struck in a depression.

Incuse countermarks cannot be graded for wear. They are graded by the clarity and completeness including the condition of the host coin which will also have more bearing on the final grade/valuation determined.

We Welcome Correspondence, but...

Thanks for your interest in our fifth edition of Unusual World Coins book. As you know, this is an ever-growing and ever-changing field. Do you have questions as to why the editors listed a particular item in a particular place? Do you know of items that we have missed and should be listed in a future edition? Do you have items that we list but are lacking proper descriptions or an illustration?

We welcome correspondence via traditional mail or e-mail.

However, we need contributions to arrive in the most practical form for immediate use.

Descriptions of items need to include diameter size in millimeters, weight in grams, metal and fineness if a precious metal. Descriptions should include design elements; identifications of portraits or events; legends as they appear on the item. Edge descriptions such as: plain, reeded or lettered, and in the case of lettering, the edge legend as it appears on the item. Mint mark, mint name, mintage, availability and pricing by grade would then round out a listing.

If we are listing an item in one location, and you feel strongly it should be listed in another area, we welcome correspondence and want to hear your views. If we have missed something entirely, we encourage your correspondence and listings. But please start with an initial contact of intent on doing something, before you work really hard on doing something that we may have already done ourselves or is being worked on by another contributor.

Scans need to be 300 dpi jpgs or tiffs and at 100% of actual size. You may send them as email attachments to: uwc@fwpubs.com or send them on a CD disc to us at: Randy Thern, F+W Publications, 700 E. State St., Iola, WI 54990 USA. Items will then be directed to the proper editors.

Do not send in actual numismatic items unsolicited. We will request items for original photography in correspondence.

HEJIRA DATE CONVERSION CHART

HEJIRA DATE CONVERSION CHART JEHIRA DATE CHART

HEJIRA (Hijira, Hegira), the name of the Muslim era (A.H. = Anno Hegirae) dates back to the Christian year 622 when Mohammed "fled" from Mecca, escaping to Medina to avoid persecution from the Koreish tribemen. Based on a lunar year the Muslim year is 11 days shorter.
*=Leap Year (Christian Calendar)

AH Hejira	AD Christian Date
1010	1601, July 2
1011	1602, June 21
1012	1603, June 11
1013	1604, May 30
1014	1605, May 19
1015	1606, May 19
1016	1607, May 9
1017	1608, April 28
1018	1609, April 6
1017	1608, April 28
1018	1609, April 6
1019	1610, March 26
1020	1611, March 16
1021	1612, March 4
1022	1613, February 21
1023	1614, February 11
1024	1615, January 31
1025	1616, January 20
1026	1617, January 9
1027	1617, December 29
1028	1618, December 19
1029	1619, December 8
1030	1620, November 26
1031	1621, November 16
1032	1622, November 5
1033	1623, October 25
1034	1624, October 14
1035	1625, October 3
1036	1626, September 22
1037	1627, Septembe 12
1038	1628, August 31
1039	1629, August 21
1040	1630, July 10
1041	1631, July 30
1042	1632, July 19
1043	1633, July 8
1044	1634, June 27
1045	1635, June 17
1046	1636, June 5
1047	1637, May 26
1048	1638, May 15
1049	1639, May 4
1050	1640, April 23
1051	1641, April 12
1052	1642, April 1
1053	1643, March 22
1054	1644, March 10
1055	1645, February 27
1056	1646, February 17
1057	1647, February 6
1058	1648, January 27
1059	1649, January 15
1060	1650, January 4
1061	1650, December 25
1062	1651, December 14
1063	1652, December 2
1064	1653, November 22
1065	1654, November 11
1066	1655, October 31
1067	1656, October 20
1068	1657, October 9
1069	1658, September 29
1070	1659, September 18
1071	1660, September 6
1072	1661, August 27
1073	1662, August 16
1074	1663, August 5
1075	1664, July 25
1076	1665, July 14
1077	1666, July 4
1078	1667, June 23
1079	1668, June 11
1080	1669, June 1
1081	1670, May 21
1082	1671, may 10
1083	1672, April 29
1084	1673, April 18
1085	1674, April 7
1086	1675, March 28
1087	1676, March 16*

AH Hejira	AD Christian Date
1088	1677, March 6
1089	1678, February 23
1090	1679, February 12
1091	1680, February 2*
1092	1681, January 21
1093	1682, January 10
1094	1682, December 31
1095	1683, December 20
1096	1684, December 8*
1097	1685, November 28
1098	1686, November 17
1099	1687, November 7
1100	1688, October 26*
1101	1689, October 15
1102	1690, October 5
1103	1691, September 24
1104	1692, September 12*
1105	1693, September 2
1106	1694, August 22
1107	1695, August 12
1108	1696, July 31*
1109	1697, July 20
1110	1698, July 10
1111	1699, June 29
1112	1700, June 18
1113	1701, June 8
1114	1702, May 28
1115	1703, May 17
1116	1704, May 6*
1117	1705, April 25
1118	1706, April 15
1119	1707, April 4
1120	1708, March 23*
1121	1709, March 13
1122	1710, March 2
1123	1711, February 19
1124	1712, Feburary 9*
1125	1713, January 28
1126	1714, January 17
1127	1715, January 7
1128	1715, December 27
1129	1716, December 16*
1130	1717, December 5
1131	1718, November 24
1132	1719, November 14
1133	1720, November 2*
1134	1721, October 22
1135	1722, October 12
1136	1723, October 1
1137	1724, September 19
1138	1725, September 9
1139	1726, August 29
1140	1727, August 19
1141	1728, August 7*
1142	1729, July 27
1143	1730, July 17
1144	1731, July 6
1145	1732, June 24*
1146	1733, June 14
1147	1734, June 3
1148	1735, May 24
1149	1736, May 12*
1150	1737, May 1
1151	1738, April 21
1152	1739, April 10
1153	1740, March 29*
1154	1741, March 19
1155	1742, March 8
1156	1743, Febuary 25
1157	1744, February 15*
1158	1745, February 3
1159	1746, January 24
1160	1747, January 13
1161	1748, January 2
1162	1748, December 22*
1163	1749, December 11
1164	1750, November 30
1165	1751, November 20
1166	1752, November 8*
1167	1753, October 29
1168	1754, October 18
1169	1755, October 7
1170	1756, September 26*
1171	1757, September 15
1172	1758, September 4
1173	1759, August 25
1174	1760, August 13*
1175	1761, August 2
1176	1762, July 23
1177	1763, July 12

AH Hejira	AD Christian Date
1178	1764, July 1*
1179	1765, June 20
1180	1766, June 9
1181	1767, May 30
1182	1768, May 18*
1183	1769, May 7
1184	1770, April 27
1185	1771, April 16
1186	1772, April 4*
1187	1773, March 25
1188	1774, March 14
1189	1775, March 4
1190	1776, February 21*
1191	1777, February 91
1192	1778, January 30
1193	1779, January 19
1194	1780, January 8*
1195	1780, December 28*
1196	1781, December 17
1197	1782, December 7
1198	1783, November 26
1199	1784, November 14*
1200	1785, November 4
1201	1786, October 24
1202	1787, October 13
1203	1788, October 2*
1204	1789, September 21
1205	1790, September 10
1206	1791, August 31
1207	1792, August 19*
1208	1793, August 9
1209	1794, July 29
1210	1795, July 18
1211	1796, July 7*
1212	1797, June 26
1213	1798, June 15
1214	1799, June 5
1215	1800, May 25
1216	1801, May 14
1217	1802, May 4
1218	1803, April 23
1219	1804, April 12*
1220	1805, April 1
1221	1806, March 21
1222	1807, March 11
1223	1808, February 28*
1224	1809, February 16
1225	1810, Febauary 6
1226	1811, January 26
1227	1812, January 16*
1228	1813, Janaury 26
1229	1813, December 24
1230	1814, December 14
1231	1815, December 3
1232	1816, November 21*
1233	1817, November 11
1234	1818, October 31
1235	1819, October 20
1236	1820, October 9*
1237	1821, September 28
1238	1822, September 18
1239	1823, September 18
1240	1824, August 26*
1241	1825, August 16
1242	1826, August 5
1243	1827, July 25
1244	1828, July 14*
1245	1829, July 3
1246	1830, June 22
1247	1831, June 12
1248	1832, May 31*
1249	1833, May 21
1250	1834, May 10
1251	1835, April 29
1252	1836, April 18*
1253	1837, April 7
1254	1838, March 27
1255	1839, March 17
1256	1840, March 5*
1257	1841, February 23
1258	1842, February 12
1259	1843, February 1
1260	1844, January 22*
1261	1845, January 10
1262	1845, December 30
1263	1846, December 20
1264	1847, December 9
1265	1848, November 27*
1266	1849, November 17
1267	1850, November 6
1268	1851, October 27
1269	1852, October 15*

AH Hejira	AD Christian Date
1270	1853, October 4
1271	1854, September 24
1272	1855, September 13
1273	1856, September 1*
1274	1857, August 22
1275	1858, August 11
1276	1859, July 31
1277	1860, July 20*
1278	1861, July 9
1279	1862, June 29
1280	1863, June 18
1281	1864, June 6*
1282	1865, May 27
1283	1866, May 16
1284	1867, May 5
1285	1868, April 24*
1286	1869, April 13
1287	1870, April 3
1288	1871, March 23
1289	1872, March 11*
1290	1873, March 1
1291	1874, February 18
1292	1875, Febuary 7
1293	1876, January 28*
1294	1877, January 16
1295	1878, January 5
1296	1878, December 26
1297	1879, December 15
1298	1880, December 4*
1299	1881, November 23
1300	1882, November 12
1301	1883, November 2
1302	1884, October 21*
1303	1885, October 10
1304	1886, September 30
1305	1887, September 19
1306	1888, September 7*
1307	1889, August 28
1308	1890, August 17
1309	1891, August 7
1310	1892, July 26*
1311	1893, July 15
1312	1894, July 5
1313	1895, June 24
1314	1896, June 12*
1315	1897, June 2
1316	1898, May 22
1317	1899, May 12
1318	1900, May 1
1319	1901, April 20
1320	1902, april 10
1321	1903, March 30
1322	1904, March 18*
1323	1905, March 8
1324	1906, February 25
1325	1907, February 14
1326	1908, February 4*
1327	1909, January 23
1328	1910, January 13
1329	1911, January 2
1330	1911, December 22
1332	1913, November 30
1333	1914, November 19
1334	1915, November 9
1335	1916, October 28*
1336	1917, October 17
1337	1918, October 7
1338	1919, September 26
1339	1920, September 15*
1340	1921, September 4
1341	1922, August 24
1342	1923, August 14
1343	1924, August 2*
1344	1925, July 22
1345	1926, July 12
1346	1927, July 1
1347	1928, June 20*
1348	1929, June 9
1349	1930, May 29
1350	1931, May 19
1351	1932, May 7*
1352	1933, April 26
1353	1934, April 16
1354	1935, April 5
1355	1936, March 24*
1356	1937, March 14
1357	1938, March 3
1358	1939, February 21
1359	1940, February 10*
1360	1941, January 29
1361	1942, January 19

AH Hejira	AD Christian Date
1362	1943, January 8
1363	1943, December 28
1364	1944, December 17*
1365	1945, December 6
1366	1946, November 25
1367	1947, November 15
1368	1948, November 3*
1369	1949, October 24
1370	1950, October 13
1371	1951, October 2
1372	1952, September 21*
1373	1953, September 10
1374	1954, August 30
1375	1955, August 20
1376	1956, August 8*
1377	1957, July 29
1378	1958, July 18
1379	1959, July 7
1380	1960, June 25*
1381	1961, June 14
1382	1962, June 4
1383	1963, May 25
1384	1964, May 13*
1385	1965, May 2
1386	1966, April 22
1387	1967, April 11
1388	1968, March 31*
1389	1969, march 20
1390	1970, March 9
1391	1971, February 27
1392	1972, February 16*
1393	1973, February 4
1394	1974, January 25
1395	1975, January 14
1396	1976, January 3*
1397	1976, December 23*
1398	1977, December 12
1399	1978, December 2
1400	1979, November 21
1401	1980, November 9*
1402	1981, October 30
1403	1982, October 19
1404	1984, October 8
1405	1984, September 27*
1406	1985, September 16
1407	1986, September 6
1409	1987, August 26
1409	1988, August 14*
1410	1989, August 3
1411	1990, July 24
1412	1991, July 13
1413	1992, July 2*
1414	1993, June 21
1415	1994, June 10
1416	1995, May 31
1417	1996, May 19*
1418	1997, May 9
1419	1998, April 28
1420	1999, April 17
1421	2000, April 6*
1422	2001, March 26
1423	2002, March 15
1424	2003, March 5
1425	2004, February 22*
1426	2005, February 10
1427	2006, January 31
1428	2007, January 20
1429	2008, January 10*
1430	2008, December 29
1431	2009, December 18
1432	2010, December 8
1433	2011, November 27*
1434	2012, November 15
1435	2013, November 5
1436	2014, October 25
1437	2015, October 15*
1438	2016, October 3
1439	2017, September 22
1440	2018, September 12
1441	2019, September 11*
1442	2020, August 20
1443	2021, August 10
1444	2022, July 30
1445	2023, July 19*
1446	2024, July 8
1447	2025, June 27
1448	2026, June 17
1449	2027, June 6*
1450	2028, May 25

STANDARD INTERNATIONAL NUMERAL SYSTEMS

Prepared especially for the ***Standard Catalog of World Coins***© 2007 by Krause Publications

Western	0	½	1	2	3	4	5	6	7	8	9	10	50	100	500	1000
Roman			I	II	III	IV	V	VI	VII	VIII	IX	X	L	C	D	M
Arabic-Turkish	٠	١/٢	١	٢	٣	٤	٥	٦	٧	٨	٩	١٠	٥٠	١٠٠	٥٠٠	١٠٠٠
Malay-Persian	٠	١/٢	۱	۲	۳	۴	۵	٦ or ۶	۷	۸	۹	۱۰	۵۰	۱۰۰	۵۰۰	۱۰۰۰
Eastern Arabic	۰	۱/۲	۱	۲	۳	۴	۵	۶	۷	۸	۹	۱۰	۵۰	۱۰۰	۵۰۰	۱۰۰۰
Hyderabad Arabic	۰	١/٢	١	٢	٣	۴	۵	۶	۷	۸	۹	۱۰	۵۰	۱۰۰	۵۰۰	۱۰۰۰
Indian (Sanskrit)	०	१/२	१	२	३	४	५	६	७	८	९	१०	५०	१००	५००	१०००
Assamese	০	১/২	১	২	৩	৪	৫	৬	৭	৮	৯	১০	৫০	১০০	৫০০	১০০০
Bengali	০	১/২	১	২	৩	৪	৫	৬	৭	৮	৯	১০	৫০	১০০	৫০০	১০০০
Gujarati	૦	૧/૨	૧	૨	૩	૪	૫	૬	૭	૮	૯	૧૦	૫૦	૧૦૦	૫૦૦	૧૦૦૦
Kutch	०	१/२	१	२	३	४	५	६	७	८	९	१०	५०	१००	५००	१०००
Devavnagri	०	१/२	१	२	३	४	५	६ or ६	७	८	९ or ९	१०	५०	१००	५००	१०००
Nepalese	०	१/२	१	२	३	४	५	६	७	८	९	१०	५०	१००	५००	१०००
Tibetan	༠	༡/༢	༡	༢	༣	༤	༥	༦	༧	༨	༩	༡༠	༥༠	༡༠༠	༥༠༠	༡༠༠༠
Mongolian	᠐	᠑/᠒	᠑	᠒	᠓	᠔	᠕	᠖	᠗	᠘	᠙	᠑᠐	᠕᠐	᠑᠐᠐	᠕᠐᠐	᠑᠐᠐᠐
Burmese	၀	၁/၂	၁	၂	၃	၄	၅	၆	၇	၈	၉	၁၀	၅၀	၁၀၀	၅၀၀	၁၀၀၀
Thai-Lao	๐	๑/๒	๑	๒	๓	๔	๕	๖	๗	๘	๙	๑๐	๕๐	๑๐๐	๕๐๐	๑๐๐๐
Lao-Laotian	໐		໑	໒	໓	໔	໕	໖	໗	໘	໙	໑໐				
Javanese	꧐		꧑	꧒	꧓	꧔	꧕	꧖	꧗	꧘	꧙	꧑꧐	꧕꧐	꧑꧐꧐	꧕꧐꧐	꧑꧐꧐꧐
Ordinary Chinese Japanese-Korean	零	半	一	二	三	四	五	六	七	八	九	十	十五	百	百五	千
Official Chinese			壹	貮	叁	肆	伍	陸	柒	捌	玖	拾	拾伍	佰	佰伍	仟
Commercial Chinese			〡	〢	〣	〤	〥	〦	〧	〨	〩	十	〥十	〡百	〥百	〡千
Korean		반	일	이	삼	사	오	육	칠	팔	구	십	오십	백	오백	천
Georgian			ა	ბ	გ	დ	ე	ვ	ზ	ჱ	თ	ი	ნ	რ	ფ	ჩ
			11 [illegible]	20 კ	30 ლ	40 მ	60 ჲ	70 ო	80 პ	90 ჟ	200 ს	300 ტ	400 ჳ	600 ქ	700 ღ	800 ყ
Ethiopian	◆		፩	፪	፫	፬	፭	፮	፯	፰	፱	፲	፶	፻	፭፻	፲፻
				20 ፳	30 ፴	40 ፵	60 ፷	70 ፸	80 ፹	90 ፺						
Hebrew			א	ב	ג	ד	ה	ו	ז	ח	ט	י	נ	ק	תק	
				20 כ	30 ל	40 מ	60 ס	70 ע	80 פ	90 צ	200 ר	300 ש	400 ת	600 תר	700 תש	800 תת
Greek			Α	Β	Γ	Δ	Ε	Τ	Ζ	Η	Θ	Ι	Ν	Ρ	Φ	Α
				20 Κ	30 Λ	40 Μ	60 Ξ	70 Ο	80 Π		200 Σ	300 Τ	400 Υ	600 Χ	700 Ψ	800 Ω

Foreign Exchange

The latest foreign exchange rates below apply to trade with banks in the country of origin. The left column shows the number of units per U.S. dollar at the official rate. The right column shows the number of units per dollar at the free market rate.

Country	#/$	#/$
Afghanistan (New Afghani)	49.9	–
Albania (Lek)	85	–
Algeria (Dinar)	70	–
Andorra uses Euro	.712	–
Angola (Readjust Kwanza)	75	–
Anguilla uses E.C. Dollar	2.68	–
Antigua uses E.C. Dollar	2.68	–
Argentina (Peso)	3.16	–
Armenia (Dram)	340	–
Aruba (Florin)	1.79	–
Australia (Dollar)	1.12	–
Austria (Euro)	.712	–
Azerbaijan (Manat)	4,600	–
Bahamas (Dollar)	1.0	–
Bahrain Is. (Dinar)	.377	–
Bangladesh (Taka)	68.7	–
Barbados (Dollar)	2.0	–
Belarus (Ruble)	2,150	–
Belgium (Euro)	.712	–
Belize (Dollar)	1.95	–
Benin uses CFA Franc West	465	–
Bermuda (Dollar)	1.0	–
Bhutan (Ngultrum)	39.5	–
Bolivia (Boliviano)	7.7	–
Bosnia-Herzegovina (Conv. marka)	1.39	–
Botswana (Pula)	6.07	–
British Virgin Islands uses U.S. Dollar	1.00	–
Brazil (Real)	1.82	–
Brunei (Dollar)	1.47	–
Bulgaria (Lev)	1.39	–
Burkina Faso uses CFA Fr.West	465	–
Burma (Kyat)	6.42	1,250
Burundi (Franc)	1,120	–
Cambodia (Riel)	4,050	–
Cameroon uses CFA Franc Central	465	–
Canada (Dollar)	.99	–
Cape Verde (Escudo)	78	–
Cayman Is.(Dollar)	0.82	–
Central African Rep.	465	–
CFA Franc Central	465	–
CFA Franc West	465	–
CFP Franc	84.8	–
Chad uses CFA Franc Central	465	–
Chile (Peso)	500	–
China, P.R. (Renminbi Yuan)	7.51	–
Colombia (Peso)	1,990	–
Comoros (Franc)	350	–
Congo uses CFA Franc Central	465	–
Congo-Dem.Rep. (Congolese Franc)	560	–
Cook Islands (Dollar)	1.73	–
Costa Rica (Colon)	518.4	–
Croatia (Kuna)	5.21	–
Cuba (Peso)	1.00	27.00
Cyprus (Pound)	.415	–
Czech Republic (Koruna)	19.6	–
Denmark (Danish Krone)	5.31	–
Djibouti (Franc)	178	–
Dominica uses E.C. Dollar	2.68	–
Dominican Republic (Peso)	33.5	–
East Caribbean (Dollar)	2.68	–
Ecuador (U.S. Dollar)	1.00	–
Egypt (Pound)	5.56	–
El Salvador (U.S. Dollar)	1.00	–
England (Sterling Pound)	.492	–
Equatorial Guinea uses CFA Franc Central	465	–
Eritrea (Nafka)	15	–
Estonia (Kroon)	11.1	–
Ethiopia (Birr)	9.08	–
Euro		.712–
Falkland Is. (Pound)	.492	–
Faroe Islands (Krona)	5.31	–
Fiji Islands (Dollar)	1.55	–
Finland (Euro)	.712	–
France (Euro)	.712	–
French Polynesia uses CFP Franc	84.8	–
Gabon (CFA Franc)	465	–
Gambia (Dalasi)	19.2	–
Georgia (Lari)	1.65	–
Germany (Euro)	.712	–
Ghana (Cedi)	9,500	–
Gibraltar (Pound)	.492	–
Greece (Euro)	.712	–
Greenland uses Danish Krone	5.31	–
Grenada uses E.C. Dollar	2.68	–
Guatemala (Quetzal)	7.75	–
Guernsey uses Sterling Pound	.492	–
Guinea Bissau (CFA Franc)	465	–
Guinea Conakry (Franc)	4,170	–
Guyana (Dollar)	205	–
Haiti (Gourde)	36	–
Honduras (Lempira)	18.9	–
Hong Kong (Dollar)	7.758	–
Hungary (Forint)	178	–
Iceland (Krona)	60.8	–
India (Rupee)	39.46	–
Indonesia (Rupiah)	9,100	–
Iran (Rial)	9,310	–
Iraq (Dinar)	1,230	–
Ireland (Euro)	.712	–
Isle of Man uses Sterling Pound	.492	–
Israel (New Sheqalim)	4.03	–
Italy (Euro)	.712	–
Ivory Coast uses CFA Franc West	465	–
Jamaica (Dollar)	71	–
Japan (Yen)	117.4	–
Jersey uses Sterling Pound	.492	–
Jordan (Dinar)	.71	–
Kazakhstan (Tenge)	121	–
Kenya (Shilling)	67	–
Kiribati uses Australian Dollar	1.12	–
Korea-PDR (Won)	2.2	465
Korea-Rep. (Won)	915	–
Kuwait (Dinar)	.282	–
Kyrgyzstan (Som)	34.6	–
Laos (Kip)	9,620	–
Latvia (Lats)	.50	–
Lebanon (Pound)	1,510	–
Lesotho (Maloti)	6.85	–
Liberia (Dollar)	62	–
Libya (Dinar)	1.24	–
Liechtenstein uses Swiss Franc	1.187	–
Lithuania (Litas)	2.46	–
Luxembourg (Euro)	.712	–
Macao (Pataca)	7.99	–
Macedonia (New Denar)	43.5	–
Madagascar (Franc)	1,835	–
Malawi (Kwacha)	140	–
Malaysia (Ringgit)	3.39	–
Maldives (Rufiya)	12.8	–
Mali uses CFA Franc West	465	–
Malta (Lira)	.31	–
Marshall Islands uses U.S.Dollar	1.00	–
Mauritania (Ouguiya)	260	–
Mauritius (Rupee)	30	–
Mexico (Peso)	10.85	–
Moldova (Leu)	11.5	–
Monaco uses Euro	.712	–
Mongolia (Tugrik)	1,185	–
Montenegro uses Euro	.712	–
Montserrat uses E.C. Dollar	2.68	–
Morocco (Dirham)	8.0	–
Mozambique (New Metical)	25.9	–
Myanmar (Burma) (Kyat)	6.42	1,250
Namibia (Rand)	6.85	–
Nauru uses Australian Dollar	1.12	–
Nepal (Rupee)	63	–
Netherlands (Euro)	.712	–
Netherlands Antilles (Gulden)	1.79	–
New Caledonia uses CFP Franc	84.8	–
New Zealand (Dollar)	1.313	–
Nicaragua (Cordoba Oro)	18.7	–
Niger uses CFA Franc West	465	–
Nigeria (Naira)	125	–
Northern Ireland uses Sterling Pound	.492	–
Norway (Krone)	5.47	–
Oman (Rial)	.385	–
Pakistan (Rupee)	60.7	–
Palau uses U.S.Dollar	1.00	–
Panama (Balboa) uses U.S.Dollar	1.00	–
Papua New Guinea (Kina)	2.88	–
Paraguay (Guarani)	4,950	–
Peru (Nuevo Sol)	3.02	–
Philippines (Peso)	44.5	–
Poland (Zloty)	2.67	–
Portugal (Euro)	.712	–
Qatar (Riyal)	3.64	–
Romania (New Leu)	2.38	–
Russia (Ruble)	25.0	–
Rwanda (Franc)	550	–
St. Helena (Pound)	.492	–
St. Kitts uses E.C. Dollar	2.68	–
St. Lucia uses E.C. Dollar	2.68	–
St. Vincent uses E.C. Dollar	2.68	–
San Marino uses Euro	.712	–
Sao Tome e Principe (Dobra)	13,750	–
Saudi Arabia (Riyal)	3.75	–
Scotland uses Sterling Pound	.492	–
Senegal uses CFA Franc West	465	–
Serbia (Dinar)	55	–
Seychelles (Rupee)	8.03	–
Sierra Leone (Leone)	2,980	–
Singapore (Dollar)	1.47	–
Slovakia (Sk. Koruna)	24	–
Slovenia (Tolar)	170	–
Solomon Is. (Dollar)	7.3	–
Somalia (Shilling)	1,355	–
Somaliland (Somali Shilling)	1,800	4,000
South Africa (Rand)	6.85	–
Spain (Euro)	.712	–
Sri Lanka (Rupee)	113	–
Sudan (Dinar)	205	300
Surinam (Dollar)	2.75	–
Swaziland (Lilangeni)	6.85	–
Sweden (Krona)	6.52	–
Switzerland (Franc)	1.187	–
Syria (Pound)	51.2	–
Taiwan (NT Dollar)	32.5	–
Tajikistan (Somoni)	3.44	–
Tanzania (Shilling)	1,210	–
Thailand (Baht)	31.5	–
Togo uses CFA Franc West	465	–
Tonga (Pa'anga)	1.94	–
Transdniestra (Ruble)	–	–
Trinidad & Tobago (Dollar)	6.25	–
Tunisia (Dinar)	1.26	–
Turkey (New Lira)	1.189	–
Turkmenistan (Manat)	5,200	–
Turks & Caicos uses U.S. Dollar	1.00	–
Tuvalu uses Australian Dollar	1.12	–
Uganda (Shilling)	1,770	–
Ukraine (Hryvnia)	5.04	–
United Arab Emirates (Dirham)	3.672	–
Uruguay (Peso Uruguayo)	22.7	–
Uzbekistan (Sum)	1,270	–
Vanuatu (Vatu)	99	–
Vatican City uses Euro	.712	–
Venezuela (Bolivar)	2,150	4,000
Vietnam (Dong)	16,100	–
Western Samoa (Tala)	2.56	–
Yemen (Rial)	200	–
Zambia (Kwacha)	3,850	–
Zimbabwe (revalued Dollar)	30,000	–

Silver Bullion Chart

Oz.	5.00	5.50	6.00	6.50	7.00	7.50	8.00	8.50	9.00	9.50	10.00	10.50	11.00	11.50	12.00	12.50	13.00	13.50	14.00	14.50	15.00
0.001	0.005	0.006	0.006	0.007	0.007	0.008	0.008	0.009	0.009	0.010	0.010	0.011	0.011	0.012	0.012	0.013	0.013	0.014	0.014	0.015	0.015
0.002	0.010	0.011	0.012	0.013	0.014	0.015	0.016	0.017	0.018	0.019	0.020	0.021	0.022	0.023	0.024	0.025	0.026	0.027	0.028	0.029	0.030
0.003	0.015	0.017	0.018	0.020	0.021	0.023	0.024	0.026	0.027	0.029	0.030	0.032	0.033	0.035	0.036	0.038	0.039	0.041	0.042	0.044	0.045
0.004	0.020	0.022	0.024	0.026	0.028	0.030	0.032	0.034	0.036	0.038	0.040	0.042	0.044	0.046	0.048	0.050	0.052	0.054	0.056	0.058	0.060
0.005	0.025	0.028	0.030	0.033	0.035	0.038	0.040	0.043	0.045	0.048	0.050	0.053	0.055	0.058	0.060	0.063	0.065	0.068	0.070	0.073	0.075
0.006	0.030	0.033	0.036	0.039	0.042	0.045	0.048	0.051	0.054	0.057	0.060	0.063	0.066	0.069	0.072	0.075	0.078	0.081	0.084	0.087	0.090
0.007	0.035	0.039	0.042	0.046	0.049	0.053	0.056	0.060	0.063	0.067	0.070	0.074	0.077	0.081	0.084	0.088	0.091	0.095	0.098	0.102	0.105
0.008	0.040	0.044	0.048	0.052	0.056	0.060	0.064	0.068	0.072	0.076	0.080	0.084	0.088	0.092	0.096	0.100	0.104	0.108	0.112	0.116	0.120
0.009	0.045	0.050	0.054	0.059	0.063	0.068	0.072	0.077	0.081	0.086	0.090	0.095	0.099	0.104	0.108	0.113	0.117	0.122	0.126	0.131	0.135
0.010	0.050	0.055	0.060	0.065	0.070	0.075	0.080	0.085	0.090	0.095	0.100	0.105	0.110	0.115	0.120	0.125	0.130	0.135	0.140	0.145	0.150
0.020	0.100	0.110	0.120	0.130	0.140	0.150	0.160	0.170	0.180	0.190	0.200	0.210	0.220	0.230	0.240	0.250	0.260	0.270	0.280	0.290	0.300
0.030	0.150	0.165	0.180	0.195	0.210	0.225	0.240	0.255	0.270	0.285	0.300	0.315	0.330	0.345	0.360	0.375	0.390	0.405	0.420	0.435	0.450
0.040	0.200	0.220	0.240	0.260	0.280	0.300	0.320	0.340	0.360	0.380	0.400	0.420	0.440	0.460	0.480	0.500	0.520	0.540	0.560	0.580	0.600
0.050	0.250	0.275	0.300	0.325	0.350	0.375	0.400	0.425	0.450	0.475	0.500	0.525	0.550	0.575	0.600	0.625	0.650	0.675	0.700	0.725	0.750
0.060	0.300	0.330	0.360	0.390	0.420	0.450	0.480	0.510	0.540	0.570	0.600	0.630	0.660	0.690	0.720	0.750	0.780	0.810	0.840	0.870	0.900
0.070	0.350	0.385	0.420	0.455	0.490	0.525	0.560	0.595	0.630	0.665	0.700	0.735	0.770	0.805	0.840	0.875	0.910	0.945	0.980	1.015	1.050
0.080	0.400	0.440	0.480	0.520	0.560	0.600	0.640	0.680	0.720	0.760	0.800	0.840	0.880	0.920	0.960	1.000	1.040	1.080	1.120	1.160	1.200
0.090	0.450	0.495	0.540	0.585	0.630	0.675	0.720	0.765	0.810	0.855	0.900	0.945	0.990	1.035	1.080	1.125	1.170	1.215	1.260	1.305	1.350
0.100	0.500	0.550	0.600	0.650	0.700	0.750	0.800	0.850	0.900	0.950	1.000	1.050	1.100	1.150	1.200	1.250	1.300	1.350	1.400	1.450	1.500
0.110	0.550	0.605	0.660	0.715	0.770	0.825	0.880	0.935	0.990	1.045	1.100	1.155	1.210	1.265	1.320	1.375	1.430	1.485	1.540	1.595	1.650
0.120	0.600	0.660	0.720	0.780	0.840	0.900	0.960	1.020	1.080	1.140	1.200	1.260	1.320	1.380	1.440	1.500	1.560	1.620	1.680	1.740	1.800
0.130	0.650	0.715	0.780	0.845	0.910	0.975	1.040	1.105	1.170	1.235	1.300	1.365	1.430	1.495	1.560	1.625	1.690	1.755	1.820	1.885	1.950
0.140	0.700	0.770	0.840	0.910	0.980	1.050	1.120	1.190	1.260	1.330	1.400	1.470	1.540	1.610	1.680	1.750	1.820	1.890	1.960	2.030	2.100
0.150	0.750	0.825	0.900	0.975	1.050	1.125	1.200	1.275	1.350	1.425	1.500	1.575	1.650	1.725	1.800	1.875	1.950	2.025	2.100	2.175	2.250
0.160	0.800	0.880	0.960	1.040	1.120	1.200	1.280	1.360	1.440	1.520	1.600	1.680	1.760	1.840	1.920	2.000	2.080	2.160	2.240	2.320	2.400
0.170	0.850	0.935	1.020	1.105	1.190	1.275	1.360	1.445	1.530	1.615	1.700	1.785	1.870	1.955	2.040	2.125	2.210	2.295	2.380	2.465	2.550
0.180	0.900	0.990	1.080	1.170	1.260	1.350	1.440	1.530	1.620	1.710	1.800	1.890	1.980	2.070	2.160	2.250	2.340	2.430	2.520	2.610	2.700
0.190	0.950	1.045	1.140	1.235	1.330	1.425	1.520	1.615	1.710	1.805	1.900	1.995	2.090	2.185	2.280	2.375	2.470	2.565	2.660	2.755	2.850
0.200	1.000	1.100	1.200	1.300	1.400	1.500	1.600	1.700	1.800	1.900	2.000	2.100	2.200	2.300	2.400	2.500	2.600	2.700	2.800	2.900	3.000
0.210	1.050	1.155	1.260	1.365	1.470	1.575	1.680	1.785	1.890	1.995	2.100	2.205	2.310	2.415	2.520	2.625	2.730	2.835	2.940	3.045	3.150
0.220	1.100	1.210	1.320	1.430	1.540	1.650	1.760	1.870	1.980	2.090	2.200	2.310	2.420	2.530	2.640	2.750	2.860	2.970	3.080	3.190	3.300
0.230	1.150	1.265	1.380	1.495	1.610	1.725	1.840	1.955	2.070	2.185	2.300	2.415	2.530	2.645	2.760	2.875	2.990	3.105	3.220	3.335	3.450
0.240	1.200	1.320	1.440	1.560	1.680	1.800	1.920	2.040	2.160	2.280	2.400	2.520	2.640	2.760	2.880	3.000	3.120	3.240	3.360	3.480	3.600
0.250	1.250	1.375	1.500	1.625	1.750	1.875	2.000	2.125	2.250	2.375	2.500	2.625	2.750	2.875	3.000	3.125	3.250	3.375	3.500	3.625	3.750
0.260	1.300	1.430	1.560	1.690	1.820	1.950	2.080	2.210	2.340	2.470	2.600	2.730	2.860	2.990	3.120	3.250	3.380	3.510	3.640	3.770	3.900
0.270	1.350	1.485	1.620	1.755	1.890	2.025	2.160	2.295	2.430	2.565	2.700	2.835	2.970	3.105	3.240	3.375	3.510	3.645	3.780	3.915	4.050
0.280	1.400	1.540	1.680	1.820	1.960	2.100	2.240	2.380	2.520	2.660	2.800	2.940	3.080	3.220	3.360	3.500	3.640	3.780	3.920	4.060	4.200
0.290	1.450	1.595	1.740	1.885	2.030	2.175	2.320	2.465	2.610	2.755	2.900	3.045	3.190	3.335	3.480	3.625	3.770	3.915	4.060	4.205	4.350
0.300	1.500	1.650	1.800	1.950	2.100	2.250	2.400	2.550	2.700	2.850	3.000	3.150	3.300	3.450	3.600	3.750	3.900	4.050	4.200	4.350	4.500
0.310	1.550	1.705	1.860	2.015	2.170	2.325	2.480	2.635	2.790	2.945	3.100	3.255	3.410	3.565	3.720	3.875	4.030	4.185	4.340	4.495	4.650
0.320	1.600	1.760	1.920	2.080	2.240	2.400	2.560	2.720	2.880	3.040	3.200	3.360	3.520	3.680	3.840	4.000	4.160	4.320	4.480	4.640	4.800
0.330	1.650	1.815	1.980	2.145	2.310	2.475	2.640	2.805	2.970	3.135	3.300	3.465	3.630	3.795	3.960	4.125	4.290	4.455	4.620	4.785	4.950
0.340	1.700	1.870	2.040	2.210	2.380	2.550	2.720	2.890	3.060	3.230	3.400	3.570	3.740	3.910	4.080	4.250	4.420	4.590	4.760	4.930	5.100
0.350	1.750	1.925	2.100	2.275	2.450	2.625	2.800	2.975	3.150	3.325	3.500	3.675	3.850	4.025	4.200	4.375	4.550	4.725	4.900	5.075	5.250
0.360	1.800	1.980	2.160	2.340	2.520	2.700	2.880	3.060	3.240	3.420	3.600	3.780	3.960	4.140	4.320	4.500	4.680	4.860	5.040	5.220	5.400
0.370	1.850	2.035	2.220	2.405	2.590	2.775	2.960	3.145	3.330	3.515	3.700	3.885	4.070	4.255	4.440	4.625	4.810	4.995	5.180	5.365	5.550
0.380	1.900	2.090	2.280	2.470	2.660	2.850	3.040	3.230	3.420	3.610	3.800	3.990	4.180	4.370	4.560	4.750	4.940	5.130	5.320	5.510	5.700
0.390	1.950	2.145	2.340	2.535	2.730	2.925	3.120	3.315	3.510	3.705	3.900	4.095	4.290	4.485	4.680	4.875	5.070	5.265	5.460	5.655	5.850
0.400	2.000	2.200	2.400	2.600	2.800	3.000	3.200	3.400	3.600	3.800	4.000	4.200	4.400	4.600	4.800	5.000	5.200	5.400	5.600	5.800	6.000
0.410	2.050	2.255	2.460	2.665	2.870	3.075	3.280	3.485	3.690	3.895	4.100	4.305	4.510	4.715	4.920	5.125	5.330	5.535	5.740	5.945	6.150
0.420	2.100	2.310	2.520	2.730	2.940	3.150	3.360	3.570	3.780	3.990	4.200	4.410	4.620	4.830	5.040	5.250	5.460	5.670	5.880	6.090	6.300
0.430	2.150	2.365	2.580	2.795	3.010	3.225	3.440	3.655	3.870	4.085	4.300	4.515	4.730	4.945	5.160	5.375	5.590	5.805	6.020	6.235	6.450
0.440	2.200	2.420	2.640	2.860	3.080	3.300	3.520	3.740	3.960	4.180	4.400	4.620	4.840	5.060	5.280	5.500	5.720	5.940	6.160	6.380	6.600

Oz.	5.00	5.50	6.00	6.50	7.00	7.50	8.00	8.50	9.00	9.50	10.00	10.50	11.00	11.50	12.00	12.50	13.00	13.50	14.00	14.50	15.00
0.450	2.250	2.475	2.700	2.925	3.150	3.375	3.600	3.825	4.050	4.275	4.500	4.725	4.950	5.175	5.400	5.625	5.850	6.075	6.300	6.525	6.750
0.460	2.300	2.530	2.760	2.990	3.220	3.450	3.680	3.910	4.140	4.370	4.600	4.830	5.060	5.290	5.520	5.750	5.980	6.210	6.440	6.670	6.900
0.470	2.350	2.585	2.820	3.055	3.290	3.525	3.760	3.995	4.230	4.465	4.700	4.935	5.170	5.405	5.640	5.875	6.110	6.345	6.580	6.815	7.050
0.480	2.400	2.640	2.880	3.120	3.360	3.600	3.840	4.080	4.320	4.560	4.800	5.040	5.280	5.520	5.760	6.000	6.240	6.480	6.720	6.960	7.200
0.490	2.450	2.695	2.940	3.185	3.430	3.675	3.920	4.165	4.410	4.655	4.900	5.145	5.390	5.635	5.880	6.125	6.370	6.615	6.860	7.105	7.350
0.500	2.500	2.750	3.000	3.250	3.500	3.750	4.000	4.250	4.500	4.750	5.000	5.250	5.500	5.750	6.000	6.250	6.500	6.750	7.000	7.250	7.500
0.510	2.550	2.805	3.060	3.315	3.570	3.825	4.080	4.335	4.590	4.845	5.100	5.355	5.610	5.865	6.120	6.375	6.630	6.885	7.140	7.395	7.650
0.520	2.600	2.860	3.120	3.380	3.640	3.900	4.160	4.420	4.680	4.940	5.200	5.460	5.720	5.980	6.240	6.500	6.760	7.020	7.280	7.540	7.800
0.530	2.650	2.915	3.180	3.445	3.710	3.975	4.240	4.505	4.770	5.035	5.300	5.565	5.830	6.095	6.360	6.625	6.890	7.155	7.420	7.685	7.950
0.540	2.700	2.970	3.240	3.510	3.780	4.050	4.320	4.590	4.860	5.130	5.400	5.670	5.940	6.210	6.480	6.750	7.020	7.290	7.560	7.830	8.100
0.550	2.750	3.025	3.300	3.575	3.850	4.125	4.400	4.675	4.950	5.225	5.500	5.775	6.050	6.325	6.600	6.875	7.150	7.425	7.700	7.975	8.250
0.560	2.800	3.080	3.360	3.640	3.920	4.200	4.480	4.760	5.040	5.320	5.600	5.880	6.160	6.440	6.720	7.000	7.280	7.560	7.840	8.120	8.400
0.570	2.850	3.135	3.420	3.705	3.990	4.275	4.560	4.845	5.130	5.415	5.700	5.985	6.270	6.555	6.840	7.125	7.410	7.695	7.980	8.265	8.550
0.580	2.900	3.190	3.480	3.770	4.060	4.350	4.640	4.930	5.220	5.510	5.800	6.090	6.380	6.670	6.960	7.250	7.540	7.830	8.120	8.410	8.700
0.590	2.950	3.245	3.540	3.835	4.130	4.425	4.720	5.015	5.310	5.605	5.900	6.195	6.490	6.785	7.080	7.375	7.670	7.965	8.260	8.555	8.850
0.600	3.000	3.300	3.600	3.900	4.200	4.500	4.800	5.100	5.400	5.700	6.000	6.300	6.600	6.900	7.200	7.500	7.800	8.100	8.400	8.700	9.000
0.610	3.050	3.355	3.660	3.965	4.270	4.575	4.880	5.185	5.490	5.795	6.100	6.405	6.710	7.015	7.320	7.625	7.930	8.235	8.540	8.845	9.150
0.620	3.100	3.410	3.720	4.030	4.340	4.650	4.960	5.270	5.580	5.890	6.200	6.510	6.820	7.130	7.440	7.750	8.060	8.370	8.680	8.990	9.300
0.630	3.150	3.465	3.780	4.095	4.410	4.725	5.040	5.355	5.670	5.985	6.300	6.615	6.930	7.245	7.560	7.875	8.190	8.505	8.820	9.135	9.450
0.640	3.200	3.520	3.840	4.160	4.480	4.800	5.120	5.440	5.760	6.080	6.400	6.720	7.040	7.360	7.680	8.000	8.320	8.640	8.960	9.280	9.600
0.650	3.250	3.575	3.900	4.225	4.550	4.875	5.200	5.525	5.850	6.175	6.500	6.825	7.150	7.475	7.800	8.125	8.450	8.775	9.100	9.425	9.750
0.660	3.300	3.630	3.960	4.290	4.620	4.950	5.280	5.610	5.940	6.270	6.600	6.930	7.260	7.590	7.920	8.250	8.580	8.910	9.240	9.570	9.900
0.670	3.350	3.685	4.020	4.355	4.690	5.025	5.360	5.695	6.030	6.365	6.700	7.035	7.370	7.705	8.040	8.375	8.710	9.045	9.380	9.715	10.050
0.680	3.400	3.740	4.080	4.420	4.760	5.100	5.440	5.780	6.120	6.460	6.800	7.140	7.480	7.820	8.160	8.500	8.840	9.180	9.520	9.860	10.200
0.690	3.450	3.795	4.140	4.485	4.830	5.175	5.520	5.865	6.210	6.555	6.900	7.245	7.590	7.935	8.280	8.625	8.970	9.315	9.660	10.005	10.350
0.700	3.500	3.850	4.200	4.550	4.900	5.250	5.600	5.950	6.300	6.650	7.000	7.350	7.700	8.050	8.400	8.750	9.100	9.450	9.800	10.150	10.500
0.710	3.550	3.905	4.260	4.615	4.970	5.325	5.680	6.035	6.390	6.745	7.100	7.455	7.810	8.165	8.520	8.875	9.230	9.585	9.940	10.295	10.650
0.720	3.600	3.960	4.320	4.680	5.040	5.400	5.760	6.120	6.480	6.840	7.200	7.560	7.920	8.280	8.640	9.000	9.360	9.720	10.080	10.440	10.800
0.730	3.650	4.015	4.380	4.745	5.110	5.475	5.840	6.205	6.570	6.935	7.300	7.665	8.030	8.395	8.760	9.125	9.490	9.855	10.220	10.585	10.950
0.740	3.700	4.070	4.440	4.810	5.180	5.550	5.920	6.290	6.660	7.030	7.400	7.770	8.140	8.510	8.880	9.250	9.620	9.990	10.360	10.730	11.100
0.750	3.750	4.125	4.500	4.875	5.250	5.625	6.000	6.375	6.750	7.125	7.500	7.875	8.250	8.625	9.000	9.375	9.750	10.125	10.500	10.875	11.250
0.760	3.800	4.180	4.560	4.940	5.320	5.700	6.080	6.460	6.840	7.220	7.600	7.980	8.360	8.740	9.120	9.500	9.880	10.260	10.640	11.020	11.400
0.770	3.850	4.235	4.620	5.005	5.390	5.775	6.160	6.545	6.930	7.315	7.700	8.085	8.470	8.855	9.240	9.625	10.010	10.395	10.780	11.165	11.550
0.780	3.900	4.290	4.680	5.070	5.460	5.850	6.240	6.630	7.020	7.410	7.800	8.190	8.580	8.970	9.360	9.750	10.140	10.530	10.920	11.310	11.700
0.790	3.950	4.345	4.740	5.135	5.530	5.925	6.320	6.715	7.110	7.505	7.900	8.295	8.690	9.085	9.480	9.875	10.270	10.665	11.060	11.455	11.850
0.800	4.000	4.400	4.800	5.200	5.600	6.000	6.400	6.800	7.200	7.600	8.000	8.400	8.800	9.200	9.600	10.000	10.400	10.800	11.200	11.600	12.000
0.810	4.050	4.455	4.860	5.265	5.670	6.075	6.480	6.885	7.290	7.695	8.100	8.505	8.910	9.315	9.720	10.125	10.530	10.935	11.340	11.745	12.150
0.820	4.100	4.510	4.920	5.330	5.740	6.150	6.560	6.970	7.380	7.790	8.200	8.610	9.020	9.430	9.840	10.250	10.660	11.070	11.480	11.890	12.300
0.830	4.150	4.565	4.980	5.395	5.810	6.225	6.640	7.055	7.470	7.885	8.300	8.715	9.130	9.545	9.960	10.375	10.790	11.205	11.620	12.035	12.450
0.840	4.200	4.620	5.040	5.460	5.880	6.300	6.720	7.140	7.560	7.980	8.400	8.820	9.240	9.660	10.080	10.500	10.920	11.340	11.760	12.180	12.600
0.850	4.250	4.675	5.100	5.525	5.950	6.375	6.800	7.225	7.650	8.075	8.500	8.925	9.350	9.775	10.200	10.625	11.050	11.475	11.900	12.325	12.750
0.860	4.300	4.730	5.160	5.590	6.020	6.450	6.880	7.310	7.740	8.170	8.600	9.030	9.460	9.890	10.320	10.750	11.180	11.610	12.040	12.470	12.900
0.870	4.350	4.785	5.220	5.655	6.090	6.525	6.960	7.395	7.830	8.265	8.700	9.135	9.570	10.005	10.440	10.875	11.310	11.745	12.180	12.615	13.050
0.880	4.400	4.840	5.280	5.720	6.160	6.600	7.040	7.480	7.920	8.360	8.800	9.240	9.680	10.120	10.560	11.000	11.440	11.880	12.320	12.760	13.200
0.890	4.450	4.895	5.340	5.785	6.230	6.675	7.120	7.565	8.010	8.455	8.900	9.345	9.790	10.235	10.680	11.125	11.570	12.015	12.460	12.905	13.350
0.900	4.500	4.950	5.400	5.850	6.300	6.750	7.200	7.650	8.100	8.550	9.000	9.450	9.900	10.350	10.800	11.250	11.700	12.150	12.600	13.050	13.500
0.910	4.550	5.005	5.460	5.915	6.370	6.825	7.280	7.735	8.190	8.645	9.100	9.555	10.010	10.465	10.920	11.375	11.830	12.285	12.740	13.195	13.650
0.920	4.600	5.060	5.520	5.980	6.440	6.900	7.360	7.820	8.280	8.740	9.200	9.660	10.120	10.580	11.040	11.500	11.960	12.420	12.880	13.340	13.800
0.930	4.650	5.115	5.580	6.045	6.510	6.975	7.440	7.905	8.370	8.835	9.300	9.765	10.230	10.695	11.160	11.625	12.090	12.555	13.020	13.485	13.950
0.940	4.700	5.170	5.640	6.110	6.580	7.050	7.520	7.990	8.460	8.930	9.400	9.870	10.340	10.810	11.280	11.750	12.220	12.690	13.160	13.630	14.100
0.950	4.750	5.225	5.700	6.175	6.650	7.125	7.600	8.075	8.550	9.025	9.500	9.975	10.450	10.925	11.400	11.875	12.350	12.825	13.300	13.775	14.250
0.960	4.800	5.280	5.760	6.240	6.720	7.200	7.680	8.160	8.640	9.120	9.600	10.080	10.560	11.040	11.520	12.000	12.480	12.960	13.440	13.920	14.400
0.970	4.850	5.335	5.820	6.305	6.790	7.275	7.760	8.245	8.730	9.215	9.700	10.185	10.670	11.155	11.640	12.125	12.610	13.095	13.580	14.065	14.550
0.980	4.900	5.390	5.880	6.370	6.860	7.350	7.840	8.330	8.820	9.310	9.800	10.290	10.780	11.270	11.760	12.250	12.740	13.230	13.720	14.210	14.700
0.990	4.950	5.445	5.940	6.435	6.930	7.425	7.920	8.415	8.910	9.405	9.900	10.395	10.890	11.385	11.880	12.375	12.870	13.365	13.860	14.355	14.850
1.000	5.000	5.500	6.000	6.500	7.000	7.500	8.000	8.500	9.000	9.500	10.000	10.500	11.000	11.500	12.000	12.500	13.000	13.500	14.000	14.500	15.000

GOLD BULLION VALUE CHART

Oz.	500.00	510.00	520.00	530.00	540.00	550.00	560.00	570.00	580.00	590.00	600.00	610.00	620.00	630.00	640.00	650.00	660.00	670.00	680.00	690.00
0.001	0.50	0.51	0.52	0.53	0.54	0.55	0.56	0.57	0.58	0.59	0.60	0.61	0.62	0.63	0.64	0.65	0.66	0.67	0.68	0.69
0.002	1.00	1.02	1.04	1.06	1.08	1.10	1.12	1.14	1.16	1.18	1.20	1.22	1.24	1.26	1.28	1.30	1.32	1.34	1.36	1.38
0.003	1.50	1.53	1.56	1.59	1.62	1.65	1.68	1.71	1.74	1.77	1.80	1.83	1.86	1.89	1.92	1.95	1.98	2.01	2.04	2.07
0.004	2.00	2.04	2.08	2.12	2.16	2.20	2.24	2.28	2.32	2.36	2.40	2.44	2.48	2.52	2.56	2.60	2.64	2.68	2.72	2.76
0.005	2.50	2.55	2.60	2.65	2.70	2.75	2.80	2.85	2.90	2.95	3.00	3.05	3.10	3.15	3.20	3.25	3.30	3.35	3.40	3.45
0.006	3.00	3.06	3.12	3.18	3.24	3.30	3.36	3.42	3.48	3.54	3.60	3.66	3.72	3.78	3.84	3.90	3.96	4.02	4.08	4.14
0.007	3.50	3.57	3.64	3.71	3.78	3.85	3.92	3.99	4.06	4.13	4.20	4.27	4.34	4.41	4.48	4.55	4.62	4.69	4.76	4.83
0.008	4.00	4.08	4.16	4.24	4.32	4.40	4.48	4.56	4.64	4.72	4.80	4.88	4.96	5.04	5.12	5.20	5.28	5.36	5.44	5.52
0.009	4.50	4.59	4.68	4.77	4.86	4.95	5.04	5.13	5.22	5.31	5.40	5.49	5.58	5.67	5.76	5.85	5.94	6.03	6.12	6.21
0.010	5.00	5.10	5.20	5.30	5.40	5.50	5.60	5.70	5.80	5.90	6.00	6.10	6.20	6.30	6.40	6.50	6.60	6.70	6.80	6.90
0.020	10.00	10.20	10.40	10.60	10.80	11.00	11.20	11.40	11.60	11.80	12.00	12.20	12.40	12.60	12.80	13.00	13.20	13.40	13.60	13.80
0.030	15.00	15.30	15.60	15.90	16.20	16.50	16.80	17.10	17.40	17.70	18.00	18.30	18.60	18.90	19.20	19.50	19.80	20.10	20.40	20.70
0.040	20.00	20.40	20.80	21.20	21.60	22.00	22.40	22.80	23.20	23.60	24.00	24.40	24.80	25.20	25.60	26.00	26.40	26.80	27.20	27.60
0.050	25.00	25.50	26.00	26.50	27.00	27.50	28.00	28.50	29.00	29.50	30.00	30.50	31.00	31.50	32.00	32.50	33.00	33.50	34.00	34.50
0.060	30.00	30.60	31.20	31.80	32.40	33.00	33.60	34.20	34.80	35.40	36.00	36.60	37.20	37.80	38.40	39.00	39.60	40.20	40.80	41.40
0.070	35.00	35.70	36.40	37.10	37.80	38.50	39.20	39.90	40.60	41.30	42.00	42.70	43.40	44.10	44.80	45.50	46.20	46.90	47.60	48.30
0.080	40.00	40.80	41.60	42.40	43.20	44.00	44.80	45.60	46.40	47.20	48.00	48.80	49.60	50.40	51.20	52.00	52.80	53.60	54.40	55.20
0.090	45.00	45.90	46.80	47.70	48.60	49.50	50.40	51.30	52.20	53.10	54.00	54.90	55.80	56.70	57.60	58.50	59.40	60.30	61.20	62.10
0.100	50.00	51.00	52.00	53.00	54.00	55.00	56.00	57.00	58.00	59.00	60.00	61.00	62.00	63.00	64.00	65.00	66.00	67.00	68.00	69.00
0.110	55.00	56.10	57.20	58.30	59.40	60.50	61.60	62.70	63.80	64.90	66.00	67.10	68.20	69.30	70.40	71.50	72.60	73.70	74.80	75.90
0.120	60.00	61.20	62.40	63.60	64.80	66.00	67.20	68.40	69.60	70.80	72.00	73.20	74.40	75.60	76.80	78.00	79.20	80.40	81.60	82.80
0.130	65.00	66.30	67.60	68.90	70.20	71.50	72.80	74.10	75.40	76.70	78.00	79.30	80.60	81.90	83.20	84.50	85.80	87.10	88.40	89.70
0.140	70.00	71.40	72.80	74.20	75.60	77.00	78.40	79.80	81.20	82.60	84.00	85.40	86.80	88.20	89.60	91.00	92.40	93.80	95.20	96.60
0.150	75.00	76.50	78.00	79.50	81.00	82.50	84.00	85.50	87.00	88.50	90.00	91.50	93.00	94.50	96.00	97.50	99.00	100.50	102.00	103.50
0.160	80.00	81.60	83.20	84.80	86.40	88.00	89.60	91.20	92.80	94.40	96.00	97.60	99.20	100.80	102.40	104.00	105.60	107.20	108.80	110.40
0.170	85.00	86.70	88.40	90.10	91.80	93.50	95.20	96.90	98.60	100.30	102.00	103.70	105.40	107.10	108.80	110.50	112.20	113.90	115.60	117.30
0.180	90.00	91.80	93.60	95.40	97.20	99.00	100.80	102.60	104.40	106.20	108.00	109.80	111.60	113.40	115.20	117.00	118.80	120.60	122.40	124.20
0.190	95.00	96.90	98.80	100.70	102.60	104.50	106.40	108.30	110.20	112.10	114.00	115.90	117.80	119.70	121.60	123.50	125.40	127.30	129.20	131.10
0.200	100.00	102.00	104.00	106.00	108.00	110.00	112.00	114.00	116.00	118.00	120.00	122.00	124.00	126.00	128.00	130.00	132.00	134.00	136.00	138.00
0.210	105.00	107.10	109.20	111.30	113.40	115.50	117.60	119.70	121.80	123.90	126.00	128.10	130.20	132.30	134.40	136.50	138.60	140.70	142.80	144.90
0.220	110.00	112.20	114.40	116.60	118.80	121.00	123.20	125.40	127.60	129.80	132.00	134.20	136.40	138.60	140.80	143.00	145.20	147.40	149.60	151.80
0.230	115.00	117.30	119.60	121.90	124.20	126.50	128.80	131.10	133.40	135.70	138.00	140.30	142.60	144.90	147.20	149.50	151.80	154.10	156.40	158.70
0.240	120.00	122.40	124.80	127.20	129.60	132.00	134.40	136.80	139.20	141.60	144.00	146.40	148.80	151.20	153.60	156.00	158.40	160.80	163.20	165.60
0.250	125.00	127.50	130.00	132.50	135.00	137.50	140.00	142.50	145.00	147.50	150.00	152.50	155.00	157.50	160.00	162.50	165.00	167.50	170.00	172.50
0.260	130.00	132.60	135.20	137.80	140.40	143.00	145.60	148.20	150.80	153.40	156.00	158.60	161.20	163.80	166.40	169.00	171.60	174.20	176.80	179.40
0.270	135.00	137.70	140.40	143.10	145.80	148.50	151.20	153.90	156.60	159.30	162.00	164.70	167.40	170.10	172.80	175.50	178.20	180.90	183.60	186.30
0.280	140.00	142.80	145.60	148.40	151.20	154.00	156.80	159.60	162.40	165.20	168.00	170.80	173.60	176.40	179.20	182.00	184.80	187.60	190.40	193.20
0.290	145.00	147.90	150.80	153.70	156.60	159.50	162.40	165.30	168.20	171.10	174.00	176.90	179.80	182.70	185.60	188.50	191.40	194.30	197.20	200.10
0.300	150.00	153.00	156.00	159.00	162.00	165.00	168.00	171.00	174.00	177.00	180.00	183.00	186.00	189.00	192.00	195.00	198.00	201.00	204.00	207.00
0.310	155.00	158.10	161.20	164.30	167.40	170.50	173.60	176.70	179.80	182.90	186.00	189.10	192.20	195.30	198.40	201.50	204.60	207.70	210.80	213.90
0.320	160.00	163.20	166.40	169.60	172.80	176.00	179.20	182.40	185.60	188.80	192.00	195.20	198.40	201.60	204.80	208.00	211.20	214.40	217.60	220.80
0.330	165.00	168.30	171.60	174.90	178.20	181.50	184.80	188.10	191.40	194.70	198.00	201.30	204.60	207.90	211.20	214.50	217.80	221.10	224.40	227.70
0.340	170.00	173.40	176.80	180.20	183.60	187.00	190.40	193.80	197.20	200.60	204.00	207.40	210.80	214.20	217.60	221.00	224.40	227.80	231.20	234.60
0.350	175.00	178.50	182.00	185.50	189.00	192.50	196.00	199.50	203.00	206.50	210.00	213.50	217.00	220.50	224.00	227.50	231.00	234.50	238.00	241.50
0.360	180.00	183.60	187.20	190.80	194.40	198.00	201.60	205.20	208.80	212.40	216.00	219.60	223.20	226.80	230.40	234.00	237.60	241.20	244.80	248.40
0.370	185.00	188.70	192.40	196.10	199.80	203.50	207.20	210.90	214.60	218.30	222.00	225.70	229.40	233.10	236.80	240.50	244.20	247.90	251.60	255.30
0.380	190.00	193.80	197.60	201.40	205.20	209.00	212.80	216.60	220.40	224.20	228.00	231.80	235.60	239.40	243.20	247.00	250.80	254.60	258.40	262.20
0.390	195.00	198.90	202.80	206.70	210.60	214.50	218.40	222.30	226.20	230.10	234.00	237.90	241.80	245.70	249.60	253.50	257.40	261.30	265.20	269.10
0.400	200.00	204.00	208.00	212.00	216.00	220.00	224.00	228.00	232.00	236.00	240.00	244.00	248.00	252.00	256.00	260.00	264.00	268.00	272.00	276.00
0.410	205.00	209.10	213.20	217.30	221.40	225.50	229.60	233.70	237.80	241.90	246.00	250.10	254.20	258.30	262.40	266.50	270.60	274.70	278.80	282.90
0.420	210.00	214.20	218.40	222.60	226.80	231.00	235.20	239.40	243.60	247.80	252.00	256.20	260.40	264.60	268.80	273.00	277.20	281.40	285.60	289.80
0.430	215.00	219.30	223.60	227.90	232.20	236.50	240.80	245.10	249.40	253.70	258.00	262.30	266.60	270.90	275.20	279.50	283.80	288.10	292.40	296.70
0.440	220.00	224.40	228.80	233.20	237.60	242.00	246.40	250.80	255.20	259.60	264.00	268.40	272.80	277.20	281.60	286.00	290.40	294.80	299.20	303.60
0.450	225.00	229.50	234.00	238.50	243.00	247.50	252.00	256.50	261.00	265.50	270.00	274.50	279.00	283.50	288.00	292.50	297.00	301.50	306.00	310.50
0.460	230.00	234.60	239.20	243.80	248.40	253.00	257.60	262.20	266.80	271.40	276.00	280.60	285.20	289.80	294.40	299.00	303.60	308.20	312.80	317.40

GOLD BULLION VALUE CHART

Oz.	500.00	510.00	520.00	530.00	540.00	550.00	560.00	570.00	580.00	590.00	600.00	610.00	620.00	630.00	640.00	650.00	660.00	670.00	680.00	690.00
0.470	235.00	239.70	244.40	249.10	253.80	258.50	263.20	267.90	272.60	277.30	282.00	286.70	291.40	296.10	300.80	305.50	310.20	314.90	319.60	324.30
0.480	240.00	244.80	249.60	254.40	259.20	264.00	268.80	273.60	278.40	283.20	288.00	292.80	297.60	302.40	307.20	312.00	316.80	321.60	326.40	331.20
0.490	245.00	249.90	254.80	259.70	264.60	269.50	274.40	279.30	284.20	289.10	294.00	298.90	303.80	308.70	313.60	318.50	323.40	328.30	333.20	338.10
0.500	250.00	255.00	260.00	265.00	270.00	275.00	280.00	285.00	290.00	295.00	300.00	305.00	310.00	315.00	320.00	325.00	330.00	335.00	340.00	345.00
0.510	255.00	260.10	265.20	270.30	275.40	280.50	285.60	290.70	295.80	300.90	306.00	311.10	316.20	321.30	326.40	331.50	336.60	341.70	346.80	351.90
0.520	260.00	265.20	270.40	275.60	280.80	286.00	291.20	296.40	301.60	306.80	312.00	317.20	322.40	327.60	332.80	338.00	343.20	348.40	353.60	358.80
0.530	265.00	270.30	275.60	280.90	286.20	291.50	296.80	302.10	307.40	312.70	318.00	323.30	328.60	333.90	339.20	344.50	349.80	355.10	360.40	365.70
0.540	270.00	275.40	280.80	286.20	291.60	297.00	302.40	307.80	313.20	318.60	324.00	329.40	334.80	340.20	345.60	351.00	356.40	361.80	367.20	372.60
0.550	275.00	280.50	286.00	291.50	297.00	302.50	308.00	313.50	319.00	324.50	330.00	335.50	341.00	346.50	352.00	357.50	363.00	368.50	374.00	379.50
0.560	280.00	285.60	291.20	296.80	302.40	308.00	313.60	319.20	324.80	330.40	336.00	341.60	347.20	352.80	358.40	364.00	369.60	375.20	380.80	386.40
0.570	285.00	290.70	296.40	302.10	307.80	313.50	319.20	324.90	330.60	336.30	342.00	347.70	353.40	359.10	364.80	370.50	376.20	381.90	387.60	393.30
0.580	290.00	295.80	301.60	307.40	313.20	319.00	324.80	330.60	336.40	342.20	348.00	353.80	359.60	365.40	371.20	377.00	382.80	388.60	394.40	400.20
0.590	295.00	300.90	306.80	312.70	318.60	324.50	330.40	336.30	342.20	348.10	354.00	359.90	365.80	371.70	377.60	383.50	389.40	395.30	401.20	407.10
0.600	300.00	306.00	312.00	318.00	324.00	330.00	336.00	342.00	348.00	354.00	360.00	366.00	372.00	378.00	384.00	390.00	396.00	402.00	408.00	414.00
0.610	305.00	311.10	317.20	323.30	329.40	335.50	341.60	347.70	353.80	359.90	366.00	372.10	378.20	384.30	390.40	396.50	402.60	408.70	414.80	420.90
0.620	310.00	316.20	322.40	328.60	334.80	341.00	347.20	353.40	359.60	365.80	372.00	378.20	384.40	390.60	396.80	403.00	409.20	415.40	421.60	427.80
0.630	315.00	321.30	327.60	333.90	340.20	346.50	352.80	359.10	365.40	371.70	378.00	384.30	390.60	396.90	403.20	409.50	415.80	422.10	428.40	434.70
0.640	320.00	326.40	332.80	339.20	345.60	352.00	358.40	364.80	371.20	377.60	384.00	390.40	396.80	403.20	409.60	416.00	422.40	428.80	435.20	441.60
0.650	325.00	331.50	338.00	344.50	351.00	357.50	364.00	370.50	377.00	383.50	390.00	396.50	403.00	409.50	416.00	422.50	429.00	435.50	442.00	448.50
0.660	330.00	336.60	343.20	349.80	356.40	363.00	369.60	376.20	382.80	389.40	396.00	402.60	409.20	415.80	422.40	429.00	435.60	442.20	448.80	455.40
0.670	335.00	341.70	348.40	355.10	361.80	368.50	375.20	381.90	388.60	395.30	402.00	408.70	415.40	422.10	428.80	435.50	442.20	448.90	455.60	462.30
0.680	340.00	346.80	353.60	360.40	367.20	374.00	380.80	387.60	394.40	401.20	408.00	414.80	421.60	428.40	435.20	442.00	448.80	455.60	462.40	469.20
0.690	345.00	351.90	358.80	365.70	372.60	379.50	386.40	393.30	400.20	407.10	414.00	420.90	427.80	434.70	441.60	448.50	455.40	462.30	469.20	476.10
0.700	350.00	357.00	364.00	371.00	378.00	385.00	392.00	399.00	406.00	413.00	420.00	427.00	434.00	441.00	448.00	455.00	462.00	469.00	476.00	483.00
0.710	355.00	362.10	369.20	376.30	383.40	390.50	397.60	404.70	411.80	418.90	426.00	433.10	440.20	447.30	454.40	461.50	468.60	475.70	482.80	489.90
0.720	360.00	367.20	374.40	381.60	388.80	396.00	403.20	410.40	417.60	424.80	432.00	439.20	446.40	453.60	460.80	468.00	475.20	482.40	489.60	496.80
0.730	365.00	372.30	379.60	386.90	394.20	401.50	408.80	416.10	423.40	430.70	438.00	445.30	452.60	459.90	467.20	474.50	481.80	489.10	496.40	503.70
0.740	370.00	377.40	384.80	392.20	399.60	407.00	414.40	421.80	429.20	436.60	444.00	451.40	458.80	466.20	473.60	481.00	488.40	495.80	503.20	510.60
0.750	375.00	382.50	390.00	397.50	405.00	412.50	420.00	427.50	435.00	442.50	450.00	457.50	465.00	472.50	480.00	487.50	495.00	502.50	510.00	517.50
0.760	380.00	387.60	395.20	402.80	410.40	418.00	425.60	433.20	440.80	448.40	456.00	463.60	471.20	478.80	486.40	494.00	501.60	509.20	516.80	524.40
0.770	385.00	392.70	400.40	408.10	415.80	423.50	431.20	438.90	446.60	454.30	462.00	469.70	477.40	485.10	492.80	500.50	508.20	515.90	523.60	531.30
0.780	390.00	397.80	405.60	413.40	421.20	429.00	436.80	444.60	452.40	460.20	468.00	475.80	483.60	491.40	499.20	507.00	514.80	522.60	530.40	538.20
0.790	395.00	402.90	410.80	418.70	426.60	434.50	442.40	450.30	458.20	466.10	474.00	481.90	489.80	497.70	505.60	513.50	521.40	529.30	537.20	545.10
0.800	400.00	408.00	416.00	424.00	432.00	440.00	448.00	456.00	464.00	472.00	480.00	488.00	496.00	504.00	512.00	520.00	528.00	536.00	544.00	552.00
0.810	405.00	413.10	421.20	429.30	437.40	445.50	453.60	461.70	469.80	477.90	486.00	494.10	502.20	510.30	518.40	526.50	534.60	542.70	550.80	558.90
0.820	410.00	418.20	426.40	434.60	442.80	451.00	459.20	467.40	475.60	483.80	492.00	500.20	508.40	516.60	524.80	533.00	541.20	549.40	557.60	565.80
0.830	415.00	423.30	431.60	439.90	448.20	456.50	464.80	473.10	481.40	489.70	498.00	506.30	514.60	522.90	531.20	539.50	547.80	556.10	564.40	572.70
0.840	420.00	428.40	436.80	445.20	453.60	462.00	470.40	478.80	487.20	495.60	504.00	512.40	520.80	529.20	537.60	546.00	554.40	562.80	571.20	579.60
0.850	425.00	433.50	442.00	450.50	459.00	467.50	476.00	484.50	493.00	501.50	510.00	518.50	527.00	535.50	544.00	552.50	561.00	569.50	578.00	586.50
0.860	430.00	438.60	447.20	455.80	464.40	473.00	481.60	490.20	498.80	507.40	516.00	524.60	533.20	541.80	550.40	559.00	567.60	576.20	584.80	593.40
0.870	435.00	443.70	452.40	461.10	469.80	478.50	487.20	495.90	504.60	513.30	522.00	530.70	539.40	548.10	556.80	565.50	574.20	582.90	591.60	600.30
0.880	440.00	448.80	457.60	466.40	475.20	484.00	492.80	501.60	510.40	519.20	528.00	536.80	545.60	554.40	563.20	572.00	580.80	589.60	598.40	607.20
0.890	445.00	453.90	462.80	471.70	480.60	489.50	498.40	507.30	516.20	525.10	534.00	542.90	551.80	560.70	569.60	578.50	587.40	596.30	605.20	614.10
0.900	450.00	459.00	468.00	477.00	486.00	495.00	504.00	513.00	522.00	531.00	540.00	549.00	558.00	567.00	576.00	585.00	594.00	603.00	612.00	621.00
0.910	455.00	464.10	473.20	482.30	491.40	500.50	509.60	518.70	527.80	536.90	546.00	555.10	564.20	573.30	582.40	591.50	600.60	609.70	618.80	627.90
0.920	460.00	469.20	478.40	487.60	496.80	506.00	515.20	524.40	533.60	542.80	552.00	561.20	570.40	579.60	588.80	598.00	607.20	616.40	625.60	634.80
0.930	465.00	474.30	483.60	492.90	502.20	511.50	520.80	530.10	539.40	548.70	558.00	567.30	576.60	585.90	595.20	604.50	613.80	623.10	632.40	641.70
0.940	470.00	479.40	488.80	498.20	507.60	517.00	526.40	535.80	545.20	554.60	564.00	573.40	582.80	592.20	601.60	611.00	620.40	629.80	639.20	648.60
0.950	475.00	484.50	494.00	503.50	513.00	522.50	532.00	541.50	551.00	560.50	570.00	579.50	589.00	598.50	608.00	617.50	627.00	636.50	646.00	655.50
0.960	480.00	489.60	499.20	508.80	518.40	528.00	537.60	547.20	556.80	566.40	576.00	585.60	595.20	604.80	614.40	624.00	633.60	643.20	652.80	662.40
0.970	485.00	494.70	504.40	514.10	523.80	533.50	543.20	552.90	562.60	572.30	582.00	591.70	601.40	611.10	620.80	630.50	640.20	649.90	659.60	669.30
0.980	490.00	499.80	509.60	519.40	529.20	539.00	548.80	558.60	568.40	578.20	588.00	597.80	607.60	617.40	627.20	637.00	646.80	656.60	666.40	676.20
0.990	495.00	504.90	514.80	524.70	534.60	544.50	554.40	564.30	574.20	584.10	594.00	603.90	613.80	623.70	633.60	643.50	653.40	663.30	673.20	683.10
1.000	500.00	510.00	520.00	530.00	540.00	550.00	560.00	570.00	580.00	590.00	600.00	610.00	620.00	630.00	640.00	650.00	660.00	670.00	680.00	690.00

GOLD BULLION VALUE CHART																					
Oz.	**700.00**	**710.00**	**720.00**	**730.00**	**740.00**	**750.00**	**760.00**	**770.00**	**780.00**	**790.00**	**800.00**	**810.00**	**820.00**	**830.00**	**840.00**	**850.00**	**860.00**	**870.00**	**880.00**	**890.00**	**900.00**
0.001	0.70	0.71	0.72	0.73	0.74	0.75	0.76	0.77	0.78	0.79	0.80	0.81	0.82	0.83	0.84	0.85	0.86	0.87	0.88	0.89	0.90
0.002	1.40	1.42	1.44	1.46	1.48	1.50	1.52	1.54	1.56	1.58	1.60	1.62	1.64	1.66	1.68	1.70	1.72	1.74	1.76	1.78	1.80
0.003	2.10	2.13	2.16	2.19	2.22	2.25	2.28	2.31	2.34	2.37	2.40	2.43	2.46	2.49	2.52	2.55	2.58	2.61	2.64	2.67	2.70
0.004	2.80	2.84	2.88	2.92	2.96	3.00	3.04	3.08	3.12	3.16	3.20	3.24	3.28	3.32	3.36	3.40	3.44	3.48	3.52	3.56	3.60
0.005	3.50	3.55	3.60	3.65	3.70	3.75	3.80	3.85	3.90	3.95	4.00	4.05	4.10	4.15	4.20	4.25	4.30	4.35	4.40	4.45	4.50
0.006	4.20	4.26	4.32	4.38	4.44	4.50	4.56	4.62	4.68	4.74	4.80	4.86	4.92	4.98	5.04	5.10	5.16	5.22	5.28	5.34	5.40
0.007	4.90	4.97	5.04	5.11	5.18	5.25	5.32	5.39	5.46	5.53	5.60	5.67	5.74	5.81	5.88	5.95	6.02	6.09	6.16	6.23	6.30
0.008	5.60	5.68	5.76	5.84	5.92	6.00	6.08	6.16	6.24	6.32	6.40	6.48	6.56	6.64	6.72	6.80	6.88	6.96	7.04	7.12	7.20
0.009	6.30	6.39	6.48	6.57	6.66	6.75	6.84	6.93	7.02	7.11	7.20	7.29	7.38	7.47	7.56	7.65	7.74	7.83	7.92	8.01	8.10
0.010	7.00	7.10	7.20	7.30	7.40	7.50	7.60	7.70	7.80	7.90	8.00	8.10	8.20	8.30	8.40	8.50	8.60	8.70	8.80	8.90	9.00
0.020	14.00	14.20	14.40	14.60	14.80	15.00	15.20	15.40	15.60	15.80	16.00	16.20	16.40	16.60	16.80	17.00	17.20	17.40	17.60	17.80	18.00
0.030	21.00	21.30	21.60	21.90	22.20	22.50	22.80	23.10	23.40	23.70	24.00	24.30	24.60	24.90	25.20	25.50	25.80	26.10	26.40	26.70	27.00
0.040	28.00	28.40	28.80	29.20	29.60	30.00	30.40	30.80	31.20	31.60	32.00	32.40	32.80	33.20	33.60	34.00	34.40	34.80	35.20	35.60	36.00
0.050	35.00	35.50	36.00	36.50	37.00	37.50	38.00	38.50	39.00	39.50	40.00	40.50	41.00	41.50	42.00	42.50	43.00	43.50	44.00	44.50	45.00
0.060	42.00	42.60	43.20	43.80	44.40	45.00	45.60	46.20	46.80	47.40	48.00	48.60	49.20	49.80	50.40	51.00	51.60	52.20	52.80	53.40	54.00
0.070	49.00	49.70	50.40	51.10	51.80	52.50	53.20	53.90	54.60	55.30	56.00	56.70	57.40	58.10	58.80	59.50	60.20	60.90	61.60	62.30	63.00
0.080	56.00	56.80	57.60	58.40	59.20	60.00	60.80	61.60	62.40	63.20	64.00	64.80	65.60	66.40	67.20	68.00	68.80	69.60	70.40	71.20	72.00
0.090	63.00	63.90	64.80	65.70	66.60	67.50	68.40	69.30	70.20	71.10	72.00	72.90	73.80	74.70	75.60	76.50	77.40	78.30	79.20	80.10	81.00
0.100	70.00	71.00	72.00	73.00	74.00	75.00	76.00	77.00	78.00	79.00	80.00	81.00	82.00	83.00	84.00	85.00	86.00	87.00	88.00	89.00	90.00
0.110	77.00	78.10	79.20	80.30	81.40	82.50	83.60	84.70	85.80	86.90	88.00	89.10	90.20	91.30	92.40	93.50	94.60	95.70	96.80	97.90	99.00
0.120	84.00	85.20	86.40	87.60	88.80	90.00	91.20	92.40	93.60	94.80	96.00	97.20	98.40	99.60	100.80	102.00	103.20	104.40	105.60	106.80	108.00
0.130	91.00	92.30	93.60	94.90	96.20	97.50	98.80	100.10	101.40	102.70	104.00	105.30	106.60	107.90	109.20	110.50	111.80	113.10	114.40	115.70	117.00
0.140	98.00	99.40	100.80	102.20	103.60	105.00	106.40	107.80	109.20	110.60	112.00	113.40	114.80	116.20	117.60	119.00	120.40	121.80	123.20	124.60	126.00
0.150	105.00	106.50	108.00	109.50	111.00	112.50	114.00	115.50	117.00	118.50	120.00	121.50	123.00	124.50	126.00	127.50	129.00	130.50	132.00	133.50	135.00
0.160	112.00	113.60	115.20	116.80	118.40	120.00	121.60	123.20	124.80	126.40	128.00	129.60	131.20	132.80	134.40	136.00	137.60	139.20	140.80	142.40	144.00
0.170	119.00	120.70	122.40	124.10	125.80	127.50	129.20	130.90	132.60	134.30	136.00	137.70	139.40	141.10	142.80	144.50	146.20	147.90	149.60	151.30	153.00
0.180	126.00	127.80	129.60	131.40	133.20	135.00	136.80	138.60	140.40	142.20	144.00	145.80	147.60	149.40	151.20	153.00	154.80	156.60	158.40	160.20	162.00
0.190	133.00	134.90	136.80	138.70	140.60	142.50	144.40	146.30	148.20	150.10	152.00	153.90	155.80	157.70	159.60	161.50	163.40	165.30	167.20	169.10	171.00
0.200	140.00	142.00	144.00	146.00	148.00	150.00	152.00	154.00	156.00	158.00	160.00	162.00	164.00	166.00	168.00	170.00	172.00	174.00	176.00	178.00	180.00
0.210	147.00	149.10	151.20	153.30	155.40	157.50	159.60	161.70	163.80	165.90	168.00	170.10	172.20	174.30	176.40	178.50	180.60	182.70	184.80	186.90	189.00
0.220	154.00	156.20	158.40	160.60	162.80	165.00	167.20	169.40	171.60	173.80	176.00	178.20	180.40	182.60	184.80	187.00	189.20	191.40	193.60	195.80	198.00
0.230	161.00	163.30	165.60	167.90	170.20	172.50	174.80	177.10	179.40	181.70	184.00	186.30	188.60	190.90	193.20	195.50	197.80	200.10	202.40	204.70	207.00
0.240	168.00	170.40	172.80	175.20	177.60	180.00	182.40	184.80	187.20	189.60	192.00	194.40	196.80	199.20	201.60	204.00	206.40	208.80	211.20	213.60	216.00
0.250	175.00	177.50	180.00	182.50	185.00	187.50	190.00	192.50	195.00	197.50	200.00	202.50	205.00	207.50	210.00	212.50	215.00	217.50	220.00	222.50	225.00
0.260	182.00	184.60	187.20	189.80	192.40	195.00	197.60	200.20	202.80	205.40	208.00	210.60	213.20	215.80	218.40	221.00	223.60	226.20	228.80	231.40	234.00
0.270	189.00	191.70	194.40	197.10	199.80	202.50	205.20	207.90	210.60	213.30	216.00	218.70	221.40	224.10	226.80	229.50	232.20	234.90	237.60	240.30	243.00
0.280	196.00	198.80	201.60	204.40	207.20	210.00	212.80	215.60	218.40	221.20	224.00	226.80	229.60	232.40	235.20	238.00	240.80	243.60	246.40	249.20	252.00
0.290	203.00	205.90	208.80	211.70	214.60	217.50	220.40	223.30	226.20	229.10	232.00	234.90	237.80	240.70	243.60	246.50	249.40	252.30	255.20	258.10	261.00
0.300	210.00	213.00	216.00	219.00	222.00	225.00	228.00	231.00	234.00	237.00	240.00	243.00	246.00	249.00	252.00	255.00	258.00	261.00	264.00	267.00	270.00
0.310	217.00	220.10	223.20	226.30	229.40	232.50	235.60	238.70	241.80	244.90	248.00	251.10	254.20	257.30	260.40	263.50	266.60	269.70	272.80	275.90	279.00
0.320	224.00	227.20	230.40	233.60	236.80	240.00	243.20	246.40	249.60	252.80	256.00	259.20	262.40	265.60	268.80	272.00	275.20	278.40	281.60	284.80	288.00
0.330	231.00	234.30	237.60	240.90	244.20	247.50	250.80	254.10	257.40	260.70	264.00	267.30	270.60	273.90	277.20	280.50	283.80	287.10	290.40	293.70	297.00
0.340	238.00	241.40	244.80	248.20	251.60	255.00	258.40	261.80	265.20	268.60	272.00	275.40	278.80	282.20	285.60	289.00	292.40	295.80	299.20	302.60	306.00
0.350	245.00	248.50	252.00	255.50	259.00	262.50	266.00	269.50	273.00	276.50	280.00	283.50	287.00	290.50	294.00	297.50	301.00	304.50	308.00	311.50	315.00
0.360	252.00	255.60	259.20	262.80	266.40	270.00	273.60	277.20	280.80	284.40	288.00	291.60	295.20	298.80	302.40	306.00	309.60	313.20	316.80	320.40	324.00
0.370	259.00	262.70	266.40	270.10	273.80	277.50	281.20	284.90	288.60	292.30	296.00	299.70	303.40	307.10	310.80	314.50	318.20	321.90	325.60	329.30	333.00
0.380	266.00	269.80	273.60	277.40	281.20	285.00	288.80	292.60	296.40	300.20	304.00	307.80	311.60	315.40	319.20	323.00	326.80	330.60	334.40	338.20	342.00
0.390	273.00	276.90	280.80	284.70	288.60	292.50	296.40	300.30	304.20	308.10	312.00	315.90	319.80	323.70	327.60	331.50	335.40	339.30	343.20	347.10	351.00
0.400	280.00	284.00	288.00	292.00	296.00	300.00	304.00	308.00	312.00	316.00	320.00	324.00	328.00	332.00	336.00	340.00	344.00	348.00	352.00	356.00	360.00
0.410	287.00	291.10	295.20	299.30	303.40	307.50	311.60	315.70	319.80	323.90	328.00	332.10	336.20	340.30	344.40	348.50	352.60	356.70	360.80	364.90	369.00
0.420	294.00	298.20	302.40	306.60	310.80	315.00	319.20	323.40	327.60	331.80	336.00	340.20	344.40	348.60	352.80	357.00	361.20	365.40	369.60	373.80	378.00
0.430	301.00	305.30	309.60	313.90	318.20	322.50	326.80	331.10	335.40	339.70	344.00	348.30	352.60	356.90	361.20	365.50	369.80	374.10	378.40	382.70	387.00
0.440	308.00	312.40	316.80	321.20	325.60	330.00	334.40	338.80	343.20	347.60	352.00	356.40	360.80	365.20	369.60	374.00	378.40	382.80	387.20	391.60	396.00
0.450	315.00	319.50	324.00	328.50	333.00	337.50	342.00	346.50	351.00	355.50	360.00	364.50	369.00	373.50	378.00	382.50	387.00	391.50	396.00	400.50	405.00
0.460	322.00	326.60	331.20	335.80	340.40	345.00	349.60	354.20	358.80	363.40	368.00	372.60	377.20	381.80	386.40	391.00	395.60	400.20	404.80	409.40	414.00

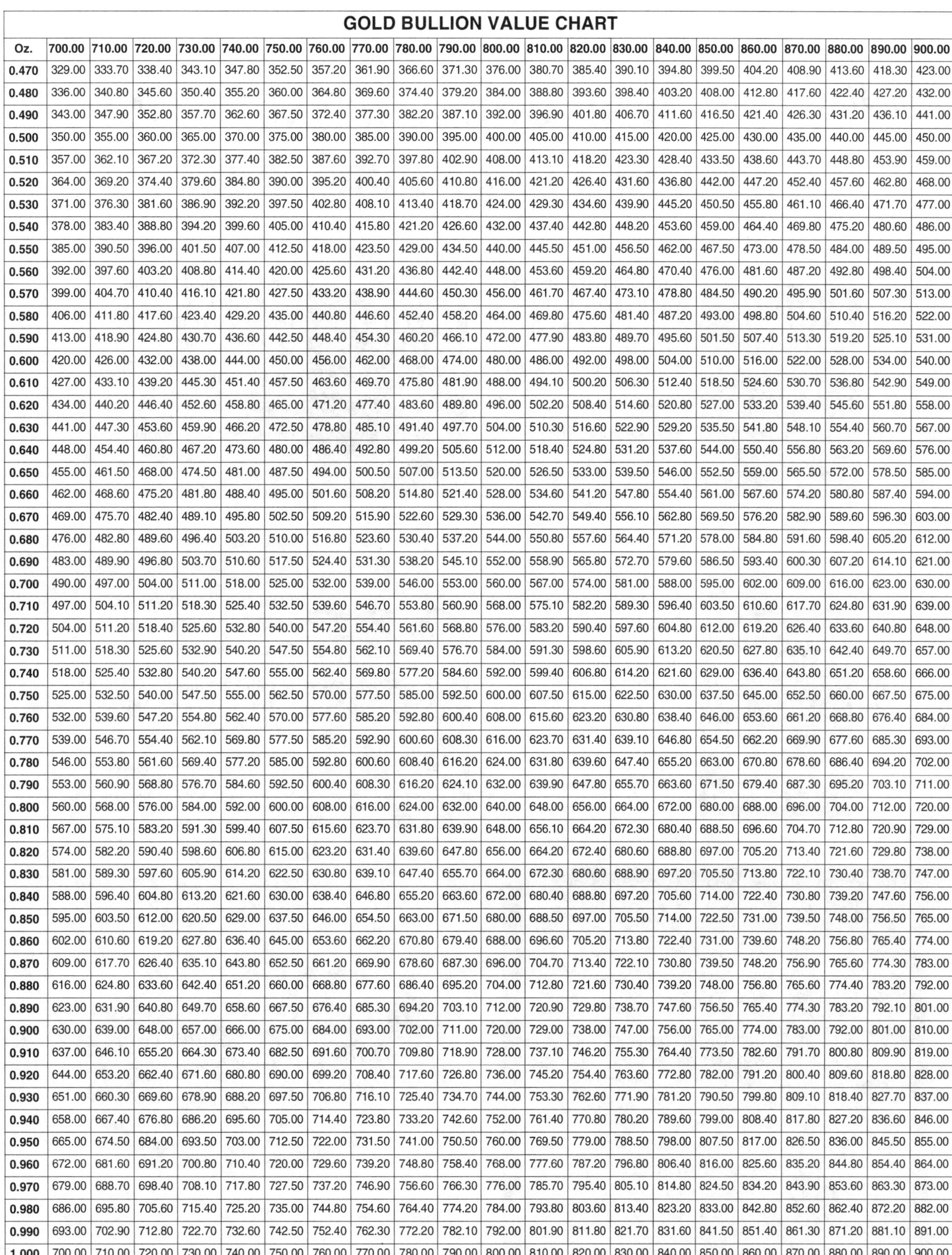

GOLD BULLION VALUE CHART

Oz.	700.00	710.00	720.00	730.00	740.00	750.00	760.00	770.00	780.00	790.00	800.00	810.00	820.00	830.00	840.00	850.00	860.00	870.00	880.00	890.00	900.00
0.470	329.00	333.70	338.40	343.10	347.80	352.50	357.20	361.90	366.60	371.30	376.00	380.70	385.40	390.10	394.80	399.50	404.20	408.90	413.60	418.30	423.00
0.480	336.00	340.80	345.60	350.40	355.20	360.00	364.80	369.60	374.40	379.20	384.00	388.80	393.60	398.40	403.20	408.00	412.80	417.60	422.40	427.20	432.00
0.490	343.00	347.90	352.80	357.70	362.60	367.50	372.40	377.30	382.20	387.10	392.00	396.90	401.80	406.70	411.60	416.50	421.40	426.30	431.20	436.10	441.00
0.500	350.00	355.00	360.00	365.00	370.00	375.00	380.00	385.00	390.00	395.00	400.00	405.00	410.00	415.00	420.00	425.00	430.00	435.00	440.00	445.00	450.00
0.510	357.00	362.10	367.20	372.30	377.40	382.50	387.60	392.70	397.80	402.90	408.00	413.10	418.20	423.30	428.40	433.50	438.60	443.70	448.80	453.90	459.00
0.520	364.00	369.20	374.40	379.60	384.80	390.00	395.20	400.40	405.60	410.80	416.00	421.20	426.40	431.60	436.80	442.00	447.20	452.40	457.60	462.80	468.00
0.530	371.00	376.30	381.60	386.90	392.20	397.50	402.80	408.10	413.40	418.70	424.00	429.30	434.60	439.90	445.20	450.50	455.80	461.10	466.40	471.70	477.00
0.540	378.00	383.40	388.80	394.20	399.60	405.00	410.40	415.80	421.20	426.60	432.00	437.40	442.80	448.20	453.60	459.00	464.40	469.80	475.20	480.60	486.00
0.550	385.00	390.50	396.00	401.50	407.00	412.50	418.00	423.50	429.00	434.50	440.00	445.50	451.00	456.50	462.00	467.50	473.00	478.50	484.00	489.50	495.00
0.560	392.00	397.60	403.20	408.80	414.40	420.00	425.60	431.20	436.80	442.40	448.00	453.60	459.20	464.80	470.40	476.00	481.60	487.20	492.80	498.40	504.00
0.570	399.00	404.70	410.40	416.10	421.80	427.50	433.20	438.90	444.60	450.30	456.00	461.70	467.40	473.10	478.80	484.50	490.20	495.90	501.60	507.30	513.00
0.580	406.00	411.80	417.60	423.40	429.20	435.00	440.80	446.60	452.40	458.20	464.00	469.80	475.60	481.40	487.20	493.00	498.80	504.60	510.40	516.20	522.00
0.590	413.00	418.90	424.80	430.70	436.60	442.50	448.40	454.30	460.20	466.10	472.00	477.90	483.80	489.70	495.60	501.50	507.40	513.30	519.20	525.10	531.00
0.600	420.00	426.00	432.00	438.00	444.00	450.00	456.00	462.00	468.00	474.00	480.00	486.00	492.00	498.00	504.00	510.00	516.00	522.00	528.00	534.00	540.00
0.610	427.00	433.10	439.20	445.30	451.40	457.50	463.60	469.70	475.80	481.90	488.00	494.10	500.20	506.30	512.40	518.50	524.60	530.70	536.80	542.90	549.00
0.620	434.00	440.20	446.40	452.60	458.80	465.00	471.20	477.40	483.60	489.80	496.00	502.20	508.40	514.60	520.80	527.00	533.20	539.40	545.60	551.80	558.00
0.630	441.00	447.30	453.60	459.90	466.20	472.50	478.80	485.10	491.40	497.70	504.00	510.30	516.60	522.90	529.20	535.50	541.80	548.10	554.40	560.70	567.00
0.640	448.00	454.40	460.80	467.20	473.60	480.00	486.40	492.80	499.20	505.60	512.00	518.40	524.80	531.20	537.60	544.00	550.40	556.80	563.20	569.60	576.00
0.650	455.00	461.50	468.00	474.50	481.00	487.50	494.00	500.50	507.00	513.50	520.00	526.50	533.00	539.50	546.00	552.50	559.00	565.50	572.00	578.50	585.00
0.660	462.00	468.60	475.20	481.80	488.40	495.00	501.60	508.20	514.80	521.40	528.00	534.60	541.20	547.80	554.40	561.00	567.60	574.20	580.80	587.40	594.00
0.670	469.00	475.70	482.40	489.10	495.80	502.50	509.20	515.90	522.60	529.30	536.00	542.70	549.40	556.10	562.80	569.50	576.20	582.90	589.60	596.30	603.00
0.680	476.00	482.80	489.60	496.40	503.20	510.00	516.80	523.60	530.40	537.20	544.00	550.80	557.60	564.40	571.20	578.00	584.80	591.60	598.40	605.20	612.00
0.690	483.00	489.90	496.80	503.70	510.60	517.50	524.40	531.30	538.20	545.10	552.00	558.90	565.80	572.70	579.60	586.50	593.40	600.30	607.20	614.10	621.00
0.700	490.00	497.00	504.00	511.00	518.00	525.00	532.00	539.00	546.00	553.00	560.00	567.00	574.00	581.00	588.00	595.00	602.00	609.00	616.00	623.00	630.00
0.710	497.00	504.10	511.20	518.30	525.40	532.50	539.60	546.70	553.80	560.90	568.00	575.10	582.20	589.30	596.40	603.50	610.60	617.70	624.80	631.90	639.00
0.720	504.00	511.20	518.40	525.60	532.80	540.00	547.20	554.40	561.60	568.80	576.00	583.20	590.40	597.60	604.80	612.00	619.20	626.40	633.60	640.80	648.00
0.730	511.00	518.30	525.60	532.90	540.20	547.50	554.80	562.10	569.40	576.70	584.00	591.30	598.60	605.90	613.20	620.50	627.80	635.10	642.40	649.70	657.00
0.740	518.00	525.40	532.80	540.20	547.60	555.00	562.40	569.80	577.20	584.60	592.00	599.40	606.80	614.20	621.60	629.00	636.40	643.80	651.20	658.60	666.00
0.750	525.00	532.50	540.00	547.50	555.00	562.50	570.00	577.50	585.00	592.50	600.00	607.50	615.00	622.50	630.00	637.50	645.00	652.50	660.00	667.50	675.00
0.760	532.00	539.60	547.20	554.80	562.40	570.00	577.60	585.20	592.80	600.40	608.00	615.60	623.20	630.80	638.40	646.00	653.60	661.20	668.80	676.40	684.00
0.770	539.00	546.70	554.40	562.10	569.80	577.50	585.20	592.90	600.60	608.30	616.00	623.70	631.40	639.10	646.80	654.50	662.20	669.90	677.60	685.30	693.00
0.780	546.00	553.80	561.60	569.40	577.20	585.00	592.80	600.60	608.40	616.20	624.00	631.80	639.60	647.40	655.20	663.00	670.80	678.60	686.40	694.20	702.00
0.790	553.00	560.90	568.80	576.70	584.60	592.50	600.40	608.30	616.20	624.10	632.00	639.90	647.80	655.70	663.60	671.50	679.40	687.30	695.20	703.10	711.00
0.800	560.00	568.00	576.00	584.00	592.00	600.00	608.00	616.00	624.00	632.00	640.00	648.00	656.00	664.00	672.00	680.00	688.00	696.00	704.00	712.00	720.00
0.810	567.00	575.10	583.20	591.30	599.40	607.50	615.60	623.70	631.80	639.90	648.00	656.10	664.20	672.30	680.40	688.50	696.60	704.70	712.80	720.90	729.00
0.820	574.00	582.20	590.40	598.60	606.80	615.00	623.20	631.40	639.60	647.80	656.00	664.20	672.40	680.60	688.80	697.00	705.20	713.40	721.60	729.80	738.00
0.830	581.00	589.30	597.60	605.90	614.20	622.50	630.80	639.10	647.40	655.70	664.00	672.30	680.60	688.90	697.20	705.50	713.80	722.10	730.40	738.70	747.00
0.840	588.00	596.40	604.80	613.20	621.60	630.00	638.40	646.80	655.20	663.60	672.00	680.40	688.80	697.20	705.60	714.00	722.40	730.80	739.20	747.60	756.00
0.850	595.00	603.50	612.00	620.50	629.00	637.50	646.00	654.50	663.00	671.50	680.00	688.50	697.00	705.50	714.00	722.50	731.00	739.50	748.00	756.50	765.00
0.860	602.00	610.60	619.20	627.80	636.40	645.00	653.60	662.20	670.80	679.40	688.00	696.60	705.20	713.80	722.40	731.00	739.60	748.20	756.80	765.40	774.00
0.870	609.00	617.70	626.40	635.10	643.80	652.50	661.20	669.90	678.60	687.30	696.00	704.70	713.40	722.10	730.80	739.50	748.20	756.90	765.60	774.30	783.00
0.880	616.00	624.80	633.60	642.40	651.20	660.00	668.80	677.60	686.40	695.20	704.00	712.80	721.60	730.40	739.20	748.00	756.80	765.60	774.40	783.20	792.00
0.890	623.00	631.90	640.80	649.70	658.60	667.50	676.40	685.30	694.20	703.10	712.00	720.90	729.80	738.70	747.60	756.50	765.40	774.30	783.20	792.10	801.00
0.900	630.00	639.00	648.00	657.00	666.00	675.00	684.00	693.00	702.00	711.00	720.00	729.00	738.00	747.00	756.00	765.00	774.00	783.00	792.00	801.00	810.00
0.910	637.00	646.10	655.20	664.30	673.40	682.50	691.60	700.70	709.80	718.90	728.00	737.10	746.20	755.30	764.40	773.50	782.60	791.70	800.80	809.90	819.00
0.920	644.00	653.20	662.40	671.60	680.80	690.00	699.20	708.40	717.60	726.80	736.00	745.20	754.40	763.60	772.80	782.00	791.20	800.40	809.60	818.80	828.00
0.930	651.00	660.30	669.60	678.90	688.20	697.50	706.80	716.10	725.40	734.70	744.00	753.30	762.60	771.90	781.20	790.50	799.80	809.10	818.40	827.70	837.00
0.940	658.00	667.40	676.80	686.20	695.60	705.00	714.40	723.80	733.20	742.60	752.00	761.40	770.80	780.20	789.60	799.00	808.40	817.80	827.20	836.60	846.00
0.950	665.00	674.50	684.00	693.50	703.00	712.50	722.00	731.50	741.00	750.50	760.00	769.50	779.00	788.50	798.00	807.50	817.00	826.50	836.00	845.50	855.00
0.960	672.00	681.60	691.20	700.80	710.40	720.00	729.60	739.20	748.80	758.40	768.00	777.60	787.20	796.80	806.40	816.00	825.60	835.20	844.80	854.40	864.00
0.970	679.00	688.70	698.40	708.10	717.80	727.50	737.20	746.90	756.60	766.30	776.00	785.70	795.40	805.10	814.80	824.50	834.20	843.90	853.60	863.30	873.00
0.980	686.00	695.80	705.60	715.40	725.20	735.00	744.80	754.60	764.40	774.20	784.00	793.80	803.60	813.40	823.20	833.00	842.80	852.60	862.40	872.20	882.00
0.990	693.00	702.90	712.80	722.70	732.60	742.50	752.40	762.30	772.20	782.10	792.00	801.90	811.80	821.70	831.60	841.50	851.40	861.30	871.20	881.10	891.00
1.000	700.00	710.00	720.00	730.00	740.00	750.00	760.00	770.00	780.00	790.00	800.00	810.00	820.00	830.00	840.00	850.00	860.00	870.00	880.00	890.00	900.00

AFGHANISTAN

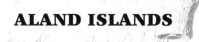

REPUBLIC

MEDALLIC BULLION

X# MB1 OUNCE
31.1340 g., 0.9990 Silver 0.9999 oz. ASW **Obv:** Arms with Koran at center **Rev:** Flag on outlined topographical map **Rev. Legend:** FREE - AFGHANISTAN

Date	Mintage	F	VF	XF	Unc	BU
1987 Proof	—	Value: 30.00				

ALAND ISLANDS

In April 1991 the Aland Islands attempted to issue their own coinage. Being a semi-autonomous territory of Finland, they intended to extend their independence to include a coinage right, but Finland strongly objected and the issue was quickly withdrawn. Mintages listed below are the official limits, but relatively few examples are known to exist.

AUTONOMOUS

STANDARD

X# 1.1 10 DALER
Bronze **Obv:** Crowned arms **Rev:** Single-masted sailing ship **Edge:** Plain **Note:** Prev. KM#1.1.

Date	Mintage	F	VF	XF	Unc	BU
1991	50,000	—	—	—	—	65.00

X# 1.2 10 DALER
Bronze **Obv:** Crowned arms **Rev:** Single-masted sailing ship **Edge Lettering:** Åland Mynt 26.04.1991. **Note:** Prev. KM#1.2.

Date	Mintage	F	VF	XF	Unc	BU
1991	Inc. above	—	—	—	—	75.00

X# 2.1 50 DALER
Copper-Nickel **Obv:** Crowned arms **Rev:** Twin-masted sailing ship **Edge:** Plain **Note:** Prev. KM#2.1.

Date	Mintage	F	VF	XF	Unc	BU
1991	25,000	—	—	—	—	200

X# 2.2 50 DALER
Copper-Nickel **Obv:** Crowned arms **Rev:** Twin-masted sailing ship **Edge Lettering:** Åland Mynt 26.04.1991. **Note:** Prev. KM#2.2.

Date	Mintage	F	VF	XF	Unc	BU
1991	Inc. above	—	—	—	—	225

X# 3.1 100 DALER
18.0000 g., 0.9250 Silver 0.5353 oz. ASW
Obv: Crowned arms **Rev:** Four-masted sailing ship **Edge:** Plain **Note:** Prev. KM#3.1.

Date	Mintage	F	VF	XF	Unc	BU
1991	25,000	—	—	—	—	375

X# 3.2 100 DALER
18.0000 g., 0.9250 Silver 0.5353 oz. ASW
Obv: Crowned arms **Rev:** Four-masted sailing ship **Edge Lettering:** Åland Mynt 26.04.1991. **Note:** Prev. KM#3.2.

Date	Mintage	F	VF	XF	Unc	BU
1991	Inc. above	—	—	—	—	400

MINT SETS

X#	Date	Mintage	Identification	Issue Price	Mkt Val
XMS1	1991 (3)	—	X1.2, X2.2, X3.2	—	700

ALBANIA

PEOPLE'S SOCIALIST REPUBLIC

1945 - 1990

ECU COINAGE

X# 1 20 ECU
31.1030 g., 0.9990 Silver 0.9989 oz. ASW, 38 mm. **Obv:** Arms **Obv. Legend:** REPUBLIKA SHQIPËRISE **Rev:** Early sailing ship **Rev. Legend:** ALBANIA **Edge:** Reeded

Date	Mintage	F	VF	XF	Unc	BU
1993 Proof	10,000	Value: 45.00				

X# 2 100 ECU
31.1030 g., 0.7500 Gold 0.7500 oz. AGW, 38 mm. **Obv:** Arms **Obv. Legend:** REPUBLIKA SHQIPËRISE **Rev:** Early sailing ship **Rev. Legend:** ALBANIA **Edge:** Reeded

Date	Mintage	F	VF	XF	Unc	BU
1993 Proof	1,000	Value: 750				

REPUBLIC

FANTASY EURO PATTERNS

X# Pn1 EURO CENT
Copper Plated Steel **Edge:** Plain

Date	Mintage	F	VF	XF	Unc	BU
2004	10,000	—	—	—	—	1.50

X# Pn2 2 EURO CENTS
Copper Plated Steel **Edge:** Plain

Date	Mintage	F	VF	XF	Unc	BU
2004	10,000	—	—	—	—	2.00

X# Pn3 5 EURO CENTS
Copper Plated Steel **Edge:** Plain

Date	Mintage	F	VF	XF	Unc	BU
2004	10,000	—	—	—	—	2.50

X# Pn4 10 EURO CENTS
Goldine **Edge:** Plain

Date	Mintage	F	VF	XF	Unc	BU
2004	10,000	—	—	—	—	3.00

X# Pn5 20 EURO CENTS
Goldine **Edge:** Plain

Date	Mintage	F	VF	XF	Unc	BU
2004	10,000	—	—	—	—	3.50

X# Pn6 50 EURO CENTS
Goldine **Edge:** Plain

Date	Mintage	F	VF	XF	Unc	BU
2004	10,000	—	—	—	—	4.00

X# Pn7 EUROP
Bi-Metallic, 22.80 mm. **Obv:** Facing bust **Rev:** Large value "1", outlined map **Edge:** Plain

Date	Mintage	F	VF	XF	Unc	BU
2004	10,000	—	—	—	—	6.00

X# Pn8 2 EUROP
Bi-Metallic, 25.70 mm. **Obv:** Capped and bearded male bust right **Rev:** Large value "2", outlined map **Edge:** Plain

Date	Mintage	F	VF	XF	Unc	BU
2004	10,000	—	—	—	—	8.00

MINT SETS

X#	Date	Mintage	Identification	Issue Price	Mkt Val
XMS1	2004 (8)	10,000	X#Pn1-Pn8	—	30.00

ALDERNEY

DEPENDENCY

FANTASY EURO PATTERNS

X# Pn1 EURO CENT
Copper Plated Steel **Ruler:** Elizabeth II **Edge:** Plain

Date	Mintage	F	VF	XF	Unc	BU
2004	10,000	—	—	—	—	1.50
2004 Proof	5,000	Value: 2.50				

X# Pn2 2 EURO CENTS
Copper Plated Steel **Ruler:** Elizabeth II **Edge:** Plain

Date	Mintage	F	VF	XF	Unc	BU
2004	10,000	—	—	—	—	2.00
2004 Proof	5,000	Value: 3.00				

X# Pn3 5 EURO CENTS
Copper Plated Steel **Ruler:** Elizabeth II **Edge:** Plain

Date	Mintage	F	VF	XF	Unc	BU
2004	10,000	—	—	—	—	2.50
2004 Proof	5,000	Value: 3.50				

X# Pn4 10 EURO CENTS
Goldine **Ruler:** Elizabeth II **Edge:** Plain

Date	Mintage	F	VF	XF	Unc	BU
2004	10,000	—	—	—	—	3.00
2004 Proof	5,000	Value: 4.00				

X# Pn5 20 EURO CENTS
Goldine **Ruler:** Elizabeth II **Edge:** Plain

Date	Mintage	F	VF	XF	Unc	BU
2004	10,000	—	—	—	—	3.50
2004 Proof	5,000	Value: 5.00				

X# Pn6 50 EURO CENTS
Goldine **Ruler:** Elizabeth II **Edge:** Plain

Date	Mintage	F	VF	XF	Unc	BU
2004	10,000	—	—	—	—	4.00
2004 Proof	5,000	Value: 6.00				

X# Pn7 EURO
Bi-Metallic, 23 mm. **Ruler:** Elizabeth II **Obv:** Allegorical female seated right **Rev:** Large value "1", seamen image **Edge:** Plain

Date	Mintage	F	VF	XF	Unc	BU
2004	10,000	—	—	—	—	6.00
2004 Proof	5,000	Value: 8.00				

X# Pn8 2 EURO
Bi-Metallic, 25.3 mm. **Ruler:** Elizabeth II **Obv:** Allegorical female seated right **Rev:** Large value "2", seamen image **Edge:** Plain

Date	Mintage	F	VF	XF	Unc	BU
2004	—	—	—	—	—	8.00
2004 Proof	—	Value: 10.00				

X# Pn9 5 EURO
Goldine **Ruler:** Elizabeth II **Edge:** Plain

Date	Mintage	F	VF	XF	Unc	BU
2004 Proof	—	Value: 12.50				

MINT SETS

X#	Date	Mintage	Identification	Issue Price	Mkt Val
XMS1	2004 (8)	10,000	X#Pn1-Pn8	—	30.00

PROOF SETS

X#	Date	Mintage	Identification	Issue Price	Mkt Val
XPS1	2004 (9)	5,000	X#Pn1-Pn9	—	50.00

ALGERIA

OTTOMAN
FANTASY COINAGE

X# 1 QUADRUBLE DE FRANCE (96 Livres)
Tin **Issuer:** Les Compagnies d'Afrique

Date	Mintage	Good	VG	F	VF	XF
1786	—	—	—	1,450	—	—

X# 2 QUADRUBLE DE FRANCE (96 Livres)
Lead **Issuer:** Les Compagnies d'Afrique

Date	Mintage	Good	VG	F	VF	XF
1788/6	—	—	—	—	—	—

ANDAMAN ISLANDS

PENAL COLONY
FANTASY COINAGE

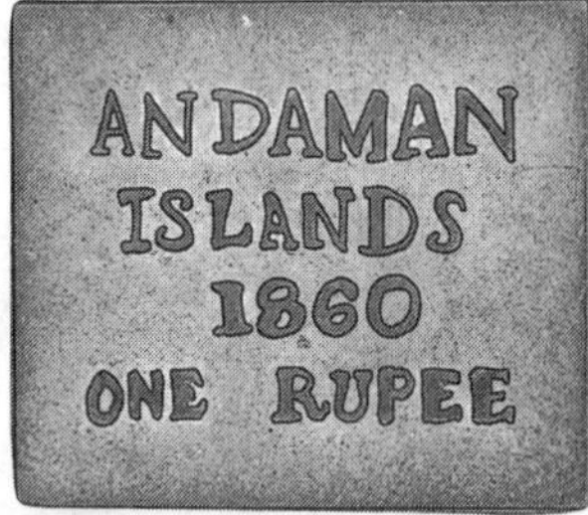

X# 1 RUPEE
Copper **Shape:** Rectangular **Note:** Uniface. A modern fantasy issue of "unknown" origin struck without any government authorization for obvious confusion of the numismatic community.

Date	Mintage	F	VF	XF	Unc	BU
1860	Est. 1,000	—	20.00	35.00	—	—

X# 1a RUPEE
Aluminum **Shape:** Rectangular **Note:** Uniface.

Date	Mintage	F	VF	XF	Unc	BU
1860	—	—	—	—	—	—

ANDEAN GROUP

ORGANIZATION
MILLED COINAGE

X# 5 PESO ANDINO
31.1600 g., 0.9990 Silver 1.0008 oz. ASW **Issuer:** BANCO MINERO DEL PERU **Obv:** Head of Simon Bolivar left **Obv. Legend:** • CREACION DEL PESO ANDINO • 17-X11-1984 **Rev:** Raised outlined map of confederation in South America **Rev. Legend:** HOMENAJE DEL BANCO MINERO DEL PERU **Edge:** Plain **Note:** The Andean Group was first organized by Bolivia, (Chile), Colombia, Ecuador, Peru and Venezuela.

Date	Mintage	F	VF	XF	Unc	BU
1984	—	—	25.00	40.00	65.00	—

ANDORRA

REPUBLIC
1873 Revolution
DECIMAL COINAGE

X# 1 5 CENTIMOS
Copper **Obv:** Crowned arms **Obv. Legend:** REPUBLICA DE LOS VALLES DE ANDORRA **Note:** Prev. KM#A1.

Date	Mintage	F	VF	XF	Unc	BU
1873	—	—	—	—	—	—

Note: Reported, not confirmed

X# 2 10 CENTIMOS
10.0000 g., Copper, 30 mm. **Obv:** Crowned arms **Obv. Legend:** REPUBLICA DE LOS VALLES DE ANDORRA **Note:** Prev. KM#B1.

Date	Mintage	F	VF	XF	Unc	BU
1873	—	—	—	250	500	—

X# 2a 10 CENTIMOS
Nickel **Obv:** Crowned arms **Obv. Legend:** REPUBLICA DE LOS VALLES DE ANDORRA

Date	Mintage	F	VF	XF	Unc	BU
1873	—	—	—	—	—	—

Note: Reported, not confirmed

PRINCIPALITY

MEDALLIC BULLION COINAGE

X# MB1 1/2 OUNCE
15.5515 g., 0.9990 Gold 0.4995 oz. AGW, 30 mm. **Obv:** Eagle alighting **Obv. Legend:** JOAN D. M. BISBE D'URGELL I PRINCEP D'ANDORRA **Rev:** Arms **Edge:** Reeded

Date	Mintage	F	VF	XF	Unc	BU
1988	3,000	—	—	—	385	—

X# MB2 OUNCE
31.1030 g., 0.9990 Gold 0.9989 oz. AGW **Obv:** Eagle alighting **Obv. Legend:** JOAN D. M. BISBE D'URGELL I PRINCEP D'ANDORRA **Rev:** Arms **Edge:** Reeded

Date	Mintage	F	VF	XF	Unc	BU
1988 Proof	—	Value: 775				

MEDALLIC COINAGE

Struck by the Bavarian State Mint, then of West Germany. Contracted for and distributed by Hans M.F. Schulman, New York, NY, U.S.A., with the approval of the Andorran Government

X# MA1 25 DINERS
14.0000 g., 0.9000 Silver 0.4051 oz. ASW **Obv:** National arms **Rev:** 1/2-length figure of Charlemagne facing left **Rev. Legend:** CAROLUS-MAGNUS **Note:** Prev. KM#M1.

Date	Mintage	F	VF	XF	Unc	BU
1960 Proof	1,350	Value: 55.00				

X# MA1a 25 DINERS
Gold **Obv:** National arms **Rev:** 1/2-length figure of Charlemagne facing left **Rev. Legend:** CAROLUS-MAGNUS

Date	Mintage	F	VF	XF	Unc	BU
1960 Proof	8	Value: 1,000				

X# MA1b 25 DINERS
Platinum APW **Obv:** National arms **Rev:** 1/2-length figure of Charlemagne facing left **Rev. Legend:** CAROLUS-MAGNUS

Date	Mintage	F	VF	XF	Unc	BU
1960 Proof	3	Value: 1,400				

X# M2 25 DINERS
14.0000 g., 0.9000 Silver 0.4051 oz. ASW **Obv:** National arms **Rev:** Bishop Benlloch of Urgel **Rev. Legend:** J.BENLLOCH•PRINCEP DE LES VALLS D'ANDORRA **Note:** Prev. KM#M3.

Date	Mintage	F	VF	XF	Unc	BU
1963 Proof	1,350	Value: 25.00				

X# M2a 25 DINERS
Gold **Obv:** National arms **Rev:** Bishop Benlloch of Urgel **Rev. Legend:** J.BENLLOCH•PRINCEP DE LES VALLS D'ANDORRA

Date	Mintage	F	VF	XF	Unc	BU
1963 Proof	8	Value: 1,000				

X# M2b 25 DINERS
Platinum APW **Obv:** National arms **Rev:** Bishop Benlloch of Urgel **Rev. Legend:** J.BENLLOCH• PRINCEP DE LES VALLS D'ANDORRA

Date	Mintage	F	VF	XF	Unc	BU
1963 Proof	3	Value: 1,400				

X# M4 25 DINERS
14.0000 g., 0.9000 Silver 0.4051 oz. ASW **Obv:** Ornate arms **Rev:** Laureate head of Napoleon left **Rev. Legend:** NAPOLEO • I • EMP • D • FRANCA • Co • PR • D • L • V • D'ANDORRA • **Note:** Prev. KM#M5. Initials under bust.

Date	Mintage	F	VF	XF	Unc	BU
1964 FM Proof	2,350	Value: 25.00				
1964 Without FM	—	Value: 350				

X# M4a 25 DINERS
Gold **Obv:** Ornate arms **Rev:** Laureate head of Napoleon left **Rev. Legend:** NAPOLEO • I • EMP • D • FRANCA • Co • PR • D • L • V • D'ANDORRA • **Note:** Prev. KM#M5a.

Date	Mintage	F	VF	XF	Unc	BU
1964 Proof	8	Value: 600				

X# M4b 25 DINERS
Platinum APW **Obv:** Ornate arms **Rev:** Laureate head of Napoleon left **Rev. Legend:** NAPOLEO • I • EMP • D • FRANCA • Co • PR • D • L • V • D'ANDORRA • **Note:** Prev. KM#M5b.

Date	Mintage	F	VF	XF	Unc	BU
1964 Proof	3	Value: 1,000				

X# M6 25 DINERS
14.0000 g., 0.9000 Silver 0.4051 oz. ASW **Obv:** National arms **Rev:** House of Council of Justice **Rev. Legend:** CASA•DE•LA•VALL•DOMVS• CONCILLI• JVSTITIAE•SEDES•/ANY•1580 **Note:** Prev. KM#M7.

Date	Mintage	F	VF	XF	Unc	BU
1965 Proof	1,350	Value: 65.00				

X# M6a 25 DINERS
Gold **Obv:** National arms **Rev:** House of Council of Justice **Rev. Legend:** CASA•DE•LA•VALL•DOMVS• CONCILLI•JVSTITIAE•SEDES•/ANY•1580

Date	Mintage	F	VF	XF	Unc	BU
1965 Proof	8	Value: 850				

X# M6b 25 DINERS
Platinum APW **Obv:** National arms **Rev:** House of Council of Justice **Rev. Legend:** CASA•DE•LA•VALL• DOMVS•CONCILLI•JVSTITIAE•SEDES•/ANY•1580

Date	Mintage	F	VF	XF	Unc	BU
1965 Proof	3	Value: 1,000				

X# M1 50 DINERS
28.0000 g., 0.9000 Silver 0.8102 oz. ASW, 38 mm. **Obv:** National arms **Rev:** 1/2-length figure of Charlemagne facing left **Rev. Legend:** CAROLUS-MAGNUS **Note:** Prev. KM#M2.

Date	Mintage	F	VF	XF	Unc	BU
1960 Proof	3,100	Value: 45.00				

X# M1a 50 DINERS
Gold, 38 mm. **Obv:** National arms **Rev:** 1/2-length figure of Charlemagne facing left **Rev. Legend:** CAROLUS-MAGNUS

Date	Mintage	F	VF	XF	Unc	BU
1960 Proof	8	Value: 1,600				

X# M1b 50 DINERS
Platinum APW, 38 mm. **Obv:** National arms **Rev:** 1/2-length figure of Charlemagne facing left **Rev. Legend:** CAROLUS-MAGNUS

Date	Mintage	F	VF	XF	Unc	BU
1960 Proof	3	Value: 3,000				

X# M3 50 DINERS
28.0000 g., 0.9000 Silver 0.8102 oz. ASW, 38 mm. **Obv:** National arms **Rev:** Bishop Benlloch of Urgel **Rev. Legend:** J.BENLLOCH•PRINCEP DE LES VALLS D'ANDORRA **Note:** Prev. KM#4.

Date	Mintage	F	VF	XF	Unc	BU
1963 Proof	3,350	Value: 35.00				

X# M3a 50 DINERS
Gold, 38 mm. **Obv:** National arms **Rev:** Bishop Benlloch of Urgel **Rev. Legend:** J.BENLLOCH• PRINCEP DE LES VALLS D'ANDORRA

Date	Mintage	F	VF	XF	Unc	BU
1963 Proof	8	Value: 1,500				

X# M3b 50 DINERS
Platinum APW, 38 mm. **Obv:** National arms **Rev:** Bishop Benlloch of Urgel **Rev. Legend:** J.BENLLOCH• PRINCEP DE LES VALLS D'ANDORRA

Date	Mintage	F	VF	XF	Unc	BU
1963 Proof	3	Value: 2,850				

X# M5 50 DINERS
28.0000 g., 0.9000 Silver 0.8102 oz. ASW, 38 mm. **Obv:** Ornate arms **Rev:** Laureate head of Napoleon left **Rev. Legend:** NAPOLEO • I • EMP • D • FRANCA • Co • PR • D • L • V • D'ANDORRA • **Note:** Prev. KM#M6. With initials under bust.

Date	Mintage	F	VF	XF	Unc	BU
1964 Proof	5,150	Value: 40.00				

X# M5a 50 DINERS
Gold, 38 mm. **Obv:** Ornate arms **Rev:** Laureate head of Napoleon left **Rev. Legend:** NAPOLEO • I • EMP • D • FRANCA • Co • PR • D • L • V • D'ANDORRA •

Date	Mintage	F	VF	XF	Unc	BU
1964 Proof	8	Value: 1,200				

X# M5b 50 DINERS
Platinum APW, 38 mm. **Obv:** Ornate arms **Rev:** Laureate head of Napoleon left **Rev. Legend:** NAPOLEO • I • EMP • D • FRANCA • Co • PR • D • L • V • D'ANDORRA •

Date	Mintage	F	VF	XF	Unc	BU
1964 Proof	3	Value: 2,500				

X# M7 50 DINERS
28.0000 g., 0.9000 Silver 0.8102 oz. ASW, 38 mm. **Obv:** National arms **Rev:** House of Council of Justice **Rev. Legend:** CASA•DE•LA•VALL•DOMVS•CONCILLI•JVSTITIAE•SEDES•/ANY•1580 **Note:** Prev. KM#M8. Many remelted.

Date	Mintage	F	VF	XF	Unc	BU
1965 Proof	2,500	Value: 60.00				

X# M7a 50 DINERS
Gold, 38 mm. **Obv:** National arms **Rev:** House of Council of Justice **Rev. Legend:** CASA•DE•LA•VALL•DOMVS•CONCILLI•JVSTITIAE•SEDES•/ANY•1580

Date	Mintage	F	VF	XF	Unc	BU
1965 Proof	8	Value: 1,300				

X# M7b 50 DINERS
Platinum APW, 38 mm. **Obv:** National arms **Rev:** House of Council of Justice **Rev. Legend:** CASA•DE•LA•VALL•DOMVS•CONCILLI•JVSTITIAE•SEDES•/ANY•1580

Date	Mintage	F	VF	XF	Unc	BU
1965 Proof	3	Value: 2,000				

FANTASY EURO PATTERNS

INA Series

X# Pn1 EURO CENT
Copper Plated Steel, 16.8 mm. **Obv:** Bishop seated facing **Rev:** Scale at right **Edge:** Plain

Date	Mintage	F	VF	XF	Unc	BU
2003	16,000	—	—	—	—	1.50
2003 Proof	14,000	Value: 2.50				

X# Pn1a EURO CENT
Silver, 16.8 mm. **Obv:** Bishop seated facing **Rev:** Scale at right **Edge:** Plain

Date	Mintage	F	VF	XF	Unc	BU
2003 Proof	1,250	Value: 6.00				

X# Pn2 2 EURO CENTS
Copper Plated Steel, 18.5 mm. **Obv:** Bishop seated facing **Rev:** Scale at right **Edge:** Plain

Date	Mintage	F	VF	XF	Unc	BU
2003	16,000	—	—	—	—	2.00
2003 Proof	14,000	Value: 3.00				

X# Pn2a 2 EURO CENTS
Silver, 18.5 mm. **Obv:** Bishop seated facing **Rev:** Scale at right **Edge:** Plain

Date	Mintage	F	VF	XF	Unc	BU
2003 Proof	1,250	Value: 7.00				

X# Pn3 5 EURO CENTS
Copper Plated Steel, 20.7 mm. **Obv:** Bishop seated facing **Rev:** Scale at right **Edge:** Plain

Date	Mintage	F	VF	XF	Unc	BU
2003	16,000	—	—	—	—	2.50
2003 Proof	14,000	Value: 3.50				

X# Pn3a 5 EURO CENTS
Silver, 20.7 mm. **Obv:** Bishop seated facing **Rev:** Scale at right **Edge:** Plain

Date	Mintage	F	VF	XF	Unc	BU
2003 Proof	1,250	Value: 8.50				

X# Pn4 10 EURO CENTS
Brass, 19.3 mm. **Obv:** Half-length crowned figure of Charlemagne with sword facing **Rev:** Dove, value in wreath of hands **Edge:** Plain

Date	Mintage	F	VF	XF	Unc	BU
2003	16,000	—	—	—	—	3.00
2003 Proof	14,000	Value: 4.00				

X# Pn4a 10 EURO CENTS
Silver, 19.3 mm. **Obv:** Half-length crowned figure of Charlemagne with sword facing **Rev:** Dove, value in wreath of hands **Edge:** Plain

Date	Mintage	F	VF	XF	Unc	BU
2003 Proof	1,250	Value: 10.00				

X# Pn5 20 EURO CENTS
Brass, 22 mm. **Obv:** Half-length crowned figure of Charlemagne with sword facing **Rev:** Dove, value in wreath of hands **Edge:** Plain

Date	Mintage	F	VF	XF	Unc	BU
2003	16,000	—	—	—	—	3.50
2003 Proof	14,000	Value: 5.00				

X# Pn5a 20 EURO CENTS
Silver, 22 mm. **Obv:** Half-length crowned figure of Charlemagne with sword facing **Rev:** Dove, value in wreath of hands **Edge:** Plain

Date	Mintage	F	VF	XF	Unc	BU
2003 Proof	1,250	Value: 12.50				

X# Pn6 50 EURO CENTS
Brass, 24.3 mm. **Obv:** Half-length crowned figure of Charlemagne with sword facing **Rev:** Dove, value in wreath of hands **Edge:** Plain

Date	Mintage	F	VF	XF	Unc	BU
2003	16,000	—	—	—	—	4.00
2003 Proof	14,000	Value: 6.00				

X# Pn6a 50 EURO CENTS
Silver, 24.3 mm. **Obv:** Half-length crowned figure of Charlemagne with sword facing **Rev:** Dove, value in wreath of hands **Edge:** Plain

Date	Mintage	F	VF	XF	Unc	BU
2003 Proof	1,250	Value: 15.00				

X# Pn7 EURO
Bi-Metallic, 22.8 mm. **Obv:** Crown above eagle in sprays **Rev:** 16th century Spanish galleon **Edge:** Plain

Date	Mintage	F	VF	XF	Unc	BU
2003	16,000	—	—	—	—	6.00
2003 Proof	14,000	Value: 8.00				

X# Pn7a EURO
Bi-Metallic Silver / Brass, 22.8 mm. **Obv:** Crown above eagle in sprays **Rev:** 16th century Spanish galleon **Edge:** Plain

Date	Mintage	F	VF	XF	Unc	BU
2003 Proof	1,250	Value: 22.50				

X# Pn8 2 EUROS
Bi-Metallic, 25.7 mm. **Obv:** Crown above eagle in sprays **Rev:** 16th century Spanish galleon

Date	Mintage	F	VF	XF	Unc	BU
2003	16,000	—	—	—	—	8.00
2003 Proof	14,000	Value: 10.00				

X# Pn8a 2 EUROS
Bi-Metallic Silver / Brass, 25.7 mm. **Obv:** Crown above eagle in sprays **Rev:** 16th century Spanish galleon **Edge:** Plain

Date	Mintage	F	VF	XF	Unc	BU
2003 Proof	1,250	Value: 28.50				

X# Pn9 5 EUROS
Brass, 36 mm. **Obv:** Half-length crowned figure of Charlemagne with sword facing **Rev:** Ski jumper **Edge:** Plain

Date	Mintage	F	VF	XF	Unc	BU
2003 Proof	14,000	Value: 12.50				

X# Pn9a 5 EUROS
Silver, 36 mm. **Obv:** Half-length crowned figure of Charlemagne with sword facing **Rev:** Ski jumper **Edge:** Plain

Date	Mintage	F	VF	XF	Unc	BU
2003 Proof	1,250	Value: 40.00				

PIEFORTS

X#	Date	Mintage	Identification	Mkt Val
P1	2003	1,000	5 Euros. Silver. X#Pn9a.	75.00

MINT SETS

X#	Date	Mintage	Identification	Issue Price	Mkt Val
XMS1	2003 (8)	16,000	X#Pn1-Pn8	—	30.00

PROOF SETS

X#	Date	Mintage	Identification	Issue Price	Mkt Val
XPS6	2003 (9)	14,000	X#Pn1-Pn9	—	50.00
XPS7	2003 (9)	1,250	X#Pn1a-Pn9a	—	150
XPS8	2003 (9)	—	X#Pn1a-Pn9a	1,250	—

ANGUILLA

PROVISIONAL GOVERNMENT

1967 and 1969

COUNTERMARKED COINAGE

Authorized by the Anguilla Island Council. Each Liberty Dollar was to have been redeemed for 10 U.S. dollars. The countermarking was privately done in San Francisco, California, U.S.A. Mintage of 6,000 of the above pieces were remelted.

X# 1 LIBERTY DOLLAR
Silver **Countermark:** ANGUILLA LIBERTY DOLLAR JULY 11, 1967 **Note:** Prev. KM#1. Countermark on Mexico 5 Pesos, KM#467. Countermark on various flattened crowns.

CM Date	Host Date	Good	VG	F	VF	XF
1967	1951-54	30.00	40.00	—	—	—

X# 2 LIBERTY DOLLAR
Silver **Countermark:** ANGUILLA LIBERTY DOLLAR July 11, 1967 **Note:** Prev. KM#2. Countermarked on Mexico 5 Pesos, KM#465.

CM Date	Host Date	Good	VG	F	VF	XF
1967	1947-48	30.00	40.00	—	—	—

X# 3 LIBERTY DOLLAR
Silver **Countermark:** ANGUILLA LIBERTY DOLLAR JULY 11, 1967 **Note:** Prev. KM#3. Countermarked on Peru Sol, KM#218.1.

CM Date	Host Date	Good	VG	F	VF	XF
1967	1923-26	28.00	32.00	—	—	—

X# 4.2 LIBERTY DOLLAR
Silver **Countermark:** ANGUILLA LIBERTY DOLLAR JULY 11, 1967 **Note:** Prev. KM#3a. Countermarked on Yemen Riyal, Y#31.

CM Date	Host Date	Good	VG	F	VF	XF
1967	AH1382 Inc. KM#4	65.00	75.00	—	—	—

X# 4.1 LIBERTY DOLLAR
Silver **Countermark:** ANGUILLA LIBERTY DOLLAR JULY 11, 1967 **Note:** Prev. KM#4. Countermarked on Yemen Ahmadi Riyal, Y#17.

CM Date	Host Date	Good	VG	F	VF	XF
1967	AH1367-81	100	125	—	—	—

X# 5 LIBERTY DOLLAR
Silver **Countermark:** ANGUILLA LIBERTY DOLLAR JULY 11, 1967 **Note:** Prev. KM#5. Countermarked on Philippines Peso, KM#172.

CM Date	Host Date	Good	VG	F	VF	XF
1967	1907-12	65.00	75.00	—	—	—

X# 6 LIBERTY DOLLAR
Silver **Countermark:** ANGUILLA LIBERTY DOLLAR JULY 11, 1967 **Note:** Prev. KM#6. Countermarked on Mexico 10 Pesos, KM#474.

CM Date	Host Date	Good	VG	F	VF	XF
1967	1955-56	40.00	50.00	—	—	—

X# 7.1 LIBERTY DOLLAR
Silver **Countermark:** ANGUILLA LIBERTY DOLLAR JULY 11, 1967 **Note:** Prev. KM#7.1. Countermarked on Panama Balboa, KM#13.

CM Date	Host Date	Good	VG	F	VF	XF
1967	1931-47	100	110	—	—	—

X# 7.2 LIBERTY DOLLAR
Silver **Countermark:** ANGUILLA LIBERTY DOLLAR JULY 11, 1967 **Note:** Prev. KM#7.2. Countermarked on Panama Balboa, KM#21.

CM Date	Host Date	Good	VG	F	VF	XF
1967	1953	100	110	—	—	—

X# 8 LIBERTY DOLLAR
Silver **Countermark:** ANGUILLA LIBERTY DOLLAR JULY 11, 1967 **Note:** Prev. KM#8. Countermarked on Ecuador Cinco Sucres, KM#79.

CM Date	Host Date	Good	VG	F	VF	XF
1967	1943-44	150	165	—	—	—

X# 9 LIBERTY DOLLAR
Silver **Countermark:** ANGUILLA LIBERTY DOLLAR JULY 11, 1967 **Note:** Prev. KM#9. Countermarked on Mexico Peso, KM#409.

CM Date	Host Date	Good	VG	F	VF	XF
1967	1901-05	185	200	—	—	—

X# 10.1 LIBERTY DOLLAR
Silver **Countermark:** ANGUILLA LIBERTY DOLLAR JULY 11, 1967 **Note:** Prev. KM#10.1. Countermarked on China Republic Yüan Shih-kai Dollar, KM#329.

CM Date	Host Date	Good	VG	F	VF	XF
1967	1914	225	240	—	—	—

X# 10.2 LIBERTY DOLLAR
Silver **Countermark:** ANGUILLA LIBERTY DOLLAR JULY 11, 1967 **Note:** Prev. KM#10.2. Countermarked on China Republic Yüan Shih-kai Dollar, KM#329.6.

CM Date	Host Date	Good	VG	F	VF	XF
1967	1920-21	225	240	—	—	—

X# 11 LIBERTY DOLLAR
Silver **Countermark:** ANGUILLA LIBERTY DOLLAR JULY 11, 1967 **Note:** Prev. KM#11. Countermarked on Mexico 5 Pesos, KM#468.

CM Date	Host Date	Good	VG	F	VF	XF
1967	1953	450	475	—	—	—

X# 12 LIBERTY DOLLAR
Silver **Countermark:** ANGUILLA LIBERTY DOLLAR JULY 11, 1967 **Note:** Prev. KM#12. Countermarked on Great Britain Trade Coinage, Y-T5.

CM Date	Host Date	Good	VG	F	VF	XF
1967	1901-35	500	525	—	—	—

X# 14 100 LIBERTY DOLLARS
Gold **Countermark:** 100 LIBERTY DOLLARS **Note:** Prev. KM#14. Countermarked on Mexico 50 Pesos, KM#481.

CM Date	Host Date	Good	VG	F	VF	XF
1967	1921-47	3,000	—	—	—	—

ARAUCANIA-PATAGONIA

KINGDOM

STANDARD COINAGE

X# 51 70 PESOS
Nickel-Silver **Ruler:** Philippe **Subject:** 70th Birthday of Prince Philippe **Obv:** Head right **Rev:** Map of Araucania - Patagonia, arms at right

Date	Mintage	F	VF	XF	Unc	BU
1997 Prooflike	—	—	—	—	20.00	—

X# 51b 70 PESOS
31.1000 g., 0.5000 Gold 0.4999 oz. AGW **Ruler:** Philippe **Subject:** 70th Birthday of Prince Philippe **Obv:** Head right **Rev:** Map of Araucania - Patagonia, arms at right

Date	Mintage	F	VF	XF	Unc	BU
1997 Proof	7	Value: 450				

X# 21 100 PESOS
Nickel-Silver **Ruler:** Philippe **Subject:** 128th Anniversary of Founding **Obv:** Head right **Rev:** Map, arms at right

Date	Mintage	F	VF	XF	Unc	BU
1988 Prooflike	—	—	—	—	25.00	—

X# 21b 100 PESOS
31.1000 g., 0.9990 Gold 0.9988 oz. AGW **Ruler:** Philippe **Subject:** 128th Anniversary of Founding **Obv:** Head right **Rev:** Value and date within wreath

Date	Mintage	F	VF	XF	Unc	BU
1988 Proof	10	Value: 600				

X# 21c 100 PESOS
31.1000 g., 0.9990 Platinum 0.9988 oz. APW **Ruler:** Philippe **Subject:** 128th Anniversary of Founding **Obv:** Head right **Rev:** Value and date within wreath

Date	Mintage	F	VF	XF	Unc	BU
1988 Proof	4	Value: 950				

X# 22 100 PESOS
Nickel-Silver **Ruler:** Philippe **Subject:** 129th Anniversary of Founding **Obv:** Head right **Rev:** Map of Araucania - Patagonia, arms at right

Date	Mintage	F	VF	XF	Unc	BU
1989 Proof	500	—	—	—	15.00	—

X# 22a 100 PESOS
31.1000 g., 0.9250 Silver 0.9249 oz. ASW **Ruler:** Philippe **Subject:** 129th Anniversary of Founding **Obv:** Head right **Rev:** Map of Araucania - Patagonia, arms at right

Date	Mintage	F	VF	XF	Unc	BU
1989 Proof	129	Value: 45.00				

X# 22b 100 PESOS
31.1000 g., 0.9990 Palladium 0.9988 oz. **Ruler:** Philippe **Subject:** 129th Anniversary of Founding **Obv:** Head right **Rev:** Map of Araucania - Patagonia, arms at right

Date	Mintage	F	VF	XF	Unc	BU
1989 Proof	10	Value: 350				

X# 22c 100 PESOS
31.1000 g., 0.9990 Gold 0.9988 oz. AGW **Ruler:** Philippe **Subject:** 129th Anniversary of Founding **Obv:** Head right **Rev:** Map of Araucania - Patagonia, arms at right

Date	Mintage	F	VF	XF	Unc	BU
1989 Proof	—	Value: 550				

X# 28 100 PESOS
Nickel-Silver **Ruler:** Philippe **Subject:** 120th Anniversary of Battleship Entrecasteaux **Obv:** Head right **Rev:** Sailing ship Entrecasteaux

Date	Mintage	F	VF	XF	Unc	BU
1990 Prooflike	500	—	—	—	25.00	—

X# 28a 100 PESOS
31.1000 g., 0.9250 Silver 0.9249 oz. ASW **Ruler:** Philippe **Subject:** 120th Anniversary of Battleship Entrecasteaux **Obv:** Head right **Rev:** Sailing ship Entrecasteaux

Date	Mintage	F	VF	XF	Unc	BU
1990 Proof	130	Value: 65.00				

X# 28b 100 PESOS

31.1000 g., 0.9990 Palladium 0.9988 oz.
Ruler: Philippe **Subject:** 120th Anniversary of Battleship Entrecasteaux **Obv:** Head right **Rev:** Sailing ship Entrecasteaux

Date	Mintage	F	VF	XF	Unc	BU
1990 Proof	10	Value: 425				

X# 28c 100 PESOS

31.1000 g., 0.9990 Gold 0.9988 oz. AGW
Ruler: Philippe **Subject:** 120th Anniversary of Battleship Entrecasteaux **Obv:** Head right **Rev:** Sailing ship Entrecasteaux

Date	Mintage	F	VF	XF	Unc	BU
1990 Proof	10	Value: 650				

X# 29b 100 PESOS

31.1000 g., 0.9250 Silver 0.9249 oz. ASW **Ruler:** Philippe **Subject:** Christmas **Obv:** Head right **Rev:** Three carrolers **Note:** Error: FELIX... Antique finish.

Date	Mintage	F	VF	XF	Unc	BU
1990	3	—	—	—	—	—

X# 31 100 PESOS

Nickel-Silver **Ruler:** Philippe **Subject:** 131st Anniversary of Founding **Obv:** Head right **Rev:** National flag

Date	Mintage	F	VF	XF	Unc	BU
1991 Prooflike	500	—	—	—	20.00	—

X# 31a 100 PESOS

31.1000 g., 0.9250 Silver 0.9249 oz. ASW
Ruler: Philippe **Subject:** 131st Anniversary of Founding **Obv:** Head right **Rev:** National flag

Date	Mintage	F	VF	XF	Unc	BU
1991 Proof	131	Value: 50.00				

X# 31b 100 PESOS

31.1000 g., 0.9990 Palladium 0.9988 oz.
Ruler: Philippe **Subject:** 131st Anniversary of Founding **Obv:** Head right **Rev:** National flag

Date	Mintage	F	VF	XF	Unc	BU
1991 Proof	10	Value: 360				

X# 31c 100 PESOS

31.1000 g., 0.9990 Gold 0.9988 oz. AGW
Ruler: Philippe **Subject:** 131st Anniversary of Founding **Obv:** Head right **Rev:** National flag

Date	Mintage	F	VF	XF	Unc	BU
1991 Proof	10	Value: 525				

X# 35 100 PESOS

Nickel-Silver **Ruler:** Philippe **Subject:** Freedom for the Mapuche Peoples (1492-1992) **Obv:** Head right **Rev:** Geronimo bust facing

Date	Mintage	F	VF	XF	Unc	BU
1992 Prooflike	500	—	—	—	20.00	—

X# 35a 100 PESOS

31.1000 g., 0.9250 Silver 0.9249 oz. ASW **Ruler:** Philippe **Subject:** Freedom for the Mapuche Peoples (1492-1992) **Obv:** Head right **Rev:** Geronimo bust facing

Date	Mintage	F	VF	XF	Unc	BU
1992 Proof	132	Value: 60.00				

X# 35b 100 PESOS

31.1000 g., 0.9990 Palladium 0.9988 oz. **Ruler:** Philippe **Subject:** Freedom for the Mapuche Peoples (1492-1992) **Obv:** Head right **Rev:** Geronimo bust facing

Date	Mintage	F	VF	XF	Unc	BU
1992 Proof	10	Value: 370				

X# 35c 100 PESOS

31.1000 g., 0.9990 Gold 0.9988 oz. AGW **Ruler:** Philippe **Subject:** Freedom for the Mapuche Peoples (1492-1992) **Obv:** Head right **Rev:** Geronimo bust facing

Date	Mintage	F	VF	XF	Unc	BU
1992 Proof	10	Value: 550				

X# 38 100 PESOS

Nickel-Silver **Ruler:** Philippe **Subject:** 133rd Anniversary of Founding **Obv:** Head right **Rev:** Map of Araucania - Patagonia, arms at right **Rev. Legend:** ... ORELIE • ANTOINE (1860-1878)

Date	Mintage	F	VF	XF	Unc	BU
1993 Prooflike	500	—	—	—	15.00	—

X# 38b 100 PESOS

31.1000 g., 0.5000 Gold 0.4999 oz. AGW **Ruler:** Philippe **Subject:** 133rd Anniversary of Founding **Obv:** Head right **Rev:** Map of Araucania - Patagonia, arms at right **Rev. Legend:** ... ORELIE • ANTOINE (1860-1878)

Date	Mintage	F	VF	XF	Unc	BU
1993 Proof	10	Value: 325				

X# 38a 100 PESOS

31.1000 g., 0.9250 Silver 0.9249 oz. ASW **Ruler:** Philippe **Subject:** 133rd Anniversary of Founding **Obv:** Head right **Rev:** Map of Araucania - Patagonia, arms at right **Rev. Legend:** ... ORELIE • ANTOINE (1860-1878)

Date	Mintage	F	VF	XF	Unc	BU
1993 Proof	133	Value: 45.00				

X# 41 100 PESOS

Nickel-Silver **Ruler:** Philippe **Subject:** 134th Anniversary of Founding **Obv:** Head right **Rev:** Map of Araucania - Patagonia, arms at right **Rev. Legend:** ... ACHILLE I (1878-1902)

Date	Mintage	F	VF	XF	Unc	BU
1994 Prooflike	500	—	—	—	15.00	—

X# 41a 100 PESOS

31.1000 g., 0.9250 Silver 0.9249 oz. ASW
Ruler: Philippe **Subject:** 134th Anniversary of Founding **Obv:** Head right **Rev:** Map of Araucania - Patagonia, arms at right **Rev. Legend:** ... ACHILLE I (1878-1902)

Date	Mintage	F	VF	XF	Unc	BU
1994 Proof	134	Value: 45.00				

X# 41b 100 PESOS

31.1000 g., 0.5000 Gold 0.4999 oz. AGW
Ruler: Philippe **Subject:** 134th Anniversary of Founding **Obv:** Head right **Rev:** Map of Araucania - Patagonia, arms at right **Rev. Legend:** ... ACHILLE I (1878-1902)

Date	Mintage	F	VF	XF	Unc	BU
1994 Proof	10	Value: 325				

X# 42a 100 PESOS

Nickel-Silver **Ruler:** Philippe **Subject:** Christmas **Obv:** Head right **Rev:** Town view, Noel below **Note:** Antique finish.

Date	Mintage	F	VF	XF	Unc	BU
1994	8	—	—	—	—	—

X# 43 100 PESOS

Nickel-Silver **Ruler:** Philippe **Subject:** 135th Anniversary of Founding **Obv:** Head right **Rev:** Map of Araucania - Patagonia, arms at right **Rev. Legend:** ... ANTOINE II (1902-1903)

Date	Mintage	F	VF	XF	Unc	BU
1995 Prooflike	500	—	—	—	15.00	—

X# 43a 100 PESOS

31.1000 g., 0.9250 Silver 0.9249 oz. ASW
Ruler: Philippe **Subject:** 135th Anniversary of Founding **Obv:** Head right **Rev:** Map of Araucania - Patagonia, arms at right **Rev. Legend:** ... ANTOINE II (1902-1903)

Date	Mintage	F	VF	XF	Unc	BU
1995 Proof	—	Value: 45.00				

X# 43b 100 PESOS

31.1000 g., 0.5000 Gold 0.4999 oz. AGW
Ruler: Philippe **Subject:** 135th Anniversary of Founding **Obv:** Head right **Rev:** Map of Araucania - Patagonia, arms at right **Rev. Legend:** ... ANTOINE II (1902-1903)

Date	Mintage	F	VF	XF	Unc	BU
1995 Proof	—	Value: 325				

X# 44b 100 PESOS

31.1000 g., 0.9250 Silver 0.9249 oz. ASW
Ruler: Philippe **Subject:** Christmas **Obv:** Head right **Rev:** Trumpeter **Note:** Antique finish.

Date	Mintage	F	VF	XF	Unc	BU
1995	23	—	—	—	—	—

X# 46 100 PESOS

Nickel-Silver **Ruler:** Philippe **Subject:** 136th Anniversary of Founding **Obv:** Head right **Rev:** Map of Araucania - Patagonia, arms at right **Rev. Legend:** ... LAURE - THERESE (1903-1916)

Date	Mintage	F	VF	XF	Unc	BU
1996 Prooflike	—	—	—	—	15.00	—

X# 46a 100 PESOS

31.1000 g., 0.9250 Silver 0.9249 oz. ASW **Ruler:** Philippe **Subject:** 136th Anniversary of Founding **Obv:** Head right **Rev:** Map of Araucania - Patagonia, arms at right **Rev. Legend:** ... LAURE - THERESE (1903-1916)

Date	Mintage	F	VF	XF	Unc	BU
1996 Proof	136	Value: 45.00				

X# 46b 100 PESOS

31.1000 g., 0.5000 Gold 0.4999 oz. AGW **Ruler:** Philippe **Subject:** 136th Anniversary of Founding **Obv:** Head right **Rev:** Map of Araucania - Patagonia, arms at right **Rev. Legend:** ... LAURE - THERESE (1903-1916)

Date	Mintage	F	VF	XF	Unc	BU
1996 Proof	—	Value: 325				

X# 47 100 PESOS

Nickel-Silver **Ruler:** Philippe **Subject:** Wedding of Prince Philippe and Princess Elizabeth **Obv:** Head right **Rev:** Map of Araucania - Patagonia, arms at right

Date	Mintage	F	VF	XF	Unc	BU
1996 Prooflike	500	—	—	—	18.00	—

X# 47a 100 PESOS
31.1000 g., 0.9250 Silver 0.9249 oz. ASW
Ruler: Philippe **Subject:** Wedding of Prince Philippe and Princess Elizabeth **Obv:** Head right **Rev:** Map of Araucania - Patagonia, arms at right

Date	Mintage	F	VF	XF	Unc	BU
1996 Proof	100	Value: 50.00				

X# 47b 100 PESOS
31.1000 g., 0.5000 Gold 0.4999 oz. AGW
Ruler: Philippe **Subject:** Wedding of Prince Philippe and Princess Elizabeth **Obv:** Head right **Rev:** Map of Araucania - Patagonia, arms at right

Date	Mintage	F	VF	XF	Unc	BU
1996 Proof	10	Value: 385				

X# 49a 100 PESOS
31.1000 g., 0.9250 Silver 0.9249 oz. ASW
Ruler: Philippe **Subject:** Christmas **Obv:** Head right **Rev:** Angel and scroll **Note:** Antique finish.

Date	Mintage	F	VF	XF	Unc	BU
1996	16	—	—	—	—	—

X# 52 100 PESOS
Nickel-Steel **Ruler:** Philippe **Subject:** 137th Anniversary of Founding **Obv:** Head right **Rev:** Map of Araucania - Patagonia, arms at right **Rev. Legend:** ... ANTOINE III (1916-1952)

Date	Mintage	F	VF	XF	Unc	BU
1997 Prooflike	500	—	—	—	15.00	—

X# 52a 100 PESOS
31.1000 g., 0.9250 Silver 0.9249 oz. ASW **Ruler:** Philippe **Subject:** 137th Anniversary of Founding **Obv:** Head right **Rev:** Map of Araucania - Patagonia, arms at right **Rev. Legend:** ... ANTOINE III (1916-1952)

Date	Mintage	F	VF	XF	Unc	BU
1997 Proof	137	Value: 45.00				

X# 52b 100 PESOS
31.1000 g., 0.5000 Gold 0.4999 oz. AGW **Ruler:** Philippe **Subject:** 137th Anniversary of Founding **Obv:** Head right **Rev:** Map of Araucania - Patagonia, arms at right **Rev. Legend:** ... ANTOINE III (1916-1952)

Date	Mintage	F	VF	XF	Unc	BU
1997 Proof	10	Value: 325				

X# 56 100 PESOS
Nickel-Silver **Ruler:** Philippe **Subject:** Christmas **Obv:** Head right **Rev:** Two bells **Note:** Antique finish.

Date	Mintage	F	VF	XF	Unc	BU
1998	138	15.00	—	—	—	—

X# 58a 100 PESOS
31.1000 g., 0.9250 Silver 0.9249 oz. ASW **Ruler:** Philippe **Subject:** Christmas **Obv:** Head right **Rev:** The Magi on camels following star **Note:** Antique finish.

Date	Mintage	F	VF	XF	Unc	BU
1998	47	55.00	—	—	—	—

X# 56a 100 PESOS
31.1000 g., 0.9250 Silver 0.9249 oz. ASW **Ruler:** Philippe **Subject:** Christmas **Obv:** Head right **Rev:** Two bells

Date	Mintage	F	VF	XF	Unc	BU
1998	46	55.00	—	—	—	—

X# 58 100 PESOS
Nickel-Silver **Ruler:** Philippe **Subject:** Christmas **Obv:** Head right **Rev:** The Magi on camels following star **Note:** Antique finish.

Date	Mintage	F	VF	XF	Unc	BU
1999	139	15.00	—	—	—	—

X# 60 100 PESOS
Nickel-Silver **Ruler:** Philippe **Subject:** 140th Anniversary of Founding **Obv:** Head right **Rev:** Peace (in 17 languages)

Date	Mintage	F	VF	XF	Unc	BU
2000 Prooflike	500	—	—	—	15.00	—

X# 60a 100 PESOS
31.1000 g., 0.9250 Silver 0.9249 oz. ASW
Ruler: Philippe **Subject:** 140th Anniversary of Founding **Obv:** Head right **Rev:** Peace (in 17 languages)

Date	Mintage	F	VF	XF	Unc	BU
2000 Proof	140	Value: 45.00				

X# 60b 100 PESOS
31.1000 g., 0.5000 Gold 0.4999 oz. AGW
Ruler: Philippe **Subject:** 140th Anniversary of Founding **Obv:** Head right **Rev:** Peace (in 17 languages)

Date	Mintage	F	VF	XF	Unc	BU
2000 Proof	10	Value: 295				

X# 61 100 PESOS
Nickel-Silver **Ruler:** Philippe **Subject:** Christmas **Obv:** Head right **Rev:** Madonna and child **Note:** Antique finish.

Date	Mintage	F	VF	XF	Unc	BU
2000	140	15.00	—	—	—	—

X# 61a 100 PESOS
31.1000 g., 0.9250 Silver 0.9249 oz. ASW
Ruler: Philippe **Subject:** Christmas **Obv:** Head right **Rev:** Madonna and child **Note:** Antique finish.

Date	Mintage	F	VF	XF	Unc	BU
2000	48	—	45.00	—	—	—

X# 64 100 PESOS
Nickel-Silver **Ruler:** Philippe **Subject:** Christmas **Obv:** Head right **Rev:** Angel **Note:** Antique finish.

Date	Mintage	F	VF	XF	Unc	BU
2001	141	15.00	—	—	—	—

X# 64a 100 PESOS
31.1000 g., 0.9250 Silver 0.9249 oz. ASW
Ruler: Philippe **Subject:** Christmas **Obv:** Head right **Rev:** Angel **Note:** Antique finish.

Date	Mintage	F	VF	XF	Unc	BU
2001	49	45.00	—	—	—	—

X# 65 100 PESOS
Nickel-Silver **Ruler:** Philippe **Subject:** Christmas **Obv:** Head right **Rev:** Snowman and pine tree **Note:** Antique finish.

Date	Mintage	F	VF	XF	Unc	BU
2002	142	15.00	—	—	—	—

X# 65a 100 PESOS
31.1000 g., 0.9250 Silver 0.9249 oz. ASW
Ruler: Philippe **Subject:** Christmas **Obv:** Head right **Rev:** Snowman and pine tree **Note:** Antique finish.

Date	Mintage	F	VF	XF	Unc	BU
2002	50	45.00	—	—	—	—

X# 66 100 PESOS
Nickel-Silver **Ruler:** Philippe **Subject:** Christmas **Obv:** Head right **Rev:** Peace dove **Note:** Antique finish.

Date	Mintage	F	VF	XF	Unc	BU
2003	143	15.00	—	—	—	—

X# 66a 100 PESOS
31.1000 g., 0.9250 Silver 0.9249 oz. ASW **Ruler:** Philippe **Subject:** Christmas **Obv:** Head right **Rev:** Peace dove **Note:** Antique finish.

Date	Mintage	F	VF	XF	Unc	BU
2003	51	45.00	—	—	—	—

X# 24 SOBERANO
Bronze **Ruler:** Philippe **Subject:** New Year **Obv:** Head right **Rev:** Hemisphere map **Note:** Antique finish.

Date	Mintage	F	VF	XF	Unc	BU
1989	100	—	—	—	—	—

X# 24a SOBERANO
Nickel-Silver **Ruler:** Philippe **Subject:** New Year **Obv:** Head right **Rev:** Hemisphere map **Note:** Antique finish.

Date	Mintage	F	VF	XF	Unc	BU
1989	40	—	—	—	—	—

X# 24b SOBERANO
31.1000 g., 0.9250 Silver 0.9249 oz. ASW
Ruler: Philippe **Subject:** New Year **Obv:** Head right **Rev:** Hemisphere map **Note:** Antique finish.

Date	Mintage	F	VF	XF	Unc	BU
1989	25	—	—	—	—	—

X# 25 SOBERANO
Bronze **Ruler:** Philippe **Subject:** Christmas **Obv:** Head right **Rev:** Graphic snowflake **Note:** Antique finish.

Date	Mintage	F	VF	XF	Unc	BU
1989	100	—	—	—	—	—

X# 25a SOBERANO
Nickel-Silver **Ruler:** Philippe **Subject:** Christmas **Obv:** Head right **Rev:** Graphic snowflake **Note:** Antique finish.

Date	Mintage	F	VF	XF	Unc	BU
1989	25	—	—	—	—	—

X# 25b SOBERANO
31.1000 g., Silver **Ruler:** Philippe **Subject:** Christmas **Obv:** Head right **Rev:** Graphic snowflake **Note:** Antique finish.

Date	Mintage	F	VF	XF	Unc	BU
1989	25	—	—	—	—	—

X# 29 SOBERANO
Bronze **Ruler:** Philippe **Subject:** Christmas **Obv:** Head right **Rev:** Three carrolers **Note:** Error: FELIX... Antique finish.

Date	Mintage	F	VF	XF	Unc	BU
1990	35	—	—	—	—	—

X# 29a SOBERANO
Nickel-Silver **Ruler:** Philippe **Subject:** Christmas **Obv:** Head right **Rev:** Three carrolers **Note:** Error: FELIX... Antique finish.

Date	Mintage	F	VF	XF	Unc	BU
1990	6	—	—	—	—	—

X# 32 SOBERANO
Nickel-Silver **Ruler:** Philippe **Subject:** Christmas **Obv:** Head right **Rev:** Madonna and child **Note:** Antique finish.

Date	Mintage	F	VF	XF	Unc	BU
1991	100	—	—	—	—	—

X# 32a SOBERANO
31.1000 g., 0.9250 Silver 0.9249 oz. ASW
Ruler: Philippe **Subject:** Christmas **Obv:** Head right **Rev:** Madonna and child

Date	Mintage	F	VF	XF	Unc	BU
1991	25	—	—	—	—	—

X# 36 SOBERANO
Bronze **Ruler:** Philippe **Subject:** Christmas **Obv:** Head right **Rev:** Tree with stars as leaves **Note:** Antique finish.

Date	Mintage	F	VF	XF	Unc	BU
1992	41	—	—	—	—	—

X# 36a SOBERANO
31.1000 g., 0.9250 Silver 0.9249 oz. ASW
Ruler: Philippe **Subject:** Christmas **Obv:** Head right **Rev:** Tree with stars as leaves

Date	Mintage	F	VF	XF	Unc	BU
1992	26	—	—	—	—	—

X# 39 SOBERANO
Copper **Ruler:** Philippe **Subject:** Christmas **Obv:** Head right **Rev:** Horsedrawn sleigh **Note:** Antique finish.

Date	Mintage	F	VF	XF	Unc	BU
1993	16	—	—	—	—	—

X# 39a SOBERANO
Nickel-Silver **Ruler:** Philippe **Subject:** Christmas **Obv:** Head right **Rev:** Horsedrawn sleigh **Note:** Antique finish.

Date	Mintage	F	VF	XF	Unc	BU
1993	8	—	—	—	—	—

X# 39b SOBERANO
31.1000 g., 0.9250 Silver 0.9249 oz. ASW
Ruler: Philippe **Subject:** Christmas **Obv:** Head right **Rev:** Horsedrawn sleigh

Date	Mintage	F	VF	XF	Unc	BU
1993	8	—	—	—	—	—

X# 42 SOBERANO
Copper **Ruler:** Philippe **Subject:** Christmas **Obv:** Head right **Rev:** Town view, Noel below **Note:** Antique finish.

Date	Mintage	F	VF	XF	Unc	BU
1994	40	—	—	—	—	—

X# 42b SOBERANO
31.1000 g., 0.9250 Silver 0.9249 oz. ASW
Ruler: Philippe **Subject:** Christmas **Obv:** Head right **Rev:** Town view, Noel below **Note:** Antique finish.

Date	Mintage	F	VF	XF	Unc	BU
1994	23	—	—	—	—	—

X# 44 SOBERANO

Copper **Ruler:** Philippe **Subject:** Christmas **Obv:** Head right **Rev:** Trumpeter **Note:** Antique finish.

Date	Mintage	F	VF	XF	Unc	BU
1995	40	—	—	—	—	—

X# 44a SOBERANO

Nickel-Silver **Ruler:** Philippe **Subject:** Christmas **Obv:** Head right **Rev:** Trumpeter **Note:** Antique finish.

Date	Mintage	F	VF	XF	Unc	BU
1995	6	—	—	—	—	—

X# 49 SOBERANO

Copper **Ruler:** Philippe **Subject:** Christmas **Obv:** Head right **Rev:** Angel and scroll **Note:** Antique finish.

Date	Mintage	F	VF	XF	Unc	BU
1996	50	—	—	—	—	—

X# 54 SOBERANO

Bronze **Ruler:** Philippe **Subject:** Christmas **Obv:** Head right **Rev:** Madonna and child **Note:** Antique finish.

Date	Mintage	F	VF	XF	Unc	BU
1997	75	—	—	—	—	—

X# 54a SOBERANO

Nickel-Silver **Ruler:** Philippe **Subject:** Christmas **Obv:** Head right **Rev:** Madonna and child **Note:** Antique finish.

Date	Mintage	F	VF	XF	Unc	BU
1997	8	—	—	—	—	—

X# 54b SOBERANO

31.1000 g., 0.9250 Silver 0.9249 oz. ASW **Ruler:** Philippe **Subject:** Christmas **Obv:** Head right **Rev:** Madonna and child **Note:** Antique finish.

Date	Mintage	F	VF	XF	Unc	BU
1997	26	—	—	—	—	—

PIEFORTS

Double thickness

X# P15 70 PESOS

62.2000 g., 0.9250 Silver 1.8497 oz. ASW **Ruler:** Philippe **Subject:** 70th Birthday of Prince Philippe **Obv:** Head right **Rev:** Map of Araucania - Patagonia, arms at right **Note:** As X#51.

Date	Mintage	F	VF	XF	Unc	BU
1997 Proof	7	—	—	—	—	—

X# P1 100 PESOS

62.2000 g., 0.9990 Silver 1.9977 oz. ASW **Ruler:** Philippe **Subject:** 128th Anniversary of Founding **Obv:** Head right **Rev:** Map, arms at right **Note:** As X#21.

Date	Mintage	F	VF	XF	Unc	BU
1988 Proof	36	Value: 165				

X# P2 100 PESOS

62.2000 g., 0.9990 Silver 1.9977 oz. ASW **Ruler:** Philippe **Subject:** 129th Anniversary of Founding **Obv:** Head right **Rev:** Map of Araucania - Patagonia, arms at right **Note:** As X#22.

Date	Mintage	F	VF	XF	Unc	BU
1989 Proof	37	Value: 85.00				

X# P3 100 PESOS

62.2000 g., 0.9990 Palladium 1.9977 oz. **Ruler:** Philippe **Subject:** 129th Anniversary of Founding **Obv:** Head right **Rev:** Map of Araucania - Patagonia, arms at right **Note:** As X#22.

Date	Mintage	F	VF	XF	Unc	BU
1989 Proof	3	—	—	—	—	—

X# P4 100 PESOS

62.2000 g., 0.9990 Silver 1.9977 oz. ASW **Ruler:** Philippe **Subject:** 120th Anniversary of Battleship Entrecasteaux **Obv:** Head right **Rev:** Sailing ship Entrecasteaux **Note:** As X#28.

Date	Mintage	F	VF	XF	Unc	BU
1990 Proof	38	Value: 150				

X# P5 100 PESOS

62.2000 g., 0.9990 Palladium 1.9977 oz. **Ruler:** Philippe **Subject:** 120th Anniversary of Battleship Entrecasteaux **Obv:** Head right **Rev:** Sailing ship Entrecasteaux **Note:** As X#28.

Date	Mintage	F	VF	XF	Unc	BU
1990 Proof	4	—	—	—	—	—

X# P6 100 PESOS

62.2000 g., 0.9990 Silver 1.9977 oz. ASW **Ruler:** Philippe **Subject:** 131st Anniversary of Founding **Obv:** Head right **Rev:** National flag

Date	Mintage	F	VF	XF	Unc	BU
1991 Proof	39	Value: 95.00				

X# P7 100 PESOS

62.2000 g., 0.9990 Palladium 1.9977 oz. **Ruler:** Philippe **Subject:** 131st Anniversary of Founding **Obv:** Head right **Rev:** National flag

Date	Mintage	F	VF	XF	Unc	BU
1991 Proof	4	—	—	—	—	—

X# P8 100 PESOS

62.2000 g., 0.9990 Silver 1.9977 oz. ASW **Ruler:** Philippe **Subject:** Freedom for the Mapuche Peoples (1492-1992) **Obv:** Head right **Rev:** Geronimo bust facing **Note:** As X#35.

Date	Mintage	F	VF	XF	Unc	BU
1992 Proof	40	Value: 95.00				

X# P9 100 PESOS

62.2000 g., 0.9990 Palladium 1.9977 oz. **Ruler:** Philippe **Subject:** Freedom for the Mapuche Peoples (1492-1992) **Obv:** Head right **Rev:** Geronimo bust facing **Note:** As X#35.

Date	Mintage	F	VF	XF	Unc	BU
1992 Proof	4	—	—	—	—	—

X# P10 100 PESOS

62.2000 g., 0.9250 Silver 1.8497 oz. ASW **Ruler:** Philippe **Subject:** 133rd Anniversary of Founding **Obv:** Head right **Rev:** Map of Araucania - Patagonia, arms at right **Rev. Legend:** ... ORELIE • ANTOINE (1860-1878)

Date	Mintage	F	VF	XF	Unc	BU
1993 Proof	41	Value: 95.00				

X# P11 100 PESOS

62.2000 g., 0.9250 Silver 1.8497 oz. ASW **Ruler:** Philippe **Subject:** 134th Anniversary of Founding **Obv:** Head right **Rev:** Map of Araucania - Patagonia, arms at right **Rev. Legend:** ... ACHILLE I (1878-1902) **Note:** As X#41.

Date	Mintage	F	VF	XF	Unc	BU
1994 Proof	42	Value: 95.00				

X# P12 100 PESOS

62.2000 g., 0.9250 Silver 1.8497 oz. ASW **Ruler:** Philippe **Subject:** 135th Anniversary of Founding **Obv:** Head right **Rev:** Map of Araucania - Patagonia, arms at right **Rev. Legend:** ... ANTOINE II (1902-1903) **Note:** As X#43.

Date	Mintage	F	VF	XF	Unc	BU
1995 Proof	43	Value: 95.00				

X# P13 100 PESOS

62.2000 g., 0.9250 Silver 1.8497 oz. ASW **Ruler:** Philippe **Subject:** 136th Anniversary of Founding **Obv:** Head right **Rev:** Map of Araucania - Patagonia, arms at right **Rev. Legend:** ... LAURE - THERESE (1903-1916) **Note:** As X#46.

Date	Mintage	F	VF	XF	Unc	BU
1996 Proof	44	Value: 95.00				

X# P14 100 PESOS

62.2000 g., 0.9250 Silver 1.8497 oz. ASW **Ruler:** Philippe **Subject:** Wedding of Prince Philippe and Princess Elizabeth **Obv:** Head right **Rev:** Map of Araucania - Patagonia, arms at right **Note:** As X#47.

Date	Mintage	F	VF	XF	Unc	BU
1996 Proof	10	—	—	—	—	—

X# P16 100 PESOS

62.2000 g., 0.9250 Silver 1.8497 oz. ASW **Ruler:** Philippe **Subject:** 137th Anniversary of Founding **Obv:** Head right **Rev:** Map of Araucania - Patagonia, arms at right **Rev. Legend:** ... ANTOINE III (1916-1952) **Note:** As X#52.

Date	Mintage	F	VF	XF	Unc	BU
1997 Proof	45	Value: 95.00				

X# P17 100 PESOS

62.2000 g., 0.9250 Silver 1.8497 oz. ASW **Ruler:** Philippe **Subject:** Christmas **Obv:** Head right **Rev:** Two bells **Note:** As X#56. Antique finish.

Date	Mintage	F	VF	XF	Unc	BU
1998	8	—	—	—	—	—

X# P18 100 PESOS

62.2000 g., 0.9250 Silver 1.8497 oz. ASW **Ruler:** Philippe **Subject:** Christmas **Obv:** Head right **Rev:** The Magi on camels following star **Note:** As X#58. Antique finish.

Date	Mintage	F	VF	XF	Unc	BU
1999	8	—	—	—	—	—

X# P19 100 PESOS

62.2000 g., 0.9250 Silver 1.8497 oz. ASW **Ruler:** Philippe **Subject:** 140th Anniversary of Founding **Obv:** Head right **Rev:** Peace (in 17 languages)

Date	Mintage	F	VF	XF	Unc	BU
2000 Proof	48	Value: 85.00				

X# P20 100 PESOS

62.2000 g., 0.9250 Silver 1.8497 oz. ASW **Ruler:** Philippe **Subject:** Christmas **Obv:** Head right **Rev:** Madonna and child **Note:** As X#61. Antique finish.

Date	Mintage	F	VF	XF	Unc	BU
2000	8	—	—	—	—	—

X# P21 100 PESOS

62.2000 g., 0.9250 Silver 1.8497 oz. ASW **Ruler:** Philippe **Subject:** Christmas **Obv:** Head right **Rev:** Angel **Note:** As X#64. Antique finish.

Date	Mintage	F	VF	XF	Unc	BU
2001	8	—	—	—	—	—

X# P22 100 PESOS

62.2000 g., 0.9250 Silver 1.8497 oz. ASW **Ruler:** Philippe **Subject:** Christmas **Obv:** Head right **Rev:** Snowman and pine tree **Note:** As X#65. Antique finish.

Date	Mintage	F	VF	XF	Unc	BU
2002	8	—	—	—	—	—

X# P23 100 PESOS

62.2000 g., 0.9250 Silver 1.8497 oz. ASW **Ruler:** Philippe **Subject:** Christmas **Obv:** Head right **Rev:** Peace dove **Note:** As X#66. Antique finish.

Date	Mintage	F	VF	XF	Unc	BU
2003	8	—	—	—	—	—

ARGENTINA

REPUBLIC

BULLION COINAGE

Morro Velho Mines Issues

X# B1.1 3 1/4 OUNCES

101.1300 g., 0.9955 Gold 3.2366 oz. AGW **Obv. Inscription:** MMV / AZ **Shape:** 40mm x 23mm rectangular **Note:** Uniface. Prev. X#B1.

Date	Mintage	F	VF	XF	Unc	BU
ND(c.1880)	—	—	—	2,450	—	—

X# B1.2 3 1/4 OUNCES
102.0000 g., 0.9954 Gold 3.2642 oz. AGW
Obv. Inscription: MMV / BC **Shape:** 42mm x 22mm rectangular **Note:** Uniface.

Date	Mintage	F	VF	XF	Unc	BU
ND(c.1880)	—	—	—	2,450	—	—

X# B2 7 OUNCES
218.0000 g., 0.9999 Gold 7.0079 oz. AGW
Obv. Inscription: MMV - FF **Shape:** 63mm x 24mm rectangular **Note:** Uniface.

Date	Mintage	F	VF	XF	Unc	BU
ND(c.1880)	—	—	—	5,250	—	—

ESSAIS

X#	Date	Mintage	Identification	Mkt Val
E1	1878	—	Centavo. Copper. Proof.	150
E2	1878	—	2 Centavos. Copper. Proof.	175

X#	Date	Mintage	Identification	Mkt Val
E3	1879	—	20 Centavos Fuertes. Silver. Proof.	1,150
E3a	1879	—	20 Centavos Fuertes. Bronze. Bronze, proof.	950

X#	Date	Mintage	Identification	Mkt Val
E4	1879	—	40 Centavos Fuertes. Silver. Proof.	1,500
E4a	1879	—	40 Centavos Fuertes. Bronze. Bronze, proof.	1,100

X#	Date	Mintage	Identification	Mkt Val
E5	1879	—	80 Centavos Fuertes. Silver. Proof.	1,650
E5a	1879	—	80 Centavos Fuertes. Bronze. Bronze, proof. Reported, not confirmed.	—
E5b	1879	—	80 Centavos Fuertes. Copper. Copper, proof.	1,100

X#	Date	Mintage	Identification	Mkt Val
E6	1879	—	Patacon. Silver. Reeded edge. Proof. Reeded edge.	4,750
E6a	1879	—	Patacon. Copper. Proof.	2,250

SALTA

PROVINCE

COUNTERMARKED COINAGE

X# 1 8 REALES
Silver **Countermark:** PATRIA monogram
Note: Countermark monogram in wreath on imitation Potosi Mint "cob" star 8 Reales. All known 8 Reales with this countermark are considered spurious by leading authorities.

CM Date	Host Date	Good	VG	F	VF	XF
ND(1817)	ND(1659)	20.00	30.00	45.00	60.00	—

TIERRA DEL FUEGO

TERRITORY

TOKEN COINAGE

X# 9 GRAMO
Gold **Issuer:** Museo del Fin del Mundo **Obv:** Legend and date **Rev:** Legend, crossed mining tools and denomination **Note:** Series 1 with USHUAIA on outer ring, struck from surviving original Buenos Aires dies in 1995.

Date	Mintage	F	VF	XF	Unc	BU
1889	100	—	—	—	—	—

X# 10 GRAMO
Gold **Issuer:** Museo del Fin del Mundo **Obv:** Legend and date **Rev:** Legend and crossed mining tools **Note:** Series 2 with USHUAIA on outer ring, struck from copy dies on larger flan after 1995.

Date	Mintage	F	VF	XF	Unc	BU
1889	100	—	—	—	125	—

ARMENIA

REPUBLIC 1918-1920

STANDARD COINAGE

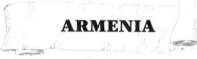

X# 1 5 RUBLES
Brass **Obv:** Eagle standing 3/4 left with wings outspread with sword **Rev:** Value in sprays
Note: Believed by most to be a 1960s fantasy.

Date	Mintage	F	VF	XF	Unc	BU
1920	—	—	—	—	—	—

REPUBLIC

MEDALLIC COINAGE

Onzas

X# 10 ONZA
31.1000 g., 0.9990 Silver 0.9988 oz. ASW **Obv:** Eagle, sun rays above, grape clusters on vines below
Rev: Stylized bell towers

Date	Mintage	F	VF	XF	Unc	BU
1989	10,000	—	—	—	—	50.00

X# 11 ONZA
3.1100 g., 0.9000 Palladium 0.0900 oz. **Obv:** Eagle, sun rays above, grape clusters on vines below
Rev: Stylized bell towers

Date	Mintage	F	VF	XF	Unc	BU
1989	1,000	—	—	—	—	75.00

X# 12 ONZA
3.1100 g., 0.9000 Gold 0.0900 oz. AGW **Obv:** Eagle, sun rays above, grape clusters on vines below
Rev: Tower, rays from different levels

Date	Mintage	F	VF	XF	Unc	BU
1989	2,500	—	—	—	—	85.00

Memorial Rubles

X# 15 RUBLE
31.1000 g., 0.9990 Silver 0.9988 oz. ASW **Obv:** Arm holding banner, crossed sword and dagger
Rev: Memorial below tower and mountain range

Date	Mintage	F	VF	XF	Unc	BU
1990 Proof	1,000	Value: 65.00				

X# 15a RUBLE
31.1000 g., 0.9990 Gold 0.9988 oz. AGW **Obv:** Arm holding banner, crossed sword and dagger
Rev: Memorial bell tower and mountain range

Date	Mintage	F	VF	XF	Unc	BU
1990 Proof	100	Value: 800				

X# 15b RUBLE
31.1000 g., 0.9990 Palladium 0.9988 oz. **Obv:** Arm holding banner, crossed sword and dagger
Rev: Memorial bell tower and mountain range

Date	Mintage	F	VF	XF	Unc	BU
1990 Proof	100	Value: 600				

X# 15c RUBLE
31.1000 g., 0.9990 Platinum 0.9988 oz. APW
Obv: Arms holding banner, crossed sword and dagger
Rev: Memorial bell tower and mountain range

Date	Mintage	F	VF	XF	Unc	BU
1990 Proof	100	Value: 1,500				

ICB Series

X# 2.1 25 DRAM
24.0000 g., 0.9250 Silver 0.7137 oz. ASW, 38 mm.
Obv: Arms **Rev:** Bust of Jesus facing **Edge:** Reeded

Date	Mintage	F	VF	XF	Unc	BU
1996 Proof	100	Value: 60.00				

X# 2.2 25 DRAM
24.0000 g., 0.9250 Silver 0.7137 oz. ASW, 38 mm.
Obv: Arms **Rev:** Bust of Jesus facing **Edge:** Plain

Date	Mintage	F	VF	XF	Unc	BU
1996 Proof	100	Value: 60.00				

X# 2a.1 25 DRAM
23.0000 g., Brass, 38 mm. **Obv:** Arms **Rev:** Bust of Jesus facing **Edge:** Reeded

Date	Mintage	F	VF	XF	Unc	BU
1996 Proof	100	Value: 35.00				

X# 2a.2 25 DRAM
23.0000 g., Brass, 38 mm. **Obv:** Arms **Rev:** Bust of Jesus facing **Edge:** Plain

Date	Mintage	F	VF	XF	Unc	BU
1996 Proof	100	Value: 35.00				

X# 2b.1 25 DRAM
20.0000 g., Gilt Alloy, 38 mm. **Obv:** Arms **Rev:** Bust of Jesus facing **Edge:** Reeded

Date	Mintage	F	VF	XF	Unc	BU
1996 Proof	100	Value: 35.00				

X# 2b.2 25 DRAM
20.0000 g., Gilt Alloy, 38 mm. **Obv:** Arms **Rev:** Bust of Jesus facing **Edge:** Plain

Date	Mintage	F	VF	XF	Unc	BU
1996 Proof	100	Value: 35.00				

X# 2c.1 25 DRAM
23.0000 g., Tri-Metallic Silvered and gilt Brass, 38 mm.
Obv: Arms **Rev:** Bust of Jesus facing **Edge:** Reeded

Date	Mintage	F	VF	XF	Unc	BU
1996 Proof	100	Value: 55.00				

X# 2c.2 25 DRAM
23.0000 g., Tri-Metallic Silvered and gilt Brass, 38 mm.
Obv: Arms **Rev:** Bust of Jesus facing **Edge:** Plain

Date	Mintage	F	VF	XF	Unc	BU
1996 Proof	100	Value: 55.00				

X# 2d.1 25 DRAM
6.0000 g., Aluminum, 38 mm. **Obv:** Arms **Rev:** Bust of Jesus facing **Edge:** Reeded

Date	Mintage	F	VF	XF	Unc	BU
1996 Proof	100	Value: 35.00				

X# 2d.2 25 DRAM
6.0000 g., Aluminum, 38 mm. **Obv:** Arms **Rev:** Bust of Jesus facing **Edge:** Plain

Date	Mintage	F	VF	XF	Unc	BU
1996 Proof	100	Value: 35.00				

X# 2e.1 25 DRAM
23.0000 g., Copper, 38 mm. **Obv:** Arms **Rev:** Bust of Jesus facing **Edge:** Reeded

Date	Mintage	F	VF	XF	Unc	BU
1996 Proof	100	Value: 35.00				

X# 2e.2 25 DRAM
23.0000 g., Copper, 38 mm. **Obv:** Arms **Rev:** Bust of Jesus facing **Edge:** Plain

Date	Mintage	F	VF	XF	Unc	BU
1996 Proof	100	Value: 35.00				

X# 2f.1 25 DRAM
20.0000 g., Copper-Nickel, 38 mm. **Obv:** Arms **Rev:** Bust of Jesus facing **Edge:** Reeded

Date	Mintage	F	VF	XF	Unc	BU
1996 Proof	100	Value: 35.00				

X# 2f.2 25 DRAM
20.0000 g., Copper-Nickel, 38 mm. **Obv:** Arms **Rev:** Bust of Jesus facing **Edge:** Plain

Date	Mintage	F	VF	XF	Unc	BU
1996 Proof	100	Value: 35.00				

FANTASY EURO PATTERNS

X# Pn1 EURO CENT
Copper Plated Steel **Edge:** Plain

Date	Mintage	F	VF	XF	Unc	BU
2004	7,000	—	—	—	—	1.50

X# Pn2 2 EURO CENTS
Copper Plated Steel **Edge:** Plain

Date	Mintage	F	VF	XF	Unc	BU
2004	7,000	—	—	—	—	2.00

X# Pn3 5 EURO CENTS
Copper Plated Steel

Date	Mintage	F	VF	XF	Unc	BU
2004	7,000	—	—	—	—	2.50

X# Pn4 10 EURO CENTS
Goldine **Edge:** Plain

Date	Mintage	F	VF	XF	Unc	BU
2004	7,000	—	—	—	—	3.00

X# Pn5 20 EURO CENTS
Goldine **Edge:** Plain

Date	Mintage	F	VF	XF	Unc	BU
2004	7,000	—	—	—	—	3.50

X# Pn6 50 EURO CENTS
Goldine **Edge:** Plain

Date	Mintage	F	VF	XF	Unc	BU
2004	7,000	—	—	—	—	4.00

X# Pn7 EURO
Bi-Metallic **Obv:** Helmeted male bust facing 3/4 right
Rev: Knight, large value "1" **Edge:** Plain

Date	Mintage	F	VF	XF	Unc	BU
2004	7,000	—	—	—	—	6.00

X# Pn8 2 EURO
Bi-Metallic **Obv:** Helmeted male bust facing 3/4 right
Rev: Knight, large value "2" **Edge:** Plain

Date	Mintage	F	VF	XF	Unc	BU
2004	—	—	—	—	—	8.00

PATTERNS

X#	Date	Mintage	Identification	Mkt Val
Pn15	1990	75	Ruble. Copper. X#15.	25.00
Pn16	1990	3	Ruble. Brass. X#15.	50.00
Pn17	1990	3	Ruble. Nickel. 31.1000 g. X#15.	60.00

PIEFORTS

X#	Date	Mintage	Identification	Mkt Val
P1	1996	—	25 Dram. 0.9250 Silver. 48.0000 g. X2.1.	85.00
P2	1996	—	25 Dram. 0.9250 Silver. 48.0000 g. X2.2.	85.00

TRIAL STRIKES

X#	Date	Mintage	Identification	Mkt Val
Ts1	1990	2	Ruble. 0.9990 Silver. 31.1000 g. Uniface obverse. X#15.	100
Ts2	1990	2	Ruble. 0.9990 Silver. 31.1000 g. Uniface reverse. X#15.	100
Ts3	1990	2	Ruble. 0.9990 Gold. 31.1000 g. Uniface obverse. X#15.	—
Ts4	1990	2	Ruble. 0.9990 Gold. 31.1000 g. Uniface reverse. X#15.	—
Ts5	1990	2	Ruble. Palladium. 31.1000 g. Uniface obverse. X#15.	—
Ts6	1990	2	Ruble. Palladium. 31.1000 g. Uniface reverse. X#15.	—
Ts7	1990	2	Ruble. Platinum. Uniface obverse. X#15.	—
Ts8	1990	2	Ruble. Platinum. Uniface reverse. X#15.	—

MINT SETS

X#	Date	Mintage	Identification	Issue Price	Mkt Val
XMS1	2004 (8)	7,000	X#Pn1-Pn8	—	30.00

ARUBA

DUTCH STATE

"Status Aparte"

FANTASY EURO PATTERNS

INA Series

X# Pn1 EURO CENT
Copper Plated Steel, 16.80 mm. **Rev:** Large value, fish, Euro stars design **Edge:** Plain

Date	Mintage	F	VF	XF	Unc	BU
2005	10,000	—	—	—	—	1.50
2005 Proof	—	Value: 2.50				

X# Pn1a EURO CENT
Silver, 16.80 mm. **Rev:** Large value, fish, EURO stars design **Edge:** Plain

Date	Mintage	F	VF	XF	Unc	BU
2005 Proof	250	Value: 6.00				

X# Pn2 2 EURO CENTS
Copper Plated Steel, 18.50 mm. **Rev:** Large value, fish, Euro stars design **Edge:** Plain

Date	Mintage	F	VF	XF	Unc	BU
2005	10,000	—	—	—	—	2.00
2005 Proof	—	Value: 3.00				

X# Pn2a 2 EURO CENTS
Silver, 18.5 mm. **Rev:** Large value, fish, EURO stars design **Edge:** Plain

Date	Mintage	F	VF	XF	Unc	BU
2005 Proof	250	Value: 7.00				

X# Pn3 5 EURO CENTS
Copper Plated Steel, 20.7 mm. **Rev:** Large value, fish **Edge:** Plain

Date	Mintage	F	VF	XF	Unc	BU
2005	10,000	—	—	—	—	2.50
2005 Proof	—	Value: 3.50				

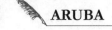

X# Pn3a 5 EURO CENTS
Silver, 20.70 mm. **Rev:** Large value, fish **Edge:** Plain

Date	Mintage	F	VF	XF	Unc	BU
2005 Proof	250	Value: 8.50				

X# Pn4 10 EURO CENTS
Goldine, 19.30 mm. **Rev:** Seahorse, large value, Euro stars design **Edge:** Plain

Date	Mintage	F	VF	XF	Unc	BU
2005	10,000	—	—	—	—	3.00
2005 Proof	—	Value: 4.00				

X# Pn4a 10 EURO CENTS
Silver, 19.3 mm. **Rev:** Seahorse, large value, EURO stars design **Edge:** Plain

Date	Mintage	F	VF	XF	Unc	BU
2005 Proof	250	Value: 10.00				

X# Pn5 20 EURO CENTS
Goldine, 22 mm. **Rev:** Seahorse, large value, Euro stars design **Edge:** Plain

Date	Mintage	F	VF	XF	Unc	BU
2005	10,000	—	—	—	—	3.50
2005 Proof	—	Value: 5.00				

X# Pn5a 20 EURO CENTS
Silver, 22 mm. **Rev:** Seahorse, large value, EURO stars design **Edge:** Plain

Date	Mintage	F	VF	XF	Unc	BU
2005 Proof	250	Value: 12.50				

X# Pn6 50 EURO CENTS
Goldine, 24.3 mm. **Rev:** Seahorse, large value, Euro stars design **Edge:** Plain

Date	Mintage	F	VF	XF	Unc	BU
2005	10,000	—	—	—	—	4.00
2005 Proof	—	Value: 6.00				

X# Pn6a 50 EURO CENTS
Silver, 24.3 mm. **Rev:** Seahorse, large value, EURO stars design **Edge:** Plain

Date	Mintage	F	VF	XF	Unc	BU
2005 Proof	250	Value: 15.00				

X# Pn7 EURO
Bi-Metallic Silver center in Goldine ring, 22.8 mm. **Rev. Designer:** Sea tortoise **Edge:** Plain

Date	Mintage	F	VF	XF	Unc	BU
2005	10,000	—	—	—	—	6.00
2005 Proof	—	Value: 8.00				

X# Pn7a EURO
Bi-Metallic Goldine center in Silver ring, 22.80 mm. **Rev:** Sea tortoise **Edge:** Plain

Date	Mintage	F	VF	XF	Unc	BU
2005 Proof	250	Value: 22.50				

X# Pn8 2 EURO
Bi-Metallic Copper-Nickel center in Goldine ring, 25.7 mm. **Rev:** Sea tortoise **Edge:** Plain

Date	Mintage	F	VF	XF	Unc	BU
2005	10,000	—	—	—	—	8.00
2005 Proof	—	Value: 10.00				

X# Pn8a 2 EURO
Bi-Metallic Goldine center in Silver ring, 25.7 mm. **Rev:** Sea tortoise **Edge:** Plain

Date	Mintage	F	VF	XF	Unc	BU
2005 Proof	250	Value: 28.50				

X# Pn9 5 EURO
Bi-Metallic **Edge:** Plain

Date	Mintage	F	VF	XF	Unc	BU
2005 Proof	—	Value: 12.50				

X# Pn9a 5 EURO
Silver **Edge:** Plain

Date	Mintage	F	VF	XF	Unc	BU
2005 Proof	250	Value: 40.00				

MINT SETS

X#	Date	Mintage	Identification	Issue Price	Mkt Val
XMS1	2005 (8)	10,000	X#Pn1-Pn8	—	30.00

PROOF SETS

X#	Date	Mintage	Identification	Issue Price	Mkt Val
XPS1	2005 (9)	—	X#Pn1-Pn9	—	50.00
XPS2	2005 (9)	250	X#Pn1a-Pn9a	—	150

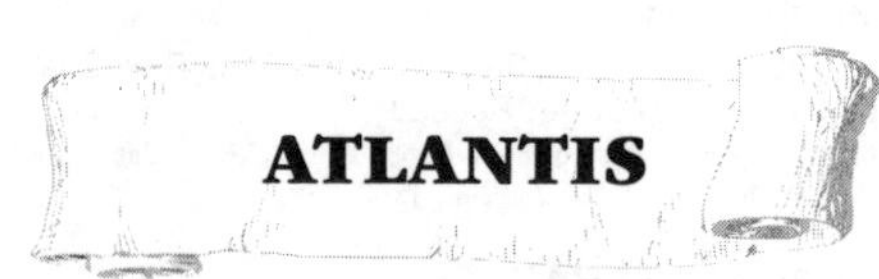

ATLANTIS

KINGDOM

STANDARD COINAGE

X# 7 DECA
9.8500 g., 0.9250 Silver 0.2929 oz. ASW, 24 mm. **Ruler:** Christiano I **Obv:** Boat steering wheel divides date **Obv. Legend:** ATLANTIS REASON • FREEDOM **Rev:** Sea sunrise **Edge:** Reeded **Note:** Intrinsic weight given as TEN GRAMS SILVER 925 FINE.

Date	Mintage	F	VF	XF	Unc	BU
1970	—	—	30.00	50.00	85.00	—

MEDALLIC COINAGE

WPNA Series

X# 10 20 ATLANTIS DOLLARS
26.5300 g., Copper, 38.9 mm. **Ruler:** Christiano I **Obv:** Young girl sitting, moutains in background **Obv. Legend:** KINGDOM OF ATLANTIS **Rev:** Poseidon standing right with trident facing Cleo standing left in front of pillars of temple entranceway **Edge:** Reeded

Date	Mintage	F	VF	XF	Unc	BU
MMIV (2004) Proof	200	Value: 30.00				

X# 12 20 ATLANTIS DOLLARS
26.4200 g., Brass, 39.12 mm. **Ruler:** Christiano I **Obv:** Two Atlantis men rowing canoe **Obv. Legend:** KINGDOM OF ATLANTIS **Rev:** Poseidon standing right with trident facing Cleo standing left in front of pillars of temple entrance way **Edge:** Reeded

Date	Mintage	F	VF	XF	Unc	BU
MMVII (2007)	150	Value: 22.50				

X# 11 100 ATLANTIS DOLLARS
31.2500 g., 0.9990 Silver 1.0037 oz. ASW, 38.9 mm. **Ruler:** Christiano I **Obv:** Young girl sitting, mountains in background **Obv. Legend:** KINGDOM OF ATLANTIS **Rev:** Poseidon standing right with trident facing Cleo standing left in front of pillars of temple entranceway **Edge:** Reeded **Edge Lettering:** FS 999

Date	Mintage	F	VF	XF	Unc	BU
MMIV (2004) Proof	50	Value: 50.00				

X# 11a 100 ATLANTIS DOLLARS
31.2500 g., 0.9990 Gold 1.0037 oz. AGW, 38.9 mm. **Ruler:** Christiano I **Obv:** Young girl sitting, mountains in background **Obv. Legend:** KINGDOM OF ATLANTIS **Rev:** Poseidon standing right with trident facing Cleo standing left in front of pillars of temple entranceway **Edge:** Reeded **Edge Lettering:** FG 999

Date	Mintage	F	VF	XF	Unc	BU
MMIV (2004) Proof	5	Value: 650				

X# 13 100 ATLANTIS DOLLARS
31.2040 g., 0.9990 Silver 1.0022 oz. ASW, 39.12 mm. **Ruler:** Christiano I **Obv:** Two Atlantis men rowing a canoe **Obv. Legend:** KINGDOM OF ATLANTIS **Rev:** Poseidon standing right with trident facing Cleo standing lft in front of pillars of temple entrance way **Edge:** Reeded with smooth area denoting fineness

Date	Mintage	F	VF	XF	Unc	BU
MMVII (2007) Proof	50	Value: 45.00				

X# 13a 100 ATLANTIS DOLLARS
31.2040 g., 0.9990 Gold 1.0022 oz. AGW, 39.12 mm. **Ruler:** Christiano I **Obv:** Two Atlantis men rowing a canoe **Obv. Legend:** KINGDOM OF ATLANTIS **Rev:** Poseidon standing right with trident facing Cleo standing left in front of pillars of temple entrance way **Edge:** Reeded

Date	Mintage	F	VF	XF	Unc	BU
MMVII (2007) Proof	4	Value: 775				

PRINCIPALITY

FANTASY COINAGE

X# 2 5 SKALOJ
Bronze **Ruler:** Christiano I

Date	Mintage	F	VF	XF	Unc	BU
1933	—	15.00	25.00	45.00	—	—

X# 4 20 SKALOJ

Silver **Ruler:** Christiano I **Note:** Possibly issued at the Century of Progress Exposition in Chicago, Illinois in 1933.

Date	Mintage	F	VF	XF	Unc	BU
1933	—	25.00	40.00	60.00	—	—

ATLANTIUM

EMPIRE

STANDARD COINAGE

X# 1 10 SOLIDI

30.5000 g., Copper Gilt, 38 mm. **Ruler:** George II **Subject:** 20th Anniversary Foundation of Emporium **Obv:** Bust facing **Obv. Legend:** EMPIRE OF ATLANTIUM - GEORGIVS II IMPERATOR ET... **Rev:** Eagle, head left, outspread wings **Rev. Legend:** 20TH ANNIVERSARY...

Date	Mintage	F	VF	XF	Unc	BU
10520 (2001)	511	—	—	—	25.00	—

PATTERNS

X#	Date	Mintage	Identification	Mkt Val
Pn1	10520 (2001)	10	10 Solidi. Copper. X1. Numbered	150
Pn3	10520 (2001)	3	10 Solidi. 0.9250 Silver. X1.	250

TRIAL STRIKES

X#	Date	Mintage	Identification	Mkt Val
TS1	10520 (2001)	1	10 Solidi. Copper. Obverse. X1.	—
TS2	10520 (2001)	1	10 Solidi. Copper. Reverse. X1.	—

AUSTRALIA

BRITISH COLONY

MILLED COINAGE

X# A1 2 POUNDS

15.9500 g., Gold **Ruler:** Victoria **Obv:** Young head left, "M" under truncation **Obv. Legend:** VICTORIA D: G: BRITANNIAR: REG: F: D: **Rev:** St. George horseback slaying dragon

Date	Mintage	F	VF	XF	Unc	BU
1879M	—	—	—	—	—	—

COMMONWEALTH OF AUSTRALIA

MEDALLIC COINAGE

X# M5 PENNY

15.5500 g., Gold **Ruler:** George V **Subject:** 80th Anniversary Commonwealth Bank **Obv:** Crowned bust left **Obv. Legend:** GEORGIVS V D.G.BRITT: OHN: REX F.D IND: IMP: **Rev:** Large value **Rev. Legend:** COMMONWEALTH OF AUSTRALIA

Date	Mintage	F	VF	XF	Unc	BU
1912	580	—	—	—	—	400

X# MB1 OUNCE

31.1030 g., 0.9990 Silver 0.9989 oz. ASW, 39.15 mm. **Obv:** Koala cub and mother **Obv. Legend:** AUSTRALIA'S TEDDY BEAR **Rev:** Crown superimposed on outline of Australia **Edge:** Reeded

Date	Mintage	F	VF	XF	Unc	BU
1991 Proof	—	Value: 11.50				

X# MB1a OUNCE

Aluminum, 39.15 mm. **Obv:** Koala cub and mother **Obv. Legend:** AUSTRALIA'S TEDDY BEAR **Rev:** Crown superimposed on outline of Australia. Marked "COPY" **Edge:** Reeded **Note:** Advertising piece

Date	Mintage	F	VF	XF	Unc	BU
1991	—	—	—	—	2.50	—

INA Series

X# M31 3 PENCE

8.2600 g., Copper-Nickel, 20.2 mm. **Ruler:** George V **Series:** INA **Obv:** Crowned bust left **Obv. Legend:** GEORGIVS V D.G. BRITT: OMN: REX **Rev:** Large "3", swan divides date **Rev. Legend:** AUSTRALIA **Edge:** Plain **Shape:** Square

Date	Mintage	F	VF	XF	Unc	BU
1920 Proof	750	—	—	—	—	—

X# M31a 3 PENCE

8.0300 g., Goldine, 20.2 mm. **Ruler:** George V **Obv:** Crowned bust left **Obv. Legend:** GEORGIVS V D.G. BRITT: OMN: REX **Rev:** Large "3", swan divides date **Rev. Legend:** AUSTRALIA **Edge:** Plain **Shape:** Square

Date	Mintage	F	VF	XF	Unc	BU
1920 Proof	750	—	—	—	—	—

X# M31b 3 PENCE

6.8500 g., Copper, 20.2 mm. **Ruler:** George V **Series:** INA **Obv:** Crowned bust left **Obv. Legend:** GEORGIVS V D.G. BRITT: OMN: REX **Rev:** Large "3", swan divides date **Rev. Legend:** AUSTRALIA **Edge:** Plain **Shape:** Square

Date	Mintage	F	VF	XF	Unc	BU
1920 Proof	750	—	—	—	—	—

X# M31c 3 PENCE

6.9300 g., Copper Bronzed, 20.2 mm. **Ruler:** George V **Series:** INA **Obv:** Crowned bust left **Obv. Legend:** GEORGIVS V D.G. BRITT: OMN: REX **Rev:** Large "3", swan divides date **Rev. Legend:** AUSTRALIA **Edge:** Plain **Shape:** Square

Date	Mintage	F	VF	XF	Unc	BU
1920 Proof	750	—	—	—	—	—

X# M35 3 PENCE

9.7000 g., Copper-Nickel, 20.2 mm. **Ruler:** George V **Obv:** Head left **Obv. Legend:** GEORGIVS V D.G. BRITT: OMN: REX **Rev:** Large "3", two whales divide date **Rev. Legend:** AUSTRALIA **Edge:** Plain

Date	Mintage	F	VF	XF	Unc	BU
1921 Proof	750	—	—	—	—	—

X# M35a 3 PENCE

8.0300 g., Goldine, 20.2 mm. **Ruler:** George V **Obv:** Head left **Obv. Legend:** GEORGIVS V D.G. BRITT: OMN: REX **Rev:** Large "3", two whales divide date **Rev. Legend:** AUSTRALIA **Edge:** Plain **Shape:** Square

Date	Mintage	F	VF	XF	Unc	BU
1921 Proof	750	—	—	—	—	—

X# M35b 3 PENCE

8.4100 g., Copper, 20.2 mm. **Ruler:** George V **Obv:** Head left **Obv. Legend:** GEORGIVS V D.G. BRITT: OMN: REX **Rev:** Large "3", two whales divide date **Rev. Legend:** AUSTRALIA **Edge:** Plain **Shape:** Square

Date	Mintage	F	VF	XF	Unc	BU
1921 Proof	750	—	—	—	—	—

X# M35c 3 PENCE

8.3600 g., Copper Bronzed, 20.2 mm. **Ruler:** George V **Obv:** Head left **Obv. Legend:** GEORGIVS V D.G. BRITT: OMN: REX **Rev:** Large "3", two whales divide date **Rev. Legend:** AUSTRALIA **Edge:** Plain **Shape:** Square

Date	Mintage	F	VF	XF	Unc	BU
1921 Proof	750	—	—	—	—	—

X# M32 SIXPENCE

9.9700 g., Copper-Nickel, 22.2 mm. **Ruler:** George V **Obv:** Crowned bust left **Obv. Legend:** GEORGIVS V D.G. BRITT: OMN: REX **Rev:** Large "6", two sharks divide date **Rev. Legend:** AUSTRALIA **Edge:** Plain **Shape:** Square

Date	Mintage	F	VF	XF	Unc	BU
1920 Proof	750	—	—	—	—	—

X# M32a SIXPENCE

9.7700 g., Goldine, 22.2 mm. **Ruler:** George V **Obv:** Crowned bust left **Obv. Legend:** GEORGIVS V D.G. BRITT: OMN: REX **Rev:** Large "6", two shark divide date **Rev. Legend:** AUSTRALIA **Edge:** Plain **Shape:** Square

Date	Mintage	F	VF	XF	Unc	BU
1920 Proof	750	—	—	—	—	—

X# M32b SIXPENCE
8.8500 g., Copper, 22.2 mm. **Ruler:** George V **Obv:** Crowned bust left **Obv. Legend:** GEORGIVS V D.G.: BRITT: OMN: REX **Rev:** Large "6", two sharks divide date **Rev. Legend:** AUSTRALIA **Edge:** Plain **Shape:** Square

Date	Mintage	F	VF	XF	Unc	BU
1920 Proof	750	—	—	—	—	—

X# M32c SIXPENCE
8.4400 g., Copper Bronzed, 22.2 mm. **Ruler:** George V **Obv:** Crowned bust left **Obv. Legend:** GEORGIVS V D.G. BRITT: OMN: REX **Rev:** Large "6", two sharks divide date **Rev. Legend:** AUSTRALIA **Edge:** Plain **Shape:** Square

Date	Mintage	F	VF	XF	Unc	BU
1920 Proof	750	—	—	—	—	—

X# M36 SIXPENCE
11.7500 g., Copper-Nickel, 22.2 mm. **Ruler:** George V **Obv:** Head left **Obv. Legend:** GEORGIVS V D.G. BRITT: OMN: REX **Rev:** Large "6", Wallaby divides date **Rev. Legend:** AUSTRALIA **Edge:** Plain **Shape:** Square

Date	Mintage	F	VF	XF	Unc	BU
1921 Proof	750	—	—	—	—	—

X# M36a SIXPENCE
9.7200 g., Goldine, 22.2 mm. **Ruler:** George V **Obv:** Head left **Obv. Legend:** GEORGIVS V D.G. BRITT: OMN: REX **Rev:** Large "6", Wallaby divides date **Rev. Legend:** AUSTRALIA **Edge:** Plain **Shape:** Square

Date	Mintage	F	VF	XF	Unc	BU
1921 Proof	750	—	—	—	—	—

X# M36b SIXPENCE
10.2300 g., Copper, 22.2 mm. **Ruler:** George V **Obv:** Head left **Obv. Legend:** GEORGIVS V D.G. BRITT: OMN: REX **Rev:** Large "6", Wallaby divides date **Rev. Legend:** AUSTRALIA **Edge:** Plain **Shape:** Square

Date	Mintage	F	VF	XF	Unc	BU
1921 Proof	750	—	—	—	—	—

X# M36c SIXPENCE
10.1600 g., Copper Bronzed, 22.2 mm. **Ruler:** George V **Obv:** Head left **Obv. Legend:** GEORGIVS V D.G. BRITT: OMN: REX **Rev:** Large "6", Wallaby divides date **Rev. Legend:** AUSTRALIA **Edge:** Plain **Shape:** Square

Date	Mintage	F	VF	XF	Unc	BU
1921 Proof	750	—	—	—	—	—

X# M33 SHILLING
11.8000 g., Copper-Nickel, 24.2 mm. **Ruler:** George V **Obv:** Crowned bust left **Obv. Legend:** GEORGIVS V D.G. BRITT: OMN: REX **Rev:** Large "1", royal spoonbill divides date **Rev. Legend:** AUSTRALIA **Edge:** Plain **Shape:** Square

Date	Mintage	F	VF	XF	Unc	BU
1920 Proof	750	—	—	—	—	—

X# M33a SHILLING
11.6300 g., Goldine, 24.2 mm. **Ruler:** George V **Obv:** Crowned bust left **Obv. Legend:** GEORGIVS V D.G. BRITT: OMN: REX **Rev:** Large "1", royal spoonbill divides date **Rev. Legend:** AUSTRALIA **Edge:** Plain **Shape:** Square

Date	Mintage	F	VF	XF	Unc	BU
1920 Proof	750	—	—	—	—	—

X# M33b SHILLING
12.0500 g., Copper, 24.2 mm. **Ruler:** George V **Obv:** Crowned bust left **Obv. Legend:** GEORGIVS V D.G. BRITT: OMN: REX **Rev:** Large "1", royal spoonbill divides date **Rev. Legend:** AUSTRALIA **Edge:** Plain **Shape:** Square

Date	Mintage	F	VF	XF	Unc	BU
1920 Proof	750	—	—	—	—	—

X# M33c SHILLING
12.0600 g., Copper Bronzed, 24.2 mm. **Ruler:** George V **Obv:** Crowned bust left **Obv. Legend:** GEORGIVS V D.G. BRITT: OMN: REX **Rev:** Large "1", royal spoonbill divides date **Rev. Legend:** AUSTRALIA **Edge:** Plain **Shape:** Square

Date	Mintage	F	VF	XF	Unc	BU
1920 Proof	750	—	—	—	—	—

X# M37 SHILLING
11.7600 g., Copper-Nickel, 24.2 mm. **Ruler:** George V **Obv:** Head left **Obv. Legend:** GEORGIVS V D.G. BRITT: OMN: REX **Rev:** Large "1", Brushtail possum divides date **Rev. Legend:** AUSTRALIA **Edge:** Plain **Shape:** Square

Date	Mintage	F	VF	XF	Unc	BU
1921 Proof	750	—	—	—	—	—

X# M37a SHILLING
11.5600 g., Goldine, 24.2 mm. **Ruler:** George V **Obv:** Head left **Obv. Legend:** GEORGIVS V D.G. BRITT: OMN: REX **Rev:** Large "1", Brushtail possum divides date **Rev. Legend:** AUSTRALIA **Edge:** Plain **Shape:** Square

Date	Mintage	F	VF	XF	Unc	BU
1921 Proof	750	—	—	—	—	—

X# M37b SHILLING
12.0600 g., Copper, 24.2 mm. **Ruler:** George V **Obv:** Head left **Obv. Legend:** GEORGIVS V D.G. BRITT: OMN: REX **Rev:** Large "1", Brushtail possum divides date **Rev. Legend:** AUSTRALIA **Edge:** Plain **Shape:** Square

Date	Mintage	F	VF	XF	Unc	BU
1921 Proof	750	—	—	—	—	—

X# M37c SHILLING
12.0600 g., Copper Bronzed, 24.2 mm. **Ruler:** George V **Obv:** Head left **Obv. Legend:** GEORGIVS V D.G. BRITT: OMN: REX **Rev:** Large "1", Brushtail possum divides date **Rev. Legend:** AUSTRALIA **Edge:** Plain **Shape:** Square

Date	Mintage	F	VF	XF	Unc	BU
1921 Proof	750	—	—	—	—	—

X# M39 FLORIN
13.7500 g., Copper-Nickel, 29.3 mm. **Ruler:** Edward VIII **Obv:** Head left **Obv. Legend:** EDWARDVS VIII D:G:BR:OMN:REX **Rev. Legend:** FID DEF E VII R•IND:IMP - AUSTRALIA **Edge:** Plain

Date	Mintage	F	VF	XF	Unc	BU
1937 Proof	—	—	—	—	—	—

X# M34 2 SHILLING
17.1300 g., Copper-Nickel, 29.7 mm. **Ruler:** George V **Obv:** Crowned bust left **Obv. Legend:** GEORGIVS V D.g. BRITT: OMN: REX **Rev:** Large "2", koala bear divides date **Rev. Legend:** AUSTRALIA **Edge:** Plain **Shape:** Square

Date	Mintage	F	VF	XF	Unc	BU
1920 Proof	750	—	—	—	—	—

X# M34a 2 SHILLING
16.8000 g., Goldine, 29.7 mm. **Ruler:** George V **Obv:** Crowned bust left **Obv. Legend:** GEORGIVS V D.G. BRITT: OMN: REX **Rev:** Large "2", koala bear divides date **Rev. Legend:** AUSTRALIA **Edge:** Plain **Shape:** Square

Date	Mintage	F	VF	XF	Unc	BU
1920 Proof	750	—	—	—	—	—

X# M34b 2 SHILLING
17.5100 g., Copper, 29.7 mm. **Ruler:** George V **Obv:** Crowned bust left **Obv. Legend:** GEORGIVS V D.G. BRITT: OMN: REX **Rev:** Large "2", koala bear divides date **Rev. Legend:** AUSTRALIA **Edge:** Plain **Shape:** Square

Date	Mintage	F	VF	XF	Unc	BU
1920 Proof	750	—	—	—	—	—

X# M34c 2 SHILLING
17.4500 g., Copper Bronzed, 29.7 mm. **Ruler:** George V **Obv:** Crowned bust left **Obv. Legend:** GEORGIVS V D.G. BRITT: OMN: REX **Rev:** Large "2", koala bear divides date **Rev. Legend:** AUSTRALIA **Edge:** Plain **Shape:** Square

Date	Mintage	F	VF	XF	Unc	BU
1920 Proof	—	—	—	—	—	—

X# M38 2 SHILLING
17.0500 g., Copper-Nickel, 29.7 mm. **Ruler:** George V **Obv:** Head left **Obv. Legend:** GEORGIVS V D.G. BRITT: OMN: REX **Rev:** Large "2", Emu divides date **Rev. Legend:** AUSTRALIA **Edge:** Plain **Shape:** Square

Date	Mintage	F	VF	XF	Unc	BU
1921 Proof	750	—	—	—	—	—

X# M38a 2 SHILLING
16.8400 g., Goldine, 29.7 mm. **Ruler:** George V **Obv:** Head left **Obv. Legend:** GEORGIVS V D.G. BRITT: OMN: REX **Rev:** Large "2", Emu divides date **Rev. Legend:** AUSTRALIA **Edge:** Plain **Shape:** Square

Date	Mintage	F	VF	XF	Unc	BU
1921 Proof	750	—	—	—	—	—

X# M38b 2 SHILLING
17.4300 g., Copper, 29.7 mm. **Ruler:** George V **Obv:** Head left **Obv. Legend:** GEORGIVS V D.G. BRITT: OMN: REX **Rev:** Large "2", Emu divides date **Rev. Legend:** AUSTRALIA **Edge:** Plain **Shape:** Square

Date	Mintage	F	VF	XF	Unc	BU
1921 Proof	750	—	—	—	—	—

X# M38c 2 SHILLING
17.5600 g., Copper Bronzed, 29.7 mm. **Ruler:** George V **Obv:** Head left **Obv. Legend:** GEORGIVS V D.G. BRITT: OMN: REX **Rev:** Large "2", Emu divides date **Rev. Legend:** AUSTRALIA **Edge:** Plain **Shape:** Square

Date	Mintage	F	VF	XF	Unc	BU
1921 Proof	750	—	—	—	—	—

GOLD BULLION COINAGE

Kangaroo Series

X# B5 100 DOLLARS
Gilt Copper **Issuer:** Monex Deposit Company **Rev:** Kangaroo standing left **Rev. Legend:** THE AUSTRALIAN NUGGET **Note:** Uniface. Salesman's sample.

Date	Mintage	F	VF	XF	Unc	BU
1994(L)	—	—	—	—	6.00	—

MEDALLIC COINAGE

1954 Geoffrey Hearn Series

X# M1 CROWN
Gilt Bronze **Ruler:** Edward VIII **Obv:** Bust left **Obv. Legend:** EDWARD•VIII•KING•&•EMPEROR **Rev:** Kangaroo standing left

Date	Mintage	F	VF	XF	Unc	BU
1936 Proof	—	Value: 100				

X# M1a CROWN
28.1000 g., Silver **Ruler:** Edward VIII **Obv:** Bust facing left **Obv. Legend:** EDWARD•VIII•KING•&•EMPEROR **Rev:** Kangaroo standing left

Date	Mintage	F	VF	XF	Unc	BU
1936 Proof	1,000	Value: 70.00				

X# M1b CROWN
28.1000 g., Silver **Ruler:** Edward VIII **Obv:** Bust facing left **Obv. Legend:** EDWARD•VIII•KING•&•EMPEROR **Rev:** Kangaroo standing left

Date	Mintage	F	VF	XF	Unc	BU
1936 Restrike; Proof	1,200	Value: 35.00				

X# M1c CROWN
Gold **Ruler:** Edward VIII **Obv:** Bust facing left **Obv. Legend:** EDWARD•VIII•KING•&•EMPEROR **Rev:** Kangaroo standing left **Note:** Restrikes known.

Date	Mintage	F	VF	XF	Unc	BU
1936 Proof	10	Value: 800				

X# M1d CROWN
Platinum APW **Ruler:** Edward VIII **Obv:** Bust facing left **Obv. Legend:** EDWARD•VIII•KING•&•EMPEROR **Rev:** Kangaroo standing left

Date	Mintage	F	VF	XF	Unc	BU
1936 Proof	10	Value: 1,600				

1967 Andor Meszaros Series

X# M2 DOLLAR
Silver

Date	Mintage	F	VF	XF	Unc	BU
1967	1,500	—	—	—	110	—
1967 Proof	750	Value: 175				
1967 2 Known, Matte Proof	—	Value: 1,650				

Note: An example realized $1,260 in Glendinings July, 1988 sale.

X# M2a DOLLAR
56.0000 g., Gold **Edge:** Plain

Date	Mintage	F	VF	XF	Unc	BU
1967 Proof	10	Value: 1,450				

Note: 3 pieces remelted

INA Retro Series

X# M11 DOUBLE FLORIN
0.9250 Silver **Ruler:** Victoria **Obv:** Veiled bust left **Obv. Legend:** VICTORIA • DEI GRATIA • IND • IMP **Rev:** Arms **Edge:** Plain

Date	Mintage	F	VF	XF	Unc	BU
1901 Proof	550	Value: 50.00				

X# M11a DOUBLE FLORIN
Bronze **Ruler:** Victoria **Obv:** Veiled bust left **Obv. Legend:** VICTORIA • DEI GRATIA • IND • IMP **Rev:** Arms **Edge:** Plain

Date	Mintage	F	VF	XF	Unc	BU
1901 Proof	550	Value: 20.00				

X# M11b DOUBLE FLORIN
Copper **Ruler:** Victoria **Obv:** Veiled bust left **Obv. Legend:** VICTORIA • DEI GRATIA • IND • IMP **Rev:** Arms **Edge:** Plain

Date	Mintage	F	VF	XF	Unc	BU
1901 Proof	550	Value: 20.00				

X# M11c.1 DOUBLE FLORIN
0.9167 Gold **Ruler:** Victoria **Obv:** Veiled bust left **Obv. Legend:** VICTORIA • DEI GRATIA • IND • IMP **Rev:** Arms **Edge:** reeded **Note:** Weight varies: 31.9-32.6 grams.

Date	Mintage	F	VF	XF	Unc	BU
1901 Matte Proof	1	—	—	—	—	—
Note: Medal alignment						
1901 Proof	1	—	—	—	—	—
Note: Coin alignment						

X# M11c.2 DOUBLE FLORIN
32.3000 g., 0.9167 Gold 0.9519 oz. AGW **Ruler:** Victoria **Obv:** Veiled bust left **Obv. Legend:** VICTORIA • DEI GRATIA • IND • IMP **Rev:** Arms **Edge:** Plain

Date	Mintage	F	VF	XF	Unc	BU
1901 Matte Proof	1	—	—	—	—	—

X# M12 DOUBLE FLORIN
32.6000 g., 0.9167 Gold 0.9608 oz. AGW **Ruler:** Victoria **Obv:** Veiled bust left **Obv. Legend:** VICTORIA • DEI GRA • BRITT • REGINA •FID • DEF • IND • IMP **Rev:** Arms **Edge:** Reeded **Note:** Medal alignment.

Date	Mintage	F	VF	XF	Unc	BU
1901 Proof	1	—	—	—	—	—

X# M13c.1 DOUBLE FLORIN
33.3000 g., 0.9167 Gold 0.9814 oz. AGW **Ruler:** Edward VII **Obv:** Crowned bust right **Obv. Legend:** EDWARDVS VII D: G: BRITT: OMN: REX F: D: IND: IMP: **Rev:** Arms **Edge:** Reeded **Note:** Medal alignment.

Date	Mintage	F	VF	XF	Unc	BU
1901 Proof	1	—	—	—	—	—

X# M13c.2 DOUBLE FLORIN
0.9167 Gold **Ruler:** Edward VII **Obv:** Crowned bust right **Obv. Legend:** EDWARDVS VII D: G: BRITT: OMN: REX F: D: IND: IMP: **Rev:** Arms **Edge:** Plain

Date	Mintage	F	VF	XF	Unc	BU
1901 Proof	1	—	—	—	—	—
Note: Medal alignment						
1901 Proof	1	—	—	—	—	—
Note: Coin alignment						

X# M13 DOUBLE FLORIN
21.9500 g., 0.9250 Silver 0.6528 oz. ASW **Ruler:** Edward VII **Obv:** Crowned bust right **Obv. Legend:** EDWARDVS VII D: G: BRITT: OMN: REX F: D: IND: IMP: **Rev:** Arms **Edge:** Plain **Note:** Medal alignment.

Date	Mintage	F	VF	XF	Unc	BU
1901 Proof	750	Value: 50.00				

X# M13a DOUBLE FLORIN
18.0200 g., Bronze **Ruler:** Edward VII **Obv:** Crowned bust right **Obv. Legend:** EDWARDVS VII D: G: BRITT: OMN: REX F: D: IND: IMP: **Rev:** Arms **Edge:** Plain **Note:** Medal alignment.

Date	Mintage	F	VF	XF	Unc	BU
1901 Proof	750	Value: 20.00				

X# M13b DOUBLE FLORIN

18.2400 g., Copper **Ruler:** Edward VII **Obv:** Crowned bust right **Obv. Legend:** EDWARDVS VII D: G: BRITT: OMN: REX F: D: IND: IMP: **Rev:** Arms **Edge:** Plain **Note:** Medal alignment.

Date	Mintage	F	VF	XF	Unc	BU
1901 Proof	750	Value: 20.00				

X# M14 DOUBLE FLORIN

33.2000 g., 0.9167 Gold 0.9784 oz. AGW **Ruler:** Edward VII **Obv:** Head right within pellet circle **Obv. Legend:** EDWARDVS VII DEI GRATIA INDIAE IMPERATOR **Rev:** Arms **Edge:** Plain **Note:** Medal alignment.

Date	Mintage	F	VF	XF	Unc	BU
1901 Proof	1	—	—	—	—	—

X# 1 5 SHILLINGS

Silver **Ruler:** George V **Obv:** Crowned bust left **Obv. Legend:** GEORGIVS V D. G. BRITT: OMN: REX **Rev:** Kookaburra in flight right below large 5 divides date **Edge:** Plain **Shape:** Square **Note:** 35 x 35mm.

Date	Mintage	F	VF	XF	Unc	BU
1920 Proof	700	Value: 50.00				

X# 1a 5 SHILLINGS

Brass **Ruler:** George V **Obv:** Crowned bust left **Obv. Designer:** GEORGIVS V D. G. BRITT: OMN: REX **Rev:** Kookaburra in flight right below large 5 divides date **Edge:** Plain **Shape:** Square **Note:** 35 x 35mm.

Date	Mintage	F	VF	XF	Unc	BU
1920 Proof	700	Value: 20.00				

X# 1b 5 SHILLINGS

Copper **Ruler:** George V **Obv:** Crowned bust left **Obv. Legend:** GEORGIVS V D. G. BRITT: OMN: REX **Rev:** Kookaburra in flight right below large 5 divides date **Edge:** Plain **Shape:** Square **Note:** 35 x 35mm.

Date	Mintage	F	VF	XF	Unc	BU
1920 Proof	700	Value: 20.00				

X# 1c 5 SHILLINGS

32.2000 g., 0.9167 Gold 0.9490 oz. AGW **Ruler:** George V **Obv:** Crowned bust left **Obv. Legend:** GEORGIVS V D. G. BRITT: OMN: REX **Rev:** Kookaburra in flight right below large 5 divides date **Edge:** Plain **Note:** 35 x 35mm.

Date	Mintage	F	VF	XF	Unc	BU
1920 Proof	1	—	—	—	650	—
Note: Coin alignment						
1920 Proof	1	—	—	—	650	—
Note: Medal alignment						

X# 1d 5 SHILLINGS

Aluminum **Ruler:** George V **Obv:** Crowned bust left **Obv. Legend:** GEORGIVS V D. G. BRITT: OMN: REX **Rev:** Kookaburra in flight right below large 5 divides date **Edge:** Plain **Shape:** Square **Note:** 35 x 35mm.

Date	Mintage	F	VF	XF	Unc	BU
1920 Proof	1	—	—	—	—	—

X# 2 5 SHILLINGS

31.8000 g., 0.9167 Gold 0.9372 oz. AGW **Ruler:** George V **Obv:** Head left **Obv. Legend:** GEORGIVS V D. G. BRITT: OMN: REX **Rev:** Kookaburra in flight right below large 5 divides date **Edge:** Plain **Shape:** Square **Note:** 35 x 35mm. Medal alignment.

Date	Mintage	F	VF	XF	Unc	BU
1920 Proof	1	—	—	—	—	—

X# 3 5 SHILLINGS

Silver **Ruler:** George V **Obv:** Head left **Obv. Legend:** GEORGIVS V D. G. BRITT: OMN: REX **Rev:** Kangaroo left in lower part of large 5 divides date **Edge:** Plain **Shape:** Square **Note:** 35 x 35mm.

Date	Mintage	F	VF	XF	Unc	BU
1921 Proof	700	Value: 50.00				

X# 3a 5 SHILLINGS

Bronze **Ruler:** George V **Obv:** Head left **Obv. Legend:** GEORGIVS V D. G. BRITT: OMN: REX **Rev:** kangaroo left in lower part of large 5 divides date **Edge:** Plain **Shape:** Square **Note:** 35 x 35mm.

Date	Mintage	F	VF	XF	Unc	BU
1921 Proof	700	Value: 20.00				

X# 3b 5 SHILLINGS

Copper **Ruler:** George V **Obv:** Head left **Obv. Legend:** GEORGIVS V D. G. BRITT: OMN: REX **Rev:** Kangaroo left in lower part of large 5 divides date **Edge:** Plain **Shape:** Square **Note:** 35 x 35mm.

Date	Mintage	F	VF	XF	Unc	BU
1921 Proof	700	Value: 20.00				

X# 3c 5 SHILLINGS

32.2000 g., 0.9167 Gold 0.9490 oz. AGW **Ruler:** George V **Obv:** Head left **Obv. Legend:** GEORGIVS V D. G. BRITT: OMN: REX **Rev:** Kangaroo left in lower part of large 5 divides date **Edge:** Plain **Shape:** Square **Note:** 35 x 35mm.

Date	Mintage	F	VF	XF	Unc	BU
1921 Matte Proof	1	—	—	—	—	—

X# 4 5 SHILLINGS

32.2000 g., 0.9167 Gold 0.9490 oz. AGW **Obv:** Crowned bust left **Obv. Legend:** GEORGIVS V D. G. BRITT: OMN: REX **Rev:** Kangaroo left in lower part of large 5 divides date **Edge:** Plain **Shape:** Square **Note:** 35 x 35mm.

Date	Mintage	F	VF	XF	Unc	BU
1921 Proof	1	—	—	—	—	—

X# M15 CROWN

0.9250 Silver **Ruler:** Edward VIII **Obv:** Head left **Obv. Legend:** EDWARDVS VIII D: G: BR: OMN: REX F: D: IND: IMP: **Rev:** Large crown **Edge:** Plain **Note:** Medal alignment.

Date	Mintage	F	VF	XF	Unc	BU
1937 Proof	675	Value: 50.00				

X# M15a CROWN

Bronze **Ruler:** Edward VIII **Obv:** Head left **Obv. Designer:** EDWARDVS VIII D: G: BR: OMN: REX F: D: IND: IMP: **Rev:** Large crown **Edge:** Plain **Note:** Medal alignment.

Date	Mintage	F	VF	XF	Unc	BU
1937 Proof	675	Value: 20.00				

X# M15b CROWN

20.2000 g., Copper **Ruler:** Edward VIII **Obv:** Head left **Obv. Legend:** EDWARDVS VIII D: G: BR: OMN: REX F: D: IND: IMP: **Rev:** Large crown **Edge:** Plain **Note:** Medal alignment.

Date	Mintage	F	VF	XF	Unc	BU
1937 Proof	675	Value: 20.00				

X# M15c.1 CROWN

39.9000 g., 0.9167 Gold 1.1759 oz. AGW **Ruler:** Edward VIII **Obv:** Head left **Obv. Legend:** EDWARDVS VIII D: G: BR: OMN: REX F: D: IND: IMP: **Rev:** Large crown **Edge:** Reeded **Note:** Medal alignment.

Date	Mintage	F	VF	XF	Unc	BU
1937 Proof	1	—	—	—	—	—

X# M15c.2 CROWN
40.0000 g., 0.9167 Gold 1.1789 oz. AGW **Ruler:** Edward VIII **Obv:** Head left **Obv. Legend:** EDWARDVS VIII D: G: BR: OMN: REX F: D: IND: IMP: **Rev:** Large crown **Edge:** Plain **Note:** Medal alignment.

Date	Mintage	F	VF	XF	Unc	BU
1937 Proof	1	—	—	—	—	—

X# M16 CROWN
23.9000 g., 0.9250 Silver 0.7107 oz. ASW, 37.90 mm. **Ruler:** Edward VIII **Obv:** Head left **Obv. Legend:** EDWARDVS VIII D: G: BR: OMN: REX **Rev:** Large crown **Edge:** Plain **Note:** Medal alignment.

Date	Mintage	F	VF	XF	Unc	BU
1937 Proof	575	Value: 50.00				

X# M16a CROWN
Bronze, 37.9 mm. **Ruler:** Edward VIII **Obv:** Head left **Obv. Legend:** EDWARDVS VIII D: G: BR: OMN: REX **Rev:** Large crown **Edge:** Plain **Note:** Medal alignment.

Date	Mintage	F	VF	XF	Unc	BU
1937 Proof	575	Value: 20.00				

X# M16b CROWN
20.0400 g., Copper, 37.9 mm. **Ruler:** Edward VIII **Obv:** Head left **Obv. Legend:** EDWARDVS VIII D: G: BR: OMN: REX **Rev:** Large crown **Edge:** Plain **Note:** Medal alignment.

Date	Mintage	F	VF	XF	Unc	BU
1937 Proof	575	Value: 20.00				

X# M16c.1 CROWN
39.9000 g., 0.9167 Gold 1.1759 oz. AGW, 37.90 mm. **Ruler:** Edward VIII **Obv:** Head left **Obv. Legend:** EDWARDVS VIII D: G: BR: OMN: REX **Rev:** Large crown **Edge:** Reeded

Date	Mintage	F	VF	XF	Unc	BU
1937 Proof	1	—	—	—	—	—
Note: Medal alignment						
1937 Proof	1	—	—	—	—	—
Note: Coin alignment						

X# M16c.2 CROWN
0.9167 Gold, 37.9 mm. **Ruler:** Edward VIII **Obv:** Head left **Obv. Legend:** EDWARDVS VIII D: G: BR: OMN: REX **Rev:** Large crown **Edge:** Plain

Date	Mintage	F	VF	XF	Unc	BU
1937 Proof	1	—	—	—	—	—

X# M17 CROWN
39.5000 g., 0.9167 Gold 1.1641 oz. AGW **Ruler:** Edward VIII **Obv:** Crowned bust left **Obv. Legend:** EDWARD VIII KING EMPEROR **Rev:** Large crown **Edge:** Plain

Date	Mintage	F	VF	XF	Unc	BU
1937 Proof	1	—	—	—	—	—

X# M18 CROWN
39.4000 g., 0.9167 Gold 1.1612 oz. AGW **Ruler:** Edward VIII **Obv:** Crowned bust left **Obv. Legend:** EDWARDVS VIII REX IMPERATOR **Rev:** Large crown **Edge:** Plain **Note:** Medal alignment.

Date	Mintage	F	VF	XF	Unc	BU
1937 Proof	1	—	—	—	—	—

Richard Lobel Series

X# M3c CROWN
Gold **Ruler:** Edward VIII **Obv:** Bust facing left **Obv. Legend:** EDWARD • VIII • KING • & • EMPEROR **Rev:** Kangaroo standing left

Date	Mintage	F	VF	XF	Unc	BU
1936 Proof	—	Value: 500				

X# M3 CROWN
Bronze **Ruler:** Edward VIII **Obv:** Bust facing left **Obv. Legend:** EDWARD • VIII • KING • & • EMPEROR **Rev:** Kangaroo standing left

Date	Mintage	F	VF	XF	Unc	BU
1936 Proof	2,000	Value: 15.00				

X# M3a CROWN
Copper-Nickel-Zinc **Ruler:** Edward VIII **Obv:** Bust facing left **Obv. Legend:** EDWARD • VIII • KING • & • EMPEROR **Rev:** Kangaroo standing left

Date	Mintage	F	VF	XF	Unc	BU
1936 Proof	3,500	Value: 15.00				

X# M3b CROWN
0.9167 Silver **Ruler:** Edward VIII **Obv:** Bust facing left **Obv. Legend:** EDWARD • VIII • KING • & • EMPEROR **Rev:** Kangaroo standing left

Date	Mintage	F	VF	XF	Unc	BU
1936 Proof	500	Value: 80.00				

X# M19 CROWN
Silver, 38 mm. **Obv:** Busts of Duke and Duchess of Windsor facing **Rev:** Kangaroo left **Edge:** Plain

Date	Mintage	F	VF	XF	Unc	BU
1936 Proof	—	Value: 45.00				

X# M41 CROWN

0.9167 Silver, 38.4 mm. **Ruler:** Edward VIII **Obv:** Bust left **Obv. Legend:** EDWARD • VIII • KING • E • EMPEROR **Rev:** Kangaroo standing left **Rev. Legend:** AUSTRALIA **Edge:** Reeded

Date	Mintage	F	VF	XF	Unc	BU
1987 Proof	100	Value: 50.00				

X# M41a CROWN

Copper-Nickel, 38.4 mm. **Ruler:** Edward VIII **Obv:** Bust left **Obv. Legend:** EDWARD • VIII • KING • E • EMPEROR **Rev:** Kangaroo standing left **Rev. Legend:** AUSTRALIA **Edge:** Reeded

Date	Mintage	F	VF	XF	Unc	BU
1987 Proof	250	Value: 20.00				

X# M41b CROWN

19.1400 g., Bronze, 38.4 mm. **Ruler:** Edward VIII E • EMPEROR **Rev:** Kangaroo standing left **Rev. Legend:** AUSTRALIA **Edge:** Reeded

Date	Mintage	F	VF	XF	Unc	BU
1987 Proof	250	Value: 20.00				

X# M4 SOVEREIGN

0.3750 Gold, 22 mm. **Ruler:** Edward VIII **Obv:** Bust facing left **Rev:** Kangaroo standing left

Date	Mintage	F	VF	XF	Unc	BU
1936 Proof	250	Value: 125				

X# M20 SOVEREIGN

Gold, 22 mm. **Obv:** Crowned bust of Victoria left **Rev:** Kangaroo left

Date	Mintage	F	VF	XF	Unc	BU
1987 Proof	—	Value: 125				

PIEFORTS

X#	Date	Mintage	Identification	Mkt Val
P1	1901	1	Double Florin. Silver. Plain edge, coin alignment, X#M11.	—
P2	1901	1	Double Florin. Silver. Plain edge, medal alignment, X#M11.	—
P3	1901	1	Double Florin. Silver. Reeded edge, coin alignment, X#M11.	—
P4	1901	1	Double Florin. Silver. Reeded edge, medal alignment, X#M11.	—
P5	1901	1	Double Florin. Silver. Plain edge, coin alignment, X#M12.	—
P6	1901	1	Double Florin. Silver. Plain edge, medal alignment, X#M12.	—
P7	1901	1	Double Florin. Silver. Reeded edge, coin alignment, X#M12.	—
P8	1901	1	Double Florin. Silver. Reeded edge, medal alignment, X#M12.	—
P9	1901	1	Double Florin. Silver. Plain edge, coin alignment, X#M13.	—
P10	1901	1	Double Florin. Silver. Plain edge, medal alignment, X#M13.	—
P11	1901	1	Double Florin. Silver. Reeded edge, coin alignment, X#M13.	—
P12	1901	1	Double Florin. Silver. Reeded edge, medal alignment, X#M13.	—
P13	1901	1	Double Florin. Silver. Plain edge, coin alignment, X#M14.	—
P14	1901	1	Double Florin. Silver. Plain edge, medal alignment, X#M14.	—
P15	1901	1	Double Florin. Silver. Reeded edge, coin alignment, X#M14.	—
P16	1901	1	Double Florin. Silver. Reeded edge, medal alignment, X#M14.	—
P17	1920	1	5 Shilling. Silver. Plain edge, coin alignment, X#1.	—
P18	1920	1	5 Shilling. Silver. Plain edge, medal alignment, X#1.	—
P19	1920	1	5 Shilling. Silver. Plain edge, coin alignment, X#2.	—
P20	1920	1	5 Shilling. Silver. Plain edge, medal alignment, X#2.	—
P21	1920	1	5 Shilling. Silver. Plain edge, coin alignment, X#3.	—
P22	1920	1	5 Shilling. Silver. Plain edge, medal alignment, X#3.	—
P23	1921	1	5 Shilling. Silver. Plain edge, coin alignment, X#4.	—
P24	1921	1	5 Shilling. Silver. Plain edge, medal alignment, X#4.	—
P25	1937	1	Crown. Silver. Plain edge, coin alignment, X#M15.	—
P26	1937	1	Crown. Silver. Plain edge, medal alignment, X#M15.	—
P27	1937	1	Crown. Silver. Reeded edge, coin alignment, X#M15.	—
P28	1937	1	Crown. Silver. Reeded edge, medal alignment, X#M15.	—
P29	1937	1	Crown. Silver. Plain edge, coin alignment, X#M16.	—
P30	1937	1	Crown. Silver. Plain edge, medal alignment, X#M16.	—
P31	1937	1	Crown. Silver. Reeded edge, coin alignment, X#M16.	—
P32	1937	1	Crown. Silver. Reeded edge, medal alignment, X#M16.	—
P33	1937	1	Crown. Silver. Plain edge, coin alignment, X#M17.	—
P34	1937	1	Crown. Silver. Plain edge, medal alignment, X#M17.	—
P35	1937	1	Crown. Silver. Reeded edge, coin alignment, X#M17.	—
P36	1937	1	Crown. Silver. Reeded edge, medal alignment, X#M17.	—
P38	1937	1	Crown. Silver. Plain edge, medal alignment, X#M18.	—
P39	1937	1	Crown. Silver. Reeded edge, coin alignment, X#M18.	—
P40	1937	1	Crown. Silver. Reeded edge, medal alignment, X#M18.	—
P41	1936	—	Crown. 0.9167 Silver. X#M3b.	100
P42	1987	25	Crown. 0.9167 Silver. X#M41.	125

VICTORIA

COLONY

PRIVATE PATTERNS

Hodgkin, Taylor and Tyndall Series

Port Phillip, Kangaroo Office

These extremely rare gold patterns originated from a commercial venture set up by Messrs. Hodgkin, Taylor and Tyndall of England. Their idea was to buy up gold dust and use it to strike their own gold of 1/4, 1/2, 1 and 2 ounces which they proposed to pass on as bullion currency from their store in Melbourne. The dies were cut by W. J. Taylor and the machinery provided. This equipment arrived at Hobson's Bay on October 23, 1853, but before it could be removed and set up at the store, known as the Kangaroo Office, the availability of the British sovereign pre-empted the venture.

X# Pn1 1/4 OUNCE

7.7900 g., Gold **Issuer:** Port Phillip, Kangaroo Office **Obv:** Kangaroo standing right **Edge:** Milled **Note:** Prev. KM#Pn1. Uniface gilt copper electrotypes of both obverses and reverses of all denominations, with the exception of the 1/2 Ounce obverse, are known to exist for Pn1-Pn4e. Values range from $100 to $200. Bonded pairs have been noted.

Date	Mintage	F	VF	XF	Unc	BU
1853 Rare	—	—	—	—	—	—

Note: P.J. Downie Sale 5-87 AXF realized $23,100

X# Pn1b 1/4 OUNCE

Copper **Issuer:** Port Phillip, Kangaroo Office **Obv:** Kangaroo standing right **Edge:** Milled **Note:** Prev. KM#Pn1b.

Date	Mintage	F	VF	XF	Unc	BU
1853	—	—	—	—	—	—

X# Pn2 1/2 OUNCE

Gold **Issuer:** Port Phillip, Kangaroo Office **Obv:** Kangaroo standing right **Edge:** Milled **Note:** Prev. KM#Pn2.

Date	Mintage	F	VF	XF	Unc	BU
1853 Rare	—	—	—	—	—	—

Note: Spink Australia Sale 10-77 XF realized $27,100

X# Pn2c 1/2 OUNCE

Copper **Issuer:** Port Phillip, Kangaroo Office **Obv:** Kangaroo standing right **Edge:** Milled **Note:** Prev. KM#Pn2c.

Date	Mintage	F	VF	XF	Unc	BU
1853	—	—	—	—	1,500	—

X# Pn2b 1/2 OUNCE

6.3300 g., Gilt **Issuer:** Port Phillip, Kangaroo Office **Obv:** Kangaroo standing right **Note:** Restrike.

Date	Mintage	F	VF	XF	Unc	BU
1853	—	—	—	—	—	—

X# Pn3 OUNCE

Gold **Issuer:** Port Phillip, Kangaroo Office **Obv:** Kangaroo standing right **Edge:** Milled **Note:** Prev. KM#Pn3.

Date	Mintage	F	VF	XF	Unc	BU
1853 Rare	—	—	—	—	—	—

X# Pn3b OUNCE

24.0800 g., Gilt Lead **Issuer:** Port Phillip, Kangaroo Office **Obv:** Kangaroo standing right **Edge:** Plain **Note:** Prev. KM#Pn3b.

Date	Mintage	F	VF	XF	Unc	BU
1853 Restrike	—	—	—	—	—	—

X# Pn3c OUNCE

Brass **Issuer:** Port Phillip, Kangaroo Office **Obv:** Kangaroo standing right **Edge:** Milled **Note:** Prev. KM#Pn3c.

Date	Mintage	F	VF	XF	Unc	BU
1853 Rare	—	—	—	—	—	—

X# Pn3d OUNCE

Copper **Issuer:** Port Phillip, Kangaroo Office **Edge:** Milled **Note:** Prev. KM#Pn3d.

Date	Mintage	F	VF	XF	Unc	BU
1853	—	—	—	—	—	—

X# Pn4 2 OUNCES

Gold **Issuer:** Port Phillip, Kangaroo Office **Obv:** Kangaroo standing right **Note:** Prev. KM#Pn4.

Date	Mintage	F	VF	XF	Unc	BU
1853 Rare	—	—	—	—	—	—

X# Pn4a 2 OUNCES

Gilt Copper **Issuer:** Port Phillip, Kangaroo Office **Obv:** Kangaroo standing right **Edge:** Plain **Note:** Prev. KM#Pn4a.

Date	Mintage	F	VF	XF	Unc	BU
1853	—	—	—	—	—	—

X# Pn4b 2 OUNCES

Copper **Issuer:** Port Phillip, Kangaroo Office **Obv:** Kangaroo standing right **Edge:** Plain **Note:** Prev. KM#Pn4b.

Date	Mintage	F	VF	XF	Unc	BU
1853 Restrike	—	—	—	—	—	—

X# Pn4c 2 OUNCES

Pewter **Issuer:** Port Phillip, Kangaroo Office **Obv:** Kangaroo standing right **Edge:** Milled **Note:** Prev. KM#Pn4c.

Date	Mintage	F	VF	XF	Unc	BU
1853	—	—	—	—	—	—

X# Pn4d 2 OUNCES

Copper **Issuer:** Port Phillip, Kangaroo Office **Obv:** Kangaroo standing right **Edge:** Milled **Note:** Prev. KM#Pn4d.

Date	Mintage	F	VF	XF	Unc	BU
1853	—	—	—	—	—	—

X# Pn4e 2 OUNCES

Lead **Issuer:** Port Phillip, Kangaroo Office **Obv:** Kangaroo standing right **Edge:** Milled **Note:** Prev. KM#Pn4e. Uniface gilt copper electrotypes of both obverses and reverses of all denominations, with the exception of the 1/2 Ounce obverse, are known to exist. Values range from $100 to $200. Bonded pairs have been noted.

Date	Mintage	F	VF	XF	Unc	BU
1853	—	—	—	—	—	—

X# Pn5 4 OUNCES

Copper **Issuer:** Port Phillip, Kangaroo Office **Obv:** Britania seated left **Note:** Prev. KM#Pn5.

Date	Mintage	F	VF	XF	Unc	BU
1853	—	—	—	—	—	—

X# Pn5a 4 PENCE

41.0000 g., Gold, 35 mm. **Issuer:** Port Phillip, Kangaroo Office **Obv:** Britania seated left

Date	Mintage	F	VF	XF	Unc	BU
ND(1855) 1 known	—	—	—	—	—	—

Note: Noble Numismatics sale No. 73, 7-03, as struck realized approximately $35,600.

W. J. Taylor Issues

X# Pn6 6 PENCE

Copper **Ruler:** Victoria **Issuer:** Port Phillip, Kangaroo Office **Obv:** Crowned head left **Edge:** Milled **Note:** Prev. KM#Pn6.

Date	Mintage	F	VF	XF	Unc	BU
ND(1855)	—	—	—	—	8,000	—

X# Pn6a 6 PENCE

Copper **Ruler:** Victoria **Issuer:** Port Phillip, Kangaroo Office **Obv:** Crowned head left **Edge:** Plain **Note:** Prev. KM#Pn6a.

Date	Mintage	F	VF	XF	Unc	BU
ND(1855)	—	—	—	—	7,500	—

X# Pn6b 6 PENCE

Copper Silvered **Ruler:** Victoria **Issuer:** Port Phillip, Kangaroo Office **Obv:** Crowned head left **Edge:** Milled **Note:** Prev. KM#Pn6b.

Date	Mintage	F	VF	XF	Unc	BU
ND(1855)	—	—	—	—	8,000	—

X# Pn6c 6 PENCE

Aluminum **Ruler:** Victoria **Issuer:** Port Phillip, Kangaroo Office **Obv:** Crowned head left **Edge:** Plain **Note:** Prev. KM#Pn6c.

Date	Mintage	F	VF	XF	Unc	BU
ND(1855)	—	—	—	—	6,000	—

X# Pn6d 6 PENCE

Silver **Ruler:** Victoria **Issuer:** Port Phillip, Kangaroo Office **Obv:** Crowned head left **Edge:** Milled **Note:** Prev. KM#Pn6d.

Date	Mintage	F	VF	XF	Unc	BU
ND(1855)	—	—	—	—	9,500	—

X# Pn6e 6 PENCE

Silver **Ruler:** Victoria **Issuer:** Port Phillip, Kangaroo Office **Obv:** Crowned head left **Edge:** Plain **Note:** Prev. KM#Pn6e.

Date	Mintage	F	VF	XF	Unc	BU
ND(1855)	—	—	—	—	—	—

X# Pn6f 6 PENCE

Gold **Ruler:** Victoria **Issuer:** Port Phillip, Kangaroo Office **Obv:** Crowned head left **Edge:** Milled

Date	Mintage	F	VF	XF	Unc	BU
ND(1855) Rare	—	—	—	—	—	—

X# Pn6g 6 PENCE

Gold **Ruler:** Victoria **Issuer:** Port Phillip, Kangaroo Office **Obv:** Crowned head left **Edge:** Plain **Note:** Prev. KM#Pn6g.

Date	Mintage	F	VF	XF	Unc	BU
ND(1855)	—	—	—	—	—	—

X# Pn7 SHILLING

Copper **Ruler:** Victoria **Issuer:** Port Phillip, Kangaroo Office **Obv:** Crowned head left **Edge:** Reeded **Note:** Prev. KM#Pn7.

Date	Mintage	F	VF	XF	Unc	BU
ND(1855)	—	—	—	—	7,500	—

X# Pn7a SHILLING

Copper **Ruler:** Victoria **Issuer:** Port Phillip, Kangaroo Office **Obv:** Crowned head left **Edge:** Plain **Note:** Prev. KM#Pn7a.

Date	Mintage	F	VF	XF	Unc	BU
ND(1855)	—	—	—	—	6,500	—

X# Pn7b SHILLING

Pewter Silvered **Ruler:** Victoria **Issuer:** Port Phillip, Kangaroo Office **Obv:** Crowned head left **Edge:** Reeded **Note:** Prev. KM#Pn7b.

Date	Mintage	F	VF	XF	Unc	BU
ND(1855)	—	—	—	—	6,000	—

X# Pn7c SHILLING

Aluminum **Ruler:** Victoria **Issuer:** Port Phillip, Kangaroo Office **Obv:** Crowned head left **Edge:** Reeded **Note:** Prev. KM#Pn7c.

Date	Mintage	F	VF	XF	Unc	BU
ND(1855)	—	—	—	—	6,000	—

X# Pn7d SHILLING

Silver **Ruler:** Victoria **Issuer:** Port Phillip, Kangaroo Office **Obv:** Crowned head left **Edge:** Reeded **Note:** Prev. KM#Pn7d.

Date	Mintage	F	VF	XF	Unc	BU
ND(1855)	—	—	—	—	9,000	—

X# Pn7e SHILLING

Silver **Ruler:** Victoria **Issuer:** Port Phillip, Kangaroo Office **Obv:** Crowned head left **Edge:** Plain **Note:** Prev. KM#Pn7e.

Date	Mintage	F	VF	XF	Unc	BU
ND(1855)	—	—	—	—	7,750	—

X# Pn7f SHILLING

Gold **Ruler:** Victoria **Issuer:** Port Phillip, Kangaroo Office **Obv:** Crowned head left **Edge:** Reeded **Note:** Prev. KM#Pn7f.

Date	Mintage	F	VF	XF	Unc	BU
ND(1855)	—	—	—	—	—	—

X# Pn7g SHILLING

Gold **Ruler:** Victoria **Issuer:** Port Phillip, Kangaroo Office **Obv:** Crowned head left **Edge:** Plain

Date	Mintage	F	VF	XF	Unc	BU
ND(1855) Reported, not Confirmed	—	—	—	—	—	—

W. J. Taylor - Wiener Issues

X# Pn8 SHILLING

Copper **Ruler:** Victoria **Issuer:** Port Phillip, Kangaroo Office **Obv:** Crowned head left **Obv. Legend:** DEI GRATIA

Date	Mintage	F	VF	XF	Unc	BU
ND(1860)	—	—	—	—	6,500	—

X# Pn9 SHILLING

Copper **Ruler:** Victoria **Issuer:** Port Phillip, Kangaroo Office **Obv:** Crowned head left **Edge:** Milled **Note:** Prev. KM#Pn9.

Date	Mintage	F	VF	XF	Unc	BU
ND(1860)	—	—	—	—	6,000	—

X# Pn9a SHILLING

Copper **Ruler:** Victoria **Issuer:** Port Phillip, Kangaroo Office **Obv:** Crowned head left **Edge:** Plain **Note:** Prev. KM#Pn9a.

Date	Mintage	F	VF	XF	Unc	BU
ND(1860)	—	—	—	—	6,000	—

X# Pn8a SHILLING
Copper **Ruler:** Victoria **Issuer:** Port Phillip, Kangaroo Office **Obv:** Crowned head left **Edge:** Plain **Note:** Prev. KM#Pn8a.

Date	Mintage	F	VF	XF	Unc	BU
ND(1860)	—	—	—	—	6,000	—

X# Pn9b SHILLING
Silver **Ruler:** Victoria **Issuer:** Port Phillip, Kangaroo Office **Obv:** Crowned head left **Obv. Legend:** DEI GRATIA **Edge:** Milled

Date	Mintage	F	VF	XF	Unc	BU
ND(1860)	—	—	—	—	7,500	—

X# Pn8b SHILLING
Silver **Ruler:** Victoria, Port Phillip, Kangaroo Office **Obv:** Crowned head left **Obv. Legend:** DEI GRATIA **Edge:** Milled

Date	Mintage	F	VF	XF	Unc	BU
ND(1860)	—	—	—	—	8,000	—

X# Pn9c SHILLING
Silver **Ruler:** Victoria **Issuer:** Port Phillip, Kangaroo Office **Obv:** Crowned head left **Edge:** Plain **Note:** Prev. KM#Pn9c.

Date	Mintage	F	VF	XF	Unc	BU
ND(1860)	—	—	—	—	6,000	—

X# Pn8c SHILLING
Silver **Ruler:** Victoria **Issuer:** Port Phillip, Kangaroo Office **Obv:** Crowned head left **Edge:** Plain **Note:** Prev. KM#Pn8c.

Date	Mintage	F	VF	XF	Unc	BU
ND(1860)	—	—	—	—	6,500	—

X# Pn8d SHILLING
Gold **Ruler:** Victoria **Issuer:** Port Phillip, Kangaroo Office **Obv:** Crowned head left **Obv. Legend:** DEI GRATIA **Edge:** Milled

Date	Mintage	F	VF	XF	Unc	BU
ND(1860) Reported, not confirmed	—	—	—	—	—	—

X# Pn9d SHILLING
Gold **Ruler:** Victoria **Issuer:** Port Phillip, Kangaroo Office **Obv:** Crowned head left **Obv. Legend:** DEI GRATIA

Date	Mintage	F	VF	XF	Unc	BU
ND(1860) Reported, not confirmed	—	—	—	—	—	—

X# Pn8e SHILLING
Gold **Ruler:** Victoria **Issuer:** Port Phillip, Kangaroo Office **Obv:** Crowned head left **Obv. Legend:** DEI GRATIA **Edge:** Plain

Date	Mintage	F	VF	XF	Unc	BU
ND(1860) Reported, not confirmed	—	—	—	—	—	—

X# Pn10 SHILLING
Silver **Ruler:** Victoria **Issuer:** Port Phillip, Kangaroo Office **Obv:** Crowned head left **Obv. Legend:** VICTORIA REGINA **Edge:** Plain

Date	Mintage	F	VF	XF	Unc	BU
ND(1860)	—	—	—	—	7,500	—

AUSTRIA

EMPIRE

MEDALLIC COINAGE

X# M1 GULDEN
12.9900 g., 0.9000 Silver 0.3759 oz. ASW
Ruler: Franz Joseph I **Subject:** Wedding of Emperor Franz Joseph **Obv:** Conjoined heads right
Obv. Legend: FRANCISC•IOS•I•D•G•AVSTRIAE IMP•ET ELISABETHA MAX•IN•BAVAR•DVCIS FIL•
Rev: Wedding vows **Note:** Prev. KM#M1.

Date	Mintage	F	VF	XF	Unc	BU
MDCCCLIV (1854)A	—	20.00	30.00	55.00	125	200

X# M3 2 GULDEN
25.9900 g., 0.9000 Silver 0.7520 oz. ASW
Ruler: Franz Joseph I **Subject:** Wedding of Emperor Franz Joseph **Obv:** Conjoined heads right **Obv. Legend:** FRANCISC•IOS•I•D•G•AVSTRIAE IMP•ET ELISABETHA MAX•IN•BAVAR•DVCIS FIL•
Rev: Wedding vows **Edge:** Denomination on edge
Note: Prev. KM#M3.

Date	Mintage	F	VF	XF	Unc	BU
MDCCCLIV (1854)A	—	60.00	120	200	300	500

X# M2 FLORIN
12.3400 g., 0.9000 Silver 0.3571 oz. ASW
Ruler: Franz Joseph I **Subject:** Fibram mine reaches 1000 meter level **Obv:** Laureate head right
Obv. Legend: FRANCISC•IOS•I•D•G•AVSTRIAE IMPERATOR **Note:** Prev. KM#M2.

Date	Mintage	F	VF	XF	Unc	BU
1875	8,000	120	180	250	400	650

X# M4 2 FLORIN
22.0000 g., 0.9000 Silver 0.6366 oz. ASW
Ruler: Franz Joseph I **Subject:** Vienna Shooting Fest
Obv: Laureate head right in sprays surrounded by 12 shields **Rev:** F. GAUL below eagle **Note:** Prev. KM#M4. The Kremnica Mint struck reproductions with "R. 1973-KOLARSKY" below eagle, 24.31 grams.

Date	Mintage	F	VF	XF	Unc	BU
1873	—	500	800	1,350	2,250	—
1873 Proof	—	Value: 2,750				

X# M5 2 FLORIN
24.6900 g., 0.9000 Silver 0.7144 oz. ASW **Ruler:** Franz Joseph I **Subject:** Silver Wedding Anniversary **Obv:** Conjoined heads right **Obv. Legend:** FRANCISC•IOS•I•D•G•AVSTRIAE IMP•ET ELISABETHA MAX•IN•BAVAR•DVCIS FIL• **Edge Lettering:** ZWEI GULDEN XLV. KET FORINT. **Note:** Prev. KM#M5. Varieties exist with and without dots in legend.

Date	Mintage	F	VF	XF	Unc	BU
MDCCCLXXIX (1879)	275,000	18.00	35.00	65.00	145	250

X# M6 2 FLORIN
24.6900 g., 0.9000 Silver 0.7144 oz. ASW **Ruler:** Franz Joseph I **Subject:** First Federal Shooting Festival
Obv: Crowned Imperial eagle surrounded by shields

Obv. Legend: I•OESTERREICHISCHES BUNDESSCHIESSEN **Note:** Prev. KM#M6.

Date	Mintage	F	VF	XF	Unc	BU
1880	—	50.00	100	150	235	—

X# M7 2 FLORIN

22.3000 g., 0.9000 Silver 0.6452 oz. ASW **Ruler:** Franz Joseph I **Subject:** Reopening of Kuttenberg Mines **Obv:** Laureate head right **Obv. Legend:** FRANCISC•IOS•I•D•G•AVSTRIAE IMPERATOR **Rev:** Church **Note:** Prev. KM#M7. The Kremnica Mint struck reproductions with "R74" below church left of shield.

Date	Mintage	F	VF	XF	Unc	BU
MDCCCLXXXVII (1887)	400	1,500	2,250	3,200	4,750	—
MDCCCLXXXVII (1887) Proof; Rare	—	Value: 5,000				

X# 15 THALER

30.8000 g., Silver **Ruler:** Rudolf II **Note:** Believed to be a late 19th century European fabrication.

Date	Mintage	F	VF	XF	Unc	BU
1606	—	—	—	—	—	—

X# M8 THALER

16.9000 g., 0.9000 Silver 0.4890 oz. ASW **Ruler:** Franz Joseph I **Subject:** Third German Shooting Festival **Obv:** Crowned Imperial eagle **Obv. Legend:** III DEUTSCHES BUNDES SCHIESSEN WIEN **Note:** Prev. KM#M8. Fein Thaler.

Date	Mintage	F	VF	XF	Unc	BU
1868	—	35.00	65.00	140	225	—

X# M9 THALER

18.5786 g., 0.9000 Silver 0.5376 oz. ASW **Ruler:** Franz Joseph I **Subject:** Opening of Mt. Raxalpe Inn **Obv:** Bust right **Note:** Prev. KM#M9. Gedenk Thaler.

Date	Mintage	F	VF	XF	Unc	BU
1877	100	1,500	2,250	3,500	5,500	—

X# M13 THALER

Silver **Subject:** 400th Anniversary of First Thaler **Rev:** Sigismund **Note:** Gedenk Thaler.

Date	Mintage	F	VF	XF	Unc	BU
1884 Rare	89	—	—	—	—	—

X# M10.1 2 THALER

37.0371 g., 0.9000 Silver 1.0716 oz. ASW **Ruler:** Franz Joseph I **Subject:** Opening of Vienna - Trieste Railway **Obv:** Laureate head right; wreath tips point between "KA" of "KAISER" **Note:** Prev. KM#M10.1.

Date	Mintage	F	VF	XF	Unc	BU
1857A	1,644	450	850	1,600	2,250	—

X# M10.2 2 THALER

37.0371 g., 0.9000 Silver 1.0716 oz. ASW **Ruler:** Franz Joseph I **Obv:** Laureate head right; wreath tips point between "AI" of "KAISER" **Note:** Prev. KM#M10.2.

Date	Mintage	F	VF	XF	Unc	BU
1857A	Inc. above	450	850	1,600	2,250	—

X# M11 DUCAT

3.5000 g., 0.9860 Gold 0.1109 oz. AGW **Subject:** Death of Franz I **Obv:** Bust right **Note:** Prev. KM#M11.

Date	Mintage	F	VF	XF	Unc	BU
1765	—	—	250	350	700	—

X# M12 4 DUCAT

14.0000 g., 0.9860 Gold 0.4438 oz. AGW **Subject:** Vienna Shooting Festival

Date	Mintage	F	VF	XF	Unc	BU
1873	—	—	—	2,750	4,500	—
1873 Proof	—	Value: 7,500				

PATTERNS

Including off metal strikes

X# Pn1 KRONE

Silver **Note:** Prev. KM#Pn40.

Date	Mintage	F	VF	XF	Unc	BU
1914 Proof	—	Value: 200				

X# Pn2 KRONE

Bronze **Note:** Prev. KM#Pn39.

Date	Mintage	F	VF	XF	Unc	BU
1914 Proof	—	Value: 100				

REPUBLIC

EURO COINAGE

European Economic Community Issues

KM# 3119 25 EURO
16.1500 g., Bi-Metallic Purple color pure Niobium 7.15g center in .900 Silver 9g, ring, 34 mm. **Subject:** 50 Years Austrian Television **Obv:** The original test pattern of the 1950's **Rev:** World globe behind "rabbit ear" antenna. Television developmental milestones from 7-1 oclock **Edge:** Plain

Date	Mintage	F	VF	XF	Unc	BU
2005 Proof	65,000	Value: 60.00				

KM# 3135 25 EURO
16.1500 g., Bi-Metallic Niobium 7.15g center in .900 Silver 9g ring, 34 mm. **Subject:** European Satellite Navigation **Obv:** Austrian Mint's global location inscribed on a compass face **Rev:** Satellites in orbit around the world globe **Edge:** Plain

Date	Mintage	F	VF	XF	Unc	BU
2006	65,000	—	—	—	—	60.00

MEDALLIC COINAGE

X# M50 10 KREUZER
31.1400 g., Silver, 39.9 mm. **Ruler:** Franz Joseph I **Obv:** Laureate bust left **Obv. Legend:** FRANC • IOS • I • D • G • AVSTRIAE IMPERATOR **Rev:** Crowned Imperial eagle **Edge:** Reeded

Date	Mintage	F	VF	XF	Unc	BU
2001	—	—	—	—	15.00	—

X# M29a 2 DUCAT
6.5100 g., Silver, 27.6 mm. **Obv:** Archduke Ferdinand Carol horseback right **Obv. Legend:** FERDIN : CAROL • D : G : ARCHID : AV : D : B : COM : TIROL : **Rev:** St. Leopold standing holding church and banner surrounded by 14 shields

Date	Mintage	F	VF	XF	Unc	BU
1963-1642 Proof	—	Value: 18.50				

X# M29 2 DUCAT
Gold **Obv:** Ferdinand Karl on horseback right divides date, city in background **Obv. Legend:** FERDIN: CAROL • D:G: ARCHID: AV: D: B: COM: TIROL: **Rev:** St. Leopold standing holding banner and church surrounded by 14 shields **Rev. Legend:** DIVVS • LEOPOL-DVS • 2 • DVGA **Note:** Restrike of 2 Ducat, 1642, KM#909.

Date	Mintage	F	VF	XF	Unc	BU
1963-1642 Proof	—	Value: 165				

X# M28 GULDINER
0.9000 Silver, 40.1 mm. **Obv:** Crowned Arch duke Sigismund of Tyrol standing facing with sword and sceptre, lion with shield at left, helmet at right **Obv. Legend:** SIGISMVNDVS ARCHDVX • AVSTRIE **Rev:** Knight with banner horseback right surrounded by 14 shields

Date	Mintage	F	VF	XF	Unc	BU
1953//1486	—	—	—	—	50.00	—

X# M31 GULDINER
34.5580 g., 0.9000 Silver 0.9999 oz. ASW
Obv. Legend: English and Latin

Date	Mintage	F	VF	XF	Unc	BU
1986//1486 *Proof FDC	1,500	Value: 45.00				

Note: *Antique or brilliant finish

X# M32 GULDINER
34.5580 g., 0.9000 Silver 0.9999 oz. ASW
Obv. Legend: French and Latin

Date	Mintage	F	VF	XF	Unc	BU
1986//1486 *Proof FDC	1,500	Value: 45.00				

Note: *Antique or brilliant finish

X# M33 GULDINER
34.5580 g., 0.9000 Silver 0.9999 oz. ASW
Obv. Legend: German and Latin

Date	Mintage	F	VF	XF	Unc	BU
1986//1486 *Proof FDC	1,500	Value: 45.00				

Note: *Antique or brilliant finish

X# M34 GULDINER
34.5580 g., 0.9000 Silver 0.9999 oz. ASW
Obv. Legend: Italian and Latin

Date	Mintage	F	VF	XF	Unc	BU
1986//1486 *Proof FDC	1,500	Value: 45.00				

Note: *Antique or brilliant finish

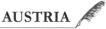

X# M35 GULDINER
34.5580 g., 0.9000 Silver 0.9999 oz. ASW
Obv. Legend: Japanese and Latin

Date	Mintage	F	VF	XF	Unc	BU
1986//1486 *Proof FDC	1,500	Value: 45.00				

Note: *Antique or brilliant finish

Euro Series

KM# M13 2-1/2 EURO
16.5000 g., Copper-Nickel, 34 mm. **Subject:** Gustav Klimt **Obv:** National arms, city view and country name in English **Rev:** Klimt's "The Kiss" **Edge:** Plain

Date	Mintage	F	VF	XF	Unc	BU
1997	50,000	—	—	—	8.00	—

X# 45 2-1/2 EURO
Copper-Nickel **Subject:** "The Kiss"

Date	Mintage	F	VF	XF	Unc	BU
1997	—	—	—	—	6.00	—

X# 38 5 EURO
Copper-Nickel **Subject:** 1000th Anniversary

Date	Mintage	F	VF	XF	Unc	BU
1996	—	—	—	—	8.50	—

X# 41 10 EURO
Silver **Subject:** Banknote

Date	Mintage	F	VF	XF	Unc	BU
1997 Proof	—	Value: 13.50				

X# 39 20 EURO
Silver **Subject:** 1000th Anniversary

Date	Mintage	F	VF	XF	Unc	BU
1996 Proof	—	Value: 16.50				

KM# M14 25 EURO
24.0000 g., 0.9250 Silver 0.7137 oz. ASW, 36.8 mm. **Subject:** Gustav Klimt **Obv:** National arms, city view and country name in English **Rev:** Klimt's "The Kiss" **Edge:** Plain

Date	Mintage	F	VF	XF	Unc	BU
1997 Proof	25,000	—	—	—	42.50	—

X# 46 25 EURO
Silver **Subject:** "The Kiss"

Date	Mintage	F	VF	XF	Unc	BU
1997 Proof	—	Value: 24.00				

KM# M15 250 EURO
Ring Composition: Silver **Center Weight:** 89.0000 g. **Center Composition:** 0.7500 Gold 2.1460 oz. AGW , 30 mm. **Subject:** Gustav Klimt **Obv:** National arms, city view and country name in English **Rev:** Klimt's "The Kiss" **Edge:** Plain

Date	Mintage	F	VF	XF	Unc	BU
1997 Proof	1,500	Value: 750				

Ecu Series

X# 48 25 EURO
Silver **Subject:** Vienna Treasury

Date	Mintage	F	VF	XF	Unc	BU
1998 Proof	—	Value: 16.50				

X# 22 5 ECU
Copper-Nickel **Subject:** Strauss

Date	Mintage	F	VF	XF	Unc	BU
1995	—	—	—	—	—	8.00

X# 24 5 ECU
Silver **Subject:** 50th Anniversary

Date	Mintage	F	VF	XF	Unc	BU
1995 Proof	—	Value: 13.50				

X# 25 5 ECU
Silver **Subject:** Membership in E.U.

Date	Mintage	F	VF	XF	Unc	BU
1995 Proof	—	Value: 13.50				

X# 27 5 ECU
Copper-Nickel **Subject:** Mozart

Date	Mintage	F	VF	XF	Unc	BU
1996	—	—	—	—	—	8.00

X# M25 10 ECU
25.0000 g., 0.9250 Silver 0.7435 oz. ASW, 38.61 mm. **Issuer:** Coin Invest Trust **Obv:** Large bell **Rev:** Large star, music chord, children at right-lower right **Rev. Inscription:** WE'HNACHT IN FRIEDEN

Date	Mintage	F	VF	XF	Unc	BU
1994 Proof	9,000	Value: 55.00				

X# 21 10 ECU
Silver **Subject:** Christmas

Date	Mintage	F	VF	XF	Unc	BU
1994 Proof	—	Value: 16.50				

X# 32 10 ECU
Silver **Subject:** Building

Date	Mintage	F	VF	XF	Unc	BU
1996 Proof	—	Value: 13.50				

X# 23 25 ECU
Silver **Subject:** Strauss

Date	Mintage	F	VF	XF	Unc	BU
1995 Proof	—	Value: 21.50				

X# 26 25 ECU
Silver **Subject:** Membership in E.U.

Date	Mintage	F	VF	XF	Unc	BU
1995 Proof	—	Value: 21.50				

X# 28 25 ECU
Silver **Subject:** Mozart

Date	Mintage	F	VF	XF	Unc	BU
1996 Proof	—	Value: 21.50				

X# 30 25 ECU
Silver **Subject:** Schubert

Date	Mintage	F	VF	XF	Unc	BU
1997 Proof	—	Value: 21.50				

MEDALIC COINAGE

Bullion

X# MB1 5 UNZEN (5 Ounces)
172.7900 g., 0.9000 Silver 4.9996 oz. ASW, 65 mm.
Obv. Legend: Inner circle English and Latin
Note: Illustration reduced.

Date	Mintage	F	VF	XF	Unc	BU
1986 Proof FDC	1,050	Value: 120				

X# MB2 5 UNZEN (5 Ounces)
155.5150 g., 0.9990 Silver 4.9947 oz. ASW, 64.90 mm. **Ruler:** Maria Theresa **Obv:** Half-length figure of Maria Theresa right **Obv. Legend:** MARIA THERESIA • D • G • REG • HUNG • BOHEM • **Rev:** Imperial eagle **Rev. Legend:** ARCHID • AVST • DUX • BURG • CO • TYR • **Edge:** Lettered **Note:** Illustration reduced.

Date	Mintage	F	VF	XF	Unc	BU
1780A (1986) Proof FDC	2,500	Value: 145				

X# MB2a 5 UNZEN (5 Ounces)
155.5150 g., 0.9990 Gold 4.9947 oz. AGW
Ruler: Maria Theresa **Obv:** Bust right **Rev:** Arms

Date	Mintage	F	VF	XF	Unc	BU
1780A (1986) Proof FDC	26	Value: 3,350				

PROOF SETS

X#	Date	Mintage	Identification	Issue Price	Mkt Val
XPS1	1986 (5)	—	XM31-XM35	295	300

GRINZING DISTRICT

REPUBLIC

TOKEN COINAGE

X# Tn1 200 SCHILLING
13.6800 g., 0.8350 Silver 0.3672 oz. ASW, 32 mm.
Issuer: Austrian National Bank **Series:** Grinzing Gulden
Obv: Medieval man standing holding bunch of grapes
Obv. Inscription: EINLÖSBAR IN / GRINZING **Rev:** Bust of Pope John Paul II 3/4 right **Edge:** Plain

Date	Mintage	F	VF	XF	Unc	BU
1983	10,000	—	—	—	35.00	—

X# Tn2 200 SCHILLING
13.6800 g., 0.8350 Silver 0.3672 oz. ASW, 32 mm.
Issuer: Austrian National Bank **Series:** Grinzing Gulden
Subject: 200 Years of Josef Buschenschank - 2000 Years of Winemaking **Obv. Inscription:** EINLÖSBAR IN / GRINZING **Rev:** Two mugs at center **Edge:** Plain

Date	Mintage	F	VF	XF	Unc	BU
1984	2,500	—	—	—	30.00	—

X# Tn3 200 SCHILLING
13.6800 g., 0.8350 Silver 0.3672 oz. ASW, 32 mm.
Issuer: Austrian National Bank **Series:** Grinzing Gulden
Obv: Medieval man standing holding bunch of grapes
Obv. Inscription: EINLÖSBAR IN / GRINZING
Rev: Bust of Beethoven left **Edge:** Plain

Date	Mintage	F	VF	XF	Unc	BU
1985	2,000	—	—	—	30.00	—

X# Tn4 200 SCHILLING
13.6800 g., 0.8350 Silver 0.3672 oz. ASW, 32 mm.
Issuer: Austrian National Bank **Series:** Grinzing Gulden
Obv: Medieval man standing holding bunch of grapes
Obv. Inscription: EINLÖSBAR IN / GRINZING **Rev:** "Goose Police" **Rev. Legend:** GRINZINGER GÄNSEPOLIZEI **Edge:** Plain

Date	Mintage	F	VF	XF	Unc	BU
1986	500	—	—	—	40.00	—

X# Tn5 200 SCHILLING
13.6800 g., 0.8350 Silver 0.3672 oz. ASW, 32 mm.
Issuer: Austrian National Bank **Series:** Grinzing Gulden
Subject: Cogwheel Railroad **Obv:** Medieval man standing holding bunch of grapes **Obv. Inscription:** EINLÖSBAR IN / GRINZING **Rev:** Steam locomotive pulling passenger car **Edge:** Plain

Date	Mintage	F	VF	XF	Unc	BU
1987	1,000	—	—	—	30.00	—

X# Tn6 200 SCHILLING
13.6800 g., 0.8350 Silver 0.3672 oz. ASW, 32 mm.
Issuer: Austrian National Bank **Series:** Grinzing Gulden
Obv: Medieval man standing holding bunch of grapes
Obv. Inscription: EINLÖSBAR IN / GRINZING **Rev:** Busts of R. Reagan and M. Gorbachev **Edge:** Plain

Date	Mintage	F	VF	XF	Unc	BU
1988	1,500	—	—	—	30.00	—

X# Tn6a 200 SCHILLING
17.4000 g., 0.9000 Gold 0.5035 oz. AGW, 32 mm.
Issuer: Austrian National Bank **Series:** Grinzing Gulden
Obv: Medieval man standing holding bunch of grapes
Obv. Inscription: EINLÖSBAR IN / GRINZING **Rev:** Busts of R. Reagan and M. Gorbachev **Edge:** Plain

Date	Mintage	F	VF	XF	Unc	BU
1988	200	—	—	—	—	—

X# Tn7 200 SCHILLING
13.6800 g., 0.8350 Silver 0.3672 oz. ASW, 32 mm.
Issuer: Austrian National Bank **Series:** Grinzing Gulden
Subject: International Olympic Committee Meeting
Obv: Medieval man standing holding bunch of grapes
Obv. Legend: EINLÖSBAR IN / GRINZING **Rev:** Torch bearer, Olympic logo **Edge:** Plain

Date	Mintage	F	VF	XF	Unc	BU
1989	1,000	—	—	—	30.00	—

X# Tn8 200 SCHILLING
13.6800 g., 0.8350 Silver 0.3672 oz. ASW, 32 mm.
Issuer: Austrian National Bank **Series:** Grinzing Gulden
Obv: Medieval man standing holding bunch of grapes
Obv. Inscription: EINLÖSBAR IN / GRINZING **Rev:** Head of local resident Bruno Kreisky facing **Edge:** Plain

Date	Mintage	F	VF	XF	Unc	BU
1990	1,000	—	—	—	30.00	—

X# Tn9 200 SCHILLING
13.6800 g., 0.8350 Silver 0.3672 oz. ASW, 32 mm.
Issuer: Austrian National Bank **Series:** Grinzing Gulden
Obv: Medieval man standing holding bunch of grapes
Obv. Inscription: EINLÖSBAR IN / GRINZING
Rev: Bust of Mozart facing 3/4 right **Edge:** Plain

Date	Mintage	F	VF	XF	Unc	BU
1991	1,000	—	—	—	30.00	—

X# Tn10 200 SCHILLING
13.6800 g., 0.8350 Silver 0.3672 oz. ASW, 32 mm.
Issuer: National Bank of Austria **Obv:** Medieval man standing holding bunch of grapes **Obv. Inscription:** EINLÖSBAR IN / GRINZIG **Rev:** Bust of Franz Wenninger, medical technician half left **Edge:** Plain

Date	Mintage	F	VF	XF	Unc	BU
1992	500	—	—	—	30.00	—

X# Tn11 200 SCHILLING
13.6800 g., 0.8350 Silver 0.3672 oz. ASW, 32 mm. **Issuer:** National Bank of Austria **Obv:** Medieval man standing holding bunch of grapes **Obv. Inscription:** EINLÖSBAR IN / GRINZIG **Rev:** Stylized sun, moon, man's head... **Edge:** Plain

Date	Mintage	F	VF	XF	Unc	BU
1993	1,000	—	—	—	30.00	—

X# Tn12 200 SCHILLING
13.6800 g., 0.8350 Silver 0.3672 oz. ASW, 32 mm. **Issuer:** National Bank of Austria **Obv:** Medieval man standing holding bunch of grapes **Obv. Inscription:** EINLÖSBAR IN / GRINZIG **Rev:** Bust of Hans Moser, film actor half right **Edge:** Plain

Date	Mintage	F	VF	XF	Unc	BU
1994	1,000	—	—	—	30.00	—

X# Tn13 200 SCHILLING
13.6800 g., 0.8350 Silver 0.3672 oz. ASW, 32 mm. **Issuer:** National Bank of Austria **Subject:** Grinzing's contribution to Austria's entry into the European Union **Obv:** Medieval man standing holding bunch of grapes **Obv. Inscription:** EINLÖSBAR IN / GRINZIG **Rev:** Woman on bull left, 12 stars at left edge, legend at right edge **Edge:** Plain

Date	Mintage	F	VF	XF	Unc	BU
1995	250	—	—	—	30.00	—

X# Tn14 200 SCHILLING
13.6800 g., 0.8350 Silver 0.3672 oz. ASW, 32 mm. **Issuer:** National Bank of Austria **Subject:** 1000 Years Austria - 2000 Years Grinzing **Obv:** Medieval man standing holding bunch of grapes **Obv. Inscription:** EINLÖSBAR IN / GRINZIG **Rev:** 2 shields of arms, legend around **Edge:** Plain

Date	Mintage	F	VF	XF	Unc	BU
1996	1,000	—	—	—	30.00	—

AUSTRIAN NETHERLANDS

KINGDOM

MEDALLIC COINAGE

X# M5 12 DUCAT
43.0000 g., Gold, 42 mm. **Ruler:** Maria Theresa with Franz I **Subject:** Royal Mint Visit **Obv:** Bust of Maria Theresa right **Obv. Legend:** M•T•D•G•R•IMP•G•H•-B•REG•A•A•D•BURG• **Rev:** Bust of Francis I right **Rev. Legend:** FRANC•D•G•R•I•S•-A•GE•IER•R•LO•B•M•H•D•

Date	Mintage	F	VF	XF	Unc	BU
ND(1751)	—	Value: 15,000				

AUSTRIAN STATES

SALZBURG

ARCHBISHOPRIC

MEDALLIC COINAGE

Largesse Money

These pieces were struck in various sizes in gold and in silver. They were to be thrown to the crowds as Wilhelmina Amalia of Brunswick-Luneburg passed through Salzburg on her way to Vienna to marry (the future Emperor) Joseph I.

X# M1 1/9 THALER
Silver, 22 mm. **Ruler:** Johann Ernst **Note:** Prev. KM#M1.

Date	Mintage	VG	F	VF	XF	Unc
MDCIC (1699)	—	60.00	120	240	385	—

X# M2 1/6 THALER
Silver, 26 mm. **Ruler:** Johann Ernst **Obv:** Crowned WAS monogram **Rev:** Crowned SR monogram **Note:** Prev. KM#M2.

Date	Mintage	VG	F	VF	XF	Unc
MDCIC (1699)	—	250	500	800	1,200	—

X# M3 1/4 THALER
Silver, 30 mm. **Ruler:** Johann Ernst **Obv:** Crowned WAS monogram **Rev:** Crowned SR monogram **Note:** Prev. KM#M3.

Date	Mintage	VG	F	VF	XF	Unc
MDCIC (1699)	—	85.00	175	300	500	—

X# M4 1/4 DUCAT
0.8750 g., 0.9860 Gold 0.0277 oz. AGW **Ruler:** Johann Ernst **Obv:** Crowned WAS monogram **Rev:** Crowned SR monogram **Note:** Prev. KM#M4.

Date	Mintage	VG	F	VF	XF	Unc
MDCIC (1699)	—	150	325	650	1,000	—

X# M5 DUCAT
3.5000 g., 0.9860 Gold 0.1109 oz. AGW **Ruler:** Johann Ernst **Obv:** Crowned WAS monogram **Rev:** Crowned SR monogram **Note:** Prev. KM#M5.

Date	Mintage	VG	F	VF	XF	Unc
MDCIC (1699)	—	225	500	1,250	2,000	—

AVRAM

DUCHY

ROYAL BANK COINAGE

X# 1 DUCAL
Goldine-Plated Metal Light and deep blue enamel, 12 mm. **Rev. Inscription:** Duchy of Avram

Date	Mintage	F	VF	XF	Unc	BU
1982	271	—	—	—	120	—
1985	250	—	—	—	60.00	—

X# 7 DUCAL
1.1400 g., Goldine-Plated Brass, 10.23 mm. **Ruler:** Prince John **Issuer:** Royal Bank of Avram **Obv:** Crowned supported arms, epoxy over light blue, pale yellow, red and black enamels **Obv. Legend:** ROYAL BANK OF AVRAM **Rev. Inscription:** GRAND / DUCHY / OF AVRAM / date **Edge:** Plain

Date	Mintage	F	VF	XF	Unc	BU
1990	250	—	—	—	30.00	—
2000	250	—	—	—	15.00	—
2005	250	—	—	—	12.00	—

X# 2 3 DUCALS
Goldine-Plated Metal Light green enamel, 16 mm. **Rev. Inscription:** Duchy of Avram

Date	Mintage	F	VF	XF	Unc	BU
1982	274	—	—	—	120	—
1985	250	—	—	—	60.00	—

X# 8 3 DUCALS
2.3500 g., Goldine-Plated Brass, 16.4 mm. **Ruler:** Prince John **Issuer:** Royal Bank of Avram **Obv:** Crown supported arms, epoxy over light green, pale yellow and multicolored enamels **Obv. Legend:** ROYAL BANK OF AVRAM **Rev. Inscription:** GRAND / DUCHY / OF AVRAM / date **Edge:** Plain

Date	Mintage	F	VF	XF	Unc	BU
1990	250	—	—	—	30.00	—
2000	250	—	—	—	15.00	—
2005	250	—	—	—	12.00	—

X# 3 7 DUCALS
Goldine-Plated Metal Orange enamel, 18 mm.
Rev. Inscription: Duchy of Avram

Date	Mintage	F	VF	XF	Unc	BU
1982	273	—	—	—	120	—
1985	250	—	—	—	60.00	—

X# 9 7 DUCALS
3.4300 g., Goldine-Plated Brass, 18.5 mm. **Ruler:** Prince John **Issuer:** Royal Bank of Avram **Obv:** Crowned and mantled arms with male supporters, epoxy over dark blue, pale yellow and multicolored enamels **Obv. Legend:** ROYAL BANK OF AVRAM **Rev. Inscription:** GRAND / DUCHY / OF AVRAM / date **Edge:** Plain

Date	Mintage	F	VF	XF	Unc	BU
1990	250	—	—	—	30.00	—
2000	250	—	—	—	15.00	—
2005	250	—	—	—	12.00	—

X# 4 15 DUCALS
Goldine-Plated Metal Pink enamel, 22 mm.
Rev. Inscription: Duchy of Avram

Date	Mintage	F	VF	XF	Unc	BU
1982	276	—	—	—	120	—
1985	250	—	—	—	60.00	—

X# 5 30 DUCALS
Goldine-Plated Metal Yellow and deep green enamel, 26 mm. **Rev. Inscription:** Duchy of Avram

Date	Mintage	F	VF	XF	Unc	BU
1982	276	—	—	—	160	—
1985	250	—	—	—	80.00	—

X# 11 30 DUCALS
6.7350 g., Goldine-Plated Brass, 26.5 mm. **Ruler:** Prince John **Issuer:** Royal Bank of Avram **Obv:** Crowned, supported arms, epoxy over orange, pale yellow and multicolored enamels **Obv. Legend:** ROYAL BANK OF AVRAM **Rev. Inscription:** GRAND / DUCHY / OF AVRAM / date **Edge:** Plain

Date	Mintage	F	VF	XF	Unc	BU
1990	250	—	—	—	40.00	—
2000	250	—	—	—	20.00	—
2005	250	—	—	—	18.00	—

X# 6 75 DUCALS
Goldine-Plated Metal Red enamel, 30 mm.
Rev. Inscription: Duchy of Avram

Date	Mintage	F	VF	XF	Unc	BU
1982	269	—	—	—	200	—
1985	250	—	—	—	100	—

X# 12 75 DUCALS
12.1300 g., Goldine-Plated Brass, 30 mm. **Ruler:** Prince John **Issuer:** Royal Bank of Avram **Obv:** Crowned and mantled arms, epoxy over red, pale yellow and multicolored arms **Obv. Legend:** ROYAL BANK OF AVRAM **Rev. Inscription:** GRAND / DUCHY / OF AVRAM / date **Edge:** Plain

Date	Mintage	F	VF	XF	Unc	BU
1990	250	—	—	—	50.00	—
2000	250	—	—	—	25.00	—
2005	250	—	—	—	22.00	—

X# 13 150 DUCALS
Goldine-Plated Brass with enamel, 34.6 mm.
: Prince John **Obv:** Crowned and mantled arms
Rev. Inscription: THE/GRAND/DUCHY/OF AVRAM
Edge: Plain

Date	Mintage	F	VF	XF	Unc	BU
2005	—	—	—	—	25.00	—

X# 14 250 DUCALS
Goldine-Plated Brass with enamel, 39.8 mm.
Ruler: Prince John **Obv:** Crowned and mantled arms
Rev. Inscription: THE/GRAND/DUCHY/OF AVRAM

Date	Mintage	F	VF	XF	Unc	BU
2005	—	—	—	—	40.00	—

AZERBAIJAN

REPUBLIC

FANTASY COINAGE

X# 1 5 RUBLES
Brass

Date	Mintage	F	VF	XF	Unc	BU
1920	—	—	—	—	—	—

Note: A modern fantasy according to leading authorities

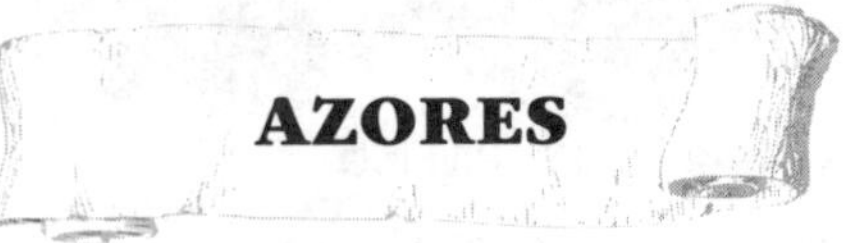

AZORES

REPUBLIC

FANTASY EURO PATTERNS

INA Issues

X# Pn1 EURO CENT
Copper, 16.9 mm. **Issuer:** INA **Obv:** Rising sun above buildings in Ponta Delgada **Obv. Legend:** REPUBLICA • PORTUGUESA • ACORES **Rev:** Scales at right **Edge:** Plain

Date	Mintage	F	VF	XF	Unc	BU
2005	—	—	—	—	—	1.50
2005 Proof	—	Value: 2.50				

X# Pn2 2 EURO CENTS
5.8000 g., Copper, 18.7 mm. **Issuer:** INA **Obv:** Rising sun above buildings in Ponta Delgada **Obv. Legend:** REPUBLICA • PORTUGUESA • ACORES **Rev:** Scales at right **Edge:** Plain

Date	Mintage	F	VF	XF	Unc	BU
2005	—	—	—	—	—	2.00
2005 Proof	—	Value: 3.00				

X# Pn3 5 EURO CENTS
7.3300 g., Copper, 21 mm. **Issuer:** INA **Obv:** Rising sun above buildings in Ponta Delgada **Obv. Legend:** REPUBLICA • PORTUGUESA • ACORES **Rev:** Scales at right **Edge:** Plain

Date	Mintage	F	VF	XF	Unc	BU
2005	—	—	—	—	—	2.50
2005 Prof	—	Value: 3.50				

X# Pn4 10 EURO CENTS
6.0200 g., Goldine, 19.3 mm. **Issuer:** INA **Obv:** National flag **Obv. Legend:** REPUBLICA • PORTUGUESA • ACORES **Rev:** Dove above value in wreath of clasped hands **Edge:** Plain

Date	Mintage	F	VF	XF	Unc	BU
2005	—	—	—	—	—	3.00
2005 Proof	—	Value: 4.00				

X# Pn5 20 EURO CENTS
7.8000 g., Goldine, 22.2 mm. **Issuer:** INA **Obv:** National flag **Obv. Legend:** REPUBLICA • PORTUGUESA • ACORES **Rev:** Dove above value in wreath of clasped hands **Edge:** Plain

Date	Mintage	F	VF	XF	Unc	BU
2005	—	—	—	—	—	3.50
2005 Proof	—	Value: 5.00				

X# Pn6 50 EURO CENTS
9.6100 g., Goldine, 24.5 mm. **Issuer:** INA **Obv:** National flag **Obv. Legend:** REPUBLICA • PORTUGUESA • ACORES **Rev:** Dove above value in wreath of clasped hands **Edge:** Plain

Date	Mintage	F	VF	XF	Unc	BU
2005	—	—	—	—	—	—
2005 Proof	—	—	—	—	—	—

X# Pn7 EURO
8.4600 g., Bi-Metallic Goldine ring, Copper-Nickel center, 22.95 mm. **Issuer:** INA **Obv:** Two dolphins leaping **Obv. Legend:** REPUBLICA • PORTUGUESA • ACORES **Rev:** Sun behind old sailing ship **Edge:** Plain

Date	Mintage	F	VF	XF	Unc	BU
2005	—	—	—	—	—	6.00
2005 Proof	—	Value: 8.00				

X# Pn8 2 EURO
10.8700 g., Bi-Metallic Copper-Nickel ring, Goldine center, 25.9 mm. **Issuer:** INA **Obv:** Two dolphins leaping **Obv. Legend:** REPUBLICA • PORTUGUES • ACORES **Rev:** Sun behind old sailing ship **Edge:** Plain

Date	Mintage	F	VF	XF	Unc	BU
2005	—	—	—	—	—	8.00
2005 Proof	—	Value: 10.00				

X# Pn9 5 EURO
25.5200 g., Goldine, 36.1 mm. **Issuer:** INA **Obv:** Two dolphins leaping **Obv. Legend:** REPUBLICA • PORTUGUESA • ACORES **Rev:** Outline map of Europe within star border **Edge:** Plain

Date	Mintage	F	VF	XF	Unc	BU
2005 Proof	—	Value: 12.50				

BAHRAIN

KINGDOM OF BAHRAIN

MEDALLIC COINAGE

X#M1 10 DINARS
16.0000 g., 0.9170 Gold 0.4717 oz. AGW
Ruler: Isa Bin Salman **Subject:** Opening of Isa Town **Obv:** Bust left **Rev:** Arms

Date	Mintage	F	VF	XF	Unc	BU
AH1388 (1968)	3,000	—	—	—	400	—

X# M2 10 DINARS
16.0000 g., 0.9170 Gold 0.4717 oz. AGW **Ruler:** Isa Bin Salman **Rev:** Independence Commemorative

Date	Mintage	F	VF	XF	Unc	BU
AH1391	3,000	—	—	—	400	—

X#M3 10 DINARS
16.0000 g., 0.9170 Gold 0.4717 oz. AGW
Ruler: Isa Bin Salman **Subject:** Opening of Hamad Town **Obv:** Bust left **Rev:** Arms

Date	Mintage	F	VF	XF	Unc	BU
AH1404-1983 Proof	—	Value: 400				

BALEARIC ISLANDS

SPANISH AUTONOMOUS COMMUNITY

FANTASY EURO PATTERNS

X# Pn1 EURO CENT
Copper Plated Steel **Edge:** Plain

Date	Mintage	F	VF	XF	Unc	BU
2004	7,000	—	—	—	—	1.50

X# Pn2 2 EURO CENTS
Copper Plated Steel **Edge:** Plain

Date	Mintage	F	VF	XF	Unc	BU
2004	7,000	—	—	—	—	2.00

X# Pn3 5 EURO CENTS
Copper Plated Steel **Edge:** Plain

Date	Mintage	F	VF	XF	Unc	BU
2004	7,000	—	—	—	—	2.50

X# Pn4 10 EURO CENTS
Goldine **Edge:** Plain

Date	Mintage	F	VF	XF	Unc	BU
2004	7,000	—	—	—	—	3.00

X# Pn5 20 EURO CENTS
Goldine **Edge:** Plain

Date	Mintage	F	VF	XF	Unc	BU
2004	7,000	—	—	—	—	3.50

X# Pn6 50 EURO CENTS
Goldine **Edge:** Plain

Date	Mintage	F	VF	XF	Unc	BU
2004	7,000	—	—	—	—	4.00

X# Pn7 EURO
Bi-Metallic **Obv:** Male head facing 3/4 right downwards **Rev:** Flower, large value "1" **Edge:** Plain

Date	Mintage	F	VF	XF	Unc	BU
2004	7,000	—	—	—	—	6.00

X# Pn8 2 EURO
Bi-Metallic **Obv:** Male head facing 3/4 right downwards **Rev:** Flower, large value "2" **Edge:** Plain

Date	Mintage	F	VF	XF	Unc	BU
2004	7,000	—	—	—	—	8.00

MINT SETS

X#	Date	Mintage	Identification	Issue Price	Mkt Val
XMS1	2004 (8)	7,000	X#Pn1-Pn8	—	30.00

BARBE ISLAND

SOVEREIGNTY

MEDALLIC COINAGE

X# M1 10 POILS
22.7500 g., Brass, 40 mm. **Ruler:** (no Ruler name) **Obv:** Island view **Obv. Legend:** ETAT SOUVERAIN DE L'ILE BARBE **Rev:** Bust of Charlemagne facing 3/4 left **Rev. Legend:** LA BARBE MEURT MAIS NE SE RASE PAS **Edge:** Reeded

Date	Mintage	F	VF	XF	Unc	BU
ND(c.1977)	—	—	—	30.00	70.00	100

BELARUS

REPUBLIC

FANTASY EURO PATTERNS

X# Pn1 EURO CENT
Copper Plated Steel **Edge:** Plain

Date	Mintage	F	VF	XF	Unc	BU
2004	7,000	—	—	—	—	1.50

X# Pn2 2 EURO CENTS
Copper Plated Steel **Edge:** Plain

Date	Mintage	F	VF	XF	Unc	BU
2004	7,000	—	—	—	—	2.00

X# Pn3 5 EURO CENTS
Copper Plated Steel **Edge:** Plain

Date	Mintage	F	VF	XF	Unc	BU
2004	7,000	—	—	—	—	2.50

X# Pn4 10 EURO CENTS
Goldine **Edge:** Plain

Date	Mintage	F	VF	XF	Unc	BU
2004	7,000	—	—	—	—	3.00

X# Pn5 20 EURO CENTS
Goldine **Edge:** Plain

Date	Mintage	F	VF	XF	Unc	BU
2004	7,000	—	—	—	—	3.50

X# Pn6 50 EURO CENTS
Goldine **Edge:** Plain

Date	Mintage	F	VF	XF	Unc	BU
2004	7,000	—	—	—	—	4.50

X# Pn7 EURO
Bi-Metallic **Obv:** Male bust facing **Edge:** Plain

Date	Mintage	F	VF	XF	Unc	BU
2004	7,000	—	—	—	—	6.50

X# Pn8 2 EURO
Bi-Metallic **Obv:** Male bust facing **Edge:** Plain

Date	Mintage	F	VF	XF	Unc	BU
2004	7,000	—	—	—	—	9.00

MINT SETS

X#	Date	Mintage	Identification	Issue Price	Mkt Val
XMS1	2004 (8)	7,000	X#Pn1-Pn8	—	35.00

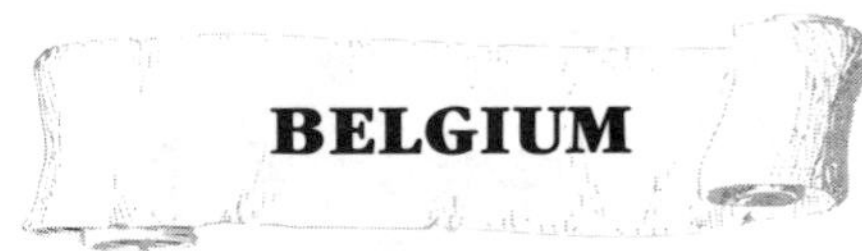

BELGIUM

KINGDOM

MEDALLIC COINAGE

X# M4 5 CENTIMES
Copper **Subject:** 25th Anniversary of Independence **Rev:** French legend **Rev. Legend:** ...DE L'INAUGURATION DU ROI **Note:** Prev. KM#M1.

Date	Mintage	F	VF	XF	Unc	BU
1856	214,000	15.00	25.00	50.00	85.00	—

X# M4a 5 CENTIMES
Bronze **Rev:** French legend **Rev. Legend:** ... DE L'INAUGURATION DU ROI **Note:** Prev. KM#M3.

Date	Mintage	F	VF	XF	Unc	BU
1856	4,776	55.00	175	350	450	—

X# M5 5 CENTIMES
Copper **Rev:** Flemish legend **Rev. Legend:** ... VAN S'KONINGS **Note:** Prev. KM#M2.

Date	Mintage	F	VF	XF	Unc	BU
1856	3,000	80.00	240	450	650	—

X# M5a 5 CENTIMES
Bronze **Rev:** Flemish legend **Rev. Legend:** ... VAN S'KONINGS **Note:** Prev. KM#M4.

Date	Mintage	F	VF	XF	Unc	BU
1856	1,160	125	250	675	1,000	—

X# M1.1 10 CENTIMES
Copper **Subject:** Marriage of Duke and Dutchess of Brabant **Note:** Prev. KM#M5.1.

Date	Mintage	F	VF	XF	Unc	BU
1853 Large date	104,000	15.00	25.00	50.00	85.00	—

X# M1.2 10 CENTIMES
Copper **Subject:** Marriage of Duke and Duchess of Brabant **Note:** Prev. KM#M5.2.

Date	Mintage	F	VF	XF	Unc	BU
1853 Small date	Inc. above	17.50	35.00	75.00	125	—

X# M6.1 2 FRANCS
10.0000 g., 0.8350 Silver 0.2684 oz. ASW **Subject:** 25th Anniversary of Independence **Rev:** French legend **Rev. Legend:** DE L'INAUGURATION DU ROI **Note:** Prev. KM#M6.1. Coin alignment.

Date	Mintage	F	VF	XF	Unc	BU
1856	12,000	75.00	150	350	650	—

X# M6.2 2 FRANCS
10.0000 g., 0.8350 Silver 0.2684 oz. ASW **Note:** Prev. KM#M6.2. Medal alignment.

Date	Mintage	F	VF	XF	Unc	BU
1856	Inc. above	100	250	500	1,000	—

X# M7.1 2 FRANCS
10.0000 g., 0.8350 Silver 0.2684 oz. ASW **Rev:** Flemish legend **Rev. Legend:** ...VAN S'KONINGS **Note:** Prev. KM#7.1. Coin alignment.

Date	Mintage	F	VF	XF	Unc	BU
1856	1,898	750	1,850	3,500	4,750	—

X# M7.2 2 FRANCS
10.0000 g., 0.8350 Silver 0.2684 oz. ASW **Note:** Prev. KM#M7.2. Medal alignment.

Date	Mintage	F	VF	XF	Unc	BU
1856	Inc. above	800	2,000	3,700	6,000	—

KM# M1 2 FRANCS
Copper, 28.2 mm. **Ruler:** Leopold II **Subject:** Mint Visit **Obv:** Inscription **Rev:** Pedro II Emperor of Brasil

Date	Mintage	F	VF	XF	Unc	BU
1871	—	—	—	—	—	—

X# M2.1 5 FRANCS
25.0000 g., 0.9000 Silver 0.7234 oz. ASW **Ruler:** Leopold I **Subject:** Marriage of the Duke and Dutchess of Brabant **Obv:** Head left **Obv. Legend:** LEOPOLD PREMIER ROI DES BELGES **Rev:** Conjoined heads right; date: 21-22 AOUT 1853 **Note:** Prev. KM#M8.1.

Date	Mintage	F	VF	XF	Unc	BU
1853	32,000	40.00	100	200	400	—

X# M2.2 5 FRANCS
25.0000 g., 0.9000 Silver 0.7234 oz. ASW **Ruler:** Leopold I **Obv:** Head left **Obv. Legend:** LEOPOLD PREMIER ROI DES BELGES **Rev:** Conjoined heads right; date: 21.22 AOUT 1853 **Note:** Prev. KM#M8.2.

Date	Mintage	F	VF	XF	Unc	BU
1853	Inc. above	40.00	100	200	400	—

X# M8 5 FRANCS
25.0000 g., 0.9000 Silver 0.7234 oz. ASW **Obv:** Conjoined heads of Leopold I and Leopold II right **Note:** Prev. KM#M9.

Date	Mintage	F	VF	XF	Unc	BU
1880	6,714	75.00	150	250	500	—

X# M8a 5 FRANCS
Copper **Obv:** Conjoined heads of Leopold I and Leopold II right **Note:** Prev. KM#M9a.

Date	Mintage	F	VF	XF	Unc	BU
1880	28,000	25.00	50.00	75.00	125	—

X# M8b 5 FRANCS
Gold **Obv:** Conjoined heads of Leopold I and Leopold II right **Note:** Prev. KM#M9b.

Date	Mintage	F	VF	XF	Unc	BU
1880 Rare	—	—	—	—	—	—

Note: Fewer than 10 pieces are known to exist

X# M9 40 FRANCS
12.9000 g., 0.9000 Gold 0.3733 oz. AGW **Subject:** 25th Anniversary of Independence **Rev:** French legend **Rev. Legend:** .... DE L'INAUGURATION **Note:** Prev. KM#M10.

Date	Mintage	F	VF	XF	Unc	BU
1856	449	—	4,000	9,000	12,000	—

X# M10 40 FRANCS
12.9000 g., 0.9000 Gold 0.3733 oz. AGW **Rev:** Flemish legend **Rev. Legend:** ... VAN S'KONINGS **Note:** Prev. KM#M12. Forgeries exist with weight: 16.8 grams.

Date	Mintage	F	VF	XF	Unc	BU
1856 Restrike	50	—	400	800	1,250	—

X# M3.1 100 FRANCS

31.6600 g., 0.9000 Gold 0.9161 oz. AGW **Ruler:** Leopold I **Subject:** Marriage of Duke and Dutchess of Brabant **Obv:** Head left **Obv. Legend:** LEOPOLD PREMIER ROI DES BELGES **Rev:** Conjoined heads right; date: 21-22 AOUT 1853 **Note:** Prev. KM#M11.1.

Date	Mintage	F	VF	XF	Unc	BU
1853	482	—	2,500	4,000	6,000	—

X# M3.2 100 FRANCS

31.6600 g., 0.9000 Gold 0.9161 oz. AGW **Ruler:** Leopold I **Obv:** Head left **Obv. Legend:** LEOPOLD PREMIER ROI DES BELGES **Rev:** Conjoined heads right; date: 21.22 AOUT 1853 **Note:** Prev. KM#M11.2. Examples without raised dot or - between 21 and 22 are restrikes.

Date	Mintage	F	VF	XF	Unc	BU
1853	Inc. above	—	2,500	4,000	6,000	—

X# M15 100 FRANCS

31.6600 g., 0.9000 Gold 0.9161 oz. AGW **Obv:** Queen Elizabeth

Date	Mintage	F	VF	XF	Unc	BU
1965 Proof	—	Value: 575				

X# M41 PATAGON

20.0000 g., 0.9250 Silver 0.5948 oz. ASW, 35 mm. **Obv:** Crown above Burgundian cross **Obv. Legend:** CAROL • II • D • G • HISP ET • INKIARVM • REX **Rev:** Crowned ams in order chain **Rev. Legend:** ARCHID • AVST • DVX BURG • BRABAN • Zc

Date	Mintage	F	VF	XF	Unc	BU
1998 Proof	1,000	Value: 45.00				

X# M42 SOUVERAIN

5.5400 g., 0.9990 Gold 0.1779 oz. AGW, 25 mm. **Obv:** Crowned rampant lion left with sword and globe **Obv. Legend:** CAROL • II • D • G • HISP • ET • IND • REX • **Rev:** Crowned arms in order chain **Rev. Legend:** ARCHID • AVST • DVX BVRG • BRABAN • Zc

Date	Mintage	F	VF	XF	Unc	BU
1996 Proof	1,000	Value: 230				
1997 Proof	1,000	Value: 215				
1998 Proof	1,000	Value: 200				

X# M20 10 LEONES

13.2400 g., Silver, 30.1 mm. **Subject:** 150th Anniversary of Kingdom **Obv:** Crowned ornate arms **Obv. Legend:** BELGIE - BELGIQUE **Rev:** Lion holding shield and sword **Rev. Legend:** • DOMINI EST REGNUM • BELGIQUE 1830-1980 BELGIE **Edge:** Plain

Date	Mintage	F	VF	XF	Unc	BU
ND(1980) Proof	—	Value: 12.50				

MEDALLIC ECU COINAGE

X# M32 ECU

6.4500 g., 0.7500 Gold 0.1555 oz. AGW, 25 mm. **Ruler:** Baudouin I **Obv:** Artistic outline of Europa and bull's head, Atomium shield below, 12 stars in circle at right, date within **Obv. Legend:** E • U • R • O • P • E • A • N • E • C • U **Rev:** Medieval copy of gold coin with King Johann III of Brabant facing, seated on throne **Rev. Legend:** BRABANCIE : DVC : MONA : 10HIS : DEI • GRA • **Edge:** Reeded

Date	Mintage	F	VF	XF	Unc	BU
1993 Proof	2,500	Value: 225				

X# M33 ECU

20.0000 g., 0.9990 Silver 0.6423 oz. ASW, 40 mm. **Ruler:** Baudouin I **Obv:** Crowned shields, large value below **Obv. Legend:** BELGIQUE **Rev:** Large B above jugate busts of Baudouin and Fabiola left in sprays **Edge:** Reeded

Date	Mintage	F	VF	XF	Unc	BU
1993 Proof	9,999	Value: 50.00				

X# M31 ECU

20.0000 g., 0.9250 Silver 0.5948 oz. ASW, 35 mm. **Ruler:** Baudouin I **Obv:** Artistic outline of Europa and bull's head, Atomium shield below, 12 stars in circle at right, date within **Obv. Legend:** E • U • R • O • P • E • A • N • E • C • U **Rev:** Medieval copy of gold coin with King Johann III of Brabant facing, seated on throne **Rev. Legend:** BRABANCIE : DVC : MONA : 10HIS : DEI • GRA • **Edge:** Reeded

Date	Mintage	F	VF	XF	Unc	BU
1993 Proof	25,000	Value: 50.00				

MINT SETS

X#	Date	Mintage	Identification	Issue Price	Mkt Val
XMS1	1853 (4)	—	XM1.1, XM1.2, XM2.2, XM3.1	—	—

BELGIUM MORESNEY

LA CALAMINE

FREE COMMUNE

FANTASY COINAGE

X# 1 2 FRANCS

Silver **Obv:** Janiform heads of Leopold I and Frederick William IV. **Edge:** Reeded **Note:** KY#161b. Uniface trial strikes exist in all metals including lead.

Date	Mintage	F	VF	XF	Unc	BU
1848	—	—	—	—	—	—

X# 1a 2 FRANCS

Silver **Obv:** Janiform heads of Leopold I and Frederick William IV. **Edge:** Plain **Note:** KY#161a. Uniface trial strikes exist in all metals including lead.

Date	Mintage	F	VF	XF	Unc	BU
1848	—	—	—	—	—	—

X# 1b 2 FRANCS

Copper **Obv:** Janiform heads of Leopold I and Frederick William IV. **Edge:** Reeded **Note:** KY#161d. Uniface trial strikes exist in all metals including lead.

Date	Mintage	F	VF	XF	Unc	BU
1848	—	—	—	—	—	—

X# 1c 2 FRANCS

Copper **Obv:** Janiform heads of Leopold I and Frederick William IV **Edge:** Plain **Note:** KY#161c. Uniface trial strikes exist in all metals including lead.

Date	Mintage	F	VF	XF	Unc	BU
1848	—	—	—	—	—	—

X# 1d 2 FRANCS

Bronze **Obv:** Janiform heads of Leopold I and Frederick William IV **Edge:** Reeded **Note:** KY#161e. Uniface trial strikes exist in all metals including lead.

Date	Mintage	F	VF	XF	Unc	BU
1848	—	—	—	—	—	—

X# 1e 2 FRANCS

Gold **Obv:** Janiform heads of Leopold I and Frederick William IV **Edge:** Plain **Note:** KY#161. Uniface trial strikes exist in all metals including lead.

Date	Mintage	F	VF	XF	Unc	BU
1848	—	—	—	—	—	—

BERMANIA

KINGDOM

MEDALLIC COINAGE

X# M2 DENAR PLUMBUM
Lead **Obv:** Long cross, "X" in angles **Obv. Legend:** ALANVS RE... **Rev:** Short cross **Rev. Legend:** ✠ BERMANIA.F...

Date	Mintage	F	VF	XF	Unc	BU
ND(1993-98)	Est. 124	—	—	—	5.00	—

X# M3 DOUBLE DENAR
0.9990 Silver **Obv:** Long cross, "X" in angles **Obv. Legend:** ALANVS RE **Rev:** Short cross **Rev. Legend:** ✠ BERMANIA . F

Date	Mintage	F	VF	XF	Unc	BU
ND(1993-98)	Est. 18	—	—	—	—	—

X# M4 5 DENARI PLUMBI
Nickel-Silver, 35 mm. **Subject:** Royal Wedding **Obv:** Crowned and mantled arms **Obv. Legend:** ALANVS • D : G : BERMANIAE • REX • ORB :... **Rev:** Bear dancing with wolf **Rev. Legend:** KINGDOM OF BERMANIA

Date	Mintage	F	VF	XF	Unc	BU
1998	1,000	—	—	—	—	12.50

X# M4a 5 DENARI PLUMBI
Aluminum, 35 mm. **Subject:** Royal Wedding **Obv:** Crowned and mantled arms **Obv. Legend:** ALANVS • D : G : BERMANIAE • REX • ORB :... **Rev:** Bear dancing with wolf **Rev. Legend:** KINGDOM OF BERMANIA

Date	Mintage	F	VF	XF	Unc	BU
1998	452	—	—	—	—	8.00

Note: Half the mintage was thrown as "largesse" to the attendees at the Royal Wedding reception

X# M4b 5 DENARI PLUMBI
0.9250 Silver, 35 mm. **Subject:** Royal Wedding **Obv:** Crowned and mantled arms **Obv. Legend:** ALANVS • D : G : BERMANIAE • REX • ORB :... **Rev:** Bear dancing with wolf **Rev. Legend:** KINGDOM OF BERMANIA

Date	Mintage	F	VF	XF	Unc	BU
1998	18	—	—	—	—	100

PATTERNS

X# Pn2 DENAR PLUMBUM
Lead **Obv:** Short cross **Obv. Legend:** ✠ ALANVS . REX... **Rev:** Short cross **Rev. Legend:** ✠ FLEISCHER

Date	Mintage	F	VF	XF	Unc	BU
ND(1993)	4	—	—	—	—	—

X# Pn1 5 DENARI PLUMBI
Lead, 35 mm. **Subject:** Royal Wedding **Obv:** Crowned and mantled arms **Obv. Legend:** ALANVS • D : G : BERMANIAE • REX • ORB :... **Rev:** Bear dancing with wolf **Rev. Legend:** KINGDOM OF BERMANIA

Date	Mintage	F	VF	XF	Unc	BU
1998	2	—	—	—	—	—

KNIGHTS OF CHRISTMAS

MEDALLIC COINAGE

X# M5 DENAR
0.9250 Silver **Ruler:** Friedrich von Belgien **Obv:** Cross of scepters **Obv. Legend:** RITTER • AVS •... **Rev:** Star of Bethlehem **Rev. Legend:** WEINACHTEN

Date	Mintage	F	VF	XF	Unc	BU
ND(2005)	Est. 100	—	—	—	—	6.00

Note: Normally partial strikes; full strikes are rare

BERMUDA

BRITISH ADMINISTRATION

MEDALLIC COINAGE

1954 Geoffrey Hearn Series

X# M1 CROWN
Gilt Bronze **Obv:** Bust of Edward VIII left **Obv. Legend:** EDWARD•VIII•KING•8•EMPEROR **Rev:** Early three-masted sailing ship

Date	Mintage	F	VF	XF	Unc	BU
1936 Proof	—	Value: 110				

X# M1a CROWN
28.1000 g., Silver **Obv:** Bust of Edward VIII left **Obv. Legend:** EDWARD•VIII•KING•8•EMPEROR **Rev:** Early three-masted sailing ship

Date	Mintage	F	VF	XF	Unc	BU
1936 Proof	1,000	Value: 65.00				

X# M1b CROWN
28.1000 g., Silver **Obv:** Bust of Edward VIII left **Obv. Legend:** EDWARD•VIII•KING•8•EMPEROR **Rev:** Early three-masted sailing ship

Date	Mintage	F	VF	XF	Unc	BU
1936 Prooflike; Restrike	750	—	—	—	35.00	—

X# M1c CROWN
Gold **Obv:** Bust of Edward VIII left **Obv. Legend:** EDWARD•VIII•KING•8•EMPEROR **Rev:** Early three-masted sailing ship

Date	Mintage	F	VF	XF	Unc	BU
1936 Proof	10	Value: 800				

Note: Restrikes known

Richard Lobel Series

X# M2 CROWN
Bronze **Obv:** Bust of Edward VIII left **Obv. Legend:** EDWARD • VIII • KING • & • EMPEROR **Rev:** Early three masted sailing ship

Date	Mintage	F	VF	XF	Unc	BU
1936 Proof	2,000	Value: 15.00				

X# M2a CROWN
Copper-Nickel-Zinc **Obv:** Bust of Edward VIII left **Obv. Legend:** EDWARD • VIII • KING • & • EMPEROR **Rev:** Early three masted sailing ship

Date	Mintage	F	VF	XF	Unc	BU
1936 Proof	3,500	Value: 15.00				

X# M2b CROWN
0.9167 Silver **Obv:** Bust of Edward VIII left **Obv. Legend:** EDWARD • VIII • KING • & • EMPEROR **Rev:** Early three masted sailing ship

Date	Mintage	F	VF	XF	Unc	BU
1936 Proof	500	Value: 50.00				

X# M2c CROWN
Gold **Obv:** Bust of Edward VIII facing left **Obv. Legend:** EDWARD • VIII • KING • & • EMPEROR **Rev:** Early three masted sailing ship

Date	Mintage	F	VF	XF	Unc	BU
1936 Proof	—	Value: 500				

X# M3 SOVEREIGN
0.3750 Gold, 22 mm. **Obv:** Bust of Edward VIII left **Obv. Legend:** EDWARD • VIII • KING • & • EMPEROR **Rev:** Early three-masted sailing ship

Date	Mintage	F	VF	XF	Unc	BU
1936 Proof	250	Value: 125				

PIEFORTS

X#	Date	Mintage	Identification	Mkt Val
P1	1936	—	Crown. 0.9167 Silver. X#2b.	100

SOMERS ISLANDS

COLONY

MEDALLIC COINAGE

X# M8 12 PENCE/DAALDER
Silver Plated Brass, 38 mm. **Obv:** Boar standing left **Obv. Legend:** * ISLANDS * SOMMER **Rev:** Sailing ship **Rev. Legend:** NIEUW • AMSTERDAM • **Edge:** Plain **Note:** Mule, obverse of New Amsterdam 1 Daalder, X#1.

Date	Mintage	F	VF	XF	Unc	BU
ND(1990)	—	—	—	—	12.50	—

X# M8a 12 PENCE/DAALDER
Copper, 38 mm. **Obv:** Boar standing left **Obv. Legend:** "ISLANDS * SOMER" **Rev:** Sailing ship **Rev. Legend:** NIEUW • AMSTERDAM **Edge:** Plain **Note:** Mule, obverse of New Amsterdam 1 Daalder, X#1.

Date	Mintage	F	VF	XF	Unc	BU
ND(1990)	—	—	—	—	—	—

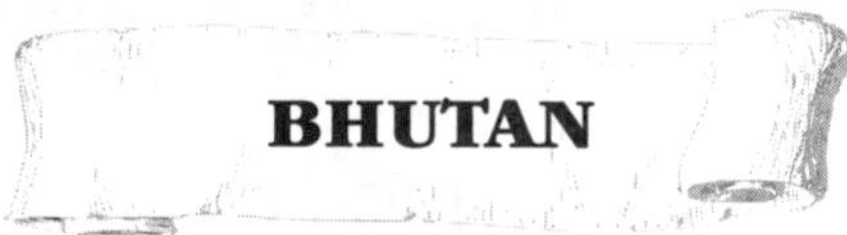

BHUTAN

KINGDOM

MEDALLIC COINAGE

X# M1 25 NGULTRUMS
Copper-Nickel **Series:** International Games **Obv. Legend:** ROYAL GOVERNMENT OF BHUTAN **Rev:** Boxing **Note:** Unofficial issue. Prev. KM#59.

Date	Mintage	F	VF	XF	Unc	BU
1984 Proof	—	Value: 12.50				

X# M2 25 NGULTRUMS
Copper-Nickel **Series:** International Games **Obv:** National emblem and legends **Obv. Legend:** ROYAL GOVERNMENT OF BHUTAN **Rev:** Shot put **Note:** Unofficial issue. Prev. KM#62.

Date	Mintage	F	VF	XF	Unc	BU
1984 Proof	—	Value: 12.50				

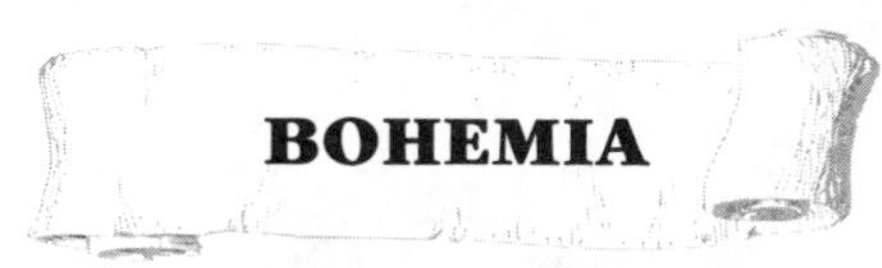

BOHEMIA

KINGDOM

MEDALLIC COINAGE

X# M10 GROSCHEN
Aluminum **Ruler:** Wladislaw II **Obv:** Crown **Obv. Legend:** KAROLVS PRIMVS DEI GRATIA REX BOEMIE **Rev:** Crowned lion rampant left **Rev. Legend:** GROSSI PRAGENSES

Date	Mintage	F	VF	XF	Unc	BU
ND	—	—	—	—	—	5.00

Note: Restrike sold in Prague's Old Town Square

X# M25 THALER
0.9000 Silver **Ruler:** Leopold I **Obv:** Crowned lion rampant left **Obv. Legend:** LVDOVICVS PRIM D GRACIA REX BO **Rev:** St. Jochim standing before shield **Rev. Legend:** AR DOMI SLI ST E7 FRACO D BA

Date	Mintage	F	VF	XF	Unc	BU
1525	—	—	—	—	—	25.00

BOLIVIA

COLONIAL

COB COINAGE

X# 10 8 ESCUDOS
Gold **Obv:** Pillars **Obv. Inscription:** PLV•SVL•TRA **Note:** The first gold pieces struck at the Potosi Mint were dated 1778. This design was first used for striking silver "cob" 8 reales in 1652.

Date	Mintage	Good	VG	F	VF	XF
(1)591 E	—	—	—	—	—	—

MILLED COINAGE

X# 1 1/4 REAL
0.7300 g., Gold **Obv:** Lion rampant left **Rev:** Crowned gate tower

Date	Mintage	Good	VG	F	VF	XF
1808 SLP monogram	—	—	—	—	—	100

REPUBLIC

MEDALLIC COINAGE

X# M1 1/2 GRAMO
0.5800 g., Gold **Rev. Legend:** POTOSI BOLIVIA

Date	Mintage	F	VF	XF	Unc	BU
1860	—	—	15.00	20.00	35.00	—

X# M3 GRAMO
1.3000 g., Gold, 13 mm. **Obv:** Nine stars surround moutain peak **Rev:** Llama standing right

Date	Mintage	F	VF	XF	Unc	BU
1852	—	—	—	30.00	45.00	—

X# M2 GRAMO
1.1500 g., Gold **Rev:** Llama

Date	Mintage	F	VF	XF	Unc	BU
1879	—	—	25.00	35.00	55.00	—

X# M4 1-1/2 GRAMOS
1.7000 g., Gold, 14.5 mm. **Obv:** Arms **Obv. Legend:** REPUBLICA DE BOLIVIA **Rev:** Llama sLtanding right **Rev. Legend:** POTOSI

Date	Mintage	F	VF	XF	Unc	BU
1846	—	—	—	30.00	45.00	—

Oruro - 1849

X# 85.1 SOL
0.6670 Silver **Obv. Legend:** ... SOCABON **Note:** Prev. KM#85.1. Weight varies: 2.60-3.60 grams, actual weight varies: .056-.077. Mint mark, Oruro in monogram. EXTREMELY RARE WITHOUT HOLE.

Date	Mintage	VG	F	VF	XF	Unc
1849 JM	—	40.00	60.00	90.00	200	—

X# 85.2 SOL
0.6670 Silver **Obv. Legend:** ... SOCN **Note:** Prev. KM#85.2. Mint mark, Oruro in monogram. EXTREMELY RARE WITHOUT HOLE.

Date	Mintage	VG	F	VF	XF	Unc
1849 JM coin rotation; Rare	—	—	—	—	—	—
1849 JM medal rotation	—	40.00	60.00	90.00	200	—

1952 - Gold Bullion Series

X# 15 3-1/2 GRAMOS (5 Bolivianos)
3.8900 g., 0.9000 Gold 0.1126 oz. AGW **Subject:** 1952 Revolution Commemorative **Note:** Prev. KM#MB1.

Date	Mintage	F	VF	XF	Unc	BU
1952(a)	29,000	—	—	—	BV+20%	—

X# 11 7 GRAMOS (10 Bolivianos)
7.7800 g., 0.9000 Gold 0.2251 oz. AGW **Subject:** 1952 Revolution Commemorative **Note:** Prev. KM#MB2.

Date	Mintage	F	VF	XF	Unc	BU
1952(a)	79,000	—	—	—	BV+15%	—

X# 12 14 GRAMOS (20 Bolivianos)
15.5600 g., 0.9000 Gold 0.4502 oz. AGW **Subject:** 1952 Revolution Commemorative **Note:** Prev. KM#MB3.

Date	Mintage	F	VF	XF	Unc	BU
1952(a)	7,142	—	—	—	BV+10%	—

X# 13 35 GRAMOS (50 Bolivianos)
38.9000 g., 0.9000 Gold 1.1256 oz. AGW
Subject: 1952 Revolution Commemorative **Note:** Prev. KM#MB4.

Date	Mintage	F	VF	XF	Unc	BU
1952(a)	2,857	—	—	—	BV+10%	—

TRIAL STRIKES

X#	Date	Mintage	Identification	Mkt Val
TS1	ND(1991)	—	Boliviano. Bronze. 19.3300 g. 38.2 mm.	15.00

MINT SETS

X#	Date	Mintage	Identification	Issue Price	Mkt Val
XMS1	1952 (4)	—	X#MB1-MB4; Market Value is BV+10%	—	—

BOPHUTHATSWANA

SOVEREIGN ENCLAVE

GOLD BULLION MEDALLIC COINAGE

X# M1 NKWE
16.9660 g., 0.9170 Gold 0.5002 oz. AGW **Subject:** 10th Anniversary of Independence **Note:** Prev. KM#M1. Similar to Lowe, KM#2.

Date	Mintage	F	VF	XF	Unc	BU
1987 Proof	—	Value: 300				

PLATINUM BULLION MEDALLIC COINAGE

X# M2 LOWE
31.2100 g., 0.9995 Platinum 1.0029 oz. APW **Subject:** 10th Anniversary of Independence **Note:** Prev. KM#M2.

Date	Mintage	F	VF	XF	Unc	BU
1987 Proof	3,000	Value: 1,100				

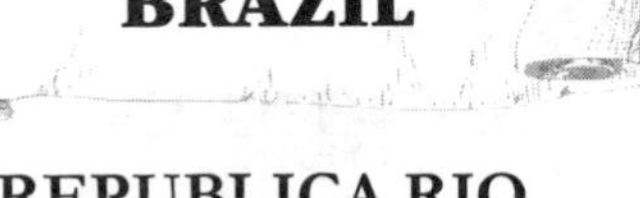

BRAZIL

REPUBLICA RIO GRANDENSSE

PESO COINAGE

X# 25 PESO
Silver **Ruler:** Alvares Machado **Obv:** Clasper hands holding sword with liberty cap and rays

Date	Mintage	F	VF	XF	Unc	BU
1835	—	—	100	150	250	—

X# 25a PESO
16.1300 g., Pewter, 37 mm. **Ruler:** Alvares Machado **Obv:** Clasper hands holding sword with liberty cap and rays

Date	Mintage	F	VF	XF	Unc	BU
1835	—	—	75.00	125	—	—

REPUBLIC COMPANHA DO OURO DE REVOLUCAO CONSTITUCIONALISTA

COUNTERMARKED COINAGE

1932 Revolution - Private Issues

X# 30 200 REIS

2.5500 g., 0.9170 Silver 0.0752 oz. ASW **Countermark:** Helmet/1932/C.O. **Note:** Prev. KM#CC1.1. Countermark on Brazil 200 Reis, KM#469.

CM Date	Host Date	Good	VG	F	VF	XF
1932	1854-67	—	—	12.00	20.00	35.00

X# 31 200 REIS

2.5000 g., 0.8350 Silver 0.0671 oz. ASW **Countermark:** Helmet/1932/C.O. **Note:** Prev. KM#CC1.2. Countermark on Brazil 200 Reis, KM#471.

CM Date	Host Date	Good	VG	F	VF	XF
1932	1867-69	—	—	18.00	35.00	60.00

X# 35 500 REIS

6.3750 g., 0.9170 Silver 0.1879 oz. ASW **Countermark:** Helmet/1932/C.O. **Note:** Prev. KM#CC1.3. Countermark on Brazil 500 Reis, KM#464.

CM Date	Host Date	Good	VG	F	VF	XF
1932	1853-67	—	—	12.00	20.00	35.00

X# 37 500 REIS

6.3750 g., 0.9170 Silver 0.1879 oz. ASW **Countermark:** Helmet/1932/C.O. **Note:** Prev. KM#CC1.5. Countermark on Brazil 500 Reis, KM#480.

CM Date	Host Date	Good	VG	F	VF	XF
1932	1876	—	—	15.00	30.00	50.00
1932	1888	—	—	12.00	20.00	35.00

X# 40 500 REIS

6.3750 g., 0.9170 Silver 0.1879 oz. ASW **Countermark:** Helmet/1932/C.O. **Note:** Prev. KM#CC1.4. Countermark on Brazil 500 Reis, KM#494.

CM Date	Host Date	Good	VG	F	VF	XF
1932	1889	—	—	15.00	25.00	45.00

X# A25.1 960 REIS

26.8900 g., 0.8950 Silver 0.7737 oz. ASW **Countermark:** Helmet/1932/C.O. **Note:** Prev. KM#CC1.6. Countermark on Brazil 960 Reis, KM#307.1.

CM Date	Host Date	Good	VG	F	VF	XF
1932	1810B-18B	—	—	40.00	60.00	90.00

X# A25.2 960 REIS

26.8900 g., 0.8950 Silver 0.7737 oz. ASW **Countermark:** Helmet/1932/C.O. **Note:** Prev. KM#CC1.7. Countermark on Brazil 960 Reis, KM#307.3.

CM Date	Host Date	Good	VG	F	VF	XF
1932	1810R-181R	—	—	40.00	60.00	90.00

X# 26 960 REIS

26.8900 g., 0.8960 Silver 0.7746 oz. ASW **Countermark:** Helmet/1932/C.O. **Note:** Prev. KM#CC1.8. Countermark on Brazil 960 Reis, KM#368.2.

CM Date	Host Date	Good	VG	F	VF	XF
1932	1824B-28B	—	—	120	200	325

X# 27 960 REIS

26.8900 g., 0.8960 Silver 0.7746 oz. ASW **Countermark:** Helmet/1932/C.O. **Note:** Countermark on 960 Reis, KM#368.1.

CM Date	Host Date	Good	VG	F	VF	XF
1932	1823R-27R	—	—	40.00	60.00	90.00

X# 43 1000 REIS

12.7500 g., 0.9167 Silver 0.3758 oz. ASW **Countermark:** Helmet/1932/C.O. **Note:** Prev. KM#CC1.12. Countermark on Brazil 1000 Reis, KM#495.

CM Date	Host Date	Good	VG	F	VF	XF
1932	1889	—	—	15.00	25.00	45.00

X# 42 1000 REIS

12.7500 g., 0.9170 Silver 0.3759 oz. ASW **Countermark:** Helmet/1932/C.O. **Note:** Prev. KM#CC1.9. Countermark on 1000 Reis, KM#459.

CM Date	Host Date	Good	VG	F	VF	XF
1932	1849-52	—	—	12.00	20.00	35.00

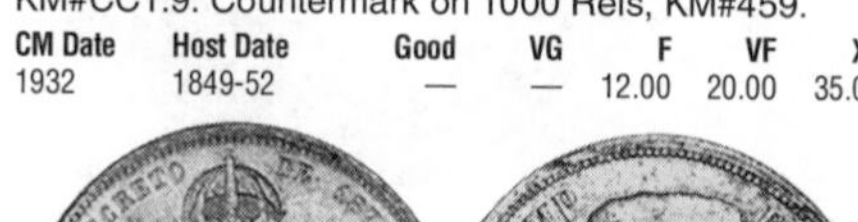

X# 39 1000 REIS

12.7500 g., 0.9167 Silver 0.3758 oz. ASW **Countermark:** Helmet / 1932 / C.O. **Note:** Countermark on Brazil 1000 Reis, KM#481.

CM Date	Host Date	Good	VG	F	VF	XF
1932	1888	10.00	17.50	25.00	35.00	—

X# 46 2000 REIS

25.5000 g., 0.9167 Silver 0.7515 oz. ASW **Countermark:** Helmet/1932/C.O. **Note:** Prev. KM#CC1.14. Countermark on Brazil 2000 Reis, KM#485.

CM Date	Host Date	Good	VG	F	VF	XF
1932	1887	—	—	30.00	60.00	90.00
1932	1888	—	—	20.00	40.00	70.00
1932	1889	—	—	20.00	40.00	70.00

X# 50 2000 REIS

7.9000 g., Silver **Countermark:** Helmet/1932/C.O. **Note:** Prev. KM#CC1.15. Countermark on Brazil 2000 Reis, KM#523 or 523a.

CM Date	Host Date	Good	VG	F	VF	XF
1932	1922	—	—	10.00	15.00	25.00

X# 44 2000 REIS

25.5000 g., 0.9170 Silver 0.7518 oz. ASW **Countermark:** Helmet/1932/C.O. **Note:** Prev. KM#CC1.13. Countermark on 2000 Reis, KM#466.

CM Date	Host Date	Good	VG	F	VF	XF
1932	1853-67	—	—	25.00	50.00	80.00

FEDERAL REPUBLIC

COUNTERMARKED AND COUNTERSTAMPED COINAGE

X# CC6.4 8 REALES

0.9030 Silver **Subject:** 400th Anniversary of Sao Paulo Brazil Numismatic Society **Note:** Counterstamped Type VI on Mexico City Mint 8 Reales, KM#377.10.

CM Date	Host Date	Good	VG	F	VF	XF
1888 MO MH	1889	—	—	—	35.00	—

X# CC13.1 40 REIS

Copper **Subject:** Opening of Santos Dumont Museum **Note:** Counterstamped Type XIII on 40 Reis, KM#319; October 1957.

CM Date	Host Date	Good	VG	F	VF	XF
1818-23	1957	—	—	—	25.00	40.00

X# CC3.1 960 REIS

0.8960 Silver **Subject:** Fourth Centennial of Sao Paulo and Numismatic Exposition **Obv:** Counterstamp: Crowned shield / S•A•N•P•E•X **Rev:** Counterstamp: "SANPEX" on globe over date **Note:** Counterstamped Type III and control number on 960 Reis, KM#307; December 1949.

CM Date	Host Date	Good	VG	F	VF	XF
1810-18	1949	—	—	—	65.00	90.00

X# CC7 960 REIS

Silver, 42.5 mm. **Subject:** Fourth Centennial of Sao Paulo and Numismatic Exposition **Obv:** Counterstamp: Crowned shield / S•A•N•P•E•X **Rev:** Counterstamp: "SANPEX" on globe over date **Note:** Counterstamp Type VI on KM#307; December 1949.

CM Date	Host Date	Good	VG	F	VF	XF
1810-18	1954	—	—	—	50.00	75.00

X# CC6.2 960 REIS

0.9030 Silver **Subject:** 400th Anniversary of Sao Paulo Brazil Numismatic Society **Note:** Countstamped Type VI on 960 Reis, KM#326.

CM Date	Host Date	Good	VG	F	VF	XF
1818-22	1954	—	—	—	60.00	90.00

X# CC6.1 960 REIS

0.8960 Silver **Subject:** 400th Anniversary of Sao Paulo Brazil Numismatic Society **Note:** Counterstamped Type VI on 960 Reis, KM#307.

CM Date	Host Date	Good	VG	F	VF	XF
1810-18	1954	—	—	—	60.00	90.00

X# CC7.1 960 REIS

0.8960 Silver **Subject:** 400th Anniversary of Sao Paulo Brazil Philatelic Society **Note:** Counterstamped Type VII on 960 Reis, KM#307.

CM Date	Host Date	Good	VG	F	VF	XF
1810-18	1954	—	—	—	60.00	90.00

X# CC7.2 960 REIS

0.9030 Silver **Subject:** 400th Anniversary of Sao Paulo Brazil Philatelic Society **Note:** Counterstamped Type VII on 960 Reis, KM#326.

CM Date	Host Date	Good	VG	F	VF	XF
1810-22	1954	—	—	—	60.00	90.00

X# CC7.3 960 REIS

0.8960 Silver **Subject:** 400th Anniversary of Sao Paulo Brazil Philatelic Society **Note:** Counterstamped Type VII on 960 Reis, KM#368.

CM Date	Host Date	Good	VG	F	VF	XF
1823-28 R	1954	—	—	—	50.00	80.00

X# CC8.1 960 REIS

0.8960 Silver **Obv:** Counterstamp: Sailing ship **Rev:** Counterstamp: SANPEX II, date around fish **Note:** Counterstamped Type VIII on 960 Reis, KM#307; January 26-31, 1955.

CM Date	Host Date	Good	VG	F	VF	XF
1810-18	1955	—	—	—	60.00	90.00

X# CC8.2 960 REIS

0.9030 Silver **Obv:** Counterstamp: Sailing ship **Rev:** Counterstamp: SANPEX II, date around fish **Note:** Counterstamped Type VIII on 960 Reis, KM#326; January 26-31, 1955.

CM Date	Host Date	Good	VG	F	VF	XF
1818-22	1955	—	—	—	60.00	90.00

X# CC10.1 960 REIS

0.8960 Silver **Subject:** XXIII Anniversary of the 1932 Revolution **Note:** Counterstamped Type X on 960 Reis, KM#307.

CM Date	Host Date	Good	VG	F	VF	XF
1810-18	1955	—	—	—	60.00	90.00

X# CC10.2 960 REIS

0.8960 Silver **Subject:** XXIII Anniversary of the 1932 Revolution **Note:** Counterstamped Type X on 960 Reis, KM#368.

CM Date	Host Date	Good	VG	F	VF	XF
1823-28 R	1955	—	—	—	50.00	80.00

X# CC9.1 960 REIS

0.8960 Silver **Subject:** 36th Eucharistic Congress **Note:** Counterstamped Type IX on 960 Reis, KM#307.

CM Date	Host Date	Good	VG	F	VF	XF
1810-18	1955	—	—	—	60.00	90.00

X# CC9.2 960 REIS

0.9030 Silver **Subject:** 36th Eucharistic Congress **Note:** Counterstamped Type IX on 960 Reis, KM#326.

CM Date	Host Date	Good	VG	F	VF	XF
1810-18	1955	—	—	—	60.00	90.00

X# CC11.1 960 REIS

0.8960 Silver **Obv:** Counterstamp: Sailing ship **Obv. Legend:** 999EXPO DG TURISMO **Rev:** Counterstamp: SANPEX III•ANO•SANTOS DUMONT around date and fsh **Note:** Counterstamped Type XI on 960 Reis, KM#307; September 1956.

CM Date	Host Date	Good	VG	F	VF	XF
1810-18	1956	—	—	—	60.00	90.00

X# CC11.2 960 REIS

0.9030 Silver **Obv:** Counterstamp: Sailing ship **Obv. Legend:** 999EXPO DG TURISMO **Rev:** Counterstamp: SANPEX III•ANO•SANTOS DUMONT around date and fsh **Note:** Counterstamped Type XI on 960 Reis, KM#326; September 1956.

CM Date	Host Date	Good	VG	F	VF	XF
1818-22	1956	—	—	—	60.00	90.00

X# CC12.1 960 REIS

0.8960 Silver **Subject:** 50th Anniversary of the Flight of Santos Dumont **Note:** Counterstamped Type XII on 960 Reis, KM#307.

CM Date	Host Date	Good	VG	F	VF	XF
1810-18	1956	—	—	—	60.00	90.00

X# CC12.2 960 REIS

0.9030 Silver **Subject:** 50th Anniversary of the Flight of Santos Dumont **Note:** Counterstamped Type XII on 960 Reis, KM#326.

CM Date	Host Date	Good	VG	F	VF	XF
1818-22	1956	—	—	—	60.00	90.00

X# CC13.2 960 REIS

0.8960 Silver **Subject:** Opening of Santos Dumont

Museum **Note:** Counterstamped Type XIII on 960 Reis, KM#307; October 1957.

CM Date	Host Date	Good	VG	F	VF	XF
1810-18	1957	—	—	—	60.00	90.00

X# CC13.3 960 REIS

0.9030 Silver **Subject:** Opening of Santos Dumont Museum **Note:** Counterstamped Type XIII on 960 Reis, KM#326; October 1957.

CM Date	Host Date	Good	VG	F	VF	XF
1818-22	1957	—	—	—	60.00	90.00

X# CC8.3 1000 REIS

0.9167 Silver **Obv:** Counterstamp: Sailing ship **Rev:** Counterstamp: SANPEX II, date around fish **Note:** Counterstamped Type VIII on 1000 Reis, KM#465; January 26-31, 1955.

CM Date	Host Date	Good	VG	F	VF	XF
1853-66	1955	—	—	—	35.00	60.00

X# CC3.2 2000 REIS

0.9167 Silver **Subject:** Fourth Centennial of Sao Paulo and Numismatic Exposition **Obv:** Counterstamp: Crowned shield / S•A•N•P•E•X **Rev:** Counterstamp: "SANPEX" on globe over date **Note:** Counterstamped Type III and control enumber on 2000 Reis, KM#485; December 1949.

CM Date	Host Date	Good	VG	F	VF	XF
1886-89	1949	—	—	—	65.00	90.00

X# CC4 2000 REIS

0.9167 Silver **Countermark:** "SANPEX" **Obv:** Countermark in fish-like outline **Note:** Countermarked Type IV and control number on 2000 Reis, KM#485; December 1949.

CM Date	Host Date	Good	VG	F	VF	XF
1886-89	1949	—	—	—	65.00	90.00

X# CC5.1 2000 REIS

0.9167 Silver **Countermark:** JUPEX **Obv:** Countermark over date **Note:** Counterstamped Type V and control number on 2000 Reis, KM#462; May 31, 1950.

CM Date	Host Date	Good	VG	F	VF	XF
1851-52	1950	—	—	—	35.00	60.00

X# CC5.2 2000 REIS

0.9167 Silver **Countermark:** JUPEX **Obv:** Countermark over date **Note:** Counterstamped Type V and control number on 2000 Reis, KM#485; May 31, 1950.

CM Date	Host Date	Good	VG	F	VF	XF
1886-89	1950	—	—	—	35.00	60.00

X# CC5.3 2000 REIS

0.9000 Silver **Countermark:** JUPEX **Obv:** Countermark over date **Note:** Counterstamped Type V and control number on 2000 Reis, KM#508; May 31, 1950.

CM Date	Host Date	Good	VG	F	VF	XF
1906-12	1950	—	—	—	30.00	85.00

X# CC6.3 2000 REIS

0.9167 Silver **Subject:** 400th Anniversary of Sao Paulo Brazil Numismatic Society **Note:** Counterstamped Type VI on 2000 Reis, KM#485.

CM Date	Host Date	Good	VG	F	VF	XF
1886-89	1954	—	—	—	35.00	60.00

X# CC11.3 2000 REIS

0.9000 Silver **Obv:** Counterstamp: Sailing ship **Obv. Legend:** 999EXPO DG TURISMO **Rev:** Counterstamp: SANPEX III•ANO•SANTOS DUMONT around date and fsh **Note:** Counterstamped Type XI on 2000 Reis, KM#508; September 1956.

CM Date	Host Date	Good	VG	F	VF	XF
1906-12	1956	—	—	—	30.00	85.00

X# CC13.4 2000 REIS

0.9000 Silver **Note:** Counterstamped Type XIII on 2000 Reis, KM#508.

CM Date	Host Date	Good	VG	F	VF	XF
1906-12	1957	—	—	—	30.00	85.00

X# CC2 5000 REIS

0.6000 Silver **Obv:** Counterstamp: 2A EXPOSICAO NUMISMATICA around triangle **Rev:** Counterstamp: BELLO HORIZONTE.GERAES. around sun behind a mountain **Note:** Counterstamped Type II and control number on 5000 Reis, KM#543; December 15, 1937.

CM Date	Host Date	Good	VG	F	VF	XF
1937	1937	—	—	—	50.00	85.00
1936	1937	—	—	—	50.00	85.00

MEDALLIC BULLION COINAGE

X# M11 12 FLORIN

Gold **Subject:** Sao Paulo 400th Anniversary / 1954 Exposition Numismatica **Obv:** Value over GWC monogram stamped "COPIA" **Rev. Inscription:** ANNO / BRASIL **Note:** Copy of Geotroyerde Westindishe Compagnie issue, KM#7.2. Klippe.

Date	Mintage	F	VF	XF	Unc	BU
1645 (1954)	—	—	—	—	—	225

X# MB1 OUNCE

31.1300 g., 0.9990 Silver 0.9998 oz. ASW, 38.9 mm. **Subject:** 500th Anniversary Discovery of Brazil **Obv:** Liberty head between two dish antennas, jet fighter below **Obv. Legend:** REPUBLICA FEDERATIVA DO BRASIL **Rev:** Weight in wreath **Rev. Legend:** ★ 5°. CENTENARIO DO DESCOBRIMENTO DO BRASIL **Edge:** Reeded

Date	Mintage	F	VF	XF	Unc	BU
ND(2000) Proof	—	—	—	—	—	—

X# MB2 OUNCE

31.1300 g., 0.9990 Silver 0.9998 oz. ASW, 38.9 mm. **Subject:** 500th Anniversary Discovery of Brazil **Obv:** Medieval sailing ship **Obv. Legend:** REPUBLICA FEDERATIVA DO BRASIL **Rev:** Weight in wreath **Rev. Legend:** ★ 5°. CENTENARIO DO DESCOBRIMENTO DO BRASIL **Edge:** Reeded

Date	Mintage	F	VF	XF	Unc	BU
ND(2000) Proof	—	—	—	—	—	—

X# MB3 OUNCE

31.1300 g., 0.9990 Silver 0.9998 oz. ASW, 38.9 mm. **Subject:** 500th Anniversary Discovery of Brazil **Obv:** Portuguese and Brazilian arms **Obv. Legend:** REPUBLICA FEDERATIVA DO BRASIL **Rev:** Pedro Alvarres Cabral standing facing with flag **Rev. Legend:** 5°. CENTENARIO DO DESCOBRIMENTO DO BRASIL **Edge:** Reeded

Date	Mintage	F	VF	XF	Unc	BU
2000 Proof	—	—	—	—	—	—

X# MB4 OUNCE
31.1300 g., 0.9990 Silver 0.9998 oz. ASW, 38.9 mm.
Subject: 500th Anniversary Discovery of Brazil
Obv: Portuguese cross **Obv. Legend:** REPUBLICA FEDERATIVA DO BRASIL **Rev:** Weight in wreath **Rev. Legend:** ★ 5°. CENTENARIO DO DESCOBRIMENTO DO BRASIL **Edge:** Reeded

Date	Mintage	F	VF	XF	Unc	BU
ND(2000) Proof	—	—	—	—	—	—

X# MB5 2 OUNCES
62.2600 g., 0.9999 Gold 2.0014 oz. AGW, 38.9 mm.
Subject: 500th Anniversary Discovery of Brazil
Obv: Liberty head between two dish antennas, jet fighter below **Obv. Legend:** REPUBLICA FEDERATIVA DO BRASIL **Rev:** Weight in wreath **Rev. Legend:** ★ 5°. CENTENARIO DO DESCOBRIMENTO DO BRASIL
Edge: Reeded

Date	Mintage	F	VF	XF	Unc	BU
ND(2000) Proof	30	—	—	—	—	—

X# MB6 2 OUNCES
62.2600 g., 0.9999 Gold 2.0014 oz. AGW, 38.9 mm.
Subject: 500th Anniversary Discovery of Brazil
Obv: Medieval sailing ship **Obv. Legend:** REPUBLICA FEDERATIVA DO BRASIL **Rev:** Weight in wreath **Rev. Legend:** ★ 5°. CENTENARIO DO DESCOBRIMENTO DO BRASIL **Edge:** Reeded

Date	Mintage	F	VF	XF	Unc	BU
ND(2000) Proof	30	—	—	—	—	—

X# MB7 2 OUNCES
62.2600 g., 0.9999 Gold 2.0014 oz. AGW, 38.9 mm.
Subject: 500th Anniversary Discovery of Brazil
Obv: Portuguese and Brazilian arms **Obv. Legend:** REPUBLICA FEDERATIVA DO BRASIL **Rev:** Pedro Alvarres Cabral standing facing with flag **Rev. Legend:** 5°. CENTENARIO DO DESCOBRIMENTO DO BRASIL
Edge: Reeded

Date	Mintage	F	VF	XF	Unc	BU
2000 Proof	25	—	—	—	—	—

X# MB8 2 OUNCES
62.2600 g., 0.9999 Gold 2.0014 oz. AGW, 38.9 mm.
Subject: 500th Anniversary Discovery of Brazil
Obv: Portuguese cross **Obv. Legend:** REPUBLICA FEDERATIVA DO BRASIL **Rev:** Weight in wreath **Rev. Legend:** ★ 5°. CENTENARIO DO DESCOBRIMENTO DO BRASIL **Edge:** Reeded

Date	Mintage	F	VF	XF	Unc	BU
ND(2000) Proof	25	—	—	—	—	—

X# MB9 5 OUNCES
155.6500 g., 0.9990 Silver 4.9991 oz. ASW, 63.6 mm.
Subject: 500th Anniversary Discovery of Brazil
Obv: Portuguese and Brazilian arms **Obv. Legend:** REPUBLICA FEDERATIVA DO BRASIL **Rev:** Pedro Alvares Carral standing facing with flag **Rev. Legend:** 5°. CENTENARIO DO DESCOBRIMENTO DO BRASIL
Edge: Alternating reeded / plain **Note:** Illustration reduced.

Date	Mintage	F	VF	XF	Unc	BU
2000 Proof	—	—	—	—	—	—

X# MB10 12 OUNCES
373.5600 g., 0.9990 Silver 11.997 oz. ASW, 89.1 mm. **Subject:** 500th Anniversary Discovery of Brazil **Obv:** Portuguese and Brazilian arms **Obv. Legend:** REPUBLICA FEDERATIVE DO BRASIL **Rev:** Pedro Alvares Carral standing facing with flag **Rev. Legend:** 5°. CENTENARIO DO DESCOBRIMENTO DO BRASIL **Edge:** Alternating reeded / plain **Note:** Illustration reduced.

Date	Mintage	F	VF	XF	Unc	BU
2000 Proof	—	—	—	—	—	—

TRIAL STRIKES

X#	Date	Mintage	Identification	Mkt Val

X#	Date	Mintage	Identification	Mkt Val
TS1	ND(2000)	50	2 Ounce. Copper. 38.9 mm. X#MB5.	—

X#	Date	Mintage	Identification	Mkt Val

TS2	ND(2000)	50	2 Ounce. Copper. 38.9 mm. X#MB6.	—

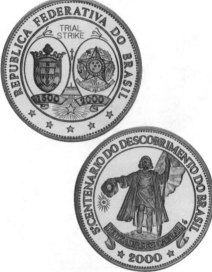

TS3	ND(2000)	50	2 Ounce. Copper. 38.9 mm. X#MB7.	—

TS4	ND(2000)	50	2 Ounce. Copper. 38.9 mm. X#MB8.	—

CEARA

STATE

COUNTERMARKED COINAGE

X# 58 20 REIS
Copper **Countermark:** "CEARA" in star **Note:** The countermark illustrated is considered false. Countermark on Brazil 20 Reis, KM#360.1.

CM Date	Host Date	Good	VG	F	VF	XF
ND(1833)	1826R	10.00	15.00	22.00	35.00	—

X# 60 2 SOLES
6.0000 g., Silver, 26 mm. **Countermark:** "CEARA" in star **Note:** Countermark on Argentina 2 Soles, KM#18.

CM Date	Host Date	Good	VG	F	VF	XF
ND(1833)	1825	20.00	30.00	50.00	75.00	—

X# 62 960 REIS
0.9030 Silver **Countermark:** "CEARA" in star **Note:** Countermark on Brazil 960 Reis, KM#307.

CM Date	Host Date	Good	VG	F	VF	XF
ND(1833)	1810-16	20.00	30.00	45.00	65.00	—

X# 64 960 REIS
0.9030 Silver **Countermark:** "CEARA" in star **Note:** Countermark on Brazil 960 Reis, KM#362.2.

CM Date	Host Date	Good	VG	F	VF	XF
ND(1833)	1819-22B	20.00	30.00	45.00	65.00	—

X# 65 960 REIS
0.8960 Silver **Countermark:** "CEARA" in star **Note:** Countermark on Brazil 960 Reis, KM#368.1.

CM Date	Host Date	Good	VG	F	VF	XF
ND(1833)	1823-28R	20.00	30.00	45.00	65.00	—

X# 66 960 REIS
0.9030 Silver **Countermark:** "CEARA" in star **Note:** Countermark on Minas Gerais 960 Reis, KM#251.2 / Potosi Mint 8 Reales, KM#73.

CM Date	Host Date	Good	VG	F	VF	XF
ND(1833)	1791-1808	35.00	50.00	65.00	100	—

X# 67 8 REALES

0.9030 Silver **Countermark:** "CEARA" in star **Note:** Countermarked on Minas Gerais 960 Reis, KM#240 / 8 Potosi Mint 8 Reales, KM#55.

CM Date	Host Date	Good	VG	F	VF	XF
ND(1833)	1773-89	—	—	—	—	—

X# 68 8 REALES

0.8960 Silver **Countermark:** "CEARA" in star **Note:** Countermark in star on Peru-Lima Mint 8 Reales, KM#106.2.

CM Date	Host Date	Good	VG	F	VF	XF
ND(1833)	1809-11	22.00	35.00	50.00	75.00	—

ICO

EMPIRE

COUNTERMARKED COINAGE

National

X# 72 80 REIS

Copper **Countermark:** IGO **Note:** Countermark on Brazil 80 Reis, KM#366.

CM Date	Host Date	Good	VG	F	VF	XF
ND(1833)	1823-31	8.00	15.00	22.00	35.00	—

X# 75 960 REIS

0.8960 Silver **Countermark:** IGO **Note:** Countermark on Brazil 960 Reis, KM#307.3.

CM Date	Host Date	Good	VG	F	VF	XF
ND(1833)	1810-18R	20.00	40.00	60.00	85.00	—

X# 77 8 REALES

0.9030 Silver **Countermark:** YCO **Note:** Countermark on Potosi Mint 8 Reales, KM#73.

CM Date	Host Date	Good	VG	F	VF	XF
ND(1833)	1791-1808	50.00	75.00	110	150	—

X# 78 8 REALES

0.9030 Silver **Countermark:** IGO **Note:** Countermark on Mexico City Mint 8 Reales, KM#110.

CM Date	Host Date	Good	VG	F	VF	XF
ND(1833)	1808-11	50.00	75.00	110	150	—

JULIANA

REPUBLIC

COUNTERMARKED COINAGE

X# 80 80 REIS

28.8400 g., Copper, 41 mm. **Countermark:** REP.JULIANA above Liberty head left **Note:** Countermark on Brazil 80 Reis, KM#366.1

CM Date	Host Date	Good	VG	F	VF	XF
1839	1829	—	—	45.00	70.00	100

X# 81 960 REIS

0.8960 Silver **Countermark:** REP.JULIANA above Liberty head left **Note:** Countermark on Brazil 960 Reis, KM#307.1.

CM Date	Host Date	Good	VG	F	VF	XF
1837	1808B-1817B	—	—	60.00	87.50	125

REPUBLIC OF PIRATINI

REPUBLIC

COUNTERMARKED COINAGE

Type I

X# 3 320 REIS
Silver **Note:** Countermark with two hands grasping a sword with Liberty Cap on point above date "1835" on Brazil 320 Reis, KM#324.2.

CM Date	Host Date	Good	VG	F	VF	XF
1835	1818-20R	10.00	18.50	25.00	42.00	—

X# 4 960 REIS
Silver **Note:** Countermark Type I on Neuva Guatemala 8 Reales, KM#53.

CM Date	Host Date	Good	VG	F	VF	XF
1835	1790-1807	32.50	55.00	80.00	125	—

X# 5 960 REIS
Silver **Note:** Countermark Type I on Peru, Lima Mint 8 Reales, KM#117.1.

CM Date	Host Date	Good	VG	F	VF	XF
1835	1811-24	20.00	35.00	50.00	80.00	—

X# 1 6400 REIS
0.9167 Gold **Note:** Countermark Type I on Brazil 6400 Reis, KM#199.

CM Date	Host Date	Good	VG	F	VF	XF
1835	1777-86	—	—	—	—	—

Type II

X# 6 20 REIS
Copper **Note:** Countermarked Type II on Brazil 20 Reis, KM#216.1.

CM Date	Host Date	Good	VG	F	VF	XF
1835	1786-99	—	—	—	—	—

X# 8 20 REIS
Copper **Note:** Countermarked on countermarked Brazil 20 Reis, KM#436.1.

CM Date	Host Date	Good	VG	F	VF	XF
1835	1823-31R	—	—	—	—	—

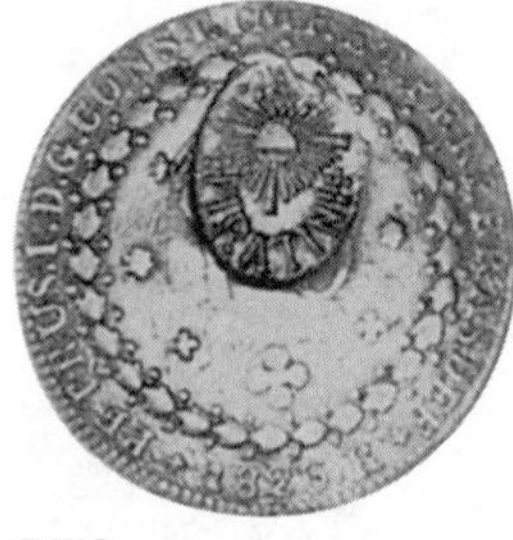

X# 7 40 REIS
Copper **Countermark:** PIRATINI **Note:** Countermark similar to Type I but with date above and countermark below sword on Brazil 40 Reis, KM#363.1.

CM Date	Host Date	Good	VG	F	VF	XF
1835	1823-31R	12.50	18.50	27.50	45.00	—

X# 10 960 REIS
Silver **Note:** Countermark Type II on Bolivia 8 Reales, KM#84.

CM Date	Host Date	Good	VG	F	VF	XF
1835	1808-25	20.00	35.00	50.00	80.00	—

X# 11 960 REIS
Silver **Note:** Countermark Type II on Brazil 960 Reis, KM#307.

CM Date	Host Date	Good	VG	F	VF	XF
1835	1810-18	20.00	40.00	60.00	—	—

X# 12 960 REIS
Silver **Note:** Countermark Type II on counterfeit Brazil 960 Reis, KM#368.1.

CM Date	Host Date	Good	VG	F	VF	XF
1835	1828R	20.00	40.00	60.00	—	—

Type III

X# 20 960 REIS
Silver **Note:** Countermark similar to Type I but sword separates date on Brazil 960 Reis, KM#368.1.

CM Date	Host Date	Good	VG	F	VF	XF
1835	1823-27R	20.00	40.00	60.00	—	—

Type IV

X# 25 8 REALES
0.9030 Silver **Note:** Countermark Type IV on countermarked Azores 1200 Reis / Mexico City Mint 8 Reales, KM#11. (Both false.)

CM Date	Host Date	Good	VG	F	VF	XF
ND(1835)	1811-1821	35.00	50.00	75.00	120	—

X# 26 20 REALES
0.9030 Silver **Countermark:** Rayed Liberty cap on straight sword held by clasped hands **Note:** Countermark Type IV on Spain, Madrid Mint 20 Reales, KM#551.2.

CM Date	Host Date	Good	VG	F	VF	XF
ND(1835)	1809-13	—	—	—	—	—

BRITISH EAST AFRICA

BRITISH ADMINISTRATION

MEDALLIC COINAGE

Pobjoy Mint Series

X# M1 CROWN
Silver **Obv:** Bust of Edward VIII left

Date	Mintage	F	VF	XF	Unc	BU
1936 Proof	—	Value: 50.00				

Richard Lobel Series

X# M2 CROWN
Bronze **Obv:** Bust of Edward VIII left **Obv. Legend:** EDWARD • VIII • KING • & • EMPEROR **Rev:** Lion standing right

Date	Mintage	F	VF	XF	Unc	BU
1936 Proof	1,000	Value: 15.00				

X# M2a CROWN
Copper-Nickel-Zinc **Obv:** Bust of Edward VIII left **Obv. Legend:** EDWARD • VIII • KING • & • EMPEROR **Rev:** Lion standing right

Date	Mintage	F	VF	XF	Unc	BU
1936 Proof	2,500	Value: 15.00				

X# M2b CROWN
0.9167 Silver **Obv:** Bust of Edward VIII left **Obv. Legend:** EDWARD • VIII • KING • & • EMPEROR **Rev:** Lion standing right

Date	Mintage	F	VF	XF	Unc	BU
1936 Proof	500	Value: 50.00				

X# M2c CROWN
Gold **Obv:** Bust of Edward VIII left **Obv. Legend:** EDWARD • VIII • KING • & • EMPEROR **Rev:** Lion standing right

Date	Mintage	F	VF	XF	Unc	BU
1936 Proof	—	Value: 500				

X# M3 SOVEREIGN
0.3750 Gold **Obv:** Bust of Edward VIII left **Obv. Legend:** EDWARD • VIII • KING • & • EMPEROR **Rev:** Lion standing left

Date	Mintage	F	VF	XF	Unc	BU
1936 Proof	250	Value: 125				

PIEFORTS

X#	Date	Mintage	Identification	Mkt Val
P1	1936	—	Crown. 0.9167 Silver. X#2b.	100

BRITISH HONDURAS

BRITISH COLONY

COUNTERMARKED COINAGE

It is generally believed that the crowned 'GR' monogram was placed on certain coins to make them acceptable as trade items with local indigenous peoples. This mark did not affect their currency status, although in light of the Revolutionary War of 1810-20 it may have been an attempt to localize and keep coins in the colony at a time when the supply of Spanish coins dwindled. This spurious Crown/'GR' countermark is believed to have been done in London ca.1915-1920. It appears on other coins also such as a Barbados penny dated 1788, Mexico Mint 8 reales dated 1797, 1/2 real dated 1774, Madrid Mint 2 reales dated 1793, Panda Potosi Mint 1/2 real dated 1808. Usually attributed to Jamaica in error. Crown over countermark in octagonal indent on English countermarked Spanish Colonial 8 Reales.

X# 3 1/2 ECU
Silver **Countermark:** GR **Note:** Crown over countermark on France 1/2 Ecu.

CM Date	Host Date	Good	VG	F	VF	XF
ND(1652)	1652	10.00	15.00	25.00	40.00	—

X# 5 ECU
Silver **Countermark:** GR **Note:** Crown over countermark on France 1 Ecu.

CM Date	Host Date	Good	VG	F	VF	XF
ND	1726	15.00	25.00	40.00	60.00	—

X# 10 8 REALES
Silver **Countermark:** GR **Note:** Market valuations are based on the English countermark being false also.

CM Date	Host Date	Good	VG	F	VF	XF
ND	1798	15.00	25.00	40.00	60.00	—

BRITISH NORTH BORNEO

BRITISH PROTECTORATE

MEDALLIC COINAGE

Richard Lobel Series

X# M1 CROWN
Bronze **Obv:** Bust of Edward VIII left **Obv. Legend:** EDWARD • VIII • KING • & • EMPEROR **Rev:** Supported arms **Rev. Legend:** BRITISH NORTH BORNEO

Date	Mintage	F	VF	XF	Unc	BU
1936 Proof	750	Value: 15.00				

X# M1a CROWN
Copper-Nickel-Zinc **Obv:** Bust of Edward VIII left **Obv. Legend:** EDWARD • VIII • KING • & • EMPEROR **Rev:** Supported arms **Rev. Legend:** BRITISH NORTH BORNEO

Date	Mintage	F	VF	XF	Unc	BU
1936 Proof	2,500	Value: 15.00				

X# M1b CROWN
0.9167 Silver **Obv:** Bust of Edward VIII left **Obv. Legend:** EDWARD • VIII • KING • & • EMPEROR **Rev:** Supported arms **Rev. Legend:** BRITISH NORTH BORNEO

Date	Mintage	F	VF	XF	Unc	BU
1936 Proof	250	Value: 50.00				

X# M1c CROWN
Gold **Obv:** Bust of Edward VIII left **Obv. Legend:** EDWARD • VIII • KING • & • EMPEROR **Rev:** Supported arms **Rev. Legend:** BRITISH NORTH BORNEO

Date	Mintage	F	VF	XF	Unc	BU
1936 Proof	—	Value: 500				

X# M2 SOVEREIGN
0.3750 Gold, 22 mm. **Obv:** Bust of Edward VIII left **Obv. Legend:** EDWARD • VIII • KING • & • EMPEROR **Rev:** Supported arms **Rev. Legend:** BRITISH NORTH BORNEO

Date	Mintage	F	VF	XF	Unc	BU
1936 Proof	250	Value: 125				

PIEFORTS

X#	Date	Mintage	Identification	Mkt Val
P1	1936	—	Crown. 0.9167 Silver. X#1b.	100

BRITISH WEST AFRICA

BRITISH COLONIES

MEDALLIC COINAGE

1972 Pobjoy Mint Series

X# M1 CROWN
33.4800 g., Silver **Subject:** Edward VIII **Obv. Legend:** EDWARD VIII BY THE GRACE OF GOD **Rev:** British lion ready to pounce

Date	Mintage	F	VF	XF	Unc	BU
1936 Proof	—	Value: 175				

X# M2 CROWN
31.2100 g., Silver **Subject:** Edward VIII **Obv:** Bust right **Obv. Legend:** EDWARD • VIII • KING • AND • EMPEROR **Rev. Designer:** British lion ready to pounce

Date	Mintage	F	VF	XF	Unc	BU
1936 Proof	—	Value: 150				

BUCK ISLAND

UNINHABITED

TOKEN COINAGE

X# TN1 1/2 BUCK
Bronze **Obv:** Island outline **Obv. Legend:** BUCK ISLAND **Rev:** Goat's head **Rev. Legend:** EIRENE

Date	Mintage	F	VF	XF	Unc	BU
ND(1958)	10,000	—	—	10.00	20.00	30.00

X# TN2 1/2 BUCK
Goldine **Obv:** Island outline **Obv. Legend:** BUCK ISLAND **Rev:** Goat's head **Rev. Legend:** EIRENE

Date	Mintage	F	VF	XF	Unc	BU
ND(1958)	Inc. above	—	—	15.00	25.00	45.00

X# TN4 BUCK
Copper-Nickel-Zinc **Obv:** Island outline **Obv. Legend:** BUCK ISLAND **Rev:** Goat's head **Rev. Legend:** EIRENE

Date	Mintage	F	VF	XF	Unc	BU
ND(1958)	350	—	—	18.00	30.00	50.00

X# TN5 BUCK

Copper-Nickel-Zinc **Obv:** Island outline **Obv. Legend:** BUCK ISLAND **Rev:** Goat's head **Rev. Legend:** EIRENE **Note:** Total mintage for this type is included in XTN1.

Date	Mintage	F	VF	XF	Unc	BU
1961	—	—	—	15.00	25.00	40.00

BULGARIA

KINGDOM

MEDALLIC COINAGE

Originally produced as a jewelry item. A similar piece with Russian legends also exists.

KM# M1 4 DUKAT

13.9600 g., 0.9860 Gold 0.4425 oz. AGW **Ruler:** Ferdinand I **Countermark:** Crown and government mark **Obv:** Military bust right **Obv. Legend:** ФЕРДИНАНДЪ I ЦАРЬ НА БЪЛГАРИЪ **Rev:** Crowned supported arms

Date	Mintage	F	VF	XF	Unc	BU
1910	—	BV	325	375	525	—
1911	—	BV	350	400	550	—
1912	—	BV	325	375	525	—
1914	—	BV	400	500	900	—
1917	—	BV	400	500	900	—
1918	—	BV	350	400	550	—
1919	—	300	400	500	900	—

Note: Values above are for holed or holed and plugged specimens; unholed specimens command 5 times the values indicated

KM# M2 4 DUKAT

13.9600 g., 0.9860 Gold 0.4425 oz. AGW **Ruler:** Boris III **Countermark:** Crown and government mark **Obv:** Military bust left **Obv. Legend:** ВОРИСЪ III ЦАРЪ НА БЪЛГАРИЪ **Rev:** Crowned supported arms

Date	Mintage	F	VF	XF	Unc	BU
ND1921	—	375	475	800	2,000	—
1926	—	375	475	800	2,000	—

Note: Values above are for holed or holed and plugged specimens; unholed specimens command 5 times the values indicated

REPUBLIC

ECU COINAGE

X# 1 25 ECU

31.1030 g., 0.9990 Silver 0.9989 oz. ASW, 38 mm. **Issuer:** Numex S.A., Madrid **Obv:** Arms **Obv. Legend:** РЕПУБЛИКА Б ЪЛГАРИЯ| **Rev:** Ancient galley, value above **Edge:** Reeded

Date	Mintage	F	VF	XF	Unc	BU
1993 Proof	8,000	Value: 40.00				

X# 2 250 ECU

31.1030 g., 0.7500 Gold 0.7500 oz. AGW, 38 mm. **Issuer:** Numex S.A., Madrid **Obv:** Arms **Obv. Legend:** РЕПУБЛИКА Б ЪЛГАРИЯ **Rev:** Ancient galley, value above **Edge:** Reeded

Date	Mintage	F	VF	XF	Unc	BU
1993 Proof	500	Value: 700				

FANTASY EURO PATTERNS

INA Series

X# Pn1 EURO CENT

4.6700 g., Copper, 16.4 mm. **Issuer:** INA **Series:** Sports **Obv:** Female broadjumping gymnast, torch below **Obv. Legend:** РЕПУБЛИКА Б ЪЛГАРИЯ **Rev:** Scales at right **Edge:** Plain

Date	Mintage	F	VF	XF	Unc	BU
2004	10,000	—	—	—	—	1.00
2004 Proof	3,000	Value: 2.00				

X# Pn1a EURO CENT

Silver, 16.4 mm. **Issuer:** INA **Series:** Sports **Obv:** Female broadjumping gymnast, torch below **Obv. Legend:** РЕПУБЛИКА Б ЪЛГАРИЯ **Rev:** Scales at right **Edge:** Plain

Date	Mintage	F	VF	XF	Unc	BU
2004 Proof	250	Value: 6.00				

X# Pn2 2 EURO CENTS

5.6300 g., Copper, 18.5 mm. **Issuer:** INA **Series:** Sports **Obv:** Female high jumping gymnast, torch below **Obv. Legend:** РЕПУБЛИКА Б ЪЛГАРИЯ **Rev:** Scales at right **Edge:** Plain

Date	Mintage	F	VF	XF	Unc	BU
2004	10,000	—	—	—	—	1.50
2004 Proof	3,000	Value: 2.50				

X# Pn2a 2 EURO CENTS

Silver, 18.5 mm. **Issuer:** INA **Series:** Sports **Obv:** Female high jumping gymnast, torch below **Obv. Legend:** РЕПУБЛИКА Б ЪЛГАРИЯ **Rev:** Scales at right **Edge:** Plain

Date	Mintage	F	VF	XF	Unc	BU
2004 Proof	250	Value: 7.00				

X# Pn3 5 EURO CENTS

7.1000 g., Copper, 21 mm. **Issuer:** INA **Series:** Sports **Obv:** Male hurdler gymnast, torch above **Obv. Legend:** РЕПУБЛИКА Б ЪЛГАРИЯ **Rev:** Scales at right **Edge:** Plain

Date	Mintage	F	VF	XF	Unc	BU
2004	10,000	—	—	—	—	2.00
2004 Proof	3,000	Value: 3.00				

X# Pn3a 5 EURO CENTS

Silver, 21 mm. **Issuer:** INA **Series:** Sports **Obv:** Male hurdler gymnast, torch above **Obv. Legend:** РЕПУБЛИКА Б ЪЛГАРИЯ **Rev:** Scales at right **Edge:** Plain

Date	Mintage	F	VF	XF	Unc	BU
2004 Proof	250	Value: 8.50				

X# Pn4 10 EURO CENTS

5.9400 g., Goldine, 19.4 mm. **Series:** Sports **Obv:** Male archer right, torch behind **Obv. Legend:** РЕПУБЛИКА Б ЪЛГАРИЯ **Rev:** Dove, value within wreath of clasped hands **Edge:** Plain

Date	Mintage	F	VF	XF	Unc	BU
2004	10,000	—	—	—	—	2.50
2004 Proof	3,000	Value: 3.50				

X# Pn4a 10 EURO CENTS

Silver, 19.4 mm. **Issuer:** INA **Series:** Sports **Obv:** Male archer right, torch behind **Obv. Legend:** РЕПУБЛИКА| Б ЪЛГАРИ Я| **Rev:** Dove, value within wreath of clasped hands **Edge:** Plain

Date	Mintage	F	VF	XF	Unc	BU
2004 Proof	250	Value: 10.00				

X# Pn5 20 EURO CENTS

7.6600 g., Goldine, 22.3 mm. **Issuer:** INA **Series:** Sports **Obv:** Sailboat, torch at right **Obv. Legend:** РЕПУБЛИКА Б ЪЛГАРИЯ **Rev:** Dove, value within wreath of clasped hands **Edge:** Plain

Date	Mintage	F	VF	XF	Unc	BU
2004	10,000	—	—	—	—	3.00
2004 Proof	3,000	Value: 4.25				

X# Pn5a 20 EURO CENTS

Silver, 22.3 mm. **Issuer:** INA **Series:** Sports **Obv:** Sailboat, torch at right **Obv. Legend:** РЕПУБЛИКА Б ЪЛГАРИЯ **Rev:** Dove, value within wreath of clasped hands **Edge:** Plain

Date	Mintage	F	VF	XF	Unc	BU
2004 Proof	250	Value: 12.50				

X# Pn6 50 EURO CENTS

9.5400 g., Goldine, 24.4 mm. **Issuer:** INA **Series:** Sports **Obv:** Weightlifter **Obv. Legend:** РЕПУБЛИКА Б ЪЛГАРИЯ **Rev:** Dove, value within wreath of clasped hands **Edge:** Plain

Date	Mintage	F	VF	XF	Unc	BU
2004	10,000	—	—	—	—	3.50
2004 Proof	3,000	Value: 5.00				

X# Pn6a 50 EURO CENTS

Silver, 24.4 mm. **Issuer:** INA **Series:** Sports **Obv:** Weightlifter **Obv. Legend:** РЕПУБЛИКА Б ЪЛГАРИЯ **Rev:** Dove, value within wreath of clasped hands **Edge:** Plain

Date	Mintage	F	VF	XF	Unc	BU
2004 Proof	250	Value: 15.00				

X# Pn7 EURO

8.4400 g., Bi-Metallic Goldine ring, Copper-Nickel center, 23.1 mm. **Issuer:** INA **Series:** Sports **Obv:** Hand putting basketball in hoop; torch at right **Obv. Legend:** РЕПУБЛИКА Б ЪЛГАРИЯ **Rev:** Large value "1", woman walking right within a ring **Edge:** Plain

Date	Mintage	F	VF	XF	Unc	BU
2004	10,000	—	—	—	—	5.50
2004 Proof	3,000	Value: 7.00				

X# Pn7a EURO

Bi-Metallic Goldine center in Silver ring, 23.1 mm. **Issuer:** INA **Series:** Sports **Obv:** Hand putting basketball in hoop **Obv. Legend:** РЕПУБЛИКА Б ЪЛГАРИЯ **Rev:** Large value "1", woman walking right within a ring **Edge:** Plain

Date	Mintage	F	VF	XF	Unc	BU
2004 Proof	250	Value: 22.50				

X# Pn8 2 EURO

Bi-Metallic Copper-Nickel ring, Goldine center **Issuer:** INA **Series:** Sports **Obv:** Cyclist right **Obv. Legend:** РЕПУБЛИКА БЪЛГАРИЯ **Rev:** Large value "2", woman walking right within ring **Edge:** Plain

Date	Mintage	F	VF	XF	Unc	BU
2004	10,000	—	—	—	—	7.00
2004 Proof	3,000	Value: 9.00				

X# Pn8a 2 EURO

Bi-Metallic Goldine center in Silver ring **Issuer:** INA **Series:** Sports **Obv:** Cyclist right **Obv. Legend:** РЕПУБЛИКА| Б ЪЛГАРИ Я| **Rev:** Large value "2", woman walking right within ring **Edge:** Plain

Date	Mintage	F	VF	XF	Unc	BU
2004 Proof	250	Value: 28.50				

X# Pn9 5 EURO

25.6000 g., Goldine, 36.2 mm. **Issuer:** INA **Series:** Sports **Subject:** Boxing **Obv:** Torch above two boxers in ring **Obv. Legend:** РЕПУБЛИКА Б ЪЛГАРИЯ **Rev:** Woman horseback right **Edge:** Plain

Date	Mintage	F	VF	XF	Unc	BU
2004 Proof	3,000	Value: 12.00				

X# Pn9a 5 EURO

Silver, 36.2 mm. **Issuer:** INA **Series:** Sports **Subject:** Boxing **Obv:** Torch above two boxers in ring **Obv. Legend:** РЕПУБЛИКА Б ЪЛГАРИЯ **Rev:** Woman horseback right **Edge:** Plain

Date	Mintage	F	VF	XF	Unc	BU
2004 Proof	250	Value: 40.00				

X# Pn10 EURO CENT

Copper Plated Steel **Edge:** Plain

Date	Mintage	F	VF	XF	Unc	BU
2004	7,000	—	—	—	—	1.00

X# Pn11 2 EURO CENTS

Copper Plated Steel **Edge:** Plain

Date	Mintage	F	VF	XF	Unc	BU
2004	7,000	—	—	—	—	1.50

X# Pn12 5 EURO CENTS

Copper Plated Steel **Edge:** Plain

Date	Mintage	F	VF	XF	Unc	BU
2004	7,000	—	—	—	—	2.00

X# Pn13 10 EURO CENTS

Goldine **Edge:** Plain

Date	Mintage	F	VF	XF	Unc	BU
2004	7,000	—	—	—	—	2.50

X# Pn14 20 EURO CENTS

Goldine **Edge:** Plain

Date	Mintage	F	VF	XF	Unc	BU
2004	7,000	—	—	—	—	3.00

X# Pn15 50 EURO CENTS

Goldine **Edge:** Plain

Date	Mintage	F	VF	XF	Unc	BU
2004	7,000	—	—	—	—	3.50

X# Pn16 EUROP

Bi-Metallic **Obv:** Scale **Rev:** Large value "1" on outlined map of Bulgaria **Edge:** Plain

Date	Mintage	F	VF	XF	Unc	BU
2004	7,000	—	—	—	—	5.50

X# Pn17 2 EUROP

Bi-Metallic **Obv:** Bust of Queen facing 3/4 right **Edge:** Plain

Date	Mintage	F	VF	XF	Unc	BU
2004	7,000	—	—	—	—	7.50

ESSAIS

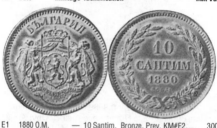

X#	Date	Mintage	Identification	Mkt Val
E1	1880 O.M.	—	10 Santim. Bronze. Prev. KM#E2.	300
E2	1887 A.B.	—	10 Santim. Bronze. Prev. KM#E3.	400

PIEFORTS

X#	Date	Mintage	Identification	Mkt Val
P1	2004	10,000	5 Euro. Goldine. X#Pn9.	—
P2	2004	175	5 Euro. Silver. X#Pn9a.	—

MINT SETS

X#	Date	Mintage	Identification	Issue Price	Mkt Val
XMS1	2004 (8)	10,000	X#Pn1-Pn8	—	26.00
XMS2	2004 (8)	7,000	X#Pn10-Pn17	—	26.00

PROOF SETS

X#	Date	Mintage	Identification	Issue Price	Mkt Val
XPS1	2004 (9)	3,000	X#Pn1-Pn9	—	45.00
XPS2	2004 (9)	250	X#Pn1a-Pn9a	—	150

BURKINA FASO

REPUBLIC

MEDALLIC BULLION COINAGE

X# MB1 OUNCE

31.1000 g., 0.9990 Silver 0.9988 oz. ASW, 38.5 mm. **Issuer:** Burkina Faso Numismatic Agency **Obv:** Arms **Obv. Inscription:** LA PATRE OU LA MORT... **Rev:** Eagle's head left and right **Edge:** Reeded

Date	Mintage	F	VF	XF	Unc	BU
1990 Proof	300	Value: 115				

X# MB1a OUNCE

31.1000 g., 0.9990 Gold 0.9988 oz. AGW, 38.5 mm. **Issuer:** Burkina Faso Numismatic Agency **Obv:** Arms **Obv. Inscription:** LA PATRE OU LA MORT... **Rev:** Eagle's head left and right **Edge:** Reeded

Date	Mintage	F	VF	XF	Unc	BU
1990 Proof	3	Value: 1,500				

X# MB1b OUNCE

Copper, 38.5 mm. **Issuer:** Burkina Faso Numismatic Agency **Obv:** Arms **Obv. Inscription:** LA PATRE OU LA MORT... **Rev:** Eagle's head left and right **Edge:** Reeded

Date	Mintage	F	VF	XF	Unc	BU
1990 Proof	30	Value: 65.00				

BURMA

UNION

COUNTERMARKED COINAGE

X# 10 8 REALES

27.0700 g., 0.7859 Silver 0.6840 oz. ASW **Note:** Countermark balance scale on various Mexico 8 Reales.

CM Date	Host Date	Good	VG	F	VF	XF
ND	ND(1970s)	10.00	13.50	18.50	25.00	—

BULLION COINAGE

Irrawaddy Counting House - Rangoon

X# 15 5 TAELS

156.3000 g., 0.9990 Silver 5.0199 oz. ASW **Obv:** Scales, anchor at lower left and lower right in oval stamp **Shape:** Rectangular **Note:** Size: 29 x 47mm.

Date	Mintage	F	VF	XF	Unc	BU
ND(1970s)	—	75.00	95.00	—	—	—

X# 14 5 TAELS

154.0000 g., 0.9990 Silver 4.9461 oz. ASW **Obv:** Scales, star at lower left and lower right in oval stamp **Shape:** Rectangular **Note:** Size: 50 x 30.

Date	Mintage	F	VF	XF	Unc	BU
ND(1970s)	—	75.00	95.00	—	—	—

X# 16 5 TAELS

0.9990 Silver **Obv:** Scales,, star at lower left and lower right in oval stamp **Shape:** Rectangular **Note:** Size: 30 x 53mm.

Date	Mintage	F	VF	XF	Unc	BU
ND(1970s)	—	75.00	95.00	—	—	—

X# 17 10 RUPEE

0.9000 Silver **Note:** Similar to 5 Taels, X15.

Date	Mintage	F	VF	XF	Unc	BU
ND	—	70.00	90.00	—	—	—

MEDALLIC COINAGE

Patriotic Rebel Liberation Army Issues

X# M3 MU

2.0000 g., 1.0000 Gold 0.0643 oz. AGW **Obv:** Legend around peacock **Obv. Legend:** UNION OF BURMA GOVERNMENT 1970-1971 **Rev. Legend:** U NU in star with SHWE MUZI below **Note:** Prev. KM#43.

Date	Mintage	F	VF	XF	Unc	BU
1970-71	—	—	—	—	125	200

X# M4 2 MU

4.0000 g., 1.0000 Gold 0.1286 oz. AGW **Note:** Prev. KM#44.

Date	Mintage	F	VF	XF	Unc	BU
1970-71	—	—	—	—	245	350

X# M5 4 MU

8.0000 g., 1.0000 Gold 0.2572 oz. AGW **Note:** Prev. KM#45.

Date	Mintage	F	VF	XF	Unc	BU
1970-71	—	—	—	—	475	550

SHAN STATES

REBEL COINAGE

Issued by guerilla rebels about 1981

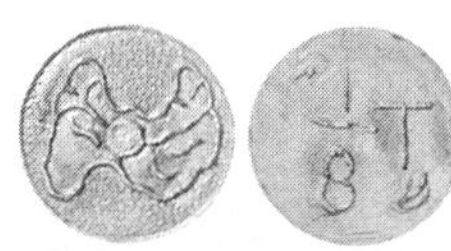

X# 1 1/8 TICAL
1.9000 g., Gold **Obv:** Crude outline map of Rebel held territories

Date	Mintage	F	VF	XF	Unc	BU
ND(c.1981)	—	—	—	100	150	—

X# 2 1/4 TICAL
3.8000 g., Gold **Obv:** Crude outline map of Rebel held territories

Date	Mintage	F	VF	XF	Unc	BU
ND(c.1981)	—	—	—	125	175	—

BRITISH COLONY

MEDALLIC COINAGE

Richard Lobel Series

X# M20 CROWN
Bronze **Subject:** Edward VIII **Obv:** Bust of Edward VIII facing left **Obv. Legend:** EDWARD • VIII • KING • & • EMPEROR **Rev:** Peacock standing with feathers fanned

Date	Mintage	F	VF	XF	Unc	BU
1936 Proof	750	Value: 20.00				

X# M20a CROWN
Copper-Nickel-Zinc **Subject:** Edward VIII **Obv:** Bust of Edward VIII facing left **Obv. Legend:** EDWARD • VIII • KING • & • EMPEROR **Rev:** Peacock standing with feathers fanned

Date	Mintage	F	VF	XF	Unc	BU
1936 Proof	2,100	Value: 20.00				

X# M20b CROWN
0.9167 Silver **Subject:** Edward VIII **Obv:** Bust of Edward VIII facing left **Obv. Legend:** EDWARD • VIII • KING • & • EMPEROR **Rev:** Peacock standing with feathers fanned

Date	Mintage	F	VF	XF	Unc	BU
1936 Proof	200	Value: 50.00				

X# M20c CROWN
Gold **Subject:** Edward VIII **Obv:** Bust of Edward VIII facing left **Obv. Legend:** EDWARD • VIII • KING • & • EMPEROR **Rev:** Peacock standing with feathers fanned

Date	Mintage	F	VF	XF	Unc	BU
1936 Proof	—	Value: 500				

X# M21 SOVEREIGN
0.3750 Gold **Subject:** Edward VIII

Date	Mintage	F	VF	XF	Unc	BU
1936 Proof	150	Value: 125				

ESSAIS

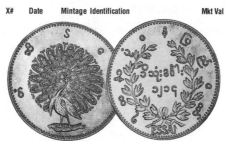

X#	Date	Mintage	Identification	Mkt Val
E1	CS1214	200	Kyat. Silver. 31mm.	25.00
E2	CS1214	40	Kyat. Copper.	15.00
E3	CS1214	15	Kyat. 0.7500 Gold.	—

PIEFORTS

X#	Date	Mintage	Identification	Mkt Val
P1	1936	—	Crown. 0.9167 Silver. X#20b.	100

TRIAL STRIKES

X#	Date	Mintage	Identification	Issue Price	Mkt Val
TSE1	CS1214	—	Kyat. Brass. A modern fantasy issue of "unknown" origin struck c.1970 without any government authorization for obvious confusion of the numismatic community.	—	22.50

BURUNDI

KINGDOM

MEDALLIC COINAGE

X# M1 10 FRANCS
1.5000 g., Billon **Subject:** 50th Anniversary - Reign of Mwambusta IV **Obv:** Portrait of late King Mwambutsa IV

Date	Mintage	F	VF	XF	Unc	BU
ND(1966) Prooflike	6,000	—	—	—	32.50	—

X# M6 10 FRANCS
1.5000 g., Billon **Subject:** Coronation of Ntare V **Obv:** Portrait of Ntare V

Date	Mintage	F	VF	XF	Unc	BU
ND(1966) Prooflike	6,000	—	—	—	35.00	—

X# M2 25 FRANCS
3.2000 g., Billon **Subject:** 50th Anniversary - Reign of Mwambutsa IV **Obv:** Portrait of late King Mwambutsa IV

Date	Mintage	F	VF	XF	Unc	BU
ND(1966) Prooflike	6,000	—	—	—	37.50	—

X# M7 25 FRANCS
3.2000 g., Billon **Subject:** Coronation of Ntare V **Obv:** Portrait of Ntare V

Date	Mintage	F	VF	XF	Unc	BU
ND(1966) Prooflike	6,000	—	—	—	40.00	—

X# M3 50 FRANCS
5.2000 g., Billon **Subject:** 50th Anniversary - Reign of Mwambutsa IV **Obv:** Portrait of late King Mwambutsa IV

Date	Mintage	F	VF	XF	Unc	BU
ND(1966) Prooflike	6,000	—	—	—	42.50	—

X# M8 50 FRANCS
5.2000 g., Billon **Subject:** Coronation of Ntare V **Obv:** Portrait of Ntare V

Date	Mintage	F	VF	XF	Unc	BU
ND(1966) Prooflike	6,000	—	—	—	45.00	—

X# M4 100 FRANCS
10.3000 g., Billon **Subject:** 50th Anniversary - Reign of Mwambutsa IV **Obv:** Portrait of late King Mwambutsa IV

Date	Mintage	F	VF	XF	Unc	BU
ND(1966) Prooflike	16,000	—	—	—	48.50	—

X# M9 100 FRANCS
10.3000 g., Billon **Subject:** Coronation of Ntare V **Obv:** Portrait of Ntare V

Date	Mintage	F	VF	XF	Unc	BU
ND(1966) Prooflike	16,000	—	—	—	50.00	—

X# M5 500 FRANCS
Billon **Subject:** 50th Anniversary - Reign of Mwambutsa IV **Obv:** Portrait of late King Mwambutsa IV

Date	Mintage	F	VF	XF	Unc	BU
ND(1966) Prooflike	—	—	—	—	80.00	—

X# M10 500 FRANCS
Billon **Subject:** Coronation of Ntare V **Obv:** Portrait of Ntare V

Date	Mintage	F	VF	XF	Unc	BU
ND(1966) Prooflike	—	—	—	—	90.00	—

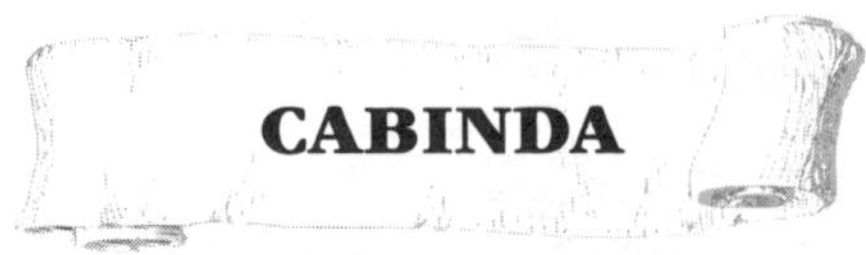

CABINDA

GOVERNMENT IN EXILE

STANDARD COINAGE

X# 1 1 CENTAVO
3.5000 g., Brass, 18 mm. **Subject:** Exile Issue **Obv:** Coat of arms **Rev:** Shrimp **Edge:** Reeded

Date	Mintage	F	VF	XF	Unc	BU
2001	—	—	—	—	0.75	1.00

X# 11 2 CENTAVOS
4.6100 g., Copper-Plated-Steel, 20.05 mm. **Obv:** National arms **Rev:** Sea shell **Edge:** Plain **Shape:** Square

Date	Mintage	F	VF	XF	Unc	BU
2006	—	—	—	—	1.50	2.00

X# 2 5 CENTAVOS
4.3000 g., Brass, 20 mm. **Obv:** Coat of arms **Rev:** Jellyfish **Edge:** Reeded

Date	Mintage	F	VF	XF	Unc	BU
2001	—	—	—	—	1.50	2.00

X# 3 10 CENTAVOS
5.5000 g., Copper-Nickel Clad Copper, 22 mm. **Obv:** Coat of arms **Rev:** Squid **Edge:** Reeded

Date	Mintage	F	VF	XF	Unc	BU
2001	—	—	—	—	2.00	2.50

X# 12 25 CENTAVOS
5.0300 g., Nickel-Clad Steel, 24.1 x 24 mm. **Obv:** National arms **Rev:** Fish **Edge:** Plain **Shape:** Six-sided

Date	Mintage	F	VF	XF	Unc	BU
2006	—	—	—	—	2.50	3.00

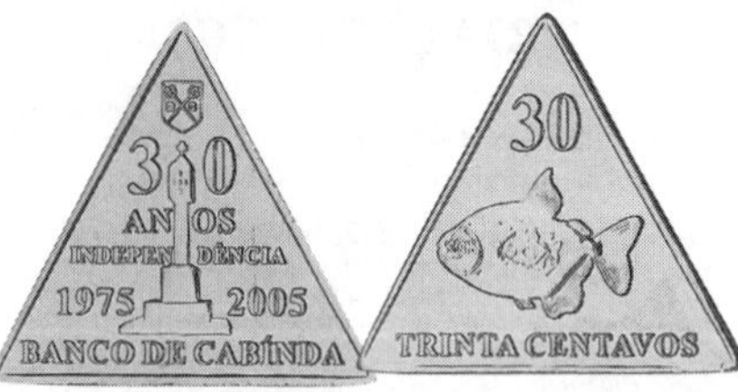

X# 9 30 CENTAVOS
5.9300 g., Copper-Nickel, 30 mm. **Subject:** 30th Anniversary of Independence **Obv:** Monument **Rev:** Fish **Edge:** Plain **Shape:** Triangle

Date	Mintage	F	VF	XF	Unc	BU
ND (2005)	—	—	—	—	6.50	7.50

X# 4 50 CENTAVOS
6.4400 g., Copper-Nickel Clad Copper, 23.9 mm. **Obv:** Coat of arms **Rev:** Stingray **Edge:** Reeded

Date	Mintage	F	VF	XF	Unc	BU
2001	—	—	—	—	2.50	3.00

X# 5 1 ESCUDO CONVERTIVEL
8.1400 g., Bi-Metallic Copper center in Brass ring, 25.9 mm. **Obv:** Coat of arms **Rev:** Fish **Edge:** Plain

Date	Mintage	F	VF	XF	Unc	BU
2003	—	—	—	—	4.00	5.00

X# 6 2.50 ESCUDO CONVERTIVEL
8.9000 g., Bi-Metallic Brass center in Copper-Nickel ring, 28.1 mm. **Obv:** Coat of arms **Rev:** Fish **Edge:** Plain

Date	Mintage	F	VF	XF	Unc	BU
2003	—	—	—	—	6.00	7.00

X# 7 5 ESCUDO CONVERTIVEL
10.3600 g., Bi-Metallic Copper-Nickel center in Brass ring, 30 mm. **Obv:** Coat of arms **Rev:** Ramora fish **Edge:** Plain

Date	Mintage	F	VF	XF	Unc	BU
2005	—	—	—	—	10.00	12.00

X# 10 5 ESCUDO CONVERTIVEL
10.3100 g., Bi-Metallic Copper-Nickel center in Brass ring, 29.6 mm. **Obv:** Monument **Rev:** Many fish above reef **Edge:** Plain **Subject:** 30th Anniversary of Independence

Date	Mintage	F	VF	XF	Unc	BU
ND(2005)	—	—	—	—	10.00	12.00

X# 8 7-1/2 ESCUDO CONVERTIVEL
35.2200 g., Brass, 60.2 x 30.5 mm. **Subject:** FAO **Obv:** Coat of arms , value and dates **Rev:** Fish, pig and rooster above produce **Edge:** Plain **Shape:** rectangle

Date	Mintage	F	VF	XF	Unc	BU
ND (2005)	—	—	—	—	14.00	16.00

X# 13 10 ESCUDOS CONVERTIVEL
46.8600 g., Bi-Metallic Copper-Nickel center in Brass ring, 49.9 mm. **Obv:** Swordfish in value **Rev:** Twelve Cabindan coin designs **Subject:** 5th Anniversary of Cabindan coinage **Edge:** Reeded

Date	Mintage	F	VF	XF	Unc	BU
ND (2006)	—	—	—	—	27.00	30.00

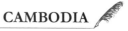

CAMBODIA

KINGDOM

TICAL COINAGE

X# 1 1/8 TICAL (1 Fuang)
Silver **Note:** A very deceptive counterfeit.

Date	Mintage	F	VF	XF	Unc	BU
ND	—	—	—	—	6.00	—

X# 1a 1/8 TICAL (1 Fuang)
Copper

Date	Mintage	F	VF	XF	Unc	BU
ND	—	—	—	—	10.00	—

X# 1b 1/8 TICAL (1 Fuang)
Gold

Date	Mintage	F	VF	XF	Unc	BU
ND	—	—	—	—	75.00	—

ESSAIS

X# E2 5 CENTIMES
Bronze **Obv:** Large bust, E left of truncation **Note:** Prev. KM#E1.

Date	Mintage	F	VF	XF	Unc	BU
1860 Proof	—	Value: 125				

X# E3 10 CENTIMES
Bronze **Obv:** Small bust, ESSAI below truncation **Note:** Prev. KM#E2.

Date	Mintage	F	VF	XF	Unc	BU
1860 Proof	—	Value: 175				

X# E3a 10 CENTIMES
Silver **Note:** Prev. KM#E2a.

Date	Mintage	F	VF	XF	Unc	BU
1860	110	Value: 400				

X# E4 10 CENTIMES
Bronze **Obv:** Large bust, E left of truncation **Note:** Prev. KM#EA3.

Date	Mintage	F	VF	XF	Unc	BU
1860 Proof	—	Value: 150				

X# E5 25 CENTIMES
Silver **Note:** Prev. KM#E3.

Date	Mintage	F	VF	XF	Unc	BU
1860 Proof	—	Value: 250				

X# E6 50 CENTIMES
Silver **Note:** Prev. KM#E4.

Date	Mintage	F	VF	XF	Unc	BU
1860 Proof	—	Value: 300				

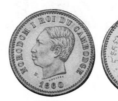

X# E7 FRANC
Silver **Note:** Prev. KM#E5.

Date	Mintage	F	VF	XF	Unc	BU
1860 Proof	—	Value: 400				

X# E8 2 FRANCS
Silver **Note:** Prev. KM#E6.

Date	Mintage	F	VF	XF	Unc	BU
1860 Proof	—	Value: 600				

X# E9 4 FRANCS
Silver **Note:** Prev. KM#E7.

Date	Mintage	F	VF	XF	Unc	BU
1860 Proof	—	Value: 1,000				

X# E10 PIASTRE
Silver **Note:** Prev. KM#E8.

Date	Mintage	F	VF	XF	Unc	BU
1860 Proof	—	Value: 5,000				

PATTERNS

Including off metal strikes

X# Pn1 10 CENTIMES
Gold **Ruler:** Norodom I **Edge:** Plain **Note:** Prev. KM#Pn3.

Date	Mintage	F	VF	XF	Unc	BU
1860 Rare	—	—	—	—	—	—

MEDALLIC COINAGE

X# 1.2 CENTIME
Bronze **Note:** Previously KM#43.2

Date	Mintage	F	VF	XF	Unc	BU
1860 Restrike	—	—	12.00	35.00	75.00	—

X# 1.3 CENTIME
Bronze **Note:** Previously KM#43.3, believed to be counterfeit.

Date	Mintage	F	VF	XF	Unc	BU
1860	—	15.00	40.00	75.00	150	—

X# 2 5 CENTIMES
Bronze **Note:** Prev. KM#42.1 or 42.2.

Date	Mintage	F	VF	XF	Unc	BU
1860	11,467,000	5.00	12.00	35.00	75.00	—
1860 Proof	—	Value: 200				
1860 Restrike	—	—	15.00	30.00	75.00	—

X# 2a 5 CENTIMES
Bronze **Note:** Prev. KM#P1. Piefort, double thickness.

Date	Mintage	F	VF	XF	Unc	BU
1860	110	—	—	—	300	—

X# 2b 5 CENTIMES
Gold **Note:** Prev. KM#Pn3.

Date	Mintage	F	VF	XF	Unc	BU
1860	—	—	—	—	—	—

X# 3 10 CENTIMES
Bronze **Note:** Prev. KM#43.1 or 43.2.

Date	Mintage	F	VF	XF	Unc	BU
1860	10,267,000	6.00	15.00	45.00	95.00	—
1860 Proof	—	Value: 300				
1860 Restrike	—	—	18.00	35.00	85.00	—

X# 3a 10 CENTIMES
Bronze **Note:** Prev. KM#P2. Piefort, double thickness.

Date	Mintage	F	VF	XF	Unc	BU
1860	110	—	—	—	400	—

X# 3b 10 CENTIMES
Gold **Note:** Prev. KM#Pn5.

Date	Mintage	F	VF	XF	Unc	BU
1860	—	—	—	—	—	—

X# 4a 20 CENTIMES
Silver **Note:** Prev. KM#P3. Piefort, double thickness.

Date	Mintage	F	VF	XF	Unc	BU
1860	—	—	—	—	600	—

X# 4 25 CENTIMES
1.2500 g., 0.9000 Silver 0.0362 oz. ASW
Ruler: Norodom I **Note:** Prev. KM#44.1.

Date	Mintage	VG	F	VF	XF	Unc
1860	—	—	10.00	30.00	100	250
1860 Proof	—	Value: 700				
1860 Restrike	—	—	—	15.00	30.00	75.00

X# 4b 25 CENTIMES
Gold **Note:** Prev. KM#Pn6.

Date	Mintage	F	VF	XF	Unc	BU
1860	—	—	—	—	—	—

X# 5 50 CENTIMES
2.5000 g., 0.9000 Silver 0.0723 oz. ASW **Note:** Prev. KM#45.1 or 45.2.

Date	Mintage	F	VF	XF	Unc	BU
1860	—	20.00	60.00	125	300	—
1860 Proof	—	Value: 800				
1860 Restrike	—	—	20.00	40.00	100	—

X# 5a 50 CENTIMES
Silver **Note:** Prev. KM#P4. Piefort, double thickness.

Date	Mintage	F	VF	XF	Unc	BU
1860	—	—	—	—	—	—

X# 5b 50 CENTIMES
Gold **Note:** Prev. KM#Pn7.

Date	Mintage	F	VF	XF	Unc	BU
1860	—	—	—	—	—	—

X# 6 FRANC
Silver **Ruler:** Norodom I **Note:** Prev. KM#46.

Date	Mintage	F	VF	XF	Unc	BU
1860	—	—	70.00	125	300	—
1860 Proof	—	Value: 650				
1860 Restrike	—	—	35.00	60.00	125	—

X# 6a FRANC
Silver **Note:** Prev. KM#P5. Piefort, double thickness.

Date	Mintage	F	VF	XF	Unc	BU
1860	—	—	—	—	900	—

X# 6b FRANC
Gold **Note:** Prev. KM#Pn8.

Date	Mintage	F	VF	XF	Unc	BU
1860	—	—	—	—	—	—

X# 7 2 FRANCS
Silver **Ruler:** Norodom I **Note:** Prev. KM#47.

Date	Mintage	F	VF	XF	Unc	BU
1860	—	—	100	200	400	—
1860 Proof	—	Value: 750				
1860 Restrike	—	—	40.00	75.00	—	—

X# 7a 2 FRANCS
Silver **Note:** Prev. KM#P6. Piefort, double thickness.

Date	Mintage	F	VF	XF	Unc	BU
1860	—	—	—	—	850	—

X# 7b 2 FRANCS
Gold **Note:** Prev. KM#Pn9.

Date	Mintage	F	VF	XF	Unc	BU
1860	—	—	—	—	—	—

X# 8 4 FRANCS
20.0000 g., 0.9000 Silver 0.5787 oz. ASW **Note:** Prev. KM#48.1 or 48.2.

Date	Mintage	F	VF	XF	Unc	BU
1860	—	85.00	225	375	700	—
1860 Proof	—	Value: 2,000				
1860 Restrike	—	—	70.00	100	225	—

X# 8a 4 FRANCS
Silver **Note:** Prev. KM#P7. Piefort, double thickness.

Date	Mintage	F	VF	XF	Unc	BU
1860	—	—	—	—	—	—

X# 8b 4 FRANCS
Gold **Note:** Prev. KM#Pn10.

Date	Mintage	F	VF	XF	Unc	BU
1860	—	—	—	—	2,250	—

X# 9 PIASTRE
27.0000 g., 0.9000 Silver 0.7812 oz. ASW **Note:** Prev. KM#49.

Date	Mintage	F	VF	XF	Unc	BU
1860	—	325	650	1,400	2,750	—
1860 Proof	—	Value: 3,250				

X# 9a PIASTRE
Silver **Note:** Prev. KM#P8. Piefort, double thickness.

Date	Mintage	F	VF	XF	Unc	BU
1860	—	—	—	—	6,000	—

X# 9b PIASTRE
Gold **Note:** Prev. KM#Pn11.

Date	Mintage	F	VF	XF	Unc	BU
1860	—	—	—	—	—	—

TEST COINAGE

X# T1 TEST COIN
25.0000 g., Silver **Ruler:** Norodom I **Rev:** St. Michael slaying the devil **Note:** Struck in Brussels, Belgium by Menning Brothers. Inscribed "Test of the Money Press of the King of Cambodia."

Date	Mintage	F	VF	XF	Unc	BU
1875	—	—	—	550	850	—

X# T2 TEST COIN
25.0000 g., Silver **Ruler:** Norodom I **Rev:** St. Michael slaying the devil **Edge:** Plain **Note:** Struck in Brussels, Belgium by Menning Brothers. Inscribed "Test of the Money Press of the King of Cambodia."

Date	Mintage	F	VF	XF	Unc	BU
1875	—	—	—	550	850	—

X# T3 TEST COIN
Bronze **Ruler:** Norodom I **Rev:** St. Michael slaying the devil **Note:** Struck in Brussels, Belgium by Menning Brothers. Inscribed "Test of the Money Press of the King of Cambodia."

Date	Mintage	F	VF	XF	Unc	BU
1875	—	—	—	250	400	—

X# T4 TEST COIN
Brass **Ruler:** Norodom I **Rev:** St. Michael slaying the devil **Note:** Struck in Brussels, Belgium by Menning Brothers. Inscribed "Test of the Money Press of the King of Cambodia."

Date	Mintage	F	VF	XF	Unc	BU
1875	—	—	—	250	400	—

X# T5 TEST COIN
Copper **Ruler:** Norodom I **Rev:** St. Michael slaying the devil **Note:** Struck in Brussels, Belgium by Menning Brothers. Inscribed "Test of the Money Press of the King of Cambodia."

Date	Mintage	F	VF	XF	Unc	BU
1875	—	—	—	250	400	—

CAMELOT

KINGDOM

FANTASY COINAGE

Issued by the Shire Post Mint.

X# 1 DOUBLE NUMMUS
5.5000 g., Copper **Ruler:** Arthur Pendragon **Obv:** Bust left, radiate and draped **Obv. Legend:** ARTORIVS DVX BELLORVM BRIT **Rev:** Winged victory advancing left holding wreath **Rev. Legend:** MONS BADONIS / PCAM

Date	Mintage	F	VF	XF	Unc	BU
ND	200	—	—	4.00	—	—

X# 3 SILIQUA
2.4000 g., 0.9000 Silver 0.0694 oz. ASW **Ruler:** Arthur Pendragon **Obv:** Bust right, radiate and draped **Obv. Legend:** ARTORIVS DVX BELLORVM BRIT **Rev:** Victory advancing left holding wreath **Rev. Legend:** MONS BADONIS / PCAM

Date	Mintage	F	VF	XF	Unc	BU
ND	500	—	—	12.00	—	—

X# 5 3 SCRIPULA
3.3000 g., 0.9167 Gold 0.0973 oz. AGW **Ruler:** Arthur Pendragon **Obv:** Bust right, radiate and draped **Obv. Legend:** ARTORIUS DVX BELLORUM BRIT **Rev:** Victory advancing left holding wreath **Rev. Legend:** MONS BADONIS / PCAM

Date	Mintage	F	VF	XF	Unc	BU
ND	12	—	—	—	150	—

CANADA

CONFEDERATION

MEDALLIC COINAGE - INA ISSUE

X# M17 50 CENTS
13.7000 g., Copper-Nickel, 29.3 mm. **Ruler:** Edward VIII **Obv:** Head left **Obv. Legend:** EDWARDVS VIII D:G:BR: OMN:REX **Rev:** Crowned supported arms **Rev. Legend:** CANADA **Edge:** Plain

Date	Mintage	F	VF	XF	Unc	BU
1937 Proof	—	—	—	—	—	—

X# M6 20 DOLLARS
24.8600 g., Silver Gilt, 38.6 mm. **Ruler:** Elizabeth II **Obv:** Tiara bust right **Obv. Legend:** ELIZABETH II - D G REGINA **Rev:** Crowned arms and supported arms **Rev. Inscription:** CANADIAN CENTENNIAL / GOLD COIN MONUMENT / SUDBURY - CANADA
Note: Purpose was for replacing medallion in proof sets as it was illegal to import the regular $20 gold proof into the USA.

Date	Mintage	F	VF	XF	Unc	BU
1967	—	—	—	—	—	32.50

MEDALLIC COINAGE - RICHARD LOBEL SERIES

X# M21 SOVEREIGN
Gold, 22 mm. **Ruler:** Edward VIII **Obv:** Bust left, dates below **Obv. Legend:** EDWARD • VIII • KING • E • EMPEROR **Rev:** Beaver right, maple leaf at left and right **Rev. Legend:** CANADA **Edge:** Plain

Date	Mintage	F	VF	XF	Unc	BU
1987 Proof	3	Value: 600				

X# M20 DOLLAR
0.9167 Silver, 38 mm. **Obv:** Bust left, dates below **Obv. Legend:** EDWARD • VIII • KING • E • EMPEROR **Rev:** Beaver right, maple leaf at left and right **Rev. Legend:** CANADA **Edge:** Plain

Date	Mintage	F	VF	XF	Unc	BU
1987 Proof	50	Value: 60.00				

X# M20a DOLLAR
20.3000 g., Copper-Nickel, 38 mm. **Ruler:** Edward VIII **Obv:** Bust left, dates below **Obv. Legend:** EDWARD • VIII • KING • E • EMPEROR **Rev:** Beaver right, maple leaf at left and right **Rev. Legend:** CANADA **Edge:** Plain

Date	Mintage	F	VF	XF	Unc	BU
1987	250	Value: 20.00				

X# M20b DOLLAR
Bronze, 38 mm. **Ruler:** Edward VIII **Obv:** Bust left, dates below **Obv. Legend:** EDWARD • VIII • KING • E • EMPEROR **Rev:** Beaver right, maple leaf at left and right **Rev. Legend:** CANADA **Edge:** Plain

Date	Mintage	F	VF	XF	Unc	BU
1987 Proof	250	Value: 20.00				

TOKEN COINAGE

X# Tn1 DOLLAR
Nickel **Issuer:** Benny Lee, Vancouver **Series:** Greenpeace **Obv:** Globe **Obv. Inscription:** GREENPEACE **Rev:** Two Timber wolves **Rev. Legend:** GREENPEACE

Date	Mintage	F	VF	XF	Unc	BU
1979	—	—	—	0.65	1.00	—

X# Tn1a DOLLAR
0.9250 Silver **Issuer:** Benny Lee, Vancouver **Series:** Greenpeace **Obv:** Globe **Obv. Inscription:** GREENPEACE **Rev:** Two Timber wolves **Rev. Legend:** GREENPEACE

Date	Mintage	F	VF	XF	Unc	BU
1979	100	—	—	4.50	6.50	—

X# Tn2 DOLLAR
Nickel **Issuer:** Benny Lee, Vancouver **Series:** Greenpeace **Obv:** Globe **Obv. Inscription:** GREENPEACE **Rev:** Two Harp seals **Rev. Legend:** GREENPEACE

Date	Mintage	F	VF	XF	Unc	BU
1979	—	—	—	0.65	1.00	—

X# Tn2a DOLLAR
0.9250 Silver **Issuer:** Benny Lee, Vancouver **Series:** Greenpeace **Obv:** Globe **Obv. Inscription:** GREENPEACE **Rev:** Two Harp seals

Date	Mintage	F	VF	XF	Unc	BU
1979	100	—	—	4.50	6.50	—

X# Tn3 DOLLAR
Nickel **Issuer:** Benny Lee, Vancouver **Series:** Greenpeace **Obv:** Globe **Obv. Inscription:** GREENPEACE **Rev:** Bald Eagle alighting **Rev. Legend:** GREENPEACE

Date	Mintage	F	VF	XF	Unc	BU
1979	—	—	—	0.65	1.00	—

X# Tn3a DOLLAR
0.9250 Silver **Issuer:** Benny Lee, Vancouver **Series:** Greenpeace **Obv:** Globe **Obv. Inscription:** GREENPEACE **Rev:** Bald Eagle alighting **Rev. Legend:** GREENPEACE

Date	Mintage	F	VF	XF	Unc	BU
1979	100	—	—	4.50	6.50	—

X# Tn4 DOLLAR
Nickel **Issuer:** Benny Lee, Vancouver **Series:** Greenpeace **Obv:** Globe **Obv. Inscription:** GREENPEACE **Rev:** Two Sperm whales **Rev. Legend:** GREENPEACE

Date	Mintage	F	VF	XF	Unc	BU
1979	—	—	—	0.65	1.00	—

X# Tn4a DOLLAR
0.9250 Silver **Issuer:** Benny Lee, Vancouver **Series:** Greenpeace **Obv:** Globe **Obv. Inscription:** GREENPEACE **Rev:** Two Sperm whales **Rev. Legend:** GREENPEACE

Date	Mintage	F	VF	XF	Unc	BU
1979	100	—	—	4.50	6.50	—

X# Tn5 DOLLAR
Nickel **Issuer:** Benny Lee, Vancouver **Series:** Greenpeace **Obv:** Globe **Obv. Inscription:** GREENPEACE **Rev:** Sisiuti **Rev. Legend:** GREENPEACE

Date	Mintage	F	VF	XF	Unc	BU
1979	—	—	—	0.65	1.00	—

X# Tn5a DOLLAR
0.9250 Silver **Issuer:** Benny Lee, Vancouver **Series:** Greenpeace **Obv:** Globe **Obv. Inscription:** GREENPEACE **Rev:** Sisiuti

Date	Mintage	F	VF	XF	Unc	BU
1979	100	—	—	4.50	6.50	—

MEDALLIC COINAGE

INA Retro Series

X# M11 DOLLAR
0.9250 Silver, 36 mm. **Ruler:** Victoria **Obv:** Veiled bust left **Obv. Legend:** VICTORIA • DEI GRATIA • IND • IMP **Rev:** Crown above maple wreath **Edge:** Plain

Date	Mintage	F	VF	XF	Unc	BU
1901 Proof	550	Value: 50.00				

X# M11a DOLLAR
Bronze, 36 mm. **Ruler:** Victoria **Obv:** Veiled bust left **Obv. Legend:** VICTORIA • DEI GRATIA • IND • IMP **Rev:** Crown above maple wreath **Edge:** Plain

Date	Mintage	F	VF	XF	Unc	BU
1901 Proof	550	Value: 20.00				

X# M11b DOLLAR
Copper, 36 mm. **Ruler:** Victoria **Obv:** Veiled bust left **Obv. Legend:** VICTORIA • DEI GRATIA • IND • IMP **Rev:** Crown above maple wreath **Edge:** Plain

Date	Mintage	F	VF	XF	Unc	BU
1901	550	Value: 20.00				

X# M11c.1 DOLLAR
0.9167 Gold, 36 mm. **Ruler:** Victoria **Obv:** Veiled bust left **Obv. Legend:** VICTORIA • DEI GRATIA • IND • IMP **Rev:** Crown above maple wreath **Edge:** Plain **Note:** Weight varies: 32.6-33.4 grams.

Date	Mintage	F	VF	XF	Unc	BU
1901 Proof	1	—	—	—	—	—
Note: Coin alignment						
1901 Proof	1	—	—	—	—	—
Note: Medal alignment						

X# M11c.2 DOLLAR
32.3000 g., 0.9167 Gold 0.9519 oz. AGW **Ruler:** Victoria **Obv:** Veiled bust left **Obv. Legend:** VICTORIA • DEI GRATIA •IND •IMP **Rev:** Crown above maple wreath **Edge:** Reeded **Note:** Medal alignment.

Date	Mintage	F	VF	XF	Unc	BU
1901 Matte Proof	1	—	—	—	—	—

X# M12 DOLLAR
22.1400 g., 0.9250 Silver 0.6584 oz. ASW **Ruler:** Edward VII **Obv:** Crowned bust right **Obv. Legend:** EDWARDVS VII D: G: BRITT: OMN: REX F: D: IND: IMP. **Rev:** Crown above maple wreath **Edge:** Plain **Note:** Medal alignment.

Date	Mintage	F	VF	XF	Unc	BU
1901 Proof	750	Value: 50.00				

X# M12a DOLLAR
18.0000 g., Bronze **Ruler:** Edward VII **Obv:** Crowned bust right **Obv. Legend:** EDWARDVS VII D: G: BRITT: OMN: REX F: D: IND: IMP. **Rev:** Crown above maple wreath **Edge:** Plain **Note:** Medal alignment.

Date	Mintage	F	VF	XF	Unc	BU
1901 Proof	750	Value: 20.00				

X# M12b DOLLAR
18.2000 g., Copper **Ruler:** Victoria **Obv:** Crowned bust right **Obv. Legend:** EDWARDVS VII D: G: BRITT: OMN: REX F: D: IND: IMP. **Rev:** Crown above maple wreath **Edge:** Plain **Note:** Medal alignment.

Date	Mintage	F	VF	XF	Unc	BU
1901 Proof	750	Value: 20.00				

X# M12c.1 DOLLAR
33.3000 g., 0.9167 Gold 0.9814 oz. AGW **Ruler:** Victoria **Obv:** Crowned bust right **Obv. Legend:** EDWARDVS VII D: G: BRITT: OMN: REX F: D: IND: IMP. **Rev:** Crown above maple wreath **Edge:** Reeded **Note:** Coin alignment

Date	Mintage	F	VF	XF	Unc	BU
1901 Proof	1	—	—	—	—	—

X# M12c.2 DOLLAR
33.3000 g., 0.9167 Gold 0.9814 oz. AGW, 36 mm. **Ruler:** Victoria **Obv:** Crowned bust right **Obv. Legend:** EDWARDVS VII D: G: BRITT: OMN: REX F: D: IND: IMP. **Rev:** Crown above maple wreath **Edge:** Plain

Date	Mintage	F	VF	XF	Unc	BU
1901 Plain	1	—	—	—	—	—
Note: Medal alignment						
1901 Proof	1	—	—	—	—	—
Note: Coin alignment						

X# M13.1 DOLLAR
33.2000 g., 0.9167 Gold 0.9784 oz. AGW **Ruler:** Edward VII **Obv:** Head right within dotted border **Obv. Legend:** EDWARDVS VII DEI GRATIA INDIAE IMPERATOR **Rev:** Crown above maple wreath **Edge:** Reeded **Note:** Medal alignment.

Date	Mintage	F	VF	XF	Unc	BU
1901 Matte Proof	1	—	—	—	—	—

X# M13.2 DOLLAR
Gold **Ruler:** Edward VII **Obv:** Head right within pellet border **Obv. Legend:** EDWARDVS VII DEI GRATIA INDIAE IMPERATOR **Rev:** Crown above maple wreath **Edge:** Plain **Note:** Medal alignment.

Date	Mintage	F	VF	XF	Unc	BU
1901 Proof	1	—	—	—	—	—

X# M14 DOLLAR
33.2000 g., 0.9167 Gold 0.9784 oz. AGW **Ruler:** Edward VII **Obv:** Bust right in suit **Obv. Legend:** EDWARDVS VII • DEI GRATIA • IND : IMP: **Rev:** Crown above maple wreath **Edge:** Reeded **Note:** Medal alignment.

Date	Mintage	F	VF	XF	Unc	BU
1901 Matte Proof	1	—	—	—	—	—

X# M15 DOLLAR
20.5100 g., 0.9250 Silver 0.6099 oz. ASW **Ruler:** Edward VIII **Obv:** Head left **Obv. Legend:** EDWARDVS VIII D: G: REX IND: IMP **Rev:** Voyageur **Edge:** Plain **Note:** Medal alignment.

Date	Mintage	F	VF	XF	Unc	BU
1937 Proof	750	Value: 50.00				

X# M15a DOLLAR
18.0600 g., Bronze **Ruler:** Edward VIII **Obv:** Head left **Obv. Legend:** EDWARDVS VIII D: G: REX IND: IMP **Rev:** Voyageur **Edge:** Plain **Note:** Medal alignment.

Date	Mintage	F	VF	XF	Unc	BU
1937 Proof	750	Value: 20.00				

X# M15b DOLLAR
18.2800 g., Copper **Ruler:** Edward VIII **Obv:** Head left **Obv. Legend:** EDWARDVS VIII D: G: REX IND: IMP **Rev:** Voyageur **Edge:** Plain **Note:** Medal alignment.

Date	Mintage	F	VF	XF	Unc	BU
1937 Proof	750	Value: 20.00				

X# M15c.1 DOLLAR
0.9167 Gold **Ruler:** Edward VIII **Obv:** Head left **Obv. Legend:** EDWARDVS VIII D: G: REX IND: IMP **Rev:** Voyageur **Edge:** Plain **Note:** Weight varies: 32.9-33.1 grams.

Date	Mintage	F	VF	XF	Unc	BU
1937 Proof	1	—	—	—	—	—
Note: Medal alignment						
1937 Proof	1	—	—	—	—	—
Note: Coin Alignment						

X# M15c.2 DOLLAR
33.1000 g., 0.9167 Gold 0.9755 oz. AGW **Ruler:** Edward VIII **Obv:** Head left **Obv. Legend:** EDWARDVS VIII D: G: REX IND: IMP **Rev:** Voyageur **Edge:** Plain

Date	Mintage	F	VF	XF	Unc	BU
1937 Matte Proof	1	—	—	—	—	—

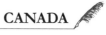

X# M16 DOLLAR
0.9250 Silver **Ruler:** Edward VIII **Obv:** Crowned bust left **Obv. Legend:** EDWARDVS VIII D: G: REX IND: IMP **Rev:** Voyageur **Edge:** Plain **Note:** Medal alignment.

Date	Mintage	F	VF	XF	Unc	BU
1937 Proof	750	Value: 50.00				

X# M16a DOLLAR
18.0000 g., Bronze, 36 mm. **Ruler:** Edward VIII **Obv:** Crowned bust left **Obv. Legend:** EDWARDVS VIII D: G: REX IND: IMP **Rev:** Voyageur **Edge:** Plain **Note:** Medal alignment.

Date	Mintage	F	VF	XF	Unc	BU
1937 Proof	750	Value: 20.00				

X# M16b DOLLAR
18.4500 g., Copper **Ruler:** Edward VIII **Obv:** Crowned bust left **Obv. Legend:** EDWARDVS VIII D: G: REX IND: IMP **Rev:** Voyageur **Edge:** Plain **Note:** Medal alignment.

Date	Mintage	F	VF	XF	Unc	BU
1937 Proof	750	Value: 20.00				

X# M16c.1 DOLLAR
33.1000 g., 0.9127 Gold 0.9712 oz. AGW **Ruler:** Edward VIII **Obv:** Crowned bust left **Obv. Legend:** EDWARDVS VIII D: G: REX IND: IMP **Rev:** Voyageur **Edge:** Reeded **Note:** Medal alignment.

Date	Mintage	F	VF	XF	Unc	BU
1937 Proof	1	—	—	—	—	—

X# M16c.2 DOLLAR
33.2000 g., 0.9167 Gold 0.9784 oz. AGW **Ruler:** Edward VIII **Obv:** Crowned bust left **Obv. Legend:** EDWARDVS VIII D: G: REX IND: IMP **Rev:** Voyageur **Edge:** Plain **Note:** Medal alignment.

Date	Mintage	F	VF	XF	Unc	BU
1937 Proof	1	—	—	—	—	—

DOMINION

BULLION COINAGE

Canada LTEE Series

X# MB26 1/10 OUNCE
3.1134 g., 0.9990 Gold 0.1000 oz. AGW **Obv:** Bust of Louis XIV of France **Rev:** Beaver on hut **Rev. Inscription:** BEAVER CASTOR **Edge:** Reeded **Note:** Prev. X#MB41.

Date	Mintage	F	VF	XF	Unc	BU
1952 Proof	—	—	—	—	—	—

X# MB20 1/20 OUNCE
1.5552 g., 0.9990 Silver 0.0499 oz. ASW, 16.1 mm. **Obv:** Crowned bust of Victoria left **Rev:** Beaver **Edge:** Reeded **Note:** Prev. X#41.

Date	Mintage	F	VF	XF	Unc	BU
1979 Proof	—	Value: 15.00				

X# MB23 1/20 OUNCE
1.5552 g., 0.9990 Silver 0.0499 oz. ASW, 16.1 mm. **Obv:** Crowned bust of Edward VII left **Rev:** Beaver **Edge:** Reeded **Note:** Prev. X#MB51.

Date	Mintage	F	VF	XF	Unc	BU
1980 Proof	1,500	Value: 12.50				

X# MB29 1/8 OUNCE
3.1103 g., 0.9990 Silver 0.0999 oz. ASW, 21.5 mm. **Obv:** Crowned bust of Victoria left **Rev:** Beaver **Edge:** Reeded **Note:** Prev. X#42.

Date	Mintage	F	VF	XF	Unc	BU
1979 Proof	—	Value: 20.00				

X# MB32 1/8 OUNCE
3.8879 g., 0.9990 Silver 0.1249 oz. ASW, 21.5 mm. **Obv:** Crowned bust of Edward VII left **Rev:** Beaver **Edge:** Reeded **Note:** Prev. X#MB52.

Date	Mintage	F	VF	XF	Unc	BU
1980 Proof	1,500	Value: 15.00				

X# MB35 1/4 OUNCE
7.7835 g., 0.9990 Gold 0.2500 oz. AGW **Obv:** Bust of Louis XIV of France **Rev:** Beaver on hut **Rev. Inscription:** BEAVER/CASTOR **Edge:** Reeded **Note:** Prev. X#MB42.

Date	Mintage	F	VF	XF	Unc	BU
1952 Proof	—	—	—	—	—	—

X# MB38 1/4 OUNCE
7.7575 g., 0.9990 Silver 0.2491 oz. ASW, 27.9 mm. **Obv:** Crowned bust of Victoria left **Rev:** Beaver **Edge:** Reeded **Note:** Prev. X#43.

Date	Mintage	F	VF	XF	Unc	BU
1979 Proof	—	Value: 30.00				

X# MB41 1/4 OUNCE
7.7575 g., 0.9999 Silver 0.2494 oz. ASW, 27.9 mm. **Obv:** Crowned bust of Edward VII left **Rev:** Beaver **Edge:** Reeded **Note:** Prev. X#MB53.

Date	Mintage	F	VF	XF	Unc	BU
1980 Proof	1,500	Value: 25.00				

X# MB44 1/2 OUNCE
15.5671 g., 0.9990 Gold 0.5000 oz. AGW **Obv:** Bust of Louis XIV of France **Rev:** Beaver on hut **Rev. Inscription:** BEAVER/CASTOR **Edge:** Reeded **Note:** Prev. X#MB43.

Date	Mintage	F	VF	XF	Unc	BU
1952 Proof	—	—	—	—	—	—

X# MB47 1/2 OUNCE
15.5150 g., 0.9990 Silver 0.4983 oz. ASW, 31 mm. **Obv:** Crowned bust of Victoria left **Rev:** Beaver **Edge:** Reeded **Note:** Prev. X#44.

Date	Mintage	F	VF	XF	Unc	BU
1979 Proof	—	Value: 50.00				

X# MB50 1/2 OUNCE
15.5150 g., 0.9990 Silver 0.4983 oz. ASW, 31 mm. **Obv:** Crowned bust of Edward VII left **Rev:** Beaver **Edge:** Reeded **Note:** Prev. X#MB54.

Date	Mintage	F	VF	XF	Unc	BU
1980 Proof	1,500	Value: 50.00				

X# MB53 OUNCE
31.1341 g., 0.9990 Gold 0.9999 oz. AGW **Obv:** Bust of Louis XIV of France **Rev:** Beaver on hut **Rev. Inscription:** BEAVER/CASTOR **Edge:** Reeded **Note:** Prev. X#MB44.

Date	Mintage	F	VF	XF	Unc	BU
1952 Proof	—	—	—	—	—	—

X# MB56 OUNCE
31.1341 g., 0.9990 Gold 0.9999 oz. AGW, 32.2 mm. **Obv:** Bust of George III in maple leaf sprays **Obv. Legend:** GEORGIUS III DEI GRATIA **Rev:** Beaver **Rev. Legend:** INTER-GOLD CANADA LTÉE **Rev. Inscription:** BEAVER/CASTOR **Edge:** Reeded **Note:** Prev. X#39.

Date	Mintage	F	VF	XF	Unc	BU
1977	10,000	—	—	—	—	750

X# MB59 OUNCE
31.1341 g., 0.9990 Gold 0.9999 oz. AGW, 32.2 mm. **Obv:** Bust of Louis XIV 3/4 left **Obv. Legend:** LUDOVICUS XIV REX CHRISTIANISSIMUS **Rev:** Beaver **Rev. Legend:** INTER-GOLD CANADA LTÉE **Rev. Inscription:** BEAVER/CASTOR **Edge:** Reeded **Note:** Prev. X#40.

Date	Mintage	F	VF	XF	Unc	BU
1978	10,000	—	—	—	—	750

X# MB65 OUNCE
31.1341 g., 0.9990 Gold 0.9999 oz. AGW **Obv:** Head of Victoria left **Obv. Legend:** VICTORIA DEI GRATIA BRITANNIARUM REGINA **Rev:** Beaver **Rev. Legend:** INTER-GOLD CANADA LTÉE **Rev. Inscription:** BEAVER/CASTOR **Edge:** Reeded **Note:** Prev. X#49.

Date	Mintage	F	VF	XF	Unc	BU
1979	10,000	—	—	—	—	750

X# MB62 OUNCE
31.1030 g., 0.9990 Silver 0.9989 oz. ASW, 45.15 mm. **Obv:** Crowned bust of Victoria left **Rev:** Beaver **Edge:** Reeded **Note:** Prev. X#45.

Date	Mintage	F	VF	XF	Unc	BU
1979 Proof	—	Value: 100				

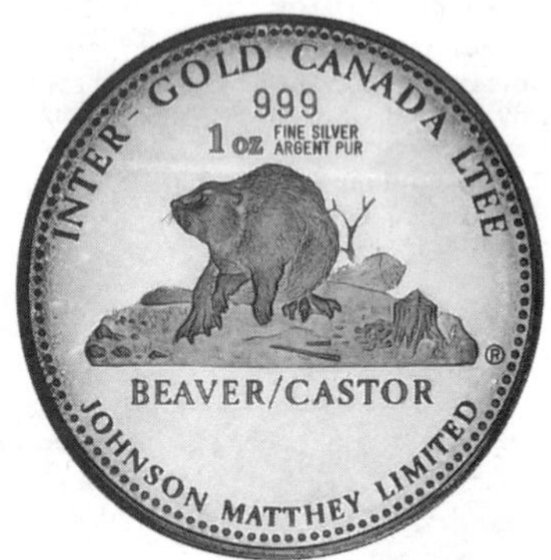

X# MB68 OUNCE
31.1030 g., 0.9990 Silver 0.9989 oz. ASW, 45.15 mm. **Obv:** Crowned bust of Edward VII left **Rev:** Beaver **Rev. Insription:** BEAVER/CASTOR **Edge:** Reeded **Note:** Prev. X#MB55.

Date	Mintage	F	VF	XF	Unc	BU
1980 Proof	1,500	Value: 100				

X# MB71 2 OUNCES
62.2683 g., 0.9990 Gold 1.9999 oz. AGW **Obv:** Bust of Louis XIV of France **Rev:** Beaver on hut **Rev. Inscription:** BEAVER/CASTOR **Edge:** Reeded **Note:** Prev. X#MB45.

Date	Mintage	F	VF	XF	Unc	BU
1952 Proof	—	—	—	—	—	—

X# MB74 2-1/2 OUNCES
77.7575 g., 0.9990 Silver 2.4974 oz. ASW, 68.5 mm. **Obv:** Crowned bust of Victoria left **Rev:** Beaver **Edge:** Reeded **Note:** Prev. X#46.

Date	Mintage	F	VF	XF	Unc	BU
1979 Proof	—	Value: 175				

X# MB77 2-1/2 OUNCES
77.7575 g., 0.9990 Silver 2.4974 oz. ASW, 68.5 mm. **Obv:** Crowned bust of Edward VII left **Rev:** Beaver **Rev. Insription:** BEAVER/CASTOR **Edge:** Reeded **Note:** Illustration reduced. Prev. X#MB56.

Date	Mintage	F	VF	XF	Unc	BU
1980 Proof	1,500	Value: 175				

X# MB80 5 OUNCES
155.6701 g., 0.9990 Gold 4.9997 oz. AGW **Obv:** Bust of Louis XIV of France **Rev:** Beaver on hut **Rev. Inscription:** BEAVER/CASTOR **Edge:** Reeded **Note:** Prev. X#MB46.

Date	Mintage	F	VF	XF	Unc	BU
1952 Proof	—	—	—	—	—	—

MEDALLIC COINAGE - NICKEL MUSEUM ISSUE

X# 301 20 DOLLARS
Bronze Or Gilt Brass **Obv:** Elizabeth II by Machin **Obv. Legend:** ELIZABETH II D. G. REGINA **Rev:** CANADIAN ARMS **Rev. Legend:** CANADA 20 DOLLARS / CANADIAN CENTENNIAL GOLD COIN MONUMENT SUNBURY CANADA **Note:** Struck at the Lombardo Mint

Date	Mintage	F	VF	XF	Unc	BU
1967	—	—	—	—	10.00	15.00

PIEFORTS

X#	Date	Mintage	Identification	Mkt Val
P1	1901	1	Dollar. Silver. Plain edge, coin alignment, X#M11.	—
P2	1901	1	Dollar. Silver. Plain edge, medal alignment, X#M11.	—
P3	1901	1	Dollar. Silver. Reeded edge, coin alignment, X#M11.	—
P4	1901	1	Dollar. Silver. Reeded edge, medal alignment, X#M11.	—
P5	1901	1	Dollar. Silver. Plain edge, couin alignment, X#M12.	—
P6	1901	1	Dollar. Silver. Plain edge, medal alignment, X#M12.	—
P7	1901	1	Dollar. Silver. Reeded edge, coin alignment, X#M12.	—
P8	1901	1	Dollar. Silver. Reeded edge, medal alignment, X#M12.	—
P9	1901	1	Dollar. Silver. Plain edge, coin alignment, X#M13.	—
P10	1901	1	Dollar. Silver. Plain edge, medal alignment, X#M13.	—
P11	1901	1	Dollar. Silver. Reeded edge, coin alignment, X#M13.	—
P12	1901	1	Dollar. Silver. Reeded edge, medal alignment, X#M13.	—
P13	1901	1	Dollar. Silver. Plain edge, coin alignment, X#M14.	—
P14	1901	1	Dollar. Silver. Plain edge, medal alignment, X#M14.	—
P15	1901	1	Dollar. Silver. Reeded edge, coin alignment, X#M14.	—
P16	1901	1	Dollar. Silver. Reeded edge, medal alignment, X#M14.	—
P17	1937	1	Dollar. Silver. Plain edge, coin alignment, X#M15.	—
P18	1937	1	Dollar. Silver. Plain edge, medal alignment, X#M15.	—
P19	1937	1	Dollar. Silver. Reeded edge, coin alignment, X#M15.	—
P20	1937	1	Dollar. Silver. Reeded edge, medal alignment, X#M15.	—
P21	1937	1	Dollar. Silver. Plain edge, coin alignment, X#M16.	—
P22	1937	1	Dollar. Silver. Plain edge, medal alignment, X#M16.	—
P23	1937	1	Dollar. Silver. Reeded edge, coin alignment, X#M16.	—
P24	1937	1	Dollar. Silver. Reeded edge, medal alignment, X#M16.	—
P25	1987	25	Dollar. 0.9167 Silver. X#M20.	125

PROOF SETS

X#	Date	Mintage	Identification	Issue Price	Mkt Val
XPS1	1952 (6)	—	X#MB41-MB46	—	—
XPS2	1979 (5)	100	X#Tn1a-Tn5a	—	40.00
XPS3	1980 (6)	1,500	X#MB51-MB56	—	110

BRITISH COLUMBIA

GABRIOLA ISLAND

SILVER MEDALLIC BULLION COINAGE

X# MB21 1/2 OUNCE
1.5567 g., 0.9990 Silver 0.0500 oz. ASW, 29.7 mm. **Issuer:** Festival Gabriola Group **Obv:** Cartoon like figure "Dancing Man" in sprays, waves in background **Obv. Legend:** GABRIOLA **Rev:** Chinese junk **Edge:** Plain

Date	Mintage	F	VF	XF	Unc	BU
1999	100	—	—	—	—	200
1999 Proof	189	Value: 75.00				

VANCOUVER ISLAND

SILVER MEDALLIC BULLION COINAGE

X# 11 1/10 OUNCE
37.8000 g., 0.9990 Silver 1.2140 oz. ASW, 42.15 mm. **Issuer:** Money Company, California **Obv:** Dragon **Obv. Legend:** VANCOUVER **Rev:** Crowned garter

Date	Mintage	F	VF	XF	Unc	BU
1992 Proof	—	Value: 15.00				

X# 9 20 DOLLARS
31.1030 g., 0.9990 Silver 0.9989 oz. ASW, 38.3 mm. **Subject:** Canadian Numismatic Assocation Convention **Obv:** Head of Queen Victoria wearing tiara left **Obv. Legend:** VANCOUVER TRADE DOLLAR **Rev:** Two totem poles behind voyagers in canoe right **Rev. Legend:** VANCOUVER - GATEWAY TO THE PACIFIC **Edge:** Reeded **Note:** Good for 20 Dollars in trade during the convention.

Date	Mintage	F	VF	XF	Unc	BU
1990 Proof	—	Value: 40.00				

TRADE COINAGE

X# T5 DOLLAR
31.1300 g., 0.9990 Silver 0.9998 oz. ASW, 36 mm. **Subject:** Canadian Numismatic Association's Convention **Obv:** Head of Queen Victoria left **Obv. Legend:** VALID IN TRADE FOR CDN $20 DURING C.N.A. **Rev:** Voyagers passing in front of totem poles **Rev. Legend:** VANCOUVER - GATEWAY TO THE PACIFIC

Date	Mintage	F	VF	XF	Unc	BU
1990 Proof	—	Value: 22.50				

PATTERNS

X# Pn5 TAEL
37.8000 g., 0.9990 Silver 1.2140 oz. ASW, 39.2 mm. **Issuer:** Sunshine Mining Co. **Obv:** Dragon **Obv. Legend:** VANCOUVER **Rev:** Rayed sun behind eagle in flight **Rev. Legend:** INTERNATIONAL BANKING & EXCHANGE TAEL

Date	Mintage	F	VF	XF	Unc	BU
1990 Proof	—	Value: 18.50				

LASQUETI ISLAND

SILVER MEDALLIC BULLION COINAGE

X# MB9 1/10 OUNCE
3.1103 g., 0.9990 Silver 0.0999 oz. ASW, 16 mm. **Subject:** Medical Marijuana **Obv:** "Lasqueti Dory" painting by Allan Farrell with beach line **Obv. Legend:** LASQUETI **Obv. Designer:** Tony Seaman **Rev:** Value in Marijuana plant sprays **Rev. Designer:** Rand Holmes **Edge:** Plain

Date	Mintage	F	VF	XF	Unc	BU
ND(2007) Proof	50	Value: 17.50				

X# MB2 1/2 OUNCE
1.5567 g., 0.9990 Silver 0.0500 oz. ASW, 29.7 mm. **Obv:** Mt. Arrowsmith, China Cloud Bay viewed through an Arbutus treee **Obv. Legend:** LASQUETI **Rev:** Chinese junk **Edge:** Plain

Date	Mintage	F	VF	XF	Unc	BU
1999 Proof	17	—	—	—	—	—

X# MB4 1/2 OUNCE
1.5567 g., 0.9990 Silver 0.0500 oz. ASW, 29.7 mm. **Obv:** Dragon **Obv. Legend:** LASQUETI **Rev:** Chinese junk **Edge:** Plain

Date	Mintage	F	VF	XF	Unc	BU
2000	169	—	—	—	—	55.00
2000 Proof	150	Value: 70.00				

X# MB7 1/2 OUNCE
1.5567 g., 0.9990 Silver 0.0500 oz. ASW, 29.7 mm. **Obv:** Dragon **Obv. Legend:** LASQUETI **Rev:** Chinese junk **Edge:** Plain

Date	Mintage	F	VF	XF	Unc	BU
2000 Dot in date	71	—	—	—	—	65.00
2000 Two dots in date	159	—	—	—	—	60.00
2000 Three dots in date	—	—	—	—	—	55.00

GOLD MEDALLIC BULLION COINAGE

X# MB1 1/10 OUNCE
3.1800 g., 0.9999 Gold 0.1022 oz. AGW, 16.6 mm. **Subject:** Medical Marijuana **Obv:** "Lasqueti Dory" painting by Allan Farrell with beach line **Obv. Legend:** LASQUETI **Obv. Designer:** Tony Seaman **Rev:** Value in Marijuana plant sprays **Rev. Designer:** Rand Holmes **Edge:** Plain

Date	Mintage	F	VF	XF	Unc	BU
MMI (2001)	38	—	—	—	—	120
MMIII (2003)	49	—	—	—	—	135
MMV (2005)	—	—	—	—	—	100

X# MB6 1/10 OUNCE
3.1800 g., 0.9999 Gold 0.1022 oz. AGW, 16.6 mm. **Subject:** Medical Marijuana **Obv:** "Lasqueti Dory" painting by Allan Farrell without beach line **Obv. Legend:** LASQUETI **Obv. Designer:** Tony Seaman **Rev:** Value in Marijuana plant sprays **Rev. Designer:** Rand Holmes **Edge:** Plain

Date	Mintage	F	VF	XF	Unc	BU
MMI (2001) Proof	38	—	—	—	—	90.00
Note: Tenth Anniversary Issue.						
MMIII (2003)	49	—	—	—	—	85.00
ND (2007)	30	—	—	—	—	—

X# MB2a 1/2 OUNCE
1.5557 g., 0.9999 Gold 0.0500 oz. AGW, 29.7 mm. **Obv:** Mt. Arrowsmith, China Cloud Bay viewed through an Arbutus tree **Rev:** Chinese junk **Edge:** Plain

Date	Mintage	F	VF	XF	Unc	BU
1999 Proof	27	—	—	—	—	—

X# MB3 1/2 OUNCE
1.5557 g., 0.9999 Gold 0.0500 oz. AGW, 27 mm. **Obv:** Busts of founders Barker and Wells left **Obv. Legend:** BARKER WELLS FOUNDERS **Rev:** Cariboo standing right **Rev. Legend:** CARIBOO GOLD **Edge:** Plain

Date	Mintage	F	VF	XF	Unc	BU
2000 Proof	53	—	—	—	—	—

X# MB5 1/2 OUNCE
1.5557 g., 0.9999 Gold 0.0500 oz. AGW, 27 mm. **Obv:** Dragon **Obv. Legend:** LASQUETI **Rev:** Chinese junk

Date	Mintage	F	VF	XF	Unc	BU
2000 Proof	29	—	—	—	—	—

DOMINION

CANADIAN CONFEDERATION

MEDALLIC COINAGE

1972 Pobjoy Mint Series

X# 2 CROWN
Silver **Subject:** Edward VIII

Date	Mintage	F	VF	XF	Unc	BU
1936 Proof	—	Value: 50.00				

X# 2a CROWN
42.1000 g., 0.9167 Gold 1.2407 oz. AGW
Subject: Edward VIII

Date	Mintage	F	VF	XF	Unc	BU
1936 Proof	—	Value: 1,000				

Richard Lobel Series

X# 3 CROWN
Bronze **Subject:** Edward VIII **Obv:** Bust of Edward VIII facing left **Obv. Legend:** EDWARD • VIII • KING • & • EMPEROR **Rev:** Beaver sitting on hut right

Date	Mintage	F	VF	XF	Unc	BU
1936 Proof	1,000	Value: 15.00				

X# 3a CROWN
Copper-Nickel-Zinc **Subject:** Edward VIII **Obv:** Bust of Edward VIII facing left **Obv. Legend:** EDWARD • VIII • KING • & • EMPEROR **Rev:** Beaver sitting on hut right

Date	Mintage	F	VF	XF	Unc	BU
1936 Proof	2,500	Value: 15.00				

X# 3b CROWN
0.9167 Silver **Subject:** Edward VIII **Obv:** Bust of Edward VIII facing left **Obv. Legend:** EDWARD • VIII • KING • & • EMPEROR **Rev:** Beaver sitting on hut right

Date	Mintage	F	VF	XF	Unc	BU
1936 Proof	200	Value: 50.00				

X# 3c CROWN
Gold **Subject:** Edward VIII **Obv:** Bust of Edward VIII facing left **Obv. Legend:** EDWARD • VIII • KING • & • EMPEROR **Rev:** Beaver sitting on hut right

Date	Mintage	F	VF	XF	Unc	BU
1936 Proof	—	Value: 500				

X# 5 CROWN
23.0000 g., 0.9167 Silver 0.6778 oz. ASW, 38 mm.
Obv: Beaver **Rev:** Duke and Duchess of Windsor
Edge: Reeded

Date	Mintage	F	VF	XF	Unc	BU
1936 Proof	—	Value: 50.00				

X# 4 SOVEREIGN
0.3750 Gold **Subject:** Edward VIII

Date	Mintage	F	VF	XF	Unc	BU
1936 Proof	200	Value: 150				

X# 6 SOVEREIGN
4.8600 g., 0.3750 Gold 0.0586 oz. AGW, 22 mm.
Obv: Beaver **Rev:** Duke and Duchess of Windsor
Edge: Reeded

Date	Mintage	F	VF	XF	Unc	BU
1936 Proof	—	Value: 125				

1967 Royal Canadian Mint Issue

X# M1 DOLLAR
24.5400 g., 0.9250 Silver 0.7298 oz. ASW
Subject: Confederation Centennial **Note:** Prev. X#1.

Date	Mintage	F	VF	XF	Unc	BU
1967 Prooflike	—	—	—	—	13.50	—

X# M1a DOLLAR
24.5400 g., 0.9250 Bronze 0.7298 oz.
Subject: Confederation Centennial **Note:** Prev. X#1a.

Date	Mintage	F	VF	XF	Unc	BU
1967 Prooflike	—	—	—	—	5.00	—

PIEFORTS

X#	Date	Mintage	Identification	Mkt Val
P25	1936	—	Crown. 0.9167 Silver. X#3b.	100

MANITOBA

CONFEDERATION

MEDALLIC COINAGE

X# 11 1/2 DOLLAR
Gold **Obv:** Buffalo on large maple leaf

Date	Mintage	F	VF	XF	Unc	BU
1898	—	—	—	175	275	—

X# 12 DOLLAR
Gold **Obv:** Buffalo on large maple leaf

Date	Mintage	F	VF	XF	Unc	BU
1898	—	—	—	300	500	—

QUEBEC

ANTICOSTI ISLAND

NATIONALIST

X# 8b 1 LYS (The lys is an heraldic symbol who is the national emblem of Quebec.)
31.1000 g., Sterling Silver **Ruler:** (No Ruler) **Issuer:** Monnaies du Québec (Coins of Quebec) **Subject:** The Flood of the Saguenay River **Note:** Commemorating the 1996 catastrophic flood of the Saguenay River; it reproduced the photo of the little house that resisted the flood and that appeared in the world press.

Date	Mintage	F	VF	XF	Unc	BU
ND (2002)	50	—	—	—	—	70.00

PATTERNS INCLUDING OFF METAL STRIKES

X# Pn1 1/8 PENNY
Copper **Ruler:** (No Ruler) **Rev:** Value within wreath, A at top **Note:** The dies were prepared at the Paris Mint possibly for Honduras. The attribution for Anticosti Island was first published by Scott Stamp and Coin Co. in their Catalogue of Canadian Coins, Medals and Tokens in 1890.

Date	Mintage	VG	F	VF	XF	Unc
1870	—	—	—	—	85.00	200

INDEPENDANTIST

NATIONALIST

X# 5b 1 LYS (The lys is an heraldic symbol who is the national emblem of Quebec.)
31.1000 g., Sterling Silver **Ruler:** (No Ruler) **Issuer:** Monnaies du Québec (Coins of Quebec) **Subject:** Upper and Lower Canada Rebellion **Note:** Commemorating the Historic 1837 — 1838 Rebellion of the upper Canada (the present day Ontario) and Lower Canada (the present day Quebec) provinces against the British imperial colonial power.

Date	Mintage	F	VF	XF	Unc	BU
ND (1987) Antique finish	25	—	—	—	75.00	—

X# 1a 1 LYS (The lys is an heraldic symbol who is the national emblem of Quebec.)
Bronze **Ruler:** (No Ruler) **Issuer:** Monnaies du Québec (Coins of Quebec) **Subject:** Parliament **Note:** Commemorating the Bicentenary of the parliamentary institution in Quebec; it reproduced the National Assembly building in Quebec City.

Date	Mintage	F	VF	XF	Unc	BU
1992 Proof	100	Value: 25.00				

X# 1b 1 LYS (The lys is an heraldic symbol who is the national emblem of Quebec.)
31.1000 g., Sterling Silver **Ruler:** (No Ruler) **Issuer:** Monnaies du Québec (Coins of Quebec) **Subject:** Parliament **Note:** Commemorating the Bicentenary of the parliamentary institution in Quebec; it reproduced the National Assembly building in Quebec City.

Date	Mintage	F	VF	XF	Unc	BU
1992 Proof	25	Value: 95.00				

X# 2a 1 LYS (The lys is an heraldic symbol who is the national emblem of Quebec.)
Brass **Ruler:** (No Ruler) **Issuer:** Monnaies du Québec (Coins of Quebec) **Subject:** Peace **Obv:** The word "Peace" is in the 5 different languages **Note:** English and Celtic language to commemorate the peace agreement between the England and Ireland (Northern Ireland and the Republic of Ireland), Hebrew and Arab, to commemorate the peace agreement between Israel and Palestine, German, to commemorate the reunification of Germany.

Date	Mintage	F	VF	XF	Unc	BU
1994 Proof	500	Value: 20.00				

X# 2b 1 LYS (The lys is an heraldic symbol who is the national emblem of Quebec.)
31.1000 g., Sterling Silver **Ruler:** (No Ruler) **Issuer:** Monnaies du Québec (Coins of Quebec) **Subject:** Peace **Obv:** The word "Peace" in the 5 different languages **Note:** English and Celtic language to commemorate the peace agreement between the England and Ireland (Northern Ireland and the Republic of Ireland), Hebrew and Arab, to commemorate the peace agreement between Israel and Palestine, German, to commemorate the reunification of Germany.

Date	Mintage	F	VF	XF	Unc	BU
1994 Proof	50	Value: 60.00				

X# 3b 1 LYS (The lys is an heraldic symbol who is the national emblem of Quebec.)
31.1000 g., Bronze **Ruler:** (No Ruler) **Issuer:** Monnaies du Québec (Coins of Quebec) **Subject:** Maisonneuve, Founder of Montreal **Note:** Only a few pieces have been struck as it was decided to change the historic dates 1640 — 1676 to those of 1612 — 1676 as more related to this historic personage himself.

Date	Mintage	F	VF	XF	Unc	BU
ND (1995) Proof	5	—	—	—	—	—

X# 3a 1 LYS (The lys is an heraldic symbol who is the national emblem of Quebec.)
Brass **Ruler:** (No Ruler) **Issuer:** Monnaies du Québec (Coins of Quebec) **Subject:** Maisonneuve, Founder of Montreal **Note:** Only a few pieces have been struck as it was decided to change the historic dates 1640 — 1676 to those of 1612 — 1676 as more related to this historic personage himself.

Date	Mintage	F	VF	XF	Unc	BU
ND (1996) Proof	5	—	—	—	—	—

X# 4b 1 LYS (The lys is an heraldic symbol who is the national emblem of Quebec.)
31.1000 g., Sterling Silver **Ruler:** (No Ruler) **Issuer:** Monnaies du Québec (Coins of Quebec) **Subject:** Maisonneuve, Founder of Montreal **Note:** As the precedent issue, commemorating the founder of Montreal, but with 1612 — 1676 as the historic dates. Bruce #254.

Date	Mintage	F	VF	XF	Unc	BU
ND (1996) Proof	64	Value: 75.00				

X# 5a 1 LYS (The lys is an heraldic symbol who is the national emblem of Quebec.)
Bronze **Ruler:** (No Ruler) **Issuer:** Monnaies du Québec (Coins of Quebec) **Subject:** Upper and Lower Canada Rebellion **Note:** Commemorating the Historic 1837 — 1838 Rebellion of the upper Canada (the present day Ontario) and Lower Canada (the present day Quebec) provinces against the British imperial colonial power.

Date	Mintage	F	VF	XF	Unc	BU
ND (1997) Matte	1,837	—	—	—	25.00	—

X# 6a 1 LYS (The lys is an heraldic symbol who is the national emblem of Quebec.)
Gold-Plated Copper **Ruler:** (No Ruler) **Issuer:** Monnaies du Québec (Coins of Quebec) **Subject:** Vlad Tepes Dracula **Note:** Commemorating the historic personage of Vlad Tepes Dracula who put a stop to the invasion of his country during the 15th century.

Date	Mintage	F	VF	XF	Unc	BU
ND (1999) Proof	1,476	Value: 20.00				

X# 6b 1 LYS (The lys is an heraldic symbol who is the national emblem of Quebec.)
31.1000 g., Sterling Silver **Ruler:** (No Ruler) **Issuer:** Monnaies du Québec (Coins of Quebec) **Subject:** Vlad Tepes Dracula **Note:** Commemorating the historic personage of Vlad Tepes Dracula who put a stop to the invasion of his country during the 15th century.

Date	Mintage	F	VF	XF	Unc	BU
ND (1999) Proof	20	Value: 75.00				

X# 7a 1 LYS (The lys is an heraldic symbol who is the national emblem of Quebec.)
Bronze **Ruler:** (No Ruler) **Issuer:** Monnaies du Québec (Coins of Quebec) **Subject:** Map and Emblem of Quebec **Note:** Reproducing the map, the heraldic symbol and the motto of Quebec

Date	Mintage	F	VF	XF	Unc	BU
ND (2000) Proof	100	Value: 25.00				

X# 7b 1 LYS (The lys is an heraldic symbol who is the national emblem of Quebec.)
31.1000 g., Sterling Silver **Ruler:** (No Ruler) **Subject:** Map and Emblem of Quebec **Note:** Reproducing the map, the heraldic symbol and the motto of Quebec

Date	Mintage	F	VF	XF	Unc	BU
ND (2000) Proof	25	Value: 65.00				

X# 8a 1 LYS (The lys is an heraldic symbol who is the national emblem of Quebec.)
Copper **Ruler:** (No Ruler) **Issuer:** Monnaies du Québec (Coins of Quebec) **Subject:** The Flood of the Saguenay River **Note:** Commemorating the 1996 catastrophic flood of the Saguenay River; it reproduced the photo of the little house that resisted the flood and that appeared in the world press.

Date	Mintage	F	VF	XF	Unc	BU
ND (2002)	1,996	—	—	—	—	20.00

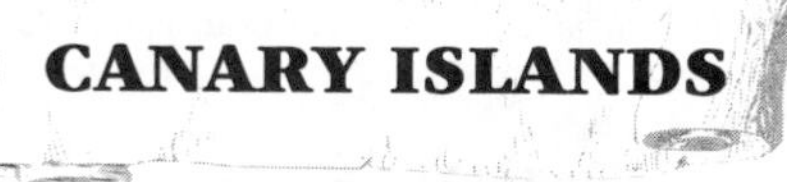

SPANISH AUTONOMOUS REGION

FANTASY EURO PATTERNS

X# Pn1 EURO CENT
Copper Plated Steel **Edge:** Plain

Date	Mintage	F	VF	XF	Unc	BU
2005	7,000	—	—	—	—	1.50

X# Pn2 2 EURO CENTS
Copper Plated Steel **Edge:** Plain

Date	Mintage	F	VF	XF	Unc	BU
2005	7,000	—	—	—	—	2.00

X# Pn3 5 EURO CENTS
Copper Plated Steel **Edge:** Plain

Date	Mintage	F	VF	XF	Unc	BU
2005	7,000	—	—	—	—	2.50

X# Pn4 10 EURO CENTS
Goldine **Edge:** Plain

Date	Mintage	F	VF	XF	Unc	BU
2005	7,000	—	—	—	—	3.00

X# Pn5 20 EURO CENTS
Goldine **Edge:** Plain

Date	Mintage	F	VF	XF	Unc	BU
2005	7,000	—	—	—	—	3.50

X# Pn6 50 EURO CENTS
Goldine **Edge:** Plain

Date	Mintage	F	VF	XF	Unc	BU
2005	7,000	—	—	—	—	4.00

X# Pn7 EURO
Bi-Metallic **Obv:** Spanish president's bust facing **Edge:** Plain

Date	Mintage	F	VF	XF	Unc	BU
2005	7,000	—	—	—	—	6.00

X# Pn8 EURO
Bi-Metallic **Obv:** Spanish president's bust facing **Edge:** Plain

Date	Mintage	F	VF	XF	Unc	BU
2005	7,000	—	—	—	—	8.00

MINT SETS

X#	Date	Mintage	Identification	Issue Price	Mkt Val
XMS1	2005 (8)	7,000	X#Pn1-Pn8	—	30.00

CAPE OF GOOD HOPE

BRITISH COLONY

MEDALLIC COINAGE

1889 L.C. Lauer Issues

X# 1 PENNY
Bronze **Obv:** Letter "I" in legend above hair ribbon **Obv. Legend:** VICTORIA D:G: BRITANNIAE REG: F: D: **Note:** Prev. KM#Pn1.

Date	Mintage	F	VF	XF	Unc	BU
1889 Proof	—	Value: 450				

X# 2 PENNY
Nickel **Obv:** Letter "I" in legend above hair ribbon **Obv. Legend:** BRITATANIA **Note:** Prev. KM#Pn2.

Date	Mintage	F	VF	XF	Unc	BU
1889 Proof	—	Value: 485				

X# 3 PENNY
Bronze **Note:** Prev. KM#Pn3.

Date	Mintage	F	VF	XF	Unc	BU
1889 Proof	—	Value: 450				

X# 4 PENNY
Copper Nickel **Note:** Prev. KM#Pn4.

Date	Mintage	F	VF	XF	Unc	BU
1889 Proof	—	Value: 485				

X# 5 PENNY
Aluminum **Note:** Prev. KM#Pn5.

Date	Mintage	F	VF	XF	Unc	BU
1889 Proof	—	Value: 600				

X# 6 PENNY
Tin **Note:** Prev. KM#Pn6.

Date	Mintage	F	VF	XF	Unc	BU
1889 Proof	—	Value: 600				

X# 7 PENNY
Silver **Note:** Prev. KM#Pn7. Also known as a Silver Penny or 1/2 Crown.

CAPE VERDE

Date	Mintage	F	VF	XF	Unc	BU
1889 Proof	—	Value: 1,500				

PORTUGUESE COLONY

FANTASY EURO PATTERNS

X# Pn1 EURO CENT
Copper Plated Steel **Edge:** Plain

Date	Mintage	F	VF	XF	Unc	BU
2004	7,000	—	—	—	—	1.50

X# Pn2 2 EURO CENTS
Copper Plated Steel **Edge:** Plain

Date	Mintage	F	VF	XF	Unc	BU
2004	7,000	—	—	—	—	2.00

X# Pn3 5 EURO CENTS
Copper Plated Steel **Edge:** Plain

Date	Mintage	F	VF	XF	Unc	BU
2004	7,000	—	—	—	—	2.50

X# Pn4 10 EURO CENTS
Goldine **Edge:** Plain

Date	Mintage	F	VF	XF	Unc	BU
2004	7,000	—	—	—	—	3.00

X# Pn5 20 EURO CENTS
Goldine **Edge:** Plain

Date	Mintage	F	VF	XF	Unc	BU
2004	7,000	—	—	—	—	3.50

X# Pn6 50 EURO CENTS
Goldine **Edge:** Plain

Date	Mintage	F	VF	XF	Unc	BU
2004	7,000	—	—	—	—	4.00

X# Pn7 EURO
Bi-Metallic **Obv:** Flag **Rev:** Value and EEU star design **Edge:** Plain

Date	Mintage	F	VF	XF	Unc	BU
2004	7,000	—	—	—	—	6.00

X# Pn8 2 EURO
Bi-Metallic **Obv:** Flag **Rev:** Value and EEU star design **Edge:** Plain

Date	Mintage	F	VF	XF	Unc	BU
2004	7,000	—	—	—	—	8.00

MINT SETS

X#	Date	Mintage	Identification	Issue Price	Mkt Val
XMS1	2004 (8)	7,000	X#Pn1-Pn8	—	30.00

CARTAGO

CARTHAGE CITY

FANTASY EURO PATTERNS

X# Pn1 EURO CENT
Copper Plated Steel

Date	Mintage	F	VF	XF	Unc	BU
2005	7,000	—	—	—	—	1.50

X# Pn2 2 EURO CENTS
Copper Plated Steel

Date	Mintage	F	VF	XF	Unc	BU
2005	7,000	—	—	—	—	2.00

X# Pn3 5 EURO CENTS
Copper Plated Steel

Date	Mintage	F	VF	XF	Unc	BU
2005	7,000	—	—	—	—	2.50

X# Pn4 10 EURO CENTS
Goldine

Date	Mintage	F	VF	XF	Unc	BU
2005	7,000	—	—	—	—	3.00

X# Pn5 20 EURO CENTS
Goldine

Date	Mintage	F	VF	XF	Unc	BU
2005	7,000	—	—	—	—	3.50

X# Pn6 50 EURO CENTS
Goldine

Date	Mintage	F	VF	XF	Unc	BU
2005	7,000	—	—	—	—	4.00

X# Pn7 EURO
Bi-Metallic Copper-Nickel center in Goldine ring **Obv:** Ancient male head 3/4 left **Rev:** Flower, large value "1"

Date	Mintage	F	VF	XF	Unc	BU
2005	7,000	—	—	—	—	6.00

X# Pn8 2 EURO
Bi-Metallic Copper-Nickel center in Goldine ring **Obv:** Ancient male head 3/4 left **Rev:** Flower, large value "2"

Date	Mintage	F	VF	XF	Unc	BU
2005	7,000	—	—	—	—	8.00

MINT SETS

X#	Date	Mintage	Identification	Issue Price	Mkt Val
XMS1	2005 (8)	7,000	X#Pn1-Pn8	—	30.00

CENTRAL AMERICA

REPUBLIC

MEDALLIC COINAGE

Banco Centroamericano Issue

X# 1 50 PESOS
20.0000 g., 0.9000 Gold 0.5787 oz. AGW **Subject:** 10th Anniversary Economic Integration **Obv:** Mountain range with radiant sun above in inner circle **Rev:** Tree with grass below and small legend above in inner circle

Date	Mintage	F	VF	XF	Unc	BU
1970 Proof	1,500	Value: 325				

CENTRAL AMERICAN STATES

REPUBLIC

MEDALLIC COINAGE

X# 11 PESO
0.9250 Silver **Subject:** 20th Anniversary of ODECA

Date	Mintage	F	VF	XF	Unc	BU
1971 Proof	—	Value: 30.00				

X# 12 2 PESOS
0.9250 Silver **Subject:** 20th Anniversary of ODECA

Date	Mintage	F	VF	XF	Unc	BU
1971 Proof	—	Value: 40.00				

X# 13 5 PESOS
0.9250 Silver **Subject:** 20th Anniversary of ODECA

Date	Mintage	F	VF	XF	Unc	BU
1971 Proof	—	Value: 65.00				

X# 14 20 PESOS
Gold **Subject:** 20th Anniversary of ODECA

Date	Mintage	F	VF	XF	Unc	BU
1971 Proof	—	Value: 400				

PROOF SETS

X#	Date	Mintage	Identification	Issue Price	Mkt Val
XPS1	1971 (4)	—	X11-X14	—	530

CENTRAL AMERICAN UNION

CONFEDERATION

ESSAIS

Central American Union Issues

X# E21 CENTAVO
Bronze **Obv:** Liberty bust left **Rev:** Value in sprays

Date	Mintage	F	VF	XF	Unc	BU
1889 Proof	—	Value: 125				

X# E22 2 CENTAVOS
Bronze **Obv:** Liberty bust left **Rev:** Value in sprays

Date	Mintage	F	VF	XF	Unc	BU
1889 Proof	—	Value: 175				

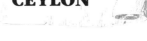

CEYLON

BRITISH COLONY

FANTASY COINAGE

A modern fantasy issue of unknown origin struck without any government authorization for the obvious confusion of the numismatic community

X# 5 4 RIXDOLLAR
Copper

Date	Mintage	F	VF	XF	Unc	BU
1812	30	—	—	125	200	—

X# 6 4 RIXDOLLAR
Silver

Date	Mintage	F	VF	XF	Unc	BU
1812	200	—	—	150	250	—

X# 7 4 RIXDOLLAR
Gold

Date	Mintage	F	VF	XF	Unc	BU
1812	—	—	—	—	900	—

MEDALLIC / INA RETRO ISSUE

X# M11 4 RIXDOLLAR
Silver, 40.98 mm. **Obv:** Laureate bust right **Obv. Legend:** GEORGIUS III DEI GRATIA REX. **Rev:** Elephant standing left in sprays **Rev. Legend:** CEYLON **Edge:** Plain

Date	Mintage	F	VF	XF	Unc	BU
1808 (2007) Proof	—	—	—	—	—	—
1808 (2007) Matte Proof	—	—	—	—	—	—

X# M11a 4 RIXDOLLAR
Copper, 40.98 mm. **Obv:** Laureate bust right **Obv. Legend:** GEORGIUS III DEI GRATIA REX. **Rev:** Elephant standing left in sprays **Rev. Legend:** CEYLON **Edge:** Plain

Date	Mintage	F	VF	XF	Unc	BU
1808 (2007) Proof	600	—	—	—	—	—

X# M11b 4 RIXDOLLAR
Aluminum, 40.98 mm. **Obv:** Laureate bust right **Obv. Legend:** GEORGIUS III DEI GRATIA REX. **Rev:** Elephant standing left in sprays **Rev. Legend:** CEYLON **Edge:** Plain

Date	Mintage	F	VF	XF	Unc	BU
1808 (2007) Proof	600	—	—	—	—	—

X# M11c 4 RIXDOLLAR
Pewter, 40.98 mm. **Obv:** Laureate bust right **Obv. Legend:** GEORGIUS III DEI GRATIA REX. **Rev:** Elephant standing left in sprays **Rev. Legend:** CEYLON **Edge:** Plain

Date	Mintage	F	VF	XF	Unc	BU
1808 (2007) Proof	600	—	—	—	—	—

X# M11d 4 RIXDOLLAR
Copper Bronzed, 40.98 mm. **Obv:** Laureate bust right **Obv. Legend:** GEORGIUS III DEI GRATIA REX. **Rev:** Elephant standing left in sprays **Rev. Legend:** CEYLON **Edge:** Plain

Date	Mintage	F	VF	XF	Unc	BU
1808 (2007) Proof	600	—	—	—	—	—

X# M11e 4 RIXDOLLAR
Nickel-Silver, 40.98 mm. **Obv:** Laureate bust right **Obv. Legend:** GEORGIUS III DEI GRATIA REX. **Rev:** Elephant standing left in sprays **Rev. Legend:** CEYLON **Edge:** Plain

Date	Mintage	F	VF	XF	Unc	BU
1808 (2007) Proof	600	—	—	—	—	—

X# M11f 4 RIXDOLLAR
Goldine, 40.98 mm. **Obv:** Laureate bust right **Obv. Legend:** GEORGIUS III DEI GRATIA REX. **Rev:** Elephant standing left in sprays **Rev. Legend:** CEYLON **Edge:** Plain

Date	Mintage	F	VF	XF	Unc	BU
1808 (2007) Proof	600	—	—	—	—	—

X# M11g 4 RIXDOLLAR
Gold, 40.98 mm. **Obv:** Laureate bust right **Obv. Legend:** GEORGIUS III DEI GRATIA REX. **Rev:** Elephant standing left in sprays **Rev. Legend:** CEYLON **Edge:** Plain

Date	Mintage	F	VF	XF	Unc	BU
1808 (2007) Proof	—	—	—	—	—	—

MEDALLIC COINAGE

1954 Geoffrey Hearn Issues

X# 1 CROWN
Gilt Bronze **Subject:** Edward VIII

Date	Mintage	F	VF	XF	Unc	BU
1936 Proof	—	Value: 100				

X# 1a CROWN
28.1000 g., Silver

Date	Mintage	F	VF	XF	Unc	BU
1936 Proof	100	Value: 85.00				

X# 1b CROWN
28.1000 g., Silver

Date	Mintage	F	VF	XF	Unc	BU
1936 Restrike; Prooflike	500	—	—	—	40.00	—

X# 1c CROWN
Gold

Date	Mintage	F	VF	XF	Unc	BU
1936 Proof	10	Value: 850				

Note: Restrikes known

Richard Lobel Issues

X# 2 CROWN
Bronze **Subject:** Edward VIII **Obv:** Bust of Edward VIII facing left **Obv. Legend:** EDWARD • VIII • KING • & • EMPEROR **Rev:** Elephant walking 3/4 right

Date	Mintage	F	VF	XF	Unc	BU
1936 Proof	1,000	Value: 25.00				

X# 2c CROWN
Gold **Subject:** Edward VIII **Obv:** Bust of Edward VIII facing left **Obv. Legend:** EDWARD • VIII • KING • & • EMPEROR **Rev:** Elephant walking 3/4 right

Date	Mintage	F	VF	XF	Unc	BU
1936 Proof	—	Value: 500				

X# 2a CROWN
Copper-Nickel-Zinc **Subject:** Edward VIII **Obv:** Bust of Edward VIII facing left **Obv. Legend:** EDWARD • VIII • KING • & • EMPEROR **Rev:** Elephant walking 3/4 right

Date	Mintage	F	VF	XF	Unc	BU
1936 Proof	2,500	Value: 20.00				

X# 2b CROWN
0.9167 Silver **Subject:** Edward VIII **Obv:** Bust of Edward VIII facing left **Obv. Legend:** EDWARD • VIII • KING • & • EMPEROR **Rev:** Elephant walking 3/4 right

Date	Mintage	F	VF	XF	Unc	BU
1936 Proof	250	Value: 75.00				

X# M3 SOVEREIGN
0.3750 Gold **Subject:** Edward VIII

Date	Mintage	F	VF	XF	Unc	BU
1936 Proof	250	Value: 125				

PIEFORTS

X#	Date	Mintage	Identification	Mkt Val
P1	1936	—	Crown. 0.9167 Silver. X#2b.	100

CHEROKEE NATION

SOVEREIGN STATE

MEDALLIC COINAGE

X# M1.1 50 EAGLES
32.7100 g., 0.9250 Silver 0.9727 oz. ASW, 41.7 mm. **Issuer:** Col. H. M. Williams **Obv:** Crossed tomahawk and peace pipe with feather behind **Rev:** Bust of Cherokee brave left **Edge:** Reeded **Note:** Without fineness stamping.

Date	Mintage	F	VF	XF	Unc	BU
1980 Proof	800	Value: 80.00				

X# M1.2 50 EAGLES
32.7100 g., 0.9250 Silver 0.9727 oz. ASW, 41.7 mm. **Issuer:** Col. H. M. Williams **Obv:** Crossed tomahawk and peace pipe with feather behind **Rev:** Bust of Cherokee brave left **Edge:** Reeded **Note:** With fineness stamping. Mintage Inc. X#1.1.

Date	Mintage	F	VF	XF	Unc	BU
1980 Proof	—	Value: 100				

X# M1a 50 EAGLES
Brass, 41.70 mm. **Issuer:** Col. H. M. Williams **Obv:** Crossed tomahawk and peace pipe with feather behind **Rev:** Bust of Cherokee brave left **Edge:** Reeded

Date	Mintage	F	VF	XF	Unc	BU
1980	—	—	—	—	—	50.00

X# M2 ADELA
31.0500 g., 0.9990 Silver 0.9972 oz. ASW, 38.8 mm. **Obv:** Seal (7-pointed star) in sprays, legend including native script **Obv. Legend:** SEAL OF THE CHEROKEE NATION - SEPT. 6. 1839 **Rev:** Bust of John Ross 3/4 left in outlined 7-pointed star, legend in native script **Edge:** Reeded

Date	Mintage	F	VF	XF	Unc	BU
2000 Proof	4,000	Value: 70.00				

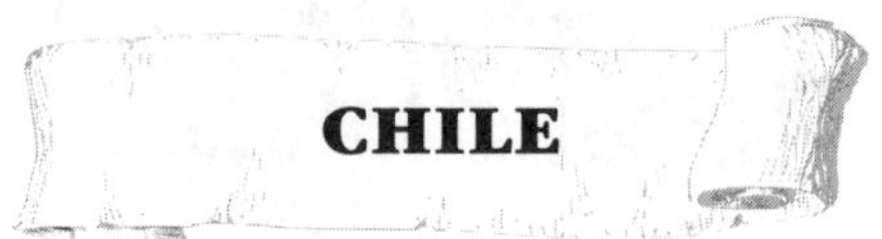

CHILE

REPUBLIC

SILVER BULLION COINAGE

X# 3 1/4 ONZA
7.7770 g., 0.9990 Silver 0.2498 oz. ASW **Subject:** 10th Anniversary of National Liberation **Note:** Prev. KM#223.

Date	Mintage	F	VF	XF	Unc	BU
ND(1983)So Proof	1,000	Value: 25.00				

X# 4 1/2 ONZA
15.5530 g., 0.9990 Silver 0.4995 oz. ASW **Subject:** 10th Anniversary of National Liberation **Note:** Prev. KM#224.

Date	Mintage	F	VF	XF	Unc	BU
ND(1983)So Proof	1,000	Value: 35.00				

X# 1a ONZA
Silver

Date	Mintage	F	VF	XF	Unc	BU
1948So	—	—	—	—	75.00	—

X# 1b ONZA
Copper

Date	Mintage	F	VF	XF	Unc	BU
1948So	—	—	—	—	30.00	—

X# 5 ONZA
31.1070 g., 0.9990 Silver 0.9991 oz. ASW **Subject:** 10th Anniversary of National Liberation **Note:** Prev. KM#5.

Date	Mintage	F	VF	XF	Unc	BU
ND(1983)So Proof	1,000	Value: 75.00				

X# 31 ONZA
31.1035 g., 0.9990 Silver 0.9990 oz. ASW **Subject:** Numismatic Association of Chile **Obv:** Similar to 4 Escudos, KM#2 **Rev:** Similar to 1/2 Real, KM#90 obverse

Date	Mintage	F	VF	XF	Unc	BU
ND(1999) Proof	75	Value: 55.00				

X# 32 ONZA
Silver **Obv:** First 1 Peso bank note of the Republica de Chile **Rev:** Chilean Numismatic Society and 1/2 Real KM#90

Date	Mintage	F	VF	XF	Unc	BU
2000 Proof	90	Value: 55.00				

X# 33 ONZA
Silver **Obv:** Nitrate Token Oficina Iberia "El Palero" Espinoza 140.10 **Rev:** Similar to KM#234

Date	Mintage	F	VF	XF	Unc	BU
2001 Proof	100	Value: 50.00				

X# 34 ONZA
Silver **Obv:** First Chilean Pattern 1819 "Peso Portales" **Rev:** Similar to KM#234

Date	Mintage	F	VF	XF	Unc	BU
2001 Proof	80	Value: 60.00				

X# 35 ONZA
Silver **Subject:** 8 Escudos Similar to KM#25 **Rev:** Similar to KM#234

Date	Mintage	F	VF	XF	Unc	BU
2002 Proof	80	Value: 55.00				

GOLD BULLION COINAGE

X# 6 1/4 ONZA
8.6400 g., 0.9000 Gold 0.2500 oz. AGW **Subject:** 10th Anniversary of National Liberation **Note:** Prev. KM#220. Similar to KM#223.

Date	Mintage	F	VF	XF	Unc	BU
ND(1983)So	1,000	—	—	—	175	—

X# 7 1/2 ONZA
17.2800 g., 0.9000 Gold 0.5000 oz. AGW **Subject:** 10th Anniversary of National Liberation **Note:** Prev. KM#221. Similar to KM#224.

Date	Mintage	F	VF	XF	Unc	BU
ND(1983)So	1,000	—	—	—	350	—

X# 1 ONZA
31.1030 g., 1.0000 Gold 0.9999 oz. AGW

Date	Mintage	F	VF	XF	Unc	BU
1948So	1,950	—	—	—	850	—

X# 2 ONZA
31.1000 g., 0.9990 Gold 0.9988 oz. AGW **Obv:** Crowned arms **Rev:** Crowned pillars and hemispheres **Note:** Prev. KM#215.

Date	Mintage	F	VF	XF	Unc	BU
1978So	—	—	—	—	750	—
1979So	1,580	—	—	—	600	—
1980So	1,730	—	—	—	600	—
1981So	200	—	—	—	700	—
1983So	999	—	—	—	650	—
1983So Proof	1	—	—	—	—	—

X# 8 ONZA
34.5590 g., 0.9000 Gold 0.9999 oz. AGW **Subject:** 10th Anniversary of National Liberation **Note:** Prev. KM#222. Similar to KM#225.

Date	Mintage	F	VF	XF	Unc	BU
1983	1,000	—	—	—	675	—

COPIAPO

BLOCKADE OF PUERTO DE CALDERA

SIEGE COINAGE

Issued during the War of 1865 with Spain

KM# 3 50 CENTAVOS
11.0000 g., 0.9700 Silver 0.3430 oz. ASW, 27 mm. **Obv:** Legend around shield, denomination flanking **Obv. Legend:** COPIAPO-CHILE **Rev:** Date

Date	Mintage	VG	F	VF	XF	Unc
1865 7 known	—	—	—	350	500	—

Note: All known 50 Centavos are restrikes made from original dies circa 1909 by Medina

KM# 4 PESO
22.0000 g., 0.9700 Silver 0.6861 oz. ASW, 35 mm.

Date	Mintage	VG	F	VF	XF	Unc
1865 Restrike	—	—	40.00	60.00	75.00	—

X# 4a PESO
Copper **Note:** Prev. KM#4a.

Date	Mintage	VG	F	VF	XF	Unc
1865	—	850	1,350	2,000	—	—

Note: Possibly a pattern, but generally thought to be a counterfeit

TARAPACA

REPUBLIC

REVOLUTIONARY COINAGE

X# 2 PESO

Copper **Note:** Prev. KM#2.

Date	Mintage	F	VF	XF	Unc	BU
1891	—	—	880	—	—	—

Note: Possible pattern, but generally thought to be a counterfeit of the originals pieces struck at Iquique by the revolutionary junta.

X# 3 PESO

Brass **Note:** Prev. KM#3.

Date	Mintage	F	VF	XF	Unc	BU
1891	—	—	700	—	—	—

Note: Possible pattern, but generally thought to be a counterfeit of the originals pieces struck at Iquique by the revolutionary junta.

EMPIRE

Based on a manuscript by Bruce Wayne Smith.

Emperors

同 治

T'ung-chih, (Mu-tsung), 2nd reign
1862-1875
Reign title: T'ung-chih T'ung-pao

德宗 光緒

Kuang-hsü (Te-tsung)
1875-1908
Reign title: Kuang-hsü T'ung-pao

宣 統

HSÜAN-T'UNG Ti

1908-1911
Reign title: Hsüan-t'ung T'ung-pao (Xuantong)

憲 洪

HUNG-HSIEN
(Yuan Shih-k'ai)
Dec. 15, 1915 - March 21, 1916
Reign title: Hung-hsien T'ung-pao

NUMERALS

NUMBER	CONVENTIONAL	FORMAL	COMMERCIAL
1	一 元	壹 弌	〡
2	二	弍 貳	〢
3	三	叁 弎	〣
4	四	肆	〤
5	五	伍	〥
6	六	陸	〦
7	七	柒	〧
8	八	捌	〨
9	九	玖	〩
10	十	拾 什	十
20	十 二 or 廿	拾貳	〢十
25	五 十 二 or 五廿	伍拾貳	〢十〥
30	十 三 or 卅	拾叁	〣十
100	百 一	佰壹	〡百
1,000	千 一	仟壹	〡千
10,000	萬 一	萬壹	〡万
100,000	萬十 億一	萬拾 億壹	十万
1,000,000	萬百一	萬佰壹	〡百万

NOTE: This table has been adapted from Chinese Bank Notes by Ward Smith and Brian Matravers.

MONETARY UNITS

Dollar Amounts		
DOLLAR (*Yuan*)	元 or 員	圓 or 圜
HALF DOLLAR (*Pan Yuan*)	圓 半	元中
50¢ (*Chiao/Hao*)	角伍	毫伍
10¢ (*Chiao/Hao*)	角壹	毫壹
1¢ (*Fen/Hsien*)	分壹	仙壹

Copper and Cash Coin Amounts

COPPER (*Mei*)	枚	CASH (*Wen*)	文

Tael Amounts	
1 TAEL (*Liang*)	兩
HALF TAEL (*Pan Liang*)	兩半
5 MACE (*Wu Ch'ien*)	錢伍
1 MACE (*I Ch'ien*)	錢壹
1 CANDEREEN (*I Fen*)	分壹

Common Prefixes

COPPER (*T'ung*)	銅	GOLD (*Chin*)	金
SILVER (*Yin*)	銀	Ku Ping (*Tael*)*	平庫

NOTE: This table has been adapted from Chinese Bank Notes by Ward Smith and Brian Matravers.

MONETARY SYSTEM

Cash Coin System

1 Tael = 800-1600 Cash*

**In theory, 1000 cash were equal to a tael of silver, but in actuality the rate varied from time to time and from place to place.*

Dollar System

10 Cash (Wen, Ch'ien) = 1 Cent (Fen, Hsien)
10 Cents = 1 Chiao (Hao)
100 Cents = 1 Dollar (Yuan)
1 Dollar = 0.72 Tael

Tael System

10 Li = 1 Fen (Candareen)
10 Fen (Candareen) = 1 Ch'ien (Mace)
10 Ch'ien (Mace) = 1 Liang (Tael)

DATING

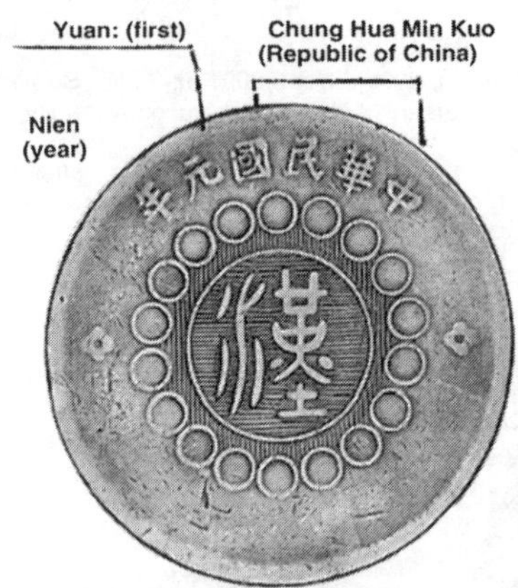

Most struck Chinese coins are dated by year within a given period, such as the regnal eras or the republican periods. A 1907 issue, for example, would be dated in the 33rd year of the Kuang Hsu era (1875 + 33 - 1 = 1907) or a 1926 issue is dated in the 15th year of the Republic (1912 + 15 - 1 = 1926). The mathematical discrepancy in both instances is accounted for by the fact that the first year is included in the elapsed time. Modern Chinese Communist coins are dated in western numerals using the western calendar, but earlier issues use conventional Chinese numerals. The coins of the Republic of China (Taiwan) are also dated in the year of the Republic, which is added to equal the calendar year. Still another method is a 60-year, repeating cycle, outlined in the table below. The date is shown by the combination of two characters, the first from the top row and the second from the column at left. In this catalog, when a cyclical date is used, the abbreviation CD appears before the AD date.

Dates not in parentheses are those which appear on the coins. For undated coins, dates appearing in parentheses are the years in which the coin was actually minted. Undated coins for which the year of minting is unknown are listed with ND (No Date) in the date or year column.

CYCLICAL DATING

	庚	辛	壬	癸	甲	乙	丙	丁	戊	己
戌	1850 1910		1862 1922		1874 1934		1886 1946		1838 1898	
亥		1851 1911		1863 1923		1875 1935		1887 1947		1839 1899
子	1840 1900		1852 1912		1864 1924		1876 1936		1888 1948	
丑		1841 1901		1853 1913		1865 1925		1877 1937		1889 1949
寅	1830 1890		1842 1902		1854 1914		1866 1926		1878 1938	
卯		1831 1891		1843 1903		1855 1915		1867 1927		1879 1939
辰	1880 1940		1832 1892		1844 1904		1856 1916		1868 1928	
巳		1881 1941		1833 1893		1845 1905		1857 1917		1869 1929
午	1870 1930		1882 1942		1834 1894		1846 1906		1858 1918	
未		1871 1931		1883 1943		1835 1895		1847 1907		1859 1919
申	1860 1920		1872 1932		1884 1944		1836 1896		1848 1908	
酉		1861 1921		1873 1933		1885 1945		1837 1897		1849 1909

NOTE: This table has been adapted from Chinese Bank Notes by Ward Smith and Brian Matravers.

REFERENCES

The following references have been used for this section:

K - Edward Kann - Illustrated Catalog of Chinese Coins.

MING DYNASTY

1368 - 1644

MEDALLIC COINAGE

Ming Emperor Hung Wu Issues

X# M285 DOLLAR

Silver **Note:** Kann#B1. Modern fantasy.

Date	Mintage	F	VF	XF	Unc
1375	—	—	35.00	65.00	100

X# M286 DOLLAR

Copper **Note:** Modern fantasy.

Date	Mintage	F	VF	XF	Unc
1375	—	—	20.00	35.00	65.00

MEDALLIC COINAGE

T'ai P'ing Rebel Issue

X# M355 DOLLAR

Gold **Note:** Kann#1483. Modern fantasy.

Date	Mintage	F	VF	XF	Unc
ND	—	—	—	—	—

CH'ING DYNASTY

Manchu, 1644 - 1911

MEDALLIC COINAGE

Empress Yun Lu and Peacock Issues

X# M180 DOLLAR

Silver **Series:** Peacock **Note:** Kann#B12.

Date	Mintage	F	VF	XF	Unc
ND(1821)/1	—	—	250	350	500

X# M181 DOLLAR

Gold **Series:** Peacock

Date	Mintage	F	VF	XF	Unc
ND(1821)/1	—	—	—	3,500	5,000

X# M185 DOLLAR

Silver **Series:** Peacock

Date	Mintage	F	VF	XF	Unc
ND(1821)/1	—	—	250	350	500

X# M190 DOLLAR

Silver **Series:** Peacock **Note:** Kann#B14.

Date	Mintage	F	VF	XF	Unc
CD1885	—	—	125	200	300

X# M191 DOLLAR

Gold **Series:** Peacock

Date	Mintage	F	VF	XF	Unc
CD1885	—	—	—	2,000	3,500

X# M192 DOLLAR

Bronze **Series:** Peacock

Date	Mintage	F	VF	XF	Unc
CD1885	—	—	100	175	275

X# M195 DOLLAR

Silver **Series:** Peacock **Obverse:** Modified design
Note: Believed to have been produced ca.1940.

Date	Mintage	F	VF	XF	Unc
CD1885	—	—	125	200	300

X# M197 DOLLAR
Silver **Series:** Peacock **Obverse:** Modified design

Date	Mintage	F	VF	XF	Unc
CD1885	—	—	125	200	300

X# M198 DOLLAR
Silver **Series:** Peacock **Obverse:** Thinner portrait

Date	Mintage	F	VF	XF	Unc
CD1885	—	—	125	200	300

MEDALLIC COINAGE

Empress and Bats Issues

X# M200 5 DOLLARS
Gold **Series:** Bats **Note:** Kann#B90.

Date	Mintage	F	VF	XF	Unc
ND	—	—	—	650	900

X# M201 5 DOLLARS
Silver **Series:** Bats **Note:** Kann#B90.

Date	Mintage	F	VF	XF	Unc
ND	—	—	125	200	300

MEDALLIC COINAGE

Empress, Peacock and Bats Issues

X# M205 DOLLAR
Silver **Series:** Peacock and Bats **Obverse:** 4 Chinese characters, "Respectfully presented by Yunnan (Province)," at bottom

Date	Mintage	F	VF	XF	Unc
ND	—	—	200	300	450

X# M210 DOLLAR
Silver **Series:** Peacock and Bats **Obverse:** Tassel at right missing **Note:** Kann#B26.

Date	Mintage	F	VF	XF	Unc
ND	—	—	200	300	450

X# M211 DOLLAR
Gold **Series:** Peacock and Bats **Obverse:** Tassel at right missing

Date	Mintage	F	VF	XF	Unc
ND	—	—	—	—	—

X# M215 DOLLAR
Silver **Series:** Peacock and Bats **Note:** Mule. Obv: XM205. Rev: XM135.

Date	Mintage	F	VF	XF	Unc
ND	—	—	200	300	450

X# M225 DOLLAR
Silver **Series:** Peacock and Bats **Obverse:** 4 Chinese characters at bottom **Obv. Legend:** "Made in Chekiang Province"

Date	Mintage	F	VF	XF	Unc
ND	—	—	150	250	400

X# M227 DOLLAR
Silver **Series:** Peacock and Bats **Obverse:** Modified design

Date	Mintage	F	VF	XF	Unc
ND	—	—	150	250	400

X# M228 DOLLAR
Silver **Series:** Peacock and Bats **Obverse:** Younger face

Date	Mintage	F	VF	XF	Unc
ND	—	—	150	250	400

X# M230 DOLLAR
Silver **Series:** Peacock and Bats **Obverse:** Modified design **Edge:** Crudely reeded

Date	Mintage	F	VF	XF	Unc
ND	—	—	150	250	400

X# M235 DOLLAR
Silver **Series:** Peacock and Bats **Obverse:** Modified design **Reverse:** Modified design **Edge:** Geometric design **Note:** Kann#B25.

Date	Mintage	F	VF	XF	Unc
ND	—	—	150	250	400

X# M236 DOLLAR
Gold **Series:** Peacock and Bats **Obverse:** Modified design **Reverse:** Modified design **Edge:** Geometric design

Date	Mintage	F	VF	XF	Unc
ND	—	—	150	250	400

MEDALLIC COINAGE

Ralph Heaton & Sons Issues

Birmingham

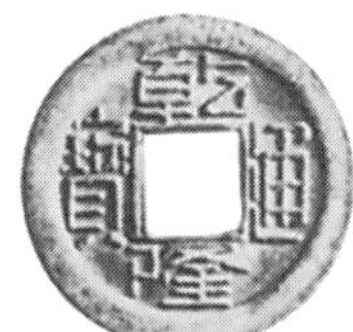

X# M238 CASH
Brass **Obverse:** "Chi en-lung T'ung Pao **Note:** An advertising token struck by this mint.

Date	Mintage	F	VF	XF	Unc
ND(1889)	—	—	—	200	500

MEDALLIC COINAGE

Horse and Dragon Issues

X# M240 DOLLAR
Silver **Obverse:** 4 Chinese characters, "Made in Kansu Province," at top **Note:** Kann#B32.

Date	Mintage	F	VF	XF	Unc
CD1905	—	—	175	250	350

X# M245 DOLLAR
Silver **Obverse:** 4 Chinese characters, "Made in Kansu Province," at top

Date	Mintage	F	VF	XF	Unc
CD1907	—	—	175	250	350

X# M250 DOLLAR
Silver **Obverse:** 4 Chinese characters, "Made in Kwangtung Province," at top **Note:** Kann#B36. Occasionally encountered with "Tung" altered to "Hsi."

Date	Mintage	F	VF	XF	Unc
CD1907	—	—	175	250	350

X# M251 DOLLAR
Silver **Obverse:** 4 Chinese characters, "Made at Kwangtung Province," at top **Note:** Kann#B36.

Date	Mintage	F	VF	XF	Unc
CD1907	—	—	175	250	350

X# M260 TAEL
Silver **Obverse:** Chinese character "Tai(wan)" at right, "Tael" at left, 4 Chinese characters, "Taiwan Military Pay," in center **Note:** Kann#B37.

Date	Mintage	F	VF	XF	Unc
ND	—	—	250	350	500

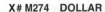

X# M265 TAEL
Silver **Obverse:** Modified design **Reverse:** Modified design

Date	Mintage	F	VF	XF	Unc
ND	—	—	250	350	500

MEDALLIC COINAGE

Emperor Hsuan T'ung Issues

X# M271 50 CENTS
Silver

Date	Mintage	F	VF	XF	Unc
ND(1909-11)	—	—	35.00	60.00	90.00

X# M272 50 CENTS
Gold **Note:** Kann#B96.

Date	Mintage	F	VF	XF	Unc
ND(1909-11)	—	—	—	1,500	2,500

X# M273 DOLLAR
Silver **Note:** Kann#B95.

Date	Mintage	F	VF	XF	Unc
ND(1909-11)	—	—	40.00	65.00	100

X# M274 DOLLAR
Gold

Date	Mintage	F	VF	XF	Unc
ND(1909-11)	—	—	—	1,000	2,000

X# M275 10 DOLLARS
Gold, 19.5 mm. **Note:** Kann#B96. Similar to XM271.

Date	Mintage	F	VF	XF	Unc
ND(1909-11)	—	—	—	1,000	2,000

X# M276 10 DOLLARS
Silver, 19.5 mm.

Date	Mintage	F	VF	XF	Unc
ND(1909-11)	—	—	40.00	65.00	100

X# M277 20 DOLLARS
Gold, 26 mm. **Note:** Kann#B97. Similar to XM271.

Date	Mintage	F	VF	XF	Unc
ND(1909-11)	—	—	—	1,200	2,500

X# M278 20 DOLLARS
Silver, 26 mm.

Date	Mintage	F	VF	XF	Unc
ND(1909-11)	—	—	40.00	65.00	100

MEDALLIC COINAGE

Li Hung-Chang Issues

X# M290 TAEL
Silver **Note:** Kann#B39.

Date	Mintage	F	VF	XF	Unc
ND	—	—	175	250	350

X# M291 TAEL
Gold

Date	Mintage	F	VF	XF	Unc
ND	—	—	—	2,500	3,500

X# M295 TAEL
Silver **Reverse:** Denomination removed at top

Date	Mintage	F	VF	XF	Unc
ND	—	—	125	200	300

X# M296 TAEL
Gold **Reverse:** Denomination removed at top

Date	Mintage	F	VF	XF	Unc
ND	—	—	—	2,500	3,500

MEDALLIC COINAGE

Miao Tribes Issues

X# M298 10 CASH
Copper **Obverse:** 2 Chinese characters, "Copper Coin," at center surrounded by 14 Chinese characters

Date	Mintage	F	VF	XF	Unc
ND	—	—	25.00	35.00	60.00

MEDALLIC COINAGE

Pan Chan Lama Issues

X# M300 DOLLAR
Silver **Rev. Legend:** "Ch'ien Lung"

Date	Mintage	F	VF	XF	Unc
ND	—	—	150	250	350

X# M302 DOLLAR
Silver **Reverse:** Blundered Tibetan characters **Note:** Kann#B74.

Date	Mintage	F	VF	XF	Unc
ND	—	—	125	200	300

X# M305 DOLLAR

Silver **Obverse:** Modified effigy

Date	Mintage	F	VF	XF	Unc
ND	—	—	125	200	300

X# M307 DOLLAR

Silver **Note:** Kann#B75.

Date	Mintage	F	VF	XF	Unc
ND	—	—	125	200	300

MEDALLIC COINAGE

Sinkiang Tael Issues

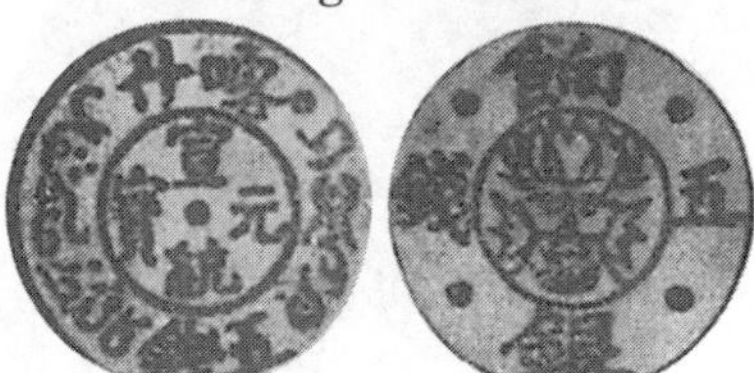

X# M325 5 MACE

Silver **Subject:** Hsuan T'ung **Note:** Kann#B88. Mint: Kashgar

Date	Mintage	F	VF	XF	Unc
ND	—	—	75.00	125	175

X# M330 TAEL

Silver **Subject:** Kuang Hsu **Note:** Kann#B83. Mint: Kashgar

Date	Mintage	F	VF	XF	Unc
ND	—	—	125	200	300

Note: Blundered date at 10 o'clock on obverse

X# M345 TAEL

Silver **Subject:** Kuang Hsu **Rev. Legend:** Error: SUNGAREI-1 TEAL. **Note:** Similar to 1 Tael, Kann #1031.

Date	Mintage	F	VF	XF	Unc
ND	—	—	175	250	350

X# M335 TAEL

Silver **Subject:** Hsuan T'ung **Note:** Kann#B81. Mint: Kashgar

Date	Mintage	F	VF	XF	Unc
AH1329(1911)	—	—	175	250	350

X# M340 TAEL

Silver **Rev. Legend:** One Tael Ration Coin **Note:** Kann#B84.

Date	Mintage	F	VF	XF	Unc
AH1329(1911)	—	—	125	200	300

MEDALLIC COINAGE

Szechuan-Tibet Dollar Issues

X# M422 10 CENTS

Silver **Subject:** Empress

Date	Mintage	F	VF	XF	Unc
ND	—	—	—	150	200

X# M423 10 CENTS

Gold **Subject:** Empress **Note:** Prev. XM450.

Date	Mintage	F	VF	XF	Unc
ND	—	—	—	500	750

X# M425 1/4 DOLLAR

Silver, 24 mm. **Note:** Similar to Dollar, XM430.

Date	Mintage	F	VF	XF	Unc
ND	—	—	—	175	225

X# M427 1/2 DOLLAR

Silver **Subject:** Empress **Note:** Kann#B28.

Date	Mintage	F	VF	XF	Unc
ND	—	—	—	200	275

X# M429 DOLLAR
Silver **Subject:** Empress Type I **Note:** Kann#B27.

Date	Mintage	F	VF	XF	Unc
ND	—	—	150	250	350

X# M430 DOLLAR
Silver **Subject:** Empress Type II

Date	Mintage	F	VF	XF	Unc
ND	—	—	150	250	350

X# M431 DOLLAR
Silver **Subject:** Empress Type III

Date	Mintage	F	VF	XF	Unc
ND	—	—	150	250	350

X# M435 DOLLAR
Silver **Obverse:** Emperor facing

Date	Mintage	F	VF	XF	Unc
ND	—	—	135	250	350

MEDALLIC COINAGE

Taiwan "Old Man" Dollar Series

X# M360 1/2 DOLLAR
Silver **Note:** Kann#B3.

Date	Mintage	F	VF	XF	Unc
ND	—	—	125	200	275

X# M363 1/2 DOLLAR
Silver **Obverse:** Modified effigy **Note:** Kann#B4.

Date	Mintage	F	VF	XF	Unc
ND	—	—	125	200	275

X# M368 DOLLAR
Silver **Reverse:** Modified effigy

Date	Mintage	F	VF	XF	Unc
ND	—	—	125	200	300

X# M370 DOLLAR
Silver **Reverse:** Outline effigy **Note:** Kann#B5.

Date	Mintage	F	VF	XF	Unc
ND	—	—	125	200	300

MEDALLIC COINAGE

Taiwan Issues

X# M373 DOLLAR
Silver **Subject:** Kuang Hsu **Note:** Kann#B36. Mint: Taiwan Central.

Date	Mintage	F	VF	XF	Unc
ND	—	—	135	225	325

X# M375 TAEL
Silver **Note:** Mint: Tainan.

Date	Mintage	F	VF	XF	Unc
ND	—	—	—	—	—

X# M377 TAEL
Silver **Obverse:** Tiger sitting in circle **Rev. Legend:** 2 Chinese characters, "One Tael," in center with 4 Chinese characters around

Date	Mintage	F	VF	XF	Unc
ND	—	—	—	—	—

MEDALLIC COINAGE

Tibet Ch'ien Lung Dollar Issues

X# M383 DOLLAR
Silver

Date	Mintage	F	VF	XF	Unc
ND	—	—	175	250	350

X# M380 DOLLAR
Silver **Note:** Kann#B2.

Date	Mintage	F	VF	XF	Unc
ND(1793)/58	—	—	175	250	350

MEDALLIC COINAGE

Tibet K'ang Hsi Tael Issues

X# M385 MACE
Silver, 25 mm. **Reverse:** 2 Chinese characters in inscription **Rev. Inscription:** "One Mace"

Date	Mintage	F	VF	XF	Unc
ND(1662)/1	—	—	—	—	—

X# M386 2 MACE
Silver, 26 mm. **Rev. Legend:** 2 Chinese characters, "Two Mace"

Date	Mintage	F	VF	XF	Unc
ND(1662)/1	—	—	—	—	—

X# M387 3 MACE
Silver, 30 mm. **Rev. Legend:** 2 Chinese characters, "Three Mace"

Date	Mintage	F	VF	XF	Unc
ND(1662)/1	—	—	—	—	—

X# M388 1/2 TAEL
Silver, 34 mm. **Rev. Legend:** 2 Chinese characters, "Half Tael"

Date	Mintage	F	VF	XF	Unc
ND(1662)/1	—	—	—	—	—

X# M389 TAEL
Silver **Rev. Legend:** 2 Chinese characters, "One Tael"

Date	Mintage	F	VF	XF	Unc
ND(1662)/1	—	—	—	—	—

MEDALLIC COINAGE

Tibet Ch'ien Lung Tael Issues

X# M395 TAEL
Silver

Date	Mintage	F	VF	XF	Unc
ND(1794)/58	—	—	—	—	—

X# M393 1/2 SHO
Gold

Date	Mintage	F	VF	XF	Unc
ND(1794)/58	—	—	—	—	—

MEDALLIC COINAGE

Tibet Chia Ching Tael Issues

X# M397 TAEL
Silver, 35 mm. **Note:** Similar to XM389.

Date	Mintage	F	VF	XF	Unc
ND(1796)/1	—	—	—	—	—

MEDALLIC COINAGE

Tibet Hsien Fêng Tael Issues

X# M400 MACE
Silver **Note:** Kann#B78.

Date	Mintage	F	VF	XF	Unc
ND(1853)/3	—	—	—	—	—

X# M401 MACE
Gold **Note:** Kann#B78.

Date	Mintage	F	VF	XF	Unc
ND(1853)/3	—	—	—	—	—

X# M405 TAEL
Gold **Note:** Kann#B108.

Date	Mintage	F	VF	XF	Unc
ND(1851)/1	—	—	—	—	—

MEDALLIC COINAGE

Tibet T'ung Chih Tael Issues

X# M410 MACE
Silver

Date	Mintage	F	VF	XF	Unc
ND(1862)/1	—	—	—	—	—

X# M455 5 TAELS

Gold **Subject:** 50th Anniversary **Note:** Kann#B102. Believed to have been struck in Shanghai ca.1919.

Date	Mintage	F	VF	XF	Unc
CD1869 Proof	—	Value: 6,000			

X# M465 5//25 TAELS

94.9000 g., Gold **Obverse:** 5 Chinese characters, "Value Five Taels Gold," at bottom

Date	Mintage	F	VF	XF	Unc
ND(1871)/10 Proof	—	Value: 7,000			

X# M470 5//25 TAELS

94.9000 g., Gold

Date	Mintage	F	VF	XF	Unc
ND(1871)/10 Proof	—	Value: 7,000			

X# M467 5//25 TAELS

94.9000 g., Gold **Reverse:** Like XM465

Date	Mintage	F	VF	XF	Unc
ND(1871)/10 Proof	—	Value: 7,000			

X# M475 50 TAELS

189.3000 g., Gold **Obverse:** 5 Chinese characters, "Value Fifty Taels Gold," at bottom

Date	Mintage	F	VF	XF	Unc
ND(1871)/10 Proof	—	Value: 10,000			

MEDALLIC COINAGE

Tibet Kuang Hsu Tael Issues

X# M415 MACE

Silver **Note:** Kann#B79.

Date	Mintage	F	VF	XF	Unc
ND(1878)/4	—	—	—	—	—

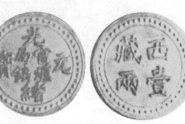

X# M417 TAEL

34.7000 g., Silver **Obverse:** 4 Chinese characters, "Made in the Official Furnace," in center **Reverse:** 4 Chinese characters, "Tibet; One Tael" **Note:** Kann#1479.

Date	Mintage	F	VF	XF	Unc
ND	—	—	60.00	100	—

X# M418 TAEL

34.7000 g., Silver **Note:** Kann#1479z. Mule. 2 obverses.

Date	Mintage	F	VF	XF	Unc
ND	—	—	60.00	100	—

X# M419 TAEL

34.7000 g., Silver **Note:** Kann#1479y. Mule. 2 reverses.

Date	Mintage	F	VF	XF	Unc
ND	—	—	60.00	100	—

MEDALLIC COINAGE

Tibet Ch'ien Lung Pagoda Tanga Series

X# M420 TANGA

Silver **Note:** Kann#B76.

Date	Mintage	F	VF	XF	Unc
ND	—	—	100	150	200

X# M421 TANGA

Copper **Note:** Kann#B76.

Date	Mintage	F	VF	XF	Unc
ND	—	—	40.00	60.00	100

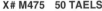

MEDALLIC COINAGE

T'ung Chih Tael Series

X# M460 5 TAELS
Gold

Date	Mintage	F	VF	XF	Unc
ND(1863)/2 Proof	—	Value: 6,500			

TAO-KUANG
Daoguang

MEDALLIC COINAGE

Emperor Tao Kuang Issues

X# M90 DOLLAR
Silver **Obverse:** Ornamental Greek border. **Reverse:** Facing dragon **Note:** Kann#B11.

Date	Mintage	F	VF	XF	Unc
CD1821	—	—	225	300	400

X# M91 DOLLAR
Gold **Obverse:** Ornamental Greek border **Reverse:** Facing dragon **Note:** Kann#B11.

Date	Mintage	F	VF	XF	Unc
CD1821	—	—	—	4,000	5,500

X# M95 DOLLAR
Silver **Obverse:** Ornamental Greek border **Reverse:** Modified facing dragon

Date	Mintage	F	VF	XF	Unc
CD1821	—	—	225	300	400

MEDALLIC COINAGE

Taiwan "Old Man" Dollar Series

X# M365 DOLLAR
Silver **Subject:** Tao Kuang

Date	Mintage	F	VF	XF	Unc
ND	—	—	125	200	300

HSIEN-FÊNG

CAST FANTASY COINAGE

X# CF105 6 CASH
Brass **Mint:** Hu-pu Board of Revenue

Date	Mintage	F	VF	XF	Unc
ND(1851-61)	—	—	—	50.00	—

X# CF106 6 CASH
Brass **Mint:** Kung-pu Board of Public Works

Date	Mintage	F	VF	XF	Unc
ND(1851-61)	—	—	—	50.00	—

X# CF110 9 CASH
Brass **Mint:** Hu-pu Board of Revenue

Date	Mintage	F	VF	XF	Unc
ND(1851-61)	—	—	—	50.00	—

X# CF111 9 CASH
Brass **Mint:** Kung-pu Board of Public Works

Date	Mintage	F	VF	XF	Unc
ND(1851-61)	—	—	—	50.00	—

X# CF115 20 CASH
Brass **Mint:** Hu-pu Board of Revenue

Date	Mintage	F	VF	XF	Unc
ND(1851-61)	—	—	—	50.00	—

X# CF116 20 CASH
Brass **Mint:** Honan

Date	Mintage	F	VF	XF	Unc
ND(1851-61)	—	—	—	50.00	—

X# CF117 20 CASH
Brass **Mint:** Hsüanfu

Date	Mintage	F	VF	XF	Unc
ND(1851-61)	—	—	—	50.00	—

X# CF118 20 CASH
Brass **Mint:** Kiangsi

Date	Mintage	F	VF	XF	Unc
ND(1851-61)	—	—	—	50.00	—

X# CF120 30 CASH
Brass **Mint:** Hu-pu Board of Revenue

Date	Mintage	F	VF	XF	Unc
ND(1851-61)	—	—	—	50.00	—

X# CF121 30 CASH
Brass **Mint:** Kung-pu Board of Public Works

Date	Mintage	F	VF	XF	Unc
ND(1851-61)	—	—	—	50.00	—

X# CF122 30 CASH
Brass **Mint:** Anhwei

Date	Mintage	F	VF	XF	Unc
ND(1851-61)	—	—	—	50.00	—

X# CF123 30 CASH
Brass **Mint:** Foochou

Date	Mintage	F	VF	XF	Unc
ND(1851-61)	—	—	—	50.00	—

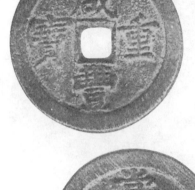

X# CF124 30 CASH
Brass **Mint:** Hsüanfu

Date	Mintage	F	VF	XF	Unc
ND(1851-61)	—	—	—	50.00	—

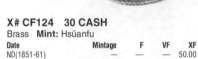

X# CF125 30 CASH
Brass **Mint:** Kiangsi

Date	Mintage	F	VF	XF	Unc
ND(1851-61)	—	—	—	50.00	—

X# CF127 40 CASH
Brass **Mint:** Hu-pu Board of Revenue

Date	Mintage	F	VF	XF	Unc
ND(1851-61)	—	—	—	50.00	—

X# CF128 40 CASH
Brass **Mint:** Foochou

Date	Mintage	F	VF	XF	Unc
ND(1851-61)	—	—	—	50.00	—

X# CF129 40 CASH
Brass **Mint:** Honan

Date	Mintage	F	VF	XF	Unc
ND(1851-61)	—	—	—	50.00	—

X# CF133 50 CASH
Brass **Mint:** Kwangtung

Date	Mintage	F	VF	XF	Unc
ND(1851-61)	—	—	—	50.00	—

X# CF139 70 CASH
Brass **Mint:** Honan

Date	Mintage	F	VF	XF	Unc
ND(1851-61)	—	—	—	50.00	—

X# CF144 80 CASH
Brass **Mint:** Kung-pu Board of Public Works

Date	Mintage	F	VF	XF	Unc
ND(1851-61)	—	—	—	50.00	—

X# CF148 90 CASH

Brass **Mint:** Hu-pu Board of Revenue

Date	Mintage	F	VF	XF	Unc
ND(1851-61)	—	—	—	50.00	—

X# CF149 90 CASH

Brass, 54 mm. **Mint:** Kung-pu Board of Public Works

Date	Mintage	F	VF	XF	Unc
ND(1851-61)	—	—	—	50.00	—

X# CF151 100 CASH

Brass **Mint:** Kansu

Date	Mintage	F	VF	XF	Unc
ND(1851-61)	—	—	—	50.00	—

X# CF152 100 CASH

Brass **Mint:** Kiangsu

Date	Mintage	F	VF	XF	Unc
ND(1851-61)	—	—	—	50.00	—

X# CF153 100 CASH

Brass **Mint:** Kwangsi

Date	Mintage	F	VF	XF	Unc
ND(1851-61)	—	—	—	50.00	—

X# CF154 100 CASH

Brass **Mint:** Shensi

Date	Mintage	F	VF	XF	Unc
ND(1851-61)	—	—	—	50.00	—

X# CF155 100 CASH

Brass **Mint:** Yarkand

Date	Mintage	F	VF	XF	Unc
ND(1851-61)	—	—	—	50.00	—

X# CF156 100 CASH

Brass **Mint:** Yünnan-fu

Date	Mintage	F	VF	XF	Unc
ND(1851-61)	—	—	—	50.00	—

X# CF157 100 CASH

Brass **Mint:** Kiangsi

Date	Mintage	F	VF	XF	Unc
ND(1851-61)	—	—	—	50.00	—

X# CF158 100 CASH

Brass **Mint:** Kweichow

Date	Mintage	F	VF	XF	Unc
ND(1851-61)	—	—	—	50.00	—

X# CF160 300 CASH

Brass **Mint:** Hu-pu Board of Revenue

Date	Mintage	F	VF	XF	Unc
ND(1851-61)	—	—	—	50.00	—

X# CF161 300 CASH

Brass **Mint:** Kiangsu

Date	Mintage	F	VF	XF	Unc
ND(1851-61)	—	—	—	50.00	—

X# CF162 300 CASH

Brass **Mint:** Kiangsi

Date	Mintage	F	VF	XF	Unc
ND(1851-61)	—	—	—	50.00	—

X# CF165 400 CASH

Brass **Mint:** Hu-pu Board of Revenue

Date	Mintage	F	VF	XF	Unc
ND(1851-61)	—	—	—	50.00	—

X# CF166 400 CASH

Brass **Mint:** Anhwei

Date	Mintage	F	VF	XF	Unc
ND(1851-61)	—	—	—	50.00	—

X# CF170 500 CASH

Brass **Mint:** Tungch'uan

Date	Mintage	F	VF	XF	Unc
ND(1851-61)	—	—	—	50.00	—

X# CF178 500 CASH

Brass **Mint:** Honan

Date	Mintage	F	VF	XF	Unc
ND(1851-61)	—	—	—	50.00	—

X# CF171 500 CASH
Brass Mint: Chengde

Date	Mintage	F	VF	XF	Unc
ND(1851-61)	—	—	—	50.00	—

X# CF172 500 CASH
Brass Mint: Foochou

Date	Mintage	F	VF	XF	Unc
ND(1851-61)	—	—	—	50.00	—

X# CF173 500 CASH
Brass Mint: Hsüanfu

Date	Mintage	F	VF	XF	Unc
ND(1851-61)	—	—	—	50.00	—

X# CF174 500 CASH
Brass Mint: Hunan

Date	Mintage	F	VF	XF	Unc
ND(1851-61)	—	—	—	50.00	—

X# CF175 500 CASH
Brass Mint: Kansu

Date	Mintage	F	VF	XF	Unc
ND(1851-61)	—	—	—	50.00	—

X# CF176 500 CASH
Brass Mint: Kwangtung

Date	Mintage	F	VF	XF	Unc
ND(1851-61)	—	—	—	50.00	—

X# CF177 500 CASH
Brass Mint: Kansu

Date	Mintage	F	VF	XF	Unc
ND(1851-61)	—	—	—	50.00	—

X# CF179 500 CASH
Brass Mint: Yünnan Fu

Date	Mintage	F	VF	XF	Unc
ND(1851-61)	—	—	—	50.00	—

X# CF180 600 CASH
Brass Mint: Hu-pu Board of Revenue

Date	Mintage	F	VF	XF	Unc
ND(1851-61)	—	—	—	50.00	—

X# CF185 700 CASH
Brass Mint: Hu-pu Board of Revenue

Date	Mintage	F	VF	XF	Unc
ND(1851-61)	—	—	—	50.00	—

X# CF190 800 CASH
Brass Mint: Hu-pu Board of Revenue

Date	Mintage	F	VF	XF	Unc
ND(1851-61)	—	—	—	50.00	—

X# CF191 800 CASH

Brass, 59 mm. **Mint:** Kung-pu Board of Public Works
Note: Illustration reduced.

Date	Mintage	F	VF	XF	Unc
ND(1851-61)	—	—	—	50.00	—

X# CF195 900 CASH

Brass **Mint:** Hu-pu Board of Revenue

Date	Mintage	F	VF	XF	Unc
ND(1851-61)	—	—	—	50.00	—

X# CF200 1000 CASH

Brass **Mint:** Chengde **Note:** Illustration reduced.

Date	Mintage	F	VF	XF	Unc
ND(1851-61)	—	—	—	50.00	—

X# CF201 1000 CASH

Brass **Mint:** Foochou

Date	Mintage	F	VF	XF	Unc
ND(1851-61)	—	—	—	50.00	—

X# CF202 1000 CASH

Brass **Mint:** Hsüanfu **Note:** Illustration reduced.

Date	Mintage	F	VF	XF	Unc
ND(1851-61)	—	—	—	50.00	—

X# CF203 1000 CASH

Brass **Mint:** Hunan

Date	Mintage	F	VF	XF	Unc
ND(1851-61)	—	—	—	50.00	—

X# CF204 1000 CASH

Brass **Mint:** Kansu

Date	Mintage	F	VF	XF	Unc
ND(1851-61)	—	—	—	50.00	—

X# CF205 1000 CASH

Brass **Mint:** Shensi

Date	Mintage	F	VF	XF	Unc
ND(1851-61)	—	—	—	50.00	—

X# CF206 1000 CASH

Brass, 64 mm. **Rev. Inscription:** "Hsin" at top **Mint:** Hu-pu Board of Revenue **Note:** Illustration reduced.

Date	Mintage	F	VF	XF	Unc
ND(1851-61)	—	—	—	50.00	—

X# CF209 1000 CASH

Brass **Mint:** Honan

Date	Mintage	F	VF	XF	Unc
ND(1851-61)	—	—	—	50.00	—

X# CF211 1000 CASH

Brass **Mint:** Shansi **Note:** Illustration reduced.

Date	Mintage	F	VF	XF	Unc
ND(1851-61)	—	—	—	50.00	—

X# CF220 4000 CASH

Brass **Mint:** Hu-pu Board of Revenue

Date	Mintage	F	VF	XF	Unc
ND(1851-61)	—	—	—	50.00	—

X# CF225 5000 CASH

Brass **Mint:** Hu-pu Board of Revenue

Date	Mintage	F	VF	XF	Unc
ND(1851-61)	—	—	—	50.00	—

T'UNG-CHIH

CAST COINAGE

X# C11 CASH

Obv. Inscription: "T'ung-chih T'ung-Pao" **Reverse:** Mint mark Chang at right. **Mint:** Changchou

Date	Mintage	Good	VG	F	VF	XF
ND	—	15.00	25.00	35.00	50.00	—

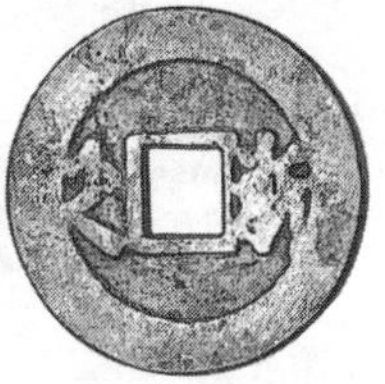

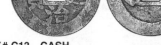

X# C13 CASH

Brass **Obv. Inscription:** "T'ung-chih T'ung Pao" **Reverse:** Mint mark Che at right **Mint:** Chêkiang

Date	Mintage	Good	VG	F	VF	XF
ND	—	15.00	25.00	35.00	50.00	—

X# C15 CASH

Brass **Obv. Inscription:** "T'ung-chih T'ung Pao" **Reverse:** Mint mark Chiang at right **Mint:** Chiangning

Date	Mintage	Good	VG	F	VF	XF
ND	—	15.00	25.00	35.00	50.00	—

X# C16 CASH

Brass **Obv. Inscription:** "T'ung-chih T'ung Pao" **Reverse:** Mint mark Fu at right **Mint:** Fuchow

Date	Mintage	Good	VG	F	VF	XF
ND	—	15.00	25.00	35.00	50.00	—

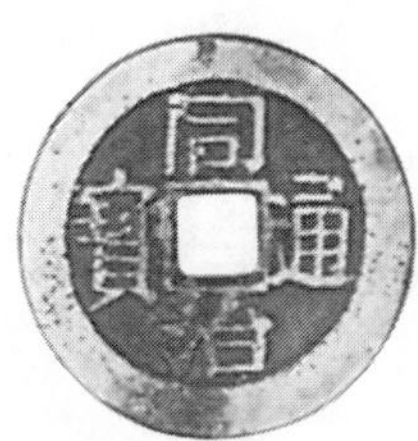

X# C19 CASH

Brass **Obv. Inscription:** "T'ung-chih T'ung Pao" **Reverse:** Mint mark Hsüan at right **Mint:** Hsüanfu

Date	Mintage	Good	VG	F	VF	XF
ND Hsuan	—	15.00	25.00	35.00	50.00	—

X# C20 CASH

Brass **Obv. Inscription:** "T'ung-chih T'ung Pao" **Reverse:** Mint mark Kwang at right **Mint:** Kuangtung

Date	Mintage	Good	VG	F	VF	XF
ND	—	15.00	25.00	35.00	50.00	—

X# C23 CASH

Brass **Obv. Inscription:** "T'ung-chih T'ung Pao" **Reverse:** Mint mark Lin at right **Mint:** Linching

Date	Mintage	Good	VG	F	VF	XF
ND	—	15.00	25.00	35.00	50.00	—

X# C24 CASH

Brass **Obv. Inscription:** "T'ung-chih T'ung Pao" **Reverse:** Mint mark Nan at right **Mint:** Hunan

Date	Mintage	Good	VG	F	VF	XF
ND	—	15.00	25.00	35.00	50.00	—

X# C29 CASH

Brass **Obv. Inscription:** "T'ung-chih T'ung Pao" **Reverse:** Mint mark Tung at right **Mint:** Shantung

Date	Mintage	Good	VG	F	VF	XF
ND	—	15.00	25.00	35.00	50.00	—

X# C31 CASH

Brass **Obv. Inscription:** "T'ung-chih T'ung Pao" **Reverse:** Mint mark Yüan at right **Mint:** T'aiyüan

Date	Mintage	Good	VG	F	VF	XF
ND	—	15.00	25.00	35.00	50.00	—

X# C32 CASH

Brass **Obv. Inscription:** "T'ung-chih T'ung Pao" **Reverse:** Mint mark Yün at right **Mint:** Yünnan Fu

Date	Mintage	Good	VG	F	VF	XF
ND	—	15.00	25.00	35.00	50.00	—

MEDALLIC COINAGE

Emperor Tung Chih Issues

X# M100 DOLLAR
Silver **Subject:** Fukien Province Congratulations to the Emperor **Note:** Type I.

Date	Mintage	F	VF	XF	Unc
ND	—	—	175	250	350

X# M105 DOLLAR
Silver **Note:** Kann#B22. Type II.

Date	Mintage	F	VF	XF	Unc
ND	—	—	175	250	350

Note: Kann mislabeled his #B22 as #B23

KUANG-HSÜ

CAST COINAGE

X# C36 CASH
Brass **Obv. Inscription:** "Kuang-hsü T'ung Pao" **Reverse:** Mint mark Chang at right **Mint:** Changchou

Date	Mintage	Good	VG	F	VF	XF
ND	—	15.00	25.00	35.00	50.00	—

X# C37 CASH
Brass **Obv. Inscription:** "Kuang-hsü T'ung Pao" **Reverse:** Mint mark Ch'ang at right **Mint:** Wuch'ang

Date	Mintage	Good	VG	F	VF	XF
ND	—	15.00	25.00	35.00	50.00	—

X# C38 CASH
Brass **Obv. Inscription:** "Kuang-hsü T'ung Pao" **Reverse:** Mint mark Che at right **Mint:** Chêkiang

Date	Mintage	Good	VG	F	VF	XF
ND	—	15.00	25.00	35.00	50.00	—

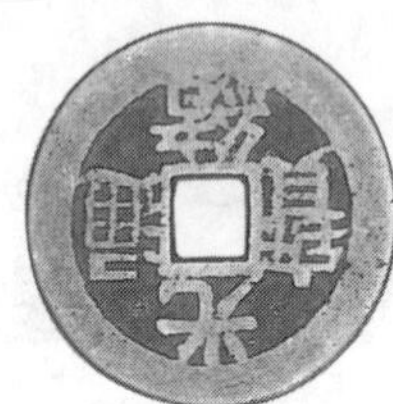

X# C39 CASH
Brass **Obv. Inscription:** "Kuang-hsü T'ung Pao" **Reverse:** Mint mark Chi at right **Mint:** Chichou

Date	Mintage	Good	VG	F	VF	XF
ND	—	15.00	25.00	35.00	50.00	—

X# C41 CASH
Brass **Obv. Inscription:** "Kuang-hsü T'ung Pao" **Reverse:** Mint mark Fu at right **Mint:** Foochou

Date	Mintage	Good	VG	F	VF	XF
ND	—	15.00	25.00	35.00	50.00	—

X# C42 CASH
Brass **Obv. Inscription:** "Kuang-hsü T'ung Pao" **Reverse:** Mint mark Ho at right **Mint:** Honan

Date	Mintage	Good	VG	F	VF	XF
ND	—	15.00	25.00	35.00	50.00	—

X# C44 CASH
Brass **Obv. Inscription:** "Kuang-hsü T'ung Pao" **Reverse:** Mint mark Hsüan at right **Mint:** Hsüanfu

Date	Mintage	Good	VG	F	VF	XF
ND	—	15.00	25.00	35.00	50.00	—

X# C45 CASH
Brass **Obv. Inscription:** "Kuang-hsü T'ung Pao" **Reverse:** Mint mark Kwang at right **Mint:** Kuangtung

Date	Mintage	Good	VG	F	VF	XF
ND	—	15.00	25.00	35.00	50.00	—

X# C46 CASH
Brass **Obv. Inscription:** "Kuang-hsü T'ung Pao" **Reverse:** Mint mark Kueilin at right **Mint:** Kueilin

Date	Mintage	Good	VG	F	VF	XF
ND	—	15.00	25.00	35.00	50.00	—

X# C48 CASH
Brass **Obv. Inscription:** "Kuang-hsü T'ung Pao" **Reverse:** Mint mark Lin at right **Mint:** Linch'ing

Date	Mintage	Good	VG	F	VF	XF
ND	—	15.00	25.00	35.00	50.00	—

X# C49 CASH
Brass **Obv. Inscription:** "Kuang-hsü T'ung Pao" **Reverse:** Mint mark Nan at right **Mint:** Hunan

Date	Mintage	Good	VG	F	VF	XF
ND	—	15.00	25.00	35.00	50.00	—

X# C50 CASH

Brass **Obv. Inscription:** "Kuang-hsü T'ung Pao" **Reverse:** Mint mark Ning at right **Mint:** Ningpo

Date	Mintage	Good	VG	F	VF	XF
ND	—	15.00	25.00	35.00	50.00	—

X# C51 CASH

Brass **Obv. Inscription:** "Kuang-hsü T'ung Pao" **Reverse:** Mint mark Shen at right **Mint:** Shensi

Date	Mintage	Good	VG	F	VF	XF
ND	—	15.00	25.00	35.00	50.00	—

X# C52 CASH

Brass **Obv. Inscription:** "Kuang-hsü T'ung Pao" **Reverse:** Mint mark Su at right **Mint:** Soochow

Date	Mintage	Good	VG	F	VF	XF
ND	—	15.00	25.00	35.00	50.00	—

X# C53 CASH

Brass **Obv. Inscription:** "Kuang-hsü T'ung Pao" **Reverse:** Mint mark T'ai at right **Mint:** T'aiwan

Date	Mintage	Good	VG	F	VF	XF
ND	—	15.00	25.00	35.00	50.00	—

X# C54 CASH

Brass **Obv. Inscription:** "Kuang-hsü T'ung Pao" **Reverse:** Mint mark T'ung at right **Mint:** Tat'ung

Date	Mintage	Good	VG	F	VF	XF
ND	—	15.00	25.00	35.00	50.00	—

X# C55 CASH

Brass **Obv. Inscription:** "Kuang-hsü T'ung Pao" **Reverse:** Mint mark at right

Date	Mintage	Good	VG	F	VF	XF
ND T'ung	—	15.00	25.00	35.00	50.00	—

X# C57 CASH

Brass **Obv. Inscription:** "Kuang-hsü T'ung Pao" **Reverse:** Mint mark Yün at right **Mint:** Miyün

Date	Mintage	Good	VG	F	VF	XF
ND	—	15.00	25.00	35.00	50.00	—

MEDALLIC COINAGE

Changchow Dollar Issues

X# M5 1/2 DOLLAR

Silver **Note:** Similar to Dollar, XM6.

Date	Mintage	F	VF	XF	Unc
ND	—	—	50.00	75.00	110

Note: Similar to Kann #6

X# M6 DOLLAR

Silver

Date	Mintage	F	VF	XF	Unc
ND	—	—	90.00	150	225

MEDALLIC COINAGE

Double Dragon Issues

X# M10 5 MACE (1/2 Tael)

Silver **Obverse:** 8 Chinese characters, "Made at Shantung Official (Mint) in 1990," around center with "Kuang-hsu Yuan Pao" **Note:** Kann#B16.

Date	Mintage	F	VF	XF	Unc
CD1900	—	—	200	325	450

X# M15 5 MACE (1/2 Tael)

Silver **Obverse:** 4 Chinese characters, "Made in Kwangtung Province" at top **Note:** Kann#B35

Date	Mintage	F	VF	XF	Unc
ND(1904)	—	—	100	150	250

X# M16 5 MACE (1/2 Tael)

Bronze **Obverse:** 4 Chinese characters, "Made in Kwangtung Province" at top

Date	Mintage	F	VF	XF	Unc
ND(1904)	—	—	45.00	75.00	100

X# M17 5 MACE (1/2 Tael)

Bronze **Obverse:** Larger bats at left and right; larger Manchu at center

Date	Mintage	F	VF	XF	Unc
ND(1904)	—	—	75.00	125	175

X# M20 TAEL

Silver **Subject:** Fengtien **Obverse:** Top center Chinese character "Nien" in seal script **Note:** Kann#B17.

Date	Mintage	F	VF	XF	Unc
ND(1894)/20	—	—	150	250	350

X# M21 TAEL

Gold **Subject:** Fengtien **Obverse:** Top center Chinese character "Nien" in seal script

Date	Mintage	F	VF	XF	Unc
ND(1894)/20	—	—	—	5,000	6,500

X# M25 TAEL

Silver **Subject:** Fengtien **Obverse:** Top center Chinese character "Nien" in regular script

Date	Mintage	F	VF	XF	Unc
ND(1894)/20	—	—	150	250	350

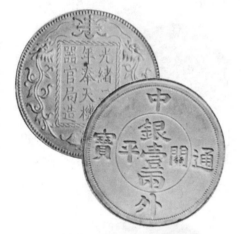

X# M30 TAEL

Silver **Obverse:** Top center Chinese character "Nien" in regular script. Mule **Reverse:** Kann #925 **Note:** (Haikwan pattern Tael).

Date	Mintage	F	VF	XF	Unc
ND(1894)/20	—	—	90.00	150	225

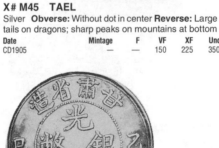

X# M35 TAEL

Silver **Obverse:** 8 Chinese characters, "Made at Shantung Official (Mint) in 1900," around center **Note:** Kann#B15.

Date	Mintage	F	VF	XF	Unc
CD1900	—	—	225	375	550

X# M40 TAEL

Silver **Obverse:** 4 Chinese characters at top, "Made in Kansu Province," date characters at left and right

Date	Mintage	F	VF	XF	Unc
CD1905	—	—	150	225	350

X# M45 TAEL

Silver **Obverse:** Without dot in center **Reverse:** Large tails on dragons; sharp peaks on mountains at bottom

Date	Mintage	F	VF	XF	Unc
CD1905	—	—	150	225	350

X# M46 TAEL

Silver **Obverse:** Without dot in center **Reverse:** Rounded peaks on mountains at bottom

Date	Mintage	F	VF	XF	Unc
CD1905	—	—	150	225	350

X# M50 TAEL

Silver **Obverse:** Plain borders **Reverse:** Plain borders **Note:** Kann#B31.

Date	Mintage	F	VF	XF	Unc
CD1905	—	—	150	225	350

X# M51 TAEL

Silver **Note:** Mule: 2 obverses of XM50.

Date	Mintage	F	VF	XF	Unc
CD1905	—	—	75.00	125	200

X# M55 TAEL

Silver **Obverse:** 4 Chinese characters, "Made in Kansu Province," at top **Reverse:** Dragons around "Yin-yang" and "Pa Kua" symbols **Note:** Kann#B33.

Date	Mintage	F	VF	XF	Unc
CD1905	—	—	150	225	350

X# M60 TAEL

Silver **Note:** Obverse similar to XM65 but beaded border. Reverse similar to XM65 but smaller round top mountains at bottom.

Date	Mintage	F	VF	XF	Unc
CD1907	—	—	150	225	350

X# M65 TAEL

Silver **Reverse:** Large tails on dragons; sharp peaks on mountains at bottom **Note:** Kann#B34.

Date	Mintage	F	VF	XF	Unc
CD1907	—	—	150	225	350

X# M66 TAEL

Silver **Note:** Mule: 2 obverses of XM65.

Date	Mintage	F	VF	XF	Unc
CD1907	—	—	75.00	125	200

X# M67 TAEL

Silver **Note:** Mule: 2 reverses of XM65.

Date	Mintage	F	VF	XF	Unc
ND(1907)	—	—	75.00	125	200

X# M68 TAEL

Silver **Reverse:** Dragons around "Yin-yang" and "Pa Kua" symbols **Note:** Mule. Obv: XM65. Rev: XM55.

Date	Mintage	F	VF	XF	Unc
CD1907	—	—	125	200	350

X# M75 TAEL

Silver **Reverse:** Rounded peaks on mountains at bottom

Date	Mintage	F	VF	XF	Unc
CD1907	—	—	175	250	350

X# M80 TAEL

Silver **Obverse:** 4 Chinese characters, "Made in Kwangtung Province," at top

Date	Mintage	F	VF	XF	Unc
CD1907	—	—	150	200	300

X# M85 TAEL

Silver **Obverse:** Beaded borders **Reverse:** Beaded borders

Date	Mintage	F	VF	XF	Unc
CD1907	—	—	150	200	300

MEDALLIC COINAGE

Emperor Kuang Hsu Issues

X# M110 1/2 DOLLAR

Silver **Note:** Similar to XM130.

Date	Mintage	F	VF	XF	Unc
ND	—	—	125	200	300

X# M115 1/2 DOLLAR

Silver **Obverse:** 6 Chinese characters, "Made in 1885 Kuang Hsu." **Reverse:** Border of Chinese character, "Shou" (long life) **Note:** Kann#B13.

Date	Mintage	F	VF	XF	Unc
CD1885	—	—	175	250	350

Note: Die varieties exist

X# M125 DOLLAR

Silver **Subject:** Kuang Hsu's Death Commemorative **Note:** Kann#B23.

Date	Mintage	F	VF	XF	Unc
ND	—	—	175	250	350

Note: Kann mislabeled #B23 as #B22

X# M126 DOLLAR

Gold **Subject:** Kuang Hsu's Death Commemorative

Date	Mintage	F	VF	XF	Unc
ND	—	—	—	1,200	2,000

X# M130 DOLLAR

Silver **Reverse:** 4 Chinese characters, "Made in Kwangtun Province," in center **Note:** Kann#B19.

Date	Mintage	F	VF	XF	Unc
ND	—	—	175	250	350

X# M131 DOLLAR

Gold **Reverse:** 4 Chinese characters, "Made in Kwangtung Province," in center

Date	Mintage	F	VF	XF	Unc
ND	—	—	—	2,500	3,500

X# M132 DOLLAR

Silver **Obverse:** Modified design

Date	Mintage	F	VF	XF	Unc
ND	—	—	125	200	300

X# M135 DOLLAR

Silver **Obverse:** 4 Chinese characters, "Respectfully submitted by Fukien (Province)" **Edge:** Reeded **Note:** Kann#B24.

Date	Mintage	F	VF	XF	Unc
ND	—	—	150	225	300

X# M136 DOLLAR

Silver **Obverse:** 4 Chinese characters, "Respectfully submitted by Fukien (Province)" **Edge:** Plain **Note:** Kann#B24.

Date	Mintage	F	VF	XF	Unc
ND	—	—	150	225	300

X# M140 DOLLAR

Silver **Obv. Legend:** Large characters **Reverse:** Symbol at bottom as 7 pointed star in center

Date	Mintage	F	VF	XF	Unc
ND	—	—	150	225	300

X# M145 DOLLAR

Silver **Obverse:** Small hat, large characters **Edge:** Reeded

Date	Mintage	F	VF	XF	Unc
ND	—	—	150	225	300

X# M150 DOLLAR

Silver **Obverse:** Small hat, small characters

Date	Mintage	F	VF	XF	Unc
ND	—	—	150	225	300

X# M116 DOLLAR

Gold **Obverse:** 6 Chinese characters, "Made in 1885 Kuang Hsu." **Reverse:** Border of Chinese character "Shou" (long life) **Note:** Kann#B13.

Date	Mintage	F	VF	XF	Unc
CD1885	—	—	—	3,500	5,000

X# M117 DOLLAR

Bronze **Obverse:** 6 Chinese characters, "Made in 1885 Kuang Hsu" **Reverse:** Border of Chinese character "Shou" (long life)

Date	Mintage	F	VF	XF	Unc
CD1885	—	—	90.00	150	225

X# M118 DOLLAR

Silvered-Bronze **Obverse:** 6 Chinese characters, "Made in 1885 Kuang Hsu" **Reverse:** Border of Chinese character "Shou" (long life)

Date	Mintage	F	VF	XF	Unc
CD1885	—	—	90.00	150	225

X# M119 DOLLAR

Silver **Obverse:** Modified design

Date	Mintage	F	VF	XF	Unc
CD1885	—	—	175	250	350

X# M120 DOLLAR
Silver **Obverse:** Modified design

Date	Mintage	F	VF	XF	Unc
CD1885	—	—	125	200	300

X# M155 5 DOLLARS
Gold **Reverse:** Facing dragons **Note:** Kann#B92.

Date	Mintage	F	VF	XF	Unc
ND	—	—	—	550	750

X# M160 5 DOLLARS
Gold **Reverse:** 5 bats **Note:** Kann#B90.

Date	Mintage	F	VF	XF	Unc
ND	—	—	—	450	650

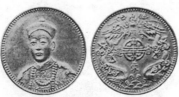

X# M165 10 DOLLARS
Gold **Reverse:** Facing dragons

Date	Mintage	F	VF	XF	Unc
ND	—	—	—	650	900

MEDALLIC COINAGE

Szechuan-Tibet Dollar Issues

X# M440 DOLLAR
Silver **Obverse:** Small bust left wearing Mandarin hat (modeled after British India Queen Victoria Rupee) **Reverse:** Inscription within flowery sprays **Rev. Inscription:** Szu-chúan Shan-tsoh **Note:** Kann #B29.

Date	Mintage	F	VF	XF	Unc
ND	—	—	125	200	300

X# M441 DOLLAR
Gold **Obverse:** Small bust left wearing Mandarin hat (modeled after British India Queen Victoria Rupee) **Reverse:** Inscription within flowery sprays **Rev. Inscription:** Szu-chúan Shan-tsoh **Note:** Kann #B29.

Date	Mintage	F	VF	XF	Unc
ND	—	—	—	1,250	1,850

X# M443 DOLLAR
Copper **Obverse:** Small bust left wearing Mandarin hat (modeled after British India Queen Victoria Rupee) **Reverse:** Inscription within flowery sprays **Rev. Inscription:** Szu-chúan Shan-tsoh

Date	Mintage	F	VF	XF	Unc
ND	—	—	—	325	450

X# M445 DOLLAR
Silver **Obverse:** Large bust left wearing Mandarin hat (modeled after British India Queen Victoria Rupee) **Reverse:** Inscription within flowery sprays **Rev. Inscription:** Szu-chúan Shan-tsoh **Note:** Prev. XM442.

Date	Mintage	F	VF	XF	Unc
ND	—	—	175	250	350

T'AI- P'ING REBELLION

CAST FANTASY COINAGE

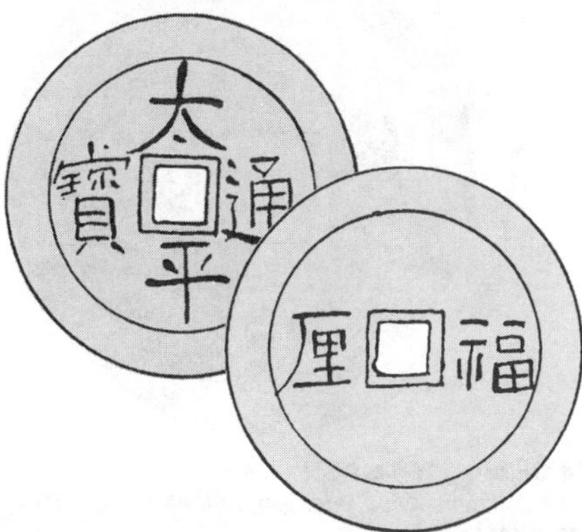

X# CF100 CASH
Copper **Obv. Inscription:** T'ai-p'ing T'ung-pao **Rev. Inscription:** Fu-li (Fukien Cash) **Note:** Schjöth #1610.

Date	Mintage	Good	VG	F	VF	XF
ND(c. 1860)	—	—	15.00	25.00	35.00	—

HSIEN-FÊNG

CAST FANTASY COINAGE

X# CF159 100 CASH
Brass, 52 mm. **Obv. Inscription:** Hsien-fêng Yüan-pao **Mint:** Shansi

Date	Mintage	F	VF	XF	Unc
ND(1851-61)	—	—	—	50.00	—

PROOF SETS

X#	Date	Mintage	Identification	Issue Price	Mkt Val
CF159	ND(1910) (4)	—	Y#23, K#219, 221, 222	—	—

FUKIEN PROVINCE

REPUBLIC

CAST COINAGE

X# M1400 10 WEN
8.6000 g., Brass, 33.3 mm. **Reverse:** Flags at left and right

Date	Mintage	F	VF	XF	Unc
ND(c.1912)	—	20.00	35.00	—	—

KANSU PROVINCE

REPUBLIC

MEDALLIC COINAGE

X# M760 DOLLAR
38.1000 g., Silver **Obverse:** Bust of Yüan Shih-kai left **Reverse:** Value in sprays **Edge:** Reeded **Note:** A modern concoction.

Date	Mintage	F	VF	XF	Unc
Yr. 3 (1914)	—	18.50	25.00	—	—

KIRIN PROVINCE

EMPIRE

MEDALLIC COINAGE

X# M321 1/2 TAEL
Silver **Obverse:** 12 seal-script characters in square **Reverse:** 4 characters (value) in small square within ornated design **Note:** Similar to Tael, Kann #914.

Date	Mintage	F	VF	XF	Unc
Yr. 8 (1882)	—	—	—	—	225

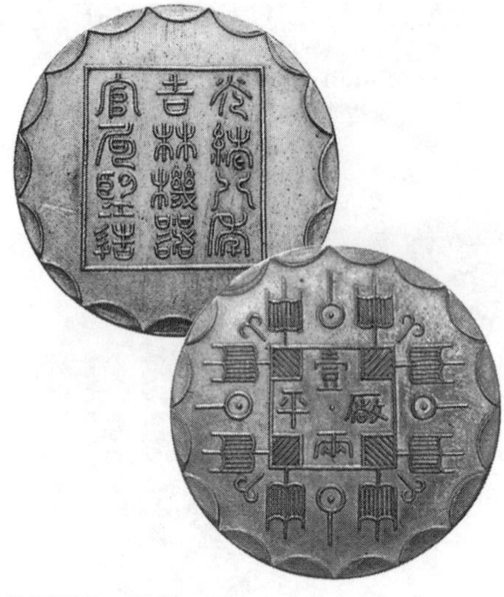

X# M322 TAEL
Silver **Obverse:** 12-seal-script characters in square **Reverse:** 4 characters (value) in small square within ornate design **Note:** Similar to Tael, Kann #914.

Date	Mintage	VG	F	VF	XF	Unc
Yr. 8 (1882)	—	—	—	—	—	300

SINKIANG PROVINCE

EMPIRE

CAST FANTASY COINAGE

X# CF230 100 CASH
Brass, 49 mm. **Obv. Inscription:** Hsien-fêng Yüan-pao **Mint:** Ushi

Date	Mintage	F	VF	XF	Unc
ND(1851-61)	—	—	—	50.00	—

X# CF228 100 CASH
Brass, 52 mm. **Obv. Inscription:** Hsien-fêng Yüan-pao **Mint:** Kashgar

Date	Mintage	F	VF	XF	Unc
ND(1851-61)	—	—	—	50.00	—

HSIEN-FÊNG

CAST FANTASY COINAGE

X# CF157 100 CASH
Brass **Mint:** Kuche

Date	Mintage	F	VF	XF	Unc
ND(1851-61)	—	—	—	50.00	—

X# CF207 1000 CASH
Brass, 62 mm. **Obv. Inscription:** Hsien-fêng Yüan-pao **Mint:** Kuche **Note:** Illustration reduced.

Date	Mintage	F	VF	XF	Unc
ND(1851-61)	—	—	—	50.00	—

YUNNAN PROVINCE

EMPIRE

FANTASY COINAGE

X# M480 20 CASH
Copper

Date	Mintage	Good	VG	F	VF	XF
ND	—	—	7.00	10.00	15.00	30.00

X# M485 RUPEE
11.5000 g., Silver **Obverse:** Szechuan style bust **Note:** Kann#599. Obviously Kann had not seen this piece and listed it as an "Essay." It is typical of the circulating Szechuan-Tibet imitations of the Indian rupee series.

Date	Mintage	Good	VG	F	VF	XF
ND	—	—	20.00	35.00	60.00	95.00

HSÜAN-T'UNG

MEDALLIC COINAGE

X# M483 DOLLAR
40.7300 g., Silver, 50.3 mm. **Obv. Inscription:** Hsüan-t'ung Yüan-pao **Reverse:** Facing dragon **Rev. Legend:** YUN-NAN PROVINCE **Edge:** Reeded **Note:** A modern concoction.

Date	Mintage	F	VF	XF	Unc
ND(1908-11)	—	18.50	25.00	—	—

FANTASY COINAGE

X# M482 DOLLAR
32.0400 g., Silver, 41.1 mm. **Obv. Inscription:** Hsüan-t'ung Yüan-pao **Reverse:** Facing dragons, ball between **Rev. Legend:** YUN-NAN-PROVINCE

Date	Mintage	F	VF	XF	Unc
ND(1908-11)	—	—	18.50	35.00	—

REPUBLIC

MEDALLIC COINAGE

X# M1390 DOLLAR
41.0700 g., Silver, 50.2 mm. **Obverse:** Bust of General T'ang Chi-yao **Reverse:** Crossed flags **Note:** A modern concoction.

Date	Mintage	F	VF	XF	Unc
ND(c.1919)	—	25.00	35.00	—	—

JAPANESE PUPPET STATES

MANCHOUKUO

JAPANESE OCCUPATION

BULLION COINAGE

These gold ingots, issued under the authority of the Japanese military, were issued and held by the Bank of Manchoukuo in the early 1930s. Although they carry Chinese legends, they were not made by or for the Chinese market.

X# 1.1 TAEL
31.2500 g., 1.0000 Gold 1.0047 oz. AGW, 30 mm. **Obverse:** Character "Fu" "Happiness" **Reverse:** 24K/1000 all in outline **Note:** Prev. KM#1.1.

Date	Mintage	VG	F	VF	XF	Unc
ND(1932)	—	—	—	800	1,600	2,000

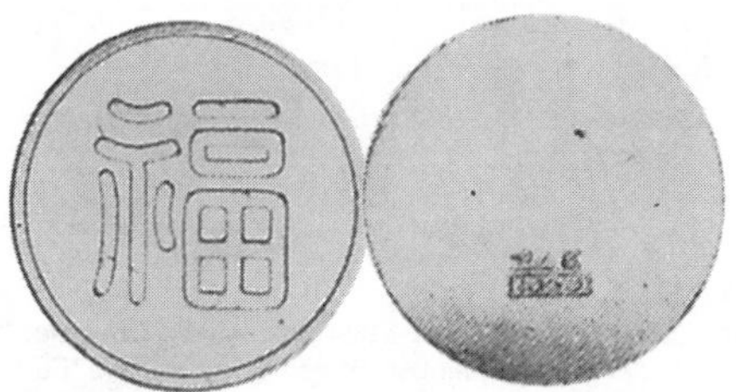

X# 1.2 TAEL
31.2500 g., 1.0000 Gold 1.0047 oz. AGW **Obverse:** Character "Fu" (happiness) **Reverse:** 1000 in outline, 24K above **Note:** Prev. KM#1.2.

Date	Mintage	VG	F	VF	XF	Unc
ND(1932)	—	—	—	800	1,600	2,000

X# 2 TAEL
Gold, 37 mm. **Obverse:** Character "Fu" (happiness) **Note:** Prev. KM#2.

Date	Mintage	VG	F	VF	XF	Unc
ND(1932)	—	—	—	1,500	2,500	3,500

X# 3 TAEL
31.2500 g., 1.0000 Gold 1.0047 oz. AGW, 30 mm.
Obverse: Character "Shuang-hsi" (Double happiness)
Note: Prev. KM#3.

Date	Mintage	VG	F	VF	XF	Unc
ND(1932)	—	—	—	2,000	3,000	4,000

X# 4 TAEL
31.2500 g., 1.0000 Gold 1.0047 oz. AGW **Obverse:** Character "Fu" (happiness) in center, characters "Fu-kuei Wan-nien" top-bottom-right-left (Richness, honor (for) 10,000 years) **Reverse:** "24K/1000" over 4 characters in frame **Note:** Prev. KM#4.

Date	Mintage	VG	F	VF	XF	Unc
ND(1932)	—	—	—	1,500	2,000	3,000

X# 5 TAEL
31.2500 g., 1.0000 Gold 1.0047 oz. AGW **Obverse:** Character "Fu" (happiness) in center, characters "Fu-kuei Wan-nien" top-bottom-right-left (richness, honor (for) 10,000 years) **Reverse:** "24K/1000" over 4 characters in frame **Note:** Prev. KM#5.

Date	Mintage	VG	F	VF	XF	Unc
ND(1932)	—	—	—	1,500	2,000	3,000

X# 6 TAEL
31.2500 g., 1.0000 Gold 1.0047 oz. AGW **Obverse:** Character "Shou" (Longevity) **Reverse:** "24K" over "'1000" in frame **Note:** Prev. KM#6.

Date	Mintage	VG	F	VF	XF	Unc
ND(1932)	—	—	—	1,500	2,000	3,000

X# 7 TAEL
Gold, 37 mm. **Obverse:** Character "Shou" (longevity) **Note:** Prev. KM#7.

Date	Mintage	VG	F	VF	XF	Unc
ND(1932)	—	—	—	2,000	2,500	3,500

X# 8 TAEL
31.2500 g., 1.0000 Gold 1.0047 oz. AGW, 30 mm. **Obverse:** Character "Lu" (Prosperity) **Note:** Prev. KM#8.

Date	Mintage	VG	F	VF	XF	Unc
ND(1932)	—	—	—	1,500	2,000	3,000

CHINA

PEOPLES REPUBLIC

TOKEN COINAGE

X# Tn1 100 PANDA DOLLARS
31.1030 g., 0.9990 Silver 0.9989 oz. ASW, 39.1 mm. **Subject:** 1989 Hong Kong International Coin Exposition **Obverse:** Facing dragon **Reverse:** Panda seated eating bamboo shoots **Edge:** Reeded

Date	Mintage	F	VF	XF	Unc
1989 Proof	—	Value: 35.00			

BI-METALLIC MEDALLIC BULLION COINAGE

Silver / Gold

X# MB67 3/8 OUNCE
7.7507 g., 0.9990 Bi-Metallic Gold center in Silver ring 0.2489 oz. **Subject:** Hong Kong International Coin Convention **Note:** Sold in a set including a similar 25 Yuan commemorative coin.

Date	Mintage	F	VF	XF	Unc
1991 Proof	2,000	Value: 300			

X# MB62 7/10 OUNCE
15.5015 g., 0.9990 Bi-Metallic Gold center in Silver ring 06.2206 oz. **Subject:** Hong Kong International Coin Convention **Note:** Sold in a set including a similar 50 Yuan commemorative coin.

Date	Mintage	F	VF	XF	Unc
1990 Proof	2,000	Value: 400			

MEDALLIC BULLION COINAGE

Silver

X# MB1 OUNCE
33.6300 g., 0.9250 Silver 1.0000 oz. ASW **Subject:** 3rd Hong Kong International Coin Exposition

Date	Mintage	F	VF	XF	Unc
1984 Proof	1,000	Value: 125			

X# MB2 OUNCE
34.6000 g., 0.9000 Silver 1.0011 oz. ASW **Subject:** 94th American Numismatic Association Convention - Great Wall

Date	Mintage	F	VF	XF	Unc
1985 Proof	500	Value: 75.00			

Note: "THE GREAT WALL" is in backward letters

X# MB26 OUNCE
34.6000 g., 0.9000 Silver 1.0011 oz. ASW **Subject:** Longevity

Date	Mintage	F	VF	XF	Unc
1987 Proof	1,600	Value: 65.00			

X# MB28 OUNCE
34.6000 g., 0.9000 Silver 1.0011 oz. ASW **Subject:** 94th American Numismatic Association Convention - Cincinnati

Date	Mintage	F	VF	XF	Unc
1988 Proof	2,000	Value: 45.00			

X# MB42 OUNCE
34.6000 g., 0.9000 Silver 1.0011 oz. ASW **Subject:** 2nd Hong Kong Coins Exposition - China Bank Building and Great Wall **Reverse:** Panda eating bamboo leaves

Date	Mintage	F	VF	XF	Unc
1989 Proof	2,300	Value: 50.00			

X# MB52 OUNCE
34.6000 g., 0.9000 Silver 1.0011 oz. ASW **Subject:** 98th American Numismatic Association Convention - Pittsburgh **Reverse:** Sleeping panda on branch

Date	Mintage	F	VF	XF	Unc
1989 Proof	1,000	Value: 55.00			

X# MB53 OUNCE
34.6000 g., 0.9000 Silver 1.0011 oz. ASW **Subject:** 18th New York International Numismatic Convention - American Horse **Obverse:** Horse galloping left, hills in background **Reverse:** Seated panda with bamboo sprig

Date	Mintage	F	VF	XF	Unc
1989 Proof	4,000	Value: 40.00			

X# MB59 OUNCE
34.6000 g., 0.9000 Silver 1.0011 oz. ASW **Subject:** Munich International Coins Fair

Date	Mintage	F	VF	XF	Unc
1990 Proof	2,000	Value: 45.00			

X# MB66 OUNCE
34.6000 g., 0.9000 Silver 1.0011 oz. ASW **Obverse:** Outline of mainland China **Reverse:** Panda

Date	Mintage	F	VF	XF	Unc
1991 Proof	—	Value: 35.00			

X# MB75 OUNCE
28.4500 g., 0.9990 Silver 0.9137 oz. ASW, 45 mm. **Obverse:** Military arms **Reverse:** Appliqué of Marshal Chen Yi bust facing **Rev. Legend:** COMMEMORATES PEOPLE'S REPUBLIC OF CHINA'S 10 GREAT MARSHALS **Rev. Inscription:** 1901-1972 Promotion 50th Anniversary **Edge:** Reeded **Note:** Complete series contains 10 varieties.

Date	Mintage	F	VF	XF	Unc
ND(2005)	—	—	—	—	—

X# MB57 3 TAELS
103.0000 g., 0.9990 Silver 3.3081 oz. ASW **Subject:** Zhao Gongming

Date	Mintage	F	VF	XF	Unc
ND Proof FDC	2,430	Value: 75.00			

X# MB3 5 OUNCES
155.5150 g., 0.9990 Silver 4.9947 oz. ASW, 70 mm.
Subject: 4th Hong Kong International Coin Exposition
Note: Prev. KM#100. Illustration reduced.

Date	Mintage	F	VF	XF	Unc
1985 Proof	2,000	Value: 200			

X# MB5 5 OUNCES
155.5150 g., 0.9990 Silver 4.9947 oz. ASW, 70 mm.
Subject: 95th American Numismatic Association Convention **Note:** Illustration reduced.

Date	Mintage	F	VF	XF	Unc
1986 Proof	2,000	Value: 150			

X# MB15 5 OUNCES
155.5150 g., 0.9990 Silver 4.9947 oz. ASW, 70 mm.
Subject: 96th American Numismatic Association Convention - Atlanta **Note:** Illustration reduced.

Date	Mintage	F	VF	XF	Unc
1987 Proof	2,500	Value: 125			

X# MB4 5 OUNCES
155.5150 g., 0.9990 Silver 4.9947 oz. ASW, 67 mm.
Subject: 30th Anniversary Sinkiang Autonomous Region **Obverse:** Government building **Note:** XMB4 was issued along with a 1 Yuan in Copper-Nickel and 10 Yuan in Silver. Illustration reduced.

Date	Mintage	F	VF	XF	Unc
1985 Proof	1,400	Value: 150			

X# MB13 5 OUNCES
155.5150 g., 0.9990 Silver 4.9947 oz. ASW, 70 mm.
Subject: Long Beach Numismatic & Philatelic Expo
Note: Illustration reduced.

Date	Mintage	F	VF	XF	Unc
1987 Proof	2,000	Value: 150			

X# MB17 5 OUNCES
155.5150 g., 0.9990 Silver 4.9947 oz. ASW, 70 mm.
Subject: 6th Hong Kong International Coin Exposition
Note: Illustration reduced.

Date	Mintage	F	VF	XF	Unc
1987 Proof	2,000	Value: 200			

X# MB22 5 OUNCES
155.5150 g., 0.9990 Silver 4.9947 oz. ASW, 70 mm. **Subject:** 7th Hong Kong International Coin Exposition **Note:** Illustration reduced.

Date	Mintage	F	VF	XF	Unc
1988 Proof	1,000	Value: 225			

X# MB24 5 OUNCES
155.5150 g., 0.9990 Silver 4.9947 oz. ASW, 69 mm. **Subject:** Munich Coin Bourse **Note:** Illustration reduced.

Date	Mintage	F	VF	XF	Unc
1988 Proof	2,000	Value: 150			

X# MB71 5 OUNCES
155.5150 g., 0.9990 Silver 4.9947 oz. ASW **Series:** Silver **Subject:** 1989 Hong Kong International Coin Exposition **Obverse:** Facing dragon **Reverse:** Panda seated eating bamboo shoots **Edge:** Reeded

Date	Mintage	F	VF	XF	Unc
1989 Proof	—	Value: 125			

X# MB45 5 OUNCES
155.5150 g., 0.9990 Silver 4.9947 oz. ASW, 69 mm. **Subject:** Bodhisattra Avalokitesvara **Note:** Illustration reduced.

Date	Mintage	F	VF	XF	Unc
1989 Proof	1,500	Value: 100			

X# MB48 5 OUNCES
155.5150 g., 0.9990 Silver 4.9947 oz. ASW, 68 mm. **Subject:** General Guan Yu **Note:** Illustration reduced.

Date	Mintage	F	VF	XF	Unc
1989 Proof	1,500	Value: 100			

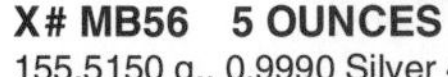

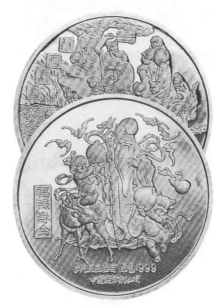

X# MB56 5 OUNCES
155.5150 g., 0.9990 Silver 4.9947 oz. ASW, 68 mm. **Subject:** Longevity **Note:** Illustration reduced.

Date	Mintage	F	VF	XF	Unc
1990 Proof	1,000	Value: 110			

X# MB6 12 OUNCES (Troy Pound)
375.2360 g., 0.9990 Silver 12.051 oz. ASW, 82 mm. **Subject:** 5th Hong Kong International Coin Exposition **Note:** Illustration reduced.

Date	Mintage	F	VF	XF	Unc
1986 Proof	1,000	Value: 550			

MEDALLIC BULLION COINAGE

Gold

X# MB12 1.5 GRAMS
1.5000 g., 0.9999 Gold 0.0482 oz. AGW **Reverse:** Yin-yang **Mint:** Singapore **Note:** Struck by the Singapore Mint.

Date	Mintage	F	VF	XF	Unc
1984SM Proof	1,500	Value: 40.00			

X# MB32 1/20 OUNCE
1.5551 g., 0.9990 Gold 0.0499 oz. AGW **Subject:** Tokyo International Coin Show - "Tong-Tong"

Date	Mintage	F	VF	XF	Unc
1987 Proof	25,025	Value: 35.00			

X# MB8 1/10 OUNCE
3.1103 g., 0.9990 Gold 0.0999 oz. AGW **Obverse:** Temple of Heaven **Reverse:** Panda with bamboo shoot **Note:** Prev. Y#40.

Date	Mintage	F	VF	XF	Unc
1982	75,000	—	—	—	—

X# MB41 1/10 OUNCE
3.1103 g., 0.9990 Gold 0.0999 oz. AGW **Subject:** Tokyo International Coin Show

Date	Mintage	F	VF	XF	Unc
1989 Proof	30,000	Value: 85.00			

X# MB39 1/4 OUNCE
7.7758 g., 0.9990 Gold 0.2497 oz. AGW **Subject:** Liu Hai and toad

Date	Mintage	F	VF	XF	Unc
ND	10,000	—	—	—	175

X# MB9 1/4 OUNCE
7.7758 g., 0.9990 Gold 0.2497 oz. AGW **Obverse:** Similar to 1 Ounce, Y#43 **Note:** Prev. Y#41.

Date	Mintage	F	VF	XF	Unc
1982	40,000	—	—	—	—

X# MB36 1/4 OUNCE
7.7758 g., 0.9990 Gold 0.2497 oz. AGW **Subject:** Mazu

Date	Mintage	F	VF	XF	Unc
1987	5,000	—	—	—	175
1987 Proof	2,000	Value: 190			

X# MB37 1/4 OUNCE
7.7758 g., 0.9990 Gold 0.2497 oz. AGW **Subject:** Sakyamnni Buddha

Date	Mintage	F	VF	XF	Unc
1988	5,000	—	—	—	175
1988 Proof	2,000	Value: 190			

X# MB38 1/4 OUNCE
7.7758 g., 0.9990 Gold 0.2497 oz. AGW **Subject:** Badhisattva Avalokitesvara

Date	Mintage	F	VF	XF	Unc
1988	5,000	—	—	—	175
1988 Proof	2,000	Value: 190			

X# MB47 1/4 OUNCE
7.7758 g., 0.9990 Gold 0.2497 oz. AGW **Subject:** Maitreya Buddha

Date	Mintage	F	VF	XF	Unc
1989	5,000	—	—	—	175
1989 Proof	2,000	Value: 190			

X# MB49 1/4 OUNCE
7.7758 g., 0.9990 Gold 0.2497 oz. AGW **Subject:** General Guan Yu

Date	Mintage	F	VF	XF	Unc
1989	5,000	—	—	—	175
1989 Proof	2,000	Value: 190			

X# MBA10 1/2 OUNCE
15.5517 g., 0.9990 Gold 0.4995 oz. AGW **Obverse:** Temple of Heaven **Reverse:** Panda with bamboo shoot

Date	Mintage	F	VF	XF	Unc
1982	13,000	—	—	—	—

X# MB43 1/2 OUNCE
15.5517 g., 0.9990 Gold 0.4995 oz. AGW **Subject:** 2nd Hong Kong Coin Exposition - Great Wall

Date	Mintage	F	VF	XF	Unc
1989 Proof	1,300	Value: 375			

 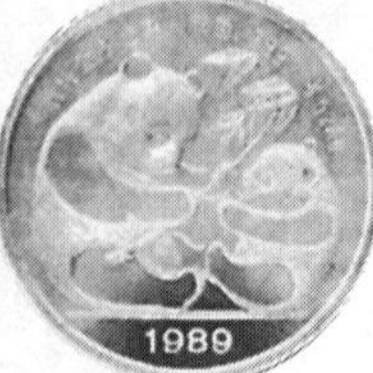

X# MB44 1/2 OUNCE
15.5517 g., 0.9990 Gold 0.4995 oz. AGW **Subject:** Munich International Coin Exposition

Date	Mintage	F	VF	XF	Unc
1989 Proof	1,500	Value: 375			

X# MB54 1/2 OUNCE
15.5517 g., 0.9990 Gold 0.4995 oz. AGW **Subject:** 18th New York International Numismatic Convention - Tang Horse

Date	Mintage	F	VF	XF	Unc
1989 Proof	5,000	Value: 365			

X# MB60 1/2 OUNCE
15.5517 g., 0.9990 Gold 0.4995 oz. AGW **Subject:** Munich International Coin Exposition

Date	Mintage	F	VF	XF	Unc
1990 Proof	1,500	Value: 375			

X# MB69 1/2 OUNCE
15.5517 g., 0.9990 Gold 0.4995 oz. AGW **Subject:** Munich International Coin Fair **Obverse:** Temple of Heaven, archway **Reverse:** Panda seated eating bamboo shoots

Date	Mintage	F	VF	XF	Unc
1991 Proof	—	Value: 400			

X# MBA11 OUNCE
31.1035 g., 0.9990 Gold 0.9990 oz. AGW **Obverse:** Temple of Heaven **Reverse:** Panda with bamboo shoot

Date	Mintage	F	VF	XF	Unc
1982	16,000	—	—	—	—

X# MB7 OUNCE
31.1035 g., 0.9990 Gold 0.9990 oz. AGW **Subject:** 1st San Francisco International Coin Expo

Date	Mintage	F	VF	XF	Unc
1987 Proof	3,000	Value: 750			

X# MB14 OUNCE
31.1035 g., 0.9990 Gold 0.9990 oz. AGW **Subject:** 96th American Numismtic Association Convention - New Orleans

Date	Mintage	F	VF	XF	Unc
1987 Proof	3,000	Value: 735			

X# MB16 OUNCE
31.1035 g., 0.9990 Gold 0.9990 oz. AGW **Subject:** Tokyo International Coin Show - "Tong-Tong"

Date	Mintage	F	VF	XF	Unc
1987 Proof	5,000	Value: 725			

X# MB18 OUNCE
31.1035 g., 0.9990 Gold 0.9990 oz. AGW **Subject:** 16th New York International Numismatic Convention

Date	Mintage	F	VF	XF	Unc
1987 Proof	2,000	Value: 735			

X# MB20 OUNCE
31.1035 g., 0.9990 Gold 0.9990 oz. AGW **Subject:** Basel International Coin Week

Date	Mintage	F	VF	XF	Unc
1988 Proof	450	Value: 900			

X# MB21 OUNCE
31.1035 g., 0.9990 Gold 0.9990 oz. AGW **Note:** Error with "Pt." (platinum die).

Date	Mintage	F	VF	XF	Unc
1988 Proof	550	Value: 900			

X# MB23 OUNCE
31.1035 g., 0.9990 Gold 0.9990 oz. AGW **Subject:** 2nd San Francisco International Coin Expo

Date	Mintage	F	VF	XF	Unc
1988 Proof	1,500	Value: 735			

X# MB25 OUNCE
31.1035 g., 0.9990 Gold 0.9990 oz. AGW **Subject:** Munich Coin Bourse

Date	Mintage	F	VF	XF	Unc
1988 Proof	2,000	Value: 725			

X# MB27 OUNCE
31.1035 g., 0.9990 Gold 0.9990 oz. AGW **Subject:** 1st Hong Kong Coin Exposition - China

Date	Mintage	F	VF	XF	Unc
1988 Proof	800	Value: 750			

X# MB29 OUNCE
31.1035 g., 0.9990 Gold 0.9990 oz. AGW **Subject:** 97th American Numismatic Association Convention - Cincinnati

Date	Mintage	F	VF	XF	Unc
1988 Proof	1,000	Value: 750			

X# MB31 OUNCE
31.1035 g., 0.9990 Gold 0.9990 oz. AGW **Subject:** American Numismatic Association Convention - New Orleans

Date	Mintage	F	VF	XF	Unc
1988 Proof	3,000	Value: 725			

X# MB70 OUNCE
31.1030 g., 0.9990 Gold 0.9989 oz. AGW **Series:** Gold **Subject:** 1989 Hong Kong International Coin Exposition **Obverse:** Facing dragon **Reverse:** Panda seated eating bamboo shoots **Edge:** Reeded

Date	Mintage	F	VF	XF	Unc
1989 Proof	—	Value: 750			

X# MB51 OUNCE
31.1035 g., 0.9990 Gold 0.9990 oz. AGW **Subject:** 3rd San Francisco International Coin Expo

Date	Mintage	F	VF	XF	Unc
1989 Proof	1,500	Value: 725			

X# MB40 5 OUNCES
155.5150 g., 0.9990 Gold 4.9947 oz. AGW, 59 mm. **Subject:** Bi Gan and the Five-Route Gods **Note:** Illustration reduced.

Date	Mintage	F	VF	XF	Unc
ND Proof	300	Value: 3,600			

X# MB33 5 OUNCES
155.5150 g., 0.9990 Gold 4.9947 oz. AGW, 69 mm. **Subject:** Tokyo International Coin Show - "Tong-Tong" **Note:** Illustration reduced.

Date	Mintage	F	VF	XF	Unc
1987 Proof	1,500	Value: 3,500			

X# MB46 5 OUNCES
155.5150 g., 0.9990 Gold 4.9947 oz. AGW **Subject:** Bodhisattva Avalokitesvara

Date	Mintage	F	VF	XF	Unc
1989 Proof	500	Value: 3,600			

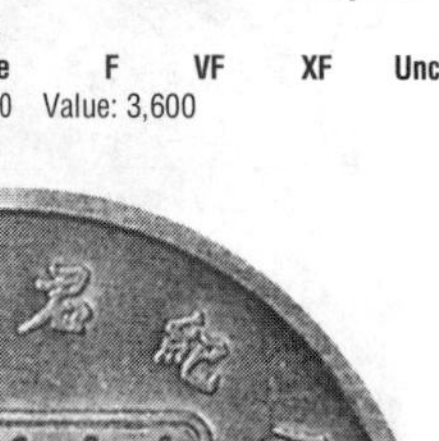

X# MB50 5 OUNCES
155.5150 g., 0.9990 Gold 4.9947 oz. AGW **Subject:** General Guan Yu

Date	Mintage	F	VF	XF	Unc
1989 Proof	500	Value: 3,600			

X# MB58 5 TAELS
156.2500 g., 0.9990 Gold 5.0183 oz. AGW **Subject:** Zhao Gongming **Note:** Illustration reduced.

Date	Mintage	F	VF	XF	Unc
ND Proof	305	Value: 3,750			

X# MB34 12 OUNCES (Troy Pound)
375.2360 g., 0.9990 Gold 12.051 oz. AGW, 79 mm. **Reverse:** Longevity **Note:** Illustration reduced.

Date	Mintage	F	VF	XF	Unc
ND(1988) Proof	200	Value: 8,500			

MEDALLIC BULLION COINAGE

Palladium

X# MB30 OUNCE
31.1030 g., 0.9990 Palladium 0.9989 oz. **Subject:** 17th New York International Numismatic Convention

Date	Mintage	F	VF	XF	Unc
1988 Proof	1,000	Value: 500			

MEDALLIC BULLION COINAGE

Platinum

X# MB19 OUNCE
31.1030 g., 1.0000 Platinum 0.9999 oz. APW **Subject:** 16th New York International Numismatic Convention

Date	Mintage	F	VF	XF	Unc
1987 Proof	1,000	Value: 1,750			

TIANANMEN SQUARE UPRISING

MEDALLIC BULLION COINAGE

Gold

X# MB61 SOVEREIGN
6.2400 g., 0.9990 Gold 0.2004 oz. AGW, 22 mm. **Obverse:** 1/2-length female student facing holding torch **Reverse:** Snake **Rev. Legend:** FREEDOM DEMOCRACY **Edge:** Reeded **Mint:** Pobjoy

Date	Mintage	F	VF	XF	Unc
1989	308	Value: 250			

MIN-CHE-KAN SOVIET

SOVIET CONTROLLED PROVINCE

MEDALLIC COINAGE

X# M1047 DOLLAR
Silver **Obverse:** Fantasy 15 character legend around globe with hammer and sickle **Note:** Prev. KM#2.

Date	Mintage	VG	F	VF	XF	Unc
1934	—	140	200	275	500	—

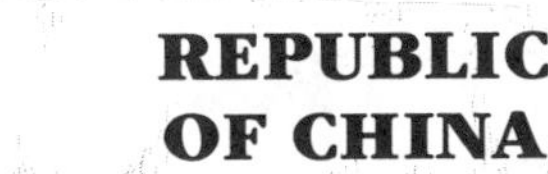

EMPIRE

HUNG-HSIEN

TRANSITIONAL COINAGE

X# 1320 10 CASH (10 Wen)
Bronze **Obv. Inscription:** Hung-hsien T'ung-pao **Note:** Prev. KM#2. Uniface. Believed to be a fantasy by some authorities.

Date	Mintage	Good	VG	F	VF	XF
ND(1916) Rare	—	—	—	—	—	—

REPUBLIC

MEDALLIC COINAGE

Allied Victory

X# M501 DOLLAR
Silver **Reverse:** Countermarked 4 Chinese characters, "T'eng Meng Sheng Li" (United Victory), at top on Sun Yat-sen Junk Dollar **Note:** The countermarked characters are filled in with colored enamels.

Date	Mintage	F	VF	XF	Unc
ND	—	—	100	175	—

Central Mint Completion Issues

X# M505 DOLLAR
Silver **Reverse:** Long rays to left of junk **Edge:** Milled **Note:** Type I.

Date	Mintage	F	VF	XF	Unc
1930//19	—	—	—	—	—

X# M506 DOLLAR
Copper-Nickel **Reverse:** Long rays to left of junk **Edge:** Milled **Note:** Type I.

Date	Mintage	F	VF	XF	Unc
1930//19	—	—	—	—	—

X# M507 DOLLAR
Copper **Reverse:** Long rays to left of junk **Edge:** Milled **Note:** Type I.

Date	Mintage	F	VF	XF	Unc
1930//19	—	—	—	—	—

X# M508 DOLLAR
Aluminum **Reverse:** Long rays to left of junk **Edge:** Milled **Note:** Type I.

Date	Mintage	F	VF	XF	Unc
1930//19	—	—	—	—	—

X# M509 DOLLAR
Copper **Reverse:** Long rays to left of junk **Edge:** Plain **Note:** Type I.

Date	Mintage	F	VF	XF	Unc
1930//19	—	—	—	—	—

X# M510 DOLLAR
Copper Gilt **Reverse:** Short rays to left of junk **Note:** Type II.

Date	Mintage	F	VF	XF	Unc
1930//19	—	—	—	—	—

Central Mint Commemorative Issues

X# M515 50 CENTS
Copper

Date	Mintage	F	VF	XF	Unc
ND(1943)/32	—	—	—	65.00	100

Chang Hsi-luan Issues

XM520-XM528 were normally issued looped with a ribbon. Many have had this removed and some even the lower legend on the reverse has been ground off (like XM528) to pass them off as coins.

X# M520 DOLLAR
Silver **Reverse:** 5 Chinese characters, "First Class Memorial," below enameled crossed flags **Edge:** Milled

Date	Mintage	F	VF	XF	Unc
ND(1912)/1	—	—	175	250	350

X# M524 DOLLAR
Silver **Reverse:** 5 Chinese characters, "Second Class Memorial," below enameled crossed flags **Edge:** Plain

Date	Mintage	F	VF	XF	Unc
ND(1912)/1	—	—	175	250	350

X# M526 DOLLAR
Silver **Reverse:** 5 Chinese characters, "Third Class Memorial," below enameled crossed flags **Edge:** Plain

Date	Mintage	F	VF	XF	Unc
ND(1912)/1	—	—	175	250	350

X# M528 DOLLAR
Silver **Reverse:** 5 Chinese characters removed below enameled crossed flags

Date	Mintage	F	VF	XF	Unc
ND(1912)/1	—	—	60.00	100	150

X# M521 DOLLAR
Copper **Reverse:** 5 Chinese characters, "First Class Memorial," below enameled crossed flags **Edge:** Milled

Date	Mintage	F	VF	XF	Unc
ND(1912)/1	—	—	75.00	125	175

Chang Hsueh-liang Issue

X# M535 50 CENTS
Silver **Rev. Legend:** "Gift of Chang Hsueh-liang" **Edge:** Plain

Date	Mintage	F	VF	XF	Unc
ND	—	—	90.00	150	225

Chang Hsun Restored Monarch Issue

X# M540 DOLLAR
Silver **Obverse:** Square emblem on chest **Reverse:** 4 Chinese characters, "Monarchy Restoration Commemorative"

Date	Mintage	F	VF	XF	Unc
ND	—	—	175	250	350

X# M541 DOLLAR
Gold **Obverse:** Square emblem on chest **Reverse:** 4 Chinese characters, "Monarchy Restoration Commemorative"

Date	Mintage	F	VF	XF	Unc
ND	—	—	—	2,500	3,500

X# M542 DOLLAR
Copper **Obverse:** Square emblem on chest **Reverse:** 4 Chinese characters, "Monarchy Restoration Commemorative"

Date	Mintage	F	VF	XF	Unc
ND	—	—	50.00	85.00	125

X# M545 DOLLAR
Silver **Obverse:** Round emblem on chest

Date	Mintage	F	VF	XF	Unc
ND	—	—	175	250	350

Chang Tso-lin Issues

X# M565 50 CENTS
Silver **Reverse:** 2 Chinese characters, "Commemorative"

Date	Mintage	F	VF	XF	Unc
ND	—	—	—	—	—

X# M550 50 CENTS
Silver **Note:** Kann#B65.

Date	Mintage	F	VF	XF	Unc
ND(1928)/17	—	—	—	—	—

X# M560 50 CENTS
Silver **Obverse:** Portrait without hat

Date	Mintage	F	VF	XF	Unc
ND(1928)/17	—	—	—	—	—

X# M555 DOLLAR
Silver **Note:** Kann#B64.

Date	Mintage	F	VF	XF	Unc
ND(1928)/17	—	—	—	—	—

General Chao Issue

X# M580 50 CENTS
Silver **Subject:** Fengtien Province

Date	Mintage	F	VF	XF	Unc
ND	—	—	150	200	300

Chiang Kai-shek Issues

X# M590 10 CASH
Copper **Reverse:** Temple of Heaven

Date	Mintage	F	VF	XF	Unc
ND	—	—	50.00	70.00	100

X# M595 10 CASH
Copper **Rev. Legend:** "Presented by Generalissimo and Madame Chiang Kai-shek" around 4 Chinese seal script characters

Date	Mintage	F	VF	XF	Unc
ND	—	—	50.00	70.00	100

X# M596 10 CASH
Silver **Rev. Legend:** "Presented by Generalissimo and Madame Chiang Kai-shek" around 4 Chinese seal script characters

Date	Mintage	F	VF	XF	Unc
ND	—	—	60.00	90.00	125

X# M600 10 CASH
Silver **Note:** Mule. Rev. XM590 with rev. KM595.

Date	Mintage	F	VF	XF	Unc
ND	—	—	50.00	70.00	100

X# M651 500 YUAN
Gold **Subject:** 70th Anniversary of the Republic

Date	Mintage	F	VF	XF	Unc
(1981)/70 Prooflike FDC	—	—	—	—	135

X# M658 500 YUAN
Gold **Subject:** 75th Anniversary of the Republic

Date	Mintage	F	VF	XF	Unc
ND(1986)/75	—	—	—	—	145

X# M630 1000 YUAN
Gold **Subject:** Chiang Kai-shek 90th Birthday

Date	Mintage	F	VF	XF	Unc
ND(1976)/65	—	—	—	—	285

X# M652 1000 YUAN
15.3700 g., Gold **Subject:** 70th Anniversary of the Republic

Date	Mintage	F	VF	XF	Unc
(1981)/70 Prooflike FDC	—	—	—	—	320

X# M659 1000 YUAN
15.3700 g., Gold **Subject:** 75th Anniversary of the Republic

Date	Mintage	F	VF	XF	Unc
ND(1986)/75	—	—	—	—	320

X# M610 2000 YUAN
Silver **Subject:** Chiang Kai-shek 80th Birthday **Reverse:** 2 Chinese characters, "Commemorative," at bottom **Note:** Similar to 2000 Yuan coin struck in gold.

Date	Mintage	F	VF	XF	Unc
ND(1966)/55	—	—	—	30.00	50.00

X# M615 2000 YUAN
Silver **Subject:** 60th Anniversary of the Republic

Date	Mintage	F	VF	XF	Unc
ND(1671)/60	—	—	14.00	18.00	25.00

X# M616 2000 YUAN
Gold **Subject:** 60th Anniversary of the Republic

Date	Mintage	F	VF	XF	Unc
ND(1971)/60	—	—	—	500	600

X# M625 2000 YUAN
17.4000 g., 0.7500 Silver 0.4195 oz. ASW **Subject:** Chiang Kai-shek 90th Birthday

Date	Mintage	F	VF	XF	Unc
ND(1976)/65	—	—	15.00	20.00	30.00

X# M635 2000 YUAN
Gold **Subject:** Chiang Kai-shek 90th Birthday

Date	Mintage	F	VF	XF	Unc
ND(1976)/65	—	—	—	550	750

X# M650 2000 YUAN
Silver **Subject:** 70th Anniversary of the Republic

Date	Mintage	F	VF	XF	Unc
ND(1981)/70	—	—	—	18.00	25.00

X# M653 2000 YUAN
Gold **Subject:** 70th Anniversary of the Republic

Date	Mintage	F	VF	XF	Unc
(1981)/70 Prooflike	—	—	—	—	750

X# M657 2000 YUAN
Silver **Subject:** 75th Anniversary of the Republic

Date	Mintage	F	VF	XF	Unc
ND(1985)/75	—	—	—	—	25.00

X# M660 2000 YUAN
29.9300 g., Gold **Subject:** 100th Anniversary of Birth **Obverse:** Bust of Chiang Kai-shek facing **Reverse:** Ornate patterns, rayed outlined map of Taiwan at center

Date	Mintage	F	VF	XF	Unc
ND(1986)/75 Proof	—	Value: 550			

MEDALLIC COINAGE

Feng Kuo-chang Issues

In 1920 the Peking government authorized the Wuchang mint in Hupeh to strike silver dollar coins with the likeness of former president Feng Kuo-chang. It is not known whether Wuchang actually made such coins, but leading numismatists living in China from the 1930s onward, have considered these as fantasies.

X# M675 DOLLAR
Silver **Edge:** Milled **Note:** Kann#B55.

Date	Mintage	F	VF	XF	Unc
ND	—	—	125	200	300

X# M676 DOLLAR
Silver **Edge:** Plain **Note:** Kann#B55.

Date	Mintage	F	VF	XF	Unc
ND	—	—	125	200	300

X# M677 DOLLAR
Gold **Edge:** Plain

Date	Mintage	F	VF	XF	Unc
ND	—	—	—	—	—

X# M670 DOLLAR
Silver **Edge:** Milled **Note:** Kann#B56.

Date	Mintage	F	VF	XF	Unc
ND(1918)/7	—	—	125	200	300

X# M671 DOLLAR
Gold **Edge:** Milled

Date	Mintage	F	VF	XF	Unc
ND(1918)/7	—	—	—	—	—

X# M680 10 DOLLARS
Gold, 20 mm. **Note:** Kann#B94.

Date	Mintage	F	VF	XF	Unc
ND	—	—	—	600	800

X# M681 10 DOLLARS
Silver

Date	Mintage	F	VF	XF	Unc
ND	—	—	—	100	150

Feng Yu-hsiang Issue

X# M690 DOLLAR
Silver **Subject:** Wu Yuan Oath

Date	Mintage	F	VF	XF	Unc
ND(1926)/15	—	—	275	450	650

Flag Issues

X# M705 5 DOLLARS
0.9170 Gold **Reverse:** Flaming sunface

Date	Mintage	F	VF	XF	Unc
ND	—	—	—	—	350

X# M700 5 DOLLARS
0.9170 Gold

Date	Mintage	F	VF	XF	Unc
1912	—	—	—	—	350

Foong Hsiang Gold & Silver Store

X# M715 OUNCE
30.7000 g., Gold **Reverse:** Peacock

Date	Mintage	F	VF	XF	Unc
ND	—	—	475	650	900

Hsiao Yueh-nan Issues

X# M720 50 CENTS
Silver, 32 mm. **Subject:** Hsiao Yueh-nan 50th Birthday **Note:** Similar to 1 Dollar, XM725.

Date	Mintage	F	VF	XF	Unc
CD1924	—	—	60.00	100	200

X# M721 50 CENTS
Copper

Date	Mintage	F	VF	XF	Unc
CD1924	—	—	25.00	40.00	60.00

X# M725 DOLLAR
Silver **Subject:** Hsiao Yueh-nan 50th Birthday

Date	Mintage	F	VF	XF	Unc
CD1924	—	—	125	200	300

Hsu Shih-chang Issue

X# M731 50 CENTS
Gold **Obverse:** 3/4 portrait of man wearing bowtie **Reverse:** 8 Chinese characters, "1919 Commemorative," above crossed flags

Date	Mintage	F	VF	XF	Unc
ND(1919)/8	—	—	—	—	—

Note: Reported, not confirmed

X# M730 50 CENTS
Silver **Obverse:** 3/4 portrait of man wearing bowtie **Reverse:** 8 Chinese characters, "1919 Commemorative," above crossed flags **Note:** Size varies: 32-33mm.

Date	Mintage	F	VF	XF	Unc
ND(1919)/8	—	—	80.00	135	200

X# M740 50 CENTS
Silver **Note:** Kann#B63.

Date	Mintage	F	VF	XF	Unc
ND(1919)/8	—	—	—	—	—

X# M741 50 CENTS
Copper **Note:** Kann#B63.

Date	Mintage	F	VF	XF	Unc
ND(1919)/8	—	—	—	—	—

X# M735 DOLLAR
Silver **Note:** Size varies: 35-36mm. Similar to 50 Cents, XM730.

Date	Mintage	F	VF	XF	Unc
ND(1919)/8	—	—	—	—	—

X# M736 DOLLAR
Gold

Date	Mintage	F	VF	XF	Unc
ND(1919)/8	—	—	—	—	—

Hupeh Military Government Issue

X# M750 50 CASH
Copper

Date	Mintage	F	VF	XF	Unc
ND(1914)/3	—	—	—	—	—

Kashgar Mint Issues

X# M770 20 CASH
Copper

Date	Mintage	F	VF	XF	Unc
ND	—	—	—	—	—

X# M780 TAEL
Silver

Date	Mintage	F	VF	XF	Unc
AH1334	—	—	—	—	—

Kiang See Province Issues

X# M790 10 CENTS
Silver

Date	Mintage	F	VF	XF	Unc
CD1912	—	—	—	—	—

Note: Reported, not confirmed

X# M795 20 CENTS
Silver

Date	Mintage	F	VF	XF	Unc
CD1912	—	—	—	—	—

Note: Reported, not confirmed

X# M800 DOLLAR
Silver **Edge:** Milled

Date	Mintage	F	VF	XF	Unc
CD1912	—	—	—	300	450

Kunming Mint Issue

X# M810 DOLLAR
Copper-Nickel

Date	Mintage	F	VF	XF	Unc
ND(1941)/30	—	—	80.00	125	200

Kweilin Mint Issues

X# M820 DOLLAR
Copper **Subject:** 1st Anniversary

Date	Mintage	F	VF	XF	Unc
ND(1939)/28	—	—	50.00	85.00	125

X# M821 DOLLAR
Silver **Subject:** 1st Anniversary

Date	Mintage	F	VF	XF	Unc
ND(1939)/28	—	—	100	150	200

X# M825 DOLLAR
Copper **Subject:** 2nd Anniversary **Reverse:** Chiang Kai-shek

Date	Mintage	F	VF	XF	Unc
ND(1940)/29	—	—	50.00	85.00	125

X# M830 DOLLAR
Copper **Subject:** 5th Anniversary

Date	Mintage	F	VF	XF	Unc
ND(1943)/32	—	—	50.00	85.00	125

X# M831 DOLLAR
Copper Nickel

Date	Mintage	F	VF	XF	Unc
ND(1943)/32	—	—	50.00	85.00	125

Lenin Issues

X# M855 DOLLAR
Silver

Date	Mintage	F	VF	XF	Unc
ND Prooflike	—	—	—	—	450

X# M856 DOLLAR
Gold

Date	Mintage	F	VF	XF	Unc
ND Prooflike	—	—	—	—	2,000

X# M850 DOLLAR
Silver **Note:** Kann#B73.

Date	Mintage	F	VF	XF	Unc
1931	—	—	150	250	350

X# M858 DOLLAR
Silver **Issuer:** Min-Che Kan Soviet **Note:** KM#1. Authenticity in doubt.

Date	Mintage	F	VF	XF	Unc
1934	—	—	—	275	375

Li Ching-lin Issues

X# M870 DOLLAR
Silver **Note:** Kann#B59.

Date	Mintage	F	VF	XF	Unc
ND(1925)/14	—	—	125	200	300

Li Yuan-hung Issues

X# M875 10 CASH
Copper

Date	Mintage	F	VF	XF	Unc
ND	—	—	300	500	750

X# M880 10 CASH
Copper

Date	Mintage	F	VF	XF	Unc
ND	—	—	300	500	750

X# M885 1/2 DOLLAR
Silver **Note:** Kann#B72.

Date	Mintage	F	VF	XF	Unc
ND	—	—	90.00	150	225

X# M886 1/2 DOLLAR
Gold **Note:** Kann#B72.

Date	Mintage	F	VF	XF	Unc
ND	—	—	—	700	1,000

X# M890 1/2 DOLLAR
Silver **Note:** Similar to 10 Cash, XM880.

Date	Mintage	F	VF	XF	Unc
ND	—	—	90.00	150	225

X# M891 1/2 DOLLAR
Gold

Date	Mintage	F	VF	XF	Unc
ND	—	—	—	700	1,000

General Lu Jung-t'ing Issues

X# M920 10 CENTS
Silver **Note:** Similar to Dollar, XM930.

Date	Mintage	F	VF	XF	Unc
ND(1916)/5	—	—	60.00	100	150

X# M925 20 CENTS
Silver **Note:** Size varies: 27-28mm. Similar to Dollar, XM930.

Date	Mintage	F	VF	XF	Unc
ND(1916)/5	—	—	50.00	85.00	125

X# M930 DOLLAR
Silver

Date	Mintage	F	VF	XF	Unc
ND(1916)/5	—	—	200	350	500

X# M932 DOLLAR
Copper

Date	Mintage	F	VF	XF	Unc
ND(1916)/5	—	—	75.00	125	175

X# M931 DOLLAR
Gold

Date	Mintage	F	VF	XF	Unc
ND(1916)/5	—	—	—	—	—

X# M935 10 DOLLARS
Gold

Date	Mintage	F	VF	XF	Unc
ND(1916)/5	—	—	—	550	775

Miao Tribes Issue

X# M945 10 CASH
Copper **Obverse:** Crossed flags within 12-pointed star **Reverse:** 2 Chinese characters, "Copper Coin," in center between branches; 4 Chinese characters, "For use by Miao People," above

Date	Mintage	F	VF	XF	Unc
ND	—	—	—	—	—

Mo Jung-hsin Issues

X# M950 10 CASH
Silver

Date	Mintage	F	VF	XF	Unc
ND(1918)/7	—	—	100	150	200

X# M951 10 CASH
Gold

Date	Mintage	F	VF	XF	Unc
ND(1918)/7	—	—	—	—	—

National Revolutionary Army Issue

X# M970 10 CASH
Copper **Subject:** An Wu Army

Date	Mintage	F	VF	XF	Unc
ND	—	—	60.00	150	200

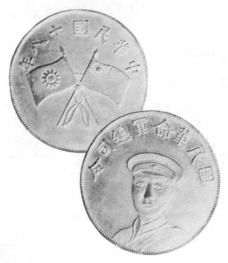

X# M960 DOLLAR
Silver **Note:** Kann#B66.

Date	Mintage	F	VF	XF	Unc
ND(1918)/7	—	—	125	225	350

Ni Szu-chung Issues

X# M971 10 CASH
Silver **Subject:** An Wu Army

Date	Mintage	F	VF	XF	Unc
ND	—	—	70.00	100	150

X# M972 10 CASH
Gold **Subject:** An Wu Army

Date	Mintage	F	VF	XF	Unc
ND	—	—	—	—	—

X# M975 10 CASH
Copper **Obverse:** Modified design

Date	Mintage	F	VF	XF	Unc
ND	—	—	70.00	90.00	125

X# M980 50 CENTS
Silver **Reverse:** 6 Chinese characters, "Made in the Anching Mint," at top; 3 five-pointed stars below center

Date	Mintage	F	VF	XF	Unc
ND(1920)/9	—	—	100	150	200

X# M990 50 CENTS
Gold **Reverse:** 3 six-pointed stars below center

Date	Mintage	F	VF	XF	Unc
ND(1920)/9	—	—	—	600	800

X# M995 DOLLAR
Silver

Date	Mintage	F	VF	XF	Unc
ND(1920)/9	—	—	150	250	350

Japanese Conquest of Shanghai Issues

X# M1000 DOLLAR
Copper, Bronze, Brass, Or Copper-Nickel

Date	Mintage	F	VF	XF	Unc
ND(1937-38)	—	—	20.00	35.00	—

X# M1001 DOLLAR
Silver Plated Brass

Date	Mintage	F	VF	XF	Unc
ND(1937-38)	—	—	—	25.00	40.00

X# M1002a DOLLAR
Copper **Subject:** Japanese Conquest of Shanghai **Obverse:** Japanese Army helmet above crossed rifle and sword **Reverse:** Junk, reverse of Dollar, Y#345

Date	Mintage	F	VF	XF	Unc
ND(1938-39)	—	—	90.00	150	225

X# M1002 DOLLAR
Brass Nickel Plated **Subject:** Japanese Conquest of Shanghai **Obverse:** Japanese Army helmet above crossed rifle and sword **Reverse:** Junk, reverse of Dollar, Y#345 **Note:** Prev. X#M1001.

Date	Mintage	F	VF	XF	Unc
ND(1938-39)	—	15.00	30.00	50.00	—

X# M1004 DOLLAR
22.6700 g., Nickel Plated Brass, 39.5 mm. **Subject:** Japanese Conquest of Shanghai **Obverse:** Japanese Army helmet above crossed rifle and sword **Reverse:** Bust Yüan Shih-kai left, obverse of Dollar, Y#329

Date	Mintage	F	VF	XF	Unc
ND(1938-39) Yr. 3	—	15.00	30.00	50.00	—

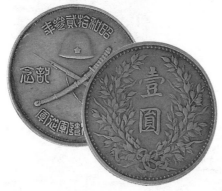

X# M1005 DOLLAR
19.0300 g., Brass Nickel Plated, 39.1 mm. **Subject:** Japanese Conquest of Shanghai **Obverse:** Japanese Army helmet above crossed rifle and sword **Reverse:** Value in sprays, reverse of Dollar, Y#329

Date	Mintage	F	VF	XF	Unc
ND(1938-39)	—	15.00	30.00	50.00	—

Shung Feng Issue

X# M1010 DOLLAR
Gold **Subject:** 35th Anniversary **Obverse:** Dragon around 2 Chinese characters "Shun Feng" **Reverse:** 2 Chinese characters, "Mei Kung" in wreath with dates "1886-1921" below

Date	Mintage	F	VF	XF	Unc
1921	—	—	—	600	800

Sinkiang Issues

X# M1020 SILVER MACE
Silver **Reverse:** 4 Chinese characters, "One Mace Ration Silver," in center **Note:** Kann#B86.

Date	Mintage	F	VF	XF	Unc
ND(1912)/1	—	—	—	—	—

X# M1021 SILVER MACE
Gold **Reverse:** 4 Chinese characters, "One Mace Ration Silver," in center **Note:** Kann#B86.

Date	Mintage	F	VF	XF	Unc
ND(1912)/1 Reported, not confirmed	—	—	—	—	—

X# M1025 2 SILVER MACE
Silver **Obverse:** Similar to XM1020 **Reverse:** 4 Chinese characters, "Two Mace Ration Silver," in center

Date	Mintage	F	VF	XF	Unc
ND(1912)/1 Reported, not confirmed	—	—	—	—	—

X# M1030 GOLD MACE
Gold **Obverse:** Similar to XM1035. **Reverse:** 4 Chinese characters, "One Mace Ration Gold," in center

Date	Mintage	F	VF	XF	Unc
ND(1912)/1	—	—	250	350	500

X# M1031 GOLD MACE
Silver **Obverse:** Similar to XM1035 **Reverse:** 4 Chinese characters, "One Mace Ration Gold," in center

Date	Mintage	F	VF	XF	Unc
ND(1912)/1 Reported, not confirmed	—	—	—	—	—

X# M1035 2 GOLD MACE
Gold **Reverse:** 4 Chinese characters, "Two Mace Ration Gold," in center

Date	Mintage	F	VF	XF	Unc
ND(1912)/1	—	—	325	450	700

X# M1036 2 GOLD MACE
Silver **Reverse:** 4 Chinese characters, "Two Mace Ration Gold," in center

Date	Mintage	F	VF	XF	Unc
ND(1912)/1 Reported, not confirmed	—	—	—	—	—

Soviet Issues

X# M1040 DOLLAR
Silver **Note:** Mule. 2 obverses.

Date	Mintage	F	VF	XF	Unc
ND	—	—	—	—	—

X# M1045 DOLLAR
Silver **Note:** Mule. Obv: XM1040. Rev: XM850.

Date	Mintage	F	VF	XF	Unc
1931	—	—	150	200	300

X# M1047 DOLLAR
Silver

Date	Mintage	F	VF	XF	Unc
1934	—	—	—	200	300

Sun Yat-sen Issues

X# M1050 10 CASH
Copper **Note:** Prev. KM#Pn4.

Date	Mintage	F	VF	XF	Unc
ND(1912)	—	—	800	1,350	2,000

X# M1052 10 CASH
Copper **Note:** Prev. KM#Pn2.

Date	Mintage	F	VF	XF	Unc
ND(1912)	—	—	400	700	1,000

X# M1054 10 CASH
Copper **Note:** Prev. KM#Pn3.

Date	Mintage	F	VF	XF	Unc
ND(1912)	—	—	400	700	1,000

X# M1060 50 CENTS
Silver **Note:** Kann#B50.

Date	Mintage	F	VF	XF	Unc
ND	—	—	—	—	—

X# M1061 50 CENTS
Gold

Date	Mintage	F	VF	XF	Unc
ND	—	—	—	—	—

X# M1065 50 CENTS
Copper Nickel **Note:** Mule. Obv: XM515. Rev: XM595.

Date	Mintage	F	VF	XF	Unc
ND(1943)/32	—	—	50.00	70.00	100

X# M1070 DOLLAR
Silver **Note:** Kann#B51.

Date	Mintage	F	VF	XF	Unc
ND	—	—	175	250	350

X# M1072 DOLLAR
Silver **Reverse:** Modified design

Date	Mintage	F	VF	XF	Unc
ND	—	—	175	250	350

X# M1080 DOLLAR
Silver **Subject:** Will Dollar **Obverse:** 4 Chinese characters **Note:** Kann#B53.

Date	Mintage	F	VF	XF	Unc
ND	—	—	—	—	—

X# M1085 DOLLAR
Silver **Obverse:** 5 Chinese characters

Date	Mintage	F	VF	XF	Unc
ND	—	—	—	—	—

X# M1090 DOLLAR
Silver **Note:** Mint: Shantung.

Date	Mintage	F	VF	XF	Unc
ND(1930)/19	—	—	—	—	—

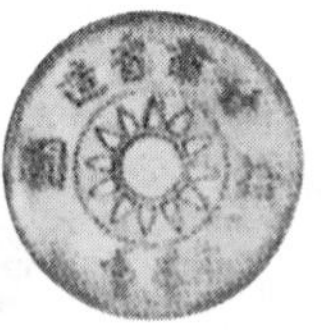

X# M760 10 DOLLARS
Gold **Note:** Kann#B101. Kansu Province.

Date	Mintage	F	VF	XF	Unc
ND(1928)/17	—	—	—	450	650

X# M1093 2000 YUAN
Silver

Date	Mintage	F	VF	XF	Unc
ND/74	—	—	—	35.00	50.00

Szechuan "Horse" Gaming Tokens

X# M1102 1/2 CENT
Copper, Bronze, Brass, Or Copper-Nickel

Date	Mintage	F	VF	XF	Unc
ND(c.1912)	—	—	40.00	70.00	100

X# M1105 CENT
Copper, Bronze, Brass, Or Copper-Nickel
Reverse: Large "1"

Date	Mintage	F	VF	XF	Unc
ND(c.1912)	—	—	40.00	70.00	100

X# M1110 5 CENTS
Copper, Bronze, Brass, Or Copper-Nickel

Date	Mintage	F	VF	XF	Unc
ND(c.1912)	—	—	40.00	70.00	100

X# M1115 5 CENTS
Copper, Bronze, Brass, Or Copper-Nickel

Date	Mintage	F	VF	XF	Unc
ND(c.1912)	—	—	35.00	75.00	130

X# M1117 5 CENTS
Copper, Bronze, Brass, Or Copper-Nickel
Note: Varieties exist.

Date	Mintage	F	VF	XF	Unc
ND(c.1912)	—	—	—	—	—

X# M1125 10 CENTS
Copper, Bronze, Brass, Or Copper-Nickel

Date	Mintage	F	VF	XF	Unc
ND(c.1912)	—	—	75.00	125	225

X# M1120 10 CENTS
Copper, Bronze, Brass, Or Copper-Nickel
Note: Varieties exist.

Date	Mintage	F	VF	XF	Unc
ND(c.1912)	—	—	75.00	125	225

Taiwan Mint Issues

X# M1150 10 CENTS
Copper, 21 mm. **Obv. Legend:** "CENTRAL MINT OF CHINA SAMPLE TAIPEI TAIWAN" **Reverse:** Similar to XM1155

Date	Mintage	F	VF	XF	Unc
ND	—	—	50.00	75.00	125

X# M1155 10 CENTS
Obv. Legend: "SAMPLE / C.M.C." (Central Mint of China)

Date	Mintage	F	VF	XF	Unc
ND	—	—	25.00	40.00	65.00

X# M1160 10 CENTS
Copper-Nickel **Obverse:** Mint facility

Date	Mintage	F	VF	XF	Unc
ND	—	—	25.00	40.00	65.00

X# M1165 50 CENTS
Silver **Subject:** Completion of New Mint Facility
Reverse: 4 coins (3 of Taiwan)

Date	Mintage	F	VF	XF	Unc
ND(1976)/65	—	—	—	—	—

X# M1170 DOLLAR
Brass **Subject:** 30th Anniversary **Note:** Also known in other metal compositions.

Date	Mintage	F	VF	XF	Unc
ND(1963)/52	—	—	45.00	75.00	125

T'an Hou-ming Issues

X# M1190 50 CENTS
Silver **Note:** Similar to 1 Dollar, XM1200.

Date	Mintage	F	VF	XF	Unc
ND(1919)/8	—	—	—	—	—

X# M1191 50 CENTS
Gold

Date	Mintage	F	VF	XF	Unc
ND(1919)/8	—	—	—	—	—

X# M1200 DOLLAR
Silver

Date	Mintage	F	VF	XF	Unc
ND(1919)/8	—	—	—	400	600

T'ang Chi Yao Issues

X# M1210 DOLLAR
Silver **Note:** Kann#B61.

Date	Mintage	F	VF	XF	Unc
ND	—	—	125	200	300

X# M1211 DOLLAR
Gold **Note:** Kann#B110.

Date	Mintage	F	VF	XF	Unc
ND	—	—	—	2,000	3,000

Tian Yee Foo - Goldsmith

X# M1215 OUNCE
31.1000 g., 0.9996 Gold 0.9994 oz. AGW
Note: Chengtu, Szechuan Province.

Date	Mintage	F	VF	XF	Unc
ND(1930)	—	—	600	750	950

Tsao Kun Issues

X# M1220 DOLLAR
Silver **Reverse:** Sash over left shoulder **Note:** 2.55mm thick. Kann#B678.

Date	Mintage	F	VF	XF	Unc
ND	—	—	175	250	350

X# M1221 DOLLAR
Gold **Note:** Kann#B1573.

Date	Mintage	F	VF	XF	Unc
ND	—	—	—	3,000	4,500

X# M1222 DOLLAR
Copper

Date	Mintage	F	VF	XF	Unc
ND	—	—	—	—	—

X# M1223 DOLLAR
Brass

Date	Mintage	F	VF	XF	Unc
ND	—	—	—	—	—

X# M1230 DOLLAR
Silver **Reverse:** Sash over right shoulder **Edge:** Milled **Note:** 4mm thick.

Date	Mintage	F	VF	XF	Unc
ND	—	—	100	150	225

X# M1231 DOLLAR
Silver **Reverse:** Sash over right shoulder **Edge:** Plain

Date	Mintage	F	VF	XF	Unc
ND	—	—	100	150	225

X# M1232 DOLLAR
Gold **Reverse:** Sash over right shoulder

Date	Mintage	F	VF	XF	Unc
ND	—	—	—	2,500	3,500

X# M1234 DOLLAR
Copper **Reverse:** Sash over right shoulder

Date	Mintage	F	VF	XF	Unc
ND	—	—	—	—	—

X# M1236 DOLLAR
Tin **Note:** Also exists looped with ribbon as a military award.

Date	Mintage	F	VF	XF	Unc
ND	—	—	—	—	—

Wang Hsing Issues

X# M1240 DOLLAR
Silver **Edge:** Plain **Note:** Kann#B60.

Date	Mintage	F	VF	XF	Unc
ND	—	—	125	200	300

X# M1245 DOLLAR

Silver **Note:** Modified design.

Date	Mintage	F	VF	XF	Unc
ND	—	—	125	200	300

Wu Pei-fu Issue

X# M1250 DOLLAR

Silver **Note:** Kann#B57.

Date	Mintage	F	VF	XF	Unc
ND	—	—	—	—	—

Yen Hsi-shan Issues

X# M1260 DOLLAR

Silver **Note:** Kann#B62.

Date	Mintage	F	VF	XF	Unc
ND(1929)/18	—	—	125	200	300

X# M1261 DOLLAR

Gold

Date	Mintage	F	VF	XF	Unc
ND(1929)/18	—	—	—	2,500	3,500

Yüan Shih-kai Series

X# 1315 20 CENTS

38.2500 g., Silver, 45.5 mm. **Obverse:** Bust of Yüan Shih-kai left **Reverse:** Value in wreath **Edge:** Reeded **Note:** A modern concoction.

Date	Mintage	F	VF	XF	Unc
Yr. 9 (1920)	—	18.50	27.50	—	—

X# M1280 1/2 DOLLAR

Silver **Reverse:** Portrait of Yuan Shih-kai in uniform facing

Date	Mintage	F	VF	XF	Unc
ND	—	—	—	—	—

X# M1281 1/2 DOLLAR

Gold

Date	Mintage	F	VF	XF	Unc
ND	—	—	—	850	1,200

X# M1295 1/2 DOLLAR

Silver

Date	Mintage	F	VF	XF	Unc
ND(1914)/3	—	—	—	—	—

X# M1287 1/2 DOLLAR

17.7800 g., Gold, 32 mm. **Obverse:** Yüan Shih-kai in plumed hat facing **Reverse:** Dragon left

Date	Mintage	F	VF	XF	Unc
Yr. 1 (1916)	—	—	—	—	—

X# M1275 DOLLAR

Copper

Date	Mintage	F	VF	XF	Unc
ND	—	—	—	—	—

X# M1300 DOLLAR

Silver **Obverse:** Rosettes at left and right **Note:** The rosettes are believed to have been added at a later date.

Date	Mintage	F	VF	XF	Unc
ND(1914)/3	—	—	—	—	—

X# 1292 DOLLAR

37.5400 g., Silver, 50.2 mm. **Obverse:** Bust of Yüan Shih-kai left, "L. GIORGI" behind **Reverse:** Value in wreath **Edge:** Reeded **Note:** A modern concoction.

Date	Mintage	F	VF	XF	Unc
Yr. 3 (1914)	—	18.50	27.50	—	—

X# 1293 DOLLAR

37.9000 g., Silver, 50.2 mm. **Obverse:** Bust of Yüan Shih-kai left, "L. GIORGI" behind **Reverse:** Value in wreath **Edge:** Reeded **Note:** A modern concoction.

Date	Mintage	F	VF	XF	Unc
Yr. 3 (1914)	—	18.50	27.50	—	—

X# M1310 DOLLAR

Silver

Date	Mintage	F	VF	XF	Unc
Yr. 5 (1916)	—	—	—	—	—

Note: Reported, not confirmed

X# M1315 DOLLAR

Silver **Obverse:** Crossed flags **Reverse:** Military bust of Yüan Shih-kai facing **Note:** Kann#B47.

Date	Mintage	F	VF	XF	Unc
Yr. 17 (1928)	—	—	—	—	—

X# M1291 5 DOLLARS

32.2500 g., Silver, 45.1 mm. **Obverse:** Bust of Yüan Shih-kai left **Reverse:** Value in sprays **Edge Lettering:** L. GIORGI - L. GIORGI and Chinese **Note:** A modern striking. Prev. X#1290.

Date	Mintage	F	VF	XF	Unc
Yr. 2 (1913)	—	18.50	27.50	—	—

X# M1305 5 DOLLARS

4.4000 g., Gold, 18 mm. **Obverse:** Bust of Yüan Shih-kai left **Reverse:** Dragon **Note:** Kann#1517.

Date	Mintage	F	VF	XF	Unc
Yr. 3 (1914)	—	—	—	2,750	4,000

X# M1290 100 DOLLARS

0.9000 Gold **Subject:** 2nd Anniversary of the Republic **Obverse:** Crossed flags **Reverse:** Bust of Yüan Shih-kai left

Date	Mintage	F	VF	XF	Unc
Yr. 2 (1913)	—	—	—	17,500	25,000

Yüan Shih-kai as Hung Hsien Series

X# M1325 10 COPPERS (100 Cash)

Copper, 32 mm. **Obverse:** 4 Chinese characters, "Hung Hsien T'ung Pao" **Reverse:** 4 Chinese characters, "Pei Yang Shih Mei," (Peiyant Mint 10 Coppers) **Note:** With centerhole.

Date	Mintage	F	VF	XF	Unc
ND(1916)	—	—	—	—	—

X# M1330 10 CENTS

Silver **Obverse:** Bust of Hung Hsienin ceremonial robe facing slightly left **Reverse:** Dragon; 4 Chinese characters, "Commemorative of 1916"

Date	Mintage	F	VF	XF	Unc
(1916)	—	—	—	150	200

X# M1331 10 CENTS

Gold **Obverse:** Bust of Hung Hsien in ceremonial robe facing slightly left **Reverse:** Dragon; 4 Chinese characters, "Commemorative of 1916"

Date	Mintage	F	VF	XF	Unc
(1916)	—	—	—	1,250	2,250

X# M1335 20 CENTS

Silver, 27 mm. **Obverse:** Bust of Hung Hsien in ceremonial robe facing slightly left **Reverse:** Dragon; 4 Chinese characters, "Commemorative of 1916" **Note:** Similar to 10 Cents, XM1330.

Date	Mintage	F	VF	XF	Unc
(1916)	—	—	—	—	—

X# M1336 20 CENTS

Gold **Obverse:** Bust of Hung Hsien in ceremonial robe facing slightly left **Reverse:** Dragon; 4 Chinese characters, "Commemorative of 1916"

Date	Mintage	F	VF	XF	Unc
(1916) Reported, not confirmed	—	—	—	—	—

X# M1340 1/2 DOLLAR
Silver **Obverse:** Bust of Hung Hsien in ceremonial robe facing **Reverse:** Dragon **Note:** Kann#B44.

Date	Mintage	F	VF	XF	Unc
(1916)	—	—	—	—	—

X# M1341 1/2 DOLLAR
Gold **Reverse:** Dragon **Note:** Kann#B104.

Date	Mintage	F	VF	XF	Unc
(1916)	—	—	—	2,000	3,500

X# M1360 1/2 DOLLAR
Silver **Obverse:** Military bust of Yüan Shih-kai facing slightly left **Reverse:** Flying dragon **Note:** Kann#B46.

Date	Mintage	F	VF	XF	Unc
Yr. 1 (1916)	—	—	—	—	—

X# M1361 1/2 DOLLAR
Gold **Reverse:** Flying dragon

Date	Mintage	F	VF	XF	Unc
Yr. 1 (1916)	—	—	—	2,000	3,500

X# M1345 DOLLAR
Silver **Obverse:** Bust of Hung Hsien in ceremonial robe facing slightly left **Reverse:** Dragon; 4 Chinese characters, "Commemorative of 1916" **Edge:** Plain **Note:** Kann#B43.

Date	Mintage	F	VF	XF	Unc
(1916)	—	—	125	200	300

X# M1346 DOLLAR
Silver **Obverse:** Bust of Hung Hsien in ceremonial robe facing slightly left **Reverse:** Dragon; 4 Chinese characters, "Commemorative of 1916" **Edge:** Milled **Note:** Kann#B43.

Date	Mintage	F	VF	XF	Unc
(1916)	—	—	125	200	300

X# M1347 DOLLAR
Gold **Obverse:** Bust of Hung Hsien in ceremonial robe facing slightly left **Reverse:** Dragon; 4 Chinese characters, "Commemorative of 1916"

Date	Mintage	F	VF	XF	Unc
(1916)	—	—	—	3,000	5,000

X# M1350 DOLLAR
Silver **Obverse:** Bust of Hung Hsien in ceremonial robe facing slightly left **Reverse:** Dragon **Note:** Modified design.

Date	Mintage	F	VF	XF	Unc
(1916)	—	—	125	200	300

X# M1355 DOLLAR
Cast Silver, 37 mm.

Date	Mintage	F	VF	XF	Unc
(1916)	—	—	—	—	—

X# M1358 DOLLAR
31.5200 g., Bronze, 40.5 mm. **Obverse:** 1/2-length bust of Yüan Shih-kai facing in ceremonial robe **Reverse:** Dragon wrapped around inscription **Rev. Inscription:** "Commemorative of 1916" **Edge:** Reeded

Date	Mintage	F	VF	XF	Unc
1916	—	—	12.50	20.00	35.00

X# M1365 DOLLAR
Silver **Subject:** Founding of the Nation **Obverse:** Bust of Hung Hsien in ceremonial robe facing **Reverse:** Facing dragon **Note:** Kann#B45.

Date	Mintage	F	VF	XF	Unc
Yr. 1 (1916)	—	—	175	250	350

X# M1380 DOLLAR
Silver **Obverse:** Bust of Hung Hsien in ceremonial robe facing 3/4 left **Reverse:** Facing dragon

Date	Mintage	F	VF	XF	Unc
Yr. 1 (1916)	—	—	200	275	400

X# M1381 DOLLAR
Gold **Note:** Kann#B103.

Date	Mintage	F	VF	XF	Unc
Yr. 1 (1916)	—	—	—	—	—

X# M1385 DOLLAR
Silver **Obverse:** Hung Hsein horseback right **Reverse:** Fortress city gate **Note:** Kann#B48.

Date	Mintage	F	VF	XF	Unc
Yr. 1 (1916)	—	—	125	200	300

X# M1390 DOLLAR
Silver **Note:** Modified design.

Date	Mintage	F	VF	XF	Unc
Yr. 1 (1916)	—	—	125	220	350

X# M1390A DOLLAR

Silver Plated Bronze **Note:** Similar to #XM1390.

Date	Mintage	F	VF	XF	Unc
ND(1916)	—	—	—	—	—

X# M1395 DOLLAR

Silver **Issuer:** Hunan Province **Obv. Legend:** Chung-hua Min-kuo **Reverse:** Dragon around value

Date	Mintage	F	VF	XF	Unc
Yr. 1 (1916)	—	—	200	375	550

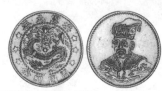

X# M1370 5 DOLLARS

3.9900 g., Gold **Obverse:** Facing dragon **Reverse:** Bust of Hung Hsien in ceremonial robe facing slightly left

Date	Mintage	F	VF	XF	Unc
Yr. 1 (1916)	—	—	—	600	800

X# M1371 5 DOLLARS

4.4000 g., Gold, 18 mm. **Series:** Y?an Shih-kai as Hung Hsien **Obverse:** Bust of Hung Hsien left **Obv. Legend:** "Beginning of Hung Hsien" **Reverse:** Dragon **Note:** KM#1518.

Date	Mintage	F	VF	XF	Unc
ND(1916)	—	—	—	2,750	4,000

X# M1372 5 DOLLARS

3.9900 g., Gold **Note:** Kann#B99. Mule. Obv: XM1370. Rev: XM1331.

Date	Mintage	F	VF	XF	Unc
Yr. 1 (1916)	—	—	—	—	—

X# M1375 10 DOLLARS

Gold, 23 mm. **Note:** Similar to 5 Dollars, XM1370.

Date	Mintage	F	VF	XF	Unc
Yr. 1 (1916)	—	—	—	900	1,200

TAIWAN

REPUBLIC

MEDALLIC COINAGE

X# M31 TAEL

37.8000 g., 0.9990 Silver 1.2140 oz. ASW, 42.15 mm. **Issuer:** Money Company, California **Obverse:** Facing dragon above clouds, horse left below **Obv. Legend:** TAIWAN **Reverse:** Crowned garter

Date	Mintage	F	VF	XF	Unc
1992 Proof	—	Value: 15.00			

CHRISTIANIA

FREE STATE

STANDARD COINAGE

X# 1 FED

Silver dark patina, 28 mm. **Obv:** End of a hash pipe, smoke forms a serpent. Three balls at left **Rev:** Two cabins and crescent moon **Rev. Legend:** CHRISTIANIA

Date	Mintage	F	VF	XF	Unc	BU
1976	Est. 200	—	—	200	300	—

Note: Thomas Holland auction prices realized in 2006

X# 2.1 FED

Silver, 31 mm. **Obv:** Triskeles as yin/yang with three balls. Sun and moon in legend **Obv. Legend:** 1 FED / CHRISTIANIA **Rev:** Three balls within flower; crossed rifle and hash pipe in legend **Rev. Legend:** CHRISTIANIA / 1977 **Note:** Thick flan 1.5mm.

Date	Mintage	F	VF	XF	Unc	BU
1977	200	—	—	—	85.00	—

X# 2.2 FED

Silver, 31 mm. **Obv:** Triskeles as yin/yang with three balls. Sun and moon in legend **Obv. Legend:** 1 FED / CHRISTIANA **Rev:** Three balls within flower; crossed rifle and hash pipe in legend **Rev. Legend:** CHRISTIANA / 1977 **Note:** Thin flan 0.8mm.

Date	Mintage	F	VF	XF	Unc	BU
1977	200	—	—	—	100	—

X# 2a FED

Copper, 31 mm. **Obv:** Triskeles as yin/yang with three balls. Sun and moon in legend **Obv. Legend:** 1 FED / CHRISTIANIA **Rev:** Three balls within flower; crossed rible and hash pipe in legend **Rev. Legend:** CHRISTIANIA / 1977

Date	Mintage	F	VF	XF	Unc	BU
1977	—	—	—	—	65.00	—

X# 7 FED

Silver **Obv:** Celtic brade pattern **Obv. Legend:** CHRISTIANIA 1 FED **Rev:** Group of twelve naked dancers on three center balls

Date	Mintage	F	VF	XF	Unc	BU
1985	200	—	—	—	130	—

X# 8 FED

Silver **Obv:** Smoking "detective" before lineup of police in riot gear **Obv. Legend:** 1 FED **Rev:** Naked couple embracing behind a seated guard dog **Rev. Legend:** CHRISTIANIA **Note:** Known as the Bogart coin.

Date	Mintage	F	VF	XF	Unc	BU
1988	200	—	—	—	65.00	—

X# 8b FED

Brass

Date	Mintage	F	VF	XF	Unc	BU
1988	—	—	—	—	120	—

X# 8a FED

Copper

Date	Mintage	F	VF	XF	Unc	BU
1988	200	—	—	—	45.00	—

X# 11 FED

Silver **Obv:** Friendly dragon, cannabis plant above, three balls below **Obv. Legend:** CHRISTIANIA 1 FED 1993 **Rev:** Three spirals inspired by the spirt of a nearby church

Date	Mintage	F	VF	XF	Unc	BU
1993	200	—	—	—	80.00	—

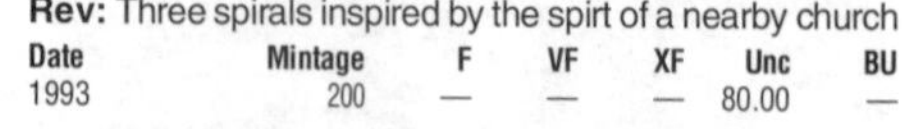

X# 14.1 FED

Silver **Obv. Inscription:** CHRISTIANIA / 1997 / 1 / FED / DANMARK (Comet Hale-Bopp at lower right **Rev:** Dragon in celtic design **Edge:** Numbered

Date	Mintage	F	VF	XF	Unc	BU
1997	200	—	—	—	50.00	—

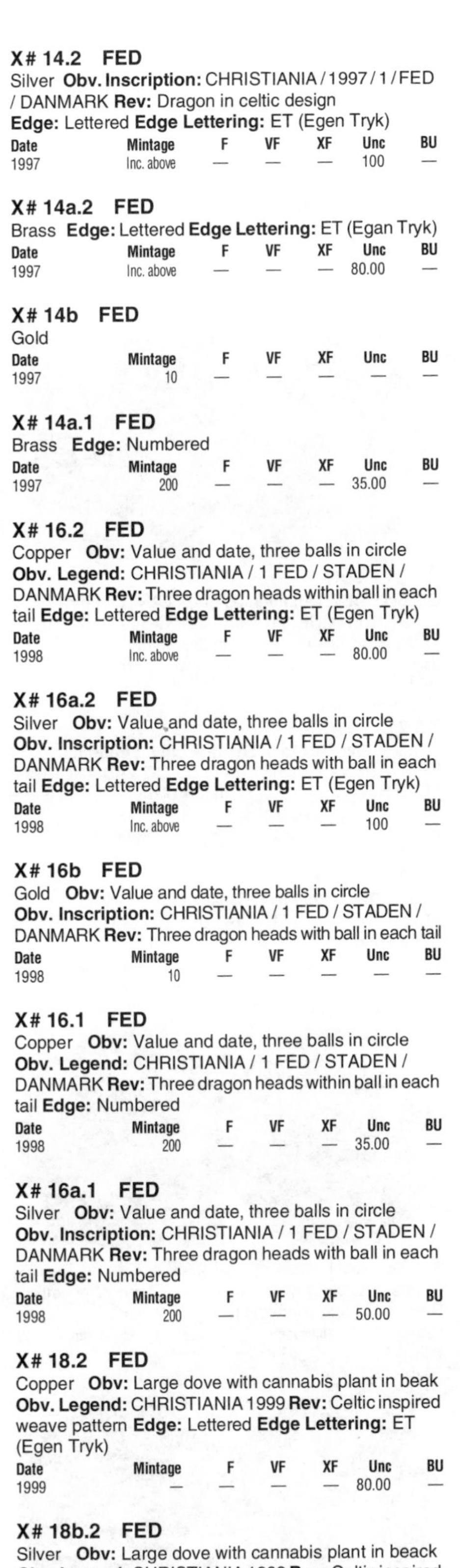

X# 14.2 FED

Silver **Obv. Inscription:** CHRISTIANIA / 1997 / 1 / FED / DANMARK **Rev:** Dragon in celtic design **Edge:** Lettered **Edge Lettering:** ET (Egen Tryk)

Date	Mintage	F	VF	XF	Unc	BU
1997	Inc. above	—	—	—	100	—

X# 14a.2 FED

Brass **Edge:** Lettered **Edge Lettering:** ET (Egan Tryk)

Date	Mintage	F	VF	XF	Unc	BU
1997	Inc. above	—	—	—	80.00	—

X# 14b FED

Gold

Date	Mintage	F	VF	XF	Unc	BU
1997	10	—	—	—	—	—

X# 14a.1 FED

Brass **Edge:** Numbered

Date	Mintage	F	VF	XF	Unc	BU
1997	200	—	—	—	35.00	—

X# 16.2 FED

Copper **Obv:** Value and date, three balls in circle **Obv. Legend:** CHRISTIANIA / 1 FED / STADEN / DANMARK **Rev:** Three dragon heads within ball in each tail **Edge:** Lettered **Edge Lettering:** ET (Egen Tryk)

Date	Mintage	F	VF	XF	Unc	BU
1998	Inc. above	—	—	—	80.00	—

X# 16a.2 FED

Silver **Obv:** Value and date, three balls in circle **Obv. Inscription:** CHRISTIANIA / 1 FED / STADEN / DANMARK **Rev:** Three dragon heads with ball in each tail **Edge:** Lettered **Edge Lettering:** ET (Egen Tryk)

Date	Mintage	F	VF	XF	Unc	BU
1998	Inc. above	—	—	—	100	—

X# 16b FED

Gold **Obv:** Value and date, three balls in circle **Obv. Inscription:** CHRISTIANIA / 1 FED / STADEN / DANMARK **Rev:** Three dragon heads with ball in each tail

Date	Mintage	F	VF	XF	Unc	BU
1998	10	—	—	—	—	—

X# 16.1 FED

Copper **Obv:** Value and date, three balls in circle **Obv. Legend:** CHRISTIANIA / 1 FED / STADEN / DANMARK **Rev:** Three dragon heads within ball in each tail **Edge:** Numbered

Date	Mintage	F	VF	XF	Unc	BU
1998	200	—	—	—	35.00	—

X# 16a.1 FED

Silver **Obv:** Value and date, three balls in circle **Obv. Inscription:** CHRISTIANIA / 1 FED / STADEN / DANMARK **Rev:** Three dragon heads with ball in each tail **Edge:** Numbered

Date	Mintage	F	VF	XF	Unc	BU
1998	200	—	—	—	50.00	—

X# 18.2 FED

Copper **Obv:** Large dove with cannabis plant in beak **Obv. Legend:** CHRISTIANIA 1999 **Rev:** Celtic inspired weave pattern **Edge:** Lettered **Edge Lettering:** ET (Egen Tryk)

Date	Mintage	F	VF	XF	Unc	BU
1999	—	—	—	—	80.00	—

X# 18b.2 FED

Silver **Obv:** Large dove with cannabis plant in beack **Obv. Legend:** CHRISTIANIA 1999 **Rev:** Celtic inspired weave pattern **Edge:** Lettered **Edge Lettering:** ET (Egen Tryk)

Date	Mintage	F	VF	XF	Unc	BU
1999	Inc. above	—	—	—	100	—

X# 18c FED

Gold **Obv:** Large dove with cannabis plant in beak **Obv. Legend:** CHRISTIANIA 1999 **Rev:** Celtic inspired weave pattern

Date	Mintage	F	VF	XF	Unc	BU
1999	10	—	—	—	—	—

X# 18.1 FED

Copper **Obv:** Inspiration from Livingstone Seagull large dove with cannabis plant in beak **Obv. Legend:** CHRISTIANIA 1999 **Rev:** Celtic inspired weave pattern **Edge:** Numbered

Date	Mintage	F	VF	XF	Unc	BU
1999	200	—	—	—	45.00	—

X# 18b.1 FED

Silver **Obv:** Inspiration from Livingstone Seagull large dove with cannabis plant in beak **Obv. Legend:** CHRISTIANIA 1999 **Rev:** Celtic inspired weave pattern **Edge:** Numbered

Date	Mintage	F	VF	XF	Unc	BU
1999	—	—	—	—	60.00	—

X# 20.2 FED

Copper **Obv:** Dragon-like bow of viking ship; bridge in background **Rev:** Cannabis plant **Rev. Legend:** CHRISTIANIA DANMARK **Edge:** Lettered **Edge Lettering:** ET (Egen Tryk)

Date	Mintage	F	VF	XF	Unc	BU
2000	Inc. above	—	—	—	80.00	—

X# 20b.2 FED

Silver **Obv:** Dragon-like bow of viking shipl bridge in background **Rev:** Cannabis plant **Rev. Legend:** CHRISTIANIA DANMARK **Edge:** Lettered **Edge Lettering:** ET (Egen Tryk)

Date	Mintage	F	VF	XF	Unc	BU
2000	Inc. above	—	—	—	100	—

X# 20c FED

Gold **Obv:** Dragon-like bow of viking ship; bridge in background **Rev:** Cannabis plant **Rev. Legend:** CHRISTIANIA DANMARK

Date	Mintage	F	VF	XF	Unc	BU
2000	10	—	—	—	—	—

X# 20.1 FED

Copper **Obv:** Dragon-like bow of viking ship; bridge in background **Rev:** Cannabis plant **Rev. Legend:** CHRISTIANIA DANMARK **Edge:** Numbered

Date	Mintage	F	VF	XF	Unc	BU
2000	200	—	—	—	45.00	—

X# 20b.1 FED

Silver **Obv:** Dragon-like bow of viking ship; bridge in background **Rev:** Cannabis plant **Rev. Legend:** CHRISTIANIA DANMARK **Edge:** Numbered

Date	Mintage	F	VF	XF	Unc	BU
2000	200	—	—	—	65.00	—

X# 23.2 FED

Copper **Obv:** Value as fancy design **Obv. Legend:** CHRISTIANIA / FRISTADEN I DANMARK **Rev:** Six people dancing as seen from above **Edge:** Lettered **Edge Lettering:** ET (Egen Tryk)

Date	Mintage	F	VF	XF	Unc	BU
2002	Inc. above	—	—	—	80.00	—

X# 23a.2 FED

Silver **Obv:** Value as fancy design **Obv. Legend:** CHRISTIANIA / FRISTADEN I DANMARK **Rev:** Six people dancing as seen from above **Edge:** Lettered **Edge Lettering:** ET (Egen Tryk)

Date	Mintage	F	VF	XF	Unc	BU
2002	Inc. above	—	—	—	100	—

X# 23b FED

Gold **Obv:** Value as fancy design **Obv. Legend:** CHRISTIANIA / FRISTADEN I DANMARK **Rev:** Six people dancing as seen from above **Edge:** Lettered **Edge Lettering:** ET (Egen Tryk)

Date	Mintage	F	VF	XF	Unc	BU
2002	10	—	—	—	950	—

X# 23.1 FED

Copper **Obv:** Value as fancy design **Obv. Legend:** CHRISTIANIA / FRISTADEN I DANMARK **Rev:** Six people dancing as seen from above **Edge:** Numbered

Date	Mintage	F	VF	XF	Unc	BU
2002	200	—	—	—	40.00	—

X# 23a.1 FED

Silver **Obv:** Value as fancy design **Obv. Legend:** CHRISTIANIA / FRISTADEN I DANMARK **Rev:** Six people dancing as seen from above **Edge:** Numbered

Date	Mintage	F	VF	XF	Unc	BU
2002	200	—	—	—	60.00	—

X# 25.2 FED

Copper **Obv:** View of Pusher Street **Obv. Legend:** CHRISTIANIA DANMARK **Rev:** Three dogs chasing each other **Edge:** Lettered **Edge Lettering:** ET (Egen Tryk)

Date	Mintage	F	VF	XF	Unc	BU
2003	Inc. above	—	—	—	80.00	—

X# 25b.2 FED

Silver **Obv:** View of Pusher Street **Obv. Legend:** CHRISTIANIA DANMARK **Rev:** Three dogs chasing each other **Edge:** Lettered **Edge Lettering:** ET (Egen Tryk)

Date	Mintage	F	VF	XF	Unc	BU
2003	Inc. above	—	—	—	100	—

X# 25c FED

Gold **Obv:** View of Pusher Street **Obv. Legend:** CHRISTIANIA DANMARK **Rev:** Three dogs chasing each other **Edge:** Lettered

Date	Mintage	F	VF	XF	Unc	BU
2003	10	—	—	—	950	—

X# 25.1 FED

Copper **Obv:** View of Pusher Street **Obv. Legend:** CHRISTIANIA DANMARK **Rev:** Three dogs chasing each other **Edge:** Numbered

Date	Mintage	F	VF	XF	Unc	BU
2003	200	—	—	—	40.00	—

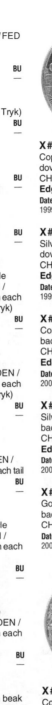

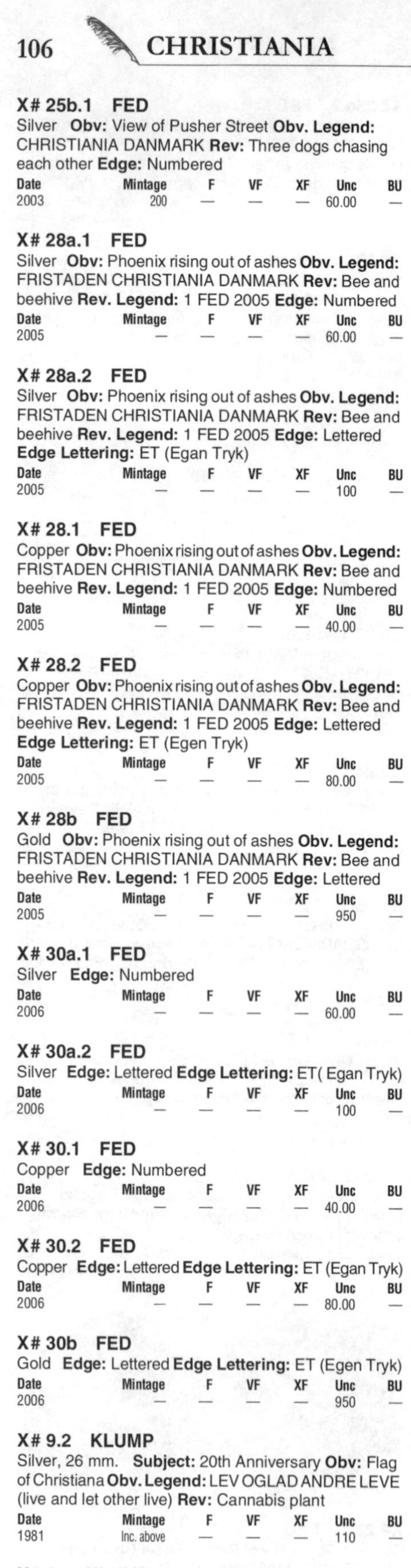

X# 25b.1 FED

Silver **Obv:** View of Pusher Street **Obv. Legend:** CHRISTIANIA DANMARK **Rev:** Three dogs chasing each other **Edge:** Numbered

Date	Mintage	F	VF	XF	Unc	BU
2003	200	—	—	—	60.00	—

X# 28a.1 FED

Silver **Obv:** Phoenix rising out of ashes **Obv. Legend:** FRISTADEN CHRISTIANIA DANMARK **Rev:** Bee and beehive **Rev. Legend:** 1 FED 2005 **Edge:** Numbered

Date	Mintage	F	VF	XF	Unc	BU
2005	—	—	—	—	60.00	—

X# 28a.2 FED

Silver **Obv:** Phoenix rising out of ashes **Obv. Legend:** FRISTADEN CHRISTIANIA DANMARK **Rev:** Bee and beehive **Rev. Legend:** 1 FED 2005 **Edge:** Lettered **Edge Lettering:** ET (Egan Tryk)

Date	Mintage	F	VF	XF	Unc	BU
2005	—	—	—	—	100	—

X# 28.1 FED

Copper **Obv:** Phoenix rising out of ashes **Obv. Legend:** FRISTADEN CHRISTIANIA DANMARK **Rev:** Bee and beehive **Rev. Legend:** 1 FED 2005 **Edge:** Numbered

Date	Mintage	F	VF	XF	Unc	BU
2005	—	—	—	—	40.00	—

X# 28.2 FED

Copper **Obv:** Phoenix rising out of ashes **Obv. Legend:** FRISTADEN CHRISTIANIA DANMARK **Rev:** Bee and beehive **Rev. Legend:** 1 FED 2005 **Edge:** Lettered **Edge Lettering:** ET (Egen Tryk)

Date	Mintage	F	VF	XF	Unc	BU
2005	—	—	—	—	80.00	—

X# 28b FED

Gold **Obv:** Phoenix rising out of ashes **Obv. Legend:** FRISTADEN CHRISTIANIA DANMARK **Rev:** Bee and beehive **Rev. Legend:** 1 FED 2005 **Edge:** Lettered

Date	Mintage	F	VF	XF	Unc	BU
2005	—	—	—	—	950	—

X# 30a.1 FED

Silver **Edge:** Numbered

Date	Mintage	F	VF	XF	Unc	BU
2006	—	—	—	—	60.00	—

X# 30a.2 FED

Silver **Edge:** Lettered **Edge Lettering:** ET(Egan Tryk)

Date	Mintage	F	VF	XF	Unc	BU
2006	—	—	—	—	100	—

X# 30.1 FED

Copper **Edge:** Numbered

Date	Mintage	F	VF	XF	Unc	BU
2006	—	—	—	—	40.00	—

X# 30.2 FED

Copper **Edge:** Lettered **Edge Lettering:** ET (Egan Tryk)

Date	Mintage	F	VF	XF	Unc	BU
2006	—	—	—	—	80.00	—

X# 30b FED

Gold **Edge:** Lettered **Edge Lettering:** ET (Egen Tryk)

Date	Mintage	F	VF	XF	Unc	BU
2006	—	—	—	—	950	—

X# 9.2 KLUMP

Silver, 26 mm. **Subject:** 20th Anniversary **Obv:** Flag of Christiana **Obv. Legend:** LEV OGLAD ANDRE LEVE (live and let other live) **Rev:** Cannabis plant

Date	Mintage	F	VF	XF	Unc	BU
1981	Inc. above	—	—	—	110	—

X# 9a KLUMP

Gold **Subject:** 20th Anniversary **Obv:** Flag of Christiana **Obv. Legend:** LEV OGLAD ANDRE LEVE (live and let other live) **Rev:** Cannabis plant

Date	Mintage	F	VF	XF	Unc	BU
1981	—	—	—	—	1,200	—

X# 9.1 KLUMP

Silver, 25 mm. **Subject:** 20th Anniversary **Obv:** Flag of Christiania **Rev:** Cannabis plant **Rev. Legend:** LEV OG LAD ANDRE LEVE (live and let others

Date	Mintage	F	VF	XF	Unc	BU
1991	Est. 100	—	—	—	110	—

X# 15 LøN

Copper **Obv:** Flag of Christiania above snail **Obv. Legend:** FRISTADEN CHRISTIANIA / LEV OG LAD ANDRE LEVE **Rev:** Value and cannabis plant

Date	Mintage	F	VF	XF	Unc	BU
1997	200	—	—	20.00	30.00	—

X# 15a LøN

Brass **Obv:** Flag of Christiania above snail **Obv. Legend:** FRISTADEN CHRISTIANIA / LEV OG LAD ANDRE LEVE **Rev:** Value and cannabis plant

Date	Mintage	F	VF	XF	Unc	BU
1997	200	—	—	20.00	30.00	—

X# 15b LøN

Silver **Obv:** Flag of Christiania above snail **Obv. Legend:** FRISTADEN CHRISTIANIA / LEV OG LAD ANDRE LEVE **Rev:** Value and cannabis plant

Date	Mintage	F	VF	XF	Unc	BU
1997	200	—	—	—	60.00	—

X# 17 LøN

Brass **Obv:** Flag of Christiania above snail **Obv. Legend:** FRISTADEN CHRISTIANIA / LEV OG LAD ANDRE LEVE **Rev:** Value and cannabis plant

Date	Mintage	F	VF	XF	Unc	BU
1998	200	—	—	20.00	30.00	—

X# 19 LøN

Copper **Obv:** Flag of Christiania above go-cart **Rev:** Value and cannabis plant

Date	Mintage	F	VF	XF	Unc	BU
1999	200	—	—	20.00	30.00	—

X# 19a LøN

Brass **Obv:** Flag of Christiania above go-cart **Rev:** Value and cannabis plant

Date	Mintage	F	VF	XF	Unc	BU
1999	200	—	—	20.00	30.00	—

X# A21 LøN

Copper **Obv:** Ornamented mask **Rev:** Value and canabis plant **Note:** Mule of obverse X#21 and reverse X#19.

Date	Mintage	F	VF	XF	Unc	BU
2000	10	—	—	—	—	—

X# A21a LøN

Brass **Obv:** Ornamented mask **Rev:** Value and canabis plant **Note:** Mule of obverse X#21 and reverse X#19.

Date	Mintage	F	VF	XF	Unc	BU
2000	10	—	—	—	—	—

X# A21b LøN

Silver **Obv:** Ornamented mask **Rev:** Value and canabis plant **Note:** Mule of obverse X#21 and reverse X#19.

Date	Mintage	F	VF	XF	Unc	BU
2000	10	—	—	—	—	—

X# 21 LøN

Copper **Obv:** Ornamented mask **Obv. Legend:** FRISTADEN CHRISTIANIA / LEV OG LAD ANDRE LEVE **Rev:** Snail below cannabis plant

Date	Mintage	F	VF	XF	Unc	BU
2000	200	—	—	20.00	30.00	—

X# 21a LøN

Brass **Obv:** Ornamented mask **Obv. Legend:** FRISTADEN CHRISTIANIA / LEV OG LAD ANDRE LEVE **Rev:** Snail below cannabis plant

Date	Mintage	F	VF	XF	Unc	BU
2000	200	—	—	20.00	30.00	—

X# 21b LøN

Silver **Obv:** Ornamented mask **Obv. Legend:** FRISTADEN CHRISTIANIA / LEV OG LAD ANDRE LEVE **Rev:** Snail below cannabis plant

Date	Mintage	F	VF	XF	Unc	BU
2000	200	—	—	—	60.00	—

X# 22 LøN

Copper **Subject:** 30th Anniversary **Obv:** Wren left **Rev:** Value and cannabis plant

Date	Mintage	F	VF	XF	Unc	BU
2001	200	—	—	—	35.00	—

X# 22a LøN

Brass **Subject:** 30th Anniversary **Obv:** Wren left **Rev:** Value and cannabis plant

Date	Mintage	F	VF	XF	Unc	BU
2001	200	—	—	—	35.00	—

X# 22b LøN

Silver **Subject:** 30th Anniversary **Obv:** Wren left **Rev:** Value and cannabis plant

Date	Mintage	F	VF	XF	Unc	BU
2001	200	—	—	—	65.00	—

X# 24 LøN

Copper **Obv:** Plant and skyline **Rev:** Value and cannabis plant

Date	Mintage	F	VF	XF	Unc	BU
2002	—	—	—	—	30.00	—

X# 24a LøN

Brass **Obv:** Plant and skyline **Rev:** Value and cannabis plant

Date	Mintage	F	VF	XF	Unc	BU
2002	200	—	—	—	30.00	—

X# 24b LøN

Silver **Obv:** Plant and skyline **Rev:** Value and cannabis plant

Date	Mintage	F	VF	XF	Unc	BU
2002	200	—	—	—	60.00	—

X# 26 LøN

Copper **Obv:** Couple embracing before buildings **Rev:** Value and cannabis plant

Date	Mintage	F	VF	XF	Unc	BU
2003	200	—	—	—	35.00	—

X# 26a LøN

Brass **Obv:** Couple embracing before buildigns **Rev:** Value and cannabis plant

Date	Mintage	F	VF	XF	Unc	BU
2003	200	—	—	—	35.00	—

X# 26b LøN

Silver **Obv:** Couple embracing before buildings **Rev:** Value and cannabis plant

Date	Mintage	F	VF	XF	Unc	BU
2003	100	—	—	—	100	—

X# 27 LøN

Copper **Obv:** Five party hats **Rev:** Value and cannabis plant

Date	Mintage	F	VF	XF	Unc	BU
2004	200	—	—	—	35.00	—

X# 27a LøN

Brass **Obv:** Five party hats **Rev:** Value and cannabis plants

Date	Mintage	F	VF	XF	Unc	BU
2004	200	—	—	—	35.00	—

X# 27b LøN

Silver **Obv:** Five party hats **Rev:** Value and cannabis plant

Date	Mintage	F	VF	XF	Unc	BU
2004	100	—	—	—	100	—

X# 29 LøN

Copper, 30 mm. **Obv:** Theatre masks **Obv. Legend:** FRISTADEN CHRISTIANIA LEV OG LAD ANDRE LEVE **Rev:** Snail below cannabis plant **Edge:** Plain

Date	Mintage	F	VF	XF	Unc	BU
2005	200	—	—	—	35.00	—

X# 29a LøN

Brass, 30 mm. **Obv:** Theatre masks **Obv. Legend:** FRISTADEN CHRISTIANIA LEV OG LAD ANDRE LEVE **Rev:** Snail below cannabis plant **Edge:** Plain

Date	Mintage	F	VF	XF	Unc	BU
2005	200	—	—	—	35.00	—

X# 29b LøN

0.9990 Silver, 30 mm. **Obv:** Theatre masks **Obv. Legend:** FRISTADEN CHRISTIANIA LEV OG LAD ANDRE LEVE **Rev:** Snail below cannabis plant **Edge:** Plain

Date	Mintage	F	VF	XF	Unc	BU
2005	100	—	—	—	100	—

X# 31 LøN

Copper, 30 mm. **Obv:** Three balls framed by buildings **Obv. Legend:** FRISTADEN CHRISTIANIA / LEV OG LAD ANDRE LEVE **Rev:** Snail below cannabis **Edge:** Plain

Date	Mintage	F	VF	XF	Unc	BU
2006	200	—	—	—	35.00	—

X# 31a LøN

Brass, 30 mm. **Obv:** Three balls framed by buildings **Obv. Legend:** FRISTADEN CHRISTIANIA / LEV OG LAD ANDRE LEVE **Rev:** Snail below cannabis **Edge:** Plain

Date	Mintage	F	VF	XF	Unc	BU
2006	200	—	—	—	35.00	—

X# 31b LøN

0.9990 Silver, 30 mm. **Obv:** Three balls framed by buildings **Obv. Legend:** FRISTADEN CHRISTIANIA / LEV OG LAD ANDRE LEVE **Rev:** Snail below cannabis **Edge:** Plain

Date	Mintage	F	VF	XF	Unc	BU
2006	100	—	—	—	100	—

X# 32 LøN

Copper, 30 mm. **Obv:** Construction **Obv. Legend:** FORNY CHRISTIANIA 1971-2006 **Rev:** Snail below cannabis **Edge:** Plain

Date	Mintage	F	VF	XF	Unc	BU
2006	200	—	—	—	35.00	—

X# 32a LøN

Brass, 30 mm. **Obv:** Construction **Obv. Legend:** FORNY CHRISTIANIA 1971-2006 **Rev:** Snail below cannabis **Edge:** Plain

Date	Mintage	F	VF	XF	Unc	BU
2006	200	—	—	—	35.00	—

X# 32b LøN

0.9990 Silver, 30 mm. **Obv:** Construction **Obv. Legend:** FORNY CHRISTIANIA 1971-2006 **Rev:** Snail below cannabis plant **Edge:** Plain

Date	Mintage	F	VF	XF	Unc	BU
2006	100	—	—	—	100	—

MEDALLIC COINAGE

X# A2 FED

Silver **Obv:** Fantasy design **Obv. Legend:** KARNEVAL / FRI FANTASIEN (English: Liberate The Fantasy)

Date	Mintage	F	VF	XF	Unc	BU
1984	—	—	—	—	65.00	—

X# A3.1 FED

Silver **Obv:** Female head left with punk hair style and earing, three balls and date below **Obv. Legend:** CHRISTIANIA DANMARKS FRISTAD **Note:** Parody of Danish coin (KM#867).

Date	Mintage	F	VF	XF	Unc	BU
1994 Uniface	—	—	—	—	65.00	—

X# M2.2 NON-DENOMINATED

Copper **Subject:** 6th Anniversary **Obv:** Rainbow above town view, date, three balls below **Obv. Legend:** CHRISTIANIA / DANMARK **Rev:** Flags flanking large 6 **Rev. Legend:** CHRISTIANIA / 6 AAR

Date	Mintage	F	VF	XF	Unc	BU
1977	—	—	—	—	65.00	—

X# M2a.2 NON-DENOMINATED

Silver **Subject:** 6th Anniversary **Obv:** Rainbow above town view, date, three balls below **Obv. Legend:** CHRISTIANIA / DANMARK **Rev:** Flags flanking large 6 **Rev. Legend:** CHRISTIANIA

Date	Mintage	F	VF	XF	Unc	BU
1977	—	—	—	—	100	—

X# M2.1 NON-DENOMINATED

Copper **Subject:** 6th Anniversary **Obv:** Rainbow above town view, date, three balls below **Obv. Legend:** CHRISTIANIA / DANMARK **Rev:** Large 6 **Rev. Legend:** CHRISTIANIA / 6 AAR

Date	Mintage	F	VF	XF	Unc	BU
1977	—	—	—	—	65.00	—

X# M2.3 NON-DENOMINATED

Copper **Subject:** 6th Anniversary **Obv:** Enameled rainbow above town view, date, three balls below **Obv. Legend:** CHRISTIANIA / DANMARK **Rev:** Flags flanking large 6 **Rev. Legend:** CHRISTIANIA / 6 AAR

Date	Mintage	F	VF	XF	Unc	BU
1977	—	—	—	—	65.00	—

X# M2a.1 NON-DENOMINATED

Silver **Subject:** 6th Anniversary **Obv:** Rainbow above town, date, three balls below **Obv. Legend:** CHRISTIANIA / DANMARK **Rev:** Large 6 **Rev. Legend:** CHRISTIANIA

Date	Mintage	F	VF	XF	Unc	BU
1977	—	—	—	—	100	—

X# M2a.3 NON-DENOMINATED

Silver **Subject:** 6th Anniversary **Obv:** Enameled rainbow above town view, date, three balls below **Obv. Legend:** CHRISTIANIA / DANMARK **Rev:** Flags flanking large 6 **Rev. Legend:** CHRISTIANIA

Date	Mintage	F	VF	XF	Unc	BU
1977	—	—	—	—	100	—

X# M3a NON-DENOMINATED

Copper **Subject:** 10th Anniversary **Obv:** Cannabis plant below 10AR **Obv. Legend:** FRISTADEN CHRISTIANIA 1971 1981 **Rev:** Skyline and cannabis plant

Date	Mintage	F	VF	XF	Unc	BU
1981	—	—	—	—	60.00	—

X# A1 NON-DENOMINATED

Silver **Subject:** 10th Anniversary **Obv:** Doghead profile left, three dancing folk below holding cannabris plant **Obv. Legend:** CHRISTIANIA 10 ÅR

Date	Mintage	F	VF	XF	Unc	BU
1981 Uniface	—	—	—	—	65.00	—

X# M3 NON-DENOMINATED

Silver **Subject:** 10th Anniversary **Obv:** Cannabis plant below 10ÅR **Obv. Legend:** FRISTADEN CHRISTIANIA 1971 1981 **Rev:** Skyline and cannabis plant **Rev. Legend:** 1981 10 År

Date	Mintage	F	VF	XF	Unc	BU
1981	—	—	—	—	80.00	—

X# M4 NON-DENOMINATED

Silver **Subject:** 20th Anniversary **Obv:** Dog (SOS in morse code around edge) **Obv. Legend:** CHRISTIANIA 1971 20 ÅR 1991 **Rev:** Celtic-like stylized heart patterns

Date	Mintage	F	VF	XF	Unc	BU
1991	—	—	—	—	80.00	—

X# M5 NON-DENOMINATED

Gold Plated Brass **Subject:** 25th Anniversary **Obv:** 25 formed by swan and dragon, three balls below **Obv. Legend:** CHRISTIANIA 1971 1996 **Rev:** Jester juggling three balls **Rev. Legend:** I KAN IKKE SLÅ OS IHJEL VI ER EN DEL AF JER SELV (you can not kill us, we are part of yourselves)

Date	Mintage	F	VF	XF	Unc	BU
1996	—	—	—	—	65.00	—

X# M5a NON-DENOMINATED

Silver **Subject:** 25th Anniversary **Obv:** 25 formed by swan and dragon, three balls below **Obv. Legend:** CHRISTIANIA 1971 1996 **Rev:** Jester juggling three balls **Rev. Legend:** I KAN IKKE SLÅ OS IHJEL VI ER EN DEL AF JER SELV (You can not kill us, we are part of yourselves)

Date	Mintage	F	VF	XF	Unc	BU
1996	—	—	—	—	110	—

X# M6 NON-DENOMINATED

Silver **Subject:** 30th Anniversary **Obv:** Large 30 **Obv. Legend:** FRISTADEN CHRISTIANIA DANMARK **Rev:** Two skateboarders

Date	Mintage	F	VF	XF	Unc	BU
2001	200	—	—	—	60.00	—

X# M6a NON-DENOMINATED

Copper **Subject:** 30th Anniversary **Obv:** Large 30 **Obv. Legend:** FRISTADEN CHRISTIANA DANMARK **Rev:** Two skateboarders

Date	Mintage	F	VF	XF	Unc	BU
2001	200	—	—	—	40.00	—

TRIAL STRIKES

X# TS2a FED

Copper **Obv:** Fantasy design **Obv. Legend:** KARNEVALS / FRI FANTASIEN

Date	Mintage	F	VF	XF	Unc	BU
1984	—	—	—	—	200	—

X# TS3.2 FED

0.9250 Silver **Obv:** Female head left with punk hair style and earing, three balls and date below **Obv. Legend:** CHRISTIANIA DANMARKS IRISTAD **Rev:** Value **Note:** Parody of Danish coin.

Date	Mintage	F	VF	XF	Unc	BU
1994	—	—	—	—	100	—

COCOS (KEELING) ISLANDS

AUSTRALIAN TERRITORY

DECIMAL COINAGE

X# 1 5 CENTS

Bronze **Obv:** Palm tree and value **Rev:** Bust of John Clunies Ross left **Note:** Prev. KM#1.

Date	Mintage	F	VF	XF	Unc	BU
1977	—	—	—	18.00	40.00	—

X# 11 5 CENTS

3.8200 g., Copper-Nickel Plated Brass, 19.7 mm. **Obv:** Palm tree **Rev:** Sea Horse **Edge:** Plain

Date	Mintage	F	VF	XF	Unc	BU
2004	10,000	—	—	—	2.50	—

X# 11a 5 CENTS

Copper-Nickel, 19.7 mm. **Obv:** Palm tree **Rev:** Sea Horse **Edge:** Plain

Date	Mintage	F	VF	XF	Unc	BU
2004	10,000	—	—	—	2.50	—

X# 2 10 CENTS

Bronze **Obv:** Palm tree and value **Rev:** Bust of John Clunies Ross left **Note:** Prev. KM#1.

Date	Mintage	F	VF	XF	Unc	BU
1977	—	—	—	20.00	45.00	—

X# 12 10 CENTS

5.7100 g., Copper-Nickel Plated Brass, 23.9 mm. **Obv:** Palm tree **Rev:** Yellow-bellied Seasnake **Edge:** Plain

Date	Mintage	F	VF	XF	Unc	BU
2004	—	—	—	—	3.00	—

X# 13 20 CENTS

7.5200 g., Copper-Nickel Plated Brass, 28.5 mm. **Obv:** Palm tree **Rev:** Lion Fish **Edge:** Plain

Date	Mintage	F	VF	XF	Unc	BU
2004	10,000	—	—	—	3.00	—

X# 13a 20 CENTS

Copper-Nickel, 28.5 mm. **Obv:** Palm tree **Rev:** Lion Fish **Edge:** Plain

Date	Mintage	F	VF	XF	Unc	BU
2004	10,000	—	—	—	3.00	—

X# 3 25 CENTS

Bronze **Obv:** Palm tree and value **Rev:** Bust of John Clunies Ross left **Note:** Prev. KM#3.

Date	Mintage	F	VF	XF	Unc	BU
1977	—	—	—	20.00	45.00	—

X# 4 50 CENTS

Bronze **Obv:** Palm tree and value **Rev:** Bust of John Clunies Ross left **Note:** Prev. KM#4.

Date	Mintage	F	VF	XF	Unc	BU
1977	—	—	—	22.00	50.00	—

X# 14 50 CENTS

10.8200 g., Copper-Nickel Plated Brass, 31.5 mm. **Obv:** Palm tree **Rev:** Ornate Butterfly fish **Edge:** Plain **Shape:** 12-sided

Date	Mintage	F	VF	XF	Unc	BU
2004	10,000	—	—	—	4.00	—

X# 14a 50 CENTS

Copper-Nickel, 31.5 mm. **Obv:** Palm tree **Rev:** Ornate Butterfly fish **Edge:** Plain **Shape:** 12-sided

Date	Mintage	F	VF	XF	Unc	BU
2004	10,000	—	—	—	4.00	—

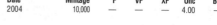

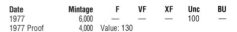

X# 15 1 DOLLAR
6.9000 g., Brass, 25.3 mm. **Obv:** Palm tree **Rev:** Black-crowned Night Heron **Edge:** Reeded

Date	Mintage	F	VF	XF	Unc	BU
2004	20,000	—	—	—	5.00	—

X# 16 2 DOLLARS
3.9500 g., Brass, 20.1 mm. **Obv:** Palm tree **Rev:** Wedge-tailed Shearwater bird in flight **Edge:** Reeded

Date	Mintage	F	VF	XF	Unc	BU
2004	20,000	—	—	—	7.00	—

X# 17 5 DOLLARS
6.7500 g., Bi-Metallic Brass center in Nickel-Steel ring, 28.5 mm. **Obv:** Palm tree **Rev:** Great White shark **Edge:** Reeded and Plain sections

Date	Mintage	F	VF	XF	Unc	BU
2004	10,000	—	—	—	15.00	—

X# 17a 5 DOLLARS
Bi-Metallic **Ring Composition:** Copper-Nickel **Center Composition:** Brass, 28.5 mm. **Obv:** Palm tree **Rev:** Great White Shark **Edge:** Reeded and plain sections

Date	Mintage	F	VF	XF	Unc	BU
2004	10,000	—	—	—	15.00	—

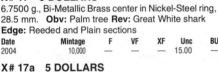

X# 18 10 DOLLARS
7.8000 g., 0.9990 Silver 0.2505 oz. ASW, 27.1 mm. **Obv:** Palm tree **Rev:** Charles Darwin **Edge:** Reeded

Date	Mintage	F	VF	XF	Unc	BU
2003 Proof	1,500	Value: 30.00				

X# 19 10 DOLLARS
7.8000 g., 0.9990 Silver 0.2505 oz. ASW **Obv:** Palm tree with additional Malay legend **Obv. Legend:** "BUKAN WANG TUNAI" **Rev:** Charles Darwin **Edge:** Reeded

Date	Mintage	F	VF	XF	Unc	BU
2003 Proof	500	Value: 40.00				

X# 20 100 DOLLARS
16.4300 g., 0.9166 Gold 0.4842 oz. AGW, 27.2 mm. **Obv:** Palm tree **Obv. Legend:** "BUKAN WANG TUNAI" **Rev:** HMS Beagle (Darwin's ship) **Edge:** Reeded

Date	Mintage	F	VF	XF	Unc	BU
2003 Proof	50	Value: 575				

X# 21 100 DOLLARS
16.4300 g., 0.9166 Gold 0.4842 oz. AGW, 27.2 mm. **Obv:** Palm tree with additional Malay legend **Rev:** HMS Beagle (Darwin's ship) **Edge:** Reeded

Date	Mintage	F	VF	XF	Unc	BU
2003 Proof	150	—	—	—	500	—

X# 5 RUPEE
Copper-Nickel **Obv:** Palm tree and value **Rev:** Bust of John Clunies Ross left **Note:** Prev. KM#5.

Date	Mintage	F	VF	XF	Unc	BU
1977	—	—	—	35.00	75.00	—

X# 6 2 RUPEES
Copper-Nickel **Obv:** Palm tree and value **Rev:** Bust of John Clunies Ross left **Note:** Prev. KM#6.

Date	Mintage	F	VF	XF	Unc	BU
1977	—	—	—	35.00	75.00	—

X# 7 5 RUPEES
Copper-Nickel **Obv:** Palm tree and value **Rev:** Bust of John Clunies Ross left **Note:** Prev. KM#7.

Date	Mintage	F	VF	XF	Unc	BU
1977	—	—	—	40.00	85.00	—

X# 8 10 RUPEES
6.5000 g., 0.9250 Silver 0.1933 oz. ASW **Subject:** 150th Anniversary - Keeling-Cocos Islands **Obv:** Palm tree and value **Rev:** Bust of John Clunies left **Note:** Prev. KM#8.

Date	Mintage	F	VF	XF	Unc	BU
1977	6,000	—	—	—	100	—
1977 Proof	4,000	Value: 130				

X# 9 25 RUPEES
16.2500 g., 0.9250 Silver 0.4832 oz. ASW **Subject:** 150th Anniversary - Keeling-Cocos Islands **Obv:** Palm tree and value **Rev:** Bust of John Clunies Ross left **Note:** Prev. KM#9.

Date	Mintage	F	VF	XF	Unc	BU
1977	6,000	—	—	—	150	—
1977 Proof	4,000	Value: 255				

X# 10 150 RUPEES
0.7500 Gold **Subject:** 150th Anniversary - Keeling-Cocos Islands **Obv:** Palm tree and value **Rev:** Bust of John Clunies Ross left **Note:** The entire issue of X#10 was stolen with only 290 pieces being recovered. Previous KM#10.

Date	Mintage	F	VF	XF	Unc	BU
ND(1977)	2,000	—	—	—	—	—
ND(1977) Proof	2,000	—	—	—	—	500

X# 10a 150 RUPEES
8.4800 g., 0.9160 Gold 0.2497 oz. AGW **Obv:** Palm tree and value **Rev:** Bust of John Clunies Ross left **Note:** Prev. KM#10a.

Date	Mintage	F	VF	XF	Unc	BU
ND(1977)	2,000	—	—	—	300	—
ND(1977) Proof	2,000	Value: 400				

MINT SETS

X#	Date	Mintage	Identification	Issue Price	Mkt Val
XMS1	1977 (7)	—	X#1-7	—	325
XMS2	1977 (2)	6,000	X#8-9	—	200
XMS3	2004 (7)	—	X#11 - 17	—	40.00
XMS4	2004 (7)	—	X#11a -14a, 15, 16, 17a	—	40.00

PROOF SETS

X#	Date	Mintage	Identification	Issue Price	Mkt Val
XPS1	1977 (2)	4,000	X#8-9	28.00	275

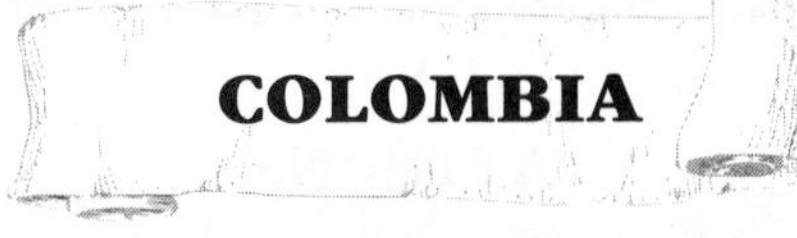

COLOMBIA

ANTIOQUIA

STATE

PATTERNS

X# 1 2 CENTAVOS
Bronze **Note:** Prev. KM#Pn1. Similar to X6.

Date	Mintage	F	VF	XF	Unc	BU
1890 Proof	—	Value: 75.00				

BOLIVAR

STATE

PATTERNS

X# 2 2 CENTAVOS
Bronze **Note:** Prev. KM#Pn1.

Date	Mintage	F	VF	XF	Unc	BU
1890 Proof	—	Value: 75.00				

BOYACA

STATE

PATTERNS

X# 3 2 CENTAVOS

Bronze **Note:** Prev. KM#Pn1. Similar to X6.

Date	Mintage	F	VF	XF	Unc	BU
1890 Proof	—	Value: 65.00				

CAUCA

STATE

PATTERNS

X# 4 2 CENTAVOS

Bronze **Note:** Prev. KM#1. Similar to X6.

Date	Mintage	F	VF	XF	Unc	BU
1890 Proof	—	Value: 65.00				

CUNDINAMARCA

STATE

PATTERNS

X# 5 2 CENTAVOS

Bronze **Note:** Prev. KM#Pn1. Similar to X6.

Date	Mintage	F	VF	XF	Unc	BU
1890 Proof	—	Value: 70.00				

MAGDALENA

STATE

PATTERNS

X# 6 2 CENTAVOS

Bronze **Note:** Prev. KM#Pn1.

Date	Mintage	F	VF	XF	Unc	BU
1890 Proof	—	Value: 250				

SANTANDER

STATE

PATTERNS

X# 7 2 CENTAVOS

Bronze **Note:** Prev. KM#Pn1. Similar to X6.

Date	Mintage	F	VF	XF	Unc	BU
1890 Proof	—	Value: 70.00				

TOLIMA

STATE

PATTERNS

X# 8 2 CENTAVOS

Bronze **Note:** Prev. KM#Pn1. Similar to X6.

Date	Mintage	F	VF	XF	Unc	BU
1890 Proof	—	Value: 65.00				

CONCH REPUBLIC

REPUBLIC

Located in Key West, Florida

BASE METAL COINAGE

X# 1 DOLLAR

21.6500 g., Tin Alloy, 35.2 mm. **Obv:** Swordfish **Rev:** Conch shell **Edge:** Plain

Date	Mintage	F	VF	XF	Unc	BU
ND (1972)	—	—	—	5.00	—	—

MEDALLIC BULLION COINAGE

X# MB1 OUNCE

31.1300 g., 0.9990 Silver 0.9998 oz. ASW, 39.2 mm. **Obv:** Conch shell, sprays below **Rev:** Flag, island outline **Rev. Legend:** LIBERTY

Date	Mintage	F	VF	XF	Unc	BU
1982	—	—	—	—	32.50	—

CORSICA ISLAND

FRENCH TERRITORY

FANTASY EURO PATTERNS

X# Pn1 EURO CENT

Copper Plated Steel **Edge:** Plain

Date	Mintage	F	VF	XF	Unc	BU
2004	—	—	—	—	—	1.50

X# Pn2 2 EURO CENT

Copper Plated Steel **Edge:** Plain

Date	Mintage	F	VF	XF	Unc	BU
2004	—	—	—	—	—	2.00

X# Pn3 5 EURO CENT

Copper Plated Steel **Edge:** Plain

Date	Mintage	F	VF	XF	Unc	BU
2004	—	—	—	—	—	2.50

X# Pn4 10 EURO CENT

Goldine **Edge:** Plain

Date	Mintage	F	VF	XF	Unc	BU
2004	—	—	—	—	—	3.00

X# Pn5 20 EURO CENT

Goldine **Edge:** Plain

Date	Mintage	F	VF	XF	Unc	BU
2004	—	—	—	—	—	3.50

X# Pn6 50 EURO CENT

Goldine **Edge:** Plain

Date	Mintage	F	VF	XF	Unc	BU
2004	—	—	—	—	—	4.00

X# Pn7 EURO

Bi-Metallic **Edge:** Plain

Date	Mintage	F	VF	XF	Unc	BU
2004	—	—	—	—	—	6.00

X# Pn8 2 EURO

Bi-Metallic **Edge:** Plain

Date	Mintage	F	VF	XF	Unc	BU
2004	—	—	—	—	—	8.00

MINT SETS

X#	Date	Mintage	Identification	Issue Price	Mkt Val
XMS1	2004 (8)	—	X#Pn1-Pn8	—	35.00

COSTA RICA

REPUBLIC

COUNTERMARKED COINAGE

1849-1850

All 1/2 and 1 dollar size coins with this countermark are considered modern fabrications. They are believed to have been created in the 1960's using authentic countermarking dies which mysteriously found their way into numismatic circles.

1889

X# 5 4 REALES

Silver **Countermark:** HABILITADA POR EL GOBIERNO **Note:** Countermark around lion in 5mm circle on U.S.A. 1/2 dollar, KM#A68.

CM Date	Host Date	Good	VG	F	VF	XF
1849	1856-66	50.00	80.00	145	225	—

X# 7 8 REALES

0.9030 Silver **Countermark:** HABILITADA POR EL GOBIERNO **Note:** Countermark around lion in 5mm circle on Mexico City Charles III 8 Reales, KM#109.

CM Date	Host Date	Good	VG	F	VF	XF
1849	1791-1808	20.00	30.00	50.00	80.00	—

X# 10 8 REALES

0.9000 Silver **Countermark:** HABILITADA POR EL GOBIERNO **Note:** Countermark around lion in 5mm circle on South Peru 1 Sol, KM#196.3.

CM Date	Host Date	Good	VG	F	VF	XF
1849	1868-75	10.00	20.00	30.00	45.00	—

X# 13 8 REALES

Silver **Countermark:** HABILITADA POR EL GOBIERNO **Note:** Countermark around lion and lion/CR in 5mm and 7mm circles on Neuva Granada 8 Reales, KM#98.

CM Date	Host Date	Good	VG	F	VF	XF
1849	1839-46	20.00	35.00	60.00	90.00	—

X# 19 8 REALES

0.9000 Silver **Countermark:** HIBILITADA POR EL GOBIERNO **Note:** Countermark around lion/CR in 5mm circle on United States 1 Dollar, KM#100.

CM Date	Host Date	Good	VG	F	VF	XF
1849	1866-73	75.00	125	200	275	—

X# 17 8 REALES

0.9000 Silver **Countermark:** HABILITADA POR EL GOBIERNO **Note:** Countermark around lion/CR in 7mm circle on Peru 1 Sol, KM#196.1.

CM Date	Host Date	Good	VG	F	VF	XF
1849	ND1864-68	10.00	20.00	30.00	45.00	—

X# 15 8 REALES

0.9030 Silver **Countermark:** HABILITADA POR EL GOBIERNO **Note:** Countermark around lion/CR in 7mm circle on Mexico Maximilian 1 Peso, KM#388.1.

CM Date	Host Date	Good	VG	F	VF	XF
1849	ND1866-67	15.00	25.00	45.00	75.00	—

X# 20 8 REALES

0.9000 Silver **Countermark:** HABILITADA POR EL GOBIERNO **Note:** Countermark around lion/CR in 7mm circle on United States Morgan 1 Dollar, KM#110.

CM Date	Host Date	Good	VG	F	VF	XF
1849	ND1878-1921	10.00	20.00	30.00	45.00	—

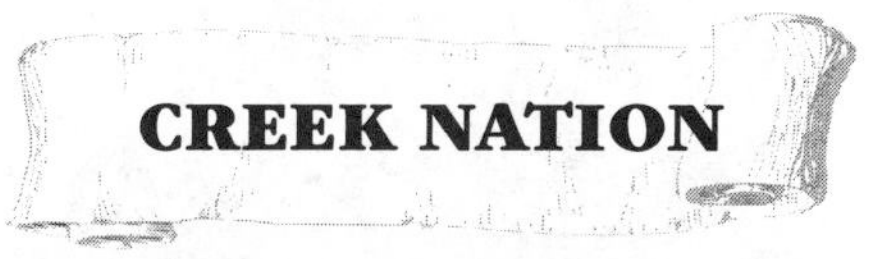

(POARCH BAND)

SOVEREIGNTY

MILLED COINAGE

X# 1 DOLLAR

31.1341 g., 0.9990 Silver 0.9999 oz. ASW, 39 mm. **Issuer:** Panda America **Subject:** Peace **Obv:** Symbol

Obv. Legend: CREEK NATION OF INDIANS
Rev: Indian horseback left **Edge:** Reeded

Date	Mintage	F	VF	XF	Unc	BU
2004	20,000	—	—	—	20.00	—
2004 Proof	10,000	Value: 40.00				

X# 2 DOLLAR

31.1341 g., 0.9990 Silver 0.9999 oz. ASW, 39 mm. **Issuer:** Panda America **Subject:** 20th Anniversary of Recognition **Obv:** Young sky dancer right, symbol **Obv. Legend:** CREEK NATION OF INDIANS **Rev:** Busts of 5 tribal chiefs, symbol below **Rev. Legend:** SOVEREIGN NATION **Edge:** Reeded

Date	Mintage	F	VF	XF	Unc	BU
2004	20,000	—	—	—	20.00	—
2004 Proof	10,000	Value: 40.00				

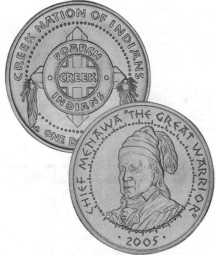

X# 7 DOLLAR

31.1400 g., 0.9990 Silver 1.0000 oz. ASW, 40.52 mm. **Obv:** Tribal seal **Obv. Legend:** CREEK NATION OF INDIANS **Obv. Designer:** A. Shagin **Rev:** Bust of Chief Menawa 3/4 left **Rev. Legend:** CHIEF MENAWA "THE GREAT WARRIOR" **Edge:** Reeded

Date	Mintage	VG	F	VF	XF	Unc
2005	20,000	—	—	—	—	30.00
2005 Proof	10,000	Value: 50.00				

X# 8 DOLLAR

31.2700 g., 0.9990 Silver 1.0043 oz. ASW, 40.55 mm. **Obv:** Tribal seal **Obv. Legend:** CREEK NATION OF INDIANS **Obv. Designer:** A. Shagin **Rev:** Tchow-ee-put-o-kaw 3/4 right **Rev. Legend:** TCOW-EE-PUT-O-KAW **Edge:** Reeded

Date	Mintage	VG	F	VF	XF	Unc
2005	20,000	—	—	—	—	30.00
2005 Proof	10,000	Value: 50.00				

X# 10 DOLLAR

31.1200 g., 0.9990 Silver 0.9995 oz. ASW, 41.61 mm. **Obv:** Dancer left at center right, a tribal seal at lower left **Obv. Legend:** CREEK NATION - OF INDIANS **Obv. Designer:** A. Shagin **Rev:** Warrior horseback 3/4 right **Rev. Legend:** SOVEREIGN NATION **Edge:** Reeded

Date	Mintage	VG	F	VF	XF	Unc
2006	20,000	—	—	—	—	30.00
2006 Proof	10,000	Value: 50.00				

X# 11 DOLLAR

31.1700 g., 0.9990 Silver 1.0011 oz. ASW, 40.58 mm. **Obv:** Tribal seal **Obv. Legend:** CREEK NATION OF INDIANS **Obv. Designer:** A. Shagin **Rev:** Facing busts of Chief Tomochichi and his son with eagle **Rev. Legend:** CHIEF TOMOCHICHI **Edge:** Reeded

Date	Mintage	VG	F	VF	XF	Unc
2006	20,000	—	—	—	—	30.00
2006 Proof	10,000	Value: 50.00				

X# 4 5 DOLLARS

0.9990 Gold, 22 mm. **Issuer:** Panda America **Subject:** Peace **Obv:** Symbol **Obv. Legend:** CREEK NATION OF INDIANS **Rev:** Indian horseback left **Edge:** Reeded

Date	Mintage	F	VF	XF	Unc	BU
2004 Proof	2,500	Value: 250				

X# 9 5 DOLLARS

6.1700 g., 0.9990 Gold 0.1982 oz. AGW, 22.18 mm. **Obv:** Tribal seal **Obv. Legend:** CREEK NATION OF INDIANS **Obv. Designer:** A. Shagin **Rev:** Busts of Chief Hopothle Mico and George Washington 3/4 left **Rev. Legend:** CHIEF HOPOTHLE MICO • GEORGE WASHINGTON **Edge:** Reeded

Date	Mintage	VG	F	VF	XF	Unc
2005 Proof	2,500	Value: 360				

X# 12 5 DOLLARS

6.1700 g., 0.9990 Gold 0.1982 oz. AGW, 22.2 mm. **Obv:** Tribal seal **Obv. Legend:** CREEK NATION OF INDIANS **Obv. Designer:** A. Shagin **Rev:** Bust of Chief Stee•Chaco•Me•Co **Rev. Legend:** CHIEF STEE • CHACO • ME • CO **Edge:** Reeded

Date	Mintage	VG	F	VF	XF	Unc
2006 Proof	2,500	Value: 320				

X# 5 10 DOLLARS

15.5515 g., 0.9995 Palladium 0.4997 oz., 30 mm. **Issuer:** Panda America **Subject:** 20th Anniversary of Recognition **Obv:** Young sky dancer right, symbol **Obv. Legend:** CREEK NATION OF INDIANS **Rev:** Busts of 5 tribal chiefs, symbol below **Rev. Legend:** SOVEREIGN NATION **Edge:** Reeded

Date	Mintage	F	VF	XF	Unc	BU
2004 Proof	250	Value: 600				

X# 6 100 DOLLARS
31.0800 g., 0.9990 Gold 0.9982 oz. AGW, 31.94 mm. **Subject:** 20th Anniversary of Treaty for Autonomy **Obv:** Native dancer right at left center, tribal seal at right **Obv. Legend:** CREEK NATION - OF INDIANS **Obv. Designer:** A. Shagin **Rev:** Five portraits left to right, tribal seal below **Rev. Legend:** • SOVEREIGN NATION • **Edge:** Reeded

Date	Mintage	VG	F	VF	XF	Unc
ND(2004) Proof	250	Value: 1,800				

CRETE

GREEK TERRITORY

FANTASY EURO PATTERNS

X# Pn1 EURO CENT
Copper Plated Steel **Edge:** Plain

Date	Mintage	F	VF	XF	Unc	BU
2004	—	—	—	—	—	1.50

X# Pn2 2 EURO CENT
Copper Plated Steel **Edge:** Plain

Date	Mintage	F	VF	XF	Unc	BU
2004	—	—	—	—	—	2.00

X# Pn3 5 EURO CENT
Copper Plated Steel **Edge:** Plain

Date	Mintage	F	VF	XF	Unc	BU
2004	—	—	—	—	—	2.50

X# Pn4 10 EURO CENT
Goldine **Edge:** Plain

Date	Mintage	F	VF	XF	Unc	BU
2004	—	—	—	—	—	3.00

X# Pn5 20 EURO CENT
Goldine **Edge:** Plain

Date	Mintage	F	VF	XF	Unc	BU
2004	—	—	—	—	—	3.50

X# Pn6 50 EURO CENT
Goldine **Edge:** Plain

Date	Mintage	F	VF	XF	Unc	BU
2004	—	—	—	—	—	4.00

X# Pn7 EURO
Bi-Metallic **Obv:** Ancient bust right **Rev:** Value, whale and EEU star design **Edge:** Plain

Date	Mintage	F	VF	XF	Unc	BU
2004	—	—	—	—	—	6.00

X# Pn8 2 EURO
Bi-Metallic **Obv:** Ancient bust right **Rev:** Value, whale, EEU star design **Edge:** Plain

Date	Mintage	F	VF	XF	Unc	BU
2004	—	—	—	—	—	8.00

MINT SETS

X#	Date	Mintage	Identification	Issue Price	Mkt Val
XMS1	2004 (8)	—	X#Pn1-Pn8	—	30.00

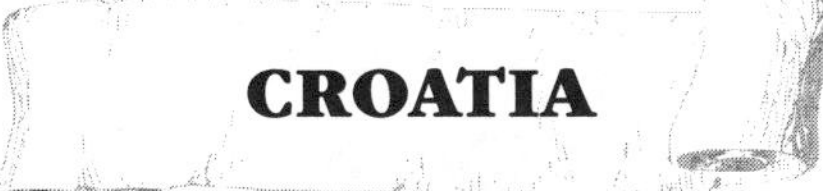

CROATIA

KINGDOM

PATTERNS

Including off metal strikes

X# 1 FORINT
9.5000 g., Silver **Obv:** Portrait right **Rev:** Star and crescent **Note:** Prev. KM#Pn1.

Date	Mintage	F	VF	XF	Unc	BU
1848 Rare	—	—	—	—	—	—

REPUBLIC

FANTASY COINAGE

Struck by Descher Sohn, Munich, Germany for Croatian Liberation Movement, Ustasa.

X# 1a 5 KUNA
0.9000 Silver **Obv:** Arms above sprays **Obv. Legend:** ZA • NEZAVISNU • DRZAVU * HRVATSKU **Rev:** Value, date in wreath **Note:** Prev. KM#Pn2.

Date	Mintage	F	VF	XF	Unc	BU
1934 Proof	—	Value: 450				

X# 1b 5 KUNA
Copper-Nickel **Obv:** Arms above sprays **Obv. Legend:** ZA • NEZAVISNU • DRZAVU * HRVATSKU **Rev:** Value, date in wreath

Date	Mintage	F	VF	XF	Unc	BU
1934 Proof	—	Value: 400				

X# 1c 5 KUNA
Zinc **Obv:** Arms above sprays **Obv. Legend:** ZA • NEZAVISNU • DRZAVU * HRVATSKU **Rev:** Value, date in wreath

Date	Mintage	F	VF	XF	Unc	BU
1934 Proof	—	Value: 400				

X# 2 50 KUNA
8.5700 g., Silver

Date	Mintage	F	VF	XF	Unc	BU
1934	Est. 100	—	—	—	25.00	60.00

Note: The 50 Kuna are a modern fantasy issue of "unknown" origin struck during 1970 without any government authorization obviously for confusion of the numismatic community.

X# 2a 50 KUNA
Copper **Obv:** Arms above sprays **Obv. Legend:** ZA • NEZAVISNU • DRZAVU * HRVATSKU **Rev:** Value, date in wreath

Date	Mintage	F	VF	XF	Unc	BU
1934	Est. 8	—	—	—	17.50	30.00

X# 2b 50 KUNA
Gold **Obv:** Arms above sprays **Obv. Legend:** ZA • NEZAVISNU • DRZAVU * HRVATSKU **Rev:** ZA • NEZAVISNU • DRZAVU * HRVATSKU

Date	Mintage	F	VF	XF	Unc	BU
1934	Est. 63	—	—	—	350	500

X# 2c 50 KUNA
Copper-Nickel **Obv:** Arms above sprays **Obv. Legend:** ZA • NEZAVISNU • DRZAVU * HRVATSKU **Rev:** Value, date in wreath

Date	Mintage	F	VF	XF	Unc	BU
1934	—	—	—	—	20.00	35.00

MEDALLIC COINAGE

X# M5 250 KUNA
5.0000 g., 0.9000 Gold 0.1447 oz. AGW **Subject:** 10th Anniversary of Death of Dr. Antle Pavelic **Note:** Struck by Descher Sohn, Munich, Germany for Croation Liberation Movement "Ustasa".

Date	Mintage	F	VF	XF	Unc	BU
1969 Proof	—	Value: 400				

X# M1 500 KUNA
9.7500 g., 0.9000 Gold 0.2821 oz. AGW **Subject:** Dr. Ante Pavelic **Note:** Prev. KM#M1.1.

Date	Mintage	F	VF	XF	Unc	BU
1941	170	—	1,750	2,250	3,000	—

X# M1a 500 KUNA
0.9000 Gold, 27 mm. **Subject:** Dr. Ante Pavelic **Note:** Prev. KM#M1.2.

Date	Mintage	F	VF	XF	Unc	BU
1941	—	—	—	—	—	—

X# M1b 500 KUNA
Nickel, 22 mm. **Subject:** Dr. Ante Pavelic **Note:** Prev. KM#1.1a.

Date	Mintage	F	VF	XF	Unc	BU
1941	—	—	—	—	—	—

X# M3 500 KUNA
Aluminum, 22 mm. **Note:** Struck unofficially by order of Dr. Ante Pavelic.

Date	Mintage	F	VF	XF	Unc	BU
1941	—	—	—	400	600	—

FANTASY EURO PATTERNS

X# Pn1 EURO CENT
Copper Plated Steel **Edge:** Plain

Date	Mintage	F	VF	XF	Unc	BU
2004	10,000	—	—	—	—	1.50

X# Pn2 2 EURO CENT
Copper Plated Steel **Edge:** Plain

Date	Mintage	F	VF	XF	Unc	BU
2004	10,000	—	—	—	—	2.00

X# Pn3 5 EURO CENT
Copper Plated Steel **Edge:** Plain

Date	Mintage	F	VF	XF	Unc	BU
2004	10,000	—	—	—	—	2.50

X# Pn4 10 EURO CENT
Goldine **Edge:** Plain

Date	Mintage	F	VF	XF	Unc	BU
2004	10,000	—	—	—	—	3.00

X# Pn5 20 EURO CENT
Goldine **Edge:** Plain

Date	Mintage	F	VF	XF	Unc	BU
2004	10,000	—	—	—	—	3.50

X# Pn6 50 EURO CENT
Goldine **Edge:** Plain

Date	Mintage	F	VF	XF	Unc	BU
2004	10,000	—	—	—	—	4.00

X# Pn7 EURO
Bi-Metallic **Obv:** Stylized castle **Obv. Legend:** Value and outline map of Croatia **Edge:** Plain

Date	Mintage	F	VF	XF	Unc	BU
2004	—	—	—	—	—	6.00

X# Pn8 2 EURO
Bi-Metallic **Obv:** Arms **Rev:** Value and outline map of Croatia **Edge:** Plain

Date	Mintage	F	VF	XF	Unc	BU
2004	10,000	—	—	—	—	8.00

MINT SETS

X#	Date	Mintage	Identification	Issue Price	Mkt Val
XMS1	2004 (8)	10,000	X#Pn1-Pn8	—	30.00

CUBA

COLONIAL

FANTASY COINAGE

The revolution was initiated at the sugar mill of Carlos Mannel de Cespedes on October 10, 1868. This issue is believed to be inspired by the Junta Central Republicana de Cuba y Puerto Rico representing the insurgents in New York City, New York, U.S.A.

X# 1 5 CENTAVOS
Silver **Note:** Prev. KM#Pn1.

Date	Mintage	F	VF	XF	Unc	BU
1870 P.-C.T. Proof	10	Value: 6,000				

X# 1a 5 CENTAVOS
Copper **Note:** Prev. KM#Pn1a.

Date	Mintage	F	VF	XF	Unc	BU
1870 P.-C.T. Proof	40	Value: 4,000				

X# 2 10 CENTAVOS
Silver **Note:** Prev. KM#Pn2.

Date	Mintage	F	VF	XF	Unc	BU
1870 P.-C.T. Proof	10	Value: 6,000				

X# 2a 10 CENTAVOS
Copper **Note:** Prev. KM#Pn2a.

Date	Mintage	F	VF	XF	Unc	BU
1870 P.-C.T. Proof	40	Value: 3,000				

X# 3 20 CENTAVOS
Silver **Note:** Prev. KM#Pn3.

Date	Mintage	F	VF	XF	Unc	BU
1870 P.-C.T. Proof	10	Value: 6,000				

X# 3a 20 CENTAVOS
Copper **Note:** Prev. KM#Pn3a.

Date	Mintage	F	VF	XF	Unc	BU
1870 P.-C.T. Proof	40	Value: 3,000				

X# 4 1/2 PESO (Medio Peso)
Silver **Note:** Prev. KM#Pn4.

Date	Mintage	F	VF	XF	Unc	BU
1870 Proof	10	Value: 6,000				

X# 4a 1/2 PESO (Medio Peso)
Bronze **Note:** Prev. KM#Pn4a.

Date	Mintage	F	VF	XF	Unc	BU
1870 P.-C.T. Proof	40	Value: 4,000				

X# 5 PESO (Un Peso)
21.4000 g., Silver **Note:** Prev. KM#Pn5.

Date	Mintage	F	VF	XF	Unc	BU
1870 P.-C.T. Proof	10	Value: 8,000				

X# 5a PESO (Un Peso)
Copper **Note:** Prev. KM#Pn5a.

Date	Mintage	F	VF	XF	Unc	BU
1870 Proof	40	Value: 6,000				

MEDALLIC COINAGE

1897 Contribution Issue

The Junta or Delegation of the Cuban Revolutionary Party established in New York City in 1892 decided to issue coins besides bonds and stamps. In 1897 the designs were created by Philip Martiny and a contract was signed with the Gorham Manufacturing Company. Because of the urgency the words UN PESO were replaced by SOUVENIR as patents were being sought. The Type I were struck at the Dunn Air-Brake Company located in Philadelphia from dies and polished flans provided by the Gorham Company. A total of 858 pieces were struck and 30 pieces were destroyed as being defective.

A total of 4,286 pieces were struck of Type II at Providence, Rhode Island as a progressive die break halted production. The balance of 4,856 pieces of Type III were struck the following day completing the original order of 10,000.

In March, 1898 the Junta authorized the Gorham Company to mint 1,000 UN PESOS.

In 1902 the balance of unsold SOUVENIR PESOS of Type III were deposited in the National Treasury and remained there for over 50 years.

X# M1 SOUVENIR PESO
22.5500 g., 0.9000 Silver 0.6525 oz. ASW **Rev:** PAT. 97 on truncation, date widely spaced **Note:** Type I.

Date	Mintage	F	VF	XF	Unc	BU
1897	828	200	400	1,500	3,200	5,000
1897 Proof	—	Value: 8,000				

X# M1a SOUVENIR PESO
Bronze **Rev:** PAT.97 on truncation, date widely spaced **Note:** Type I.

Date	Mintage	F	VF	XF	Unc	BU
1897	—	—	—	—	3,000	5,000

X# M2 SOUVENIR PESO
22.5500 g., 0.9000 Silver 0.6525 oz. ASW **Rev:** Date closely spaced, star below 97 baseline **Note:** Type II.

Date	Mintage	F	VF	XF	Unc	BU
1897	4,286	60.00	100	200	600	1,000
1897 Proof	—	Value: 900				

X# M2a SOUVENIR PESO
Bronze **Rev:** Date closely spaced, star below 97 baseline **Note:** Type II.

Date	Mintage	F	VF	XF	Unc	BU
1897 Matte proof	—	—	—	750	1,250	2,000

X# M3 SOUVENIR PESO
22.5500 g., 0.9000 Silver 0.6525 oz. ASW **Rev:** Date closely spaced, star above 97 baseline **Note:** Type III.

Date	Mintage	F	VF	XF	Unc	BU
1897	4,856	60.00	100	200	700	1,000
1897 Matte proof	—	Value: 1,000				

X# M3a SOUVENIR PESO
Bronze **Rev:** Date closely spaced, star above 97 baseline **Note:** Type III.

Date	Mintage	F	VF	XF	Unc	BU
1897 Matte proof	—	—	—	750	1,250	2,000

1898 Contribution Issues

X# M14 20 CENTAVOS
6.6500 g., 0.9000 Silver 0.1924 oz. ASW

Date	Mintage	F	VF	XF	Unc	BU
1898	—	—	—	600	900	—

X# M15 PESO
22.6000 g., 0.9000 Silver 0.6539 oz. ASW **Obv:** Arms **Rev:** Bust, date below

Date	Mintage	F	VF	XF	Unc	BU
1898	1,000	300	750	1,650	3,200	4,000
1898 Matte proof	—	Value: 6,100				

X# M15a PESO
Copper

Date	Mintage	F	VF	XF	Unc	BU
1898 Matte Proof	—	Value: 5,000				

SECOND REPUBLIC

1962 - Present

MEDALLIC BULLION

Cuban Numismatic Association (USA) Issue

X# MB7 OUNCE
31.3300 g., 0.9990 Silver 1.0062 oz. ASW **Obv:** Arms **Rev:** Star **Rev. Legend:** CUBAN NUMISMATIC ASSOCIATION - FOUNDED JANUARY 9, 2004 **Edge:** Reeded

Date	Mintage	F	VF	XF	Unc	BU
ND(2006) Proof	—	Value: 30.00				

Note: With handstamped serial #001-150

Date	Mintage	F	VF	XF	Unc	BU
ND(2006) Proof	—	Value: 25.00				

Note: Without serial #

MEDALLIC COINAGE

Souvenir Peso

X# M5.2 SOUVENIR PESO
0.9250 g., Silver, 38.3 mm. **Subject:** Cubans in Exile **Obv:** Arms **Obv. Legend:** CUBANOS EN EXILIO **Rev:** Liberty head right **Rev. Legend:** PATRIA Y LIBERTAD **Edge:** Plain **Note:** With British Assay Office hallmark (required with the return of certain pieces from an outside of England dealership).

Date	Mintage	F	VF	XF	Unc	BU
1965 Proof	—	Value: 115				

X# M31 PESO
41.0000 g., 0.9990 Gold 1.3168 oz. AGW, 40 mm. **Issuer:** Central de Numismática y Medallística de Mexico **Obv:** Arms **Obv. Legend:** REPUBLICA **Rev:** Bust of Ernesto Che Cuevara **Rev. Legend:** PATRIA O MUERTE - HASTA LA VICTORIA I SIEMPRE

Date	Mintage	F	VF	XF	Unc	BU
1970	—	—	—	—	—	—

X# M31a PESO
24.0000 g., 0.9250 Silver 0.7137 oz. ASW, 40 mm. **Issuer:** Central de Numismática y Medallistíca de Mexico **Obv:** Arms **Obv. Legend:** REPUBLICA **Rev:** Bust of Ernesto Che Guevara **Rev. Legend:** PATRIA O MUERTE - HASTA LA VICTORIA I SIEMPRE

Date	Mintage	F	VF	XF	Unc	BU
1970	—	—	—	—	—	—

ICB Ltd. Issues

X# 19 PESO
16.0000 g., Copper-Nickel, 32.5 mm. **Issuer:** ICB Ltd. **Series:** Piratas del Caribe **Obv:** Arms **Obv. Legend:** REPUBLICA DE CUBA **Rev:** Bust of Sir Francis Drake, sailing ship in colored foil

Date	Mintage	F	VF	XF	Unc	BU
1995 Proof	100	Value: 100				

X# 11 10 PESOS
24.0000 g., 0.9250 Silver 0.7137 oz. ASW, 38 mm.
Issuer: ICB Ltd. **Series:** Mariposas del Caribe
Obv: Arms **Obv. Legend:** REPUBLICA DE CUBA - .999 SILVER - 20 GRAMS (error) **Obv. Inscription:** Anartia Amatha ("Coolie") butterfly **Edge:** Reeded

Date	Mintage	F	VF	XF	Unc	BU
1995 Proof	33	Value: 85.00				

X# 12 10 PESOS
24.0000 g., 0.9250 Silver 0.7137 oz. ASW, 38 mm.
Issuer: ICB Ltd. **Series:** Mariposas del Caribe
Obv: Arms **Obv. Legend:** REPUBLICA DE CUBA - .999 SILVER - 20 GRAMS (error) **Rev:** Phoebis Avellaneda butterfly **Edge:** Reeded

Date	Mintage	F	VF	XF	Unc	BU
1995 Proof	33	Value: 85.00				

X# 13 10 PESOS
24.0000 g., 0.9250 Silver 0.7137 oz. ASW, 38 mm.
Issuer: ICB Ltd. **Series:** Mariposas del Caribe
Obv: Arms **Obv. Legend:** REPUBLICA DE CUBA - .999 SILVER - 20 GRAMS (error) **Rev:** Psedolycaena Marsyas butterfly **Edge:** Reeded

Date	Mintage	F	VF	XF	Unc	BU
1995 Proof	33	Value: 85.00				

X# 13.2 10 PESOS
24.0000 g., 0.9250 Silver 0.7137 oz. ASW, 38 mm.
Issuer: ICB Ltd. **Series:** Mariposas del Caribe
Obv: Arms **Obv. Legend:** REPUBLICA DE CUBA - .999 SILVER - 20 GRAMS (error) **Rev:** Psedolycaena Marsyas butterfly **Edge:** Plain

Date	Mintage	F	VF	XF	Unc	BU
1995 Proof	33	Value: 85.00				

X# 14 10 PESOS
24.0000 g., 0.9250 Silver 0.7137 oz. ASW, 38 mm.
Issuer: ICB Ltd. **Series:** Mariposas del Caribe
Obv: Arms **Obv. Legend:** REPUBLICA DE CUBA - .999 SILVER - 20 GRAMS (error) **Rev:** Danaus Plexippus butterfly **Edge:** Reeded

Date	Mintage	F	VF	XF	Unc	BU
1995 Proof	33	Value: 85.00				

X# 15 10 PESOS
24.0000 g., 0.9250 Silver 0.7137 oz. ASW, 38 mm.
Issuer: ICB Ltd. **Series:** Mariposas del Caribe
Obv: Arms **Obv. Legend:** REPUBLICA DE CUBA - .999 SILVER - 20 GRAMS (error) **Rev:** Hypolimnas Misippus butterfly **Edge:** Reeded

Date	Mintage	F	VF	XF	Unc	BU
1995 Proof	33	Value: 85.00				

X# 16 10 PESOS
24.0000 g., 0.9250 Silver 0.7137 oz. ASW, 38 mm.
Issuer: ICB Ltd. **Series:** Mariposas del Caribe
Obv: Arms **Obv. Legend:** REPUBLICA DE CUBA - .999 SILVER - 20 GRAMS (error) **Rev:** Siproeta Stelenes butterfly **Edge:** Reeded

Date	Mintage	F	VF	XF	Unc	BU
1995 Proof	33	Value: 85.00				

X# 17 50 PESOS
155.5000 g., 0.9990 Silver 4.9942 oz. ASW, 66 mm.
Issuer: ICB Ltd. **Obv:** Arms **Rev:** Three butterflies, Siproeta Stelenes, Anartia Amathea (small spots) and Hypolimnus **Rev. Designer:** Misippus **Note:** Illustration reduced.

Date	Mintage	F	VF	XF	Unc	BU
1995 Proof	61	Value: 75.00				

X# 18 50 PESOS
155.5000 g., 0.9990 Silver 4.9942 oz. ASW, 66 mm.
Issuer: ICB Ltd. **Obv:** Arms **Rev:** Three butterflies, Danaus Plexippus (large spots), Phoebis Avellaneda and Psedolycaena **Rev. Designer:** Marsyas **Note:** Illustration reduced.

Date	Mintage	F	VF	XF	Unc	BU
1995 Proof	61	Value: 75.00				

1965 Exile Issues

Originally struck for the Agency for Cuban Numismatists in exile sponsored by Alpha 66, a group of anti-Castro Cubans.

X# M4 SOUVENIR PESO
0.9250 Silver, 38.3 mm. **Subject:** Cubans in Exile **Obv:** Arms **Obv. Legend:** CUBANOS EN EXILIO **Rev:** Liberty head right **Rev. Legend:** PATRIA Y LIBERTAD **Edge:** Reeded

Date	Mintage	F	VF	XF	Unc	BU
1965 Proof	—	Value: 50.00				

X# M5.1 SOUVENIR PESO
0.9250 Silver, 38.3 mm. **Subject:** Cubans in Exile **Obv:** Arms **Obv. Legend:** CUBANOS EN EXILIO **Rev:** Liberty head right **Rev. Legend:** PATRIA Y LIBERTAD **Edge:** Plain

Date	Mintage	F	VF	XF	Unc	BU
1965 Proof	—	Value: 60.00				

X# M6 SOUVENIR PESO
0.9250 Silver, 38.3 mm. **Subject:** Cubans in Exile **Obv:** Arms **Obv. Legend:** CUBANOS EN EXILIO **Rev:** Liberty head right **Rev. Legend:** PATRIA Y LIBERTAD **Edge:** Lettered

Date	Mintage	F	VF	XF	Unc	BU
1965 Proof	—	Value: 90.00				

X# M16 SOUVENIR PESO
29.3400 g., 0.9250 Silver 0.8725 oz. ASW, 38.9 mm. **Obv:** Arms **Obv. Legend:** CUBANOS EN EXILIO **Rev:** Liberty head right **Rev. Legend:** PATRIA Y LIBERTAD **Edge:** Three types: Reeded, Plain and Lettered **Note:** Modern imitation of X#M4.

Date	Mintage	F	VF	XF	Unc	BU
1965 Prooflike	—	—	—	—	25.00	—

Richard Lobel Issues

X# M7 SOUVENIR PESO
Copper-Nickel-Zinc **Subject:** 20th Anniversary Cubans in Exile **Obv:** Arms **Obv. Legend:** CUBANOS EN EXILIO **Rev:** Short neck Type I, Liberty head right **Rev. Legend:** * PATRIA Y LIBERTAD * SOUVENIR

Date	Mintage	F	VF	XF	Unc	BU
1985 Proof	500	Value: 25.00				

X# M8 SOUVENIR PESO
0.9250 Silver **Subject:** 20th Anniversary Cubans in Exile **Obv:** Arms **Obv. Legend:** CUBANOS EN EXILIO **Rev:** Short neck Type I, Liberty head right **Rev. Legend:** * PATRIA Y LIBERTAD * SOUVENIR

Date	Mintage	F	VF	XF	Unc	BU
1985 Proof	50	Value: 95.00				

X# M9 SOUVENIR PESO
0.5830 Gold **Subject:** 20th Anniversary Cubans in Exile **Obv:** Arms **Obv. Legend:** CUBANOS EN EXILIO **Rev:** Short neck Type I, Liberty head right **Rev. Legend:** * PATRIA Y LIBERTAD * SOUVENIR

Date	Mintage	F	VF	XF	Unc	BU
1985 Proof	5	Value: 700				

X# M10 SOUVENIR PESO
Copper-Nickel-Zinc **Subject:** 20th Anniversary Cubans in Exile **Obv:** Arms **Obv. Legend:** CUBANOS EN EXILIO **Rev:** Long neck Type II, Liberty head right **Rev. Legend:** * PATRIA Y LIBERTAD * SOUVENIR

Date	Mintage	F	VF	XF	Unc	BU
1985 Proof	1,000	Value: 20.00				

X# M11 SOUVENIR PESO
Bronze **Subject:** 20th Anniversary Cubans in Exile **Obv:** Arms **Obv. Legend:** CUBANOS EN EXILIO **Rev:** Long neck Type II, Liberty head right **Rev. Legend:** * PATRIA Y LIBERTAD * SOUVENIR

Date	Mintage	F	VF	XF	Unc	BU
1985 Proof	500	Value: 10.00				

X# M12 SOUVENIR PESO
0.9250 Silver **Subject:** 20th Anniversary Cubans in Exile **Obv:** Arms **Obv. Legend:** CUBANOS EN EXILIO **Rev:** Long neck Type II, Liberty head right **Rev. Legend:** * PATRIA Y LIBERTAD * SOUVENIR

Date	Mintage	F	VF	XF	Unc	BU
1985 Proof	200	Value: 40.00				

X# M13 SOUVENIR PESO
0.5830 Gold **Subject:** 20th Anniversary Cubans in Exile **Obv:** Arms **Obv. Legend:** CUBANOS EN EXILIO **Rev:** Long neck Type II, Liberty head right **Rev. Legend:** * PATRIA Y LIBERTAD * SOUVENIR

Date	Mintage	F	VF	XF	Unc	BU
1985 Proof	5	Value: 700				

MEDALLIC BULLION COINAGE

X# MB1 ONZA
31.1035 g., 0.9999 Silver 0.9999 oz. ASW **Obv:** Bust of the Statue of Liberty in mourning right **Obv. Legend:** EMPRESSA CUBANA DE ACUÑACIONES **Rev:** Liberty head right **Rev. Legend:** PATRIA Y LIBERTAD • SOUVENIR •

Date	Mintage	F	VF	XF	Unc	BU
1986	2,000	—	—	—	25.00	—

X# MB5 ONZA
31.1000 g., 0.9990 Silver 0.9988 oz. ASW, 38.3 mm. **Subject:** Discovery of America **Obv:** Three sailing ships of Columbus **Obv. Legend:** EN ALTA MAR. RVMBO OESTE **Rev:** Columbus preparing for departure **Rev. Legend:** SALDA DEL PUERTO DE PALOS **Note:** Prev. KM#MB5.

Date	Mintage	F	VF	XF	Unc	BU
1987	—	—	—	—	20.00	—

X# MB6 ONZA
31.1000 g., 0.9990 Silver 0.9988 oz. ASW **Subject:** Zunzuncito - Hummingbird

Date	Mintage	F	VF	XF	Unc	BU
1999	12	—	—	—	300	—
1999 Proof	—	Value: 30.00				

X# MB10 5 ONZAS
155.5175 g., 0.9999 Silver 4.9993 oz. ASW, 65 mm. **Subject:** Discovery of America **Obv:** Rayed star **Obv. Legend:** PATRIA Y LIBERTAD **Rev:** Columbus' ship Santa Maria **Rev. Legend:** DESCUBRIMIENTO DE AMERICA **Note:** Illustration reduced.

Date	Mintage	F	VF	XF	Unc	BU
1987 Proof	—	Value: 90.00				

MEDALLIC COINAGE

1969 Patriotic Issues

X# M17 PESO

30.0000 g., Gold **Obv:** Arms **Obv. Legend:** REPUBLICA DE CUBA EN ARMAS **Rev:** Bust 3/4 left **Rev. Legend:** GENERAL ANTONIO MACEO

Date	Mintage	F	VF	XF	Unc	BU
1969	—	—	—	—	800	—

X# M18 2 PESOS

Gold **Obv:** Arms **Obv. Legend:** CUBA ENEL EXILIO **Rev:** Bust of Jose Marti right

Date	Mintage	F	VF	XF	Unc	BU
1969	—	—	—	—	120	—

X# M19 4 PESOS

Gold **Obv:** Arms **Obv. Legend:** CUBA ENEL EXILIO **Rev:** Bust of Jose Marti right

Date	Mintage	F	VF	XF	Unc	BU
1969	—	—	—	—	175	—

X# M20 5 PESOS

Gold **Obv:** Arms **Obv. Legend:** CUBA ENEL EXILIO **Rev:** Bust of Jose Marti right

Date	Mintage	F	VF	XF	Unc	BU
1969	—	—	—	—	250	—

X# M21 10 PESOS

Gold **Obv:** Arms **Obv. Legend:** CUBA ENEL EXILIO **Rev:** Bust of Jose Marti right

Date	Mintage	F	VF	XF	Unc	BU
1969	—	—	—	—	375	—

X# M22 SOUVENIR 5 PESOS

Gold **Obv:** Arms **Obv. Legend:** REPUBLICA DE CUBA **Rev:** Bust of Jose Marti right **Rev. Legend:** PATRIA Y LIBERTAD

Date	Mintage	F	VF	XF	Unc	BU
1966	—	—	—	—	—	—

PATTERNS

Including off metal strikes

X#	Date	Mintage	Identification	Mkt Val
Pn1	1995	—	10 Pesos. Platinum. 44.0000 g.	—
Pn2	1995	—	10 Pesos. 0.9250 Silver. 24.0000 g. Reeded edge.	85.00
Pn3	1995	—	10 Pesos. 0.9250 Silver. 24.0000 g. Plain edge.	85.00
Pn4	1995	—	10 Pesos. Brass. 23.0000 g. Reeded edge.	65.00

X#	Date	Mintage	Identification	Mkt Val
Pn5	1995	—	10 Pesos. Brass. 23.0000 g. Plain edge.	65.00
Pn6	1995	—	10 Pesos. Gilt Alloy. 20.0000 g. Reeded edge.	75.00
Pn7	1995	—	10 Pesos. Gilt Alloy. 20.0000 g. Plain edge.	75.00
Pn8	1995	—	10 Pesos. Tri-Metallic. 23.0000 g. Reeded edge.	85.00
Pn9	1995	—	10 Pesos. Tri-Metallic. 23.0000 g. Plain edge.	85.00
Pn10	1995	—	10 Pesos. Aluminum. 6.0000 g. Reeded edge.	65.00
Pn11	1995	—	10 Pesos. Aluminum. 6.0000 g. Plain edge.	65.00
Pn12	1995	—	10 Pesos. Copper. 23.0000 g. Reeded edge.	65.00
Pn13	1995	—	10 Pesos. Copper. 23.0000 g. Plain edge.	65.00
Pn14	1995	—	10 Pesos. Copper-Nickel. 20.0000 g. Reeded edge.	65.00
Pn15	1995	—	10 Pesos. Copper-Nickel. 20.0000 g. Plain edge.	65.00
Pn16	1995	—	10 Pesos. Brass. 23.0000 g. Reeded edge. X#11.1.	65.00
Pn17	1995	—	10 Pesos. Brass. 23.0000 g. Plain edge. X#11.2.	65.00
Pn18	1995	—	10 Pesos. Gilt Alloy. 20.0000 g. Reeded edge. X#11.1.	75.00
Pn19	1995	—	10 Pesos. Gilt Alloy. 20.0000 g. Plain edge. X#11.2.	75.00
Pn20	1995	—	10 Pesos. Tri-Metallic. 23.0000 g. Reeded edge. X#11.1.	85.00
Pn21	1995	—	10 Pesos. Tri-Metallic. 23.0000 g. Plain edge. X#11.2.	85.00
Pn22	1995	—	10 Pesos. Aluminum. 6.0000 g. Reeded edge. X#11.1.	65.00
Pn23	1995	—	10 Pesos. Aluminum. 6.0000 g. Plain edge. X#11.2.	65.00
Pn24	1995	—	10 Pesos. Copper. 23.0000 g. Reeded edge. X#11.1.	65.00
Pn25	1995	—	10 Pesos. Copper. 23.0000 g. Plain edge. X#11.2.	65.00
Pn26	1995	—	10 Pesos. Copper-Nickel. 20.0000 g. Reeded edge. X#11.1.	65.00
Pn27	1995	—	10 Pesos. Copper-Nickel. 20.0000 g. Plain edge. X#11.2.	65.00
Pn28	1995	—	10 Pesos. Brass. 23.0000 g. Reeded edge. X#12.1.	65.00
Pn29	1995	—	10 Pesos. Brass. 23.0000 g. Plain edge. X#12.2.	65.00
Pn30	1995	—	10 Pesos. Gilt Alloy. 20.0000 g. Reeded edge. X#12.1.	75.00
Pn31	1995	—	10 Pesos. Gilt Alloy. 20.0000 g. Plain edge. X#12.2.	75.00
Pn32	1995	—	10 Pesos. Tri-Metallic. 23.0000 g. Reeded edge. X#12.1.	85.00
Pn33	1995	—	10 Pesos. Tri-Metallic. 23.0000 g. Plain edge. X#12.2.	85.00
Pn34	1995	—	10 Pesos. Aluminum. 6.0000 g. Reeded edge. X#12.1.	65.00
Pn35	1995	—	10 Pesos. Aluminum. 6.0000 g. Plain edge. X#12.2.	65.00
Pn36	1995	—	10 Pesos. Copper. 23.0000 g. Reeded edge. X#12.1.	65.00
Pn37	1995	—	10 Pesos. Copper. 23.0000 g. Plain edge. X#12.2.	65.00
Pn38	1995	—	10 Pesos. Copper-Nickel. 20.0000 g. Reeded edge. X#12.1.	65.00
Pn39	1995	—	10 Pesos. Copper-Nickel. 20.0000 g. Plain edge. X#12.2.	65.00
Pn40	1995	—	10 Pesos. Brass. 23.0000 g. Reeded edge. X#13.1.	65.00
Pn41	1995	—	10 Pesos. Brass. 23.0000 g. Plain edge. X#13.2.	65.00
Pn43	1995	—	10 Pesos. Gilt Alloy. 20.0000 g. Plain edge. X#13.2.	75.00
Pn44	1995	—	10 Pesos. Tri-Metallic. 23.0000 g. Reeded edge. X#13.1.	85.00
Pn45	1995	—	10 Pesos. Tri-Metallic. 23.0000 g. Plain edge. X#13.2.	85.00
Pn46	1995	—	10 Pesos. Aluminum. 6.0000 g. Reeded edge. X#13.1.	65.00
Pn47	1995	—	10 Pesos. Aluminum. 6.0000 g. Plain edge. X#13.2.	65.00
Pn48	1995	—	10 Pesos. Copper. 23.0000 g. Reeded edge. X#13.1.	65.00
Pn49	1995	—	10 Pesos. Copper. 23.0000 g. Plain edge. X#13.2.	65.00
Pn50	1995	—	10 Pesos. Copper-Nickel. 20.0000 g. Reeded edge. X#13.1.	65.00
Pn51	1995	—	10 Pesos. Copper-Nickel. 20.0000 g. Plain edge. X#13.2.	65.00
Pn52	1995	—	10 Pesos. Brass. 23.0000 g. Reeded edge. X#14.1.	65.00
Pn53	1995	—	10 Pesos. Brass. 23.0000 g. Plain edge. X#14.2.	65.00
Pn54	1995	—	10 Pesos. Gilt Alloy. 20.0000 g. Reeded edge. X#14.1.	75.00
Pn55	1995	—	10 Pesos. Gilt Alloy. 20.0000 g. Plain edge. X#14.2	75.00
Pn56	1995	—	10 Pesos. Tri-Metallic. 23.0000 g. Reeded edge. X#14.1.	85.00
Pn57	1995	—	10 Pesos. Tri-Metallic. 23.0000 g. Plain edge. X#14.2.	85.00
Pn58	1995	—	10 Pesos. Aluminum. 6.0000 g. Reeded edge. X#14.1.	65.00
Pn59	1995	—	10 Pesos. Aluminum. 6.0000 g. Plain edge. X#14.2.	65.00
Pn60	1995	—	10 Pesos. Copper. 23.0000 g. Reeded edge. X#14.1.	65.00
Pn61	1995	—	10 Pesos. Copper. 23.0000 g. Plain edge. X#14.2.	65.00
Pn62	1995	—	10 Pesos. Copper-Nickel. 20.0000 g. Reeded edge. X#14.1.	65.00
Pn63	1995	—	10 Pesos. Copper-Nickel. 20.0000 g. Plain edge. X#14.2.	65.00
Pn64	1995	—	10 Pesos. Brass. 23.0000 g. Reeded edge. X#15.1.	65.00
Pn65	1995	—	10 Pesos. Brass. 23.0000 g. Plain edge. X#15.2.	65.00
Pn66	1995	—	10 Pesos. Gilt Alloy. 20.0000 g. Reeded edge. X#15.1.	75.00
Pn67	1995	—	10 Pesos. Gilt Alloy. 20.0000 g. Plain edge. X#15.2.	75.00

X#	Date	Mintage	Identification	Mkt Val
Pn68	1995	—	10 Pesos. Tri-Metallic. 23.0000 g. Reeded edge. X#15.1.	85.00
Pn69	1995	—	10 Pesos. Tri-Metallic. 23.0000 g. Plain edge. X#15.2.	85.00
Pn70	1995	—	10 Pesos. Aluminum. 6.0000 g. Reeded edge. X#15.1.	65.00
Pn71	1995	—	10 Pesos. Aluminum. 6.0000 g. Plain edge. X#15.2.	65.00
Pn72	1995	—	10 Pesos. Copper. 23.0000 g. Reeded edge. X#15.1.	65.00
Pn73	1995	—	10 Pesos. Copper. 23.0000 g. Plain edge. X#15.2.	65.00
Pn74	1995	—	10 Pesos. Copper-Nickel. 20.0000 g. Reeded edge. X#15.1.	65.00
Pn75	1995	—	10 Pesos. Copper-Nickel. 20.0000 g. Plain edge. X#15.2.	65.00

X#	Date	Mintage	Identification	Mkt Val
Pn76	1995	—	10 Pesos. Brass. 23.0000 g. Reeded edge. X#16.1.	65.00
Pn77	1995	—	10 Pesos. Brass. 23.0000 g. Plain edge. X#16.2.	65.00
Pn78	1995	—	10 Pesos. Gilt Alloy. 20.0000 g. Reeded edge. X#16.1.	75.00
Pn79	1995	—	10 Pesos. Gilt Alloy. 20.0000 g. Plain edge. X#16.2.	75.00
Pn80	1995	—	10 Pesos. Tri-Metallic. 23.0000 g. Reeded edge. X#16.1.	85.00
Pn81	1995	—	10 Pesos. Tri-Metallic. 23.0000 g. Plain edge. X#16.2.	85.00
Pn82	1995	—	10 Pesos. Aluminum. 6.0000 g. Reeded edge. X#16.1.	65.00
Pn83	1995	—	10 Pesos. Aluminum. 6.0000 g. Plain edge. X#16.2.	65.00
Pn84	1995	—	10 Pesos. Copper. 23.0000 g. Reeded edge. X#16.1.	65.00
Pn85	1995	—	10 Pesos. Copper. 23.0000 g. Plain edge. X#16.2.	65.00
Pn86	1995	—	10 Pesos. Copper-Nickel. 20.0000 g. Reeded edge. X#16.1.	65.00
Pn87	1995	—	10 Pesos. Copper-Nickel. 20.0000 g. Plain edge. X#16.2.	65.00

X#	Date	Mintage	Identification	Mkt Val
Pn88	1995	—	10 Pesos. Brass. 23.0000 g. Reeded edge.	65.00
Pn89	1995	—	10 Pesos. Brass. 23.0000 g. Plain edge.	65.00
Pn90	1995	—	10 Pesos. Gilt Alloy. 20.0000 g. Reeded edge.	75.00
Pn91	1995	—	10 Pesos. Gilt Alloy. 20.0000 g. Plain edge.	75.00
Pn92	1995	—	10 Pesos. Tri-Metallic. 23.0000 g. Reeded edge.	85.00
Pn93	1995	—	10 Pesos. Tri-Metallic. 23.0000 g. Plain edge.	85.00
Pn94	1995	—	10 Pesos. Aluminum. 6.0000 g. Reeded edge.	65.00
Pn95	1995	—	10 Pesos. Aluminum. 6.0000 g. Plain edge.	65.00
Pn96	1995	—	10 Pesos. Copper. 23.0000 g. Reeded edge.	65.00
Pn97	1995	—	10 Pesos. Copper. 23.0000 g. Plain edge.	65.00
Pn98	1995	—	10 Pesos. Copper-Nickel. 20.0000 g. Reeded edge.	65.00
Pn99	1995	—	10 Pesos. Copper-Nickel. 20.0000 g. Plain edge.	65.00

X#	Date	Mintage	Identification	Mkt Val
Pn100	1995	—	10 Pesos. Brass. 23.0000 g. Reeded edge.	65.00
Pn101	1995	—	10 Pesos. Brass. 23.0000 g. Plain edge.	65.00
Pn102	1995	—	10 Pesos. Gilt Alloy. 20.0000 g. Reeded edge.	75.00
Pn103	1995	—	10 Pesos. Gilt Alloy. 20.0000 g. Plain edge.	75.00
Pn104	1995	—	10 Pesos. Tri-Metallic. 23.0000 g. Reeded edge.	85.00
Pn105	1995	—	10 Pesos. Tri-Metallic. 23.0000 g. Plain edge.	85.00
Pn106	1995	—	10 Pesos. Aluminum. 6.0000 g. Reeded edge.	65.00
Pn107	1995	—	10 Pesos. Aluminum. 6.0000 g. Plain edge.	65.00
Pn108	1995	—	10 Pesos. Copper. 23.0000 g. Reeded edge.	65.00
Pn109	1995	—	10 Pesos. Copper. 23.0000 g. Plain edge.	65.00
Pn110	1995	—	10 Pesos. Copper-Nickel. 20.0000 g. Reeded edge.	65.00
Pn111	1995	—	10 Pesos. Copper-Nickel. 20.0000 g. Plain edge.	65.00

X#	Date	Mintage	Identification	Mkt Val
Pn112	1995	—	10 Pesos. Brass. 23.0000 g. Reeded edge.	65.00
Pn113	1995	—	10 Pesos. Brass. 23.0000 g. Plain edge.	65.00
Pn114	1995	—	10 Pesos. Gilt Alloy. 20.0000 g. Reeded edge.	75.00
Pn115	1995	—	10 Pesos. Gilt Alloy. 20.0000 g. Plain edge.	75.00
Pn116	1995	—	10 Pesos. Tri-Metallic. 23.0000 g. Reeded edge.	85.00
Pn117	1995	—	10 Pesos. Tri-Metallic. 23.0000 g. Plain edge.	85.00
Pn118	1995	—	10 Pesos. Aluminum. 6.0000 g. Reeded edge.	65.00
Pn119	1995	—	10 Pesos. Aluminum. 6.0000 g. Plain edge.	65.00
Pn120	1995	—	10 Pesos. Copper. 23.0000 g. Reeded edge.	65.00
Pn121	1995	—	10 Pesos. Copper. 23.0000 g. Plain edge.	65.00
Pn122	1995	—	10 Pesos. Copper-Nickel. 20.0000 g. Reeded edge.	65.00
Pn123	1995	—	10 Pesos. Copper-Nickel. 20.0000 g. Plain edge.	65.00

X#	Date	Mintage	Identification	Mkt Val
Pn124	1995	—	10 Pesos. Brass. 23.0000 g. Reeded edge.	65.00
Pn125	1995	—	10 Pesos. Brass. 23.0000 g. Plain edge.	65.00
Pn126	1995	—	10 Pesos. Gilt Alloy. 20.0000 g. Reeded edge.	75.00
Pn127	1995	—	10 Pesos. Gilt Alloy. 20.0000 g. Plain edge.	75.00
Pn128	1995	—	10 Pesos. Tri-Metallic. 23.0000 g. Reeded edge.	85.00
Pn129	1995	—	10 Pesos. Tri-Metallic. 23.0000 g. Plain edge.	85.00
Pn130	1995	—	10 Pesos. Aluminum. 6.0000 g. Reeded edge.	65.00
Pn131	1995	—	10 Pesos. Aluminum. 6.0000 g. Plain edge.	65.00
Pn132	1995	—	10 Pesos. Copper. 23.0000 g. Reeded edge.	65.00
Pn133	1995	—	10 Pesos. Copper. 23.0000 g. Plain edge.	65.00
Pn134	1995	—	10 Pesos. Copper-Nickel. 20.0000 g. Reeded edge.	65.00
Pn135	1995	—	10 Pesos. Copper-Nickel. 20.0000 g. Plain edge.	65.00

X#	Date	Mintage	Identification	Mkt Val
Pn136	1995	—	10 Pesos. Brass. 23.0000 g. Reeded edge.	65.00
Pn137	1995	—	10 Pesos. Brass. 23.0000 g. Plain edge.	65.00
Pn138	1995	—	10 Pesos. Gilt Alloy. 20.0000 g. Reeded edge.	75.00
Pn139	1995	—	10 Pesos. Gilt Alloy. 20.0000 g. Plain edge.	39.00
Pn140	1995	—	10 Pesos. Tri-Metallic. 23.0000 g. Reeded edge.	85.00
Pn141	1995	—	10 Pesos. Tri-Metallic. 23.0000 g. Plain edge.	85.00
Pn142	1995	—	10 Pesos. Aluminum. 6.0000 g. Reeded edge.	65.00
Pn143	1995	—	10 Pesos. Aluminum. 6.0000 g. Plain edge.	65.00
Pn144	1995	—	10 Pesos. Copper. 23.0000 g. Reeded edge.	65.00
Pn145	1995	—	10 Pesos. Copper. 23.0000 g. Plain edge.	65.00
Pn146	1995	—	10 Pesos. Copper-Nickel. 20.0000 g. Reeded edge.	65.00
Pn147	1995	—	10 Pesos. Copper-Nickel. 20.0000 g. Plain edge.	65.00
Pn148	1995	—	10 Pesos. Brass. 23.0000 g. Reeded edge.	65.00
Pn149	1995	—	10 Pesos. Brass. 23.0000 g. Plain edge.	65.00
Pn150	1995	—	10 Pesos. Gilt Alloy. 20.0000 g. Reeded edge.	75.00
Pn152	1995	—	10 Pesos. Tri-Metallic. 23.0000 g. Reeded edge.	85.00
Pn153	1995	—	10 Pesos. Tri-Metallic. 23.0000 g. Plain edge.	85.00
Pn154	1995	—	10 Pesos. Aluminum. 6.0000 g. Reeded edge.	65.00
Pn155	1995	—	10 Pesos. Aluminum. 6.0000 g. Plain edge.	65.00
Pn156	1995	—	10 Pesos. Copper. 23.0000 g. Reeded edge.	65.00
Pn157	1995	—	10 Pesos. Copper. 23.0000 g. Plain edge.	65.00
Pn158	1995	—	10 Pesos. Copper-Nickel. 20.0000 g. Reeded edge.	65.00
Pn159	1995	—	10 Pesos. Copper-Nickel. 20.0000 g. Plain edge.	65.00

PIEFORTS

X#	Date	Mintage	Identification	Mkt Val
P5a	1870 P.-C.T.	—	Peso. Copper.	3,750
P5	1980 P.-C.T.	—	Peso. Silver. Prev. KM#Pn5b.	7,500

X#	Date	Mintage	Identification	Mkt Val
P11	1995	—	10 Pesos. 0.9250 Silver. 48.0000 g. Reeded edge.	145
P12	1995	—	10 Pesos. 0.9250 Silver. 48.0000 g. Plain edge.	145

X#	Date	Mintage	Identification	Mkt Val
P13	1995	—	50 Pesos. Gilt Alloy. Reeded edge.	75.00
P14	1995	—	10 Pesos. 0.9250 Silver. 48.0000 g. Reeded edge. X#11.1.	175
P15	1995	—	10 Pesos. 0.9250 Silver. 48.0000 g. Plain edge. X#11.2.	175
P16	1995	—	10 Pesos. 0.9250 Silver. 48.0000 g. Reeded edge. X#12.1.	175
P17	1995	—	10 Pesos. 0.9250 Silver. 48.0000 g. Plain edge. X#12.2.	175
P18	1995	—	10 Pesos. 0.9250 Silver. 48.0000 g. Reeded edge. X#13.1.	175
P19	1995	—	10 Pesos. 0.9250 Silver. 48.0000 g. Plain edge. X#13.2.	175
P20	1995	—	10 Pesos. 0.9250 Silver. 48.0000 g. Reeded edge. X#14.1.	175
P21	1995	—	10 Pesos. 0.9250 Silver. 48.0000 g. Proof edge. X#14.2.	175
P22	1995	—	10 Pesos. 0.9250 Silver. 48.0000 g. Reeded edge. X#15.1.	175
P23	1995	—	10 Pesos. 0.9250 Silver. 48.0000 g. Plain edge. X#15.2.	175
P24	1995	—	10 Pesos. 0.9250 Silver. 48.0000 g. Reeded edge. X#16.1.	175
P25	1995	—	10 Pesos. 0.9250 Silver. 48.0000 g. Plain edge. X#16.2.	145
P26	1995	—	50 Pesos. Gilt Alloy. Reeded edge.	75.00
P27	1995	—	50 Pesos. Gilt Alloy. Plain edge.	75.00
P28	1995	—	50 Pesos. Gilt Alloy. Reeded edge.	75.00
P29	1995	—	50 Pesos. Gilt Alloy. Plain edge.	75.00
P30	1995	—	50 Pesos. Gilt Alloy. Reeded edge.	75.00
P31	1995	—	50 Pesos. Gilt Alloy. Plain edge.	75.00
P32	1995	—	50 Pesos. Gilt Alloy. Reeded edge.	75.00
P34	1995	—	50 Pesos. Gilt Alloy. Reeded edge.	75.00
P35	1995	—	50 Pesos. Gilt Alloy.	75.00
P36	1995	—	50 Pesos. Gilt Alloy. Piet Heyn	100
P37	1995	—	50 Pesos. Gilt Alloy. Piet Heyn	100

TRIAL STRIKE SPLASHES

X#	Date	Mintage	Identification	Mkt Val
TS1	1965	—	Souvenir Peso. Lead. Obv. XM#4.	—
TS2	1965	—	Souvenir Peso. Lead. Rev. XM#4.	—

PROOF SETS

X#	Date	Mintage	Identification	Issue Price	Mkt Val
XPS1	1870 P.-C.T. (5)	40	X1a-X5a	—	9,000

CYPRUS

BRITISH COLONY

MEDALLIC COINAGE

INA Retro Issues

X# M11 36 PIASTRES

0.9250 Silver **Obv:** Veiled bust left **Obv. Legend:** VICTORIA • DEI GRATIA • IND • IMP **Rev:** Crowned shield with lion rampant left, divides date **Edge:** Plain

Date	Mintage	F	VF	XF	Unc	BU
1901 Proof	450	Value: 45.00				

X# M11a 36 PIASTRES

Bronze **Obv:** Veiled bust left **Obv. Legend:** VICTORIA • DEI GRATIA • IND • IMP **Rev:** Crowned shield with lion rampant left, divides date **Edge:** Plain

Date	Mintage	F	VF	XF	Unc	BU
1901 Proof	450	Value: 25.00				

X# M11b 36 PIASTRES

Copper **Obv:** Veiled bust left **Obv. Legend:** VICTORIA • DEI GRATIA • IND • IMP **Rev:** Crowned shield with lion rampant left, divides date **Edge:** Plain

Date	Mintage	F	VF	XF	Unc	BU
1901 Proof	450	Value: 25.00				

X# M11c.1 36 PIASTRES

Gold **Obv:** Veiled bust left **Obv. Legend:** VICTORIA • DEI GRATIA • IND • IMP **Rev:** Crowned shield with lion rampant left, divides date **Edge:** Reeded **Note:** Medal alignment.

Date	Mintage	F	VF	XF	Unc	BU
1901 Proof	1	—	—	—	—	—

X# M11c.2 36 PIASTRES

32.2000 g., 0.9167 Gold 0.9490 oz. AGW **Obv:** Veiled bust left **Obv. Legend:** VICTORIA • DEI GRATIA • IND • IMP **Rev:** Crowned shield with lion rampant left, divides date **Edge:** Plain

Date	Mintage	F	VF	XF	Unc	BU
1901 Proof	1	—	—	—	—	—
Note: Coin alignment						
1901 Proof	1	—	—	—	—	—
Note: Medal alignment						

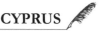

X# M12.1 36 PIASTRES
32.3000 g., 0.9167 Gold 0.9519 oz. AGW **Obv:** Veiled bust left **Obv. Legend:** VICTORIA • DEI • GRA BRITT • REGINA • FID • DEF • IND • IMP • **Rev:** Crowned shield with lion rampant left, divides date **Edge:** Reeded **Note:** Medal alignment.

Date	Mintage	F	VF	XF	Unc	BU
1901 Proof	1	—	—	—	—	—

X# M12.2 36 PIASTRES
31.7000 g., 0.9167 Gold 0.9342 oz. AGW **Obv:** Veiled bust left **Obv. Legend:** VICTORIA • DEI • GRA BRITT • REGINA • FID • DEF • IND • IMP • **Rev:** Crowned shield with lion rampant left, divides date **Edge:** Plain **Note:** Medal alignment.

Date	Mintage	F	VF	XF	Unc	BU
1901 Proof	1	—	—	—	—	—

X# M13 36 PIASTRES
Silver **Obv:** Crowned bust right **Obv. Legend:** EDWARDS VII D: G: BRITT: OMN: REX F: D: IND: IMP. **Rev:** Crowned shield with lion rampant left, divides date **Edge:** Plain **Note:** Medal alignment.

Date	Mintage	F	VF	XF	Unc	BU
1901 Proof	450	Value: 45.00				

X# M13a 36 PIASTRES
Bronze **Obv:** Crowned bust right **Obv. Legend:** EDWARDVS VII D: G: BRITT: OMN: REX F: D: IND: IMP. **Rev:** Crowned shield with lion rampant left, divides date **Edge:** Plain **Note:** Medal alignment.

Date	Mintage	F	VF	XF	Unc	BU
1901 Proof	450	Value: 25.00				

X# M13b 36 PIASTRES
Copper **Obv:** Crowned bust right **Obv. Legend:** EDWARDVS VII D: G: BRITT: OMN: REX F: D: IND: IMP. **Rev:** Crowned shield with lion rampant left, divides date **Edge:** Plain **Note:** Medal alignment.

Date	Mintage	F	VF	XF	Unc	BU
1901 Proof	450	Value: 25.00				

X# M13c.1 36 PIASTRES
32.7000 g., 0.9167 Gold 0.9637 oz. AGW **Obv:** Crowned bust right **Obv. Legend:** EDWARDVS VII D: G: BRITT: OMN: REX F: D: IND: IMP. **Rev:** Crowned shield with lion rampant left, divides date **Edge:** Reeded **Note:** Medal alignment.

Date	Mintage	F	VF	XF	Unc	BU
1901 Proof	1	—	—	—	—	—

X# M13c.2 36 PIASTRES
0.9167 Gold **Obv:** Crowned bust right **Obv. Legend:** EDWARDVS VII D: G: BRITT: OMN: REX F: D: IND: IMP. **Rev:** Crowned shield with lion rampant left, divides date **Edge:** Plain **Note:** Weight varies: 32-32.4 grams.

Date	Mintage	F	VF	XF	Unc	BU
1901 Proof	1	—	—	—	—	—
Note: Medal alignment						
1901 Proof	1	—	—	—	—	—
Note: Coin alignment						

X# M14 36 PIASTRES
22.1500 g., 0.9250 Silver 0.6587 oz. ASW **Obv:** Head right within beaded circle **Obv. Legend:** EDWARDVS VII DEI GRATIA INDIAE IMPERATOR **Rev:** Crowned shield with lion rampant left divides date **Edge:** Plain

Date	Mintage	F	VF	XF	Unc	BU
1901 Proof	120	Value: 45.00				

X# M14a 36 PIASTRES
17.9500 g., Bronze **Obv:** Head right within beaded circle **Obv. Legend:** EDWARDVS VII DEI GRATIA INDIAE IMPERATOR **Rev:** Crowned shield with lion rampant left divides date **Edge:** Plain

Date	Mintage	F	VF	XF	Unc	BU
1901 Proof	120	Value: 25.00				

X# M14b 36 PIASTRES
18.0200 g., Copper **Obv:** Head right within beaded circle **Obv. Legend:** EDWARDVS VII DEI GRATIA INDIAE IMPERATOR **Rev:** Crowned shield with lion rampant left divides date **Edge:** Plain

Date	Mintage	F	VF	XF	Unc	BU
1901 Proof	120	Value: 25.00				

X# M14c.1 36 PIASTRES
32.2000 g., 0.9167 Gold 0.9490 oz. AGW **Obv:** Head right within beaded circle **Obv. Legend:** EDWARDVS VII DEI GRATIA INDIAE IMPERATOR **Rev:** Crowned shield with lion rampant left divides date **Edge:** Reeded **Note:** Medal alignment.

Date	Mintage	F	VF	XF	Unc	BU
1901 Proof	1	—	—	—	—	—

X# M14c.2 36 PIASTRES
32.5000 g., 0.9167 Gold 0.9578 oz. AGW **Obv:** Head right within beaded circle **Obv. Legend:** EDWARDVS VII DEI GRATIA INDIAE IMPERATOR **Rev:** Crowned shield with lion rampant left divides date **Edge:** Plain **Note:** Medal alignment.

Date	Mintage	F	VF	XF	Unc	BU
1901 Proof	1	—	—	—	—	—

X# M15 45 PIASTRES
24.2800 g., 0.9250 Silver 0.7220 oz. ASW **Obv:** Head left **Obv. Legend:** EDWARDVS VIII D: G: BR: OMN: REX F: D: IND: IMP. **Rev:** Two lions left, heads facing **Edge:** Plain

Date	Mintage	F	VF	XF	Unc	BU
1937 Proof	550	Value: 45.00				

X# M15c.1 45 PIASTRES
39.9000 g., 0.9167 Gold 1.1759 oz. AGW **Obv:** Head left **Obv. Legend:** EDWARDVS VIII DEI GRATIA INDIAE IMPERATOR **Rev:** Two lions left, heads facing **Edge:** Reeded

Date	Mintage	F	VF	XF	Unc	BU
1937 Proof, medal alignment	1	—	—	—	—	—
1937 Proof, coin alignment	1	—	—	—	—	—

X# M15a 45 PIASTRES
19.4200 g., Bronze **Obv:** Head left **Obv. Legend:** EDWARDVS VII DEI GRATIA INDIAE IMPERATOR **Rev:** Two lions left, heads facing **Edge:** Plain **Note:** Medal alignment.

Date	Mintage	F	VF	XF	Unc	BU
1937 Proof	550	Value: 25.00				

X# M15b 45 PIASTRES
19.4800 g., Copper **Obv:** Head left **Obv. Legend:** EDWARDVS VII DEI GRATIA INDIAE IMPERATOR **Rev:** Two lions left, heads facing **Edge:** Plain **Note:** Medal alignment.

Date	Mintage	F	VF	XF	Unc	BU
1937 Proof	550	Value: 25.00				

X# M15c.2 45 PIASTRES
40.0000 g., 0.9167 Gold 1.1789 oz. AGW **Obv:** Head left **Obv. Legend:** EDWARDVS VIII DEI GRATIA INDIAE IMPERATOR **Rev:** Two lions left, heads facing **Edge:** Plain **Note:** Medal alignment.

Date	Mintage	F	VF	XF	Unc	BU
1937 Proof	1	—	—	—	—	—

X# M16 45 PIASTRES
0.9167 Gold **Obv:** Crowned bust left **Obv. Legend:** EDWARD VIII KING EMPEROR **Rev:** Two lions left, heads facing **Edge:** Plain **Note:** Weight varies: 39.4-39.8 grams.

Date	Mintage	F	VF	XF	Unc	BU
1937 Proof	1	—	—	—	—	—
Note: Medal alignment						
1937 Proof	1	—	—	—	—	—
Note: Coin alignment						

Richard Lobel Issues

X# M1 CROWN
Bronze **Subject:** Edward VIII **Obv:** Bust of Edward VIII facing left **Obv. Legend:** EDWARD • VIII • KING • & • EMPEROR **Rev:** Crowned shield

Date	Mintage	F	VF	XF	Unc	BU
1936 Proof	750	Value: 15.00				

X# M1a CROWN
Copper-Nickel-Zinc **Subject:** Edward VIII **Obv:** Bust of Edward VIII facing left **Obv. Legend:** EDWARD • VIII • KING • & • EMPEROR **Rev:** Crowned shield

Date	Mintage	F	VF	XF	Unc	BU
1936 Proof	2,250	Value: 15.00				

X# M1b CROWN
0.9167 Silver **Subject:** Edward VIII **Obv:** Bust of Edward VIII facing left **Obv. Legend:** EDWARD • VIII • KING • & • EMPEROR **Rev:** Crowned shield

Date	Mintage	F	VF	XF	Unc	BU
1936 Proof	200	Value: 50.00				

X# M1c CROWN
Gold **Subject:** Edward VIII **Obv:** Bust of Edward VIII facing left **Obv. Legend:** EDWARD • VIII • KING • & • EMPEROR **Rev:** Crowned shield

Date	Mintage	F	VF	XF	Unc	BU
1936 Proof	—	Value: 500				

X# M2 SOVEREIGN
0.3750 Gold **Subject:** Edward VIII

Date	Mintage	F	VF	XF	Unc	BU
1936 Proof	200	Value: 125				

REPUBLIC

REFORM COINAGE

100 Cents = 1 Pound

KM# 75a POUND
28.2800 g., 0.9250 Silver 0.8410 oz. ASW, 38.6 mm. **Subject:** Cyprus Joins the European Union **Obv:** National arms **Rev:** Map and Triton trumpeting through a sea shell **Edge:** Plain

Date	Mintage	F	VF	XF	Unc	BU
2004 Proof	3,000	Value: 45.00				

MEDALLIC COINAGE

Archbishop Makarios Fund Issues

Struck at the Paris Mint, France.

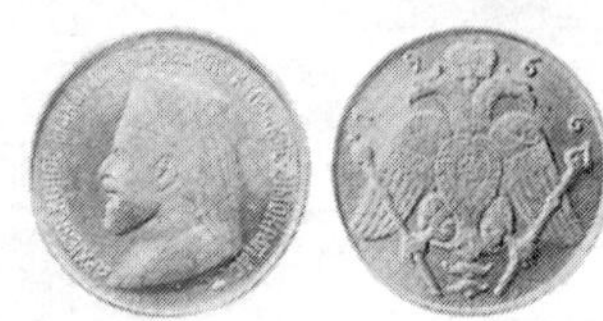

X# M3 1/2 SOVEREIGN
3.9940 g., 0.9167 Gold 0.1177 oz. AGW **Obv:** Bust of Archbishop Makarios III left **Note:** Prev. KM#M1.

Date	Mintage	F	VF	XF	Unc	BU
1966 Proof	25,000	Value: 125				

X# M4 SOVEREIGN
7.9881 g., 0.9167 Gold 0.2354 oz. AGW **Obv:** Bust of Archbishop Makarios III left **Note:** Prev. KM#M2.

Date	Mintage	F	VF	XF	Unc	BU
1966 Proof	50,000	Value: 200				

X# M8 3 POUNDS
7.5000 g., 0.9250 Silver 0.2230 oz. ASW **Obv:** Bust of Archbishop Makarios III left **Note:** Struck at the Paris Mint, France.

Date	Mintage	F	VF	XF	Unc	BU
1974	—	—	—	—	35.00	75.00

X# M5.1 5 POUNDS
40.0000 g., 0.9170 Gold 1.1792 oz. AGW **Obv:** Bust of Archbishop Makarios III left **Note:** Prev. KM#M3.

Date	Mintage	F	VF	XF	Unc	BU
1966	1,500	—	—	1,200	1,750	—

X# M5.2 5 POUNDS
40.0000 g., 0.9170 Gold 1.1792 oz. AGW **Obv:** Bust of Archbishop Makarios III left **Edge:** Plain **Note:** Serial number added. Prev. KM#M4.

Date	Mintage	F	VF	XF	Unc	BU
1966	200	—	—	2,500	3,500	—

X# M6 6 POUNDS
15.0000 g., 0.9250 Silver 0.4461 oz. ASW **Obv:** Bust of Archbishop Makarios III left

Date	Mintage	F	VF	XF	Unc	BU
1974	—	—	—	—	50.00	100

X# M9 12 POUNDS
30.0000 g., 0.9250 Silver 0.8921 oz. ASW **Obv:** Bust of Archbishop Makarios III left

Date	Mintage	F	VF	XF	Unc	BU
1974	—	—	—	—	85.00	165

FANTASY EURO PATTERNS

INA Issues

X# Pn1 EURO CENT
Copper Plated Steel, 16.8 mm. **Obv:** Moufflon leaping left **Rev:** Scale at right **Edge:** Plain

Date	Mintage	F	VF	XF	Unc	BU
2004	18,000	—	—	—	—	1.50
2004 Proof	12,500	Value: 2.50				

X# Pn1a EURO CENT
Silver, 16.8 mm. **Obv:** Mouflon leaping left **Rev:** Scale at right **Edge:** Plain

Date	Mintage	F	VF	XF	Unc	BU
2004 Proof	400	Value: 6.00				

X# Pn2 2 EURO CENT
Copper Plated Steel, 18.5 mm. **Obv:** Moufflon leaping left **Rev:** Scale at right **Edge:** Plain

Date	Mintage	F	VF	XF	Unc	BU
2004	18,000	—	—	—	—	2.00
2004 Proof	12,500	Value: 3.00				

X# Pn2a 2 EURO CENT
Silver, 18.5 mm. **Obv:** Moufflon leaping left **Rev:** Scale at right **Edge:** Plain

Date	Mintage	F	VF	XF	Unc	BU
2004 Proof	400	Value: 7.00				

X# Pn3 5 EURO CENT
Copper Plated Steel, 20.7 mm. **Obv:** Moufflon leaping left **Rev:** Scale at right **Edge:** Plain

Date	Mintage	F	VF	XF	Unc	BU
2004	1,800	—	—	—	2.50	—
2004 Proof	12,500	Value: 3.50				

X# Pn3a 5 EURO CENT
Silver, 20.7 mm. **Obv:** Moufflon leaping left **Rev:** Scale at right **Edge:** Plain

Date	Mintage	F	VF	XF	Unc	BU
2004 Proof	400	Value: 8.50				

X# Pn4 10 EURO CENT
Goldine, 19.3 mm. **Obv:** Ancient gallery **Rev:** Dove, value in wreath of hands **Edge:** Plain

Date	Mintage	F	VF	XF	Unc	BU
2004	18,000	—	—	—	—	3.00
2004 Proof	12,500	Value: 4.00				

X# Pn4a 10 EURO CENT
Silver, 19.3 mm. **Obv:** Ancient galley **Rev:** Dove, value in wreath of hands **Edge:** Plain

Date	Mintage	F	VF	XF	Unc	BU
2004 Proof	400	Value: 10.00				

X# Pn5 20 EURO CENT

Goldine, 22 mm. **Obv:** Ancient galley **Rev:** Dove, value in wreath of hands **Edge:** Plain

Date	Mintage	F	VF	XF	Unc	BU
2004	18,000	—	—	—	—	3.50
2004 Proof	12,500	Value: 5.00				

X# Pn5a 20 EURO CENT

Silver, 22 mm. **Obv:** Ancient galley **Rev:** Dove, value in wreath of hands **Edge:** Plain

Date	Mintage	F	VF	XF	Unc	BU
2004 Proof	400	Value: 12.50				

X# Pn6 50 EURO CENT

Goldine, 24.3 mm. **Obv:** Ancient galley **Rev:** Dove, value in wreath of hands **Edge:** Plain

Date	Mintage	F	VF	XF	Unc	BU
2004	18,000	—	—	—	—	4.00
2004 Proof	12,500	Value: 6.00				

X# Pn6a 50 EURO CENT

Silver, 24.3 mm. **Obv:** Ancient galley **Rev:** Dove, value in wreath of hands **Edge:** Plain

Date	Mintage	F	VF	XF	Unc	BU
2004 Proof	400	Value: 15.00				

X# Pn7 EURO

Bi-Metallic, 22.8 mm. **Obv:** Arms in pentagon **Rev:** Ancient galley **Edge:** Plain

Date	Mintage	F	VF	XF	Unc	BU
2004	18,000	—	—	—	—	6.00
2004 Proof	12,500	Value: 8.00				

X# Pn7a EURO

Bi-Metallic Brass center in Silver ring, 22.8 mm. **Obv:** Arms in pentagon **Rev:** Ancient galley **Edge:** Plain

Date	Mintage	F	VF	XF	Unc	BU
2004 Proof	400	Value: 22.50				

X# Pn8 2 EURO

Bi-Metallic, 25.7 mm. **Obv:** Arms in pentagon **Rev:** Ancient galley **Edge:** Plain

Date	Mintage	F	VF	XF	Unc	BU
2004	18,000	—	—	—	—	8.00
2004 Proof	12,500	Value: 10.00				

X# Pn8a 2 EURO

Bi-Metallic Brass center in Silver ring, 25.7 mm. **Obv:** Arms in pentagon **Rev:** Ancient galley **Edge:** Plain

Date	Mintage	F	VF	XF	Unc	BU
2004 Proof	400	Value: 28.50				

X# Pn9 5 EURO

Goldine, 36 mm. **Obv:** Arms in pentagon **Rev:** Ancient Greek statue before temple **Edge:** Plain

Date	Mintage	F	VF	XF	Unc	BU
2004 Proof	12,500	Value: 12.50				

X# Pn9a 5 EURO

Silver, 36 mm. **Obv:** Arms in pentagon **Rev:** Ancient Greek statue before temple **Edge:** Plain

Date	Mintage	F	VF	XF	Unc	BU
2004 Proof	400	Value: 40.00				

PIEFORTS

X#	Date	Mintage	Identification	Mkt Val
P1	1901	1	36 Piastres. Silver. Plain edge, coin alignment, X#M11.	—
P2	1901	1	36 Piastres. Silver. Plain edge, medal alignment, X#M11.	—
P3	1901	1	36 Piastres. Silver. Reeded edge, coin alignment, X#M11.	—
P4	1901	1	36 Piastres. Silver. Reeded edge, medal alignment, X#M11.	—
P5	1901	1	36 Piastres. Silver. Plain edge, coin alignment, X#M12.	—
P6	1901	1	36 Piastres. Silver. Plain edge, medal alignment, X#M12.	—
P7	1901	1	36 Piastres. Silver. Reeded edge, coin alignment, X#M12.	—
P8	1901	1	36 Piastres. Silver. Reeded edge, medal alignment, X#M12.	—
P9	1901	1	36 Piastres. Silver. Plain edge, coin alignment, X#M13.	—
P10	1901	1	36 Piastres. Silver. Plain edge, medal alignment, X#M13.	—
P11	1901	1	36 Piastres. Silver. Reeded edge, coin alignment, X#M13.	—
P12	1901	1	36 Piastres. Silver. Reeded edge, medal alignment, X#M13.	—
P13	1901	1	36 Piastres. Silver. Plain edge, coin alignment, X#M14.	—
P14	1901	1	36 Piastres. Silver. Plain edge, medal alignment, X#M14.	—
P15	1901	1	36 Piastres. Silver. Reeded edge, coin alignment, X#M14.	—
P16	1901	1	36 Piastres. Silver. Reeded edge, medal alignment, X#M14.	—
P17	1937	1	45 Piastres. Silver. Plain edge, coin alignment, X#M15.	—
P18	1937	1	45 Piastres. Silver. Plain edge, medal alignment, X#M15.	—
P19	1937	1	45 Piastres. Silver. Reeded edge, coin alignment, X#M15.	—
P20	1937	1	45 Piastres. Silver. Reeded edge, medal alignment, X#M15.	—
P21	1937	1	45 Piastres. Silver. Plain edge, coin alignment, X#M16.	—
P22	1937	1	45 Piastres. Silver. Plain edge, medal alignment, X#M16.	—
P23	1937	1	45 Piastres. Silver. Reeded edge, coin alignment, X#M16.	—
P24	1937	1	45 Piastres. Silver. Reeded edge, medal alignment, X#M16.	—
P25	2004	400	5 Euro. Silver. X#Pn9a.	—
P26	1936	—	Crown. 0.9167 Silver. X#M1b.	100

MINT SETS

X#	Date	Mintage	Identification	Issue Price	Mkt Val
XMS1	2004 (8)	18,000	X#Pn1-Pn8	—	30.00

PROOF SETS

X#	Date	Mintage	Identification	Issue Price	Mkt Val
XPS1	2004 (9)	12,500	X#Pn1-Pn9	—	45.00
XPS2	2004 (9)	400	X#Pn1a-Pn9a	—	150

CZECH REPUBLIC

REPUBLIC

MEDALLIC COINAGE

KM# M1 DUCAT

3.5000 g., 0.9860 Gold 0.1109 oz. AGW, 20 mm. **Subject:** Architectural Montage of Czech & Moravian Cities **Obv:** Crowned Bohemian lion rampant left **Edge:** Plain

Date	Mintage	F	VF	XF	Unc	BU
1993(m) Proof	1,000	Value: 135				

KM# M1a DUCAT

2.9600 g., 0.9990 Silver 0.0951 oz. ASW, 20 mm. **Obv:** Crowned Bohemian lion rampant lion **Edge:** Plain

Date	Mintage	F	VF	XF	Unc	BU
1993 Proof	1,000	Value: 17.50				

KM# M3 DUCAT

3.5000 g., 0.9860 Gold 0.1109 oz. AGW, 20 mm. **Obv:** Crowned Bohemian lion rampant left **Rev:** Cathedral **Edge:** Plain **Note:** Similar to 5 Ducat, X#4.

Date	Mintage	F	VF	XF	Unc	BU
1994 Proof	620	Value: 200				

KM# M5 DUCAT

3.5000 g., 0.9860 Gold 0.1109 oz. AGW, 20 mm. **Obv:** Crowned Bohemian lion rampant left **Rev:** Plzen city view **Edge:** Plain **Note:** Similar to 5 Ducats, X#M6a.

Date	Mintage	F	VF	XF	Unc	BU
1995 Proof	—	Value: 200				

KM# M7 DUCAT

3.5000 g., 0.9860 Gold 0.1109 oz. AGW, 20 mm. **Obv:** Crowned Bohemian lion rampant left **Rev:** Karlstein Castle **Edge:** Plain **Note:** Similar to 5 Ducats, X#M8.

Date	Mintage	F	VF	XF	Unc	BU
1996 Proof	—	Value: 200				

KM# M9 DUCAT

3.5000 g., 0.9860 Gold 0.1109 oz. AGW, 20 mm. **Obv:** Crowned Bohemian lion rampant left **Edge:** Plain **Note:** Similar to 5 Ducats, X#M10.

Date	Mintage	F	VF	XF	Unc	BU
1997 Proof	—	Value: 200				

KM# M11 DUCAT

3.5000 g., 0.9850 Gold 0.1108 oz. AGW, 20 mm. **Obv:** Crowned Bohemian lion rampant left **Rev:** Haloed king **Edge:** Plain **Note:** Similar to 5 Ducats, X#M13

Date	Mintage	F	VF	XF	Unc	BU
1998 Proof	Est. 1,500	Value: 150				

KM# M17a DUCAT

14.9000 g., 0.9990 Silver 0.4785 oz. ASW, 20 mm. **Obv:** Crowned Bohemian lion rampant left **Edge:** Plain

Date	Mintage	F	VF	XF	Unc	BU
1999 Proof	Est. 5,000	Value: 20.00				

KM# M15 DUCAT

3.5000 g., 0.9850 Gold 0.1108 oz. AGW, 20 mm. **Obv:** Crowned Bohemian lion rampant left **Rev:** St. Barbara's Cathedral **Edge:** Plain

Date	Mintage	F	VF	XF	Unc	BU
1999 Proof	Est. 1,500	Value: 150				

KM# M12 2 DUCAT

7.0000 g., 0.9860 Gold 0.2219 oz. AGW, 35.3 mm. **Subject:** St. Wenceslav **Obv:** Crowned Bohemian lion rampant left **Rev:** Haloed King **Edge:** Reeded **Note:** Similar to 5 Ducats, X#M13.

Date	Mintage	F	VF	XF	Unc	BU
1998 Proof	Est. 1,500	Value: 200				

KM# M16 2 DUCAT

7.0000 g., 0.9860 Gold 0.2219 oz. AGW, 35.30 mm. **Obv:** Crowned Bohemian lion rampant left **Rev:** St. Barbara's Cathedral **Edge:** Reeded

Date	Mintage	F	VF	XF	Unc	BU
1999 Proof	Est. 1,500	Value: 200				

KM# M2 5 DUCAT

17.5000 g., 0.9860 Gold 0.5547 oz. AGW, 35.3 mm. **Subject:** Architectural Montage of Czech & Moravian Cities **Obv:** Crowned Bohemian lion rampant left **Edge:** Reeded

Date	Mintage	F	VF	XF	Unc	BU
1993 Proof	128	Value: 675				

KM# M2a 5 DUCAT

14.8400 g., 0.9999 Silver 0.4770 oz. ASW, 35.30 mm. **Obv:** Crowned Bohemian lion rampant left **Edge:** Reeded

Date	Mintage	F	VF	XF	Unc	BU
1993(m) Proof	10,000	Value: 25.00				

KM# M4 5 DUCAT
17.5000 g., 0.9860 Gold 0.5547 oz. AGW, 35.3 mm.
Obv: Crowned Bohemian lion rampant left
Rev: Cathedral **Edge:** Reeded

Date	Mintage	F	VF	XF	Unc	BU
1994 Proof	40	Value: 830				

KM# M4a 5 DUCAT
14.8400 g., 0.9990 Silver 0.4766 oz. ASW, 35.3 mm.
Obv: Crowned Bohemian lion rampant left
Edge: Reeded

Date	Mintage	F	VF	XF	Unc	BU
1994 Proof	5,000	Value: 25.00				

KM# M6 5 DUCAT
17.5000 g., 0.9860 Gold 0.5547 oz. AGW, 35.3 mm.
Obv: Crowned Bohemian lion rampant left **Rev:** Plzen city view **Edge:** Reeded **Note:** Similar to KM#M6a.

Date	Mintage	F	VF	XF	Unc	BU
1995 Proof	—	Value: 830				

KM# M6a 5 DUCAT
14.8400 g., 0.9990 Silver 0.4766 oz. ASW, 35.3 mm.
Obv: Crowned Bohemian lion rampant left **Edge:** Reeded

Date	Mintage	F	VF	XF	Unc	BU
1995 Proof	5,000	Value: 25.00				

KM# M8 5 DUCAT
17.5000 g., 0.9860 Gold 0.5547 oz. AGW, 35.3 mm.
Obv: Crowned Bohemian lion rampant left
Rev: Karlstein Castle **Edge:** Reeded

Date	Mintage	F	VF	XF	Unc	BU
1996 Proof	—	Value: 830				

KM# M8a 5 DUCAT
14.8400 g., 0.9990 Silver 0.4766 oz. ASW, 35.3 mm.
Obv: Crowned Bohemian lion rampant left
Rev: Karlstein Castle **Edge:** Reeded

Date	Mintage	F	VF	XF	Unc	BU
1996 Proof	—	Value: 25.00				

KM# M10a 5 DUCAT
14.8400 g., 0.9990 Silver 0.4766 oz. ASW, 35.3 mm.
Obv: Crowned Bohemian lion rampant left **Edge:** Reeded

Date	Mintage	F	VF	XF	Unc	BU
1997 Proof	—	Value: 20.00				

KM# M10 5 DUCAT
17.5000 g., 0.9860 Gold 0.5547 oz. AGW, 35.3 mm.
Obv: Crowned Bohemian lion rampant left **Rev:** Arch above Rudolph II monogram **Edge:** Reeded

Date	Mintage	F	VF	XF	Unc	BU
1997 Proof	—	Value: 830				

KM# M13 5 DUCAT
17.5000 g., 0.9860 Gold 0.5547 oz. AGW, 35.3 mm.
Subject: St. Wenceslav **Obv:** Crowned Bohemian lion rampant left **Rev:** Haloed king **Edge:** Reeded

Date	Mintage	F	VF	XF	Unc	BU
1998 Proof	Est. 1,500	Value: 800				

KM# M13a 5 DUCAT
14.8400 g., 0.9990 Silver 0.4766 oz. ASW, 35.3 mm.
Obv: Crowned Bohemian lion rampant left **Edge:** Reeded

Date	Mintage	F	VF	XF	Unc	BU
1998 Proof	Est. 5,000	Value: 20.00				

KM# M17 5 DUCAT
17.5000 g., 0.9860 Gold 0.5547 oz. AGW, 35.3 mm.
Obv: Crowned Bohemian lion rampant left **Rev:** St. Barbara's Cathedral **Edge:** Reeded

Date	Mintage	F	VF	XF	Unc	BU
1999 Proof	Est. 1,500	Value: 800				

KM# M14 10 DUCAT
35.0000 g., 0.9999 Silver 1.1251 oz. ASW, 35.3 mm.
Subject: St. Wenceslav **Obv:** Crowned Bohemian lion rampant left **Rev:** Haloed king **Edge:** Reeded
Note: Similar to 5 Ducats, KM#M13.

Date	Mintage	F	VF	XF	Unc	BU
1998 Proof	Est. 1,500	Value: 1,000				

KM# M18 10 DUCAT
35.0000 g., 0.9999 Silver 1.1251 oz. ASW, 35.3 mm.
Obv: Crowned Bohemian lion rampant left **Rev:** St. Barbar's Cathedral **Edge:** Reeded

Date	Mintage	F	VF	XF	Unc	BU
1999 Proof	Est. 1,500	Value: 1,000				

FANTASY EURO PATTERNS

INA Issues

X# Pn1 EURO CENT
Copper Plated Steel, 16.8 mm. **Issuer:** INA
Obv: Statue, buildings in Telc **Obv. Legend:** CESKÁ REPUBLIKA **Rev:** Large value, crown, Euro stars design **Edge:** Plain

Date	Mintage	F	VF	XF	Unc	BU
2004	14,000	—	—	—	—	1.50
2004 Proof	3,000	Value: 2.50				

X# Pn1a EURO CENT
Silver **Obv:** Statue, buildings in Telc **Obv. Legend:** CESKÁ REPUBLIKA **Rev:** Large value, crown, Euro stars design

Date	Mintage	F	VF	XF	Unc	BU
2004 Proof	250	Value: 6.00				

X# Pn2 2 EURO CENT
Copper Plated Steel, 18.5 mm. **Issuer:** INA **Obv:** Statue, buildings in Telc **Obv. Legend:** CESKÁ REPUBLIKA **Rev:** Large value, crown, Euro stars design **Edge:** Plain

Date	Mintage	F	VF	XF	Unc	BU
2004	14,000	—	—	—	—	2.00
2004 Proof	3,000	Value: 3.00				

X# Pn2a 2 EURO CENT
Silver **Obv:** Statue, buildings in Telc **Obv. Legend:** CESKÁ REPUBLIKA **Rev:** Large value, crown, Euro stars design

Date	Mintage	F	VF	XF	Unc	BU
2004 Proof	250	Value: 7.00				

X# Pn3 5 EURO CENT
Copper Plated Steel, 20.7 mm. **Issuer:** INA
Obv: Statue, buildings in Telc **Obv. Legend:** CESKÁ REPUBLIKA **Rev:** Large value, crown, Euro stars design **Edge:** Plain

Date	Mintage	F	VF	XF	Unc	BU
2004	14,000	—	—	—	—	2.50
2004 Proof	3,000	Value: 3.50				

X# Pn3a 5 EURO CENT
Silver **Obv:** Statue, buildings in Telc **Obv. Legend:** CESKÁ REPUBLIKA **Rev:** Large value, crown, Euro stars design

Date	Mintage	F	VF	XF	Unc	BU
2004 Proof	250	Value: 8.50				

X# Pn4 10 EURO CENT
Goldine, 19.3 mm. **Issuer:** INA **Obv:** Ploskovice Chateau **Obv. Legend:** CESKÁ REPUBLIKA **Rev:** Rampant lion, Euro stars design, large value **Edge:** Plain

Date	Mintage	F	VF	XF	Unc	BU
2004	14,000	—	—	—	—	3.00
2004 Proof	3,000	Value: 4.00				

X# Pn4a 10 EURO CENT
Silver **Obv:** Ploskovice Chateau **Obv. Legend:** CESKÁ REPUBLIKA **Rev:** Rampant lion, Euro stars design, large value

Date	Mintage	F	VF	XF	Unc	BU
2004 Proof	250	Value: 10.00				

X# Pn5 20 EURO CENT
Goldine **Issuer:** INA **Obv:** Ploskovice Chateau **Obv. Legend:** CESKÁ REPUBLIKA **Rev:** Rampant lion left, Euro stars design, large value **Edge:** Plain

Date	Mintage	F	VF	XF	Unc	BU
2004	14,000	—	—	—	—	3.50
2004 Proof	3,000	Value: 5.00				

X# Pn5a 20 EURO CENT
Silver **Obv:** Ploskovice Chateau **Obv. Legend:** CESKÁ REPUBLIKA **Rev:** Rampant lion left, Euro stars design, large value

Date	Mintage	F	VF	XF	Unc	BU
2004 Proof	250	Value: 12.50				

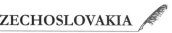

X# Pn6 50 EURO CENT
Goldine **Issuer:** INA **Obv:** Ploskovice Chateau **Obv. Legend:** CESKÁ REPUBLIKA **Rev:** Rampant lion left, Euro stars design, large value **Edge:** Plain

Date	Mintage	F	VF	XF	Unc	BU
2004	14,000	—	—	—	—	4.00
2004 Proof	3,000	Value: 6.00				

X# Pn6a 50 EURO CENT
Silver **Obv:** Ploskovice Chateau **Obv. Legend:** CESKÁ REPUBLIKA **Rev:** Rampant lion left, Euro stars desing, large value

Date	Mintage	F	VF	XF	Unc	BU
2004 Proof	250	Value: 15.00				

X# Pn7 EURO
Bi-Metallic Goldine center, Copper-Nickel ring, 22.8 mm. **Issuer:** INA **Obv:** Starometske Namesti Square **Obv. Legend:** CESKÁ REPUBLIKA **Rev:** Large value, horseman, Euro stars design **Edge:** Plain

Date	Mintage	F	VF	XF	Unc	BU
2004	14,000	—	—	—	—	6.00
2004 Proof	3,000	Value: 8.00				

X# Pn7a EURO
Bi-Metallic Goldine center in Silver ring **Obv:** Starometske Namesti square **Obv. Legend:** CESKÁ REPUBLIKA **Rev:** Large value, horseman, Euro stars design

Date	Mintage	F	VF	XF	Unc	BU
2004 Proof	250	Value: 22.50				

X# Pn8 2 EURO
Bi-Metallic Copper-Nickel center, Goldine ring, 25.7 mm. **Issuer:** INA **Obv:** Starometske Namesti Square **Obv. Legend:** CESKÁ REPUBLIKA **Rev:** Large value, horseman, Euro stars design **Edge:** Plain

Date	Mintage	F	VF	XF	Unc	BU
2004	14,000	—	—	—	—	8.00
2004 Proof	3,000	Value: 10.00				

X# Pn8a 2 EURO
Bi-Metallic Goldine center in silver ring **Obv:** Starometske Namesti Square **Obv. Legend:** CESKÁ REPUBLIKA **Rev:** Large value, horseman, Euro stars design

Date	Mintage	F	VF	XF	Unc	BU
2004 Proof	250	Value: 28.50				

X# Pn9 5 EURO
Goldine **Issuer:** INA **Obv. Legend:** CESKÁ REPUBLIKA **Edge:** Plain

Date	Mintage	F	VF	XF	Unc	BU
2004 Proof	3,000	Value: 12.50				

X# Pn9a 5 EURO
Silver **Obv. Legend:** CESKÁ REPUBLIKA

Date	Mintage	F	VF	XF	Unc	BU
2004 Proof	250	Value: 40.00				

X# Pn10 EURO CENT
Copper Plated Steel **Edge:** Plain

Date	Mintage	F	VF	XF	Unc	BU
2004	—	—	—	—	—	1.00

X# Pn11 2 EURO CENT
Copper Plated Steel **Edge:** Plain

Date	Mintage	F	VF	XF	Unc	BU
2004	—	—	—	—	—	1.50

X# Pn12 5 EURO CENT
Copper Plated Steel **Edge:** Plain

Date	Mintage	F	VF	XF	Unc	BU
2004	—	—	—	—	—	2.00

X# Pn13 10 EURO CENT
Goldine **Edge:** Plain

Date	Mintage	F	VF	XF	Unc	BU
2004	—	—	—	—	—	2.50

X# Pn14 20 EURO CENT
Goldine **Edge:** Plain

Date	Mintage	F	VF	XF	Unc	BU
2004	—	—	—	—	—	3.00

X# Pn15 50 EURO CENT
Goldine **Edge:** Plain

Date	Mintage	F	VF	XF	Unc	BU
2004	—	—	—	—	—	3.50

X# Pn16 EURO
Bi-Metallic **Obv:** Medieval male bust 3/4 left **Rev:** Large value on outline map of Czech Republic

Date	Mintage	F	VF	XF	Unc	BU
2004	—	—	—	—	—	5.50

X# Pn17 2 EURO
Bi-Metallic **Obv:** Prague's Town Hall Astrological clock **Rev:** Large value on outline map of Czech Republic

Date	Mintage	F	VF	XF	Unc	BU
2004	—	—	—	—	—	7.50

MINT SETS

X#	Date	Mintage	Identification	Issue Price	Mkt Val
XMS1	2004 (8)	14,000	X#Pn1-Pn8	—	30.00
XMS2	2004 (8)	—	X#Pn10-Pn17.	—	26.00

PROOF SETS

X#	Date	Mintage	Identification	Issue Price	Mkt Val
XPS1	2004 (9)	3,000	X#Pn1-Pn9	—	50.00
XPS2	2004 (9)	250	X#Pn1a-Pn9a	—	150

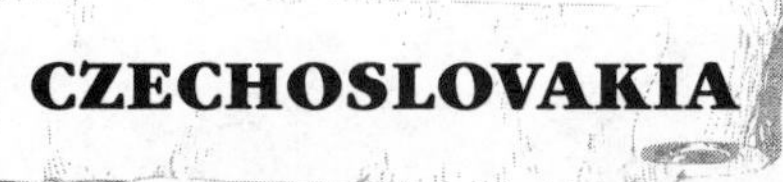

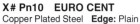

CZECHOSLOVAKIA

REPUBLIC

SILVER MEDALLIC COINAGE

X# M1 5 DUKATEN
19.8900 g., 0.9870 Silver 0.6311 oz. ASW, 34.5 mm. **Subject:** 10th Anniversary of Republic

Date	Mintage	F	VF	XF	Unc	BU
ND(1928)	—	—	—	30.00	50.00	—

X# M5 5 DUKATEN
15.0300 g., Silver, 29 mm. **Subject:** 1000th Anniversary - Christianity in Bohemia

Date	Mintage	F	VF	XF	Unc	BU
ND(1929)	—	—	—	45.00	75.00	—

X# M2 10 DUKATEN
19.8900 g., 0.9870 Silver 0.6311 oz. ASW, 40 mm. **Subject:** 10th Anniversary of Republic

Date	Mintage	F	VF	XF	Unc	BU
ND(1928)	32,000	—	—	35.00	60.00	—

X# M6 10 DUKATEN
30.0500 g., 0.9870 Silver 0.9535 oz. ASW **Subject:** 1000th Anniversary - Christianity in Bohemia

Date	Mintage	F	VF	XF	Unc	BU
ND(1929)	3,259	—	—	60.00	100	—

X# M21a 10 DUKATEN
30.0500 g., 0.9870 Silver 0.9535 oz. ASW, 40 mm. **Subject:** Reopening of Kremnica Mines

Date	Mintage	F	VF	XF	Unc	BU
1934	—	—	—	—	—	—

GOLD MEDALLIC COINAGE

X# M7 DUKAT
4.0000 g., 0.9860 Gold 0.1268 oz. AGW **Subject:** 1000th Anniversary - Christianity in Bohemia

Date	Mintage	F	VF	XF	Unc	BU
ND(1929)	1,631	—	—	400	550	—

X# M12 DUKAT
3.4900 g., 0.9860 Gold 0.1106 oz. AGW **Subject:** Tyrs - Sokol Movement **Note:** Prev. KM#M10.

Date	Mintage	F	VF	XF	Unc	BU
1932	1,742	—	—	300	450	—

X# M15 DUKAT

3.4900 g., 0.9860 Gold 0.1106 oz. AGW **Obv:** Dr. Antonin Svehla

Date	Mintage	F	VF	XF	Unc	BU
1933	1,000	—	—	300	450	—

X# M16 DUKAT

3.4900 g., 0.9860 Gold 0.1106 oz. AGW **Obv:** Dr. Antonin Svehla **Rev:** Cross above date

Date	Mintage	F	VF	XF	Unc	BU
1933	Inc. above	—	—	350	550	—

X# M14.1 DUKAT

3.4900 g., 0.9860 Gold 0.1106 oz. AGW
Subject: Reopening of Kremnica Mines

Date	Mintage	F	VF	XF	Unc	BU
1934	288	—	—	700	950	—

Note: See X#14.2 for the 1971 dated restrike.

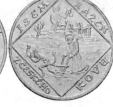

X# M14.2 DUKAT

3.4900 g., 0.9860 Gold 0.1106 oz. AGW
Subject: Reopening of Kremnica Mines

Date	Mintage	F	VF	XF	Unc	BU
1971	—	—	—	—	90.00	—

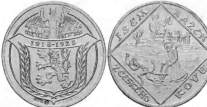

X# M3 2 DUKATEN

6.9800 g., 0.9860 Gold 0.2213 oz. AGW **Subject:** 10th Anniversary of Republic

Date	Mintage	F	VF	XF	Unc	BU
ND(1928)	—	—	—	250	350	—
ND(1928) Restrike (1973)	—	—	—	—	300	—

X# M19 2 DUKATEN

6.9800 g., 0.9860 Gold 0.2213 oz. AGW **Subject:** Reopening of Kremnica Mines

Date	Mintage	F	VF	XF	Unc	BU
1934	159	—	—	1,250	1,650	—

X# M8 3 DUKATEN

12.0000 g., 0.9860 Gold 0.3804 oz. AGW
Subject: 1000th Anniversary - Christianity in Bohemia

Date	Mintage	F	VF	XF	Unc	BU
ND(1929)	1,058	—	—	750	1,000	—

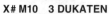

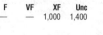

X# M10 3 DUKATEN

10.0000 g., 0.9860 Gold 0.3170 oz. AGW
Subject: 1000th Anniversary - Death of St. Wenzel
Note: Prev. KM#M21.

Date	Mintage	F	VF	XF	Unc	BU
ND(1929)	750	—	—	1,000	1,400	—

X# M4 4 DUKATEN

13.9600 g., 0.9860 Gold 0.4425 oz. AGW
Subject: 10th Anniversary of Republic

Date	Mintage	F	VF	XF	Unc	BU
ND(1928)	—	—	—	350	500	—
ND(1928)	—	—	—	—	400	—

Note: Restrike (1973)

X# M9 5 DUKATEN

20.0000 g., 0.9860 Gold 0.6340 oz. AGW
Subject: 1000th Anniversary - Christianity in Bohemia

Date	Mintage	F	VF	XF	Unc	BU
ND(1929)	787	—	—	1,400	1,750	—

X# M20 5 DUKATEN

17.4500 g., 0.9860 Gold 0.5532 oz. AGW
Subject: Reopening of Kremnica Mine

Date	Mintage	F	VF	XF	Unc	BU
1934	70	—	—	4,000	5,500	—

X# M21 10 DUKATEN

34.9000 g., 0.9860 Gold 1.1063 oz. AGW
Subject: Reopening of Kremnica Mine

Date	Mintage	F	VF	XF	Unc	BU
1934	68	—	—	6,500	8,500	—

PEOPLES REPUBLIC

SILVER MEDALLIC COINAGE

X# M35 5 DUCAT

0.9990 Silver **Obv:** Dubcek bust left **Obv. Legend:** PRAVDA VITEZI — VERITAS VINCET / ALEXANDER DUBCEK **Rev:** Hus bust left in rays **Rev. Legend:** M. JOANES HUS **Edge:** Reeded

Date	Mintage	F	VF	XF	Unc	BU
ND	5,000	—	—	—	—	—

X# M36 10 DUCAT
1.0000 g., 0.9990 Silver 0.0321 oz. ASW
Obv: Conjoined busts of Svoboda and Dubcek
Obv. Legend: PRAVDA VITEZI — VERITAS VINCIT / L. SVOBODA — A. DUBCEK **Rev:** St. Wenceslaus statue **Rev. Legend:** SANCTUS VENCESLAUS

Date	Mintage	F	VF	XF	Unc	BU
ND Proof	5,000	—	—	—	—	—

GOLD MEDALLIC COINAGE

X# M37 5 DUCAT
17.5000 g., 0.9860 Gold 0.5547 oz. AGW **Obv:** Dobcek bust left **Obv. Legend:** PRAVDA VITEZI — VERITAS VINCET / ALEXANDER DUBCEK **Rev:** Hus bust left in rays **Rev. Legend:** M. JOANES HUS.

Date	Mintage	F	VF	XF	Unc	BU
ND Proof	5,000	—	—	—	—	—

X# M38 10 DUCAT
35.0000 g., 0.9860 Gold 1.1095 oz. AGW **Obv:** Conjoined busts of Svoboda and Dubcek **Obv. Legend:** PRAVDA VITEZI — VERITAS VINCIT / L. SVOBODA — A. DUBCEK **Rev:** St. Wenceslaus statue **Rev. Legend:** SANCTUS VENCESLAUS **Edge:** Reeded

Date	Mintage	F	VF	XF	Unc	BU
ND Proof	5,000	—	—	—	—	—

SOCIALIST REPUBLIC

GOLD MEDALLIC COINAGE

X# M28 DUKAT
3.4900 g., 0.9860 Gold 0.1106 oz. AGW
Subject: 600th Anniversary Death of Charles IV

Date	Mintage	F	VF	XF	Unc	BU
1978	20,000	—	—	90.00	125	—
1979	10,000	—	—	145	—	—
1980	10,000	—	—	145	—	—
1981	10,000	—	—	145	—	—
1982	10,000	—	—	145	—	—

X# M29 2 DUKATEN
6.9800 g., 0.9860 Gold 0.2213 oz. AGW
Subject: 600th Anniversary Death of Charles IV

Date	Mintage	F	VF	XF	Unc	BU
1978	10,000	—	—	180	250	—

X# M30 5 DUKATEN
17.4500 g., 0.9860 Gold 0.5532 oz. AGW
Subject: 600th Anniversary Death of Charles IV

Date	Mintage	F	VF	XF	Unc	BU
1978	10,000	—	—	425	600	—

X# M31 10 DUKATEN
34.9000 g., 0.9860 Gold 1.1063 oz. AGW
Subject: 600th Anniversary Death of Charles IV

Date	Mintage	F	VF	XF	Unc	BU
1978	10,000	—	—	850	1,200	—

CZECH SLOVAK FEDERAL REPUBLIC

MEDALLIC COINAGE

Numex S.A. Madrid

X# 41 20 ECU
31.1030 g., 0.9990 Silver 0.9989 oz. ASW, 38 mm. **Obv:** Arms **Obv. Legend:** CESKA' A SLOVENSKA FEDERATIVNI REPUBLIKA **Rev:** Charlemagne facing seated on throne **Rev. Legend:** KVIMPRAVSVSTVS KAROLVSMAGNVS ROMANO **Edge:** Reeded

Date	Mintage	F	VF	XF	Unc	BU
1992 Proof	8,000	Value: 40.00				

X# 42 200 ECU
31.1030 g., 0.8150 Gold 0.8150 oz. AGW, 38 mm. **Obv:** Arms **Obv. Legend:** CESKA' A SLOVENSKA FEDERATIVNI REPUBLIKA **Rev:** Charlemagne facing seated on throne **Rev. Legend:** KVIMPRAVSVSTVS KAROLVSMAGNVS ROMANO **Edge:** Reeded

Date	Mintage	F	VF	XF	Unc	BU
1992 Proof	800	Value: 550				

WALLENSTEIN

REPUBLIC

MEDALLIC ISSUES

X# 1 5 DUCATS
17.5000 g., 0.9860 Gold 0.5547 oz. AGW
Subject: 300th Anniversary of Assassination of Albrecht von Wallenstein

Date	Mintage	F	VF	XF	Unc	BU
ND(1972) Proof; Restrike	—	Value: 1,000				

X# 3 10 DUCATS
35.0000 g., 0.9860 Gold 1.1095 oz. AGW
Subject: 300th Anniversary of Assassination of Albrecht von Wallenstein

Date	Mintage	F	VF	XF	Unc	BU
ND(1972) Proof; Restrike	—	Value: 2,200				

DAMANHUR

FEDERATION

TOKEN COINAGE

Lire Equivalents

X# 1 10 CALI
Terra-Cotta yellow glaze **Obv:** Legend around value **Rev:** Graphic image

Date	Mintage	F	VF	XF	Unc	BU
ND(1986)	—	—	—	—	—	—

X# 16 10 CALI
5.9000 g., Silver, 20.5 mm. **Obv:** Large value and graphic **Rev:** Graphic

Date	Mintage	F	VF	XF	Unc	BU
1995	—	—	—	90.00	—	—

X# 17 10 CALI
Terra-Cotta red glaze **Obv:** Legend around value **Rev:** Graphic image, date below

Date	Mintage	F	VF	XF	Unc	BU
XXIII (1998)	—	—	—	—	—	—

X# 2 20 CALI
Terra-Cotta yellow glaze

Date	Mintage	F	VF	XF	Unc	BU
ND(1986)	—	—	—	—	—	—

X# 18 20 CALI
Terra-Cotta red color **Obv:** Legend around value **Rev:** Graphic image, date below

Date	Mintage	F	VF	XF	Unc	BU
XXIII (1998)	—	—	—	—	—	—

X# 19 25 CALI
Terra-Cotta yellow glaze **Obv:** Legend around value **Rev:** Graphic image above date

Date	Mintage	F	VF	XF	Unc	BU
XXIII (1998)	—	—	—	—	—	—

X# 20 50 CALI
Terra-Cotta red color **Obv:** Legend around value **Rev:** Graphic image, date above

Date	Mintage	F	VF	XF	Unc	BU
XXIII (1998)	—	—	—	—	—	—

X# 4 CREDITO
Terra-Cotta red color **Obv:** Large value

Date	Mintage	F	VF	XF	Unc	BU
ND(1986)	—	—	—	—	—	—

X# 21 CREDITO
Terra-Cotta red color **Obv:** Value above graphic image **Rev:** Date above graphic image

Date	Mintage	F	VF	XF	Unc	BU
XXIII (1986)	—	—	—	—	—	—

X# 5 2 CREDITI
Terra-Cotta red color

Date	Mintage	F	VF	XF	Unc	BU
ND(1986)	—	—	—	—	—	—

X# 22 2 CREDITI
Terra-Cotta red color **Obv:** Value within graphic square **Rev:** Date below graphic image

Date	Mintage	F	VF	XF	Unc	BU
XXIII (1998)	—	—	—	—	—	—

X# 13 5 CREDITI
Copper-Nickel dark patina **Obv:** Owl and value **Rev:** Graphic image and value within linear square and diamond

Date	Mintage	F	VF	XF	Unc	BU
Yr. XXIII (1998)	—	—	—	—	—	—

X# 7 10 CREDITI
3.6000 g., Silver **Obv:** Large value **Rev:** Face

Date	Mintage	F	VF	XF	Unc	BU
1986	—	—	—	65.00	—	—

X# 12 10 CREDITI
3.7000 g., Silver, 19 mm.

Date	Mintage	F	VF	XF	Unc	BU
1989	—	—	—	65.00	—	—

X# 14 10 CREDITI
3.7000 g., Silver, 19 mm. **Obv:** Large value **Rev:** Face

Date	Mintage	F	VF	XF	Unc	BU
1995	—	—	—	55.00	—	—

X# 8 25 CREDITI
11.3000 g., Silver, 25 mm. **Obv:** Graphic image **Rev:** Two faces kissing

Date	Mintage	F	VF	XF	Unc	BU
1986	—	—	—	70.00	—	—

X# 15 25 CREDITI
11.5000 g., Silver, 11.5 mm. **Obv:** Graphic image **Rev:** Two faces kissing

Date	Mintage	F	VF	XF	Unc	BU
1995	—	—	—	65.00	—	—

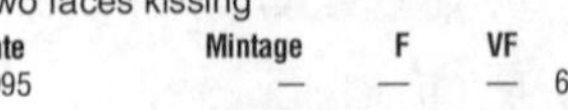

X# 10 50 CREDITI
5.8000 g., Silver, 20.5 mm. **Obv:** Value within graphic **Rev:** Logo

Date	Mintage	F	VF	XF	Unc	BU
ND(1986)	—	—	—	—	—	—

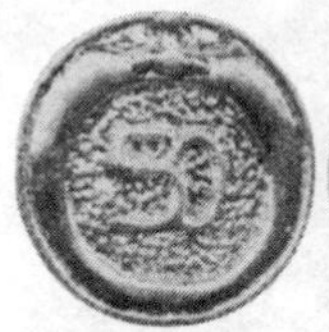

X# 9 50 CREDITI
5.8000 g., Silver, 20.5 mm. **Obv:** Large value within open mouth **Rev:** crab and graphic

Date	Mintage	F	VF	XF	Unc	BU
1986	—	—	—	—	—	—

X# 11 100 CREDITI
Gold

Date	Mintage	F	VF	XF	Unc	BU
1986	—	—	—	—	—	—

Euro Equivalents

X# 23 10 CALI
1.8000 g., Aluminum, 15 mm. **Obv:** Value within linear square and diamond **Rev:** Butterfly

Date	Mintage	F	VF	XF	Unc	BU
1999	—	—	—	—	15.00	—

X# 24 20 CALI
2.0000 g., Aluminum, 17 mm. **Obv:** Value within linear square and diamond **Rev:** Crab

Date	Mintage	F	VF	XF	Unc	BU
1999	—	—	—	—	16.50	—
2001	—	—	—	—	16.50	—

X# 25 50 CALI
2.5000 g., Aluminum, 20 mm. **Obv:** Value within linear square and diamond **Rev:** Snail shell

Date	Mintage	F	VF	XF	Unc	BU
1999	—	—	—	—	18.00	—
2001	—	—	—	—	18.00	—

X# 26 CREDITO
3.5000 g., Bronzital, 21.5 mm. **Obv:** Value and large leaf **Rev:** Plant

Date	Mintage	F	VF	XF	Unc	BU
1999	—	—	—	—	28.00	—
2000	—	—	—	—	28.00	—
2002	—	—	—	—	28.00	—

X# 27 2 CREDITI
5.7000 g., Copper, 24 mm. **Obv:** Value within leaves **Rev:** Linear designs

Date	Mintage	F	VF	XF	Unc	BU
1999	—	—	—	—	22.50	—
2002	—	—	—	—	22.50	—

X# 28 5 CREDITI
6.1000 g., Bronzital, 25 mm. **Obv:** Three flags and value **Rev:** Large chalice flanked by columns

Date	Mintage	F	VF	XF	Unc	BU
1999	—	—	—	—	25.00	—
2000	—	—	—	—	25.00	—

X# 29 10 CREDITI
9.6000 g., Copper Nickel, 27 mm. **Obv:** Value within linear design **Rev:** Nude female advancing right

Date	Mintage	F	VF	XF	Unc	BU
1999	—	—	—	—	28.00	—
2002	—	—	—	—	28.00	—

X# 30 20 CREDITI
8.7500 g., Bi-Metallic Nickel-Silver center in Bronzital ring, 27 mm. **Obv:** Value within linear wreath design **Rev:** Three dancing figures

Date	Mintage	F	VF	XF	Unc	BU
1999	—	—	—	—	35.00	—
2003	—	—	—	—	35.00	—

DANISH WEST INDIES

DANISH COLONY

COUNTERMARKED COINAGE

Barbados Series

X# 35 PENNY
Copper **Countermark:** Crowned FRVII **Note:** Prev. KM#35. Countermark on Barbados penny, KM#Tn8.

CM Date	Host Date	Good	VG	F	VF	XF
ND(1850)	1788	—	—	—	—	—

Brazil Series

X# 36 10 REIS
Copper **Countermark:** Crowned FRVII **Note:** Prev. KM#36. Countermark on Brazil 10/XX Reis, KM#423.1.

CM Date	Host Date	Good	VG	F	VF	XF
ND(1850)	1830	—	—	—	—	—

X# 31 40 REIS
Copper **Countermark:** Crowned FRVII **Note:** Prev. KM#31. Countermark on Brazil 40 Reis.

CM Date	Host Date	Good	VG	F	VF	XF
ND(1850)	1826	—	—	—	—	—

X# 32.1 960 REIS
Silver **Countermark:** Crowned FRVII **Note:** Prev. KM#32.1. Countermark on Brazil 960 Reis, KM#307.

CM Date	Host Date	Good	VG	F	VF	XF
ND(1850)	1814	350	550	850	1,250	—

X# 32.2 960 REIS
Silver **Countermark:** Crowned FRVII **Note:** Prev. KM#32.2. Countermark on Brazil 960 Reis, KM#326.1

CM Date	Host Date	Good	VG	F	VF	XF
ND(1850)	1818	350	550	850	1,250	—
ND(1850)	1819	350	550	850	1,250	—

British West Indies Series

X# 71 1/8 DOLLAR
0.8920 Silver **Countermark:** Crowned FRVII **Note:** Countermark on British West Indies 1/8 Dollar, KM#2.

CM Date	Host Date	Good	VG	F	VF	XF
ND(1850)	1822	—	—	—	—	—

X# 72 1/4 DOLLAR
0.8920 Silver **Countermark:** Crowned FRVII **Note:** Countermark on British West Indies 1/4 Dollar, KM#3.

CM Date	Host Date	Good	VG	F	VF	XF
ND(1850)	1822	—	—	—	—	—

English Series

X# 64 DOLLAR
0.9030 Silver **Countermark:** Crowned FRVII **Note:** Countermark on Bank of England Dollar, KM#Tn1.

CM Date	Host Date	Good	VG	F	VF	XF
ND(1850)	1804	—	—	—	—	—

X# 37 PENNY
Copper **Countermark:** Crowned FRVII **Note:** Prev. KM#37. Countermark on English Penny, KM#618.

CM Date	Host Date	Good	VG	F	VF	XF
ND(1850)	1797	60.00	90.00	150	250	—

X# 33 1/2 PENNY
Copper **Countermark:** Crowned FRVII **Note:** Countermark of Hull, Yorkshire 1/2 Penny "Condor" token.

CM Date	Host Date	Good	VG	F	VF	XF
ND(1850)	1791	—	—	—	—	—

X# 40 1/2 PENNY
Copper **Countermark:** Crowned FRVII **Note:** Prev. KM#40. Countermark on English 1/2 Penny, KM#662.

CM Date	Host Date	Good	VG	F	VF	XF
ND(1850)	1806	—	—	—	—	—
ND(1850)	1807	—	—	—	—	—

X# 38 1/2 PENNY
Copper **Countermark:** Crowned FRVII **Note:** Prev. KM#38. Countermark on English Penny, KM#662.

CM Date	Host Date	Good	VG	F	VF	XF
ND(1850)	1807	—	—	—	—	—

X# 65 1/2 PENNY
Copper **Countermark:** Crowned FRVII
Note: Countermark English 1/2 Penny, KM#692.

CM Date	Host Date	Good	VG	F	VF	XF
ND(1850)	1826	—	—	—	—	—

X# 41 2 PENCE
Copper **Countermark:** Crowned FRVII **Note:** Prev. KM#41. Countermark on English 2 Pence, KM#619.

CM Date	Host Date	Good	VG	F	VF	XF
ND(1850)	1797	—	—	—	—	—

X# 60 6 PENCE
0.9250 Silver **Countermark:** Crowned FRVII
Note: Countermark on English 6 Pence, KM#582.3.

CM Date	Host Date	Good	VG	F	VF	XF
ND(1850)	1746	—	—	—	—	—

X# 67 6 PENCE
0.9250 Silver **Countermark:** Crowned FRVII
Note: Countermark on English 6 Pence, KM#733.1.

CM Date	Host Date	Good	VG	F	VF	XF
ND(1850)	1838-48	—	—	—	—	—

X# 58 1/2 CROWN
0.9250 Silver **Countermark:** Crowned FRVII
Note: Countermark on English 1/2 Crown of George III.

CM Date	Host Date	Good	VG	F	VF	XF
ND(1850)	1690s	—	—	—	—	—

X# 63 1/2 CROWN
0.9250 Silver **Countermark:** Crowned FRVII
Note: Countermark on English 1/2 Crown, KM#672.

CM Date	Host Date	Good	VG	F	VF	XF
ND(1850)	1818	—	—	—	—	—

X# 61 SHILLING
0.9250 Silver **Countermark:** Crowned FRVII
Note: Countermark on English Shilling, KM#583.2.

CM Date	Host Date	Good	VG	F	VF	XF
ND(1850)	1745	—	—	—	—	—

X# 62 SHILLING
0.9250 Silver **Countermark:** Crowned FRVII
Note: Countermark on English Shilling, KM#666.

CM Date	Host Date	Good	VG	F	VF	XF
ND(1850)	1816	—	—	—	—	—

X# 66 SHILLING
0.9250 Silver **Countermark:** Crowned FRVII
Note: Countermark on English Shilling, KM#713.

CM Date	Host Date	Good	VG	F	VF	XF
ND(1850)	1834-37	—	—	—	—	—

X# 68 SHILLING
0.9250 Silver **Countermark:** Crowned FRVII
Note: Countermark on English Shilling, KM#734.1.

CM Date	Host Date	Good	VG	F	VF	XF
ND(1850)	1838-48	—	—	—	—	—

French Series

X# 81 1/2 FRANC
Silver **Countermark:** Crowned FRVII
Note: Countermark on France 1/2 Franc, KM#723.

CM Date	Host Date	Good	VG	F	VF	XF
ND(1850)	1825-30	—	—	—	—	—

X# 82 1/2 FRANC
0.9000 Silver **Countermark:** Crowned FRVII
Note: Countermark on France 1/2 Franc, KM#741.

CM Date	Host Date	Good	VG	F	VF	XF
ND(1850)	1831-45	—	—	—	—	—

X# 80 1/12 ECU
0.9167 Silver **Note:** Countermark on France 1/12 Ecu, KM#132.1.

CM Date	Host Date	Good	VG	F	VF	XF
ND(1850)	1643	—	—	—	—	—

Haiti Series

X# 39 6-1/4 CENTIMES
Copper **Countermark:** Crowned FRVII **Note:** Prev. KM#39. Countermark on Haiti 6-1/4 Centimes, KM#38.

CM Date	Host Date	Good	VG	F	VF	XF
ND(1850)	1850	—	—	—	—	—

Ireland Series

X# 42 1/2 PENNY
Copper **Countermark:** Crowned FRVII **Note:** Prev. KM#42. Countermark on Ireland 1/2 Penny, KM#147.

CM Date	Host Date	Good	VG	F	VF	XF
ND(1850)	1805	—	—	—	—	—

Isle of Man Series

X# 43 PENNY
Copper **Countermark:** Crowned FRVII **Note:** Prev. KM#43. Countermark on Isle of Man Penny, KM#11.

CM Date	Host Date	Good	VG	F	VF	XF
ND(1850)	1813	—	—	—	—	—

Mexican Series

X# 75 8 REALES
0.9030 Silver **Countermark:** Crowned FRVII
Note: Countermark on Mexico 8 Reales, KM#377.

CM Date	Host Date	Good	VG	F	VF	XF
ND(1850)	1825-48	—	—	—	—	—

Netherlands Series

X# 85 25 CENTS
0.5690 Silver **Countermark:** Crowned FRVII
Note: Countermark on Netherlands 25 Cents, KM#48.

CM Date	Host Date	Good	VG	F	VF	XF
ND(1850)	1825	—	—	—	—	—

Peru Series

X# 44 4 REALES
Copper **Countermark:** Crowned FRVII **Note:** Prev. KM#44. Countermark on South Peru 4 Reales, KM#172.

CM Date	Host Date	Good	VG	F	VF	XF
ND(1850)	1838	—	—	—	—	—

X# 47 8 REALES
Copper **Countermark:** Crowned FRVII **Note:** Prev. KM#47. Countermark on South Peru 4 Reales, KM#170.4.

CM Date	Host Date	Good	VG	F	VF	XF
ND(1850)	1838	—	—	—	—	—

Spanish Colonial Series

X# 46 REALE
3.3834 g., Silver **Countermark:** Crowned FRVII
Note: Countermark on Lima Mint Reale, KM#75.

CM Date	Host Date	Good	VG	F	VF	XF
ND(1850)	1782 LIMAE MI	—	—	—	—	—

X# 45 2 REALES
6.7668 g., Silver **Countermark:** Crowned FRVII
Note: Countermark on Lima Mint 2 Reales, KM#62.

CM Date	Host Date	Good	VG	F	VF	XF
ND(1850)	ND1761 LM JM	—	—	—	—	—

X# 50 2 REALES
6.7700 g., Silver **Countermark:** Crowned FRVII
Note: Countermark on Spanish Colonial 2 Reales.

CM Date	Host Date	Good	VG	F	VF	XF
ND(1850)	1796	—	—	—	—	—

X# 48 4 REALES
13.5400 g., Silver **Countermark:** Crowned FRVII
Note: Countermark on Spanish Colonial 4 Reales.

CM Date	Host Date	Good	VG	F	VF	XF
ND(1850)	1778	—	—	—	—	—

X# 51 4 REALES
13.5400 g., Silver **Countermark:** Crowned FRVII
Note: Countermark on Spanish Colonial 4 Reales.

CM Date	Host Date	Good	VG	F	VF	XF
ND(1850)	1806	—	—	—	—	—

Spanish Series

X# 90 4 MARAVEDIS

Copper **Countermark:** Crowned FRVII
Note: Countermark on Spain 4 Maravedi.

CM Date	Host Date	Good	VG	F	VF	XF
ND(1850)	ND	—	—	—	—	—

U.S. Colonial Virginia Series

Only the U.S. quarters dated 1849 and half dollars dated 1848-1850 are considered legitimate issues. The following listings are all believed to be spurious countermarks on a variety of host coins. The few genuine countermarked pieces are currently listed in the "Standard Catalog of World Coins, 1801-1900."

X# 29 1/2 PENNY

Copper **Countermark:** Crowned FRVII **Note:** Prev. KM#29. Countermark on Virginia 1/2 Penny, C#7.

CM Date	Host Date	Good	VG	F	VF	XF
ND(1850)	1773	—	—	—	—	—

U.S. Series

X# 24.1 1/2 CENT

Copper **Countermark:** Crowned FRVII **Note:** Prev. KM#24.1. Countermark on U.S.A. 1/2 Cent, KM#33.

CM Date	Host Date	Good	VG	F	VF	XF
ND(1850)	1808	—	—	—	—	—

X# 24.2 1/2 CENT

Copper **Countermark:** Crowned FRVII **Note:** Prev. KM#24.2. Countermark on U.S.A. 1/2 Cent, KM#41.

CM Date	Host Date	Good	VG	F	VF	XF
ND(1850)	1809	—	—	—	—	—
ND(1850)	1832	—	—	—	—	—
ND(1850)	1834	—	—	—	—	—

X# 25.1 CENT

Copper **Countermark:** Crowned FRVII **Note:** Prev. KM#25.1. Countermark on U.S.A. Large Cent, C#16.

CM Date	Host Date	Good	VG	F	VF	XF
ND(1850)	1795	250	450	750	1,200	—

X# 25.2 CENT

Copper **Countermark:** Crowned FRVII **Note:** Prev. KM#25.2. Countermark on U.S.A. Large Cent, KM#22.

CM Date	Host Date	Good	VG	F	VF	XF
ND(1850)	1797	220	425	650	1,000	—
ND(1850)	1800	220	425	650	1,000	—
ND(1850)	1801	220	425	650	1,000	—
ND(1850)	1803	220	425	650	1,000	—
ND(1850)	1805	220	425	650	1,000	—
ND(1850)	1807	220	425	650	1,000	—

X# 25.3 CENT

Copper **Countermark:** Crowned FRVII **Note:** Prev. KM#25.3. Countermark on U.S.A. Large Cent, KM#45.

CM Date	Host Date	Good	VG	F	VF	XF
ND(1850)	1816	150	300	450	700	—
ND(1850)	1818	150	300	450	700	—
ND(1850)	1819	150	300	450	700	—
ND(1850)	1822	150	300	450	700	—
ND(1850)	1826	150	300	450	700	—
ND(1850)	1831	150	300	450	700	—
ND(1850)	1832	150	300	450	700	—
ND(1850)	1833	150	300	450	700	—
ND(1850)	1835	150	300	450	700	—
ND(1850)	1836	150	300	450	700	—
ND(1850)	1837	150	300	450	700	—
ND(1850)	1838	150	300	450	700	—
ND(1850)	1839	150	300	450	700	—

X# 25.4 CENT

Copper **Countermark:** Crowned FRVII **Note:** Prev. included with KM#25.3. Countermark on U.S.A. Large Cent, KM#67.

CM Date	Host Date	Good	VG	F	VF	XF
ND(1850)	ND	150	300	450	700	—
ND(1850)	ND	150	300	450	700	—
ND(1850)	ND	150	300	450	700	—
ND(1850)	ND	150	300	450	700	—
ND(1850)	ND	150	300	450	700	—
ND(1850)	ND	150	300	450	700	—
ND(1850)	ND	150	300	450	700	—
ND(1850)	ND	150	300	450	700	—

X# 26.1 25 CENTS

Silver **Countermark:** Crowned FRVII **Note:** Prev. KM#26.1. Countermark on U.S.A. Liberty Bust 25 Cent, KM#44.

CM Date	Host Date	Good	VG	F	VF	XF
ND(1850)	1821	—	—	—	—	—

X# 26.2 25 CENTS

Silver **Countermark:** Crowned FRVII **Note:** Prev. KM#26.2. Countermark on U.S.A. Liberty Bust 25 Cent, KM#55.

CM Date	Host Date	Good	VG	F	VF	XF
ND(1850)	1832	—	—	—	—	—

X# 26.3 25 CENTS

0.9000 Silver **Countermark:** Crowned FRVII
Note: Prev. KM#26.3. Countermark on U.S.A. Liberty Seated 25 Cent, KM#64.2.

CM Date	Host Date	Good	VG	F	VF	XF
ND(1850)	1841	600	1,200	1,850	2,800	—
ND(1850)	1845	600	1,200	1,850	2,800	—
ND(1850)	1847	600	1,200	1,850	2,800	—

X# 27.1 50 CENTS

Silver **Countermark:** Crowned FRVII **Note:** Prev. KM#27.1. Countermark on U.S.A. Liberty Bust 50 Cent, KM#37.

CM Date	Host Date	Good	VG	F	VF	XF
ND(1850)	1810	600	1,200	1,850	2,800	—
ND(1850)	1812	600	1,200	1,850	2,800	—
ND(1850)	1823	600	1,200	1,850	2,800	—
ND(1850)	1824	600	1,200	1,850	2,800	—
ND(1850)	1826	600	1,200	1,850	2,800	—
ND(1850)	1830	600	1,200	1,850	2,800	—
ND(1850)	1831	600	1,200	1,850	2,800	—
ND(1850)	1833	600	1,200	1,850	2,800	—
ND(1850)	1834	600	1,200	1,850	2,800	—
ND(1850)	1836	600	1,200	1,850	2,800	—

X# 27.2 50 CENTS

0.9000 Silver **Countermark:** Crowned FRVII
Note: Prev. KM#27.2. Countermark on U.S.A. Liberty Seated 50 Cent, KM#68.

CM Date	Host Date	Good	VG	F	VF	XF
ND(1850)	1848	650	1,300	2,150	3,250	—
ND(1850)	ND1849	650	1,300	2,150	3,250	—

X# 28 DOLLAR

Silver **Countermark:** Crowned FRVII **Note:** Prev. KM#28. Countermark on U.S.A. Liberty Seated dollar, KM#68.

CM Date	Host Date	Good	VG	F	VF	XF
ND(1850)	1841	1,000	2,000	3,000	4,500	—
ND(1850)	1842	1,000	2,000	3,000	4,500	—
ND(1850)	1843	1,000	2,000	3,000	4,500	—
ND(1850)	1847	1,000	2,000	3,000	4,500	—

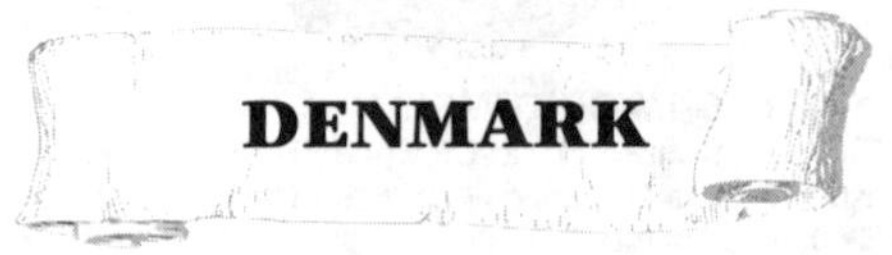

DENMARK

KINGDOM

MEDALLIC COINAGE

The Medallic Issues are similar to circulation coinage except they are without a denomination.

X# A1 2 KRONER

Gold **Subject:** Golden Wedding Anniversary

Date	Mintage	F	VF	XF	Unc	BU
1892	2	—	—	—	13,500	—

X# 1 2 KRONER

15.0000 g., 0.8000 Silver 0.3858 oz. ASW
Ruler: Christian IX **Subject:** 40th Anniversary of Reign
Note: Prev. KM#M1.

Date	Mintage	F	VF	XF	Unc	BU
1903(h) P Proof	—	Value: 2,000				

X# 2 2 KRONER

15.0000 g., 0.8000 Silver 0.3858 oz. ASW
Ruler: Christian X **Subject:** Silver Wedding Anniversary **Note:** Prev. KM#M2.

Date	Mintage	F	VF	XF	Unc	BU
1923(h) HCN Proof	—	Value: 3,000				

X# 3 2 KRONER

15.0000 g., 0.8000 Silver 0.3858 oz. ASW
Ruler: Christian X **Subject:** King's 60th Birthday
Note: Prev. KM#M3.

Date	Mintage	F	VF	XF	Unc	BU
1930(h) N Proof	—	Value: 2,750				

X# 4 2 KRONER

15.0000 g., 0.8000 Silver 0.3858 oz. ASW
Ruler: Christian X **Subject:** 25th Anniversary of Reign
Note: Prev. KM#M4.

Date	Mintage	F	VF	XF	Unc	BU
1937(h) N; S Proof	—	Value: 3,500				

X# 5 2 KRONER
15.0000 g., 0.8000 Silver 0.3858 oz. ASW
Ruler: Christian X **Subject:** King's 75th Birthday
Note: Prev. KM#M5.

Date	Mintage	F	VF	XF	Unc	BU
1945(h) N; S Proof	—	Value: 1,350				

X# 6 2 KRONER
15.0000 g., 0.8000 Silver 0.3858 oz. ASW
Ruler: Frederik IX **Note:** Prev. KM#M6. Greenland Commemorative.

Date	Mintage	F	VF	XF	Unc	BU
1953(h) N; S Proof	—	Value: 3,150				

X# 7 2 KRONER
15.0000 g., 0.8000 Silver 0.3858 oz. ASW **Ruler:** Frederik IX **Subject:** Princess Margrethe's 18th Birthday **Note:** Prev. KM#M7.

Date	Mintage	F	VF	XF	Unc	BU
ND(1958)(h) C; S Proof	110	Value: 350				

X# 8 5 KRONER
17.0000 g., 0.8000 Silver 0.4372 oz. ASW
Ruler: Frederik IX **Subject:** Silver Wedding Anniversary **Note:** Prev. KM#M8.

Date	Mintage	F	VF	XF	Unc	BU
1960(h) C; S Proof	250	Value: 245				

X# 9 5 KRONER
17.0000 g., 0.8000 Silver 0.4372 oz. ASW
Ruler: Frederik IX **Subject:** Wedding of Princess Anne Marie **Note:** Prev. KM#M9.

Date	Mintage	F	VF	XF	Unc	BU
1964(h) C; S Proof	100	Value: 365				

X# 10 10 KRONER
20.4000 g., 0.8000 Silver 0.5247 oz. ASW
Ruler: Frederik IX **Subject:** Wedding of Princess Margrethe **Note:** Prev. KM#M10.

Date	Mintage	F	VF	XF	Unc	BU
1967(h) C; S Proof	100	Value: 385				

X# 11 10 KRONER
20.4000 g., 0.8000 Silver 0.5247 oz. ASW **Ruler:** Frederik IX **Subject:** Wedding of Princess Benedikte **Note:** Prev. KM#M11.

Date	Mintage	F	VF	XF	Unc	BU
1968(h) C; S Proof	100	Value: 375				

X# 12 10 KRONER
20.4000 g., 0.8000 Silver 0.5247 oz. ASW
Ruler: Frederik IX **Subject:** Death of Frederik IX and Accession of Margrethe II **Note:** Prev. KM#M12.

Date	Mintage	F	VF	XF	Unc	BU
1972(h) S; S Proof	100	Value: 375				

ECU COINAGE

X# 21 ECU
28.2800 g., 0.9250 Silver 0.8410 oz. ASW, 38.6 mm.
Ruler: Margrethe II **Obv:** Map of Europe
Obv. Legend: • DENMARK • EUROPE - EUROPA
Rev: Medeival sailing boat **Edge:** Reeded

Date	Mintage	F	VF	XF	Unc	BU
ND(1992)PM Proof	10,000	Value: 30.00				

X# 22 ECU
20.0000 g., 0.9990 Silver 0.6423 oz. ASW, 40 mm.
Ruler: Margrethe II **Obv:** Bronze statue of nude young lady on a boulder **Obv. Legend:** DANMARK KØBENHAVN **Rev:** Circular outer band with 12 stars, early Viking ship divides date, large value superimposed across it's sail **Edge:** Reeded

Date	Mintage	F	VF	XF	Unc	BU
1993 Proof	9,999	Value: 25.00				

X# 30 5 ECU
26.3300 g., Copper-Nickel, 38 mm. **Subject:** 550th Anniversary Founding of Copenhaven **Obv:** City shield **Obv. Legend:** DANMARK - KØBENHAVN - DÄNEMARK **Rev:** Exchange Building in Copenhaven **Rev. Legend:** BØRSEN AF KØBENHAVN **Edge:** Reeded

Date	Mintage	F	VF	XF	Unc	BU
1995	—	—	—	—	12.50	—

X# 31 20 ECU
25.0000 g., 0.9250 Silver 0.7435 oz. ASW, 38.61 mm.
Ruler: Margrethe II **Issuer:** Coin Invest Trust

Subject: 550th Anniversary of Copenhagen **Obv:** Arms **Obv. Legend:** DANMARK - KØBENHAVN - DÄNEMARK **Rev:** Young female nude "Den Lille Havfrue" sitting on boulder (Hans Christian Anderson)

Date	Mintage	F	VF	XF	Unc	BU
1995 Proof	—	Value: 25.00				

FANTASY EURO PATTERNS

INA Issues

X# Pn1 EURO CENT

Copper, 16.8 mm. **Ruler:** Margrethe II **Obv:** Mermaid of Copenhagen sitting left, sailing ship in background **Rev:** Scale at right **Edge:** Plain

Date	Mintage	F	VF	XF	Unc	BU
2002	23,000	—	—	—	—	1.50
2002 Proof	20,000	Value: 2.50				

X# Pn1a EURO CENT

Silver, 16.8 mm. **Ruler:** Margrethe II **Obv:** Mermaid of Copenhagen sitting left, sailing ship in background **Rev:** Scale at right **Edge:** Plain

Date	Mintage	F	VF	XF	Unc	BU
2002 Proof	4,500	Value: 6.00				

X# Pn2 2 EURO CENT

Copper, 18.5 mm. **Ruler:** Margrethe II **Obv:** Mermaid of Copenhagen sitting left, sailing ship in background **Rev:** Scale at right **Edge:** Plain

Date	Mintage	F	VF	XF	Unc	BU
2002	23,000	—	—	—	—	2.00
2002 Proof	20,000	Value: 3.00				

X# Pn2a 2 EURO CENT

Silver, 18.5 mm. **Ruler:** Margrethe II **Obv:** Mermaid of Copenhagen sitting left, sailing ship in background **Rev:** Scale at right **Edge:** Plain

Date	Mintage	F	VF	XF	Unc	BU
2002 Proof	4,500	Value: 7.00				

X# Pn3 5 EURO CENT

Copper, 20.7 mm. **Ruler:** Margrethe II **Obv:** Mermaid of Copenhagen sitting left, sailing ship in background **Rev:** Scale at right **Edge:** Plain

Date	Mintage	F	VF	XF	Unc	BU
2002	23,000	—	—	—	—	2.50
2002 Proof	20,000	Value: 3.50				

X# Pn3a 5 EURO CENT

Silver, 20.7 mm. **Ruler:** Margrethe II **Obv:** Mermaid of Copenhagen sitting left, sailing ship in background **Rev:** Scale at right **Edge:** Plain

Date	Mintage	F	VF	XF	Unc	BU
2002 Proof	4,500	Value: 8.50				

X# Pn4 10 EURO CENT

Brass, 19.3 mm. **Ruler:** Margrethe II **Obv:** Bust with tiara right **Rev:** Dove in flight **Edge:** Plain

Date	Mintage	F	VF	XF	Unc	BU
2002	23,000	—	—	—	—	3.00
2002 Proof	20,000	Value: 4.00				

X# Pn4a 10 EURO CENT

Silver, 19.3 mm. **Ruler:** Margrethe II **Obv:** Bust wearing tiara right **Rev:** Dove in flight **Edge:** Plain

Date	Mintage	F	VF	XF	Unc	BU
2002 Proof	4,500	Value: 10.00				

X# Pn5 20 EURO CENT

Brass, 22 mm. **Ruler:** Margrethe II **Obv:** Bust with tiara right **Rev:** Dove in flight **Edge:** Plain

Date	Mintage	F	VF	XF	Unc	BU
2002	23,000	—	—	—	—	3.50
2002 Proof	20,000	Value: 5.00				

X# Pn5a 20 EURO CENT

Silver, 22 mm. **Ruler:** Margrethe II **Obv:** Bust wearing tiara right **Rev:** Dove in flight **Edge:** Plain

Date	Mintage	F	VF	XF	Unc	BU
2002 Proof	4,500	Value: 12.50				

X# Pn6 50 EURO CENT

Brass, 24.3 mm. **Ruler:** Margrethe II **Obv:** Bust with tiara right **Rev:** Dove in flight **Edge:** Plain

Date	Mintage	F	VF	XF	Unc	BU
2002	23,000	—	—	—	—	4.00
2002 Proof	20,000	Value: 6.00				

X# Pn6a 50 EURO CENT

Silver, 24.3 mm. **Ruler:** Margrethe II **Obv:** Bust wearing tiara right **Rev:** Dove in flight

Date	Mintage	F	VF	XF	Unc	BU
2002 Proof	4,500	Value: 15.00				

X# Pn7 EURO

Bi-Metallic, 22.8 mm. **Ruler:** Margrethe II **Obv:** Bust with tiara right **Rev:** Medieval sailing ship at right **Edge:** Plain

Date	Mintage	F	VF	XF	Unc	BU
2002	23,000	—	—	—	—	6.00
2002 Proof	20,000	Value: 8.00				

X# Pn7a EURO

Bi-Metallic Silver/Brass, 22.8 mm. **Ruler:** Margrethe II **Obv:** Bust wearing tiara right **Rev:** Medieval sailing ship at right **Edge:** Plain

Date	Mintage	F	VF	XF	Unc	BU
2002 Proof	4,500	Value: 22.50				

X# Pn8 2 EURO

Bi-Metallic, 25.7 mm. **Ruler:** Margrethe II **Obv:** Bust with tiara right **Rev:** Medieval sailing ship at right **Edge:** Plain

Date	Mintage	F	VF	XF	Unc	BU
2002	23,000	—	—	—	—	8.00
2002 Proof	20,000	Value: 10.00				

X# Pn8a 2 EURO

Bi-Metallic Silver/Brass, 25.7 mm. **Ruler:** Margrethe II **Obv:** Bust wearing tiara right **Rev:** Medieval sailing ship at right **Edge:** Plain

Date	Mintage	F	VF	XF	Unc	BU
2002 Proof	4,500	Value: 28.50				

X# Pn9 5 EURO

Goldine, 36 mm. **Ruler:** Margrethe II **Obv:** Bust with tiara right **Rev:** Female seated 3/4 left with Danish shield at right, sailing ship "Viking" at left **Edge:** Plain

Date	Mintage	F	VF	XF	Unc	BU
2002 Proof	20,000	Value: 12.50				

X# Pn9a 5 EURO

Silver, 36 mm. **Ruler:** Margrethe II **Obv:** Bust wearing tiara right **Rev:** Female seated 3/4 left with Danish shield at right, sailing ship "Viking" at left **Edge:** Plain

Date	Mintage	F	VF	XF	Unc	BU
2002 Proof	4,500	Value: 40.00				

PIEFORTS

X#	Date	Mintage	Identification	Mkt Val
P1	2002	2,500	5 Euro. 0.9250 Silver. 34.5000 g. X#Pn9a.	65.00

MINT SETS

X#	Date	Mintage	Identification	Issue Price	Mkt Val
XMS1	2002 (8)	23,000	X#Pn1-Pn8	—	30.00

PROOF SETS

X#	Date	Mintage	Identification	Issue Price	Mkt Val
XPS1	2002 (9)	23,000	X#Pn1-Pn9	—	50.00
XPS2	2002 (9)	20,000	X#Pn1a-Pn9a	—	150

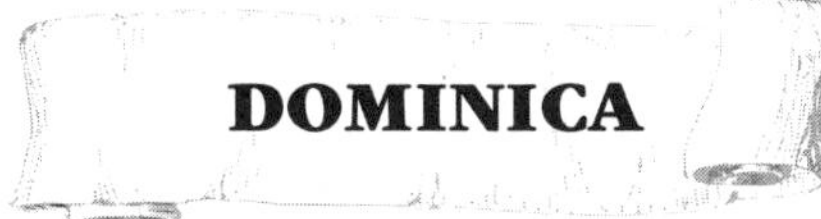

DOMINICA

BRITISH COLONY

TOKEN COINAGE

X# Tn1 10 CENTS
Brass **Obv:** Denomination **Rev:** Denomination **Note:** Prev. KM#Tn1.

Date	Mintage	VG	F	VF	XF	Unc
ND	—	10.00	20.00	40.00	60.00	75.00

DOMINICAN REPUBLIC

REPUBLIC

MEDALLIC COINAGE

X# 6 50 PESOS
31.1000 g., 0.9250 Silver 0.9249 oz. ASW **Subject:** 500th Anniversary - Discovery and Evangelization of America **Obv:** Arms **Obv. Legend:** REPUBLICA DOMINICANA **Rev:** Bust of Columbus between Santa Maria and commercial jet airplane

Date	Mintage	F	VF	XF	Unc	BU
1984 Proof	Est. 10	Value: 350				

X# 6a 50 PESOS
Brass **Subject:** 500th Anniversary - Discovery and Evangelization of America **Obv:** Arms **Obv. Legend:** REPUBLICA DOMINICANA **Rev:** Bust of Columbus between Santa Maria and commercial jet airplane

Date	Mintage	F	VF	XF	Unc	BU
1984 Proof	Est. 10	Value: 200				

X# 6b 50 PESOS
Gilt Brass **Subject:** 500th Anniversary - Discovery and Evangelization of America **Obv:** Arms **Obv. Legend:** REPUBLICA DOMINICANA **Rev:** Bust of Columbus between Santa Maria and commercial jet airplane

Date	Mintage	F	VF	XF	Unc	BU
1984 Proof	Est. 10	Value: 200				

X# 6c 50 PESOS
Aluminum **Subject:** 500th Anniversary - Discovery and Evangelization of America **Obv:** Arms **Obv. Legend:** REPUBLICA DOMINICANA **Rev:** Bust of Columbus between Santa Maria and commercial jet airplane

Date	Mintage	F	VF	XF	Unc	BU
1984 Proof	Est. 10	Value: 200				

X# 3 100 PESOS (Troy Onza)
31.1000 g., 0.9990 Gold 0.9988 oz. AGW **Subject:** Enriquillo **Note:** Prev. KM#M3.

Date	Mintage	F	VF	XF	Unc	BU
1980 Proof	Est. 15	Value: 1,500				

X# 3a 100 PESOS (Troy Onza)
Silver **Subject:** Enriquillo **Note:** Prev. KM#3.

Date	Mintage	F	VF	XF	Unc	BU
1980 Proof	Est. 40	Value: 75.00				

X# 3b 100 PESOS (Troy Onza)
Bronze **Subject:** Enriquillo **Note:** Prev. KM#M3b.

Date	Mintage	F	VF	XF	Unc	BU
1980 Proof	Est. 40	Value: 35.00				

X# 3c 100 PESOS (Troy Onza)
Aluminum **Note:** Prev. KM#M3b.

Date	Mintage	F	VF	XF	Unc	BU
1980 Proof	40	Value: 25.00				

X# 4.1 100 PESOS (Troy Onza)
10.0000 g., 0.9000 Silver 0.2893 oz. ASW **Subject:** Human Rights **Note:** Prev. KM#M4.

Date	Mintage	F	VF	XF	Unc	BU
1983 Proof	Est. 12	Value: 45.00				

X# 4a 100 PESOS (Troy Onza)
0.9000 Gold **Subject:** Human Rights

Date	Mintage	F	VF	XF	Unc	BU
1983 Proof	—	—	—	—	—	—

X# 2 200 PESOS
31.1000 g., 0.9000 Gold 0.8999 oz. AGW, 38 mm. **Subject:** 100th Anniversary - Discovery of Columbus' Remains **Obv:** Arms in sprays **Rev:** Portrait of Colombus, sprays below at left, church at right **Rev. Legend:** CENTENARIO DEL HALLAZGO DE LOS RESTOS DE COLON **Edge:** Reeded **Note:** Prev. KM#M2a.

Date	Mintage	F	VF	XF	Unc	BU
1977 Proof	Est. 10	Value: 750				

X# 2a 200 PESOS
31.1000 g., 0.9000 Silver 0.8999 oz. ASW, 38 mm. **Subject:** 100th Anniversary - Discovery of Columbus' Remains **Obv:** Arms in sprays **Rev:** Portrait of Columbus, sprays below at left, church at right **Rev. Legend:** CENTENARIO DEL HALLAZGO DE LOS RESTOS DE COLON **Edge:** Reeded **Note:** Prev. KM#M2.

Date	Mintage	F	VF	XF	Unc	BU
1977 Proof	Est. 40	Value: 70.00				

X# 2b 200 PESOS
Bronze, 38 mm. **Subject:** 100th Anniversary - Discovery of Columbus' Remains **Obv:** Arms in sprays **Rev:** Portrait of Columbus, sprays below at left, church at right **Rev. Legend:** CENTENARIO DEL HALLAZGO DE LOS RESTOS DE COLON **Edge:** Reeded **Note:** Prev. KM#M2b.

Date	Mintage	F	VF	XF	Unc	BU
1977 Proof	Est. 40	Value: 35.00				

X# 2c 200 PESOS
Aluminum, 38 mm. **Subject:** 100th Anniversary - Discovery of Columbus' Remains **Obv:** Arms in sprays **Rev:** Portrait of Columbus, sprays below at left, church at right **Rev. Legend:** CENTENARIO DEL HALLAZGO DE LOS RESTOS DE COLON **Edge:** Reeded **Note:** Prev. KM#M2c.

Date	Mintage	F	VF	XF	Unc	BU
1977 Proof	Est. 40	Value: 25.00				

X# 2d 200 PESOS
31.1000 g., 0.9000 Platinum 0.8999 oz. APW, 38 mm. **Obv:** Arms in sprays **Rev:** Portrait of Columbus, sprays below at left, church at right **Rev. Legend:** CENTENARIO DEL HALLAZGO DE LOS RESTOS DE COLON **Edge:** Reeded

Date	Mintage	F	VF	XF	Unc	BU
1977 Proof	—	Value: 1,750				

Note: Estimated mintage 5-10

X# 5 300 PESOS
Silver, 30 mm. **Subject:** Human Rights **Obv:** Arms **Obv. Legend:** * REPUBLICA DOMINICANA

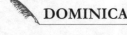

Rev: Three jugate heads right **Rev. Legend:** * CUNA DE LOS DERECHOS HUMANOS * - MUNTE SIMOS * ENRIQUILLO * LEMBA

Date	Mintage	F	VF	XF	Unc	BU
1983 Proof	—	Value: 65.00				

X# 5a 300 PESOS

Silver, 30 mm. **Subject:** Human Rights **Obv:** Arms **Obv. Legend:** * REPUBLICA DOMINICANA **Rev:** Three jugate heads right **Rev. Legend:** * CUNA DE LOS DERECHOS HUMANOS * - MUNTE SIMOS * ENRIQUILLO * LEMBA **Note:** Prev. KM#M5.

Date	Mintage	F	VF	XF	Unc	BU
1983 Proof	—	Value: 65.00				

X# 5b 300 PESOS

Copper, 30 mm. **Subject:** Human Rights **Obv:** Arms **Obv. Legend:** * REPUBLICA DOMINICANA **Rev:** Three jugate heads right **Rev. Legend:** * CUNA DE LOS DERECHOS HUMANOS * - MUNTE SIMOS * ENRIQUILLO * LEMBA **Note:** Piefort.

Date	Mintage	F	VF	XF	Unc	BU
1983 Proof	—	Value: 80.00				

X# 5c 300 PESOS

Silver, 30 mm. **Subject:** Human Rights **Obv:** Arms **Obv. Legend:** * REPUBLICA DOMINICANA **Rev:** Three jugate heads right **Rev. Legend:** * CUNA DE LOS DERECHOS HUMANOS * - MUNTE SIMOS * ENRIQUILLO * LEMBA **Note:** Piefort.

Date	Mintage	F	VF	XF	Unc	BU
1983 Proof	—	Value: 110				

X# 1 500 PESOS

Gold, 40.1 mm. **Subject:** Visit of Juan Carlos and Sofia of Spain **Obv:** Arms **Obv. Legend:** REPUBLICA DOMINICANA **Rev:** Jugate busts left **Rev. Legend:** JUAN CARLOS I Y SOFIA / REYES DE ESPAÑA-PRIMER VIAJE A AMERICA / SANTO DOMINGO - MAYO 1976 **Note:** Prev. KM#M1a.

Date	Mintage	F	VF	XF	Unc	BU
1976 Proof	Est. 10	Value: 800				

X# 1a 500 PESOS

Silver, 40.1 mm. **Subject:** Visit of Juan Carlos and Sofia of Spain **Obv:** Arms **Obv. Legend:** REPUBLICA DOMINICANA **Rev:** Jugate busts left **Rev. Legend:** JUAN CARLOS I Y SOFIA / REYES DE ESPAÑA-PRIMER VIAJE A AMERICA / SANTO DOMINGO - MAYO 1976 **Note:** Prev. KM#M1.

Date	Mintage	F	VF	XF	Unc	BU
1976 Proof	Est. 40	Value: 75.00				

X# 1b 500 PESOS

Bronze, 40.1 mm. **Subject:** Visit of Juan Carlos and Sofia of Spain **Obv:** Arms **Obv. Legend:** REPUBLICA DOMINICANA **Rev:** Jugate busts left **Rev. Legend:** JUAN CARLOS I Y SOFIA / REYES DE ESPAÑA-PRIMER VIAJE A AMERICA / SANTO DOMINGO - MAYO 1976 **Note:** Prev. KM#M1c.

Date	Mintage	F	VF	XF	Unc	BU
1976 Proof	Est. 40	Value: 30.00				

X# 1c 500 PESOS

Aluminum, 40.1 mm. **Subject:** Visit of Juan Carlos and Sofia of Spain **Obv:** Arms **Obv. Legend:** REPUBLICA DOMINICANA **Rev:** Jugate busts left **Rev. Legend:** JUAN CARLOS I Y SOFIA / REYES DE ESPAÑA-PRIMER VIAJE A AMERICA / SANTO DOMINGO - MAYO 1976 **Note:** Prev. KM#M1d.

Date	Mintage	F	VF	XF	Unc	BU
1976 Proof	Est. 40	Value: 20.00				

X# 1d 500 PESOS

Platinum APW, 40.1 mm. **Subject:** Visit of Juan Carlos and Sofia of Spain **Obv:** Arms **Obv. Legend:** REPUBLICA DOMINICANA **Rev:** Jugate busts left **Rev. Legend:** JUAN CARLOS I Y SOFIA / REYES DE ESPAÑA-PRIMER VIAJE A AMERICA / SANTO DOMINGO - MAYO 1976 **Note:** Prev. KM#M1b.

Date	Mintage	F	VF	XF	Unc	BU
1976 Proof	—	—	—	—	—	—

X# 7 500 PESOS

0.9000 Gold **Subject:** 500th Anniversary - Discovery of America **Obv:** Arms **Rev:** Bust of Columbus right **Note:** Similar to KM#M6.

Date	Mintage	F	VF	XF	Unc	BU
1984 Proof	Est. 10	Value: 800				

X# 7a 500 PESOS

Aluminum **Subject:** 500th Anniversary - Discovery of America **Obv:** Arms **Rev:** Bust of Columbus right **Note:** Similar to KM#M6.

Date	Mintage	F	VF	XF	Unc	BU
1984 Proof	Est. 10	Value: 250				

MEDALLIC BULLION COINAGE

X# 25 5 OUNCES

155.5150 g., 0.9990 Silver 4.9947 oz. ASW, 68 mm. **Subject:** 500th Anniversary Columbus Discovers America **Note:** Illustration reduced.

Date	Mintage	F	VF	XF	Unc	BU
1987Mo Proof	—	Value: 165				

PIEFORTS

X#	Date	Mintage	Identification	Mkt Val
P1	1976	10	500 Pesos. Silver. X1.	145
P2	1976	10	500 Pesos. Goldine. X1.	110
P3	1976	—	500 Pesos. Copper. X1.	100
P4	1977	10	200 Pesos. Silver. Plain edge. X2.	130
P5	1977	—	200 Pesos. Goldine. Plain edge. X2.	120
P6	1980	10	100 Pesos. Silver. Plain edge. X3.	150

TRIAL STRIKES

With "PRUEBA"

X#	Date	Mintage	Identification	Mkt Val
TS1	1983	—	100 Pesos. Silver. Obverse. X4.	50.00
TS2	1983	—	100 Pesos. Silver. Reverse. X4.	50.00
TS3	1983	—	100 Pesos. Copper. Obverse. X4.	30.00
TS4	1983	—	100 Pesos. Copper. Obverse. X4.	30.00
TS5	1983	—	300 Pesos. Silver. Obverse. X5.	60.00
TS6	1983	—	300 Pesos. Silver. Reverse. X5.	60.00
TS7	1983	—	300 Pesos. Copper. Obverse. X5.	35.00
TS8	1983	—	300 Pesos. Copper. Reverse. X5.	35.00

EAST CARIBBEAN STATES

BRITISH CARIBBEAN TERRITORIES

TRIAL STRIKES

X# ts2 10 CENTS

20.1400 g., Copper-Nickel, 37.8 mm. **Ruler:** Elizabeth II **Rev:** Sir Francis Drake's ship "Golden Hind" **Edge:** Plain **Note:** With "Model".

Date	Mintage	F	VF	XF	Unc	BU
1955 (1991) Proof	—	Value: 20.00				

X# TS1 10 CENTS

18.8100 g., Bronze, 37.9 mm. **Ruler:** Elizabeth II **Rev:** Sir Francis Drake's ship "Golden Hind" **Edge:** Plain **Note:** With "MODEL"

Date	Mintage	F	VF	XF	Unc	BU
1955 (1991) Proof	—	Value: 15.00				

ECUADOR

REPUBLIC

MEDALLIC BULLION

X# MB5 50 REALES / 5 OUNCE

155.5150 g., 0.9990 Silver 4.9947 oz. ASW, 65 mm. **Obv:** Oval arms **Obv. Legend:** ISLAS GALAPAGOS **Rev:** Galapagos tortoise **Note:** Illustration reduced.

Date	Mintage	F	VF	XF	Unc	BU
1987 Proof	—	Value: 135				

EGYPT

OTTOMAN EMPIRE

1595 - 1914AD

AHMED III

AH1115-1143/1703-1730AD

MEDALLIC COINAGE

Mint: Misr

X# M1 1-1/2 JEDID ZHEIRLI

6.0800 g., Gold, 33 mm. **Obv:** Toughra in beaded circle above foliage **Rev:** Mint name in beaded circle above foliage **Note:** Created as jewelry.

Date	Mintage	VG	F	VF	XF	Unc
AH1115 Rare	—	—	—	—	—	—

Mint: Misr

X# M2 4 FINDIK

13.3400 g., Gold, 51 mm. **Obv:** Large toughra surrounded by six smaller toughras, all in beaded circles **Rev:** Large mint name surrounded by six smaller mint names, all in beaded circles **Note:** Created as jewelry.

Date	Mintage	VG	F	VF	XF	Unc
AH1115 Rare	—	—	—	—	—	—

OTTOMAN EMPIRE

Resumed

TOKEN COINAGE

Borel Lavalley et Cie

Mint: Without Mint Name

X# Tn31 5 FRANCS

Brass **Obv:** Clipper ship **Obv. Legend:** TRAVANX DU CANAL DE SUEZ - EGYPTE **Rev:** Large value "5" **Rev. Legend:** BOREL LAVALLEY ET COMPLE **Note:** A modern copy.

Date	Mintage	VG	F	VF	XF	Unc
1865 (1970)	400	—	—	—	20.00	—

Mint: Without Mint Name

X# Tn31a 5 FRANCS

Bronze **Obv:** Clipper ship **Obv. Legend:** TRAVANX DU CANAL DE SUEZ - EGYPTE **Rev:** Large value "5" **Rev. Legend:** BOREL LAVALLEY ET COMPLE **Note:** A modern copy.

Date	Mintage	VG	F	VF	XF	Unc
1865 (1970)	200	—	—	—	35.00	50.00

BRITISH OCCUPATION

AH1333-1341 / 1914-1922AD

FUAD I

As Sultan, AH1335-1341/1917-1922AD

TOKEN COINAGE

Mint: Without Mint Name

X# Tn15 8 REALES

24.8300 g., Silver, 41 mm. **Issuer:** Saga-Saad Meawad **Obv:** Laureate bust of Ferdinand VII right **Obv. Legend:** FERDIN•VII•DEI•GRATIA **Rev:** Crowned arms between pillars **Note:** Imitation of Spanish Colonial 8 Reales.

Date	Mintage	Good	VG	F	VF	XF
1920	—	25.00	60.00	150	250	—

KINGDOM

AH1341-1372 / 1922-1952AD

TOKEN COINAGE

Mint: Without Mint Name

X# Tn25 2 REALES

Silver, 28.5 mm. **Obv:** Laureate bust of Charles IV right **Obv. Legend:** CAROLUS IIII DEI GRATIA **Rev:** Crowned arms between pillars **Rev. Legend:** • HISPAN • ET IND • REX • **Note:** Imitation of Spanish Colonial Lima Mint 2 Reales. Hallmarked: cat, "b"--20.

Date	Mintage	Good	VG	F	VF	XF
1799JJ LIMEA monogram	—	12.50	25.00	45.00	75.00	—

Mint: Without Mint Name

X# Tn27 8 REALES

Brass, 41 mm. **Issuer:** Mahmod Rashed, Cairo **Obv:** Laureate bust of Ferdinand VII right **Obv. Legend:** FERDIN VII DEI GRATIA **Rev:** Crowned arms between pillars **Rev. Legend:** MAHMOD RASHED CAIRO SAGA (retrograde S) **Note:** Imitation of Spanish Colonial 8 Reales.

Date	Mintage	F	VF	XF	Unc
1990 retrograde 9's	—	75.00	125	—	—

Mint: Without Mint Name

X# Tn23 8 REALES

Silver, 41 mm. **Issuer:** Saad Meawad, Cairo **Obv:** Laureate bust of Ferdinand VII right **Obv. Legend:** FERDIN (retrograde N) VII DEI GRATIA **Rev:** Crowned arms between pillars **Rev. Legend:** CAIRO SAGA SAAD MEAWAD **Note:** Imitation of Spanish Colonial 8 Reales.

Date	Mintage	Good	VG	F	VF	XF
1920	—	25.00	60.00	150	250	—

Mint: Without Mint Name
X# Tn19 2 REALES
2.4000 g., Billon, 28.15 mm. **Issuer:** Saad Meawad, Cairo **Obv:** Laureate bust of Ferdinand VII right **Obv. Legend:** SAAD - MEAWAD.CAIRO. **Rev:** Crowned arms between pillars **Rev. Legend:** MEDAILLE • FANTAISIL • **Edge:** Plain **Note:** Imitation of Spanish Colonial 2 Reales.

Date	Mintage	Good	VG	F	VF	XF
ND	—	12.50	25.00	45.00	75.00	—

Mint: Without Mint Name
X# Tn17 2 REALES
3.4800 g., Billon, 28.63 mm. **Issuer:** Akhouan Nassi, Cairo **Obv:** Laureate bust of Charles III right **Obv. Legend:** AKHOUAN • NASSI • CAIRE • SA **Rev:** Crowned arms between pillars **Rev. Legend:** MEDAILLE • ... • ET CAIRE **Edge:** Plain **Note:** Imitation of Spanish Colonial 2 Reales. Hallmarked.

Date	Mintage	Good	VG	F	VF	XF
ND	—	12.50	25.00	45.00	75.00	—

Mint: Without Mint Name
X# Tn21 2 REALES
4.4300 g., Billon, 28.62 mm. **Issuer:** Sdim Moussa Levy **Obv:** Laureate bust of Charles IV right **Obv. Legend:** SELIM • MOUSSA • LEVY • **Rev:** Crowned arms between pillars **Rev. Legend:** • MEDAILLE FANTAISIE • ETC • **Edge:** Plain **Note:** Imitation of Spanish Colonial 2 Reales. Hallmarked.

Date	Mintage	Good	VG	F	VF	XF
ND	—	12.50	25.00	45.00	75.00	—

ARAB REPUBLIC

AH1391- / 1971- AD

MEDALLIC BULLION COINAGE

Mint: Without Mint Name
X# MB11 60 PIASTRES
5.8000 g., Gold, 21.7 mm. **Obv:** Bust of Queen Nefertiti right **Rev:** Rising sun, palm trees, pyramids **Edge:** Reeded

Date	Mintage	F	VF	XF	Unc
ND	—	—	—	—	—

Note: Very unusual unidentifiable legends

Mint: Cairo
X# MB2 5 OUNCES
155.5150 g., 0.9990 Silver 4.9947 oz. ASW, 67 mm. **Subject:** Ancient Rulers **Obv:** Ancient stylized eagle **Rev:** Bust of Cleopatra VII left **Note:** Illustration reduced

Date	Mintage	F	VF	XF	Unc
AH1407(1987)	—	—	—	—	100

Mint: Cairo
X# MB1 5 OUNCES
155.5150 g., 0.9990 Silver 4.9947 oz. ASW, 67 mm. **Subject:** Ancient Rulers **Obv:** Ancient stylized eagle **Rev:** Mask of Tutankhamen **Note:** Illustration reduced.

Date	Mintage	F	VF	XF	Unc
AH1407(1987)	—	—	—	—	100

Mint: Cairo
X# MB3 5 OUNCES
155.5150 g., 0.9990 Silver 4.9947 oz. ASW, 67 mm. **Subject:** Ancient Rulers **Obv:** Ancient stylized eagle **Rev:** Bust of Nefertiti right **Note:** Illustration reduced

Date	Mintage	F	VF	XF	Unc
AH1407 (1987)	—	—	—	—	100

EL SALVADOR

SANTA ANA LA GRANDE

MEDALLIC COINAGE

X# M1 REAL
Silver **Note:** Prev. KM#M1. Struck for Ferdinand VII as the new king of Spain while he was under Napoleonic French guard.

Date	Mintage	F	VF	XF	Unc	BU
1808	—	35.00	60.00	100	185	—

VICE-ROYALTY OF NEW SPAIN

MEDALLIC COINAGE

X# M2 REAL
Silver **Obv. Legend:** FERNANDO • VII • REY • DE •

ESP • IN DIAS • * **Rev. Legend:** PROCLAMADO • EN • S • SALVADOR • DE • G • **Note:** Prev. KM#M2.

Date	Mintage	F	VF	XF	Unc	BU
1808	—	30.00	55.00	90.00	175	—

X# M3 2 REALES

Silver **Obv. Legend:** A FERNANDO * VII * ANO * I * DE SU REINA * **Rev. Legend:** PROCLAMADO EN LA • N • C • DES • SALVADOR • EN GUATEM • **Note:** Prev. KM#M3.

Date	Mintage	F	VF	XF	Unc	BU
1808 PGA	—	30.00	55.00	95.00	180	—

X# M4 2 REALES

Silver **Obv. Legend:** A FERNANDO * VII * ANO * I * DE SU REYN * **Rev. Legend:** PROCLAMADO EN LA • N • C • DES • SALVADOR • EN GUATEM * **Note:** Prev. KM#M4.

Date	Mintage	F	VF	XF	Unc	BU
1808 PGA	—	35.00	60.00	100	185	—

REPUBLIC OF EL SALVADOR

MEDALLIC COINAGE

General Barrios Series

Originals were struck in Bronze and silver in 1861. These restrikes were produced about 1971.

X# 5 PESO

Copper **Subject:** General Barrios **Obv:** Arms **Rev:** Head right

Date	Mintage	F	VF	XF	Unc	BU
1861 Proof	—	Value: 125				

X# 5a PESO

Aluminum **Subject:** General Barrios **Edge:** Reeded

Date	Mintage	F	VF	XF	Unc	BU
1861 Proof	—	Value: 85.00				

X# 5b PESO

Aluminum **Subject:** General Barrios **Edge:** Plain

Date	Mintage	F	VF	XF	Unc	BU
1861 Proof	—	Value: 85.00				

X# 5c PESO

Silver **Subject:** General Barrios

Date	Mintage	F	VF	XF	Unc	BU
1861 Proof	—	Value: 150				

X# 5d PESO

Gold **Subject:** General Barrios

Date	Mintage	F	VF	XF	Unc	BU
1861 Proof; Rare	—	—	—	—	—	—

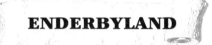

ENDERBYLAND

AUSTRALIAN ANTARCTIC TERRITORY

FANTASY COINAGE

X# 1 SOVEREIGN

Brass, 25.5 mm. **Obv:** Arrowed symbol **Obv. Legend:** ANTARCTIC TERRITORY **Obv. Designer:** Fred Zinkann **Rev:** Enflamed Runic symbol **Edge:** Plain

Date	Mintage	F	VF	XF	Unc	BU
1990	250	—	—	9.50	30.00	—

X# 1a SOVEREIGN

Aluminum, 26.1 mm. **Obv:** Arrowed symbol **Obv. Legend:** ANTARCTIC TERRITORY **Obv. Designer:** Fred Zinkann **Rev:** Enflamed Runic symbol **Edge:** Plain

Date	Mintage	F	VF	XF	Unc	BU
1990 (2004 restrike)	250	—	—	10.00	20.00	—

X# 1b SOVEREIGN

Copper, 25.35 mm. **Obv:** Arrowed symbol **Obv. Legend:** ANTARCTIC TERRITORY **Obv. Designer:** Fred Zinkann **Rev:** Enflamed Runic symbol **Edge:** Plain

Date	Mintage	F	VF	XF	Unc	BU
1990 (2004 restrike)	250	—	—	9.50	25.00	—

X# 2 SOVEREIGN

Copper-Nickel Clad Copper, 25.5 mm. **Obv:** Arrowed symbol **Obv. Legend:** ANTARCTIC TERRITORY **Obv. Designer:** Fred Zinkann **Rev:** Enflamed Runic symbol **Edge:** Plain **Note:** Counterstamped on U.S. quarter dollar.

Date	Mintage	F	VF	XF	Unc	BU
1990	—	—	—	12.50	15.00	—

PATTERNS

X#	Date	Mintage	Identification	Mkt Val
Pn1	1990	5	Sovereign. Copper Alloys. X#1.	50.00
Pn2	1990	5	Sovereign. Copper-Nickel. X#1.	50.00
Pn3	1990	5	Sovereign. 0.9950 Molybdenum. X#1.	125
Pn4	1990	1	Sovereign. Niobium. X#1.	—
Pn5	1990	5	Sovereign. Palladium. X#1.	200
Pn6	1990	3	Sovereign. Titanium. X#1.	110
Pn7	1990	5	Sovereign. 0.9990 Silver. X#1.	85.00
Pn8	1990	1	Sovereign. 0.7500 Gold. X#1.	—
Pn9	1990	—	Sovereign. Steel. X#1.	—

TRIAL STRIKES

X#	Date	Mintage	Identification	Mkt Val
TS1	1990	30	Sovereign. 0.9950 Molybdenum. Obverse, X#1.	15.00
TS2	ND(1990)	30	Sovereign. 0.9950 Molybdenum. Reverse, X#1.	15.00

EQUATORIAL GUINEA

REPUBLIC

MEDALLIC COINAGE

Banco Central Issues

X# M1 1000 BIPKWELE

12.5900 g., 0.9250 Silver 0.3744 oz. ASW, 34.4 mm. **Subject:** 1979 Spanish Royalty Visit **Obv:** Arms **Obv. Legend:** REPUBLICA DE GUINEA ECUATORIAL **Rev:** Jugate busts of Juan Carlos and Sofia left **Rev. Legend:** S.S.M.M. LOS REYES DE ESPÃNA VISTAN GUINEA **Note:** Previous KM#M1.

Date	Mintage	F	VF	XF	Unc	BU
(19)80	5,125	—	—	—	20.00	—
(19)80 Proof	3,000	Value: 27.50				

X# M5 1000 BIPKWELE

12.5900 g., 0.9250 Silver 0.3744 oz. ASW, 34.4 mm. **Subject:** 1979 Spanish Royalty Visit **Obv:** Arms **Obv. Legend:** REPUBLICA DE GUINEA ECUATORIAL **Rev:** Bust of Juan Carlos left **Rev. Legend:** S.M. DON JUAN CARLOS I VISITA GUINEA **Note:** Previous KM#M2.

Date	Mintage	F	VF	XF	Unc	BU
(19)80	5,125	—	—	—	20.00	—
(19)80 Proof	3,000	Value: 27.50				

X# M2 2000 BIPKWELE

25.0000 g., 0.9250 Silver 0.7435 oz. ASW, 40.7 mm. **Subject:** 1979 Spanish Royalty Visit **Obv:** Arms **Obv. Legend:** REPUBLICA DE GUINEA ECUATORIAL **Rev:** Jugate busts of Juan Carlos and Sofia left **Rev. Legend:** S.S.M.M. LOS REYES DE ESPAÑA VISITAN GUINEA **Note:** Previous KM#M3.

Date	Mintage	F	VF	XF	Unc	BU
(19)80	5,125	—	—	—	25.00	—
(19)80 Proof	3,000	Value: 30.00				

X# M6 2000 BIPKWELE
25.0000 g., 0.9250 Silver 0.7435 oz. ASW, 40.7 mm. **Subject:** 1979 Spanish Royalty Visit **Obv:** Arms **Obv. Legend:** REPUBLICA DE GUINEA ECUATORIAL **Rev:** Bust of Juan Carlos left **Rev. Legend:** S.M. DON JUAN CARLOS I VISITA GUINEA **Note:** Prev. KM#M4.

Date	Mintage	F	VF	XF	Unc	BU
(19)80	5,125	—	—	—	25.00	—
(19)80 Proof	3,000	Value: 30.00				

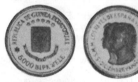

X# M3 5000 BIPKWELE
4.0000 g., 0.9170 Gold 0.1179 oz. AGW, 20 mm. **Subject:** 1979 Spanish Royalty Visit **Obv:** Arms **Rev:** Jugate busts of Juan Carlos and Sofia left **Rev. Legend:** S.S.M.LOS REYES DE ESPAÑA VISITAN GUINEA **Note:** Previous KM#M5.

Date	Mintage	F	VF	XF	Unc	BU
(19)80	4,250	—	—	—	110	—
(19)80 Proof	2,000	Value: 150				

X# M7 5000 BIPKWELE
4.0000 g., 0.9170 Gold 0.1179 oz. AGW, 20 mm. **Subject:** 1979 Spanish Royalty Visit **Obv:** Arms **Obv. Legend:** REPUBLICA DE GUINEA ECUATORIAL **Rev:** Bust of Juan Carlos left **Note:** Prev. KM#M6.

Date	Mintage	F	VF	XF	Unc	BU
(19)80	4,250	—	—	—	110	—
(19)80 Proof	2,000	Value: 150				

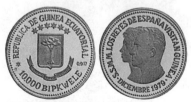

X# M4 10000 BIPKWELE
8.0000 g., 0.9170 Gold 0.2358 oz. AGW, 24 mm. **Subject:** 1979 Spanish Royalty Visit **Obv:** Arms **Obv. Legend:** REPUBLICA DE GUINEA ECUATORIAL **Rev:** Jugate busts of Juan Carlos and Sofia left **Rev. Legend:** S.S.M.M.LOS REYES DE ESPAÑA VISITAN GUINEA **Note:** Prev. KM#M7.

Date	Mintage	F	VF	XF	Unc	BU
(19)80	4,250	—	—	—	220	—
(19)80 Proof	2,000	Value: 300				

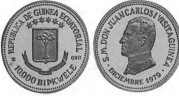

X# M8 10000 BIPKWELE
8.0000 g., 0.9170 Gold 0.2358 oz. AGW, 24 mm. **Subject:** 1979 Spanish Royalty Visit **Obv:** Arms **Obv. Legend:** REPUBLICA DE GUINEA ECUATORIAL **Rev:** Bust of Juan Carlos left **Rev. Legend:** S.M. DON JUAN CARLOS I VISITA GUINEA **Note:** Prev. KM#M8.

Date	Mintage	F	VF	XF	Unc	BU
(19)80	4,250	—	—	—	220	—
(19)80 Proof	2,000	Value: 300				

PATTERNS

Including off metal strikes

KM# Pn17 1000 FRANCOS
26.4000 g., Copper-Nickel, 38.2 mm. **Subject:** UN 50 Years **Obv:** National arms **Rev:** Large "UN" letters with German inscription on UN logo **Edge:** Reeded **Note:** First reported in World Coin News Round-up in August 2003

Date	Mintage	F	VF	XF	Unc	BU
1995 Proof	—	Value: 100				

PATTERNS

Including off metal strikes

X#	Date	Mintage	Identification	Mkt Val
Pn1	(19)80	—	1000 Bipkwele. Copper. X#M1.	20.00
Pn2	(19)80	—	1000 Bipkwele. Aluminum. X#M1.	15.00
Pn3	(19)80	—	1000 Bipkwele. 0.9170 Gold. X#M1.	125
Pn4	(19)80	—	1000 Bipkwele. Copper. X#M5.	20.00
Pn5	(19)80	—	1000 Bipkwele. Aluminum. X#M5.	—
Pn6	(19)80	—	1000 Bipkwele. 0.9170 Gold. X#M5.	125
Pn7	(19)80	—	2000 Bipkwele. Copper. X#M2.	30.00
Pn8	(19)80	—	2000 Bipkwele. Aluminum. X#M2.	25.00
Pn9	(19)80	—	2000 Bipkwele. 0.9170 Gold. X#M2.	—
Pn10	(19)80	—	2000 Bipkwele. Copper. X#M6.	30.00
Pn11	(19)80	—	2000 Bipkwele. Aluminum. X#M6.	20.00
Pn12	(19)80	—	2000 Bipkwele. 0.9170 Gold. X#M6.	—
Pn13	(19)80	—	5000 Bipkwele. Copper. 34 mm. Juan Carlos and Sofia.	35.00
Pn14	(19)80	—	5000 Bipkwele. Aluminum. 34 mm. Juan Carlos and Sofia.	25.00
Pn15	(19)80	—	5000 Bipkwele. Copper. 34 mm. Juan Carlos.	35.00
Pn16	(19)80	—	5000 Bipkwele. Aluminum. 34 mm. Juan Carlos.	25.00
Pn17	(19)80	—	5000 Bipkwele. Copper. X#M3.	20.00
Pn18	(19)80	—	5000 Bipkwele. Aluminum. X#M3.	15.00
Pn19	(19)80	—	5000 Bipkwele. Copper. X#M7.	20.00
Pn20	(19)80	—	5000 Bipkwele. Aluminum. X#M7.	15.00
Pn21	(19)80	—	10000 Bipkwele. Copper. 40.7 mm. Juan Carlos and Sofia.	30.00
Pn22	(19)80	—	10000 Bipkwele. Aluminum. 40.7 mm. Juan Carlos and Sofia.	20.00

X#	Date	Mintage	Identification	Mkt Val
Pn23	(19)80	—	10000 Bipkwele. Copper. 40.7 mm. Juan Carlos.	30.00
Pn24	(19)80	—	10000 Bipkwele. Aluminum. 40.7 mm. Juan Carlos.	20.00
Pn25	(19)80	—	10000 Bipkwele. Copper. X#M4.	30.00
Pn26	(19)80	—	10000 Bipkwele. Aluminum. X#M4.	20.00
Pn27	(19)80	—	10000 Bipkwele. Copper. X#M8.	—
Pn28	(19)80	—	10000 Bipkwele. Aluminum. X#M8.	20.00

PIEFORTS

X#	Date	Mintage	Identification	Issue Price	Mkt Val
P48	(19)80	—	5000 Bipkwele. Goldine/Copper. 34 mm. Juan Carlos. Plain edge.	—	—

X#	Date	Mintage	Identification	Issue Price	Mkt Val
P21	(19)80	—	1000 Bipkwele. 0.9250 Silver. 25.4900 g. Reeded edge. X#M1.	—	65.00
P22	(19)80	—	1000 Bipkwele. 0.9250 Silver. 25.4900 g. Plain edge. X#M1.	—	65.00
P23	(19)80	—	1000 Bipkwele. 0.9170 Gold. 25.5000 g. X#M1.	—	475
P24	(19)80	—	1000 Bipkwele. Copper. Reeded edge. X#M1.	—	35.00
P25	(19)80	—	1000 Bipkwele. Copper. Plain edge. X#M1.	—	35.00
P26	(19)80	—	1000 Bipkwele. Goldine/Copper. X#M1.	—	35.00
P27	(19)80	—	1000 Bipkwele. 0.9250 Silver. 25.4900 g. Reeded edge. X#M5.	—	65.00
P28	(19)80	—	1000 Bipkwele. 0.9250 Silver. 25.4900 g. Plain edge. X#M5.	—	65.00
P29	(19)80	—	1000 Bipkwele. 0.9170 Gold. 25.5000 g. X#M5.	—	475
P30	(19)80	—	1000 Bipkwele. Copper. Reeded edge. X#M5.	—	35.00
P31	(19)80	—	1000 Bipkwele. Copper. Plain edge. X#M5.	—	35.00
P32	(19)80	—	1000 Bipkwele. Goldine/Copper. X#M5.	—	35.00

X#	Date	Mintage	Identification	Issue Price	Mkt Val
P33	(19)80	—	2000 Bipkwele. 0.9250 Silver. Reeded edge. X#M2.	—	125
P34	(19)80	—	2000 Bipkwele. 0.9250 Silver. Plain edge. X#M2.	—	125
P35	(19)80	—	2000 Bipkwele. 0.9170 Gold. X#M2.	—	875
P36	(19)80	—	2000 Bipkwele. Copper. Reeded edge. X#M2.	—	55.00
P37	(19)80	—	2000 Bipkwele. Copper. Plain edge. X#M2.	—	55.00
P38	(19)80	—	2000 Bipkwele. Goldine/Copper. X#M2.	—	55.00
P39	(19)80	—	2000 Bipkwele. 0.9250 Silver. Reeded edge. X#M6.	—	125
P40	(19)80	—	2000 Bipkwele. 0.9250 Silver. Plain edge. X#M6.	—	125
P41	(19)80	—	2000 Bipkwele. Gold. X#M6.	—	875
P42	(19)80	—	2000 Bipkwele. Copper. Reeded edge. X#M6.	—	55.00
P43	(19)80	—	2000 Bipkwele. Copper. Plain edge. X#M6.	—	55.00
P44	(19)80	—	2000 Bipkwele. Goldine/Copper. X#M6.	—	55.00
P45	(19)80	—	5000 Bipkwele. 0.9250 Silver. 34 mm. Juan Carlos and Sofia. Plain edge.	—	125
P46	(19)80	—	5000 Bipkwele. Goldine/Copper. 34 mm. Juan Carlos and Sofia. Plain edge.	—	55.00
P47	(19)80	—	5000 Bipkwele. 0.9250 Silver. 34 mm. Juan Carlos. Plain edge.	—	55.00
P49	(19)80	750	5000 Bipkwele. 0.9170 Gold. X#M3.	—	400
P50	(19)80	—	5000 Bipkwele. 0.9170 Gold. X#M3.	—	70.00
P51	(19)80	—	5000 Bipkwele. 0.9170 Gold. X#M7.	—	400
P52	(19)80	—	5000 Bipkwele. Copper. X#M7.	—	70.00
P53	(19)80	—	10000 Bipkwele. 0.9250 Silver. 40.6 mm. Juan Carlos and Sofia. Plain edge.	—	200
P54	(19)80	—	10000 Bipkwele. Goldine/Copper. 40.6 mm. Juan Carlos and Sofia. Plain edge.	—	90.00
P55	(19)80	—	10000 Bipkwele. 0.9250 Silver. 40.6 mm. Juan Carlos. Plain edge.	—	200
P56	(19)80	—	10000 Bipkwele. Goldine/Copper. 40.6 mm. Juan Carlos. Plain edge.	—	90.00
P57	(19)80	—	10000 Bipkwele. 0.9170 Gold. X#M4.	—	700
P58	(19)80	—	10000 Bipkwele. Copper. X#M4.	—	85.00
P59	(19)80	—	10000 Bipkwele. 0.9170 Gold. X#M8.	—	700
P60	(19)80	—	10000 Bipkwele. Copper. X#M8.	—	85.00

TRIAL STRIKES

X#	Date	Mintage	Identification	Issue Price	Mkt Val
TS54	(19)80	—	5000 Bipkwele. 0.9250 Silver. Reverse X#M6, with PRUEBA.	—	—
TS11	(19)80	—	1000 Bipkwele. 0.9250 Silver. Obverse X#M1, with PRUEBA.	—	25.00
TS12	(19)80	—	1000 Bipkwele. 0.9250 Silver. Reverse X#M1, with PRUEBA.	—	25.00
TS13	(19)80	—	1000 Bipkwele. 0.9250 Silver. Obverse X#M1, without PRUEBA.	—	25.00
TS14	(19)80	—	1000 Bipkwele. 0.9250 Silver. Reverse X#M1, without PRUEBA.	—	25.00
TS15	(19)80	—	1000 Bipkwele. Copper. Obverse X#M1, with PRUEBA.	—	20.00
TS16	(19)80	—	1000 Bipkwele. Copper. Reverse X#M1, with PRUEBA.	—	20.00
TS17	(19)80	—	1000 Bipkwele. 0.9250 Silver. Obverse X#M5, with PRUEBA.	—	25.00
TS18	(19)80	—	1000 Bipkwele. 0.9250 Silver. Reverse X#M5, with PRUEBA.	—	25.00
TS19	(19)80	—	1000 Bipkwele. 0.9250 Silver. Obverse X#M5, without PRUEBA.	—	25.00
TS20	(19)80	—	1000 Bipkwele. 0.9250 Silver. Reverse X#M5, without PRUEBA.	—	25.00
TS21	(19)80	—	1000 Bipkwele. Copper. Obverse X#M5, with PRUEBA.	—	20.00
TS22	(19)80	—	1000 Bipkwele. Copper. Reverse X#M5, with PRUEBA.	—	20.00
TS23	(19)80	—	2000 Bipkwele. 0.9250 Silver. Obverse X#M2, with PRUEBA.	—	35.00
TS24	(19)80	—	2000 Bipkwele. 0.9250 Silver. Reverse X#M2, with PRUEBA.	—	35.00
TS25	(19)80	—	2000 Bipkwele. 0.9250 Silver. Obverse X#M2, without PRUEBA.	—	35.00
TS26	(19)80	—	2000 Bipkwele. 0.9250 Silver. Reverse X#M2, without PRUEBA.	—	35.00
TS27	(19)80	—	2000 Bipkwele. Copper. Obverse X#M2, with PRUEBA.	—	27.50
TS28	(19)80	—	2000 Bipkwele. Copper. Reverse X#M2, with PRUEBA.	—	27.50
TS29	(19)80	—	2000 Bipkwele. 0.9250 Silver. Obverse X#M6, with PRUEBA.	—	35.00
TS30	(19)80	—	2000 Bipkwele. 0.9250 Silver. Reverse X#M6, with PRUEBA.	—	35.00
TS31	(19)80	—	2000 Bipkwele. 0.9250 Silver. Obverse X#M6, without PRUEBA.	—	35.00
TS32	(19)80	—	2000 Bipkwele. 0.9250 Silver. Reverse X#M6, without PRUEBA.	—	35.00
TS33	(19)80	—	2000 Bipkwele. Copper. Obverse X#M6, with PRUEBA.	—	27.50
TS34	(19)80	—	2000 Bipkwele. Copper. Reverse X#M6, with PRUEBA.	—	27.50
TS35	(19)80	—	5000 Bipkwele. 0.9250 Silver. 34 mm. Obverse arms, with PRUEBA.	—	50.00
TS36	(19)80	—	5000 Bipkwele. 0.9250 Silver. 34 mm. Reverse Juan and Sofia, with PRUEBA.	—	50.00
TS37	(19)80	—	5000 Bipkwele. 0.9250 Silver. 34 mm. Obverse arms, without PRUEBA.	—	50.00
TS38	(19)80	—	5000 Bipkwele. 0.9250 Silver. 34 mm. Reverse Juan and Sofia, without PRUEBA.	—	50.00
TS39	(19)80	—	5000 Bipkwele. Copper. 34 mm. Obverse arms, with PRUEBA.	—	40.00
TS40	(19)80	—	5000 Bipkwele. Copper. 34 mm. Reverse Juan and Sofia, with PRUEBA.	—	40.00
TS41	(19)80	—	5000 Bipkwele. 0.9250 Silver. 34 mm. Obverse arms, with PRUEBA.	—	50.00
TS42	(19)80	—	5000 Bipkwele. 0.9250 Silver. 34 mm. Reverse Juan Carlos, with PRUEBA.	—	50.00
TS43	(19)80	—	5000 Bipkwele. 0.9250 Silver. 34 mm. Obverse arms, without PRUEBA.	—	50.00
TS44	(19)80	—	5000 Bipkwele. 0.9250 Silver. 34 mm. Reverse Juan Carlos, without PRUEBA.	—	50.00
TS45	(19)80	—	5000 Bipkwele. Copper. 34 mm. Obverse arms, with PRUEBA.	—	40.00
TS46	(19)80	—	5000 Bipkwele. Copper. 34 mm. Reverse Juan Carlos, with PRUEBA.	—	40.00
TS47	(19)80	—	5000 Bipkwele. 0.9250 Silver. Obverse X#M3, with PRUEBA.	—	25.00
TS48	(19)80	—	5000 Bipkwele. 0.9250 Silver. Reverse X#M3, with PRUEBA.	—	25.00
TS49	(19)80	—	5000 Bipkwele. 0.9250 Silver. Obverse X#M3, without PRUEBA.	—	25.00
TS50	(19)80	—	5000 Bipkwele. 0.9250 Silver. Reverse X#M3, without PRUEBA.	—	25.00
TS51	(19)80	—	5000 Bipkwele. Copper. Obverse X#M3, with PRUEBA.	—	20.00
TS52	(19)80	—	5000 Bipkwele. Copper. Reverse X#M3, with PRUEBA.	—	20.00
TS53	(19)80	—	5000 Bipkwele. 0.9250 Silver. Obverse X#M6, with PRUEBA.	—	25.00
TS55	(19)80	—	5000 Bipkwele. 0.9250 Silver. Obverse X#M6, without PRUEBA.	—	25.00
TS56	(19)80	—	5000 Bipkwele. 0.9250 Silver. Reverse X#M6, without PRUEBA.	—	25.00
TS57	(19)80	—	5000 Bipkwele. Copper. Obverse X#M6, with PRUEBA.	—	20.00
TS58	(19)80	—	5000 Bipkwele. Copper. Reverse X#M6, with PRUEBA.	—	20.00
TS59	(19)80	—	10000 Bipkwele. 0.9250 Silver. 40.6 mm. Obverse arms, with PRUEBA.	—	50.00
TS60	(19)80	—	10000 Bipkwele. 0.9250 Silver. 40.6 mm. Reverse Juan and Sofia, with PRUEBA.	—	50.00
TS61	(19)80	—	10000 Bipkwele. 0.9250 Silver. 40.6 mm. Obverse arms, without PRUEBA.	—	50.00
TS62	(19)80	—	10000 Bipkwele. 0.9250 Silver. 40.6 mm. Reverse Juan and Sofia, without PRUEBA.	—	50.00
TS63	(19)80	—	10000 Bipkwele. Copper. 40.6 mm. Obverse arms, with PRUEBA.	—	40.00

X#	Date	Mintage	Identification	Issue Price	Mkt Val
TS64	(19)80	—	10000 Bipkwele. Copper. 40.6 mm. Reverse Juan and Sofia, with PRUEBA.	—	40.00
TS65	(19)80	—	10000 Bipkwele. 0.9250 Silver. 40.6 mm. Obverse arms, with PRUEBA.	—	50.00
TS66	(19)80	—	10000 Bipkwele. 0.9250 Silver. 40.6 mm. Reverse Juan Carlos, with PRUEBA.	—	50.00
TS67	(19)80	—	10000 Bipkwele. 0.9250 Silver. 40.6 mm. Obverse arms, without PRUEBA.	—	50.00
TS68	(19)80	—	10000 Bipkwele. 0.9250 Silver. 40.6 mm. Reverse Juan Carlos, without PRUEBA.	—	50.00
TS69	(19)80	—	10000 Bipkwele. Copper. 40.6 mm. Obverse arms, with PRUEBA.	—	40.00
TS70	(19)80	—	10000 Bipkwele. Copper. 40.6 mm. Reverse Juan Carlos, with PRUEBA.	—	40.00
TS71	(19)80	—	10000 Bipkwele. 0.9250 Silver. Obverse X#M4, with PRUEBA.	—	35.00
TS72	(19)80	—	10000 Bipkwele. 0.9250 Silver. Reverse X#M4, with PRUEBA.	—	35.00
TS73	(19)80	—	10000 Bipkwele. 0.9250 Silver. Obverse X#M4, without PRUEBA.	—	35.00
TS74	(19)80	—	10000 Bipkwele. 0.9250 Silver. Reverse X#M4, without PRUEBA.	—	35.00
TS75	(19)80	—	10000 Bipkwele. Copper. Obverse X#M4, with PRUEBA.	—	27.50
TS76	(19)80	—	10000 Bipkwele. Copper. Reverse X#M4, with PRUEBA.	—	27.50
TS77	(19)80	—	10000 Bipkwele. 0.9250 Silver. Obverse X#M8, with PRUEBA.	—	35.00
TS78	(19)80	—	10000 Bipkwele. 0.9250 Silver. Reverse X#M8, with PRUEBA.	—	35.00
TS79	(19)80	—	10000 Bipkwele. 0.9250 Silver. Obverse X#M8, without PRUEBA.	—	35.00
TS80	(19)80	—	10000 Bipkwele. 0.9250 Silver. Reverse X#M8, without PRUEBA.	—	35.00
TS81	(19)80	—	10000 Bipkwele. Copper. Obverse X#M8, with PRUEBA.	—	27.50
TS82	(19)80	—	10000 Bipkwele. Copper. Reverse X#M8, with PRUEBA.	—	27.50

ESPERANTO

INTERNATIONAL LANGUAGE

FANTASY COINAGE

Spesmilo Series

X# 1 SPESMILO

Silver **Subject:** 25th Anniversary - First Publication of the Language **Note:** Struck at Holy Freres, Switzerland. Prev. KY#11.

Date	Mintage	F	VF	XF	Unc	BU
1912	—	—	—	70.00	100	—

X# 2 2 SPESMILOJ

Silver **Subject:** 25th Anniversary - First Publication of the Language **Note:** Struck at Holy Freres, Switzerland. Prev. KY#12.

Date	Mintage	F	VF	XF	Unc	BU
1912	—	—	—	125	175	—

UNIVERSAL LEAGUE

An Esperanto organization based in the Netherlands. Coins minted at Utrecht.

X# 3 STELO

Bronze, 20 mm. **Obv:** Shield with star w/rays **Obv. Legend:** UNO MONDO • UNU LINGVO • UNO MONO **Rev:** Star behind value **Rev. Legend:** UNIVERSALA LIGO **Edge:** Plain **Note:** Minted in 1960.

Date	Mintage	F	VF	XF	Unc	BU
1959 (u)	10,000	—	—	—	10.00	—

X# 4 5 STELOJ

Aluminum-Bronze **Note:** Minted in 1960.

Date	Mintage	F	VF	XF	Unc	BU
1959 (u)	10,000	—	—	—	10.00	—

X# 5 10 STELOJ

Copper-Nickel **Obv:** Bust of Dr. Zamen Hof left **Obv. Legend:** D•RO L.L.ZAMEHOF KREINTO DE ESPERANTO **Rev. Legend:** UNIVERSALA LIGO **Note:** Minted in 1960.

Date	Mintage	F	VF	XF	Unc	BU
1959 (u)	10,000	—	—	—	15.00	—

X# 6 25 STELOJ

25.0000 g., 0.9000 Silver 0.7234 oz. ASW **Obv:** Bust of Dr. Zamen Hof left **Obv. Legend:** D•RO L.L.ZAMEHOF KREINTO DE ESPERANTO **Rev. Legend:** UNIVERSALA LIGO

Date	Mintage	F	VF	XF	Unc	BU
1965 (u) Proof	5,000	Value: 50.00				

X# 7 25 STELOJ

19.0000 g., Copper-Nickel **Obv:** Bust of Dr. Zamen Hof left **Obv. Legend:** D•RO L.L.ZAMEHOF KREINTO DE ESPERANTO **Rev. Legend:** UNIVERSALA LIGO **Note:** Without "PROOF" under portrait.

Date	Mintage	F	VF	XF	Unc	BU
1965 (u) Proof	1,000	Value: 25.00				

X# 8 25 STELOJ

50.0000 g., 0.9830 Gold 1.5801 oz. AGW **Obv:** Bust of Dr. Zamen Hof left **Obv. Legend:** D•RO L.L.ZAMEHOF KREINTO DE ESPERANTO **Rev. Legend:** UNIVERSALA LIGO

Date	Mintage	F	VF	XF	Unc	BU
1965	10	—	—	—	—	1,500

Note: Individually edge numbered.

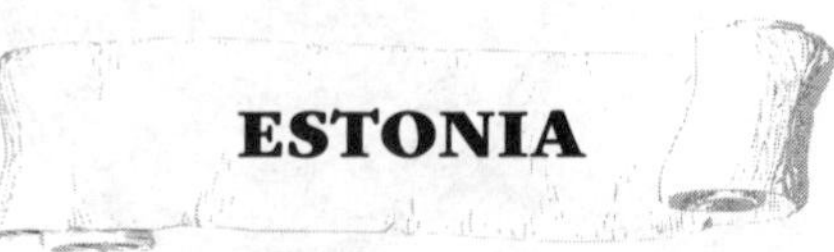

ESTONIA

GOVERNMENT IN EXILE

FANTASY COINAGE

X# 1 10 KROONI

18.0000 g., 0.9250 Silver 0.5353 oz. ASW **Subject:** General Johan Laidoner **Note:** Laidoner was Commander of the Estonian army in their 1918 War for Independence.

Date	Mintage	F	VF	XF	Unc	BU
1974	950	—	—	—	100	—

X# 2 DUCAT

3.5000 g., 0.9000 Gold 0.1013 oz. AGW **Subject:** Konstantine Paets

Date	Mintage	F	VF	XF	Unc	BU
1974	950	—	—	—	210	—

X# 2a DUCAT

Aluminum-Bronze **Subject:** Konstantine Paets

Date	Mintage	F	VF	XF	Unc	BU
1974	—	—	—	—	—	—

X# 3 DUCAT

3.5000 g., 0.9000 Gold 0.1013 oz. AGW **Subject:** Joan Tonisson

Date	Mintage	F	VF	XF	Unc	BU
1974	950	—	—	—	210	—

TOKEN COINAGE

X# Tn4 KROON

Silvered-Bronze **Obv:** Arms **Rev:** Archaic sailing ship

Date	Mintage	F	VF	XF	Unc	BU
1990	—	—	—	—	20.00	—

X# Tn5 KROON
Gilt Bronze

Date	Mintage	F	VF	XF	Unc	BU
1990	—	—	—	—	20.00	—

X# Tn6 KROON
Obv: Arms **Rev:** Archaic sailing ship

Date	Mintage	F	VF	XF	Unc	BU
1990	—	—	—	—	25.00	—

X# Tn8 25 KROONI
Copper-Nickel **Subject:** Tallinn Songfest

Date	Mintage	F	VF	XF	Unc	BU
1990	—	—	—	—	30.00	—

X# Tn9 50 KROONI
Copper-Nickel **Subject:** Tallinn Songfest

Date	Mintage	F	VF	XF	Unc	BU
1990	—	—	—	—	35.00	—

X# Tn10 100 KROONI
Copper-Nickel **Subject:** Tallinn Songfest **Note:** The Tallinn series for the songfest were issued on par with the Swedish Kronor.

Date	Mintage	F	VF	XF	Unc	BU
1990	—	—	—	—	55.00	—

MODERN REPUBLIC

1991 - present

FANTASY EURO PATTERNS

INA Series

X# Pn1 EURO CENT
4.8200 g., Copper, 16.8 mm. **Issuer:** INA **Obv:** Stars at left, arms at right **Obv. Inscription:** EESTI **Rev:** Scales at right **Edge:** Plain

Date	Mintage	F	VF	XF	Unc	BU
2004	12,500	—	—	—	—	3.00
2004 Proof	3,000	Value: 2.50				

X# Pn1a EURO CENT
Silver, 16.8 mm. **Issuer:** INA **Obv:** Stars at left, arms at right **Obv. Inscription:** EESTI **Rev:** Scales at right **Edge:** Plain

Date	Mintage	F	VF	XF	Unc	BU
2004 Proof	175	Value: 6.00				

X# Pn2 2 EURO CENT
5.7700 g., Copper, 18.5 mm. **Issuer:** INA **Obv:** Stars at left, arms at right **Obv. Inscription:** EESTI **Rev:** Scales at right **Edge:** Plain

Date	Mintage	F	VF	XF	Unc	BU
2004	12,500	—	—	—	—	4.00
2004 Proof	3,000	Value: 3.00				

X# Pn2a 2 EURO CENT
Silver, 18.5 mm. **Issuer:** INA **Obv:** Stars at left, arms at right **Obv. Inscription:** EESTI **Rev:** Scales at right **Edge:** Plain

Date	Mintage	F	VF	XF	Unc	BU
2004 Proof	175	Value: 7.00				

X# Pn3 5 EURO CENT
7.3000 g., Copper, 20.7 mm. **Issuer:** INA **Obv:** Stars at left, arms at right **Obv. Inscription:** EESTI **Rev:** Scales at right **Edge:** Plain

Date	Mintage	F	VF	XF	Unc	BU
2004	12,500	—	—	—	—	5.00
2004 Proof	3,000	Value: 3.50				

X# Pn3a 5 EURO CENT
Silver, 20.7 mm. **Issuer:** INA **Obv:** Stars at left, arms at right **Obv. Inscription:** EESTI **Rev:** Scales at right **Edge:** Plain

Date	Mintage	F	VF	XF	Unc	BU
2004 Proof	175	Value: 8.50				

X# Pn4 10 EURO CENT
6.0500 g., Goldine, 19.3 mm. **Issuer:** INA **Obv:** Bust of Karl Ernst Von Baer slightly right divides date **Obv. Legend:** EESTI VABARIIK **Rev:** Dove, value in wreath of clasped hands **Edge:** Plain

Date	Mintage	F	VF	XF	Unc	BU
2004	12,500	—	—	—	—	6.00
2004 Proof	3,000	Value: 4.00				

X# Pn4a 10 EURO CENT
Silver, 19.3 mm. **Issuer:** INA **Obv:** Bust of Karl Ernst Von Baer slightly right divides date **Obv. Legend:** EESTI VABARIIK **Rev:** Dove, value in wreath of clasped hands **Edge:** Plain

Date	Mintage	F	VF	XF	Unc	BU
2004 Proof	175	Value: 10.00				

X# Pn5 20 EURO CENT
7.7500 g., Goldine, 22 mm. **Issuer:** INA **Obv:** Bust of Karl Ernst Von Baer slightly right divides date **Obv. Legend:** EESTI VABARIIK **Rev:** Dove, value in wreath of clasped hands **Edge:** Plain

Date	Mintage	F	VF	XF	Unc	BU
2004	12,500	—	—	—	—	8.00
2004 Proof	3,000	Value: 5.00				

X# Pn5a 20 EURO CENT
Silver, 22 mm. **Issuer:** INA **Obv:** Bust of Karl Ernst Von Baer slightly right divides date **Obv. Legend:** EESTI VABARIIK **Rev:** Dove, value in wreath of clasped hands **Edge:** Plain

Date	Mintage	F	VF	XF	Unc	BU
2004 Proof	175	Value: 12.50				

X# Pn6 50 EURO CENT
9.5600 g., Goldine, 24.3 mm. **Issuer:** INA **Obv:** Bust of Karl Ernst Von Baer slightly right divides date **Obv. Legend:** EESTI VABARIIK **Rev:** Dove, value in wreath of clasped hands **Edge:** Plain

Date	Mintage	F	VF	XF	Unc	BU
2004	12,500	—	—	—	—	10.00
2004 Proof	3,000	Value: 6.00				

X# Pn6a 50 EURO CENT
Silver, 24.3 mm. **Issuer:** INA **Obv:** Bust of Karl Ernst Von Baer slightly right divides date **Obv. Legend:** EESTI VABARIIK **Rev:** Dove, value in wreath of clasped hands **Edge:** Plain

Date	Mintage	F	VF	XF	Unc	BU
2004 Proof	175	Value: 15.00				

X# Pn7 EURO
8.5000 g., Bi-Metallic Goldine / Copper-Nickel, 22.8 mm. **Issuer:** INA **Obv:** Barn swallow in flight **Obv. Legend:** EESTI VABARIIK **Rev:** Medieval sailing ship, EEU star design and outlined map of Estonia at right **Edge:** Plain

Date	Mintage	F	VF	XF	Unc	BU
2004	12,500	—	—	—	—	14.00
2004 Proof	3,000	Value: 8.00				

X# Pn7a EURO
Bi-Metallic Goldine-Silver, 22.8 mm. **Issuer:** INA **Obv:** Barn swallow in flight **Rev:** Medieval sailing ship, EEU star design and outlined map of Estonia at right **Edge:** Plain

Date	Mintage	F	VF	XF	Unc	BU
2004 Proof	175	Value: 22.50				

X# Pn8 2 EURO

10.8500 g., Bi-Metallic Copper-Nickel/Goldine, 25.7 mm. **Issuer:** INA **Obv:** Two barn swallows in flight **Obv. Legend:** EESTI VABARIIK **Rev:** Values, medieval sailing ship, EEU star design and medieval outlined map of Estonia at right **Edge:** Plain

Date	Mintage	F	VF	XF	Unc	BU
2004	12,500	—	—	—	—	17.00
2004 Proof	3,000	Value: 10.00				

X# Pn8a 2 EURO

Bi-Metallic Silver/Goldine, 25.7 mm. **Obv:** Two barn swallows in flight **Obv. Legend:** EESTI VABARIIK **Rev:** Value, medieval sailing ship, EEU star design and medieval outlined map of Estonia at right

Date	Mintage	F	VF	XF	Unc	BU
2004 Proof	175	Value: 28.50				

X# Pn9 5 EURO

Goldine, 36 mm. **Issuer:** INA **Obv:** Bust of Karl Ernst Von Baer slightly right divides date **Obv. Legend:** EESTI VABARIIK **Rev:** Five barn swallows on shield divides date, stars above and below **Edge:** Plain

Date	Mintage	F	VF	XF	Unc	BU
2004 Proof	3,000	Value: 12.50				

X# Pn9a 5 EURO

Silver, 36 mm. **Issuer:** INA **Obv:** Bust of Karl Ernst von Baer slightly right divides date **Obv. Legend:** EESTI VABARIIK **Rev:** Five barn swallows on shield divides date, stars above and below **Edge:** Plain

Date	Mintage	F	VF	XF	Unc	BU
2004 Proof	175	Value: 40.00				

Anonymous Issue

X# Pn10 EURO CENT

Copper Plated Steel **Obv:** Three stylized deer heads right **Rev:** Large value, scales **Edge:** Plain

Date	Mintage	F	VF	XF	Unc	BU
2004	—	—	—	—	—	3.00

X# Pn11 2 EURO CENT

Copper Plated Steel **Obv:** Three stylized deer heads right **Rev:** Large value, scales

Date	Mintage	F	VF	XF	Unc	BU
2004	—	—	—	—	—	5.00

X# Pn12 5 EURO CENT

Copper Plated Steel **Obv:** Three stylized deer heads right **Rev:** Large value, scales **Edge:** Plain

Date	Mintage	F	VF	XF	Unc	BU
2004	—	—	—	—	—	7.00

X# Pn13 10 EURO CENT

Goldine **Obv:** Bust of Vabariik facing **Rev:** Large value in wreath of clasped hands **Edge:** Plain

Date	Mintage	F	VF	XF	Unc	BU
2004	—	—	—	—	—	9.00

X# Pn14 20 EURO CENT

Goldine **Obv:** Bust of Vabariik facing **Rev:** Large value in wreath of clasped hands **Edge:** Plain

Date	Mintage	F	VF	XF	Unc	BU
2004	—	—	—	—	—	12.00

X# Pn15 50 EURO CENT

Goldine **Obv:** Bust of Vabariik facing **Rev:** Large value in wreath of clasped hands **Edge:** Plain

Date	Mintage	F	VF	XF	Unc	BU
2004	—	—	—	—	—	15.00

X# Pn16 EURO

Bi-Metallic **Obv:** Bust of Bellinghausen facing 3/4 right, swallow in flight left **Rev:** Large value, viking boat

Date	Mintage	F	VF	XF	Unc	BU
2004	—	—	—	—	—	18.00

X# Pn17 2 EURO

Bi-Metallic **Obv:** Bust of Bellinghausen facing 3/4 right, two swallows in flight **Rev:** Large value, viking boat

Date	Mintage	F	VF	XF	Unc	BU
2004	—	—	—	—	—	22.00

MINT SETS

X#	Date	Mintage	Identification	Issue Price	Mkt Val
XMS1	2004 (8)	12,500	X#Pn1-Pn8	—	70.00
XMS2	2004 (8)	—	X#Pn10-Pn17.	—	30.00

PROOF SETS

X#	Date	Mintage	Identification	Issue Price	Mkt Val
XPS1	2004 (9)	3,000	X#Pn1-Pn9	—	100
XPS2	2004 (9)	175	X#Pn1a-Pn9a.	—	150

ETHIOPIA

EMPIRE OF ETHIOPIA

MEDALLIC COINAGE

Birr / Talari Series

X# 3.1 1/8 BIRR

Gold **Obv:** Empress Zauditu **Rev:** Denomination obliterated

Date	Mintage	F	VF	XF	Unc	BU
EE1917 (1925)	—	—	500	900	1,800	—

X# 3.2 1/8 BIRR

Gold **Rev:** Denomination clear

Date	Mintage	F	VF	XF	Unc	BU
EE1917 (1925)	—	—	—	1,250	—	—

X# 4.1 1/4 BIRR

Gold **Obv:** Empress Zauditu **Rev:** Denomination obliterated

Date	Mintage	F	VF	XF	Unc	BU
EE1917 (1924)	—	—	750	1,700	3,000	—

X# 4.2 1/4 BIRR

Gold **Rev:** Denomination clear

Date	Mintage	F	VF	XF	Unc	BU
EE1917 (1925)	—	—	—	1,750	2,800	—

X# 5 1/2 BIRR

Gold **Obv:** Empress Zauditu **Rev:** Denomination obliterated **Note:** Prev. KM#M3 (Y#24).

Date	Mintage	F	VF	XF	Unc	BU
EE1916 (1924)	—	—	2,500	3,500	5,500	—

X# 5a.1 1/2 BIRR

Silver **Rev:** Denomination obliterated

Date	Mintage	F	VF	XF	Unc	BU
EE1917 (1925)	—	—	1,800	2,500	3,500	—

X# 5a.2 1/2 BIRR

Silver **Rev:** Denomination clear

Date	Mintage	F	VF	XF	Unc	BU
EE1917 (1925)	—	—	2,000	2,800	3,900	—

X# 6 BIRR

Gold **Obv:** Empress Zauditu **Rev:** Denomination obliterated **Note:** Prev. KM#M4.

Date	Mintage	F	VF	XF	Unc	BU
EE1916 (1924) Rare	2	—	—	—	—	—

Note: Bowers and Merena GUIA sale 3-88 AU realized $15,400

X# 11 1/4 TALARI

6.2900 g., Gold, 25 mm. **Subject:** Coronation of Haile Selassie I **Note:** Similar to Talari, XM12.

Date	Mintage	F	VF	XF	Unc	BU
EE1923 (1931) Prooflike	—	—	—	—	275	—

X# 18 1/2 TALARI

6.2900 g., Gold **Subject:** Coronation of Haile Selassie I **Note:** Weight varies: 16.7-20.6 grams.

Date	Mintage	F	VF	XF	Unc	BU
EE1923 Prooflike	—	—	—	—	550	—

X# 19 1/2 TALARI

19.8000 g., Gold **Subject:** Coronation of Haile Selassie I

Date	Mintage	F	VF	XF	Unc	BU
EE1923 (1931)	—	—	600	850	1,250	—

X# 20 1/2 TALARI

13.8000 g., Gold **Subject:** 25th Anniversary of Reign

Date	Mintage	F	VF	XF	Unc	BU
EE1948 (1956)	—	—	—	375	575	—

X# 1 TALARI

40.2000 g., Gold **Subject:** Menelik II

Date	Mintage	F	VF	XF	Unc	BU
EE1889 (1897) Proof	—	Value: 800				

X# 2 TALARI

Silver **Subject:** Menelik II

Date	Mintage	F	VF	XF	Unc	BU
EE1889 (1897) Proof	—	Value: 65.00				

X# 17 TALARI

23.3000 g., Gold **Subject:** Ras Tafari

Date	Mintage	F	VF	XF	Unc	BU
EE1911 (1919)	—	—	550	750	1,100	—

X# 7 TALARI

Gold **Subject:** Haile Selassie I **Note:** Weight varies: 38.19-39.95 grams. Mintage figure per Kreisberg/Schulman sale Jan. 1963. Struck for Geoffrey Hearn by John Pinches, London, England.

Date	Mintage	F	VF	XF	Unc	BU
EE1923 (1931) Proof	10	Value: 1,000				

X# 10 TALARI

Silver **Subject:** Coronation of Haile Selassie I

Date	Mintage	F	VF	XF	Unc	BU
EE1923 (1931)	—	—	100	175	275	—

X# 8 TALARI

Silver **Subject:** Haile Selassie I

Date	Mintage	F	VF	XF	Unc	BU
EE1923 (1931) Proof	—	Value: 200				

X# 9 TALARI

Gold **Subject:** Coronation of Haile Selassie I

Date	Mintage	F	VF	XF	Unc	BU
EE1923 (1931)	—	—	1,500	2,500	4,500	—

X# 12 TALARI

29.4000 g., Gold **Subject:** Coronation of Haile Selassie I

Date	Mintage	F	VF	XF	Unc	BU
EE1923 (1931) Prooflike	—	—	—	—	850	—

X# 12a TALARI

Gold **Subject:** Coronation of Haile Selassie I **Note:** Weight varies: 43.20-47.60 grams.

Date	Mintage	F	VF	XF	Unc	BU
EE1923 (1931) Prooflike	—	—	—	—	1,000	—

Crown Series

Struck by the Franklin Mint, Pennsylvania, U.S.A. Sold at the Ethiopian Pavilion at EXPO 1967.

X# 13 CROWN

Bronze **Subject:** Haile Selassie I - 75th Birthday Commemorative **Obv:** Head facing 3/4 left

Obv. Legend: H.I.M. HAILE SELASSIE I **Rev:** Crowned and mantled arms

Date	Mintage	F	VF	XF	Unc	BU
1967	3,061	—	—	—	15.00	—
1967 Prooflike	501	—	—	—	—	30.00

X# 14 CROWN

0.9250 Silver **Subject:** Haile Selassie I - 75th Birthday Commemorative **Obv:** Head facing 3/4 left **Obv. Legend:** H.I.M. HAILE SELASSIE I **Rev:** Crowned and mantled arms

Date	Mintage	F	VF	XF	Unc	BU
1967 Proof	600	Value: 65.00				

X# 15 CROWN

0.9990 Silver **Subject:** Haile Selassie I - 75th Birthday Commemorative **Obv:** Head facing 3/4 left **Obv. Legend:** H.I.M. HAILE SELASSIE I **Rev:** Crowned and mantled arms

Date	Mintage	F	VF	XF	Unc	BU
1967 Proof	400	Value: 75.00				

X# 16 CROWN

0.7500 Gold **Obv:** Head facing 3/4 left **Obv. Legend:** H.I.M. HAILE SELASSIE I **Rev:** Crowned and mantled arms

Date	Mintage	F	VF	XF	Unc	BU
1967 Proof; Unique	—	—	—	—	—	—

MINT VISIT MEDALS

X# 21 BIRR

Silver **Ruler:** Empress Zauditu (Waizero) EE1909-1923 / 1916-1930AD **Subject:** Prince Regent, Ras Taffari's Visit to Paris Mint **Obv:** Crowned bust right **Rev:** Inscription

Date	Mintage	F	VF	XF	Unc	BU
1924 Matte Proof	—	Value: 500				

X# 22 BIRR

Gold **Ruler:** Empress Zauditu (Waizero) EE1909-1923 / 1916-1930AD **Obv:** Legend similar to rev. legend of KM#16 **Rev:** Crowned lion right, right foreleg raised holding ribboned cross

Date	Mintage	F	VF	XF	Unc	BU
1924 Unique	—	—	—	—	—	—

EUROPA

FEDERATED STATES

EUROPA COINAGE

X# 1 1/10 EUROPA

12.0000 g., Bronze, 31.5 mm. **Obv. Legend:** ETATS FEDERES D'EUROPE **Rev:** Bust right **Rev. Legend:** LOUIS PASTEUR **Edge:** Plain

Date	Mintage	F	VF	XF	Unc	BU
1928	—	150	250	350	—	—

X# 1a 1/10 EUROPA

Aluminum **Obv. Legend:** ETATS FEDERES D'EUROPE **Rev:** Bust right **Rev. Legend:** LOUIS PASTEUR **Edge:** Plain

Date	Mintage	F	VF	XF	Unc	BU
1928	—	—	—	—	—	—

X# 2 EUROPA

27.0000 g., Silver **Obv. Legend:** ETATS FEDERES D'EUROPE **Rev:** Bust right **Rev. Legend:** LOUIS PASTEUR **Edge:** Plain

Date	Mintage	F	VF	XF	Unc	BU
1928	—	—	—	225	350	—

X# 2a EUROPA

Bronze **Obv. Legend:** ETATS FEDERES D'EUROPE **Rev:** Bust right **Rev. Legend:** LOUIS PASTEUR **Edge:** Plain

Date	Mintage	F	VF	XF	Unc	BU
1928	—	—	—	—	—	—

X# 2b EUROPA

Silver Plated Brass **Obv. Legend:** ETATS FEDERES D'EUROPE **Rev:** Bust right **Rev. Legend:** LOUIS PASTEUR **Edge:** Plain

Date	Mintage	F	VF	XF	Unc	BU
1928	—	—	—	—	—	—

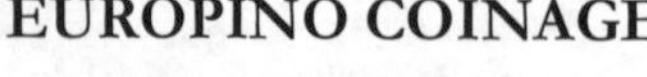

EUROPINO COINAGE

X# 11 2 1/2 EUROPINOS

12.5000 g., 0.9000 Silver 0.3617 oz. ASW **Subject:** Eisenhower **Note:** Prev. KY#19.

Date	Mintage	F	VF	XF	Unc	BU
1952HM	10,000	—	—	—	25.00	—
1959	—	—	—	—	—	—

X# 12 2 1/2 EUROPINOS

Aluminum **Subject:** Eisenhower **Note:** Prev. KY#19b.

Date	Mintage	F	VF	XF	Unc	BU
1952HM	2	—	—	—	—	—

X# 13 2 1/2 EUROPINOS

Gold **Note:** Prev. KY#19c.

Date	Mintage	F	VF	XF	Unc	BU
1952HM Unique	—	—	—	—	—	—

X# 14 2 1/2 EUROPINOS

Platinum APW

Date	Mintage	F	VF	XF	Unc	BU
1952HM Unique	—	—	—	—	—	—

X# 15 2 1/2 EUROPINOS

Silver **Note:** Piefort.

Date	Mintage	F	VF	XF	Unc	BU
1952HM	—	—	—	—	65.00	—

X# 17 5 EUROPINOS

0.9000 Silver, 36 mm. **Edge:** Reeded **Note:** Prev. KY#18.

Date	Mintage	F	VF	XF	Unc	BU
1952HM Proof	300	Value: 120				

X# 18 5 EUROPINOS

Gold **Edge:** Reeded **Note:** Prev. KY#18b.

Date	Mintage	F	VF	XF	Unc	BU
1952HM Proof	—	Value: 2,000				

X# 19 5 EUROPINOS

Platinum APW

Date	Mintage	F	VF	XF	Unc	BU
1952HM Proof; Rare	—	—	—	—	—	—

X# 20 5 EUROPINOS

Silver **Edge:** Plain **Note:** Prev. KY#18a. Piefort.

Date	Mintage	F	VF	XF	Unc	BU
1952HM Proof	—	Value: 225				

X# 21 5 EUROPINOS

Gold **Edge:** Plain **Note:** Prev. KY#18c. Piefort.

Date	Mintage	F	VF	XF	Unc	BU
1952HM Proof	—	—	—	—	—	—

X# 22 5 EUROPINOS

Copper **Edge:** Plain **Note:** Prev. KY#18d. Piefort.

Date	Mintage	F	VF	XF	Unc	BU
1952HM Proof	—	Value: 100				

X# 23 5 EUROPINOS

Lead

Date	Mintage	F	VF	XF	Unc	BU
1952HM Proof	—	Value: 75.00				

X# A1 5 EUROPINOS
Silver, 28.1 mm. **Obv:** Flag **Rev:** Torch **Rev. Legend:** LIBERTAS **Edge:** Plain

Date	Mintage	F	VF	XF	Unc	BU
1965	—	—	—	—	25.00	—

INTERNATIONAL FEDERATION

EUROPA COINAGE

X# 5 1/20 FLORIN
14.6300 g., 0.9990 Silver 0.4699 oz. ASW, 35 mm. **Obv:** Young Girl **Rev:** Wheat ear and value **Edge:** Plain **Note:** Issued by Begeer of Voorschoten, Netherlands.

Date	Mintage	F	VF	XF	Unc	BU
ND(1934)	—	—	—	75.00	125	—

X# 5a 1/20 FLORIN
Bronze **Obv:** Young Girl **Rev:** Wheat ear and value

Date	Mintage	F	VF	XF	Unc	BU
ND(1934)	—	—	—	50.00	75.00	—

X# 6 FLORIN
5.8300 g., Gold **Note:** Prev. KY#14.

Date	Mintage	F	VF	XF	Unc	BU
ND(1934)	—	—	—	225	300	—

X# 6a FLORIN
Bronze

Date	Mintage	F	VF	XF	Unc	BU
ND(1934)	—	—	—	30.00	50.00	—

EUROPEAN PAYMENTS UNION

TRADE COINAGE

Struck at the Bavarian State Mint, Munich, West Germany.

X# 9 5 DUKATEN
17.4600 g., Gold, 25.1 mm. **Subject:** 10th Anniversary **Obv:** Europa riding a bull 3/4 left **Obv. Legend:** MDCCCCIL • EUROPA - RAT • MDCCCCLIX **Rev:** Member nation's names in German text below tree **Rev. Inscription:** EUROPA **Edge:** Plain

Date	Mintage	F	VF	XF	Unc	BU
ND(1959)	—	—	250	350	500	—

X# 7 10 DUCATEN
50.0000 g., 1.0000 Silver 1.6075 oz. ASW **Subject:** 7th Anniversary of EPU **Note:** Prev. #X5. Struck at the Bavarian State Mint, Munich, West Germany.

Date	Mintage	F	VF	XF	Unc	BU
1957	—	—	—	75.00	125	—

EUROPEAN UNION

MEDALLIC COINAGE

Berolina Medaillenvertriess Series

X# 225 ECU
23.0000 g., 0.6250 Silver 0.4621 oz. ASW, 40 mm. **Subject:** ECU - European Currency Mint **Obv:** Large "E" within 12 stars and sprays **Obv. Legend:** 22me ÉCU d'EUROPE... **Rev:** French ecu of 1664, obverse and reverse **Rev. Legend:** EUROPÄISCHE WÄHRUNG SEINHEIT **Edge:** Plain

Date	Mintage	F	VF	XF	Unc	BU
1981 Proof	7,500	Value: 30.00				

X# 266 ECU
23.0000 g., 0.6250 Silver 0.4621 oz. ASW, 40 mm. **Obv:** Large "E" within 12 stars and sprays **Obv. Legend:** 42me ÉCU d'EUROPE... **Edge:** Plain

Date	Mintage	F	VF	XF	Unc	BU
1991 Proof	—	Value: 25.00				

X# 267 ECU
23.0000 g., 0.9990 Silver 0.7387 oz. ASW, 40 mm. **Obv:** Large "E" within 12 stars and sprays **Obv. Legend:** 42me ÉCU d'EUROPE... **Edge:** Plain

Date	Mintage	F	VF	XF	Unc	BU
1991 Proof	—	Value: 30.00				

X# 268 ECU
23.0000 g., 0.6250 Silver 0.4621 oz. ASW, 40 mm. **Obv:** Large "E" within 12 stars and sprays **Obv. Legend:** 43me ÉCU d'EUROPE... **Rev:** Outer circle of 12 national coins, small map of Euorpe in center **Rev. Legend:** • EUROPAISCHE • WÄHRUNG **Edge:** Plain

Date	Mintage	F	VF	XF	Unc	BU
1992 Proof	5,000	Value: 25.00				

X# 269 ECU
23.0000 g., 0.9990 Silver 0.7387 oz. ASW, 40 mm. **Obv:** Large "E" within 12 stars and sprays **Obv. Legend:** 43me ÉCU d'EUROPE... **Rev:** Outer circle of 12 national coins, small map of Euorpe in center **Edge:** Plain

Date	Mintage	F	VF	XF	Unc	BU
1992 Proof	5,000	Value: 30.00				

X# 201 THALER
26.0000 g., 0.9250 Silver 0.7732 oz. ASW **Subject:** Robert Schuman

Date	Mintage	F	VF	XF	Unc	BU
1971 Proof	30,000	Value: 30.00				

X# 202 THALER
26.0000 g., 0.9250 Silver 0.7732 oz. ASW
Subject: Konrad Adenauer

Date	Mintage	F	VF	XF	Unc	BU
1971 Proof	30,000	Value: 25.00				

X# 203 THALER
26.0000 g., 0.9250 Silver 0.7732 oz. ASW **Subject:** Alcide de Gasperi

Date	Mintage	F	VF	XF	Unc	BU
1972 Proof	30,000	Value: 25.00				

X# 204 THALER
26.0000 g., 0.9250 Silver 0.7732 oz. ASW
Subject: Winston Churchill

Date	Mintage	F	VF	XF	Unc	BU
1972 Proof	30,000	Value: 25.00				

X# 205 THALER
26.0000 g., 0.9250 Silver 0.7732 oz. ASW
Subject: Paul-Henri Spaak

Date	Mintage	F	VF	XF	Unc	BU
1973 Proof	50,000	Value: 25.00				

X# 206 THALER
26.0000 g., 0.9250 Silver 0.7732 oz. ASW
Subject: Heinrich von Brentano

Date	Mintage	F	VF	XF	Unc	BU
1973 Proof	50,000	Value: 25.00				

X# 207 THALER
26.0000 g., 0.9250 Silver 0.7732 oz. ASW
Subject: 25th Anniversary Europa Council

Date	Mintage	F	VF	XF	Unc	BU
1974 Proof	75,000	Value: 20.00				

X# 208 THALER
26.0000 g., 0.9250 Silver 0.7732 oz. ASW
Subject: Georges Pompidou

Date	Mintage	F	VF	XF	Unc	BU
1974 Proof	50,000	Value: 25.00				

X# 209 THALER
26.0000 g., 0.9250 Silver 0.7732 oz. ASW
Subject: Berlaymont in Brussels

Date	Mintage	F	VF	XF	Unc	BU
1975 Proof	50,000	Value: 20.00				

X# 210 THALER
26.0000 g., 0.9250 Silver 0.7732 oz. ASW
Subject: Schumann and Adenauer

Date	Mintage	F	VF	XF	Unc	BU
1975 Proof	75,000	Value: 25.00				

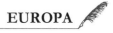

X# 211 THALER

26.0000 g., 0.9250 Silver 0.7732 oz. ASW
Subject: Guy Hollet

Date	Mintage	F	VF	XF	Unc	BU
1976 Proof	75,000	Value: 25.00				

X# 212 THALER

26.0000 g., 0.9250 Silver 0.7732 oz. ASW
Subject: Strassburg Palace

Date	Mintage	F	VF	XF	Unc	BU
1976 Proof	50,000	Value: 20.00				

X# 213 THALER

26.0000 g., 0.9250 Silver 0.7732 oz. ASW
Subject: Joseph Bech

Date	Mintage	F	VF	XF	Unc	BU
1977 Proof	50,000	Value: 25.00				

X# 214 THALER

26.0000 g., 0.9250 Silver 0.7732 oz. ASW
Subject: 20th Anniversary Treaties of Rome

Date	Mintage	F	VF	XF	Unc	BU
1977 Proof	50,000	Value: 20.00				

X# 215 THALER

26.0000 g., 0.9250 Silver 0.7732 oz. ASW
Subject: Europa Election

Date	Mintage	F	VF	XF	Unc	BU
1978 Proof	50,000	Value: 25.00				

X# 216 THALER

26.0000 g., 0.9250 Silver 0.7732 oz. ASW
Subject: Gustav Stresemann

Date	Mintage	F	VF	XF	Unc	BU
1978 Proof	50,000	Value: 25.00				

X# 217 THALER

26.0000 g., 0.9250 Silver 0.7732 oz. ASW
Subject: Europa Tree

Date	Mintage	F	VF	XF	Unc	BU
1979 Proof	50,000	Value: 20.00				

X# 218 THALER

26.0000 g., 0.9250 Silver 0.7732 oz. ASW
Subject: Simone Veill

Date	Mintage	F	VF	XF	Unc	BU
1979 Proof	50,000	Value: 25.00				

X# 219 THALER

23.0000 g., 0.6250 Silver 0.4621 oz. ASW
Subject: Carlo Schmid

Date	Mintage	F	VF	XF	Unc	BU
1980 Proof	7,500	Value: 25.00				

X# 220 THALER

26.0000 g., 0.9250 Silver 0.7732 oz. ASW

Date	Mintage	F	VF	XF	Unc	BU
1980 Proof	5,000	Value: 30.00				

X# 221 THALER

23.0000 g., 0.6250 Silver 0.4621 oz. ASW
Subject: Europa Riding the Bull

Date	Mintage	F	VF	XF	Unc	BU
1980 Proof	7,500	Value: 35.00				

X# 222 THALER

26.0000 g., 0.9250 Silver 0.7732 oz. ASW

Date	Mintage	F	VF	XF	Unc	BU
1980 Proof	7,500	Value: 40.00				

X# 223 THALER

23.0000 g., 0.6250 Silver 0.4621 oz. ASW
Subject: Aristide Briand

Date	Mintage	F	VF	XF	Unc	BU
1981 Proof	7,500	Value: 25.00				

X# 224 THALER

26.0000 g., 0.9250 Silver 0.7732 oz. ASW

Date	Mintage	F	VF	XF	Unc	BU
1981 Proof	7,500	Value: 30.00				

X# 226 THALER

26.0000 g., 0.9250 Silver 0.7732 oz. ASW

Date	Mintage	F	VF	XF	Unc	BU
1981 Proof	7,500	Value: 30.00				

X# 227 THALER

23.0000 g., 0.6250 Silver 0.4621 oz. ASW
Subject: George C. Marshall

Date	Mintage	F	VF	XF	Unc	BU
1982 Proof	7,500	Value: 25.00				

X# 228 THALER

26.0000 g., 0.9250 Silver 0.7732 oz. ASW

Date	Mintage	F	VF	XF	Unc	BU
1982 Proof	7,500	Value: 30.00				

X# 229 THALER

23.0000 g., 0.6250 Silver 0.4621 oz. ASW
Subject: Walter Hallstein

Date	Mintage	F	VF	XF	Unc	BU
1982 Proof	6,000	Value: 25.00				

X# 230 THALER

26.0000 g., 0.9250 Silver 0.7732 oz. ASW

Date	Mintage	F	VF	XF	Unc	BU
1982 Proof	6,000	Value: 30.00				

X# 231 THALER

23.0000 g., 0.6250 Silver 0.4621 oz. ASW
Subject: Youth Sees Europe

Date	Mintage	F	VF	XF	Unc	BU
1983 Proof	6,000	Value: 20.00				

X# 232 THALER

26.0000 g., 0.9250 Silver 0.7732 oz. ASW

Date	Mintage	F	VF	XF	Unc	BU
1983 Proof	6,000	Value: 25.00				

X# 233 THALER

23.0000 g., 0.6250 Silver 0.4621 oz. ASW
Subject: Jean Monnet

Date	Mintage	F	VF	XF	Unc	BU
1983 Proof	5,000	Value: 30.00				

X# 234 THALER

26.0000 g., 0.9250 Silver 0.7732 oz. ASW

Date	Mintage	F	VF	XF	Unc	BU
1983 Proof	5,000	Value: 30.00				

X# 235 THALER

23.0000 g., 0.6250 Silver 0.4621 oz. ASW
Subject: Europa Election

Date	Mintage	F	VF	XF	Unc	BU
1984 Proof	5,000	Value: 30.00				

X# 236 THALER

26.0000 g., 0.9250 Silver 0.7732 oz. ASW

Date	Mintage	F	VF	XF	Unc	BU
1984 Proof	5,000	Value: 30.00				

X# 237 THALER

23.0000 g., 0.6250 Silver 0.4621 oz. ASW
Subject: Antonio Segni

Date	Mintage	F	VF	XF	Unc	BU
1984 Proof	5,000	Value: 25.00				

X# 238 THALER

26.0000 g., 0.9250 Silver 0.7732 oz. ASW

Date	Mintage	F	VF	XF	Unc	BU
1984 Proof	5,000	Value: 30.00				

X# 239 THALER

23.0000 g., 0.6250 Silver 0.4621 oz. ASW
Subject: Year of Music

Date	Mintage	F	VF	XF	Unc	BU
1985 Proof	5,000	Value: 25.00				

X# 240 THALER

26.0000 g., 0.9250 Silver 0.7732 oz. ASW

Date	Mintage	F	VF	XF	Unc	BU
1985 Proof	5,000	Value: 30.00				

X# 241 THALER

23.0000 g., 0.6250 Silver 0.4621 oz. ASW **Subject:** 25th Anniversary Unified European Postal System

Date	Mintage	F	VF	XF	Unc	BU
1985 Proof	5,000	Value: 25.00				

X# 242 THALER

26.0000 g., 0.9250 Silver 0.7732 oz. ASW

Date	Mintage	F	VF	XF	Unc	BU
1985 Proof	5,000	Value: 30.00				

X# 243 THALER

23.0000 g., 0.6250 Silver 0.4621 oz. ASW
Subject: Admission of Spain and Portugal into The Common Market

Date	Mintage	F	VF	XF	Unc	BU
1986 Proof	5,000	Value: 25.00				

X# 244 THALER

26.0000 g., 0.9250 Silver 0.7732 oz. ASW

Date	Mintage	F	VF	XF	Unc	BU
1986 Proof	5,000	Value: 30.00				

X# 245 THALER

23.0000 g., 0.6250 Silver 0.4621 oz. ASW
Subject: Year of Traffic Safety

Date	Mintage	F	VF	XF	Unc	BU
1986 Proof	5,000	Value: 25.00				

X# 246 THALER

26.0000 g., 0.9250 Silver 0.7732 oz. ASW

Date	Mintage	F	VF	XF	Unc	BU
1986 Proof	5,000	Value: 30.00				

X# 247 THALER

23.0000 g., 0.6250 Silver 0.4621 oz. ASW
Subject: Year of the Environment

Date	Mintage	F	VF	XF	Unc	BU
1987 Proof	5,000	Value: 25.00				

X# 248 THALER

26.0000 g., 0.9250 Silver 0.7732 oz. ASW

Date	Mintage	F	VF	XF	Unc	BU
1987 Proof	5,000	Value: 30.00				

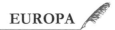

X# 249 THALER

23.0000 g., 0.6250 Silver 0.4621 oz. ASW
Subject: Altiero Spinelli

Date	Mintage	F	VF	XF	Unc	BU
1987 Proof	5,000	Value: 25.00				

X# 250 THALER

26.0000 g., 0.9250 Silver 0.7732 oz. ASW

Date	Mintage	F	VF	XF	Unc	BU
1987 Proof	5,000	Value: 30.00				

X# 252 THALER

23.0000 g., 1.0000 Silver 0.7394 oz. ASW

Date	Mintage	F	VF	XF	Unc	BU
1988 Proof	5,000	Value: 25.00				

X# 253 THALER

23.0000 g., 0.6250 Silver 0.4621 oz. ASW
Subject: 40th Anniversary the Hague Conference

Date	Mintage	F	VF	XF	Unc	BU
1988 Proof	5,000	Value: 25.00				

X# 254 THALER

26.0000 g., 0.9250 Silver 0.7732 oz. ASW

Date	Mintage	F	VF	XF	Unc	BU
1988 Proof	5,000	Value: 30.00				

X# 256 THALER

23.0000 g., 0.6250 Silver 0.4621 oz. ASW **Subject:** European Parliament Elections

Date	Mintage	F	VF	XF	Unc	BU
1989 Proof	5,000	Value: 30.00				

X# 257 THALER

23.0000 g., 0.9990 Silver 0.7387 oz. ASW

Date	Mintage	F	VF	XF	Unc	BU
1989 Proof	5,000	Value: 30.00				

X# 258 THALER

23.0000 g., 0.6250 Silver 0.4621 oz. ASW
Subject: 25 Years of European Space Flight

Date	Mintage	F	VF	XF	Unc	BU
1989 Proof	—	Value: 25.00				

X# 259 THALER

23.0000 g., 1.0000 Silver 0.7394 oz. ASW

Date	Mintage	F	VF	XF	Unc	BU
1989 Proof	—	Value: 30.00				

X# 260 THALER

23.0000 g., 0.6250 Silver 0.4621 oz. ASW
Subject: European Unification

Date	Mintage	F	VF	XF	Unc	BU
1990 Proof	—	Value: 30.00				

X# 261 THALER

23.0000 g., 1.0000 Silver 0.7394 oz. ASW

Date	Mintage	F	VF	XF	Unc	BU
1990 Proof	—	Value: 30.00				

X# 262 THALER

23.0000 g., 0.6250 Silver 0.4621 oz. ASW **Subject:** European Conference for Security and Cooperation

Date	Mintage	F	VF	XF	Unc	BU
1990 Proof	—	Value: 25.00				

X# 263 THALER

23.0000 g., 1.0000 Silver 0.7394 oz. ASW

Date	Mintage	F	VF	XF	Unc	BU
1990 Proof	—	Value: 30.00				

X# 264 THALER

23.0000 g., 0.6250 Silver 0.4621 oz. ASW
Subject: Jacques Delors

Date	Mintage	F	VF	XF	Unc	BU
ND(1991) Proof	—	Value: 25.00				

X# 265 THALER

23.0000 g., 1.0000 Silver 0.7394 oz. ASW

Date	Mintage	F	VF	XF	Unc	BU
ND(1991) Proof	—	Value: 30.00				

X# 251 THALER

23.0000 g., 0.6250 Silver 0.4621 oz. ASW
Subject: Film and Television Industry

Date	Mintage	F	VF	XF	Unc	BU
1988 Proof	5,000	Value: 25.00				

PANEUROPEAN UNION

Confederatio Europea - Bruxelles

ECU COINAGE

X# 170 ECU
4.0000 g., 0.9250 Silver 0.1190 oz. ASW
Subject: Carolus Magnus **Note:** Prev. X#40.

Date	Mintage	F	VF	XF	Unc	BU
1972 Prooflike	10,000	—	—	—	25.00	—

X# 86 ECU
7.0000 g., 0.9250 Silver 0.2082 oz. ASW, 24 mm.

Date	Mintage	F	VF	XF	Unc	BU
1979 Prooflike	50,000	—	—	—	17.50	—

X# 145 ECU
4.0000 g., 0.9250 Silver 0.1190 oz. ASW, 20 mm.
Note: Prev. X#115.

Date	Mintage	F	VF	XF	Unc	BU
1984 IPZS Proof	7,500	Value: 25.00				

X# 131 ECU
4.5000 g., 0.9250 Silver 0.1338 oz. ASW, 20 mm.
Subject: 40th Anniversary Europa **Obv:** Large "40" above 12 stars in flat circle **Obv. Legend:** CONFEDERATIO EUROPA **Rev:** Three outlined youth's heads left **Rev. Legend:** JEUNESSE / YOUTH **Rev. Designer:** R. Politi **Edge:** Reeded

Date	Mintage	F	VF	XF	Unc	BU
1989 Proof	264	Value: 70.00				

X# 171 2 ECU
8.6000 g., 0.9250 Silver 0.2557 oz. ASW, 26 mm.
Subject: Carolus V **Note:** Prev. X#41.

Date	Mintage	F	VF	XF	Unc	BU
1972 Prooflike	10,000	—	—	—	30.00	—

X# 172 5 ECU
20.0000 g., 0.9250 Silver 0.5948 oz. ASW, 36 mm.
Subject: Napoleon Bonaparte **Note:** Prev. X#42.

Date	Mintage	F	VF	XF	Unc	BU
1972 Prooflike	10,000	—	—	—	50.00	—

X# 146 5 ECU
9.0000 g., 0.9250 Silver 0.2676 oz. ASW, 24 mm.
Note: Prev. X#116.

Date	Mintage	F	VF	XF	Unc	BU
1984 IPZS Prooflike	2,500	—	—	—	40.00	—

X# 121 5 ECU
9.0000 g., 0.9250 Silver 0.2676 oz. ASW, 24 mm.
Subject: Europe's Year of Music **Obv:** Bust of Johann Sebastion Bach facing 3/4 right **Obv. Legend:** CONFEDERATIO • EUROPA **Rev:** Paneuropa emblem above Europa in quadriga left, value below **Edge:** Plain

Date	Mintage	F	VF	XF	Unc	BU
1985 Proof	6,500	Value: 30.00				

X# 122 5 ECU
9.0000 g., 0.9250 Silver 0.2676 oz. ASW, 24 mm.
Subject: Europe's Year of Music **Obv:** Bust of Georg Friedrich Händel facing 3/4 right **Obv. Legend:** CONFEDERATIO • EUROPA **Rev:** Paneuropa emblem above Europa in quadriga left, value below **Edge:** Plain

Date	Mintage	F	VF	XF	Unc	BU
1985 Proof	6,500	Value: 30.00				

X# 123 5 ECU
0.9000 g., 0.9250 Silver 0.0268 oz. ASW, 24 mm.
Subject: Europe's Year of Music **Obv:** Bust of Domenico Scarlatti facing slightly right **Obv. Legend:** CONFEDERATIO • EUROPA **Rev:** Paneuropa emblem above Europa in quadriga left, value below **Edge:** Plain

Date	Mintage	F	VF	XF	Unc	BU
1985 Proof	6,500	Value: 30.00				

X# 132 5 ECU
9.0000 g., 0.9250 Silver 0.2676 oz. ASW, 26 mm.
Subject: 40th Anniversary Europa **Obv:** Large "40" above 12 stars in flat circle **Obv. Legend:** CONFEDERATIO EUROPA **Rev:** Modernistic outlined head right **Rev. Legend:** CULTURE / CULTURE **Rev. Designer:** R. Politi **Edge:** Reeded

Date	Mintage	F	VF	XF	Unc	BU
1989 Proof	264	Value: 100				

X# 173 10 ECU
3.0000 g., 0.9000 Gold 0.0868 oz. AGW, 18 mm.
Subject: Richard de Condenhove-Kalergi **Note:** Prev. X#43.

Date	Mintage	F	VF	XF	Unc	BU
1972 Prooflike	10,000	—	—	—	120	—

X# 87 10 ECU
14.0000 g., 0.9250 Silver 0.4163 oz. ASW, 30 mm.

Date	Mintage	F	VF	XF	Unc	BU
1979 Prooflike	20,000	—	—	—	45.00	—

X# 91 10 ECU
21.6200 g., 0.9250 Silver 0.6429 oz. ASW, 35 mm.
Subject: 60th Anniversary Paneuropa Movement **Obv:** Paneuropa emblem above value **Obv. Legend:** CONFEDERATIO EUROPA **Rev:** Bust of R. Coudenhove-Kalergi right **Rev. Legend:** RICHARD COUDENHOVE-KALERGI **Edge:** Reeded

Date	Mintage	F	VF	XF	Unc	BU
1982 Proof	5,200	Value: 45.00				

X# 92 10 ECU
21.6200 g., 0.9250 Silver 0.6429 oz. ASW, 35 mm.
Subject: 60th Anniversary Paneuropa Movement **Obv:** Paneuropa emblem above value **Obv. Legend:** CONFEDERATIO EUROPA **Rev:** Head of Sir W. Churchill facing slightly left **Rev. Legend:** WINSTON CHURCHILL • LET EUROPE ARISE **Edge:** Reeded

Date	Mintage	F	VF	XF	Unc	BU
1982 Proof	5,200	Value: 45.00				

X# 147 10 ECU
18.0000 g., 0.9250 Silver 0.5353 oz. ASW **Note:** Prev. X#117.

Date	Mintage	F	VF	XF	Unc	BU
1984 IPZS Proof	2,500	Value: 60.00				

X# 133 10 ECU
18.0000 g., 0.9250 Silver 0.5353 oz. ASW, 32 mm.
Subject: 40th Anniversary Europa **Obv:** Large "40" above 12 stars in flat circle **Obv. Legend:** CONFEDERATIO EUROPA **Rev:** Modernistic plant and architecture **Rev. Legend:** PATRIMOINE NATUREL ET ARCHITECTONIOUE / NATURAL AND ARCHITECTURAL **Rev. Designer:** R. Politi **Edge:** Reeded

Date	Mintage	F	VF	XF	Unc	BU
1989 Proof	264	Value: 120				

X# 174 20 ECU

6.0000 g., 0.9000 Gold 0.1736 oz. AGW **Subject:** Jean Monnet and Paul Henri Spaak **Note:** Prev. X#44.

Date	Mintage	F	VF	XF	Unc	BU
1972	10,000	—	—	—	220	—

X# 88 20 ECU

28.0000 g., 0.9250 Silver 0.8327 oz. ASW, 36 mm.

Date	Mintage	F	VF	XF	Unc	BU
1979 Proof	15,000	Value: 65.00				

X# 175 50 ECU

15.0000 g., 0.9000 Gold 0.4340 oz. AGW, 30 mm. **Subject:** Winston Churchill and Edward Heath **Note:** Prev. X#45.

Date	Mintage	F	VF	XF	Unc	BU
1972 Prooflike	10,000	—	—	—	325	—

X# 89 50 ECU

5.5000 g., 0.9000 Gold 0.1591 oz. AGW, 22. mm.

Date	Mintage	F	VF	XF	Unc	BU
1979 Prooflike	10,000	—	—	—	250	—

X# 148 50 ECU

5.0000 g., 0.9000 Gold 0.1447 oz. AGW **Note:** Prev. X#118.

Date	Mintage	F	VF	XF	Unc	BU
1984 IPZS Proof	2,000	Value: 250				

X# 124 50 ECU

5.5000 g., 0.9000 Gold 0.1591 oz. AGW, 20 mm. **Subject:** Europe's Year of Music **Obv:** Bust of Johann Sebastion Bach facing 3/4 right **Obv. Legend:** CONFEDERATIO • EUROPA **Rev:** Greek temple, value below in sprays **Edge:** Plain

Date	Mintage	F	VF	XF	Unc	BU
1985 Proof	3,000	Value: 175				

X# 125 50 ECU

5.5000 g., 0.9000 Gold 0.1591 oz. AGW, 20 mm. **Subject:** Europe's Year of Music **Obv:** Bust of Georg Friedrich Händel facing 3/4 right **Obv. Legend:** CONFEDERATIO • EUROPA **Rev:** Greek temple, value below in sprays **Edge:** Plain

Date	Mintage	F	VF	XF	Unc	BU
1985 Proof	3,000	Value: 175				

X# 126 50 ECU

5.5000 g., 0.9000 Gold 0.1591 oz. AGW, 20 mm. **Subject:** Europe's Year of Music **Obv:** Bust of Domenico Scarlatti facing slightly right **Obv. Legend:** CONFEDERATIO • EUROPA **Rev:** Greek temple, value below in sprays **Edge:** Plain

Date	Mintage	F	VF	XF	Unc	BU
1985 Proof	3,000	Value: 175				

X# 134 50 ECU

7.0000 g., 0.9000 Gold 0.2025 oz. AGW, 24 mm. **Subject:** 40th Anniversary Europa **Obv:** Large "40" above 12 stars in flat circle **Obv. Legend:** CONFEDERATIO EUROPA **Rev:** Solidarity symbol **Rev. Legend:** SOLIDARITE / SOLIDARITY **Edge:** Reeded

Date	Mintage	F	VF	XF	Unc	BU
1989 Proof	—	Value: 350				

X# 176 100 ECU

30.0000 g., 0.9000 Gold 0.8680 oz. AGW **Subject:** K. Andenauer, A. De Gasperi and R. Schuman **Note:** Prev. X#46.

Date	Mintage	F	VF	XF	Unc	BU
1972 Prooflike	10,000	—	—	—	675	—

X# 90 100 ECU

11.0000 g., 0.9000 Gold 0.3183 oz. AGW, 28 mm.

Date	Mintage	F	VF	XF	Unc	BU
1979 Prooflike	5,000	—	—	—	400	—

X# 93 100 ECU

11.1100 g., 0.9000 Gold 0.3215 oz. AGW, 27 mm. **Subject:** 60th Anniversary Paneuropa Movement **Obv:** Paneuropa emblem above value **Obv. Legend:** CONFEDERATIO EUROPA **Rev:** Head of R. Coudenhove-Kalergi right **Rev. Legend:** RICHARD COUDENHOVE-KALERGI **Edge:** Reeded

Date	Mintage	F	VF	XF	Unc	BU
1982 Proof	700	Value: 500				

X# 94 100 ECU

11.1100 g., 0.9000 Gold 0.3215 oz. AGW, 27 mm. **Subject:** 60th Anniversary Paneuropa Movement **Obv:** Paneuropa emblem above value **Obv. Legend:** CONFEDERATIO EUROPA **Rev:** Head of Sir W. Churchill facing slightly left **Rev. Legend:** WINSTON CHURCHILL • LET EUROPE ARISE **Edge:** Reeded

Date	Mintage	F	VF	XF	Unc	BU
1982 Proof	700	Value: 500				

X# 149 100 ECU

9.0000 g., 0.9000 Gold 0.2604 oz. AGW **Note:** Prev. X#119.

Date	Mintage	F	VF	XF	Unc	BU
1984 IPZS Proof	1,000	Value: 500				

X# 127 100 ECU

11.0000 g., 0.9000 Gold 0.3183 oz. AGW, 26 mm. **Subject:** Europe's Year of Music **Obv:** Head of Ludwig van Beethoven left **Obv. Legend:** CONFEDERATIO • EUROPA **Rev:** Europa standing before bars of music, value below **Rev. Legend:** AN DIE FREUDE **Edge:** Plain

Date	Mintage	F	VF	XF	Unc	BU
1985 Proof	—	Value: 550				

X# 135 100 ECU

14.0000 g., 0.9000 Gold 0.4051 oz. AGW, 28 mm. **Subject:** 40th Anniversary Europa **Obv:** Large "40" above 12 stars in flat circle **Obv. Legend:** CONFEDERATIO EUROPA **Rev:** Human rights symbol **Rev. Legend:** DROITS DE L'HOMME / HUMAN RIGHTS **Rev. Designer:** D. Grieco **Edge:** Reeded

Date	Mintage	F	VF	XF	Unc	BU
1989 Proof	—	Value: 650				

EUROPEAN ECONOMIC COMMUNITY

ECU COINAGE

X# 31 ECU

40.0000 g., 0.9250 Silver 1.1895 oz. ASW

Date	Mintage	F	VF	XF	Unc	BU
1979(a) Prooflike	6,000	—	—	—	75.00	—

X# 32 ECU

50.0000 g., 0.9200 Gold 1.4789 oz. AGW

Date	Mintage	F	VF	XF	Unc	BU
1979(a) Prooflike	1,460	—	—	—	1,750	—

X# 33 ECU

Bronze

Date	Mintage	F	VF	XF	Unc	BU
1979(a) Prooflike	—	—	—	—	20.00	—

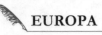

X# 33a ECU

Gilt Bronze

Date	Mintage	F	VF	XF	Unc	BU
1979(a) Prooflike	—	—	—	—	25.00	—

X# 35 ECU

50.0000 g., 0.9200 Gold 1.4789 oz. AGW **Subject:** 1st Anniversary of Ecu

Date	Mintage	F	VF	XF	Unc	BU
1980(a) Prooflike	1,900	—	—	—	1,350	—

X# 36 ECU

Gilt Bronze **Subject:** 1st Anniversary of Ecu

Date	Mintage	F	VF	XF	Unc	BU
1980(a) Prooflike	50,000	—	—	—	20.00	—

X# 34 ECU

40.0000 g., 0.9250 Silver 1.1895 oz. ASW **Subject:** 1st Anniversary of Ecu

Date	Mintage	F	VF	XF	Unc	BU
1980(a) Prooflike	20,000	—	—	—	45.00	—

X# 37 ECU

40.0000 g., 0.9250 Silver 1.1895 oz. ASW **Subject:** Greece Enters European Economic Community

Date	Mintage	F	VF	XF	Unc	BU
1981(a) Prooflike	20,000	—	—	—	45.00	—

X# 38 ECU

50.0000 g., 0.9200 Gold 1.4789 oz. AGW **Subject:** Greece Enters European Economic Community

Date	Mintage	F	VF	XF	Unc	BU
1981(a) Prooflike	2,000	—	—	—	1,200	—

X# 39 ECU

Bronze **Subject:** Greece Enters European Economic Community

Date	Mintage	F	VF	XF	Unc	BU
1981(a) Prooflike	50,000	—	—	—	20.00	—

X# 40 ECU

40.0000 g., 0.9250 Silver 1.1895 oz. ASW, 41 mm. **Subject:** 25th Anniversary European Economic Community

Date	Mintage	F	VF	XF	Unc	BU
1982(a) Prooflike	20,000	—	—	—	45.00	—

X# 41 ECU

50.0000 g., 0.9200 Gold 1.4789 oz. AGW **Subject:** 25th Anniversary European Economic Community

Date	Mintage	F	VF	XF	Unc	BU
1982(a) Prooflike	2,000	—	—	—	1,200	—

X# 42 ECU

Bronze **Subject:** 25th Anniversary European Economic Community

Date	Mintage	F	VF	XF	Unc	BU
1982(a) Prooflike	50,000	—	—	—	20.00	—

X# 43 ECU

40.0000 g., 0.9250 Silver 1.1895 oz. ASW

Date	Mintage	F	VF	XF	Unc	BU
1983(a) Prooflike	20,000	—	—	—	45.00	—

X# 44 ECU

50.0000 g., 0.9200 Gold 1.4789 oz. AGW

Date	Mintage	F	VF	XF	Unc	BU
1983(a) Prooflike	2,000	—	—	—	1,200	—

X# 45 ECU

Bronze

Date	Mintage	F	VF	XF	Unc	BU
1983(a) Prooflike	50,000	—	—	—	20.00	—

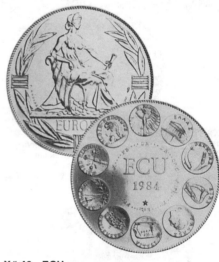

X# 46 ECU

40.0000 g., 0.9250 Silver 1.1895 oz. ASW

Date	Mintage	F	VF	XF	Unc	BU
1984(a) Prooflike	20,000	—	—	—	45.00	—

X# 47 ECU

50.0000 g., 0.9200 Gold 1.4789 oz. AGW

Date	Mintage	F	VF	XF	Unc	BU
1984(a) Prooflike	2,000	—	—	—	1,200	—

X# 48 ECU

Bronze

Date	Mintage	F	VF	XF	Unc	BU
1984(a) Prooflike	50,000	—	—	—	20.00	—

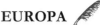

X# 49 ECU

40.0000 g., 0.9250 Silver 1.1895 oz. ASW

Date	Mintage	F	VF	XF	Unc	BU
1985(a) Prooflike	20,000	—	—	—	45.00	—

X# 50 ECU

50.0000 g., 0.9200 Gold 1.4789 oz. AGW

Date	Mintage	F	VF	XF	Unc	BU
1985(a) Prooflike	2,000	—	—	—	1,200	—

X# 51 ECU

Bronze

Date	Mintage	F	VF	XF	Unc	BU
1985(a) Prooflike	50,000	—	—	—	20.00	—

X# 52 ECU

40.0000 g., 0.9250 Silver 1.1895 oz. ASW

Date	Mintage	F	VF	XF	Unc	BU
1986(a) Prooflike	20,000	—	—	—	45.00	—
1987(a) Prooflike	20,000	—	—	—	50.00	—
1988(a) Prooflike	20,000	—	—	—	55.00	—

X# 53 ECU

50.0000 g., 0.9200 Gold 1.4789 oz. AGW

Date	Mintage	F	VF	XF	Unc	BU
1986(a) Prooflike	2,000	—	—	—	1,200	—
1987(a) Prooflike	2,000	—	—	—	1,200	—
1988(a) Prooflike	2,000	—	—	—	1,400	—

X# 54 ECU

Bronze

Date	Mintage	F	VF	XF	Unc	BU
1986(a) Prooflike	50,000	—	—	—	20.00	—
1987(a) Prooflike	50,000	—	—	—	20.00	—
1988(a) Prooflike	50,000	—	—	—	20.00	—

X# 55 ECU

10.0000 g., 0.9500 Silver 0.3054 oz. ASW, 23 mm. **Obv:** Laureate bust of Europa left in sprays **Obv. Inscription:** EUROPA **Rev:** Letters ECU forming cross, date in angles, 12 abbreviated currencies in dotted outer circle **Edge:** Reeded

Date	Mintage	F	VF	XF	Unc	BU
1987(a) Prooflike	15,000	—	—	—	50.00	—

X# 55a ECU

12.5000 g., 0.9200 Gold 0.3697 oz. AGW, 23 mm. **Obv:** Laureate bust of Europa left in sprays **Obv. Inscription:** EUROPA **Rev:** Lettters ECU forming cross, date in angles **Edge:** Reeded

Date	Mintage	F	VF	XF	Unc	BU
1987(a) Prooflike	5,000	—	—	—	425	—

X# 55b ECU

13.7500 g., 0.9990 Platinum 0.4416 oz. APW, 23 mm. **Obv:** Laureate bust of Europa left in sprays **Obv. Inscription:** EUROPA **Rev:** Letters ECU forming cross, date in angles **Edge:** Reeded

Date	Mintage	F	VF	XF	Unc	BU
1987(a) Prooflike	1,000	—	—	—	750	—

X# 58 ECU

40.0000 g., 0.9250 Silver 1.1895 oz. ASW
Subject: 30th Anniversary of the European Economic Community

Date	Mintage	F	VF	XF	Unc	BU
1988(a) Prooflike	20,000	—	—	—	65.00	—

X# 61 ECU

40.0000 g., 0.9250 Silver 1.1895 oz. ASW

Date	Mintage	F	VF	XF	Unc	BU
1989(a) Prooflike	—	—	—	—	65.00	—

X# 62 ECU

50.0000 g., 0.9200 Gold 1.4789 oz. AGW

Date	Mintage	F	VF	XF	Unc	BU
1989(a) Prooflike	—	—	—	—	1,500	—

X# 63 ECU

Bronze

Date	Mintage	F	VF	XF	Unc	BU
1989(a) Prooflike	—	—	—	—	20.00	—

X# 64 ECU

40.0000 g., 0.9250 Silver 1.1895 oz. ASW

Date	Mintage	F	VF	XF	Unc	BU
1990(a) Prooflike	5,900	—	—	—	100	—
1991(a) Prooflike	5,900	—	—	—	100	—

X# 65 ECU

50.0000 g., 0.9200 Gold 1.4789 oz. AGW

Date	Mintage	F	VF	XF	Unc	BU
1990(a) Prooflike	1,450	—	—	—	1,750	—
1991(a) Prooflike	1,450	—	—	—	1,750	—

X# 66 ECU

Bronze

Date	Mintage	F	VF	XF	Unc	BU
1990(a) Prooflike	45,000	—	—	—	15.00	—
1991(a) Prooflike	45,000	—	—	—	15.00	—

X# 67 ECU

7.5000 g., Aluminum-Bronze, 23 mm. **Obv:** Laureate bust of Europa left in sprays **Obv. Inscription:** EUROPA **Rev:** Letters ECU forming cross, date in angles, 12 abbreviated currencies in dotted outer circle **Edge:** Reeded

Date	Mintage	F	VF	XF	Unc	BU
1990(a) Prooflike	—	—	—	—	6.00	—

X# 70 ECU

33.0000 g., Aluminum-Bronze, 41 mm. **Obv:** Laureate bust of Europa left in sprays **Obv. Inscription:** EUROPA **Rev:** Twelve coin like designs representing members in outer circle, date and value in center **Edge:** Reeded

Date	Mintage	F	VF	XF	Unc	BU
1992(a) Prooflike	45,000	—	—	—	25.00	—
1992(a) Prooflike	45,000	—	—	—	25.00	—

X# 101 ECU

Bronze, 40 mm. **Obv:** Europa leaning against kneeling bull, arch of 12 stars above **Rev:** Ten coin like national symbols outside circle of currencies, two symbols within, value above, date below **Edge:** Plain

Date	Mintage	F	VF	XF	Unc	BU
1992 Proof	—	Value: 25.00				
1993 Proof	9,999	Value: 25.00				

X# 68 ECU

40.0000 g., 0.9250 Silver 1.1895 oz. ASW, 41 mm. **Obv:** Laureate bust of Europa left in sprays **Obv. Inscription:** EUROPA **Rev:** Twelve coin like designs representing members in outer circles, date and value in center **Edge:** Reeded

Date	Mintage	F	VF	XF	Unc	BU
1992(a) Prooflike	5,900	—	—	—	150	—

X# 69 ECU

50.0000 g., 0.9200 Gold 1.4789 oz. AGW, 41 mm. **Obv:** Laureate bust of Europa left in sprays **Obv. Inscription:** EUROPA **Rev:** Twelve coin like designs representing members in outer circle, date and value in center **Edge:** Reeded

Date	Mintage	F	VF	XF	Unc	BU
1992(a) Prooflike	—	—	—	—	1,650	—

X# 101a ECU

0.9990 Silver, 40 mm. **Obv:** Europe leaning against kneeling bull, arch of 12 stars above **Obv. Legend:** EUROPA **Rev:** Ten coin like national symbolds outside circle of currencies, two symbols within, value above, date below **Edge:** Plain

Date	Mintage	F	VF	XF	Unc	BU
1992 Proof	—	Value: 50.00				

X# 71 ECU

Aluminum-Bronze, 23 mm. **Obv:** Laureate bust of Europa left in sprays **Obv. Inscription:** EUROPA **Rev:** Letters ECU forming cross, date in angles, 12 abbreviated currencies in dotted outer circle **Edge:** Reeded

Date	Mintage	F	VF	XF	Unc	BU
1993(a) Prooflike	400,000	—	—	—	4.00	—

X# 72 ECU

40.0000 g., 0.9250 Silver 1.1895 oz. ASW, 41 mm. **Obv:** Laureate bust of Europa left in sprays **Obv. Inscription:** EUROPA **Rev:** Twelve coin like designs representing members in outer circle, date and value in center **Edge:** Reeded

Date	Mintage	F	VF	XF	Unc	BU
1993(a) Prooflike	5,900	—	—	—	150	—

X# 73 ECU

50.0000 g., 0.9200 Gold 1.4789 oz. AGW, 41 mm. **Obv:** Laureate bust of Europa left in sprays **Obv. Inscription:** EUROPA **Rev:** Twelve coin like designs representing members in outer circle, date and value in center **Edge:** Reeded

Date	Mintage	F	VF	XF	Unc	BU
1993(a) Prooflike	1,450	—	—	—	1,750	—

X# 74 ECU

33.0000 g., Aluminum-Bronze, 41 mm. **Obv:** Laureate bust of Europa left in sprays **Obv. Inscription:** EUROPA **Rev:** Twelve coin like designs representing members in outer circle, date and value in center **Edge:** Reeded

Date	Mintage	F	VF	XF	Unc	BU
1993(a) Prooflike	45,000	—	—	—	27.50	—

X# 75 ECU

33.0000 g., Copper-Nickel-Zinc, 41 mm. **Obv:** Laureate bust of Europa left in sprays **Obv. Inscription:** EUROPA **Rev:** Twelve coin like designs representing members in outer circle, date and value in center **Edge:** Reeded

Date	Mintage	F	VF	XF	Unc	BU
1993(a) Prooflike	—	—	—	—	20.00	—

X# 102 ECU

32.5000 g., Bronze, 40 mm. **Obv:** Large EUROPA over map of Europe **Rev:** Large ECU above Europa riding a bull, date below **Edge:** Plain

Date	Mintage	F	VF	XF	Unc	BU
1993 Proof	9,999	Value: 17.50				

X# 103 ECU

33.0000 g., Bronze, 41 mm. **Obv:** Twelve national shields in circle surround 12-pointed emblem with large "E" **Rev:** Twelve stars in outer circle surround value, date **Shape:** 12-sided

Date	Mintage	F	VF	XF	Unc	BU
1993 Proof	9,999	Value: 17.50				

X# 100 5 ECU

26.5000 g., Bronze, 38 mm. **Obv:** Outer ring of 12 stars, inner ring of modernistic people surrounding value, date **Rev:** Twelve-sided circular band with 12 stars surrounding map of Europe **Edge:** Plain

Date	Mintage	F	VF	XF	Unc	BU
1992 Proof	12	—	—	—	—	—

X# 100a 5 ECU

26.0000 g., 0.9250 Silver 0.7732 oz. ASW, 38 mm. **Obv:** Outer ring of 12 stars, inner ring of modernistic people surrounding value, date **Rev:** Twelve-sided circular band with 12 stars surrounding map of Europe **Edge:** Plain

Date	Mintage	F	VF	XF	Unc	BU
1992 Proof	—	Value: 45.00				

INTERNATIONAL NUMISMATIC CONGRESS

Nova Europae

TRADE COINAGE

Struck at the Bavarian State Mint, Munich, West Germany.

X# 155.1 ECU

4.2500 g., Copper **Subject:** XI International Numismatic Congress **Edge:** Reeded

Date	Mintage	F	VF	XF	Unc	BU
1991	7,000	—	—	—	20.00	—

X# 155.2 ECU

4.2500 g., Copper, 20 mm. **Subject:** XI International Numismatic Congress **Edge:** Plain

Date	Mintage	F	VF	XF	Unc	BU
1991	4,000	—	—	—	25.00	—

X# 156.1 2 ECU

5.2500 g., Copper-Nickel-Zinc, 23 mm. **Subject:** XI International Numismatic Congress **Edge:** Reeded

Date	Mintage	F	VF	XF	Unc	BU
1991	2,000	—	—	—	60.00	—

X# 156.2 2 ECU

5.2500 g., Copper-Nickel-Zinc, 23 mm. **Subject:** XI International Numismatic Congress **Edge:** Plain

Date	Mintage	F	VF	XF	Unc	BU
1991	4,000	—	—	—	25.00	—

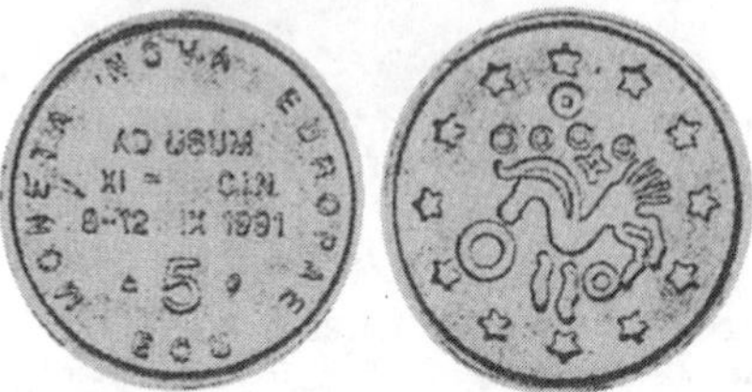

X# 157.1 5 ECU

7.2500 g., Bronze, 27 mm. **Subject:** XI International Numismatic Congress **Edge:** Reeded

Date	Mintage	F	VF	XF	Unc	BU
1991	2,000	—	—	—	75.00	—

X# 157.2 5 ECU

7.2500 g., Bronze, 27 mm. **Subject:** XI International Numismatic Congress **Edge:** Plain

Date	Mintage	F	VF	XF	Unc	BU
1991	4,000	—	—	—	25.00	—

X# 158.1 10 ECU

Copper-Nickel-Zinc **Subject:** XI International Numismatic Congress **Edge:** Reeded

Date	Mintage	F	VF	XF	Unc	BU
1991	500	—	—	—	200	—

X# 158.2 10 ECU

Copper-Nickel-Zinc **Subject:** XI International Numismatic Congress **Edge:** Plain

Date	Mintage	F	VF	XF	Unc	BU
1991	4,000	—	—	—	25.00	—

ESSAIS

X#	Date	Mintage	Identification	Mkt Val
E1	1980(a)	100	Ecu. 0.9200 Gold. 50.0000 g.	2,000
E2	1981(a)	100	Ecu. 0.9200 Gold. 50.0000 g.	2,000

X#	Date	Mintage	Identification	Mkt Val

X#	Date	Mintage	Identification	Mkt Val
E3	1982(a)	100	Ecu. 0.9990 Platinum. 55.0000 g. 40 mm.	2,450

X#	Date	Mintage	Identification	Mkt Val
E4	1983(a)	100	Ecu. 0.9990 Platinum. 55.0000 g. 40 mm.	2,500

X#	Date	Mintage	Identification	Mkt Val
E5	1984(a)	100	Ecu. 0.9990 Platinum. 55.0000 g. 40 mm.	2,500

X#	Date	Mintage	Identification	Mkt Val
E6	1985(a)	100	Ecu. 0.9990 Platinum. 55.0000 g. 40 mm.	2,500
E7	1986(a)	100	Ecu. 0.9990 Platinum. 55.0000 g.	2,500
E8	1987(a)	100	Ecu. 0.9990 Platinum. 55.0000 g.	2,500
E9	1988(a)	100	Ecu. 0.9990 Platinum. 55.0000 g.	2,500
E10	1989(a)	—	Ecu. 0.9990 Platinum. 55.0000 g.	2,750
E11	1990(a)	90	Ecu. 0.9990 Platinum. 55.0000 g.	2,800
E12	1991(a)	85	Ecu. 0.9990 Platinum.	2,800
E13	1992(a)	85	Ecu. 0.9990 Platinum. 55.0000 g. 41 mm.	2,800
E14	1993(a)	85	Ecu. 0.9990 Platinum. 55.0000 g. 41 mm.	2,800

TRIAL STRIKES

X#	Date	Mintage	Identification	Mkt Val
TS2	ND(1952)	—	5 Europinos. Bronze. Uniface obverse.	100

PROOF SETS

X#	Date	Mintage	Identification	Issue Price	Mkt Val
XPS1	1979 (5)	5,000	X86-X90	—	725
XPS2	1979 (3)	15,000	X86-X88	—	125
XPS3	1982 (4)	200	X91-X94	—	1,100
XPS4	1984 (5)	—	X115-X119	805	850
XPS5	1984 (3)	—	X115-X117	117	125
XPS6	1984 (2)	—	X118-X119	695	725
XPS7	1985 (5)	500	X121-X127	—	1,150
XPS8	1985 (4)	2,500	X121-X123, X127	—	600
XPS9	1985 (3)	3,500	X121-X123	—	90.00
XPS10	1985 (3)	1,000	X124-X126	—	525
XPS11	1989 (5)	—	X131-X135	—	1,300
XPS12	1989 (3)	—	X131-X133	—	300
XPS15	1991 (4)	4,000	X#155.2-158.2	—	100

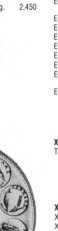

EUTOPIA

UTOPIA

PATTERNS

X#	Date	Mintage	Identification	Mkt Val
Pn1	1886	—	Dollar. Gold center. Silver ring. 0.8400 g. 13.3600 g.	—

FAEROE ISLANDS

DANISH STATE

FANTASY EURO PATTERNS

X# Pn1 EURO CENT
Copper Plated Steel **Edge:** Plain

Date	Mintage	F	VF	XF	Unc	BU
2004	12,500	—	—	—	—	1.00

X# Pn2 2 EURO CENT
Copper Plated Steel **Edge:** Plain

Date	Mintage	F	VF	XF	Unc	BU
2004	12,500	—	—	—	—	1.50

X# Pn3 5 EURO CENT
Copper Plated Steel **Edge:** Plain

Date	Mintage	F	VF	XF	Unc	BU
2004	12,500	—	—	—	—	2.00

X# Pn4 10 EURO CENT
Goldine **Edge:** Plain

Date	Mintage	F	VF	XF	Unc	BU
2004	12,500	—	—	—	—	2.50

X# Pn5 20 EURO CENT
Goldine **Edge:** Plain

Date	Mintage	F	VF	XF	Unc	BU
2004	12,500	—	—	—	—	3.00

X# Pn6 50 EURO CENT
Goldine **Edge:** Plain

Date	Mintage	F	VF	XF	Unc	BU
2004	12,500	—	—	—	—	3.50

X# Pn7 EURO
Bi-Metallic **Edge:** Plain

Date	Mintage	F	VF	XF	Unc	BU
2004	12,500	—	—	—	—	5.50

X# Pn8 2 EURO
Bi-Metallic **Edge:** Plain

Date	Mintage	F	VF	XF	Unc	BU
2004	12,500	—	—	—	—	7.50

MINT SETS

X#	Date	Mintage	Identification	Issue Price	Mkt Val
XMS1	2004 (8)	12,500	X#Pn1-Pn8	—	26.00

FALKLAND ISLANDS

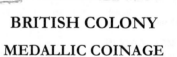

BRITISH COLONY

MEDALLIC COINAGE

1972 Pobjoy Mint Issue

X# M1 CROWN
Silver **Ruler:** Elizabeth II **Subject:** Edward VIII

Date	Mintage	F	VF	XF	Unc	BU
1936	—	—	—	—	—	—

Note: Reported, not confirmed

Geoffrey Hearn Series - 'By the Grace of God' Issue

X# M2 CROWN
33.4800 g., Silver **Ruler:** Elizabeth II **Subject:** Edward VIII **Obv:** Bust left **Obv. Legend:** EDWARD • VIII • KING • & • EMPEROR

Date	Mintage	F	VF	XF	Unc	BU
1936 Proof	—	Value: 175				

Richard Lobel Series

X# M3 CROWN
Bronze, 38.17 mm. **Ruler:** Elizabeth II **Subject:** Edward VIII **Obv:** Bust left **Obv. Legend:** EDWARD • VIII • KING • & • EMPEROR **Rev:** Penguin standing right **Edge:** Plain

Date	Mintage	F	VF	XF	Unc	BU
1936 Proof	1,000	Value: 15.00				

X# M3a CROWN
Copper-Nickel-Zinc, 38.17 mm. **Ruler:** Elizabeth II **Subject:** Edward VIII **Obv:** Bust left **Obv. Legend:** EDWARD • VIII • KING • & • EMPEROR **Rev:** Penguin standing right **Edge:** Plain

Date	Mintage	F	VF	XF	Unc	BU
1936 Proof	2,500	Value: 15.00				

X# M3b CROWN
0.9167 Silver, 38.17 mm. **Ruler:** Elizabeth II **Subject:** Edward VIII **Obv:** Bust left **Obv. Legend:** EDWARD • VIII • KING • & • EMPEROR **Rev:** Penguin standing right **Edge:** Plain

Date	Mintage	F	VF	XF	Unc	BU
1936 Proof	200	Value: 50.00				

X# M3c CROWN
Gold, 38.17 mm. **Ruler:** Elizabeth II **Subject:** Edward VIII **Obv:** Bust left **Obv. Legend:** EDWARD • VIII • KING • & • EMPEROR **Rev:** Penguin standing right **Edge:** Plain

Date	Mintage	F	VF	XF	Unc	BU
1936 Proof	—	Value: 500				

X# M5 CROWN
23.1100 g., 0.9167 Silver 0.6811 oz. ASW, 38.15 mm. **Ruler:** Elizabeth II **Obv:** Head of Duchess, bust of Duke facing **Obv. Legend:** DUKE & DUCHESS OF WINDSOR **Rev:** Penguin standing right **Edge:** Reeded

Date	Mintage	F	VF	XF	Unc	BU
1987 Proof	—	—	—	—	—	—

X# M4 SOVEREIGN
0.3750 Gold, 21.98 mm. **Ruler:** Elizabeth II **Subject:** Edward VIII **Obv:** Bust left **Obv. Legend:** EDWARD • VIII • KING • & • EMPEROR **Rev:** Penguin standing right **Edge:** Plain

Date	Mintage	F	VF	XF	Unc	BU
1936 Proof	200	Value: 125				

X# M4a SOVEREIGN
4.4200 g., Silver, 21.98 mm. **Ruler:** Elizabeth II **Subject:** Edward VIII **Obv:** Bust left **Obv. Legend:** EDWARD • VIII • KING • & • EMPEROR **Rev:** Penguin walking right **Edge:** Plain

Date	Mintage	F	VF	XF	Unc	BU
1936 Proof	—	Value: 10.00				

X# M6 SOVEREIGN
0.3750 Gold, 21.98 mm. **Ruler:** Elizabeth II **Obv:** Head of Duchess, bust of Duke facing **Obv. Legend:** DUKE & DUCHESS OF WINDSOR **Rev:** Penguin standing right **Edge:** Reeded

Date	Mintage	F	VF	XF	Unc	BU
1987 Proof	—	—	—	—	—	—

X# M6a SOVEREIGN
4.4200 g., Silver, 21.98 mm. **Ruler:** Elizabeth II **Obv:** Head of Duchess, bust of Duke facing **Obv. Legend:** DUKE & DUCHESS OF WINDSOR **Rev:** Penguin standing right **Edge:** Reeded

Date	Mintage	F	VF	XF	Unc	BU
1987 Proof	—	—	—	—	—	—

PIEFORTS

X#	Date	Mintage	Identification	Mkt Val
P1	1936	—	Crown. 0.9167 Silver. X#M3b.	100

FINLAND

GRAND DUCHY

DECIMAL COINAGE

X# A1 75 PENNIA
Silver, 29 mm. **Ruler:** Alexander II **Obv:** Crowned imperial eagle **Rev:** Value date in oak sprays **Note:** Struck illegally as "favors" by the Helsinki Mint Director P.U. Helle. Mintage 20-30 pieces.

Date	Mintage	F	VF	XF	Unc	BU
1865 (1953)	—	—	—	—	—	—

CIVIL WAR COINAGE

Liberated Finnish Government Issue

X# B1 5 PENNIA
2.5000 g., Copper, 17.9 mm. **Obv:** 3 trumpets **Obv. Legend:** • KANSAN TYÖ, KANSAN VALTA • - SUOMI - FINLAND **Rev:** Large value, wreath knot above second 1 in 1918 **Note:** This variety was unofficially struck outside of Finland in the early 1920's. Prev. KM#21.2.

Date	Mintage	F	VF	XF	Unc	BU
1920	—	—	—	—	—	—

REPUBLIC

MEDALLIC COINAGE

Ecu Series

X# 1 5 ECU
Copper-Nickel, 38.61 mm. **Issuer:** Coin Invest Trust **Subject:** CSCE / KFZE Conference 20th Anniversary **Obv:** Artwork, head of Jean Sibelius **Rev:** Landscape, modern buildings **Edge:** Reeded

Date	Mintage	F	VF	XF	Unc	BU
1992	Est. 10,000	—	—	—	15.00	—

X# 18 5 ECU
27.0000 g., Copper-Nickel, 38.61 mm. **Obv:** Lapplander with reindeer **Rev:** Rovaniemi shield above bridge scene **Rev. Legend:** LAPIN PÄÄKAUPUNKI • ROVANIEMI - HAUPTSTADT LAPPLANDS **Edge:** Reeded

Date	Mintage	F	VF	XF	Unc	BU
1994	3,500	—	—	—	—	15.00

X# 2 20 ECU
25.0000 g., 0.9250 Silver 0.7435 oz. ASW, 38.61 mm. **Issuer:** Coin Invest Trust **Subject:** CSCE / KFZE Conference 20th Anniversary **Obv:** Artwork, head of Jean Sibelius **Rev:** Landscape, modern buildings **Edge:** Reeded

Date	Mintage	F	VF	XF	Unc	BU
1992 Proof	Est. 7,500	Value: 35.00				

X# 17 20 ECU
25.0000 g., 0.9250 Silver 0.7435 oz. ASW, 38.61 mm. **Obv:** Lapplander with reindeer **Rev:** Rovaniemi shield above bridge scene **Rev. Legend:** LAPIN PÄÄKAUPUNKI • ROVANIEMI - HAUPTSTADT LAPPLANDS **Edge:** Reeded

Date	Mintage	F	VF	XF	Unc	BU
1994 Proof	3,500	Value: 35.00				

X# 19 20 ECU
25.0000 g., 0.9250 Silver 0.7435 oz. ASW, 38.6 mm. **Obv:** Two reindeer below wreath of 12 stars **Rev:** Bust of Johan Ludvig Runeberg 3/4 left **Edge:** Lettered

Date	Mintage	F	VF	XF	Unc	BU
1995 Proof	—	Value: 35.00				

X# 4 20 ECU
27.0000 g., 0.9250 Silver 0.8029 oz. ASW **Rev:** Castle of Turku

Date	Mintage	F	VF	XF	Unc	BU
1996 Proof	25,000	Value: 30.00				

X# 36 20 ECU
27.2000 g., 0.9250 Silver 0.8089 oz. ASW, 38.5 mm. **Obv:** Upper part of crowned lion left wielding sword **Rev:** Early sailing ship, castle, arch with 12 stars **Rev. Legend:** HANSE • PORTTI EUROOPPAAN **Edge:** Lettered **Edge Lettering:** Translated "Not legal tender"

Date	Mintage	F	VF	XF	Unc	BU
1996 Proof	—	Value: 40.00				

X# 7 20 ECU
27.0000 g., 0.9250 Silver 0.8029 oz. ASW **Obv:** Upper part of crowned lion left wielding sword **Rev:** Aurora Borealis **Edge:** Lettered

Date	Mintage	F	VF	XF	Unc	BU
1997 Proof	20,000	Value: 40.00				

X# 8 20 ECU
27.0000 g., 0.9250 Silver 0.8029 oz. ASW **Rev:** Castle of Häme and Ingeborg Aakentytar Tott **Note:** Castle of Häme

Date	Mintage	F	VF	XF	Unc	BU
1997 Proof	20,000	Value: 30.00				

X# 11 20 ECU
27.0000 g., 0.9250 Silver 0.8029 oz. ASW **Note:** Zacharius Topelius.

Date	Mintage	F	VF	XF	Unc	BU
1998 Proof	20,000	Value: 30.00				

X# 3 150 ECU
6.7200 g., 0.7500 Gold 0.1620 oz. AGW, 23 mm. **Issuer:** Coin Invest Trust **Subject:** CSCE / KFZE Conference 20th Anniversary **Obv:** Artwork, head of Jean Sibelius **Rev:** Landscape, modern buildings **Edge:** Reeded **Note:** Similar to 5 Ecu, KM#M1.

Date	Mintage	F	VF	XF	Unc	BU
1992 Proof	Est. 1,000	Value: 200				

X# 16 150 ECU
6.7200 g., 0.7500 Gold 0.1620 oz. AGW, 23 mm. **Obv:** Lapplander with reindeer **Rev:** Rovaniemi shield above bridge scene **Rev. Legend:** LAPIN PÄÄKAUPUNKI • ROVANIEMI - HAUPTSTADT LAPPLANDS **Edge:** Reeded

Date	Mintage	F	VF	XF	Unc	BU
1994 Proof	250	Value: 300				

Euro Series

X# 20 5 EURO
Ring Weight: 23.1500 g. **Ring Composition:** Copper-Nickel **Center Composition:** Brass, 38.6 mm. **Obv:** Upper part of crowned lion left wielding sword **Rev:** Olavinlinna Castle **Edge:** Lettered **Edge Lettering:** Translated "Not lawful payment"

Date	Mintage	F	VF	XF	Unc	BU
1996 Proof	—	Value: 18.50				

X# 44 5 EURO
Bi-Metallic Brass center in Nickel ring, 38.5 mm. **Subject:** First World Air Games in Turkey **Obv:** Monoplane, sky surfers and parachutist **Rev:** Monoplane, hot air balloon, handglider **Rev. Legend:** FÉDÉRATION AÉRONAUTIQUE INTERNATIONALE **Edge:** Lettered

Date	Mintage	F	VF	XF	Unc	BU
ND(19)96 error	—	—	—	—	—	25.00
ND(19)97	—	—	—	—	—	20.00

X# 43 5 EURO
Bi-Metallic Brass center in Nickel ring, 38.5 mm. **Series:** FAI **Subject:** First World Air Games in Turkey **Obv:** Helicopter, glider, monoplane **Rev:** Monoplane, hot air balloon, hand glider **Rev. Legend:** FÉDÉRATION AÉRONAUTIQUE INTERNATIONALE **Edge:** Lettered

Date	Mintage	F	VF	XF	Unc	BU
(19)97	—	—	—	—	—	20.00

X# 5 10 EURO
14.4000 g., 0.9250 Silver 0.4282 oz. ASW **Rev:** Castle of Olavinlinna

Date	Mintage	F	VF	XF	Unc	BU
1996	25,000	—	—	—	15.00	—

X# 21 10 EURO
23.1500 g., Copper-Nickel, 38.6 mm. **Obv:** Upper part of crowned lion left, wielding sword **Rev:** Olavinlinna Castle **Edge:** Lettered **Edge Lettering:** Translated "Not lawful payment" **Note:** Prev. X#M5.

Date	Mintage	F	VF	XF	Unc	BU
1996 Proof	—	Value: 18.50				

X# 46 10 EURO
Silver, 38.5 mm. **Subject:** First World Air Games in Turkey **Obv:** Hot air balloons **Rev:** Monoplane, hot air balloon, hand glider **Rev. Legend:** FÉDÉRATION AÉRONAUTIQUE INTERNATIONALE **Edge:** Lettered

Date	Mintage	F	VF	XF	Unc	BU
ND(19)97 Proof	—	Value: 42.50				

X# 6 10 EURO
27.0000 g., 0.9250 Silver 0.8029 oz. ASW **Subject:** 75 Years of Åland Self-government

Date	Mintage	F	VF	XF	Unc	BU
1997	10,000	—	—	—	20.00	—

X# 9 10 EURO
27.0000 g., 0.9250 Silver 0.8029 oz. ASW
Subject: Nagano Games **Rev:** Cross Country Skiing

Date	Mintage	F	VF	XF	Unc	BU
1998 Proof	30,000	Value: 22.50				

X# 10 10 EURO
27.0000 g., 0.9250 Silver 0.8029 oz. ASW
Subject: Nagano Games **Rev:** Alpine skiing

Date	Mintage	F	VF	XF	Unc	BU
1998 Proof	30,000	Value: 22.50				

X# 22 20 EURO
Silver, 38.5 mm. **Obv:** Upper part of crowned lion left wielding sword **Rev:** Olavinlinna Castle **Edge:** Lettered **Edge Lettering:** Translated "Not lawful payment"

Date	Mintage	F	VF	XF	Unc	BU
1996 Proof	—	Value: 35.00				

X# 12 50 EURO
8.6400 g., 0.9000 Gold 0.2500 oz. AGW
Subject: Nagano Games **Rev:** Cross country skiing

Date	Mintage	F	VF	XF	Unc	BU
1998 Proof	5,000	Value: 200				

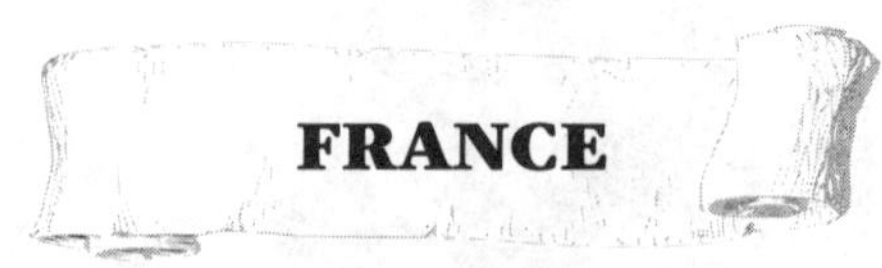

FRANCE

KINGDOM

MEDALLIC COINAGE

X# M50 1-1/4 ECU D'OR
4.3700 g., Gold, 24.5 mm. **Subject:** Wedding to Ferdinand, Archduke of Austria **Obv:** Bust of Marie Antoinette right **Obv. Legend:** M • ANOT • A • A • LUDO • FRANCIA DELP.SPONSA **Rev:** Woman right receiving wreath from angel at left **Rev. Legend:** CONCORD • NOVO • SANG • VIN • NEX • FIRM • **Rev. Inscription:** NVPT.CEL.VIEN.PROCV./FERD.A • A.19 APR.

Date	Mintage	F	VF	XF	Unc	BU
1770	—	—	—	—	—	—

X# M50a 1-1/4 ECU D'OR
3.9600 g., Silver, 24.5 mm. **Obv:** Bust of Marie Antoinette right **Obv. Legend:** M • ANTO • A • A • LUDO • FRANCIA DELP.SPONSA **Rev:** Woman right receiving wreath from angel at left **Rev. Legend:** CONCORD • NOVO • SANG • VIN • NEX.FIRM. **Rev. Inscription:** NVPT.CEL.VIEN.PROCV./FED.A•A.19 APR.

Date	Mintage	F	VF	XF	Unc	BU
1770	—	100	175	300	—	—

FIRST REPUBLIC

1793-1794, L'An 2

PRETENDER COINAGE

X# 2 6 DENIERS
Bronze **Ruler:** Louis XVII **Obv:** L above, Roman numeral XVII below **Obv. Legend:** FLEUR DELYS **Rev:** Shield divides value **Note:** Prev. KM#PT2.

Date	Mintage	F	VF	XF	Unc	BU
ND(1794)	—	150	275	550	1,300	—

X# 3 12 DENIERS
Copper **Ruler:** Louis XVII **Note:** Prev. KM#PT3.

Date	Mintage	F	VF	XF	Unc	BU
ND(1794)	—	85.00	200	450	1,000	—

PRETENDER COINAGE WITH ESSAI

X# E4 6 DENIERS
Bronze **Ruler:** Louis XVII **Obv:** Bust left; ESSAI below **Note:** Prev. KM#PTE4.

Date	Mintage	F	VF	XF	Unc	BU
ND	—	—	100	200	600	—

X# E5 12 DENIERS
Copper **Ruler:** Louis XVII **Rev:** Date in wreath **Rev. Legend:** PIECE D'ESSAI **Note:** Prev. KM#PTE5. These pieces are considered souvenir issues produced by Royalist Partisans.

Date	Mintage	F	VF	XF	Unc	BU
1792	—	150	275	550	1,250	—

X# E1 30 SOLS
Bronze **Ruler:** Louis XVII **Obv:** Bust left; ESSAI below **Rev:** Value in wreath

Date	Mintage	F	VF	XF	Unc	BU
ND(1792)	—	200	400	800	1,400	—

CONSULSHIP

Napoleon as First Consul

MEDALLIC COINAGE

KM# M9 5 FRANCS
Pewter **Subject:** Napoleon as First Consul Visit to Paris Mint

Date	Mintage	F	VF	XF	Unc	BU
1803(ANXI) Restrike	—	—	50.00	125	250	—

KM# M9a 5 FRANCS
25.0000 g., 0.9000 Silver 0.7234 oz. ASW, 36.5 mm.
Subject: Napoleon as First Consul Visit to Paris Mint

Date	Mintage	F	VF	XF	Unc	BU
1803(ANXI)	—	—	750	1,500	2,100	—
1803(ANXI) Restrike	—	—	150	300	500	—

KM# M9b 5 FRANCS
Gold, 36.5 mm. **Subject:** Napoleon as First Consul Visit to Paris Mint

Date	Mintage	F	VF	XF	Unc	BU
1803(ANXI) Unique	—	—	—	—	—	—
1803(ANXI) Restrike	—	—	—	—	—	—

GALLIA REDDITA EUROPAE

MEDALLIC COINAGE

X# M1 2 FRANCS
Bronze **Series:** Austrian **Obv:** Similar to 5 Francs, XM3 **Rev. Legend:** FRANCOIS I • EMP • D'AUTRICHE **Edge:** Plain

Date	Mintage	F	VF	XF	Unc	BU
1814	150	—	—	125	225	—

X# M2 2 FRANCS
Silver **Series:** Austrian **Edge Lettering:** DIEU PROTEGEN LA FRANCE

Date	Mintage	F	VF	XF	Unc	BU
1814	1,500	—	—	40.00	80.00	—

X# M5 2 FRANCS
Bronze **Series:** Prussian **Obv:** Similar to 5 Francs, XM3 **Rev. Legend:** FREDERIC GUILLAUME III • ROI DE PRUSSE **Edge:** Plain

Date	Mintage	F	VF	XF	Unc	BU
1814	150	—	—	45.00	90.00	—

X# M6 2 FRANCS
Silver **Series:** Prussian **Edge Lettering:** DIEU PROTEGE LA FRANCE

Date	Mintage	F	VF	XF	Unc	BU
1814	1,800	—	—	35.00	70.00	—

X# M9 2 FRANCS
Bronze **Series:** Russian **Edge:** Plain

Date	Mintage	F	VF	XF	Unc	BU
1814	150	—	—	45.00	100	—

X# M11 2 FRANCS
Silver **Series:** Russian **Rev. Legend:** AU PACIFICATEUR DE L'EUROPE

Date	Mintage	F	VF	XF	Unc	BU
1814	1,500	—	—	50.00	245	—

X# M10 2 FRANCS
Bronze **Series:** Russian **Edge:** Reeded **Note:** Circular design in relief

Date	Mintage	F	VF	XF	Unc	BU
1814	300	—	—	35.00	70.00	—

X# M3 5 FRANCS
Bronze **Series:** Austrian **Edge:** Plain

Date	Mintage	F	VF	XF	Unc	BU
1814	250	—	—	85.00	175	—

X# M4 5 FRANCS
Silver **Series:** Austrian **Edge Lettering:** DIEU PROTEGE LA FRANCE

Date	Mintage	F	VF	XF	Unc	BU
1814	3,000	—	—	150	250	—

X# M7 5 FRANCS
Silver **Series:** Prussian **Obv. Legend:** GALLIA REDDITA EUROPAE / APRILE 1814 **Rev. Legend:** FREDERIC GUILLAUME III • ROI DE PRUSSE. **Rev. Inscription:** ANGE / DE / PAIS. / PARIS. **Edge:** Plain

Date	Mintage	F	VF	XF	Unc	BU
1814	4,000	—	—	125	225	—

X# M8 5 FRANCS
Silver **Series:** Prussian **Edge Lettering:** DIEU PROTEGE LA FRANCE

Date	Mintage	F	VF	XF	Unc	BU
1814	4,000	—	—	125	225	—

X# M12 5 FRANCS
Bronze **Series:** Russian **Edge:** Plain

Date	Mintage	F	VF	XF	Unc	BU
1814	250	—	—	120	250	—

X# M13 5 FRANCS
Bronze **Series:** Russian **Edge Lettering:** DIEU PROTEGE LA FRANCE

Date	Mintage	F	VF	XF	Unc	BU
1814	3,000	—	—	150	275	—

X# M14 5 FRANCS
Silver **Series:** Russian **Rev. Legend:** AU PACIFICATEUR DE L'EUROPE

Date	Mintage	F	VF	XF	Unc	BU
1814	3,500	—	—	125	250	—

X# M15 5 FRANCS
Bronze **Series:** Russian **Edge Lettering:** DOMINE SALVULM...

Date	Mintage	F	VF	XF	Unc	BU
1814	3,500	—	—	120	250	—

FIRST EMPIRE

Napoleon as Emperor

MEDALLIC COINAGE

KM# M1 2 FRANCS
Pewter **Subject:** Prince Charles of Baden Visit to Paris Mint **Obv:** Two shields of arms in branches **Rev:** Six-line inscription

Date	Mintage	F	VF	XF	Unc	BU
1806	—	—	75.00	150	300	—

KM# M1a 2 FRANCS
Bronze **Subject:** Visit of Prince Charles of Baden to Paris Mint **Obv:** 2 shields of arms in branches **Rev:** Six-line inscription

Date	Mintage	F	VF	XF	Unc	BU
1806	—	—	75.00	150	300	—

KM# M1b 2 FRANCS
10.0000 g., 0.9000 Silver 0.2893 oz. ASW **Subject:** Visit of Prince Charles of Baden to Paris Mint **Obv:** 2 shields of arms in branches **Rev:** Six-line inscription

Date	Mintage	F	VF	XF	Unc	BU
1806	—	—	200	300	625	—

KM# M2 2 FRANCS
10.0000 g., 0.9000 Bronze 0.2893 oz. **Subject:** Visit of Prince Ludwig of Bavaria to Paris Mint **Obv:** Uniformed bust of Max. Josef right **Rev:** 6-line legend

Date	Mintage	F	VF	XF	Unc	BU
1806	—	—	75.00	150	300	—

KM# M2a 2 FRANCS
10.0000 g., 0.9000 Silver 0.2893 oz. ASW **Subject:** Visit of Prince Ludwig of Bavaria to Paris Mint

Date	Mintage	F	VF	XF	Unc	BU
1806	—	—	200	300	600	—

KM# M3 2 FRANCS
Bronze **Subject:** King of Saxony Visit to Paris Mint

Date	Mintage	F	VF	XF	Unc	BU
1809	—	—	75.00	150	300	—

KM# M3a 2 FRANCS
10.0000 g., 0.9000 Silver 0.2893 oz. ASW **Subject:** King of Saxony Visit to Paris Mint

Date	Mintage	F	VF	XF	Unc	BU
1809	—	—	150	300	525	—

KM# M3b 2 FRANCS
Gold **Subject:** King of Saxony Visit to Paris Mint

Date	Mintage	F	VF	XF	Unc	BU
1809	—	—	750	1,500	2,400	—

KM# M4 2 FRANCS
Bronze **Subject:** King of Württemberg Visit to Paris Mint

Date	Mintage	F	VF	XF	Unc	BU
1809	—	—	75.00	150	300	—

KM# M4a 2 FRANCS
10.0000 g., 0.9000 Silver 0.2893 oz. ASW **Subject:** King of Württemberg Visit to Paris Mint

Date	Mintage	F	VF	XF	Unc	BU
1809	—	—	150	300	500	—

KM# M4b 2 FRANCS
Gold **Subject:** King of Württemberg Visit to Paris Mint

Date	Mintage	F	VF	XF	Unc	BU
1809	—	—	750	1,600	2,800	—

KM# M5 2 FRANCS
Bronze **Subject:** King of Württemberg Visit to Paris Mint

Date	Mintage	F	VF	XF	Unc	BU
1809	—	—	75.00	150	250	—

KM# M5a 2 FRANCS
10.0000 g., 0.9000 Silver 0.2893 oz. ASW
Subject: King of Württemberg Visit to Paris Mint

Date	Mintage	F	VF	XF	Unc	BU
1809	—	—	150	300	500	—

KM# M6 2 FRANCS
Bronze **Subject:** King and Queen of Bavaria Visit to Paris Mint

Date	Mintage	F	VF	XF	Unc	BU
1810	—	—	75.00	150	300	—

KM# M6a 2 FRANCS
10.0000 g., 0.9000 Silver 0.2893 oz. ASW
Subject: King and Queen of Bavaria Visit to Paris Mint

Date	Mintage	F	VF	XF	Unc	BU
1810	—	—	200	300	500	—

KM# M6b 2 FRANCS
Gold **Subject:** King and Queen of Bavaria Visit to Paris Mint

Date	Mintage	F	VF	XF	Unc	BU
1810	—	—	1,000	1,750	3,500	—

SECOND KINGDOM

MILLED - COUNTERFEIT ISSUE

X# 1 20 FRANCS
6.4516 g., 0.9000 Gold 0.1867 oz. AGW **Issuer:** British Government **Obv:** Bust right **Obv. Legend:** Louis XVIII ROI DE FRANCE **Obv. Designer:** T. Wyon Jr. **Rev:** Crowned arms in sprays **Rev. Legend:** PIECE DE - 20 FRANCS **Note:** Prev. KM#707. Privy mark: Fleur-de-lis.

Date	Mintage	Good	VG	F	VF	XF
1815R	—	135	200	300	400	1,000

Note: In 1815 the British Government counterfeited a similar French Gold 20 Francs of that year with the bust of Louis XVIII on them. The difference is that the British counterfeits had an 'R' mint mark and unusual reverse legend. They were made to pay the troops, who then could pay for what they wanted in a currency that the locals would accept.

MEDALLIC COINAGE

KM# M7 2 FRANCS
Bronze **Subject:** Duke and Duchess de Berry Visit to Paris Mint

Date	Mintage	F	VF	XF	Unc	BU
1817	—	—	75.00	125	225	—

KM# M7a 2 FRANCS
10.0000 g., 0.9000 Silver 0.2893 oz. ASW **Subject:** Duke and Duchess de Berry Visit to Paris Mint

Date	Mintage	F	VF	XF	Unc	BU
1817	—	—	200	400	850	—

KM# M7b 2 FRANCS
Pewter **Subject:** Duke and Duchess de Berry Visit to Paris Mint

Date	Mintage	F	VF	XF	Unc	BU
1817	—	—	50.00	100	250	—

KM# M8 2 FRANCS
Bronze **Subject:** Prince and Princess of Denmark Visit to Paris Mint **Obv:** Crowned shields of arms **Rev:** Seven-line inscription

Date	Mintage	F	VF	XF	Unc	BU
1822	—	—	75.00	125	225	—

KM# M8a 2 FRANCS
10.0000 g., 0.9000 Silver 0.2893 oz. ASW **Subject:** Prince and Princess of Denmark Visit to Paris Mint **Obv:** Crowned shields of arms **Rev:** Seven-line inscription

Date	Mintage	F	VF	XF	Unc	BU
1822	—	—	200	300	600	—

KM# M10 5 FRANCS
Bronze **Subject:** Duke de Berry Visit to Paris Mint **Obv:** Uniformed bust of Louis XVIII **Rev:** Six-line inscription

Date	Mintage	F	VF	XF	Unc	BU
1814	—	—	75.00	150	300	—

KM# M10a 5 FRANCS
25.0000 g., 0.9000 Silver 0.7234 oz. ASW **Subject:** Duke de Berry Visit to Paris Mint **Obv:** Uniformed bust of Louis XVIII **Rev:** Six-line inscription

Date	Mintage	F	VF	XF	Unc	BU
1814	—	—	350	600	950	—

Note: Exist with smooth and engraved edges

KM# M11 5 FRANCS
Bronze **Subject:** Comte D'Artois Visit to Marseille Mint **Obv:** Uniformed bust of Louis XVIII **Rev:** Six-line inscription

Date	Mintage	F	VF	XF	Unc	BU
1814	—	—	75.00	125	225	—

KM# M11a 5 FRANCS
25.0000 g., 0.9000 Silver 0.7234 oz. ASW **Subject:** Comte D'Artois Visit to Marseille Mint **Obv:** Uniformed bust of Louis XVIII **Rev:** Six-line inscription

Date	Mintage	F	VF	XF	Unc	BU
1814	60	—	250	350	800	—

KM# M11b 5 FRANCS
Gold **Subject:** Comte D'Artois Visit to Marseille Mint **Obv:** Uniformed bust of Louis XVIII **Rev:** Six-line inscription

Date	Mintage	F	VF	XF	Unc	BU
1814 Unique	1	—	—	—	—	—

KM# M12 5 FRANCS
Pewter **Subject:** Duchess D'Angouleme Visit to Paris Mint

Date	Mintage	F	VF	XF	Unc	BU
1817	—	—	75.00	125	250	—

KM# M12a 5 FRANCS
Bronze **Subject:** Duchess D'Angouleme Visit to Paris Mint

Date	Mintage	F	VF	XF	Unc	BU
1817	—	—	75.00	125	225	—

KM# M12b 5 FRANCS
Gilt Bronze **Subject:** Duchess D'Angouleme Visit to Paris Mint

Date	Mintage	F	VF	XF	Unc	BU
1817	—	—	75.00	150	250	—

KM# M12c 5 FRANCS
25.0000 g., 0.9000 Silver 0.7234 oz. ASW
Subject: Duchess D'Angouleme Visit to Paris Mint

Date	Mintage	F	VF	XF	Unc	BU
1817	—	—	250	400	750	—

KM# M12d 5 FRANCS
Gold **Subject:** Duchess D'Angouleme Visit to Paris Mint

Date	Mintage	F	VF	XF	Unc	BU
1817	—	—	—	—	12,500	—

Note: Three known

KM# M13 5 FRANCS
Pewter **Subject:** Duke D'Angouleme Visit to La Rochelle mint

Date	Mintage	F	VF	XF	Unc	BU
1817	—	—	75.00	150	275	—

KM# M13a 5 FRANCS
25.0000 g., 0.9000 Silver 0.7234 oz. ASW **Subject:** Duke D'Angouleme Visit to La Rochelle mint

Date	Mintage	F	VF	XF	Unc	BU
1817	—	—	300	450	750	—

KM# M14 5 FRANCS
Bronze **Subject:** Visit of the Duke and Duchess de Berry to Paris Mint

Date	Mintage	F	VF	XF	Unc	BU
1817	—	—	50.00	100	200	—

KM# M14a 5 FRANCS
25.0000 g., 0.9000 Silver 0.7234 oz. ASW **Subject:** Visit of the Duke and Duchess de Berry to Paris Mint

Date	Mintage	F	VF	XF	Unc	BU
1817	—	—	300	450	750	—

KM# MA25 5 FRANCS
25.0000 g., 0.9000 Silver 0.7234 oz. ASW **Subject:** Count of Corvetto Visit to Paris Mint

Date	Mintage	F	VF	XF	Unc	BU
1817	—	—	350	450	750	—

KM# M15 5 FRANCS
Pewter **Subject:** Charles Philippe (later Charles X) Visit to Paris Mint

Date	Mintage	F	VF	XF	Unc	BU
1818	—	—	75.00	150	300	—

KM# M15a 5 FRANCS
Bronze **Subject:** Charles Philippe (later Charles X) Visit to Paris Mint

Date	Mintage	F	VF	XF	Unc	BU
1818	—	—	75.00	175	300	—

KM# M15b 5 FRANCS
25.0000 g., 0.9000 Silver 0.7234 oz. ASW **Subject:** Charles Philippe (later Charles X) Visit to Paris Mint

Date	Mintage	F	VF	XF	Unc	BU
1818	—	—	400	600	1,100	—

KM# M15c 5 FRANCS
Gold **Subject:** Charles Philippe (later Charles X) Visit to Paris Mint

Date	Mintage	F	VF	XF	Unc	BU
1818	—	—	—	—	10,000	—

KM# M16 5 FRANCS
Bronze **Subject:** Prince of Salerno and Duchess de Berry Visit to Paris Mint **Obv:** Head of Charles X left **Rev:** Eight-line inscription

Date	Mintage	F	VF	XF	Unc	BU
1825	—	—	75.00	125	250	—

KM# M16a 5 FRANCS
25.0000 g., 0.9000 Silver 0.7234 oz. ASW **Subject:** Prince of Salerno and Duchess de Berry Visit to Paris Mint **Obv:** Head of Charles X left **Rev:** Eight-line inscription

Date	Mintage	F	VF	XF	Unc	BU
1825	—	—	400	600	900	—

KM# M17 5 FRANCS
Bronze **Subject:** Visit of the King to Lille Mint **Obv:** Head of Charles X left **Rev:** Seven-line inscription

Date	Mintage	F	VF	XF	Unc	BU
1827	—	—	75.00	125	250	—

KM# M17a 5 FRANCS
25.0000 g., 0.9000 Silver 0.7234 oz. ASW **Subject:** Visit of the King to Lille Mint **Obv:** Head of Charles X left **Rev:** Seven-line inscription

Date	Mintage	F	VF	XF	Unc	BU
1827	—	—	300	500	750	—

KM# M17b 5 FRANCS
Gold **Subject:** Visit of the King to Lille Mint **Obv:** Head of Charles X left **Rev:** Seven-line inscription

Date	Mintage	F	VF	XF	Unc	BU
1827 Unique	—	—	—	—	—	—

KM# M18 5 FRANCS
Bronze **Subject:** Duke de Bordeaux (later Pretender Henri V) Visit to Paris Mint **Obv:** Crowned arms in branches **Rev:** Seven-line inscription

Date	Mintage	F	VF	XF	Unc	BU
1828	50	—	100	200	500	—

KM# M18a 5 FRANCS
25.0000 g., 0.9000 Silver 0.7234 oz. ASW **Subject:** Duke de Bordeaux (later Pretender Henri V) Visit to Paris Mint **Obv:** Crowned arms in branches **Rev:** 7-line legend

Date	Mintage	F	VF	XF	Unc	BU
1828	50	—	300	500	1,100	—

KM# M19 5 FRANCS
Bronze **Subject:** King and Queen of the Two Sicilies to Paris Mint **Obv:** Crowned shields of arms in branches **Rev:** Seven-line inscription

Date	Mintage	F	VF	XF	Unc	BU
1830	200	—	75.00	125	225	—

KM# M19a 5 FRANCS
Silvered Bronze **Subject:** King and Queen of the Two Sicilies to Paris Mint **Obv:** Crowned shields of arms in branches **Rev:** 7-line inscription

Date	Mintage	F	VF	XF	Unc	BU
1830	—	—	75.00	150	250	—

KM# M19b 5 FRANCS
25.0000 g., 0.9000 Silvered Copper Alloy 0.7234 oz. **Subject:** King and Queen of the Two Sicilies to Paris Mint **Obv:** Crowned shields of arms in branches **Rev:** 7-line inscription

Date	Mintage	F	VF	XF	Unc	BU
1830	197	—	300	500	750	—

KM# M19c 5 FRANCS
Gold **Subject:** King and Queen of the Two Sicilies to Paris Mint **Obv:** Crowned shields of arms in branches **Rev:** 7-line inscription

Date	Mintage	F	VF	XF	Unc	BU
1830	13	—	—	—	7,500	—

KM# M20 5 FRANCS
Pewter **Subject:** Visit of King Louis Philippe I to Rouen mint

Date	Mintage	F	VF	XF	Unc	BU
1831	—	—	75.00	125	225	—

KM# M20a 5 FRANCS
Bronze **Subject:** Visit of King Louis Philippe I to Rouen mint

Date	Mintage	F	VF	XF	Unc	BU
1831	50	—	75.00	150	275	—

KM# M20b 5 FRANCS
25.0000 g., 0.9000 Silver 0.7234 oz. ASW **Subject:** Visit of King Louis Philippe I to Rouen mint

Date	Mintage	F	VF	XF	Unc	BU
1831	—	—	150	300	400	—

KM# M20c 5 FRANCS
Gold **Subject:** Visit of King Louis Philippe I to Rouen mint

Date	Mintage	F	VF	XF	Unc	BU
1831	—	—	—	—	—	—

KM# M21 5 FRANCS
Gold **Subject:** Prince of Salerno Visit to Paris Mint **Obv:** Laureate head of Louis Philippe I right **Rev:** Seven-line inscription

Date	Mintage	F	VF	XF	Unc	BU
1846	50	—	—	650	950	—

KM# M21a 5 FRANCS
25.0000 g., 0.9000 Silver 0.7234 oz. ASW **Subject:** Prince of Salerno Visit to Paris Mint **Obv:** Laureate head of Louis Philippe I right **Rev:** 7-line inscription

Date	Mintage	F	VF	XF	Unc	BU
1846	12	—	300	500	900	—

KM# M22 5 FRANCS
Bronze **Subject:** Ibrahim Pasha Visit to Paris Mint **Obv:** Laureate head of Louis Philippe I right **Rev:** Six-line inscription

Date	Mintage	F	VF	XF	Unc	BU
1846	20	—	125	200	400	—

KM# M22a 5 FRANCS
25.0000 g., 0.9000 Silver 0.7234 oz. ASW **Subject:** Ibrahim Pasha Visit to Paris Mint **Obv:** Laureate head of Louis Philippe I right **Rev:** 6-line inscription

Date	Mintage	F	VF	XF	Unc	BU
1846	4	—	—	1,000	2,000	—

PRETENDER COINAGE

X# A15 2-1/2 CENTIMES
Bronze **Ruler:** Henry V **Note:** Prev. KM#PTE49.

Date	Mintage	F	VF	XF	Unc	BU
ND	—	—	150	250	425	—

X# A15a 2-1/2 CENTIMES
Lead **Ruler:** Henry V **Note:** Prev. KM#PTE49a.

Date	Mintage	F	VF	XF	Unc	BU
ND	—	—	125	225	400	—

X# 15 5 CENTIMES
Silver **Ruler:** Henry V **Obv:** Small uniformed bust left **Note:** Prev. KM#PT15.

Date	Mintage	F	VF	XF	Unc	BU
1832	—	50.00	100	300	500	—

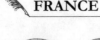

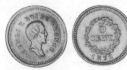

X# 16 5 CENTIMES
Silver **Ruler:** Henry V **Obv:** Head right **Note:** Prev. KM#PT16.

Date	Mintage	F	VF	XF	Unc	BU
1832	—	50.00	125	350	550	—

X# 17 5 CENTIMES
Silver **Ruler:** Henry V **Rev:** Value; date below divided by lys **Note:** Prev. KM#PT17. Reduced size.

Date	Mintage	F	VF	XF	Unc	BU
1832	—	50.00	100	200	350	—

X# 18 10 CENTIMES
Silver **Ruler:** Henry V **Obv:** Small uniformed bust left **Note:** Prev. KM#PT18.

Date	Mintage	F	VF	XF	Unc	BU
1832	—	50.00	100	200	450	—

X# 19 10 CENTIMES
Silver **Ruler:** Henry V **Obv:** Larger uniformed bust left **Note:** Prev. KM#PT19.

Date	Mintage	F	VF	XF	Unc	BU
1832	—	50.00	100	200	450	—

X# 20 10 CENTIMES
Silver **Ruler:** Henry V **Obv:** Head left **Note:** Prev. KM#PT20.

Date	Mintage	F	VF	XF	Unc	BU
1832	—	50.00	100	200	450	—

X# 21 10 CENTIMES
Silver **Ruler:** Henry V **Rev:** Value; date below divided by lys **Note:** Prev. KM#PT21. Reduced size.

Date	Mintage	F	VF	XF	Unc	BU
1832	—	55.00	100	225	500	—

X# 22 1/4 FRANC
Silver **Ruler:** Henry V **Edge:** Plain **Note:** Prev. KM#PT22.

Date	Mintage	F	VF	XF	Unc	BU
1832	—	60.00	100	175	350	—
1833	—	75.00	120	200	400	—

X# 23 1/2 FRANC
Silver **Ruler:** Henry V **Note:** Prev. KM#PT23.

Date	Mintage	F	VF	XF	Unc	BU
1832	—	50.00	100	175	300	—
1833	—	50.00	100	175	300	—

X# 23a 1/2 FRANC
Bronze **Ruler:** Henry V **Note:** Prev. KM#PT23a.

Date	Mintage	F	VF	XF	Unc	BU
1833	—	35.00	55.00	85.00	150	—

X# 24 1/2 FRANC
Bronze **Ruler:** Henry V **Obv:** Uniformed bust left, child's head **Note:** Prev. KM#PT24.

Date	Mintage	F	VF	XF	Unc	BU
1833	—	50.00	85.00	150	250	—

X# 25 1/2 FRANC
Bronze **Ruler:** Henry V **Obv:** Small uniformed bust left **Note:** Prev. KM#PT25.

Date	Mintage	F	VF	XF	Unc	BU
1833	—	50.00	85.00	150	250	—

X# 26 1/2 FRANC
Bronze **Ruler:** Henry V **Note:** Prev. KM#PT26.

Date	Mintage	F	VF	XF	Unc	BU
1858A	—	75.00	125	200	400	—

X# 27 FRANC
Silver **Ruler:** Henry V **Obv:** Large bust **Note:** Prev. KM#PT27.

Date	Mintage	F	VF	XF	Unc	BU
1831	—	35.00	60.00	125	250	—

X# 28.1 FRANC
4.4000 g., Silver, 23.3 mm. **Ruler:** Henry V **Obv:** Small bust **Edge:** Plain **Note:** Prev. KM#PT28.1.

Date	Mintage	F	VF	XF	Unc	BU
1831	—	35.00	60.00	125	250	—

X# 28.2 FRANC
4.4000 g., Silver, 23.3 mm. **Ruler:** Henry V **Edge:** Reeded **Note:** Prev. KM#PT28.2.

Date	Mintage	F	VF	XF	Unc	BU
1831	—	35.00	60.00	125	200	—
1832	—	35.00	60.00	125	200	—

X# 28.1a FRANC
Gold **Ruler:** Henry V **Note:** Prev. KM#PTP28.1a. Piefort.

Date	Mintage	F	VF	XF	Unc	BU
1832	—	—	750	1,250	2,000	—

X# 28.1b FRANC
Bronze **Ruler:** Henry V **Note:** Prev. KM#PTP28.1b. Piefort.

Date	Mintage	F	VF	XF	Unc	BU
1832	—	75.00	125	250	400	—

X# 28.1c FRANC
8.9800 g., Bronze **Ruler:** Henry V **Edge:** Plain **Note:** Prev. KM#PTP28.1c. Piefort.

Date	Mintage	F	VF	XF	Unc	BU
1832	—	—	—	250	450	—

X# 28.1d FRANC
8.5000 g., Silver **Ruler:** Henry V **Edge:** Plain **Note:** Prev. KM#PTP28.1d. Double Piefort (quadruple thickness).

Date	Mintage	F	VF	XF	Unc	BU
1832	—	125	200	400	1,000	—

X# 28.1e FRANC
12.0000 g., Silver **Ruler:** Henry V **Edge:** Plain **Note:** Prev. KM#PTP28.1e. Piefort.

Date	Mintage	F	VF	XF	Unc	BU
1832	—	—	—	400	750	—

X# 29 FRANC
Silver **Ruler:** Henry V **Edge:** Plain **Note:** Prev. KM#P29. T.W.I. below bust.

Date	Mintage	F	VF	XF	Unc	BU
1832	—	—	75.00	150	350	—

X# 31.1 2 FRANCS
Silver **Ruler:** Henry V **Edge:** Reeded **Note:** Prev. KM#PT31.1.

Date	Mintage	F	VF	XF	Unc	BU
1831	—	150	250	400	600	—
1832	—	150	250	400	600	—
1833	—	150	250	400	600	—

X# 31.3a 2 FRANCS
19.1200 g., Gold **Ruler:** Henry V **Edge:** Lettered **Note:** Prev. KM#PTP31.3a.

Date	Mintage	F	VF	XF	Unc	BU
1832	—	—	—	2,000	4,250	—

X# 31.3c 2 FRANCS
Silver **Ruler:** Henry V **Note:** Prev. KM#PTP31.3c. Piefort.

Date	Mintage	F	VF	XF	Unc	BU
1832	—	—	400	600	1,000	—

X# 31.3d 2 FRANCS
39.8100 g., Silver **Ruler:** Henry V **Note:** Prev. KM#PTP31.3d. Double Piefort (quadruple thickness).

Date	Mintage	F	VF	XF	Unc	BU
1832	—	—	—	1,000	2,000	—

X# 50 2 FRANCS
34.6400 g., Silver **Ruler:** Henry V **Note:** Prev. KM#PTP50. Double Piefort.

Date	Mintage	F	VF	XF	Unc	BU
1833	—	—	—	600	1,600	—

X# 31.2 2 FRANCS

Silver **Ruler:** Henry V **Edge:** Lettered **Note:** Prev. KM#PT31.2.

Date	Mintage	F	VF	XF	Unc	BU
1833	—	150	250	300	700	—

X# 31.3b 2 FRANCS

Bronze **Ruler:** Henry V **Edge:** Plain **Note:** Prev. KM#PT31.3b.

Date	Mintage	F	VF	XF	Unc	BU
1833	—	40.00	100	200	300	—

X# 32 5 FRANCS

Silver **Ruler:** Henry V **Note:** Prev. KM#PT32.

Date	Mintage	F	VF	XF	Unc	BU
1830	—	175	250	375	775	—

X# 32a 5 FRANCS

Bronze **Ruler:** Henry V **Note:** Prev. KM#PT32a.

Date	Mintage	F	VF	XF	Unc	BU
1830	—	50.00	125	225	350	—

X# 32b 5 FRANCS

Pewter **Ruler:** Henry V **Note:** Prev. KM#PT32b.

Date	Mintage	F	VF	XF	Unc	BU
1830	—	50.00	85.00	150	300	—

X# 33 5 FRANCS

17.1900 g., Bronze **Ruler:** Henry V **Obv:** Head left **Rev:** Crowned arms in wreath; date below **Note:** Prev. KM#PT33.

Date	Mintage	F	VF	XF	Unc	BU
1831	—	75.00	125	225	400	—

X# 33a 5 FRANCS

Pewter **Ruler:** Henry V **Note:** Prev. KM#PT33a.

Date	Mintage	F	VF	XF	Unc	BU
1831	—	50.00	85.00	175	300	—

X# 35 5 FRANCS

33.3500 g., Silver **Ruler:** Henry V **Note:** Prev. KM#PT35.

Date	Mintage	F	VF	XF	Unc	BU
1831	—	175	300	450	700	—
1832	—	175	300	450	700	—

X# 35b 5 FRANCS

Bronze **Ruler:** Henry V **Note:** Prev. KM#PT35b.

Date	Mintage	F	VF	XF	Unc	BU
1831	—	50.00	100	175	250	—

X# 35a 5 FRANCS

27.4000 g., Gold **Ruler:** Henry V **Edge:** Plain **Note:** Prev. KM#PT35a.

Date	Mintage	F	VF	XF	Unc	BU
1832	—	—	—	—	12,000	—

X# 35c 5 FRANCS

58.7900 g., Silver **Ruler:** Henry V **Edge:** Plain **Note:** Prev. KM#PTP35c. Piefort.

Date	Mintage	F	VF	XF	Unc	BU
1832	—	300	500	800	2,000	—

X# 35d 5 FRANCS

109.4600 g., Silver **Ruler:** Henry V **Note:** Prev. KM#PTP35d. Double Piedfort (quadruple thickness).

Date	Mintage	F	VF	XF	Unc	BU
1832	—	400	600	1,250	3,500	—

X# 35e 5 FRANCS

109.4600 g., Silver **Ruler:** Henry V **Note:** Prev. KM#PTP35e. Quadruple Piefort (octuple thickness).

Date	Mintage	F	VF	XF	Unc	BU
1832	—	—	—	—	6,000	—

X# 35f 5 FRANCS

33.3200 g., Bronze **Ruler:** Henry V **Note:** Prev. KM#PTP35f. Piefort.

Date	Mintage	F	VF	XF	Unc	BU
1832	—	—	150	250	500	—

X# 35g 5 FRANCS

71.9900 g., Gold Piefort **Ruler:** Henry V **Obv:** Bust left **Rev:** Denomination flanks arms, date below **Edge:** Plain **Note:** Only a few specimens known

Date	Mintage	F	VF	XF	Unc	BU
1832	—	—	—	—	16,000	—

X# 36 5 FRANCS

Bronze **Ruler:** Henry V **Subject:** Visit of Henry V to England **Note:** Prev. KM#PT36.

Date	Mintage	F	VF	XF	Unc	BU
1843	—	—	—	250	450	—

X# 36a 5 FRANCS

29.4500 g., Silver **Ruler:** Henry V **Note:** Prev. KM#PT36a.

Date	Mintage	F	VF	XF	Unc	BU
1843	—	—	—	600	1,000	—

X# 36b 5 FRANCS

Gold **Ruler:** Henry V **Note:** Prev. KM#PT36b.

Date	Mintage	F	VF	XF	Unc	BU
1843	—	—	—	4,250	6,500	—

PRETENDER COINAGE WITH ESSAI

X# E6 CENTIME

2.8500 g., Bronze **Ruler:** Napoleon II **Note:** Prev. KM#PTE6.

Date	Mintage	F	VF	XF	Unc	BU
1816	—	50.00	75.00	150	250	—

X# E7 3 CENTIMES

7.0700 g., Bronze **Ruler:** Napoleon II **Note:** Prev. KM#PTE7.

Date	Mintage	F	VF	XF	Unc	BU
1816	—	50.00	75.00	150	250	—

X# E8 5 CENTIMES

10.6700 g., Bronze **Ruler:** Napoleon II **Note:** Prev. KM#PTE8.

Date	Mintage	F	VF	XF	Unc	BU
1816	—	85.00	125	175	250	—

X# E9 10 CENTIMES

13.9000 g., Bronze **Ruler:** Napoleon II **Note:** Prev. KM#PTE9.

Date	Mintage	F	VF	XF	Unc	BU
1816	—	85.00	125	200	300	—

X# E10 1/4 FRANC

1.2400 g., Silver **Ruler:** Napoleon II **Note:** Prev. KM#PTE10.

Date	Mintage	F	VF	XF	Unc	BU
1816	—	75.00	125	200	350	—

X# E10a 1/4 FRANC

Bronze **Ruler:** Napoleon II **Note:** Prev. KM#PTE10a.

Date	Mintage	F	VF	XF	Unc	BU
1816	—	35.00	55.00	90.00	175	—

X# 22c 1/4 FRANC

Gilt Bronze **Ruler:** Henry V **Note:** Piedfort. Prev. KM#PTP22c.

Date	Mintage	F	VF	XF	Unc	BU
1833	—	70.00	125	200	400	—

X# 22a 1/4 FRANC

Bronze **Ruler:** Henry V **Note:** Prev. KM#PT22a.

Date	Mintage	F	VF	XF	Unc	BU
1833	—	30.00	50.00	100	200	—

X# 22b 1/4 FRANC

Silver **Ruler:** Henry V **Note:** Prev. KM#PTP22b. Piefort.

Date	Mintage	F	VF	XF	Unc	BU
1833	—	125	200	300	550	—

X# E11 1/2 FRANC

2.3500 g., Silver **Ruler:** Napoleon II **Note:** Prev. KM#PTE11.

Date	Mintage	F	VF	XF	Unc	BU
1816	—	75.00	125	250	400	—

X# E11a 1/2 FRANC

Bronze **Ruler:** Napoleon II **Note:** Prev. KM#PTE11a.

Date	Mintage	F	VF	XF	Unc	BU
1816	—	50.00	75.00	125	250	—

X# E12 FRANC

Silver **Ruler:** Napoleon II **Note:** Prev. KM#PTE12.

Date	Mintage	F	VF	XF	Unc	BU
1816	—	100	150	250	450	—

X# E12a FRANC

Bronze **Ruler:** Napoleon II **Note:** Prev. KM#PTE12a.

Date	Mintage	F	VF	XF	Unc	BU
1816	—	50.00	85.00	150	250	—

X# A29 FRANC

12.0000 g., Silver **Ruler:** Henry V **Edge:** Plain **Note:** T.W.I. below bust. Prev. KM#PT29.

Date	Mintage	F	VF	XF	Unc	BU
1832	—	50.00	75.00	150	400	—

X# E13 2 FRANCS

Silver **Ruler:** Napoleon II **Note:** Prev. KM#PTE13.

Date	Mintage	F	VF	XF	Unc	BU
1816	—	150	250	400	750	—

X# E13a 2 FRANCS

Bronze **Ruler:** Napoleon II **Note:** Prev. KM#PTE13a.

Date	Mintage	F	VF	XF	Unc	BU
1816	—	50.00	100	175	300	—

X# E13b 2 FRANCS

White Metal **Ruler:** Napoleon II **Note:** Prev. KM#PTE13b.

Date	Mintage	F	VF	XF	Unc	BU
1816	—	30.00	50.00	75.00	150	—

X# E30 2 FRANCS

Silver **Ruler:** Henry V **Note:** Prev. KM#PTE30.

Date	Mintage	F	VF	XF	Unc	BU
ND	—	80.00	150	250	400	—

X# E30a 2 FRANCS

Bronze Or Gilt Brass **Ruler:** Henry V **Note:** Prev. KM#PTE30a.

Date	Mintage	F	VF	XF	Unc	BU
ND	—	35.00	65.00	125	175	—

X# E30b 2 FRANCS

34.6400 g., Silver **Ruler:** Henry V **Note:** Prev. KM#PTE30b. Double Piefort.

Date	Mintage	F	VF	XF	Unc	BU
ND	—	—	350	600	1,200	—

X# E14 5 FRANCS

21.1700 g., Silver **Ruler:** Napoleon II **Note:** Prev. KM#PTE14.

Date	Mintage	F	VF	XF	Unc	BU
1816	—	275	550	950	1,600	—

X# E14a 5 FRANCS

Bronze **Ruler:** Napoleon II **Note:** Prev. KM#PTE14a.

Date	Mintage	F	VF	XF	Unc	BU
1816	—	125	200	350	600	—

X# E14b 5 FRANCS

Gold **Ruler:** Napoleon II **Note:** Prev. KM#PTE14b. Unofficial pieces (patterns?) struck during the reign of Napoleon III, possibly to give continuity to the dynasty.

Date	Mintage	F	VF	XF	Unc	BU
1816 Rare	—	—	—	—	—	—

X# E48 20 FRANCS

Lead **Ruler:** Napoleon II **Note:** Prev. KM#PTE48.

Date	Mintage	F	VF	XF	Unc	BU
1815	—	—	—	300	500	—

SECOND EMPIRE

Napoleon III as Emperor

MEDALLIC COINAGE

KM# M23b 5 CENTIMES

Gold **Subject:** Emperor and Empress visit to the Bourse

Date	Mintage	F	VF	XF	Unc	BU
1853 (w)	—	350	500	900	1,800	—

KM# M23 5 CENTIMES

Bronze **Subject:** Emperor and Empress visit to the Bourse **Note:** Struck at Lille

Date	Mintage	F	VF	XF	Unc	BU
1853 (w)	2,000	20.00	30.00	50.00	150	—

KM# M23a 5 CENTIMES

Silver **Subject:** Emperor and Empress visit to the Bourse **Note:** Struck at Lille.

Date	Mintage	F	VF	XF	Unc	BU
1853 (w)	—	75.00	125	200	350	—

KM# M24b 10 CENTIMES

Gold **Subject:** Emperor and Empress visit to the Bourse

Date	Mintage	F	VF	XF	Unc	BU
1853 (w) Rare	2	—	—	—	—	—

KM# M24 10 CENTIMES

Bronze **Subject:** Emperor and Empress visit to the Bourse **Note:** Struck at Lille.

Date	Mintage	F	VF	XF	Unc	BU
1853 (w)	1,000	20.00	30.00	50.00	150	—

KM# M24a 10 CENTIMES

Silver **Subject:** Emperor and Empress visit to the Bourse **Note:** Struck at Lille.

Date	Mintage	F	VF	XF	Unc	BU
1853 (w)	100	75.00	150	250	400	—

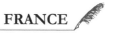

KM# M25 10 CENTIMES
Bronze **Note:** Struck at Paris.

Date	Mintage	F	VF	XF	Unc	BU
1854 (w)	—	25.00	50.00	100	265	—

KM# M25a 10 CENTIMES
Silver **Subject:** Monument of Napoleon I erected

Date	Mintage	F	VF	XF	Unc	BU
1854 (w)	—	100	200	350	550	—

KM# M25b 10 CENTIMES
Gold **Subject:** Monument of Napoleon I erected

Date	Mintage	F	VF	XF	Unc	BU
1854 (w)	—	400	800	1,250	2,150	—

KM# M26 10 CENTIMES
Bronze **Subject:** Napoleon III vist to the Paris mint

Date	Mintage	F	VF	XF	Unc	BU
1854 (a)	—	20.00	40.00	75.00	150	—

KM# M26a 10 CENTIMES
Silver **Subject:** Napoleon III visit to the Paris mint

Date	Mintage	F	VF	XF	Unc	BU
1854 (a)	—	75.00	125	200	350	—

KM# M26b 10 CENTIMES
Gold **Subject:** Napoleon III to the mint

Date	Mintage	F	VF	XF	Unc	BU
1854 (a)	—	400	700	1,200	2,000	—

MODERN REPUBLICS
1870-

MEDALLIC COINAGE

KM# M27 20 FRANCS
Silver **Subject:** President of Rene Coty Visit **Obv:** Head of Republic **Rev:** Coin press

Date	Mintage	F	VF	XF	Unc	BU
1955	—	—	50.00	100	200	—

KM# M27a 20 FRANCS
Gold **Subject:** President of Rene Coty Visit **Obv:** Head of Republic **Rev:** Coin press

Date	Mintage	F	VF	XF	Unc	BU
1955	—	—	300	350	550	—

KM# M28 20 FRANCS
Silver **Subject:** Visit by President of Rene Coty **Obv:** Head of Republic **Rev:** Coin press

Date	Mintage	F	VF	XF	Unc	BU
1955	—	—	50.00	100	200	—

KM# M28a 20 FRANCS
Gold **Subject:** Visit by President of Rene Coty **Obv:** Head of Republic **Rev:** Coin press

Date	Mintage	F	VF	XF	Unc	BU
1955	—	—	300	350	550	—

PRETENDER COINAGE

X# 39 10 CENTIMES
9.6100 g., Bronze **Ruler:** Napoleon IV **Note:** Prev. KM#PT39.

Date	Mintage	F	VF	XF	Unc	BU
1874	—	—	50.00	75.00	160	—

X# 45 10 CENTIMES
Copper **Ruler:** Ernest I **Note:** Prev. KY#96.

Date	Mintage	F	VF	XF	Unc	BU
1888	—	—	—	—	—	—

X# 37.1 5 FRANCS
Silver **Ruler:** Henry V **Edge:** Plain **Note:** Prev. KM#PTE37.1.

Date	Mintage	F	VF	XF	Unc	BU
1871	—	250	350	600	1,200	—

X# 37.2 5 FRANCS
25.1700 g., Silver **Ruler:** Henry V **Edge:** Reeded **Note:** Prev. KM#PTE37.2.

Date	Mintage	F	VF	XF	Unc	BU
1871	—	200	300	600	1,200	—

X# 37.2a 5 FRANCS
Bronze **Ruler:** Henry V **Note:** Prev. KM#PTE37.2a.

Date	Mintage	F	VF	XF	Unc	BU
1871	—	50.00	90.00	175	400	—

X# 37.2b 5 FRANCS
Gold **Ruler:** Henry V **Edge:** Reeded **Note:** Prev. KM#PTE37.2b.

Date	Mintage	F	VF	XF	Unc	BU
1871	—	—	—	4,500	7,000	—

X# 37.3 5 FRANCS
24.8700 g., Silver **Ruler:** Henry V **Edge:** Lettered **Note:** Prev. KM#PTE37.3.

Date	Mintage	F	VF	XF	Unc	BU
1871	—	—	—	1,350	2,700	—

X# 38 5 FRANCS
23.6300 g., Silver **Ruler:** Henry V **Edge:** Plain **Note:** Prev. KM#PT38.

Date	Mintage	F	VF	XF	Unc	BU
1873	—	—	—	1,000	2,000	—

X# 38a 5 FRANCS
Bronze **Ruler:** Henry V **Note:** Prev. KM#PT38a.

Date	Mintage	F	VF	XF	Unc	BU
1873	—	—	—	300	600	—

X# 38b 5 FRANCS
47.5400 g., Silver **Ruler:** Henry V **Note:** Prev. KM#PT38b. Piefort (double thickness).

Date	Mintage	F	VF	XF	Unc	BU
1873	—	—	—	1,900	3,750	—

X# M1a 5 FRANCS
Bronze **Ruler:** Ernest I

Date	Mintage	F	VF	XF	Unc	BU
1888	—	—	—	—	—	—

X# M1b 5 FRANCS
Ruler: Ernest I **Note:** Silver foiled paper.

Date	Mintage	F	VF	XF	Unc	BU
1888	—	—	—	—	—	—

PRETENDER COINAGE WITH ESSAI

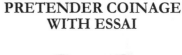

X# E40 20 CENTIMES
Silver **Ruler:** Napoleon IV **Obv:** Head left **Rev:** Crown above value and date **Note:** Prev. KM#PTE40.

Date	Mintage	F	VF	XF	Unc	BU
1874	—	—	40.00	80.00	175	—

X# E41 50 CENTIMES
Silver **Ruler:** Napoleon IV **Obv:** Head left **Rev:** Crown above value and date **Note:** Prev. KM#PTE41.

Date	Mintage	F	VF	XF	Unc	BU
1874	—	—	60.00	100	200	—

X# E42 FRANC
Silver **Ruler:** Napoleon IV **Note:** Prev. KM#PTE42.

Date	Mintage	F	VF	XF	Unc	BU
1874	—	—	100	175	350	—

X# E43 2 FRANCS
10.0700 g., Silver **Ruler:** Napoleon IV **Note:** Prev. KM#PTE43.

Date	Mintage	F	VF	XF	Unc	BU
1874	—	—	150	300	500	—

X# E44.1 5 FRANCS
25.6200 g., Silver **Ruler:** Napoleon IV **Rev:** Eagle in circle **Edge:** Plain **Note:** Prev. KM#PTE45.1.

Date	Mintage	F	VF	XF	Unc	BU
1870	—	—	750	1,500	2,000	—

X# E44.2 5 FRANCS
26.0700 g., Silver **Ruler:** Napoleon IV **Rev:** Eagle in square **Edge:** Reeded **Note:** Prev. KM#PTE45.2.

Date	Mintage	F	VF	XF	Unc	BU
1874	—	—	600	900	1,250	—

X# E44a 5 FRANCS
49.3800 g., Silver **Ruler:** Napoleon IV **Note:** Prev. KM#PTP45.2a. Piefort.

Date	Mintage	F	VF	XF	Unc	BU
1874	—	—	850	1,700	2,750	—

EURO COINAGE

European Union Issues

KM# 1371 5 EURO
24.9000 g., Bi-Metallic Gold And Silver .750 Gold 2.7 g insert on .900 Silver 22.2g planchet, 37 mm. **Obv:** The seed sower on gold insert **Rev:** French face map and denomination **Edge:** Plain

Date	Mintage	F	VF	XF	Unc	BU
2004 Proof	3,000	Value: 475				

SATIRICAL COINAGE

Gambetta 1870

X# 47.1 5 FRANCS
Silver **Edge:** Plain **Note:** Prev. KY#99.

Date	Mintage	F	VF	XF	Unc	BU
ND(1870) Proof	—	Value: 425				

X# 47.2 5 FRANCS
Silver **Edge:** Reeded **Note:** Prev. KY#99.

Date	Mintage	F	VF	XF	Unc	BU
ND(1870) Proof	—	Value: 425				

X# 47a 5 FRANCS
Bronze

Date	Mintage	F	VF	XF	Unc	BU
ND(1870) Proof	—	Value: 200				

X# 47b 5 FRANCS
Iron

Date	Mintage	F	VF	XF	Unc	BU
ND(1870) Proof	—	Value: 300				

X# 47c 5 FRANCS
Silver **Note:** Piefort.

Date	Mintage	F	VF	XF	Unc	BU
ND(1870) Proof	—	Value: 850				

Thiers 1872

X# 48.1 5 FRANCS
Silver **Edge:** Plain **Note:** Prev. KY#97.

Date	Mintage	F	VF	XF	Unc	BU
1872 Proof	—	Value: 625				

X# 48.2 5 FRANCS
Silver **Edge:** Reeded **Note:** Prev. KY#97.

Date	Mintage	F	VF	XF	Unc	BU
1872 Proof	—	Value: 625				

X# 48a 5 FRANCS
Bronze **Note:** Prev. KY#97a.

Date	Mintage	F	VF	XF	Unc	BU
1872 Proof; Restrike	—	Value: 300				

Mac-Mahon I 1874

X# E51 5 FRANCS
25.4500 g., Silver **Ruler:** Henry IV **Series:** Mac-Mahon I **Obv:** Head left, NAPOLEON F. below **Obv. Legend:** MAC-MAHON I — SEPTENNAT **Rev. Inscription:** ESSAI / MONETAIRE

Date	Mintage	F	VF	XF	Unc	BU
1874	—	—	—	—	—	—

X# 49 5 FRANCS
Silver **Obv:** Head left, NAPOLEON F. below **Obv. Legend:** MAC-MAHON I — SEPTENNAT **Rev:** Hatted and crowned arms, Order of the Golden Fleece below, ESSAI at lower right **Rev. Legend:** REPUBLIQUE FRANÇAISE **Note:** Prev. KY#98.

Date	Mintage	F	VF	XF	Unc	BU
1874 Proof	—	Value: 800				

X# E50 5 FRANCS
Silver **Obv:** Head left, NAPOLEON F. below **Obv. Legend:** MAC-MAHON I — SEPTENNAT **Rev:** Hatted and crowned arms with Order of the Golden Fleece below, ESSAI at lower right **Rev. Legend:** REPUBLIQUE FRANÇAISE **Edge:** Lettered **Note:** Prev. KY#98a.

Date	Mintage	F	VF	XF	Unc	BU
1874 Proof	—	Value: 650				

X# E50a 5 FRANCS
Gold **Obv:** Head left, NAPOLEON F. below **Obv. Legend:** MAC-MAHON I — SEPTENNAT **Rev:** Hatted and crowned arms with Order of the Golden Fleece below, ESSAI at lower right **Rev. Legend:** REPUBLIQUE FRANÇAISE **Edge:** Plain **Note:** Prev. KY#98b.

Date	Mintage	F	VF	XF	Unc	BU
1874 Proof	—	Value: 2,750				

X# E50b 5 FRANCS
Bronze **Obv:** Head left, NAPOLEON F. below **Obv. Legend:** MAC-MAHON I — SEPTENNAT **Rev:** Hatted and crowned arms with Order of the Golden Fleece below, ESSAI at lower right **Rev. Legend:** REPUBLIQUE FRANÇAISE **Edge:** Plain **Note:** Prev. KY#98c.

Date	Mintage	F	VF	XF	Unc	BU
1874 Proof	—	Value: 325				

X# E50c 5 FRANCS
Iron **Obv:** Head left, NAPOLEON F. below **Obv. Legend:** MAC-MAHON I — SEPTENNAT **Rev:** Hatted and crowned arms with Order of the Golden Fleece below, ESSAI at lower right **Rev. Legend:** REPUBLIQUE FRANÇAISE **Edge:** Plain

Date	Mintage	F	VF	XF	Unc	BU
1874 Proof	—	Value: 625				

MODERN ECU COINAGE

X# 61 ECU
5.0000 g., 0.9990 Silver 0.1606 oz. ASW, 20 mm. **Issuer:** Göde GmbH, Waldaschaff **Obv:** 6 stars, date above large "ECU", 6 stars below **Obv. Legend:** • LIBERTE • EGALITE • FRATERNITE • REPUBLIQUE FRANÇAISE **Rev:** Charlemagne horseback 3/4 left **Rev. Legend:** • CHARLE - MAGNE • 747 - 814 **Edge:** Reeded

Date	Mintage	F	VF	XF	Unc	BU
1993 Proof	9,999	Value: 9.00				

X# 62 ECU
8.5000 g., 0.9990 Silver 0.2730 oz. ASW, 30 mm. **Issuer:** Göde GmbH, Waldaschaff **Obv:** 6 stars, date above large "ECU", 6 stars below **Obv. Legend:** • LIBERTE • EGALITE • FRATERNITE • REPUBLIQUE FRANÇAISE **Rev:** Charlemagne horseback 3/4 left **Rev. Legend:** • CHARLE - MAGNE • 747 - 814 **Edge:** Reeded

Date	Mintage	F	VF	XF	Unc	BU
1993 Proof	9,999	Value: 15.00				

X# 63 ECU
20.0000 g., 0.9990 Silver 0.6423 oz. ASW, 40 mm. **Issuer:** Göde GmbH, Waldaschaff **Obv:** 6 stars, date above large "ECU", 6 stars below **Obv. Legend:** • LIBERTE • EGALITE • FRATERNITE • REPUBLIQUE FRANÇAISE **Rev:** Charlemagne horseback 3/4 left **Rev. Legend:** • CHARLE - MAGNE • 747 - 814 **Edge:** Reeded

Date	Mintage	F	VF	XF	Unc	BU
1993 Proof	9,999	Value: 35.00				

EURO COINAGE

ICB Issue

X# 91 20 EURO
Bronze **Obv:** Framed painting **Obv. Legend:** REPUBLIQUE-FRANCAISE **Rev:** Bust of Henri Matisse facing 3/4 left

Date	Mintage	VG	F	VF	XF	Unc
1997	—	—	—	—	—	8.50

AQUITAINE

KINGDOM

SATIRICAL COINAGE

Produced by B. Forgeals to ridicule the reactionary spirit of the Bordelais

X# 1 GASCON
Silver **Note:** Prev. KY#101.

Date	Mintage	F	VF	XF	Unc	BU
1848 Proof	—	Value: 350				

X# 1a GASCON
White Metal **Note:** Prev. KY#101a.

Date	Mintage	F	VF	XF	Unc	BU
1848 Proof	—	Value: 175				

X# 1b GASCON
Copper **Note:** Prev. KY#101b.

Date	Mintage	F	VF	XF	Unc	BU
1848 Proof	—	Value: 200				

X# 1c GASCON
Gilt Copper **Note:** Prev. KY#101c.

Date	Mintage	F	VF	XF	Unc	BU
1848 Proof	—	Value: 220				

BOUILLON

DUCHY

Admiral Philip of Auvergne

ECU COINAGE

X# 1.1 ECU
Silver **Ruler:** Phillippe d' Auvergne **Edge:** Plain **Note:** Prev. KY#100.

Date	Mintage	F	VF	XF	Unc	BU
1815 A Proof	—	Value: 400				

X# 1.1a ECU
Copper **Ruler:** Phillippe d' Auvergne **Subject:** Philippe D'Auvergne **Edge:** Plain **Note:** Prev. KY#100c.

Date	Mintage	F	VF	XF	Unc	BU
1815 A	—	—	—	—	—	—

Note: Reported, not confirmed

X# 1.1b ECU
Gold **Ruler:** Phillippe d' Auvergne **Edge:** Plain **Note:** Prev. KY#100a.

Date	Mintage	F	VF	XF	Unc	BU
1815 A Proof	—	—	—	—	—	—

X# 1.2 ECU
Gold **Ruler:** Phillippe d' Auvergne **Edge:** Lettered **Note:** Prev. KY#100b. Struck ca. 1870-1880.

Date	Mintage	F	VF	XF	Unc	BU
1815 A Proof	—	—	—	—	—	—

FREEDONIA

PRINCIPALITY

MEDALLIC COINAGE

X# M5 50 DOLLARS
31.1300 g., 0.9990 Silver 0.9998 oz. ASW **Ruler:** Prince John I **Obv:** Crowned arms **Obv. Legend:** SUPERIBIMUS **Rev:** Large "50"

Date	Mintage	F	VF	XF	Unc	BU
1998 Proof	—	Value: 20.00				

FRENCH ANTILLES

SAINT MARTIN

ESSAIS

X# E11 1/4 EURO
7.8000 g., 0.9990 Silver 0.2505 oz. ASW, 27.2 mm. **Series:** Euro **Obv:** Bust of Louis Oscar Roty almost left **Rev:** Liberte et Science (medal 1896) **Edge:** Reeded

Date	Mintage	F	VF	XF	Unc	BU
2004 Proof	2,000	Value: 24.00				

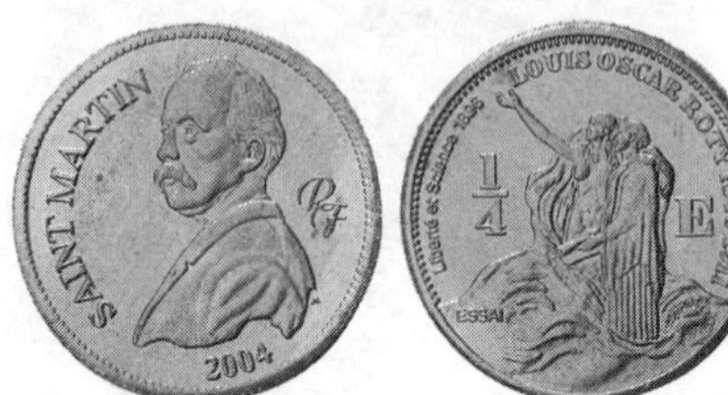

X# E11a 1/4 EURO
10.3500 g., Copper **Obv:** Bust of Louis Oscar Roty half left **Rev:** Liberte et Science (medal 1896)

Date	Mintage	F	VF	XF	Unc	BU
2004	30	—	—	—	50.00	50.00

X# E12 1-1/2 EURO
31.1400 g., 0.9990 Silver 1.0000 oz. ASW, 38.6 mm. **Series:** Euro **Obv:** Arms **Obv. Legend:** RÉPUBLIQUE FRANÇAISE **Rev:** Sailing ship La Ville de Paris, 1764-1782 **Rev. Legend:** HISTORIRE DE LA MARINE FRANÇAISE **Edge:** Reeded

Date	Mintage	F	VF	XF	Unc	BU
2004 Proof	2,000	Value: 35.00				

X# E13 1-1/2 EURO
25.7500 g., Brass Brass, 39.13 mm. **Series:** Euro **Obv:** Arms **Obv. Legend:** RÉPUBLIQUE FRANÇAISE **Rev:** Sailing ship La Ville de Paris, 1764-1782 **Rev. Legend:** HISTORIRE DE LA MARINE FRANÇAISE **Edge:** Reeded

Date	Mintage	F	VF	XF	Unc	BU
2004	25	—	—	—	75.00	—

X# E14 1-1/2 EURO
Lead, 38.6 mm. **Series:** Euro **Obv:** Arms **Obv. Legend:** RÉPUBLIQUE FRANÇAISE **Rev:** Sailing ship La Ville de Paris, 1764-1782 **Rev. Legend:** HISTORIRE DE LA MARINE FRANÇAISE **Edge:** Reeded

Date	Mintage	F	VF	XF	Unc	BU
2004	—	—	—	—	75.00	—

X# E15 EURO
0.8530 g., 0.9167 Gold 0.0251 oz. AGW, 27.18 mm. **Series:** Euro **Obv:** Arms **Rev:** Balbuzard pêcheur with fish in claw in flight **Rev. Legend:** Protection de la Faune **Edge:** Plain

Date	Mintage	F	VF	XF	Unc	BU
2004 Proof	300	Value: 250				

X# E15a 20 EURO
10.3300 g., Copper **Obv:** Arms **Rev:** Balbuzard Pêcheur with fish in claw in flight **Rev. Legend:** protection de la faune **Edge:** Plain

Date	Mintage	F	VF	XF	Unc	BU
2004	30	—	—	—	50.00	50.00

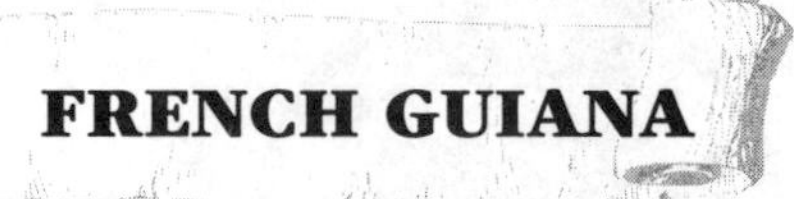

FRENCH GUIANA

REPUBLIC

ESSAIS

X# E1 10 CENTIMES
Bronze **Obv:** Cross **Obv. Legend:** REPUBLIQUE DE LA GUYANNE INDEPENDANTE **Rev. Legend:** LIBERTE ★ JUSTICE **Note:** Prev. KM#E1.

Date	Mintage	F	VF	XF	Unc	BU
1887	—	—	90.00	175	285	450

X# E5 10 CENTIMES
Bronze **Obv:** Bust of Liberty right **Obv. Legend:** REPUBLIQUE DE LA GUYANNAE INDEPENDANTE **Rev. Legend:** LIBERTE ★ JUSTICE **Note:** Prev. KM#E5.

Date	Mintage	F	VF	XF	Unc	BU
1889	—	—	110	350	550	—

X# E2 20 CENTIMES
Copper-Nickel **Obv:** Head of Liberty left **Obv. Legend:** REPUBLIQUE DE LA GUYANNE INDEPENDANTE **Rev:** Cross **Rev. Legend:** LIBERTE ★ JUSTICE **Note:** Prev. KM#E2.

Date	Mintage	F	VF	XF	Unc	BU
1887	—	—	80.00	165	275	—

X# E3 5 FRANCS
25.3000 g., 0.9000 Silver 0.7320 oz. ASW **Obv:** Head of Liberty left **Obv. Legend:** REPUBLIQUE DE LA

GUYANNE INDEPENDANTE **Rev:** Cross **Rev. Legend:** LIBERTE ★ JUSTICE **Note:** Prev. KM#E3.

Date	Mintage	F	VF	XF	Unc	BU
1887	—	—	800	1,850	2,600	—

X# E4 5 FRANCS
White Metal **Obv:** Head of Liberty left **Obv. Legend:** REPUBLIQUE DE LA GUYANNE INDEPENDANTE **Rev:** Cross **Rev. Legend:** LIBERTE ★ JUSTICE **Note:** Prev. KM#E4.

Date	Mintage	F	VF	XF	Unc	BU
1887	—	—	220	500	700	—

FRENCH COLONY

ESSAIS

X# E11 1/4 EURO
7.8000 g., 0.9990 Silver 0.2505 oz. ASW, 27.2 mm. **Series:** Euro **Obv:** Bust of Louis Oscar Roty almost left **Obv. Legend:** GUYANE FRANÇAISE **Rev:** Chrstofle (1892 medal) **Edge:** Reeded

Date	Mintage	F	VF	XF	Unc	BU
2004 Proof	2,000	Value: 20.00				

X# E11a 1/4 EURO
10.3300 g., Copper **Obv:** Bust of Louis Oscar Roty half left **Obv. Legend:** GUYANE FRANÇAISE **Rev:** Christofle (1892 medal) **Edge:** Reeded

Date	Mintage	F	VF	XF	Unc	BU
2004	30	—	—	—	50.00	50.00

X# E12 1-1/2 EURO
31.1400 g., 0.9990 Silver 1.0000 oz. ASW, 38.6 mm. **Series:** Euro **Obv:** Arms **Obv. Legend:** RÉPUBLIQUE FRANÇAISE **Obv. Inscription:** GUYANE FRANÇAISE **Rev:** Sailing ship "Le Soleil Royal" 1670-1692 **Rev. Legend:** HISTORIRE DE LA MARINE FRANÇAISE **Edge:** Reeded

Date	Mintage	F	VF	XF	Unc	BU
2004 Proof	2,000	Value: 30.00				

X# E13 1-1/2 EURO
26.5200 g., Brass, 38.6 mm. **Series:** Euro **Obv:** Arms **Obv. Legend:** RÉPUBLIQUE FRANÇAISE **Obv. Inscription:** GUYANE FRANÇAIS **Rev:** Sailing ship "Le Soleil Royal" 1670-1692 **Rev. Legend:** HISTORIRE DE LA MARINE FRANÇAISE **Edge:** Reeded

Date	Mintage	F	VF	XF	Unc	BU
2004	25	—	—	—	75.00	—

X# E14 1-1/2 EURO
25.5000 g., Lead, 38.6 mm. **Series:** Euro **Obv:** Arms **Obv. Legend:** RÉPUBLIQUE FRANÇAISE **Obv. Inscription:** GUYANE FRANÇAIS **Rev:** Sailing ship "Le Soleil Royal" 1670-1692 **Rev. Legend:** HISTORIRE DE LA MARINE FRANÇAISE **Edge:** Reeded

Date	Mintage	F	VF	XF	Unc	BU
2004	1	—	—	—	—	—

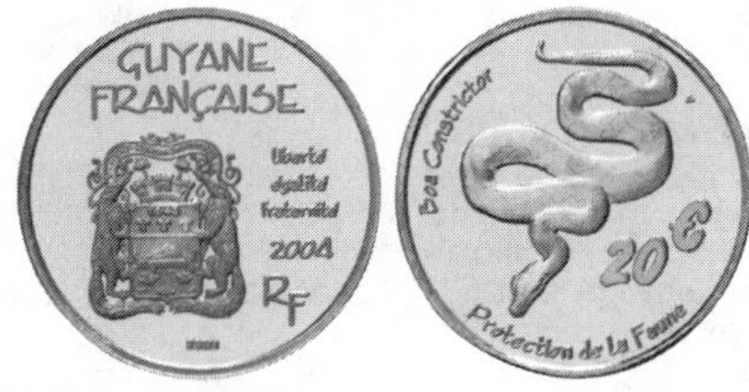

X# E15 20 EURO
8.5300 g., 0.9167 Gold 0.2514 oz. AGW, 27.1 mm. **Series:** Euro **Obv:** Arms **Obv. Legend:** GUYANE FRANÇAISE **Rev:** Boa constrictor **Rev. Legend:** Protection de la Faune **Edge:** Plain

Date	Mintage	F	VF	XF	Unc	BU
2004 Proof	300	Value: 295				

X# E15a 20 EURO
10.3100 g., Copper **Obv:** Arms **Obv. Legend:** GUYANE FRANÇAISE **Rev:** Boa Constrictor **Rev. Legend:** Protection de la Faune **Edge:** Plain

Date	Mintage	F	VF	XF	Unc	BU
2004	30	—	—	—	50.00	50.00

TRIAL STRIKES

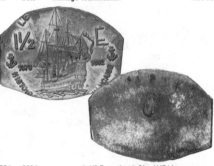

X#	Date	Mintage	Identification	Mkt Val
TS1	2004	—	1-1/2 Euro. Lead. Obv. X#E14.	—

ILE CRESCENT

FRENCH OVERSEAS TERRITORY

DECIMAL COINAGE

X# 1 500 POA
Blue Acrylic, 38 mm. **Obv:** Two palm trees, island **Obv. Legend:** ILE CRESCENT **Note:** Uniface, 5mm thick.

Date	Mintage	VG	F	VF	XF	Unc
2006	—	—	—	—	—	20.00

X# 2 1000 POA
Green Acrylic, 38 mm. **Obv:** Two palm trees, island **Obv. Legend:** ILE CRESCENT **Note:** Uniface, 5mm thick.

Date	Mintage	VG	F	VF	XF	Unc
2006	—	—	—	—	—	20.00

X# 3 5000 POA
Yellow Acrylic, 38 mm. **Obv:** Two palm trees, island **Obv. Legend:** ILE CRESCENT **Note:** Uniface, 5mm thick.

Date	Mintage	VG	F	VF	XF	Unc
2006	—	—	—	—	—	20.00

FRENCH SOMALILAND

OBOCK

CAPITAL CITY

COUNTERMARKED COINAGE

"In the name of God, the Merciful, the Compassionate; struck at Obokh (fineness) 92.6"

X# 16 1/2 RUPEE
5.8300 g., 0.9167 Silver 0.1718 oz. ASW
Edge: Reeded **Note:** Countermark Arabic inscription in rectangle on India-British 1/2 Rupee, KM#491.

CM Date	Host Date	Good	VG	F	VF	XF
ND(c.1880s)	1877-80	—	60.00	85.00	150	225

X# 12 RUPEE
11.6600 g., 0.9167 Silver 0.3436 oz. ASW
Edge: Reeded **Note:** Countermark Arabic inscription in rectangle on India-British Rupee, KM#458.

CM Date	Host Date	Good	VG	F	VF	XF
ND(c.1880s)	1840	—	60.00	85.00	150	300

X# 15 RUPEE
11.6600 g., 0.9167 Silver 0.3436 oz. ASW
Edge: Reeded **Note:** Countermark Arabic inscription in rectangle on India-British Rupee, KM#473.1.

CM Date	Host Date	Good	VG	F	VF	XF
ND(c.1880s)	1862	—	60.00	85.00	150	225

X# 17 RUPEE
11.6600 g., 0.9167 Silver 0.3436 oz. ASW
Edge: Reeded **Note:** Countermark Arabic inscription in rectangle on India-British Rupee, KM#492.

CM Date	Host Date	Good	VG	F	VF	XF
ND(c.1880s)	1877-80	—	60.00	85.00	150	225

X# 11 RUPEE
11.6600 g., 0.9167 Silver 0.3436 oz. ASW
Edge: Reeded **Note:** Countermark Arabic inscription in rectangle on India-British Rupee, KM#457.

CM Date	Host Date	Good	VG	F	VF	XF
NDc.1880s	1835	—	65.00	100	165	300
ND(c.1880s)	1840	—	65.00	100	165	300

X# 13 THALER
28.0668 g., 0.8333 Silver 0.7519 oz. ASW
Edge: Lettered **Note:** Countermark Arabic inscription in rectangle on Austria M.T. Thaler, KM#T1.

CM Date	Host Date	Good	VG	F	VF	XF
ND(c.1880s)	1780	—	100	150	200	350

FRENCH SOUTHERN & ANTARCTIC TERRITORIES

FRENCH TERRITORY

ESSAIS

X# E11 1/4 EURO
7.8000 g., 0.9990 Silver 0.2505 oz. ASW, 27.2 mm.
Obv: Bust of Louis Oscar Roty almost left **Obv. Legend:** TERRES AUSTRALES et / ANTARCTIQUES / FRANÇAISE **Rev:** "Semense" (medal, 1898) **Edge:** Reeded

Date	Mintage	F	VF	XF	Unc	BU
2004 Proof	2,000	Value: 24.00				

X# E11a 1/4 EURO
10.3400 g., Copper, 27.24 mm. **Obv:** Bust of Louis Oscar Roty half left **Obv. Inscription:** TERRES AUSTRALES et / ANTARCTIQUES / FRANÇAISE **Rev:** Walking "Semense" left **Edge:** Reeded

Date	Mintage	F	VF	XF	Unc	BU
2004	30	—	—	—	50.00	50.00

X# E12 1-1/2 EURO
31.1400 g., 0.9990 Silver 1.0000 oz. ASW, 38.6 mm.
Obv: Arms **Obv. Legend:** RÉPUBLIQUE FRANÇAISE **Rev:** Corvette L'Astrolabe, 1811-1851
Rev. Legend: HISTOIRE DE LA MARINE FRANÇAISE **Edge:** Reeded

Date	Mintage	F	VF	XF	Unc	BU
2004 Proof	2,000	Value: 35.00				

X# E13 1-1/2 EURO
26.1200 g., Brass Antiqued, 39.15 mm. **Obv:** Arms **Obv. Legend:** RÉPUBLIQUE FRANÇAISE **Rev:** Corvette L'Astrolabe, 1811-1851 **Rev. Legend:** HISTOIRE DE LA MARINE FRANÇAISE **Edge:** Reeded

Date	Mintage	F	VF	XF	Unc	BU
2004	25	Value: 75.00				

X# E15 20 EURO
8.5300 g., 0.9167 Gold 0.2514 oz. AGW, 27.1 mm.
Obv: Arms **Rev:** Emperor Penguin with chick
Edge: Plain

Date	Mintage	F	VF	XF	Unc	BU
2004 Proof	300	Value: 250				

X# E15a 20 EURO
10.3400 g., Copper, 27.20 mm. **Obv:** Arms
Rev: Emperor Penguin with chick **Edge:** Plain

Date	Mintage	F	VF	XF	Unc	BU
2004	30	—	—	—	50.00	50.00

ILES DE AMSTERDAM & ST. PAUL

FRENCH TERRITORY

MEDALLIC COINAGE

Zinkann Series

X# M1 5 EURO
5.3000 g., Copper-Nickel, 25 mm. **Ruler:** no ruler
Obv: Large Lis above stylized peaks **Obv. Inscription:** AMSTERDAM & / ST. PAUL iles **Obv. Designer:** Fred Zinkann **Rev:** Stylized crowned arms divides date
Rev. Legend: BON ancrer GRÉS **Edge:** Plain

Date	Mintage	F	VF	XF	Unc	BU
2007 frz Proof	50	Value: 12.50				

X# M1a 5 EURO
5.2000 g., Brass, 25 mm. **Ruler:** no ruler **Obv:** Large Lis above stylized peaks **Obv. Inscription:** AMSTERDAM & / ST. PAUL iles **Obv. Designer:** Fred Zinkann **Rev:** Stylized crowned arms divides date
Rev. Legend: BON ancrer GRÉS **Edge:** Plain

Date	Mintage	F	VF	XF	Unc	BU
2007 frz Proof	25	Value: 10.00				

X# M1b 5 EURO
6.6000 g., 0.9990 Silver 0.2120 oz. ASW, 25 mm. **Ruler:** no ruler **Obv:** Large Lis above stylized peaks **Obv. Inscription:** AMSTERDAM & / ST. PAUL iles **Obv. Designer:** Fred Zinkann **Rev:** Stylized crowned arms divides date **Rev. Legend:** BON ancrer GRÉS **Edge:** Plain

Date	Mintage	F	VF	XF	Unc	BU
2007 frz Proof	25	Value: 17.50				

X# M1c 5 EURO
8.1000 g., 0.7500 Gold 0.1953 oz. AGW, 25 mm. **Ruler:** no ruler **Obv:** Large Lis above stylized peaks **Obv. Inscription:** AMSTERDAM & / ST. PAUL iles **Obv. Designer:** Fred Zinkann **Rev:** Stylized crowned arms divides date **Rev. Legend:** BON ancrer GRÉS **Edge:** Plain

Date	Mintage	F	VF	XF	Unc	BU
2007 frz Proof	5	Value: 200				

FRIULI-VENEZIA GIULIA

AUTONOMOUS REGION

Friuli (former Duchy)

MEDALLIC COINAGE

X# 1 100 FURLANS
7.1600 g., Copper, 25.98 mm. **Subject:** 900th Anniversary **Obv:** Seated figure - Lombard man, denomination below **Obv. Legend:** UN MODON PAROMP E O'TORNARIN A PLOMP **Rev:** Bishops chair and sword **Rev. Legend:** NASCITE DE PATRIE DAL FRIUL **Edge:** Plain

Date	Mintage	F	VF	XF	Unc	BU
ND(1977)	—	—	—	—	25.00	—

X# 2 200 FURLANS
8.7500 g., Stainless Steel, 27.22 mm. **Subject:** 900th Anniversary **Obv:** Man and lion wrestling, denomination below **Obv. Legend:** UN MODON PAROMP E O'TORNARIN A PLOMP **Rev:** Henry IV granting sovereignty for Friuli to Patriarch Sigeardo of Aquileia **Rev. Legend:** NASCITE DE PATRIE DAL FRIUL **Edge:** Reeded **Note:** Struck at I.P.Z.S. (Italian mint)

Date	Mintage	F	VF	XF	Unc	BU
ND(1977)	—	—	—	—	30.00	—

X# 3 1000 FURLANS
10.6600 g., Bronze, 29.22 mm. **Subject:** 1000th Anniversary **Obv:** Landmarks of the Friuli city of Udine, denomination below **Obv. Legend:** PAR RICVARDA 1 MIL AGNS DI VDIN **Rev:** Otto II and Patriarch Rodoaldus of Aquileia **Edge:** Reeded **Note:** Struck at I.P.Z.S. (Italian mint)

Date	Mintage	F	VF	XF	Unc	BU
ND(1983)	—	—	—	—	50.00	—

FUJAIRAH

EMIRATE

PATTERNS

X# Pn1 250 FILS
4.5900 g., Silver **Ruler:** Muhammad bin Hamad al-Sharqi **Obv:** Mohammad bin Hamad al-Sharqi **Rev:** Bird left

Date	Mintage	F	VF	XF	Unc	BU
1968 Proof	15	Value: 400				

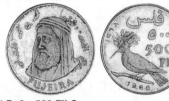

X# Pn2 500 FILS
7.8500 g., Silver **Ruler:** Muhammad bin Hamad al-Sharqi **Obv:** Mohammad bin Hamad al-Sharqi **Rev:** Bird left

Date	Mintage	F	VF	XF	Unc	BU
1968 Proof	15	Value: 450				

X# Pn3 750 FILS
11.9000 g., Silver **Ruler:** Muhammad bin Hamad al-Sharqi **Obv:** Mohammad bin Hamad al-Sharqi **Rev:** Bird left

Date	Mintage	F	VF	XF	Unc	BU
1968 Proof	15	Value: 550				

X# Pn4 DINAR
21.6400 g., Silver **Ruler:** Muhammad bin Hamad al-Sharqi **Obv:** Mohammad bin Hamad al-Sharqi **Note:** Often encountered in a red leatherette case by Pinches or an Asprey case.

Date	Mintage	F	VF	XF	Unc	BU
1968 Proof	50	Value: 675				
1968 Matte Proof	1	Value: 1,200				

TRIAL STRIKES

X#	Date	Mintage	Identification	Issue Price	Mkt Val
TS1	1968	1	500 Fils. Silver. Prev. KM#TS1. Uniface rev. X#Pn2.	—	350
TS2	1968	1	750 Fils. Silver. Prev. KM#TS2. Uniface rev. X#Pn3.	—	350
TS3	1968	1	Dinar. Silver. Prev. KM#TS3. Uniface obv. X#Pn4.	—	400
TS4	1968	1	Dinar. Silver. Prev. KM#TS4. Uniface obv. X#Pn4.	—	400

PROOF SETS

X#	Date	Mintage	Identification	Issue Price	Mkt Val
XPS1	1968 (4)	15	X#Pn1-Pn4	—	2,000

GEORGIA

REPUBLIC

FANTASY EURO PATTERNS

X# Pn1 EURO CENT
Copper Plated Steel **Edge:** Plain

Date	Mintage	F	VF	XF	Unc	BU
2004	—	—	—	—	—	1.50

X# Pn2 2 EURO CENT
Copper Plated Steel **Edge:** Plain

Date	Mintage	F	VF	XF	Unc	BU
2004	—	—	—	—	—	2.00

X# Pn3 5 EURO CENT
Copper Plated Steel **Edge:** Plain

Date	Mintage	F	VF	XF	Unc	BU
2004	—	—	—	—	—	2.50

X# Pn4 10 EURO CENT
Goldine **Edge:** Plain

Date	Mintage	F	VF	XF	Unc	BU
2004	—	—	—	—	—	3.00

X# Pn5 20 EURO CENT
Goldine **Edge:** Plain

Date	Mintage	F	VF	XF	Unc	BU
2004	—	—	—	—	—	3.50

X# Pn6 50 EURO CENT
Goldine **Edge:** Plain

Date	Mintage	F	VF	XF	Unc	BU
2004	—	—	—	—	—	4.00

X# Pn7 EURO
Bi-Metallic **Edge:** Plain

Date	Mintage	F	VF	XF	Unc	BU
2004	—	—	—	—	—	6.00

X# Pn8 2 EURO
Bi-Metallic **Edge:** Plain

Date	Mintage	F	VF	XF	Unc	BU
2004	—	—	—	—	—	8.00

MINT SETS

X#	Date	Mintage	Identification	Issue Price	Mkt Val
XMS1	2004 (8)	—	X#Pn1-Pn8	—	30.00

GERMAN STATES

AUGSBURG

FREE CITY

MEDALLIC COINAGE

X# M5 1-1/2 DUCAT
5.0500 g., Gold **Subject:** Coronation of Joseph (I) at King of Hungary **Obv:** Imperial crown between two kneeling cherubs **Obv. Inscription:** JOSEPHUS / REX HUNGARIAR / CORONATUS / IN REGE ROMANORV / AUGUSTAE **Rev:** Vertical sword wrapped in laurel sprays, rays from Eye of God above **Rev. Legend:** AMORE •E-T •TIMORE • **Note:** Fr.#80.

Date	Mintage	VG	F	VF	XF	Unc
1690	—	—	—	—	—	—

BADEN

BADEN-DURLACH LINE

Grand Duchy

MEDALLIC COINAGE

X# M4 DUCAT
3.5000 g., 0.9860 Gold 0.1109 oz. AGW **Subject:** Homage of Baden Weiler **Obv:** Crowned arms with griffon supporters **Rev:** Column with arms of badenweiler at left, female figure at right, date in exergue **Note:** Prev. KM#M4.

Date	Mintage	F	VF	XF	Unc	BU
1738 H	260	550	950	1,750	2,650	—

X# M4a DUCAT
Silver **Subject:** Homage of Baden Weiler **Obv:** Crowned arms with griffon supporters **Rev:** Column with arms of badenweiler at left, female figure at right, date in exergue **Note:** Prev. KM#M4a.

Date	Mintage	F	VF	XF	Unc	BU
1738 H	—	—	—	—	—	—

X# M5 DUCAT
3.5000 g., 0.9860 Gold 0.1109 oz. AGW **Subject:** Homage of Baden-Hachberg **Rev:** Altar with two shields of arms on front topped by flaming urn, date in exergue **Note:** Prev. KM#M5.

Date	Mintage	F	VF	XF	Unc	BU
1738 H	380	550	950	1,750	2,650	—

X# M5a DUCAT
Silver **Subject:** Homage of Baden-Hachberg **Rev:** Altar with two shields of arms on front topped by flaming urn, date in exergue **Note:** Prev. KM#M5a.

Date	Mintage	F	VF	XF	Unc	BU
1738 H	—	—	—	—	—	—

X# M6 DUCAT
3.5000 g., 0.9860 Gold 0.1109 oz. AGW
Subject: Homage of Rotteln **Rev:** Round altar with two shields of arms topped by flame, date in exergue **Note:** Prev. KM#M6.

Date	Mintage	F	VF	XF	Unc	BU
1738 H	650	450	850	1,500	2,500	—

X# 6a DUCAT
Silver **Subject:** Homage of Rottein **Rev:** Round altar with two shields of arms topped by flame, date in exergue **Note:** Prev. KM#M6a.

Date	Mintage	F	VF	XF	Unc	BU
1738 H	—	—	—	—	—	—

UNITED BADEN LINE

MEDALLIC COINAGE

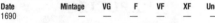

X# M1 KREUZER
Copper **Subject:** Recovery of Grand Duchess Sophie **Note:** Prev. KM#M1.

Date	Mintage	F	VF	XF	Unc	BU
1832	—	25.00	50.00	70.00	120	—

X# M2 KREUZER
Copper **Subject:** Evangelical Church at Eppingan **Note:** Prev. KM#M2.

Date	Mintage	F	VF	XF	Unc	BU
1879	—	20.00	40.00	60.00	110	—

X# M3 KREUZER
Copper **Subject:** Evangelical Church at Feudenheim **Note:** Prev. KM#M3.

Date	Mintage	F	VF	XF	Unc	BU
1889	—	20.00	40.00	60.00	110	—

BAVARIA

KINGDOM

MEDALLIC COINAGE

Karl Goetz Series

X# M1 2 MARK
8.2000 g., Silver **Ruler:** Ludwig III **Obv:** Bust left **Rev:** Crowned eagle above shield

Date	Mintage	F	VF	XF	Unc	BU
1913 Proof	—	Value: 150				

X# M1a 2 MARK
9.7800 g., Copper **Ruler:** Ludwig III **Obv:** Bust left **Rev:** Crowned eagle above shield

Date	Mintage	F	VF	XF	Unc	BU
1913 Proof	—	Value: 50.00				

X# M1b 2 MARK
9.0300 g., Bronze **Ruler:** Ludwig III **Obv:** Bust left **Rev:** Crowned eagle above shield

Date	Mintage	F	VF	XF	Unc	BU
1913 Proof	—	Value: 50.00				

X# M1c 2 MARK
Nickel **Ruler:** Ludwig III **Obv:** Bust left **Rev:** Crowned eagle above shield

Date	Mintage	F	VF	XF	Unc	BU
1913 Proof	—	Value: 60.00				

X# M1d 2 MARK
Gold **Ruler:** Ludwig III **Obv:** Bust left **Rev:** Crowned eagle above shield

Date	Mintage	F	VF	XF	Unc	BU
1913 Proof	—	Value: 400				

X# M1e 2 MARK
Platinum APW **Ruler:** Ludwig III **Obv:** Bust left **Rev:** Crowned eagle above shield

Date	Mintage	F	VF	XF	Unc	BU
1913 Proof	—	Value: 1,500				

X# M2 3 MARK
13.3000 g., 0.8850 Silver 0.3784 oz. ASW
Ruler: Ludwig III **Obv:** Head left **Rev:** Eagle, wing over crowned shield

Date	Mintage	F	VF	XF	Unc	BU
1913 Proof	—	Value: 100				

X# M2a 3 MARK
14.3500 g., Copper **Ruler:** Ludwig III **Obv:** Head left **Rev:** Eagle, wing over crowned shield

Date	Mintage	F	VF	XF	Unc	BU
1913 Proof	—	Value: 70.00				

X# M2b 3 MARK
Gold **Ruler:** Ludwig III **Obv:** Head left **Rev:** Eagle, wing over crowned shield

Date	Mintage	F	VF	XF	Unc	BU
1913 Proof	—	Value: 550				

X# M2c 3 MARK
12.7400 g., Copper-Plated Silver **Ruler:** Ludwig III **Obv:** Head left **Rev:** Eagle, wing over crowned shield

Date	Mintage	F	VF	XF	Unc	BU
1913 Proof	—	Value: 110				

X# M3 5 MARK
17.8000 g., Silver **Ruler:** Ludwig III **Obv:** Bust left **Rev:** Eagle with wings spread over crown at left, shield below

Date	Mintage	F	VF	XF	Unc	BU
1913 Prooflike	—	—	—	—	220	—

X# M3a 5 MARK
Copper **Ruler:** Ludwig III **Obv:** Bust left **Rev:** Eagle with wings spread over crown at left, shield below

Date	Mintage	F	VF	XF	Unc	BU
1913 Prooflike	—	—	—	—	125	—

X# M3b 5 MARK
Bronze **Ruler:** Ludwig III **Obv:** Bust left **Rev:** Eagle with wings spread over crown at left, shield below

Date	Mintage	F	VF	XF	Unc	BU
1913 Prooflike	—	—	—	—	125	—

X# M3c 5 MARK
33.7500 g., Gold **Ruler:** Ludwig III **Obv:** Bust left **Rev:** Eagle with wings spread over crown at left, shield below

Date	Mintage	F	VF	XF	Unc	BU
1913 Prooflike	—	—	—	—	975	—

X# M3d 5 MARK
56.2000 g., Platinum APW **Ruler:** Ludwig III **Obv:** Bust left **Rev:** Eagle with wings spread over crown at left, shield below

Date	Mintage	F	VF	XF	Unc	BU
1913 Prooflike	2	—	—	—	2,800	—

X# M3e 5 MARK
20.7000 g., Copper-Plated Silver **Ruler:** Ludwig III **Obv:** Bust left **Rev:** Eagle with wings spread over crown at left, shield below

Date	Mintage	F	VF	XF	Unc	BU
1913 Prooflike	—	—	—	—	160	—

X# M4 10 MARK
Gold **Ruler:** Ludwig III **Obv:** Bust left **Rev:** Crown, sceptre below

Date	Mintage	F	VF	XF	Unc	BU
1913 Proof	—	Value: 320				

X# M4a 10 MARK
3.6300 g., Copper **Ruler:** Ludwig III **Obv:** Bust left **Rev:** Crown, sceptre below

Date	Mintage	F	VF	XF	Unc	BU
1913 Proof	—	Value: 45.00				

X# M4b 10 MARK
Gilt Copper **Ruler:** Ludwig III **Obv:** Bust left **Rev:** Crown, sceptre below

Date	Mintage	F	VF	XF	Unc	BU
1913 Proof	—	Value: 60.00				

X# M4c 10 MARK
3.3800 g., Bronze **Ruler:** Ludwig III **Obv:** Bust left **Rev:** Crown, sceptre below

Date	Mintage	F	VF	XF	Unc	BU
1913 Proof	—	Value: 50.00				

X# M4d 10 MARK
Brass **Ruler:** Ludwig III **Obv:** Bust left **Rev:** Crown, sceptre below

Date	Mintage	F	VF	XF	Unc	BU
1913 Proof	—	Value: 50.00				

X# M4e 10 MARK
3.6000 g., Silver **Ruler:** Ludwig III **Obv:** Bust left **Rev:** Crown, sceptre below

Date	Mintage	F	VF	XF	Unc	BU
1913 Proof	—	Value: 100				

X# M5 20 MARK
8.5000 g., Gold **Ruler:** Ludwig III **Obv:** Bust left **Rev:** Allegorical male supporting crown, eagle at his feet

Date	Mintage	F	VF	XF	Unc	BU
1913 Proof	—	Value: 320				

X# M5a 20 MARK
Copper **Ruler:** Ludwig III **Obv:** Bust left **Rev:** Allegorical male supporting crown, eagle at his feet

Date	Mintage	F	VF	XF	Unc	BU
1913 Proof	—	Value: 50.00				

X# M5b 20 MARK
Gilt Copper **Ruler:** Ludwig III **Obv:** Bust left **Rev:** Allegorical male supporting crown, eagle at his feet

Date	Mintage	F	VF	XF	Unc	BU
1913 Proof	—	Value: 60.00				

X# M5c 20 MARK
Bronze **Ruler:** Ludwig III **Obv:** Bust left **Rev:** Allegorical male supporting crown, eagle at his feet

Date	Mintage	F	VF	XF	Unc	BU
1913 Proof	—	Value: 50.00				

X# M5d 20 MARK
Gilt Brass **Ruler:** Ludwig III **Obv:** Bust left **Rev:** Allegorical male supporting crown, eagle at his feet

Date	Mintage	F	VF	XF	Unc	BU
1913 Proof	—	Value: 60.00				

X# M5e 20 MARK
Aluminum **Ruler:** Ludwig III **Obv:** Bust left **Rev:** Allegorical male supporting crown, eagle at his feet

Date	Mintage	F	VF	XF	Unc	BU
1913 Proof	—	Value: 50.00				

X# M5f 20 MARK
4.3000 g., Silver **Ruler:** Ludwig III **Obv:** Bust left **Rev:** Allegorical male supporting crown, eagle at his feet

Date	Mintage	F	VF	XF	Unc	BU
1913 Proof	—	Value: 125				

X# M5g 20 MARK
16.0000 g., Platinum APW **Ruler:** Ludwig III

Date	Mintage	F	VF	XF	Unc	BU
1913 Proof	—	Value: 950				

TRIAL STRIKES

X#	Date	Mintage	Identification	Issue Price	Mkt Val
TS1	ND	—	5 Mark. Obverse.	—	—

PROOF SETS

X#	Date	Mintage	Identification	Issue Price	Mkt Val
XPS1	1913 (5)	—	X1a-X5a	—	350
XPS2	1913 (10)	—	Combined set of Bavaria X#1a-5a and Prussia X#2a-6a.	—	625

BREMEN

FREE CITY

MEDALLIC COINAGE

X# M1 GEDENKTHALER
17.5390 g., 0.9860 Silver 0.5560 oz. ASW, 33 mm.
Subject: Opening of New Business Exchange

Date	Mintage	F	VF	XF	Unc	BU
1864 B	5,000	—	100	150	225	—

CORVEY

BENEDICTINE ABBEY

REGULAR COINAGE

KM# A86 MARIENGROSCHEN
Silver **Ruler:** Christof von Bellinghausen **Obv:** Crowned arms **Obv. Legend:** CHRISTO • II • G • AB • COR • IMP **Rev. Legend:** SACRI • ROM • IMP • PR

Date	Mintage	Good	VG	F	VF	XF
1683	—	—	—	—	—	—

FRANKFURT AM MAIN

FREE CITY

MEDALLIC ISSUES

X# 1 DUCAT
3.5000 g., 0.9860 Gold 0.1109 oz. AGW **Subject:** 300th Anniversary of the Reformation **Note:** Prev. KM#302; KM#M1.

Date	Mintage	F	VF	XF	Unc	BU
1817	—	850	130	200	350	—

X# 1a DUCAT
Silver **Subject:** Reformation **Note:** Prev. Pn49. Similar to M1.

Date	Mintage	F	VF	XF	Unc	BU
1817	—	—	—	—	—	—

X# M21 2 DUCAT
Gold **Subject:** Coronation of Matthias II **Obv:** Laureate armored bust right with ruffled collar **Obv. Legend:** MATTHIAS II•D•G•H•B•REX CORO IN REG•ROM **Rev:** Large Imperial crown, rayed sunface at upper left, rayed moon at lower right **Rev. Legend:** CONCORDI - LVMINE MAIOR **Note:** Fr.#950.

Date	Mintage	VG	F	VF	XF	Unc
1612	—	—	—	—	—	—

X# 2 2 DUCAT
7.0000 g., 0.9860 Gold 0.2219 oz. AGW **Subject:** 300th Anniversary of the Reformation **Note:** Prev. KM#303; KM#M2.

Date	Mintage	F	VF	XF	Unc	BU
1817	—	—	—	—	—	—

HAMBURG

FREE CITY

MEDALLIC COINAGE

X# M1 10 DUCAT (Portugalöser)
35.0000 g., 0.9860 Gold 1.1095 oz. AGW **Obv:** "God" in clouds shining down on early city harbor view **Obv. Legend:** SUB UMBRA ALARUM TUARUM **Rev:** Four ornate shields **Rev. Legend:** BANCHORUM IN EUROPA BONO CUM DEO ERECTORUM MEMORIA **Note:** Prev. KM#123.

Date	Mintage	F	VF	XF	Unc	BU
M•DC•LXXXIX (1689)	—	—	—	4,000	5,500	—

PATTERNS

Maximilian Issues

Struck in Munich, Bavaria

X# 1 20 MARK
Bronze, 22.7 mm. **Obv:** Medieval sailing ship **Rev:** Eagle standing right **Edge:** Plain

Date	Mintage	F	VF	XF	Unc	BU
1907	—	—	—	40.00	70.00	—

X# 1a 20 MARK
Bronze, 22.7 mm. **Obv:** Medieval sailing ship **Rev:** Eagle standing right **Edge:** Plain

Date	Mintage	F	VF	XF	Unc	BU
1907	—	—	—	40.00	70.00	—

X# 2 20 MARK
Bronze **Obv:** Medieval sailing ship **Rev:** Crowned arms

Date	Mintage	F	VF	XF	Unc	BU
1907	—	—	—	40.00	70.00	—

HANNOVER

KINGDOM

MEDALLIC COINAGE

X# 1 THALER
16.8500 g., Silver **Subject:** Shooting Festival **Obv:** Supported helmeted arms **Rev:** Germania seated holding wreath and sword, shield at right **Note:** Prev. KM#M1.

Date	Mintage	F	VF	XF	Unc	BU
1872	6,317	—	65.00	120	185	—

HESSE-DARMSTADT

GRAND DUCHY

REGULAR COINAGE

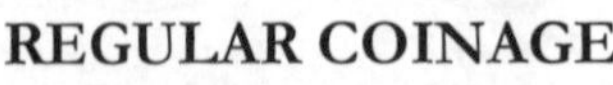

X# M10 GULDEN
10.6000 g., 0.9000 Silver 0.3067 oz. ASW **Ruler:** Ludwig II **Subject:** Public Freedom Through German Parliament **Obv:** Head left **Obv. Legend:** LUDWIG ERBGROSH.U.MITREGENT V. HESSEN **Rev:** Inscription **Rev. Legend:** PRESSEFREIHEIT... **Note:** Prev. KM#327.

Date	Mintage	F	VF	XF	Unc	BU
1848	—	—	250	400	600	—

MEDALLIC COINAGE

X# 7 6 KREUZER
Billon **Ruler:** Ludwig II **Subject:** Visit of Princes Ludwig and Heinrich to Darmstadt Mint **Note:** Prev. KM#M7.

Date	Mintage	F	VF	XF	Unc	BU
ND(1848)	—	—	350	500	750	—

X# 8 6 KREUZER
Billon **Ruler:** Ludwig II **Subject:** Visit of Prince Wilhelm and Princess ANna to Darmstadt Mint **Note:** Prev. KM#M8.

Date	Mintage	F	VF	XF	Unc	BU
1859	—	—	350	500	750	—

X# 9 1/2 JAGOTHALER
Silver

Date	Mintage	F	VF	XF	Unc	BU
ND	—	—	—	—	—	—

X# 1 DUCAT
3.5000 g., 0.9860 Gold 0.1109 oz. AGW **Ruler:** Ludwig VIII **Obv:** Crowned double L monogram **Rev:** City of Darmstadt and horse **Note:** Prev. KM#M1.

Date	Mintage	F	VF	XF	Unc	BU
ND	—	600	1,000	1,800	3,000	—

X# 1a DUCAT
Silver **Ruler:** Ludwig VIII **Note:** Prev. KM#M1a.

Date	Mintage	F	VF	XF	Unc	BU
ND	—	35.00	65.00	100	175	—

X# 2 DUCAT
3.5000 g., 0.9860 Gold 0.1109 oz. AGW **Ruler:** Ludwig VIII **Rev:** Reclining lion holding shield with monogram **Note:** Prev. KM#M2.

Date	Mintage	F	VF	XF	Unc	BU
ND	—	—	1,200	2,000	3,500	—

X# 3 DUCAT
3.5000 g., 0.9860 Gold 0.1109 oz. AGW **Ruler:** Ludwig VIII **Obv:** City of Darmstadt and horse **Rev:** Rampant lion holding shield with monogram **Note:** Prev. KM#M3.

Date	Mintage	F	VF	XF	Unc	BU
1741	—	600	1,000	1,800	3,000	—

X# 6 2 DUCAT
7.0000 g., 0.9860 Gold 0.2219 oz. AGW
Ruler: Ludwig VIII **Obv:** Stag and hunter **Rev:** Stag and dogs **Note:** Prev. KM#M6.

Date	Mintage	F	VF	XF	Unc	BU
ND	—	1,000	2,500	4,000	6,500	—

X# 6a 2 DUCAT
Silver **Ruler:** Ludwig VIII **Note:** Prev. KM#M6a.

Date	Mintage	F	VF	XF	Unc	BU
ND	—	65.00	130	200	350	—

X# M5 DUCATEN
3.5000 g., 0.9860 Gold 0.1109 oz. AGW
Ruler: Ludwig VIII **Rev:** Boar **Note:** Prev. KM#M5.

Date	Mintage	F	VF	XF	Unc	BU
ND(1739-68)	—	600	1,000	1,800	3,000	—

X# 5a DUCATEN
Copper **Ruler:** Ludwig VIII **Note:** Prev. KM#M5a.

Date	Mintage	F	VF	XF	Unc	BU
ND	—	15.00	30.00	50.00	80.00	—

X# 5b DUCATEN
Silver **Ruler:** Ludwig VIII **Note:** Prev. KM#M5b.

Date	Mintage	F	VF	XF	Unc	BU
ND	—	35.00	65.00	100	175	—

X# 4 DUCATEN
3.5000 g., 0.9860 Gold 0.1109 oz. AGW **Ruler:** Ludwig VIII **Note:** Prev. KM#M4.

Date	Mintage	F	VF	XF	Unc	BU
ND	—	500	800	1,500	2,500	—

X# 4a DUCATEN
Copper **Ruler:** Ludwig VIII **Note:** Prev. KM#M4a.

Date	Mintage	F	VF	XF	Unc	BU
ND	—	15.00	30.00	50.00	80.00	—

X# 4b DUCATEN
Silver **Ruler:** Ludwig VIII **Note:** Prev. KM#M4b.

Date	Mintage	F	VF	XF	Unc	BU
ND	—	35.00	65.00	100	175	—

ISENBURG

COUNTY

MEDALLIC COINAGE

X# 1 HELLER (Snipe Heller)
Copper **Obv:** In laurel wreath, ECGJ in script monogram **Rev:** Snipe standing left in grass

Date	Mintage	VG	F	VF	XF	Unc
ND(1824)	—	15.00	25.00	50.00	75.00	—

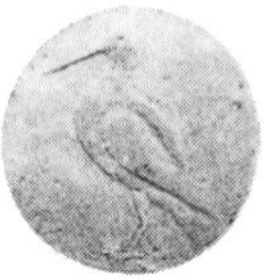

X# 2 HELLER (Snipe Heller)
Copper **Obv:** ECGY monogram **Rev:** Without grass

Date	Mintage	VG	F	VF	XF	Unc
ND(1828)	—	15.00	25.00	50.00	75.00	—

X# 3 HELLER (Snipe Heller)
Copper **Obv:** ECFzY monogram **Rev:** Snipe on mound

Date	Mintage	VG	F	VF	XF	Unc
ND(1840)	—	15.00	25.00	50.00	75.00	—

X# 4 HELLER (Snipe Heller)
Copper **Obv:** AJ script monogram in laurel wreath

Date	Mintage	VG	F	VF	XF	Unc
ND(1847)	—	15.00	25.00	50.00	75.00	—

X# 5 HELLER (Snipe Heller)
Copper **Obv:** BFzY in laurel wreath

Date	Mintage	VG	F	VF	XF	Unc
ND(1861)	—	15.00	25.00	50.00	75.00	—
ND(1861) Proof	—	Value: 120				

X# 6 HELLER (Snipe Heller)
Copper **Obv:** WFzY monogram **Rev:** Snipe standing right in grass

Date	Mintage	VG	F	VF	XF	Unc
ND	—	20.00	30.00	60.00	90.00	—
ND Proof	—	Value: 150				

MANSFELD-EISLEBEN

PRINCIPALITY

MEDALLIC COINAGE

X# M1 1/2 THALER
Silver, 46 mm. **Subject:** 100th Anniversary Naumburger Convention **Obv:** Bust of Martin Luther facing 3/4 right **Obv. Legend:** Mart • Luther • der • H Schrifft D: Weiland Pred • u: Prof: Z: Wittenb. **Rev:** City view, Mansfeld arms below **Rev. Legend:** Gottes wort • u: Luthers Lehr Vergeht nun: U • nimmermehr • Islebie

Date	Mintage	VG	F	VF	XF	Unc
1661 Swan	—	—	—	—	—	—

X# M2 3/4 THALER
Silver, 46 mm. **Subject:** 100th Anniversary Naumburger Convention **Obv:** Bust of Martin Luther facing 3/4 right **Obv. Legend:** Mart • Luther • der • H Schrifft D: Weiland Pred • u: Prof: Z: Wittenb. **Rev:** City view, Mansfeld arms below **Rev. Legend:** Gottes wort • u: Luthers Lehr Vergeht nun: U • nimmermehr • Islebie

Date	Mintage	VG	F	VF	XF	Unc
1661 Clover	—	—	—	—	—	—

X# M3 1-1/2 THALER
Silver, 46 mm. **Subject:** 100th Anniversary Naumburger Convention **Obv:** Bust of Martin Luther facing 3/4 right **Obv. Legend:** Mart • Luther • der • H Schrifft D: Weiland Pred • u: Prof: Z: Wittenb. **Rev:** City view, Mansfeld arms below **Rev. Legend:** Gottes Wort • u: Luthers Lehr Vergeht nun: U • nimmermehr • Islebie

Date	Mintage	VG	F	VF	XF	Unc
1661 Clover	—	—	—	—	—	—

MECKLENBURG-STRELITZ

GRAND DUCHY

MEDALLIC COINAGE

X# M1 THALER
Silver **Subject:** 200th Anniversary - Promulgation of Luther's Thesis **Obv:** Bust of Adolph Friedrich III right **Rev:** Religion with anchor before a temple, inscription and date in exergue below **Note:** Dav.#2444. Prev. KM#M1.

Date	Mintage	F	VF	XF	Unc	BU
1717 J.C.A.	—	550	1,000	1,650	2,500	—

X# M2 THALER

Silver **Subject:** 200th anniversary - promulgation of Luther's thesis **Rev:** Walled city with forest in foreground **Note:** Dav.#2445. Prev. KM#M2.

Date	Mintage	F	VF	XF	Unc	BU
1717 J.C.A.	—	400	800	1,250	2,000	—

X# M3 THALER

Silver **Subject:** 200th Anniversary - Promulgation of Luther's Thesis **Rev:** Temple on an island **Note:** Dav.#2446. Prev. KM#M3.

Date	Mintage	F	VF	XF	Unc	BU
1717 J.C.A.	—	400	800	1,250	2,000	—

X# M4 2 THALER

Silver **Subject:** 200th Anniversary - Promulgation of Luther's Thesis **Note:** Similar to Thaler (KM#M1). Prev. KM#M4.

Date	Mintage	F	VF	XF	Unc	BU
1717 J.C.A. Rare	—	—	—	—	—	—

MUNSTER

BISHOPRIC

MEDALLIC COINAGE

X# M1 REGIMENTS THALER

Silver **Ruler:** Clemens August von Bayern **Obv:** St. Paul in circle of shields **Rev:** Charlemagne **Note:** Prev. KM#1.

Date	Mintage	F	VF	XF	Unc	BU
1761	—	50.00	90.00	150	250	—

X# M2 1-1/2 THALER

Silver **Ruler:** Clemens August von Bayern **Note:** Prev. KM#2.

Date	Mintage	F	VF	XF	Unc	BU
1719	—	75.00	145	250	450	—

X# M3 1-1/2 THALER

Silver **Ruler:** Clemens August von Bayern **Note:** Prev. KM#M3.

Date	Mintage	F	VF	XF	Unc	BU
1719	—	65.00	120	200	350	—

MILLED COINAGE

X# M11 1 1/4 SHAU THALER

35.8800 g., Silver, 51 mm. **Ruler:** Ferdinand von Bayern **Subject:** Peace of Westphalia **Obv:** Two angels above city view **Obv. Legend:** HINC • TOTI • PAX • INSONAT • ORBI **Obv. Inscription:** MONASTERIVM / WESTPHA **Rev:** Clasped hands, cornucopia **Note:** Date on reverse in Roman numerals, MDCXXXVVVIII.

Date	Mintage	F	VF	XF	Unc	BU
1648	—	—	850	1,200	—	—

NASSAU

DUCHY

Nassau-Usingen

MEDALLIC COINAGE

X# 1 THALER

28.0600 g., 0.0833 Silver 0.0751 oz. ASW **Subject:** Patriot Nicolaus Fischer **Obv:** Similar to 1 Thaler, C#12c

Date	Mintage	F	VF	XF	Unc	BU
1812	—	—	—	7,000	10,000	—

NURNBERG

BISHOPRIC

MEDALLIC COINAGE

X# M5 DUCAT

Gold, 22 mm. **Subject:** New Years **Obv:** City view **Rev. Inscription:** PROSET / DAS / NEUE / IAHR in sprays

Date	Mintage	F	VF	XF	Unc	BU
ND(ca.1760) Proof	—	—	—	—	—	—

FREE CITY

TOKEN COINAGE

X# Tn5 2/3 GOLDGULDEN
2.2600 g., Gold, 21 mm. **Obv:** 3 shields **Obv. Legend:** ANNO DOMINI... **Rev:** Ornate ribbon border **Rev. Legend:** NVMMVS / AVREVS / PRO AERARIO / REIPVBL / NORIBERG **Note:** City government tax accounting token. Fr. #1816.

Date	Mintage	F	VF	XF	Unc	BU
MDCXXI (1621)	—	—	—	—	—	—

MEDALLIC COINAGE

X# M11 60 KREUZER
Silver **Obv:** Two shields of arms, larve "V" below **Obv. Inscription:** RESPUB: / NURENBERG: **Rev:** Crowned imperial eagle, 60 in orb on eagles breast **Note:** Atax token. Kellner #352, Dav. #100.

Date	Mintage	Good	VG	F	VF	XF
ND(c.1632)	—	—	—	—	—	—

X# M6 1/8 THALER
Silver, 22 mm. **Subject:** Peace of Westphalia **Obv:** Hobby horse rider left divides date **Obv. Legend:** FRIEDEN GEDACHT NUS. IN NURNB: **Rev:** Small crowned imperial eagle above inscription **Rev. Legend:** VIVAT / FERDINAND 9 / III: ROM: / IMP: / VIVAT **Shape:** Klippe **Note:** Fr.#1840.

Date	Mintage	VG	F	VF	XF	Unc
1650	—	—	—	—	—	—

X# M1 GOLDGULDEN
3.5000 g., 0.9860 Gold 0.1109 oz. AGW **Subject:** Centennial of the Reformation **Rev:** Date in chronogram

Date	Mintage	VG	F	VF	XF	Unc
ND(1617)	—	450	800	1,200	1,800	—

X# M7 DUCAT
Gold, 22 mm. **Subject:** Peace of Westphalia **Obv:** Hobby horse rider left divides date **Obv. Legend:** FRIEDEN GEDACHTNUS. IN NURNB: **Rev:** Small crowned imperial eagle above inscription **Rev. Legend:** VIVAT / FERDINAND 9 / III: ROM: / IMP: / VIVAT **Shape:** Klippe

Date	Mintage	VG	F	VF	XF	Unc
1650	—	—	900	1,500	2,800	—

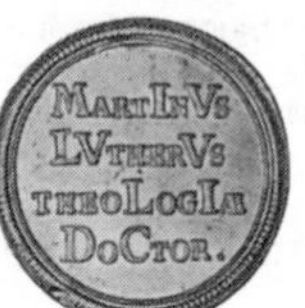

X# M2 DUCAT
3.5000 g., 0.9860 Gold 0.1109 oz. AGW **Subject:** 2nd Centennial of the Reformation **Obv:** Hand holding shade above candle **Rev:** Four-line inscription, date in chronogram **Note:** Prev. KM#M2.

Date	Mintage	VG	F	VF	XF	Unc
ND(1717)	—	300	600	1,100	1,650	—

X# M2a DUCAT
Silver **Note:** Prev. KM#M2a.

Date	Mintage	VG	F	VF	XF	Unc
ND(1717)	—	—	—	75.00	125	—

X# M3 2 DUCAT
7.0000 g., 0.9860 Gold 0.2219 oz. AGW **Subject:** 2nd Centennial of the Reformation **Obv:** Arm and hand holding basket above lighted candle in inner circle **Rev:** 4-line inscription, date in chronogram **Note:** Klippe. Prev. KM#M3.

Date	Mintage	VG	F	VF	XF	Unc
ND(1717)	—	850	1,750	3,250	5,500	—

X# M4 3 DUCAT
3.5000 g., 0.9860 Gold 0.1109 oz. AGW **Obv:** Two figures before altar with crucifix **Rev:** Two figures standing beside Christ

Date	Mintage	F	VF	XF	Unc	BU
ND	—	275	525	1,000	1,600	—

OSNABRUCK

BISHOPRIC

MEDALLIC COINAGE

KM# 257 THALER
Silver **Subject:** Sede Vacante **Note:** Regiments Thaler. Prev. KM#M1.

Date	Mintage	F	VF	XF	Unc	BU
1728	—	—	—	150	250	—

X# M2 THALER
Silver **Subject:** Sede Vacante **Obv:** Bust of St. Peter facing 3/4 right within 12 shields in border **Rev:** Bust of CAROL.M.FVN almost facing holding sword and orb **Note:** Regiments Thaler.

Date	Mintage	F	VF	XF	Unc	BU
1761	—	—	—	135	225	—

PADERBORN

BISHOPRIC

MEDALLIC COINAGE

X# M1 THALER
Silver **Ruler:** Clemens August **Subject:** Sede Vacante **Note:** Regiments Thaler. Prev. KM#M1.

Date	Mintage	F	VF	XF	Unc	BU
1719	—	65.00	125	200	350	—

X# M2 THALER
Silver **Ruler:** Sede Vacante **Subject:** Sede Vacante **Note:** Prev. KM#M2.

Date	Mintage	F	VF	XF	Unc	BU
1761	—	75.00	135	225	375	—

X# M3 THALER
Silver **Ruler:** Wilhelm Anton **Subject:** Election of Wilhelm Anton **Rev:** 8-line inscription **Note:** Dav.#2946. Prev. KM#M3.

Date	Mintage	VG	F	VF	XF	Unc
1763	—	225	525	1,000	1,750	—

POMERANIA

SWEDISH OCCUPATION

MEDALLIC COINAGE

X# M2 THALER
Silver **Rev:** Without palm branches around candle **Note:** Dav. #1872. Prev. KM#M2.

Date	Mintage	VG	F	VF	XF	Unc
1709 IM	—	300	600	1,200	1,800	—

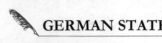

X# M1 THALER
Silver **Note:** Reichsthaler. Dav. #1872. Prev. KM#M1.

Date	Mintage	VG	F	VF	XF	Unc
1709 IM	—	200	400	800	1,200	—

X# M5 2 DUCAT
7.0000 g., 0.9860 Gold 0.2219 oz. AGW **Obv:** 1/2-length figure of Karl XII right **Rev:** Lion between falling columns, date below **Note:** Prev. KM#M5.

Date	Mintage	VG	F	VF	XF	Unc
1706	—	650	1,300	3,500	6,000	—

X# M6 2 DUCAT
7.0000 g., 0.9860 Gold 0.2219 oz. AGW **Rev:** Five-line inscription in branches **Note:** Prev. KM#M6.

Date	Mintage	VG	F	VF	XF	Unc
1706	—	1,450	2,850	5,000	8,500	—

PRUSSIA

KINGDOM

REGULAR COINAGE

A series of counterfeit Prussian 5, 10 and 20 Mark gold pieces all dated 1887A were being marketed in the early 1970's. They were created by a dentist in Bonn, West Germany and the previously unknown date listed above aroused the curiousity of the numismatic community and eventually exposed the scam.

X# 20 5 MARK
3.9825 g., 0.9000 Gold 0.1152 oz. AGW

Date	Mintage	F	VF	XF	Unc	BU
1887A	—	—	—	—	BV	—

X# 21 10 MARK
7.9650 g., 0.9000 Gold 0.2305 oz. AGW

Date	Mintage	F	VF	XF	Unc	BU
1887A	—	—	—	—	BV	—

X# 22 20 MARK
15.9300 g., 0.9000 Gold 0.4609 oz. AGW

Date	Mintage	F	VF	XF	Unc	BU
1887A	—	—	—	—	BV	—

MEDALLIC COINAGE

X# M21 GEDENKTHALER
Silver **Ruler:** Wilhelm II **Subject:** Visit to Palestine **Obv:** Jugate busts right **Obv. Legend:** GEDENKTHALER ZUR PALÄSTINAFAHRT DES DEUTSCHEN KAISERPAARES **Rev:** Palestinian lady facing, dancing with wreaths **Rev. Legend:** GOTT DER ALLMÄCHTIGE, GAB SEIN GELEITE! - RUCKKUNFT / 28 NOV. 1898

Date	Mintage	F	VF	XF	Unc	BU
1898 Proof	—	Value: 175				

X# M10 DUCAT
3.5000 g., 0.9860 Gold 0.1109 oz. AGW
Ruler: Friedrich Wilhelm I **Subject:** Coronation of Friedrich Wilhelm **Rev:** 6-line inscription and date **Note:** Prev. KM#M1.

Date	Mintage	VG	F	VF	XF	Unc
1714 IFS	—	175	325	750	1,500	—

X# M11 DUCAT
3.5000 g., 0.9860 Gold 0.1109 oz. AGW
Ruler: Friedrich Wilhelm I **Subject:** Coronation of Friedrich Wilhelm at Konigsberg **Obv:** Different armored bust of Friedrich Wilhelm right **Note:** Prev. KM#M2.

Date	Mintage	VG	F	VF	XF	Unc
1714 M/CG	—	175	325	750	1,500	—

X# M12 DUCAT
3.5000 g., 0.9860 Gold 0.1109 oz. AGW
Ruler: Friedrich Wilhelm I **Subject:** Coronation of Friedrich Wilhelm at Konigsberg **Obv:** Head laureate right **Rev:** FELICITAS POPVLI around Goddess of Good Fortune **Note:** Prev. KM#M3.

Date	Mintage	VG	F	VF	XF	Unc
1740	—	150	350	650	1,150	—

X# M13 DUCAT
3.5000 g., 0.9860 Gold 0.1109 oz. AGW **Ruler:** Friedrich Wilhelm I **Rev. Legend:** VERITATI ET IVSTITIAE **Note:** Prev. KM#M4.

Date	Mintage	VG	F	VF	XF	Unc
1740	—	120	200	450	800	—

PATTERNS

Karl Goetz Issues

Struck in Munich, Bavaria

X# 2a 2 MARK
9.7600 g., Copper, 28.2 mm. **Subject:** Wilhelm II

Date	Mintage	F	VF	XF	Unc	BU
1913 Proof	—	Value: 50.00				

X# 2b 2 MARK
8.9600 g., Silver Plated Copper, 28.2 mm.
Subject: Wilhelm II

Date	Mintage	F	VF	XF	Unc	BU
1913 Proof	—	Value: 65.00				

X# 2c 2 MARK
24.4400 g., Platinum APW, 28.2 mm. **Subject:** Wilhelm II

Date	Mintage	F	VF	XF	Unc	BU
1913 Proof	—	Value: 950				

X# 3 3 MARK
12.4000 g., Silver **Subject:** Wilhelm II

Date	Mintage	F	VF	XF	Unc	BU
1913 Proof	—	Value: 175				

X# 3a 3 MARK
13.0000 g., Copper **Subject:** Wilhelm II

Date	Mintage	F	VF	XF	Unc	BU
1913 Proof	—	Value: 50.00				

X# 3b 3 MARK
Bronze **Subject:** Wilhelm II

Date	Mintage	F	VF	XF	Unc	BU
1913 Proof	—	Value: 50.00				

X# 3c 3 MARK
11.7200 g., Silver Plated Copper **Subject:** Wilhelm II

Date	Mintage	F	VF	XF	Unc	BU
1913 Proof	—	Value: 65.00				

X# 4 5 MARK
19.0000 g., Silver **Subject:** Wilhelm II

Date	Mintage	F	VF	XF	Unc	BU
1913 Proof	—	Value: 250				

X# 4a 5 MARK
19.1500 g., Copper **Subject:** Wilhelm II

Date	Mintage	F	VF	XF	Unc	BU
1913 Proof	—	Value: 85.00				

X# 4b 5 MARK
Bronze **Subject:** Wilhelm II

Date	Mintage	F	VF	XF	Unc	BU
1913 Proof	—	Value: 100				

X# 4c 5 MARK
Gold **Subject:** Wilhelm II

Date	Mintage	F	VF	XF	Unc	BU
1913 Proof	—	—	—	—	—	—

X# 4d 5 MARK
56.5700 g., Platinum APW **Subject:** Wilhelm II

Date	Mintage	F	VF	XF	Unc	BU
1913 Proof	—	Value: 2,850				

X# 5 10 MARK
2.8000 g., Gold **Subject:** Wilhelm II

Date	Mintage	F	VF	XF	Unc	BU
1913 Proof	—	—	—	—	—	—

X# 5a 10 MARK
3.3600 g., Copper **Subject:** Wilhelm II

Date	Mintage	F	VF	XF	Unc	BU
1913 Proof	—	Value: 50.00				

X# 5b 10 MARK
Gilt Copper **Subject:** Wilhelm II

Date	Mintage	F	VF	XF	Unc	BU
1913 Proof	—	Value: 60.00				

X# 5c 10 MARK
3.3100 g., Bronze **Subject:** Wilhelm II

Date	Mintage	F	VF	XF	Unc	BU
1913 Proof	—	Value: 55.00				

X# 5d 10 MARK
3.5900 g., Silver **Subject:** Wilhelm II

Date	Mintage	F	VF	XF	Unc	BU
1913 Proof	—	Value: 120				

X# 6 20 MARK
4.2000 g., Gold **Subject:** Wilhelm II

Date	Mintage	F	VF	XF	Unc	BU
1913 Proof	—	—	—	—	—	—

X# 6a 20 MARK
4.2400 g., Copper **Subject:** Wilhelm II

Date	Mintage	F	VF	XF	Unc	BU
1913 Proof	—	Value: 50.00				

X# 6b 20 MARK
Gilt Copper **Subject:** Wilhelm II

Date	Mintage	F	VF	XF	Unc	BU
1913 Proof	—	Value: 60.00				

X# 6c 20 MARK
Bronze **Subject:** Wilhelm II

Date	Mintage	F	VF	XF	Unc	BU
1913 Proof	—	Value: 75.00				

X# 6d 20 MARK
Gilt Silver **Subject:** Wilhelm II

Date	Mintage	F	VF	XF	Unc	BU
1913 Proof	—	Value: 90.00				

X# 6e 20 MARK
4.2000 g., Silver **Subject:** Wilhelm II

Date	Mintage	F	VF	XF	Unc	BU
1913 Proof	—	Value: 120				

PATTERNS

Karl Goetz Issues

Struck in Munich, Bavaria

X#	Date	Mintage	Identification	Mkt Val
2	1913	—	2 Mark. Silver. 9.1000 g. 28 mm. Bust left. Eagle with wings spread, arms below. Plain edge. Prev. KM#Pn50.	—

PROOF SETS

X#	Date	Mintage	Identification	Issue Price	Mkt Val
XPS1	1913 (5)	—	X2a-X6a	—	285
XPS2	1913 (10)	—	Prussia X#2a-6a and Bavaria X#1a-5a combined set.	—	625

SAXE-MEININGEN

DUCHY

MEDALLIC COINAGE

X# M5 THALER
Silver **Obv:** Bust of Martin Luther right **Obv. Legend:** MARTINVS LVTHERVS THEOLOGIAE DOCTOR **Rev:** Bust of Catharina von Bora left **Rev. Legend:** CATHARINA VON BORA•D•LVTHERS FRAV

Date	Mintage	VG	F	VF	XF	Unc
MDCLLVVVII (1717)	—	—	—	—	—	—

SAXE-SAALFELD

DUCHY

TRADE COINAGE

X# M1 DUCAT
7.0000 g., 0.9860 Gold 0.2219 oz. AGW, 22 mm. **Ruler:** Christian Ernst and Franz Josias **Subject:** Death of the Duke **Obv:** Man on cross at left, man kneeling at right **Rev:** Radiant sun at upper right, bird in flight and clouds at left **Note:** Prev. Fr.#3010.

Date	Mintage	VG	F	VF	XF	Unc
ND(1745)	—	350	650	1,250	2,000	—

X# M2 2 DUCAT
7.0000 g., 0.9860 Gold 0.2219 oz. AGW **Ruler:** Christian Ernst and Franz Josias **Subject:** Death of the Duke **Note:** Prev. Fr.#3009.

Date	Mintage	VG	F	VF	XF	Unc
ND(1745)	—	350	650	1,250	2,000	—

SAXONY

DUCHY AND ELECTORATE

MEDALLIC COINAGE

X# 5 DUCAT
3.5000 g., 0.9860 Gold 0.1109 oz. AGW
Note: Originally issued for the mother of Johann Georg I at Christmas. The popularity of this issue resulted in restriking until 1872.

Date	Mintage	F	VF	XF	Unc	BU
1616	—	—	250	350	500	—

KINGDOM

MEDALLIC COINAGE

X# 12 2 MARK
Silver **Ruler:** Albert **Subject:** Muldner Hutte Mint Visit of King Albert

Date	Mintage	F	VF	XF	Unc	BU
1892	—	—	—	600	900	—
1892 Proof	—	Value: 1,000				

X# 13 2 MARK
Silver **Ruler:** Georg **Subject:** Visit of King George

Date	Mintage	F	VF	XF	Unc	BU
1903 Proof	—	Value: 1,250				

X# 14 2 MARK
Silver **Ruler:** Friedrich August III **Subject:** Visit of King Friedrich August

Date	Mintage	F	VF	XF	Unc	BU
1905 Proof	—	Value: 1,200				

WOLGAST

CITY

MEDALLIC COINAGE

Largesse Money

X# M2 1/2 THALER
Silver, 37.5 mm. **Subject:** Death of Gustavus Adolphus **Obv:** Gustavus Adolphus lying in state with battle in backgournd **Rev:** King in chariot crushing enemies below

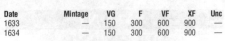

Date	Mintage	VG	F	VF	XF	Unc
1633	—	150	300	600	900	—
1634	—	150	300	600	900	—

X# M16 5 THALER
Silver, 77 mm. **Note:** Dav. #LS275A. Illustration reduced. Prev. KM #M16.

Date	Mintage	VG	F	VF	XF	Unc
1633	—	—	—	2,000	3,000	—

WURTTEMBERG

DUCHY

MEDALLIC COINAGE

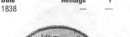

X# 11 1/2 GULDEN
4.4700 g., Gold Plated Silver, 23.9 mm. **Obv:** Bust of Karl Heinrich Knorr facing 3/4 left **Rev:** Value, date in sprays **Edge:** Plain

Date	Mintage	F	VF	XF	Unc	BU
1838	—	—	—	—	—	—

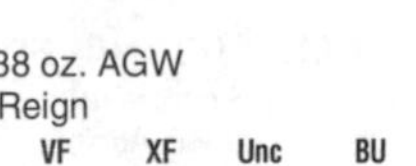

X# 1 4 DUCAT
14.0000 g., 0.9860 Gold 0.4438 oz. AGW
Subject: 25th Anniversary of Reign

Date	Mintage	F	VF	XF	Unc	BU
1841	6,236	600	1,000	1,600	2,400	—

X# 3 4 DUCAT
14.0000 g., 0.9860 Gold 0.4438 oz. AGW
Subject: Visit of King Wilhelm to Mint

Date	Mintage	F	VF	XF	Unc	BU
1844	17	—	—	12,000	20,000	—

WURZBURG

BISHOPRIC

MEDALLIC COINAGE

X# M2 GOLDGULDEN
3.2500 g., 0.7700 Gold 0.0805 oz. AGW

Date	Mintage	VG	F	VF	XF	Unc
ND(1719)	—	200	450	950	1,750	—

X# M1 GOLDGULDEN
3.2500 g., 0.7700 Gold 0.0805 oz. AGW
Obv: Crowned and mantled arms **Rev:** Shield on front of altar, flaming urn on top **Note:** Prev. KM#M1.

Date	Mintage	VG	F	VF	XF	Unc
ND(1719)	—	200	450	950	1,750	—

X# M3 GOLDGULDEN
3.2500 g., 0.7700 Gold 0.0805 oz. AGW **Note:** Prev. KM#M3.

Date	Mintage	VG	F	VF	XF	Unc
1724	—	200	450	950	1,750	—

X# M4 GOLDGULDEN
3.2500 g., 0.7700 Gold 0.0805 oz. AGW **Obv:** Bust of Friedrich Karl right **Rev:** Banner arms in ornamental cartouche **Note:** Prev. KM#M4.

Date	Mintage	VG	F	VF	XF	Unc
ND(1729)	—	225	500	1,100	2,000	—

X# M5 GOLDGULDEN
3.2500 g., 0.7700 Gold 0.0805 oz. AGW **Rev:** Flowers hanging from different ornamental cartouche **Note:** Prev. KM#M5.

Date	Mintage	VG	F	VF	XF	Unc
ND(1729)	—	225	500	1,100	2,000	—

X# M6 GOLDGULDEN
3.2500 g., 0.7700 Gold 0.0805 oz. AGW **Note:** Prev. KM#M6.

Date	Mintage	VG	F	VF	XF	Unc
ND(1746)	—	175	350	750	1,400	2,250

X# M7 GOLDGULDEN
3.2500 g., 0.7700 Gold 0.0805 oz. AGW **Obv:** Head of Maximilian Joseph right **Rev:** Palm above Wurzburg coat-of-arms, value and date, with full inscription **Note:** Prev. KM#M7.

Date	Mintage	VG	F	VF	XF	Unc
1803	—	—	2,250	3,500	5,000	—

X# M8 GOLDGULDEN
3.2500 g., 0.7700 Gold 0.0805 oz. AGW **Rev:** Palm above Wurzburg coat-of-arms and S. P. - Q. W., abbreviated inscription **Note:** Prev. KM#M8.

Date	Mintage	VG	F	VF	XF	Unc
1803	—	—	1,500	2,500	3,500	—

X# M9 GOLDGULDEN
3.2500 g., 0.7700 Gold 0.0805 oz. AGW **Obv:** Head of Maximilian Joseph left **Rev:** City view of Wurzburg **Note:** Prev. KM#M9.

Date	Mintage	VG	F	VF	XF	Unc
1815	—	—	1,250	2,000	3,000	—

X# M10 GOLDGULDEN
3.2500 g., 0.7700 Gold 0.0805 oz. AGW **Rev:** Coat-of-arms, value **Note:** Prev. KM#M10.

Date	Mintage	VG	F	VF	XF	Unc
1817	—	—	2,000	3,500	5,000	—

X# M11 GOLDGULDEN
3.2500 g., 0.7700 Gold 0.0805 oz. AGW **Note:** Prev. KM#M11.

Date	Mintage	VG	F	VF	XF	Unc
ND(1817)	—	—	1,250	2,000	3,000	—

X# M12 GOLDGULDEN
3.2500 g., 0.7700 Gold 0.0805 oz. AGW **Obv:** Head of Ludwig left **Rev:** 6-line inscription **Note:** Prev. KM#M12.

Date	Mintage	VG	F	VF	XF	Unc
1826 Rare	65	—	—	—	—	—

X# M13 GOLDGULDEN
3.2500 g., 0.7700 Gold 0.0805 oz. AGW **Rev:** View of Wurzburg, value and date **Note:** Prev. KM#M13.

Date	Mintage	VG	F	VF	XF	Unc
ND(1827)	—	—	1,750	3,000	4,500	—

X# M14 GOLDGULDEN
3.2500 g., 0.7700 Gold 0.0805 oz. AGW **Note:** Prev. KM#M14. Roman I follows king's name.

Date	Mintage	VG	F	VF	XF	Unc
ND(ca.1835)	—	—	1,250	2,000	3,000	—

X# M15 GOLDGULDEN
3.2500 g., 0.7700 Gold 0.0805 oz. AGW **Rev:** City view of Wurzburg **Note:** Prev. KM#M15.

Date	Mintage	VG	F	VF	XF	Unc
ND(ca.1843)	—	—	1,500	2,500	3,500	—

X# M16 GOLDGULDEN
3.2500 g., 0.7700 Gold 0.0805 oz. AGW **Rev:** Arms in sprays **Edge:** Slant reeded **Note:** Prev. KM#M16.

Date	Mintage	VG	F	VF	XF	Unc
ND(ca.1843)	—	—	1,500	2,500	3,500	—

X# M17 GOLDGULDEN
3.2500 g., 0.7700 Gold 0.0805 oz. AGW **Edge:** Straight reeded **Note:** Prev. KM#M17.

Date	Mintage	VG	F	VF	XF	Unc
ND(ca.1843)	—	—	2,000	3,500	5,000	—

X# M18 GOLDGULDEN
3.2500 g., 0.7700 Gold 0.0805 oz. AGW **Obv:** Head of Ludwig right **Rev:** City view of Wurzburg **Note:** Prev. KM#M18.

Date	Mintage	VG	F	VF	XF	Unc
ND	300	—	1,250	2,000	3,000	—

X# M19 GOLDGULDEN
3.2500 g., 0.7700 Gold 0.0805 oz. AGW **Rev:** Arms in sprays, value GOLD GULDEN **Note:** Prev. KM#M19.

Date	Mintage	VG	F	VF	XF	Unc
ND	Inc. above	—	1,250	2,000	3,000	—

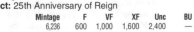

X# M20 GOLDGULDEN
3.2500 g., 0.7700 Gold 0.0805 oz. AGW **Rev:** Value: GOLDGULDEN **Note:** Prev. KM#M20.

Date	Mintage	VG	F	VF	XF	Unc
ND	Inc. above	—	1,250	2,250	3,500	—

X# M21 GOLDGULDEN
3.2500 g., 0.7700 Gold 0.0805 oz. AGW **Obv:** Head of Maximilian right **Obv. Legend:** ....KOENIG **Note:** Prev. KM#M21.

Date	Mintage	VG	F	VF	XF	Unc
ND(1850)	215	—	1,250	2,000	3,000	—

X# M22 GOLDGULDEN
3.2500 g., 0.7700 Gold 0.0805 oz. AGW **Obv. Legend:** ... REX **Note:** Prev. KM#M22.

Date	Mintage	VG	F	VF	XF	Unc
ND(1850)	Inc. above	—	1,250	2,250	3,500	—

X# M23 GOLDGULDEN
3.2500 g., 0.7700 Gold 0.0805 oz. AGW **Obv. Legend:** ...KOENIG **Rev:** City view of Wurzburg **Note:** Prev. KM#M23.

Date	Mintage	VG	F	VF	XF	Unc
ND(1850)	Inc. above	—	1,250	2,000	3,000	—

X# M24 GOLDGULDEN
3.2500 g., 0.7700 Gold 0.0805 oz. AGW **Obv. Legend:** ...REX **Note:** Prev. KM#M24.

Date	Mintage	VG	F	VF	XF	Unc
ND(1850)	Inc. above	—	1,250	2,250	3,500	—

X# M25 GOLDGULDEN
3.2500 g., 0.7700 Gold 0.0805 oz. AGW **Obv:** Head of Ludwig II right **Edge:** Reeded **Note:** Prev. KM#M25.

Date	Mintage	VG	F	VF	XF	Unc
ND(1864)	350	—	1,250	2,000	3,000	—

X# M26 GOLDGULDEN
3.2500 g., 0.7700 Gold 0.0805 oz. AGW **Edge:** Plain **Note:** Prev. KM#M26.

Date	Mintage	VG	F	VF	XF	Unc
ND(1864)	Inc. above	—	1,250	2,250	3,500	—

X# M27 GOLDGULDEN
3.2500 g., 0.7700 Gold 0.0805 oz. AGW **Obv:** Head of Ludwig II right **Rev:** Wurzburg coat-of-arms **Edge:** Reeded **Note:** Prev. KM#M27.

Date	Mintage	VG	F	VF	XF	Unc
ND(1864)	350	—	1,250	2,100	3,250	—

X# M28 GOLDGULDEN
3.2500 g., 0.7700 Gold 0.0805 oz. AGW **Edge:** Plain **Note:** Prev. KM#M28.

Date	Mintage	VG	F	VF	XF	Unc
ND	Inc. above	—	1,350	2,500	3,750	—

X# M29 GOLDGULDEN
5.3000 g., 0.7700 Gold 0.1312 oz. AGW **Obv:** Ludwig III **Rev:** St. Kilian and value **Note:** Prev. KM#M29.

Date	Mintage	VG	F	VF	XF	Unc
ND(1916) Unique	—	—	—	—	—	—

GERMANY

DEMORILIZED REPUBLIC

MEDALLIC COINAGE

X# 11 20 MARK
18.1500 g., Copper-Nickel, 33.2 mm. **Obv:** DDR arms **Obv. Legend:** DEUTSCHE DEMORALISCHE REPUBLIC **Rev:** Two outstretched arms, flag behind in oval banner **Rev. Legend:** PARTEI DER STASI "ERINNERUGEN AN DIE ZUKUNF" **Edge:** Plain

Date	Mintage	F	VF	XF	Unc	BU
1990 Proof	—	Value: 15.00				

GERMANY-FEDERAL REPUBLIC

FEDERAL REPUBLIC

MEDALLIC COINAGE

X# M360 THALER
29.2500 g., Silver, 42.75 mm. **Series:** Münich Thaler **Subject:** 800th Anniversary of Founding **Obv:** City gate, saint in doorway, crowned rampant lion left above **Obv. Legend:** ACHTHUNDERT JAHRE - 1158 MÜNCHEN 1958 **Rev:** Medieval city view **Edge:** Plain

Date	Mintage	F	VF	XF	Unc	BU
ND(1958)	—	—	—	—	85.00	—

Argenteus Issues

X# M33 SILVER DUCAT
15.0000 g., 1.0000 Silver 0.4822 oz. ASW, 35.2 mm. **Obv:** Value "I" in center of 6-pointed cross, lilies in angles **Obv. Legend:** PRO PROSPERITATE MUNDI **Rev:** Bust of Maria Theresa left divides dates 1717 - 1780 **Rev. Legend:** MARIA • THERESIA IMPERATRIX • GER • **Edge:** Plain

Date	Mintage	F	VF	XF	Unc	BU
1957 Proof	—	Value: 16.50				

X# M38 SILVER DUCAT
15.0000 g., 1.0000 Silver 0.4822 oz. ASW, 35.2 mm. **Obv:** Value "I" in center of 6-pointed cross, lilies in angles **Obv. Legend:** PRO PROSPERITATE MUNDI **Rev:** Bust of Pope Pius XII left **Rev. Legend:** PIUS XII.PONTIFEX MAXIMUS 1876 - 1958 **Edge:** Plain

Date	Mintage	F	VF	XF	Unc	BU
1958 Proof	—	Value: 20.00				

X# M42 SILVER DUCAT
15.0000 g., 1.0000 Silver 0.4822 oz. ASW, 35.2 mm. **Obv:** Value "I" in center of 6-pointed cross, lilies in angles **Obv. Legend:** PRO PROSPERITATE MUNDI **Rev:** Head of Nefertiti left **Rev. Legend:** MATER OPERUM ATQUE ARTIFICIORUM • AEGYPTUS • **Edge:** Plain

Date	Mintage	F	VF	XF	Unc	BU
1958 Proof	—	Value: 20.00				

X# M73 SILVER DUCAT
15.0000 g., 1.0000 Silver 0.4822 oz. ASW, 35.2 mm. **Subject:** 10th Anniversary, 1st President, F.R.P. **Obv:** Value "I" in center of 6-pointed cross, lilies in angles **Obv. Legend:** PRO PROSPERITATE MUNDI **Rev:** Bust of Heuss left, shield at bottom **Rev. Legend:** • THEODORUS HEUSS MOD.P.P.GERMAN • **Edge:** Plain

Date	Mintage	F	VF	XF	Unc	BU
ND(1959) Proof	—	Value: 16.50				

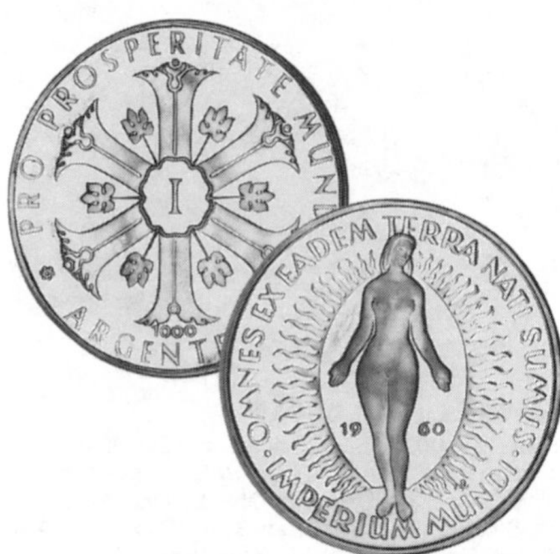

X# M79 SILVER DUCAT
15.0000 g., 1.0000 Silver 0.4822 oz. ASW, 35.2 mm. **Series:** Type II: Imperial Currency **Subject:** Children of Earth **Obv:** Value "I" in center of 6-pointed cross, lilies in angles **Obv. Legend:** PRO PROSPERITATE MUNDI

Rev: Radiant nude female standing facing, head 3/4 right **Rev. Legend:** OMNES EX EADEM TERRA NATI SUMUS • IMPERIUM MUNDI • **Edge:** Plain

Date	Mintage	F	VF	XF	Unc	BU
1960 Proof	—	Value: 20.00				

X# M98 SILVER DUCAT

15.0000 g., 1.0000 Silver 0.4822 oz. ASW, 35.2 mm. **Subject:** Battle of Marathon **Obv:** Value "I" in center of 6-pointed cross, lilies in angles **Obv. Legend:** PRO PROSPERITATE MUNDI **Rev:** Athenian owl above helmeted head of Minerva left **Rev. Legend:** GRAECIA • ANNO A.CHR.N.CDXC... **Edge:** Plain

Date	Mintage	F	VF	XF	Unc	BU
1960 Proof	—	Value: 20.00				

X# M76 SILVER DUCAT

15.0000 g., 1.0000 Silver 0.4822 oz. ASW, 35.2 mm. **Subject:** 1960 Rome Olympics **Obv:** Value "I" in center of 6-pointed cross, lilies in angles **Obv. Legend:** PRO PROSPERITATE MUNDI **Rev:** Head of Roma right **Rev. Legend:** OLYMPIA ROMA **Edge:** Plain

Date	Mintage	F	VF	XF	Unc	BU
1960 Proof	—	Value: 16.50				

X# M84 SILVER DUCAT

15.0000 g., 1.0000 Silver 0.4822 oz. ASW, 35.2 mm. **Subject:** Holy Mother Mary with Child **Obv:** Value "I" in center of 6-pointed cross, lilies in angles **Obv. Legend:** PRO PROSPERITATE MUNDI **Rev:** Crowned Holy Mother Mary with Child **Rev. Legend:** + SANCTA MARIA MONACHII **Edge:** Plain

Date	Mintage	F	VF	XF	Unc	BU
1960 Proof	—	Value: 16.50				

X# M88 SILVER DUCAT

15.0000 g., 1.0000 Silver 0.4822 oz. ASW, 35.2 mm. **Subject:** Pope John XXIII **Obv:** Value "I" in center of 6-pointed cross, lilies in angles **Obv. Legend:** PRO PROSPERITATE MUNDI **Rev:** Bust of Pope John XXIII left **Rev. Legend:** IOANNES XXIII PONTIFEX MAXIMUS **Edge:** Plain

Date	Mintage	F	VF	XF	Unc	BU
1960 Proof	—	Value: 20.00				

X# M92 SILVER DUCAT

14.9067 g., 1.0000 Silver 0.4792 oz. ASW **Subject:** Prince Eugene of Austria

Date	Mintage	F	VF	XF	Unc	BU
1960 Proof	—	Value: 16.50				

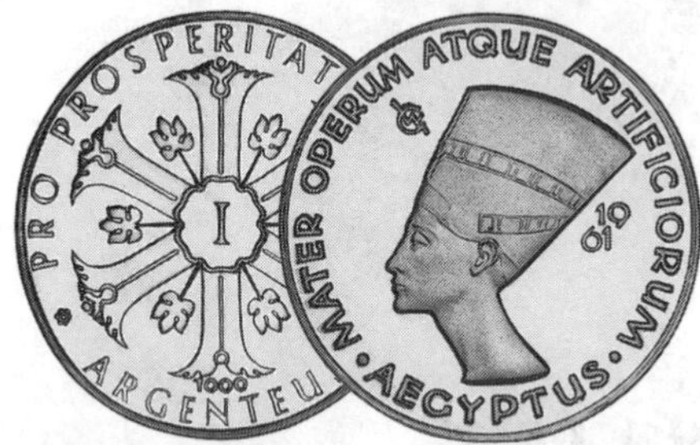

X# M96 SILVER DUCAT

15.0000 g., 1.0000 Silver 0.4822 oz. ASW, 35.2 mm. **Subject:** Queen Nefertiti of Egypt **Obv:** Value "I" in center of 6-pointed cross, lilies in angles **Obv. Legend:** PRO PROSPERITATE MUNDI **Rev:** Head of Nefertiti left **Rev. Legend:** MATER OPERUM ATIQUE ARTIFICIORUM • AEGYPTUS **Edge:** Plain

Date	Mintage	F	VF	XF	Unc	BU
1960 Proof	—	Value: 20.00				

X# M111 SILVER DUCAT

15.0000 g., 1.0000 Silver 0.4822 oz. ASW, 35.2 mm. **Obv:** Value "I" in center of 6-pointed cross, lilies in angles **Obv. Legend:** PRO PROSPERITATE MUNDI **Rev:** Crowned bust of Germania facing 3/4 left divides date **Rev. Legend:** GERMANIA AETERNA **Edge:** Plain

Date	Mintage	F	VF	XF	Unc	BU
1961 Proof	—	Value: 16.50				

X# M115 SILVER DUCAT

15.0000 g., 1.0000 Silver 0.4822 oz. ASW, 35.2 mm. **Obv:** Value "I" in center of 6-pointed cross, lilies in angles **Obv. Legend:** PRO PROSPERITATE MUNDI **Rev:** Bust of Adenauer left **Rev. Legend:** CONRAD ADENAUER PATER PATRIAE GERMAN **Edge:** Plain

Date	Mintage	F	VF	XF	Unc	BU
1961 Proof	—	Value: 16.50				

X# M119 SILVER DUCAT

15.0000 g., 1.0000 Silver 0.4822 oz. ASW, 35.2 mm. **Subject:** Reunion, Life For Germany **Obv:** Value "I" in center of 6-pointed cross, lilies in angles **Obv. Legend:** PRO PROSPERITATE MUNDI **Rev:** Germania kneeling between two children **Rev. Legend:** CONCORDIA SALUS **Edge:** Plain

Date	Mintage	F	VF	XF	Unc	BU
1961 Proof	—	Value: 16.50				

X# M124 SILVER DUCAT

15.0000 g., 1.0000 Silver 0.4822 oz. ASW, 35.2 mm. **Subject:** Vatican Council **Obv:** Value "I" in center of 6-arm cross **Obv. Legend:** PRO PROSPERITATE MUNDI **Rev:** Busts of Popes John XXIII and Paul VI left **Rev. Legend:** CONCILIUM VATICANUM **Edge:** Plain

Date	Mintage	F	VF	XF	Unc	BU
1963 Proof	—	Value: 20.00				

X# M150 SILVER DUCAT

15.0000 g., 1.0000 Silver 0.4822 oz. ASW, 35.2 mm. **Subject:** President Ludwig Erhard's Inauguration **Obv:** Value "I" in center of 6-pointed cross, lilies in angles **Obv. Legend:** PRO PROSPERITATE MUNDI **Rev:** Bust of Erhard left, small shield at bottom **Rev. Legend:** L. ERHARD KANZLER DER BUNDESREP. DEUTSCHLAND **Edge:** Plain

Date	Mintage	F	VF	XF	Unc	BU
1963 Proof	—	Value: 16.50				

X# M142 SILVER DUCAT

15.0000 g., 1.0000 Silver 0.4822 oz. ASW, 35.2 mm. **Subject:** Investiture of Pope Paul VI **Obv:** Value "I" in center of 6-pointed cross, lilies in angles **Obv. Legend:** PRO PROSPERITATE MUNDI **Rev:** Bust of Pope Paul VI left **Rev. Legend:** PAULUS VI • PONTIFEX MAXIMUS • **Edge:** Plain

Date	Mintage	F	VF	XF	Unc	BU
1963 Proof	—	Value: 20.00				

X# M153 SILVER DUCAT

15.0000 g., 1.0000 Silver 0.4822 oz. ASW, 35.2 mm. **Obv:** Value "I" in center of 6-pointed cross, lilies in angles **Obv. Legend:** PRO PROSPERITATE MUNDI **Rev:** Bust of Cleopatra left **Rev. Legend:** AEGYPTUS **Edge:** Plain

Date	Mintage	F	VF	XF	Unc	BU
1963 Proof	—	Value: 16.50				

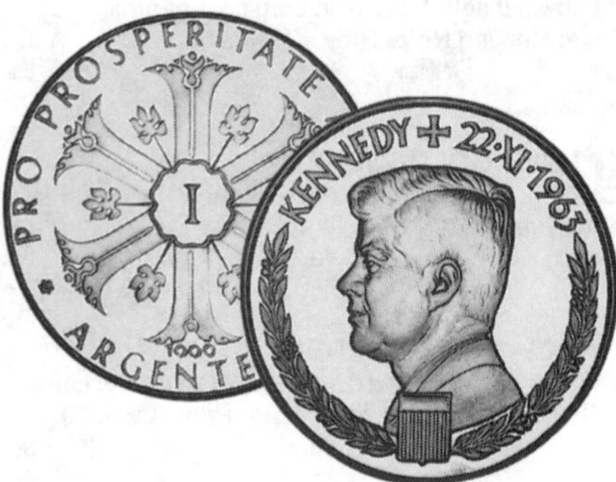

X# M161 SILVER DUCAT

15.0000 g., 1.0000 Silver 0.4822 oz. ASW, 35.2 mm. **Subject:** JFK's Death **Obv:** Value "I" in center of 6-arm cross **Obv. Legend:** PRO PROSPERITATE MUNDI **Rev:** Bust of Kennedy left in sprays **Rev. Legend:** KENNEDY + 22 • X1 • 1963 **Edge:** Plain

Date	Mintage	F	VF	XF	Unc	BU
ND(1963) Proof	—	Value: 20.00				

X# M170 SILVER DUCAT
15.0000 g., 1.0000 Silver 0.4822 oz. ASW, 35.2 mm. **Obv:** Value "I" in center of 6-pointed cross, lilies in angles **Obv. Legend:** PRO PROSPERITATE MUNDI **Rev:** Prince Eugene of Austria horseback right **Edge:** Plain **Note:** Prev. X#M92.

Date	Mintage	F	VF	XF	Unc	BU
1963 Proof	—	Value: 16.50				

X# M236 SILVER DUCAT
15.0000 g., 1.0000 Silver 0.4822 oz. ASW, 35.2 mm. **Subject:** 1964 Tokyo Olympics **Obv:** Value "I" in center of 6-pointed cross, lilies in angles **Obv. Legend:** PRO PROSPERITATE MUNDI **Rev:** Crowned Budha head left **Edge:** Plain

Date	Mintage	F	VF	XF	Unc	BU
1964 Proof	—	Value: 20.00				

X# M241 SILVER DUCAT
15.0000 g., 1.0000 Silver 0.4822 oz. ASW, 35.2 mm. **Obv:** Value "I" in center of 6-pointed cross, lilies in angles **Obv. Legend:** PRO PROSPERITATE MUNDI **Rev:** Goddess of Motherhood with child **Rev. Legend:** MAGNA MATER **Edge:** Plain

Date	Mintage	F	VF	XF	Unc	BU
1964 Proof	—	Value: 16.50				

X# M175 SILVER DUCAT
15.0000 g., 1.0000 Silver 0.4822 oz. ASW, 35.2 mm. **Obv:** Value "I" in center of 6-pointed cross, lilies in angles **Obv. Legend:** PRO PROSPERITATE MUNDI **Rev:** Helmeted Patron Saint of Bavaria standing, facing **Edge:** Plain

Date	Mintage	F	VF	XF	Unc	BU
1964 Proof	—	Value: 16.50				

X# M185 SILVER DUCAT
15.0000 g., 1.0000 Silver 0.4822 oz. ASW, 35.2 mm. **Obv:** Value "I" in center of 6-pointed cross, lilies in angles **Obv. Legend:** PRO PROSPERITATE MUNDI **Rev:** Port of Hamburg, cargo ship **Rev. Legend:** HAMBURGUM - PORTUS MUNDI **Edge:** Plain

Date	Mintage	F	VF	XF	Unc	BU
1965 Proof	—	Value: 16.50				

X# M195 SILVER DUCAT
15.0000 g., 1.0000 Silver 0.4822 oz. ASW, 35.2 mm. **Subject:** Twenty Years of Reconstruction **Obv:** Value "I" in center of 6-pointed cross, lilies in angles **Obv. Legend:** PRO PROSPERITATE MUNDI **Rev:** City view **Rev. Inscription:** MONACHIUM **Edge:** Plain

Date	Mintage	F	VF	XF	Unc	BU
1965 Proof	—	Value: 16.50				

X# M180 SILVER DUCAT
15.0000 g., 1.0000 Silver 0.4822 oz. ASW, 35.2 mm. **Subject:** Cologne **Obv:** Value "I" in center of 6-pointed cross, lilies in angles **Obv. Legend:** PRO PROSPERITATE MUNDI **Rev:** Cologne Cathedral, shield at upper right **Rev. Inscription:** COLONIA **Edge:** Plain

Date	Mintage	F	VF	XF	Unc	BU
1965 Proof	—	Value: 16.50				

X# M190 SILVER DUCAT
15.0000 g., 1.0000 Silver 0.4822 oz. ASW, 35.2 mm. **Subject:** Albert Schweitzer **Obv:** Value "I" in center of 6-pointed cross, lilies in angles **Obv. Legend:** PRO PROSPERITATE MUNDI **Rev:** Bust of Albert Schweitzer right **Rev. Legend:** SERVATOR GENERIS HUMANI **Edge:** Plain

Date	Mintage	F	VF	XF	Unc	BU
1965 Proof	—	Value: 16.50				

X# M198 SILVER DUCAT
15.0000 g., 1.0000 Silver 0.4822 oz. ASW, 35.2 mm. **Subject:** Dutch Naval Heroes **Obv:** Value "I" in center of 6-pointed cross, lilies in angles **Obv. Legend:** PRO PROSPERITATE MUNDI **Rev:** Busts of Johan and Cornelis Evertsen 3/4 right, crowned shield at bottom **Rev. Legend:** • NEDERLAND • JOHAN EN CORNELIS EVERTSEN • **Edge:** Plain

Date	Mintage	F	VF	XF	Unc	BU
1966 Proof	—	Value: 16.50				

X# M201 SILVER DUCAT
15.0000 g., 1.0000 Silver 0.4822 oz. ASW, 35.2 mm. **Obv:** Value "I" in center of 6-pointed cross, lilies in angles **Obv. Legend:** PRO PROSPERITATE MUNDI **Rev:** Crowned head of St. Adelheid, H.R.E. left **Rev. Legend:** SANCTA ADELHEID IMPERATRIX + 999 **Edge:** Plain

Date	Mintage	F	VF	XF	Unc	BU
ND(1967) Proof	—	Value: 16.50				

X# M209 SILVER DUCAT
15.0000 g., 1.0000 Silver 0.4822 oz. ASW, 35.2 mm. **Subject:** 250th Anniversary Coronation of Maria Theresa of Austria **Obv:** Value "I" in center of 6-pointed cross, lilies in angles **Obv. Legend:** PRO PROSPERITATE MUNDI **Rev:** Bust of Maria Theresa left divides dates 1717-1780 **Rev. Legend:** MARIA • THERESIA IMPERATRIX • GER • **Edge:** Plain

Date	Mintage	F	VF	XF	Unc	BU
1967 Proof	—	Value: 16.50				

X# M205 SILVER DUCAT
15.0000 g., 1.0000 Silver 0.4822 oz. ASW, 35.2 mm. **Subject:** Canada's Centennial **Obv:** Value "I" in center of 6-pointed cross, lilies in angles **Obv. Legend:** PRO PROSPERITATE MUNDI **Rev:** Bust of Indian maiden right **Rev. Legend:** CANADA PATRIA NOSTRA **Edge:** Plain

Date	Mintage	F	VF	XF	Unc	BU
ND(1967) Proof	—	Value: 16.50				

X# M230 SILVER DUCAT
15.0000 g., 1.0000 Silver 0.4822 oz. ASW, 35.20 mm. **Subject:** 1968 Mexico Olympics **Obv:** Value "I" in center of 6-pointed cross, lilies in angles **Obv. Legend:** PRO PROSPERITATE MUNDI **Rev:** Rayed ancient head facing **Edge:** Plain

Date	Mintage	F	VF	XF	Unc	BU
1968 Proof	—	Value: 20.00				

X# M214 SILVER DUCAT
15.0000 g., 1.0000 Silver 0.4822 oz. ASW, 35.2 mm. **Subject:** RFK's Death **Obv:** Value "I" in center of 6-pointed cross, lilies in angles **Obv. Legend:** PRO PROSPERITATE MUNDI **Rev:** Bust of Kennedy right between crosses **Rev. Legend:** ROBERT F. KENNEDY + 6 • VI • 1968 **Edge:** Plain

Date	Mintage	F	VF	XF	Unc	BU
ND(1968) Proof	—	Value: 20.00				

X# M259 SILVER DUCAT
15.0000 g., 1.0000 Silver 0.4822 oz. ASW, 35.2 mm. **Obv:** Value "I" in center of 6-pointed cross, lilies in angles **Obv. Legend:** PRO PROSPERITATE MUNDI **Rev:** Nude female crouching **Rev. Legend:** AURUM DIVINUM **Edge:** Plain

Date	Mintage	F	VF	XF	Unc	BU
ND(1970) Proof	—	Value: 20.00				

X# M269 SILVER DUCAT
15.0000 g., 1.0000 Silver 0.4822 oz. ASW, 35.2 mm. **Subject:** Montreal Olympics **Obv:** Value "I" in center of 6-pointed cross, lilies in angles **Obv. Legend:** PRO PROSPERITATE MUNDI **Rev:** Head of Greek left, Maple leaves below **Edge:** Plain

Date	Mintage	F	VF	XF	Unc	BU
1976 Proof	—	Value: 20.00				

X# M127 SILVER DUCAT
15.0000 g., 1.0000 Silver 0.4822 oz. ASW **Obv:** Value "I" in center of 6-arm cross **Obv. Legend:** PRO PROSPERITATE MUNDI **Rev:** Helmeted bust of Joan of Arc left **Rev. Legend:** IOHANNA ★ 1412 GALLIA 1962 **Edge:** Plain

Date	Mintage	F	VF	XF	Unc	BU
ND(1962) Proof	—	Value: 16.50				

X# 34 3 SILVER DUCAT
45.0000 g., 1.0000 Silver 1.4467 oz. ASW, 50 mm. **Obv:** Value "III" in center of 6-pointed cross, lilies in angles **Obv. Legend:** PRO PROSPERITATE MUNDI **Rev:** Bust of Maria Theresa left divides dates 1717 - 1780 **Rev. Legend:** MARIA • THERESIA IMPERATRIX • GER **Edge:** Plain

Date	Mintage	F	VF	XF	Unc	BU
1957 Proof	—	Value: 35.00				

X# M43 3 SILVER DUCAT
45.0000 g., 1.0000 Silver 1.4467 oz. ASW, 50 mm. **Obv:** Value "III" in center of 6-pointed cross, lilies in angles **Obv. Legend:** PRO PROSPERITATE MUNDI **Rev:** Head of Nefertiti left **Rev. Legend:** MATER OPERUM ATQUE ARTIFICIORUM • AEGYPTUS • **Edge:** Plain

Date	Mintage	F	VF	XF	Unc	BU
1958 Proof	—	Value: 50.00				

X# M39 3 SILVER DUCAT
45.0000 g., 1.0000 Silver 1.4467 oz. ASW, 50 mm. **Obv:** Value "III" in center of 6-pointed cross, lilies in angles **Obv. Legend:** PRO PROSPERITATE MUNDI **Rev:** Bust of Pope Pius XII left **Rev. Legend:** PIUS XII.PONTIFEX MAXIMUS **Edge:** Plain

Date	Mintage	F	VF	XF	Unc	BU
1958 Proof	—	Value: 50.00				

X# M74 3 SILVER DUCAT

45.0000 g., 1.0000 Silver 1.4467 oz. ASW, 50 mm. **Subject:** 10th Anniversary, 1st President, F.R.P. **Obv:** Value "III" in center of 6-pointed cross, lilies in angles **Obv. Legend:** PRO PROSPERITATE MUNDI **Rev:** Bust of Heuss left, shield at bottom **Rev. Legend:** • THEODORUS HEUSS MOD.P.P.GERMAN • **Edge:** Plain

Date	Mintage	F	VF	XF	Unc	BU
ND(1959) Proof	—	Value: 35.00				

X# M77 3 SILVER DUCAT

45.0000 g., 1.0000 Silver 1.4467 oz. ASW, 50 mm. **Subject:** 1960 Rome Olympics **Obv:** Value "III" in center of 6-pointed cross, lilies in angles **Obv. Legend:** PRO PROSPERITATE MUNDI **Rev:** Head of Rome right **Rev. Legend:** OLYMPIA ROMA **Edge:** Plain

Date	Mintage	F	VF	XF	Unc	BU
1960 Proof	—	Value: 50.00				

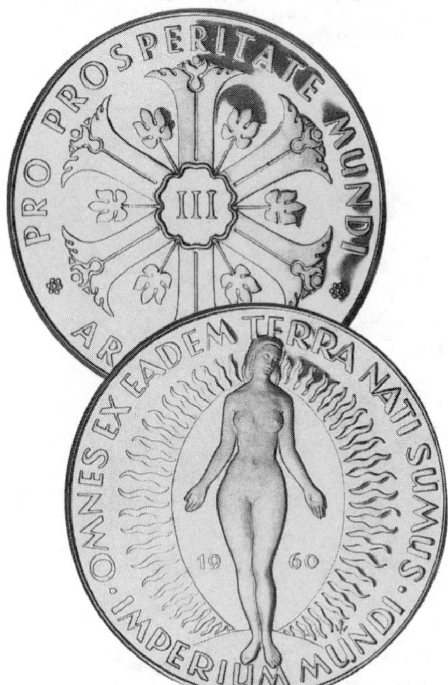

X# M80 3 SILVER DUCAT

45.0000 g., 1.0000 Silver 1.4467 oz. ASW, 50 mm. **Series:** Type II: Imperial Currency **Subject:** Children of Earth **Obv:** Value "III" in center of 6-pointed cross, lilies in angles **Obv. Legend:** PRO PROSPERITATE MUNDI **Rev:** Radiant nude female standing facing, head 3/4 right **Rev. Legend:** OMNES EX EADEM TERRA NATI SUMUS • IMPERIUM MUNDI • **Edge:** Plain

Date	Mintage	F	VF	XF	Unc	BU
1960 Proof	—	Value: 50.00				

X# M89 3 SILVER DUCAT

45.0000 g., 1.0000 Silver 1.4467 oz. ASW, 50 mm. **Obv:** Value "III" in center of 6-pointed cross, lilies in angles **Obv. Legend:** PRO PROSPERITATE MUNDI **Rev:** Bust of Pope John XXIII left **Rev. Legend:** IOANNES XXIII PONTIFEX MAXIMUS **Edge:** Plain

Date	Mintage	F	VF	XF	Unc	BU
1960 Proof	—	Value: 50.00				

X# M99 3 SILVER DUCAT

45.0000 g., 1.0000 Silver 1.4467 oz. ASW, 50 mm. **Subject:** Battle of Marathon **Obv:** Value "III" in center of 6-pointed cross, lilies in angles **Obv. Legend:** PRO PROSPERITATE MUNDI **Rev:** Athenian owl above helmeted head of Minerva left **Rev. Legend:** GRAECIA • ANNO A.CHR.N.CDXC... **Edge:** Plain

Date	Mintage	F	VF	XF	Unc	BU
1960 Proof	—	Value: 50.00				

X# M85 3 SILVER DUCAT

45.0000 g., 1.0000 Silver 1.4467 oz. ASW, 50 mm. **Subject:** Holy Mother Mary with Child **Obv:** Value "III" in center of 6-pointed cross, lilies in angles **Obv. Legend:** PRO PROSPERITATE MUNDI **Rev:** Crowned Holy Mother Mary with Child **Rev. Legend:** + SANCTA MARIA MONACHII **Edge:** Plain

Date	Mintage	F	VF	XF	Unc	BU
1960 Proof	—	Value: 35.00				

X# M112 3 SILVER DUCAT

45.0000 g., 1.0000 Silver 1.4467 oz. ASW, 50 mm. **Obv:** Value "III" in center of 6-pointed cross, lilies in angles **Obv. Legend:** PRO PROSPERITATE MUNDI **Rev:** Crowned bust of Germania facing 3/4 left divides date **Rev. Legend:** GERMANIA AETERNA **Edge:** Plain

Date	Mintage	F	VF	XF	Unc	BU
1961 Proof	—	Value: 35.00				

X# M116 3 SILVER DUCAT

45.0000 g., 1.0000 Silver 1.4467 oz. ASW, 50 mm. **Obv:** Value "II" in center of 6-pointed cross, lilies in angles **Obv. Legend:** PRO PROSPERITATE MUNDI **Rev:** Bust of Adenauer left **Rev. Legend:** CONRAD ADENAUER PATER PATRIAE GERMAN. **Edge:** Plain

Date	Mintage	F	VF	XF	Unc	BU
1961 Proof	—	Value: 35.00				

X# M120 3 SILVER DUCAT

45.0000 g., 1.0000 Silver 1.4467 oz. ASW, 50 mm. **Subject:** Reunion, Life For Germany **Obv:** Value "III" in center of 6-pointed cross, lilies in angles **Obv. Legend:** PRO PROSPERITATE MUNDI **Rev:** Germania kneeling between two children **Rev. Legend:** CONCORDIA SALUS **Edge:** Plain

Date	Mintage	F	VF	XF	Unc	BU
1961 Proof	—	Value: 35.00				

X# M97 3 SILVER DUCAT

45.0000 g., 1.0000 Silver 1.4467 oz. ASW, 50 mm. **Obv:** Value "III" in center of 6-pointed cross, lilies in angles **Obv. Legend:** PRO PROSPERITATE MUNDI **Rev:** Head of Nefertiti left **Rev. Legend:** MATER OPERUM ATQUE ARTIFICIORUM • AEGYPTUS • **Edge:** Plain

Date	Mintage	F	VF	XF	Unc	BU
1961 Proof	—	Value: 50.00				

X# M128 3 SILVER DUCAT

45.0000 g., 1.0000 Silver 1.4467 oz. ASW, 50 mm. **Obv:** Value "III" in center of 6-arm cross **Obv. Legend:** PRO PROSPERITATE MUNDI **Rev:** Helmeted bust of Joan of Arc left **Rev. Legend:** IOHANNA ★ 1412 GALLIA **Edge:** Plain

Date	Mintage	F	VF	XF	Unc	BU
ND(1962) Proof	—	Value: 35.00				

X# M143 3 SILVER DUCAT

45.0000 g., 1.0000 Silver 1.4467 oz. ASW, 50 mm. **Obv:** Value "III" in center of 6-pointed cross, lilies in angles **Obv. Legend:** PRO PROSPERITATE MUNDI **Rev:** Bust of Pope Paul VI left **Rev. Legend:** PAULUS VI • PONTIFEX MAXIMUS • **Edge:** Plain

Date	Mintage	F	VF	XF	Unc	BU
1963 Proof	—	Value: 50.00				

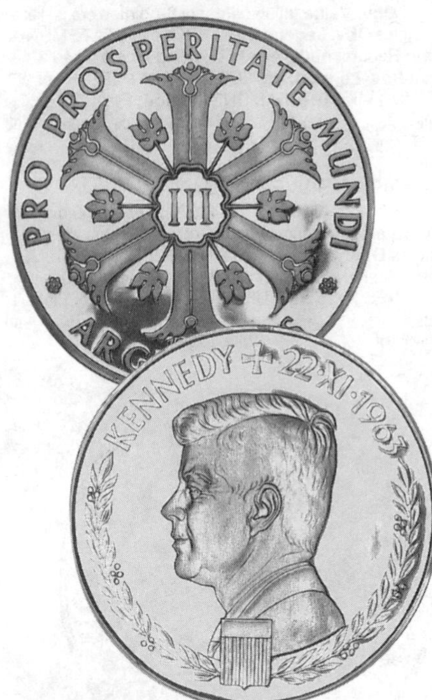

X# M162 3 SILVER DUCAT

45.0000 g., 1.0000 Silver 1.4467 oz. ASW, 50 mm. **Subject:** JFK's Death **Obv:** Value "III" in center of 6-arm cross **Obv. Legend:** PRO PROSPERITATE MUNDI **Rev:** Bust of Kennedy left in sprays **Rev. Legend:** KENNEDY + 22.X1.1963 **Edge:** Plain

Date	Mintage	F	VF	XF	Unc	BU
ND(1963) Proof	—	Value: 50.00				

X# M125 3 SILVER DUCAT

45.0000 g., 1.0000 Silver 1.4467 oz. ASW, 50 mm. **Subject:** Second Vatican Council **Obv:** Value "III" in center of 6-arm cross **Obv. Legend:** PRO PROSPERITATE MUNDI **Rev:** Busts of Popes John XXIII and Paul VI left **Rev. Legend:** CONCILIUM VATICANUM **Edge:** Plain

Date	Mintage	F	VF	XF	Unc	BU
1963 Proof	—	Value: 50.00				

X# M134 3 SILVER DUCAT

15.0000 g., 1.0000 Silver 0.4822 oz. ASW, 35.2 mm. **Subject:** JFK Visits Europe **Obv:** Value "I" in center of 6-pointed cross, lilies in angles **Obv. Legend:** PRO PROSPERITATE MUNDI **Rev:** Bust of Kennedy left, shield below in sprays **Rev. Legend:** U.S. PRESIDENT J. F. KENNEDY VISITS EUROPE **Edge:** Plain

Date	Mintage	F	VF	XF	Unc	BU
1963 Proof	—	Value: 50.00				

X# M151 3 SILVER DUCAT

45.0000 g., 1.0000 Silver 1.4467 oz. ASW, 50 mm. **Subject:** President Ludwig Erhard's Inauguration **Obv:** Value "III" in center of 6-pointed cross, lilies in angles **Obv. Legend:** PRO PROSPERITATE MUNDI **Rev:** Bust of Erhard left, small shield at bottom **Rev. Legend:** L. ERHARD KANZLER DER BUNDESREP.DEUTSCHLAND **Edge:** Plain

Date	Mintage	F	VF	XF	Unc	BU
1963 Proof	—	Value: 35.00				

X# M171 3 SILVER DUCAT

45.0000 g., 1.0000 Silver 1.4467 oz. ASW, 50 mm. **Obv:** Value "III" in center of 6-pointed cross, lilies in angles **Obv. Legend:** PRO PROSPERITATE MUNDI **Rev:** Prince Eugene of Austria horseback right **Rev. Legend:** EUGENIUS PRINC• - AUSTRIA **Edge:** Plain

Date	Mintage	F	VF	XF	Unc	BU
1963 Proof	—	Value: 35.00				

X# M154 3 SILVER DUCAT

45.0000 g., 1.0000 Silver 1.4467 oz. ASW, 50.1 mm. **Obv:** Value "III" in center of 6-pointed cross, lilies in angles **Obv. Legend:** PRO PROSPERITATE MUNDI **Rev:** Bust of Cleopatra left **Rev. Legend:** AEGYPTUS **Edge:** Plain

Date	Mintage	F	VF	XF	Unc	BU
1963 Proof	—	Value: 35.00				

X# M284 3 SILVER DUCAT

45.0000 g., 1.0000 Silver 1.4467 oz. ASW, 50 mm. **Series:** Argenteus **Obv:** Value "III" in center of 6-pointed cross, lilies in angles **Obv. Legend:** PRO

PROSPERITATE MUNDI **Rev:** Head left **Rev. Legend:** * POETA GERMAORUM - 1488 ULRICUS HUTTEN 1525 **Edge:** Plain

Date	Mintage	F	VF	XF	Unc	BU
1963 Proof	—	Value: 35.00				

X# M135 3 SILVER DUCAT

45.0000 g., 1.0000 Silver 1.4467 oz. ASW, 50 mm. **Subject:** JFK Visits Europe **Obv:** Value "III" in center of 6-pointed cross, lilies in angles **Obv. Legend:** PRO PROSPERITATE MUNDI **Rev:** Bust of Kennedy left, shield below in sprays **Rev. Legend:** U.S. PRESIDENT J. F. KENNEDY VISITS EUROPE **Edge:** Plain **Note:** Prev. X#138.

Date	Mintage	F	VF	XF	Unc	BU
1963 Proof	—	Value: 50.00				

X# M289 3 SILVER DUCAT

45.0000 g., 1.0000 Silver 1.4467 oz. ASW, 50 mm. **Obv:** Value "III" in center of 6-pointed cross, lillies in angles **Obv. Legend:** PRO PROSPERITATE MUNDI **Rev:** Mother with child **Rev. Legend:** MAGNA MATER **Edge:** Plain

Date	Mintage	F	VF	XF	Unc	BU
1964 Proof	—	Value: 40.00				

X# M237 3 SILVER DUCAT

45.0000 g., 1.0000 Silver 1.4467 oz. ASW, 50 mm. **Subject:** 1964 Tokyo Olympics **Obv:** Value "III" in center of 6-pointed cross, lilies in angles **Obv. Legend:** PRO PROSPERITATE MUNDI **Rev:** Crowned Buddha head left **Edge:** Plain

Date	Mintage	F	VF	XF	Unc	BU
1964 Proof	—	Value: 50.00				

X# M176 3 SILVER DUCAT

45.0000 g., 1.0000 Silver 1.4467 oz. ASW, 50 mm. **Obv:** Value "III" in center of 6-pointed cross, lilies in angles **Obv. Legend:** PRO PROSPERITATE MUNDI **Rev:** Helmeted Patron Saint of Bavaria standing, facing **Edge:** Plain

Date	Mintage	F	VF	XF	Unc	BU
1964 Proof	—	Value: 50.00				

X# M181 3 SILVER DUCAT

45.0000 g., 1.0000 Silver 1.4467 oz. ASW, 50 mm. **Obv:** Value "III" in center of 6-pointed cross, lilies in angles **Obv. Legend:** PRO PROSPERITATE MUNDI **Rev:** Cologne Cathedral, shield at upper right **Rev. Inscription:** COLONIA **Edge:** Plain

Date	Mintage	F	VF	XF	Unc	BU
1965 Proof	—	Value: 35.00				

X# M186 3 SILVER DUCAT

45.0000 g., 1.0000 Silver 1.4467 oz. ASW, 50 mm. **Obv:** Value "III" in center of 6-pointed cross, lilies in angles **Obv. Legend:** PRO PROSPERITATE MUNDI **Rev:** Port of Hamburg, cargo ship **Rev. Legend:** HAMBURGUM - PORTUS MUNDI **Edge:** Plain

Date	Mintage	F	VF	XF	Unc	BU
1965 Proof	—	Value: 35.00				

X# M191 3 SILVER DUCAT

45.0000 g., 1.0000 Silver 1.4467 oz. ASW, 50 mm. **Obv:** Value "III" in center of 6-pointed cross, lilies in angles **Obv. Legend:** PRO PROSPERITATE MUNDI **Rev:** Bust of Albert Schweitzer right **Rev. Legend:** SERVATOR GENERIS HUMANI **Edge:** Plain

Date	Mintage	F	VF	XF	Unc	BU
1965 Proof	—	Value: 35.00				

X# M196 3 SILVER DUCAT

45.0000 g., 1.0000 Silver 1.4467 oz. ASW, 50 mm. **Subject:** Twenty Years of Reconstruction **Obv:** Value "III" in center of 6-pointed cross, lilies in angles **Obv. Legend:** PRO PROSPERITATE MUNDI **Rev:** City view **Rev. Inscription:** MONACHIUM **Edge:** Plain

Date	Mintage	F	VF	XF	Unc	BU
1965 Proof	—	Value: 35.00				

X# M199 3 SILVER DUCAT

45.0000 g., 1.0000 Silver 1.4467 oz. ASW, 50 mm. **Obv:** Value "III" in center of 6-pointed cross, lilies in angles **Obv. Legend:** PRO PROSPERITATE MUNDI **Rev:** Busts of Johan and Cornelis Evertsen 3/4 right, crowned shield at bottom **Rev. Legend:** • NEDERLAND • JOHAN EN CORNELIS EVERTSEN • **Edge:** Plain

Date	Mintage	F	VF	XF	Unc	BU
1966 Proof	—	Value: 35.00				

X# M202 3 SILVER DUCAT

45.0000 g., 1.0000 Silver 1.4467 oz. ASW, 50 mm. **Obv:** Value "III" in center of 6-pointed cross, lilies in angles **Obv. Legend:** PRO PROSPERITATE MUNDI **Rev:** Crowned head of St. Adelheid, H.R.E. left **Rev. Legend:** SANCTA ADELHEID IMPERATRIX + 999 **Edge:** Plain

Date	Mintage	F	VF	XF	Unc	BU
ND(1967) Proof	—	Value: 35.00				

X# M206 3 SILVER DUCAT

45.0000 g., 1.0000 Silver 1.4467 oz. ASW, 50 mm. **Subject:** Canada's Centennial **Obv:** Value "III" in center of 6-pointed cross, lilies in angles **Obv. Legend:** PRO PROSPERITATE MUNDI **Rev:** Bust of Indian maiden right **Rev. Legend:** CANADA PATRIA NOSTRA **Edge:** Plain

Date	Mintage	F	VF	XF	Unc	BU
ND(1967) Proof	—	Value: 35.00				

X# M210 3 SILVER DUCAT

45.0000 g., 1.0000 Silver 1.4467 oz. ASW, 50 mm. **Obv:** Value "III" in center of 6-pointed cross, lilies in angles **Obv. Legend:** PRO PROSPERITATE MUNDI **Rev:** Bust of Maria Theresa left divides dates 1717-1780 **Rev. Legend:** MARIA • THERESIA IMPERATRIX • GER • **Edge:** Plain

Date	Mintage	F	VF	XF	Unc	BU
1967 Proof	—	Value: 35.00				

X# M285 3 SILVER DUCAT

45.0000 g., 1.0000 Silver 1.4467 oz. ASW, 50 mm. **Series:** Argenteus **Obv:** Value "III" in center of 6-pointed cross, lilies in angles **Obv. Legend:** PRO PROSPERITATE MUNDI **Rev:** Head right **Rev. Legend:** ANNOA • CH • N • CCCXXXIII ALEXANDER APUD ISSUM VICIT **Edge:** Plain

Date	Mintage	F	VF	XF	Unc	BU
1967 Proof	—	Value: 35.00				

X# M286 3 SILVER DUCAT

45.0000 g., 1.0000 Silver 1.4467 oz. ASW, 50 mm. **Series:** Argenteus **Obv:** Value "III" in center of 6-pointed cross, lilies in angles **Obv. Legend:** PRO PROSPERITATE MUNDI **Rev:** Bust of Germania 3/4 right **Rev. Legend:** DUCIT AMOR GERMANIAE **Edge:** Plain

Date	Mintage	F	VF	XF	Unc	BU
1967 Proof	—	Value: 35.00				

X# M215 3 SILVER DUCAT

45.0000 g., 1.0000 Silver 1.4467 oz. ASW, 50 mm. **Subject:** RFK's Death **Obv:** Value "III" in center of 6-pointed cross, lilies in angles **Obv. Legend:** PRO PROSPERITATE MUNDI **Rev:** Bust of Kennedy right between crosses **Rev. Legend:** ROBERT F. KENNEDY + 6 • VI • 1968 **Edge:** Plain

Date	Mintage	F	VF	XF	Unc	BU
ND(1968) Proof	—	Value: 35.00				

X# M231 3 SILVER DUCAT

45.0000 g., 1.0000 Silver 1.4467 oz. ASW, 50 mm. **Subject:** 1968 Mexico Olympics **Obv:** Value "III" in center of 6-pointed cross, lilies in angles **Obv. Legend:** PRO PROSPERITATE MUNDI **Rev:** Rayed ancient head facing **Edge:** Plain

Date	Mintage	F	VF	XF	Unc	BU
1968 Proof	—	Value: 35.00				

X# M253 3 SILVER DUCAT

45.0000 g., 1.0000 Silver 1.4467 oz. ASW, 50 mm. **Obv:** Value "III" in center of 6-pointed cross, lilies in angles **Obv. Legend:** PRO PROSPERITATE MUNDI **Rev:** Lunar landing, earth, capsule, astronaut **Rev. Legend:** LUNAM CALCAVIT 21.VII.1969 **Edge:** Plain

Date	Mintage	F	VF	XF	Unc	BU
1969 Proof	—	Value: 35.00				

X# M255 3 SILVER DUCAT

45.0000 g., 1.0000 Silver 1.4467 oz. ASW, 50 mm. **Subject:** Apollo XI **Obv:** Value "III" in center of 6-pointed cross, lilies in angles **Obv. Legend:** PRO PROSPERITATE MUNDI **Rev:** Busts of 3 astronauts left **Rev. Legend:** COLLINS / ALDRIN / ARMSTRONG **Edge:** Plain

Date	Mintage	F	VF	XF	Unc	BU
ND(1969) Proof	—	Value: 35.00				

X# M287 3 SILVER DUCAT

45.0000 g., 1.0000 Silver 1.4467 oz. ASW, 50 mm. **Series:** Argenteus **Obv:** Old city view **Obv. Legend:**

NÜRNBERG **Rev:** Bust 3/4 right **Rev. Legend:** ALBRECHT DÜRER ★ 1471 ZU NURNBERG • 1971

Date	Mintage	F	VF	XF	Unc	BU
1971 Proof	—	Value: 35.00				

X# M288 3 SILVER DUCAT
45.0000 g., 1.0000 Silver 1.4467 oz. ASW, 50 mm. **Series:** Argenteus **Obv:** Church towers in Munich **Obv. Legend:** MÜNCHEN / OLYMPIASTADT **Rev:** Laureate Greek head left, columns with statues at left, building at right **Rev. Inscription:** OLYMPIA

Date	Mintage	F	VF	XF	Unc	BU
1972 Proof	—	Value: 35.00				

X# M270 3 SILVER DUCAT
15.0000 g., 1.0000 Shell Casing Brass 0.4822 oz., 50 mm. **Obv:** Value "III" in center of 6-pointed cross, lilies in angles **Obv. Legend:** PRO PROSPERITATE MUNDI **Rev:** Head of Greek left, Maple leaves below **Edge:** Plain

Date	Mintage	F	VF	XF	Unc	BU
1976 Proof	—	Value: 35.00				

X# M280 3 SILVER DUCAT
45.0000 g., 1.0000 Silver 1.4467 oz. ASW, 50 mm. **Subject:** 600th Anniversary Death of Charles IV of Luxemburg **Obv:** Value "III" in center of 6-arm cross **Obv. Legend:** PRO PROSPERITATE MUNDI **Rev:** Crowned Charles IV seated on throne flanked by large birds and shields **Rev. Legend:** Karolus Quarius Dioina Faoente...... **Edge:** Plain

Date	Mintage	F	VF	XF	Unc	BU
1978 Proof	—	Value: 35.00				

X# M300 3 SILVER DUCAT
45.0000 g., 1.0000 Silver 1.4467 oz. ASW, 50 mm. **Obv:** Value "III" in center of 6-pointed cross, lilies in angles **Obv. Legend:** PRO PROSPERITATE MUNDI **Rev:** Knight horseback left (painting by Durer) **Edge:** Plain **Note:** Prev. X#M330.

Date	Mintage	F	VF	XF	Unc	BU
1981 Proof	—	Value: 35.00				

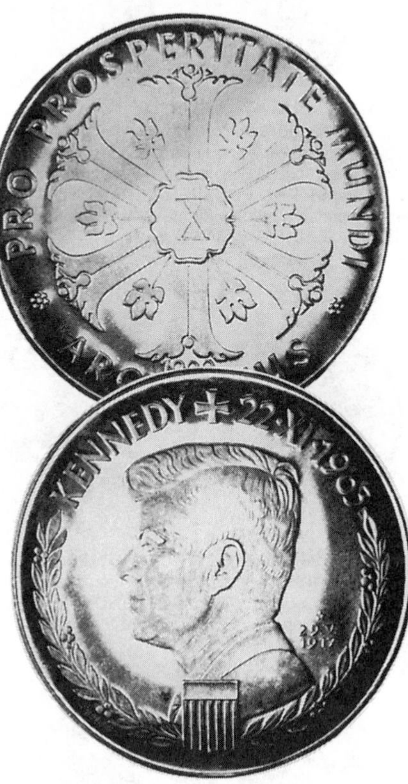

X# M166 10 SILVER DUCAT
150.0000 g., 1.0000 Silver 4.8224 oz. ASW, 80 mm. **Subject:** JFK's Death **Obv:** Value "X" in center of 6-pointed cross, lilies in angles **Obv. Legend:** PRO PROSPERITATE MUNDI **Rev:** Bust of Kennedy left in sprays **Rev. Legend:** KENNEDY + 22.X1.1963 **Edge:** Plain **Note:** Illustration reduced. Prev. X#M135. Numbered on edge.

Date	Mintage	F	VF	XF	Unc	BU
ND(1963) Proof	2,000	Value: 75.00				

Aureus Magnus Issues

Private medals struck for Werner Graul (Aureus Magnus), West Germany by the Vienna, Austria and Hamburg, West Germany mints. These are currently struck for Dr. Jurgen Graul, his son

X# M211 1/2 DUCAT
1.7250 g., 0.9800 Gold 0.0543 oz. AGW, 15.5 mm. **Obv:** Value "S" in center of 6-pointed cross, lilies in angles **Obv. Legend:** PRO PROSPERITATE MUNDI **Rev:** Bust of Maria Theresa left divides dates 1717-1780 **Rev. Legend:** MARIA • THERESIA IMPERATRIX • GER • **Edge:** Plain

Date	Mintage	F	VF	XF	Unc	BU
1967 Proof	—	Value: 40.00				

X# M40 DUCAT
3.4500 g., 0.9800 Gold 0.1087 oz. AGW, 20 mm. **Obv:** Value "I" in center of 6-arm cross **Obv. Legend:** PRO PROSPERITATE MUNDI **Rev:** Bust of Pope Pius XII left **Rev. Legend:** PIUS XII.PONTIFEX MAXIMUS **Edge:** Plain

Date	Mintage	F	VF	XF	Unc	BU
1958 Proof	—	Value: 80.00				

X# M44 DUCAT
3.4500 g., 0.9800 Gold 0.1087 oz. AGW, 20 mm. **Subject:** Queen Nefertiti of Egypt **Obv:** Value "I" in center of 6-pointed cross, lilies in angles **Obv. Legend:** PRO PROSPERITATE MUNDI **Rev:** Head of Nefertiti left **Rev. Legend:** MATER OPERUM ATQUE ARTIFICIORUM • AEGYPTUS • **Edge:** Plain

Date	Mintage	F	VF	XF	Unc	BU
1958 Proof	—	Value: 80.00				

X# M100 DUCAT
3.4500 g., 0.9800 Gold 0.1087 oz. AGW, 20 mm. **Subject:** Battle of Marathon **Obv:** Value "I" in center of 6-pointed cross, lilies in angles **Obv. Legend:** PRO PROSPERITATE MUNDI **Rev:** Athenian owl above helmeted head of Minerva left **Rev. Legend:** GRAECIA • ANNO A.CHR.N.CDXC. **Edge:** Plain

Date	Mintage	F	VF	XF	Unc	BU
ND(1960) Proof	—	Value: 80.00				

X# M81 DUCAT

3.4500 g., 0.9800 Gold 0.1087 oz. AGW, 20.1 mm. **Series:** Type II: Imperial currency **Subject:** Children of Earth **Obv:** Value "I" in center of 6-pointed cross, lilies in angles **Obv. Legend:** PRO PROSPERITATE MUNDI **Rev:** Radiant nude female standing facing, head 3/4 right **Rev. Legend:** OMNES EX EADEM TERRA NATI SUMUS • IMPERIUM MUNDI • **Edge:** Plain **Note:** Prev. X#M103.

Date	Mintage	F	VF	XF	Unc	BU
1960 Proof	—	Value: 80.00				

X# M86 DUCAT

3.4500 g., 0.9800 Gold 0.1087 oz. AGW, 20.1 mm. **Obv:** Value "I" in center of 6-pointed cross, lilies in angles **Obv. Legend:** PRO PROSPERITATE MUNDI **Rev:** Crowned Holy Mother Mary with Child **Rev. Legend:** + SANCTA MARIA MONACHII **Edge:** Plain **Note:** Prev. X#M85.

Date	Mintage	F	VF	XF	Unc	BU
1960 Proof	—	Value: 80.00				

X# M163 DUCAT

3.4500 g., 0.9800 Gold 0.1087 oz. AGW, 20.1 mm. **Subject:** JFK's Death **Obv:** Value "I" in center of 6-pointed cross, lilies in angles **Obv. Legend:** PRO PROSPERITATE MUNDI **Rev:** Bust of Kennedy left in sprays **Rev. Legend:** KENNEDY + 22 • X1 • 1963 **Edge:** Plain **Note:** Prev. X#M136.

Date	Mintage	F	VF	XF	Unc	BU
ND(1963) Proof	—	Value: 80.00				

X# M155 DUCAT

3.4500 g., 0.9800 Gold 0.1087 oz. AGW, 20.1 mm. **Subject:** Queen Cleopatra of Egypt **Obv:** Value "I" in center of 6-pointed cross, lilies in angles **Obv. Legend:** PRO PROSPERITATE MUNDI **Rev:** Bust of Cleopatra left **Rev. Legend:** AEGYPTUS **Edge:** Plain

Date	Mintage	F	VF	XF	Unc	BU
1963 Proof	—	Value: 80.00				

X# M244 DUCAT

3.3800 g., 0.9800 Gold 0.1065 oz. AGW, 20.15 mm. **Obv:** Value "I" in center of 6-pointed cross, lilies in angles **Obv. Legend:** PRO PROSPERITATE MUNDI **Rev:** Goddess of Motherhood with child **Rev. Legend:** MAGNA MATER **Edge:** Plain

Date	Mintage	F	VF	XF	Unc	BU
1964 Proof	—	Value: 80.00				

X# M207 DUCAT

3.4500 g., 0.9800 Gold 0.1087 oz. AGW, 21.7 mm. **Subject:** Canada's Centennial **Obv:** Value "I" in center of 6-pointed cross, lilies in angles **Obv. Legend:** PRO PROSPERITATE MUNDI **Rev:** Bust of Indian maiden right **Rev. Legend:** CANADA PATRIA NOSTRA **Edge:** Plain

Date	Mintage	F	VF	XF	Unc	BU
ND(1967) Proof	—	Value: 80.00				

X# M212 DUCAT

3.4500 g., 0.9860 Gold 0.1094 oz. AGW, 19.7 mm. **Obv:** Crown above 6-pointed cross **Obv. Legend:** CORONA AUREA CUSUS IN AUSTRIA **Rev:** Bust of Maria Theresa left, divides dates 1717-1780 **Rev. Legend:** MARIA • THERESIA IMPERATRIX • GER • **Edge:** Plain **Note:** Prev. X#M209.

Date	Mintage	F	VF	XF	Unc	BU
1967 Proof	—	Value: 80.00				

X# M129 DUCAT

3.4500 g., 0.9800 Gold 0.1087 oz. AGW, 20.1 mm. **Subject:** 450th Anniversary Birth of Joan of Arc of France **Obv:** Value "I" in center of 6-arm cross **Obv. Legend:** PRO PROSPERITATE MUNDI **Rev:** Helmeted bust of Joan of Arc left **Rev. Legend:** IOHANNA ★ 1412 GALLIA **Edge:** Plain

Date	Mintage	F	VF	XF	Unc	BU
1992 Proof	—	Value: 80.00				

X# M290 2-1/2 DUCAT

8.6250 g., 0.9800 Gold 0.2717 oz. AGW, 26 mm. **Obv:** Value "IIS" in center of 6-pointed cross, lillies in angles **Obv. Legend:** PRO PROSPERITATE MUNDI **Rev:** Bust of Pope Pius XII left **Edge:** Plain

Date	Mintage	F	VF	XF	Unc	BU
1958 Proof	—	Value: 160				

X# M78 2-1/2 DUCAT

8.6250 g., 0.9800 Gold 0.2717 oz. AGW, 26 mm. **Subject:** 1960 Rome Olympics **Obv:** Value "XXS" in center of 6-arm cross **Obv. Legend:** PRO PROSPERITATE MUNDI **Rev:** Head of Rome right **Rev. Legend:** OLYMPIA ROMA **Edge:** Plain

Date	Mintage	F	VF	XF	Unc	BU
1960 Proof	—	Value: 200				

X# M164 2-1/2 DUCAT

8.6250 g., 0.9800 Gold 0.2717 oz. AGW, 26 mm. **Subject:** JFK's Death **Obv:** Value "IIS" in center of 6-pointed cross, lilies in angles **Obv. Legend:** PRO PROSPERITATE MUNDI **Rev:** Bust of Kennedy left in sprays **Rev. Legend:** KENNEDY + 22 • X1 • 1963 **Edge:** Plain

Date	Mintage	F	VF	XF	Unc	BU
ND(1963) Proof	—	Value: 200				

X# M291 2-1/2 DUCAT

8.6250 g., 0.9800 Gold 0.2717 oz. AGW, 26 mm. **Obv:** Value "IIS" in center of 6-pointed cross, lillies in angles **Obv. Legend:** PRO PROSPERITATE MUNDI **Rev:** Bust of Pope Paul VI left **Edge:** Plain

Date	Mintage	F	VF	XF	Unc	BU
1963 Proof	—	Value: 160				

X# M137 2-1/2 DUCAT

8.6250 g., 0.9800 Gold 0.2717 oz. AGW, 26 mm. **Subject:** JFK Visits Europe **Obv:** Value "IIS" in center of 6-pointed cross, lilies in angles **Obv. Legend:** PRO PROSPERITATE MUNDI **Rev:** Bust of Kennedy left, shield below in sprays **Rev. Legend:** U.S. PRESIDENT J. F. KENNEDY VISITS EUROPE **Edge:** Plain

Date	Mintage	F	VF	XF	Unc	BU
1963 Proof	—	Value: 200				

X# M208 2-1/2 DUCAT

8.6250 g., 0.9800 Gold 0.2717 oz. AGW, 26 mm. **Subject:** Canada's Centennial **Obv:** Value "IIS" in center of 6-arm cross **Obv. Legend:** PRO PROSPERITATE MUNDI **Rev:** Bust of Indian maiden left **Rev. Legend:** CANADA PATRIA NOSTRA **Edge:** Plain

Date	Mintage	F	VF	XF	Unc	BU
ND(1967) Proof	—	Value: 200				

X# M5 5 DUCAT

17.5000 g., 0.9800 Gold 0.5514 oz. AGW, 35.20 mm. **Series:** Rome, Eternal City **Obv:** Value "V" in center of 6-pointed cross, lilies in angles **Obv. Legend:** PRO PROSPERITATE MUNDI **Rev:** Archways **Rev. Legend:** FAMA PERENIS ERIT - ROMA AETERNA **Edge:** Plain **Note:** Prev. X#M6.

Date	Mintage	F	VF	XF	Unc	BU
1947 Proof	—	Value: 400				

X# M13 5 DUCAT

17.2500 g., 0.9800 Gold 0.5435 oz. AGW, 35.2 mm. **Subject:** 800th Anniversary Coronation of Henry II of Austria **Obv:** Value "V" in center of 6-pointed cross, lilies in angles **Obv. Legend:** PRO PROSPERITATE MUNDI **Rev:** Crowned Henry II standing facing, head left, holding church and sword **Rev. Legend:** A • D • MCLVI AUSTRIA DUCATUS INSTAURATUS • HEINRICH JOSOMIR GOTT • **Edge:** Plain

Date	Mintage	F	VF	XF	Unc	BU
1956 Proof	—	Value: 400				

X# M9 5 DUCAT

17.2500 g., 0.9800 Gold 0.5435 oz. AGW **Subject:** 200th Anniversary Alcea Castle **Obv:** Value "V" in center of 6-pointed cross, lilies in angles **Obv. Legend:** PRO PROSPERITATE MUNDI **Rev:** Castle, shield at bottom **Rev. Legend:** CASTRUM ALCEA **Edge:** Plain

Date	Mintage	F	VF	XF	Unc	BU
ND(1957) Proof	—	Value: 400				

X# M36 5 DUCAT

17.2500 g., 0.9800 Gold 0.5435 oz. AGW, 35.2 mm. **Obv:** Value "V" in center of 6-pointed cross, lilies in angles **Obv. Legend:** PRO PROSPERITATE MUNDI **Rev:** Bust of Maria Theresa left divides dates 1717 - 1780 **Rev. Legend:** MARIA • THERESA **Edge:** Plain

Date	Mintage	F	VF	XF	Unc	BU
1957 Proof	—	Value: 400				

X# M71 5 DUCAT

17.2500 g., 0.9800 Gold 0.5435 oz. AGW, 35.2 mm. **Series:** Type I: Imperial Currency **Subject:** Children of Earth **Obv:** Value "V" in center of 6-pointed cross, lilies in angles **Obv. Legend:** PRO PROSPERITATE MUNDI **Rev:** Female nude standing facing, head 3/4 right **Rev. Legend:** OMNES EX EADEM TERRA NATI SUMUS • IMPERIUM MUNDI • **Edge:** Plain

Date	Mintage	F	VF	XF	Unc	BU
1959 Proof	—	Value: 400				

X# M82 5 DUCAT

17.2500 g., 0.9800 Gold 0.5435 oz. AGW **Series:** Type II: Imperial Currency **Subject:** Children of Earth **Obv:** Value "V" in center of 6-pointed cross, lilies in angles **Obv. Legend:** PRO PROSPERITATE MUNDI **Rev:** Radiant nude female standing facing, head 3/4 right **Rev. Legend:** OMNES EX EADEM TERRA NATI SUMUS • IMPERIUM MUNDI • **Edge:** Plain

Date	Mintage	F	VF	XF	Unc	BU
1960 Proof	—	Value: 400				

X# M102 5 DUCAT

17.2500 g., 0.9800 Gold 0.5435 oz. AGW, 35.2 mm. **Subject:** Battle of Marathon **Obv:** Value "V" in center of 6-arm cross **Obv. Legend:** PRO PROSPERITATE MUNDI **Rev:** Athentian owl above helmeted head of Minerva left **Rev. Legend:** GRACIA • ANNO A.CHR.N.CDXC...... **Edge:** Plain **Note:** Prev. X#M101.

Date	Mintage	F	VF	XF	Unc	BU
1960 Proof	—	Value: 400				

X# M91 5 DUCAT

17.2500 g., 0.9800 Gold 0.5435 oz. AGW, 35.2 mm. **Obv:** Value "V" in center of 6-pointed cross, lilies in angles **Obv. Legend:** PRO PROSPERITATE MUNDI **Rev:** Bust of Pope John XXIII left **Rev. Legend:** IOANNES XXIII PONTIFEX MAXIMUS **Edge:** Plain **Note:** Prev. X#M109.

Date	Mintage	F	VF	XF	Unc	BU
1960 Proof	—	Value: 400				

X# M165 5 DUCAT

17.2500 g., 0.9800 Gold 0.5435 oz. AGW, 35.2 mm. **Subject:** JFK's Death **Obv:** Value "V" in center of 6-arm cross **Obv. Legend:** PRO PROSPERITATE MUNDI **Rev:** Bust of Kennedy left in sprays **Rev. Legend:** KENNEDY + 22.X1.1963 **Edge:** Plain **Note:** Prev. X#M138.

Date	Mintage	F	VF	XF	Unc	BU
ND(1963) Proof	—	Value: 400				

X# M138 5 DUCAT

17.5000 g., 0.9800 Gold 0.5514 oz. AGW, 35.2 mm. **Subject:** JFK Visits Europe **Obv:** Value "V" in center of 6-pointed cross, lilies in angles **Obv. Legend:** PRO PROSPERITATE MUNDI **Rev:** Bust of Kennedy left, shield in sprays below **Rev. Legend:** U.S. PRESIDENT J. F. KENNEDY VISITS EUROPE **Edge:** Plain

Date	Mintage	F	VF	XF	Unc	BU
1963 Proof	—	Value: 400				

X# M6 10 DUCAT

39.9600 g., 0.9800 Gold 1.2590 oz. AGW, 50 mm. **Obv:** Value "X" in center of 6-pointed cross, lilies in angles **Obv. Legend:** PRO PROSPERITATE MUNDI **Rev:** Archways **Rev. Legend:** FAMA PERENNIS ERIT - ROMA ÆTERNA **Edge:** Plain

Date	Mintage	F	VF	XF	Unc	BU
1947 Proof	—	Value: 925				

X# M7 10 DUCAT

35.3400 g., 0.9800 Gold 1.1134 oz. AGW, 51 mm. **Subject:** Liberation of West Germany **Obv:** Value "X" in center of 6-pointed cross, lilies in angles **Obv. Legend:** * SIGNATUS AD PRETIUM AURI CONSERVANDUM * **Rev:** Old sailing ship **Rev. Legend:** GERMANIA LIBERTATEM RECUPERAVIT **Edge:** Plain

Date	Mintage	F	VF	XF	Unc	BU
1955 Proof	—	Value: 825				

X# M16 10 DUCAT

35.3400 g., 0.9800 Gold 1.1134 oz. AGW, 51 mm. **Obv:** Value "X" in center of 6-pointed cross, lilies in angles **Obv. Legend:** SIGNATUS AD PRETIUM AURI CONSERVANDUM **Rev:** Old sailing ship **Rev. Legend:** GERMANIA PACEMET LIBERTATEM AMAT **Edge:** Plain

Date	Mintage	F	VF	XF	Unc	BU
1956 Proof	—	Value: 825				

X# M11 10 DUCAT

34.5000 g., 0.9800 Gold 1.0870 oz. AGW, 50 mm. **Obv:** Value "X" in center of 6-pointed cross, liles in angles **Obv. Legend:** * AVORUM NON MORITURA VIRTUS * **Rev:** Prince Ludvig Wilhelm of Baden horseback left **Rev. Legend:** LUDOVICUS WILHELMUS PRINCEPS BADENSIS **Edge:** Plain

Date	Mintage	F	VF	XF	Unc	BU
1955 Proof	—	Value: 800				

X# M14 10 DUCAT

34.5000 g., 0.9800 Gold 1.0870 oz. AGW, 50 mm. **Subject:** 800th Anniversary Coronation of Henry II of Austria **Obv:** Value "X" in center of 6-pointed cross, lilies in angles **Obv. Legend:** PRO PROSPERITATE MUNDI **Rev:** Crowned Henry II standing facing, head left, holding church and sword **Rev. Legend:** A • D • MCLVI AUSTRIA DUCATUS INSTAURATUS • HEINRICH JOSOMIR GOTT **Edge:** Plain

Date	Mintage	F	VF	XF	Unc	BU
1956 Proof	—	Value: 800				

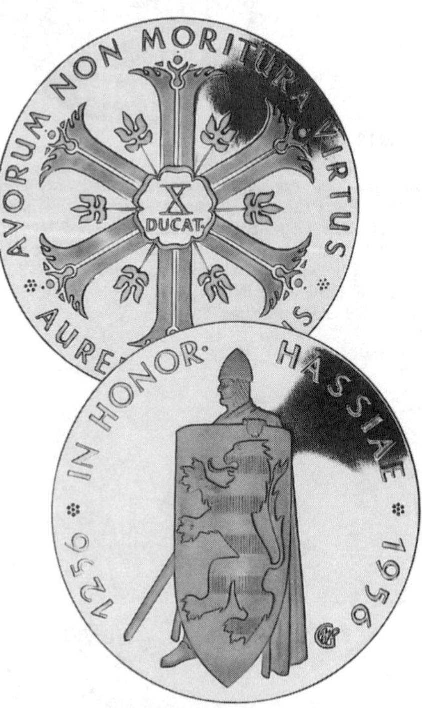

X# M19 10 DUCAT

34.5000 g., 0.9800 Gold 1.0870 oz. AGW, 50 mm. **Subject:** 700th Anniversary Hessen **Obv:** Value "X" in center of 6-pointed cross, lilies in angles **Obv. Legend:** PRO PROSPERITATE MUNDI **Rev:** Knight standing left with sword and Hessen shield **Rev. Legend:** * IN HONOR • HASSIAE * **Edge:** Plain

Date	Mintage	F	VF	XF	Unc	BU
1956 Proof	—	Value: 800				

X# M8 10 DUCAT
34.5000 g., 0.9800 Gold 1.0870 oz. AGW, 50 mm.
Subject: 400th Anniversary Hall in Swabia **Obv:** Value "X" in center of 6-pointed cross, lilies in angles **Obv. Legend:** * AVORUM NON MORITURA VIRTUS * **Rev:** City view, 2 shields above **Rev. Legend:** IN HONOREM HALAE SUEVICAE **Edge:** Plain

Date	Mintage	F	VF	XF	Unc	BU
ND(1956) Proof	—	Value: 800				

X# M21 10 DUCAT
34.5000 g., 0.9800 Gold 1.0870 oz. AGW, 50 mm.
Subject: Denmark **Obv:** Value "X" in center of 6-pointed cross, lilies in angles **Obv. Legend:** * AVORUM NON MORITURA VIRTUS * **Rev:** Sailing ship **Rev. Legend:** DANEBROG DANIAE DECUS **Edge:** Plain

Date	Mintage	F	VF	XF	Unc	BU
1957 Proof	—	Value: 800				

X# M24 10 DUCAT
34.8700 g., 0.9800 Gold 1.0986 oz. AGW, 50 mm.
Subject: Return of Saarland to West Germany
Obv: Eagle with shield on breast **Rev:** 11 shields around value **Rev. Legend:** • RÜCKKEHR DER SAAR • 1.JANUAR 1957

Date	Mintage	F	VF	XF	Unc	BU
1957 Proof	—	Value: 800				

X# M37 10 DUCAT
34.5000 g., 0.9800 Gold 1.0870 oz. AGW, 44.5 mm.
Obv: Value "X" in center of 6-pointed cross, lilies in angles **Obv. Legend:** PRO PROSPERITATE MUNDI **Rev:** Bust of Maria Theresa left divides dates 1717-1780 **Rev. Legend:** MARIA • THERESIA IMPERATRIX • GER • **Edge:** Plain

Date	Mintage	F	VF	XF	Unc	BU
1957 Proof	—	Value: 800				

X# M22 10 DUCAT
34.5000 g., 0.9800 Gold 1.0870 oz. AGW, 50 mm.
Subject: Peace and Liberation of West Germany
Obv: Value "X" in center of 6-pointed cross, lilies in angles
Obv. Legend: * AVORUM NON MORITURA VIRTUS *
Rev: Sailing ship, shield at left **Rev. Legend:** GERMANIA PACEM ET LIBERTATEM AMAT **Edge:** Plain

Date	Mintage	F	VF	XF	Unc	BU
1957 Proof	—	Value: 800				

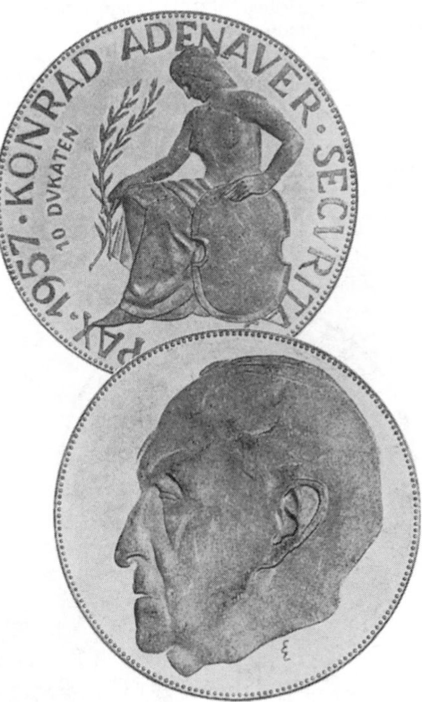

X# M28 10 DUCAT
34.5000 g., 0.9800 Gold 1.0870 oz. AGW, 50 mm.
Subject: Security and Peace **Obv:** Germania seated left with shield and sprigs **Obv. Legend:** • KONRAD ADENAVER • SECVRITAS • ET • PAX. **Rev:** Head of Adenauer left **Edge:** Plain

Date	Mintage	F	VF	XF	Unc	BU
1957 Proof	—	Value: 800				

X# M32 10 DUCAT
34.5000 g., 0.9800 Gold 1.0870 oz. AGW, 50 mm. **Subject:** Founding of Eltz Castle **Obv:** Value "X" in center of 6-pointed cross, lilies in angles **Rev:** Eltz castle **Edge:** Plain

Date	Mintage	F	VF	XF	Unc	BU
1957 Proof	—	Value: 800				

X# M48 10 DUCAT
34.5000 g., 0.9800 Gold 1.0870 oz. AGW, 50 mm. **Subject:** 400th Anniversary Elizabeth I Coronation **Obv:** Value "X" in center of 6-pointed cross, lilies in angles **Obv. Legend:** * AVORUN NON MORITURA VIRTUS * **Rev:** The Fight for Freedom on the High Seas **Rev. Legend:** ELIZABETH I.1558 - 1603 • IN MEM.REGNI ANGLIAE REGINAE **Edge:** Plain

Date	Mintage	F	VF	XF	Unc	BU
1958 Proof	—	Value: 800				

X# M46 10 DUCAT
34.5000 g., 0.9800 Gold 1.0870 oz. AGW, 50 mm. **Subject:** Queen Nefertiti of Egypt **Obv:** Value "X" in center of 6-pointed cross, lilies in angles **Obv. Legend:** PRO PROSPERITATE MUNDI **Rev:** Head of Nefertiti left **Rev. Legend:** MATER OPERUM ATQUE ARTIFICIORUM • AEGYPTUS • **Edge:** Plain

Date	Mintage	F	VF	XF	Unc	BU
1958 Proof	—	Value: 800				

X# M52 10 DUCAT
34.7200 g., 0.9800 Gold 1.0939 oz. AGW, 50 mm. **Subject:** 1000th Anniversary **Obv:** Value "X" in center of 6-pointed cross, lilies in angles **Obv. Legend:** * PRO PROSPERITATE MUNDI * **Rev:** Free Market, City of Trier **Rev. Legend:** FORUM CIVITATIS TREVERENSIS **Edge:** Plain

Date	Mintage	F	VF	XF	Unc	BU
1958 Proof	—	Value: 800				

X# M56 10 DUCAT
34.5000 g., 0.9800 Gold 1.0870 oz. AGW, 50 mm. **Subject:** Free City of Hamburg, Germany **Obv:** Value "X" in center of 6-pointed cross, lilies in angles **Obv. Legend:** * AVORUM NON MORITURA VIRTUS * **Rev:** City view **Rev. Legend:** HAMBURGUM - CIV • HANSEAT • **Edge:** Plain

Date	Mintage	F	VF	XF	Unc	BU
1958 Proof	—	Value: 800				

X# M60 10 DUCAT
34.5000 g., 0.9800 Gold 1.0870 oz. AGW, 50 mm. **Subject:** 800th Anniversary of Lubeck **Obv:** Value "X" in center of 6-pointed cross, lilies in angles **Obv. Legend:** * AVORUM NON MORITURA VIRTUS * **Rev:** Shield above castle **Rev. Legend:** IN HONOREM LUBECA **Rev. Inscription:** CONCORDIA DOMI/FORIS PAX **Edge:** Plain

Date	Mintage	F	VF	XF	Unc	BU
1958 Proof	—	Value: 800				

X# M64 10 DUCAT
34.8400 g., 0.9800 Gold 1.0977 oz. AGW **Subject:** Free City of Bremen, Member of Hanseatic League **Obv:** Value "X" in center of 6-pointed cross, lilies in angles **Obv. Legend:** * AVORUM NON MORITURA VIRTUS * **Rev:** Knight standing with sword and shield between buildings **Rev. Legend:** CIVITAS HANSEATICA - BREMA **Edge:** Plain

Date	Mintage	F	VF	XF	Unc	BU
1958 Proof	—	Value: 800				

X# M50 10 DUCAT
34.5000 g., 0.9800 Gold 1.0870 oz. AGW, 50 mm. **Subject:** 1400th Anniversary City of Paris **Obv:** Value "X" in center of 6-pointed cross, lilies in angles **Obv. Legend:** * AVORUM NON MORITURA VIRTUS * **Rev:** City view, shield at bottom **Rev. Legend:** LUTETIA PARISIORUM CAPUT GALLIAE **Edge:** Plain

Date	Mintage	F	VF	XF	Unc	BU
1958 Proof	—	Value: 800				

X# M54 10 DUCAT

34.5000 g., 0.9800 Gold 1.0870 oz. AGW, 50 mm. **Subject:** Augusburg **Obv:** Value "X" in center of 6-pointed cross, lilies in angles **Rev:** City view **Edge:** Plain

Date	Mintage	F	VF	XF	Unc	BU
1958 Proof	—	Value: 800				

X# M58 10 DUCAT

34.5000 g., 0.9800 Gold 1.0870 oz. AGW, 50 mm. **Subject:** Luneberg **Obv:** Value "X" in center of 6-pointed cross, lilies in angles **Rev:** City view **Edge:** Plain

Date	Mintage	F	VF	XF	Unc	BU
1958 Proof	300	Value: 800				

X# M62 10 DUCAT

34.5000 g., 0.9800 Gold 1.0870 oz. AGW, 50 mm. **Subject:** 800th Anniversary of Munich **Obv:** Value "X" in center of 6-pointed cross, lilies in angles **Obv. Legend:** * AVORUM NON MORITURA VIRTUS * **Rev:** City view, shield at bottom **Rev. Legend:** IN HONOREM CIVITATIS MONACENCIS **Edge:** Plain

Date	Mintage	F	VF	XF	Unc	BU
1958 Proof	—	Value: 800				

X# M68 10 DUCAT

34.5000 g., 0.9800 Gold 1.0870 oz. AGW, 50 mm. **Subject:** 350th Anniversary Hudson in Manhattan **Obv:** Value "X" in center of 6-pointed cross, lilies in angles **Obv. Legend:** * AVORUM NON MORITURA VIRTUS * **Rev:** Hudson's ship **Rev. Legend:** A • D • MDCIX HENRICUS HUDSON INSULAM MANHATTAN APERUIT **Edge:** Plain

Date	Mintage	F	VF	XF	Unc	BU
1959 Proof	—	Value: 800				

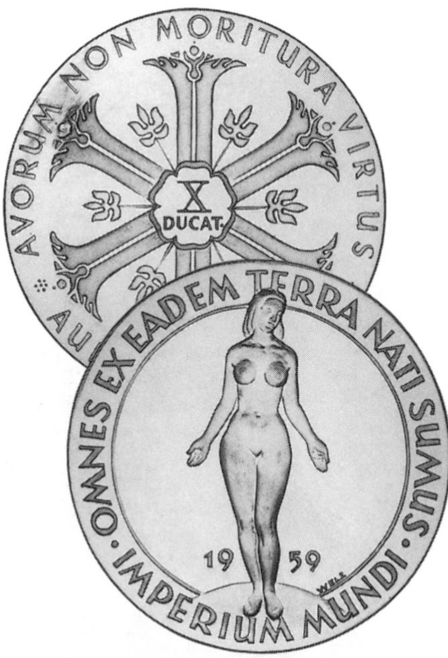

X# M72 10 DUCAT

34.5000 g., 0.9800 Gold 1.0870 oz. AGW, 50 mm. **Series:** Type I: Imperial Currency **Subject:** Children of Earth **Obv:** Value "X" in center of 6-pointed cross, lilies in angles **Obv. Legend:** PRO PROSPERITATE MUNDI **Rev:** Female nude standing facing, head 3/4 right **Rev. Legend:** OMNES EX EADEM TERRA NATI SUMUS • IMPERIUM MUNDI • **Edge:** Plain

Date	Mintage	F	VF	XF	Unc	BU
1959 Proof	—	Value: 800				

X# M83 10 DUCAT

34.5000 g., 0.9800 Gold 1.0870 oz. AGW, 50 mm. **Series:** Type II: Imperial Currency **Subject:** Children of Earth **Obv:** Value "X" in center of 6-pointed cross, lilies in angles **Obv. Legend:** PRO PROSPERITATE MUNDI **Rev:** Radiant nude female standing facing, head 3/4 right **Rev. Legend:** OMNES EX EADEM TERRA NATI SUMUS • IMPERIUM MUNDI • **Edge:** Plain

Date	Mintage	F	VF	XF	Unc	BU
1960 Proof	—	Value: 800				

X# M113 10 DUCAT

34.5000 g., 0.9800 Gold 1.0870 oz. AGW, 44.50 mm. **Subject:** Germania (Germany) - Eternally **Obv:** Value "X" in center of 6-pointed cross, lilies in angles **Obv. Legend:** PRO PROSPERITATE MUNDI **Rev:** Crowned bust of Germania facing 3/4 left, divides date **Rev. Legend:** GERMANIA AETERNA **Edge:** Plain

Date	Mintage	F	VF	XF	Unc	BU
1961 Proof	—	Value: 800				

X# M123 10 DUCAT

34.5000 g., 0.9800 Gold 1.0870 oz. AGW, 44.5 mm. **Subject:** Reunion, Life For Germany **Obv:** Value "X" in center of 6-pointed cross, lilies in angles **Obv. Legend:** PRO PROSPERITATE MUNDI **Rev:** Germania kneeling between two children **Rev. Legend:** CONCORDIA SALUS **Edge:** Plain

Date	Mintage	F	VF	XF	Unc	BU
1961 Proof	—	Value: 800				

X# M139 10 DUCAT

34.5000 g., 0.9800 Gold 1.0870 oz. AGW, 50 mm. **Subject:** JFK Visits Europe **Obv:** Value "X" in center of 6-pointed cross, lilies in angles **Obv. Legend:** PRO PROSPERITATE MUNDI **Rev:** Bust of Kennedy left, shield in sprays below **Rev. Legend:** U.S. PRESIDENT J. F. KENNEDY VISITS EUROPE **Edge:** Plain

Date	Mintage	F	VF	XF	Unc	BU
1963 Proof	—	Value: 800				

X# M25 20 DUCAT
69.0000 g., 0.9800 Gold 2.1739 oz. AGW, 50 mm. **Subject:** Return of Saarland to West Germany **Obv:** Eagle with shield on breast **Rev:** 11 shields around value **Rev. Legend:** • RÜCKKEHR DER SAAR • 1.JANUAR 1957

Date	Mintage	F	VF	XF	Unc	BU
1957 Proof	—	Value: 1,550				

X# M29 20 DUCAT
69.0000 g., 0.9800 Gold 2.1739 oz. AGW, 50 mm. **Subject:** Security and Peace **Obv:** Germania seated left with shield and sprigs **Obv. Legend:** • KONRAD ADENAVER • SECVRITAS • ET • PAX • **Rev:** Head of Adenauer left **Edge:** Plain

Date	Mintage	F	VF	XF	Unc	BU
1957 Proof	—	Value: 1,550				

X# M69 20 DUCAT
69.0000 g., 0.9800 Gold 2.1739 oz. AGW, 50 mm. **Subject:** 350th Anniversary Hudson in Manhattan **Obv:** Value "XX" in center of 6-pointed cross, lilies in angles **Obv. Legend:** * AVORUM NON MORITURA VIRTUS * **Rev:** Hudson's ship **Rev. Legend:** A • D • MDCIX HENRICUS HUDSON INSULAM MANHATTAN APERUIT **Edge:** Plain

Date	Mintage	F	VF	XF	Unc	BU
1959 Proof	—	Value: 1,550				

X# M167 20 DUCAT
69.0000 g., 0.9800 Gold 2.1739 oz. AGW, 50 mm. **Subject:** JFK's Death **Obv:** Value "XX" in center of 6-pointed cross, lilies in angles **Obv. Legend:** PRO PROSPERITATE MUNDI **Rev:** Bust of Kennedy left in sprays **Rev. Legend:** KENNEDY + 22.X1.1963 **Edge:** Plain **Note:** Prev. KM#M35.

Date	Mintage	F	VF	XF	Unc	BU
ND(1963) Proof	—	Value: 1,550				

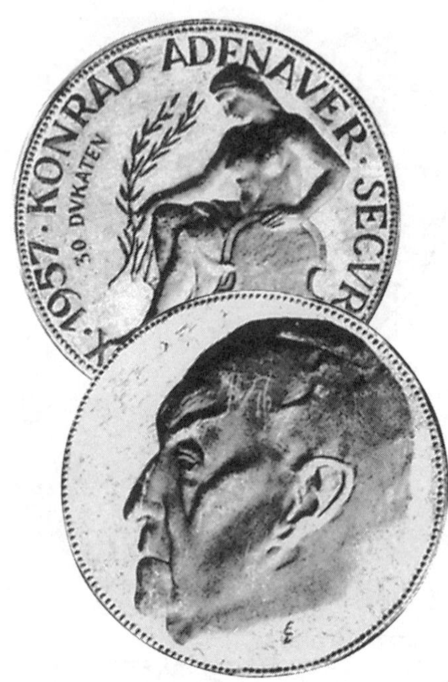

X# M30 30 DUCAT
103.5000 g., 0.9800 Gold 3.2609 oz. AGW, 50 mm. **Subject:** Security and Peace **Obv:** Germania seated left with shield and sprigs **Obv. Legend:** • KONRAD ADENAVER • SECVRITAS • ET • PAX. **Rev. Designer:** Head of Adenauer left **Edge:** Plain **Note:** Prev. Bruce #XM26.

Date	Mintage	F	VF	XF	Unc	BU
1957 Proof	—	Value: 2,350				

X# M70 30 DUCAT
103.5000 g., 0.9800 Gold 3.2609 oz. AGW, 50 mm. **Subject:** 350th Anniversary Hudson in Manhattan **Obv:** Value XX in center of 6-pointed cross, lilies in angles **Obv. Legend:** ★ AVORUM NON MORITURA VIRTUS ★ **Rev:** Hudson's ship **Rev. Legend:** A • D • MDCIX HENRICUS HUDSON INSULAM MANHATTAN APERUIT **Edge:** Plain

Date	Mintage	F	VF	XF	Unc	BU
1959 Proof	—	Value: 2,350				

X# M168 30 DUCAT
103.5000 g., 0.9800 Gold 3.2609 oz. AGW, 50 mm. **Subject:** JFK's Death **Obv:** Value "XXX" in center of 6-pointed cross, lilies in angles **Obv. Legend:** PRO PROSPERITATE MUNDI **Rev:** Bust of Kennedy left in sprays **Rev. Legend:** KENNEDY + 22.X1.1963 **Edge:** Plain **Note:** Prev. X#M141.

Date	Mintage	F	VF	XF	Unc	BU
ND(1963) Proof	—	Value: 2,350				

Berlin Thaler Issues

X# M375 THALER
23.0000 g., 1.0000 Silver 0.7394 oz. ASW

Date	Mintage	F	VF	XF	Unc	BU
1990 Proof	—	Value: 40.00				

X# M376 THALER
Gilt Brass

Date	Mintage	F	VF	XF	Unc	BU
1990 Proof	—	Value: 20.00				

X# M377 THALER
Bronze Antique

Date	Mintage	F	VF	XF	Unc	BU
1990 Proof	—	Value: 13.50				

Hamburg Mint Issues

X# M351 5 REICHSMARK
155.6706 g., 0.9990 Silver 4.9997 oz. ASW, 71 mm. **Subject:** 160th Anniversary Bremerhaven Harbor Facility **Note:** Illustration reduced.

Date	Mintage	F	VF	XF	Unc	BU
1987	1,500	—	—	—	—	200

X# M352 5 REICHSMARK
373.6096 g., 0.9990 Gold 11.999 oz. AGW, 71 mm. **Subject:** 160th Anniversary Bremerhaven Harbor Facility **Note:** Illustration reduced.

Date	Mintage	F	VF	XF	Unc	BU
1987	250	—	—	—	—	9,500

Square Deal Productions Issues

X# M401 MARK
8.5000 g., 0.9990 Silver 0.2730 oz. ASW **Issuer:** Münzprägstatt München (Munich) **Obv:** Arms **Obv. Legend:** BUNDESREPUBLIK DEUTSCHLAND **Rev:** Large value between oak leaves **Edge:** Plain **Shape:** Square **Note:** 23.7x23.7mm.

Date	Mintage	F	VF	XF	Unc	BU
2001 Proof	10,000	Value: 60.00				

X# M401a MARK
0.5800 Gold **Issuer:** Münsprägstatt München (Munich) **Obv:** Arms **Obv. Legend:** BUNDESREPUBLIK DEUTSCHLAND **Rev:** Large value between oak leaves **Edge:** Plain **Shape:** Square **Note:** 23.7x23.7mm.

Date	Mintage	F	VF	XF	Unc	BU
2001 Proof	2,500	Value: 350				

PATTERNS

INA Issues

X# Pn101 PFENNIG
Copper **Obv:** Oak leaf sprig **Obv. Legend:** BUNDESREPUBLIK DEUTSCHLAND **Rev:** Large value "1" in sprays on country outline **Edge:** Plain

Date	Mintage	F	VF	XF	Unc	BU
2005 Prooflike	—	—	—	—	—	1.50

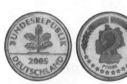

X# Pn102 2 PFENNIG
Copper **Obv:** Oak leaf sprig **Obv. Legend:** BUNDESREPUBLIK DEUTSCHLAND **Rev:** Large value "2" in sprays on country outline **Edge:** Plain

Date	Mintage	F	VF	XF	Unc	BU
2005 Prooflike	—	—	—	—	—	2.00

X# Pn103 5 PFENNIG
Brass **Obv:** Oak leaf sprig **Obv. Legend:** BUNDESREPUBLIK DEUTSCHLAND **Rev:** Large value "5" in sprays on country outline **Edge:** Plain

Date	Mintage	F	VF	XF	Unc	BU
2005 Prooflike	—	—	—	—	—	2.50

X# Pn104 10 PFENNIG
Brass **Obv:** Oak leaf sprig **Obv. Legend:** BUNDESEPUBLIK DEUTSCHLAND **Rev:** Large value "10" in sprays on country outline

Date	Mintage	F	VF	XF	Unc	BU
2005 Prooflike	—	—	—	—	—	3.00

X# Pn105 50 PFENNIG
Copper-Nickel **Obv:** Large value "50" **Obv. Legend:** ★ BUNDESREPUBLIK ★ DEUTSCHLAND **Rev:** Woman kneeling planting oak tree **Edge:** Plain

Date	Mintage	F	VF	XF	Unc	BU
2005 Prooflike	—	—	—	—	—	3.50

X# Pn106 MARK
Copper-Nickel **Subject:** 125th Anniversary of Colgne Cathedral **Obv:** Eagle **Obv. Legend:** BUNDESREPUBLIK DEUTSCHLAND **Rev:** Cologne Cathedral **Rev. Legend:** DER KOLNER DOM 125 JAHRE VOLIENDET

Date	Mintage	F	VF	XF	Unc	BU
2005 Prooflike	—	—	—	—	—	4.00

X# Pn107 2 MARK
Copper-Nickel **Subject:** 350th Anniversary Birth of Ludwig von Baden **Obv:** Eagle **Obv. Legend:** BUNDERSREPUBLIK DEUTSCHLAND **Rev:** Armored bust of Ludwig von Baden right **Rev. Legend:** LUDWIG WILHELM MARKGRAF VON BADEN **Edge:** Plain

Date	Mintage	F	VF	XF	Unc	BU
2005 Prooflike	—	—	—	—	—	6.00

X# Pn108 5 MARK
Copper-Nickel **Subject:** 200th Anniversary Death of Johann C. F. von Schiller **Obv:** Eagle **Obv. Inscription:**

BUNDESREPUBLIK / DEUTSCHLAND **Rev:** Portrait of Schiller right **Rev. Inscription:** FRIEDRICH - VON - SCHILLER **Edge:** Plain

Date	Mintage	F	VF	XF	Unc	BU
2005 Prooflike	—	—	—	—	—	8.00

MEDALLIC COINAGE

Aureus Magnus Issues

Private medals struck for Werner Graul (Aureus Magnus), West Germany by the Vienna, Austria and Hamburg, West Germany mints. These are currently struck for Dr. Jurgen Graul, his son

MINT SETS

X#	Date	Mintage	Identification	Issue Price	Mkt Val
XMS21	2005 (8)	—	X#Pn1-Pn8	—	20.00

GERMANY, THIRD REICH

THIRD REICH

MEDALLIC COINAGE

X# 27 2 REICHSMARK
18.1200 g., Silver Plated Brass, 24.9 mm. **Obv:** Head of Hitler left **Rev:** Eagle, swastika below **Edge:** Plain

Date	Mintage	F	VF	XF	Unc	BU
1938	—	—	—	—	—	35.00

PATTERNS

Including off metal strikes

X# Pn23 5 REICHSMARK
Silver **Obv:** Bust of Adolf Hitler left **Rev:** Eagle, swastika below **Edge:** Plain

Date	Mintage	F	VF	XF	Unc	BU
1934	—	—	—	—	—	—

X# Pn24 5 REICHSMARK
Gold **Obv:** Bust of Adolf Hitler left **Rev:** Eagle, swastika below **Edge:** Plain

Date	Mintage	F	VF	XF	Unc	BU
1934	—	—	—	—	—	—

X# Pn25 5 REICHSMARK
Platinum APW **Obv:** Bust of Adolf Hitler left **Rev:** Eagle, swastika below **Edge:** Plain

Date	Mintage	F	VF	XF	Unc	BU
1934	—	—	—	—	—	—

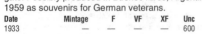

X# Pn21 20 REICHSMARK
6.4100 g., Gold **Obv:** Head of Hitler left **Rev:** Brandenburg gate **Note:** Error "PRODE" at left under gate. Possibly produced in Buenos Aires, Argentina in 1959 as souvenirs for German veterans.

Date	Mintage	F	VF	XF	Unc	BU
1933	—	—	—	—	600	—

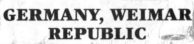

X# Pn22 100 REICHSMARK
0.3330 Gold **Obv:** Head of Hitler left **Rev:** Brandenburg gate **Note:** Prev. X#94. Error "PRODE" at left under gate. Possibly produced in Buenos Aires, Argentina in 1959 as souvenirs for German veterans.

Date	Mintage	F	VF	XF	Unc	BU
1933 Proof	—	Value: 2,000				

GERMANY, WEIMAR REPUBLIC

WEIMAR REPUBLIC

PATTERNS

Josef Wild Issues

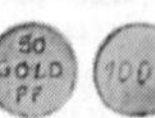

X# 101 50 GOLD PFENNIG
0.1700 g., 1.0000 Gold 0.0055 oz. AGW, 6 mm. **Obv. Inscription:** 50 / GOLD / PF **Rev. Inscription:** "1000"

Date	Mintage	F	VF	XF	Unc	BU
ND(1923)	—	—	—	—	300	—

X# 108 GOLD MARK
0.3700 g., 1.0000 Gold 0.0119 oz. AGW **Obv:** Arms **Obv. Legend:** DUSSELDORF **Rev. Inscription:** 1 / GOLD / M

Date	Mintage	F	VF	XF	Unc	BU
ND(1923)	—	—	—	—	425	—

X# 111 GOLD MARK
0.3600 g., 1.0000 Gold 0.0116 oz. AGW, 9.5 mm. **Obv:** Arms **Obv. Legend:** HANNOVER **Rev. Inscription:** 1 / GOLD / M

Date	Mintage	F	VF	XF	Unc	BU
ND(1923)	—	—	—	—	450	—

X# 113 GOLD MARK
0.3600 g., 1.0000 Gold 0.0116 oz. AGW, 9.5 mm. **Obv:** Munich child standing facing **Obv. Legend:** MÜNICH **Rev. Inscription:** 1 / GOLD / M

Date	Mintage	F	VF	XF	Unc	BU
ND(1923)	—	—	—	—	425	—

X# 114 GOLD MARK
0.3700 g., 1.0000 Gold 0.0119 oz. AGW, 9.5 mm. **Obv:** Eagle **Obv. Legend:** NÜRNBERG **Rev. Inscription:** 1 / GOLD / M

Date	Mintage	F	VF	XF	Unc	BU
ND(1923)	—	—	—	—	450	—

X# 115 GOLD MARK
0.3000 g., 1.0000 Gold 0.0096 oz. AGW, 9.5 mm. **Obv:** Arms **Obv. Legend:** REGENSBURG **Rev. Inscription:** 1 / GOLD / M

Date	Mintage	F	VF	XF	Unc	BU
ND(1924)	—	—	—	—	500	—

X# 116 GOLD MARK
0.3300 g., 1.0000 Gold 0.0106 oz. AGW, 9.5 mm. **Obv:** Arms **Obv. Legend:** ROTHENBURG **Rev. Inscription:** 1 / GOLD / M

Date	Mintage	F	VF	XF	Unc	BU
ND(1924)	—	—	—	—	450	—

X# 112 GOLD MARK
0.3400 g., 1.0000 Gold 0.0109 oz. AGW, 9.5 mm. **Obv:** Arms **Obv. Legend:** LÜBECK **Rev. Inscription:** 1 / GOLD / M

Date	Mintage	F	VF	XF	Unc	BU
ND(1924)	—	—	—	—	450	—

X# 107 GOLD MARK
0.3500 g., 1.0000 Gold 0.0113 oz. AGW, 9.5 mm. **Obv:** Arms **Obv. Legend:** BREMEN **Rev. Inscription:** 1 / GOLD / MARK

Date	Mintage	F	VF	XF	Unc	BU
ND(1924)	—	—	—	—	—	—

X# 110 GOLD MARK
0.3200 g., 1.0000 Gold 0.0103 oz. AGW, 9.5 mm. **Obv:** Arms **Obv. Legend:** HAMBURG **Rev. Inscription:** 1 / GOLD / M

Date	Mintage	F	VF	XF	Unc	BU
ND(1924)	—	—	—	—	425	—

X# 106 GOLD MARK
0.3600 g., 1.0000 Gold 0.0116 oz. AGW, 9 mm. **Obv:** Arms **Obv. Legend:** BAYREUTH **Rev. Inscription:** 1 / GOLD / M

Date	Mintage	F	VF	XF	Unc	BU
ND(1924)	—	—	—	—	425	—

X# 104 GOLD MARK
0.3700 g., 1.0000 Gold 0.0119 oz. AGW, 9 mm. **Obv:** Arms **Obv. Legend:** AUGSBURG **Rev. Inscription:** 1 / GOLD / M

Date	Mintage	F	VF	XF	Unc	BU
ND(1924)	—	—	—	—	500	—

X# 105 GOLD MARK
0.3700 g., 1.0000 Gold 0.0119 oz. AGW, 9.5 mm. **Obv:** Arms **Obv. Legend:** BAD KISSINGEN **Rev. Inscription:** 1 / GOLD / M

Date	Mintage	F	VF	XF	Unc	BU
ND(1925)	—	—	—	—	500	—

X# 109 GOLD MARK
0.3400 g., 1.0000 Gold 0.0109 oz. AGW, 9.5 mm.
Obv: Arms **Obv. Legend:** FRANKFURT M.
Rev. Inscription: 1 / GOLD / M

Date	Mintage	F	VF	XF	Unc	BU
ND(1925)	—	—	—	—	425	—

X# 117 GOLD MARK
0.3500 g., 1.0000 Gold 0.0113 oz. AGW, 9.5 mm.
Obv: Horse left rearing **Obv. Legend:** STUTTGART
Rev. Inscription: 1 / GOLD / M

Date	Mintage	F	VF	XF	Unc	BU
ND(1925)	—	—	—	—	450	—

X# 118 3 GOLD MARK
1.0900 g., 1.0000 Gold 0.0350 oz. AGW, 11.5 mm.
Obv: Stylized eagle **Obv. Legend:** JOS. WILD NÜRNBERG **Rev. Inscription:** 3 / GOLD / M

Date	Mintage	F	VF	XF	Unc	BU
1923	—	—	—	—	600	—

X# 119 5 GOLD MARK
1.8000 g., 1.0000 Gold 0.0579 oz. AGW, 14 mm.
Obv: Stylized eagle **Obv. Legend:** JOS. WILD NÜRNBERG **Rev. Inscription:** 5 / GOLD / M

Date	Mintage	F	VF	XF	Unc	BU
1923	—	—	—	—	650	—

X# 103 20 GOLD MARK
7.1400 g., 1.0000 Gold 0.2295 oz. AGW, 21.4 mm.
Obv: Radiant sun **Obv. Legend:** KURSFÄHIGES GOLD **Rev. Inscription:** 20 / GOLDMARK

Date	Mintage	F	VF	XF	Unc	BU
ND(1923)	—	—	—	—	1,200	—

X# 122 20 GOLD MARK
7.1300 g., 1.0000 Gold 0.2292 oz. AGW, 21.5 mm.
Obv: City view **Obv. Legend:** NÜRNBERG **Rev. Inscription:** 20 / GOLDMARK / 7.14 GRAMM / 1000-FEIN

Date	Mintage	F	VF	XF	Unc	BU
1927	—	—	—	—	1,000	—
1928	—	—	—	—	1,200	—

X# 120 1/32 DUCAT
0.1100 g., 1.0000 Gold 0.0035 oz. AGW, 5 mm.
Obv: Crowned arms **Rev:** Paschal lamb left

Date	Mintage	F	VF	XF	Unc	BU
ND(1925)	—	—	—	—	450	—

X# 102 DUCAT-10 GOLD MARK
3.5700 g., 1.0000 Gold 0.1148 oz. AGW, 21.4 mm.
Obv: Radiant sun **Obv. Legend:** KURSFÄHIGES GOLD **Rev. Inscription:** 1 / GOLD-DUKATEN / ODER / 10 / GOLD-MARK

Date	Mintage	F	VF	XF	Unc	BU
ND(1924)	—	—	—	—	1,000	—

X# 121 DUCAT
3.4300 g., 1.0000 Gold 0.1103 oz. AGW, 21.5 mm.
Subject: Octoberfest **Obv:** Munich child standing facing **Rev:** Church of Our Lady

Date	Mintage	F	VF	XF	Unc	BU
1926	—	—	—	—	1,500	—

Karl Goetz Issues

Struck in Munich, Bavaria

X# 18a 50 PFENNIG
2.5000 g., 0.5000 Silver 0.0402 oz. ASW

Date	Mintage	F	VF	XF	Unc	BU
1925D Proof	—	Value: 175				

X# 18b 50 PFENNIG
6.9100 g., Gold

Date	Mintage	F	VF	XF	Unc	BU
1925D Proof	—	Value: 250				

X# 18c 50 PFENNIG
13.3900 g., Platinum APW

Date	Mintage	F	VF	XF	Unc	BU
1925D Proof	2	—	—	—	—	—

X# 19a 50 PFENNIG
Aluminum

Date	Mintage	F	VF	XF	Unc	BU
1925D	—	—	—	—	—	—

X# 19 50 PFENNIG
2.5000 g., 0.5000 Silver 0.0402 oz. ASW

Date	Mintage	F	VF	XF	Unc	BU
1925D	—	—	—	100	200	—

X# 20 50 PFENNIG
2.5000 g., 0.5000 Silver 0.0402 oz. ASW

Date	Mintage	F	VF	XF	Unc	BU
1925D Proof	—	Value: 175				

X# 20a 50 PFENNIG
Aluminum

Date	Mintage	F	VF	XF	Unc	BU
1925D Proof	—	Value: 100				

X# 20b 50 PFENNIG
6.9100 g., Gold

Date	Mintage	F	VF	XF	Unc	BU
1925D Proof	—	Value: 450				

X# 20c 50 PFENNIG
Platinum APW

Date	Mintage	F	VF	XF	Unc	BU
1925D Proof	2	Value: 750				

X# 21 50 PFENNIG
2.3000 g., 0.5000 Silver 0.0370 oz. ASW

Date	Mintage	F	VF	XF	Unc	BU
1925D Proof	—	Value: 125				

X# 21a 50 PFENNIG
Aluminum

Date	Mintage	F	VF	XF	Unc	BU
1925D Proof	—	Value: 100				

X# 18 50 PFENNIG
Aluminum **Note:** Prev. KM#PnA265.

Date	Mintage	F	VF	XF	Unc	BU
1925D Proof	—	Value: 125				

X# 22 MARK
4.9000 g., 1.0000 Silver 0.1575 oz. ASW

Date	Mintage	F	VF	XF	Unc	BU
1926D Proof	—	Value: 125				

X# 23 2 MARK
10.2000 g., 1.0000 Silver 0.3279 oz. ASW

Date	Mintage	F	VF	XF	Unc	BU
1926D Proof	—	Value: 200				

X# 23a 2 MARK
17.6500 g., Platinum APW

Date	Mintage	F	VF	XF	Unc	BU
1926D Proof	—	Value: 800				

X# 24 3 MARK
16.1000 g., 1.0000 Silver 0.5176 oz. ASW
Subject: Bavaria

Date	Mintage	F	VF	XF	Unc	BU
1925 Proof	—	Value: 200				

X# 24a 3 MARK
Bronze **Subject:** Bavaria

Date	Mintage	F	VF	XF	Unc	BU
1925 Proof	—	Value: 125				

X# 24b 3 MARK
Nickel **Subject:** Bavaria

Date	Mintage	F	VF	XF	Unc	BU
1925 Proof	—	Value: 150				

X# 24c 3 MARK
Platinum APW **Subject:** Bavaria

Date	Mintage	F	VF	XF	Unc	BU
1925 Proof	—	Value: 1,150				

X# 59 3 MARK
28.2300 g., Platinum APW

Date	Mintage	F	VF	XF	Unc	BU
1925 Proof	—	Value: 1,150				

X# 25 3 MARK
Silver Plated Bronze

Date	Mintage	F	VF	XF	Unc	BU
1925D Proof	—	Value: 85.00				

X# 26 3 MARK
Silver Plated Bronze

Date	Mintage	F	VF	XF	Unc	BU
1925D Proof	—	Value: 85.00				

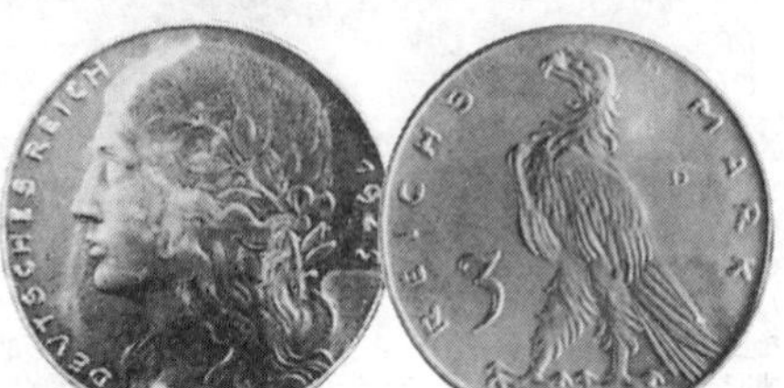

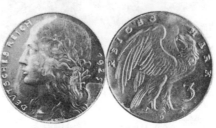

X# 27 3 MARK
Silver Plated Bronze

Date	Mintage	F	VF	XF	Unc	BU
1925D Proof	—	Value: 85.00				

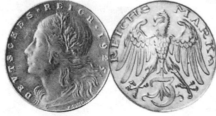

X# 28 3 MARK
Silver Plated Bronze

Date	Mintage	F	VF	XF	Unc	BU
1925D Proof	—	Value: 85.00				

X# 29 3 MARK
Silver Plated Bronze

Date	Mintage	F	VF	XF	Unc	BU
1925D Proof	—	Value: 85.00				

X# 30 3 MARK
Silver Plated Bronze

Date	Mintage	F	VF	XF	Unc	BU
1925D Proof	—	Value: 85.00				

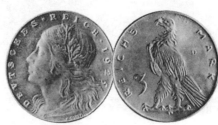

X# 31 3 MARK
Silver Plated Bronze

Date	Mintage	F	VF	XF	Unc	BU
1925D Proof	—	Value: 85.00				

X# 32 3 MARK
Silver Plated Bronze

Date	Mintage	F	VF	XF	Unc	BU
1925D Proof	—	Value: 85.00				

X# 32a 3 MARK
17.4300 g., Gold

Date	Mintage	F	VF	XF	Unc	BU
1925D Proof	—	Value: 550				

X# 45 3 MARK
Silver

Date	Mintage	F	VF	XF	Unc	BU
1925D Proof	—	Value: 150				

X# 33 3 MARK
Silver Plated Bronze

Date	Mintage	F	VF	XF	Unc	BU
1925D Proof	—	Value: 85.00				

X# 34 3 MARK
Silver Plated Bronze

Date	Mintage	F	VF	XF	Unc	BU
1925D Proof	—	Value: 85.00				

X# 35 3 MARK

Silver Plated Bronze

Date	Mintage	F	VF	XF	Unc	BU
1925D Proof	—	Value: 85.00				

X# 36 3 MARK

Silver Plated Bronze

Date	Mintage	F	VF	XF	Unc	BU
1925D Proof	—	Value: 85.00				

X# 37 3 MARK

Silver Plated Bronze

Date	Mintage	F	VF	XF	Unc	BU
1925D Proof	—	Value: 85.00				

X# 38 3 MARK

Silver Plated Bronze

Date	Mintage	F	VF	XF	Unc	BU
1925D Proof	—	Value: 85.00				

X# 39 3 MARK

Silver Plated Bronze

Date	Mintage	F	VF	XF	Unc	BU
1925D Proof	—	Value: 85.00				

X# 40 3 MARK

Silver Plated Bronze

Date	Mintage	F	VF	XF	Unc	BU
1925D Proof	—	Value: 85.00				

X# 40a 3 MARK

Bronze

Date	Mintage	F	VF	XF	Unc	BU
1925D Proof	—	Value: 75.00				

X# 41 3 MARK

Silver Plated Bronze

Date	Mintage	F	VF	XF	Unc	BU
1925D Proof	—	Value: 85.00				

X# 42 3 MARK

Silver Plated Bronze

Date	Mintage	F	VF	XF	Unc	BU
1925D Proof	—	Value: 85.00				

X# 43 3 MARK

Silver Plated Bronze

Date	Mintage	F	VF	XF	Unc	BU
1925D Proof	—	Value: 85.00				

X# 44 3 MARK

Silver Plated Bronze

Date	Mintage	F	VF	XF	Unc	BU
1925D Proof	—	Value: 85.00				

X# 49 3 MARK

Silver Plated Bronze

Date	Mintage	F	VF	XF	Unc	BU
1926D Proof	—	Value: 85.00				

X# 49a 3 MARK

Gold

Date	Mintage	F	VF	XF	Unc	BU
1926D Proof	—	Value: 800				

X# 50 3 MARK

Silver Plated Bronze

Date	Mintage	F	VF	XF	Unc	BU
1926D Proof	—	Value: 85.00				

X# 50a 3 MARK

Gold

Date	Mintage	F	VF	XF	Unc	BU
1926D Proof	—	Value: 800				

X# 51 3 MARK

Silver Plated Bronze

Date	Mintage	F	VF	XF	Unc	BU
1926D Proof	—	Value: 85.00				

X# 51a 3 MARK

Gold

Date	Mintage	F	VF	XF	Unc	BU
1926D Proof	—	Value: 800				

X# 52 3 MARK

Silver Plated Bronze

Date	Mintage	F	VF	XF	Unc	BU
1926D Proof	—	Value: 85.00				

X# 52a 3 MARK

Gold

Date	Mintage	F	VF	XF	Unc	BU
1926D Proof	—	Value: 800				

X# 61 3 MARK
Gold

Date	Mintage	F	VF	XF	Unc	BU
1926D Proof	—	Value: 750				

X# 57 3 MARK
14.8000 g., Silver

Date	Mintage	F	VF	XF	Unc	BU
1926D Proof	—	Value: 125				

X# 58 3 MARK
15.1000 g., Silver

Date	Mintage	F	VF	XF	Unc	BU
1926D Proof	—	Value: 125				

X# 63 5 MARK
Silvered Bronze

Date	Mintage	F	VF	XF	Unc	BU
1925D Proof	—	Value: 150				

X# 63a 5 MARK
Silver

Date	Mintage	F	VF	XF	Unc	BU
1925D Proof	—	Value: 225				

X# 64 5 MARK
Silvered Bronze

Date	Mintage	F	VF	XF	Unc	BU
1925D Proof	—	Value: 150				

X# 64a 5 MARK
Silver

Date	Mintage	F	VF	XF	Unc	BU
1925D Proof	—	Value: 225				

X# 65 5 MARK
Silvered Bronze

Date	Mintage	F	VF	XF	Unc	BU
1925D Proof	—	Value: 150				

X# 65a 5 MARK
Silver

Date	Mintage	F	VF	XF	Unc	BU
1925D Proof	—	Value: 225				

X# 66 5 MARK
Silvered Bronze

Date	Mintage	F	VF	XF	Unc	BU
1925D Proof	—	Value: 150				

X# 66a 5 MARK
Silver

Date	Mintage	F	VF	XF	Unc	BU
1925D Proof	—	Value: 225				

X# 66b 5 MARK
28.6200 g., Gold

Date	Mintage	F	VF	XF	Unc	BU
1925D Proof	—	Value: 850				

X# 67 5 MARK
Silvered Bronze

Date	Mintage	F	VF	XF	Unc	BU
1925D Proof	—	Value: 150				

X# 67a 5 MARK
Silver

Date	Mintage	F	VF	XF	Unc	BU
1925D Proof	—	Value: 225				

X# 68 5 MARK
Silvered Bronze

Date	Mintage	F	VF	XF	Unc	BU
1925D Proof	—	Value: 150				

X# 68a 5 MARK
Silver

Date	Mintage	F	VF	XF	Unc	BU
1925D Proof	—	Value: 225				

X# 68b 5 MARK
40.6000 g., Platinum APW

Date	Mintage	F	VF	XF	Unc	BU
1925D Proof	2	Value: 1,750				

X# 69 5 MARK
Silvered Bronze

Date	Mintage	F	VF	XF	Unc	BU
1925D Proof	—	Value: 150				

X# 69a 5 MARK
Silver

Date	Mintage	F	VF	XF	Unc	BU
1925D Proof	—	Value: 225				

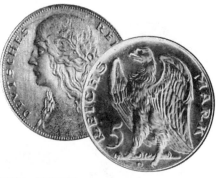

X# 70 5 MARK
Silvered Bronze

Date	Mintage	F	VF	XF	Unc	BU
1925D Proof	—	Value: 150				

X# 70a 5 MARK
Silver

Date	Mintage	F	VF	XF	Unc	BU
1925D Proof	—	Value: 225				

X# 70b 5 MARK
17.4300 g., Gold

Date	Mintage	F	VF	XF	Unc	BU
1925D Proof	—	Value: 850				

X# 71 5 MARK
Silvered Bronze

Date	Mintage	F	VF	XF	Unc	BU
1925D Proof	—	Value: 150				

X# 71a 5 MARK
Silver

Date	Mintage	F	VF	XF	Unc	BU
1925D Proof	—	Value: 225				

X# 72 5 MARK
Silvered Bronze

Date	Mintage	F	VF	XF	Unc	BU
1925D Proof	—	Value: 150				

X# 72a 5 MARK
Silver

Date	Mintage	F	VF	XF	Unc	BU
1925D Proof	—	Value: 225				

X# 73 5 MARK
Silvered Bronze

Date	Mintage	F	VF	XF	Unc	BU
1925D Proof	—	Value: 150				

X# 73a 5 MARK
Silver

Date	Mintage	F	VF	XF	Unc	BU
1925D Proof	—	Value: 225				

X# 74 5 MARK
Silvered Bronze

Date	Mintage	F	VF	XF	Unc	BU
1925D Proof	—	Value: 150				

X# 74a 5 MARK
Silver

Date	Mintage	F	VF	XF	Unc	BU
1925D Proof	—	Value: 225				

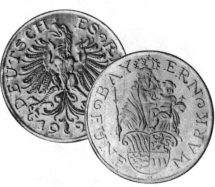

X# 79 5 MARK
24.9000 g., Silver

Date	Mintage	F	VF	XF	Unc	BU
1925D Proof	—	Value: 225				

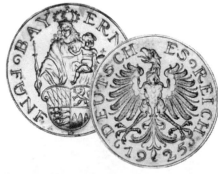

X# 79a 5 MARK
Platinum APW

Date	Mintage	F	VF	XF	Unc	BU
1925D Proof	2	Value: 1,800				

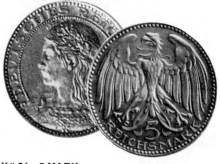

X# 81 5 MARK
23.6000 g., Silver

Date	Mintage	F	VF	XF	Unc	BU
1926D Proof	—	Value: 225				

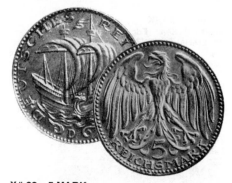

X# 82 5 MARK
24.3000 g., Silver

Date	Mintage	F	VF	XF	Unc	BU
1926D Proof	—	Value: 225				

X# 83 5 MARK
34.8500 g., Gold

Date	Mintage	F	VF	XF	Unc	BU
1926D Proof	—	Value: 1,100				

X# 83a 5 MARK
40.6100 g., Platinum APW

Date	Mintage	F	VF	XF	Unc	BU
1926D Proof	3	Value: 2,000				

X# 84 5 MARK
24.5000 g., Silver **Subject:** Von Hindenburg **Rev:** Legend below truncation **Rev. Legend:** PROBE **Edge:** Plain

Date	Mintage	F	VF	XF	Unc	BU
1927D	—	—	—	—	35.00	—

X# 85 5 MARK
24.5000 g., Silver **Rev:** Without "PROBE"

Date	Mintage	F	VF	XF	Unc	BU
1927D	—	—	—	—	30.00	—

X# 87 5 MARK
24.5000 g., Silver **Rev:** Without "PROBE" or mint mark **Edge:** Plain **Note:** Hallmarked as #X86.

Date	Mintage	F	VF	XF	Unc	BU
1927	—	—	—	—	30.00	—

X# 86 5 MARK
24.5000 g., Silver **Edge:** Plain **Note:** Hallmarked: BAYER.HAUPTMUNZAMT·FEINSILBER

Date	Mintage	F	VF	XF	Unc	BU
1927D	—	—	—	—	—	—

Karl Schmidt Issues

X# 88 5 MARK
31.1000 g., Silver **Subject:** Unity

Date	Mintage	F	VF	XF	Unc	BU
1927	—	—	—	—	125	—

X# 88a 5 MARK
31.1000 g., Silver **Subject:** Unity

Date	Mintage	F	VF	XF	Unc	BU
1927	—	—	—	—	125	—

X# 90 5 MARK
24.7000 g., Silver **Subject:** E. Basserman

Date	Mintage	F	VF	XF	Unc	BU
1927	—	—	—	—	150	—

X# 91 5 MARK
24.7000 g., Silver **Subject:** Seating of the Reichstag

Date	Mintage	F	VF	XF	Unc	BU
1927	—	—	—	—	125	—

X# 92 5 MARK
30.4000 g., Silver **Subject:** Constitution Day

Date	Mintage	F	VF	XF	Unc	BU
1927	—	—	—	—	125	—

X# 89 5 MARK
Silver **Note:** Prev. KM#Pn333.

Date	Mintage	F	VF	XF	Unc	BU
1927A	—	—	—	—	145	—

MEDALLIC COINAGE

Karl Goetz Issues

Struck in Munich, Bavaria

X# 1 5 MARK
Silver **Subject:** Von Hindenburg **Note:** Prev. KM#M1.

Date	Mintage	F	VF	XF	Unc	BU
1927D	—	—	—	—	30.00	—

X# 1a 5 MARK
22.4700 g., Gold **Subject:** Von Hindenburg **Note:** Prev. KM#M1a.

Date	Mintage	F	VF	XF	Unc	BU
1927D	—	—	—	—	600	—

X# 1b 5 MARK
43.2600 g., Platinum APW **Note:** Prev. KM#M1b.

Date	Mintage	F	VF	XF	Unc	BU
1927D	—	—	—	—	1,650	—

X# 2 10 MARK
Gold **Subject:** Von Hindenburg **Note:** Prev. KM#M5.

Date	Mintage	F	VF	XF	Unc	BU
1928 Proof	—	Value: 300				

X# 2a 10 MARK
Silver **Note:** Prev. KM#M5a.

Date	Mintage	F	VF	XF	Unc	BU
1928	—	—	—	—	35.00	—

X# 3 20 MARK
6.4900 g., Gold **Subject:** Von Hindenburg **Note:** Prev. KM#M6.

Date	Mintage	F	VF	XF	Unc	BU
1928 Proof	—	Value: 325				

X# 3a 20 MARK
Silver **Note:** Prev. KM#M6a.

Date	Mintage	F	VF	XF	Unc	BU
1928	—	—	—	—	45.00	—

X# 7 25 MARK
6.9400 g., Gold **Note:** Prev. KM#M7.

Date	Mintage	F	VF	XF	Unc	BU
1932	—	—	—	—	325	—

X# 7a 25 MARK
10.1500 g., Platinum APW **Note:** Prev. KM#M7a.

Date	Mintage	F	VF	XF	Unc	BU
1932	5	—	—	—	950	—

Bernhart Issues

X# 4 5 MARK
Silver **Subject:** Von Hindenburg **Note:** Prev. KM#M2.

Date	Mintage	F	VF	XF	Unc	BU
1928 Proof	—	Value: 30.00				

X# 4a 5 MARK
23.0000 g., Gold **Subject:** Von Hindenburg **Note:** Prev. KM#M2a.

Date	Mintage	F	VF	XF	Unc	BU
1928 Proof	—	Value: 650				

X# M5 10 MARK
3.4200 g., 0.7500 Gold 0.0825 oz. AGW, 19.5 mm. **Subject:** Von Hindenburg **Obv:** Helmeted arms **Rev:** Head left **Note:** Prev. KM#M3.

Date	Mintage	F	VF	XF	Unc	BU
1928 Proof	—	Value: 200				

X# 5a 10 MARK
Silver **Obv:** Helmeted arms **Rev:** Head left **Note:** Prev. KM#M3a.

Date	Mintage	F	VF	XF	Unc	BU
1928 Proof	—	Value: 25.00				

X# 6 20 MARK
6.3900 g., 0.7500 Gold 0.1541 oz. AGW, 22.5 mm. **Subject:** Von Hindenburg **Obv:** Helmeted arms **Rev:** Head left **Note:** Prev. KM#M4.

Date	Mintage	F	VF	XF	Unc	BU
1928 Proof	—	Value: 220				

X# 6a 20 MARK
Silver **Obv:** Helmeted arms **Rev:** Head left **Note:** Prev. KM#M4a.

Date	Mintage	F	VF	XF	Unc	BU
1928 Proof	—	Value: 35.00				

GERMANY-EMPIRE

EMPIRE

PATTERNS

Karl Goetz Issues

X# 1 25 PFENNIG
Nickel

Date	Mintage	F	VF	XF	Unc	BU
1908	—	—	—	—	—	85.00

X# 1a 25 PFENNIG
Copper

Date	Mintage	F	VF	XF	Unc	BU
1908	—	—	—	—	—	65.00

X# 1b 25 PFENNIG
Silver

Date	Mintage	F	VF	XF	Unc	BU
1908	—	—	—	—	—	110

X# 1c 25 PFENNIG
12.2000 g., Platinum APW

Date	Mintage	F	VF	XF	Unc	BU
1908	2	—	—	—	—	675

X# 2 25 PFENNIG
Nickel

Date	Mintage	F	VF	XF	Unc	BU
1908D	—	—	—	—	—	85.00

X# 2a 25 PFENNIG
Copper

Date	Mintage	F	VF	XF	Unc	BU
1908D	—	—	—	—	—	60.00

X# 2b 25 PFENNIG
Bronze

Date	Mintage	F	VF	XF	Unc	BU
1908D	—	—	—	—	—	70.00

X# 2c 25 PFENNIG
4.1000 g., 1.0000 Silver 0.1318 oz. ASW

Date	Mintage	F	VF	XF	Unc	BU
1908D	—	—	—	—	—	110

X# 3 25 PFENNIG
Silver

Date	Mintage	F	VF	XF	Unc	BU
1908D	—	—	—	—	—	110

X# 4 25 PFENNIG
Nickel

Date	Mintage	F	VF	XF	Unc	BU
1908D	—	—	—	—	—	85.00

X# 4a 25 PFENNIG
Copper

Date	Mintage	F	VF	XF	Unc	BU
1908D	—	—	—	—	—	65.00

X# 4b 25 PFENNIG
Bronze

Date	Mintage	F	VF	XF	Unc	BU
1908D	—	—	—	—	—	65.00

X# 4c 25 PFENNIG
Silver Plated Bronze

Date	Mintage	F	VF	XF	Unc	BU
1908D	—	—	—	—	—	75.00

X# 4d 25 PFENNIG
Nickel

Date	Mintage	F	VF	XF	Unc	BU
1908D	—	—	—	—	—	75.00

X# 4e 25 PFENNIG
Silver

Date	Mintage	F	VF	XF	Unc	BU
1908D	—	—	—	—	—	110

X# 5 25 PFENNIG
Copper-Nickel

Date	Mintage	F	VF	XF	Unc	BU
1908D	—	—	—	—	—	80.00

X# 5a 25 PFENNIG
Copper

Date	Mintage	F	VF	XF	Unc	BU
1908D	—	—	—	—	—	65.00

X# 5b 25 PFENNIG
Bronze

Date	Mintage	F	VF	XF	Unc	BU
1908D	—	—	—	—	—	70.00

X# 60 25 PFENNIG
6.9300 g., Gold

Date	Mintage	F	VF	XF	Unc	BU
1908D	—	—	—	—	—	285

X# 60a 25 PFENNIG
Platinum APW

Date	Mintage	F	VF	XF	Unc	BU
1908D	—	—	—	—	—	675

X# 6 25 PFENNIG
Copper

Date	Mintage	F	VF	XF	Unc	BU
1908D	—	—	—	—	—	65.00

X# 6a 25 PFENNIG
Silver

Date	Mintage	F	VF	XF	Unc	BU
1908D	—	—	—	—	—	120

X# 7 25 PFENNIG
Copper-Nickel

Date	Mintage	F	VF	XF	Unc	BU
1908D	—	—	—	—	—	80.00

X# 7a 25 PFENNIG
Nickel

Date	Mintage	F	VF	XF	Unc	BU
1908D	—	—	—	—	—	80.00

X# 8 25 PFENNIG
Copper-Nickel

Date	Mintage	F	VF	XF	Unc	BU
1908D	—	—	—	—	—	75.00

X# 8a 25 PFENNIG
Nickel

Date	Mintage	F	VF	XF	Unc	BU
1908D	—	—	—	—	—	75.00

X# 8b 25 PFENNIG
Bronze

Date	Mintage	F	VF	XF	Unc	BU
1908D	—	—	—	—	—	60.00

X# 8c 25 PFENNIG
4.0000 g., 1.0000 Silver 0.1286 oz. ASW

Date	Mintage	F	VF	XF	Unc	BU
1908D	—	—	—	—	—	110

X# 5c 25 PFENNIG
Silver **Note:** Weight varies: 4.10-5.00 grams.

Date	Mintage	F	VF	XF	Unc	BU
1908D	—	—	—	—	—	120

X# 9 25 PFENNIG
5.9000 g., Silver **Note:** Prev. KM#Pn164. Legend over value.

Date	Mintage	F	VF	XF	Unc	BU
1909A	—	—	—	—	—	135

X# 10 25 PFENNIG
Silver **Note:** Prev. KM#Pn165. Standing eagle right.

Date	Mintage	F	VF	XF	Unc	BU
1909A	—	—	—	—	—	135

X# 12 25 PFENNIG
Silver Plated Bronze **Note:** Prev. KM#Pn166.

Date	Mintage	F	VF	XF	Unc	BU
1909A	—	—	—	—	—	85.00

Maximilian Dasio Issues

X# 13 MARK
Silver **Obv:** Crown/1/Mark **Rev:** Crowned eagle right looking left with wings outspread

Date	Mintage	F	VF	XF	Unc	BU
ND	—	—	—	—	—	—

X# 13a MARK
Silver Plated Copper **Obv:** Crown/1/Mark **Rev:** Crowned eagle right looking left with wings outspread

Date	Mintage	F	VF	XF	Unc	BU
ND	—	—	—	—	100	200	—

X# 14 MARK
Silver **Obv:** Warrior facing looking right with sword and shield **Rev:** Crown/1 'Mark'

Date	Mintage	F	VF	XF	Unc	BU
ND	—	—	—	—	—	—

X# 14a MARK
Silver Plated Copper **Obv:** Warrior facing looking right with sword and shield **Rev:** Crown/1 'Mark'

Date	Mintage	F	VF	XF	Unc	BU
ND	—	—	—	—	—	—

Hch. Schmidt Issues

Struck at the C. Drentwert Mint in Augsburg, Bavaria

X# 15 4 MARK (Thaler)
22.1000 g., Silver **Obv:** Legend below truncation **Obv. Legend:** VERSUCH

Date	Mintage	F	VF	XF	Unc	BU
1904 Proof	—	Value: 500				

X# 16 4 MARK (Thaler)
20.6000 g., 0.8000 Silver 0.5298 oz. ASW **Obv:** Legend below truncation **Obv. Legend:** GES. GESCH

Date	Mintage	F	VF	XF	Unc	BU
1904 Proof	—	—	—	—	—	—

X# 17 4 MARK (Thaler)
20.6000 g., 0.8000 Silver 0.5298 oz. ASW **Obv:** Without name below truncation **Note:** This proposed 4 Mark coin was a "Contribution to Numismatics" collector's pieces wishing well to the departed Thaler (equal to 3 Mark) and the 5 Mark issue of the newer coinage.

Date	Mintage	F	VF	XF	Unc	BU
1904 Proof	—	—	—	—	—	—

GHANA

REPUBLIC

MEDALLIC COINAGE

X# 2 CROWN
Copper-Nickel **Subject:** OAU summit meeting **Note:** Prev. KM#M1.

Date	Mintage	F	VF	XF	Unc	BU
1965 Proof	10,000	Value: 16.50				

X# 3 CROWN

28.2800 g., 0.9250 Silver 0.8410 oz. ASW **Note:** Prev. KM#M2.

Date	Mintage	F	VF	XF	Unc	BU
1965 Proof	1,000	Value: 40.00				

X# 4 CROWN

28.2800 g., 0.9170 Gold 0.8337 oz. AGW **Note:** Prev. KM#M3.

Date	Mintage	F	VF	XF	Unc	BU
1965 Proof	50	Value: 800				

X# 1 2 POUNDS

15.9800 g., 0.9170 Gold 0.4711 oz. AGW **Subject:** Republic Day **Note:** Prev. KM#M5.

Date	Mintage	F	VF	XF	Unc	BU
ND(1960) Proof	15,000	Value: 350				

X# 5 2 POUNDS

15.9800 g., 0.9170 Gold 0.4711 oz. AGW **Subject:** OAU Summit Meeting **Note:** Prev. KM#M4.

Date	Mintage	F	VF	XF	Unc	BU
1965 Proof	2,020	Value: 375				

X# 6 2 POUNDS

15.9800 g., 0.9170 Gold 0.4711 oz. AGW **Subject:** Kotoka **Obv:** Arms with date below **Rev:** Bust of Kotoka 1/2 left **Note:** Prev. KM#M6.

Date	Mintage	F	VF	XF	Unc	BU
1968 Proof	2,000	Value: 375				

X# 7 2 POUNDS

15.9800 g., 0.9170 Gold 0.4711 oz. AGW **Subject:** Freedom in Unity **Note:** Prev. KM#M7.

Date	Mintage	F	VF	XF	Unc	BU
1973 Proof	2,000	Value: 375				

X# 8 2 POUNDS

15.9800 g., 0.9170 Gold 0.4711 oz. AGW **Subject:** Operation Feed Yourself **Obv:** Native planting crops **Rev:** Arms and date **Note:** Prev. KM#M8.

Date	Mintage	F	VF	XF	Unc	BU
1975 Proof	—	Value: 350				

X# 9 2 POUNDS

19.6700 g., 0.9170 Gold 0.5799 oz. AGW **Subject:** 20th Anniversary of Independence **Note:** Prev. KM#M9.

Date	Mintage	F	VF	XF	Unc	BU
ND(1977) Proof	4,397	Value: 450				

X# 9a 2 POUNDS

11.8800 g., Silver **Subject:** 20th Anniversary of Independence **Note:** Prev. KM#M9a.

Date	Mintage	F	VF	XF	Unc	BU
ND(1977) Proof	—	Value: 25.00				

X# 10 4 POUNDS

39.5400 g., 0.9170 Gold 1.1657 oz. AGW **Subject:** 20th Anniversary of Independence **Note:** Prev. KM#M10.

Date	Mintage	F	VF	XF	Unc	BU
ND(1977) Proof	300	Value: 1,350				

X# 22 10 SIKA

26.1000 g., Copper-Nickel, 38.5 mm. **Subject:** Marine Life Protection **Obv:** National arms **Rev:** Multicolor fish scene **Edge:** Reeded

Date	Mintage	F	VF	XF	Unc	BU
1997	—	—	—	—	30.00	—

X# 23 10 SIKA

26.1000 g., Copper-Nickel, 38.5 mm. **Subject:** Marine Life Protection **Obv:** National arms **Rev:** Multicolor fish scene **Edge:** Reeded

Date	Mintage	F	VF	XF	Unc	BU
2000	—	—	—	—	30.00	—

X# 37 10 SIKA

25.3000 g., Copper-Nickel, 38.6 mm. **Obv:** National arms **Rev:** Two multicolor fish **Edge:** Reeded

Date	Mintage	F	VF	XF	Unc	BU
2000 Proof	—	Value: 30.00				

X# 15 100 SIKA

25.0500 g., 0.9990 Silver 0.8045 oz. ASW, 38.6 mm. **Subject:** Marine Life Protection **Obv:** National arms **Rev:** Multicolor fish scene **Edge:** Reeded

Date	Mintage	F	VF	XF	Unc	BU
1997 Proof	—	Value: 50.00				

X# 24 100 SIKA

19.8400 g., 0.9990 Silver 0.6372 oz. ASW, 40.5 mm. **Subject:** The Santa Maria **Obv:** National arms **Rev:** Sail ship **Edge:** Reeded

Date	Mintage	F	VF	XF	Unc	BU
2000 Proof	—	Value: 40.00				

X# 25 100 SIKA
31.0200 g., 0.9990 Silver 0.9963 oz. ASW, 38.6 mm. **Obv:** National arms **Rev:** Uniformed General Acheampong **Edge:** Reeded

Date	Mintage	F	VF	XF	Unc	BU
2002	—	—	—	—	35.00	45.00

X# 26 100 SIKA
31.1100 g., 0.9990 Silver 0.9992 oz. ASW, 38.7 mm. **Subject:** Year of the Horse **Obv:** Chinese building **Rev:** Gold plated horse facing right **Edge:** Reeded

Date	Mintage	F	VF	XF	Unc	BU
ND(2002) Proof	—	Value: 50.00				

X# 27 100 SIKA
31.1100 g., 0.9990 Silver 0.9992 oz. ASW, 38.7 mm. **Subject:** Year of the Horse **Obv:** Chinese building **Rev:** Gold plated horse facing left **Edge:** Reeded

Date	Mintage	F	VF	XF	Unc	BU
ND(2002) Proof	—	Value: 50.00				

X# 31 100 SIKA
25.0000 g., Copper-Nickel, 38.6 mm. **Subject:** 50th Anniversary of Elizabeth II's Coronation **Obv:** Queen Elizabeth II above Ghana's national arms **Rev:** Young Q. Elizabeth II below small crown **Edge:** Reeded

Date	Mintage	F	VF	XF	Unc	BU
ND(2003)	—	—	—	—	9.00	10.00

X# 33 100 SIKA
25.0000 g., Copper-Nickel, 38.6 mm. **Obv:** Queen Elizabeth II above Ghana's national arms **Rev:** Prince William working a computor mouse **Edge:** Reeded

Date	Mintage	F	VF	XF	Unc	BU
2003	—	—	—	—	9.00	10.00

X# 35 100 SIKA
25.0000 g., Copper-Nickel, 38.6 mm. **Obv:** Queen Elizabeth II above Ghana's national arms **Rev:** Queen Mother **Edge:** Reeded

Date	Mintage	F	VF	XF	Unc	BU
ND(2003)	—	—	—	—	9.00	10.00

X# 19 500 SIKA
31.1035 g., 0.9990 Silver 0.9990 oz. ASW, 40 mm. **Subject:** 2004 Olympics **Obv:** National arms **Rev:** High relief chariot **Edge:** Reeded

Date	Mintage	F	VF	XF	Unc	BU
2001 Antique Finish	15,000	—	—	—	50.00	—

X# 20 500 SIKA
26.0000 g., 0.9990 Gold Plated Silver 0.8350 oz. ASW AGW, 22 mm. **Subject:** Japanese Royal Baby **Obv:** Queen Elizabeth's portrait above national arms **Rev:** Red heart shaped crystal in hollowed out surface **Edge:** Plain

Date	Mintage	F	VF	XF	Unc	BU
2001	2,000	—	—	—	140	—

X# 30 500 SIKA
25.0000 g., 0.9250 Silver 0.7435 oz. ASW, 38.6 mm. **Obv:** Queen Elizabeth II above Ghana's national arms **Rev:** Queen Elizabeth II, Crown Prince Charles, Prince William **Edge:** Reeded

Date	Mintage	F	VF	XF	Unc	BU
2001 Proof	5,000	Value: 50.00				

X# 16 500 SIKA
4.9500 g., 0.3750 Gold 0.0597 oz. AGW, 22 mm. **Subject:** Queen Elizabeth's Golden Jubilee **Obv:** St. George **Rev:** Young multicolor portrait of the Queen **Edge:** Reeded

Date	Mintage	F	VF	XF	Unc	BU
2002 Proof	10,000	Value: 85.00				

X# 17 500 SIKA
24.9300 g., 0.9000 Silver 0.7213 oz. ASW, 38.6 mm. **Subject:** Ancient Navigator's **Obv:** National arms below Queen Elizabeth's head right **Rev:** Ancient Egyptian boat with rowers **Edge:** Reeded

Date	Mintage	F	VF	XF	Unc	BU
2002 Proof	—	Value: 55.00				

X# 18 500 SIKA
24.9300 g., 0.9000 Silver 0.7213 oz. ASW, 38.6 mm.
Subject: Ancient Navigators **Obv:** National arms below Queen Elizabeth's head right **Rev:** Ancient Phoenician ship **Edge:** Reeded

Date	Mintage	F	VF	XF	Unc	BU
2002 Proof	—	Value: 55.00				

X# 21 500 SIKA
31.1000 g., 0.9990 Silver 0.9988 oz. ASW, 40 mm.
Subject: Olympics **Obv:** National arms **Rev:** Ancient athlete raised design **Edge:** Plain **Note:** Design fits into the 10 francs KM-91 coin design of the Democratic Republic of the Congo

Date	Mintage	F	VF	XF	Unc	BU
2002 Antiqued finish	—	—	—	—	45.00	—

X# 29 500 SIKA
15.2200 g., 0.9000 Silver 0.4404 oz. ASW, 34 mm.
Obv: Queen Elizabeth II above small national arms
Rev: Bull elephant **Edge:** Reeded

Date	Mintage	F	VF	XF	Unc	BU
2002 Proof	—	Value: 25.00				

X# 32 500 SIKA
25.0000 g., 0.9250 Silver 0.7435 oz. ASW, 38.6 mm.
Subject: 50th Anniversary of Elizabeth II's Coronation
Obv: Queen Elizabeth II above Ghana's national arms
Rev: Young Elizabeth II below small crown **Edge:** Reeded

Date	Mintage	F	VF	XF	Unc	BU
ND(2003) Proof	5,000	Value: 45.00				

X# 34 500 SIKA
25.0000 g., 0.9250 Silver 0.7435 oz. ASW, 38.6 mm.
Obv: Queen Elizabeth II above Ghana's national arms
Rev: Prince William working a computer mouse
Edge: Reeded

Date	Mintage	F	VF	XF	Unc	BU
2003 Proof	5,000	Value: 45.00				

X# 36 500 SIKA
25.0000 g., 0.9250 Silver 0.7435 oz. ASW, 38.6 mm.
Obv: Queen Elizabeth II above Ghana's national arms
Rev: Queen Mother **Edge:** Reeded

Date	Mintage	F	VF	XF	Unc	BU
ND(2003) Proof	5,000	Value: 45.00				

X# 28 500 SIKA
26.1000 g., 0.9250 Silver 0.7762 oz. ASW, 40 mm.
Obv: National arms **Rev:** Leatherback sea turtle
Edge: Reeded

Date	Mintage	F	VF	XF	Unc	BU
2003 Proof	5,000	Value: 37.50				

BRITISH COLONY

MEDALLIC / INA RETRO ISSUE

X# M6 10 REALES
Silver, 40.98 mm. **Obv:** Laureate bust right
Obv. Legend: GEORGIUS III DEI GRATIA REX.
Rev: Hibernia seated left with shield, key below
Rev. Legend: GIBRALTAR **Edge:** Plain

Date	Mintage	F	VF	XF	Unc	BU
1808 (2007) Proof	—	—	—	—	—	—
1808 (2007) Matte Proof	—	—	—	—	—	—

X# M6a 10 REALES
Copper, 40.98 mm. **Obv:** Laureate bust right
Obv. Legend: GEORGIUS III DEI GRATIA REX.
Rev: Hibernia seated left with shield, key below
Rev. Legend: GIBRALTAR **Edge:** Plain

Date	Mintage	F	VF	XF	Unc	BU
1808 (2007) Proof	500	—	—	—	—	—

X# M6b 10 REALES
Aluminum, 40.98 mm. **Obv:** Laureate bust right
Obv. Legend: GEORGIUS III DEI GRATIA REX.
Rev: Hibernia seated left with shield, key below
Rev. Legend: GIBRALTAR **Edge:** Plain

Date	Mintage	F	VF	XF	Unc	BU
1808 (2007) Proof	500	—	—	—	—	—

X# M6c 10 REALES
Pewter, 40.98 mm. **Obv:** Laureate bust right
Obv. Legend: GEORGIUS III DEI GRATIA REX.
Rev: Hibernia seated left with shield, key below
Rev. Legend: GIBRALTAR **Edge:** Plain

Date	Mintage	F	VF	XF	Unc	BU
1808 (2007) Proof	500	—	—	—	—	—

X# M6d 10 REALES
Copper Bronzed, 40.98 mm. **Obv:** Laureate bust right
Obv. Legend: GEORGIUS III DEI GRATIA REX.
Rev: Hibernia seated left with shield, key below
Rev. Legend: GIBRALTAR **Edge:** Plain

Date	Mintage	F	VF	XF	Unc	BU
1808 (2007) Proof	500	—	—	—	—	—

X# M6e 10 REALES
Nickel-Silver, 40.98 mm. **Obv:** Laureate bust right
Obv. Legend: GEORGIUS III DEI GRATIA REX.
Rev: Hibernia seated left with shield, key below
Rev. Legend: GIBRALTAR **Edge:** Plain

Date	Mintage	F	VF	XF	Unc	BU
1808 (2007) Proof	500	—	—	—	—	—

X# M6f 10 REALES
Goldine, 40.98 mm. **Obv:** Laureate bust right
Obv. Legend: GEORGIUS III DEI GRATIA REX.
Rev: Hibernia seated left with shield, key below
Rev. Legend: GIBRALTAR **Edge:** Plain

Date	Mintage	F	VF	XF	Unc	BU
1808 (2007) Proof	500	—	—	—	—	—

X# M6g 10 REALES
Gold, 40.98 mm. **Obv:** Laureate bust right
Obv. Legend: GEORGIUS III DEI GRATIA REX.
Rev: Hibernia seated left with shield, key below
Rev. Legend: GIBRALTAR **Edge:** Plain

Date	Mintage	F	VF	XF	Unc	BU
1808 (2007) Proof	—	—	—	—	—	—

MEDALLIC COINAGE

Richard Lobel Series

X# M1 CROWN
Bronze, 38.17 mm. **Subject:** Edward VIII **Obv:** Bust left **Obv. Legend:** EDWARD • VIII • KING • & • EMPEROR **Rev:** Castle, lion left with key **Edge:** Plain

Date	Mintage	F	VF	XF	Unc	BU
1936 Proof	1,000	Value: 15.00				

X# M1a CROWN
Copper-Nickel-Zinc, 38.17 mm. **Subject:** Edward VIII **Obv:** Bust left **Obv. Legend:** EDWARD • VIII • KING • & • EMPEROR **Rev:** Castle, lion left with key **Edge:** Plain

Date	Mintage	F	VF	XF	Unc	BU
1936 Proof	2,000	Value: 15.00				

X# M1b CROWN
0.9167 Silver, 38.17 mm. **Subject:** Edward VIII **Obv:** Bust left **Obv. Legend:** EDWARD • VIII • KING • & • EMPEROR **Rev:** Castle, lion left with key **Edge:** Plain

Date	Mintage	F	VF	XF	Unc	BU
1936 Proof	200	Value: 50.00				

X# M1c CROWN
Gold, 38.17 mm. **Subject:** Edward VIII **Obv:** Bust left **Obv. Legend:** EDWARD • VIII • KING • & • EMPEROR **Rev:** Castle, lion left with key **Edge:** Plain

Date	Mintage	F	VF	XF	Unc	BU
1936 Proof	—	Value: 500				

X# M2 SOVEREIGN
0.3750 Gold, 21.98 mm. **Subject:** Edward VIII **Obv:** Bust left **Obv. Legend:** EDWARD • VIII • KING • & • EMPEROR **Rev:** Castle, lion left with key **Edge:** Plain

Date	Mintage	F	VF	XF	Unc	BU
1936 Proof	200	Value: 125				

X# M2a SOVEREIGN
4.4200 g., Silver, 21.98 mm. **Subject:** Edward VIII **Obv:** Bust left **Obv. Legend:** EDWARD • VIII • KING • & • EMPEROR **Rev:** Castle, lion left with key **Edge:** Plain

Date	Mintage	F	VF	XF	Unc	BU
1936 Proof	—	Value: 10.00				

FANTASY EURO PATTERNS

X# Pn1 EURO CENT
Copper Plated Steel, 16.8 mm. **Obv:** Anchor leaning on cargo **Rev:** Rayed head facing **Edge:** Plain

Date	Mintage	F	VF	XF	Unc	BU
2004	10,000	—	—	—	—	1.50
2004 Proof	5,000	Value: 2.50				

X# Pn1a EURO CENT
Silver, 16.8 mm. **Obv:** Anchor leaning on cargo **Rev:** Rayed head facing **Edge:** Plain

Date	Mintage	F	VF	XF	Unc	BU
2004 Proof	300	Value: 6.00				

X# Pn2 2 EURO CENT
Copper Plated Steel, 18.5 mm. **Obv:** Anchor leaning on cargo **Rev:** Rayed head facing **Edge:** Plain

Date	Mintage	F	VF	XF	Unc	BU
2004	10,000	—	—	—	—	2.00
2004 Proof	5,000	Value: 3.00				

X# Pn2a 2 EURO CENT
Silver, 18.5 mm. **Obv:** Anchor leaning on cargo **Rev:** Rayed head facing **Edge:** Plain

Date	Mintage	F	VF	XF	Unc	BU
2004 Proof	300	Value: 7.00				

X# Pn3 5 EURO CENT
Copper Plated Steel, 20.7 mm. **Obv:** Anchor leaning on cargo **Rev:** Rayed head facing

Date	Mintage	F	VF	XF	Unc	BU
2004	10,000	—	—	—	—	2.50
2004 Proof	5,000	Value: 3.50				

X# Pn3a 5 EURO CENT
Silver, 20.7 mm. **Obv:** Anchor leaning on cargo **Rev:** Rayed head facing **Edge:** Plain

Date	Mintage	F	VF	XF	Unc	BU
2004 Proof	300	Value: 8.50				

X# Pn4 10 EURO CENT
Goldine, 19.3 mm. **Obv:** Medieval sailing ship **Rev:** Crowned lion upright with sword and shield at left **Edge:** Plain

Date	Mintage	F	VF	XF	Unc	BU
2004	10,000	—	—	—	—	3.00
2004 Proof	5,000	Value: 4.00				

X# Pn4a 10 EURO CENT
Silver, 19.3 mm. **Obv:** Medieval sailing ship **Rev:** Crowned lion upright with sword and shield at left **Edge:** Plain

Date	Mintage	F	VF	XF	Unc	BU
2004 Proof	300	Value: 10.00				

X# Pn5 20 EURO CENT
Goldine, 22 mm. **Obv:** Medieval sailing ship **Rev:** Crowned lion upright with sword and shield at left **Edge:** Plain

Date	Mintage	F	VF	XF	Unc	BU
2004	10,000	—	—	—	—	3.50
2004 Proof	5,000	Value: 5.00				

X# Pn5a 20 EURO CENT
Silver, 22 mm. **Obv:** Medieval sailing ship **Rev:** Crowned lion upright with sword and shield at left **Edge:** Plain

Date	Mintage	F	VF	XF	Unc	BU
2004 Proof	300	Value: 12.50				

X# Pn6 50 EURO CENT
Goldine, 24.3 mm. **Obv:** Medieval sailing ship **Rev:** Crowned lion upright with sword and shield at left **Edge:** Plain

Date	Mintage	F	VF	XF	Unc	BU
2004	10,000	—	—	—	—	4.00
2004 Proof	5,000	Value: 6.00				

X# Pn6a 50 EURO CENT
Silver, 24.3 mm. **Obv:** Medieval sailing ship **Rev:** Crowned lion upright with sword and shield at left **Edge:** Plain

Date	Mintage	F	VF	XF	Unc	BU
2004 Proof	300	Value: 15.00				

X# Pn7 EURO
Bi-Metallic Nickel center in Goldine ring, 22.8 mm. **Obv:** Spanish Colonial arms - "PLVS VLTRA" **Rev:** Woman standing behind seated man facing right - at right **Edge:** Plain

Date	Mintage	F	VF	XF	Unc	BU
2004	10,000	—	—	—	—	6.00
2004 Proof	5,000	Value: 7.50				

X# Pn7a EURO
Bi-Metallic Brass/Silver, 22.8 mm. **Obv:** Spanish Colonial arms - "PLVS VLTA" **Rev:** Woman standing behind seated man facing right - at right **Edge:** Plain

Date	Mintage	F	VF	XF	Unc	BU
2004 Proof	300	Value: 22.50				

X# Pn8 2 EURO
Bi-Metallic Goldine center in Nickel ring, 25.7 mm. **Obv:** Spanish Colonial arms - "PLVS VLTRA" **Rev:** Woman standing behind seated man facing right - at right **Edge:** Plain

Date	Mintage	F	VF	XF	Unc	BU
2004	10,000	—	—	—	—	8.00
2004 Proof	5,000	Value: 10.00				

X# Pn8a 2 EURO
Bi-Metallic Silver/Brass, 25.7 mm. **Obv:** Spanish Colonial arms - "PLVS VLTRA" **Rev:** Woman standing behind seated man facing right - at right **Edge:** Plain

Date	Mintage	F	VF	XF	Unc	BU
2004 Proof	300	Value: 28.50				

X# Pn9 5 EURO
Goldine, 36 mm. **Obv:** Spanish Colonial arms - "PLVS VLTRA" **Rev:** Justice seated facing right - at right **Edge:** Plain

Date	Mintage	F	VF	XF	Unc	BU
2004 Proof	5,000	Value: 12.50				

X# Pn9a 5 EURO
Silver, 36 mm. **Obv:** Spanish Colonial arms - "PLVS VLTRA" **Rev:** Justice seated facing right - at right **Edge:** Plain

Date	Mintage	F	VF	XF	Unc	BU
2004 Proof	300	Value: 40.00				

PIEFORTS

X#	Date	Mintage	Identification	Mkt Val
P1	2004	300	5 Euro. Silver. X#Pn9a.	65.00
P2	1936	—	Crown. 0.9167 Silver. X#M1b.	100

MINT SETS

X#	Date	Mintage	Identification	Issue Price	Mkt Val
XMS1	2004 (8)	10,000	X#Pn1-Pn8	—	30.00

PROOF SETS

X#	Date	Mintage	Identification	Issue Price	Mkt Val
XPS1	2004 (9)	5,000	X#Pn1-Pn9	—	50.00
XPS2	2004 (9)	300	X#Pn1a-Pn9a	—	150

GOLD COAST

BRITISH OUTPOST

MEDALLIC COINAGE - RICHARD LOBEL SERIES

X# 1 CROWN
Bronze **Subject:** Edward VIII **Obv:** Bust left **Obv. Legend:** EDWARD • VIII • KING • & • EMPEROR **Rev:** Supported arms **Edge:** Plain **Note:** Prev. X#1.

Date	Mintage	F	VF	XF	Unc	BU
1936 Proof	450	Value: 20.00				

X# 1a CROWN
Copper-Nickel-Zinc **Subject:** Edward VIII **Obv:** Bust left **Obv. Legend:** EDWARD • VIII • KING • & • EMPEROR **Rev:** Supported arms **Edge:** Plain

Date	Mintage	F	VF	XF	Unc	BU
1936 Proof	1,500	Value: 15.00				

X# 1b CROWN
0.9167 Silver **Subject:** Edward VIII **Obv:** Bust left **Obv. Legend:** EDWARD • VIII • KING • & • EMPEROR **Rev:** Supported arms **Edge:** Plain

Date	Mintage	F	VF	XF	Unc	BU
1936 Proof	150	Value: 50.00				

X# 1c CROWN
Gold **Subject:** Edward VIII **Obv:** Bust left **Obv. Legend:** EDWARD • VIII • KING • & • EMPEROR **Rev:** Supported arms **Edge:** Plain

Date	Mintage	F	VF	XF	Unc	BU
1936 Proof	—	Value: 500				

X# 2a SOVEREIGN
4.4200 g., Silver, 21.98 mm. **Subject:** Edward VIII **Obv:** Bust left **Obv. Legend:** EDWARD • VIII • KING • & • EMPEROR **Rev:** Supported arms **Rev. Legend:** GOLD COAST **Edge:** Plain

Date	Mintage	F	VF	XF	Unc	BU
1936 Proof	—	Value: 10.00				

X# 2 SOVEREIGN
0.3750 Gold, 21.98 mm. **Subject:** Edward VIII **Obv:** Bust left **Obv. Legend:** EDWARD • VIII • KING • & • EMPEROR **Rev:** Supported arms **Edge:** Reeded **Edge Lettering:** Plain **Note:** Prev. X#2.

Date	Mintage	F	VF	XF	Unc	BU
1936 Proof	—	Value: 125				

X# 3 SOVEREIGN
Gold, 21.98 mm. **Obv:** Head of Duchess, bust of Duke facing **Obv. Legend:** DUKE & DUCHESS OF WINDSOR **Rev:** Supported arms **Edge:** Reeded

Date	Mintage	F	VF	XF	Unc	BU
1987 Proof	—	Value: 125				

X# 3a SOVEREIGN
4.4200 g., Silver, 21.98 mm. **Obv:** Head of Duchess, bust of Duke facing **Obv. Legend:** DUKE & DUCHESS OF WINDSOR **Rev:** Supported arms **Edge:** Reeded

Date	Mintage	F	VF	XF	Unc	BU
1987 Proof	—	Value: 10.00				

PIEFORTS

X#	Date	Mintage	Identification	Mkt Val
P1	1936	—	Crown. 0.9167 Silver. X#1b.	100

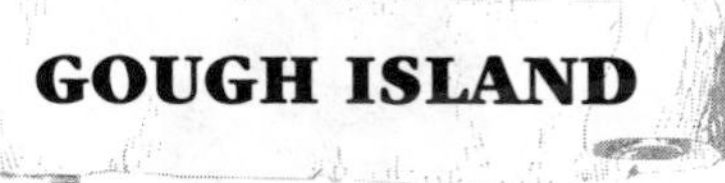

GOUGH ISLAND

BRITISH DEPENDENCY

COLLECTOR COINAGE

Milled

X# 1.1 CROWN
28.2800 g., Copper-Nickel, 39 mm. **Obv:** Elizabeth II **Rev:** Two doves above world with rising sun background **Edge:** Reeded

Date	Mintage	F	VF	XF	Unc	BU
2005	—	—	—	—	12.00	—

X# 1.2 CROWN
28.2800 g., 0.9000 Silver 0.8183 oz. ASW, 39 mm. **Obv:** Elizabeth II **Rev:** Two doves above world with rising sun background **Edge:** Reeded

Date	Mintage	F	VF	XF	Unc	BU
2005	—	—	—	—	32.50	—

X# 1 CROWN
Copper-Nickel **Ruler:** Elizabeth II **Subject:** 60th Anniversary - Victory in World War II **Obv:** Bust right **Rev:** Rising sun between 2 doves in flight above upper globe **Rev. Legend:** 1945 - VICTORY - 2005

Date	Mintage	VG	F	VF	XF	Unc
2005	—	—	—	—	—	10.00

X# 1a CROWN
Silver **Ruler:** Elizabeth II **Subject:** 60th Anniversary - Victory in World War II **Obv:** Bust right **Rev:** Rising sun between two doves in flight above upper globe **Rev. Legend:** 1945 - VICTORY - 2005

Date	Mintage	VG	F	VF	XF	Unc
2005	—	—	—	—	—	35.00

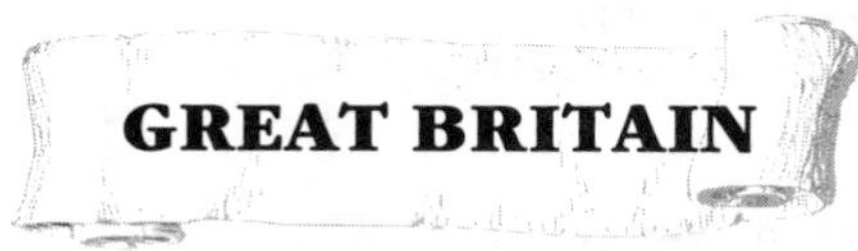

GREAT BRITAIN

WIZARD REALM

WIZARD COINAGE

X# 125 KNUT
7.0000 g., Copper, 25 mm. **Obv:** Druid bust left **Obv. Inscription:** GRINGOTTS BANK **Rev:** Goat left **Rev. Legend:** UNUM KNUT

Date	Mintage	F	VF	XF	Unc	BU
ND	—	—	—	—	7.50	—

X# 126 SICKLE
11.3000 g., Nickel Alloy, 32 mm. **Obv:** Druid bust left **Obv. Legend:** GRINGOTTS BANK **Rev:** Dragon in flight right **Rev. Legend:** UNUM SICKLE

Date	Mintage	F	VF	XF	Unc	BU
ND	—	—	—	—	—	12.50

X# 127 GALLEON
28.2800 g., Gold Plated, 38.6 mm. **Obv:** Druid bust left **Obv. Legend:** GRINGOTTS BANK **Rev:** Dragon in flight **Rev. Legend:** UNUM GALEON

Date	Mintage	F	VF	XF	Unc	BU
ND	—	—	—	—	—	20.00

KINGDOM

Resumed

TRADE COINAGE

Britannia Issues

Issued to facilitate British trade in the Orient, the reverse design incorporated the denomination in Chinese characters and Malay script.

This issue was struck at the Bombay (B) and Calcutta (C) Mints in India, except for 1925 and 1930 issues which were struck at London. Through error the mint marks did not appear on some early (1895-1900) issues as indicated.

X# TC1 DOLLAR
Silver **Obv. Legend:** FOR JEWELRY

Date	Mintage	F	VF	XF	Unc	BU
1908	—	—	8.50	13.50	22.00	—

FANTASY COINAGE

Prince of Wales

Other 'MODEL' series such as this one exist, but are considered game counters and of little commercial value. Many exist with the name of LAUER, a German medal and token manufacturer.

X# 30 1/2 SOVEREIGN
Bronze, 19.5 mm. **Ruler:** Victoria **Obv:** Bust left **Obv. Legend:** VICTORIA QUEEN OF GREAT BRITAIN **Rev:** Crowned equestrian left in garter **Rev. Legend:** THE PRINCE OF WALES MODEL SOVE

Date	Mintage	VG	F	VF	XF	Unc
1849	—	1.50	3.50	6.00	10.00	—

X# 31 1/2 SOVEREIGN
Bronze, 19.5 mm. **Ruler:** Victoria **Obv:** Bust left **Obv. Legend:** VICTORIA QUEEN OF GREAT BRITAIN **Rev:** Crowned plumes in garter **Rev. Legend:** THE PRINCE OF WALES MODEL SOVE

Date	Mintage	VG	F	VF	XF	Unc
ND(1849)	—	1.50	3.50	6.00	10.00	—

Joseph Moore

Struck by Allen & Moore of Birmingham. Brilliant uncirculated examples command a premium of 50-60%

X# 1 1/32 FARTHING
Copper **Obv:** Youthful portrait of Victoria

Date	Mintage	F	VF	XF	Unc	BU
1848	—	2.00	4.00	10.00	25.00	—

X# 2 1/16 FARTHING
Copper **Obv:** Youthful portrait of Victoria

Date	Mintage	F	VF	XF	Unc	BU
1848	—	2.00	4.00	10.00	25.00	—

X# 3 1/8 FARTHING
Copper **Obv:** Youthful portrait of Victoria

Date	Mintage	F	VF	XF	Unc	BU
1848	—	2.00	4.00	10.00	25.00	—

X# 4 1/4 FARTHING
Copper **Obv:** Youthful portrait of Victoria **Note:** X1-X4 were sold as a set in a case.

Date	Mintage	F	VF	XF	Unc	BU
1848	—	2.00	4.00	10.00	25.00	—

X# 5 1/2 FARTHING
Copper

Date	Mintage	F	VF	XF	Unc	BU
1848	—	1.50	2.50	7.00	20.00	—

X# 6 MILLE
Copper

Date	Mintage	F	VF	XF	Unc	BU
1854	—	2.00	4.00	10.00	25.00	—

X# 7 1/2 PENNY
Silver **Obv:** V-R

Date	Mintage	F	VF	XF	Unc	BU
ND(1844)	—	60.00	100	150	275	—

X# 7a 1/2 PENNY
Copper Plated White Metal **Obv:** V-R

Date	Mintage	F	VF	XF	Unc	BU
ND(1844)	—	8.00	15.00	30.00	75.00	—

X# 8 1/2 PENNY
Copper **Obv:** V-R

Date	Mintage	F	VF	XF	Unc	BU
ND(1844)	—	8.00	15.00	30.00	75.00	—

X# 8a 1/2 PENNY
Copper And Brass **Obv:** V-R

Date	Mintage	F	VF	XF	Unc	BU
ND(1844)	—	8.00	15.00	30.00	75.00	—

X# 8b 1/2 PENNY
Copper Plated White Metal **Obv:** V-R

Date	Mintage	F	VF	XF	Unc	BU
ND(1844)	—	8.00	15.00	30.00	75.00	—

X# 21 1/2 PENNY
Copper

Date	Mintage	F	VF	XF	Unc	BU
1848	—	2.00	4.00	10.00	30.00	—

X# 9 PENNY
Silver

Date	Mintage	F	VF	XF	Unc	BU
ND(1844)	—	60.00	100	170	250	400

X# 9a PENNY
Copper

Date	Mintage	F	VF	XF	Unc	BU
ND(1844)	—	6.00	10.00	20.00	45.00	85.00

X# 9b PENNY
Copper And Brass

Date	Mintage	F	VF	XF	Unc	BU
ND(1844)	—	6.00	10.00	20.00	45.00	85.00

X# 9c PENNY
Copper Plated White Metal

Date	Mintage	F	VF	XF	Unc	BU
ND(1844)	—	6.00	10.00	20.00	45.00	85.00

X# 10 PENNY
Copper Plated White Metal **Obv. Legend:** ONE PENNEY (error)

Date	Mintage	F	VF	XF	Unc	BU
ND(1844)	—	—	—	—	—	—

X# 11 PENNY
Brass

Date	Mintage	F	VF	XF	Unc	BU
1844	—	6.00	10.00	20.00	45.00	75.00

X# 11a PENNY
Copper Plated White Metal

Date	Mintage	F	VF	XF	Unc	BU
1844	—	6.00	10.00	20.00	45.00	75.00

X# 22 PENNY
Copper

Date	Mintage	F	VF	XF	Unc	BU
1848	—	2.00	4.00	10.00	30.00	—

X# 28 FLORIN
Silver Plated Brass

Date	Mintage	F	VF	XF	Unc	BU
1849	—	—	—	150	300	450

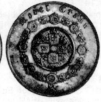

X# 23 CROWN
Copper Silvered and Gilt **Obv:** Without legend

Date	Mintage	F	VF	XF	Unc	BU
1848	—	—	30.00	60.00	125	200

X# 24 CROWN
Copper Silvered and Gilt **Obv. Legend:** VICTORIA QUEEN OF GREAT BRITAIN

Date	Mintage	F	VF	XF	Unc	BU
1848	—	6.00	12.00	20.00	45.00	—

X# 25 CROWN
Copper Silvered and Gilt **Obv. Legend:** VICTORIA REGINA

Date	Mintage	F	VF	XF	Unc	BU
ND(1848)	—	50.00	75.00	150	250	350

PATTERNS

Including off metal strikes

X# Pn147 POUND
9.5000 g., 0.9250 Silver 0.2825 oz. ASW, 22.5 mm. **Ruler:** Elizabeth II **Obv:** Queen Elizabeth II **Rev:** Forth Railway Bridge **Edge:** Plain

Date	Mintage	F	VF	XF	Unc	BU
2003 Proof	7,500	Value: 45.00				

X# Pn148 POUND
19.6190 g., 0.9166 Gold 0.5781 oz. AGW, 22.5 mm. **Ruler:** Elizabeth II **Obv:** Queen Elizabeth II **Rev:** Forth Railway Bridge **Edge:** Plain

Date	Mintage	F	VF	XF	Unc	BU
2003 Proof	3,000	Value: 450				

X# Pn149 POUND
9.5000 g., 0.9250 Silver 0.2825 oz. ASW, 22.5 mm. **Ruler:** Elizabeth II **Obv:** Queen Elizabeth II **Rev:** Menai Straits Bridge **Edge:** Plain

Date	Mintage	F	VF	XF	Unc	BU
2003 Proof	7,500	Value: 45.00				

X# Pn150 POUND
19.6190 g., 0.9166 Gold 0.5781 oz. AGW, 22.5 mm. **Ruler:** Elizabeth II **Obv:** Queen Elizabeth II **Rev:** Menai Straits Bridge **Edge:** Plain

Date	Mintage	F	VF	XF	Unc	BU
2003 Proof	3,000	Value: 450				

X# Pn151 POUND
9.5000 g., 0.9250 Silver 0.2825 oz. ASW, 22.5 mm.
Ruler: Elizabeth II **Obv:** Queen Elizabeth II
Rev: Egyptian Arch Bridge **Edge:** Plain

Date	Mintage	F	VF	XF	Unc	BU
2003 Proof	7,500	Value: 45.00				

X# Pn152 POUND
19.6190 g., 0.9166 Gold 0.5781 oz. AGW, 22.5 mm.
Ruler: Elizabeth II **Obv:** Queen Elizabeth II
Rev: Egyptian Arch Bridge **Edge:** Plain

Date	Mintage	F	VF	XF	Unc	BU
2003 Proof	3,000	Value: 450				

X# Pn153 POUND
9.5000 g., 0.9250 Silver 0.2825 oz. ASW, 22.5 mm.
Ruler: Elizabeth II **Obv:** Queen Elizabeth II
Rev: Millennium Bridge **Edge:** Plain

Date	Mintage	F	VF	XF	Unc	BU
2003 Proof	7,500	Value: 45.00				

X# Pn154 POUND
19.6190 g., 0.9166 Gold 0.5781 oz. AGW, 22.5 mm.
Ruler: Elizabeth II **Obv:** Queen Elizabeth II
Rev: Millennium Bridge **Edge:** Plain

Date	Mintage	F	VF	XF	Unc	BU
2003 Proof	3,000	Value: 450				

X# Pn155 POUND
9.5000 g., 0.9250 Silver 0.2825 oz. ASW, 22.5 mm.
Ruler: Elizabeth II **Obv:** Queen Elizabeth II
Rev: English Lion **Edge:** Plain

Date	Mintage	F	VF	XF	Unc	BU
2004 Proof	5,000	Value: 38.00				

X# Pn156 POUND
19.6190 g., 0.9166 Gold 0.5781 oz. AGW, 22.5 mm.
Ruler: Elizabeth II **Obv:** Queen Elizabeth II
Rev: English Lion **Edge:** Plain

Date	Mintage	F	VF	XF	Unc	BU
2004 Proof	2,250	Value: 450				

X# Pn157 POUND
9.5000 g., 0.9250 Silver 0.2825 oz. ASW, 22.5 mm.
Ruler: Elizabeth II **Obv:** Queen Elizabeth II **Rev:** Welsh Dragon **Edge:** Plain

Date	Mintage	F	VF	XF	Unc	BU
2004 Proof	2,250	Value: 38.00				

X# Pn158 POUND
19.6190 g., 0.9166 Gold 0.5781 oz. AGW, 22.5 mm.
Ruler: Elizabeth II **Obv:** Queen Elizabeth II **Rev:** Welsh Dragon **Edge:** Plain

Date	Mintage	F	VF	XF	Unc	BU
2004 Proof	2,250	Value: 450				

X# Pn159 POUND
9.5000 g., 0.9250 Silver 0.2825 oz. ASW, 22.5 mm.
Ruler: Elizabeth II **Obv:** Queen Elizabeth II
Rev: Northern Irish Hart **Edge:** Plain

Date	Mintage	F	VF	XF	Unc	BU
2004 Proof	5,000	Value: 38.00				

X# Pn160 POUND
19.6190 g., 0.9166 Gold 0.5781 oz. AGW, 22.5 mm.
Ruler: Elizabeth II **Obv:** Queen Elizabeth II
Rev: Northern Irish Hart **Edge:** Plain

Date	Mintage	F	VF	XF	Unc	BU
2004 Proof	2,250	Value: 450				

X# Pn161 POUND
9.5000 g., 0.9250 Silver 0.2825 oz. ASW, 22.5 mm.
Ruler: Elizabeth II **Obv:** Queen Elizabeth II
Rev: Scottish Unicorn **Edge:** Plain

Date	Mintage	F	VF	XF	Unc	BU
2004 Proof	5,000	Value: 38.00				

X# Pn162 POUND
19.6190 g., 0.9166 Gold 0.5781 oz. AGW, 22.5 mm.
Ruler: Elizabeth II **Obv:** Queen Elizabeth II
Rev: Scottish Unicorn **Edge:** Plain

Date	Mintage	F	VF	XF	Unc	BU
2004 Proof	2,250	Value: 450				

FANTASY PATTERNS

X# Pn3 TESTOON
Silver **Issuer:** Emery **Subject:** Lady Jane Grey **Obv:** Crowned bust 3/4 left **Obv. Legend:** IOAN:D G: ANG: FR: ET: HIB: REGINA **Rev:** Crowned rose divides crowned I - crowned R

Date	Mintage	F	VF	XF	Unc	BU
MDLIII (1553)	—	—	—	500	700	—

TOKEN COINAGE

X# Tn11 GUINEA
Brass, 26 mm. **Ruler:** George III **Obv:** Laureate bust right **Obv. Legend:** GEORGIVS III DEI GRATIA
Rev: Crowned "spade" shaped arms **Rev. Legend:** IN MEMORY OF THE GOOD OLD DAYS

Date	Mintage	VG	F	VF	XF	Unc
1797	—	0.75	1.75	3.00	5.00	10.00

MEDALLIC COINAGE

Sterling Issues

X# 34 FARTHING
Copper **Ruler:** Victoria **Edge:** Milled **Note:** Prev. KM#PPn40.

Date	Mintage	F	VF	XF	Unc	BU
1860 Proof	—	Value: 375				

X# 34a FARTHING
Bronzed Copper **Ruler:** Victoria **Edge:** Milled **Note:** Prev. KM#PPn41.

Date	Mintage	F	VF	XF	Unc	BU
1860 Proof	—	Value: 375				

X# 34b FARTHING
Aluminum **Ruler:** Victoria **Edge:** Milled **Note:** Prev. KM#PPn42.

Date	Mintage	F	VF	XF	Unc	BU
1860 Proof	—	Value: 350				

X# 34c FARTHING
Silver **Ruler:** Victoria **Edge:** Milled **Note:** Prev. KM#PPn43.

Date	Mintage	F	VF	XF	Unc	BU
1860 Proof	—	Value: 550				

X# 34d FARTHING
Gold **Ruler:** Victoria **Obv:** Young head left **Edge:** Milled **Note:** Prev. KM#PPn44.

Date	Mintage	F	VF	XF	Unc	BU
1860 Proof	—	Value: 2,200				

X# 35 FARTHING
Copper **Ruler:** Victoria **Rev:** Four crowned shields form cross **Edge:** Plain **Note:** Prev. KM#PPn45.

Date	Mintage	F	VF	XF	Unc	BU
1860 Proof	—	Value: 375				

X# 35a FARTHING
Bronzed Copper **Ruler:** Victoria **Rev:** Four crowned shields form cross **Edge:** Plain **Note:** Prev. KM#PPn46.

Date	Mintage	F	VF	XF	Unc	BU
1860 Proof	—	Value: 375				

X# 35b FARTHING
Aluminum **Ruler:** Victoria **Rev:** Four crowned shields form cross **Edge:** Plain **Note:** Prev. KM#PPn47.

Date	Mintage	F	VF	XF	Unc	BU
1860 Proof	—	Value: 350				

X# 35c FARTHING
Silver **Ruler:** Victoria **Rev:** Four crowned shields form cross **Edge:** Plain **Note:** Prev. KM#PPn48.

Date	Mintage	F	VF	XF	Unc	BU
1860 Proof	—	Value: 650				

X# 35d FARTHING

Gold **Ruler:** Victoria **Rev:** Four crowned shields form cross **Edge:** Plain **Note:** Prev. KM#PPn49.

Date	Mintage	F	VF	XF	Unc	BU
1860 Proof	—	Value: 2,200				

X# 40 FARTHING

Copper **Ruler:** Victoria **Obv:** Crowned veiled bust left **Rev:** Four crowned shields form cross **Edge:** Milled **Note:** Prev. KM#PPn70.

Date	Mintage	F	VF	XF	Unc	BU
1887 Proof	—	Value: 375				

X# 40a FARTHING

Bronzed Copper **Ruler:** Victoria **Obv:** Crowned veiled bust left **Rev:** Four crowned shields form cross **Edge:** Milled **Note:** Prev. KM#PPn71.

Date	Mintage	F	VF	XF	Unc	BU
1887 Proof	—	Value: 375				

X# 40b FARTHING

Aluminum **Ruler:** Victoria **Obv:** Crowned veiled bust left **Rev:** Four crowned shields form cross **Edge:** Milled **Note:** Prev. KM#PPn72.

Date	Mintage	F	VF	XF	Unc	BU
1887 Proof	—	Value: 350				

X# 40c FARTHING

Silver **Ruler:** Victoria **Obv:** Crowned veiled bust left **Rev:** Four crowned shields form cross **Edge:** Milled **Note:** Prev. KM#PPn73.

Date	Mintage	F	VF	XF	Unc	BU
1887 Proof	—	Value: 650				

X# 40d FARTHING

Gold **Ruler:** Victoria **Obv:** Crowned veiled bust left **Rev:** Four crowned shields form cross **Edge:** Milled **Note:** Prev. KM#PPn74.

Date	Mintage	F	VF	XF	Unc	BU
1887 Proof	—	Value: 2,000				

X# 41 FARTHING

Copper **Ruler:** Victoria **Edge:** Plain **Note:** Prev. KM#PPn75.

Date	Mintage	F	VF	XF	Unc	BU
1887 Proof	—	Value: 375				

X# 41a FARTHING

Bronzed Copper **Ruler:** Victoria **Edge:** Plain **Note:** Prev. KM#PPn76.

Date	Mintage	F	VF	XF	Unc	BU
1887 Proof	—	Value: 375				

X# 41b FARTHING

Aluminum **Ruler:** Victoria **Edge:** Plain **Note:** Prev. KM#PPn77.

Date	Mintage	F	VF	XF	Unc	BU
1887 Proof	—	Value: 350				

X# 41c FARTHING

Silver **Ruler:** Victoria **Edge:** Plain **Note:** Prev. KM#PPn78.

Date	Mintage	F	VF	XF	Unc	BU
1887 Proof	—	Value: 650				

X# 41d FARTHING

Gold **Ruler:** Victoria **Edge:** Plain **Note:** Prev. KM#PPn79.

Date	Mintage	F	VF	XF	Unc	BU
1887 Proof	—	Value: 2,000				

X# 36 1/2 PENNY

Copper **Ruler:** Victoria **Obv:** Young head left **Rev:** Four crowned shields form cross **Edge:** Milled **Note:** Prev. KM#PPn50.

Date	Mintage	F	VF	XF	Unc	BU
1860 Proof	—	Value: 425				

X# 36a 1/2 PENNY

Bronzed Copper **Ruler:** Victoria **Obv:** Young head left **Rev:** Four crowned shields form cross **Edge:** Milled **Note:** Prev. KM#PPn51.

Date	Mintage	F	VF	XF	Unc	BU
1860 Proof	—	Value: 425				

X# 36c 1/2 PENNY

Silver **Ruler:** Victoria **Obv:** Young head left **Rev:** Four crowned shields form cross **Edge:** Milled **Note:** Prev. KM#PPn53.

Date	Mintage	F	VF	XF	Unc	BU
1860 Proof	—	Value: 650				

X# 36d 1/2 PENNY

Gold **Ruler:** Victoria **Obv:** Young head left **Rev:** Four crowned shields form cross **Edge:** Milled **Note:** Prev. KM#PPn54.

Date	Mintage	F	VF	XF	Unc	BU
1860 Proof	2,200	Value: 2,400				

X# 37 1/2 PENNY

Copper **Ruler:** Victoria **Edge:** Plain **Note:** Prev. KM#PPn55.

Date	Mintage	F	VF	XF	Unc	BU
1860 Proof	—	Value: 425				

X# 37a 1/2 PENNY

Bronzed Copper **Ruler:** Victoria **Edge:** Plain **Note:** Prev. KM#PPn56.

Date	Mintage	F	VF	XF	Unc	BU
1860 Proof	—	Value: 425				

X# 37b 1/2 PENNY

Aluminum **Ruler:** Victoria **Edge:** Plain **Note:** Prev. KM#PPn57.

Date	Mintage	F	VF	XF	Unc	BU
1860 Proof	—	Value: 350				

X# 37c 1/2 PENNY

Silver **Ruler:** Victoria **Edge:** Plain **Note:** Prev. KM#PPn58.

Date	Mintage	F	VF	XF	Unc	BU
1860 Proof	—	Value: 650				

X# 37d 1/2 PENNY

Gold **Ruler:** Victoria **Edge:** Plain **Note:** Prev. KM#PPn59.

Date	Mintage	F	VF	XF	Unc	BU
1860 Proof	—	Value: 2,400				

X# 36b 1/2 PENNY

Aluminum **Ruler:** Victoria **Obv:** Young head left **Rev:** Four crowned shields form cross **Edge:** Milled **Note:** Prev. KM#PPn52.

Date	Mintage	F	VF	XF	Unc	BU
1860 Proof	—	Value: 350				

X# 42 1/2 PENNY

Copper **Ruler:** Victoria **Obv:** Crowned bust left **Rev:** Four crowned shields form cross **Edge:** Milled **Note:** Prev. KM#PPn80.

Date	Mintage	F	VF	XF	Unc	BU
1887 Proof	—	Value: 425				

X# 42a 1/2 PENNY

Bronzed Copper **Ruler:** Victoria **Obv:** Crowned bust left **Rev:** Four crowned shields form cross **Edge:** Milled **Note:** Prev. KM#PPn81.

Date	Mintage	F	VF	XF	Unc	BU
1887 Proof	—	Value: 425				

X# 42b 1/2 PENNY

Aluminum **Ruler:** Victoria **Obv:** Crowned bust left **Rev:** Four crowned shields form cross **Edge:** Milled **Note:** Prev. KM#PPn82.

Date	Mintage	F	VF	XF	Unc	BU
1887 Proof	—	Value: 350				

X# 42c 1/2 PENNY

Silver **Ruler:** Victoria **Obv:** Crowned bust left **Rev:** Four crowned shields form cross **Edge:** Milled **Note:** Prev. KM#PPn83.

Date	Mintage	F	VF	XF	Unc	BU
1887 Proof	—	Value: 850				

X# 42d 1/2 PENNY

Gold **Ruler:** Victoria **Obv:** Crowned bust left **Rev:** Four crowned shields form cross **Edge:** Milled **Note:** Prev. KM#PPn84.

Date	Mintage	F	VF	XF	Unc	BU
1887 Proof	—	Value: 3,200				

X# 43 1/2 PENNY

Copper **Ruler:** Victoria **Edge:** Plain **Note:** Prev. KM#PPn85.

Date	Mintage	F	VF	XF	Unc	BU
1887 Proof	—	Value: 425				

X# 43a 1/2 PENNY

Bronzed Copper **Ruler:** Victoria **Edge:** Plain **Note:** Prev. KM#PPn86.

Date	Mintage	F	VF	XF	Unc	BU
1887 Proof	—	Value: 425				

X# 43b 1/2 PENNY

Aluminum **Ruler:** Victoria **Edge:** Plain **Note:** Prev. KM#PPn87.

Date	Mintage	F	VF	XF	Unc	BU
1887 Proof	—	Value: 350				

X# 43c 1/2 PENNY

Silver **Ruler:** Victoria **Edge:** Plain **Note:** Prev. KM#PPn88.

Date	Mintage	F	VF	XF	Unc	BU
1887 Proof	—	Value: 350				

X# 43d 1/2 PENNY

Gold **Ruler:** Victoria **Edge:** Plain **Note:** Prev. KM#PPn89.

Date	Mintage	F	VF	XF	Unc	BU
1887 Proof	—	Value: 3,200				

X# 38 PENNY

Copper **Ruler:** Victoria **Obv:** Young head left **Rev:** Four crowned shields form cross **Edge:** Milled **Note:** Prev. KM#PPn60.

Date	Mintage	F	VF	XF	Unc	BU
1860 Proof	—	Value: 475				

X# 38a PENNY

Bronzed Copper **Ruler:** Victoria **Obv:** Young head left **Rev:** Four crowned shields form cross **Edge:** Milled **Note:** Prev. KM#PPn61.

Date	Mintage	F	VF	XF	Unc	BU
1860 Proof	—	Value: 475				

X# 38b PENNY
Aluminum **Ruler:** Victoria **Obv:** Young head left **Rev:** Four crowned shields form cross **Edge:** Milled **Note:** Prev. KM#PPn62.

Date	Mintage	F	VF	XF	Unc	BU
1860 Proof	—	Value: 400				

X# 38c PENNY
Silver **Ruler:** Victoria **Obv:** Young head left **Rev:** Four crowned shields form cross **Edge:** Milled **Note:** Prev. KM#PPn63.

Date	Mintage	F	VF	XF	Unc	BU
1860 Proof	—	Value: 950				

X# 38d PENNY
Gold **Ruler:** Victoria **Obv:** Young head left **Rev:** Four crowned shields form cross **Edge:** Milled **Note:** Prev. KM#PPn64.

Date	Mintage	F	VF	XF	Unc	BU
1860 Proof	—	Value: 3,600				

X# 39 PENNY
Copper **Ruler:** Victoria **Edge:** Plain **Note:** Prev. KM#PPn39.

Date	Mintage	F	VF	XF	Unc	BU
1860 Proof	—	Value: 475				

X# 39a PENNY
Bronzed Copper **Ruler:** Victoria **Edge:** Plain **Note:** Prev. KM#PPn66.

Date	Mintage	F	VF	XF	Unc	BU
1860 Proof	—	Value: 475				

X# 39b PENNY
Aluminum **Ruler:** Victoria **Edge:** Plain **Note:** Prev. KM#PPn67.

Date	Mintage	F	VF	XF	Unc	BU
1860 Proof	—	Value: 400				

X# 39c PENNY
Silver **Ruler:** Victoria **Edge:** Plain **Note:** Prev. KM#PPn68.

Date	Mintage	F	VF	XF	Unc	BU
1860 Proof	—	Value: 950				

X# 39d PENNY
Gold **Ruler:** Victoria **Edge:** Plain **Note:** Prev. KM#PPn69.

Date	Mintage	F	VF	XF	Unc	BU
1860 Proof	—	Value: 3,600				

X# 44 PENNY
Copper **Ruler:** Victoria **Obv:** Crowned veiled bust left **Rev:** Four crowned shields form cross **Edge:** Milled **Note:** Prev. KM#PPn90.

Date	Mintage	F	VF	XF	Unc	BU
1887 Proof	—	Value: 475				

X# 44a PENNY
Bronzed Copper **Ruler:** Victoria **Obv:** Crowned veiled bust left **Rev:** Four crowned shields form cross **Edge:** Milled **Note:** Prev. KM#PPn91.

Date	Mintage	F	VF	XF	Unc	BU
1887 Proof	—	Value: 475				

X# 44b PENNY
Aluminum **Ruler:** Victoria **Obv:** Crowned veiled bust left **Rev:** Four crowned shields form cross **Edge:** Milled **Note:** Prev. KM#PPn92.

Date	Mintage	F	VF	XF	Unc	BU
1887 Proof	—	Value: 400				

X# 44c PENNY
Silver **Ruler:** Victoria **Obv:** Crowned veiled bust left **Rev:** Four crowned shields form cross **Edge:** Milled **Note:** Prev. KM#PPn93.

Date	Mintage	F	VF	XF	Unc	BU
1887 Proof	—	Value: 950				

X# 44d PENNY
Gold **Ruler:** Victoria **Obv:** Crowned veiled bust left **Rev:** Four crowned shields form cross **Edge:** Milled **Note:** Prev. KM#PPn94.

Date	Mintage	F	VF	XF	Unc	BU
1887 Proof	—	Value: 3,600				

X# 45 PENNY
Copper **Ruler:** Victoria **Edge:** Plain **Note:** Prev. KM#PPn95.

Date	Mintage	F	VF	XF	Unc	BU
1887 Proof	—	Value: 475				

X# 45a PENNY
Bronzed Copper **Ruler:** Victoria **Edge:** Plain **Note:** Prev. KM#PPn96.

Date	Mintage	F	VF	XF	Unc	BU
1887 Proof	—	Value: 475				

X# 45b PENNY
Aluminum **Ruler:** Victoria **Edge:** Plain **Note:** Prev. KM#PPn97.

Date	Mintage	F	VF	XF	Unc	BU
1887 Proof	—	Value: 400				

X# 45c PENNY
Silver **Ruler:** Victoria **Edge:** Plain **Note:** Prev. KM#PPn98.

Date	Mintage	F	VF	XF	Unc	BU
1887 Proof	—	Value: 950				

X# 45d PENNY
Gold **Ruler:** Victoria **Edge:** Plain **Note:** Prev. KM#PPn99.

Date	Mintage	F	VF	XF	Unc	BU
1887 Proof	—	Value: 3,600				

PRIVATE PATTERNS

Smith on Decimal Currency Issues

X# 46 CENT
Copper **Ruler:** Victoria **Obv:** Young bust left **Note:** Prev. KM#PPn27.

Date	Mintage	F	VF	XF	Unc	BU
1846 Proof	—	Value: 275				

X# 46a CENT
Bronzed Copper **Ruler:** Victoria **Obv:** Young bust left **Note:** Prev. KM#PPnA27.

Date	Mintage	F	VF	XF	Unc	BU
1846 Proof	—	Value: 250				

X# 47 CENTUM
Copper **Ruler:** Victoria **Obv:** Young bust left **Note:** Prev. KM#PPn28.

Date	Mintage	F	VF	XF	Unc	BU
1846 Proof	—	Value: 275				

X# 47a CENTUM
White Metal **Ruler:** Victoria **Obv:** Young bust left **Note:** Prev. KM#PPnA28.

Date	Mintage	F	VF	XF	Unc	BU
1846 Proof	—	Value: 250				

X# 48 2 CENTS
Copper **Ruler:** Victoria **Obv:** Young bust left **Note:** Prev. KM#PPn29.

Date	Mintage	F	VF	XF	Unc	BU
1846	—	—	—	—	—	—

X# 48a 2 CENTS
Bronzed Copper **Ruler:** Victoria **Obv:** Young bust left **Note:** Prev. KM#PPnA29.

Date	Mintage	F	VF	XF	Unc	BU
1846 Proof	—	Value: 250				

X# 48b 2 CENTS
White Metal **Ruler:** Victoria **Obv:** Young bust left **Note:** Prev. KM#PPn30.

Date	Mintage	F	VF	XF	Unc	BU
1846 Proof; Restrike	—	Value: 250				

X# 48c 2 CENTS
Silver **Ruler:** Victoria **Obv:** Young bust left **Note:** Prev. KM#PPn31.

Date	Mintage	F	VF	XF	Unc	BU
1846 Proof; Restrike	—	Value: 650				

X# 48d 2 CENTS
Gold **Ruler:** Victoria **Obv:** Young bust left **Note:** Prev. KM#PPn32.

Date	Mintage	F	VF	XF	Unc	BU
1846 Proof; Restrike	—	Value: 2,250				

X# 49 5 CENTS
Copper **Ruler:** Victoria **Obv:** Young bust left **Note:** Prev. KM#PPn33.

Date	Mintage	F	VF	XF	Unc	BU
1846 Proof	—	Value: 400				

X# 49a 5 CENTS
Bronzed Copper **Ruler:** Victoria **Obv:** Young bust left **Note:** Prev. KM#PPn34.

Date	Mintage	F	VF	XF	Unc	BU
1846 Proof	—	Value: 350				

X# 50 10 CENTS
Copper **Ruler:** Victoria **Obv:** Young bust left **Note:** Prev. KM#PPn35.

Date	Mintage	F	VF	XF	Unc	BU
1846 Proof	—	Value: 600				

X# 50a 10 CENTS
White Metal **Ruler:** Victoria **Obv:** Young bust left **Note:** Prev. KM#PPn36.

Date	Mintage	F	VF	XF	Unc	BU
1846 Proof; Restrike	—	Value: 600				

X# 50b 10 CENTS
Copper **Ruler:** Victoria **Obv:** Young bust left **Note:** Prev. KM#PPn37.

Date	Mintage	F	VF	XF	Unc	BU
1846 Proof; Restrike	—	Value: 450				

X# 50c 10 CENTS
Bronzed Copper **Ruler:** Victoria **Obv:** Young bust left **Note:** Prev. KM#PPn38.

Date	Mintage	F	VF	XF	Unc	BU
1846 Proof; Restrike	—	Value: 500				

X# 50d 10 CENTS
Silver **Ruler:** Victoria **Obv:** Young bust left **Note:** Prev. KM#PPn39.

Date	Mintage	F	VF	XF	Unc	BU
1846 Proof; Restrike	—	Value: 1,200				

Mills-Whiteaves Issues

X# 51 CROWN
Silver **Ruler:** George IV **Obv:** Large head left **Rev:** Supported helmed arms **Edge:** Plain **Note:** Without necktie.

Date	Mintage	F	VF	XF	Unc	BU
1820 Proof	—	Value: 8,500				

X# 51a CROWN
Gold **Ruler:** George IV **Obv:** Large head left **Rev:** Supported helmed arms **Edge:** Plain **Note:** Prev. KM#PPn14.

Date	Mintage	F	VF	XF	Unc	BU
1820 Proof	—	Value: 35,000				

X# 52 CROWN
Silver **Ruler:** George IV **Obv:** Large head with necktie left **Edge:** Plain **Note:** Prev. KM#PPn15.

Date	Mintage	F	VF	XF	Unc	BU
1820 Proof	—	Value: 8,500				

Bonomi-Thomas Issues

X# 53 CROWN
Silver **Ruler:** Victoria **Obv:** Young bust with tiara left **Obv. Legend:** VICTORIA REG DEL GRATIA **Rev:** Helmeted Minerva standing right with trident and shield releasing dove **Rev. Inscription:** BRITT / MINERVA - VICTRIX / FID DEF **Edge:** Plain **Note:** Prev. KM#PPn16.

Date	Mintage	F	VF	XF	Unc	BU
1837 Proof	150	Value: 2,500				

Note: Numbered T1-T150 on edge

X# 53a CROWN
Gold **Ruler:** Victoria **Obv:** Young bust with tiara left **Obv. Legend:** VICTORIA REG DEL GRATIA **Rev:** Helmeted Minerva standing right with trident and shield releasing Nike **Rev. Inscription:** BRITT / MINERVA - VICTRIX / FID DEF **Edge:** Plain **Note:** Prev. KM#PPn17.

Date	Mintage	F	VF	XF	Unc	BU
1837 Proof	6	Value: 8,500				

Note: Numbered T1-T6 on edge

X# 53b CROWN
Copper **Ruler:** Victoria **Obv:** Young bust with tiara left **Obv. Legend:** VICTORIA REG DEL GRATIA **Rev:** Helmeted Minerva standing right with trident and shield releasing Nike **Rev. Inscription:** BRITT / MINERVA - VICTRIX / FID DEF **Edge:** Plain **Note:** Prev. KM#PPnA18.

Date	Mintage	F	VF	XF	Unc	BU
1837 Proof	10	Value: 1,250				

Note: Numbered T1-T6 on edge

X# 53c CROWN
Bronze **Ruler:** Victoria **Obv:** Young bust with tiara left **Obv. Legend:** VICTORIA REG DEL GRATIA **Rev:** Helmeted Minerva standing right with trident and shild releasing Nike **Rev. Inscription:** BRITT / MINERVA - VICTRIX / FID DEF **Edge:** Plain **Note:** Prev. KM#PPn18.

Date	Mintage	F	VF	XF	Unc	BU
1837 Proof	10	Value: 1,250				

X# 53d CROWN
Tin **Ruler:** Victoria **Obv:** Young bust with tiara left **Obv. Legend:** VICTORIA REG DEL GRATIA **Rev:** Helmeted Minerva standing right with trident and shield releasing Nike **Rev. Inscription:** BRITT / MINERVA - VICTRIX / FID DEF **Edge:** Plain **Note:** Prev. KM#PPn19.

Date	Mintage	F	VF	XF	Unc	BU
1837 Proof	10	Value: 850				

X# 53e CROWN
Aluminum **Ruler:** Victoria **Obv:** Young bust with tiara left **Obv. Legend:** VICTORIA REG DEL GRATIA **Rev:** Helmeted Minerva standing right with trident and shield releasing Nike **Rev. Inscription:** BRITT / MINERVA - VICTRIX / FID DEF **Edge:** Plain **Note:** Prev. KM#PPn20.

Date	Mintage	F	VF	XF	Unc	BU
1837 Proof	10	Value: 850				

X# 53f CROWN
White Metal **Ruler:** Victoria **Obv:** Young bust with tiara left **Obv. Legend:** VICTORIA REG DEL GRATIA **Rev:** Helmeted Minerva standing right with trident and shield releasing Nike **Rev. Inscription:** BRITT / MINERVA - VICTRIX / FID DEF **Edge:** Plain **Note:** Prev. KM#PPn21.

Date	Mintage	F	VF	XF	Unc	BU
1837 Proof	—	Value: 850				

X# 53g CROWN
Lead **Ruler:** Victoria **Obv:** Young bust with tiara left **Obv. Legend:** VICTORIA REG DEL GRATIA **Rev:** Helmeted Minerva standing right with trident and shield releasing Nike **Rev. Inscription:** BRITT / MINERVA - VICTRIX / FID DEF **Edge:** Plain **Note:** Prev. KM#PPn22.

Date	Mintage	F	VF	XF	Unc	BU
1837 Proof	—	Value: 850				

X# 53h CROWN
Copper **Ruler:** Victoria **Obv:** Young bust with tiara left **Obv. Legend:** VICTORIA REG DEL GRATIA **Rev:** Helmeted Minerva standing right with trident and shield releasing Nike **Rev. Inscription:** BRITT / MINERVA - VICTRIX / FID DEF **Edge:** Reeded **Note:** Prev. KM#PPn23.

Date	Mintage	F	VF	XF	Unc	BU
1837 Proof	—	Value: 850				

X# 53i CROWN
White Metal **Ruler:** Victoria **Obv:** Young bust with tiara left **Obv. Legend:** VICTORIA REG DEL GRATIA **Rev:** Helmeted Minerva standing right with trident and shild releasing Nike **Rev. Inscription:** BRITT / MINERVA - VICTRIX / FID DEF **Edge:** Reeded **Note:** Prev. KM#PPn24.

Date	Mintage	F	VF	XF	Unc	BU
1837 Proof	—	Value: 850				

X# 53j CROWN
Lead **Ruler:** Victoria **Obv:** Young bust with tiara left **Obv. Legend:** VICTORIA REG DEL GRATIA **Rev:** Helmeted Minerva standing right with trident and shield releasing Nike **Rev. Inscription:** BRITT / MINERVA - VICTRIX / FID DEF **Edge:** Reeded **Note:** Prev. KM#PPn25.

Date	Mintage	F	VF	XF	Unc	BU
1837 Proof	—	Value: 850				

X# 54 CROWN
White Metal **Ruler:** Victoria **Obv:** Young bust with tiara left **Rev:** Royal arms **Note:** Prev. KM#PPn26.

Date	Mintage	F	VF	XF	Unc	BU
1837 Proof	—	Value: 850				

Spink & Sons Issues

X# 55 6 PENCE
Silver **Ruler:** Victoria **Obv:** Crowned veiled bust left **Rev:** Crowned supported arms **Edge:** Plain **Note:** Date in Roman numerals; MDCCCLXXXVII. Prev. KM#PPn100.

Date	Mintage	F	VF	XF	Unc	BU
1887 Proof	64	Value: 600				

X# 55a 6 PENCE
Gold **Ruler:** Victoria **Obv:** Crowned veiled bust left **Rev:** Crowned supported arms **Note:** Date in Roman numerals; MDCCCLXXXVII. Prev. KM#PPn101.

Date	Mintage	F	VF	XF	Unc	BU
1887 Proof	15	Value: 1,750				

X# 55b 6 PENCE
Copper **Ruler:** Victoria **Obv:** Crowned veiled bust left **Rev:** Crowned supported arms **Note:** Date in Roman numerals; MDCCCLXXXVII. Prev. KM#PPn102.

Date	Mintage	F	VF	XF	Unc	BU
1887 Proof	10	Value: 450				

X# 55c 6 PENCE
Aluminum **Ruler:** Victoria **Obv:** Crowned veiled bust left **Rev:** Crowned supported arms **Note:** Date in Roman numerals; MDCCCLXXXVII. Prev. KM#PPn103.

Date	Mintage	F	VF	XF	Unc	BU
1887 Proof	20	Value: 350				

X# 55d 6 PENCE
Tin **Ruler:** Victoria **Obv:** Crowned veiled bust left **Rev:** Crowned supported arms **Note:** Date in Roman numerals; MDCCCLXXXVII. Prev. KM#PPn104.

Date	Mintage	F	VF	XF	Unc	BU
1887 Proof	9	Value: 400				

X# 56 CROWN
Silver **Ruler:** Victoria **Obv:** Crowned veiled bust left, "J.R.T." on truncatiion **Rev:** Crowned supported arms **Edge:** Plain **Note:** Date in Roman numerals; MDCCCLXXXVII. Prev. KM#PPn105.

Date	Mintage	F	VF	XF	Unc	BU
1887 Proof	—	Value: 2,000				

X# 57 CROWN
Silver **Ruler:** Victoria **Obv:** Crowned veiled bust left, "SPINK & SON" on truncation **Rev:** Crowned supported arms **Note:** Date in Roman numerals; MDCCCLXXXVII. Prev. KM#PPn106.

Date	Mintage	F	VF	XF	Unc	BU
1887 Proof	32	Value: 2,000				

X# 58 CROWN
Silver **Ruler:** Victoria **Obv:** Crowned veiled bust left, without signature **Rev:** Crowned supported arms **Note:** Date in Roman numerals; MDCCCLXXXVII. Prev. KM#PPn107.

Date	Mintage	F	VF	XF	Unc	BU
1887 Proof	—	Value: 2,000				

X# 59 CROWN
Silver **Ruler:** Victoria **Obv:** Crowned veiled bust left **Rev:** Crowned supported arms, SPINK & SON at bottom **Note:** Date in Roman numerals; MDCCCLXXXVII. Prev. KM#PPn108.

Date	Mintage	F	VF	XF	Unc	BU
1887 Proof	—	Value: 2,000				

X# 59a CROWN
Gold **Ruler:** Victoria **Obv:** Crowned veiled bust left **Rev:** Crowned supported arms **Edge:** Plain **Note:** Date in Roman numerals; MDCCCLXXXVII. Prev. KM#PPn109.

Date	Mintage	F	VF	XF	Unc	BU
1887 Proof	6	Value: 6,500				

X# 59b CROWN
Copper **Ruler:** Victoria **Obv:** Crowned veiled bust left **Rev:** Crowned supported arms **Edge:** Plain **Note:** Date in Roman numerals; MDCCCLXXXVII. Prev. KM#PPn110.

Date	Mintage	F	VF	XF	Unc	BU
1887 Proof	5	Value: 1,500				

X# 59c CROWN
Aluminum **Ruler:** Victoria **Obv:** Crowned veiled bust left **Rev:** Crowned supported arms **Note:** Date in Roman numerals; MDCCCLXXXVII. Prev. KM#PPn111.

Date	Mintage	F	VF	XF	Unc	BU
1887 Proof	10	Value: 1,500				

X# 59d CROWN
Pewter **Ruler:** Victoria **Obv:** Crowned veiled bust left **Rev:** Crowned supported arms **Edge:** Plain **Note:** Date in Roman numerals; MDCCCLXXXVII. Prev. KM#PPn112.

Date	Mintage	F	VF	XF	Unc	BU
1887 Proof	—	Value: 1,350				

X# 59e CROWN
Lead **Ruler:** Victoria **Obv:** Crowned veiled bust left **Rev:** Crowned supported arms **Edge:** Plain **Note:** Date in Roman numerals; MDCCCLXXXVII. Prev. KM#PPn113.

Date	Mintage	F	VF	XF	Unc	BU
1887 Proof	—	Value: 900				

X# 59f CROWN
Silver **Ruler:** Victoria **Obv:** Crowned veiled bust left **Rev:** Crowned supported arms **Edge:** Reeded **Note:** Date in Roman numerals; MDCCCLXXXVII. Prev. KM#PPn114.

Date	Mintage	F	VF	XF	Unc	BU
1887 Proof	—	Value: 2,000				

X# 59g CROWN
Gold **Ruler:** Victoria **Obv:** Crowned veiled bust left **Rev:** Crowned supported arms **Edge:** Reeded **Note:** Date in Roman numerals; MDCCCLXXXVII. Prev. KM#PPn115.

Date	Mintage	F	VF	XF	Unc	BU
1887 Proof	6	Value: 6,500				

X# 60 CROWN
Copper **Ruler:** Victoria **Obv:** Crowned veiled bust left **Rev:** Crowned supported arms **Edge Lettering:** MADE IN BAVARIA **Note:** Date in Roman numerals; MDCCCLXXXVII. Prev. KM#PPn116.

Date	Mintage	F	VF	XF	Unc	BU
1887 Proof	—	Value: 1,500				

X# 60a CROWN
Pewter **Ruler:** Victoria **Obv:** Crowned veiled bust left **Rev:** Crowned supported arms **Note:** Date in Roman numerals; MDCCCLXXXVII. Prev. KM#PPn117.

Date	Mintage	F	VF	XF	Unc	BU
1887 Proof	—	Value: 1,250				

X# 60b CROWN
Aluminum **Ruler:** Victoria **Obv:** Crowned veiled bust left **Rev:** Crowned supported arms **Note:** Date in Roman numerals; MDCCCLXXXVII. Prev. KM#PPn118.

Date	Mintage	F	VF	XF	Unc	BU
1887 Proof	—	Value: 1,250				

X# 61 CROWN
32.1400 g., Silver **Ruler:** Edward VII **Issuer:** Spink

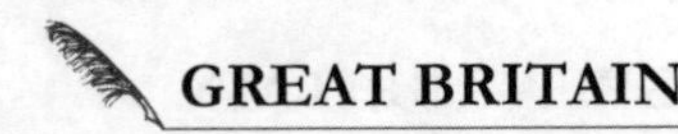

Obv: King horseback left **Rev:** Oval arms **Edge:** Plain **Note:** Prev. KM#PPn119.

Date	Mintage	F	VF	XF	Unc	BU
1902 Proof	—	Value: 1,850				

X# 61a CROWN

Gold **Ruler:** Edward VII **Obv:** King horseback left **Rev:** Oval arms **Edge:** Plain **Note:** Prev. KM#PPn120.

Date	Mintage	F	VF	XF	Unc	BU
1902 Proof	—	Value: 5,500				

X# 62 1/2 POUND

64.2800 g., Silver **Ruler:** Edward VII **Issuer:** Spink **Obv:** King horseback left **Rev:** Oval arms **Edge:** Plain **Note:** Prev. KM#PPn121.

Date	Mintage	F	VF	XF	Unc	BU
1902 Proof	—	Value: 4,500				

X# 63 POUND

128.5600 g., Silver **Ruler:** Edward VII **Issuer:** Spink **Obv:** King horseback left **Rev:** Oval arms **Edge:** Plain **Note:** Prev. KM#PPn122.

Date	Mintage	F	VF	XF	Unc	BU
1902 Proof	—	Value: 3,500				

A. G. Wyon Issues

X# 69 CROWN

27.4800 g., Silver **Ruler:** George V **Obv:** Head left **Rev:** St. George horseback left slaying dragon **Edge:** Plain

Date	Mintage	F	VF	XF	Unc	BU
MDCDX (1910)	10	—	—	—	5,000	—

X# 69a CROWN

27.4800 g., Silver **Ruler:** George V **Obv:** Head left **Rev:** St. George horseback left slaying dragon **Edge:** Milled

Date	Mintage	F	VF	XF	Unc	BU
MDCDX (1910)	10	—	—	—	5,000	—

X# 69b CROWN

Gold **Ruler:** George V **Obv:** Head left **Rev:** St. George horseback left slaying dragon **Edge:** Plain

Date	Mintage	F	VF	XF	Unc	BU
MDCDX (1910) Rare	—	—	—	—	—	—

X# 69c CROWN

Gold **Ruler:** George V **Obv:** Head left **Rev:** St. George horseback left slaying dragon **Edge:** Milled

Date	Mintage	F	VF	XF	Unc	BU
MDCDX (1910) Rare	—	—	—	—	—	—

X# 69d CROWN

Copper **Ruler:** George V **Obv:** Head left **Rev:** St. George horseback left slaying dragon

Date	Mintage	F	VF	XF	Unc	BU
MDCDX (1910) Matte	—	—	—	—	—	—

X# 69e CROWN

Silver Plated Copper **Ruler:** George V **Obv:** Head left **Rev:** St. George horseback left slaying dragon

Date	Mintage	F	VF	XF	Unc	BU
MDCDX (1910)	2	—	—	—	—	—

X# 70.1 CROWN

32.5300 g., Silver **Ruler:** George V **Obv:** Head left **Rev:** St. George horseback left slaying dragon **Edge:** Plain **Note:** Prev. KM#PPn120a.

Date	Mintage	F	VF	XF	Unc	BU
1910	10	—	—	—	5,000	—

X# 70.2 CROWN

32.6300 g., Silver **Ruler:** George V **Obv:** Head left **Rev:** St. George horseback left slaying dragon **Edge:** Milled

Date	Mintage	F	VF	XF	Unc	BU
1910	10	—	—	—	5,000	—

X# 70b CROWN

Silver **Ruler:** George V **Obv:** Head left **Rev:** St. George horseback left slaying dragon **Note:** Weight varies: 27.54-28.38 grams.

Date	Mintage	F	VF	XF	Unc	BU
1910 Matte	—	—	—	—	—	—

X# 70c CROWN

Gold **Ruler:** George V **Obv:** Head left **Rev:** St. George horseback left slaying dragon **Edge:** Plain **Note:** Prev. KM#PPn120.

Date	Mintage	F	VF	XF	Unc	BU
1910 Rare	—	—	—	—	—	—

X# 70d CROWN

Gold **Ruler:** George V **Obv:** Head left **Rev:** St. George horseback left slaying dragon **Edge:** Milled

Date	Mintage	F	VF	XF	Unc	BU
1910 Rare	—	—	—	—	—	—

X# 70e CROWN

Copper **Ruler:** George V **Obv:** Head left **Rev:** St. George horseback left slaying dragon

Date	Mintage	F	VF	XF	Unc	BU
1910	—	—	—	—	—	—

Reginald Huth Issues

X# 67 8 PENCE

Silver **Ruler:** George V **Issuer:** Huth **Obv:** Draped bust left **Rev:** Four crowned shields form cross **Edge:** Reeded **Note:** Prev. KM#PPn131.

Date	Mintage	F	VF	XF	Unc	BU
1913 Proof	—	Value: 600				

X# 67a 8 PENCE

Gold **Ruler:** George V **Obv:** Draped bust left **Rev:** Four crowned shields form cross **Edge:** Reeded **Note:** Prev. KM#PPn132.

Date	Mintage	F	VF	XF	Unc	BU
1913 Proof	—	Value: 2,000				

X# 67b 8 PENCE

8.2000 g., Platinum APW **Ruler:** George V **Obv:** Draped bust left **Rev:** Four crowned shields form cross **Edge:** Reeded **Note:** Prev. KM#PPn133.

Date	Mintage	F	VF	XF	Unc	BU
1913 Proof	—	Value: 2,250				

X# 67c 8 PENCE

Copper **Ruler:** George V **Obv:** Draped bust left **Rev:** Four crowned shields form cross **Edge:** Reeded **Note:** Prev. KM#PPn134.

Date	Mintage	F	VF	XF	Unc	BU
1913 Proof	—	Value: 400				

X# 67d 8 PENCE

Nickel **Ruler:** George V **Obv:** Draped bust left **Rev:** Four crowned shields form cross **Edge:** Reeded **Note:** Prev. KM#PPn135.

Date	Mintage	F	VF	XF	Unc	BU
1913 Proof	—	Value: 400				

X# 64 DOUBLE FLORIN

Silver **Ruler:** George V **Issuer:** Huth **Obv:** Draped bust left **Rev:** Four crowned shields form cross **Rev. Legend:** BRI. 19 11 REX **Edge:** Plain **Note:** Prev. KM#PPn123.

Date	Mintage	F	VF	XF	Unc	BU
1911 Proof	—	Value: 850				

X# 64a DOUBLE FLORIN

Silver **Ruler:** George V **Obv:** Draped bust left **Rev:** Four crowned shields form cross **Edge:** Reeded **Note:** Prev. KM#PPn124.

Date	Mintage	F	VF	XF	Unc	BU
1911 Proof	—	Value: 850				

X# 65 DOUBLE FLORIN

Silver **Ruler:** George V **Obv:** Draped bust left **Rev:** Four crowned shields form cross **Rev. Legend:** REX 19 11 BRI. TANI **Edge:** Plain **Note:** Prev. KM#PPn125.

Date	Mintage	F	VF	XF	Unc	BU
1911 Proof	—	Value: 850				

X# 66.1 DOUBLE FLORIN

Copper **Ruler:** George V **Obv:** Draped bust left **Rev:** Four crowned shields form cross **Note:** Countermark: ANGLESEY COPPER below bust. Overstruck on an Anglesey penny.

Date	Mintage	F	VF	XF	Unc	BU
1911	—	—	—	250	450	—

X# 66.2 DOUBLE FLORIN

Copper **Ruler:** George V **Obv:** Draped bust left **Rev:** Four crowned shields form cross **Note:** Countermark: CORNISH COPPER below bust.

Date	Mintage	F	VF	XF	Unc	BU
1911	—	—	—	250	450	—

X# 66.3 DOUBLE FLORIN

Copper **Ruler:** George V **Obv:** Draped bust left **Rev:** Four crowned shields form cross **Note:** Countermark: PHOSPHOR COPPER below bust

Date	Mintage	F	VF	XF	Unc	BU
1911	—	—	—	250	450	—

X# 66 OCTORINO
Silver **Ruler:** George V **Issuer:** Huth **Obv:** Draped bust left **Rev:** Four crowned shields form cross **Edge:** Reeded **Note:** Prev. KM#PPn126.

Date	Mintage	F	VF	XF	Unc	BU
1913 Proof	—	Value: 650				

X# 66a OCTORINO
Gold **Ruler:** George V **Obv:** Draped bust left **Rev:** Four crowned shields form cross **Edge:** Reeded **Note:** Prev. KM#PPn127.

Date	Mintage	F	VF	XF	Unc	BU
1913 Proof	—	Value: 2,000				

X# 66b OCTORINO
8.0000 g., Platinum APW **Ruler:** George V **Obv:** Draped bust left **Rev:** Four crowned shields form cross **Edge:** Reeded **Note:** Prev. KM#PPn128.

Date	Mintage	F	VF	XF	Unc	BU
1913 Proof	—	Value: 2,250				

X# 66c OCTORINO
Copper **Ruler:** George V **Obv:** Draped bust left **Rev:** Four crowned shields form cross **Edge:** Reeded **Note:** Prev. KM#PPn129.

Date	Mintage	F	VF	XF	Unc	BU
1913 Proof	—	Value: 400				

X# 66d OCTORINO
Lead **Ruler:** George V **Obv:** Draped bust left **Rev:** Four crowned shields form cross **Edge:** Plain **Note:** Prev. KM#PPn130.

Date	Mintage	F	VF	XF	Unc	BU
1913 Proof	—	Value: 350				

X# 66e OCTORINO
Iron **Ruler:** George V **Obv:** Draped bust left **Rev:** Four crowned shields form cross **Note:** Prev. KM#PPnA130.

Date	Mintage	F	VF	XF	Unc	BU
1913 Proof	—	Value: 400				

X# 68 12 GROATS
Silver **Ruler:** George V **Issuer:** Huth **Obv:** Draped bust left **Rev:** Four crowned shields form cross **Edge:** Plain **Note:** Prev. KM#PPn136.

Date	Mintage	F	VF	XF	Unc	BU
1914 Proof	—	Value: 850				

X# 68a 12 GROATS
Silver **Ruler:** George V **Obv:** Draped bust left **Rev:** Four crowned shields form cross **Edge:** Reeded

Date	Mintage	F	VF	XF	Unc	BU
1914 Proof	—	Value: 850				

X# 68b 12 GROATS
Platinum APW **Ruler:** George V **Obv:** Draped bust left **Rev:** Four crowned shields form cross

Date	Mintage	F	VF	XF	Unc	BU
1914 Proof	—	Value: 3,500				

X# 68c 12 GROATS
Gold **Ruler:** George V **Obv:** Draped bust left **Rev:** Four crowned shields form cross **Edge:** Reeded **Note:** Prev. KM#PPn139.

Date	Mintage	F	VF	XF	Unc	BU
1914 Proof	—	Value: 2,750				

MEDALLIC COINAGE

1954 Geoffrey Hearn Issues

X# M1 CROWN
Gilt Bronze **Ruler:** Edward VIII **Subject:** Edward VIII **Obv:** Bust left **Rev:** St. George horseback right slaying dragon

Date	Mintage	F	VF	XF	Unc	BU
1936 Proof	—	Value: 500				

X# M1a CROWN
28.1000 g., Silver **Ruler:** Edward VIII **Subject:** Edward VIII **Obv:** Bust left **Rev:** St. George horseback right slaying dragon

Date	Mintage	F	VF	XF	Unc	BU
1936 Proof	100	Value: 350				

X# M1c CROWN
Gold **Ruler:** Edward VIII **Obv:** Bust left **Rev:** St. George horseback right slaying dragon **Note:** Restrikes known.

Date	Mintage	F	VF	XF	Unc	BU
1936 Proof	10	Value: 1,650				

1946 Issues

X# M2 CROWN
Gilt Bronze **Ruler:** Edward VIII **Subject:** Edward VIII **Obv:** Bust left **Rev:** St. George horseback left slaying dragon

Date	Mintage	F	VF	XF	Unc	BU
1936 Proof	—	Value: 400				

X# M2a CROWN
28.1000 g., Silver **Ruler:** Edward VIII **Obv:** Bust left **Rev:** St. George horseback left slaying dragon

Date	Mintage	F	VF	XF	Unc	BU
1936 Proof	100	Value: 85.00				

X# M2b CROWN
28.1000 g., Silver **Ruler:** Edward VIII **Obv:** Bust left **Rev:** St. George horseback left slaying dragon

Date	Mintage	F	VF	XF	Unc	BU
1936 Prooflike; Restrike	1,000	—	—	—	45.00	—

X# M2d CROWN
Platinum APW **Ruler:** Edward VIII **Obv:** Bust left **Rev:** St. George horseback left slaying dragon

Date	Mintage	F	VF	XF	Unc	BU
1936 Proof	—	Value: 1,500				

X# M2c CROWN
Gold **Ruler:** Edward VIII **Obv:** Bust left **Rev:** St. George horseback left slaying dragon **Note:** Restrikes known.

Date	Mintage	F	VF	XF	Unc	BU
1936 Proof	10	Value: 800				

Unknown Mint Issues

X# 150 PENNY
1.5300 g., Silver Blackened metal possibly silver, 17 mm. **Ruler:** Elizabeth II **Obv:** King Arthur **Rev:** Hand with extended middle finger

Date	Mintage	F	VF	XF	Unc	BU
ND (1970-2006)	—	—	—	—	—	—

X# M3 1/2 CROWN
Silver **Ruler:** Edward VIII **Subject:** Edward VIII **Obv:** Bust left **Obv. Legend:** EDWARD • VIII • KING • & • EMPEROR **Rev:** St. George horseback left slaying dragon

Date	Mintage	F	VF	XF	Unc	BU
1936 Proof	—	Value: 65.00				

1972 Pobjoy Mint Issues

X# M4 CROWN
28.9200 g., Silver **Ruler:** Edward VIII **Subject:** Edward VIII **Obv:** Bust right **Obv. Legend:** EDWARD • VIII •

KING • & • EMPEROR **Rev:** St. George horseback left slaying dragon **Note:** Weight varies: 28.92-31.21 grams.

Date	Mintage	F	VF	XF	Unc	BU
1936 Proof	—	Value: 50.00				

X# M4a CROWN
Gold **Ruler:** Edward VIII **Obv:** Bust right **Rev:** St. George horseback left slaying dragon

Date	Mintage	F	VF	XF	Unc	BU
1937 Proof	—	Value: 700				

X# M10 CROWN
Silver, 38 mm. **Ruler:** Edward VIII **Series:** 1972 Pobjoy Mint **Obv:** Head left **Obv. Legend:** EDWARD VIII BY THE GRACE OF GOD **Rev:** St. George horseback right slaying dragon

Date	Mintage	F	VF	XF	Unc	BU
1936 Proof	—	Value: 100				

X# M11 CROWN
Silver, 38 mm. **Ruler:** Edward VIII **Series:** 1972 Pobjoy Mint **Obv:** Head left **Obv. Legend:** EDWARD VIII BY THE GRACE OF GOD **Rev:** St. George horseback right slaying dragon

Date	Mintage	F	VF	XF	Unc	BU
1936 Proof	—	Value: 100				

Richard Lobel Series

X# M5 CROWN
Bronze, 38.10 mm. **Subject:** Edward VIII **Obv:** Bust left **Obv. Legend:** EDWARD • VIII • KING • & • EMPEROR **Rev:** St. George horseback left slaying dragon **Edge:** Plain

Date	Mintage	F	VF	XF	Unc	BU
1936 Proof	2,000	Value: 15.00				

X# M5a CROWN
Copper-Nickel-Zinc, 38.10 mm. **Subject:** Edward VIII **Obv:** Bust left **Obv. Legend:** EDWARD • VIII • KING • & • EMPEROR **Rev:** St. George horseback left slaying dragon **Edge:** Plain

Date	Mintage	F	VF	XF	Unc	BU
1936 Proof	4,000	Value: 15.00				

X# M5b CROWN
0.9167 Silver, 38.10 mm. **Subject:** Edward VIII **Obv:** Bust left **Obv. Legend:** EDWARD • VIII • KING • & • EMPEROR **Rev:** St. George horseback left slaying dragon **Edge:** Plain

Date	Mintage	F	VF	XF	Unc	BU
1936 Proof	500	Value: 75.00				

X# M5c CROWN
Gold, 38.10 mm. **Subject:** Edward VIII **Obv:** Bust left **Obv. Legend:** EDWARD • VIII • KING • & • EMPEROR **Rev:** St. George horseback left slaying dragon **Edge:** Plain

Date	Mintage	F	VF	XF	Unc	BU
1936 Proof	—	Value: 500				

X# M15 CROWN
Silver, 38.6 mm. **Obv:** Head of Dutchess and bust of Duke facing **Obv. Legend:** DUKE & DUTCHESS OF WINDSOR **Rev:** St. George horseback left slaying dragon **Edge:** Plain

Date	Mintage	F	VF	XF	Unc	BU
1987 Proof	25	Value: 60.00				

X# M15a CROWN
Copper-Nickel, 38.6 mm. **Obv:** Head of Dutchess and bust of Duke facing **Obv. Legend:** DUKE & DUTCHESS OF WINDSOR **Rev:** St. George horseback left slaying dragon **Edge:** Plain

Date	Mintage	F	VF	XF	Unc	BU
1987 Proof	100	Value: 30.00				

X# M15b CROWN
Bronze, 38.6 mm. **Obv:** Head of Dutchess and bust of Duke facing **Obv. Legend:** DUKE & DUTCHESS OF WINDSOR **Rev:** St. George horseback left slaying dragon **Edge:** Plain

Date	Mintage	F	VF	XF	Unc	BU
1987 Proof	50	Value: 30.00				

X# M13 CROWN
23.8400 g., 0.9167 Silver 0.7026 oz. ASW, 38.05 mm. **Obv:** Bust left, dates below **Obv. Legend:** EDWARD • VIII • KING • E• EMPEROR **Rev:** St. George horseback left, slaying dragon **Edge:** Plain

Date	Mintage	F	VF	XF	Unc	BU
1987 Proof	100	Value: 50.00				

X# M13a CROWN
20.0300 g., Copper-Nickel, 38.05 mm. **Subject:** Edward VIII **Obv:** Bust left, dates below **Obv. Legend:** EDWARD • VIII • KING • E • EMPEROR **Rev:** St. George horseback left, slaying dragon **Edge:** Plain

Date	Mintage	F	VF	XF	Unc	BU
1987 Proof	500	Value: 20.00				

X# M13b CROWN
18.8400 g., Bronze, 38.05 mm. **Subject:** Edward VIII **Obv:** Bust left, dates below **Obv. Legend:** EDWARD • VIII • KING • E • EMPEROR **Rev:** St. George horseback left, slaying dragon **Edge:** Plain

Date	Mintage	F	VF	XF	Unc	BU
1987 Proof	250	Value: 20.00				

X# M15c CROWN
Gold, 38.6 mm. **Subject:** Edward VIII **Obv:** Head of Dutchess and bust of Duke facing **Obv. Legend:** DUKE & DUTCHESS OF WINDSOR **Rev:** St. George horseback left slaying dragon **Edge:** Plain

Date	Mintage	F	VF	XF	Unc	BU
1987 Proof	2	Value: 775				

X# M6 SOVEREIGN
0.3750 Gold **Subject:** Edward VIII **Obv:** Bust left **Rev:** St. George horseback left slaying dragon

Date	Mintage	F	VF	XF	Unc	BU
1936 Proof	500	Value: 150				

X# M16 SOVEREIGN
Gold, 22 mm. **Subject:** Edward VIII **Obv:** Head of Dutchess and bust of Duke facing **Obv. Legend:** DUKE & DUTCHESS OF WINDSOR **Rev:** St. George horseback left slaying dragon **Edge:** Plain

Date	Mintage	F	VF	XF	Unc	BU
1987 Proof	—	—	—	—	—	—

X# M14 SOVEREIGN
Gold, 22 mm. **Subject:** Edward VIII **Obv:** Bust left, dates below **Obv. Legend:** EDWARD • VIII • KING • E • EMPEROR **Rev:** St. George horseback left, slaying dragon **Edge:** Plain

Date	Mintage	F	VF	XF	Unc	BU
1987 Proof	3	Value: 600				

X# M16a SOVEREIGN
4.4000 g., Silver, 22 mm. **Subject:** Edward VIII **Obv:** Head of Dutchess and bust of Duke facing **Obv. Legend:** DUKE & DUTCHESS OF WINDSOR **Rev:** St. George horseback left slaying dragon **Edge:** Plain

Date	Mintage	F	VF	XF	Unc	BU
1987 Proof	—	Value: 10.00				

MEDALLIC SILVER BULLION COINAGE

1987 B.N.T.A. Issue

X# MB1 5 OUNCES
155.5150 g., 1.0000 Silver 4.9997 oz. ASW, 65 mm. **Subject:** 150th Anniversary of Coronation of Queen Victoria **Note:** Illustration reduced.

Date	Mintage	F	VF	XF	Unc	BU
1987 Proof	—	Value: 150				

MEDALLIC / INA RETRO ISSUE

X# M125 CROWN
Silver, 40.97 mm. **Obv:** Laureate bust right
Obv. Legend: GEORGIUS III DEI GRATIA REX.
Rev: Crowned arms with small crowned shield at center
Rev. Legend: INCORRUPTA FIDES VERITASQUE
Edge: Plain

Date	Mintage	F	VF	XF	Unc	BU
1808 (2007) Proof	—	—	—	—	—	—
1808 (2007) Matte Proof	—	—	—	—	—	—

X# M125a CROWN
Copper, 40.97 mm. **Obv:** Laureate bust right
Obv. Legend: GEORGIUS III DEI GRATIA REX.
Rev: Crowned arms with small crowned shield at center
Rev. Legend: INCORRUPTA FIDES VERITASQUE
Edge: Plain

Date	Mintage	F	VF	XF	Unc	BU
1808 (2007) Proof	1,250	—	—	—	—	—

X# M125b CROWN
Aluminum, 40.97 mm. **Obv:** Laureate bust right
Obv. Legend: GEORGIUS III DEI GRATIA REX.
Rev: Crowned arms with small crowned shield at center
Rev. Legend: INCORRUPTA FIDES VERITASQUE
Edge: Plain

Date	Mintage	F	VF	XF	Unc	BU
1808 (2007) Proof	1,250	—	—	—	—	—

X# M125c CROWN
Pewter, 40.97 mm. **Obv:** Laureate bust right
Obv. Legend: GEORGIUS III DEI GRATIA REX.
Rev: Crowned arms with small crowned shield at center
Rev. Legend: INCORRUPTA FIDES VERITASQUE
Edge: Plain

Date	Mintage	F	VF	XF	Unc	BU
1808 (2007) Proof	1,250	—	—	—	—	—

X# M125e CROWN
Nickel-Silver, 40.97 mm. **Obv:** Laureate bust right
Obv. Legend: GEORGIUS III DEI GRATIA REX.
Rev: Crowned arms with small crowned shield at center
Rev. Legend: INCORRUPTA FIDES VERITASQUE
Edge: Plain

Date	Mintage	F	VF	XF	Unc	BU
1808 (2007) Proof	1,250	—	—	—	—	—

X# M125f CROWN
Goldine, 40.97 mm. **Obv:** Laureate bust right
Obv. Legend: GEORGIUS III DEI GRATIA REX.
Rev: Crowned arms with small crowned shield at center
Rev. Legend: INCORRUPTA FIDES VERITASQUE
Edge: Plain

Date	Mintage	F	VF	XF	Unc	BU
1808 (2007) Proof	1,250	—	—	—	—	—

X# M125g CROWN
Gold, 40.97 mm. **Obv:** Laureate bust right **Obv. Legend:** GEORGIUS III DEI GRATIA REX. **Rev:** Crowned arms with small crowned shield at center **Rev. Legend:** INCORRUPTA FIDES VERITASQUE **Edge:** Plain

Date	Mintage	F	VF	XF	Unc	BU
1808 (2007) Proof	—	—	—	—	—	—

MEDALLIC COINAGE

NIB Maundy Retro Issues

X# 111 PENNY
0.0470 g., 0.9250 Silver 0.0014 oz. ASW **Ruler:** Edward VIII **Obv:** Head left **Obv. Legend:** EDWARD VIII D: G: REX: FID: DEF **Rev:** Crowned value within wreath **Edge:** Plain

Date	Mintage	F	VF	XF	Unc	BU
1936 Proof	—	Value: 18.50				

X# 112 2 PENCE
0.9500 g., 0.9250 Silver 0.0283 oz. ASW **Ruler:** Edward VIII **Obv:** Head left **Obv. Legend:** EDWARD VIII: D: G: REX: FID: DEF **Rev:** Crowned value within wreath **Edge:** Plain

Date	Mintage	F	VF	XF	Unc	BU
1936 Proof	—	Value: 18.50				

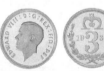

X# 113 3 PENCE
1.4400 g., 0.9250 Silver 0.0428 oz. ASW **Ruler:** Edward VIII **Obv:** Head left **Obv. Legend:** EDWARD VIII: D: G: REX: FID: DEF **Rev:** Crowned value within wreath **Edge:** Plain

Date	Mintage	F	VF	XF	Unc	BU
1936 Proof	—	Value: 18.50				

X# 114 4 PENCE
1.9500 g., 0.9250 Silver 0.0580 oz. ASW **Ruler:** Edward VIII **Obv:** Head left **Obv. Legend:** EDWARD VIII: D: G: REX: FID: DEF **Rev:** Crowned value within wreath **Edge:** Plain

Date	Mintage	F	VF	XF	Unc	BU
1937 Proof	—	—	—	—	—	—

X# M9 SOVEREIGN
Gold, 22 mm. **Ruler:** Victoria **Obv:** Crowned bust left **Obv. Legend:** Victoria Dei Gratia - Britanniar • reg • f • d **Rev:** Four crowned shields forming a cross **Rev. Legend:** TVEATVR VNITA DEVS...

Date	Mintage	F	VF	XF	Unc	BU
MDCCCXLVII Proof	—	Value: 175				

X# M8 SOVEREIGN
Gold, 22 mm. **Ruler:** Edward VIII **Obv:** Head left **Obv. Legend:** EDWARD VIII : D : G : REX : FID : DEF **Rev:** St. George horseback right slaying dragon

Date	Mintage	F	VF	XF	Unc	BU
1936 Proof	—	Value: 175				

X# 151 GALLEON
9.3200 g., Silver, 29.3 mm. **Ruler:** Elizabeth II **Obv:** Crowned arms **Obv. Legend:** "HABET DIVITIAS EUROPE" **Rev:** Ship design copied from the Noble gold coins of the 1300's **Rev. Legend:** "XX DOCTUS : IN : SE : SEMPER : " **Edge:** Iregular plain

Date	Mintage	F	VF	XF	Unc	BU
ND (1975-2006)	—	—	—	—	—	—

Historic Coin Co. Ltd. Retro Issues

X# 115 3 PENCE
0.9250 Silver **Ruler:** Edward VIII **Obv:** Head left **Obv. Legend:** EDWARDVS VIII DEI GRA: BRITT: OMN REX **Rev:** Thistle plant

Date	Mintage	F	VF	XF	Unc	BU
1937 Proof	3,500	Value: 15.00				

X# 116 3 PENCE
0.9250 Silver **Ruler:** Edward VIII **Obv:** Head left **Obv. Legend:** EDWARDVS VIII DEI GRA: BRITT: OMN REX **Rev:** Crowned E-R divides date

Date	Mintage	F	VF	XF	Unc	BU
1937 Proof	3,500	Value: 15.00				

X# 117 6 PENCE
0.9250 Silver **Ruler:** Edward VIII **Obv:** Head left **Obv. Legend:** EDWARDVS VIII DEI GRA: BRITT: OMN REX **Rev:** Lion on crown

Date	Mintage	F	VF	XF	Unc	BU
1937 Proof	3,500	Value: 17.50				

X# 118 SHILLING
0.9250 Silver **Ruler:** Edward VIII **Obv:** Head left **Obv. Legend:** EDWARDVS VIII DEI GRA: BRITT: OMN REX **Rev:** Crowned arms

Date	Mintage	F	VF	XF	Unc	BU
1937 Proof	3,500	Value: 20.00				

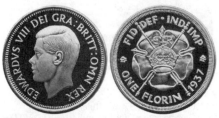

X# 119 FLORIN
0.9250 Silver **Ruler:** Edward VIII **Obv:** Head left **Obv. Legend:** EDWARDVS VIII DEI GRA: BRITT: OMN REX **Rev:** Crown above crossed sceptres, flower below

Date	Mintage	F	VF	XF	Unc	BU
1937 Proof	3,500	Value: 40.00				

X# 120 1/2 CROWN
0.9250 Silver **Ruler:** Edward VIII **Obv:** Head left **Obv. Legend:** EDWARDVS VIII DEI GRA: BRITT: OMN REX **Rev:** Shield within garter, crowned and supported

Date	Mintage	F	VF	XF	Unc	BU
1937 Proof	3,500	Value: 30.00				

X# 121 5 SHILLING
0.9250 Silver **Ruler:** Edward VIII **Obv:** Head left **Obv. Legend:** EDWARDVS VIII DEI GRA: BRITT: OMN REX **Rev:** St. George slaying dragon, Garter motto above, value and date below

Date	Mintage	F	VF	XF	Unc	BU
1937 Proof	3,500	Value: 50.00				

Euro Issues

X# M31a 25 EURO
Copper-Nickel **Obv:** Helmeted Britannia right **Obv. Legend:** Britanniarum Dei Gratia **Rev:** Oval portrait Lord Nelson upper right of H.M.S. Victory **Edge:** Reeded

Date	Mintage	F	VF	XF	Unc	BU
1996	—	—	—	—	15.00	—

IRON BRIDGE MUSEUM

X# 301 FARTHING
Copper **Obv:** Ironbridge and horse **Obv. Legend:** IRONBIDGE GORGE MUSEUM TOKEN **Rev:** Britannia seated, date below **Rev. Legend:** FARTHING

Date	Mintage	F	VF	XF	Unc	BU
1987H	—	—	—	—	1.50	2.50

X# 302 1/2 PENNY
Copper **Obv:** Ironbridge and horse **Obv. Legend:** IRONBRIDGE GORGE MUSEUM TOKEN **Rev:** Britannia seated, date below **Rev. Legend:** HALF PENNY

Date	Mintage	F	VF	XF	Unc	BU
1987H	—	—	—	—	2.00	3.50

X# 303 PENNY
Copper **Obv:** Ironbradge and horse **Obv. Legend:** IRONBRIDGE GORGE MUSEUM TOKEN **Rev:** Britannia seated, date below **Rev. Legend:** ONE PENNY

Date	Mintage	F	VF	XF	Unc	BU
1987H	—	—	—	—	3.50	5.00

X# 304 3 PENCE
Silver **Obv:** Ironbridge and horse **Obv. Legend:** IRONBRODGE GORGE MUSEUM TOKEN **Rev. Legend:** THREE PENCE

Date	Mintage	F	VF	XF	Unc	BU
1987	—	—	—	—	7.50	10.00

PIEFORTS

X#	Date	Mintage	Identification	Mkt Val
P1	1879	1	Crown. Silver. Plain edge, coin alignment, X#81.	—
P2	1879	1	Crown. Silver. Plain edge, medal alignment, X#81.	—
P3	1879	1	Crown. Silver. Reeded edge, coin alignment, X#81.	—
P4	1879	1	Crown. Silver. Reeded edge, medal alignment, X#81.	—
P5	1879	1	Crown. Silver. Plain edge, coin alignment, X#82.	—
P6	1879	1	Crown. Silver. Plain edge, medal alignment, X#82.	—
P7	1879	1	Crown. Silver. Reeded edge, coin alignment, X#82.	—
P8	1879	1	Crown. Silver. Reeded edge, medal alignment, X#82.	—
P9	1879	1	Crown. Silver. Plain edge, coin alignment, X#83.	—
P10	1879	1	Crown. Silver. Plain edge, medal alignment, X#83.	—
P11	1879	—	Crown. Silver. Reeded edge, coin alignment, X#83.	—
P12	1879	1	Crown. Silver. Reeded edge, coin alignment, X#83.	—
P13	1893	1	Double Florin. Silver. Plain edge, coin alignment, X#84.	—
P14	1893	1	Double Florin. Silver. Plain edge, medal alignment, X#84.	—
P15	1893	1	Double Florin. Silver. Reeded edge, coin alignment, X#84.	—
P16	1893	1	Double Florin. Silver. Reeded edge, medal alignment, X#84.	—
P17	1893	1	Double Florin. Silver. Plain edge, coin alignment, X#85.	—
P18	1893	1	Double Florin. Silver. Plain edge, medal alignment, X#85.	—
P19	1893	1	Double Florin. Silver. Reeded edge, coin alignment, X#85.	—
P20	1893	1	Double Florin. Silver. Reeded edge, medal alignment, X#85.	—
P21	1902	1	Double Florin. Silver. Plain edge, coin alignment, X#86.	—
P22	1902	1	Double Florin. Silver. Plain edge, medal alignment, X#86.	—
P23	1902	1	Double Florin. Silver. Reeded edge, coin alignment, X#86.	—
P24	1902	1	Double Florin. Silver. Reeded edge, medal alignment, X#86.	—
P25	1902	1	Double Florin. Silver. Plain edge, coin alignment, X#87.	—
P26	1902	1	Double Florin. Silver. Plain edge, medal alignment, X#87.	—
P27	1902	1	Double Florin. Silver. Reeded edge, coin alignment, X#87.	—
P28	1902	1	Double Florin. Silver. Reeded edge, medal alignment, X#87.	—
P29	1902	1	Double Florin. Silver. Plain edge, coin alignment, X#89.	—
P30	1902	1	Double Florin. Silver. Plain edge, medal alignment, X#89.	—
P31	1902	1	Double Florin. Silver. Reeded edge, coin alignment, X#89.	—
P32	1902	1	Double Florin. Silver. Reeded edge, medal alignment, X#89.	—
P33	1910	1	Double Florin. Silver. Plain edge, coin alignment, X#87.	—
P34	1910	1	Double Florin. Silver. Plain edge, medal alignment, X#87.	—
P35	1910	1	Double Florin. Silver. Reeded edge, coin alignment, X#87.	—
P36	1910	1	Double Florin. Silver. Reeded edge, coin alignment, X#87.	—
P37	1910	1	Double Florin. Silver. Plain edge, coin alignment, X#89.	—
P38	1910	1	Double Florin. Silver. Plain edge, medal alignment, X#89.	—
P39	1910	1	Double Florin. Silver. Reeded edge, coin alignment, X#89.	—
P40	1910	1	Double Florin. Silver. Reeded edge, medal alignment, X#89.	—
P41	MDCDX (1910)	1	Crown. Silver. Plain edge, coin alignment, X#92.	—
P42	MDCDX (1910)	1	Crown. Silver. Plain edge, medal alignment, X#92.	—
P43	MDCDX (1910)	1	Crown. Silver. Reeded edge, coin alignment, X#92.	—
P44	MDCDX (1910)	1	Crown. Silver. Reeded edge, medal alignment, X#92.	—
P45	1910	1	Double Florin. Silver. Plain edge, coin alignment, X#93.	—
P46	1910	1	Double Florin. Silver. Plain edge, medal alignment, X#93.	—
P47	1910	1	Double Florin. Silver. Reeded edge, coin alignment, X#93.	—

X#	Date	Mintage	Identification	Mkt Val
P48	1910	1	Double Florin. Silver. Reeded edge, medal alignment, X#93.	—
P49	1911	1	Crown. Silver. Plain edge, coin alignment, X#94.	—
P50	1911	1	Crown. Silver. Plain edge, medal alignment, X#94.	—
P51	1911	1	Crown. Silver. Reeded edge, coin alignment, X#94.	—
P52	1911	1	Crown. Silver. Reeded edge, medal alignment, X#94.	—
P53	MDCDXI (1911)	1	Crown. Silver. Plain edge, coin alignment, X#95.	—
P54	MDCDXI (1911)	1	Crown. Silver. Plain edge, medal alignment, X#95.	—
P55	MDCDXI (1911)	1	Crown. Silver. Reeded edge, coin alignment, X#95.	—
P56	MDCDXI (1911)	1	Crown. Silver. Reeded edge, medal alignment, X#95.	—
P57	MDCDXI (1911)	1	Crown. Silver. Plain edge, coin alignment, X#96.	—
P58	MDCDXI (1911)	1	Crown. Silver. Plain edge, medal alignment, X#96.	—
P59	MDCDXI (1911)	1	Crown. Silver. Reeded edge, coin alignment, X#96.	—
P60	MDCDXI (1911)	1	Crown. Silver. Reeded edge, medal alignment, X#96.	—
P61	MDCDXI (1911)	1	Crown. Silver. Plain edge, coin alignment, X#97.	—
P62	MDCDXI (1911)	1	Crown. Silver. Plain edge, medal alignment, X#97.	—
P64	MDCDXI (1911)	1	Crown. Silver. Reeded edge, medal alignment, X#97.	—
P65	1911	1	Crown. Silver. Plain edge, coin alignment, X#98.	—
P66	1911	1	Crown. Silver. Plain edge, medal alignment, X#98.	—
P67	1911	1	Crown. Silver. Reeded edge, coin alignment, X#98.	—
P68	1911	1	Crown. Silver. Reeded edge, medal alignment, X#98.	—
P69	1936	1	Crown. Silver. Plain edge, coin alignment, X#99.	—
P70	1936	1	Crown. Silver. Plain edge, medal alignment, X#99.	—
P71	1936	1	Crown. Silver. Reeded edge, coin alignment, X#99.	—
P72	1936	1	Crown. Silver. Reeded edge, medal alignment, X#99.	—
P73	1936	1	Crown. Silver. Plain edge, coin alignment, X#100.	—
P74	1936	1	Crown. Silver. Plain edge, medal alignment, X#100.	—
P75	1936	1	Crown. Silver. Reeded edge, coin alignment, X#100.	—
P76	1936	1	Crown. Silver. Reeded edge, medal alignment, X#100.	—
P77	1937	1	Double Florin. Silver. Plain edge, coin alignment, X#101.	—
P78	1937	1	Double Florin. Silver. Plain edge, medal alignment, X#101.	—
P79	1937	1	Double Florin. Silver. Reeded edge, coin alignment, X#101.	—
P80	1937	1	Double Florin. Silver. Reeded edge, medal alignment, X#101.	—
P81	1937	1	Crown. Silver. Plain edge, coin alignment, X#102.	—
P82	1937	1	Crown. Silver. Plain edge, medal alignment, X#102.	—
P83	1937	1	Crown. Silver. Reeded edge, coin alignment, X#102.	—
P84	1937	1	Crown. Silver. Reeded edge, medal alignment, X#102.	—
P85	1937	1	Crown. Silver. Plain edge, coin alignment, X#103.	—
P86	1937	1	Crown. Silver. Plain edge, medal alignment, X#103.	—
P87	1937	1	Crown. Silver. Reeded edge, coin alignment, X#103.	—
P88	1937	1	Crown. Silver. Reeded edge, medal alignment, X#103.	—
P89	1937	1	Double Florin. Silver. Plain edge, coin alignment, X#104.	—
P90	1937	1	Double Florin. Silver. Plain edge, medal alignment, X#104.	—
P91	1937	1	Double Florin. Silver. Reeded edge, coin alignment, X#104.	—
P92	1937	1	Double Florin. Silver. Reeded edge, medal alignment, X#104.	—
P93	1953	1	Double Florin. Silver. Plain edge, coin alignment, X#105.	—
P94	1953	1	Double Florin. Silver. Plain edge, medal alignment, X#105.	—
P95	1953	1	Double Florin. Silver. Reeded edge, coin alignment, X#105.	—
P96	1953	1	Double Florin. Silver. Reeded edge, medal alignment, X#105.	—

X#	Date	Mintage	Identification	Mkt Val
P101	1996	—	25 Euro. 0.9990 Silver. 41.7100 g. X#M31.	85.00
P111	1936	—	Crown. 0.9167 Silver. X#M5b.	100
P112	1987	25	Crown. 0.9167 Silver. X#M7.	125
P113	1987	10	Crown. 0.9167 Silver. 31.0300 g. X#M15.	125

TRIAL STRIKES

X#	Date	Mintage	Identification	Mkt Val
TS1	ND(1972)	—	25 New Pence. Silver. 30.4500 g. 39 mm. Head facing right. MODEL in middle of coin.	30.00

ENGLAND

KINGDOM

ECU COINAGE

X# 11 ECU

20.3400 g., Copper-Nickel-Zinc, 38 mm. **Ruler:** Elizabeth II **Obv:** Neptune and Europa standing flanking circular outlined map of Europe **Obv. Legend:** • EUROPE ★ EUROPA • ENGLAND **Obv. Designer:** R. D. Maklouf **Rev:** Three Graces standing

Date	Mintage	F	VF	XF	Unc	BU
1992	—	—	—	—	6.50	—

X# 11a ECU

23.0000 g., 0.9250 Silver 0.6840 oz. ASW, 38 mm. **Ruler:** Elizabeth II **Obv:** Neptune and Europa standing flanking circular outlined map of Europe **Obv. Legend:** • EUROPE ★ EUROPA • ENGLAND **Obv. Designer:** R. D. Maklouf **Rev:** Three Graces standing

Date	Mintage	F	VF	XF	Unc	BU
1992 Proof	500	Value: 65.00				

X# 12a ECU

38.0000 g., 0.9167 Gold 1.1199 oz. AGW, 38 mm. **Ruler:** Elizabeth II **Obv:** Neptune and Europa standing flanking circular outlined map of Europe **Obv. Legend:** • EUROPE ★ EUROPA • ENGLAND **Obv. Designer:** R. D. Maklouf **Rev:** Three Graces standing

Date	Mintage	F	VF	XF	Unc	BU
1992 Proof	25	—	—	—	—	—

X# 12 ECU

3.0000 g., 0.7500 Gold 0.0723 oz. AGW, 22.5 mm. **Ruler:** Elizabeth II **Obv:** Neptune and Europa standing flanking circular outlined map of Europe **Obv. Legend:** • EUROPE ★ EUROPA • ENGLAND **Obv. Designer:** R. D. Maklouf **Rev:** Three Graces standing

Date	Mintage	F	VF	XF	Unc	BU
1992 Proof	500	Value: 200				

X# 14 25 ECU

23.0000 g., 0.9250 Silver 0.6840 oz. ASW, 38 mm. **Ruler:** Elizabeth II **Obv:** Neptune and Europa standing flanking circular outlined map of Europe **Obv. Legend:** • EUROPE ★ EUROPA • ENGLAND **Obv. Designer:** R. D. Maklouf **Rev:** Three Graces standing

Date	Mintage	F	VF	XF	Unc	BU
1992 Proof	500	Value: 65.00				

X# 14a 25 ECU

38.0000 g., 0.9167 Gold 1.1199 oz. AGW, 38 mm. **Ruler:** Elizabeth II **Obv:** Neptune and Europa standing flanking circular outlined map of Europe **Obv. Legend:** • EUROPE ★ EUROPA • ENGLAND **Obv. Designer:** R. D. Maklouf **Rev:** Three Graces standing

Date	Mintage	F	VF	XF	Unc	BU
1992 Proof	25	—	—	—	—	—

X# 14b 25 ECU

20.3400 g., Copper-Nickel-Zinc, 38 mm. **Ruler:** Elizabeth II **Obv:** Neptune and Europa standing flanking circular outlined map of Europe **Obv. Legend:** • EUROPE ★ EUROPA • ENGLAND **Obv. Designer:** R. D. Maklouf **Rev:** Three Graces standing

Date	Mintage	F	VF	XF	Unc	BU
1992	—	—	—	—	6.50	—

PIEFORTS

X#	Date	Mintage	Identification	Mkt Val
P1	1992	500	Ecu. 0.7500 Gold. 6.0000 g. X#12.	—
P2	1992	100	Ecu. 0.9250 Silver. 46.0000 g. X#11a.	—
P3	1992	500	25 Ecu. 0.9250 Silver. 46.0000 g. X#14.	—
P4	1992	25	25 Ecu. 0.9167 Gold. 76.0000 g. X#14a.	—

WALES

KINGDOM

MEDALLIC / INA RETRO ISSUE

X# M1 CROWN

Silver, 40.98 mm. **Obv:** Laureate bust right **Obv. Legend:** GEORGIUS III DEI GRATIA REX. **Rev:** Plumes in crown **Rev. Legend:** HONI • SOIT • QUI • MAL • Y • PENSE / WALES • CYMRU **Edge:** Plain

Date	Mintage	F	VF	XF	Unc	BU
1808 (2007) Proof	—	—	—	—	—	—
1808 (2007) Matte Proof	—	—	—	—	—	—

X# M1a CROWN
Copper, 40.98 mm. **Obv:** Laureate bust right **Obv. Legend:** GEORGIUS III DEI GRATIA REX. **Rev:** Plumes in Crown **Rev. Legend:** HONI • SOIT • QUI • MAL • Y • PENSE / WALES • CYMRU **Edge:** Plain

Date	Mintage	F	VF	XF	Unc	BU
1808 (2007) Proof	700	—	—	—	—	—

X# M1b CROWN
Aluminum, 40.98 mm. **Obv:** Laureate bust right **Obv. Legend:** GEORGIUS III DEI GRATIA REX. **Rev:** Plumes in crown **Rev. Legend:** HONI • SOIT • QUI • MAL • Y • PENSE / WALES • CYMRU **Edge:** Plain

Date	Mintage	F	VF	XF	Unc	BU
1808 (2007) Proof	700	—	—	—	—	—

X# M1c CROWN
Pewter, 40.98 mm. **Obv:** Laureate bust right **Obv. Legend:** GEORGIUS III DEI GRATIA REX. **Rev:** Plumes in crown **Rev. Legend:** HONI • SOIT • QUI • MAL • Y • PENSE / WALES • CYMRU **Edge:** Plain

Date	Mintage	F	VF	XF	Unc	BU
1808 (2007) Proof	700	—	—	—	—	—

X# M1d CROWN
Copper Bronzed, 40.98 mm. **Obv:** Laureate bust right **Obv. Legend:** GEORGIUS III DEI GRATIA REX. **Rev:** Plumes in crown **Rev. Legend:** HONI • SOIT • QUI • MAL • Y • PENSE / WALES • CYMRU **Edge:** Plain

Date	Mintage	F	VF	XF	Unc	BU
1808 (2007) Proof	700	—	—	—	—	—

X# M1e CROWN
Nickel-Silver, 40.98 mm. **Obv:** Laureate bust right **Obv. Legend:** GEORGIUS III DEI GRATIA REX. **Rev:** Plumes in crown **Rev. Legend:** HONI • SOIT • QUI • MAL • Y • PENSE / WALES • CYMRU **Edge:** Plain

Date	Mintage	F	VF	XF	Unc	BU
1808 (2007) Proof	700	—	—	—	—	—

X# M1f CROWN
Goldine, 40.98 mm. **Obv:** Laureate bust right **Obv. Legend:** GEORGIUS III DEI GRATIA REX. **Rev:** Plumes in crown **Rev. Legend:** HONI • SOIT • QUI • MAL • Y • PENSE / WALES • CYMRU **Edge:** Plain

Date	Mintage	F	VF	XF	Unc	BU
1808 (2007) Proof	700	—	—	—	—	—

X# M1g CROWN
Gold, 40.98 mm. **Obv:** Laureate bust right **Obv. Legend:** GEORGIUS III DEI GRATIA REX. **Rev:** Plumes in crown **Rev. Legend:** HONI • SOIT • QUI • MAL • Y • PENSE / WALES • CYMRU **Edge:** Plain

Date	Mintage	F	VF	XF	Unc	BU
1808 (2007) Proof	—	—	—	—	—	—

ECU COINAGE

International Currency Bureau Issues

X# 1 ECU
20.3400 g., Copper-Nickel-Zinc, 38.0 mm. **Ruler:** Elizabeth II **Obv:** Neptune and Europa standing flanking circular outlined map of Europe **Obv. Legend:** • EUROPE ★ EUROPA • WALES **Obv. Designer:** R. D. Maklouf **Rev:** Helmeted bust of Edward the Black Prince facing

Date	Mintage	F	VF	XF	Unc	BU
1992	—	—	—	—	—	10.00

X# 1a ECU
23.0000 g., 0.9250 Silver 0.6840 oz. ASW, 38 mm. **Ruler:** Elizabeth II **Obv:** Neptune and Europa standing flanking circular outlined map of Europe **Obv. Legend:** • EUROPE ★ EUROPA • WALES **Obv. Designer:** R. D. Maklouf **Rev:** Helmeted bust of Edward the Black Prince facing

Date	Mintage	F	VF	XF	Unc	BU
1992 Proof	500	Value: 65.00				

X# 2 ECU
3.0000 g., 0.7500 Gold 0.0723 oz. AGW, 22.5 mm. **Ruler:** Elizabeth II **Obv:** Neptune and Europa standing flanking circular outlined map of Europe **Obv. Legend:** • EUROPE ★ EUORPA • WALES **Obv. Designer:** R. D. Maklouf **Rev:** Helmeted bust of Edward the Black Prince facing

Date	Mintage	F	VF	XF	Unc	BU
1992 Proof	500	Value: 200				

X# 1c ECU
38.0000 g., 0.9167 Gold 1.1199 oz. AGW, 38 mm. **Ruler:** Elizabeth II **Obv:** Neptune and Europa standing flanking circular outlined map of Europe **Obv. Legend:** • EUROPE ★ EUROPA • WALES **Obv. Designer:** R. D. Maklouf **Rev:** Helmeted bust of Edward the Black Prince facing **Note:** Prev. #X2a.

Date	Mintage	F	VF	XF	Unc	BU
1992 Proof	25	—	—	—	—	—

X# 3 ECU
28.2800 g., 0.9250 Silver 0.8410 oz. ASW, 38.6 mm. **Ruler:** Elizabeth II **Obv:** Map of Europe **Obv. Legend:** • WALES • EUROPE - EUROPA **Rev:** Dragon standing left **Rev. Legend:** Y • DDRAIG • GOCH • DDYRY • CYCHWYN

Date	Mintage	F	VF	XF	Unc	BU
ND(1992)PM Proof	10,000	Value: 35.00				

X# 4c 25 ECU
Goldine, 38 mm. **Ruler:** Elizabeth II **Obv:** Neptune and Europa standing flanking circular outlined map of Europe **Obv. Legend:** • EUROPE ★ EUROPA • WALES **Obv. Designer:** R. D. Maklouf **Rev:** Helmeted bust of Edward the Black Prince facing **Note:** Prev. #X4.

Date	Mintage	F	VF	XF	Unc	BU
1992	—	—	—	—	—	15.00

X# 4d 25 ECU
0.3750 Gold, 38 mm. **Ruler:** Elizabeth II **Obv:** Neptune and Europa standing flanking circular outlined map of Europe **Obv. Legend:** • EUROPE ★ EUROPA • WALES **Obv. Designer:** R. D. Maklouf **Rev:** Helmeted bust of Edward the Black Prince facing

Date	Mintage	F	VF	XF	Unc	BU
1992 Proof	10	Value: 400				

X# 4b 25 ECU
20.3400 g., Copper-Nickel-Zinc, 38 mm. **Ruler:** Elizabeth II **Obv:** Neptune and Europa standing flanking circular outlined map of Europe **Obv. Legend:** • EUROPE ★ EUROPA • WALES **Obv. Designer:** R. D. Maklouf **Rev:** Helmeted bust of Edward the Black Prince facing

Date	Mintage	F	VF	XF	Unc	BU
1992	—	—	—	—	—	15.00

FANTASY EURO PATTERNS

X# Pn1 EURO CENT
Copper Plated Steel **Edge:** Plain

Date	Mintage	F	VF	XF	Unc	BU
2004	—	—	—	—	—	1.50

X# Pn2 2 EURO CENT
Copper Plated Steel **Edge:** Plain

Date	Mintage	F	VF	XF	Unc	BU
2004	—	—	—	—	—	2.00

X# Pn3 5 EURO CENT
Copper Clad Steel **Edge:** Plain

Date	Mintage	F	VF	XF	Unc	BU
2004	—	—	—	—	—	2.50

X# Pn4 10 EURO CENT
Goldine **Edge:** Plain

Date	Mintage	F	VF	XF	Unc	BU
2004	—	—	—	—	—	3.00

X# Pn6 50 EURO CENT
Goldine **Edge:** Plain

Date	Mintage	F	VF	XF	Unc	BU
2004	—	—	—	—	—	4.00

X# Pn7 EURO
Bi-Metallic **Obv:** Bust of William Burges left **Rev:** Artistic sailing ship, large value "1" **Edge:** Plain

Date	Mintage	F	VF	XF	Unc	BU
2004	—	—	—	—	—	6.00

X# Pn8 2 EURO
Bi-Metallic, 26 mm. **Obv:** Bust of William Burges left **Rev:** Artistic sailing ship, large value "2" **Edge:** Plain **Note:** Error in name "W(B)URGES

Date	Mintage	F	VF	XF	Unc	BU
2004	—	—	—	—	—	8.00

PIEFORTS

X#	Date	Mintage	Identification	Mkt Val
P1	1992	500	Ecu. 0.7500 Gold. 6.0000 g. X#2.	—
P2	1992	100	Ecu. 0.9250 Silver. 46.0000 g. X#1a.	125
P3	1992	500	25 Ecu. 0.9250 Silver. 46.0000 g. X#4.	100
P4	1992	25	25 Ecu. 0.9167 Gold. 76.0000 g. X#4a.	—

MINT SETS

X#	Date	Mintage	Identification	Issue Price	Mkt Val
XMS1	2004 (8)	—	X#Pn1-Pn8	—	30.00

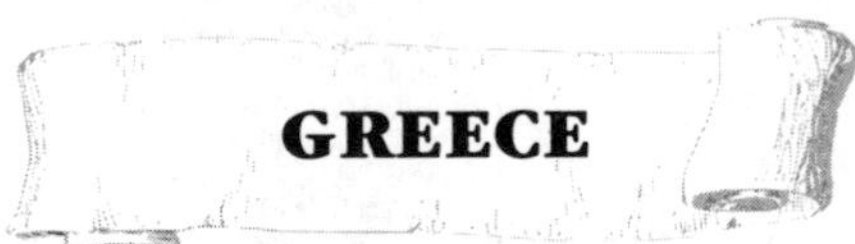

GREECE

KINGDOM

MEDALLIC COINAGE

Private political issues created for use in suspension jewelry. These pieces are most often found holed, with jewelry mounts, or with traces of mounts having been removed. Values listed below are for original pieces with little or no detracting features. Holed pieces and examples with extensive damage from mounting maintain lower values.

X# M5 2 DUCAT
Gold, 30.5 mm. **Subject:** Prime Minister Eleftherios Venizelos **Obv:** Double headed eagle with shield on breast, date in legend **Rev:** Bust 3/4 right

Date	Mintage	F	VF	XF	Unc	BU
1912	—	300	450	750	—	—

X# M1 2 DUCAT
5.2600 g., Gold **Subject:** Prime Minister Eleftherios Venizelos **Obv:** Crowned double headed eagle with shield on breast, anniversary date below **Rev:** Bust left

Date	Mintage	F	VF	XF	Unc	BU
ND(1919)	—	250	350	500	—	—
ND Restrike	—	—	—	—BV+20%		—

X# M2 4 DUCAT
10.7900 g., Gold **Subject:** Prime Minister Eleftherios Venizelos **Obv:** Crowned double headed eagle with shield on breast, anniversary date below **Rev:** Bust left

Date	Mintage	F	VF	XF	Unc	BU
ND(1919)	—	400	700	1,200	—	—
ND Restrike	—	—	—	—	BV+15%	—

X# M4 4 DUCAT
10.7900 g., Gold, 40 mm. **Subject:** Prime Minister Eleftherios Venizelos **Obv:** Crowned double headed eagle with shield on breast, date below **Rev:** Bust left

Date	Mintage	F	VF	XF	Unc	BU
1919	—	450	750	1,250	—	—

X# M3 4 DUCAT
11.0200 g., 0.9167 Gold 0.3248 oz. AGW, 39.5 mm. **Subject:** Prime Minister Eleftherios Venizelos **Obv:** Crowned double headed eagle with shield on breast, date below **Rev:** Bust right

Date	Mintage	F	VF	XF	Unc	BU
1919	—	450	750	1,250	—	—

X# M6 4 DUCAT
Gold, 40 mm. **Ruler:** Constantine I **Subject:** Constantine I **Obv:** Triple crowned double headed eagle with shield on breast, date below **Rev:** Bust left

Date	Mintage	F	VF	XF	Unc	BU
1920	—	600	1,000	1,750	—	—

REPUBLIC

MEDALLIC COINAGE

Euro Issues

X# 55 10 EURO
Silver **Subject:** Banknote

Date	Mintage	F	VF	XF	Unc	BU
1997 Proof	—	Value: 13.50				

X# 53 10 EURO
Silver **Subject:** Music

Date	Mintage	F	VF	XF	Unc	BU
1997 Proof	—	Value: 13.50				

ECU COINAGE

X# 10 ECU
6.0000 g., 0.9990 Silver 0.1927 oz. ASW, 21 mm. **Obv:** Greek goddess seated left **Rev:** 11 cubes in unusual formation **Rev. Inscription:** EUROPA

Date	Mintage	F	VF	XF	Unc	BU
1981 Proof	20,000	Value: 25.00				

X# 30 ECU
28.2800 g., 0.9250 Silver 0.8410 oz. ASW, 38.6 mm. **Obv:** Map of Europe with large "ECU" at center **Obv. Legend:** • GREECE • EUROPE - EUROPA **Rev:** Ancient Greek galley, 5 stars above, 5 stars below **Edge:** Reeded

Date	Mintage	F	VF	XF	Unc	BU
ND(1992)PM Proof	10,000	Value: 30.00				

X# 32 ECU
20.5000 g., Copper-Nickel, 38 mm. **Issuer:** Chelsea Coins, London **Obv:** Ancient galley above Greek flag within 12 stars **Rev:** Head of Alexander the Great of Macedonia right **Edge:** Plain

Date	Mintage	F	VF	XF	Unc	BU
1993	900	—	—	—	15.00	—

X# 44 ECU
20.0000 g., 0.9990 Silver 0.6423 oz. ASW **Issuer:** Göde GmbH **Obv:** Acropolis, large ECU below **Rev:** Bust of Homer 3/4 left **Edge:** Reeded

Date	Mintage	F	VF	XF	Unc	BU
ND(1993) Proof	9,999	Value: 40.00				

X# 32a ECU
23.0000 g., 0.9250 Silver 0.6840 oz. ASW **Issuer:** Chelsea Coins, London **Obv:** Ancient gallery above Greek flag within 12 stars **Rev:** Head of Alexander the Great of Macedonia right **Edge:** Plain

Date	Mintage	F	VF	XF	Unc	BU
1993 Proof	280	Value: 60.00				

X# 37 ECU
23.0000 g., 0.9250 Silver 0.6840 oz. ASW, 38 mm. **Issuer:** Chelsea Coins, London **Obv:** Ancient galley above Greek flag within 12 stars **Rev:** Alexander the Great of Macedonia horseback right, 12 stars above **Edge:** Reeded

Date	Mintage	F	VF	XF	Unc	BU
1994 Proof	1,000	Value: 50.00				

X# 41 ECU
8.0000 g., Gold **Issuer:** Chelsea Coins, London **Obv:** Ancient galley above Greek flag within 12 stars **Rev:** Alexander the Great of Macedonia horseback right, 12 stars above **Edge:** Reeded

Date	Mintage	F	VF	XF	Unc	BU
1994 Proof	150	—	—	—	—	—

X# 35 ECU
Silver **Subject:** European Summit Meeting on Corfu Island **Obv:** Prow of ancient galley **Rev:** Stylistic Greek flag, 12 stars **Rev. Legend:** HELLENIC PRESIDENCY

Date	Mintage	F	VF	XF	Unc	BU
1994	—	—	—	—	25.00	—

X# 38 5 ECU
Copper-Nickel, 38 mm. **Issuer:** Chelsea Coins, London **Obv:** Ancient galley above Greek flag within 12 stars **Rev:** Alexander the Great of Macedonia horseback right, 12 stars above **Edge:** Reeded

Date	Mintage	F	VF	XF	Unc	BU
1994	—	—	—	—	20.00	—

X# 21 10 ECU
10.0000 g., 0.9990 Silver 0.3212 oz. ASW, 28.2 mm. **Obv:** Pegasus rearing left **Rev:** Cornucopia within 12 stars **Edge:** Reeded

Date	Mintage	F	VF	XF	Unc	BU
1991 Proof	1,000	—	—	—	—	—
1992 Proof	11,500	Value: 40.00				

X# 31 10 ECU
28.2800 g., 0.9250 Silver 0.8410 oz. ASW, 38.6 mm. **Obv:** Map of Europe with large "ECU" at center **Obv. Legend:** • GREECE • EUROPE - EUROPA **Rev:** Ancient Greek galley, 5 stars above, 5 stars below **Edge:** Reeded

Date	Mintage	F	VF	XF	Unc	BU
ND(1992)PM Proof	10,000	Value: 30.00				

X# 24 10 ECU
28.0000 g., 0.9990 Silver 0.8993 oz. ASW **Obv:** Owl facing, perched on branch **Rev:** Cornucopia within 12 stars **Edge:** Reeded

Date	Mintage	F	VF	XF	Unc	BU
1993 Proof	2,500	Value: 35.00				

X# 33 20 ECU
20.5000 g., Copper-Nickel, 38 mm. **Issuer:** Chelsea Coins, London **Obv:** Ancient gallery above Greek flag within 12 stars **Rev:** Head of Alexander the Great of Macedonia right **Edge:** Plain

Date	Mintage	F	VF	XF	Unc	BU
1993	3,000	—	—	—	12.50	—

X# 33a 20 ECU
23.0000 g., 0.9250 Silver 0.6840 oz. ASW, 38 mm. **Issuer:** Chelsea Coins, London **Obv:** Ancient galley above Greek flag within 12 stars **Rev:** Head of Alexander the Great of Macedonia right **Edge:** Plain

Date	Mintage	F	VF	XF	Unc	BU
1993 Proof	300	Value: 60.00				

X# 33b 20 ECU
38.0000 g., 0.9167 Gold 1.1199 oz. AGW, 38 mm. **Issuer:** Chelsea Coins, London **Obv:** Ancient galley above Greek flag within 12 stars **Rev:** Head of Alexander the Great of Macedonia right **Edge:** Plain

Date	Mintage	F	VF	XF	Unc	BU
1993 Proof	10	—	—	—	—	—

X# 39 20 ECU
23.0000 g., 0.9250 Silver 0.6840 oz. ASW, 38 mm. **Issuer:** Chelsea Coins, London **Obv:** Ancient galley above Greek flag within 12 stars **Rev:** Alexander the Great of Macedonia horseback right, 12 stars above **Edge:** Reeded

Date	Mintage	F	VF	XF	Unc	BU
1994 Proof	2,900	Value: 50.00				

X# 22 25 ECU
28.0000 g., 0.9990 Silver 0.8993 oz. ASW, 37.2 mm. **Obv:** Pegasus rearing left **Rev:** Cornucopia within 12 stars **Edge:** Reeded

Date	Mintage	F	VF	XF	Unc	BU
1991 Proof	1,000	—	—	—	—	—
1992 Proof	11,500	Value: 60.00				

X# 25 25 ECU
28.0000 g., 0.9990 Silver 0.8993 oz. ASW, 37.2 mm. **Obv:** Owl facing, perched on branch **Rev:** Cornucopia within 12 stars **Edge:** Reeded

Date	Mintage	F	VF	XF	Unc	BU
1993 Proof	2,500	Value: 55.00				

X# 23 150 ECU

6.7200 g., 0.7500 Gold 0.1620 oz. AGW, 20 mm.
Obv: Pegasus rearing left **Rev:** Cornucopia within 12 stars **Edge:** Reeded

Date	Mintage	F	VF	XF	Unc	BU
1991 Proof	250	—	—	—	—	—
1992 Proof	1,500	Value: 275				

X# 26 150 ECU

6.7200 g., 0.7500 Gold 0.1620 oz. AGW, 20 mm.
Obv: Owl facing, perched on branch **Rev:** Cornucopia within 12 stars **Edge:** Reeded

Date	Mintage	F	VF	XF	Unc	BU
1993 Proof	500	Value: 275				

X# 40 150 ECU

Bi-Metallic Silver/Gold **Issuer:** Chelsea Coins, London **Obv:** Ancient galley above Greek flag within 12 stars **Rev:** Alexander the Great of Macedonia horseback right, 12 stars above **Edge:** Reeded

Date	Mintage	F	VF	XF	Unc	BU
1994 Proof	400	—	—	—	—	—

X# 34 200 ECU

6.0000 g., 0.7500 Gold 0.1447 oz. AGW, 22.05 mm. **Issuer:** Chelsea Coins, London **Obv:** Ancient galley above Greek flag within 12 stars **Rev:** Head of Alexander the Great of Macedonia right **Edge:** Plain

Date	Mintage	F	VF	XF	Unc	BU
1993 Proof	100	Value: 300				

FANTASY EURO

ICB Issue

X# 60 10 EURO

Bronze **Subject:** 1996 Olympics **Obv:** Stylized sailing ship, stylized flag below **Obv. Legend:** HELLAS - EUROPA (in Greek) **Rev:** Olympic athletes **Rev. Legend:** OLYMPUS (in Greek)

Date	Mintage	VG	F	VF	XF	Unc
1996	—	—	—	—	—	8.50

PIEFORTS

X#	Date	Mintage	Identification	Mkt Val
P1	1991	500	10 Ecu. 0.9990 Silver. 20.0000 g. X21.	—
P2	1991	500	25 Ecu. 0.9990 Silver. 56.0000 g. X22.	—
P3	1992	1,000	10 Ecu. 0.9990 Silver. 20.0000 g. X21.	60.00
P4	1992	1,000	25 Ecu. 0.9990 Silver. 56.0000 g. X22.	90.00
P5	1993	1,000	10 Ecu. 0.9990 Silver. 20.0000 g. X24.	60.00
P6	1993	1,000	25 Ecu. 0.9990 Silver. 56.0000 g. X25.	90.00
P7	1993	140	Ecu. 0.9250 Silver. 46.0000 g. X32a.	120
P8	1993	150	20 Ecu. 0.9250 Silver. 46.0000 g. X33a.	120
P9	1993	5	20 Ecu. 0.9167 Gold. 76.0000 g. X33b.	—
X#	Date	Mintage	Identification	Mkt Val

P10	1995	—	Ecu. Silver. 38.0000 g.	40.00

PROOF SETS

X#	Date	Mintage	Identification	Issue Price	Mkt Val
XPS1	1991 (3)	250	X21-X23	—	—
XPS2	1991 (2)	750	X21, X22	—	—
XPS3	1991 (2)	250	XP1, XP2	—	—
XPS4	1992 (3)	1,500	X21-X23	—	350
XPS5	1992 (2)	10,000	X21, X22	—	100
XPS6	1992 (2)	1,000	XP3, XP4	—	150
XPS7	1993 (3)	500	X24-26	—	350
XPS8	1993 (2)	2,000	X24, X25	—	100
XPS9	1993 (2)	1,000	XP5, XP6	—	150

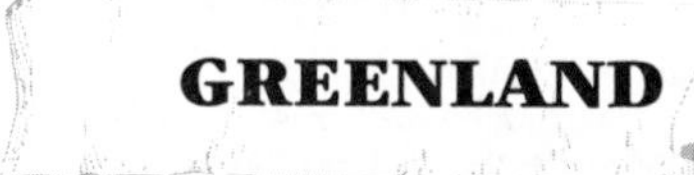

GREENLAND

PRIVATE ISSUE

BULLION COINAGE

X# 5 PIASTER

31.1030 g., 0.9990 Silver 0.9989 oz. ASW, 32 mm.
Obv: Personification of Greenland sitting on throne left **Obv. Legend:** KALAALLIT NUNAAT **Rev:** Polar bear standing left **Rev. Legend:** GRØNLAND

Date	Mintage	F	VF	XF	Unc	BU
1987 Proof	1,000	Value: 60.00				
1989 Proof	500	Value: 65.00				

X# 6 5 PIASTER

155.5150 g., 0.9990 Silver 4.9947 oz. ASW, 65 mm.
Obv: Personification of Greenland sitting on throne left **Obv. Legend:** KALAALLIT NUNAAT **Rev:** Polar bear standing left **Rev. Legend:** GRØNLAND **Note:** Struck by Valcambi, Lelocle, Switzerland. Illustration reduced.

Date	Mintage	F	VF	XF	Unc	BU
1987 Proof	—	Value: 140				

STATE

ECU COINAGE

X# 11 25 ECU

0.9990 Silver, 38 mm. **Ruler:** Margrethe II **Issuer:** Numex S.A., Madrid **Obv:** Crowned Danish arms **Obv. Legend:** GRØNLANDS HJEMMESTYRE **Rev:** Polar bear with cub walking left **Edge:** Reeded

Date	Mintage	F	VF	XF	Unc	BU
1831	2,273,000	100	250	750	3,000	—

X# 12 150 ECU

Gold, 38 mm. **Ruler:** Margrethe II **Issuer:** Numex S.A., Madrid **Obv:** Crowned Danish arms **Obv. Legend:** GRØNLANDS HJEMMESTYRE **Rev:** Polar bear with cub walking left **Edge:** Reeded

Date	Mintage	F	VF	XF	Unc	BU
1993 Proof	500	Value: 750				

FANTASY EURO PATTERNS

X# Pn1 EURO CENT
Copper Plated Steel **Edge:** Plain

Date	Mintage	F	VF	XF	Unc	BU
2004	12,500	—	—	—	—	1.50
2004 Proof	5,000	Value: 2.50				

X# Pn2 2 EURO CENT
Copper Plated Steel

Date	Mintage	F	VF	XF	Unc	BU
2004	12,500	—	—	—	—	2.00
2004 Proof	5,000	Value: 3.00				

X# Pn3 5 EURO CENT
Copper Plated Steel **Edge:** Plain

Date	Mintage	F	VF	XF	Unc	BU
2004	12,500	—	—	—	—	2.50
2004 Proof	5,000	Value: 3.50				

X# Pn4 10 EURO CENT
Goldine **Edge:** Plain

Date	Mintage	F	VF	XF	Unc	BU
2004	12,500	—	—	—	—	3.00
2004 Proof	5,000	Value: 4.00				

X# Pn5 20 EURO CENT
Goldine **Edge:** Plain

Date	Mintage	F	VF	XF	Unc	BU
2004	12,500	—	—	—	—	3.50
2004 Proof	5,000	Value: 5.00				

X# Pn6 50 EURO CENT
Goldine **Edge:** Plain

Date	Mintage	F	VF	XF	Unc	BU
2004	12,500	—	—	—	—	4.00
2004 Proof	5,000	Value: 6.00				

X# Pn7 EURO
Bi-Metallic **Obv:** Zeppelin behind male head left **Rev:** Value and outline map of Greenland **Edge:** Plain

Date	Mintage	F	VF	XF	Unc	BU
2004	12,500	—	—	—	—	6.00
2004 Proof	5,000	Value: 8.00				

X# Pn8 2 EURO
Bi-Metallic **Obv:** Sailing ship **Rev:** Value on outline map of Greenland **Edge:** Plain

Date	Mintage	F	VF	XF	Unc	BU
2004	12,500	—	—	—	—	8.00
2004 Proof	5,000	Value: 10.00				

X# Pn9 5 EURO
Tri-Metallic **Obv:** Bird above rabbit **Rev:** Value on outline map of Greenland

Date	Mintage	F	VF	XF	Unc	BU
2004 Proof	5,000	Value: 12.50				

MINT SETS

X#	Date	Mintage	Identification	Issue Price	Mkt Val
XMS1	2004 (8)	12,500	X#Pn1-Pn8	—	20.00

PROOF SETS

X#	Date	Mintage	Identification	Issue Price	Mkt Val
XPS1	2004	5,000	X#Pn1-Pn9	—	35.00

GRENADA

INDEPENDENT STATE
Commonwealth of Nations
MEDALLIC COINAGE

X# M1 25 DOLLARS
29.9700 g., 0.9990 Silver 0.9626 oz. ASW **Subject:** Carifta Exposition - Premier Eric Gairy **Note:** Prev. KM#M1.

Date	Mintage	F	VF	XF	Unc	BU
1969 Proof	—	Value: 100				

X# M2 200 DOLLARS
37.9400 g., 0.9160 Gold 1.1173 oz. AGW **Subject:** Carifta Exposition - Premier Eric Gairy **Note:** Prev. KM#M2.

Date	Mintage	F	VF	XF	Unc	BU
1969 Proof	—	Value: 1,000				

GRIQUATOWN

GRIQUATOWN
BRITISH COLONY
TOKEN COINAGE
1815 - 1816 Missionary Series

X# Tn1 1/4 PENNY
Copper **Note:** Prev. KM#Tn1.

Date	Mintage	F	VF	XF	Unc	BU
ND(1815-16)	—	—	450	650	1,200	—
ND(1815-16) Proof	—	Value: 1,500				

X# Tn2 1/2 PENNY
Copper **Note:** Prev. KM#Tn2.

Date	Mintage	F	VF	XF	Unc	BU
ND(1815-16)	—	—	500	750	1,500	—
ND(1815-16) Proof	—	Value: 1,700				

X# Tn4 5 PENCE
Silver **Note:** Prev. KM#Tn4.

Date	Mintage	F	VF	XF	Unc	BU
ND(1815-16)	—	—	500	900	1,750	—
ND(1815-16) Proof	—	Value: 1,950				

X# Tn5 10 PENCE
Silver **Note:** Prev. KM#Tn5.

Date	Mintage	F	VF	XF	Unc	BU
ND(1815-16)	—	—	650	1,100	2,200	—
ND(1815-16) Proof	—	Value: 2,500				

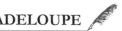

1890 L. C. Lauer Series

Struck by Messrs. Otto Nolte & Co., Berlin, Germany

X# 8 PENNY

Copper **Note:** Prev. Bruce#X5 and KM#Pn5.

Date	Mintage	F	VF	XF	Unc	BU
1890 Proof	—	Value: 550				

X# 9 PENNY

Copper **Note:** Prev. Bruce#X6 and KM#Pn6.

Date	Mintage	F	VF	XF	Unc	BU
ND(1890) Proof	—	Value: 450				

X# 10 PENNY

Nickel **Note:** Prev. Bruce#X7 and KM#Pn7.

Date	Mintage	F	VF	XF	Unc	BU
ND(1890) Rare	—	—	—	—	—	—

Fantasy Missionary Issues

The 100 Pence is a modern fantasy issue of unknown origin struck without any government authorization for obvious confusion of the numismatic community

X# 1 100 PENCE

Silver

Date	Mintage	F	VF	XF	Unc	BU
ND	—	—	—	—	25.00	—

X# 2 100 PENCE

Copper

Date	Mintage	F	VF	XF	Unc	BU
ND	—	—	—	—	15.00	—

X# 3 100 PENCE

Silver **Note:** Piefort.

Date	Mintage	F	VF	XF	Unc	BU
ND	—	—	—	—	35.00	—

GUADELOUPE

FRENCH OCCUPATION

COUNTERMARKED COINAGE

X# 3 3 SOLS 9 DENIERS

Copper **Countermark:** "RF" **Note:** Countermark in oval on French 1/2 Sol of Louis XVI.

CM Date	Host Date	Good	VG	F	VF	XF
1767	ND(1774-91)	—	6.00	12.00	25.00	40.00

X# 2 2 BITS

4.3400 g., Silver **Countermark:** "RF" and "GR"
Note: Countermark in oval on 1/4 cut of Spanish Colonial bust type 8 Reales with a crowned script and countermark in rectangular indent for British Honduras.

CM Date	Host Date	Good	VG	F	VF	XF
1767	ND(1774-91)	—	12.50	20.00	35.00	60.00

RF Countermark

This countermark was only authorized in 1793 to be struck only on French Colonies 12 Deniers dated 1767. The following are modern concoctions

X# 4 3 SOLS 9 DENIERS

Copper **Countermark:** "RF" **Note:** Countermark in oval on French 1 Sol of Louis XVI.

CM Date	Host Date	Good	VG	F	VF	XF
1767	ND(1774-91)	—	6.00	12.00	25.00	40.00

X# 1 2 BITS

4.3400 g., Silver **Countermark:** "RF"
Note: Countermark in oval on 1/6 cut of Spanish Colonial pillar type 8 Reales.

CM Date	Host Date	Good	VG	F	VF	XF
1767	ND(1774-91)	—	12.50	20.00	35.00	60.00

X# 5 ECU

Silver **Countermark:** "RF" **Note:** Countermark in oval on France Ecu of Louis XVI.

CM Date	Host Date	Good	VG	F	VF	XF
1767	ND(1774-91)	—	35.00	50.00	90.00	150

G & Crowned G Countermark

The punch for the small crowned ""G"" has a filled crown while the genuine punches have an open crown. The sunburst ""G"" countermark is now considered to be spurious by leading authorities

X# 9 12 DENIERS

Bronze **Countermark:** "G" **Note:** Countermark in 15-pointed sunburst indent on French Colonies 12 Deniers.

CM Date	Host Date	Good	VG	F	VF	XF
1767	ND(1767)	—	8.00	15.00	22.00	35.00

X# 6 2 SOUS

Bronze **Countermark:** "G" **Note:** Countermark in 15-pointed sunburst indent on France 2 Sols.

CM Date	Host Date	Good	VG	F	VF	XF
1767	ND(1792-93)	—	8.00	15.00	22.00	35.00

X# 8 25 SOUS

Silver **Countermark:** "G" **Note:** Countermark in outlined 8-sided indent on quartered France 1/2 Ecu.

CM Date	Host Date	Good	VG	F	VF	XF
1767	ND(1792-93)	—	6.00	12.00	20.00	30.00

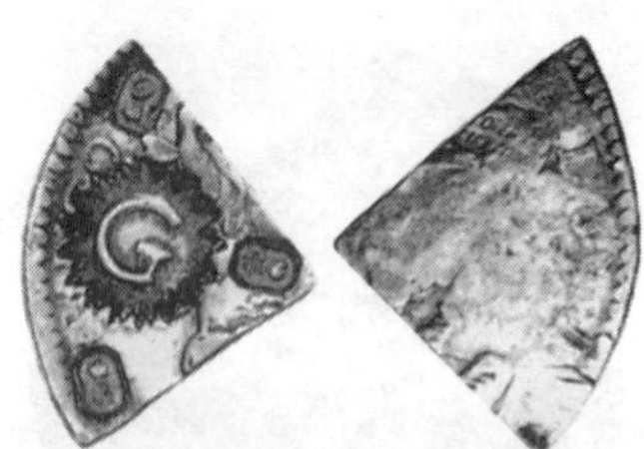

X# 11 50 SOUS
Silver **Countermark:** Additional "G" **Note:** Countermark in 15-pointed sunburst indent on X#10.

CM Date	Host Date	Good	VG	F	VF	XF
1767	ND(1792-93)	—	6.00	12.00	20.00	30.00

X# 13 50 SOUS
Silver **Countermark:** Crowned "G" **Note:** Countermark in outlined 8-sided indent on halved France 1/2 Ecu.

CM Date	Host Date	Good	VG	F	VF	XF
1767	ND(1774-90)	—	10.00	20.00	30.00	45.00

X# 10 50 SOUS
Silver **Countermark:** Crowned "G" **Note:** Countermark in outlined 8-sided indent on quartered France Ecu.

CM Date	Host Date	Good	VG	F	VF	XF
1767	ND(1792-93)	—	6.00	12.00	20.00	30.00

X# 16 22 LIVRES
0.9170 Gold **Countermark:** "G" **Note:** Countermark in 15-pointed sunburst indent on Brazil 6400 Reis of John V.

CM Date	Host Date	Good	VG	F	VF	XF
1767	ND(1727-50)	—	—	—	—	—

X# 17 22 LIVRES
0.9170 Gold **Countermark:** "G" **Note:** Countermark in 15-pointed sunburst indent on Brazil 6400 Reis of Maria I and Pedro III.

CM Date	Host Date	Good	VG	F	VF	XF
1767	ND(1777-86)	—	—	—	—	—

X# 18 22 LIVRES
0.9170 Gold **Countermark:** "G" **Note:** Countermark in 15-pointed sunburst indent on Brazil 6400 Reis of Maria I.

CM Date	Host Date	Good	VG	F	VF	XF
1767	ND(1789-1805)	—	—	—	—	—

X# 20 5 FRANCS
Note: Countermark in outlined 8-sided indent on France 5 Francs dated 1834. An obvious modern concoction.

CM Date	Host Date	Good	VG	F	VF	XF
1834	ND(1834)	—	12.50	20.00	30.00	45.00

FRENCH COLONY

ESSAIS

X# E11 1/4 EURO
7.8000 g., 0.9990 Silver 0.2505 oz. ASW, 27.2 mm. **Series:** Euro **Obv:** Bust of Louis Oscar Roty almost left **Obv. Legend:** GUADELOUPE **Rev:** Lyon (1892 medal) **Edge:** Reeded

Date	Mintage	F	VF	XF	Unc	BU
2004 Proof	2,000	—	—	—	—	20.00

X# E11a 1/4 EURO
10.3100 g., Copper, 27.25 mm. **Obv:** Bust of Louis Oscar Roty half left **Obv. Legend:** GUADELOUPE **Rev:** Lyon (1892 medal) **Edge:** Reeded

Date	Mintage	F	VF	XF	Unc	BU
2004	30	—	—	—	50.00	50.00

X# E12 1-1/2 EURO
31.1400 g., 0.9990 Silver 1.0000 oz. ASW, 38.6 mm. **Series:** Euro **Obv:** Arms **Obv. Legend:** RÉPUBLIQUE FRANÇAISE **Obv. Inscription:** Liberté / égalité / fraternité **Rev:** Battleship Gloire, 1860-1879 **Rev. Legend:** HISTOIRE DE LA MARINE FRANÇAISE **Edge:** Reeded

Date	Mintage	F	VF	XF	Unc	BU
2004 Proof	2,000	Value: 35.00				

X# E13 1-1/2 EURO
26.0700 g., Brass antiqued, 39.18 mm. **Series:** Euro **Obv:** Arms **Obv. Legend:** RÉPUBLIQUE FRANÇAISE **Rev:** Battleship Gloire, 1860-1879 **Rev. Legend:** HISTOIRE DE LA MARINE FRANÇAISE **Edge:** Reeded

Date	Mintage	F	VF	XF	Unc	BU
2004 Proof	25	Value: 50.00				

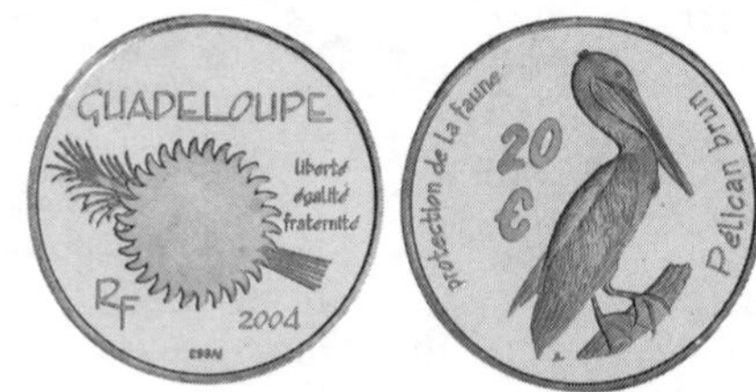

X# E15 20 EURO
8.5300 g., 0.9167 Gold 0.2514 oz. AGW, 27.1 mm. **Series:** Euro **Obv:** Arms **Obv. Inscription:** Liberté/égalité/fratenité **Rev:** Brown pelican **Rev. Legend:** Protection de la Faune **Edge:** Plain

Date	Mintage	F	VF	XF	Unc	BU
2004 Proof	300	Value: 285				

X# E15a 20 EURO
10.3300 g., Copper, 27.19 mm. **Obv:** Arms **Obv. Inscription:** Liberté / égalité / fratenité **Rev:** Brown pelican **Rev. Legend:** Protection de la Faune **Edge:** Plain

Date	Mintage	F	VF	XF	Unc	BU
2004	30	—	—	—	50.00	50.00

FANTASY EURO PATTERNS

X# Pn1 EURO CENT
Copper Plated Steel

Date	Mintage	F	VF	XF	Unc	BU
2005	2,500	—	—	—	—	1.50

X# Pn2 2 EURO CENT
Copper Plated Steel

Date	Mintage	F	VF	XF	Unc	BU
2005	2,500	—	—	—	—	2.00

X# Pn3 5 EURO CENT
Copper Plated Steel

Date	Mintage	F	VF	XF	Unc	BU
2005	2,500	—	—	—	—	2.50

X# Pn4 10 EURO CENT
Goldine

Date	Mintage	F	VF	XF	Unc	BU
2005	2,500	—	—	—	—	3.00

X# Pn5 20 EURO CENT
Goldine

Date	Mintage	F	VF	XF	Unc	BU
2005	2,500	—	—	—	—	3.50

X# Pn6 50 EURO CENT
Goldine

Date	Mintage	F	VF	XF	Unc	BU
2005	2,500	—	—	—	—	4.00

X# Pn7 EURO
Bi-Metallic

Date	Mintage	F	VF	XF	Unc	BU
2005	2,500	—	—	—	—	6.00

X# Pn8 2 EURO
Bi-Metallic

Date	Mintage	F	VF	XF	Unc	BU
2005	2,500	—	—	—	—	8.00

FRENCH OVERSEAS DEPARTMENT

ESSAIS

X# E6 1/4 EURO
7.8000 g., 0.9990 Silver 0.2505 oz. ASW, 27.2 mm. **Obv:** Louis O. Roty **Rev:** Seated angel **Edge:** Reeded

Date	Mintage	F	VF	XF	Unc	BU
2004 Proof	2,000	Value: 30.00				

X# E7 1-1/2 EURO
31.6000 g., 0.9990 Silver 1.0149 oz. ASW, 39.1 mm. **Obv:** Sun across sugar cane **Rev:** Sail ship Cuirasse Gloire **Edge:** Reeded and lettered **Edge Lettering:** "NWTM ONE OZ..999"

Date	Mintage	F	VF	XF	Unc	BU
2004 Proof	2,000	Value: 40.00				

MINT SETS

X#	Date	Mintage	Identification	Issue Price	Mkt Val
XMS1	2005 (8)	2,500	X#Pn1-Pn8	—	30.00

GRANDE TERRE

FRENCH COLONY

COUNTERMARKED COINAGE

X# 9 NON-DENOMINATED
Note: Countermark in dentilated rectangle on worn coins. Prev. Craig #41.

CM Date	Host Date	Good	VG	F	VF	XF
	ND	10.00	20.00	35.00	—	—

X# 13 NON-DENOMINATED
Countermark: "GT" **Note:** Countermark monogram on worn coins.

CM Date	Host Date	Good	VG	F	VF	XF
	ND	10.00	20.00	35.00	—	—

X# 11 NON-DENOMINATED
Note: Countermark punched on worn coins. Prev. Craig #43.

CM Date	Host Date	Good	VG	F	VF	XF
	ND	10.00	20.00	35.00	—	—

ISLE DESIRADE

FRENCH COLONY

COUNTERSTAMPED COINAGE

X# 1 NON-DENOMINATED
Counterstamp: "GLD" (Guadeloupe La Desirade) **Note:** Counterstamp on French 12 Deniers. Prev. Craig #51.

CS Date	Host Date	Good	VG	F	VF	XF
ND	ND	—	—	—	—	—

X# 6 NON-DENOMINATED Counterstamp: "ID" (Isle Desirade) **Note:** Counterstamp separated by fleur de lis on worn coins. Prev. Craig #33.

CS Date	Host Date	Good	VG	F	VF	XF
ND	ND	—	—	—	—	—

LES SAINTES

FRENCH COLONY

COUNTERSTAMPED COINAGE

X# 10 NON-DENOMINATED
Counterstamp: "IG" (Isle Guadeloupe) on obverse. "LS" (Les Saintes) on reverse **Note:** Counterstamp in heart shape on obvervse. Counterstamp in denteated rectangle on worn coins on reverse. Prev. Craig #51.

CS Date	Host Date	Good	VG	F	VF	XF
	ND	15.00	25.00	50.00	—	—

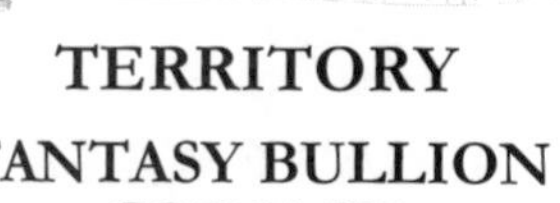

GUAM

TERRITORY

FANTASY BULLION COINAGE

X# 10 1/10 OUNCE
3.1106 g., 0.9999 Gold 0.1000 oz. AGW, 17.7 mm. **Ruler:** Guahan **Issuer:** Bernard von Nothaus

Obv: Native male, bust right **Obv. Legend:** MAGA' LAHI MATA' PANG- GUAHAN **Rev:** Palm tree, island **Rev. Legend:** HALE'-TA TANO' TA **Rev. Inscription:** GUAM **Edge:** Reeded

Date	Mintage	F	VF	XF	Unc	BU
1994 Proof	—	Value: 75.00				

X# 11 OUNCE

31.1341 g., 0.9990 Gold 0.9999 oz. AGW
Ruler: Guahan **Issuer:** Bernard von Nothaus
Subject: Head right **Obv. Legend:** MAGA' LAHI MATA' PANG **Rev:** Large palm tree, island in eliptical outline **Rev. Inscription:** GUAN **Edge:** Reeded

Date	Mintage	F	VF	XF	Unc	BU
1994 Proof	—	Value: 750				

X# 11a OUNCE

Bronze **Ruler:** Guahan **Issuer:** Bernard von Nothaus **Obv:** Head right **Obv. Legend:** MAGA' LAHI MATA' PANG **Rev:** Large palm tree, island in eliptical outline **Edge:** Reeded

Date	Mintage	F	VF	XF	Unc	BU
1994 Proof	—	Value: 20.00				

MEDALLIC COINAGE

X# 5 DOLLAR

23.8700 g., Silver, 38.3 mm. **Obv:** Island, key hole with palm tree **Obv. Legend:** WHERE AMERICA'S DAY BEGINS **Rev:** Magellan standing right, sailing ship in background **Rev. Legend:** GUAM DOLLAR - AGANA **Note:** Individually numbered in the right obverse field.

Date	Mintage	F	VF	XF	Unc	BU
1974	—	—	—	—	45.00	—

X# 5a DOLLAR

23.8700 g., Silver with Silver gilt, 38.3 mm. **Obv:** Island, key hole with palm tree **Obv. Legend:** WHERE AMERICA'S DAY BEGINS **Rev:** Magellan standing right, sailing ship in background **Rev. Legend:** GUAM DOLLAR - AGANA **Note:** Individually numbered in the right obverse field.

Date	Mintage	F	VF	XF	Unc	BU
1974	—	—	—	—	45.00	—

GUATEMALA

SPANISH COLONY

MEDALLIC COINAGE

Vice Royalty of New Spain

Proclamation issues were struck for Ferdinand VII as the new king of Spain while he was under Napoleonic French guard.

X# M2 REAL

Silver **Issuer:** Nueva Guatemala **Obv:** Bust right **Obv. Legend:** FERDIN • HISP • VIII • GUAT • II • **Rev:** Crowned shield **Rev. Legend:** * INTER * SUSPIRIA * FIDES *

Date	Mintage	F	VF	XF	Unc	BU
1808	—	75.00	100	175	250	—
1808 PGA	—	75.00	100	175	250	—

X# M1 REAL

Silver **Issuer:** Nueva Guatemala **Obv. Legend:** FERNANDO • VII... **Note:** Prev. KM#M1.

Date	Mintage	F	VF	XF	Unc	BU
1808	—	75.00	100	175	250	—

X# M6 REAL

Silver **Issuer:** Quetzaltenango **Note:** Prev. KM#M6.

Date	Mintage	F	VF	XF	Unc	BU
1808	—	75.00	100	175	250	—

X# M3 2 REALES

6.6000 g., Silver **Issuer:** Nueva Guatemala **Subject:** 1st Year of Reign **Obv. Legend:** ....DE SU REYN **Note:** Prev. KM#M3.

Date	Mintage	F	VF	XF	Unc	BU
1808	—	90.00	125	225	350	—

X# M4 2 REALES

6.6000 g., Silver **Issuer:** Nueva Guatemala **Obv. Legend:** ....DE SU REINA **Note:** Prev. KM#M4.

Date	Mintage	F	VF	XF	Unc	BU
1808	—	90.00	125	225	350	—

X# M5 2 REALES

9.3000 g., Silver **Issuer:** Nueva Guatemala **Edge:** Plain **Note:** Prev. KM#M5.

Date	Mintage	F	VF	XF	Unc	BU
1808	—	125	175	300	450	—

X# M7 2 REALES

Silver **Issuer:** Quetzaltenango **Obv. Legend:** ... ANO / I / DE / SU / REYNA / **Note:** Prev. KM#M7.

Date	Mintage	F	VF	XF	Unc	BU
1808	—	90.00	125	225	350	—

X# M8 2 REALES

Silver **Issuer:** Quetzaltenango **Obv. Legend:** DE • ESP • E • IND • **Note:** Prev. KM#M8. For similar medallic issues see El Salvador and Honduras listings.

Date	Mintage	F	VF	XF	Unc	BU
1808	—	90.00	125	225	350	—

REPUBLIC

MEDALLIC COINAGE

X# M21 4/5 OUNCE

27.9500 g., 0.9000 Gold 0.8087 oz. AGW, 30.9 mm. **Series:** National Heroes **Obv:** Arms **Obv. Legend:** REPUBLICA DE GUATEMALA **Rev:** Bust of Tecun Uman wearing ornate headdress left **Edge:** Plain

Date	Mintage	F	VF	XF	Unc	BU
1965	—	—	—	600	700	—

ICB Issues

X# 1.1 QUETZAL

24.0000 g., 0.9250 Silver 0.7137 oz. ASW, 38 mm. **Obv:** Arms **Obv. Legend:** REPUBLICA DE GUATEMALA **Rev:** Juan Fernandez Firecrown hummingbird in flight, Lake Atitlan, volcanos in background **Edge:** Reeded

Date	Mintage	F	VF	XF	Unc	BU
1995 Proof	150	Value: 60.00				

X# 1.2 QUETZAL

24.0000 g., 0.9250 Silver 0.7137 oz. ASW, 38 mm. **Obv:** Arms **Obv. Legend:** REPUBLICA DE GUATEMALA **Rev:** Juan Fernandez Firecrown hummingbird in flight, Lake Atitlan, volcanos in background **Edge:** Plain

Date	Mintage	F	VF	XF	Unc	BU
1995 Proof	150	Value: 60.00				

X# 1a.1 QUETZAL

23.0000 g., Brass, 38 mm. **Obv:** Arms **Obv. Legend:** REPUBLICA DE GUATEMALA **Rev:** Juan Fernandez Firecrown hummingbird in flight, Lake Atitlan, volcanos in background **Edge:** Reeded

Date	Mintage	F	VF	XF	Unc	BU
1995 Proof	150	Value: 45.00				

X# 1a.2 QUETZAL

23.0000 g., Brass, 38 mm. **Obv:** Arms **Obv. Legend:** REPUBLICA DE GUATEMALA **Rev:** Juan Fernandez Firecrown hummingbird in flight, Lake Atitlan, volcanos in background **Edge:** Plain

Date	Mintage	F	VF	XF	Unc	BU
1995 Proof	150	Value: 45.00				

X# 1b.1 QUETZAL

20.0000 g., Gilt Alloy, 38 mm. **Obv:** Arms **Obv. Legend:** REPUBLICA DE GUATEMALA **Rev:** Juan Fernandez Firecrown hummingbird in flight, Lake Atitlan, volcanos in background **Edge:** Reeded

Date	Mintage	F	VF	XF	Unc	BU
1995 Proof	150	Value: 45.00				

X# 1b.2 QUETZAL

20.0000 g., Gilt Alloy, 38 mm. **Obv:** Arms **Obv. Legend:** REPUBLICA DE GUATEMALA **Rev:** Juan Fernandez Firecrown hummingbird in flight, Lake Atitlan, volcanos in background **Edge:** Plain

Date	Mintage	F	VF	XF	Unc	BU
1995 Proof	150	Value: 45.00				

X# 1c.1 QUETZAL

23.0000 g., Tri-Metallic, 38 mm. **Obv:** Arms **Obv. Legend:** REPUBLICA DE GUATEMALA **Rev:** Juan Fernandez Firecrown hummingbird in flight, Lake Atitlan, volcanos in background **Edge:** Reeded

Date	Mintage	F	VF	XF	Unc	BU
1995 Proof	150	Value: 75.00				

X# 1c.2 QUETZAL

23.0000 g., Tri-Metallic, 38 mm. **Obv:** Arms **Obv. Legend:** REPUBLICA DE GUATEMALA **Rev:** Juan Fernandez Firecrown hummingbird in flight, Lake Atitlan, volcanos in background **Edge:** Plain

Date	Mintage	F	VF	XF	Unc	BU
1995 Proof	150	Value: 75.00				

X# 1c.3 QUETZAL

23.0000 g., Tri-Metallic, 38 mm. **Obv:** Arms **Obv. Legend:** REPUBLICA DE GUATEMALA **Rev:** Juan Fernandez Firecrown hummingbird in flight, Lake Atitlan, volcanos in background **Edge:** Reeded

Date	Mintage	F	VF	XF	Unc	BU
1995 Matte Proof	150	Value: 65.00				

X# 1c.4 QUETZAL

23.0000 g., Tri-Metallic, 38 mm. **Obv:** Arms **Obv. Legend:** REPUBLICA DE GUATEMALA **Rev:** Juan Fernandez Firecrown hummingbird in flight, Lake Atitlan, volcanos in background **Edge:** Plain

Date	Mintage	F	VF	XF	Unc	BU
1995 Matte Proof	150	Value: 65.00				

X# 1d.1 QUETZAL

6.0000 g., Aluminum, 38 mm. **Obv:** Arms **Obv. Legend:** REPUBLICA DE GUATEMALA **Rev:** Juan Fernandez Firecrown hummingbird in flight, Lake Atitlan, volcanos in background **Edge:** Reeded

Date	Mintage	F	VF	XF	Unc	BU
1995 Proof	150	Value: 50.00				

X# 1d.2 QUETZAL

6.0000 g., Aluminum, 38 mm. **Obv:** Arms **Obv. Legend:** REPUBLICA DE GUATEMALA **Rev:** Juan Fernandez Firecrown hummingbird in flight, Lake Atitlan, volcanos in background **Edge:** Plain

Date	Mintage	F	VF	XF	Unc	BU
1995 Proof	150	Value: 50.00				

X# 1e.1 QUETZAL

23.0000 g., Copper, 38 mm. **Obv:** Arms **Obv. Legend:** REPUBLICA DE GUATEMALA **Rev:** Juan Fernandez Firecrown hummingbird in flight, Lake Atitlan, volcanos in background **Edge:** Reeded

Date	Mintage	F	VF	XF	Unc	BU
1995 Proof	150	Value: 50.00				

X# 1e.2 QUETZAL

23.0000 g., Copper, 38 mm. **Obv:** Arms **Obv. Legend:** REPUBLICA DE GUATEMALA **Rev:** Juan Fernandez Firecrown hummingbird in flight, Lake Atitlan, volcanos in background **Edge:** Plain

Date	Mintage	F	VF	XF	Unc	BU
1995 Proof	150	Value: 50.00				

X# 1f.1 QUETZAL

20.0000 g., Copper-Nickel, 38 mm. **Obv:** Arms **Obv. Legend:** REPUBLICA DE GUATEMALA **Rev:** Juan Fernandez Firecrown hummingbird in flight, Lake Atitlan, volcanos in background **Edge:** Reeded

Date	Mintage	F	VF	XF	Unc	BU
1995 Proof	150	Value: 50.00				

X# 1f.2 QUETZAL

20.0000 g., Copper-Nickel, 38 mm. **Obv:** Arms **Obv. Legend:** REPUBLICA DE GUATEMALA **Rev:** Juan Fernandez Firecrown hummingbird in flight, Lake Atitlan, volcanos in background **Edge:** Plain

Date	Mintage	F	VF	XF	Unc	BU
1995 Proof	150	Value: 50.00				

X# 2.2 10 QUETZALES

24.0000 g., 0.9250 Silver 0.7137 oz. ASW, 38 mm. **Obv:** Arms **Obv. Legend:** REPUBLICA DE GUATEMALA **Rev:** Quetzal bird in flight, Temple Tikal at left in background **Edge:** Plain

Date	Mintage	F	VF	XF	Unc	BU
1995 Proof	150	Value: 60.00				

X# 2a.1 10 QUETZALES

23.0000 g., Brass, 38 mm. **Obv:** Arms **Obv. Legend:** REPUBLICA DE GUATEMALA **Rev:** Quetzal bird in flight, Temple Tikal at left in background **Edge:** Reeded

Date	Mintage	F	VF	XF	Unc	BU
1995 Proof	150	Value: 50.00				

X# 2a.2 10 QUETZALES

23.0000 g., Brass, 38 mm. **Obv:** Arms **Obv. Legend:** REPUBLICA DE GUATEMALA **Rev:** Quetzal bird in flight, Temple Tikal at left in background **Edge:** Plain

Date	Mintage	F	VF	XF	Unc	BU
1995 Proof	150	Value: 50.00				

X# 2b.1 10 QUETZALES

20.0000 g., Gilt Alloy, 38 mm. **Obv:** Arms **Obv. Legend:** REPUBLICA DE GUATEMALA **Rev:** Quetzal bird in flight, Temple Tikal at left in background **Edge:** Reeded

Date	Mintage	F	VF	XF	Unc	BU
1995 Proof	150	Value: 50.00				

X# 2b.2 10 QUETZALES

20.0000 g., Gilt Alloy, 38 mm. **Obv:** Arms **Obv. Legend:** REPUBLICA DE GUATEMALA **Rev:** Quetzal bird in flight, Temple Tikal at left in background **Edge:** Plain

Date	Mintage	F	VF	XF	Unc	BU
1995 Proof	150	Value: 50.00				

X# 2c.1 10 QUETZALES

23.0000 g., Tri-Metallic, 38 mm. **Obv:** Arms **Obv. Legend:** REPUBLICA DE GUATEMALA **Rev:** Quetzal bird in flight, Temple Tikal at left in background **Edge:** Reeded

Date	Mintage	F	VF	XF	Unc	BU
1995 Proof	150	Value: 65.00				

X# 2c.2 10 QUETZALES

23.0000 g., Tri-Metallic, 38 mm. **Obv:** Arms **Obv. Legend:** REPUBLICA DE GUATEMALA **Rev:** Quetzal bird in flight, Temple Tikal at left in background **Edge:** Plain

Date	Mintage	F	VF	XF	Unc	BU
1995 Proof	150	Value: 65.00				

X# 2d.1 10 QUETZALES

6.0000 g., Aluminum, 38 mm. **Obv:** Arms **Obv. Legend:** REPUBLICA DE GUATEMALA **Rev:** Quetzal bird in flight, Temple Tikal at left in background **Edge:** Reeded

Date	Mintage	F	VF	XF	Unc	BU
1995 Proof	150	Value: 50.00				

X# 2d.2 10 QUETZALES

6.0000 g., Aluminum, 38 mm. **Obv:** Arms **Obv. Legend:** REPUBLICA DE GUATEMALA **Rev:** Quetzal bird in flight, Temple Tikal at left in background **Edge:** Plain

Date	Mintage	F	VF	XF	Unc	BU
1995 Proof	150	Value: 50.00				

X# 2e.1 10 QUETZALES

23.0000 g., Copper, 38 mm. **Obv:** Arms **Obv. Legend:** REPUBLICA DE GUATEMALA **Rev:** Quetzal bird in flight, Temple Tikal at left in background **Edge:** Reeded

Date	Mintage	F	VF	XF	Unc	BU
1995 Proof	150	Value: 50.00				

X# 2e.2 10 QUETZALES

23.0000 g., Copper, 38 mm. **Obv:** Arms **Obv. Legend:** REPUBLICA DE GUATEMALA **Rev:** Quetzal bird in flight, Temple Tikal at left in background **Edge:** Plain

Date	Mintage	F	VF	XF	Unc	BU
1995 Proof	150	Value: 50.00				

X# 2f.1 10 QUETZALES

20.0000 g., Copper-Nickel, 38 mm. **Obv:** Arms **Obv. Legend:** REPUBLICA DE GUATEMALA **Rev:** Quetzal bird in flight, Temple Tikal at left in background **Edge:** Reeded

Date	Mintage	F	VF	XF	Unc	BU
1995 Proof	150	Value: 50.00				

X# 2f.2 10 QUETZALES

20.0000 g., Copper-Nickel, 38 mm. **Obv:** Arms **Obv. Legend:** REPUBLICA DE GUATEMALA **Rev:** Quetzal bird in flight, Temple Tikal at left in background **Edge:** Plain

Date	Mintage	F	VF	XF	Unc	BU
1995 Proof	150	Value: 50.00				

X# 3.1 50 QUETZALES
24.0000 g., 0.9250 Silver 0.7137 oz. ASW, 38 mm. **Obv:** Arms **Obv. Legend:** REPUBLICA DE GUATEMALA **Rev:** Guacamaya parrot perched on branch, Antigua Guatemala at left in background **Edge:** Reeded

Date	Mintage	F	VF	XF	Unc	BU
1995 Proof	150	Value: 60.00				

X# 3.2 50 QUETZALES
24.0000 g., 0.9250 Silver 0.7137 oz. ASW, 38 mm. **Obv:** Arms **Obv. Legend:** REPUBLICA DE GUATEMALA**Rev:** Guacamaya parrot perched on branch, Antigua Guatemala at left in background **Edge:** Plain

Date	Mintage	F	VF	XF	Unc	BU
1995 Proof	150	Value: 60.00				

X# 3a.1 50 QUETZALES
23.0000 g., Brass, 38 mm. **Obv:** Arms **Obv. Legend:** REPUBLICA DE GUATEMALA **Rev:** Guacamaya parrot perched on branch, Antigua Guatemala at left in background **Edge:** Reeded

Date	Mintage	F	VF	XF	Unc	BU
1995 Proof	150	Value: 45.00				

X# 3a.2 50 QUETZALES
23.0000 g., Brass, 38 mm. **Obv:** Arms **Obv. Legend:** REPUBLICA DE GUATEMALA **Rev:** Guacamaya parrot perched on branch, Antigua Guatemala at left in background **Edge:** Plain

Date	Mintage	F	VF	XF	Unc	BU
1995 Proof	150	Value: 45.00				

X# 3b.1 50 QUETZALES
20.0000 g., Gilt Alloy, 38 mm. **Obv:** Arms **Obv. Legend:** REPUBLICA DE GUATEMALA **Rev:** Guacamaya parrot perched on branch, Antigua Guatemala at left in background **Edge:** Reeded

Date	Mintage	F	VF	XF	Unc	BU
1995 Proof	150	Value: 45.00				

X# 3b.2 50 QUETZALES
20.0000 g., Gilt Alloy, 38 mm. **Obv:** Arms **Obv. Legend:** REPUBLICA DE GUATEMALA **Rev:** Guacamaya parrot perched on branch, Antigua Guatemala at left in background **Edge:** Plain

Date	Mintage	F	VF	XF	Unc	BU
1995 Proof	150	Value: 45.00				

X# 3c.1 50 QUETZALES
23.0000 g., Tri-Metallic, 38 mm. **Obv:** Arms **Obv. Legend:** REPUBLICA DE GUATEMALA **Rev:** Guacamaya parrot perched on branch, Antigua Guatemala at left in background **Edge:** Reeded

Date	Mintage	F	VF	XF	Unc	BU
1995 Proof	150	Value: 65.00				

X# 3c.2 50 QUETZALES
23.0000 g., Tri-Metallic, 38 mm. **Obv:** Arms **Obv. Legend:** REPUBLICA DE GUATEMALA **Rev:** Guacamaya parrot perched on branch, Antigua Guatemala at left in background **Edge:** Plain

Date	Mintage	F	VF	XF	Unc	BU
1995 Proof	150	Value: 65.00				

X# 3d.1 50 QUETZALES
6.0000 g., Aluminum, 38 mm. **Obv:** Arms **Obv. Legend:** REPUBLICA DE GUATEMALA **Rev:** Guacamaya parrot perched on branch, Antigua Guatemala at left in background **Edge:** Reeded

Date	Mintage	F	VF	XF	Unc	BU
1995 Proof	150	Value: 45.00				

X# 3d.2 50 QUETZALES
6.0000 g., Aluminum, 38 mm. **Obv:** Arms **Obv. Legend:** REPUBLICA DE GUATEMALA **Rev:** Guacamaya parrot perched on branch, Antigua Guatemala at left in background **Edge:** Plain

Date	Mintage	F	VF	XF	Unc	BU
1995 Proof	150	Value: 45.00				

X# 3e.1 50 QUETZALES
23.0000 g., Copper, 38 mm. **Obv:** Arms **Obv. Legend:** REPUBLICA DE GUATEMALA **Rev:** Guacamaya parrot perched on branch, Antigua Guatemala at left in background **Edge:** Reeded

Date	Mintage	F	VF	XF	Unc	BU
1995 Proof	150	Value: 45.00				

X# 3e.2 50 QUETZALES
23.0000 g., Copper, 38 mm. **Obv:** Arms **Obv. Legend:** REPUBLICA DE GUATEMALA **Rev:** Guacamaya parrot perched on branch, Antigua Guatemala at left in background **Edge:** Plain

Date	Mintage	F	VF	XF	Unc	BU
1995 Proof	150	Value: 45.00				

X# 3f.1 50 QUETZALES
20.0000 g., Copper-Nickel, 38 mm. **Obv:** Arms **Obv. Legend:** REPUBLICA DE GUATEMALA **Rev:** Guacamaya parrot perched on branch, Antigua Guatemala at left in background **Edge:** Reeded

Date	Mintage	F	VF	XF	Unc	BU
1995 Proof	150	Value: 45.00				

X# 3f.2 50 QUETZALES
20.0000 g., Copper-Nickel, 38 mm. **Obv:** Arms **Obv. Legend:** REPUBLICA DE GUATEMALA **Rev:** Guacamaya parrot perched on branch, Antiqua Guatemala at left in background **Edge:** Plain

Date	Mintage	F	VF	XF	Unc	BU
1995 Proof	150	Value: 45.00				

STANDARD COINAGE

8 Reales = 1 Peso

KM# 1 2 REALES
6.8000 g., Silver, 26 mm. **Subject:** Jury Duty **Obv:** Radiant sun above altar of justice **Rev:** Allegorical woman

Date	Mintage	F	VF	XF	Unc	BU
1837	—	—	—	—	—	—

PIEFORTS

X#	Date	Mintage	Identification	Mkt Val
P1	1995	—	Quetzal. 0.9250 Silver. 48.0000 g. Reeded edge. X1.1.	125
P2	1995	—	Quetzal. 0.9250 Silver. 48.0000 g. Plain edge. X1.2.	125
P3	1995	—	10 Quetzales. 0.9250 Silver. 48.0000 g. Reeded edge. X2.1.	125
P4	1995	—	10 Quetzales. 0.9250 Silver. 48.0000 g. Plain edge. X2.2.	125
P5	1995	—	50 Quetzales. 0.9250 Silver. 48.0000 g. Reeded edge. X3.1.	125
P6	1995	—	50 Quetzales. 0.9250 Silver. 48.0000 g. Plain edge. X3.2.	125

TRIAL STRIKES

X#	Date	Mintage	Identification	Mkt Val
TS1	1995	—	50 Quetzales. Copper-Nickel. 45 mm. Guacamaya Parrot.	—
TS2	1995	—	50 Quetzales. Bronze. 45 mm. Guacamaya Parrot.	—
TS3	1995	—	50 Quetzales. Gilt. 45 mm. Guacamaya Parrot.	—
TS4	1995	—	50 Quetzales. Silver. 45 mm. Guacamaya Parrot.	—

PATTERNS

Including off metal strikes

X#	Date	Mintage	Identification	Mkt Val
Pn1	1995	—	Quetzal. 0.9167 Gold. 40.3000 g. Reeded edge. X1.	3,000
Pn2	1995	—	Quetzal. 0.9167 Gold. 40.8000 g. Plain edge. X1.	3,000
Pn3	1995	—	Quetzal. 0.9167 Gold. 40.1000 g. Reeded edge. X1.	3,000
Pn4	1995	—	Quetzal. 0.9167 Gold. 40.2000 g. Plain edge. X1.	3,000
Pn5	1995	—	Quetzal. 0.9167 Gold. 40.3000 g. Reeded edge. Mule, Obv. X1, Rev. 10 Quetzal X2.	3,000
Pn6	1995	—	10 Quetzales. 0.9167 Gold. 40.3000 g. Reeded edge. X2.	3,000
Pn7	1995	—	10 Quetzales. 0.9167 Gold. 40.8000 g. Plain edge. X2.	3,000
Pn8	1995	—	10 Quetzales. 0.9167 Gold. 40.1000 g. Reeded edge. X2.	3,000
Pn9	1995	—	10 Quetzales. 0.9167 Gold. 40.2000 g. Plain edge. X2.	3,000
Pn10	1995	—	10 Quetzales. 0.9167 Gold. 40.3000 g. Reeded edge. Mule, Obv. X2, Rev. Quetzal X1.	3,000
Pn11	1995	—	50 Quetzales. Platinum. 44.0000 g. Reeded edge. X3.	10,000

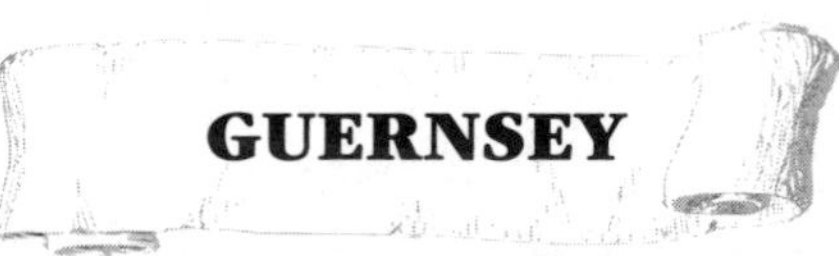

GUERNSEY

BRITISH DEPENDENCY

ECU COINAGE

X# 1 ECU
28.2800 g., 0.9250 Silver 0.8410 oz. ASW, 38.6 mm. **Ruler:** Elizabeth II **Obv:** Map of Europe **Obv. Legend:** • GUERNSEY • EUROPE - EUROPA **Rev:** Arms **Rev. Legend:** S. BALLIVIE INSVIE DEGERNEREVE

Date	Mintage	F	VF	XF	Unc	BU
ND(1992)PM Proof	10,000	Value: 25.00				

FANTASY EURO PATTERNS

X# Pn1 EURO CENT
Copper Plated Steel, 16.8 mm. **Ruler:** Elizabeth II **Obv:** Ship's wheel and anchor **Rev:** Radiant head facing **Edge:** Plain

Date	Mintage	F	VF	XF	Unc	BU
2004	10,000	—	—	—	—	1.50
2004 Proof	4,000	Value: 2.50				

X# Pn1a EURO CENT
Silver, 16.8 mm. **Ruler:** Elizabeth II **Obv:** Ship's wheel and anchor **Rev:** Radiant head facing **Edge:** Plain

Date	Mintage	F	VF	XF	Unc	BU
2004 Proof	300	Value: 6.00				

X# Pn2 2 EURO CENT

Copper Plated Steel, 18.5 mm. **Ruler:** Elizabeth II **Obv:** Ship's wheel and anchor **Rev:** Radiant head facing **Edge:** Plain

Date	Mintage	F	VF	XF	Unc	BU
2004	10,000	—	—	—	—	2.00
2004 Proof	4,000	Value: 3.00				

X# Pn2a 2 EURO CENT

Silver, 18.5 mm. **Ruler:** Elizabeth II **Obv:** Ship's wheel and anchor **Rev:** Radiant head facing **Edge:** Plain

Date	Mintage	F	VF	XF	Unc	BU
2004 Proof	300	Value: 7.00				

X# Pn3 5 EURO CENT

Copper Plated Steel, 20.7 mm. **Ruler:** Elizabeth II **Obv:** Ship's wheel and anchor **Rev:** Radiant head facing **Edge:** Plain

Date	Mintage	F	VF	XF	Unc	BU
2004	10,000	—	—	—	—	2.50
2004 Proof	4,000	Value: 3.50				

X# Pn3a 5 EURO CENT

Silver, 20.7 mm. **Ruler:** Elizabeth II **Obv:** Ship's wheel and anchor **Rev:** Radiant head facing **Edge:** Plain

Date	Mintage	F	VF	XF	Unc	BU
2004 Proof	300	Value: 8.50				

X# Pn4 10 EURO CENT

Goldine, 19.3 mm. **Ruler:** Elizabeth II **Obv:** Sailing ship **Rev:** Crowned lion upright with sword and shield at left **Edge:** Plain

Date	Mintage	F	VF	XF	Unc	BU
2004	10,000	—	—	—	—	3.00
2004 Proof	4,000	Value: 4.00				

X# Pn4a 10 EURO CENT

Silver, 19.3 mm. **Ruler:** Elizabeth II **Obv:** Sailing ship **Rev:** Crowned lion upright with sword and shield at left **Edge:** Plain

Date	Mintage	F	VF	XF	Unc	BU
2004 Proof	300	Value: 10.00				

X# Pn5 20 EURO CENT

Goldine, 22 mm. **Ruler:** Elizabeth II **Obv:** Sailing ship **Rev:** Crowned lion upright with sword and shield at left **Edge:** Plain

Date	Mintage	F	VF	XF	Unc	BU
2004	10,000	—	—	—	—	3.50
2004 Proof	4,000	Value: 5.00				

X# Pn5a 20 EURO CENT

Silver, 22 mm. **Ruler:** Elizabeth II **Obv:** Sailing ship **Rev:** Crowned lion upright with sword and shield at left **Edge:** Plain

Date	Mintage	F	VF	XF	Unc	BU
2004 Proof	300	Value: 12.50				

X# Pn6 50 EURO CENT

Goldine, 24.3 mm. **Ruler:** Elizabeth II **Obv:** Sailing ship **Rev:** Crowned lion upright with sword and shield at left **Edge:** Plain

Date	Mintage	F	VF	XF	Unc	BU
2004	10,000	—	—	—	—	4.00
2004 Proof	4,000	Value: 6.00				

X# Pn6a 50 EURO CENT

Silver, 24.3 mm. **Ruler:** Elizabeth II **Obv:** Sailing ship **Rev:** Crowned lion upright with sword and shield at left **Edge:** Plain

Date	Mintage	F	VF	XF	Unc	BU
2004 Proof	300	Value: 15.00				

X# Pn7 EURO

Bi-Metallic Copper-Nickel center in Goldine ring, 22.8 mm. **Ruler:** Elizabeth II **Obv:** Goddess of sea 3/4 left **Rev:** Woman standing behind man seated facing right - at right **Edge:** Plain

Date	Mintage	F	VF	XF	Unc	BU
2004	10,000	—	—	—	—	6.00
2004 Proof	4,000	Value: 8.00				

X# Pn7a EURO

Bi-Metallic Brass/Silver, 22.8 mm. **Ruler:** Elizabeth II **Obv:** Goddess of sea 3/4 left **Rev:** Woman standing behind man seated facing right - at right **Edge:** Plain

Date	Mintage	F	VF	XF	Unc	BU
2004 Proof	300	Value: 22.50				

X# Pn8 2 EURO

Bi-Metallic Goldine center in Copper-Nickel ring, 25.7 mm. **Ruler:** Elizabeth II **Obv:** Goddess of sea 3/4 left **Rev:** Woman standing behind man seated facing right - at right **Edge:** Plain

Date	Mintage	F	VF	XF	Unc	BU
2004	10,000	—	—	—	—	8.00
2004 Proof	4,000	Value: 10.00				

X# Pn8a 2 EURO

Bi-Metallic Brass/Silver, 25.7 mm. **Ruler:** Elizabeth II **Obv:** Goddess of sea 3/4 left **Rev:** Woman standing behind man seated facing right - at right **Edge:** Plain

Date	Mintage	F	VF	XF	Unc	BU
2004 Proof	300	Value: 28.50				

X# Pn9 5 EURO

Goldine, 36 mm. **Ruler:** Elizabeth II **Obv:** Goddess of sea 3/4 left **Rev:** Justice seated right - at right **Edge:** Plain

Date	Mintage	F	VF	XF	Unc	BU
2004 Proof	4,000	Value: 12.50				

X# Pn9a 5 EURO

Silver, 36 mm. **Ruler:** Elizabeth II **Obv:** Goddess of sea 3/4 left **Rev:** Justice seated right - at right **Edge:** Plain

Date	Mintage	F	VF	XF	Unc	BU
2004 Proof	300	Value: 40.00				

PIEFORTS

X#	Date	Mintage	Identification	Mkt Val
P1	2004	300	5 Euro. Silver. X#Pn9a.	65.00

MINT SETS

X#	Date	Mintage	Identification	Issue Price	Mkt Val
XMS1	2004 (8)	10,000	X#Pn1-Pn8	—	30.00

PROOF SETS

X#	Date	Mintage	Identification	Issue Price	Mkt Val
XPS1	2004 (9)	4,000	X#Pn1-Pn9	—	50.00
XPS2	2004 (9)	300	X#Pn1a-Pn9a	—	150

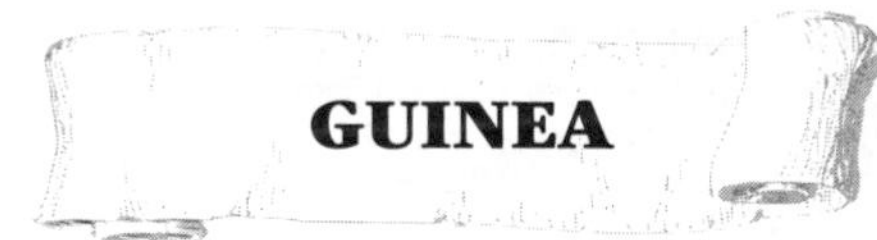

GUINEA

REPUBLIC

MEDALLIC COINAGE

X# 1 200 SYLI

Copper-Nickel **Subject:** International Games **Rev:** Race walking

Date	Mintage	F	VF	XF	Unc	BU
1984 Plain proof	—	Value: 20.00				
1984 Frosted pr	—	Value: 18.50				

X# 2 500 SYLI

31.0600 g., 0.9990 Silver 0.9976 oz. ASW **Subject:** International Games **Rev:** Race walking

Date	Mintage	F	VF	XF	Unc	BU
1984 Proof	—	Value: 42.50				

TRIAL STRIKES

X#	Date	Mintage	Identification	Mkt Val
TS6	ND(1984)	—	200 Syli. Lead. X#1.	35.00

FOUTAH DJALON

COUNTSHIP

MEDALLIC COINAGE

Struck for the French entrepreneur Count (Aime) Olivier de Sanderval while he was trying to establish a domain

X# 1 5 FRANCS

Copper **Ruler:** (Aime) Olivier de Sanderval

Date	Mintage	F	VF	XF	Unc	BU
1879 Proof	—	Value: 2,400				

X# 2 5 FRANCS
25.0000 g., 0.9500 Silver 0.7635 oz. ASW **Ruler:** (Aime) Olivier de Sanderval **Note:** Prev. Dav.#512.

Date	Mintage	F	VF	XF	Unc	BU
1879 Proof	—	Value: 2,250				

X# 3 5 FRANCS
25.0000 g., 0.9500 Silver 0.7635 oz. ASW **Ruler:** (Aime) Olivier de Sanderval **Note:** Prev. Dav. #513.

Date	Mintage	F	VF	XF	Unc	BU
1894 Proof	—	Value: 2,350				

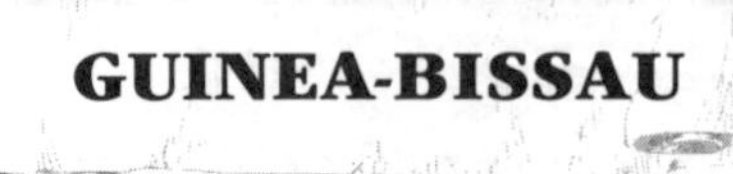

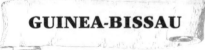

GUINEA-BISSAU

REPUBLIC

MEDALLIC COINAGE

X# 1.1 250 PESOS
Copper-Nickel **Rev:** International Games - Balance Beam; engraver's initials on balance beam

Date	Mintage	F	VF	XF	Unc	BU
1984 Proof	—	Value: 15.00				

X# 1.2 250 PESOS
Copper-Nickel **Rev:** Without initials on balance beam

Date	Mintage	F	VF	XF	Unc	BU
1984 Proof	—	Value: 29.50				

X# 2 250 PESOS
Copper-Nickel **Rev:** International Games - Horizontal Bar

Date	Mintage	F	VF	XF	Unc	BU
1984 Proof	—	Value: 27.50				

X# 3 1000 PESOS
31.2400 g., Silver **Rev:** International Games - Balance Beam **Note:** According to official information released by the Bank National of Guinea-Bissau, KM#M1-M3 are not legal tender and were issued without the authorization of their government.

Date	Mintage	F	VF	XF	Unc	BU
1984 Proof	—	Value: 55.00				

TRIAL STRIKES

X#	Date	Mintage	Identification	Mkt Val
TS1	1984	—	250 Pesos. Lead. X#1.	65.00

HAITI

NORTHERN KINGDOM

MEDALLIC COINAGE

X# 11 CROWN
Silver, 38 mm. **Ruler:** King Henri **Obv:** Laureate armored bust right **Obv. Legend:** HENRICUS DEI GRATIA HAITI REX **Rev:** Crowned shield with rising phoenix **Rev. Legend:** DEUS. CAUSA. ATQUE GLADIUS MEUS.

Date	Mintage	F	VF	XF	Unc	BU
1811 // AN 8	—	—	—	—	1,500	—

X# 12 CROWN

Silver **Ruler:** King Henri **Obv:** Laureate armored bust right **Obv. Legend:** HENRICUS DEI GRATIA HAITI REX **Rev:** Crowned shield with rising phoenix **Rev. Legend:** DEUS. CAUSA. ATQUE GLADIUS MEUS.

Date	Mintage	F	VF	XF	Unc	BU
1811 // AN 8 Proof; Restrike	—	Value: 550				

X# 12a CROWN

56.7500 g., Platinum APW **Ruler:** King Henri **Obv:** Laureate armored bust right **Obv. Legend:** HENRICUS DEI GRATIA HAITI REX **Rev:** Crowned shield with rising phoenix **Rev. Legend:** DEUS. CAUSA. ATQUE GLADIUS MEUS.

Date	Mintage	F	VF	XF	Unc	BU
1811 // AN 8 Proof; Restrike	—	Value: 3,000				

X# 12b CROWN

Copper **Ruler:** King Henri **Obv:** Laureate armored bust right **Obv. Legend:** HENRICUS DEI GRATIA HAITI REX **Rev:** Crowned shield with rising phoenix **Rev. Legend:** DEUS. CAUSA. ATQUE GLADIUS MEUS.

Date	Mintage	F	VF	XF	Unc	BU
1811 // AN 8 Proof; Restrike	—	Value: 375				

X# 15 CROWN

Silver **Ruler:** King Henri **Obv:** Armored bust left **Obv. Legend:** HENRICUS DEI GRATIA HAITI REX **Rev:** Crowned shield with rising phoenix **Rev. Legend:** DEUS. CAUSA. ATQUE GLADIUS MEUS.

Date	Mintage	F	VF	XF	Unc	BU
1811 // AN 8	—	—	—	—	3,000	—

X# 10 CROWN

24.4000 g., Silver **Ruler:** King Henri **Obv:** Laureate armored bust right **Obv. Legend:** HENRICUS DEI GRATIA HAITI REX **Rev:** Crowned shield with rising phoenix **Rev. Legend:** DEUS. CAUSA. ATQUE GLADIUS MEUS. **Note:** Prev. Bruce#XM11.

Date	Mintage	F	VF	XF	Unc	BU
1811 // AN 8	—	—	—	—	1,750	—

X# 10a CROWN

Copper **Ruler:** King Henri **Obv:** Laureate armored bust right **Obv. Legend:** HENRICUS DEI GRATIA HAITI REX **Rev:** Crowned shield with rising phoenix **Rev. Legend:** DEUS. CAUSA. ATQUE GLADIUS MEUS. **Note:** Prev. Bruce#XM11a.

Date	Mintage	F	VF	XF	Unc	BU
1811 // AN 8	—	—	—	—	600	—

X# 11a CROWN

Copper, 38 mm. **Ruler:** King Henri **Obv:** Laureate armored bust right **Obv. Legend:** HENRICUS DEI GRATIA HAITI REX **Rev:** Crowned shield with rising phoenix **Rev. Legend:** DEUS. CAUSA. ATQUE GLADIUS MEUS.

Date	Mintage	F	VF	XF	Unc	BU
1811 // AN8	—	—	—	—	450	—

INA Retro Issue

X# 13 CROWN

24.3000 g., 0.9250 Silver 0.7226 oz. ASW **Ruler:** King Henri **Obv:** Laureate armored bust right **Obv. Legend:** HENRICUS DEI GRATIA HAITI REX. **Rev:** Crowned shield with rising phoenix **Rev. Legend:** DEUS. CAUSA. ATQUE GLADIUS MEUS. **Edge:** Plain

Date	Mintage	F	VF	XF	Unc	BU
1811//Lan8 Proof	—	Value: 50.00				

X# 13a CROWN

19.7700 g., Bronze **Ruler:** King Henri **Obv:** Laureate armored bust right **Obv. Legend:** HENRICUS DEI GRATIA HAITI REX **Rev:** Crowned shield with rising phoenix **Rev. Legend:** DEUS. CAUSA. ATQUE GLADIUS MEUS. **Edge:** Plain

Date	Mintage	F	VF	XF	Unc	BU
1811//Lan8 Proof	—	Value: 25.00				

X# 13c CROWN

20.5800 g., Gold Plated **Ruler:** King Henri **Obv:** Laureate armored bust right **Obv. Legend:** HENRICUS DEI GRATIA HAITI REX **Rev:** Crowned shield with rising phoenix **Rev. Legend:** DEUS. CAUSA. ATQUE GLADIUS MEUS. **Edge:** Plain

Date	Mintage	F	VF	XF	Unc	BU
1811//Lan8 Proof	—	Value: 30.00				

X# 13b CROWN

20.0100 g., Copper **Ruler:** King Henri **Obv:** Laureate armored bust right **Obv. Legend:** HENRICUS DEI GRATIA HAITI REX **Rev:** Crowned shield with rising phoenix **Rev. Legend:** DEUS. CAUSA. ATQUE GLADIUS MEUS. **Edge:** Plain

Date	Mintage	F	VF	XF	Unc	BU
1811//Lan8 Proof	—	Value: 25.00				

HAWAII

KINGDOM

LILIUOKALANI MEDALLIC ISSUES

Reginald Huth Pattern Issues

The Liliuokalani patterns have no official status. They were struck at the private order of wealthy English collector Huth by Pinches and Company of London and first appeared in Honolulu about 1901.

X# M1 DOLLAR (Akahi Dala)

Silver

Date	Mintage	F	VF	XF	Unc	BU
1891(93) Proof	50	Value: 8,000				

Note: Two recent replicas of the Liliuokalani dollar exist. One is a 32mm sterling silver piece. The originals have a 38mm diameter which copies the original obverse and reverse devices, with the word COPY added incuse near the rim on the reverse. The second is a 39mm, gold anodized aluminum piece produced for sale to tourists and featuring a representation of the obverse, with the initials RHM added in the field, in combination with the 1883 dollar reverse design.

X# M2 20 DOLLARS (20 Dala)
Gold

Date	Mintage	F	VF	XF	Unc	BU
1893 Proof	4	Value: 75,000				

X# M3 DOLLAR
Silver **Obv:** One dolphin **Note:** Replicas exist in gold anodized aluminum featuring a representation of the obverse, with the initials RHM added in the field, in combination with the 1883 dollar reverse design.

Date	Mintage	F	VF	XF	Unc	BU
MDCCCXCIII (1893) Proof	20	Value: 9,000				

X# M3a DOLLAR
Bronze

Date	Mintage	F	VF	XF	Unc	BU
MDCCCXCIII (1893)	—	—	—	—	—	—

X# M4 DOLLAR
Silver **Obv:** Four dolphins around head facing right

Date	Mintage	F	VF	XF	Unc	BU
MDCCCXCIII (1893) Proof	30	Value: 9,000				

X# M4a DOLLAR
Iron **Obv:** Four dolphins around head facing right

Date	Mintage	F	VF	XF	Unc	BU
MDCCCXCIII (1893) Proof	3	Value: 12,000				

X# M4b DOLLAR
Bronze **Obv:** Four dolphins around head facing right

Date	Mintage	F	VF	XF	Unc	BU
MDCCCXCIII (1893) Proof	2	Value: 15,000				

X# M4c DOLLAR
Tin **Obv:** Four dolphins around head facing right

Date	Mintage	F	VF	XF	Unc	BU
MDCCCXCIII (1893) Unique; Proof	—	Value: 15,000				

X# M4d DOLLAR
Gold **Obv:** Four dolphins around head facing right

Date	Mintage	F	VF	XF	Unc	BU
MDCCCXCIII (1893) Unique; Proof	—	Value: 100,000				

MEDALLIC COINAGE

Kaiulani Issues

X# 5 DOLLAR
Silver

Date	Mintage	F	VF	XF	Unc	BU
1895 Four dolphins on obverse	Est. 30	Value: 6,000				

X# 6 DOLLAR
Iron

Date	Mintage	F	VF	XF	Unc	BU
1895	3	Value: 7,500				

X# 7 DOLLAR
Bronze

Date	Mintage	F	VF	XF	Unc	BU
1895	2	Value: 9,000				

X# 8 DOLLAR
Tin

Date	Mintage	F	VF	XF	Unc	BU
1895 Unique	—	Value: 10,000				

X# 9 DOLLAR
Gold

Date	Mintage	F	VF	XF	Unc	BU
1895 Unique	—	Value: 75,000				

PATTERNS

Unauthorized Silver Issues

X# Pn9 1/8 DOLLAR (Hapawalu)
Bronze **Ruler:** Kalakaua I **Obv:** Head right **Rev:** Crown above denomination in sprays

Date	Mintage	F	VF	XF	Unc	BU
1883	—	Value: 2,000				

X# Pn10 1/8 DOLLAR (Hapawalu)
Nickel **Ruler:** Kalakaua I **Obv:** Head right **Rev:** Crown above denomination in sprays

Date	Mintage	F	VF	XF	Unc	BU
1883	—	Value: 2,000				

X# Pn11 1/8 DOLLAR (Hapawalu)
Gold **Ruler:** Kalakaua I **Obv:** Head right **Rev:** Crown above denomination in sprays

Date	Mintage	F	VF	XF	Unc	BU
1883	—	Value: 20,000				

X# Pn12 1/8 DOLLAR (Hapawalu)
Platinum APW **Ruler:** Kalakaua I **Obv:** Head right **Rev:** Crown above denomination in sprays

Date	Mintage	F	VF	XF	Unc	BU
1883	3	Value: 10,000				

X# Pn13 1/4 DOLLAR (Hapaha)
Bronze

Date	Mintage	F	VF	XF	Unc	BU
1884	—	Value: 1,500				

X# Pn14 1/4 DOLLAR (Hapaha)
Brass

Date	Mintage	F	VF	XF	Unc	BU
1884 Unique	—	Value: 1,500				

X# Pn15 1/4 DOLLAR (Hapaha)
Oride

Date	Mintage	F	VF	XF	Unc	BU
1884 Unique	—	Value: 1,500				

X# Pn16 1/4 DOLLAR (Hapaha)
Gold

Date	Mintage	F	VF	XF	Unc	BU
1884	—	Value: 15,000				

X# Pn17 1/4 DOLLAR (Hapaha)
Platinum APW

Date	Mintage	F	VF	XF	Unc	BU
1884	—	Value: 5,000				

X# Pn18 1/2 DOLLAR (Hapalua)
Bronze

Date	Mintage	F	VF	XF	Unc	BU
1884	—	Value: 3,000				

X# Pn19 1/2 DOLLAR (Hapalua)
Gold

Date	Mintage	F	VF	XF	Unc	BU
1884 2 pieces known	—	Value: 15,000				

X# Pn20 1/2 DOLLAR (Hapalua)
Platinum APW

Date	Mintage	F	VF	XF	Unc	BU
1884	—	Value: 7,000				

Note: All of the patterns in this section are of spurious origin. It is thought they were produced clandestinely by a workman at the Philadelphia mint, where the original die making tools were still preserved, in the early 1900's. The "unathorized" 1/8 Dollar Patterns may be distinguished from the "official" pieces by the presence of flowing "lazy" eights in the date, as contrasted to the "block" eights used on regular Hawaiian coinage.

UNITED STATES TERRITORY

TOKEN COINAGE

X# Tn1 TOKEN TRADE DALA
Bronze **Subject:** Royal Hawaiian Mint

Date	Mintage	F	VF	XF	Unc	BU
1990	2,000	—	—	—	3.00	—

STATE

LILIUOKALANI MEDALLIC ISSUES

Reginald Huth Pattern Issues

The Liliuokalani patterns have no official status. They were struck at the private order of wealthy English collector Huth by Pinches and Company of London and first appeared in Honolulu about 1901.

X# 12 AKAHI DALA
31.1400 g., 0.9990 Silver 1.0000 oz. ASW, 38.5 mm.
Obv: Bust left **Obv. Legend:** LILIUOKALANI HAWAII **Rev:** Map of islands **Rev. Legend:** QUEEN OF HAWAII **Edge:** Reeded

Date	Mintage	F	VF	XF	Unc	BU
1891 Proof	—	Value: 40.00				

MEDALLIC COINAGE

X# 20 ALOHA DALA
Bronze, 32 mm. **Subject:** 50th Anniversary of Festivals **Obv:** Bust Kamehameha right **Obv. Legend:** ALOHA FESTIVALS HAWAII **Rev:** Island group **Rev. Legend:** HALIA ALOHA TREASURED MEMORIES **Edge:** Reeded

Date	Mintage	F	VF	XF	Unc	BU
ND(1996)	—	—	—	—	4.00	—

MEDALLIC SILVER COINAGE

Bernard von NotHaus Issues

Essentially bullion issues

X# MB109 1/20 OUNCE
1.5552 g., 0.9990 Silver 0.0499 oz. ASW, 14 mm.
Obv: Head right **Obv. Legend:** PRINCESS VICTORIA KAIULANI...... **Rev:** Crown above value in sprays **Rev. Legend:** ROYAL HAWAIIAN SILVER - HAPAIWAKALUA **Edge:** Reeded

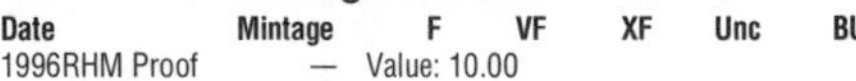

Date	Mintage	F	VF	XF	Unc	BU
1996RHM Proof	—	Value: 10.00				

X# MB77 1/10 OUNCE
3.1103 g., 0.9990 Silver 0.0999 oz. ASW, 19 mm.
Obv: Head right **Obv. Legend:** PRINCESS VICTORIA KAIULANI...... **Rev:** Crowned arms **Rev. Legend:** ROYAL HAWAIIAN SILVER **Edge:** Reeded

Date	Mintage	F	VF	XF	Unc	BU
1991RHM Proof	100	Value: 20.00				

X# MB76 1/10 OUNCE
3.1103 g., 0.9990 Silver 0.0999 oz. ASW, 19 mm.
Obv: Bust left **Obv. Legend:** LILIUOKALANI QUEEN OF HAWAII **Rev:** Crowned arms **Rev. Legend:** ROYAL HAWAIIAN SILVER **Edge:** Reeded

Date	Mintage	F	VF	XF	Unc	BU
1991RHM Proof	100	Value: 20.00				

X# MB75 1/10 OUNCE
3.1103 g., 0.9990 Silver 0.0999 oz. ASW, 19 mm.
Obv: Head right **Obv. Legend:** KALAKAUA I KING OF HAWAII **Rev:** Crowned arms **Rev. Legend:** ROYAL HAWAIIAN SILVER **Edge:** Reeded

Date	Mintage	F	VF	XF	Unc	BU
1991RHM Proof	100	Value: 20.00				

X# MB110 1/10 OUNCE
3.1103 g., 0.9990 Silver 0.0999 oz. ASW, 19 mm.
Obv: Bust left **Obv. Legend:** LILIUOKALANI QUEEN OF HAWAII **Rev:** Crowned arms **Rev. Legend:** ROYAL HAWAIIAN SILVER - HAPAHUMI **Edge:** Reeded

Date	Mintage	F	VF	XF	Unc	BU
1996RHM Proof	—	Value: 20.00				

X# MB111 1/4 OUNCE
7.7758 g., 0.9990 Silver 0.2497 oz. ASW, 26.5 mm.
Subject: 200th Anniversary of Kingdom **Obv:** Bust right holding spear **Obv. Legend:** 200 LA HO 'OMANA 'O **Rev:** Crowned arms **Rev. Legend:** ROYAL HAWAIIAN SILVER - HAPAHA **Edge:** Reeded

Date	Mintage	F	VF	XF	Unc	BU
1996RHM Proof	—	Value: 35.00				

X# MB62 1/2 OUNCE
15.5515 g., 0.9990 Silver 0.4995 oz. ASW
Subject: Robbers Roost

Date	Mintage	F	VF	XF	Unc	BU
1991 Proof	1,000	Value: 100				

X# MB112 1/2 OUNCE
15.5515 g., 0.9990 Silver 0.4995 oz. ASW, 32 mm.
Obv: Head right **Obv. Legend:** KALAKAUA I KING OF HAWAII **Rev:** Crowned arms **Rev. Legend:** ROYAL HAWAIIAN SILVER - HAPALUA **Edge:** Reeded

Date	Mintage	F	VF	XF	Unc	BU
1996RHM Proof	—	Value: 50.00				

X# MB4 OUNCE (Kala Dala)
31.1030 g., 0.9990 Silver 0.9989 oz. ASW **Obv:** Head right **Obv. Legend:** KALAKAUA I KING OF HAWAII **Rev:** Crowned arms **Rev. Legend:** UA MAU KE EA O KA - AINA I KA PONO, KALAKALA below

Date	Mintage	F	VF	XF	Unc	BU
ND(1982)THM Proof	3,200	Value: 85.00				

Note: First day counterstamp valued at $150

X# MB4a OUNCE (Kala Dala)
Bronze **Obv:** Head right **Obv. Legend:** KALAKAUA I KING OF HAWAII **Rev:** Crowned arms **Rev. Legend:** UA MAU KE EA O KA - AINA I KA PONO, KALA DALA below

Date	Mintage	F	VF	XF	Unc	BU
ND(1982)THM Proof	50	Value: 50.00				

X# MB6a OUNCE (Dala)
Bronze **Obv:** Head right **Obv. Legend:** KALAKAUA I KING OF HAWAII **Rev:** Crowned arms **Rev. Legend:** UA MAU KE EA O KA - AINA I KA PONO, CENTENNIAL DALA below

Date	Mintage	F	VF	XF	Unc	BU
1983 Proof	50	Value: 40.00				

X# MB6 OUNCE (Dala)
31.1030 g., 0.9990 Silver 0.9989 oz. ASW **Subject:** Centennial of First Coinage **Obv:** Head right **Obv. Legend:** KALAKAUA I KING OF HAWAII **Rev:** Crowned arms **Rev. Legend:** UA MAU KE EA O KA - AINA I KA PONO, CENTENNIAL DALA below **Note:** 300 pieces were countermarked with first day of issue date - "12-4-82".

Date	Mintage	F	VF	XF	Unc	BU
ND(1983) Proof	10,000	Value: 75.00				

X# MB8 OUNCE (Dala)
31.1030 g., 0.9990 Silver 0.9989 oz. ASW
Subject: Statehood Silver Jubilee **Obv:** Bust with tiara left **Obv. Legend:** LILIUOKALANI — • HAWAII • **Rev:** Crowned arms **Rev. Legend:** HAWAIIAN STATEHOOD - SILVER JUBILEE, -ADMISSION DAY DALA below

Date	Mintage	F	VF	XF	Unc	BU
1984THM Proof	9,819	Value: 150				

X# MB10 OUNCE (Dala)
Bronze

Date	Mintage	F	VF	XF	Unc	BU
1984THM Proof	6,874	Value: 12.50				

X# MB11 OUNCE (Dala)
31.1030 g., 0.9990 Silver 0.9989 oz. ASW **Subject:** Statehood Silver Jubilee

Date	Mintage	F	VF	XF	Unc	BU
1984THM Proof	—	Value: 110				

X# MB13 OUNCE (Dala)
Bronze

Date	Mintage	F	VF	XF	Unc	BU
1984THM Proof	3,500	Value: 15.00				

X# MB14 OUNCE (Akahi (1) Dala)
31.1030 g., 0.9990 Silver 0.9989 oz. ASW **Obv:** Bust with tiara left **Obv. Legend:** LILIUOKALANI —• HAWAII • **Rev:** Crowned arms **Rev. Legend:** ONE TROY OUNCE - .999 FINE SILVER, • AKAHI DALA • below

Date	Mintage	F	VF	XF	Unc	BU
ND(1985) Proof	1,358	Value: 75.00				

X# MB14a OUNCE (Akahi (1) Dala)
Bronze

Date	Mintage	F	VF	XF	Unc	BU
ND(1985) Proof	50	Value: 40.00				

X# MB15 OUNCE (Akahi (1) Dala)
31.1030 g., 0.9990 Silver 0.9989 oz. ASW
Rev: Legend with large lettering

Date	Mintage	F	VF	XF	Unc	BU
1985 Proof	—	Value: 75.00				

X# MB15a OUNCE (Akahi (1) Dala)
Bronze

Date	Mintage	F	VF	XF	Unc	BU
1985 Proof	50	Value: 40.00				

X# MB18 OUNCE (Akahi (1) Dala)
31.1030 g., 0.9990 Silver 0.9989 oz. ASW
Rev: Legend with small lettering

Date	Mintage	F	VF	XF	Unc	BU
1986THM	920	—	—	—	45.00	—
1986THM Proof	740	Value: 85.00				

X# MB18a OUNCE (Akahi (1) Dala)
Bronze

Date	Mintage	F	VF	XF	Unc	BU
1986THM Proof	50	Value: 40.00				

X# MB19 OUNCE (Akahi (1) Dala)
31.1030 g., 0.9990 Silver 0.9989 oz. ASW
Subject: Kamehameha I

Date	Mintage	F	VF	XF	Unc	BU
1986RHM Proof	500	Value: 65.00				

X# MB19a OUNCE (Akahi (1) Dala)
Bronze

Date	Mintage	F	VF	XF	Unc	BU
1986RHM Proof	50	Value: 28.00				

X# MB21 OUNCE (Akahi (1) Dala)
31.1030 g., 0.9990 Silver 0.9989 oz. ASW
Subject: Year of the Hawaiian

Date	Mintage	F	VF	XF	Unc	BU
1987 Proof	—	Value: 55.00				

X# MB23 OUNCE (Akahi (1) Dala)
Bronze

Date	Mintage	F	VF	XF	Unc	BU
1987 Proof	—	Value: 20.00				

X# MB31 OUNCE (Akahi (1) Dala)
31.1030 g., 0.9990 Silver 0.9989 oz. ASW
Subject: Kamehameha I

Date	Mintage	F	VF	XF	Unc	BU
1988RHM	2,800	—	—	—	20.00	—

X# MB53 OUNCE (Akahi (1) Dala)
31.1030 g., 0.9990 Silver 0.9989 oz. ASW
Subject: Kalakaua I

Date	Mintage	F	VF	XF	Unc	BU
1990RHM Proof	1,500	Value: 50.00				

X# MB64 OUNCE (Akahi (1) Dala)
31.1030 g., 0.9990 Silver 0.9989 oz. ASW
Subject: Kalakaua I

Date	Mintage	F	VF	XF	Unc	BU
1991RHM Proof	900	Value: 40.00				

X# MB44 OUNCE (Akahi (1) Dala)
31.1030 g., 0.9990 Silver 0.9989 oz. ASW
Subject: 30th Anniversary Hawaiian Statehood

Date	Mintage	F	VF	XF	Unc	BU
1989BVN	2,200	—	—	—	40.00	—

X# MB54 OUNCE (Akahi (1) Dala)
31.1030 g., 0.9990 Silver 0.9989 oz. ASW
Subject: Liliuokalani

Date	Mintage	F	VF	XF	Unc	BU
1990RHM Proof	1,500	Value: 50.00				

X# MB67 OUNCE (Akahi (1) Dala)
31.1030 g., 0.9990 Silver 0.9989 oz. ASW
Subject: 50th Anniversary Pearl Harbor - Type I

Date	Mintage	F	VF	XF	Unc	BU
1991 Proof	1,367	Value: 65.00				

X# MB51 OUNCE (Akahi (1) Dala)
31.1030 g., 0.9990 Silver 0.9989 oz. ASW
Subject: Honolulu Dala

Date	Mintage	F	VF	XF	Unc	BU
1990RHM	1,940	—	—	—	25.00	—
1991RHM	2,200	—	—	—	25.00	—

X# MB55 OUNCE (Akahi (1) Dala)
31.1030 g., 0.9990 Silver 0.9989 oz. ASW
Subject: Princess Victoria

Date	Mintage	F	VF	XF	Unc	BU
1991RHM Proof	1,000	Value: 60.00				

X# MB68 OUNCE (Akahi (1) Dala)
31.1030 g., 0.9990 Silver 0.9989 oz. ASW
Subject: 50th Anniversary Pearl Harbor - Type II

Date	Mintage	F	VF	XF	Unc	BU
1991 Proof	—	Value: 45.00				

X# MB68a OUNCE (Akahi (1) Dala)

Bronze **Subject:** 50th Anniversary Pearl Harbor - Type II

Date	Mintage	F	VF	XF	Unc	BU
1991 Proof	—	Value: 25.00				

X# MB73 OUNCE

31.1030 g., 0.9990 Silver 0.9989 oz. ASW, 39 mm. **Issuer:** Pacific Bullion Exchange **Obv:** Crowned, mantled and supported arms in sprays **Obv. Legend:** kala • o • ka • aina - UA MAU KE EA O KA AINA I KA PONO **Rev:** Iolani Palace **Rev. Legend:** HONOLULU, HAWAII **Edge:** Reeded

Date	Mintage	F	VF	XF	Unc	BU
1974 Proof	—	Value: 25.00				

X# MB37 OUNCE

31.1030 g., 0.9990 Silver 0.9989 oz. ASW **Subject:** 30th Anniversary Deak - Hawaii

Date	Mintage	F	VF	XF	Unc	BU
1987 Proof	200	Value: 65.00				

X# MB85 OUNCE

31.1030 g., 0.9990 Silver 0.9989 oz. ASW, 39 mm. **Obv:** Kamehameha statue **Obv. Inscription:** KIING KAMEHAMEHA - SOVEREIGN HAWAII **Rev:** Native canoe, shield at center **Rev. Legend:** UA MAU KE EA O KA 'AINA I KA PONO **Edge:** Reeded

Date	Mintage	F	VF	XF	Unc	BU
1993RHM Proof	—	Value: 75.00				

X# MB100 OUNCE

31.1030 g., 0.9990 Silver 0.9989 oz. ASW, 39 mm. **Subject:** Bicentennial of Kingdom **Obv:** Bust right holding spear **Obv. Legend:** 200 LA HO 'OMANA 'O - 200th ANNIVERSARY **Rev:** Wooden dagger, canoe, island group **Rev. Legend:** FOUNDING THE KINGDOM OF HAWAII **Rev. Inscription:** UNIFICATION **Edge:** Reeded

Date	Mintage	F	VF	XF	Unc	BU
ND(1995)RHM Proof	—	Value: 55.00				

X# MB101 8 OUNCES

248.8240 g., 0.9990 Silver 7.9915 oz. ASW, 89 mm. **Subject:** Bicentennial of Kingdom **Obv:** Bust right holding spear **Obv. Legend:** 200 LA HO 'OMANA 'O - 200th ANNIVERSARY **Rev:** Wooden dagger, canoe, island group **Rev. Legend:** FOUNDING THE KINGDOM OF HAWAII **Rev. Inscription:** UNIFICATION **Edge:** Reeded

Date	Mintage	F	VF	XF	Unc	BU
ND(1995)RHM Proof	—	Value: 250				

X# MB83 DALA

31.1030 g., 0.9990 Silver 0.9989 oz. ASW, 39 mm. **Subject:** 100th Anniversary of Overthrow **Obv:** Bust of Liliuokolani facing slightly left **Obv. Legend:** OH HONEST AMERICANS AS CHRISTIANS HEAR ME **Rev:** Crowned garter, monogram in center

Date	Mintage	F	VF	XF	Unc	BU
1993 Proof	—	Value: 60.00				

X# MB150 10 DALA

0.9990 Silver, 38 mm. **Obv:** Head right **Obv. Legend:** • PRINCESS VICTORIA • KAIULANI...... **Rev:** Crowned and mantled arms **Rev. Legend:** TEN HAWAII SILVER DOLLARS **Edge:** Reeded **Note:** A premium issue at $10.00 each, one per month.

Date	Mintage	F	VF	XF	Unc	BU
1994(2004)RHM Proof	30	Value: 150				

X# MB152 10 DALA

0.9990 Silver, 38 mm. **Obv:** Bust left **Obv. Legend:** LILIUOKALANI QUEEN OF HAWAII **Rev:** Crowned and mantled arms **Rev. Legend:** TEN HAWAII SILVER DOLLARS **Edge:** Reeded **Note:** A premium issue at $10.00 each, one per month.

Date	Mintage	F	VF	XF	Unc	BU
1996(2004)RHM Proof	30	Value: 150				

X# MB153 10 DALA

0.9990 Silver, 38 mm. **Obv:** Head right **Obv. Legend:** KALAKAUA I KING OF HAWAII **Rev:** Crowned and mantled arms **Rev. Legend:** TEN HAWAII SILVER DOLLARS **Edge:** Reeded **Note:** A premium issue at $10.00 each, one per month.

Date	Mintage	F	VF	XF	Unc	BU
1996(2004)RHM Proof	30	Value: 150				

X# MB155 10 DALA
0.9990 Silver, 38 mm. **Subject:** 2000th Anniversary of Founding **Obv:** Two native portraits **Obv. Legend:** LA HO'OMANA 'O 2000 **Rev:** Crowned and mantled arms **Rev. Legend:** TEN HAWAII SILVER DOLLARS **Edge:** Reeded **Note:** A premium issue at $10.00 each, one per month.

Date	Mintage	F	VF	XF	Unc	BU
ND(2004)RHM Proof	30	Value: 150				

X# MB154 10 DALA
0.9990 Silver, 38 mm. **Obv:** Statue of Kamehameha **Obv. Inscription:** KING KAMEHAMEHA - SOVEREIGN HAWAII **Rev:** Crowned and mantled arms **Rev. Legend:** TEN HAWAII SILVER DOLLARS **Edge:** Reeded **Note:** A premium issue of $10.00 each, one per month.

Date	Mintage	F	VF	XF	Unc	BU
ND(2004)RHM Proof	30	Value: 150				

X# MB151 10 DALA
0.9990 Silver, 38 mm. **Subject:** 200th Anniversary of Kingdom **Obv:** Bust of Kamehameha I right holding spear **Obv. Legend:** 200 LA HO 'OMANA 'O **Rev:** Crowned and mantled arms **Rev. Legend:** TEN HAWAII SILVER DOLLARS **Edge:** Reeded **Note:** A premium issue at $10.00 each, one per month.

Date	Mintage	F	VF	XF	Unc	BU
ND(2004)RHM Proof	30	Value: 150				

X# MB91 ALOHA DALA
31.1030 g., 0.9990 Silver 0.9989 oz. ASW, 39 mm. **Obv:** Bust left **Obv. Legend:** LILIUOKALANI QUEEN OF HAWAII **Rev:** Crowned and mantled arms **Rev. Legend:** ROYAL HAWAIIAN SILVER **Note:** Serial # on reverse.

Date	Mintage	F	VF	XF	Unc	BU
1994 Proof	—	Value: 30.00				

X# MB107 ALOHA DALA
31.1030 g., 0.9990 Silver 0.9989 oz. ASW **Obv:** Hula dancer **Obv. Legend:** HAWAII **Obv. Inscription:** Islands of / ALOHA **Rev:** Palm tree at left, volcano at center **Edge:** Reeded

Date	Mintage	F	VF	XF	Unc	BU
1995RHM	—	—	—	—	30.00	—

X# MB114 ALOHA DALA
31.1030 g., 0.9990 Silver 0.9989 oz. ASW, 39 mm. **Subject:** 50th Anniversary of Festivals **Obv:** Bust Kamehameha right **Obv. Legend:** ALOHA FESTIVALS HAWAII **Rev:** Island group **Rev. Legend:** HALIA ALOHA TREASURED MEMORIES **Edge:** Reeded

Date	Mintage	F	VF	XF	Unc	BU
ND(1996) Proof	—	Value: 50.00				

X# 11 AKAHI DALA
31.1400 g., 0.9990 Silver 1.0000 oz. ASW, 38.5 mm. **Obv:** Head right **Obv. Legend:** KALAKAUA I KING OF HAWAII **Rev:** Crowned and mantled arms **Rev. Legend:** UA MAU KE EA OKA AINA I KA PONO. **Edge:** Reeded

Date	Mintage	F	VF	XF	Unc	BU
1883 Proof	—	Value: 45.00				

X# MB113 AKAHI DALA
31.1030 g., 0.9990 Silver 0.9989 oz. ASW, 39 mm. **Obv:** Kamehameha statue **Obv. Legend:** KING

KAMEHAMEHA - SOVEREIGN HAWAII **Rev:** Crowned and mantled arms **Rev. Legend:** ROYAL HAWAIIAN SILVER **Edge:** Reeded

Date	Mintage	F	VF	XF	Unc	BU
1996RHM Proof	—	Value: 40.00				

X# MB71 HONOLULU DALA
31.1030 g., 0.9990 Silver 0.9989 oz. ASW, 39 mm. **Obv:** Kamehameha statue **Obv. Legend:** KING KAMEHAMEHA KINGDOM OF HAWAII **Rev:** Palm tree at left, volcano at center

Date	Mintage	F	VF	XF	Unc	BU
1992RHM	—	—	—	—	25.00	—

X# MB80 MIDWAY DALA
31.1030 g., 0.9990 Silver 0.9989 oz. ASW, 39 mm. **Subject:** 50th Anniversary Battle of Midway **Obv:** Two U.S. Navy aircraft **Rev:** American flag at left, four Japanese flags vertically at right **Rev. Legend:** AMERICA EVENS THE SCORE **Edge:** Reeded

Date	Mintage	F	VF	XF	Unc	BU
ND(1992) Proof	—	Value: 45.00				

X# MB80a MIDWAY DALA
Bronze, 39 mm. **Subject:** 50th Anniversary Battle of Midway **Obv:** Two U.S. Navy aircraft **Rev:** American flag at left, four Japanese flags vertically at right **Rev. Legend:** AMERICA EVENS THE SCORE **Edge:** Reeded

Date	Mintage	F	VF	XF	Unc	BU
ND(1992) Proof	—	Value: 25.00				

X# 16 MAHALO DALA
Bronze, 39 mm. **Obv:** Bust left **Obv. Legend:** LILIUOKALANI QUEEN OF HAWAII **Rev:** Crowned and mantled arms **Rev. Legend:** ROYAL HAWAIIAN MINT

Date	Mintage	F	VF	XF	Unc	BU
1996 Proof	—	Value: 12.00				

X# 17 MAHALO DALA
Bronze, 39 mm. **Obv:** Kamehamehah statue **Obv. Legend:** KING KAMEHAMEHA - SOVEREIGN HAWAII **Rev:** Crowned and mantled arms **Rev. Legend:** ROYAL HAWAIIAN MINT

Date	Mintage	F	VF	XF	Unc	BU
1996 Proof	—	Value: 12.00				

X# MB120 WAIKIKI DALA
31.1030 g., 0.9990 Silver 0.9989 oz. ASW **Obv:** Hula dancer **Obv. Inscription:** Islands of / ALOHA **Rev:** Two palm trees at left, volcano at center **Rev. Inscription:** ALOHA **Edge:** Reeded

Date	Mintage	F	VF	XF	Unc	BU
1997RHM	—	—	—	—	30.00	—
1997RHM Proof	500	Value: 40.00				

MEDALLIC GOLD COINAGE

Bernard von NotHaus Issues

Essentially bullion issues

X# MB86 1/20 OUNCE
1.5552 g., 0.9999 Gold 0.0500 oz. AGW, 13.8 mm. **Obv:** Kamehameha statue **Obv. Inscription:** KING KAMEHAMEHA - SOVEREIGN HAWAII **Rev:** Native sailboat, shield at center **Rev. Legend:** UA MAU KE EA O KA 'AINA I KA PONO **Edge:** Reeded

Date	Mintage	F	VF	XF	Unc	BU
1993RHM Proof	400	Value: 90.00				

X# MB102 1/20 OUNCE
1.5552 g., 0.9999 Gold 0.0500 oz. AGW **Subject:** Bicentennial of Kingdom **Obv:** Bust right holding spear **Obv. Legend:** 200 LA HO 'OMANA 'O - 200th ANNIVERSARY **Rev:** Wooden dagger, canoe, island group **Rev. Legend:** FOUNDING THE KINGDOM OF HAWAII **Rev. Inscription:** UNIFICATION **Edge:** Reeded

Date	Mintage	F	VF	XF	Unc	BU
ND(1995)RHM Proof	—	Value: 90.00				

X# MB16 1/20 OUNCE
(Hapaiwakalua (1/20) Crown)
1.5555 g., 0.9999 Gold 0.0500 oz. AGW
Subject: Liliuokalani

Date	Mintage	F	VF	XF	Unc	BU
ND(1985)THM Proof	117	Value: 125				

X# MB17 1/20 OUNCE
(Hapaiwakalua (1/20) Crown)
1.5555 g., 0.9999 Gold 0.0500 oz. AGW
Subject: Kalakaua I

Date	Mintage	F	VF	XF	Unc	BU
ND(1985)THM Proof	234	Value: 125				

X# MB24 1/20 OUNCE
(Hapaiwakalua (1/20) Crown)
1.5555 g., 0.9999 Gold 0.0500 oz. AGW **Subject:** Kalakaua I

Date	Mintage	F	VF	XF	Unc	BU
1987THM Proof	—	Value: 90.00				

X# MB32 1/20 OUNCE
(Hapaiwakalua (1/20) Crown)
1.5555 g., 0.9999 Gold 0.0500 oz. AGW
Subject: Kalakaua I

Date	Mintage	F	VF	XF	Unc	BU
1988BVN Proof	—	Value: 90.00				

X# MB38 1/20 OUNCE
(Hapaiwakalua (1/20) Crown)
1.5555 g., 0.9999 Gold 0.0500 oz. AGW
Subject: Kalakaua I

Date	Mintage	F	VF	XF	Unc	BU
1989BVNH	725	—	—	—	65.00	—
1989BVNH Proof	400	Value: 150				

X# MB45 1/20 OUNCE
(Hapaiwakalua (1/20) Crown)
1.5555 g., 0.9999 Gold 0.0500 oz. AGW
Subject: Liliuokalani

Date	Mintage	F	VF	XF	Unc	BU
1989BVNH	950	—	—	—	45.00	—
1989BVNH Proof	400	Value: 60.00				

X# MB56 1/20 OUNCE
(Hapaiwakalua (1/20) Crown)
1.5555 g., 0.9999 Gold 0.0500 oz. AGW
Subject: Princess Victoria

Date	Mintage	F	VF	XF	Unc	BU
1991RHM	—	—	—	—	60.00	—
1991RHM Proof	400	Value: 80.00				

X# MB81 1/10 OUNCE
3.1103 g., 0.9999 Gold 0.1000 oz. AGW, 14 mm.
Subject: 50th Anniversary Battle of Midway
Obv: Liberty head left **Rev:** American flag at left, four Japanese flags vertically at right **Edge:** Reeded

Date	Mintage	F	VF	XF	Unc	BU
ND(1992) Proof	—	Value: 175				

X# MB87 1/10 OUNCE
3.1103 g., 0.9999 Gold 0.1000 oz. AGW, 16.5 mm.
Obv: Kamehameha statue **Obv. Inscription:** KING KAMEHAMEHA - SOVEREIGN HAWAII **Rev:** Native canoe, shield at center **Rev. Legend:** UA MAU KE EA O KA 'AINA I KA PONO **Edge:** Reeded

Date	Mintage	F	VF	XF	Unc	BU
1993RHM Proof	400	Value: 150				

X# MB103 1/10 OUNCE
3.1103 g., 0.9999 Gold 0.1000 oz. AGW
Subject: Bicentennial of Kingdom **Obv:** Bust right holding spear **Obv. Legend:** 200 LA HO 'OMANA 'O - 200th ANNIVERSARY **Rev:** Wooden dagger, canoe, island group **Rev. Legend:** FOUNDING THE KINGDOM OF HAWAII **Edge:** Reeded

Date	Mintage	F	VF	XF	Unc	BU
ND(1995)RHM Proof	—	Value: 165				

X# MB115 1/10 OUNCE
3.1103 g., 0.9999 Gold 0.1000 oz. AGW, 18 mm.
Subject: 50th Anniversary of Festivals **Obv:** Bust Kamehameha right **Obv. Legend:** ALOHA FESTIVALS HAWAII **Rev:** Island group **Rev. Legend:** HALIA ALOHA TREASURED MEMORIES **Edge:** Reeded

Date	Mintage	F	VF	XF	Unc	BU
ND(1996) Proof	—	Value: 150				

X# MB25 1/10 OUNCE
(Hapa'umi (1/10) Crown)
3.1103 g., 0.9999 Gold 0.1000 oz. AGW
Subject: Kalakaua I

Date	Mintage	F	VF	XF	Unc	BU
1987RHM Proof	—	Value: 150				

X# MB26 1/10 OUNCE
(Hapa'umi (1/10) Crown)
3.1103 g., 0.9999 Gold 0.1000 oz. AGW
Subject: Liliuokalani

Date	Mintage	F	VF	XF	Unc	BU
1987RHM Proof	—	Value: 150				

X# MB33 1/10 OUNCE
(Hapa'umi (1/10) Crown)
3.1103 g., 0.9999 Gold 0.1000 oz. AGW
Subject: Kalakaua I

Date	Mintage	F	VF	XF	Unc	BU
1988BVN Proof	—	Value: 165				

X# MB39 1/10 OUNCE
(Hapa'umi (1/10) Crown)
3.1103 g., 0.9999 Gold 0.1000 oz. AGW
Subject: Kalakaua I

Date	Mintage	F	VF	XF	Unc	BU
1989BVNH	350	—	—	—	90.00	—
1989BVNH Proof	400	Value: 150				

X# MB46 1/10 OUNCE
(Hapa'umi (1/10) Crown)
3.1103 g., 0.9999 Gold 0.1000 oz. AGW
Subject: Liliuokalani

Date	Mintage	F	VF	XF	Unc	BU
1989BVNH	475	—	—	—	90.00	—
1989BVNH Proof	400	Value: 125				

X# MB57 1/10 OUNCE
(Hapa'umi (1/10) Crown)
3.1103 g., 0.9999 Gold 0.1000 oz. AGW
Subject: Princess Victoria

Date	Mintage	F	VF	XF	Unc	BU
1991RHM	—	—	—	—	90.00	—
1991RHM Proof	400	Value: 125				

X# MB65 1/10 OUNCE
(Hapa'umi (1/10) Crown)
3.1103 g., 0.9999 Gold 0.1000 oz. AGW
Subject: Liliuokalani

Date	Mintage	F	VF	XF	Unc	BU
1991RHM Proof	900	Value: 125				

X# MB66 1/10 OUNCE (Gold Dala)
3.1103 g., 0.9999 Gold 0.1000 oz. AGW **Subject:** Liberty - 50th Anniversary Pearl Harbor - Memorial

Date	Mintage	F	VF	XF	Unc	BU
1991 Proof	—	Value: 125				

X# MB88 1/4 OUNCE
7.7758 g., 0.9999 Gold 0.2500 oz. AGW, 22 mm.
Obv: Kamehameha statue **Obv. Inscription:** KING KAMEHAMEHA - SOVEREIGN HAWAII **Rev:** Native sailboat, shield at center **Rev. Legend:** UA MAU KE EA O KA 'AINA I KA PONO **Edge:** Reeded

Date	Mintage	F	VF	XF	Unc	BU
1993RHM Proof	400	Value: 250				

X# MB104 1/4 OUNCE
7.7758 g., 0.9999 Gold 0.2500 oz. AGW, 22 mm.
Subject: Bicentennial of Kingdom **Obv:** Bust right holding spear **Obv. Legend:** 200 LA HO 'OMANA 'O - 200th ANNIVERSARY **Rev:** Wooden dagger, canoe, island group **Rev. Legend:** FOUNDING THE KINGDOM OF HAWAII **Edge:** Reeded

Date	Mintage	F	VF	XF	Unc	BU
ND(1995)RHM Proof	—	Value: 250				

X# MB1 1/4 OUNCE (Hapaha (1/4) Crown)
12.4412 g., 0.9990 Gold 0.3996 oz. AGW **Subject:** Kalakaua I

Date	Mintage	F	VF	XF	Unc	BU
1980THM Proof	78	Value: 700				

X# MB2 1/4 OUNCE (Hapaha (1/4) Crown)
12.4412 g., 0.9990 Gold 0.3996 oz. AGW **Subject:** Liliuokalani

Date	Mintage	F	VF	XF	Unc	BU
1981THM Proof	974	Value: 400				

X# MB2a 1/4 OUNCE (Hapaha (1/4) Crown)
Bronze **Subject:** Liliuokalani

Date	Mintage	F	VF	XF	Unc	BU
1981THM Proof	50	Value: 40.00				

X# MB3 1/4 OUNCE (Hapaha (1/4) Crown)
7.7758 g., 0.9990 Gold 0.2497 oz. AGW **Subject:** Kalakaua I

Date	Mintage	F	VF	XF	Unc	BU
1981THM Proof	653	Value: 400				

X# MB3a 1/4 OUNCE (Hapaha (1/4) Crown)
Bronze **Subject:** Kalakaua I

Date	Mintage	F	VF	XF	Unc	BU
1981THM Proof	50	Value: 40.00				

X# MB27 1/4 OUNCE (Hapaha (1/4) Crown)
12.4412 g., 0.9990 Gold 0.3996 oz. AGW **Subject:** Liliuokalani

Date	Mintage	F	VF	XF	Unc	BU
1987RHM Proof	—	Value: 400				

X# MB28 1/4 OUNCE (Hapaha (1/4) Crown)
12.4412 g., 0.9990 Gold 0.3996 oz. AGW **Subject:** Kalakaua I

Date	Mintage	F	VF	XF	Unc	BU
1987RHM Proof	—	Value: 400				

X# MB34 1/4 OUNCE (Hapaha (1/4) Crown)
12.4412 g., 0.9990 Gold 0.3996 oz. AGW **Subject:** Kalakaua I

Date	Mintage	F	VF	XF	Unc	BU
1988BVN Proof	400	Value: 400				

X# MB40 1/4 OUNCE (Hapaha (1/4) Crown)
12.4412 g., 0.9990 Gold 0.3996 oz. AGW **Subject:** Kalakaua I

Date	Mintage	F	VF	XF	Unc	BU
1989BVNH	185	—	—	—	200	—
1989BVNH Proof	400	Value: 400				

X# MB47 1/4 OUNCE (Hapaha (1/4) Crown)
12.4412 g., 0.9990 Gold 0.3996 oz. AGW **Subject:** Liliuokalani

Date	Mintage	F	VF	XF	Unc	BU
1989BVNH	225	—	—	—	200	—
1989BVNH Proof	400	Value: 250				

X# MB58 1/4 OUNCE (Hapaha (1/4) Crown)
12.4412 g., 0.9990 Gold 0.3996 oz. AGW **Subject:** Princess Victoria

Date	Mintage	F	VF	XF	Unc	BU
1991RHM	—	—	—	—	200	—
1991RHM Proof	400	Value: 250				

X# MB82 1/2 OUNCE
1.5400 g., 0.9990 Gold 0.0495 oz. AGW, 13.1 mm. **Obv:** Liberty head left **Obv. Legend:** LIBERTY **Obv. Inscription:** HAWAII **Rev:** Eagle in flight right **Rev. Legend:** LIBERTY FROM EAST TO WEST **Rev. Inscription:** SALUTE TO AMERICA

Date	Mintage	F	VF	XF	Unc	BU
1992RHM Proof	—	Value: 45.00				

X# MB89 1/2 OUNCE
15.5515 g., 0.9999 Gold 0.4999 oz. AGW **Obv:** Kamahameha statue **Obv. Inscription:** KING KAMEHAMEHA - SOVEREIGN HAWAII **Rev:** Native sailboat, shield at center **Rev. Legend:** UA MAU KE EA O KA 'AINA I KA PONO **Edge:** Reeded

Date	Mintage	F	VF	XF	Unc	BU
1993RHM Proof	400	Value: 400				

X# MB105 1/2 OUNCE
15.5515 g., 0.9999 Gold 0.4999 oz. AGW **Subject:** Bicentennial of Kingdom **Obv:** Bust right holding spear **Obv. Legend:** 200 LA HO 'OMANA 'O - 200th ANNIVERSARY **Rev:** Wooden dagger, canoe, island group **Rev. Legend:** FOUNDING THE KINGDOM OF HAWAII **Edge:** Reeded

Date	Mintage	F	VF	XF	Unc	BU
ND(1995)RHM Proof	—	Value: 400				

X# MB29 1/2 OUNCE (Hapalua (1/2) Crown)
15.5515 g., 0.9999 Gold 0.4999 oz. AGW **Subject:** Kalakaua I

Date	Mintage	F	VF	XF	Unc	BU
1987RHM Proof	—	Value: 475				

X# MB35 1/2 OUNCE (Hapalua (1/2) Crown)
15.5515 g., 0.9999 Gold 0.4999 oz. AGW **Subject:** Kalakaua I

Date	Mintage	F	VF	XF	Unc	BU
1988BVN Proof	—	Value: 500				

X# MB41 1/2 OUNCE (Hapalua (1/2) Crown)
15.5515 g., 0.9999 Gold 0.4999 oz. AGW **Subject:** Kalakaua I

Date	Mintage	F	VF	XF	Unc	BU
1989BVNH	65	—	—	—	275	—
1989BVNH Proof	400	Value: 450				

X# MB48 1/2 OUNCE (Hapalua (1/2) Crown)
15.5515 g., 0.9999 Gold 0.4999 oz. AGW **Subject:** Liliuokalaui

Date	Mintage	F	VF	XF	Unc	BU
1989BVNH	47	—	—	—	275	—
1989BVNH Proof	400	Value: 450				

X# MB59 1/2 OUNCE (Hapalua (1/2) Crown)
15.5515 g., 0.9999 Gold 0.4999 oz. AGW **Subject:** Princess Victoria

Date	Mintage	F	VF	XF	Unc	BU
1991RHM	—	—	—	—	275	—
1991RHM Proof	400	Value: 450				

X# MB7 OUNCE (Crown)
31.1030 g., 0.9990 Gold 0.9989 oz. AGW
Subject: Centennial of First Coinage

Date	Mintage	F	VF	XF	Unc	BU
1983THM Proof	384	Value: 1,000				

X# MB7a OUNCE (Crown)
Bronze **Subject:** Centennial of First Coinage

Date	Mintage	F	VF	XF	Unc	BU
1983THM Proof	50	Value: 50.00				

X# MB20 OUNCE (Akahi (1) Crown)
31.1030 g., 0.9999 Gold 0.9998 oz. AGW **Subject:** Kalakaua I

Date	Mintage	F	VF	XF	Unc	BU
1986JM Proof	107	Value: 1,000				

X# MB20a OUNCE (Akahi (1) Crown)
Bronze **Subject:** Kalakaua I

Date	Mintage	F	VF	XF	Unc	BU
1986JM Proof	50	Value: 40.00				

X# MB30 OUNCE (Akahi (1) Crown)
31.1030 g., 0.9999 Gold 0.9998 oz. AGW **Subject:** Liliuokalani

Date	Mintage	F	VF	XF	Unc	BU
1987RHM Proof	—	Value: 1,000				

X# MB36 OUNCE (Akahi (1) Crown)
31.1030 g., 0.9999 Gold 0.9998 oz. AGW
Subject: Kalakaua I

Date	Mintage	F	VF	XF	Unc	BU
1988BVN Proof	—	Value: 1,000				

X# MB36a OUNCE (Akahi (1) Crown)
Silver **Subject:** Kalakaua I

Date	Mintage	F	VF	XF	Unc	BU
1988BVN Proof	8	—	—	—	—	—

X# MB42 OUNCE (Akahi (1) Crown)
31.1030 g., 0.9999 Gold 0.9998 oz. AGW
Subject: Kalakaua I

Date	Mintage	F	VF	XF	Unc	BU
1989BVNH	95	—	—	—	800	—

X# MB43 OUNCE (Akahi (1) Crown)
31.1030 g., 0.9999 Gold 0.9998 oz. AGW **Subject:** Kalakaua I **Rev:** With serial number in panel

Date	Mintage	F	VF	XF	Unc	BU
1989BVNH Proof	400	Value: 900				

X# MB49 OUNCE (Akahi (1) Crown)
31.1030 g., 0.9999 Gold 0.9998 oz. AGW
Subject: Liliuokalaui

Date	Mintage	F	VF	XF	Unc	BU
1989BVNH	115	—	—	—	600	—

X# MB50 OUNCE (Akahi (1) Crown)
31.1030 g., 0.9999 Gold 0.9998 oz. AGW **Subject:** Liliuokalaui **Rev:** With serial number in panel

Date	Mintage	F	VF	XF	Unc	BU
1989BVNH Proof	400	Value: 1,000				

X# MB60 OUNCE (Akahi (1) Crown)
31.1030 g., 0.9999 Gold 0.9998 oz. AGW, 34.3 mm.
Subject: Princess Victoria

Date	Mintage	F	VF	XF	Unc	BU
1991RHM	—	—	—	—	900	—

X# MB61 OUNCE (Akahi (1) Crown)
31.1030 g., 0.9999 Gold 0.9998 oz. AGW, 34.3 mm.
Subject: Princess Victoria **Rev:** With serial number in panel

Date	Mintage	F	VF	XF	Unc	BU
1991 RHM Proof	400	Value: 1,000				

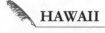

X# MB9 OUNCE (Dala)
31.1030 g., 0.9990 Gold 0.9989 oz. AGW

Date	Mintage	F	VF	XF	Unc	BU
1984THM Proof	296	Value: 850				

X# MB12 OUNCE (Dala)
31.1030 g., 0.9990 Gold 0.9989 oz. AGW

Date	Mintage	F	VF	XF	Unc	BU
1984THM Proof	187	Value: 875				

X# MB22 OUNCE (Akahi (1) Dala)
31.1030 g., 0.9990 Gold 0.9989 oz. AGW

Date	Mintage	F	VF	XF	Unc	BU
1987 Proof	—	Value: 1,000				

X# MB90 OUNCE
31.1030 g., 0.9999 Gold 0.9998 oz. AGW
Obv: Kamehamehah statue **Obv. Inscription:** KING KAMEHAMEHA - SOVEREIGN HAWAII **Rev:** Native sailboat, shield at center **Rev. Legend:** UA MAU KE EA O KA 'AINA I KA PONO **Edge:** Reeded

Date	Mintage	F	VF	XF	Unc	BU
1993RHM Proof	400	Value: 1,000				

X# MB106 OUNCE
31.1030 g., 0.9999 Gold 0.9998 oz. AGW
Subject: Bicentennial of Kingdom **Obv:** Bust right holding spear **Obv. Legend:** 200 LA HO 'OMANA 'O - 200th ANNIVERSARY **Rev:** Wooden dagger, canoe, island group **Rev. Legend:** FOUNDING THE KINGDOM OF HAWAII **Edge:** Reeded

Date	Mintage	F	VF	XF	Unc	BU
ND(1995)RHM Proof	—	Value: 1,000				

X# MB84 DALA
3.1103 g., 0.9999 Gold 0.1000 oz. AGW, 16 mm.
Subject: 100th Anniversary of Overthrow **Obv:** Bust of Liliuokolani facing slightly left **Obv. Legend:** OH HONEST AMERICANS AS CHRISTIANS HEAR ME
Rev: Crowned garter, monogram, in center

Date	Mintage	F	VF	XF	Unc	BU
1993 Proof	—	Value: 160				

X# MB92 1/20 CROWN
1.5552 g., 0.9999 Gold 0.0500 oz. AGW, 13.9 mm.
Obv: Bust left **Obv. Legend:** LILIUOKALANI QUEEN OF HAWAII **Rev:** Crown **Rev. Legend:** ROYAL HAWAIIAN GOLD **Edge:** Reeded

Date	Mintage	F	VF	XF	Unc	BU
1994 Proof	—	Value: 90.00				

X# MB93 1/10 CROWN
3.1103 g., 0.9999 Gold 0.1000 oz. AGW, 17.7 mm.
Obv: Bust left **Obv. Legend:** LILIUOKALANI QUEEN OF HAWAII **Rev:** Crown **Rev. Legend:** ROYAL HAWAIIAN GOLD **Edge:** Reeded

Date	Mintage	F	VF	XF	Unc	BU
1994 Proof	—	Value: 150				

X# MB94 1/4 CROWN
7.7758 g., 0.9999 Gold 0.2500 oz. AGW, 21.9 mm.
Obv: Bust left **Obv. Legend:** LILIUOKALANI QUEEN OF HAWAII **Rev:** Crown **Rev. Legend:** ROYAL HAWAIIAN GOLD **Edge:** Reeded

Date	Mintage	F	VF	XF	Unc	BU
1994 Proof	—	Value: 300				

X# MB95 1/2 CROWN
15.5515 g., 0.9999 Gold 0.4999 oz. AGW **Obv:** Bust left **Obv. Legend:** LILIUOKALANI QUEEN OF HAWAII **Rev:** Crown **Rev. Legend:** ROYAL HAWAIIAN GOLD **Edge:** Reeded

Date	Mintage	F	VF	XF	Unc	BU
1994 Proof	—	Value: 600				

X# MB96 CROWN
31.1030 g., 0.9999 Gold 0.9998 oz. AGW **Obv:** Bust left **Obv. Legend:** LILIUOKALANI QUEEN OF HAWAII **Rev:** Crown **Rev. Legend:** ROYAL HAWAIIAN GOLD **Edge:** Reeded

Date	Mintage	F	VF	XF	Unc	BU
1994 Proof	—	Value: 675				

MEDALLIC PLATINUM COINAGE

Bernard von NotHaus Issues

Essentially bullion issues

X# MB63 1/10 OUNCE (Hapaumi Puela)
Platinum APW **Subject:** Princess Victoria

Date	Mintage	F	VF	XF	Unc	BU
1991RHM Proof	900	Value: 200				

X# MB127 AKAHI PUELA
31.1030 g., 0.9990 Platinum 0.9989 oz. APW
Obv: Head right **Rev:** Puela (shield) in Taro leaves **Rev. Legend:** ROYAI HAWAIIAN PLATINUM **Edge:** Reeded

Date	Mintage	F	VF	XF	Unc	BU
1997 Proof	—	Value: 1,800				

X# MB123 1/20 PUELA
1.5552 g., 0.9990 Platinum 0.0499 oz. APW **Obv:** Head right **Obv. Legend:** KALAKAUA I KING OF HAWAII **Rev:** Puela (shield) in Taro leaves **Rev. Legend:** ROYAL HAWAIIAN PLATINUM **Edge:** Reeded

Date	Mintage	F	VF	XF	Unc	BU
1997 Proof	—	Value: 200				

X# MB124 1/10 PUELA
3.1103 g., 0.9990 Platinum 0.0999 oz. APW **Obv:** Head right **Obv. Legend:** KALAKAUA I KING OF HAWAII **Rev:** Puela (shield) in Taro leaves **Rev. Legend:** ROYAL HAWAIIAN PLATINUM **Edge:** Reeded

Date	Mintage	F	VF	XF	Unc	BU
1997 Proof	—	Value: 400				

X# MB125 1/4 PUELA
7.7758 g., 0.9990 Platinum 0.2497 oz. APW **Obv:** Head right **Obv. Legend:** KALAKAUA I KING OF HAWAII **Rev:** Puela (shield) in Taro leaves **Rev. Legend:** ROYAL HAWAIIAN PLATINUM **Edge:** Reeded

Date	Mintage	F	VF	XF	Unc	BU
1997 Proof	—	Value: 650				

X# MB126 1/2 PUELA
15.5515 g., 0.9990 Platinum 0.4995 oz. APW
Obv: Head right **Obv. Legend:** KALAKAUA I KING OF HAWAII **Rev:** Puela (shield) in Taro leaves
Rev. Legend: ROYAL HAWAIIAN PLATINUM
Edge: Reeded

Date	Mintage	F	VF	XF	Unc	BU
1997 Proof	—	Value: 900				

COUNTERSTAMPED COINAGE

X# MB5 OUNCE (Kala Dala)
31.1030 g., 0.9990 Silver 0.9989 oz. ASW
Counterstamp: Queen Liliuokalani // crowned ornate arms **Note:** 47 pieces counterstamped.

CS Date	Host Date	Good	VG	F	VF	XF
1883THM Proof	Value: 100					

X# MB52 OUNCE (Akahi (1) Dala)
31.1030 g., 0.9990 Silver 0.9989 oz. ASW
Counterstamp: Obv: RHM Grand Opening 6-9-90. Rev: Queen Liliuokalani. **Note:** 850 pieces counterstamped on X#MB51.

CS Date	Host Date	Good	VG	F	VF	XF
1990	1990RHM	—	—	—	—	—

X# MB74 DOLLAR

26.7300 g., 0.9000 Silver 0.7734 oz. ASW, 38.1 mm. **Counterstamp:** Royal Hawaiian Mint Dollar // Aloha Money **Note:** Counterstamp on US dollar, KM#110.

CS Date	Host Date	Good	VG	F	VF	XF
(1993)	1883	—	—	—	—	—

X# MB69 DOLLAR

31.1030 g., 0.9990 Silver 0.9989 oz. ASW, 40.60 mm. **Counterstamp:** Kalakaua I // PEARL HARBOR DALA **Note:** Counterstamp on U.S. Dollar/Ounce, KM#273.

CS Date	Host Date	Good	VG	F	VF	XF
1991	1991	—	—	—	—	—

X# MB72 DOLLAR

31.1030 g., 0.9990 Silver 0.9989 oz. ASW, 40.6 mm. **Counterstamp:** Royal Hawaiian Mint Dollar // Aloha Money **Note:** Counterstamped on US dollar, KM#273.

CS Date	Host Date	Good	VG	F	VF	XF
1993	ND(1993)	—	—	—	—	—

X# MB70 DALA

3.1103 g., 0.9990 Silver 0.0999 oz. ASW **Subject:** First Day of Issue 3-9-91 **Countermark:** Queen Liliuokalana // First Day of Issue **Note:** Counterstamped on X#MB55.

CS Date	Host Date	Good	VG	F	VF	XF
1991RHM Proof	Value: 55.00					

TOKEN COINAGE

X# Tn2 ALOHA DALA

11.0000 g., Brass, 32 mm. **Subject:** Aloha Festivals 50th Anniversary **Obv:** Kamehameha **Rev:** Like X20 but with additional "token" legend **Edge:** Reeded

Date	Mintage	F	VF	XF	Unc	BU
ND (1996)RHM	—	—	—	—	5.00	—

TRADE COINAGE

X# T1 MAUI TRADE DOLLAR

25.5700 g., Copper-Nickel, 39.2 mm. **Issuer:** Maui Trade Dollar Association **Obv:** Pineapple, flowers, whale, rising sun **Obv. Inscription:** MAUI / NO KA OI **Obv. Designer:** S. T. Wurmser **Rev:** Large ornate value ONE / 1 **Rev. Legend:** THE VALLEY ISLE **Edge:** Reeded

Date	Mintage	F	VF	XF	Unc	BU
1992	100,000	—	—	—	7.50	—

X# T2 MAUI TRADE DOLLAR

25.5700 g., Copper-Nickel, 39.2 mm. **Issuer:** Maui Trade Dollar Association **Obv:** Flowers, two whales, rising sun **Obv. Legend:** MAUI NO KA OI **Obv. Designer:** S. T. Wurmser **Rev:** Large ornate value ONE / 1 **Rev. Legend:** THE VALLEY ISLE **Edge:** Reeded

Date	Mintage	F	VF	XF	Unc	BU
1993	100,000	—	—	—	7.50	—

X# T3 MAUI TRADE DOLLAR

25.5700 g., Copper-Nickel, 39.2 mm. **Issuer:** Maui Trade Dollar Association **Obv:** Flowers, two dolphins **Obv. Inscription:** MAUI / NO KA OI **Obv. Designer:** S. T. Wurmser **Rev:** Large ornate value ONE / 1 **Rev. Legend:** THE VALLEY ISLE **Edge:** Reeded

Date	Mintage	F	VF	XF	Unc	BU
1994	135,000	—	—	—	7.50	—

X# T4 MAUI TRADE DOLLAR

25.5700 g., Copper-Nickel, 39.2 mm. **Issuer:** Maui Trade Dollar Association **Obv:** Sea tortoise, tropical fish, rising sun **Obv. Inscription:** MAUI / NO KA OI **Obv. Designer:** S. T. Wurmser **Rev:** Large ornate value ONE / 1 **Rev. Legend:** THE VALLEY ISLE **Edge:** Reeded

Date	Mintage	F	VF	XF	Unc	BU
1995	115,000	—	—	—	6.50	—

X# T5 MAUI TRADE DOLLAR

25.5700 g., Copper-Nickel, 39.2 mm. **Issuer:** Maui Trade Dollar Association **Obv:** Trees, parrot

Obv. Inscription: MAUI / NO KA OI **Obv. Designer:** S. T. Wurmser **Rev:** Large ornate value ONE / 1 **Rev. Legend:** THE VALLEY ISLE **Edge:** Reeded

Date	Mintage	F	VF	XF	Unc	BU
1996	105,000	—	—	—	7.50	—

X# T6 MAUI TRADE DOLLAR

25.5700 g., Copper-Nickel, 39.2 mm. **Issuer:** Maui Trade Dollar Association **Obv:** Three whales, rising sun **Obv. Legend:** MAUI NO KA OI **Obv. Designer:** S. T. Wurmser **Rev:** Large ornate value ONE / 1 **Rev. Legend:** THE VALLEY ISLE **Edge:** Reeded

Date	Mintage	F	VF	XF	Unc	BU
1997	100,000	—	—	—	7.50	—

X# T7 MAUI TRADE DOLLAR

25.5700 g., Copper-Nickel, 39.2 mm. **Issuer:** Maui Trade Dollar Association **Obv:** Birds, tropical fish, sea tortoise, whale, rising sun **Obv. Inscription:** MAUI / NO KA OI **Obv. Designer:** S. T. Wurmser **Rev:** Large ornate value ONE / 1 **Rev. Legend:** THE VALLEY ISLE **Edge:** Reeded

Date	Mintage	F	VF	XF	Unc	BU
1998	100,000	—	—	—	6.50	—

X# T8 MAUI TRADE DOLLAR

25.5700 g., Copper-Nickel, 39.2 mm. **Issuer:** Maui Trade Dollar Association **Obv:** Whale, birds, plant, rising sun **Obv. Inscription:** MAUI / NO KA OI **Obv. Designer:** S. T. Wurmser **Rev:** Large ornate value ONE / 1 **Rev. Legend:** THE VALLEY ISLE **Edge:** Reeded

Date	Mintage	F	VF	XF	Unc	BU
1999	95,000	—	—	—	6.50	—

X# T9 MAUI TRADE DOLLAR

25.5700 g., Copper-Nickel, 39.2 mm. **Issuer:** Maui Trade Dollar Association **Obv:** Three porpoises, rising sun **Obv. Inscription:** MAUI / NO KA OI **Obv. Designer:** S. T. Wurmser **Rev:** Large ornate value ONE / 1 **Rev. Legend:** THE VALLEY ISLE **Edge:** Reeded

Date	Mintage	F	VF	XF	Unc	BU
2000	140,000	—	—	—	7.50	—

X# T10 MAUI TRADE DOLLAR

25.5700 g., Copper-Nickel, 39.2 mm. **Issuer:** Maui Trade Dollar Association **Obv:** Whale, bird, palm trees, rising sun **Obv. Inscription:** MAUI / NO KA OI **Obv. Designer:** S. T. Wurmser **Rev:** Large ornate value ONE / 1 **Rev. Legend:** THE VALLEY ISLE **Edge:** Reeded

Date	Mintage	F	VF	XF	Unc	BU
2001	120,000	—	—	—	7.50	—

X# T11 MAUI TRADE DOLLAR

25.5700 g., Copper-Nickel, 39.2 mm. **Issuer:** Maui Trade Dollar Association **Obv:** Birds, two whales, rising sun **Obv. Legend:** MAUI / NO KA OI **Obv. Designer:** S. T. Wurmser **Rev:** Large ornate value ONE / 1 **Rev. Legend:** THE VALLEY ISLE **Edge:** Reeded

Date	Mintage	F	VF	XF	Unc	BU
2002	—	—	—	—	7.50	—

X# T12 MAUI TRADE DOLLAR

25.5700 g., Copper-Nickel, 39.2 mm. **Issuer:** Maui Trade Dollar Association **Obv:** Dolphin, sea lion, birds, rising sun **Obv. Legend:** MAUI NO KA OI **Obv. Designer:** S. T. Wurmser **Rev:** Large ornate value ONE / 1 **Rev. Legend:** THE VALLEY ISLE **Edge:** Reeded

Date	Mintage	F	VF	XF	Unc	BU
2003	—	—	—	—	7.00	—

X# T13 MAUI TRADE DOLLAR

25.5700 g., Copper-Nickel, 39.2 mm. **Issuer:** Maui Trade Dollar Association **Obv:** Flowers, sea tortoise, tropical fish, rising sun **Obv. Inscription:** MAUI / NO KA OI **Obv. Designer:** S. T. Wurmser **Rev:** Large ornate value ONE / 1 **Rev. Legend:** THE VALLEY ISLE **Edge:** Reeded

Date	Mintage	F	VF	XF	Unc	BU
2004	—	—	—	—	6.00	—

X# T14 MAUI TRADE DOLLAR
25.5700 g., Copper-Nickel, 39.2 mm. **Issuer:** Maui Trade Dollar Association **Obv:** Palm tree, rising sun, three sting rays **Obv. Inscription:** MAUI / NO KA OI **Obv. Designer:** S. T. Wurmser **Rev:** Large ornate value ONE / 1 **Rev. Legend:** THE VALLEY ISLE **Edge:** Reeded

Date	Mintage	F	VF	XF	Unc	BU
2005	—	—	—	—	6.00	—

X# T15 KONA DOLLAR
20.8500 g., Bronze, 39.2 mm. **Obv:** Arms **Obv. Legend:** KONA COAST CHAMBER OF COMMERCE **Obv. Inscription:** UA MAUKE EA O KA AINA I KA POND **Rev:** Coastal scene with church, building, palm trees, volcanoin distance **Rev. Legend:** ALOHA **Rev. Inscription:** HAWAII **Edge:** Reeded

Date	Mintage	VG	F	VF	XF	Unc
1983	—	—	—	—	—	12.50

MEDALLIC SILVER BULLION

Scenic Series

X# MB140 OUNCE (Dala)
31.1341 g., 0.9990 Silver 0.9999 oz. ASW **Obv:** Seven Sacred Pools **Obv. Legend:** HAWAIIAN SCENIC SERIES NO. 5 - SEVEN SACRED POOLS, HANA, MAUI **Rev:** Three natives, pineapple plant **Rev. Inscription:** "Aloha" from Hawaii

Date	Mintage	F	VF	XF	Unc	BU
1989 Proof	—	Value: 18.50				

X# MB141 OUNCE (Dala)
31.1341 g., 0.9990 Silver 0.9999 oz. ASW **Obv:** Shore line **Obv. Legend:** HAWAIIAN SCENIC SERIES NO. 6 - KALAWAO, MOLOKAI **Rev:** Native woman crafting **Rev. Inscription:** "Aloha" from Hawaii

Date	Mintage	F	VF	XF	Unc	BU
1990 Proof	—	Value: 18.50				

X# MB142 OUNCE (Dala)
31.1341 g., 0.9990 Silver 0.9999 oz. ASW **Obv:** 1959 Volcanic eruption **Obv. Legend:** HAWAIIAN SCENIC SERIES NO. 7 - KILAUEA IKI, HAWAII **Rev:** Native seated at left, flowers at right **Rev. Inscription:** "Aloha" from Hawaii

Date	Mintage	F	VF	XF	Unc	BU
1990 Proof	—	Value: 18.50				

X# MB143 OUNCE (Dala)
31.1341 g., 0.9990 Silver 0.9999 oz. ASW **Obv:** Palm tree, shore line **Obv. Legend:** HAWAIIAN SCENIC SERIES NO. 8 - WINDWARD, OAHU **Rev:** Surfer, plants **Rev. Inscription:** "Aloha" from Hawaii

Date	Mintage	F	VF	XF	Unc	BU
1991 Proof	—	Value: 18.50				

X# MB144 OUNCE (Dala)
31.1341 g., 0.9990 Silver 0.9999 oz. ASW **Obv:** Valey, Needle Point **Obv. Legend:** HAWAIIAN SCENIC SERIES NO. 9 - IAO VALLEY NEEDLE POINT, MAUI **Rev:** Native climbing palm tree, flowers **Rev. Inscription:** "Aloha" from Hawaii

Date	Mintage	F	VF	XF	Unc	BU
1991 Proof	—	Value: 18.50				

X# MB145 OUNCE (Dala)
31.1341 g., 0.9990 Silver 0.9999 oz. ASW **Obv:** Pinapple field, mountains in distance **Obv. Legend:** HAWAIIAN SCENIC SERIES NO. 10 - LANAI CITY, LANAI **Rev:** Fish, diver **Rev. Inscription:** "Aloha" from Hawaii

Date	Mintage	F	VF	XF	Unc	BU
1991 Proof	—	Value: 18.50				

PATTERNS

X# 1 GRAM
1.0000 g., 0.9990 Gold 0.0321 oz. AGW
Issuer: Ahualoa Land Bank Issue

Date	Mintage	F	VF	XF	Unc	BU
1976 N	100	—	—	—	65.00	—

X# 4 GRAM

1.0000 g., 0.9990 Gold 0.0321 oz. AGW
Issuer: Ahualoa Land Bank Issue

Date	Mintage	F	VF	XF	Unc	BU
1989RHM	55	—	—	—	50.00	—

X# 2 2-1/2 GRAMS

2.5000 g., 0.9990 Gold 0.0803 oz. AGW **Issuer:** Volcano Island Bank Issue **Obv:** Bust of Madame Pele left

Date	Mintage	F	VF	XF	Unc	BU
1977 N	100	—	—	—	100	—

X# 3 5 GRAMS

5.0000 g., 0.9990 Gold 0.1606 oz. AGW **Issuer:** Kona Coast Bank Issue **Obv:** Bust of Captain Cook right **Rev:** Ships wheel

Date	Mintage	F	VF	XF	Unc	BU
1978 N	100	—	—	—	175	—

PROOF SETS

X#	Date	Mintage	Identification	Issue Price	Mkt Val
XPS1	1988BVN (5)	400	X#MB32-X#MB36	—	—
XPS2	1989BVNH (5)	400	X#MB38-X#MB41, X#MB43	1,492	3,500
XPS3	1989BVNH (5)	400	X#MB45-X#MB48, X#MB50	1,489	1,500
XPS4	1991 (3)	900	X#MB61-X#MB62, X#MB64	495	700
XPS5	1991 (3)	—	X#MB66, X#MB68, X#MB68a	199	400
XPS8	1991 (3)	100	X#MB75-X#MB77	25.00	80.00
XPS9	ND(1992) (3)	—	X#MB80, X#MB80a, X#MB81	199	300
XPS10	1993 (5)	—	X#MB86-X#MB90	1,495	3,500
XPS11	1993 (3)	—	X#MB83-X#MB85	179	350
XPS12	1993 (2)	—	X#MB83, X#MB85	53.00	75.00
XPS13	1994 (5)	—	X#MB92-X#MB96	—	2,500
XPS14	1995 (5)	—	X#MB102-X#MB106	1,750	3,000
XPS15	1995 (3)	1,000	X#MB100, X#MB101, X#MB104	745	1,000
XPS16	1996 (5)	—	X#MB109-X#MB113	79.00	150
XPS17	1997 (5)	—	X#MB123-X#MB127	2,950	5,000

HEJAZ

KINGDOM

COUNTERMARKED COINAGE

These spurious or questionable countermarks found on Maria Theresa restrike thalers appeared in the numismatic market in the early 1970s. Many of these are much larger than the official countermark. There does not appear to be any signs of heavy circulation wear on the reverses, merely flattened designs from the heavy countermarking.

X# 11 THALER

28.0600 g., 0.8333 Silver 0.7517 oz. ASW
Ruler: al Husain Ibn Ali AH1334-42/1916-24AD
Countermark: "al-Hejas" **Note:** Type II Countermark on Austria MT Thaler, KM#T1.

CM Date	Host Date	Good	VG	F	VF	XF
ND(1916-20)	1780 Restrike	125	175	250	350	—

X# 12 THALER

28.0600 g., 0.8333 Silver 0.7517 oz. ASW
Ruler: al Husain Ibn Ali AH1334-42/1916-24AD
Countermark: "al-Hejas" **Note:** Type III Countermark on Austria MT Thaler, KM#T1.

CM Date	Host Date	Good	VG	F	VF	XF
ND(1916-20)	1780 Restrike	125	175	250	350	—

X# 13 THALER

28.0600 g., 0.8333 Silver 0.7517 oz. ASW
Ruler: al Husain Ibn Ali AH1334-42/1916-24AD
Countermark: "al-Hejas" **Note:** Type IV Countermark on Austria MT Thaler, KM#T1.

CM Date	Host Date	Good	VG	F	VF	XF
ND(1916-20)	1780 Restrike	125	175	250	350	—

X# 14 THALER

28.0600 g., 0.8333 Silver 0.7517 oz. ASW
Ruler: al Husain Ibn Ali AH1334-42/1916-24AD
Countermark: "al-Hejas" **Note:** Type V Countermark on Austria MT Thaler, KM#T1.

CM Date	Host Date	Good	VG	F	VF	XF
ND(1916-20)	1780 Restrike	125	175	250	350	—

X# 15 THALER

28.0600 g., 0.8333 Silver 0.7517 oz. ASW **Ruler:** al Husain Ibn Ali AH1334-42/1916-24AD **Countermark:** "al-Hejas" **Note:** Type VI Countermark on Austria MT Thaler, KM#T1.

CM Date	Host Date	Good	VG	F	VF	XF
ND(1916-20)	ND Restrike	125	175	250	350	—

X# 16 THALER

28.0600 g., 0.8333 Silver 0.7517 oz. ASW, 41 mm. **Ruler:** al Husain Ibn Ali AH1334-42/1916-24AD **Countermark:** "al-Hejas" **Note:** Type VII countermark on Austria MT Thaler, KM#T1.

CM Date	Host Date	Good	VG	F	VF	XF
ND(1916-20)	1780 Restrike	150	165	185	200	—

X# 17 THALER

28.0600 g., 0.8333 Silver 0.7517 oz. ASW, 41 mm. **Ruler:** al Husain Ibn Ali AH1334-42/1916-24AD **Countermark:** "al-Hejas" **Note:** Type VIII countermarked on Austria MT Thaler, KM#T1.

CM Date	Host Date	Good	VG	F	VF	XF
ND(1916-20)	1780 Restrike	150	165	185	200	—

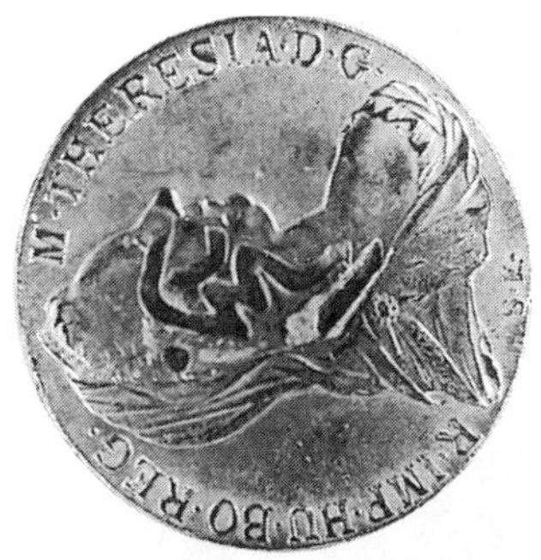

X# 18 THALER

28.0600 g., 0.8333 Silver 0.7517 oz. ASW, 41 mm. **Ruler:** al Husain Ibn Ali AH1334-42/1916-24AD **Countermark:** "al-Hejas" **Note:** Type IX countermark n Austria MT Thaler, KM#T1.

CM Date	Host Date	Good	VG	F	VF	XF
ND(1916-20)	1780 Restrike	150	165	185	200	—

X# 25 1/10 IMADI RIYAL

Silver **Ruler:** al Husain Ibn Ali AH1334-42/1916-24AD **Countermark:** Hejaz **Note:** Countermark on Yemen 1/10 Imadi Riyal, Y#5.

CM Date	Host Date	Good	VG	F	VF	XF
ND(1916-20)	AH1322 (Accession)	—	—	—	—	—

X# 6 RUPEE

0.9170 Silver **Note:** Countermark "Hejas" on India rupee, KM#473.1.

CM Date	Host Date	Good	VG	F	VF	XF
ND(1916-20)	1862	25.00	75.00	175	350	—

MEDALLIC COINAGE

X# 2 10 PIASTRES

9.8300 g., 0.9250 Silver 0.2923 oz. ASW, 27.8 mm. **Obv:** Legends and inscriptions in 1 circle and 2 cartouches **Rev:** Legends and inscriptions in 3 circles and 2 cartouches **Edge:** Reeded **Note:** Copy struck in recent times by a private mint located in the U.S.A.

Date	Mintage	F	VF	XF	Unc	BU
AH1334//8 Prooflike	Est. 20	—	—	—	300	—

COUNTERMARKED COINAGE

Silver Coins

Silver coins of various sizes were also countermarked al-Hejaz. The most common host coins include the Maria Theresa Thaler of Austria, and 5, 10, and 20 Kurush or Qirsh of Turkey and Egypt. The countermark occurs in various sizes and styles of script. These countermarks may have been applied by local silversmiths to discourage re-exportation of the badly needed hard currency and silver of known fineness.

Some crown-sized examples exist with both the al-Hejaz and Nejd countermarks. The authenticity of the silver countermarked coins has long been discussed, and it is likely that most were privately produced. Other host coins are considered controversial.

X# 7 2 PIASTRES

Silver **Countermark:** "Hejaz" **Note:** Prev. KM#7. Countermark on Turkey 2 Kurush, KM#749. Accession date: 1327.

CM Date	Host Date	Good	VG	F	VF	XF
ND(1916-20)	ND(AH1327//1-6)	12.50	20.00	40.00	75.00	—

X# 8 2 PIASTRES

Silver **Countermark:** "Hejaz" **Note:** Prev. KM#8. Countermark on Turkey 2 Kurush, KM#770. Accession date: 1327.

CM Date	Host Date	Good	VG	F	VF	XF
ND(1916-20)	ND(AH1327//7-9)	12.50	20.00	40.00	75.00	—

X# 9 2 PIASTRES

Silver **Countermark:** "Hejaz" **Note:** Prev. KM#9. Countermark on Egypt 2 Qirsh, KM#307. Accession date: 1327.

CM Date	Host Date	Good	VG	F	VF	XF
ND(1916-20)	ND(AH1327//2H, 3H)	12.50	20.00	40.00	75.00	—

FANTASY COINAGE

X# 1 RYAL

Copper, 36.50 mm. **Ruler:** al Husain Ibn Ali AH1334-42/1916-24AD **Note:** A fantasy issue struck in various metals in recent times by a private mint located in the U.S.A. for distribution at the Mardi Gras celebration in New Orleans.

Date	Mintage	F	VF	XF	Unc	BU
AH1340 Prooflike	—	—	—	—	45.00	—

X# 1a RYAL

Brass **Ruler:** al Husain Ibn Ali AH1334-42/1916-24AD **Edge:** Reeded

Date	Mintage	F	VF	XF	Unc	BU
AH1340 Prooflike	—	—	—	—	75.00	—

X# 1b RYAL

Copper-Nickel **Ruler:** al Husain Ibn Ali AH1334-42/1916-24AD **Edge:** Reeded

Date	Mintage	F	VF	XF	Unc	BU
AH1340 Prooflike	—	—	—	—	150	—

X# 1c RYAL

Silver **Ruler:** al Husain Ibn Ali AH1334-42/1916-24AD **Edge:** Reeded

Date	Mintage	F	VF	XF	Unc	BU
AH1340 Prooflike	Est. 10	—	—	—	400	—

X# 1d RYAL

Aluminum, 36.5 mm. **Ruler:** al Husain Ibn Ali AH1334-42/1916-24AD

Date	Mintage	F	VF	XF	Unc	BU
AH1340 Prooflike	—	—	—	—	150	—

Note: These are not to be confused with the original pattern struck by the Birmingham Mint as these were struck in the late 1960's by a private mint in the U.S.A.

ISLE OF HELIOPOLIS

LEAGUE OF THE SUN'S SONS AND DAUGHTERS

MEDALLIC COINAGE

X# 1 5 ÇOLES
Copper, 39.2 mm. **Obv:** Large value "5" above circular design **Obv. Legend:** LIGUE DES FILS ET FILLES DU SOLEIL **Rev:** Stylized sun-children, mountains, sun in background **Rev. Legend:** SONNENMÜNZE DER SONNENKINDER **Edge:** Reeded **Note:** Thickness: 3.08mm.

Date	Mintage	F	VF	XF	Unc	BU
2004 Proof	50	—	—	—	40.00	—

X# 1a 5 ÇOLES
Silver, 39.2 mm. **Obv:** Large value "5" above circular design **Obv. Legend:** LIGUE DES FILS ET FILLES DU SOLEIL **Rev:** Stylized sun-children, mountains, sun in background **Rev. Legend:** SONNENMÜNZE DER SONNENKINDER **Edge:** Reeded **Note:** Thickness: 3.08mm.

Date	Mintage	F	VF	XF	Unc	BU
2004 Proof	5	—	—	—	90.00	—

HONDURAS

REPUBLIC

FANTASY COINAGE

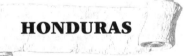

X# 2 8 PESOS
Silver **Obv:** Arms **Obv. Legend:** *MONEDA PROVISIONAL DEL ESTADO DE HONDURAS **Rev:** Tree **Rev. Legend:** LIBRE CREZCA FECUNDO **Note:** A modern concoction.

Date	Mintage	F	VF	XF	Unc	BU
1862T A	—	—	—	—	—	40.00

MEDALLIC COINAGE

ICB Issue

X# 1.1 10 LEMPIRAS
24.0000 g., 0.9250 Silver 0.7137 oz. ASW, 38 mm. **Obv:** Arms **Obv. Legend:** REPUBLICA DE HONDURAS **Rev:** Head of Lempira right **Edge:** Reeded

Date	Mintage	F	VF	XF	Unc	BU
1995 Proof	150	Value: 70.00				

X# 1.2 10 LEMPIRAS
24.0000 g., 0.9250 Silver 0.7137 oz. ASW, 38 mm. **Obv:** Arms **Obv. Legend:** REPUBLICA DE HONDURAS **Rev:** Head of Lempira right **Edge:** Plain

Date	Mintage	F	VF	XF	Unc	BU
1995 Proof	150	—	—	—	—	—

X# 1a.1 10 LEMPIRAS
23.0000 g., Brass, 38 mm. **Obv:** Arms **Obv. Legend:** REPUBLICA DE HONDURAS **Rev:** Head of Lempira right **Edge:** Reeded

Date	Mintage	F	VF	XF	Unc	BU
1995 Proof	150	—	—	—	—	—

X# 1a.2 10 LEMPIRAS
23.0000 g., Brass, 38 mm. **Obv:** Arms **Obv. Legend:** REPUBLICA DE HONDURAS **Rev:** Head of Lempira right **Edge:** Plain

Date	Mintage	F	VF	XF	Unc	BU
1995 Proof	150	—	—	—	—	—

X# 1b.1 10 LEMPIRAS
20.0000 g., Gilt Alloy, 38 mm. **Obv:** Arms **Obv. Legend:** REPUBLICA DE HONDURAS **Rev:** Head of Lempira right **Edge:** Reeded

Date	Mintage	F	VF	XF	Unc	BU
1995 Proof	150	Value: 50.00				

X# 1b.2 10 LEMPIRAS
20.0000 g., Gilt Alloy, 38 mm. **Obv:** Arms **Obv. Legend:** REPUBLICA DE HONDURAS **Rev:** Head of Lempira right **Edge:** Plain

Date	Mintage	F	VF	XF	Unc	BU
1995 Proof	150	Value: 50.00				

X# 1c.1 10 LEMPIRAS
23.0000 g., Tri-Metallic, 38 mm. **Obv:** Arms **Obv. Legend:** REPUBLICA DE HONDURAS **Rev:** Head of Lempira right **Edge:** Reeded

Date	Mintage	F	VF	XF	Unc	BU
1995 Proof	150	Value: 85.00				

X# 1c.2 10 LEMPIRAS
23.0000 g., Tri-Metallic, 38 mm. **Obv:** Arms **Obv. Legend:** REPUBLICA DE HONDURAS **Rev:** Head of Lempira right **Edge:** Plain

Date	Mintage	F	VF	XF	Unc	BU
1995 Proof	150	Value: 85.00				

X# 1d.1 10 LEMPIRAS
6.0000 g., Aluminum, 38 mm. **Obv:** Arms **Obv. Legend:** REPUBLICA DE HONDURAS **Rev:** Head of Lempira right **Edge:** Reeded

Date	Mintage	F	VF	XF	Unc	BU
1995 Proof	150	Value: 50.00				

X# 1d.2 10 LEMPIRAS
6.0000 g., Aluminum, 38 mm. **Obv:** Arms **Obv. Legend:** REPUBLICA DE HONDURAS **Rev:** Head of Lempira right **Edge:** Plain

Date	Mintage	F	VF	XF	Unc	BU
1995 Proof	150	Value: 50.00				

X# 1e.1 10 LEMPIRAS
23.0000 g., Copper, 38 mm. **Obv:** Arms **Obv. Legend:** REPUBLICA DE HONDURAS **Rev:** Head of Lempira right **Edge:** Reeded

Date	Mintage	F	VF	XF	Unc	BU
1995 Proof	150	Value: 50.00				

X# 1e.2 10 LEMPIRAS
23.0000 g., Copper, 38 mm. **Obv:** Arms **Obv. Legend:** REPUBLICA DE HONDURAS **Rev:** Head of Lempira right **Edge:** Plain

Date	Mintage	F	VF	XF	Unc	BU
1995 Proof	150	Value: 50.00				

X# 1f.1 10 LEMPIRAS
20.0000 g., Copper-Nickel, 38 mm. **Obv:** Arms **Obv. Legend:** REPUBLICA DE HONDURAS **Rev:** Head of Lempira right **Edge:** Reeded

Date	Mintage	F	VF	XF	Unc	BU
1995 Proof	150	Value: 50.00				

X# 1f.2 10 LEMPIRAS
20.0000 g., Copper-Nickel, 38 mm. **Obv:** Arms **Obv. Legend:** REPUBLICA DE HONDURAS **Rev:** Head of Lempira right **Edge:** Plain

Date	Mintage	F	VF	XF	Unc	BU
1995 Proof	150	Value: 50.00				

PATTERNS

Including off metal strikes

Rosettes separate legends on Pn1-Pn5a.

X#	Date	Mintage	Identification	Mkt Val
Pn1	1995	—	10 Lempiras. Platinum. 44.0000 g. Reeded edge. X1.1.	9,000
Pn2	1995	—	10 Lempiras. 0.9167 Gold. 40.4000 g. Reeded edge. X1.1.	2,000
Pn3	1995	—	10 Lempiras. 0.9167 Gold. 40.1000 g. Plain edge. X1.2.	2,000
Pn4	1995	—	10 Lempiras. 0.9167 Gold. 40.3000 g. Reeded edge. X1.	2,000
Pn5	1995	—	10 Lempiras. 0.9167 Gold. 40.0000 g. Plain edge. X1.	2,000

PIEFORTS

X#	Date	Mintage	Identification	Mkt Val
P1	1995	—	10 Lempiras. 0.9250 Silver. 48.0000 g. Reeded edge. X1.1.	150
P2	1995	—	10 Lempiras. 0.9250 Silver. 48.0000 g. Plain edge. X1.2.	150

HONG KONG

BRITISH COLONY

BULLION COINAGE

X# B21 1/2 TAEL
18.8100 g., 0.9990 Gold 0.6041 oz. AGW, 19 mm. **Obv. Inscription:** Four Chinese characters, "500" below **Rev:** Uniface **Edge:** Plain **Note:** Issuer unknown.

Date	Mintage	F	VF	XF	Unc	BU
ND(1930s)	—	BV	285	325	—	—

Pak Cheuk, Jeweler

X# B19 TAEL
37.3236 g., 1.0000 Gold 1.1999 oz. AGW, 22 mm. **Obv:** Chinese inscriptions, "1000" **Rev:** Uniface **Edge:** Plain

Date	Mintage	F	VF	XF	Unc	BU
ND(1930s)	—	BV	900	1,300	—	—

King Fook, Gold dealer

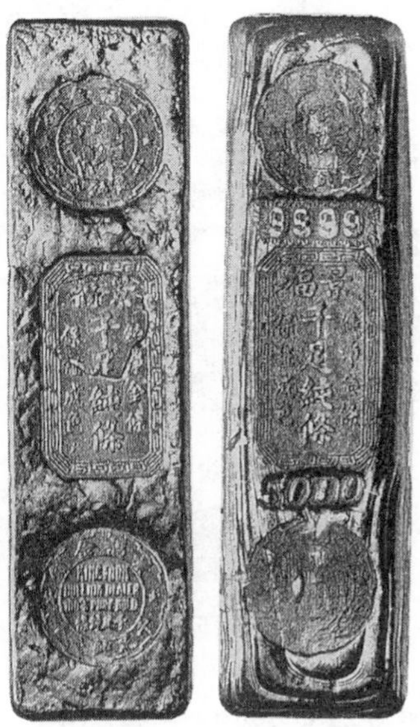

X# B22 6 OUNCES
187.1200 g., 0.9999 Gold 6.0152 oz. AGW
Issuer: King Fook **Obv:** 2 circular, 1 rectangular stamps
Obv. Inscription: King Fook / Bullion Dealer...
Rev: 2 circular, 1 rectangular; 9999 and 5000 stamps
Note: 21.5mm x 80mm

Date	Mintage	F	VF	XF	Unc	BU
ND(c.1950)	—	—	5,140	7,500	—	—

Lee Cheong, Gold dealer

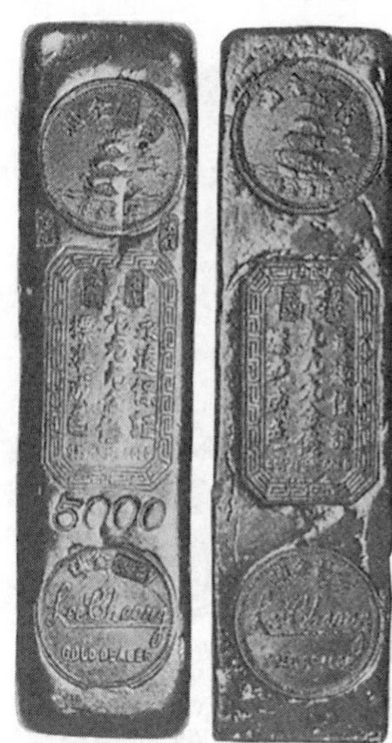

X# B20 6 OUNCES
187.0000 g., 0.9990 Gold 6.0059 oz. AGW **Obv:** 2 circular, 1 rectangular stamps **Obv. Inscription:** Lee Cheong **Rev:** 2 circular, 1 rectangular stamps
Shape: Rectangular **Note:** 19.5mm x 77mm

Date	Mintage	F	VF	XF	Unc	BU
ND(c.1950)	—	—	5,140	7,500	—	—

Hong Kong Electro Metallurgical Company

Electrolytic pure silver bar

X# B3 NON-DENOMINATED
36.9000 g., 0.9999 Silver 1.1862 oz. ASW **Issuer:** Hong Kong Electro Metallurgical Co. **Obv:** Three Chinese stampings **Note:** Uniface. Size: 20.00 x 45.50mm.

Date	Mintage	Good	VG	F	VF	XF
ND(1960s)	—	—	—	30.00	45.00	65.00

Hong Kong - Shanghai Specie Office

A mysterious series of spurious silver bars of recent manufacture

X# B13 5 DOLLARS
Silver **Countermark:** Without "FIVE DOLLARS" **Note:** Fineness varies: .999-.9999. Weight varies: 155-160 grams.

Date	Mintage	F	VF	XF	Unc	BU
ND(1970s)	—	—	85.00	115	—	—

X# B14 5 DOLLARS
Silver **Countermark:** "STERLING" **Note:** Fineness varies: .999-.9999. Weight varies: 155-160 grams.

Date	Mintage	F	VF	XF	Unc	BU
ND(1970s)	—	—	85.00	115	—	—

X# B11 5 DOLLARS
Silver **Subject:** Queen Victoria **Note:** Weight varies: 155-160 grams. Fineness varies: .999-.9999. Chinese characters "Tsu Yin" (pure silver). A spurious issue.

Date	Mintage	F	VF	XF	Unc	BU
ND(1970)	—	—	85.00	115	—	—

Fung Lai Chun, Gold dealer

X# B16 TAEL
37.4000 g., Gold, 26 mm. **Ruler:** George V **Obv:** Ancient "pu", tablet with inscriptions **Rev:** Lion **Rev. Legend:** FUNG LAI CHUN GOLD DEALER **Edge:** Plain

Date	Mintage	F	VF	XF	Unc	BU
ND(1930s)	—	BV	900	1,300	—	—

Chow Sang Sang Co. Ltd.

X# B17 TAEL
Gold, 24 mm. **Ruler:** George V **Obv:** Chinese legend and inscription **Rev. Legend:** CHOW SONG SONG CO. LTD. **Edge:** Plain

Date	Mintage	F	VF	XF	Unc	BU
ND(1930s)	—	BV	850	950	—	—

Nam Shing Co.

X# B18 TAEL
1.0000 Gold, 24 mm. **Ruler:** George V **Obv:** Chinese inscriptions, "1000" **Rev:** Uniface, small Chinese hallmark **Edge:** Plain

Date	Mintage	F	VF	XF	Unc	BU
ND(1930s)	—	BV	900	1,300	—	—

BULLION COINAGE / CHOU TA-FU JEWELRY STORE

X# B32 TAEL
0.9999 Gold **Ruler:** Elizabeth II **Obv. Inscription:** Chou Ta-fu... Chin Hang **Rev. Inscription:** ONE TAEL / 9999

Date	Mintage	VG	F	VF	XF	Unc
ND(ca. 1970)	—	—	—	—	850	1,300

BULLION COINAGE - HSIN HANG

X# B25 OUNCE
33.8400 g., Gold **Obv. Inscription:** Hsin Hang **Shape:** Oblong **Note:** Uniface, 21.5 x 29.3 mm.

Date	Mintage	F	VF	XF	Unc	BU
ND(1930-39)	—	—	900	1,300	—	—

MEDALLIC COINAGE

INA Retro Issues

X# 1 DOLLAR
0.9250 Silver **Ruler:** Victoria **Obv:** Veiled bust left **Obv. Legend:** VICTORIA • DEI GRATIA • IND • IMP **Rev:** Large 1 within oriental design **Edge:** Proof

Date	Mintage	F	VF	XF	Unc	BU
1901 Proof	360	Value: 75.00				

X# 1a DOLLAR
Bronze **Ruler:** Victoria **Obv:** Veiled bust left **Obv. Legend:** VICTORIA • DEI GRATIA • IND • IMP **Rev:** Large 1 within oriental design **Edge:** Plain

Date	Mintage	F	VF	XF	Unc	BU
1901 Proof	360	Value: 40.00				

X# 1b DOLLAR
Copper **Ruler:** Victoria **Obv:** Veiled bust left **Obv. Legend:** VICTORIA • DEI GRATIA • IND • IMP **Rev:** Large 1 within oriental design **Edge:** Plain

Date	Mintage	F	VF	XF	Unc	BU
1901 Proof	360	Value: 40.00				

X# 1c DOLLAR
0.9167 Gold **Ruler:** Victoria **Obv:** Veiled bust left **Obv. Legend:** VICTORIA • DEI GRATIA • IND • IMP **Rev:** Large 1 within oriental design **Edge:** Plain

Date	Mintage	F	VF	XF	Unc	BU
1901 Proof	1	—	—	—	—	—

X# 1d DOLLAR
Aluminum **Ruler:** Victoria **Obv:** Veiled bust left **Obv. Legend:** VICTORIA • DEI GRATIA • IND • IMP **Rev:** Large 1 within oriental design **Edge:** Plain

Date	Mintage	F	VF	XF	Unc	BU
1901	1	—	—	—	—	—

X# 2.2 DOLLAR
32.3000 g., 0.9167 Gold 0.9519 oz. AGW **Ruler:** Victoria **Obv:** Veiled bust left **Obv. Legend:** VICTORIA • DEI • GRA BRITT • REGINA • FID • DEF IND • IMP • **Rev:** Large 1 within oriental design **Edge:** Plain

Date	Mintage	F	VF	XF	Unc	BU
1901 Proof	1	—	—	—	—	—

X# 2.1 DOLLAR
32.5000 g., 0.9167 Gold 0.9578 oz. AGW **Ruler:** Victoria **Obv:** Veiled bust left **Obv. Legend:** VICTORIA • DEI • GRA BRITT • REGINA • FID • DEF IND • IMP • **Rev:** Large 1 within oriental design **Edge:** Plain **Note:** Medal alignment

Date	Mintage	F	VF	XF	Unc	BU
1901 Proof	1	—	—	—	—	—

X# 3 DOLLAR
22.4200 g., 0.9250 Silver 0.6667 oz. ASW **Ruler:** Edward VII **Obv:** Crowned bust right **Obv. Legend:** EDWARDVS VII D: G: BRITT: OMN: REX F: D: IND: IMP. **Rev:** Large 1 within oriental design **Edge:** Plain

Date	Mintage	F	VF	XF	Unc	BU
1901 Proof	450	Value: 75.00				

X# 3a DOLLAR
17.9000 g., Bronze **Ruler:** Edward VII **Obv:** Crowned bust right **Obv. Legend:** EDWARDVS VII D: G: BRITT: OMN: REX F: D: IND: IMP. **Rev:** Large 1 within oriental design **Edge:** Plain

Date	Mintage	F	VF	XF	Unc	BU
1901 Proof	450	Value: 40.00				

X# 3c.2 DOLLAR
33.4000 g., 0.9167 Gold 0.9843 oz. AGW **Ruler:** Edward VII **Obv:** Crowned bust right **Obv. Legend:** EDWARDVS VII D: G: BRITT: OMN: REX F: D: IND: IMP. **Rev:** Large 1 within oriental design **Edge:** Plain

Date	Mintage	F	VF	XF	Unc	BU
1901 Proof	1	—	—	—	—	—

X# 3b DOLLAR
18.3600 g., Copper **Obv:** Crowned bust right **Obv. Legend:** EDWARDVS VII D: G: BRITT: OMN: REX F: D: IND: IMP. **Rev:** Large 1 within oriental design **Edge:** Plain

Date	Mintage	F	VF	XF	Unc	BU
1901 Proof	450	Value: 40.00				

X# 3c.1 DOLLAR
33.3000 g., 0.9167 Gold 0.9814 oz. AGW **Ruler:** Edward VII **Obv:** Crowned bust right **Obv. Legend:** EDWARDVS VII D: G: BRITT: OMN: REX F: D: IND: IMP. **Rev:** Large 1 within oriental design **Edge:** Reeded

Date	Mintage	F	VF	XF	Unc	BU
1901 Proof	1	—	—	—	—	—

X# 4 DOLLAR
33.3000 g., 0.9167 Gold 0.9814 oz. AGW **Ruler:** Edward VII **Obv:** Head right within beaded border **Obv. Legend:** EDWARDVS VII DEI GRATIA INDIAE IMPERATOR **Rev:** Large 1 within oriental design **Edge:** Plain

Date	Mintage	F	VF	XF	Unc	BU
1901 Proof	1	—	—	—	—	—
Note: Coin alignment						
1901 Proof	1	—	—	—	—	—
Note: Medal alignment						

Richard Lobel Issues

X# M7 CROWN
Bronze **Subject:** Edward VIII **Obv:** Bust left **Obv. Legend:** EDWARD • VIII • KING • & • EMPEROR **Rev:** Stylized junk **Edge:** Plain

Date	Mintage	F	VF	XF	Unc	BU
1936 Proof	1,000	Value: 20.00				

X# M7a CROWN

Copper-Nickel-Zinc **Subject:** Edward VIII **Obv:** Bust left **Obv. Legend:** EDWARD • VIII • KING • & • EMPEROR **Rev:** Stylized junk **Edge:** Plain

Date	Mintage	F	VF	XF	Unc	BU
1936 Proof	2,000	Value: 20.00				

X# M7b CROWN

0.9167 Silver **Subject:** Edward VIII **Obv:** Bust left **Obv. Legend:** EDWARD • VIII • KING • & • EMPEROR **Rev:** Stylized junk **Edge:** Plain

Date	Mintage	F	VF	XF	Unc	BU
1936 Proof	200	Value: 50.00				

X# M7c CROWN

Gold **Subject:** Edward VIII **Obv:** Bust left **Obv. Legend:** EDWARD • VIII • KING • & • EMPEROR **Rev:** Stylized junk **Edge:** Plain

Date	Mintage	F	VF	XF	Unc	BU
1936 Proof	—	Value: 500				

X# M7d CROWN

Copper **Subject:** Edward VIII **Obv:** Bust left **Obv. Legend:** EDWARD • VIII • KING • & • EMPEROR **Rev:** Stylized junk **Edge:** Plain **Note:** Struck in error

Date	Mintage	F	VF	XF	Unc	BU
1936 Proof	—	Value: 20.00				

X# M8 SOVEREIGN

0.3750 Gold **Subject:** Edward VIII **Obv:** Bust left **Obv. Legend:** EDWARD • VIII • KING • & • EMPEROR **Rev:** Stylized junk **Edge:** Plain

Date	Mintage	F	VF	XF	Unc	BU
1936 Proof	200	Value: 125				

X# M8a SOVEREIGN

4.4200 g., Silver **Subject:** Edward VIII **Obv:** Bust left **Obv. Legend:** EDWARD • VIII • KING • & • EMPEROR **Rev:** Stylized junk **Edge:** Plain

Date	Mintage	F	VF	XF	Unc	BU
1936 Proof	—	Value: 10.00				

MEDALLIC BULLION COINAGE

X# MB1 OUNCE

31.1030 g., 0.9990 Silver 0.9989 oz. ASW **Subject:** 1985 Hong Kong International Coin Expo **Rev:** Year of the Ox **Note:** Struck by a private mint located in the U.S.A. Refer also to China-Peoples Republic listings for other Hong Kong show issues.

Date	Mintage	F	VF	XF	Unc	BU
1985 Proof	—	Value: 25.00				

X# B31 TAEL

37.8000 g., 0.9990 Silver 1.2140 oz. ASW, 42.15 mm. **Ruler:** Elizabeth II **Obv:** Facing dragons **Rev:** Crowned garter around shield with "Gin"

Date	Mintage	F	VF	XF	Unc	BU
1992 Proof	—	Value: 15.00				

PIEFORTS

X#	Date	Mintage	Identification	Mkt Val
P1	1901	1	Dollar. Silver. Plain edge, coin alignment, X#1.	—
P2	1901	1	Dollar. Silver. Plain edge, medal alignment, X#1.	—
P3	1901	1	Dollar. Silver. Reeded edge, coin alignment, X#1.	—
P4	1901	1	Dollar. Silver. Reeded edge, medal alignment, X#1.	—
P5	1901	1	Dollar. Silver. Plain edge, coin alignment, X#2.	—
P6	1901	1	Dollar. Silver. Plain edge, medal alignment, X#2.	—
P7	1901	1	Dollar. Silver. Reeded edge, coin alignment, X#2.	—
P8	1901	1	Dollar. Silver. Reeded edge, medal alignment, X#2.	—
P9	1901	1	Dollar. Silver. Plain edge, coin alignment, X#3.	—
P10	1901	1	Dollar. Silver. Plain edge, medal alignment, X#3.	—
P11	1901	1	Dollar. Silver. Reeded edge, coin alignment, X#3.	—
P12	1901	1	Dollar. Silver. Reeded edge, medal alignment, X#3.	—
P13	1901	1	Dollar. Silver. Plain edge, coin alignment, X#4.	—
P14	1901	1	Dollar. Silver. Plain edge, medal alignment, X#4.	—
P15	1901	1	Dollar. Silver. Reeded edge, coin alignment, X#4.	—
P16	1901	1	Dollar. Silver. Reeded edge, medal alignment, X#4.	—
P17	1936	—	Crown. 0.9167 Silver. X#M7b.	100

HUNGARY

KINGDOM

MEDALLIC COINAGE

X# M11 3/4 DUCAT

2.6000 g., Gold, 20 mm. **Ruler:** Franz II **Subject:** Coronation **Obv:** Crown above 5-line inscription, date **Obv. Inscription:** FRANCIS CVS • / D • G • HVN • BOH • REX • / ARCHID... **Rev:** White lion upright left holding Hungarian cross and Austrian shield **Rev. Legend:** LEGE • ET • FIDE •

Date	Mintage	F	VF	XF	Unc	BU
MDCCXCII (1792)	—	—	250	425	600	—

X# M13 3/4 DUCAT

2.6000 g., Gold, 20.5 mm. **Ruler:** Franz II **Subject:** Coronation of Maria Luisa in Hungary **Obv:** Flower **Obv. Legend:** RECTE ET CANDIDE **Rev:** Crown over 5-line inscription **Rev. Legend:** MARIA LVDOVICA AVG • ...

Date	Mintage	F	VF	XF	Unc	BU
MDCCCVIII (1808)	—	—	80.00	135	—	—

X# M14 1-1/4 DUCAT

4.3700 g., Gold, 24.95 mm. **Ruler:** Franz II **Subject:** Coronation of Maria Luisa in Hungary **Obv:** Flower **Obv. Legend:** RECTE ET CANDIDE **Rev:** Crown over 5-line inscription **Rev. Inscription:** MARIA LVDOVICA AVG • ...

Date	Mintage	F	VF	XF	Unc	BU
MDCCCVIII (1808)	—	—	120	200	—	—

X# M1c FORINT

Gold **Note:** Prev. KM#M1c.

Date	Mintage	F	VF	XF	Unc	BU
1878 Rare	3	—	—	—	—	—

X# M1 FORINT

12.3457 g., 0.9000 Silver 0.3572 oz. ASW **Ruler:** Franz Joseph I **Subject:** Reopening of the Joseph II Mine at Schemnitz **Obv:** Laureate head right **Rev:** Two dates within beaded circle **Note:** Prev. KM#M1.

Date	Mintage	F	VF	XF	Unc	BU
1878KB	400	—	700	1,250	2,200	—

X# M1a FORINT

Copper **Ruler:** Franz Joseph I **Subject:** Reopening of the Joseph II Mine at Schemnitz **Obv:** Laureate head right **Rev:** Two dates within beaded circle **Note:** Prev. KM#M1a.

Date	Mintage	F	VF	XF	Unc	BU
1878 Rare	3	—	—	—	—	—

X# M1b FORINT

Bronze **Ruler:** Franz Joseph I **Subject:** Reopening of the Joseph II Mine at Schemnitz **Obv:** Laureate head right **Rev:** Two dates within beaded circle **Note:** Prev. KM#M1b.

Date	Mintage	F	VF	XF	Unc	BU
1878 Reported, not confirmed	—	—	—	—	—	—

SOUVENIR COINAGE

1000th Anniversary of the Kingdom of Hungary

Struck on demand using some earlier coin designs with new legends of Francis Joseph and dated 1896. In 1965 restrikes were produced of certain types.

X# 1 BRACTEATE

0.2500 g., Silver **Note:** Type of Bela IV (1235-1270 AD).

Date	Mintage	F	VF	XF	Unc	BU
1896	—	—	—	—	—	—

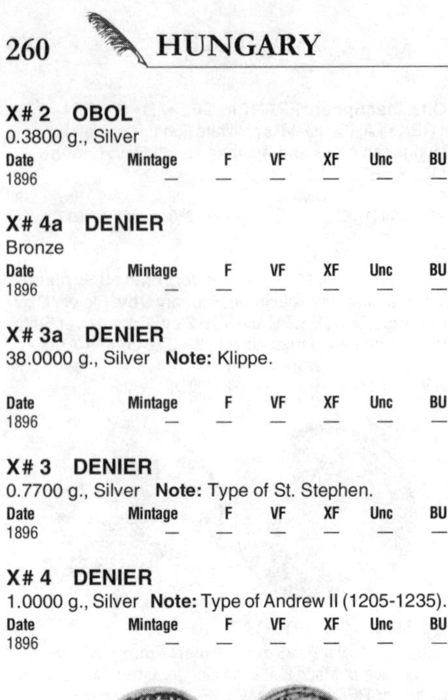

X# 2 OBOL

0.3800 g., Silver

Date	Mintage	F	VF	XF	Unc	BU
1896	—	—	—	—	—	—

X# 4a DENIER

Bronze

Date	Mintage	F	VF	XF	Unc	BU
1896	—	—	—	—	—	—

X# 3a DENIER

38.0000 g., Silver **Note:** Klippe.

Date	Mintage	F	VF	XF	Unc	BU
1896	—	—	—	—	—	—

X# 3 DENIER

0.7700 g., Silver **Note:** Type of St. Stephen.

Date	Mintage	F	VF	XF	Unc	BU
1896	—	—	—	—	—	—

X# 4 DENIER

1.0000 g., Silver **Note:** Type of Andrew II (1205-1235).

Date	Mintage	F	VF	XF	Unc	BU
1896	—	—	—	—	—	—

X# 5 DENIER

0.6100 g., Silver **Note:** Type of Matthias Hunyadi.

Date	Mintage	F	VF	XF	Unc	BU
1896KB	—	—	—	—	—	—

X# 9 GOLDGULDEN

3.5600 g., Gold **Note:** Style of Karl Robert.

Date	Mintage	F	VF	XF	Unc	BU
1896	100	—	—	1,350	2,250	—

X# 6 GROSCHEN

3.4100 g., Silver **Note:** Type of Louis The Great.

Date	Mintage	F	VF	XF	Unc	BU
1896	—	—	—	—	—	—

X# 10 GROSCHEN

3.4100 g., Silver **Note:** Style of Karl Robert.

Date	Mintage	F	VF	XF	Unc	BU
1896	—	—	—	—	—	—

X# 10a GROSCHEN

Copper

Date	Mintage	F	VF	XF	Unc	BU
1896	—	—	—	—	—	—

X# 7 DENAR

Silver **Note:** Klippe.

Date	Mintage	F	VF	XF	Unc	BU
1896	—	—	—	—	—	—

X# 7a DENAR

Silver **Note:** Klippe.

Date	Mintage	F	VF	XF	Unc	BU
1896	—	—	—	—	—	—

X# 13 THALER

Silver **Obv:** 1/2-length figure right holding sceptre and orb **Rev:** Madonna and child above shield

Date	Mintage	F	VF	XF	Unc	BU
1896 KB Proof	—	Value: 600				
1896 KB-UP Proof; Restrike	—	Value: 120				

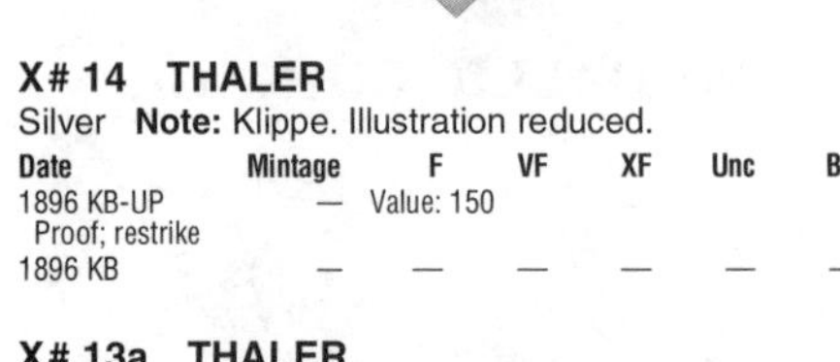

X# 14 THALER

Silver **Note:** Klippe. Illustration reduced.

Date	Mintage	F	VF	XF	Unc	BU
1896 KB-UP Proof; restrike	—	Value: 150				
1896 KB	—	—	—	—	—	—

X# 13a THALER

30.0800 g., Gold **Rev:** Madonna and child above shield **Note:** Franz Joseph I.

Date	Mintage	F	VF	XF	Unc	BU
1896 KB	100	—	—	—	—	—

X# 16 THALER

Silver **Obv:** St. George on horseback slaying dragon **Note:** This particular design was struck as a religious medal in various sizes for many years.

Date	Mintage	F	VF	XF	Unc	BU
ND(1896) Prooflike	—	—	—	—	650	—

X# 8.1a 9 DUCAT

30.0800 g., Gold

Date	Mintage	F	VF	XF	Unc	BU
1896KB Prooflike	100	—	—	—	4,250	—

X# 11 5 KORONA

24.0000 g., 0.9000 Silver 0.6944 oz. ASW **Obv:** Bust of Franz Joseph right **Rev:** Arpad horseback

Date	Mintage	F	VF	XF	Unc	BU
1896 KB	—	—	—	—	—	—
1896 KB-UP Restrike	—	—	—	—	75.00	—

X# 12 5 KORONA

Silver **Note:** Klippe.

Date	Mintage	F	VF	XF	Unc	BU
1896 KB-UP Proof; Restrike	—	Value: 120				

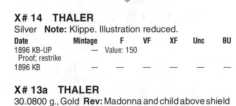

PATTERNS

1965 Commercial Series

Struck especially for a U.S. numismatic firm located in Ohio using pattern designs with additional U.P.(utanvert probaveret) letters.

X# Pn11.2 2 PENGO
20.2600 g., Silver **Note:** Klippe. Restruck 1965.

Date	Mintage	F	VF	XF	Unc	BU
1935BP UP Proof; Restrike	—	Value: 100				

X# Pn10.1 2 PENGO
10.0100 g., Silver **Subject:** Pazmany **Note:** Original patterns exist without "UP" below arms.

Date	Mintage	F	VF	XF	Unc	BU
1935BP UP Proof; Restrike	—	Value: 45.00				

X# Pn10.2 2 PENGO
20.1900 g., Silver **Note:** Klippe. Restruck 1965.

Date	Mintage	F	VF	XF	Unc	BU
1935BP UP Proof; Restrike	—	Value: 100				

X# Pn11.1 2 PENGO
9.9900 g., Silver **Subject:** 200th Anniversary of Death of Rakoczi **Note:** Original patterns exist without "UP" at lower left and right of crowned arms.

Date	Mintage	F	VF	XF	Unc	BU
1935BP UP Proof; Restrike	—	Value: 45.00				

X# Pn12.1 5 PENGO
25.2700 g., Silver **Subject:** St. Ladislav **Note:** Original patterns exist without "UP" under the crown.

Date	Mintage	F	VF	XF	Unc	BU
1929BP UP Proof; Restrike	—	Value: 75.00				

X# Pn12.2 5 PENGO
50.3000 g., Silver **Shape:** Square **Note:** Klippe. 45 x 45mm. Illustration reduced.

Date	Mintage	F	VF	XF	Unc	BU
1929BP UP Proof; Restrike	—	Value: 125				

X# Pn13.2 5 PENGO
50.1200 g., Silver **Shape:** Square **Note:** Klippe. 45 x 45mm. Restruck 1965. Illustration reduced.

Date	Mintage	F	VF	XF	Unc	BU
1938BP UP Proof; Restrike	—	Value: 125				

X# Pn13.1 5 PENGO
24.8500 g., Silver **Subject:** St. Stephen **Note:** Original patterns exist without "U-P" at left and right of crowned arms.

Date	Mintage	F	VF	XF	Unc	BU
1938BP UP Proof; Restrike	—	Value: 75.00				

X# Pn40 40 PENGO
11.6200 g., Gold, 27 mm. **Subject:** 200th Anniversary of Death of Rakoczi **Obv:** Crowned arms in order chain **Obv. Legend:** ★ MAGYAR KIRALYSAG ★ **Rev:** Franz Rakoczi horseback right **Rev. Legend:** RAKOCZI FERENC

Date	Mintage	F	VF	XF	Unc	BU
1935BP UP Restrike	—	—	—	—	BV+10%	—

X# Pn41 100 PENGO
Gold **Note:** A modern fantasy according to leading authorities.

Date	Mintage	F	VF	XF	Unc	BU
1938BP Proof	—	—	—	—	BV+10%	—

PEOPLES REPUBLIC

1949-1989

DECIMAL COINAGE

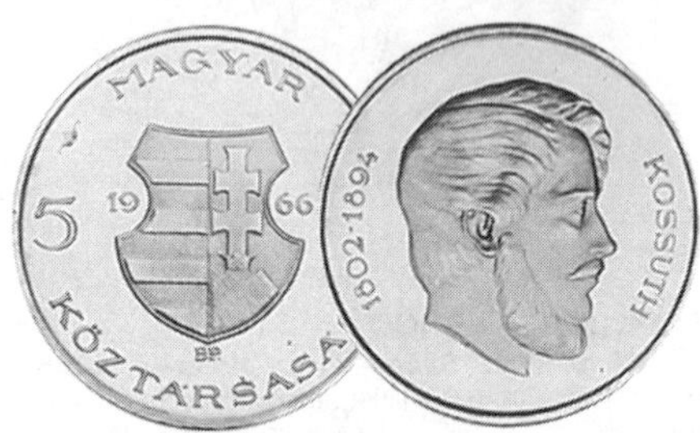

X# 15 5 FORINT
13.0000 g., 0.8350 Silver 0.3490 oz. ASW **Obv:** Arms of the Republic **Rev:** Lajos Kossuth **Note:** Prev. KM#534b. Issued in 8-piece proof sets along with 7 minor coins of the Peoples' Republic.

Date	Mintage	F	VF	XF	Unc	BU
1966 Proof	5,006	Value: 22.50				
1967 Proof	5,015	Value: 22.50				

MEDALLIC BULLION COINAGE

X# MB5 1/10 UNCIA
3.0700 g., Gold, 13 mm. **Obv:** Large crown **Obv. Legend:** MAGYARORSZAG **Rev:** Madonna and child **Rev. Legend:** S. MARIA MATER DEI PATRONA HUNGARIAE **Edge:** Reeded

Date	Mintage	F	VF	XF	Unc	BU
1985 Proof	—	—	—	—	BV+40%	—

X# MB6 1/4 UNCIA
7.8200 g., Gold, 18 mm. **Obv:** Large crown **Obv. Legend:** MAGYARORSZAG **Rev:** Madonna and child **Rev. Legend:** S. MARIA MATER DEI PATRONA HUNGARIAE **Edge:** Reeded

Date	Mintage	F	VF	XF	Unc	BU
1985 Proof	—	—	—	—	BV+30%	—

X# MB7 1/2 UNCIA
15.6100 g., Gold, 22.8 mm. **Obv:** Large crown **Obv. Legend:** MAGYARORSZAG **Rev:** Madonna and child **Rev. Legend:** S. MARIA MATER DEI PATRONA HUNGARIAE **Edge:** Reeded

Date	Mintage	F	VF	XF	Unc	BU
1985 Proof	—	—	—	—	BV+25%	—

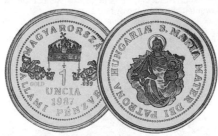

X# MB8 UNCIA
31.0400 g., Gold, 32.2 mm. **Obv:** Large crown **Obv. Legend:** MAGYARORSZAG **Rev:** Madonna and child **Rev. Legend:** S. MARIA MATER DEI PATRONA HUNGARIAE **Edge:** Reeded

Date	Mintage	F	VF	XF	Unc	BU
1985 Proof	—	—	—	—	BV+20%	—

X# MB1 5 UNCIA (5 Ounces)
155.5150 g., 0.9990 Silver 4.9947 oz. ASW, 62 mm. **Subject:** Madonna and Child **Note:** Illustration reduced.

Date	Mintage	F	VF	XF	Unc	BU
1986BP BGY Proof	—	Value: 150				

X# MB2 5 UNCIA (5 Ounces)
155.5150 g., 0.9990 Silver 4.9947 oz. ASW, 67 mm. **Subject:** Hungary - United States Exhibitions **Rev:** Treasures of Hungary **Note:** Illustration reduced.

Date	Mintage	F	VF	XF	Unc	BU
1986BP BGY Proof	1,000	Value: 135				

SECOND REPUBLIC

1989-present

ECU COINAGE

Numex S.A., Madrid

X# 21 40 ECU
31.1030 g., 0.9000 Silver 0.8999 oz. ASW, 38 mm. **Obv:** Crowned arms **Obv. Legend:** MAGYAR KÖZTÁRSASÁG **Rev:** Knights armored arms holding sword blade in wreath upright **Edge:** Reeded

Date	Mintage	F	VF	XF	Unc	BU
1993 Proof	—	Value: 45.00				

FANTASY EURO PATTERNS

INA Issues

X# Pn1 EURO CENT
Copper Plated Steel, 16.8 mm. **Issuer:** INA **Obv:** Bust of Sándor Petőfi facing 3/4 left **Obv. Legend:** MAGYAR KÖZTÁRSASÁG **Rev:** Large value, balance scale, Euro stars design **Edge:** Plain

Date	Mintage	F	VF	XF	Unc	BU
2004	12,500	—	—	—	—	1.50
2004 Proof	3,000	Value: 2.50				

X# Pn1a EURO CENT
Silver **Obv:** Bust of Sandor Petofi facing 3/4 left **Obv. Legend:** MAGYAR KÖZTÁRSASÁG **Rev:** Large value, balance scale, Euro stars design

Date	Mintage	F	VF	XF	Unc	BU
2004 Proof	250	Value: 6.00				

X# Pn2 2 EURO CENT
Copper Plated Steel, 18.50 mm. **Issuer:** INA **Obv:** Bust of Sándor Petöfi facing 3/4 left **Obv. Legend:** MAGYAR KÖZTÁRSASÁG **Rev:** Large value, balance scale, Euro stars design **Edge:** Plain

Date	Mintage	F	VF	XF	Unc	BU
2004	12,500	—	—	—	—	2.00
2004 Proof	3,000	Value: 3.00				

X# Pn2a 2 EURO CENT
Silver **Obv:** Bust of Sandor Petofi facing 3/4 left **Obv. Legend:** MAGYAR KÖZTÁRSASÁG **Rev:** Large value, balance scale, Euro stars design

Date	Mintage	F	VF	XF	Unc	BU
2004 Proof	—	Value: 7.00				

X# Pn3 5 EURO CENT
Copper Plated Steel, 20.7 mm. **Issuer:** INA **Obv:** Bust of Sándor Petöfi facing 3/4 left **Obv. Legend:** MAGYAR KÖZTÁRSASÁG **Rev:** Large value, balance scale, Euro stars design **Edge:** Plain

Date	Mintage	F	VF	XF	Unc	BU
2004	12,500	—	—	—	—	2.50
2004 Proof	3,000	Value: 3.50				

X# Pn3a 5 EURO CENT
Silver **Obv:** Bust of Sandor Petofi facing 3/4 left **Obv. Legend:** MAGYAR KÖZTÁRSASÁG **Rev:** Large value, balance scale, Euro stars design

Date	Mintage	F	VF	XF	Unc	BU
2004 Proof	250	Value: 8.50				

X# Pn4 10 EURO CENT
Goldine, 19.3 mm. **Issuer:** INA **Obv:** Bust of Kossuth facing **Obv. Legend:** MAGYAR KÖZTÁRSASÁG **Rev:** Dove, value in wreath of clasped hands **Edge:** Plain

Date	Mintage	F	VF	XF	Unc	BU
2004	12,500	—	—	—	—	3.00
2004 Proof	3,000	Value: 4.00				

X# Pn4a 10 EURO CENT
Silver **Obv:** Bust of Kossuth facing **Obv. Legend:** MAGYAR KÖZTÁRSASÁG **Rev:** Dove, value in wreath of clasped hands

Date	Mintage	F	VF	XF	Unc	BU
2004 Proof	250	Value: 10.00				

X# Pn5 20 EURO CENT
Goldine, 22 mm. **Issuer:** INA **Obv:** Bust of Kossuth facing **Obv. Legend:** MAGYAR KÖZTÁRSASÁG **Rev:** Dove, value in wreath of clasped hands **Edge:** Plain

Date	Mintage	F	VF	XF	Unc	BU
2004	12,500	—	—	—	—	3.50
2004 Proof	3,000	Value: 5.00				

X# Pn5a 20 EURO CENT
Silver **Obv:** Bust of Kossuth facing **Obv. Legend:** MAGYAR KÖZTÁRSASÁG **Rev:** Dove, value in wreath of clasped hands

Date	Mintage	F	VF	XF	Unc	BU
2004 Proof	250	Value: 12.50				

X# Pn6 50 EURO CENT
Goldine, 24.3 mm. **Issuer:** INA **Obv:** Bust of Kossuth facing **Obv. Legend:** MAGYAR KÖZTÁRSASÁG **Rev:** Dove, value in wreath of clasped hands **Edge:** Plain

Date	Mintage	F	VF	XF	Unc	BU
2004	12,500	—	—	—	—	4.00
2004 Proof	3,000	Value: 6.00				

X# Pn6a 50 EURO CENT
Silver **Obv:** Bust of Kossuth facing **Obv. Legend:** MAGYAR KÖZTÁRSASÁG **Rev:** Dove, value in wreath of clasped hands

Date	Mintage	F	VF	XF	Unc	BU
2004 Proof	250	Value: 15.00				

X# Pn7 EURO
Bi-Metallic Copper-Nickel center in Goldine ring, 22.8 mm. **Issuer:** INA **Obv:** Crowned bust of King Stephen facing 3/4 left **Obv. Legend:** MAGYAR KÖZTÁRSASÁG **Rev:** Large value, sailing ship Phoenix, Euro stars design **Edge:** Plain

Date	Mintage	F	VF	XF	Unc	BU
2004	12,500	—	—	—	—	6.00
2004 Proof	3,000	Value: 8.00				

X# Pn7a EURO
Bi-Metallic Silver center in Goldine ring **Obv:** Crowned bust of King Stephen facing 3/4 left **Obv. Legend:** MAGYAR KÖZTÁRSASÁG **Rev:** Large value, sailing ship Phoenix, Euro stars design

Date	Mintage	F	VF	XF	Unc	BU
2004 Proof	250	Value: 22.50				

X# Pn8 2 EURO
Bi-Metallic Goldine center in Copper-Nickel ring, 25.7 mm. **Issuer:** INA **Obv:** Conjugate busts of King Mathias and Queen Beatrix facing 3/4 right **Obv. Legend:** MAGYAR KÖZTÁRSASÁG **Rev:** Large value, sailing ship Phoenix, Euro stars design **Edge:** Plain

Date	Mintage	F	VF	XF	Unc	BU
2004	12,500	—	—	—	—	8.00
2004 Proof	3,000	Value: 10.00				

X# Pn8a 2 EURO
Bi-Metallic Goldine center in Silver ring **Obv:** Conjoint busts of King Mathias and Queen Beatrix facing 3/4 right **Obv. Legend:** MAGYAR KÖZTÁRSASÁG **Rev:** Large value, sailing ship Phoenix, Euro stars design

Date	Mintage	F	VF	XF	Unc	BU
2004 Proof	250	Value: 28.50				

X# Pn9 5 EURO
Goldine **Issuer:** INA **Obv. Legend:** MAGYAR KÖZTÁRSASÁG **Edge:** Plain

Date	Mintage	F	VF	XF	Unc	BU
2004 Proof	3,000	Value: 12.50				

X# Pn9a 5 EURO
Silver **Edge:** Plain

Date	Mintage	F	VF	XF	Unc	BU
2004 Proof	250	Value: 40.00				

Unknown Issuer

X# Pn14 EURO CENT
Copper Plated Steel **Obv. Legend:** MAGYAR KÖZTÁRSASÁG **Rev. Inscription:** SPECIMEN **Edge:** Plain

Date	Mintage	F	VF	XF	Unc	BU
2003	30,000	—	—	—	—	1.00

X# Pn15 2 EURO CENT
Copper Plated Steel **Obv. Legend:** MAGYAR KÖZTÁRSASÁG **Rev. Legend:** SPECIMEN **Edge:** Plain

Date	Mintage	F	VF	XF	Unc	BU
2003	30,000	—	—	—	—	1.50

X# Pn16 5 EURO CENT
Copper Plated Steel **Obv. Legend:** MAGYAR KÖZTÁRSASÁG **Rev. Legend:** SPECIMEN

Date	Mintage	F	VF	XF	Unc	BU
2003	30,000	—	—	—	—	2.00

X# Pn17 10 EURO CENT
Goldine **Obv. Legend:** MAGYAR KÖZTÁRSASÁG **Rev. Legend:** SPECIMEN

Date	Mintage	F	VF	XF	Unc	BU
2003	30,000	—	—	—	—	2.50

X# Pn18 20 EURO CENT
Goldine **Obv. Legend:** MAGYAR KÖZTÁRSASÁG **Rev. Legend:** SPECIMEN

Date	Mintage	F	VF	XF	Unc	BU
2003	30,000	—	—	—	—	3.00

X# Pn19 50 EURO CENT
Goldine **Obv. Legend:** MAGYAR KÖZTÁRSASÁG **Rev. Legend:** SPECIMEN

Date	Mintage	F	VF	XF	Unc	BU
2003	30,000	—	—	—	—	3.50

X# Pn20 EURO
Bi-Metallic **Obv:** Cathedral **Obv. Legend:** MAGYAR KÖZTÁRSASÁG **Rev:** Allegorical female seated right, EEU star design **Rev. Legend:** SPECIMEN

Date	Mintage	F	VF	XF	Unc	BU
2003	30,000	—	—	—	—	5.50

X# Pn21 2 EURO
Bi-Metallic **Obv:** Cathedral **Obv. Legend:** MAGYAR KÖZTÁRSASÁG **Rev:** Allegorical female seated right, EEU star design **Rev. Legend:** SPECIMEN

Date	Mintage	F	VF	XF	Unc	BU
2003	30,000	—	—	—	—	7.50

ND (2004) Issue

X# Pn22 EURO CENT
Copper Plated Steel **Obv. Legend:** HUNGARY **Edge:** Plain

Date	Mintage	F	VF	XF	Unc	BU
ND(2004)	—	—	—	—	—	1.00

X# Pn23 2 EURO CENT
Copper Plated Steel **Obv. Legend:** HUNGARY **Edge:** Plain

Date	Mintage	F	VF	XF	Unc	BU
ND(2004)	—	—	—	—	—	1.50

X# Pn24 5 EURO CENT
Copper Plated Steel **Obv. Legend:** HUNGARY

Date	Mintage	F	VF	XF	Unc	BU
ND(2004)	—	—	—	—	—	2.00

X# Pn25 10 EURO CENT

Goldine **Obv. Legend:** HUNGARY

Date	Mintage	F	VF	XF	Unc	BU
ND(2004)	—	—	—	—	—	2.50

X# Pn26 20 EURO CENT

Goldine **Obv. Legend:** HUNGARY

Date	Mintage	F	VF	XF	Unc	BU
ND(2004)	—	—	—	—	—	3.00

X# Pn27 50 EURO CENT

Goldine **Obv. Legend:** HUNGARY

Date	Mintage	F	VF	XF	Unc	BU
ND(2004)	—	—	—	—	—	3.50

X# Pn28 EURO

Bi-Metallic **Obv:** Bust of L. Kossuth facing 3/4 left **Obv. Legend:** HUNGARY **Rev:** Two stylized doves, large value, EEU star design

Date	Mintage	F	VF	XF	Unc	BU
ND(2004)	—	—	—	—	—	5.50

X# Pn29 2 EURO

Bi-Metallic **Obv:** Bust of L. Kossuth facing 3/4 left **Obv. Legend:** HUNGARY **Rev:** Two stylized doves, large value, EEU star design

Date	Mintage	F	VF	XF	Unc	BU
ND(2004)	—	—	—	—	—	7.50

MINT SETS

X#	Date	Mintage	Identification	Issue Price	Mkt Val
XMS2	2003 (8)	30,000	X#Pn14-Pn21	—	26.00
XMS1	2004 (8)	15,000	X#Pn1-Pn8	—	30.00
XMS3	ND(2004) (8)	—	X#Pn22-Pn29.	—	26.00

PROOF SETS

X#	Date	Mintage	Identification	Issue Price	Mkt Val
XPS1	2004 (9)	5,000	X#Pn1-Pn9	—	50.00
XPS2	2004 (9)	500	X#Pn1a-Pn9a	—	150

HUTT RIVER PROVINCE

PRINCIPALITY

Struck for "Hutt River Province", a wheat farm of 18,000 acres called a "Principality" by this self-proclaimed prince in Western Australia

DECIMAL COINAGE

Prince Leonard Issues

X# 1 5 CENTS

Aluminum **Ruler:** Prince Leonard

Date	Mintage	F	VF	XF	Unc	BU
1976	5,000	—	—	—	1.50	—
1976 Proof	2,000	Value: 2.00				
1977	—	—	—	—	1.50	—
1977 Proof	1,000	Value: 2.00				
1978 Proof	500	Value: 3.00				

X# 2 10 CENTS

Bronze **Ruler:** Prince Leonard

Date	Mintage	F	VF	XF	Unc	BU
1976	5,000	—	—	—	1.50	—
1976 Proof	2,000	Value: 2.50				
1977	—	—	—	—	1.50	—
1977 Proof	1,000	Value: 2.50				
1978 Proof	500	Value: 3.50				

X# 3 20 CENTS

Brass **Ruler:** Prince Leonard

Date	Mintage	F	VF	XF	Unc	BU
1976	5,000	—	—	—	2.00	—
1976 Proof	2,000	Value: 3.00				
1977	—	—	—	—	2.00	—
1977 Proof	1,000	Value: 3.00				
1978 Proof	500	Value: 4.00				

X# 4 50 CENTS

Copper-Nickel-Zinc **Ruler:** Prince Leonard

Date	Mintage	F	VF	XF	Unc	BU
1976	5,000	—	—	—	2.50	—
1976 Proof	2,000	Value: 4.00				
1977	—	—	—	—	2.50	—
1977 Proof	1,000	Value: 4.00				
1978 Proof	500	Value: 5.00				

X# 7 DOLLAR

Nickel Silvered Copper **Ruler:** Prince Leonard **Subject:** Queen Elizabeth II Silver Jubilee

Date	Mintage	F	VF	XF	Unc	BU
1977 Proof	1,000	Value: 10.00				
1978 Proof	500	Value: 10.00				

X# 28 5 DOLLARS

31.1030 g., 0.9990 Silver 0.9989 oz. ASW **Ruler:** Prince Leonard **Subject:** Koala

Date	Mintage	F	VF	XF	Unc	BU
1990 Proof	—	Value: 8.50				

X# 243 5 DOLLARS

Copper-Nickel, 39 mm. **Ruler:** Prince Leonard **Obv:** Arms of the United States **Rev:** Head of President Bill Clinton left **Rev. Inscription:** PROTECT DEFEND **Edge:** Reeded

Date	Mintage	F	VF	XF	Unc	BU
1993	—	—	—	—	7.00	—
1993 Proof	50,000	Value: 10.00				

X# 243a 5 DOLLARS

31.1341 g., 0.9990 Gold 0.9999 oz. AGW, 39 mm. **Ruler:** Prince Leonard **Obv:** Arms of the United States **Rev:** Head of President Bill Clinton left **Rev. Inscription:** PROTECT DEFEND **Edge:** Reeded

Date	Mintage	F	VF	XF	Unc	BU
1993 Proof	10	—	—	—	—	—

X# 250 5 DOLLARS

Brass, 44 mm. **Ruler:** Prince Leonard **Subject:** 50th Anniversary D-Day Landings **Obv:** Crown over value on native design **Obv. Designer:** Hal Reed **Rev:** Soldier pointing, large "V" in background **Rev. Legend:** D • DAY • JUNE 6, 1944 **Edge:** Reeded

Date	Mintage	F	VF	XF	Unc	BU
ND(1994)	—	—	—	—	—	—

X# 251 5 DOLLARS

Bronze, 39 mm. **Ruler:** Prince Leonard **Subject:** 50th Anniversary D-Day Landings **Obv:** Crown over value on native design **Obv. Designer:** Hal Reed **Rev:** Soldier pointing, large "V" in background **Rev. Legend:** D • DAY • JUNE 6, 1944 **Edge:** Reeded

Date	Mintage	F	VF	XF	Unc	BU
ND(1994) Proof	10,000	Value: 10.00				

X# 244 10 DOLLARS

31.1341 g., 0.9990 Silver 0.9999 oz. ASW, 39 mm. **Ruler:** Prince Leonard **Obv:** Arms of the United States

Rev: Head of President Bill Clinton left **Rev. Inscription:** PROTECT DEFEND **Edge:** Reeded

Date	Mintage	F	VF	XF	Unc	BU
1993 Proof	15,000	Value: 25.00				

X# 248 10 DOLLARS

Silver Plated Brass, 44 mm. **Ruler:** Prince Leonard **Obv:** Crown over value on native design **Obv. Designer:** Alex Shagin **Rev:** Supersaurus Dinosaurs **Edge:** Reeded

Date	Mintage	F	VF	XF	Unc	BU
1993	—	—	—	—	12.50	—

X# 245 20 DOLLARS

Gold Plated Copper-Nickel, 39 mm. **Ruler:** Prince Leonard **Obv:** Arms of the United States **Obv. Designer:** Hal Reed **Rev:** Head of President Bill Clinton left **Rev. Inscription:** PROTECT DEFEND **Edge:** Reeded

Date	Mintage	F	VF	XF	Unc	BU
1993 Proof	—	—	—	—	—	—

X# 252 20 DOLLARS

Gold Plated Bronze, 39 mm. **Ruler:** Prince Leonard **Subject:** 50th Anniversary D-Day Landings **Obv:** Crown over value on native design **Obv. Designer:** Hal Reed **Rev:** Soldier pointing, large "V" in background **Rev. Legend:** D • DAY • JUNE 6, 1944 **Edge:** Reeded

Date	Mintage	F	VF	XF	Unc	BU
ND(1994) Proof	10,000	Value: 25.00				

X# 255 20 DOLLARS

Gold Plated Bronze, 39 mm. **Ruler:** Prince Leonard **Subject:** Los Angeles Games **Obv:** Crown over value on native design **Obv. Designer:** Hal Reed **Rev:** Soccer player **Rev. Legend:** LIBERTY

Date	Mintage	F	VF	XF	Unc	BU
1994 Proof	10,000	Value: 20.00				

X# 14 25 DOLLARS

31.1030 g., 0.9990 Silver 0.9989 oz. ASW **Ruler:** Prince Leonard **Rev:** George Orwell

Date	Mintage	F	VF	XF	Unc	BU
1984	1,984	—	—	—	45.00	—

X# 15 25 DOLLARS

31.2500 g., 0.9990 Silver 1.0037 oz. ASW **Ruler:** Prince Leonard **Rev:** Conjoined heads of President and Mrs. Ronald Reagan right

Date	Mintage	F	VF	XF	Unc	BU
1985JM Proof	5,000	Value: 37.50				

X# 16 25 DOLLARS

31.2500 g., 0.9990 Silver 1.0037 oz. ASW **Ruler:** Prince Leonard **Rev:** Automobile Centennial

Date	Mintage	F	VF	XF	Unc	BU
1985 Proof	5,000	Value: 40.00				

X# 19 25 DOLLARS

31.2500 g., 0.9990 Silver 1.0037 oz. ASW **Ruler:** Prince Leonard **Rev:** Statue of Liberty Centennial

Date	Mintage	F	VF	XF	Unc	BU
1986 Proof	25,000	Value: 35.00				

X# 23 25 DOLLARS

31.1030 g., 0.9990 Silver 0.9989 oz. ASW **Ruler:** Prince Leonard **Rev:** George Washington Inaugural Bicentennial

Date	Mintage	F	VF	XF	Unc	BU
1989 Proof	3,000	Value: 40.00				

X# 253 25 DOLLARS

31.1341 g., 0.9990 Silver 0.9999 oz. ASW, 39 mm. **Ruler:** Prince Leonard **Subject:** 50th Anniversary D-Day Landings **Obv:** Crown over value on native design **Obv. Designer:** Hal Reed **Rev:** Soldier pointing, large "V" in background **Rev. Legend:** D • DAY • JUNE 6, 1944 **Edge:** Reeded

Date	Mintage	F	VF	XF	Unc	BU
ND(1994) Proof	10,000	Value: 30.00				

X# 5 30 DOLLARS

32.8000 g., 0.9990 Silver 1.0534 oz. ASW **Ruler:** Prince Leonard

Date	Mintage	F	VF	XF	Unc	BU
1976 Proof	1,000	Value: 40.00				

X# 8 30 DOLLARS
32.8000 g., 0.9990 Silver 1.0534 oz. ASW
Ruler: Prince Leonard **Rev:** Red Robin

Date	Mintage	F	VF	XF	Unc	BU
1977 Proof	1,000	Value: 45.00				

X# 9 30 DOLLARS
32.8000 g., 0.9990 Silver 1.0534 oz. ASW **Ruler:** Prince Leonard **Subject:** Bicentennial of Captain Cook's Discovery of Hawaii **Rev:** H.M.S. Resolution

Date	Mintage	F	VF	XF	Unc	BU
1978 Proof	500	Value: 60.00				

X# 11 30 DOLLARS
32.8000 g., 0.9990 Silver 1.0534 oz. ASW **Ruler:** Prince Leonard **Rev:** Fall of Skylab

Date	Mintage	F	VF	XF	Unc	BU
1979 Proof	500	Value: 50.00				

X# 246 50 DOLLARS
124.5364 g., 0.9990 Silver 3.9998 oz. ASW
Ruler: Prince Leonard **Obv:** Arms of the United States **Obv. Designer:** Hal Reed **Rev:** Head of President Bill Clinton left **Rev. Inscription:** PROTECT DEFEND **Edge:** Reeded

Date	Mintage	F	VF	XF	Unc	BU
1993 Proof	—	—	—	—	—	—

X# 249 50 DOLLARS
124.5364 g., 0.9990 Silver 3.9998 oz. ASW, 65 mm.
Ruler: Prince Leonard **Obv:** Crown over value on native design **Obv. Designer:** Alex Shagin **Rev:** Supersaurus Dinosaurs **Edge:** Reeded **Note:** Illustration reduced.

Date	Mintage	F	VF	XF	Unc	BU
1993 Proof	5,000	Value: 65.00				

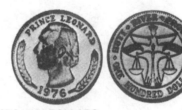

X# 6 100 DOLLARS
9.0000 g., 1.0000 Gold 0.2893 oz. AGW
Ruler: Prince Leonard

Date	Mintage	F	VF	XF	Unc	BU
1976 Proof	500	Value: 250				

X# A9 100 DOLLARS
9.0000 g., 1.0000 Gold 0.2893 oz. AGW
Ruler: Prince Leonard **Rev:** Wedge-tailed Eagle

Date	Mintage	F	VF	XF	Unc	BU
1977 Proof	500	Value: 300				

X# 10 100 DOLLARS
9.0000 g., 1.0000 Gold 0.2893 oz. AGW **Ruler:** Prince Leonard **Subject:** Bicentennial of Captain Cook's Discovery of Hawaii **Rev:** H.M.S. Resolution

Date	Mintage	F	VF	XF	Unc	BU
1978 Proof	500	Value: 275				

X# 12 100 DOLLARS
9.0000 g., 1.0000 Gold 0.2893 oz. AGW **Ruler:** Prince Leonard **Rev:** Fall of Skylab

Date	Mintage	F	VF	XF	Unc	BU
1979 Proof	500	Value: 260				

X# 13 100 DOLLARS
9.0000 g., 1.0000 Gold 0.2893 oz. AGW **Ruler:** Prince Leonard **Rev:** 80th Birthday of Queen Mother

Date	Mintage	F	VF	XF	Unc	BU
1980PM Proof	18	Value: 495				

X# 17 100 DOLLARS
186.6180 g., 0.9990 Silver 5.9937 oz. ASW, 64.5 mm.
Ruler: Prince Leonard **Rev:** Statue of Liberty Centennial **Note:** Illustration reduced.

Date	Mintage	F	VF	XF	Unc	BU
1986 Proof	—	Value: 150				

X# 21 100 DOLLARS
186.6180 g., 0.9990 Silver 5.9937 oz. ASW, 64.5 mm. **Ruler:** Prince Leonard **Rev:** America's Cup **Note:** Struck by Johnson Matthey, Toronto, Ontario, Canada. Illustration reduced.

Date	Mintage	F	VF	XF	Unc	BU
1987 Proof	1,000	Value: 150				

X# 22 100 DOLLARS
186.6200 g., 0.9990 Silver 5.9937 oz. ASW, 64.5 mm. **Ruler:** Prince Leonard **Rev:** Seoul Olympics **Note:** Illustration reduced.

Date	Mintage	F	VF	XF	Unc	BU
1988JM Proof	1,000	—	—	—	—	—

X# 24 100 DOLLARS
186.6200 g., 0.9990 Silver 5.9937 oz. ASW, 64.5 mm. **Ruler:** Prince Leonard **Obv:** Koala bear on branch at bottom, 2 kangaroos upper right going left **Rev:** George Washington Inaugural Bicentennial **Note:** Illustration reduced.

Date	Mintage	F	VF	XF	Unc	BU
1989 Proof	1,500	Value: 160				

X# 25 100 DOLLARS
31.1030 g., 0.9990 Palladium 0.9989 oz. **Ruler:** Prince Leonard **Subject:** Nuclear Fusion Experiments **Obv:** Koala and kangaroos **Rev:** Chemistry, physics-industry

Date	Mintage	F	VF	XF	Unc	BU
1989 Proof	—	Value: 400				

X# 247 100 DOLLARS
3.1134 g., 0.9990 Gold 0.1000 oz. AGW, 16.5 mm. **Ruler:** Prince Leonard **Obv:** Arms of the United States **Obv. Designer:** Hal Reed **Rev:** Head of President Bill Clinton left **Rev. Inscription:** PROTECT DEFEND **Edge:** Reeded

Date	Mintage	F	VF	XF	Unc	BU
1993 Proof	2,500	Value: 125				

X# 305 100 DOLLARS
8.0000 g., 0.9999 Gold 0.2572 oz. AGW, 24 mm. **Ruler:** Prince Leonard **Subject:** 30th Anniversary of HRP **Obv:** Biblical Stone Gateway monument **Obv. Designer:** Allan Sterling **Rev:** Crown over value on native design **Edge:** Plain

Date	Mintage	F	VF	XF	Unc	BU
2000W Proof	25	Value: 185				

X# 18 SOVEREIGN
7.9881 g., 0.9170 Gold 0.2355 oz. AGW **Ruler:** Prince Leonard **Rev:** Automobile Centennial

Date	Mintage	F	VF	XF	Unc	BU
1985 Proof	2,000	Value: 235				

X# 20 SOVEREIGN
7.9881 g., 0.9170 Gold 0.2355 oz. AGW **Ruler:** Prince Leonard **Rev:** Statue of Liberty Centennial

Date	Mintage	F	VF	XF	Unc	BU
1986 Proof	10,000	Value: 225				

Desert Storm Series

X# 29 5 DOLLARS
31.1030 g., 0.9990 Silver 0.9989 oz. ASW **Ruler:** Prince Leonard **Obv:** Crown over value on native design **Rev:** U.S. Jeep - Type I

Date	Mintage	F	VF	XF	Unc	BU
1990NQM	Est. 4,500	—	—	—	16.00	—

X# 30 5 DOLLARS
31.1030 g., 0.9990 Silver 0.9989 oz. ASW **Ruler:** Prince Leonard **Obv:** Crown over value on native design **Rev:** U.S. Jeep - Type II with "IN GOD WE TRUST" added

Date	Mintage	F	VF	XF	Unc	BU
1990NQM	Est. 46,000	—	—	—	12.00	—

X# 31 5 DOLLARS
26.3200 g., Copper-Nickel-Zinc, 38.95 mm. **Ruler:** Prince Leonard **Obv:** Crown over value on native design **Rev:** U.S. AH-64 Apache Attack Helicopter **Edge:** Reeded

Date	Mintage	F	VF	XF	Unc	BU
1991	—	—	—	—	7.00	—
1991 Proof	—	Value: 10.00				

X# 65 5 DOLLARS
26.3200 g., Copper-Nickel-Zinc, 38.95 mm. **Ruler:** Prince Leonard **Obv:** Crown over value on native design **Rev:** M-998 Hummer (HMMWV) **Edge:** Reeded

Date	Mintage	F	VF	XF	Unc	BU
1991 Proof	—	Value: 10.00				
1991	—	—	—	—	7.00	—

X# 59 5 DOLLARS
26.3200 g., Copper-Nickel-Zinc, 38.95 mm. **Ruler:** Prince Leonard **Obv:** Crown over value on native design **Rev:** Submarines, the "Silent Service" **Edge:** Reeded

Date	Mintage	F	VF	XF	Unc	BU
1991 Proof	—	—	—	—	—	—
1991	—	—	—	—	7.00	—

X# 32 5 DOLLARS
26.3200 g., Copper-Nickel-Zinc, 38.95 mm. **Ruler:** Prince Leonard **Obv:** Crown over value on native design **Rev:** U.S. F-117A Stealth Jet Fighter **Edge:** Reeded

Date	Mintage	F	VF	XF	Unc	BU
1991	—	—	—	—	7.00	—
1991 Proof	—	Value: 10.00				

X# 33 5 DOLLARS
26.3200 g., Copper-Nickel-Zinc, 38.95 mm. **Ruler:** Prince Leonard **Obv:** Crown over value on native design **Rev:** U.S. M-551 Sheridan Tank **Edge:** Reeded

Date	Mintage	F	VF	XF	Unc	BU
1991	—	—	—	—	7.00	—
1991 Proof	—	Value: 10.00				

X# 34 5 DOLLARS
26.3200 g., Copper-Nickel-Zinc, 38.95 mm. **Ruler:** Prince Leonard **Obv:** Crown over value on native design **Rev:** U.S. Airborne Troops **Edge:** Reeded

Date	Mintage	F	VF	XF	Unc	BU
1991	—	—	—	—	7.00	—
1991 Proof	—	Value: 10.00				

X# 35 5 DOLLARS
26.3200 g., Copper-Nickel-Zinc, 38.95 mm. **Ruler:** Prince Leonard **Obv:** Crown over value on native design **Rev:** U.S. Patriot Missile Batteries **Edge:** Reeded

Date	Mintage	F	VF	XF	Unc	BU
1991	—	—	—	—	7.00	—
1991 Proof	—	Value: 10.00				

X# 36 5 DOLLARS
26.3200 g., Copper-Nickel-Zinc, 38.95 mm. **Ruler:** Prince Leonard **Obv:** Crown over value on native design **Rev:** U.S. Marines **Edge:** Reeded

Date	Mintage	F	VF	XF	Unc	BU
1991	—	—	—	—	7.00	—
1991 Proof	—	Value: 10.00				

X# 37 5 DOLLARS
26.3200 g., Copper-Nickel-Zinc, 38.95 mm. **Ruler:** Prince Leonard **Obv:** Crown over value on native design **Rev:** U.S. F4-G Phanthom "Wild Weasel" Jet Fighter **Edge:** Reeded

Date	Mintage	F	VF	XF	Unc	BU
1991	—	—	—	—	7.00	—
1991 Proof	—	Value: 10.00				

X# 38 5 DOLLARS

26.3200 g., Copper-Nickel-Zinc, 38.95 mm. **Ruler:** Prince Leonard **Obv:** Crown over value on native design **Rev:** U.S. Guided Missile Destroyer **Edge:** Reeded

Date	Mintage	F	VF	XF	Unc	BU
1991	—	—	—	—	7.00	—
1991 Proof	—	Value: 10.00				

X# 39 5 DOLLARS

26.3200 g., Copper-Nickel-Zinc, 38.95 mm. **Ruler:** Prince Leonard **Obv:** Crown over value on native design **Rev:** U.S. MGM-52C Lance Guided Missile **Edge:** Reeded

Date	Mintage	F	VF	XF	Unc	BU
1991	—	—	—	—	7.00	—
1991 Proof	—	Value: 10.00				

X# 40 5 DOLLARS

26.3200 g., Copper-Nickel-Zinc, 38.95 mm. **Ruler:** Prince Leonard **Obv:** Crown over value on native design **Rev:** Battleship U.S.S. Missouri **Edge:** Reeded

Date	Mintage	F	VF	XF	Unc	BU
1991	—	—	—	—	7.00	—
1991 Proof	—	Value: 10.00				

X# 41 5 DOLLARS

26.3200 g., Copper-Nickel-Zinc, 38.95 mm. **Ruler:** Prince Leonard **Obv:** Crown over value on native design **Rev:** U.S. Bradley Vehicle **Edge:** Reeded

Date	Mintage	F	VF	XF	Unc	BU
1991	—	—	—	—	7.00	—
1991 Proof	—	Value: 10.00				

X# 42 5 DOLLARS

26.3200 g., Copper-Nickel-Zinc, 38.95 mm. **Ruler:** Prince Leonard **Obv:** Crown over value on native design **Rev:** U.S. A-6E Intruder Attack Jet **Edge:** Reeded

Date	Mintage	F	VF	XF	Unc	BU
1991	—	—	—	—	7.00	—
1991 Proof	—	—	—	—	—	—

X# 43 5 DOLLARS

26.3200 g., Copper-Nickel-Zinc, 38.95 mm. **Ruler:** Prince Leonard **Obv:** Crown over value on native design **Rev:** U.S. BGM-109 Cruise Guided Missile **Edge:** Reeded

Date	Mintage	F	VF	XF	Unc	BU
1991	—	—	—	—	7.00	—
1991 Proof	—	Value: 10.00				

X# 44 5 DOLLARS

26.3200 g., Copper-Nickel-Zinc, 38.95 mm. **Ruler:** Prince Leonard **Obv:** Crown over value on native design **Rev:** U.S. M-1 Abrams Tank **Edge:** Reeded

Date	Mintage	F	VF	XF	Unc	BU
1991	—	—	—	—	7.00	—
1991 Proof	—	Value: 10.00				

X# 45 5 DOLLARS

26.3200 g., Copper-Nickel-Zinc, 38.95 mm. **Ruler:** Prince Leonard **Obv:** Crown over value on native design **Rev:** U.S. A-10 Thunderbolt II "Warthog" Attack Jet **Edge:** Reeded

Date	Mintage	F	VF	XF	Unc	BU
1991	—	—	—	—	7.00	—
1991 Proof	—	Value: 10.00				

X# 46 5 DOLLARS

26.3200 g., Copper-Nickel-Zinc, 38.95 mm. **Ruler:** Prince Leonard **Obv:** Crown over value on native design **Rev:** Aircraft Carrier - U.S.S. John F. Kennedy **Edge:** Reeded

Date	Mintage	F	VF	XF	Unc	BU
1991	—	—	—	—	7.00	—
1991 Proof	—	Value: 10.00				

X# 47 5 DOLLARS

26.3200 g., Copper-Nickel-Zinc, 38.95 mm. **Ruler:** Prince Leonard **Obv:** Crown over value on native design **Rev:** U.S. AIM-9 "Sidewinder" Guided Missile **Edge:** Reeded

Date	Mintage	F	VF	XF	Unc	BU
1991	—	—	—	—	7.00	—
1991 Proof	—	Value: 10.00				

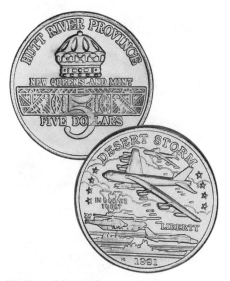

X# 48 5 DOLLARS

26.3200 g., Copper-Nickel-Zinc, 38.95 mm. **Ruler:** Prince Leonard **Obv:** Crown over value on native design **Rev:** U.S. B-52 Stratofortress Jet Bomber **Edge:** Reeded

Date	Mintage	F	VF	XF	Unc	BU
1991	—	—	—	—	7.00	—
1991 Proof	—	Value: 10.00				

X# 49 5 DOLLARS
26.3200 g., Copper-Nickel-Zinc, 38.95 mm.
Ruler: Prince Leonard **Obv:** Crown over value on native design **Rev. Designer:** U.S. M-163 Vulcan Cannon
Edge: Reeded

Date	Mintage	F	VF	XF	Unc	BU
1991	—	—	—	—	7.00	—
1991 Proof	—	Value: 10.00				

X# 50 5 DOLLARS
26.3200 g., Copper-Nickel-Zinc, 38.95 mm. **Ruler:** Prince Leonard **Obv:** Crown over value on native design **Rev:** Woman's Armed Forces **Edge:** Reeded

Date	Mintage	F	VF	XF	Unc	BU
1991	—	—	—	—	7.00	—
1991 Proof	—	Value: 10.00				

X# 51 5 DOLLARS
26.3200 g., Copper-Nickel-Zinc, 38.95 mm. **Ruler:** Prince Leonard **Obv:** Crown over value on native design **Rev:** U.S. Infantry - Tow Missile **Edge:** Reeded

Date	Mintage	F	VF	XF	Unc	BU
1991	—	—	—	—	7.00	—
1991 Proof	—	Value: 10.00				

X# 52 5 DOLLARS
26.3200 g., Copper-Nickel-Zinc, 38.95 mm. **Ruler:** Prince Leonard **Obv:** Crown over value on native design **Rev:** U.S. F-14 Tomcat Jet Fighter **Edge:** Reeded

Date	Mintage	F	VF	XF	Unc	BU
1991	—	—	—	—	7.00	—
1991 Proof	—	Value: 10.00				

X# 53 5 DOLLARS
26.3200 g., Copper-Nickel-Zinc, 38.95 mm. **Ruler:** Prince Leonard **Obv:** Crown over value on native design **Rev:** U.S. M-60A3 Tank **Edge:** Reeded

Date	Mintage	F	VF	XF	Unc	BU
1991	—	—	—	—	7.00	—
1991 Proof	—	Value: 10.00				

X# 54 5 DOLLARS
26.3200 g., Copper-Nickel-Zinc, 38.95 mm. **Ruler:** Prince Leonard **Obv:** Crown over value on native design **Rev:** U.S. Army Mortar Squad **Edge:** Reeded

Date	Mintage	F	VF	XF	Unc	BU
1991	—	—	—	—	7.00	—
1991 Proof	—	Value: 10.00				

X# 55 5 DOLLARS
26.3200 g., Copper-Nickel-Zinc, 38.95 mm. **Ruler:** Prince Leonard **Obv:** Crown over value on native design **Rev:** U.S. "Dragon" Anti-tank Weapon **Edge:** Reeded

Date	Mintage	F	VF	XF	Unc	BU
1991	—	—	—	—	7.00	—
1991 Proof	—	Value: 10.00				

X# 56 5 DOLLARS
26.3200 g., Copper-Nickel-Zinc, 38.95 mm.
Ruler: Prince Leonard **Obv:** Crown over value on native design **Rev:** U.S. F-16C "Fighting Falcon" Jet Fighter
Edge: Reeded

Date	Mintage	F	VF	XF	Unc	BU
1991	—	—	—	—	7.00	—
1991 Proof	—	Value: 10.00				

X# 57 5 DOLLARS

26.3200 g., Copper-Nickel-Zinc, 38.95 mm. **Ruler:** Prince Leonard **Obv:** Crown over value on native design **Rev:** U.S. Multi-launch Rocket System **Edge:** Reeded

Date	Mintage	F	VF	XF	Unc	BU
1991	—	—	—	—	7.00	—
1991 Proof	—	Value: 10.00				

X# 58 5 DOLLARS

26.3200 g., Copper-Nickel-Zinc, 38.95 mm. **Ruler:** Prince Leonard **Obv:** Crown over value on native design **Rev:** Chemical warfare **Edge:** Reeded

Date	Mintage	F	VF	XF	Unc	BU
1991	—	—	—	—	7.00	—
1991 Proof	—	Value: 10.00				

X# 60 5 DOLLARS

26.3200 g., Copper-Nickel-Zinc, 38.95 mm. **Ruler:** Prince Leonard **Obv:** Crown over value on native design **Rev:** U.S. F-15E "Strike Eagle" Jet Fighter **Edge:** Reeded

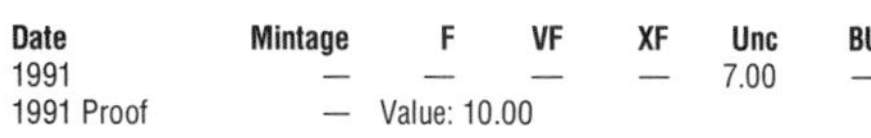

Date	Mintage	F	VF	XF	Unc	BU
1991	—	—	—	—	7.00	—
1991 Proof	—	Value: 10.00				

X# 61 5 DOLLARS

26.3200 g., Copper-Nickel-Zinc, 38.95 mm. **Ruler:** Prince Leonard **Obv:** Crown over value on native design **Rev:** U.S. M-1198 155mm Towed Howitzer **Edge:** Reeded

Date	Mintage	F	VF	XF	Unc	BU
1991	—	—	—	—	7.00	—
1991 Proof	—	—	—	—	—	—

X# 62 5 DOLLARS

26.3200 g., Copper-Nickel-Zinc, 38.95 mm. **Ruler:** Prince Leonard **Obv:** Crown over value on native design **Rev:** Top Secret War **Edge:** Reeded

Date	Mintage	F	VF	XF	Unc	BU
1991	—	—	—	—	7.00	—
1991 Proof	—	Value: 10.00				

X# 63 5 DOLLARS

26.3200 g., Copper-Nickel-Zinc, 38.95 mm. **Ruler:** Prince Leonard **Obv:** Crown over value on native design **Rev:** U.S. MIM-23 "Hawk" Surface to Air Guided Missile **Edge:** Reeded

Date	Mintage	F	VF	XF	Unc	BU
1991	—	—	—	—	7.00	—
1991 Proof	—	Value: 10.00				

X# 64 5 DOLLARS

26.3200 g., Copper-Nickel-Zinc, 38.95 mm. **Ruler:** Prince Leonard **Obv:** Crown over value on native design **Rev:** English AV-8B "Harrier" Jump Jet **Edge:** Reeded

Date	Mintage	F	VF	XF	Unc	BU
1991	—	—	—	—	7.00	—
1991 Proof	—	Value: 10.00				

X# 66 5 DOLLARS

26.3200 g., Copper-Nickel-Zinc, 38.95 mm. **Ruler:** Prince Leonard **Obv:** Crown over value on native design **Rev:** U.S. Coast Guard Support **Edge:** Reeded

Date	Mintage	F	VF	XF	Unc	BU
1991	—	—	—	—	7.00	—
1991 Proof	—	Value: 10.00				

X# 67 5 DOLLARS
26.3200 g., Copper-Nickel-Zinc, 38.95 mm.
Ruler: Prince Leonard **Obv:** Crown over value on native design **Rev:** U.S. FIM-91A "Stinger" Anti-aircraft Missile System **Edge:** Reeded

Date	Mintage	F	VF	XF	Unc	BU
1991	—	—	—	—	7.00	—
1991 Proof	—	Value: 10.00				

X# 68 5 DOLLARS
26.3200 g., Copper-Nickel-Zinc, 38.95 mm. **Ruler:** Prince Leonard **Obv:** Crown over value on native design **Rev:** U.S. F-18 "Hornet" Jet Fighter **Edge:** Reeded

Date	Mintage	F	VF	XF	Unc	BU
1991	—	—	—	—	7.00	—
1991 Proof	—	Value: 10.00				

X# 69 5 DOLLARS
26.3200 g., Copper-Nickel-Zinc, 38.95 mm. **Ruler:** Prince Leonard **Obv:** Crown over value on native design **Rev:** U.S. M-109 Self-propelled Howitzer **Edge:** Reeded

Date	Mintage	F	VF	XF	Unc	BU
1991	—	—	—	—	7.00	—
1991 Proof	—	Value: 10.00				

X# 70 5 DOLLARS
26.3200 g., Copper-Nickel-Zinc, 38.95 mm.
Ruler: Prince Leonard **Obv:** Crown over value on native design **Rev:** U.S. Tactical Missile Systems (TACMS) **Edge:** Reeded

Date	Mintage	F	VF	XF	Unc	BU
1991	—	—	—	—	7.00	—
1991 Proof	—	Value: 10.00				

X# 71 5 DOLLARS
26.3200 g., Copper-Nickel-Zinc, 38.95 mm. **Ruler:** Prince Leonard **Obv:** Crown over value on native design **Rev:** U.S. Tiger Anti-tank Brigade **Edge:** Reeded

Date	Mintage	F	VF	XF	Unc	BU
1991	—	—	—	—	7.00	—
1991 Proof	—	Value: 10.00				

X# 72 5 DOLLARS
26.3200 g., Copper-Nickel-Zinc, 38.95 mm. **Ruler:** Prince Leonard **Obv:** Crown over value on native design **Rev:** U.S. AH-15 Hughes "Cobra" Helicopter ("Huey") **Edge:** Reeded

Date	Mintage	F	VF	XF	Unc	BU
1991	—	—	—	—	7.00	—
1991 Proof	—	Value: 10.00				

X# 73 5 DOLLARS
26.3200 g., Copper-Nickel-Zinc, 38.95 mm.
Ruler: Prince Leonard **Obv:** Crown over value on native design **Rev:** Desert Patrol **Edge:** Reeded

Date	Mintage	F	VF	XF	Unc	BU
1991	—	—	—	—	7.00	—
1991 Proof	—	Value: 10.00				

X# 74 5 DOLLARS
26.3200 g., Copper-Nickel-Zinc, 38.95 mm. **Ruler:** Prince Leonard **Obv:** Crown over value on native design **Rev:** U.S. E-3 "Sentry" (AWACS) **Edge:** Reeded

Date	Mintage	F	VF	XF	Unc	BU
1991	—	—	—	—	7.00	—
1991 Proof	—	Value: 10.00				

X# 75 5 DOLLARS
26.3200 g., Copper-Nickel-Zinc, 38.95 mm. **Ruler:** Prince Leonard **Obv:** Crown over value on native design **Rev:** Coming Home **Edge:** Reeded

Date	Mintage	F	VF	XF	Unc	BU
1991	—	—	—	—	7.00	—
1991 Proof	—	Value: 10.00				

X# 76 20 DOLLARS

Gold Plated Copper-Nickel-Zinc, 38.95 mm. **Ruler:** Prince Leonard **Obv:** Crown over value on native design **Edge:** Reeded

Date	Mintage	F	VF	XF	Unc	BU
1991 Proof	—	Value: 12.00				

X# 77 20 DOLLARS

Gold Plated Bronze, 38.95 mm. **Ruler:** Prince Leonard **Obv:** Crown over value on native design **Rev:** U.S. F-117A Stealth Jet Fighter **Edge:** Reeded

Date	Mintage	F	VF	XF	Unc	BU
1991 Proof	—	Value: 12.00				

X# 82 20 DOLLARS

Gold Plated Bronze, 38.95 mm. **Ruler:** Prince Leonard **Obv:** Crown over value on native design **Rev:** U.S. F4-G Phanthom "Wild Weasel" Jet Fighter **Edge:** Reeded

Date	Mintage	F	VF	XF	Unc	BU
1991 Proof	—	Value: 12.00				

X# 93 20 DOLLARS

Gold Plated Bronze, 38.95 mm. **Ruler:** Prince Leonard **Obv:** Crown over value on native design **Rev:** U.S. B-52 Stratofortress Jet Bomber **Edge:** Reeded

Date	Mintage	F	VF	XF	Unc	BU
1991 Proof	—	Value: 12.00				

X# 97 20 DOLLARS

Gold Plated Bronze, 38.95 mm. **Ruler:** Prince Leonard **Obv:** Crown over value on native design **Rev:** U.S. F-14 Tomcat Jet Fighter **Edge:** Reeded

Date	Mintage	F	VF	XF	Unc	BU
1991 Proof	—	Value: 12.00				

X# 101 20 DOLLARS

Gold Plated Bronze, 38.95 mm. **Ruler:** Prince Leonard **Obv:** Crown over value on native design **Rev:** U.S. F-16C "Fighting Falcon" Jet Fighter **Edge:** Reeded

Date	Mintage	F	VF	XF	Unc	BU
1991 Proof	—	Value: 12.00				

X# 105 20 DOLLARS

Gold Plated Bronze, 38.95 mm. **Ruler:** Prince Leonard **Obv:** Crown over value on other native design **Rev:** U.S. F-15E "Strike Eagle" Jet Fighter **Edge:** Reeded

Date	Mintage	F	VF	XF	Unc	BU
1991 Proof	—	Value: 12.00				

X# 109 20 DOLLARS

Gold Plated Bronze, 38.95 mm. **Ruler:** Prince Leonard **Obv:** Crown over value on native design **Rev:** English AV-8B "Harrier" Jump Jet **Edge:** Reeded

Date	Mintage	F	VF	XF	Unc	BU
1991 Proof	—	Value: 12.00				

X# 113 20 DOLLARS

Gold Plated Bronze, 38.95 mm. **Ruler:** Prince Leonard **Obv:** Crown over value on native design **Rev:** U.S. F-18 "Hornet" Jet Fighter **Edge:** Reeded

Date	Mintage	F	VF	XF	Unc	BU
1991 Proof	—	Value: 12.00				

X# 117 20 DOLLARS

Gold Plated Bronze, 38.95 mm. **Ruler:** Prince Leonard **Obv:** Crown over value on native design **Rev:** U.S. Hughes "Cobra" Helicopter ("Huey") **Edge:** Reeded

Date	Mintage	F	VF	XF	Unc	BU
1991 Proof	—	Value: 12.00				

X# 121 25 DOLLARS

31.1341 g., 0.9990 Silver 0.9999 oz. ASW, 38.95 mm. **Ruler:** Prince Leonard **Obv:** Crown over value on native design **Rev:** U.S. AH-64 Apache Attack Helicopter **Edge:** Reeded **Note:** Prev. X#76.

Date	Mintage	F	VF	XF	Unc	BU
1991 Proof	—	Value: 35.00				

X# 122 25 DOLLARS

31.1341 g., 0.9990 Silver 0.9999 oz. ASW, 38.95 mm. **Ruler:** Prince Leonard **Obv:** Crown over value on native design **Rev:** U.S. F-117A Stealth Jet Fighter **Edge:** Reeded

Date	Mintage	F	VF	XF	Unc	BU
1991 Proof	—	Value: 28.50				

X# 123 25 DOLLARS

31.1341 g., 0.9990 Silver 0.9999 oz. ASW, 38.95 mm. **Ruler:** Prince Leonard **Obv:** Crown over value on native design **Rev:** U.S. M-551 Sheridan Tank **Edge:** Reeded

Date	Mintage	F	VF	XF	Unc	BU
1991 Proof	—	Value: 28.50				

X# 124 25 DOLLARS

31.1341 g., 0.9990 Silver 0.9999 oz. ASW, 38.95 mm. **Ruler:** Prince Leonard **Obv:** Crown over value on native design **Rev:** U.S. Airborne Troops **Edge:** Reeded

Date	Mintage	F	VF	XF	Unc	BU
1991 Proof	—	Value: 28.50				

X# 125 25 DOLLARS

31.1341 g., 0.9990 Silver 0.9999 oz. ASW, 38.95 mm. **Ruler:** Prince Leonard **Obv:** Crown over value on native design **Rev:** U.S. Patriot Missile Batteries **Edge:** Reeded

Date	Mintage	F	VF	XF	Unc	BU
1991 Proof	—	Value: 28.50				

X# 126 25 DOLLARS

31.1341 g., 0.9990 Silver 0.9999 oz. ASW, 38.95 mm. **Ruler:** Prince Leonard **Obv:** Crown over value on native design **Rev:** U.S. Marines **Edge:** Reeded

Date	Mintage	F	VF	XF	Unc	BU
1991 Proof	—	Value: 28.50				

X# 127 25 DOLLARS

31.1341 g., 0.9990 Silver 0.9999 oz. ASW, 38.95 mm. **Ruler:** Prince Leonard **Obv:** Crown over value on native design **Rev:** U.S. F4-G Phanthom "Wild Weasel" Jet Fighter **Edge:** Reeded

Date	Mintage	F	VF	XF	Unc	BU
1991 Proof	—	Value: 28.50				

X# 128 25 DOLLARS

31.1341 g., 0.9990 Silver 0.9999 oz. ASW, 38.95 mm. **Ruler:** Prince Leonard **Obv:** Crown over value on native design **Rev:** U.S. Guided Missile Destroyer **Edge:** Reeded

Date	Mintage	F	VF	XF	Unc	BU
1991 Proof	—	Value: 28.50				

X# 129 25 DOLLARS

31.1341 g., 0.9990 Silver 0.9999 oz. ASW, 38.95 mm. **Ruler:** Prince Leonard **Obv:** Crown over value on native design **Rev:** U.S. MGM-52G Lance Guided Missile **Edge:** Reeded

Date	Mintage	F	VF	XF	Unc	BU
1991 Proof	—	Value: 28.50				

X# 130 25 DOLLARS

31.1341 g., 0.9990 Silver 0.9999 oz. ASW, 38.95 mm. **Ruler:** Prince Leonard **Obv:** Crown over value on native design **Rev:** Battleship U.S.S. Missouri **Edge:** Reeded

Date	Mintage	F	VF	XF	Unc	BU
1991 Proof	—	Value: 28.50				

X# 131 25 DOLLARS

31.1341 g., 0.9990 Silver 0.9999 oz. ASW, 38.95 mm. **Ruler:** Prince Leonard **Obv:** Crown over value on native design **Rev:** U.S. Bradley vehicle **Edge:** Reeded

Date	Mintage	F	VF	XF	Unc	BU
1991 Proof	—	Value: 28.50				

X# 132 25 DOLLARS

31.1341 g., 0.9990 Silver 0.9999 oz. ASW, 38.95 mm. **Ruler:** Prince Leonard **Obv:** Crown over value on native design **Rev:** U.S. A-6E Intruder Attack Jet **Edge:** Reeded

Date	Mintage	F	VF	XF	Unc	BU
1991 Proof	—	Value: 28.50				

X# 133 25 DOLLARS

31.1341 g., 0.9990 Silver 0.9999 oz. ASW, 38.95 mm. **Ruler:** Prince Leonard **Obv:** Crown over value on native design **Rev:** U.S. BGM-109 Cruise Guided Missile **Edge:** Reeded

Date	Mintage	F	VF	XF	Unc	BU
1991 Proof	—	Value: 28.50				

X# 134 25 DOLLARS

31.1341 g., 0.9990 Silver 0.9999 oz. ASW, 38.95 mm. **Ruler:** Prince Leonard **Obv:** Crown over value on native design **Rev:** U.S. M-1 Abrams Tank **Edge:** Reeded

Date	Mintage	F	VF	XF	Unc	BU
1991 Proof	—	Value: 28.50				

X# 135 25 DOLLARS

31.1341 g., 0.9990 Silver 0.9999 oz. ASW, 38.95 mm. **Ruler:** Prince Leonard **Obv:** Crown over value on native design **Rev:** U.S. A-10 Thunderbolt II "Warthog" Attack Jet **Edge:** Reeded

Date	Mintage	F	VF	XF	Unc	BU
1991 Proof	—	Value: 28.50				

X# 136 25 DOLLARS

31.1341 g., 0.9990 Silver 0.9999 oz. ASW, 38.95 mm. **Ruler:** Prince Leonard **Obv:** Crown over value on native design **Rev:** Aircraft Carrier - U.S.S. J.F. Kennedy **Edge:** Reeded

Date	Mintage	F	VF	XF	Unc	BU
1991 Proof	—	Value: 28.50				

X# 137 25 DOLLARS

31.1341 g., 0.9990 Silver 0.9999 oz. ASW, 38.95 mm. **Ruler:** Prince Leonard **Obv:** Crown over value on native design **Rev:** U.S. AIM-9 "Sidewinder" Guided Missile **Edge:** Reeded

Date	Mintage	F	VF	XF	Unc	BU
1991 Proof	—	Value: 28.50				

X# 138 25 DOLLARS

31.1341 g., 0.9990 Silver 0.9999 oz. ASW, 38.95 mm. **Ruler:** Prince Leonard **Obv:** Crown over value on native design **Rev:** U.S. B-52 Stratofortress Jet Bomber **Edge:** Reeded

Date	Mintage	F	VF	XF	Unc	BU
1991 Proof	—	Value: 28.50				

X# 139 25 DOLLARS

31.1341 g., 0.9990 Silver 0.9999 oz. ASW, 38.95 mm. **Ruler:** Prince Leonard **Obv:** Crown over value on native design **Rev:** U.S. M-163 Vulcan Cannon **Edge:** Reeded

Date	Mintage	F	VF	XF	Unc	BU
1991 Proof	—	Value: 28.50				

X# 140 25 DOLLARS

31.1341 g., 0.9990 Silver 0.9999 oz. ASW, 38.95 mm. **Ruler:** Prince Leonard **Obv:** Crown over value on native design **Rev:** Woman's Armed Forces **Edge:** Reeded

Date	Mintage	F	VF	XF	Unc	BU
1991 Proof	—	Value: 28.50				

X# 141 25 DOLLARS

31.1341 g., 0.9990 Silver 0.9999 oz. ASW, 38.95 mm. **Ruler:** Prince Leonard **Obv:** Crown over value on native design **Rev:** U.S. Infantry - Tow Missile **Edge:** Reeded

Date	Mintage	F	VF	XF	Unc	BU
1991 Proof	—	Value: 28.50				

X# 142 25 DOLLARS

31.1341 g., 0.9990 Silver 0.9999 oz. ASW, 38.95 mm. **Ruler:** Prince Leonard **Obv:** Crown over value on native design **Rev:** U.S. F-14 Tomcat Jet Fighter **Edge:** Reeded

Date	Mintage	F	VF	XF	Unc	BU
1991 Proof	—	Value: 28.50				

X# 143 25 DOLLARS
31.1341 g., 0.9990 Silver 0.9999 oz. ASW, 38.95 mm. **Ruler:** Prince Leonard **Obv:** Crown over value on native design **Rev:** U.S. M60A3 Tank **Edge:** Reeded

Date	Mintage	F	VF	XF	Unc	BU
1991 Proof	—	Value: 28.50				

X# 144 25 DOLLARS
31.1341 g., 0.9990 Silver 0.9999 oz. ASW, 38.95 mm. **Ruler:** Prince Leonard **Obv:** Crown over value on native design **Rev:** U.S. Army Mortar Attack **Edge:** Reeded

Date	Mintage	F	VF	XF	Unc	BU
1991 Proof	—	Value: 28.50				

X# 145 25 DOLLARS
31.1341 g., 0.9990 Silver 0.9999 oz. ASW, 38.95 mm. **Ruler:** Prince Leonard **Obv:** Crown over value on native design **Rev:** U.S. "Dragon" Anti-tank weapon **Edge:** Reeded

Date	Mintage	F	VF	XF	Unc	BU
1991 Proof	—	Value: 28.50				

X# 146 25 DOLLARS
31.1341 g., 0.9990 Silver 0.9999 oz. ASW, 38.95 mm. **Ruler:** Prince Leonard **Obv:** Crown over value on native design **Rev:** U.S. F-16C "Fighting Falcon" Jet Fighter **Edge:** Reeded

Date	Mintage	F	VF	XF	Unc	BU
1991 Proof	—	Value: 28.50				

X# 147 25 DOLLARS
31.1341 g., 0.9990 Silver 0.9999 oz. ASW, 38.95 mm. **Ruler:** Prince Leonard **Obv:** Crown over value on native design **Rev:** U.S. Multi-launch Rocket System **Edge:** Reeded

Date	Mintage	F	VF	XF	Unc	BU
1991 Proof	—	Value: 28.50				

X# 148 25 DOLLARS
31.1341 g., 0.9990 Silver 0.9999 oz. ASW, 38.95 mm. **Ruler:** Prince Leonard **Obv:** Crown over value on native design **Rev:** Chemical warfare **Edge:** Reeded

Date	Mintage	F	VF	XF	Unc	BU
1991 Proof	—	Value: 28.50				

X# 149 25 DOLLARS
31.1341 g., 0.9990 Silver 0.9999 oz. ASW, 38.95 mm. **Ruler:** Prince Leonard **Obv:** Crown over value on native design **Rev:** Submarines, the "Silent Service" **Edge:** Reeded

Date	Mintage	F	VF	XF	Unc	BU
1991 Proof	—	Value: 28.50				

X# 150 25 DOLLARS
31.1341 g., 0.9990 Silver 0.9999 oz. ASW, 38.95 mm. **Ruler:** Prince Leonard **Obv:** Crown over value on native design **Rev:** U.S. F-15E "Strike Eagle" Jet Fighter **Edge:** Reeded

Date	Mintage	F	VF	XF	Unc	BU
1991 Proof	—	Value: 28.50				

X# 151 25 DOLLARS
31.1341 g., 0.9990 Silver 0.9999 oz. ASW, 38.95 mm. **Ruler:** Prince Leonard **Obv:** Crown over value on native design **Rev:** U.S. M-1198 155mm Towed Howitzer **Edge:** Reeded

Date	Mintage	F	VF	XF	Unc	BU
1991 Proof	—	Value: 28.50				

X# 152 25 DOLLARS
31.1341 g., 0.9990 Silver 0.9999 oz. ASW, 38.95 mm. **Ruler:** Prince Leonard **Obv:** Crown over value on native design **Rev:** Top Secret War **Edge:** Reeded

Date	Mintage	F	VF	XF	Unc	BU
1991 Proof	—	Value: 28.50				

X# 153 25 DOLLARS
31.1341 g., 0.9990 Silver 0.9999 oz. ASW, 38.95 mm. **Ruler:** Prince Leonard **Obv:** Crown over value on native design **Rev:** U.S. MIM-23 "Hawk" Surface To Air Guided Missile **Edge:** Reeded

Date	Mintage	F	VF	XF	Unc	BU
1991 Proof	—	Value: 28.50				

X# 154 25 DOLLARS
31.1341 g., 0.9990 Silver 0.9999 oz. ASW, 38.95 mm. **Ruler:** Prince Leonard **Obv:** Crown over value on native design **Rev:** English AV-8B "Harrier" Jump Jet **Edge:** Reeded

Date	Mintage	F	VF	XF	Unc	BU
1991 Proof	—	Value: 28.50				

X# 155 25 DOLLARS
31.1341 g., 0.9990 Silver 0.9999 oz. ASW, 38.95 mm. **Ruler:** Prince Leonard **Obv:** Crown over value on native design **Rev:** U.S. M-998 "Hummer" (HMMWV) **Edge:** Reeded

Date	Mintage	F	VF	XF	Unc	BU
1991 Proof	—	Value: 28.50				

X# 156 25 DOLLARS
31.1341 g., 0.9990 Silver 0.9999 oz. ASW, 38.95 mm. **Ruler:** Prince Leonard **Obv:** Crown over value on native design **Rev:** U.S. Coast Guard Support **Edge:** Reeded

Date	Mintage	F	VF	XF	Unc	BU
1991 Proof	—	Value: 28.50				

X# 157 25 DOLLARS
31.1341 g., 0.9990 Silver 0.9999 oz. ASW, 38.95 mm. **Ruler:** Prince Leonard **Obv:** Crown over value on native design **Rev:** U.S. FIM-91A "Stinger" Anti-aircraft Missile System **Edge:** Reeded

Date	Mintage	F	VF	XF	Unc	BU
1991 Proof	—	Value: 28.50				

X# 158 25 DOLLARS
31.1341 g., 0.9990 Silver 0.9999 oz. ASW, 38.95 mm. **Ruler:** Prince Leonard **Obv:** Crown over value on native design **Rev:** U.S. F-18 "Hornet" Jet Fighter **Edge:** Reeded

Date	Mintage	F	VF	XF	Unc	BU
1991 Proof	—	Value: 28.50				

X# 159 25 DOLLARS
31.1341 g., 0.9990 Silver 0.9999 oz. ASW, 38.95 mm. **Ruler:** Prince Leonard **Obv:** Crown over value on native design **Rev:** U.S. M-109 Self-propelled Howitzer **Edge:** Reeded

Date	Mintage	F	VF	XF	Unc	BU
1991 Proof	—	Value: 28.50				

X# 160 25 DOLLARS
31.1341 g., 0.9990 Silver 0.9999 oz. ASW, 38.95 mm. **Ruler:** Prince Leonard **Obv:** Crown over value on native design **Rev:** U.S. Tactical Missile Systems (TACMS) **Edge:** Reeded

Date	Mintage	F	VF	XF	Unc	BU
1991 Proof	—	Value: 28.50				

X# 161 25 DOLLARS
31.1341 g., 0.9990 Silver 0.9999 oz. ASW, 38.95 mm. **Ruler:** Prince Leonard **Obv:** Crown over value on native design **Rev:** U.S. Tiger Anti-tank Brigade **Edge:** Reeded

Date	Mintage	F	VF	XF	Unc	BU
1991 Proof	—	Value: 28.50				

X# 162 25 DOLLARS
31.1341 g., 0.9990 Silver 0.9999 oz. ASW, 38.95 mm. **Ruler:** Prince Leonard **Obv:** Crown over value on native design **Rev:** U.S. Hughes "Cobra" Helicopter ("Huey") **Edge:** Reeded

Date	Mintage	F	VF	XF	Unc	BU
1991 Proof	—	Value: 28.50				

X# 163 25 DOLLARS
31.1341 g., 0.9990 Silver 0.9999 oz. ASW, 38.95 mm. **Ruler:** Prince Leonard **Obv:** Crown over value on native design **Rev:** Desert Patrol **Edge:** Reeded

Date	Mintage	F	VF	XF	Unc	BU
1991 Proof	—	Value: 28.50				

X# 164 25 DOLLARS
31.1341 g., 0.9990 Silver 0.9999 oz. ASW, 38.95 mm. **Ruler:** Prince Leonard **Obv:** Crown over value on native design **Rev:** U.S. E-3 "Sentry" (AWACS) **Edge:** Reeded

Date	Mintage	F	VF	XF	Unc	BU
1991 Proof	—	Value: 28.50				

X# 165 25 DOLLARS
31.1341 g., 0.9990 Silver 0.9999 oz. ASW, 38.95 mm. **Ruler:** Prince Leonard **Obv:** Crown over value on native design **Rev:** Coming Home **Edge:** Reeded

Date	Mintage	F	VF	XF	Unc	BU
1991 Proof	—	Value: 28.50				

World War II Series

X# 167 5 DOLLARS
Copper-Nickel-Zinc, 39 mm. **Ruler:** Prince Leonard **Obv:** Crown over value on native design **Rev:** Air Battle of Britain **Edge:** Reeded

Date	Mintage	F	VF	XF	Unc	BU
1992	—	—	—	—	6.00	—

X# 168 5 DOLLARS
Copper-Nickel-Zinc, 39 mm. **Ruler:** Prince Leonard **Obv:** Crown over value on native design **Rev:** Sinking of the German battleship Bismark **Edge:** Reeded

Date	Mintage	F	VF	XF	Unc	BU
1992	—	—	—	—	6.00	—

X# 169 5 DOLLARS
Copper-Nickel-Zinc, 39 mm. **Ruler:** Prince Leonard **Obv:** Crown over value on native design **Rev:** U.S.M.C. "Black Sheep" Squadron **Edge:** Reeded

Date	Mintage	F	VF	XF	Unc	BU
1992	—	—	—	—	6.00	—

X# 170 5 DOLLARS
Copper-Nickel-Zinc, 39 mm. **Ruler:** Prince Leonard **Obv:** Crown over value on native design **Rev:** North African campaign **Edge:** Reeded

Date	Mintage	F	VF	XF	Unc	BU
1992	—	—	—	—	6.00	—

X# 171 5 DOLLARS
Copper-Nickel-Zinc, 39 mm. **Ruler:** Prince Leonard **Obv:** Crown over value on native design **Rev:** Attack on Pearl Harbor **Edge:** Reeded

Date	Mintage	F	VF	XF	Unc	BU
1992	—	—	—	—	6.00	—

X# 172 5 DOLLARS
Copper-Nickel-Zinc, 39 mm. **Ruler:** Prince Leonard **Obv:** Crown over value on native design **Rev:** Battle of the North Atlantic **Edge:** Reeded

Date	Mintage	F	VF	XF	Unc	BU
1992	—	—	—	—	6.00	—

X# 173 5 DOLLARS
Copper-Nickel-Zinc, 39 mm. **Ruler:** Prince Leonard **Obv:** Crown over value on native design **Rev:** CBI Theatre - Flying Tigers **Edge:** Reeded

Date	Mintage	F	VF	XF	Unc	BU
1992	—	—	—	—	6.00	—

X# 174 5 DOLLARS
Copper-Nickel-Zinc, 39 mm. **Ruler:** Prince Leonard **Obv:** Crown over value on native design **Rev:** Coast Guard Commando Raid **Edge:** Reeded

Date	Mintage	F	VF	XF	Unc	BU
1992	—	—	—	—	6.00	—

X# 175 5 DOLLARS
Copper-Nickel-Zinc, 39 mm. **Ruler:** Prince Leonard **Obv:** Crown over value on native design **Rev:** Lt. Col. Doolittle's Air Raid on Tokyo **Edge:** Reeded

Date	Mintage	F	VF	XF	Unc	BU
1992	—	—	—	—	6.00	—

X# 176 5 DOLLARS
Copper-Nickel-Zinc, 39 mm. **Ruler:** Prince Leonard **Obv:** Crown over value on native design **Rev:** Flying the "Hump" supplying China **Edge:** Reeded

Date	Mintage	F	VF	XF	Unc	BU
1992	—	—	—	—	6.00	—

X# 177 5 DOLLARS
Copper-Nickel-Zinc, 39 mm. **Ruler:** Prince Leonard **Obv:** Crown over value on native design **Rev:** Battle of Midway **Edge:** Reeded

Date	Mintage	F	VF	XF	Unc	BU
1992	—	—	—	—	6.00	—

X# 178 5 DOLLARS
Copper-Nickel-Zinc, 39 mm. **Ruler:** Prince Leonard **Obv:** Crown over value on native design **Rev:** Air Rescue at Sea **Edge:** Reeded

Date	Mintage	F	VF	XF	Unc	BU
1992	—	—	—	—	6.00	—

X# 179 5 DOLLARS
Copper-Nickel-Zinc, 39 mm. **Ruler:** Prince Leonard **Obv:** Crown over value on native design **Rev:** Battle of Guadalcanal **Edge:** Reeded

Date	Mintage	F	VF	XF	Unc	BU
1992	—	—	—	—	6.00	—

X# 180 5 DOLLARS
Copper-Nickel-Zinc, 39 mm. **Ruler:** Prince Leonard **Obv:** Crown over value on native design **Rev:** Sting of the Mosquito Boats **Edge:** Reeded

Date	Mintage	F	VF	XF	Unc	BU
1992	—	—	—	—	6.00	—

X# 181 5 DOLLARS
Copper-Nickel-Zinc, 39 mm. **Ruler:** Prince Leonard **Obv:** Crown over value on native design **Rev:** Battle for Burma **Edge:** Reeded

Date	Mintage	F	VF	XF	Unc	BU
1992	—	—	—	—	6.00	—

X# 182 5 DOLLARS
Copper-Nickel-Zinc, 39 mm. **Ruler:** Prince Leonard **Obv:** Crown over value on native design **Rev:** Alaska at War **Edge:** Reeded

Date	Mintage	F	VF	XF	Unc	BU
1992	—	—	—	—	6.00	—

X# 183 5 DOLLARS

Copper-Nickel-Zinc, 39 mm. **Ruler:** Prince Leonard **Obv:** Crown over value on native design **Rev:** Air war over Europe **Edge:** Reeded

Date	Mintage	F	VF	XF	Unc	BU
1992	—	—	—	—	6.00	—

X# 184 5 DOLLARS

Copper-Nickel-Zinc, 39 mm. **Ruler:** Prince Leonard **Obv:** Crown over value on native design **Rev:** Bombing Ploest Oil Refineries **Edge:** Reeded

Date	Mintage	F	VF	XF	Unc	BU
1992	—	—	—	—	6.00	—

X# 185 5 DOLLARS

Copper-Nickel-Zinc, 39 mm. **Ruler:** Prince Leonard **Obv:** Crown over value on native design **Rev:** Battle of the Bismark Sea **Edge:** Reeded

Date	Mintage	F	VF	XF	Unc	BU
1992	—	—	—	—	6.00	—

X# 186 5 DOLLARS

Copper-Nickel-Zinc, 39 mm. **Ruler:** Prince Leonard **Obv:** Crown over value on native design **Rev:** Downing of Admiral Yamamoto **Edge:** Reeded

Date	Mintage	F	VF	XF	Unc	BU
1992	—	—	—	—	6.00	—

X# 187 5 DOLLARS

Copper-Nickel-Zinc, 39 mm. **Ruler:** Prince Leonard **Obv:** Crown over value on native design **Rev:** Landing on the Marshall Islands **Edge:** Reeded

Date	Mintage	F	VF	XF	Unc	BU
1992	—	—	—	—	6.00	—

X# 188 5 DOLLARS

Copper-Nickel-Zinc, 39 mm. **Ruler:** Prince Leonard **Obv:** Crown over value on native design **Rev:** B-17 Flying Fortress forging victory **Edge:** Reeded

Date	Mintage	F	VF	XF	Unc	BU
1992	—	—	—	—	6.00	—

X# 193 5 DOLLARS

Copper-Nickel-Zinc, 39 mm. **Ruler:** Prince Leonard **Obv:** Crown over value on native design **Rev:** Operation Overlord - D-Day Landings **Edge:** Reeded

Date	Mintage	F	VF	XF	Unc	BU
1992	—	—	—	—	6.00	—

X# 189 5 DOLLARS

Copper-Nickel-Zinc, 39 mm. **Ruler:** Prince Leonard **Obv:** Crown over value on native design **Rev:** U.S.M.C. landing on Leyte Island **Edge:** Reeded

Date	Mintage	F	VF	XF	Unc	BU
1992	—	—	—	—	6.00	—

X# 190 5 DOLLARS

Copper-Nickel-Zinc, 39 mm. **Ruler:** Prince Leonard **Obv:** Crown over value on native design **Rev:** Battle of Leyte Gulf **Edge:** Reeded

Date	Mintage	F	VF	XF	Unc	BU
1992	—	—	—	—	6.00	—

X# 191 5 DOLLARS

Copper-Nickel-Zinc, 39 mm. **Ruler:** Prince Leonard **Obv:** Crown over value on native design **Rev:** Glider Landings in Normandy **Edge:** Reeded

Date	Mintage	F	VF	XF	Unc	BU
1992	—	—	—	—	6.00	—

X# 192 5 DOLLARS

Copper-Nickel-Zinc, 39 mm. **Ruler:** Prince Leonard **Obv:** Crown over value on native design **Rev:** Battle for Omaha Beach **Edge:** Reeded

Date	Mintage	F	VF	XF	Unc	BU
1992	—	—	—	—	6.00	—

X# 194 5 DOLLARS

Copper-Nickel-Zinc, 39 mm. **Ruler:** Prince Leonard **Obv:** Crown over value on native design **Rev:** Battle of the Philippine Sea **Edge:** Reeded

Date	Mintage	F	VF	XF	Unc	BU
1992	—	—	—	—	6.00	—

X# 195 5 DOLLARS
Copper-Nickel-Zinc, 39 mm. **Ruler:** Prince Leonard **Obv:** Crown over value on native design **Rev:** Break-out at Saint Lo, France **Edge:** Reeded

Date	Mintage	F	VF	XF	Unc	BU
1992	—	—	—	—	6.00	—

X# 196 5 DOLLARS
Copper-Nickel-Zinc, 39 mm. **Ruler:** Prince Leonard **Obv:** Crown over value on native design **Rev:** Capture of Cherbourg **Edge:** Reeded

Date	Mintage	F	VF	XF	Unc	BU
1992	—	—	—	—	6.00	—

X# 197 5 DOLLARS
Copper-Nickel-Zinc, 39 mm. **Ruler:** Prince Leonard **Subject:** World War II **Obv:** Crown over value on native design **Rev:** Bridge at Remagen **Edge:** Reeded

Date	Mintage	F	VF	XF	Unc	BU
1992	—	—	—	—	6.00	—

X# 198 5 DOLLARS
Copper-Nickel-Zinc, 39 mm. **Ruler:** Prince Leonard **Obv:** Crown over value on native design **Rev:** Submarine Warfare in the Pacific **Edge:** Reeded

Date	Mintage	F	VF	XF	Unc	BU
1992	—	—	—	—	6.00	—

X# 199 5 DOLLARS
Copper-Nickel-Zinc, 39 mm. **Ruler:** Prince Leonard **Obv:** Crown over value on native design **Rev:** Mustang Fighters Flying Cover on Bombay missions **Edge:** Reeded

Date	Mintage	F	VF	XF	Unc	BU
1992	—	—	—	—	6.00	—

X# 200 5 DOLLARS
Copper-Nickel-Zinc, 39 mm. **Ruler:** Prince Leonard **Obv:** Crown over value on native design **Rev:** Battle for Monte Cassino in Italy **Edge:** Reeded

Date	Mintage	F	VF	XF	Unc	BU
1992	—	—	—	—	6.00	—

X# 201 5 DOLLARS
Copper-Nickel-Zinc, 39 mm. **Ruler:** Prince Leonard **Obv:** Crown over value on native design **Rev:** Battered Bastards of Bastogne - General McAuliffe's reply of "Nuts!" **Edge:** Reeded

Date	Mintage	F	VF	XF	Unc	BU
1992	—	—	—	—	6.00	—

X# 202 5 DOLLARS
Copper-Nickel-Zinc, 39 mm. **Ruler:** Prince Leonard **Obv:** Crown over value on native design **Rev:** Battle of the Bulge **Edge:** Reeded

Date	Mintage	F	VF	XF	Unc	BU
1992	—	—	—	—	6.00	—

X# 203 5 DOLLARS
Copper-Nickel-Zinc, 39 mm. **Ruler:** Prince Leonard **Obv:** Crown over value on native design **Rev:** V-1 "buzz" bombs over Britain **Edge:** Reeded

Date	Mintage	F	VF	XF	Unc	BU
1992	—	—	—	—	6.00	—

X# 204 5 DOLLARS
Copper-Nickel-Zinc, 39 mm. **Ruler:** Prince Leonard **Obv:** Crown over value on native design **Rev:** General MacArthur's Return to the Philippine Islands **Edge:** Reeded

Date	Mintage	F	VF	XF	Unc	BU
1992	—	—	—	—	6.00	—

X# 205 5 DOLLARS
Copper-Nickel-Zinc, 39 mm. **Ruler:** Prince Leonard **Obv:** Crown over value on native design **Rev:** Fight for Iwo Jima - Flagraising on Mt. Suribachi **Edge:** Reeded

Date	Mintage	F	VF	XF	Unc	BU
1992	—	—	—	—	6.00	—

X# 206 5 DOLLARS
Copper-Nickel-Zinc, 39 mm. **Ruler:** Prince Leonard **Obv:** Crown over value on native design **Rev:** Landings on Okinawa **Edge:** Reeded

Date	Mintage	F	VF	XF	Unc	BU
1992	—	—	—	—	6.00	—

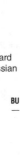

X# 207 5 DOLLARS
Copper-Nickel-Zinc, 39 mm. **Ruler:** Prince Leonard **Obv:** Crown over value on native design **Rev:** Russian and American troops link up at the Elbe River **Edge:** Reeded

Date	Mintage	F	VF	XF	Unc	BU
1992	—	—	—	—	6.00	—

X# 208 5 DOLLARS
Copper-Nickel-Zinc, 39 mm. **Ruler:** Prince Leonard **Obv:** Crown over value on native design **Rev:** Kamikaze - Flying Bomb **Edge:** Reeded

Date	Mintage	F	VF	XF	Unc	BU
1992	—	—	—	—	6.00	—

X# 209 5 DOLLARS
Copper-Nickel-Zinc, 39 mm. **Ruler:** Prince Leonard **Obv:** Crown over value on native design **Rev:** Search and Rescue Helicopter **Edge:** Reeded

Date	Mintage	F	VF	XF	Unc	BU
1992	—	—	—	—	6.00	—

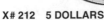

X# 210 5 DOLLARS
Copper-Nickel-Zinc, 39 mm. **Ruler:** Prince Leonard **Obv:** Crown over value on native design **Rev:** Releasing the Atomic Bomb - Euola Gay Mission **Edge:** Reeded

Date	Mintage	F	VF	XF	Unc	BU
1992	—	—	—	—	6.00	—

X# 211 5 DOLLARS
Copper-Nickel-Zinc, 39 mm. **Ruler:** Prince Leonard **Obv:** Crown over value on native design **Rev:** VJ Day - Surrender signing aboard U.S.S. Missouri **Edge:** Reeded

Date	Mintage	F	VF	XF	Unc	BU
1992	—	—	—	—	6.00	—

X# 212 5 DOLLARS
Copper-Nickel-Zinc, 39 mm. **Ruler:** Prince Leonard **Obv:** Crown over value on native design **Rev:** Liberty standing facing holding torch and shield **Edge:** Reeded

Date	Mintage	F	VF	XF	Unc	BU
ND(1992)	—	—	—	—	6.00	—

X# 257 10 DOLLARS
Brass, 44 mm. **Ruler:** Prince Leonard **Obv:** Crown over value on native design **Obv. Designer:** Hal Reed **Rev:** Air Battle of Britain **Edge:** Reeded

Date	Mintage	F	VF	XF	Unc	BU
ND(1995)	—	—	—	—	10.00	—

X# 258 10 DOLLARS
Brass, 44 mm. **Ruler:** Prince Leonard **Obv:** Crown over value on native design **Obv. Designer:** Hal Reed **Rev:** Sinking of the German battleship Bismark **Edge:** Reeded

Date	Mintage	F	VF	XF	Unc	BU
ND(1995)	—	—	—	—	10.00	—

X# 259 10 DOLLARS
Brass, 44 mm. **Ruler:** Prince Leonard **Obv:** Crown over value on native design **Obv. Designer:** Hal Reed **Rev:** U.S.M.C. "Black Sheep" Squadron **Edge:** Reeded

Date	Mintage	F	VF	XF	Unc	BU
ND(1995)	—	—	—	—	10.00	—

X# 260 10 DOLLARS
Brass, 44 mm. **Ruler:** Prince Leonard **Obv:** Crown over value on native design **Obv. Designer:** Hal Reed **Rev:** North African campaign **Edge:** Reeded

Date	Mintage	F	VF	XF	Unc	BU
ND(1995)	—	—	—	—	10.00	—

X# 261 10 DOLLARS
Brass, 44 mm. **Ruler:** Prince Leonard **Obv:** Crown over value on native design **Obv. Designer:** Hal Reed **Rev:** Attack on Pearl Harbor **Edge:** Reeded

Date	Mintage	F	VF	XF	Unc	BU
ND(1995)	—	—	—	—	10.00	—

X# 262 10 DOLLARS
Brass, 44 mm. **Ruler:** Prince Leonard **Obv:** Crown over value on native design **Obv. Designer:** Hal Reed **Rev:** Battle of the North Atlantic **Edge:** Reeded

Date	Mintage	F	VF	XF	Unc	BU
ND(1995)	—	—	—	—	10.00	—

X# 263 10 DOLLARS
Brass, 44 mm. **Ruler:** Prince Leonard **Obv:** Crown over value on native design **Obv. Designer:** Hal Reed **Rev:** CBI Theatre - Flying Tigers **Edge:** Reeded

Date	Mintage	F	VF	XF	Unc	BU
ND(1995)	—	—	—	—	10.00	—

X# 264 10 DOLLARS
Brass, 44 mm. **Ruler:** Prince Leonard **Obv:** Crown over value on native design **Obv. Designer:** Hal Reed **Rev:** Coast Guard Commando Raid **Edge:** Reeded

Date	Mintage	F	VF	XF	Unc	BU
ND(1995)	—	—	—	—	10.00	—

X# 265 10 DOLLARS
Brass, 44 mm. **Ruler:** Prince Leonard **Obv:** Crown over value on native design **Obv. Designer:** Hal Reed **Rev:** Lt. Col. Doolittle's Air Raid on Tokyo **Edge:** Reeded

Date	Mintage	F	VF	XF	Unc	BU
ND(1995)	—	—	—	—	10.00	—

X# 266 10 DOLLARS
Brass, 44 mm. **Ruler:** Prince Leonard **Obv:** Crown over value on native design **Obv. Designer:** Hal Reed **Rev:** Flying the "Hump" supplying China **Edge:** Reeded

Date	Mintage	F	VF	XF	Unc	BU
ND(1995)	—	—	—	—	10.00	—

X# 267 10 DOLLARS
Brass, 44 mm. **Ruler:** Prince Leonard **Obv:** Crown over value on native design **Obv. Designer:** Hal Reed **Rev:** Battle of Midway **Edge:** Reeded

Date	Mintage	F	VF	XF	Unc	BU
ND(1995)	—	—	—	—	10.00	—

X# 268 10 DOLLARS
Brass, 44 mm. **Ruler:** Prince Leonard **Obv:** Crown over value on native design **Obv. Designer:** Hal Reed **Rev:** Air Rescue at Sea **Edge:** Reeded

Date	Mintage	F	VF	XF	Unc	BU
ND(1995)	—	—	—	—	10.00	—

X# 269 10 DOLLARS
Brass, 44 mm. **Ruler:** Prince Leonard **Obv:** Crown over value on native design **Obv. Designer:** Hal Reed **Rev:** Battle of Guadalcanal **Edge:** Reeded

Date	Mintage	F	VF	XF	Unc	BU
ND(1995)	—	—	—	—	10.00	—

X# 270 10 DOLLARS
Brass, 44 mm. **Ruler:** Prince Leonard **Obv:** Crown over value on native design **Obv. Designer:** Hal Reed **Rev:** Sting of the Mosquito Boats **Edge:** Reeded

Date	Mintage	F	VF	XF	Unc	BU
ND(1995)	—	—	—	—	10.00	—

X# 271 10 DOLLARS
Brass, 44 mm. **Ruler:** Prince Leonard **Obv:** Crown over value on native design **Obv. Designer:** Hal Reed **Rev:** Battle for Burma **Edge:** Reeded

Date	Mintage	F	VF	XF	Unc	BU
ND(1995)	—	—	—	—	10.00	—

X# 272 10 DOLLARS
Brass, 44 mm. **Ruler:** Prince Leonard **Obv:** Crown over value on native design **Obv. Designer:** Hal Reed **Rev:** Alaska at war **Edge:** Reeded

Date	Mintage	F	VF	XF	Unc	BU
ND(1995)	—	—	—	—	10.00	—

X# 273 10 DOLLARS
Brass, 44 mm. **Ruler:** Prince Leonard **Obv:** Crown over value on native design **Obv. Designer:** Hal Reed **Rev:** Air war over Europe **Edge:** Reeded

Date	Mintage	F	VF	XF	Unc	BU
ND(1995)	—	—	—	—	10.00	—

X# 274 10 DOLLARS
Brass, 44 mm. **Ruler:** Prince Leonard **Obv:** Crown over value on native design **Obv. Designer:** Hal Reed **Rev:** Bombing Ploest Oil Refneries **Edge:** Reeded

Date	Mintage	F	VF	XF	Unc	BU
ND(1995)	—	—	—	—	10.00	—

X# 275 10 DOLLARS

Brass, 44 mm. **Ruler:** Prince Leonard **Obv:** Crown over value on native design **Obv. Designer:** Hal Reed **Rev:** Battle of the Bismark Sea **Edge:** Reeded

Date	Mintage	F	VF	XF	Unc	BU
ND(1995)	—	—	—	—	10.00	—

X# 276 10 DOLLARS

Brass, 44 mm. **Ruler:** Prince Leonard **Obv:** Crown over value on native design **Obv. Designer:** Hal Reed **Rev:** Downing of Admiral Yamamoto **Edge:** Reeded

Date	Mintage	F	VF	XF	Unc	BU
ND(1995)	—	—	—	—	10.00	—

X# 277 10 DOLLARS

Brass, 44 mm. **Ruler:** Prince Leonard **Obv:** Crown over value on native design **Obv. Designer:** Hal Reed **Rev:** Landing on the Marshall Islands **Edge:** Reeded

Date	Mintage	F	VF	XF	Unc	BU
ND(1995)	—	—	—	—	10.00	—

X# 278 10 DOLLARS

Brass, 44 mm. **Ruler:** Prince Leonard **Obv:** Crown over value on native design **Obv. Designer:** Hal Reed **Rev:** B-17 Flying Fortress forging victory **Edge:** Reeded

Date	Mintage	F	VF	XF	Unc	BU
ND(1995)	—	—	—	—	10.00	—

X# 279 10 DOLLARS

Brass, 44 mm. **Ruler:** Prince Leonard **Obv:** Crown over value on native design **Obv. Designer:** Hal Reed **Rev:** U.S.M.C. landing on Leyte Island **Edge:** Reeded

Date	Mintage	F	VF	XF	Unc	BU
ND(1995)	—	—	—	—	10.00	—

X# 280 10 DOLLARS

Brass, 44 mm. **Ruler:** Prince Leonard **Obv:** Crown over value on native design **Obv. Designer:** Hal Reed **Rev:** Battle of Leyte Gulf **Edge:** Reeded

Date	Mintage	F	VF	XF	Unc	BU
ND(1995)	—	—	—	—	10.00	—

X# 281 10 DOLLARS

Brass, 44 mm. **Ruler:** Prince Leonard **Obv:** Crown over value on native design **Obv. Designer:** Hal Reed **Rev:** Glider Landings in Normandy **Edge:** Reeded

Date	Mintage	F	VF	XF	Unc	BU
ND(1995)	—	—	—	—	10.00	—

X# 282 10 DOLLARS

Brass, 44 mm. **Ruler:** Prince Leonard **Obv:** Crown over value on native design **Obv. Designer:** Hal Reed **Rev:** Battle for Omaha Beach **Edge:** Reeded

Date	Mintage	F	VF	XF	Unc	BU
ND(1995)	—	—	—	—	10.00	—

X# 283 10 DOLLARS

Brass, 44 mm. **Ruler:** Prince Leonard **Obv:** Crown over value on native design **Obv. Designer:** Hal Reed **Rev:** Operation Overlord - D-Day Landings **Edge:** Reeded

Date	Mintage	F	VF	XF	Unc	BU
ND(1995)	—	—	—	—	10.00	—

X# 284 10 DOLLARS

Brass, 44 mm. **Ruler:** Prince Leonard **Obv:** Crown over value on native design **Obv. Designer:** Hal Reed **Rev:** Battle of the Philippine Sea **Edge:** Reeded

Date	Mintage	F	VF	XF	Unc	BU
ND(1995)	—	—	—	—	10.00	—

X# 285 10 DOLLARS

Brass, 44 mm. **Ruler:** Prince Leonard **Obv:** Crown over value on native design **Obv. Designer:** Hal Reed **Rev:** Break-out at Saint Lo, France **Edge:** Reeded

Date	Mintage	F	VF	XF	Unc	BU
ND(1995)	—	—	—	—	10.00	—

X# 286 10 DOLLARS

Brass, 44 mm. **Ruler:** Prince Leonard **Obv:** Crown over value on native design **Obv. Designer:** Hal Reed **Rev:** Capture of Cherbourg **Edge:** Reeded

Date	Mintage	F	VF	XF	Unc	BU
ND(1995)	—	—	—	—	10.00	—

X# 287 10 DOLLARS

Brass, 44 mm. **Ruler:** Prince Leonard **Obv:** Crown over value on native design **Obv. Designer:** Hal Reed **Rev:** Bridge at Remagen **Edge:** Reeded

Date	Mintage	F	VF	XF	Unc	BU
ND(1995)	—	—	—	—	10.00	—

X# 288 10 DOLLARS

Brass, 44 mm. **Ruler:** Prince Leonard **Obv:** Crown over value on native design **Obv. Designer:** Hal Reed **Rev:** Submarine Warfare in the Pacific **Edge:** Reeded

Date	Mintage	F	VF	XF	Unc	BU
ND(1995)	—	—	—	—	10.00	—

X# 289 10 DOLLARS

Brass, 44 mm. **Ruler:** Prince Leonard **Obv:** Crown over value on native design **Obv. Designer:** Hal Reed **Rev:** Mustang Fighters Flying Cover on bombing missions **Edge:** Reeded

Date	Mintage	F	VF	XF	Unc	BU
ND(1995)	—	—	—	—	10.00	—

X# 290 10 DOLLARS

Brass, 44 mm. **Ruler:** Prince Leonard **Obv:** Crown over value on native design **Obv. Designer:** Hal Reed **Rev:** Battle for Monte Cassino in Italy **Edge:** Reeded

Date	Mintage	F	VF	XF	Unc	BU
ND(1995)	—	—	—	—	10.00	—

X# 291 10 DOLLARS

Brass, 44 mm. **Ruler:** Prince Leonard **Obv:** Crown over value on native design **Obv. Designer:** Hal Reed **Rev:** Battered Bastards of Bastogne - General McAuliffe's reply of "Nuts!" **Edge:** Reeded

Date	Mintage	F	VF	XF	Unc	BU
ND(1995)	—	—	—	—	10.00	—

X# 292 10 DOLLARS

Brass, 44 mm. **Ruler:** Prince Leonard **Obv:** Crown over value on native design **Obv. Designer:** Hal Reed **Rev:** Battle of the Bulge **Edge:** Reeded

Date	Mintage	F	VF	XF	Unc	BU
ND(1995)	—	—	—	—	10.00	—

X# 293 10 DOLLARS

Brass, 44 mm. **Ruler:** Prince Leonard **Obv:** Crown over value on native design **Obv. Designer:** Hal Reed **Rev:** V-1 "buzz" bombs over Britain **Edge:** Reeded

Date	Mintage	F	VF	XF	Unc	BU
ND(1995)	—	—	—	—	10.00	—

X# 294 10 DOLLARS

Brass, 44 mm. **Ruler:** Prince Leonard **Obv:** Crown over value on native design **Obv. Designer:** Hal Reed **Rev:** General MacArthur's return to the Philippine Islands **Edge:** Reeded

Date	Mintage	F	VF	XF	Unc	BU
ND(1995)	—	—	—	—	10.00	—

X# 295 10 DOLLARS

Brass, 44 mm. **Ruler:** Prince Leonard **Obv:** Crown over value on native design **Obv. Designer:** Hal Reed **Rev:** Fight for Iwo Jima - Flagraising on Mt. Suribachi **Edge:** Reeded

Date	Mintage	F	VF	XF	Unc	BU
ND(1995)	—	—	—	—	10.00	—

X# 296 10 DOLLARS

Brass, 44 mm. **Ruler:** Prince Leonard **Obv:** Crown over value on native design **Obv. Designer:** Hal Reed **Rev:** Landings on Okinawa **Edge:** Reeded

Date	Mintage	F	VF	XF	Unc	BU
ND(1995)	—	—	—	—	10.00	—

X# 297 10 DOLLARS

Brass, 44 mm. **Ruler:** Prince Leonard **Obv:** Crown over value on native design **Obv. Designer:** Hal Reed **Rev:** Russian and American troops link up at the Elbe River **Edge:** Reeded

Date	Mintage	F	VF	XF	Unc	BU
ND(1995)	—	—	—	—	10.00	—

X# 298 10 DOLLARS

Brass, 44 mm. **Ruler:** Prince Leonard **Obv:** Crown over value on native design **Obv. Designer:** Hal Reed **Rev:** Kamikaze - Flying Bomb **Edge:** Reeded

Date	Mintage	F	VF	XF	Unc	BU
ND(1995)	—	—	—	—	10.00	—

X# 299 10 DOLLARS

Brass, 44 mm. **Ruler:** Prince Leonard **Obv:** Crown over value on native design **Obv. Designer:** Hal Reed **Rev:** Search and Rescue Helicopter **Edge:** Reeded

Date	Mintage	F	VF	XF	Unc	BU
ND(1995)	—	—	—	—	10.00	—

X# 300 10 DOLLARS

Brass, 44 mm. **Ruler:** Prince Leonard **Obv:** Crown over value on native design **Obv. Designer:** Hal Reed **Rev:** Releasing the Atomic Bomb - Enola Gay Mission **Edge:** Reeded

Date	Mintage	F	VF	XF	Unc	BU
ND(1995)	—	—	—	—	10.00	—

X# 301 10 DOLLARS

Brass, 44 mm. **Ruler:** Prince Leonard **Obv:** Crown over value on native design **Obv. Designer:** Hal Reed **Rev:** VJ Day - Surrender signing aboard the U.S.S. Missouri **Edge:** Reeded

Date	Mintage	F	VF	XF	Unc	BU
ND(1995)	—	—	—	—	10.00	—

X# 302 10 DOLLARS

Brass, 44 mm. **Ruler:** Prince Leonard **Obv:** Crown over value on native design **Obv. Designer:** Hal Reed **Rev:** Liberty standing facing holding torch and shield **Edge:** Reeded

Date	Mintage	F	VF	XF	Unc	BU
ND(1995)	—	—	—	—	10.00	—

X# 166 20 DOLLARS

Gold Plated Copper-Nickel-Zinc, 39 mm. **Ruler:** Prince Leonard **Obv:** Crown over value on native design **Rev:** Sinking of the U.S.S. Arizona **Rev. Legend:** STARS AND STRIPES FOREVER **Edge:** Reeded

Date	Mintage	F	VF	XF	Unc	BU
1991 Proof	—	Value: 22.50				

Fathers of Baseball Series

X# 213 5 DOLLARS
25.1000 g., Copper-Nickel-Zinc, 39 mm.
Ruler: Prince Leonard **Obv:** Bust of Alexander Cartwright facing **Obv. Designer:** Hal Reed **Rev:** Batter in diamond shaped frame **Edge:** Reeded

Date	Mintage	F	VF	XF	Unc	BU
1992	—	—	—	—	7.00	—
1992 Proof	—	Value: 10.00				

X# 213a 5 DOLLARS
31.1341 g., 0.9990 Silver 0.9999 oz. ASW, 39 mm.
Ruler: Prince Leonard **Obv:** Bust of Alexander Cartwright facing **Obv. Designer:** Hal Reed **Rev:** Batter in diamond shaped frame **Edge:** Reeded

Date	Mintage	F	VF	XF	Unc	BU
1992 Proof	10,000	Value: 45.00				

X# 214 5 DOLLARS
25.1000 g., Copper-Nickel-Zinc, 39 mm.
Ruler: Prince Leonard **Obv:** Bust of Henry Chadwick facing **Obv. Designer:** Hal Reed **Rev:** Baseball manual **Edge:** Reeded

Date	Mintage	F	VF	XF	Unc	BU
1992	—	—	—	—	7.00	—
1992 Proof	—	Value: 10.00				

X# 214a 5 DOLLARS
31.1341 g., 0.9990 Silver 0.9999 oz. ASW, 39 mm.
Ruler: Prince Leonard **Obv:** Bust of Henry Chadwick facing **Obv. Designer:** Hal Reed **Rev:** Baseball manual **Edge:** Reeded

Date	Mintage	F	VF	XF	Unc	BU
1992 Proof	10,000	Value: 45.00				

X# 215 5 DOLLARS
25.1000 g., Copper-Nickel-Zinc, 39 mm.
Ruler: Prince Leonard **Obv:** Bust of Harry Wright facing 3/4 left **Obv. Designer:** Hal Reed **Rev:** Fielder in diamond frame **Edge:** Reeded

Date	Mintage	F	VF	XF	Unc	BU
1992	—	—	—	—	7.00	—
1992 Proof	—	Value: 10.00				

X# 215a 5 DOLLARS
31.1341 g., 0.9990 Silver 0.9999 oz. ASW, 39 mm.
Ruler: Prince Leonard **Obv:** Bust of Harry Wright facing 3/4 left **Obv. Designer:** Hal Reed **Rev:** Fielder in diamond frame **Edge:** Reeded

Date	Mintage	F	VF	XF	Unc	BU
1992 Proof	10,000	Value: 45.00				

X# 216 5 DOLLARS
25.1000 g., Copper-Nickel-Zinc, 39 mm. **Ruler:** Prince Leonard **Obv:** Bust of Abner Doubleday facing 3/4 left **Obv. Designer:** Hal Reed **Rev:** Batter and catcher **Edge:** Reeded

Date	Mintage	F	VF	XF	Unc	BU
1992	—	—	—	—	7.00	—
1992 Proof	—	Value: 10.00				

X# 216a 5 DOLLARS
31.1341 g., 0.9990 Silver 0.9999 oz. ASW, 39 mm.
Ruler: Prince Leonard **Obv:** Bust of Abner Doubleday facing 3/4 left **Obv. Designer:** Hal Reed **Rev:** Batter and catcher **Edge:** Reeded

Date	Mintage	F	VF	XF	Unc	BU
1992 Proof	10,000	Value: 45.00				

X# 217 5 DOLLARS
25.1000 g., Copper-Nickel-Zinc, 39 mm.
Ruler: Prince Leonard **Obv:** Bust of Albert Spaulding facing **Obv. Designer:** Hal Reed **Rev:** Pitcher in diamond frame **Edge:** Reeded

Date	Mintage	F	VF	XF	Unc	BU
1992	—	—	—	—	7.00	—
1992 Proof	—	Value: 10.00				

X# 217a 5 DOLLARS
31.1341 g., 0.9990 Silver 0.9999 oz. ASW, 39 mm.
Ruler: Prince Leonard **Obv:** Bust of Albert Spaulding facing **Obv. Designer:** Hal Reed **Rev:** Pitcher in diamond frame **Edge:** Reeded

Date	Mintage	F	VF	XF	Unc	BU
1992 Proof	10,000	Value: 45.00				

X# 223 5 DOLLARS
Copper-Nickel, 39 mm. **Ruler:** Prince Leonard **Obv:** Baseball game **Obv. Designer:** Hal Reed **Rev:** Bust of Charles Comiskey facing 3/4 left **Edge:** Reeded

Date	Mintage	F	VF	XF	Unc	BU
1993	—	—	—	—	7.00	—

X# 224 5 DOLLARS

Copper-Nickel, 39 mm. **Ruler:** Prince Leonard **Obv:** Baseball game **Obv. Designer:** Hal Reed **Rev:** Bust of Adrian "Cap" Anson facing 3/4 left **Edge:** Reeded

Date	Mintage	F	VF	XF	Unc	BU
1993	—	—	—	—	7.00	—

X# 227 5 DOLLARS

Copper-Nickel, 39 mm. **Ruler:** Prince Leonard **Obv:** Baseball game **Obv. Designer:** Hal Reed **Rev:** Bust of Mike (King) Kelly facing **Edge:** Reeded

Date	Mintage	F	VF	XF	Unc	BU
1993	—	—	—	—	7.00	—

X# 230 5 DOLLARS

Copper-Nickel, 39 mm. **Ruler:** Prince Leonard **Obv:** Baseball game **Obv. Designer:** Hal Reed **Rev:** Bust of Tommy McCarthy facing **Edge:** Reeded

Date	Mintage	F	VF	XF	Unc	BU
1993	—	—	—	—	7.00	—

X# 225 5 DOLLARS

Copper-Nickel, 39 mm. **Ruler:** Prince Leonard **Obv:** Baseball game **Obv. Designer:** Hal Reed **Rev:** Bust of Buck Ewing facing **Edge:** Reeded

Date	Mintage	F	VF	XF	Unc	BU
1993	—	—	—	—	7.00	—

X# 228 5 DOLLARS

Copper-Nickel, 39 mm. **Ruler:** Prince Leonard **Obv:** Baseball game **Obv. Designer:** Hal Reed **Rev:** Bust of Charley Radbourne facing 3/4 left **Edge:** Reeded

Date	Mintage	F	VF	XF	Unc	BU
1993	—	—	—	—	7.00	—

X# 231 5 DOLLARS

Copper-Nickel, 39 mm. **Ruler:** Prince Leonard **Obv:** Baseball game **Obv. Designer:** Hal Reed **Rev:** Bust of Moses Walker facing **Edge:** Reeded

Date	Mintage	F	VF	XF	Unc	BU
1993	—	—	—	—	7.00	—

X# 226 5 DOLLARS

Copper-Nickel, 39 mm. **Ruler:** Prince Leonard **Obv:** Baseball game **Obv. Designer:** Hal Reed **Rev:** Bust of W.A. "Candy" Cummings facing 3/4 right **Edge:** Reeded

Date	Mintage	F	VF	XF	Unc	BU
1993	—	—	—	—	7.00	—

X# 229 5 DOLLARS

Copper-Nickel, 39 mm. **Ruler:** Prince Leonard **Obv:** Baseball game **Obv. Designer:** Hal Reed **Rev:** Bust of Amos Rusie facing 3/4 left **Edge:** Reeded

Date	Mintage	F	VF	XF	Unc	BU
1993	—	—	—	—	7.00	—

X# 232 5 DOLLARS

Copper-Nickel, 39 mm. **Ruler:** Prince Leonard **Obv:** Baseball game **Obv. Designer:** Hal Reed **Rev:** Bust of "Shoeless Joe" Jackson facing **Edge:** Reeded

Date	Mintage	F	VF	XF	Unc	BU
1993	—	—	—	—	7.00	—

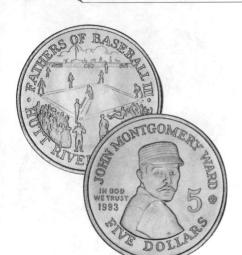

X# 233 5 DOLLARS
Copper-Nickel, 39 mm. **Ruler:** Prince Leonard **Obv:** Baseball game **Obv. Designer:** Hal Reed **Rev:** Sideview bust of John Montgomery Ward - facing **Edge:** Reeded

Date	Mintage	F	VF	XF	Unc	BU
1993	—	—	—	—	7.00	—

X# 236 5 DOLLARS
Copper-Nickel, 39 mm. **Ruler:** Prince Leonard **Obv:** Baseball game **Obv. Designer:** Hal Reed **Rev:** Bust of Time Keefe facing 3/4 left **Edge:** Reeded

Date	Mintage	F	VF	XF	Unc	BU
1993	—	—	—	—	7.00	—

X# 239 5 DOLLARS
Copper-Nickel, 39 mm. **Ruler:** Prince Leonard **Obv:** Baseball game **Obv. Designer:** Hal Reed **Rev:** Bust of Napoleon Lajoie facing **Edge:** Reeded

Date	Mintage	F	VF	XF	Unc	BU
1993	—	—	—	—	7.00	—

X# 234 5 DOLLARS
Copper-Nickel, 39 mm. **Ruler:** Prince Leonard **Obv:** Baseball game **Obv. Designer:** Hal Reed **Rev:** Bust of Dan Brouthers facing slightly right **Edge:** Reeded

Date	Mintage	F	VF	XF	Unc	BU
1993	—	—	—	—	7.00	—

X# 237 5 DOLLARS
Copper-Nickel, 39 mm. **Ruler:** Prince Leonard **Obv:** Baseball game **Obv. Designer:** Hal Reed **Rev:** Bust of Billy Sunday facing **Edge:** Reeded

Date	Mintage	F	VF	XF	Unc	BU
1993	—	—	—	—	7.00	—

X# 240 5 DOLLARS
Copper-Nickel, 39 mm. **Ruler:** Prince Leonard **Obv:** Baseball game **Obv. Designer:** Hal Reed **Rev:** Bust of Judge Landis facing slightly left **Edge:** Reeded

Date	Mintage	F	VF	XF	Unc	BU
1993	—	—	—	—	7.00	—

X# 235 5 DOLLARS
Copper-Nickel, 39 mm. **Ruler:** Prince Leonard **Obv:** Baseball game **Obv. Designer:** Hal Reed **Rev:** Bust of John McGraw facing 3/4 left **Edge:** Reeded

Date	Mintage	F	VF	XF	Unc	BU
1993	—	—	—	—	7.00	—

X# 238 5 DOLLARS
Copper-Nickel, 39 mm. **Ruler:** Prince Leonard **Obv:** Baseball game **Obv. Designer:** Hal Reed **Rev:** Bust of Billy Hamilton facing **Edge:** Reeded

Date	Mintage	F	VF	XF	Unc	BU
1993	—	—	—	—	7.00	—

X# 241 5 DOLLARS
Copper-Nickel, 39 mm. **Ruler:** Prince Leonard **Obv:** Baseball game **Obv. Designer:** Hal Reed **Rev:** Bust of Ed Delahanty facing slightly right **Edge:** Reeded

Date	Mintage	F	VF	XF	Unc	BU
1993	—	—	—	—	7.00	—

X# 242 5 DOLLARS
Copper-Nickel, 39 mm. **Ruler:** Prince Leonard **Obv:** Baseball game **Obv. Designer:** Hal Reed **Rev:** Bust of Jake Beckley facing slightly left **Edge:** Reeded

Date	Mintage	F	VF	XF	Unc	BU
1993	—	—	—	—	7.00	—

X# 218 100 DOLLARS
3.1134 g., 0.9990 Gold 0.1000 oz. AGW, 18 mm. **Ruler:** Prince Leonard **Obv:** Bust of Alexander Cartwright facing **Obv. Designer:** Hal Reed **Rev:** Batter in diamond shaped frame

Date	Mintage	F	VF	XF	Unc	BU
1992 Proof	—	Value: 150				

X# 219 100 DOLLARS
3.1134 g., 0.9990 Gold 0.1000 oz. AGW, 18 mm. **Ruler:** Prince Leonard **Obv:** Bust of Henry Chadwick facing **Obv. Designer:** Hal Reed **Rev:** Baseball manual **Edge:** Reeded

Date	Mintage	F	VF	XF	Unc	BU
1992 Proof	—	Value: 150				

X# 220 100 DOLLARS
3.1134 g., 0.9990 Gold 0.1000 oz. AGW, 18 mm. **Ruler:** Prince Leonard **Obv:** Bust of Harry Wright facing 3/4 left **Obv. Designer:** Hal Reed **Rev:** Fielder in diamond frame **Edge:** Reeded

Date	Mintage	F	VF	XF	Unc	BU
1992 Proof	—	Value: 150				

X# 221 100 DOLLARS
3.1134 g., 0.9990 Gold 0.1000 oz. AGW, 18 mm. **Ruler:** Prince Leonard **Obv:** Bust of Abner Doubleday facing 3/4 left **Obv. Designer:** Hal Reed **Rev:** Batter and catcher **Edge:** Reeded

Date	Mintage	F	VF	XF	Unc	BU
1992 Proof	—	Value: 150				

X# 222 100 DOLLARS
3.1134 g., 0.9990 Gold 0.1000 oz. AGW, 18 mm. **Ruler:** Prince Leonard **Obv:** Bust of Albert Spaulding facing **Obv. Designer:** Hal Reed **Rev:** Pitcher in diamond frame **Edge:** Reeded

Date	Mintage	F	VF	XF	Unc	BU
1992 Proof	—	Value: 150				

ESSAIS

X# E4 5 DOLLARS
Bronze, 39 mm. **Ruler:** Prince Leonard **Subject:** Fathers of Baseball **Obv. Inscription:** "HALL REED" / serial # **Rev:** Batter in diamond shaped frame **Edge:** Reeded

Date	Mintage	F	VF	XF	Unc	BU
1992 Proof	500	—	—	—	—	—

X# E5 5 DOLLARS
Bronze, 39 mm. **Ruler:** Prince Leonard **Subject:** Fathers of Baseball **Obv. Inscription:** "HALL REED" / serial # **Rev:** Baseball manual **Edge:** Reeded

Date	Mintage	F	VF	XF	Unc	BU
1992 Proof	500	—	—	—	—	—

X# E6 5 DOLLARS
Bronze, 39 mm. **Ruler:** Prince Leonard **Subject:** Fathers of Baseball **Obv. Inscription:** "HALL REED" / serial # **Rev:** Fielder in diamond frame **Edge:** Reeded

Date	Mintage	F	VF	XF	Unc	BU
1992 Proof	—	—	—	—	—	—

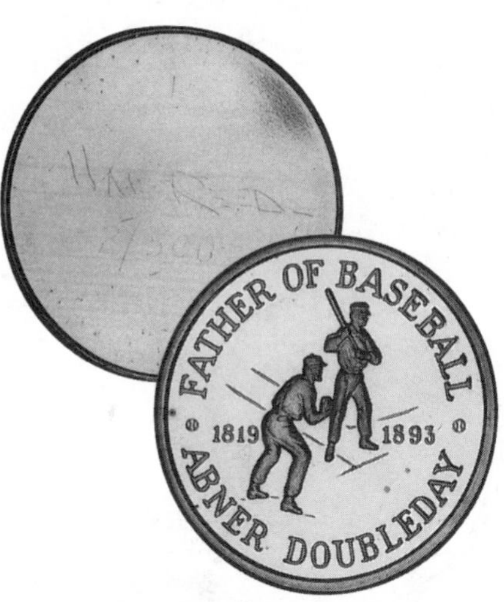

X# E7 5 DOLLARS
Bronze, 39 mm. **Ruler:** Prince Leonard **Subject:** Fathers of Baseball **Obv. Inscription:** "HALL REED" / serial # **Rev:** Batter and catcher **Edge:** Reeded

Date	Mintage	F	VF	XF	Unc	BU
1992 Proof	500	—	—	—	—	—

X# E1 25 DOLLARS
Copper, 39 mm. **Ruler:** Prince Leonard **Obv. Inscription:** A. SHAGIN / Serial # **Rev:** George Orwell

Date	Mintage	F	VF	XF	Unc	BU
1984 Proof	1,984	Value: 100				

X# E2 25 DOLLARS
31.1340 g., 0.9990 Silver 0.9999 oz. ASW, 39 mm. **Ruler:** Prince Leonard **Obv. Inscription:** A. SHAGIN / Serial # **Rev:** Head of George Orwell in profile right **Edge:** Reeded

Date	Mintage	F	VF	XF	Unc	BU
1984 Proof	—	—	—	—	—	—

X# E3 25 DOLLARS
Bronze, 39 mm. **Ruler:** Prince Leonard **Obv. Inscription:** A. SHAGIN / Serial # **Rev:** Head of George Orwell in profile right **Edge:** Plain

Date	Mintage	F	VF	XF	Unc	BU
1984 Proof	—	—	—	—	—	—

PATTERNS

#Pn1-Pn12 Commemorate the 75th Anniversary of World War I

X#	Date	Mintage	Identification	Mkt Val
PnA1	ND(1984)	—	5 Dollars. Brass. 25th Anniversary Moon Landing	—
Pn1	1993	—	10 Dollars. Brass. 44 mm. Sinking of the Lusitania	—
Pn2	1993	—	10 Dollars. Brass. 44 mm. Aerial Combat	—
Pn3	1993	—	10 Dollars. Brass. 44 mm. Trench Warfare	—
Pn4	1993	—	10 Dollars. Brass. 44 mm. Field Artillery	—
Pn5	1993	—	10 Dollars. Brass. 44 mm. Aerial Bombardment	—
Pn6	1993	—	10 Dollars. Brass. 44 mm. Manfrid von Richofen, the "Red Barron"	—
Pn7	1993	—	10 Dollars. Brass. 44 mm. Tank	—
Pn8	1993	—	10 Dollars. Brass. 44 mm. Zeppelin Destroyed	—
Pn9	1993	—	10 Dollars. Brass. 44 mm. Naval Engagement	—
Pn10	1993	—	10 Dollars. Brass. 44 mm. Allied Artillery	—
Pn11	1993	—	10 Dollars. Brass. 44 mm. German Artillery	—
Pn12	1993	—	10 Dollars. Brass. 44 mm. Laurence of Arabia	—

X#	Date	Mintage	Identification	Mkt Val
Pn13	1997	—	5 Dollars. Copper-Nickel. 39 mm. Princess Diana	—
Pn14	2000	2	100 Dollars. 0.9990 Silver. X#305.	—

MINT SETS

X#	Date	Mintage	Identification	Issue Price	Mkt Val
XMS1	1977 (4)	—	X1-X4	—	2.50
XMS2	1984 (2)	1,984	X14, XE1	49.50	—

PROOF SETS

X#	Date	Mintage	Identification	Issue Price	Mkt Val
XPS1	1976 (5)	1,000	X1-X5	50.00	37.00
XPS2	1976 (4)	1,000	X1-X4	10.00	7.00
XPS3	1977 (6)	1,000	X1-X4, X7, X8	58.00	52.00
XPS4	1978 (6)	500	X1-X4, X7, X9	58.00	52.00

ICELAND

KINGDOM

MEDALLIC COINAGE

X# M1 2 KRONUR
20.0000 g., Bronze, 35.5 mm. **Subject:** 1000 Years Althing **Obv. Designer:** BB - Baldvin Bjornsson **Rev. Designer:** TM - Tryggvi Magnusson **Note:** Prev. KM#M1. Struck privately by the Saxon State Mint, Muldenhutten, Germany, at the instigation of a Parliamentary committee. Denominations on edges.

Date	Mintage	F	VF	XF	Unc	BU
1930	20,000	—	20.00	35.00	75.00	—
1930 With box	—	—	25.00	40.00	70.00	—

X# M2 5 KRONUR
20.0000 g., Silver, 35.5 mm. **Subject:** 1000 Years Althing **Obv. Designer:** BB - Baldvin Bjornsson **Rev. Designer:** GE - Gudmundur Einarsson **Note:** Prev. KM#M2.

Date	Mintage	F	VF	XF	Unc	BU
1930	10,000	—	45.00	75.00	140	—
1930 With box	—	—	50.00	80.00	125	—

X# M3 10 KRONUR
45.0000 g., Silver **Subject:** 1000 Years Althing **Obv. Designer:** EJ - Einar Jonsson **Rev. Designer:** BB - Baldvin Bjornsson **Note:** Prev. KM#M3. FH stands for Friedrich Hornlein, the engraver. Struck privately by the Saxon State Mint, Muldenhutten, Germany, at the instigation of a Parliamentary committee.

Date	Mintage	F	VF	XF	Unc	BU
1930 FH	10,000	—	60.00	120	250	—
1930 With box	—	—	65.00	125	210	—

REPUBLIC

ECU COINAGE

Numex S.A., Madrid

X# 11 50 ECU
31.1030 g., 0.9990 Silver 0.9989 oz. ASW, 40 mm. **Obv:** Crowned supported arms **Rev:** Viking ship, seagull approaching **Rev. Legend:** ISLAND **Edge:** Plain

Date	Mintage	F	VF	XF	Unc	BU
1993 Proof	5,000	Value: 45.00				

X# 12 500 ECU
31.1030 g., 0.7500 Gold 0.7500 oz. AGW, 40 mm. **Obv:** Crowned supported arms **Rev:** Viking ship, seagull approaching **Rev. Legend:** ISLAND **Edge:** Plain

Date	Mintage	F	VF	XF	Unc	BU
1993 Proof	250	Value: 650				

FANTASY EURO PATTERNS

X# Pn1 CEROS
Copper Plated Steel, 16.8 mm. **Obv:** Seal's head facing **Edge:** Plain

Date	Mintage	F	VF	XF	Unc	BU
2004	15,000	—	—	—	—	1.50
2004 Proof	5,000	Value: 2.50				

X# Pn1a CEROS
Silver, 16.8 mm. **Obv:** Seal's head facing **Edge:** Plain

Date	Mintage	F	VF	XF	Unc	BU
2004 Proof	500	Value: 6.00				

X# Pn2 2 CEROS
Copper Plated Steel, 18.5 mm. **Obv:** Two birds left **Rev:** Plants **Edge:** Plain

Date	Mintage	F	VF	XF	Unc	BU
2004	15,000	—	—	—	—	2.00
2004 Proof	5,000	Value: 3.00				

X# Pn2a 2 CEROS
Silver, 18.5 mm. **Obv:** Two birds left **Rev:** Plants **Edge:** Plain

Date	Mintage	F	VF	XF	Unc	BU
2004 Proof	500	Value: 7.00				

X# Pn3 5 CEROS
Copper Plated Steel, 20.7 mm. **Obv:** Wolf's head facing **Rev:** Plants **Edge:** Plain

Date	Mintage	F	VF	XF	Unc	BU
2004	15,000	—	—	—	—	2.50
2004 Proof	5,000	Value: 3.50				

X# Pn3a 5 CEROS
Silver, 20.7 mm. **Obv:** Wolf's head facing **Rev:** Plants **Edge:** Plain

Date	Mintage	F	VF	XF	Unc	BU
2004 Proof	500	Value: 8.50				

X# Pn4 10 CEROS
Goldine, 19.3 mm. **Obv:** Male bust facing **Edge:** Plain

Date	Mintage	F	VF	XF	Unc	BU
2004	15,000	—	—	—	—	3.00
2004 Proof	5,000	Value: 4.00				

X# Pn4a 10 CEROS
Silver, 19.3 mm. **Obv:** Male bust facing **Edge:** Plain

Date	Mintage	F	VF	XF	Unc	BU
2004 Proof	500	Value: 10.00				

X# Pn5 20 CEROS
Goldine, 22 mm. **Obv:** Mythical bust facing **Rev:** Horse head left at right **Edge:** Plain

Date	Mintage	F	VF	XF	Unc	BU
2004	15,000	—	—	—	—	3.50
2004 Proof	5,000	Value: 5.00				

X# Pn5a 20 CEROS
Silver, 22 mm. **Obv:** Mythical bust facing **Rev:** Horse head left at right **Edge:** Plain

Date	Mintage	F	VF	XF	Unc	BU
2004 Proof	500	Value: 12.50				

X# Pn6 50 CEROS
Goldine, 24.3 mm. **Obv:** Crescent moon with face right with winged child hunched down left **Rev:** Pony at right **Edge:** Plain

Date	Mintage	F	VF	XF	Unc	BU
2004	15,000	—	—	—	—	4.00
2004 Proof	5,000	Value: 6.00				

X# Pn6a 50 CEROS
Silver, 24.3 mm. **Obv:** Crescent moon with face right with winged child hunched down left **Rev:** Pony at right **Edge:** Plain

Date	Mintage	F	VF	XF	Unc	BU
2004 Proof	500	Value: 15.00				

X# Pn7 EUROP
Bi-Metallic Copper-Nickel center in Goldine ring, 22.8 mm. **Edge:** Plain

Date	Mintage	F	VF	XF	Unc	BU
2004	15,000	—	—	—	—	6.00
2004 Proof	5,000	Value: 8.00				

X# Pn7a EUROP
Bi-Metallic Brass/Silver, 22.8 mm. **Edge:** Plain

Date	Mintage	F	VF	XF	Unc	BU
2004 Proof	500	Value: 22.50				

X# Pn8 2 EUROP
Bi-Metallic Goldine center in Copper-Nickel ring, 25.7 mm. **Obv:** Bust of mythical male 3/4 left **Edge:** Plain

Date	Mintage	F	VF	XF	Unc	BU
2004	15,000	—	—	—	—	8.00
2004 Proof	5,000	Value: 10.00				

X# Pn8a 2 EUROP
Bi-Metallic Silver/Brass, 25.7 mm. **Obv:** Bust of mythical male 3/4 left **Edge:** Plain

Date	Mintage	F	VF	XF	Unc	BU
2004 Proof	500	Value: 28.50				

X# Pn9 5 EUROP
Tri-Metallic Copper center, Nickel ring, Brass outer ring, 36 mm. **Obv:** 3/4-length woman standing with shield facing **Edge:** Plain

Date	Mintage	F	VF	XF	Unc	BU
2004 Proof	5,000	Value: 12.50				

X# Pn9a 5 EUROP
Silver **Obv:** 3/4-length woman standing with shield facing **Edge:** Plain

Date	Mintage	F	VF	XF	Unc	BU
2004 Proof	500	Value: 40.00				

PIEFORTS

X#	Date	Mintage	Identification	Mkt Val
P1	2004	500	5 Europ. Silver. X#Pn9a.	60.00

MINT SETS

X#	Date	Mintage	Identification	Issue Price	Mkt Val
XMS1	1930 (3)	—	XM1-XM3	—	400
XMS1a	1930 (3)	—	With case of issue	—	425
XMS2	2004 (8)	1,500	X#Pn1-Pn8	—	30.00

PROOF SETS

X#	Date	Mintage	Identification	Issue Price	Mkt Val
XPS1	2004 (9)	5,000	X#Pn1-Pn9	—	50.00
XPS2	2004 (9)	500	X#Pn1a-Pn9a	—	150

INDIA-INDEPENDENT KINGDOMS

KUTCH

KINGDOM

MEDALLIC COINAGE

In the last years of its coinage history, Kutch struck some non-circulating coins which state denomination. At least one was a pattern which wasn't approved for circulation strikes and the others were probably presentation pieces.

X# M1 2-1/2 KORI
6.9350 g., 0.9370 Silver 0.2089 oz. ASW **Ruler:** Madanasinghji VS2004-2005 / 1947-1948AD

Date	Mintage	VG	F	VF	XF	Unc
VS1984 Rare	—	—	—	—	—	—
VS1984 Rare	—	—	—	—	—	—

X# M2 5 KORI
Silver **Ruler:** Madanasinghji VS2004-2005 / 1947-1948AD **Obv:** Small bust of Khengarji III left **Rev. Inscription:** George V...

Date	Mintage	VG	F	VF	XF	Unc
VS1985	—	—	—	—	450	600

X# M3 5 KORI
Silver **Ruler:** Madanasinghji VS2004-2005 / 1947-1948AD **Obv:** Large bust of Khengarji III left **Rev. Inscription:** George V

Date	Mintage	VG	F	VF	XF	Unc
VS1985	—	—	—	—	450	600

X# M4 10 KORI
Silver **Ruler:** Madanasinghji VS2004-2005 / 1947-1948AD

Date	Mintage	VG	F	VF	XF	Unc
VS1998//1941 Rare	—	—	—	—	—	—

X# M4a 10 KORI
Gold **Ruler:** Madanasinghji VS2004-2005 / 1947-1948AD

Date	Mintage	Good	VG	F	VF	XF
VS1998/1941 Rare	—	—	—	—	—	—

X# M6 10 KORI
Silver **Ruler:** Madanasinghji VS2004-2005 / 1947-1948AD **Obv:** Small bust of Khengarji III left

Date	Mintage	VG	F	VF	XF	Unc
VS1998/1942 Rare	—	—	—	—	—	—

X# M6a 10 KORI
Gold **Ruler:** Madanasinghji VS2004-2005 / 1947-1948AD **Obv:** Small bust of Khengarji III left

Date	Mintage	VG	F	VF	XF	Unc
VS1998/1942 Rare	—	—	—	—	—	—

X# M7 GOLD KORI
7.3600 g., Gold **Ruler:** Madanasinghji VS2004-2005 / 1947-1948AD **Subject:** Coronation of Madanasinghji

Date	Mintage	VG	F	VF	XF	Unc
VS2004/1947	—	—	—	—	550	850

X# M9 GOLD KORI
7.3600 g., Gold **Ruler:** Pragmalji III & Maharani Prittdevi VS2048- / 1991AD- **Subject:** Coronation of Pragmalji III and Maharani Pritidevi

Date	Mintage	VG	F	VF	XF	Unc
VS2048/1991	—	—	—	—	550	850

X# M8 MOHUR
18.7300 g., Gold **Ruler:** Madanasinghji VS2004-2005 / 1947-1948AD **Subject:** Coronation of Maharani Pritidevi **Rev:** Turreted gateway

Date	Mintage	VG	F	VF	XF	Unc
VS2004/1947	30	—	—	—	3,500	5,000

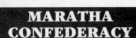

MARATHA CONFEDERACY

INDEPENDENT KINGDOM

TRADE COINAGE

X# T1 DUCAT
Gold **Obv:** Two female deities with trident between **Rev:** Siva standing **Note:** Imitation of Venetian Ducat.

Date	Mintage	Good	VG	F	VF	XF
ND(1600)	—	—	—	100	175	300

SIKH EMPIRE

EMPIRE

FANTASY COINAGE

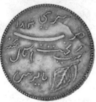

X# 1 PAISA
Copper **Note:** Once thought to be a pattern it is now considered a contemporary fantasy.

Date	Mintage	F	VF	XF	Unc	BU
1830	—	—	12.00	18.00	—	—

TRIPURA

KINGDOM

MEDALLIC COINAGE

X# 7 RUPEE
Silver, 30.6 mm. **Ruler:** Vira Vikrama Kishore Manikya TE1333-1357 / 1923-1947AD **Obv:** Bust of Vira Vikrama Kishore left **Rev:** Rampant lion left **Edge:** Milled **Note:** 11.30-11.90 grams. Varieties exist. Prev. KM#406.

Date	Mintage	VG	F	VF	XF	Unc
TE1337(1930)	—	20.00	30.00	45.00	65.00	110

X# 8 RUPEE
Silver, 29.6 mm. **Ruler:** Vira Vikrama Kishore Manikya TE1333-1357 / 1923-1947AD **Obv:** Rampant lion left **Rev. Legend:** With "Sri Srimati Maharani Kanchan Prabha Maha Devi" **Edge:** Milled **Note:** Prev. KM#409.

Date	Mintage	VG	F	VF	XF	Unc
TE1338(1931)	—	35.00	50.00	85.00	125	200
TE1341(1934)	—	17.50	27.50	37.50	60.00	100

X# 9 RUPEE
Silver **Ruler:** Vira Vikrama Kishore Manikya TE1333-1357 / 1923-1947AD **Rev. Legend:** With "Queen Kirti Mani" **Note:** Prev. KM#408.

Date	Mintage	VG	F	VF	XF	Unc
TE1341(1934)	—	50.00	85.00	125	200	350

X# 5 MOHUR
11.5000 g., Gold **Ruler:** Virendra Kishore Manikya TE1319-1333 / 1909-1923AD **Rev. Legend:** With "Queen Prabhavati" **Edge:** Milled **Note:** Prev. KM#396.

Date	Mintage	VG	F	VF	XF	Unc
TE1319(1909) Rare	—	—	—	1,000	1,250	1,500

X# 6 MOHUR
Gold **Ruler:** Virendra Kishore Manikya TE1319-1333 / 1909-1923AD **Rev. Legend:** With "Queen Jivankumari Devi" **Edge:** Milled **Note:** Prev. KM#397.

Date	Mintage	Good	VG	F	VF	XF
TE1319 (1909) Rare	—	—	—	—	1,000	1,250

X# 10 MOHUR
11.5000 g., Gold **Ruler:** Vira Vikrama Kishore Manikya TE1333-1357 / 1923-1947AD **Obv:** Rampant lion left **Rev. Legend:** With "Sri Srimati Maharani Kanchan Prabha Maha Devi" **Edge:** Milled **Note:** Prev. KM#412.

Date	Mintage	VG	F	VF	XF	Unc
TE1341 (1934)	—	—	—	—	1,200	1,800

INDIA - PRINCELY STATES

AWADH

KINGDOM

MEDALLIC COINAGE

X# 1 NON-DENOMINATED
78.3300 g., Silver, 69 mm. **Subject:** Ghazi ud-Din Haidar Coronation **Note:** Illustration reduced.

Date	Mintage	F	VF	XF	Unc	BU
AH1234(1819)	—	—	850	1,650	2,250	—

BAHAWALPUR

PRINCELY STATE

MEDALLIC COINAGE

X# M10 NAZARANA RUPEE
12.3000 g., Silver **Ruler:** Sir Sadiq Muhammad Khan V AH1325-1365 / 1907-1947AD **Obv:** Bust of Muhammad Bahawal Khan V left **Rev:** Ornate helmeted arms **Note:** Design prepared for the nawab by Spink & Son Ltd., London. Prev. Y#10.

Date	Mintage	VG	F	VF	XF	Unc
AH1343	—	—	—	250	325	400

X# M11b ASHRAFI
Silver, 22.5 mm. **Ruler:** Sadiq Muhammad Khan V AH1325-65 / 1907-47AD **Obv:** Bust of Muhammad Bahawal Khan V left **Rev:** Ornate helmeted arms **Note:** Design prepared for the nawab by Spink & Son Ltd., London. Prev. Y#11b.

Date	Mintage	F	VF	XF	Unc	BU
AH1343 Prooflike; Rare	—	—	—	—	—	—

X# M11 ASHRAFI
7.0000 g., Gold, 22.5 mm. **Ruler:** Sir Sadiq Muhammad Khan V AH1325-1365 / 1907-1947AD **Obv:** Bust of Muhammad Bahawal Khan V left **Rev:** Ornate helmeted arms **Note:** Fr. #1030. Design prepared for the nawab by Spink & Son Ltd., London. Prev. Y#11.

Date	Mintage	VG	F	VF	XF	Unc
AH1343	—	—	—	400	500	650

BARODA

PRINCELY STATE

MILLED COINAGE

X# M40 1/3 MOHUR
Gold, 18 mm. **Ruler:** Pratap Singh VS1995-2008 / 1938-1951AD **Obv:** Bust of Pratap Singh right **Note:** Weight varies: 2.07-2.13 grams. Prev. Y#40.

Date	Mintage	F	VF	XF	Unc	BU
VS1995 (1938)	—	—	400	600	1,000	—

X# M41 MOHUR
Gold, 21 mm. **Ruler:** Pratap Singh VS1995-2008 / 1938-1951AD **Obv:** Bust of Pratap Singh right **Note:** Weight varies: 6.20-6.40 grams. Prev. Y#41.

Date	Mintage	F	VF	XF	Unc	BU
VS1995 (1938)	—	—	400	600	1,000	—

BHADRANATH

STATE

MEDALLIC COINAGE

X# 1 1/2 MOHUR
Gold

Date	Mintage	F	VF	XF	Unc	BU
1872	—	—	—	—	—	—

X# 2 MOHUR
Gold

Date	Mintage	F	VF	XF	Unc	BU
1872	—	—	—	—	—	—

BIKANIR

PRINCELY STATE

MEDALLIC COINAGE

X# M1 NAZARANA RUPEE
Silver **Ruler:** Ganga Singh VS1944-1999 / 1887-1942AD **Subject:** 50th Anniversary of Reign **Obv:** Bust of Ganga Singh facing **Rev:** Crowned monogram **Note:** Prev. KM#73.

Date	Mintage	F	VF	XF	Unc	BU
VS1994(1937)	—	—	20.00	30.00	45.00	—
VS1994(1937) Restrike; Prooflike	—	—	—	—	20.00	—

X# M1a NAZARANA RUPEE
Gold **Ruler:** Ganga Singh VS1944-1999 / 1887-1942AD **Subject:** 50th Anniversary of Reign **Obv:** Bust of Ganga Singh facing **Rev:** Crowned monogram

Date	Mintage	VG	F	VF	XF	Unc
VS1994 Prooflike; Restrike; Rare	—	—	—	—	—	—

X# M2a NAZARANA 1/2 MOHUR
Silver **Ruler:** Ganga Singh VS1944-1999 / 1887-1942AD **Subject:** 50th Anniversary of Reign **Obv:** Bust of Ganga Singh facing **Rev:** Crowned monogram **Note:** Prev. KM#74a.

Date	Mintage	F	VF	XF	Unc	BU
VS1994(1937) Restrike; Prooflike	—	—	—	—	45.00	—

X# M2 NAZARANA 1/2 MOHUR
Gold, 17 mm. **Ruler:** Ganga Singh VS1944-1999 / 1887-1942AD **Subject:** 50th Anniversary of Reign **Obv:** Bust of Ganga Singh facing **Rev:** Crowned monogram **Note:** Prev. KM#74.

Date	Mintage	VG	F	VF	XF	Unc
VS1994(1937)	—	—	—	175	225	300
VS1994(1937) Restrike; Prooflike	—	—	—	—	—	225

X# M3a NAZARANA MOHUR
Silver **Ruler:** Ganga Singh VS1944-1999 / 1887-1942AD **Subject:** 50th Anniversary of Reign **Obv:** Bust of Ganga Singh facing **Rev:** Crowned monogram **Note:** Prev. KM#75a.

Date	Mintage	F	VF	XF	Unc	BU
VS1994(1937) Restrike; Prooflike	—	—	—	—	45.00	—

X# M3 NAZARANA MOHUR
Gold **Ruler:** Ganga Singh VS1944-1999 / 1887-1942AD **Subject:** 50th Anniversary of Reign **Obv:** Bust of Ganga Singh facing **Rev:** Crowned monogram **Note:** Prev. KM#75.

Date	Mintage	VG	F	VF	XF	Unc
VS1994(1937)	—	—	—	250	325	450
VS1994(1937) Restrike; Prooflike	—	—	—	—	—	325

X# M4 NAZARANA MOHUR
8.6800 g., Gold **Ruler:** Sadul Singh AH1361-1367 / 1942-1947AD **Subject:** 50th Anniversary of Reign **Obv:** Bust of Ganga Singh facing **Rev:** Crowned monogram

Date	Mintage	VG	F	VF	XF	Unc
VS1999	—	—	—	—	1,000	2,000

COOCH BEHAR

BRITISH PROTECTORATE

MEDALLIC COINAGE

X# M7 NAZARANA 1/2 RUPEE
4.7000 g., Silver **Ruler:** Raja Rajendra Narayan SE1833-1835 / 1911-1913AD **Obv:** Arms **Note:** Prev. KM#195.

Date	Mintage	F	VF	XF	Unc	BU
CB402(1912)	1,001	25.00	50.00	70.00	100	—

X# M9 NAZARANA 1/2 RUPEE
4.7000 g., Silver **Ruler:** Jitendra Narayan SE1835-1844 / 1913-1922AD **Obv:** Arms **Note:** Prev. KM#210.

Date	Mintage	F	VF	XF	Unc	BU
CB404(1914)	1,004	25.00	50.00	70.00	100	—

X# M11 NAZARANA 1/2 RUPEE
5.4000 g., Silver **Ruler:** Jagaddipendra Narayan SE1844-1871 / 1922-1949AD **Obv:** Arms **Note:** Prev. KM#225.

Date	Mintage	F	VF	XF	Unc	BU
CB413(1923)	—	17.50	35.00	50.00	70.00	—

X# M13 NAZARANA MOHUR
8.0000 g., Gold **Ruler:** Jagaddipendra Narayan SE1844-1871 / 1922-1949AD

Date	Mintage	F	VF	XF	Unc	BU
CB413 (-1923) Rare	—	—	—	—	—	—

X# M8 NAZARANA MOHUR
8.5000 g., Gold **Ruler:** Raja Rajendra Narayan SE1833-1835 / 1911-1913AD **Obv:** Arms **Note:** Prev. KM#200.

Date	Mintage	F	VF	XF	Unc	BU
CB402(1912)	100	—	—	1,200	1,800	—

X# M10 NAZARANA MOHUR
8.0000 g., Gold **Ruler:** Jitendra Narayan SE1835-1844 / 1913-1922AD **Obv:** Arms **Note:** Prev. KM#215.

Date	Mintage	F	VF	XF	Unc	BU
CB404(1914)	100	—	—	1,200	1,800	—

X# M12 NAZARANA MOHUR
8.7000 g., Gold **Ruler:** Jagaddipendra Narayan SE1844-1871 / 1922-1949AD **Obv:** Arms **Note:** Prev. KM#230.

Date	Mintage	F	VF	XF	Unc	BU
CB413 (1923)	—	—	—	1,200	1,800	—

DATIA

BRITISH PROTECTORATE

MEDALLIC COINAGE

X# 1 NAZARANA 1/2 MOHUR
Gold **Ruler:** Govind Singh 1907-1948AD **Obv:** Bust of Govind Singh 3/4 right **Rev:** Arms **Note:** Prev. KM#M1. Weight varies: 5.35-5.78 grams.

Date	Mintage	F	VF	XF	Unc	BU
ND(ca. 1940s)	—	—	750	1,500	2,500	—

DHAR

BRITISH PROTECTORATE

MEDALLIC COINAGE

X# M10 MOHUR
6.4000 g., Gold, 20 mm. **Obv:** Coat of Arms, English legend above, Persian legend below **Obv. Legend:** DHAR STATE...ZARB PIRAN DHAR **Note:** Previous KM#10.

Date	Mintage	VG	F	VF	XF	Unc
1943	—	1,000	1,300	1,600	2,000	—

X# 1 NAZARANA MOHUR
Gold **Ruler:** Anand Rao IV AH1363-1368 / 1943-1948AD **Note:** Prev. KM#M1.

Date	Mintage	F	VF	XF	Unc	BU
1943	—	—	600	900	1,800	—

FARIDKOT

PRINCELY STATE

MEDALLIC COINAGE

X# M1 NAZARANA 1/2 RUPEE
Silver **Ruler:** Harindar Singh **Obv:** Bust of Harinder Singh left **Rev:** Arms **Note:** Prev. KM#M1.

Date	Mintage	F	VF	XF	Unc	BU
1941	—	—	—	—	—	—

X# M2 NAZARANA RUPEE
Silver **Ruler:** Harindar Singh **Obv:** Bust of Harinder Singh left **Rev:** Arms **Note:** Prev. KM#M2.

Date	Mintage	F	VF	XF	Unc	BU
1941 Rare	—	—	—	—	—	—

X# M10 5 RUPEES
58.0000 g., Silver, 51 mm. **Ruler:** Harindar Singh **Note:** Previous KM#10.

Date	Mintage	F	VF	XF	Unc	BU
1941 Unique	—	—	—	—	—	—

X# M3 NAZARANA 1/3 MOHUR
Gold **Ruler:** Harindar Singh **Obv:** Bust of Harinder Singh left **Rev:** Arms **Note:** Prev. KM#M3. Weight varies: 3.57-3.80 grams.

Date	Mintage	F	VF	XF	Unc	BU
1941	—	—	750	1,200	1,650	—

JIND

BRITISH PROTECTORATE

MEDALLIC COINAGE

X# M1 NAZARANA RUPEE
Silver **Ruler:** Ranbir Singh VS1943 - / 1886 - AD **Subject:** 50th Anniversary of Reign **Obv:** Persian inscription **Rev:** Persian inscription **Note:** Prev. KM#M1. Weight varies: 10.70-11.60 grams.

Date	Mintage	Good	VG	F	VF	XF
VS1993 (1937)	—	50.00	100	175	250	350

X# M2 NAZARANA RUPEE
Silver **Ruler:** Ranbir Singh VS1943 - / 1886 - AD **Subject:** 50th anniversary of reign **Obv:** Persian inscription **Rev:** Persian inscription **Note:** Weight varies: 10.7 - 11.6 grams; countermarked with "1".

Date	Mintage	Good	VG	F	VF	XF
VS1993 (1937)	—	50.00	150	200	250	350

JUBBAL

PRINCELY STATE

MEDALLIC COINAGE

X# 1 1/2 MOHUR
5.5800 g., Gold **Ruler:** Raja Bhayay Chandra Bahadur VS1967-2004/1910-1947AD **Obv:** Supported arms **Rev:** "Shri" in hexagram

Date	Mintage	VG	F	VF	XF	Unc
VS1988(1931)	—	—	—	—	950	1,250

X# 2 MOHUR
11.5900 g., Gold **Ruler:** Raja Bhayay Chandra Bahadur VS1967-2004/1910-1947AD **Obv:** Supported Arms **Rev. Designer:** "Shri" in hexagram

Date	Mintage	VG	F	VF	XF	Unc
VS1988(1931)	—	—	—	—	1,200	1,500

KARAULI

KINGDOM, BRITISH PROTECTORATE

MEDALLIC COINAGE

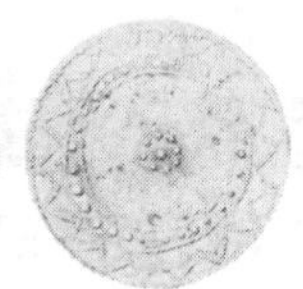

X# 2 MOHUR
10.9500 g., Gold

Date	Mintage	Good	VG	F	VF	XF
ND//2 (1886) Rare	—	—	—	—	—	—

X# 1 1/2 MOHUR
5.4800 g., Gold

Date	Mintage	Good	VG	F	VF	XF
ND//2 (1886) Rare	—	—	—	—	—	—

KISHANGARH

KINGDOM

HAMMERED COINAGE

X# 1 1/4 RUPEE
Silver **Ruler:** Muhammad Shah AH1131-1161 / 1719-1748AD **Note:** A modern concoction. Weight varies: 2.675-2.90 grams.

Date	Mintage	F	VF	XF	Unc	BU
AH1151	—	—	1.00	1.25	—	—

X# 2 1/2 RUPEE
Silver **Ruler:** Muhammad Shah AH1131-1161 / 1719-1748AD **Note:** A modern concoction. Weight varies: 5.35-5.80 grams.

Date	Mintage	F	VF	XF	Unc	BU
AH1151	—	—	2.00	2.50	—	—

X# 3 RUPEE
Silver **Ruler:** Muhammad Shah AH1131-1161 / 1719-1748AD **Note:** A modern concoction. Weight varies: 10.70-11.60 grams.

Date	Mintage	F	VF	XF	Unc	BU
AH1151	—	—	4.00	5.00	—	—

RAJKOT

PRINCELY STATE

MEDALLIC COINAGE

X# 1 MOHUR

7.8800 g., Gold **Ruler:** Dharmendra Singhji **Obv:** Sunrise **Rev:** Arms **Note:** Prev. KM#M1.

Date	Mintage	F	VF	XF	Unc	BU
1945	54	—	—	350	550	—

Note: Mintage figure is from original records.

Date	Mintage	F	VF	XF	Unc	BU
1954 Restrike	—	—	—	200	300	—

Note: Restrikes have sun slightly higher above the water, as pictured above.

X# 1a MOHUR

Silver **Ruler:** Dharmendra Singhji **Obv:** Sunrise **Rev:** Arms **Note:** Prev. KM#M1a.

Date	Mintage	F	VF	XF	Unc	BU
1945 Restrike	1,000	—	—	25.00	35.00	—

Note: Although originally considered a quasi legitimate issue by some authorities, the silver pieces were produced in recent times for the collector market

RATLAM

BRITISH PROTECTORATE

TOKEN COINAGE

X# Tn1 PAISA

7.0500 g., Bronze, 25.6 mm. **Obv:** Hanuman standing **Rev:** Scales

Date	Mintage	Good	VG	F	VF	XF
VS1911	—	12.00	15.00	20.00	35.00	—

REWA

BRITISH PROTECTORATE

MEDALLIC COINAGE

X# M1 1/2 RUPEE

Silver **Ruler:** Gulab Singh VS1975-2003 / 1918-1946AD **Subject:** Accession **Obv:** Arms with small lion supporters **Note:** Thin flan. Prev. KM#29.

Date	Mintage	VG	F	VF	XF	Unc
VS1975(1918)	—	21.50	42.50	70.00	100	—

X# M2 RUPEE

Silver **Ruler:** Gulab Singh VS1975-2003 / 1918-1946AD **Subject:** Accession **Obv:** Arms with small lion supporters **Note:** Thick flan. Prev.KM#31.

Date	Mintage	VG	F	VF	XF	Unc
VS1975(1918)	—	75.00	150	375	700	—

X# M3 1/2 MOHUR

Gold **Ruler:** Gulab Singh VS1975-2003 / 1918-1946AD **Subject:** Accession **Obv:** Arms with small lion supporters **Note:** Weight varies: 4.40-5.40 grams. Prev.KM#33.

Date	Mintage	VG	F	VF	XF	Unc
VS1975(1918)	—	250	375	550	800	—

X# M7 3/4 MOHUR

8.8000 g., Gold **Ruler:** Gulab Singh VS1975-2003 / 1918-1946AD **Obv:** Arms with large lion supporters in sprays **Rev:** Sprays in inner circle, date at top **Note:** Prev.KM#40.

Date	Mintage	VG	F	VF	XF	Unc
VS1977(1920)	—	250	375	550	800	—

X# M4 MOHUR

Gold **Ruler:** Gulab Singh VS1975-2003 / 1918-1946AD **Subject:** Accession **Obv:** Arms with small lion supporters **Note:** Weight varies: 10.70-11.71 grams. Prev.KM#35.

Date	Mintage	VG	F	VF	XF	Unc
VS1975(1918)	—	250	375	550	800	—

X# M5 MOHUR

Gold **Ruler:** Gulab Singh VS1975-2003/ 1918-1946AD **Subject:** Accession **Obv:** Arms with small lion supporters, large katar below, legend connected **Rev:** Legend and inscription connected **Note:** Weight varies: 10.70-11.71 grams. Prev.KM#36.

Date	Mintage	VG	F	VF	XF	Unc
VS1975(1918)	—	250	375	550	800	—

TRAVANCORE

KINGDOM

TULABHARAM MEDALLIC COINAGE

These presentation coins were struck prior to the weighing in ceremony of the Maharajah. The balance of his weight in these gold coins were distributed amongst the learned Brahmins and are referred to as Tulabhara Kasu. The legend reads - Sri Patmanabha - , the National Deity.

X# 1 1/4 PAGODA

0.6300 g., Gold, 8.8 mm. **Obv:** Tamil legend in 3 lines **Note:** Uniface. Prev. KM#M1.

Date	Mintage	F	VF	XF	Unc	BU
ND(1829, 47)	—	—	70.00	100	150	—

X# 5 1/4 PAGODA

0.6300 g., Gold, 12.7 mm. **Obv:** Tamil legend in 3 lines **Note:** Uniface. Prev. KM#M5.

Date	Mintage	F	VF	XF	Unc	BU
ND(1850, 55)	—	—	70.00	100	150	—

X# 9 1/4 PAGODA

0.6400 g., Gold **Obv:** Inscription: Tamil in three lines in sprays **Rev:** Sankha (conch shell) in sprays **Note:** Prev. KM#M9. Size varies: 10.9-12.7mm.

Date	Mintage	F	VF	XF	Unc	BU
ND(1870-1931)	—	45.00	65.00	90.00	135	—

X# 2 1/2 PAGODA

1.2700 g., Gold, 10.9 mm. **Obv:** Tamil legend in 3 lines **Note:** Uniface. Prev. KM#M2.

Date	Mintage	F	VF	XF	Unc	BU
ND(1829, 47)	—	50.00	80.00	115	175	—

X# 6 1/2 PAGODA

1.2700 g., Gold, 14.5 mm. **Obv:** Tamil legend in 3 lines

Date	Mintage	F	VF	XF	Unc	BU
ND(1850, 55)	—	50.00	80.00	115	175	—

X# 10 1/2 PAGODA

1.2800 g., Gold **Obv:** Inscription: Tamil in three lines in sprays **Rev:** Sankha (conch shell) in sprays **Note:** Prev. KM#M10.

Date	Mintage	F	VF	XF	Unc	BU
ND(1870-1931)	—	55.00	85.00	120	175	—

X# 3 PAGODA

2.5400 g., Gold, 13 mm. **Obv:** Tamil legend in 3 lines **Note:** Uniface. Prev. KM#M3.

Date	Mintage	F	VF	XF	Unc	BU
ND(1829, 47)	—	80.00	135	185	275	—

X# 7 PAGODA

2.5400 g., Gold, 17 mm. **Obv:** Tamil legend in 3 lines **Note:** Uniface. Prev. KM#M7.

Date	Mintage	F	VF	XF	Unc	BU
ND(1850, 55)	—	80.00	135	185	275	—

X# 11 PAGODA
2.5400 g., Gold **Obv:** Inscription: Tamil in three lines in sprays **Rev:** Sankha (conch shell) in sprays
Note: Prev. KM#M11.

Date	Mintage	F	VF	XF	Unc	BU
ND(1870-1931)	—	85.00	140	200	285	—

X# 4 2 PAGODA
5.0600 g., Gold, 15.4 mm. **Obv:** Tamil legend in 3 lines
Note: Uniface. Prev. KM#M4.

Date	Mintage	F	VF	XF	Unc	BU
ND(1829, 47)	—	120	200	280	400	—

X# 8 2 PAGODA
5.0600 g., Gold, 20.3 mm. **Obv:** Tamil legend in 3 lines
Note: Prev. KM#M8.

Date	Mintage	F	VF	XF	Unc	BU
ND(1850, 55)	—	120	200	280	400	—

X# 12 2 PAGODA
5.0900 g., Gold **Obv:** Inscription: Tamil in three lines in sprays **Rev:** Sankha (conch shell) in sprays
Note: Prev. KM#M12. Size varies: 20.0-23.9mm.

Date	Mintage	F	VF	XF	Unc	BU
ND(1870-1931)	—	125	210	300	425	—

INDIA-BRITISH

BRITISH

BULLION - TOLA ISSUE - RAM DUE RAI RAGHO SAVAN-TIGER BRAND

X# 85 TOLA
Gold **Obv:** Tiger walking left, palm tree behind **Obv. Legend:** RAM DUE RAI RAGHO SARAN • CALCUTTA
Rev: Crossed rifles **Rev. Legend:** TIGER BRAND

Date	Mintage	F	VF	XF	Unc	BU
ND	—	—	—	200	250	—

BULLION COINAGE

Tola Issue - M. S. Manilal Chimanlal & Co. - Bombay

X# 38 1/4 TOLA
2.9400 g., 0.9950 Gold 0.0940 oz. AGW **Obv:** 8-pointed badge **Obv. Legend:** M.S. MANILAL CHIMANLAL & CO. - BOMBAY **Rev. Legend:** *Diamond - Find Gold*

Date	Mintage	F	VF	XF	Unc	BU
ND(1940s)	—	—	BV	65.00	80.00	—

COLONIAL

BULLION COINAGE

East India Company

Struck in imitation of the AH1202 Year 19 1/2 and 1 Mohurs. Usually the date AH1202 is replaced by dots or initials and the name of the jeweler appears on the obverse at bottom. Many varieties exist including those struck in silver.

X# 35 RUPEE
11.4500 g., Silver, 28.22 mm. **Obv:** Initials "GR" **Rev:** Mint name Murshidabad below "19" **Edge:** Oblique milling

Date	Mintage	VG	F	VF	XF	Unc
AH(1202)/R.Y.19	—	10.00	17.50	27.50	45.00	—

MEDALLIC COINAGE

Richard Lobel Series

X# M93a SOVEREIGN
4.4200 g., Silver, 21.98 mm. **Obv:** Head of Duchess, bust of Duke facing **Obv. Legend:** DUKE & DUCHESS OF WINDSOR **Rev:** Tiger walking left **Edge:** Reeded

Date	Mintage	F	VF	XF	Unc	BU
1987 Proof	—	Value: 10.00				

COLONY

BULLION COINAGE

Jeweler's Series

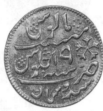

X# 18 MOHUR
Gold **Obv. Inscription:** ...... Hala(t)abad (?) **Rev. Inscription:** ...... Darb Sadusan (?)

Date	Mintage	VG	F	VF	XF	Unc
AH(1202)/R.Y.19	—	—	—	275	300	350

MILLED COINAGE

X# 20 1/2 ANNA
12.8100 g., Bronze, 32.7 mm. **Issuer:** East India Company **Obv:** Ganesha seated in ornate frame **Rev:** Value, date in sprays **Rev. Legend:** EAST INDIA COMPANY **Edge:** Reeded **Note:** A modern tourist token.

Date	Mintage	F	VF	XF	Unc	BU
1839	—	1.00	2.00	5.00	10.00	—

X# 17 RUPEE
Silver **Ruler:** Victoria **Obv:** Crowned bust left
Obv. Legend: VICTORIA EMPRESS **Rev:** Ornate border **Rev. Inscription:** ONE / RUPEE / INDIA
Note: An oriental imitation.

Date	Mintage	VG	F	VF	XF	Unc
1920	—	5.00	9.00	15.00	25.00	—

BULLION COINAGE

Private bullion issues have been recorded in weights of 1/4, 1/2, 1, 5, 10, 20 and 25 Tolas in gold and silver. The actual weight of the Tola is based on the obsolete English Guinea.

X# 31 3/4 MOHUR
8.8400 g., Gold, 27 mm. **Obv:** Initials "AR"

Date	Mintage	F	VF	XF	Unc	BU
AH1202//19	—	BV	225	275	—	—

X# 16.2 MOHUR
Gold **Obv. Inscription:** "F M" large letters

Date	Mintage	VG	F	VF	XF	Unc
AH(1202)//19	—	—	—	275	300	350

X# 16.1 MOHUR
Gold **Obv. Inscription:** "F M" small letters **Note:** Prev. X#16.

Date	Mintage	VG	F	VF	XF	Unc
AH(1202)//19	—	—	—	275	300	350

X# 44 1/4 TOLA
2.9400 g., 0.9950 Gold 0.0940 oz. AGW **Series:** Tola - M.S. Manilal Chimanlal & Co. - Bombay **Obv:** Eight-pointed rayed star **Rev. Legend:** *Diamond - Fine Gold*

Date	Mintage	F	VF	XF	Unc	BU
ND	—	—	BV	70.00	—	—

X# 78 TOLA
11.6600 g., 0.9950 Gold 0.3730 oz. AGW, 22 mm.
Obv: Elephant walking left **Rev:** Large value "1" **Rev. Legend:** ★ GUARANTEED FINE ★ ELEPHANT

Date	Mintage	F	VF	XF	Unc	BU
ND	—	—	BV	185	245	—

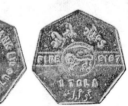

X# 61 TOLA
11.7000 g., 0.9167 Gold 0.3448 oz. AGW **Issuer:** Habib Bank Ltd. **Obv:** Symbol above large "HB" in circle

Obv. Legend: + HABIB BANK Ltd. + GUINEA GOLD **Rev:** Lion left in center circle, "Guinea gold" in Gujarati above, in Urdu below value

Date	Mintage	F	VF	XF	Unc	BU
ND	—	BV	245	265	300	—

X# 27 3 TOLAS
34.9800 g., 0.9999 Gold 1.1245 oz. AGW, 33 mm. **Issuer:** Bombay Mint for Indian Mines

Date	Mintage	F	VF	XF	Unc	BU
NDB	—	BV	800	850	925	—

X# 42.2 5 TOLAS
58.3000 g., 0.9950 Gold 1.8649 oz. AGW
Obv: Modified die, 8-pointed star with jewel in center
Rev: Modified die

Date	Mintage	F	VF	XF	Unc	BU
ND	—	—	BV	1,275	1,400	—

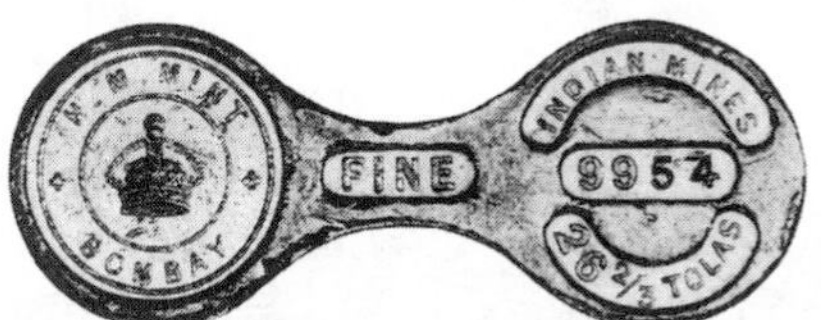

X# 28 26-2/3 TOLAS
311.0000 g., 0.9954 Gold 9.9525 oz. AGW **Issuer:** Bombay Mint for Indian Mines **Shape:** Dog-bone

Date	Mintage	F	VF	XF	Unc	BU
ND	—	—	—	7,000	—	—

East India Company

Struck in imitation of the AH1202 Year 19 1/2 and 1 Mohurs. Usually the date AH1202 is replaced by dots or initials and the name of the jeweler appears on the obverse at bottom. Many varieties exist including those struck in silver.

X# 2 1/2 RUPEE
Silver **Obv:** Initials BD **Rev:** Initials K.L. **Edge:** Plain

Date	Mintage	VG	F	VF	XF	Unc
AH(1202) / R.Y.19	—	12.00	20.00	35.00	55.00	85.00

X# 29 RUPEE
Silver, 27.18 mm. **Series:** Jeweler's **Obv. Inscription:** "MA" **Rev. Inscription:** Murshidabad **Edge:** Oblique milling

Date	Mintage	VG	F	VF	XF	Unc
AH1202//19	—	10.00	16.50	27.50	45.00	—

X# 30 RUPEE
Silver, 26.3 mm. **Series:** Jeweler's **Obv. Inscription:** Lala Bijnatha Manalal **Rev:** Flower at left

Date	Mintage	VG	F	VF	XF	Unc
AH(1202)//1911	—	10.00	16.50	27.50	45.00	—

X# 3 RUPEE
Silver, 27.5 mm. **Series:** Jeweler's **Obv. Inscription:** Lala Mahraj Mal Juli **Rev. Inscription:** Kaupur **Edge:** Oblique milling

Date	Mintage	VG	F	VF	XF	Unc
AH(1202) / R.Y. 19	—	10.00	16.50	27.50	45.00	—

X# 4 RUPEE
12.2000 Silver **Series:** Jeweler's **Obv. Inscription:** Ni jan al-din, registered jewelry merchant in Delhi **Edge:** Plain

Date	Mintage	VG	F	VF	XF	Unc
AH(1202) / R.Y. 19	—	10.00	16.50	27.50	45.00	—

X# 5 RUPEE
10.8500 g., Silver, 28 mm. **Series:** Jeweler's **Rev. Inscription:** Gurus das (?) **Edge:** Plain

Date	Mintage	VG	F	VF	XF	Unc
AH(1202) / R.Y. 19	—	10.00	16.50	27.50	45.00	—

X# 6 RUPEE
10.4200 g., Silver, 26.9 mm. **Series:** Jeweler's **Rev. Inscription:** Ramchandras Shadiram **Edge:** Oblique milling

Date	Mintage	VG	F	VF	XF	Unc
AH(1202) / R.Y. 19	—	10.00	16.50	27.50	45.00	—

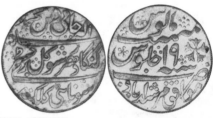

X# 7 RUPEE
12.9500 g., Silver, 27.7 mm. **Series:** Jeweler's **Obv. Inscription:** Gauja Dharar Shakal **Edge:** Oblique milling

Date	Mintage	VG	F	VF	XF	Unc
AH(1202) / R.Y.19	—	10.00	16.50	27.50	45.00	—

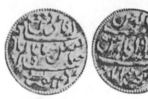

X# 8 1/2 MOHUR
6.1800 g., Gold **Note:** Prev. Bruce#X1.

Date	Mintage	VG	F	VF	XF	Unc
AH(1202)/R.Y.19	—	—	—	125	150	200

X# 11 MOHUR
13.2600 g., Gold **Obv:** Legend at bottom **Obv. Legend:** "Chiraq ud din Masawan" **Note:** Prev. KM#M102x.

Date	Mintage	VG	F	VF	XF	Unc
AH(1202)/R.Y.19	—	—	—	275	300	350

X# 12 MOHUR
13.2600 g., Gold **Obv:** Initials CD

Date	Mintage	VG	F	VF	XF	Unc
AH(1202)/R.Y. 19	—	—	—	275	300	350

X# 13 MOHUR
13.2600 g., Gold **Obv:** Initials RN

Date	Mintage	VG	F	VF	XF	Unc
AH(1202)/R.Y. 19	—	—	—	275	300	350

X# 14 MOHUR
13.2600 g., Gold **Rev:** 6-pointed star

Date	Mintage	VG	F	VF	XF	Unc
AH(1202)/R.Y. 19	—	—	—	275	300	350

Tola Issue - Central Bank of India

X# 21 TOLA
11.6600 g., 0.9960 Gold 0.3734 oz. AGW

Date	Mintage	F	VF	XF	Unc	BU
ND	—	—	BV	275	325	—

X# 22 5 TOLAS
58.3000 g., 0.9957 Gold 1.8663 oz. AGW

Date	Mintage	F	VF	XF	Unc	BU
ND	—	—	BV	1,300	1,450	—

X# 23 10 TOLAS
116.6000 g., 0.9956 Gold 3.7321 oz. AGW **Note:** Uniface.

Date	Mintage	F	VF	XF	Unc	BU
ND	—	—	BV	2,650	3,000	—

X# 24 10 TOLAS
0.9957 Gold

Date	Mintage	F	VF	XF	Unc	BU
ND	—	—	BV	2,650	3,000	—

Tola Issue - M. S. Manilal Chimanlal & Co. - Bombay

X# 40 1/2 TOLA
5.8800 g., 0.9950 Gold 0.1881 oz. AGW
Obv: 8-pointed badge **Obv. Legend:** M.S. MANICAL CHIMANLAL & CO. - BOMBAY

Date	Mintage	F	VF	XF	Unc	BU
ND(1940s)	—	—	BV	135	175	—

X# 41 TOLA
11.6600 g., 0.9950 Gold 0.3730 oz. AGW **Obv:** Outline of India **Rev. Inscription:** GATEWAY OF INDIA / BOMBAY

Date	Mintage	F	VF	XF	Unc	BU
ND	—	—	BV	265	320	—

X# 45 TOLA
11.6500 g., 0.9950 Gold 0.3727 oz. AGW, 23 mm.
Obv: 8-pointed radiant star

Date	Mintage	F	VF	XF	Unc	BU
ND	—	—	BV	275	300	—

X# 32 5 TOLAS
58.3000 g., 0.9990 Silver 1.8724 oz. ASW
Subject: Gateway of India

Date	Mintage	F	VF	XF	Unc	BU
ND	—	—	28.00	38.00	55.00	—

X# 42.1 5 TOLAS
58.3000 g., 0.9950 Gold 1.8649 oz. AGW
Obv: 8-pointed star with jewel in center

Date	Mintage	F	VF	XF	Unc	BU
ND	—	—	BV	1,275	1,400	—

X# 43 5 TOLAS
58.3000 g., 0.9950 Gold 1.8649 oz. AGW

Date	Mintage	F	VF	XF	Unc	BU
ND	—	—	BV	1,275	1,400	—

X# 33 10 TOLAS
116.6000 g., 0.9990 Silver 3.7449 oz. ASW
Note: Uniface.

Date	Mintage	F	VF	XF	Unc	BU
ND	—	—	50.00	70.00	100	—

X# 34 25 TOLAS

291.5000 g., 0.9990 Silver 9.3622 oz. ASW

Note: Similar to 5 Tolas, XM32.

Date	Mintage	F	VF	XF	Unc	BU
ND	—	—	100	125	165	—

X# 39 GUINEA

11.6600 g., 0.9166 Gold 0.3436 oz. AGW

Date	Mintage	F	VF	XF	Unc	BU
ND	—	—	BV	240	300	—

Tola Issue - Habib Bank Ltd.

X# 54 1/2 TOLA

5.8500 g., 0.9950 Gold 0.1871 oz. AGW

Date	Mintage	F	VF	XF	Unc	BU
ND	—	—	BV	140	180	—

X# 56.1 TOLA

11.6500 g., 0.9950 Gold 0.3727 oz. AGW, 23.2 mm.

Obv: Lion left holding sword, rays behind **Rev:** Large lettering

Date	Mintage	F	VF	XF	Unc	BU
ND	—	—	BV	185	245	—

X# 56.2 TOLA

11.6500 g., 0.9950 Gold 0.3727 oz. AGW, 23.2 mm.

Obv: Lion left holding sword, rays behind **Rev:** Small lettering

Date	Mintage	F	VF	XF	Unc	BU
ND	—	—	BV	185	245	—

X# 55 TOLA

11.6600 g., 0.9950 Gold 0.3730 oz. AGW

Date	Mintage	F	VF	XF	Unc	BU
ND	—	—	BV	285	325	—

X# 52 5 TOLAS

58.3000 g., 0.9990 Silver 1.8724 oz. ASW

Date	Mintage	F	VF	XF	Unc	BU
ND	—	—	60.00	80.00	120	—

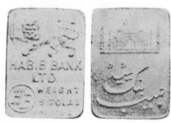

X# 58 5 TOLAS

58.3000 g., 0.9950 Gold 1.8649 oz. AGW

Date	Mintage	F	VF	XF	Unc	BU
ND	—	—	BV	1,300	1,450	—

Tola Issue - Devkaran Nanjee - Bombay

Struck by H.M. Mint, Bombay. For later issues of I.G. Mint see Republic listing #X14 and X15.

X# 75 10 TOLAS

116.6000 g., 0.9990 Silver 3.7449 oz. ASW

Note: Fineness will vary slightly.

Date	Mintage	F	VF	XF	Unc	BU
NDB	—	—	65.00	85.00	125	—

X# 76 20 TOLAS

233.2000 g., 0.9992 Silver 7.4912 oz. ASW **Note:** Fineness will vary slightly. Illustration reduced. 78 x 35mm.

Date	Mintage	F	VF	XF	Unc	BU
NDB	—	—	100	120	165	—

Tola Issue - M/S Rattanchand Rikhabdas Jain - Bombay

X# 80 TOLA

11.6600 g., 0.9950 Gold 0.3730 oz. AGW

Date	Mintage	F	VF	XF	Unc	BU
ND	—	—	BV	275	325	—

Tola Issue - Shewpujan Roy Indra San Roy - Star Brand

X# 83 TOLA

11.6600 g., 0.9950 Gold 0.3730 oz. AGW

Date	Mintage	F	VF	XF	Unc	BU
ND	—	—	BV	275	325	—

Tola Issue - M/S Kirtilal Jeshinglal & Co. - Bombay

X# 57 TOLA
11.6700 g., Gold, 23.8 mm. **Obv:** Elephant standing left

Date	Mintage	F	VF	XF	Unc	BU
ND	—	—	BV	200	275	—

Tola Issue - Hanuman Roy - Baldeu Roy

X# 77 1/2 TOLA
5.8200 g., 0.9950 Gold 0.1862 oz. AGW, 20 mm.
Obv: Crossed flags of Republic of India

Date	Mintage	F	VF	XF	Unc	BU
ND	—	—	BV	125	160	—

Tola Issue - B.J. Raya Guru

X# 79 1/2 TOLA
5.8200 g., Gold, 22 mm. **Obv:** Lion left, rays behind
Shape: Scalloped

Date	Mintage	F	VF	XF	Unc	BU
ND	—	—	BV	125	160	—

Tola Issue - L. Kashi Nath Seth Bankers - Bombay

X# 82 TOLA
11.6700 g., 0.9960 Gold 0.3737 oz. AGW, 23.5 mm.

Date	Mintage	F	VF	XF	Unc	BU
ND	—	—	BV	190	240	—

Tola Issue - Kamal Narayau - Mysore

X# 86 1/4 TOLA
Gold **Rev:** Tiger left

Date	Mintage	F	VF	XF	Unc	BU
ND	—	—	BV	65.00	85.00	—

X# 88 TOLA
Gold **Rev:** Tiger left

Date	Mintage	F	VF	XF	Unc	BU
ND	—	—	BV	200	275	—

PATTERNS

Bank of Jaipur

X# Pn65 40 GRAMMES
40.0000 g., 0.9990 Silver 1.2847 oz. ASW **Rev:** Flower

Date	Mintage	F	VF	XF	Unc	BU
ND(c.1900)	—	—	—	45.00	65.00	—

X# Pn66 40 GRAMMES
50.0000 g., 0.9990 Silver 1.6059 oz. ASW **Note:** Countermarked: 3 characters.

Date	Mintage	F	VF	XF	Unc	BU
ND(c.1900)	—	—	—	50.00	75.00	—

X# Pn67 40 GRAMMES
60.0000 g., 0.9990 Silver 1.9270 oz. ASW
Note: Countermarked: 3 characters.

Date	Mintage	F	VF	XF	Unc	BU
ND(c.1900)	—	—	—	65.00	95.00	—

TOKEN COINAGE

The British Indian Government introduced a special series of tokens for use by Famine Relief Officials as part of a policy to deal with great famine disasters in Bengal in 1874 and in Southern India in 1876.

X# Tn6 1/2 ANNA
Nickel-Brass, 19 mm. **Ruler:** George VI **Series:** Calcutta Mint Issue **Obv:** Small crown **Obv. Legend:** H.M.MINT • CALCUTTA + **Rev:** Large value "• 1/2 •" **Edge:** Plain **Note:** Mint employee canteen token

Date	Mintage	F	VF	XF	Unc	BU
ND(c.1940)	—	5.00	10.00	18.00	30.00	40.00

X# Tn10 1/2 ANNA
Copper, 26 mm. **Ruler:** George VI **Series:** Lahore Mint Issue **Obv:** Small crown **Obv. Legend:** H. M's MINT - LAHORE **Obv. Inscription:** + AN 1/2 NA +
Rev. Inscription: TOKEN **Edge:** Plain **Note:** Mint employee canteen token, Prid. #175.

Date	Mintage	F	VF	XF	Unc	BU
ND(1943)	—	8.00	15.00	25.00	50.00	60.00

X# Tn7 ANNA
Nickel-Brass, 19 mm. **Ruler:** Edward VIII **Series:** Calcutta Mint Issue **Obv:** Small crown **Obv. Legend:** H.M.MINT • CALCUTTA + **Rev:** Large value "• 1 •" **Edge:** Plain **Note:** Mint employee canteen token

Date	Mintage	F	VF	XF	Unc	BU
ND(c.1940)	—	5.00	10.00	18.00	30.00	40.00

X# Tn11 ANNA
Copper, 26 mm. **Ruler:** George VI **Series:** Lahore Mint Issue **Obv:** Small crown **Obv. Legend:** H. M's MINT - LAHORE **Obv. Inscription:** + AN 1 NA + **Rev. Inscription:** TOKEN **Edge:** Plain **Note:** Mint employee canteen token, Prid. #174.

Date	Mintage	F	VF	XF	Unc	BU
ND(1943)	—	8.00	15.00	25.00	50.00	60.00

X# Tn8 2 ANNAS
Nickel-Brass, 19 mm. **Ruler:** George VI **Series:** Calcutta Mint Issue **Obv:** Small crown **Obv. Legend:** H.M. MINT • CALCUTTA + **Rev:** Large value "• 2 •" **Edge:** Plain **Note:** Mint employee canteen token

Date	Mintage	F	VF	XF	Unc	BU
ND(c.1940)	—	8.00	15.00	25.00	50.00	60.00

X# Tn12 2 ANNAS
Copper, 26 mm. **Ruler:** George VI **Series:** Lahore Mint Issue **Obv:** Small crown **Obv. Legend:** H. M's MINT - LAHORE **Obv. Inscription:** + AN 2 NA +
Rev. Inscription: TOKEN **Edge:** Plain **Note:** Mint employee canteen token, Prid. #173.

Date	Mintage	F	VF	XF	Unc	BU
ND(1943)	—	9.00	13.00	22.00	45.00	55.00

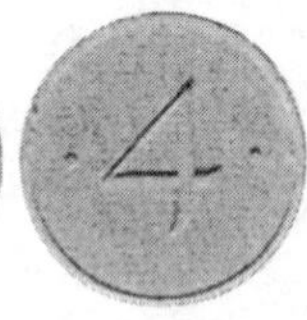

X# Tn9 4 ANNAS
Nickel-Brass, 19 mm. **Ruler:** George VI **Series:** Calcutta Mint Issue **Obv:** Small crown **Obv. Legend:** H.M.MINT • CALCUTTA + **Rev:** Large value "• 4 •" **Edge:** Plain **Note:** Mint employee canteen token, Prid. #171.

Date	Mintage	F	VF	XF	Unc	BU
ND(c.1940)	—	10.00	18.00	30.00	55.00	65.00

X# Tn13 4 ANNAS
Copper, 26 mm. **Ruler:** George VI **Series:** Lahore Mint Issue **Obv:** Small crown **Obv. Legend:** H. M's MINT - LAHORE **Obv. Inscription:** + AN 4 NA +
Rev. Inscription: TOKEN **Edge:** Plain **Note:** Mint employee canteen token, Prid. #172.

Date	Mintage	F	VF	XF	Unc	BU
ND(1943)	—	10.00	18.00	30.00	55.00	65.00

MEDALLIC COINAGE

Richard Lobel Series

X# M90 CROWN
Bronze **Subject:** Edward VIII **Obv:** Bust left **Obv. Legend:** EDWARD • VIII • KING • & • EMPEROR **Rev:** Tiger walking left **Edge:** Plain

Date	Mintage	F	VF	XF	Unc	BU
1936 Proof	650	Value: 20.00				

X# M90a CROWN
Copper-Nickel-Zinc **Subject:** Edward VII **Obv:** Bust left **Obv. Legend:** EDWARD • VIII • KING • & • EMPEROR **Rev:** Tiger walking left **Edge:** Plain

Date	Mintage	F	VF	XF	Unc	BU
1936 Proof	1,550	Value: 20.00				

X# M90b CROWN
0.9167 Silver **Subject:** Edward VIII **Obv:** Bust left **Obv. Legend:** EDWARD • VIII • KING • & • EMPEROR **Rev:** Tiger walking left **Edge:** Plain

Date	Mintage	F	VF	XF	Unc	BU
1936 Proof	200	Value: 75.00				

X# M90c CROWN
Gold **Subject:** Edward VIII **Obv:** Bust left **Obv. Legend:** EDWARD • VIII • KING • & • EMPEROR **Rev:** Tiger walking left **Edge:** Plain

Date	Mintage	F	VF	XF	Unc	BU
1936 Proof	—	Value: 700				

X# M90d CROWN
Copper **Subject:** Edward VIII **Obv:** Bust left **Obv. Legend:** EDWARD • VIII • KING • & • EMPEROR **Rev:** Tiger walking left **Edge:** Plain **Note:** Struck in error

Date	Mintage	F	VF	XF	Unc	BU
1936 Proof	100	Value: 30.00				

X# M92 CROWN
23.0200 g., 0.9167 Silver 0.6784 oz. ASW, 38 mm. **Obv:** Head of Duchess, bust of Duke facing **Obv. Legend:** DUKE & DUCHESS OF WINDSOR **Rev:** Tiger walking left **Edge:** Reeded

Date	Mintage	F	VF	XF	Unc	BU
1987 Proof	—	Value: 75.00				

X# M91 SOVEREIGN
0.3750 Gold, 21.98 mm. **Subject:** Edward VIII **Obv:** Bust left **Obv. Legend:** EDWARD • VIII • KING • & • EMPEROR **Rev:** Tiger walking left **Edge:** Plain

Date	Mintage	F	VF	XF	Unc	BU
1936 Proof	200	Value: 150				

X# M91a SOVEREIGN
4.4200 g., Silver, 21.98 mm. **Obv:** Bust left **Obv. Legend:** EDWARD • VIII • KING • & • EMPEROR **Rev:** Tiger walking left **Edge:** Plain

Date	Mintage	F	VF	XF	Unc	BU
1936 Proof	—	Value: 10.00				

X# M93 SOVEREIGN
Gold, 21.98 mm. **Obv:** Head of Duchess, bust of Duke facing **Obv. Legend:** DUKE & DUCHESS OF WINDSOR **Rev:** Tiger walking left **Edge:** Reeded

Date	Mintage	F	VF	XF	Unc	BU
1987 Proof	—	Value: 125				

AZAD HIND PROVISIONAL GOVERNMENT

MILLED COINAGE

X# 95 RUPAYA
11.6000 g., Silver **Subject:** 100th Anniversary of Birth **Obv:** Bust of Subhash Chandra Bose 3/4 left **Obv. Legend:** ★ UNITY • FAITH • SACRIFICE ★ 23rd. JANUARY, 1897 **Rev:** Leaping tiger, large "1" behind **Rev. Legend:** AARZI HUKUMAT AZAD HIND **Rev. Inscription:** JAI HIND **Note:** Prev. X#45.

Date	Mintage	F	VF	XF	Unc	BU
1943 (1997) Proof	—	Value: 35.00				

PIEFORTS

X#	Date	Mintage	Identification	Mkt Val
P1	1936	—	Crown. 0.9167 Silver. X#M90b.	150

REPUBLIC

BULLION COINAGE

X# 127 1/2 RUPEE
5.8500 g., 0.9990 Silver 0.1879 oz. ASW, 23.5 mm. **Issuer:** NR **Obv:** Ganesha seated facing, mouse below **Rev:** Large "Shri" on spokes

Date	Mintage	F	VF	XF	Unc	BU
ND(ca.1980) Proof	—	Value: 6.00				

X# 128 RUPEE
11.6300 g., 0.9990 Silver 0.3735 oz. ASW, 26.45 mm. **Obv:** Lakshmi (Goddess of Wealth) seated facing in lotus flower

Date	Mintage	F	VF	XF	Unc	BU
ND(ca.1980) Proof	—	Value: 7.50				

X# 111 5 GRAMMES
4.9900 g., 0.9990 Silver 0.1603 oz. ASW, 23.9 mm. **Issuer:** Unknown **Obv:** Ganesha seated facing on stool, mouse below **Rev:** Large "Shri" on spokes

Date	Mintage	F	VF	XF	Unc	BU
ND(ca.1980) Proof	—	Value: 6.00				

X# 116 5 GRAMMES
4.9600 g., 0.9990 Silver 0.1593 oz. ASW, 23.9 mm. **Issuer:** NR **Obv:** Lakshmi (Goddess of Wealth) standing facing, swans at left, elephant lying at right **Rev:** Large "Shri" on spokes

Date	Mintage	F	VF	XF	Unc	BU
ND(ca.1980) Proof	—	Value: 6.00				

X# 112 10 GRAMMES
9.9800 g., 0.9990 Silver 0.3205 oz. ASW, 31.65 mm. **Issuer:** Unknown **Obv:** Ganesha facing seated on stool, mouse below **Rev:** Large "Shri" on spokes

Date	Mintage	F	VF	XF	Unc	BU
ND(ca.1980) Proof	—	Value: 10.00				

X# 117 10 GRAMMES
10.0300 g., 0.9990 Silver 0.3221 oz. ASW, 31.7 mm. **Issuer:** NR **Obv:** Lakshmi (Goddess of Wealth) standing facing, swans at left, elephant lying at right **Rev:** Large "Shri" on spokes

Date	Mintage	F	VF	XF	Unc	BU
ND(ca.1980) Proof	—	Value: 10.00				

MEDALLIC COINAGE

X# 125 10 GRAMMES
9.9800 g., 0.9990 Silver 0.3205 oz. ASW, 31 mm. **Issuer:** M/S. Roshanlal Girdharilal Jain & Co. • Bombay • **Obv:** Lakshmi (Goddess of Wealth) standing facing, swans at left, elephant lying at right **Rev:** 8-pointed star

Date	Mintage	F	VF	XF	Unc	BU
ND(ca.1980) Proof	—	Value: 10.00				

X# 113 25 GRAMMES
25.0100 g., 0.9990 Silver 0.8033 oz. ASW, 37.9 mm. **Issuer:** Unknown **Obv:** Ganesha facing seated on stool, mouse below **Rev:** Large "Shri" on spokes

Date	Mintage	F	VF	XF	Unc	BU
ND(ca.1980) Proof	—	Value: 20.00				

X# 118 25 GRAMMES
25.0100 g., 0.9990 Silver 0.8033 oz. ASW, 37.9 mm. **Issuer:** NR **Obv:** Lakshmi (Goddess of Wealth) standing facing, swans at left, elephant lying at right **Rev:** Large "Shri" on spokes

Date	Mintage	F	VF	XF	Unc	BU
ND(ca.1980) Proof	—	Value: 20.00				

X# 104 2 ANNAS
Copper-Nickel, 22 mm. **Subject:** Independence Commemorative **Obv:** Outline map of India **Rev:** Republic flag **Edge:** Plain **Shape:** Square
Note: Although non-denominated being struck on 2 Annas flans many circulated freely.

Date	Mintage	VG	F	VF	XF	Unc
1947	—	1.00	1.75	3.75	7.50	15.00

X# 101 GOLD RUPEE
10.0000 g., 0.9999 Gold 0.3215 oz. AGW, 27.1 mm. **Subject:** 50th Anniversary Indian Independence **Obv:** Chart **Obv. Inscription:** GOLDEN ANNIVERSARY **Rev:** Bust of Gandhi 3/4 right **Edge:** Reeded

Date	Mintage	F	VF	XF	Unc	BU
1997 Proof	—	Value: 225				

X# 102 GOLD RUPEE
10.0000 g., 0.9999 Gold 0.3215 oz. AGW, 27.1 mm. **Subject:** 50th Anniversary Indian Independence **Obv:** Asoka column **Rev:** Goddess Laksmi **Edge:** Reeded

Date	Mintage	F	VF	XF	Unc	BU
1997 Proof	—	Value: 225				

X# 103 GOLD RUPEE
10.0000 g., 0.9999 Gold 0.3215 oz. AGW, 27.1 mm. **Subject:** 50th Anniversary Indian Independence **Obv:** Asoka column in sprays **Rev:** Elephant deity Ganesha riding a mouse **Edge:** Reeded

Date	Mintage	F	VF	XF	Unc	BU
1997 Proof	—	Value: 225				

BULLION COINAGE

Devkaran Nanjee / Dena Bank - Bombay

Struck by the Indian Government Mint, Bombay. For earliest issues of H.M. Mint - Bombay see Colonial listings #X75 and X76.

X# 9 50 GRAMMES
50.0000 g., 0.9985 Silver 1.6051 oz. ASW
Note: Fineness will vary slightly.

Date	Mintage	F	VF	XF	Unc	BU
ND	—	—	18.00	28.00	45.00	—

X# 10 100 GRAMMES
100.0000 g., 0.9985 Silver 3.2101 oz. ASW
Note: Fineness will vary slightly.

Date	Mintage	F	VF	XF	Unc	BU
ND	—	—	30.00	45.00	70.00	—

X# 14 10 TOLAS
116.6000 g., 0.9991 Silver 3.7452 oz. ASW
Note: Fineness will vary slightly.

Date	Mintage	F	VF	XF	Unc	BU
ND	—	—	40.00	60.00	85.00	—

X# 15 20 TOLAS
233.2000 g., 0.9991 Silver 7.4905 oz. ASW **Note:** Similar to 10 Tolas, X14. Fineness will vary slightly.

Date	Mintage	F	VF	XF	Unc	BU
ND	—	—	70.00	90.00	135	—

Narrondass Manordass Refiners - Bombay

X# 35 10 TOLAS
116.6000 g., 0.9990 Silver 3.7449 oz. ASW

Date	Mintage	F	VF	XF	Unc	BU
ND	—	—	35.00	50.00	75.00	—

Jagadambarai Jwalaprasad Issue

X# 106 TOLA
11.6100 g., 0.9990 Gold 0.3729 oz. AGW, 23.2 mm.
Series: Aeroplane Brand **Obv:** Airplane **Obv. Legend:** JAGADAMBARI • JWALAPRASAD **Rev. Legend:** AEROPLANE BRAND **Edge:** Plain

Date	Mintage	F	VF	XF	Unc	BU
ND(c.1970)	—	—	—	285	325	—

INDONESIA

REPUBLIC

MEDALLIC COINAGE

X# 1 25 RUPIAH
Gold **Subject:** Prince Diponegoro **Note:** Prev. KM#M1. For earlier issues see Netherlands East Indies listings.

Date	Mintage	F	VF	XF	Unc	BU
ND(1952)(u)	36,000	—	—	225	300	—

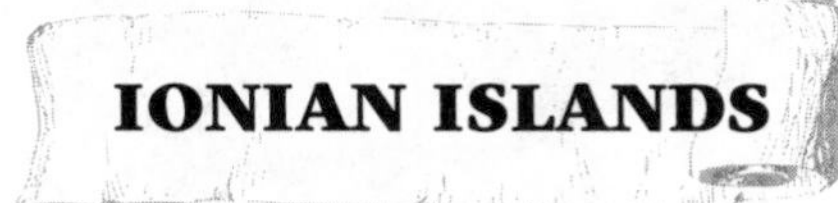

IONIAN ISLANDS

ZANTE

SOVEREIGN ORDER OF ST. DENNIS OF ZANTE

FANTASY COINAGE

X# 1 50 ASPRA
Franklinium Silver-Clad

Date	Mintage	F	VF	XF	Unc	BU
1966 Proof	2,202	Value: 15.00				

X# 2 100 ASPRA
Copper-Nickel Silvered **Subject:** St. Dennis of Zante

Date	Mintage	F	VF	XF	Unc	BU
1966 Proof	2,202	Value: 25.00				

X# 2a 100 ASPRA
Bronze **Subject:** St. Dennis of Zante

Date	Mintage	F	VF	XF	Unc	BU
1966 Proof	3	Value: 125				

X# 2b 100 ASPRA
Brass **Subject:** St. Dennis of Zante

Date	Mintage	F	VF	XF	Unc	BU
1966 Proof	3	Value: 125				

X# 2c 100 ASPRA
Franklinium **Subject:** St. Dennis of Zante

Date	Mintage	F	VF	XF	Unc	BU
1966 Proof	3	Value: 160				

X# 2d 100 ASPRA
0.9250 Silver **Subject:** St. Dennis of Zante

Date	Mintage	F	VF	XF	Unc	BU
1966 Proof	3	Value: 250				

X# 2e 100 ASPRA
0.9990 Silver **Subject:** St. Dennis of Zante

Date	Mintage	F	VF	XF	Unc	BU
1966 Proof	3	Value: 275				

X# 2f 100 ASPRA
Platinum APW **Subject:** St. Dennis of Zante

Date	Mintage	F	VF	XF	Unc	BU
1966 Proof	1	—	—	—	—	—

PROOF SETS

X#	Date	Mintage	Identification	Issue Price	Mkt Val
XPS1	1966 (2)	2,202	X1, X2	—	40.00

IRAN

KINGDOM

MEDALS OF VALOR

Similar medals have also been reported for AH1325. These are often confused and cataloged as actual coins, and many of the earlier types actually circulated along side regular coinage. Examples with mountings removed sell for 60-80% of the valuations given

X# MV16 NON-DENOMINATED
Silver **Obverse:** Sun rising behind lion lying left in sprays **Reverse:** Shah's inscription in sprays

Date	Mintage	F	VF	XF	Unc
AH1209 (error 1290)	—	75.00	125	200	300

NASIR AL-DIN SHAH

AH1264-1313 / 1848-1896AD

MEDALLIC COINAGE

The following were most likely intended for presentation purposes rather than as a circulation medium

X# M20 5 KRANS
Silver **Subject:** 30th Anniversary of Reign

Date	Mintage	F	VF	XF	Unc
AH1293	—	—	1,650	2,750	3,500

X# M11 5 KRANS
23.0251 g., 0.9000 Silver 0.6662 oz. ASW **Subject:** 50th Anniversary of Reign **Note:** Prev. KM#M3.

Date	Mintage	F	VF	XF	Unc
AH1313 Without loop	—	—	2,750	3,250	3,750
AH1313 With loop	—	—	1,350	1,650	—

X# M7 10 KRANS
45.0501 g., 0.9000 Silver 1.3035 oz. ASW **Note:** Prev. Y#15.

Date	Mintage	F	VF	XF	Unc
AH1301B	—	—	2,000	3,000	4,000

X# M9 10 KRANS
45.0501 g., 0.9000 Silver 1.3035 oz. ASW
Subject: Shah's Return From Europe **Note:** Similar to XM10. Prev. KM#M11.

Date	Mintage	F	VF	XF	Unc
AH1307	—	—	2,000	3,000	4,000

X# M12 10 KRANS
45.7000 g., Silver **Subject:** 50th Anniversary of Reign **Note:** Prev. KM#M4.

Date	Mintage	F	VF	XF	Unc
AH1313	—	—	2,000	3,000	4,000

X# M11a 5 TOMAN
28.5500 g., Gold **Note:** Prev. KM#M12.

Date	Mintage	F	VF	XF	Unc
AH1313	—	—	1,000	1,800	2,600

Note: Modern reproductions exist.

X# M6 10 TOMAN
28.7440 g., 0.9000 Gold 0.8317 oz. AGW
Obverse: Legend First Nasir type **Reverse:** Lion and sun **Note:** Prev. KM#M8.

Date	Mintage	F	VF	XF	Unc
AH1293 Rare	—	—	—	—	—

X# M14 10 TOMAN
28.7440 g., 0.9000 Gold 0.8317 oz. AGW
Subject: 50th Anniversary of Reign of Nasir al-Din **Note:** Prev. KM#M12.

Date	Mintage	F	VF	XF	Unc
AH1313	—	—	4,500	6,500	8,000

X# M8 25 TOMAN
71.7400 g., 0.9000 Gold 2.0758 oz. AGW, 50 mm.
Note: Prev. KM#M5.

Date	Mintage	F	VF	XF	Unc
AH1301B	—	—	15,000	17,500	22,000

X# M10 25 TOMAN
72.2700 g., 0.9000 Gold 2.0911 oz. AGW **Subject:** Shah's Return From Europe **Note:** Prev. KM#M6.

Date	Mintage	F	VF	XF	Unc
AH1307	—	—	12,500	15,000	20,000

MEDALS OF VALOR

Similar medals have also been reported for AH1325. These are often confused and cataloged as actual coins, and many of the earlier types actually circulated along side regular coinage. Examples with mountings removed sell for 60-80% of the valuations given

X# MV12 NON-DENOMINATED
11.0000 g., Silver **Obverse:** Sun rising behind lion standing left holding sword in sprays **Reverse:** Outer legend in four cartouches around Shah's inscription

Date	Mintage	F	VF	XF	Unc
ND(1848-55)	—	150	225	350	—

X# MV11 NON-DENOMINATED
9.7200 g., Gold **Subject:** Nazir al-Din Shah
Obverse: Sun rising behind lion standing left holding sword in sprays **Reverse:** Outer legend in four cartouches around Shah's inscription

Date	Mintage	F	VF	XF	Unc
ND(1848-55)	—	400	600	900	—

X# MV10 NON-DENOMINATED
Silver, 37 mm. **Obverse:** Inscription at left of crown above sun rising above lion standing left on shelf holding sword within sprays **Edge:** Plain

Date	Mintage	VG	F	VF	XF	Unc
AH1270 (1853)	—	—	—	—	—	—

X# MV13 NON-DENOMINATED
Silver **Obverse:** Sun rising behind lion left in sprays **Reverse:** Continuous legend around Shah's inscription

Date	Mintage	F	VF	XF	Unc
AH1273	—	150	225	350	—

X# MV17 NON-DENOMINATED

27.8000 g., Gold **Obverse:** Sun rising behind lion lying left in sprays **Reverse:** Shah's inscription in sprays

Date	Mintage	F	VF	XF	Unc
AH1209 (error 1290)	—	600	950	1,350	—

X# MV18 NON-DENOMINATED

Gold **Subject:** Nazir al-Din Shah **Obverse:** Sun rising above lion standing left on shelf holding sword in sprays **Reverse:** Continuous legend around Shah's inscription

Date	Mintage	F	VF	XF	Unc
AH1297	—	500	700	1,000	—

X# MV19 NON-DENOMINATED

Silver **Obverse:** Sun rising above lion standing left on shelf holding sword in sprays **Reverse:** Continuous legend around Shah's inscription

Date	Mintage	F	VF	XF	Unc
AH1297	—	60.00	100	150	225

X# MV15 NON-DENOMINATED

13.9800 g., Gold, 34.9 mm. **Obverse:** Sun rising above lion standing left on shelf holding sword in sprays **Reverse:** Continuous legend around Shah's inscription

Date	Mintage	VG	F	VF	XF	Unc
AH1298	—	—	400	650	800	1,000

X# MV21 NON-DENOMINATED

Silver **Obverse:** Sun rising behind lion standing left on shelf holding sword in sprays **Reverse:** Continuous legend around Shah's inscription

Date	Mintage	F	VF	XF	Unc
AH1300	—	60.00	100	150	225

X# MV22 NON-DENOMINATED

Bronze **Obverse:** Sun behind lion standing left on shelf holding sword in sprays **Reverse:** Continuous legend around Shah's inscription

Date	Mintage	F	VF	XF	Unc
AH1300	—	20.00	40.00	65.00	90.00

X# MV20 NON-DENOMINATED

13.5700 g., Gold, 34.9 mm. **Obverse:** Sun rising behind lion standing left on shelf holding sword in sprays **Reverse:** Continuous legend around Shah's inscription **Note:** Weight varies: 13.57 - 14.40 g

Date	Mintage	F	VF	XF	Unc
AH1300	—	400	650	800	1,000

X# MV23 NON-DENOMINATED

14.0500 g., Gold **Obverse:** Sun behind lion standing left on shelf holding sword in sprays **Reverse:** Continuous legend around Shsh's inscription

Date	Mintage	F	VF	XF	Unc
AH1311	—	400	650	800	1,000

X# MV24 NON-DENOMINATED

Silver **Obverse:** Sun behind lion standing left on shelf holding sword in sprays **Reverse:** Continuous legend around Shah's inscription

Date	Mintage	F	VF	XF	Unc
AH1311	—	60.00	100	150	225

MUZAFFAR AL-DIN SHAH

AH1313-1324 / 1896-1907AD

MEDALLIC COINAGE

The following were most likely intended for presentation purposes rather than as a circulation medium

X# M21 5 KRANS

Silver **Subject:** Shah's Visit to Brussels Mint **Obverse:** Military uniformed bust facing 3/4 right

Date	Mintage	F	VF	XF	Unc
AH1318	—	—	2,250	3,000	3,750

X# M22 5 KRANS

Silvered Bronze **Obverse:** Military uniformed bust facing 3/4 right

Date	Mintage	F	VF	XF	Unc
AH1318	—	—	2,000	2,750	3,500

X# M23 10 TOMAN

Gold **Subject:** Shah's Visit to Brussels Mint **Obverse:** Military uniformed bust facing 3/4 right **Note:** Similar to X#M21. Weight varies: 30.97-31.03 grams.

Date	Mintage	F	VF	XF	Unc
AH1318	—	—	10,000	12,000	15,000

MEDALS OF VALOR

Similar medals have also been reported for AH1325. These are often confused and cataloged as actual coins, and many of the earlier types actually circulated along side regular coinage. Examples with mountings removed sell for 60-80% of the valuations given

X# MV26 NON-DENOMINATED

Silver **Obverse:** Sun behind lion standing left on shelf holding sword in sprays **Reverse:** Continuous legend around Shah's inscription

Date	Mintage	F	VF	XF	Unc
AH1315	—	65.00	100	150	225

X# MV30 NON-DENOMINATED

Silver **Obverse:** Sun behind lion standing left on shelf holding sword in sprays **Reverse:** Continuous legend around Shah's inscription

Date	Mintage	F	VF	XF	Unc
AH1317	—	40.00	60.00	90.00	135

X# MV31 NON-DENOMINATED

Bronze **Obverse:** Sun behind lion standing left on shelf holding sword in sprays **Reverse:** Continuous legend around Shah's inscription

Date	Mintage	F	VF	XF	Unc
AH1317	—	20.00	40.00	65.00	90.00

X# MV29 NON-DENOMINATED

13.5400 g., Gold **Subject:** Muzzafer al-Din Shah **Obverse:** Sun behind lion standing left on shelf holding sword in sprays **Reverse:** Continuous legend around Shah's inscription **Note:** Typical ribbon mounting.

Date	Mintage	F	VF	XF	Unc
AH1317	—	350	550	750	900

X# MV33 NON-DENOMINATED

15.9300 g., Silver, 37.6 mm. **Obverse:** Sun behind lion standing left on shelf holding sword in sprays **Reverse:** Continuous legend around Shah's inscription

Date	Mintage	F	VF	XF	Unc
AH1318	—	300	450	600	750

MUHAMMAD ALI SHAH
AH1324-1327 / 1907-1909AD

MEDALLIC COINAGE

The following were most likely intended for presentation purposes rather than as a circulation medium

X# M27 5 KRANS

Silver

Date	Mintage	F	VF	XF	Unc
AH1327	—	—	2,250	3,000	3,900

X# M25 5 TOMAN

14.3000 g., 0.9000 Gold 0.4138 oz. AGW **Note:** Prev. KM#M10.

Date	Mintage	F	VF	XF	Unc
AH1326	—	—	—	2,250	3,750

SULTAN AHMAD SHAH
AH1327-1344 / 1909-1925AD

MEDALS OF VALOR

Similar medals have also been reported for AH1325. These are often confused and cataloged as actual coins, and many of the earlier types actually circulated along side regular coinage. Examples with mountings removed sell for 60-80% of the valuations given

X# MV40 NON-DENOMINATED

11.2800 g., Silver, 30.9 mm. **Obverse:** Bust 3/4-left in sprays **Reverse:** Crown above sun rising above lion standing left on shelf holding sword within inner circle, bow below **Edge:** Plain

Date	Mintage	F	VF	XF	Unc
AH1337 (1918)	—	60.00	100	150	225

REZA SHAH
AH1344-1360 / 1925-1941AD

MEDALLIC COINAGE

The following were most likely intended for presentation purposes rather than as a circulation medium

X# M35 TOMAN

2.8700 g., Gold **Subject:** Reza's First New Year Celebration **Note:** Prev. Y#119.

Date	Mintage	F	VF	XF	Unc
SH1305	—	—	—	125	200

MUHAMMAD REZA PAHLAVI SHAH
SH1320-1358 / 1941-1979AD

MEDALLIC COINAGE

The following were most likely intended for presentation purposes rather than as a circulation medium

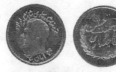

X# M49 1/4 PAHLAVI

1.9650 g., 0.9000 Gold 0.0569 oz. AGW **Subject:** Coronation **Obverse:** Head left, 4 Aban 46 below **Reverse:** Inscription in sprays

Date	Mintage	Good	VG	F	VF	XF
SH1346	—	—	—	—	—	—

X# M51 1/2 PAHLAVI

3.9300 g., 0.9000 Gold 0.1137 oz. AGW, 19.7 mm. **Obverse:** Bust of Empress Farah Diba left **Reverse:** Empress crest

Date	Mintage	F	VF	XF	Unc
SH1351 Proof	—	Value: 400			
SH1352 Proof	—	Value: 400			
SH1353 Proof	—	Value: 400			
SH1354 Proof	—	Value: 400			
SH1355 Proof	—	Value: 400			
MS2536 Proof	—	Value: 400			
MS2537 Proof	—	Value: 400			

X# M50 1/2 PAHLAVI

3.9300 g., 0.9000 Gold 0.1137 oz. AGW, 19.7 mm. **Obverse:** Military bust left **Reverse:** Royal arms

Date	Mintage	F	VF	XF	Unc
SH1351 Proof	—	Value: 400			
SH1352 Proof	—	Value: 400			
SH1353 Proof	—	Value: 400			
SH1354 Proof	—	Value: 400			
SH1355 Proof	—	Value: 400			
MS2536 Proof	—	Value: 400			
MS2537 Proof	—	Value: 400			

X# M53 PAHLAVI

8.0000 g., 0.9000 Gold 0.2315 oz. AGW, 26 mm. **Obverse:** Bust of Empress Farah Diba left **Reverse:** Empress crest

Date	Mintage	F	VF	XF	Unc
SH1352 Proof	—	Value: 500			
SH1352 Proof	—	Value: 500			
SH1353 Proof	—	Value: 500			
SH1354 Proof	—	Value: 500			
SH1355 Proof	—	Value: 500			
MS2536 Proof	—	Value: 500			
MS2537 Proof	—	Value: 500			

X# M54 3 PAHLAVI
25.0000 g., 0.9000 Gold 0.7234 oz. AGW, 40.2 mm. **Obverse:** Military bust left **Reverse:** Royal arms

Date	Mintage	F	VF	XF	Unc
SH1351 Proof	—	Value: 1,500			
SH1352 Proof	—	Value: 1,500			
SH1353 Proof	—	Value: 1,500			
SH1354 Proof	—	Value: 1,500			
SH1355 Proof	—	Value: 1,500			
MS2536 Proof	—	Value: 1,500			
MS2537 Proof	—	Value: 1,500			

X# M55 3 PAHLAVI
25.0000 g., 0.9000 Gold 0.7234 oz. AGW, 40.2 mm. **Obverse:** Bust of Empress Farah Diba left **Reverse:** Empress crest

Date	Mintage	F	VF	XF	Unc
SH1351 Proof	—	Value: 1,500			
SH1352 Proof	—	Value: 1,500			
SH1353 Proof	—	Value: 1,500			
SH1354 Proof	—	Value: 1,500			
SH1355 Proof	—	Value: 1,500			
MS2536 Proof	—	Value: 1,500			
MS2537 Proof	—	Value: 1,500			

X# M56 12 PAHLAVI
100.0000 g., 0.9000 Gold 2.8934 oz. AGW **Obverse:** Military bust left **Reverse:** Royal arms **Note:** Illustration reduced, actual size 60mm.

Date	Mintage	F	VF	XF	Unc
MS2537 Proof	—	Value: 3,000			

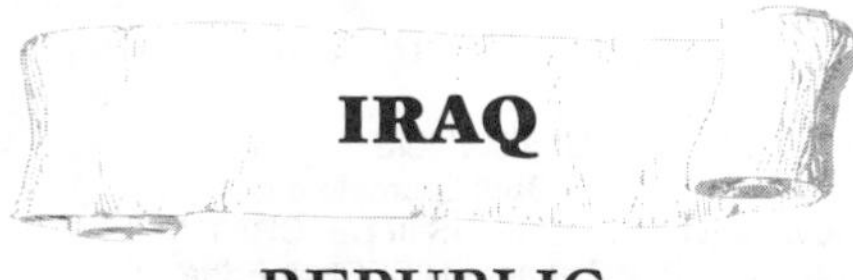

IRAQ

REPUBLIC
MEDALLIC COINAGE

X# 1 500 FILS
45.0000 g., Silver **Subject:** 1st Anniversary of the Republic **Obverse:** Bust of General Abdul Karim Kassem **Note:** Prev. KM#M1.

Date	Mintage	F	VF	XF	Unc
1959	500,000	—	12.00	25.00	40.00
1959 Proof	—	Value: 60.00			

X# 3 50 DINARS
16.9650 g., 0.9170 Gold 0.5001 oz. AGW **Subject:** 1st Anniversary of Hussein as President **Obverse:** Bust 3/4 left above Legend **Reverse:** Arabic legend

Date	Mintage	F	VF	XF	Unc
1980 Proof	10,000	Value: 400			

X# 2 100 DINARS
38.0000 g., 0.9170 Gold 1.1203 oz. AGW **Subject:** Battle of Gadissyiat **Obverse:** Bust of Saddam Hussein

Date	Mintage	F	VF	XF	Unc
1980	—	—	—	—	825

IRELAND

KINGDOM

MEDALLIC COINAGE

Thomas L. Elder Issue

Brian Boru (926-1014 A.D.) was King of Ireland from 1002-1014 A.D. and is referred to as the ""George Washington of Ireland"". At the age of 88 he broke the Danish power in Ireland at the battle of Clontarf April 23, 1014 where he was slain.

X# 7 CROWN
Aluminum **Subject:** Brian Boru **Edge:** Plain

Date	Mintage	F	VF	XF	Unc	BU
ND(1960)	225	—	70.00	145	285	—

X# 7a CROWN
Bronze **Subject:** Brian Boru **Edge:** Plain

Date	Mintage	F	VF	XF	Unc	BU
ND(1960)	8	—	—	400	850	—

X# 7b CROWN

Silver **Subject:** Brian Boru **Edge:** Lettered

Date	Mintage	F	VF	XF	Unc	BU
ND(1960)	75	—	85.00	175	350	—

1900 Reginald Huth Issues

Commemorating the visit of Queen Victoria to Ireland; struck by John Pinches, London, England

X# 2 3 SHILLING

Silver **Note:** Prev. KM#M2.

Date	Mintage	F	VF	XF	Unc	BU
MCM (1900) Proof	—	Value: 550				

X# 2a 3 SHILLING

Gold **Note:** Prev. KM#M2a.

Date	Mintage	F	VF	XF	Unc	BU
MCM (1900) Possibly Unique	—	—	—	—	—	—

X# 3 3 SHILLING

Silver **Rev:** With III above and Oct: below crown **Note:** Prev. KM#M3.

Date	Mintage	F	VF	XF	Unc	BU
MCM (1900) Proof	—	Value: 950				

X# 3a 3 SHILLING

Gold **Rev:** With III above and Oct: below crown **Note:** Prev. KM#M3a.

Date	Mintage	F	VF	XF	Unc	BU
MCM (1900) Possibly Unique	—	—	—	—	—	—

X# 4 3 SHILLING

Silver **Rev:** With III above and Sep: below crown **Note:** Prev. KM#M4.

Date	Mintage	F	VF	XF	Unc	BU
MCM (1900) Proof	—	Value: 950				

X# 4a 3 SHILLING

Gold **Rev:** With III above and Sep: below crown **Note:** Prev. KM#M4a.

Date	Mintage	F	VF	XF	Unc	BU
MCM (1900) Possibly Unique	—	—	—	—	—	—

X# 1 40 PENCE

18.8100 g., Silver **Rev:** With XL above and Sep: below crown **Note:** Prev. KM#M1.

Date	Mintage	F	VF	XF	Unc	BU
1900 Proof	—	Value: 900				

X# 5 2 FLORIN

Silver **Note:** Prev. KM#M5. Weight varies: 19.25-22.60 g.

Date	Mintage	F	VF	XF	Unc	BU
1900 Proof	—	Value: 650				

X# 5a 2 FLORIN

31.8200 g., Gold **Note:** Prev. KM#M5a.

Date	Mintage	F	VF	XF	Unc	BU
1900 Possibly Unique	—	—	—	—	—	—

INA Retro Issue

X# M18 60 SCHILLINGS

Silver, 40.99 mm. **Obv:** Laureate bust right **Obv. Legend:** GEORGIUS III DEI GRATIA REX. **Rev:** Harp **Rev. Legend:** HIBERNIA **Edge:** Plain

Date	Mintage	F	VF	XF	Unc	BU
1808 (2007) Proof	50	—	—	—	—	—
1808 (2007) Matte Proof	50	—	—	—	—	—

X# M18a 60 SCHILLINGS

Copper, 40.99 mm. **Obv:** Laureate bust right **Obv. Legend:** GEORGIUS III DEI GRATIA REX. **Rev:** Harp **Rev. Legend:** HIBERNIA **Edge:** Plain

Date	Mintage	F	VF	XF	Unc	BU
1808 (2007) Proof	1,000	—	—	—	—	—

X# M18b 60 SCHILLINGS

Aluminum, 40.99 mm. **Obv:** Laureate bust right **Obv. Legend:** GEORGIUS III DEI GRATIA REX. **Rev:** Harp **Rev. Legend:** HIBERNIA **Edge:** Plain

Date	Mintage	F	VF	XF	Unc	BU
1808 (2007) Proof	1,000	—	—	—	—	—

X# M18c 60 SCHILLINGS

Pewter, 40.99 mm. **Obv:** Laureate bust right **Obv. Legend:** GEORGIUS III DEI GRATIA REX. **Rev:** Harp **Rev. Legend:** HIBERNIA **Edge:** Plain

Date	Mintage	F	VF	XF	Unc	BU
1808 (2007) Proof	1,000	—	—	—	—	—

X# M18d 60 SCHILLINGS

Copper Bronzed, 40.99 mm. **Obv:** Laureate bust right **Obv. Legend:** GEORGIUS III DEI GRATIA REX. **Rev:** Harp **Rev. Legend:** HIBERNIA **Edge:** Plain

Date	Mintage	F	VF	XF	Unc	BU
1808 (2007) Proof	1,000	—	—	—	—	—

X# M18e 60 SCHILLINGS

Nickel-Silver, 40.99 mm. **Obv:** Laureate bust right **Obv. Legend:** GEORGIUS III DEI GRATIA REX. **Rev:** Harp **Rev. Legend:** HIBERNIA **Edge:** Plain

Date	Mintage	F	VF	XF	Unc	BU
1808 (2007) Proof	1,000	—	—	—	—	—

X# M18f 60 SCHILLINGS

Goldine, 40.99 mm. **Obv:** Laureate bust right **Obv. Legend:** GEORGIUS III DEI GRATIA REX. **Rev:** Harp **Rev. Legend:** HIBERNIA **Edge:** Plain

Date	Mintage	F	VF	XF	Unc	BU
1808 (2007) Proof	1,000	—	—	—	—	—

X# M18g 60 SCHILLINGS

Gold, 40.97 mm. **Obv:** Laureate bust right **Obv. Legend:** GEORGIUS III DEI GRATIA REX. **Rev:** Harp **Rev. Legend:** HIBERNIA **Edge:** Plain

Date	Mintage	F	VF	XF	Unc	BU
1808 (2007) Proof	—	—	—	—	—	—

X# 11b 48 PENCE

18.2500 g., Copper **Obv:** Veiled bust left **Obv. Legend:** VICTORIA • DEI GRATIA • IND • IMP **Rev:** Crowned harp within quatrilobe **Rev. Legend:** HIBERNIA **Edge:** Plain

Date	Mintage	F	VF	XF	Unc	BU
1901 Proof	360	Value: 40.00				

X# 11 48 PENCE

0.9250 Silver **Obv:** Veiled bust left **Obv. Legend:** VICTORIA • DEI GRATIA • IND • IMP **Rev:** Crowned harp within quatrilobe **Rev. Legend:** HIBERNIA **Edge:** Plain

Date	Mintage	F	VF	XF	Unc	BU
1901 Proof	360	Value: 75.00				

X# 11c.1 48 PENCE

0.9167 Gold **Obv:** Veiled bust left **Obv. Legend:** VICTORIA • DEI GRATIA • IND • IMP **Rev:** Crowned harp within quatrilobe **Rev. Legend:** HIBERNIA **Edge:** Plain **Note:** Weight varies: 33.10, 33.20, 48.90 g.

Date	Mintage	F	VF	XF	Unc	BU
1901 Proof	2	—	—	—	—	—
Note: Medal alignment						
1901 Proof	1	—	—	—	—	—
Note: Coin alignment						

X# 11c.2 48 PENCE

0.9167 Gold **Obv:** Veiled bust left **Obv. Legend:** VICTORIA • DEI GRATIA • IND • IMP **Rev:** Crowned harp within quatrilobe **Rev. Legend:** HIBERNIA **Edge:** Reeded

Date	Mintage	F	VF	XF	Unc	BU
1901 Proof	1	—	—	—	—	—

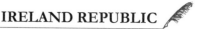

X# 11a 48 PENCE

18.0300 g., Bronze **Obv:** Veiled bust left **Obv. Legend:** VICTORIA • DEI GRATIA • IND • IMP **Rev:** Crowned harp within quatrilobe **Rev. Legend:** HIBERNIA **Edge:** Plain

Date	Mintage	F	VF	XF	Unc	BU
1901 Proof	360	Value: 40.00				

X# 12.2 48 PENCE

33.1000 g., 0.9167 Gold 0.9755 oz. AGW **Obv:** Veiled bust left **Obv. Legend:** VICTORIA • DEI • GRA BRITT • REGINA • FID • DEF IND • IMP • **Rev:** Crowned harp within quatrilobe **Rev. Legend:** HIBERNIA **Edge:** Plain **Note:** Medal alignment

Date	Mintage	F	VF	XF	Unc	BU
1901 Proof	1	—	—	—	—	—

X# 12.1 48 PENCE

0.9756 g., 0.9167 Gold 0.0288 oz. AGW **Obv:** Veiled bust left **Obv. Legend:** VICTORIA • DEI • GRA BRITT • REGINA • FID • DEF IND • IMP • **Rev:** Crowned harp within quatrilobe **Rev. Legend:** HIBERNIA **Edge:** Reeded

Date	Mintage	F	VF	XF	Unc	BU
1901 Proof	1	—	—	—	—	—

X# 13 48 PENCE

0.9250 Silver **Obv:** Crowned bust right **Obv. Legend:** EDWARDVS VII D: G: BRITT: OMN: REX F: D: IND: IMP. **Rev:** Crowned harp within quatrilobe **Rev. Legend:** HIBERNIA **Edge:** Plain

Date	Mintage	F	VF	XF	Unc	BU
1901 Proof	425	Value: 75.00				

X# 13b 48 PENCE

Copper **Obv:** Crowned bust right **Obv. Legend:** EDWARDVS VII D: G: BRITT: OMN: REX F: D: IND: IMP. **Rev:** Crowned harp within quatrilobe **Rev. Legend:** HIBERNIA **Edge:** Plain

Date	Mintage	F	VF	XF	Unc	BU
1901 Proof	425	Value: 40.00				

X# 13c.2 48 PENCE

0.9167 Gold **Obv:** Crowned bust right **Obv. Legend:** EDWARDVS VII D: G: BRITT: OMN: REX F: D: IND: IMP. **Rev:** Crowned harp within quatrilobe **Rev. Legend:** HIBERNIA **Edge:** Plain **Note:** Weight varies: 32.40 or 32.60 g.

Date	Mintage	F	VF	XF	Unc	BU
1901 Proof	1	—	—	—	—	—
Note: Medal alignment						
1901 Proof	1	—	—	—	—	—
Note: Coin alignment						

X# 13c.1 48 PENCE

32.0000 g., 0.9167 Gold 0.9431 oz. AGW **Obv:** Crowned bust right **Obv. Legend:** EDWARDVS VII D: G: BRITT: OMN: REX F: D: IND: IMP. **Rev:** Crowned harp within quatrilobe **Rev. Legend:** HIBERNIA **Edge:** Reeded **Note:** Medal alignment

Date	Mintage	F	VF	XF	Unc	BU
1901 Proof	1	—	—	—	—	—

X# 13a 48 PENCE

Bronze **Obv:** Crowned bust right **Obv. Legend:** EDWARDVS VII D: G: BRITT: OMN: REX F: D: IND: IMP. **Rev:** Crowned harp within quatrilobe **Rev. Legend:** HIBERNIA **Edge:** Plain

Date	Mintage	F	VF	XF	Unc	BU
1901 Proof	425	Value: 40.00				

X# 14c 48 PENCE

33.0000 g., 0.9167 Gold 0.9726 oz. AGW **Obv:** Head right within pellet border **Obv. Legend:** EDWARDVS VII DEI GRATIA INDIAE IMPERATOR **Rev:** Crowned harp within quatrilobe **Rev. Legend:** HIBERNIA **Edge:** Reeded **Note:** Medal alignment

Date	Mintage	F	VF	XF	Unc	BU
1901 Proof	1	—	—	—	—	—

X# 14b 48 PENCE

Copper **Obv:** Head right within pellet border **Obv. Legend:** EDWARDVS VII DEI GRATIA INDIAE IMPERATOR **Rev:** Crowned harp within quatrilobe **Rev. Legend:** HIBERNIA **Edge:** Plain

Date	Mintage	F	VF	XF	Unc	BU
1901 Proof	120	Value: 40.00				

X# 14 48 PENCE

0.9250 Silver **Obv:** Head right within pellet border **Obv. Legend:** EDWARDVS VII DEI GRATIA INDIAE IMPERATOR **Rev:** Crowned harp within quatrilobe **Rev. Legend:** HIBERNIA **Edge:** Plain

Date	Mintage	F	VF	XF	Unc	BU
1901 Proof	120	Value: 80.00				

X# 14a 48 PENCE

Bronze **Obv:** Head right within pellet border **Obv. Legend:** EDWARDVS VII DEI GRATIA INDIAE IMPERATOR **Rev:** Crowned harp within quatrilobe **Rev. Legend:** HIBERNIA **Edge:** Plain

Date	Mintage	F	VF	XF	Unc	BU
1901 Proof	120	Value: 40.00				

PIEFORTS

X#	Date	Mintage	Identification	Mkt Val
P1	1901	1	48 Pence. Silver. Plain edge, coin alignment, X#11.	—
P2	1901	1	48 Pence. Silver. Plain edge, medal alignment, X#11.	—
P3	1901	1	48 Pence. Silver. Reeded edge, coin alignment, X#11.	—
P4	1901	1	48 Pence. Silver. Reeded edge, medal alignment, X#11.	—
P5	1901	1	48 Pence. Silver. Plain edge, coin alignment, X#12.	—
P6	1901	1	48 Pence. Silver. Plain edge, medal alignment, X#12.	—
P7	1901	1	48 Pence. Silver. Reeded edge, coin alignment, X#12.	—
P8	1901	1	48 Pence. Silver. Reeded edge, medal alignment, X#12.	—
P9	1901	1	48 Pence. Silver. Plain edge, coin alignment, X#13.	—
P10	1901	1	48 Pence. Silver. Plain edge, medal alignment, X#13.	—
P11	1901	1	48 Pence. Silver. Reeded edge, coin alignment, X#13.	—
P12	1901	1	48 Pence. Silver. Reeded edge, medal alignment, X#13.	—
P13	1901	1	48 Pence. Silver. Plain edge, coin alignment, X#14.	—
P14	1901	1	48 Pence. Silver. Plain edge, medal alignment, X#14.	—
P15	1901	1	48 Pence. Silver. Reeded edge, coin alignment, X#14.	—
P16	1901	1	48 Pence. Silver. Reeded edge, medal alignment, X#14.	—

IRELAND REPUBLIC

BRITISH ADMINISTRATION

PIEFORTS

X# P11 25 EURO

47.2500 g., Silver, 38 mm. **Obv:** Harp **Rev:** Multicolor Red Squirrel **Edge:** Reeded

Date	Mintage	F	VF	XF	Unc	BU
1996 Proof	—	Value: 125				

REPUBLIC

MEDALLIC COINAGE

European Currency Unit - ECU

X# 25 ECU
28.2800 g., 0.9250 Silver 0.8410 oz. ASW, 38.6 mm. **Obv:** Large "ECU", map of Europe **Obv. Legend:** • EIRE • EUROPE - EUROPA **Rev:** Harp **Rev. Legend:** SAORSTAT ÉIREANN **Edge:** Reeded

Date	Mintage	F	VF	XF	Unc	BU
ND(1992)PM Proof	10,000	Value: 35.00				

X# 30 ECU
20.0000 g., 0.9990 Silver 0.6423 oz. ASW, 40 mm. **Issuer:** Göde GmbH, Munich **Obv:** Two stags standing **Obv. Legend:** éire **Rev:** Large "ECU", harp, 12 stars along edge **Edge:** Reeded

Date	Mintage	F	VF	XF	Unc	BU
1993 Proof	9,999	Value: 70.00				

X# 1 5 ECU
10.0000 g., 0.9250 Silver 0.2974 oz. ASW, 28 mm. **Subject:** EEC Council Meeting in Dublin **Rev. Designer:** Thomas Ryan **Edge:** Reeded

Date	Mintage	F	VF	XF	Unc	BU
1990 Proof	20,000	Value: 35.00				

X# 35 5 ECU
6.0500 g., Bi-Metallic Brass center in Copper-Nickel ring, 38.5 mm. **Obv:** Harp **Obv. Legend:** Irland éire Ireland **Obv. Inscription:** Brian Borù Harp **Rev:** Bust of St. Patrick facing **Rev. Legend:** Bodroig St. Patrick **Edge:** Reeded

Date	Mintage	F	VF	XF	Unc	BU
1995 Proof	—	Value: 15.00				

X# 2 10 ECU
28.0000 g., 0.9250 Silver 0.8327 oz. ASW, 37.5 mm. **Subject:** EEC Council Meeting in Dublin **Rev. Designer:** Thomas Ryan **Edge:** Reeded

Date	Mintage	F	VF	XF	Unc	BU
1990 Proof	20,000	Value: 75.00				

X# 38 25 ECU
Silver, 38.6 mm. **Obv:** Cat sitting, facing backwards **Obv. Legend:** éire **Rev:** Harp, 12 stars in outer ring

Date	Mintage	F	VF	XF	Unc	BU
1995 Proof	—	Value: 50.00				

X# 43 25 ECU
Bi-Metallic **Obv:** Cat sitting, facing backwards **Obv. Legend:** éire **Rev:** Harp, 12 stars in outer ring

Date	Mintage	F	VF	XF	Unc	BU
1997	—	—	—	—	15.00	—

X# 3 50 ECU
15.0000 g., 0.9170 Gold 0.4422 oz. AGW, 28 mm. **Subject:** EEC Council Meeting in Dublin **Rev. Designer:** Thomas Ryan **Edge:** Reeded

Date	Mintage	F	VF	XF	Unc	BU
1990 Proof	5,000	Value: 475				

Euro Coinage

X# 41 25 EURO
Bi-Metallic **Obv:** Squirrel standing right, eating **Obv. Legend:** éire **Rev:** Harp, 12 stars in outer ring

Date	Mintage	F	VF	XF	Unc	BU
1997	—	—	—	—	15.00	—

X# 42 25 EURO
Copper-Nickel **Obv:** Dormouse perched right **Obv. Legend:** éire **Rev:** Harp, 12 stars in outer ring

Date	Mintage	F	VF	XF	Unc	BU
1997	—	—	—	—	15.00	—

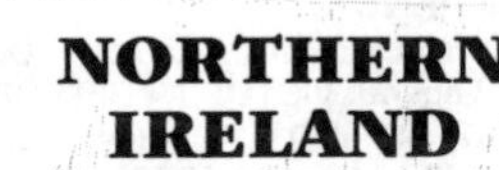

NORTHERN IRELAND

KINGDOM

ECU COINAGE

X# 1a.2 ECU
6.0000 g., 0.7500 Gold 0.1447 oz. AGW, 22.5 mm. **Ruler:** Elizabeth II **Issuer:** Spink London **Obv:** Neptune and Europa standing flanking oval outlined map of Europe **Obv. Legend:** • EUROPE ★ EUROPA • N. IRELAND **Obv. Designer:** R.D. Maklouf **Rev:** Hibernia kneeling with harp **Note:** Fineness ".750" added.

Date	Mintage	F	VF	XF	Unc	BU
1992SRH Proof	Inc. above	Value: 200				

X# 1 ECU
5.2000 g., Copper-Nickel-Zinc, 22.5 mm. **Ruler:** Elizabeth II **Issuer:** Spink London **Obv:** Neptune and Europa standing flanking oval outlined map of Europe **Obv. Legend:** • EUROPE ★ EUROPA • N. IRELAND **Obv. Designer:** R.D. Maklouf **Rev:** Hibernia kneeling with harp

Date	Mintage	F	VF	XF	Unc	BU
1992	—	—	—	—	6.50	—

X# 1a.1 ECU
6.0000 g., 0.7500 Gold 0.1447 oz. AGW, 22.5 mm. **Ruler:** Elizabeth II **Issuer:** Spink London **Obv:** Neptune and Europa standing flanking oval outlined map of Europe **Obv. Legend:** • EUROPE ★ EUROPA • N. IRELAND **Obv. Designer:** R.D. Maklouf **Rev:** Hibernia kneeling with harp

Date	Mintage	F	VF	XF	Unc	BU
1992 Proof	2,500	Value: 200				

X# 2.1 ECU
23.0000 g., 0.9250 Silver 0.6840 oz. ASW, 38 mm. **Ruler:** Elizabeth II **Issuer:** Spink London **Obv:** Neptune and Europa standing flanking circular outlined map of Europe **Obv. Legend:** • EUROPE ★ EUROPA • N. IRELAND **Obv. Designer:** R.D. Maklouf **Rev:** Hibernia kneeling with harp

Date	Mintage	F	VF	XF	Unc	BU
1992 Proof	10,000	Value: 40.00				

X# 2.2 ECU
23.0000 g., 0.9250 Silver 0.6840 oz. ASW, 38 mm. **Ruler:** Elizabeth II **Issuer:** Spink London **Obv:** Neptune and Europa standing flanking circular outlined map of Euorpe **Obv. Legend:** • EUROPE ★ EUROPA • N. IRELAND **Obv. Designer:** R.D. Maklouf **Rev:** Hibernia kneeling with harp **Note:** Fineness ".925" added.

Date	Mintage	F	VF	XF	Unc	BU
1992SRH Proof	Inc. above	Value: 40.00				

X# 3.1 25 ECU
23.0000 g., 0.9250 Silver 0.6840 oz. ASW, 38 mm. **Ruler:** Elizabeth II **Issuer:** Spink London **Obv:** Neptune and Europa standing flanking circular outlined map of Europe **Obv. Legend:** • EUROPE ★ EUROPA • N. IRELAND **Obv. Designer:** R.D. Maklouf **Rev:** Hibernia kneeling with harp

Date	Mintage	F	VF	XF	Unc	BU
1992 Proof	15,000	Value: 50.00				

X# 3.2 25 ECU
23.0000 g., 0.9250 Silver 0.6840 oz. ASW, 38 mm. **Ruler:** Elizabeth II **Issuer:** Spink London **Obv:** Neptune and Europa standing flanking circular outlined map of Europe **Obv. Legend:** • EUROPE ★ EUROPA • N. IRELAND **Obv. Designer:** R.D. Maklouf **Rev:** Hibernia kneeling with harp **Note:** Fineness ".925" added.

Date	Mintage	F	VF	XF	Unc	BU
1992SRH Proof	Inc. above	Value: 50.00				

X# 3a 25 ECU
38.0000 g., 0.9167 Gold 1.1199 oz. AGW, 38 mm. **Ruler:** Elizabeth II **Issuer:** Spink London **Obv:** Neptune and Europa standing flanking circular outlined map of Europe **Obv. Legend:** • EUROPE ★ EUROPA • N. IRELAND **Obv. Designer:** R.D. Maklouf **Rev:** Hibernia kneeling with harp

Date	Mintage	F	VF	XF	Unc	BU
1992 Proof	25	—	—	—	—	—

PIEFORTS

X#	Date	Mintage	Identification	Mkt Val
P1	1992	1,000	Ecu. 0.9250 Silver. 47.1000 g. X#2.1.	80.00
P2	1992SRH	I.A.	Ecu. 0.9250 Silver. 46.0000 g. X#2.2.	—
P3	1992	4,000	25 Ecu. 0.9250 Silver. 46.0000 g. X#3.1.	100
P4	1992SRH	I.A.	25 Ecu. 0.9250 Silver. 46.0000 g. X#3.2.	100
P5	1992	25	25 Ecu. 0.9167 Gold. 76.0000 g. X#3a.	—

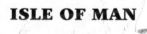

ISLE OF MAN

CROWN COLONY

MEDALLIC / INA RETRO ISSUE

X# M17 5 SHILLING
Silver, 40.94 mm. **Obv:** Laureate bust right **Obv. Legend:** GEORGIUS III DEI GRATIA REX. **Rev:** Triskeles on outlined map **Rev. Legend:** STABIT / QVOCVNQVE / IECERIS **Edge:** Plain

Date	Mintage	F	VF	XF	Unc	BU
1808 (2007) Proof	—	—	—	—	—	—
1808 (2007) Matte Proof	—	—	—	—	—	—

X# M17a 5 SHILLING
Copper, 40.94 mm. **Obv:** Laureate bust right **Obv. Legend:** GEORGIUS III DEI GRATIA REX. **Rev:** Triskeles on outlined map **Rev. Legend:** STABIT / QVOCVNQVE / IECERIS **Edge:** Plain

Date	Mintage	F	VF	XF	Unc	BU
1808 (2007) Proof	500	—	—	—	—	—

X# M17b 5 SHILLING
Aluminum, 40.94 mm. **Obv:** Laureate bust right **Obv. Legend:** GEORGIUS III DEI GRATIA REX. **Rev:** Triskeles on outlined map **Rev. Legend:** STABIT / QVOCVNQVE / IECERIS **Edge:** Plain

Date	Mintage	F	VF	XF	Unc	BU
1808 (2007) Proof	500	—	—	—	—	—

X# M17c 5 SHILLING
Pewter, 40.94 mm. **Obv:** Laureate bust right **Obv. Legend:** GEORGIUS III DEI GRATIA REX. **Rev:** Triskeles on outlined map **Rev. Legend:** STABIT / QVOCVNQVE / IECERIS **Edge:** Plain

Date	Mintage	F	VF	XF	Unc	BU
1808 (2007) Proof	500	—	—	—	—	—

X# M17d 5 SHILLING
Copper Bronzed, 40.94 mm. **Obv:** Laureate bust right **Obv. Legend:** GEORGIUS III DEI GRATIA REX. **Rev:** Triskeles on outlined map **Rev. Legend:** STABIT / QVOCVNQVE / IECERIS **Edge:** Plain

Date	Mintage	F	VF	XF	Unc	BU
1808 (2007) Proof	500	—	—	—	—	—

X# M17e 5 SHILLING
Nickel-Silver, 40.94 mm. **Obv:** Laureate bust right **Obv. Legend:** GEORGIUS III DEI GRATIA REX. **Rev:** Triskeles on outlined map **Rev. Legend:** STABIT / QVOCVNQVE / IECERIS **Edge:** Plain

Date	Mintage	F	VF	XF	Unc	BU
1808 (2007) Proof	500	—	—	—	—	—

X# M17f 5 SHILLING
Goldine, 40.94 mm. **Obv:** Laureate bust right **Obv. Legend:** GEORGIUS III DEI GRATIA REX. **Rev:** Triskeles on outlined map **Rev. Legend:** STABIT / QVOCVNQVE / IECERIS **Edge:** Plain

Date	Mintage	F	VF	XF	Unc	BU
1808 (2007) Proof	500	—	—	—	—	—

X# M17g 5 SHILLING
Gold, 40.94 mm. **Obv:** Laureate bust right **Obv. Legend:** GEORGIUS III DEI GRATIA REX. **Rev:** Triskeles on outlined map **Rev. Legend:** STABIT / QVOCVNQVE / IECERIS **Edge:** Plain

Date	Mintage	F	VF	XF	Unc	BU
1808 (2007) Proof	—	—	—	—	—	—

BRITISH DEPENDENCY

MEDALLIC COINAGE

Unknown Mint Issues

X# 3 18 PENCE
8.1200 g., 0.8330 Silver 0.2175 oz. ASW **Subject:** Edward VIII **Obv:** Bust left **Obv. Legend:** EDWARD • VIII • KING • & • EMPEROR **Rev:** Triskeles **Rev. Legend:** JECERIS STABIT QUOCUNQUE

Date	Mintage	F	VF	XF	Unc	BU
ND	—	—	—	—	35.00	—

Richard Lobel Issues

X# 2 SOVEREIGN
0.3750 Gold, 21.98 mm. **Subject:** Edward VIII **Obv:** Bust left **Obv. Legend:** EDWARD • VIII • KING • & • EMPEROR **Rev:** Peel Castle

Date	Mintage	F	VF	XF	Unc	BU
1936 Proof	165	Value: 125				

X# 2a SOVEREIGN
4.4200 g., Silver, 21.98 mm. **Subject:** Edward VIII **Obv:** Bust left **Obv. Legend:** EDWARD • VIII • KING • & • EMPEROR **Rev:** Peel Castle

Date	Mintage	F	VF	XF	Unc	BU
1936 Proof	—	Value: 10.00				

X# 1 CROWN
Bronze, 38.10 mm. **Subject:** Edward VIII **Obv:** Bust left **Obv. Legend:** EDWARD • VIII • KING • & • EMPEROR **Rev:** Peel Castle **Edge:** Plain

Date	Mintage	F	VF	XF	Unc	BU
1936 Proof	650	Value: 15.00				

X# 1a CROWN
Copper-Nickel-Zinc, 38.10 mm. **Subject:** Edward VIII **Obv:** Bust left **Obv. Legend:** EDWARD • VIII • KING • & • EMPEROR **Rev:** Peel Castle **Edge:** Plain

Date	Mintage	F	VF	XF	Unc	BU
1936 Proof	1,500	Value: 15.00				

X# 1b CROWN
0.9167 Silver, 38.10 mm. **Subject:** Edward VIII **Obv:** Bust left **Obv. Legend:** EDWARD • VIII • KING • & • EMPEROR **Rev:** Peel Castle **Edge:** Plain

Date	Mintage	F	VF	XF	Unc	BU
1936 Proof	165	Value: 50.00				

X# 1c CROWN
Gold, 38.10 mm. **Subject:** Edward VIII **Obv:** Bust left **Obv. Legend:** EDWARD • VIII • KING • & • EMPEROR **Rev:** Peel Castle **Edge:** Plain

Date	Mintage	F	VF	XF	Unc	BU
1936 Proof	—	Value: 500				

FANTASY EURO PATTERNS

X# Pn1 EURO CENT
Copper Plated Steel **Ruler:** Elizabeth II **Edge:** Plain

Date	Mintage	F	VF	XF	Unc	BU
2004	10,000	—	—	—	—	1.50
2004 Proof	5,000	Value: 2.50				

X# Pn2 2 EURO CENT
Copper Plated Steel **Ruler:** Elizabeth II **Edge:** Plain

Date	Mintage	F	VF	XF	Unc	BU
2004	10,000	—	—	—	—	2.00
2004 Proof	5,000	Value: 3.00				

X# Pn3 5 EURO CENT
Copper Plated Steel **Ruler:** Elizabeth II **Edge:** Plain

Date	Mintage	F	VF	XF	Unc	BU
2004	10,000	—	—	—	—	2.50
2004 Proof	5,000	Value: 3.50				

X# Pn4 10 EURO CENT
Goldine **Ruler:** Elizabeth II **Edge:** Plain

Date	Mintage	F	VF	XF	Unc	BU
2004	10,000	—	—	—	—	3.00
2004 Proof	5,000	Value: 4.00				

X# Pn5 20 EURO CENT
Goldine **Ruler:** Elizabeth II **Edge:** Plain

Date	Mintage	F	VF	XF	Unc	BU
2004	10,000	—	—	—	—	3.50
2004 Proof	5,000	Value: 5.00				

X# Pn6 50 EURO CENT
Goldine **Ruler:** Elizabeth II **Edge:** Plain

Date	Mintage	F	VF	XF	Unc	BU
2004	10,000	—	—	—	—	4.00
2004 Proof	5,000	Value: 6.00				

X# Pn7 EURO
Bi-Metallic **Ruler:** Elizabeth II **Obv:** Nude helmeted allegorical female warrior advancing right with sword and shield **Rev:** Allegorical woman standing right behind seated male **Edge:** Plain

Date	Mintage	F	VF	XF	Unc	BU
2004	10,000	—	—	—	—	6.00
2004 Proof	5,000	Value: 8.00				

X# Pn8 2 EURO
Bi-Metallic **Ruler:** Elizabeth II **Obv:** Nude helmeted allegorical female warrior advancing right with sword and shield **Rev:** Allegorical woman standing right behind seated male **Edge:** Plain

Date	Mintage	F	VF	XF	Unc	BU
2004	10,000	—	—	—	—	8.00
2004 Proof	5,000	Value: 10.00				

X# Pn9 5 EURO
Goldine **Ruler:** Elizabeth II **Edge:** Plain

Date	Mintage	F	VF	XF	Unc	BU
2004 Proof	5,000	Value: 12.50				

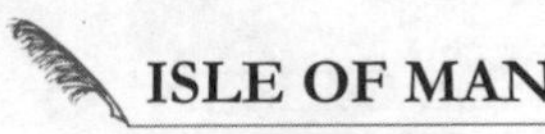

PIEFORTS

X#	Date	Mintage	Identification	Mkt Val
P1	1901	1	4 Shilling. Silver. Plain edge, coin alignment, X#M11.	—
P2	1901	1	4 Shilling. Silver. Plain edge, medal alignment, X#M11.	—
P3	1901	1	4 Shilling. Silver. Reeded edge, coin alignment, X#M11.	—
P4	1901	1	4 Shilling. Silver. Reeded edge, medal alignment, X#M11.	—
P5	1901	1	4 Shilling. Silver-Billon. Plain edge, coin alignment, X#M12.	—
P6	1901	1	4 Shilling. Silver. Plain edge, medal alignment, X#M12.	—
P7	1901	1	4 Shilling. Silver. Reeded edge, coin alignment, X#M12.	—
P8	1901	1	4 Shilling. Silver. Reeded edge, medal alignment, X#M12.	—
P9	1901	1	4 Shilling. Silver. Plain edge, coin alignment, X#M13.	—
P10	1901	1	4 Shilling. Silver. Plain edge, medal alignment, X#M13.	—
P11	1901	1	4 Shilling. Silver. Reeded edge, coin alignment, X#M13.	—
P12	1901	1	4 Shilling. Silver. Reeded edge, medal alignment, X#M13.	—
P13	1901	1	4 Shilling. Silver. Plain edge, coin alignment, X#M14.	—
P14	1901	1	4 Shilling. Silver. Plain edge, medal alignment, X#M14.	—
	1901	1	4 Shilling. Silver. Plain edge, medal alignment, X#M14.	—
P15	1901	1	4 Shilling. Silver. Reeded edge, coin alignment, X#M14.	—
P16	1901	1	4 Shilling. Silver. Reeded edge, medal alignment, X#M14.	—
P17	1936	—	Crown. 0.9167 Silver. X#1b.	100

MINT SETS

X#	Date	Mintage	Identification	Issue Price	Mkt Val
XMS1	2004 (8)	10,000	X#Pn1-Pn8	—	30.00

PROOF SETS

X#	Date	Mintage	Identification	Issue Price	Mkt Val
XPS1	2004 (9)	5,000	X#Pn1-Pn9	—	50.00

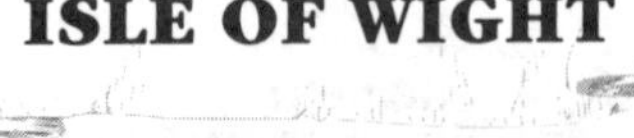

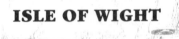

ISLE OF WIGHT

COUNTY

MEDALLIC COINAGE

Ecu / Pound Series

X# 11 3 ECUS-2 POUNDS
28.2800 g., Copper-Nickel, 38.6 mm. **Obv:** Crowned and supported arms **Rev:** Victoria above Osborne House **Edge:** Reeded

Date	Mintage	Good	VG	F	VF	XF
1996PM Proof	—	Value: 12.50				

X# 11a 3 ECUS-2 POUNDS
28.2800 g., 0.9250 Silver 0.8410 oz. ASW, 38.6 mm. **Obv:** Crowned and supported arms **Rev:** Victoria above Osborne House **Edge:** Reeded

Date	Mintage	Good	VG	F	VF	XF
1996PM Proof	30,000	Value: 22.50				

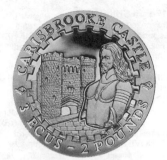

X# 12 3 ECUS-2 POUNDS
28.2800 g., Copper-Nickel, 38.6 mm. **Obv:** Crowned and supported arms **Rev:** Carisbrooke Castle at left, Charles I at right **Edge:** Reeded

Date	Mintage	Good	VG	F	VF	XF
1996PM Proof	—	Value: 12.50				

X# 12a 3 ECUS-2 POUNDS
28.2800 g., 0.9250 Silver 0.8410 oz. ASW, 38.6 mm. **Obv:** Crowned and supported arms **Rev:** Carisbrooke Castle at left, Charles I at right **Edge:** Reeded

Date	Mintage	Good	VG	F	VF	XF
1996PM Proof	30,000	Value: 22.50				

X# 13 3 ECUS-2 POUNDS
28.2800 g., Copper-Nickel, 38.6 mm. **Subject:** Cowes Week Regatta **Obv:** Crowned and supported arms **Rev:** Early yacht at left, speedboat at right **Edge:** Reeded

Date	Mintage	Good	VG	F	VF	XF
1996PM Proof	—	Value: 12.50				

X# 13a 3 ECUS-2 POUNDS
28.2800 g., 0.9250 Silver 0.8410 oz. ASW, 38.6 mm. **Subject:** Cowes Week Regatta **Obv:** Crowned and supported arms **Rev:** Early yacht at left, speedboat at right **Edge:** Reeded

Date	Mintage	Good	VG	F	VF	XF
1996PM Proof	30,000	Value: 22.50				

X# 14 3 ECUS-2 POUNDS
28.2800 g., Copper-Nickel, 38.6 mm. **Obv:** Crowned and supported arms **Rev:** Three Germany city shields **Rev. Legend:** CIVIC TWINS **Edge:** Reeded

Date	Mintage	Good	VG	F	VF	XF
1996PM Proof	—	Value: 12.50				

X# 14a 3 ECUS-2 POUNDS
28.2800 g., 0.9250 Silver 0.8410 oz. ASW, 38.6 mm. **Obv:** Crowned and supported arms **Rev:** Three German city shields **Rev. Legend:** CIVIC TWINS **Edge:** Reeded

Date	Mintage	Good	VG	F	VF	XF
1996PM Proof	30,000	Value: 22.50				

EURO Series

X# 22 10 EURO CENT
1.7300 g., Base Metal Brass Plated, 17 mm. **Obv:** Crowned supported arms **Rev:** Eiffel Tower **Edge:** Reeded

Date	Mintage	Good	VG	F	VF	XF
1999 Proof	10,000	Value: 6.00				

X# 23 20 EURO CENT
3.4300 g., Base Metal Brass Plated, 21.5 mm. **Obv:** Crowned supported arms **Rev:** Brandenburg Gate **Edge:** Reeded

Date	Mintage	Good	VG	F	VF	XF
1999 Proof	10,000	Value: 6.00				

X# 24 50 EURO CENT
4.0000 g., Virenium, 22 mm. **Obv:** Crowned supported arms **Rev:** Big Ben **Edge:** Reeded

Date	Mintage	Good	VG	F	VF	XF
1999 Proof	10,000	Value: 6.00				

X# 15 EURO
28.2800 g., Copper-Nickel, 38.6 mm. **Subject:** 44th Anniversary Britannia at Cowes Regatta **Obv:** Crowned supported arms **Rev:** Royal Yacht Britannia **Edge:** Reeded

Date	Mintage	Good	VG	F	VF	XF
1997 Proof	—	Value: 13.50				

X# 15a EURO
28.2800 g., 0.9250 Silver 0.8410 oz. ASW, 38.6 mm. **Subject:** 44th Anniversary Britannia at Cowes Regatta **Obv:** Crowned supported arms **Rev:** Royal Yacht Britannia **Edge:** Reeded

Date	Mintage	Good	VG	F	VF	XF
1997 Proof	5,000	Value: 27.50				

X# 16 EURO
28.2800 g., Copper-Nickel, 38.6 mm. **Subject:** The Lost World **Obv:** Crowned supported arms **Rev:** Tyrannosaurus Rex and Stegosaurus **Edge:** Reeded

Date	Mintage	Good	VG	F	VF	XF
1997 Proof	—	Value: 6.00				

X# 16a EURO

28.2800 g., 0.9250 Silver 0.8410 oz. ASW, 38.6 mm. **Subject:** The Lost World **Obv:** Crowned supported arms **Rev:** Tyrannosaurus Rex and Stegosaurus **Edge:** Reeded

Date	Mintage	Good	VG	F	VF	XF
1997 Proof	5,000	Value: 22.50				

X# 25 EURO

8.0000 g., Steel Nickel Plated, 27.1 mm. **Obv:** Crowned supported arms **Rev:** European continent **Edge:** Reeded

Date	Mintage	Good	VG	F	VF	XF
1999 Proof	10,000	Value: 7.50				

X# 26 2 EURO

9.8000 g., Copper-Nickel, 30.5 mm. **Obv:** Crowned supported arms **Edge:** Reeded

Date	Mintage	Good	VG	F	VF	XF
1999 Proof	10,000	Value: 10.00				

PROOF SETS

X#	Date	Mintage	Identification	Issue Price	Mkt Val
XPS1	1999 (5)	10,000	X22-X26	—	35.00

ISRAEL

REPUBLIC

MEDALLIC COINAGE

X# 7 100 SHEKELS

11.9400 g., 0.9167 Gold 0.3519 oz. AGW, 28.9 mm. **Issuer:** Numismatic Center of Mexico **Obv:** Crowned bust of King Solomon right **Rev:** Menorah in sprays with 12 circular symbols **Edge:** Plain

Date	Mintage	F	VF	XF	Unc	BU
JE5722-1962 Proof	—	Value: 275				

X# 8 100 SHEKELS

11.8800 g., 0.9167 Gold 0.3501 oz. AGW, 28.9 mm. **Issuer:** Numismatic Center of Mexico **Obv:** Crowned bust of King David right **Rev:** Menorah in sprays with 12 circular symbols **Edge:** Plain

Date	Mintage	F	VF	XF	Unc	BU
JE5722-1962 Proof	—	Value: 275				

X# 11 100 SHEKELS

40.0000 g., 0.9800 Silver 1.2603 oz. ASW, 42 mm. **Issuer:** Numismatic Center of Mexico **Subject:** Year of the Shekel 1964 - 1965 **Obv:** Crowned bust of King David left **Rev:** Menorah in sprays

Date	Mintage	F	VF	XF	Unc	BU
ND(1964)	—	—	—	—	45.00	—

X# 11a 100 SHEKELS

45.0000 g., 0.9167 Gold 1.3262 oz. AGW, 42 mm. **Issuer:** Numismatic Center of Mexico **Subject:** Year of the Shekel 1964 - 1965 **Obv:** Crowned bust of King David left **Rev:** Menorah in sprays

Date	Mintage	F	VF	XF	Unc	BU
ND(1964)	—	—	—	—	975	—

X# 21 5 EURO

Copper-Nickel **Obv:** Bust of Yitzhak Rabin facing, 3 doves above **Rev:** Israeli and Euro flags

Date	Mintage	F	VF	XF	Unc	BU
1997 Proof	—	Value: 10.00				

X# 19 50 EURO

Silver **Subject:** Golda Meir

Date	Mintage	F	VF	XF	Unc	BU
1996 Proof	—	Value: 25.00				

X# 22 50 EURO

0.9250 Silver **Obv:** Bust of Yitzhak Rabin facing, 3 doves above **Rev:** Israeli and Euro flags

Date	Mintage	F	VF	XF	Unc	BU
1997 Proof	—	Value: 30.00				

X# 23 100 EURO

3.5000 g., 0.9167 Gold 0.1031 oz. AGW, 21 mm. **Obv:** Bust of Yitzhak Rabin facing, 3 doves above **Rev:** Israeli and Euro flags

Date	Mintage	F	VF	XF	Unc	BU
1997 Proof	—	Value: 200				

ITALIAN STATES

MILAN

AUSTRIAN ADMINISTRATION

MEDALLIC COINAGE

X# M1 MEZZA (1/2) LIRA

Silver **Subject:** Investiture as Duchess **Obv:** Seven-line inscription **Rev:** Lion with arms **Note:** Medal struck on planchet having 10 Scudi value. Prev. KM#M1.

Date	Mintage	VG	F	VF	XF	Unc
1741	—	50.00	100	180	375	—

X# M2 UNA (1) LIRA

Silver **Subject:** Investiture as Duchess **Obv:** Three-line inscription **Rev:** Lion with arms **Note:** Medal struck on planchet having 20 Scudi value. Prev. KM#M2.

Date	Mintage	VG	F	VF	XF	Unc
1741	—	60.00	120	220	450	—

PAPAL STATES

FANTASY PAPACY

FANTASY COINAGE

X# 21 3 DUCAT

7.8500 g., 0.9990 Silver 0.2521 oz. ASW, 25 mm. **Ruler:** Mathew **Obv:** Arms **Obv. Legend:** MATTHAEUS PONT MAX AN.I • GAUDI • **Obv. Designer:** Fred Zinkann **Rev:** Stylized dove above in ray of light **Rev. Inscription:** • CARITAS - VERITAS • / VENI - LUX **Edge:** Plain **Note:** Struck by Mintmasters, Franklin Park, IL, U.S.A.

Date	Mintage	F	VF	XF	Unc	BU
1 (1989) Proof	50	Value: 35.00				

X# 21a 3 DUCAT

7.5500 g., 0.9990 Silver 0.2425 oz. ASW, 25 mm. **Ruler:** Mathew **Obv:** Arms **Obv. Legend:** MATTHAEUS PONT MAX AN.I • GAUDI • **Obv. Designer:** Fred Zinkann **Rev:** Stylized dove above in ray of light **Rev. Inscription:** • CARITAS - VERITAS • / VENI - LUX **Edge:** Plain **Note:** Mintage Inc. X#21.

Date	Mintage	F	VF	XF	Unc	BU
1 (1989) Proof	—	Value: 35.00				

X# 21b 3 DUCAT

8.0000 g., Copper-Nickel, 25 mm. **Ruler:** Mathew **Obv:** Arms **Obv. Legend:** MATTHAEUS PONT MAX AN.I • GAUDI • **Obv. Designer:** Fred Zinkann **Rev:** Stylized dove above in ray of light **Rev. Inscription:** • CARITAS - VERITAS • / VENI - LUX **Edge:** Plain

Date	Mintage	F	VF	XF	Unc	BU
1 (1989) Proof	25	Value: 30.00				

X# 21c 3 DUCAT

8.0000 g., Copper, 25 mm. **Ruler:** Mathew **Obv:** Arms **Obv. Legend:** MATTHAEUS PONT MAX AN.I • GAUDI • **Obv. Designer:** Fred Zinkann **Rev:** Stylized dove above in ray of light **Rev. Inscription:** • CARITAS - VERITAS • / VENI - LUX **Edge:** Plain

Date	Mintage	F	VF	XF	Unc	BU
1 (1989) Proof	10	Value: 25.00				

PAPACY

MEDALLIC COINAGE

X# 5 5 LIRE
Silver **Obv:** Bust of Pope Pius IX in suit left **Obv. Legend:** PIVS IX PONT. MAX. **Rev:** Value in sprays **Rev. Legend:** STATO PONTIFECIO

Date	Mintage	F	VF	XF	Unc	BU
XXV//1870	—	—	125	200	325	—

X# 2 5 LIRE
25.4000 g., Silver **Ruler:** Leo XIII **Obv:** Bust facing slightly right **Obv. Legend:** LEO XIII PONTIFEX MAXIMUS **Rev:** Arms of Pecci family

Date	Mintage	F	VF	XF	Unc	BU
1//1878B	—	—	—	350	500	—

X# 1 5 LIRE
25.1000 g., Silver **Ruler:** Leo XIII **Obv:** Bust facing slightly right **Obv. Legend:** LEO XIII PONTIFEX MAXIMUS **Rev:** Arms of Pecci family **Note:** Prev. KY#167 also Prev. KM#Pn6.

Date	Mintage	F	VF	XF	Unc	BU
1//1878B	—	—	—	350	500	—

PATTERNS

Including off metal strikes

X#	Date	Mintage	Identification	Issue Price	Mkt Val
Pn11	1 (1989)	4	3 Ducat. Hafnium. X#21.	—	300
Pn12	1 (1989)	3	3 Ducat. Titanium. X#21.	—	300
Pn13	1 (1989)	3	3 Ducat. Rhenium. X#21.	—	300
Pn14	1 (1989)	3	3 Ducat. Chromium. X#21.	—	300
Pn15	1 (1989)	2	3 Ducat. Gold. X#21.	—	400
Pn16	1 (1989)	1	3 Ducat. Tantalum. X#21.	—	500

PAPAL STATES-BOLOGNA

CITY

MEDALLIC COINAGE

KM# M1 SCUDO (9 Giulii)
Silver **Ruler:** Benedict XIV **Obv:** Capped bust left **Obv. Legend:** BENEDICTVS • XIV • P • M • ET • ARCH • BON • **Rev:** Inscription **Rev. Inscription:** PASTORI / ET / PRINCIPI. / SENATUS / BONONIENSIS / MDCCXLI **Note:** Dav. #1458.

Date	Mintage	VG	F	VF	XF	Unc
1741//MDCCXLI	—	475	650	800	1,500	—

KM# M2 SCUDO (9 Giulii)
Silver **Ruler:** Benedict XIV **Obv:** Capped bust, right **Obv. Legend:** B E N E D I C T • X I V • P • M • B O N O N • A • X V I I **Rev:** Inscription **Rev. Inscription:** VNVM / OMNIVM VOTVM / SALVS / PRINCIPIS / S.P.Q.B. **Note:** Dav. #1460.

Date	Mintage	VG	F	VF	XF	Unc
ND(1756)//XVII	—	1,000	1,250	1,800	3,500	—

KM# M3 SCUDO (9 Giulii)
Silver **Ruler:** Benedict XIV **Obv:** Capped bust right **Obv. Legend:** B E N E D I C T • X I V • P • M • B O N O N • A • X V I I **Rev:** Inscription **Rev. Inscription:** PATRIA / ET / SCIENTIARVM / INSTITVTO / MAGNIFICE / AVCTO / S.P.Q.B. **Note:** Dav. #1461.

Date	Mintage	VG	F	VF	XF	Unc
ND(1756)//XVII	—	1,000	1,250	1,800	3,500	—

KM# M4 10 SCUDI
Gold **Ruler:** Benedict XIV **Obv:** Capped bust right **Rev:** Inscription **Rev. Inscription:** VNVM... **Note:** Struck with 1 Scudo dies, KM#M2 (Dav. #1460).

Date	Mintage	VG	F	VF	XF	Unc
1756//XVII Unique	—	—	—	—	—	—

PAPAL STATES-GAETA

STATE

FANTASY COINAGE

Private issue struck for Pope Pius IX

X# 1 2 BAIOCCHI
Copper **Obv:** Arms

Date	Mintage	F	VF	XF	Unc	BU
1848G	—	—	—	—	220	—

X# 1a 2 BAIOCCHI
Copper Brassed **Obv:** Arms

Date	Mintage	F	VF	XF	Unc	BU
1848G	—	—	—	—	250	—

X# 2 3 BAIOCCHI
Copper **Obv:** Arms

Date	Mintage	F	VF	XF	Unc	BU
1848G	—	—	—	—	260	—

X# 3 10 BAIOCCHI
Brass **Countermark:** Tiara

Date	Mintage	F	VF	XF	Unc	BU
1848G	—	—	—	—	200	—

X# 3a 10 BAIOCCHI
Silvered Copper **Countermark:** Tiara

Date	Mintage	F	VF	XF	Unc	BU
1848G	—	—	—	—	250	—

X# 4 20 BAIOCCHI
Copper **Countermark:** Tiara **Obv:** Arms

Date	Mintage	F	VF	XF	Unc	BU
1848G	—	—	—	—	200	—

X# 4a 20 BAIOCCHI
Silvered Copper **Countermark:** Tiara **Obv:** Arms

Date	Mintage	F	VF	XF	Unc	BU
1848G	—	—	—	—	200	—

X# 5 SCUDO
Brass Silvered **Countermark:** Tiara **Obv:** Arms

Date	Mintage	F	VF	XF	Unc	BU
1848	—	—	—	—	350	—

X# 5a SCUDO
Silvered Bronze **Countermark:** Tiara **Obv:** Arms

Date	Mintage	F	VF	XF	Unc	BU
1848	—	—	—	—	350	—

X# 5b SCUDO
Copper Bronzed **Countermark:** Tiara **Obv:** Arms

Date	Mintage	F	VF	XF	Unc	BU
1848	—	—	—	—	300	—

X# 6 ZECCHINO
Copper **Countermark:** Tiara **Obv:** Bust right

Date	Mintage	F	VF	XF	Unc	BU
1848G	—	—	—	—	200	—

X# 6a ZECCHINO
Copper Bronzed **Countermark:** Tiara **Obv:** Bust right

Date	Mintage	F	VF	XF	Unc	BU
1848G	—	—	—	—	225	—

X# 6b ZECCHINO
White Metal **Countermark:** Tiara **Obv:** Bust right

Date	Mintage	F	VF	XF	Unc	BU
1848G	—	—	—	—	250	—

X# 6c ZECCHINO
Silver Gilt **Countermark:** Tiara **Obv:** Bust right

Date	Mintage	F	VF	XF	Unc	BU
1848G	—	—	—	—	350	—

ROMAN REPUBLIC

FIRST REPUBLIC

1798-1799

MEDALLIC COINAGE

X# 1 SCUDO
21.4500 g., Silver **Obv:** Small Eagle in wreath perched on fasces on podium, banner at left wing with "REP. ROMANA" **Rev. Inscription:** ALLE / SPERANZE / DELLA. GIOUENTV / LV.PATRIA **Note:** Dav. #1483.

Date	Mintage	VG	F	VF	XF	Unc
A.6. (1798) (1798)	—	—	—	1,500	3,000	—

X# 1a SCUDO
Bronze **Obv:** Small Eagle in wreath perched on fasces on podium, banner at left wing with "REP. ROMANA" **Rev. Inscription:** ALLE / SPERANZE / DELA. GIOUENTV / LA. PATRIA

Date	Mintage	VG	F	VF	XF	Unc
A.6. (1798) (1798)	—	—	—	250	500	—

X# 2 SCUDO
27.0000 g., Silver **Obv:** Large eagle in wreath on podium, banner at right with "REPUBLIC/ROMANA" **Rev. Legend:** GIORNO CHE VALE DI TANTI ANNI IL PIANTO **Rev. Inscription:** LIBERTA/ROMANA/XXVII/PIOVOSO **Note:** Dav. #1484.

Date	Mintage	VG	F	VF	XF	Unc
AN. VII (1799)	—	—	—	1,000	2,000	—

X# 2a SCUDO
Bronze **Obv:** Large eagle in wreath on podium, banner at right with "REPUBLIC/ROMANA" **Rev. Legend:** GIORNO CHE VALE DI TANTI ANNI IL PIANTO **Rev. Inscription:** LIBERTA/ROMANA/XXVII/PIOVOSO

Date	Mintage	VG	F	VF	XF	Unc
AN. VII (1799)	—	—	—	200	400	—

X# 3 SCUDO
21.7000 g., Silver **Obv:** Small eagle in wreath perched on fasces on podium, banner at left wing with "REP. ROMANA" **Rev. Legend:** GIORNO CHE VALE DI TANTI ANNI IL PIANTO **Rev. Inscription:** LIBERTA/ROMANA/27/PIOVOSO **Note:** Dav. #1485.

Date	Mintage	VG	F	VF	XF	Unc
ND(1798)	—	—	—	1,000	2,000	—

X# 3a SCUDO
Bronze **Obv:** Small eagle in wreath perched on fasces on podium, banner at left wing with "REP. ROMANA" **Rev. Legend:** GIORNO CHE VALE DI TANTI ANNI IL PIANTO **Rev. Inscription:** LIBERTA/ROMANA/27/PIOVOSO **Note:** Dav. #1485.

Date	Mintage	VG	F	VF	XF	Unc
ND(1798)	—	—	—	175	350	—

French Siege of Rome - 1849

Coins struck ca. late 1800s

X# 10 5 BAIOCCHI
1.9000 g., Billon

Date	Mintage	F	VF	XF	Unc	BU
1849	—	—	—	—	—	—

X# 11 10 BAIOCCHI
5.0000 g., Billon

Date	Mintage	F	VF	XF	Unc	BU
1849	—	—	—	—	—	—

X# 12 20 BAIOCCHI
Billon

Date	Mintage	F	VF	XF	Unc	BU
1849	—	—	—	—	—	—

X# 13 40 BAIOCCHI
Billon

Date	Mintage	F	VF	XF	Unc	BU
1849	—	—	—	—	—	—

VENICE

REPUBLIC

MEDALLIC COINAGE

X# 201 14 ZECCHINI
49.2200 g., Gold, 68 mm. **Obv:** Doge kneeling before Christ, ornate border **Obv. Legend:** SM VENET - PAVLO RAINER • **Rev:** Christ standing facing surrounded by stars, flowery border **Rev. Legend:** • SIT • T • XPE • DAT • Q • TV • • REGIS • ISTE • DVCAT • **Note:** An Indian copy of Venetian multiple zecchini of Paolo Rainier. Illustration reduced.

Date	Mintage	F	VF	XF	Unc	BU
ND(1779-89)	—	—	1,150	—	—	—

ITALY

KINGDOM

FANTASY COINAGE

Vittorio Emmanuel III

The following are all considered fantasy types

X# 1 100 LIRE
30.0000 g., Gold **Obv:** Fascist **Rev:** Bust of Vittorio Emmanuel III left wearing helmet

Date	Mintage	F	VF	XF	Unc	BU
1928	—	—	—	—	650	—

Benito Mussolini

The following are all considered fantasy types struck ca. 1970

X# 2 20 LIRE
17.5000 g., Silver **Rev:** Bust of Mussolini left wearing helmet **Rev. Legend:** MVSSOLINI MCMXLIII

Date	Mintage	F	VF	XF	Unc	BU
(1943) Prooflike	—	—	—	—	—	25.00

X# 2a 20 LIRE
Silvered-Bronze

Date	Mintage	F	VF	XF	Unc	BU
(1943) Prooflike	—	—	—	—	—	10.00

X# 2b 20 LIRE
Brass

Date	Mintage	F	VF	XF	Unc	BU
(1943) Prooflike	—	—	—	—	—	4.00

X# 2c 20 LIRE
31.0000 g., Gold

Date	Mintage	F	VF	XF	Unc	BU
(1943) Prooflike	—	—	—	—	—	450

X# 3 20 LIRE
0.5000 Gold, 20 mm.

Date	Mintage	F	VF	XF	Unc	BU
(1943) Prooflike	—	—	—	—	—	145

X# 4 20 LIRE
0.5000 Gold, 17 mm.

Date	Mintage	F	VF	XF	Unc	BU
(1943) Prooflike	—	—	—	—	—	120

X# 8 20 LIRE
Silvered Brass, 35.5 mm. **Obv:** Fasces, lion head right **Obv. Legend:** ITALIA **Rev:** Bust of B. Mussolini right below large "1945" **Rev. Legend:** MUSSOLINI **Edge:** Reeded

Date	Mintage	F	VF	XF	Unc	BU
1945	—	—	—	8.00	10.00	12.00

X# 5 50 LIRE
Gold **Obv:** Fascist **Rev:** Bust of Mussolini left wearing helmet **Rev. Legend:** MVSSOLINI MCMXLIII

Date	Mintage	F	VF	XF	Unc	BU
(1943)	—	—	—	—	—	275

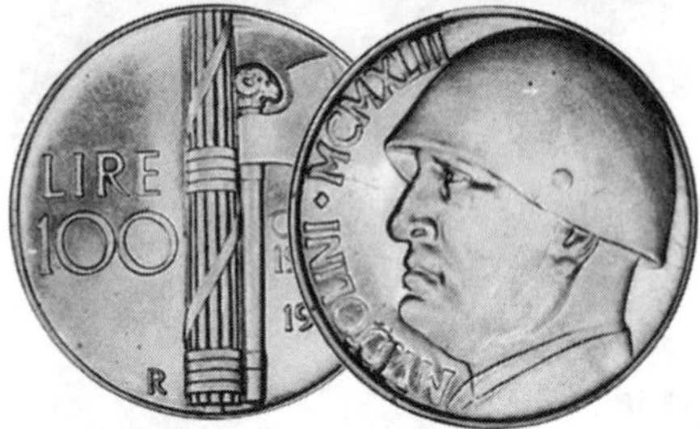

X# 6 100 LIRE
Gold **Rev:** Bust of Mussolini left wearing helmet **Rev. Legend:** MVSSOLINI MCMXLIII **Note:** Type I.

Date	Mintage	F	VF	XF	Unc	BU
(1943) Prooflike	—	—	—	—	—	500

X# 6a 100 LIRE

Silver Plated Brass **Note:** Type I.

Date	Mintage	F	VF	XF	Unc	BU
(1943)	—	—	—	—	—	8.00

X# 7 100 LIRE

Gold **Rev:** Bust of Mussolini left wearing helmut **Rev. Legend:** MVSSOLINI MCMXLIII **Note:** Type II.

Date	Mintage	F	VF	XF	Unc	BU
(1943) Prooflike	—	—	—	—	—	500

MEDALLIC COINAGE

Umberto II

The following are all considered fantasy types struck ca. 1970

X# M1a 20 LIRE

Silvered Brass **Ruler:** Umberto II

Date	Mintage	F	VF	XF	Unc	BU
1946	—	—	—	10.00	15.00	20.00

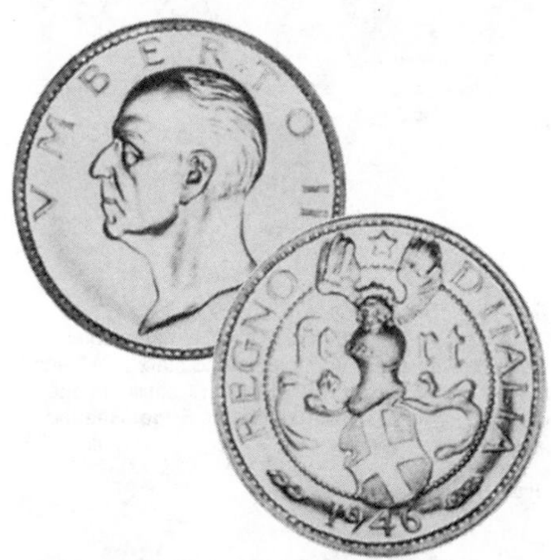

X# M1 20 LIRE

24.9500 g., Silver, 37.15 mm. **Ruler:** Umberto II **Obv:** Helmeted arms divides fe-rt **Rev:** Head of Umberto II left **Note:** Presumed to have been struck in the 1960's.

Date	Mintage	F	VF	XF	Unc	BU
1946	—	—	—	—	120	200

X# m3 100 LIRE

Platinum APW, 37.15 mm. **Ruler:** Umberto II **Obv:** Head left **Rev:** Helmeted arms divide fe - rt **Note:** Weight varies: 31.71-32.09 grams. Presumed to have been struck in the 1960's.

Date	Mintage	F	VF	XF	Unc	BU
1946	5	—	—	—	—	1,850

Note: All five know pieces were sold in the Superior Galleries - Edwards Metcalf and Buddy Ebsen Collection auction of June 1987.

X# M2 100 LIRE

Gold, 37.15 mm. **Ruler:** Umberto II **Obv:** Head left **Rev:** Helmeted arms divide fe - rt **Note:** Weight varies: 31.72-32.12 grams. Presumed to have been struck in the 1960's.

Date	Mintage	F	VF	XF	Unc	BU
1946	—	—	—	—	850	1,250

REPUBLIC

MEDALLIC COINAGE

ICB Series

X# 101 20 EURO

Goldine **Obv:** Portrait painting of Mona Lisa divides date and 12 stars **Obv. Legend:** ITALIA **Rev:** Bust of Leonardo da Vinci 3/4 right

Date	Mintage	F	VF	XF	Unc	BU
1997	—	—	—	—	6.00	—

X# 101a 20 EURO

Copper-Nickel **Obv:** Portrait painting of Mona Lisa divides date and 12 stars **Obv. Legend:** ITALIA **Rev. Designer:** Bust of Leonardo da Vinci 3/4 right

Date	Mintage	F	VF	XF	Unc	BU
1997	—	—	—	—	6.00	—

X# 101b 20 EURO

Silver **Obv:** Portrait painting of Mona Lisa divides date and 12 stars **Obv. Legend:** ITALIA **Rev:** Bust of Leonardo da Vinci 3/4 right

Date	Mintage	F	VF	XF	Unc	BU
1997	—	—	—	—	20.00	—

Ecu Series

X# 18 ECU

23.0000 g., Copper-Nickel, 38.6 mm. **Issuer:** CITV **Subject:** 35th Anniversary Founding E.E.C. **Obv:** Globe, Tower with E.C.C. flag **Obv. Legend:** ITALIA **Rev:** Senate Palace in Rome **Rev. Legend:** 35 ANNIVERSARIO FONDAZIONE C.E.E. **Edge:** Reeded

Date	Mintage	F	VF	XF	Unc	BU
1992	15,000	—	—	—	—	13.50

X# 19 ECU

25.0000 g., 0.9250 Silver 0.7435 oz. ASW, 38.6 mm. **Issuer:** CITV **Subject:** 35th Anniversary Foudning E.E.C. **Obv:** Globe, Tower with E.C.C. flag **Obv. Legend:** ITALIA **Rev:** Senate Palace in Rome **Rev. Legend:** 35 ANNIVERSARIO FONDAZIONE C.E.E. **Edge:** Reeded

Date	Mintage	F	VF	XF	Unc	BU
1992 Proof	7,500	Value: 40.00				

X# 20 ECU

6.7200 g., 0.7500 Gold 0.1620 oz. AGW, 22.5 mm. **Issuer:** CITV **Subject:** 35th Anniversary Founding E.E.C. **Obv:** Globe, Tower with E.C.C. flag **Obv. Legend:** ITALIA **Rev:** Senate Palace in Rome **Rev. Legend:** 35 ANNIVERSARIO FONDAZIONE C.E.E. **Edge:** Reeded

Date	Mintage	F	VF	XF	Unc	BU
1992 Proof	1,250	Value: 250				

X# 31 ECU

31.1030 g., 0.9250 Silver 0.9249 oz. ASW, 40 mm. **Issuer:** Intercoins S.p.A., Milan **Obv:** Early sailing ship with large "ECU" and date on sails **Obv. Legend:** ITALIE • ITALIEN • ITALY **Obv. Inscription:** ITALIA **Rev:** Head of Europa left **Edge:** Reeded

Date	Mintage	F	VF	XF	Unc	BU
1993 Proof	10,000	Value: 27.50				

X# 33 ECU
28.2800 g., 0.9250 Silver 0.8410 oz. ASW, 38.6 mm. **Obv:** Large "ECU" on map of Europe **Obv. Legend:** • ITALY • EUROPE - EUROPA **Rev:** Laureate head of Julius Caesar right, 12 stars **Rev. Legend:** REPUBLICA ITALIANA **Edge:** Reeded

Date	Mintage	F	VF	XF	Unc	BU
ND(1993) Proof	10,000	Value: 27.50				

X# 35 ECU
20.0000 g., 0.9990 Silver 0.6423 oz. ASW **Issuer:** Göde GmbH, Waldaschaff **Obv:** Venetian lion standing left on stone block with large "ECU" **Obv. Legend:** REPUBBLICA ITALIANA **Rev:** Bust of Galileo 3/4 right **Rev. Legend:** GALILAEUS GALILAEI **Edge:** Reeded

Date	Mintage	F	VF	XF	Unc	BU
ND(1993) Proof	9,999	Value: 60.00				

X# 36 ECU
32.5000 g., Brass, 40 mm. **Issuer:** Göde Gmbh, Waldaschaff **Obv:** 12 stars in arch above large "ITALIA", Roma suckling twins below **Rev:** Large "ECU" above Europa riding steer right **Edge:** Reeded **Note:** Gold and blue enameling.

Date	Mintage	F	VF	XF	Unc	BU
1993 Proof	9,999	Value: 30.00				

X# 21 5 ECU
18.0000 g., 0.9861 Silver 0.5706 oz. ASW, 35 mm. **Issuer:** Euronummus S.r.l., Milan **Obv:** Value in center of 12 stars **Obv. Legend:** COMUNITA ECONOMICA EUROPEA • ITALIA • **Obv. Designer:** R. Mauri **Rev:** Europa riding steer right **Rev. Legend:** ISTITUTO POLIGRAFICO E ZECCA DELO STATO **Rev. Designer:** M. Landi **Edge:** Plain

Date	Mintage	F	VF	XF	Unc	BU
1993 Proof	20,000	Value: 35.00				

X# 22 10 ECU
4.0000 g., 0.9167 Gold 0.1179 oz. AGW, 16 mm. **Issuer:** Euronummus S.r.l., Milan **Obv:** Value in center of 12 stars **Obv. Legend:** COMUNITA ECONOMICA EUROPEA • ITALIA • **Obv. Designer:** R. Mauri **Rev:** Europa riding steer right **Rev. Legend:** ISTITUTO POLIGRAFICO E ZECCA DELLO STATO **Rev. Designer:** M. Landi **Edge:** Plain

Date	Mintage	F	VF	XF	Unc	BU
1993 Proof	7,500	Value: 125				

X# 60 20 ECU
23.3200 g., Silver, 38 mm. **Obv:** Roman soldier standing with spear and standard, 6 stars at left and 6 at right **Obv. Legend:** ITALIA **Rev:** Coinlike image of Julius Caesar right, 12 stars in outer ring **Edge:** Reeded

Date	Mintage	F	VF	XF	Unc	BU
MCMXCV (1995) Proof	—	Value: 30.00				

X# 61 20 ECU
23.3200 g., Silver, 38 mm. **Obv:** Roman soldier standing with spear and standard, 6 stars at left and 6 at right **Obv. Legend:** ITALIA **Rev:** Coinlike image of Octavian right, 12 stars in outer ring **Edge:** Reeded

Date	Mintage	F	VF	XF	Unc	BU
MCMXCV (1995) Proof	—	Value: 30.00				

X# 62 20 ECU
23.3200 g., Silver, 38 mm. **Obv:** Roman soldier standing with spear and standard, 6 stars at left and 6 at right **Obv. Legend:** ITALIA **Rev:** Coinlike image of Tiberins right, 12 stars in outer ring **Edge:** Reeded

Date	Mintage	F	VF	XF	Unc	BU
MCMXCV (1995) Proof	—	Value: 30.00				

X# 51 20 ECU
23.3200 g., Silver, 38 mm. **Obv:** Roman soldier standing with spear and standard, 6 stars at left and 6 at right **Obv. Legend:** ITALIA **Rev:** Coinlike image of Caligula right, 12 stars in outer ring **Edge:** Reeded

Date	Mintage	F	VF	XF	Unc	BU
MCMXCV (1995) Proof	—	Value: 30.00				

X# 52 20 ECU
23.3200 g., Silver, 38 mm. **Obv:** Roman soldier standing with spear and standard, 6 stars at left and 6

at right **Obv. Legend:** ITALIA **Rev:** Coinlike image of Claudius right, 12 stars in outer ring **Edge:** Reeded

Date	Mintage	F	VF	XF	Unc	BU
MCMXCV (1995) Proof	—	Value: 30.00				

X# 53 20 ECU
23.3200 g., Silver, 38 mm. **Obv:** Roman soldier standing with spear and standard, 6 stars at left and 6 at right **Obv. Legend:** ITALIA **Rev:** Coinlike image of Nero left, 12 stars in outer ring **Edge:** Reeded

Date	Mintage	F	VF	XF	Unc	BU
MCMXCV (1995) Proof	—	Value: 30.00				

X# 54 20 ECU
23.3200 g., Silver, 38 mm. **Obv:** Roman soldier standing with spear and standard, 6 stars at left and 6 at right **Obv. Legend:** ITALIA **Rev:** Coinlike image of Galba right, 12 stars in outer ring **Edge:** Reeded

Date	Mintage	F	VF	XF	Unc	BU
MCMXCV (1995) Proof	—	Value: 30.00				

X# 55 20 ECU
23.3200 g., Silver, 38 mm. **Obv:** Roman soldier standing with spear and standard, 6 stars at left and 6

at right **Obv. Legend:** ITALIA **Rev:** Coinlike image of Otho right, 12 stars in out ring **Edge:** Reeded

Date	Mintage	F	VF	XF	Unc	BU
MCMXCV (1995) Proof	—	Value: 30.00				

X# 56 20 ECU
23.3200 g., Silver, 38 mm. **Obv:** Roman soldier standing with spear and standard, 6 stars at left and 6 at right **Obv. Legend:** ITALIA **Rev:** Coinlike image of Vitellius right, 12 stars in outer ring **Edge:** Reeded

Date	Mintage	F	VF	XF	Unc	BU
MCMXCV (1995) Proof	—	Value: 30.00				

X# 57 20 ECU
23.3200 g., Silver, 38 mm. **Obv:** Roman soldier standing with spear and standard, 6 stars at left and 6 at right **Obv. Legend:** ITALIA **Rev:** Coinlike image of Vespasian right, 12 stars in outer ring **Edge:** Reeded

Date	Mintage	F	VF	XF	Unc	BU
MCMXCV (1995) Proof	—	Value: 30.00				

X# 58 20 ECU
23.3200 g., Silver, 38 mm. **Obv:** Roman soldier standing with spear and standard, 6 stars at left and 6

at right **Obv. Legend:** ITALIA **Rev:** Coinlike image of Titus left, 12 stars in outer ring **Edge:** Reeded

Date	Mintage	F	VF	XF	Unc	BU
MCMXCV (1995) Proof	—	Value: 30.00				

X# 59 20 ECU
23.3200 g., Silver, 38 mm. **Obv:** Roman soldier standing with spear and standard, 6 stars at left and 6 at right **Obv. Legend:** ITALIA **Rev:** Coinlike image of Domitian right, 12 stars in outer ring **Edge:** Reeded

Date	Mintage	F	VF	XF	Unc	BU
MCMXCV (1995) Proof	—	Value: 30.00				

X# 23 25 ECU
8.0000 g., 0.9167 Gold 0.2358 oz. AGW, 22 mm. **Issuer:** Euronummus S.r.l., Milan **Obv:** Value in center of 12 stars **Obv. Legend:** COMUNITA ECONOMICA EUROPEA • ITALIA • **Obv. Designer:** R. Mauri **Rev:** Europa riding steer right **Rev. Legend:** ISTITUTO POLIGRAFICO E ZECCA DELLO STATO **Rev. Designer:** M. Landi **Edge:** Plain

Date	Mintage	F	VF	XF	Unc	BU
1993 Proof	5,500	Value: 250				

X# 24 50 ECU
14.0000 g., 0.9167 Gold 0.4126 oz. AGW, 30 mm. **Issuer:** Euronummus S.r.l., Milan **Obv:** Value in center of 12 stars **Obv. Legend:** COMUNITA ECONOMICA EUROPEA • ITALIA • **Obv. Designer:** R. Mauri **Rev:** Europa riding steer right **Rev. Legend:** ISTITUTO POLIGRAFICO E ZECCA DELLO STATO **Rev. Designer:** M. Landi **Edge:** Plain

Date	Mintage	F	VF	XF	Unc	BU
1993 Proof	3,500	Value: 400				

X# 25 75 ECU
15.5500 g., Bi-Metallic .9167 Gold/.950 Platinum, 22 mm. **Issuer:** Euronummus S.r.l., Milan **Obv:** Value in center of 12 stars **Obv. Legend:** COMUNITA ECONOMICA EUROPEA • ITALIA • **Obv. Designer:** R. Mauri **Rev:** Europa riding steer right **Rev. Legend:** ISTITUTO POLIGRAFICO E ZECCA DELLO STATO **Rev. Designer:** M. Landi **Edge:** Plain

Date	Mintage	F	VF	XF	Unc	BU
1993 Proof	1,000	Value: 550				

X# 26 100 ECU
25.0000 g., 0.9167 Gold 0.7368 oz. AGW, 35 mm. **Issuer:** Euronummus S.r.l., Milan **Obv:** Value in center of 12 stars **Obv. Legend:** COMUNITA ECONOMICA EUROPEA • ITALIA • **Obv. Designer:** R. Mauri **Rev:** Europa riding steer right **Rev. Legend:** ISTITUTO POLIGRAFICO E ZECCA DELLO STATO **Rev. Designer:** M. Landi **Edge:** Plain

Date	Mintage	F	VF	XF	Unc	BU
1993 Proof	2,000	Value: 650				

X# 27 150 ECU
31.1030 g., Bi-Metallic .9167 Gold/.950 Platinum, 32 mm. **Issuer:** Euronummus S.r.l., Milan **Obv:** Value in center of 12 stars **Obv. Legend:** COMUNITA ECONOMICA EUROPEA • ITALIA • **Obv. Designer:** R. Mauri **Rev:** Europa riding steer right **Rev. Legend:** ISTITUTO POLIGRAFICO E ZECCA DELLO STATO **Rev. Designer:** M. Landi **Edge:** Plain

Date	Mintage	F	VF	XF	Unc	BU
1993 Proof	1,000	Value: 1,000				

X# 28 200 ECU
50.0000 g., 0.9167 Gold 1.4736 oz. AGW, 40 mm. **Issuer:** Euronummus S.r.l., Milan **Obv:** Value in center of 12 stars **Obv. Legend:** COMUNITA ECONOMICA EUROPEA • ITALIA • **Obv. Designer:** R. Mauri **Rev:** Europa riding steer right **Rev. Legend:** ISTITUTO POLIGRAFICO E ZECCA DELLO STATO **Rev. Designer:** M. Landi **Edge:** Plain

Date	Mintage	F	VF	XF	Unc	BU
1993 Proof	1,500	Value: 1,250				

PIEFORTS (P)

X#	Date	Mintage	Identification	Mkt Val
P1	1992	900	Ecu. 0.9250 Silver. 50.0000 g. X19.	125
P2	1997	—	20 Euro. Silver. X#101b.	40.00

PROOF SETS

X#	Date	Mintage	Identification	Issue Price	Mkt Val
XPS1	1993 (5)	500	X22-X24, X26, X28	—	2,650
XPS2	1993 (3)	1,000	X22-X24	—	750

ALGHERO

COMMUNE

TOKEN COINAGE

X# Tn11 MARENGO
Silver, 30.4 mm. **Obv:** Sunface in order chain **Rev:** Castle with eight shields, name above **Edge:** Plain

Date	Mintage	F	VF	XF	Unc	BU
ND(1998)	—	—	—	—	50.00	65.00

X# Tn12 10 MARENGHI
0.9000 Gold, 21 mm. **Obv:** Denomination **Obv. Legend:** ALGHERO **Edge:** Plain

Date	Mintage	F	VF	XF	Unc	BU
ND(1998) Proof	—	Value: 185				

X# Tn13 20 MARENGHI
10.0000 g., 0.9000 Gold 0.2893 oz. AGW, 26 mm. **Obv:** Crowned arms above denomination **Obv. Legend:** ALGHERO **Edge:** Plain

Date	Mintage	F	VF	XF	Unc	BU
ND(1998) Proof	—	Value: 200				

ASIAGO

COMMUNE

TOKEN COINAGE

X# Tn11 MARENGO
Silver, 30.4 mm. **Obv:** Sunface in order chain **Obv. Legend:** ITALIA **Rev:** Castle with 8 shields **Edge:** Plain

Date	Mintage	F	VF	XF	Unc	BU
ND(1998)	—	—	—	—	50.00	65.00

X# Tn12 10 MARENGHI
0.9000 Gold, 21 mm. **Obv:** Church, observatory **Obv. Legend:** ASIAGO **Rev:** Nude female fountain **Edge:** Plain

Date	Mintage	F	VF	XF	Unc	BU
ND(1998) Proof	—	Value: 185				

X# Tn13 20 MARENGHI
10.0000 g., 0.9000 Gold 0.2893 oz. AGW, 26 mm. **Obv:** City arms, golf club and golf ball **Obv. Legend:** ASIAGO **Rev:** Nude female fountain **Edge:** Plain

Date	Mintage	F	VF	XF	Unc	BU
ND(1998) Proof	—	Value: 200				

ISOLA D'ELBA

COMMUNE

TOKEN COINAGE

X# Tn11 MARENGO
Silver, 30.4 mm. **Obv:** Sunface in order chain **Rev:** Castle with eight shields, name above **Edge:** Plain

Date	Mintage	F	VF	XF	Unc	BU
ND(1998)	—	—	—	—	50.00	65.00

X# Tn12 10 MARENGHI
0.9000 Gold, 21 mm. **Obv:** Denomination **Obv. Legend:** ISOLA D'ELBA **Edge:** Plain

Date	Mintage	F	VF	XF	Unc	BU
ND(1998) Proof	—	Value: 185				

X# Tn13 20 MARENGHI
10.0000 g., 0.9000 Gold 0.2893 oz. AGW, 26 mm. **Obv:** Standing figure with staff breaks denomination **Obv. Legend:** ISOLA D'ELBA **Edge:** Plain

Date	Mintage	F	VF	XF	Unc	BU
ND(1998) Proof	—	Value: 200				

LAINO D'INTELVI

COMMUNE

EURO TOKEN COINAGE

X# 1 50 EURO CENT
Brass, 25 mm. **Obv:** Outlined subject **Obv. Legend:** COMUNE DI LAINO D'INTELVI • COMO **Rev:** Euro map and stars design, large value

Date	Mintage	F	VF	XF	Unc	BU
1999	5,000	—	—	—	16.00	20.00

X# 1a 50 EURO CENT
0.9990 Silver, 25 mm. **Obv:** Outlined subject **Obv. Legend:** COMUNE DI LAINO D'INTELVI • COMO **Rev:** Euro map and stars design, large value

Date	Mintage	F	VF	XF	Unc	BU
1999	—	—	—	—	—	75.00

X# 2 EURO
Bi-Metallic Copper-Nickel center in Brass ring, 28 mm. **Obv:** Outlined subject **Obv. Legend:** COMUNE DI LAINO D'INTELVI • COMO **Rev:** Large value, Euro map and stars design

Date	Mintage	F	VF	XF	Unc	BU
1999	5,000	—	—	—	22.00	28.00

X# 2a EURO
0.9990 Silver, 28 mm. **Obv. Legend:** COMUNE DI LAINO D'INTELVI • COMO **Rev:** Large value, Euro map and stars design

Date	Mintage	F	VF	XF	Unc	BU
1999	—	—	—	—	—	100

MIGLIANICO

COMMUNE

EURO TOKEN COINAGE

X# 1 EURO
Bi-Metallic Copper-Nickel center in Brass ring, 28 mm. **Obv:** Crowned arms in sprays **Obv. Legend:** ★ ★ ★ MIGLIANICO (CH) ★ COMUNE D'EUROPA **Rev:** Large value, Euro map and stars design

Date	Mintage	F	VF	XF	Unc	BU
ND(1998)	2,000	—	—	—	75.00	125

X# 1a EURO
0.9990 Silver, 28 mm. **Obv:** Crowned arms in sprays **Obv. Legend:** ★ ★ ★ MIGLIANICO (CH) ★ COMUNE D'EUROPA **Rev:** Large value, Euro map and stars design

Date	Mintage	F	VF	XF	Unc	BU
ND(1998)	60	—	—	—	—	250

MONTECATINI

COMMUNE

TOKEN COINAGE

X# Tn11 MARENGO
Silver, 30.4 mm. **Obv:** Sunface in order chain **Rev:** Castle with eight shields, name above **Edge:** Plain

Date	Mintage	F	VF	XF	Unc	BU
ND(1998)	—	—	—	—	50.00	65.00

X# Tn12 10 MARENGHI
0.9000 Gold, 21 mm. **Obv:** Denomination **Obv. Legend:** MONTECATINI **Edge:** Plain

Date	Mintage	F	VF	XF	Unc	BU
ND(1998) Proof	—	Value: 185				

X# Tn13 20 MARENGHI
10.0000 g., 0.9000 Gold 0.2893 oz. AGW, 26 mm. **Obv:** Crowned arms above buildings and denomination **Obv. Legend:** MONTECATINI **Edge:** Plain

Date	Mintage	F	VF	XF	Unc	BU
ND(1998) Proof	—	Value: 200				

MONTESILVANO COMMUNE

COMMUNE

EURO TOKEN COINAGE

X# 1 EURO
Bi-Metallic Copper-Nickel center in Brass ring, 28 mm. **Obv:** Ornate arms **Obv. Legend:** COMITATO PROVINCIALE ERO • PESCARA • **Rev:** Large value, Euro map and star design

Date	Mintage	F	VF	XF	Unc	BU
ND(1998)	10,000	—	—	—	15.00	20.00

X# 1a EURO
0.9990 Silver, 28 mm. **Obv:** Crowned arms **Obv. Legend:** COMITATO PROVINCIALE ERO • PESCARA • **Rev:** Large value, Euro map and star design

Date	Mintage	F	VF	XF	Unc	BU
ND(1998)	100	—	—	—	—	50.00

MINT SETS

X#	Date	Mintage	Identification	Issue Price	Mkt Val
XMS1	ND(1998) (2)	100	X#1, 1a	—	70.00

NAPOLI

COMMUNE

EURO TOKEN COINAGE

X# 1 50 EURO CENT
Bronzital **Obv:** Castle **Rev:** Value and EEC map

Date	Mintage	F	VF	XF	Unc	BU
ND(1999)	5,000	—	—	—	8.00	10.00

X# 2 EURO
Bi-Metallic Nickel-Silver in Brass ring

Date	Mintage	F	VF	XF	Unc	BU
ND(1999)	5,000	—	—	—	10.00	12.50

ORTIESI ST. ULRICH

COMMUNE

TOKEN COINAGE

X# Tn11 MARENGO
Silver, 30.4 mm. **Obv:** Sunface in order chain **Rev:** Castle with eight shields, name above **Edge:** Plain

Date	Mintage	F	VF	XF	Unc	BU
ND(1998)	—	—	—	—	50.00	65.00

X# Tn12 10 MARENGHI
0.9000 Gold, 21 mm. **Obv:** Denomination **Obv. Legend:** ORTISEI ST. ULRICH **Edge:** Plain

Date	Mintage	F	VF	XF	Unc	BU
ND(1998) Proof	—	Value: 185				

X# Tn13 20 MARENGHI
10.0000 g., 0.9000 Gold 0.2893 oz. AGW, 26 mm. **Obv:** Horse with rider above shields, denomination to right **Obv. Legend:** ORTISEI ST. ULRICH **Edge:** Plain

Date	Mintage	F	VF	XF	Unc	BU
ND(1998) Proof	—	Value: 200				

RIMINI

COMMUNE

TOKEN COINAGE

X# Tn11 MARENGO
Silver, 30.4 mm. **Obv:** Sunface in order chain **Rev:** Castle with eight shields, name above **Edge:** Plain

Date	Mintage	F	VF	XF	Unc	BU
ND(1998)	—	—	—	—	50.00	65.00

X# Tn12 10 MARENGHI
0.9000 Gold, 21 mm. **Obv:** Denomination **Obv. Legend:** RIMINI **Edge:** Plain

Date	Mintage	F	VF	XF	Unc	BU
ND(1998) Proof	—	Value: 185				

X# Tn13 20 MARENGHI
10.0000 g., 0.9000 Gold 0.2893 oz. AGW, 26 mm. **Obv:** Quartered devices with denomination in lower right section **Obv. Legend:** RIMINI **Edge:** Plain

Date	Mintage	F	VF	XF	Unc	BU
ND(1998) Proof	—	Value: 200				

SAN RAFFAELE CIMENA COMMUNE

COMMUNE

EURO TOKEN COINAGE

X# 1 EURO
Bi-Metallic Copper-Nickel center in Brass ring, 28 mm. **Obv:** Crowned arms in sprays **Obv. Legend:** COMUNE DI SAN RAFFAELE CIMENA (TO) **Rev:** Large value, Euro map and star design

Date	Mintage	F	VF	XF	Unc	BU
ND(1998)	50	—	—	—	—	75.00

X# 1a EURO
0.9990 Silver, 28 mm. **Obv:** Crowned arms in sprays **Obv. Legend:** COMUNE DI SAN RAFFAELE CIMENA (TO) **Rev:** Large value, Euro map and star design

Date	Mintage	F	VF	XF	Unc	BU
ND(1998)	50	—	—	—	—	50.00

MINT SETS

X#	Date	Mintage	Identification	Issue Price	Mkt Val
XMS1	ND(1998) (2)	50	X#1, 1a	—	125

SAN REMO

COMMUNE

TOKEN COINAGE

X# Tn11 MARENGO
Silver, 30.4 mm. **Obv:** Sunface in order chain **Rev:** Castle with eight shields, name above **Edge:** Plain

Date	Mintage	F	VF	XF	Unc	BU
ND(1998)	—	—	—	—	50.00	65.00

X# Tn12 10 MARENGHI
0.9000 Gold, 21 mm. **Obv:** Denomination
Obv. Legend: SAN REMO **Edge:** Plain

Date	Mintage	F	VF	XF	Unc	BU
ND(1998) Proof	—	Value: 185				

X# Tn13 20 MARENGHI
10.0000 g., 0.9000 Gold 0.2893 oz. AGW, 26 mm.
Obv: Church above shield and denomination
Obv. Legend: SAN REMO **Edge:** Plain

Date	Mintage	F	VF	XF	Unc	BU
ND(1998) Proof	—	Value: 200				

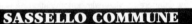

SASSELLO COMMUNE

COMMUNE

EURO TOKEN COINAGE

X# 1 10 EURO CENT
Brass, 18 mm. **Obv:** Ornate arms **Obv. Legend:** COMUNE DI SASSELLO (LIGURIA) **Rev:** Euro map and star design, large value

Date	Mintage	F	VF	XF	Unc	BU
ND(1998)	2,500	—	—	—	25.00	35.00

X# 1a 10 EURO CENT
0.9990 Silver, 18 mm. **Obv:** Ornate arms
Obv. Legend: COMUNE DI SASSELLO (LIGURIA)
Rev: Euro map and star design, large value

Date	Mintage	F	VF	XF	Unc	BU
ND(1998)	50	—	—	—	—	100

X# 2 20 EURO CENT
Brass, 21 mm. **Obv:** Ornate arms **Obv. Legend:** COMUNE DI SASSELLO (LIGURIA) **Rev:** Euro map and star design, large value

Date	Mintage	F	VF	XF	Unc	BU
ND(1998)	—	—	—	—	30.00	40.00

X# 2a 20 EURO CENT
Silver, 21 mm. **Obv:** Ornate arms **Obv. Legend:** COMUNE DI SASSELLO (LIGURIA) **Rev:** Euro map and star design

Date	Mintage	F	VF	XF	Unc	BU
ND(1998)	50	—	—	—	—	100

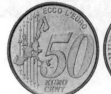

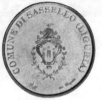

X# 3 50 EURO CENT
Brass, 25 mm. **Obv:** Ornate arms **Obv. Legend:** COMUNE DE SASSELO (LIGURIA) **Rev:** Euro map and star design, large value

Date	Mintage	F	VF	XF	Unc	BU
ND(1998)	16,000	—	—	—	8.00	10.00

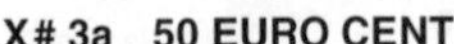

X# 3a 50 EURO CENT
0.9990 Silver, 25 mm. **Obv:** Ornate arms
Obv. Legend: COMUNE DE SASSELO (LIGURIA)
Rev: Euro map and star design, large value

Date	Mintage	F	VF	XF	Unc	BU
ND(1998)	100	—	—	—	—	25.00

X# 4 EURO
Bi-Metallic Copper-Nickel center in Brass ring, 28 mm.
Obv: Ornate arms **Obv. Legend:** COMUNE DE SASSELO (LIGURIA) **Rev:** Large value, Euro map and star design

Date	Mintage	F	VF	XF	Unc	BU
ND(1998)	16,000	—	—	—	10.00	12.50

X# 4a EURO
0.9990 Silver, 28 mm. **Obv:** Ornate arms
Obv. Legend: COMUNE DE SASSELO (LIGURIA)
Rev: Large value, Euro map and star design

Date	Mintage	F	VF	XF	Unc	BU
ND(1998)	100	—	—	—	—	35.00

X# 5 2 EURO
Bi-Metallic Brass center in Copper-Nickel ring, 26 mm.
Obv: Ornate arms **Obv. Legend:** COMUNE DI SASSELLO (LIGURIA) **Rev:** Euro map and star design

Date	Mintage	F	VF	XF	Unc	BU
ND(1998)	2,500	—	—	—	45.00	60.00

X# 5a 2 EURO
0.9990 Silver, 26 mm. **Obv:** Ornate arms
Obv. Legend: COMUNE DI SASSELLO (LIGURIA)
Rev: Euro map and star design

Date	Mintage	F	VF	XF	Unc	BU
ND(1998)	50	—	—	—	—	150

MINT SETS

X#	Date	Mintage	Identification	Issue Price	Mkt Val
XMS1	ND(1998) (2)	100	X#1, 2	—	60.00

SETTIMO TORINESE CITY

CITY

EURO TOKEN COINAGE

X# 1 5 EURO CENT
Copper, 20 mm. **Obv:** Crowned arms in sprays
Obv. Legend: CITTA' DI SETTIMO TORINESE
Rev: Large value, Euro map and stars design

Date	Mintage	F	VF	XF	Unc	BU
ND(1999)	6,000	—	—	—	10.00	12.50

X# 2 10 EURO CENT
Brass, 18.5 mm. **Obv. Legend:** CITTA' DI SETTIMO TORINESE **Obv. Inscription:** EURO / LA NOBILTA / DELLA / MONETA **Rev:** Euro map and stars design, large value

Date	Mintage	F	VF	XF	Unc	BU
1999	6,000	—	—	—	12.50	15.00

X# 3 20 EURO CENT
Brass, 21 mm. **Obv:** Castle gate tower **Obv. Legend:** CITTA' DI SETTIMO TORINESE **Rev:** Euro map and stars design, large value

Date	Mintage	F	VF	XF	Unc	BU
ND(1999)	6,000	—	—	—	12.50	15.00

X# 4 50 EURO CENT
Brass, 25 mm. **Obv:** Crowned arms in sprays
Obv. Legend: CITTA' DI SETTIMO TORINESE **Rev:** Euro map and stars design, large value

Date	Mintage	F	VF	XF	Unc	BU
1999	6,000	—	—	—	15.00	18.00

X# 6 2 EURO
Bi-Metallic Brass center in Copper-Nickel ring, 25 mm.
Obv: Crowned arms in sprays **Obv. Legend:** CITTA' DI SETTIMO TORINESE **Rev:** Large value, Euro map and stars design

Date	Mintage	F	VF	XF	Unc	BU
1999	6,000	—	—	—	30.00	35.00

SIRMIONE

COMMUNE

TOKEN COINAGE

X# Tn11 MARENGO
Silver, 30.4 mm. **Obv:** Sunface in order chain **Rev:** Castle with eight shields, name above **Edge:** Plain

Date	Mintage	F	VF	XF	Unc	BU
ND(1998)	—	—	—	—	50.00	65.00

X# Tn12 10 MARENGHI
0.9000 Gold, 21 mm. **Obv:** Denomination **Obv. Legend:** SIRMIONE **Edge:** Plain

Date	Mintage	F	VF	XF	Unc	BU
ND(1998) Proof	—	Value: 185				

X# Tn13 20 MARENGHI
10.0000 g., 0.9000 Gold 0.2893 oz. AGW, 26 mm. **Obv:** Head right, denomination below **Obv. Legend:** SIRMIONE **Edge:** Plain

Date	Mintage	F	VF	XF	Unc	BU
ND(1998) Proof	—	Value: 200				

SORRENTO

COMMUNE

TOKEN COINAGE

X# Tn11 MARENGO
Silver, 30.4 mm. **Obv:** Sunface in order chain **Rev:** Castle with eight shields, name above **Edge:** Plain

Date	Mintage	F	VF	XF	Unc	BU
ND(1998)	—	—	—	—	50.00	65.00

X# Tn12 10 MARENGHI
0.9000 Gold, 21 mm. **Obv:** Denomination **Obv. Legend:** SORRENTO **Edge:** Plain

Date	Mintage	F	VF	XF	Unc	BU
ND(1998) Proof	—	Value: 185				

X# Tn13 20 MARENGHI
10.0000 g., 0.9000 Gold 0.2893 oz. AGW, 26 mm. **Obv:** Trees and lake, denomination below **Obv. Legend:** SORRENTO **Edge:** Plain

Date	Mintage	F	VF	XF	Unc	BU
ND(1998) Proof	—	Value: 200				

TAORMINA

COMMUNE

TOKEN COINAGE

X# Tn11 MARENGO
Silver, 30.4 mm. **Obv:** Sunface in order chain **Rev:** Castle with eight shields, name above **Edge:** Plain

Date	Mintage	F	VF	XF	Unc	BU
ND(1998)	—	—	—	—	50.00	65.00

X# Tn12 10 MARENGHI
0.9000 Gold, 21 mm. **Obv:** Denomination **Obv. Legend:** TAORMINA **Edge:** Plain

Date	Mintage	F	VF	XF	Unc	BU
ND(1998) Proof	—	Value: 185				

X# Tn13 20 MARENGHI
10.0000 g., 0.9000 Gold 0.2893 oz. AGW, 26 mm. **Obv:** Denomination over triangular mountain island, boats below **Obv. Legend:** TAORMINA **Edge:** Plain

Date	Mintage	F	VF	XF	Unc	BU
ND(1998) Proof	—	Value: 200				

JAPAN

EMPIRE

CAST COINAGE

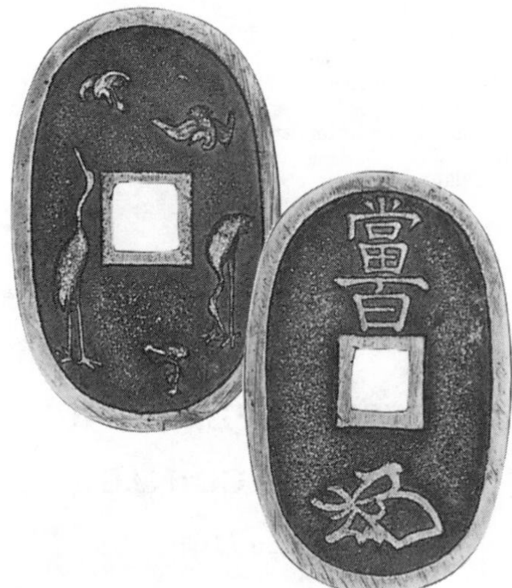

X# 5 100 MON
Bronze **Obv:** Five birds **Rev. Inscription:** 100 MON **Shape:** Oval **Note:** Amulet. Size 31.2x48.

Date	Mintage	Good	VG	F	VF	XF
ND	—	—	—	12.50	20.00	35.00

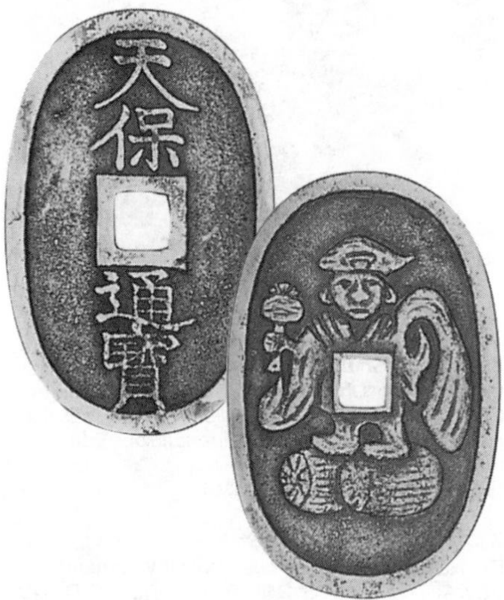

X# 3 100 MON
Bronze **Obv. Inscription:** Ten-ho Tsu-ho **Rev:** God of Plenty standing on two barrels **Shape:** Oval **Note:** Amulet. Size 32x47.5.

Date	Mintage	Good	VG	F	VF	XF
ND	—	—	—	12.50	20.00	35.00

X# 4 100 MON
Bronze **Obv:** Bird standing at waters edge, tree behind **Rev. Inscription:** 100 MON **Shape:** Oval **Note:** Amulet. Size 32x48.5.

Date	Mintage	Good	VG	F	VF	XF
ND	—	—	—	12.50	20.00	35.00

X# 6 100 MON
Bronze **Obv:** Three bats in circle above square hole **Shape:** Oval **Note:** Uniface amulet. Size 35x53.

Date	Mintage	Good	VG	F	VF	XF
ND	—	—	—	12.50	20.00	35.00

X# 10 NON-DENOMINATED
14.6500 g., Billon **Obv:** Various chopmarks **Rev:** Various chopmarks

Date	Mintage	F	VF	XF	Unc	BU
ND	—	—	—	—	—	—

FANTASY COINAGE

X# 15 YEN
29.4800 g., Copper-Nickel, 39.8 mm. **Obv:** Dragon **Obv. Legend:** "Dai Nippon" **Rev:** Crossed flags in inner circle, sprays **Edge:** Reeded

Date	Mintage	F	VF	XF	Unc	BU
Yr.3(1870)	—	7.50	12.50	20.00	—	—

X# 21 YEN
26.9568 g., 0.9000 Silver 0.7800 oz. ASW

Date	Mintage	F	VF	XF	Unc	BU
Yr. 4 (1915) Unique; Rare	—	—	—	—	—	—

Port Authority Tokyo (Edo) - Shinagawa Fort Office

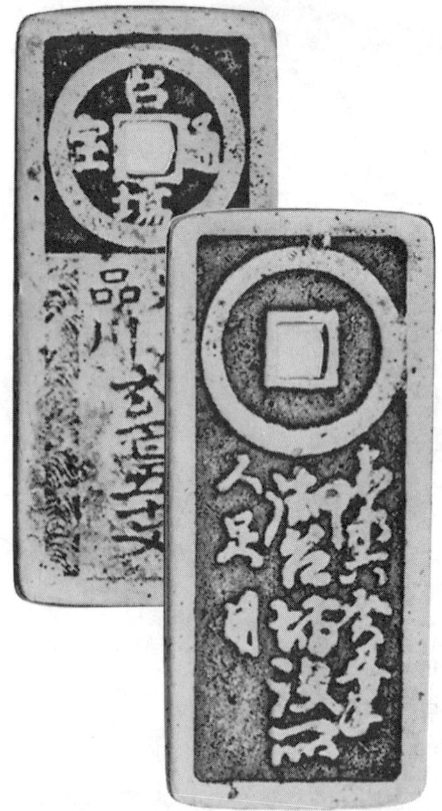

X# 51 250 MON
Bronze **Note:** One of 3 fantasy pieces produced by Otabelchoro ca.1920's.

Date	Mintage	Good	VG	F	VF	XF
ND	—	6.00	10.00	15.00	25.00	—

MEDALLIC COINAGE

Square Deal Productions Issue

X# 71 YEN
8.0000 g., 0.9990 Silver 0.2569 oz. ASW **Issuer:** B.H. Mayermint, Munich **Obv:** Sprig, value below **Obv. Legend:** "Nippon-koku" **Obv. Designer:** Andor Orand **Rev:** Large "1" over year of reign **Edge:** Reeded **Shape:** Square **Note:** Size: 24x24mm.

Date	Mintage	F	VF	XF	Unc	BU
Yr. 50 (1975) Proof	—	Value: 70.00				

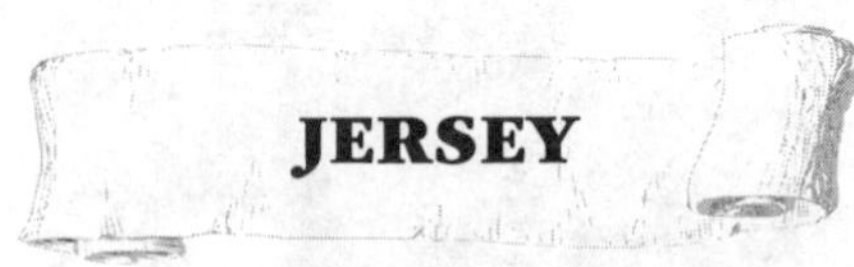

JERSEY

BRITISH DEPENDENCY

MEDALLIC COINAGE

INA Retro Issue

X# M1 4 SHILLINGS
0.9250 Silver **Obv:** Crowned bust right **Obv. Legend:** EDWARDVS VII D: G: BRITT: OMN: REX: F: D: IND: IMP. **Rev:** Crowned shield within quadrilobe **Edge:** Plain

Date	Mintage	F	VF	XF	Unc	BU
1910 Proof	360	Value: 50.00				

X# M1a 4 SHILLINGS
Bronze **Obv:** Crowned bust right **Obv. Legend:** EDWARDVS VII D: G: BRITT: OMN: REX: F: D: IND: IMP. **Rev:** Crowned shield within quadrilobe **Edge:** Plain

Date	Mintage	F	VF	XF	Unc	BU
1910 Proof	360	Value: 25.00				

X# M1b 4 SHILLINGS
Copper **Obv:** Crowned bust right **Obv. Legend:** EDWARDVS VII D: G: BRITT: OMN: REX: F: D: IND: IMP. **Rev:** Crowned shield within quatrilobe **Edge:** Plain

Date	Mintage	F	VF	XF	Unc	BU
1910 Proof	360	Value: 25.00				

X# M1c.1 4 SHILLINGS
33.2000 g., 0.9167 Gold 0.9784 oz. AGW
Obv: Crowned bust right **Obv. Legend:** EDWARDVS VII D: G: BRITT: OMN: REX: F: D: IND: IMP.
Rev: Crowned shield within quatrilobe **Edge:** Reeded

Date	Mintage	F	VF	XF	Unc	BU
1910 Proof	1	—	—	—	—	—
Note: Medal alignment						
1910 Proof	1	—	—	—	—	—
Note: Coin alignment						

X# M1c.2 4 SHILLINGS
0.9167 Gold **Obv:** Crowned bust right **Obv. Legend:** EDWARDVS VII D: G: BRITT: OMN: REX: F: D: IND: IMP. **Rev:** Crowned shield within quadrilobe **Edge:** Plain **Note:** Weight varies: 33.1-33.4 grams.

Date	Mintage	F	VF	XF	Unc	BU
1910 Plain	1	—	—	—	—	—
Note: Medal alignment						
1910 Proof	1	—	—	—	—	—
Note: Coin alignment						

X# M2.1 4 SHILLINGS
33.3000 g., 0.9167 Gold 0.9814 oz. AGW **Obv:** Head right within pellet circle **Obv. Legend:** EDWARDVS VII DEI GRATIA INDIAE IMPERATOR **Rev:** Crowned shield within quatrilobe **Edge:** Reeded **Note:** Medal alignment.

Date	Mintage	F	VF	XF	Unc	BU
1910 Proof	1	—	—	—	—	—

X# M2.2 4 SHILLINGS
33.3000 g., 0.9167 Gold 0.9814 oz. AGW **Obv:** head right within pellet circle **Obv. Legend:** EDWARDVS VII DEI GRATIA INDIAE IMPERATOR **Rev:** Crowned shield within quatrilobe **Edge:** Plain **Note:** Medal alignment

Date	Mintage	F	VF	XF	Unc	BU
1910 Proof	1	—	—	—	—	—

X# M3 4 SHILLINGS
0.9250 Silver **Obv:** Head left **Obv. Legend:** GEORGIVS V DEI GRATIA INDIAE IMPERATOR **Rev:** Crowned shield within quatrilobe **Edge:** Plain

Date	Mintage	F	VF	XF	Unc	BU
1910 Proof	360	Value: 50.00				

X# M3a 4 SHILLINGS
Bronze **Obv:** Head left **Obv. Legend:** GEORGIVS V DEI GRATIA INDIAE IMPERATOR **Rev:** Crowned shield within quatrilobe **Edge:** Plain

Date	Mintage	F	VF	XF	Unc	BU
1910 Proof	360	Value: 25.00				

X# M3b 4 SHILLINGS
Copper **Obv:** Head left **Obv. Legend:** GEORGIVS V DEI GRATIA INDIAE IMPERATOR **Rev:** Crowned shield within quatrilobe **Edge:** Plain

Date	Mintage	F	VF	XF	Unc	BU
1910 Proof	360	Value: 25.00				

X# M3c.1 4 SHILLINGS
32.7000 g., 0.9167 Gold 0.9637 oz. AGW **Obv:** Head left **Obv. Legend:** GEORGIVS V DEI GRATIA INDIAE IMPERATOR **Rev:** Crowned shield within quatrilobe **Edge:** Plain

Date	Mintage	F	VF	XF	Unc	BU
1910 Proof	1	—	—	—	—	—
Note: Medal alignment						
1910 Proof	1	—	—	—	—	—
Note: Coin alignment						

X# M3c.2 4 SHILLINGS
0.9167 Gold **Obv:** Head left **Obv. Legend:** GEORGIVS V DEI GRATIA INDIAE IMPERATOR **Rev:** Crowned shield within quatrilobe **Edge:** Plain **Note:** Medal alignment

Date	Mintage	F	VF	XF	Unc	BU
1910 Proof	1	—	—	—	—	—

X# M4 4 SHILLINGS
22.0000 g., 0.9250 Silver 0.6542 oz. ASW, 36.17 mm. **Obv:** Crowned bust left **Obv. Legend:** EDWARDVS VIII D: G: REX IND: IMP **Rev:** Shield divides date **Edge:** Plain **Note:** Medal alignment.

Date	Mintage	F	VF	XF	Unc	BU
1937 Proof	360	Value: 50.00				

X# M4a 4 SHILLINGS
Bronze, 36.17 mm. **Obv:** Crowned bust left **Obv. Legend:** EDWARDVS VIII D: G: REX IND: IMP **Rev:** Shield divides date **Edge:** Plain **Note:** Medal alignment.

Date	Mintage	F	VF	XF	Unc	BU
1937 Proof	360	Value: 25.00				

X# M4b 4 SHILLINGS
18.2300 g., Copper, 36.17 mm. **Obv:** Crowned bust left **Obv. Legend:** EDWARDVS VIII D: G: REX IND: IMP **Rev:** Shield divides date **Edge:** Plain **Note:** Medal alignment.

Date	Mintage	F	VF	XF	Unc	BU
1937 Proof	360	Value: 25.00				

X# M4c.1 4 SHILLINGS
0.9167 Gold, 36.17 mm. **Obv:** Crowned bust left **Obv. Legend:** EDWARDVS VIII D: G: REX IND: IMP **Rev:** Shield divides date **Edge:** Reeded **Note:** Weight varies: 33.2-33.1 grams.

Date	Mintage	F	VF	XF	Unc	BU
1937 Proof	1	—	—	—	—	—
Note: Medal alignment						
1937 Matte Proof	1	—	—	—	—	—
Note: Coin alignment						

X# M4c.2 4 SHILLINGS
33.2000 g., 0.9167 Gold 0.9784 oz. AGW **Obv:** Crowned bust left **Obv. Legend:** EDWARDVS VIII D: G: REX IND: IMP **Rev:** Shield divides date **Edge:** Plain **Note:** Medal alignment.

Date	Mintage	F	VF	XF	Unc	BU
1937 Proof	1	—	—	—	—	—

X# M5 4 SHILLINGS
0.9250 Silver **Obv:** Head left **Obv. Legend:** EDWARDVS VIII D: G: REX IND: IMP **Rev:** Shield divides date **Edge:** Plain **Note:** Medal alignment.

Date	Mintage	F	VF	XF	Unc	BU
1937 Proof	260	Value: 50.00				

X# M5a 4 SHILLINGS
Bronze **Obv:** Head left **Obv. Legend:** EDWARDVS VIII D: G: REX IND: IMP **Rev:** Sheild divides date **Edge:** Plain **Note:** Medal alignment.

Date	Mintage	F	VF	XF	Unc	BU
1937 Proof	260	Value: 25.00				

X# M5b 4 SHILLINGS
18.2300 g., Copper **Obv:** Head left **Obv. Legend:** EDWARDVS VIII D: G: REX IND: IMP **Rev:** Shield divides date **Edge:** Plain **Note:** Medal alignment.

Date	Mintage	F	VF	XF	Unc	BU
1937 Proof	260	Value: 25.00				

X# M5c.1 4 SHILLINGS
0.9167 Gold **Obv:** Head left **Obv. Legend:** EDWARDVS VIII D: G: REX IND: IMP **Rev:** Shield divides date **Edge:** Reeded **Note:** Weight varies: 33.2-33.3. grams.

Date	Mintage	F	VF	XF	Unc	BU
1937 Proof	1	—	—	—	—	—
Note: Medal alignment						
1937 Matte Proof	1	—	—	—	—	—
Note: Coin alignment						

X# M5c.2 4 SHILLINGS
33.2000 g., 0.9167 Gold 0.9784 oz. AGW, 36.17 mm. **Obv:** Head left **Obv. Legend:** EDWARDVS VIII D: G: REX IND: IMP **Rev:** Shield divides date **Edge:** Plain **Note:** Medal alignment.

Date	Mintage	F	VF	XF	Unc	BU
1937 Proof	1	—	—	—	—	—

X# M6 4 SHILLINGS
0.9250 Silver **Obv:** Head left **Obv. Legend:** GEORGIVS VI DEI GRATIA INDIAE IMPERATOR **Rev:** Shield divides date **Edge:** Plain

Date	Mintage	F	VF	XF	Unc	BU
1937 Proof	360	Value: 50.00				

X# M6a 4 SHILLINGS
Bronze, 36.17 mm. **Obv:** Head left **Obv. Legend:** GEORGIVS VI DEI GRATIA INDIAE IMPERATOR **Obv. Designer:** Donald R. Golder / H. Paget **Rev:** Shield divides date **Rev. Legend:** STATES OF JERSEY **Edge:** Plain

Date	Mintage	F	VF	XF	Unc	BU
1937 Proof	360	Value: 25.00				

X# M6b 4 SHILLINGS
Copper **Obv:** Head left **Obv. Legend:** GEORGIVS VI DEI GRATIA INDIAE IMPERATOR **Rev:** Shield divides date **Edge:** Plain

Date	Mintage	F	VF	XF	Unc	BU
1937 Proof	360	Value: 25.00				

X# M6c.1 4 SHILLINGS
0.9167 Gold **Obv:** Head left **Obv. Legend:** GEORGIVS VI DEI GRATIA INDIAE IMPERATOR **Rev:** Shield divides date **Edge:** Reeded **Note:** Weight varies: 33.3-33.5 grams.

Date	Mintage	F	VF	XF	Unc	BU
1937 Proof	1	—	—	—	—	—
Note: Medal alignment						
1937 Proof	1	—	—	—	—	—
Note: Coin alignment						

X# M6c.2 4 SHILLINGS
32.0000 g., 0.9167 Gold 0.9431 oz. AGW **Obv:** Head left **Obv. Legend:** GEORGIVS VI DEI GRATIA INDIAE IMPERATOR **Rev:** Shield divides date **Edge:** Plain **Note:** Medal alignment.

Date	Mintage	F	VF	XF	Unc	BU
1937 Proof	1	—	—	—	—	—

X# M8 5 SHILLING
Silver, 40.96 mm. **Obv:** Laureate bust right **Obv. Legend:** GEORGIUS III DEI GRATIA REX. **Rev:** GR monogram above arms in quadralobe **Rev. Legend:** STATES OF JERSEY **Edge:** Plain

Date	Mintage	F	VF	XF	Unc	BU
1808 (2007) Proof	—	—	—	—	—	—
1808 (2007) Matte Proof	—	—	—	—	—	—

X# M8a 5 SHILLING
Copper, 40.96 mm. **Obv:** Laureate bust right **Obv. Legend:** GEORGIUS III DEI GRATIA REX. **Rev:** GR monogram above arms in quadralobe **Rev. Legend:** STATES OF JERSEY **Edge:** Plain

Date	Mintage	F	VF	XF	Unc	BU
1808 (2007) Proof	500	—	—	—	—	—

X# M8b 5 SHILLING
Aluminum, 40.96 mm. **Obv:** Laureate bust right **Obv. Legend:** GEORGIUS III DEI GRATIA REX. **Rev:** GR monogram above arms in quadralobe **Rev. Legend:** STATES OF JERSEY **Edge:** Plain

Date	Mintage	F	VF	XF	Unc	BU
1808 (2007) Proof	500	—	—	—	—	—

X# M8c 5 SHILLING
Pewter, 40.96 mm. **Obv:** Laureate bust right **Obv. Legend:** GEORGIUS III DEI GRATIA REX. **Rev:** GR monogram above arms in quadralobe **Rev. Legend:** STATES OF JERSEY **Edge:** Plain

Date	Mintage	F	VF	XF	Unc	BU
1808 (2007) Proof	500	—	—	—	—	—

X# M8d 5 SHILLING
Copper Bronzed, 40.96 mm. **Obv:** Laureate bust right **Obv. Legend:** GEORGIUS III DEI GRATIA REX. **Rev:** GR monogram above arms in quadralobe **Rev. Legend:** STATES OF JERSEY **Edge:** Plain

Date	Mintage	F	VF	XF	Unc	BU
1808 (2007) Proof	500	—	—	—	—	—

X# M8e 5 SHILLING
Nickel-Silver, 40.96 mm. **Obv:** Laureate bust right **Obv. Legend:** GEORGIUS III DEI GRATIA REX. **Rev:** GR monogram above arms in quadralobe **Rev. Legend:** STATES OF JERSEY **Edge:** Plain

Date	Mintage	F	VF	XF	Unc	BU
1808 (2007) Proof	500	—	—	—	—	—

X# M8f 5 SHILLING
Goldine, 40.96 mm. **Obv:** Laureate bust right **Obv. Legend:** GEORGIUS III DEI GRATIA REX. **Rev:** GR monogram above arms in quadralobe **Rev. Legend:** STATES OF JERSEY **Edge:** Plain

Date	Mintage	F	VF	XF	Unc	BU
1808 (2007) Proof	500	—	—	—	—	—

X# M8g 5 SHILLING
Gold, 40.96 mm. **Obv:** Laureate bust right **Obv. Legend:** GEORGIUS III DEI GRATIA REX. **Rev:** GR monogram above arms in quadralobe **Rev. Legend:** STATES OF JERSEY **Edge:** Plain

Date	Mintage	F	VF	XF	Unc	BU
1808 (2007) Proof	—	—	—	—	—	—

FANTASY EURO PATTERNS

X# Pn1 EURO CENT
Copper Plated Steel **Ruler:** Elizabeth II

Date	Mintage	F	VF	XF	Unc	BU
2004	10,000	—	—	—	—	1.50
2004 Proof	—	Value: 2.50				

X# Pn1a EURO CENT
Silver

Date	Mintage	F	VF	XF	Unc	BU
2004 Proof	—	Value: 6.00				

X# Pn2 2 EURO CENT
Copper Plated Steel **Ruler:** Elizabeth II

Date	Mintage	F	VF	XF	Unc	BU
2004	10,000	—	—	—	—	2.00
2004 Proof	—	Value: 3.00				

X# Pn2a 2 EURO CENT
Silver

Date	Mintage	F	VF	XF	Unc	BU
2004 Proof	—	Value: 7.00				

X# Pn3 5 EURO CENT
Copper Plated Steel **Ruler:** Elizabeth II

Date	Mintage	F	VF	XF	Unc	BU
2004	10,000	—	—	—	—	2.50
2004 Proof	—	Value: 3.50				

X# Pn3a 5 EURO CENT
Silver

Date	Mintage	F	VF	XF	Unc	BU
2004 Proof	—	Value: 8.50				

X# Pn4a 10 EURO CENT
Silver

Date	Mintage	F	VF	XF	Unc	BU
2004 Proof	—	Value: 10.00				

X# Pn4 10 EURO CENT
Goldine **Ruler:** Elizabeth II

Date	Mintage	F	VF	XF	Unc	BU
2004	10,000	—	—	—	—	3.00
2004 Proof	—	Value: 4.00				

X# Pn5 20 EURO CENT
Goldine **Ruler:** Elizabeth II

Date	Mintage	F	VF	XF	Unc	BU
2004	10,000	—	—	—	—	3.50
2004 Proof	—	Value: 5.00				

X# Pn5a 20 EURO CENT
Silver

Date	Mintage	F	VF	XF	Unc	BU
2004 Proof	—	Value: 12.50				

X# Pn6a 50 EURO CENT
Silver

Date	Mintage	F	VF	XF	Unc	BU
2004 Proof	—	Value: 15.00				

X# Pn6 50 EURO CENT
Goldine **Ruler:** Elizabeth II

Date	Mintage	F	VF	XF	Unc	BU
2004	10,000	—	—	—	—	4.00
2004 Proof	—	Value: 6.00				

X# Pn7 EURO
Bi-Metallic **Ruler:** Elizabeth II **Obv:** Britannia standing right holding branch between lighthouse and sailing ship **Rev:** Large value, allegorical woman standing right behind seated male

Date	Mintage	F	VF	XF	Unc	BU
2004	10,000	—	—	—	—	6.00
2004 Proof	—	Value: 8.00				

X# Pn7a EURO
Silver **Obv:** Britannia standing right holding branch between lighthouse and sailing ship **Rev:** Large value, allegorical woman standing right behind seated male

Date	Mintage	F	VF	XF	Unc	BU
2004 Proof	—	Value: 22.50				

X# Pn8 2 EURO
Bi-Metallic **Ruler:** Elizabeth II **Obv:** Britannia standing right holding branch between lighthouse and sailing ship **Rev:** Large value, allegorical woman standing right behind seated male

Date	Mintage	F	VF	XF	Unc	BU
2004	10,000	—	—	—	—	8.00
2004 Proof	—	Value: 10.00				

X# Pn8a 2 EURO
Silver **Obv:** Britannia standing right holding branch between lighthouse and sailing ship **Rev:** Larve value, allegorical woman standing right behind seated male

Date	Mintage	F	VF	XF	Unc	BU
2004 Proof	—	Value: 28.50				

X# Pn9 5 EURO

Date	Mintage	F	VF	XF	Unc	BU
2004 Proof	—	Value: 12.50				

X# Pn9a 5 EURO
Silver

Date	Mintage	F	VF	XF	Unc	BU
2004 Proof	—	Value: 40.00				

PIEFORTS

X#	Date	Mintage	Identification	Mkt Val
P1	1910	1	4 Shillings. Silver. Plain edge, coin alignment, X#M1.	—
P2	1910	1	4 Shillings. Silver. Plain edge, medal alignment, X#M1.	—
P3	1910	1	4 Shillings. Silver. Reeded edge, coin alignment, X#M1.	—
P4	1910	1	4 Shillings. Silver. Reeded edge, medal alignment, X#M1.	—
P5	1910	1	4 Shillings. Silver. Plain edge, coin alignment, X#M2.	—
P6	1910	1	4 Shillings. Silver. Plain edge, medal alignment, X#M2.	—
P7	1910	1	4 Shillings. Silver. Reeded edge, coin alignment, X#M2.	—
P8	1910	1	4 Shillings. Silver. Reeded edge, medal alignment, X#M2.	—
P9	1910	1	4 Shillings. Silver. Plain edge, coin alignment, X#M3.	—
P10	1910	1	4 Shillings. Silver. Plain edge, medal alignment, X#M3.	—
P11	1910	1	4 Shillings. Silver. Reeded edge, coin alignment, X#M3.	—
P12	1910	1	4 Shillings. Silver. Reeded edge, medal alignment, X#M3.	—
P13	1937	1	4 Shillings. Silver. Plain edge, coin alignment, X#M4.	—
P14	1937	1	4 Shillings. Silver. Plain edge, medal alignment, X#M4.	—
P15	1937	1	4 Shillings. Silver. Reeded edge, coin alignment, X#M4.	—
P16	1937	1	4 Shillings. Silver. Reeded edge, medal alignment, X#M4.	—
P17	1937	1	4 Shillings. Silver. Plain edge, coin alignment, X#M5.	—
P18	1937	1	4 Shillings. Silver. Plain edge, medal alignment, X#M5.	—
P19	1937	1	4 Shillings. Silver. Reeded edge, coin alignment, X#M5.	—
P20	1937	1	4 Shillings. Silver. Reeded edge, medal alignment, X#M5.	—
P21	1937	1	4 Shillings. Silver. Plain edge, coin alignment, X#M6.	—
P22	1937	1	4 Shillings. Silver. Plain edge, medal alignment, X#M6.	—
P23	1937	1	4 Shillings. Silver. Reeded edge, coin alignment, X#M6.	—
P24	1937	1	4 Shillings. Silver. Reeded edge, medal alignment, X#M6.	—

MINT SETS

X#	Date	Mintage	Identification	Issue Price	Mkt Val
XMS1	2004 (8)	10,000	X#Pn1-Pn8	—	30.00

PROOF SETS

X#	Date	Mintage	Identification	Issue Price	Mkt Val
XPS1	2004 (9)	—	X#Pn1-Pn9	—	50.00
XPS2	2004 (9)	—	X#Pn1a-Pn9a	—	150

KAMBERRA ISLAND

KINGDOM

FANTASY COINAGE

X# 1 NUMISMA
7.2500 g., Bi-Metallic center Alpaca within Nical ring, 26.75 mm. **Ruler:** Franck I **Obv:** Bust left **Obv. Legend:** FRANK I REY DE KAMBERRA **Rev:** Large value "1", crowned and mantled arms **Rev. Legend:** LIBRE / FUERTE / GRANDE **Edge:** Reeded

Date	Mintage	F	VF	XF	Unc	BU
2004	1,000	—	—	—	—	15.00

X# 1a NUMISMA
Brass, 26.75 mm. **Ruler:** Franck I **Obv:** Bust left **Obv. Legend:** FRANK I REY DE KAMBERRA **Rev:** Large value "1", crowned and mantled arms **Rev. Legend:** LIBRE / FUERTE / GRANDE **Edge:** Reeded

Date	Mintage	F	VF	XF	Unc	BU
2004	50	—	—	—	—	45.00

X# 1b NUMISMA
Copper-Nickel-Zinc, 26.75 mm. **Ruler:** Franck I **Obv:** Bust left **Obv. Legend:** FRANK I REY DE KAMBERRA **Rev:** Large value "1", crowned and mantled arms **Rev. Legend:** LIBRE / FUERTE / GRANDE **Edge:** Reeded

Date	Mintage	F	VF	XF	Unc	BU
2004	50	—	—	—	—	45.00

X# 1c NUMISMA
Copper, 26.75 mm. **Ruler:** Franck I **Obv:** Bust left **Obv. Legend:** FRANK I REY DE KAMBERRA **Rev:** Large value "1", crowned and mantled arms **Rev. Legend:** LIBRE / FUERTE / GRANDE **Edge:** Reeded

Date	Mintage	F	VF	XF	Unc	BU
2004	50	—	—	—	—	45.00

X# 2 2 NUMISMAS
7.2500g., Bi-Metallic center bronze withn brass ring, 26.75 mm. **Ruler:** Franck I **Obv:** Bust left **Obv. Legend:** FRANK I REY DE KAMBERRA **Rev:** Large value "2", crowned and mantled arms **Rev. Legend:** LIBRE / FUERTE / GRANDE **Edge:** Plain

Date	Mintage	F	VF	XF	Unc	BU
2005	200	—	—	—	—	15.00

X# 2a 2 NUMISMAS
7.2500g., Bi-Metallic center bronze withn copper-nickel ring, 26.75 mm. **Ruler:** Franck I **Obv:** Bust left **Obv. Legend:** FRANK I REY DE KAMBERRA **Rev:** Large value "2", crowned and mantled arms **Rev. Legend:** LIBRE / FUERTE / GRANDE **Edge:** Plain

Date	Mintage	F	VF	XF	Unc	BU
2005	25	—	—	—	—	40.00

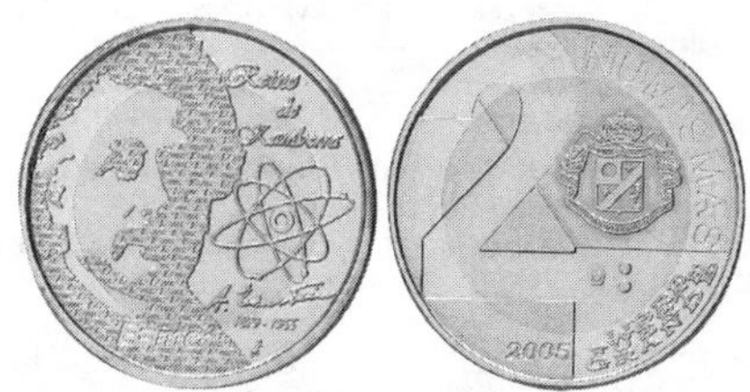

X# 3 2 NUMISMAS
7.2500g., Bi-Metallic Copper alloy within brass ring, 26.75 mm. **Ruler:** Franck I **Obv:** Outlined map, left center, atomicsymbol, Einstein's signature at right, formula E=MC2 below **Obv. Inscription:** "Reino de Kamberra" **Rev:** Crowned and draped arms to right of large value 2 **Rev. Legend:** LIBRE / FUERTE / GRANDE **Edge:** Plain

Date	Mintage	F	VF	XF	Unc	BU
2005	300	—	—	—	—	15.00

X# 3a 2 NUMISMAS
7.2500g., Bi-Metallic Copper alloy within copper-nickel-zinc ring, 26.75 mm. **Ruler:** Franck I **Obv:** Outlined map, left center atomic symbol, Einstein's signature at right, formula E=MC2 below **Obv. Inscription:** "Reino de Kamberra" **Rev:** Crowned and draped arms to right of large value 2 **Rev. Legend:** LIBRE / FUERTE / GRANDE **Edge:** Plain

Date	Mintage	F	VF	XF	Unc	BU
2005	50	—	—	—	—	40.00

X# 3b 2 NUMISMAS
7.2500g., Bi-Metallic Copper alloy within copper alloy ring, 26.75 mm. **Ruler:** Franck I **Obv:** Outlined map, left center atomic symbol, Einstein's signature at right, formula E=MC2 below **Obv. Inscription:** "Reino de Kamberra" **Rev:** Crowned and draped arms to right of large value 2 **Rev. Legend:** LIBRE / FUERTE / GRANDE **Edge:** Plain Note: Not released.

Date	Mintage	F	VF	XF	Unc	BU
2005	50	—	—	—	—	—

KAYLESS

EMPIRE

FANTASY COINAGE

X# 1 K'HLUK
34.0000 g., Copper **Ruler:** Kayless **Obv:** Head facing of Kayless (Klingon cultural hero) **Rev:** Old Klingon Empire 3-pointed star symbol **Note:** Also known on a 17 gram planchet, holed for pendant use.

Date	Mintage	F	VF	XF	Unc	BU
ND	200	—	—	16.00	—	—

TRIAL STRIKES

X# Ts1 K'HLUK
Aluminum **Ruler:** Kayless **Obv:** Head facing **Note:** Oversize flan. X #1.

Date	Mintage	F	VF	XF	Unc	BU
ND	—	—	—	—	—	—

KERGUELEN ISLANDS

FRENCH TERRITORY

ESSAI

X# E2 20 FRANCS
8.5000 g., Tantalum, 22 mm. **Obv:** Double pointed arrow below field of 13 stars **Obv. Inscription:** iles-ker-/gue-len **Obv. Designer:** Fred Zinkann **Rev:** Stylized enflamed crown **Rev. Legend:** VINGT • FRANCS • AUSTRALE • REGIES **Rev. Inscription:** • TANTALIUM • / QUATRIEME • OZ. **Edge:** Reeded

Date	Mintage	F	VF	XF	Unc	BU
2003 Proof	3	—	—	—	45.00	—

X# E3 20 FRANCS
5.5000 g., 0.9990 Silver 0.1766 oz. ASW, 22 mm. **Obv:** Double pointed arrow below field of 13 stars **Obv. Inscription:** iles-ker-/gue-len **Obv. Designer:** Fred Zinkann **Rev:** Stylized enflamed crown **Rev. Legend:** VINGT • FRANCS • AUSTRALE • REGIES **Rev. Inscription:** • TANTALIUM • / QUATRIEME • OZ. **Edge:** Reeded

Date	Mintage	F	VF	XF	Unc	BU
2003 Proof	90	Value: 35.00				

X# E4 20 FRANCS
4.9500 g., 0.2100 Gold 0.0334 oz. AGW, 22 mm. **Obv:** Double pointed arrow below field of 13 stars **Obv. Inscription:** iles-ker-/gue-len **Obv. Designer:** Fred Zinkann **Rev:** Stylized enflamed crown **Rev. Legend:** VINGT • FRANCS • AUSTRALE • REGIES **Rev. Inscription:** • TANTALIUM • / QUATRIEME • OZ. **Edge:** Reeded

Date	Mintage	F	VF	XF	Unc	BU
2003 Proof	—	—	—	—	75.00	—

X# E5 20 FRANCS
6.6000 g., 0.9990 Silver 0.2120 oz. ASW, 22 mm. **Obv:** Double pointed arrow below field of 13 stars **Obv. Inscription:** iles-ker-/gue-len **Obv. Designer:** Fred Zinkann **Rev:** Stylized enflamed crown **Rev. Legend:** VINGT • FRANCS • AUSTRALE • REGIES **Rev. Inscription:** • TANTALIUM • / QUATRIEME • OZ. **Edge:** Reeded

Date	Mintage	F	VF	XF	Unc	BU
2004 Proof	108	Value: 25.00				

X# E6 20 FRANCS
6.5000 g., 0.9950 Tantalum 0.2079 oz., 22 mm. **Obv:** Double pointed arrow below field of 13 stars **Obv. Inscription:** iles-ker-/gue-len **Obv. Designer:** Fred Zinkann **Rev:** Stylized enflamed crown **Rev. Legend:** VINGT • FRANCS • AUSTRALE • REGIES **Rev. Inscription:** • TANTALIUM • / QUATRIEME • OZ. **Edge:** Reeded

Date	Mintage	F	VF	XF	Unc	BU
2004 Proof	38	Value: 75.00				

X# E7 20 FRANCS
4.9000 g., 0.2100 Gold 0.0331 oz. AGW, 22 mm. **Obv:** Double pointed arrow below field of 13 stars **Obv. Inscription:** iles-ker-/gue-len **Obv. Designer:** Fred Zinkann **Rev:** Stylized enflamed crown **Rev. Legend:** VINGT • FRANCS • AUSTRALE • REGIES **Rev. Inscription:** • TANTALIUM • / QUATRIEME • OZ. **Edge:** Reeded

Date	Mintage	F	VF	XF	Unc	BU
2004 Proof	1	—	—	—	—	—

X# E8 20 FRANCS
5.8000 g., 0.7500 Gold 0.1398 oz. AGW, 22 mm. **Obv:** Double pointed arrow below field of 13 stars **Obv. Inscription:** iles-ker-/gue-len **Obv. Designer:** Fred Zinkann **Rev:** Stylized enflamed crown **Rev. Legend:** VINGT • FRANCS • AUSTRALE • REGIES **Rev. Inscription:** • TANTALIUM • / QUATRUEME • OZ. **Edge:** Reeded

Date	Mintage	F	VF	XF	Unc	BU
2004 Proof	4	—	—	—	—	—

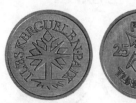

X# E1 25 FRANCS
11.9200 g., Tungsten, 23.5 mm. **Obv:** Stylized tree **Obv. Legend:** ILES KERGUELEN • PAIX **Obv. Designer:** Fred Zinkann **Rev:** Crossed double pointed arrows behind pointed and heart ended arrow **Rev. Legend:** TUNGSTEN

Date	Mintage	F	VF	XF	Unc	BU
ND(1981)FRZ Proof	3	—	—	—	—	—

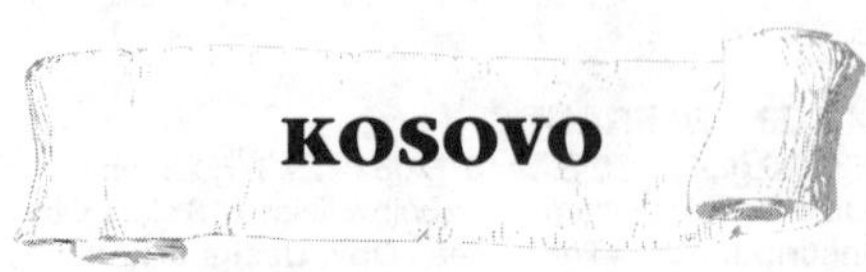

PROVINCE

FANTASY EURO PATTERNS

X# Pn1 EURO CENT
Copper Plated Steel

Date	Mintage	F	VF	XF	Unc	BU
2005	7,000	—	—	—	—	1.00

X# Pn2 2 EURO CENT
Copper Plated Steel

Date	Mintage	F	VF	XF	Unc	BU
2005	7,000	—	—	—	—	1.50

X# Pn3 5 EURO CENT
Copper Plated Steel

Date	Mintage	F	VF	XF	Unc	BU
2005	7,000	—	—	—	—	2.00

X# Pn4 10 EURO CENT
Goldine

Date	Mintage	F	VF	XF	Unc	BU
2005	7,000	—	—	—	—	2.50

X# Pn5 20 EURO CENT
Goldine

Date	Mintage	F	VF	XF	Unc	BU
2005	7,000	—	—	—	—	3.00

X# Pn6 50 EURO CENT
Goldine

Date	Mintage	F	VF	XF	Unc	BU
2005	7,000	—	—	—	—	3.50

X# Pn7 EURO
Bi-Metallic **Obv:** Old woman facing wearing scarf **Rev:** Three stars, large value, EEU star design

Date	Mintage	F	VF	XF	Unc	BU
2005	7,000	—	—	—	—	5.50

X# Pn8 2 EURO
Bi-Metallic **Obv:** Old woman facing wearing scarf **Rev:** Three stars, large value, EEU star design

Date	Mintage	F	VF	XF	Unc	BU
2005	7,000	—	—	—	—	7.50

MINT SETS

X#	Date	Mintage	Identification	Issue Price	Mkt Val
XMS1	2005 (8)	7,000	X#Pn1-Pn8	25.00	26.00

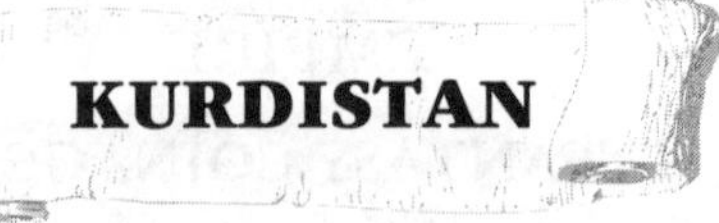

GOVERNMENT IN EXILE

MILLED COINAGE

X# 1.1 DINAR
8.2500 g., Bronze-Plated Zinc, 27 mm. **Obv:** Sun over mountains and "DEWLETA KURDISTANE" with incorrect Arabic for "Kurdistan" **Rev:** Saladin on horse with modern Kurd flag **Edge:** Plain **Note:** Prev. KM#1.

Date	Mintage	F	VF	XF	Unc	BU
2003-AH1424	300	—	—	—	35.00	—

X# 1.2 DINAR
8.2500 g., Bronze-Plated Zinc, 27 mm. **Obv:** Sun over mountains and "DEWLETA KURDISTAN" with correct Arabic for "Kurdistan" **Rev:** Saladin on horse with modern Kurd flag **Edge:** Pain

Date	Mintage	F	VF	XF	Unc	BU
2003-AH1424	4,700	—	—	—	7.50	—

X# 2.1 10 DINARS
26.1600 g., Copper-Nickel, 39 mm. **Obv:** Sun over mountains and "DEWLETA KURDISTAN" with incorrect Arabic for "Kurdistan" below **Rev:** Persian Fallow Deer and value **Edge:** Reeded

Date	Mintage	F	VF	XF	Unc	BU
2003-AH1424	300	—	—	—	45.00	—

X# 2.2 10 DINARS
26.1600 g., Copper-Nickel, 39 mm. **Obv:** Sun over mountains and "DEWLETA KURDISTAN" with corrected Arabic for "Kurdistan" **Rev:** Persian Fallow Deer and value **Edge:** Reeded

Date	Mintage	F	VF	XF	Unc	BU
2003-AH1424	4,700	—	—	—	15.00	—

X# 7 25 DINAR
2.0000 g., Copper, 17.5 mm. **Obv:** Mountain and sun **Rev:** Grey partridge **Edge:** Plain

Date	Mintage	F	VF	XF	Unc	BU
AH1427-2006	6,500	—	—	—	1.25	—

X# 8 50 DINARS
4.0000 g., Brass, 23.5 mm. **Obv:** Mountain and sun **Rev:** European grey heron **Edge:** Plain

Date	Mintage	F	VF	XF	Unc	BU
AH1427-2006	8,500	—	—	—	2.00	—

X# 3 100 DINARS
0.2500 g., 0.9990 Silver 0.0080 oz. ASW, 27 mm. **Obv:** Sun over mountains **Rev:** Lesser Kestrel, *Falco naumanni* **Edge:** Plain

Date	Mintage	F	VF	XF	Unc	BU
AH1424 (2003) Proof	800	Value: 30.00				

X# 9 100 DINARS
4.3000 g., Copper-Nickel, 22 mm. **Obv:** Mountain and sun **Rev:** Red fox **Edge:** Reeded

Date	Mintage	F	VF	XF	Unc	BU
AH1427-2006	6,500	—	—	—	3.00	—

X# 10 250 DINARS
7.0000 g., Copper-Nickel, 28 mm. **Obv:** Mountain and sun **Rev:** Eurasian Lynx **Edge:** Reeded **Shape:** 8-sided

Date	Mintage	F	VF	XF	Unc	BU
AH1427-2006	8,500	—	—	—	4.00	—

X# 11 500 DINARS
10.5000 g., Copper-Nickel, 35 mm. **Obv:** Mountain and sun **Rev:** Wild goat **Edge:** Reeded

Date	Mintage	F	VF	XF	Unc	BU
AH1427-2006	6,500	—	—	—	5.00	—

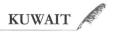

X# 4 1000 DINARS

0.4990 g., 0.9170 Gold 0.0147 oz. AGW, 27 mm. **Obv:** Sun over mountains **Rev:** Saladin on horseback holding the modern Kurdish flag **Edge:** Plain

Date	Mintage	F	VF	XF	Unc	BU
AH1424 (2003) Proof	100	Value: 425				

X# 12 1000 DINARS

8.0000 g., Bronze-Plated Zinc, 27 mm. **Obv:** Mountain and sun **Rev:** Mustafa Barzani **Edge:** Reeded

Date	Mintage	F	VF	XF	Unc	BU
AH1427-2006	8,500	—	—	—	6.00	—

X# 13 2500 DINARS

7.7500 g., Bi-Metallic Copper out ring, Brass inner ring, 30 mm. **Obv:** Mountain and sun **Rev:** Oil refinery

Date	Mintage	F	VF	XF	Unc	BU
AH1427-2006	9,500	—	—	—	10.00	—

X# 5 10000 DINAR

0.9990 Silver **Obv:** Mountains **Rev:** Merlin (falco columbarius)

Date	Mintage	F	VF	XF	Unc	BU
2006/AH Proof	1,200	Value: 25.00				

X# 6 100000 DINAR

8.4900 g., 0.9166 Gold 0.2502 oz. AGW **Obv:** Mountains **Rev:** Saladin bust facing

Date	Mintage	F	VF	XF	Unc	BU
AH1427-2006 Proof	150	Value: 325				

PATTERNS

X#	Date	Mintage	Identification	Mkt Val
Pn3	2003-AH1424	30	Dinar. Zinc. 8.3500 g. 27.19 mm. X#1.2.	50.00

X#	Date	Mintage	Identification	Mkt Val
Pn4	2003-AH1424	30	100 Dinars. Copper. 10.3100 g. 27.22 mm. Plain edge. X#3.	50.00

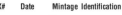

X#	Date	Mintage	Identification	Mkt Val
Pn5	2003-AH1424	30	1000 Dinars. Copper. 10.3100 g. 27.25 mm. Plain edge. X#4.	50.00
Pn1	2003-AH1424	38	10 Dinars. Brass. 26.3000 g. 38.44 mm. Reeded edge. KM#2.	80.00
Pn2	2003-AH1424	5	10 Dinars. Silver. KM#2.	250
Pn6	AH1427-2006	30	1000 Dinars. Copper. 8.3300 g. 27.22 mm. Plain edge. X#12.	50.00

X#	Date	Mintage	Identification	Mkt Val
Pn7	AH1427-2006	30	10000 Dinar. Copper. 10.3100 g. 27.28 mm. Reeded edge. X#5.	50.00

X#	Date	Mintage	Identification	Mkt Val
Pn8	AH1427-2006	30	100000 Dinar. Copper. 10.3100 g. 27.16 mm. Plain edge. X#6.	50.00

TRIAL STRIKES

X#	Date	Mintage	Identification	Mkt Val
TS1	2003-AH1424	—	10 Dinars. Lead. KM#2. Spelling error *Kurdistan* in Arabic.	—

X#	Date	Mintage	Identification	Mkt Val
TS2	2003-AH1424	—	10 Dinars. Lead. KM#2A. Sharp right antler tips.	—

X#	Date	Mintage	Identification	Mkt Val
TS3	2003-AH1424	—	10 Dinars. Lead. KM#2A. Blunt right antler tips.	—

KUWAIT

STATE OF KUWAIT

MEDALLIC COINAGE

X# 9 5 DINARS

28.2800 g., 0.9250 Silver 0.8410 oz. ASW **Subject:** 35th Anniversary of National Day **Obv:** Palace **Rev:** Flag and building

Date	Mintage	F	VF	XF	Unc	BU
ND (1985)	—	—	—	—	65.00	—

X# 13 5 DINARS

28.2800 g., 0.9250 Silver 0.8410 oz. ASW **Subject:** 50th Anniversary of Exporting 1st Oil Shipment **Obv:** State seal, pump and tankers **Rev:** Oil well and tanks

Date	Mintage	F	VF	XF	Unc	BU
ND (1985)	—	—	—	—	65.00	—

X# 6 5 DINARS

33.6250 g., 0.9250 Silver 0.9999 oz. ASW **Subject:** 5th Islamic Summit Conference **Obv:** Arabic, English and French legend, crescent and minaret. **Rev:** Arms

Date	Mintage	F	VF	XF	Unc	BU
ND (1987) Proof	—	—	—	—	—	—

X# 5 5 DINARS

28.2800 g., 0.9250 Silver 0.8410 oz. ASW **Subject:** Liberation of Kuwait **Obv:** Legend in center circle and three inner rings **Rev:** "Kuwait is free", row of buildings

Date	Mintage	F	VF	XF	Unc	BU
ND (1991)	—	Value: 65.00				
ND(AH1407) (1991) Proof	—	Value: 60.00				

X# 8 5 DINARS

72.5000 g., 0.9250 Silver 2.1560 oz. ASW **Subject:** 25th Anniversary - Central Bank **Obv:** Falcon, ship and building **Rev:** Inscription

Date	Mintage	F	VF	XF	Unc	BU
ND (1994)	—	—	—	—	120	—

X# 11 5 DINARS

28.2800 g., 0.9250 Silver 0.8410 oz. ASW **Subject:** 5th Liberation Day **Obv:** State seal **Rev:** Finger print

Date	Mintage	F	VF	XF	Unc	BU
AH1406 (1996)	—	—	—	—	65.00	—

X# 15 5 DINARS

28.2800 g., 0.9250 Silver 0.8410 oz. ASW **Subject:** 30th Anniversary - Kuwait University **Obv:** Coat of arms

Date	Mintage	F	VF	XF	Unc	BU
ND (1996) Proof	—	Value: 75.00				

X# 12 50 DINARS

16.9660 g., 0.9170 Gold 0.5002 oz. AGW **Subject:** 5th Liberation Day **Obv:** State seal **Rev:** Finger print

Date	Mintage	F	VF	XF	Unc	BU
ND (1985) Proof	—	Value: 450				

X# 7 50 DINARS

16.9660 g., 0.9170 Gold 0.5002 oz. AGW **Subject:** 5th Islamic Summit Conference **Obv:** Arabic, English and French legend, crescent and minaret **Rev:** Dhow

Date	Mintage	F	VF	XF	Unc	BU
ND (1987) Proof	—	Value: 475				

X# 16 50 DINARS

16.9660 g., 0.9170 Gold 0.5002 oz. AGW **Subject:** 1st Anniversary - Liberation Day **Obv:** Concentric legends **Rev:** Building

Date	Mintage	F	VF	XF	Unc	BU
ND (1991) Proof	—	Value: 450				

X# 10 50 DINARS

16.9660 g., 0.9170 Gold 0.5002 oz. AGW **Subject:** 35th Anniversary of the National Day **Obv:** Palace **Rev:** Flag on builiding

Date	Mintage	F	VF	XF	Unc	BU
ND (1996)	—	—	—	—	—	425

X# 14 50 DINARS

16.9660 g., 0.9170 Gold 0.5002 oz. AGW **Subject:** 50th Anniversary of Exporting 1st Oil Shipment **Obv:** State seal, pump and tankers **Rev:** Well and tanks

Date	Mintage	F	VF	XF	Unc	BU
ND (1996)	—	—	—	—	—	425

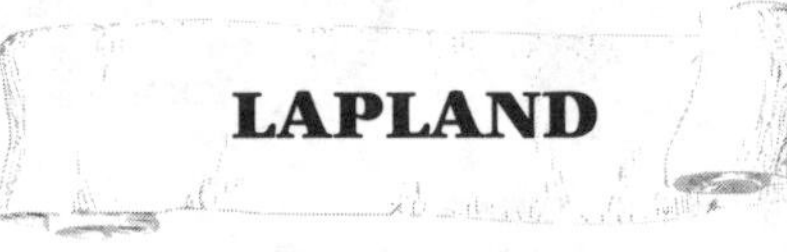

NORTHERN SCANDINAVIA

FANTASY EURO PATTERNS

X# Pn1 EURO CENT

Copper Plated Steel

Date	Mintage	F	VF	XF	Unc	BU
2005	7,000	—	—	—	—	1.00

X# Pn2 2 EURO CENT

Copper Plated Steel

Date	Mintage	F	VF	XF	Unc	BU
2005	7,000	—	—	—	—	1.50

X# Pn3 5 EURO CENT

Copper Plated Steel

Date	Mintage	F	VF	XF	Unc	BU
2005	7,000	—	—	—	—	2.00

X# Pn4 10 EURO CENT

Goldine

Date	Mintage	F	VF	XF	Unc	BU
2005	7,000	—	—	—	—	2.50

X# Pn5 20 EURO CENT
Goldine

Date	Mintage	F	VF	XF	Unc	BU
2005	7,000	—	—	—	—	3.00

X# Pn6 50 EURO CENT
Goldine

Date	Mintage	F	VF	XF	Unc	BU
2005	7,000	—	—	—	—	3.50

X# Pn7 EURO
Bi-Metallic **Obv:** Male bust facing **Rev:** Stylized leaf, large value, EEU star design

Date	Mintage	F	VF	XF	Unc	BU
2005	7,000	—	—	—	—	5.50

X# Pn8 2 EURO
Bi-Metallic **Obv:** Male bust facing **Rev:** Stylized leaf, alrge value, EEU star design

Date	Mintage	F	VF	XF	Unc	BU
2005	7,000	—	—	—	—	7.50

MINT SETS

X#	Date	Mintage	Identification	Issue Price	Mkt Val
XMS1	2005 (8)	7,000	X#Pn1-Pn8	—	26.00

LATVIA

FIRST REPUBLIC

1918-1939

FANTASY COINAGE

X# 1 10 GULDEN
Silver **Edge:** Plain

Date	Mintage	F	VF	XF	Unc	BU
ND(1936)	—	—	—	30.00	60.00	80.00

X# 2 10 GULDEN
Silver Plated Bronze **Note:** Designed by E. Telcs. Struck by Begeer's Mint, the Netherlands.

Date	Mintage	F	VF	XF	Unc	BU
ND(1936)	—	—	—	15.00	30.00	40.00

MODERN REPUBLIC

1991-present

ECU COINAGE

X# 11 15 ECU
31.1030 g., 0.9990 Silver 0.9989 oz. ASW, 38 mm. **Issuer:** Numex S.A., Madrid **Obv:** Supported arms **Rev:** Lynx standing right, facing **Rev. Legend:** LATVIJAS REPUBLIKA

Date	Mintage	F	VF	XF	Unc	BU
1993 Proof	6,000	Value: 40.00				

X# 12 150 ECU
31.1030 g., 0.8150 Gold 0.8150 oz. AGW, 38 mm. **Issuer:** Numex S.A., Madrid **Obv:** Supported arms **Rev:** Lynx standing right, facing **Rev. Legend:** LATVIJAS REPUBLIKA

Date	Mintage	F	VF	XF	Unc	BU
1993 Proof	600	Value: 625				

MEDALLIC COINAGE

Legation Series

X# 5b OUNCE
Bronze, 38.25 mm. **Issuer:** Legation of Latvia **Subject:** 70th Anniversary of Independence **Obv:** Supported arms **Obv. Legend:** LATVIJAS REPUBLIKA **Rev:** Sun, monument **Rev. Legend:** 1918 / 1988

Date	Mintage	F	VF	XF	Unc	BU
ND(1988) Proof	—	Value: 22.50				

X# 5 OUNCE
Silver, 38.25 mm. **Issuer:** Legation of Latvia **Subject:** 70th Anniversary of Independence **Obv:** Supported arms **Obv. Legend:** LATVIJAS REPUBLIKA **Rev:** Sun, monument **Rev. Legend:** 1918 / 1988

Date	Mintage	F	VF	XF	Unc	BU
ND(1988) Proof	7,000	Value: 45.00				

X# 5a OUNCE
0.9990 Gold 1 ounce AGW, 38.25 mm.
Issuer: Legation of Latvia **Subject:** 70th Anniversary of Independence **Obv:** Supported arms **Obv. Legend:** LATVIJAS REPUBLIKA **Rev:** Sun, monument **Rev. Legend:** 1918 / 1988

Date	Mintage	F	VF	XF	Unc	BU
ND(1988) Proof	700	Value: 800				

X# 10 OUNCE
31.1000 g., 0.9990 Silver 0.9988 oz. ASW
Obv: Supported arms **Rev:** Ship

Date	Mintage	F	VF	XF	Unc	BU
1989 Proof	3,500	Value: 60.00				

X# 10a OUNCE
31.1000 g., 0.9990 Gold 1 ounce AGW 0.9988 oz. AGW
Obv: Supported arms **Rev:** Ship

Date	Mintage	F	VF	XF	Unc	BU
1989 Proof	350	Value: 850				

X# 10b OUNCE
31.1000 g., 0.9990 Palladium 0.9988 oz.
Obv: Supported arms **Rev:** Ship

Date	Mintage	F	VF	XF	Unc	BU
1989 Proof	350	Value: 500				

X# 10c OUNCE
24.0000 g., Copper, 38.4 mm.

Date	Mintage	F	VF	XF	Unc	BU
1989	—	—	—	—	—	25.00

FANTASY EURO PATTERNS

INA Series

X# Pn1 EURO CENT
Copper, 16.8 mm. **Obv:** Freedom Monument, Liberty holding up 3 stars, divides date **Obv. Legend:** LATVIJAS REPUBLIKA **Rev:** Scales at right **Edge:** Plain

Date	Mintage	F	VF	XF	Unc	BU
2004	Inc. above	—	—	—	—	3.00
2004 Proof	3,000	Value: 2.50				

X# Pn1a EURO CENT
Silver **Obv:** Freedom Monument, Liberty holding up 3 stars, divides date **Obv. Legend:** LATVIJAS REPUBLIKA **Rev:** Scales at right

Date	Mintage	F	VF	XF	Unc	BU
2004 Proof	175	Value: 6.00				

X# Pn2 2 EURO CENT
5.7200 g., Copper, 18.5 mm. **Obv:** Freedom Monument, Liberty holding up 3 stars, divides date **Obv. Legend:** LATVIJAS REPUBLIKA **Rev:** Scales at right **Edge:** Plain

Date	Mintage	F	VF	XF	Unc	BU
2004	12,500	—	—	—	—	5.00
2004 Proof	3,000	Value: 3.00				

X# Pn2a 2 EURO CENT
Silver **Obv:** Freedom Monument, Liberty holding up 3 stars, divides date **Obv. Legend:** LATVIJAS REPUBLIKA **Rev:** Scales at right

Date	Mintage	F	VF	XF	Unc	BU
2004 Proof	175	Value: 7.00				

X# Pn3 5 EURO CENT

Copper, 20.7 mm. **Obv:** Freedom Monument, Liberty holding up 3 stars, divides date **Obv. Legend:** LATVIJAS REPUBLIKA **Rev:** Scales at right **Edge:** Plain

Date	Mintage	F	VF	XF	Unc	BU
2004	12,500	—	—	—	—	7.00
2004 Proof	3,000	Value: 3.50				

X# Pn3a 5 EURO CENT

Silver **Obv:** Freedom Monument, Liberty holding up 3 stars, divides date **Obv. Legend:** LATVIJAS REPUBLIKA **Rev:** Scales at right

Date	Mintage	F	VF	XF	Unc	BU
2004 Proof	175	Value: 8.50				

X# Pn4 10 EURO CENT

5.9500 g., Goldine, 19.3 mm. **Obv:** Medieval sailing ship **Obv. Legend:** LATVIJAS REPUBLIKA **Rev:** Dove, value in wreath of clasped hands **Edge:** Plain

Date	Mintage	F	VF	XF	Unc	BU
2004	12,500	—	—	—	—	10.00
2004 Proof	3,000	Value: 4.00				

X# Pn4a 10 EURO CENT

Silver **Obv:** Medieval sailing ship **Obv. Legend:** LATVIJAS REPUBLIKA **Rev:** Dove, value in wreath of clasped hands

Date	Mintage	F	VF	XF	Unc	BU
2004 Proof	175	Value: 10.00				

X# Pn5 20 EURO CENT

7.7400 g., Goldine, 22 mm. **Obv:** Medieval sailing ship **Obv. Legend:** LATVIJAS REPUBLIKA **Rev:** Dove, value in wreath of clasped hands **Edge:** Plain

Date	Mintage	F	VF	XF	Unc	BU
2004	12,500	—	—	—	—	12.00
2004 Proof	3,000	Value: 5.00				

X# Pn5a 20 EURO CENT

Silver **Obv:** Medieval sailing ship **Obv. Legend:** LATVIJAS REPUBLIKA **Rev:** Dove, value in wreath of clasped hands

Date	Mintage	F	VF	XF	Unc	BU
2004 Proof	175	Value: 12.50				

X# Pn6 50 EURO CENT

9.4600 g., Goldine, 24.3 mm. **Obv:** Medieval sailing ship **Obv. Legend:** LATVIJAS REPUBLIKA **Rev:** Dove, value in wreath of clasped hands **Edge:** Plain

Date	Mintage	F	VF	XF	Unc	BU
2004	12,500	—	—	—	—	15.00
2004 Proof	3,000	Value: 6.00				

X# Pn6a 50 EURO CENT

Silver **Obv:** Medieval sailing ship **Obv. Legend:** LATVIJAS REPUBLIKA **Rev:** Dove, value in wreath of clasped hands

Date	Mintage	F	VF	XF	Unc	BU
2004 Proof	175	Value: 15.00				

X# Pn7 EURO

8.3300 g., Bi-Metallic Goldine ring, Copper-Nickel center, 22.8 mm. **Obv:** Crowned crossed keys above castle gateway divides date **Obv. Legend:** LATVIJAS REPUBLIKA **Rev:** Large value, sailing ship "Julia Maria" **Edge:** Plain

Date	Mintage	F	VF	XF	Unc	BU
2004	12,500	—	—	—	—	18.00
2004 Proof	3,000	Value: 8.00				

X# Pn7a EURO

Bi-Metallic Goldine center in Silver ring **Obv:** Crowned crossed keys above castle gateway divides date **Obv. Legend:** LATVIJAS REPUBLIKA **Rev:** Large value, sailing ship "Julia Maria"

Date	Mintage	F	VF	XF	Unc	BU
2004 Proof	175	Value: 22.50				

X# Pn8 2 EURO

10.6600 g., Bi-Metallic Copper-Nickel ring, Goldine center, 25.7 mm. **Obv:** Crowned crossed keys above castle gateway divides date **Obv. Legend:** LATVIJAS REPUBLIKA **Rev:** Large value, sailing ship "Julia Maria" **Edge:** Plain

Date	Mintage	F	VF	XF	Unc	BU
2004	12,500	—	—	—	—	25.00
2004 Proof	3,000	Value: 10.00				

X# Pn8a 2 EURO

Bi-Metallic **Obv:** Crowned crossed keys above castle gateway divides date **Obv. Legend:** LATVIJAS REPUBLIKA **Rev:** Large value, sailing ship "Julia Maria"

Date	Mintage	F	VF	XF	Unc	BU
2004 Proof	175	Value: 28.50				

X# Pn9 5 EURO

25.6000 g., Goldine, 36.1 mm. **Obv:** Arms of Regal, crowned crossed keys above castle gateway divides date **Obv. Legend:** LATVIJAS REPUBLIKA **Rev:** Large value, sailing ship "Julia Maria"

Date	Mintage	F	VF	XF	Unc	BU
2004 Proof	3,000	Value: 12.50				

X# Pn9a 5 EURO

Silver **Obv:** Arms of Regal, crowned crossed keys above castle gateway divides date **Obv. Legend:** LATVIJAS REPUBLIKA **Rev:** Large value, sailing ship "Julia Maria"

Date	Mintage	F	VF	XF	Unc	BU
2004 Proof	175	Value: 40.00				

Unknown Issuer

X# Pn10 EURO CENT

Copper Plated Steel **Obv. Legend:** LATVIA **Edge:** Plain

Date	Mintage	F	VF	XF	Unc	BU
ND(2004)	7,500	—	—	—	—	4.00

X# Pn11 2 EURO CENT

Copper Plated Steel **Obv. Legend:** LATVIA **Edge:** Plain

Date	Mintage	F	VF	XF	Unc	BU
ND(2004)	7,500	—	—	—	—	6.00

X# Pn12 5 EURO CENT

Copper Plated Steel **Obv. Legend:** LATVIA

Date	Mintage	F	VF	XF	Unc	BU
ND(2004)	7,500	—	—	—	—	8.00

X# Pn13 10 EURO CENT

Goldine **Obv. Legend:** LATVIA

Date	Mintage	F	VF	XF	Unc	BU
ND(2004)	7,500	—	—	—	—	10.00

X# Pn14 20 EURO CENT

Goldine **Obv. Legend:** LATVIA

Date	Mintage	F	VF	XF	Unc	BU
ND(2004)	7,500	—	—	—	—	12.00

X# Pn15 50 EURO CENT

Goldine **Obv. Legend:** LATVIA

Date	Mintage	F	VF	XF	Unc	BU
ND(2004)	7,500	—	—	—	—	15.00

X# Pn16 EURO

Bi-Metallic **Obv:** Bust of Janis Painis facing 3/4 right **Obv. Legend:** LATVIA **Rev:** Three stars, large value, EEU star design

Date	Mintage	F	VF	XF	Unc	BU
ND(2004)	7,500	—	—	—	—	18.00

X# Pn17 2 EURO

Bi-Metallic **Obv:** Bust of Janis Painis facing 3/4 right **Obv. Legend:** LATVIA **Rev:** Three stars, large value, EEU star design

Date	Mintage	F	VF	XF	Unc	BU
ND(2004)	7,500	—	—	—	—	22.00

PIEFORTS

X#	Date	Mintage	Identification	Mkt Val
P1	ND(1988)	70	Ounce. Silver. 62.2100 g. X#B5.	90.00
P2	ND(1988)	7	Ounce. Gold. 93.3100 g. X#B5a. Triple weight.	2,500
P3	1989	50	Ounce. 0.9990 Silver. 62.2000 g. X#10.	110
P4	1989	5	Ounce. Palladium. 62.2000 g. X#10b.	975
P5	1989	5	Ounce. 31.1000 Gold. 93.3000 g. X#10a. Triple weight.	2,500

TRIAL STRIKES

X#	Date	Mintage	Identification	Mkt Val
TS1	1989	10	Ounce. Copper. Uniface obverse. X#10.	—
TS2	1989	35	Ounce. Nickel. Uniface obverse. X#10.	—
TS3	1988	78	Ounce. Bronze. X#10. Legend spelling as TEVZEMEJ.	25.00
TS4	1988	49	Ounce. Pure Silver. 31.1g. As X#5 but with the word "Tevzemei" mispelled as "Tevzemej".	—

Note: The original strike was of 500 pieces but 451 were melted when the error was discovered.

X#	Date	Mintage	Identification	Mkt Val
TS5	1988	43	Ounce. Pure Silver. 62.2g. As X#5 but with the word "Tevzemei" mispelled as "Tevzemej".	—

Note: The original strike was of 70 Pieforts but 27 were melted when the error was discovered.

MINT SETS

X#	Date	Mintage	Identification	Issue Price	Mkt Val
XMS1	2004 (8)	12,500	X#Pn1-Pn8	—	90.00

X#	Date	Mintage	Identification	Issue Price	Mkt Val
XMS2	ND(2004) (8)	7,500	X#Pn10-Pn17	—	26.00

PROOF SETS

X#	Date	Mintage	Identification	Issue Price	Mkt Val
XPS1	2004 (9)	3,000	X#Pn1-Pn9	—	110
XPS2	2004 (9)	175	X#Pn1a-Pn9a	—	150

LEAGUE OF NATIONS

INTERNATIONAL SOCIETY

Geneva, Switzerland

FANTASY COINAGE

X# 1 FRANC
0.3226 g., 0.9000 Gold 0.0093 oz. AGW **Obv:** Date, S.of.N. **Rev:** Denomination

Date	Mintage	F	VF	XF	Unc	BU
1921 Unique	—	—	—	—	—	—

LESOTHO

KINGDOM

MEDALLIC COINAGE

X# 1 10 MALOTI
Copper-Nickel **Ruler:** Moshoeshoe II **Series:** International Games **Rev:** Field hockey

Date	Mintage	F	VF	XF	Unc	BU
1984 Proof	—	Value: 12.00				

X# 2 10 MALOTI
Copper-Nickel **Ruler:** Moshoeshoe II
Series: International Games **Rev:** Hurdler

Date	Mintage	F	VF	XF	Unc	BU
1984 Proof	—	Value: 18.00				

X# 3 25 MALOTI
28.3500 g., Silver **Ruler:** Moshoeshoe II **Series:** International Games **Rev:** Hurdler

Date	Mintage	F	VF	XF	Unc	BU
1984 Proof	—	Value: 25.00				

LIBERIA

REPUBLIC

COUNTERMARKED COINAGE

X# 12 DOLLAR
27.0200 g., 0.8350 Silver 0.7253 oz. ASW, 37.6 mm.
Countermark: Liberty head left in 17mm circle
Note: Countermarked on Columbia 8 Reales, KM#89.

CM Date	Host Date	Good	VG	F	VF	XF
1847	1835	—	—	—	—	100

MEDALLIC COINAGE

X# 1 10 DOLLARS
Copper-Nickel, 38.2 mm. **Series:** International Games
Obv: Arms **Rev:** Weight Lifter

Date	Mintage	F	VF	XF	Unc	BU
1984 Proof	—	Value: 12.00				

X# 2 10 DOLLARS
Copper-Nickel, 37.9 mm. **Series:** International Games
Obv: Arms **Rev:** Basketball

Date	Mintage	F	VF	XF	Unc	BU
1984 Proof	—	Value: 15.00				

X# 14 10 DOLLARS
31.1035 g., 0.9990 Silver 0.9990 oz. ASW, 39 mm.
Obv: Heraldic Eagle **Rev:** Type I Standing Liberty Quarter design **Edge:** Reeded

Date	Mintage	F	VF	XF	Unc	BU
2000 Proof	—	Value: 40.00				

X# 15 10 DOLLARS

31.1035 g., 0.9990 Silver 0.9990 oz. ASW, 39 mm. **Obv:** Heraldic Eagle **Rev:** Seated Liberty Dollar design **Edge:** Reeded

Date	Mintage	F	VF	XF	Unc	BU
2000 Proof	—	Value: 40.00				

X# 16 10 DOLLARS

31.1035 g., 0.9990 Silver 0.9990 oz. ASW, 39 mm. **Obv:** Heraldic Eagle **Rev:** Peace Liberty dollar design **Edge:** Reeded

Date	Mintage	F	VF	XF	Unc	BU
2000 Proof	—	Value: 40.00				

X# 3 25 DOLLARS

31.3700 g., Silver, 38.7 mm. **Series:** International Games **Obv:** Arms **Rev:** Basketball

Date	Mintage	F	VF	XF	Unc	BU
1984 Proof	—	Value: 100				

PATTERNS

Including off metal strikes

X# Pn1 CENT

Bronze **Obv:** Liberty head left **Rev:** Shield **Rev. Legend:** IN GOD WE TRUST **Note:** Prev. KM#Pn47.

Date	Mintage	F	VF	XF	Unc	BU
1890 Proof	—	Value: 45.00				

X# Pn2 CENT

Bronze **Obv:** Liberty head left **Rev:** Shield in sprays **Rev. Legend:** IN GOD WE TRUST **Note:** Prev. KM#Pn48.

Date	Mintage	F	VF	XF	Unc	BU
1890 Proof	—	Value: 175				

X# Pn3 CENT

Bronze **Obv:** Liberty head left **Rev:** Value ONE / CENT / date in sprays **Rev. Legend:** IN GOD WE TRUST **Note:** Prev. KM#Pn49.

Date	Mintage	F	VF	XF	Unc	BU
1890 Proof	—	Value: 150				

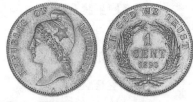

X# Pn4 CENT

Bronze **Obv:** Liberty head left **Rev:** 1 / CENT / date in sprays **Rev. Legend:** IN GOD WE TRUST **Note:** Prev. KM#Pn50.

Date	Mintage	F	VF	XF	Unc	BU
1890 Proof	—	Value: 175				

X# Pn5 2 CENTS

Bronze **Obv:** Liberty head left **Rev:** Shield **Rev. Legend:** IN GOD WE TRUST **Note:** Prev. KM#Pn51.

Date	Mintage	F	VF	XF	Unc	BU
1890 Proof	—	Value: 250				

X# Pn6 2 CENTS

Bronze **Obv:** Liberty head left **Rev:** Shield in sprays **Rev. Legend:** IN GOD WE TRUST **Note:** Prev. KM#Pn52.

Date	Mintage	F	VF	XF	Unc	BU
1890 Proof	—	Value: 225				

X# Pn7 2 CENTS

Bronze **Obv:** Liberty head left **Rev:** Value TWO / CENTS / date in sprays **Rev. Legend:** IN GOD WE TRUST **Note:** Prev. KM#Pn53.

Date	Mintage	F	VF	XF	Unc	BU
1890 Proof	—	Value: 185				

X# Pn8 2 CENTS

Bronze **Obv:** Liberty head left **Rev:** Value 2 / CENTS / date in sprays **Rev. Legend:** IN GOD WE TRUST **Note:** Prev. KM#Pn54.

Date	Mintage	F	VF	XF	Unc	BU
1890 Proof	—	Value: 225				

LIBYA

SOCIALIST PEOPLE'S REPUBLIC

MEDALLIC COINAGE

X# 4 NON-DENOMINATED
28.1600 g., Silver, 40 mm. **Subject:** 10th Anniversary as President **Obv:** Bust of Colonel Qaddafi 3/4 right **Rev:** Ancient Fortress

Date	Mintage	F	VF	XF	Unc	BU
MS(1979)	—	—	—	40.00	65.00	—

X# 5 NON-DENOMINATED
15.9600 g., Gold, 27 mm. **Subject:** Qaddafi - 10th Anniversary as President **Obv:** Bust of Colonel Qaddafi 3/4 right **Rev:** Ancient Fortress

Date	Mintage	F	VF	XF	Unc	BU
ND(1979)	—	—	—	350	500	—

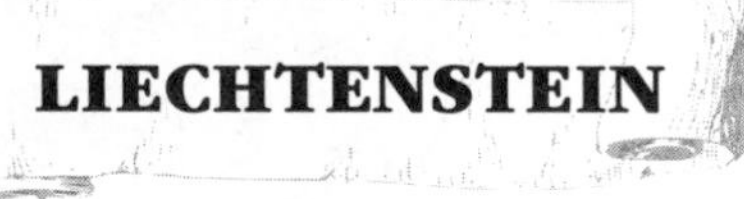

LIECHTENSTEIN

PRINCIPALITY

FANTASY EURO PATTERNS

X# Pn1 CEROS
Copper Plated Steel, 16.8 mm. **Obv:** Wine barrel **Edge:** Plain

Date	Mintage	F	VF	XF	Unc	BU
2004	10,000	—	—	—	—	1.50
2004 Proof	5,000	Value: 2.50				

X# Pn1a CEROS
Silver, 16.8 mm. **Obv:** Wine barrel **Edge:** Plain

Date	Mintage	F	VF	XF	Unc	BU
2004 Proof	500	Value: 6.00				

X# Pn2 2 CEROS
Copper Plated Steel, 18.5 mm. **Obv:** Plant **Rev:** Flower **Edge:** Plain

Date	Mintage	F	VF	XF	Unc	BU
2004	10,000	—	—	—	—	2.00
2004 Proof	5,000	Value: 3.00				

X# Pn2a 2 CEROS
Silver, 18.5 mm. **Obv:** Plant **Rev:** Flower **Edge:** Plain

Date	Mintage	F	VF	XF	Unc	BU
2004 Proof	500	Value: 7.00				

X# Pn3 5 CEROS
Copper Plated Steel, 20.7 mm. **Obv:** Screw press **Rev:** Flower **Edge:** Plain

Date	Mintage	F	VF	XF	Unc	BU
2004	10,000	—	—	—	—	2.50
2004 Proof	5,000	Value: 3.50				

X# Pn3a 5 CEROS
Silver, 20.7 mm. **Obv:** Screw press **Rev:** Flower **Edge:** Plain

Date	Mintage	F	VF	XF	Unc	BU
2004 Proof	500	Value: 8.50				

X# Pn4 10 CEROS
Goldine, 19.3 mm. **Obv:** Crowned and mantled arms **Rev:** Male portrait **Edge:** Plain

Date	Mintage	F	VF	XF	Unc	BU
2004	10,000	—	—	—	—	3.00
2004 Proof	5,000	Value: 4.00				

X# Pn4a 10 CEROS
Silver, 19.3 mm. **Obv:** Crowned and mantled arms **Rev:** Male portrait **Edge:** Plain

Date	Mintage	F	VF	XF	Unc	BU
2004 Proof	500	Value: 10.00				

X# Pn5 20 CEROS
Goldine, 22 mm. **Obv:** Crowned and mantled arms **Rev:** Portrait **Edge:** Plain

Date	Mintage	F	VF	XF	Unc	BU
2004	10,000	—	—	—	—	3.50
2004 Proof	5,000	Value: 5.00				

X# Pn5a 20 CEROS
Silver, 22 mm. **Obv:** Crowned and mantled arms **Rev:** Portrait **Edge:** Plain

Date	Mintage	F	VF	XF	Unc	BU
2004 Proof	500	Value: 12.50				

X# Pn6 50 CEROS
Goldine, 24.3 mm. **Obv:** Crowned and mantled arms **Rev:** Female portrait **Edge:** Plain

Date	Mintage	F	VF	XF	Unc	BU
2004	10,000	—	—	—	—	4.00
2004 Proof	5,000	Value: 6.00				

X# Pn6a 50 CEROS
Silver, 24.3 mm. **Obv:** Crowned and mantled arms **Rev:** Female portrait **Edge:** Plain

Date	Mintage	F	VF	XF	Unc	BU
2004 Proof	500	Value: 15.00				

X# Pn7 EUROP
Bi-Metallic Copper-Nickel center in Goldine ring, 22.8 mm. **Obv:** Castle **Rev:** Large value over outline map of Liechtenstein **Edge:** Plain

Date	Mintage	F	VF	XF	Unc	BU
2004	10,000	—	—	—	—	6.00
2004 Proof	5,000	Value: 8.00				

X# Pn7a EUROP
Bi-Metallic Silver center in Brass ring, 22.8 mm. **Obv:** Castle **Rev:** Large value over outline map of Liechtenstein **Edge:** Plain

Date	Mintage	F	VF	XF	Unc	BU
2004 Proof	500	Value: 22.50				

X# Pn8 2 EUROP
Bi-Metallic Goldine center in Copper-Nickel ring, 25.7 mm. **Obv:** Castle **Rev:** Large value over outline map of Liechtenstein **Edge:** Plain

Date	Mintage	F	VF	XF	Unc	BU
2004	10,000	—	—	—	—	8.00
2004 Proof	5,000	Value: 10.00				

X# Pn8a 2 EUROP
Bi-Metallic Brass center in Silver ring, 25.7 mm. **Obv:** Castle **Rev:** Large value over outline map of Liechtenstein **Edge:** Plain

Date	Mintage	F	VF	XF	Unc	BU
2004 Proof	500	Value: 28.50				

X# Pn9 5 EUROP
Tri-Metallic Goldine / Copper-Nickel / Copper, 36 mm. **Obv:** Virgin Mary seated facing with child **Rev:** Large value over outline map of Liechtenstein **Edge:** Plain

Date	Mintage	F	VF	XF	Unc	BU
2004 Proof	5,000	Value: 12.50				

X# Pn9a 5 EUROP
Tri-Metallic Goldine / Silver / Copper, 36 mm. **Obv:** Virgin Mary seated facing with child **Rev:** Large value over outlined map of Liechtenstein **Edge:** Plain

Date	Mintage	F	VF	XF	Unc	BU
2004 Proof	—	Value: 40.00				

MEDALLIC COINAGE

X# 7 5 FRANKEN
14.7000 g., 0.9000 Silver 0.4253 oz. ASW, 35.2 mm. **Subject:** Marriage of Crown Prince Johann Adam and Maria **Obv:** Crowned and mantled arms **Obv. Legend:** FELICITER CONJUNCTI + VADUZ 30.JUL.1967 **Rev:** Crown above facing heads **Rev. Legend:** JOHAN • ADAM • PRINC • HEPED • DE LIECHTENSTEIN + MARIA COMT • KINSKY+

Date	Mintage	F	VF	XF	Unc	BU
1967 Proof	—	Value: 35.00				

X# 7a 5 FRANKEN
Gold, 35.2 mm. **Subject:** Marriage of Crown Prince Johann Adam and Maria **Obv:** Crowned and mantled arms **Obv. Legend:** FELICITER CONJUNCTI + VADUZ 30.JULI.1967 **Rev:** Crown above facing heads **Rev. Legend:** JOHANN • ADAM • PRINC • HEPED • DE LIECHTENSTEIN + MARIA COMT • KINSKY +

Date	Mintage	F	VF	XF	Unc	BU
1967 Proof	—	Value: 400				

X# 5 20 FRANKEN
7.0000 g., Gold **Ruler:** Prince Franz Josef II **Subject:** 60th birthday of Franz Joseph II **Note:** Prev. KM#M5.

Date	Mintage	F	VF	XF	Unc	BU
ND(1966) Proof	—	Value: 165				

X# 6 20 FRANKEN

6.9600 g., Gold **Ruler:** Prince Franz Josef II **Subject:** Marriage of Crown Prince Johann Adam and Maria **Note:** Prev. KM#M6.

Date	Mintage	F	VF	XF	Unc	BU
1967 Proof	—	Value: 165				

MEDALLIC BULLION COINAGE

Struck at the Vienna Mint, Austria

X# MB1 10 TALER

155.5150 g., 0.9990 Silver 4.9947 oz. ASW, 65 mm. **Ruler:** Josef Johann Adam **Subject:** Vaduz Palace **Note:** Illustration reduced.

Date	Mintage	F	VF	XF	Unc	BU
1986 Proof	2,500	Value: 85.00				

ECU COINAGE

X# 21 5 ECU

26.0000 g., Copper-Nickel, 38.61 mm. **Ruler:** Hans Adam II **Issuer:** CITV **Obv:** Crowned and mantled arms **Obv. Legend:** FURSTENTUM LIECHTENSTEIN **Rev:** Gutenberg Castle **Rev. Legend:** LIECHTENSTEIN IM HERZEN EUROPAS **Edge:** Reeded **Edge Lettering:** Médaille

Date	Mintage	F	VF	XF	Unc	BU
1993	10,000	—	—	—	—	12.00

X# 22 20 ECU

31.1030 g., 0.9990 Silver 0.9989 oz. ASW, 38.61 mm. **Ruler:** Hans Adam II **Issuer:** CITV **Obv:** Crowned and mantled arms **Obv. Legend:** FURSTENTUM LIECHTENSTEIN **Rev:** Vaduz Castle **Rev. Legend:** LIECHTENSTEIN IM HERZEN EUROPAS **Edge:** Reeded **Edge Lettering:** Médaille

Date	Mintage	F	VF	XF	Unc	BU
1993 Proof	7,500	Value: 50.00				

X# 23 150 ECU

6.7200 g., 0.7500 Gold 0.1620 oz. AGW, 38.61 mm. **Ruler:** Hans Adam II **Issuer:** CITV **Obv:** Crowned and mantled arms **Obv. Legend:** FURSTENTUM LIECHTENSTEIN **Rev:** Castle **Rev. Legend:** LIECHENSTEIN IM HERZEN EUROPAS **Edge:** Reeded **Edge Lettering:** Médaille

Date	Mintage	F	VF	XF	Unc	BU
1993 Proof	750	Value: 250				

EURO COINAGE

X# 35 5 EURO

31.0000 g., Copper-Nickel, 38.61 mm. **Subject:** 125th Anniversary of Liechtenstein's Railroads **Obv:** Crowned and mantled arms **Obv. Legend:** FURSTENTUM LIECHTENSTEIN **Rev:** Modern electric locomotive **Rev. Legend:** 125 JAHRE EISENBAHN IN LIECHTENSTEIN **Edge:** Reeded

Date	Mintage	F	VF	XF	Unc	BU
1997	10,000	—	—	—	12.00	—

X# 37 5 EURO

31.0000 g., Copper Nickel, 38.61 mm. **Subject:** Heidiland **Obv:** Crowned and mantled arms **Obv. Legend:** FURSTENTUM LIECHTENSTEIN **Rev:** Heidi with young dog

Date	Mintage	F	VF	XF	Unc	BU
1998	—	—	—	—	—	12.00

X# 38 20 EURO

25.0000 g., 0.9250 Silver 0.7435 oz. ASW, 38.61 mm. **Subject:** Heidiland **Obv:** Crowned and mantled arms **Obv. Legend:** FURSTENTUM LIECHTENSTEIN **Rev:** Heidi with young dog

Date	Mintage	F	VF	XF	Unc	BU
1998 Proof	—	Value: 35.00				

X# 36 40 EURO

25.0000 g., 0.9250 Silver 0.7435 oz. ASW, 38.61 mm. **Subject:** 125th Anniversary of Liechtenstein's Railroads **Obv:** Crowned and mantled arms **Obv. Legend:** FURSTENTUM LIECHTENSTEIN **Rev:** Modern electric locomotive **Rev. Legend:** 125 JAHRE EISENBAHN in LIECHTENSTEIN **Edge:** Reeded

Date	Mintage	F	VF	XF	Unc	BU
1997 Proof	7,500	Value: 30.00				

X# 39 40 EURO

50.0000 g., 0.9250 Silver 1.4869 oz. ASW, 38.61 mm. **Subject:** Heidiland **Obv:** Crowned and mantled arms **Obv. Legend:** FURSTENTUM LIECHTENSTEIN **Rev:** Heidi with young dog

Date	Mintage	F	VF	XF	Unc	BU
1998 Proof	—	Value: 75.00				

PIEFORTS

X#	Date	Mintage	Identification	Mkt Val
P1	1993	1,400	20 Ecu. 0.9990 Silver. 62.2000 g. Mint mark and .925 at upper left on rev., X22.	100

X#	Date	Mintage	Identification	Mkt Val
P2	1993	100	20 Ecu. 0.9990 Silver. 62.2000 g. Mint mark and .999 at base of mountains on rev., X22.	120
P3	1997	350	40 Euro. 0.9250 Silver. 50.0000 g. 38.61 mm.	—
P4	2004	500	5 Europ. Silver. X#Pn9a.	—

MINT SETS

X#	Date	Mintage	Identification	Issue Price	Mkt Val
XMS1	2004 (8)	10,000	X#Pn1-Pn8	—	30.00

PROOF SETS

X#	Date	Mintage	Identification	Issue Price	Mkt Val
XPS1	2004 (9)	5,000	X#Pn1-Pn9	—	50.00
XPS2	2004 (9)	500	X#Pn1a-Pn9a	—	150

LIEGE

PRINCIPALITY

MEDALLIC COINAGE

X# M11 10 DENARII

13.1100 g., Silver, 30.1 mm. **Subject:** Millennium of Principality **Obv:** Shield in spray **Obv. Legend:** MILLENNIUM VAN HET PRINSBISDOM LUIK ... **Rev:** St. Lambert standing facing **Rev. Legend:** PATRONIS LEODIENSIS SANCTUS LAMBERTUS **Edge:** Plain

Date	Mintage	F	VF	XF	Unc	BU
ND(1980) Proof	—	Value: 12.50				

LITHUANIA

MODERN REPUBLIC

1991-present

FANTASY EURO PATTERNS

INA Issues

X# Pn1 EURO CENT

4.7000 g., Copper, 16.80 mm. **Issuer:** INA **Obv:** Knight horseback left **Obv. Legend:** LIETUVA **Rev:** Scales at right **Edge:** Plain

Date	Mintage	F	VF	XF	Unc	BU
2004	12,500	—	—	—	—	1.50
2004 Proof	3,000	Value: 2.50				

X# Pn1a EURO CENT

Silver **Issuer:** INA **Obv:** Knight horseback left **Obv. Legend:** LIETUVA **Rev:** Scales at right

Date	Mintage	F	VF	XF	Unc	BU
2004 Proof	175	Value: 6.00				

X# Pn2 2 EURO CENT

5.6300 g., Copper, 18.5 mm. **Issuer:** INA **Obv:** Knight horseback left **Obv. Legend:** LIETUVA **Rev:** Scales at right **Edge:** Plain

Date	Mintage	F	VF	XF	Unc	BU
2004	12,500	—	—	—	—	2.00
2004 Proof	3,000	Value: 3.00				

X# Pn2a 2 EURO CENT

Silver **Issuer:** INA **Obv:** Knight horseback left **Obv. Legend:** LIETUVA **Rev:** Scales at right

Date	Mintage	F	VF	XF	Unc	BU
2004 Proof	175	Value: 7.00				

X# Pn3 5 EURO CENT

7.2000 g., Copper, 20.7 mm. **Issuer:** INA **Obv:** Knight horseback left **Obv. Inscription:** LIETUVA **Rev:** Scales at right **Edge:** Plain

Date	Mintage	F	VF	XF	Unc	BU
2004	12,500	—	—	—	—	2.50
2004 Proof	3,000	Value: 3.50				

X# Pn3a 5 EURO CENT

Silver **Issuer:** INA **Obv:** Knight horseback left **Obv. Legend:** LIETUVA **Rev:** Scales at right

Date	Mintage	F	VF	XF	Unc	BU
2004 Proof	175	Value: 8.50				

X# Pn4 10 EURO CENT

5.9500 g., Goldine, 19.85 mm. **Issuer:** INA **Obv:** Knight horseback left **Obv. Legend:** LIETUVA **Rev:** Dove above value in wreath of clapsed hands **Edge:** Plain

Date	Mintage	F	VF	XF	Unc	BU
2004	12,500	—	—	—	—	3.00
2004 Proof	3,000	Value: 4.00				

X# Pn4a 10 EURO CENT

Silver **Issuer:** INA **Obv:** Knight horseback left **Obv. Legend:** LIETUVA **Rev:** Dove above value in wreath of clasped hands

Date	Mintage	F	VF	XF	Unc	BU
2004 Proof	175	Value: 10.00				

X# Pn5 20 EURO CENT

7.7500 g., Goldine, 22 mm. **Issuer:** INA **Obv:** Knight horseback left **Obv. Legend:** LIETUVA **Rev:** Dove above value in wreath of clasped hands **Edge:** Plain

Date	Mintage	F	VF	XF	Unc	BU
2004	12,500	—	—	—	—	6.00
2004 Proof	3,000	Value: 5.00				

X# Pn5a 20 EURO CENT

Silver **Issuer:** INA **Obv:** Knight horseback left **Obv. Legend:** LIETUVA **Rev:** Dove above value in wreath of clasped hands

Date	Mintage	F	VF	XF	Unc	BU
2004 Proof	175	Value: 12.50				

X# Pn6 50 EURO CENT

9.5500 g., Goldine, 24.3 mm. **Issuer:** INA **Obv:** Knight horseback left **Obv. Legend:** LIETUVA **Rev:** Dove above value in wreath of clasped hands **Edge:** Plain

Date	Mintage	F	VF	XF	Unc	BU
2004	12,500	—	—	—	—	15.00
2004 Proof	3,000	Value: 6.00				

X# Pn6a 50 EURO CENT

Silver **Issuer:** INA **Obv:** Knight horseback left **Obv. Legend:** LIETUVA **Rev:** Dove above value in wreath of clasped hands

Date	Mintage	F	VF	XF	Unc	BU
2004 Proof	175	Value: 15.00				

X# Pn7 EURO

8.2200 g., Bi-Metallic Copper-Nickel center in Golding ring, 22.8 mm. **Issuer:** INA **Obv:** Crowned bust with sword right **Obv. Legend:** LIETUVA **Rev:** Large value, owl alighting **Edge:** Plain

Date	Mintage	F	VF	XF	Unc	BU
2004	12,500	—	—	—	—	25.00
2004 Proof	3,000	Value: 8.00				

X# Pn7a EURO

Bi-Metallic Goldine center in Silver ring **Issuer:** INA **Obv:** Crowned bust of Vytautus with sword upright to right **Obv. Legend:** LIETUVA **Rev:** Large value, owl alighting

Date	Mintage	F	VF	XF	Unc	BU
2004 Proof	175	Value: 22.50				

X# Pn8 2 EURO

10.5400 g., Bi-Metallic Goldine center in Copper-Nickel ring, 25.7 mm. **Issuer:** INA **Obv:** Crowned bust of Vytautus with sword upright to right **Obv. Legend:** LIETUVA **Rev:** Large value, owl alighting **Edge:** Plain

Date	Mintage	F	VF	XF	Unc	BU
2004	12,500	—	—	—	—	35.00
2004 Proof	3,000	Value: 10.00				

X# Pn8a 2 EURO

Silver **Issuer:** INA **Obv:** Crowned bust of Vytautus with sword upright to right **Obv. Legend:** LIETUVA **Rev:** Large value, owl alighting

Date	Mintage	F	VF	XF	Unc	BU
2004 Proof	175	Value: 28.50				

X# Pn9 5 EURO

25.6000 g., Goldine, 36 mm. **Issuer:** INA **Obv:** Crowned bust of Vytautus with sword upright to right **Obv. Legend:** LIETUVA **Rev:** Large value, owl alighting **Edge:** Plain

Date	Mintage	F	VF	XF	Unc	BU
ND(2004) Proof	3,000	Value: 12.50				

X# Pn9a 5 EURO

Silver **Issuer:** INA **Obv:** Crowned bust of Vytautus with sword upright to right **Obv. Legend:** LIETUVA **Rev:** Large value, owl alighting

Date	Mintage	F	VF	XF	Unc	BU
ND(2004) Proof	175	Value: 40.00				

Unknown Issuer

X# Pn10 EURO CENT

Copper Plated Steel **Obv. Legend:** LITHUANIA

Date	Mintage	F	VF	XF	Unc	BU
ND(2004)	7,500	—	—	—	—	3.00

X# Pn11 2 EURO CENT

Copper Plated Steel **Obv. Legend:** LITHUANIA

Date	Mintage	F	VF	XF	Unc	BU
ND(2004)	7,500	—	—	—	—	6.00

X# Pn12 5 EURO CENT

Copper Plated Steel **Obv. Legend:** LITHUANIA

Date	Mintage	F	VF	XF	Unc	BU
ND(2004)	7,500	—	—	—	—	10.00

X# Pn13 10 EURO CENT

Goldine **Obv. Legend:** LITHUANIA

Date	Mintage	F	VF	XF	Unc	BU
ND(2004)	7,500	—	—	—	—	14.00

X# Pn14 20 EURO CENT

Goldine **Obv. Legend:** LITHUANIA

Date	Mintage	F	VF	XF	Unc	BU
ND(2004)	7,500	—	—	—	—	20.00

X# Pn15 50 EURO CENT

Goldine **Obv. Legend:** LITHUANIA

Date	Mintage	F	VF	XF	Unc	BU
ND(2004)	7,500	—	—	—	—	30.00

X# Pn16 EURO

Bi-Metallic **Obv:** Bust 3/4 right **Obv. Legend:** LITHUANIA **Rev:** Arms, large value, EEU stars design

Date	Mintage	F	VF	XF	Unc	BU
ND(2004)	7,500	—	—	—	—	40.00

X# Pn17 2 EURO

Bi-Metallic **Obv:** Bust 3/4 right **Obv. Legend:** LITHUANIA **Rev:** Arms, large value, EEU stars design

Date	Mintage	F	VF	XF	Unc	BU
ND(2004)	7,500	—	—	—	—	7.50

MINT SETS

X#	Date	Mintage	Identification	Issue Price	Mkt Val
XMS1	2004 (8)	12,500	X#Pn1-Pn8	—	50.00
XMS2	NS(2004) (8)	7,500	X#Pn10-Pn17	—	40.00

PROOF SETS

X#	Date	Mintage	Identification	Issue Price	Mkt Val
XPS1	2004 (9)	3,000	X#Pn1-Pn9	—	120
XPS2	2004	175	X#Pn1a-9a	—	150

LUNDY

BRITISH ADMINISTRATION

PATTERNS

Including off metal strikes

X# Pn1 PUFFIN

Bronze **Edge:** Plain **Note:** Prev. KM#Pn1. Large planchet.

Date	Mintage	F	VF	XF	Unc	BU
1929	—	—	—	—	150	—

TOKEN COINAGE

X# Tn1 1/2 PUFFIN

Bronze **Note:** Prev. KM#Tn1. Similar to KM#Tn3.

Date	Mintage	F	VF	XF	Unc	BU
1929	50,000	2.50	5.00	12.00	25.00	50.00

X# Tn3 1/2 PUFFIN

Bronze **Note:** Prev. KM#Tn3.

Date	Mintage	F	VF	XF	Unc	BU
1965 Proof	3,000	Value: 18.00				

X# Tn5 1/2 PUFFIN

Nickel-Brass **Note:** Prev. KM#Tn3a.

Date	Mintage	F	VF	XF	Unc	BU
1965 Proof	3,000	Value: 18.00				

X# Tn7 1/2 PUFFIN

Gold **Note:** Prev. KM#Tn3b.

Date	Mintage	F	VF	XF	Unc	BU
1965 Proof	50	Value: 1,500				

X# Tn2 PUFFIN

Bronze **Note:** Prev. KM#Tn2.

Date	Mintage	F	VF	XF	Unc	BU
1929	50,000	3.00	6.00	15.00	27.50	60.00

X# Tn4 PUFFIN

Bronze **Note:** Prev. KM#Tn4.

Date	Mintage	F	VF	XF	Unc	BU
1965 Proof	3,000	Value: 22.00				

X# Tn6 PUFFIN

Nickel-Brass **Note:** Prev. KM#Tn4a.

Date	Mintage	F	VF	XF	Unc	BU
1965 Proof	3,000	Value: 22.00				

X# Tn8 PUFFIN

Gold **Note:** Prev. KM#Tn4b.

Date	Mintage	F	VF	XF	Unc	BU
1965 Proof	50	Value: 2,500				

PROOF SETS

X#	Date	Mintage	Identification	Issue Price	Mkt Val
XPS1	1965 (4)	3,000	XTn3-XTn6	—	170
XPS2	1965 (4)	25	XTn7, XTn8 (2 each)	—	8,000

LUXEMBOURG

GRAND DUCHY

ECU COINAGE

X# 25 ECU

28.2800 g., 0.9250 Silver 0.8410 oz. ASW **Ruler:** Jean **Obv:** Crowned rampant lion left **Obv. Legend:** GRAND - DUCHE DE LUXEMBOURG **Rev:** Large "ECU" on map of Europe **Rev. Legend:** • LUXEMBOURG • EUROPE - EUROPA **Edge:** Reeded

Date	Mintage	F	VF	XF	Unc	BU
ND(1992)PM Proof	10,000	Value: 35.00				

X# 40 ECU

20.0000 g., 0.9990 Silver 0.6423 oz. ASW, 40 mm. **Ruler:** Jean **Issuer:** Göde GmbH, Waldaschaff **Obv:** Facing bust of Charles IV, shield at left and at right **Obv. Legend:** CHARLES IV. • 1316-1378 COMTE DE LUXEMBOURG...

Rev: 12 members arms in circle, large "ECU" in center of band with 12 stars **Edge:** Reeded

Date	Mintage	F	VF	XF	Unc	BU
ND(1993) Proof	9,999	Value: 55.00				

X# 21 5 ECU

23.0000 g., Copper-Nickel, 38.6 mm. **Ruler:** Jean **Issuer:** CITV **Subject:** 40th Anniversary European Parliament **Obv:** Crowned bust of Charles IV facing **Obv. Legend:** CHARLES IV, COMTE DE LUXEMBOURG,... **Rev:** Charlotte bridge **Rev. Legend:** 40 ANS PARLEMENT EUROPÉEN **Edge:** Reeded

Date	Mintage	F	VF	XF	Unc	BU
1992	20,000	—	—	—	—	10.00

X# 28 5 ECU

23.0000 g., Copper-Nickel, 38.6 mm. **Ruler:** Jean **Issuer:** CITV **Subject:** 35th Anniversary European Investmentbank **Obv:** Crowned bust of Henry VII right **Obv. Legend:** HENRI VII., COMTE DE LUXEMBOURG... **Rev:** Bank complex **Rev. Legend:** BANQUE EUROPEENNE D'INVESTISSEMENT **Edge:** Reeded

Date	Mintage	F	VF	XF	Unc	BU
1993	10,000	—	—	—	—	10.00

X# 35 5 ECU

22.7000 g., Copper-Nickel, 37.5 mm. **Ruler:** Jean **Issuer:** Sertons International B.V., Elst **Obv:** Castle wall above arms **Obv. Inscription:** LËTZEBUERG **Obv. Designer:** D. J. Hegeman **Rev:** Bust of Joseph Bech 3/4 left at right **Rev. Legend:** GRAND • DUCHE DE LUXEMBOURG **Rev. Designer:** I. Rank-Broadley **Edge:** Plain **Edge Lettering:** Sans cours légal

Date	Mintage	F	VF	XF	Unc	BU
1993	75,000	—	—	—	—	12.50

X# 43 5 ECU

Copper-Nickel, 38.61 mm. **Subject:** Eurocontrol - Air Traffic Control **Obv:** Airplane over map of Europe **Rev:** John the Blind on throne

Date	Mintage	F	VF	XF	Unc	BU
1996	3,500	—	—	—	—	12.50

X# 22 20 ECU

25.0000 g., 0.9250 Silver 0.7435 oz. ASW, 38.6 mm. **Ruler:** Joseph II **Issuer:** CITV **Subject:** 40th

Anniversary European Parliament **Obv:** Crowned bust of Charles IV facing **Obv. Legend:** CHARLES IV, COMTE DE LUXEMBOURG,... **Rev:** Charlotte bridge **Rev. Legend:** 40 ANS PARLEMENT EUROPÉEN **Edge:** Reeded

Date	Mintage	F	VF	XF	Unc	BU
1992 Proof	25,000	Value: 40.00				

X# 29 20 ECU

25.0000 g., 0.9250 Silver 0.7435 oz. ASW, 38.6 mm. **Ruler:** Jean **Issuer:** CITV **Subject:** 35th Anniversary European Investmentbank **Obv:** Crowned bust of Henry VII right **Obv. Legend:** HENRI VII., COMTE DE LUXEMBOURG... **Rev:** Bank complex **Rev. Legend:** BANQUE EUROPEENNE D'INVESTISSEMENT **Edge:** Reeded

Date	Mintage	F	VF	XF	Unc	BU
1993 Proof	7,500	Value: 40.00				

X# 44 20 ECU

25.0000 g., 0.9250 Silver 0.7435 oz. ASW, 38.61 mm. **Subject:** Eurocontrol - Air Traffic Control **Obv:** Airplane over map of Europe **Rev:** John the Blind on throne

Date	Mintage	F	VF	XF	Unc	BU
1996 Proof	2,750	Value: 45.00				

X# 36 25 ECU

22.8500 g., 0.9250 Silver 0.6795 oz. ASW, 37 mm. **Ruler:** Jean **Issuer:** Sertons International B.V., Elst **Obv:** Castle wall above arms **Obv. Inscription:** LËTZEBUERG **Obv. Designer:** D. J. Hegeman **Rev:** Bust of Joseph Bech 3/4 left at right **Rev. Legend:** GRAND • DUCHE DE LUXEMBOURG **Rev. Designer:** I. Rank-Broadley **Edge:** Plain **Edge Lettering:** Sans cours légal

Date	Mintage	F	VF	XF	Unc	BU
1993 Proof	20,000	Value: 42.50				

X# 45 50 ECU

155.5000 g., 0.9990 Silver 4.9942 oz. ASW, 63 mm. **Subject:** Eurocontrol - Air Traffic Control **Obv:** Airplane over map of Europe **Rev:** John the Blind on throne

Date	Mintage	F	VF	XF	Unc	BU
1996 Proof	650	Value: 150				

X# 37 100 ECU

8.6400 g., 0.9000 Gold 0.2500 oz. AGW, 21 mm. **Ruler:** Jean **Issuer:** Sertons International B.V., Elst **Obv:** Castle wall above arms **Obv. Inscription:** LËTZEBUERG **Obv. Designer:** D. J. Hegeman **Rev:** Bust of Joseph Bech 3/4 left at right **Rev. Legend:** GRAND • DUCHE DE LUXEMBOURG **Rev. Designer:** I. Rank-Broadley **Edge:** Plain **Edge Lettering:** Sans cours légal

Date	Mintage	F	VF	XF	Unc	BU
1993 Proof	1,000	Value: 275				

X# 23 150 ECU

6.7200 g., 0.7500 Gold 0.1620 oz. AGW, 22.5 mm. **Ruler:** Jean **Issuer:** CITV **Subject:** 40th Anniversary European Parliament **Obv:** Crowned bust of Charles IV facing **Obv. Legend:** CHARLES IV, COMTE DE LUXEMBOURG,... **Rev:** Charlotte bridge **Rev. Legend:** 40 ANS PARLEMENT EUROPÉEN **Edge:** Reeded

Date	Mintage	F	VF	XF	Unc	BU
1992 Proof	2,500	Value: 250				

X# 30 150 ECU

6.7200 g., 0.7500 Gold 0.1620 oz. AGW, 22.5 mm. **Ruler:** Jean **Issuer:** CITV **Subject:** 35th Anniversary European Investmentbank **Obv:** Crowned bust of Henry VII right **Obv. Legend:** HENRI VII., COMTE DE LUXEMBOURG... **Rev:** Bank complex **Rev. Legend:** BANQUE EUROPEENNE D'INVESTISSEMENT **Edge:** Reeded

Date	Mintage	F	VF	XF	Unc	BU
1993 Proof	700	Value: 250				

X# 38 250 ECU

17.2700 g., 0.9000 Gold 0.4997 oz. AGW, 29 mm. **Ruler:** Jean **Issuer:** Sertons International B.V., Elst **Obv:** Castle wall above arms **Obv. Inscription:** LËTZEBUERG **Obv. Designer:** D. J. Hegeman **Rev:** Bust of Joseph Bech 3/4 left at right **Rev. Legend:** GRAND • DUCHE DE LUXEMBOURG... **Rev. Designer:** I. Rank-Broadley **Edge:** Plain **Edge Lettering:** Sans cours légal

Date	Mintage	F	VF	XF	Unc	BU
1993 Proof	1,000	Value: 400				

MEDALLIC COINAGE

X# MA1 5 FRANCS

25.1500 g., Silver **Issuer:** Banque de Bruxelles **Subject:** Princess Ermesinde **Note:** Prev. KM#M14.

Date	Mintage	F	VF	XF	Unc	BU
ND(1963)(b)	—	—	—	—	—	30.00

X# MA1a 5 FRANCS

21.8000 g., Bronze **Issuer:** Banque de Bruxelles **Subject:** Princess Ermesinde **Note:** Prev. KM#M14a.

Date	Mintage	F	VF	XF	Unc	BU
ND(1963)(b)	—	—	—	—	—	16.50

X# MA1b 5 FRANCS

41.9000 g., Gold **Issuer:** Banque du Bruxelles. **Subject:** Princess Ermesinde **Note:** Prev. KM#M14b. With ESSAI.

Date	Mintage	F	VF	XF	Unc	BU
ND(1963)(b)	—	—	—	—	—	900

X# M1 20 FRANCS

6.4516 g., 0.9000 Gold 0.1867 oz. AGW **Subject:** Marriage Commemorative - Prince Jean and Princess Josephine Charlotte **Note:** Prev. KM#M1.

Date	Mintage	F	VF	XF	Unc	BU
1953(b)	25,573	—	—	125	150	225

X# M2 20 FRANCS
Copper **Subject:** 100th Anniversary of Luxembourg **Note:** Prev. KM#M2.

Date	Mintage	F	VF	XF	Unc	BU
1963(b)	—	—	—	—	20.00	30.00

X# M2a 20 FRANCS
Copper-Nickel **Subject:** 100th Anniversary of Luxembourg **Note:** Prev. KM#M2a.

Date	Mintage	F	VF	XF	Unc	BU
1963(b)	—	—	—	—	25.00	35.00

X# M2b 20 FRANCS
6.4516 g., 0.9000 Gold 0.1867 oz. AGW
Subject: 100th Anniversary of Luxembourg **Note:** Prev. KM#M2b. With ESSAI.

Date	Mintage	F	VF	XF	Unc	BU
1963(b)	25,263	—	—	135	150	250

X# M4 20 FRANCS
Bronze **Subject:** Coronation **Note:** Prev. KM#M4.

Date	Mintage	F	VF	XF	Unc	BU
1964(b)	—	—	—	—	20.00	30.00

X# M4a 20 FRANCS
Copper-Nickel **Subject:** Coronation **Note:** Prev. KM#M4a.

Date	Mintage	F	VF	XF	Unc	BU
1964(b)	—	—	—	—	25.00	35.00

X# M4b 20 FRANCS
6.4516 g., 0.9000 Gold 0.1867 oz. AGW **Subject:** Coronation **Note:** Prev. KM#M4b. With ESSAI.

Date	Mintage	F	VF	XF	Unc	BU
1964(b)	200	—	—	—	170	260

X# M4c 20 FRANCS
6.4516 g., 0.9000 Gold 0.1867 oz. AGW
Subject: Coronation

Date	Mintage	F	VF	XF	Unc	BU
1964(b)	25,050	—	—	135	150	260

X# M31 20 FRANCS
6.4516 g., 0.9000 Gold 0.1867 oz. AGW **Subject:** 100th Anniversary - Death of Poet Michel Lentz

Date	Mintage	F	VF	XF	Unc	BU
1993 Proof	500	Value: 300				

X# M3 40 FRANCS
Silver **Issuer:** Banque de Bruxelles **Subject:** Princess Ermesinde **Note:** Prev. KM#M3.

Date	Mintage	F	VF	XF	Unc	BU
ND(1963)(b)	—	—	—	—	—	20.00

X# M3a 40 FRANCS
Copper-Nickel **Issuer:** Banque de Bruxelles
Subject: Princess Ermesinde **Note:** Prev. KM#M3a.

Date	Mintage	F	VF	XF	Unc	BU
ND(1963)(b)	—	—	—	—	—	12.50

X# M3b 40 FRANCS
Bronze **Issuer:** Banque de Bruxelles **Subject:** Princess Ermesinde **Note:** Prev. KM#M3b.

Date	Mintage	F	VF	XF	Unc	BU
ND(1963)(b)	—	—	—	—	—	12.50

X# M3c 40 FRANCS
12.9032 g., 0.9000 Gold 0.3733 oz. AGW **Issuer:** Banque de Bruxelles **Subject:** Princess Ermesinde **Note:** Prev. KM#M3c. With ESSAI.

Date	Mintage	F	VF	XF	Unc	BU
ND(1963)(b)	5,000	—	—	450	500	600

X# M5 40 FRANCS
12.9032 g., 0.9000 Gold 0.3733 oz. AGW **Obv:** Grand Duchess Charlotte head facing left **Note:** Prev. KM#M5.

Date	Mintage	F	VF	XF	Unc	BU
1964(b)	3,000	—	—	450	500	600

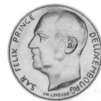

X# M6 40 FRANCS
12.9032 g., 0.9000 Gold 0.3733 oz. AGW **Obv:** Prince Felix head facing left **Note:** Prev. KM#M6.

Date	Mintage	F	VF	XF	Unc	BU
1964(b)	3,000	—	—	450	500	600

X# M7 40 FRANCS
12.9032 g., 0.9000 Gold 0.3733 oz. AGW **Obv:** Grand Duke Jean head facing left **Note:** Prev. KM#M7.

Date	Mintage	F	VF	XF	Unc	BU
1964(b)	3,000	—	—	450	500	600

X# M8 40 FRANCS
12.9032 g., 0.9000 Gold 0.3733 oz. AGW **Obv:** Grand Duchess Josephine Charlotte head facing left
Note: Prev. KM#M8.

Date	Mintage	F	VF	XF	Unc	BU
1964(b)	3,000	—	—	450	500	600

X# M9 40 FRANCS
Copper-Nickel **Subject:** 300th Anniversary of Patron Saint **Note:** Prev. KM#M9.

Date	Mintage	F	VF	XF	Unc	BU
1966	—	—	—	—	10.00	15.00

X# M9a 40 FRANCS
Silver **Subject:** 300th Anniversary of Patron Saint **Note:** Prev. KM#M9a.

Date	Mintage	F	VF	XF	Unc	BU
1966	—	—	—	—	20.00	30.00

X# M9b 40 FRANCS
12.9032 g., 0.9000 Gold 0.3733 oz. AGW
Subject: 300th Anniversary of Patron Saint (Virgin Mary) **Note:** Prev. KM#M9b. With ESSAI.

Date	Mintage	F	VF	XF	Unc	BU
1966	5,000	—	—	450	500	600

X# M10 40 FRANCS
Silver **Subject:** 100th Anniversary of London Treaty

Date	Mintage	F	VF	XF	Unc	BU
1967	—	—	—	—	20.00	30.00

X# M10a 40 FRANCS
Bronze **Subject:** 100th Anniversary of London Treaty **Note:** Prev. KM#M10a.

Date	Mintage	F	VF	XF	Unc	BU
1967	—	—	—	—	10.00	15.00

X# M10b 40 FRANCS
Copper-Nickel **Subject:** 100th Anniversary of London Treaty **Note:** Prev. KM#M10b.

Date	Mintage	F	VF	XF	Unc	BU
1967	—	—	—	—	12.00	20.00

X# M10c 40 FRANCS
12.9032 g., 0.9000 Gold 0.3733 oz. AGW
Subject: 100th Anniversary of London Treaty
Obv: Henry and Amalia conjoined heads facing left
Note: Prev. KM#M10c. With ESSAI.

Date	Mintage	F	VF	XF	Unc	BU
1967	5,000	—	—	450	500	600

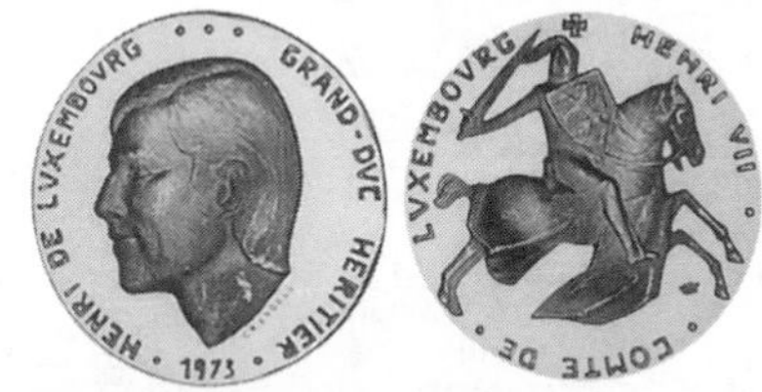

X# M11 40 FRANCS
12.9032 g., 0.9000 Gold 0.3733 oz. AGW
Subject: Grand Duke Henry VII **Rev:** Prince Henri charging on horseback **Note:** Prev. KM#M11.

Date	Mintage	F	VF	XF	Unc	BU
1973 (a) Proof	5,000	Value: 300				

X# M12 40 FRANCS
12.9032 g., 0.9000 Gold 0.3733 oz. AGW
Subject: 80th Birthday of Princess Josephine Charlotte
Rev: Fischbach Castle **Note:** Prev. KM#M12.

Date	Mintage	F	VF	XF	Unc	BU
1976 (a) Proof	6,500	Value: 300				

X# M13 40 FRANCS
12.9032 g., 0.9000 Gold 0.3733 oz. AGW **Subject:** Silver Wedding, 1953-1978 **Note:** Prev. KM#M13.

Date	Mintage	F	VF	XF	Unc	BU
ND(1978) Proof	3,000	Value: 300				

X# M18 40 FRANCS
12.9032 g., 0.9000 Gold 0.3733 oz. AGW
Subject: Grand Duke Adolph

Date	Mintage	F	VF	XF	Unc	BU
1982 Proof	1,000	Value: 300				

X# M19 40 FRANCS
12.9032 g., 0.9000 Gold 0.3733 oz. AGW
Subject: Grand Duke Guillaume

Date	Mintage	F	VF	XF	Unc	BU
1982 Proof	1,000	Value: 300				

X# M20 40 FRANCS
12.9032 g., 0.9000 Gold 0.3733 oz. AGW
Subject: Grand Duchess Marie - Adelaide

Date	Mintage	F	VF	XF	Unc	BU
1982 Proof	1,000	Value: 300				

X# M21 40 FRANCS
12.9032 g., 0.9000 Gold 0.3733 oz. AGW
Subject: Grand Duchess Charlotte

Date	Mintage	F	VF	XF	Unc	BU
1982 Proof	1,000	Value: 300				

X# M22 40 FRANCS
12.9032 g., 0.9000 Gold 0.3733 oz. AGW
Subject: Grand Duke Jean

Date	Mintage	F	VF	XF	Unc	BU
1982 Proof	1,000	Value: 300				

X# M23 40 FRANCS
12.9032 g., 0.9000 Gold 0.3733 oz. AGW
Subject: Grand Duchess Josephine - Charlotte

Date	Mintage	F	VF	XF	Unc	BU
1982 Proof	1,000	Value: 300				

X# M24 40 FRANCS
12.9032 g., 0.9000 Gold 0.3733 oz. AGW
Subject: Prince Henri

Date	Mintage	F	VF	XF	Unc	BU
1982 Proof	1,000	Value: 300				

X# M25 40 FRANCS
12.9032 g., 0.9000 Gold 0.3733 oz. AGW
Subject: Princess Maria Theresa

Date	Mintage	F	VF	XF	Unc	BU
1982 Proof	1,000	Value: 300				

X# M26 40 FRANCS
12.9032 g., 0.9000 Gold 0.3733 oz. AGW
Subject: Count Henry VII

Date	Mintage	F	VF	XF	Unc	BU
1984 Proof	2,000	Value: 350				

X# M27 40 FRANCS
12.9032 g., 0.9000 Gold 0.3733 oz. AGW
Subject: Visit of Pope John Paul II

Date	Mintage	F	VF	XF	Unc	BU
1985 Proof	1,575	Value: 400				

X# M28 40 FRANCS
12.9032 g., 0.9000 Gold 0.3733 oz. AGW
Subject: Rebuilding of the souvenir monument

Date	Mintage	F	VF	XF	Unc	BU
1985 Proof	200	Value: 500				

X# M29 40 FRANCS
12.9032 g., 0.9000 Gold 0.3733 oz. AGW
Subject: Death of Grand Duchess Charlotte

Date	Mintage	F	VF	XF	Unc	BU
1985 Proof	470	Value: 450				

X# M30 40 FRANCS
12.9032 g., 0.9000 Gold 0.3733 oz. AGW
Subject: 25th Anniversary - London Treaty

Date	Mintage	F	VF	XF	Unc	BU
1992 Proof	1,200	Value: 300				

X# M32 40 FRANCS
12.9032 g., 0.9000 Gold 0.3733 oz. AGW
Subject: 40th Wedding Anniversary, 1953-1993

Date	Mintage	F	VF	XF	Unc	BU
ND(1993) Proof	700	Value: 400				

X# M33 40 FRANCS
12.9032 g., 0.9000 Gold 0.3733 oz. AGW
Subject: 30th Anniversary of Reign, 1964-1994

Date	Mintage	F	VF	XF	Unc	BU
ND(1994) Proof	700	Value: 400				

X# M34 40 FRANCS
12.9032 g., 0.9000 Gold 0.3733 oz. AGW **Subject:** 100th Anniversary - Birth of Grand Duchess Charlotte, 1896-1985 **Rev:** Berg Castle

Date	Mintage	F	VF	XF	Unc	BU
ND(1996) Proof	600	Value: 425				

X# M35 40 FRANCS
12.9032 g., 0.9000 Gold 0.3733 oz. AGW **Subject:** 550th Anniversary - Henri V as Count, 1247-1281

Date	Mintage	F	VF	XF	Unc	BU
ND(1997) Proof	600	Value: 425				

X# M36 40 FRANCS
12.9032 g., 0.9000 Gold 0.3733 oz. AGW
Subject: Grand Duke Henri **Obv:** Portrait **Rev:** Arms

Date	Mintage	F	VF	XF	Unc	BU
ND(1997) Proof	600	Value: 425				

ESSAIS

X#	Date	Mintage	Identification	Mkt Val
E1	1964(b)	—	20 Francs. Brass. XM4.	32.50
E2	1964(b)	—	40 Francs. Silver. XM5.	65.00
E3	1964(b)	—	40 Francs. Brass. XM5.	45.00
E4	1964(b)	—	40 Francs. Silver. XM6.	65.00
E5	1964(b)	—	40 Francs. Brass. XM6.	45.00
E6	1964(b)	—	40 Francs. Silver. XM7.	65.00
E7	1964(b)	—	40 Francs. Brass. XM7.	45.00
E8	1964(b)	—	40 Francs. Silver. XM8.	57.50
E9	1964(b)	—	40 Francs. Brass. XM8.	45.00
E10	1967	—	40 Francs. Silver. XM10.	65.00
E11	1967	—	40 Francs. Copper-Nickel. XM10.	45.00
E12	1967	—	40 Francs. Brass. XM10.	32.50

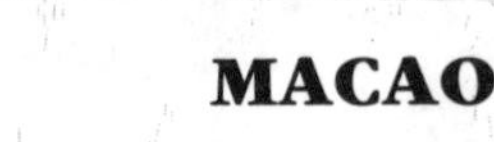

MACAO

PORTUGUESE COLONY

BULLION COINAGE

On Wing (Wing-on) Bank

X# 4 1/2 OUNCE
15.5000 g., 0.9990 Gold 0.4978 oz. AGW

Date	Mintage	F	VF	XF	Unc	BU
ND(c.1950)	—	—	BV	450	650	—

X# 5 OUNCE
31.1000 g., 0.9990 Gold 0.9988 oz. AGW

Date	Mintage	F	VF	XF	Unc	BU
ND(c.1950)	—	—	BV	800	1,300	—

SILGOLD COINAGE

X# 11 400 SILGOLD
0.9990 Bi-Metallic 373.242 Silver/6.2207 Gold, 85 mm. **Issuer:** Money Co., California **Subject:** 35th Macao Grand Prix **Obv:** Fireball between facing dragons **Rev:** Two coin images, colony outline **Rev. Legend:** • MACAU GRANDE PRÉMIO 1988 • XXXV ANIVERSÃRIO **Note:** Illustration reduced.

Date	Mintage	F	VF	XF	Unc	BU
1988 Proof	250	Value: 750				

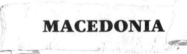

MACEDONIA

REPUBLIC

FANTASY EURO PATTERNS

X# Pn1 EURO CENT
Copper Plated Steel **Edge:** Plain

Date	Mintage	F	VF	XF	Unc	BU
2005	7,000	—	—	—	—	1.00

X# Pn2 2 EURO CENT
Copper Plated Steel **Edge:** Plain

Date	Mintage	F	VF	XF	Unc	BU
2005	7,000	—	—	—	—	1.50

X# Pn3 5 EURO CENT
Copper Plated Steel **Edge:** Plain

Date	Mintage	F	VF	XF	Unc	BU
2005	7,000	—	—	—	—	2.00

X# Pn4 10 EURO CENT
Goldine **Edge:** Plain

Date	Mintage	F	VF	XF	Unc	BU
2005	7,000	—	—	—	—	2.50

X# Pn5 20 EURO CENT
Goldine **Edge:** Plain

Date	Mintage	F	VF	XF	Unc	BU
2005	7,000	—	—	—	—	3.00

X# Pn6 50 EURO CENT
Goldine **Edge:** Plain

Date	Mintage	F	VF	XF	Unc	BU
2005	7,000	—	—	—	—	3.50

X# Pn7 EURO
Bi-Metallic **Obv:** Stylized farmers, horse **Rev:** Stylized flower, large value, EEU star design **Edge:** Plain

Date	Mintage	F	VF	XF	Unc	BU
2005	7,000	—	—	—	—	5.50

X# Pn8 2 EURO
Bi-Metallic **Obv:** Stylized farmers, horse **Rev:** Stylized flower, large value, EEU star design **Edge:** Plain

Date	Mintage	F	VF	XF	Unc	BU
2005	7,000	—	—	—	—	7.50

MINT SETS

X#	Date	Mintage	Identification	Issue Price	Mkt Val
XMS1	2005 (8)	7,000	X#Pn1-Pn8	—	26.00

MADAGASCAR

KINGDOM

FANTASY COINAGE

X# 1 10 CENTIMES
Bronze **Subject:** Ranavalona III **Note:** Prev. KY#153.

Date	Mintage	F	VF	XF	Unc	BU
1883	—	—	—	125	200	275

X# 4 KIROBO
6.8000 g., Silver **Subject:** Ranavalona III **Note:** Prev. KY#155.

Date	Mintage	F	VF	XF	Unc	BU
1888	—	—	—	300	400	800

X# 4a KIROBO
Bronze **Subject:** Ranavalona III **Note:** Prev. KY#155a.

Date	Mintage	F	VF	XF	Unc	BU
1888	—	—	—	150	225	300

X# 4b KIROBO
Aluminum **Subject:** Ranavalona III **Edge:** Plain **Note:** Prev. KY#155b.

Date	Mintage	F	VF	XF	Unc	BU
1888	—	—	—	100	150	200

X# 4c KIROBO
Aluminum **Subject:** Ranavalona III **Edge:** Reeded **Note:** Prev. KY#155c.

Date	Mintage	F	VF	XF	Unc	BU
1888	—	—	—	100	150	200

X# 2a 5 FRANCS
Bronze **Subject:** Ranavalomanjaka **Obv:** Legend with small lettering

Date	Mintage	F	VF	XF	Unc	BU
1883	—	—	—	125	200	300

X# 2 5 FRANCS
Silver **Subject:** Ranavalomanjaka **Obv:** Legend with small lettering

Date	Mintage	F	VF	XF	Unc	BU
1883	—	—	—	350	500	800

X# 2b 5 FRANCS
Aluminum **Subject:** Ranavalomanjaka **Obv:** Legend with small lettering **Edge:** Plain

Date	Mintage	F	VF	XF	Unc	BU
1883	—	—	—	85.00	165	275

X# 2c 5 FRANCS
Aluminum **Subject:** Ranavalomanjaka **Obv:** Legend with small lettering **Edge:** Reeded

Date	Mintage	F	VF	XF	Unc	BU
1883	—	—	—	85.00	165	275

X# 3 5 FRANCS
Silver **Subject:** Ranavalomanjaka **Obv:** Legend with large lettering **Note:** Prev. KY#154.

Date	Mintage	F	VF	XF	Unc	BU
1883	—	—	—	350	500	800

X# 3a 5 FRANCS
Bronze **Subject:** Ranavalomanjaka **Obv:** Legend with large lettering **Note:** Prev. KY#154a.

Date	Mintage	F	VF	XF	Unc	BU
1883	—	—	—	125	200	300

X# 3b 5 FRANCS
Aluminum **Subject:** Ranavalomanjaka **Obv:** Legend with large lettering **Edge:** Plain **Note:** Prev. KY#154b.

Date	Mintage	F	VF	XF	Unc	BU
1883	—	—	—	85.00	165	275

X# 3c 5 FRANCS
Aluminum **Subject:** Ranavalomanjaka **Obv:** Legend with large lettering **Edge:** Reeded **Note:** Prev. KY#154c.

Date	Mintage	F	VF	XF	Unc	BU
1883	—	—	—	85.00	165	275

X# 3d 5 FRANCS
Tin **Subject:** Ranavalomanjaka **Obv:** Legend with large lettering

Date	Mintage	F	VF	XF	Unc	BU
1883	—	—	—	85.00	165	275

MEDALLIC COINAGE

X# M1b 5 FRANCS
Aluminum **Subject:** Ranavona III **Note:** Prev. KY#152b.

Date	Mintage	F	VF	XF	Unc	BU
1885	—	—	—	75.00	150	250

X# M2 5 FRANCS
Silver **Subject:** Ranavalona III

Date	Mintage	F	VF	XF	Unc	BU
ND	—	—	—	425	675	850

X# M2a 5 FRANCS
Bronze **Subject:** Ranavalona III

Date	Mintage	F	VF	XF	Unc	BU
ND	—	—	—	200	350	500

X# M2b 5 FRANCS
Tin **Subject:** Ranavalona III

Date	Mintage	F	VF	XF	Unc	BU
ND	—	—	—	200	350	500

X# M1 5 FRANCS
Silver **Subject:** Ranavona III **Note:** Prev. KY#152.

Date	Mintage	F	VF	XF	Unc	BU
1886	—	—	—	400	600	800

X# M1a 5 FRANCS
Bronze **Subject:** Ranavona III **Note:** Prev. KY#152a.

Date	Mintage	F	VF	XF	Unc	BU
1886	—	—	—	125	200	300

1895 Dr. Reginald Huth Series

Struck in London, England

X# M3d DOLLAR
Platinum APW **Subject:** Ranavalo Manjaka III **Note:** Type I. Prev. KY#156.

Date	Mintage	F	VF	XF	Unc	BU
1895 Unique; Proof	—	Value: 5,000				

X# M3c DOLLAR
Gold **Subject:** Ranavalo Manjaka III **Note:** Type I. Prev. KY#156a.

Date	Mintage	F	VF	XF	Unc	BU
1895 Unique; Rare	—	—	—	—	—	—

X# M3 DOLLAR
Silver **Subject:** Ranavalo Manjaka III **Note:** Type I. Prev. KY#156b.

Date	Mintage	F	VF	XF	Unc	BU
1895 Proof	25	Value: 800				

X# M3b DOLLAR
Copper **Subject:** Ranavalo Manjaka III **Note:** Type I. Prev. KY#156c.

Date	Mintage	F	VF	XF	Unc	BU
1895 Unique; Rare	—	—	—	—	—	—

X# M3a DOLLAR
Iron **Subject:** Ranavalo Manjaka III **Note:** Type I. Prev. KY#156d.

Date	Mintage	F	VF	XF	Unc	BU
1895 Rare	2	—	—	—	—	—

X# M4d DOLLAR
Platinum APW **Subject:** Ranavalo Manjaka III **Note:** Type II. Prev. KY#157.

Date	Mintage	F	VF	XF	Unc	BU
1895 Unique	—	—	—	—	—	—

X# M4c DOLLAR
Gold **Subject:** Ranavalo Manjaka III **Note:** Type II. Prev. KY#157a.

Date	Mintage	F	VF	XF	Unc	BU
1895 Unique	—	—	—	—	—	—

X# M4e DOLLAR
Palladium **Subject:** Ranavalo Manjaka III **Note:** Type II. Prev. KY#157b.

Date	Mintage	F	VF	XF	Unc	BU
1895 Unique	—	—	—	—	—	—

X# M4 DOLLAR
Silver **Subject:** Ranavalo Manjaka III **Note:** Type II. Prev. KY#157c.

Date	Mintage	F	VF	XF	Unc	BU
1895 Proof	25	Value: 750				

X# M4b DOLLAR
Copper **Subject:** Ranavalo Manjaka III **Note:** Type II. Prev. KY#157d.

Date	Mintage	F	VF	XF	Unc	BU
1895 Unique	—	—	—	—	—	—

X# M4a DOLLAR
Iron **Subject:** Ranavalo Manjaka III **Note:** Type II. Prev. KY#157e.

Date	Mintage	F	VF	XF	Unc	BU
1895 Unique	—	—	—	—	—	—

MADEIRA ISLANDS

AUTONOMOUS REGION

ECU COINAGE

X# 11 14 ECUS
10.0000 g., 0.9250 Silver 0.2974 oz. ASW, 30 mm. **Subject:** 20th Anniversary of Autonomy **Obv:** 12 stars in outer ring, arms with seal supporters at center **Obv. Legend:** MADEIRA **Obv. Designer:** L. L. Palhao **Rev:** Statue, landscape **Rev. Legend:** AUTONOMIA A RECONSTRUÇÃO DE PORTUGAL NO ATLÂNTICO **Edge:** Reeded

Date	Mintage	F	VF	XF	Unc	BU
1994 Proof	20,000	Value: 40.00				

X# 12 21 ECUS
19.2000 g., 0.9250 Silver 0.5710 oz. ASW, 38.6 mm. **Subject:** 20th Anniversary of Autonomy **Obv. Designer:** L. L. Palhao **Rev:** Statue, portal, seascape **Rev. Legend:** ILHAS DA MADEIRA E DO PORTO SANTO 1976-1996 **Edge:** Reeded

Date	Mintage	F	VF	XF	Unc	BU
1994 Proof	15,000	Value: 55.00				

X# 13 70 ECUS
6.2200 g., 0.9990 Gold 0.1998 oz. AGW, 22 mm. **Subject:** 20th Anniversary of Autonomy **Obv. Designer:** L. L. Palhao **Rev:** Statue **Rev. Legend:** AUTONOMIA A RECONSTRUÇÃO NO ATLÂNTICO **Edge:** Reeded

Date	Mintage	F	VF	XF	Unc	BU
1994 Proof	5,000	Value: 175				

FANTASY EURO PATTERNS

INA Series

X# Pn1 EURO CENT
4.7300 g., Copper, 16.8 mm. **Obv:** Shark, shield below **Obv. Legend:** REPUBLICA PORTUGUESA REGIAO AUTÔNOMA DA MADEIRA **Rev:** Scales at right

Date	Mintage	F	VF	XF	Unc	BU
2005	—	—	—	—	—	1.50
2005 Proof	—	Value: 2.50				

X# Pn2 2 EURO CENT
5.8000 g., Copper, 18.7 mm. **Obv:** Shark, shield below **Obv. Legend:** REPUBLICA PORTUGUESA REGIAO AUTÔNOMA DA MADEIRA **Rev:** Scales at right

Date	Mintage	F	VF	XF	Unc	BU
2005	—	—	—	—	—	2.00
2005 Proof	—	Value: 3.00				

X# Pn3 5 EURO CENT
7.2500 g., Copper, 20.8 mm. **Obv:** Shark, shield below **Obv. Legend:** REPUBLICA PORTUGUESA REGIAO AUTÔNOMA DA MADEIRA **Rev:** Scales at right

Date	Mintage	F	VF	XF	Unc	BU
2005	—	—	—	—	—	2.50
2005 Proof	—	Value: 3.50				

X# Pn4 10 EURO CENT

6.0000 g., Goldine, 19.3 mm. **Obv:** Two glasses of wine, stylized sun, shield below **Obv. Legend:** REPUBLICA PORTUGUESA REGIAO AUTÔNOMA DA MADEIRA **Rev:** Dove above value within wreath of clasped hands

Date	Mintage	F	VF	XF	Unc	BU
2005	—	—	—	—	—	3.00
2005 Proof	2,005	Value: 4.00				

X# Pn5 20 EURO CENT

7.8400 g., Goldine, 22.1 mm. **Obv:** Two glasses of wine, stylized sun, shield below **Obv. Legend:** REPUBLICA PORTUGUESA REGIAO AUTÔNOMA DE MADEIRA **Rev:** Dove above value within wreath of clasped hands

Date	Mintage	F	VF	XF	Unc	BU
2005	—	—	—	—	—	3.50
2005 Proof	—	Value: 5.00				

X# Pn6 50 EURO CENT

9.5600 g., Goldine, 24.5 mm. **Obv:** Two glasses of wine, stylized sun, shield below **Obv. Legend:** REPUBLICA PORTUGUESA REGIAO AUTÔNOMA DE MADEIRA **Rev:** Dove above value within wreath of clasped hands

Date	Mintage	F	VF	XF	Unc	BU
2005	—	—	—	—	—	4.00
2005 Proof	—	Value: 6.00				

X# Pn7 EURO

8.4500 g., Bi-Metallic Goldine ring, copper-nickel center, 23 mm. **Obv:** Bust of João Goncalves Zarco facing, shield at right **Obv. Legend:** REPUBLICA PORTUGUESA REGIAO AUTÔNOMA DE MADEIRA **Rev:** Sun above old sailing ship **Edge:** Plain

Date	Mintage	F	VF	XF	Unc	BU
2005	—	—	—	—	—	6.00
2005 Proof	—	Value: 8.00				

X# Pn8 2 EURO

Bi-Metallic Copper-nickel ring, goldine center, 25.8 mm. **Obv:** Bust f João Goncalves Zarco facing, shield at right **Obv. Legend:** REPUBLICA PORTUGUESA REGIAO AUTÔNOMA DE MADEIRA **Rev:** Sun above old sailing ship **Edge:** Plain

Date	Mintage	F	VF	XF	Unc	BU
2005	—	—	—	—	—	8.00
2005 Proof	—	Value: 10.00				

FANTASY EURO PATTERNS

INA Series

MINT SETS

X#	Date	Mintage	Identification	Issue Price	Mkt Val
XMS1	2005 (8)	—	X#Pn1-Pn8	—	30.00

PROOF SETS

X#	Date	Mintage	Identification	Issue Price	Mkt Val
XPS1	2005 (9)	—	X-Pn1-Pn9	—	50.00

MALAYA

KELANTAN

SULTANATE

ISLAMIC GOLD BULLION

X# 1 1/4 DINAR

0.5000 g., 0.9166 Gold 0.0147 oz. AGW, 21 mm.

Date	Mintage	F	VF	XF	Unc	BU
AH1427	—	—	—	—	—	27.00

X# 2 1/2 DINAR

1.0600 g., 0.9166 Gold 0.0312 oz. AGW, 20 mm.

Date	Mintage	F	VF	XF	Unc	BU
AH1427	—	—	—	—	—	48.00

X# 3 DINAR

4.2500 g., 0.9166 Gold 0.1252 oz. AGW, 23 mm.

Date	Mintage	F	VF	XF	Unc	BU
AH1427	—	—	—	—	—	90.00

MALDIVE ISLANDS

2ND REPUBLIC

MEDALLIC COINAGE

X# MA1 25 RUFIYAA

Copper-Nickel **Subject:** International Games - soccer **Obv:** National emblem - crescent moon, star and palm tree flanked by 2 flags. **Rev:** 2 Soccer players **Note:** Prev. KM#M1.

Date	Mintage	F	VF	XF	Unc	BU
AH1405 Proof	—	Value: 12.50				

X# MA2 25 RUFIYAA

Copper-Nickel, Swimmer mm. **Subject:** International Games - swimming **Obv:** National emblem - crescent moon, star and palm tree flanked by 2 flags. **Note:** Prev. KM#M2.

Date	Mintage	F	VF	XF	Unc	BU
AH1405 Proof	—	Value: 18.50				

ICB Ltd. Issues

X# 1 250 RUFIYAA

24.0000 g., 0.9250 Silver 0.7137 oz. ASW, 38 mm. **Obv:** Arms **Rev:** Early sailing ship, island in background at left, tropical fish in color below **Rev. Legend:** BEAUTIFUL MALDIVES

Date	Mintage	F	VF	XF	Unc	BU
1996 Proof	10	Value: 125				

X# 1a.1 250 RUFIYAA

23.0000 g., Brass, 38 mm. **Obv:** Arms **Rev:** Early sailing ship, island in background at left, tropical fish in color below **Rev. Legend:** BEAUTIFUL MALDIVES **Edge:** Reeded

Date	Mintage	F	VF	XF	Unc	BU
1996 Proof	100	Value: 45.00				

X# 1a.2 250 RUFIYAA

23.0000 g., Brass, 38 mm. **Obv:** Arms **Rev:** Early sailing ship, island in background at left, tropical fish in color below **Rev. Legend:** BEAUTIFUL MALDIVES **Edge:** Plain

Date	Mintage	F	VF	XF	Unc	BU
1996 Proof	100	Value: 45.00				

X# 1b.1 250 RUFIYAA

20.0000 g., Gilt Alloy, 38 mm. **Obv:** Arms **Rev:** Early sailing ship, island in background at left, tropical fish in color below **Rev. Legend:** BEAUTIFUL MALDIVES **Edge:** Reeded

Date	Mintage	F	VF	XF	Unc	BU
1996 Proof	100	Value: 45.00				

X# 1b.2 250 RUFIYAA

20.0000 g., Gilt Alloy, 38 mm. **Obv:** Arms **Rev:** Early sailing ship, island in background at left, tropical fish in color below **Rev. Legend:** BEAUTIFUL MALDIVES **Edge:** Plain

Date	Mintage	F	VF	XF	Unc	BU
1996 Proof	100	Value: 45.00				

X# 1c.1 250 RUFIYAA

23.0000 g., Tri-Metallic Silvered and gilt Brass, 38 mm. **Obv:** Arms **Rev:** Early sailing ship, island in background at left, tropical fish in color below **Rev. Legend:** BEAUTIFUL MALDIVES **Edge:** Reeded

Date	Mintage	F	VF	XF	Unc	BU
1996 Proof	100	Value: 60.00				

X# 1c.2 250 RUFIYAA

23.0000 g., Tri-Metallic Silvered and gilt Brass, 38 mm. **Obv:** Arms **Rev:** Early sailing ship, island in background at left, tropical fish in color below **Edge:** Plain

Date	Mintage	F	VF	XF	Unc	BU
1996 Proof	100	Value: 60.00				

X# 1d.1 250 RUFIYAA

6.0000 g., Aluminum, 38 mm. **Obv:** Arms **Rev:** Early sailing ship, island in background at left, tropical fish in color below **Rev. Legend:** BEAUTIFUL MALDIVES **Edge:** Reeded

Date	Mintage	F	VF	XF	Unc	BU
1996 Proof	100	Value: 45.00				

X# 1d.2 250 RUFIYAA

6.0000 g., Aluminum, 38 mm. **Obv:** Arms **Rev:** Early sailing ship, island in background at left, tropical fish in color below **Rev. Legend:** BEAUTIFUL MALDIVES **Edge:** Plain

Date	Mintage	F	VF	XF	Unc	BU
1996 Proof	100	Value: 45.00				

X# 1e.1 250 RUFIYAA

23.0000 g., Copper, 38 mm. **Obv:** Arms **Rev:** Early sailing ship, island in background at left, tropical fish in color below **Rev. Legend:** BEAUTIFUL MALDIVES **Edge:** Reeded

Date	Mintage	F	VF	XF	Unc	BU
1996 Proof	100	Value: 45.00				

X# 1e.2 250 RUFIYAA

23.0000 g., Copper, 38 mm. **Obv:** Arms **Rev:** Early sailing ship, island in background at left, tropical fish in color below **Rev. Legend:** BEAUTIFUL MALDIVES **Edge:** Plain

Date	Mintage	F	VF	XF	Unc	BU
1996 Proof	100	Value: 45.00				

X# 1f.1 250 RUFIYAA

20.0000 g., Copper-Nickel, 38 mm. **Obv:** Arms **Rev:** Early sailing ship, island in background at left, tropical fish in color below **Rev. Legend:** BEAUTIFUL MALDIVES **Edge:** Reeded

Date	Mintage	F	VF	XF	Unc	BU
1996 Proof	100	Value: 45.00				

X# 1f.2 250 RUFIYAA

20.0000 g., Copper-Nickel, 38 mm. **Obv:** Arms **Rev:** Early sailing ship, island in background at left, tropical fish in color below **Rev. Legend:** BEAUTIFUL MALDIVES **Edge:** Plain

Date	Mintage	F	VF	XF	Unc	BU
1996 Proof	100	Value: 45.00				

X# 2.1 250 RUFIYAA

24.0000 g., 0.9250 Silver 0.7137 oz. ASW, 38 mm. **Obv:** Arms **Rev:** Early sailing ship, island in background at left, tropical fish below **Rev. Legend:** BEAUTIFUL MALDIVES **Edge:** Reeded

Date	Mintage	F	VF	XF	Unc	BU
1996 Proof	100	Value: 60.00				

X# 2.2 250 RUFIYAA

24.0000 g., 0.9250 Silver 0.7137 oz. ASW, 38 mm. **Obv:** Arms **Rev:** Early sailing ship, island in background at left, tropical fish below **Rev. Legend:** BEAUTIFUL MALDIVES **Edge:** Plain

Date	Mintage	F	VF	XF	Unc	BU
1996 Proof	100	Value: 60.00				

X# 2a.1 250 RUFIYAA

23.0000 g., Brass, 38 mm. **Obv:** Arms **Rev:** Early sailing ship, island in background at left, tropical fish below **Rev. Legend:** BEAUTIFUL MALDIVES **Edge:** Reeded

Date	Mintage	F	VF	XF	Unc	BU
1996 Proof	100	Value: 45.00				

X# 2a.2 250 RUFIYAA

23.0000 g., Brass, 38 mm. **Obv:** Arms **Rev:** Early sailing ship, island in background at left, tropical fish below **Rev. Legend:** BEAUTIFUL MALDIVES **Edge:** Reeded

Date	Mintage	F	VF	XF	Unc	BU
1996 Proof	100	Value: 45.00				

X# 2b.1 250 RUFIYAA

20.0000 g., Gilt Alloy, 38 mm. **Obv:** Arms **Rev:** Early sailing ship, island in background at left, tropical fish below **Rev. Legend:** BEAUTIFUL MALDIVES **Edge:** Reeded

Date	Mintage	F	VF	XF	Unc	BU
1996 Proof	100	Value: 45.00				

X# 2b.2 250 RUFIYAA

20.0000 g., Gilt Alloy, 38 mm. **Obv:** Arms **Rev:** Early sailing ship, island in background at left, tropical fish below **Rev. Legend:** BEAUTIFUL MALDIVES **Edge:** Plain

Date	Mintage	F	VF	XF	Unc	BU
1996 Proof	100	Value: 45.00				

X# 2c.1 250 RUFIYAA

23.0000 g., Tri-Metallic Silvered and gilt Brass, 38 mm. **Obv:** Arms **Rev:** Early sailing ship, island in background at left, tropical fish below **Rev. Legend:** BEAUTIFUL MALDIVES **Edge:** Reeded

Date	Mintage	F	VF	XF	Unc	BU
1996 Proof	100	Value: 60.00				

X# 2c.2 250 RUFIYAA

Tri-Metallic Silvered and gilt Brass, 38 mm. **Obv:** Arms **Rev:** Early sailing ship, island in background at left, tropical fish below **Rev. Legend:** BEAUTIFUL MALDIVES **Edge:** Plain

Date	Mintage	F	VF	XF	Unc	BU
1996 Proof	100	Value: 60.00				

X# 2d.1 250 RUFIYAA

6.0000 g., Aluminum, 38 mm. **Obv:** Arms **Rev:** Early sailing ship, island in background at left, tropical fish below **Rev. Legend:** BEAUTIFUL MALDIVES **Edge:** Reeded

Date	Mintage	F	VF	XF	Unc	BU
1996 Proof	100	Value: 45.00				

X# 2d.2 250 RUFIYAA

6.0000 g., Aluminum, 38 mm. **Obv:** Arms **Rev:** Early sailing ship, island in background at left, tropical fish below **Rev. Legend:** BEAUTIFUL MALDIVES **Edge:** Plain

Date	Mintage	F	VF	XF	Unc	BU
1996 Proof	100	Value: 45.00				

X# 2e.1 250 RUFIYAA

23.0000 g., Copper, 38 mm. **Obv:** Arms **Rev:** Early sailing ship, island in background at left, tropical fish below **Rev. Legend:** BEAUTIFUL MALDIVES **Edge:** Reeded

Date	Mintage	F	VF	XF	Unc	BU
1996 Proof	100	Value: 45.00				

X# 2e.2 250 RUFIYAA

23.0000 g., Copper, 38 mm. **Obv:** Arms **Rev:** Early sailing ship, island in background at left, tropical fish below **Rev. Legend:** BEAUTIFUL MALDIVES **Edge:** Plain

Date	Mintage	F	VF	XF	Unc	BU
1996 Proof	100	Value: 45.00				

X# 2f.1 250 RUFIYAA

20.0000 g., Copper-Nickel, 38 mm. **Obv:** Arms **Rev:** Early sailing ship, island in background at left, tropical fish below **Rev. Legend:** BEAUTIFUL MALDIVES **Edge:** Reeded

Date	Mintage	F	VF	XF	Unc	BU
1996 Proof	100	Value: 45.00				

X# 2f.2 250 RUFIYAA

20.0000 g., Copper-Nickel, 38 mm. **Obv:** Arms **Rev:** Early sailing ship, island in background at left, tropical fish below **Rev. Legend:** BEAUTIFUL MALDIVES **Edge:** Plain

Date	Mintage	F	VF	XF	Unc	BU
1996 Proof	100	Value: 45.00				

PIEFORTS

X#	Date	Mintage	Identification	Mkt Val
P1	1996	—	250 Rufiyaa. 0.9250 Silver. 48.0000 g. X1.	175
P2	1996	—	250 Rufiyaa. 0.9250 Silver. 48.0000 g. X2.	150

MALTA

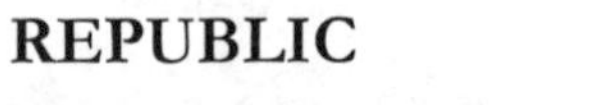

REPUBLIC

FANTASY EURO PATTERNS

2003 Issue

X# Pn10 EURO CENT

Copper Plated Steel **Obv. Legend:** MALTA **Edge:** Plain

Date	Mintage	F	VF	XF	Unc	BU
2003	—	—	—	—	—	1.00

X# Pn11 2 EURO CENT

Copper Plated Steel **Obv. Legend:** MALTA **Edge:** Plain

Date	Mintage	F	VF	XF	Unc	BU
2003	—	—	—	—	—	1.50

X# Pn12 5 EURO CENT

Copper Plated Steel **Obv. Legend:** MALTA

Date	Mintage	F	VF	XF	Unc	BU
2003	—	—	—	—	—	2.00

X# Pn13 10 EURO CENT

Goldine **Obv. Legend:** MALTA

Date	Mintage	F	VF	XF	Unc	BU
2003	—	—	—	—	—	2.50

X# Pn14 20 EURO CENT

Goldine **Obv. Legend:** MALTA

Date	Mintage	F	VF	XF	Unc	BU
2003	—	—	—	—	—	3.00

X# Pn15 50 EURO CENT

Goldine **Obv. Legend:** MALTA

Date	Mintage	F	VF	XF	Unc	BU
2003	—	—	—	—	—	3.50

X# Pn16 EURO

Bi-Metallic **Obv:** Armored bust of Jean Parisot de la Valette facing 3/4 left **Obv. Legend:** MALTA **Rev:** Allegorical woman seated right, large value, EEC star design

Date	Mintage	F	VF	XF	Unc	BU
2003	—	—	—	—	—	5.50

X# Pn17 2 EURO

Bi-Metallic **Obv:** Armored bust of Jean Parisot de la Valette facing 3/4 left **Obv. Legend:** MALTA **Rev:** Allegorical woman seated right, large value, EEC star design

Date	Mintage	F	VF	XF	Unc	BU
2003	—	—	—	—	—	7.50

INA Issues

X# Pn1 EURO CENT

Copper Plated Steel, 16.8 mm. **Obv:** George Cross **Rev:** Scale at right **Edge:** Plain

Date	Mintage	F	VF	XF	Unc	BU
2004	17,500	—	—	—	—	1.50
2004 Proof	3,500	Value: 2.50				

X# Pn1a EURO CENT

Silver, 16.8 mm. **Obv:** George Cross **Rev:** Scale at right **Edge:** Plain

Date	Mintage	F	VF	XF	Unc	BU
2004 Proof	150	Value: 6.00				

X# Pn2 2 EURO CENT

Copper Plated Steel, 18.5 mm. **Obv:** George Cross **Rev:** Scale at right **Edge:** Plain

Date	Mintage	F	VF	XF	Unc	BU
2004	17,500	—	—	—	—	2.00
2004 Proof	3,500	Value: 3.00				

X# Pn2a 2 EURO CENT

Silver, 18.5 mm. **Obv:** George Cross **Rev:** Scale at right **Edge:** Plain

Date	Mintage	F	VF	XF	Unc	BU
2004 Proof	150	Value: 7.00				

X# Pn3 5 EURO CENT

Copper Plated Steel, 20.7 mm. **Obv:** George Cross **Rev:** Scale at right **Edge:** Plain

Date	Mintage	F	VF	XF	Unc	BU
2004	17,500	—	—	—	—	2.50
2004 Proof	3,500	Value: 3.50				

X# Pn3a 5 EURO CENT

Silver, 20.7 mm. **Obv:** George Cross **Rev:** Scale at right **Edge:** Plain

Date	Mintage	F	VF	XF	Unc	BU
2004 Proof	150	Value: 8.50				

X# Pn4 10 EURO CENT

Goldine, 19.3 mm. **Obv:** Tal-Imdina Gate **Rev:** Dove, value in wreath of hands **Edge:** Plain

Date	Mintage	F	VF	XF	Unc	BU
2004	17,500	—	—	—	—	3.00
2004 Proof	3,500	Value: 4.00				

X# Pn4a 10 EURO CENT

Silver, 19.3 mm. **Obv:** Tal-Imdina Gate **Rev:** Dove, value in wreath of hands **Edge:** Plain

Date	Mintage	F	VF	XF	Unc	BU
2004 Proof	150	Value: 10.00				

X# Pn5 20 EURO CENT

Goldine, 22 mm. **Obv:** Tal-Imdina Gate **Rev:** Dove, value in wreath of hands **Edge:** Plain

Date	Mintage	F	VF	XF	Unc	BU
2004	17,500	—	—	—	—	3.50
2004 Proof	3,500	Value: 5.00				

X# Pn5a 20 EURO CENT

Silver, 22 mm. **Obv:** Tal-Imdina Gate **Rev:** Dove, value in wreath of hands **Edge:** Plain

Date	Mintage	F	VF	XF	Unc	BU
2004 Proof	150	Value: 12.50				

X# Pn6 50 EURO CENT

Goldine, 24.3 mm. **Obv:** Tal-Imdina Gate **Rev:** Dove, value in wreath of hands **Edge:** Plain

Date	Mintage	F	VF	XF	Unc	BU
2004	17,500	—	—	—	—	4.00
2004 Proof	3,500	Value: 6.00				

X# Pn6a 50 EURO CENT

Silver, 24.3 mm. **Obv:** Tal-Imdina Gate **Rev:** Dove, value in wreath of hands **Edge:** Plain

Date	Mintage	F	VF	XF	Unc	BU
2004 Proof	150	Value: 15.00				

X# Pn7 EURO

Bi-Metallic, 22.8 mm. **Obv:** Great Siege Monument **Rev:** Sailing ship near Valetta **Edge:** Plain

Date	Mintage	F	VF	XF	Unc	BU
2004	17,500	—	—	—	—	6.00
2004 Proof	3,500	Value: 8.00				

X# Pn7a EURO

Bi-Metallic Brass center in Silver ring, 22.8 mm. **Obv:** Great Siege Monument **Rev:** Sailing ship near Valetta **Edge:** Plain

Date	Mintage	F	VF	XF	Unc	BU
2004 Proof	150	Value: 22.50				

X# Pn8 2 EURO

Bi-Metallic, 25.7 mm. **Obv:** Great Siege Monument **Rev:** Sailing ship near Valetta **Edge:** Plain

Date	Mintage	F	VF	XF	Unc	BU
2004	17,500	—	—	—	—	8.00
2004 Proof	3,500	Value: 10.00				

X# Pn8a 2 EURO

Bi-Metallic Brass center in Silver ring, 25.7 mm. **Obv:** Great Siege Monument **Rev:** Sailing ship near Valetta **Edge:** Plain

Date	Mintage	F	VF	XF	Unc	BU
2004 Proof	150	Value: 28.50				

X# Pn9 5 EURO

25.8000 g., Goldine, 36 mm. **Obv:** Great Siege Monument **Rev:** Dolphin leaping, islands behind **Edge:** Plain

Date	Mintage	F	VF	XF	Unc	BU
2004 Proof	3,500	Value: 15.00				

X# Pn9a 5 EURO

Silver, 36 mm. **Obv:** Great Siege Monument **Rev:** Dolphin leaping, islands behind **Edge:** Plain

Date	Mintage	F	VF	XF	Unc	BU
2004 Proof	150	Value: 40.00				

ND Issue

X# Pn18 EURO CENT

Copper Plated Steel **Obv. Legend:** MALTA

Date	Mintage	F	VF	XF	Unc	BU
ND(2004)	—	—	—	—	—	1.00

X# Pn19 2 EURO CENT

Copper Plated Steel **Obv. Legend:** MALTA

Date	Mintage	F	VF	XF	Unc	BU
ND(2004)	—	—	—	—	—	1.50

X# Pn20 5 EURO CENT

Copper Plated Steel **Obv. Legend:** MALTA

Date	Mintage	F	VF	XF	Unc	BU
ND(2004)	—	—	—	—	—	2.00

X# Pn21 10 EURO CENT

Goldine **Obv. Legend:** MALTA

Date	Mintage	F	VF	XF	Unc	BU
ND(2004)	—	—	—	—	—	2.50

X# Pn22 20 EURO CENT

Goldine **Obv. Legend:** MALTA

Date	Mintage	F	VF	XF	Unc	BU
ND(2004)	—	—	—	—	—	3.00

X# Pn23 50 EURO CENT

Goldine **Obv. Legend:** MALTA

Date	Mintage	F	VF	XF	Unc	BU
(2004)	—	—	—	—	—	3.50

X# Pn24 EURO

Bi-Metallic **Obv:** Jane de la Vallette bust robed right **Rev:** Medieval sailing ship, large value, EEC star design

Date	Mintage	F	VF	XF	Unc	BU
ND(2004)	—	—	—	—	—	5.50

X# Pn25 2 EURO

Bi-Metallic **Obv:** Jean de la Vallette bust robed right **Obv. Legend:** MALTA **Rev:** Medieval sailing ship, large value, EEC star design

Date	Mintage	F	VF	XF	Unc	BU
ND(2004)	—	—	—	—	—	7.50

PIEFORTS

X#	Date	Mintage	Identification	Mkt Val
P1	2004	150	5 Euro. Silver. X#Pn9a.	—

MINT SETS

X#	Date	Mintage	Identification	Issue Price	Mkt Val
XMS1	2003 (8)	—	X#Pn10-Pn17	—	26.00
XMS2	2004 (8)	17,500	X#Pn1-Pn8	—	30.00
XMS3	ND(2004) (8)	—	X#Pn18-Pn25	—	26.00

PROOF SETS

X#	Date	Mintage	Identification	Issue Price	Mkt Val
XPS1	2004 (9)	3,500	X#Pn1-Pn9	—	50.00
XPS2	2004 (9)	150	X#Pn1a-Pn9a	—	150

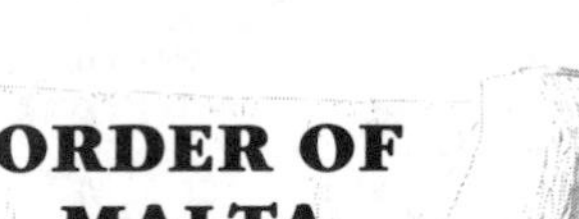

ORDER OF MALTA

SOVEREIGN ORDER

MEDALLIC COINAGE

X# 17 10 GRANI
Bronze **Ruler:** Angelo de Mojana di Cologna
Obv: Crowned Maltese cross **Rev:** Maltese cross above clasped hands **Note:** Prev. KM#M17.

Date	Mintage	F	VF	XF	Unc	BU
1967 Proof	10,000	Value: 12.50				

X# 29 10 GRANI
Bronze **Ruler:** Angelo de Mojana di Cologna
Obv: Crowned Maltese cross **Rev:** Maltese cross above clasped hands **Note:** Prev. KM#M29.

Date	Mintage	F	VF	XF	Unc	BU
1969 Proof	3,000	Value: 15.00				

X# 35 10 GRANI
Bronze **Ruler:** Angelo de Mojana di Cologna
Obv: Crown above two shields **Rev:** Maltese cross above clasped hands **Note:** Prev. KM#35.

Date	Mintage	F	VF	XF	Unc	BU
1970 Proof	3,000	Value: 15.00				

X# 40 10 GRANI
Bronze **Ruler:** Angelo de Mojana di Cologna
Obv: Crowned ornate arms **Obv. Legend:** F. ANGELVS DE MOJANA • M • M • H • H **Rev:** Maltese cross above clasped hands **Note:** Prev. KM#M40.

Date	Mintage	F	VF	XF	Unc	BU
1971 Proof	3,000	Value: 15.00				

X# 46 10 GRANI
Bronze, 30 mm. **Ruler:** Angelo de Mojana di Cologna
Subject: 400th Anniversary - Sea Battle of Lepanto, 1571 **Obv:** Bust right **Rev:** Naval battle scene
Note: Prev. KM#M46.

Date	Mintage	F	VF	XF	Unc	BU
1971 Proof	5,000	Value: 15.00				

X# 48 10 GRANI
Bronze, 29.50 mm. **Ruler:** Angelo de Mojana di Cologna **Obv:** Fr. Angelvs de Mojana bust facing left **Rev:** Maltese cross above clasped hands **Rev. Legend:** ✠ SOVRANO • MILITARE • ORDINE • DI • MALTA **Note:** Prev. KM#M48.

Date	Mintage	F	VF	XF	Unc	BU
1972 Proof	3,000	Value: 15.00				
1973 Proof	3,000	Value: 15.00				

X# 56 10 GRANI
Bronze **Ruler:** Angelo de Mojana di Cologna **Obv:** Bust left **Rev:** Head of St. John **Note:** Prev. KM#M56.

Date	Mintage	F	VF	XF	Unc	BU
1974 Proof	3,000	Value: 15.00				
1975 Proof	3,000	Value: 15.00				
1976 Proof	3,000	Value: 15.00				
1977 Proof	3,000	Value: 15.00				

X# 70 10 GRANI
Bronze, 30 mm. **Ruler:** Angelo de Mojana di Cologna
Obv: Bust left **Rev:** Medieval galley **Note:** Prev. KM#M70.

Date	Mintage	F	VF	XF	Unc	BU
1978 Proof	3,000	Value: 15.00				

X# 74 10 GRANI
Bronze **Ruler:** Angelo de Mojana di Cologna
Obv: Bust right **Rev:** War galley **Note:** Prev. KM#M74.

Date	Mintage	F	VF	XF	Unc	BU
1979 Proof	3,000	Value: 15.00				

X# 80 10 GRANI
Bronze **Ruler:** Angelo de Mojana di Cologna
Obv: Bust right **Rev:** Maltese cross **Rev. Legend:** IN • HOC • SIGNO • MILITAMVS **Note:** Prev. KM#M80.

Date	Mintage	F	VF	XF	Unc	BU
1980 Proof	3,000	Value: 16.50				

X# 85 10 GRANI
Bronze **Ruler:** Angelo de Mojana di Cologna
Series: International Year of Disabled Persons
Obv: Bust left **Note:** Prev. KM#M85.

Date	Mintage	F	VF	XF	Unc	BU
1981 Proof	3,000	Value: 16.50				

X# 90 10 GRANI
Bronze **Ruler:** Angelo de Mojana di Cologna
Subject: 20th Anniversary of Fr. A. de Mojana

Obv: Bust left **Rev:** Crowned ornate arms **Rev. Legend:** * VICESIMO • AB • EIVS • ELECTIONE • FELICITER • REDEVNTE * **Note:** Prev. KM#M90.

Date	Mintage	F	VF	XF	Unc	BU
ND(1982) Proof	2,000	Value: 18.50				

X# 96 10 GRANI

Bronze **Ruler:** Angelo de Mojana di Cologna **Obv:** Bust left **Rev:** Large Maltese cross **Rev. Legend:** IN • HOC • SIGNO • MILITAMVS **Note:** Prev. KM#M96.

Date	Mintage	F	VF	XF	Unc	BU
1983 Proof	2,000	Value: 18.50				

X# 102 10 GRANI

Bronze **Ruler:** Angelo de Mojana di Cologna **Subject:** Piranesi **Obv:** Bust left **Rev:** Ancient male figure **Note:** Prev. KM#M102.

Date	Mintage	F	VF	XF	Unc	BU
1984 Proof	2,000	Value: 18.50				

X# 108 10 GRANI

Bronze **Ruler:** Angelo de Mojana di Cologna **Obv:** Bust left **Rev:** Large Maltese cross **Rev. Legend:** IN • HOC • SIGNO • MILITAMVS **Note:** Prev. KM#M108.

Date	Mintage	F	VF	XF	Unc	BU
1985 Proof	2,000	Value: 18.50				

X# 113 10 GRANI

Bronze, 30 mm. **Ruler:** Angelo de Mojana di Cologna **Obv:** Bust left **Rev:** Grotto of Apparitions at Lourdes **Note:** Prev. KM#M113.

Date	Mintage	F	VF	XF	Unc	BU
1986 Proof	2,000	Value: 18.50				

X# 118 10 GRANI

Bronze **Ruler:** Angelo de Mojana di Cologna **Subject:** 25th Anniversary of Fr. A. de Mojana **Obv:** Bust left **Rev:** Crowned ornate arms **Note:** Prev. KM#M118.

Date	Mintage	F	VF	XF	Unc	BU
1987 Proof	2,000	Value: 18.50				

X# 124 10 GRANI

Bronze, 30 mm. **Ruler:** Angelo de Mojana di Cologna **Obv:** Bust left **Rev:** Medieval galley **Note:** Prev. KM#M124.

Date	Mintage	F	VF	XF	Unc	BU
1988 Proof	2,000	Value: 18.50				

X# 130 10 GRANI

Bronze, 30 mm. **Ruler:** Giancarlo Pallavicini **Subject:** Interregnum **Obv:** Maltese cross **Obv. Legend:** SVB • HOC • SIGNO • MILITAMVS **Rev:** St. John the Baptist holding banner, Paschal Lamb at his feet **Rev. Legend:** NON SURREXIT MAIOR **Note:** Prev. KM#M130.

Date	Mintage	F	VF	XF	Unc	BU
1988 Proof	2,000	Value: 18.50				

X# 136 10 GRANI

Bronze, 30 mm. **Ruler:** Andreas Bertie **Obv:** Fr. Andreas Bertie bust left **Rev:** Crowned and mantled arms **Rev. Legend:** VIRTVS ARIETE FORTIOR **Note:** Prev. KM#M136.

Date	Mintage	F	VF	XF	Unc	BU
1988 Proof	Inc. above	Value: 18.50				

X# 142 10 GRANI

Bronze, 30 mm. **Ruler:** Andreas Bertie **Obv:** Bust left **Rev:** Fra. Gerardo welcoming a beggar **Note:** Prev. KM#M142.

Date	Mintage	F	VF	XF	Unc	BU
1989 Proof	2,000	Value: 18.50				

X# 148 10 GRANI

Bronze, 30 mm. **Ruler:** Andreas Bertie **Obv:** Bust left **Rev:** St. John the Baptist seated 3/4 left **Rev. Legend:** SAN IOANNES BAPTISTA **Note:** Prev. KM#M148.

Date	Mintage	F	VF	XF	Unc	BU
1990 Proof	2,000	Value: 18.50				

X# 153 10 GRANI

Bronze, 30 mm. **Ruler:** Andreas Bertie **Obv:** Bust left **Rev:** St. John the Baptist, kneeling left, praying **Note:** Prev. KM#M153.

Date	Mintage	F	VF	XF	Unc	BU
1991 Proof	2,000	Value: 18.50				

X# 158 10 GRANI

Bronze **Ruler:** Andreas Bertie **Note:** Prev. KM#M158.

Date	Mintage	F	VF	XF	Unc	BU
1992 Proof	2,000	Value: 18.50				

X# 164 10 GRANI

Bronze **Ruler:** Andreas Bertie **Note:** Prev. KM#M164.

Date	Mintage	F	VF	XF	Unc	BU
1993 Proof	2,000	Value: 18.50				

X# 170 10 GRANI

Bronze, 30 mm. **Ruler:** Andreas Bertie **Obv:** Bust left **Rev:** Head of St. John the Baptist **Rev. Legend:** S. JOAN BAPT ORA PRO NOBIS **Note:** Prev. KM#M170.

Date	Mintage	F	VF	XF	Unc	BU
1994 Proof	2,000	Value: 18.50				

X# 176 10 GRANI

Bronze **Ruler:** Andreas Bertie **Note:** Prev. KM#M176.

Date	Mintage	F	VF	XF	Unc	BU
1995 Proof	2,000	Value: 18.50				

X# 181 10 GRANI

8.0000 g., Bronze, 30 mm. **Ruler:** Andreas Bertie **Obv:** Bust left **Rev:** Allegorical scene "assisting a beggar"

Date	Mintage	F	VF	XF	Unc	BU
1996 Proof	—	Value: 18.50				

X# 186 10 GRANI

8.0000 g., Bronze, 30 mm. **Ruler:** Andreas Bertie **Obv:** Bust left **Rev:** Dome of St. Peter's Basilica in ornate frame **Rev. Legend:** SCTA MARIA AVENTINENSIS

Date	Mintage	F	VF	XF	Unc	BU
1997 Proof	—	Value: 18.50				

X# 191 10 GRANI

8.0000 g., Bronze, 30 mm. **Ruler:** Andreas Bertie **Obv:** Bust left **Rev:** Crowned and mantled arms **Rev. Legend:** ELECTIONIS DECENNIUM SUAE IN DOMINO CELEBRANS

Date	Mintage	F	VF	XF	Unc	BU
1998 Proof	1,000	Value: 18.50				

X# 197 10 GRANI

8.0000 g., Bronze, 30 mm. **Ruler:** Andreas Bertie **Subject:** 900th Anniversary of Founding of the Order **Obv:** Bust left **Rev. Legend:** NOVE SECOLI DI VITA DEL SOVRANO MILITARE ORDINE DI MALTA **Edge:** Reeded

Date	Mintage	F	VF	XF	Unc	BU
1999 Proof	1,000	Value: 18.50				

X# 203 10 GRANI

8.0000 g., Bronze, 30 mm. **Ruler:** Andreas Bertie **Obv:** Bust left **Rev:** Allegorical scene - helping a beggar

Date	Mintage	F	VF	XF	Unc	BU
2000 Proof	1,000	Value: 18.50				

X# 210 10 GRANI

8.0000 g., Bronze, 30 mm. **Ruler:** Andreas Bertie **Subject:** Christmas 2001 **Obv:** Bust left **Rev:** Madonna with child, Saint Joseph **Rev. Legend:** NATIVITAS DOMINI NOSTRI IESU CHRISTI

Date	Mintage	F	VF	XF	Unc	BU
2001 Proof	1,000	Value: 18.50				

X# 215 10 GRANI

8.0000 g., Bronze, 30 mm. **Ruler:** Andreas Bertie **Subject:** Christmas 2002 **Obv:** Bust left **Rev:** Madonna with child **Rev. Legend:** NATIVITAS DOMINI NOSTRI IESU CHRISTI

Date	Mintage	F	VF	XF	Unc	BU
2002 Proof	1,000	Value: 18.50				

X# 218 10 GRANI

8.0000 g., Bronze, 30 mm. **Ruler:** Andreas Bertie **Subject:** Christmas 2003 **Obv:** Bust left **Rev:** Madonna with child **Rev. Legend:** NATIVITAS DOMINI NOSTRI IESU CHRISTI

Date	Mintage	F	VF	XF	Unc	BU
2003 Proof	1,000	Value: 18.50				

X# 221 10 GRANI

8.0000 g., Bronze, 30 mm. **Ruler:** Andreas Bertie **Obv:** Bust left **Rev:** Ornate Madonna with child **Rev. Legend:** NATIVITAS DOMINI NOSTRI IESU CHRISTI **Edge:** Reeded

Date	Mintage	F	VF	XF	Unc	BU
2004 Proof	1,000	Value: 18.50				

X# 23 2 TARI

Bronze **Ruler:** Angelo de Mojana di Cologna **Series:** F.A.O. **Obv:** Maltese cross above clasped hands **Rev:** Globe in grain stalks **Rev. Legend:** FIAT • PANIS **Note:** 1 millimeter thick. Prev. KM#M23.1.

Date	Mintage	F	VF	XF	Unc	BU
1968 Proof	20,000	Value: 12.50				

X# 23a 2 TARI

Bronze **Ruler:** Angelo de Mojana di Cologna **Series:** F.A.O. **Note:** 2 millimeters thick. Prev. KM#M23.2.

Date	Mintage	F	VF	XF	Unc	BU
1968 Proof	Inc. above	Value: 13.50				

X# 18 9 TARI

9.0000 g., 0.9000 Silver 0.2604 oz. ASW **Ruler:** Angelo de Mojana di Cologna **Obv:** Crowned ornate arms **Obv. Legend:** F. ANGELVS DE MOJANA ... **Rev:** Large Maltese cross **Rev. Legend:** SVB • HOC • SIGNO • MILITAMVS **Note:** Prev. KM#M18.

Date	Mintage	F	VF	XF	Unc	BU
1967 Proof	10,000	Value: 25.00				

X# 30 9 TARI

9.0000 g., 0.9000 Silver 0.2604 oz. ASW **Ruler:** Angelo de Mojana di Cologna **Obv:** Crowned ornate arms **Rev:** Paschal Lamb standing left, holding banner **Rev. Legend:** ✠ ECCE • AGNVS • DEI • QVI • TOLLIT • PECCATA • MVNDI **Note:** Prev. KM#M30.

Date	Mintage	F	VF	XF	Unc	BU
1969 Proof	3,000	Value: 25.00				

X# 36 9 TARI

9.0000 g., 0.9000 Silver 0.2604 oz. ASW, 29.50 mm. **Ruler:** Angelo de Mojana di Cologna **Obv:** Crowned ornate arms **Rev:** Head of St. John the Baptist **Note:** Prev. KM#M36.

Date	Mintage	F	VF	XF	Unc	BU
1970 Proof	3,000	Value: 25.00				

X# 41 9 TARI

9.0000 g., 0.9000 Silver 0.2604 oz. ASW, 30 mm. **Ruler:** Angelo de Mojana di Cologna **Obv:** Bust left **Rev:** Head of St. John the Baptist **Rev. Legend:** S • IOAN • BAPT • ORA • PRO • NOBIS **Note:** Prev. KM#M41.

Date	Mintage	F	VF	XF	Unc	BU
1971 Proof	3,000	Value: 25.00				

X# 47 9 TARI

9.0000 g., 0.9000 Silver 0.2604 oz. ASW, 30 mm. **Ruler:** Angelo de Mojana di Cologna **Subject:** 400th Anniversary - Battle of Lepanto, 1571 **Obv:** Crown above two shields **Rev:** Naval battle scene **Note:** Prev. KM#M47.

Date	Mintage	F	VF	XF	Unc	BU
1971 Proof	5,000	Value: 25.00				

X# 49 9 TARI

9.0000 g., 0.9000 Silver 0.2604 oz. ASW **Ruler:** Angelo de Mojana di Cologna **Obv:** Fr. Angelvs de Mojana bust facing left **Rev:** Crowned ornate shields **Note:** Prev. KM#M49.

Date	Mintage	F	VF	XF	Unc	BU
1972 Proof	3,000	Value: 25.00				

X# 53 9 TARI

9.0000 g., 0.9000 Silver 0.2604 oz. ASW **Ruler:** Angelo de Mojana di Cologna **Obv:** Bust left **Rev:** Head of St. John the Baptist **Rev. Legend:** S • IOAN • BAPT • ORA • PRO • NOBIS **Note:** Prev. KM#M53.

Date	Mintage	F	VF	XF	Unc	BU
1973 Proof	3,000	Value: 25.00				

X# 57 9 TARI

9.0000 g., 0.9000 Silver 0.2604 oz. ASW **Ruler:** Angelo de Mojana di Cologna **Obv:** Bust left **Rev:** Maltese cross above clasped hands **Rev. Legend:** OVRANO • MILITARE • ORDINE • DI • MALTA **Note:** Prev. KM#M57.

Date	Mintage	F	VF	XF	Unc	BU
1974 Proof	3,000	Value: 25.00				
1975 Proof	3,000	Value: 25.00				
1976 Proof	3,000	Value: 25.00				
1977 Proof	3,000	Value: 25.00				

X# 71 9 TARI

9.0000 g., 0.9000 Silver 0.2604 oz. ASW **Ruler:** Angelo de Mojana di Cologna **Obv:** Bust left **Rev:** Medieval galley **Note:** Prev. KM#M71.

Date	Mintage	F	VF	XF	Unc	BU
1978 Proof	3,000	Value: 25.00				

X# 75 9 TARI

9.0000 g., 0.9000 Silver 0.2604 oz. ASW **Ruler:** Angelo de Mojana di Cologna **Obv:** Bust right **Rev:** Medieval galley **Note:** Prev. KM#M75.

Date	Mintage	F	VF	XF	Unc	BU
1979 Proof	3,000	Value: 25.00				

X# 81 9 TARI
9.0000 g., 0.9000 Silver 0.2604 oz. ASW **Ruler:** Angelo de Mojana di Cologna **Obv:** Bust right **Rev:** Head of St. John the Baptist on a platter **Rev. Legend:** S JOAN • BAPT • ORA • PRO • NOBIS **Note:** Prev. KM#M81.

Date	Mintage	F	VF	XF	Unc	BU
1980 Proof	3,000	Value: 25.00				

X# 86 9 TARI
9.0000 g., 0.9000 Silver 0.2604 oz. ASW **Ruler:** Angelo de Mojana di Cologna **Series:** International Year of Disabled Persons **Obv:** Bust left **Rev:** St. John the Baptist reaching for person in wheelchair **Note:** Prev. KM#M86.

Date	Mintage	F	VF	XF	Unc	BU
1981 Proof	3,000	Value: 25.00				

X# 91 9 TARI
9.0000 g., 0.9000 Silver 0.2604 oz. ASW **Ruler:** Angelo de Mojana di Cologna **Subject:** 20th Anniversary of Fr. A. de Mojana **Obv:** Bust left **Rev:** Crowned ornate arms **Rev. Legend:** VICESIMO • AB • ELECTIONE • FELICITER • REDEVNTE **Note:** Prev. KM#M91.

Date	Mintage	F	VF	XF	Unc	BU
1982 Proof	2,000	Value: 30.00				

X# 97 9 TARI
9.0000 g., 0.9000 Silver 0.2604 oz. ASW **Ruler:** Angelo de Mojana di Cologna **Obv:** Bust left **Rev:** Head of St. John the Baptist on a platter **Note:** Prev. KM#M97.

Date	Mintage	F	VF	XF	Unc	BU
1983 Proof	2,000	Value: 30.00				

X# 103 9 TARI
9.0000 g., 0.9000 Silver 0.2604 oz. ASW, 30 mm. **Ruler:** Angelo de Mojana di Cologna **Obv:** Bust left **Rev:** Building **Note:** Prev. KM#M103.

Date	Mintage	F	VF	XF	Unc	BU
1984 Proof	2,000	Value: 30.00				

X# 109 9 TARI
9.0000 g., 0.9000 Silver 0.2604 oz. ASW **Ruler:** Angelo de Mojana di Cologna **Obv:** Bust left **Rev:** Head of St. John the Baptist on a platter **Note:** Prev. KM#M109.

Date	Mintage	F	VF	XF	Unc	BU
1985 Proof	2,000	Value: 30.00				

X# 114 9 TARI
9.0000 g., 0.9000 Silver 0.2604 oz. ASW, 30 mm. **Ruler:** Angelo de Mojana di Cologna **Obv:** Bust left **Rev:** Basilica at Lourdes **Note:** Prev. KM#M114.

Date	Mintage	F	VF	XF	Unc	BU
1986 Proof	2,000	Value: 30.00				

X# 119 9 TARI
9.0000 g., 0.9000 Silver 0.2604 oz. ASW **Ruler:** Angelo de Mojana di Cologna **Subject:** 25th Anniversary of Fr. A. de Mojana **Obv:** Bust left **Rev:** Crowned ornate arms **Note:** Prev. KM#M119.

Date	Mintage	F	VF	XF	Unc	BU
1987 Proof	2,000	Value: 30.00				

X# 125 9 TARI
9.0000 g., 0.9000 Silver 0.2604 oz. ASW, 30 mm. **Ruler:** Angelo de Mojana di Cologna **Obv:** Bust left **Rev:** Medieval galley **Note:** Prev. KM#M125.

Date	Mintage	F	VF	XF	Unc	BU
1988 Proof	2,000	Value: 30.00				

X# 131 9 TARI
9.0000 g., 0.9000 Silver 0.2604 oz. ASW, 30 mm. **Ruler:** Giancarlo Pallavicini **Subject:** Interregnum **Obv:** Large Maltese cross **Obv. Legend:** ✠ SVB • HOC • SIGNO • MILITAMVS **Rev:** St. John the Baptist standing facing holding banner, Paschal Lamb at his feet **Note:** Prev. KM#M131.

Date	Mintage	F	VF	XF	Unc	BU
1988 Proof	—	Value: 30.00				

X# 137 9 TARI
9.0000 g., 0.9000 Silver 0.2604 oz. ASW, 30 mm. **Ruler:** Andreas Bertie **Obv:** Bust left **Rev:** Crowned and mantled arms **Rev. Legend:** VIRTVS ARIETE FORTIOR **Note:** Prev. KM#M137.

Date	Mintage	F	VF	XF	Unc	BU
1988 Proof	—	Value: 30.00				

X# 143 9 TARI
9.0000 g., 0.9000 Silver 0.2604 oz. ASW, 30 mm. **Ruler:** Andreas Bertie **Obv:** Bust left **Rev:** Head of St. John the Baptist on a platter **Rev. Legend:** S • IOAN • BAPT • ORA PRO NOBIS **Note:** Prev. KM#M143.

Date	Mintage	F	VF	XF	Unc	BU
1989 Proof	2,000	Value: 30.00				

X# 149 9 TARI
8.0000 g., 0.9860 Silver 0.2536 oz. ASW **Ruler:** Andreas Bertie **Obv:** Bust left **Rev:** St. John the Baptist baptising a person **Rev. Legend:** FILIVS MEVS DILECTVS **Note:** Prev. KM#M149.

Date	Mintage	F	VF	XF	Unc	BU
1990 Proof	2,000	Value: 32.50				

X# 154 9 TARI
8.0000 g., 0.9860 Silver 0.2536 oz. ASW, 30 mm. **Ruler:** Andreas Bertie **Obv:** Bust left **Rev:** St. John the Baptist welcoming group of people **Note:** Prev. KM#M154.

Date	Mintage	F	VF	XF	Unc	BU
1991 Proof	2,000	Value: 32.50				

X# 159 9 TARI
8.0000 g., 0.9860 Silver 0.2536 oz. ASW **Ruler:** Andreas Bertie **Note:** Prev. KM#M159.

Date	Mintage	F	VF	XF	Unc	BU
1992 Proof	2,000	Value: 32.50				

X# 165 9 TARI
8.0000 g., 0.9860 Silver 0.2536 oz. ASW **Ruler:** Andreas Bertie **Note:** Prev. KM#M165.

Date	Mintage	F	VF	XF	Unc	BU
1993 Proof	2,000	Value: 32.50				

X# 171 9 TARI
8.0000 g., 0.9860 Silver 0.2536 oz. ASW, 30 mm. **Ruler:** Andreas Bertie **Obv:** Bust left **Rev:** Church of Saint Maria all'Aventino **Note:** Prev. KM#M171.

Date	Mintage	F	VF	XF	Unc	BU
1994 Proof	2,000	Value: 32.50				

X# 177 9 TARI
8.0000 g., 0.9860 Silver 0.2536 oz. ASW **Ruler:** Andreas Bertie **Note:** Prev. KM#M177.

Date	Mintage	F	VF	XF	Unc	BU
1995 Proof	2,000	Value: 32.50				

X# 182 9 TARI
9.0000 g., 0.9860 Silver 0.2853 oz. ASW **Ruler:** Andreas Bertie **Obv:** Bust left **Rev:** Fra' Gerardo assisting a pilgrim **Rev. Legend:** FRA GERARDO 1120

Date	Mintage	F	VF	XF	Unc	BU
1996 Proof	—	Value: 32.50				

X# 187 9 TARI

Silver, 30 mm. **Ruler:** Andreas Bertie **Obv:** Bust left **Rev:** Facade of St. Maria's Church in Aventino

Date	Mintage	F	VF	XF	Unc	BU
1997 Proof	—	Value: 32.50				

X# 192 9 TARI

9.0000 g., 0.9860 Silver 0.2853 oz. ASW, 30 mm. **Ruler:** Andreas Bertie **Obv:** Bust left **Rev:** Crowned and mantled arms **Rev. Legend:** ELECTIONIS DECENNIUM SUAE IN DOMINO CELEBRANS

Date	Mintage	F	VF	XF	Unc	BU
1998 Proof	—	Value: 32.50				

X# 198 9 TARI

9.0000 g., 0.9860 Silver 0.2853 oz. ASW, 30 mm. **Ruler:** Andreas Bertie **Subject:** 900th Anniversary of Founding of the Order **Obv:** Bust left **Rev. Legend:** NOVE SECOLI DI VITA DEL SOVRANO MILITARE ORDINE DI MALTA **Edge:** Reeded

Date	Mintage	F	VF	XF	Unc	BU
1999 Proof	2,000	Value: 32.50				

X# 204 9 TARI

9.0000 g., 0.9860 Silver 0.2853 oz. ASW, 30 mm. **Ruler:** Andreas Bertie **Obv:** Bust left **Rev:** St. John the Baptist **Rev. Legend:** FILIUS MEUS DILECTUS

Date	Mintage	F	VF	XF	Unc	BU
2000 Proof	1,000	Value: 32.50				

X# 211 9 TARI

9.0000 g., 0.9860 Silver 0.2853 oz. ASW, 30 mm. **Ruler:** Andreas Bertie **Subject:** Christmas 2001 **Obv:** Bust left **Rev:** Madonna with child, Saint Joseph **Rev. Legend:** NATIVITAS DOMINI NOSTRI IESU CHRISTI

Date	Mintage	F	VF	XF	Unc	BU
2001 Proof	—	Value: 32.50				

X# 216 9 TARI

9.0000 g., 0.9860 Silver 0.2853 oz. ASW, 30 mm. **Ruler:** Andreas Bertie **Subject:** Christmas 2002 **Obv:** Head left **Rev:** Madonna with child **Rev. Legend:** NATIVITAS DOMINI NOSTRI IESU CHRISTI

Date	Mintage	F	VF	XF	Unc	BU
2002 Proof	1,000	Value: 32.50				

X# 219 9 TARI

9.0000 g., 0.9860 Silver 0.2853 oz. ASW, 30 mm. **Ruler:** Andreas Bertie **Subject:** Christmas 2003 **Obv:** Bust left **Rev:** Madonna with child **Rev. Legend:** NATIVITAS DOMINI NOSTRI IESU CHRISTI

Date	Mintage	F	VF	XF	Unc	BU
2003 Proof	1,000	Value: 32.50				

X# 222 9 TARI

9.0000 g., 0.9860 Silver 0.2853 oz. ASW, 30 mm. **Ruler:** Andreas Bertie **Obv:** Bust left **Rev:** Ornate Madonna with child **Rev. Legend:** NATIVITAS DOMINI NOSTRI IESU CHRISTI

Date	Mintage	F	VF	XF	Unc	BU
2004 Proof	1,000	Value: 32.50				

X# 1 SCUDO

12.0000 g., 0.9860 Silver 0.3804 oz. ASW **Ruler:** Ernesto Paterno-Castello di Carcaci **Obv:** Maltese cross **Rev:** Paschal Lamb left with Order banner **Note:** Prev. KM#M1.

Date	Mintage	F	VF	XF	Unc	BU
1961 Proof	1,200	Value: 25.00				

X# 5 SCUDO

12.0000 g., 0.9860 Silver 0.3804 oz. ASW, 32 mm. **Ruler:** Angelo de Mojana di Cologna **Obv:** Crowned ornate arms **Obv. Legend:** F. ANGELVS DE MOJANA ... **Rev:** Head of St. John the Baptist **Rev. Legend:** S • IOAN • BAPT • ORA • PRO • NOBIS **Note:** Prev. KM#M5.

Date	Mintage	F	VF	XF	Unc	BU
1962 Proof	200	Value: 125				
1963 Proof	600	Value: 65.00				

X# 9 SCUDO

12.0000 g., 0.9860 Silver 0.3804 oz. ASW **Ruler:** Angelo de Mojana di Cologna **Obv:** Bust 3/4 left **Rev:** Head of St. John the Baptist **Rev. Legend:** S • IOAN • BAPT • ORA • PRO • NOBIS **Note:** Prev. KM#M9.

Date	Mintage	F	VF	XF	Unc	BU
1964	4,000	—	—	—	15.00	—
1964 Proof	1,000	Value: 25.00				

X# 13 SCUDO

12.0000 g., 0.9860 Silver 0.3804 oz. ASW, 32 mm. **Ruler:** Angelo de Mojana di Cologna **Obv:** Bust 3/4 left **Rev:** Paschal Lamb left, with banner **Rev. Legend:** ECCE • AGNVS • DEI • QVI • TOLLIT • PECCATA • MVNDI **Note:** Prev. KM#M13.

Date	Mintage	F	VF	XF	Unc	BU
1965 Proof	3,000	Value: 25.00				
1966 Proof	3,000	Value: 25.00				

X# 19 SCUDO

12.0000 g., 0.9860 Silver 0.3804 oz. ASW **Ruler:** Angelo de Mojana di Cologna **Obv:** Bust left **Rev:** Crowned Maltese cross in Order chain **Note:** Prev. KM#M19.

Date	Mintage	F	VF	XF	Unc	BU
1967 Proof	3,000	Value: 25.00				

X# 24 SCUDO

12.0000 g., 0.9860 Silver 0.3804 oz. ASW **Ruler:** Angelo de Mojana di Cologna **Obv:** Bust right **Rev:** St. John standing facing holding banner, Paschal Lamb at his feet **Rev. Legend:** NON • SVRREXIT • MAIOR **Note:** Prev. KM#M24.

Date	Mintage	F	VF	XF	Unc	BU
1968 Proof	3,000	Value: 25.00				

X# 31 SCUDO

12.0000 g., 0.9860 Silver 0.3804 oz. ASW, 32 mm. **Ruler:** Angelo de Mojana di Cologna **Obv:** Bust left **Rev:** St. John the Baptist standing holding Order banner, Paschal Lamb at his feet **Note:** Prev. KM#M31.

Date	Mintage	F	VF	XF	Unc	BU
1969 Proof	3,000	Value: 25.00				

X# 37 SCUDO

12.0000 g., 0.9860 Silver 0.3804 oz. ASW **Ruler:** Angelo de Mojana di Cologna **Obv:** Bust left **Rev:** Crowned shields **Note:** Prev. KM#M37.

Date	Mintage	F	VF	XF	Unc	BU
MCMLXX Proof	3,000	Value: 25.00				

X# 42 SCUDO

12.0000 g., 0.9860 Silver 0.3804 oz. ASW **Ruler:** Angelo de Mojana di Cologna **Obv:** Bust left **Rev:** Crowned shields **Note:** Prev. KM#M42.

Date	Mintage	F	VF	XF	Unc	BU
1971 Proof	3,000	Value: 25.00				
1973 Proof	3,000	Value: 25.00				

X# 50 SCUDO

12.0000 g., 0.9860 Silver 0.3804 oz. ASW
Ruler: Angelo de Mojana di Cologna **Obv:** Bust left
Rev: Maltese cross **Rev. Legend:** SVB • HOC • SIGNO • MILITAMVS **Note:** Prev. KM#M50.

Date	Mintage	F	VF	XF	Unc	BU
1972 Proof	3,000	Value: 25.00				

X# 58 SCUDO

12.0000 g., 0.9860 Silver 0.3804 oz. ASW
Ruler: Angelo de Mojana di Cologna **Obv:** Bust left
Rev: Paschal Lamb standing left, holds banner
Rev. Legend: ✠ ECCE • AGNVS • DEI • QVI • TOLLIT • PECCATA • MVNDI **Note:** Prev. KM#M58.

Date	Mintage	F	VF	XF	Unc	BU
1974 Proof	3,000	Value: 25.00				
1975 Proof	3,000	Value: 25.00				

X# 64 SCUDO

12.0000 g., 0.9860 Silver 0.3804 oz. ASW
Ruler: Angelo de Mojana di Cologna **Obv:** Bust left
Rev: Paschal Lamb standing left, holds banner
Rev. Legend: ✠ ECCE • AGNVS • DEI • QVI • TOLLIT • PECCATA • MVNDI **Note:** Prev. KM#M64.

Date	Mintage	F	VF	XF	Unc	BU
1976 Proof	3,000	Value: 25.00				

X# 67 SCUDO

12.0000 g., 0.9860 Silver 0.3804 oz. ASW
Ruler: Angelo de Mojana di Cologna **Obv:** Bust left
Rev: Building facade **Note:** Prev. KM#M67.

Date	Mintage	F	VF	XF	Unc	BU
1977 Proof	3,000	Value: 25.00				

X# 72 SCUDO

12.0000 g., 0.9860 Silver 0.3804 oz. ASW
Ruler: Angelo de Mojana di Cologna **Obv:** Bust left
Rev: Medieval galley **Note:** Prev. KM#M72.

Date	Mintage	F	VF	XF	Unc	BU
1978 Proof	3,000	Value: 25.00				

X# 76 SCUDO

12.0000 g., 0.9860 Silver 0.3804 oz. ASW
Ruler: Angelo de Mojana di Cologna **Obv:** Bust right
Rev: Castle in Magione, Italy **Note:** Prev. KM#M76.

Date	Mintage	F	VF	XF	Unc	BU
1979 Proof	3,000	Value: 25.00				

X# 82 SCUDO

12.0000 g., 0.9860 Silver 0.3804 oz. ASW
Ruler: Angelo de Mojana di Cologna **Obv:** Bust right
Rev: Crowned arms in Order chain **Note:** Prev. KM#M82.

Date	Mintage	F	VF	XF	Unc	BU
1980 Proof	2,000	Value: 25.00				

X# 87 SCUDO

12.0000 g., 0.9860 Silver 0.3804 oz. ASW
Ruler: Angelo de Mojana di Cologna **Series:** World Food Day **Obv:** Bust left **Rev:** Person wrestling with large locust **Note:** Prev. KM#M87.

Date	Mintage	F	VF	XF	Unc	BU
ND(1981) Proof	2,000	Value: 30.00				

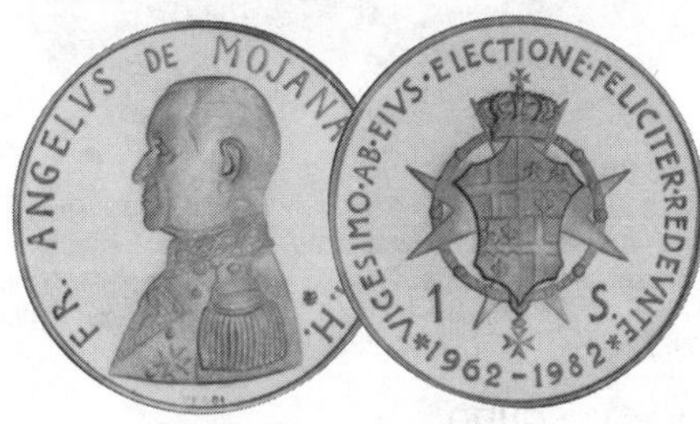

X# 92 SCUDO

12.0000 g., 0.9860 Silver 0.3804 oz. ASW
Ruler: Angelo de Mojana di Cologna **Subject:** 20th Anniversary of Fr. A. de Mojana **Obv:** Bust left
Rev: Crowned arms on Maltese cross in Order chain
Rev. Legend: VIGESIMO • AB • EIVS • ELECTIONE • FELICITER • REDEVENTE **Note:** Prev. KM#M92.

Date	Mintage	F	VF	XF	Unc	BU
ND(1982) Proof	2,000	Value: 30.00				

X# 98 SCUDO

12.0000 g., 0.9860 Silver 0.3804 oz. ASW, 32 mm.
Ruler: Angelo de Mojana di Cologna **Obv:** Bust left
Rev: Paschal Lamb standing left with banner
Rev. Legend: ✠ ECCE • AGNVS • DEI • QVI • TOLLIT • PECCATA • MVNDI **Note:** Prev. KM#M98.

Date	Mintage	F	VF	XF	Unc	BU
1983 Proof	2,000	Value: 30.00				

X# 104 SCUDO

12.0000 g., 0.9860 Silver 0.3804 oz. ASW, 32 mm.
Ruler: Angelo de Mojana di Cologna **Obv:** Bust left
Rev: Building **Note:** Prev. KM#M104.

Date	Mintage	F	VF	XF	Unc	BU
1984 Proof	2,000	Value: 25.00				

X# 110 SCUDO

12.0000 g., 0.9860 Silver 0.3804 oz. ASW
Ruler: Angelo de Mojana di Cologna **Obv:** Bust left
Rev: Crowned ornate arms in Order chain **Note:** Prev. KM#M110.

Date	Mintage	F	VF	XF	Unc	BU
1985 Proof	2,000	Value: 25.00				

X# 115 SCUDO

12.0000 g., 0.9860 Silver 0.3804 oz. ASW, 33 mm.
Ruler: Angelo de Mojana di Cologna **Obv:** Bust left **Rev:** Grotto of Apparitions at Lourdes **Note:** Prev. KM#M115.

Date	Mintage	F	VF	XF	Unc	BU
1986 Proof	2,000	Value: 25.00				

X# 120 SCUDO

12.0000 g., 0.9860 Silver 0.3804 oz. ASW, 33 mm. **Ruler:** Angelo de Mojana di Cologna **Subject:** 25th Anniversary of Fr. A. de Mojana **Obv:** Bust left **Rev:** Crowned ornate arms **Rev. Legend:** FELICE VIGESIMO QVINTO ANNO PRINCIPATVS SVI **Note:** Prev. KM#M120.

Date	Mintage	F	VF	XF	Unc	BU
1987 Proof	2,000	Value: 25.00				

X# 126 SCUDO

12.0000 g., 0.9860 Silver 0.3804 oz. ASW, 32 mm. **Ruler:** Angelo de Mojana di Cologna **Obv:** Bust left **Rev:** Building facade **Note:** Prev. KM#M126.

Date	Mintage	F	VF	XF	Unc	BU
1988 Proof	2,000	Value: 25.00				

X# 138 SCUDO

12.0000 g., 0.9860 Silver 0.3804 oz. ASW **Ruler:** Andreas Bertie **Obv:** Fr. Andreas Bertie bust facing left **Rev:** Crowned and mantled arms **Rev. Legend:** VIRTVS ARIETE FORTIOR **Note:** Prev. KM#M138.

Date	Mintage	F	VF	XF	Unc	BU
1988 Proof	1,000	Value: 30.00				

X# 132 SCUDO

12.0000 g., 0.9860 Silver 0.3804 oz. ASW **Ruler:** Giancarlo Pallavicini **Subject:** Interregnum **Obv:** Maltese cross **Rev:** St. John the Baptist **Rev. Legend:** SUB. HOC ... **Note:** Prev. KM#M132.

Date	Mintage	F	VF	XF	Unc	BU
1988 Proof	Inc. above	Value: 30.00				

X# 144 SCUDO

12.0000 g., 0.9860 Silver 0.3804 oz. ASW, 33 mm. **Ruler:** Andreas Bertie **Obv:** Bust left **Rev:** St. John walking with child and beggar **Note:** Prev. KM#M144.

Date	Mintage	F	VF	XF	Unc	BU
1989 Proof	2,000	Value: 27.50				

X# 150 SCUDO

12.0000 g., 0.9860 Silver 0.3804 oz. ASW **Ruler:** Andreas Bertie **Obv:** Bust left **Rev:** St. John the Baptist seated 3/4 left **Note:** Prev. KM#M150.

Date	Mintage	F	VF	XF	Unc	BU
1990 Proof	2,000	Value: 27.50				

X# 155 SCUDO

12.0000 g., 0.9860 Silver 0.3804 oz. ASW, 33 mm. **Ruler:** Andreas Bertie **Obv:** Bust left **Rev:** Dome of St. Mary's Basilica in ornamental frame **Rev. Legend:** SCTA • MARIA • AVENTINENSIS **Note:** Prev. KM#M155.

Date	Mintage	F	VF	XF	Unc	BU
1991 Proof	2,000	Value: 27.50				

X# 160 SCUDO

12.0000 g., 0.9860 Silver 0.3804 oz. ASW **Ruler:** Andreas Bertie **Note:** Prev. KM#M160.

Date	Mintage	F	VF	XF	Unc	BU
1992 Proof	2,000	Value: 27.50				

X# 166 SCUDO

12.0000 g., 0.9860 Silver 0.3804 oz. ASW **Ruler:** Andreas Bertie **Note:** Prev. KM#M166.

Date	Mintage	F	VF	XF	Unc	BU
1993 Proof	2,000	Value: 27.50				

X# 172 SCUDO

12.0000 g., 0.9860 Silver 0.3804 oz. ASW, 33 mm. **Ruler:** Andreas Bertie **Obv:** Bust left **Rev:** Paschal Lamb left **Rev. Legend:** ✠ ECCE • AGNVS • DEI • QVI • TOLLIT • PECCATA • **Note:** Prev. KM#M172.

Date	Mintage	F	VF	XF	Unc	BU
1994 Proof	2,000	Value: 27.50				

X# 178 SCUDO

12.0000 g., 0.9860 Silver 0.3804 oz. ASW, 33 mm. **Ruler:** Andreas Bertie **Obv:** Bust left **Rev:** Crowned and mantled arms **Rev. Legend:** VIRTUS ARIETE FORTIOR **Note:** Prev. KM#M178.

Date	Mintage	F	VF	XF	Unc	BU
1995 Proof	2,000	Value: 27.50				

X# 183 SCUDO

12.0000 g., 0.9860 Silver 0.3804 oz. ASW, 33 mm. **Ruler:** Andreas Bertie **Obv:** Bust left **Rev:** Grand Cross

Date	Mintage	F	VF	XF	Unc	BU
1996 Proof	2,000	Value: 27.50				
2002 Proof	—	Value: 27.50				

X# 188 SCUDO

12.0000 g., 0.9860 Silver 0.3804 oz. ASW, 32 mm. **Ruler:** Andreas Bertie **Obv:** Portrait left **Rev:** Galley Veneta - Battle of Lepanto **Edge:** Reeded **Note:** Prev. KM#M189.

Date	Mintage	F	VF	XF	Unc	BU
1997 Proof	2,000	Value: 30.00				

X# 193 SCUDO

12.0000 g., 0.9860 Silver 0.3804 oz. ASW, 33 mm. **Ruler:** Andreas Bertie **Obv:** Bust left **Rev:** Crowned and mantled arms **Rev. Legend:** ELECTIONIS DECENNIUM SUAE IN DOMINO CELEBRANS

Date	Mintage	F	VF	XF	Unc	BU
1998 Proof	1,000	Value: 30.00				

X# 199 SCUDO

12.0000 g., 0.9860 Silver 0.3804 oz. ASW, 33 mm. **Ruler:** Andreas Bertie **Subject:** 900th Anniversary of Founding of the Order **Obv:** Bust left **Rev. Legend:** NOVE SECOLI DI VITA DEL SOVRANO MILITARE ORDINE DI MALTA **Edge:** Reeded

Date	Mintage	F	VF	XF	Unc	BU
1999 Proof	1,000	Value: 30.00				

X# 205 SCUDO

12.0000 g., 0.9860 Silver 0.3804 oz. ASW **Ruler:** Andreas Bertie **Obv:** Bust left **Rev:** Residence in Rome

Date	Mintage	F	VF	XF	Unc	BU
2000 Proof	1,000	Value: 30.00				
2004 Proof	—	Value: 30.00				

X# 212 SCUDO

12.0000 g., 0.9860 Silver 0.3804 oz. ASW, 33 mm. **Ruler:** Andreas Bertie **Obv:** Bust left **Rev:** Crowned and mantled arms **Rev. Legend:** VIRTUS ARIETE FORTIOR

Date	Mintage	F	VF	XF	Unc	BU
2001 Proof	1,000	Value: 30.00				

X# 220 SCUDO

12.0000 g., 0.9860 Silver 0.3804 oz. ASW, 40 mm. **Ruler:** Andreas Bertie **Obv:** Bust left **Rev:** Allegorical scene - helping a beggar

Date	Mintage	F	VF	XF	Unc	BU
2003 Proof	1,000	Value: 30.00				

X# 2 2 SCUDI

24.0000 g., 0.9860 Silver 0.7608 oz. ASW **Ruler:** Ernesto Paterno-Castello di Carcaci **Obv:** Maltese cross **Obv. Legend:** SVB • HOC • SIGNO • MILITAMVS **Rev:** Head of St. John the Baptist **Rev. Legend:** S • IOAN • BAPT • ORA • PRO • NOBIS **Note:** Prev. KM#M2.

Date	Mintage	F	VF	XF	Unc	BU
1961 Proof	1,200	Value: 45.00				

X# 6 2 SCUDI

24.0000 g., 0.9860 Silver 0.7608 oz. ASW **Ruler:** Angelo de Mojana di Cologna **Obv:** Crowned ornate arms **Obv. Legend:** F. ANGELVS DE MOJANA ... **Rev:** Grand Master kneeling before St. John the Baptist accepting Order banner **Note:** Prev. KM#M6.

Date	Mintage	F	VF	XF	Unc	BU
1962 Proof	200	Value: 200				
1963 Proof	600	Value: 90.00				

X# 10 2 SCUDI
24.0000 g., 0.9860 Silver 0.7608 oz. ASW
Ruler: Angelo de Mojana di Cologna **Obv:** Bust 3/4 left **Rev:** Crowned ornate arms **Note:** Prev. KM#M10.

Date	Mintage	F	VF	XF	Unc	BU
1964	4,000	—	—	—	30.00	—
1964 Proof	1,000	Value: 50.00				

X# 14 2 SCUDI
24.0000 g., 0.9860 Silver 0.7608 oz. ASW **Ruler:** Angelo de Mojana di Cologna **Obv:** Bust facing 3/4 left **Rev:** St. John the Baptist standing holding banner, Paschal Lamb at his feet **Note:** Prev. KM#M14.

Date	Mintage	F	VF	XF	Unc	BU
1965 Proof	3,000	Value: 45.00				
1966 Proof	3,000	Value: 45.00				

X# 20 2 SCUDI
24.0000 g., 0.9860 Silver 0.7608 oz. ASW
Ruler: Angelo de Mojana di Cologna **Obv:** Bust left **Rev:** Crowned ornate arms **Note:** Prev. KM#M20.

Date	Mintage	F	VF	XF	Unc	BU
1967 Proof	3,000	Value: 45.00				

X# 25 2 SCUDI
24.0000 g., 0.9860 Silver 0.7608 oz. ASW **Ruler:** Angelo de Mojana di Cologna **Obv:** Bust right **Rev:** Crowned Maltese cross **Note:** Prev. KM#M25.

Date	Mintage	F	VF	XF	Unc	BU
1968 Proof	3,000	Value: 35.00				

X# 32 2 SCUDI
24.0000 g., 0.9860 Silver 0.7608 oz. ASW **Ruler:** Angelo de Mojana di Cologna **Obv:** Bust left **Rev:** Crowned ornate arms **Note:** Prev. KM#M32.

Date	Mintage	F	VF	XF	Unc	BU
1969 Proof	3,000	Value: 35.00				

X# 38 2 SCUDI
24.0000 g., 0.9860 Silver 0.7608 oz. ASW
Ruler: Angelo de Mojana di Cologna **Obv:** Bust left **Rev:** Paschal Lamb standing left with banner **Note:** Prev. KM#M38.

Date	Mintage	F	VF	XF	Unc	BU
MCMLXX (1970) Proof	3,000	Value: 35.00				

X# 43 2 SCUDI
24.0000 g., 0.9860 Silver 0.7608 oz. ASW **Ruler:** Angelo de Mojana di Cologna **Obv:** Bust left **Rev:** St. John the Baptist standing facing holding banner, Paschal Lamb at his feet **Note:** Prev. KM#M43.

Date	Mintage	F	VF	XF	Unc	BU
1971 Proof	3,000	Value: 35.00				
1973 Proof	3,000	Value: 35.00				

X# 51 2 SCUDI
24.0000 g., 0.9860 Silver 0.7608 oz. ASW
Ruler: Angelo de Mojana di Cologna **Obv:** Bust left **Rev:** Paschal Lamb left with banner standing on globe **Rev. Legend:** ECCE • AGNVS • DEI • QVI • TOLLIT • PECCATA • MVNDI **Note:** Prev. KM#M51.

Date	Mintage	F	VF	XF	Unc	BU
1972 Proof	3,000	Value: 35.00				

X# 59 2 SCUDI
24.0000 g., 0.9860 Silver 0.7608 oz. ASW **Ruler:** Angelo de Mojana di Cologna **Obv:** Bust left **Rev:** Crowned arms in Order chain **Note:** Prev. KM#M59.

Date	Mintage	F	VF	XF	Unc	BU
1974 Proof	3,000	Value: 35.00				

X# 60 2 SCUDI

24.0000 g., 0.9860 Silver 0.7608 oz. ASW **Ruler:** Angelo de Mojana di Cologna **Obv:** Bust left **Rev:** Head of St. John the Baptist **Rev. Legend:** S • IOAN • BAPT • ORA • PRO • NOBIS **Note:** Prev. KM#M60.

Date	Mintage	F	VF	XF	Unc	BU
1975 Proof	3,000	Value: 35.00				

X# 65 2 SCUDI

24.0000 g., 0.9860 Silver 0.7608 oz. ASW **Ruler:** Angelo de Mojana di Cologna **Obv:** Bust left **Rev:** St. John baptising Christ holding lamp **Note:** Prev. KM#M65.

Date	Mintage	F	VF	XF	Unc	BU
1976 Proof	3,000	Value: 35.00				

X# 68 2 SCUDI

24.0000 g., 0.9860 Silver 0.7608 oz. ASW **Ruler:** Angelo de Mojana di Cologna **Obv:** Bust left **Rev:** Palace **Note:** Prev. KM#M68.

Date	Mintage	F	VF	XF	Unc	BU
1977 Proof	3,000	Value: 35.00				

X# 73 2 SCUDI

24.0000 g., 0.9860 Silver 0.7608 oz. ASW **Ruler:** Angelo de Mojana di Cologna **Obv:** Bust left **Rev:** Medieval galley **Note:** Prev. KM#M73.

Date	Mintage	F	VF	XF	Unc	BU
1978 Proof	3,000	Value: 35.00				

X# 77 2 SCUDI

24.0000 g., 0.9860 Silver 0.7608 oz. ASW **Ruler:** Angelo de Mojana di Cologna **Rev:** Castle in Ipplis Premariacco, Italy **Note:** Prev. KM#M77.

Date	Mintage	F	VF	XF	Unc	BU
1979 Proof	3,000	Value: 35.00				

X# 83 2 SCUDI

24.0000 g., 0.9860 Silver 0.7608 oz. ASW **Ruler:** Angelo de Mojana di Cologna **Obv:** Bust left **Rev:** Paschal Lamb standing left with banner **Note:** Prev. KM#M83.

Date	Mintage	F	VF	XF	Unc	BU
1980 Proof	2,000	Value: 55.00				

X# 88 2 SCUDI

24.0000 g., 0.9860 Silver 0.7608 oz. ASW **Ruler:** Angelo de Mojana di Cologna **Series:** World Food Day **Obv:** Bust left **Rev:** Distributing cooked food **Note:** Prev. KM#M88.

Date	Mintage	F	VF	XF	Unc	BU
1981 Proof	2,000	Value: 55.00				

X# 93 2 SCUDI

24.0000 g., 0.9860 Silver 0.7608 oz. ASW **Ruler:** Angelo de Mojana di Cologna **Subject:** 20th Anniversary of Fr. A. de Mojana **Obv:** Bust left **Rev:** Crowned arms in Order chain **Note:** Prev. KM#M93.

Date	Mintage	F	VF	XF	Unc	BU
ND(1982) Proof	2,000	Value: 55.00				

X# 99 2 SCUDI

24.0000 g., 0.9860 Silver 0.7608 oz. ASW **Ruler:** Angelo de Mojana di Cologna **Obv:** Bust left **Rev:** Crowned ornate arms in Order chain **Note:** Prev. KM#M99.

Date	Mintage	F	VF	XF	Unc	BU
1983 Proof	2,000	Value: 55.00				

X# 106 2 SCUDI
24.0000 g., 0.9860 Silver 0.7608 oz. ASW
Ruler: Angelo de Mojana di Cologna **Obv:** Bust left **Rev:** Palace **Note:** Prev. KM#M105.

Date	Mintage	F	VF	XF	Unc	BU
1984 Proof	2,000	Value: 55.00				

X# 111 2 SCUDI
24.0000 g., 0.9860 Silver 0.7608 oz. ASW **Ruler:** Angelo de Mojana di Cologna **Obv:** Bust left **Rev:** St. John the Baptist baptising a person **Note:** Prev. KM#M111.

Date	Mintage	F	VF	XF	Unc	BU
1985 Proof	2,000	Value: 55.00				

X# 116 2 SCUDI
24.0000 g., 0.9860 Silver 0.7608 oz. ASW **Ruler:** Angelo de Mojana di Cologna **Obv:** Bust left **Rev:** Grotto of Apparitions at Lourdes **Note:** Prev. KM#M116.

Date	Mintage	F	VF	XF	Unc	BU
1986 Proof	2,000	Value: 55.00				

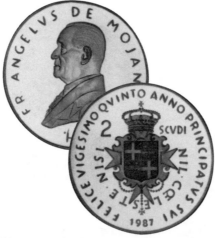

X# 121 2 SCUDI
24.0000 g., 0.9860 Silver 0.7608 oz. ASW **Ruler:** Angelo de Mojana di Cologna **Subject:** 20th Anniversary of Fr. A. de Mojana **Obv:** Bust left **Rev:** Crowned ornate arms **Rev. Legend:** FELICE VIGESIMO QVINTO ANNO PRINCIPATVS SVI **Note:** Prev. KM#M121.

Date	Mintage	F	VF	XF	Unc	BU
1987 Proof	2,000	Value: 55.00				

X# 127 2 SCUDI
24.0000 g., 0.9860 Silver 0.7608 oz. ASW
Ruler: Angelo de Mojana di Cologna **Obv:** Bust left **Rev:** Crowned ornate arms in Order chain **Note:** Prev. KM#M127.

Date	Mintage	F	VF	XF	Unc	BU
1988 Proof	2,000	Value: 60.00				

X# 133 2 SCUDI
24.0000 g., 0.9860 Silver 0.7608 oz. ASW **Ruler:** Giancarlo Pallavicini **Subject:** Interregnum **Obv:** Maltese cross with legend SVB. HOC ... **Rev:** St. John the Baptist **Note:** Prev. KM#M133.

Date	Mintage	F	VF	XF	Unc	BU
1988 Proof	Inc. above	Value: 60.00				

X# 139 2 SCUDI
24.0000 g., 0.9860 Silver 0.7608 oz. ASW
Ruler: Andreas Bertie **Obv:** Bust left **Rev:** Crowned and mantled arms **Note:** Prev. KM#M139.

Date	Mintage	F	VF	XF	Unc	BU
1988 Proof	1,000	Value: 60.00				

X# 145 2 SCUDI
24.0000 g., 0.9860 Silver 0.7608 oz. ASW, 40 mm.
Ruler: Andreas Bertie **Obv:** Bust left **Rev:** St. John the Baptist walking left in highwinds, Paschal Lamb at his feet **Note:** Prev. KM#M145.

Date	Mintage	F	VF	XF	Unc	BU
1989 Proof	2,000	Value: 55.00				

X# 151 2 SCUDI
24.0000 g., 0.9860 Silver 0.7608 oz. ASW, 40 mm.
Ruler: Andreas Bertie **Obv:** Bust left **Rev:** St. John the Baptist baptising a person **Rev. Legend:** FILIVS MEVS DILECTVS **Note:** Prev. KM#M151.

Date	Mintage	F	VF	XF	Unc	BU
1990 Proof	2,000	Value: 55.00				

X# 156 2 SCUDI
24.0000 g., 0.9860 Silver 0.7608 oz. ASW, 40 mm.
Ruler: Andreas Bertie **Obv:** Bust left **Rev:** Order of Malta Palace **Note:** Prev. KM#M156.

Date	Mintage	F	VF	XF	Unc	BU
1991 Proof	2,000	Value: 55.00				

X# 161 2 SCUDI
24.0000 g., 0.9860 Silver 0.7608 oz. ASW
Ruler: Andreas Bertie **Note:** Prev. KM#M161.

Date	Mintage	F	VF	XF	Unc	BU
1992 Proof	2,000	Value: 55.00				

X# 167 2 SCUDI
24.0000 g., 0.9860 Silver 0.7608 oz. ASW
Ruler: Andreas Bertie **Note:** Prev. KM#M167.

Date	Mintage	F	VF	XF	Unc	BU
1993 Proof	2,000	Value: 55.00				

X# 173 2 SCUDI
24.0000 g., 0.9860 Silver 0.7608 oz. ASW, 40 mm. **Ruler:** Andreas Bertie **Obv:** Bust left **Note:** Prev. KM#M173.

Date	Mintage	F	VF	XF	Unc	BU
1994 Proof	2,000	Value: 55.00				

X# 179 2 SCUDI
24.0000 g., 0.9860 Silver 0.7608 oz. ASW, 40 mm. **Ruler:** Andreas Bertie **Obv:** Bust left **Rev:** Early minting scene **Rev. Legend:** SOVRANO MILITARE ORDINE DI MALTA **Note:** Prev. KM#M179.

Date	Mintage	F	VF	XF	Unc	BU
1995 Proof	2,000	Value: 55.00				

X# 184 2 SCUDI
24.0000 g., 0.9860 Silver 0.7608 oz. ASW, 40 mm. **Ruler:** Andreas Bertie **Obv:** Bust left **Rev:** St. John the Baptist walking left preaching the Divine Word **Rev. Legend:** NON SURREXIT MAIOR

Date	Mintage	F	VF	XF	Unc	BU
1996 Proof	—	Value: 55.00				

X# 189 2 SCUDI
24.0000 g., 0.9860 Silver 0.7608 oz. ASW, 40 mm. **Ruler:** Andreas Bertie **Obv:** Bust left **Rev:** Grand Master's Galley ca.1790

Date	Mintage	F	VF	XF	Unc	BU
1997 Proof	2,000	Value: 55.00				

X# 194 2 SCUDI
24.0000 g., 0.9860 Silver 0.7608 oz. ASW, 40 mm. **Ruler:** Andreas Bertie **Obv:** Bust left **Rev:** Crowned and mantled arms **Rev. Legend:** ELECTIONIS DECENNIUM SUAE IN DOMINO CELEBRANS

Date	Mintage	F	VF	XF	Unc	BU
1998 Proof	—	Value: 55.00				
2003 Proof	—	Value: 55.00				

X# 200 2 SCUDI
24.0000 g., 0.9860 Silver 0.7608 oz. ASW, 40 mm. **Ruler:** Andreas Bertie **Subject:** 900th Anniversary of Founding of the Order **Obv:** Bust left **Rev. Legend:** NOVE SECOLI DI VITA DEL SOVRANO MILITARE ORDINE DI MALTA **Edge:** Reeded

Date	Mintage	F	VF	XF	Unc	BU
1999 Proof	1,000	Value: 55.00				

X# 209 2 SCUDI
24.0000 g., 0.9860 Silver 0.7608 oz. ASW, 40 mm. **Ruler:** Andreas Bertie **Subject:** Jubilee Year of the Patron Saint **Obv:** Bust left **Rev:** Dome of St. Peter's Basilica in ornate frame **Rev. Legend:** ANNUS IUBILAEI MM

Date	Mintage	F	VF	XF	Unc	BU
2000 Proof	2,000	Value: 55.00				

X# 206 2 SCUDI
24.0000 g., 0.9860 Silver 0.7608 oz. ASW, 40 mm. **Ruler:** Andreas Bertie **Obv:** Bust left **Rev:** Malta Palace **Rev. Legend:** PALAZZO MALTA

Date	Mintage	F	VF	XF	Unc	BU
2000 Proof	1,000	Value: 55.00				

X# 213 2 SCUDI
24.0000 g., 0.9860 Silver 0.7608 oz. ASW **Ruler:** Andreas Bertie **Obv:** Bust left **Rev:** St. John the Baptist preaching the Divine Word **Rev. Legend:** NO N SURREXIT MAIOR

Date	Mintage	F	VF	XF	Unc	BU
2001 Proof	2,000	Value: 55.00				

X# 217 2 SCUDI
24.0000 g., 0.9860 Silver 0.7608 oz. ASW, 40 mm. **Ruler:** Andreas Bertie **Obv:** Head left **Rev:** Maltese cross

Date	Mintage	F	VF	XF	Unc	BU
2002 Proof	2,000	Value: 55.00				

X# 223 2 SCUDI
24.0000 g., 0.9860 Silver 0.7608 oz. ASW, 40 mm. **Ruler:** Andreas Bertie **Obv:** Bust left **Rev:** Villa Aventino

Date	Mintage	F	VF	XF	Unc	BU
2004 Proof	2,000	Value: 55.00				

X# 26 3 SCUDI
12.0000 g., 0.8000 Silver 0.3086 oz. ASW **Ruler:** Angelo de Mojana di Cologna **Series:** F.A.O. **Obv:** Crowned ornate arms **Rev:** St. John standing with banner, Paschal Lamb lying at his feet **Note:** Prev. KM#M26.

Date	Mintage	F	VF	XF	Unc	BU
1968 Proof	20,000	Value: 20.00				

X# 3 5 SCUDI
4.0000 g., 0.9160 Gold 0.1178 oz. AGW **Ruler:** Ernesto Paterno-Castello di Carcaci **Obv:** Large Maltese cross **Obv. Legend:** SUB • HOC • MILITAMVS **Rev:** St. John the Baptist standing with banner, Paschal Lamb at his feet **Note:** Prev. KM#M3.

Date	Mintage	F	VF	XF	Unc	BU
1961 Proof	1,200	Value: 120				

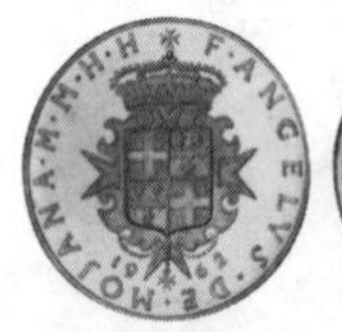 

X# 7 5 SCUDI
4.0000 g., 0.9200 Gold 0.1183 oz. AGW **Ruler:** Angelo de Mojana di Cologna **Obv:** Crowned ornate arms **Rev:** St. John the Baptist standing with banner, Paschal Lamb lying at his feet **Note:** Prev. KM#M7.

Date	Mintage	F	VF	XF	Unc	BU
1962 Proof	200	Value: 400				
1963 Proof	600	Value: 200				

X# 11 5 SCUDI
4.0000 g., 0.9000 Gold 0.1157 oz. AGW **Ruler:** Angelo de Mojana di Cologna **Obv:** Bust 3/4 left **Rev:** St. John the Baptist standing with banner, Paschal Lamb lying at his feet **Note:** Prev. KM#M11.

Date	Mintage	F	VF	XF	Unc	BU
1964 Proof	1,000	Value: 125				

X# 15 5 SCUDI
4.0000 g., 0.9000 Gold 0.1157 oz. AGW **Ruler:** Angelo de Mojana di Cologna **Obv:** Bust 3/4 left **Rev:** St. John the Baptist giving banner to kneeling Grand Master **Note:** Prev. KM#M15.

Date	Mintage	F	VF	XF	Unc	BU
1965 Proof	1,000	Value: 125				
1966 Proof	600	Value: 200				

X# 21 5 SCUDI
4.0000 g., 0.9000 Gold 0.1157 oz. AGW **Ruler:** Angelo de Mojana di Cologna **Obv:** Bust left **Rev:** St. John the Baptist giving banner to kneeling Grand Master **Note:** Prev. KM#M21.

Date	Mintage	F	VF	XF	Unc	BU
1967 Proof	1,000	Value: 125				

X# 27 5 SCUDI
4.0000 g., 0.9000 Gold 0.1157 oz. AGW **Ruler:** Angelo de Mojana di Cologna **Obv:** Bust right **Rev:** St. John the Baptist giving banner to kneeling Grand Master **Note:** Prev. KM#M27.

Date	Mintage	F	VF	XF	Unc	BU
1968 Proof	1,000	Value: 125				

X# 33.1 5 SCUDI
4.0000 g., 0.9000 Gold 0.1157 oz. AGW **Ruler:** Angelo de Mojana di Cologna **Obv:** Bust left **Rev:** Crowned Maltese cross **Note:** Prev. KM#M33.1.

Date	Mintage	F	VF	XF	Unc	BU
1969 Proof	1,000	Value: 125				

X# 33.2 5 SCUDI
4.0000 g., 0.9000 Gold 0.1157 oz. AGW **Ruler:** Angelo de Mojana di Cologna **Obv:** Bust left **Rev:** Crowned Maltese cross **Note:** Prev. KM#M33.2.

Date	Mintage	F	VF	XF	Unc	BU
MCMLXX Proof	1,000	Value: 125				

X# 44 5 SCUDI
4.0000 g., 0.9000 Gold 0.1157 oz. AGW **Ruler:** Angelo de Mojana di Cologna **Obv:** Bust left **Rev:** St. John standing giving a banner to kneeling Grand Master **Rev. Legend:** SVB • HOC • SI - GNO • MILITAMVS **Note:** Prev. KM#M44.

Date	Mintage	F	VF	XF	Unc	BU
1971 Proof	1,000	Value: 125				
1972 Proof	1,000	Value: 125				
1973 Proof	1,000	Value: 125				
1974 Proof	1,000	Value: 125				
1975 Proof	1,000	Value: 125				

X# 66 5 SCUDI
4.0000 g., 0.9000 Gold 0.1157 oz. AGW **Ruler:** Angelo de Mojana di Cologna **Obv:** Bust left **Rev:** St. John the Baptist giving banner to kneeling Grand Master **Note:** Prev. KM#M66.

Date	Mintage	F	VF	XF	Unc	BU
1976 Proof	1,000	Value: 125				
1977 Proof	1,000	Value: 125				
1978 Proof	1,000	Value: 125				

X# 78 5 SCUDI
4.0000 g., 0.9000 Gold 0.1157 oz. AGW **Ruler:** Angelo de Mojana di Cologna **Obv:** Bust right **Rev:** St. John the Baptist giving banner to kneeling Grand Master **Note:** Prev. KM#M78.

Date	Mintage	F	VF	XF	Unc	BU
1979 Proof	1,000	Value: 125				
1980 Proof	600	Value: 185				
1981 Proof	1,000	Value: 135				

X# 94 5 SCUDI
4.0000 g., 0.9000 Gold 0.1157 oz. AGW, 20 mm. **Ruler:** Angelo de Mojana di Cologna **Subject:** 20th Anniversary of Fr. A. de Mojana **Obv:** Bust left **Rev:** Crowned ornate arms in Order chain **Note:** Prev. KM#M94.

Date	Mintage	F	VF	XF	Unc	BU
ND(1982) Proof	600	Value: 200				

X# 100 5 SCUDI
4.0000 g., 0.9000 Gold 0.1157 oz. AGW
Ruler: Angelo de Mojana di Cologna **Obv:** Bust left **Rev:** St. John the Baptist giving banner to kneeling Grand Master **Note:** Prev. KM#M100.

Date	Mintage	F	VF	XF	Unc	BU
1983 Proof	600	Value: 175				

X# 107 5 SCUDI
4.0000 g., 0.9000 Gold 0.1157 oz. AGW
Ruler: Angelo de Mojana di Cologna **Obv:** Bust left **Rev:** St. John the Baptist giving banner to kneeling Grand Master **Note:** Prev. KM#M106.

Date	Mintage	F	VF	XF	Unc	BU
ND(1984-86) Proof	600	Value: 175				

X# 122 5 SCUDI
4.0000 g., 0.9000 Gold 0.1157 oz. AGW
Ruler: Angelo de Mojana di Cologna **Subject:** 25th Anniversary of Fr. A. de Mojana **Obv:** Bust left **Rev:** Crowned ornate arms **Note:** Prev. KM#M122.

Date	Mintage	F	VF	XF	Unc	BU
1987 Proof	600	Value: 175				

X# 128 5 SCUDI
4.0000 g., 0.9000 Gold 0.1157 oz. AGW
Ruler: Angelo de Mojana di Cologna **Obv:** Bust left **Rev:** St. John the Baptist giving banner to kneeling Grand Master **Note:** Prev. KM#M128.

Date	Mintage	F	VF	XF	Unc	BU
1988 Proof	600	Value: 185				

X# 134 5 SCUDI
4.0000 g., 0.9000 Gold 0.1157 oz. AGW
Ruler: Giancarlo Pallavicini **Subject:** Interregnum **Obv:** Maltese cross with legend SVB. HOC ... **Rev:** St. John the Baptist **Note:** Prev. KM#M134.

Date	Mintage	F	VF	XF	Unc	BU
1988 Proof	Inc. above	Value: 185				

X# 140 5 SCUDI
4.0000 g., 0.9000 Gold 0.1157 oz. AGW
Ruler: Andreas Bertie **Obv:** Bust left **Rev:** Crowned and mantled arms **Note:** Prev. KM#M140.

Date	Mintage	F	VF	XF	Unc	BU
1988 Proof	500	Value: 200				

X# 146 5 SCUDI
4.0000 g., 0.9000 Gold 0.1157 oz. AGW, 20 mm.
Ruler: Andreas Bertie **Obv:** Bust left **Rev:** St. John the Baptist giving banner to kneeling Grand Master **Note:** Prev. KM#M146.

Date	Mintage	F	VF	XF	Unc	BU
1989 Proof	600	Value: 125				
1990 Proof	600	Value: 125				
1991 Proof	600	Value: 125				

X# 162 5 SCUDI
4.0000 g., 0.9000 Gold 0.1157 oz. AGW
Ruler: Andreas Bertie **Note:** Prev. KM#M162.

Date	Mintage	F	VF	XF	Unc	BU
1992 Proof	600	Value: 125				

X# 168 5 SCUDI
4.0000 g., 0.9000 Gold 0.1157 oz. AGW
Ruler: Andreas Bertie **Note:** Prev. KM#M168.

Date	Mintage	F	VF	XF	Unc	BU
1993 Proof	600	Value: 125				

X# 175 5 SCUDI
4.0000 g., 0.9000 Gold 0.1157 oz. AGW, 20 mm.
Ruler: Andreas Bertie **Obv:** Bust left **Obv. Designer:** F. Pioli **Rev:** St. John the Baptist presenting standard of the order to the Grand Master kneeling **Rev. Legend:** SUB HOC SIGNO MILITAMUS

Date	Mintage	F	VF	XF	Unc	BU
1994 Proof	600	Value: 125				
1995 Proof	600	Value: 125				
1996 Proof	—	Value: 125				
1997 Proof	—	Value: 125				
2001 Proof	—	Value: 125				
2002 Proof	—	Value: 125				
2003 Proof	—	Value: 125				
2004 Proof	—	Value: 125				

X# 195 5 SCUDI
4.0000 g., 0.9000 Gold 0.1157 oz. AGW, 20 mm.
Ruler: Andreas Bertie **Obv:** Bust left **Rev:** Crowned and mantled arms **Rev. Legend:** ELECTIONIS DECENNIUM SUAE IN DOMINO CELEBRANS

Date	Mintage	F	VF	XF	Unc	BU
1998 Proof	—	Value: 125				

X# 201 5 SCUDI
4.0000 g., 0.9000 Gold 0.1157 oz. AGW, 20 mm.
Ruler: Andreas Bertie **Subject:** 900th Anniversary of Founding of the Order **Obv:** Bust left **Rev. Legend:** NOVE SECOLI DI VITA DEL SOVRANO MILITARE ORDINE DI MALTA **Edge:** Reeded

Date	Mintage	F	VF	XF	Unc	BU
1999 Proof	—	Value: 125				

X# 207 5 SCUDI
4.0000 g., 0.9000 Gold 0.1157 oz. AGW, 20 mm.
Ruler: Andreas Bertie **Obv:** Bust left **Rev:** Grand Master receiving standard from St. John the Baptist **Rev. Legend:** SUB HOC SIGNO MILITAMUS

Date	Mintage	F	VF	XF	Unc	BU
2000 Proof	—	Value: 125				

X# 4 10 SCUDI
8.0000 g., 0.9160 Gold 0.2356 oz. AGW **Ruler:** Ernesto Paterno-Castello di Carcaci **Obv:** Large Maltese cross **Rev:** St. John the Baptist standing facing with banner, Paschal Lamb at his feet **Note:** Prev. KM#M4.

Date	Mintage	F	VF	XF	Unc	BU
1961 Proof	1,200	Value: 230				

X# 8 10 SCUDI
8.0000 g., 0.9200 Gold 0.2366 oz. AGW
Ruler: Angelo de Mojana di Cologna **Obv:** Crowned ornate arms **Rev:** Paschal Lamb standing left with banner **Note:** Prev. KM#M8.

Date	Mintage	F	VF	XF	Unc	BU
1962 Proof	200	Value: 500				
1963 Proof	600	Value: 235				

X# 12 10 SCUDI
8.0000 g., 0.9000 Gold 0.2315 oz. AGW
Ruler: Angelo de Mojana di Cologna **Obv:** Bust 3/4 left **Rev:** Paschal Lamb standing left with banner **Rev. Legend:** ✠ ECCE • AGNVS • DEI • QVI • TOLLIT • PECCATA • MVNOI **Note:** Prev. KM#M12.

Date	Mintage	F	VF	XF	Unc	BU
1964 Proof	1,000	Value: 220				

X# 16 10 SCUDI
8.0000 g., 0.9000 Gold 0.2315 oz. AGW **Ruler:** Angelo de Mojana di Cologna **Note:** Prev. KM#M16.

Date	Mintage	F	VF	XF	Unc	BU
1965 Proof	1,000	Value: 220				
1966 Proof	600	Value: 235				

X# 22 10 SCUDI
8.0000 g., 0.9000 Gold 0.2315 oz. AGW
Ruler: Angelo de Mojana di Cologna **Obv:** Bust left **Rev:** Crowned ornate arms **Note:** Prev. KM#M22.

Date	Mintage	F	VF	XF	Unc	BU
1967 Proof	1,000	Value: 220				

X# 28 10 SCUDI
8.0000 g., 0.9000 Gold 0.2315 oz. AGW
Ruler: Angelo de Mojana di Cologna **Obv:** Bust right **Rev:** Crowned ornate shields **Note:** Prev. KM#M28.

Date	Mintage	F	VF	XF	Unc	BU
1968 Proof	1,000	Value: 220				

X# 34 10 SCUDI
8.0000 g., 0.9000 Gold 0.2315 oz. AGW
Ruler: Angelo de Mojana di Cologna **Obv:** Bust left **Rev:** St. John the Baptist giving banner to kneeling Grand Master **Rev. Legend:** SVB • HOC • SIGNO • MILITAMVS **Note:** Prev. KM#M34.

Date	Mintage	F	VF	XF	Unc	BU
1969 Proof	1,000	Value: 200				
1970 Proof	1,000	Value: 200				

X# 45 10 SCUDI
8.0000 g., 0.9000 Gold 0.2315 oz. AGW
Ruler: Angelo de Mojana di Cologna **Obv:** Bust of Fr. A. de Mojana left **Rev:** Paschal Lamb with banner **Note:** Prev. KM#M45.

Date	Mintage	F	VF	XF	Unc	BU
1971 Proof	1,000	Value: 200				

X# 52 10 SCUDI
8.0000 g., 0.9000 Gold 0.2315 oz. AGW
Ruler: Angelo de Mojana di Cologna **Obv:** Bust left **Rev:** St. John standing with banner, sheep lying at his feet **Rev. Legend:** NON • SVRREXIT • MAIOR

Date	Mintage	F	VF	XF	Unc	BU
1972 Proof	1,000	Value: 200				
1974 Proof	1,000	Value: 200				

X# 55 10 SCUDI
8.0000 g., 0.9000 Gold 0.2315 oz. AGW
Ruler: Angelo de Mojana di Cologna **Obv:** Bust left **Rev:** Paschal Lamb standing left with banner on globe **Rev. Legend:** ECCA • AGNVS • DEI • QVI • TOLLIT • PECCATA • MVNDI **Note:** Prev. KM#M55.

Date	Mintage	F	VF	XF	Unc	BU
1973 Proof	1,000	Value: 220				

X# 61 10 SCUDI
8.0000 g., 0.9000 Gold 0.2315 oz. AGW
Ruler: Angelo de Mojana di Cologna **Obv:** Bust left **Rev:** Crowned ornate arms **Note:** Prev. KM#M61.

Date	Mintage	F	VF	XF	Unc	BU
1975 Proof	1,000	Value: 220				
1976 Proof	1,000	Value: 220				

X# 69 10 SCUDI
8.0000 g., 0.9000 Gold 0.2315 oz. AGW, 25 mm. **Ruler:** Angelo de Mojana di Cologna **Obv:** Bust left **Rev:** St. John the Baptist baptising a person **Note:** Prev. KM#M69.

Date	Mintage	F	VF	XF	Unc	BU
1977 Proof	1,000	Value: 220				
1978 Proof	1,000	Value: 220				

X# 79 10 SCUDI
8.0000 g., 0.9000 Gold 0.2315 oz. AGW, 25 mm.
Ruler: Angelo de Mojana di Cologna **Obv:** Bust right **Rev:** Palace **Note:** Prev. KM#M79.

Date	Mintage	F	VF	XF	Unc	BU
1979 Proof	1,000	Value: 220				

X# 84 10 SCUDI
8.0000 g., 0.9000 Gold 0.2315 oz. AGW, 25 mm.
Ruler: Angelo de Mojana di Cologna **Obv:** Bust right **Rev:** Maltese cross above clasped hands **Note:** Prev. KM#M84.

Date	Mintage	F	VF	XF	Unc	BU
1980 Proof	600	Value: 300				

X# 89 10 SCUDI
8.0000 g., 0.9000 Gold 0.2315 oz. AGW, 25 mm.
Ruler: Angelo de Mojana di Cologna **Series:** World Food Day **Obv:** Bust left **Rev:** Basket of corn ears **Note:** Prev. KM#M89.

Date	Mintage	F	VF	XF	Unc	BU
1981 Proof	1,000	Value: 275				

X# 95 10 SCUDI
8.0000 g., 0.9000 Gold 0.2315 oz. AGW, 25 mm.
Ruler: Angelo de Mojana di Cologna **Subject:** 20th Anniversary of Fr. A. de Mojana **Obv:** Bust left **Rev:** Crowned ornate arms in Order chain **Note:** Prev. KM#M95.

Date	Mintage	F	VF	XF	Unc	BU
ND(1982) Proof	600	Value: 300				

X# 101 10 SCUDI
8.0000 g., 0.9000 Gold 0.2315 oz. AGW, 25 mm.
Ruler: Angelo de Mojana di Cologna **Obv:** Bust left **Note:** Prev. KM#M101.

Date	Mintage	F	VF	XF	Unc	BU
1983 Proof	600	Value: 300				

X# A107 10 SCUDI
8.0000 g., 0.9000 Gold 0.2315 oz. AGW, 25 mm.
Ruler: Angelo de Mojana di Cologna **Obv:** Bust left **Rev:** Altar of Chiesa di Santa Maria al Aventino **Note:** Prev. KM#M107.

Date	Mintage	F	VF	XF	Unc	BU
1984 Proof	600	Value: 300				

X# 112 10 SCUDI
8.0000 g., 0.9000 Gold 0.2315 oz. AGW, 25 mm. **Ruler:** Angelo de Mojana di Cologna **Obv:** Bust left **Rev:** Maltese cross above clasped hands **Note:** Prev. KM#M112.

Date	Mintage	F	VF	XF	Unc	BU
1985 Proof	600	Value: 300				

X# 117 10 SCUDI
8.0000 g., 0.9000 Gold 0.2315 oz. AGW
Ruler: Angelo de Mojana di Cologna **Obv:** Bust left **Rev:** Large Maltese cross **Note:** Prev. KM#M117.

Date	Mintage	F	VF	XF	Unc	BU
1986 Proof	600	Value: 300				

X# 123 10 SCUDI
8.0000 g., 0.9000 Gold 0.2315 oz. AGW
Ruler: Angelo de Mojana di Cologna **Subject:** 25th Anniversary of Fr. A. de Mojana **Obv:** Bust left **Rev:** Crowned ornate arms **Note:** Prev. KM#M123.

Date	Mintage	F	VF	XF	Unc	BU
1987 Proof	600	Value: 300				

X# 129 10 SCUDI
8.0000 g., 0.9000 Gold 0.2315 oz. AGW
Ruler: Angelo de Mojana di Cologna **Obv:** Shoulder-length portrait of Fr. A. Mojana left **Rev:** Similar to KM#M112 **Note:** Prev. KM#M129.

Date	Mintage	F	VF	XF	Unc	BU
1988 Proof	600	Value: 300				

X# 135 10 SCUDI
8.0000 g., 0.9000 Gold 0.2315 oz. AGW
Ruler: Giancarlo Pallavicini **Subject:** Interregnum **Obv:** Maltese cross with legend SVB. HOC ... **Rev:** St. John the Baptist **Note:** Prev. KM#M135.

Date	Mintage	F	VF	XF	Unc	BU
1988 Proof	Inc. above	Value: 300				

X# 141 10 SCUDI
8.0000 g., 0.9000 Gold 0.2315 oz. AGW
Ruler: Giancarlo Pallavicini **Obv:** Fr. Andreas Bertie bust facing left **Rev:** Crowned and mantled arms **Note:** Prev. KM#M141.

Date	Mintage	F	VF	XF	Unc	BU
1988 Proof	500	Value: 300				

X# 147 10 SCUDI
8.0000 g., 0.9000 Gold 0.2315 oz. AGW, 25 mm.
Ruler: Andreas Bertie **Obv:** Bust left **Rev:** Head of St. John the Baptist on a platter **Note:** Prev. KM#M147.

Date	Mintage	F	VF	XF	Unc	BU
1989 Proof	600	Value: 270				

X# 152 10 SCUDI
8.0000 g., 0.9000 Gold 0.2315 oz. AGW, 25 mm.
Ruler: Andreas Bertie **Obv:** Bust left **Rev:** Crowned and mantled arms **Note:** Prev. KM#M152.

Date	Mintage	F	VF	XF	Unc	BU
1990 Proof	600	Value: 270				

X# 157 10 SCUDI
8.0000 g., 0.9000 Gold 0.2315 oz. AGW, 25 mm.
Ruler: Andreas Bertie **Obv:** Bust left **Rev:** St. John the Baptist tending the sick **Note:** Prev. KM#M157.

Date	Mintage	F	VF	XF	Unc	BU
1991 Proof	600	Value: 270				

X# 163 10 SCUDI
8.0000 g., 0.9000 Gold 0.2315 oz. AGW
Ruler: Andreas Bertie **Note:** Prev. KM#M163.

Date	Mintage	F	VF	XF	Unc	BU
1992 Proof	600	Value: 270				

X# 169 10 SCUDI
8.0000 g., 0.9000 Gold 0.2315 oz. AGW
Ruler: Andreas Bertie **Note:** Prev. KM#M169.

Date	Mintage	F	VF	XF	Unc	BU
1993 Proof	600	Value: 270				

X# 174 10 SCUDI
8.0000 g., 0.9000 Gold 0.2315 oz. AGW, 25 mm.
Ruler: Andreas Bertie **Obv:** Bust left **Rev:** Maltese cross above clasped hands **Note:** Prev. KM#M174.

Date	Mintage	F	VF	XF	Unc	BU
1994 Proof	600	Value: 270				

X# 180 10 SCUDI
8.0000 g., 0.9000 Gold 0.2315 oz. AGW, 25 mm.
Ruler: Andreas Bertie **Obv:** Bust left **Rev:** Scene of providing medical assistance **Rev. Legend:** INFIRMIS SERVIRE **Note:** Prev. KM#M180.

Date	Mintage	F	VF	XF	Unc	BU
1995 Proof	600	Value: 270				
2002 Proof	—	Value: 270				

X# 185 10 SCUDI
8.0000 g., 0.9000 Gold 0.2315 oz. AGW, 25 mm.
Ruler: Andreas Bertie **Obv:** Bust left **Rev:** St. John the Baptist aiding an ill man **Rev. Legend:** INFIRMIS SERVIRE FIRMISSIMUM REGNAR

Date	Mintage	F	VF	XF	Unc	BU
1996 Proof	—	Value: 270				
2003 Proof	—	Value: 270				

X# 190 10 SCUDI
8.0000 g., 0.9000 Gold 0.2315 oz. AGW, 25 mm.
Ruler: Andreas Bertie **Obv:** Bust left **Rev:** Galley of Grand Master Emmanuel Pinto de Fonseca, 1741-1773

Date	Mintage	F	VF	XF	Unc	BU
1997 Proof	—	Value: 270				

X# 196 10 SCUDI
8.0000 g., 0.9000 Gold 0.2315 oz. AGW, 25 mm.
Ruler: Andreas Bertie **Obv:** Bust left **Rev:** Crowned and mantled arms **Rev. Legend:** ELECTIONIS DECENNIUM SUAE IN DOMINO CELBRANS

Date	Mintage	F	VF	XF	Unc	BU
1998 Proof	—	Value: 270				

X# 202 10 SCUDI
8.0000 g., 0.9000 Gold 0.2315 oz. AGW, 25 mm.
Ruler: Andreas Bertie **Subject:** 900th Anniversary of Founding of the Order **Obv:** Bust left **Rev. Legend:** NOVE SECOLI DI VITA DEL SOVRANO MILITARE ORDINE DI MALTA **Edge:** Reeded

Date	Mintage	F	VF	XF	Unc	BU
1999 Proof	—	Value: 270				

X# 208 10 SCUDI
8.0000 g., 0.9000 Gold 0.2315 oz. AGW, 25 mm.
Ruler: Andreas Bertie **Obv:** Bust left **Rev:** Maltese cross

Date	Mintage	F	VF	XF	Unc	BU
2000 Proof	—	Value: 270				

X# 214 10 SCUDI
4.0000 g., 0.9000 Gold 0.1157 oz. AGW, 25 mm.
Ruler: Andreas Bertie **Obv:** Bust left **Rev:** Maltese cross above clasped hands

Date	Mintage	F	VF	XF	Unc	BU
2001 Proof	—	Value: 250				

X# 224 10 SCUDI
8.0000 g., 0.9000 Gold 0.2315 oz. AGW
Ruler: Andreas Bertie **Obv:** Bust left **Rev:** Altar in St. Marys Church

Date	Mintage	F	VF	XF	Unc	BU
2004 Proof	—	Value: 270				

X# 39 SOVRANO
8.0500 g., 0.9000 Gold 0.2329 oz. AGW
Ruler: Angelo de Mojana di Cologna **Obv:** Bust left **Rev:** Crowned and mantled arms **Rev. Legend:** SOVRANO • MILITARE • ORDINE • DI • MALTA **Note:** Prev. KM#M39.

Date	Mintage	F	VF	XF	Unc	BU
1970 Proof	15,000	Value: 245				

ORDER OF ST. JOHN OF JERUSALEM

MEDALLIC COINAGE

X# 401 TARI
Brass **Subject:** 400th Anniversary of Great Siege

Date	Mintage	F	VF	XF	Unc	BU
1965 Proof	3,315	Value: 6.50				

X# 402 25 TARI
Franklinium **Subject:** 400th Anniversary of Great Siege

Date	Mintage	F	VF	XF	Unc	BU
1965 Proof	3,316	Value: 12.50				

X# 403 50 TARI
Franklinium **Subject:** 400th Anniversary of Great Siege

Date	Mintage	F	VF	XF	Unc	BU
1965 Proof	3,379	Value: 25.00				

X# 404 ZECCHINO
Copper-Nickel Silvered **Subject:** 400th Anniversary of Great Siege

Date	Mintage	F	VF	XF	Unc	BU
1965 Proof	3,315	Value: 35.00				

X# 404a ZECCHINO
Bronze **Subject:** 400th Anniversary of Great Siege

Date	Mintage	F	VF	XF	Unc	BU
1965 Proof	3	—	—	—	—	—

X# 404b ZECCHINO
Brass **Subject:** 400th Anniversary of Great Siege

Date	Mintage	F	VF	XF	Unc	BU
1965 Proof	3	—	—	—	—	—

X# 404c ZECCHINO
Franklinium **Subject:** 400th Anniversary of Great Siege

Date	Mintage	F	VF	XF	Unc	BU
1965 Proof	3	Value: 250				

X# 404d ZECCHINO
0.9250 Silver **Subject:** 400th Anniversary of Great Siege

Date	Mintage	F	VF	XF	Unc	BU
1965 Proof	3	Value: 350				

X# 404e ZECCHINO
0.9990 Silver **Subject:** 400th Anniversary of Great Siege

Date	Mintage	F	VF	XF	Unc	BU
1965 Proof	3	Value: 350				

X# 404f ZECCHINO
Platinum APW **Subject:** 400th Anniversary of Great Siege

Date	Mintage	F	VF	XF	Unc	BU
1965 Proof	1	—	—	—	—	—

HOSPITALLIER ORDER

FANTASY COINAGE

X# 321 LIRA
7.5000 g., Copper-Nickel, 24.25 mm. **Obv:** Crowned arms **Obv. Legend:** SOVRANO OSPEDALIERO ORDINE DI MALTA **Rev:** Bust of Pope John Paul II left **Rev. Legend:** 10 ANNES PAULUS II **Edge:** Plain

Date	Mintage	VG	F	VF	XF	Unc
2005	—	—	—	—	—	3.50

X# 322 LIRA
7.5000 g., Copper-Nickel, 24.25 mm. **Obv:** Crowned arms **Obv. Legend:** SOVRANO OSPEDALIERO ORDINE DI MALTA **Rev:** Pope John Paul II standing praying at the Wailing Wall **Rev. Legend:** SOLI DEO GLORIA **Edge:** Plain

Date	Mintage	VG	F	VF	XF	Unc
2005	—	—	—	—	—	3.50

X# 323 LIRA
7.5000 g., Copper-Nickel, 24.25 mm. **Obv:** Crowned arms **Obv. Legend:** SOVRANO OSPEDALIERO ORDINE DI MALTA **Rev:** Vatican facade, bust of Pope John Paul II at right **Rev. Legend:** 1978 HABEMUS PAPAM **Edge:** Plain

Date	Mintage	VG	F	VF	XF	Unc
2005	—	—	—	—	—	3.50

X# 324 LIRA
7.5000 g., Copper-Nickel, 24.25 mm. **Obv:** Crowned arms **Obv. Legend:** SOVRANO OSPEDALIERO ORDINE DI MALTA **Rev:** Pope John Paul II descending from airplane in Poland **Rev. Legend:** AD MAIOREM DEI GLORIA **Edge:** Plain

Date	Mintage	VG	F	VF	XF	Unc
2005	—	—	—	—	—	3.50

X# 325 LIRA
7.5000 g., Copper-Nickel, 24.25 mm. **Obv:** Crowned arms **Obv. Legend:** SOVRANO OSPEDALIERO ORDINE DI MALTA **Rev:** Arms at left, Pope John Paul II in prayer at center right **Rev. Legend:** EX CATHEDRA PETRI **Edge:** Plain

Date	Mintage	VG	F	VF	XF	Unc
2005	—	—	—	—	—	3.50

X# 312 25 LIRAS
7.8300 g., 0.9000 Silver 0.2266 oz. ASW, 25.9 mm. **Obv:** Crowned arms **Obv. Legend:** SOVRANO

OSPEDALIERO ORDINE DI MALTA **Rev:** Bust of Pope John Paul II left **Edge:** Reeded

Date	Mintage	F	VF	XF	Unc	BU
2004 Proof	—	Value: 25.00				

X# 301 100 LIRAS

24.6000 g., Copper-Nickel, 38.6 mm. **Subject:** Marine Life Protection **Obv:** Crowned arms **Obv. Legend:** SOVRANO OSPEDALIERO ORDINE DI MALTA **Rev:** Multicolor fish scene **Edge:** Reeded

Date	Mintage	F	VF	XF	Unc	BU
1999 Proof	—	Value: 27.50				

X# 303 100 LIRAS

24.6000 g., Copper-Nickel, 38.6 mm. **Subject:** Marine Life Protection **Obv:** Crowned arms **Obv. Legend:** SOVRANO OSPEDALIERO ORDINE DI MALTA **Rev:** Multicolor fish scene **Edge:** Reeded **Note:** Prev. X#3.

Date	Mintage	F	VF	XF	Unc	BU
2000 Proof	—	Value: 27.50				

X# 305 100 LIRAS

31.1700 g., 0.9990 Silver 1.0011 oz. ASW, 38.5 mm. **Subject:** European Union **Obv:** Crowned arms **Obv. Legend:** SOVRANO OSPEDALIERO ORDINE DI MALTA **Rev:** Poseidon with two horses **Edge:** Reeded **Note:** Prev. KM#M4.

Date	Mintage	F	VF	XF	Unc	BU
2001 Proof	—	Value: 30.00				

X# 302 500 LIRAS

31.2000 g., 0.9990 Silver 1.0021 oz. ASW, 38.6 mm. **Subject:** Alexander the Great **Obv:** Crowned arms **Obv. Legend:** SOVRANO OSPEDALIERO ORDINE DI MALTA **Rev:** Portrait and map **Edge:** Reeded **Note:** Prev. X#5.

Date	Mintage	F	VF	XF	Unc	BU
1999 Proof	—	Value: 45.00				

X# 304 500 LIRAS

31.2000 g., 0.9990 Silver 1.0021 oz. ASW, 38.6 mm. **Subject:** Siege of 1565 **Obv:** Crowned arms **Obv. Legend:** SOVRANO OSPEDALIERO ORDINE DI MALTA **Rev:** Ship and castle **Edge:** Reeded **Note:** Prev. X#6.

Date	Mintage	F	VF	XF	Unc	BU
2000 Proof	—	Value: 45.00				

X# 308 500 LIRAS

32.5000 g., 0.9990 Silver 1.0438 oz. ASW **Subject:** Live in Truth **Obv:** Crowned arms **Obv. Legend:** SOVRANO OSPEDALIERO ORDINE DI MALTA

Date	Mintage	F	VF	XF	Unc	BU
2000 Proof	—	Value: 45.00				

X# 315 500 LIRAS

Gold **Obv:** Crowned arms **Obv. Legend:** SOVRANO OSPEDALIERO ORDINE DI MALTA **Rev:** Bust of Pope John Paul II left

Date	Mintage	F	VF	XF	Unc	BU
2004 Proof	1,000	—	—	—	—	—
2005 Proof	2,000	—	—	—	—	—

X# 316 1000 LIRAS

Gold **Obv:** Crowned arms **Obv. Legend:** SOVRANO OSPEDALIERO ORDINE DI MALTA **Rev:** Pope John Paul II at stone wall

Date	Mintage	F	VF	XF	Unc	BU
2004 Proof	1,000	—	—	—	—	—
2005 Proof	2,000	—	—	—	—	—

X# 306 2500 LIRAS

13.0000 g., 0.9990 Gold 0.4175 oz. AGW, 36.6 mm. **Subject:** 100th Birthday of Emperor Hirohito **Obv:** Crowned arms **Obv. Legend:** SOVRANO OSPEDALIERO ORDINE DI MALTA **Rev:** Hirohito's portrait **Edge:** Reeded **Note:** Mint: B. H. Mayer.

Date	Mintage	F	VF	XF	Unc	BU
2001 Proof	2,001	Value: 325				

X# 317 2500 LIRAS

Gold **Obv:** Crowned arms **Obv. Legend:** SOVRANO OSPEDALIERO ORDINE DI MALTA **Rev:** Papal arms at left, 1/2-length figure of Pope John Paul II facing holding cross

Date	Mintage	F	VF	XF	Unc	BU
2004 Proof	1,000	Value: 325				
2005 Proof	2,000	Value: 325				

X# 318 5000 LIRAS

Gold **Obv:** Crowned arms **Obv. Legend:** SOVRANO OSPEDALIERO ORDINE DI MALTA **Rev:** Saint standing between Pope John Paul II and Archbishop seated

Date	Mintage	F	VF	XF	Unc	BU
2004 Proof	1,000	—	—	—	—	—
2005 Proof	2,000	—	—	—	—	—

X# 319 10000 LIRAS

Gold, 32 mm. **Obv:** Crowned arms **Obv. Legend:** SOVRANO OSPEDALIERO ORDINE DI MALTA **Rev:** Pope John Paul II facing waving, Vatican Guards in foreground

Date	Mintage	F	VF	XF	Unc	BU
2004 Proof	1,000	—	—	—	—	—
2005 Proof	2,000	—	—	—	—	—

PROVAS

X#	Date	Mintage	Identification	Mkt Val
PR1	1961	—	Scudo. M1.	75.00
PR2	1961	—	2 Scudi. M2.	125
PR3	1961	—	5 Scudi. M3.	245
PR4	1961	—	10 Scudi. M4.	350
PR5	1968	—	2 Tari. M23.	25.00
PR6	1968	—	3 Scudi. M26.	50.00

MINT SETS

X#	Date	Mintage	Identification	Issue Price	Mkt Val
XMS1	1964 (2)	4,000	X#9, X#10	—	35.00
XMS2	2005 (5)	—	X#321-325	—	17.50

PROOF SETS

X#	Date	Mintage	Identification	Issue Price	Mkt Val
XPS1	1961 (4)	1,200	X#1-4	—	400
XPS3	1962 (4)	200	X#5-8	—	1,250
XPS4	1963 (4)	600	X#5-8	—	575
XPS6	1964 (4)	1,000	X#9-12	—	400
XPS7	1965 (4)	1,000	X#13-16	—	400
XPS8	1965 (2)	2,000	X#13-14	—	60.00
XPS9	1966 (4)	600	X#13-16	—	500
XPS10	1966 (2)	2,400	X#13-14	—	60.00
XPS11	1967 (4)	1,000	X#19-22	62.50	400
XPS12	1967 (2)	2,000	X#19-20	14.00	60.00
XPS13	1967 (2)	10,000	X#17-18	3.50	35.00
XPS14	1968 (4)	1,000	X#24, 25, 27, 28	62.50	375
XPS15	1968 (2)	2,000	X#24-25	14.00	50.00
XPS16	1968 (2)	20,000	X#23, 26	3.00	30.00
XPS17	1969 (2)	1,000	X#31, 34	75.00	225
XPS18	1969 (2)	2,000	X#31-32	17.00	50.00
XPS19	1969 (2)	10,000	X#29-30	3.00	40.00
XPS20	1970 (4)	1,000	X#33.2, 34, 37, 38	75.00	375
XPS21	1970 (2)	2,000	X#37-38	17.00	50.00
XPS22	1970 (2)	3,000	X#35-36	3.00	40.00
XPS23	1971 (6)	1,000	X#40-45	78.00	420
XPS24	1971 (2)	2,000	X#42-43	17.00	50.00
XPS25	1971 (2)	2,000	X#40-41	3.00	40.00
XPS26	1971 (2)	5,000	X#46-47	5.00	22.50
XPS27	1972 (4)	1,000	X#44, 50-52	82.00	375
XPS28	1972 (2)	2,000	X#50-51	18.00	50.00
XPS29	1972 (2)	3,000	X#49-50	5.00	40.00
XPS30	1973 (6)	1,000	X#42-44, 48, 53, 55	110	420
XPS31	1973 (2)	2,000	X#42, 43	12.00	50.00
XPS32	1973 (2)	3,000	X#48, 53	6.00	37.50
XPS33	1974 (6)	1,000	X#44, 52, 56-59	170	420
XPS34	1974 (2)	3,000	X#58-59	33.00	50.00
XPS35	1974 (2)	2,000	X#56-57	8.00	37.50
XPS36	1975 (4)	1,000	X#44, 58, 60, 61	170	375
XPS37	1975 (2)	2,000	X#58, 60	30.00	50.00
XPS38	1975 (2)	3,000	X#56-57	8.00	37.50
XPS39	1976 (4)	1,000	X#61, 64-66	180	375
XPS40	1976 (2)	2,000	X#64-65	35.00	50.00
XPS41	1976 (2)	3,000	X#56-57	10.00	37.50
XPS42	1977 (4)	1,000	X#66-69	—	375
XPS43	1977 (2)	2,000	X#67-68	—	50.00
XPS44	1977 (2)	3,000	X#56-57	—	37.50
XPS45	1978 (4)	1,000	X#66, 69, 72, 73	—	375
XPS46	1978 (2)	2,000	X#72-73	—	50.00
XPS47	1978 (2)	3,000	X#70-71	—	37.50
XPS48	1979 (3)	1,000	X#76-79	—	375
XPS49	1979 (2)	2,000	X#76-77	—	50.00
XPS50	1979 (2)	3,000	X#74-75	—	37.50
XPS51	1980 (4)	600	X#78, 82-84	—	575
XPS52	1980 (2)	1,400	X#82-83	—	80.00
XPS53	1980 (2)	3,000	X#80-81	—	40.00
XPS54	1981 (4)	1,000	X#78, 87-89	—	500
XPS55	1981 (2)	1,000	X#87-88	—	85.00
XPS56	1981 (2)	3,000	X#85-86	—	42.50
XPS57	1982 (4)	600	X#92-95	—	585
XPS58	1982 (2)	1,400	X#92-93	—	85.00
XPS59	1982 (2)	2,000	X#90-91	—	50.00
XPS60	1983 (4)	600	X#98-101	—	560
XPS61	1983 (2)	1,400	X#98-99	—	85.00
XPS62	1983 (2)	2,000	X#96-97	—	50.00
XPS63	1984 (4)	600	X#104, 106, 107, A107	—	550
XPS64	1984 (2)	1,400	X#104, 106	—	75.00
XPS65	1984 (2)	2,000	X#102-103	—	47.50
XPS66	1985 (4)	600	X#107, 110-112	—	550
XPS67	1985 (2)	2,000	X#110-111	—	75.00
XPS68	1985 (2)	2,000	X#108-109	—	47.50
XPS69	1986 (4)	600	X#107, 115-117	200	550
XPS70	1986 (2)	2,000	X#115-116	40.00	75.00
XPS71	1986 (2)	2,000	X#113-114	18.00	47.50
XPS72	1987 (2)	600	X#122-123	—	475
XPS73	1987 (2)	2,000	X#120-121	—	75.00
XPS74	1987 (2)	2,000	X#118-119	—	47.50
XPS75	1988 (2)	600	X#128-129	—	485
XPS76	1988 (2)	2,000	X#126-127	—	80.00
XPS77	1988 (2)	2,000	X#124-125	—	47.50
XPS78	1988 (2)	—	X#134-135	—	485
XPS79	1988 (2)	—	X#132-133	—	90.00
XPS80	1988 (2)	—	X#130-131	—	47.50
XPS81	1988 (2)	500	X#140-141	—	500
XPS82	1988 (2)	1,000	X#138-139	—	90.00
XPS83	1988 (2)	—	X#136-137	—	47.50
XPS84	1989 (6)	—	X#142-147	—	500
XPS85	1989 (2)	—	X#146-147	—	375
XPS86	1989 (2)	—	X#144-145	—	85.00
XPS87	1989 (2)	—	X#142-143	—	47.50
XPS88	1990 (4)	—	X#146, 150-152	—	450
XPS89	1990 (2)	—	X#148-149	—	50.00
XPS90	1990 (2)	—	X#150-151	—	85.00
XPS91	1991 (4)	—	X#146, 155-157	—	450
XPS92	1991 (2)	—	X#153-154	—	50.00
XPS93	1991 (2)	—	X#155-156	—	85.00
XPS94	1992 (2)	—	X#160-163	—	450
XPS95	1992 (2)	—	X#158-159	—	50.00
XPS96	1992 (2)	—	X#160-161	—	85.00

X#	Date	Mintage	Identification	Issue Price	Mkt Val
XPS97	1993 (4)	—	X#166-169	—	450
XPS98	1993 (2)	—	X#164-165	—	50.00
XPS99	1993 (2)	—	X#166-167	—	82.50
XPS100	1994 (4)	—	X#172, 173, A174, 175	—	450
XPS101	1994 (2)	—	X#170-171	—	50.00
XPS102	1994 (2)	—	X#172-173	—	85.00
XPS103	1995 (4)	—	X#175, 178-180	—	450
XPS104	1995 (2)	—	X#176-177	—	50.00
XPS105	1995 (2)	—	X#178-179	—	85.00
XPS106	1996 (4)	—	X#175, 183-185	—	450
XPS107	1996 (2)	—	X#181-182	—	50.00
XPS108	1996 (2)	—	X#183-184	—	85.00
XPS109	1997 (4)	—	X#175, M188-M190	—	460
XPS110	1997 (2)	—	X#186-187	—	50.00
XPS111	1997 (2)	—	X#188-189	—	85.00
XPS112	1998 (4)	—	X#193-196	—	460
XPS113	1998 (2)	—	X#191-192	—	50.00
XPS114	1998 (2)	—	X#193-194	—	85.00
XPS115	1999 (4)	—	X#199-202	—	460
XPS116	1999 (2)	—	X#197-198	—	50.00
XPS117	1999 (2)	—	X#199-200	—	85.00
XPS118	2000 (4)	—	X#205-208	—	460
XPS119	2000 (2)	—	X#203-204	—	50.00
XPS120	2000 (2)	—	X#205-206	—	85.00
XPS124	2001 (4)	—	X#175, 212-214	—	460
XPS125	2001 (2)	—	X#210-211	—	50.00
XPS126	2001 (2)	—	X#212-213	—	85.00
XPS127	2002 (4)	—	X#175, 180, 183, 187	—	435
XPS128	2002 (2)	—	X#215-216	—	50.00
XPS129	2002 (2)	—	X#183, 217	—	85.00
XPS130	2003 (4)	—	X#175, 185, 194, 220	—	460
XPS131	2003 (2)	—	X#218-219	—	50.00
XPS132	2003 (2)	—	X#194, 220	—	85.00
XPS133	2004 (4)	—	X#175, 205, 223, 224	—	460
XPS134	2004 (2)	—	X#221-222	—	50.00
XPS135	2004 (2)	—	X#205, 223	—	85.00
XPS136	2004 (6)	1,000	X#315-319 Including bronze medal	—	—
XPS137	2005 (6)	2,000	X#315-319 Including bronze medal	—	—

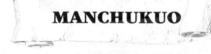

MANCHUKUO

JAPANESE OCCUPATION

World War II

FANTASY COINAGE

Believed to be a modern fabrication

X# 10 CHIEN

Copper **Ruler:** Ta T'ung **Obv:** Crossed flags, florals at left and right **Rev:** Two dragons facing, value between

Date	Mintage	F	VF	XF	Unc	BU
Yr. 5 (1938)	—	—	15.00	20.00	30.00	—

X# 9 CHIEN

Copper **Ruler:** Ta T'ung **Obv:** Crossed flags, florals at left and right **Rev:** Facing dragon

Date	Mintage	VG	F	VF	XF	Unc
Yr. 5 (1938)	—	—	—	15.00	20.00	30.00

MARTINIQUE

FRENCH COLONY

CUT AND COUNTER-MARKED COINAGE

1793-1801

AR = Mr. Ruffy, goldsmith at St. Pierre

FA = Francois Arnsud, goldsmith at Fort Royal

22 or 20 = Fineness of gold

Eagle = Mr. Costet, goldsmith at St. Pierre

X# 5 1/2 BIT

10.0000 g., Bronze **Countermark:** Crowned heart in rectangle **Note:** Countermark on France 5 Centimes, KM#640.2. A modern concoction.

CM Date	Host Date	Good	VG	F	VF	XF
ND	LAN 5 (1796-97) AA	—	—	—	—	—

ESSAIS

Standard thickness

X# E11a 1/4 EURO

10.3100 g., Copper, 27.26 mm. **Obv:** Bust of Louis Oscar Roty half left **Obv. Legend:** MARTINIQUE **Rev:** Electricit? - woman dancing **Edge:** Reeded

Date	Mintage	F	VF	XF	Unc	BU
2004	30	—	—	—	50.00	50.00

X# E15a 20 EURO

10.3200 g., Copper, 27.20 mm. **Obv:** 4 shields of arms with cobras on shields **Obv. Inscription:** MARTINIQUE **Rev:** Great egret **Rev. Legend:** Protectin de la Faune **Edge:** Plain

Date	Mintage	F	VF	XF	Unc	BU
2004	50	—	—	—	50.00	50.00

X# E11 1/4 EURO

7.8000 g., 0.9990 Silver 0.2505 oz. ASW, 27.2 mm. **Series:** Euro **Obv:** Bust of Louis Oscar Roty almost left **Obv. Legend:** MARTINIQUE **Rev:** Electricité (1882 medal) **Edge:** Reeded

Date	Mintage	F	VF	XF	Unc	BU
2004 Proof	2,000	Value: 25.00				

X# E12 1-1/2 EURO

31.1400 g., 0.9990 Silver 1.0000 oz. ASW, 38.6 mm. **Series:** Euro **Obv:** Arms **Obv. Legend:** RÉPUBLIQUE FRANÇAISE **Obv. Inscription:** MARTINIQUE **Rev:** Warship Cuirasé Dunkerque **Rev. Legend:** HISTORIRE DE LA MARINE FRANÇAISE **Edge:** Reeded

Date	Mintage	F	VF	XF	Unc	BU
2004 Proof	2,000	Value: 45.00				

X# E13 1-1/2 EURO

26.0400 g., Brass, 38.6 mm. **Series:** Euro **Obv:** Arms **Obv. Legend:** RÉPUBLIQUE FRANÇAISE **Obv. Inscription:** MARTINIQUE **Rev:** Warship Cuirassé Dunkerque **Rev. Legend:** HISTORIRE DE LA MARINE FRANÇAISE **Edge:** Reeded

Date	Mintage	F	VF	XF	Unc	BU
2004	25	—	—	—	75.00	75.00

X# E15 20 EURO
8.5300 g., 0.9167 Gold 0.2514 oz. AGW, 27.1 mm. **Series:** Euro **Obv:** Arms **Obv. Inscription:** MARTINIQUE **Rev:** Great Egret **Rev. Legend:** Protection de la Faune **Edge:** Plain

Date	Mintage	F	VF	XF	Unc	BU
2004 Proof	300	Value: 280				

FANTASY EURO PATTERNS

European Pattern Collection

X# Pn1 EURO CENT
Copper Plated Steel **Edge:** Plain

Date	Mintage	F	VF	XF	Unc	BU
2005	5,000	—	—	—	—	1.50

X# Pn2 2 EURO CENT
Copper Plated Steel **Edge:** Plain

Date	Mintage	F	VF	XF	Unc	BU
2005	5,000	—	—	—	—	2.00

X# Pn3 5 EURO CENT
Copper Plated Steel **Edge:** Plain

Date	Mintage	F	VF	XF	Unc	BU
2005	5,000	—	—	—	—	2.50

X# Pn4 10 EURO CENT
Goldine **Edge:** Plain

Date	Mintage	F	VF	XF	Unc	BU
2005	5,000	—	—	—	—	3.00

X# Pn5 20 EURO CENT
Goldine **Edge:** Plain

Date	Mintage	F	VF	XF	Unc	BU
2005	5,000	—	—	—	—	3.50

X# Pn6 50 EURO CENT
Goldine **Edge:** Plain

Date	Mintage	F	VF	XF	Unc	BU
2005	5,000	—	—	—	—	4.00

X# Pn7 EURO
Bi-Metallic **Obv:** Outlined map of Martinique, palm trees around rim **Obv. Legend:** *"Martinique"* **Rev:** Large value "1", palm trees around rim **Rev. Legend:** *"Les Antilles"* **Edge:** Plain

Date	Mintage	F	VF	XF	Unc	BU
2005	5,000	—	—	—	—	6.00

X# Pn8 2 EURO
Bi-Metallic **Obv:** Outlined map of Martinique, palm trees around rim **Obv. Legend:** *"Martinique"* **Rev:** Large value "2", palm trees around rim **Rev. Legend:** *"Les Antilles"* **Edge:** Plain

Date	Mintage	F	VF	XF	Unc	BU
2005	5,000	—	—	—	—	8.00

MINT SETS

X#	Date	Mintage	Identification	Issue Price	Mkt Val
XMS1	2005 (8)	5,000	X#Pn1-Pn8	—	30.00

MAURITANIA

REPUBLIC

MEDALLIC COINAGE

X# 1.1 500 OUGUIYA
Copper-Nickel **Subject:** International Athletics - Runners **Rev:** Full baseline

Date	Mintage	F	VF	XF	Unc	BU
1984 Proof	—	Value: 20.00				

X# 1.2 500 OUGUIYA
Copper-Nickel **Subject:** International Athletics - Runners **Rev:** Tapered baseline

Date	Mintage	F	VF	XF	Unc	BU
1984 Proof	—	Value: 20.00				

X# 2 500 OUGUIYA
Copper-Nickel **Subject:** International Athletics - Fencing

Date	Mintage	F	VF	XF	Unc	BU
1984 Proof	—	Value: 30.00				

MAURITIUS

CROWN COLONY

MEDALLIC COINAGE

Richard Lobel Series

X# M1 CROWN
Bronze, 38.10 mm. **Subject:** Edward VIII **Obv:** Bust left **Obv. Legend:** EDWARD • VIII • KING • & • EMPEROR **Rev:** Dodo bird left **Edge:** Plain

Date	Mintage	F	VF	XF	Unc	BU
1936 Proof	500	Value: 20.00				

X# M1a CROWN
Copper-Nickel-Zinc, 38.10 mm. **Subject:** Edward VIII **Obv:** Bust left **Obv. Legend:** EDWARD • VIII • KING • & • EMPEROR **Rev:** Dodo bird left **Edge:** Plain

Date	Mintage	F	VF	XF	Unc	BU
1936 Proof	1,550	Value: 20.00				

X# M1b CROWN
0.9167 Silver, 38.10 mm. **Subject:** Edward VIII **Obv:** Bust left **Obv. Legend:** EDWARD • VIII • KING • & • EMPEROR **Rev:** Dodo bird left **Edge:** Plain

Date	Mintage	F	VF	XF	Unc	BU
1936 Proof	150	Value: 50.00				

X# M1c CROWN
Gold, 38.10 mm. **Subject:** Edward VIII **Obv:** Bust left **Obv. Legend:** EDWARD • VIII • KING • & • EMPEROR **Rev:** Dodo bird left **Edge:** Plain

Date	Mintage	F	VF	XF	Unc	BU
1936 Proof	—	Value: 500				

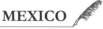

X# M2 SOVEREIGN
0.3750 Gold, 21.98 mm. **Subject:** Edward VIII
Obv: Bust left **Obv. Legend:** EDWARD • VIII • KING • & • EMPEROR **Rev:** Dodo bird left **Edge:** Plain

Date	Mintage	F	VF	XF	Unc	BU
1936 Proof	150	Value: 175				

X# M2a SOVEREIGN
4.4200 g., Silver, 21.98 mm. **Subject:** Edward VIII
Obv: Bust left **Obv. Legend:** EDWARD • VIII • KING • & • EMPEROR **Rev:** Dodo bird left **Edge:** Plain

Date	Mintage	F	VF	XF	Unc	BU
1936 Proof	—	Value: 10.00				

PIEFORTS

X#	Date	Mintage	Identification	Mkt Val
P1	1936	—	Crown. 0.9167 Silver. X#M1b.	100

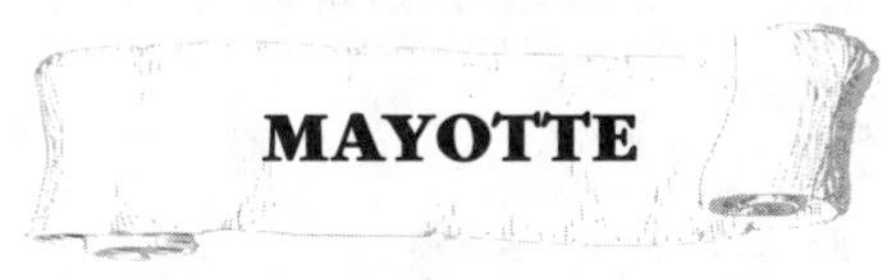

MAYOTTE

FRENCH TERRITORY

ESSAIS

Euro Coinage

X# E11 1/4 EURO
7.8000 g., 0.9990 Silver 0.2505 oz. ASW, 27.2 mm.
Obv: Bust of Louis Oscar Roty almost left **Obv. Legend:** MAYOTTE **Rev:** Maternité (1893 medal) **Edge:** Reeded

Date	Mintage	F	VF	XF	Unc	BU
2004 Proof	2,000	Value: 25.00				

X# E11a 1/4 EURO
10.3400 g., Copper, 27.23 mm. **Obv:** Bust of Louis Oscar Roty half left **Obv. Legend:** MAYOTTE
Rev: Maternité (1893 medal) **Edge:** Reeded

Date	Mintage	F	VF	XF	Unc	BU
2004	30	—	—	—	50.00	50.00

X# E12 1-1/2 EURO
31.1400 g., 0.9990 Silver 1.0000 oz. ASW, 38.6 mm.
Obv: Arms **Obv. Legend:** RÉPUBLIQUE FRANÇAISE
Rev: Ship **Rev. Legend:** HISTORIRE DE LA MARINE FRANÇAISE **Edge:** Reeded

Date	Mintage	F	VF	XF	Unc	BU
2004 Proof	2,000	Value: 45.00				

X# E13 1-1/2 EURO
26.2000 g., Brass antiqued, 39.15 mm. **Obv:** Arms
Obv. Legend: R?PUBLIQUE FRAN?AISE **Rev:** Ship
Rev. Legend: HISTORIRE DE LA MARINE FRAN?AISE **Edge:** Reeded

Date	Mintage	F	VF	XF	Unc	BU
2004	25	—	—	—	75.00	75.00

X# E15 20 EURO
8.5300 g., 0.9167 Gold 0.2514 oz. AGW, 27.1 mm.
Obv: Arms **Obv. Inscription:** Liberté/égalité/fratenité
Rev: Two brown lemurs on branches **Rev. Legend:** PROTECTION DE LA FAUNE **Edge:** Plain

Date	Mintage	F	VF	XF	Unc	BU
2004 Proof	300	Value: 280				

X# E15a 20 EURO
10.3400 g., Copper, 27.15 mm. **Obv:** Shield of arms
Obv. Legend: Liberte / Egalite / Fratenité **Rev:** 2 brown lemurs on branches **Rev. Legend:** PROTECTION DE LA FAUNE **Edge:** Plain

Date	Mintage	F	VF	XF	Unc	BU
2004	30	—	—	—	50.00	50.00

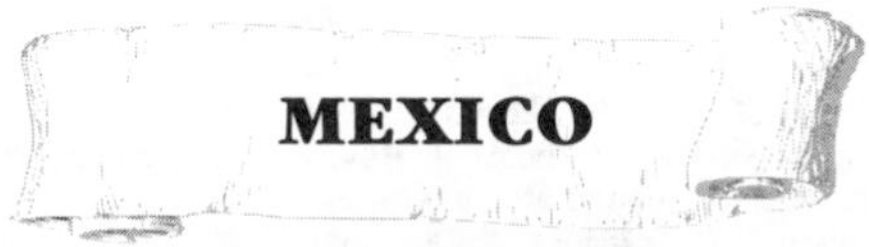

MEXICO

WAR OF INDEPENDENCE

Hidalgo State

FANTASY COINAGE

X# 2 4 REALES
Silver **Countermark:** 4R. / MON.PROV / DI / HIDALGO / Mo **Note:** Countermark on religious medal of "N.S.D. S.JUAN D LOS LAGOS."

Date	Mintage	Good	VG	F	VF	XF
ND(ca.1810)	—	25.00	35.00	60.00	90.00	—

FANTASY COUNTER-MARKED COINAGE

X# 1 4 REALES
0.9030 Silver **Countermark:** 4R. / MON.PROV / DI / HIDALGO / Mo **Note:** Countermark on cut segment of Spanish Colonial 8 Reales.

Date	Mintage	Good	VG	F	VF	XF
ND(ca.1810)	—	40.00	60.00	90.00	145	—

REPUBLIC

First

FANTASY COINAGE

X# 31 8 REALES
29.3200 g., Copper-Nickel, 39.8 mm. **Obv:** Eagle, branch in beak, wings outspread, facing, perched on rock **Obv. Legend:** UNITED MAXXICO AMERICA **Rev:** Rising sun, sea **Edge:** Reeded **Note:** An unusual oriental fabrication.

Date	Mintage	F	VF	XF	Unc	BU
1884Zs	—	4.00	6.00	10.00	—	—

TOKEN COINAGE

Gaming Token

X# Tn12 NON-DENOMINATED (20 Pesos)
Copper **Obv:** Mexican Republic 20 Pesos **Rev:** United States 20 Dollars

Date	Mintage	F	VF	XF	Unc	BU
1878	—	—	10.00	20.00	35.00	50.00

REPUBLIC

Second

NON-CIRCULATING COINAGE

Privately Produced

X# NC1 1/4 REAL (Una Quartilla)
Brass **Obv:** Liberty bust right **Rev:** Curved inscription within inner circle

Date	Mintage	F	VF	XF	Unc	BU
1838CA	—	—	250	500	850	—

X# NC1a 1/4 REAL (Una Quartilla)
Silver **Obv:** Liberty bust right **Rev:** Curved inscription within inner circle

Date	Mintage	F	VF	XF	Unc	BU
1838CA	—	—	500	1,000	1,500	—

X# NC2 1/4 REAL (Una Quartilla)
Copper **Obv:** Liberty bust right **Rev:** Standing indian facing with arrow in right hand, bow in left

Date	Mintage	F	VF	XF	Unc	BU
1838	—	—	250	500	850	—

X# NC2a 1/4 REAL (Una Quartilla)
Brass **Obv:** Liberty bust right **Rev:** Standing facing indian holding arrow in right hand, bow in left

Date	Mintage	F	VF	XF	Unc	BU
1838	—	—	250	500	850	—

X# NC3 1/4 REAL (Una Quartilla)
Brass **Obv:** Liberty bust right **Rev:** Curved value above mint mark, sprigs below, flowers scattered around

Date	Mintage	F	VF	XF	Unc	BU
1838Do	—	—	250	500	850	—

X# NC4 1/4 REAL (Una Quartilla)
Brass **Obv:** Liberty bust right **Rev:** Straight line value within fancy frame

Date	Mintage	F	VF	XF	Unc	BU
1838Ga	—	—	250	500	850	—

X# NC5 1/4 REAL (Una Quartilla)
Brass **Obv:** Liberty bust right **Rev:** Curved value within sprays

Date	Mintage	F	VF	XF	Unc	BU
1838Go	—	—	250	500	850	—

X# NC6 1/4 REAL (Una Quartilla)
Brass **Obv:** Liberty bust right **Rev:** Curved value above mint mark within sprays

Date	Mintage	F	VF	XF	Unc	BU
1838Mo	—	—	175	375	750	—

X# NC7 1/4 REAL (Una Quartilla)
Brass **Obv:** Liberty bust right **Rev:** Straight line value above mint mark, beads around border

Date	Mintage	F	VF	XF	Unc	BU
1838Mo	—	—	175	375	750	—

X# NC8 1/4 REAL (Una Quartilla)
Brass **Obv:** Liberty bust right **Rev:** Victory column with flying eagle above in sprays

Date	Mintage	F	VF	XF	Unc	BU
1838	—	—	250	500	850	—

X# NC9 1/4 REAL (Una Quartilla)
Brass **Obv:** Liberty bust right **Rev:** Value within beaded inner circle, legend around

Date	Mintage	F	VF	XF	Unc	BU
1838SLP	—	—	250	500	850	—

X# NC10 1/4 REAL (Una Quartilla)
Copper **Obv:** Liberty bust right **Rev:** Arms **Rev. Legend:** CANTON DE TUXTLA

Date	Mintage	F	VF	XF	Unc	BU
1838	—	—	30.00	60.00	100	—

X# NC11 1/4 REAL (Una Quartilla)
Brass **Obv:** Liberty bust right **Rev:** Curved value above mint mark within sprays

Date	Mintage	F	VF	XF	Unc	BU
1838Zs	—	—	250	500	850	—

X# NC11a 1/4 REAL (Una Quartilla)
Silver **Obv:** Liberty bust right **Rev:** Curved inscription within sprays

Date	Mintage	F	VF	XF	Unc	BU
1838Zs	—	—	500	1,000	1,500	—

X# NC12 2 CENTAVOS
Bronze **Obv:** Liberty bust left **Rev:** Straight line value within circle of stars **Rev. Legend:** ESTADO DE CAMPECHE **Note:** Struck by L. Chr. Lauer, Nurnberg, Germany.

Date	Mintage	F	VF	XF	Unc	BU
1890	—	—	20.00	40.00	70.00	—

X# NC12a 2 CENTAVOS
Copper Nickel **Obv:** Liberty bust left **Rev:** Straight line value within circle of stars **Rev. Legend:** ESTADO DE CAMPECHE **Note:** Struck by L. Chr. Lauer, Nurnberg, Germany

Date	Mintage	F	VF	XF	Unc	BU
1890	—	—	50.00	100	150	—

X# NC13 2 CENTAVOS
Bronze **Obv:** Liberty bust left **Rev. Legend:** ESTADO DE COAHUILA **Note:** Similar to NC15. Struck by L. Chr. Lauer, Nurnberg, Germany

Date	Mintage	F	VF	XF	Unc	BU
1890	—	—	20.00	40.00	70.00	—

X# NC13a 2 CENTAVOS
Copper-Nickel **Obv:** Liberty bust left **Rev. Legend:** ESTADO DE COAHUILA **Note:** Similar to NC15. Struck by L. Chr. Lauer, Nurnberg, Germany

Date	Mintage	F	VF	XF	Unc	BU
1890	—	—	50.00	100	150	—

X# NC14 2 CENTAVOS
Bronze **Obv:** Liberty bust left **Rev. Legend:** ESTADO DE MEXICO **Note:** Similar to NC15. Struck by L. Chr. Lauer, Nurnberg, Germany

Date	Mintage	F	VF	XF	Unc	BU
1890	—	—	20.00	40.00	70.00	—

X# NC14a 2 CENTAVOS
Copper-Nickel **Obv:** Liberty bust left **Rev. Legend:** ESTADO DE MEXICO **Note:** Similar to NC15. Struck by L. Chr. Lauer, Nurnberg, Germany

Date	Mintage	F	VF	XF	Unc	BU
1890	—	—	50.00	100	150	—

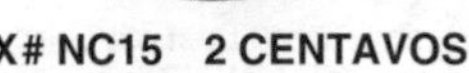

X# NC15 2 CENTAVOS
Bronze **Obv:** Liberty bust left **Rev:** Straight line value above small star within inner circle **Rev. Legend:** ESTADO DE NUEVO LEON **Note:** Struck by L. Chr. Lauer, Nurnberg, Germany

Date	Mintage	F	VF	XF	Unc	BU
1890	—	—	20.00	40.00	70.00	—

X# NC15a 2 CENTAVOS
Copper-Nickel **Obv:** Liberty bust left **Rev:** Straight line value above small star, within inner circle **Rev. Legend:** ESTADO DE NUEVO LEON **Note:** Struck by L. Chr. Lauer, Nurnberg, Germany

Date	Mintage	F	VF	XF	Unc	BU
1890	—	—	50.00	100	150	—

X# NC16 2 CENTAVOS

Bronze **Obv:** Liberty bust left **Rev:** Straight line value within inner circle of stars **Rev. Legend:** ESTADO DE PUEBLA **Note:** Struck by L. Chr. Lauer, Nurnberg, Germany

Date	Mintage	F	VF	XF	Unc	BU
1890	—	—	20.00	40.00	70.00	—

X# NC16a 2 CENTAVOS

Copper-Nickel **Obv:** Liberty bust left **Rev:** Straight line value within inner circle above date **Rev. Legend:** ESTADO DE PUEBLA **Note:** Struck by L. Chr. Lauer, Nurnberg, Germany

Date	Mintage	F	VF	XF	Unc	BU
1890	—	—	50.00	100	150	—

X# NC17 2 CENTAVOS

Bronze **Obv:** Liberty bust left **Rev:** Straight line value above small star within inner circle **Rev. Legend:** ESTADO DE QUERETARO **Note:** Struck by L. Chr. Lauer, Nurnberg, Germany

Date	Mintage	F	VF	XF	Unc	BU
1890	—	—	20.00	40.00	70.00	—

X# NC17a 2 CENTAVOS

Copper-Nickel **Obv:** Liberty bust left **Rev:** Straight line value within inner circle **Rev. Legend:** ESTADO DE QUERETARO **Note:** Struck by L. Chr. Lauer, Nurnberg, Germany

Date	Mintage	F	VF	XF	Unc	BU
1890	—	—	50.00	100	150	—

X# NC18 2 CENTAVOS

Bronze **Obv:** Liberty bust left **Rev:** Straight line value within circle of stars **Rev. Legend:** ESTADO DE SANS - LUIS - POTOSI **Note:** Struck by L. Chr. Lauer, Nurnberg, Germany

Date	Mintage	F	VF	XF	Unc	BU
1890	—	—	20.00	40.00	70.00	—

X# NC18a 2 CENTAVOS

Copper-Nickel **Obv:** Liberty bust left **Rev:** Straight line value within circle of stars **Rev. Legend:** ESTADO DE SANS - LUIS - POTOSI **Note:** Struck by L. Chr. Lauer, Nurnberg, Germany

Date	Mintage	F	VF	XF	Unc	BU
1890	—	—	50.00	100	150	—

X# NC19 2 CENTAVOS

Bronze **Obv:** Liberty bust left **Rev:** Straight line value within circle **Rev. Legend:** ESTADO DE TLAXCALA **Note:** Struck by L. Chr. Lauer, Nurnberg, Germany

Date	Mintage	F	VF	XF	Unc	BU
1890	—	—	20.00	40.00	70.00	—

X# NC19a 2 CENTAVOS

Copper-Nickel **Obv:** Liberty bust left **Rev:** Straight line value within inner circle **Rev. Legend:** ESTADO DE TLAXCALA **Note:** Struck by L. Chr. Lauer, Nurnberg, Germany

Date	Mintage	F	VF	XF	Unc	BU
1890	—	—	50.00	100	150	—

X# NC20 2 CENTAVOS

Bronze **Obv:** Liberty bust left **Rev:** Straight line value within inner circle of stars **Rev. Legend:** ESTADO DE ZACATECAS **Note:** Struck by L. Chr. Lauer, Nurnberg, Germany

Date	Mintage	F	VF	XF	Unc	BU
1890	—	—	20.00	40.00	70.00	—

X# NC20a 2 CENTAVOS

Copper-Nickel **Issuer:** Zacatecas **Obv:** Liberty bust left **Rev:** Straight line value above small star within inner circle **Rev. Legend:** ESTADO DE ZACATECAS **Note:** Struck by L. Chr. Lauer, Nurnberg, Germany

Date	Mintage	F	VF	XF	Unc	BU
1890	—	—	50.00	100	150	—

X# NC21 2 CENTAVOS

Bronze **Subject:** 80th Anniversary of Independence **Obv:** Liberty bust left **Note:** Medallic Issue.

Date	Mintage	F	VF	XF	Unc	BU
1890	—	—	40.00	80.00	120	—

X# NC21a 2 CENTAVOS

Silvered Bronze **Subject:** 80th Anniversary of Independence **Obv:** Liberty bust left **Note:** Medallic Issue.

Date	Mintage	F	VF	XF	Unc	BU
1890	—	—	65.00	125	180	—

X# NC21b 2 CENTAVOS

Copper-Nickel **Subject:** 80th Anniversary of Independence **Obv:** Liberty bust left **Note:** Medallic Issue.

Date	Mintage	F	VF	XF	Unc	BU
1890	—	—	100	200	250	—

PRIVATE COINAGE - REPUBLIC OF NORTH MEXICO

KM# NC22 2 CENTS

Bronze **Note:** Medallic Issue.

Date	Mintage	F	VF	XF	Unc	BU
1890	—	—	75.00	150	225	—

PRIVATE COINAGE - REPUBLIC OF THE RIO GRANDE

KM# NC23 2 CENTS

Bronze **Note:** Medallic Issue.

Date	Mintage	F	VF	XF	Unc	BU
1890	—	—	100	200	300	—

UNITED STATES

SILVER BULLION COINAGE

Libertad Series

KM# 542 1/20 ONZA
(1/20 Troy Ounce of Silver)

1.5551 g., 0.9990 Silver 0.0499 oz. ASW **Obv:** National arms, eagle left **Rev:** Winged Victory

Date	Mintage	F	VF	XF	Unc	BU
1991Mo	50,017	—	—	—	—	5.50
1992Mo	295,783	—	—	—	—	4.50
1992Mo Proof	5,000	Value: 10.00				
1993Mo	100,000	—	—	—	—	4.50
1993Mo Proof	—	Value: 10.00				
1994Mo	90,100	—	—	—	—	4.50
1994Mo Proof	10,000	Value: 10.00				
1995Mo	50,000	—	—	—	—	5.50
1995Mo Proof	2,000	Value: 12.00				

KM# 609 1/20 ONZA
(1/20 Troy Ounce of Silver)

1.5551 g., 0.9990 Silver 0.0499 oz. ASW **Obv:** National arms, eagle left **Rev:** Winged Victory

Date	Mintage	F	VF	XF	Unc	BU
1996Mo	50,000	—	—	—	—	10.00
1996Mo Proof	1,000	Value: 15.00				
1997Mo	20,000	—	—	—	—	10.00
1997Mo Proof	800	Value: 15.00				
1998Mo	6,400	—	—	—	—	10.00
1998Mo Proof	300	Value: 18.50				
1999Mo	8,001	—	—	—	—	12.00
1999Mo Proof	600	Value: 16.50				
2000Mo	57,500	—	—	—	—	12.00
2000Mo Proof	900	Value: 16.50				
2001Mo	25,000	—	—	—	—	12.00
2001Mo Proof	1,500	Value: 15.00				
2002Mo	45,000	—	—	—	—	8.00
2002Mo Proof	2,800	Value: 13.00				
2003Mo	—	—	—	—	—	8.00
2003Mo Proof	—	Value: 13.00				
2004Mo	—	—	—	—	—	8.00
2004Mo Proof	—	Value: 13.00				
2005Mo	—	—	—	—	—	8.00
2005Mo Proof	—	Value: 12.00				
2006Mo	—	—	—	—	—	8.00
2006Mo Proof	—	Value: 12.00				
2007Mo	—	—	—	—	—	—
2007Mo Proof	—	—	—	—	—	—

KM# 543 1/10 ONZA
(1/10 Troy Ounce of Silver)

3.1103 g., 0.9990 Silver 0.0999 oz. ASW **Obv:** National arms, eagle left **Rev:** Winged Victory

Date	Mintage	F	VF	XF	Unc	BU
1991Mo	50,017	—	—	—	—	7.50
1992Mo	299,983	—	—	—	—	6.50
1992Mo Proof	5,000	Value: 12.00				
1993Mo	100,000	—	—	—	—	6.50
1993Mo Proof	—	Value: 12.00				
1994Mo	90,100	—	—	—	—	6.50
1994Mo Proof	10,000	Value: 12.00				
1995Mo	50,000	—	—	—	—	7.50
1995Mo Proof	2,000	Value: 13.50				

KM# 610 1/10 ONZA
(1/10 Troy Ounce of Silver)

3.1103 g., 0.9990 Silver 0.0999 oz. ASW **Obv:** National arms, eagle left **Rev:** Winged Victory

Date	Mintage	F	VF	XF	Unc	BU
1996Mo	50,000	—	—	—	—	12.00
1996Mo Proof	1,000	Value: 17.50				
1997Mo	20,000	—	—	—	—	12.00
1997Mo Proof	800	Value: 17.50				
1998Mo	6,400	—	—	—	—	12.00
1998Mo Proof	300	Value: 22.50				
1999Mo	8,000	—	—	—	—	14.00
1999Mo Proof	600	Value: 20.00				

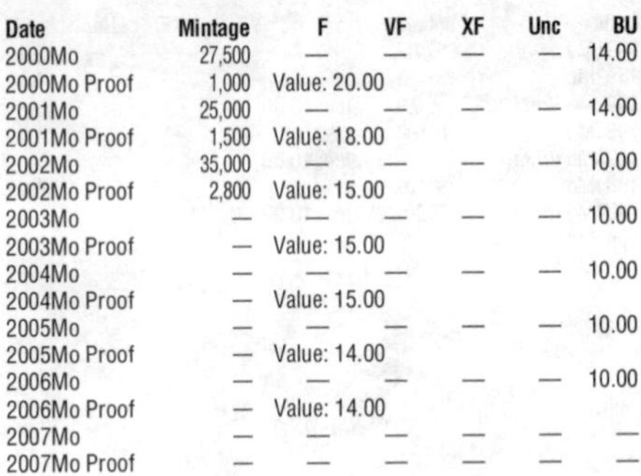

Date	Mintage	F	VF	XF	Unc	BU
2000Mo	27,500	—	—	—	—	14.00
2000Mo Proof	1,000	Value: 20.00				
2001Mo	25,000	—	—	—	—	14.00
2001Mo Proof	1,500	Value: 18.00				
2002Mo	35,000	—	—	—	—	10.00
2002Mo Proof	2,800	Value: 15.00				
2003Mo	—	—	—	—	—	10.00
2003Mo Proof	—	Value: 15.00				
2004Mo	—	—	—	—	—	10.00
2004Mo Proof	—	Value: 15.00				
2005Mo	—	—	—	—	—	10.00
2005Mo Proof	—	Value: 14.00				
2006Mo	—	—	—	—	—	10.00
2006Mo Proof	—	Value: 14.00				
2007Mo	—	—	—	—	—	—
2007Mo Proof	—	—	—	—	—	—

KM# 544 1/4 ONZA
(1/4 Troy Ounce of Silver)

7.7758 g., 0.9990 Silver 0.2497 oz. ASW **Obv:** National arms, eagle left **Rev:** Winged Victory

Date	Mintage	F	VF	XF	Unc	BU
1991Mo	50,017	—	—	—	—	9.00
1992Mo	104,000	—	—	—	—	7.50
1992Mo Proof	5,000	Value: 15.00				
1993Mo	86,500	—	—	—	—	7.50
1993Mo Proof	—	Value: 15.00				
1994Mo	90,100	—	—	—	—	7.50
1994Mo Proof	15,000	Value: 15.00				
1995Mo	50,000	—	—	—	—	9.00
1995Mo Proof	2,000	Value: 16.50				

KM# 611 1/4 ONZA
(1/4 Troy Ounce of Silver)

7.7758 g., 0.9990 Silver 0.2497 oz. ASW **Obv:** National arms, eagle left **Rev:** Winged Victory

Date	Mintage	F	VF	XF	Unc	BU
1996Mo	50,000	—	—	—	—	15.00
1996Mo Proof	1,000	Value: 20.00				
1997Mo	20,000	—	—	—	—	15.00
1997Mo Proof	800	Value: 20.00				
1998Mo	6,400	—	—	—	—	15.00
1998Mo Proof	300	Value: 32.50				
1999Mo	7,000	—	—	—	—	18.00
1999Mo Proof	600	Value: 25.00				
2000Mo	21,000	—	—	—	—	18.00
2000Mo Proof	700	Value: 25.00				
2001Mo	25,000	—	—	—	—	18.00
2001Mo Proof	1,000	Value: 22.00				
2002Mo	35,000	—	—	—	—	13.50
2002Mo Proof	2,800	Value: 20.00				
2003Mo	—	—	—	—	—	13.50
2003Mo Proof	—	Value: 20.00				
2004Mo	—	—	—	—	—	13.50
2004Mo Proof	—	Value: 20.00				
2005Mo	—	—	—	—	—	13.50
2005Mo Proof	—	Value: 18.50				
2006Mo	—	—	—	—	—	13.00
2006Mo Proof	—	Value: 18.50				
2007Mo	—	—	—	—	—	—
2007Mo Proof	—	—	—	—	—	—

KM# 545 1/2 ONZA
(1/2 Troy Ounce of Silver)

15.5517 g., 0.9990 Silver 0.4995 oz. ASW
Obv: National arms, eagle left **Rev:** Winged Victory

Date	Mintage	F	VF	XF	Unc	BU
1991Mo	50,618	—	—	—	—	12.00
1992Mo	119,000	—	—	—	—	10.00
1992Mo Proof	5,000	Value: 17.50				
1993Mo	71,500	—	—	—	—	10.00
1993Mo Proof	—	Value: 17.50				
1994Mo	90,100	—	—	—	—	10.00
1994Mo Proof	15,000	Value: 17.50				
1995Mo	50,000	—	—	—	—	10.00
1995Mo Proof	2,000	Value: 18.50				

KM# 612 1/2 ONZA
(1/2 Troy Ounce of Silver)

15.5517 g., 0.9990 Silver 0.4995 oz. ASW
Obv: National arms, eagle left **Rev:** Winged Victory

Date	Mintage	F	VF	XF	Unc	BU
1996Mo	50,000	—	—	—	—	20.00
1996Mo Proof	1,000	Value: 30.00				
1997Mo	20,000	—	—	—	—	20.00
1997Mo Proof	800	Value: 30.00				
1998Mo	6,400	—	—	—	—	22.00
1998Mo Proof	300	Value: 45.00				
1999Mo	7,000	—	—	—	—	22.00
1999Mo Proof	600	Value: 35.00				
2000Mo	20,000	—	—	—	—	22.00
2000Mo Proof	700	Value: 35.00				
2001Mo	20,000	—	—	—	—	22.00
2001Mo Proof	1,000	Value: 30.00				
2002Mo	35,000	—	—	—	—	18.00
2002Mo Proof	2,800	Value: 25.00				
2003Mo	—	—	—	—	—	18.00
2003Mo Proof	—	Value: 25.00				
2004Mo	—	—	—	—	—	18.00
2004Mo Proof	—	Value: 25.00				
2005Mo	—	—	—	—	—	18.00
2005Mo Proof	—	Value: 22.00				
2006Mo	—	—	—	—	—	18.00
2006Mo Proof	—	Value: 22.00				
2007Mo	—	—	—	—	—	—
2007Mo Proof	—	—	—	—	—	—

KM# 494.1 ONZA (Troy Ounce of Silver)

31.1000 g., 0.9990 Silver 0.9988 oz. ASW **Subject:** Libertad **Obv:** National arms, eagle left **Rev:** Winged Victory

Date	Mintage	F	VF	XF	Unc	BU
1982Mo	1,049,680	—	—	—	BV	17.50
1983Mo	1,001,768	—	—	—	BV	17.50
1983Mo Proof	998	Value: 225				
1984Mo	1,014,000	—	—	—	BV	17.50
1985Mo	2,017,000	—	—	—	BV	17.50
1986Mo	1,699,426	—	—	—	BV	17.50
1986Mo Proof	30,006	Value: 30.00				
1987Mo	500,000	—	—	—	BV	50.00
1987Mo Proof	12,000	Value: 38.00				
1987Mo Proof doubled date	Inc. above	Value: 45.00				
1988Mo	1,500,500	—	—	—	BV	47.00
1989Mo	1,396,500	—	—	—	BV	27.00
1989Mo Proof	10,000	Value: 70.00				

KM# 494.2 ONZA (Troy Ounce of Silver)

31.1000 g., 0.9990 Silver 0.9988 oz. ASW
Obv: National arms, eagle left **Rev:** Winged Victory
Edge: Reeded

Date	Mintage	F	VF	XF	Unc	BU
1988Mo Proof	10,000	Value: 75.00				
1990Mo	1,200,000	—	—	—	BV	17.50
1990Mo Proof	10,000	Value: 63.00				
1991Mo	1,650,518	—	—	—	BV	30.00

KM# 494.5 ONZA (Troy Ounce of Silver)

31.1000 g., 0.9990 Silver 0.9988 oz. ASW
Subject: Libertad **Obv:** National arms, eagle left
Rev: Winged Victory **Edge:** Reeded edge **Note:** Mule

Date	Mintage	F	VF	XF	Unc	BU
1991Mo Proof	10,000	Value: 57.00				

KM# 494.3 ONZA (Troy Ounce of Silver)

31.1000 g., 0.9990 Silver 0.9988 oz. ASW
Subject: Libertad **Obv:** National arms, eagle left
Rev: Winged Victory with revised design and lettering
Edge: Reeded edge **Note:** Mule

Date	Mintage	F	VF	XF	Unc	BU
1991Mo	Inc. above	—	—	—	BV	45.00
1992Mo	2,458,000	—	—	—	BV	30.00
1992Mo Proof	10,000	Value: 53.00				

KM# 494.4 ONZA (Troy Ounce of Silver)

31.1000 g., 0.9990 Silver 0.9988 oz. ASW
Subject: Libertad **Obv:** National arms, eagle left
Rev: Winged Victory with revised design and lettering
Edge: Reeded edge **Note:** Mule

Date	Mintage	F	VF	XF	Unc	BU
1993Mo	1,000,000	—	—	—	BV	20.00
1993Mo Proof	—	Value: 57.00				

Date	Mintage	F	VF	XF	Unc	BU
1994Mo	400,000	—	—	—	BV	25.00
1994Mo Proof	10,000	Value: 57.00				
1995Mo	500,000	—	—	—	BV	25.00
1995Mo Proof	2,000	Value: 57.00				

KM# 613 ONZA (Troy Ounce of Silver)
33.6250 g., 0.9250 Silver 0.9999 oz. ASW
Obv: National arms, eagle left **Rev:** Winged Victory

Date	Mintage	F	VF	XF	Unc	BU
1996Mo	300,000	—	—	—	—	27.00
1996Mo Proof	2,000	Value: 60.00				
1997Mo	100,000	—	—	—	—	27.00
1997Mo Proof	1,500	Value: 60.00				
1998Mo	67,000	—	—	—	—	42.00
1998Mo Proof	500	Value: 85.00				
1999Mo	95,000	—	—	—	—	27.00
1999Mo Proof	600	Value: 70.00				

KM# 639 ONZA (Troy Ounce of Silver)
31.1000 g., 0.9990 Silver 0.9988 oz. ASW
Subject: Libertad **Obv:** National arms, eagle left within center of past and present arms **Rev:** Winged Victory
Edge: Reeded edge **Note:** Mule

Date	Mintage	F	VF	XF	Unc	BU
2000Mo	340,000	—	—	—	—	25.00
2000Mo Proof	1,600	Value: 52.00				
2001Mo	650,000	—	—	—	—	20.00
2001Mo Proof	2,000	Value: 52.00				
2002Mo	850,000	—	—	—	—	18.00
2002Mo Proof	3,800	Value: 52.00				
2003Mo	—	—	—	—	—	18.00
2003Mo Proof	—	Value: 52.00				
2004Mo	—	—	—	—	—	18.00
2004Mo Proof	—	Value: 47.50				
2005Mo	—	—	—	—	—	18.00
2005Mo Proof	—	Value: 47.50				
2006Mo	—	—	—	—	—	18.00
2006Mo Proof	—	Value: 52.00				
2007Mo	—	—	—	—	—	—
2007Mo Proof	—	—	—	—	—	—

KM# 614 2 ONZAS (2 Troy Ounces of Silver)
62.2070 g., 0.9990 Silver 1.9979 oz. ASW **Subject:** Libertad **Obv:** National arms, eagle left within center of past and present arms **Rev:** Winged Victory

Date	Mintage	F	VF	XF	Unc	BU
1996Mo	50,000	—	—	—	—	35.00
1996Mo Proof	1,200	Value: 65.00				
1997Mo	15,000	—	—	—	—	35.00
1997Mo Proof	1,300	Value: 70.00				
1998Mo	7,000	—	—	—	—	45.00
1998Mo Proof	400	Value: 100				
1999Mo	5,000	—	—	—	—	60.00
1999Mo Proof	280	Value: 175				
2000Mo	7,500	—	—	—	—	60.00
2000Mo Proof	500	Value: 75.00				
2001Mo	1,700	—	—	—	—	60.00
2001Mo Proof	500	Value: 75.00				
2002Mo	8,700	—	—	—	—	55.00
2002Mo Proof	1,000	Value: 70.00				
2003Mo	—	—	—	—	—	55.00
2003Mo Proof	—	Value: 70.00				
2004Mo	—	—	—	—	—	45.00
2004Mo Proof	—	Value: 70.00				
2005Mo	—	—	—	—	—	45.00
2005Mo Proof	—	Value: 70.00				
2006Mo	—	—	—	—	—	45.00
2006Mo Proof	—	Value: 70.00				
2007Mo	—	—	—	—	—	—
2007Mo Proof	—	—	—	—	—	—

KM# 615 5 ONZAS (5 Troy Ounces of Silver)
155.5175 g., 0.9990 Silver 4.9948 oz. ASW **Subject:** Libertad **Obv:** National arms, eagle left within center of past and present arms **Rev:** Winged Victory

Date	Mintage	F	VF	XF	Unc	BU
1996Mo	20,000	—	—	—	—	110
1996Mo Proof	1,200	Value: 200				
1997Mo	10,000	—	—	—	—	110
1997Mo Proof	1,300	Value: 200				
1998Mo	3,500	—	—	—	—	220
1998Mo Proof	400	Value: 400				
1999Mo	2,800	—	—	—	—	100
1999Mo Proof	100	Value: 500				
2000Mo	4,000	—	—	—	—	100
2000Mo Proof	500	Value: 200				
2001Mo	4,000	—	—	—	—	95.00
2001Mo Proof	600	Value: 200				
2002Mo	5,200	—	—	—	—	95.00
2002Mo Proof	1,000	Value: 200				
2003Mo	—	—	—	—	—	85.00
2003Mo Proof	—	Value: 115				
2004Mo	—	—	—	—	—	90.00
2004Mo Proof	—	Value: 135				
2005Mo	—	—	—	—	—	85.00
2005Mo Proof	—	Value: 125				
2006Mo	—	—	—	—	—	85.00
2006Mo Proof	—	Value: 125				
2007Mo	—	—	—	—	—	—
2007Mo Proof	—	—	—	—	—	—

KM# 677 KILO (32.15 Troy Ounces of Silver)
999.9775 g., 0.9990 Silver 32.116 oz. ASW, 110 mm.
Subject: Collector Bullion **Obv:** National arms in center of past and present arms **Rev:** Winged Victory
Edge: Reeded

Date	Mintage	F	VF	XF	Unc	BU
2002Mo Prooflike	1,100	—	—	—	—	750
2003Mo Proof	3,000	Value: 650				
2004Mo Prooflike	—	—	—	—	—	650
2005Mo Proof	—	Value: 675				

GOLD BULLION COINAGE

KM# 530 1/20 ONZA
(1/20 Ounce of Pure Gold)
1.7500 g., 0.9000 Gold 0.0506 oz. AGW **Obv:** Winged Victory **Rev:** Calendar stone

Date	Mintage	F	VF	XF	Unc	BU
1987Mo	—	—	—	—	—	275
1988Mo	—	—	—	—	—	—

KM# 589 1/20 ONZA
(1/20 Ounce of Pure Gold)
1.5551 g., 0.9990 Gold 0.0499 oz. AGW **Obv:** Winged Victory **Rev:** National arms, eagle left

Date	Mintage	F	VF	XF	Unc	BU
1991Mo	10,000	—	—	—	—	BV+30%
1992Mo	65,225	—	—	—	—	BV+30%
1993Mo	10,000	—	—	—	—	BV+30%
1994Mo	10,000	—	—	—	—	BV+30%

KM# 642 1/20 ONZA
(1/20 Ounce of Pure Gold)
1.5551 g., 0.9990 Gold 0.0499 oz. AGW **Obv:** National arms, eagle left **Rev:** Native working

Date	Mintage	F	VF	XF	Unc	BU
2000Mo Proof	—	Value: 50.00				

KM# 671 1/20 ONZA
(1/20 Ounce of Pure Gold)
1.5551 g., 0.9990 Gold 0.0499 oz. AGW, 16 mm.
Obv: National arms, eagle left **Rev:** Winged Victory
Edge: Reeded **Note:** Design similar to KM#609. Value estimates do not include the high taxes and surcharges added to the issue prices by the Mexican Government.

Date	Mintage	F	VF	XF	Unc	BU
2000Mo	5,300	—	—	—	BV+30%	—
2002Mo	5,000	—	—	—	BV+30%	—
2004Mo	—	—	—	—	BV+30%	—
2005Mo	—	—	—	—	BV+30%	—
2006Mo	—	—	—	—	BV+30%	—
2007Mo	—	—	—	—	—	—

KM# 628 1/15 ONZA (1/15 Ounce of Pure Gold)

0.9990 Gold **Obv:** Winged Victory above legend **Rev:** National arms, eagle left within circle

Date	Mintage	F	VF	XF	Unc	BU
1987Mo	—	—	—	—	—	275

KM# 541 1/10 ONZA (1/10 Ounce of Pure Gold)

3.1103 g., 0.9990 Gold 0.0999 oz. AGW **Obv:** National arms, eagle left **Rev:** Winged Victory

Date	Mintage	F	VF	XF	Unc	BU
1991Mo	10,000	—	—	—	—	BV+20%
1992Mo	50,777	—	—	—	—	BV+20%
1993Mo	10,000	—	—	—	—	BV+20%
1994Mo	10,000	—	—	—	—	BV+20%

KM# 672 1/10 ONZA (1/10 Ounce of Pure Gold)

3.1103 g., 0.9990 Gold 0.0999 oz. AGW, 20 mm. **Obv:** National arms, eagle left **Rev:** Winged Victory **Edge:** Reeded **Note:** Design similar to KM#610. Value estimates do not include the high taxes and surcharges added to the issue prices by the Mexican Government.

Date	Mintage	F	VF	XF	Unc	BU
2000Mo	3,500	—	—	—	BV+20%	—
2002Mo	5,000	—	—	—	BV+20%	—
2004Mo	—	—	—	—	BV+20%	—
2005Mo	—	—	—	—	BV+20%	—
2006Mo	—	—	—	—	BV+20%	—
2007Mo	—	—	—	—	—	—

KM# 487 1/4 ONZA (1/4 Ounce of Pure Gold)

8.6396 g., 0.9000 Gold 0.2500 oz. AGW **Obv:** National arms, eagle left **Rev:** Winged Victory **Note:** Similar to KM#488.

Date	Mintage	F	VF	XF	Unc	BU
1981Mo	313,000	—	—	—	—	BV+11%
1982Mo	—	—	—	—	—	BV+11%

KM# 590 1/4 ONZA (1/4 Ounce of Pure Gold)

7.7758 g., 0.9990 Gold 0.2497 oz. AGW **Obv:** Winged Victory above legend **Rev:** National arms, eagle left

Date	Mintage	F	VF	XF	Unc	BU
1991Mo	10,000	—	—	—	—	BV+11%
1992Mo	28,106	—	—	—	—	BV+11%
1993Mo	2,500	—	—	—	—	BV+11%
1994Mo	2,500	—	—	—	—	BV+11%

KM# 673 1/4 ONZA (1/4 Ounce of Pure Gold)

7.7758 g., 0.9990 Gold 0.2497 oz. AGW, 26.9 mm. **Obv:** National arms, eagle left **Rev:** Winged Victory **Edge:** Reeded **Note:** Design similar to KM#611. Value estimates do not include the high taxes and surcharges added to the issue prices by the Mexican Government.

Date	Mintage	F	VF	XF	Unc	BU
2000Mo	2,500	—	—	—	BV+12%	—
2002Mo	—	—	—	—	BV+12%	—
2004Mo	—	—	—	—	BV+12%	—
2005Mo	—	—	—	—	BV+12%	—
2006Mo	—	—	—	—	BV+15%	—
2007Mo	—	—	—	—	—	—

KM# 488 1/2 ONZA (1/2 Ounce of Pure Gold)

17.2792 g., 0.9000 Gold 0.5000 oz. AGW **Obv:** National arms, eagle left **Rev:** Winged Victory

Date	Mintage	F	VF	XF	Unc	BU
1981Mo	193,000	—	—	—	—	BV+8%
1982Mo	—	—	—	—	—	BV+8%
1989Mo Proof	704	Value: 500				

KM# 591 1/2 ONZA (1/2 Ounce of Pure Gold)

15.5517 g., 0.9990 Gold 0.4995 oz. AGW **Obv:** Winged Victory above legend **Rev:** National arms, eagle left

Date	Mintage	F	VF	XF	Unc	BU
1991Mo	10,000	—	—	—	—	BV+8%
1992Mo	25,220	—	—	—	—	BV+8%
1993Mo	2,500	—	—	—	—	BV+8%
1994Mo	2,500	—	—	—	—	BV+8%

KM# 674 1/2 ONZA (1/2 Ounce of Pure Gold)

15.5517 g., 0.9990 Gold 0.4995 oz. AGW, 32.9 mm. **Obv:** National arms, eagle left **Rev:** Winged Victory **Edge:** Reeded **Note:** Design similar to KM#612. Value estimates do not include the high taxes and surcharges added to the issue prices by the Mexican Government.

Date	Mintage	F	VF	XF	Unc	BU
2000Mo	1,500	—	—	—	BV+8%	—
2002Mo	—	—	—	—	BV+8%	—
2004Mo	—	—	—	—	BV+8%	—
2005Mo	—	—	—	—	BV+8%	—
2006Mo	—	—	—	—	BV+8%	—
2007Mo	—	—	—	—	—	—

KM# 489 ONZA (Ounce of Pure Gold)

34.5585 g., 0.9000 Gold 0.9999 oz. AGW **Obv:** National arms, eagle left **Rev:** Winged Victory **Note:** Similar to KM#488.

Date	Mintage	F	VF	XF	Unc	BU
1981Mo	596,000	—	—	—	—	BV+3%
1985Mo	—	—	—	—	—	BV+3%
1988Mo	—	—	—	—	—	BV+3%

KM# 592 ONZA (Ounce of Pure Gold)

31.1035 g., 0.9990 Gold 0.9990 oz. AGW **Obv:** Winged Victory above legend **Rev:** National arms, eagle left

Date	Mintage	F	VF	XF	Unc	BU
1991Mo	109,193	—	—	—	—	BV+3%
1992Mo	46,281	—	—	—	—	BV+3%
1993Mo	10,000	—	—	—	—	BV+3%
1994Mo	1,000	—	—	—	—	BV+3%

KM# 675 ONZA (Ounce of Pure Gold)

31.1035 g., 0.9990 Gold 0.9990 oz. AGW, 40 mm. **Obv:** National arms, eagle left **Rev:** Winged Victory **Edge:** Reeded **Note:** Design similar to KM#639. Value estimates do not include the high taxes and surcharges added to the issue prices by the Mexican Government.

Date	Mintage	F	VF	XF	Unc	BU
2000Mo	2,730	—	—	—	BV+3%	—
2002Mo	—	—	—	—	BV+3%	—
2004Mo	—	—	—	—	BV+3%	—
2005Mo	—	—	—	—	BV+3%	—
2006Mo	—	—	—	—	BV+3%	—

PLATINUM BULLION COINAGE

KM# 538 1/4 ONZA (1/4 Ounce)

7.7775 g., 0.9990 Platinum 0.2498 oz. APW **Obv:** National arms, eagle left **Rev:** Winged Victory

Date	Mintage	F	VF	XF	Unc	BU
1989Mo	704	Value: 400				

MEDALLIC SILVER BULLION COINAGE

X# MB45 1/10 ONZA

0.9990 Silver **Series:** Pillar Dollar **Subject:** 14th International Numismatic Convention Mexico City **Obv:** Crowned Spanish arms **Obv. Legend:** PHILIP • V•D•G•HISPAN•ET IND•REX **Rev:** Spanish Colonial arms **Rev. Legend:** + VTRAQUE VNUM *

Date	Mintage	F	VF	XF	Unc	BU
1987Mo Proof	—	Value: 25.00				

X# MB34 1/10 ONZA

3.1100 g., 0.9990 Silver 0.0999 oz. ASW, 21 mm. **Subject:** 96th American Numismatic Association Convention **Obv:** Old screw coining press **Obv. Legend:** CASA DE MONEDA DE MEXICO **Rev:** ANA logo - oil lamp **Note:** Prev. X#MB6.

Date	Mintage	F	VF	XF	Unc	BU
1987Mo Proof	—	Value: 15.00				

X# MB46 1/4 ONZA

0.9990 Silver **Series:** Pillar Dollar **Subject:** 14th International Numismatic Convention Mexico City **Obv:** Crowned Spanish arms **Obv. Legend:** PHILIP • V•D•G•HISPAN•ET IND•REX **Rev:** Spanish Colonial arms **Rev. Legend:** + VTRAQUE VNUM *

Date	Mintage	F	VF	XF	Unc	BU
1732 (1987)Mo Proof	—	Value: 35.00				

X# MB47 1/2 ONZA

0.9990 Silver **Series:** Pillar Dollar **Subject:** 14th International Numismatic Convention Mexico City **Obv:** Crowned Spanish arms **Obv. Legend:** PHILIP • V•D•G•HISPAN•ET IND•REX **Rev:** Spanish Colonial arms **Rev. Legend:** + VTRAQUE VNUM *

Date	Mintage	F	VF	XF	Unc	BU
1732 (1987)Mo Proof	—	Value: 50.00				

X# MB48 ONZA

0.9990 Silver **Series:** Pillar Dollar **Subject:** 14th International Numismatic Convention Mexico City **Obv:** Crowned Spanish arms **Obv. Legend:** PHILIP • V•D•G•HISPAN•ET IND•REX **Rev:** Spanish Colonial arms **Rev. Legend:** + VTRAQUE VNUM *

Date	Mintage	F	VF	XF	Unc	BU
1732 (1987)Mo Proof	—	Value: 65.00				

KM# M49a ONZA

33.6250 g., 0.9250 Silver 0.9999 oz. ASW **Obv:** Mint mark above coin press

Date	Mintage	F	VF	XF	Unc	BU
1949	1,000,000	—	12.00	13.50	17.50	27.50

KM# M49b.1 ONZA

33.6250 g., 0.9250 Silver 0.9999 oz. ASW **Obv:** Wide spacing between DE MONEDA **Rev:** Mint mark below balance scale **Note:** Type I

Date	Mintage	F	VF	XF	Unc	BU
1978Mo	280,000	—	—	BV	11.50	13.50

KM# M49b.2 ONZA

33.6250 g., 0.9250 Silver 0.9999 oz. ASW **Obv:** Close spacing between DE MONEDA **Rev:** Mint mark below balance scale **Note:** Type II

Date	Mintage	F	VF	XF	Unc	BU
1978Mo	Inc. above	—	—	BV	17.50	22.50

KM# M49b.3 ONZA

33.6250 g., 0.9250 Silver 0.9999 oz. ASW **Obv:** Close spacing between DE MONEDA **Rev:** Left scale pan points to U in UNA **Note:** Type III

Date	Mintage	F	VF	XF	Unc	BU
1979Mo	4,508,000	—	—	BV	16.50	20.00

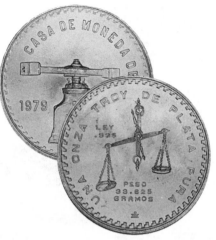

KM# M49b.4 ONZA

33.6250 g., 0.9250 Silver 0.9999 oz. ASW **Obv:** Close spacing between DE MONEDA **Rev:** Left scale pan points between U and N of UNA **Note:** Type IV

Date	Mintage	F	VF	XF	Unc	BU
1979Mo	Inc. above	—	—	BV	16.50	20.00

KM# M49b.5 ONZA

33.6250 g., 0.9250 Silver 0.9999 oz. ASW **Obv:** Close spacing between DE MONEDA **Rev:** Left scale pan points between U and N of UNA **Note:** Type V

Date	Mintage	F	VF	XF	Unc	BU
1980Mo	6,104,000	—	—	BV	16.50	20.00
1980/70Mo	Inc. above	—	—	BV	16.50	25.00

X# MB9 ONZA

0.9990 Silver, 40 mm. **Obv. Inscription:** "Viva Mexico" **Rev:** Liberty cap in rays

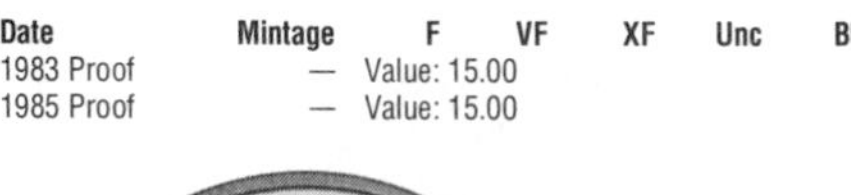

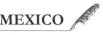

Date	Mintage	F	VF	XF	Unc	BU
1983 Proof	—	Value: 15.00				
1985 Proof	—	Value: 15.00				

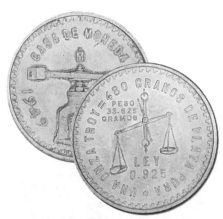

X# MB11 ONZA

0.9990 Silver, 40 mm. **Obv. Inscription:** "Viva Mexico" **Rev:** Olmeca stone head facing 3/4 right

Date	Mintage	F	VF	XF	Unc	BU
1984 Proof	—	Value: 15.00				

X# MB10 ONZA

0.9990 Silver, 40 mm. **Obv. Inscription:** "Viva Mexico" **Rev:** "Caballito" left in rays

Date	Mintage	F	VF	XF	Unc	BU
1984 Proof	—	Value: 15.00				
1985 Proof	—	Value: 15.00				

X# MB17 ONZA

0.9990 Silver, 40 mm. **Obv. Inscription:** "Viva Mexico" **Rev:** Bust of Cuauhtemoc left

Date	Mintage	F	VF	XF	Unc	BU
1984 Proof	—	Value: 15.00				

X# MB15 ONZA

0.9990 Silver, 40 mm. **Obv. Inscription:** "Viva Mexico" **Rev:** Mayan culture

Date	Mintage	F	VF	XF	Unc	BU
1984 Proof	—	Value: 15.00				

X# MB14 ONZA

0.9990 Silver, 40 mm. **Obv. Inscription:** "Viva Mexico" **Rev:** Imperial Eagle of Iturbide perched on cactus, head right

Date	Mintage	F	VF	XF	Unc	BU
1984 Proof	—	Value: 15.00				

X# MB13 ONZA

0.9990 Silver, 40 mm. **Obv. Inscription:** "Viva Mexico" **Rev:** Liberty statue facing divides dates 1821-1921 **Rev. Legend:** MDCCCXXI - MCMXXI

Date	Mintage	F	VF	XF	Unc	BU
1984 Proof	—	Value: 15.00				

X# MB12 ONZA

0.9990 Silver, 40 mm. **Obv. Inscription:** "Viva Mexico" **Rev:** "Quetzalcoatl" head left

Date	Mintage	F	VF	XF	Unc	BU
1984 Proof	—	Value: 15.00				

X# MB37 ONZA

31.3000 g., 0.9990 Silver 1.0053 oz. ASW, 38 mm. **Subject:** 200th Anniversary of U.S.A. Constitution **Obv:** Old screw coining press **Obv. Legend:** CASA DE MONEDA DE MEXICO **Rev:** Franklin, Washington and Jefferson seated at table

Date	Mintage	F	VF	XF	Unc	BU
1987Mo Proof	5,000	Value: 25.00				

X# MB51 2 ONZAS

62.2060 g., 0.9990 Silver 1.9979 oz. ASW, 49 mm. **Subject:** 1998 Seoul Summer Games **Obv:** Old screw coining press **Obv. Legend:** CASA DE MONEDA DE MEXICO **Rev:** Ancient coin surrounded by 12 modern events

Date	Mintage	F	VF	XF	Unc	BU
1988Mo Proof	—	Value: 65.00				

X# MB49 5 ONZAS

155.5150 g., 0.9990 Silver 4.9947 oz. ASW, 65.10 mm. **Series:** Pillar Dollar **Subject:** 14th International Numismatic Convention Mexico City **Obv:** Crowned Spanish arms **Obv. Legend:** PHILIP • V • D • G • HISPAN • ET IND • REX **Rev:** Spanish Colonial arms **Rev. Legend:** + VTRAQUE VNUM * **Edge:** 40 REALES **Note:** Illustration reduced. Prev. X#MB2.

Date	Mintage	F	VF	XF	Unc	BU
1987Mo Proof	4,800	Value: 125				

Note: 192 pieces had two Thai countermarks added. Refer to Thailand listings

X# MB20 5 ONZAS
155.5150 g., 0.9990 Silver 4.9947 oz. ASW, 65.10 mm. **Subject:** 450th Anniversary of Mexico City Mint **Obv:** Old screw type coining press **Obv. Legend:** CASA DE MONEDA DE MEXICO **Rev:** Balance scale **Rev. Legend:** 450 AÑOS DE LA PRIMERA ACUÑACION **Edge:** Reeded **Note:** Serial number on edge. Illustration reduced. Prev. X#MB1.

Date	Mintage	F	VF	XF	Unc	BU
1986Mo Proof	10,000	Value: 65.00				

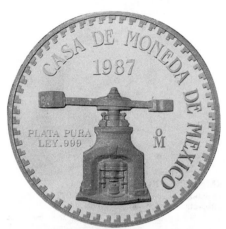

X# MB23 5 ONZAS
0.9990 Silver, 64.9 mm. **Subject:** 5th Birthday of North American born Panda - Tohui **Obv:** Old screw type coining press **Obv. Legend:** CASA DE MONEDA DE MEXICO **Rev:** Mother seated with cub **Rev. Legend:** 5° aniversario del panda **Edge:** Reeded **Note:** Illustration reduced. Serial number on edge.

Date	Mintage	F	VF	XF	Unc	BU
1987Mo Proof	—	Value: 100				

X# MB38 5 ONZAS
155.5200 g., 0.9990 Silver 4.9949 oz. ASW, 69 mm. **Subject:** 200th Anniversary of U.S.A. Constitution **Obv:** Old screw coining press **Obv. Legend:** CASA DE MONEDA DE MEXICO **Rev:** Franklin, Washington and Jefferson seated at table **Note:** Illustration reduced.

Date	Mintage	F	VF	XF	Unc	BU
1987Mo Proof	5,000	Value: 85.00				

X# MB33.1 5 ONZAS
155.5150 g., 0.9990 Silver 4.9947 oz. ASW, 65.10 mm. **Subject:** Ixtaccihuati and Popocatepeti **Obv:** Arms **Obv. Legend:** ESTADOS UNIDOS MEXICANOS **Rev:** Ixtaccihuati and Popocatepeti, mountains in background **Edge:** Plain **Note:** Illustration reduced. Prev. X#MB5.1.

Date	Mintage	F	VF	XF	Unc	BU
1987Mo Proof	500	Value: 75.00				

X# MB33.2 5 ONZAS
155.5150 g., 0.9990 Silver 4.9947 oz. ASW **Subject:** Ixtaccihuati and Popocatepeti **Obv:** Arms **Obv. Legend:** ESTADOS UNIDOS MEXICANOS **Rev:** Ixtaccihuati and Popocatepeti, mountains in background **Edge:** Reeded **Note:** Prev. X#MB5.2.

Date	Mintage	F	VF	XF	Unc	BU
1987Mo Proof	500	Value: 75.00				

X# MB35 5 ONZAS
155.5150 g., 0.9995 Silver 4.9972 oz. ASW, 65.10 mm. **Subject:** 96th American Numismatic Convention **Obv:** Arms **Obv. Legend:** ESTADOS UNIDOS MEXICANOS **Rev:** Butterfly migration in North America, ANA logo above **Note:** Illustration reduced. Prev. X#MB7.

Date	Mintage	F	VF	XF	Unc	BU
1987Mo Proof	2,000	Value: 85.00				

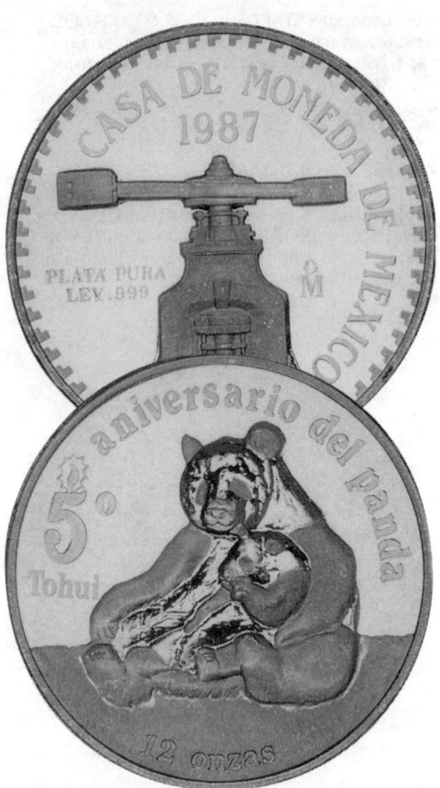

X# MB24 12 ONZAS
373.2360 g., 0.9990 Silver 11.987 oz. ASW **Subject:** 5th Birthday of North American Born Panda - Tohui **Obv:** Old screw type coining press **Obv. Legend:** CASA DE MONEDA DE MEXICO **Rev:** Mother seated with cub **Rev. Legend:** 5° aniversario del panda **Note:** Illustration reduced.

Date	Mintage	F	VF	XF	Unc	BU
1987Mo Proof	5,000	Value: 250				

X# MB39 12 ONZAS
0.9990 Silver, 80 mm. **Subject:** 200th Anniversary of U.S.A. Constitution **Obv:** Old screw coining press **Obv. Legend:** CASA DE MONEDA DE MEXICO **Rev:** Franklin, Washington and Jefferson seated at table **Note:** Illustration reduced.

Date	Mintage	F	VF	XF	Unc	BU
1987Mo Proof	250	Value: 125				

X# MB50 12 ONZAS
373.2360 g., 0.9990 Silver 11.987 oz. ASW **Series:** Pillar Dollar **Subject:** 14th International Numismatic Convention Mexico City **Obv:** Crowned Spanish arms **Obv. Legend:** PHILIP • V • D • G • HISPAN • ET IND • REX **Rev:** Spanish Colonial arms **Rev. Legend:** + VTRAQUE VNUM * **Note:** Illustration reduced. Prev. X#MB2.

Date	Mintage	F	VF	XF	Unc	BU
1987Mo Proof	4,800	—	—	—	—	—

Note: Reported, not confirmed

X# MB52 12 ONZAS
0.9990 Silver **Subject:** 1988 Seoul Summer Games **Obv:** Old screw coining press **Obv. Legend:** CASA DE MONEDA DE MEXICO **Rev:** Ancient coin surrounded by 12 modern events **Note:** Illustration reduced.

Date	Mintage	F	VF	XF	Unc	BU
1998Mo Proof	—	Value: 250				

MEDALLIC GOLD COINAGE

KM# M91a 10 PESOS
8.3333 g., 0.9000 Gold 0.2411 oz. AGW **Subject:** 200th Anniversary - Birth of Hidalgo

Date	Mintage	F	VF	XF	Unc	BU
1953	—	—	—	—	BV	175

KM# M123a 10 PESOS
8.3333 g., 0.9000 Gold 0.2411 oz. AGW
Subject: Centennial of Constitution

Date	Mintage	F	VF	XF	Unc	BU
1957	Est. 73,000	—	—	—	BV	175

Note: Mintage includes #M122a

KM# M92a 20 PESOS
16.6666 g., 0.9000 Gold 0.4822 oz. AGW
Subject: 200th Anniversary - Birth of Hidalgo

Date	Mintage	F	VF	XF	Unc	BU
1953	—	—	—	—	BV	345

KM# M122a 50 PESOS
41.6666 g., 0.9000 Gold 1.2056 oz. AGW **Subject:** Centennial of Constitution

Date	Mintage	F	VF	XF	Unc	BU
1957 Inc. M123a	—	—	—	—	BV	850

MEDALLIC GOLD BULLION COINAGE

X# MB26 1/10 ONZA
0.9990 Gold **Subject:** 5th Birthday of North American born Panda - Tohui **Obv:** Old screw type coining press **Obv. Legend:** CASA DE MONEDA DE MEXICO **Rev:** Mother seated with cub **Rev. Legend:** 5° aniversario del panda

Date	Mintage	F	VF	XF	Unc	BU
1987Mo Proof	—	—	—	—	—	—

Note: Reported, not confirmed

X# MB58 1/4 ONZA
0.9990 Gold **Obv:** Bust of Philip V right **Obv. Legend:** * PHILIP • V • D • G • HISPAN • ET IND • REX * **Rev:** Crowned Spanish arms **Rev. Legend:** * INITIUM SAPIENTIAE TIMOR DOMINI *

Date	Mintage	F	VF	XF	Unc	BU
1732//1888Mo	—	—	—	—	—	—

X# MB40 1/4 ONZA

0.9990 Gold **Subject:** 200th Anniversary U.S.A. Constitution **Obv:** Old screw coining press **Obv. Legend:** CASA DE MONEDA DE MEXICO **Rev:** Franklin, Washington and Jefferson seated at table

Date	Mintage	F	VF	XF	Unc	BU
1987Mo Proof	5,000	Value: 250				

X# MB27 1/4 ONZA

0.9990 Gold **Subject:** 5th Birthday of North American born Panda - Tohui **Obv:** Old screw type coining press **Obv. Legend:** CASA DE MONEDA DE MEXICO **Rev:** Mother seated with cub **Rev. Legend:** 5° aniversario del panda

Date	Mintage	F	VF	XF	Unc	BU
1987Mo Proof	—	—	—	—	—	—

Note: Reported, not confirmed

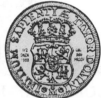

X# MB59 1/2 ONZA

0.9990 Gold **Obv:** Bust of Philip V right **Obv. Legend:** * PHILIP • V • D • G • HISPAN • ET IND • REX * **Rev:** Crowned Spanish arms **Rev. Legend:** * INITIUM SAPIENTIAE TIMOR DOMINI *

Date	Mintage	F	VF	XF	Unc	BU
1732//1888Mo	—	—	—	—	—	—

X# MB28 1/2 ONZA

0.9990 Gold **Subject:** 5th Birthday of North American born Panda - Tohui **Obv:** Old screw type coining press **Obv. Legend:** CASA DE MONEDA DE MEXICO **Rev:** Mother seated with cub **Rev. Legend:** 5° aniversario del panda

Date	Mintage	F	VF	XF	Unc	BU
1987Mo Proof	—	—	—	—	—	—

Note: Reported, not confirmed

X# MB60 ONZA

0.9990 Gold, 31 mm. **Obv:** Bust of Philip V right **Obv. Legend:** * PHILIP • V • D • G • HISPAN • ET IND • REX * **Rev:** Crowned Spanish arms **Rev. Legend:** * INITIUM SAPIENTIAE TIMOR DOMINI *

Date	Mintage	F	VF	XF	Unc	BU
1732//1888Mo	—	—	—	—	—	—

X# MB61 ONZA

Gold, 65.1 mm. **Obv:** Bust of Philip V right **Obv. Legend:** * PHILIP • V • D • G • HISPAN • ET IND • REX * **Rev:** Crowned Spanish arms **Rev. Legend:** * INITIUM SAPIENTIAE TIMOR DOMINI * **Note:** Illustration reduced.

Date	Mintage	F	VF	XF	Unc	BU
1732//1888Mo	—	—	—	—	—	—

X# MB29 ONZA

Gold **Subject:** 5th Birthday of North American born Panda - Tohui **Obv:** Old screw type coining press **Obv. Legend:** CASA DE MONEDA DE MEXICO **Rev:** Mother seated with cub **Rev. Legend:** 5° aniversario del panda

Date	Mintage	F	VF	XF	Unc	BU
1987Mo Proof	—	—	—	—	—	—

Note: Reported, not confirmed

X# MB53 2 ONZAS

0.9990 Gold **Subject:** 1988 Seoul Summer Games **Obv:** Old screw coining press **Obv. Legend:** CASA DE MONEDA DE MEXICO **Rev:** Ancient coin surrounded by 12 modern events

Date	Mintage	F	VF	XF	Unc	BU
1988Mo	—	—	—	—	—	—

X# MB30 5 ONZAS

0.9990 Gold **Subject:** 5th Birthday of North American born Panda - Tohui **Obv:** Old screw type coining press **Obv. Legend:** CASA DE MONEDA DE MEXICO **Rev:** Mother seated with cub **Rev. Legend:** 5° aniversario del panda

Date	Mintage	F	VF	XF	Unc	BU
1987Mo Proof	—	—	—	—	—	—

Note: Reported, not confirmed

X# MB31 12 ONZAS

373.2360 g., 0.9990 Gold 11.987 oz. AGW **Subject:** 5th Birthday of North American born Panda - Tohui **Obv:** Old screw type coining press **Obv. Legend:** CASA DE MONEDA DE MEXICO **Rev:** Mother seated with cub **Rev. Legend:** 5° aniversario del panda

Date	Mintage	F	VF	XF	Unc	BU
1987Mo Proof	100	—	—	—	—	—

X# MB41 12 ONZAS

0.9990 Gold **Subject:** 200th Anniversary of U.S.A. Constitution **Obv:** Old screw coining press **Obv. Legend:** CASA DE MONEDA DE MEXICO **Rev:** Franklin, Washington and Jefferson seated at table

Date	Mintage	F	VF	XF	Unc	BU
1987Mo Proof	5,000	Value: 6,000				

MEDALLIC PLATINUM BULLION COINAGE

X# MB22 ONZA

31.1030 g., 0.9995 Platinum 0.9994 oz. APW, 32 mm. **Obv:** Arms **Obv. Legend:** REPUBLICA MEXICANA **Rev:** Old screw coining press **Rev. Legend:** CASA DE MONEDA DE MEXICO **Edge:** Reeded **Note:** Prev. X#MB14.

Date	Mintage	F	VF	XF	Unc	BU
1987Mo P Proof	—	Value: 1,200				

X# MB32 12 ONZAS

0.9990 Platinum APW, 60 mm. **Subject:** 5th Birthday of North American born Panda - Tohui **Obv:** Old screw type coining press **Obv. Legend:** CASA DE MONEDA DE MEXICO **Rev:** Mother seated with cub **Rev. Legend:** 5° aniversario del panda **Note:** Illustration reduced.

Date	Mintage	F	VF	XF	Unc	BU
1987Mo Proof	—	—	—	—	—	—

Note: Reported, not confirmed

X# MB42 12 ONZAS
0.9990 Platinum APW, 65 mm. **Subject:** 200th Anniversary of U.S.A. Constitution **Obv:** Old screw coining press **Obv. Legend:** CASA DE MONEDA DE MEXICO **Rev:** Franklin, Washington and Jefferson seated at table **Note:** Illustration reduced. Prev. X#MB14.

Date	Mintage	F	VF	XF	Unc	BU
1987Mo Proof	—	—	—	—	—	—

PIEFORTS

X# P11 5 ONZAS
311.0300 g., 0.9990 Silver 9.9894 oz. ASW **Series:** Pillar Dollar **Subject:** 14th International Numismatic Convention Mexico City - 1987 **Obv:** Crowned Spanish arms **Obv. Legend:** PHILIP • V • D • G • HISPAN • ET IND • REX **Rev:** Spanish Colonial arms **Rev. Legend:** + VTRAQUE VNUM + **Edge:** Plain

Date	Mintage	F	VF	XF	Unc	BU
1987Mo Proof	200	Value: 200				

PATTERNS

Including off metal strikes

X#	Date	Mintage	Identification	Mkt Val
	1950Mo	—	5 Pesos. Silver. Arms/Hidalgo.	1,650
	1951Mo	2	Onza. Silver. Elephant facing right. Bust with helmet left. Miner/ Elephant.	4,000
Pn1	1987Mo	—	1/10 Onza. Bronze. X#MB26. 15mm.	100
Pn2	1987Mo	—	1/4 Onza. Bronze. X#MB27. 20mm.	125
Pn3	1987Mo	—	1/2 Onza. Bronze. X#MB28. 26mm.	150
Pn4	1987Mo	—	Onza. Bronze. X#MB29. 31.5mm.	175
Pn5	1987Mo	—	5 Onzas. Bronze. X#MB30. Stamped "PRUEBA LATON."	150
Pn6	1987Mo	—	12 Onzas. 0.9990 Silver. X#MB31.	250
Pn11	1987Mo	—	12 Onzas. 0.9990 Silver. X#MB42.	85.00

PROOF SETS

X#	Date	Mintage	Identification	Issue Price	Mkt Val
XPS1	1987Mo (2)	—	X#MB34, 35	—	—
XPS2	1988Mo (5)	—	X#MB45-MB49	—	300
XPS3	1988Mo (5)	—	X#MB57-MB61	—	—

DURANGO

WAR OF INDEPENDENCE

COUNTERMARKED COINAGE

X# 5 20 PESOS
Cast Brass **Countermark:** Script GCM or JCM
Obv: Monogram countermark on Liberty cap

CM Date	Host Date	Good	VG	F	VF	XF
	1914	—	—	—	—	—

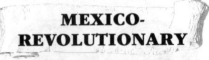

MEXICO-REVOLUTIONARY

DURANGO

CONSTITUTIONAL ARMY

Cuencame

FANTASY COINAGE

X# 1 20 PESOS
0.5833 Gold **Obv:** National arms **Obv. Legend:** MUERA HUERTA (Death to Huerta) **Rev:** Radiant Liberty cap

Date	Mintage	F	VF	XF	Unc	BU
1914	—	—	—	—	—	—

X# 2 20 PESOS
27.8000 g., 0.9000 Gold 0.8044 oz. AGW

Date	Mintage	F	VF	XF	Unc	BU
1914	—	—	—	—	—	—

X# 3 20 PESOS
Silver

Date	Mintage	F	VF	XF	Unc	BU
1914	—	—	—	—	—	—

X# 4 20 PESOS
Copper **Note:** A modern fantasy issue.

Date	Mintage	F	VF	XF	Unc	BU
1914	—	—	—	—	—	—

COUNTERMARKED COINAGE

X# 5 20 PESOS
Cast Brass **Countermark:** Script GCM or JCM
Obv: Monogram countermark on Liberty Cap

CM Date	Host Date	Good	VG	F	VF	XF
ND	1914	—	—	—	—	—

JALISCO

INSTITUTIONAL REPUBLIC

Issued by the Cristeros during their brief religious uprising.

FANTASY COINAGE

X# 22 PESO
Silver

Date	Mintage	F	VF	XF	Unc	BU
1935	—	—	300	450	600	—

MIDDLE EARTH

Middle Earth was the creation of J.R.R. Tolkien as the location of the epic The Lord of the Rings. The races, language and genealogy he created as a base for the characters in the story have given generations of readers fertile ground for exploration into the world of fantasy. Called a trilogy, it is really six books, and for a fuller story one must add The Hobbit as well as The Silmarillion.

Inspired by the rich texture of such a fantasy world, Tom Maringer of Springdale, Arkansas, has taken but three mentions of coinage in the epic and has developed a coinage system not only for the Hobbits, but also for many of the other races in the book such as the immortal elves, the sturdy dwarf lords, the hardy horsemen and even the folk from the far south who use strange elephantine beasts in war and commerce. On his website, Maringer has changed the names of the folk who use these coin types from those used in the Lord of the Rings.

ANGBAND

Angband is the stronghold of Melkor. Morgouth is the name given Melkor after the theft of the Silmarils. The full sense of the name is "Dark Enemy of the world."

WIZARD'S STRONGHOLD

STANDARD COINAGE

Issued by the Shire Post Mint.

X# 1 CROWN
13.5000 g., Iron, 28 mm. **Obv:** Crown of Melkor
Rev: Ancalagon the Black, a dragon, perched on a tower

Date	Mintage	F	VF	XF	Unc	BU
ND	900	—	—	—	12.00	—

X# 2 CROWN
6.2000 g., Silver **Obv:** Crown of Melkor **Rev:** Ancalagon the Black, a dragon, perched on a tower
Note: Examples were also holed and used as pendants.

Date	Mintage	F	VF	XF	Unc	BU
ND	120	—	—	—	12.00	—

X# 3 CROWN
6.2000 g., Niobium **Obv:** Crown of Melkor
Rev: Ancalagon the Black, a dragon, perched on a tower
Note: Purple in tone.

Date	Mintage	F	VF	XF	Unc	BU
ND	36	—	—	—	24.00	—

X# 4 CROWN
11.0000 g., 0.9000 Gold 0.3183 oz. AGW **Obv:** Crown of Melkor **Rev:** Ancalagon the Black, a dragon, perched on a tower

Date	Mintage	F	VF	XF	Unc	BU
ND	3	—	—	—	250	—

DALE TOWN

Dale is the city-kingdom and home to men who lived under the Lonely Mountain. It was built on wooden piers over the lake; destroyed by fire started by the dragon Smaug. It was later rebuilt under King Bard.

MUNICIPALITY

STANDARD COINAGE

X# 1 PENNY
3.1000 g., Copper, 20 mm. **Obv:** Raven of Dale
Rev: Short cross, bee and bird in angles
Rev. Inscription: (Land of milk and honey) in runes

Date	Mintage	F	VF	XF	Unc	BU
2769 TA	1,000	—	—	—	2.00	—

X# 2 PENNY
2.5000 g., 0.9000 Silver 0.0723 oz. ASW, 20 mm.
Obv: Raven of Dale **Rev:** Short cross, bee and birds in angles **Rev. Legend:** (Land of milk and honey)

Date	Mintage	F	VF	XF	Unc	BU
2769 TA	300	—	—	—	6.00	—

X# 3 PENNY
1.9000 g., Titanium **Obv:** Raven of Dale **Rev:** Short cross, bee and bird in angles **Rev. Legend:** (Land of milk and honey) **Note:** Anodized a pale blue

Date	Mintage	F	VF	XF	Unc	BU
2769 TA	20	—	—	—	12.00	—

X# 4 PENNY
2.4000 g., Niobium **Obv:** Raven of Dale **Rev:** Short cross, bee and birds in angles **Rev. Legend:** (Land of milk and honey) **Note:** Anodized a light reddish purple

Date	Mintage	F	VF	XF	Unc	BU
2769 TA	20	—	—	—	12.00	—

X# 5 DALER
31.1050 g., 0.9990 Silver 0.9990 oz. ASW
Subject: Centennial of the slaying of the dragon
Obv: Archer slaying dragon Smaug in flight **Rev:** Village of Dale and Lonely Mountain in background

Date	Mintage	F	VF	XF	Unc	BU
FA 20	—	—	—	—	—	75.00

EREGION

Eregion is a Second Age realm settled by Elven-folk.

KINGDOM

STANDARD COINAGE

X# 1 ONE LADY
Copper **Obv:** Profile left of the Lady of the Goldenwood within flora **Rev:** Stylized map of the Goldenwood, 18 spearheads pointing outwards as border **Note:** Struck on an untrimmed planchet. Also exist holed for pendants.

Date	Mintage	F	VF	XF	Unc	BU
ND	400	—	—	—	10.00	—

X# 5.1 SPRING LEAF
7.1000 g., Niobium **Obv:** Leaf veins with legend verse of a Noldoran verse ancestral to the Hymn of Rivendell written in the Beleriand mode of Tengwar
Obv. Inscription: GILTHONIETH, A! ELBERIN! / SILITHREN PENDAAR MIRUIN / MENELLO CALMAUR ELENHOTH ! (Star-kindler, O Elbereth! white shining slants down like the Silmarils from the heavens - the radiance of the star-hos **Rev:** Leaf veins with legend in Noldorin written in the Angerthas Moria
Rev. Inscription: DI-CELEBRIMBOR ARAN EREGION TEGILBOR NIN ECHANT CORONOR MINEGRAASTEN IEN NELEDHEN (Under Celebrimbor, lord of Eregion Tegilbor made me in the eleventieth year of the third yen) **Note:** Green anodized.

Date	Mintage	F	VF	XF	Unc	BU
420 SA	140	—	—	—	—	25.00

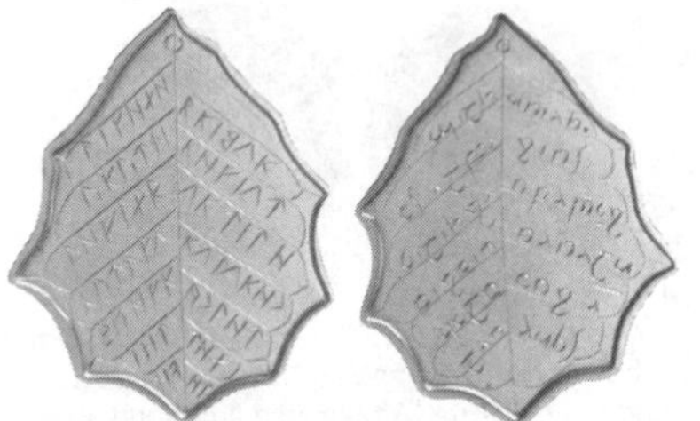

X# 5.2 SUMMER LEAF
5.3000 g., Brass **Obv:** Leaf veins with legend verse of a Noldoran verse ancestral to the Hymn of Rivendell written in the Beleriand mode of Tengwar **Obv. Inscription:** GILTHONIETH, A! ELBERIN! / SILITHREN PENDAAR MIRUIN / MENELLO CALMAUR ELENHOTH ! (Star-kindler, O Elbereth! white shining slants down like the Silmarils from the heavens - the radiance of the star-hos
Rev: Leaf veins with legend in Noldorin written in the Angerthas Moria **Rev. Inscription:** DI-CELEBRIMBOR ARAN EREGION TEGILBOR NIN ECHANT CORONOR MINEGRAASTEN IEN NELEDHEN (Under Celebrimbor, lord of Eregion Tegilbor made me in the eleventieth year of the third yen) **Note:** Bright yellow tone.

Date	Mintage	F	VF	XF	Unc	BU
420	500	—	—	—	—	10.00

X# 5.3 FALL LEAF
7.0000 g., Copper **Obv:** Leaf veins with legend verse of a Noldoran verse ancestral to the Hymn of Rivendell writeein in the Beleriand mode of Tengwar **Obv. Inscription:** GILTHONIETH, A! ELBERIN! / SILITHREN PENDAAR MIRUIN / MENELLO CALMAUR ELENHOTH ! (Star-kindler, O Elbereth! white shining slants down like the Silmarils from the heavens - the radiance of the star-hos **Rev:** Leaf veins with legend in Noldorin written in the Angerthas Moria **Rev. Inscription:** DI-CELEBRIMBOR ARAN EREGION TEGILBOR NIN ECHANT CORONOR MINEGRAASTEN IEN NELEDHEN (Under Celebrimbor, lord of Eregion Tegilbor made me in the eleventieth year of the third yen) **Note:** Brown tone patina.

Date	Mintage	F	VF	XF	Unc	BU
420 SA	700	—	—	—	10.00	—

X# 5.4 WINTER LEAF
7.9000 g., 0.9250 Silver 0.2349 oz. ASW **Obv:** Leaf veins with legend verse of a Noldoran verse ancestral to the Hymn of Rivendell written in the Beleriand mode of Tengwar **Obv. Inscription:** GILTHONIETH, A! ELBERIN! / SILITHREN PENDAAR MIRUIN / MENELLO CALMAUR ELENHOTH ! (Star-kindler, O Elbereth! white shining slants down like the Silmarils from the heavens - the radiance of the star-hos
Rev: Leaf veins with legend in Noldorin written in the Angerthas Moria **Rev. Inscription:** DI-CELEBRIMBOR ARAN EREGION TEGILBOR NIN ECHANT CORONOR MINEGRAASTEN IEN NELEDHEN (Under Celebrimbor, lord of Eregion Tegilbor made me in the eleventieth year of the third yen) **Note:** Bright white tone.

Date	Mintage	F	VF	XF	Unc	BU
420 SA	120	—	—	—	—	—

FAR HARAUD

Far Haraud is the southern part of Harad. The men of Far Harad were allied with Sauron in the War of the Ring. They used the oliophaunt for labor and warfare.

EVIL EMPIRE

STANDARD COINAGE

X# 1 OLIOPHAUNT
5.0000 g., Copper **Obv:** Oliphaunt left **Rev:** Inscription "PALAN HARAD" **Note:** Round flan, octagonal field

Date	Mintage	F	VF	XF	Unc	BU
ND	200	—	—	—	8.00	—

X# 2 MUMAKIL
15.5000 g., Copper, 22 mm. **Obv:** Oliphaunt right, war tower on back, serpent below **Rev:** "PALAN HARAD" **Note:** Octagonal planchet, hand trimmed, thick!

Date	Mintage	F	VF	XF	Unc	BU
ND	200	—	—	—	18.00	—

X# 3 MUMAK
16.0000 g., Copper, 24 mm. **Obv:** Oliphaunt left, war tower on back **Rev:** "PALAN HARAD" **Note:** Octagonal border on round planchet

Date	Mintage	F	VF	XF	Unc	BU
ND	300	—	—	—	12.00	—

GONDOR

KINGDOM

STANDARD COINAGE

X# 7 KASTAR ((4 Tharni))
12.4000 g., 0.9250 Silver 0.3688 oz. ASW
Ruler: Aragorn **Subject:** Coronation of Elessar
Obv: King on horseback right with banner of Arwen
Rev: Crowned, mantled and supported arms.

Date	Mintage	F	VF	XF	Unc	BU
year 1 FA	—	—	—	—	—	—

X# 5 THARNI
2.4000 g., 0.9000 Silver 0.0694 oz. ASW **Ruler:** Aragorn **Obv:** King Eleussar on horseback left, holding banner of Gondor **Obv. Legend:** Eleussar, Aruwen, Gondour **Rev:** Seal of Gondor; Tree and sword Andauril

Date	Mintage	F	VF	XF	Unc	BU
yr. 1 of 4th Age	—	—	—	—	10.00	—

IZAN GAARDA

Isengard is the fortress built by Gondor. It consisted of a natural circular stone wall surrounding a broad plane, in the center of which was the tower of Orthanc. Saruman made the fortress his own and replaced its grass and trees with stone and machinery. He housed orcs, men and wolves there until it was attacked and demolished by the Ents during the War of the Ring.

WIZARD'S STRONGHOLD

STANDARD COINAGE

X# 2 RED HAND
5.5000 g., Copper, 21 mm. **Obv:** Bird above fortress
Obv. Legend: YZAN GAARDA **Rev:** The white hand
Rev. Legend: SHARKU MANO (Hand of the old man)

Date	Mintage	F	VF	XF	Unc	BU
ND	120	—	—	—	3.00	—

X# 1 WHITE HAND

6.1000 g., 0.9000 Silver 0.1765 oz. ASW, 21.5 mm. **Obv:** Bird above fortress **Obv. Legend:** YZAN GAARDA **Rev:** The white hand **Rev. Legend:** SHARKU MANO (Hand of the old man)

Date	Mintage	F	VF	XF	Unc	BU
ND	240	—	—	—	10.00	—

MORDAUR

Mordor is the wasteland in the south of Middle Earth where the dark lord, Sauron lives in the stronghold tower of Barad-dur. It is also the location of Orodruin, sometimes called Mount Doom, from whose fire the rings of power were forged and where the one-ring must be destroyed. Sauron's eye is all seeing and its' gaze is powerful and controlling. He controls the Black riders and the Ringwraiths - Nazgul as well as Orcs.

WIZARD'S STRONGHOLD

STANDARD COINAGE

X# 1 EYE

6.0000 g., Iron, 24 mm. **Ruler:** Sauron **Obv:** Eye of Sauron **Obv. Legend:** (Obey / Mordaur) **Rev:** Fiery Mountain

Date	Mintage	F	VF	XF	Unc	BU
2905 TA	600	—	—	—	6.00	—

X# 2 EYE

5.0000 g., 0.3500 Silver 0.0563 oz. ASW **Ruler:** Sauron **Obv:** Eye of Sauron **Rev:** Fiery Mountain **Rev. Legend:** (Obey / Mordaur) **Note:** Examples were also holed for use as pendants.

Date	Mintage	F	VF	XF	Unc	BU
2905 TA	240	—	—	—	6.00	—

MOURIA

The Great Halls and Mines of Mouria were built by Durin's Folk under the mountains. It had a great hall called Khazad-dum. The dwarves excavated a vast underground domain. During the time of the War of the Ring, the halls were long abandoned by the dwarves, and they became home to cave trolls, goblins, orcs and the evil Balrog who does battle with Gandalf the Grey.

KINGDOM

STANDARD COINAGE

X# 1 AXE

9.0000 g., Copper, 28 mm. **Ruler:** Daurin **Obv:** Head left within vertical oval **Obv. Legend:** (Daurin Lord of Mouria) **Rev:** Double-headed axe

Date	Mintage	F	VF	XF	Unc	BU
ND	2,000	—	—	—	6.00	—

X# 1a AXE

40.0000 g., 0.9250 Silver 1.1895 oz. ASW **Ruler:** Daurin **Obv:** Head left within vertical oval **Obv. Legend:** (Daurin Lord of Mouria) **Rev:** Double-headed axe

Date	Mintage	F	VF	XF	Unc	BU
ND	48	—	—	—	—	26.00

X# 1b AXE

31.1000 g., 0.9990 Gold 0.9988 oz. AGW **Ruler:** Daurin **Obv:** Head left within vertical oval **Obv. Legend:** (Daurin Lord of Mouria) **Rev:** Double-headed axe

Date	Mintage	F	VF	XF	Unc	BU
ND	7	—	—	—	700	—

X# 5 AXE

24.0000 g., 0.9990 Copper 0.7708 oz. **Ruler:** Thrayne **Obv:** Star above anvil **Obv. Legend:** "Thrayne Turgul Y'Erebor (Thrayne, King under this Mountain) **Rev:** Double headed axe head **Rev. Legend:** "Baruk Khauzad" (Axes of the Dwarves)

Date	Mintage	F	VF	XF	Unc	BU
2800	—	—	—	—	16.00	—

X# 5a AXE

Silver **Ruler:** Thrayne **Obv:** Star above anvil **Rev:** Double headed axe head

Date	Mintage	F	VF	XF	Unc	BU
2800	—	—	—	—	—	—

X# 5b AXE

Gold **Ruler:** Thrayne **Obv:** Star above anvil **Rev:** Double headed axe head

Date	Mintage	F	VF	XF	Unc	BU
2800	—	—	—	—	—	—

X# 4 PIECES OF SEVEN

Copper **Ruler:** Daurin **Obv:** Head within vertical oval **Rev:** Double-headed axe **Note:** 7 pieces of 5g. copper struck at one time forming one design of the axe, 35 g. total. Dies of Bruce #X1.

Date	Mintage	F	VF	XF	Unc	BU
ND	20	—	—	—	20.00	—

ROHAUN

The Kingdom of the Rohirrim was once a province of Gondor, and the land was was given to men in return for their aid in the Battle of the Fields of Celebrant. The Rohirrim farmed and raised horses. The riders of Rohan played a crucial role at the battle of the Pelennor Fields during the War of the Ring.

KINGDOM

STANDARD COINAGE

X# 1 FOAL

Copper **Ruler:** Theodun **Obv. Inscription:** THEODUN KONG EORLINGAS (Theodun King of the Eorlings) **Rev:** Mearas, king of the horses, galloping left **Rev. Legend:** EUDORAS / 3014 **Note:** Oval die on large, untrimmed planchet, 25x19mm.

Date	Mintage	F	VF	XF	Unc	BU
3014 TA	1,000	—	—	—	4.00	—

X# 3 1/2 DRAM

2.4000 g., 0.9000 Silver 0.0694 oz. ASW **Ruler:** Theodun **Obv. Legend:** THEODUN KONG EORLINGAS (Theodun King of the Eorlings) **Rev:** Mearas, king of the horses, galloping left **Rev. Legend:** EUDORAS / 3017 **Note:** Irregular shaped planchet (open collar strike). Same dies as Bruce#X5.

Date	Mintage	F	VF	XF	Unc	BU
3017 TA	140	—	—	—	7.00	—

X# 5 DRAM

6.0000 g., 0.9000 Silver 0.1736 oz. ASW, 25 mm. **Ruler:** Theodun **Obv. Inscription:** THEODUN KONG

EORLINGAS (Theodun King of the Eorlings)
Rev: Mearas, king of the horses, galloping left **Rev. Legend:** EUDORAS / 3017 **Note:** Thick (dump) flan.

Date	Mintage	F	VF	XF	Unc	BU
3017 TA	90	—	—	—	14.00	—

SHIRE

The Shire is the abode the Hobbit. It is divided into four Farthings, which are further divided into a number of folklands. There are several towns within each that play a part in the story of the Lord of the Rings. Bilbo and Frodo Baggins live in Hobbittown at a house called Bag End. There were a few members of the landed genty, who did not need to work, but most Hobbits were farmers, tradesmen or laborers. The Shire was primarily agricultural.

PEACEFUL ANARCHY

STANDARD COINAGE

X# 1 FARTHING
Copper **Obv:** Tree, date flanking **Rev:** Quartered circle **Note:** Struck from center of Penny die Bruce#X4.

Date	Mintage	F	VF	XF	Unc	BU
1401 SR	500	—	—	—	—	6.00

X# 1a FARTHING
Brass **Obv:** Tree, date flanking **Rev:** Quartered circle

Date	Mintage	F	VF	XF	Unc	BU
1401 SR	100	—	—	—	—	6.00

X# 2 FARTHING
Copper, 10 mm. **Obv:** Tree, date flanking **Rev:** Quartered circle **Note:** Struck from center of Penny die KM#X5.

Date	Mintage	F	VF	XF	Unc	BU
1401 SR	200	—	—	—	2.00	—

X# 2a FARTHING
0.5500 g., Copper **Obv:** Tree, date flanking **Rev:** Quartered circle **Note:** Center of penny die KM#X5. Heavy restrike of 1403.

Date	Mintage	F	VF	XF	Unc	BU
1401 (1403) SR	200	—	—	—	2.00	—

X# 15 FARTHING
0.5700 g., Copper, 10 mm. **Obv:** Pine tree within pellet circle **Rev:** Large "F" (h) direction, Tengwa for north (formon)

Date	Mintage	F	VF	XF	Unc	BU
1402 SR	200	—	—	—	3.00	—

X# 15a FARTHING
Brass, 10 mm. **Obv:** Pine tree in pellet circle **Rev:** Large "F" (h) direction, Tengwa for north (formon)

Date	Mintage	F	VF	XF	Unc	BU
1402 SR	600	—	—	—	2.00	—

X# 15b FARTHING
0.7700 g., 0.9250 Silver 0.0229 oz. ASW, 10 mm. **Obv:** Pine tree in pellet circle **Rev:** Large "F" (h) direction, Tengwa for north (formon) **Note:** Equivalant to a penny

Date	Mintage	F	VF	XF	Unc	BU
1402 SR	50	—	—	—	6.00	—

X# 16 FARTHING
0.5700 g., Copper, 10 mm. **Obv:** Elm tree within pellet circle **Rev:** Large "R" (y) direction, tengwa for east (romen)

Date	Mintage	F	VF	XF	Unc	BU
1402 SR	200	—	—	—	3.00	—

X# 16a FARTHING
Brass, 10 mm. **Obv:** Elm tree within pellet circle **Rev:** Large "R" (y) direction, tengwa for east (romen)

Date	Mintage	F	VF	XF	Unc	BU
1402 SR	600	—	—	—	2.00	—

X# 16b FARTHING
0.7700 g., 0.9250 Silver 0.0229 oz. ASW, 10 mm. **Obv:** Elm tree within pellet circle **Rev:** Large "R" (y) direction, tengwa for east (romen) **Note:** Equivalent to a penny.

Date	Mintage	F	VF	XF	Unc	BU
1402 SR	50	—	—	—	6.00	—

X# 17 FARTHING
0.5700 g., Copper, 10 mm. **Obv:** Willow tree within pellet circle **Rev:** Large "H" (inverted y) direction, tengwa for south (hyarmon)

Date	Mintage	F	VF	XF	Unc	BU
1402 SR	200	—	—	—	3.00	—

X# 17a FARTHING
Brass **Obv:** Willow tree within pellet circle **Rev:** Large "H" (inverted y) direction, tengwa for south (hyarmon)

Date	Mintage	F	VF	XF	Unc	BU
1402 SR	600	—	—	—	2.00	—

X# 17b FARTHING
0.7700 g., 0.9250 Silver 0.0229 oz. ASW, 10 mm. **Obv:** Willow tree within pellet circle **Rev:** Large "H" (inverted y) direction, tengwa for south (hyarmon) **Note:** Equivalent to a penny.

Date	Mintage	F	VF	XF	Unc	BU
1402 SR	50	—	—	—	6.00	—

X# 18 FARTHING
0.5700 g., Copper, 10 mm. **Obv:** Oak tree within pellet circle **Rev:** Large "N" (m) direction tengwa for west (numen)

Date	Mintage	F	VF	XF	Unc	BU
1402 SR	200	—	—	—	3.00	—

X# 18a FARTHING
Brass, 10 mm. **Obv:** Oak tree within pellet circle **Rev:** Large "N" (m) direction tengwa for west (numen)

Date	Mintage	F	VF	XF	Unc	BU
1402 SR	600	—	—	—	2.00	—

X# 18b FARTHING
0.7700 g., 0.9250 Silver 0.0229 oz. ASW, 10 mm. **Obv:** Oak tree within pellet circle **Rev:** Large "N" (m) direction tengwa for west (numen) **Note:** Equivalent to a penny.

Date	Mintage	F	VF	XF	Unc	BU
1402 SR	50	—	—	—	6.00	—

X# 20 1/2 PENNY
2.0000 g., Bronze, 17 mm. **Obv:** Water oak within pellet circle **Rev:** Quartered circle

Date	Mintage	F	VF	XF	Unc	BU
1402 SR	2,800	—	3.00	5.00	8.00	—

X# 21 1/2 PENNY
1.7000 g., Copper **Obv:** Water oak within pellet circle **Obv. Legend:** "PERKELEBRIS I SUZA BAR KUDUK" **Rev:** Quartered circle **Rev. Legend:** "BELEGROTH SUZA YEN 1402"

Date	Mintage	F	VF	XF	Unc	BU
1402 SR	600	—	—	2.00	—	—

X# 21a 1/2 PENNY
1.7000 g., Brass **Obv:** Water oak within pellet circle **Rev:** Quartered circle

Date	Mintage	F	VF	XF	Unc	BU
1402	300	—	—	2.00	—	—

X# 3 PENNY
Copper **Obv:** Tree **Obv. Legend:** THE / SHIRE **Rev:** Quartered circle **Rev. Legend:** ONE / PENNY **Note:** Struck from rough acid etched dies.

Date	Mintage	F	VF	XF	Unc	BU
ND(1401)	16	—	—	—	225	—

X# 3a PENNY
6.2000 g., 0.9000 Silver 0.1794 oz. ASW **Obv:** Tree **Obv. Legend:** THE / SHIRE **Rev:** Quartered circle **Rev. Legend:** ONE / PENNY **Note:** Struck from rough acid etched dies. Silver penny equals a shilling.

Date	Mintage	F	VF	XF	Unc	BU
ND(1401)	40	—	—	—	325	—

X# 4 PENNY
Copper **Obv:** Tree, date flanking **Obv. Legend:** THE SHIRE **Rev:** Quartered circle **Rev. Legend:** ONE PENNY **Note:** Wider and deeper lettering, dentilated outer circle

Date	Mintage	F	VF	XF	Unc	BU
1401 SR	136	—	—	—	45.00	—

X# 4a PENNY
Gold **Obv:** Tree, date flanking **Obv. Legend:** THE SHIRE **Rev:** Quartered circle **Rev. Legend:** ONE PENNY **Note:** Special presentation strike.

Date	Mintage	F	VF	XF	Unc	BU
1401	1	—	—	—	—	—

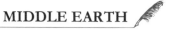

X# 5 PENNY

Copper **Obv:** Tree, date flanking **Obv. Legend:** THE / SHIRE **Rev:** Quartered circle **Rev. Legend:** ONE / PENNY **Note:** Better diework.

Date	Mintage	F	VF	XF	Unc	BU
1401 SR	800	—	—	—	8.00	—

X# 5a PENNY

6.2000 g., 0.9000 Silver 0.1794 oz. ASW **Obv:** Tree, date flanking **Obv. Legend:** THE / SHIRE **Rev:** Quartered circle **Rev. Legend:** ONE / PENNY

Date	Mintage	F	VF	XF	Unc	BU
1401	40	—	—	—	45.00	—

X# 5.1 PENNY

5.5000 g., Copper, 20 mm. **Obv:** Tree, date flanking **Rev:** Quartered circle **Note:** Thick planchet, raised central area. Heavy restrike done at the Tri-Lakes Coin Show, January 2003.

Date	Mintage	F	VF	XF	Unc	BU
1401 SR	200	—	—	—	6.00	—

X# 6 PENNY

Copper **Obv:** Tree, date flanking **Obv. Legend:** THE / SHIRE **Rev:** Quartered circle **Rev. Legend:** ONE / PENNY **Note:** Raised rim

Date	Mintage	F	VF	XF	Unc	BU
1401 SR	800	—	—	—	6.00	—

X# 21.1 PENNY

2.5000 g., Copper, 20 mm. **Obv:** Tree **Obv. Legend:** ER KELEBRIS / SUZA BAR KUDUK (One Penny / Shire abode of the Halflings) **Rev:** Quartered circle **Shape:** 12-sided

Date	Mintage	F	VF	XF	Unc	BU
1402 SR	800	—	—	—	16.00	—

X# 21.2 PENNY

3.1000 g., Copper, 20 mm. **Obv:** Tree **Obv. Legend:** ER KELEBRIS / SUZA BAR KUDUK (One Penny / Shire abode of the Halflings) **Rev:** Quartered circle **Shape:** Round

Date	Mintage	F	VF	XF	Unc	BU
1402 SR	6,200	—	—	—	4.00	—

X# 21.2a PENNY

Iron **Obv:** Tree **Obv. Legend:** ER KELEBRIS / SUZA BAR KUDUK (One Penny / Shire abode of the Halflings) **Rev:** Quartered circle **Note:** Issued during a copper shortage.

Date	Mintage	F	VF	XF	Unc	BU
1402	64	—	—	—	15.00	—

X# 21.3 PENNY

5.5000 g., Copper **Obv:** Tree **Obv. Legend:** ER KELEBRIS / SUZA BAR KUDUK (One Penny / Shire abode of the Halflings) **Rev:** Quartered circle **Note:** Struck on a thick planchet.

Date	Mintage	F	VF	XF	Unc	BU
1402 SR	200	—	—	—	4.00	—

X# 33 PENNY

3.1000 g., Copper, 20 mm. **Obv:** Pine tree within pellet circle **Obv. Legend:** ER KELEBRIS / SUZA BAR KUDUK (One Penny / Shire abode of the Halflings) **Rev:** Quartered circle **Note:** Bright finish or dark patina varieties exist.

Date	Mintage	F	VF	XF	Unc	BU
1403 SR	10,200	—	—	—	2.00	—

X# 33a PENNY

2.4000 g., 0.9000 Silver 0.0694 oz. ASW **Obv:** Pine tree within pellet circle **Obv. Legend:** ER KELEBRIS / SUZA BAR KUDUK (One Penny / Shire abode of the Halflings) **Rev:** Quartered circle **Edge:** Reeded **Note:** Silver Penny is equal to a Shilling.

Date	Mintage	F	VF	XF	Unc	BU
1403 SR	100	—	—	—	10.00	—

X# 33b PENNY

6.0000 g., 0.9000 Silver 0.1736 oz. ASW **Obv:** Pine tree within pellet circle **Obv. Legend:** ER KELEBRIS / SUZA BAR KUDUK (One Penny / Shire abode of the Halflings) **Rev:** Quartered circle **Note:** Silver Penny is equal to a Shilling.

Date	Mintage	F	VF	XF	Unc	BU
1403 SR	24	—	—	—	16.00	—

X# 8 3 PENCE

4.2000 g., Brass **Obv:** Tree **Obv. Legend:** THE / SHIRE **Rev:** Large 3 flanked by a pair of "Balantine" rings **Rev. Legend:** THREE / PENCE **Note:** Obverse die from Bruce #X3.1

Date	Mintage	F	VF	XF	Unc	BU
ND(1401)	40	—	—	—	45.00	—

X# 9 3 PENCE

4.2000 g., Brass, 17 mm. **Obv:** Tree **Obv. Legend:** THE SHIRE / SUZA BAR KUDUK (Shire, abode of the Halflings) **Rev:** III and date in center **Rev. Legend:** THREE PENCE / NELDE KELEBRISI **Note:** Thick planchet.

Date	Mintage	F	VF	XF	Unc	BU
1401 SR	240	—	—	—	8.00	—

X# 24 3 PENCE

8.0000 g., Copper **Obv:** Plum tree in full fruit, date flanking **Rev:** Large 3 **Rev. Legend:** NELDE KELEBRIS / SUZA BAR KUDUK (Three Pence / Shire abode of the Halflings) **Note:** Octagon shaped high relief rim within round planchet

Date	Mintage	F	VF	XF	Unc	BU
1402 SR	2,000	—	—	—	4.00	—

X# 24a 3 PENCE

7.0000 g., Copper **Obv:** Plum tree in full fruit, date flanking **Rev:** Large 3 **Rev. Legend:** NELDE KELEBRIS / SUZA BAR KUDUK (Three Pence / Shire abode of the Halflings) **Shape:** 8-sided **Note:** Same as #24, but hand trimed edges. Used as a presentation piece.

Date	Mintage	F	VF	XF	Unc	BU
1402 SR	—	—	—	—	8.00	—

X# 10 6 PENCE

2.5000 g., 0.9000 Silver 0.0723 oz. ASW, 19 mm. **Obv:** Tree, date flanking **Obv. Legend:** THE / SHIRE **Rev:** Bridge of Stonebows **Rev. Legend:** SIX / PENCE

Date	Mintage	F	VF	XF	Unc	BU
1401	52	—	—	—	60.00	—

X# 11 6 PENCE

2.5000 g., 0.9000 Silver 0.0723 oz. ASW **Obv:** Tree, date flanking **Obv. Legend:** THE / SHIRE **Rev:** Bridge of Stonebows **Rev. Legend:** SIX / 6 / PENCE

Date	Mintage	F	VF	XF	Unc	BU
1401	200	—	—	—	10.00	—

X# 22 6 PENCE

3.1000 g., 0.9000 Silver 0.0897 oz. ASW, 18 mm. **Obv:** Water oak tree with acorn **Obv. Inscription:** "PERKELEBRIS I SUZA BAR KUDUK" **Rev:** Quartered circle **Rev. Legend:** "BELEGROTH SUZA YEN 1402" **Note:** Provisional 6 Pence struck with dies of Half Penny Bruce #X20.

Date	Mintage	F	VF	XF	Unc	BU
1402 SR	40	—	—	—	12.00	—

X# 25 6 PENCE

16.0000 g., Copper **Obv:** White oak tree with acorns **Rev:** Quartered circle **Note:** Very thick. Struck from the same dies as Bruce #X23. Provisional 6 Pence.

Date	Mintage	F	VF	XF	Unc	BU
1402 SR	160	—	—	8.00	10.00	—

X# 26 6 PENCE

2.5000 g., 0.9000 Silver 0.0723 oz. ASW, 19 mm. **Obv:** Spruce tree, date above **Rev:** Bridge at Stonebows **Rev. Legend:** PERMALTRIS / SUZA BAR KUDUK (One Half Shilling, Shire abode of the Halflings) **Edge:** Reeded

Date	Mintage	F	VF	XF	Unc	BU
1402 SR	1,000	—	6.00	8.00	12.00	—

X# 23 SHILLING

6.2000 g., 0.9000 Silver 0.1794 oz. ASW, 26 mm. **Obv:** White oak tree with acorns **Obv. Legend:** ER MALTRIS SUZA BAR KUDUK (One Shilling - Shire abode of the Halflings) **Rev:** Quartered circle **Rev. Legend:** SUZA YEN 1402 (Shire year 1402)

Date	Mintage	F	VF	XF	Unc	BU
1402 SR	600	—	12.00	14.00	16.00	—

X# 12 1/4 CROWN (6 Shillings)

3.3000 g., 0.9167 Gold 0.0973 oz. AGW **Obv:** Tree, date flanking **Obv. Legend:** THE / SHIRE **Rev:** Tall crown within beaded circle **Rev. Legend:** ONE / QUARTER **Edge:** Reeded

Date	Mintage	F	VF	XF	Unc	BU
1401	24	—	—	—	125	—

X# 30 1/2 CROWN

7.9881 g., 0.9167 Gold 0.2354 oz. AGW **Obv:** Chestnut tree **Rev:** Crown **Rev. Legend:** PERIMALTRINA SUZA BAR KUDUK (Half Crown of the Shire abode of the Halflings) **Edge:** Reeded

Date	Mintage	F	VF	XF	Unc	BU
1402 SR	24	—	—	—	200	—

MONETARY REFORM OF 1404

Hlokarpeni = old farthing; Banapeni = old 1/2 penny; Hlokartharantiin/peni = old penny; Bantharantiin = 1/8 Kastar; tharantiin = 1/4 kastar; bankastar = 1/2 kastar.

X# 35 HLOKARPENI

0.7000 g., Brass **Obv:** Pine tree in pellet circle **Rev:** Large "F" (h) direction tengwa for north (formen)

Date	Mintage	F	VF	XF	Unc	BU
1404 SR	200	—	—	—	1.00	—

X# 36 HLOKARPENI

0.7000 g., Brass **Obv:** Elm tree in pellet circle **Rev:** Large "R" (y)direction tengwa for east (romen)

Date	Mintage	F	VF	XF	Unc	BU
1404 SR	200	—	—	—	1.00	—

X# 37 HLOKARPENI

0.7000 g., Brass **Obv:** Willow tree within pellet circle **Rev:** Large "H" (inverted y) direction tengwa for south (hyarmen)

Date	Mintage	F	VF	XF	Unc	BU
1404 SR	200	—	—	—	1.00	—

X# 38 HLOKARPENI

0.7000 g., Brass **Obv:** Oak tree within pellet circle **Rev:** Large "N" (m) direction tengwa for west (numen)

Date	Mintage	F	VF	XF	Unc	BU
1404 SR	200	—	—	—	1.00	—

X# 39 HLOKARTHARANTIIN/PENI

3.1000 g., Copper **Obv:** Elm tree, leafless **Obv. Legend:** HLOKARTHARANTIIN SUZANT (Quarter Tharantum of the Shire, S.Y. 4041) **Rev:** Quartered circle

Date	Mintage	F	VF	XF	Unc	BU
1404 SR	Est. 2,000	—	—	—	2.00	—

X# 39a HLOKARTHARANTIIN/PENI

2.6000 g., Bronze **Obv:** Elm tree, leafless **Obv. Legend:** HLOKARTHARANTIIN SUZANAT (Quarter Tharantum of the Shire, S.Y. 4041) **Rev:** Quartered circle

Date	Mintage	F	VF	XF	Unc	BU
1404 SR	600	—	—	—	4.00	—

X# 39b HLOKARTHARANTIIN/PENI

2.4000 g., Niobium **Obv:** Elm tree, leafless **Obv. Legend:** HLOKARTHARANTIIN SUZANAT (Quarter Tharantum of the Shire, S.Y. 4041) **Rev:** Quartered circle **Note:** Green tone.

Date	Mintage	F	VF	XF	Unc	BU
1404 SR	72	—	—	—	12.00	—

X# 41 HLOKARTHARANTIIN/PENI

3.1000 g., Copper **Obv:** Willow tree, bare **Obv. Legend:** HLOKARTHARANTIIN SUZANAT (Quarter Tharantum of the Shire, S.Y. 4041) **Rev:** Quartered circle

Date	Mintage	F	VF	XF	Unc	BU
1405 SR	Est. 2,000	—	—	—	2.00	—

X# 41a HLOKARTHARANTIIN/PENI

2.6000 g., Bronze **Obv:** Willow tree, bare **Obv. Legend:** HLOKARTHARANTIIN SUZANAT (Quarter Tharantum of the Shire, S.Y. 4041) **Rev:** Quartered circle

Date	Mintage	F	VF	XF	Unc	BU
1405 SR	600	—	—	—	4.00	—

X# 41b HLOKARTHARANTIIN/PENI

2.4000 g., Niobium **Obv:** Willow tree, bare **Obv. Legend:** HLOKARTHARANTIIN SUZANAT (Quarter Tharantum of the Shire, S.Y. 4041) **Rev:** Quartered circle

Date	Mintage	F	VF	XF	Unc	BU
1405 SR	72	—	—	—	12.00	—

X# 40 THARANTIIN

2.4000 g., 0.9000 Silver 0.0694 oz. ASW **Obv:** Elm tree in full leaf **Obv. Legend:** HLOKARTHARANTIIN SUZANAT (Quarter Tharantum of the Shire, S.Y. 4041) **Rev:** Quartered circle

Date	Mintage	F	VF	XF	Unc	BU
1404 SR	Est. 576	—	—	—	10.00	—

X# 42 THARANTIIN

2.4000 g., 0.9000 Silver 0.0694 oz. ASW **Obv:** Willow tree in full leaf **Obv. Legend:** HLOKARTHARANTIIN SUZANAT (Quarter Tharantum of the Shire, S.Y. 4041) **Rev:** Quartered circle

Date	Mintage	F	VF	XF	Unc	BU
1405 SR	Est. 576	—	—	—	10.00	—

COUNTERMARKED COINAGE

X# 27 6 PENCE

16.0000 g., Copper **Obv:** White oak tree with acorns **Rev:** Quartered circle **Note:** Counterstamped "6" on obverse of Bruce #X25, which was struck using dies of Bruce #X21.

CM Date	Host Date	Good	VG	F	VF	XF
ND(1402 SR)	1402	—	—	—	—	—

Note: After consultation with the mintmaster, this counterstamp was deemed false, not an official product of the mint.

YULETIDE PRESENTATION ISSUES

X# YT1 SHILLING

35.0000 g., Copper **Obv:** Chestnut tree **Rev:** Crown **Note:** Very thick, square planchet, 27x27mm. Struck from dies of Bruce #X30.

Date	Mintage	F	VF	XF	Unc	BU
1402 SR	60	—	—	—	60.00	—

X# YT2 SHILLING

35.0000 g., Copper **Obv:** White Oak Tree, die of Bruce #X23 **Rev:** Quartered circle, die of Bruce #X23. **Note:** Very thick, square planchet oriented as a diamond. 27x27mm.

Date	Mintage	F	VF	XF	Unc	BU
1403 SR	66	—	—	—	26.00	—

X# YT3 SHILLING

35.0000 g., 0.9990 Copper 1.1241 oz. **Obv:** Four reverse farthing die impressions around central farthing obverse, Bruce #X35-38 **Rev:** Modified impression of sixpence, Bruce #X26 reverse, showing bridge **Note:** Untrimmed planchet

Date	Mintage	F	VF	XF	Unc	BU
1405 SR	—	—	—	—	25.00	—

BIRTHDAY ISSUES

X# Tn1 MATHOM

2.5000 g., Bronze **Obv:** Tree **Obv. Legend:** THE / PARTY / 1 WIN / SR 1401 **Rev:** Present with ribbon bow **Rev. Legend:** ONE / MATHOM

Date	Mintage	F	VF	XF	Unc	BU
1401 SR	144	—	—	—	45.00	—

X# Tn2 MATHOM

3.1000 g., Bronze **Obv:** Legend around date **Obv. Legend:** THE HUNDRED WEIGHT FEAST / 30th HALIMATH SR 1402 **Rev:** Present wrapped in ribbon **Rev. Legend:** ONE / MATHOM

Date	Mintage	F	VF	XF	Unc	BU
1402 SR	164	—	—	—	10.00	—

X# Tn3 MATHOM

5.5000 g., Copper **Obv:** Head left wearing cap **Obv. Legend:** ONE MATHOM **Rev:** Wooden Barrel in center **Rev. Legend:** BAGGINS BIRTHDAY BASH / SR 1403

Date	Mintage	F	VF	XF	Unc	BU
1403 SR	460	—	—	4.00	—	—

TOKEN COINAGE

X# Tn52 PENNY

3.1000 g., Copper **Obv:** Dragonfly **Rev:** H / O-P / E

Date	Mintage	F	VF	XF	Unc	BU
ND	800	—	—	—	2.00	—

X# Tn53 PENNY

3.1000 g., Copper **Obv:** Dragon in flight **Obv. Legend:** WAR OF THE RING • NET **Rev:** Axe and three flowers within hexagon shield, rays to edge **Note:** Issued to support the website.

Date	Mintage	F	VF	XF	Unc	BU
ND	200	—	—	—	20.00	—

X# Tn54 PENNY

5.0000 g., Copper **Obv:** Skyline of Toronto **Obv. Legend:** A LONG EXPECTED PARTY / GOTF / TORONTO / 2003 **Rev:** Bridge **Note:** Issued to Gathering of the Fellowship party workers at the Toronto opening of part 3 of the film.

Date	Mintage	F	VF	XF	Unc	BU
2003	100	—	—	10.00	—	—

X# Tn51 ONE

5.5000 g., Copper **Obv:** Butterfly **Obv. Legend:** WAR NO MORE **Rev:** ONE within rays **Note:** Struck on heavy planchet, rounded edge.

Date	Mintage	F	VF	XF	Unc	BU
ND	100	—	—	—	2.00	—

X# Tn51a ONE

3.1000 g., Copper **Obv:** Butterfly **Rev:** ONE within rays **Edge:** Smooth

Date	Mintage	F	VF	XF	Unc	BU
ND	400	—	—	2.00	—	—

X# Tn55 6 PENCE

2.5000 g., 0.9000 Silver 0.0723 oz. ASW **Obv:** Skyline of Toronto **Obv. Legend:** ALONG EXPECTED PARTY / GOTF / TORONTO / 2003 **Rev:** Bridge of Stonebows **Note:** Issued at the Toronto opening of part 3 of the film.

Date	Mintage	F	VF	XF	Unc	BU
2003	350	—	—	12.00	—	—

TRIAL STRIKES

X# Ts1 FARTHING
Aluminum **Note:** Four Farthing designs on one large planchet for die alignment.

Date	Mintage	F	VF	XF	Unc	BU
1402 SR	15	—	—	—	—	—

X# Ts2 FARTHING
Aluminum **Note:** Four Farthing designs on one large planchet for die alignment.

Date	Mintage	F	VF	XF	Unc	BU
1404	6	—	—	—	—	—

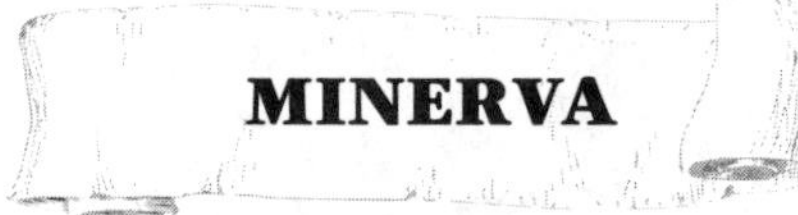

MINERVA

On January 19, 1972, the North and South Minerva Reefs (situated 400 miles south of Fiji, and previously unclaimed by any nation) were occupied and claimed under international law by the founders of the State of Minerva. These men immediately began a bold, sophisticated plan of landfill and seawall development to literally create from one barren reef the land needed for a city-state of 30,000 inhabitants.

The Republic of Minerva was dedicated to the principles of capitalism and free enterprise. Its government was limited to the protection of its citizens against force and fraud. Other world governments were officially notified of the existence of the newly created island and its government. Landfill operations were proceeding apace, and recognition had been received from the first of the world's countries - when disaster struck.

On June 21, 1972, Minerva was forcibly invaded by the Kingdom of Tonga, its nearest neighbor (260 miles distant). Unable to defend the island effectively, its government was forced into exile pending resolution of the conflict.

REPUBLIC

FANTASY COINAGE

Morris Davis Issue

X# 1 35 DOLLARS
24.0000 g., 0.9990 Silver 0.7708 oz. ASW, 39 mm. **Obv:** Bust of Minerva 3/4 left **Obv. Legend:** REPUBLIC OF MINERVA - SOUTH PACIFIC OCEAN **Rev:** Torch **Edge:** Reeded **Note:** Examples with a "cloudy" field surface are worth 50% less. .999 Silver, 24.0000 grams/1.0000 Gold, .65 grams.

Date	Mintage	F	VF	XF	Unc	BU
1973 LM Proof	10,500	—	—	—	—	110

MOLDOVA

REPUBLIC

FANTASY EURO PATTERNS

X# Pn1 EURO CENT
Copper Plated Steel **Edge:** Plain

Date	Mintage	F	VF	XF	Unc	BU
2004	7,000	—	—	—	—	1.50

X# Pn2 2 EURO CENT
Copper Plated Steel **Edge:** Plain

Date	Mintage	F	VF	XF	Unc	BU
2004	7,000	—	—	—	—	2.00

X# Pn3 5 EURO CENT
Copper Plated Steel **Edge:** Plain

Date	Mintage	F	VF	XF	Unc	BU
2004	7,000	—	—	—	—	2.50

X# Pn4 10 EURO CENT
Goldine **Edge:** Plain

Date	Mintage	F	VF	XF	Unc	BU
2004	7,000	—	—	—	—	3.00

X# Pn5 20 EURO CENT
Goldine **Edge:** Plain

Date	Mintage	F	VF	XF	Unc	BU
2004	7,000	—	—	—	—	3.50

X# Pn6 50 EURO CENT
Goldine **Edge:** Plain

Date	Mintage	F	VF	XF	Unc	BU
2004	7,000	—	—	—	—	4.00

X# Pn7 EURO
Bi-Metallic **Obv:** Male bust facing 3/4 right **Rev:** Floral design, large value "1", EEU star design **Edge:** Plain

Date	Mintage	F	VF	XF	Unc	BU
2004	7,000	—	—	—	—	6.00

X# Pn8 2 EURO
Bi-Metallic **Obv:** Male bust facing 3/4 right **Rev:** Floral design, large value "2", EEU star design **Edge:** Plain

Date	Mintage	F	VF	XF	Unc	BU
2004	7,000	—	—	—	—	8.00

MINT SETS

X#	Date	Mintage	Identification	Issue Price	Mkt Val
XMS1	2004 (8)	7,000	X#Pn1-Pn8	—	30.00

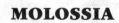

MOLOSSIA

REPUBLIC

MEDALLIC COINAGE

X# M1 50 VALORA
Nickel-Plated Steel, 39 mm. **Subject:** 30th Anniversary of Founding a Treaty **Obv:** Lesser arms of Molossia, feathered crowned badge with rearing horse **Obv. Legend:** REPUBLIC OF MOLOSSIA - Nothing Ventured, Nothing Gained **Rev:** Crown and rearing horse on quartered flag background **Rev. Legend:** Treaty of Friendship between Westarctica and Molossia

Date	Mintage	F	VF	XF	Unc	BU
2006	100	—	—	—	—	15.00

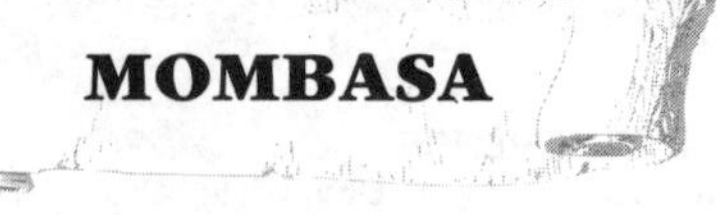

MOMBASA

BRITISH COLONY

FANTASY COINAGE

Imperial British East Africa Company

X# 1 KROON
Silver **Countermark:** "I.B.E.A.Co/balance scales/1888" on Orange Free State pattern 1 Kroon 1887.

Date	Mintage	F	VF	XF	Unc	BU
1888 Unique		—	—	—	—	—

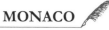

MONACO

PRINCIPALITY

MEDALLIC COINAGE

1966 Spink Issues

Struck by the Paris Mint for Spink and Sons, Ltd. of London

X# M1 10 FRANCS
25.0000 g., 0.9000 Silver 0.7234 oz. ASW **Subject:** 10th Wedding Anniversary **Note:** Prev. KM#M1.

Date	Mintage	F	VF	XF	Unc	BU
1966 (a)	24,000	—	—	—	22.00	35.00
1966 (a) Proof	1,000	Value: 100				

X# M2 200 FRANCS
32.0000 g., 0.9200 Gold 0.9465 oz. AGW **Subject:** 10th Wedding Anniversary **Note:** Prev. KM#M2.

Date	Mintage	F	VF	XF	Unc	BU
1966 (a)	5,000	—	—	—	675	—
1966 (a) Proof	1,000	Value: 900				

1974 Paris Issues

X# M3 100 FRANCS
37.0400 g., 0.9990 Silver 1.1896 oz. ASW **Subject:** 25th Anniversary of Reign **Note:** Prev. KM#M3.

Date	Mintage	F	VF	XF	Unc	BU
1974 (a) Proof	25,000	Value: 185				

Note: It is estimated that more than 10% were melted.

X# M4 1000 FRANCS
0.9970 Platinum APW **Subject:** 25th Anniversary of Reign **Note:** Prev. KM#M4.

Date	Mintage	F	VF	XF	Unc	BU
1974 (a) Proof	10,000	Value: 1,500				

Note: It is estimated that more than 10% were melted.

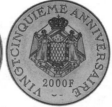

X# M5 2000 FRANCS
0.9970 Platinum APW **Subject:** 25th Anniversary of Reign **Note:** Prev. KM#M5.

Date	Mintage	F	VF	XF	Unc	BU
1974 (a) Proof	10,000	Value: 1,750				

Note: It is estimated that more than 10% were melted.

X# M6 3000 FRANCS
0.9990 Gold **Subject:** 25th Anniversary of Reign **Note:** Prev. KM#M6.

Date	Mintage	F	VF	XF	Unc	BU
1974 (a) Proof	5,000	Value: 950				

Note: It is estimated that more than 10% were melted.

ECU COINAGE

Victor Gadoury Merchant Token

X# M11 ECU
27.0000 g., Aluminum-Bronze, 35 mm. **Ruler:** Rainier III **Issuer:** V. Gadoury, Monte-Carlo **Subject:** 20th Anniversary French Coin Catalog **Obv:** Canadian Maple leaf with "VG" **Obv. Legend:** VICTOR GADOURY - MONACO **Rev:** French coin catalog **Rev. Legend:** • 1973 • 20e ANNIVERSAIRE • 1993 • V. Gadoury, numismatist, was born in Canada **Edge:** Reeded

Date	Mintage	F	VF	XF	Unc	BU
ND(1993)	1,000	—	—	—	—	8.50

X# M11a ECU
35.0000 g., 0.9250 Silver 1.0408 oz. ASW, 35 mm. **Ruler:** Rainier III **Issuer:** V. Gadoury, Monte-Carlo **Subject:** 20th Anniversary French Coin Catalog **Obv:** Canadian Maple leaf with "VG" **Obv. Legend:** VICTOR GADOURY - MONACO **Rev:** French coin catalog **Rev. Legend:** • 1973 • 20e ANNIVERSAIRE • 1993 • **Edge:** Reeded

Date	Mintage	F	VF	XF	Unc	BU
ND(1993)	50	—	—	—	—	100

X# M11b ECU
35.0000 g., 0.9250 Silver Gilt 1.0408 oz. ASW, 35 mm. **Ruler:** Rainier III **Issuer:** V. Gadoury, Monte-Carlo **Subject:** 20th Anniversary French Coin Catalog **Obv:** Canadian Maple leaf with "VG" **Obv. Legend:** VICTOR GADOURY - MONACO **Rev:** French coin catalog **Rev. Legend:** • 1973 • 20e ANNIVERSAIRE • 1993 • **Edge:** Reeded

Date	Mintage	F	VF	XF	Unc	BU
ND(1993)	10	—	—	—	—	150

ICB Private Issue

X# 21 ECU
20.0000 g., 0.9250 Silver 0.5948 oz. ASW
Subject: Montgolfier brothers first flight, 1783 **Obv:** Early French hot air balloon **Obv. Legend:** PRINCIPAUTE DE MONACO **Rev:** Ancient and early sailing ships, hot air balloon, 12 stars in outer rims **Rev. Legend:** EUROPE EUROPA **Edge:** Reeded

Date	Mintage	F	VF	XF	Unc	BU
1994 Proof	5,000	Value: 35.00				

X# 21a ECU
Goldine **Subject:** Montgolfier brothers first flight, 1783 **Obv:** Early French hot air balloon **Obv. Legend:** PRINCIPAUTE DE MONACO **Rev:** Ancient and early sailing ships, hot air balloon, 12 stars in outer rims **Rev. Legend:** EUROPE EUROPA **Edge:** Plain

Date	Mintage	F	VF	XF	Unc	BU
1994	—	—	—	—	—	11.50

X# 21b ECU
Copper-Nickel **Subject:** Montgolfier brothers first flight, 1783 **Obv:** Early French hot air balloon **Obv. Legend:** PRINCIPAUTE DE MONACO **Rev:** Ancient and early sailing ships, hot air balloons, 12 stars in outer rims **Rev. Legend:** EUROPE EUROPA

Date	Mintage	F	VF	XF	Unc	BU
1994	—	—	—	—	—	8.50

X# 21c ECU
Bi-Metallic **Subject:** Montgolfier brothers first flight, 1783 **Obv:** Early French hot air ballon **Obv. Legend:** PRINCIPAUTE DE MONACO **Rev:** Ancient and early sailing ships, hot air balloon, 12 stars in outer rims **Rev. Legend:** EUROPE EUROPA **Edge:** Plain

Date	Mintage	F	VF	XF	Unc	BU
1994	—	—	—	—	—	17.50

FANTASY EURO PATTERNS

X# Pn1 EURO CENT
Copper Plated Steel **Ruler:** Rainier III **Subject:** 75th Grand Prix **Edge:** Plain

Date	Mintage	F	VF	XF	Unc	BU
2004	3,999	—	—	—	—	1.50
2004 Proof	999	Value: 2.50				

X# Pn2 2 EURO CENT

Copper Plated Steel **Ruler:** Rainier III **Subject:** 75th Grand Prix **Edge:** Plain

Date	Mintage	F	VF	XF	Unc	BU
2004	3,999	—	—	—	—	2.00
2004 Proof	999	Value: 3.00				

X# Pn3 5 EURO CENT

Copper Plated Steel **Ruler:** Rainier III **Subject:** 75th Grand Prix **Edge:** Plain

Date	Mintage	F	VF	XF	Unc	BU
2004	3,999	—	—	—	—	2.50
2004 Proof	999	Value: 3.50				

X# Pn4 10 EURO CENT

Goldine **Ruler:** Rainier III **Subject:** 75th Grand Prix **Edge:** Plain

Date	Mintage	F	VF	XF	Unc	BU
2004	3,999	—	—	—	—	3.00
2004 Proof	999	Value: 4.00				

X# Pn5 20 EURO CENT

Goldine **Ruler:** Rainier III **Subject:** 75th Grand Prix **Edge:** Plain

Date	Mintage	F	VF	XF	Unc	BU
2004	3,999	—	—	—	—	3.50
2004 Proof	999	Value: 5.00				

X# Pn6 50 EURO CENT

Goldine **Ruler:** Rainier III **Subject:** 75th Grand Prix **Edge:** Plain

Date	Mintage	F	VF	XF	Unc	BU
2004	3,999	—	—	—	—	4.00
2004 Proof	999	Value: 10.00				

X# Pn7 EURO

Bi-Metallic **Ruler:** Rainier III **Subject:** 75th Grand Prix **Obv:** Vintage race car, palm trees **Rev:** Large value on fan milled background **Edge:** Plain

Date	Mintage	F	VF	XF	Unc	BU
2004	3,999	—	—	—	—	6.00
2004 Proof	999	Value: 15.00				

X# Pn8 2 EURO

Bi-Metallic **Ruler:** Rainier III **Subject:** 75th Grand Prix **Obv:** Vintage race car, palm trees **Rev:** Large value, fan milled background **Edge:** Plain

Date	Mintage	F	VF	XF	Unc	BU
2004	3,999	—	—	—	—	8.00
2004 Proof	999	Value: 20.00				

X# Pn9 5 EURO

Ruler: Rainier III **Subject:** 75th Grand Prix

Date	Mintage	F	VF	XF	Unc	BU
2004 Proof	999	Value: 25.00				

PIEFORTS

Double thickness; Standard metals unless otherwise stated

X#	Date	Mintage	Identification	Mkt Val
P1	1994	3,000	Ecu. 0.9250 Silver Gilt. 40.0000 g. Early French hot air ballon colored. PRINCIPAUTE DE MONACO. Ancient and early sailing ships, hot air balloons, 12 stars in outer rims. EUROPE EUROPA. Colored balloon	95.00

MINT SETS

X#	Date	Mintage	Identification	Issue Price	Mkt Val
XMS1	2004 (8)	3,999	X#Pn1-Pn8	—	30.00

PROOF SETS

X#	Date	Mintage	Identification	Issue Price	Mkt Val
XPS1	1974 (4)	—	X#M3-XM6	—	1,575
XPS2	2004 (9)	999	X#Pn1-Pn9	—	50.00

PEOPLE'S REPUBLIC

FANTASY EURO PATTERNS

X# Pn1 EURO CENT

Copper Plated Steel **Edge:** Plain

Date	Mintage	F	VF	XF	Unc	BU
2005	7,000	—	—	—	—	1.50

X# Pn2 2 EURO CENT

Copper Plated Steel **Edge:** Plain

Date	Mintage	F	VF	XF	Unc	BU
2005	7,000	—	—	—	—	2.00

X# Pn3 5 EURO CENT

Copper Clad Steel **Edge:** Plain

Date	Mintage	F	VF	XF	Unc	BU
2005	7,000	—	—	—	—	2.50

X# Pn4 10 EURO CENT

Goldine **Edge:** Plain

Date	Mintage	F	VF	XF	Unc	BU
2005	7,000	—	—	—	—	3.00

X# Pn5 20 EURO CENT

Goldine **Edge:** Plain

Date	Mintage	F	VF	XF	Unc	BU
2005	7,000	—	—	—	—	3.50

X# Pn6 50 EURO CENT

Goldine **Edge:** Plain

Date	Mintage	F	VF	XF	Unc	BU
2005	7,000	—	—	—	—	4.00

X# Pn7 EURO

Bi-Metallic **Obv:** Helmeted head of Kublai Khan facing 3/4 right **Rev:** Flower, large value "1", EEU star design **Edge:** Plain

Date	Mintage	F	VF	XF	Unc	BU
2005	7,000	—	—	—	—	6.00

X# Pn8 2 EURO

Bi-Metallic **Obv:** Helmeted head of Kublai Khan facing 3/4 right **Rev:** Flower, large value "2", EEU star design **Edge:** Plain

Date	Mintage	F	VF	XF	Unc	BU
2005	7,000	—	—	—	—	8.00

STATE

MEDALLIC COINAGE

X# 1 10 TUGRIK

Copper Nickel, 38.7 mm. **Subject:** International games - Archery **Obv:** Arms in sprays **Rev:** Archer right

Date	Mintage	F	VF	XF	Unc	BU
1984 Proof	—	Value: 18.50				

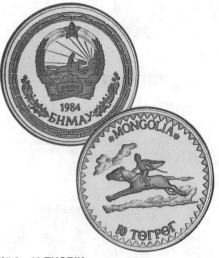

X# 2 10 TUGRIK

Copper Nickel, 38.3 mm. **Subject:** International games - Equestrian **Obv:** Arms in sprays

Date	Mintage	F	VF	XF	Unc	BU
1984 Proof	—	Value: 19.50				

MINT SETS

X#	Date	Mintage	Identification	Issue Price	Mkt Val
XMS1	2005 (8)	7,000	X#Pn1-Pn8	—	30.00

PROVISIONAL REVOLUTIONARY REPUBLIC

MILLED COINAGE

X# 2 SOLDO

29.0000 g., Copper-Nickel Silver Plated, 39.4 mm. **Obv:** Cristo Falcon perched on peak, flag below **Obv. Legend:** GOVERNO PROVVISORIO DELLA REPUBBLICA RIVOLUZIONARIA DI **Obv. Inscription:** MONTE CRISTO **Rev:** General Secretary's "3 Sparrows" crest **Rev. Inscription:** Goberno In Esilio **Edge:** Reeded

Date	Mintage	F	VF	XF	Unc	BU
2006 Proof	100	Value: 40.00				

X# 1 10 SOLDI

36.7600 g., Copper-Nickel Black and multicolored enamels 44.5 mm. **Subject:** Memorial to Pope John Paul II **Obv:** Multicolored knight named Dragut on horseback right **Obv. Inscription:** GOVERNO PROVVISORIO DELLA / REPUBBLICA RIVOLUZIONARIA DI / MONTE CRISTO **Rev:** Crowned Polish eagle with wings outspread **Rev. Inscription:** IN MEMORIAM / 10 ANNES PAULUS II **Edge:** Plain

Date	Mintage	F	VF	XF	Unc	BU
MMV	100	—	—	—	—	25.00

MONTENEGRO

REPUBLIC

FANTASY EURO PATTERNS

X# Pn1 EURO CENT
Copper Plated Steel **Edge:** Plain

Date	Mintage	F	VF	XF	Unc	BU
2005	7,000	—	—	—	—	1.50

X# Pn2 2 EURO CENT
Copper Plated Steel **Edge:** Plain

Date	Mintage	F	VF	XF	Unc	BU
2005	7,000	—	—	—	—	2.00

X# Pn3 5 EURO CENT
Copper Plated Steel **Edge:** Plain

Date	Mintage	F	VF	XF	Unc	BU
2005	7,000	—	—	—	—	2.50

X# Pn4 10 EURO CENT
Goldine **Edge:** Plain

Date	Mintage	F	VF	XF	Unc	BU
2005	7,000	—	—	—	—	3.00

X# Pn5 20 EURO CENT
Goldine **Edge:** Plain

Date	Mintage	F	VF	XF	Unc	BU
2005	7,000	—	—	—	—	3.50

X# Pn6 50 EURO CENT
Goldine **Edge:** Plain

Date	Mintage	F	VF	XF	Unc	BU
2005	7,000	—	—	—	—	4.00

X# Pn7 EURO
Bi-Metallic **Obv:** Male bust facing 3/4 left **Rev:** Two stylized doves, large value, EEU star design **Edge:** Plain

Date	Mintage	F	VF	XF	Unc	BU
2005	7,000	—	—	—	—	6.00

X# Pn8 2 EURO
Bi-Metallic **Obv:** Male bust facing 3/4 left **Rev:** Two stylized doves, large value, EEU star design **Edge:** Plain

Date	Mintage	F	VF	XF	Unc	BU
2005	7,000	—	—	—	—	8.00

MINT SETS

X#	Date	Mintage	Identification	Issue Price	Mkt Val
XMS1	2005 (8)	7,000	X#Pn1-Pn8	—	30.00

MOON

MILLED COINAGE

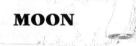

X# 1 PENNY
Bronze, 20 mm. **Series:** Green Cheese **Obv:** Landing craft **Obv. Legend:** MOON MONEY **Rev:** Cow jumping over the moon **Edge:** Plain

Date	Mintage	F	VF	XF	Unc	BU
ND(1969)	—	—	—	—	—	3.00

X# 2 NICKEL
Brass, 20 mm. **Series:** Green Cheese **Obv:** Half-length figure of astronaut Armstrong facing **Obv. Legend:** ALL AMERICAN BOY — NEIL A. ARMSTRONG **Rev:** Footprint in moon surface **Rev. Inscription:** Man's first / footprint / on the moon

Date	Mintage	F	VF	XF	Unc	BU
ND(1969)	—	—	—	—	—	5.00

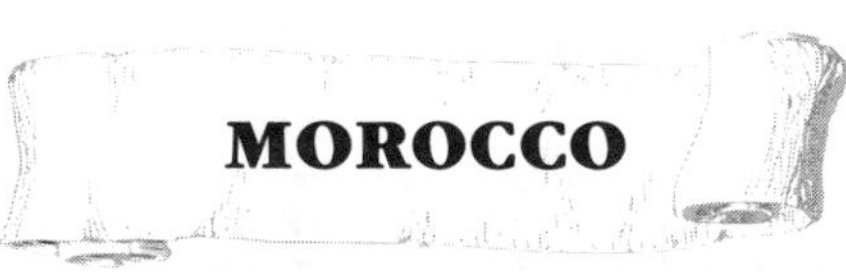

MOROCCO

FRENCH PROTECTORATE

BULLION COINAGE

X# 12 500 DIRHAMS
31.1031 g., 0.9170 Gold 0.9170 oz. AGW **Ruler:** Mohammed V AH1346-1381 / 1927-1962AD **Issuer:** First Banking Corporation, Tangier **Obv:** Hercules standing, facing 3/4 right, holding club and hide **Obv. Legend:** FIRST • BANKING • CO - PORATION • TANGIER **Note:** Refiners: N. M. Rothschild & Sons; prev. Y#250.

Date	Mintage	F	VF	XF	Unc	BU
ND(1954)	—	—	—	475	650	—

FANTASY COINAGE

X# 3 SOVEREIGN
7.9800 g., 0.9167 Gold 0.2352 oz. AGW **Subject:** 25th Anniversary of Accession

Date	Mintage	F	VF	XF	Unc	BU
AH1371 (1951)	200	—	—	650	850	—

X# 1 2 SOVEREIGNS
15.9760 g., 0.9167 Gold 0.4708 oz. AGW **Ruler:** Abu'l-'Abbas Ahmad II AH986-1012/1578-1603AD
Note: Weight varies: 15.95-16.04 grams.

Date	Mintage	F	VF	XF	Unc	BU
AH1372 (1952)	—	—	—	400	525	—

KINGDOM

Resumed

FANTASY COINAGE

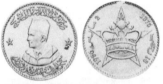

X# 4 NON-DENOMINATED
Gold, 18 mm. **Subject:** Restoration of Monarchy **Edge:** Plain

Date	Mintage	F	VF	XF	Unc	BU
AH1375	—	—	—	85.00	125	175

X# 5 NON-DENOMINATED
Gold **Subject:** Restoration of Monarchy **Note:** Weight varies: 3.97-4.95 grams.

Date	Mintage	F	VF	XF	Unc	BU
AH1375	—	—	120	160	200	—

X# 6 NON-DENOMINATED
19.8200 g., Gold, 36 mm. **Subject:** Restoration of Monarchy

Date	Mintage	F	VF	XF	Unc	BU
AH1375	—	—	575	750	900	—

MOZAMBIQUE

REPUBLIC

PATTERNS

Including off metal strikes

X# 1 100 MATADES
31.1000 g., 0.9990 Silver 0.9988 oz. ASW, 39 mm. **Subject:** Free Mozambique **Obv:** Soldier **Rev:** Arrows **Edge:** Reeded

Date	Mintage	F	VF	XF	Unc	BU
1987 Proof	—	Value: 50.00				

NAMIBIA

REPUBLIC

1920 - present

MEDALLIC BULLION COINAGE

X# MB3 OUNCE
0.9990 Silver **Issuer:** Namibian Miuters (Pty.) Ltd.
Subject: Independence **Obv:** Supported arms
Rev: Bust of President Sam Nujoma facing

Date	Mintage	F	VF	XF	Unc	BU
1990 Proof	5,000	Value: 40.00				

X# MB4 OUNCE
0.9167 Gold **Issuer:** Namibian Miuters (Pty.) Ltd.
Subject: Independence **Obv:** Supported arms
Rev: Bust of President Sam Nujoma facing

Date	Mintage	F	VF	XF	Unc	BU
1990 Proof	5,000	Value: 675				

GERMAN ADMINISTRATION

MEDALLIC BULLION COINAGE

X# MB2 5 UNZEN
155.5150 g., 0.9990 Gold 4.9947 oz. AGW, 65 mm.
Subject: 75th Anniversary Reiter Monument Horseman "Bushriders" of the German Colonial Army **Rev:** Tree, elephants walking left

Date	Mintage	F	VF	XF	Unc	BU
ND(1987)BP Proof	10	Value: 3,750				

X# MB1 5 UNZEN
155.5150 g., 0.9990 Silver 4.9947 oz. ASW, 65 mm.
Subject: 75th Anniversary Reiter Monument Horseman "Bushriders" of the German Colonial Army **Rev:** Tree, elephants walking left **Note:** Illustration reduced.

Date	Mintage	F	VF	XF	Unc	BU
ND(1987)BP Proof	2,000	Value: 150				

ESSAIS

Rand Coinage

X# E1 100 RAND
6.4500 g., 0.9000 Gold 0.1866 oz. AGW **Subject:** 75th Anniversary Reiter Monument Horseman "Bushriders" of the German Colonial Army

Date	Mintage	F	VF	XF	Unc	BU
ND(1987)BP Proof	15	Value: 1,000				

X# E2 100 RAND
Silver **Subject:** 75th Anniversary Reiter Monument Horseman "Bushriders" of the German Colonial Army

Date	Mintage	F	VF	XF	Unc	BU
ND(1987)BP Proof	1,000	Value: 20.00				

Dollar Coinage

Struck by the Budapest Mint in Hungary for the Money Company located in Tarzana, California, U.S.A.

X# E3 DOLLAR
Copper-Nickel **Issuer:** Money Co., California
Obv: Supported arms **Rev:** Native archer aiming right

Date	Mintage	F	VF	XF	Unc	BU
1990	1,000	—	—	—	15.00	—

X# E4 10 DOLLARS
25.0600 g., 0.9000 Silver 0.7251 oz. ASW
Issuer: Money Co., California **Obv:** Supported arms
Rev: Native archer aiming right **Edge:** Reeded

Date	Mintage	F	VF	XF	Unc	BU
1990 Proof	1,000	Value: 42.50				

Mark Coinage

X# E5 MARK
Copper-Nickel **Issuer:** Money Co., California
Obv: Supported arms **Rev:** Male lion seated left

Date	Mintage	F	VF	XF	Unc	BU
1990	1,000	—	—	—	15.00	—

X# E6 10 MARK
25.2400 g., 0.9000 Silver 0.7303 oz. ASW, 38 mm.
Issuer: Money Co., California **Obv:** Supported arms
Rev: Male lion seated left **Edge:** Reeded

Date	Mintage	F	VF	XF	Unc	BU
1990 Proof	1,000	Value: 42.50				

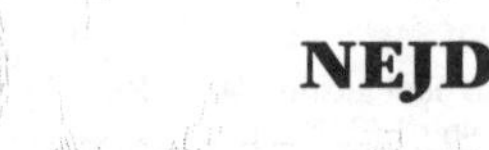

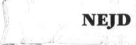

NEJD

KINGDOM

Abd Al-Aziz bin Saud

COUNTERMARKED COINAGE

Silver Coins

Following the defeat of the Ottomans in 1916, silver coins of various sizes were also countermarked 'Nejd'. The most common host coins include the Maria Theresa thalers of Austria, British India Rupees, and 5, 10, and 20 Kurush or Qirsh of Turkey and Egypt. The countermark occurs in various sizes and styles of script. These countermarks may have been applied by local silversmiths to discourage re-exportation of the badly needed hard currency and silver of known fineness.

Some crown-sized examples exist with both the 'al-Hejaz' and 'Nejd' countermarks. The authenticity of the silver countermarked coins has long been discussed, and it is likely that most were privately produced. Other host coins are considered controversial.

X# 1 5 PIASTRES
Silver **Ruler:** Abd Al-Aziz Bin Sa'ud **Countermark:** *Nejd* **Note:** Accession date: AH1327. **Countermark** on Egypt 5 Piastres, KM#308. Prev. KM#1.

CM Date	Host Date	Good	VG	F	VF	XF
ND(1918)	AH1327/2H	—	—	175	250	—
ND(1918)	AH1327/3H	—	—	175	250	—
ND(1918)	AH1327/4H	—	—	175	250	—
ND(1918)	AH1327/6H	—	—	175	250	—

X# 2.1 5 PIASTRES
Silver **Countermark:** "Nejd" **Note:** Countermark on Egypt 5 Piastres, KM#318.1. Accession date: AH1335. Prev. KM#2.1.

CM Date	Host Date	Good	VG	F	VF	XF
ND(1918)	AH1335-1916	—	—	175	250	—
ND(1918)	AH1335-1917	—	—	175	250	—

X# 2.2 5 PIASTRES
Silver **Ruler:** Abd Al-Aziz Bin Sa'ud **Countermark:** "Nejd" **Note:** Countermark on Egypt 5 Piastres, KM#318.2. Accession date: AH1333. Prev. KM#2.2.

CM Date	Host Date	Good	VG	F	VF	XF
ND(1918)	AH1335-1917H	—	—	175	250	—

X# 3 5 PIASTRES
Silver **Ruler:** Abd Al-Aziz Bin Sa'ud **Countermark:** *Nejd* **Note:** Countermark on Turkey 5 Kurush, KM#750. Accession date: AH1327. Prev. KM#3.

CM Date	Host Date	Good	VG	F	VF	XF
ND(1918)	AH1327/1-7	—	—	175	250	—

X# 4 5 PIASTRES
Silver **Ruler:** Abd Al-Aziz Bin Sa'ud **Countermark:** "Nejd" **Note:** Countermark on Turkey 5 Kurush, KM#771. Accession date: AH1327. Prev. KM#4.

CM Date	Host Date	Good	VG	F	VF	XF
ND(1918)	AH1327/7-9	—	—	175	250	—

X# 5 RUPEE
Silver **Ruler:** Abd Al-Aziz Bin Sa'ud **Countermark:** "Nejd" **Note:** Countermark on India Rupee, KM#450. Prev. KM#5.

CM Date	Host Date	Good	VG	F	VF	XF
ND(1918)	1835	—	—	265	350	—

X# 6 RUPEE
Silver **Ruler:** Abd Al-Aziz Bin Sa'ud **Countermark:** "Nejd" **Note:** Countermark on India Rupee, KM#457. Prev. KM#6.

CM Date	Host Date	Good	VG	F	VF	XF
ND(1918)	1840	—	—	265	350	—

X# 7 RUPEE
Silver **Ruler:** Abd Al-Aziz Bin Sa'ud **Countermark:** "Nejd" **Note:** Countermark on India Rupee, KM#458. Prev.KM#7.

CM Date	Host Date	Good	VG	F	VF	XF
ND(1918)	1840	—	—	265	350	—

X# 8.1 RUPEE
Silver **Ruler:** Abd Al-Aziz Bin Sa'ud **Countermark:** "Nejd" **Note:** Countermark on India Rupee, KM#473. Prev. KM#8.

CM Date	Host Date	Good	VG	F	VF	XF
ND(1918)	1862-76	—	—	265	350	—

X# 8.2 RUPEE
Silver **Ruler:** Abd Al-Aziz Bin Sa'ud **Countermark:** "Nejd" **Note:** Countermark on India Rupee, KM#492. Prev. KM#A9.

CM Date	Host Date	Good	VG	F	VF	XF
ND(1918)	1877-1901	—	—	265	350	—

X# 9 10 PIASTRES
Silver **Ruler:** Abd Al-Aziz Bin Sa'ud **Countermark:** "Nejd" **Note:** Countermark on Egypt 10 Qirsh, KM#295. Accession date: AH1293. Prev. KM#9.

CM Date	Host Date	Good	VG	F	VF	XF
(1918)	AH1293/27 w	—	—	200	285	—
ND(1918)	AH1293/29 w	—	—	200	285	—
ND(1918)	AH1293/29H	—	—	200	285	—
ND(1918)	AH1293/30H	—	—	200	285	—
ND(1918)	AH1293/31H	—	—	200	285	—
ND(1918)	AH1293/32H	—	—	200	285	—
ND(1918)	AH1293/33H	—	—	200	285	—

X# 15.1 10 PIASTRES
Silver **Ruler:** Abd Al-Aziz Bin Sa'ud **Countermark:** "Nejd" **Note:** Countermark on Egypt 10 Piastres, KM#319. Accession date: AH1333. Prev. KM#A11.1.

CM Date	Host Date	Good	VG	F	VF	XF
ND(1918)	AH1335-1916	—	—	200	285	—
ND(1918)	AH1335-1917	—	—	200	285	—

X# 15.2 10 PIASTRES
Silver **Ruler:** Abd Al-Aziz Bin Sa'ud **Countermark:** "Nejd" **Note:** Countermark on Egypt 10 Piastres, KM#320. Accession date: AH1333. Prev. KM#A11.2.

CM Date	Host Date	Good	VG	F	VF	XF
ND(1918)	AH1335-1917H	—	—	200	285	—

X# 11 10 PIASTRES
Silver **Ruler:** Abd Al-Aziz Bin Sa'ud **Countermark:** "Nejd" **Note:** Countermark on Turkey 10 Kurush, KM#772. Accession date: AH1327. Prev. KM#11.

CM Date	Host Date	Good	VG	F	VF	XF
ND(1918)	AH1327/7-10	—	—	200	285	—

X# 14.2 20 PIASTRES
28.0600 g., 0.8333 Silver 0.7517 oz. ASW, 41 mm. **Ruler:** Ibn Sa'ud **Countermark:** Type II "Nejd" **Note:** Countermarked on Austria MT Thaler, KM#T1. Prev. KM#12.

CM Date	Host Date	Good	VG	F	VF	XF
ND(1916-20)	1780 Restrike	100	—	—	350	435

X# 20 20 PIASTRES
27.0700 g., 0.9030 Silver 0.7859 oz. ASW **Ruler:** Ibn Sa'ud **Countermark:** al-Hejaz and Nejd **Note:** Countermarks "al-Hejaz" and "Nejd" on Austria MT Thaler, KM#T1.

CM Date	Host Date	Good	VG	F	VF	XF
ND(1916-23)	1780 Restrike	175	200	250	300	—

X# 16 20 PIASTRES
27.0700 g., 0.9030 Silver 0.7859 oz. ASW **Ruler:** Ibn Sa'ud **Countermark:** "Nejd" **Note:** Privately countermarked "Nejd" on Mexico City Mint 8 Reales, KM#109. Prev. KM#15.

CM Date	Host Date	Good	VG	F	VF	XF
ND(1916-23)	1808TH	—	125	200	300	—

X# 12.1 20 PIASTRES
0.8333 Silver **Ruler:** Abd Al-Aziz Bin Sa'ud **Countermark:** Nejd **Note:** Countermark on Egypt 20 Piastres, KM#296.

CM Date	Host Date	Good	VG	F	VF	XF
AH1292/20	ND(1918) W	—	—	275	350	—

X# A13.1 20 PIASTRES
Silver **Ruler:** Abd Al-Aziz Bin Sa'ud **Countermark:** Nejd **Note:** Countermarked on Egypt 20 Piastres, KM#321.

CM Date	Host Date	Good	VG	F	VF	XF
ND(1918-1919)	ND	—	125	200	300	—

X# 13.1 20 PIASTRES
Silver **Ruler:** Abd Al-Aziz Bin Sa'ud **Countermark:** "Nejd" **Note:** Countermark on Turkey 20 Kurush, KM#675. Accession date: AH1255. Prev. KM#B12.1.

CM Date	Host Date	Good	VG	F	VF	XF
ND(1918)	AH1255/6-15	—	—	350	450	—

X# 13.2 20 PIASTRES
Silver **Ruler:** Abd Al-Aziz Bin Sa'ud **Countermark:** "Nejd" **Note:** Countermark on Turkey 20 Kurush, KM#676. Accession date: AH1255. Prev. KM#B12.2.

CM Date	Host Date	Good	VG	F	VF	XF
ND(1918)	AH1255/15-23	—	—	350	450	—

X# 13.3 20 PIASTRES
Silver **Ruler:** Abd Al-Aziz Bin Sa'ud **Countermark:** "Nejd" **Note:** Countermark on Turkey 20 Kurush, KM#693. Accession date: AH1277. Prev. KM#C12.

CM Date	Host Date	Good	VG	F	VF	XF
ND(1918)	AH1277/1-15	—	—	350	450	—

X# 13.4 20 PIASTRES
Silver **Ruler:** Abd Al-Aziz Bin Sa'ud **Countermark:** "Nejd" **Note:** Countermark on Turkey 20 Kurush, KM#722. Accession date: AH1293. Prev. KM#A12.

CM Date	Host Date	Good	VG	F	VF	XF
ND(1918)	AH1293/1-3	—	—	350	450	—

X# 12.3 20 PIASTRES
Silver **Ruler:** Abd Al-Aziz Bin Sa'ud **Countermark:** "Nejd" **Note:** Countermark on Egypt 20 Piastres, KM#321. Accession date: 1333. Prev. KM#A13.1.

CM Date	Host Date	Good	VG	F	VF	XF
ND(1918)	AH1335-1916	—	—	350	450	—
ND(1918)	AH1335-1917	—	—	350	450	—

X# 12.4 20 PIASTRES
Silver **Ruler:** Abd Al-Aziz Bin Sa'ud **Countermark:** "Nejd" **Note:** Countermark on Egypt 20 Piastres, KM#322. Accession date: 1333. Prev. KM#A13.2.

CM Date	Host Date	Good	VG	F	VF	XF
ND(1918)	AH1335-1917H	—	—	350	450	—

X# 13.5 20 PIASTRES
Silver **Ruler:** Abd Al-Aziz Bin Sa'ud **Countermark:** "Nejd" **Note:** Countermark on Turkey 20 Kurush, KM#780. Accession date: AH1327. Prev. KM#13.

CM Date	Host Date	Good	VG	F	VF	XF
ND(1918)	AH1327/8-10	—	—	350	450	—

X# 14.1 20 PIASTRES
Silver **Ruler:** Abd Al-Aziz Bin Sa'ud **Countermark:** "Nejd" **Note:** Countermark on Austria Maria Theresa Thaler, KM#T1. Prev. KM#14.

CM Date	Host Date	Good	VG	F	VF	XF
ND(1918)	1780 Restrike	—	—	—	350	435

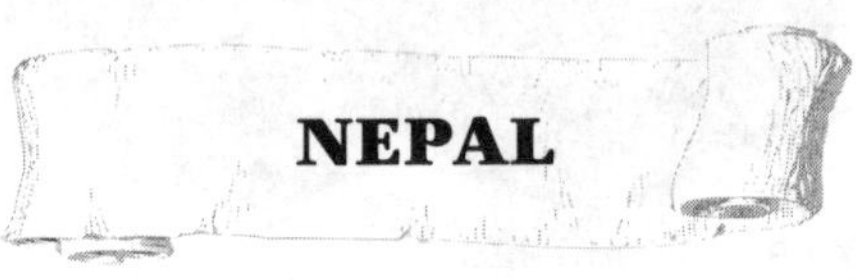

NEPAL

KINGDOM

Shah Dynasty

BULLION COINAGE

Tola Series - Sham-Lal-Sen

X# 19 1/4 TOLA
1.2930 g., 0.9950 Gold 0.0414 oz. AGW, 15 mm.
Rev: Deer running left, sunrise, mountains behind

Date	Mintage	F	VF	XF	Unc	BU
ND	—	—	BV	65.00	85.00	—

X# 21 TOLA
11.6800 g., 0.9950 Gold 0.3736 oz. AGW, 23.8 mm.
Obv: Value in sprays **Rev:** Deer running left, sunrise, mountains behind

Date	Mintage	F	VF	XF	Unc	BU
ND(1960)	—	—	—	275	350	—

CAMPAIGN MEDALS

Third Nepal - Tibet War, 1855-1856

X# CM1 NON-DENOMINATED
Silver, 38 mm. **Ruler:** Surendra Vikrama SE1769-1803 / 1847-1881AD **Subject:** Sri Natha Paltan **Note:** Prev. X#1. Normally issued looped. Sixteen other regiment issues exist.

Date	Mintage	F	VF	XF	Unc	BU
VS1912//1855	—	—	250	350	500	—

NETHERLANDS

KINGDOM OF THE NETHERLANDS

MEDALLIC BULLION COINAGE

X# MB1 5 DAALDER
155.5150 g., 0.9990 Silver 4.9947 oz. ASW, 63 mm.
Subject: 400th Anniversary of Utrecht Ducat
Note: Illustration reduced.

Date	Mintage	F	VF	XF	Unc	BU
1986 (u) Proof	—	Value: 125				

MEDALLIC COINAGE

X# 8 5 CENTS

5.1500 g., Copper-Nickel-Zinc **Ruler:** Beatrix **Subject:** 25th Anniversary Liberation WWII **Obv:** Jugate busts of Queens Juliana and Wilhelmina 3/4 right and right **Obv. Legend:** 5 MEI NEDERLAND 25 JAAR VRIJ... **Rev:** Large "5" in ornate frame **Edge:** Plain **Shape:** Square **Note:** 19 x 19mm.

Date	Mintage	F	VF	XF	Unc	BU
ND(1970)//1940	—	—	1.50	2.00	4.00	—

X# 2 5 CENTS

5.2100 g., Copper-Nickel-Zinc **Ruler:** Beatrix **Obv:** Bust of Wilhelmina **Obv. Legend:** WILHELMINA MOEDER DES VADERLANDS **Rev:** Large "5" in ornate frame **Edge:** Plain **Shape:** Square **Note:** 19.6 x 19.6mm.

Date	Mintage	F	VF	XF	Unc	BU
1945//1948 (sic)	—	—	1.50	2.50	4.00	—

X# 3 5 CENTS

5.0800 g., Copper-Nickel-Zinc **Ruler:** Beatrix **Subject:** 30th Anniversary of Reign **Obv:** Jugate busts of Juliana and Wilhelmina **Obv. Legend:** 5 MEI NEDERLAND 30 JAAR VRIJ - KONINGIN JULIANA KONINGIN **Rev:** Large "5" in ornate frame **Shape:** Square **Note:** 19.3x19.3mm.

Date	Mintage	F	VF	XF	Unc	BU
ND(1975)//1940	—	—	1.50	2.50	4.00	—

X# 4 5 CENTS

4.6200 g., Copper-Nickel-Zinc **Ruler:** Beatrix **Subject:** 70th Birthday **Obv:** Bust of Juliana left **Obv. Legend:** • JULIANA KONINGIN DER NEDERLANDEN • **Rev:** Large "5" in ornate frame **Edge:** Plain **Shape:** Square **Note:** 19.2x19.2mm.

Date	Mintage	F	VF	XF	Unc	BU
1979	—	—	1.50	2.50	4.00	—

X# 5 5 CENTS

4.4100 g., Copper-Nickel-Zinc **Ruler:** Beatrix **Subject:** Coronation **Obv:** Bust of Beatrix facing 3/4 right **Obv. Legend:** BEATRIX KONINGEN DER NEDERLANDEN 30.4.1980 **Rev:** Large "5" in ornate frame **Edge:** Plain **Shape:** Square **Note:** 19.25x19.25mm.

Date	Mintage	F	VF	XF	Unc	BU
1980	—	—	1.50	2.50	4.00	—

X# 9 5 CENTS

5.0600 g., Copper-Nickel-Zinc **Ruler:** Beatrix **Subject:** 32nd Anniversary of Reign **Obv:** Bust of Juliana left **Obv. Legend:** JULIANA KONINGIN DER NEDERLANDEN **Rev:** Large "5" in ornate frame **Edge:** Plain **Shape:** Square **Note:** 19.55x19.55mm.

Date	Mintage	F	VF	XF	Unc	BU
ND(1980)//1948	—	—	—	—	—	—

X# 7 5 CENTS

5.1300 g., Copper-Nickel-Zinc **Ruler:** Beatrix **Subject:** Wedding Anniversary **Obv:** Facing busts of Beatrix and Prince Claus **Obv. Legend:** BEATRIX EN CLAUS KONINGEN EN PRINS DER NEDERLANDEN **Rev:** Large "5" in ornate frame **Edge:** Plain **Shape:** Square **Note:** 19.65x19.65mm.

Date	Mintage	F	VF	XF	Unc	BU
1980//1938	—	—	1.50	2.50	4.00	—

X# 6 5 CENTS

5.2000 g., Copper-Nickel-Zinc **Ruler:** Beatrix **Obv:** Bust of Beatrix left **Obv. Legend:** KONINGEN BEATRIX **Rev:** Large "5" in ornate frame **Edge:** Plain **Shape:** Square **Note:** 19.6x19.6mm.

Date	Mintage	F	VF	XF	Unc	BU
1980//1938	—	—	1.50	2.50	4.00	—

X# A47 50 DAALDERS

25.0000 g., Silver, 38 mm. **Subject:** 25th Birthday of Prince **Obv:** Bust of Prince of Orange right, modern building behind **Rev:** Crowned arms at center, outline of galleon behind

Date	Mintage	F	VF	XF	Unc	BU
1992 Proof	—	—	—	—	—	—

Ecu Series

X# 52 2-1/2 ECU CENT

2.2500 g., Brass Plated Nickel, 16 mm. **Ruler:** Beatrix **Series:** Land of flowers **Obv:** Flowers **Obv. Inscription:** DE NEDERLANDEN **Rev:** Value on sail of medieval ship, 12 stars in arc above **Edge:** Plain

Date	Mintage	F	VF	XF	Unc	BU
1992	25,000	—	—	—	—	6.50

X# 53 5 ECU CENT

2.7000 g., Brass Plated Nickel, 18 mm. **Ruler:** Beatrix **Series:** Land of flowers **Obv:** Flowers **Obv. Inscription:** DE NEDERLANDEN **Rev:** Value on sail of medieval ship, 12 stars in arc above **Edge:** Plain

Date	Mintage	F	VF	XF	Unc	BU
1992	25,000	—	—	—	—	6.50

X# 54 10 ECU CENT

3.5000 g., Brass Plated Nickel, 20 mm. **Ruler:** Beatrix **Series:** Land of flowers **Obv:** Flowers **Obv. Inscription:** DE NEDERLANDEN **Rev:** Value on sail of medieval ship, 12 stars in arc above **Edge:** Plain

Date	Mintage	F	VF	XF	Unc	BU
1992	25,000	—	—	—	—	6.50

X# 55 25 ECU CENT

6.5000 g., Brass Plated Nickel, 26 mm. **Ruler:** Beatrix **Series:** Land of flowers **Obv:** Flowers **Obv. Inscription:** DE NEDERLANDEN **Rev:** Value on sail of medieval ship, 12 stars in arc above **Edge:** Plain

Date	Mintage	F	VF	XF	Unc	BU
1992	25,000	—	—	—	—	6.50

X# 58a 50 ECU CENT

7.0000 g., 0.9250 Silver 0.2082 oz. ASW **Subject:** 12-1/2 Anniversary of Coronation and Visit to Aruba and the Netherlands Antilles **Obv:** Medieval ship with denomination on sail **Rev:** Heads of five royal family right **Rev. Legend:** BEZOEK KON.FAM.NED. ANTILLEN EN ARUBA... **Edge:** Plain **Shape:** Square **Note:** 24 x 24mm.

Date	Mintage	F	VF	XF	Unc	BU
1992 Proof	—	—	—	—	—	—

X# 56 50 ECU CENT

5.0000 g., Steel Copper-tin plated **Ruler:** Beatrix **Series:** Land of flowers **Obv:** Flowers **Obv. Inscription:** DE NEDERLANDEN **Rev:** Value on sail of medieval ship, 12 stars in arc above **Edge:** Plain **Shape:** Square **Note:** 24 x 24mm.

Date	Mintage	F	VF	XF	Unc	BU
1992	25,000	—	—	—	—	12.50

X# 56a 50 ECU CENT

5.0000 g., Steel Nickel plated **Ruler:** Beatrix **Series:** Land of flowers **Obv:** Flowers **Obv. Inscription:** DE NEDERLANDEN **Rev:** Value on sail of medieval ship, 12 stars in arc above **Edge:** Plain **Shape:** Square **Note:** 24 x 24mm.

Date	Mintage	F	VF	XF	Unc	BU
1992	7,500	—	—	—	—	18.50

X# 56b 50 ECU CENT

7.0000 g., 0.9250 Silver 0.2082 oz. ASW **Ruler:** Beatrix **Series:** Land of flowers **Obv:** Flowers **Obv. Inscription:** DE NEDERLANDEN **Rev:** Value on sail of medieval ship, 12 stars in arc above **Edge:** Plain **Shape:** Square **Note:** 24 x 24mm.

Date	Mintage	F	VF	XF	Unc	BU
1992 Proof	1,500	Value: 45.00				

X# 58 50 ECU CENT

5.0000 g., Steel Bronze plated **Ruler:** Beatrix **Subject:** 12-1/2 Anniversary of Coronation and Visit to Aruba and the Netherlands Antilles **Obv:** Medieval ship with denomination on sail **Rev:** Heads of five royal family right **Rev. Legend:** BEZOEK KON.FAM.NED. ANTILLEN EN ARUBA... **Edge:** Plain **Shape:** Square **Note:** 24 x 24mm.

Date	Mintage	F	VF	XF	Unc	BU
1992	50,000	—	—	—	—	18.50

X# 64 50 ECU CENT

7.0000 g., 0.9250 Silver 0.2082 oz. ASW
Ruler: Beatrix **Obv:** Medieval ship with denomination on sail **Rev:** Bust of Jan A. Leeghwater 3/4 right, water, windmills and pumping stations in background
Edge: Plain **Shape:** Square **Note:** 24 x 24mm.

Date	Mintage	F	VF	XF	Unc	BU
1993 Proof	1,500	Value: 60.00				

X# 57 100 ECU CENT

9.0000 g., Brass Nickel plated, 30 mm. **Ruler:** Beatrix **Series:** Land of flowers **Obv:** Flowers **Obv. Inscription:** DE NEDERLANDEN **Rev:** Value on sail of medieval ship, 12 stars in arc above **Edge:** Plain

Date	Mintage	F	VF	XF	Unc	BU
1992	25,000	—	—	—	—	12.50

X# 11.1 ECU

28.5000 g., Copper-Nickel-Zinc, 38 mm. **Ruler:** Beatrix **Issuer:** Mauquoy - Tramaux & Co. B.v.b.a., Grobbendonk **Obv:** Charlemagne horseback left **Obv. Legend:** DE NEDERLANDEN **Rev:** Large circular "E-C-U" in 12 link circular chain **Edge:** Reeded **Note:** Prev. X#1.

Date	Mintage	F	VF	XF	Unc	BU
MCMLXXXVIII (1988)M	7,500	—	—	—	—	65.00

X# 11.2 ECU

28.5000 g., Copper-Nickel-Zinc, 38 mm. **Ruler:** Beatrix **Issuer:** Mauquoy - Tramaux & Co. B.v.b.a., Grobbendonk **Obv:** Charlemagne horseback left **Obv. Legend:** DE NEDERLANDEN **Rev:** Large circular "E-C-U" in 12 link circular chain **Edge:** Plain **Note:** Prev. X#1. Mintage Inc. X#11.1.

Date	Mintage	F	VF	XF	Unc	BU
MCMLXXXVIII (1988)M	—	—	—	—	—	65.00

X# 12 ECU

15.5520 g., 0.9990 Silver 0.4995 oz. ASW, 30 mm. **Ruler:** Beatrix **Issuer:** Mauquoy - Tramaux & Co. B.v.b.a., Grobbendonk **Subject:** Chevalier
Obv: Charlemagne horseback left **Obv. Legend:** DE NEDERLANDEN **Rev:** Large circular "E-C-U" in 12 link circular chain **Edge:** Plain **Note:** Prev. X#2.

Date	Mintage	F	VF	XF	Unc	BU
MCMLXXXVIII (1988)M Proof	500	Value: 350				

X# 13.1 ECU

33.7000 g., 0.9250 Silver 1.0022 oz. ASW, 38 mm. **Ruler:** Beatrix **Issuer:** Mauquoy - Tramaux & Co. B.v.b.a., Grobbendonk **Obv:** Charlemagne horseback left **Obv. Legend:** DE NEDERLANDEN **Obv. Inscription:** AG 1 OZ **Rev:** Large circular "E-C-U" in 12 link circular chain **Edge:** Reeded **Note:** Prev. X#3.

Date	Mintage	F	VF	XF	Unc	BU
MCMLXXXVIII (1988)M Prooflike	2,500	—	—	—	—	160

X# 13.2 ECU

33.7000 g., 0.9250 Silver 1.0022 oz. ASW, 38 mm. **Ruler:** Beatrix **Issuer:** Mauquoy - Tramaux & Co. B.v.b.a., Grobbendonk **Obv:** Charlemagne horseback left **Obv. Legend:** DE NEDERLANDEN **Rev:** Large circular "E-C-U" in 12 link circular chain **Edge:** Plain **Note:** Prev. X#3. Mintage: Inc. X#13.1.

Date	Mintage	F	VF	XF	Unc	BU
MCMLXXXVIII (1988)M Prooflike	—	—	—	—	—	110

X# 14 ECU

17.0250 g., 0.9160 Gold 0.5014 oz. AGW, 29 mm. **Ruler:** Beatrix **Issuer:** Mauquoy - Tramaux & Co. B.v.b.a., Grobbendonk **Subject:** Chevalier **Obv:** Charlemagne horseback left **Obv. Legend:** DE NEDERLANDEN **Rev:** Large circular "E-C-U" in 12 link circular chain **Edge:** Plain **Note:** Prev. X#4.

Date	Mintage	F	VF	XF	Unc	BU
MCMLXXXVIII (1988)M Prooflike	750	—	—	—	—	750

X# 20 ECU

6.0000 g., Brass, 26 mm. **Ruler:** Beatrix **Issuer:** Mauquoy - Tramaux & Co. B.v.b.a., Grobbendonk **Subject:** Deventer Mint 1000th Anniversary **Obv:** Large "ECU", medieval sailing ship, 12 stars in ribbon border **Obv. Legend:** DE NEDER - LANDEN **Rev:** Otto III pfennig above mint emblem at left, crowned arms at right **Rev. Legend:** ★ 1000 J.MUNTSLAG ★ **Edge:** Reeded **Note:** Prev. X#10.

Date	Mintage	F	VF	XF	Unc	BU
1990	11,049	—	—	—	—	25.00

X# 20a ECU

7.2000 g., 0.9250 Silver 0.2141 oz. ASW, 26 mm. **Ruler:** Beatrix **Issuer:** Mauquoy - Tramaux & Co. B.v.b.a., Grobbendonk **Subject:** Deventer Mint 1000th Anniversary **Obv:** Large "ECU", medieval sailing ship, 12 stars in ribbon border **Obv. Legend:** DE NEDER - LANDEN **Rev:** Otto III pfennig above mint emblem at left, crowned arms at right **Rev. Legend:** DEVENTER ★ 1000 J.MUNTSLAG **Edge:** Reeded **Note:** Prev. X#11. With fineness.

Date	Mintage	F	VF	XF	Unc	BU
1990 Proof	1,500	Value: 95.00				

X# 22 ECU

6.0000 g., Brass, 26 mm. **Ruler:** Beatrix **Issuer:** Mauquoy - Tramaux & Co. B.v.b.a., Grobbendonk **Subject:** Europa Week **Obv:** Large "ECU", medieval sailing ship, 12 stars in ribbon border **Obv. Legend:** DE NEDER - LANDEN **Rev:** RGER Emblem, 12 stars on stem at left, crowned arms at right **Rev. Legend:** ZOETERMEER, WAAR ANDERS! **Edge:** Reeded

Date	Mintage	F	VF	XF	Unc	BU
1990	20,000	—	—	—	—	20.00

X# 22a ECU

7.2500 g., 0.9250 Silver 0.2156 oz. ASW, 26 mm. **Ruler:** Beatrix **Issuer:** Mauquoy - Tramaux & Co. B.v.b.a., Grobbendonk **Subject:** Europa Week **Obv:** Large "ECU", medieval sailing ship, 12 stars in ribbon border **Obv. Legend:** DE NEDER - LANDEN **Rev:** RGER Emblem, 12 stars on stem at left, crowned arms at right **Rev. Legend:** ZOETERMEER, WAAR ANDERS! **Edge:** Reeded **Note:** Prev. X#13.

Date	Mintage	F	VF	XF	Unc	BU
1990 Proof	1,500	Value: 95.00				

X# 24 ECU

6.0000 g., Brass, 26 mm. **Ruler:** Beatrix **Issuer:** Mauquoy - Tramaux & Co. B.v.b.a., Grobbendonk **Subject:** 800th Anniversary Zutpher Charter **Obv:** Large "ECU", medieval sailing ship, 12 stars in ribbon border **Obv. Legend:** DE NEDER - LANDEN **Rev:** Stylized state shield at left, crowned arms at right **Rev. Legend:** ZUTPHEN ★ 800 JAARSTAD **Edge:** Reeded **Note:** Prev. X#14.

Date	Mintage	F	VF	XF	Unc	BU
1990	20,000	—	—	—	—	20.00

X# 24a ECU

7.2000 g., 0.9250 Silver 0.2141 oz. ASW, 26 mm. **Ruler:** Beatrix **Issuer:** Mauquoy - Tramaux & Co. B.v.b.a., Grobbendonk **Subject:** 800th Anniversary Zutphen Charter **Obv:** Large "ECU", medieval sailing ship, 12 stars in ribbon border **Obv. Legend:** DE NEDER - LANDEN **Rev:** Stylized state shield at left, crowned arms at right **Rev. Legend:** ZUTPHEN ★ 800 JAARSTAD **Edge:** Reeded **Note:** Prev. X#15.

Date	Mintage	F	VF	XF	Unc	BU
1990 Proof	1,500	Value: 95.00				

X# 201 ECU

Copper-Nickel, 30 mm. **Ruler:** Beatrix **Subject:** Moon Landing **Rev:** Astronaut descending ladder to moon's surface **Rev. Legend:** EERSTE MENS 1969 OP DE MAAN 1994 **Edge:** Plain

Date	Mintage	F	VF	XF	Unc	BU
1994	—	—	—	—	6.50	—

X# 201a ECU

Silver, 30 mm. **Ruler:** Beatrix **Subject:** Moon Landing **Rev:** Astronaut descending ladder to moon's surface **Rev. Legend:** EERSTE MENS 1969 OP DE MAAN 1994 **Edge:** Plain

Date	Mintage	F	VF	XF	Unc	BU
1994 Proof	—	Value: 20.00				

X# 202 ECU

Copper-Nickel, 30 mm. **Ruler:** Beatrix **Rev:** Sailing ship, Brandaris lighthouse, Ameland **Rev. Legend:** TOT WAARSCHOUWINGE ALLER SEEVARENDE DE GOD BEHOEDE **Rev. Inscription:** NEDERLANDSE / VUURTORENS **Edge:** Plain

Date	Mintage	F	VF	XF	Unc	BU
1994	—	—	—	—	6.50	—

X# 202a ECU
Silver, 30 mm. **Ruler:** Beatrix **Rev:** Sailing ship, Brandaris lighthouse, Ameland **Rev. Legend:** TOT WAARSCHOUWINGE ALLER SEEVARENDE DE GOD BEHOEDE **Rev. Inscription:** NEDERLANDSE / VUURTORENS **Edge:** Plain

Date	Mintage	F	VF	XF	Unc	BU
1994 Proof	—	Value: 20.00				

X# 203 ECU
Copper-Nickel, 30 mm. **Ruler:** Beatrix **Rev:** Mauritius Dodo bird **Edge:** Plain

Date	Mintage	F	VF	XF	Unc	BU
1995	—	—	—	—	6.50	—

X# 203a ECU
Silver, 30 mm. **Ruler:** Beatrix **Rev:** Mauritius Dodo bird **Edge:** Plain

Date	Mintage	F	VF	XF	Unc	BU
1995 Proof	—	Value: 20.00				

X# 204 ECU
Copper-Nickel, 30 mm. **Ruler:** Beatrix **Subject:** 100th Anniversary of Film Making **Edge:** Plain

Date	Mintage	F	VF	XF	Unc	BU
1995	—	—	—	—	6.50	—

X# 204a ECU
Silver, 30 mm. **Ruler:** Beatrix **Subject:** 100th Anniversary of Film Making **Edge:** Plain

Date	Mintage	F	VF	XF	Unc	BU
1995 Proof	—	Value: 20.00				

X# 205 ECU
Copper-Nickel, 30 mm. **Ruler:** Beatrix **Subject:** 40th Anniversary Victory WWII **Rev:** Queen Wilhelmina **Edge:** Plain

Date	Mintage	F	VF	XF	Unc	BU
1995	—	—	—	—	6.50	—

X# 205a ECU
Silver, 30 mm. **Ruler:** Beatrix **Subject:** 40th Anniversary Victory WWII **Rev:** Queen Wilhelmina **Edge:** Plain

Date	Mintage	F	VF	XF	Unc	BU
1995 Proof	—	Value: 20.00				

X# 206 ECU
Copper-Nickel, 30 mm. **Ruler:** Beatrix **Subject:** 50th Anniversary United Nations **Edge:** Plain

Date	Mintage	F	VF	XF	Unc	BU
1995	—	—	—	—	6.50	—

X# 206a ECU
Silver, 30 mm. **Ruler:** Beatrix **Subject:** 50th Anniversary United Nations **Edge:** Plain

Date	Mintage	F	VF	XF	Unc	BU
1995 Proof	—	Value: 20.00				

X# 207 ECU
Copper-Nickel, 30 mm. **Ruler:** Beatrix **Subject:** SAIL Amsterdam **Rev:** Sailing ships **Edge:** Plain

Date	Mintage	F	VF	XF	Unc	BU
1995	—	—	—	—	6.50	—

X# 207a ECU
Silver, 30 mm. **Ruler:** Beatrix **Subject:** SAIL Amsterdam **Rev:** Sailing ships **Edge:** Plain

Date	Mintage	F	VF	XF	Unc	BU
1995 Proof	—	Value: 20.00				

X# 208 ECU
Copper-Nickel, 30 mm. **Ruler:** Beatrix **Subject:** Birds of Prey **Rev:** Falcon **Edge:** Plain

Date	Mintage	F	VF	XF	Unc	BU
1995	—	—	—	—	6.50	—

X# 208a ECU
Silver, 30 mm. **Ruler:** Beatrix **Subject:** Birds of Prey **Rev:** Falcon **Edge:** Plain

Date	Mintage	F	VF	XF	Unc	BU
1995 Proof	—	Value: 20.00				

X# 209 ECU
Copper-Nickel, 30 mm. **Ruler:** Beatrix **Subject:** Nobel Prize **Rev:** Portrait of Jan Tinbergen **Edge:** Plain

Date	Mintage	F	VF	XF	Unc	BU
1995	—	—	—	—	6.50	—

X# 209a ECU
Silver, 30 mm. **Ruler:** Beatrix **Subject:** Nobel Prize **Rev:** Portrait of Jan Tinbergen **Edge:** Plain

Date	Mintage	F	VF	XF	Unc	BU
1995 Proof	—	Value: 20.00				

X# 210 ECU
Copper-Nickel, 30 mm. **Ruler:** Beatrix **Subject:** Christmas **Rev:** Children holding large stars by Dick Bruna **Edge:** Plain

Date	Mintage	F	VF	XF	Unc	BU
1995	—	—	—	—	6.50	—

X# 210a ECU
Silver, 30 mm. **Ruler:** Beatrix **Subject:** Christmas **Rev:** Children holding large stars by Dick Bruna **Edge:** Plain

Date	Mintage	F	VF	XF	Unc	BU
1995 Proof	—	Value: 20.00				

X# 211 ECU
Copper-Nickel, 30 mm. **Ruler:** Beatrix **Rev:** Scene from painting by Johannes Vermeer, 1632-1675 **Edge:** Plain

Date	Mintage	F	VF	XF	Unc	BU
1996	—	—	—	—	6.50	—

X# 211a ECU
Silver, 30 mm. **Ruler:** Beatrix **Rev:** Scene from painting by Johannes Vermeer, 1632-1675 **Edge:** Plain

Date	Mintage	F	VF	XF	Unc	BU
1996 Proof	—	Value: 20.00				

X# 212 ECU
Copper-Nickel, 30 mm. **Ruler:** Beatrix **Subject:** Spring Flowers **Rev:** Vase of flowers **Rev. Legend:** VOOR JAARS BLOEMEN **Edge:** Plain

Date	Mintage	F	VF	XF	Unc	BU
1996	—	—	—	—	6.50	—

X# 212a ECU
Silver, 30 mm. **Ruler:** Beatrix **Subject:** Spring Flowers **Rev:** Vase of flowers **Rev. Legend:** VOOR JAARS BLOEMEN **Edge:** Plain

Date	Mintage	F	VF	XF	Unc	BU
1996 Proof	—	Value: 20.00				

X# 213 ECU
Copper-Nickel, 30 mm. **Ruler:** Beatrix **Rev:** Oliver B. Bommel and Tom Poes walking right, cartoon bear and cat by Maarten Toonda **Edge:** Plain

Date	Mintage	F	VF	XF	Unc	BU
1996	—	—	—	—	6.50	—

X# 213a ECU
Silver, 30 mm. **Ruler:** Beatrix **Rev:** Oliver B. Bommel and Tom Poes walking right, cartoon bear and cat by Maarten Toonda **Edge:** Plain

Date	Mintage	F	VF	XF	Unc	BU
1996 Proof	—	Value: 20.00				

X# 214 ECU
Copper-Nickel, 30 mm. **Ruler:** Beatrix **Subject:** Vacation **Rev:** Family heading to the beach **Rev. Legend:** VAKANTE **Edge:** Plain

Date	Mintage	F	VF	XF	Unc	BU
1996	—	—	—	—	6.50	—

X# 214a ECU
Silver, 30 mm. **Ruler:** Beatrix **Subject:** Vacation **Rev:** Family heading to the beach **Rev. Legend:** VAKANTE **Edge:** Plain

Date	Mintage	F	VF	XF	Unc	BU
1996 Proof	—	Value: 20.00				

X# 215 ECU
Copper-Nickel, 30 mm. **Ruler:** Beatrix **Subject:** Cycling Tour of France **Rev:** 5 cyclists **Rev. Legend:** TOUR DE FRANCE **Edge:** Plain

Date	Mintage	F	VF	XF	Unc	BU
1996	—	—	—	—	6.50	—

X# 215a ECU
Silver, 30 mm. **Ruler:** Beatrix **Subject:** Cycling Tour of France **Rev:** 5 cyclists **Rev. Legend:** TOUR DE FRANCE **Edge:** Plain

Date	Mintage	F	VF	XF	Unc	BU
1996 Proof	—	Value: 20.00				

X# 216 ECU

Copper-Nickel, 30 mm. **Ruler:** Beatrix **Subject:** Atlantic Olympic Games **Rev:** Sprinters **Rev. Inscription:** XXVI / OLYMPIADE / ATLANTA **Edge:** Plain

Date	Mintage	F	VF	XF	Unc	BU
1996	—	—	—	—	6.50	—

X# 216a ECU

Silver, 30 mm. **Ruler:** Beatrix **Subject:** Atlantic Olympic Games **Rev:** Sprinters **Rev. Legend:** XXVI / OLYMPIADE / ATLANTA **Edge:** Plain

Date	Mintage	F	VF	XF	Unc	BU
1996 Proof	—	Value: 20.00				

X# 217 ECU

Copper-Nickel, 30 mm. **Ruler:** Beatrix **Subject:** 50th Anniversary of UNICEF **Rev:** Children dancing in circle **Edge:** Plain

Date	Mintage	F	VF	XF	Unc	BU
1996	—	—	—	—	6.50	—

X# 217a ECU

Silver, 30 mm. **Ruler:** Beatrix **Subject:** 50th Anniversary of UNICEF **Rev:** Children dancing in circle **Edge:** Plain

Date	Mintage	F	VF	XF	Unc	BU
1996 Proof	—	Value: 20.00				

X# 218 ECU

Copper-Nickel, 30 mm. **Ruler:** Beatrix **Subject:** Discoveries **Edge:** Plain

Date	Mintage	F	VF	XF	Unc	BU
1996	—	—	—	—	6.50	—

X# 219 ECU

Copper-Nickel, 30 mm. **Ruler:** Beatrix **Subject:** Nature and Conservation **Rev:** Pony **Edge:** Plain

Date	Mintage	F	VF	XF	Unc	BU
1997	—	—	—	—	6.50	—

X# 219a ECU

Silver, 30 mm. **Ruler:** Beatrix **Subject:** Nature and Conservation **Rev:** Pony **Edge:** Plain

Date	Mintage	F	VF	XF	Unc	BU
1997 Proof	—	Value: 20.00				

X# 220 ECU

Copper-Nickel, 30 mm. **Ruler:** Beatrix **Rev:** Suske and Wiske cartoon figures **Edge:** Plain

Date	Mintage	F	VF	XF	Unc	BU
1997	—	—	—	—	6.50	—

X# 220a ECU

Silver, 30 mm. **Ruler:** Beatrix **Rev:** Suske and Wiske cartoon figures **Edge:** Plain

Date	Mintage	F	VF	XF	Unc	BU
1997 Proof	—	Value: 20.00				

X# 221 ECU

Copper-Nickel, 30 mm. **Ruler:** Beatrix **Subject:** 50th Anniversary Marshall Plan **Rev:** Package, $ sign **Edge:** Plain

Date	Mintage	F	VF	XF	Unc	BU
1997	—	—	—	—	6.50	—

X# 221a ECU

Silver, 30 mm. **Ruler:** Beatrix **Subject:** 50th Anniversary Marshall Plan **Rev:** Package, $ sign **Edge:** Plain

Date	Mintage	F	VF	XF	Unc	BU
1997 Proof	—	Value: 20.00				

X# 222 ECU

Copper-Nickel, 30 mm. **Ruler:** Beatrix **Subject:** European Union **Rev:** Symbols **Edge:** Plain

Date	Mintage	F	VF	XF	Unc	BU
1997	—	—	—	—	6.50	—

X# 222a ECU

Silver, 30 mm. **Ruler:** Beatrix **Subject:** European Union **Rev:** Symbols **Edge:** Plain

Date	Mintage	F	VF	XF	Unc	BU
1997 Proof	—	Value: 20.00				

X# 223 ECU

Copper-Nickel, 30 mm. **Ruler:** Beatrix **Rev:** Sailboat Skûtsjesile **Edge:** Plain

Date	Mintage	F	VF	XF	Unc	BU
1997	—	—	—	—	6.50	—

X# 223a ECU

Silver, 30 mm. **Ruler:** Beatrix **Rev:** Sailboat Skûtsjesile **Edge:** Plain

Date	Mintage	F	VF	XF	Unc	BU
1997 Proof	—	Value: 20.00				

X# 224 ECU

Copper-Nickel, 30 mm. **Ruler:** Beatrix **Subject:** 200th Anniversary Shubert **Rev:** Hands playing piano **Edge:** Plain

Date	Mintage	F	VF	XF	Unc	BU
1997	—	—	—	—	6.50	—

X# 224a ECU

Silver, 30 mm. **Ruler:** Beatrix **Subject:** 200th Anniversary Shubert **Rev:** Hands playing piano **Edge:** Plain

Date	Mintage	F	VF	XF	Unc	BU
1997 Proof	—	Value: 20.00				

X# 225 ECU

Copper-Nickel, 30 mm. **Ruler:** Beatrix **Subject:** Youth Trends **Rev:** Cross of C-O-O-L, kids on rollerblades in angles **Edge:** Plain

Date	Mintage	F	VF	XF	Unc	BU
1997	—	—	—	—	6.50	—

X# 225a ECU

Silver, 30 mm. **Ruler:** Beatrix **Subject:** Youth Trends **Rev:** Cross of C-O-O-L, kids on rollerblades in angles **Edge:** Plain

Date	Mintage	F	VF	XF	Unc	BU
1997 Proof	—	Value: 20.00				

X# 226 ECU

Copper-Nickel, 30 mm. **Ruler:** Beatrix **Subject:** Birth **Rev:** Baby in blanket **Edge:** Plain

Date	Mintage	F	VF	XF	Unc	BU
1997	—	—	—	—	6.50	—

X# 226a ECU

Silver, 30 mm. **Ruler:** Beatrix **Subject:** Birth **Rev:** Baby in blanket **Edge:** Plain

Date	Mintage	F	VF	XF	Unc	BU
1997 Proof	—	Value: 20.00				

X# 227 ECU

Copper-Nickel, 30 mm. **Ruler:** Beatrix **Subject:** Four Seasons **Rev:** Symbolic tree **Edge:** Plain

Date	Mintage	F	VF	XF	Unc	BU
1998	—	—	—	—	6.50	—

X# 227a ECU

Silver, 30 mm. **Ruler:** Beatrix **Subject:** Four Seasons **Rev:** Symbolic tree **Edge:** Plain

Date	Mintage	F	VF	XF	Unc	BU
1998 Proof	—	Value: 20.00				

X# 228 ECU

Copper-Nickel, 30 mm. **Ruler:** Beatrix **Subject:** Münster Peace Treaty **Edge:** Plain

Date	Mintage	F	VF	XF	Unc	BU
1998	—	—	—	—	6.50	—

X# 228a ECU

Silver, 30 mm. **Ruler:** Beatrix **Subject:** Münster Peace Treaty **Edge:** Plain

Date	Mintage	F	VF	XF	Unc	BU
1998 Proof	—	Value: 20.00				

X# 229 ECU

Copper-Nickel, 30 mm. **Ruler:** Beatrix **Subject:** 100th Anniversary KNHB **Rev:** Hockey **Edge:** Plain

Date	Mintage	F	VF	XF	Unc	BU
1998	—	—	—	—	6.50	—

X# 229a ECU

Silver, 30 mm. **Ruler:** Beatrix **Subject:** 100th Anniversary KNHB **Rev:** Hockey **Edge:** Plain

Date	Mintage	F	VF	XF	Unc	BU
1998 Proof	—	Value: 20.00				

X# 230 ECU

Copper-Nickel, 30 mm. **Ruler:** Beatrix **Subject:** Netherlands Wetlands **Rev:** Dykes and windmills **Edge:** Plain

Date	Mintage	F	VF	XF	Unc	BU
1998	—	—	—	—	6.50	—

X# 230a ECU

Silver, 30 mm. **Ruler:** Beatrix **Subject:** Netherlands Wetlands **Rev:** Dykes and windmills **Edge:** Plain

Date	Mintage	F	VF	XF	Unc	BU
1998 Proof	—	Value: 20.00				

X# 231 ECU

Copper-Nickel, 30 mm. **Ruler:** Beatrix **Rev:** Theme from "Swans and Scenery" M. C. Escher **Edge:** Plain

Date	Mintage	F	VF	XF	Unc	BU
1998	—	—	—	—	6.50	—

X# 231a ECU

Silver, 30 mm. **Ruler:** Beatrix **Rev:** Theme from "Swans and Scenery" M. C. Escher **Edge:** Plain

Date	Mintage	F	VF	XF	Unc	BU
1998 Proof	—	Value: 20.00				

X# 232 ECU

Copper-Nickel, 30 mm. **Ruler:** Beatrix **Rev:** Royal Golden carriage **Edge:** Plain

Date	Mintage	F	VF	XF	Unc	BU
1998	—	—	—	—	6.50	—

X# 232a ECU

Silver, 30 mm. **Ruler:** Beatrix **Rev:** Royal Golden carriage **Edge:** Plain

Date	Mintage	F	VF	XF	Unc	BU
1998 Proof	—	Value: 20.00				

X# 233 ECU

Copper-Nickel, 30 mm. **Ruler:** Beatrix **Subject:** Pets **Rev:** Pets playing **Edge:** Plain

Date	Mintage	F	VF	XF	Unc	BU
1998	—	—	—	—	6.50	—

X# 233a ECU

Silver, 30 mm. **Ruler:** Beatrix **Subject:** Pets **Rev:** Pets playing **Edge:** Plain

Date	Mintage	F	VF	XF	Unc	BU
1998 Proof	—	Value: 20.00				

X# 234 ECU
Copper-Nickel, 30 mm. **Ruler:** Beatrix **Rev:** Jan, Jans and children, cartoon characters **Edge:** Plain

Date	Mintage	F	VF	XF	Unc	BU
1998	—	—	—	—	6.50	—

X# 234a ECU
Silver, 30 mm. **Ruler:** Beatrix **Rev:** Jan, Jans and children, cartoon characters **Edge:** Plain

Date	Mintage	F	VF	XF	Unc	BU
1998 Proof	—	Value: 20.00				

X# 235 ECU
Copper-Nickel, 30 mm. **Ruler:** Beatrix **Edge:** Plain

Date	Mintage	F	VF	XF	Unc	BU
1999	—	—	—	—	6.50	—

X# 235a ECU
Silver, 30 mm. **Ruler:** Beatrix **Edge:** Plain

Date	Mintage	F	VF	XF	Unc	BU
1999 Proof	—	Value: 20.00				

X# 236 ECU
Copper-Nickel, 30 mm. **Ruler:** Beatrix **Subject:** 100th Anniversary KNLTB **Rev:** Tennis **Edge:** Plain

Date	Mintage	F	VF	XF	Unc	BU
1999	—	—	—	—	6.50	—

X# 236a ECU
Silver, 30 mm. **Ruler:** Beatrix **Subject:** 100th Anniversary KNLTB **Rev:** Tennis **Edge:** Plain

Date	Mintage	F	VF	XF	Unc	BU
1999 Proof	—	Value: 20.00				

X# 237 ECU
Copper-Nickel, 30 mm. **Ruler:** Beatrix **Edge:** Plain

Date	Mintage	F	VF	XF	Unc	BU
1999	—	—	—	—	6.50	—

X# 237a ECU
Silver, 30 mm. **Ruler:** Beatrix **Edge:** Plain

Date	Mintage	F	VF	XF	Unc	BU
1999 Proof	—	Value: 20.00				

X# 238 ECU
Copper-Nickel, 30 mm. **Ruler:** Beatrix **Edge:** Plain

Date	Mintage	F	VF	XF	Unc	BU
1999	—	—	—	—	6.50	—

X# 238a ECU
Silver, 30 mm. **Ruler:** Beatrix **Edge:** Plain

Date	Mintage	F	VF	XF	Unc	BU
1999 Proof	—	Value: 20.00				

X# 239 ECU
Copper-Nickel, 30 mm. **Ruler:** Beatrix **Edge:** Plain

Date	Mintage	F	VF	XF	Unc	BU
1999	—	—	—	—	6.50	—

X# 239a ECU
Silver, 30 mm. **Ruler:** Beatrix **Edge:** Plain

Date	Mintage	F	VF	XF	Unc	BU
1999 Proof	—	Value: 20.00				

X# 240 ECU
Copper-Nickel, 30 mm. **Ruler:** Beatrix **Edge:** Plain

Date	Mintage	F	VF	XF	Unc	BU
1999	—	—	—	—	6.50	—

X# 240a ECU
Silver, 30 mm. **Ruler:** Beatrix **Edge:** Plain

Date	Mintage	F	VF	XF	Unc	BU
1999 Proof	—	Value: 20.00				

X# 241 ECU
Copper-Nickel, 30 mm. **Ruler:** Beatrix **Edge:** Plain

Date	Mintage	F	VF	XF	Unc	BU
1999	—	—	—	—	6.50	—

X# 241a ECU
Silver, 30 mm. **Ruler:** Beatrix **Edge:** Plain

Date	Mintage	F	VF	XF	Unc	BU
1999 Proof	—	Value: 20.00				

X# 242 ECU
Copper-Nickel, 30 mm. **Ruler:** Beatrix **Rev:** Jip and Janneke, cartoon characters **Edge:** Plain

Date	Mintage	F	VF	XF	Unc	BU
1999	—	—	—	—	6.50	—

X# 242a ECU
Silver, 30 mm. **Ruler:** Beatrix **Rev:** Jip and Janneke, cartoon characters **Edge:** Plain

Date	Mintage	F	VF	XF	Unc	BU
1999 Proof	—	Value: 20.00				

X# 94 2 ECU
Copper-Nickel, 30 mm. **Ruler:** Beatrix **Subject:** Sail 95 Amsterdam **Obv:** Rampant lion left with sword and bundle of arrows **Obv. Legend:** KONINKRIJK DER NEDERLAND **Rev:** V.O.C. sailing ship "Amsterdam"

Date	Mintage	F	VF	XF	Unc	BU
1995	30,000	—	—	—	—	6.50

X# 95 2 ECU
Copper-Nickel, 30 mm. **Ruler:** Beatrix **Subject:** Sail 95 Amsterdam **Obv:** Rampant lion left with sword and bundle of arrows **Obv. Legend:** KONINKRIJK DER NEDERLANDEN **Rev:** City view above V.O.C. sailing ship "Batavia" sails **Edge:** Plain

Date	Mintage	F	VF	XF	Unc	BU
1995	30,000	—	—	—	—	6.50

X# 96 2 ECU
Copper-Nickel, 30 mm. **Ruler:** Beatrix **Subject:** Sail 95 Amsterdam **Obv:** Rampant lion left with sword and bundle of arrows **Obv. Legend:** KONINKRIJK DER NEDERLANDEN **Rev:** Schooner "Eendracht" **Edge:** Plain

Date	Mintage	F	VF	XF	Unc	BU
1995	30,000	—	—	—	—	6.50

X# 97 2 ECU
Copper-Nickel, 30 mm. **Ruler:** Beatrix **Subject:** Sail 95 Amsterdam **Obv:** Rampant lion left with sword and bundle of arrows **Obv. Legend:** KONINKRIJK DER NEDERLANDEN **Rev:** Training ship "Sagres" **Edge:** Plain

Date	Mintage	F	VF	XF	Unc	BU
1995	30,000	—	—	—	—	6.50

X# 98 2 ECU
Copper-Nickel, 30 mm. **Ruler:** Beatrix **Subject:** Sail 95 Amsterdam **Obv:** Rampant lion left with sword and bundle of arrows **Obv. Legend:** KONINKRIJK DER NEDERLANDEN **Rev:** Frisian "Tjotter-type" sailboats **Edge:** Plain

Date	Mintage	F	VF	XF	Unc	BU
1995	30,000	—	—	—	—	6.50

X# 16 2-1/2 ECU
15.0000 g., Copper-Nickel-Zinc, 33 mm. **Ruler:** Beatrix **Issuer:** Mauquoy - Tramaux & Co. B.v.b.a., Grobbendonk **Obv:** Large "ECU", medieval sailing ship, 12 stars in ribbon border **Obv. Legend:** DE NEDER - LANDEN **Rev:** Jugate busts of Constantijn and Christiaan Huygens right **Rev. Legend:** ADMOVERE OCULIS DISTANTIA SIDERA NOSTRIS **Edge:** Reeded **Note:** Prev. X#5.

Date	Mintage	F	VF	XF	Unc	BU
1989M	18,608	—	—	—	—	25.00

X# 16a 2-1/2 ECU
20.0000 g., 0.9250 Silver 0.5948 oz. ASW, 33 mm. **Ruler:** Beatrix **Issuer:** Mauquoy - Tramaux & Co. B.v.b.a., Grobbendonk **Series:** Europa **Obv:** Large "ECU", medieval sailing ship, 12 stars in ribbon border **Obv. Legend:** DE NEDER - LANDEN **Rev:** Jugate busts of Constantijn and Christiaan Huygens right **Rev. Legend:** ADMOVERE OCULIS DISTANTIA SIDERA NOSTRIS **Edge:** Plain **Note:** Prev. X#6.

Date	Mintage	F	VF	XF	Unc	BU
1989M Prooflike	1,500	—	—	—	—	100

X# 26 2-1/2 ECU
15.0000 g., Copper-Nickel-Zinc, 33 mm. **Ruler:** Beatrix **Issuer:** Mauquoy - Tramaux & Co. B.v.b.a., Grobbendonk **Subject:** Geert Groote **Obv:** Large "ECU", medieval sailing ship, 12 stars in ribbon border **Obv. Legend:** DE NEDER - LANDEN **Rev:** Geert Groote seated at left facing left **Rev. Inscription:** HAEC ARMA / STRENUITAS / SEVERITAS / BENIGNITAS **Edge:** Plain **Note:** Prev. X#16.

Date	Mintage	F	VF	XF	Unc	BU
1990	50,000	—	—	—	—	12.50

X# 26a 2-1/2 ECU
17.0000 g., 0.9250 Silver 0.5055 oz. ASW, 33 mm. **Ruler:** Beatrix **Issuer:** Mauquoy - Tramaux & Co. B.v.b.a., Grobbendonk **Obv:** Large "ECU", medieval sailing ship, 12 stars in ribbon border **Obv. Legend:** DE NEDER - LANDEN **Rev:** Geert Groote seated at left facing left **Rev. Inscription:** HAEC ARMA / STRENUITAS / SEVERITAS / BENIGNITAS **Edge:** Plain **Note:** Prev. X#17.

Date	Mintage	F	VF	XF	Unc	BU
1990 Proof	1,500	Value: 110				

X# 32 2-1/2 ECU
15.0000 g., Copper-Nickel, 33 mm. **Ruler:** Beatrix **Issuer:** Mauquoy - Tramaux & Co. B.v.b.a., Grobbendonk **Subject:** Potato City Week **Obv:** Large "ECU", medieval sailing ship, 12 stars in ribbon border **Obv. Legend:** DE NEDER - LANDEN **Rev:** REGR Emblem, stylized potato plant, Emmeloord seal at left, crowned arms of Noordoostpolder at right **Edge:** Plain **Note:** Prev. X#22.

Date	Mintage	F	VF	XF	Unc	BU
1990	5,000	—	—	—	—	50.00

X# 36 2-1/2 ECU
15.0000 g., Copper Nickel, 33 mm. **Ruler:** Beatrix **Issuer:** Mauquoy - Tramaux & Co. B.v.b.a., Grobbendonk **Subject:** 25th Wedding Anniversary **Obv:** Large "ECU", medieval sailing ship, 12 stars in

ribbon border **Obv. Legend:** DE NEDER - LANDEN **Rev:** Jugate busts of Beatrix and Prince Claus left **Rev. Legend:** ZILVEREN HUWELIJK KONINGIN BEATRIX EN PRINS KLAUS **Rev. Inscription:** eenkeus van het hart **Edge:** Plain

Date	Mintage	F	VF	XF	Unc	BU
1991	25,000	—	—	—	—	25.00

X# 36a 2-1/2 ECU

17.0000 g., 0.9250 Silver 0.5055 oz. ASW, 33 mm. **Ruler:** Beatrix **Issuer:** Mauquoy - Tramaux & Co. B.v.b.a., Grobbendonk **Subject:** 25th Wedding Anniversary **Obv:** Large "ECU", medieval sailing ship, 12 stars in ribbon border **Obv. Legend:** DE NEDER - LANDEN **Rev:** Jugate busts of Beatrix and Prince Claus left **Rev. Legend:** ZILVEREN HUWELIJK KONINGIN BEATRIX EN PRINS KLAUS **Rev. Inscription:** eenkeus van het hart **Edge:** Plain

Date	Mintage	F	VF	XF	Unc	BU
1991 Proof	750	Value: 160				

X# 39 2-1/2 ECU

15.0000 g., Copper-Nickel, 33 mm. **Ruler:** Beatrix **Issuer:** Mauquoy - Tramaux & Co. B.v.b.a., Grobbendonk **Obv:** Large "ECU", medieval sailing ship, 12 stars in ribbon border **Obv. Legend:** DE NEDER - LANDEN **Rev:** Church at left, crowned arms at right **Rev. Legend:** ARNHEM, EURO - STADT AAN DE RIJN **Edge:** Plain

Date	Mintage	F	VF	XF	Unc	BU
1991	26,361	—	—	—	—	18.50

X# 39a 2-1/2 ECU

17.0000 g., 0.9250 Silver 0.5055 oz. ASW, 33 mm. **Ruler:** Beatrix **Issuer:** Mauquoy - Tramaux & Co. B.v.b.a., Grobbendonk **Obv:** Large "ECU", medieval sailing ship, 12 stars in ribbon border **Obv. Legend:** DE NEDER - LANDEN **Rev:** Church at left, crowned arms at right **Rev. Legend:** ARNHEM, EURO - STADT AAN DE RIJN **Edge:** Plain

Date	Mintage	F	VF	XF	Unc	BU
1991 Proof	500	Value: 175				

X# 41 2-1/2 ECU

15.0000 g., Copper-Nickel, 33 mm. **Ruler:** Beatrix **Issuer:** Mauquoy - Tramaux & Co. B.v.b.a., Grobbendonk **Subject:** 75th Four Day March **Obv:** Large "ECU", medieval sailing ship, 12 stars in ribbon border **Obv. Legend:** DE NEDER - LANDEN **Rev:** Stylized art, legs walking in center strip at left, crowned arms at right **Rev. Legend:** 75E INT.VIERDAAGSE • NIJMEGEN **Edge:** Plain

Date	Mintage	F	VF	XF	Unc	BU
1991	40,000	—	—	—	—	18.50

X# 41a 2-1/2 ECU

17.0000 g., 0.9250 Silver 0.5055 oz. ASW, 33 mm. **Ruler:** Beatrix **Issuer:** Mauquoy - Tramaux & Co. B.v.b.a., Grobbendonk **Subject:** 75th Four Day March **Obv:** Large "ECU", medieval sailing ship, 12 stars in ribbon border **Obv. Legend:** DE NEDER - LANDEN **Rev:** Stylized art, legs walking in center strip at left, crowned arms at right **Rev. Legend:** 75E INT.VIERDAAGSE • NIJMEGEN **Edge:** Plain

Date	Mintage	F	VF	XF	Unc	BU
1991 Proof	500	Value: 175				

X# 43 2-1/2 ECU

15.0000 g., Copper-Nickel, 33 mm. **Ruler:** Beatrix **Issuer:** Mauquoy - Tramaux & Co. B.v.b.a., Grobbendonk **Obv:** Large "ECU", medieval sailing ship, 12 stars in ribbon border **Obv. Legend:** DE NEDER - LANDEN **Rev:** Bust of Desiderius Erasmus von Rotterdam at left (H. Holbein portrait) **Rev. Inscription:** ME / VELLE / ESSE / TOTIUS / MUNDI / NON / UNIMUS / OPPIDI **Edge:** Plain

Date	Mintage	F	VF	XF	Unc	BU
1991	64,932	—	—	—	—	8.00

X# 43a 2-1/2 ECU

17.0000 g., 0.9250 Silver 0.5055 oz. ASW, 33 mm. **Ruler:** Beatrix **Issuer:** Mauquoy - Tramaux & Co. B.v.b.a., Grobbendonk **Obv:** Large "ECU", medieval sailing ship, 12 stars in ribbon border **Obv. Legend:** DE NEDER - LANDEN **Rev:** Bust of Desiderius Erasmus von Rotterdam at left (H. Holbein portrait) **Rev. Inscription:** ME / VELLE / ESSE / TOTIUS / MUNDI / NON / UNIMUS / OPPIDI **Edge:** Plain

Date	Mintage	F	VF	XF	Unc	BU
1991 Proof	1,500	Value: 180				

X# 47 2-1/2 ECU

15.0000 g., Copper-Nickel, 33 mm. **Ruler:** Beatrix **Issuer:** Mauquoy - Tramaux & Co. B.v.b.a., Grobbendonk **Obv:** Large "ECU", medieval sailing ship, 12 stars in ribbon border **Obv. Legend:** DE NEDER - LANDEN **Rev:** Bust of Willem I. Frederik 3/4 right at left, three emblems at right **Rev. Inscription:** UITBREIDUNG / VAN HET / VERKEER MET / ALLE VOLKEN **Edge:** Plain

Date	Mintage	F	VF	XF	Unc	BU
1992	65,000	—	—	—	—	8.00

X# 47a 2-1/2 ECU

17.0000 g., 0.9250 Silver 0.5055 oz. ASW, 33 mm. **Ruler:** Beatrix **Issuer:** Mauquoy - Tramaux & Co. B.v.b.a., Grobbendonk **Obv:** Large "ECU", medieval sailing ship, 12 stars in ribbon border **Obv. Legend:** DE NEDER - LANDEN **Rev:** Bust of Willem I. Frederik 3/4 right at left, three emblems at right **Rev. Inscription:** UITBREIDUNG / VAN HET / VERKEER MET / ALLE VOLKEN **Edge:** Plain **Note:** With fineness.

Date	Mintage	F	VF	XF	Unc	BU
1992 Proof	1,500	Value: 95.00				

X# 59 2-1/2 ECU

15.0000 g., Copper-Nickel, 33 mm. **Ruler:** Beatrix **Subject:** 12-1/2 Anniversary of Coronation and Visit to Aruba and the Neterlands Antilles **Obv:** Medieval sailing ship with state shields **Obv. Legend:** KONINKRIJK DER NEDERLANDEN **Rev:** Heads of five royal family right **Rev. Legend:** BEZOEK KON.FAM.NED. ANTILLEN EN ARUBA... **Edge:** Plain

Date	Mintage	F	VF	XF	Unc	BU
1992	50,000	—	—	—	—	9.00

X# 59a 2-1/2 ECU

17.0000 g., 0.9250 Silver 0.5055 oz. ASW, 33 mm. **Ruler:** Beatrix **Subject:** 12-1/2 Anniversary of Coronation and Visit to Aruba and the Netherlands Antilles **Obv:** Medieval sailing ship with state shields **Obv. Legend:** KONINKRIJK DER NEDERLANDEN **Rev:** Heads of five royal family right **Rev. Legend:** BEZOEK KON.FAM.NED.ANTILLEN EN ARUBA... **Edge:** Plain

Date	Mintage	F	VF	XF	Unc	BU
1992 Proof	1,500	Value: 80.00				

X# 65 2-1/2 ECU

15.0000 g., Copper-Nickel, 33 mm. **Ruler:** Beatrix **Obv:** Large "ECU", medieval sailing ship, 12 stars in ribbon border **Obv. Legend:** DE NEDER - LANDEN **Rev:** Bust of Jan A. Leeghwater 3/4 right, water, windmills and pumping stations in background **Rev. Inscription:** EXPERIEN- /TIA DOCET **Edge:** Plain

Date	Mintage	F	VF	XF	Unc	BU
1993	65,000	—	—	—	—	9.00

X# 65a 2-1/2 ECU

17.0000 g., 0.9250 Silver 0.5055 oz. ASW, 33 mm. **Ruler:** Beatrix **Obv:** Large "ECU", medieval sailing ship, 12 stars in ribbon border **Obv. Legend:** DE NEDER - LANDEN **Rev:** Bust of Jan A. Leeghwater 3/4 right, water, windmills and pumping stations in background **Rev. Inscription:** EXPERIEN- /TIA DOCET **Edge:** Plain

Date	Mintage	F	VF	XF	Unc	BU
1993 Proof	1,500	Value: 80.00				

X# 69 2-1/2 ECU

15.0000 g., Copper-Nickel, 33 mm. **Ruler:** Beatrix **Obv:** Large "ECU", medieval sailing ship, 12 stars in ribbon border **Obv. Legend:** DE NEDER - LANDEN **Rev:** Stylized bridge over Maas River, St. Servatius' keys, large "E" above **Rev. Legend:** MAAS - TRICHT **Edge:** Plain

Date	Mintage	F	VF	XF	Unc	BU
1993	50,000	—	—	—	—	9.00

X# 69a 2-1/2 ECU
17.0000 g., 0.9250 Silver 0.5055 oz. ASW, 33 mm. **Ruler:** Beatrix **Obv:** Large "ECU", medieval sailing ship, 12 stars in ribbon border **Obv. Legend:** DE NEDER - LANDEN **Rev:** Stylized bridge over Maas River, St. Servatius' keys, large "E" above **Rev. Legend:** MAAS - TRICHT **Edge:** Plain **Note:** With fineness.

Date	Mintage	F	VF	XF	Unc	BU
1993 Proof	1,500	Value: 80.00				

X# 73 2-1/2 ECU
15.0000 g., Copper-Nickel, 33 mm. **Ruler:** Beatrix **Subject:** 85th Birthday of Queen Mother, 50th Anniversary Prince Bernhard's Being Commander of Armed Force **Obv:** Rampant lion left with sword and bundle of arrows, 12 stars around **Obv. Inscription:** KONINKRIJK / NEDERLANDEN **Rev:** Jugate busts of Princess Juliana and Prince Bernhardt right **Rev. Inscription:** "IN / SAMEN- / WERKING / LIGT DE / SLEUTEL VOOR DE / TOEKOMST" **Edge:** Plain

Date	Mintage	F	VF	XF	Unc	BU
1994	50,000	—	—	—	—	8.50

X# 73a 2-1/2 ECU
17.0000 g., 0.9250 Silver 0.5055 oz. ASW, 33 mm. **Ruler:** Beatrix **Subject:** 85th Birthday of Queen Mother, 50th Anniversary Prince Bernhard's Being Commander of Armed Force **Obv:** Rampant lion left with sword and bundle of arrows, 12 stars around **Obv. Inscription:** KONINKRIJK / NEDERLANDEN **Rev:** Jugate busts of Princess Juliana and Prince Bernhardt right **Rev. Inscription:** "IN / SAMEN- / WERKING / LIGT DE / SLEUTEL VOOR DE / TOEKOMST" **Edge:** Plain **Note:** With fineness.

Date	Mintage	F	VF	XF	Unc	BU
1994 Proof	1,500	Value: 80.00				

X# 81 2-1/2 ECU
15.0000 g., Copper-Nickel, 33 mm. **Ruler:** Beatrix **Subject:** F. D. Roosevelt **Obv:** Rampant lion left with sword and bundle of arrows, 12 stars around **Obv. Inscription:** KONINKRIJK DER NEDERLANDEN **Edge:** Plain

Date	Mintage	F	VF	XF	Unc	BU
1994	50,000	—	—	—	—	10.00

X# 81a 2-1/2 ECU
20.0000 g., 0.9250 Silver 0.5948 oz. ASW, 33 mm. **Ruler:** Beatrix **Subject:** F. D. Roosevelt **Obv:** Rampant lion left with sword and bundle of arrows, 12 stars around **Obv. Inscription:** KONINKRIJK DER NEDERLANDEN **Edge:** Plain **Note:** With fineness.

Date	Mintage	F	VF	XF	Unc	BU
1994 Proof	1,500	Value: 80.00				

X# 85 2-1/2 ECU
15.0000 g., Copper-Nickel, 33 mm. **Ruler:** Beatrix **Subject:** Grotius **Obv:** Rampant lion left with sword and bundle of arrows **Obv. Legend:** KONINKRIJK DER NEDERLANDEN **Edge:** Plain

Date	Mintage	F	VF	XF	Unc	BU
1995	50,000	—	—	—	—	8.50

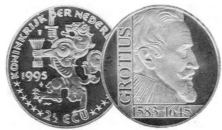

X# 85a 2-1/2 ECU
20.0000 g., 0.9250 Silver 0.5948 oz. ASW, 33 mm. **Ruler:** Beatrix **Subject:** Grotius **Obv:** Rampant lion left with sword and bundle of arms **Obv. Legend:** KONINKRIJK DER NEDERLANDEN **Edge:** Plain **Note:** With fineness.

Date	Mintage	F	VF	XF	Unc	BU
1995 Proof	1,500	Value: 80.00				

X# 89 2-1/2 ECU
15.0000 g., Copper-Nickel, 33 mm. **Ruler:** Beatrix **Subject:** Wilhelmina / 40th Anniversary Liberation WWII **Obv:** Rampant lion left with sword and bundle of arrows **Obv. Legend:** KONINKRIJK DER NEDERLANzDEN **Edge:** Plain

Date	Mintage	F	VF	XF	Unc	BU
1995	50,000	—	—	—	—	8.50

X# 89a 2-1/2 ECU
20.0000 g., 0.9250 Silver 0.5948 oz. ASW, 33 mm. **Ruler:** Beatrix **Subject:** Wilhelmina / 40th Anniversary Liberation WWII **Obv:** Rampant lion left with sword and bundle of arrows **Obv. Legend:** KONINKRIJK DER NEDERLANDEN **Note:** With fineness.

Date	Mintage	F	VF	XF	Unc	BU
1995 Proof	1,500	Value: 80.00				

X# 99 2-1/2 ECU
15.0000 g., Copper-Nickel, 33 mm. **Ruler:** Beatrix **Subject:** Johannes Vermeer **Edge:** Plain

Date	Mintage	F	VF	XF	Unc	BU
1996	50,000	—	—	—	—	8.50

X# 99a 2-1/2 ECU
20.0000 g., 0.9250 Silver 0.5948 oz. ASW, 33 mm. **Ruler:** Beatrix **Rev:** Johannes Vermeer **Edge:** Plain

Date	Mintage	F	VF	XF	Unc	BU
1996 Proof	1,500	Value: 80.00				

X# 103 2-1/2 ECU
15.0000 g., Copper-Nickel, 33 mm. **Ruler:** Beatrix **Subject:** Jacob van Kampen **Edge:** Plain

Date	Mintage	F	VF	XF	Unc	BU
1996	50,000	—	—	—	—	8.50

X# 103a 2-1/2 ECU
20.0000 g., 0.9250 Silver 0.5948 oz. ASW, 33 mm. **Ruler:** Beatrix **Subject:** Jacob van Kampen **Edge:** Plain

Date	Mintage	F	VF	XF	Unc	BU
1996 Proof	1,500	Value: 80.00				

X# 107 2-1/2 ECU
15.0000 g., Copper-Nickel, 33 mm. **Ruler:** Beatrix **Subject:** 300th Anniversary Johan Maurits van Nassau-Sieggen **Obv:** Bust 3/4 right, youth riding elephant, anteater **Edge:** Plain

Date	Mintage	F	VF	XF	Unc	BU
1997	50,000	—	—	—	—	8.50

X# 107a 2-1/2 ECU
20.0000 g., 0.9250 Silver 0.5948 oz. ASW, 33 mm. **Ruler:** Beatrix **Subject:** 300th Anniversary Johan Maurits van Nassau-Sieggen **Obv:** Bust 3/4 right, youth riding elephant, anteater **Edge:** Plain **Note:** With fineness.

Date	Mintage	F	VF	XF	Unc	BU
1997 Proof	1,500	Value: 80.00				

X# 111 2-1/2 ECU
15.0000 g., Copper-Nickel, 33 mm. **Ruler:** Beatrix **Subject:** 400 Years Diplomatic Contact with Russia **Rev:** Busts of Tsar Peter I left, Beatrix facing 3/4 left **Rev. Legend:** NEDERLAND - RUSLAND **Edge:** Plain

Date	Mintage	F	VF	XF	Unc	BU
1997	50,000	—	—	—	—	8.50

X# 111a 2-1/2 ECU

20.0000 g., 0.9250 Silver 0.5948 oz. ASW, 33 mm. **Ruler:** Beatrix **Subject:** 400 Years Diplomatic Contact with Russia **Rev:** Busts of Tsar Peter I left, Beatrix facing 3/4 left **Rev. Inscription:** NEDERLAND - RUSLAND **Edge:** Plain **Note:** With fineness.

Date	Mintage	F	VF	XF	Unc	BU
1997 Proof	1,500	Value: 80.00				

X# 115 2-1/2 ECU

15.0000 g., Copper-Nickel, 33 mm. **Ruler:** Beatrix **Subject:** 200th Anniversary Birth of Johan Rudolf Thorbecke **Rev:** Head left, buildings behind **Edge:** Plain

Date	Mintage	F	VF	XF	Unc	BU
1998	50,000	—	—	—	—	10.00

X# 115a 2-1/2 ECU

20.0000 g., 0.9250 Silver 0.5948 oz. ASW, 33 mm. **Ruler:** Beatrix **Subject:** 200th Anniversary Birth of Johan Rudolf Thorbecke **Rev:** Head left, buildings behind **Edge:** Plain **Note:** With fineness.

Date	Mintage	F	VF	XF	Unc	BU
1998 Proof	1,500	Value: 90.00				

X# 48 5 ECU

5.0000 g., Brass, 23 mm. **Ruler:** Beatrix **Issuer:** Mauquoy - Tramaux & Co. B.v.b.a., Grobbendonk **Obv:** Large "ECU", medieval sailing ship, 12 stars in ribbon border **Obv. Legend:** DE NEDER - LANDEN **Rev:** Bust of Willem I. Frederik 3/4 right at left, three emblems at right **Rev. Inscription:** UITBREIDUNG / VAN HET / VERKEER MET / ALLE VOLKEN **Edge:** Plain

Date	Mintage	F	VF	XF	Unc	BU
1992	25,000	—	—	—	—	16.00

X# 48a 5 ECU

7.0000 g., 0.9250 Silver 0.2082 oz. ASW, 23 mm. **Ruler:** Beatrix **Issuer:** Mauquoy - Tramaux & Co. B.v.b.a., Grobbendonk **Obv:** Large "ECU", medieval sailing ship, 12 stars in ribbon border **Obv. Legend:** DE NEDER - LANDEN **Rev:** Bust of Willem I. Frederik 3/4 right at left, three emblems at right **Rev. Inscription:** UITBREIDUNG / VAN HET / VERKEER MET / ALLE VOLKEN **Edge:** Plain

Date	Mintage	F	VF	XF	Unc	BU
1992 Proof	1,500	Value: 95.00				

X# 60 5 ECU

5.0000 g., Brass, 23 mm. **Ruler:** Beatrix **Subject:** 12-1/2 Anniversary of Coronation and Visit to Aruba and the Netherlands Antilles **Obv:** Medieval sailing ship with state shields **Obv. Legend:** KONINKRIJK DER NEDERLANDEN **Rev:** Heads of five royal family right **Rev. Legend:** BEZOEK KON . FAM . NED . ANTILLEN EN ARUBA... **Edge:** Plain

Date	Mintage	F	VF	XF	Unc	BU
1992 Proof	5,000	—	—	—	—	16.00

X# 60a 5 ECU

6.5000 g., 0.9250 Silver 0.1933 oz. ASW, 23 mm. **Subject:** 12-1/2 Anniversary of Coronation and Visit to Aruba and the Netherlands Antilles **Obv:** Medieval sailing ship with state shields **Obv. Legend:** KONINKRIJK DER NEDERLANDEN **Rev:** Heads of five royal family right **Rev. Legend:** BEZOEK KON. FAM. NED. ANTILLEN EN ARUBA... **Edge:** Plain

Date	Mintage	F	VF	XF	Unc	BU
1992 Proof	1,500	Value: 80.00				

X# 17.1 10 ECU

20.0000 g., Copper-Nickel-Zinc, 37.95 mm. **Ruler:** Beatrix **Issuer:** Mauquoy - Tramaux & Co. B.v.b.a., Grobbendonk **Series:** Europa **Obv:** Large "ECU", medieval sailing ship, 12 stars in ribbon border **Obv. Legend:** DE NEDER - LANDEN **Rev:** Jugate busts of Constantijn and Christiaan Huygens right **Rev. Legend:** ADMOVERE OCULIS DISTANTIA SIDERA NOSTRIS **Edge:** Reeded **Note:** Prev. X#7.

Date	Mintage	F	VF	XF	Unc	BU
1989M	10,000	—	—	—	—	50.00

X# 17.1a 10 ECU

25.0000 g., 0.9250 Silver 0.7435 oz. ASW, 37.95 mm. **Ruler:** Beatrix **Issuer:** Mauquoy - Tramaux & Co. B.v.b.a., Grobbendonk **Series:** Europa **Obv:** Large "ECU", medieval sailing ship, 12 stars in ribbon border **Obv. Legend:** DE NEDER - LANDEN **Rev:** Jugate busts of Constantijn and Christiaan Huygens right **Rev. Legend:** ADMOVERE OCULIS DISTANTIA SIDERA NOSTRIS

Date	Mintage	F	VF	XF	Unc	BU
1989M Prooflike	50	—	—	—	—	975

X# 17.2 10 ECU

20.0000 g., Copper-Nickel-Zinc, 37.95 mm. **Ruler:** Beatrix **Issuer:** Mauquoy - Tramaux & Co. B.v.b.a., Grobbendonk **Series:** Europa **Obv:** Large "ECU", medieval sailing ship, 12 stars in ribbon border **Obv. Legend:** DE NEDER - LANDEN **Rev:** Jugate busts of Constantijn and Christiaan Huygens right **Rev. Legend:** ADMOVERE OCULIS DISTANTIA SIDERA NOSTRIS **Edge:** Plain **Note:** Prev. X#7. Mintage: Inc. X#17.1.

Date	Mintage	F	VF	XF	Unc	BU
1989M	—	—	—	—	—	32.50

X# 27.1a 10 ECU

25.0000 g., 0.9250 Silver 0.7435 oz. ASW, 38 mm. **Ruler:** Beatrix **Issuer:** Mauquoy - Tramaux & Co. B.v.b.a., Grobbendonk **Subject:** Large "ECU", medieval sailing ship, 12 stars in ribbon border **Obv. Designer:** DE NEDER - LANDEN **Rev:** Geert Groote seated at left facing left **Rev. Inscription:** HAEC ARMA / STRENUITAS / SEVERITAS / BENIGNITAS **Edge:** Reeded **Note:** Prev. X#19.

Date	Mintage	F	VF	XF	Unc	BU
1990 Proof	1,447	Value: 120				
1991 Proof	53	—	—	—	—	—

Note: 250 examples were struck dated 1991, 197 were remelted.

X# 27.1 10 ECU

20.0000 g., Copper-Nickel, 38 mm. **Ruler:** Beatrix **Issuer:** Mauquoy - Tramaux & Co. B.v.b.a., Grobbendonk **Obv:** Large "ECU", medieval sailing ship, 12 stars in ribbon border **Obv. Legend:** DE NEDER - LANDEN **Rev:** Geert Groote seated at left facing left **Rev. Inscription:** HAEC ARMA / STRENUITAS / SEVERITAS / BENIGNITAS **Edge:** Reeded **Note:** Prev. X#18.

Date	Mintage	F	VF	XF	Unc	BU
1990	25,000	—	—	—	—	25.00

X# 27.2 10 ECU

20.0000 g., Copper-Nickel, 38 mm. **Ruler:** Beatrix **Issuer:** Mauquoy - Tramaux & Co. B.v.b.a., Grobbendonk **Obv:** Large "ECU", medieval sailing ship, 12 stars in ribbon border **Obv. Legend:** DE NEDER - LANDEN **Rev:** Geert Groote seated at left facing left **Rev. Inscription:** HAEC ARMA / STRENUITAS / SEVERITAS / BENIGNITAS **Edge:** Plain **Note:** Prev. X#18. Mintage: Inc. X#27.1.

Date	Mintage	F	VF	XF	Unc	BU
1990	—	—	—	—	—	25.00

X# 28 10 ECU

25.0000 g., 0.9250 Silver 0.7435 oz. ASW, 38 mm. **Ruler:** Beatrix **Issuer:** Mauquoy - Tramaux & Co. B.v.b.a., Grobbendonk **Subject:** Geert Groote **Obv:** Large "ECU", medieval sailing ship, 12 stars in ribbon border **Obv. Legend:** DE NEDER - LANDEN **Rev:** Geert Groote seated at left facing left **Rev. Inscription:** HAEC ARMA / STRENUITAS / SEVERITAS / BENIGNITAS **Edge:** Plain **Note:** Prev. X#20.

Date	Mintage	F	VF	XF	Unc	BU
1990 Proof	25,000	Value: 65.00				

X# 29 10 ECU

6.7200 g., 0.7500 Gold 0.1620 oz. AGW, 22.5 mm. **Ruler:** Beatrix **Issuer:** Mauquoy - Tramaux & Co. B.v.b.a., Grobbendonk **Subject:** Geert Groote **Obv:** Large "ECU", medieval sailing ship, 12 stars in ribbon border **Obv. Legend:** DE NEDER - LANDEN **Rev:** Geert Groote seated at left facing left **Rev. Inscription:** HAEC ARMA / STRENUITAS / SEVERITAS / BENIGNITAS **Edge:** Reeded **Note:** Prev. X#21.

Date	Mintage	F	VF	XF	Unc	BU
1990 Proof	2,500	Value: 325				

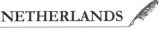

X# 44 10 ECU

20.0000 g., Copper-Nickel, 38 mm. **Ruler:** Beatrix **Issuer:** Mauquoy - Tramaux & Co. B.v.b.a., Grobbendonk **Obv:** Large "ECU", medieval sailing ship, 12 stars in ribbon border **Obv. Legend:** DE NEDER - LANDEN **Rev:** Bust of Desiderius Erasmus von Rotterdam at left (H. Holbein portrait) **Rev. Inscription:** ME / VELLE / ESSE / TOTIUS / MUNDI / NON / UNIMUS / OPPIDI **Edge:** Plain

Date	Mintage	F	VF	XF	Unc	BU
1991	25,000	—	—	—	—	18.50

X# 44a 10 ECU

25.0000 g., 0.9250 Silver 0.7435 oz. ASW, 38 mm. **Ruler:** Beatrix **Issuer:** Mauquoy - Tramaux & Co. B.v.b.a., Grobbendonk **Obv:** Large "ECU", medieval sailing ship, 12 stars in ribbon border **Obv. Legend:** DE NEDER - LANDEN **Rev:** Bust of Desiderius Erasmus von Rotterdam at left (H. Holbein portrait) **Rev. Inscription:** ME / VELLE / ESSE / TOTIUS / MUNDI / NON / UNIMUS / OPPIDI **Edge:** Plain **Note:** With fineness.

Date	Mintage	F	VF	XF	Unc	BU
1991 Proof	1,500	Value: 95.00				

X# 49 10 ECU

20.0000 g., Copper-Nickel, 38 mm. **Ruler:** Beatrix **Issuer:** Mauquoy - Tramaux & Co. B.v.b.a., Grobbendonk **Obv:** Large "ECU", medieval sailing ship, 12 stars in ribbon border **Obv. Legend:** DE NEDER - LANDEN **Rev:** Bust of Willem I. Frederik 3/4 right at left, three emblems at right **Rev. Inscription:** UITBREIDUNG / VAN HET / VERKEER MET / ALLE VOLKEN **Edge:** Plain

Date	Mintage	F	VF	XF	Unc	BU
1992	25,000	—	—	—	—	18.50

X# 49a 10 ECU

25.0000 g., 0.9250 Silver 0.7435 oz. ASW, 38 mm. **Ruler:** Beatrix **Issuer:** Mauquoy - Tramaux & Co. B.v.b.a., Grobbendonk **Obv:** Large "ECU", medieval sailing ship, 12 stars in ribbon border **Obv. Legend:** DE NEDER - LANDEN **Rev:** Bust of Willem I. Frederik 3/4 right at left, three emblems at right **Rev. Inscription:** UITBREIDUNG / VAN HET / VERKEER MET / ALLE VOLKEN **Edge:** Plain **Note:** With fineness.

Date	Mintage	F	VF	XF	Unc	BU
1992 Proof	1,495	Value: 80.00				

X# 61 10 ECU

20.0000 g., Copper-Nickel, 38 mm. **Ruler:** Beatrix **Subject:** 12-1/2 Anniversary of Coronation and Visit to Aruba and the Netherlands Antilles **Obv:** Medieval sailing ship with state shields **Obv. Legend:** KONINKRIJK DER NEDERLANDEN **Rev:** Heads of five royal family right **Rev. Legend:** BEZOEK KON.FAM.NED.ANTILLEN EN ARUBA... **Edge:** Plain

Date	Mintage	F	VF	XF	Unc	BU
1992	25,000	—	—	—	—	18.50

X# 61a 10 ECU

20.0000 g., 0.9250 Silver 0.5948 oz. ASW, 38 mm. **Ruler:** Beatrix **Subject:** 12-1/2 Anniversary of Coronation and Visit to Aruba and the Netherlands Antilles **Obv:** Medieval sailing ship with state shields **Obv. Legend:** KONINKRIJK DER NEDERLANDEN **Rev:** Heads of five royal family right **Rev. Legend:** BEZOEK KON.FAM.NED.ANTILLEN EN ARUBA... **Edge:** Plain

Date	Mintage	F	VF	XF	Unc	BU
1992 Proof	1,500	Value: 80.00				

X# 66 10 ECU

20.0000 g., Copper-Nickel, 38 mm. **Ruler:** Beatrix **Obv:** Large "ECU", medieval sailing ship, 12 stars in ribbon border **Obv. Legend:** DE NEDER - LANDEN **Rev:** Bust of Jan A. Leeghwater 3/4 right, water, windmills and pumping stations in background **Rev. Inscription:** EXPERIEN- /TIA DOCET **Edge:** Plain

Date	Mintage	F	VF	XF	Unc	BU
1993	25,000	—	—	—	—	18.50

X# 66a 10 ECU

25.0000 g., 0.9250 Silver 0.7435 oz. ASW, 38 mm. **Ruler:** Beatrix **Obv:** Large "ECU", medieval sailing ship, 12 stars in ribbon border **Obv. Legend:** DE NEDER - LANDEN **Rev:** Bust of Jan A. Leeghwater 3/4 right, water, windmills and pumping stations in background **Rev. Inscription:** EXPERIEN- /TIA DOCET **Edge:** Plain

Date	Mintage	F	VF	XF	Unc	BU
1993 Proof	1,500	Value: 80.00				

X# 70 10 ECU

20.0000 g., Copper-Nickel, 38 mm. **Ruler:** Beatrix **Obv:** Large "ECU", medieval sailing ship, 12 stars in ribbon border **Obv. Legend:** DE NEDER - LANDEN **Rev:** Stylized border over Maas River, St. Servatius' keys, large "E" above **Rev. Legend:** MAAS - TRICHT **Edge:** Plain

Date	Mintage	F	VF	XF	Unc	BU
1993	25,000	—	—	—	—	18.50

X# 70a 10 ECU

25.0000 g., 0.9250 Silver 0.7435 oz. ASW, 38 mm. **Ruler:** Beatrix **Obv:** Large "ECU", medieval sailing ship, 12 stars in ribbon border **Obv. Legend:** DE NEDER - LANDEN **Rev:** Stylized bridge over Maas River, St. Servatius' keys, large "E" above **Rev. Legend:** MAAS - TRICHT **Edge:** Plain **Note:** With fineness.

Date	Mintage	F	VF	XF	Unc	BU
1993 Proof	1,500	Value: 80.00				

X# 74 10 ECU

20.0000 g., Copper-Nickel, 38 mm. **Ruler:** Beatrix **Subject:** 85th Birthday of Queen Mother, 50th Anniversary Prince Bernhard's Being Commander Armed Force **Obv:** Rampant lion left with sword and bundle of arrows, 12 stars around **Obv. Inscription:** KONINKRIJK / NEDERLANDEN **Rev:** Jugate busts of Princess Juliana and Prince Bernhard right **Rev. Inscription:** "IN / SAMEN- / WERKING / LIGT DE / SLEUTEL VOOR DE / TOEKOMST" **Edge:** Plain

Date	Mintage	F	VF	XF	Unc	BU
1994	25,000	—	—	—	—	15.00

X# 74a 10 ECU

25.0000 g., 0.9250 Silver 0.7435 oz. ASW, 38 mm. **Ruler:** Beatrix **Subject:** 85th Birthday of Queen Mother, 50th Anniversary Prince Bernhard's Being Commander of Armed Force **Obv:** Rampant lion left with sword and bundle of arrows, 12 stars around **Obv. Inscription:** KONINKRIJK / NEDERLANDEN **Rev:** Jugate busts of Princess Juliana and Prince Bernhard right **Rev. Inscription:** "IN / SAMEN- / WERKING / LIGT DE / SLEUTEL VOOR DE / TOEKOMST" **Edge:** Plain **Note:** With fineness.

Date	Mintage	F	VF	XF	Unc	BU
1994 Proof	1,500	Value: 80.00				

X# 82 10 ECU

20.0000 g., Copper-Nickel, 38 mm. **Ruler:** Beatrix **Subject:** F. D. Roosevelt **Obv:** Rampant lion left with sword and bundle of arrows, 12 stars around **Obv. Inscription:** KONINKRIJK DER NEDERLANDEN **Edge:** Plain

Date	Mintage	F	VF	XF	Unc	BU
1994	25,000	—	—	—	—	20.00

X# 82a 10 ECU

25.0000 g., 0.9250 Silver 0.7435 oz. ASW, 38 mm. **Ruler:** Beatrix **Subject:** F. D. Roosevelt **Obv:** Rampant lion left with sword and bundle of arrows, 12 stars around **Obv. Inscription:** KONINKRIJK DER NEDERLANDEN **Edge:** Plain

Date	Mintage	F	VF	XF	Unc	BU
1994 Proof	1,500	Value: 80.00				

X# 86 10 ECU

20.0000 g., Copper-Nickel, 38 mm. **Ruler:** Beatrix **Subject:** Grotius **Obv:** Rampant lion left with sword and bundle of arrows **Obv. Legend:** KONINKRIJK DER NEDERLANDEN **Edge:** Plain

Date	Mintage	F	VF	XF	Unc	BU
1995	25,000	—	—	—	—	16.00

X# 86a 10 ECU

25.0000 g., 0.9250 Silver 0.7435 oz. ASW, 38 mm. **Ruler:** Beatrix **Subject:** Grotius **Obv:** Rampant lion left with sword and bundle of arrows **Obv. Legend:** KONINKRIJK DER NEDERLANDEN **Note:** With fineness.

Date	Mintage	F	VF	XF	Unc	BU
1995 Proof	1,500	Value: 80.00				

X# 90 10 ECU

20.0000 g., Copper-Nickel, 38 mm. **Ruler:** Beatrix **Subject:** Wilhelmina / 40th Anniversary Liberation WWII **Obv:** Rampant lion left with sword and bundle of arrows **Obv. Legend:** KONINKRIJK DER NEDERLANDEN **Edge:** Plain

Date	Mintage	F	VF	XF	Unc	BU
1995	25,000	—	—	—	—	15.00

X# 90a 10 ECU

25.0000 g., 0.9250 Silver 0.7435 oz. ASW, 38 mm. **Ruler:** Beatrix **Subject:** Wilhelmina / 40th Anniversary Liberation WWII **Obv:** Rampant lion left with sword and bundle of arrows **Obv. Legend:** KONINKRIJK DER NEDERLANDEN **Edge:** Plain **Note:** With fineness.

Date	Mintage	F	VF	XF	Unc	BU
1995 Proof	1,500	Value: 80.00				

X# 100 10 ECU

20.0000 g., Copper-Nickel, 38 mm. **Ruler:** Beatrix **Subject:** Johannes Vermeer **Edge:** Plain

Date	Mintage	F	VF	XF	Unc	BU
1996 Proof	25,000	Value: 16.00				

X# 100a 10 ECU

25.0000 g., 0.9250 Silver 0.7435 oz. ASW, 38 mm. **Ruler:** Beatrix **Subject:** Johannes Vermeer **Edge:** Plain **Note:** With fineness.

Date	Mintage	F	VF	XF	Unc	BU
1996 Proof	1,500	Value: 80.00				

X# 104 10 ECU

20.0000 g., Copper-Nickel, 38 mm. **Ruler:** Beatrix **Subject:** Jacob van Kampen **Edge:** Plain

Date	Mintage	F	VF	XF	Unc	BU
1996	25,000	—	—	—	—	16.00

X# 104a 10 ECU

25.0000 g., 0.9250 Silver 0.7435 oz. ASW, 38 mm. **Ruler:** Beatrix **Subject:** Jacob van Kampen **Edge:** Plain

Date	Mintage	F	VF	XF	Unc	BU
1996 Proof	1,500	Value: 80.00				

X# 108 10 ECU

20.0000 g., Copper-Nickel, 38 mm. **Ruler:** Beatrix **Subject:** 300th Anniversary Johan Maurits van Nassau-Sieggen **Obv:** Bust 3/4 right, youth riding elephant, anteater **Edge:** Plain

Date	Mintage	F	VF	XF	Unc	BU
1997	25,000	—	—	—	—	16.00

X# 108a 10 ECU

25.0000 g., 0.9250 Silver 0.7435 oz. ASW, 38 mm. **Ruler:** Beatrix **Subject:** 300th Anniversary Johan Maurits van Nassau-Sieggen **Obv:** Bust 3/4 right, youth riding elephant, anteater **Edge:** Plain **Note:** With fineness.

Date	Mintage	F	VF	XF	Unc	BU
1997 Proof	1,500	Value: 80.00				

X# 112 10 ECU

20.0000 g., Copper-Nickel, 38 mm. **Ruler:** Beatrix **Subject:** 400 Years Diplomatic Contact with Russia **Rev:** Busts of Tsar Peter I left, Beatrix facing 3/4 left **Rev. Inscription:** NEDERLAND - RUSLAND **Edge:** Plain

Date	Mintage	F	VF	XF	Unc	BU
1997	25,000	—	—	—	—	16.00

X# 112a 10 ECU

25.0000 g., 0.9250 Silver 0.7435 oz. ASW, 38 mm. **Ruler:** Beatrix **Subject:** 400 Years Diplomatic Contact with Russia **Rev:** Busts of Tsar Peter I left, Beatrix facing 3/4 left **Rev. Inscription:** NEDERLAND - RUSLAND **Edge:** Plain **Note:** With fineness.

Date	Mintage	F	VF	XF	Unc	BU
1997 Proof	1,500	Value: 80.00				

X# 116 10 ECU

20.0000 g., Copper-Nickel, 38 mm. **Ruler:** Beatrix **Subject:** 200th Anniversary Birth of Johan Rudolf Thorbecke **Rev:** Head left, buildings behind **Edge:** Plain

Date	Mintage	F	VF	XF	Unc	BU
1998	25,000	—	—	—	—	20.00

X# 116a 10 ECU

25.0000 g., 0.9250 Silver 0.7435 oz. ASW, 38 mm. **Ruler:** Beatrix **Subject:** 200th Anniversary Birth of Johan Rudolf Thorbecke **Rev:** Head left, building behind **Edge:** Plain **Note:** With fineness.

Date	Mintage	F	VF	XF	Unc	BU
1998 Proof	1,500	Value: 80.00				

X# 18.1 25 ECU

25.0000 g., 0.9250 Silver 0.7435 oz. ASW, 38 mm. **Ruler:** Beatrix **Issuer:** Mauquoy - Tramaux & Co. B.v.b.a., Grobbendonk **Series:** Europa **Obv:** Large "ECU", medieval sailing ship, 12 stars in ribbon border **Obv. Legend:** DE NEDER - LANDEN **Rev:** Jugate busts of Constantijn and Christiaan Huygens right **Rev. Legend:** ADMOVERE OCULIS DISTANTIA SIDERA NOSTRIS **Edge:** Reeded **Note:** Prev. X#8.

Date	Mintage	F	VF	XF	Unc	BU
1989M Prooflike	5,000	—	—	—	—	100

X# 18.2 25 ECU

25.0000 g., 0.9250 Silver 0.7435 oz. ASW, 37.95 mm. **Ruler:** Beatrix **Issuer:** Mauquoy - Tramaux & Co. B.v.b.a., Grobbendonk **Series:** Europa **Obv:** Large "ECU", medieval sailing ship, 12 stars in ribbon border **Obv. Legend:** DE NEDER - LANDEN **Rev:** Jugate busts of Constantijn and Christiaan Huygens right **Rev. Legend:** ADMOVERE OCULIS DISTANTIA SIDERA NOSTRIS **Edge:** Plain **Note:** Prev. X#8. Mintage: Inc. X#18.1.

Date	Mintage	F	VF	XF	Unc	BU
1989M Prooflike	—	—	—	—	—	100

X# 33 25 ECU

25.0000 g., 0.9250 Silver 0.7435 oz. ASW, 38 mm. **Ruler:** Beatrix **Issuer:** Mauquoy - Tramaux & Co. B.v.b.a., Grobbendonk **Subject:** Potato City Week **Obv:** Large "ECU", medieval sailing ship, 12 stars in ribbon border **Obv. Legend:** DE NEDER - LANDEN **Rev:** REGR Emblem, stylized potato plant, Emmeloord seal at left, crowned arms of Noordoostpolder at right **Edge:** Plain **Note:** Prev. X#23.

Date	Mintage	F	VF	XF	Unc	BU
1990 Proof	1,500	Value: 160				

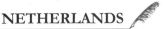

X# 34 25 ECU
25.0000 g., 0.9250 Silver 0.7435 oz. ASW, 38 mm. **Ruler:** Beatrix **Issuer:** Mauquoy - Tramaux & Co. B.v.b.a., Grobbendonk **Subject:** 1990 Europa Conference in Amsterdam **Obv:** Large "ECU", medieval sailing ship, 12 stars in ribbon border **Obv. Legend:** AMSTELOD - CIVIT.EUROP. **Rev:** Half-length figure of Benedictus de Spinoza facing at right **Rev. Legend:** 50th ASSEMBLY - AMSTERDAM **Rev. Inscription:** FINIS / REI PU - / BLICAE / LIBERTAS / EST **Edge:** Plain **Note:** Prev. X#24.

Date	Mintage	F	VF	XF	Unc	BU
1990 Proof	1,600	Value: 225				

X# 35 25 ECU
25.0000 g., 0.9250 Silver 0.7435 oz. ASW, 38 mm. **Ruler:** Beatrix **Issuer:** Mauquoy - Tramaux & Co. B.v.b.a., Grobbendonk **Subject:** 1990 Europa Conference in Amsterdam **Obv:** Large "ECU", medieval sailing ship, 12 stars in ribbon border **Obv. Legend:** DE NEDER - LANDEN **Rev:** Half-length figure of Benedictus de Spinoza facing at right **Rev. Legend:** 50th ASSEMBLY - AMSTERDAM **Rev. Inscription:** FINIS / REI PU - / BLICAE / LIBERTAS / EST **Edge:** Plain

Date	Mintage	F	VF	XF	Unc	BU
1990 Proof	900	Value: 250				

X# 37.1 25 ECU
25.0000 g., 0.9250 Silver 0.7435 oz. ASW, 38 mm. **Ruler:** Beatrix **Issuer:** Mauquoy - Tramaux & Co. B.v.b.a., Grobbendonk **Subject:** 25th Wedding Anniversary **Obv:** Large "ECU", medieval sailing ship, 12 stars in ribbon border **Obv. Legend:** DE NEDER - LANDEN **Rev:** Jugate busts of Beatrix and Prince Claus left **Rev. Legend:** ZILVEREN HUWELIJK KONINGIN BEATRIX EN PRINS KLAUS **Rev. Inscription:** eenkeus van het hart **Edge:** Plain **Note:** elke generatie. With fineness. Prev. X#25.

Date	Mintage	F	VF	XF	Unc	BU
1991 Proof	25,000	Value: 65.00				

X# 37.2 25 ECU
25.0000 g., 0.9250 Silver 0.7435 oz. ASW, 38 mm. **Ruler:** Beatrix **Issuer:** Mauquoy - Tramaux & Co. B.v.b.a., Grobbendonk **Subject:** 25th Wedding Anniversary **Obv:** Large "ECU", medieval sailing ship, 12 stars in ribbon border **Obv. Legend:** DE NEDER - LANDEN **Rev:** Jugate busts of Beatrix and Prince Claus left **Rev. Legend:** ZILVEREN HUWELIJK KONINGIN BEATRIX EN PRINS KLAUS **Rev. Inscription:** eenkeus van het hart **Edge:** Plain **Note:** elke generatie. Without fineness. Prev. X#25. Mintage: Inc. X#27.1.

Date	Mintage	F	VF	XF	Unc	BU
1991 Proof	—	Value: 65.00				

X# 40 25 ECU
25.0000 g., 0.9250 Silver 0.7435 oz. ASW, 38 mm. **Ruler:** Beatrix **Issuer:** Mauquoy - Tramaux & Co. B.v.b.a., Grobbendonk **Obv:** Large "ECU", medieval sailing ship, 12 stars in ribbon border **Obv. Legend:** DE NEDER - LANDEN **Rev:** Church at left, crowned arms at right **Rev. Legend:** ARNHEM, EURO - STADT AAN DE RIJN **Edge:** Plain

Date	Mintage	F	VF	XF	Unc	BU
1991 Proof	1,500	Value: 160				

X# 42 25 ECU
25.0000 g., 0.9250 Silver 0.7435 oz. ASW, 38 mm. **Ruler:** Beatrix **Issuer:** Mauquoy - Tramaux & Co. B.v.b.a., Grobbendonk **Subject:** 75th Four Day March **Obv:** Large "ECU", medieval sailing ship, 12 stars in ribbon border **Obv. Legend:** DE NEDER - LANDEN **Rev:** Stylized art, legs walking in center strip at left, crowned arms at right **Rev. Legend:** 75E INT.VIERDAAGSE • NIJMEGEN **Edge:** Plain

Date	Mintage	F	VF	XF	Unc	BU
1991 Proof	2,750	Value: 125				

X# 45.1 25 ECU
25.0000 g., 0.9250 Silver 0.7435 oz. ASW, 38 mm. **Ruler:** Beatrix **Issuer:** Mauquoy - Tramaux & Co. B.v.b.a., Grobbendonk **Obv:** Large "ECU", medieval sailing ship, 12 stars in ribbon border **Obv. Legend:** DE NEDER - LANDEN **Rev:** Bust of Desiderius Erasmus von Rotterdam at left (H. Holbein portrait), with fineness **Rev. Inscription:** ME / VELLE / ESSE / TOTIUS / MUNDI / NON / UNIMUS / OPPIDI **Edge:** Plain **Note:** With fineness.

Date	Mintage	F	VF	XF	Unc	BU
1991 Proof	29,998	Value: 50.00				

X# 45.2 25 ECU
25.0000 g., 0.9250 Silver 0.7435 oz. ASW, 38 mm. **Ruler:** Beatrix **Issuer:** Mauquoy - Tramaux & Co. B.v.b.a., Grobbendonk **Obv:** Large "ECU", medieval sailing ship, 12 stars in ribbon border **Obv. Legend:** DE NEDER - LANDEN **Rev:** Bust of Desiderius Erasmus von Rotterdam at left (H. Holbein portrait), without fineness **Rev. Inscription:** ME / VELLE / ESSE / TOTIUS / MUNDI / NON / UNIMUS / OPPIDI **Edge:** Plain **Note:** Without fineness. Mintage Inc. X#45.1.

Date	Mintage	F	VF	XF	Unc	BU
1991 Proof	—	Value: 50.00				

X# 50.1 25 ECU
25.0000 g., 0.9250 Silver 0.7435 oz. ASW, 38 mm. **Ruler:** Beatrix **Issuer:** Mauquoy - Tramaux & Co. B.v.b.a., Grobbendonk **Obv:** Large "ECU", medieval sailing ship, 12 stars in ribbon border **Obv. Legend:** DE NEDER - LANDEN **Rev:** Bust of Willem I. Frederik 3/4 right at left, three emblems at right **Rev. Inscription:** UITBREIDUNG / VAN HET / VERKEER MET / ALLE VOLKEN **Edge:** Plain **Note:** With fineness.

Date	Mintage	F	VF	XF	Unc	BU
1992 Proof	28,493	Value: 57.50				

X# 50.2 25 ECU
25.0000 g., 0.9250 Silver 0.7435 oz. ASW, 38 mm. **Ruler:** Beatrix **Issuer:** Mauquoy - Tramaux & Co. B.v.b.a., Grobbendonk **Obv:** Large "ECU", medieval sailing ship, 12 strs in ribbon border **Obv. Legend:** DE NEDER - LANDEN **Rev:** Bust of Willem I. Frederik 3/4 right at left, three emblems at right **Rev. Inscription:** UITBREIDUNG / VAN HET / VERKEER MET / ALLE VOLKEN **Edge:** Plain **Note:** Without fineness. Mintage: Inc. X#50.1.

Date	Mintage	F	VF	XF	Unc	BU
1992 Proof	—	Value: 57.50				

X# 50.3 25 ECU

25.0000 g., 0.9250 Silver 0.7435 oz. ASW, 38 mm. **Ruler:** Beatrix **Issuer:** Mauquoy - Tramaux & Co. B.v.b.a., Grobbendonk **Subject:** 100th Anniversary Royal Dutch Numismatic Society **Obv:** Large "ECU", medieval sailing ship, 12 stars in ribbon border **Obv. Legend:** DE NEDER - LANDEN **Rev:** Bust of Willem I. Frederik 3/4 right at left, three emblems at right **Rev. Inscription:** UITBREIDUNG / VAN HET / VERKEER MET / ALLE VOLKEN **Edge Lettering:** Kon.Ned.Genootschap voor Munt-en Penningkunde 100 jaar

Date	Mintage	F	VF	XF	Unc	BU
1992 Proof	1,507	Value: 190				

X# 62.1 25 ECU

25.0000 g., 0.9250 Silver 0.7435 oz. ASW, 38 mm. **Ruler:** Beatrix **Subject:** 12-1/2 Anniversary of Coronation and Visit to Aruba and the Netherlands Antilles **Obv:** Medieval sailing ship with state shields **Obv. Legend:** KONINKRIJK DER NEDERLANDEN **Rev:** Heads of five royal family right **Rev. Legend:** BEZOEK KON.FAM.NED.ANTILLEN EN ARUBA... **Edge:** Plain **Note:** With fineness.

Date	Mintage	F	VF	XF	Unc	BU
1992 Proof	30,000	Value: 50.00				

X# 62.2 25 ECU

25.0000 g., 0.9250 Silver 0.7435 oz. ASW, 38 mm. **Ruler:** Beatrix **Subject:** 12-1/2 Anniversary of Coronation and Visit to Aruba and the Netherlands Antilles **Obv:** Medieval sailing ship with state shields **Obv. Legend:** KONINKRIJK DER NEDERLANDEN **Rev:** Heads of five royal family right **Rev. Legend:** BEZOEK KON.FAM.NED.ANTILLEN EN ARUBA... **Edge:** Plain **Note:** Without fineness. Mintage Inc. X#62.1.

Date	Mintage	F	VF	XF	Unc	BU
1992 Proof	—	Value: 50.00				

X# 67.1 25 ECU

25.0000 g., 0.9250 Silver 0.7435 oz. ASW, 38 mm. **Ruler:** Beatrix **Obv:** Large "ECU", medieval sailing ship, 12 stars in ribbon border **Obv. Legend:** DE NEDER - LANDEN **Rev:** Bust of Jan A. Leeghwater 3/4 right, water, windmills and pumping stations in background **Rev. Inscription:** EXPERIEN- /TIA DOCET **Note:** With fineness.

Date	Mintage	F	VF	XF	Unc	BU
1993 Proof	25,000	Value: 50.00				

X# 67.2 25 ECU

25.0000 g., 0.9250 Silver 0.7435 oz. ASW, 38 mm. **Ruler:** Beatrix **Obv:** Large "ECU", medieval sailing ship, 12 stars in ribbon border **Obv. Legend:** DE NEDER - LANDEN **Rev:** Bust of Jan A. Leeghwater 3/4 right, water, windmills and pumping stations in background **Rev. Inscription:** EXPERIEN- /TIA DOCET **Note:** Without fineness. Mintage X#67.1.

Date	Mintage	F	VF	XF	Unc	BU
1993 Proof	—	Value: 50.00				

X# 71.1 25 ECU

25.0000 g., 0.9250 Silver 0.7435 oz. ASW, 38 mm. **Ruler:** Beatrix **Obv:** Large "ECU", medieval sailing ship, 12 stars in ribbon border **Obv. Legend:** DE NEDER - LANDEN **Rev:** Stylized bridge over Maas River, St. Servatius' keys, large "E" above **Rev. Legend:** MAAS - TRICHT **Edge:** Plain **Note:** With fineness.

Date	Mintage	F	VF	XF	Unc	BU
1993 Proof	25,000	Value: 50.00				

X# 71.2 25 ECU

25.0000 g., 0.9250 Silver 0.7435 oz. ASW, 38 mm. **Ruler:** Beatrix **Obv:** Large "ECU", medieval sailing ship, 12 stars in ribbon border **Obv. Legend:** DE NEDER - LANDEN **Rev:** Stylized bridge over Maas River, St. Servatius' keys, large "E" above **Rev. Legend:** MAAS - TRICHT **Edge:** Plain **Note:** Without fineness. Mintage: Inc. X#71.1.

Date	Mintage	F	VF	XF	Unc	BU
1993 Proof	—	Value: 50.00				

X# 75 25 ECU

25.0000 g., 0.9250 Silver 0.7435 oz. ASW, 38 mm. **Ruler:** Beatrix **Subject:** 85th Birthday of Queen Mother, 50th Anniversary Prince Bernhard's Being Commander of Armed Force **Obv:** Rampant lion left with sword and bundle of arrows, 12 stars around **Obv. Inscription:** KONINKRIJK / NEDERLANDEN **Rev:** Jugate busts of Princess Juliana and Prince Bernhard right **Rev. Inscription:** "IN / SAMEN- / WERKING / LIGT DE / SLEUTEL VOOR DE / TOEKOMST" **Edge:** Plain

Date	Mintage	F	VF	XF	Unc	BU
1994 Proof	25,000	Value: 27.50				

X# 75.1 25 ECU

25.0000 g., 0.9250 Silver 0.7435 oz. ASW, 38 mm. **Ruler:** Beatrix **Subject:** 85th Birthday of Queen Mother, 50th Anniversary Prince Bernhard's being Commander of Armed Force **Obv:** Rampant lion left with sword and bundle of arrows, 12 stars around **Obv. Inscription:** KONINKRIJK / NEDERLANDEN **Rev:** Jugate busts of Princess Juliana and Prince Bernhard right **Rev. Inscription:** "IN / SAMEN- / WERKING / LIGT DE / SLEUTEL VOOR DE / TOEKOMST" **Edge:** Plain **Note:** With fineness.

Date	Mintage	F	VF	XF	Unc	BU
1994 Proof	25,000	Value: 45.00				

X# 75.2 25 ECU

25.0000 g., 0.9250 Silver 0.7435 oz. ASW, 38 mm. **Ruler:** Beatrix **Subject:** 85th Birthday of Queen Mother, 50th Anniversary Prince Bernhard's being Commander of Armed Force **Obv:** Rampant lion left with sword and bundle of arrows, 12 stars around **Obv. Inscription:** KONINKRIJK / NEDERLANDEN **Rev:** Jugate busts of Princess Juliana and Prince Bernhardt right **Rev. Inscription:** "IN / SAMEN- / WERKING / LIGT DE / SLEUTEL VOOR DE / TOEKOMST" **Edge:** Plain **Note:** Without fineness. Mintage Inc. X#75.1.

Date	Mintage	F	VF	XF	Unc	BU
1994 Proof	—	Value: 45.00				

X# 83.1 25 ECU

25.0000 g., 0.9250 Silver 0.7435 oz. ASW, 38 mm. **Ruler:** Beatrix **Subject:** F. D. Roosevelt **Obv:** Rampant lion left with sword and bundle of arrows, 12 stars around **Obv. Inscription:** KONINKRIJK DER NEDERLANDEN **Edge:** Plain **Note:** With fineness.

Date	Mintage	F	VF	XF	Unc	BU
1994 Proof	25,000	Value: 50.00				

X# 83.2 25 ECU

25.0000 g., 0.9250 Silver 0.7435 oz. ASW, 38 mm. **Ruler:** Beatrix **Subject:** F. D. Roosevelt **Obv:** Rampant lion left with sword and bundle of arrows, 12 stars around **Obv. Inscription:** KONINKRIJK DER NEDERLANDEN **Edge:** Plain **Note:** Without fineness. Mintage Inc. X#83.1.

Date	Mintage	F	VF	XF	Unc	BU
1994 Proof	—	Value: 50.00				

X# 87.1 25 ECU

25.0000 g., 0.9250 Silver 0.7435 oz. ASW, 38 mm. **Ruler:** Beatrix **Subject:** Grotius **Obv:** Rampant lion left with sword and bundle of arrows **Obv. Legend:** KONINKRIJK DER NEDERLANDEN **Edge:** Plain **Note:** With fineness.

Date	Mintage	F	VF	XF	Unc	BU
1995 Proof	25,000	Value: 40.00				

X# 87.2 25 ECU
25.0000 g., 0.9250 Silver 0.7435 oz. ASW, 38 mm. **Ruler:** Beatrix **Subject:** Grotius **Obv:** Rampant lion left with sword and bundle of arrows **Obv. Legend:** KONINKRIJK DER NEDERLANDEN **Edge:** Plain **Note:** Without fineness. Mintage Inc. X#87.1.

Date	Mintage	F	VF	XF	Unc	BU
1995 Proof	—	Value: 40.00				

X# 91.1 25 ECU
25.0000 g., 0.9250 Silver 0.7435 oz. ASW, 38 mm. **Ruler:** Beatrix **Subject:** Wilhelmina / 40th Anniversary Liberation WWII **Obv:** Rampant lion left with sword and bundle of arrows **Obv. Legend:** KONINKRIJK DER NEDERLANDEN **Edge:** Plain **Note:** With fineness.

Date	Mintage	F	VF	XF	Unc	BU
1995 Proof	25,000	Value: 40.00				

X# 91.2 25 ECU
25.0000 g., 0.9250 Silver 0.7435 oz. ASW, 38 mm. **Ruler:** Beatrix **Subject:** Wilhelmina / 40th Anniversary Liberation WWii **Obv:** Rampant lion left with sword and bundle of arrows **Obv. Legend:** KONINKRIJK DER NEDERLANDEN **Edge:** Plain **Note:** Mintage Inc. X#91.1.

Date	Mintage	F	VF	XF	Unc	BU
1995 Proof	—	Value: 40.00				

X# 101 25 ECU
25.0000 g., 0.9250 Silver 0.7435 oz. ASW, 38 mm. **Ruler:** Beatrix **Subject:** Johannes Vermeer **Edge:** Plain

Date	Mintage	F	VF	XF	Unc	BU
1996 Proof	25,000	Value: 40.00				

X# 105 25 ECU
25.0000 g., 0.9250 Silver 0.7435 oz. ASW, 38 mm. **Ruler:** Beatrix **Subject:** Jacob van Kampen **Edge:** Plain

Date	Mintage	F	VF	XF	Unc	BU
1996 Proof	25,000	Value: 40.00				

X# 109 25 ECU
25.0000 g., 0.9250 Silver 0.7435 oz. ASW, 38 mm. **Ruler:** Beatrix **Subject:** 300th Anniversary Johan Maurits van Nassau-Sieggen **Rev:** Bust 3/4 right, youth riding elephant, anteater **Edge:** Plain

Date	Mintage	F	VF	XF	Unc	BU
1997 Proof	25,000	Value: 60.00				

X# 113 25 ECU
25.0000 g., 0.9250 Silver 0.7435 oz. ASW, 38 mm. **Ruler:** Beatrix **Subject:** 400 Years Diplomatic Contact with Russia **Rev:** Busts of Tsar Peter I left, Beatrix facing 3/4 left **Rev. Inscription:** NEDERLAND - RUSLAND **Edge:** Plain **Note:** With fineness.

Date	Mintage	F	VF	XF	Unc	BU
1997 Proof	25,000	Value: 40.00				

X# 117 25 ECU
25.0000 g., 0.9250 Silver 0.7435 oz. ASW, 38 mm. **Ruler:** Beatrix **Subject:** 200th Anniversary Birth of Johan Rudolf Thorbecke **Rev:** Head left, buildings behind **Edge:** Plain **Note:** With fineness.

Date	Mintage	F	VF	XF	Unc	BU
1998 Proof	25,000	Value: 50.00				

X# 38 100 ECU
3.3600 g., 0.9160 Gold 0.0989 oz. AGW, 18 mm. **Ruler:** Beatrix **Issuer:** Mauquoy - Tramaux & Co. B.v.b.a., Grobbendonk **Subject:** 25th Wedding Anniversary **Obv:** Large "ECU", medieval sailing ship, 12 stars in ribbon border **Obv. Legend:** DE NEDER - LANDEN **Rev:** Jugate busts of Beatrix and Prince Klaus left **Rev. Legend:** ZILVEREN HUWELIJK KONINGIN BEATRIX EN PRINS KLAUS **Rev. Inscription:** eenkeus van het hart **Edge:** Plain

Date	Mintage	F	VF	XF	Unc	BU
1991 Proof	1,250	Value: 225				

X# 63 100 ECU
3.3600 g., 0.9167 Gold 0.0990 oz. AGW, 18 mm. **Ruler:** Beatrix **Subject:** 12-1/2 Anniversary of Coronation and Visit to Aruba and the Netherlands Antilles **Obv:** Medieval sailing ship with state shields **Obv. Legend:** KONINKRIJK DER NEDERLANDEN **Rev:** Heads of five royal family right **Rev. Legend:** BEZOEK KON.FAM.NED.ANTILLEN EN ARUBA... **Edge:** Plain

Date	Mintage	F	VF	XF	Unc	BU
1992 Proof	3,000	Value: 200				

X# 68.1 100 ECU
6.7200 g., 0.7500 Gold 0.1620 oz. AGW, 22.5 mm. **Ruler:** Beatrix **Obv:** Large "ECU", medieval sailing ship, 12 stars in ribbon border **Obv. Legend:** DE NEDER - LANDEN **Rev:** Bust of Jan A. Leeghwater 3/4 right, water, windmills and pumping stations in background **Rev. Inscription:** EXPERIEN- /TIA DOCET **Edge:** Reeded **Note:** With fineness.

Date	Mintage	F	VF	XF	Unc	BU
1993 Proof	3,000	Value: 200				

X# 68.2 100 ECU

6.7200 g., 0.7500 Gold 0.1620 oz. AGW, 22.5 mm. **Ruler:** Beatrix **Obv:** Large "ECU", medieval sailing ship, 12 stars in ribbon border **Obv. Legend:** DE NEDER - LANDEN **Rev:** Bust of Jan A. Leeghwater 3/4 right, water, windmills and pumping stations in background **Rev. Inscription:** EXPERIEN- /TIA DOCET **Edge:** Reeded **Note:** Without fineness. Mintage: Inc. X#68.1.

Date	Mintage	F	VF	XF	Unc	BU
1993 Proof	—	Value: 200				

X# 72 100 ECU

3.3600 g., 0.9167 Gold 0.0990 oz. AGW, 18 mm. **Ruler:** Beatrix **Obv:** Large "ECU", medieval sailing ship, 12 stars in ribbon border **Obv. Legend:** DE NEDER - LANDEN **Rev:** Stylized bridge over Maas River, St. Servatius' keys, large "E" above **Rev. Legend:** MAAS - TRICHT **Edge:** Reeded

Date	Mintage	F	VF	XF	Unc	BU
1993 Proof	1,500	Value: 200				

X# 76 100 ECU

3.3600 g., 0.9160 Gold 0.0989 oz. AGW, 18 mm. **Ruler:** Beatrix **Subject:** 85th Birthday of Queen Mother, 50th Anniversary Prince Bernhard's Being Commander of Armed Force **Obv:** Rampant lion left with sword and bundle of arrows, 12 stars around **Obv. Inscription:** KONINKRIJK / NEDERLANDEN **Rev:** Jugate busts of Princess Juliana and Prince Bernhardt right **Rev. Inscription:** "IN / SAMEN- / WERKING / LIGT DE / SLEUTEL VOOR DE / TOEKOMST" **Edge:** Reeded

Date	Mintage	F	VF	XF	Unc	BU
1994 Proof	3,000	Value: 195				

X# 84 100 ECU

3.3600 g., 0.9167 Gold 0.0990 oz. AGW, 18 mm. **Ruler:** Beatrix **Subject:** F. D. Roosevelt **Obv:** Rampant lion left with sword and bundle of arrows, 12 stars around **Obv. Inscription:** KONINKRIJK DER NEDERLANDEN **Edge:** Reeded

Date	Mintage	F	VF	XF	Unc	BU
1994 Proof	3,000	Value: 200				

X# 88 100 ECU

3.3600 g., 0.9167 Gold 0.0990 oz. AGW, 18 mm. **Ruler:** Beatrix **Subject:** Grotius **Obv:** Rampant lion left with sword and bundle of arrows **Obv. Legend:** KONINKRIJK DER NEDERLANDEN **Edge:** Reeded

Date	Mintage	F	VF	XF	Unc	BU
1995 Proof	2,500	Value: 200				

X# 92 100 ECU

3.3600 g., 0.9167 Gold 0.0990 oz. AGW, 18 mm. **Ruler:** Beatrix **Subject:** Wilhelmina / 40th Anniversary Liberation WWII **Obv:** Rampant lion left with sword and bundle of arrows **Obv. Legend:** KONINKRIJK DER NEDERLANDEN **Edge:** Reeded

Date	Mintage	F	VF	XF	Unc	BU
1995 Proof	2,500	Value: 200				

X# 102 100 ECU

3.3600 g., 0.9167 Gold 0.0990 oz. AGW, 18 mm. **Ruler:** Beatrix **Subject:** Johannes Vermeer **Edge:** Reeded

Date	Mintage	F	VF	XF	Unc	BU
1996 Proof	2,500	Value: 200				

X# 106 100 ECU

3.3600 g., 0.9167 Gold 0.0990 oz. AGW, 18 mm. **Ruler:** Beatrix **Subject:** Jacob van Kampen **Edge:** Reeded

Date	Mintage	F	VF	XF	Unc	BU
1996 Proof	2,500	Value: 200				

X# 110 100 ECU

3.3600 g., 0.9167 Gold 0.0990 oz. AGW, 18 mm. **Ruler:** Beatrix **Subject:** 300th Anniversary Johan Maurits van Nassau-Sieggen **Rev:** Bust 3/4 right, youth riding elephant, anteater **Edge:** Reeded

Date	Mintage	F	VF	XF	Unc	BU
1997 Proof	2,500	Value: 200				

X# 114 100 ECU

3.3600 g., 0.9167 Gold 0.0990 oz. AGW, 18 mm. **Ruler:** Beatrix **Subject:** 400 Years Diplomatic Contact with Russia **Rev:** Busts of Tsar Peter I left, Beatrix facing 3/4 left **Rev. Inscription:** NEDERLAND - RUSLAND **Edge:** Reeded

Date	Mintage	F	VF	XF	Unc	BU
1997 Proof	2,500	Value: 200				

X# 118 100 ECU

3.3600 g., 0.9167 Gold 0.0990 oz. AGW, 18 mm. **Ruler:** Beatrix **Subject:** 200th Anniversary Birth of Johan Rudolf Thorbecke **Rev:** Head left, buildings behind **Edge:** Reeded

Date	Mintage	F	VF	XF	Unc	BU
1998 Proof	2,500	Value: 210				

X# 19.1 200 ECU

6.7200 g., 0.7500 Gold 0.1620 oz. AGW, 22.5 mm. **Ruler:** Beatrix **Issuer:** Mauquoy - Tramaux & Co. B.v.b.a., Grobbendonk **Obv:** Large "ECU," medieval sailing ship, 12 stars in ribbon border **Obv. Legend:** DE NEDER - LANDEN **Rev:** Jugate busts of Constantijn and Christian Haygens right **Rev. Legend:** ADMOVERE OCULIS DISTANTIA SIDERA NOSTRIS **Edge:** Reeded **Note:** Prev. X#19.

Date	Mintage	F	VF	XF	Unc	BU
1989M Prooflike	1,000	—	—	—	—	450

X# 19.2 200 ECU

6.7200 g., 0.7500 Gold 0.1620 oz. AGW, 22.50 mm. **Ruler:** Beatrix **Issuer:** Mauquoy - Tramaux & Co. B.v.b.a., Grobbendonk **Series:** Europa **Subject:** Huygens **Obv:** Large "ECU", medieval sailing ship, 12 stars in ribbon border **Obv. Legend:** DE NEDER - LANDEN **Rev:** Jugate busts of Constantijn and Christiaan Huygens right **Rev. Legend:** ADMOVERE OCULIS DISTANTIA SIDERA NOSTRIS **Edge:** Plain **Note:** Prev. X#19. Mintage included X#19.1.

Date	Mintage	F	VF	XF	Unc	BU
1989M Prooflike	1,000	—	—	—	—	450

X# 31 200 ECU

6.7000 g., 0.8250 Gold 0.1777 oz. AGW **Subject:** Geert Groote **Note:** Prev. X#21.

Date	Mintage	F	VF	XF	Unc	BU
1990 Proof	2,500	—	—	—	—	—

X# 46 200 ECU

6.7200 g., 0.7500 Gold 0.1620 oz. AGW, 22.5 mm. **Ruler:** Beatrix **Issuer:** Mauquoy - Tramaux & Co. B.v.b.a., Grobbendonk **Obv:** Large "ECU", medieval sailing ship, 12 stars in ribbon border **Obv. Legend:** DE NEDER - LANDEN **Rev:** Bust of Desiderius Erasmus von Rotterdam at left (H. Holbein portrait) **Rev. Inscription:** ME / VELLE / ESSE / TOTIUS / MUNDI / NON / UNIMUS / OPPIDI **Edge:** Plain

Date	Mintage	F	VF	XF	Unc	BU
1991 Proof	3,000	Value: 285				

X# 51.1 200 ECU

6.7200 g., 0.7500 Gold 0.1620 oz. AGW, 22.5 mm. **Ruler:** Beatrix **Issuer:** Mauquoy - Tramaux & Co. B.v.b.a., Grobbendonk **Obv:** Large "ECU", medieval sailing ship, 12 stars in ribbon border **Obv. Legend:** DE NEDER - LANDEN **Rev:** Bust of Willem I. Frederik 3/4 right at left, three emblems at righ **Rev. Inscription:** UITBREIDUNG / VAN HET / VERKEER MET / ALLE VOLKEN **Edge:** Reeded **Note:** With fineness ".585". Mintage: Inc. X#51.2.

Date	Mintage	F	VF	XF	Unc	BU
1992 Proof	—	Value: 285				

X# 51.2 200 ECU

6.7200 g., 0.7500 Gold 0.1620 oz. AGW, 22.5 mm. **Ruler:** Beatrix **Issuer:** Mauquoy - Tramaux & Co. B.v.b.a., Grobbendonk **Obv:** Large "ECU", medieval sailing ship, 12 stars in ribbon border **Obv. Legend:** DE NEDER - LANDEN **Rev:** Bust of Willem I. Frederik 3/4 right at left, three emblems at right **Rev. Inscription:** UITBREIDUNG / VAN HET / VERKEER MET / ALLE VOLKEN **Edge:** Reeded **Note:** With fineness ".750".

Date	Mintage	F	VF	XF	Unc	BU
1992tulip Proof	3,000	Value: 285				

X# 51.3 200 ECU

6.7200 g., 0.7500 Gold 0.1620 oz. AGW, 22.5 mm. **Ruler:** Beatrix **Issuer:** Mauquoy - Tramaux & Co. B.v.b.a., Grobbendonk **Obv:** Large "ECU", medieval sailing ship, 12 stars in ribbon border **Obv. Legend:** DE NEDER - LANDEN **Rev:** Bust of Willem I. Frederik 3/4 right at left, three emblems at right **Rev. Inscription:** UITBREIDUNG / VAN HET / VERKEER MET / ALLE VOLKEN **Edge:** Reeded **Note:** Without fineness. Inc. #X#51.2.

Date	Mintage	F	VF	XF	Unc	BU
1992 Proof	—	Value: 285				

Euro Series

X# 121 5 EURO
15.5000 g., Copper-Nickel, 33 mm. **Ruler:** Beatrix **Subject:** Willem Barentsz **Obv. Legend:** KONINKRIJK DER NEDERLANDEN

Date	Mintage	F	VF	XF	Unc	BU
1996	100,000	—	—	—	15.00	—

X# 126 5 EURO
15.5000 g., Copper-Nickel, 33 mm. **Ruler:** Beatrix **Subject:** Constantijn Huygens

Date	Mintage	F	VF	XF	Unc	BU
1996	100,000	—	—	—	11.50	—

X# 132 5 EURO
15.5000 g., Copper-Nickel, 33 mm. **Ruler:** Beatrix **Subject:** Pieter Cornelisz Hooft

Date	Mintage	F	VF	XF	Unc	BU
1997	100,000	—	—	—	8.50	—

X# 138 5 EURO
15.5000 g., Copper-Nickel, 33 mm. **Ruler:** Beatrix **Subject:** Johan van Oldenbarnevelt

Date	Mintage	F	VF	XF	Unc	BU
1997	100,000	—	—	—	7.00	—

X# 144 5 EURO
15.5000 g., Copper-Nickel, 33 mm. **Ruler:** Beatrix **Subject:** Maarten Tromp

Date	Mintage	F	VF	XF	Unc	BU
1998	100,000	—	—	—	6.50	—

X# 150 5 EURO
15.5000 g., Copper-Nickel, 33 mm. **Ruler:** Beatrix **Subject:** M. C. Escher

Date	Mintage	F	VF	XF	Unc	BU
1998	100,000	—	—	—	11.00	—

X# 122 10 EURO
10.4200 g., Bi-Metallic Copper-Nickel/Monedor I, 30.1 mm. **Ruler:** Beatrix **Subject:** Willem Barentsz
Obv: Stylized dove in flight left, arms above
Obv. Legend: KONINKRIJK DER NEDERLANDEN
Rev: Bust facing 3/4 right at lower left, sailing ship at upper right **Edge:** Reeded

Date	Mintage	F	VF	XF	Unc	BU
1996	50,000	—	—	—	—	22.50

X# 127 10 EURO
10.4200 g., Bi-Metallic Copper-Nickel/Monedor I, 30.1 mm. **Ruler:** Beatrix **Subject:** Constantijn Huygens
Obv: Stylized dove in flight left, arms above **Rev:** Sailing ship at left, bust facing 3/4 left at right **Edge:** Reeded

Date	Mintage	F	VF	XF	Unc	BU
1996	50,000	—	—	—	—	20.00

X# 139 10 EURO
14.0000 g., Bi-Metallic .999 Silver/Copper, gilt, 30 mm. **Ruler:** Beatrix **Subject:** Johan van Oldenbarnevelt

Date	Mintage	F	VF	XF	Unc	BU
1997	25,000	—	—	—	—	20.00

X# 145 10 EURO
14.0000 g., Bi-Metallic .999 Silver/Copper, gilt, 30 mm. **Ruler:** Beatrix **Subject:** Maarten Tromp

Date	Mintage	F	VF	XF	Unc	BU
1998	25,000	—	—	—	—	16.00

X# 151 10 EURO
14.0000 g., Bi-Metallic .999 Silver/Copper, gilt, 30 mm. **Ruler:** Beatrix **Subject:** M. C. Escher

Date	Mintage	F	VF	XF	Unc	BU
1998	25,000	—	—	—	—	22.50

X# 123 20 EURO
15.0000 g., 0.8000 Silver 0.3858 oz. ASW, 33 mm. **Ruler:** Beatrix **Subject:** Willem Barentsz

Date	Mintage	F	VF	XF	Unc	BU
1996 Prooflike	—	—	—	—	—	35.00

X# 128.1 20 EURO
15.0000 g., 0.8000 Silver 0.3858 oz. ASW, 33 mm. **Ruler:** Beatrix **Subject:** Constantijn Huygens
Note: With fineness.

Date	Mintage	F	VF	XF	Unc	BU
1996 Proof	25,000	—	—	—	—	30.00

X# 128.2 20 EURO
15.0000 g., 0.8000 Silver 0.3858 oz. ASW, 33 mm. **Ruler:** Beatrix **Subject:** Constantijn Huygens
Note: Without fineness. Mintage Inc. X#128.1.

Date	Mintage	F	VF	XF	Unc	BU
1996 Prooflike	—	—	—	—	—	35.00

X# 134 20 EURO
15.0000 g., 0.8000 Silver 0.3858 oz. ASW, 33 mm. **Ruler:** Beatrix **Subject:** Pieter Cornelisz Hooft

Date	Mintage	F	VF	XF	Unc	BU
1997 Prooflike	—	—	—	—	—	28.50

X# 140 20 EURO
15.0000 g., 0.8000 Silver 0.3858 oz. ASW, 33 mm.
Ruler: Beatrix **Subject:** Johan van Oldenbarnevelt

Date	Mintage	F	VF	XF	Unc	BU
1997	25,000	—	—	—	—	25.00

X# 146 20 EURO
15.0000 g., 0.8000 Silver 0.3858 oz. ASW, 33 mm.
Ruler: Beatrix **Subject:** Maarten Tromp

Date	Mintage	F	VF	XF	Unc	BU
1998 Prooflike	25,000	—	—	—	—	22.50

X# 152 20 EURO
15.0000 g., 0.8000 Silver 0.3858 oz. ASW, 33 mm.
Ruler: Beatrix **Subject:** M. C. Escher

Date	Mintage	F	VF	XF	Unc	BU
1998 Prooflike	—	—	—	—	—	65.00

X# 124 50 EURO
25.0000 g., 0.8000 Silver 0.6430 oz. ASW
Ruler: Beatrix **Subject:** Willem Barentsz

Date	Mintage	F	VF	XF	Unc	BU
1996 Prooflike	20,000	—	—	—	—	95.00

X# 129 50 EURO
25.0000 g., 0.9250 Silver 0.7435 oz. ASW, 38 mm.
Ruler: Beatrix **Subject:** Constantijn Huygens

Date	Mintage	F	VF	XF	Unc	BU
1996 Proof	20,000	Value: 95.00				

X# 135 50 EURO
25.0000 g., 0.9250 Silver 0.7435 oz. ASW, 38 mm.
Ruler: Beatrix **Subject:** Pieter Cornelisz Hooft

Date	Mintage	F	VF	XF	Unc	BU
1997 Prooflike	20,000	—	—	—	—	90.00

X# 141 50 EURO
25.0000 g., 0.9250 Silver 0.7435 oz. ASW, 38 mm.
Ruler: Beatrix **Subject:** Johan van Oldenbarnevelt

Date	Mintage	F	VF	XF	Unc	BU
1997 Prooflike	—	—	—	—	—	75.00

X# 147 50 EURO
25.0000 g., 0.9250 Silver 0.7435 oz. ASW, 38 mm.
Ruler: Beatrix **Subject:** Maarten Tromp

Date	Mintage	F	VF	XF	Unc	BU
1998 Prooflike	20,000	—	—	—	—	57.50

X# 153 50 EURO
25.0000 g., 0.9250 Silver 0.7435 oz. ASW, 38 mm.
Ruler: Beatrix **Subject:** M. C. Escher

Date	Mintage	F	VF	XF	Unc	BU
1998 Prooflike	20,000	—	—	—	—	125

X# 125 100 EURO
3.4940 g., 0.9830 Gold 0.1104 oz. AGW, 20.8 mm.
Ruler: Beatrix **Subject:** Willem Barentsz

Date	Mintage	F	VF	XF	Unc	BU
1996 Prooflike	2,000	—	—	—	—	—

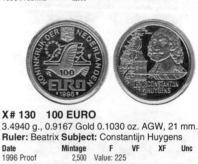

X# 130 100 EURO
3.4940 g., 0.9167 Gold 0.1030 oz. AGW, 21 mm.
Ruler: Beatrix **Subject:** Constantijn Huygens

Date	Mintage	F	VF	XF	Unc	BU
1996 Proof	2,500	Value: 225				

X# 136 100 EURO
3.4940 g., 0.9167 Gold 0.1030 oz. AGW, 21 mm.
Ruler: Beatrix **Subject:** Pieter Cornelisz Hooft

Date	Mintage	F	VF	XF	Unc	BU
1997 Proof	3,000	Value: 225				

X# 142 100 EURO

3.4940 g., 0.9167 Gold 0.1030 oz. AGW, 21 mm.
Ruler: Beatrix **Subject:** Johan van Oldenbarnevelt

Date	Mintage	F	VF	XF	Unc	BU
1997 Proof	3,000	Value: 200				

X# 148 100 EURO

3.4940 g., 0.9167 Gold 0.1030 oz. AGW, 21 mm.
Ruler: Beatrix **Subject:** Maarten Tromp

Date	Mintage	F	VF	XF	Unc	BU
1998 Proof	3,000	Value: 150				

X# 154 100 EURO

3.4940 g., 0.9167 Gold 0.1030 oz. AGW, 21 mm.
Ruler: Beatrix **Subject:** M. C. Escher

Date	Mintage	F	VF	XF	Unc	BU
1998 Proof	3,000	Value: 175				

X# 143 200 EURO

Bi-Metallic 155.50 Silver with 2.00 Gold hologram, 65 mm. **Ruler:** Beatrix **Subject:** Luxemburg
Note: Illustration reduced.

Date	Mintage	F	VF	XF	Unc	BU
1997 Proof	2,000	Value: 300				

X# 137 200 EURO

155.5000 g., Silver with 2.00 Gold Hologram, 65 mm.
Ruler: Beatrix **Subject:** Jan Pietersz Sweelinck/ Amsterdam **Note:** 155.50 Silver with 2.00 Gold hologram. Illustration reduced.

Date	Mintage	F	VF	XF	Unc	BU
1997 Proof	2,000	Value: 285				

X# 149 200 EURO

Bi-Metallic 155.50 Silver with 2.00 Gold hologram, 65 mm. **Ruler:** Beatrix **Subject:** London

Date	Mintage	F	VF	XF	Unc	BU
1998 Proof	2,000	Value: 300				

X# 155 200 EURO

Bi-Metallic, 65 mm. **Ruler:** Beatrix **Subject:** Vienna
Note: 155.50 Silver with 2.00 Gold hologram.

Date	Mintage	F	VF	XF	Unc	BU
1998 Proof	2,000	Value: 285				

X# 157 200 EURO

Bi-Metallic, 65 mm. **Ruler:** Beatrix **Subject:** Helsinki
Note: 155.50 Silver with 2.00 Gold hologram.

Date	Mintage	F	VF	XF	Unc	BU
1999 Proof	2,000	Value: 285				

X# 156 200 EURO

Bi-Metallic, 65 mm. **Ruler:** Beatrix **Subject:** Berlin
Note: 155.50 Silver with 2.00 Gold hologram

Date	Mintage	F	VF	XF	Unc	BU
1999 Proof	2,000	Value: 285				

PATTERNS

Including off metal strikes

X#	Date	Mintage	Identification	Mkt Val
Pn1	MCMLXXXVIII (1988)	—	Ecu. 0.9250 Silver. 33.7000 g. 38 mm. Reeded edge. X#11.1.	—
Pn2	MCMLXXXVIII (1988)	2	Ecu. Lead. 38 mm. Plain edge. X#13.2.	—
Pn3	MCMLXXXVII (1957)	2	Ecu. 0.9250 Silver. 10.0000 g. 29 mm. Plain edge. X#14.	—
Pn4	MCMLXXXVII (1957)	5	Ecu. 0.9200 Gold. 33.8200 g. 38 mm. Reeded edge. Similar to X#13.1 but with "AU 1 OZ" on reverse.	—
Pn5	1989M	—	10 Ecu. 0.9250 Silver. 25.0000 g. X#17.1.	—
Pn6	1989M	5	25 Ecu. 0.9000 Gold. 334.5585 g. 37.95 mm. X#18.	—
Pn7	1990	5	25 Ecu. 0.9160 Gold. 39.0600 g. 38 mm. X#28.	—
Pn8	1990	5	25 Ecu. 0.9160 Gold. 39.0600 g. 38 mm. X#33.	—
Pn9	1990	5	25 Ecu. 0.9160 Gold. 39.0600 g. 38 mm. X#34.	—
Pn10	1990	5	25 Ecu. 0.9250 Silver. 25.0000 g. 38 mm. Mule, Obv. X#24, Rev. X#28.	—
Pn11	1990	2	25 Ecu. 0.9250 Silver. 25.0000 g. 38 mm. X#45.1.	—
Pn12	1991	5	25 Ecu. 0.9160 Gold. 39.0600 g. 38 mm. X#37.	—
Pn13	1991	10	2-1/2 Ecu. Copper-Nickel. X#39.	—
Pn14	1991	5	25 Ecu. 0.9160 Gold. 39.0600 g. 38 mm. X#40.	—
Pn15	1991	5	25 Ecu. 0.9160 Gold. 39.0600 g. 38 mm. X#42.	—
Pn16	1991	5	25 Ecu. 0.9160 Gold. 39.0600 g. 38 mm. X#45.1.	—
Pn19	1992	5	25 Ecu. 0.9160 Gold. 39.0600 g. 38 mm.	—
Pn17	1992	5	25 Ecu. 0.9160 Gold. 39.0600 g. 38 mm. X#50.	—
Pn18	1992	5	25 Ecu. 0.9160 Gold. 39.0600 g. 38 mm. X#62.1.	—
Pn20	1993	5	25 Ecu. 0.9160 Gold. 39.0600 g. 38 mm. X#67.1.	—
Pn21	1993	5	25 Ecu. 0.9160 Gold. 39.0600 g. 38 mm. X#71.1.	—
Pn22	1994	5	25 Ecu. 0.9160 Gold. 39.0600 g. 38 mm. X#75.	—

TRIAL STRIKES

X#	Date	Mintage	Identification	Mkt Val
TS1	MCMLXXXVIII (1988)	1	Ecu. 0.9990 Silver. Obverse X#12.	—
TS2	MCMLXXXVIII (1988)	1	Ecu. 0.9990 Silver. Reverse X#12.	—

MINT SETS

X#	Date	Mintage	Identification	Issue Price	Mkt Val
XMS1	1995 (5)	30,000	X#94-98	40.00	40.00
XMS2	2005 (7)	—	X#Pn23-29	—	30.00

PROOF SETS

X#	Date	Mintage	Identification	Issue Price	Mkt Val
XPS3	1990 (6)	—	X#20a, 22a, 24a, 26a, 27.1a, 28	—	—
XPS4	1991 (4)	—	X#36-38 including medal of Wilhelm I	—	300
XPS5	1991 (4)	—	X#43-44, 45.1, 46	—	250
XPS6	1992 (4)	—	X#47, 49, 50.1, 50.2	—	250
XPS7	1992 (7)	—	X#52-56, 56a, 56b, 57	—	27.50
XPS8	1993 (4)	—	X#69-70, 71.1, 72	—	200

FRIESLAND

AUTONOMY MOVEMENT

MEDALLIC COINAGE

X# M6 29 STUIVERS

0.8350 Silver, 35 mm. **Obv:** Crowned arms divides date and value **Obv. Legend:** POPVLVM FRISIAE GVBERNAVT **Rev:** Bust of William Louis Nass facing 3/4 left **Rev. Legend:** GVILELMVS LVDOVICVS NASS: **Edge:** Plain

Date	Mintage	F	VF	XF	Unc	BU
1984 Proof	10,000	Value: 15.00				

X# M6a 29 STUIVERS

0.5833 Gold, 35 mm. **Obv:** Crowned arms divides date and value **Obv. Legend:** POPVLVM FRISIAE GVBERNAVT **Rev:** Bust of William Louis Nass facing 3/4 left **Rev. Legend:** GVILELMVS LVDOVICVS NASS: **Edge:** Plain

Date	Mintage	F	VF	XF	Unc	BU
1984 Proof	10,000	Value: 425				

X# M2 1/2 DAALDER

Silver Plated, 30 mm. **Subject:** Quote by Grote Pier **Obv:** Sword upright **Obv. Legend:** BUTTER (leaf) BREA (leaf) EN (leaf) GRIENE (leaf) TSIIS (Butter, Bread and Green Cheese) **Obv. Designer:** L. Jansma **Rev:** Skûtsje sailboat, pompeblad leaf to right **Rev. Inscription:** IT SKUTSJE **Edge:** Plain

Date	Mintage	F	VF	XF	Unc	BU
ND(1983)	—	—	—	—	8.00	—

X# M1 DAALDER
8.0000 g., 0.9250 Silver 0.2379 oz. ASW, 25 mm. **Issuer:** Lykele Jansma **Subject:** 1435 Battle at Warns **Obv:** Crowned arms **Obv. Inscription:** FRYSLAN **Obv. Designer:** L. Jansma **Rev:** Plompeblad leaf with value **Rev. Legend:** (leaf) LEAVER (leaf) DEA (leaf) AS (leaf) SLAAF (rather dead than a slave) **Edge:** Plain

Date	Mintage	F	VF	XF	Unc	BU
1982	10,000	—	—	—	25.00	—

X# M3 DAALDER
Silver Plated, 30 mm. **Subject:** Quote by Grote Pier **Obv:** Sword upright **Obv. Legend:** BUTTER (leaf) BREA (leaf) EN (leaf) GRIENE (leaf) TSIIS (Butter, Bread and Green Cheese) **Obv. Designer:** L. Jansma **Rev:** Skûtsje sailboat, pompeblade leaf to right **Rev. Inscription:** IT SKUTSJE **Edge:** Plain

Date	Mintage	F	VF	XF	Unc	BU
ND(1983)	—	—	—	—	8.00	—

X# M4 2 DAALDER
Silver Plated, 30 mm. **Subject:** Quote by Grote Pier **Obv:** Sword upright **Obv. Legend:** BUTTER (leaf) BREA (leaf) EN (leaf) GRIENE (leaf) TSIIS (Butter, Bread and Green Cheese) **Obv. Designer:** L. Jansma **Rev:** Skûtsje sailboat, pompeblade leaf to right **Rev. Inscription:** IT SKUTSJE **Edge:** Plain

Date	Mintage	F	VF	XF	Unc	BU
ND(1983)	—	—	—	—	8.00	—

X# M5 2-1/2 DAALDER
Silver Plated, 30 mm. **Subject:** Quote by Grote Pier **Obv:** Sword upright **Obv. Legend:** BUTTER (leaf) BREA (leaf) EN (leaf) GRIENE (leaf) TSIIS (Butter, Bread and Green Cheese) **Obv. Designer:** L. Jansma **Rev:** Skûtsje sailboat, pompeblad leaf to right **Rev. Inscription:** IT SKUTSJE **Edge:** Plain

Date	Mintage	F	VF	XF	Unc	BU
ND(1983)	—	—	—	—	8.00	—

X# M7 SULVEREN
12.0000 g., 0.9990 Silver 0.3854 oz. ASW, 30 mm. **Obv:** Cubic background **Obv. Designer:** Aizo Betlen **Rev:** Male skating right, cubic background **Rev. Legend:** ien fryske sulveren rider

Date	Mintage	F	VF	XF	Unc	BU
1985 Prooflike	10,000	—	—	—	—	35.00
1986 Prooflike	10,000	—	—	—	—	35.00

X# M8 1/2 KROAN
Brass, 30 mm. **Subject:** Small Nations Olympics - Cross Country Skating **Obv:** Five oak leaf star **Obv. Legend:** (leaf) eala (leaf) frya (leaf) fresona (leaf) **Rev. Legend:** OLYMPYSKE SPULLEN LYTES NAASJES **Edge:** Plain

Date	Mintage	F	VF	XF	Unc	BU
1985	2,010	—	—	—	10.00	—

X# M9 KROAN
Copper-Nickel, 30 mm. **Subject:** Small Nations Olympics - Cross Country Skating **Obv:** Five oak leaf star **Obv. Legend:** (leaf) eala (leaf) frya (leaf) fresona (leaf) **Rev. Legend:** OLYMPYSKE SPULLEN LYTES NAASJES **Edge:** Plain

Date	Mintage	F	VF	XF	Unc	BU
1985	2,010	—	—	—	10.00	—

X# M10 2 KROANEN
Copper-Nickel, 30 mm. **Subject:** Small Nations Olympics - Cross Country Skating **Obv:** Five oak leaf star **Obv. Legend:** (leaf) eala (leaf) frya (leaf) fresona (leaf) **Rev. Legend:** OLYMPYSKE SPULLEN LYTES NAASJES **Edge:** Plain

Date	Mintage	F	VF	XF	Unc	BU
1985	2,010	—	—	—	10.00	—

X# M11 2-1/2 KROANEN
Copper-Nickel, 30 mm. **Subject:** Small Nations Olympics - Cross Country Skating **Obv:** Five oak leaf star **Obv. Legend:** (leaf) eala (leaf) frya (leaf) fresona (leaf) **Rev. Legend:** OLYMPYSKE SPULLEN LYTES NAASJES **Edge:** Plain

Date	Mintage	F	VF	XF	Unc	BU
1985	2,010	—	—	—	10.00	—

X# M12 5 KROANEN
Copper-Nickel, 30 mm. **Subject:** Small Nations Olympics - Cross Counry Skating **Obv:** FIve oak leaf star **Obv. Legend:** (leaf) eala (leaf) frya (leaf) fresona (leaf) **Rev. Legend:** OLYMPYSKE SPULLEN LYTES NAASJES **Edge:** Plain

Date	Mintage	F	VF	XF	Unc	BU
1985	2,010	—	—	—	10.00	—

X# M12a 5 KROANEN
0.9990 Silver, 30 mm. **Subject:** Small Nations Olympics - Cross Country Skating **Obv:** Five oak leaf star **Obv. Legend:** (leaf) eala (leaf) frya (leaf) fresona (leaf) **Rev. Legend:** OLYMPYSKE SPULLEN LYTES NAASJES **Edge:** Plain

Date	Mintage	F	VF	XF	Unc	BU
1985	—	—	—	—	35.00	—

X# M13 10 KROANEN
Gold, 30 mm. **Subject:** Small Nations Olympics - Cross Country Skating **Obv:** Five oak leaf star **Obv. Legend:** (leaf) eala (leaf) frya (leaf) fresona (leaf) **Rev. Legend:** OLYMPYSKE SPULLEN LYTES NAASJES **Edge:** Plain

Date	Mintage	F	VF	XF	Unc	BU
1985	2,010	—	—	—	350	—

ZEELAND

PROVINCE

SIEGE COINAGE

Middelburg - 1573

FR# 162 4 DUCAT
Gold **Countermark:** Zeeland shield and Middelburg shield **Obv. Legend:** DEO / REGI / ... / MIDDELB: **Note:** Klippe, uniface

Date	Mintage	F	VF	XF	Unc	BU
1573 Rare	—	—	—	—	—	—

NETHERLANDS ANTILLES

KINGDOM

FANTASY EURO PATTERNS

X# Pn1 EURO CENT
Copper Plated Steel, 16.8 mm. **Ruler:** Beatrix **Issuer:** INA **Obv:** Head of Juliana right **Rev:** Tropical fish left at right **Edge:** Plain

Date	Mintage	F	VF	XF	Unc	BU
2004	10,000	—	—	—	—	1.50
2004 Proof	—	Value: 2.50				

X# Pn1a EURO CENT
Silver, 16.8 mm. **Ruler:** Beatrix **Issuer:** INA **Obv:** Head of Juliana right **Rev:** Tropical fish left at right **Edge:** Plain

Date	Mintage	F	VF	XF	Unc	BU
2004 Proof	275	Value: 6.00				

X# Pn2 2 EURO CENT
Copper Plated Steel, 18.5 mm. **Ruler:** Beatrix **Issuer:** INA **Obv:** Head of Juliana right **Rev:** Tropical fish left at right **Edge:** Plain

Date	Mintage	F	VF	XF	Unc	BU
2004	10,000	—	—	—	—	2.00
2004 Proof	—	Value: 3.00				

X# Pn2a 2 EURO CENT
Silver, 18.5 mm. **Ruler:** Beatrix **Issuer:** INA **Obv:** Head of Juliana right **Rev:** Tropical fish left at right **Edge:** Plain

Date	Mintage	F	VF	XF	Unc	BU
2004 Proof	275	Value: 7.00				

X# Pn3 5 EURO CENT
Copper Plated Steel, 20.7 mm. **Ruler:** Beatrix **Issuer:** INA **Obv:** Head of Juliana right **Rev:** Tropical fish left at right **Edge:** Plain

Date	Mintage	F	VF	XF	Unc	BU
2004	10,000	—	—	—	—	2.50
2004 Proof	—	Value: 3.50				

X# Pn3a 5 EURO CENT
Silver, 20.7 mm. **Ruler:** Beatrix **Issuer:** INA **Obv:** Head of Juliana right **Rev:** Tropical fish left at right **Edge:** Plain

Date	Mintage	F	VF	XF	Unc	BU
2004 Proof	275	Value: 8.50				

X# Pn4 10 EURO CENT
Goldine, 19.3 mm. **Ruler:** Beatrix **Issuer:** INA **Obv:** Head of Juliana right **Rev:** Sea horse **Edge:** Plain

Date	Mintage	F	VF	XF	Unc	BU
2004	10,000	—	—	—	—	3.00
2004 Proof	—	Value: 4.00				

X# Pn4a 10 EURO CENT
Silver, 19.3 mm. **Ruler:** Beatrix **Issuer:** INA **Obv:** Head of Juliana right **Rev:** Sea horse **Edge:** Plain

Date	Mintage	F	VF	XF	Unc	BU
2004 Proof	275	Value: 10.00				

X# Pn5 20 EURO CENT
Goldine, 22 mm. **Ruler:** Beatrix **Issuer:** INA **Obv:** Bust of Juliana right **Rev:** Sea horse **Edge:** Plain

Date	Mintage	F	VF	XF	Unc	BU
2004	10,000	—	—	—	—	3.50
2004 Proof	—	Value: 5.00				

X# Pn5a 20 EURO CENT
Silver, 22 mm. **Ruler:** Beatrix **Issuer:** INA **Obv:** Bust of Juliana right **Rev:** Sea horse **Edge:** Plain

Date	Mintage	F	VF	XF	Unc	BU
2004 Proof	—	Value: 12.50				

X# Pn6 50 EURO CENT
Goldine, 24.3 mm. **Ruler:** Beatrix **Issuer:** INA **Obv:** Bust of Juliana right **Rev:** Sea horse **Edge:** Plain

Date	Mintage	F	VF	XF	Unc	BU
2004	10,000	—	—	—	—	4.00
2004 Proof	—	Value: 6.00				

X# Pn6a 50 EURO CENT
Silver, 24.3 mm. **Ruler:** Beatrix **Issuer:** INA **Obv:** Bust of Juliana right **Rev:** Sea horse **Edge:** Plain

Date	Mintage	F	VF	XF	Unc	BU
2004 Proof	—	Value: 15.00				

X# Pn7 EURO
Bi-Metallic Copper-Nickel center in Goldine ring, 22.8 mm. **Ruler:** Beatrix **Issuer:** INA **Obv:** Bust of Juliana right **Rev:** Sun above flamingo **Edge:** Plain

Date	Mintage	F	VF	XF	Unc	BU
2004	10,000	—	—	—	—	6.00
2004 Proof	—	Value: 8.00				

X# Pn7a EURO
Bi-Metallic Silver center in Goldine ring, 22.8 mm. **Ruler:** Beatrix **Issuer:** INA **Obv:** Bust of Juliana right **Rev:** Sun above flamingo **Edge:** Plain

Date	Mintage	F	VF	XF	Unc	BU
2004 Proof	275	Value: 22.50				

X# Pn8 2 EURO
Bi-Metallic Goldine center in Copper-Nickel ring, 25.7 mm. **Ruler:** Beatrix **Issuer:** INA **Obv:** Bust of Juliana right **Rev:** Sun above flamingo **Edge:** Plain

Date	Mintage	F	VF	XF	Unc	BU
2004	10,000	—	—	—	—	8.00
2004 Proof	—	Value: 10.00				

X# Pn8a 2 EURO
Bi-Metallic Silver center in Goldine ring, 25.7 mm. **Ruler:** Beatrix **Issuer:** INA **Obv:** Bust of Juliana right **Rev:** Sun above flamingo **Edge:** Plain

Date	Mintage	F	VF	XF	Unc	BU
2004 Proof	275	Value: 28.50				

X# Pn9 5 EURO
Goldine **Ruler:** Beatrix **Issuer:** INA **Obv:** Head of Juliana right **Edge:** Plain

Date	Mintage	F	VF	XF	Unc	BU
2004 Proof	—	Value: 12.50				

X# Pn9a 5 EURO
Silver **Ruler:** Beatrix **Issuer:** INA **Obv:** Head of Juliana right **Edge:** Plain

Date	Mintage	F	VF	XF	Unc	BU
2004 Proof	275	Value: 40.00				

MINT SETS

X#	Date	Mintage	Identification	Issue Price	Mkt Val
XMS1	2004 (8)	10,000	X#Pn1-Pn8	—	30.00

PROOF SETS

X#	Date	Mintage	Identification	Issue Price	Mkt Val
XPS1	2004 (9)	—	X#Pn1-Pn9	—	50.00
XPS2	2004 (9)	275	X#Pn1a-Pn9a	—	150

SAINT MARTIN

KINGDOM

FANTASY EURO COINAGE

X# Pn1 EURO CENT
Copper Plated Steel **Ruler:** Beatrix

Date	Mintage	F	VF	XF	Unc	BU
2005	2,500	—	—	—	—	1.50

X# Pn2 2 EURO CENT
Copper Plated Steel **Ruler:** Beatrix

Date	Mintage	F	VF	XF	Unc	BU
2005	2,500	—	—	—	—	2.00

X# Pn3 5 EURO CENT
Copper Plated Steel **Ruler:** Beatrix

Date	Mintage	F	VF	XF	Unc	BU
2005	2,500	—	—	—	—	2.50

X# Pn4 10 EURO CENT
Goldine **Ruler:** Beatrix

Date	Mintage	F	VF	XF	Unc	BU
2005	2,500	—	—	—	—	3.00

X# Pn5 20 EURO CENT
Goldine **Ruler:** Beatrix

Date	Mintage	F	VF	XF	Unc	BU
2005	2,500	—	—	—	—	3.50

X# Pn6 50 EURO CENT
Goldine **Ruler:** Beatrix

Date	Mintage	F	VF	XF	Unc	BU
2005	2,500	—	—	—	—	4.00

X# Pn7 EURO
Bi-Metallic **Ruler:** Beatrix

Date	Mintage	F	VF	XF	Unc	BU
2005	2,500	—	—	—	—	6.00

X# Pn8 2 EURO
Bi-Metallic **Ruler:** Beatrix

Date	Mintage	F	VF	XF	Unc	BU
2005	2,500	—	—	—	—	8.00

MINT SETS

X#	Date	Mintage	Identification	Issue Price	Mkt Val
XMS1	2005 (8)	2,500	X#Pn1-Pn8	—	30.00

NETHERLANDS EAST INDIES

FRENCH OCCUPATION

Kingdom of Holland 1806 - 1810

FANTASY COINAGE

X# 1 1/2 DUCAT
Silver **Countermark:** "JAVA" and "1809" on Netherlands 1/2 Silver Ducats **Note:** A fantasy issue produced supposedly for Count Ferrard circa 1900-1920.

Date	Mintage	Good	VG	F	VF	XF
1762	—	35.00	60.00	100	175	—

JAPANESE OCCUPATION

World War II

BULLION COINAGE

R. T. Braakensiek Assaying & Refining Workshops, Ltd., Djakarta, Batavia

X# 11 SATOE TAEL
54.0000 g., 0.9990 Silver 1.7343 oz. ASW
Rev: Refinery worker carrying load left

Date	Mintage	F	VF	XF	Unc	BU
ND	—	450	750	1,100	—	—

NEW CALEDONIA

FRENCH OVERSEAS TERRITORY

TOKEN COINAGE

Nickel Societe Anonyme

A series of tokens struck for the exploitation of nickel ore from New Caledonia

X# Tn1 5 CENTIMES
Copper-Nickel-Zinc

Date	Mintage	F	VF	XF	Unc	BU
1881	—	—	—	175	250	425

X# Tn2 10 CENTIMES
Copper-Nickel-Zinc

Date	Mintage	F	VF	XF	Unc	BU
1881	—	—	—	175	250	425

X# Tn3 25 CENTIMES
Copper-Nickel-Zinc

Date	Mintage	F	VF	XF	Unc	BU
1881	—	—	—	175	250	455

Societe Franco-Australienne Gomen Digeon & Co.

X# Tn4 5 FRANCS
Copper-Nickel

Date	Mintage	F	VF	XF	Unc	BU
1882	—	—	—	150	250	500

NEW FRANCE

MONARCHY

Araucania and Patagonia

FANTASY COINAGE

X# 1 2 CENTAVOS
Bronze **Ruler:** Orlie-Antoine de Tounens **Note:** Prev. KY#170.

Date	Mintage	F	VF	XF	Unc	BU
1874 Proof	—	Value: 1,000				

X# 13 PESO
Silver **Ruler:** Orlie-Antoine de Tounens **Rev:** "UN PESO" **Note:** Prev. KY#168. Type III. Piefort.

Date	Mintage	F	VF	XF	Unc	BU
1874 Proof	—	Value: 3,000				

X# 5 PESO
Silver **Ruler:** Orlie-Antoine de Tounens **Note:** Type I. Piefort.

Date	Mintage	F	VF	XF	Unc	BU
1874 E Proof	—	Value: 3,000				

X# 2 PESO
Silver **Ruler:** Orlie-Antoine de Tounens **Rev:** Small "1 PESO" **Edge:** Plain **Note:** Type I. Prev. KY#168b.

Date	Mintage	F	VF	XF	Unc	BU
1874 E Proof	—	Value: 2,000				

X# 3 PESO
Silver **Ruler:** Orlie-Antoine de Tounens **Rev:** Small "1 PESO" **Edge:** Reeded **Note:** Type I. Prev. KY#168b.

Date	Mintage	F	VF	XF	Unc	BU
1874 E Proof	—	Value: 2,000				

X# 4 PESO
Bronze **Ruler:** Orlie-Antoine de Tounens **Rev:** Small "1 PESO" **Note:** Type I. Prev. KY#168c.

Date	Mintage	F	VF	XF	Unc	BU
1874 E Proof	—	Value: 1,000				

X# 9 PESO
Silver **Ruler:** Orlie-Antoine de Tounens **Note:** Type II. Piefort.

Date	Mintage	F	VF	XF	Unc	BU
1874 Proof	—	Value: 3,000				

X# 6 PESO
Silver **Ruler:** Orlie-Antoine de Tounens **Rev:** Large "1 PESO" without E **Edge:** Plain **Note:** Type II. Prev. KY#169.

Date	Mintage	F	VF	XF	Unc	BU
1874 Proof	—	Value: 2,850				

X# 7 PESO
Silver **Ruler:** Orlie-Antoine de Tounens **Rev:** Large "1 PESO" without E **Edge:** Reeded **Note:** Type II. Prev. KY#169.

Date	Mintage	F	VF	XF	Unc	BU
1874 Proof	—	Value: 2,000				

X# 8 PESO
Bronze **Ruler:** Orlie-Antoine de Tounens **Rev:** Large "1 PESO" without E **Note:** Type II. Prev. KY#169a.

Date	Mintage	F	VF	XF	Unc	BU
1874 Proof	—	Value: 1,000				

X# 10 PESO
Silver **Ruler:** Orlie-Antoine de Tounens **Rev:** "UN PESO" **Edge:** Plain **Note:** Type III.

Date	Mintage	F	VF	XF	Unc	BU
1874 Proof	—	Value: 2,000				

X# 11 PESO
Silver **Ruler:** Orlie-Antoine de Tounens **Rev:** "UN PESO" **Edge:** Reeded **Note:** Type III.

Date	Mintage	F	VF	XF	Unc	BU
1874 Proof	—	Value: 2,000				

X# 12 PESO
Bronze **Ruler:** Orlie-Antoine de Tounens **Rev:** "UN PESO" **Note:** Type III. Prev. KY#168a.

Date	Mintage	F	VF	XF	Unc	BU
1874 Proof	—	Value: 1,000				

X# 14 PESO
Silver **Ruler:** Orlie-Antoine de Tounens **Rev:** Small "1 PESO" without E **Note:** Type IV.

Date	Mintage	F	VF	XF	Unc	BU
1874 Proof	—	Value: 2,750				

X# 21 100 PESOS
Copper-Nickel-Zinc **Ruler:** Orlie-Antoine de Tounens **Subject:** 128th Anniversary of Founding

Date	Mintage	F	VF	XF	Unc	BU
1988 Prooflike	2,000	—	—	—	30.00	—

X# 22 100 PESOS
31.1030 g., 1.0000 Palladium 0.9999 oz. **Ruler:** Orlie-Antoine de Tounens **Subject:** 128th Anniversary of Founding

Date	Mintage	F	VF	XF	Unc	BU
1988 Proof	128	Value: 495				

X# 23 100 PESOS
31.1030 g., 1.0000 Gold 0.9999 oz. AGW **Ruler:** Orlie-Antoine de Tounens **Subject:** 128th Anniversary of Founding

Date	Mintage	F	VF	XF	Unc	BU
1988 Proof	128	Value: 750				

X# 24 100 PESOS
31.1030 g., 1.0000 Platinum 0.9999 oz. APW **Ruler:** Orlie-Antoine de Tounens **Subject:** 128th Anniversary of Founding

Date	Mintage	F	VF	XF	Unc	BU
1988 Proof	128	Value: 1,000				

X# 25 100 PESOS
62.2060 g., 1.0000 Silver 1.9999 oz. ASW **Ruler:** Orlie-Antoine de Tounens **Subject:** 128th Anniversary of Founding **Note:** Piefort.

Date	Mintage	F	VF	XF	Unc	BU
1988 Proof	38	Value: 300				

FANTASY KINGDOMS

ISLE DU MASSACRE

Issued by the Shire Post Mint

X# 51 SOL
9.0000 g., Copper **Ruler:** Louis XIV **Obv:** Louis XIV bust right **Obv. Legend:** LUD• XIIII • D • G • FRA • ET• NAV • REX **Rev:** Three skulls within crowned shield **Rev. Legend:** ISLE DU MASSACRE 1699

Date	Mintage	F	VF	XF	Unc	BU
1699	200	—	—	25.00	—	—

X# 52 1/4 ECU
6.0000 g., Silver **Ruler:** Louis XIV **Obv:** Louis XIV bust right **Rev:** Three skulls within crowned shield

Date	Mintage	F	VF	XF	Unc	BU
1699	24	—	—	32.00	—	—

ISLE DAUPHIN

Issued by the Shire Post Mint

X# 55 SOL
9.0000 g., Copper **Ruler:** Louis XIV **Obv:** Louis XIV bust right **Rev:** Crowned dolphin with three fleur-de-lis around **Rev. Legend:** ISLE DAUPHIN

Date	Mintage	F	VF	XF	Unc	BU
1707	100	—	—	20.00	—	—

X# 56 ECU
6.0000 g., Silver **Ruler:** Louis XIV **Obv:** Louis XIV bust right **Rev:** Crowned dolphin with three fleur de lis around

Date	Mintage	F	VF	XF	Unc	BU
1707	24	—	—	25.00	—	—

POST AUX AKANSAS

Issued by the Shire Post Mint

X# 60 SOL
9.0000 g., Copper **Ruler:** Louis XIV **Obv:** Louis XIV bust right **Rev:** Crowned bow-and-arrow, three fleur-de-lis around **Rev. Legend:** POSTE AUX AKANSAS

Date	Mintage	F	VF	XF	Unc	BU
1690	60	—	—	25.00	—	—

X# 61 1/4 ECU
6.0000 g., Silver **Ruler:** Louis XIV **Obv:** Louis XIV bust right **Rev:** Crowned bow-and-arrow flanked by three fleur-de-lis

Date	Mintage	F	VF	XF	Unc	BU
1690	20	—	—	35.00	—	—

X# 62 LOUIS D'OR
6.0000 g., 0.9000 Gold 0.1736 oz. AGW **Ruler:** Louis XIV **Obv:** Louis XIV bust right **Rev:** Crowned bow-and-arrow, three fleur-de-lis flanking

Date	Mintage	F	VF	XF	Unc	BU
1690	1	—	—	—	—	—

LA NOUVELLE FRANCE

Issued by the Shire Post Mint

X# 65 5 CENTIMES
9.0000 g., Copper **Ruler:** Napoleon **Obv:** Crowned N **Obv. Legend:** LA NOUVELLE FRANCE **Rev:** Value and date within oak wreath

Date	Mintage	F	VF	XF	Unc	BU
1803	—	—	—	10.00	—	—

NEW GUINEA

AUSTRALIAN ADMINISTRATION

1914-1973

MEDALLIC COINAGE

Richard Lobel Series

X# M1 CROWN
Bronze, 38.10 mm. **Subject:** Edward VIII **Obv:** Bust left **Obv. Legend:** EDWARD • VIII • KING • & • EMPEROR **Rev:** Bird of Paradise **Edge:** Plain

Date	Mintage	F	VF	XF	Unc	BU
1936 Proof	500	Value: 20.00				

X# M1a CROWN
Copper-Nickel-Zinc, 38.10 mm. **Subject:** Edward VIII **Obv:** Bust left **Obv. Legend:** EDWARD • VIII • KING • & • EMPEROR **Rev:** Bird of Paradise **Edge:** Plain

Date	Mintage	F	VF	XF	Unc	BU
1936 Proof	1,550	Value: 20.00				

X# M1b CROWN
0.9167 Silver, 38.10 mm. **Subject:** Edward VIII **Obv:** Bust left **Obv. Legend:** EDWARD • VIII • KING • & • EMPEROR **Rev:** Bird of Paradise **Edge:** Plain

Date	Mintage	F	VF	XF	Unc	BU
1936 Proof	200	Value: 55.00				

X# M1c CROWN
Gold, 38.10 mm. **Subject:** Edward VIII **Obv:** Bust left **Obv. Legend:** EDWARD • VIII • KING • & • EMPEROR **Rev:** Bird of Paradise **Edge:** Plain

Date	Mintage	F	VF	XF	Unc	BU
1936 Proof	—	Value: 500				

X# M2 SOVEREIGN
0.3750 Gold, 21.98 mm. **Subject:** Edward VIII **Obv:** Bust left **Obv. Legend:** EDWARD • VIII • KING • & • EMPEROR **Rev:** Bird of Paradise **Edge:** Plain

Date	Mintage	F	VF	XF	Unc	BU
1936 Proof	150	Value: 200				

X# M2a SOVEREIGN
4.4200 g., Silver, 21.98 mm. **Subject:** Edward VIII **Obv:** Bust left **Obv. Legend:** EDWARD • VIII • KING • & • EMPEROR **Rev:** Bird of Paradise **Edge:** Plain

Date	Mintage	F	VF	XF	Unc	BU
1936 Proof	—	Value: 10.00				

PIEFORTS

X#	Date	Mintage	Identification	Mkt Val
P1	1936	—	Crown. 0.9167 Silver. X#M1b.	100

NEW HEBRIDES

FRENCH/BRITISH CONDOMINIUM

(Jointly Governed Territory)

FANTASY COINAGE

X# 1 500 FRANCS
19.4400 g., 0.9250 Silver 0.5781 oz. ASW **Subject:** Year of the Child

Date	Mintage	F	VF	XF	Unc	BU
1979 Proof	500	Value: 150				

X# 2 500 FRANCS
Nickel-Brass **Subject:** Year of the Child

Date	Mintage	F	VF	XF	Unc	BU
1979 Proof	—	Value: 200				

X# 3 500 FRANCS
Copper-Nickel-Aluminum **Subject:** Year of the Child

Date	Mintage	F	VF	XF	Unc	BU
1979 Proof	—	Value: 200				

NEW ISLAND

COMMONWEALTH MEDALLIC COINAGE

X# 1 ROGER
12.4700 g., Brass, 30.05 mm. **Issuer:** Lee Mothes **Obv:** Bird in flight left **Obv. Legend:** COMMONWEALTH OF NEW ISLAND **Rev:** Female dancing **Rev. Legend:** JOY **Rev. Inscription:** We Are One **Edge:** Reeded **Note:** Medal alignment. Redeemable at Oceans and Dreams Studio, Kaukauna, WI.

Date	Mintage	VG	F	VF	XF	Unc
2003	1,000	—	—	—	—	22.50

X# 1a ROGER
13.5000 g., 0.9990 Silver 0.4336 oz. ASW, 30.05 mm. **Issuer:** Lee Mothes **Obv:** Bird in flight left **Obv. Legend:** COMMONWEALTH OF NEW ISLAND **Rev:** Female dancing **Rev. Legend:** JOY **Rev. Inscription:** We Are One **Edge:** Reeded **Note:** Coin alignment.

Date	Mintage	VG	F	VF	XF	Unc
2003	100	—	—	—	—	55.00

NEW YORK

GARDINER'S ISLAND

PRIVATE ISLAND PATTERN TRIAL

X# PT1 NON-DENOMINATED
Silver Clad

Date	Mintage	F	VF	XF	Unc	BU
1965FM Proof	3,000	Value: 30.00				

X# PT2 NON-DENOMINATED
Franklinium

Date	Mintage	F	VF	XF	Unc	BU
1965FM Proof	3,000	Value: 25.00				

X# PT3 NON-DENOMINATED
Nicon Franklinium II

Date	Mintage	F	VF	XF	Unc	BU
1965FM Proof	3,000	Value: 25.00				

X# PT4 NON-DENOMINATED
54.1200 g., Platinum APW

Date	Mintage	F	VF	XF	Unc	BU
1965FM Proof	2	Value: 1,850				

PROOF SETS

X#	Date	Mintage	Identification	Issue Price	Mkt Val
XPS1	1965 (3)	3,000	X#PT1-X#PT3	19.95	80.00

NEW ZEALAND

BRITISH PARLIAMENTARY STATE

MEDALLIC COINAGE

Richard Lobel Series

Struck by John Pinches, London, England

X# 16 SOVEREIGN
0.3750 Gold, 21.98 mm. **Obv:** Head of Duchess, bust of Duke facing **Obv. Legend:** DUKE & DUCHESS OF WINDSOR **Rev:** Kiwi bird walking right **Edge:** Plain

Date	Mintage	F	VF	XF	Unc	BU
1936 Proof	—	Value: 150				

X# M16a SOVEREIGN
4.4200 g., Silver, 21.98 mm. **Obv:** Head of Duchess, bust of Duke facing **Obv. Legend:** DUKE & DUCHESS OF WINDSOR **Rev:** Kiwi bird walking right **Edge:** Plain

Date	Mintage	F	VF	XF	Unc	BU
1936 Proof	—	Value: 10.00				

MEDALLIC COINAGE - INA ISSUE

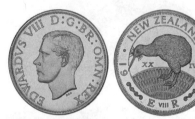

X# M15 24 PENCE
13.7000 g., Copper-Nickel, 29.3 mm. **Obv:** Head left **Obv. Legend:** EDWARDVS VIII D: G: BR: OMN: REX **Rev:** Kiwi standing left on ornamental sphere **Rev. Legend:** NEW ZEALAND **Edge:** Plain

Date	Mintage	F	VF	XF	Unc	BU
1937 Proof	—	—	—	—	—	—

STATE

1907 - present

MEDALLIC COINAGE

1954 Geoffrey Hearn Issues

X# M1 CROWN
Bronze Gilt **Subject:** Edward VIII **Note:** Restrikes unknown.

Date	Mintage	F	VF	XF	Unc	BU
1936 Proof	5	Value: 150				

X# M1a CROWN
28.1200 g., Silver **Subject:** Edward VIII

Date	Mintage	F	VF	XF	Unc	BU
1936 Proof	100	Value: 120				

X# M1b CROWN
28.1200 g., Silver **Subject:** Edward VIII

Date	Mintage	F	VF	XF	Unc	BU
1936 Restrike; Prooflike	—	—	—	—	45.00	—

X# M1c CROWN
Gold **Note:** Restrikes known.

Date	Mintage	F	VF	XF	Unc	BU
1936 Proof	5	Value: 850				

1972 Pobjoy Mint Issues

X# M2 CROWN
30.4600 g., Silver **Subject:** Edward VIII

Date	Mintage	F	VF	XF	Unc	BU
1936 Proof	—	Value: 95.00				

Richard Lobel Series

Struck by John Pinches, London, England

X# M3 CROWN
Bronze, 38.10 mm. **Subject:** Edward VIII **Obv:** Bust left **Obv. Legend:** EDWARD • VIII • KING • & • EMPEROR **Rev:** Kiwi bird walking right **Edge:** Plain

Date	Mintage	F	VF	XF	Unc	BU
1936 Proof	1,000	Value: 20.00				

X# M3a CROWN
Copper-Nickel-Zinc, 38.10 mm. **Subject:** Edward VIII **Obv:** Bust left **Obv. Legend:** EDWARD • VIII • KING • & • EMPEROR **Rev:** Kiwi bird walking right **Edge:** Plain

Date	Mintage	F	VF	XF	Unc	BU
1936 Proof	1,500	Value: 20.00				

X# M3b CROWN
0.9167 Silver, 38.10 mm. **Subject:** Edward VIII **Obv:** Bust left **Obv. Legend:** EDWARD • VIII • KING • & • EMPEROR **Rev:** Kiwi bird walking right **Edge:** Plain

Date	Mintage	F	VF	XF	Unc	BU
1936 Proof	250	Value: 50.00				

X# M3c CROWN
Gold, 38.10 mm. **Subject:** Edward VIII **Obv:** Bust left **Obv. Legend:** EDWARD • VIII • KING • & • EMPEROR **Rev:** Kiwi bird walking right **Edge:** Plain

Date	Mintage	F	VF	XF	Unc	BU
1936 Proof	—	Value: 500				

X# M4 SOVEREIGN
0.3750 Gold, 21.98 mm. **Subject:** Edward VIII **Obv:** Bust left **Obv. Legend:** EDWARD • VIII • KING • & • EMPEROR **Rev:** Kiwi bird walking right **Edge:** Plain

Date	Mintage	F	VF	XF	Unc	BU
1936 Proof	250	Value: 200				

X# M4a SOVEREIGN
4.4200 g., Silver, 21.98 mm. **Subject:** Edward VIII **Obv:** Bust left **Obv. Legend:** EDWARD • VIII • KING • & • EMPEROR **Rev:** Kiwi bird walking right **Edge:** Plain

Date	Mintage	F	VF	XF	Unc	BU
1936 Proof	—	Value: 10.00				

1984 Olympic Appeal Fund Issues

X# M5 5 DOLLARS
29.0000 g., 0.9250 Silver 0.8624 oz. ASW **Subject:** XXIII Olympiad Los Angeles **Obv:** Stylized runners

Date	Mintage	F	VF	XF	Unc	BU
1984 Proof	20,000	Value: 60.00				

X# M6 20 DOLLARS
29.5000 g., 0.9167 Gold 0.8694 oz. AGW **Subject:** XXIII Olympiad Los Angeles **Obv:** Stylized runners

Date	Mintage	F	VF	XF	Unc	BU
1984 Proof	500	Value: 475				

INA Retro Issues

X# M11 CROWN
0.9250 Silver **Obv:** Crowned bust left **Obv. Legend:** EDWARD VIII KING EMPEROR **Rev:** Crowned shield **Edge:** Plain

Date	Mintage	F	VF	XF	Unc	BU
1937 Proof	175	Value: 45.00				

X# M11a CROWN
Bronze **Obv:** Crowned bust left **Obv. Legend:** EDWARD VIII KING EMPEROR **Rev:** Crowned shield **Edge:** Plain

Date	Mintage	F	VF	XF	Unc	BU
1937 Proof	175	Value: 25.00				

X# M11b CROWN
Copper **Obv:** Crowned bust left **Obv. Legend:** EDWARD VIII KING EMPEROR **Rev:** Crowned shield **Edge:** Plain

Date	Mintage	F	VF	XF	Unc	BU
1937 Proof	175	Value: 25.00				

X# M11c.1 CROWN
39.9000 g., 0.9167 Gold 1.1759 oz. AGW **Obv:** Crowned bust left **Obv. Legend:** EDWARD VIII KING EMPEROR **Rev:** Crowned shield **Edge:** Reeded **Note:** Coin alignment.

Date	Mintage	F	VF	XF	Unc	BU
1937 Proof	1	—	—	—	—	—

X# M11c.2 CROWN
39.9000 g., 0.9167 Gold 1.1759 oz. AGW **Obv:** Crowned bust left **Obv. Legend:** EDWARD VIII KING EMPEROR **Rev:** Crowned shield **Edge:** Plain **Note:** Medal alignment.

Date	Mintage	F	VF	XF	Unc	BU
1937 Proof	1	—	—	—	—	—

X# M12 CROWN
39.6000 g., 0.9167 Gold 1.1671 oz. AGW **Obv:** Crowned bust left **Obv. Legend:** EDWARDVS VIII REX IMPERATOR **Rev:** Crowned shield **Edge:** Plain

Date	Mintage	F	VF	XF	Unc	BU
1937 Proof	1	—	—	—	—	—

X# M13 CROWN
0.9250 Silver **Obv:** Head left **Obv. Legend:** EDWARDVS VIII D: G: BR: OMN: REX **Rev:** Crowned shield **Edge:** Plain

Date	Mintage	F	VF	XF	Unc	BU
1937 Proof	475	Value: 45.00				

X# M13a CROWN
Bronze **Obv:** Head left **Obv. Legend:** EDWARDVS VIII D: G: BR: OMN: REX **Rev:** Crowned shield **Edge:** Plain

Date	Mintage	F	VF	XF	Unc	BU
1937 Proof	475	Value: 25.00				

X# M13b CROWN
Copper **Obv:** Head left **Obv. Legend:** EDWARDVS VIII D: G: BR: OMN: REX **Rev:** Crowned shield **Edge:** Plain

Date	Mintage	F	VF	XF	Unc	BU
1937 Proof	475	Value: 25.00				

X# M13c.1 CROWN
40.0000 g., 0.9167 Gold 1.1789 oz. AGW **Obv:** Head left **Obv. Legend:** EDWARDVS VIII D: G: BR: OMN: REX **Rev:** Crowned shield **Edge:** Reeded **Note:** Medal alignment.

Date	Mintage	F	VF	XF	Unc	BU
1937 Proof	1	—	—	—	—	—

X# M13c.2 CROWN
40.0000 g., 0.9167 Gold 1.1789 oz. AGW **Obv:** Head left **Obv. Legend:** EDWARDVS VIII D: G: BR: OMN: REX **Rev:** Crowned shield **Edge:** Plain **Note:** Medal alignment.

Date	Mintage	F	VF	XF	Unc	BU
1937 Proof	1	—	—	—	—	—

MEDALLIC GOLD BULLION COINAGE

Struck for Auckland Coin and Bullion Exchange, Ltd., Auckland, New Zealand

X# MB1 1/4 OUNCE
7.7757 g., 0.9999 Gold 0.2500 oz. AGW **Obv:** Kiwi **Rev:** Map

Date	Mintage	F	VF	XF	Unc	BU
1985	—	—	—	—	BV+ 30%	—

X# MB2 OUNCE
31.1030 g., 0.9999 Gold 0.9998 oz. AGW **Obv:** Kiwi **Rev:** Map

Date	Mintage	F	VF	XF	Unc	BU
1985	—	—	—	—	BV+ 12 %	—

PATTERNS

Including off metal strikes

X# Pn1 PENNY
Bronze **Note:** Prev. KM#Pn1.

Date	Mintage	F	VF	XF	Unc	BU
1879 Proof	—	Value: 2,250				

PIEFORTS

X#	Date	Mintage	Identification	Mkt Val
P1	1937	1	Crown. Silver. Plain edge, coin alignment, X#M11.	—
P2	1937	1	Crown. Silver. Plain edge, medal alignment, X#M11.	—
P3	1937	1	Crown. Silver. Reeded edge, coin alignment, X#M11.	—
P4	1937	1	Crown. Silver. Reeded edge, medal alignment, X#M11.	—
P5	1937	1	Crown. Silver. Plain edge, coin alignment, X#M12.	—
P6	1937	1	Crown. Silver. Plain edge, medal alignment, X#M12.	—
P7	1937	1	Crown. Silver. Reeded edge, coin alignment, X#M12.	—
P8	1937	1	Crown. Silver. Reeded edge, medal alignment, X#M12.	—
P9	1937	1	Crown. Silver. Plain edge, coin alignment, X#M13.	—
P10	1937	1	Crown. Silver. Plain edge, medal alignment, X#M13.	—
P11	1937	1	Crown. Silver. Reeded edge, coin alignment, X#M13.	—
P12	1937	1	Crown. Silver. Reeded edge, medal alignment, X#M13.	—
P13	1936	—	Crown. 0.9167 Silver. X#M3b.	100

NEWFOUNDLAND

PROVINCE

MEDALLIC COINAGE

Richard Lobel Series

X# M1 CROWN
Bronze, 38.10 mm. **Subject:** Edward VIII **Obv:** Bust left **Obv. Legend:** EDWARD • VIII • KING • & • EMPEROR **Rev:** Early sailing ship **Edge:** Plain

Date	Mintage	F	VF	XF	Unc	BU
1936 Proof	750	Value: 20.00				

X# M1a CROWN
Copper-Nickel-Zinc, 38.10 mm. **Subject:** Edward VIII **Obv:** Bust left **Obv. Legend:** EDWARD • VIII • KING • & • EMPEROR **Rev:** Early sailing ship **Edge:** Plain

Date	Mintage	F	VF	XF	Unc	BU
1936 Proof	1,550	Value: 20.00				

X# M1b CROWN
0.9167 Silver, 38.10 mm. **Subject:** Edward VIII **Obv:** Bust left **Obv. Legend:** EDWARD •VIII • KING • & • EMPEROR **Rev:** Early sailing ship **Edge:** Plain

Date	Mintage	F	VF	XF	Unc	BU
1936 Proof	200	Value: 60.00				

X# M1c CROWN
Gold, 38.10 mm. **Subject:** Edward VIII **Obv:** Bust left **Obv. Legend:** EDWARD • VIII • KING • & • EMPEROR **Rev:** Early sailing ship **Edge:** Plain

Date	Mintage	F	VF	XF	Unc	BU
1936 Proof	10	Value: 500				

X# M2 SOVEREIGN
0.3750 Gold, 21.98 mm. **Subject:** Edward VIII **Obv:** Bust left **Obv. Legend:** EDWARD • VIII • KING • & • EMPEROR **Rev:** Early sailing ship **Edge:** Plain

Date	Mintage	F	VF	XF	Unc	BU
1936 Proof	200	Value: 125				

X# M2a SOVEREIGN
4.4200 g., Silver, 21.98 mm. **Subject:** Edward VIII **Obv:** Bust left **Obv. Legend:** EDWARD • VIII • KING • & • EMPEROR **Rev:** Early sailing ship **Edge:** Plain

Date	Mintage	F	VF	XF	Unc	BU
1936 Proof	—	Value: 10.00				

PIEFORTS

X#	Date	Mintage	Identification	Mkt Val
P1	1936	—	Crown. 0.9167 Silver. X#M1b.	100

NICARAGUA

SPANISH COLONY

MEDALLIC COINAGE

KM# M1 REAL
Silver **Note:** This was a proclamation issue, struck at the Guatemala City mint for Ferdinand VII as the new King of Spain while he was under Napoleonic French Guard.

Date	Mintage	F	VF	XF	Unc	BU
1808	1,600	85.00	135	225	525	—

KM# M2 REAL
Silver **Note:** This was a proclamation issue, most likely struck at the Guatemala City mint for Augustin I Iturbide, Emperor during the brief period that Central America was part of the short-lived Mexican Empire.

Date	Mintage	F	VF	XF	Unc	BU
1822	—	125	250	450	750	—

NICHTSBURG-ZILCHSTADT

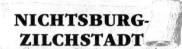

FANTASY

MILLED COINAGE

X# 1 MIDEN
Copper, 30 mm. **Obv:** Large 1, ornamentation below **Obv. Inscription:** NICHTSBURG ZILCHSTADT **Rev:** Stylized son **Rev. Legend:** EX NIHILO NIHIL FIT **Rev. Inscription:** ZERO - MACNAUGHT **Note:** Thickness: 3mm.

Date	Mintage	F	VF	XF	Unc	BU
MMIII (2003)	65	—	—	20.00	25.00	—

X# 1a MIDEN
0.9990 Silver, 30 mm. **Obv:** Large 1, ornamentation below **Obv. Inscription:** NICHTSBURG ZILCHSTADT **Rev:** Stylized son **Rev. Legend:** EX NIHILO NIHIL FIT **Rev. Inscription:** ZERO - MACNAUGHT **Edge:** Plain **Note:** Thickness: 3mm.

Date	Mintage	F	VF	XF	Unc	BU
MMIII (2003)	10	—	—	—	50.00	—

X# 2 11 MIDENIKA
Copper-Nickel, 38 mm. **Obv:** Stylized N = Z rotated **Obv. Legend:** Shûnya **Obv. Inscription:** ZILCHSTADT - NICHTSBURG - ZILCHSTADT - NICHTSBURG **Rev. Legend:** ayin me'yesh - yesh me'ayin **Rev. Inscription:** Kyo - mu **Edge:** Reeded **Note:** Thickness: 2.30mm.

Date	Mintage	F	VF	XF	Unc	BU
MMV (2005)	51	—	—	—	18.00	—

X# 2a 11 MIDENIKA
0.9990 Silver, 38 mm. **Obv:** Stylized N = Z rotated **Obv. Legend:** Shûnya **Obv. Inscription:** ZILCHSTADT - NICHTSBURG - ZILCHSTADT - NICHTSBURG **Rev. Legend:** ayin me'yesh - yesh me'ayin **Rev. Inscription:** Kyo - mu **Edge:** Plain **Note:** Thickness: 2.30mm.

Date	Mintage	F	VF	XF	Unc	BU
MMV (2005)	5	—	—	—	75.00	—

PATTERNS

Including off metal strikes

X#	Date	Mintage	Identification	Mkt Val
Pn1	MMV (2005)	1	11 Midenika. Bronze. X#2.	100
Pn2	MMV (2005)	1	11 Midenika. Brass. X#2.	100
Pn3	MMV (2005)	1	11 Midenika. Gilt Brass. X#2.	100

NIGERIAN SCAMS

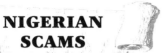

REPUBLIC

FANTASY COINAGE

X# 1 2 SKAMS
Brass, 24 mm. **Obv:** Arms **Obv. Legend:** REPUBLIC of NIGERIAN SCAMS **Rev:** Peanuts above value, stylized pyramid

Date	Mintage	F	VF	XF	Unc	BU
2992	—	—	—	—	—	—

NIGHTINGALE ISLAND

BRITISH ADMINISTRATION

COLLECTOR COINAGE

X# 1 CROWN
28.2800 g., Copper-Nickel, 39 mm. **Obv:** Elizabeth II **Rev:** Multicolor portrait of Queen Mother as a young girl **Edge:** Reeded

Date	Mintage	F	VF	XF	Unc	BU
2005	—	—	—	—	14.00	—

X# 2 CROWN
28.2800 g., Copper-Nickel, 39 mm. **Obv:** Elizabeth II **Rev:** Multicolor portrait of Queen Mother in blue dress **Edge:** Reeded

Date	Mintage	F	VF	XF	Unc	BU
2005	—	—	—	—	14.00	—

X# 3 CROWN
28.2800 g., Copper-Nickel, 39 mm. **Obv:** Elizabeth II **Rev:** Multicolor portrait of Queen Mother in green dress **Edge:** Reeded

Date	Mintage	F	VF	XF	Unc	BU
2005	—	—	—	—	14.00	—

X# 4 CROWN
28.2800 g., Copper-Nickel, 39 mm. **Obv:** Elizabeth II **Rev:** Multicolor portrait of Queen Mother in a light blue outfit **Edge:** Reeded

Date	Mintage	F	VF	XF	Unc	BU
2005	—	—	—	—	14.00	—

X# 5 CROWN
28.2800 g., Copper-Nickel, 39 mm. **Obv:** Elizabeth II **Rev:** Multicolor portrait of Queen Mother in pink outfit **Edge:** Reeded

Date	Mintage	F	VF	XF	Unc	BU
2005	—	—	—	—	14.00	—

NORD

REPUBLIC

TOKEN COINAGE

Northern League Political Party (Italy)

X# 1 LEGA
12.3500 g., Copper, 35 mm. **Obv:** Albert da Guissan standing with shield and sword **Obv. Legend:** • REPUBBLICA DEL NORD • AI POPOLI **Rev:** Two bent bars

Date	Mintage	F	VF	XF	Unc	BU
1992 Large date	—	—	—	—	—	10.00
1992 Small date	—	—	—	—	—	8.00

X# 2 2 LEGHE
Nickel-Steel, 35 mm. **Obv:** Albert da Guissan standing with shield and sword **Rev:** Two bent bars

Date	Mintage	F	VF	XF	Unc	BU
1992	—	—	—	—	—	10.00

X# 3 5 LEGHE
12.2000 g., Brass, 35 mm. **Obv:** Albert da Guissan standing with shield and sword **Rev:** Two bent bars

Date	Mintage	F	VF	XF	Unc	BU
1992 Large date	—	—	—	—	—	12.00
1992 Small date	—	—	—	—	—	10.00

X# 4 10 LEGHE
Nickel-Steel, 35 mm. **Obv:** Albert da Guissan standing with shield and sword **Rev:** Two bent bars

Date	Mintage	F	VF	XF	Unc	BU
1992	—	—	—	—	—	15.00

X# 5 50 LIGHE
26.5000 g., 0.9250 Silver 0.7881 oz. ASW, 40 mm. **Obv:** Radiant Albert da Guissan standing with shield and sword **Obv. Legend:** * REPUBLICA DÉL NORD * NATHION VENETA **Rev:** Lion of St. Mark with sword

Date	Mintage	F	VF	XF	Unc	BU
1992	—	—	—	—	—	50.00

NORTH MEXICO

REPUBLIC

NON-CIRCULATING COINAGE

X# NC22 2 CENTS
Bronze **Ruler:** (no Ruler name) **Obv:** Flag **Rev. Legend:** In God We Trust

Date	Mintage	F	VF	XF	Unc	BU
1890	—	—	75.00	150	225	—

NORTHERN MARIANA ISLANDS

COMMONWEALTH

US Administration

MEDALLIC COINAGE

X# 1 5 DOLLARS
25.0000 g., 0.9250 Silver 0.7435 oz. ASW, 38.6 mm. **Subject:** Discovered by Ferdinand Magellan **Obv:** Emblem above eagle **Rev:** Spanish galleon **Edge:** Reeded

Date	Mintage	F	VF	XF	Unc	BU
2004 Proof	7,500	Value: 32.50				

X# 2 5 DOLLARS
1.2440 g., 0.9999 Gold 0.0400 oz. AGW, 13.92 mm. **Subject:** Discovered by Ferdinand Magellen **Obv:** Emblem above eagle **Rev:** Spanish galleon **Edge:** Reeded

Date	Mintage	F	VF	XF	Unc	BU
2004 Proof	25,000	Value: 45.00				

X# 3 5 DOLLARS
25.0000 g., 0.9250 Silver 0.7435 oz. ASW, 38.6 mm. **Obv:** Emblem above eagle **Rev:** Bust of Pope John Paul II facing **Edge:** Reeded

Date	Mintage	F	VF	XF	Unc	BU
2004 Proof	5,000	Value: 35.00				

X# 4 5 DOLLARS
1.2440 g., 0.9999 Gold 0.0400 oz. AGW, 13.92 mm. **Obv:** Emblem above eagle **Rev:** Bust of Pope John Paul II facing **Edge:** Reeded

Date	Mintage	F	VF	XF	Unc	BU
2004 Proof	15,000	Value: 50.00				

X# 5 5 DOLLARS
25.0000 g., 0.9250 Silver 0.7435 oz. ASW, 38.6 mm. **Obv:** Emblem above eagle **Rev:** Holographic picture of Albert Einstein with and without tongue sticking out **Edge:** Reeded

Date	Mintage	F	VF	XF	Unc	BU
ND(2004) Proof	25,000	Value: 60.00				

X# 6 5 DOLLARS
1.2440 g., 0.9999 Gold 0.0400 oz. AGW, 13.92 mm. **Obv:** Emblem above eagle **Rev:** Einstein sticking his tongue out **Edge:** Reeded

Date	Mintage	F	VF	XF	Unc	BU
2004 Proof	25,000	Value: 50.00				

X# 7 5 DOLLARS
25.0000 g., 0.9250 Silver 0.7435 oz. ASW, 37 mm. **Issuer:** CITV **Obv:** Arms **Rev:** Two angels resting on colored rose bud with three colored roses at right **Rev. Legend:** "Endless Love" **Shape:** Heart

Date	Mintage	F	VF	XF	Unc	BU
2005 Proof	1,888	Value: 60.00				

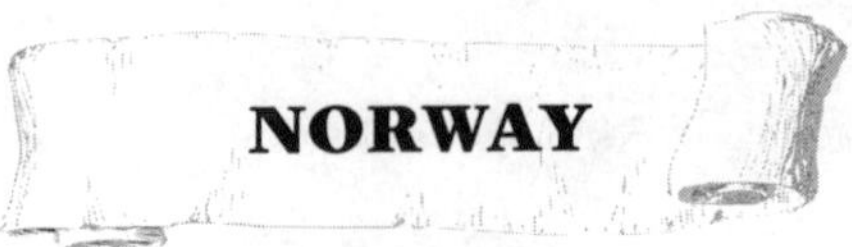

NORWAY

KINGDOM

DECIMAL COINAGE

KM# 479 20 KRONER
9.7300 g., Copper-Zinc-Nickel, 27.4 mm. **Ruler:** Harald V **Obv:** Harold V **Edge:** Plain

Date	Mintage	F	VF	XF	Unc	BU
2006	10,000	—	—	—	—	12.50

LARGESSE COINAGE

X# M1 4 MARK
11.0000 g., 0.8780 Silver 0.3105 oz. ASW **Subject:** Coronation of Charles XIV John **Obv:** Crowned bust right **Obv. Legend:** CARL XIV JOHAN SV OG NORG K.KRON **Rev. Inscription:** FOLKETS / KJAERLIGHED / MIN / BELONNING **Note:** Prev. KM#M1. For similar issues refer to Sweden listings.

Date	Mintage	F	VF	XF	Unc	BU
1818	—	—	60.00	125	200	—

KM# A107.1 1/4 SPECIE DALER
7.2200 g., 0.8750 Silver 0.2031 oz. ASW **Subject:** Royal Visti to Norway **Obv. Legend:** CVRDNVG IN MEMORIAM

Date	Mintage	VG	F	VF	XF	Unc
1685 Rare	—	—	—	—	—	—

KM# A107.2 1/4 SPECIE DALER
7.2200 g., 0.8750 Silver 0.2031 oz. ASW **Obv. Legend:** CVRDNVG TERPAMARI

Date	Mintage	VG	F	VF	XF	Unc
1685 Rare	—	—	—	—	—	—

ECU COINAGE

X# 11 5 ECU
Copper-Nickel, 38.6 mm. **Ruler:** Harald V **Issuer:** CITV, Vaduz **Subject:** 100th Anniversary Polar Exploration by F. Nansen **Obv:** Ship **Obv. Legend:** la POLAR EXPEDITION 1893/1993 **Rev:** Dogsled - bust of F. Nansen facing **Rev. Legend:** FRIDTJOF NANSEN 100 ANNIVERSARY **Edge:** Reeded

Date	Mintage	F	VF	XF	Unc	BU
ND(1993)	5,000	—	—	—	—	12.50

X# 14 5 ECU
26.5000 g., Copper-Nickel, 38.6 mm. **Ruler:** Harald V **Obv:** Bergem arms **Obv. Legend:** 925 YEARS BERGEN BRYGGE **Rev:** Large value **Edge:** Reeded

Date	Mintage	F	VF	XF	Unc	BU
1994	—	—	—	—	—	12.50

X# 12 20 ECU
25.0000 g., 0.9250 Silver 0.7435 oz. ASW, 38.6 mm. **Ruler:** Harald V **Issuer:** CITV, Vaduz **Subject:** 100th Anniversary Polar Exploration by F. Nansen **Obv:** Ship **Obv. Legend:** la POLAR EXPEDITION 1893/1993 **Rev:** Dogsled - bust of F. Nansen facing **Rev. Legend:** FRIDTJOF NANSEN 100 ANNIVERSARY **Edge:** Reeded

Date	Mintage	F	VF	XF	Unc	BU
ND(1993) Proof	3,500	Value: 42.50				

X# 15 20 ECU
25.0000 g., 0.9250 Silver 0.7435 oz. ASW, 38.6 mm. **Ruler:** Harald V **Obv:** Bergen arms **Obv. Legend:** 925 YEARS BERGEN BRYGGE **Rev:** Large value **Edge:** Reeded

Date	Mintage	F	VF	XF	Unc	BU
1994 Proof	—	Value: 40.00				

X# 31 25 ECU
Brass **Ruler:** Harald V **Issuer:** ICF **Obv:** Norwegian arms on map of Europe, 12 stars in circle **Obv. Legend:** NORGE OG EUROPA **Rev:** Cat standing left, facing **Rev. Legend:** KONGERIKET NORGE

Date	Mintage	F	VF	XF	Unc	BU
1996	—	—	—	—	15.00	—

X# 13 150 ECU
6.7200 g., 0.7500 Gold 0.1620 oz. AGW, 23 mm. **Ruler:** Harald V **Issuer:** CITV, Vaduz **Subject:** 100th Anniversary Polar Exploration by F. Nansen **Obv:** Ship **Obv. Legend:** la POLAR EXPEDITION 1893/1993 **Rev:** Dogsled - bust of F. Nansen facing **Rev. Legend:** FRIDTJOF NANSEN 100 ANNIVERSARY **Edge:** Reeded

Date	Mintage	F	VF	XF	Unc	BU
ND(1993) Proof	500	Value: 250				

X# 16 150 ECU
6.7200 g., 0.7500 Gold 0.1620 oz. AGW, 23 mm. **Ruler:** Harald V **Obv:** Bergen arms **Obv. Legend:** 925 YEARS BERGEN BRYGGE **Rev:** Large value **Edge:** Reeded

Date	Mintage	F	VF	XF	Unc	BU
1994 Proof	—	Value: 250				

ICF Issues

X# 17 ECU
19.2000 g., Bi-Metallic Brass/Copper, 38 mm. **Ruler:** Harald V **Subject:** XVII Winter Olympics in Lillehammer **Obv:** Norwegian arms on map of Europe, 12 stars in circle **Obv. Legend:** NORGE OG EUROPA **Rev:** Skier, hockey player **Rev. Legend:** LILLEHAMMER VINTER LEKER **Edge:** Plain

Date	Mintage	F	VF	XF	Unc	BU
1994 Proof	2,000	Value: 12.50				

X# 17a ECU
22.0000 g., 0.9250 Silver 0.6542 oz. ASW, 38 mm. **Ruler:** Harald V **Subject:** XVII Winter Olympics in Lillehammer **Obv:** Norwegian arms on map of Europe, 12 stars in circle **Obv. Legend:** NORGE OG EUROPA **Rev:** Skier, hockey player **Rev. Legend:** LILLEHAMMER VINTER LEKER **Edge:** Plain

Date	Mintage	F	VF	XF	Unc	BU
1994 Proof	2,000	Value: 40.00				

X# 18 10 ECU
19.2000 g., Bi-Metallic Brass Brass, gilt/Copper, 38 mm. **Ruler:** Harald V **Subject:** XVII Winter Olympics in Lillehammer **Obv:** Norwegian arms on map of Europe, 12 stars in circle **Obv. Legend:** NORGE OG EUROPA **Rev:** Skier, hockey player **Rev. Legend:** LILLEHAMMER VINTER LEKER **Edge:** Plain

Date	Mintage	F	VF	XF	Unc	BU
1994 Proof	12,500	Value: 15.00				

X# 19 25 ECU
22.0000 g., 0.9250 Silver 0.6542 oz. ASW, 38 mm. **Ruler:** Harald V **Subject:** XVII Winter Olympics in Lillehammer **Obv:** Norwegian arms on map of Europe, 12 stars in circle **Obv. Legend:** NORGE OG EUROPA **Rev:** Skier, hockey player **Rev. Legend:** LILLEHAMMER VINTER LEKER **Edge:** Plain

Date	Mintage	F	VF	XF	Unc	BU
1994 Proof	12,500	Value: 40.00				

X# 20 200 ECU
6.0000 g., 0.7500 Gold 0.1447 oz. AGW, 22.05 mm. **Ruler:** Harald V **Subject:** XVII Winter Olympics in Lillehammer **Obv:** Norwegian arms on map of Europe, 12 stars in circle **Obv. Legend:** NORGE OG EUROPA **Rev:** Skier, hockey player **Rev. Legend:** LILLEHAMMER VINTER LEKER **Edge:** Plain

Date	Mintage	F	VF	XF	Unc	BU
1994 Proof	1,500	Value: 240				

FANTASY EURO PATTERNS

X# Pn1 EURO CENT
Copper Plated Steel, 16.8 mm. **Ruler:** Harald V **Edge:** Plain

Date	Mintage	F	VF	XF	Unc	BU
2004	15,000	—	—	—	—	1.50
2004 Proof	5,000	Value: 2.50				

X# Pn1a EURO CENT
Silver, 16.8 mm. **Ruler:** Harald V **Edge:** Plain

Date	Mintage	F	VF	XF	Unc	BU
2004 Proof	500	Value: 6.00				

X# Pn2 2 EURO CENT
Copper Plated Steel, 18.5 mm. **Ruler:** Harald V **Edge:** Plain

Date	Mintage	F	VF	XF	Unc	BU
2004	15,000	—	—	—	—	2.00
2004 Proof	5,000	Value: 3.00				

X# Pn2a 2 EURO CENT
Silver, 18.5 mm. **Ruler:** Harald V **Edge:** Plain

Date	Mintage	F	VF	XF	Unc	BU
2004 Proof	500	Value: 7.00				

X# Pn3 5 EURO CENT
Copper Plated Steel, 20.7 mm. **Ruler:** Harald V **Edge:** Plain

Date	Mintage	F	VF	XF	Unc	BU
2004	15,000	—	—	—	—	2.50
2004 Proof	5,000	Value: 3.50				

X# Pn3a 5 EURO CENT
Silver, 20.70 mm. **Ruler:** Harald V **Edge:** Plain

Date	Mintage	F	VF	XF	Unc	BU
2004 Proof	500	Value: 8.50				

X# Pn4 10 EURO CENT
Goldine **Ruler:** Harald V **Edge:** Plain

Date	Mintage	F	VF	XF	Unc	BU
2004	15,000	—	—	—	—	3.00
2004 Proof	5,000	Value: 4.00				

X# Pn4a 10 EURO CENT
Silver **Ruler:** Harald V **Edge:** Plain

Date	Mintage	F	VF	XF	Unc	BU
2004 Proof	500	Value: 10.00				

X# Pn5 20 EURO CENT
Goldine, 22 mm. **Ruler:** Harald V **Edge:** Plain

Date	Mintage	F	VF	XF	Unc	BU
2004	15,000	—	—	—	—	3.50
2004 Proof	5,000	Value: 5.00				

X# Pn5a 20 EURO CENT
Silver, 22 mm. **Ruler:** Harald V **Edge:** Plain

Date	Mintage	F	VF	XF	Unc	BU
2004 Proof	500	Value: 12.50				

X# Pn6 50 EURO CENT
Goldine, 24.3 mm. **Ruler:** Harald V **Edge:** Plain

Date	Mintage	F	VF	XF	Unc	BU
2004	15,000	—	—	—	—	4.00
2004 Proof	5,000	Value: 6.00				

X# Pn6a 50 EURO CENT
Silver, 24.3 mm. **Ruler:** Harald V **Edge:** Plain

Date	Mintage	F	VF	XF	Unc	BU
2004 Proof	500	Value: 15.00				

X# Pn10 25 EURO
Brass, 38 mm. **Obv:** Norwegian arms on map of Europe, 12 stars in circle **Obv. Legend:** NORGE OG EUROPE **Rev:** Cat divides date, denomination below **Rev. Legend:** KONGERIKET NORGE

Date	Mintage	F	VF	XF	Unc	BU
1996	—	—	—	—	—	5.00

X# Pn7 EUROP
Bi-Metallic, 23.50 mm. **Ruler:** Harald V **Obv:** Building, moose around rim **Rev:** Large value "1", moose around rim **Edge:** Plain

Date	Mintage	F	VF	XF	Unc	BU
2004	15,000	—	—	—	—	6.00
2004 Proof	5,000	Value: 8.00				

X# Pn7a EUROP
Bi-Metallic Goldine center in Silver ring, 23.5 mm. **Ruler:** Harald V **Obv:** Building, moose around rim **Rev:** Large value "1", moose around rim **Edge:** Plain

Date	Mintage	F	VF	XF	Unc	BU
2004 Proof	500	Value: 22.50				

X# Pn8 2 EUROP
Bi-Metallic, 26.50 mm. **Ruler:** Harald V **Obv:** Equestrian figure, right moose around rim **Rev:** Large value "2", moose around rim **Edge:** Plain

Date	Mintage	F	VF	XF	Unc	BU
2004	15,000	—	—	—	—	8.00
2004 Proof	—	Value: 10.00				

X# Pn8a 2 EUROP
Bi-Metallic Goldine center in Silver ring, 26.5 mm. **Ruler:** Harald V **Obv:** Equestrian figure right, moose around rim **Rev:** Large value "2", moose around rim **Edge:** Plain

Date	Mintage	F	VF	XF	Unc	BU
2004 Proof	500	Value: 28.50				

X# Pn9 5 EUROP
Tri-Metallic Goldine, Copper-Nickel **Obv:** Archaic sail boat, moose around rim **Rev:** Large value "5", moose around rim **Edge:** Plain

Date	Mintage	F	VF	XF	Unc	BU
2004 Proof	5,000	Value: 12.50				

X# Pn9a 5 EUROP
Silver **Ruler:** Harald V **Obv:** Archaic sail boat, moose around rim **Rev:** Large value "5", moose around rim **Edge:** Plain

Date	Mintage	F	VF	XF	Unc	BU
2004 Proof	500	Value: 40.00				

TRIAL STRIKES

X# TS1 1/3 RIKSDALER
0.9030 Silver **Note:** Counterstamped on Mexico City Mint 8 Reales, KM#106.2.

Date	Mintage	Good	VG	F	VF	XF
1777	—	—	—	—	275	450

PIEFORTS

X#	Date	Mintage	Identification	Mkt Val
P1	1994	5,000	25 Ecu. 0.9250 Silver. 44.0000 g. X19.	75.00

MINT SETS

X#	Date	Mintage	Identification	Issue Price	Mkt Val
XMS1	2004 (8)	15,000	X#Pn1-Pn8	—	30.00

PROOF SETS

X#	Date	Mintage	Identification	Issue Price	Mkt Val
XPS1	2004 (9)	5,000	X#Pn1-Pn9	—	50.00
XPS2	2004 (9)	500	X#Pn1a-Pn9a	—	150

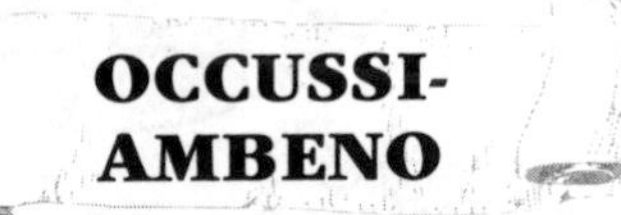

OCCUSSI-AMBENO

SULTANATE

MEDALLIC COINAGE

X# 3 DOLLAR
31.3000 g., 0.9990 Silver 1.0053 oz. ASW, 38.6 mm. **Issuer:** State Bank **Subject:** First directly elected President of Taiwan **Obv:** Crown **Rev:** Bust of President Lee Teng-hui facing **Edge:** Reeded

Date	Mintage	F	VF	XF	Unc	BU
1996 Proof	10,600	Value: 62.50				

X# 4 DOLLAR
31.3000 g., 0.9990 Silver 1.0053 oz. ASW, 38.6 mm. **Issuer:** State Bank **Subject:** First directly elected Vice-president of Taiwan **Obv:** Crown **Rev:** Bust of Vice-president facing **Edge:** Reeded

Date	Mintage	F	VF	XF	Unc	BU
1996 Proof	10,600	Value: 62.50				

X# 5 DOLLAR
31.3000 g., 0.9990 Silver 1.0053 oz. ASW, 38.6 mm. **Issuer:** State Bank **Subject:** Year of the Ox **Obv:** Crown **Rev:** Ox standing left **Edge:** Reeded

Date	Mintage	F	VF	XF	Unc	BU
1997 Proof	4,000	Value: 62.50				

X# 6 DOLLAR
31.3000 g., 0.9990 Silver 1.0053 oz. ASW, 38.6 mm. **Issuer:** State Bank **Subject:** Year of the Ox **Rev:** Two oxen walking left **Edge:** Reeded

Date	Mintage	F	VF	XF	Unc	BU
1997 Proof	4,000	Value: 62.50				

X# 7 15 DOLLARS
3.1300 g., 0.9999 Gold 0.1006 oz. AGW, 18 mm. **Issuer:** State Bank **Subject:** First directly elected President and Vice-president of Taiwan **Obv:** Crown **Rev:** Bust of President and Vice-president facing **Edge:** Reeded

Date	Mintage	F	VF	XF	Unc	BU
1996 Proof	5,100	Value: 295				

X# 8 15 DOLLARS
500.0000 g., 0.9990 Silver 16.058 oz. ASW, 100 mm. **Issuer:** State Bank **Subject:** Year of the Ox **Obv:** Crown **Rev:** Ox drinking water **Edge:** Reeded

Date	Mintage	F	VF	XF	Unc	BU
1997 Proof	500	Value: 185				

X# 9 15 DOLLARS
3.1300 g., 0.9999 Gold 0.1006 oz. AGW, 18 mm. **Issuer:** State Bank **Subject:** Year of the Ox **Obv:** Crown **Rev:** Ox drinking water **Edge:** Reeded

Date	Mintage	F	VF	XF	Unc	BU
1997 Proof	3,000	Value: 295				

X# 10 25 DOLLARS
7.7400 g., 0.9999 Gold 0.2488 oz. AGW, 22.9 mm. **Issuer:** State Bank **Subject:** First directly elected President and Vice-president of Taiwan **Obv:** Crown **Rev:** Busts of President and Vice-president facing **Edge:** Reeded

Date	Mintage	F	VF	XF	Unc	BU
1996 Proof	3,100	Value: 325				

X# 11 50 DOLLARS
15.5100 g., 0.9999 Gold 0.4986 oz. AGW, 30 mm. **Issuer:** State Bank **Subject:** First directly elected President and Vice-president of Taiwan **Obv:** Crown **Rev:** Busts of President and Vice-president facing **Edge:** Reeded

Date	Mintage	F	VF	XF	Unc	BU
1996 Proof	5,100	Value: 525				

X# 12 50 DOLLARS
15.5100 g., 0.9999 Gold 0.4986 oz. AGW, 30 mm. **Issuer:** State Bank **Subject:** Year of the Ox **Obv:** Crown **Rev:** Water buffalo cow lying with calf **Edge:** Reeded

Date	Mintage	F	VF	XF	Unc	BU
1997 Proof	3,000	Value: 525				

X# 1 100 DOLLARS
31.5000 g., 0.9250 Silver 0.9368 oz. ASW, 39.8 mm. **Issuer:** State Bank **Mint:** Valcambi **Obv:** Crown **Rev:** Nude painting by Velázquez **Edge:** Reeded

Date	Mintage	F	VF	XF	Unc	BU
1990 Proof	2,000	Value: 75.00				

X# 2 100 DOLLARS
31.5000 g., 0.9250 Silver 0.9368 oz. ASW, 39.8 mm. **Issuer:** State Bank **Mint:** Valcambi **Obv:** Crown **Rev:** Nude painting by Goya **Edge:** Reeded

Date	Mintage	F	VF	XF	Unc	BU
1990 Proof	2,000	Value: 75.00				

OMAN

SULTANATE

MEDALLIC COINAGE

A series of 3 silver and 4 gold medallic coins were produced in AH1391/1971AD and are inscribed STATE OF OMAN (Dawlat Uman). These were issued by the exile government of Imam Ghalib Ibn Ali in Dammam, Saudi Arabia, and distributed from a post box in Amman, Jordan. The Imamate had enjoyed effective autonomy in the interior of Oman from 1920-54, at which time the Sultan resumed direct control. Imamist forces in Oman were finally driven out in 1959. The Imam has been in exile since 1955.

X# M1 5 RYALS
4.0000 g., 0.9250 Silver 0.1190 oz. ASW **Obv:** Star and crescent above crossed flags and 2 swords **Rev:** Flower between English and Arabic denominations **Note:** Prev. KM#M1.

Date	Mintage	F	VF	XF	Unc	BU
AH1391	4,000	—	—	—	30.00	—

X# M2 10 RYALS
8.0000 g., 0.9250 Silver 0.2379 oz. ASW **Obv:** Star and crescent above crossed flags and 2 swords **Rev:** Secretary bird with snake in claws **Note:** Prev. KM#M2.

Date	Mintage	F	VF	XF	Unc	BU
AH1391	4,000	—	—	—	40.00	—

X# M3 20 RYALS
16.0000 g., 0.9250 Silver 0.4758 oz. ASW **Obv:** Star and crescent above crossed flags and 2 swords **Rev:** Mosque **Note:** Prev. KM#M3.

Date	Mintage	F	VF	XF	Unc	BU
AH1391	4,000	—	—	—	60.00	—

X# M4 50 RYALS
4.0000 g., 0.9170 Gold 0.1179 oz. AGW **Obv:** Star and crescent above crossed flags and 2 swords **Rev:** Sailboat and rocky coast **Note:** Prev. KM#M4.

Date	Mintage	F	VF	XF	Unc	BU
AH1391	4,000	—	—	—	185	—

X# M5 100 RYALS
8.0000 g., 0.9170 Gold 0.2358 oz. AGW **Obv:** Star and crescent above crossed flags and 2 swords **Rev:** Flower **Note:** Prev. KM#M5.

Date	Mintage	F	VF	XF	Unc	BU
AH1391	4,000	—	—	—	250	—

X# M6 200 RYALS
16.0000 g., 0.9170 Gold 0.4717 oz. AGW **Obv:** Star and crescent above crossed flags and 2 swords **Rev:** Secretary bird **Note:** Prev. KM#M6.

Date	Mintage	F	VF	XF	Unc	BU
AH1391	4,000	—	—	—	400	—

X# M7 500 RYALS
40.0000 g., 0.9170 Gold 1.1792 oz. AGW **Obv:** Star and crescent above crossed flags and 2 swords **Rev:** Mosque **Note:** Prev. KM#M7.

Date	Mintage	F	VF	XF	Unc	BU
AH1391	4,000	—	—	—	900	—

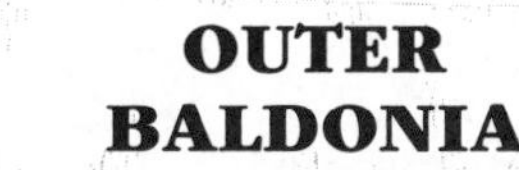

OUTER BALDONIA

PRINCIPALITY

FANTASY COINAGE

X# 1 10 TUNAR
0.8260 Gold **Subject:** Arundel

Date	Mintage	F	VF	XF	Unc	BU
1948	50	—	—	550	700	—

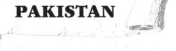

PAKISTAN

ISLAMIC REPUBLIC

BULLION COINAGE

Mohammed Farooq & Sons - Karachi

X# 5 TOLA
0.9985 Gold **Subject:** Springbok

Date	Mintage	F	VF	XF	Unc	BU
ND	—	—	BV	275	350	—

PALESTINE

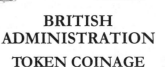

BRITISH ADMINISTRATION

TOKEN COINAGE

X# Tn4 MIL
Brass **Obv:** Date 5699 on either side of shield, legend around **Obv. Legend:** 1/2 MILL...KOFER HAYISHUV...BAR TAV **Rev:** INcuse impress of the obverse with the shiled in a higher relief **Note:** Uniface.

Called the "Hagana Defence Token." Struck in the Plitz factory in Holon.

Date	Mintage	F	VF	XF	Unc	BU
JE5699 (1938-39)	—	—	4.50	7.50	12.50	—

Note: The British Government did not object to the issue of these tokens which circulated until the 1950s as coins.

X# Tn1 SOUVENIR MIL

6.8000 g., Bronze **Note:** Thin planchet, 'Y' in Holyland not fully engraved. Same beading on both sides. On top two berries, the right is higher. Hebrew Mill does not touch circle.

Date	Mintage	F	VF	XF	Unc	BU
1927	—	—	100	175	300	—

Note: This souvenir which incorporates an appropriate reproduction of a 1927 1 Mil coin of Palestine was privately created for sale to pilgrims as a souvenir of their visit to the Holy Land; The Arabic translates to Souvenir of the Holy Land. It is not known who produced them nor how many were produced

X# Tn2 SOUVENIR MIL

8.7100 g., Bronze **Note:** Thick planchet. 'C' in Historical is re-engraved. Obverse beading is longer. Of top two berries, left one is higher. Hebrew "Mil" extends past circle.

Date	Mintage	F	VF	XF	Unc	BU
1927	—	—	100	175	300	—

X# Tn3 SOUVENIR MIL

6.8000 g., Bronze **Note:** Similar to X#Tn2 but struck on a thin planchet.

Date	Mintage	F	VF	XF	Unc	BU
1927	—	—	200	350	700	—

MEDALLIC COINAGE

Richard Lobel Series

X# M1 CROWN

Bronze, 38.10 mm. **Subject:** Edward VIII **Obv:** Bust left **Obv. Legend:** EDWARD • VIII • KING • & • EMPEROR **Rev:** Six coins from Palestine **Edge:** Plain

Date	Mintage	F	VF	XF	Unc	BU
1936 Proof	750	Value: 20.00				

X# M1a CROWN

Copper-Nickel-Zinc, 38.10 mm. **Subject:** Edward VIII **Obv:** Bust left **Obv. Legend:** EDWARD • VIII • KING • & • EMPEROR **Rev:** Six coins from Palestine **Edge:** Plain

Date	Mintage	F	VF	XF	Unc	BU
1936 Proof	2,500	Value: 20.00				

X# M1b CROWN

0.9167 Silver, 38.10 mm. **Subject:** Edward VIII **Obv:** Bust left **Obv. Legend:** EDWARD • VIII • KING • & • EMPEROR **Rev:** Six coins from Palestine **Edge:** Plain

Date	Mintage	F	VF	XF	Unc	BU
1936 Proof	250	Value: 75.00				

X# M1c CROWN

Gold, 38.10 mm. **Subject:** Edward VIII **Obv:** Bust left **Obv. Legend:** EDWARD • VIII • KING • & • EMPEROR **Rev:** Six coins from Palestine **Edge:** Plain

Date	Mintage	F	VF	XF	Unc	BU
1936 Proof	—	Value: 800				

X# M2 SOVEREIGN

0.3750 Gold, 21.98 mm. **Subject:** Edward VIII **Obv:** Bust left **Obv. Legend:** EDWARD • VIII • KING • & • EMPEROR **Rev:** Six coins from Palestine **Edge:** Plain

Date	Mintage	F	VF	XF	Unc	BU
1936 Proof	250	Value: 175				

X# M2a SOVEREIGN

4.4200 g., Silver, 21.98 mm. **Subject:** Edward VIII **Obv:** Bust left **Obv. Legend:** EDWARD • VIII • KING • & • EMPEROR **Rev:** Six coins of Palestine **Edge:** Plain

Date	Mintage	F	VF	XF	Unc	BU
1936 Proof	—	Value: 10.00				

X# M3 SOVEREIGN

0.3750 Gold, 21.98 mm. **Obv:** Head of Duchess, bust of Duke facing **Obv. Legend:** DUKE & DUCHESS OF WINDSOR **Rev:** Kiwi bird walking right **Edge:** Plain

Date	Mintage	F	VF	XF	Unc	BU
1936 Proof	—	Value: 150				

X# M3a SOVEREIGN

4.4200 g., Silver, 21.98 mm. **Obv:** Head of Duchess, bust of Duke facing **Obv. Legend:** DUKE & DUCHESS OF WINDSOR **Rev:** Kiwi bird walking right **Edge:** Plain

Date	Mintage	F	VF	XF	Unc	BU
1936 Proof	—	Value: 10.00				

PIEFORTS

X#	Date	Mintage	Identification	Mkt Val
P1	1936	—	Crown. 0.9167 Silver. X#M1b.	150

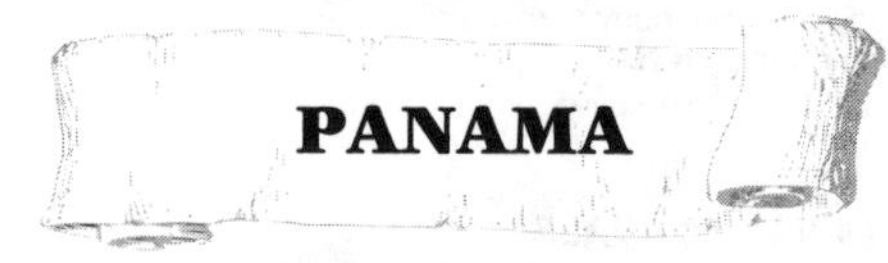

REPUBLIC

MILLED COINAGE

X# 11 2-1/2 CENTESIMOS

Brass, 21.25 mm. **Obv:** Arms **Rev:** Value

Date	Mintage	F	VF	XF	Unc	BU
ND(c.1920)	—	0.60	5.00	10.00	25.00	100

SILVER CURRENCY COINAGE

Liberty Dollar Org.

X# 21 20 LIBERTY DOLLARS

31.1900 g., 0.9990 Silver 1.0017 oz. ASW, 39 mm. **Obv:** Banner at center **Obv. Legend:** PANAMA **Obv. Inscription:** MI PAIS - "Liberty Dollar" **Rev:** Liberty head left **Rev. Legend:** LIBERTAD* **Rev. Inscription:** CONFIE EN DIOS **Edge:** Reeded

Date	Mintage	F	VF	XF	Unc	BU
2007 Proof	—	Value: 22.50				

MEDALLIC COINAGE

The following have been declared illegal and unauthorized by the Finance Minister of the current Government of Panama. The issues were marketed in Germany, but mintage limits were not fulfilled

X# M1 BALBOA

Copper-Nickel, 32 mm. **Subject:** Calgary Olympics **Obv:** Arms **Rev:** Ski jumper

Date	Mintage	F	VF	XF	Unc	BU
1988 Proof	Est. 50,000	Value: 25.00				

X# M1a BALBOA

15.0000 g., 1.0000 Silver 0.4822 oz. ASW, 32 mm. **Subject:** Calgary Olympics **Obv:** Arms **Rev:** Ski jumper

Date	Mintage	F	VF	XF	Unc	BU
1988 Proof	Est. 20,000	Value: 45.00				

X# M2 BALBOA

Copper-Nickel, 32 mm. **Subject:** Calgary Olympics **Obv:** Arms **Rev:** Free-Style skier

Date	Mintage	F	VF	XF	Unc	BU
1988 Proof	Est. 50,000	Value: 25.00				

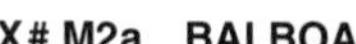

X# M2a BALBOA

15.0000 g., 1.0000 Silver 0.4822 oz. ASW, 32 mm.
Subject: Calgary Olympics **Obv:** Arms **Rev:** Free-style skater

Date	Mintage	F	VF	XF	Unc	BU
1988 Proof	Est. 20,000	Value: 45.00				

X# M3 BALBOA

Copper-Nickel, 32 mm. **Subject:** Calgary Olympics
Obv: Arms **Rev:** Biathlon skier shooting

Date	Mintage	F	VF	XF	Unc	BU
1988 Proof	Est. 50,000	Value: 25.00				

X# M3a BALBOA

15.0000 g., 1.0000 Silver 0.4822 oz. ASW, 32 mm.
Subject: Calgary Olympics - Biathlon Skier **Obv:** Arms **Rev:** Biathlon skier shooting

Date	Mintage	F	VF	XF	Unc	BU
1988 Proof	Est. 20,000	Value: 45.00				

X# M4 BALBOA

Copper-Nickel, 32 mm. **Subject:** Calgary Olympics
Obv: Arms **Rev:** Ice Hockey players

Date	Mintage	F	VF	XF	Unc	BU
1988 Proof	Est. 50,000	Value: 25.00				

X# M4a BALBOA

15.0000 g., 1.0000 Silver 0.4822 oz. ASW, 32 mm.
Subject: Calgary Olympics **Obv:** Arms **Rev:** Ice Hockey players

Date	Mintage	F	VF	XF	Unc	BU
1988 Proof	Est. 20,000	Value: 45.00				

X# M5 BALBOA

Copper-Nickel, 32 mm. **Subject:** Seoul Olympics
Obv: Arms **Rev:** 2 fencers

Date	Mintage	F	VF	XF	Unc	BU
1988 Proof	Est. 50,000	Value: 25.00				

X# M5a BALBOA

15.0000 g., 1.0000 Silver 0.4822 oz. ASW, 32 mm.
Subject: Seoul Olympics **Obv:** Arms **Rev:** 2 fencers

Date	Mintage	F	VF	XF	Unc	BU
1988 Proof	Est. 20,000	Value: 45.00				

X# M6 BALBOA

Copper-Nickel, 32 mm. **Subject:** Seoul Olympics
Obv: Arms **Rev:** Woman tennis player

Date	Mintage	F	VF	XF	Unc	BU
1988 Proof	Est. 50,000	Value: 25.00				

X# M6a BALBOA

15.0000 g., 1.0000 Silver 0.4822 oz. ASW, 32 mm.
Subject: Seoul Olympics **Obv:** Arms **Rev:** Woman tennis player

Date	Mintage	F	VF	XF	Unc	BU
1988 Proof	Est. 20,000	Value: 45.00				

X# M7 BALBOA

Copper-Nickel, 32 mm. **Subject:** Seoul Olympics
Obv: Arms **Rev:** Mounted woman competing in the equestrian event

Date	Mintage	F	VF	XF	Unc	BU
1988 Proof	Est. 50,000	Value: 25.00				

X# M7a BALBOA

15.0000 g., 1.0000 Silver 0.4822 oz. ASW, 32 mm.
Subject: Seoul Olympics **Obv:** Arms **Rev:** Mounted woman competing in the equestrian event

Date	Mintage	F	VF	XF	Unc	BU
1988 Proof	Est. 20,000	Value: 45.00				

X# M8 BALBOA

Copper-Nickel, 32 mm. **Subject:** Seoul Olympics
Obv: Arms **Rev:** Gymnast on parallel bars

Date	Mintage	F	VF	XF	Unc	BU
1988 Proof	Inc. above	Value: 25.00				

X# M8a BALBOA

15.0000 g., 1.0000 Silver 0.4822 oz. ASW, 32 mm.
Subject: Seoul Olympics **Obv:** Arms **Rev:** Gymnast on parallel bars

Date	Mintage	F	VF	XF	Unc	BU
1988 Proof	Est. 20,000	Value: 45.00				

X# M11 BALBOA

Copper-Nickel, 33.10 mm. **Obv:** Arms **Rev:** Head of Martin Luther King at right, church at left

Date	Mintage	F	VF	XF	Unc	BU
1988 Proof	Est. 50,000	Value: 15.00				

X# M11a BALBOA

15.0000 g., 1.0000 Silver 0.4822 oz. ASW, 32 mm.
Obv: Arms **Rev:** Head of Martin Luther King at right, church at left

Date	Mintage	F	VF	XF	Unc	BU
1988 Proof	Est. 20,000	Value: 40.00				

X# M12 BALBOA

Copper-Nickel, 33.10 mm. **Obv:** Arms **Rev:** Head of John F. Kennedy at lower right, Liberty bell at upper left

Date	Mintage	F	VF	XF	Unc	BU
1988 Proof	Est. 50,000	Value: 15.00				

X# M12a BALBOA

15.0000 g., 0.9990 Silver 0.4818 oz. ASW, 33.10 mm.
Obv: Arms **Rev:** Head of John F. Kennedy at lower right, Liberty bell at upper left

Date	Mintage	F	VF	XF	Unc	BU
1988 Proof	Est. 20,000	Value: 40.00				

X# M13 5 BALBOAS

31.1000 g., 0.9990 Silver 0.9988 oz. ASW, 39.90 mm.
Obv: Arms **Rev:** 3/4-length figure of Baron Manfred von Richthofen at right, triplane at left in background

Date	Mintage	F	VF	XF	Unc	BU
1988 Proof	Est. 30,000	Value: 100				

X# M9 50 BALBOAS
8.4000 g., 0.5850 Gold 0.1580 oz. AGW, 24.50 mm. **Subject:** Calgary Olympics **Obv:** Arms **Rev:** Woman figure skater

Date	Mintage	F	VF	XF	Unc	BU
1988 Proof	Est. 5,000	Value: 225				

X# M10 50 BALBOAS
8.4000 g., 0.5850 Gold 0.1580 oz. AGW, 24.50 mm. **Subject:** Seoul Olympics **Obv:** Arms **Rev:** Woman gymnast performing a ribbon dance routine

Date	Mintage	F	VF	XF	Unc	BU
1988 Proof	Est. 5,000	Value: 500				

X# M15 100 BALBOAS
8.1600 g., 0.9000 Gold 0.2361 oz. AGW **Obv:** Arms **Rev:** Baron Manfred von Richthofen, the Red Baron, Fokker

Date	Mintage	F	VF	XF	Unc	BU
1988 Proof	Est. 10,000	Value: 300				

X# M16 200 BALBOAS
15.5500 g., 0.9990 Gold 0.4994 oz. AGW, 28 mm. **Obv:** Arms **Rev:** Head of John F. Kennedy at right facing left, Statue of Liberty at upper left

Date	Mintage	F	VF	XF	Unc	BU
1988 Proof	Est. 10,000	Value: 400				

X# M14 25 BALBOAS
155.5150 g., 0.9990 Silver 4.9947 oz. ASW, 65 mm. **Obv:** Arms **Rev:** Baron Manfred von Richthofen in a dogfight over clouds **Note:** Illustration reduced.

Date	Mintage	F	VF	XF	Unc	BU
1988 Proof	Est. 20,000	Value: 250				

X# M17 1000 BALBOAS
373.2400 g., 0.9990 Gold 11.987 oz. AGW, 65 mm. **Obv:** Arms **Rev:** Head of John F. Kennedy at right facing 3/4 left, Capitol building at upper right **Note:** Illustration reduced.

Date	Mintage	F	VF	XF	Unc	BU
1988 Proof	30	Value: 8,500				

X# M18 1500 BALBOAS
373.2400 g., 0.9990 Platinum 11.987 oz. APW, 65 mm. **Obv:** Arms **Rev:** Head of John F. Kennedy at right facing 3/4 left, Statue of Liberty at upper left **Note:** Illustration reduced.

Date	Mintage	F	VF	XF	Unc	BU
1988 Proof	Est. 200	Value: 17,500				

PARADISE

PRINCIPALITY

MEDALLIC COINAGE

X# M1a DUPEE
26.4400 g., Silver, 37.2 mm. **Ruler:** Prince Lonnie Hammargren **Obv:** Facing bust **Obv. Legend:** ★ ★ IN GOD WE TRUST ★ ★ PRINCIPAL LONNIE HAMMAGREN **Rev:** Stylized Bird of Paradise **Rev. Legend:** PRINCIPALITY OF PARADISE - E Pluribus Unum **Edge:** Reeded

Date	Mintage	F	VF	XF	Unc	BU
1990 Proof	—	Value: 17.50				

X# M1 DUPEE
Copper-Nickel, 37.2 mm. **Ruler:** Prince Lonnie Hammargren **Obv:** Facing bust **Obv. Legend:** ★ ★ IN GOD WE TRUST ★ ★ PRINCIPAL LONNIE HAMMARGREN **Rev:** Stylized Bird of Paradise **Rev. Legend:** PRINCIPALITY OF PARADISE - E Pluribus Unum **Note:** A privately made casino gaming token.

Date	Mintage	F	VF	XF	Unc	BU
1990	—	—	—	—	6.00	—

PARAGUAY

REPUBLIC

COUNTERMARKED COINAGE

1858 - 1868

X# 1 2 REALES
Silver **Countermark:** Lion sitting, facing, liberty cap on staff divides date **Note:** Countermark on Argentina 4 Soles, KM#22.

CM Date	Host Date	Good	VG	F	VF	XF
1858	1828	35.00	50.00	85.00	175	—

X# 5 2 REALES
Silver **Countermark:** Lion sitting, facing, liberty cap on staff divides date **Note:** Countermark on Guatemala 2 Reales, KM#139.

CM Date	Host Date	Good	VG	F	VF	XF
1868	1862-65	12.50	20.00	35.00	65.00	—

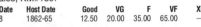

X# 7 2 REALES
Silver **Countermark:** Lion sitting, facing, liberty cap on staff divides date **Note:** Countermark on Lima, Peru 2 Reales, KM#141.1.

CM Date	Host Date	Good	VG	F	VF	XF
1868	1825-40	12.50	20.00	35.00	65.00	—

X# 10 CENT
Copper **Countermark:** Lion sitting, facing, liberty cap on staff divides date **Note:** Countermark on United States Cent, KM#67.

CM Date	Host Date	Good	VG	F	VF	XF
1868	1840-57	20.00	35.00	50.00	70.00	—

X# 19 4 SOLES
13.5000 g., 0.6667 Silver 0.2894 oz. ASW
Countermark: Lion sitting, facing, Liberty cap on staff **Note:** Countermark on Bolivia 4 Soles, KM#96a.

CM Date	Host Date	Good	VG	F	VF	XF
ND(1858)	1830 PTS	—	—	50.00	70.00	100

X# 20 4 SOLES
13.5000 g., 0.6667 Silver 0.2894 oz. ASW
Countermark: Lion sitting, facing, Liberty cap on staff **Note:** Countermark on Bolivia 4 Soles, KM#123.2.

CM Date	Host Date	Good	VG	F	VF	XF
ND(1858)	1853-58 PTS	—	—	50.00	70.00	100

MEDALLIC COINAGE

X# M127 300 GUARANIES
Gold **Subject:** General A. Stroessner

Date	Mintage	Good	VG	F	VF	XF
ND	—	—	—	15.00	20.00	—

PEMBA

BRITISH COLONY

COUNTERMARKED COINAGE

X# 5 1/2 RUPEE
Silver **Countermark:** Arabic inscription in clove design **Note:** Countermark on Mewar 1/2 Rupee.

CM Date	Host Date	Good	VG	F	VF	XF
ND	ND	60.00	90.00	150	200	—

X# 8 1/2 RUPEE
Silver **Countermark:** Arabic inscription in clove design **Note:** Countermark on British Indian 1/2 Rupee.

CM Date	Host Date	Good	VG	F	VF	XF
ND	1877-1900	45.00	65.00	100	150	—

X# 10 RUPEE
Silver **Countermark:** Arabic inscription in clove design **Note:** Countermark on British India-Bengal Murshidabad Mint 1 Rupee.

CM Date	Host Date	Good	VG	F	VF	XF
ND	R.Y.19	60.00	90.00	150	200	—

X# 12 RUPEE
Silver **Countermark:** Arabic inscription in clove design **Note:** Countermark on East India Company Rupee, KM#450.3.

CM Date	Host Date	Good	VG	F	VF	XF
ND	1835	70.00	100	185	250	—

X# 13 RUPEE
Silver **Countermark:** Arabic inscription in clove design **Note:** Countermark on East India Company 1 Rupee, KM#457.

CM Date	Host Date	Good	VG	F	VF	XF
ND	1840	70.00	100	185	250	—

X# 14 RUPEE
Silver **Countermark:** Arabic inscription in clove design **Note:** Countermark on British India Rupee, KM#492.

CM Date	Host Date	Good	VG	F	VF	XF
ND	1877-1901	70.00	100	185	250	—

X# 17 THALER
Silver **Countermark:** Arabic inscription in clove design **Note:** Countermark on Austria-Gunzberg Mint 1 Thaler.

CM Date	Host Date	Good	VG	F	VF	XF
ND	1765SC	120	200	325	450	—

X# 18 THALER
Silver **Countermark:** Arabic inscription in clove design **Note:** Countermark on Austria-Burgau-Gunzberg Mint 1 Thaler.

CM Date	Host Date	Good	VG	F	VF	XF
ND	1780	120	200	325	450	—

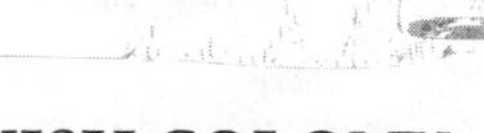

PERU

SPANISH COLONY

COUNTERMARKED COINAGE

Fantasy

X# 1 8 REALES
0.9030 Silver **Countermark:** "Shepard" on Peru Lima Mint 8 Reales, KM#117.1

CM Date	Host Date	Good	VG	F	VF	XF
ND	(1811-24)	25.00	35.00	50.00	75.00	—

REPUBLIC

MEDALLIC COINAGE

Thonnellier Patterns

Proposed patterns struck in France by Thonnelier and brought to the Cuzco Mint by their agent Allier.

X# 7 8 REALES
Silver **Obv:** Arms in sprays **Obv. Legend:** • REPUB • PERUANA • CUZCO • **Rev. Legend:** FIRME Y FELIZ POR LA UNION **Rev. Inscription:** PRENSA / PARA MONEDA / DE / THONNELLIER... **Edge:** Plain

Date	Mintage	F	VF	XF	Unc	BU
1835CUZCO B	—	—	—	400	550	—

X# 7a 8 REALES
Copper **Obv:** Arms in sprays **Obv. Legend:** • REPUB • PERUANA • CUZCO • **Rev. Legend:** FIRME Y FELIZ POR LA UNION **Rev. Inscription:** PRENSA / PARA MONEDA / DE / THONNELLIER... **Edge:** Plain

Date	Mintage	F	VF	XF	Unc	BU
1835CUZCO B	—	—	—	250	350	—

X# 7b 8 REALES
Silver Plated Copper **Obv:** Arms in sprays **Obv. Legend:** • REPUB • PERUANA • CUZCO • **Rev. Legend:** FIRME Y FELIZ POR LA UNION **Rev. Inscription:** PRENSA / PARA MONEDA / DE / THONNELLIER... **Edge:** Plain

Date	Mintage	F	VF	XF	Unc	BU
1835CUZCO B	—	—	—	300	450	—

X# 8 8 REALES
Silver **Obv:** Arms in sprays **Obv. Legend:** • REPUB • PERUANA • CUZCO • **Rev. Legend:** FIRME Y FELIZ POR LA UNION **Rev. Inscription:** PRENSA / PARA MONEDA / DE / THONNELLIER... **Edge:** Incuse leaf pattern

Date	Mintage	F	VF	XF	Unc	BU
1835CUZCO B	—	—	—	450	600	—

X# 8a 8 REALES
Copper **Obv:** Arms in sprays **Obv. Legend:** • REPUB • PERUANA • CUZCO • **Rev. Legend:** FIRME Y FELIZ POR LA UNION **Rev. Inscription:** PRENSA / PARA MONEDA / DE / THONNELLIER... **Edge:** Incuse leaf pattern

Date	Mintage	F	VF	XF	Unc	BU
1835CUZCO B	—	—	—	275	400	—

X# 8b 8 REALES
Silver Plated Copper **Obv:** Arms in sprays **Obv. Legend:** • REPUB • PERUANA • CUZCO • **Rev. Legend:** FIRME Y FELIZ POR LA UNION **Rev. Inscription:** PRENSA / PARA MONEDA / DE / THONNELLIER... **Edge:** Incuse leaf pattern

Date	Mintage	F	VF	XF	Unc	BU
1835CUZCO B	—	—	—	350	500	—

ICB Series

X# 11.1 20 NUEVOS SOLES
24.0000 g., 0.9250 Silver 0.7137 oz. ASW, 38 mm. **Subject:** XXVI Olympics - Atlanta - 1896 Olympics, Athens **Obv:** Arms **Obv. Legend:** BANCO CENTRAL DE RESERVA DEL PERU **Rev:** Robert Garrett poised with discus right **Edge:** Reed

Date	Mintage	F	VF	XF	Unc	BU
1996 Proof	25	Value: 75.00				

X# 11.2 20 NUEVOS SOLES
24.0000 g., 0.9250 Silver 0.7137 oz. ASW, 38 mm. **Subject:** XXVI Olympics - Atlanta - 1896 Olympics, Athens **Obv:** Arms **Obv. Legend:** BANCO CENTRAL DE RESERVA DEL PERU **Rev:** Robert Garrett poised with discus right **Edge:** Plain

Date	Mintage	F	VF	XF	Unc	BU
1996 Proof	25	Value: 75.00				

X# 11a.1 20 NUEVOS SOLES
23.0000 g., Brass, 38 mm. **Subject:** XXVI Olympics - Atlanta - 1896 Olympics, Athens **Obv:** Arms **Obv. Legend:** BANCO CENTRAL DE RESERVA DEL PERU **Rev:** Robert Garrett poised with discus right **Edge:** Reeded

Date	Mintage	F	VF	XF	Unc	BU
1996 Proof	25	Value: 50.00				

X# 11a.2 20 NUEVOS SOLES
23.0000 g., Brass, 38 mm. **Subject:** XXVI Olympics - Atlanta - 1896 Olympics, Athens **Obv:** Arms **Obv. Legend:** BANCO CENTRAL DE RESERVA DEL PERU **Rev:** Robert Garrett poised with discus right **Edge:** Plain

Date	Mintage	F	VF	XF	Unc	BU
1996 Proof	25	Value: 50.00				

X# 11b.1 20 NUEVOS SOLES
20.0000 g., Gilt Alloy, 38 mm. **Subject:** XXVI Olympics - Atlanta - 1896 Olympics, Athens **Obv:** Arms **Obv. Legend:** BANCO CENTRAL DE RESERVA DEL PERU **Rev:** Robert Garrett poised with discus right **Edge:** Reeded

Date	Mintage	F	VF	XF	Unc	BU
1996 Proof	25	Value: 50.00				

X# 11b.2 20 NUEVOS SOLES
20.0000 g., Gilt Alloy, 38 mm. **Subject:** XXVI Olympics - Atlanta - 1896 Olympics, Athens **Obv:** Arms **Obv. Legend:** BANCO CENTRAL DE RESERVA DEL PERU **Rev:** Robert Garrett poised with discus right **Edge:** Plain

Date	Mintage	F	VF	XF	Unc	BU
1996 Proof	25	Value: 50.00				

X# 11c.1 20 NUEVOS SOLES
23.0000 g., Tri-Metallic Silvered and gilt Brass, 38 mm. **Subject:** XXVI Olympics - Atlanta - 1896 Olympics, Athens **Obv:** Arms **Obv. Legend:** BANCO CENTRAL DE RESERVA DEL PERU **Rev:** Robert Garrett poised with discus right **Edge:** Reeded

Date	Mintage	F	VF	XF	Unc	BU
1996 Proof	25	Value: 75.00				

X# 11c.2 20 NUEVOS SOLES
Tri-Metallic Silvered and gilt Brass, 38 mm. **Subject:** XXVI Olympics - Atlanta - 1896 Olympics, Athens **Obv:** Arms **Obv. Legend:** BANCO CENTRAL DE RESERVA DEL PERU **Rev:** Robert Garrett poised with discus right **Edge:** Plain

Date	Mintage	F	VF	XF	Unc	BU
1996 Proof	25	Value: 75.00				

X# 11d.1 20 NUEVOS SOLES
6.0000 g., Aluminum, 38 mm. **Subject:** XXVI Olympics - Atlanta - 1896 Olympics, Athens **Obv:** Arms **Obv. Legend:** BANCO CENTRAL DE RESERVA DEL PERU **Rev:** Robert Garrett poised with discus right **Edge:** Reeded

Date	Mintage	F	VF	XF	Unc	BU
1996 Proof	25	Value: 50.00				

X# 11d.2 20 NUEVOS SOLES
6.0000 g., Aluminum, 38 mm. **Subject:** XXVI Olympics - Atlanta - 1896 Olympics, Athens **Obv:** Arms **Obv. Legend:** BANCO CENTRAL DE RESERVA DEL PERU **Rev:** Robert Garrett poised with discus right **Edge:** Plain

Date	Mintage	F	VF	XF	Unc	BU
1996 Proof	25	Value: 50.00				

X# 11e.1 20 NUEVOS SOLES
23.0000 g., Copper, 38 mm. **Subject:** XXVI Olympics - Atlanta - 1896 Olympics, Athens **Obv:** Arms **Obv. Legend:** BANCO CENTRAL DE RESERVA DEL PERU **Rev:** Robert Garrett poised with discus right **Edge:** Reeded

Date	Mintage	F	VF	XF	Unc	BU
1996 Proof	25	Value: 50.00				

X# 11e.2 20 NUEVOS SOLES
23.0000 g., Copper, 38 mm. **Subject:** XXVI Olympics - Atlanta - 1896 Olympics, Athens **Obv:** Arms **Obv. Legend:** BANCO CENTRAL DE RESERVA DEL PERU **Rev:** Robert Garrett poised with discus right **Edge:** Plain

Date	Mintage	F	VF	XF	Unc	BU
1996 Proof	25	Value: 50.00				

X# 11f.1 20 NUEVOS SOLES
20.0000 g., Copper-Nickel, 38 mm. **Subject:** XXVI Olympics - Atlanta - 1896 Olympics, Athens **Obv:** Arms **Obv. Legend:** BANCO CENTRAL DE RESERVA DEL PERU **Rev:** Robert Garrett poised with discus right **Edge:** Reeded

Date	Mintage	F	VF	XF	Unc	BU
1996 Proof	25	Value: 50.00				

X# 11f.2 20 NUEVOS SOLES
20.0000 g., Copper-Nickel, 38 mm. **Subject:** XXVI Olympics - Atlanta - 1896 Olympics, Athens **Obv:** Arms **Obv. Legend:** BANCO CENTRAL DE RESERVA DEL PERU **Rev:** Robert Garrett poised with discus right **Edge:** Plain

Date	Mintage	F	VF	XF	Unc	BU
1996 Proof	25	Value: 50.00				

X# 12.1 20 NUEVOS SOLES
24.0000 g., 0.9250 Silver 0.7137 oz. ASW, 38 mm. **Subject:** XXVI Olympics - Atlanta - 1908 Olympics,

London **Obv:** Arms **Obv. Legend:** BANCO CENTRAL DE RESERVA DEL PERU **Rev:** Boxer Albert Oldham standing right **Edge:** Reeded

Date	Mintage	F	VF	XF	Unc	BU
1996 Proof	25	Value: 75.00				

X# 12.2 20 NUEVOS SOLES
24.0000 g., 0.9250 Silver 0.7137 oz. ASW, 38 mm. **Subject:** XXVI Olympics - Atlanta - 1908 Olympics, London **Obv:** Arms **Obv. Legend:** BANCO CENTRAL DE RESERVA DEL PERU **Rev:** Boxer Albert Oldham standing right **Edge:** Plain

Date	Mintage	F	VF	XF	Unc	BU
1996 Proof	25	Value: 75.00				

X# 12a.1 20 NUEVOS SOLES
23.0000 g., Brass, 38 mm. **Subject:** XXVI Olympics - Atlanta - 1908 Olympics, London **Obv:** Arms **Obv. Legend:** BANCO CENTRAL DE RESERVA DEL PERU **Rev:** Boxer Albert Oldham standing right **Edge:** Reeded

Date	Mintage	F	VF	XF	Unc	BU
1996 Proof	25	Value: 50.00				

X# 12a.2 20 NUEVOS SOLES
23.0000 g., Brass, 38 mm. **Subject:** XXVI Olympics - Atlanta - 1908 Olympics, London **Obv:** Arms **Obv. Legend:** BANCO CENTRAL DE RESERVA DEL PERU **Rev:** Boxer Albert Oldham standing right **Edge:** Plain

Date	Mintage	F	VF	XF	Unc	BU
1996 Proof	25	Value: 50.00				

X# 12b.1 20 NUEVOS SOLES
20.0000 g., Gilt Alloy, 38 mm. **Subject:** XXVI Olympics - Atlanta - 1908 Olympics, London **Obv:** Arms **Obv. Legend:** BANCO CENTRAL DE RESERVA DEL PERU **Rev:** Boxer Albert Oldham standing right **Edge:** Reeded

Date	Mintage	F	VF	XF	Unc	BU
1996 Proof	25	Value: 50.00				

X# 12b.2 20 NUEVOS SOLES
20.0000 g., Gilt Alloy, 38 mm. **Subject:** XXVI Olympics - Atlanta - 1908 Olympics, London **Obv:** Arms **Obv. Legend:** BANCO CENTRAL DE RESERVA DEL PERU **Rev:** Boxer Albert Oldham standing right **Edge:** Plain

Date	Mintage	F	VF	XF	Unc	BU
1996 Proof	25	Value: 50.00				

X# 12c.1 20 NUEVOS SOLES
23.0000 g., Tri-Metallic Silvered and gilt Brass, 38 mm. **Subject:** XXVI Olympics - Atlanta - 1908 Olympics, London **Obv:** Arms **Obv. Legend:** BANCO CENTRAL DE RESERVA DEL PERU **Rev:** Boxer Albert Oldham standing right **Edge:** Reeded

Date	Mintage	F	VF	XF	Unc	BU
1996 Proof	25	Value: 50.00				

X# 12c.2 20 NUEVOS SOLES
23.0000 g., Tri-Metallic Silvered and gilt Brass, 38 mm. **Subject:** XXVI Olympics - Atlanta - 1908 Olympics, London **Obv:** Arms **Obv. Legend:** BANCO CENTRAL DE RESERVA DEL PERU **Rev:** Boxer Albert Oldham standing right **Edge:** Plain

Date	Mintage	F	VF	XF	Unc	BU
1996 Proof	25	Value: 50.00				

X# 12d.1 20 NUEVOS SOLES
6.0000 g., Aluminum, 38 mm. **Subject:** XXVI Olympics - Atlanta - 1908 Olympics, London **Obv:** Arms **Obv. Legend:** BANCO CENTRAL DE RESERVA DEL PERU **Rev:** Boxer Albert Oldham standing right **Edge:** Reeded

Date	Mintage	F	VF	XF	Unc	BU
1996 Proof	25	Value: 50.00				

X# 12d.2 20 NUEVOS SOLES
6.0000 g., Aluminum, 38 mm. **Subject:** XXVI Olympics - Atlanta - 1908 Olympics, London **Obv:** Arms **Obv. Legend:** BANCO CENTRAL DE RESERVA DEL PERU **Rev:** Boxer Albert Oldham standing right **Edge:** Plain

Date	Mintage	F	VF	XF	Unc	BU
1996 Proof	25	Value: 50.00				

X# 12e.1 20 NUEVOS SOLES
23.0000 g., Copper, 38 mm. **Subject:** XXVI Olympics - Atlanta - 1908 Olympics, London **Obv:** Arms **Obv. Legend:** BANCO CENTRAL DE RESERVA DEL PERU **Rev:** Boxer Albert Oldham standing right **Edge:** Reeded

Date	Mintage	F	VF	XF	Unc	BU
1996 Proof	25	Value: 50.00				

X# 12f.1 20 NUEVOS SOLES
20.0000 g., Copper-Nickel, 38 mm. **Subject:** XXVI Olympics - Atlanta - 1908 Olympics, London **Obv:** Arms **Obv. Legend:** BANCO CENTRAL DE RESERVA DEL PERU **Rev:** Boxer Albert Oldham standing right **Edge:** Reeded

Date	Mintage	F	VF	XF	Unc	BU
1996 Proof	25	Value: 50.00				

X# 12f.2 20 NUEVOS SOLES
20.0000 g., Copper-Nickel, 38 mm. **Subject:** XXVI Olympics - Atlanta - 1908 Olympics, London **Obv:** Arms **Obv. Legend:** BANCO CENTRAL DE RESERVA DEL PERU **Rev:** Boxer Albert Oldham standing right **Edge:** Plain

Date	Mintage	F	VF	XF	Unc	BU
1996 Proof	25	Value: 50.00				

X# 13.1 20 NUEVOS SOLES
24.0000 g., 0.9250 Silver 0.7137 oz. ASW, 38 mm. **Subject:** XXVI Olympics - Atlanta - 1932 Olympics, Los Angeles **Obv:** Arms **Obv. Legend:** BANCO CENTRAL DE RESERVA DEL PERU **Rev:** Matti Jarvinen poised right with javelin **Edge:** Reeded

Date	Mintage	F	VF	XF	Unc	BU
1996 Proof	25	Value: 75.00				

X# 13.2 20 NUEVOS SOLES
24.0000 g., 0.9250 Silver 0.7137 oz. ASW, 38 mm. **Subject:** XXVI Olympics - Atlanta - 1932 Olympics, Los Angeles **Obv:** Arms **Obv. Legend:** BANCO CENTRAL DE RESERVA DEL PERU **Rev:** Matti Jarvinen poised right with javelin **Edge:** Plain

Date	Mintage	F	VF	XF	Unc	BU
1996 Proof	25	Value: 75.00				

X# 13a.1 20 NUEVOS SOLES
23.0000 g., Brass, 38 mm. **Subject:** XXVI Olympics - Atlanta - 1932 Olympics, Los Angeles **Obv:** Arms **Obv. Legend:** BANCO CENTRAL DE RESERVA DEL PERU **Rev:** Matti Jarvinen poised right with javelin **Edge:** Reeded

Date	Mintage	F	VF	XF	Unc	BU
1996 Proof	25	Value: 50.00				

X# 13a.2 20 NUEVOS SOLES
23.0000 g., Brass, 38 mm. **Subject:** XXVI Olympics - Atlanta - 1932 Olympics, Los Angeles **Obv:** Arms **Obv. Legend:** BANCO CENTRAL DE RESERVA DEL PERU **Rev:** Matti Jarvinen poised right with javelin **Edge:** Plain

Date	Mintage	F	VF	XF	Unc	BU
1996 Proof	25	Value: 50.00				

X# 13b.1 20 NUEVOS SOLES
20.0000 g., Gilt Alloy, 38 mm. **Subject:** XXVI Olympics - Atlanta - 1932 Olympics, Los Angeles **Obv:** Arms **Obv. Legend:** BANCO CENTRAL DE RESERVA DEL PERU **Rev:** Matti Jarvinen poised right with javelin **Edge:** Reeded

Date	Mintage	F	VF	XF	Unc	BU
1996 Proof	25	Value: 50.00				

X# 13b.2 20 NUEVOS SOLES
20.0000 g., Gilt Alloy, 38 mm. **Subject:** XXVI Olympics - Atlanta - 1932 Olympics, Los Angeles **Obv:** Arms **Obv. Legend:** BANCO CENTRAL DE RESERVA DEL PERU **Rev:** Matti Jarvinen poised right with javelin **Edge:** Plain

Date	Mintage	F	VF	XF	Unc	BU
1996 Proof	25	Value: 50.00				

X# 13c.1 20 NUEVOS SOLES
23.0000 g., Tri-Metallic Silvered and gilt Brass, 38 mm. **Subject:** XXVI Olympics - Atlanta - 1932 Olympics, Los Angeles **Obv:** Arms **Obv. Legend:** BANCO CENTRAL DE RESERVA DEL PERU **Rev:** Matti Jarvinen poised right with javelin **Edge:** Reeded

Date	Mintage	F	VF	XF	Unc	BU
1996 Proof	25	Value: 75.00				

X# 13c.2 20 NUEVOS SOLES
23.0000 g., Tri-Metallic Silvered and gilt Brass, 38 mm. **Subject:** XXVI Olympics - Atlanta - 1932 Olympics, Los Angeles **Obv:** Arms **Obv. Legend:** BANCO CENTRAL DE RESERVA DEL PERU **Rev:** Matti Jarvinen poised right with javelin **Edge:** Plain

Date	Mintage	F	VF	XF	Unc	BU
1996 Proof	25	Value: 75.00				

X# 13d.1 20 NUEVOS SOLES
6.0000 g., Aluminum, 38 mm. **Subject:** XXVI Olympics - Atlanta - 1932 Olympics, Los Angeles **Obv:** Arms **Obv. Legend:** BANCO CENTRAL DE RESERVA DEL PERU **Rev:** Matti Jarvinen poised right with javelin **Edge:** Reeded

Date	Mintage	F	VF	XF	Unc	BU
1996 Proof	25	Value: 50.00				

X# 13d.2 20 NUEVOS SOLES
6.0000 g., Aluminum, 38 mm. **Subject:** XXVI Olympics - Atlanta - 1932 Olympics, Los Angeles **Obv:** Arms **Obv. Legend:** BANCO CENTRAL DE RESERVA DEL PERU **Rev:** Matti Jarvinen poised right with javelin **Edge:** Plain

Date	Mintage	F	VF	XF	Unc	BU
1996 Proof	25	Value: 50.00				

X# 13e.1 20 NUEVOS SOLES
23.0000 g., Copper, 38 mm. **Subject:** XXVI Olympics - Atlanta - 1932 Olympics, Los Angeles **Obv:** Arms **Obv. Legend:** BANCO CENTRAL DE RESERVA DEL PERU **Rev:** Matti Jarvinen poised right with javelin **Edge:** Reeded

Date	Mintage	F	VF	XF	Unc	BU
1996 Proof	25	Value: 50.00				

X# 13e.2 20 NUEVOS SOLES
23.0000 g., Copper, 38 mm. **Subject:** XXVI Olympics - Atlanta - 1932 Olympics, Los Angeles **Obv:** Arms **Obv. Legend:** BANCO CENTRAL DE RESERVA DEL PERU **Rev:** Matti Jarvinen poised right with javelin **Edge:** Plain

Date	Mintage	F	VF	XF	Unc	BU
1996 Proof	25	Value: 50.00				

X# 13f.1 20 NUEVOS SOLES
20.0000 g., Copper-Nickel, 38 mm. **Subject:** XXVI Olympics - Atlanta - 1932 Olympics, Los Angeles **Obv:** Arms **Obv. Legend:** BANCO CENTRAL DE RESERVA DEL PERU **Rev:** Matti Jarvinen poised right with javelin **Edge:** Reeded

Date	Mintage	F	VF	XF	Unc	BU
1996 Proof	25	Value: 50.00				

X# 13f.2 20 NUEVOS SOLES
20.0000 g., Copper-Nickel, 38 mm. **Subject:** XXVI Olympics - Atlanta - 1932 Olympics, Los Angeles **Obv:** Arms **Obv. Legend:** BANCO CENTRAL DE RESERVA DEL PERU **Rev:** Matti Jarvinen poised right with javelin **Edge:** Plain

Date	Mintage	F	VF	XF	Unc	BU
1996 Proof	25	Value: 50.00				

X# 14.1 20 NUEVOS SOLES
24.0000 g., 0.9250 Silver 0.7137 oz. ASW, 38 mm. **Subject:** XXVI Olympics - Atlanta - 1936 Olympics, Berlin **Obv:** Arms **Obv. Legend:** BANCO CENTRAL DE RESERVA DEL PERU **Rev:** Torchbearer running, facing **Edge:** Reeded

Date	Mintage	F	VF	XF	Unc	BU
1996 Proof	25	Value: 75.00				

X# 14.2 20 NUEVOS SOLES
24.0000 g., 0.9250 Silver 0.7137 oz. ASW, 38 mm. **Subject:** XXVI Olympics - Atlanta - 1936 Olympics, Berlin **Obv:** Arms **Obv. Legend:** BANCO CENTRAL DE RESERVA DEL PERU **Rev:** Torchbearer running, facing **Edge:** Plain

Date	Mintage	F	VF	XF	Unc	BU
1996 Proof	25	Value: 75.00				

X# 14a.1 20 NUEVOS SOLES
23.0000 g., Brass, 38 mm. **Subject:** XXVI Olympics - Atlanta - 1936 Olympics, Berlin **Obv:** Arms **Obv. Legend:** BANCO CENTRAL DE RESERVA DEL PERU **Rev:** Torchbearer running, facing **Edge:** Reeded

Date	Mintage	F	VF	XF	Unc	BU
1996 Proof	25	Value: 50.00				

X# 14a.2 20 NUEVOS SOLES
23.0000 g., Brass, 38 mm. **Subject:** XXVI Olympics - Atlanta - 1936 Olympics, Berlin **Obv:** Arms **Obv. Legend:** BANCO CENTRAL DE RESERVA DEL PERU **Rev:** Torchbearer running, facing **Edge:** Plain

Date	Mintage	F	VF	XF	Unc	BU
1996 Proof	25	Value: 50.00				

X# 14b.2 20 NUEVOS SOLES
20.0000 g., Gilt Alloy, 38 mm. **Subject:** XXVI Olympics - Atlanta - 1936 Olympics, Berlin **Obv:** Arms **Obv. Legend:** BANCO CENTRAL DE RESERVA DEL PERU **Rev:** Torchbearer running, facing **Edge:** Plain

Date	Mintage	F	VF	XF	Unc	BU
1996 Proof	25	Value: 50.00				

X# 14c.1 20 NUEVOS SOLES
23.0000 g., Tri-Metallic Silvered and gilt Brass, 38 mm. **Subject:** XXVI Olympics - Atlanta - 1936 Olympics, Berlin **Obv:** Arms **Obv. Legend:** BANCO CENTRAL DE RESERVA DEL PERU **Rev:** Torchbearer running, facing **Edge:** Reeded

Date	Mintage	F	VF	XF	Unc	BU
1996 Proof	25	Value: 75.00				

X# 14c.2 20 NUEVOS SOLES
23.0000 g., Tri-Metallic Silvered and gilt Brass, 38 mm. **Subject:** XXVI Olympics - Atlanta - 1936 Olympics, Berlin **Obv:** Arms **Obv. Legend:** BANCO CENTRAL DE RESERVA DEL PERU **Rev:** Torchbearer running, facing **Edge:** Plain

Date	Mintage	F	VF	XF	Unc	BU
1996 Proof	25	Value: 75.00				

X# 14d.1 20 NUEVOS SOLES
6.0000 g., Aluminum, 38 mm. **Subject:** XXVI Olympics - Atlanta - 1936 Olympics, Berlin **Obv:** Arms **Obv. Legend:** BANCO CENTRAL DE RESERVA DEL PERU **Rev:** Torchbearer running, facing **Edge:** Reeded

Date	Mintage	F	VF	XF	Unc	BU
1996 Proof	25	Value: 50.00				

X# 14d.2 20 NUEVOS SOLES
6.0000 g., Aluminum, 38 mm. **Subject:** XXVI Olympics - Atlanta - 1936 Olympics, Berlin **Obv:** Arms **Obv. Legend:** BANCO CENTRAL DE RESERVA DEL PERU **Rev:** Torchbearer running, facing **Edge:** Plain

Date	Mintage	F	VF	XF	Unc	BU
1996 Proof	25	Value: 50.00				

X# 14e.1 20 NUEVOS SOLES
23.0000 g., Copper, 38 mm. **Subject:** XXVI Olympics - Atlanta - 1936 Olympics, Berlin **Obv:** Arms **Obv. Legend:** BANCO CENTRAL DE RESERVA DEL PERU **Rev:** Torchbearer running, facing **Edge:** Reeded

Date	Mintage	F	VF	XF	Unc	BU
1996 Proof	25	Value: 50.00				

X# 14e.2 20 NUEVOS SOLES
23.0000 g., Copper, 38 mm. **Subject:** XXVI Olympics - Atlanta - 1936 Olympics, Berlin **Obv:** Arms **Obv. Legend:** BANCO CENTRAL DE RESERVA DEL PERU **Rev:** Torchbearer running, facing **Edge:** Plain

Date	Mintage	F	VF	XF	Unc	BU
1996 Proof	25	Value: 50.00				

X# 14f.1 20 NUEVOS SOLES
20.0000 g., Copper-Nickel, 38 mm. **Subject:** XXVI Olympics - Atlanta - 1936 Olympics, Berlin **Obv:** Arms **Obv. Legend:** BANCO CENTRAL DE RESERVA DEL PERU **Rev:** Torchbearer running, facing **Edge:** Reeded

Date	Mintage	F	VF	XF	Unc	BU
1996 Proof	25	Value: 50.00				

X# 14f.2 20 NUEVOS SOLES
20.0000 g., Copper-Nickel, 38 mm. **Subject:** XXVI Olympics - Atlanta - 1936 Olympics, Berlin **Obv:** Arms **Obv. Legend:** BANCO CENTRAL DE RESERVA DEL PERU **Rev:** Torchbearer running, facing **Edge:** Plain

Date	Mintage	F	VF	XF	Unc	BU
1996 Proof	25	Value: 50.00				

X# 15.1 20 NUEVOS SOLES
24.0000 g., 0.9250 Silver 0.7137 oz. ASW, 38 mm. **Subject:** XXVI Olympics - Atlanta - 1968 Olympics, Mexico City **Obv:** Arms **Obv. Legend:** BANCO CENTRAL DE RESERVA DEL PERU **Rev:** Sprinter Tommie Smith running right **Edge:** Reeded

Date	Mintage	F	VF	XF	Unc	BU
1996 Proof	25	Value: 75.00				

X# 15.2 20 NUEVOS SOLES
24.0000 g., 0.9250 Silver 0.7137 oz. ASW, 38 mm. **Subject:** XXVI Olympics - Atlanta - 1968 Olympics, Mexico City **Obv:** Arms **Obv. Legend:** BANCO CENTRAL DE RESERVA DEL PERU **Rev:** Sprinter Tommie Smith running right **Edge:** Plain

Date	Mintage	F	VF	XF	Unc	BU
1996 Proof	25	Value: 75.00				

X# 15a.1 20 NUEVOS SOLES
23.0000 g., Brass, 38 mm. **Subject:** XXVI Olympics - Atlanta - 1968 Olympics, Mexico City **Obv:** Arms **Obv. Legend:** BANCO CENTRAL DE RESERVA DEL PERU **Rev:** Sprinter Tommie Smith running right **Edge:** Reeded

Date	Mintage	F	VF	XF	Unc	BU
1996 Proof	25	Value: 50.00				

X# 15a.2 20 NUEVOS SOLES
23.0000 g., Brass, 38 mm. **Subject:** XXVI Olympics - Atlanta - 1968 Olympics, Mexico City **Obv:** Arms **Obv. Legend:** BANCO CENTRAL DE RESERVA DEL PERU **Rev:** Sprinter Tommie Smith running right **Edge:** Plain

Date	Mintage	F	VF	XF	Unc	BU
1996 Proof	25	Value: 50.00				

X# 15b.1 20 NUEVOS SOLES
20.0000 g., Gilt Alloy, 38 mm. **Subject:** XXVI Olympics - Atlanta - 1968 Olympics, Mexico City **Obv:** Arms **Obv. Legend:** BANCO CENTRAL DE RESERVA DEL PERU **Rev:** Sprinter Tommie Smith running right **Edge:** Reeded

Date	Mintage	F	VF	XF	Unc	BU
1996 Proof	25	Value: 50.00				

X# 15b.2 20 NUEVOS SOLES
20.0000 g., Gilt Alloy, 38 mm. **Subject:** XXVI Olympics - Atlanta - 1968 Olympics, Mexico City **Obv:** Arms **Obv. Legend:** BANCO CENTRAL DE RESERVA DEL PERU **Rev:** Sprinter Tommie Smith running right **Edge:** Plain

Date	Mintage	F	VF	XF	Unc	BU
1996 Proof	25	Value: 50.00				

X# 15c.1 20 NUEVOS SOLES
23.0000 g., Tri-Metallic Silvered and gilt Brass, 38 mm. **Subject:** XXVI Olympics - Atlanta - 1968 Olympics, Mexico City **Obv:** Arms **Obv. Legend:** BANCO CENTRAL DE RESERVA DEL PERU **Rev:** Sprinter Tommie Smith running right **Edge:** Reeded

Date	Mintage	F	VF	XF	Unc	BU
1996 Proof	25	Value: 75.00				

X# 15c.2 20 NUEVOS SOLES
23.0000 g., Tri-Metallic Silvered and gilt Brass, 38 mm. **Subject:** XXVI Olympics - Atlanta - 1968 Olympics, Mexico City **Obv:** Arms **Obv. Legend:** BANCO CENTRAL DE RESERVA DEL PERU **Rev:** Sprinter Tommie Smith running right **Edge:** Plain

Date	Mintage	F	VF	XF	Unc	BU
1996 Proof	25	Value: 75.00				

X# 15d.1 20 NUEVOS SOLES
6.0000 g., Aluminum, 38 mm. **Subject:** XXVI Olympics - Atlanta - 1968 Olympics, Mexico City **Obv:** Arms **Obv. Legend:** BANCO CENTRAL DE RESERVA DEL PERU **Rev:** Sprinter Tommie Smith running right **Edge:** Reeded

Date	Mintage	F	VF	XF	Unc	BU
1996 Proof	25	Value: 50.00				

X# 15d.2 20 NUEVOS SOLES
6.0000 g., Aluminum, 38 mm. **Subject:** XXVI Olympics - Atlanta - 1968 Olympics, Mexico City **Obv:** Arms **Obv. Legend:** BANCO CENTRAL DE RESERVA DEL PERU **Rev:** Sprinter Tommie Smith running right **Edge:** Plain

Date	Mintage	F	VF	XF	Unc	BU
1996 Proof	25	Value: 50.00				

X# 15e.1 20 NUEVOS SOLES
23.0000 g., Copper, 38 mm. **Subject:** XXVI Olympics - Atlanta - 1968 Olympics, Mexico City **Obv:** Arms **Obv. Legend:** BANCO CENTRAL DE RESERVA DEL PERU **Rev:** Sprinter Tommie Smith running right **Edge:** Reeded

Date	Mintage	F	VF	XF	Unc	BU
1996 Proof	25	Value: 50.00				

X# 15e.2 20 NUEVOS SOLES
23.0000 g., Copper, 38 mm. **Subject:** XXVI Olympics - Atlanta - 1968 Olympics, Mexico City **Obv:** Arms **Obv. Legend:** BANCO CENTRAL DE RESERVA DEL PERU **Rev:** Sprinter Tommie Smith running right **Edge:** Plain

Date	Mintage	F	VF	XF	Unc	BU
1996 Proof	25	Value: 50.00				

X# 15f.1 20 NUEVOS SOLES
20.0000 g., Copper-Nickel, 38 mm. **Subject:** XXVI Olympics - Atlanta - 1968 Olympics, Mexico City **Obv:** Arms **Obv. Legend:** BANCO CENTRAL DE RESERVA DEL PERU **Rev:** Sprinter Tommie Smith running right **Edge:** Reeded

Date	Mintage	F	VF	XF	Unc	BU
1996 Proof	25	Value: 50.00				

X# 15f.2 20 NUEVOS SOLES

20.0000 g., Copper-Nickel, 38 mm. **Subject:** XXVI Olympics - Atlanta - 1968 Olympics, Mexico City **Obv:** Arms **Obv. Legend:** BANCO CENTRAL DE RESERVA DEL PERU **Rev:** Sprinter Tommie Smith running right **Edge:** Plain

Date	Mintage	F	VF	XF	Unc	BU
1996 Proof	25	Value: 50.00				

X# 16.1 20 NUEVOS SOLES

24.0000 g., 0.9250 Silver 0.7137 oz. ASW, 38 mm. **Subject:** XXVI Olympics - Atlanta - 1988 Olympics, Seoul **Obv:** Arms **Obv. Legend:** BANCO CENTRAL DE RESERVA DEL PERU **Rev:** Pole vaulter Sergei Bubka ascending **Edge:** Reeded

Date	Mintage	F	VF	XF	Unc	BU
1996 Proof	25	Value: 75.00				

X# 16.2 20 NUEVOS SOLES

24.0000 g., 0.9250 Silver 0.7137 oz. ASW, 38 mm. **Subject:** XXVI Olympics - Atlanta - 1988 Olympics, Seoul **Obv:** Arms **Obv. Legend:** BANCO CENTRAL DE RESERVA DEL PERU **Rev:** Pole vaulter Sergei Bubka ascending **Edge:** Plain

Date	Mintage	F	VF	XF	Unc	BU
1996 Proof	25	Value: 75.00				

X# 16a.1 20 NUEVOS SOLES

23.0000 g., Brass, 38 mm. **Subject:** XXVI Olympics - Atlanta - 1988 Olympics, Seoul **Obv:** Arms **Obv. Legend:** BANCO CENTRAL DE RESERVA DEL PERU **Rev:** Pole vaulter Sergei Bubka ascending **Edge:** Reeded

Date	Mintage	F	VF	XF	Unc	BU
1996 Proof	25	Value: 50.00				

X# 16a.2 20 NUEVOS SOLES

23.0000 g., Brass, 38 mm. **Subject:** XXVI Olympics - Atlanta - 1988 Olympics, Seoul **Obv:** Arms **Obv. Legend:** BANCO CENTRAL DE RESERVA DEL PERU **Rev:** Pole vaulter Sergei Bubka ascending **Edge:** Plain

Date	Mintage	F	VF	XF	Unc	BU
1996 Proof	25	Value: 50.00				

X# 16b.1 20 NUEVOS SOLES

20.0000 g., Gilt Alloy, 38 mm. **Subject:** XXVI Olympics - Atlanta - 1988 Olympics, Seoul **Obv:** Arms **Obv. Legend:** BANCO CENTRAL DE RESERVA DEL PERU **Rev:** Pole vaulter Sergei Bubka ascending **Edge:** Reeded

Date	Mintage	F	VF	XF	Unc	BU
1996 Proof	25	Value: 50.00				

X# 16b.2 20 NUEVOS SOLES

20.0000 g., Gilt Alloy, 38 mm. **Subject:** XXVI Olympics - Atlanta - 1988 Olympics, Seoul **Obv:** Arms **Obv. Legend:** BANCO CENTRAL DE RESERVA DEL PERU **Rev:** Pole vaulter Sergei Bubka ascending **Edge:** Plain

Date	Mintage	F	VF	XF	Unc	BU
1996 Proof	25	Value: 50.00				

X# 16c.1 20 NUEVOS SOLES

23.0000 g., Tri-Metallic Silvered and gilt Brass, 38 mm. **Subject:** XXVI Olympics - Atlanta - 1988 Olympics, Seoul **Obv:** Arms **Obv. Legend:** BANCO CENTRAL DE RESERVA DEL PERU **Rev:** Pole vaulter Sergei Bubka ascending **Edge:** Reeded

Date	Mintage	F	VF	XF	Unc	BU
1996 Proof	25	Value: 75.00				

X# 16c.2 20 NUEVOS SOLES

23.0000 g., Tri-Metallic Silvered and gilt Brass, 38 mm. **Subject:** XXVI Olympics - Atlanta - 1988 Olympics, Seoul **Obv:** Arms **Obv. Legend:** BANCO CENTRAL DE RESERVA DEL PERU **Rev:** Pole vaulter Sergei Bubka ascending **Edge:** Plain

Date	Mintage	F	VF	XF	Unc	BU
1996 Proof	25	Value: 75.00				

X# 16d.1 20 NUEVOS SOLES

6.0000 g., Aluminum, 38 mm. **Subject:** XXVI Olympics - Atlanta - 1988 Olympics, Seoul **Obv:** Arms **Obv. Legend:** BANCO CENTRAL DE RESERVA DEL PERU **Rev:** Pole vaulter Sergei Bubka ascending **Edge:** Reeded

Date	Mintage	F	VF	XF	Unc	BU
1996 Proof	25	Value: 50.00				

X# 16d.2 20 NUEVOS SOLES

6.0000 g., Aluminum, 38 mm. **Subject:** XXVI Olympics - Atlanta - 1988 Olympics, Seoul **Obv:** Arms **Obv. Legend:** BANCO CENTRAL DE RESERVA DEL PERU **Rev:** Pole vaulter Sergei Bubka ascending **Edge:** Plain

Date	Mintage	F	VF	XF	Unc	BU
1996 Proof	25	Value: 50.00				

X# 16e.1 20 NUEVOS SOLES

23.0000 g., Copper, 38 mm. **Subject:** XXVI Olympics - Atlanta - 1988 Olympics, Seoul **Obv:** Arms **Obv. Legend:** BANCO CENTRAL DE RESERVA DEL PERU **Rev:** Pole vaulter Sergei Bubka ascending **Edge:** Reeded

Date	Mintage	F	VF	XF	Unc	BU
1996 Proof	25	Value: 50.00				

X# 16e.2 20 NUEVOS SOLES

23.0000 g., Copper, 38 mm. **Subject:** XXVI Olympics - Atlanta - 1988 Olympics, Seoul **Obv:** Arms **Obv. Legend:** BANCO CENTRAL DE RESERVA DEL PERU **Rev:** Pole vaulter Sergei Bubka ascending **Edge:** Plain

Date	Mintage	F	VF	XF	Unc	BU
1996 Proof	25	Value: 50.00				

X# 16f.1 20 NUEVOS SOLES

20.0000 g., Copper-Nickel, 38 mm. **Subject:** XXVI Olympics - Atlanta - 1988 Olympics, Seoul **Obv:** Arms **Obv. Legend:** BANCO CENTRAL DE RESERVA DEL PERU **Rev:** Pole vaulter Sergei Bubka ascending **Edge:** Reeded

Date	Mintage	F	VF	XF	Unc	BU
1996 Proof	25	Value: 50.00				

X# 16f.2 20 NUEVOS SOLES

20.0000 g., Copper-Nickel, 38 mm. **Subject:** XXVI Olympics - Atlanta - 1988 Olympics, Seoul **Obv:** Arms **Obv. Legend:** BANCO CENTRAL DE RESERVA DEL PERU **Rev:** Pole vaulter Sergei Bubka ascending **Edge:** Plain

Date	Mintage	F	VF	XF	Unc	BU
1996 Proof	25	Value: 50.00				

X# 17.1 20 NUEVOS SOLES

24.0000 g., 0.9250 Silver 0.7137 oz. ASW, 38 mm. **Subject:** XXVI Olympics - Atlanta - 1896 Olympics, Athens **Obv:** Small Liberty seated right with shield and staff, Phrygian cap atop **Obv. Legend:** BANCO CENTRAL DE RESERVA DEL PERU **Rev:** Robert Garrett poised with discus right **Edge:** Reeded

Date	Mintage	F	VF	XF	Unc	BU
1996 Proof	100	Value: 50.00				

X# 17.2 20 NUEVOS SOLES

24.0000 g., 0.9250 Silver 0.7137 oz. ASW, 38 mm. **Subject:** XXVI Olympics - Atlanta - 1896 Olympics, Athens **Obv:** Small Liberty seated right with shield and staff, Phrygian cap atop **Obv. Legend:** BANCO CENTRAL DE RESERVA DEL PERU **Rev:** Robert Garrett poised with discus right **Edge:** Plain

Date	Mintage	F	VF	XF	Unc	BU
1996 Proof	100	Value: 50.00				

X# 17a.1 20 NUEVOS SOLES

23.0000 g., Brass, 38 mm. **Subject:** XXVI Olympics - Atlanta - 1896 Olympics, Athens **Obv:** Small Liberty seated right with shield and staff, Phrygian cap atop **Obv. Legend:** BANCO CENTRAL DE RESERVA DEL PERU **Rev:** Robert Garrett poised with discus right **Edge:** Reeded

Date	Mintage	F	VF	XF	Unc	BU
1996 Proof	100	Value: 30.00				

X# 17a.2 20 NUEVOS SOLES

23.0000 g., Brass, 38 mm. **Subject:** XXVI Olympics - Atlanta - 1896 Olympics, Athens **Obv:** Small Liberty seated right with shield and staff, Phrygian cap atop **Obv. Legend:** BANCO CENTRAL DE RESERVA DEL PERU **Rev:** Robert Garrett poised with discus right **Edge:** Plain

Date	Mintage	F	VF	XF	Unc	BU
1996 Proof	100	Value: 30.00				

X# 17b.1 20 NUEVOS SOLES

20.0000 g., Gilt Alloy, 38 mm. **Subject:** XXVI Olympics - Atlanta - 1896 Olympics, Athens **Obv:** Small Liberty seated right with shield and staff, Phrygian cap atop **Obv. Legend:** BANCO CENTRAL DE RESERVA DEL PERU **Rev:** Robert Garrett poised with discus right **Edge:** Reeded

Date	Mintage	F	VF	XF	Unc	BU
1996 Proof	100	Value: 30.00				

X# 17b.2 20 NUEVOS SOLES

Gilt Alloy, 38 mm. **Subject:** XXVI Olympics - Atlanta - 1896 Olympics, Athens **Obv:** Small Liberty seated right with shield and staff, Phrygian cap atop **Obv. Legend:** BANCO CENTRAL DE RESERVA DEL PERU **Rev:** Robert Garrett poised with discus right **Edge:** Plain

Date	Mintage	F	VF	XF	Unc	BU
1996 Proof	100	Value: 30.00				

X# 17c.1 20 NUEVOS SOLES

23.0000 g., Tri-Metallic Silvered and gilt Brass, 38 mm. **Subject:** XXVI Olympics - Atlanta - 1896 Olympics, Athens **Obv:** Small Liberty seated right with shield and staff, Phrygian cap atop **Obv. Legend:** BANCO CENTRAL DE RESERVA DEL PERU **Rev:** Robert Garrett poised with discus right **Edge:** Reeded

Date	Mintage	F	VF	XF	Unc	BU
1996 Proof	25	Value: 75.00				

X# 17c.2 20 NUEVOS SOLES

23.0000 g., Tri-Metallic Silvered and gilt Brass, 38 mm. **Subject:** XXVI Olympics - Atlanta - 1896 Olympics, Athens **Obv:** Small Liberty seated right with shield and staff, Phrygian cap atop **Obv. Legend:** BANCO CENTRAL DE RESERVA DEL PERU **Rev:** Robert Garrett poised with discus right **Edge:** Plain

Date	Mintage	F	VF	XF	Unc	BU
1996 Proof	25	Value: 75.00				

X# 17d.1 20 NUEVOS SOLES

6.0000 g., Aluminum, 38 mm. **Subject:** XXVI Olympics - Atlanta - 1896 Olympics, Athens **Obv:** Small Liberty seated right with shield and staff, Phrygian cap atop **Obv. Legend:** BANCO CENTRAL DE RESERVA DEL PERU **Rev:** Robert Garrett poised with discus right **Edge:** Reeded

Date	Mintage	F	VF	XF	Unc	BU
1996 Proof	100	Value: 30.00				

X# 17d.2 20 NUEVOS SOLES
6.0000 g., Aluminum, 38 mm. **Subject:** XXVI Olympics - Atlanta - 1896 Olympics, Athens **Obv:** Small Liberty seated right with shield and staff, Phrygian cap atop **Obv. Legend:** BANCO CENTRAL DE RESERVA DEL PERU **Rev:** Robert Garrett poised with discus right **Edge:** Plain

Date	Mintage	F	VF	XF	Unc	BU
1996 Proof	100	Value: 30.00				

X# 17e.1 20 NUEVOS SOLES
23.0000 g., Copper, 38 mm. **Subject:** XXVI Olympics - Atlanta - 1896 Olympics, Athens **Obv:** Small Liberty seated right with shield and staff, Phrygian cap atop **Obv. Legend:** BANCO CENTRAL DE RESERVA DEL PERU **Rev:** Robert Garrett poised with discus right **Edge:** Reeded

Date	Mintage	F	VF	XF	Unc	BU
1996 Proof	100	Value: 30.00				

X# 17e.2 20 NUEVOS SOLES
23.0000 g., Copper, 38 mm. **Subject:** XXVI Olympics - Atlanta - 1896 Olympics, Athens **Obv:** Small Liberty seated right with shield and staff, Phrygian cap atop **Obv. Legend:** BANCO CENTRAL DE RESERVA DEL PERU **Rev:** Robert Garrett poised with discus right **Edge:** Plain

Date	Mintage	F	VF	XF	Unc	BU
1996 Proof	100	Value: 30.00				

X# 17f.1 20 NUEVOS SOLES
20.0000 g., Copper-Nickel, 38 mm. **Subject:** XXVI Olympics - Atlanta - 1896 Olympics, Athens **Obv:** Small Liberty seated right with shield and staff, Phrygian cap atop **Obv. Legend:** BANCO CENTRAL DE RESERVA DEL PERU **Rev:** Robert Garrett poised with discus right **Edge:** Reeded

Date	Mintage	F	VF	XF	Unc	BU
1996 Proof	100	Value: 30.00				

X# 17f.2 20 NUEVOS SOLES
20.0000 g., Copper-Nickel, 38 mm. **Subject:** XXVI Olympics - Atlanta - 1896 Olympics, Athens **Obv:** Small Liberty seated right with shield and staff, Phrygian cap atop **Obv. Legend:** BANCO CENTRAL DE RESERVA DEL PERU **Rev:** Robert Garrett poised with discus right **Edge:** Plain

Date	Mintage	F	VF	XF	Unc	BU
1996 Proof	100	Value: 30.00				

X# 18.1 20 NUEVOS SOLES
24.0000 g., 0.9250 Silver 0.7137 oz. ASW, 38 mm. **Subject:** XXVI Olympics - Atlanta - 1908 Olympics, London **Obv:** Small Liberty seated right with shield and staff, Phrygian cap atop **Obv. Legend:** BANCO CENTRAL DE RESERVA DEL PERU **Rev:** Boxer Albert Oldham standing right **Edge:** Reeded

Date	Mintage	F	VF	XF	Unc	BU
1996 Proof	100	Value: 50.00				

X# 18.2 20 NUEVOS SOLES
24.0000 g., 0.9250 Silver 0.7137 oz. ASW, 38 mm. **Subject:** XXVI Olympics - Atlanta - 1908 Olympics, London **Obv:** Small Liberty seated right with shield and staff, Phrygian cap atop **Obv. Legend:** BANCO CENTRAL DE RESERVA DEL PERU **Rev:** Boxer Albert Oldham standing right **Edge:** Plain

Date	Mintage	F	VF	XF	Unc	BU
1996 Proof	100	Value: 50.00				

X# 18a.1 20 NUEVOS SOLES
23.0000 g., Brass, 38 mm. **Subject:** XXVI Olympics - Atlanta - 1908 Olympics, London **Obv:** Small Liberty seated right with shield and staff, Phrygian cap atop **Obv. Legend:** BANCO CENTRAL DE RESERVA DEL PERU **Rev:** Boxer Albert Oldham standing right **Edge:** Reeded

Date	Mintage	F	VF	XF	Unc	BU
1996 Proof	100	Value: 35.00				

X# 18a.2 20 NUEVOS SOLES
23.0000 g., Brass **Subject:** XXVI Olympics - Atlanta - 1908 Olympics, London **Obv:** Small Liberty seated right with shield and staff, Phrygian cap atop **Obv. Legend:** BANCO CENTRAL DE RESERVA DEL PERU **Rev:** Boxer Albert Oldham standing right **Edge:** Plain

Date	Mintage	F	VF	XF	Unc	BU
1996 Proof	100	Value: 35.00				

X# 18b.1 20 NUEVOS SOLES
20.0000 g., Gilt Alloy, 38 mm. **Subject:** XXVI Olympics - Atlanta - 1908 Olympics, London **Obv:** Small Liberty seated right with shield and staff, Phrygian cap atop **Obv. Legend:** BANCO CENTRAL DE RESERVA DEL PERU **Rev:** Boxer Albert Oldham standing right **Edge:** Reeded

Date	Mintage	F	VF	XF	Unc	BU
1996 Proof	100	Value: 35.00				

X# 18b.2 20 NUEVOS SOLES
20.0000 g., Gilt Alloy, 38 mm. **Subject:** XXVI Olympics - Atlanta - 1908 Olympics, London **Obv:** Small Liberty seated right with shield and staff, Phrygian cap atop **Obv. Legend:** BANCO CENTRAL DE RESERVA DEL PERU **Rev:** Boxer Albert Oldham standing right **Edge:** Plain

Date	Mintage	F	VF	XF	Unc	BU
1996 Proof	100	Value: 35.00				

X# 18c.1 20 NUEVOS SOLES
23.0000 g., Tri-Metallic Silvered and gilt Brass, 38 mm. **Subject:** XXVI Olympics - Atlanta - 1908 Olympics, London **Obv:** Small Liberty seated right with shield and staff, Phrygian cap atop **Obv. Legend:** BANCO CENTRAL DE RESERVA DEL PERU **Rev:** Boxer Albert Oldham standing right **Edge:** Reeded

Date	Mintage	F	VF	XF	Unc	BU
1996 Proof	25	Value: 75.00				

X# 18c.2 20 NUEVOS SOLES
23.0000 g., Tri-Metallic Silvered and gilt Brass, 38 mm. **Subject:** XXVI Olympics - Atlanta - 1908 Olympics, London **Obv:** Small Liberty seated right with shield and staff, Phrygian cap atop **Obv. Legend:** BANCO CENTRAL DE RESERVA DEL PERU **Rev:** Boxer Albert Oldham standing right **Edge:** Plain

Date	Mintage	F	VF	XF	Unc	BU
1996 Proof	25	Value: 75.00				

X# 18d.1 20 NUEVOS SOLES
6.0000 g., Aluminum, 38 mm. **Subject:** XXVI Olympics - Atlanta - 1908 Olympics, London **Obv:** Small Liberty seated right with shield and staff, Phrygian cap atop **Obv. Legend:** BANCO CENTRAL DE RESERVA DEL PERU **Rev:** Boxer Albert Oldham standing right **Edge:** Reeded

Date	Mintage	F	VF	XF	Unc	BU
1996 Proof	100	Value: 32.00				

X# 18d.2 20 NUEVOS SOLES
6.0000 g., Aluminum, 38 mm. **Subject:** XXVI Olympics - Atlanta - 1908 Olympics, London **Obv:** Small Liberty seated right with shield and staff, Phrygian cap atop **Obv. Legend:** BANCO CENTRAL DE RESERVA DEL PERU **Rev:** Boxer Albert Oldham standing right **Edge:** Plain

Date	Mintage	F	VF	XF	Unc	BU
1996 Proof	100	Value: 32.00				

X# 18e.1 20 NUEVOS SOLES
23.0000 g., Copper, 38 mm. **Subject:** XXVI Olympics - Atlanta - 1908 Olympics, London **Obv:** Small Liberty seated right with shield and staff, Phrygian cap atop **Obv. Legend:** BANCO CENTRAL DE RESERVA DEL PERU **Rev:** Boxer Albert Oldham standing right **Edge:** Reeded

Date	Mintage	F	VF	XF	Unc	BU
1996 Proof	100	Value: 35.00				

X# 18e.2 20 NUEVOS SOLES
23.0000 g., Copper, 38 mm. **Subject:** XXVI Olympics - Atlanta - 1908 Olympics, London **Obv:** Small Liberty seated right with shield and staff, Phrygian cap atop **Obv. Legend:** BANCO CENTRAL DE RESERVA DEL PERU **Rev:** Boxer Albert Oldham standing right **Edge:** Plain

Date	Mintage	F	VF	XF	Unc	BU
1996 Proof	100	Value: 35.00				

X# 18f.1 20 NUEVOS SOLES
20.0000 g., Copper-Nickel, 38 mm. **Subject:** XXVI Olympics - Atlanta - 1908 Olympics, London **Obv:** Small Liberty seated right with shield and staff, Phrygian cap atop **Obv. Legend:** BANCO CENTRAL DE RESERVA DEL PERU **Rev:** Boxer Albert Oldham standing right **Edge:** Reeded

Date	Mintage	F	VF	XF	Unc	BU
1996 Proof	100	Value: 35.00				

X# 18f.2 20 NUEVOS SOLES
20.0000 g., Copper-Nickel, 38 mm. **Subject:** XXVI Olympics - Atlanta - 1908 Olympics, London **Obv:** Small Liberty seated right with shield and staff, Phrygian cap atop **Obv. Legend:** BANCO CENTRAL DE RESERVA DEL PERU **Rev:** Boxer Albert Oldham standing right **Edge:** Plain

Date	Mintage	F	VF	XF	Unc	BU
1996 Proof	100	Value: 35.00				

X# 19.1 20 NUEVOS SOLES
24.0000 g., 0.9250 Silver 0.7137 oz. ASW, 38 mm. **Subject:** XXVI Olympics - Atlanta - 1932 Olympics, Los Angeles **Obv:** Small Liberty seated right with shield and staff, Phrygian cap atop **Obv. Legend:** BANCO CENTRAL DE RESERVA DEL PERU **Rev:** Matti Jarvinen poised right with javelin **Edge:** Reeded

Date	Mintage	F	VF	XF	Unc	BU
1996 Proof	100	Value: 50.00				

X# 19.2 20 NUEVOS SOLES
24.0000 g., 0.9250 Silver 0.7137 oz. ASW, 38 mm. **Subject:** XXVI Olympics - Atlanta - 1932 Olympics, Los Angeles **Obv:** Small Liberty seated right with shield and staff, Phrygian cap atop **Obv. Legend:** BANCO CENTRAL DE RESERVA DEL PERU **Rev:** Matti Jarvinen poised right with javelin **Edge:** Plain

Date	Mintage	F	VF	XF	Unc	BU
1996 Proof	100	Value: 50.00				

X# 19a.1 20 NUEVOS SOLES
23.0000 g., Brass, 38 mm. **Subject:** XXVI Olympics - Atlanta - 1932 Olympics, Los Angeles **Obv:** Small Liberty seated right with shield and staff, Phrygian cap atop **Obv. Legend:** BANCO CENTRAL DE RESERVA DEL PERU **Rev:** Matti Jarvinen poised right with javelin **Edge:** Reeded

Date	Mintage	F	VF	XF	Unc	BU
1996 Proof	100	Value: 30.00				

X# 19a.2 20 NUEVOS SOLES

23.0000 g., Brass, 38 mm. **Subject:** XXVI Olympics - Atlanta, 1932 Olympics, Los Angeles **Obv:** Small Liberty seated right with shield and staff, Phrygian cap atop **Obv. Legend:** BANCO CENTRAL DE RESERVA DEL PERU **Rev:** Matti Jarvinen poised right with javelin **Edge:** Plain

Date	Mintage	F	VF	XF	Unc	BU
1996 Proof	100	Value: 30.00				

X# 19b.1 20 NUEVOS SOLES

20.0000 g., Gilt Alloy, 38 mm. **Subject:** XXVI Olympics - Atlanta - 1932 Olympics, Los Angeles **Obv:** Small Liberty seated right with shield and staff, Phrygian cap atop **Obv. Legend:** BANCO CENTRAL DE RESERVA DEL PERU **Rev:** Matti Jarvinen poised right with javelin **Edge:** Reeded

Date	Mintage	F	VF	XF	Unc	BU
1996 Proof	100	Value: 30.00				

X# 19b.2 20 NUEVOS SOLES

20.0000 g., Gilt Alloy, 38 mm. **Subject:** XXVI Olympics - Atlanta - 1932 Olympics, Los Angeles **Obv:** Small Liberty seated right with shield and staff, Phrygian cap atop **Obv. Legend:** BANCO CENTRAL DE RESERVA DEL PERU **Rev:** Matti Jarvinen poised right with javelin **Edge:** Plain

Date	Mintage	F	VF	XF	Unc	BU
1996 Proof	100	Value: 30.00				

X# 19c.1 20 NUEVOS SOLES

23.0000 g., Tri-Metallic Silvered and gilt Brass, 38 mm. **Subject:** XXVI Olympics - Atlanta - 1932 Olympics, Los Angeles **Obv:** Small Liberty seated right with shield and staff, Phrygian cap atop **Obv. Legend:** BANCO CENTRAL DE RESERVA DEL PERU **Rev:** Matti Jarvinen poised right with javelin **Edge:** Reeded

Date	Mintage	F	VF	XF	Unc	BU
1996 Proof	25	Value: 75.00				

X# 19c.2 20 NUEVOS SOLES

Tri-Metallic Silvered and gilt Brass, 38 mm. **Subject:** XXVI Olympics - Atlanta - 1932 Olympics, Los Angeles **Obv:** Small Liberty seated right with shield and staff, Phrygian cap atop **Obv. Legend:** BANCO CENTRAL DE RESERVA DEL PERU **Rev:** Matti Jarvinen poised right with javelin **Edge:** Plain

Date	Mintage	F	VF	XF	Unc	BU
1996 Proof	25	Value: 75.00				

X# 19d.1 20 NUEVOS SOLES

6.0000 g., Aluminum, 38 mm. **Subject:** XXVI Olympics - Atlanta - 1932 Olympics, Los Angeles **Obv:** Small Liberty seated right with shield and staff, Phrygian cap atop **Obv. Legend:** BANCO CENTRAL DE RESERVA DEL PERU **Rev:** Matti Jarvinen poised right with javelin **Edge:** Reeded

Date	Mintage	F	VF	XF	Unc	BU
1996 Proof	100	Value: 30.00				

X# 19d.2 20 NUEVOS SOLES

6.0000 g., Aluminum, 38 mm. **Subject:** XXVI Olympics - Atlanta - 1932 Olympics, Los Angeles **Obv:** Small Liberty seated right with shield and staff, Phrygian cap atop **Obv. Legend:** BANCO CENTRAL DE RESERVA DEL PERU **Rev:** Matti Jarvinen poised right with javelin **Edge:** Plain

Date	Mintage	F	VF	XF	Unc	BU
1996 Proof	100	Value: 30.00				

X# 19e.1 20 NUEVOS SOLES

23.0000 g., Copper, 38 mm. **Subject:** XXVI Olympics - Atlanta - 1932 Olympics, Los Angeles **Obv:** Small Liberty seated right with shield and staff, Phrygian cap atop **Obv. Legend:** BANCO CENTRAL DE RESERVA DEL PERU **Rev:** Matti Jarvinen poised right with javelin **Edge:** Reeded

Date	Mintage	F	VF	XF	Unc	BU
1996 Proof	100	Value: 30.00				

X# 19e.2 20 NUEVOS SOLES

23.0000 g., Copper, 38 mm. **Subject:** XXVI Olympics - Atlanta - 1932 Olympics, Los Angeles **Obv:** Small Liberty seated right with shield and staff, Phrygian cap atop **Obv. Legend:** BANCO CENTRAL DE RESERVA DEL PERU **Rev:** Matti Jarvinen poised right with javelin **Edge:** Plain

Date	Mintage	F	VF	XF	Unc	BU
1996 Proof	100	Value: 30.00				

X# 19f.1 20 NUEVOS SOLES

20.0000 g., Copper-Nickel, 38 mm. **Subject:** XXVI Olympics - Atlanta - 1932 Olympics, Los Angeles **Obv:** Small Liberty seated right with shield and staff, Phrygian cap atop **Obv. Legend:** BANCO CENTRAL DE RESEVA DEL PERU **Rev:** Matti Jarvinen poised right with javelin **Edge:** Reeded

Date	Mintage	F	VF	XF	Unc	BU
1996 Proof	100	Value: 30.00				

X# 19f.2 20 NUEVOS SOLES

20.0000 g., Copper-Nickel, 38 mm. **Subject:** XXVI Olympics - Atlanta - 1932 Olympics, Los Angeles **Obv:** Small Liberty seated right with shield and staff, Phrygian cap atop **Obv. Legend:** BANCO CENTRAL DE RESERVA DEL PERU **Rev:** Matti Jarvinen poised right with javelin **Edge:** Plain

Date	Mintage	F	VF	XF	Unc	BU
1996 Proof	100	Value: 30.00				

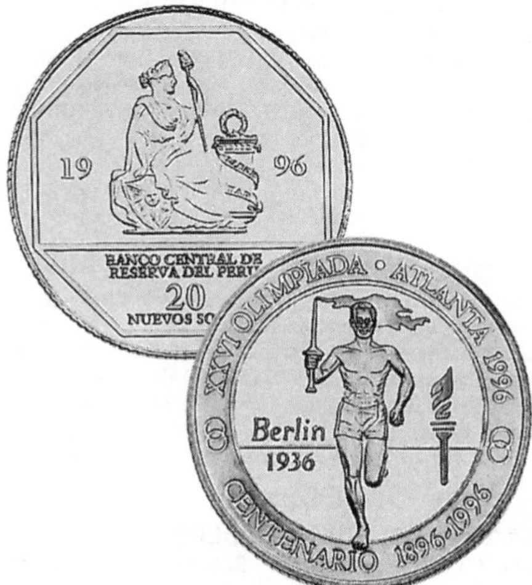

X# 20.1 20 NUEVOS SOLES

24.0000 g., 0.9250 Silver 0.7137 oz. ASW, 38 mm. **Subject:** XXVI Olympics - Atlanta - 1936 Olympics, Berlin **Obv:** Small Liberty seated right with shield and staff, Phrygian cap atop **Obv. Legend:** BANCO CENTRAL DE RESERVA DEL PERU **Rev:** Torchbearer running, facing **Edge:** Reeded

Date	Mintage	F	VF	XF	Unc	BU
1996 Proof	100	Value: 50.00				

X# 20.2 20 NUEVOS SOLES

24.0000 g., 0.9250 Silver 0.7137 oz. ASW, 38 mm. **Subject:** XXVI Olympics - Atlanta - 1936 Olympics, Berlin **Obv:** Small Liberty seated right with shield and staff, Phrygian cap atop **Obv. Legend:** BANCO CENTRAL DE RESERVA DEL PERU **Rev:** Torchbearer running, facing **Edge:** Plain

Date	Mintage	F	VF	XF	Unc	BU
1996 Proof	100	Value: 50.00				

X# 20a.1 20 NUEVOS SOLES

23.0000 g., Brass, 38 mm. **Subject:** XXVI Olympics - Atlanta - 1936 Olympics, Berlin **Obv:** Small Liberty seated right with shield and staff, Phrygian cap atop **Obv. Legend:** BANCO CENTRAL DE RESERVA DEL PERU **Rev:** Torchbearer running, facing **Edge:** Reeded

Date	Mintage	F	VF	XF	Unc	BU
1996 Proof	100	Value: 30.00				

X# 20a.2 20 NUEVOS SOLES

23.0000 g., Brass, 38 mm. **Subject:** XXVI Olympics - Atlanta - 1936 Olympics, Berlin **Obv:** Small Liberty seated right with shield and staff, Phrygian cap atop **Obv. Legend:** BANCO CENTRAL DE RESERVA DEL PERU **Rev:** Torchbearer running, facing **Edge:** Plain

Date	Mintage	F	VF	XF	Unc	BU
1996 Proof	100	Value: 30.00				

X# 20b.1 20 NUEVOS SOLES

20.0000 g., Gilt Alloy, 38 mm. **Subject:** XXVI Olympics - Atlanta - 1936 Olympics, Berlin **Obv:** Small Liberty seated right with shield and staff, Phrygian cap atop **Obv. Legend:** BANCO CENTRAL DE RESERVA DEL PERU **Rev:** Torchbearer running, facing **Edge:** Reeded

Date	Mintage	F	VF	XF	Unc	BU
1996 Proof	100	Value: 30.00				

X# 20b.2 20 NUEVOS SOLES

20.0000 g., Gilt Alloy, 38 mm. **Subject:** XXVI Olympics - Atlanta - 1936 Olympics, Berlin **Obv:** Small Liberty seated right with shield and staff, Phrygian cap atop **Obv. Legend:** BANCO CENTRAL DE RESERVA DEL PERU **Rev:** Torchbearer running, facing **Edge:** Plain

Date	Mintage	F	VF	XF	Unc	BU
1996 Proof	100	Value: 30.00				

X# 20c.1 20 NUEVOS SOLES

Tri-Metallic Silvered and gilt Brass, 38 mm. **Subject:** XXVI Olympics - Atlanta - 1936 Olympics, Berlin **Obv:** Small Liberty seated right with shield and staff, Phrygian cap atop **Obv. Legend:** BANCO CENTRAL DE RESERVA DEL PERU **Rev:** Torchbearer running, facing **Edge:** Reeded

Date	Mintage	F	VF	XF	Unc	BU
1996 Proof	25	Value: 75.00				

X# 20c.2 20 NUEVOS SOLES

Tri-Metallic Silvered and gilt Brass, 38 mm. **Subject:** XXVI Olympics - Atlanta - 1936 Olympics, Berlin **Obv:** Small Liberty seated right with shield and staff, Phrygian cap atop **Obv. Legend:** BANCO CENTRAL DE RESERVA DEL PERU **Rev:** Torchbearer running, facing **Edge:** Plain

Date	Mintage	F	VF	XF	Unc	BU
1996 Proof	25	Value: 75.00				

X# 20d.1 20 NUEVOS SOLES

6.0000 g., Aluminum, 38 mm. **Subject:** XXVI Olympics - Atlanta - 1936 Olympics, Berlin **Obv:** Small Liberty seated right with shield and staff, Phrygian cap atop **Obv. Legend:** BANCO CENTRAL DE RESERVA DEL PERU **Rev:** Torchbearer running, facing **Edge:** Reeded

Date	Mintage	F	VF	XF	Unc	BU
1996 Proof	100	Value: 30.00				

X# 20d.2 20 NUEVOS SOLES

6.0000 g., Aluminum, 38 mm. **Subject:** XXVI Olympics - Atlanta - 1936 Olympics, Berlin **Obv:** Small Liberty seated right with shield and staff, Phrygian cap atop **Obv. Legend:** BANCO CENTRAL DE RESERVA DEL PERU **Rev:** Torchbearer running, facing **Edge:** Plain

Date	Mintage	F	VF	XF	Unc	BU
1996 Proof	100	Value: 30.00				

X# 20e.1 20 NUEVOS SOLES

23.0000 g., Copper, 38 mm. **Subject:** XXVI Olympics - Atlanta - 1936 Olympics, Berlin **Obv:** Small Liberty seated right with shield and staff, Phrygian cap atop **Obv. Legend:** BANCO CENTRAL DE RESERVA DEL PERU **Rev:** Torchbearer running, facing **Edge:** Reeded

Date	Mintage	F	VF	XF	Unc	BU
1996 Proof	100	Value: 30.00				

X# 20e.2 20 NUEVOS SOLES

23.0000 g., Copper, 38 mm. **Subject:** XXVI Olympics - Atlanta - 1936 Olympics, Berlin **Obv:** Small Liberty seated right with shield and staff, Phrygian cap atop **Obv. Legend:** BANCO CENTRAL DE RESERVA DEL PERU **Rev:** Torchbearer running, facing **Edge:** Plain

Date	Mintage	F	VF	XF	Unc	BU
1996 Proof	100	Value: 30.00				

X# 20f.1 20 NUEVOS SOLES

20.0000 g., Copper-Nickel, 38 mm. **Subject:** XXVI Olympics - Atlanta - 1936 Olympics, Berlin **Obv:** Small Liberty seated right with shield and staff, Phrygian cap atop **Obv. Legend:** BANCO CENTRAL DE RESERVA DEL PERU **Rev:** Torchbearer running, facing **Edge:** Reeded

Date	Mintage	F	VF	XF	Unc	BU
1996 Proof	100	Value: 30.00				

X# 20f.2 20 NUEVOS SOLES
20.0000 g., Copper-Nickel, 38 mm. **Subject:** XXVI Olympics - Atlanta - 1936 Olympics, Berlin **Obv:** Small Liberty seated right with shield and staff, Phrygian cap atop **Obv. Legend:** BANCO CENTRAL DE RESERVA DEL PERU **Rev:** Torchbearer running, facing **Edge:** Plain

Date	Mintage	F	VF	XF	Unc	BU
1996 Proof	100	Value: 30.00				

X# 21.1 20 NUEVOS SOLES
24.0000 g., 0.9250 Silver 0.7137 oz. ASW, 38 mm. **Subject:** XXVI Olympics - Atlanta - 1968 Olympics, Mexico City **Obv:** Small Liberty seated right with shield and staff, Phrygian cap atop **Obv. Legend:** BANCO CENTRAL DE RESERVA DEL PERU **Rev:** Sprinter Tommie Smith running right **Edge:** Reeded

Date	Mintage	F	VF	XF	Unc	BU
1996 Proof	100	Value: 50.00				

X# 21.2 20 NUEVOS SOLES
24.0000 g., 0.9250 Silver 0.7137 oz. ASW, 38 mm. **Subject:** XXVI Olympics - Atlanta - 1968 Olympics, Mexico City **Obv:** Small Liberty seated right with shield and staff, Phrygian cap atop **Obv. Legend:** BANCO CENTRAL DE RESERVA DEL PERU **Rev:** Sprinter Tommie Smith running right **Edge:** Reeded

Date	Mintage	F	VF	XF	Unc	BU
1996 Proof	100	Value: 50.00				

X# 21a.1 20 NUEVOS SOLES
23.0000 g., Brass, 38 mm. **Subject:** XXVI Olympics - Atlanta - 1968 Olympics, Mexico City **Obv:** Small Liberty seated right with shield and staff, Phrygian cap atop **Obv. Legend:** BANCO CENTRAL DE RESERVA DEL PERU **Rev:** Sprinter Tommie Smith running right **Edge:** Reeded

Date	Mintage	F	VF	XF	Unc	BU
1996 Proof	100	Value: 30.00				

X# 21a.2 20 NUEVOS SOLES
23.0000 g., Brass, 38 mm. **Subject:** XXVI Olympics - Atlanta - 1968 Olympics, Mexico City **Obv:** Small Liberty seated right with shield and staff, Phrygian cap atop **Obv. Legend:** BANCO CENTRAL DE RESERVA DEL PERU **Rev:** Sprinter Tommie Smith running right **Edge:** Plain

Date	Mintage	F	VF	XF	Unc	BU
1996 Proof	100	Value: 30.00				

X# 21b.1 20 NUEVOS SOLES
20.0000 g., Gilt Alloy, 38 mm. **Subject:** XXVI Olympics - Atlanta - 1968 Olympics, Mexico City **Obv:** Small Liberty seated right with shield and staff, Phrygian cap atop **Obv. Legend:** BANCO CENTRAL DE RESERVA DEL PERU **Rev:** Sprinter Tommie Smith running right **Edge:** Reeded

Date	Mintage	F	VF	XF	Unc	BU
1996 Plain	100	Value: 30.00				

X# 21b.2 20 NUEVOS SOLES
20.0000 g., Gilt Alloy, 38 mm. **Subject:** XXVI Olympics - Atlanta - 1968 Olympics, Mexico City **Obv:** Small Liberty seated right with shield and staff, Phrygian cap atop **Obv. Legend:** BANCO CENTRAL DE RESERVA DEL PERU **Rev:** Sprinter Tommie Smith running right **Edge:** Plain

Date	Mintage	F	VF	XF	Unc	BU
1996 Proof	100	Value: 30.00				

X# 21c.1 20 NUEVOS SOLES
23.0000 g., Tri-Metallic Silvered and gilt Brass, 38 mm. **Subject:** XXVI Olympics - Atlanta - 1968 Olympics, Mexico City **Obv:** Small Liberty seated right with shield and staff, Phrygian cap atop **Obv. Legend:** BANCO CENTRAL DE RESERVA DEL PERU **Rev:** Sprinter Tommie Smith running right **Edge:** Reeded

Date	Mintage	F	VF	XF	Unc	BU
1996 Proof	25	Value: 75.00				

X# 21c.2 20 NUEVOS SOLES
23.0000 g., Tri-Metallic Silvered and gilt Brass, 38 mm. **Subject:** XXVI Olympics - Atlanta - 1968 Olympics, Mexico City **Obv:** Small Liberty seated right with shield and staff, Phrygian cap atop **Obv. Legend:** BANCO CENTRAL DE RESERVA DEL PERU **Rev:** Sprinter Tommie Smith running right **Edge:** Plain

Date	Mintage	F	VF	XF	Unc	BU
1996 Proof	25	Value: 75.00				

X# 21d.1 20 NUEVOS SOLES
6.0000 g., Aluminum, 38 mm. **Subject:** XXVI Olympics - Atlanta - 1968 Olympics, Mexico City **Obv:** Small Liberty seated right with shield and staff, Phrygian cap atop **Obv. Legend:** BANCO CENTRAL DE RESERVA DEL PERU **Rev:** Sprinter Tommie Smith running right **Edge:** Reeded

Date	Mintage	F	VF	XF	Unc	BU
1996 Proof	100	Value: 30.00				

X# 21d.2 20 NUEVOS SOLES
6.0000 g., Aluminum, 38 mm. **Subject:** XXVI Olympics - Atlanta - 1968 Olympics, Mexico City **Obv:** Small Liberty seated right with shield and staff, Phrygian cap atop **Obv. Legend:** BANCO CENTRAL DE RESERVA DEL PERU **Rev:** Sprinter Tommie Smith running right **Edge:** Plain

Date	Mintage	F	VF	XF	Unc	BU
1996 Proof	100	Value: 30.00				

X# 21e.1 20 NUEVOS SOLES
23.0000 g., Copper, 38 mm. **Subject:** XXVI Olympics - Atlanta - 1968 Olympics, Mexico City **Obv:** Small Liberty seated right with shield and staff, Phrygian cap atop **Obv. Legend:** BANCO CENTRAL DE RESERVA DEL PERU **Rev:** Sprinter Tommie Smith running right **Edge:** Reeded

Date	Mintage	F	VF	XF	Unc	BU
1996 Proof	100	Value: 30.00				

X# 21e.2 20 NUEVOS SOLES
23.0000 g., Copper, 38 mm. **Subject:** XXVI Olympics - Atlanta - 1968 Olympics, Mexico City **Obv:** Small Liberty seated right with shield and staff, Phrygian cap atop **Obv. Legend:** BANCO CENTRAL DE RESERVA DEL PERU **Rev:** Sprinter Tommie Smith running right **Edge:** Plain

Date	Mintage	F	VF	XF	Unc	BU
1996 Proof	100	Value: 30.00				

X# 21f.1 20 NUEVOS SOLES
20.0000 g., Copper-Nickel, 38 mm. **Subject:** XXVI Olympics - Atlanta - 1968 Olympics, Mexico City **Obv:** Small Liberty seated right with shield and staff, Phrygian cap atop **Obv. Legend:** BANCO CENTRAL DE RESERVA DEL PERU **Rev:** Sprinter Tommie Smith running right **Edge:** Reeded

Date	Mintage	F	VF	XF	Unc	BU
1996 Proof	100	Value: 30.00				

X# 21f.2 20 NUEVOS SOLES
20.0000 g., Copper-Nickel, 38 mm. **Subject:** XXVI Olympics - Atlanta - 1968 Olympics, Mexico City **Obv:** Small Liberty seated right with shield and staff, Phrygian cap atop **Obv. Legend:** BANCO CENTRAL DE RESERVA DEL PERU **Rev:** Sprinter Tommie Smith running right **Edge:** Plain

Date	Mintage	F	VF	XF	Unc	BU
1996 Proof	100	Value: 30.00				

X# 22.1 20 NUEVOS SOLES
24.0000 g., 0.9250 Silver 0.7137 oz. ASW, 38 mm. **Subject:** XXVI Olympics - Atlanta - 1988 Olympics, Seoul **Obv:** Small Liberty seated right with shield and staff, Phrygian cap atop **Obv. Legend:** BANCO CENTRAL DE RESERVA DEL PERU **Rev:** Pole vaulter Sergei Bubka ascending **Edge:** Reeded

Date	Mintage	F	VF	XF	Unc	BU
1996 Proof	100	Value: 50.00				

X# 22.2 20 NUEVOS SOLES
24.0000 g., 0.9250 Silver 0.7137 oz. ASW, 38 mm. **Subject:** XXVI Olympics - Atlanta - 1988 Olympics, Seoul **Obv:** Small Liberty seated right with shield and staff, Phrygian cap atop **Obv. Legend:** BANCO CENTRAL DE RESERVA DEL PERU **Rev:** Pole vaulter Sergei Bubka ascending **Edge:** Plain

Date	Mintage	F	VF	XF	Unc	BU
1996 Proof	100	Value: 50.00				

X# 22a.1 20 NUEVOS SOLES
23.0000 g., Brass, 38 mm. **Subject:** XXVI Olympics - Atlanta - 1988 Olympics, Seoul **Obv:** Small Liberty seated right with shield and staff, Phrygian cap atop **Obv. Legend:** BANCO CENTRAL DE RESERVA DEL PERU **Rev:** Pole vaulter Sergei Bubka ascending **Edge:** Reeded

Date	Mintage	F	VF	XF	Unc	BU
1996 Proof	100	Value: 30.00				

X# 22a.2 20 NUEVOS SOLES
23.0000 g., Brass, 38 mm. **Subject:** XXVI Olympics - Atlanta - 1988 Olympics, Seoul **Obv:** Small Liberty seated right with shield and staff, Phrygian cap atop **Obv. Legend:** BANCO CENTRAL DE RESERVA DEL PERU **Rev:** Pole vaulter Sergei Bubka ascending **Edge:** Plain

Date	Mintage	F	VF	XF	Unc	BU
1996 Proof	100	Value: 30.00				

X# 22b.1 20 NUEVOS SOLES
20.0000 g., Gilt Alloy, 38 mm. **Subject:** XXVI Olympics - Atlanta - 1988 Olympics, Seoul **Obv:** Small Liberty seated right with shield and staff, Phrygian cap atop **Obv. Legend:** BANCO CENTRAL DE RESERVA DEL PERU **Rev:** Pole vaulter Sergei Bubka ascending **Edge:** Reeded

Date	Mintage	F	VF	XF	Unc	BU
1996 Proof	100	Value: 30.00				

X# 22b.2 20 NUEVOS SOLES
20.0000 g., Gilt Alloy, 38 mm. **Subject:** XXVI Olympics - Atlanta - 1988 Olympics, Seoul **Obv:** Small Liberty seated right with shield and staff, Phrygian cap atop **Obv. Legend:** BANCO CENTRAL DE RESERVA DEL PERU **Rev:** Pole vaulter Sergei Bubka ascending **Edge:** Plain

Date	Mintage	F	VF	XF	Unc	BU
1996 Proof	100	Value: 30.00				

X# 22c.1 20 NUEVOS SOLES
Tri-Metallic Silvered and gilt Brass, 38 mm. **Subject:** XXVI Olympics - Atlanta - 1988 Olympics, Seoul **Obv:** Small Liberty seated right with shield and staff, Phrygian cap atop **Obv. Legend:** BANCO CENTRAL DE RESERVA DEL PERU **Rev:** Pole vaulter Sergei Bubka ascending **Edge:** Reeded

Date	Mintage	F	VF	XF	Unc	BU
1996 Proof	25	Value: 75.00				

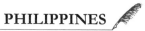

X# 22c.2 20 NUEVOS SOLES
Tri-Metallic Silvered and gilt Brass, 38 mm.
Subject: XXVI Olympics - Atlanta - 1988 Olympics, Seoul **Obv:** Small Liberty seated right with shield and staff, Phrygian cap atop **Obv. Legend:** BANCO CENTRAL DE RESERVA DEL PERU **Rev:** Pole vaulter Sergei Bubka ascending **Edge:** Plain

Date	Mintage	F	VF	XF	Unc	BU
1996 Proof	25	Value: 75.00				

X# 22d.1 20 NUEVOS SOLES
6.0000 g., Aluminum, 38 mm. **Subject:** XXVI Olympics - Atlanta - 1988 Olympics, Seoul **Obv:** Small Liberty seated right with shield and staff, Phrygian cap atop **Obv. Legend:** BANCO CENTRAL DE RESERVA DEL PERU **Rev:** Pole vaulter Sergei Bubka ascending **Edge:** Reeded

Date	Mintage	F	VF	XF	Unc	BU
1996 Proof	100	Value: 30.00				

X# 22d.2 20 NUEVOS SOLES
6.0000 g., Aluminum, 38 mm. **Subject:** XXVI Olympics - Atlanta - 1988 Olympics, Seoul **Obv:** Small Liberty seated right with shield and staff, Phrygian cap atop **Obv. Legend:** BANCO CENTRAL DE RESERVA DEL PERU **Rev:** Pole vaulter Sergei Bubka ascending **Edge:** Plain

Date	Mintage	F	VF	XF	Unc	BU
1996 Proof	100	Value: 30.00				

X# 22e.1 20 NUEVOS SOLES
23.0000 g., Copper, 38 mm. **Subject:** XXVI Olympics - Atlanta - 1988 Olympics, Seoul **Obv:** Small Liberty seated right with shield and staff, Phrygian cap atop **Obv. Legend:** BANCO CENTRAL DE RESERVA DEL PERU **Rev:** Pole vaulter Sergei Bubka ascending **Edge:** Reeded

Date	Mintage	F	VF	XF	Unc	BU
1996 Proof	100	Value: 30.00				

X# 22e.2 20 NUEVOS SOLES
Copper, 38 mm. **Subject:** XXVI Olympics - Atlanta - 1988 Olympics, Seoul **Obv:** Small Liberty seated right with shield and staff, Phrygian cap atop **Obv. Legend:** BANCO CENTRAL DE RESERVA DEL PERU **Rev:** Pole vaulter Sergei Bubka ascending **Edge:** Plain

Date	Mintage	F	VF	XF	Unc	BU
1996 Proof	100	Value: 30.00				

X# 22f.1 20 NUEVOS SOLES
Copper-Nickel, 38 mm. **Subject:** XXVI Olympics - Atlanta - 1988 Olympics, Seoul **Obv:** Small Liberty seated right with shield and staff, Phrygian cap atop **Obv. Legend:** BANCO CENTRAL DE RESERVA DEL PERU **Rev:** Pole vaulter Sergei Bubka ascending **Edge:** Reeded

Date	Mintage	F	VF	XF	Unc	BU
1996 Proof	100	Value: 30.00				

X# 22f.2 20 NUEVOS SOLES
Copper-Nickel, 38 mm. **Subject:** XXVI Olympics - Atlanta - 1988 Olympics, Seoul **Obv:** Small Liberty seated right with shield and staff, Phrygian cap atop **Obv. Legend:** BANCO CENTRAL DE RESERVA DEL PERU **Rev:** Pole vaulter Sergei Bubka ascending **Edge:** Plain

Date	Mintage	F	VF	XF	Unc	BU
1996 Proof	100	Value: 30.00				

PATTERNS

Including off metal strikes

X#	Date	Mintage	Identification	Mkt Val
Pn1	1996	—	20 Nuevos Soles. 0.9250 Silver. 24.0000 g. Reeded edge.	50.00
Pn2	1996	—	20 Nuevos Soles. 0.9250 Silver. 24.0000 g. Plain edge.	50.00
Pn3	1996	—	20 Nuevos Soles. Brass. 23.0000 g. Reeded edge.	30.00
Pn4	1996	—	20 Nuevos Soles. Brass. 23.0000 g. Plain edge.	30.00
Pn5	1996	—	20 Nuevos Soles. Gilt Alloy. 20.0000 g. Reeded edge.	30.00
Pn6	1996	—	20 Nuevos Soles. Gilt Alloy. 20.0000 g. Plain edge.	30.00
Pn7	1996	—	20 Nuevos Soles. Tri-Metallic. 23.0000 g. Reeded edge.	50.00
Pn8	1996	—	20 Nuevos Soles. Tri-Metallic. 23.0000 g. Plain edge.	50.00
Pn9	1996	—	20 Nuevos Soles. Aluminum. 6.0000 g. Reeded edge.	30.00
Pn10	1996	—	20 Nuevos Soles. Aluminum. 6.0000 g. Plain edge.	30.00
Pn11	1996	—	20 Nuevos Soles. Copper. 23.0000 g. Reeded edge.	30.00
Pn12	1996	—	20 Nuevos Soles. Copper. 23.0000 g. Plain edge.	30.00
Pn13	1996	—	20 Nuevos Soles. Copper-Nickel. 20.0000 g. Reeded edge.	30.00
Pn14	1996	—	20 Nuevos Soles. Copper-Nickel. 20.0000 g. Plain edge.	30.00
Pn15	1996	100	20 Nuevos Soles. 0.9250 Silver. 24.0000 g. Reeded edge.	50.00
Pn16	1996	—	20 Nuevos Soles. 0.9250 Silver. 24.0000 g. Plain edge.	50.00
Pn17	1996	—	20 Nuevos Soles. Brass. 23.0000 g. Reeded edge.	30.00
Pn18	1996	—	20 Nuevos Soles. Brass. 23.0000 g. Plain edge.	30.00
Pn19	1996	—	20 Nuevos Soles. Gilt Alloy. 20.0000 g. Reeded edge.	30.00
Pn20	1996	—	20 Nuevos Soles. Gilt Alloy. 20.0000 g. Plain edge.	30.00
Pn21	1996	—	20 Nuevos Soles. Tri-Metallic. 23.0000 g. Reeded edge.	50.00
Pn22	1996	—	20 Nuevos Soles. Tri-Metallic. 23.0000 g. Plain edge.	50.00
Pn23	1996	—	20 Nuevos Soles. Aluminum. 6.0000 g.	30.00
Pn24	1996	—	20 Nuevos Soles. Aluminum. 6.0000 g. Plain edge.	30.00
Pn25	1996	—	20 Nuevos Soles. Copper. 23.0000 g. Reeded edge.	30.00
Pn26	1996	—	20 Nuevos Soles. Copper. 23.0000 g. Plain edge.	30.00
Pn27	1996	—	20 Nuevos Soles. Copper-Nickel. 20.0000 g. Reeded edge.	30.00
Pn28	1996	—	20 Nuevos Soles. Copper-Nickel. 20.0000 g. Plain edge.	30.00

PIEFORTS

X#	Date	Mintage	Identification	Mkt Val
P1	1996	—	20 Nuevos Soles. 0.9250 Silver. 48.0000 g. X11.1.	120
P2	1996	—	20 Nuevos Soles. 0.9250 Silver. 48.0000 g. X11.2.	120
P3	1996	—	20 Nuevos Soles. 0.9250 Silver. 48.0000 g. X12.1.	120
P4	1996	—	20 Nuevos Soles. 0.9250 Silver. 48.0000 g. X12.2.	120
P5	1996	—	20 Nuevos Soles. 0.9250 Silver. 48.0000 g. X13.1.	120
P6	1996	—	20 Nuevos Soles. 0.9250 Silver. 48.0000 g. X13.2.	120
P7	1996	—	20 Nuevos Soles. 0.9250 Silver. 48.0000 g. X14.1.	120
P8	1996	—	20 Nuevos Soles. 0.9250 Silver. 48.0000 g. X14.2.	120
P9	1996	—	20 Nuevos Soles. 0.9250 Silver. 48.0000 g. X15.1.	120
P10	1996	—	20 Nuevos Soles. 0.9250 Silver. 48.0000 g. X15.2.	120
P11	1996	—	20 Nuevos Soles. 0.9250 Silver. 48.0000 g. X16.1.	120
P12	1996	—	20 Nuevos Soles. 0.9250 Silver. 48.0000 g. X16.2.	120
P13	1996	—	20 Nuevos Soles. 0.9250 Silver. 48.0000 g. X17.1.	125
P14	1996	—	20 Nuevos Soles. 0.9250 Silver. 48.0000 g. X17.2.	125
P15	1996	—	20 Nuevos Soles. 0.9250 Silver. 48.0000 g. X18.1.	125
P16	1996	—	20 Nuevos Soles. 0.9250 Silver. 48.0000 g. X18.2.	125
P17	1996	—	20 Nuevos Soles. 0.9250 Silver. 48.0000 g. X19.1.	125
P18	1996	—	20 Nuevos Soles. 0.9250 Silver. 48.0000 g. X19.2.	125
P19	1996	—	20 Nuevos Soles. 0.9250 Silver. 48.0000 g. X20.1.	125
P20	1996	—	20 Nuevos Soles. 0.9250 Silver. 48.0000 g. X20.2.	125
P22	1996	—	20 Nuevos Soles. 0.9250 Silver. 48.0000 g. X21.2.	125
P23	1996	—	20 Nuevos Soles. 0.9250 Silver. 48.0000 g. X22.1.	125
P24	1996	—	20 Nuevos Soles. 0.9250 Silver. 48.0000 g. X22.2.	125
P25	1996	—	20 Nuevos Soles. 0.9250 Silver. 48.0000 g. XPn1.	75.00
P26	1996	—	20 Nuevos Soles. 0.9250 Silver. 48.0000 g. XPn2.	75.00
P27	1996	—	20 Nuevos Soles. 0.9250 Silver. 48.0000 g. XPn15.	75.00
P28	1996	—	20 Nuevos Soles. 0.9250 Silver. 48.0000 g. XPn16.	75.00

CHINCHA ISLANDS

REPUBLIC

LOCAL COINAGE

X# 1 20 CENTAVOS
Copper **Obv:** 5-pointed star with ornaments below **Rev:** Large 20, value **Note:** Prev. KY#41.

Date	Mintage	F	VF	XF	Unc	BU
1889 Proof	—	Value: 125				

PHILIPPINES

SPANISH COLONY

ESSAIS

X# Pn3 20 REAUX
Copper **Note:** Prev. KM#Pn5. Struck at the Paris Mint.

Date	Mintage	F	VF	XF	Unc	BU
1859 Paris Proof	—	Value: 1,000				

X# Pn4 40 REAUX
Copper **Note:** Prev. KM#Pn6. Struck at the Paris Mint.

Date	Mintage	F	VF	XF	Unc	BU
1859 Paris Proof	—	Value: 1,400				

X# Pn5 80 REAUX
Copper **Note:** Prev. KM#Pn7. Struck at the Paris Mint.

Date	Mintage	F	VF	XF	Unc	BU
1859 Paris Proof	—	Value: 800				

TOKEN COINAGE

X# Tn1 2 DOLLARS
1.8500 g., Gold, 15 mm.

Date	Mintage	F	VF	XF	Unc	BU
1946	—	—	—	125	250	—

PATTERNS

Struck in Paris, France

X# Pn1 2 CENTAVOS

Copper

Date	Mintage	F	VF	XF	Unc	BU
1859	—	—	—	300	450	—

Note: Prev. KM#Pn4

Date	Mintage	
1859 Proof	—	Value: 600

Note: Prev. KM#Pn4a

X# Pn2 5 PESETAS

25.3500 g., Silver **Subject:** Isabel II **Note:** Prev. KM#Pn1.

Date	Mintage	
1855 Proof	—	Value: 15,000

COMMONWEALTH

MEDALLIC COINAGE

X# 11 DOLLAR

Silver, 38 mm. **Subject:** Opening of the Manila Mint **Obv:** Bust of President Wilson left **Obv. Legend:** PRESIDENT OF THE UNITED STATES **Obv. Designer:** Clifford Hewitt **Rev:** Justice kneeling left, cherub in front **Rev. Legend:** TO COMMEMORATE THE OPENING OF THE MINT **Edge:** Plain

Date	Mintage	F	VF	XF	Unc	BU
1920	2,200	—	200	250	500	825

Note: Many pieces were dumped into Manila Bay just prior to the Japanese Occupation

X# 11a DOLLAR

Bronze, 38 mm. **Subject:** Opening of the Manila Mint **Obv:** Bust of President Wilson left **Obv. Legend:** PRESIDENT OF THE UNITED STATES **Obv. Designer:** Clifford Hewitt **Rev:** Justice kneeling left, cherub in front **Rev. Legend:** TO COMMEMORATE THE OPENING OF THE MINT **Edge:** Plain

Date	Mintage	F	VF	XF	Unc	BU
1920	3,700	—	—	175	500	1,800

Note: Many pieces were dumped into Manila Bay just prior to the Japanese Occupation. Sea salvaged pieces are available at $15.00.

X# 11b DOLLAR

Gold, 38 mm. **Subject:** Opening of the Manila Mint **Obv:** Bust of President Wilson left **Obv. Legend:** PRESIDENT OF THE UNITED STATES **Obv. Designer:** Clifford Hewitt **Rev:** Justice kneeling left, cherub in front **Rev. Legend:** TO COMMEMORATE THE OPENING OF THE MINT **Edge:** Plain

Date	Mintage	F	VF	XF	Unc	BU
1920	8	—	—	12,500	20,000	27,500

REPUBLIC

PRETENDER COINAGE

Charles VII of Spain

X# PT1 5 PESETAS

Copper **Obv:** Laureated head of Charles right, date below **Rev:** Value in branches **Note:** Prev. KM#PT1.

Date	Mintage	F	VF	XF	Unc	BU
1874(b) Unique; Proof	—	—	—	—	—	—

TRIAL STRIKES

X#	Date	Mintage	Identification	Issue Price	Mkt Val
TS1	1874(b)	—	5 Pesetas. Bronze. Prev. KM#TS7. Reverse of XPT1.	—	—

POLAND

KINGDOM

FANTASY COINAGE

X# 1 THALER

Silver **Note:** A fantasy thaler "originally" struck in 1836 and later restruck.

Date	Mintage	F	VF	XF	Unc	BU
1547	—	—	200	300	—	—
1547 Restrike	—	—	25.00	40.00	—	—

X# 3 8 ZLOTYCH

Silver **Ruler:** Sigismund I **Obv:** Crowned bust of Sigismund right **Obv. Legend:** SIGISMVNDVS • RRIM • REX • POLONIE **Rev:** Crowned arms surrounded by four shields **Rev. Legend:** * DEVS • IN • VIRTVTE • TVA • LETABITVR REX **Note:** Fantasy similar to a 6 groschen of the period.

Date	Mintage	F	VF	XF	Unc	BU
15Z9	—	—	100	175	—	—

MEDALLIC COINAGE

X# M1 THALER (Gedenktaler)

Silver **Ruler:** Sigismund III **Obv:** Crowned monogram STR within wreath **Rev:** Date within wreath **Note:** Dav. #4317.

Date	Mintage	F	VF	XF	Unc	BU
1623 Rare	—	—	—	—	—	—
1625 Rare	—	—	—	—	—	—
1626 Rare	—	—	—	—	—	—
1627 Rare	—	—	—	—	—	—
1628 Rare	—	—	—	—	—	—

X# M2 THALER (Gedenktaler)

Silver **Ruler:** Sigismund III **Rev:** Five crowned shields in cruciform patterm **Note:** Dav. #4318.

Date	Mintage	F	VF	XF	Unc	BU
1628 Rare	—	—	—	—	—	—
1629 Rare	—	—	—	—	—	—

X# M3 THALER (Gedenktaler)

Silver **Ruler:** Sigismund III **Obv:** Angels on both sides of crowned monogram **Rev:** Five shields, lions on both sides of central shield **Note:** Dav. #4319.

Date	Mintage	F	VF	XF	Unc	BU
1630 Rare	—	—	—	—	—	—

X# M5 2 DUCAT

7.0000 g., Gold **Ruler:** Johann III Sobieski **Obv:** Laureate bust right **Obv. Legend:** IOAN•III D.G.REX.POL•M:D:LIT•R•PR• **Rev:** Sun above crowed eagle in flight **Rev. Legend:** SIO MVNITA TVBIOR

Date	Mintage	F	VF	XF	Unc	BU
ND(1674)	—	—	—	—	—	—

X# M4 2 DUCAT

Gold, 23 mm. **Obv:** Bust of Princess Isabelle right **Obv. Legend:** ISABELEA.PRINCEPS. CZARTORYSKA. **Rev:** Crowned and mantled arms **Rev. Legend:** NAT:COM:DE.FLEMING.DOMINA.IN BORKLO. **Note:** Polish patriot.

Date	Mintage	F	VF	XF	Unc	BU
1772	—	—	475	600	—	—

REPUBLIC

MEDALLIC COINAGE

X# M10 GROSZ

1.5000 g., Bronze **Subject:** Mint Dedication **Rev:** 21.V below GROSZ

Date	Mintage	F	VF	XF	Unc	BU
1925(w)	1,000	1.75	3.50	6.00	12.00	—

X# M7 GROSZ

Bronze **Rev:** 21.V below GROSZ **Note:** Prev. KM#M1.

Date	Mintage	F	VF	XF	Unc	BU
1925(w)	1,000	2.50	5.00	10.00	20.00	—

X# M11 2 GROSZE

2.0000 g., Bronze **Subject:** Visit of President I Moscickiego **Rev:** 27/x IM26 below GROSZE

Date	Mintage	F	VF	XF	Unc	BU
1926(w)	600	5.00	8.00	13.50	27.50	—

X# M8 2 GROSZE

Bronze **Rev:** 27 x 26 below GROSZE **Note:** Prev. KM#M2.

Date	Mintage	F	VF	XF	Unc	BU
1926(w)	600	6.00	10.00	20.00	40.00	—

X# M12 5 GROSZY

3.5000 g., Brass **Subject:** Visit of President St. Wojciechowski **Rev:** 12/IV SW 24 below GROSZY

Date	Mintage	F	VF	XF	Unc	BU
1923	500	3.00	6.00	10.00	20.00	—

X# M6 5 GROSZY

Brass **Rev:** 12/IV SW 24 below GROSZY **Note:** Prev. KM#M3.

Date	Mintage	F	VF	XF	Unc	BU
1923(w)	500	5.00	8.50	17.50	35.00	—

X# M9 5 GROSZY

Bronze **Subject:** 2nd Polish Numismatic and Medallographic Society Conference at Posen on June 3, 1929 **Note:** 98 pieces were officially destroyed.

Date	Mintage	F	VF	XF	Unc	BU
1929(w)	Est. 200	40.00	60.00	100	175	—

X# M13 5 GROSZY

Brass **Subject:** 2nd Polish Numismatic and Medallographic Society Meeting at Posen on June 3, 1929

Date	Mintage	F	VF	XF	Unc	BU
1929(w)	45	50.00	75.00	120	200	—

X# M14 5 ZLOTYCH

25.0000 g., Silver **Obv:** SW and WG monograms and 3/V **Rev:** 100 pears in circle

Date	Mintage	F	VF	XF	Unc	BU
1925	100	250	450	800	1,250	—

X# M14a 5 ZLOTYCH

Gold

Date	Mintage	F	VF	XF	Unc	BU
1925 Rare	2	—	—	—	—	—

WWII GERMAN OCCUPATION

FANTASY TOKEN COINAGE

Lodz Ghetto 1942-1944

Lodz was a major industrial city in western Poland before World War II and site of the first wartime ghetto under German occupation (May 1940). It was also the last ghetto to close during the war (August 1944). Legitimate token coinage was struck in 1942 and 1943, in the name of the Jewish Elders of Litzmannstadt. This genuine series can be found listed in the Standard Catalog of World Coins. Most of the real pieces have seen very little circulation, but are commonly found in conditions from slightly to badly corroded. The badly corroded specimens have the appearance of zinc. This fantasy token is of a denomination never used for the original issues.

X# Tn1 50 MARK

11.0000 g., Aluminum-Bronze, 30 mm. **Obv. Legend:** DER AELTESTE DER JUDEN IN LITZMANNSTADT **Rev:** Large Star of David **Rev. Inscription:** GETTO

Date	Mintage	F	VF	XF	Unc	BU
1943	—	—	—	10.00	15.00	—

REPUBLIC

Democratic

ECU COINAGE

X# 22 ECU

31.1030 g., 0.7500 Gold 0.7500 oz. AGW, 38 mm. **Issuer:** Numex S.A., Madrid **Obv:** Arms **Obv. Legend:** RZECZPOSPOLITA POLSKA **Rev:** Bust of Pope John Paul II left **Rev. Legend:** "VERITATIS SPLENDOR" **Edge:** Reeded

Date	Mintage	F	VF	XF	Unc	BU
1993 Proof	250	Value: 800				

X# 21 30 ECU

31.1030 g., 0.9990 Silver 0.9989 oz. ASW, 38 mm. **Issuer:** Numex S.A., Madrid **Obv:** Arms **Obv. Legend:** RZECZPOSPOLITA POLSKA **Rev:** Bust of Pope John Paul II left **Rev. Legend:** "VERITATIS SPLENDOR" **Edge:** Reeded

Date	Mintage	F	VF	XF	Unc	BU
1993 Proof	5,000	Value: 45.00				

FANTASY EURO PATTERNS

X# Pn1 EURO CENT

Copper, 16.8 mm. **Issuer:** INA **Obv:** Bust of Frederic Chopin left **Rev:** Scale at right **Edge:** Plain

Date	Mintage	F	VF	XF	Unc	BU
2004	20,000	—	—	—	—	1.50
2004 Proof	20,000	Value: 2.50				

X# Pn1a EURO CENT

Silver, 16.8 mm. **Issuer:** INA **Obv:** Bust of Frederic Chopin left **Rev:** Scale at right **Edge:** Plain

Date	Mintage	F	VF	XF	Unc	BU
2004 Proof	2,500	Value: 6.00				

X# Pn2 2 EURO CENT

Copper, 18.5 mm. **Issuer:** INA **Obv:** Bust of Frederic Chopin left **Rev:** Scale at right **Edge:** Plain

Date	Mintage	F	VF	XF	Unc	BU
2004	20,000	—	—	—	—	2.00
2004 Proof	20,000	Value: 3.00				

X# Pn2a 2 EURO CENT

Silver, 18.5 mm. **Issuer:** INA **Obv:** Bust of Frederic Chopin left **Rev:** Scale at right **Edge:** Plain

Date	Mintage	F	VF	XF	Unc	BU
2004 Proof	2,500	Value: 7.00				

X# Pn3 5 EURO CENT

Copper, 20.7 mm. **Issuer:** INA **Obv:** Bust of Frederic Chopin left **Rev:** Scale at right **Edge:** Plain

Date	Mintage	F	VF	XF	Unc	BU
2004	20,000	—	—	—	—	2.50
2004 Proof	20,000	Value: 3.50				

X# Pn3a 5 EURO CENT

Silver, 20.7 mm. **Issuer:** INA **Obv:** Bust of Frederic Chopin left **Rev:** Scale at right **Edge:** Plain

Date	Mintage	F	VF	XF	Unc	BU
2004 Proof	2,500	Value: 8.50				

X# Pn4 10 EURO CENT

Brass, 19.3 mm. **Issuer:** INA **Obv:** Bust of Nicolaus Copernicus 3/4 left **Rev:** Dove, value in wreath of hands **Edge:** Plain

Date	Mintage	F	VF	XF	Unc	BU
2004	20,000	—	—	—	—	3.00
2004 Proof	20,000	Value: 4.00				

X# Pn4a 10 EURO CENT

Silver, 19.3 mm. **Issuer:** INA **Obv:** Bust of Nicolaus Copernicus 3/4 left **Rev:** Dove, value in wreath of hands **Edge:** Plain

Date	Mintage	F	VF	XF	Unc	BU
2004 Proof	2,500	Value: 10.00				

X# Pn5 20 EURO CENT

Brass, 22 mm. **Issuer:** INA **Obv:** Bust of Nicolaus Copernicus 3/4 left **Rev:** Dove, value in wreath of hands **Edge:** Plain

Date	Mintage	F	VF	XF	Unc	BU
2004	20,000	—	—	—	—	3.50
2004 Proof	20,000	Value: 5.00				

X# Pn5a 20 EURO CENT

Silver, 22 mm. **Issuer:** INA **Obv:** Bust of Nicolaus Copernicus 3/4 left **Rev:** Dove, value in wreath of hands **Edge:** Plain

Date	Mintage	F	VF	XF	Unc	BU
2004 Proof	2,500	Value: 12.50				

X# Pn6 50 EURO CENT

Brass, 24.3 mm. **Issuer:** INA **Obv:** Bust of Nicolaus Copernicus 3/4 left **Rev:** Dove, value in wreath of hands **Edge:** Plain

Date	Mintage	F	VF	XF	Unc	BU
2004	20,000	—	—	—	—	4.00
2004 Proof	20,000	Value: 6.00				

X# Pn6a 50 EURO CENT

Silver, 24.3 mm. **Issuer:** INA **Obv:** Bust of Nicolaus Copernicus 3/4 left **Rev:** Dove, value in wreath of hands **Edge:** Plain

Date	Mintage	F	VF	XF	Unc	BU
2004 Proof	2,500	Value: 15.00				

X# Pn7 EURO

Bi-Metallic, 22.8 mm. **Issuer:** INA **Obv:** Bust of Nicolaus Copernicus 3/4 left **Rev:** Spanish galleon **Edge:** Plain

Date	Mintage	F	VF	XF	Unc	BU
2004	Est. 500	—	—	—	—	35.00

X# Pn8 EURO

Bi-Metallic, 22.8 mm. **Issuer:** INA **Obv:** Bust of Pope John Paul II 3/4 left, Polish eagle behind **Rev:** Spanish galleon **Edge:** Plain

Date	Mintage	F	VF	XF	Unc	BU
2004	Est. 19,500	—	—	—	—	6.00
2004 Proof	20,000	Value: 8.00				

X# Pn8a EURO

Bi-Metallic Silver/Brass, 22.8 mm. **Issuer:** INA **Obv:** Bust of Pope John Paul II 3/4 left, Polish eagle behind **Rev:** Spanish galleon **Edge:** Plain

Date	Mintage	F	VF	XF	Unc	BU
2004 Proof	2,500	Value: 22.50				

X# Pn9 2 EURO

Bi-Metallic, 25.7 mm. **Issuer:** INA **Obv:** Bust of Pope John Paul II 3/4 left, Polish eagle behind **Rev:** Spanish galleon **Edge:** Plain

Date	Mintage	F	VF	XF	Unc	BU
2004	20,000	—	—	—	—	8.00
2004 Proof	20,000	Value: 10.00				

X# Pn9a 2 EURO

Bi-Metallic Silver/Brass, 25.7 mm. **Issuer:** INA **Obv:** Bust of Pope John Paul II 3/4 left, Polish eagle behind **Rev:** Spanish galleon **Edge:** Plain

Date	Mintage	F	VF	XF	Unc	BU
2004 Proof	2,500	Value: 28.50				

X# Pn10 5 EURO

Brass, 36 mm. **Issuer:** INA **Obv:** Bust of Pope John Paul II 3/4 left, Polish eagle behind **Rev:** Ancient Greeks in front of temple **Edge:** Plain

Date	Mintage	F	VF	XF	Unc	BU
2004 Proof	20,000	Value: 12.50				

X# Pn10a 5 EURO

Silver, 36 mm. **Issuer:** INA **Obv:** Bust of Pope John Paul II 3/4 left, Polish eagle behind **Rev:** Ancient Greeks in front of temple **Edge:** Plain

Date	Mintage	F	VF	XF	Unc	BU
2004 Proof	2,500	Value: 40.00				

BULLION COINAGE

X# M21 NO DENOMINATION

15.5520 g., 0.9990 Gold 0.4995 oz. AGW, 27 mm. **Obv:** Pope John Paul II half-length figure left, cross in background **Obv. Designer:** Eva Olszewska-Borys **Rev:** Papal arms **Rev. Legend:** JAN PAWEL II PAPIEZ POLAK

Date	Mintage	F	VF	XF	Unc	BU
1987 Proof	200	—	—	—	—	—

METALLIC BULLION

X# M20 NO DENOMINATION

7.7857 g., 0.9990 Gold 0.2501 oz. AGW, 18 mm. **Obv:** Pope John Paul II half-length figure within wide circle **Obv. Designer:** Eva Olszewska-Borys **Rev:** Papal arms **Rev. Legend:** JAN PAWEL II PAPIEZ POLAK

Date	Mintage	F	VF	XF	Unc	BU
1986 Proof	—	—	—	—	—	—

X# M22 NO DENOMINATION

31.1050 g., 0.9990 Platinum 0.9990 oz. APW, 32 mm. **Obv:** Pope John Paul II half-length figure left, cross in background **Obv. Designer:** Eva Olszewska-Borys **Rev:** Papal arms **Rev. Legend:** JAN PAWEL II PAPIEZ POLAK

Date	Mintage	F	VF	XF	Unc	BU
1987 Proof	200	—	—	—	—	—

PIEFORTS

X#	Date	Mintage	Identification	Mkt Val
P1	2004	5,000	5 Euro. Silver. X#Pn10a.	—

MINT SETS

X#	Date	Mintage	Identification	Issue Price	Mkt Val
XMS1	2004 (8)	500	X#Pn1-Pn7, Pn9	—	65.00
XMS2	2004 (8)	19,500	X#Pn1-Pn6, Pn8, Pn9	—	30.00

PROOF SETS

X#	Date	Mintage	Identification	Issue Price	Mkt Val
XPS1	2004 (8)	500	X#Pn1-Pn6, Pn8, Pn9	—	45.00
XPS2	2004 (9)	2,500	X#Pn1a-Pn6a, Pn8a, Pn9a, Pn10a	—	150
XPS3	2004 (9)	2,500	X#Pn1a-Pn7a, Pn9a, Pn10a	—	—

DANZIG

CITY

FANTASY EURO PATTERNS

X# Pn1 EURO CENT

Copper Plated Steel **Edge:** Plain

Date	Mintage	F	VF	XF	Unc	BU
2005	7,000	—	—	—	—	1.50

X# Pn2 2 EURO CENT

Copper Plated Steel **Edge:** Plain

Date	Mintage	F	VF	XF	Unc	BU
2005	7,000	—	—	—	—	2.00

X# Pn3 5 EURO CENT

Copper Plated Steel **Edge:** Plain

Date	Mintage	F	VF	XF	Unc	BU
2005	7,000	—	—	—	—	2.50

X# Pn4 10 EURO CENT

Goldine **Edge:** Plain

Date	Mintage	F	VF	XF	Unc	BU
2005	7,000	—	—	—	—	3.00

X# Pn5 20 EURO CENT

Goldine **Edge:** Plain

Date	Mintage	F	VF	XF	Unc	BU
2005	7,000	—	—	—	—	3.50

X# Pn6 50 EURO CENT

Goldine **Edge:** Plain

Date	Mintage	F	VF	XF	Unc	BU
2005	7,000	—	—	—	—	4.00

X# Pn7 EURO

Bi-Metallic

Date	Mintage	F	VF	XF	Unc	BU
2005	7,000	—	—	—	—	6.00

X# Pn8 2 EURO

Bi-Metallic

Date	Mintage	F	VF	XF	Unc	BU
2005	7,000	—	—	—	—	8.00

MINT SETS

X#	Date	Mintage	Identification	Issue Price	Mkt Val
XMS1	2005 (8)	7,000	X#Pn1-Pn8	—	30.00

PORTUGAL

KINGDOM

COUNTERMARKED COINAGE

X# 11 THALER

28.0600 g., 0.8330 Silver 0.7515 oz. ASW, 40 mm. **Ruler:** Maria II **Countermark:** Large crowned arms **Obv:** Bust of Maria Theresa right **Rev:** Crowned imperial eagle **Note:** c/m on Austrian thaler, KM#T1. A smaller crowned arms countermark was applied to legalize circulating Spanish, Spanish Colonial and Brazilian coins in 1834.

CM Date	Host Date	Good	VG	F	VF	XF
ND(1834)	1780	—	—	12.50	25.00	—

REPUBLIC

ECU COINAGE

X# 38 ECU

32.5000 g., Brass, 40 mm. **Issuer:** Göde GmbH, Waldaschaff **Obv:** Early sailing ship at left, bust of Vasco da Gama at right below arch of 12 stars, arch of large "PORTUGAL" with gold and blue enamels **Rev:** Europa riding a steer **Edge:** Plain

Date	Mintage	F	VF	XF	Unc	BU
1993 Proof	9,999	Value: 50.00				

X# 21 2-1/2 ECU

16.5000 g., Copper-Nickel, 34 mm. **Series:** Navigators **Subject:** Modern arms, early sailing craft **Obv. Designer:** PORTUGAL **Rev:** Bust of Henry at left, early sailing ship at right **Rev. Legend:** EUROPA E OS NOVOS MUNDOS **Edge:** Reeded

Date	Mintage	F	VF	XF	Unc	BU
1991INCM	40,000	—	—	—	—	9.00

X# 24 2-1/2 ECU

16.5000 g., Copper-Nickel, 34 mm. **Series:** Navigators **Obv:** Modern arms, early sailing craft **Obv. Legend:** PORTUGAL **Rev:** Early sailing ship at left, bust of João II at right **Rev. Legend:** EUROPA E OS NOVOS MUNDOS **Edge:** Reeded

Date	Mintage	F	VF	XF	Unc	BU
1992INCM	40,000	—	—	—	—	9.00

X# 28 2-1/2 ECU

16.5000 g., Copper-Nickel, 34 mm. **Series:** Navigators **Obv:** Modern arms, early sailing craft **Obv. Legend:** PORTUGAL **Rev:** Bartolomeu Dias with astrolobe, early sailing ship **Rev. Legend:** EUROPA E OS NOVOS MUNDOS **Edge:** Reeded

Date	Mintage	F	VF	XF	Unc	BU
1993INCM	40,000	—	—	—	—	9.00

X# 33 2-1/2 ECU

16.5000 g., Copper-Nickel, 34 mm. **Series:** Navigators **Obv:** Modern arms, early sailing craft **Obv. Legend:** PORTUGAL **Rev:** Manuel I **Rev. Legend:** EUROPA E OS NOVOS MUNDOS **Edge:** Reeded

Date	Mintage	F	VF	XF	Unc	BU
1993INCM	40,000	—	—	—	—	9.00

X# 48 2-1/2 ECU

16.5000 g., Copper-Nickel, 34 mm. **Series:** Navigators **Obv:** Modern arms, early sailing craft **Obv. Legend:** PORTUGAL **Rev:** Bust of Vasco da Gama facing at left, early sailing ship at center right **Rev. Legend:** EUROPA E OS NOVOS MUNDOS **Edge:** Reeded

Date	Mintage	F	VF	XF	Unc	BU
1995INCM	—	—	—	—	—	9.00

X# 52 2-1/2 ECU

16.5000 g., Copper-Nickel, 34 mm. **Series:** Navigators **Obv:** Modern arms, early sailing craft **Obv. Legend:** PORTUGAL **Rev:** Early sailing ship at left, bust of Cabral facing 3/4 left at right **Rev. Legend:** EUROPA E OS NOVOS MUNDOS **Edge:** Reeded

Date	Mintage	F	VF	XF	Unc	BU
1996	—	—	—	—	—	9.00

X# 57 2-1/2 ECU

Copper-Nickel, 34 mm. **Series:** Navigators **Obv:** Modern arms, early sailing craft **Obv. Legend:** PORTUGAL **Rev:** Bust of Magalhaes facing 3/4 right at left, early sailing ship at center **Rev. Legend:** EUROPA E OS NOVOS MUNDOS **Edge:** Reeded

Date	Mintage	F	VF	XF	Unc	BU
1997	—	—	—	—	—	9.00

X# 61 2-1/2 ECU

16.5000 g., Copper-Nickel, 34 mm. **Series:** Navigators **Obv:** Modern arms, early sailing craft **Obv. Legend:** PORTUGAL **Rev:** Early sailing ship at center, bust of Albuquerque facing 3/4 left at right **Rev. Legend:** EUROPA E OS NOVOS MUNDOS **Edge:** Reeded

Date	Mintage	F	VF	XF	Unc	BU
1998INCM	—	—	—	—	—	9.00

X# 71 2-1/2 ECU

14.8000 g., Copper-Nickel, 33.1 mm. **Obv:** Shield, sailboat, rays **Rev:** Busts of Leonor of Portugal and Frederik III of Prussia at left facing right, sailing ship at right **Rev. Legend:** AS MÃES DA EUROPA **Edge:** Reeded

Date	Mintage	F	VF	XF	Unc	BU
1998	—	—	—	—	5.00	—

X# 22 25 ECU

28.0000 g., 0.9250 Silver 0.8327 oz. ASW, 37 mm. **Series:** Navigators **Obv:** Modern arms, early sailing craft **Obv. Legend:** PORTUGAL **Rev:** Bust of Henry at left, early sailing ship at right **Rev. Legend:** EUROPA E OS NOVOS MUNDOS **Edge:** Reeded

Date	Mintage	F	VF	XF	Unc	BU
1991INCM Proof	20,000	Value: 50.00				

X# 25 25 ECU

28.0000 g., 0.9250 Silver 0.8327 oz. ASW, 37 mm. **Series:** Navigators **Obv:** Modern arms, early sailing craft **Obv. Legend:** PORTUGAL **Rev:** Early sailing ship at left, bust of João II at right **Rev. Legend:** EUROPA E OS NOVOS MUNDOS **Edge:** Reeded

Date	Mintage	F	VF	XF	Unc	BU
1992INCM Proof	20,000	Value: 40.00				

X# 29 25 ECU

28.0000 g., 0.9250 Silver 0.8327 oz. ASW, 37 mm. **Series:** Navigators **Obv:** Modern arms, early sailing craft **Obv. Legend:** PORTUGAL **Rev:** Bartholomeu Dias with astrolobe, early sailing ship **Rev. Legend:** EUROPA E OS NOVOS MUNDOS **Edge:** Reeded

Date	Mintage	F	VF	XF	Unc	BU
1993INCM Proof	20,000	Value: 40.00				

X# 34 25 ECU

28.0000 g., 0.9250 Silver 0.8327 oz. ASW, 37 mm. **Series:** Navigators **Obv:** Modern arms, early sailing craft **Obv. Legend:** PORTUGAL **Rev:** Manuel I **Rev. Legend:** EUROPA E OS NOVOS MUNDOS **Edge:** Reeded

Date	Mintage	F	VF	XF	Unc	BU
1993INCM Proof	20,000	Value: 40.00				

X# 49 25 ECU

28.0000 g., 0.9250 Silver 0.8327 oz. ASW **Series:** Navigators **Obv:** Modern arms, early sailing craft **Obv. Legend:** PORTUGAL **Rev:** Bust of Vasco da Gama facing at left, early sailing ship at center right **Rev. Legend:** EUROPA E OS NOVOS MUNDOS **Edge:** Reeded

Date	Mintage	F	VF	XF	Unc	BU
1995INCM Proof	—	Value: 40.00				

X# 53 25 ECU

28.0000 g., 0.9250 Silver 0.8327 oz. ASW, 37 mm. **Series:** Navigators **Obv:** Modern arms, early sailing craft **Obv. Legend:** PORTUGAL **Rev:** Early sailing ship at left, bust of Cabral facing 3/4 left at right **Rev. Legend:** EUROPA E OS NOVOS MUNDOS **Edge:** Reeded

Date	Mintage	F	VF	XF	Unc	BU
1996 Proof	—	Value: 40.00				

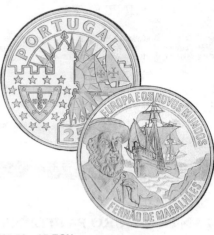

X# 58 25 ECU

28.0000 g., 0.9250 Silver 0.8327 oz. ASW, 37 mm. **Series:** Navigators **Obv:** Modern arms, early sailing craft **Obv. Legend:** PORTUGAL **Rev:** Bust of Magalhaes facing 3/4 right at left, early sailing ship at center **Rev. Legend:** EUROPA E OS NOVOS MUNDOS **Edge:** Reeded

Date	Mintage	F	VF	XF	Unc	BU
1997 Proof	—	Value: 40.00				

X# 62 25 ECU

28.0000 g., 0.9250 Silver 0.8327 oz. ASW, 37 mm. **Series:** Navigators **Obv:** Modern arms, early sailing craft **Obv. Legend:** PORTUGAL **Rev:** Early sailing ship at center, but of Albuquerque facing 3/4 left at right **Rev. Legend:** EUROPA E OS NOVOS MUNDOS **Edge:** Reeded

Date	Mintage	F	VF	XF	Unc	BU
1998INCM Proof	—	Value: 40.00				

X# 23 200 ECU

8.4850 g., 0.9167 Gold 0.2501 oz. AGW **Series:** Navigators **Obv:** Modern arms, early sailing craft **Obv. Legend:** PORTUGAL **Rev:** Bust of Henry at left, early sailing ship at right **Rev. Legend:** EUROPA E OS NOVOS MUNDOS **Edge:** Reeded **Note:** This was originally reported as a 250 Ecu KM#654 & then declared not legal tender by the Lisbon Mint which minted this series!

Date	Mintage	F	VF	XF	Unc	BU
1991INCM Proof	2,500	Value: 300				

X# 26 200 ECU
8.4850 g., 0.9167 Gold 0.2501 oz. AGW, 23.5 mm. **Series:** Navigators **Obv:** Modern arms, early sailing craft **Obv. Legend:** PORTUGAL **Rev:** Early sailing ship at left, bust of João II at right **Rev. Legend:** EUROPA E OS NOVOS MUNDOS **Edge:** Reeded

Date	Mintage	F	VF	XF	Unc	BU
1992INCM Proof	2,500	Value: 300				

X# 30 200 ECU
8.4850 g., 0.9167 Gold 0.2501 oz. AGW, 23.5 mm. **Series:** Navigators **Obv:** Modern arms, early sailing craft **Obv. Legend:** PORTUGAL **Rev:** Bartholomeu Dias with astrolobe, early sailing ship **Rev. Legend:** EUROPA E OS NOVOS MUNDOS **Edge:** Reeded

Date	Mintage	F	VF	XF	Unc	BU
1993INCM Proof	2,500	Value: 300				

X# 35 200 ECU
8.4850 g., 0.9167 Gold 0.2501 oz. AGW, 23.5 mm. **Series:** Navigators **Obv:** Modern arms, early sailing craft **Obv. Legend:** PORTUGAL **Rev:** Manuel I **Rev. Legend:** EUROPA E OS NOVOS MUNDOS **Edge:** Reeded

Date	Mintage	F	VF	XF	Unc	BU
1993INCM Proof	2,500	Value: 300				

X# 50 200 ECU
8.4250 g., 0.9167 Gold 0.2483 oz. AGW, 23.5 mm. **Series:** Navigators **Obv:** Modern arms, early sailing craft **Obv. Legend:** PORTUGAL **Rev:** Bust of Vasco da Gama facing at left, early sailing ship at center right **Rev. Legend:** EUROPA E OS NOVOS MUNDOS **Edge:** Reeded

Date	Mintage	F	VF	XF	Unc	BU
1995INCM Proof	—	Value: 300				

X# 54 200 ECU
8.4250 g., 0.9167 Gold 0.2483 oz. AGW **Obv:** Modern arms, early sailing craft **Obv. Legend:** PORTUGAL **Rev:** Early sailing ship at left, bust of Cabral facing 3/4 left at right **Rev. Legend:** EUROPA E OS NOVOS MUNDOS **Edge:** Reeded

Date	Mintage	F	VF	XF	Unc	BU
1996 Proof	—	Value: 300				

X# 59 200 ECU
8.4250 g., 0.9167 Gold 0.2483 oz. AGW, 23.5 mm. **Series:** Navigators **Obv:** Modern arms, early sailing craft **Obv. Legend:** PORTUGAL **Rev. Legend:** EUROPA E OS NOVOS MUNDOS **Edge:** Reeded

Date	Mintage	F	VF	XF	Unc	BU
1997 Proof	—	Value: 300				

X# 63 200 ECU
8.4250 g., 0.9167 Gold 0.2483 oz. AGW, 23.5 mm. **Series:** Navigators **Obv:** Modern arms, early sailing craft **Obv. Legend:** PORTUGAL **Rev:** Early sailing ship at center, bust of Albuquerque facing 3/4 left at right **Rev. Legend:** EUROPA E OS NOVOS MUNDOS **Edge:** Reeded

Date	Mintage	F	VF	XF	Unc	BU
1998 Proof	—	Value: 300				

EURO COINAGE

European Economic Community Issues

X# 72 5 EURO
15.0400 g., Copper-Nickel, 33.1 mm. **Obv:** Shield, sailboat, rays **Rev:** Sailing ship at center, bust of Alphonso de Albuquerque at right facing 3/4 left **Rev. Legend:** EUROPA E OS NOVOS MUNDOS **Edge:** Reeded

Date	Mintage	F	VF	XF	Unc	BU
1998	—	—	—	—	6.00	—

PUERTO RICO

COMMONWEALTH

MILLED COINAGE

X# 1 10 PESOS
86.4660 g., 0.9990 Silver 2.7771 oz. ASW, 49 mm. **Issuer:** Puerto Rican Nationalist Party **Subject:** Centenary of Birth **Obv:** Flag on sunburst **Obv. Legend:** REPUBLICA DE PUERTO RICO **Rev:** Bust of Pedro Albizu Campos 3/4 left

Date	Mintage	F	VF	XF	Unc	BU
ND(1992)	100	—	—	—	—	—

X# 1a 10 PESOS
Bronze, 49 mm. **Issuer:** Puerto Rican Nationalist Party **Subject:** Centenary of Birth **Obv:** Flag on sunburst **Obv. Legend:** REPUBLICA DE PUERTO RICO **Rev:** Bust of Pedro Albizu Campos 3/4 left

Date	Mintage	F	VF	XF	Unc	BU
ND(1992)	1,000	—	—	—	35.00	—

X# 1b 10 PESOS
123.7899 g., 0.7500 Gold 2.9848 oz. AGW, 49 mm. **Issuer:** Puerto Rican Nationalist Party **Subject:** Centenary of Birth **Obv:** Flag on sunburst **Obv. Legend:** REPUBLICA DE PUERTO RICO **Rev:** Bust of Pedro Albizu Campos 3/4 left

Date	Mintage	F	VF	XF	Unc	BU
ND(1992)	5	—	—	—	—	—

SILVER CURRENCY COINAGE

Liberty Dollar Org. Issues

X# 11 20 LIBERTY DOLLARS
31.1600 g., 0.9990 Silver 1.0008 oz. ASW, 38.94 mm. **Obv:** Liberty head left **Obv. Legend:** LIBERTAD **Obv. Inscription:** CONFIB EN / DIOS **Rev:** Panama penant at center **Rev. Legend:** PUERTO RICO **Rev. Inscription:** MI PAIS **Edge:** Reeded

Date	Mintage	F	VF	XF	Unc	BU
2007 Proof	—	Value: 22.50				

SPANISH COLONY

PATTERNS

Including off metal strikes

X# Pn1 10 CENTIMOS
Copper **Ruler:** Alfonso XIII **Note:** Prev. KM#Pn1.

Date	Mintage	F	VF	XF	Unc	BU
1890	—	—	—	—	1,650	—

PURPLE SHAFTIEULAND

SATIRICAL

MEDALLIC COINAGE

Bob Kolosa Issue

X# M1 NUDGE
Brass, 16 mm. **Ruler:** Chief Weeskee Rooyoo Kissieutieu **Rev. Inscription:** IN / FORINADE / WE TRUST

Date	Mintage	F	VF	XF	Unc	BU
1970	1,000	—	—	1.00	1.50	—

X# M1a NUDGE
Aluminum, 16 mm. **Ruler:** Chief Weeskee Rooyoo Kissieutieu **Rev. Inscription:** IN / FORINADE / WE TRUST

Date	Mintage	F	VF	XF	Unc	BU
1970	1,000	—	—	0.75	1.25	—

X# M2 TWIST
Brass, 22 mm. **Ruler:** Chief Weeskee Rooyoo Kissieutieu **Obv:** Pretzel **Rev. Inscription:** IN / FORINADE / WE TRUST

Date	Mintage	F	VF	XF	Unc	BU
1970	1,000	—	—	1.00	1.50	—

X# M2a TWIST
Aluminum, 22 mm. **Ruler:** Chief Weeskee Rooyoo Kissieutieu **Rev. Inscription:** IN / FORINADE / WE TRUST

Date	Mintage	F	VF	XF	Unc	BU
1970	1,000	—	—	1.25	1.75	—

X# M3 1/4 SHAFT
Brass, 38 mm. **Ruler:** Chief Weeskee Rooyoo Kissieutieu **Obv:** Four 1/4 shaft segments
Rev. Inscription: IN / FORINADE / WE TRUST

Date	Mintage	F	VF	XF	Unc	BU
1970	1,000	—	—	1.50	2.00	—

X# M3a 1/4 SHAFT
Aluminum, 38 mm. **Ruler:** Chief Weeskee Rooyoo Kissieutieu **Obv:** Four 1/4 shaft segments
Rev. Inscription: IN / FORINADE / WE TRUST

Date	Mintage	F	VF	XF	Unc	BU
1970	1,000	—	—	1.25	1.75	—

X# M4 1/2 SHAFT
Brass, 38 mm. **Ruler:** Chief Weeskee Rooyoo Kissieutieu **Obv:** Two 1/2 shaft segments
Rev. Inscription: IN / FORINADE / WE TRUST

Date	Mintage	F	VF	XF	Unc	BU
1970	1,000	—	—	2.00	2.50	—

X# M4a 1/2 SHAFT
Aluminum, 38 mm. **Ruler:** Chief Weeskee Rooyoo Kissieutieu **Obv:** Two 1/2 shaft segments
Rev. Inscription: IN / FORINADE / WE TRUST

Date	Mintage	F	VF	XF	Unc	BU
1970	1,000	—	—	1.75	2.25	—

X# M5 SHAFT
Brass, 38 mm. **Ruler:** Chief Weeskee Rooyoo Kissieutieu **Obv:** Bow on shaft
Rev. Inscription: IN / FORINADE / WE TRUST

Date	Mintage	F	VF	XF	Unc	BU
1970	1,000	—	—	2.50	3.00	—

X# M5a SHAFT
Aluminum, 38 mm. **Ruler:** Chief Weeskee Rooyoo Kissieutieu **Obv:** Bow on shaft
Rev. Inscription: IN / FORINADE / WE TRUST

Date	Mintage	F	VF	XF	Unc	BU
1970	1,000	—	—	2.00	2.50	—

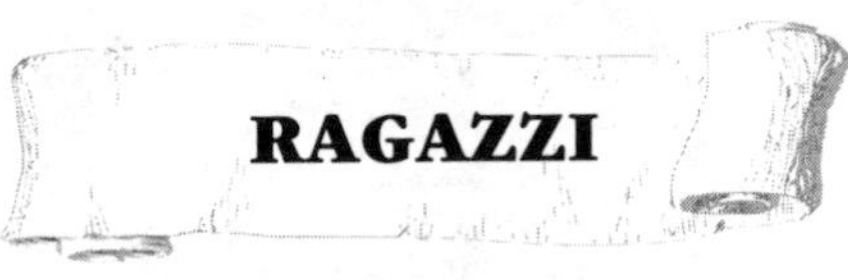

REPUBBLICA DEI RAGAZZI

Charity Children's Home

TOKEN COINAGE

X# Tn1 MERITO
2.0100 g., Aluminum, 24.3 mm. **Obv:** Coat of arms
Rev: Tower and fisherman **Edge:** Plain

Date	Mintage	F	VF	XF	Unc	BU
ND(1955)	—	—	—	—	12.00	15.00

X# Tn2 2 MERITI
2.1500 g., Aluminum, 25.7 mm. **Obv:** Coat of arms
Rev: Teacher with two children **Edge:** Plain

Date	Mintage	F	VF	XF	Unc	BU
ND(1955)	—	—	—	—	12.00	15.00

X# Tn3 5 MERITI
2.8100 g., Aluminum, 28.1 mm. **Obv:** Coat of arms
Rev: Adult comforting two children **Edge:** Plain

Date	Mintage	F	VF	XF	Unc	BU
ND(1955)	—	—	—	—	13.00	16.00

X# Tn4 10 MERITI
3.2200 g., Aluminum, 30.2 mm. **Obv:** Coat of arms **Rev:** Adult settling dispute between two children **Edge:** Plain

Date	Mintage	F	VF	XF	Unc	BU
ND(1955)	—	—	—	—	15.00	18.00

X# Tn5 50 MERITI
4.0000 g., Aluminum, 32.3 mm. **Obv:** Coat of arms
Rev: Adult teaching the concept of Libert to two children **Edge:** Plain

Date	Mintage	F	VF	XF	Unc	BU
ND(1955)	—	—	—	—	15.00	18.00

X# Tn6 100 MERITI
4.9600 g., Aluminum, 35.3 mm. **Obv:** Coat of arms **Rev:** Adult watching an act of charity by a youth **Edge:** Plain

Date	Mintage	F	VF	XF	Unc	BU
ND(1955)	—	—	—	—	17.00	20.00

X# Tn7 200 MERITI
10.1000 g., 0.9990 Silver 0.3244 oz. ASW, 7.2 mm.
Obv: Coat of arms **Rev:** Adult teaching work ethic to three youths **Edge:** Plain

Date	Mintage	F	VF	XF	Unc	BU
ND(1955)	—	—	—	—	35.00	50.00

X# Tn8 500 MERITI
24.8500 g., 0.9990 Silver 0.7981 oz. ASW, 37.3 mm.
Obv: Coat of arms **Rev:** Parents with child **Edge:** Plain

Date	Mintage	F	VF	XF	Unc	BU
ND(1955)	—	—	—	—	85.00	100

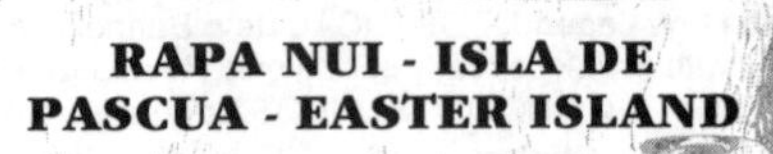

CHILEAN DEPENDENCY

FANTASY COINAGE

Issued by Joe Lang

X# 1 PESO
1.8000 g., Nickel Plated Brass, 16.49 mm. **Obv:** Stone monolithic head left **Obv. Legend:** RAPA NUI — ISLA DE PASCUA **Rev:** Bonito Fish left — "au hopu" **Edge:** Plain

Date	Mintage	F	VF	XF	Unc	BU
2007	9,000	—	—	—	—	1.00

X# 2 5 PESOS
4.5000 g., Brass, 20.24 mm. **Obv:** Stone monolithic head left **Obv. Legend:** RAPA NUI — ISLA DE PASCUA **Rev:** Forceps Fish — " tipitipi hoe" **Edge:** Plain

Date	Mintage	F	VF	XF	Unc	BU
2007	9,000	—	—	—	—	2.00

X# 3 10 PESOS
5.5100 g., Brass, 25.75 mm. **Obv:** Stone monolithic head right **Obv. Legend:** RAPA NUI — ISLA DE PASCUA **Rev:** Mythical creature "Birdman Cult" — "tangata manu" crouching right **Edge:** Plain **Shape:** 11-sided

Date	Mintage	F	VF	XF	Unc	BU
2007	7,000	—	—	—	—	3.00

X# 4 50 PESOS
5.2300 g., Copper-Plated Brass, 24.94 mm. **Obv:** Stone monolithic head right **Obv. Legend:** RAPA NUI — ISLA DE PASCUA **Rev:** Moray Eel "koreha toko ari", plants below **Edge:** Plain

Date	Mintage	F	VF	XF	Unc	BU
2007	9,000	—	—	—	—	4.00

X# 5 100 PESOS
6.7300 g., Copper-Plated Brass, 29.25 mm. **Obv:** Stone monolithic head right **Obv. Legend:** RAPA NUI — ISLA DE PASCUA **Rev:** Polynesian Sailing double canoe — "vaka" **Edge:** Plain **Shape:** 11-sided

Date	Mintage	F	VF	XF	Unc	BU
2007	7,000	—	—	—	—	5.00

X# 6 200 PESOS
4.7500 g., Bi-Metallic **Ring Composition:** Yellow Brass **Center Composition:** Nickel, 24.99 mm. **Obv:** Statue seated "Makemake" **Obv. Legend:** RAPA NUI — ISLA DE PASCUA **Rev:** Hammerhead Shark — "niuhi tapaka'i" **Edge:** Reeded

Date	Mintage	F	VF	XF	Unc	BU
2007	9,000	—	—	—	—	6.00

X# 7 500 PESOS
5.8300 g., Bi-Metallic **Ring Composition:** Red Brass **Center Composition:** Nickel, 27.22 mm. **Obv:** Statue seated "Makemake" **Obv. Legend:** RAPA NUI — ISLA DE PASCUA **Rev:** Row of stone monolithic statues — "Moai" **Edge:** Reeded

Date	Mintage	F	VF	XF	Unc	BU
2007	9,000	—	—	—	—	10.00

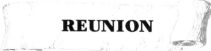

REUNION

FRENCH DEPARTMENT

ESSAIS

Standard metals unless otherwise noted

X# E11 1/4 EURO
7.8000 g., 0.9990 Silver 0.2505 oz. ASW, 27.2 mm. **Series:** Euro **Obv:** Bust of Louis Oscar Roty almost left **Obv. Legend:** RÉUNION **Rev:** La Femiére (medal, 1888) **Edge:** Reeded

Date	Mintage	F	VF	XF	Unc	BU
2004 Proof	2,000	Value: 25.00				

X# E11a 1/4 EURO
10.3400 g., Copper, 27.22 mm. **Obv:** Bust of Louis Oscar Roty half left **Obv. Legend:** R?UNION **Rev:** La Femi?re (medal, 1888) **Edge:** Reeded

Date	Mintage	F	VF	XF	Unc	BU
2004	30	—	—	—	50.00	50.00

X# E12 1-1/2 EURO
31.1400 g., 0.9990 Silver 1.0000 oz. ASW, 38.6 mm. **Series:** Euro **Obv:** Arms **Obv. Legend:** RÉPUBLIQUE FRANÇAISE **Rev:** Aircraft carrier, Charles de Gaulle, 2000- **Rev. Legend:** HISTORIRE DE LA MARINE FRANÇAISE **Edge:** Reeded

Date	Mintage	F	VF	XF	Unc	BU
2004 Proof	2,000	Value: 45.00				

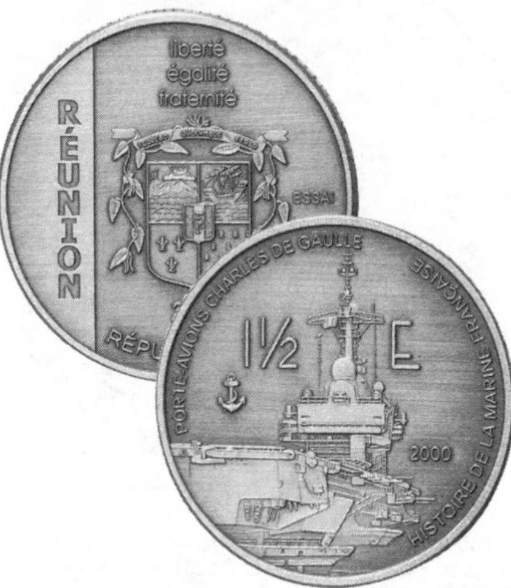

X# E13 1-1/2 EURO
26.5200 g., Brass antiqued, 39.13 mm. **Series:** Euro **Obv:** Arms **Obv. Legend:** R?PUBLIQUE FRAN?AISE **Rev:** Aircraft carrier, Charles de Gaulle, 2000- **Rev. Legend:** HISTORIRE DE LA MARINE FRAN?AISE **Edge:** Reeded

Date	Mintage	F	VF	XF	Unc	BU
2004	25	Value: 75.00				

X# E15 20 EURO
8.5300 g., 0.9167 Gold 0.2514 oz. AGW, 27.1 mm. **Series:** Euro **Obv:** Arms **Rev:** Yellow-nosed Albatros **Rev. Legend:** Protecton de la Faune **Edge:** Plain

Date	Mintage	F	VF	XF	Unc	BU
2004 Proof	300	Value: 325				

X# E15a 20 EURO
10.3300 g., Copper, 27.19 mm. **Obv:** Shield of arms **Rev:** Yellow-nosed albatross **Rev. Legend:** protection de la faune **Edge:** Plain

Date	Mintage	F	VF	XF	Unc	BU
2004	30	—	—	—	50.00	50.00

RIO GRANDE

REPUBLIC

NON-CIRCULATING COINAGE

X# NC23 2 CENTS
Bronze

Date	Mintage	F	VF	XF	Unc	BU
1890	—	—	100	200	300	—

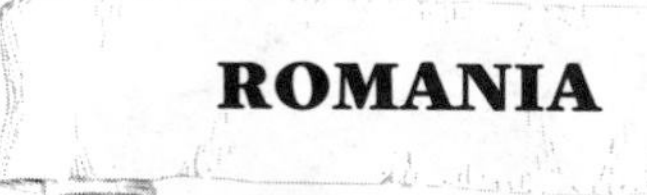

ROMANIA

KINGDOM

MEDALLIC COINAGE

X# M1 20 LEI
6.4516 g., 0.9000 Gold 0.1867 oz. AGW **Ruler:** Ferdinand I **Subject:** Ferdinand I Coronation **Note:** Prev. KM#M1.

Date	Mintage	F	VF	XF	Unc	BU
1922(a)	300,000	150	250	450	650	—

X# M5 20 LEI
6.4516 g., 0.9000 Gold 0.1867 oz. AGW **Ruler:** Carol II **Subject:** Centennial - Birth of Carol I **Note:** Prev. KM#M2.

Date	Mintage	F	VF	XF	Unc	BU
1939C	—	150	250	600	850	—

X# M6 20 LEI
6.4516 g., 0.9000 Gold 0.1867 oz. AGW **Ruler:** Carol II **Note:** Prev. KM#M3.

Date	Mintage	F	VF	XF	Unc	BU
1939C	—	150	250	600	850	—

X# M9 20 LEI
6.4516 g., 0.9000 Gold 0.1867 oz. AGW **Ruler:** Carol II **Subject:** Carol II 10th Anniversary **Note:** Prev. KM#M4.

Date	Mintage	F	VF	XF	Unc	BU
1940C	—	150	250	600	850	—

X# M10 20 LEI
6.4516 g., 0.9000 Gold 0.1867 oz. AGW **Ruler:** Carol II **Note:** Prev. KM#M5.

Date	Mintage	F	VF	XF	Unc	BU
1940C	—	150	250	600	850	—

X# M13 20 LEI
6.5500 g., 0.9000 Gold 0.1895 oz. AGW **Ruler:** Mihai I **Subject:** Romanian Kings **Note:** Prev. KM#M6.

Date	Mintage	F	VF	XF	Unc	BU
1944	1,000,000	—	BV	BV	175	225

X# M2 25 LEI
8.0645 g., 0.9000 Gold 0.2333 oz. AGW
Ruler: Ferdinand I **Subject:** Ferdinand I Coronation
Note: Prev. KM#M7.

Date	Mintage	F	VF	XF	Unc	BU
1922	150,000	250	400	600	900	—

X# M3 50 LEI
16.1290 g., 0.9000 Gold 0.4667 oz. AGW
Ruler: Ferdinand I **Subject:** Ferdinand I Coronation
Note: Prev. KM#M8.

Date	Mintage	F	VF	XF	Unc	BU
1922	105,000	400	600	950	1,450	—

X# M4 100 LEI
32.2580 g., 0.9000 Gold 0.9334 oz. AGW
Ruler: Ferdinand I **Subject:** Ferdinand I Coronation
Note: Prev. KM#M9.

Date	Mintage	F	VF	XF	Unc	BU
1922	30,000	750	1,250	2,000	3,500	5,000

X# M7 100 LEI
32.5000 g., 0.9000 Gold 0.9404 oz. AGW **Ruler:** Carol II **Subject:** Centennial - Birth of Carol I **Note:** Prev. KM#M10.

Date	Mintage	F	VF	XF	Unc	BU
1939C	—	1,500	2,500	3,750	6,000	—

X# M8 100 LEI
32.5000 g., 0.9000 Gold 0.9404 oz. AGW
Ruler: Carol II **Note:** Prev. KM#M11.

Date	Mintage	F	VF	XF	Unc	BU
1939C	—	1,500	2,500	3,750	6,000	—

X# M11 100 LEI
32.5000 g., 0.9000 Gold 0.9404 oz. AGW
Ruler: Carol II **Subject:** Carol II 10th Anniversary
Note: Prev. KM#M12.

Date	Mintage	F	VF	XF	Unc	BU
1940C	—	1,250	2,000	3,250	5,000	—

X# M12 100 LEI
32.5000 g., 0.9000 Gold 0.9404 oz. AGW
Ruler: Carol II **Note:** Prev. KM#M14.

Date	Mintage	F	VF	XF	Unc	BU
1940C	—	1,250	2,000	3,250	5,000	—

Galbeni Issues

The medals listed below were issued with the commemorative gold coins listed earlier in this section. These are referred to as Galbeni.

X# MG1 100 LEI
42.0000 g., 0.9000 Gold 1.2152 oz. AGW
Ruler: Carol II **Note:** Prev. KM#M15.

Date	Mintage	F	VF	XF	Unc	BU
1939	—	—	—	1,150	1,800	—

X# MG2 100 LEI
42.0000 g., 0.9000 Gold 1.2152 oz. AGW
Ruler: Carol II **Note:** Prev. KM#M16.

Date	Mintage	F	VF	XF	Unc	BU
1939	—	—	—	1,150	1,800	—

X# MG3 100 LEI
42.0000 g., 0.9000 Gold 1.2152 oz. AGW
Ruler: Carol II **Subject:** Carol II 10th Anniversary
Note: Similar to KM#M16. Prev. KM#M17.

Date	Mintage	F	VF	XF	Unc	BU
1940	—	—	—	1,750	3,000	—

X# MG4 100 LEI
42.0000 g., 0.9000 Gold 1.2152 oz. AGW **Ruler:** Carol II
Rev: Mounted horse facing right **Note:** Prev. KM#M18.

Date	Mintage	F	VF	XF	Unc	BU
1940	—	—	—	3,250	5,000	—

REPUBLIC

MEDALLIC COINAGE

ICB Issues

X# 1 100 LEI
27.0000 g., 0.9250 Silver 0.8029 oz. ASW, 37 mm.
Subject: XXVI Olympiad - Atlanta **Obv:** Arms
Obv. Legend: ROMANIA **Rev:** Female gymnast Lavinia Milosovici posing left **Edge:** Plain
Edge Lettering: 100 LEI

Date	Mintage	F	VF	XF	Unc	BU
1996 Proof	125	Value: 45.00				

X# 1a 100 LEI
20.0000 g., Brass, 37 mm. **Subject:** XXVI Olympiad - Atlanta **Obv:** Arms **Obv. Legend:** ROMANIA
Rev: Female gymnast Lavinia Milosovici posing left
Edge: Plain **Edge Lettering:** 100 LEI

Date	Mintage	F	VF	XF	Unc	BU
1996 Proof	125	Value: 25.00				

X# 1b 100 LEI
20.0000 g. Nickel center in Brass ringr, 37 mm.. **Subject:** XXVI Olympiad - Atlanta **Obv:** Arms **Obv. Legend:** ROMANIA **Rev:** Female gymnast Lavinia Milosovici posing left **Edge:** Plain **Edge Lettering:** 100 LEI

Date	Mintage	F	VF	XF	Unc	BU
1996 Proof	125	Value: 45.00				

X# 1c 100 LEI
Aluminum, 37 mm. **Subject:** XXVI Olympic - Atlanta
Obv: Arms **Obv. Legend:** ROMANIA **Rev:** Female gymnast Lavinia Milosovici posing left **Edge:** Plain
Edge Lettering: 100 LEI

Date	Mintage	F	VF	XF	Unc	BU
1996 Proof	125	Value: 25.00				

X# 1d 100 LEI
Copper, 37 mm. **Subject:** XXVI Olympiad - Atlanta
Obv: Arms **Obv. Legend:** ROMANIA **Rev:** Female gymnast Lavinia Milosovici posing left **Edge:** Plain
Edge Lettering: 100 LEI

Date	Mintage	F	VF	XF	Unc	BU
1996 Proof	125	Value: 25.00				

X# 2 100 LEI
27.0000 g., 0.9250 Silver 0.8029 oz. ASW, 37 mm.
Subject: XXVI Olympiad - Atlanta **Obv:** Arms
Obv. Legend: ROMANIA **Rev:** Male tennis player
Edge: Plain **Edge Lettering:** 100 LEI

Date	Mintage	F	VF	XF	Unc	BU
1996 Proof	125	Value: 45.00				

X# 2a 100 LEI
20.0000 g., Brass, 37 mm. **Subject:** XXVI Olympiad - Atlanta **Obv:** Arms **Obv. Legend:** ROMANIA **Rev:** Male tennis player **Edge:** Plain **Edge Lettering:** 100 LEI

Date	Mintage	F	VF	XF	Unc	BU
1996 Proof	125	Value: 25.00				

X# 2b 100 LEI
20.0000 g. Nickel center in Brass ringr, 37 mm.
Subject: XXVI Olympiad - Atlanta **Obv:** Arms
Obv. Legend: ROMANIA **Rev:** Male tennis player
Edge: Plain **Edge Lettering:** 100 LEI

Date	Mintage	F	VF	XF	Unc	BU
1996 Proof	125	Value: 45.00				

X# 2c 100 LEI

6.0000 g., Aluminum, 37 mm. **Subject:** XXVI Olympiad - Atlanta **Obv:** Arms **Obv. Legend:** ROMANIA **Rev:** Male tennis player **Edge:** Plain **Edge Lettering:** 100 LEI

Date	Mintage	F	VF	XF	Unc	BU
1996 Proof	125	Value: 25.00				

X# 2d 100 LEI

21.0000 g., Copper, 37 mm. **Subject:** XXVI Olympiad - Atlanta **Obv:** Arms **Obv. Legend:** ROMANIA **Rev:** Male tennis player **Edge:** Plain **Edge Lettering:** 100 LEI

Date	Mintage	F	VF	XF	Unc	BU
1996 Proof	125	Value: 25.00				

X# 3 100 LEI

27.0000 g., 0.9250 Silver 0.8029 oz. ASW, 37 mm. **Ruler:** Carol I **Subject:** XXVI Olympiad - Atlanta **Obv:** Arms **Obv. Legend:** ROMANIA **Rev:** Two opposing basketball players jumpring at the hoop **Edge:** Plain **Edge Lettering:** 100 LEI

Date	Mintage	F	VF	XF	Unc	BU
1996 Proof	125	Value: 45.00				

X# 3a 100 LEI

20.0000 g., Brass, 37 mm. **Subject:** XXVI Olympiad - Atlanta **Obv:** Arms **Obv. Legend:** ROMANIA **Rev:** Two opposing basketball players jumping at the hoop **Edge:** Plain **Edge Lettering:** 100 LEI

Date	Mintage	F	VF	XF	Unc	BU
1996 Proof	125	Value: 25.00				

X# 3b 100 LEI

20.0000 g. Nickel center in Brass ringr, 37 mm. **Subject:** XXVI Olympiad - Atlanta **Obv:** Arms **Obv. Legend:** ROMANIA **Rev:** Two opposing basketball players jumping at the hoop **Edge:** Plain **Edge Lettering:** 100 LEI

Date	Mintage	F	VF	XF	Unc	BU
1996 Proof	125	Value: 45.00				

X# 3c 100 LEI

6.0000 g., Aluminum, 37 mm. **Subject:** XXVI Olympiad - Atlanta **Obv:** Arms **Obv. Legend:** ROMANIA **Rev:** Two opposing basketball players jumping at the hoop **Edge:** Plain **Edge Lettering:** 100 LEI

Date	Mintage	F	VF	XF	Unc	BU
1996 Proof	125	Value: 25.00				

X# 3d 100 LEI

21.0000 g., Copper, 37 mm. **Subject:** XXVI Olympiad - Atlanta **Obv:** Arms **Obv. Legend:** ROMANIA **Rev:** Two opposing basketball players jumping at the hoop **Edge:** Plain **Edge Lettering:** 100 LEI

Date	Mintage	F	VF	XF	Unc	BU
1996 Proof	125	Value: 25.00				

X# 4 100 LEI

27.0000 g., 0.9250 Silver 0.8029 oz. ASW, 37 mm. **Subject:** XXVI Olympiad - Atlanta **Obv:** Arms **Obv. Legend:** ROMANIA **Rev:** Marksman kneeling with rifle facing, target image at left **Edge:** Plain **Edge Lettering:** 100 LEI

Date	Mintage	F	VF	XF	Unc	BU
1996 Proof	125	Value: 45.00				

X# 4a 100 LEI

20.0000 g., Brass, 37 mm. **Subject:** XXVI Olympiad - Atlanta **Obv:** Arms **Obv. Legend:** ROMANIA **Rev:** Marksman kneeling with rifle facing, target image at left **Edge:** Plain **Edge Lettering:** 100 LEI

Date	Mintage	F	VF	XF	Unc	BU
1996 Proof	125	Value: 25.00				

X# 4b 100 LEI

20.0000 g. Nickel center in Brass ringr, 37 mm. **Subject:** XXVI Olympiad - Atlanta **Obv:** Arms **Obv. Legend:** ROMANIA **Rev:** Marksman kneeling with rifle facing, target image at left **Edge:** Plain **Edge Lettering:** 100 LEI

Date	Mintage	F	VF	XF	Unc	BU
1996 Proof	125	Value: 45.00				

X# 4c 100 LEI

12.0000 g., Aluminum, 37 mm. **Subject:** XXVI Olympiad - Atlanta **Obv:** Arms **Obv. Legend:** ROMANIA **Rev:** Marksman kneeling with rifle facing, target image at left **Edge:** Plain **Edge Lettering:** 100 LEI

Date	Mintage	F	VF	XF	Unc	BU
1996 Proof	125	Value: 25.00				

X# 4d 100 LEI

21.0000 g., Copper, 37 mm. **Subject:** XXVI Olympiad - Atlanta **Obv:** Arms **Obv. Legend:** ROMANIA **Rev:** Marksman kneeling with rifle facing, target image at left **Edge:** Plain **Edge Lettering:** 100 LEI

Date	Mintage	F	VF	XF	Unc	BU
1996 Proof	125	Value: 25.00				

X# 5 100 LEI

27.0000 g., 0.9250 Silver 0.8029 oz. ASW, 37 mm. **Subject:** XXVI Olympiad - Atlanta **Obv:** Arms **Obv. Legend:** ROMANIA **Rev:** Male "equestrian" racing left **Edge:** Plain **Edge Lettering:** 100 LEI

Date	Mintage	F	VF	XF	Unc	BU
1996 Proof	125	Value: 45.00				

X# 5a 100 LEI

20.0000 g., Brass, 37 mm. **Subject:** XXVI Olympiad - Atlanta **Obv:** Arms **Obv. Legend:** ROMANIA **Rev:** Male "equestrian" racing left **Edge:** Plain **Edge Lettering:** 100 LEI

Date	Mintage	F	VF	XF	Unc	BU
1996 Proof	125	Value: 25.00				

X# 5b 100 LEI

20.0000 g. Nickel center in Brass ringr, 37 mm. **Subject:** XXVI Olympiad - Atlanta **Obv:** Arms **Obv. Legend:** ROMANIA **Rev:** Male "equestrian" racing left **Edge:** Plain **Edge Lettering:** 100 LEI

Date	Mintage	F	VF	XF	Unc	BU
1996 Proof	125	Value: 45.00				

X# 5c 100 LEI

6.0000 g., Aluminum, 37 mm. **Subject:** XXVI Olympiad - Atlanta **Obv:** Arms **Obv. Legend:** ROMANIA **Rev:** Male "equestrian" racing left **Edge:** Plain **Edge Lettering:** 100 LEI

Date	Mintage	F	VF	XF	Unc	BU
1996 Proof	125	Value: 25.00				

X# 5d 100 LEI

21.0000 g., Copper, 37 mm. **Subject:** XXVI Olympiad - Atlanta **Obv:** Arms **Obv. Legend:** ROMANIA **Rev:** Male "equestrian" racing left **Edge:** Plain **Edge Lettering:** 100 LEI

Date	Mintage	F	VF	XF	Unc	BU
1996 Proof	125	Value: 25.00				

X# 6 100 LEI

27.0000 g., 0.9250 Silver 0.8029 oz. ASW, 37 mm. **Subject:** XIX Winter Olympics - Nagano **Obv:** Arms **Obv. Legend:** ROMANIA **Rev:** Male speed skater facing turning left **Edge:** Plain **Edge Lettering:** 100 LEI

Date	Mintage	F	VF	XF	Unc	BU
1998 Proof	125	Value: 45.00				

X# 6a 100 LEI

20.0000 g., Brass, 37 mm. **Subject:** XIX Winter Olympics - Nagano **Obv:** Arms **Obv. Legend:** ROMANIA **Rev:** Male speed skater facing turning left **Edge:** Plain **Edge Lettering:** 100 LEI

Date	Mintage	F	VF	XF	Unc	BU
1998 Proof	125	Value: 25.00				

X# 6b 100 LEI

Nickel center in Brass ringr, 37 mm. **Subject:** XIX Winter Olympics - Nagano **Obv:** Arms **Obv. Legend:** ROMANIA **Rev:** Male speed skater facing turning left **Edge:** Plain **Edge Lettering:** 100 LEI

Date	Mintage	F	VF	XF	Unc	BU
1998 Proof	125	Value: 45.00				

X# 6c 100 LEI

6.0000 g., Aluminum, 37 mm. **Subject:** XIX Winter Olympics - Nagano **Obv:** Arms **Obv. Legend:** ROMANIA **Rev:** Male speed skater facing turning left **Edge:** Plain **Edge Lettering:** 100 LEI

Date	Mintage	F	VF	XF	Unc	BU
1998 Proof	125	Value: 25.00				

X# 6d 100 LEI

21.0000 g., Copper, 37 mm. **Subject:** XIX Winter Olympics - Nagano **Obv:** Arms **Obv. Legend:** ROMANIA **Rev:** Male speed skater facing turning left **Edge:** Plain **Edge Lettering:** 100 LEI

Date	Mintage	F	VF	XF	Unc	BU
1998 Proof	125	Value: 25.00				

X# 7 100 LEI

27.0000 g., 0.9250 Silver 0.8029 oz. ASW, 37 mm. **Subject:** XIX Winter Olympics - Nagano **Obv:** Arms **Obv. Legend:** ROMANIA **Rev:** Two male hockey players facing off **Edge:** Plain **Edge Lettering:** 100 LEI

Date	Mintage	F	VF	XF	Unc	BU
1998 Proof	125	Value: 45.00				

X# 7a 100 LEI

20.0000 g., Brass, 37 mm. **Subject:** XIX Winter Olympics - Nagano **Obv:** Arms **Obv. Legend:** ROMANIA **Rev:** Two male hockey players facing off **Edge:** Plain **Edge Lettering:** 100 LEI

Date	Mintage	F	VF	XF	Unc	BU
1998 Proof	125	Value: 25.00				

X# 7b 100 LEI

Nickel center in Brass ringr, 37 mm. **Subject:** XIX Winter Olympics - Nagano **Obv:** Arms **Obv. Legend:** ROMANIA **Rev:** Two male hockey players facing off **Edge:** Plain **Edge Lettering:** 100 LEI

Date	Mintage	F	VF	XF	Unc	BU
1998 Proof	125	Value: 45.00				

X# 7c 100 LEI

6.0000 g., Aluminum, 37 mm. **Subject:** XIX Winter Olympics - Nagano **Obv:** Arms **Obv. Legend:** ROMANIA **Rev:** Two male hockey players facing off **Edge:** Plain **Edge Lettering:** 100 LEI

Date	Mintage	F	VF	XF	Unc	BU
1998 Proof	125	Value: 25.00				

X# 7d 100 LEI

21.0000 g., Copper, 37 mm. **Subject:** XIX Winter Olympics - Nagano **Obv:** Arms **Obv. Legend:** ROMANIA **Rev:** Two male hockey players facing off **Edge:** Plain **Edge Lettering:** 100 LEI

Date	Mintage	F	VF	XF	Unc	BU
1998 Proof	125	Value: 25.00				

X# 8 100 LEI

27.0000 g., 0.9250 Silver 0.8029 oz. ASW, 37 mm. **Subject:** XIX Winter Olympics - Nagano **Obv:** Arms **Obv. Legend:** ROMANIA **Rev:** Male skier in flight left **Edge:** Plain **Edge Lettering:** 100 LEI

Date	Mintage	F	VF	XF	Unc	BU
1998 Proof	125	Value: 45.00				

X# 8a 100 LEI

20.0000 g., Brass, 37 mm. **Subject:** XIX Winter Olympics - Nagano **Obv:** Arms **Obv. Legend:** ROMANIA **Rev:** Male skier in flight left **Edge:** Plain **Edge Lettering:** 100 LEI

Date	Mintage	F	VF	XF	Unc	BU
1998 Proof	125	Value: 25.00				

X# 8b 100 LEI

20.0000 g. Nickel center in Brass ringr, 37 mm. **Subject:** XIX Winter Olympics - Nagano **Obv:** Arms **Obv. Legend:** ROMANIA **Rev:** Male skier in flight left **Edge:** Plain **Edge Lettering:** 100 LEI

Date	Mintage	F	VF	XF	Unc	BU
1998 Proof	125	Value: 45.00				

X# 8c 100 LEI

6.0000 g., Aluminum, 37 mm. **Subject:** XIX Winter Olympics - Nagano **Obv:** Arms **Obv. Legend:** ROMANIA **Rev:** Male skier in flight left **Edge:** Plain **Edge Lettering:** 100 LEI

Date	Mintage	F	VF	XF	Unc	BU
1998 Proof	125	Value: 25.00				

X# 8d 100 LEI

21.0000 g., Copper, 37 mm. **Subject:** XIX Winter Olympics - Nagano **Obv:** Arms **Obv. Legend:** ROMANIA **Rev:** Male skier in flight left **Edge:** Plain **Edge Lettering:** 100 LEI

Date	Mintage	F	VF	XF	Unc	BU
1998 Proof	125	Value: 25.00				

X# 9 100 LEI

27.0000 g., 0.9250 Silver 0.8029 oz. ASW, 37 mm. **Subject:** XIX Winter Olympics - Nagano **Obv:** Arms **Obv. Legend:** ROMANIA **Rev:** Figure skating couple facing **Edge:** Plain **Edge Lettering:** 100 LEI

Date	Mintage	F	VF	XF	Unc	BU
1998 Proof	125	Value: 45.00				

X# 9a 100 LEI

20.0000 g., Brass, 37 mm. **Subject:** XIX Winter Olympics - Nagano **Obv:** Arms **Obv. Legend:** ROMANIA **Rev:** Figure skating couple facing **Edge:** Plain **Edge Lettering:** 100 LEI

Date	Mintage	F	VF	XF	Unc	BU
1998 Proof	125	Value: 25.00				

X# 9b 100 LEI

Ring Weight: 20.0000 g. **Ring Composition:** Brass **Center Composition:** Nickel, 37 mm. **Subject:** XIX Winter Olympics - Nagano **Obv:** Arms **Obv. Legend:** ROMANIA **Rev:** Figure skating couple facing **Edge:** Plain **Edge Lettering:** 100 LEI

Date	Mintage	F	VF	XF	Unc	BU
1998 Proof	125	Value: 45.00				

X# 9c 100 LEI

6.0000 g., Aluminum, 37 mm. **Subject:** XIX Winter Olympics - Nagano **Obv:** Arms **Obv. Legend:** ROMANIA **Rev:** Figure skating couple facing **Edge:** Plain **Edge Lettering:** 100 LEI

Date	Mintage	F	VF	XF	Unc	BU
1998 Proof	125	Value: 25.00				

X# 9d 100 LEI

21.0000 g., Copper, 37 mm. **Subject:** XIX Winter Olympics - Nagano **Obv:** Arms **Obv. Legend:** ROMANIA **Rev:** Figure skating couple facing **Edge:** Plain **Edge Lettering:** 100 LEI

Date	Mintage	F	VF	XF	Unc	BU
1998 Proof	125	Value: 25.00				

FANTASY EURO PATTERNS

X# Pn11 EURO CENT

Copper Plated Steel **Ruler:** Carol I **Edge:** Plain

Date	Mintage	F	VF	XF	Unc	BU
2004	—	—	—	—	—	1.50

X# Pn12 2 EURO CENT

Copper Plated Steel **Ruler:** Carol I **Edge:** Plain

Date	Mintage	F	VF	XF	Unc	BU
2004	—	—	—	—	—	2.00

X# Pn13 5 EURO CENT

Copper Plated Steel **Ruler:** Carol I **Edge:** Plain

Date	Mintage	F	VF	XF	Unc	BU
2004	—	—	—	—	—	2.50

X# Pn14 10 EURO CENT

Goldine **Ruler:** Carol I **Edge:** Plain

Date	Mintage	F	VF	XF	Unc	BU
2004	—	—	—	—	—	3.00

X# Pn15 20 EURO CENT

Goldine **Ruler:** Carol I **Edge:** Plain

Date	Mintage	F	VF	XF	Unc	BU
2004	—	—	—	—	—	3.50

X# Pn16 50 EURO CENT

Goldine **Ruler:** Carol I **Edge:** Plain

Date	Mintage	F	VF	XF	Unc	BU
2004	—	—	—	—	—	4.00

X# Pn17 EUROP

Bi-Metallic **Ruler:** Carol I **Edge:** Plain

Date	Mintage	F	VF	XF	Unc	BU
2004	—	—	—	—	—	6.00

X# Pn18 2 EUROP

Bi-Metallic **Ruler:** Carol I **Edge:** Plain

Date	Mintage	F	VF	XF	Unc	BU
2004	—	—	—	—	—	8.00

PIEFORTS

X#	Date	Mintage	Identification	Mkt Val
P1	1996	—	100 Lei. 0.9250 Silver. 54.0000 g. X#1.	75.00
P2	1996	—	100 Lei. Brass. 40.0000 g. X#1a.	40.00
P3	1996	—	100 Lei. 40.0000 g. X#1b.	75.00
P4	1996	—	100 Lei. Aluminum. 12.0000 g. X#1c.	40.00
P5	1996	—	100 Lei. Copper. 42.0000 g. X#1d.	40.00
P6	1996	—	100 Lei. Silver. 54.0000 g. X#2.	75.00
P7	1996	—	100 Lei. Brass. 40.0000 g. X#2a.	40.00
P8	1996	—	100 Lei. 40.0000 g. X#2b.	75.00
P9	1996	—	100 Lei. Aluminum. 12.0000 g. X#2c.	40.00
P10	1996	—	100 Lei. Copper. 42.0000 g. X#2d.	40.00
P11	1996	—	100 Lei. 0.9250 Silver. 54.0000 g. X#3.	75.00
P12	1996	—	100 Lei. Brass. 40.0000 g. X#3a.	40.00
P13	1996	—	100 Lei. X#3b.	75.00
P14	1996	—	100 Lei. Aluminum. 12.0000 g. X#3c.	40.00
P15	1996	—	100 Lei. Copper. 42.0000 g. X#3d.	40.00
P16	1996	—	100 Lei. 0.9250 Silver. 54.0000 g. X#4.	75.00
P17	1996	—	100 Lei. Brass. 40.0000 g. X#4a.	40.00
P18	1996	—	100 Lei. 40.0000 g. X#4b.	75.00
P19	1996	—	100 Lei. Aluminum. 12.0000 g. X#4c.	40.00
P20	1996	—	100 Lei. Copper. 42.0000 g. X#4d.	40.00
P21	1996	—	100 Lei. 0.9250 Silver. 54.0000 g. X#5.	75.00
P22	1996	—	100 Lei. Brass. 40.0000 g. X#5a.	40.00
P23	1996	—	100 Lei. 40.0000 g. X#5b.	75.00
P24	1996	—	100 Lei. Aluminum. 12.0000 g. X#5c.	40.00
P25	1996	—	100 Lei. Copper. 21.0000 g. X#5d.	40.00
P26	1998	—	100 Lei. 0.9250 Silver. 54.0000 g. X#6.	75.00
P27	1998	—	100 Lei. Brass. 40.0000 g. X#6a.	40.00
P28	1998	—	100 Lei. 40.0000 g. X#6b.	75.00
P29	1998	—	100 Lei. Aluminum. 12.0000 g. X#6c.	40.00
P30	1998	—	100 Lei. Copper. 42.0000 g. X#6d.	40.00
P31	1998	—	100 Lei. 0.9250 Silver. 54.0000 g. X#7.	75.00
P32	1998	—	100 Lei. Brass. 40.0000 g. X#7a.	40.00
P33	1998	—	100 Lei. X#7b.	75.00
P34	1998	—	100 Lei. Aluminum. 12.0000 g. X#7c.	40.00
P35	1998	—	100 Lei. Copper. 42.0000 g. X#7d.	40.00
P36	1998	—	100 Lei. 0.9250 Silver. 54.0000 g. X#8.	75.00
P37	1998	—	100 Lei. Brass. 40.0000 g. X#8a.	40.00

X#	Date	Mintage	Identification	Mkt Val
P38	1998	—	100 Lei. 40.0000 g. X#8b.	75.00
P39	1998	—	100 Lei. Aluminum. 12.0000 g. X#8c.	40.00
P40	1998	—	100 Lei. Copper. 42.0000 g. X#8d.	40.00
P41	1998	—	100 Lei. 0.9250 Silver. 54.0000 g. X#9.	75.00
P42	1998	—	100 Lei. Brass. 40.0000 g. X#9a.	40.00
P43	1998	—	200 Lei. 40.0000 g. X#9b.	75.00
P44	1998	—	100 Lei. Aluminum. 12.0000 g. X#9c.	40.00
P45	1998	—	100 Lei. Copper. 42.0000 g. X#9d.	40.00

MINT SETS

X#	Date	Mintage	Identification	Issue Price	Mkt Val
XMS1	2004 (8)	—	X#Pn1-Pn8	—	30.00

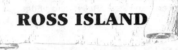

ROSS ISLAND

MCMURDO

NEW ZEALAND DEPENDENCY

U.S. Antarctic Weather Station

MEDALLIC COINAGE

X# 1 10 DOLLARS
8.1000 g., 0.9990 Silver 0.2601 oz. ASW, 25.5 mm. **Subject:** 30th Anniversary IGY **Obv:** Stylized winds above three mountain peaks - "Antarctic Landscape" **Obv. Inscription:** McMURDO **Obv. Designer:** Fred Zinkann **Rev:** Ornate hexagon "atom" design in rays - "Ice Crown" **Rev. Legend:** WHERE ALL DOMINIONS AND DIRECTIONS MEET THROUGH WIND AND ICE UMBRAGE **Rev. Inscription:** ANTARCTICA **Edge:** Plain **Edge Lettering:** SILVER

Date	Mintage	F	VF	XF	Unc	BU
ND(1987) Proof	75	Value: 40.00				

X# 1a 10 DOLLARS
5.0000 g., Pewter, 25.5 mm. **Subject:** 30th Anniversary IGY **Obv:** Stylized winds above three mountain peaks - "Antarctic Landscape" **Obv. Inscription:** McMURDO **Obv. Designer:** Fred Zinkann **Rev:** Ornate hexagon "atom" design in rays - "Ice Crown" **Rev. Legend:** WHERE ALL DOMINIONS AND DIRECTIONS MEET THROUGH WIND AND ICE UMBRAGE **Rev. Inscription:** ANTARCTICA **Edge:** Plain

Date	Mintage	F	VF	XF	Unc	BU
ND(1987) Proof	75	Value: 20.00				

X# 1b 10 DOLLARS
10.0000 g., 0.9950 Tantalum 0.3199 oz., 25.5 mm. **Subject:** 30th Anniversary IGY **Obv:** Stylized winds above three mountain peaks - "Antarctic Landscape" **Obv. Inscription:** McMURDO **Obv. Designer:** Fred Zinkann **Rev:** Ornate hexagon "atom" design in rays - "Ice Crown" **Rev. Legend:** WHERE ALL DOMINIONS AND DIRECTIONS MEET THROUGH WIND AND ICE UMBRAGE **Rev. Inscription:** ANTARCTICA **Edge:** Plain

Date	Mintage	F	VF	XF	Unc	BU
ND(1987) Proof	18	Value: 250				

X# 1c 10 DOLLARS
3.5000 g., 0.9990 Niobium 0.1124 oz., 25.5 mm. **Subject:** 30th Anniversary IGY **Obv:** Stylized winds above three mountain peaks - "Antarctic Landscape" **Obv. Inscription:** McMURDO **Obv. Designer:** Fred Zinkann **Rev:** Ornate hexagon "atom" design in rays - "Ice Crown" **Rev. Legend:** WHERE ALL DOMINIONS AND DIRECTIONS MEETTHROUGH WIND AND ICE UMBRAGE **Rev. Inscription:** ANTARCTICA **Edge:** Plain

Date	Mintage	F	VF	XF	Unc	BU
ND(1987) Restrike	19	—	—	—	20.00	—

X# 1d 10 DOLLARS
4.5000 g., Copper Nickel, 25.5 mm. **Subject:** 30th Anniversary IGY **Obv:** Stylized winds above three mountainpeaks-"AntarcticLandscape" **Obv. Inscription:** McMURDO **Obv. Designer:** Fred Zinkann **Rev:** Ornate hexagon "atom" design in rays - "Ice Crown" **Rev. Legend:** WHERE ALL DOMINIONS AND DIRECTIONS MEET THROUGH WIND AND ICE UMBRAGE **Rev. Inscription:** ANTARCTICA **Edge:** Plain

Date	Mintage	F	VF	XF	Unc	BU
ND(1987)	25	—	—	—	10.00	—

PIEFORTS

X#	Date	Mintage	Identification	Mkt Val
P1	ND(1987)	5	10 Dollars. 0.9990 Silver. 16.0000 g. X#1.	150

RUSSIA

RUSSIAN FANTASY FEDERATION

FANTASY EURO PATTERNS

X# Pn1 EURO CENT
Copper Plated Steel **Obv:** Crowned arms in order chain **Rev:** Leaf sprig with berries at left, value at right **Edge:** Plain

Date	Mintage	F	VF	XF	Unc	BU
2004	8,000	—	—	—	—	3.00

X# Pn2 2 EURO CENT
Copper Plated Steel **Obv:** Crowned arms in order chain **Rev:** Leaf sprig with berries at left, value at right **Edge:** Plain

Date	Mintage	F	VF	XF	Unc	BU
2004	8,000	—	—	—	—	4.00

X# Pn3 5 EURO CENT
Copper Plated Steel **Obv:** Crowned arms in order chain **Rev:** Leaf sprig with berries at left, value at right **Edge:** Plain

Date	Mintage	F	VF	XF	Unc	BU
2004	8,000	—	—	—	—	6.00

X# Pn4 10 EURO CENT
Goldine **Obv:** Crowned arms in order chain **Rev:** Leaf sprig with berries at left, value at right **Edge:** Plain

Date	Mintage	F	VF	XF	Unc	BU
2004	8,000	—	—	—	—	7.00

X# Pn5 20 EURO CENT
Goldine **Obv:** Crowned arms in order chain **Rev:** Leaf sprig with berries at left, value at right **Edge:** Plain

Date	Mintage	F	VF	XF	Unc	BU
2004	8,000	—	—	—	—	9.00

X# Pn6 50 EURO CENT
Goldine **Obv:** Crowned arms in order chain **Rev:** Leaf sprig with berries at left, value at right **Edge:** Plain

Date	Mintage	F	VF	XF	Unc	BU
2004	8,000	—	—	—	—	11.00

X# Pn7 EURO
Bi-Metallic **Obv:** Crowned arms in order chain **Obv. Legend:** RUSSIAN FEDERATION **Rev:** Leaf sprig with berries at left, value at right **Edge:** Plain

Date	Mintage	F	VF	XF	Unc	BU
2004	7,000	—	—	—	—	15.00

X# Pn9 EURO
Bi-Metallic Copper-Nickel center in Goldine ring **Obv:** Head of Czar Nicholas II left **Obv. Legend:** RUSSIAN FEDERATION **Rev:** Leaf sprig with berries at left, value at right

Date	Mintage	F	VF	XF	Unc	BU
2004	1,000	—	—	—	—	30.00

X# Pn8 2 EURO
Bi-Metallic **Obv:** Crowned arms in order chain **Obv. Legend:** RUSSIAN FEDERATION **Rev:** Leaf sprig with berries at left, value at right **Edge:** Plain

Date	Mintage	F	VF	XF	Unc	BU
2004	7,000	—	—	—	—	15.00

X# Pn10 2 EURO
Bi-Metallic Copper-Nickel center in Goldine ring **Obv:** Head of Czar Nicholas II left **Obv. Legend:** RUSSIAN FEDERATION **Rev:** Leaf sprig with berries at left, value at right

Date	Mintage	F	VF	XF	Unc	BU
2004	1,000	—	—	—	—	35.00

EMPIRE

CAST COINAGE

X# 6 POLTINA
White Metal **Ruler:** Peter III **Obv:** Imperial eagle, value below **Note:** Posthumous issue.

Date	Mintage	F	VF	XF	Unc	BU
1771	—	—	—	—	—	—

X# 10 ROUBLE
White Metal **Ruler:** Peter III **Obv:** Bust of Peter left in Cossack general's uniform **Rev:** Peter with scepter, horseback right **Note:** Posthumous issue.

Date	Mintage	F	VF	XF	Unc	BU
177?	—	120	175	—	—	—

X# 7 ROUBLE

White Metal **Ruler:** Peter III **Obv:** Bust left in Cossack general's uniform in sprays **Rev:** Value above date in center **Note:** Posthumous issue.

Date	Mintage	F	VF	XF	Unc	BU
1771	—	170	250	—	—	—

X# 8 ROUBLE

White Metal **Ruler:** Peter III **Obv:** Bust of Peter left in Cossack general's uniform **Rev:** 8-pointed cross divides date, value above **Note:** Posthumous issue.

Date	Mintage	F	VF	XF	Unc	BU
1772	—	145	175	—	—	—

X# 9 ROUBLE

White Metal **Ruler:** Peter III **Obv:** Bust of Peter left in Cossack general's uniform **Rev:** 8-pointed cross, date below **Note:** Posthumous issue. A modern copy exists struck over a piatak of Catherine II.

Date	Mintage	F	VF	XF	Unc	BU
1773	—	120	150	—	—	—

X# 4 GRIVNA

White Metal **Ruler:** Peter III **Obv:** Crowned П / 3 **Rev:** Cross, letters in angles **Rev. Inscription:** ГРИВНА **Note:** Posthumous issue.

Date	Mintage	F	VF	XF	Unc	BU
1771	—	—	—	—	—	—

X# 5 2 GRIVENNIK

White Metal **Ruler:** Peter III **Obv:** Crowned П / III above sprays, value below **Rev:** Cross, dotted border in angles **Note:** Posthumous issue.

Date	Mintage	F	VF	XF	Unc	BU
1771	—	—	—	—	—	—

GOLD MINE INGOTS

During the late 19th and early 20th century, Russian law provided that gold mine owners who supplied gold to the mints should receive back whatever silver was recovered during refining of the gold. The silver was returned in the form of circular ingots of various weights which resembled coins. These pieces have often been erroneously described as Russian trade coins for use in Mongolia, China, and Turkestan.

Note: Both the Doyla and the Zolotnik are weights, not denominations.

KM# 1 24 DOLYA

1.0664 g., 0.9900 Silver 0.0339 oz. ASW
Ruler: Nicholas II **Obv:** Crowned double headed eagle within circle **Rev:** Value

Date	Mintage	F	VF	XF	Unc	BU
ND(1901)	—	—	350	450	650	—

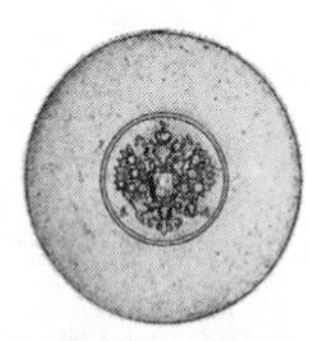

KM# 2 ZOLOTNIK

4.2656 g., 0.9900 Silver 0.1358 oz. ASW
Ruler: Nicholas II **Obv:** Crowned double headed eagle within small circle **Rev:** Value

Date	Mintage	F	VF	XF	Unc	BU
ND(1901)	—	—	300	400	600	—

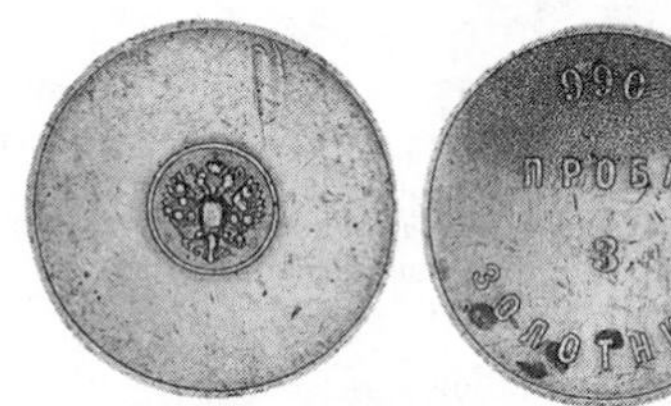

KM# 3 3 ZOLOTNIKS

12.7969 g., 0.9900 Silver 0.4073 oz. ASW
Ruler: Nicholas II **Obv:** Crowned double headed eagle within small circle **Rev:** Value

Date	Mintage	F	VF	XF	Unc	BU
ND(1901)	—	—	1,000	1,500	2,000	—

KM# 4 10 ZOLOTNIKS

42.6563 g., 0.9900 Silver 1.3577 oz. ASW
Ruler: Nicholas II **Obv:** Crowned double headed eagle within small circle **Rev:** Value

Date	Mintage	F	VF	XF	Unc	BU
ND(1901)	—	—	350	550	900	—

TRADE COINAGE

X# 1 4 DUCAT

Gold **Subject:** Alexander II **Note:** A private fantasy normally encountered holed and countermarked.

Date	Mintage	F	VF	XF	Unc	BU
1905	—	—	550	700	900	—

MEDALLIC COINAGE

Supreme Monarchical Council

X# M12c ROUBLE

Nickel **Obv:** Head of Nicholas II left **Rev:** Imperial eagle with shields on wings **Edge:** Reeded

Date	Mintage	F	VF	XF	Unc	BU
1990	5,000	—	—	—	—	15.00

X# M12b ROUBLE

31.1341 g., 0.9990 Pure Gold 0.9999 oz. **Obv:** Head of Nicholas II left **Rev:** Imperial Eagle with shields on wings **Edge:** Reeded

Date	Mintage	F	VF	XF	Unc	BU
1991 Proof	100	Value: 800				

X# M12 ROUBLE

31.1341 g., 0.9990 Silver 0.9999 oz. ASW, 38.25 mm. **Obv:** Head of Nicholas II left **Rev:** Imperial Eagle with shields on wings **Edge:** Reeded

Date	Mintage	F	VF	XF	Unc	BU
1990 Proof	1,000	Value: 55.00				

X# M12a ROUBLE

31.1341 g., 0.9990 Pure Palladium 0.9999 oz., 38.25 mm. **Obv:** Head of Nicholas II left **Rev:** Imperial Eagle with shields on wings **Edge:** Reeded

Date	Mintage	F	VF	XF	Unc	BU
ND(1990) Proof	100	Value: 495				

CCCP (U.S.S.R.)

(Union of Soviet Socialist Republics)

MILLED COINAGE

X# 40 5000 ROUBLES
Copper-Nickel **Issuer:** All Russian Exchange Bank **Series:** Deposit Certificate **Obv:** Bank monogram **Obv. Legend:** ДЕН@ @ILГИ - СРЕДСТВО АЕЛI@ @IL - СОЗИДАНИЕ **Rev. Legend:** ВСЕРОССИИСКИИ БИРЖЕВОИ **Edge:** Reeded **Note:** Redemption at 5000 Roubles until December 30, 1996; 10,000 Roubles after.

Date	Mintage	F	VF	XF	Unc	BU
1991	10,000	—	—	—	—	—

MEDALLIC SILVER BULLION COINAGE

1987 Gillio Issue

Struck at the Leningrad Mint

X# MB1 5 OUNCES
156.4500 g., 0.9990 Silver 5.0247 oz. ASW, 66 mm. **Issuer:** American Bullion and Coin **Subject:** "Glasnost" Russian-American Peace and Cooperation **Rev:** Defense of Nature-Polar bears **Note:** For earlier Imperial issues see Russia. Illustration reduced.

Date	Mintage	F	VF	XF	Unc	BU
1987 Proof	10,000	Value: 500				

BULLION COINAGE

X# MB2 5 OUNCES
156.4500 g., 0.9990 Silver 5.0247 oz. ASW, 59.85 mm. **Issuer:** American Bullion and Coin **Subject:** USA - USSR INF Treaty **Obv:** Flags above clasped hands, sprays below **Rev:** Two nation's capital buildings **Note:** Illustration reduced.

Date	Mintage	F	VF	XF	Unc	BU
1987 Proof	1,000	Value: 500				

X# MB3 5 OUNCES
156.4500 g., 0.9990 Silver 5.0247 oz. ASW **Issuer:** Bank for Foreign Economic Affairs **Subject:** Millennium of Russian Christianity **Obv:** Head of Christ facing between dates 988-1988 **Rev:** Cyrillic inscription between two church figures **Note:** Illustration reduced.

Date	Mintage	F	VF	XF	Unc	BU
1988 Proof	1,000	Value: 500				

X# MB4 5 OUNCES
156.4500 g., 0.9990 Silver 5.0247 oz. ASW, 59.85 mm. **Issuer:** Bank for Foreign Economic Affairs **Subject:** Millennium of First Russian Coin **Obv:** Earliest coin **Rev:** Three Medieval coining scenes **Note:** Illustration reduced.

Date	Mintage	F	VF	XF	Unc	BU
1988 Proof	1,000	Value: 500				

MEDALLIC COINAGE

X# M11d ROUBLE
23.5000 g., Copper **Subject:** 60th Anniversary Czarist Russian Government in Exile **Obv:** Head of Czar Nicholas II left **Rev:** Imperial eagle on broad sword **Edge:** Plain

Date	Mintage	F	VF	XF	Unc	BU
1989	10,000	—	—	—	—	20.00

X# 11c ROUBLE
31.1000 g., Pure Gold **Subject:** 60th Anniversary Czarist Russian Government in Exile **Obv:** Head of Czar Nicholas II left **Rev:** Imperial eagle, sword behind **Edge:** Plain

Date	Mintage	F	VF	XF	Unc	BU
1989 Proof	100	Value: 850				

X# M11 ROUBLE
31.1000 g., 0.9990 Pure Platinum 0.9988 oz., 38.25 mm. **Subject:** 60th Anniversary Czarist Russian Government in Exile **Obv:** Head of Nicholas II left

Rev: Imperial eagle, sword behind **Edge:** Plain **Note:** Hallmarked ".999".

Date	Mintage	F	VF	XF	Unc	BU
ND(1989)Proof	10	Value: 1,750				

X# M11a ROUBLE

23.5000 g., Platinum APW, 38.25 mm. **Subject:** 60th Anniversary Czarist Russian Government in Exile **Obv:** Head of Nicholas II left **Rev:** Imperial eagle, sword behind **Edge:** Plain

Date	Mintage	F	VF	XF	Unc	BU
ND(1989) Proof	10,000	Value: 120				

X# M11b ROUBLE

31.1000 g., 0.9990 Pure Silver 0.9988 oz., 38.25 mm. **Subject:** 60th Anniversary Czarist Russian Government in Exile **Obv:** Head of Czar Nicholas II left **Rev:** Imperial eagle, sword behind **Edge:** Plain **Note:** Hallmarked ".999".

Date	Mintage	F	VF	XF	Unc	BU
ND(1989)Proof	1,000	Value: 75.00				

X# M21 RUBLE/DOLLAR

Scrap Metal **Issuer:** Soviet Peace Committee **Subject:** USA - USSR INF Treaty **Obv:** Bell shape **Rev:** Large "1", olive sprig

Date	Mintage	F	VF	XF	Unc	BU
1988	—	—	—	—	10.00	—

RUSSIAN FEDERATION

Issued by БАНК РОССИИ (Bank Russia)

REFORM COINAGE

January 1, 1998

1,000 Old Roubles = 1 New Rouble

Y# 847 3 ROUBLES

34.5600 g., 0.9000 Silver 100000 oz. ASW, 39 mm. **Rev:** St. Trinity Monastery

Date	Mintage	F	VF	XF	Unc	BU
2003(sp) Proof	10,000	Value: 40.00				

DISPLAY MODELS

X# DM1 3 ROUBLES

23.2300 g., Pewter Specific gravity: 7.368, 38.7 mm. **Subject:** Uniface Bank Display Model **Obv:** Double-headed eagle **Rev:** The word "Model" in raised Cyrillic letters **Edge:** Reeded **Note:** Prev. KM#DM1.

Date	Mintage	F	VF	XF	Unc	BU
1999(m) Proof	—	—	—	—	—	—

X# DM2 3 ROUBLES

15.2200 g., Lead And Tin Alloy Specific gravity :9.280, 38.7 mm. **Subject:** Uniface Bank Display Model **Obv:** The word "Model" in incuse Cyrillic letters **Rev:** Design of Y-638 **Edge:** Reeded **Note:** Prev. KM#DM2.

Date	Mintage	F	VF	XF	Unc	BU
1999(m) Proof	—	—	—	—	—	—

X# DM3 3 ROUBLES

15.2200 g., Lead And Tin Alloy, 38.7 mm. **Subject:** Uniface Bank Display Model **Obv:** The word "Model" in incuse Cyrillic letters **Rev:** Design of Y-639 **Edge:** Reeded **Note:** Prev. KM#DM3.

Date	Mintage	F	VF	XF	Unc	BU
1999(m) Proof	—	—	—	—	—	—

ECU COINAGE

X# 31 50 ECU

31.1030 g., 0.9990 Silver 0.9989 oz. ASW, 38 mm. **Issuer:** Numex S.A., Madrid **Obv:** Double headed eagle **Obv. Legend:** РОССИИСКА Я ФЕДЕРААИЯ **Rev:** Kremlin complex **Edge:** Reeded

Date	Mintage	F	VF	XF	Unc	BU
1993 Proof	7,500	Value: 40.00				

X# 32 150 ECU

31.1030 g., 0.8150 Gold 0.8150 oz. AGW, 38 mm. **Issuer:** Numex S.A., Madrid **Obv:** Double headed eagle **Obv. Legend:** РОССИИСКА Я ФЕДЕРААИЯ **Rev:** Kremlin complex **Edge:** Reeded

Date	Mintage	F	VF	XF	Unc	BU
1993 Proof	1,500	Value: 800				

PIEFORTS

X#	Date	Mintage	Identification	Issue Price	Mkt Val
P1	1989	1	Rouble. Platinum. X#M11. 93.3090 g. (triple thickness and three ounces)	—	—
P2	1989	60	Rouble. Silver. X#M11b. Weight 62.2060 g.	—	—
P3	ND(1989)	60	Rouble. Platinum. X#M11a. Weight 47.0 g.	—	—
P4	1989	60	Rouble. Copper. X#M11d. Weight 47.0 g.	—	—
P5	1989	6	Rouble. Pure Gold. X#M11c. 93.3g., (triple thickness and three ounces)	—	—
P6	1990	70	Rouble. Pure Silver. X#M12. 62.2g.	—	—
P7	1990	7	Rouble. Pure Palladium. X#M12a. 62.2g.	—	—
P8	1990	7	Rouble. Pure Gold. X#M12b. 93.3g. (triple thickness and three ounces).	—	—
P11	ND(1991)	100	Rouble. Silver. X#12. 2.00 oz.	—	100
P12	ND(1991)	7	Rouble. Palladium. X#12a. 2.00 oz.	—	—
P12	ND(1991)	7	Rouble. Palladium. X#12a. 2.00 oz.	—	—
P13	ND(1991)	7	Rouble. Gold. X#12b. 2.00 oz.	—	—

MINT SETS

X#	Date	Mintage	Identification	Issue Price	Mkt Val
XMS1	2004 (8)	7,000	X#Pn1-Pn8	—	35.00
XMS2	2004 (8)	1,000	X#Pn1-Pn6, Pn9, Pn10	—	70.00

RUSSIA (KALININGRAD)

ENCLAVE (OBLAST)

MEDALLIC COINAGE

X# 1 MARKA

7.6000 g., Bronze, 28 mm. **Series:** Glory of Russian Arms **Obv:** Value in sprays **Obv. Legend:** ЗАЛАДНЫИ АНКЛАВ РОССИИ - КАЛИНИГРАД **Rev:** Kalachnikov AK-47 Assault Rifle **Rev. Legend:** ★ ★ ★ РУССОГО ОРУЖИЯ ★ ★ ★ **Rev. Inscription:** СЛАВА **Edge:** Plain

Date	Mintage	F	VF	XF	Unc	BU
2002 Proof	400	Value: 50.00				

X# 4 MARKA

7.6000 g., Bronze, 28 mm. **Series:** Glory of Russian Arms **Obv:** Value in sprays **Obv. Legend:** ЗАЛАДНЫИ АНКЛАВ РОССИИ - КАЛИНИГРАД **Rev:** K-50 Helicopter **Rev. Legend:** ★ ★ ★ РУССОГО ОРУЖИЯ ★ ★ ★ **Rev. Inscription:** СЛАВА **Edge:** Reeded

Date	Mintage	F	VF	XF	Unc	BU
2003 Proof	400	Value: 50.00				

X# 7 MARKA
7.6000 g., Bronze, 28 mm. **Series:** Glory of Russian Arms **Obv:** Value in sprays **Obv. Legend:** ЗАЛАДНЫИ АНКЛАВ РОССИИ - КАЛИНИГРАД **Rev:** T-34 Tank **Rev. Legend:** ★ ★ ★ РУССОГО ОРУЖИЯ ★ ★ ★ **Rev. Inscription:** СЛАВА **Edge:** Reeded

Date	Mintage	F	VF	XF	Unc	BU
2003 Proof	400	Value: 50.00				

X# 10 MARKA
7.6000 g., Bronze, 28 mm. **Series:** Glory of Russian Arms **Obv:** Value in sprays **Obv. Legend:** ЗАЛАДНЫИ АНКЛАВ РОССИИ - КАЛИНИГРАД **Rev:** MiG-29 Jet Fighter **Rev. Legend:** ★ ★ ★ РУССОГО ОРУЖИЯ ★ ★ ★ **Rev. Inscription:** СЛАВА **Edge:** Reeded

Date	Mintage	F	VF	XF	Unc	BU
2003 Proof	400	Value: 50.00				

X# 13 MARKA
7.6000 g., Bronze, 28 mm. **Series:** Glory of Russian Arms **Obv:** Value in sprays **Obv. Legend:** ЗАЛАДНЫИ АНКЛАВ РОССИИ - КАЛИНИГРАД **Rev:** Katyusha Rocket Launcher **Rev. Legend:** ★ ★ ★ РУССОГО ОРУЖИЯ ★ ★ ★ **Rev. Inscription:** СЛАВА **Edge:** Reeded

Date	Mintage	F	VF	XF	Unc	BU
2003 Proof	400	Value: 50.00				

X# 16 MARKA
7.6000 g., Bronze, 28 mm. **Series:** Glory of Russian Arms **Obv:** Value in sprays **Obv. Legend:** ЗАЛАДНЫИ АНКЛАВ РОССИИ - КАЛИНИГРАД **Rev:** S-13 Submarine **Rev. Legend:** ★ ★ ★ РУССОГО ОРУЖИЯ ★ ★ ★ **Rev. Inscription:** СЛАВА **Edge:** Reeded

Date	Mintage	F	VF	XF	Unc	BU
2003 Proof	400	Value: 50.00				

X# 19 MARKA
7.6000 g., Bronze, 28 mm. **Series:** Glory of Russian Arms **Subject:** Value in sprays **Obv. Legend:** ЗАЛАДНЫИ АНКЛАВ РОССИИ - КАЛИНИГРАД **Rev:** BTR-80 Armored Personel Carrier **Rev. Legend:** ★ ★ ★ РУССОГО ОРУЖИЯ ★ ★ ★ **Rev. Inscription:** СЛАВА **Edge:** Reeded

Date	Mintage	F	VF	XF	Unc	BU
2003 Proof	400	Value: 50.00				

X# 22 MARKA
7.6000 g., Bronze, 28 mm. **Series:** Glory of Russian Arms **Obv:** Value in sprays **Obv. Legend:** ЗАЛАДНЫИ АНКЛАВ РОССИИ - КАЛИНИГРАД **Rev:** Su-37 Jet Fighter **Rev. Legend:** ★ ★ ★ РУССОГО ОРУЖИЯ ★ ★ ★ **Rev. Inscription:** СЛАВА **Edge:** Reeded

Date	Mintage	F	VF	XF	Unc	BU
2003 Proof	400	Value: 50.00				

X# 25 MARKA
7.6000 g., Bronze, 28 mm. **Series:** Glory of Russian Arms **Obv:** Value in sprays **Obv. Legend:** ЗАЛАДНЫИ АНКЛАВ РОССИИ - КАЛИНИГРАД **Rev:** 45mm Field Cannon **Rev. Legend:** ★ ★ ★ РУССОГО ОРУЖИЯ ★ ★ ★ **Rev. Inscription:** СЛАВА **Edge:** Reeded

Date	Mintage	F	VF	XF	Unc	BU
2003 Proof	400	Value: 50.00				

X# 2.1 3 MARKI
9.4500 g., 0.9250 Silver 0.2810 oz. ASW, 28 mm. **Series:** Glory of Russian Arms **Obv:** Value in sprays **Obv. Legend:** ЗАЛАДНЫИ АНКЛАВ РОССИИ - КАЛИНИГРАД **Rev:** Kalachnikov AK-47 Assault Rifle **Rev. Legend:** ★ ★ ★ РУССОГО ОРУЖИЯ ★ ★ ★ **Rev. Inscription:** СЛАВА **Edge:** Plain

Date	Mintage	F	VF	XF	Unc	BU
2002 Proof	225	Value: 100				

X# 2.2 3 MARKI
9.4500 g., 0.9250 Silver 0.2810 oz. ASW, 28 mm. **Series:** Glory of Russian Arms **Obv:** Value in sprays **Obv. Legend:** ЗАЛАДНЫИ АНКЛАВ РОССИИ - КАЛИНИГРАД **Rev:** Kalachnikov AK-47 Assault Rifle **Rev. Legend:** ★ ★ ★ РУССОГО ОРУЖИЯ ★ ★ ★ **Rev. Inscription:** СЛАВА **Edge:** Reeded

Date	Mintage	F	VF	XF	Unc	BU
2003 Proof	25	Value: 350				

X# 5 3 MARKI
9.4500 g., 0.9250 Silver 0.2810 oz. ASW, 28 mm. **Series:** Glory of Russian Arms **Obv:** Value in sprays **Obv. Legend:** ЗАЛАДНЫИ АНКЛАВ РОССИИ - КАЛИНИГРАД **Rev:** K-50 Helicopter **Rev. Legend:** ★ ★ ★ РУССОГО ОРУЖИЯ ★ ★ ★ **Rev. Inscription:** СЛАВА **Edge:** Reeded

Date	Mintage	F	VF	XF	Unc	BU
2003 Proof	250	Value: 100				

X# 8 3 MARKI
9.4500 g., 0.9250 Silver 0.2810 oz. ASW, 28 mm. **Series:** Glory of Russian Arms **Obv:** Value in sprays **Obv. Legend:** ЗАЛАДНЫИ АНКЛАВ РОССИИ - КАЛИНИГРАД **Rev:** T-34 Tank **Rev. Legend:** ★ ★ ★ РУССОГО ОРУЖИЯ ★ ★ ★ **Rev. Inscription:** СЛАВА **Edge:** Reeded

Date	Mintage	F	VF	XF	Unc	BU
2003 Proof	250	Value: 100				

X# 11 3 MARKI
9.4500 g., 0.9250 Silver 0.2810 oz. ASW, 28 mm. **Series:** Glory of Russian Arms **Obv:** Value in sprays **Obv. Legend:** ЗАЛАДНЫИ АНКЛАВ РОССИИ - КАЛИНИГРАД **Rev:** MiG-29 Jet Fighter **Rev. Legend:** ★ ★ ★ РУССОГО ОРУЖИЯ ★ ★ ★ **Rev. Inscription:** СЛАВА **Edge:** Reeded

Date	Mintage	F	VF	XF	Unc	BU
2003 Proof	250	Value: 100				

X# 14 3 MARKI
9.4500 g., 0.9250 Silver 0.2810 oz. ASW, 28 mm. **Series:** Glory of Russian Arms **Obv:** Value in sprays **Obv. Legend:** ЗАЛАДНЫИ АНКЛАВ РОССИИ - КАЛИНИГРАД **Rev:** Katyusha Rocket Launcher **Rev. Legend:** ★ ★ ★ РУССОГО ОРУЖИЯ ★ ★ ★ **Rev. Inscription:** СЛАВА **Edge:** Reeded

Date	Mintage	F	VF	XF	Unc	BU
2003 Proof	250	Value: 100				

X# 17 3 MARKI
9.4500 g., 0.9250 Silver 0.2810 oz. ASW, 28 mm. **Series:** Glory of Russian Arms **Obv:** Value in sprays **Obv. Legend:** ЗАЛАДНЫИ АНКЛАВ РОССИИ - КАЛИНИГРАД **Rev:** S-13 Submarine **Rev. Legend:** ★ ★ ★ РУССОГО ОРУЖИЯ ★ ★ ★ **Rev. Inscription:** СЛАВА **Edge:** Reeded

Date	Mintage	F	VF	XF	Unc	BU
2003 Proof	—	Value: 100				

X# 20 3 MARKI
9.4500 g., 0.9250 Silver 0.2810 oz. ASW, 28 mm. **Series:** Glory of Russian Arms **Obv:** Value in sprays **Obv. Legend:** ЗАЛАДНЫИ АНКЛАВ РОССИИ - КАЛИНИГРАД **Rev:** BTR Armored Personnel Carrier **Rev. Legend:** ★ ★ ★ РУССОГО ОРУЖИЯ ★ ★ ★ **Rev. Inscription:** СЛАВА **Edge:** Reeded

Date	Mintage	F	VF	XF	Unc	BU
2003 Proof	250	Value: 100				

X# 23 3 MARKI
9.4500 g., 0.9250 Silver 0.2810 oz. ASW, 28 mm. **Series:** Glory of Russian Arms **Obv:** Value in sprays **Obv. Legend:** ЗАЛАДНЫИ АНКЛАВ РОССИИ - КАЛИНИГРАД **Rev:** Su-37 Jet Fighter **Rev. Legend:** ★ ★ ★ РУССОГО ОРУЖИЯ ★ ★ ★ **Rev. Inscription:** СЛАВА **Edge:** Reeded

Date	Mintage	F	VF	XF	Unc	BU
2003 Proof	250	Value: 100				

X# 26 3 MARKI
9.4500 g., 0.9250 Silver 0.2810 oz. ASW, 28 mm. **Series:** Glory of Russian Arms **Obv:** Value in sprays **Obv. Legend:** ЗАЛАДНЫИ АНКЛАВ РОССИИ - КАЛИНИГРАД **Rev:** 45mm Field Cannon **Rev. Legend:** ★ ★ ★ РУССОГО ОРУЖИЯ ★ ★ ★ **Rev. Inscription:** СЛАВА **Edge:** Reeded

Date	Mintage	F	VF	XF	Unc	BU
2003 Proof	250	Value: 100				

X# 3 20 MAROK
12.1000 g., 0.5850 Gold 0.2276 oz. AGW, 28 mm. **Series:** Glory of Russian Arms **Obv:** Value in sprays **Obv. Legend:** ЗАЛАДНЫИ АНКЛАВ РОССИИ - КАЛИНИГРАД **Rev:** Kalachnikov AK-47 Assault Rifle **Rev. Legend:** ★ ★ ★ РУССОГО ОРУЖИЯ ★ ★ ★ **Rev. Inscription:** СЛАВА **Edge:** Plain

Date	Mintage	F	VF	XF	Unc	BU
2002 Proof	8	Value: 1,250				

X# 6 20 MAROK
11.6000 g., 0.5850 Gold 0.2182 oz. AGW, 28 mm. **Series:** Glory of Russian Arms **Obv:** Value in sprays **Obv. Legend:** ЗАЛАДНЫИ АНКЛАВ РОССИИ - КАЛИНИГРАД **Rev:** K-50 Helicopter **Rev. Legend:** ★ ★ ★ РУССОГО ОРУЖИЯ ★ ★ ★ **Rev. Inscription:** СЛАВА **Edge:** Reeded

Date	Mintage	F	VF	XF	Unc	BU
2003 Proof	8	Value: 1,250				

X# 9 20 MAROK
11.6000 g., 0.5850 Gold 0.2182 oz. AGW, 28 mm. **Series:** Glory of Russian Arms **Obv:** Value in sprays **Obv. Legend:** ЗАЛАДНЫИ АНКЛАВ РОССИИ - КАЛИНИГРАД **Rev:** T-34 Tank **Rev. Legend:** ★ ★ ★ РУССОГО ОРУЖИЯ ★ ★ ★ **Rev. Inscription:** СЛАВА

Date	Mintage	F	VF	XF	Unc	BU
2003 Proof	8	Value: 1,250				

X# 12 20 MAROK
11.6000 g., 0.5850 Gold 0.2182 oz. AGW, 28 mm. **Series:** Glory of Russian Arms **Obv:** Value in sprays **Obv. Legend:** ЗАЛАДНЫИ АНКЛАВ РОССИИ - КАЛИНИГРАД **Rev:** MiG-29 Jet Fighter **Rev. Legend:** ★ ★ ★ РУССОГО ОРУЖИЯ ★ ★ ★ **Rev. Inscription:** СЛАВА **Edge:** Reeded

Date	Mintage	F	VF	XF	Unc	BU
2003 Proof	8	Value: 1,250				

X# 18 20 MAROK
11.6000 g., 0.5850 Gold 0.2182 oz. AGW, 28 mm. **Series:** Glory of Russian Arms **Obv:** Value in sprays **Obv. Legend:** ЗАЛАДНЫИ АНКЛАВ РОССИИ - КАЛИНИГРАД **Rev:** S-13 Submarine **Rev. Legend:** ★ ★ ★ РУССОГО ОРУЖИЯ ★ ★ ★ **Rev. Inscription:** СЛАВА **Edge:** Reeded

Date	Mintage	F	VF	XF	Unc	BU
2003 Proof	8	Value: 1,250				

X# 21 20 MAROK
11.6000 g., 0.5850 Gold 0.2182 oz. AGW, 28 mm. **Series:** Glory of Russian Arms **Obv:** Value in sprays **Obv. Legend:** ЗАЛАДНЫИ АНКЛАВ РОССИИ - КАЛИНИГРАД **Rev:** BTR Armored Personel Carrier **Rev. Legend:** ★ ★ ★ РУССОГО ОРУЖИЯ ★ ★ ★ **Rev. Inscription:** СЛАВА **Edge:** Reeded

Date	Mintage	F	VF	XF	Unc	BU
2003 Proof	8	Value: 1,250				

X# 24 20 MAROK
9.4500 g., 0.9250 Silver 0.2810 oz. ASW, 28 mm. **Series:** Glory of Russian Arms **Subject:** Value in sprays **Obv. Legend:** ЗАЛАДНЫИ АНКЛАВ РОССИИ - КАЛИНИГРАД **Rev:** Su-37 Jet Fighter **Rev. Legend:** ★ ★ ★ РУССОГО ОРУЖИЯ ★ ★ ★ **Rev. Inscription:** СЛАВА **Edge:** Reeded

Date	Mintage	F	VF	XF	Unc	BU
2003 Proof	250	Value: 120				

X# 27 20 MAROK
11.6000 g., 0.5850 Gold 0.2182 oz. AGW, 28 mm. **Series:** Glory of Russian Arms **Obv:** Value in sprays **Obv. Legend:** ЗАЛАДНЫИ АНКЛАВ РОССИИ - КАЛИНИГРАД **Rev:** 45mm Field Cannon **Rev. Legend:** ★ ★ ★ РУССОГО ОРУЖИЯ ★ ★ ★ **Rev. Inscription:** СЛАВА **Edge:** Reeded

Date	Mintage	F	VF	XF	Unc	BU
2003 Proof	8	Value: 1,250				

RUSSIAN CAUCASIA

CHECHNYA

REPUBLIC

STANDARD COINAGE

X# 1 25 SOM (2-1/2 Toman)
Copper **Note:** Quite recently one specimen has been reported from Russia.

Date	Mintage	F	VF	XF	Unc	BU
AH1338(1919) Rare	—	—	—	—	—	—

X# 2 5 TOMAN
Brass

Date	Mintage	F	VF	XF	Unc	BU
AH1338(1919)	—	—	—	—	—	—

X# 3 10 TOMAN
Brass **Obv:** Crowned balance scale, banner, rifle and sabre, crescent below **Rev:** Arabian inscription **Note:** According to reliable sources, all 10 Toman coins were released to circulation.

Date	Mintage	F	VF	XF	Unc	BU
AH1338(1919)	—	—	—	—	—	—

X# 4 10 TOMAN
Copper **Obv:** Crowned balance scale, crescent below **Rev:** Arabian denomination and date **Note:** Struck over Russia 2 Kopek, Y#10. Modern forgeries exist.

Date	Mintage	F	VF	XF	Unc	BU
AH1338(1919)	—	—	—	—	—	—

FANTASY EURO PATTERNS

X# Pn1 EURO CENT
Steel Copper plated, 16.8 mm. **Edge:** Plain

Date	Mintage	F	VF	XF	Unc	BU
2005	7,000	—	—	—	—	2.00

X# Pn2 2 EURO CENT
Steel Copper plated, 18.5 mm. **Edge:** Plain

Date	Mintage	F	VF	XF	Unc	BU
2005	7,000	—	—	—	—	3.00

X# Pn3 5 EURO CENT
Steel Copper plated, 20.7 mm. **Edge:** Plain

Date	Mintage	F	VF	XF	Unc	BU
2005	7,000	—	—	—	—	3.50

X# Pn4 10 EURO CENT
Goldine, 19.3 mm. **Edge:** Plain

Date	Mintage	F	VF	XF	Unc	BU
2005	7,000	—	—	—	—	4.00

X# Pn5 20 EURO CENT
Goldine, 22 mm. **Edge:** Plain

Date	Mintage	F	VF	XF	Unc	BU
2005	7,000	—	—	—	—	5.00

X# Pn6 50 EURO CENT
Goldine, 24.3 mm. **Edge:** Plain

Date	Mintage	F	VF	XF	Unc	BU
2005	7,000	—	—	—	—	6.00

X# Pn7 EURO
Bi-Metallic, 22.8 mm. **Edge:** Plain

Date	Mintage	F	VF	XF	Unc	BU
2005	7,000	—	—	—	—	8.50

X# Pn8 2 EURO
Bi-Metallic, 25.7 mm. **Edge:** Plain

Date	Mintage	F	VF	XF	Unc	BU
2005	7,000	—	—	—	—	10.00

MINT SETS

X#	Date	Mintage	Identification	Issue Price	Mkt Val
XMS1	2005 (8)	7,000	X#Pn1-Pn8	—	50.00

SAINT BARTHELEMY

FRENCH COLONY

MEDALLIC COINAGE

X# 1 50 FRANCS/50 RIKSDALER
Nickel, 27 mm. **Obv:** Supported arms **Rev:** Stylized arms

Date	Mintage	F	VF	XF	Unc	BU
1988	20,000	—	—	—	15.00	25.00

X# 11 100 FRANCS / 100 RIKSDALER
Nickel **Obv:** Supported arms **Rev:** Stylized arms

Date	Mintage	F	VF	XF	Unc	BU
1993	—	—	—	—	20.00	35.00

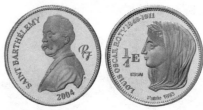

X# 13 100 FRANCS / 100 DALER
Nickel **Obv:** Bust of Marius Stackelborough left **Rev:** Crowned Swedish arms in order chain

Date	Mintage	F	VF	XF	Unc	BU
1995	—	—	—	—	30.00	50.00

X# 12 200 FRANCS / 200 RIKSDALER
Nickel **Obv:** Supported arms **Rev:** Stylized arms

Date	Mintage	F	VF	XF	Unc	BU
1994	—	—	—	—	25.00	45.00

X# 2 500 FRANCS/500 RIKSDALER

Date	Mintage	F	VF	XF	Unc	BU
1988	—	—	—	—	—	—

EMERGENCY COINAGE

X# 10 SHILLING
Silvered Brass **Issuer:** Robert Miles Reincke **Obv:** Laureate bust of Robert Miles Reincke right **Obv. Legend:** AMORE - FACET MILESIUS REXUS URINUS **Rev:** Ornate arms **Rev. Legend:** LES CASTELETS • VILLAGE A LURIN **Note:** Struck at the Lombardo Mint, Canada.

Date	Mintage	F	VF	XF	Unc	BU
1970	516	—	—	—	85.00	—

Note: Issued during a coin shortage. 211 pieces were redeemed

ESSAIS

X# E11 1/4 EURO
7.8000 g., 0.9990 Silver 0.2505 oz. ASW, 27.2 mm. **Series:** Euro **Obv:** Bust of Louis Oscar Roty almost left **Obv. Legend:** SAINT BARTHÉLEMY **Rev:** Patrie (medal 1893) **Edge:** Reeded

Date	Mintage	F	VF	XF	Unc	BU
2004 Proof	2,000	Value: 25.00				

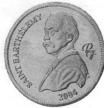

X# E11a 1/4 EURO
10.3400 g., Copper, 27.23 mm. **Obv:** Bust of Louis Oscar Roty half left **Obv. Legend:** BARTH?LEMY **Rev:** Patrie (medal 1893) **Edge:** Plain

Date	Mintage	F	VF	XF	Unc	BU
2004	30	—	—	—	50.00	50.00

X# E12 1-1/2 EURO
31.1400 g., 0.9990 Silver 1.0000 oz. ASW, 38.6 mm. **Series:** Euro **Obv:** Arms **Obv. Legend:** RÉPUBLIQUE FRANÇAISE **Rev:** Frigate Hermione, 1779-1793 **Rev. Legend:** HISTORIRE DE LA MARINE FRANÇAISE **Edge:** Reeded

Date	Mintage	F	VF	XF	Unc	BU
2004 Proof	2,000	Value: 45.00				

X# E13 1-1/2 EURO
29.1100 g., Bronze antiqued, 39.13 mm. **Series:** Euro **Obv:** Arms **Obv. Legend:** R?PUBLIQUE FRAN?AISE **Rev:** Frigate Hermione, 1779-1793 **Rev. Legend:** HISTORIRE DE LA MARINE FRAN?AISE **Edge:** Reeded

Date	Mintage	F	VF	XF	Unc	BU
2004	25	—	—	—	75.00	—

X# E15 20 EURO
8.5300 g., 0.9167 Gold 0.2514 oz. AGW, 27.1 mm. **Series:** Euro **Obv:** Arms **Rev:** Pied-billed Grebe **Rev. Legend:** Protection de la Faune **Edge:** Plain

Date	Mintage	F	VF	XF	Unc	BU
2004 Proof	300	Value: 300				

X# E15a 20 EURO
10.3500 g., Copper, 27.19 mm. **Obv:** Shield of arms **Rev:** Pied-billed Grebe **Rev. Legend:** Protection de la Faune **Edge:** Plain

Date	Mintage	F	VF	XF	Unc	BU
2004	30	—	—	—	—	50.00

PATTERNS WITH ESSAIS

X# E14 1-1/2 EURO
Brass, 38.6 mm. **Series:** Euro **Obv:** Arms **Obv. Legend:** RÉPUBLIQUE FRANÇAISE **Rev:** Frigate Hermione, 1779-1793 **Rev. Legend:** HISTORIRE DE LA MARINE FRANÇAISE **Edge:** Reeded

Date	Mintage	F	VF	XF	Unc	BU
2004	Est. 50	—	—	—	—	—

SWEDISH OCCUPATION

COUNTERMARKED COINAGE

X# 25 1/2 PENNY
Copper **Countermark:** Type IV Crown **Counterstamp:** Host **Note:** Countermark on Great Britain 1/2 Penny, KM#662.

CM Date	Host Date	Good	VG	F	VF	XF
ND(1834)	1806	—	—	—	—	—

Note: A modern concoction

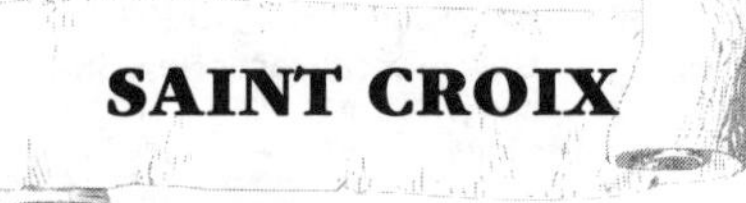

SAINT CROIX

DANISH COLONY

COUNTERMARKED COINAGE

1798-1813

X# 1 1/4 DOLLAR
0.9030 Silver **Countermark:** STC **Note:** Prev. KM#1. Countermark on Mexico City 2 reales, KM#90.

CM Date	Host Date	Good	VG	F	VF	XF
ND(1798-1813)	ND1790	—	—	—	—	—

X# 2 1/4 DOLLAR
0.9030 Silver **Countermark:** STC **Note:** Prev. KM#2. Countermark on Mexico City 2 reales, KM#91.

CM Date	Host Date	Good	VG	F	VF	XF
ND(1798-1813)	ND1792-1808	—	—	—	—	—

X# 3 1/2 DOLLAR
0.9030 Silver **Countermark:** STC **Note:** Prev. KM#3. Countermark Bolivia (Potosi) 4 Reales, KM#72.

CM Date	Host Date	Good	VG	F	VF	XF
ND(1798-1813)	ND1791-1809	—	—	—	—	—

X# 6 DOLLAR
0.9030 Silver **Countermark:** STC **Note:** Prev. KM#6. Countermark on Mexico City 8 Reales, KM#107.

CM Date	Host Date	Good	VG	F	VF	XF
ND(1798-1813)	ND1789-90	—	—	—	—	—

X# 4 DOLLAR
0.9030 Silver **Countermark:** STC **Note:** Prev. KM#4. Countermark on Mexico City 8 Reales, KM#109.

CM Date	Host Date	Good	VG	F	VF	XF
ND(1798-1813)	ND1791-1808	—	—	—	—	—

X# 5 DOLLAR
0.9030 Silver **Countermark:** STC **Note:** Prev. KM#5. Countermark on Mexico City 8 Reales, KM#110.

CM Date	Host Date	Good	VG	F	VF	XF
ND(1798-1813)	ND1808-11	—	—	—	—	—

SAINT HELENA

BRITISH COLONY

FANTASY EURO PATTERNS

X# Pn1 EURO CENT
Copper Plated Steel **Ruler:** Elizabeth II **Edge:** Plain

Date	Mintage	F	VF	XF	Unc	BU
2004	10,000	—	—	—	—	1.50
2004 Proof	4,000	Value: 2.50				

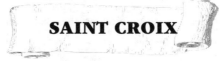

X# Pn1a EURO CENT
Silver **Ruler:** Elizabeth II **Edge:** Plain

Date	Mintage	F	VF	XF	Unc	BU
2004 Proof	250	Value: 6.00				

X# Pn2 2 EURO CENT
Copper Plated Steel **Ruler:** Elizabeth II **Edge:** Plain

Date	Mintage	F	VF	XF	Unc	BU
2004	10,000	—	—	—	—	2.00
2004 Proof	4,000	Value: 3.00				

X# Pn2a 2 EURO CENT
Silver **Ruler:** Elizabeth II **Edge:** Plain

Date	Mintage	F	VF	XF	Unc	BU
2004 Proof	250	Value: 7.00				

X# Pn3 5 EURO CENT
Copper Plated Steel **Ruler:** Elizabeth II **Edge:** Plain

Date	Mintage	F	VF	XF	Unc	BU
2004	10,000	—	—	—	—	2.50
2004 Proof	4,000	Value: 3.50				

X# Pn3a 5 EURO CENT
Silver **Ruler:** Elizabeth II **Edge:** Plain

Date	Mintage	F	VF	XF	Unc	BU
2004 Proof	250	Value: 8.50				

X# Pn4 10 EURO CENT
Goldine **Ruler:** Elizabeth II **Edge:** Plain

Date	Mintage	F	VF	XF	Unc	BU
2004	10,000	—	—	—	—	3.00
2004 Proof	4,000	Value: 4.00				

X# Pn4a 10 EURO CENT
Silver **Ruler:** Elizabeth II **Edge:** Plain

Date	Mintage	F	VF	XF	Unc	BU
2004 Proof	250	Value: 10.00				

X# Pn5 20 EURO CENT
Goldine **Ruler:** Elizabeth II **Edge:** Plain

Date	Mintage	F	VF	XF	Unc	BU
2004	10,000	—	—	—	—	3.50
2004 Proof	4,000	Value: 5.00				

X# Pn5a 20 EURO CENT
Silver **Ruler:** Elizabeth II **Edge:** Plain

Date	Mintage	F	VF	XF	Unc	BU
2004 Proof	250	Value: 12.50				

X# Pn6 50 EURO CENT
Goldine **Ruler:** Elizabeth II **Edge:** Plain

Date	Mintage	F	VF	XF	Unc	BU
2004	10,000	—	—	—	—	4.00
2004 Proof	4,000	Value: 6.00				

X# Pn6a 50 EURO CENT
Silver **Ruler:** Elizabeth II **Edge:** Plain

Date	Mintage	F	VF	XF	Unc	BU
2004 Proof	250	Value: 15.00				

X# Pn7 EURO
Bi-Metallic **Ruler:** Elizabeth II **Obv:** Laureate head of Napoleon right **Rev:** Large value "1", woman standing right behind man seated right **Edge:** Plain

Date	Mintage	F	VF	XF	Unc	BU
2004	—	—	—	—	—	6.00
2004 Proof	4,000	Value: 8.00				

X# Pn7a EURO
Bi-Metallic Goldine/Silver **Ruler:** Elizabeth II **Edge:** Plain

Date	Mintage	F	VF	XF	Unc	BU
2004 Proof	250	Value: 22.50				

X# Pn8 2 EURO
Bi-Metallic **Ruler:** Elizabeth II **Obv:** Laureate head of Napoleon right **Rev:** Large value "2", woman standing right behind man seated right **Edge:** Plain

Date	Mintage	F	VF	XF	Unc	BU
2004	—	—	—	—	—	8.00
2004 Proof	—	Value: 10.00				

X# Pn8a 2 EURO
Bi-Metallic Goldine/Silver **Ruler:** Elizabeth II **Edge:** Plain

Date	Mintage	F	VF	XF	Unc	BU
2004 Proof	250	Value: 28.50				

X# Pn9 5 EURO
Goldine **Ruler:** Elizabeth II **Edge:** Plain

Date	Mintage	F	VF	XF	Unc	BU
2004 Proof	—	Value: 12.50				

X# Pn9a 5 EURO
Silver **Ruler:** Elizabeth II **Edge:** Plain

Date	Mintage	F	VF	XF	Unc	BU
2004 Proof	250	Value: 40.00				

MINT SETS

X#	Date	Mintage	Identification	Issue Price	Mkt Val
XMS1	2004 (8)	10,000	X#Pn1-Pn8	—	30.00

PROOF SETS

X#	Date	Mintage	Identification	Issue Price	Mkt Val
XPS1	2004 (9)	4,000	X#Pn1-Pn9	—	50.00
XPS2	2004 (9)	250	X#Pn1a-Pn9a	—	150

SAINT HILDEGARD

COINAGE OF THE REALM

STANDARD COINAGE

One dollar tokens for circulation at renaissance faires and events of the Society for Creative Anachronism.

X# 1a FOLLIS
Copper **Obv:** Large +H monogram in low relief **Obv. Legend:** SANCTA HILDEGARDENSIS **Rev:** Bust facing **Rev. Legend:** BARAK BASILEUS AN TIR

Date	Mintage	F	VF	XF	Unc	BU
ND(1994) VV IC	—	—	4.00	6.00	—	—

X# 1b FOLLIS
Copper **Obv:** Large +H monogram in high relief **Obv. Legend:** SANCTA HILDEGARDENSIS **Rev:** Bust facing **Rev. Legend:** BARAK BASILEUS AN TIR

Date	Mintage	F	VF	XF	Unc	BU
ND(1998) IC	—	—	3.00	5.00	—	—

X# 2a FOLLIS
Copper **Subject:** King Barak and Queen Lao, patrons of St. Hildegard **Obv:** Large +H monogram in low relief **Rev:** Standing figures of man and woman **Rev. Legend:** BARAK ET LAO PATRONI, A.S. XXX

Date	Mintage	F	VF	XF	Unc	BU
ND(1994)	—	—	—	—	—	—

X# 2 FOLLIS
Copper **Subject:** 30th year celebration **Obv:** Large +H monogram in low relief **Obv. Legend:** SANCTA HILDEGARDENSIS **Rev:** Two figures standing, facing **Rev. Legend:** BARAK ET LAO PATRONI AS XXX

Date	Mintage	F	VF	XF	Unc	BU
ND VV IC	—	—	—	—	—	—

X# 3a FOLLIS
Copper **Subject:** Ravensfuri Brothers, King Skepti and Jarl Barak - Patrons of St. Hildegard **Obv:** Large +H monogram in low relief **Obv. Legend:** SANCTA HILDEGARDENSIS **Rev:** Two figures standing, facing, one with sword upright **Rev. Legend:** SKEPTI BARAK AS XXXI

Date	Mintage	F	VF	XF	Unc	BU
ND(1996) VV IC	—	—	4.00	6.00	—	—

X# 4a FOLLIS
Copper **Subject:** Estrella War XIAIII **Obv:** Large +H monogram in low relief **Obv. Legend:** SANCTA HILDEGARDENSIS **Rev:** Large X with Is and star in angles **Rev. Legend:** ERICK + NICHELLE AT ENVELDT

Date	Mintage	F	VF	XF	Unc	BU
ND(1997) VV IC	—	—	4.00	6.00	—	—

X# 5a FOLLIS
Copper **Subject:** Gulf War VI **Obv:** Large +H monogram in low relief **Obv. Legend:** SANCTA HILDEGARDENSIS **Rev:** Mounted rider left with banner with device of the Kingdom of Meridies **Rev. Legend:** GARETH RHIANNON VI

Date	Mintage	F	VF	XF	Unc	BU
ND(1997) VV IC	—	—	4.00	6.00	—	—

X# 2b FOLLIS
Copper **Subject:** King Barak adn Queen Lao, patrons of St. Hildegard **Obv:** Large +H monogram in high relief **Rev:** Standing figures of man and woman **Rev. Legend:** BARAK ET LAO PATRONI, A.S. XXX

Date	Mintage	F	VF	XF	Unc	BU
ND(1998)	—	—	—	—	—	—

X# 6a FOLLIS
Copper **Subject:** Year 32 **Obv:** Large +H monogram in low relief **Obv. Legend:** SANCTA HILDEGARDENSIS **Rev:** Two figures seated, facing **Rev. Legend:** DARIVS ET MORGAINE AS XXXII

Date	Mintage	F	VF	XF	Unc	BU
ND(1998) VV IC	—	—	4.00	6.00	—	—

X# 6b FOLLIS
Copper **Subject:** Year 32 **Obv:** Large +H monogram in high releif **Obv. Legend:** SANCTA HILDEGARDENSIS **Rev:** Two figures seated, facing **Rev. Legend:** DARIVS ET MORGAINE AS XXXII

Date	Mintage	F	VF	XF	Unc	BU
ND(1998) IC	—	—	3.00	5.00	—	—

X# 7a FOLLIS
Copper **Subject:** Estrella WAR XIV **Obv:** Large +H monogram in low relief **Obv. Legend:** SANCTA HILDEGARDENSIS **Rev:** Large X, IV flanking, crown above, star below **Rev. Legend:** ARTHVR + TAMIRA (crown) ATENVEIDT

Date	Mintage	F	VF	XF	Unc	BU
ND(1998) VV IC	—	—	3.00	5.00	—	—

X# 7b FOLLIS
Copper **Subject:** Estrella War XIV **Obv:** Large +H monogram in high relief **Obv. Legend:** SANCTA HILDEGARDENSIS **Rev:** Large X, IV flanking, crown above, star below **Rev. Legend:** ARTHVR + TAMIRA (crown) ATENVELDT

Date	Mintage	F	VF	XF	Unc	BU
ND(1998) IC	—	—	3.00	5.00	—	—

X# 8a FOLLIS
Copper **Subject:** Honoring SCA Kingdom of Ansteorra (Texas) **Obv:** Large +H monogram in low relief **Obv. Legend:** SANCTA HILDEGARDENSIS **Rev:** Two five-pointed stars superimposed **Rev. Legend:** RICHARD + GLADWEN (crown) ANSTEORRA

Date	Mintage	F	VF	XF	Unc	BU
ND(1998) VV IC	—	—	4.00	6.00	—	—

X# 8b FOLLIS
Copper **Subject:** Honoring SCA Kingdom of Ansteorra **Obv:** Large +H monogram in high relief **Obv. Legend:** SANCTA HILDEGARDENSIS **Rev:** Two five-pointed stars superimposed **Rev. Legend:** RICHARD + GLADWEN (crown) ANSTEORRA

Date	Mintage	F	VF	XF	Unc	BU
ND(1998) IC	—	—	3.00	5.00	—	—

X# 9a FOLLIS
Copper **Subject:** Honoring SCA Kingdom of Trimaris **Obv:** Large +H monogram in low relief **Obv. Legend:** SANCTA HILDEGARDENSIS **Rev:** Trimaris **Rev. Legend:** STROMEK + ALIANORE (crown) TRIMARIS

Date	Mintage	F	VF	XF	Unc	BU
ND(1998) VV IC	—	—	4.00	6.00	—	—

X# 9b FOLLIS
Copper **Subject:** Honoring SCA Kingdom of Trimaris **Obv:** Large +H monogram in high relief **Obv. Legend:** SANCTA HILDEGARDENSIS **Rev:** Trimaris **Rev. Legend:** STROMEK + ALIANORE (crown) TRIMARIS

Date	Mintage	F	VF	XF	Unc	BU
ND(1998) IC	—	—	3.00	5.00	—	—

X# 10 FOLLIS

Copper **Subject:** Honoring SCA Kingdom of Calontir (Plains states) **Obv:** Large +H monogram in high relief **Obv. Legend:** SANCTA HILDEGARDENSIS **Rev:** Cross of Calatrava **Rev. Legend:** VALENS + SUSANAN (crown) CALONTIR

Date	Mintage	F	VF	XF	Unc	BU
ND(1998) IC	—	—	3.00	5.00	—	—

X# 11 FOLLIS

Copper **Subject:** Year 33, a postumous strike for Duke Jafar of the Midrealm (Michigan, upper midwest) **Obv:** Large +H monogram in high relief **Obv. Legend:** SANCTA HILDEGARDENSIS **Rev:** Bust 3/4 facing, spear over shoulder, shield with dragon device of the Midrealm on his shoulder **Rev. Legend:** JAFAR XXXIII KENNA

Date	Mintage	F	VF	XF	Unc	BU
ND(1998) IC	—	—	5.00	8.00	—	—

X# 12 FOLLIS

Copper **Subject:** Honoring SCA Kingdom of An Tir (Pacific Northwest) **Obv:** Large +H monogram in high relief **Obv. Legend:** SANCTA HILDEGARDENSIS **Rev:** Facing lion's head, badge of An Tir **Rev. Legend:** BRENDAN ARYANA / AN TIR

Date	Mintage	F	VF	XF	Unc	BU
ND(1998) IC	—	—	3.00	5.00	—	—

X# 13 FOLLIS

Copper **Subject:** Kingdom of the West **Obv:** Large +H monogram in high relief **Obv. Legend:** SANCTA HILDEGARDENSIS **Rev:** Helmeted bust facing,with badge of the Kingdom of the West on shiled on his shoulder and holding globus cruciger w/St. Hildegard emblem **Rev. Legend:** HAVOC ETAINE

Date	Mintage	F	VF	XF	Unc	BU
ND(1998) IC	—	—	4.00	6.00	—	—

X# 14 FOLLIS

Copper **Subject:** John Kane, Bookseller **Obv:** Large +H monogram in high relief **Obv. Legend:** SANCTA HILDEGARDENSIS **Rev:** Pentagram **Rev. Legend:** IOHN KANE BOOK SELLER

Date	Mintage	F	VF	XF	Unc	BU
ND(1998) IC	—	—	5.00	8.00	—	—

X# 15 FOLLIS

Copper **Subject:** Kingdom of the Outlands **Obv:** Large +H monogram in high relief **Obv. Legend:** SANCTA HILDEGARDENSIS **Rev:** Leaping stag left **Rev. Legend:** EX TER

Date	Mintage	F	VF	XF	Unc	BU
ND(1998) IC	—	—	3.00	5.00	—	—

X# 16 FOLLIS

Copper **Subject:** Caravan of the High Silk Road, SCA merchant household **Obv:** Large +H monogram in high relief **Obv. Legend:** SANCTA HILDEGARDENSIS **Rev:** Palm Tree **Rev. Legend:** Caravan of the High Silk Road (in script)

Date	Mintage	F	VF	XF	Unc	BU
ND(1998) IC	—	—	4.00	6.00	—	—

X# 17 FOLLIS

Copper **Subject:** Kingdom of Caid **Obv:** Large +H monogram in high relief **Obv. Legend:** SANCTA HILDEGARDENSIS **Rev:** Three crescents **Rev. Legend:** AL TOMUKI + LVCIANA (crown) CAÏD

Date	Mintage	F	VF	XF	Unc	BU
ND(1998) IC	—	—	3.00	5.00	—	—

X# 21 FOLLIS

Copper **Subject:** Greenwood Players **Obv:** Large +H monogram in high relief **Obv. Legend:** SANCTA HILDEGARDENSIS **Rev:** Fool **Rev. Legend:** GREENWOOD PLAYERS

Date	Mintage	F	VF	XF	Unc	BU
ND(1998) IC	—	—	4.00	6.00	—	—

X# 23 FOLLIS

Copper **Subject:** Golde Lemon **Obv:** Large +H monogram in high relief **Obv. Legend:** SANCTA HILDEGARDENSIS **Rev:** Open sliced lemon, drip between **Rev. Legend:** GOLDEN LEMON AN TIR

Date	Mintage	F	VF	XF	Unc	BU
ND(1998) IC	—	—	4.00	6.00	—	—

X# 18 FOLLIS

Copper **Subject:** Kingdom of Artemesia **Obv:** Large +H monogram in high releif **Obv. Legend:** SANCTA HILDEGARDENSIS **Rev:** Griffen seated left, holding wreath in raised left paw **Rev. Legend:** SEAN KASSANDRA / ARTEMESIA

Date	Mintage	F	VF	XF	Unc	BU
ND(1999) IC	—	—	4.00	6.00	—	—

X# 19 FOLLIS

Copper **Subject:** Kingdom of Atlantia **Obv:** Large +H monogram in high relief **Obv. Legend:** SANCTA HILDEGARDENSIS **Rev:** Scallop shell **Rev. Legend:** LVNED (rose) NIOBE / ATLANTIA

Date	Mintage	F	VF	XF	Unc	BU
ND(1999) IC	—	—	4.00	6.00	—	—

X# 20 FOLLIS

Copper **Subject:** Pillaged Village, SCA merchant **Obv:** Large +H monogram in high relief **Obv. Legend:** SANCTA HILDEGARDENSIS **Rev:** Three warriors, two with shields, one with bag of loot over his shoulder, one with spear, one with sword; anguished villager in house at right **Rev. Legend:** PILLAGED / VILLAGE

Date	Mintage	F	VF	XF	Unc	BU
ND(1999) IC	—	—	4.00	6.00	—	—

X# 22 FOLLIS

Copper **Subject:** Year 34 **Obv:** Large +H monogram in high relief **Obv. Legend:** SANCTA HILDEGARDENSIS **Rev:** Two shields **Rev. Legend:** BIO GRIFFEN : MELISSA A. S. 34 **Note:** Honors the medics and waterbearers

Date	Mintage	F	VF	XF	Unc	BU
ND(1999) IC	—	—	3.00	5.00	—	—

X# 24 FOLLIS

Copper **Subject:** Principality of Gleann Abhann **Obv:** Large +H monogram in high relief **Obv. Legend:** SANCTA HILDEGARDENSIS **Rev:** Rampant ram **Rev. Legend:** GLEANN ABHANN HONOR ABOVE ALL

Date	Mintage	F	VF	XF	Unc	BU
ND(2000) IC	—	—	3.00	5.00	—	—

X# 25 FOLLIS

Copper **Subject:** Gig Harbor Renaissance Faire and Gothic Fantasy **Obv:** Large +H monogram in high relief **Obv. Legend:** SANCTA HILDEGARDENSIS **Rev:** Knight on horseback right **Rev. Legend:** SEATLE KNIGHTS GIG HARBOR WA

Date	Mintage	F	VF	XF	Unc	BU
ND(2000) IC	—	—	3.00	5.00	—	—

X# 26 FOLLIS

Copper **Subject:** Ambrose and Marian (Prince and Princess of the) Summits Principality (South Oregon) **Obv:** Large +H monogram in high relief **Obv. Legend:** SANCTA HILDEGARDENSIS **Rev:** Summits shield supported by Oscar the Otter, mascot of the household

Date	Mintage	F	VF	XF	Unc	BU
ND(2000) IC	—	—	3.00	5.00	—	—

X# 27 FOLLIS

Copper **Subject:** Elfrida of Greenwalls (Marion Zimmer Bradley) **Obv:** Large +H monogram in high relief **Obv. Legend:** SANCTA HILDEGARDENSIS **Rev:** Crowned female bust holding celestial sphere and plume **Rev. Legend:** ELFRIDA MZB AS XXXV

Date	Mintage	F	VF	XF	Unc	BU
ND(2000) IC	—	—	4.00	6.00	—	—

X# 29 FOLLIS

Copper **Subject:** Honoring the SCA Kingdom of Atenvelot (Arizona) **Obv:** Large +H monogram in high relief **Obv. Legend:** SANCTA HILDEGARDENSIS **Rev:** Sun, face within **Rev. Legend:** JOHNATHAN + ETAIN (crown) ATENVELDT

Date	Mintage	F	VF	XF	Unc	BU
ND(2001) IC	—	—	3.00	5.00	—	—

X# 30 FOLLIS

Copper **Subject:** House of the Silver Winds, SCA and RenFaire merchant and instrument maker **Obv:** Large +H monogram in high relief **Obv. Legend:** SANCTA HILDEGARDENSIS **Rev:** Musical treble cleff **Rev. Legend:** HOUSE OF THE SILVERWINDS

Date	Mintage	F	VF	XF	Unc	BU
ND(2001) IC	—	—	3.00	5.00	—	—

X# 31 FOLLIS

Copper **Subject:** 20th Anniversary of the SCA Kingdom of Atlantia (mid-Atlantic states) **Obv:** Large +H monogram in high relief **Obv. Legend:** SANCTA HILDEGARDENSIS **Rev:** "Sea unicorn", XX flanking **Rev. Legend:** HAVORDH + MARYGRACE (crown) ATLANTIA

Date	Mintage	F	VF	XF	Unc	BU
ND(2001) IC	—	—	3.00	5.00	—	—

X# 32 FOLLIS

Copper **Subject:** Commemorating the Marriage of the head of the Household Platypi **Obv:** Large +H monogram in high relief **Obv. Legend:** SANCTA HILDEGARDENSIS **Rev:** Platypus right **Rev. Legend:** JANOS - RACHEL / HOUSE PLATYPI

Date	Mintage	F	VF	XF	Unc	BU
ND(2001) IC	—	—	4.00	6.00	—	—

X# 33 FOLLIS

Copper **Subject:** Honoring the SCA Barony of Aquaterra (Everett, WA) **Obv:** Large +H monogram in high relief **Obv. Legend:** SANCTA HILDEGARDENSIS **Rev:** Shield, three wreaths above three waves **Rev. Legend:** IVLIAN + ARIANNE (coronet) AQVATERRA

Date	Mintage	F	VF	XF	Unc	BU
ND(2001) IC	—	—	3.00	5.00	—	—

X# 37 FOLLIS

Copper **Subject:** Glastonbury Renaissance Faire **Obv:** Large +H monogram in high relief **Obv. Legend:** SANCTA HILDEGARDENSIS **Rev:** OCCA mirror image (for oregon Coast Council of the Arts, faire sponsor) in style of Northwest Coast Indian owl mask design **Rev. Legend:** GLADSTONBURY REN' FAIRE

Date	Mintage	F	VF	XF	Unc	BU
ND(2002) IC	—	—	3.00	5.00	—	—

X# 34 FOLLIS

Copper **Subject:** RingCon I **Obv:** Large +H monogram in high relief **Obv. Legend:** SANCTA HILDEGARDENSIS **Rev:** Dragon grasping flaming ring **Rev. Legend:** "One ring to bring them" in Tengwar

Date	Mintage	F	VF	XF	Unc	BU
ND(2002) IC	—	—	3.00	5.00	—	—

X# 35 FOLLIS

Copper **Subject:** Shasta Highlands Renaissance Faire and Celtic Festival **Obv:** Large +H monogram in high relief **Obv. Legend:** SANCTA HILDEGARDENSIS **Rev:** Double headed eagle with shield (view of Mt. Shasta) on breast **Rev. Legend:** SHASTA HIGHLANDS FAIRE

Date	Mintage	F	VF	XF	Unc	BU
ND(2002) IC	—	—	4.00	6.00	—	—

X# 28 FOLLIS

Copper **Subject:** RingCon II - Argonath **Obv:** Large +H monogram in high relief **Obv. Legend:** SANCTA HILDEGARDENSIS **Rev:** Head and outstretched hand of Guardian statue **Rev. Legend:** RC II

Date	Mintage	F	VF	XF	Unc	BU
ND(2003) IC	—	—	3.00	5.00	—	—

X# 36 FOLLIS

Copper **Obv:** Large +H monogram in high relief **Obv. Legend:** SANCTA HILDEGARDENSIS **Rev:** Stonehedge **Rev. Legend:** STONE / GARDEN

Date	Mintage	F	VF	XF	Unc	BU
ND(2003) IC	200	—	5.00	8.00	—	—
Note: Error: retrograde A in GARDEN						
ND(2003) IC	—	—	3.00	5.00	—	—
Note: Corrected A in GARDEN						

X# 38 FOLLIS
Copper **Subject:** Ragnarok (combat event) **Obv:** Large +H monogram in high relief **Obv. Legend:** SANCTA HILDEGARDENSIS **Rev:** Norse Battle Raven **Rev. Legend:** RAGNAROK, DAVIN, GROA (in runes)

Date	Mintage	F	VF	XF	Unc	BU
ND(2003) IC	—	—	3.00	5.00	—	—

X# 40 FOLLIS
Copper **Subject:** Gig Harbor RenFaire fantasy location **Obv:** Large +H monogram in high relief **Obv. Legend:** SANCTA HILDEGARDENSIS **Rev:** Rose, thistle and lis in angles of pointed trefoil **Rev. Legend:** HOLY GLEN SHIRE

Date	Mintage	F	VF	XF	Unc	BU
ND(2003) IC	—	—	3.00	5.00	—	—

X# 41 FOLLIS
Copper **Subject:** RingCon III - Rohirrim **Obv:** Large +H monogram in high relief **Obv. Legend:** SANCTA HILDEGARDENSIS **Rev:** Horse advancing left **Rev. Legend:** THEODEN EORLINGAS RC III (in Tengwar)

Date	Mintage	F	VF	XF	Unc	BU
ND(2003) IC	—	—	3.00	5.00	—	—

X# 42 FOLLIS
Copper **Subject:** Lucets - Lynn the Wear, SCA merchant **Obv:** Large +H monogram in high releif **Rev:** "Lucet" braiding tool **Rev. Legend:** LUCETS - LYNN THE WEAVER

Date	Mintage	F	VF	XF	Unc	BU
ND(2004)	—	—	—	—	—	—

X# 43 FOLLIS
Copper **Subject:** 30th Annual Egil's Tourney (near Eugene, Oregon) **Obv:** Large +H monogram in high relief **Rev:** Serpet knot **Rev. Legend:** EGILS (in runes) XXX

Date	Mintage	F	VF	XF	Unc	BU
ND(2004)	—	—	—	—	—	—

X# 44 FOLLIS
Copper **Subject:** Ravenswood Leather, SCA and Ren Faire merchant **Obv:** Large +H monogram in high relief **Rev:** Raven in flight as seen from below, over a knotwork panel **Rev. Legend:** RAVENSWOOD LEATHER

Date	Mintage	F	VF	XF	Unc	BU
ND(2004)	—	—	—	—	—	—

MEDALLIC COINAGE

X# M1 FOLLIS
Copper **Obv:** Bust facing **Obv. Designer:** BARAK BASILEUS AN TIR **Rev. Inscription:** SECULA MEDIA CURRENS in four lines

Date	Mintage	F	VF	XF	Unc	BU
ND(1993)	100	—	4.00	6.00	—	—

IAN CNULLE - MONEY CHANGER

These are the personal trade tokens minted and issued by Ian Cnulle (modernly known as G.P. Franck-Weiby) as "money changer" at the larger SCA events in the Pacific Northwest, since 1994.

TRADE COINAGE

One dollar tokens for circulation at renaissance faires and events of the Society for Creative Anachronism.

X# 151 PENNY
0.9990 Silver, 19.7 mm. **Obv:** King's head facing **Obv. Legend:** SECVLA • MED • PRES **Rev:** Long cross, three pellets in center angles **Rev. Legend:** IAN ON VIL ARG

Date	Mintage	F	VF	XF	Unc	BU
ND(1994-99)	—	—	—	—	7.00	—

X# 152 PENNY
0.9990 Silver, 20.0 mm. **Obv:** King's head facing **Obv. Legend:** SECVLA • MED • PRES **Rev:** Short cross, two pellets in each angle **Rev. Legend:** VILLA • ARGENS •

Date	Mintage	F	VF	XF	Unc	BU
ND(1999-2004)	—	—	—	—	7.00	—

X# 160 4 PENNY
Silver **Obv:** Crowned bust facing within nine-lobed inner circle **Obv. Legend:** SECVLA • MEDIA • PRAESENS : IAN • CNVLE **Rev:** Long cross, three pellets in angles **Rev. Legend:** POSVI •IAH • ADIVTROE • MEVM • / VI ILA ARG ENS

Date	Mintage	F	VF	XF	Unc	BU
ND(2004)	—	—	—	—	28.00	—

X# 155 FLEUR D'ARGENT
0.9990 Silver, 25.2 mm. **Obv:** Castle **Obv. Legend:** SENESCIT • MVNDVS **Rev:** Lis within double legend **Rev. Legend:** REIVVENESCIT : MVNDVS : / SECVLA : MEDIPRESENS

Date	Mintage	F	VF	XF	Unc	BU
ND(1995-2004)	—	—	—	—	15.00	—

X# 165 TREMISSIS
1.5500 g., 0.9990 Gold 0.0498 oz. AGW, 14.5 mm. **Obv:** Bust right **Obv. Legend:** SECVLA MED PRES **Rev:** Victory standing with wreath and chalice **Rev. Legend:** AVRVM PVRVM XXIVK / VAOB

Date	Mintage	F	VF	XF	Unc	BU
ND(1995-2005)	57	—	—	—	50.00	—

X# 167 TREMISSIS
2.2000 g., 0.9990 Gold 0.0707 oz. AGW, 15.7 mm. **Obv:** Crowned bust right **Rev:** Bust right within wreath and pellet border **Rev. Legend:** RAS TAFARI / FASHAKHA WA SALAMA LA KNAZABA (Joy and Peace to the People, in Gheez)

Date	Mintage	F	VF	XF	Unc	BU
ND(1997-2005)	67	—	—	—	65.00	—

X# 170 FLORIN D'OR
3.7400 g., 0.9990 Gold 0.1201 oz. AGW, 21.6 mm. **Obv:** King standing holding halberd and chalice **Obv. Legend:** SECVLA MEDIA PRESN **Rev:** Lis **Rev. Legend:** AVRVM PVRVM

Date	Mintage	F	VF	XF	Unc	BU
ND(1993-2000)	51	—	—	—	115	—

SAINT LUCIA

FRENCH COLONY

COUNTERMARKED COINAGE

Series of 1813

X# 3 11 SOUS 6 DENIERS
Silver **Note:** Countermarked on 1/3 outer cut of Spanish or Spanish Colonial 2 Reales.

CM Date	Host Date	Good	VG	F	VF	XF
ND(1813)	1773-1808	—	—	—	—	—

X# 4 17 SOUS 3 DENIERS
Silver **Note:** Countermarked on 1/2 cut of Spanish or Spanish Colonial 2 Reales.

CM Date	Host Date	Good	VG	F	VF	XF
ND(1813)	1773-1808	—	—	—	—	—

SAINT PIERRE & MIQUELON

FRENCH TERRITORY

ESSAIS

X# E11 1/4 EURO
7.8000 g., 0.9990 Silver 0.2505 oz. ASW, 27.2 mm. **Series:** Euro **Obv:** Bust of Louis Oscar Roty almost left **Rev:** "Marianne" (medal 1893) **Edge:** Reeded

Date	Mintage	F	VF	XF	Unc	BU
2004 Proof	2,000	Value: 25.00				

X# E12 1-1/2 EURO
31.1400 g., 0.9990 Silver 1.0000 oz. ASW, 38.6 mm. **Series:** Euro **Obv:** Arms **Obv. Legend:** RÉPUBLIQUE FRANÇAISE **Rev:** Corvette Mimosa, 1941-1942 **Rev. Legend:** HISTORIRE DE LA MARINE FRANÇAISE **Edge:** Reeded

Date	Mintage	F	VF	XF	Unc	BU
2004 Proof	2,000	Value: 45.00				

X# E13 1-1/2 EURO
29.5000 g., Bronze antiqued, 39.14 mm. **Series:** Euro **Obv:** Arms **Obv. Legend:** R?PUBLIQUE FRAN?AISE **Rev:** Corvette Mimosa, 1941-1942 **Rev. Legend:** HISTORIRE DE LA MARINE FRAN?AISE **Edge:** Reeded

Date	Mintage	F	VF	XF	Unc	BU
2004	25	—	—	—	75.00	—

X# E15 20 EURO
8.5300 g., 0.9167 Gold 0.2514 oz. AGW, 27.1 mm. **Series:** Euro **Obv:** Arms **Rev:** Great Blue Heron **Rev. Legend:** Protection de la Faune **Edge:** Plain

Date	Mintage	F	VF	XF	Unc	BU
2004 Proof	300	Value: 300				

X# E15a 20 EURO
10.3300 g., Copper, 27.15 mm. **Obv:** Shield of arms **Rev:** Great Blue Heron **Rev. Legend:** Protection de la Faune **Edge:** Plain

Date	Mintage	F	VF	XF	Unc	BU
2004	30	—	—	—	50.00	50.00

X# E11a 1/4 EURO
10.3000 g., Copper, 27.25 mm. **Obv:** Bust of Louis Oscar Roty half left **Rev:** Marianne (medal 1893) **Edge:** Reeded

Date	Mintage	F	VF	XF	Unc	BU
2004	30	—	—	—	50.00	50.00

PATTERNS WITH ESSAIS

X# E14 1-1/2 EURO
Brass **Series:** Euro **Subject:** Arms **Obv. Designer:** RÉPUBLIQUE FRANÇAISE **Rev:** Corvette Mimosa, 1941-1942 **Rev. Legend:** HISTORIRE DE LA MARINE FRANÇAISE

Date	Mintage	F	VF	XF	Unc	BU
2004	Est. 50	—	—	—	—	—

SAINT THOMAS & PRINCE ISLAND

DEMOCRATIC REPUBLIC

MEDALLIC COINAGE

X# M1 20 DOBRAS
Copper-Nickel **Subject:** International Games **Rev:** Gymnast

Date	Mintage	F	VF	XF	Unc	BU
1984 Proof	—	Value: 17.50				

SAN MARINO

REPUBLIC

FANTASY EURO PATTERNS

X# Pn1 EURO CENT
Subject: Grand Prix **Obv:** Crowned arms **Rev:** Race car

Date	Mintage	F	VF	XF	Unc	BU
2005	—	—	—	—	—	1.50
2005 Proof	—	Value: 2.50				

X# Pn2 2 EURO CENT
Subject: Grand Prix **Obv:** Crowned arms **Rev:** Race car

Date	Mintage	F	VF	XF	Unc	BU
2005	—	—	—	—	—	2.00
2005 Proof	—	Value: 3.00				

X# Pn3 5 EURO CENT
Subject: Grand Prix **Obv:** Crowned arms **Rev:** Race car

Date	Mintage	F	VF	XF	Unc	BU
2005	—	—	—	—	—	2.50
2005 Proof	—	Value: 3.50				

X# Pn4 10 EURO CENT
Subject: Grand Prix **Obv:** Crowned arms **Rev:** Race car

Date	Mintage	F	VF	XF	Unc	BU
2005	—	—	—	—	—	3.00
2005 Proof	—	Value: 4.00				

X# Pn5 20 EURO CENT
Subject: Grand Prix **Obv:** Crowned arms **Rev:** Race car

Date	Mintage	F	VF	XF	Unc	BU
2005	—	—	—	—	—	3.50
2005 Proof	—	Value: 5.00				

X# Pn6 50 EURO CENT
Subject: Grand Prix **Obv:** Crowned arms **Rev:** Race car

Date	Mintage	F	VF	XF	Unc	BU
2005	—	—	—	—	—	4.00
2005 Proof	—	Value: 6.00				

X# Pn7 EURO
Subject: Grand Prix **Obv:** Crowned arms **Rev:** Race car

Date	Mintage	F	VF	XF	Unc	BU
2005	—	—	—	—	—	6.00
2005 Proof	—	Value: 8.00				

X# Pn8 2 EURO
Subject: Grand Prix **Obv:** Crowned arms **Rev:** Race car

Date	Mintage	F	VF	XF	Unc	BU
2005	—	—	—	—	—	8.00
2005 Proof	—	Value: 10.00				

X# Pn9 5 EURO
Subject: Grand Prix **Obv:** Crowned arms **Rev:** Race car

Date	Mintage	F	VF	XF	Unc	BU
2005 Proof	—	Value: 12.50				

MINT SETS

X#	Date	Mintage	Identification	Issue Price	Mkt Val
XMS1	2005 (8)	—	X#Pn1-Pn8	—	30.00

PROOF SETS

X#	Date	Mintage	Identification	Issue Price	Mkt Val
XPS1	2005 (9)	—	X#Pn1-Pn9	—	50.00

SAN SERRIFFE

REPUBLIC

FANTASY COINAGE

Struck for the Bird & Bull Press, Newtown, Pennslyvania

X# 1 100 CORONAS
31.1030 g., 0.9990 Silver 0.9989 oz. ASW **Subject:** 30th Anniversary of Bird & Bull Press **Obv:** Athenian Owl

Date	Mintage	F	VF	XF	Unc	BU
1988 Proof	425	Value: 90.00				

X# 2 100 CORONAS
Bronze

Date	Mintage	F	VF	XF	Unc	BU
1988 Proof	90	Value: 15.00				

X# 3 100 CORONAS
Aluminum

Date	Mintage	F	VF	XF	Unc	BU
1988 Proof	90	Value: 15.00				

PROOF SETS

X#	Date	Mintage	Identification	Issue Price	Mkt Val
XPS1	1988 (3)	90	X1-X3	100	120

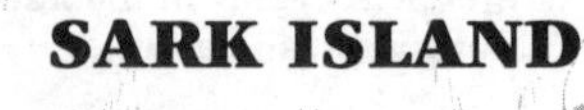

SARK ISLAND

FEUDALISTIC SOCIETY

MEDALLIC COINAGE

X# M1 4 GRAMS
Silver, 20.10 mm. **Obv:** Supported arms **Obv. Legend:** ISLAND — OF SARK 1565 1965 **Rev:** Arms within ribbon motto **Rev. Legend:** FOURTH CENTENARY 1965 1565 **Edge:** Plain

Date	Mintage	F	VF	XF	Unc	BU
1965 Prooflike	1,000	—	—	—	—	15.00

X# M2 7 GRAMS
Silver, 22.62 mm. **Obv:** Supported arms **Obv. Legend:** ISLAND — OF SARK 1565 1965 **Rev:** Arms within ribbon motto **Rev. Legend:** FOURTH — CENTENARY 1965 1565 **Edge:** Plain

Date	Mintage	F	VF	XF	Unc	BU
1965 Prooflike	1,000	—	—	—	—	25.00

X# M3 12 GRAMS
Silver, 30.07 mm. **Obv:** Supported arms **Obv. Legend:** ISLAND — OF SARK 1565 1965 **Rev:** Arms within ribbon motto **Rev. Legend:** FOURTH — CENTENARY 1965 1565 **Edge:** Plain

Date	Mintage	F	VF	XF	Unc	BU
1965 Prooflike	1,000	—	—	—	—	35.00

PROOF-LIKE SETS (PL)

X#	Date	Mintage	Identification	Issue Price	Mkt Val
XPL1	1965(3) (3)	1,000	XM1-XM3	—	75.00

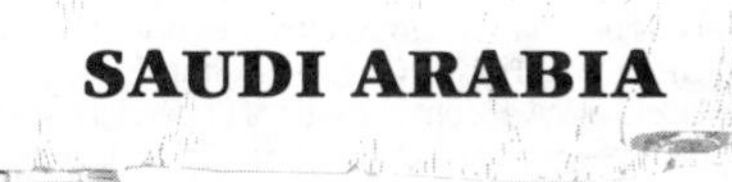

SAUDI ARABIA

UNITED KINGDOMS

KINGDOM

TRADE COINAGE

X# 21 GUINEA
8.0000 g., Gold, 21.8 mm. **Obv. Inscription:** "R22", "22" or no notation on obverse **Rev. Inscription:** "MDM22" at left **Note:** Commercial copy of 1 Guinea, KM#36.

Date	Mintage	F	VF	XF	Unc	BU
AH1370 (1950)	—	—	—	—	BV+10%	—

FANTASY COINAGE

X# 11 DIRHAM
3.0000 g., 0.9990 Silver 0.0964 oz. ASW, 25 mm. **Issuer:** Umar Ibrahim Vadillo **Obv:** Legend around Kalima **Rev:** Kaaba

Date	Mintage	F	VF	XF	Unc	BU
ND(1999) Proof	—	Value: 15.00				

X# 12 5 DIRHAM
15.0000 g., 0.9990 Silver 0.4818 oz. ASW, 27 mm. **Issuer:** Umar Ibrahim Vadillo **Obv:** Legend around Kalima **Rev:** Kaaba

Date	Mintage	F	VF	XF	Unc	BU
ND(1999) Proof	—	Value: 15.00				

X# 13 DINAR
4.3000 g., 0.9170 Gold 0.1268 oz. AGW, 23 mm. **Issuer:** Umar Ibrahim Vadillo **Obv:** Legend around Kalima **Rev:** Domed tomb, mineret

Date	Mintage	F	VF	XF	Unc	BU
ND(1999) Proof	—	Value: 200				

X# 14 HEAVY DINAR
8.6000 g., 0.9170 Gold 0.2535 oz. AGW, 26 mm. **Issuer:** Umar Ibrahim Vadillo **Obv:** Legend around Kalima **Rev:** Domed tomb, mineret

Date	Mintage	F	VF	XF	Unc	BU
ND(1999) Proof	—	Value: 300				

PATTERNS

Including off metal strikes

X# Pn1 GHIRSH
7.1300 g., Copper-Nickel, 26 mm. **Ruler:** Abd Al-Aziz Bin Sa'ud (Ibn Sa'ud) AH1344-73/1926-53AD **Obv:** Toughra, legend below **Note:** Believed to have been struck in recent times by a private mint located in the U.S.A.

Date	Mintage	F	VF	XF	Unc	BU
AH1345(1926)Proof	—	Value: 175				

SCOTLAND

KINGDOM

FANTASY HAMMERED COINAGE

X# 1 TESTOON
Silver **Ruler:** Francis and Mary **Issuer:** Emery **Obv:** Facing busts **Obv. Legend:** FRANC • ET MARIA • ... **Rev:** Crowned arms **Rev. Legend:** ...• PACEM...

Date	Mintage	Good	VG	F	VF	XF
15xx	—	—	75.00	135	225	—

MEDALLIC / INA RETRO ISSUE

X# M11 CROWN
Silver, 40.97 mm. **Obv:** Laureate bust right **Obv. Legend:** GEORGIUS III DEI GRATIA REX. **Rev:** Crown above sword and sceptre between thistles **Rev. Legend:** QUAE DEUS CONIUNXIT NEMO SEPARET / • SCOTLAND • **Edge:** Plain

Date	Mintage	F	VF	XF	Unc	BU
1808 (2007)Proof	—					
1808 (2007)Matte Proof	—					

X# M11a CROWN
Copper, 40.97 mm. **Obv:** Laureate bust right **Obv. Legend:** GEORGIUS III DEI GRATIA REX. **Rev:** Crown above sword and sceptre between thistles **Rev. Legend:** QUAE DEUS CONIUNXIT NEMO SEPARET / • SCOTLAND • **Edge:** Plain

Date	Mintage	F	VF	XF	Unc	BU
1808 (2007) Proof	1,000	—	—	—	—	—

X# M11b CROWN
Aluminum, 40.97 mm. **Obv:** Laureate bust right **Obv. Legend:** GEORGIUS III DEI GRATIA REX. **Rev:** Crown above sword and sceptre between thistles **Rev. Legend:** QUAE DEUS CONIUNXIT NEMO SEPARET / • SCOTLAND • **Edge:** Plain

Date	Mintage	F	VF	XF	Unc	BU
1808 (2007) Proof	1,000	—	—	—	—	—

X# M11c CROWN
Pewter, 40.97 mm. **Obv:** Laureate bust right **Obv. Legend:** GEORGIUS III DEI GRATIA REX. **Rev:** Crown above sword and sceptre between thistles **Rev. Legend:** QUAE DEUS CONIUNXIT NEMO SEPARET / • SCOTLAND • **Edge:** Plain

Date	Mintage	F	VF	XF	Unc	BU
1808 (2007) Proof	1,000	—	—	—	—	—

X# M11d CROWN
Copper Bronzed, 40.97 mm. **Obv:** Laureate bust right **Obv. Legend:** GEORGIUS III DEI GRATIA REX. **Rev:** Crown above sword and sceptre between thistles **Rev. Legend:** QUAE DEUS CONIUNXIT NEMO SEPARET / • SCOTLAND • **Edge:** Plain

Date	Mintage	F	VF	XF	Unc	BU
1808 (2007) Proof	1,000	—	—	—	—	—

X# M11e CROWN

Nickel-Silver, 40.97 mm. **Obv:** Laureate bust right **Obv. Legend:** GEORGIUS III DEI GRATIA REX. **Rev:** Crown above sword and sceptre between thistles **Rev. Legend:** QUAE DEUS CONIUNXIT NEMO SEPARET / • SCOTLAND • **Edge:** Plain

Date	Mintage	F	VF	XF	Unc	BU
1808 (2007) Proof	1,000	—	—	—	—	—

X# M11f CROWN

Goldine, 40.97 mm. **Obv:** Laureate bust right **Obv. Legend:** GEORGIUS III DEI GRATIA REX. **Rev:** Crown above sword and sceptre between thistles **Rev. Legend:** QUAE DEUS CONIUNXIT NEMO SEPARET / • SCOTLAND • **Edge:** Plain

Date	Mintage	F	VF	XF	Unc	BU
1808 (2007) Proof	1,000	—	—	—	—	—

X# M11g CROWN

Gold, 40.97 mm. **Obv:** Laureate bust right **Obv. Legend:** GEORGIUS III DEI GRATIA REX. **Rev:** Crown above sword and sceptre between thistles **Rev. Legend:** QUAE DEUS CONIUNXIT NEMO SEPARET / • SCOTLAND • **Edge:** Plain

Date	Mintage	F	VF	XF	Unc	BU
1808 (2007) Proof	—	—	—	—	—	—

MEDALLIC COINAGE

X# M1 60 SHILLING

Silver **Obv:** Laureate bust of James II (VII) right, value below bust **Rev:** Crowned arms in collar of the Order of the Thistle, crown divides date

Date	Mintage	VG	F	VF	XF	Unc
1688 Proof	—	Value: 2,000				

Note: Struck in 1828 by Matthew Young

X# M1a 60 SHILLING

Gold **Obv:** Laureate bust of James II (VII) right, value below bust **Rev:** Crowned arms in collar of the Order of the Thistle, crown divides date

Date	Mintage	VG	F	VF	XF	Unc
1688 Rare	—	—	—	—	—	—

Note: Struck in 1828 by Matthew Young

PRETENDER COINAGE

With the death of James II on September 16, 1701, James Francis Edward Stuart became the Stuart claimant to the throne of England and Scotland. He was to become known in Jacobite circles as James III of England and James VIII of Scotland. He attempted two invasions of England - one in 1708 and another in 1715.

Norbert Roettiers prepared dies on two occassions for coins for the would-be king. One set was for an English crown of 1709 and the second group was for a crown and a guinea of 1716 for Scotland and a 1716 guinea for England. No comtemporary strikings are known for the 1716 dies. The dies came into the hands of one Matthew Young and in 1828, Young struck various pieces, after which the dies were destroyed. (Modern copies of this restrike do exist.)

X# PT1 CROWN

Silver **Obv:** Laureate bust of James III right **Obv. Legend:** IACOBVS III ... **Rev:** Crowned oval arms

Date	Mintage	F	VF	XF	Unc	BU
1709 Unique	—	—	—	—	—	—

X# PT2 CROWN

Silver **Ruler:** James VIII **Obv:** Laureate bust right **Obv. Legend:** IACOBVS VIII - DEL • GRATIA **Rev:** Crowned arms **Rev. Legend:** SCOT • ANGL • FRAN • ET • HIB • REX **Note:** Prev. KM#PT2.

Date	Mintage	F	VF	XF	Unc	BU
1716	—	—	—	1,250	2,500	—

X# PT2a CROWN

Bronze **Ruler:** James VIII **Obv:** Laureate bust right **Obv. Legend:** IACOBVS VIII - DEL • GRATIA **Rev:** Crowned arms **Rev. Legend:** SCOT • ANGL • FRAN • ET • HIB • REX **Note:** Prev. KM#PT2a.

Date	Mintage	F	VF	XF	Unc	BU
1716 Rare	—	—	—	—	—	—

X# PT2b CROWN

White Metal **Ruler:** James VIII **Obv:** Laureate bust right **Obv. Legend:** IACOBVS VIII - DEL • GRATIA **Rev:** Crowned arms **Rev. Legend:** SCOT • ANGL • FRAN • ET • HIB • REX **Note:** Prev. KM#PT2b.

Date	Mintage	F	VF	XF	Unc	BU
1716	—	—	—	700	1,250	—

X# PT2c CROWN

Gold **Ruler:** James VIII **Obv:** Laureate bust right **Obv. Legend:** IACOBVS VIII - DEL • GRATIA **Rev:** Crowned square arms **Rev. Legend:** SCOT • ANGL • FRAN • ET • HIB • REX **Note:** Prev. KM#PT2c.

Date	Mintage	F	VF	XF	Unc	BU
1716 Rare	—	—	—	—	—	—

X# PT3 GUINEA

Silver **Obv:** Young laureate bust of James III left **Obv. Legend:** IACOBVS TERTIUS **Rev:** Similar to PT4 **Note:** Prev. KM#PT3.

Date	Mintage	F	VF	XF	Unc	BU
1716	—	—	—	1,000	1,850	—

X# PT3a GUINEA

Bronze **Note:** Prev. KM#PT3a.

Date	Mintage	F	VF	XF	Unc	BU
1716 Rare	—	—	—	—	—	—

X# PT4 GUINEA

11.0900 g., Gold **Obv:** Older laureate bust of James VIII right **Obv. Legend:** IACOBVS VIII **Note:** Prev. KM#PT4.

Date	Mintage	F	VF	XF	Unc	BU
1716 Rare	—	—	—	—	—	—

X# PT4a GUINEA

Silver **Note:** Prev. KM#PT4a.

Date	Mintage	F	VF	XF	Unc	BU
1716	—	—	—	950	1,750	—

X# PT4b GUINEA

Bronze **Note:** Prev. KM#PT4b.

Date	Mintage	F	VF	XF	Unc	BU
1716 Rare	—	—	—	—	—	—

ECU COINAGE

X# 10 ECU

5.2000 g., Copper-Nickel-Zinc, 22.5 mm. **Ruler:** Elizabeth II **Obv:** Neptune and Europa standing flanking circular outlined map of Europe **Obv. Legend:** • EUROPE * EUROPA • SCOTLAND **Obv. Designer:** R. D. Maklouf **Rev:** Shield at lower center, thistle at upper right, unicorn and St. Andrew's cross behind **Edge:** Spink, London

Date	Mintage	F	VF	XF	Unc	BU
1992	—	—	—	—	6.50	—

X# 13 ECU

28.2800 g., 0.9250 Silver 0.8410 oz. ASW, 38.6 mm. **Ruler:** Elizabeth II **Obv:** Map of Europe **Obv. Legend:** • SCOTLAND • EUROPE - EUROPA **Rev:** Laureate bust of King Jacob left **Rev. Legend:** JACOBVS : D : G : ANG : SCOT : FRAN : ET : HIB : REX

Date	Mintage	F	VF	XF	Unc	BU
ND(1992)PM Proof	10,000	Value: 35.00				

X# 11 25 ECU

Tri-Metallic, 38 mm. **Ruler:** Elizabeth II **Issuer:** Spink, London **Obv:** Neptune and Europa standing flanking circular outlined map of Europe **Obv. Legend:** • EUROPE * EUROPA • SCOTLAND **Obv. Designer:** R. D. Maklouf **Rev:** Shield at lower center, thistle at upper right, unicorn and St. Andrew's cross behind

Date	Mintage	F	VF	XF	Unc	BU
1992 Proof	250	Value: 65.00				

X# 11a 25 ECU

23.0000 g., 0.9250 Silver 0.6840 oz. ASW, 38 mm. **Ruler:** Elizabeth II **Issuer:** Spink, London **Obv:** Neptune and Europa standing flanking circular outlined map of Europe **Obv. Legend:** • EUROPE * EUROPA • SCOTLAND **Obv. Designer:** R. D. Maklouf **Rev:** Shield at lower center, thistle at upper right, unicorn and St. Andrew's cross behind

Date	Mintage	F	VF	XF	Unc	BU
1992 Proof	250	Value: 65.00				

X# 15 25 ECU
23.0000 g., 0.9250 Silver 0.6840 oz. ASW, 38 mm. **Ruler:** Elizabeth II **Obv:** Neptune and Europa standing flanking circular outlined map of Europe **Obv. Legend:** • EUROPE * EUROPA • SCOTLAND **Obv. Designer:** R. D. Maklouf **Rev:** Shield at lower center, thistle at upper right, unicorn and St. Andrew's cross behind

Date	Mintage	F	VF	XF	Unc	BU
1992 Proof	500	Value: 50.00				

X# 15a 25 ECU
38.0000 g., 0.9167 Gold 1.1199 oz. AGW, 38 mm. **Ruler:** Elizabeth II **Obv:** Neptune and Europa standing flanking circular outlined map of Europe **Obv. Legend:** • EUROPE * EUROPA • SCOTLAND **Obv. Designer:** R. D. Maklouf **Rev:** Shield at lower center, thistle at upper right, unicorn and St. Andrew's cross behind

Date	Mintage	F	VF	XF	Unc	BU
1992 Proof	25	—	—	—	—	—

X# 12 200 ECU
3.0000 g., 0.7500 Gold 0.0723 oz. AGW, 22.50 mm. **Ruler:** Elizabeth II **Issuer:** Spink, London **Obv:** Neptune and Europa standing flanking circular outlined map of Europe **Obv. Legend:** • EUROPE * EUROPA • SCOTLAND **Obv. Designer:** R. D. Maklouf **Rev:** Shield at lower center, thistle at upper right, unicorn and St. Andrew's cross behind

Date	Mintage	F	VF	XF	Unc	BU
1992 Proof	500	Value: 135				

PIEFORTS

X#	Date	Mintage	Identification	Mkt Val
P1	1992	500	200 Ecu. 0.7500 Gold. 6.0000 g. X#12.	300
P2	1992	100	25 Ecu. 0.9250 Silver. 46.0000 g. X#11a.	125
P3	1992	500	25 Ecu. 0.9250 Silver. 46.0000 g. X#15.	125
P4	1992	25	25 Ecu. 0.9167 Gold. 76.0000 g. X#15a.	—

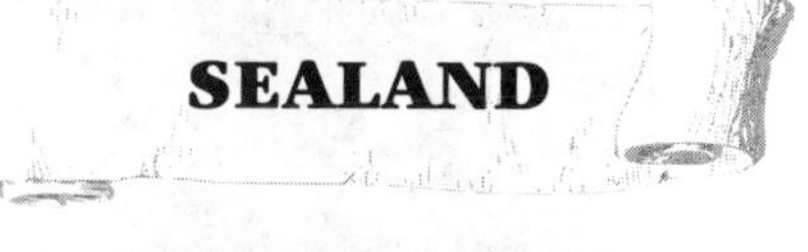

SEALAND

PRINCIPALITY

STANDARD COINAGE

X# 7a.1 25 CENTS
15.5670 g., 0.9990 Silver 0.5000 oz. ASW, 31.8 mm. **Ruler:** Prince Roy **Issuer:** Money Company **Series:** Treasures of the Sea **Obv:** Arms, panel below **Obv. Legend:** PRINCIPALITY OF SEALAND **Rev:** Orcha whale **Rev. Legend:** TREASURES OF THE SEA **Edge:** Reeded **Note:** AG prefix with three digit serial number.

Date	Mintage	F	VF	XF	Unc	BU
1994 Proof	500	Value: 15.00				

X# 7 25 CENTS
Bronze, 31.8 mm. **Ruler:** Prince Roy **Issuer:** Money Company **Series:** Treasures of the Sea **Obv:** Arms, panel below **Obv. Legend:** PRINCIPALITY OF SEALAND **Rev:** Orcha whale **Rev. Legend:** TREASURES OF THE SEA **Edge:** Reeded **Note:** Four digit serial number on panel.

Date	Mintage	F	VF	XF	Unc	BU
1994 Proof	1,111	—	—	—	—	—

X# 7a.2 25 CENTS
15.5670 g., 0.9990 Silver 0.5000 oz. ASW, 31.8 mm. **Ruler:** Prince Roy **Issuer:** Money Company **Series:** Treasures of the Sea **Obv:** Arms, panel below **Obv. Legend:** PRINCIPALITY OF SEALAND **Rev:** Orcha whale **Rev. Legend:** TREASURES OF THE SEA **Edge:** Reeded **Note:** WCE prefix with three digit serial number for West Coast Expo.

Date	Mintage	F	VF	XF	Unc	BU
1994 Proof	500	Value: 20.00				

X# 8.1 1/2 DOLLAR
Copper-Nickel, 39 mm. **Ruler:** Prince Roy **Issuer:** Money Company **Series:** Treasures of the Sea **Obv:** Arms **Obv. Legend:** PRINCIPALITY OF SEALAND **Rev:** Orcha whale **Rev. Legend:** TREASURES OF THE SEA **Edge:** Reeded

Date	Mintage	F	VF	XF	Unc	BU
1994 Proof	1,111	Value: 30.00				

X# 8.1a 1/2 DOLLAR
15.5670 g., 0.9990 Silver 0.5000 oz. ASW, 39 mm. **Ruler:** Prince Roy **Issuer:** Money Company **Series:** Treasures of the Sea **Obv:** Arms **Obv. Legend:** PRINCIPALITY OF SEALAND **Rev:** Orcha whale **Rev. Legend:** TREASURES OF THE SEA **Edge:** Reeded

Date	Mintage	F	VF	XF	Unc	BU
1994 Proof	500	Value: 35.00				

X# 8.2 1/2 DOLLAR
Copper-Nickel, 39 mm. **Ruler:** Prince Roy **Issuer:** Money Company **Series:** Treasures of the Sea **Obv:** Arms **Obv. Legend:** PRINCIPALITY OF SEALAND **Rev:** Orcha whale **Rev. Legend:** TREASURES OF THE SEA **Edge:** Scalloped

Date	Mintage	F	VF	XF	Unc	BU
1994 Proof	150	Value: 30.00				

X# 9 DOLLAR
31.1340 g., 0.9990 Silver 0.9999 oz. ASW, 39 mm. **Ruler:** Prince Roy **Series:** Treasures of the Sea **Obv:** Arms **Obv. Legend:** PRINCIPALITY OF SEALAND **Rev:** Dolphins **Rev. Legend:** TREASURES OF THE SEA **Edge:** Reeded

Date	Mintage	F	VF	XF	Unc	BU
1994 Proof	20,000	Value: 45.00				

X# 10 DOLLAR
3.1134 g., 0.9990 Gold 0.1000 oz. AGW, 10.1 mm. **Ruler:** Prince Roy **Issuer:** Money Company **Series:** Treasures of the Sea **Obv:** Arms **Obv. Legend:** PRINCIPALITY OF SEALAND **Rev:** Orca whale **Rev. Legend:** TREASURES OF THE SEA **Edge:** Reeded

Date	Mintage	F	VF	XF	Unc	BU
1994 Proof	1,111	Value: 145				

X# 11 2-1/2 DOLLARS
Bronze, 63.7 mm. **Ruler:** Prince Roy **Issuer:** Money Company **Series:** Treasures of the Sea **Obv:** Arms **Obv. Legend:** PRINCIPALITY OF SEALAND **Rev:** Orcha whale **Rev. Legend:** TREASURES OF THE SEA **Edge:** Reeded

Date	Mintage	F	VF	XF	Unc	BU
1994 Proof	10,000	Value: 35.00				

X# 11a 2-1/2 DOLLARS
Silver, 63.7 mm. **Ruler:** Prince Roy **Issuer:** Money Company **Series:** Treasures of the Sea **Obv:** Arms **Obv. Legend:** PRINCIPALITY OF SEALAND **Rev:** Orcha whale **Rev. Legend:** TREASURES OF THE SEA **Edge:** Reeded

Date	Mintage	F	VF	XF	Unc	BU
1994 Proof	500	Value: 250				

X# 12 2-1/2 DOLLARS
0.9990 Gold, 13.8 mm. **Ruler:** Prince Roy **Issuer:** Money Company **Series:** Treasures of the Sea **Obv:** Arms **Obv. Legend:** PRINCIPALITY OF SEALAND **Rev:** Orca whale **Rev. Legend:** TREASURES OF THE SEA **Edge:** Reeded

Date	Mintage	F	VF	XF	Unc	BU
1994 Proof	1,111	Value: 175				

X# 13 5 DOLLARS
3.1134 g., 0.9990 Gold 0.1000 oz. AGW, 16.5 mm. **Ruler:** Prince Roy **Issuer:** Money Company **Series:** Treasures of the Sea **Obv:** Arms **Obv. Legend:** PRINCIPALITY OF SEALAND **Rev:** Orca whale **Rev. Legend:** TREASURES OF THE SEA **Edge:** Reeded

Date	Mintage	F	VF	XF	Unc	BU
1994 Proof	2,500	Value: 75.00				

X# 1 10 DOLLARS
25.1500 g., 0.9250 Silver 0.7479 oz. ASW, 40.6 mm. **Ruler:** Prince Roy **Obv:** Head of Princess Joan left **Obv. Legend:** PRINCIPALITY OF SEALAND **Rev:** Clipper ship **Rev. Legend:** HEART WITHIN AND GOD OVERHEAD **Edge:** Reeded

Date	Mintage	F	VF	XF	Unc	BU
1972 Proof	2,000	Value: 60.00				

X# 3.1 10 DOLLARS
12.3000 g., 0.9250 Silver 0.3658 oz. ASW, 30.1 mm. **Ruler:** Prince Roy **Issuer:** Josef Baier **Series:** 10 Year Jubilee **Obv:** Arms **Obv. Legend:** PRINCIPALITY OF SEALAND **Rev:** Bust of Joan right **Rev. Legend:** PRINCESS JOAN **Edge:** Reeded

Date	Mintage	F	VF	XF	Unc	BU
1977 Proof	2,000	Value: 35.00				

X# 3.2 10 DOLLARS
12.3000 g., 0.9250 Silver 0.3658 oz. ASW, 30.2 mm. **Ruler:** Prince Roy **Issuer:** Josef Baier **Series:** 10 Year Jubilee **Obv:** Arms, .925 below **Obv. Legend:** PRINCIPALITY OF SEALAND **Rev:** Bust of Joan right **Rev. Legend:** Princess Joan **Edge:** Plain

Date	Mintage	F	VF	XF	Unc	BU
1977 Proof	25	Value: 65.00				

X# 4.1 10 DOLLARS
12.3000 g., 0.9250 Silver 0.3658 oz. ASW, 30.1 mm. **Ruler:** Prince Roy **Issuer:** Josef Baier **Series:** 10 Year Jubilee **Obv:** Arms **Obv. Legend:** PRINCIPALITY OF SEALAND **Rev:** Bust left **Rev. Legend:** ROY OF SEALAND **Edge:** Reeded

Date	Mintage	F	VF	XF	Unc	BU
1977 Proof	2,000	Value: 35.00				

X# 4.2 10 DOLLARS
12.3000 g., 0.9250 Silver 0.3658 oz. ASW, 30.1 mm. **Ruler:** Prince Roy **Issuer:** Josef Baier **Series:** 10 Year Jubilee **Obv:** Arms **Obv. Legend:** PRINCIPALITY OF SEALAND **Rev:** Bust left **Rev. Legend:** ROY OF SEALAND **Edge:** Plain

Date	Mintage	F	VF	XF	Unc	BU
1977 Proof	25	Value: 65.00				

X# 2 20 DOLLARS
25.0000 g., Silver **Ruler:** Prince Roy **Obv:** Arms **Obv. Legend:** *Principality of Sealand* **Rev:** Head of Princess Joan left

Date	Mintage	F	VF	XF	Unc	BU
1975 Proof	—	Value: 60.00				

X# 5 100 DOLLARS
14.4000 g., 0.9000 Gold 0.4167 oz. AGW, 38.3 mm. **Ruler:** Prince Roy **Issuer:** Josef Baier **Subject:** 10 Year Jubilee **Obv:** Arms **Obv. Legend:** PRINCIPALITY OF SEALAND **Rev:** Small cameo bust of Joan right at left, WWII radar platform in sprays at center, small cameo bust of Roy left at right **Edge:** Reeded

Date	Mintage	F	VF	XF	Unc	BU
1977 Proof	2,000	Value: 380				

X# 5a 100 DOLLARS
19.4500 g., Brass, 38.3 mm. **Ruler:** Prince Roy **Subject:** 10 Year Jubilee **Obv:** Arms **Obv. Legend:** PRINCIPALITY OF SEALAND **Rev:** Small cameo bust of Joan right at left, Roy left at right, WWII radar platform in sprays at center **Edge:** Reeded

Date	Mintage	F	VF	XF	Unc	BU
1977 Proof	—	Value: 65.00				

X# 6 100 DOLLARS
Silver antiqued, 38.6 mm. **Obv:** Arms **Obv. Legend:** PRINCIPALITY OF SEALAND **Rev:** Bust of Johannes Seiger left **Rev. Legend:** PRIME MINISTER OF SEALAND **Note:** Rebel issue.

Date	Mintage	F	VF	XF	Unc	BU
1991 Proof	1,000	Value: 37.50				

TRIAL STRIKES

X#	Date	Mintage	Identification	Mkt Val
TS1	1994	99	1/2 Dollar. Copper-Nickel. Obverse X8.1.	—

X#	Date	Mintage	Identification	Mkt Val
TS2	1994	99	1/2 Dollar. Copper-Nickel. Reverse X8.1.	—

X#	Date	Mintage	Identification	Mkt Val
TS3	1994	99	Dollar. Silver. Obverse X9.	—

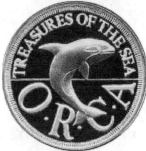

X#	Date	Mintage	Identification	Mkt Val
TS4	1994	99	Dollar. Silver. Reverse X9.	—
TS5	1994	250	Dollar. Bronze. Obverse X9.	—

X#	Date	Mintage	Identification	Mkt Val
TS6	1994	250	Dollar. Bronze. Reverse X9.	—

PROOF SETS

X#	Date	Mintage	Identification	Issue Price	Mkt Val
XPS1	1977 (3)	2,000	X3.1, X4.1,X5	300	500
XPS2	1994 (4)	1,111	X7a.1, X8.1, X9, X13	140	—

SEBORGA

PRINCIPALITY

DECIMAL COINAGE

X# 1 5 CENTESIMI

Copper-Nickel, 19.5 mm. **Ruler:** Prince Giorgio I **Obv:** Bust right **Obv. Legend:** GIORGIO I PRINCIPE DI SEBORGA **Rev:** Sword in stone **Rev. Legend:** PRINCIPATO DI SEBORGA **Edge:** Plain

Date	Mintage	F	VF	XF	Unc	BU
1995	—	—	—	—	25.00	—

X# 7 10 CENTESIMI

Brass, 25.5 mm. **Ruler:** Prince Giorgio I **Obv:** Bust of St. Bernard 3/4 right **Obv. Legend:** PRINCIPATO DI SEBORGA **Rev:** Arms of St. Bernard **Rev. Legend:** PAUPERA MILITIA CHRISTI **Edge:** Plain

Date	Mintage	F	VF	XF	Unc	BU
1996	—	—	—	—	25.00	—

X# 8 10 CENTESIMI

0.9990 Silver, 25.5 mm. **Ruler:** Prince Giorgio I **Obv:** Bust of St. Bernard 3/4 right **Obv. Legend:** PRINCIPATO DI SEBORGA **Rev:** Arms of St. Bernard **Rev. Legend:** PAUPERA MILITIA CHRISTI **Edge:** Plain

Date	Mintage	F	VF	XF	Unc	BU
1996	—	—	—	—	30.00	—

X# 2 15 CENTESIMI

Copper-Nickel, 26.2 mm. **Ruler:** Prince Giorgio I **Edge:** Plain

Date	Mintage	F	VF	XF	Unc	BU
1995	—	—	—	—	35.00	—

X# 9 15 CENTESIMI

Copper-Nickel, 26 mm. **Ruler:** Prince Giorgio I **Obv:** Bust right **Obv. Legend:** GIORGIO I • PRINCIPE DI SEBORGA **Rev:** Shield of Order of St. Bernard **Rev. Legend:** PRINCIPATO DI SEBORGA **Edge:** Plain

Date	Mintage	F	VF	XF	Unc	BU
1996	30,000	—	—	—	15.00	—

X# 3 1/2 LUIGINO

8.5300 g., Brass In Copper-Nickel, 30.1 mm. **Ruler:** Prince Giorgio I **Obv:** Bust right **Obv. Legend:** GIORGIO I • PRINCIPE DI SEBORGA **Rev:** San Marino Plaza **Rev. Legend:** PRINCIPATO DI SEBORGA **Edge:** Plain

Date	Mintage	F	VF	XF	Unc	BU
1995	21,000	—	—	—	15.00	—

X# 4 LUIGI

13.0400 g., Bronze, 28 mm. **Ruler:** Prince Giorgio I **Obv:** Bust right **Obv. Legend:** GIORGIO I PRINCIPE DE SEBORGA **Rev:** Crowned mantled arms **Rev. Legend:** PRINCIPATO DE SEBORGA **Edge:** Plain

Date	Mintage	F	VF	XF	Unc	BU
1995	10,700	—	—	—	30.00	—

X# 10 LUIGI

Bronze, 28 mm. **Ruler:** Prince Giorgio I **Obv:** Bust right **Obv. Legend:** GIORGIO I • PRINCIPE DI SEBORGA **Rev:** Crowned mantled arms **Rev. Legend:** PRINCIPATO DI SEBORGA **Edge:** Plain

Date	Mintage	F	VF	XF	Unc	BU
1996	10,700	—	—	—	30.00	—

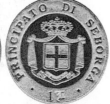

X# 11 LUIGI

0.9990 Silver, 28 mm. **Ruler:** Prince Giorgio I **Obv:** Bust right **Obv. Legend:** GIORGIO I • PRINCIPE DE SEBORGA **Rev:** Crowned mantled arms **Rev. Legend:** PRINCIPATO DI SEBORGA **Edge:** Plain

Date	Mintage	F	VF	XF	Unc	BU
1996 Proof	1,918	Value: 45.00				

X# 12 2 LUIGI

Brass In Copper-Nickel, 28 mm. **Ruler:** Prince Giorgio I **Series:** Independence **Obv:** Bust facing **Obv. Legend:** PRINCIPATO DI SEBORGA **Rev:** Crowned shield, value **Rev. Legend:** PROCLAMAZIONE D'INDIPENDENZE • 20 AGOSTO 1996 **Edge:** Plain

Date	Mintage	F	VF	XF	Unc	BU
1996	—	—	—	—	30.00	—

X# 13 2 LUIGI

0.9990 Silver, 28 mm. **Ruler:** Prince Giorgio I **Series:** Independence **Obv:** Bust facing **Obv. Legend:** PRINCIPATO DI SEBORGA **Rev:** Crowned shield, value **Edge:** Plain

Date	Mintage	F	VF	XF	Unc	BU
1996	—	—	—	—	50.00	—

X# 5 7-1/2 LUIGI

31.1200 g., 0.9990 Silver 0.9995 oz. ASW, 36.9 mm. **Ruler:** Prince Giorgio I **Obv:** Bust right **Obv. Legend:** GIORGIO I PRINCIPE DI SEBORGA **Rev:** Crowned mantled arms **Rev. Legend:** PRINCIPATO DE SEBORGA **Edge:** Plain

Date	Mintage	F	VF	XF	Unc	BU
1995	150	—	—	—	—	—

X# 6 7-1/2 LUIGI

0.9990 Silver, 37 mm. **Ruler:** Prince Giorgio I **Obv:** Bust right **Obv. Legend:** GIORGIO I • PRINCIPE DE SEBORGA **Rev:** Three shields above sword in stone **Rev. Legend:** PRINCIPATO DE SEBORGA **Edge:** Plain

Date	Mintage	F	VF	XF	Unc	BU
1995 Proof	1,000	Value: 60.00				

PROVAS

X#	Date	Mintage	Identification	Mkt Val
Pr1	1994	50	Luigi. Nickel.	150
Pr2	1994	50	Luigi. Brass.	120
Pr3	1994	50	Luigi. Nickel-Silver.	150
Pr4	1994	50	Luigi. Brass.	120
Pr5	1994	50	Luigi. Aluminum.	100
Pr6	1994	50	Luigi. Copper.	100
Pr7	1994	50	Luigi. Lead.	100
Pr8	1994	50	Luigi. Stainless Steel.	120
Pr9	1994	50	Luigi. Iron-Plated Nickel.	125
Pr10	1994	50	Luigi. Stainless Steel.	120
Pr11	1994	50	Luigi. Brass.	120
Pr12	1994	50	Luigi. 0.9990 Silver.	200
Pr13	1994	50	Luigi. Copper-Nickel.	150
Pr14	1994	50	Luigi. Gold.	—
Pr15	1994	50	Luigi. Platinum.	—

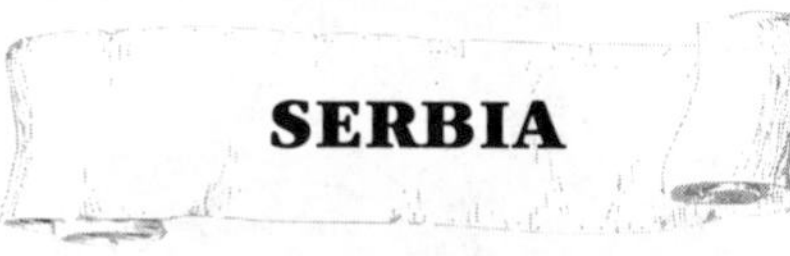

SERBIA

REPUBLIC

FANTASY EURO PATTERNS

X# Pn1 EURO CENT

Copper Plated Steel **Edge:** Plain

Date	Mintage	F	VF	XF	Unc	BU
2005	—	—	—	—	—	1.00

X# Pn2 2 EURO CENT

Copper Plated Steel **Edge:** Plain

Date	Mintage	F	VF	XF	Unc	BU
2005	—	—	—	—	—	1.50

X# Pn3 5 EURO CENT
Copper Plated Steel **Edge:** Plain

Date	Mintage	F	VF	XF	Unc	BU
2005	—	—	—	—	—	2.00

X# Pn4 10 EURO CENT
Goldine **Edge:** Plain

Date	Mintage	F	VF	XF	Unc	BU
2005	—	—	—	—	—	2.50

X# Pn5 20 EURO CENT
Goldine **Edge:** Plain

Date	Mintage	F	VF	XF	Unc	BU
2005	—	—	—	—	—	3.00

X# Pn6 50 EURO CENT
Goldine **Edge:** Plain

Date	Mintage	F	VF	XF	Unc	BU
2005	—	—	—	—	—	3.50

X# Pn7 EUROP
Bi-Metallic **Edge:** Plain

Date	Mintage	F	VF	XF	Unc	BU
2005	—	—	—	—	—	5.50

X# Pn8 2 EUROP
Bi-Metallic **Edge:** Plain

Date	Mintage	F	VF	XF	Unc	BU
2005	—	—	—	—	—	7.50

MINT SETS

X#	Date	Mintage	Identification	Issue Price	Mkt Val
XMS1	2005 (8)	—	X#Pn1-Pn8	—	26.00

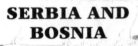

SERBIA AND BOSNIA

SERBIA AND BOSNIA

ROYAL GOVERNMENT

(In Exile)

FANTASY COINAGE

Authorized by J. B. Count of Mitrovica of the Royal and Imperial House of Serbia and Bosnia, Department of the Monetary Authority

X# 10 DINAR
Copper-Nickel-Zinc **Subject:** Commemorating the 1912 Balkan War

Date	Mintage	F	VF	XF	Unc	BU
1987	1,912	—	—	—	—	12.00

X# 1 5 DINARA
24.2000 g., 0.9250 Silver 0.7197 oz. ASW
Subject: 100th Anniversary of the Throne

Date	Mintage	F	VF	XF	Unc	BU
1982 Proof	1,999	Value: 60.00				

X# 2 5 DINARA
Copper-Nickel Alloy **Note:** Color is similar to gold.

Date	Mintage	F	VF	XF	Unc	BU
1982 Proof	100	Value: 45.00				

X# 3 5 DINARA
33.0000 g., 0.9990 Platinum 1.0599 oz. APW

Date	Mintage	F	VF	XF	Unc	BU
1982 Proof	1	Value: 3,500				

X# 7 5 DINARA
22.1000 g., Gold

Date	Mintage	F	VF	XF	Unc	BU
1982 Proof	—	Value: 2,500				

X# 4 10 DINARA
3.5000 g., 0.5850 Gold 0.0658 oz. AGW **Subject:** 25th Anniversary of Coronation H.H. Marziano II

Date	Mintage	F	VF	XF	Unc	BU
1981 Proof	—	Value: 90.00				

X# 5 10 DINARA
Silver **Note:** Piefort.

Date	Mintage	F	VF	XF	Unc	BU
1981 Proof	100	Value: 45.00				

X# 6 10 DINARA
5.3400 g., 0.9990 Platinum 0.1715 oz. APW

Date	Mintage	F	VF	XF	Unc	BU
1981 Proof	1	Value: 650				

PIEFORTS

X#	Date	Mintage	Identification	Mkt Val
P2	1987	—	Dinar. Gold. (.500 Fine)	—
P1	1987	75	Dinar. Sterling Silver. 31.1g.	—

FANTASY COINAGE

Authorized by J. B. Count of Mitrovica of the Royal and Imperial House of Serbia and Bosnia, Department of the Monetary Authority

X#	Date	Mintage	Identification	Mkt Val
Pn1	1987	28	Dinar. Copper-Nickel-Zinc. X10	—
Pn2	1987	—	Dinar. Sterling Silver. X#P1. 31.1g.	—
Pn3	1987	—	Dinar. Sterling Silver. Uniface. X#10 reverse. 31.1g.	—

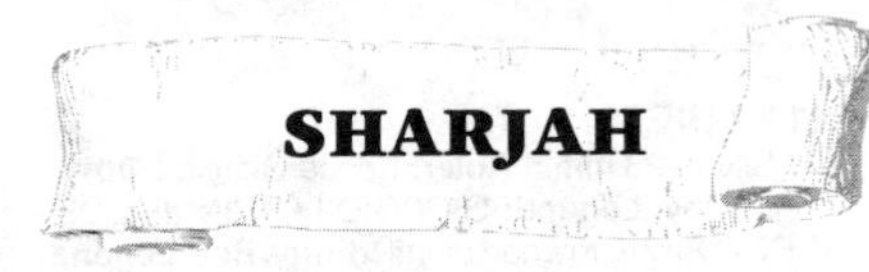

SHARJAH

EMIRATE

FANTASY COINAGE

This coinage was ordered by the Sheik who, according to the British, had no authority to issue it

X# 1 5 RUPEE
25.0000 g., 0.7200 Silver 0.5787 oz. ASW, 36 mm.
Ruler: Khalid bin Muhammad al-Qasimi **Subject:** President John F. Kennedy Memorial
Obv: National arms **Note:** Prev. KM#1. 18,100 remelted in 1966.

Date	Mintage	F	VF	XF	Unc	BU
AH1383	33,000	—	—	—	20.00	—

X# 2 5 RUPEE
25.0000 g., 0.7200 Silver 0.5787 oz. ASW, 36 mm.
Ruler: Khalid bin Muhammad al-Qasimi **Subject:** President John F. Kennedy Memorial **Obv:** "PROOF" below flags **Note:** Prev. KM#1.

Date	Mintage	F	VF	XF	Unc	BU
AH1383 Proof	10,000	Value: 35.00				

SHAWNEE TRIBAL NATION

AMERICAN INDIAN TRIBAL RESERVATION

TOKEN COINAGE

KM# Tn1 DOLLAR
31.2600 g., 0.9990 Silver 1.0040 oz. ASW, 40 mm.
Obv: Tribal emblem **Rev:** Chief Tecumseh (1768-1813)
Edge: Reeded **Note:** "Legal Tender" on reservation only

Date	Mintage	F	VF	XF	Unc	BU
2002	50,000	—	—	—	—	—
2002 Proof	20,000	Value: 40.00				

SOVEREIGN NATION

MILLED COINAGE

X# 2 5 DOLLARS
6.2200 g., 0.9999 Gold 0.1999 oz. AGW, 20 mm.
Obv: Arms **Obv. Legend:** THE SOVEREIGN NATION OF THE SHAWNEE TRIBE **Obv. Designer:** Alex Shagin **Rev:** Bust of Tecumseh "Shooting Star" 3/4 left
Edge: Reeded

Date	Mintage	F	VF	XF	Unc	BU
2002 Proof	5,000	Value: 250				

X# 4 5 DOLLARS
6.2200 g., 0.9999 Gold 0.1999 oz. AGW, 22.5 mm. **Issuer:** PandaAmerica **Obv:** Arms **Obv. Legend:** THE SOVEREIGN NATION OF THE SHAWNEE TRIBE **Obv. Designer:** Alex Shagin **Rev:** Bust of George Drouillard 3/4 right **Rev. Legend:** GEORGE DROUILLARD SIGN TALKER

Date	Mintage	F	VF	XF	Unc	BU
2003 Proof	5,000	Value: 225				

X# 6 5 DOLLARS
6.2207 g., 0.9990 Gold 0.1998 oz. AGW, 22 mm. **Obv:** Arms **Rev:** Sacagawea with child and horse **Edge:** Reeded

Date	Mintage	F	VF	XF	Unc	BU
2004 Proof	5,000	Value: 200				

SOVEREIGNTY

MILLED COINAGE

X# 1 DOLLAR
31.2000 g., 0.9999 Silver 1.0030 oz. ASW, 39 mm. **Issuer:** PandaAmerica **Obv:** Tribal seal **Obv. Legend:** THE SOVEREIGN NATION OF THE SHAWNEE TRIBE **Obv. Designer:** Alex Shagin **Rev:** Bust of Chief "Shooting Star" Tecumseh "The Prophet" 3/4 right **Edge:** Reeded **Note:** Mintage figures given are for total limits.

Date	Mintage	F	VF	XF	Unc	BU
2002	50,000	—	—	—	—	20.00
2002 Proof	20,000	Value: 40.00				

X# 3 DOLLAR
31.2000 g., 0.9999 Silver 1.0030 oz. ASW, 39 mm. **Obv:** Tribal seal **Obv. Legend:** THE SOVEREIGN NATION OF THE SHAWNEE TRIBE **Obv. Designer:** Alex Shagin **Rev:** Lewis, Clark and Drouillard scouting **Edge:** Reeded **Note:** Mintage figures given are for total limits.

Date	Mintage	F	VF	XF	Unc	BU
2003	50,000	—	—	—	—	25.00
2003 Proof	20,000	Value: 45.00				

X# 5 DOLLAR
31.2000 g., 0.9999 Silver 1.0030 oz. ASW, 39 mm. **Obv:** Tribal seal **Obv. Legend:** THE SOVEREIGN NATION OF THE SHAWNEE TRIBE **Obv. Designer:** Alex Shagin **Rev:** Flag behing Indian Chief and Thomas Jefferson standing, eagle on shield at their feet **Edge:** Reeded **Note:** Mintage figures given are for total limits.

Date	Mintage	F	VF	XF	Unc	BU
2004	50,000	—	—	—	—	20.00
2004 Proof	20,000	Value: 40.00				

X# 15 DOLLAR
31.3100 g., 0.9990 Silver 1.0056 oz. ASW, 40.6 mm. **Obv:** Tribal seal **Obv. Inscription:** THE SOVEREIGN NATION OF THE SHAWNEE TRIBE **Obv. Designer:** A. Shagin **Rev:** Lewis, Clark, Dromillard and Sacagawea in a canoe **Rev. Legend:** EXPEDITION OF DISCOVERY **Edge:** Reeded

Date	Mintage	F	VF	XF	Unc	BU
2005	50,000	—	—	—	30.00	—
2005 Proof	20,000	Value: 45.00				

X# 20 DOLLAR
31.2100 g., 0.9999 Silver 1.0033 oz. ASW, 40.6 mm. **Obv:** Tribal seal **Obv. Inscription:** THE SOVEREIGN NATION OF THE SHAWNEE TRIBE **Obv. Designer:** A. Shagin **Rev:** 1/2 length figure of Tenskwatawa "the prophet" 3/4 left **Rev. Legend:** PROPHET TENSKWATAWA **Edge:** Reeded

Date	Mintage	F	VF	XF	Unc	BU
2006	50,000	—	—	—	30.00	—
2006 Proof	20,000	Value: 45.00				

X# 16 5 DOLLARS
6.3000 g., 0.9999 Gold 0.2025 oz. AGW, 22.5 mm. **Obv:** Tribal seal **Obv. Inscription:** THE SOVEREIGN NATION OF THE SHAWNEE TRIBE **Obv. Designer:** A. Shagin **Rev:** Sacagawea with papoose on horseback right **Rev. Legend:** EXPEDITION OF DISCOVERY **Edge:** Reeded

Date	Mintage	F	VF	XF	Unc	BU
2005 Proof	5,000	Value: 325				

X# 21 5 DOLLARS
6.2500 g., 0.9999 Gold 0.2009 oz. AGW, 22.5 mm. **Obv:** Tribal seal **Obv. Legend:** THE SOVEREIGN NATION OF THE SHAWNEE TRIBE **Obv. Designer:** A. Shagin **Rev:** Bust of Chief Tecumseh 3/4 right **Rev. Legend:** TECVMSEH **Edge:** Reeded

Date	Mintage	F	VF	XF	Unc	BU
2006 Proof	5,000	Value: 325				

X# 17 50 DOLLARS
15.5500 g., 0.9999 Gold 0.4999 oz. AGW, 30.1 mm. **Obv:** Tribal seal **Obv. Inscription:** THE SOVEREIGN NATION

OF THE SHAWNEE TRIBE **Obv. Designer:** A. Shagin **Rev:** Sacagawea with papoose on horseback right **Rev. Legend:** EXPEDITION OF DISCOVERY **Edge:** Reeded

Date	Mintage	F	VF	XF	Unc	BU
2005 Proof	999	Value: 600				

X# 8 100 DOLLARS

30.9100 g., 0.9999 Gold 0.9936 oz. AGW, 38.9 mm. **Obv:** Tribal seal **Obv. Legend:** THE SOVEREIGN NATION OF THE SHAWNEE TRIBE **Obv. Designer:** A. Shagin **Rev:** Bust of "Sign Talker" 3/4 right **Rev. Legend:** GEORGE DROILLARD "SIGN TÁLKER" **Edge:** Milled

Date	Mintage	F	VF	XF	Unc	BU
2003 Proof	999	Value: 1,200				

X# 9 500 DOLLARS

92.5500 g., 0.9999 Gold 2.9751 oz. AGW **Obv:** Tribal seal **Obv. Legend:** THE SOVEREIGN NATION OF THE SHAWNEE TRIBE **Obv. Designer:** A. Shagin **Rev:** Lewis, Clark and Drouillard scouting **Rev. Legend:** LEWIS • CLARK • DROUILLARD **Edge:** Reeded

Date	Mintage	F	VF	XF	Unc	BU
2003 Proof	300	Value: 4,500				

X# 13 500 DOLLARS

15.5400 g., 0.9990 Platinum 0.4991 oz. APW, 30 mm. **Obv:** Tribal seal **Obv. Legend:** THE SOVEREIGN NATION OF THE SHAWNEE TRIBE **Obv. Designer:** A. Shagin **Rev:** Flag and shield between indian and present **Rev. Legend:** EXPEDITION OF DISCOVERY **Edge:** Reeded

Date	Mintage	F	VF	XF	Unc	BU
2004 Proof	999	Value: 950				

X# 14 1000 DOLLARS

31.0000 g., 0.9999 Platinum 0.9965 oz. APW, 38.7 mm. **Obv:** Tribal seal **Obv. Legend:** THE SOVEREIGN NATION OF THE SHAWNEE TRIBE **Obv. Designer:** A. Shagin **Rev:** Flag and shield between indian and present **Rev. Legend:** EXPEDITION OF DISCOVERY **Edge:** Reeded

Date	Mintage	F	VF	XF	Unc	BU
2004 Proof	300	Value: 2,750				

TOKEN COINAGE

X# Tn2 DOLLAR

31.2600 g., 0.9990 Silver 1.0040 oz. ASW, 40 mm. **Obv:** Tribal seal **Rev:** Figures of Lewis, Clark and Drouillard with muskets **Edge:** Reeded **Note:** "Legal Tender" on reservation only

Date	Mintage	F	VF	XF	Unc	BU
2003	50,000	—	—	—	20.00	—
2003 Proof	20,000	Value: 40.00				

X# Tn3 DOLLAR

31.2600 g., 0.9990 Silver 1.0040 oz. ASW, 40 mm. **Obv:** Tribal seal **Rev:** Standing figures of Thomas Jefferson and an Indian Chief(?) **Edge:** Reeded **Note:** "Legal Tender" on reservation only

Date	Mintage	F	VF	XF	Unc	BU
2004	50,000	—	—	—	20.00	—
2004 Proof	20,000	Value: 40.00				

X# Tn4 5 DOLLARS

6.2207 g., 0.9990 Gold 0.1998 oz. AGW, 22 mm. **Obv:** Tribal seal **Rev:** "The Prophet" (1778-1837) **Edge:** Reeded **Note:** "Legal Tender" on reservation only

Date	Mintage	F	VF	XF	Unc	BU
2002 Proof	5,000	Value: 200				

X# Tn5 5 DOLLARS

6.2207 g., 0.9990 Gold 0.1998 oz. AGW, 22 mm. **Obv:** Tribal seal **Rev:** George Drouillard **Edge:** Reeded **Note:** "Legal Tender" on reservation only

Date	Mintage	F	VF	XF	Unc	BU
2003 Proof	5,000	Value: 200				

SCOTTISH ADMINISTRATION

MEDALLIC COINAGE

X# 1 KRONER

Copper-Nickel, 38 mm. **Issuer:** Sail Shetland Ltd. **Subject:** Cutty Sark Tall Ships' Races **Obv:** Sailing ship Alexander von Humboldt (Germany) **Obv. Designer:** Barry Williams **Rev:** Outline map of race course, 5 national flags below **Edge:** Reeded

Date	Mintage	F	VF	XF	Unc	BU
1999 Proof	1,000	Value: 17.50				

X# 1a KRONER

0.9250 Silver, 38 mm. **Issuer:** Sail Shetland Ltd. **Subject:** Cutty Sark Tall Ships' Races **Obv:** Sailing ship Alexander von Humboldt (Germany) **Obv. Designer:** Barry Williams **Rev:** Outline map of race course, 5 national flags below **Edge:** Plain

Date	Mintage	F	VF	XF	Unc	BU
1999 Proof	250	Value: 50.00				

X# 1b KRONER

0.9250 Gilt Silver, 38 mm. **Issuer:** Sail Shetland Ltd. **Subject:** Cutty Sark Tall Ships' Races **Obv:** Sailing ship Alexander von Humboldt (Germany) **Obv. Designer:** Barry Williams **Rev:** Outline map of race course, 5 national flags below **Edge:** Plain

Date	Mintage	F	VF	XF	Unc	BU
1999 Proof	250	Value: 60.00				

X# 2 KRONER

Copper-Nickel, 38 mm. **Issuer:** Sail Shetland Ltd. **Subject:** Cutty Sark Tall Ships' Races **Obv:** Sailing ship Christian Radich (Norway) **Obv. Designer:** Barry Williams **Rev:** Outline map of race course, 5 national flags below **Edge:** Reeded

Date	Mintage	F	VF	XF	Unc	BU
1999 Proof	1,000	Value: 17.50				

X# 2a KRONER

0.9250 Silver, 38 mm. **Issuer:** Sail Shetland Ltd. **Subject:** Cutty Sark Tall Ships' Races **Obv:** Sailing ship Christian Radich (Norway) **Obv. Designer:** Barry Williams **Rev:** Outline map of race course, 5 national flags below **Edge:** Plain

Date	Mintage	F	VF	XF	Unc	BU
1999 Proof	250	Value: 50.00				

X# 2b KRONER

0.9250 Gilt Silver, 38 mm. **Issuer:** Sail Shetland Ltd. **Subject:** Cutty Sark Tall Ships' Races **Obv:** Sailing ship Christian Radich (Norway) **Obv. Designer:** Barry Williams **Rev:** Outline map of race course, 5 national flags below **Edge:** Plain

Date	Mintage	F	VF	XF	Unc	BU
1999 Proof	250	Value: 60.00				

X# 3 KRONER

Copper-Nickel, 38 mm. **Issuer:** Sail Shetland Ltd. **Subject:** Cutty Sark Tall Ships' Races **Obv:** Sailing ship Cuauhtemoc (Mexico) **Obv. Designer:** Barry Williams **Rev:** Outline map of race course, 5 national flags below **Edge:** Reeded

Date	Mintage	F	VF	XF	Unc	BU
1999 Proof	1,000	Value: 17.50				

X# 3a KRONER

0.9250 Silver, 38 mm. **Issuer:** Sail Shetland Ltd. **Subject:** Cutty Sark Tall Ships' Races **Obv:** Sailing ship Cuauhtemoc (Mexico) **Obv. Designer:** Barry Williams **Rev:** Outline map of race course, 5 national flags below **Edge:** Plain

Date	Mintage	F	VF	XF	Unc	BU
1999 Proof	250	Value: 50.00				

X# 3b KRONER

0.9250 Gilt Silver, 38 mm. **Issuer:** Sail Shetland Ltd. **Subject:** Cutty Sark Tall Ships' Races **Obv:** Sailing ship Cuauhtemoc (Mexico) **Obv. Designer:** Barry Williams **Rev:** Outline map of race course, 5 national flags below **Edge:** Plain

Date	Mintage	F	VF	XF	Unc	BU
1999 Proof	250	Value: 60.00				

X# 4 KRONER

Copper-Nickel, 38 mm. **Issuer:** Sail Shetland Ltd. **Subject:** Cutty Sark Tall Ships' Races **Obv:** Sailing ship Danmark (Denmark) **Obv. Designer:** Barry Williams **Rev:** Outline map of race course, 5 national flags below **Edge:** Reeded

Date	Mintage	F	VF	XF	Unc	BU
1999 Proof	1,000	Value: 17.50				

X# 4a KRONER

0.9250 Silver, 38 mm. **Issuer:** Sail Shetland Ltd. **Subject:** Cutty Sark Tall Ships' Races **Obv:** Sailing ship Danmark (Denmark) **Rev:** Outline map of race course, 5 national flags below **Edge:** Plain

Date	Mintage	F	VF	XF	Unc	BU
1999 Proof	250	Value: 50.00				

X# 4b KRONER

0.9250 Gilt Silver, 38 mm. **Issuer:** Sail Shetland Ltd. **Subject:** Cutty Sark Tall Ships' Races **Obv:** Sailing ship Danmark (Denmark) **Obv. Designer:** Barry Williams **Rev:** Outline map of race course, 5 national flags below **Edge:** Plain

Date	Mintage	F	VF	XF	Unc	BU
1999 Proof	250	Value: 60.00				

X# 5 KRONER

Copper-Nickel, 38 mm. **Issuer:** Sail Shetland Ltd. **Subject:** Cutty Sark Tall Ships' Races **Obv:** Sailing ship Eendracht (Netherlands) **Obv. Designer:** Barry Williams **Rev:** Outline map of race course, 5 national flags below **Edge:** Reeded

Date	Mintage	F	VF	XF	Unc	BU
1999 Proof	1,000	Value: 17.50				

X# 5a KRONER

0.9250 Silver, 38 mm. **Issuer:** Sail Shetland Ltd. **Subject:** Cutty Sark Tall Ships' Races **Obv:** Sailing ship Eendracht (Netherlands) **Obv. Designer:** Barry Williams **Rev:** Outline map of race course, 5 national flags below **Edge:** Plain

Date	Mintage	F	VF	XF	Unc	BU
1999 Proof	250	Value: 50.00				

X# 5b KRONER

0.9250 Gilt Silver, 38 mm. **Issuer:** Sail Shetland Ltd. **Subject:** Cutty Sark Tall Ships' Races **Obv:** Sailing ship Eendracht (Netherlands) **Obv. Designer:** Barry Williams **Rev:** Outline map of race course, 5 national flags below **Edge:** Plain

Date	Mintage	F	VF	XF	Unc	BU
1999 Proof	250	Value: 60.00				

X# 6 KRONER

, 38 mm. **Issuer:** Sail Shetland Ltd. **Subject:** Cutty Sark Tall Ships' Races **Obv:** Sailing ship Kruzenshtern (Russia) **Obv. Designer:** Barry Williams **Rev:** Outline map of race course, 5 national flags below **Edge:** Reeded

Date	Mintage	F	VF	XF	Unc	BU
1999 Proof	1,000	—	—	—	—	—

X# 6a KRONER

0.9250 Silver, 38 mm. **Issuer:** Sail Shetland Ltd. **Subject:** Cutty Sark Tall Ships' Races **Obv:** Sailing ship Kruzenshtern (Russia) **Obv. Designer:** Barry Williams **Rev:** Outline map of race course, 5 national flags below **Edge:** Plain

Date	Mintage	F	VF	XF	Unc	BU
1999 Proof	250	Value: 50.00				

X# 6b KRONER

0.9250 Gilt Silver, 38 mm. **Issuer:** Sail Shetland Ltd. **Subject:** Cutty Sark Tall Ships' Races **Obv:** Sailing ship Kruzenshtern (Russia) **Obv. Designer:** Barry Williams **Rev:** Outline map of race course, 5 national flags below **Edge:** Plain

Date	Mintage	F	VF	XF	Unc	BU
1999 Proof	250	Value: 60.00				

X# 7 KRONER

Copper-Nickel, 38 mm. **Issuer:** Sail Shetland Ltd. **Subject:** Cutty Sark Tall Ships' Races **Obv:** Sailing ship Pogoria (Poland) **Obv. Designer:** Barry Williams **Rev:** Outline map of race course, 5 national flags below **Edge:** Reeded

Date	Mintage	F	VF	XF	Unc	BU
1999 Proof	1,000	Value: 17.50				

X# 7a KRONER

0.9250 Silver, 38 mm. **Issuer:** Sail Shetland Ltd. **Subject:** Cutty Sark Tall Ships' Races **Obv:** Sailing ship Pogoria (Poland) **Obv. Designer:** Barry Williams **Rev:** Outline map of race course, 5 national flags below **Edge:** Plain

Date	Mintage	F	VF	XF	Unc	BU
1999 Proof	250	Value: 50.00				

X# 7b KRONER

0.9250 Gilt Silver, 38 mm. **Issuer:** Sail Shetland Ltd. **Subject:** Cutty Sark Tall Ships' Races **Obv:** Sailing ship Pogoria (Poland) **Obv. Designer:** Barry Williams **Rev:** Outline map of race course, 5 national flags below **Edge:** Plain

Date	Mintage	F	VF	XF	Unc	BU
1999 Proof	250	Value: 60.00				

X# 8 KRONER

Copper-Nickel, 38 mm. **Issuer:** Sail Shetland Ltd. **Subject:** Cutty Sark Tall Ships' Races **Obv:** Sailing ship Statsraad Lehmkuhl (Norway) **Obv. Designer:** Barry Williams **Rev:** Outline map of race course, 5 national flags below **Edge:** Reeded

Date	Mintage	F	VF	XF	Unc	BU
1999 Proof	1,000	Value: 17.50				

X# 8a KRONER

0.9250 Silver, 38 mm. **Issuer:** Sail Shetland Ltd. **Subject:** Cutty Sark Tall Ships' Races **Obv:** Sailing ship Statsraad Lehmkuhl (Norway) **Obv. Designer:** Barry Williams **Rev:** Outline map of race course, 5 national flags below **Edge:** Plain

Date	Mintage	F	VF	XF	Unc	BU
1999 Proof	250	Value: 50.00				

X# 8b KRONER

0.9250 Gilt Silver, 38 mm. **Issuer:** Sail Shetland Ltd. **Subject:** Cutty Sark Tall Ships' Races **Obv:** Sailing ship Statsraad Lehmkuhl **Obv. Designer:** Barry Williams **Rev:** Outline map of race course, 5 national flags below **Edge:** Plain

Date	Mintage	F	VF	XF	Unc	BU
1999 Proof	250	Value: 60.00				

X# 9 KRONER

Copper-Nickel, 38 mm. **Issuer:** Sail Shetland Ltd. **Subject:** Cutty Sark Tall Ships' Races **Obv:** Sailing ship Swan Fan Makkum (Netherlands) **Obv. Designer:** Barry Williams **Rev:** Outline map of race course, 5 national flags below **Edge:** Reeded

Date	Mintage	F	VF	XF	Unc	BU
1999 Proof	1,000	Value: 17.50				

X# 9a KRONER

0.9250 Silver, 38 mm. **Issuer:** Sail Shetland Ltd. **Subject:** Cutty Sark Tall Ships' Races **Obv:** Sailing ship Swan Fan Makkum (Netherlands) **Obv. Designer:** Barry Williams **Rev:** Outline map of race course, 5 national flags below **Edge:** Plain

Date	Mintage	F	VF	XF	Unc	BU
1999 Proof	250	Value: 50.00				

X# 9b KRONER

0.9250 Gilt Silver, 38 mm. **Issuer:** Sail Shetland Ltd. **Subject:** Cutty Sark Tall Ships' Races **Obv:** Sailing ship Swan Fan Makkum (Netherlands) **Obv. Designer:** Barry Williams **Rev:** Outline map of race course, 5 national flags below **Edge:** Plain

Date	Mintage	F	VF	XF	Unc	BU
1999 Proof	250	Value: 60.00				

X# 10 KRONER

Copper-Nickel, 38 mm. **Issuer:** Sail Shetland Ltd. **Subject:** Cutty Sark Tall Ships' Races **Obv:** Sailing ship Sorlander (Norway) **Obv. Designer:** Barry Williams **Rev:** Outline map of race course, 5 national flags below **Edge:** Reeded

Date	Mintage	F	VF	XF	Unc	BU
1999 Proof	1,000	Value: 17.50				

X# 10a KRONER

0.9250 Silver, 38 mm. **Issuer:** Sail Shetland Ltd. **Subject:** Cutty Sark Tall Ships' Races **Obv:** Sailing ship Sorlander (Norway) **Obv. Designer:** Barry Williams **Rev:** Outline map of race course, 5 national flags below **Edge:** Plain

Date	Mintage	F	VF	XF	Unc	BU
1999 Proof	250	Value: 50.00				

X# 10b KRONER

Gilt Silver, 38 mm. **Issuer:** Sail Shetland Ltd. **Subject:** Cutty Sark Tall Ships' Races **Obv:** Sailing ship Sorlander (Norway) **Obv. Designer:** Barry Williams **Rev:** Outline map of race course, 5 national flags below **Edge:** Plain

Date	Mintage	F	VF	XF	Unc	BU
1999 Proof	250	Value: 60.00				

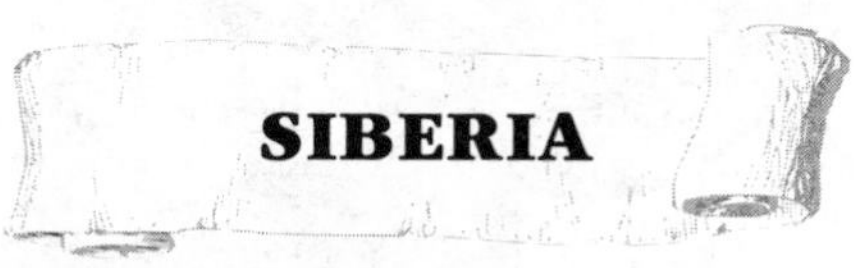

SIBERIA

REGION

FANTASY EURO PATTERNS

X# Pn1 EURO CENT

Copper Plated Steel **Obv:** Head of Siberian Tiger left

Date	Mintage	F	VF	XF	Unc	BU
2005	7,000	—	—	—	—	2.00

X# Pn2 2 EURO CENT

Copper Plated Steel **Obv:** Head of Siberian Tiger left **Edge:** Plain

Date	Mintage	F	VF	XF	Unc	BU
2005	7,000	—	—	—	—	3.00

X# Pn3 5 EURO CENT

Copper Plated Steel **Obv:** Head of Siberian Tiger left **Edge:** Plain

Date	Mintage	F	VF	XF	Unc	BU
2005	7,000	—	—	—	—	3.50

X# Pn4 10 EURO CENT

Goldine **Obv:** Head of Siberian Tiger facing **Edge:** Plain

Date	Mintage	F	VF	XF	Unc	BU
2005	7,000	—	—	—	—	4.00

X# Pn5 20 EURO CENT

Goldine **Obv:** Head of Siberian Tiger facing **Edge:** Plain

Date	Mintage	F	VF	XF	Unc	BU
2005	7,000	—	—	—	—	5.00

X# Pn6 50 EURO CENT

Goldine **Obv:** Head of Siberian Tiger facing **Edge:** Plain

Date	Mintage	F	VF	XF	Unc	BU
2005	7,000	—	—	—	—	6.00

X# Pn7 EURO

Bi-Metallic **Obv:** Head of Catherine II facing **Rev:** Oak leaves, large value "1" **Edge:** Plain

Date	Mintage	F	VF	XF	Unc	BU
2005	7,000	—	—	—	—	8.50

X# Pn8 2 EURO

Bi-Metallic **Obv:** Head of Catherine II facing **Rev:** Oak leaves, large value "2" **Edge:** Plain

Date	Mintage	F	VF	XF	Unc	BU
2005	7,000	—	—	—	—	10.00

MINT SETS

X#	Date	Mintage	Identification	Issue Price	Mkt Val
XMS1	2005 (8)	7,000	X#Pn1-Pn8	—	50.00

SIERRA LEONE

BRITISH COLONY

Sierra Leone Company

DOLLAR DENOMINATED COINAGE

KM# 6 DOLLAR

0.9020 Silver **Obv:** Lion, Africa below **Obv. Legend:** SIERRA LEONE COMPANY **Rev:** Clasped hands flanked by value, date below, written value as legend

Date	Mintage	F	VF	XF	Unc	BU
1791	6,560	400	1,000	2,200	4,500	—
1791 Proof	40	Value: 10,000				

KM# 6a DOLLAR

Copper **Obv:** Lion, Africa below **Obv. Legend:** SIERRA LEONE COMPANY **Rev:** Clasped hands flanked by value, date below, written value as legend

Date	Mintage	F	VF	XF	Unc	BU
1791 Proof	—	Value: 1,500				

KM# 6b DOLLAR

Gilt Copper **Obv:** Lion, Africa below **Obv. Legend:** SIERRA LEONE COMPANY **Rev:** Clasped hands flanked by value, date below, written value as legend

Date	Mintage	F	VF	XF	Unc	BU
1791 Proof	—	Value: 3,500				

KM# 7 DOLLAR

0.9020 Silver **Obv:** Lion, Africa below **Obv. Legend:** SIERRA LEONE COMPANY **Rev:** Clasped hands flanked by value, date below, written value as legend

Date	Mintage	F	VF	XF	Unc	BU
1791	800	650	1,500	3,500	5,500	—
1791 Proof	5	—	—	—	—	—

KM# 7a DOLLAR

Copper **Obv:** Lion, Africa below **Obv. Legend:** SIERRA LEONE COMPANY **Rev:** Clasped hands flanked by value, date below, written value as legend

Date	Mintage	F	VF	XF	Unc	BU
1791 Proof	—	—	—	—	—	—

KM# 7b DOLLAR

Gilt Copper **Obv:** Lion, Africa below **Obv. Legend:** SIERRA LEONE COMPANY **Rev:** Clasped hands flanked by value, date below, written value as legend

Date	Mintage	F	VF	XF	Unc	BU
1791 Proof	—	Value: 4,000				

MEDALLIC COINAGE

Richard Lobel Series

X# M1 CROWN

Bronze, 38.10 mm. **Subject:** Edward VIII **Obv:** Bust left **Obv. Legend:** EDWARD • VIII • KING • & • EMPEROR **Rev:** Lion crouched 3/4 left **Rev. Inscription:** AFRICA **Edge:** Plain

Date	Mintage	F	VF	XF	Unc	BU
1936 Proof	500	Value: 15.00				

X# M1a CROWN

Copper-Nickel-Zinc, 38.10 mm. **Subject:** Edward VIII **Obv:** Bust left **Obv. Legend:** EDWARD • VIII • KING • & • EMPEROR **Rev:** Lion crouched 3/4 left **Rev. Inscription:** AFRICA **Edge:** Plain

Date	Mintage	F	VF	XF	Unc	BU
1936 Proof	1,500	Value: 15.00				

X# M1b CROWN

0.9167 Silver, 38.10 mm. **Subject:** Edward VIII **Obv:** Bust left **Obv. Legend:** EDWARD • VIII • KING • & • EMPEROR **Rev:** Lion crouched 3/4 left **Rev. Inscription:** AFRICA **Edge:** Plain

Date	Mintage	F	VF	XF	Unc	BU
1936 Proof	150	Value: 50.00				

X# M1c CROWN

Gold, 38.10 mm. **Subject:** Edward VIII **Obv:** Bust left **Obv. Legend:** EDWARD • VIII • KING • & • EMPEROR **Rev:** Lion crouched 3/4 left **Rev. Inscription:** AFRICA **Edge:** Plain

Date	Mintage	F	VF	XF	Unc	BU
1936 Proof	—	Value: 500				

X# M1d CROWN

Copper, 38.10 mm. **Subject:** Edward VIII **Obv:** Bust left **Obv. Legend:** EDWARD • VIII • KING • & • EMPEROR **Rev:** Lion crouched 3/4 left **Edge:** Plain **Note:** Struck in error

Date	Mintage	F	VF	XF	Unc	BU
1936 Proof	100	Value: 30.00				

X# M2 SOVEREIGN

0.3750 Gold, 21.98 mm. **Subject:** Edward VIII **Obv:** Bust left **Obv. Legend:** EDWARD • VIII • KING • & • EMPEROR **Rev:** Lion crouched 3/4 left **Rev. Inscription:** AFRICA **Edge:** Plain

Date	Mintage	F	VF	XF	Unc	BU
1936 Proof	150	Value: 125				

X# M2a SOVEREIGN

4.4200 g., Silver, 21.98 mm. **Subject:** Edward VIII **Obv:** Bust left **Obv. Legend:** EDWARD • VIII • KING • & • EMPEROR **Rev:** Lion crouched 3/4 left **Rev. Inscription:** AFRICA **Edge:** Plain

Date	Mintage	F	VF	XF	Unc	BU
1936 Proof	—	Value: 10.00				

REPUBLIC

DOLLAR DENOMINATED COINAGE

KM# 47 DOLLAR

Copper-Nickel **Obv:** Arms **Rev:** Crowned lion

Date	Mintage	F	VF	XF	Unc	BU
1997	—	—	—	—	7.50	9.00

KM# 48 DOLLAR

Copper-Nickel **Obv:** Arms **Rev:** Unicorn

Date	Mintage	F	VF	XF	Unc	BU
1997	—	—	—	—	7.50	9.00

KM# 53 DOLLAR

Copper-Nickel **Subject:** Golden Wedding Anniversary **Obv:** Arms **Rev:** E and P monogram

Date	Mintage	F	VF	XF	Unc	BU
1997	—	—	—	—	10.00	12.00

KM# 56 DOLLAR

Copper-Nickel **Subject:** Golden Wedding Anniversary **Obv:** Arms **Rev:** Royal yacht

Date	Mintage	F	VF	XF	Unc	BU
1997	—	—	—	—	7.00	8.50

KM# 59 DOLLAR

Copper-Nickel **Subject:** Golden Wedding Anniversary **Obv:** Arms **Rev:** Royal couple

Date	Mintage	F	VF	XF	Unc	BU
1997	—	—	—	—	7.00	8.50

KM# 62 DOLLAR

Copper-Nickel **Subject:** Golden Wedding Anniversary **Obv:** Arms **Rev:** Fireworks above palace

Date	Mintage	F	VF	XF	Unc	BU
1997	—	—	—	—	7.00	8.50

KM# 65 DOLLAR

Copper-Nickel **Subject:** Golden Wedding Anniversary **Obv:** Arms **Rev:** Queen with two children

Date	Mintage	F	VF	XF	Unc	BU
1997	—	—	—	—	7.00	8.50

KM# 68 DOLLAR

Copper-Nickel **Subject:** Golden Wedding Anniversary **Obv:** Arms **Rev:** Royal couple with two children

Date	Mintage	F	VF	XF	Unc	BU
1997	—	—	—	—	7.00	8.50

KM# 71 DOLLAR

Copper-Nickel **Subject:** Diana - The Peoples' Princess **Obv:** Arms **Rev:** Head 1/4 right

Date	Mintage	F	VF	XF	Unc	BU
1997	—	—	—	—	8.00	9.00

KM# 77 DOLLAR

Copper-Nickel **Subject:** Diana - The Peoples' Princess **Obv:** Arms **Rev:** Diana with Mother Theresa

Date	Mintage	F	VF	XF	Unc	BU
1997	—	—	—	—	9.00	10.00

KM# 83 DOLLAR

Copper-Nickel **Subject:** Diana - The Peoples' Princess **Obv:** Arms **Rev:** Diana and AIDS patient

Date	Mintage	F	VF	XF	Unc	BU
1997	—	—	—	—	8.00	9.00

KM# 89 DOLLAR

Copper-Nickel **Subject:** Diana - The Peoples' Princess **Obv:** Arms **Rev:** Diana with sons William and Harry

Date	Mintage	F	VF	XF	Unc	BU
1997	—	—	—	—	8.00	9.00

KM# 95 DOLLAR

Copper-Nickel **Subject:** Jurassic Park **Obv:** Arms **Rev:** Velociraptor

Date	Mintage	F	VF	XF	Unc	BU
1997	—	—	—	—	15.00	—

KM# 103 DOLLAR

Copper-Nickel **Subject:** In Memoriam, Diana - The Peoples' Princess **Obv:** Arms **Rev:** Head 1/4 left

Date	Mintage	F	VF	XF	Unc	BU
1998	—	—	—	—	8.00	9.00

KM# 109 DOLLAR

Copper-Nickel **Subject:** Dr. Livingston **Obv:** Arms **Rev:** Half length bust of David Livingstone at right above natives in longboat

Date	Mintage	F	VF	XF	Unc	BU
1998	—	—	—	—	8.00	9.00

KM# 118 DOLLAR

Copper-Nickel **Subject:** China 2000 Series **Obv:** Arms **Rev:** Kneeling terracotta warrior

Date	Mintage	F	VF	XF	Unc	BU
1999	—	—	—	—	8.50	10.00

KM# 112 DOLLAR

Copper-Nickel **Subject:** Amerigo Vespucci **Obv:** Arms **Rev:** Ship and mountainous portrait

Date	Mintage	F	VF	XF	Unc	BU
1999	—	—	—	—	8.00	9.00

KM# 115 DOLLAR

Copper-Nickel **Subject:** Charles Darwin **Obv:** Arms **Rev:** Ship at left, bust at right

Date	Mintage	F	VF	XF	Unc	BU
1999	—	—	—	—	8.00	9.00

KM# 121 DOLLAR

Copper-Nickel **Subject:** China 2000 Series - Ming Dynasty **Obv:** Arms **Rev:** Temple of Heaven

Date	Mintage	F	VF	XF	Unc	BU
1999	—	—	—	—	8.50	10.00

KM# 124 DOLLAR

Copper-Nickel **Subject:** China 2000 Series **Obv:** Arms **Rev:** Portion of the Great Wall

Date	Mintage	F	VF	XF	Unc	BU
1999	—	—	—	—	8.50	10.00

KM# 127 DOLLAR

Copper-Nickel **Subject:** China 2000 Series **Obv:** Arms **Rev:** Bronze chariot

Date	Mintage	F	VF	XF	Unc	BU
1999	—	—	—	—	8.50	10.00

KM# 130 DOLLAR

Copper-Nickel **Subject:** China 2000 Series **Obv:** Arms **Rev:** First century armillary sphere

Date	Mintage	F	VF	XF	Unc	BU
1999	—	—	—	—	8.50	10.00

KM# 133 DOLLAR

Copper-Nickel **Subject:** China 2000 Series **Obv:** Arms **Rev:** Tang Dynasty Royal Horse

Date	Mintage	F	VF	XF	Unc	BU
1999	—	—	—	—	8.50	10.00

KM# 136 DOLLAR

Copper-Nickel **Subject:** Macau returns to China **Obv:** Arms **Rev:** Church, car, roulette wheel, and hands shaking

Date	Mintage	F	VF	XF	Unc	BU
1999	—	—	—	—	9.50	11.00

KM# 139 DOLLAR

Copper-Nickel **Subject:** Prince Edward's Wedding **Obv:** Arms **Rev:** Symbolic wedding design

Date	Mintage	F	VF	XF	Unc	BU
1999	—	—	—	—	8.50	10.00

KM# 152 DOLLAR

28.4300 g., Copper-Nickel, 38.7 mm. **Obv:** Arms **Rev:** Chinese unicorn within circle **Edge:** Reeded

Date	Mintage	F	VF	XF	Unc	BU
2000	—	—	—	—	10.00	12.00
1999	—	—	—	—	10.00	12.00

Note: Reported as an error date resulting from muled dies

KM# 142 DOLLAR

Copper-Nickel **Subject:** Year of the Dragon **Obv:** Arms **Rev:** Dragon

Date	Mintage	F	VF	XF	Unc	BU
2000	—	—	—	—	10.00	13.00

KM# 150 DOLLAR

28.2800 g., Copper-Nickel **Obv:** Arms **Rev:** Two Phoenix birds **Edge:** Reeded

Date	Mintage	F	VF	XF	Unc	BU
2000	—	—	—	—	10.00	13.00

KM# 151 DOLLAR
Copper-Nickel **Obv:** Arms **Rev:** Chinese dragon

Date	Mintage	F	VF	XF	Unc	BU
2000	—	—	—	—	10.00	13.00

KM# 174 DOLLAR
Copper-Nickel **Subject:** Buddha **Obv:** Arms **Rev:** Seated Buddha

Date	Mintage	F	VF	XF	Unc	BU
2000	—	—	—	—	8.50	10.00

KM# 175 DOLLAR
Copper-Nickel **Obv:** Arms **Rev:** Goddess of Mercy

Date	Mintage	F	VF	XF	Unc	BU
2000	—	—	—	—	8.50	10.00

KM# 176 DOLLAR
Copper-Nickel **Obv:** Arms **Rev:** Tzai-yen holding scroll

Date	Mintage	F	VF	XF	Unc	BU
2000	—	—	—	—	10.00	12.00

KM# 198 DOLLAR
28.2800 g., Copper-Nickel, 38.6 mm. **Subject:** Year of the Snake **Obv:** National arms **Rev:** Snake **Edge:** Reeded

Date	Mintage	F	VF	XF	Unc	BU
2001	—	—	—	—	10.00	12.00

KM# 206 DOLLAR
Copper-Nickel **Subject:** P'an Ku **Obv:** National arms **Rev:** Dragon

Date	Mintage	F	VF	XF	Unc	BU
2001	—	—	—	—	10.00	12.00

KM# 214 DOLLAR
Copper-Nickel **Subject:** P'an Ku **Obv:** National arms **Rev:** Dragon and three animals

Date	Mintage	F	VF	XF	Unc	BU
2001	—	—	—	—	10.00	12.00

KM# 222 DOLLAR
28.2800 g., Copper-Nickel, 38.6 mm. **Series:** The Big Five **Obv:** National arms **Rev:** Rhino **Edge:** Reeded

Date	Mintage	F	VF	XF	Unc	BU
2001	—	—	—	—	10.00	12.00

KM# 225 DOLLAR
28.2800 g., Copper-Nickel **Series:** The Big Five **Obv:** National arms **Rev:** Lion

Date	Mintage	F	VF	XF	Unc	BU
2001	—	—	—	—	10.00	12.00

KM# 228 DOLLAR
28.2800 g., Copper-Nickel **Series:** The Big Five **Obv:** National arms **Rev:** Leopard

Date	Mintage	F	VF	XF	Unc	BU
2001	—	—	—	—	10.00	12.00

KM# 231 DOLLAR
28.2800 g., Copper-Nickel **Series:** The Big Five **Obv:** National arms **Rev:** Elephants

Date	Mintage	F	VF	XF	Unc	BU
2001	—	—	—	—	10.00	12.00

KM# 234 DOLLAR
28.2800 g., Copper-Nickel **Series:** The Big Five **Obv:** National arms **Rev:** Buffalo

Date	Mintage	F	VF	XF	Unc	BU
2001	—	—	—	—	10.00	12.00

KM# 237 DOLLAR
28.2800 g., Copper-Nickel **Series:** The Big Five **Obv:** National arms **Rev:** All five animals

Date	Mintage	F	VF	XF	Unc	BU
2001	—	—	—	—	10.00	12.00

KM# 241 DOLLAR
28.2800 g., Copper-Nickel, 38.6 mm. **Series:** Big Cats **Obv:** National arms **Rev:** Male and female lions **Edge:** Reeded

Date	Mintage	F	VF	XF	Unc	BU
2001	—	—	—	—	12.50	15.00

KM# 241a DOLLAR
28.2800 g., Copper-Nickel, 38.6 mm. **Series:** Big Cats **Obv:** National arms **Rev:** Male and female lions **Edge:** Reeded

Date	Mintage	F	VF	XF	Unc	BU
2001	—	—	—	—	—	15.00

KM# 242 DOLLAR
28.2800 g., Copper-Nickel, 38.6 mm. **Series:** Big Cats **Obv:** National arms **Rev:** Tiger **Edge:** Reeded

Date	Mintage	F	VF	XF	Unc	BU
2001	—	—	—	—	10.00	12.00

KM# 242a DOLLAR
28.2800 g., Copper-Nickel, 38.6 mm. **Series:** Big Cats **Obv:** National arms **Rev:** Tiger **Edge:** Reeded

Date	Mintage	F	VF	XF	Unc	BU
2001	—	—	—	—	—	15.00

KM# 243 DOLLAR
28.2800 g., Copper-Nickel, 38.6 mm. **Series:** Big Cats **Obv:** National arms **Rev:** Cheetah **Edge:** Reeded

Date	Mintage	F	VF	XF	Unc	BU
2001	—	—	—	—	10.00	12.00

KM# 243a DOLLAR
28.2800 g., Copper-Nickel, 38.6 mm. **Series:** Big Cats **Obv:** National arms **Rev:** Cheetah **Edge:** Reeded

Date	Mintage	F	VF	XF	Unc	BU
2001	—	—	—	—	—	15.00

KM# 244 DOLLAR
28.2800 g., Copper-Nickel, 38.6 mm. **Series:** Big Cats **Obv:** National arms **Rev:** Cougar **Edge:** Reeded

Date	Mintage	F	VF	XF	Unc	BU
2001	—	—	—	—	10.00	12.00

KM# 244a DOLLAR
28.2800 g., Copper-Nickel, 38.6 mm. **Series:** Big Cats **Obv:** National arms **Rev:** Cougar **Edge:** Reeded

Date	Mintage	F	VF	XF	Unc	BU
2001	—	—	—	—	—	15.00

KM# 245 DOLLAR
28.2800 g., Copper-Nickel, 38.6 mm. **Series:** Big Cats **Obv:** National arms **Rev:** Black panther **Edge:** Reeded

Date	Mintage	F	VF	XF	Unc	BU
2001	—	—	—	—	10.00	12.00

KM# 245a DOLLAR
28.2800 g., Copper-Nickel, 38.6 mm. **Series:** Big Cats **Obv:** National arms **Rev:** Black panther **Edge:** Reeded

Date	Mintage	F	VF	XF	Unc	BU
2001	—	—	—	—	—	15.00

KM# 256 DOLLAR
28.2800 g., Copper-Nickel, 38.6 mm. **Subject:** Year of the Horse **Obv:** National arms **Rev:** Horse **Edge:** Reeded

Date	Mintage	F	VF	XF	Unc	BU
2002	—	—	—	—	10.00	12.00

KM# 264 DOLLAR
28.2800 g., Copper-Nickel, 38.6 mm. **Subject:** RMS Titanic **Obv:** National arms **Rev:** Titanic at dock **Edge:** Reeded

Date	Mintage	F	VF	XF	Unc	BU
2002	—	—	—	—	10.00	12.00

KM# 268 DOLLAR
28.2800 g., Copper-Nickel, 38.6 mm. **Subject:** Queen's Golden Jubilee **Obv:** National arms **Rev:** Queen Elizabeth II and Prince Philip visiting blacksmiths in Sierra Leone **Edge:** Reeded

Date	Mintage	F	VF	XF	Unc	BU
2002	—	—	—	—	10.00	12.00

KM# 269 DOLLAR
28.2800 g., Copper-Nickel, 38.6 mm. **Subject:** Queen's Golden Jubilee **Obv:** National arms **Rev:** Queen Elizabeth II with her two sons **Edge:** Reeded

Date	Mintage	F	VF	XF	Unc	BU
2002	—	—	—	—	10.00	12.00

KM# 276 DOLLAR
28.2800 g., Copper-Nickel, 38.6 mm. **Subject:** British Queen Mother **Obv:** National arms **Rev:** Queen Mother with dog in garden **Edge:** Reeded

Date	Mintage	F	VF	XF	Unc	BU
2002	—	—	—	—	10.00	12.00

KM# 279 DOLLAR
28.2800 g., Copper-Nickel, 38.6 mm. **Subject:** British Queen Mother **Obv:** National arms **Rev:** Queen Mother with daughters **Edge:** Reeded

Date	Mintage	F	VF	XF	Unc	BU
2002	—	—	—	—	10.00	12.00

KM# 282 DOLLAR
28.2800 g., Copper-Nickel, 38.6 mm. **Subject:** Queen Elizabeth's Golden Jubilee **Obv:** National arms **Rev:** The Queen and a young Prince Charles **Edge:** Reeded

Date	Mintage	F	VF	XF	Unc	BU
2002	—	—	—	—	10.00	12.00

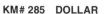

KM# 285 DOLLAR

28.2800 g., Copper-Nickel, 38.6 mm. **Subject:** Queen Elizabeth's Golden Jubilee **Obv:** National arms **Rev:** Queen and Prince Philip **Edge:** Reeded

Date	Mintage	F	VF	XF	Unc	BU
2002	—	—	—	—	10.00	12.00

KM# 291 DOLLAR

28.2800 g., Copper-Nickel, 38.6 mm. **Subject:** Olympics **Obv:** National arms **Rev:** Ancient archer **Edge:** Reeded

Date	Mintage	F	VF	XF	Unc	BU
2003	—	—	—	—	10.00	12.00
2004	—	—	—	—	10.00	12.00

KM# 288 DOLLAR

28.2800 g., Copper-Nickel, 38.6 mm. **Subject:** Olympics **Obv:** National arms **Rev:** Victory goddess Nike **Edge:** Reeded **Note:** The Leone is the official currency of Sierra Leone

Date	Mintage	F	VF	XF	Unc	BU
2003	—	—	—	—	10.00	12.00
2004	—	—	—	—	10.00	12.00

KM# 297 DOLLAR

28.2800 g., Copper-Nickel, 38.6 mm. **Obv:** National arms **Rev:** Nelson Mandela **Edge:** Reeded

Date	Mintage	F	VF	XF	Unc	BU
2004	—	—	—	—	15.00	16.50

KM# 300 DOLLAR

28.2800 g., Copper-Nickel, 38.6 mm. **Obv:** National arms **Rev:** Ronald Reagan **Edge:** Reeded

Date	Mintage	F	VF	XF	Unc	BU
2004	—	—	—	—	15.00	16.50

KM# 304 DOLLAR

28.4200 g., Copper-Nickel, 38.6 mm. **Obv:** National arms **Rev:** Giraffe **Edge:** Reeded

Date	Mintage	F	VF	XF	Unc	BU
2005	—	—	—	—	10.00	12.00

KM# 305 DOLLAR

28.4200 g., Copper-Nickel, 38.6 mm. **Obv:** National arms **Rev:** Crocodile **Edge:** Reeded

Date	Mintage	F	VF	XF	Unc	BU
2005	—	—	—	—	10.00	12.00

KM# 306 DOLLAR

28.4200 g., Copper-Nickel, 38.6 mm. **Obv:** National arms **Rev:** Hippo in water **Edge:** Reeded

Date	Mintage	F	VF	XF	Unc	BU
2005	—	—	—	—	10.00	12.00

KM# 307 DOLLAR

28.6200 g., 0.9250 Silver 0.8511 oz. ASW, 38.5 mm. **Obv:** National arms **Rev:** Giraffe **Edge:** Reeded

Date	Mintage	F	VF	XF	Unc	BU
2005 Proof	—	Value: 50.00				

KM# 317 DOLLAR

Copper-Nickel **Subject:** Battle of El Alamen **Rev:** Tank, plane and ground troops

Date	Mintage	F	VF	XF	Unc	BU
2005	—	—	—	—	10.00	12.00

KM# 316 DOLLAR

Copper-Nickel **Subject:** The Battle of the Atlantic **Rev:** Plane and ship convoy

Date	Mintage	F	VF	XF	Unc	BU
2005	—	—	—	—	10.00	12.00

KM# 319 DOLLAR

Copper-Nickel **Subject:** The Battle of Berlin **Rev:** Berlin city view, tank

Date	Mintage	F	VF	XF	Unc	BU
2005	—	—	—	—	10.00	12.00

KM# 315 DOLLAR
Copper-Nickel **Subject:** Battle of Britian **Rev:** Planes in flight

Date	Mintage	F	VF	XF	Unc	BU
2005	—	—	—	—	10.00	12.00

KM# 318 DOLLAR
Copper-Nickel **Subject:** Battle of the Bulge **Rev:** Forest battle scene

Date	Mintage	F	VF	XF	Unc	BU
2005	—	—	—	—	10.00	12.00

KM# 320 DOLLAR
Copper-Nickel **Subject:** The Heavy Water Raids **Rev:** Troops on skies, factory in ruins

Date	Mintage	F	VF	XF	Unc	BU
2005	—	—	—	—	10.00	12.00

KM# 321 DOLLAR
Copper-Nickel **Obv:** National Arms **Rev:** Gorillia

Date	Mintage	F	VF	XF	Unc	BU
2005	—	—	—	—	10.00	12.00

KM# 322 DOLLAR
Copper-Nickel **Rev:** John Paul II head left, within ring of the Stations of the Cross

Date	Mintage	F	VF	XF	Unc	BU
2005	—	—	—	—	10.00	12.00

KM# 323 DOLLAR
Copper-Nickel **Rev:** Benedict XVI and St. Peter's

Date	Mintage	F	VF	XF	Unc	BU
2005	—	—	—	—	10.00	12.00

KM# 324 DOLLAR
Copper-Nickel **Obv:** National Arms **Rev:** Brontosaurus

Date	Mintage	F	VF	XF	Unc	BU
2006	—	—	—	—	10.00	12.00

KM# 308 DOLLAR
28.3700 g., Copper-Nickel, 38.5 mm. **Obv:** National arms **Rev:** Stegosaurus **Edge:** Reeded

Date	Mintage	F	VF	XF	Unc	BU
2006	—	—	—	—	—	9.00

KM# 309 DOLLAR
28.3700 g., Copper-Nickel, 38.5 mm. **Obv:** National arms **Rev:** Tyrannosaurus Rex **Edge:** Reeded

Date	Mintage	F	VF	XF	Unc	BU
2006	—	—	—	—	—	9.00

KM# 310 DOLLAR
28.3700 g., Copper-Nickel, 38.5 mm. **Obv:** National arms **Rev:** Triceratops **Edge:** Reeded

Date	Mintage	F	VF	XF	Unc	BU
2006	—	—	—	—	—	9.00

KM# 311 DOLLAR
28.3700 g., Copper-Nickel, 38.5 mm. **Obv:** National arms **Rev:** Lion **Edge:** Reeded

Date	Mintage	F	VF	XF	Unc	BU
2006	—	—	—	—	—	9.00

KM# 312 DOLLAR
28.3700 g., Copper-Nickel, 38.5 mm. **Obv:** National arms **Rev:** Camel **Edge:** Reeded

Date	Mintage	F	VF	XF	Unc	BU
2006	—	—	—	—	—	9.00

KM# 313 DOLLAR
28.3700 g., Copper-Nickel, 38.5 mm. **Obv:** National arms **Rev:** Chimpanzee **Edge:** Reeded

Date	Mintage	F	VF	XF	Unc	BU
2006	—	—	—	—	—	9.00

KM# 314 DOLLAR
28.3700 g., Copper-Nickel, 38.5 mm. **Obv:** National arms **Rev:** Gazelle **Edge:** Reeded

Date	Mintage	F	VF	XF	Unc	BU
2006	—	—	—	—	—	9.00

KM# 326 DOLLAR
Copper-Nickel **Rev:** Cheetah

Date	Mintage	F	VF	XF	Unc	BU
2007	—	—	—	—	15.00	—

KM# 327 DOLLAR
Copper-Nickel **Rev:** Zebra

Date	Mintage	F	VF	XF	Unc	BU
2007	—	—	—	—	15.00	—

KM# 328 DOLLAR
Copper-Nickel **Rev:** Rhino

Date	Mintage	F	VF	XF	Unc	BU
2007	—	—	—	—	15.00	—

KM# 329 DOLLAR
Copper-Nickel **Obv:** Arms **Rev:** African elephant

Date	Mintage	F	VF	XF	Unc	BU
2007	—	—	—	—	17.50	—

KM# 98 5 DOLLARS
15.5517 g., 0.9990 Silver 0.4995 oz. ASW
Subject: Shanghai Coin and Stamp Exposition
Obv: Arms **Rev:** Standing crowned lion right

Date	Mintage	F	VF	XF	Unc	BU
1997 Proof	Est. 10,000	Value: 30.00				

KM# 99 5 DOLLARS
15.5517 g., 0.9990 Silver 0.4995 oz. ASW
Subject: Shanghai Coin and Stamp Exposition
Obv: Arms **Rev:** Standing unicorm left

Date	Mintage	F	VF	XF	Unc	BU
1997 Proof	Est. 10,000	Value: 30.00				

KM# 101 5 DOLLARS
15.5517 g., 0.9990 Silver 0.4995 oz. ASW **Subject:** Visit of President Clinton to China **Obv:** Arms **Rev:** Bust 1/4 right, tower at right

Date	Mintage	F	VF	XF	Unc	BU
1998 Proof	Est. 10,000	Value: 30.00				

KM# 102 5 DOLLARS
15.5517 g., 0.9990 Silver 0.4995 oz. ASW
Subject: Visit of President Clinton to Beijing **Obv:** Arms **Rev:** Great Wall at left, bust 1/4 left

Date	Mintage	F	VF	XF	Unc	BU
1998 Proof	Est. 10,000	Value: 30.00				

KM# 49 10 DOLLARS
28.2800 g., 0.9250 Silver 0.8410 oz. ASW **Obv:** Arms **Rev:** Standing crowned lion right

Date	Mintage	F	VF	XF	Unc	BU
1997 Proof	Est. 10,000	Value: 45.00				

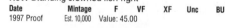

KM# 50 10 DOLLARS
28.2800 g., 0.9250 Silver 0.8410 oz. ASW **Obv:** Arms **Rev:** Standing unicorn left

Date	Mintage	F	VF	XF	Unc	BU
1997 Proof	Est. 10,000	Value: 45.00				

KM# 54 10 DOLLARS
28.2800 g., 0.9250 Silver 0.8410 oz. ASW
Subject: Golden Wedding Anniversary **Obv:** Arms
Rev: E and P monogram within flower circle

Date	Mintage	F	VF	XF	Unc	BU
1997 Proof	Est. 10,000	Value: 47.50				

KM# 57 10 DOLLARS
28.2800 g., 0.9250 Silver 0.8410 oz. ASW
Subject: Golden Wedding Anniversary **Obv:** Arms
Rev: Royal Yacht with cameo head facing at upper left

Date	Mintage	F	VF	XF	Unc	BU
1997 Proof	Est. 10,000	Value: 47.50				

KM# 60 10 DOLLARS
28.2800 g., 0.9250 Silver 0.8410 oz. ASW
Subject: Golden Wedding Anniversary **Obv:** Arms
Rev: Royal couple

Date	Mintage	F	VF	XF	Unc	BU
1997 Proof	Est. 10,000	Value: 47.50				

KM# 63 10 DOLLARS
28.2800 g., 0.9250 Silver 0.8410 oz. ASW
Subject: Golden Wedding Anniversary **Obv:** Arms
Rev: Fireworks above palace

Date	Mintage	F	VF	XF	Unc	BU
1997 Proof	Est. 10,000	Value: 47.50				

KM# 66 10 DOLLARS
28.2800 g., 0.9250 Silver 0.8410 oz. ASW
Subject: Golden Wedding Anniversary **Obv:** Arms
Rev: Queen with two children

Date	Mintage	F	VF	XF	Unc	BU
1997 Proof	Est. 10,000	Value: 47.50				

KM# 69 10 DOLLARS
28.2800 g., 0.9250 Silver 0.8410 oz. ASW
Subject: Golden Wedding Anniversary **Obv:** Arms
Rev: Royal couple with two children

Date	Mintage	F	VF	XF	Unc	BU
1997 Proof	Est. 10,000	Value: 47.50				

KM# 72 10 DOLLARS
28.2800 g., 0.9250 Silver 0.8410 oz. ASW
Subject: Diana - The Peoples' Princess **Obv:** Arms
Rev: Head facing

Date	Mintage	F	VF	XF	Unc	BU
1997 Proof	Est. 10,000	Value: 30.00				

KM# 78 10 DOLLARS
28.2800 g., 0.9250 Silver 0.8410 oz. ASW **Subject:** Diana - The Peoples' Princess **Obv:** Arms **Rev:** Diana with Mother Theresa

Date	Mintage	F	VF	XF	Unc	BU
1997	Est. 10,000	Value: 42.50				

KM# 84 10 DOLLARS
28.2800 g., 0.9250 Silver 0.8410 oz. ASW **Subject:** Diana - The Peoples' Princess **Obv:** Arms **Rev:** Diana and AIDS patient

Date	Mintage	F	VF	XF	Unc	BU
1997 Proof	Est. 10,000	Value: 25.00				

KM# 90 10 DOLLARS
28.2800 g., 0.9250 Silver 0.8410 oz. ASW
Subject: Diana - The Peoples' Princess **Obv:** Arms
Rev: Diana with sons William and Harry

Date	Mintage	F	VF	XF	Unc	BU
1997 Proof	Est. 10,000	Value: 27.50				

KM# 96 10 DOLLARS
28.2800 g., 0.9250 Silver 0.8410 oz. ASW
Subject: Jurassic Park **Obv:** Arms **Rev:** Velociraptor

Date	Mintage	F	VF	XF	Unc	BU
1997 Proof	Est. 10,000	Value: 45.00				

KM# 104 10 DOLLARS
28.2800 g., 0.9250 Silver 0.8410 oz. ASW **Subject:** In Memoriam, Diana - The Peoples' Princess **Obv:** Arms **Rev:** Head 1/4 left

Date	Mintage	F	VF	XF	Unc	BU
1998 Proof	Est. 10,000	Value: 37.50				

KM# A110 10 DOLLARS
28.2800 g., 0.9250 Silver 0.8410 oz. ASW
Subject: Dr. Livingstone **Obv:** Arms **Rev:** Standing figures rowing ancient boat, bust 1/4 left at upper right
Note: Prev. KM#110.

Date	Mintage	F	VF	XF	Unc	BU
1998 Proof	Est. 10,000	Value: 50.00				

KM# 113 10 DOLLARS
28.2800 g., 0.9250 Silver 0.8410 oz. ASW
Subject: Amerigo Vespucci **Obv:** Arms **Rev:** Ship and Vespucci portrait

Date	Mintage	F	VF	XF	Unc	BU
1999 Proof	Est. 10,000	Value: 50.00				

KM# 119 10 DOLLARS
28.2800 g., 0.9250 Silver 0.8410 oz. ASW
Subject: China 2000 Series **Obv:** Arms **Rev:** Kneeling Terracotta warrior

Date	Mintage	F	VF	XF	Unc	BU
1999 Proof	Est. 10,000	Value: 47.50				

KM# 122 10 DOLLARS
28.2800 g., 0.9250 Silver 0.8410 oz. ASW
Subject: China 2000 Series - Ming Dynasty **Obv:** Arms **Rev:** Temple of Heaven

Date	Mintage	F	VF	XF	Unc	BU
1999 Proof	Est. 10,000	Value: 47.50				

KM# 125 10 DOLLARS
28.2800 g., 0.9250 Silver 0.8410 oz. ASW
Subject: China 2000 Series **Obv:** Arms **Rev:** Portion of the Great Wall

Date	Mintage	F	VF	XF	Unc	BU
1999 Proof	Est. 10,000	Value: 47.50				

KM# 128 10 DOLLARS
28.2800 g., 0.9250 Silver 0.8410 oz. ASW **Subject:** China 2000 Series **Obv:** Arms **Rev:** Bronze chariot

Date	Mintage	F	VF	XF	Unc	BU
1999 Proof	Est. 10,000	Value: 47.50				

KM# 131 10 DOLLARS
28.2800 g., 0.9250 Silver 0.8410 oz. ASW
Subject: China 2000 Series **Obv:** Arms **Rev:** First century armillary sphere

Date	Mintage	F	VF	XF	Unc	BU
1999 Proof	Est. 10,000	Value: 47.50				

KM# 134 10 DOLLARS
28.2800 g., 0.9250 Silver 0.8410 oz. ASW
Subject: China 2000 Series **Obv:** Arms **Rev:** Tang Dynasty royal horse

Date	Mintage	F	VF	XF	Unc	BU
1999 Proof	Est. 10,000	Value: 47.50				

KM# 137 10 DOLLARS
28.2800 g., 0.9250 Silver 0.8410 oz. ASW
Subject: Macau Return to China **Obv:** Arms **Rev:** Church, car, roulette wheel and clasped hands below

Date	Mintage	F	VF	XF	Unc	BU
1999 Proof	Est. 10,000	Value: 50.00				

KM# 140 10 DOLLARS
28.2800 g., 0.9250 Silver 0.8410 oz. ASW
Subject: Prince Edward's Wedding **Obv:** Arms
Rev: Symbolic wedding design

Date	Mintage	F	VF	XF	Unc	BU
1999 Proof	Est. 10,000	Value: 50.00				

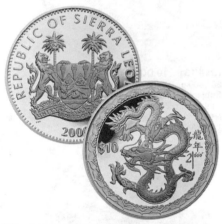

KM# 143 10 DOLLARS
28.2800 g., 0.9250 Silver 0.8410 oz. ASW
Subject: Year of the Dragon **Obv:** Arms **Rev:** Dragon

Date	Mintage	F	VF	XF	Unc	BU
2000 Proof	Est. 25,000	Value: 45.00				

KM# 153 10 DOLLARS
28.2800 g., 0.9250 Silver 0.8410 oz. ASW **Obv:** Arms
Rev: Two Phoenix birds

Date	Mintage	F	VF	XF	Unc	BU
2000 Proof	Est. 10,000	Value: 45.00				

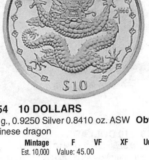

KM# 154 10 DOLLARS
28.2800 g., 0.9250 Silver 0.8410 oz. ASW **Obv:** Arms
Rev: Chinese dragon

Date	Mintage	F	VF	XF	Unc	BU
2000 Proof	Est. 10,000	Value: 45.00				

KM# 155 10 DOLLARS
28.2800 g., 0.9250 Silver 0.8410 oz. ASW **Obv:** Arms
Rev: Chinese unicorn within circle

Date	Mintage	F	VF	XF	Unc	BU
2000 Proof	Est. 10,000	Value: 45.00				

KM# 177 10 DOLLARS
28.2800 g., 0.9250 Silver 0.8410 oz. ASW **Obv:** Arms
Rev: Seated Buddha

Date	Mintage	F	VF	XF	Unc	BU
2000 Proof	Est. 25,000	Value: 47.50				

KM# 178 10 DOLLARS
28.2800 g., 0.9250 Silver 0.8410 oz. ASW **Obv:** Arms
Rev: Goddess of Mercy

Date	Mintage	F	VF	XF	Unc	BU
2000 Proof	Est. 25,000	Value: 47.50				

KM# 179 10 DOLLARS
28.2800 g., 0.9250 Silver 0.8410 oz. ASW **Obv:** Arms
Rev: Tzai-yen holding scroll

Date	Mintage	F	VF	XF	Unc	BU
2000 Proof	Est. 25,000	Value: 47.50				

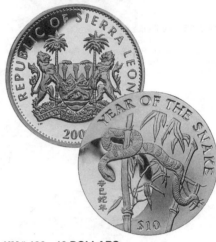

KM# 199 10 DOLLARS
28.2800 g., 0.9250 Silver 0.8410 oz. ASW, 38.6 mm.
Subject: Year of the Snake **Obv:** National arms
Rev: Snake on bamboo **Edge:** Reeded

Date	Mintage	F	VF	XF	Unc	BU
2001 Proof	Est. 25,000	Value: 50.00				

KM# 207 10 DOLLARS
28.2800 g., 0.9250 Silver 0.8410 oz. ASW
Subject: P'an Ku **Obv:** National arms **Rev:** Dragon

Date	Mintage	F	VF	XF	Unc	BU
2001 Proof	Est. 5,000	Value: 47.50				

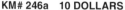

KM# 215 10 DOLLARS
28.2800 g., 0.9250 Silver 0.8410 oz. ASW **Subject:** P'an Ku **Obv:** National arms **Rev:** Dragon and three animals

Date	Mintage	F	VF	XF	Unc	BU
2001 Proof	Est. 5,000	Value: 47.50				

KM# 223 10 DOLLARS
28.2800 g., 0.9250 Silver 0.8410 oz. ASW, 38.6 mm. **Series:** The Big Five **Obv:** National arms **Rev:** Rhino and value within circle **Edge:** Reeded

Date	Mintage	F	VF	XF	Unc	BU
2001 Proof	—	Value: 45.00				

KM# 226 10 DOLLARS
28.2800 g., 0.9250 Silver 0.8410 oz. ASW **Series:** The Big Five **Obv:** National arms **Rev:** Lion head and value within circle

Date	Mintage	F	VF	XF	Unc	BU
2001 Proof	Est. 10,000	Value: 45.00				

KM# 229 10 DOLLARS
28.2800 g., 0.9250 Silver 0.8410 oz. ASW **Series:** The Big Five **Obv:** National arms **Rev:** Leopard and value within circle

Date	Mintage	F	VF	XF	Unc	BU
2001 Proof	Est. 10,000	Value: 45.00				

KM# 232 10 DOLLARS
28.2800 g., 0.9250 Silver 0.8410 oz. ASW **Series:** The Big Five **Obv:** National arms **Rev:** Elephants and value within circle

Date	Mintage	F	VF	XF	Unc	BU
2001 Proof	Est. 10,000	Value: 45.00				

KM# 235 10 DOLLARS
28.2800 g., 0.9250 Silver 0.8410 oz. ASW **Series:** The Big Five **Obv:** National arms **Rev:** Buffalo and value within circle

Date	Mintage	F	VF	XF	Unc	BU
2001 Proof	Est. 10,000	Value: 45.00				

KM# 238 10 DOLLARS
28.2800 g., 0.9250 Silver 0.8410 oz. ASW **Series:** The Big Five **Obv:** National arms **Rev:** All five animals within circle

Date	Mintage	F	VF	XF	Unc	BU
2001 Proof	Est. 10,000	Value: 45.00				

KM# 246 10 DOLLARS
28.2800 g., 0.9250 Silver 0.8410 oz. ASW, 38.6 mm. **Series:** Big Cats **Obv:** National arms **Rev:** Male and female lions **Edge:** Reeded

Date	Mintage	F	VF	XF	Unc	BU
2001 Proof	10,000	Value: 45.00				

KM# 246a 10 DOLLARS
28.2800 g., 0.9250 Silver 0.8410 oz. ASW, 38.6 mm. **Series:** Big Cats **Obv:** National arms **Rev:** Male and female lions **Edge:** Reeded

Date	Mintage	F	VF	XF	Unc	BU
2001 Proof	—	Value: 50.00				

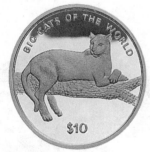

KM# 247 10 DOLLARS
28.2800 g., 0.9250 Silver 0.8410 oz. ASW, 38.6 mm. **Series:** Big Cats **Obv:** National arms **Rev:** Tiger **Edge:** Reeded

Date	Mintage	F	VF	XF	Unc	BU
2001 Proof	—	Value: 45.00				

KM# 247a 10 DOLLARS
28.2800 g., 0.9250 Silver 0.8410 oz. ASW, 38.6 mm. **Series:** Big Cats **Obv:** National arms **Rev:** Tiger **Edge:** Reeded

Date	Mintage	F	VF	XF	Unc	BU
2001 Proof	—	Value: 50.00				

KM# 248 10 DOLLARS
28.2800 g., 0.9250 Silver 0.8410 oz. ASW, 38.6 mm. **Series:** Big Cats **Obv:** National arms **Rev:** Cheetah head facing **Edge:** Reeded

Date	Mintage	F	VF	XF	Unc	BU
2001 Proof	10,000	Value: 45.00				

KM# 248a 10 DOLLARS
28.2800 g., 0.9250 Silver 0.8410 oz. ASW, 38.6 mm. **Series:** Big Cats **Obv:** National arms **Rev:** Cheetah head facing **Edge:** Reeded

Date	Mintage	F	VF	XF	Unc	BU
2001 Proof	—	Value: 50.00				

BIG CATS OF THE WORLD
$10

KM# 249 10 DOLLARS
28.2800 g., 0.9250 Silver 0.8410 oz. ASW, 38.6 mm. **Series:** Big Cats **Obv:** National arms **Rev:** Cougar **Edge:** Reeded

Date	Mintage	F	VF	XF	Unc	BU
2001 Proof	10,000	Value: 45.00				

KM# 249a 10 DOLLARS
28.2800 g., 0.9250 Silver 0.8410 oz. ASW, 38.6 mm. **Series:** Big Cats **Obv:** National arms **Rev:** Cougar **Edge:** Reeded

Date	Mintage	F	VF	XF	Unc	BU
2001 Proof	—	Value: 50.00				

KM# 250 10 DOLLARS
28.2800 g., 0.9250 Silver 0.8410 oz. ASW, 38.6 mm. **Series:** Big Cats **Obv:** National arms **Rev:** Leopard **Edge:** Reeded

Date	Mintage	F	VF	XF	Unc	BU
2001 Proof	10,000	Value: 45.00				

KM# 250a 10 DOLLARS
28.2800 g., 0.9250 Silver 0.8410 oz. ASW, 38.6 mm. **Series:** Big Cats **Obv:** National arms **Rev:** Leopard **Edge:** Reeded

Date	Mintage	F	VF	XF	Unc	BU
2001 Proof	—	Value: 50.00				

KM# 265 10 DOLLARS
28.2800 g., 0.9250 Silver 0.8410 oz. ASW, 38.6 mm. **Subject:** RMS Titanic **Obv:** National arms **Rev:** Titanic at dock **Edge:** Reeded

Date	Mintage	F	VF	XF	Unc	BU
2002 Proof	10,000	Value: 47.50				

KM# 270 10 DOLLARS
28.2800 g., 0.9250 Gold Clad Silver 0.8410 oz., 38.6 mm. **Subject:** Queen's Golden Jubilee **Obv:** National arms **Rev:** Queen Elizabeth II and Prince Philip visiting blacksmiths in Sierra Leone **Edge:** Reeded

Date	Mintage	F	VF	XF	Unc	BU
2002 Proof	10,000	Value: 50.00				

KM# 271 10 DOLLARS
28.2800 g., 0.9250 Gold Clad Silver 0.8410 oz., 38.6 mm. **Subject:** Queen's Golden Jubilee **Obv:** National arms **Rev:** Queen Elizabeth II, Prince Charles and Princess Anne **Edge:** Reeded

Date	Mintage	F	VF	XF	Unc	BU
2002 Proof	10,000	Value: 50.00				

KM# 283 10 DOLLARS
28.2800 g., 0.9250 Gold Clad Silver 0.8410 oz., 38.6 mm. **Subject:** Queen Elizabeth's Golden Jubilee **Obv:** National arms **Rev:** Queen and young Prince Charles **Edge:** Reeded

Date	Mintage	F	VF	XF	Unc	BU
2002 Proof	10,000	Value: 47.50				

KM# 286 10 DOLLARS
28.2800 g., 0.9250 Gold Clad Silver 0.8410 oz., 38.6 mm. **Subject:** Queen Elizabeth's Golden Jubilee **Obv:** National arms **Rev:** Queen and Prince Philip **Edge:** Reeded

Date	Mintage	F	VF	XF	Unc	BU
2002 Proof	10,000	Value: 47.50				

KM# 257 10 DOLLARS
28.2800 g., 0.9250 Silver 0.8410 oz. ASW, 38.6 mm. **Subject:** Year of the Horse **Obv:** National arms **Rev:** Horse divides circle **Edge:** Reeded

Date	Mintage	F	VF	XF	Unc	BU
2002 Proof	5,000	Value: 50.00				

KM# 277 10 DOLLARS
28.2800 g., 0.9250 Gold Clad Silver 0.8410 oz., 38.6 mm. **Subject:** British Queen Mother **Obv:** National arms **Rev:** Bust facing in garden with dog within sprigs **Edge:** Reeded

Date	Mintage	F	VF	XF	Unc	BU
2002 Proof	10,000	Value: 47.50				

KM# 280 10 DOLLARS
28.2800 g., 0.9250 Gold Clad Silver 0.8410 oz., 38.6 mm. **Subject:** British Queen Mother **Obv:** National arms **Rev:** Conjoined busts facing within sprigs **Edge:** Reeded

Date	Mintage	F	VF	XF	Unc	BU
2002 Proof	10,000	Value: 47.50				

KM# 289 10 DOLLARS
28.2800 g., 0.9250 Silver 0.8410 oz. ASW, 38.6 mm. **Subject:** Olympics **Obv:** National arms **Rev:** Victory goddess Nike **Edge:** Reeded **Note:** The leone is the official currency of Sierra Leone

Date	Mintage	F	VF	XF	Unc	BU
2003 Proof	10,000	Value: 45.00				
2004 Proof	10,000	Value: 45.00				

KM# 292 10 DOLLARS
28.2800 g., 0.9250 Silver 0.8410 oz. ASW, 38.6 mm. **Subject:** Olympics **Obv:** National arms **Rev:** Ancient archer **Edge:** Reeded

Date	Mintage	F	VF	XF	Unc	BU
2003 Proof	10,000	Value: 45.00				
2004 Proof	10,000	Value: 45.00				

KM# 298 10 DOLLARS
28.2800 g., 0.9250 Silver 0.8410 oz. ASW, 38.6 mm. **Obv:** National arms **Rev:** Nelson Mandela **Edge:** Reeded

Date	Mintage	F	VF	XF	Unc	BU
2004 Proof	10,000	Value: 50.00				

KM# 301 10 DOLLARS
28.2800 g., 0.9250 Silver 0.8410 oz. ASW, 38.6 mm. **Obv:** National arms **Rev:** Ronald Reagan **Edge:** Reeded

Date	Mintage	F	VF	XF	Unc	BU
2004 Proof	10,000	Value: 50.00				

KM# 330 10 DOLLARS
0.9167 Silver **Series:** Crown Jewels **Obv:** Arms **Obv. Legend:** REPUBLIC OF SIERRA LEONE **Rev:** Imperial State crown with ruby setting **Rev. Legend:** CROWN JEWELS **Edge:** Reeded

Date	Mintage	F	VF	XF	Unc	BU
2006 Proof	—	Value: 120				

KM# 331 10 DOLLARS
0.9167 Silver **Series:** Crown Jewels **Obv:** Arms **Obv. Legend:** REPUBLIC OF SIERRA LEONE **Rev:** Sword of State with sapphire setting **Rev. Legend:** CROWN JEWELS **Edge:** Reeded

Date	Mintage	F	VF	XF	Unc	BU
2006 Proof	—	Value: 120				

KM# 332 10 DOLLARS
0.9167 Silver **Series:** Crown Jewels **Obv:** Arms **Obv. Legend:** REPUBLIC OF SIERRA LEONE **Rev:** St. Edward's Crown with emerald setting **Rev. Legend:** CROWN JEWELS **Edge:** Reeded

Date	Mintage	F	VF	XF	Unc	BU
2006 Proof	—	Value: 120				

KM# 333 10 DOLLARS
0.9167 Silver **Series:** Crown Jewels **Obv:** Arms **Obv. Legend:** REPUBLIC OF SIERRA LEONE **Rev:** Orb and Sceptre with the cross with diamond setting **Rev. Legend:** CROWN JEWELS **Edge:** Reeded

Date	Mintage	F	VF	XF	Unc	BU
2006 Proof	—	Value: 120				

KM# 334 10 DOLLARS
Copper-Nickel **Subject:** 80th Birthday of Queen Elizabeth II **Obv:** Arms **Obv. Legend:** REPUBLIC OF SIERRA LEONE **Rev:** Elizabeth II seated giving Christmas message **Rev. Legend:** 80th Birthday of H.M. Queen Elizabeth II **Edge:** Reeded

Date	Mintage	F	VF	XF	Unc	BU
2006	—	—	—	—	16.50	18.50

KM# 334a 10 DOLLARS
Silver **Subject:** 80th Birthday of Queen Elizabeth II **Obv:** Arms **Obv. Legend:** REPUBLIC OF SIERRA LEONE **Rev:** Elizabeth II seated giving Christmas Message **Rev. Legend:** 80th Birthday of H.M. Queen Elizabeth II **Edge:** Reeded

Date	Mintage	F	VF	XF	Unc	BU
2006 Proof	—	Value: 75.00				

KM# 335 10 DOLLARS
Copper-Nickel **Subject:** 80th Bithday of Queen Elizabeth II **Obv:** Arms **Obv. Legend:** REPUBLIC OF SIERRA LEONE **Rev:** Elizabeth II at 2002 Golden Jubilee celebrations in London, Concorde and Red Arrows doing flypass over Buckingham Palace **Rev. Legend:** 80th Birthday of H.M. Queen Elizabeth II **Edge:** Reeded

Date	Mintage	F	VF	XF	Unc	BU
2006	—	—	—	—	16.50	18.50

KM# 335a 10 DOLLARS
0.9167 Silver **Subject:** 80th Birthday of Queen Elizabeth Ii **Obv:** Arms **Obv. Legend:** RIPUBLIC OF SIERRA LEONE **Rev:** Elizabeth II at 2002 Golden Jubilee celebrations in London, Concorde and Red Arrows doing flypass over Buckingham Palace **Rev. Legend:** 80th Birthday of H.M. Queen Elizabeth II **Edge:** Reeded

Date	Mintage	F	VF	XF	Unc	BU
2006 Proof	—	Value: 75.00				

KM# 336 10 DOLLARS
Copper-Nickel **Subject:** 80th Birthday of Queen Elizabeth II **Obv:** Arms **Obv. Legend:** REPUBLIC OF SIERRA LEONE **Rev:** Elizabeth II presenting 1966 Football World Cup to English team **Rev. Legend:** 80th Birthday of H.M. Queen Elizabeth II **Edge:** Reeded

Date	Mintage	F	VF	XF	Unc	BU
2006	—	—	—	—	16.50	18.50

KM# 336a 10 DOLLARS
0.9167 Silver **Subject:** 80th Birthday of Queen Elizabeth II **Obv:** Arms **Obv. Legend:** REPUBLIC OF SIERRA LEONE **Rev:** Elizabeth II presenting 1966 Football World Cup to English team **Rev. Legend:** 80th Birthday of H.M. Queen Elizabeth II **Edge:** Reeded

Date	Mintage	F	VF	XF	Unc	BU
2006 Proof	—	Value: 75.00				

KM# 337 10 DOLLARS
Copper-Nickel **Subject:** 80th Birthday of Queen Elizabeth II **Obv:** Arms **Obv. Legend:** REPUBLIC OF SIERRA LEONE **Rev:** Investiture of Charles as Prince of Wales in 1969 **Rev. Legend:** 80th Birthday of H.M. Queen Elizabeth II **Edge:** Reeded

Date	Mintage	F	VF	XF	Unc	BU
2006	—	—	—	—	16.50	18.50

KM# 337a 10 DOLLARS
0.9167 Silver **Subject:** 80th Birthday of Queen Elizabeth II **Obv:** Arms **Obv. Legend:** REPUBLIC OF SIERRA LEONE **Rev:** Investiture of Charles as Prince of Wales in 1969 **Rev. Legend:** 80th Birthday of H.M. Queen Elizabeth II **Edge:** Reeded

Date	Mintage	F	VF	XF	Unc	BU
2006 Proof	—	Value: 75.00				

KM# 338 10 DOLLARS
Copper-Nickel **Subject:** 10th Anniversary Death of Princess Diana **Obv:** Arms **Obv. Legend:** REPUBLIC OF SIERRA LEONE **Rev:** Diana with sons, Prince William and Prince Harry facing **Rev. Legend:** DIANA — PRINCESS OF WALES **Edge:** Reeded

Date	Mintage	F	VF	XF	Unc	BU
2007	—	—	—	—	16.50	18.50

KM# 338a 10 DOLLARS
0.9167 Silver **Subject:** 10th Anniversary Death of Princess Diana **Obv:** Arms **Obv. Legend:** REPUBLIC OF SIERRA LEONE **Rev:** Diana with sons, Prince William and Prince Harry facing **Rev. Legend:** DIANA — PRINCESS OF WALES **Edge:** Reeded

Date	Mintage	F	VF	XF	Unc	BU
2007 Proof	—	Value: 75.00				

KM# 73 20 DOLLARS
1.2441 g., 0.9990 Gold 0.0400 oz. AGW **Subject:** Diana - The Peoples' Princess **Obv:** Arms **Rev:** Head facing

Date	Mintage	F	VF	XF	Unc	BU
1997 Proof	Est. 101,000	Value: 47.50				

KM# 79 20 DOLLARS
1.2441 g., 0.9990 Gold 0.0400 oz. AGW **Subject:** Diana - The Peoples' Princess **Obv:** Arms **Rev:** Lady Diana and Mother Theresa

Date	Mintage	F	VF	XF	Unc	BU
1997 Proof	Est. 101,000	Value: 55.00				

KM# 85 20 DOLLARS
1.2441 g., 0.9990 Gold 0.0400 oz. AGW **Subject:** Diana - The Peoples' Princess **Obv:** Arms **Rev:** Lady Diana and AIDS patient

Date	Mintage	F	VF	XF	Unc	BU
1997 Proof	Est. 101,000	Value: 42.50				

KM# 91 20 DOLLARS
1.2441 g., 0.9990 Gold 0.0400 oz. AGW **Subject:** Diana - The Peoples' Princess **Obv:** Arms **Rev:** With sons William and Harry

Date	Mintage	F	VF	XF	Unc	BU
1997 Proof	Est. 101,000	Value: 45.00				

KM# 105 20 DOLLARS
1.2441 g., 0.9990 Gold 0.0400 oz. AGW **Subject:** In Memorium **Obv:** Arms **Rev:** Lady Diana

Date	Mintage	F	VF	XF	Unc	BU
1998 Proof	Est. 10,000	Value: 50.00				

KM# 144 20 DOLLARS
1.2441 g., 0.9990 Gold 0.0400 oz. AGW **Subject:** Year of the Dragon **Obv:** Arms **Rev:** Dragon

Date	Mintage	F	VF	XF	Unc	BU
2000 Proof	Est. 15,000	Value: 55.00				

KM# 180 20 DOLLARS
1.2400 g., 0.9990 Gold 0.0398 oz. AGW **Subject:** Buddha **Obv:** Arms **Rev:** Seated Buddha **Edge:** Reeded **Note:** Struck at Pobjoy Mint.

Date	Mintage	F	VF	XF	Unc	BU
2000 Proof	Est. 5,000	Value: 55.00				

KM# 181 20 DOLLARS
1.2400 g., 0.9990 Gold 0.0398 oz. AGW **Obv:** Arms **Rev:** Goddess of Mercy

Date	Mintage	F	VF	XF	Unc	BU
2000 Proof	Est. 5,000	Value: 55.00				

KM# 182 20 DOLLARS
1.2400 g., 0.9990 Gold 0.0398 oz. AGW **Obv:** Arms **Rev:** Tzai-yen holding scroll

Date	Mintage	F	VF	XF	Unc	BU
2000 Proof	Est. 5,000	Value: 55.00				

KM# 200 20 DOLLARS
1.2441 g., 0.9990 Gold 0.0400 oz. AGW, 13.9 mm. **Subject:** Year of the Snake **Obv:** National arms **Rev:** Snake **Edge:** Reeded

Date	Mintage	F	VF	XF	Unc	BU
2001 Proof	Est. 50,000	Value: 60.00				

KM# 208 20 DOLLARS
1.2441 g., 0.9990 Gold 0.0400 oz. AGW **Subject:** P'an Ku **Obv:** National arms **Rev:** Dragon

Date	Mintage	F	VF	XF	Unc	BU
2001 Proof	Est. 5,000	Value: 60.00				

KM# 216 20 DOLLARS
1.2441 g., 0.9990 Gold 0.0400 oz. AGW **Subject:** P'an Ku **Obv:** National arms **Rev:** Dragon and three animals

Date	Mintage	F	VF	XF	Unc	BU
2001 Proof	Est. 5,000	Value: 60.00				

KM# 258 20 DOLLARS
1.2400 g., 0.9990 Gold 0.0398 oz. AGW, 13.92 mm. **Subject:** Year of the Horse **Obv:** National arms **Rev:** Horse **Edge:** Reeded

Date	Mintage	F	VF	XF	Unc	BU
2002 Proof	5,000	Value: 55.00				

KM# 272 30 DOLLARS
6.2200 g., 0.3750 Gold 0.0750 oz. AGW, 22 mm.
Subject: Queen's Golden Jubilee **Obv:** National arms
Rev: Queen Elizabeth II and Prince Philip **Edge:** Reeded

Date	Mintage	F	VF	XF	Unc	BU
2002 Proof	5,000	Value: 95.00				

KM# 273 30 DOLLARS
6.2200 g., 0.3750 Gold 0.0750 oz. AGW, 22 mm.
Subject: Queen's Golden Jubilee **Obv:** National arms
Rev: Queen Elizabeth II, Prince Charles and Princess Anne **Edge:** Reeded

Date	Mintage	F	VF	XF	Unc	BU
2002 Proof	5,000	Value: 95.00				

KM# 74 50 DOLLARS
3.1100 g., 0.9990 Gold 0.0999 oz. AGW
Subject: Diana - The Peoples' Princess **Obv:** Arms
Rev: Portrait of Lady Diana

Date	Mintage	F	VF	XF	Unc	BU
1997 Proof	Est. 7,500	Value: 85.00				

KM# 80 50 DOLLARS
3.1100 g., 0.9990 Gold 0.0999 oz. AGW
Subject: Diana - The Peoples' Princess **Obv:** Arms
Rev: Lady Diana and Mother Theresa

Date	Mintage	F	VF	XF	Unc	BU
1997 Proof	Est. 7,500	Value: 90.00				

KM# 86 50 DOLLARS
3.1100 g., 0.9990 Gold 0.0999 oz. AGW
Subject: Diana - The Peoples' Princess **Obv:** Arms
Rev: Lady Diana and AIDS patient

Date	Mintage	F	VF	XF	Unc	BU
1997 Proof	Est. 7,500	Value: 80.00				

KM# 92 50 DOLLARS
3.1100 g., 0.9990 Gold 0.0999 oz. AGW
Subject: Diana - The Peoples' Princess **Obv:** Arms
Rev: With sons William and Harry

Date	Mintage	F	VF	XF	Unc	BU
1997 Proof	Est. 7,500	Value: 85.00				

KM# 106 50 DOLLARS
3.1100 g., 0.9990 Gold 0.0999 oz. AGW
Subject: Diana - The Peoples' Princess **Obv:** Arms
Rev: Portrait of Lady Diana

Date	Mintage	F	VF	XF	Unc	BU
1998 Proof	Est. 7,500	Value: 90.00				

KM# 184 50 DOLLARS
3.1100 g., 0.9990 Gold 0.0999 oz. AGW **Obv:** Arms
Rev: Goddess of Mercy

Date	Mintage	F	VF	XF	Unc	BU
2000 Proof	Est. 5,000	Value: 95.00				

KM# 145 50 DOLLARS
3.1100 g., 0.9990 Gold 0.0999 oz. AGW **Subject:** Year of the Dragon **Obv:** Arms **Rev:** Dragon

Date	Mintage	F	VF	XF	Unc	BU
2000 Proof	Est. 20,000	Value: 90.00				

KM# 183 50 DOLLARS
3.1100 g., 0.9990 Gold 0.0999 oz. AGW **Obv:** Arms
Rev: Seated Buddha **Edge:** Reeded

Date	Mintage	F	VF	XF	Unc	BU
2000 Proof	Est. 5,000	Value: 95.00				

KM# 185 50 DOLLARS
3.1100 g., 0.9990 Gold 0.0999 oz. AGW **Obv:** Arms
Rev: Tzai-yen holding scroll

Date	Mintage	F	VF	XF	Unc	BU
2000 Proof	Est. 5,000	Value: 95.00				

KM# 201 50 DOLLARS
3.1103 g., 0.9990 Gold 0.0999 oz. AGW, 18 mm.
Subject: Year of the Snake **Obv:** National arms
Rev: Snake **Edge:** Reeded

Date	Mintage	F	VF	XF	Unc	BU
2001 Proof	Est. 10,000	Value: 95.00				

KM# 209 50 DOLLARS
3.1103 g., 0.9990 Gold 0.0999 oz. AGW **Subject:** P'an Ku **Obv:** National arms **Rev:** Dragon

Date	Mintage	F	VF	XF	Unc	BU
2001 Proof	Est. 5,000	Value: 95.00				

KM# 217 50 DOLLARS
3.1103 g., 0.9990 Gold 0.0999 oz. AGW **Subject:** P'an Ku **Obv:** National arms **Rev:** Dragon and three animals

Date	Mintage	F	VF	XF	Unc	BU
2001 Proof	Est. 5,000	Value: 95.00				

KM# 266 50 DOLLARS
155.5500 g., 0.9999 Silver 5.0003 oz. ASW, 65 mm.
Subject: RMS Titanic **Obv:** National arms **Rev:** Titanic at dock **Edge:** Reeded

Date	Mintage	F	VF	XF	Unc	BU
2002 Proof	2,000	Value: 150				

KM# 259 50 DOLLARS
3.1100 g., 0.9990 Gold 0.0999 oz. AGW, 17.95 mm.
Subject: Year of the Horse **Obv:** National arms
Rev: Horse **Edge:** Reeded

Date	Mintage	F	VF	XF	Unc	BU
2002 Proof	5,000	Value: 95.00				

KM# 51 100 DOLLARS
6.2200 g., 0.9999 Gold 0.1999 oz. AGW
Subject: Shanghai Coin and Stamp Exposition
Obv: Arms **Rev:** Crowned lion

Date	Mintage	F	VF	XF	Unc	BU
1997 Proof	Est. 5,000	Value: 175				

KM# 52 100 DOLLARS
6.2200 g., 0.9999 Gold 0.1999 oz. AGW
Subject: Shanghai Coin and Stamp Exposition
Obv: Arms **Rev:** Crowned lion

Date	Mintage	F	VF	XF	Unc	BU
1997 Proof	Est. 5,000	Value: 175				

KM# 55 100 DOLLARS
6.2200 g., 0.9999 Gold 0.1999 oz. AGW
Subject: Golden Wedding Anniversary **Obv:** Arms
Rev: E and P monogram

Date	Mintage	F	VF	XF	Unc	BU
1997 Proof	Est. 3,500	Value: 175				

KM# 58 100 DOLLARS
6.2200 g., 0.9999 Gold 0.1999 oz. AGW **Subject:** Golden Wedding Anniversary **Obv:** Arms **Rev:** Yacht

Date	Mintage	F	VF	XF	Unc	BU
1997 Proof	Est. 3,500	Value: 175				

KM# 61 100 DOLLARS
6.2200 g., 0.9999 Gold 0.1999 oz. AGW **Subject:** Golden Wedding Anniversary **Obv:** Arms **Rev:** Royal couple

Date	Mintage	F	VF	XF	Unc	BU
1997 Proof	Est. 10,000	Value: 175				

KM# 64 100 DOLLARS
6.2200 g., 0.9999 Gold 0.1999 oz. AGW
Subject: Golden Wedding Anniversary **Obv:** Arms
Rev: Fireworks above palace

Date	Mintage	F	VF	XF	Unc	BU
1997 Proof	Est. 3,500	Value: 175				

KM# 67 100 DOLLARS
6.2200 g., 0.9999 Gold 0.1999 oz. AGW
Subject: Golden Wedding Anniversary **Obv:** Arms
Rev: Queen with two children

Date	Mintage	F	VF	XF	Unc	BU
1997 Proof	Est. 3,500	Value: 175				

KM# 70 100 DOLLARS
6.2200 g., 0.9999 Gold 0.1999 oz. AGW
Subject: Golden Wedding Anniversary **Obv:** Arms
Rev: Royal couple with two children

Date	Mintage	F	VF	XF	Unc	BU
1997 Proof	Est. 3,500	Value: 175				

KM# 75 100 DOLLARS
6.2200 g., 0.9999 Gold 0.1999 oz. AGW
Subject: Diana - The Peoples' Princess **Obv:** Arms
Rev: Portrait of Lady Diana

Date	Mintage	F	VF	XF	Unc	BU
1997 Proof	Est. 5,000	Value: 165				

KM# 81 100 DOLLARS
6.2200 g., 0.9999 Gold 0.1999 oz. AGW
Subject: Diana - The Peoples' Princess **Obv:** Arms with supporters **Rev:** Diana with Mother Theresa

Date	Mintage	F	VF	XF	Unc	BU
1997 Proof	Est. 5,000	Value: 175				

KM# 87 100 DOLLARS
6.2200 g., 0.9999 Gold 0.1999 oz. AGW
Subject: Diana - The Peoples' Princess **Obv:** Arms
Rev: Lady Diana and AIDS patient

Date	Mintage	F	VF	XF	Unc	BU
1997 Proof	Est. 5,000	Value: 155				

KM# 93 100 DOLLARS
6.2200 g., 0.9999 Gold 0.1999 oz. AGW
Subject: Diana - The Peoples' Princess **Obv:** Arms
Rev: With sons William and Harry

Date	Mintage	F	VF	XF	Unc	BU
1997 Proof	Est. 5,000	Value: 160				

KM# 97 100 DOLLARS
6.2200 g., 0.9999 Gold 0.1999 oz. AGW
Subject: Jurassic Park **Obv:** Arms **Rev:** Velociraptor

Date	Mintage	F	VF	XF	Unc	BU
1997 Proof	Est. 5,000	Value: 175				

KM# 100 100 DOLLARS
6.2200 g., 0.9999 Gold 0.1999 oz. AGW **Subject:** Queen Victoria's Diamond Jubilee Centennial **Obv:** Arms **Rev:** Crowned bust with diamond necklace facing

Date	Mintage	F	VF	XF	Unc	BU
1997 Proof	Est. 3,500	Value: 200				

KM# 107 100 DOLLARS
6.2200 g., 0.9999 Gold 0.1999 oz. AGW **Subject:** Diana - The People's Princess **Obv:** Arms **Rev:** Head half left

Date	Mintage	F	VF	XF	Unc	BU
1998 Proof	Est. 5,000	Value: 165				

KM# 111 100 DOLLARS
6.2200 g., 0.9999 Gold 0.1999 oz. AGW **Subject:** Dr. Livingstone **Obv:** Arms **Rev:** Dr. Livingstone above figures in boat

Date	Mintage	F	VF	XF	Unc	BU
1998 Proof	Est. 5,000	Value: 170				

KM# 114 100 DOLLARS
6.2200 g., 0.9999 Gold 0.1999 oz. AGW
Subject: Amerigo Vespucci **Obv:** Arms **Rev:** Ship and mountainous portrait

Date	Mintage	F	VF	XF	Unc	BU
1999 Proof	Est. 5,000	Value: 175				

KM# 117 100 DOLLARS
6.2200 g., 0.9999 Gold 0.1999 oz. AGW **Subject:** Charles Darwin **Obv:** Arms **Rev:** Ship and portrait

Date	Mintage	F	VF	XF	Unc	BU
1999 Proof	Est. 5,000	Value: 175				

KM# 120 100 DOLLARS
6.2200 g., 0.9999 Gold 0.1999 oz. AGW **Subject:** China 2000 Series **Obv:** Arms **Rev:** Kneeling terra cotta warrior

Date	Mintage	F	VF	XF	Unc	BU
1999 Proof	Est. 5,000	Value: 165				

KM# 123 100 DOLLARS

6.2200 g., 0.9999 Gold 0.1999 oz. AGW
Subject: China 2000 Series - Ming Dynasty **Obv:** Arms **Rev:** Temple of Heaven

Date	Mintage	F	VF	XF	Unc	BU
1999 Proof	Est. 5,000	Value: 165				

KM# 126 100 DOLLARS

6.2200 g., 0.9999 Gold 0.1999 oz. AGW **Subject:** China 2000 Series **Obv:** Arms **Rev:** Portion of the Great Wall

Date	Mintage	F	VF	XF	Unc	BU
1999 Proof	Est. 5,000	Value: 165				

KM# 129 100 DOLLARS

6.2200 g., 0.9999 Gold 0.1999 oz. AGW **Series:** China 2000 **Obv:** Arms **Rev:** Bronze chariot

Date	Mintage	F	VF	XF	Unc	BU
1999 Proof	Est. 5,000	Value: 165				

KM# 132 100 DOLLARS

6.2200 g., 0.9999 Gold 0.1999 oz. AGW **Series:** China 2000 **Obv:** Arms **Rev:** First century armillary sphere

Date	Mintage	F	VF	XF	Unc	BU
1999 Proof	Est. 5,000	Value: 165				

KM# 135 100 DOLLARS

6.2200 g., 0.9999 Gold 0.1999 oz. AGW **Series:** China 2000 **Obv:** Arms **Rev:** Tang Dynasty royal horse

Date	Mintage	F	VF	XF	Unc	BU
1999 Proof	Est. 5,000	Value: 165				

KM# 138 100 DOLLARS

6.2200 g., 0.9999 Gold 0.1999 oz. AGW
Subject: Macau Return to China **Obv:** Arms
Rev: Church, car, roulette wheel, and hands shaking

Date	Mintage	F	VF	XF	Unc	BU
1999 Proof	Est. 5,000	Value: 175				

KM# 141 100 DOLLARS

6.2200 g., 0.9999 Gold 0.1999 oz. AGW
Subject: Prince Edward's Wedding **Obv:** Arms
Rev: Symbolic wedding design

Date	Mintage	F	VF	XF	Unc	BU
1999 Proof	Est. 5,000	Value: 175				

KM# 146 100 DOLLARS

6.2200 g., 0.9999 Gold 0.1999 oz. AGW **Subject:** Year of the Dragon **Obv:** Arms **Rev:** Dragon

Date	Mintage	F	VF	XF	Unc	BU
2000 Proof	Est. 20,000	Value: 165				

KM# 186 100 DOLLARS

6.2200 g., 0.9999 Gold 0.1999 oz. AGW **Obv:** Arms
Rev: Seated Buddha **Edge:** Reeded

Date	Mintage	F	VF	XF	Unc	BU
2000	Est. 5,000	Value: 175				

KM# 187 100 DOLLARS

6.2200 g., 0.9999 Gold 0.1999 oz. AGW **Obv:** Arms
Rev: Goddess of Mercy

Date	Mintage	F	VF	XF	Unc	BU
2000 Proof	Est. 5,000	Value: 175				

KM# 188 100 DOLLARS

6.2200 g., 0.9999 Gold 0.1999 oz. AGW **Obv:** Arms
Rev: Tzai-yen holding scroll

Date	Mintage	F	VF	XF	Unc	BU
2000 Proof	Est. 5,000	Value: 175				

KM# 202 100 DOLLARS

6.2200 g., 0.9990 Gold 0.1998 oz. AGW, 22 mm.
Subject: Year of the Snake **Obv:** National arms
Rev: Snake **Edge:** Reeded

Date	Mintage	F	VF	XF	Unc	BU
2001 Proof	—	Value: 175				

KM# 210 100 DOLLARS

6.2200 g., 0.9990 Gold 0.1998 oz. AGW **Subject:** P'an Ku **Obv:** National arms **Rev:** Dragon

Date	Mintage	F	VF	XF	Unc	BU
2001 Proof	Est. 10,000	Value: 175				

KM# 218 100 DOLLARS

6.2200 g., 0.9990 Gold 0.1998 oz. AGW **Subject:** P'an Ku **Obv:** National arms **Rev:** Dragon and three animals

Date	Mintage	F	VF	XF	Unc	BU
2001 Proof	Est. 10,000	Value: 175				

KM# 224 100 DOLLARS

6.2200 g., 0.9990 Gold 0.1998 oz. AGW, 22 mm.
Series: The Big Five **Obv:** National arms **Rev:** Rhino **Edge:** Reeded

Date	Mintage	F	VF	XF	Unc	BU
2001 Proof	Est. 5,000	Value: 175				

KM# 227 100 DOLLARS

6.2200 g., 0.9990 Gold 0.1998 oz. AGW **Series:** The Big Five **Obv:** National arms **Rev:** Lion

Date	Mintage	F	VF	XF	Unc	BU
2001 Proof	Est. 5,000	Value: 175				

KM# 230 100 DOLLARS

6.2200 g., 0.9990 Gold 0.1998 oz. AGW **Series:** The Big Five **Obv:** National arms **Rev:** Leopard

Date	Mintage	F	VF	XF	Unc	BU
2001 Proof	Est. 5,000	Value: 175				

KM# 233 100 DOLLARS

6.2200 g., 0.9990 Gold 0.1998 oz. AGW **Series:** The Big Five **Obv:** National arms **Rev:** Elephants

Date	Mintage	F	VF	XF	Unc	BU
2001 Proof	Est. 5,000	Value: 175				

KM# 236 100 DOLLARS

6.2200 g., 0.9990 Gold 0.1998 oz. AGW **Series:** The Big Five **Obv:** National arms **Rev:** Buffalo

Date	Mintage	F	VF	XF	Unc	BU
2001 Proof	Est. 5,000	Value: 175				

KM# 239 100 DOLLARS

6.2200 g., 0.9990 Gold 0.1998 oz. AGW **Series:** The Big Five **Obv:** National arms **Rev:** All five animals

Date	Mintage	F	VF	XF	Unc	BU
2001 Proof	Est. 5,000	Value: 175				

KM# 251 100 DOLLARS

6.2200 g., 0.9990 Gold 0.1998 oz. AGW, 22 mm.
Series: Big Cats **Obv:** National arms **Rev:** Male and female lions **Edge:** Reeded

Date	Mintage	F	VF	XF	Unc	BU
2001 Proof	5,000	Value: 175				

KM# 252 100 DOLLARS

6.2200 g., 0.9990 Gold 0.1998 oz. AGW, 22 mm.
Series: Big Cats **Rev:** Tiger **Edge:** Reeded

Date	Mintage	F	VF	XF	Unc	BU
2001 Proof	5,000	Value: 175				

KM# 253 100 DOLLARS

6.2200 g., 0.9990 Gold 0.1998 oz. AGW, 22 mm.
Series: Big Cats **Rev:** Cheetah **Edge:** Reeded

Date	Mintage	F	VF	XF	Unc	BU
2001 Proof	5,000	Value: 175				

KM# 254 100 DOLLARS

6.2200 g., 0.9990 Gold 0.1998 oz. AGW, 22 mm.
Series: Big Cats **Rev:** Cougar **Edge:** Reeded

Date	Mintage	F	VF	XF	Unc	BU
2001 Proof	5,000	Value: 175				

KM# 255 100 DOLLARS

6.2200 g., 0.9990 Gold 0.1998 oz. AGW, 22 mm.
Series: Big Cats **Rev:** Black panther **Edge:** Reeded

Date	Mintage	F	VF	XF	Unc	BU
2001 Proof	5,000	Value: 175				

KM# 274 100 DOLLARS

6.2200 g., 0.9999 Gold 0.1999 oz. AGW, 22 mm.
Subject: Queen's Golden Jubilee **Obv:** National arms
Rev: Queen Elizabeth II and Prince Philip **Edge:** Reeded

Date	Mintage	F	VF	XF	Unc	BU
2002 Proof	2,002	Value: 175				

KM# 275 100 DOLLARS

6.2200 g., 0.9999 Gold 0.1999 oz. AGW, 22 mm.
Subject: Queen's Golden Jubilee **Obv:** National arms
Rev: Queen Elizabeth II, Prince Charles and Princess Anne **Edge:** Reeded

Date	Mintage	F	VF	XF	Unc	BU
2002 Proof	5,000	Value: 175				

KM# 284 100 DOLLARS

6.2200 g., 0.9999 Gold 0.1999 oz. AGW, 22 mm.
Subject: Queen Elizabeth's Golden Jubilee
Obv: National arms **Rev:** Queen and young Prince Charles **Edge:** Reeded

Date	Mintage	F	VF	XF	Unc	BU
2002 Proof	2,002	Value: 175				

KM# 287 100 DOLLARS

6.2200 g., 0.9999 Gold 0.1999 oz. AGW, 22 mm.
Subject: Queen Elizabeth's Golden Jubilee **Obv:** National arms **Rev:** Queen and Prince Philip **Edge:** Reeded

Date	Mintage	F	VF	XF	Unc	BU
2002 Proof	2,002	Value: 175				

KM# 260 100 DOLLARS

6.2200 g., 0.9990 Gold 0.1998 oz. AGW, 22 mm.
Subject: Year of the Horse **Obv:** National arms
Rev: Horse **Edge:** Reeded

Date	Mintage	F	VF	XF	Unc	BU
2002 Proof	2,000	Value: 175				

KM# 278 100 DOLLARS

6.2200 g., 0.9999 Gold 0.1999 oz. AGW, 22 mm.
Subject: British Queen Mother **Obv:** National arms
Rev: Queen Mother in garden with dog **Edge:** Reeded

Date	Mintage	F	VF	XF	Unc	BU
2002 Proof	2,000	Value: 175				

KM# 281 100 DOLLARS

6.2200 g., 0.9999 Gold 0.1999 oz. AGW, 22 mm.
Subject: British Queen Mother **Obv:** National arms
Rev: Queen Mother with daughters **Edge:** Reeded

Date	Mintage	F	VF	XF	Unc	BU
2002 Proof	2,000	Value: 175				

KM# 293 100 DOLLARS

6.2200 g., 0.9999 Gold 0.1999 oz. AGW, 22 mm.
Subject: Olympics **Obv:** National arms **Rev:** Ancient archer **Edge:** Reeded

Date	Mintage	F	VF	XF	Unc	BU
2003 Proof	5,000	Value: 175				
2004 Proof	5,000	Value: 175				

KM# 290 100 DOLLARS

6.2200 g., 0.9999 Gold 0.1999 oz. AGW, 22 mm.
Subject: Olympics **Obv:** National arms **Rev:** Victory goddess Nike **Edge:** Reeded **Note:** The leone is the official currency of Sierra Leone

Date	Mintage	F	VF	XF	Unc	BU
2003 Proof	5,000	Value: 175				
2004 Proof	5,000	Value: 175				

KM# 267 150 DOLLARS

1000.0000 g., 0.9999 Silver 32.146 oz. ASW, 85 mm.
Subject: RMS Titanic **Obv:** National arms **Rev:** Titanic at dock **Edge:** Reeded

Date	Mintage	F	VF	XF	Unc	BU
2002 Proof	500	Value: 525				

KM# 240 250 DOLLARS

15.5500 g., 0.9999 Gold 0.4999 oz. AGW, 29.9 mm.
Subject: Centennial of Queen Victoria's Diamond Jubilee
Obv: Arms **Rev:** Crowned bust with diamond necklace facing **Edge:** Reeded **Note:** This denomination was never offered to the public. The entire issue is reported to have been commissioned by and sold to a single purchaser.

Date	Mintage	F	VF	XF	Unc	BU
1997 Proof	Est. 1,000	Value: 375				

KM# 76 250 DOLLARS

15.5000 g., 0.9990 Gold 0.4978 oz. AGW **Subject:** Diana - The Peoples' Princess **Obv:** Arms **Rev:** Portrait of Lady Diana

Date	Mintage	F	VF	XF	Unc	BU
1997 Proof	Est. 3,000	Value: 370				

KM# 82 250 DOLLARS
15.5000 g., 0.9990 Gold 0.4978 oz. AGW
Subject: Diana - The Peoples' Princess **Obv:** Arms
Rev: Mother Theresa and Lady Diana

Date	Mintage	F	VF	XF	Unc	BU
1997 Proof	Est. 3,000	Value: 385				

KM# 88 250 DOLLARS
15.5000 g., 0.9990 Gold 0.4978 oz. AGW
Subject: Diana - The Peoples' Princess **Obv:** Arms
Rev: Lady Diana with AIDS patient

Date	Mintage	F	VF	XF	Unc	BU
1997 Proof	Est. 3,000	Value: 360				

KM# 94 250 DOLLARS
15.5000 g., 0.9990 Gold 0.4978 oz. AGW
Subject: Diana - The Peoples' Princess **Obv:** Arms
Rev: Lady Diana with sons William and Harry

Date	Mintage	F	VF	XF	Unc	BU
1997 Proof	Est. 3,000	Value: 365				

KM# 108 250 DOLLARS
15.5000 g., 0.9990 Gold 0.4978 oz. AGW **Subject:** Diana - The Peoples' Princess **Obv:** Arms **Rev:** Head half left

Date	Mintage	F	VF	XF	Unc	BU
1998 Proof	Est. 3,000	Value: 370				

KM# 147 250 DOLLARS
15.5000 g., 0.9990 Gold 0.4978 oz. AGW
Subject: Year of the Dragon **Obv:** Arms **Rev:** Dragon

Date	Mintage	F	VF	XF	Unc	BU
2000 Proof	Est. 5,000	Value: 370				

KM# 189 250 DOLLARS
15.5000 g., 0.9990 Gold 0.4978 oz. AGW **Obv:** Arms
Rev: Seated Buddha

Date	Mintage	F	VF	XF	Unc	BU
2000 Proof	Est. 5,000	Value: 385				

KM# 190 250 DOLLARS
15.5500 g., 0.9990 Gold 0.4994 oz. AGW **Obv:** Arms
Rev: Goddess of Mercy

Date	Mintage	F	VF	XF	Unc	BU
2000 Proof	Est. 5,000	Value: 385				

KM# 191 250 DOLLARS
15.5500 g., 0.9990 Gold 0.4994 oz. AGW **Obv:** Arms
Rev: Tzai-yen holding scroll

Date	Mintage	F	VF	XF	Unc	BU
2000 Proof	Est. 5,000	Value: 385				

KM# 203 250 DOLLARS
15.5118 g., 0.9990 Gold 0.4982 oz. AGW, 30 mm.
Subject: Year of the Snake **Obv:** National arms
Rev: Snake **Edge:** Reeded

Date	Mintage	F	VF	XF	Unc	BU
2001 Proof	Est. 5,000	Value: 375				

KM# 211 250 DOLLARS
15.5518 g., 0.9990 Gold 0.4995 oz. AGW **Subject:** P'an Ku **Obv:** National arms **Rev:** Dragon

Date	Mintage	F	VF	XF	Unc	BU
2001 Proof	Est. 2,000	Value: 385				

KM# 219 250 DOLLARS
15.5518 g., 0.9990 Gold 0.4995 oz. AGW **Subject:** P'an Ku **Obv:** National arms **Rev:** Dragon and three animals

Date	Mintage	F	VF	XF	Unc	BU
2001 Proof	Est. 2,000	Value: 385				

KM# 261 250 DOLLARS
15.5500 g., 0.9990 Gold 0.4994 oz. AGW, 30 mm.
Subject: Year of the Horse **Obv:** National arms
Rev: Horse **Edge:** Reeded

Date	Mintage	F	VF	XF	Unc	BU
2002 Proof	2,000	Value: 385				

KM# 148 500 DOLLARS
31.1035 g., 0.9990 Gold 0.9990 oz. AGW
Subject: Year of the Dragon **Obv:** Arms **Rev:** Dragon
Note: Similar to 10 Dollars, KM#143.

Date	Mintage	F	VF	XF	Unc	BU
2000 Proof	Est. 1,000	Value: 765				

KM# 192 500 DOLLARS
31.1035 g., 0.9990 Gold 0.9990 oz. AGW **Obv:** Arms
Rev: Seated Buddha **Edge:** Reeded **Note:** Struck at Pobjoy Mint.

Date	Mintage	F	VF	XF	Unc	BU
2000 Proof	Est. 5,000	Value: 740				

KM# 193 500 DOLLARS
31.1035 g., 0.9990 Gold 0.9990 oz. AGW **Obv:** Arms
Rev: Goddess of Mercy

Date	Mintage	F	VF	XF	Unc	BU
2000 Proof	Est. 5,000	Value: 740				

KM# 194 500 DOLLARS
31.1035 g., 0.9990 Gold 0.9990 oz. AGW **Obv:** Arms
Rev: Tzai-yen holding scroll

Date	Mintage	F	VF	XF	Unc	BU
2000 Proof	Est. 5,000	Value: 740				

KM# 204 500 DOLLARS
31.1035 g., 0.9990 Gold 0.9990 oz. AGW, 32.7 mm.
Subject: Year of the Snake **Obv:** National arms
Rev: Snake **Edge:** Reeded

Date	Mintage	F	VF	XF	Unc	BU
2001 Proof	Est. 1,000	Value: 765				

KM# 212 500 DOLLARS
31.1035 g., 0.9990 Gold 0.9990 oz. AGW
Subject: P'an Ku **Obv:** National arms **Rev:** Dragon

Date	Mintage	F	VF	XF	Unc	BU
2001 Proof	Est. 1,000	Value: 765				

KM# 220 500 DOLLARS
31.1035 g., 0.9990 Gold 0.9990 oz. AGW **Subject:** P'an Ku **Obv:** National arms **Rev:** Dragon and three animals

Date	Mintage	F	VF	XF	Unc	BU
2001 Proof	Est. 1,000	Value: 765				

KM# 262 500 DOLLARS
31.1000 g., 0.9990 Gold 0.9988 oz. AGW, 32.7 mm.
Subject: Year of the Horse **Obv:** National arms
Rev: Horse **Edge:** Reeded

Date	Mintage	F	VF	XF	Unc	BU
2002 Proof	1,000	Value: 765				

KM# 294 500 DOLLARS
31.1000 g., 0.9999 Gold 0.9997 oz. AGW, 32.7 mm. **Obv:** National arms **Rev:** Multicolor Astro Boy cartoon **Edge:** Reeded **Note:** The leone is Sierra Leone's official currency

Date	Mintage	F	VF	XF	Unc	BU
2003 Proof	2,003	Value: 750				

KM# 299 500 DOLLARS
31.1035 g., 0.9999 Gold 0.9999 oz. AGW, 32.7 mm.
Obv: National arms **Rev:** Nelson Mandela **Edge:** Reeded

Date	Mintage	F	VF	XF	Unc	BU
2004 Proof	—	Value: 750				

KM# 149 2500 DOLLARS
155.5175 g., 0.9990 Gold 4.9948 oz. AGW
Subject: Year of the Dragon **Obv:** Arms **Rev:** Dragon

Date	Mintage	F	VF	XF	Unc	BU
2000 Proof	250	Value: 3,500				

KM# 195 2500 DOLLARS
155.5175 g., 0.9990 Gold 4.9948 oz. AGW **Obv:** Arms
Rev: Seated Buddha **Edge:** Reeded

Date	Mintage	F	VF	XF	Unc	BU
2000 Proof	Est. 250	Value: 3,500				

KM# 196 2500 DOLLARS
155.5175 g., 0.9990 Gold 4.9948 oz. AGW **Obv:** Arms
Rev: Goddess of Mercy

Date	Mintage	F	VF	XF	Unc	BU
2000 Proof	Est. 250	Value: 3,500				

KM# 197 2500 DOLLARS
155.5175 g., 0.9990 Gold 4.9948 oz. AGW **Obv:** Arms
Rev: Tzai-yen holding scroll

Date	Mintage	F	VF	XF	Unc	BU
2000 Proof	Est. 250	Value: 3,500				

KM# 205 2500 DOLLARS
155.5175 g., 0.9990 Gold 4.9948 oz. AGW, 50 mm.
Subject: Year of the Snake **Obv:** National arms
Rev: Snake **Edge:** Reeded

Date	Mintage	F	VF	XF	Unc	BU
2001 Proof	Est. 250	Value: 3,550				

KM# 213 2500 DOLLARS
155.5175 g., 0.9990 Gold 4.9948 oz. AGW
Subject: P'an Ku **Obv:** National arms **Rev:** Dragon

Date	Mintage	F	VF	XF	Unc	BU
2001 Proof	Est. 250	Value: 3,550				

KM# 263 2500 DOLLARS
155.5100 g., 0.9990 Gold 4.9946 oz. AGW, 50 mm.
Subject: Year of the Horse **Obv:** National arms
Rev: Horse **Edge:** Reeded

Date	Mintage	F	VF	XF	Unc	BU
2002 Proof	250	Value: 3,550				

MEDALLIC / INA RETRO ISSUE

X# M6 2 DOLLARS
Silver, 40.97 mm. **Obv:** Laureate bust right **Obv. Legend:** GEORGIUS III DEI GRATIA REX. **Rev:** Clasped hands above lion standing left **Rev. Legend:** SIERRA LEONE **Rev. Inscription:** AFRICA **Edge:** Plain

Date	Mintage	F	VF	XF	Unc	BU
1808 (2007) Proof	—	—	—	—	—	—
1808 (2007) Matte Proof	—	—	—	—	—	—

X# M6a 2 DOLLARS
Copper, 40.97 mm. **Obv:** Laureate bust right **Obv. Legend:** GEORGIUS III DEI GRATIA REX. **Rev:** Clasped hands above lion standing left **Rev. Legend:** SIERRA LEONE **Rev. Inscription:** AFRICA **Edge:** Plain

Date	Mintage	F	VF	XF	Unc	BU
1808 (2007) Proof	500	—	—	—	—	—

X# M6b 2 DOLLARS
Aluminum, 40.97 mm. **Obv:** Laureate bust right **Obv. Legend:** GEORGIUS III DEI GRATIA REX. **Rev:** Clasped hands above lion standing left **Rev. Legend:** SIERRA LEONE **Rev. Inscription:** AFRICA **Edge:** Plain

Date	Mintage	F	VF	XF	Unc	BU
1808 (2007) Proof	500	—	—	—	—	—

X# M6c 2 DOLLARS
Pewter, 40.97 mm. **Obv:** Laureate bust right **Obv. Legend:** GEORGIUS III DEI GRATIA REX. **Rev:** Clasped hands above lion standing left **Rev. Legend:** SIERRA LEONE **Rev. Inscription:** AFRICA **Edge:** Plain

Date	Mintage	F	VF	XF	Unc	BU
1808 (2007) Proof	500	—	—	—	—	—

X# M6d 2 DOLLARS
Copper Bronzed, 40.97 mm. **Obv:** Laureate bust right **Obv. Legend:** GEORGIUS III DEI GRATIA REX. **Rev:** Clasped hands above lion standing left **Rev. Legend:** SIERRA LEONE **Edge:** Plain

Date	Mintage	F	VF	XF	Unc	BU
1808 (2007) Proof	500	—	—	—	—	—

X# M6e 2 DOLLARS
Nickel-Silver, 40.97 mm. **Obv:** Laureate bust right **Obv. Legend:** GEORGIUS III DEI GRATIA REX. **Rev:** Clasped hands above lion standing left **Rev. Legend:** SIERRA LEONE **Rev. Inscription:** AFRICA **Edge:** Plain

Date	Mintage	F	VF	XF	Unc	BU
1808 (2007) Proof	500	—	—	—	—	—

X# M6f 2 DOLLARS
Goldine, 40.97 mm. **Obv:** Laureate bust right **Obv. Legend:** GEORGIUS III DEI GRATIA REX. **Rev:** Clasped hands above lion standing left **Rev. Legend:** SIERRA LEONE **Rev. Inscription:** AFRICA **Edge:** Plain

Date	Mintage	F	VF	XF	Unc	BU
1808 (2007) Proof	500	—	—	—	—	—

X# M6g 2 DOLLARS
Gold, 40.97 mm. **Obv:** Laureate bust right **Obv. Legend:** GEORGIUS III DEI GRATIA REX. **Rev:** Clasped hands above lion standing left **Rev. Legend:** SIERRA LEONE **Rev. Inscription:** AFRICA **Edge:** Plain

Date	Mintage	F	VF	XF	Unc	BU
1808 (2007) Proof	—	—	—	—	—	—

PIEFORTS

X#	Date	Mintage	Identification	Mkt Val
P1	1936	—	Crown. 0.9167 Silver. X#M1b.	100

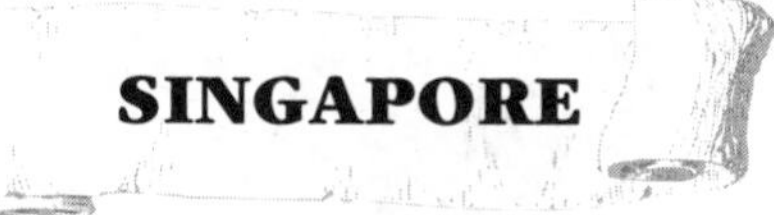

REPUBLIC

MEDALLIC SILVER BULLION COINAGE

X# MBA2 OUNCE
31.1341 g., 0.9990 Silver 0.9999 oz. ASW, 38.7 mm. **Series:** Chinese Lunar Year **Subject:** Year of the Rat **Obv:** Four Chinese characters - "Happiness, heavens, life, knowing and being aware" **Obv. Legend:** REPUBLIC OF SINGAPORE **Rev:** Rat left **Edge:** Reeded

Date	Mintage	F	VF	XF	Unc	BU
1984sm Proof	—	Value: 30.00				

X# MBA6 OUNCE
31.1341 g., 0.9990 Silver 0.9999 oz. ASW, 38.7 mm. **Series:** Chinese Lunar Year **Subject:** Year of the Ox **Obv:** Four Chinese characters - "Success through industry" **Obv. Legend:** REPUBLIC OF SINGAPORE **Rev:** Child riding ox right **Edge:** Reeded

Date	Mintage	F	VF	XF	Unc	BU
1985sm Proof	20,000	Value: 30.00				

X# MB11 OUNCE
31.1341 g., 0.9990 Silver 0.9999 oz. ASW, 38.7 mm. **Series:** Double Dragon **Obv:** Keying Junk **Obv. Legend:** REPUBLIC OF SINGAPORE **Rev:** Two facing dragons **Edge:** Reeded

Date	Mintage	F	VF	XF	Unc	BU
1985sm Proof	2,000	Value: 32.50				

X# MB13 OUNCE
31.1341 g., 0.9990 Silver 0.9999 oz. ASW, 38.7 mm. **Series:** Chinese Lunar Year **Subject:** Year of the Tiger **Obv:** Four Chinese characters - "Awe-inspiring power and might" **Obv. Legend:** REPUBLIC OF SINGAPORE **Rev:** Tiger prowling **Edge:** Reeded

Date	Mintage	F	VF	XF	Unc	BU
1986sm Proof	10,000	Value: 35.00				

X# MB21 OUNCE
31.1341 g., 0.9990 Silver 0.9999 oz. ASW, 38.7 mm. **Subject:** Return of Halley's Comet **Obv:** Comet in space **Obv. Legend:** REPUBLIC OF SINGAPORE **Rev:** Lion standing left under fan **Edge:** Reeded

Date	Mintage	F	VF	XF	Unc	BU
1986sm Proof	2,000	Value: 27.50				

X# MB23 OUNCE
31.1341 g., 0.9990 Silver 0.9999 oz. ASW, 38.7 mm. **Series:** Double Dragon **Subject:** Century of Singapore-Malaysia Railroad **Obv:** Steam locomotive crossing bridge **Obv. Legend:** REPUBLIC OF SINGAPORE **Rev:** Two facing dragons **Edge:** Reeded

Date	Mintage	F	VF	XF	Unc	BU
1986sm Proof	1,500	Value: 35.00				

X# MB25 OUNCE
31.1341 g., 0.9990 Silver 0.9999 oz. ASW, 38.7 mm. **Series:** Chinese Lunar Year **Subject:** Year of the Rabbit **Obv:** Four Chinese characters - "Amiable countenance" **Obv. Legend:** REPUBLIC OF SINGAPORE **Rev:** Rabbit hopping 3/4 right **Edge:** Reeded

Date	Mintage	F	VF	XF	Unc	BU
1987sm Proof	20,000	Value: 22.50				

X# MB45 OUNCE
31.1341 g., 0.9990 Silver 0.9999 oz. ASW, 38.7 mm. **Series:** Double Dragons **Subject:** First Aeroplane Flight in Singapore **Obv:** Antique aeroplane in flight **Obv. Legend:** REPUBLIC OF SINGAPORE **Rev:** Two facing dragons **Edge:** Reeded

Date	Mintage	F	VF	XF	Unc	BU
1987sm Proof	1,500	Value: 30.00				

X# MB34 OUNCE
31.1341 g., 0.9990 Silver 0.9999 oz. ASW, 38.7 mm. **Series:** Chinese Lunar Year **Subject:** Year of the Dragon **Obv:** Four Chinese characters - "Success and prosperity" **Obv. Legend:** REPUBLIC OF SINGAPORE **Rev:** Flying dragon **Edge:** Reeded

Date	Mintage	F	VF	XF	Unc	BU
1988sm Proof	10,000	Value: 28.00				

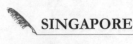

X# MB48 OUNCE
31.1341 g., 0.9990 Silver 0.9999 oz. ASW, 38.7 mm. **Series:** Chinese Lunar Year **Subject:** Year of the Snake **Obv:** Four Chinese characters - "Grace, wisdom and sprite" **Obv. Legend:** REPUBLIC OF SINGAPORE **Rev:** Snake poised upright behind lady **Edge:** Reeded

Date	Mintage	F	VF	XF	Unc	BU
1989sm Proof	2,500	Value: 35.00				

X# MB55 OUNCE
31.1030 g., 0.9250 Silver 0.9249 oz. ASW, 38.7 mm. **Series:** Chinese Lunar Year **Subject:** Year of the Horse **Obv:** Four Chinese characters - "Reward and success" **Obv. Legend:** REPUBLIC OF SINGAPORE **Rev:** Two horses at water's edge **Edge:** Reeded

Date	Mintage	F	VF	XF	Unc	BU
1990sm Proof	5,000	Value: 25.00				

X# MB67 OUNCE
31.1341 g., 0.9990 Silver 0.9999 oz. ASW, 38.7 mm. **Series:** Chinese Lunar Year **Subject:** Year of the Goat **Obv:** Four Chinese characters - "The sun, it's peace and warmth during spring" **Obv. Legend:** REPUBLIC OF SINGAPORE **Rev:** Goat with kid **Edge:** Reeded

Date	Mintage	F	VF	XF	Unc	BU
1991sm Proof	5,000	Value: 22.50				

X# MB80 OUNCE
31.1030 g., 0.9250 Silver 0.9249 oz. ASW, 38.7 mm. **Series:** Chinese Lunar Year **Subject:** Year of the Monkey **Obv:** Four Chinese characters - "Intelligent, enthusiastic and witty" **Obv. Legend:** REPUBLIC OF SINGAPORE **Rev:** Golden Hair monkey left perched on branch **Edge:** Reeded

Date	Mintage	F	VF	XF	Unc	BU
1992sm Proof	5,000	Value: 22.50				

X# MB91 OUNCE
31.1030 g., 0.9250 Silver 0.9249 oz. ASW, 38.7 mm. **Series:** Chinese Lunar Year **Subject:** Year of the Rooster **Obv:** Four Chinese characters - "Confidence and bravity" **Obv. Legend:** REPUBLIC OF SINGAPORE **Rev:** Rooster right standing on one leg facing left **Edge:** Reeded

Date	Mintage	F	VF	XF	Unc	BU
1993sm Proof	3,800	Value: 28.00				

X# MB101 OUNCE
31.1030 g., 0.9250 Silver 0.9249 oz. ASW, 38.7 mm. **Series:** Chinese Lunar Year **Subject:** Year of the Dog **Obv:** Four Chinese characters - "Loyalty, comradeship, strength and faithfulness" **Obv. Legend:** REPUBLIC OF SINGAPORE **Rev:** Two Alsation dogs, laying and sitting **Edge:** Reeded

Date	Mintage	F	VF	XF	Unc	BU
1994sm Proof	3,800	Value: 28.00				

X# MB112 OUNCE
31.1030 g., 0.9250 Silver 0.9249 oz. ASW, 38.7 mm. **Series:** Chinese Lunar Year **Subject:** Year of the Boar **Obv:** Four Chinese characters - "Boundless prosperity and happiness" **Obv. Legend:** REPUBLIC OF SINGAPORE **Rev:** Sow and two piglets **Rev. Designer:** Artist James Koh **Edge:** Reeded

Date	Mintage	F	VF	XF	Unc	BU
1995sm Proof	1,000	Value: 25.00				

X# MB12 5 OUNCES
155.6706 g., 0.9990 Silver 4.9997 oz. ASW, 65 mm. **Series:** Double Dragon **Obv:** Keying Junk **Obv. Legend:** REPUBLIC OF SINGAPORE **Rev:** Two facing dragons **Edge:** Reeded **Note:** Illustration reduced.

Date	Mintage	F	VF	XF	Unc	BU
1985sm Proof	500	Value: 185				

X# MB14 5 OUNCES
155.6706 g., 0.9990 Silver 4.9997 oz. ASW, 65 mm. **Series:** Chinese Lunar Year **Subject:** Year of the Tiger **Obv:** Four Chinese characters - "Awe-inspiring power and might" **Obv. Legend:** REPUBLIC OF SINGAPORE **Rev:** Tiger prowling **Edge:** Reeded **Note:** Illustration reduced.

Date	Mintage	F	VF	XF	Unc	BU
1986sm Proof	5,500	Value: 75.00				

X# MB22 5 OUNCES
155.6706 g., 0.9990 Silver 4.9997 oz. ASW, 65 mm. **Subject:** Return of Halley's Comet **Obv:** Comet in space **Obv. Legend:** REPUBLIC OF SINGAPORE **Rev:** Lion standing left under fan **Edge:** Reeded **Note:** Illustration reduced.

Date	Mintage	F	VF	XF	Unc	BU
1986sm Proof	1,000	Value: 100				

X# MB24 5 OUNCES
155.6706 g., 0.9990 Silver 4.9997 oz. ASW, 65 mm. **Series:** Double Dragon **Subject:** Century of Singapore-Malaysia Railroad **Obv:** Steam locomotive crossing bridge **Obv. Legend:** REPUBLIC OF SINGAPORE **Rev:** Two facing dragons **Edge:** Reeded **Note:** Illustration reduced.

Date	Mintage	F	VF	XF	Unc	BU
1986sm Proof	650	Value: 120				

X# MBA26 5 OUNCES
155.5150 g., 0.9990 Silver 4.9947 oz. ASW, 65 mm. **Series:** Chinese Lunar Year **Subject:** Year of the Rabbit **Obv:** Four Chinese characters - "Amiable countenance" **Obv. Legend:** REPUBLIC OF SINGAPORE **Rev:** Rabbit hopping 3/4 right **Edge:** Reeded

Date	Mintage	F	VF	XF	Unc	BU
1987sm Proof	5,000	Value: 85.00				

X# MB46 5 OUNCES

155.6706 g., 0.9990 Silver 4.9997 oz. ASW, 65 mm. **Series:** Double Dragons **Subject:** First Aeroplane Flight in Singapore **Obv:** Antique Aeroplane in Flight **Obv. Legend:** REPUBLIC OF SINGAPORE **Rev:** Two facing dragons **Edge:** Reeded

Date	Mintage	F	VF	XF	Unc	BU
1987sm Proof	650	Value: 145				

X# MB35 5 OUNCES

155.6706 g., 0.9990 Silver 4.9997 oz. ASW, 65 mm. **Series:** Chinese Lunar Year **Subject:** Year of the Dragon **Obv:** Four Chinese characters **Obv. Legend:** REPUBLIC OF SINGAPORE **Rev:** Two dragons flying **Edge:** Reeded **Note:** Illustration reduced.

Date	Mintage	F	VF	XF	Unc	BU
1988sm Proof	5,000	Value: 75.00				

X# MBA49 5 OUNCES

155.6707 g., 0.9990 Silver 4.9997 oz. ASW, 65 mm. **Series:** Chinese Lunar Year **Subject:** Year of the Snake **Obv:** Four Chinese characters - "Grace, wisdom and sprite" **Obv. Legend:** REPUBLIC OF SINGAPORE **Rev:** Snake wrapped around lady **Edge:** Reeded

Date	Mintage	F	VF	XF	Unc	BU
1989sm Proof	1,000	Value: 90.00				

X# MBA55 5 OUNCES

155.5150 g., 0.9250 Silver 4.6247 oz. ASW, 65 mm. **Subject:** Singapore International Coin Convention **Obv:** Peaches of Immortality **Obv. Legend:** REPUBLIC OF SINGAPORE **Rev:** Gods of Prosperity, Luck and Longevity **Edge:** Reeded

Date	Mintage	F	VF	XF	Unc	BU
1989sm Proof	500	Value: 100				

X# MBA56 5 OUNCES

155.5150 g., 0.9250 Silver 4.6247 oz. ASW, 65 mm. **Series:** Chinese Lunar Year **Subject:** Year of the Horse **Obv:** Four Chinese characters - "Reward and success" **Obv. Legend:** REPUBLIC OF SINGAPORE **Rev:** Two horses at water's edge **Edge:** Reeded

Date	Mintage	F	VF	XF	Unc	BU
1990sm Proof	1,000	Value: 80.00				

X# MB68 5 OUNCES

155.6707 g., 0.9990 Silver 4.9997 oz. ASW, 65 mm. **Series:** Chinese Lunar Year **Subject:** Year of the Goat **Obv:** Four Chinese characters - "The sun, it's peace and warmth during spring" **Obv. Legend:** REPUBLIC OF SINGAPORE **Rev:** Goat with kid **Edge:** Reeded

Date	Mintage	F	VF	XF	Unc	BU
1991sm Proof	2,000	Value: 70.00				

X# MB75 5 OUNCES

155.1500 g., 0.9250 Silver 4.6139 oz. ASW, 65 mm. **Subject:** Singapore International Coin Convention **Obv:** Eight Chinese characters - "Accomplishment by emulation of the Eight Immortals" **Obv. Legend:** REPUBLIC OF SINGAPORE **Rev:** Eight Immortals, two geese above **Edge:** Reeded

Date	Mintage	F	VF	XF	Unc	BU
1991sm Proof	500	Value: 85.00				

X# MB81 5 OUNCES

155.5150 g., 0.9250 Silver 4.6247 oz. ASW, 65 mm. **Series:** Chinese Lunar Year **Subject:** Year of the Monkey **Obv:** Four Chinese characters - "Intelligent, enthusiastic and witty" **Obv. Legend:** REPUBLIC OF SINGAPORE **Rev:** Golden Hair monkey left perched on branch **Edge:** Reeded

Date	Mintage	F	VF	XF	Unc	BU
1992sm Proof	1,000	Value: 75.00				

X# MB88 5 OUNCES

155.5150 g., 0.9250 Silver 4.6247 oz. ASW, 65 mm. **Subject:** Singapore International Coin Convention **Obv:** Four Chinese characters - "Good wishes to one and all" **Obv. Legend:** REPUBLIC OF SINGAPORE **Rev. Legend:** "Lord Maitreya" **Edge:** Reeded

Date	Mintage	F	VF	XF	Unc	BU
1992sm Proof	500	Value: 85.00				

X# MB92 5 OUNCES

155.5150 g., 0.9250 Silver 4.6247 oz. ASW, 65 mm. **Series:** Chinese Lunar Year **Subject:** Year of the Rooster **Obv:** Four Chinese characters - "Confidence and bravity" **Obv. Legend:** REPUBLIC OF SINGAPORE **Rev:** Rooster right standing on one leg facing left **Edge:** Reeded

Date	Mintage	F	VF	XF	Unc	BU
1993sm Proof	2,000	Value: 70.00				

X# MB99 5 OUNCES

155.5150 g., 0.9250 Silver 4.6247 oz. ASW, 65 mm. **Subject:** Singapore International Coin Convention **Obv:** Archaic Chinese Liu Hai seated, one of the immortals of Taoism within four Chinese characters **Obv. Inscription:** "Wealth entering from all directions" **Rev:** Archaic Chinese Bi Gan, God of Literature and Wealth standing between two children **Edge:** Reeded

Date	Mintage	F	VF	XF	Unc	BU
1993sm Proof	500	Value: 85.00				

X# MB102 5 OUNCES

155.5150 g., 0.9250 Silver 4.6247 oz. ASW, 65 mm. **Series:** Chinese Lunar Year **Subject:** Year of the Dog **Obv:** Four Chinese characters - "Loyalty, comradeship, strength and faithfulness" **Obv. Legend:** REPUBLIC OF SINGAPORE **Rev:** Two Alsation dogs, laying and sitting **Edge:** Reeded

Date	Mintage	F	VF	XF	Unc	BU
1994sm Proof	1,800	Value: 75.00				

X# MB110 5 OUNCES

155.5150 g., 0.9250 Silver 4.6247 oz. ASW, 65 mm. **Subject:** Singapore-Taisei International Coin Convention **Obv:** Facing dragons **Rev:** Archaic Chinese hero Kwan Yu horseback 3/4 right **Edge:** Reeded

Date	Mintage	F	VF	XF	Unc	BU
1994sm Proof	388	Value: 95.00				

X# MB113 5 OUNCES

155.5150 g., 0.9250 Silver 4.6247 oz. ASW, 65 mm. **Series:** Chinese Lunar Year **Subject:** Year of the Boar **Obv:** Four Chinese characters - "Boundless prosperity and happiness" **Obv. Legend:** REPUBLIC OF SINGAPORE **Rev:** Family of five pigs **Rev. Designer:** Artist James Koh **Edge:** Reeded

Date	Mintage	F	VF	XF	Unc	BU
1995sm Proof	1,000	Value: 75.00				

X# MB33 12 OUNCES

373.6092 g., 0.9990 Silver 11.999 oz. ASW **Subject:** Singapore International Coin Convention **Obv:** Orchids at left, Singapore City in background, statue of Sir Stamford Raffles left at right **Obv. Legend:** REPUBLIC OF SINGAPORE **Rev:** Lion head left in center of circular blades **Rev. Legend:** SINGAPORE INTERNATIONAL COIN CONVENTION **Edge:** Reeded

Date	Mintage	F	VF	XF	Unc	BU
1987sm Prooflike	188	—	—	—	—	175

X# MB36 12 OUNCES

373.6092 g., 0.9990 Silver 11.999 oz. ASW **Subject:** Singapore International Coin Convention **Obv:** Archaic Chinese character for "Dragon" **Obv. Legend:** REPUBLIC OF SINGAPORE **Rev:** Pearl between five facing dragons **Edge:** Reeded

Date	Mintage	F	VF	XF	Unc	BU
1988sm Prooflike	1,500	—	—	—	—	125

X# MB89 12 OUNCES

373.6096 g., 0.9990 Silver 11.999 oz. ASW, 65 mm. **Subject:** Singapore International Coin Convention **Obv:** Four Chinese characters - "Good wishes to one and all" **Obv. Legend:** REPUBLIC OF SINGAPORE **Rev. Legend:** "Lord Maitreya" **Edge:** Reeded

Date	Mintage	F	VF	XF	Unc	BU
1992sm Proof	500	Value: 145				

X# MB1 10 SINGOLLAR/OUNCE

31.1341 g., 0.9990 Silver 0.9999 oz. ASW, 38.7 mm. **Subject:** Year of the Rat **Obv:** Four Chinese characters - "Happiness, heavens, life, knowing and being aware" **Obv. Legend:** REPUBLIC OF SINGAPORE **Rev:** Rat left **Edge:** Reeded

Date	Mintage	F	VF	XF	Unc	BU
1984sm Proof	20,000	Value: 27.50				

X# MB6 10 SINGOLLAR/OUNCE
31.1341 g., 0.9990 Silver 0.9999 oz. ASW, 38.7 mm. **Series:** Chinese Lunar Year **Subject:** Year of the Ox **Obv:** Four Chinese characters - "Success through industry" **Obv. Legend:** REPUBLIC OF SINGAPORE **Rev:** Child riding ox right **Edge:** Reeded

Date	Mintage	F	VF	XF	Unc	BU
1985sm Proof	20,000	Value: 27.50				

MEDALLIC GOLD BULLION COINAGE

X# MB90 1/2 OUNCE
15.5670 g., 0.9999 Gold 0.5004 oz. AGW, 27 mm. **Subject:** Singapore International Coin Convention **Obv:** Four Chinese characters - "Good wishes to one and all" **Obv. Legend:** REPUBLIC OF SINGAPORE **Obv. Inscription:** "Good wishes to one and all" **Rev. Legend:** "Lord Maitreya" **Edge:** Reeded

Date	Mintage	F	VF	XF	Unc	BU
1992sm Proof	500	—	—	—	—	BV+20%

X# MB100 1/2 OUNCE
15.5500 g., 0.9999 Gold 0.4999 oz. AGW, 27 mm. **Subject:** Singapore International Coin Convention **Obv:** Archaic Chinese Liu Hai seated, one of the immortals of Taoism, within four Chinese characters **Obv. Inscription:** "Wealth entering from all directions" **Rev:** Archaic Chinese Bi Gan, God of Literature and Wealth standing between two children **Edge:** Reeded

Date	Mintage	F	VF	XF	Unc	BU
1993sm Proof	500	—	—	—	—	BV+20%

X# MB111 1/2 OUNCE
15.5500 g., 0.9999 Gold 0.4999 oz. AGW, 28.5 mm. **Subject:** Singapore-Taisei International Coin Convention **Obv:** Facing dragons **Rev:** Archaic Chinese hero Kwan Yu horseback 3/4 right **Edge:** Reeded

Date	Mintage	F	VF	XF	Unc	BU
1994sm Proof	288	—	—	—	—	BV+25%

X# MB47 OUNCE
31.1106 g., 0.9999 Gold 1.0000 oz. AGW, 32.1 mm. **Subject:** National Coin Fair **Obv:** Archaic Chinese character -"Dragon" **Obv. Legend:** REPUBLIC OF SINGAPORE **Rev:** Pearl between two facing dragons **Edge:** Reeded

Date	Mintage	F	VF	XF	Unc	BU
1988sm Proof	500	—	—	—	—	BV+15%

X# MBB55 OUNCE
31.1100 g., 0.9999 Gold 1.0000 oz. AGW, 32.05 mm. **Subject:** Singapore International Coin Convention **Obv:** Peaches of Immortality **Obv. Legend:** REPUBLIC OF SINGAPORE **Rev:** Gods of Prosperity, Luck and Longevity **Edge:** Reeded

Date	Mintage	F	VF	XF	Unc	BU
1989sm Proof	250	—	—	—	—	BV+20%

X# MB27 5 SINGOLD
1.5553 g., 0.9999 Gold 0.0500 oz. AGW, 13.92 mm. **Series:** Chinese Lunar Year **Subject:** Year of the Rabbit **Obv:** Four Chinese characters - "Amiable countenance" **Obv. Legend:** REPUBLIC OF SINGAPORE **Rev:** Rabbit hopping 3/4 right **Edge:** Reeded

Date	Mintage	F	VF	XF	Unc	BU
1987sm	8,000	—	—	—	—	BV+25%
1987sm proof	1,000	—	—	—	—	BV+30%

X# MB37 5 SINGOLD
1.5553 g., 0.9999 Gold 0.0500 oz. AGW, 13.92 mm. **Series:** Chinese Lunar Year **Subject:** Year of the Dragon **Obv:** Four Chinese characters - "Goodwill, success and prosperity" **Obv. Legend:** REPUBLIC OF SINGAPORE **Rev:** Flying dragon facing left **Edge:** Reeded

Date	Mintage	F	VF	XF	Unc	BU
1988sm	10,000	—	—	—	—	BV+25%
1988sm Proof	500	—	—	—	—	BV+30%

X# MB28 10 SINGOLD
3.1106 g., 0.9999 Gold 0.1000 oz. AGW, 17.92 mm. **Series:** Chinese Lunar Year **Subject:** Year of the Rabbit **Obv:** Four Chinese characters - "Amiable countenance" **Obv. Legend:** REPUBLIC OF SINGAPORE **Rev:** Rabbit hopping 3/4 right **Edge:** Reeded

Date	Mintage	F	VF	XF	Unc	BU
1987sm	8,000	—	—	—	—	BV+20%
1987sm Proof	1,000	—	—	—	—	BV+25%

X# MB38 10 SINGOLD
3.1106 g., 0.9999 Gold 0.1000 oz. AGW, 17.95 mm. **Series:** Chinese Lunar Year **Subject:** Year of the Dragon **Obv:** Four Chinese characters - "Goodwill, success and prosperity" **Obv. Legend:** REPUBLIC OF SINGAPORE **Rev:** Flying dragon facing left **Edge:** Reeded

Date	Mintage	F	VF	XF	Unc	BU
1988sm	10,000	—	—	—	—	BV+20%
1988sm Proof	500	—	—	—	—	BV+25%

X# MB29 25 SINGOLD
7.7765 g., 0.9999 Gold 0.2500 oz. AGW, 21.95 mm. **Series:** Chinese Lunar Year **Subject:** Year of the Rabbit **Obv:** Four Chinese characters - "Amiable countenance" **Obv. Legend:** REPUBLIC OF SINGAPORE **Rev:** Rabbit hopping 3/4 right **Edge:** Reeded

Date	Mintage	F	VF	XF	Unc	BU
1987sm	8,000	—	—	—	—	BV+20%
1987sm Proof	1,000	—	—	—	—	BV+25%

X# MB39 25 SINGOLD
7.7765 g., 0.9990 Gold 0.2498 oz. AGW, 21.95 mm. **Series:** Chinese Lunar Year **Subject:** Year of the Dragon **Obv:** Four Chinese characters - "Goodwill, success and prosperity" **Obv. Legend:** REPUBLIC OF SINGAPORE **Rev:** Flying dragon facing left **Edge:** Reeded

Date	Mintage	F	VF	XF	Unc	BU
1988sm	10,000	—	—	—	—	BV+20%
1988sm Proof	500	—	—	—	—	BV+25%

X# MB30 50 SINGOLD
15.5530 g., 0.9999 Gold 0.5000 oz. AGW, 27 mm. **Series:** Chinese Lunar Year **Subject:** Year of the Rabbit **Obv:** Four Chinese characters - "Amiable countenance" **Obv. Legend:** REPUBLIC OF SINGAPORE **Rev:** Rabbit hopping 3/4 right **Edge:** Reeded

Date	Mintage	F	VF	XF	Unc	BU
1987sm	8,000	—	—	—	—	BV+15%
1987sm Proof	1,000	—	—	—	—	BV+20%

X# MB40 50 SINGOLD
15.5530 g., 0.9999 Gold 0.5000 oz. AGW, 27 mm. **Series:** Chinese Lunar Year **Subject:** Year of the Dragon **Obv:** Four Chinese characters - "Goodwill, success and prosperity" **Obv. Legend:** REPUBLIC OF SINGAPORE **Rev:** Flying dragon facing left **Edge:** Reeded

Date	Mintage	F	VF	XF	Unc	BU
1988sm	10,000	—	—	—	—	BV+15%
1988sm Proof	500	—	—	—	—	BV+20%

X# MB31 100 SINGOLD
31.1061 g., 0.9999 Gold 0.9999 oz. AGW, 32.1 mm. **Series:** Chinese Lunar Year **Subject:** Year of the Rabbit **Obv:** Four Chinese characters - "Amiable countenance" **Obv. Legend:** REPUBLIC OF SINGAPORE **Rev:** Rabbit hopping 3/4 right **Edge:** Reeded

Date	Mintage	F	VF	XF	Unc	BU
1987sm	10,000	—	—	—	—	BV+15%
1987sm Proof	1,000	—	—	—	—	BV+20%

X# MB41 100 SINGOLD
31.1061 g., 0.9990 Gold 0.9990 oz. AGW, 32.1 mm. **Series:** Chinese Lunar Year **Subject:** Year of the Dragon **Obv:** Four Chinese characters - "Goodwill, success and prosperity" **Obv. Legend:** REPUBLIC OF SINGAPORE **Rev:** Flying dragon facing left **Edge:** Reeded

Date	Mintage	F	VF	XF	Unc	BU
1988sm	15,000	—	—	—	—	BV+15%
1988sm Proof	1,000	—	—	—	—	BV+20%

X# MB42 (500) SINGOLD/5 OUNCES
155.5306 g., 0.9999 Gold 4.9997 oz. AGW
Series: Chinese Lunar Year **Subject:** Year of the Dragon **Obv:** Four Chinese characters - "Goodwill, success and prosperity" **Obv. Legend:** REPUBLIC OF SINGAPORE **Rev:** Pearl between two facing dragons **Edge:** Reeded

Date	Mintage	F	VF	XF	Unc	BU
1988sm Proof	500	—	—	—	—	BV+20%

X# MB20 (1200) SINGOLD/12 OUNCES
373.2733 g., 0.9999 Gold 11.999 oz. AGW, 65 mm.
Series: Chinese Lunar Year **Subject:** Year of the Tiger **Obv:** Four Chinese characters - "Awe-inspiring power and might" **Obv. Legend:** REPUBLIC OF SINGAPORE **Rev:** Tiger prowling **Edge:** Reeded

Date	Mintage	F	VF	XF	Unc	BU
1986sm Proof	250	—	—	—	—	BV+20%

X# MB32 (1200) SINGOLD/12 OUNCES
373.2733 g., 0.9999 Gold 11.999 oz. AGW, 76 mm.
Series: Chinese Lunar Year **Subject:** Year of the Rabbit **Obv:** Four Chinese characters - "Amiable countenance" **Obv. Legend:** REPUBLIC OF SINGAPORE **Rev:** Rabbit hopping 3/4 right **Edge:** Reeded **Note:** Illustration reduced.

Date	Mintage	F	VF	XF	Unc	BU
1987sm Proof	250	—	—	—	—	BV+20%

X# MB43 (1200) SINGOLD/12 OUNCES
373.2733 g., 0.9999 Gold 11.999 oz. AGW, 65 mm.
Series: Chinese Lunar Year **Subject:** Year of the Dragon **Obv:** Four Chinese characters - "Goodwill, success and prosperity" **Obv. Legend:** REPUBLIC OF SINGAPORE **Rev:** Pearl between five facing dragons **Edge:** Reeded **Note:** Illustration reduced.

Date	Mintage	F	VF	XF	Unc	BU
1988sm Proof	200	—	—	—	—	BV+20%

X# MB54 (1200) SINGOLD/12 OUNCES
373.2733 g., 0.9999 Gold 11.999 oz. AGW, 65 mm.
Series: Chinese Lunar Year **Subject:** Year of the Snake **Obv:** Four Chinese characters - "Grace, wisdom and sprite" **Obv. Legend:** REPUBLIC OF SINGAPORE **Rev:** Snake wrapped around lady **Edge:** Reeded

Date	Mintage	F	VF	XF	Unc	BU
1989sm Proof	50	—	—	—	—	BV+30%

X# MB61 (1200) SINGOLD/12 OUNCES
373.2733 g., 0.9999 Gold 11.999 oz. AGW, 65 mm.
Series: Chinese Lunar Year **Subject:** Year of the Horse **Obv:** Four Chinese characters - "Reward and success" **Obv. Legend:** REPUBLIC OF SINGAPORE **Rev:** Two horses at water's edge **Edge:** Reeded

Date	Mintage	F	VF	XF	Unc	BU
1990sm Proof	50	—	—	—	—	BV+30%

X# MB74 (1200) SINGOLD/12 OUNCES
373.2733 g., 0.9999 Gold 11.999 oz. AGW, 65 mm.
Series: Chinese Lunar Year **Subject:** Year of the Goat **Obv:** Four Chinese characters - "The sun, it's peace and warmth during spring" **Obv. Legend:** REPUBLIC OF SINGAPORE **Rev:** Goat standing 3/4 right **Edge:** Reeded

Date	Mintage	F	VF	XF	Unc	BU
1991sm Proof	50	—	—	—	—	BV+30%

X# MB87 (1200) SINGOLD/12 OUNCES
373.2733 g., 0.9999 Gold 11.999 oz. AGW, 65 mm.
Series: Chinese Lunar Year **Subject:** Year of the Monkey **Obv:** Four Chinese characters - "Intelligent, enthusiastic and witty" **Obv. Legend:** REPUBLIC OF SINGAPORE **Rev:** Two Golden Hair monkeys perched on branch **Edge:** Reeded

Date	Mintage	F	VF	XF	Unc	BU
1992sm Proof	50	—	—	—	—	BV+30%

X# MB98 (1200) SINGOLD/12 OUNCES
373.2733 g., 0.9999 Gold 11.999 oz. AGW
Series: Chinese Lunar Year **Subject:** Year of the Rooster **Obv:** Four Chinese characters - "Confidence and bravity" **Obv. Legend:** REPUBLIC OF SINGAPORE **Rev:** Rooster right standing on one leg facing left **Edge:** Reeded

Date	Mintage	F	VF	XF	Unc	BU
1993sm Proof	50	—	—	—	—	BV+30%

X# MB108 (1200) SINGOLD/12 OUNCES
373.2733 g., 0.9999 Gold 11.999 oz. AGW, 65 mm.
Series: Chinese Lunar Year **Subject:** Year of the Dog **Obv:** Four Chinese characters - "Loyalty, comradeship, strength and faithfulness" **Obv. Legend:** REPUBLIC OF SINGAPORE **Rev:** Dog left under peach tree **Rev. Designer:** Artist Lang Shihnung **Edge:** Reeded

Date	Mintage	F	VF	XF	Unc	BU
1994sm Proof	50	—	—	—	—	BV+30%

X# MB119 (1200) SINGOLD/12 OUNCES
373.2733 g., 0.9999 Gold 11.999 oz. AGW, 65 mm.
Series: Chinese Lunar Year **Subject:** Year of the Boar **Obv:** Four Chinese characters - "Boundless prosperity and happiness" **Obv. Legend:** REPUBLIC OF SINGAPORE **Edge:** Reeded

Date	Mintage	F	VF	XF	Unc	BU
1995sm Proof	50	—	—	—	—	BV+30%

X# MB2 5 SINGOLD (1/20 Ounce)
1.5553 g., 0.9990 Gold 0.0500 oz. AGW, 13.92 mm.
Series: Chinese Lunar Year **Subject:** Year of the Rat **Obv:** Chinese character - "Life" **Obv. Legend:** REPUBLIC OF SINGAPORE **Rev:** Rat left **Edge:** Reeded

Date	Mintage	F	VF	XF	Unc	BU
1984sm	5,000	—	—	—	—	BV+20%

X# MB7 5 SINGOLD (1/20 Ounce)
1.5553 g., 0.9999 Gold 0.0500 oz. AGW, 13.92 mm.
Series: Chinese Lunar Year **Subject:** Year of the Ox
Obv: Four Chinese characters - "Success through industry" **Obv. Legend:** REPUBLIC OF SINGAPORE
Rev: Child riding ox right **Edge:** Reeded

Date	Mintage	F	VF	XF	Unc	BU
1985sm	5,000	—	—	—	—	BV+20%

X# MB15 5 SINGOLD (1/20 Ounce)
1.5553 g., 0.9999 Gold 0.0500 oz. AGW, 13.92 mm.
Series: Chinese Lunar Year **Subject:** Year of the Tiger
Obv: Four Chinese characters - "Awe-inspiring power and might **Obv. Legend:** REPUBLIC OF SINGAPORE
Rev: Tiger prowling **Edge:** Reeded

Date	Mintage	F	VF	XF	Unc	BU
1986sm	20,000	—	—	—	—	BV+20%

X# MB49 5 SINGOLD (1/20 Ounce)
1.5553 g., 0.9999 Gold 0.0500 oz. AGW, 13.92 mm.
Series: Chinese Lunar Year **Subject:** Year of the Snake
Obv: Four Chinese characters - "Grace, wisdom and sprite" **Obv. Legend:** REPUBLIC OF SINGAPORE
Rev: Snake poised upright behind lady **Edge:** Reeded

Date	Mintage	F	VF	XF	Unc	BU
1989sm	5,000	—	—	—	—	BV+20%
1989sm Proof	200	—	—	—	—	BV+30%

X# MB52 5 SINGOLD (1/20 Ounce)
15.5530 g., 0.9999 Gold 0.5000 oz. AGW, 27 mm.
Series: Chinese Lunar Year **Subject:** Year of the Snake
Obv: Four Chinese characters - "Grace, wisdom and sprite" **Obv. Legend:** REPUBLIC OF SINGAPORE
Rev: Snake poised upright behind lady **Edge:** Reeded

Date	Mintage	F	VF	XF	Unc	BU
1989sm	2,500	—	—	—	—	BV+20%
1989sm Proof	200	—	—	—	—	BV+30%

X# MB56 5 SINGOLD (1/20 Ounce)
1.5553 g., 0.9999 Gold 0.0500 oz. AGW, 13.92 mm.
Series: Chinese Lunar Year **Subject:** Year of the Horse
Obv: Four Chinese characters - "Reward and success"
Obv. Legend: REPUBLIC OF SINGAPORE
Rev: Horse rearing left **Edge:** Reeded

Date	Mintage	F	VF	XF	Unc	BU
1990sm	30,000	—	—	—	—	BV+20%
1990sm Proof	200	—	—	—	—	BV+30%

X# MB59 5 SINGOLD (1/20 Ounce)
15.5530 g., 0.9999 Gold 0.5000 oz. AGW, 27 mm.
Series: Chinese Lunar Year **Subject:** Year of the Horse
Obv: Four Chinese characters - "Reward and success"
Obv. Legend: REPUBLIC OF SINGAPORE
Rev: Horse rearing left **Edge:** Reeded

Date	Mintage	F	VF	XF	Unc	BU
1990sm	5,000	—	—	—	—	BV+20%
1990sm Proof	200	—	—	—	—	BV+30%

X# MB69 5 SINGOLD (1/20 Ounce)
1.5553 g., 0.9999 Gold 0.0500 oz. AGW, 13.92 mm.
Series: Chinese Lunar Year **Subject:** Year of the Goat
Obv: Four Chinese characters - "The sun, it's peace and warmth during spring" **Obv. Legend:** REPUBLIC OF SINGAPORE **Rev:** Goat standing 3/4 right **Edge:** Reeded

Date	Mintage	F	VF	XF	Unc	BU
1991sm	30,000	—	—	—	—	BV+20%
1991sm Proof	250	—	—	—	—	BV+30%

X# MB82 5 SINGOLD (1/20 Ounce)
1.5553 g., 0.9999 Gold 0.0500 oz. AGW, 13.92 mm.
Series: Chinese Lunar Year **Subject:** Year of the Monkey **Obv:** Four Chinese characters - "Intelligent, enthusiastic and witty" **Obv. Legend:** REPUBLIC OF SINGAPORE **Rev:** Golden Hair monkey left perched on branch **Edge:** Reeded

Date	Mintage	F	VF	XF	Unc	BU
1992sm	30,000	—	—	—	—	BV+20%
1992sm Proof	250	—	—	—	—	BV+30%

X# MB93 5 SINGOLD (1/20 Ounce)
1.5553 g., 0.9999 Gold 0.0500 oz. AGW, 13.92 mm.
Series: Chinese Lunar Year **Subject:** Year of the Rooster
Obv: Four Chinese characters - "Confidence and bravity"
Obv. Legend: REPUBLIC OF SINGAPORE **Rev:** Rooster right standing on one leg facing left **Edge:** Reeded

Date	Mintage	F	VF	XF	Unc	BU
1993sm	15,000	—	—	—	—	BV+20%
1993sm Proof	500	—	—	—	—	BV+30%

X# MB103 5 SINGOLD (1/20 Ounce)
1.5553 g., 0.9999 Gold 0.0500 oz. AGW, 13.92 mm.
Series: Chinese Lunar Year **Subject:** Year of the Dog
Obv: Four Chinese characters - "Loyalty, comradeship, strength and faithfulness" **Obv. Legend:** REPUBLIC OF SINGAPORE **Rev:** Dog left under peach tree
Rev. Designer: Artist Lang Shihning **Edge:** Reeded

Date	Mintage	F	VF	XF	Unc	BU
1994sm	15,000	—	—	—	—	BV+20%
1994sm Proof	500	—	—	—	—	BV+30%

X# MB106 5 SINGOLD (1/20 Ounce)
1.5553 g., 0.9999 Gold 0.0500 oz. AGW, 27 mm.
Series: Chinese Lunar Year **Subject:** Year of the Dog
Obv: Four Chinese characters - "Loyalty, comradeship, strength and faithfulness" **Obv. Legend:** REPUBLIC OF SINGAPORE **Rev:** Dog left under peach tree
Rev. Designer: Artist Lang Shihning **Edge:** Reeded

Date	Mintage	F	VF	XF	Unc	BU
1994sm	3,000	—	—	—	—	BV+20%
1994sm Proof	500	—	—	—	—	BV+30%

X# MB114 5 SINGOLD (1/20 Ounce)
1.5553 g., 0.9999 Gold 0.0500 oz. AGW, 13.92 mm.
Series: Chinese Lunar Year **Subject:** Year of the Boar
Obv: Four Chinese characters - "Boundless prosperity and happiness" **Obv. Legend:** REPUBLIC OF SINGAPORE **Rev:** Sow and two piglets
Rev. Designer: Artist James Koh **Edge:** Reeded

Date	Mintage	F	VF	XF	Unc	BU
1995sm	15,000	—	—	—	—	BV+20%
1995sm Proof	500	—	—	—	—	BV+30%

X# MB3 10 SINGOLD (1/10 Ounce)
3.1106 g., 0.9999 Gold 0.1000 oz. AGW, 17.95 mm.
Series: Chinese Lunar Year **Subject:** Year of the Rat
Obv: Chinese character - "Knowing and being aware"
Obv. Legend: REPUBLIC OF SINGAPORE **Rev:** Rat left **Edge:** Reeded

Date	Mintage	F	VF	XF	Unc	BU
1984sm	5,000	—	—	—	—	BV+15%

X# MB8 10 SINGOLD (1/10 Ounce)
3.1106 g., 0.9999 Gold 0.1000 oz. AGW, 17.95 mm.
Series: Chinese Lunar Year **Subject:** Year of the Ox
Obv: Four Chinese characters - "Success through industry" **Obv. Legend:** REPUBLIC OF SINGAPORE
Rev: Child riding ox right **Edge:** Reeded

Date	Mintage	F	VF	XF	Unc	BU
1985sm	5,000	—	—	—	—	BV+15%

X# MB16 10 SINGOLD (1/10 Ounce)
3.1106 g., 0.9999 Gold 0.1000 oz. AGW, 17.95 mm.
Series: Chinese Lunar Year **Subject:** Year of the Tiger
Obv: Four Chinese characters - "Awe-inspiring power and might **Obv. Legend:** REPUBLIC OF SINGAPORE
Rev: Tiger prowling **Edge:** Reeded

Date	Mintage	F	VF	XF	Unc	BU
1986sm	—	—	—	—	—	BV+15%

X# MB50 10 SINGOLD (1/10 Ounce)
3.1106 g., 0.9999 Gold 0.1000 oz. AGW, 17.95 mm.
Series: Chinese Lunar Year **Subject:** Year of the Snake
Obv: Four Chinese characters - "Grace, wisdom and sprite" **Obv. Legend:** REPUBLIC OF SINGAPORE
Rev: Snake poised upright behind lady **Edge:** Reeded

Date	Mintage	F	VF	XF	Unc	BU
1989sm	5,000	—	—	—	—	BV+15%
1989smProof	200	—	—	—	—	BV+25%

X# MB57 10 SINGOLD (1/10 Ounce)
3.1106 g., 0.9999 Gold 0.1000 oz. AGW, 17.95 mm.
Series: Chinese Lunar Year **Subject:** Year of the Horse
Obv: Four Chinese characters - "Reward and success"
Obv. Legend: REPUBLIC OF SINGAPORE
Rev: Horse rearing left **Edge:** Reeded

Date	Mintage	F	VF	XF	Unc	BU
1990sm	15,000	—	—	—	—	BV+15%
1990sm Proof	200	—	—	—	—	BV+25%

X# MB70 10 SINGOLD (1/10 Ounce)
3.1106 g., 0.9999 Gold 0.1000 oz. AGW, 17.95 mm.
Series: Chinese Lunar Year **Subject:** Year of the Goat
Obv: Four Chinese characters - "The sun, it's peace and warmth during spring" **Obv. Legend:** REPUBLIC OF SINGAPORE **Rev:** Goat standing 3/4 right **Edge:** Reeded

Date	Mintage	F	VF	XF	Unc	BU
1991sm	15,000	—	—	—	—	BV+15%
1991sm Proof	250	—	—	—	—	BV+25%

X# MB83 10 SINGOLD (1/10 Ounce)
3.1106 g., 0.9999 Gold 0.1000 oz. AGW, 17.95 mm.
Series: Chinese Lunar Year **Subject:** Year of the Monkey **Obv:** Four Chinese characters - "Intelligent, enthusiastic and witty" **Obv. Legend:** REPUBLIC OF SINGAPORE **Rev:** Golden Hair monkey perched on branch **Edge:** Reeded

Date	Mintage	F	VF	XF	Unc	BU
1992sm	15,000	—	—	—	—	BV+15%
1992sm Proof	250	—	—	—	—	BV+25%

X# MB94 10 SINGOLD (1/10 Ounce)
3.1106 g., 0.9999 Gold 0.1000 oz. AGW, 17.95 mm.
Series: Chinese Lunar Year **Subject:** Year of the Rooster **Obv:** Four Chinese characters - "Confidence and bravity" **Obv. Legend:** REPUBLIC OF SINGAPORE **Rev:** Rooster right standing on one leg facing left **Edge:** Reeded

Date	Mintage	F	VF	XF	Unc	BU
1993sm	10,000	—	—	—	—	BV+15%
1993sm Proof	500	—	—	—	—	BV+25%

X# MB104 10 SINGOLD (1/10 Ounce)
3.1106 g., 0.9999 Gold 0.1000 oz. AGW, 17.95 mm.
Series: Chinese Lunar Year **Subject:** Year of the Dog
Obv: Four Chinese characters - "Loyalty, comradeship, strength and faithfulness" **Obv. Legend:** REPUBLIC OF SINGAPORE **Rev:** Dog left under peach tree **Rev. Designer:** Artist Lang Shihning **Edge:** Reeded

Date	Mintage	F	VF	XF	Unc	BU
1994sm	10,000	—	—	—	—	BV+15%
1994sm Proof	500	—	—	—	—	BV+25%

X# MB115 10 SINGOLD (1/10 Ounce)
3.1106 g., 0.9999 Gold 0.1000 oz. AGW, 17.95 mm.
Series: Chinese Lunar Year **Subject:** Year of the Boar
Obv: Four Chinese characters - "Boundless prosperity and happiness" **Obv. Legend:** REPUBLIC OF SINGAPORE **Rev:** Sow and two piglets
Rev. Designer: Artist James Koh **Edge:** Reeded

Date	Mintage	F	VF	XF	Unc	BU
1995sm	10,000	—	—	—	—	BV+15%
1995sm Proof	500	—	—	—	—	BV+25%

X# MB4 25 SINGOLD (1/4 Ounce)
7.7765 g., 0.9999 Gold 0.2500 oz. AGW, 21.95 mm.
Series: Chinese Lunar Year **Subject:** Year of the Rat
Obv: Chinese character - "Heavens" **Obv. Legend:** REPUBLIC OF SINGAPORE **Rev:** Rat left **Edge:** Reeded

Date	Mintage	F	VF	XF	Unc	BU
1984sm	2,500	—	—	—	—	BV+15%

X# MB9 25 SINGOLD (1/4 Ounce)
7.7765 g., 0.9999 Gold 0.2500 oz. AGW, 21.95 mm. **Series:** Chinese Lunar Year **Subject:** Year of the Ox **Obv:** Four Chinese characters - "Success through industry" **Obv. Legend:** REPUBLIC OF SINGAPORE **Rev:** Child riding ox right **Edge:** Reeded

Date	Mintage	F	VF	XF	Unc	BU
1985sm	2,500	—	—	—	—	BV+15%

X# MB17 25 SINGOLD (1/4 Ounce)
7.7765 g., 0.9999 Gold 0.2500 oz. AGW, 21.95 mm. **Series:** Chinese Lunar Year **Subject:** Year of the Tiger **Obv:** Four Chinese characters - "Awe-inspiring power and might" **Obv. Legend:** REPUBLIC OF SINGAPORE **Rev:** Tiger prowling **Edge:** Reeded

Date	Mintage	F	VF	XF	Unc	BU
1986sm	10,000	—	—	—	—	BV+15%

X# MB51 25 SINGOLD (1/4 Ounce)
7.7765 g., 0.9999 Gold 0.2500 oz. AGW, 21.95 mm. **Series:** Chinese Lunar Year **Subject:** Year of the Snake **Obv:** Four Chinese characters - "Grace, wisdom and sprite" **Obv. Legend:** REPUBLIC OF SINGAPORE **Rev:** Snake poised upright behind lady **Edge:** Reeded

Date	Mintage	F	VF	XF	Unc	BU
1989sm	2,500	—	—	—	—	BV+15%
1989sm Proof	200	—	—	—	—	BV+25%

X# MB58 25 SINGOLD (1/4 Ounce)
7.7765 g., 0.9999 Gold 0.2500 oz. AGW, 21.95 mm. **Subject:** Year of the Horse **Obv:** Four Chinese characters - "Reward and success" **Obv. Legend:** REPUBLIC OF SINGAPORE **Rev:** Horse rearing left **Edge:** Reeded

Date	Mintage	F	VF	XF	Unc	BU
1990sm	5,000	—	—	—	—	BV+15%
1990sm Proof	200	—	—	—	—	BV+25%

X# MB71 25 SINGOLD (1/4 Ounce)
7.7765 g., 0.9999 Gold 0.2500 oz. AGW, 21.95 mm. **Series:** Chinese Lunar Year **Subject:** Year of the Goat **Obv:** Four Chinese characters - "The sun, it's peace and warmth during spring" **Obv. Legend:** REPUBLIC OF SINGAPORE **Rev:** Goat standing 3/4 right **Edge:** Reeded

Date	Mintage	F	VF	XF	Unc	BU
1991sm	4,000	—	—	—	—	BV+15%
1991sm Proof	250	—	—	—	—	BV+25%

X# MB84 25 SINGOLD (1/4 Ounce)
7.7765 g., 0.9999 Gold 0.2500 oz. AGW, 21.95 mm. **Series:** Chinese Lunar Year **Subject:** Year of the Monkey **Obv:** Four Chinese characters - "Intelligent, enthusiastic and witty" **Obv. Legend:** REPUBLIC OF SINGAPORE **Rev:** Golden Hair monkey perched on branch **Edge:** Reeded

Date	Mintage	F	VF	XF	Unc	BU
1992sm	4,000	—	—	—	—	BV+15%
1992sm Proof	250	—	—	—	—	BV+25%

X# MB95 25 SINGOLD (1/4 Ounce)
7.7765 g., 0.9999 Gold 0.2500 oz. AGW, 21.95 mm. **Series:** Chinese Lunar Year **Subject:** Year of the Rooster **Obv:** Four Chinese characters - "Confidence and bravity" **Obv. Legend:** REPUBLIC OF SINGAPORE **Rev:** Rooster right standing on one leg facing left **Edge:** Reeded

Date	Mintage	F	VF	XF	Unc	BU
1993sm	6,000	—	—	—	—	BV+15%
1993sm Proof	500	—	—	—	—	BV+25%

X# MB105 25 SINGOLD (1/4 Ounce)
7.7765 g., 0.9999 Gold 0.2500 oz. AGW, 21.95 mm. **Series:** Chinese Lunar Year **Subject:** Year of the Dog **Obv:** Four Chinese characters - "Loyalty, comradeship, strength and faithfulness" **Obv. Legend:** REPUBLIC OF SINGAPORE **Rev:** Dog left under peach tree **Rev. Designer:** Artist Lang Shihning **Edge:** Reeded

Date	Mintage	F	VF	XF	Unc	BU
1994sm	6,000	—	—	—	—	BV+15%
1994sm Proof	500	—	—	—	—	BV+25%

X# MB116 25 SINGOLD (1/4 Ounce)
7.7765 g., 0.9999 Gold 0.2500 oz. AGW, 21.95 mm. **Series:** Chinese Lunar Year **Subject:** Year of the Boar **Obv:** Four Chinese characters - "Boundless prosperity and happiness" **Obv. Legend:** REPUBLIC OF SINGAPORE **Rev:** Sow and two piglets **Rev. Designer:** Artist James Koh **Edge:** Reeded

Date	Mintage	F	VF	XF	Unc	BU
1995sm	6,000	—	—	—	—	BV+15%
1995sm Proof	500	—	—	—	—	BV+25%

X# MB5 50 SINGOLD (1/2 Ounce)
15.5530 g., 0.9999 Gold 0.5000 oz. AGW, 27 mm. **Series:** Chinese Lunar Year **Subject:** Year of the Rat **Obv:** Chinese character - "Happiness" **Obv. Legend:** REPUBLIC OF SINGAPORE **Rev:** Rat left **Edge:** Reeded

Date	Mintage	F	VF	XF	Unc	BU
1984sm	2,500	—	—	—	—	BV+10%

X# MB10 50 SINGOLD (1/2 Ounce)
15.5530 g., 0.9999 Gold 0.5000 oz. AGW, 27 mm. **Series:** Chinese Lunar Year **Subject:** Year of the Ox **Obv:** Four Chinese characters - "Success through industry" **Obv. Legend:** REPUBLIC OF SINGAPORE **Rev:** Child riding ox right **Edge:** Reeded

Date	Mintage	F	VF	XF	Unc	BU
1985sm	2,500	—	—	—	—	BV+10%

X# MB18 50 SINGOLD (1/2 Ounce)
15.5530 g., 0.9999 Gold 0.5000 oz. AGW, 27 mm. **Series:** Chinese Lunar Year **Subject:** Year of the Tiger **Obv:** Four Chinese characters **Obv. Legend:** REPUBLIC OF SINGAPORE **Rev:** Tiger prowling **Edge:** Reeded

Date	Mintage	F	VF	XF	Unc	BU
1986sm	15,000	—	—	—	—	BV+10%

X# MB72 50 SINGOLD (1/2 Ounce)
15.5530 g., 0.9999 Gold 0.5000 oz. AGW **Series:** Chinese Lunar Year **Subject:** Year of the Goat **Obv:** Four Chinese characters - "The sun, it's peace and warmth during spring" **Obv. Legend:** REPUBLIC OF SINGAPORE **Rev:** Goat standing 3/4 right **Edge:** Reeded

Date	Mintage	F	VF	XF	Unc	BU
1991sm	4,000	—	—	—	—	BV+10%
1991sm Proof	250	—	—	—	—	BV+20%

X# MB85 50 SINGOLD (1/2 Ounce)
15.5530 g., 0.9999 Gold 0.5000 oz. AGW, 27 mm. **Series:** Chinese Lunar Year **Subject:** Year of the Monkey **Obv:** Four Chinese characters - "Intelligent, enthusiastic and witty" **Obv. Legend:** REPUBLIC OF SINGAPORE **Edge:** Reeded

Date	Mintage	F	VF	XF	Unc	BU
1992sm	4,000	—	—	—	—	BV+10%
1992sm Proof	250	—	—	—	—	BV+20%

X# MB96 50 SINGOLD (1/2 Ounce)
15.5530 g., 0.9999 Gold 0.5000 oz. AGW, 27 mm. **Series:** Chinese Lunar Year **Subject:** Year of the Rooster **Obv:** Four Chinese characters - "Confidence and bravity" **Obv. Legend:** REPUBLIC OF SINGAPORE **Rev:** Rooster right standing on one leg facing left **Edge:** Reeded

Date	Mintage	F	VF	XF	Unc	BU
1993sm	3,000	—	—	—	—	BV+10%
1993sm Proof	500	—	—	—	—	BV+20%

X# MB117 50 SINGOLD (1/2 Ounce)
15.5530 g., 0.9999 Gold 0.5000 oz. AGW, 27 mm. **Series:** Chinese Lunar Year **Subject:** Year of the Boar **Obv:** Four Chinese characters - "Boundless prosperity and happiness" **Obv. Legend:** REPUBLIC OF SINGAPORE **Rev:** Sow and two piglets **Rev. Designer:** Artist James Koh **Edge:** Reeded

Date	Mintage	F	VF	XF	Unc	BU
1995sm	3,000	—	—	—	—	BV+10%
1995sm Proof	500	—	—	—	—	BV+20%

X# MB19 100 SINGOLD (1 Ounce)
31.1061 g., 0.9999 Gold 0.9999 oz. AGW, 32.1 mm. **Series:** Chinese Lunar Year **Subject:** Year of the Tiger **Obv:** Four Chinese characters - "Awe-inspiring power and might **Obv. Legend:** REPUBLIC OF SINGAPORE **Rev:** Tiger prowling **Edge:** Reeded

Date	Mintage	F	VF	XF	Unc	BU
1986sm	15,000	—	—	—	—	BV+10%

X# MB53 100 SINGOLD (1 Ounce)
31.1061 g., 0.9999 Gold 0.9999 oz. AGW, 32.1 mm. **Series:** Chinese Lunar Year **Subject:** Year of the Snake **Obv:** Four Chinese characters - "Grace, wisdom and sprite" **Obv. Legend:** REPUBLIC OF SINGAPORE **Rev:** Snake poised upright behind lady **Edge:** Reeded

Date	Mintage	F	VF	XF	Unc	BU
1989sm	2,500	—	—	—	—	BV+10%
1989sm Proof	200	—	—	—	—	BV+20%

X# MB60 100 SINGOLD (1 Ounce)
31.1061 g., 0.9999 Gold 0.9999 oz. AGW, 32.1 mm. **Series:** Chinese Lunar Year **Subject:** Year of the Horse **Obv:** Four Chinese characters - "Reward and success" **Obv. Legend:** REPUBLIC OF SINGAPORE **Rev:** Horse rearing left **Edge:** Reeded

Date	Mintage	F	VF	XF	Unc	BU
1990sm	5,000	—	—	—	—	BV+10%
1990sm Proof	200	—	—	—	—	BV+20%

X# MB73 100 SINGOLD (1 Ounce)
31.1061 g., 0.9999 Gold 0.9999 oz. AGW, 32.1 mm. **Series:** Chinese Lunar Year **Subject:** Year of the Goat **Obv:** Four Chinese characters - "The sun, it's peace and warmth during spring" **Obv. Legend:** REPUBLIC OF SINGAPORE **Rev:** Goat standing 3/4 right **Edge:** Reeded

Date	Mintage	F	VF	XF	Unc	BU
1991sm	4,000	—	—	—	—	BV+10%
1991sm Proof	250	—	—	—	—	BV+20%

X# MB86 100 SINGOLD (1 Ounce)
31.1061 g., 0.9999 Gold 0.9999 oz. AGW, 32.1 mm. **Series:** Chinese Lunar Year **Subject:** Year of the Monkey **Obv:** Four Chinese characters - "Intelligent, enthusiastic and witty" **Obv. Legend:** REPUBLIC OF SINGAPORE **Rev:** Golden Hair monkey left perched on branch **Edge:** Reeded

Date	Mintage	F	VF	XF	Unc	BU
1992sm	4,000	—	—	—	—	BV+10%
1992sm Proof	250	—	—	—	—	BV+20%

X# MB97 100 SINGOLD (1 Ounce)
31.1061 g., 0.9999 Gold 0.9999 oz. AGW, 32.1 mm. **Series:** Chinese Lunar Year **Subject:** Year of the Rooster **Obv:** Four Chinese characters - "Confidence and bravity" **Obv. Legend:** REPUBLIC OF SINGAPORE **Rev:** Rooster right standing on one leg facing left **Edge:** Reeded

Date	Mintage	F	VF	XF	Unc	BU
1993sm	4,000	—	—	—	—	BV+10%
1993sm Proof	500	—	—	—	—	BV+20%

X# MB107 100 SINGOLD (1 Ounce)
31.1061 g., 0.9999 Gold 0.9999 oz. AGW, 32.1 mm. **Series:** Chinese Lunar Year **Subject:** Year of the Dog **Obv:** Four Chinese characters - "Loyalty, comradeship, strength and faithfulness" **Obv. Legend:** REPUBLIC OF SINGAPORE **Rev:** Dog left under peach tree **Rev. Designer:** Artist Lang Shihning **Edge:** Reeded

Date	Mintage	F	VF	XF	Unc	BU
1994sm	3,000	—	—	—	—	BV+10%
1994sm Proof	500	—	—	—	—	BV+20%

X# MB118 100 SINGOLD (1 Ounce)
31.1061 g., 0.9999 Gold 0.9999 oz. AGW, 32.1 mm. **Series:** Chinese Lunar Year **Subject:** Year of the Boar **Obv:** Four Chinese characters - "Boundless prosperity and happiness" **Obv. Legend:** REPUBLIC OF SINGAPORE **Rev:** Sow and two piglets **Rev. Designer:** Artist James **Edge:** Reeded

Date	Mintage	F	VF	XF	Unc	BU
1995sm	3,000	—	—	—	—	BV+10%
1995sm Proof	500	—	—	—	—	BV+20%

X# MB62 5 GRAMS
5.0000 g., 0.9999 Gold 0.1607 oz. AGW, 19.41 mm. **Obv:** Six Chinese characters - "Accomplishment by emulation of the Eight Immortals" **Obv. Legend:** REPUBLIC OF SINGAPORE **Rev:** Tsao Guojn standing **Edge:** Reeded

Date	Mintage	F	VF	XF	Unc	BU
1990sm Proof	500	—	—	—	—	BV+20%

X# MB63 5 GRAMS
5.0000 g., 0.9999 Gold 0.1607 oz. AGW, 19.41 mm. **Obv:** Six Chinese characters - "Accomplishment by emulation of the Eight Immortals" **Obv. Legend:** REPUBLIC OF SINGAPORE **Rev:** Han Zhongli standing **Edge:** Reeded

Date	Mintage	F	VF	XF	Unc	BU
1990sm Proof	500	—	—	—	—	BV+20%

X# MB64 5 GRAMS
5.0000 g., 0.9999 Gold 0.1607 oz. AGW, 19.41 mm. **Obv:** Six Chinese characters - "Accomplishment by emulation of the Eight Immortals" **Obv. Legend:** REPUBLIC OF SINGAPORE **Rev:** Lu Dongbin standing **Edge:** Reeded

Date	Mintage	F	VF	XF	Unc	BU
1990sm Proof	500	—	—	—	—	BV+20%

X# MB65 5 GRAMS
5.0000 g., 0.9999 Gold 0.1607 oz. AGW, 19.41 mm. **Obv:** Six Chinese characters - "Accomplishment by emulation of the Eight Immortals" **Obv. Legend:** REPUBLIC OF SINGAPORE **Rev:** Zhang Guolao **Edge:** Reeded

Date	Mintage	F	VF	XF	Unc	BU
1990sm Proof	500	—	—	—	—	BV+20%

X# MB76 5 GRAMS
5.0000 g., 0.9999 Gold 0.1607 oz. AGW, 19.41 mm. **Subject:** Singapore International Coin Convention **Obv:** Eight Chinese characters - "Accomplishment by emulation of the Eight Immortals" **Obv. Legend:** REPUBLIC OF SINGAPORE **Rev:** Li Tieguai **Edge:** Reeded

Date	Mintage	F	VF	XF	Unc	BU
1991sm Proof	500	—	—	—	—	BV+20%

X# MB77 5 GRAMS
5.0000 g., 0.9999 Gold 0.1607 oz. AGW **Subject:** Singapore International Coin Convention **Obv:** Eight Chinese characters - "Accomplishment by emulation of the Eight Immortals" **Obv. Legend:** REPUBLIC OF SINGAPORE **Rev:** Lan Tsaiho **Edge:** Reeded

Date	Mintage	F	VF	XF	Unc	BU
1991sm Proof	500	—	—	—	—	BV+20%

X# MB78 5 GRAMS
5.0000 g., 0.9999 Gold 0.1607 oz. AGW, 19.41 mm. **Subject:** Singapore International Coin Convention **Obv:** Eight Chinese characters - "Accomplishment by emulation of the Eight Immortals" **Obv. Legend:** REPUBLIC OF SINGAPORE **Rev:** He Shiangu **Edge:** Reeded

Date	Mintage	F	VF	XF	Unc	BU
1991sm Proof	500	—	—	—	—	BV+20%

X# MB79 5 GRAMS
5.0000 g., 0.9999 Gold 0.1607 oz. AGW, 19.41 mm. **Subject:** Singapore International Coin Convention **Obv:** Eight Chinese characters - "Accomplishment by emulation of the Eight Immortals" **Obv. Legend:** REPUBLIC OF SINGAPORE **Rev:** Han Shiangzi **Edge:** Reeded

Date	Mintage	F	VF	XF	Unc	BU
1991sm Proof	500	—	—	—	—	BV+20%

MEDALLIC PLATINUM BULLION COINAGE

X# MBA21 OUNCE
31.1186 g., 0.9995 Platinum 0.9999 oz. APW, 32 mm. **Series:** Chinese Lunar Year **Subject:** Year of the Tiger **Obv:** Four Chinese characters - "Awe-inspiring power and might" **Obv. Legend:** REPUBLIC OF SINGAPORE **Rev:** Tiger prowling **Edge:** Reeded

Date	Mintage	F	VF	XF	Unc	BU
1986sm Prooflike	1,000	—	—	—	—	BV+10%

X# MB44 OUNCE
31.1186 g., 0.9995 Platinum 0.9999 oz. APW, 32 mm. **Series:** Chinese Lunar Year **Subject:** Year of the Dragon **Obv:** Four Chinese characters - "Goodwill, success and prosperity" **Obv. Legend:** REPUBLIC OF SINGAPORE **Rev:** Flying dragon, pearl at left **Edge:** Reeded

Date	Mintage	F	VF	XF	Unc	BU
1988sm	1,500	—	—	—	—	BV+10%

PROOF SETS

X#	Date	Mintage	Identification	Issue Price	Mkt Val
XPS1	1987sm (5)	500	XMB27-31	—	—
XPS2	1988sm (5)	1,000	XMB37-41	—	—
XPS3	1989sm (5)	200	XMB49-53	—	—
XPS4	1990sm (4)	500	XMB62-65	—	—
XPS5	1990sm (5)	200	XMB56-60	—	—
XPS6	1991sm (4)	500	XMB76-79	—	—
XPS7	1991sm (5)	250	XMB69-73	—	—
XPS8	1992sm (5)	250	XMB82-86	—	—
XPS9	1993sm (5)	500	XMB93-97, 20 g gold plated silver ingot	—	—
XPS10	1994sm (2)	188	XMB110, 111	—	—
XPS11	1994sm (2)	—	XMB101, 102, 23 g silver ingot	—	—
XPS12	1994sm (5)	500	XMB103-107, 20 g gold plated silver ingot	—	—
XPS13	1995sm (5)	500	XMB114-118, 23 g silver ingot	—	—
XPS14	1995sm (2)	—	XMB112, 113, 23 g silver ingot	—	—

SLOVAKIA

REPUBLIC

FANTASY EURO PATTERNS

INA Issues

X# Pn1 EURO CENT
Copper Plated Steel, 16.8 mm. **Issuer:** INA **Obv:** Statue in Kluch Palace, Nitra **Obv. Legend:** SLOVENSKÁ REPUBLIKA **Rev:** Large value, shield, Euro stars design **Edge:** Plain

Date	Mintage	F	VF	XF	Unc	BU
2004	12,500	—	—	—	—	1.50
2004 Proof	3,000	Value: 2.50				

X# Pn1a EURO CENT
Silver, 16.8 mm. **Issuer:** INA **Obv:** Statue in Kluch Palace, Nitra **Obv. Legend:** SLOVENSKÁ REPUBLIKA **Rev:** Large value, shield, Euro stars design **Edge:** Plain

Date	Mintage	F	VF	XF	Unc	BU
2004 Proof	250	Value: 6.00				

X# Pn2 2 EURO CENT
Copper Plated Steel, 18.5 mm. **Issuer:** INA **Obv:** Statue in Kluch Palace, Nitra **Obv. Legend:** SLOVENSKÁ REPUBLIKA **Rev:** Large value, shield, Euro stars design **Edge:** Plain

Date	Mintage	F	VF	XF	Unc	BU
2004	12,500	—	—	—	—	2.00
2004 Proof	3,000	Value: 3.00				

X# Pn2a 2 EURO CENT

Silver, 18.5 mm. **Issuer:** INA **Obv:** Statue in Kluch Palace, Nitra **Obv. Legend:** SLOVENSKÁ REPUBLIKA **Rev:** Large value, shield, Euro stars design **Edge:** Plain

Date	Mintage	F	VF	XF	Unc	BU
2004 Proof	250	Value: 7.00				

X# Pn3 5 EURO CENT

Copper Plated Steel, 20.7 mm. **Issuer:** INA **Obv:** Statue in Kluch Palace, Nitra **Obv. Legend:** SLOVENSKÁ REPUBLIKA **Rev:** Large value, shield, Euro stars design **Edge:** Plain

Date	Mintage	F	VF	XF	Unc	BU
2004	12,500	—	—	—	—	2.50
2004 Proof	3,000	Value: 3.50				

X# Pn3a 5 EURO CENT

Silver, 20.7 mm. **Issuer:** INA **Obv:** Statue in Kluch Palace, Nitra **Obv. Legend:** SLOVENSKÁ REPUBLIKA **Rev:** Large value, shield, Euro stars design **Edge:** Plain

Date	Mintage	F	VF	XF	Unc	BU
2004 Proof	250	Value: 8.50				

X# Pn4 10 EURO CENT

Goldine, 19.3 mm. **Issuer:** INA **Obv:** Levoca Town Hall **Obv. Legend:** SLOVENSKÁ REPUBLIKA **Rev:** Castle, Euro stars design, large value **Edge:** Plain

Date	Mintage	F	VF	XF	Unc	BU
2004	12,500	—	—	—	—	3.00
2004 Proof	3,000	Value: 4.00				

X# Pn4a 10 EURO CENT

Silver, 19.3 mm. **Issuer:** INA **Obv:** Levoca Town Hall **Obv. Legend:** SLOVENSKÁ REPUBLIKA **Rev:** Castle, Euro stars design, large value **Edge:** Plain

Date	Mintage	F	VF	XF	Unc	BU
2004 Proof	250	Value: 10.00				

X# Pn5 20 EURO CENT

Goldine, 22 mm. **Issuer:** INA **Obv:** Levoca Town Hall **Obv. Legend:** SLOVENSKÁ REPUBLIKA **Rev:** Castle, Euro stars design, large value **Edge:** Plain

Date	Mintage	F	VF	XF	Unc	BU
2004	12,500	—	—	—	—	3.50
2004 Proof	3,000	Value: 5.00				

X# Pn5a 20 EURO CENT

Silver, 22 mm. **Issuer:** INA **Obv:** Levoca Town Hall **Obv. Legend:** SLOVENSKÁ REPUBLIKA **Rev:** Castle, Euro stars design, large value **Edge:** Plain

Date	Mintage	F	VF	XF	Unc	BU
2004 Proof	250	Value: 12.50				

X# Pn6 50 EURO CENT

Goldine, 24.3 mm. **Issuer:** INA **Obv:** Levoca Town Hall **Obv. Legend:** SLOVENSKÁ REPUBLIKA **Rev:** Castle, Euro stars design, large value **Edge:** Plain

Date	Mintage	F	VF	XF	Unc	BU
2004	12,500	—	—	—	—	4.00
2004 Proof	3,000	Value: 6.00				

X# Pn6a 50 EURO CENT

Silver, 24.3 mm. **Issuer:** INA **Obv:** Levoca Town Hall **Obv. Legend:** SLOVENSKÁ REPUBLIKA **Rev:** Castle, Euro stars design, large value **Edge:** Plain

Date	Mintage	F	VF	XF	Unc	BU
2004 Proof	250	Value: 15.00				

X# Pn7 EURO

Bi-Metallic Copper-Nickel center in Goldine ring, 22.8 mm. **Issuer:** INA **Obv:** Bratislava National Theatre **Obv. Legend:** SLOVENSKÁ REPUBLIKA **Rev:** Large value, woman harvesting wheat **Edge:** Plain

Date	Mintage	F	VF	XF	Unc	BU
2004	12,500	—	—	—	—	6.00
2004 Proof	3,000	Value: 8.00				

X# Pn7a EURO

Bi-Metallic Silver center in Goldine ring, 22.8 mm. **Issuer:** INA **Obv:** Bratislava National Theatre **Obv. Legend:** SLOVENSKÁ REPUBLIKA **Rev:** Large value, woman harvesting wheat **Edge:** Plain

Date	Mintage	F	VF	XF	Unc	BU
2004 Proof	—	Value: 22.50				

X# Pn8 2 EURO

Bi-Metallic Goldine center in Copper-Nickel ring, 25.7 mm. **Issuer:** INA **Obv:** Bratislava National Theatre **Obv. Legend:** SLOVENSKÁ REPUBLIKA **Rev:** Large value, woman harvesting wheat **Edge:** Plain

Date	Mintage	F	VF	XF	Unc	BU
2004	12,500	—	—	—	—	8.00
2004 Proof	3,000	Value: 10.00				

X# Pn8a 2 EURO

Bi-Metallic Silver center in Goldine ring, 25.7 mm. **Issuer:** INA **Obv:** Bratislava National Theatre **Obv. Legend:** SLOVENSKÁ REPUBLIKA **Rev:** Large value, woman harvesting wheat **Edge:** Plain

Date	Mintage	F	VF	XF	Unc	BU
2004 Proof	250	Value: 28.50				

X# Pn9 5 EURO

Goldine **Issuer:** INA **Obv:** Bratislava National Theatre **Obv. Legend:** SLOVENSKÁ REPUBLIKA **Edge:** Plain

Date	Mintage	F	VF	XF	Unc	BU
2004 Proof	3,000	Value: 12.50				

X# Pn9a 5 EURO

Silver **Issuer:** INA **Obv:** Bratislava National Theatre **Obv. Legend:** SLOVENSKÁ REPUBLIKA **Edge:** Plain

Date	Mintage	F	VF	XF	Unc	BU
2004 Proof	250	Value: 40.00				

Unknown Issuer

X# Pn11 EURO CENT

Copper Plated Steel **Edge:** Plain

Date	Mintage	F	VF	XF	Unc	BU
2005	15,000	—	—	—	—	1.00

X# Pn12 2 EURO CENT

Copper Plated Steel **Edge:** Plain

Date	Mintage	F	VF	XF	Unc	BU
2005	15,000	—	—	—	—	1.50

X# Pn13 5 EURO CENT

Copper Plated Steel **Edge:** Plain

Date	Mintage	F	VF	XF	Unc	BU
2005	15,000	—	—	—	—	2.00

X# Pn14 10 EURO CENT

Goldine **Edge:** Plain

Date	Mintage	F	VF	XF	Unc	BU
2005	15,000	—	—	—	—	2.50

X# Pn15 20 EURO CENT

Goldine **Edge:** Plain

Date	Mintage	F	VF	XF	Unc	BU
2005	15,000	—	—	—	—	3.00

X# Pn16 50 EURO CENT

Goldine **Edge:** Plain

Date	Mintage	F	VF	XF	Unc	BU
2005	15,000	—	—	—	—	3.50

X# Pn17 EURO

Bi-Metallic **Edge:** Plain

Date	Mintage	F	VF	XF	Unc	BU
2005	15,000	—	—	—	—	5.50

X# Pn18 2 EURO

Bi-Metallic **Edge:** Plain

Date	Mintage	F	VF	XF	Unc	BU
2005	15,000	—	—	—	—	7.50

MINT SETS

X#	Date	Mintage	Identification	Issue Price	Mkt Val
XMS1	2004 (8)	—	X#Pn1-Pn8	—	30.00
XMS2	2005 (13)	15,000	X#Pn11-Pn18, KM#11.1, 12-14, 35	—	26.00

PROOF SETS

X#	Date	Mintage	Identification	Issue Price	Mkt Val
XPS1	2004 (9)	3,000	X#Pn1-Pn9	—	50.00
XPS2	2004 (9)	250	X#Pn1a-Pn9a	—	150

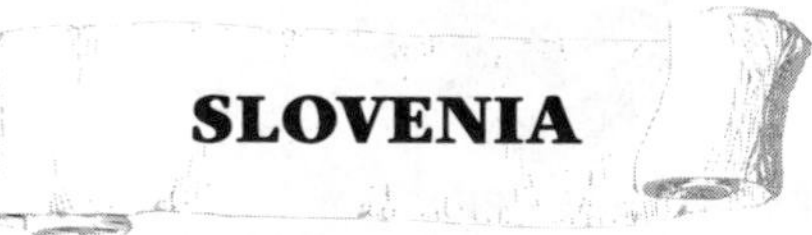

REPUBLIC

TOKEN COINAGE

Lipa Holding, Ljubljana Series

100 Vinar = 1 Lipa

X# Tn1 VINAR

11.0000 g., Copper-Zinc, 29 mm. **Obv:** Large value "1" on pedestal in sprays **Obv. Legend:** Republika Slovenija **Rev:** Monument in sprays **Edge:** Lettered **Note:** Prev. KM#Tn1.

Date	Mintage	F	VF	XF	Unc	BU
1990	6,000	—	—	25.00	35.00	50.00

X# Tn4 2/1000 LIPE

3.1400 g., Copper-Zinc, 18.10 mm. **Obv. Legend:** REPUBLIKA SLOVENIJA (incuse) **Rev:** Value (incuse) **Note:** Prev. KM#Tn4.

Date	Mintage	F	VF	XF	Unc	BU
1991	—	—	—	—	—	—

Note: Fewer than five known

X# Tn11 0.02 LIPE

Brass, 18.10 mm. **Obv:** Bunch of grapes **Obv. Legend:** REPUBLIKA SLOVENIJA **Edge:** Plain **Note:** Prev. KM#Tn11.

Date	Mintage	F	VF	XF	Unc	BU
1992	—	—	—	—	4.00	—

X# Tn5 0.02 LIPE

Brass, 18.70 mm. **Obv:** Corn crib **Obv. Legend:** ★ REPUBLIKA ★ SLOVENIJA **Note:** Prev. KM#Tn5. Some examples of KM#Tn5 have been found struck over Yugoslavian 10 Para 1990, KM#139.

Date	Mintage	F	VF	XF	Unc	BU
1992	—	—	—	—	3.00	—

X# Tn6 0.05 LIPE

Copper-Nickel-Zinc, 19.50 mm. **Obv:** Grape leaves **Obv. Legend:** ★ REPUBLIKA ★ SLOVENIJA **Edge:** Plain **Note:** Prev. KM#Tn6.

Date	Mintage	F	VF	XF	Unc	BU
1991	5,000	—	—	—	6.00	—

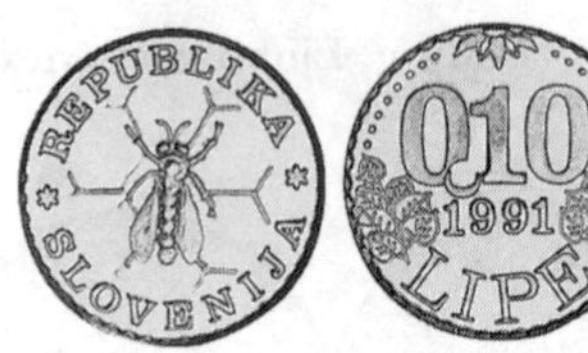

X# Tn7 0.10 LIPE

4.6100 g., Brass, 21.90 mm. **Obv:** Bee **Obv. Legend:** ★ REPUBLIKA ★ SLOVENIJA **Edge:** Plain **Note:** Prev. KM#Tn7.

Date	Mintage	F	VF	XF	Unc	BU
1991	5,000	—	—	—	8.00	—

X# Tn8 0.20 LIPE

Copper-Nickel, 23.10 mm. **Obv. Legend:** REPUBLIKA SLOVENIJA **Rev:** Insect **Edge:** Plain **Note:** Prev. KM#Tn8.

Date	Mintage	F	VF	XF	Unc	BU
1991	5,000	—	—	—	12.00	—

X# Tn9 0.50 LIPE

Copper-Nickel **Note:** Prev. KM#Tn9.

Date	Mintage	F	VF	XF	Unc	BU
1991	—	—	—	—	15.00	—

X# Tn2 LIPA

11.0000 g., 0.9250 Silver 0.3271 oz. ASW, 27 mm. **Obv. Legend:** REPUBLIKA SLOVENIJA **Rev:** Bust of Dr. France Preseren facing **Note:** Prev. KM#Tn2.

Date	Mintage	F	VF	XF	Unc	BU
1990 Proof	10,000	Value: 50.00				

X# Tn10 10 LIP

6.7500 g., 0.9000 Gold 0.1953 oz. AGW, 21 mm. **Obv. Legend:** REPUBLIKA SLOVENIJA **Rev:** Bust of Ivan Cankar left **Note:** Prev. KM#Tn10.

Date	Mintage	F	VF	XF	Unc	BU
1991 Proof	273	Value: 325				

X# Tn3 50 LIP

11.0000 g., 0.9000 Gold 0.3183 oz. AGW, 27 mm. **Obv. Legend:** REPUBLIKA SLOVENIJA **Rev:** Bust of Ivan Cankar facing **Note:** Prev. KM#Tn3.

Date	Mintage	F	VF	XF	Unc	BU
1990 Proof	400	Value: 400				

MEDALLIC COINAGE

X# M1 VINAR

Brass, 29 mm. **Obv:** Large "1" on pedestal in sprays **Obv. Legend:** Republic Slovenija **Rev:** Monument in sprays **Edge:** Lettered

Date	Mintage	F	VF	XF	Unc	BU
1990	—	—	—	—	—	—

FANTASY EURO PATTERNS

INA Issue

X# Pn1 EURO CENT

Copper Plated Steel, 16.8 mm. **Issuer:** INA **Obv:** Lippizaner horse with rider left **Rev:** Scale at left **Edge:** Plain

Date	Mintage	F	VF	XF	Unc	BU
2004	—	—	—	—	—	1.50
2004 Proof	17,500	Value: 2.50				

X# Pn1a EURO CENT

Silver, 16.8 mm. **Issuer:** INA **Obv:** Lippizaner horse with rider left **Rev:** Scale at left **Edge:** Plain

Date	Mintage	F	VF	XF	Unc	BU
2004 Proof	150	Value: 6.00				

X# Pn2 2 EURO CENT

Copper Plated Steel, 18.5 mm. **Issuer:** INA **Obv:** Lippizaner horse with rider left **Rev:** Scale at left **Edge:** Plain

Date	Mintage	F	VF	XF	Unc	BU
2004	17,500	—	—	—	—	2.00
2004 Proof	17,500	Value: 3.00				

X# Pn2a 2 EURO CENT

Silver, 18.5 mm. **Issuer:** INA **Obv:** Lippizaner horse with rider left **Rev:** Scale at left **Edge:** Plain

Date	Mintage	F	VF	XF	Unc	BU
2004 Proof	150	Value: 7.00				

X# Pn3 5 EURO CENT

Copper Plated Steel, 20.7 mm. **Issuer:** INA **Obv:** Lippizaner horse with rider left **Rev:** Scale at left **Edge:** Plain

Date	Mintage	F	VF	XF	Unc	BU
2004	—	—	—	—	—	2.50
2004 Proof	17,500	Value: 3.50				

X# Pn3a 5 EURO CENT

Silver, 20.7 mm. **Issuer:** INA **Obv:** Lippizaner horse with rider left **Rev:** Scale at left **Edge:** Plain

Date	Mintage	F	VF	XF	Unc	BU
2004 Proof	150	Value: 8.50				

X# Pn4 10 EURO CENT

Goldine, 19.3 mm. **Issuer:** INA **Obv:** Carniolan gray bee left **Rev:** Dove, value in wreath of hands **Edge:** Plain

Date	Mintage	F	VF	XF	Unc	BU
2004	—	—	—	—	—	3.00
2004 Proof	17,500	Value: 4.00				

X# Pn4a 10 EURO CENT

Silver, 19.3 mm. **Issuer:** INA **Obv:** Carniolan gray bee left **Rev:** Dove, value in wreath of hands **Edge:** Plain

Date	Mintage	F	VF	XF	Unc	BU
2004 Proof	150	Value: 10.00				

X# Pn5 20 EURO CENT

Goldine, 22 mm. **Issuer:** INA **Obv:** Carniolan gray bee left **Rev:** Dove, value in wreath of hands **Edge:** Plain

Date	Mintage	F	VF	XF	Unc	BU
2004	—	—	—	—	—	3.50
2004 Proof	17,500	Value: 5.00				

X# Pn5a 20 EURO CENT

Silver, 22 mm. **Issuer:** INA **Obv:** Carniolan gray bee left **Rev:** Dove, value in wreath of hands **Edge:** Plain

Date	Mintage	F	VF	XF	Unc	BU
2004 Proof	150	Value: 12.50				

X# Pn6 50 EURO CENT

Goldine, 24.3 mm. **Issuer:** INA **Obv:** Carniolan gray bee left **Rev:** Dove, value in wreath of hands **Edge:** Plain

Date	Mintage	F	VF	XF	Unc	BU
2004	—	—	—	—	—	5.00
2004 Proof	17,500	Value: 6.00				

X# Pn6a 50 EURO CENT

Silver, 24.3 mm. **Issuer:** INA **Obv:** Carniolan gray bee left **Rev:** Dove, value in wreath of hands **Edge:** Plain

Date	Mintage	F	VF	XF	Unc	BU
2004 Proof	150	Value: 15.00				

X# Pn7 EURO

Bi-Metallic, 22.8 mm. **Issuer:** INA **Obv:** Brown bear walking left **Rev:** Church **Edge:** Plain

Date	Mintage	F	VF	XF	Unc	BU
2004	—	—	—	—	—	7.50
2004 Proof	17,500	Value: 8.00				

X# Pn7a EURO

Bi-Metallic Brass center in Silver ring, 22.8 mm. **Issuer:** INA **Obv:** Brown bear walking left **Rev:** Church **Edge:** Plain

Date	Mintage	F	VF	XF	Unc	BU
2004 Proof	150	Value: 22.50				

X# Pn8 2 EURO

Bi-Metallic, 25.7 mm. **Issuer:** INA **Obv:** Ziatog (mythical chamois) standing 3/4 right **Rev:** Church **Edge:** Plain

Date	Mintage	F	VF	XF	Unc	BU
2004	—	—	—	—	—	8.00
2004 Proof	17,500	Value: 10.00				

X# Pn8a 2 EURO

Bi-Metallic Brass center in Silver ring, 25.7 mm. **Issuer:** INA **Obv:** Ziatog (mythical chamois) standing 3/4 right **Rev:** Church **Edge:** Plain

Date	Mintage	F	VF	XF	Unc	BU
2004 Proof	150	Value: 28.50				

X# Pn9 5 EURO

Brass, 36 mm. **Issuer:** INA **Obv:** Ziatog (mythical chamois) standing 3/4 right **Rev:** Janez Vajkard Valvasor facing portrait **Edge:** Plain

Date	Mintage	F	VF	XF	Unc	BU
2004 Proof	17,500	Value: 15.00				

X# Pn9a 5 EURO
Silver, 36 mm. **Issuer:** INA **Obv:** Ziatog (mythical chamois) standing 3/4 right **Rev:** Janez Vajkard Valvasor facing portrait **Edge:** Plain

Date	Mintage	F	VF	XF	Unc	BU
2004 Proof	150	Value: 40.00				

PIEFORTS

X#	Date	Mintage	Identification	Mkt Val
P1	2004	150	5 Euro. Silver. X#Pn9a.	65.00

MINT SETS

X#	Date	Mintage	Identification	Issue Price	Mkt Val
XMS1	2004 (8)	—	X#Pn1-Pn8	—	30.00

PROOF SETS

X#	Date	Mintage	Identification	Issue Price	Mkt Val
XPS1	2004 (9)	17,500	X#Pn1-Pn9	—	50.00
XPS2	2004 (9)	150	X#Pn1a-Pn9a	—	150

SOLOMON ISLANDS

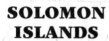

COMMONWEALTH NATION

FANTASY COINAGE

X# 1 30 DOLLARS
0.9990 Gold Plated Silver **Rev:** Cuscus

Date	Mintage	F	VF	XF	Unc	BU
1975 Proof	40,000	Value: 85.00				

X# 2 30 DOLLARS
0.9990 Gold Plated Silver **Rev:** Solomon Mamaloni
Note: A 100 Dollar coin dated 1975 of .900 gold with mintage of 10,000 has been reported, not confirmed.

Date	Mintage	F	VF	XF	Unc	BU
1975 Proof	—	Value: 95.00				

SOMALIA

REPUBLIC OF SOMALIA

FANTASY COINAGE

X# 8 DOLLAR
26.8000 g., Copper-Nickel, 39 mm. **Obv:** Arms **Obv. Legend:** SOMALIA REPUBLIC **Rev:** Peace dove in flight in sprays, globe in background **Rev. Legend:** WORLD PEACE FOR THE THIRD MILLENNIUM **Edge:** Reeded

Date	Mintage	F	VF	XF	Unc	BU
2000	—	—	—	—	7.50	—

X# 1a 5 DOLLARS
31.2000 g., 0.9990 Silver 1.0021 oz. ASW, 39.1 mm. **Obv:** National arms **Rev:** Titanic underway **Edge:** Partially reeded with metal content from 5-7 o'clock

Date	Mintage	F	VF	XF	Unc	BU
1998 Proof	200	Value: 55.00				

TRIAL STRIKES

X# TS1 20 DOLLARS
26.2200 g., Gilt Bronze, 38.9 mm. **Obv:** National arms **Rev:** "TRIAL STRIKE BRONZE" **Edge:** Reeded

Date	Mintage	F	VF	XF	Unc	BU
1998 Proof	—	—	—	—	—	—

X# TS2 20 DOLLARS
26.2100 g., Gilt Bronze, 38.9 mm. **Obv:** "TRIAL STRIKE BRONZE" **Rev:** Titanic under way **Edge:** Reeded

Date	Mintage	F	VF	XF	Unc	BU
ND (1998) Proof	—	—	—	—	—	—

X# TS3 20 DOLLARS
26.3600 g., Copper-Nickel, 38.9 mm. **Obv:** National arms **Rev:** "TRIAL STRIKE CUPRO-NICKLE" **Edge:** Reeded

Date	Mintage	F	VF	XF	Unc	BU
1998	—	—	—	—	—	—

X# TS4 20 DOLLARS

26.5200 g., Copper-Nickel, 38.9 mm. **Obv:** "TRIAL STRIKE CUPRO-NICKLE" **Rev:** Titanic under way **Edge:** Reeded

Date	Mintage	F	VF	XF	Unc	BU
ND (1998) Proof	—	—	—	—	—	—

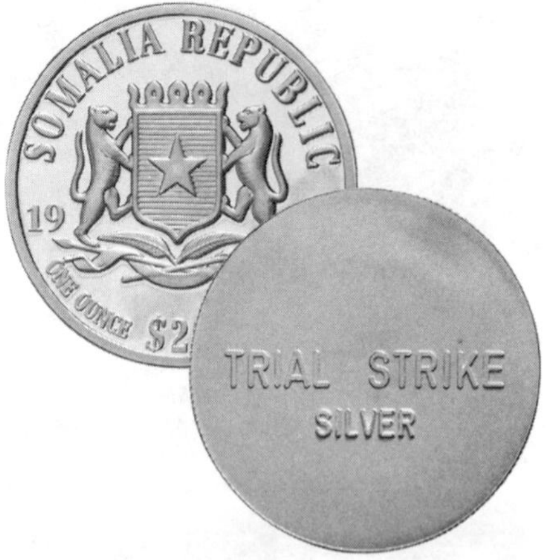

X# TS5 20 DOLLARS

31.2700 g., 0.9990 Silver 1.0043 oz. ASW, 38.9 mm. **Obv:** National arms **Rev:** "TRIAL STRIKE SILVER" **Edge:** Reeded

Date	Mintage	F	VF	XF	Unc	BU
1998 Proof	—	—	—	—	—	—

X# TS6 20 DOLLARS

31.2500 g., 0.9990 Silver 1.0037 oz. ASW, 38.9 mm. **Obv:** "TRIAL STRIKE SILVER" **Rev:** Titanic under way **Edge:** Reeded

Date	Mintage	F	VF	XF	Unc	BU
ND (1998) Proof	—	—	—	—	—	—

REPUBLIC OF SOMALI

FANTASY COINAGE

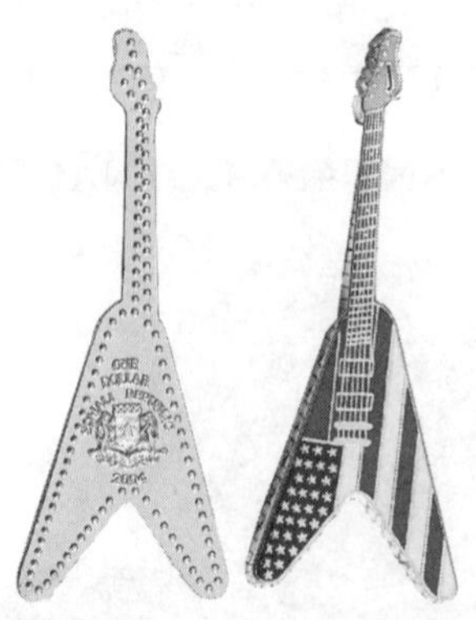

X# 61 DOLLAR

3.0900 g., 0.9990 Copper-Nickel Silver plated with multi-color enameling 0.0992 oz., 17.42x45.19 mm. **Subject:** 50th Anniversary of Rock and Roll **Obv:** Value above supported arms **Obv. Legend:** SOMALI REPUBLIC **Rev:** American flag guitar **Edge:** plain **Shape:** Guitar **Note:** Prev. X#33.

Date	Mintage	F	VF	XF	Unc	BU
2004	—	—	—	—	30.00	—

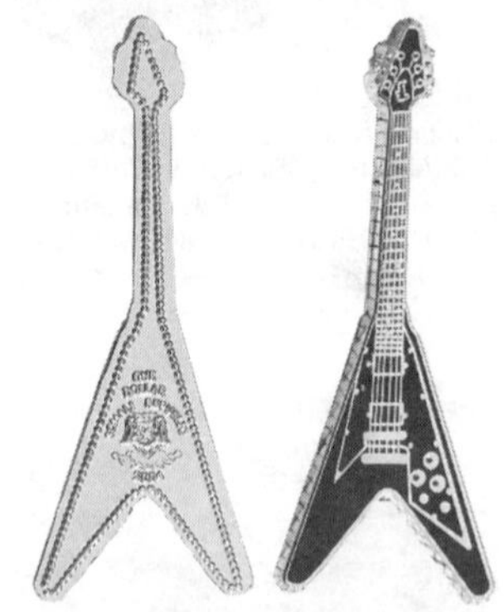

X# 62 DOLLAR

3.2200 g., Copper-Nickel Silver plated with black enameling, 17.77x44.98 mm. **Subject:** 50th Anniversary of Rock and Roll **Obv:** Value above supported arms **Obv. Legend:** SOMALI REPUBLIC **Rev:** Flying "V" guitar **Edge:** Plain **Shape:** Guitar

Date	Mintage	F	VF	XF	Unc	BU
2004	—	—	—	—	—	10.00

X# 63 DOLLAR

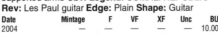

4.1500 g., Copper-Nickel Silver plated with red and white enameling, 18.65x45.79 mm. **Subject:** 50th Anniversary of Rock and Roll **Obv:** Value above supported arms **Obv. Legend:** SOMALI REPUBLIC **Rev:** Les Paul guitar **Edge:** Plain **Shape:** Guitar

Date	Mintage	F	VF	XF	Unc	BU
2004	—	—	—	—	—	10.00

X# 64 DOLLAR

3.6300 g., Copper-Nickel Silver plated with dark blue and white enameling, 17.03x45.90 mm. **Subject:** 50th Anniversary of Rock and Roll **Obv:** Value above supported arms **Obv. Legend:** SOMALI REPUBLIC **Rev:** Explorer guitar **Edge:** Plain **Shape:** Guitar

Date	Mintage	F	VF	XF	Unc	BU
2004	—	—	—	—	—	10.00

X# 65 DOLLAR

3.7000 g., Copper-Nickel Silver plated with pink enameling, 22.86x45.22 mm. **Subject:** 50th Annivesary of Rock and Roll **Obv:** Value above supported arms **Obv. Legend:** SOMALI REPUBLIC **Rev:** Star guitar **Edge:** Plain **Shape:** Guitar

Date	Mintage	F	VF	XF	Unc	BU
2004	—	—	—	—	—	10.00

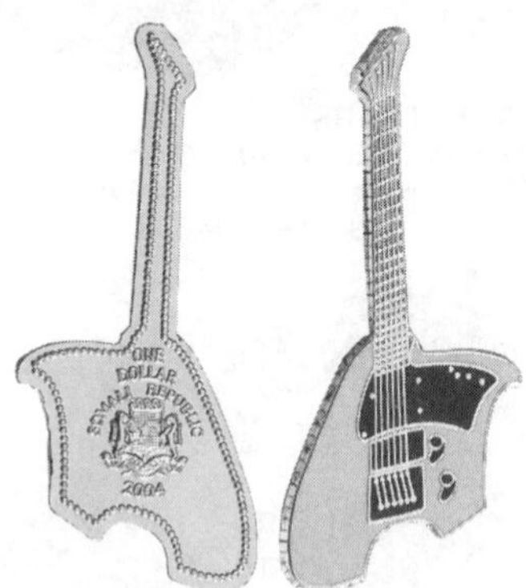

X# 66 DOLLAR

3.9500 g., Copper-Nickel Silver plated with yellow and black enameling, 20.54x45.90 mm. **Subject:** 50th Anniversary of Rock and Roll **Obv:** Value above supported arms **Obv. Legend:** SOMALI REPUBLIC **Rev:** Klein guitar **Edge:** Plain **Shape:** Guitar

Date	Mintage	F	VF	XF	Unc	BU
2004	—	—	—	—	—	10.00

X# 21 DOLLAR

Copper-Nickel, 39 mm. **Subject:** Life of Pope John Paul II **Obv:** Arms **Obv. Legend:** SOMALI REPUBLIC **Rev:** Multi-colored photo scene of Pope John Paul II as an infant

Date	Mintage	F	VF	XF	Unc	BU
2005 Proof	—	Value: 13.50				

X# 22 DOLLAR

Copper-Nickel, 39 mm. **Subject:** Life of Pope John Paul II **Obv:** Arms **Obv. Legend:** SOMALI REPUBLIC **Rev:** Multi-colored photo scene of Pope John Paul II's ordination photo

Date	Mintage	F	VF	XF	Unc	BU
2005 Proof	—	Value: 13.50				

X# 23 DOLLAR

Copper-Nickel, 39 mm. **Subject:** Life of Pope John Paul II **Obv:** Arms **Obv. Legend:** SOMALI REPUBLIC **Rev:** Multi-colored photo scene of Pope John Paul II in a casual hiking scene

Date	Mintage	F	VF	XF	Unc	BU
2005 Proof	—	Value: 13.50				

X# 24 DOLLAR

Copper-Nickel, 39 mm. **Subject:** Life of Pope John Paul II **Obv:** Arms **Obv. Legend:** SOMALI REPUBLIC **Rev:** Multi-colored photo scene of Pope John Paul II profile as bishop

Date	Mintage	F	VF	XF	Unc	BU
2005 Proof	—	Value: 13.50				

X# 25 DOLLAR

Copper-Nickel, 39 mm. **Subject:** Life of Pope John Paul II **Obv:** Arms **Obv. Legend:** SOMALI REPUBLIC **Rev:** Multi-colored photo scene of Pope John Paul II as pope, with outstretched arms

Date	Mintage	F	VF	XF	Unc	BU
2005 Proof	—	Value: 13.50				

X# 26 DOLLAR

Copper-Nickel, 39 mm. **Subject:** Life of Pope John Paul II **Obv:** Arms **Obv. Legend:** SOMALI REPUBLIC **Rev:** Multi-colored photo scene of Pope John Paul II as pope, raised fist

Date	Mintage	F	VF	XF	Unc	BU
2005 Proof	—	Value: 13.50				

X# 27 DOLLAR

Copper-Nickel, 39 mm. **Subject:** Life of Pope John Paul II **Obv:** Arms **Obv. Legend:** SOMALI REPUBLIC **Rev:** Multi-colored photo scene of Pope John Paul II with Mother Theresa

Date	Mintage	F	VF	XF	Unc	BU
2005 Proof	—	Value: 13.50				

X# 28 DOLLAR

Copper-Nickel, 39 mm. **Subject:** Life of Pope John Paul II **Obv:** Arms **Obv. Legend:** SOMALI REPUBLIC **Rev:** Multi-colored photo scene of Pope John Paul II in mass vestments

Date	Mintage	F	VF	XF	Unc	BU
2005 Proof	—	Value: 13.50				

X# 29 DOLLAR

Copper-Nickel, 39 mm. **Subject:** Life of Pope John Paul II **Obv:** Arms **Obv. Legend:** SOMALI REPUBLIC **Rev:** Multi-colored photo scene of Pope John Paul II signing a document

Date	Mintage	F	VF	XF	Unc	BU
2005 Proof	—	Value: 13.50				

X# 30 DOLLAR
Copper-Nickel, 39 mm. **Subject:** Life of Pope John Paul II **Obv:** Arms **Obv. Legend:** SOMALI REPUBLIC **Rev:** Multi-colored photo scene of Somalian youth holding poster of Pope John Paul II

Date	Mintage	F	VF	XF	Unc	BU
2005 Proof	—	Value: 13.50				

X# 31 DOLLAR
Copper-Nickel, 39 mm. **Subject:** Life of Pope John Paul II **Obv:** Arms **Obv. Legend:** SOMALI REPUBLIC **Rev:** Multi-colored photo scene with Pope John Paul II kissing the ground

Date	Mintage	F	VF	XF	Unc	BU
2005 Proof	—	Value: 13.50				

X# 32 DOLLAR
Copper-Nickel, 39 mm. **Subject:** Life of Pope John Paul II **Obv:** Arms **Obv. Legend:** SOMALI REPUBLIC **Rev:** Multi-colored photo scene of Pope John Paul II blessing a child

Date	Mintage	F	VF	XF	Unc	BU
2005 Proof	—	Value: 13.50				

X# 40 DOLLAR
7.5000 g., Copper-Nickel, 24 mm. **Obv:** Crowned supported arms **Obv. Legend:** SOMALI REPUBLIC **Rev:** 1/2 length figure of Cardinal Ratzinger facing 3/4 right at left, Freising Cathedral at right, shield above **Rev. Legend:** PATRIAE BAVARIAE SEMPER OBLIGATUM **Edge:** Plain

Date	Mintage	VG	F	VF	XF	Unc
2006	30,000	—	—	—	—	3.50

X# 41 DOLLAR
7.5000 g., Copper-Nickel, 24 mm. **Obv:** Crowned supported arms **Obv. Legend:** SOMALI REPUBLIC **Rev:** Conjoined busts of Cardinal Ratzinger and Pope John Paul II right **Rev. Legend:** + 10 ANNES PAULUS 11. + IOSEPHUS RATZINGER **Edge:** Plain

Date	Mintage	VG	F	VF	XF	Unc
2006	30,000	—	—	—	—	3.50

X# 42 DOLLAR
7.5000 g., Copper-Nickel, 24 mm. **Obv:** Crowned supported arms **Obv. Legend:** SOMALI REPUBLIC **Rev:** Arms at left, bust of Pope Benedictus XVI facing 3/4 right **Rev. Legend:** HABEMUS PAPAM BENEDICTUS XVI **Edge:** Plain

Date	Mintage	VG	F	VF	XF	Unc
2006	30,000	—	—	—	—	3.50

X# 43 DOLLAR
7.5000 g., Copper-Nickel, 24 mm. **Obv:** Crowned supported arms **Obv. Legend:** SOMALI REPUBLIC **Rev:** Rays above and raised hand wearing the fisherman's ring **Rev. Legend:** BENEDICTUS XVI - ANULUM PISCATORIS **Edge:** Plain

Date	Mintage	VG	F	VF	XF	Unc
2006	30,000	—	—	—	—	3.50

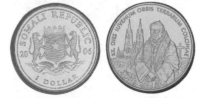

X# 44 DOLLAR
7.5000 g., Copper-Nickel, 24 mm. **Subject:** World Youth Day **Obv:** Crowned supported arms **Obv. Legend:** SOMALI REPUBLIC **Rev:** Cologne Cathedral in background at left, 1/2 length fiure of Pope Benedictus XVI facing at center right **Rev. Legend:** XX . DIES IUVENUM ORBIS TERRARUM COLONIAE **Edge:** Plain

Date	Mintage	VG	F	VF	XF	Unc
2006	30,000	—	—	—	—	3.50

X# 50 DOLLAR
6.8800 g., Copper-Nickel Silver plated, reverse with reddish brown and black enameling, 26x44.94 mm. **Obv:** Value above supported arms **Obv. Legend:** FEDERAL REPUBLIC OF SOMALIA **Rev:** Motorcycle **Edge:** Plain **Shape:** Motorcycle

Date	Mintage	F	VF	XF	Unc	BU
2007	—	—	—	—	—	10.00

X# 51 DOLLAR
7.0000 g., Copper-Nickel Silver plated, reverse with red and black enameling, 28.52x45.22 mm. **Obv:** Value above supported arms **Obv. Legend:** FEDERAL REPUBLIC OF SOMALIA **Rev:** Motorcycle **Edge:** Plain

Date	Mintage	F	VF	XF	Unc	BU
2007	—	—	—	—	—	10.00

X# 52 DOLLAR
7.4600 g., Copper-Nickel Silver plated, reverse with green and black enameling, 25.91x44.92 mm. **Obv:** Value above supported arms **Obv. Legend:** FEDERAL

REPUBLIC OF SOMALIA **Rev:** Motorcycle **Edge:** Plain **Shape:** Motorcycle

Date	Mintage	F	VF	XF	Unc	BU
2007	—	—	—	—	—	10.00

X# 53 DOLLAR

7.0900 g., Copper-Nickel Silver plated, reverse with blue and black enameling, 28.51x45.02 mm. **Obv:** Value above supported arms **Obv. Legend:** FEDERAL REPUBLIC OF SOMALIA **Rev:** Motorcycle **Edge:** Plain **Shape:** Motorcycle

Date	Mintage	F	VF	XF	Unc	BU
2007	—	—	—	—	—	10.00

X# 54 DOLLAR

7.9500 g., Copper-Nickel Silver plated, reverse with yellow and black enameling, 27.15x44.83 mm. **Obv:** Value above supported arms **Obv. Legend:** FEDERAL REPUBLIC OF SOMALIA **Rev:** Motorcycle **Edge:** Plain **Shape:** Motorcycle

Date	Mintage	F	VF	XF	Unc	BU
2007	—	—	—	—	—	10.00

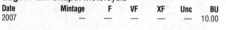

X# 55 DOLLAR

7.0500 g., Copper-Nickel Silver plated, reverse with purple and black enameling, 29.18x45.33 mm. **Obv:** Value above supported arms **Obv. Legend:** FEDERAL REPUBLIC OF SOMALIA **Rev:** Motorcycle **Edge:** Plain **Shape:** Motorcycle

Date	Mintage	F	VF	XF	Unc	BU
2007	—	—	—	—	—	10.00

X# 1 5 DOLLARS

25.5700 g., Copper-Nickel, 39 mm. **Obv:** Arms **Obv. Legend:** SOMALI REPUBLIC **Rev:** R.M.S. Titanic in passage **Edge:** Reeded

Date	Mintage	F	VF	XF	Unc	BU
1998	—	—	—	—	15.00	—

X# 3 5 DOLLARS

26.2400 g., Copper-Nickel, 40 mm. **Subject:** Oscar Winner **Obv:** Arms **Obv. Legend:** SOMALI REPUBLIC **Rev:** Half-length figure of Roberto Benigni facing holding Oscar award **Rev. Legend:** OSCAR WINNER 1999 **Edge:** Plain

Date	Mintage	F	VF	XF	Unc	BU
1999 Proof	—	Value: 20.00				

X# 9 10 DOLLARS

31.2000 g., 0.9990 Silver 1.0021 oz. ASW, 40.5 mm. **Obv:** Outlined map of Africa, with trees huts and amimals, arms at lower left **Rev:** Chimpanzee **Edge:** Reeded

Date	Mintage	F	VF	XF	Unc	BU
1998	—	—	—	—	18.50	—

X# 2 10 DOLLARS

31.1341 g., 0.9990 Silver 0.9999 oz. ASW, 39 mm. **Obv:** Arms **Obv. Legend:** SOMALI REPUBLIC **Rev:** R.M.S. Titanic in passage **Edge:** Reeded

Date	Mintage	F	VF	XF	Unc	BU
1999 Proof	10,000	Value: 37.50				

X# 5 10 DOLLARS

25.7700 g., Copper-Nickel, 38.6 mm. **Series:** Marine-Life Protection **Obv:** Arms **Obv. Legend:** SOMALI REPUBLIC **Rev:** Multi-colored underwater ocean marine life scene **Rev. Legend:** MARINE - LIFE PROTECTION **Edge:** Reeded

Date	Mintage	F	VF	XF	Unc	BU
1998 Proof	10,000	Value: 25.00				

X# 6 10 DOLLARS

25.7700 g., Copper-Nickel, 38.6 mm. **Series:** Marine-Life Protection **Obv:** Arms **Obv. Legend:** SOMALI REPUBLIC **Rev:** Multi-colored fresh water fish scene **Rev. Legend:** MARINE - LIFE PROTECTION **Edge:** Reeded

Date	Mintage	F	VF	XF	Unc	BU
1999 Proof	10,000	Value: 25.00				

X# 7 10 DOLLARS

25.0000 g., 0.9250 Silver 0.7435 oz. ASW, 38.7 mm. **Subject:** Year of the Dragon **Obv:** Arms **Obv. Legend:** SOMALI REPUBLIC **Rev:** Multi-colored maiden, dragon head emerging upright **Edge:** Reeded

Date	Mintage	F	VF	XF	Unc	BU
2000 Proof	2,000	Value: 35.00				

X# 11 10 DOLLARS

31.2000 g., 0.9990 Silver 1.0021 oz. ASW, 40.8 mm. **Obv:** Outlined map of Africa, with trees, huts and animals, arms at lower left **Rev:** Two African Chimpanzees facing **Edge:** Reeded

Date	Mintage	F	VF	XF	Unc	BU
2000	—	—	—	—	18.50	—

X# 10 10 DOLLARS
31.2400 g., 0.9990 Silver 1.0033 oz. ASW, 40.6 mm. **Obv:** Outlined map of Africa, with trees, huts and animals, arms at lower left **Rev:** The three monkeys: "hear, see and speak no evil" s **Edge:** Reeded

Date	Mintage	F	VF	XF	Unc	BU
2001	—	—	—	—	25.00	—

X# 12 10 DOLLARS
31.3100 g., 0.9250 Silver 0.9311 oz. ASW, 40.5 mm. **Obv:** National arms and pictorial map of Africa **Rev:** Seated monkey **Edge:** Reeded

Date	Mintage	F	VF	XF	Unc	BU
2002	—	—	—	—	20.00	—

X# 4 20 DOLLARS
20.1700 g., 0.8330 Silver 0.5402 oz. ASW, 40.3 mm. **Subject:** Oscar Winner **Obv:** Arms **Obv. Legend:** SOMALI REPUBLIC **Rev:** Half-length figure of Roberto Benigni facing holding Oscar award **Rev. Legend:** OSCAR WINNER 1999 **Edge:** Reeded

Date	Mintage	F	VF	XF	Unc	BU
1999 Proof	—	Value: 40.00				

X# 34 25 DOLLARS
0.9000 Silver **Obv:** National arms **Rev:** Multicolor ocean fish scene

Date	Mintage	F	VF	XF	Unc	BU
1998 Proof	3,000	Value: 35.00				

X# 35 25 DOLLARS
0.9000 Silver **Obv:** National arms **Rev:** Multicolor fresh water fish scene

Date	Mintage	F	VF	XF	Unc	BU
1999 Proof	3,000	Value: 35.00				

X# 36 150 DOLLARS
0.9990 Silver **Obv:** National arms **Rev:** Multicolor ocean fish scene

Date	Mintage	F	VF	XF	Unc	BU
1998 Proof	1,000	—	—	—	—	—

X# 37 150 DOLLARS
0.9990 Silver **Obv:** National arms **Rev:** Multicolor fresh water fish scene

Date	Mintage	F	VF	XF	Unc	BU
1999 Proof	1,000	—	—	—	—	—

MINT SETS

X#	Date	Mintage	Identification	Issue Price	Mkt Val
XMS1	2006 (5)	30,000	X#40-44	—	17.50

PROOF SETS

X#	Date	Mintage	Identification	Issue Price	Mkt Val
XPS1	2005 (12)	—	X#21-32	—	165

SOMALILAND

REPUBLIC

DOLLAR COINAGE

X# 2 5 DOLLARS
25.5600 g., Copper-Nickel, 42.5 mm. **Obv:** Arms **Obv. Legend:** REPUBLIC OF SOMALILAND **Rev:** Sinking of Titanic **Rev. Legend:** R.M.S. Titanic **Edge:** Plain

Date	Mintage	F	VF	XF	Unc	BU
1998	—	—	—	—	8.00	—
2002	—	—	—	—	8.00	—

X# 3 5 DOLLARS
21.5000 g., Stainless Steel, 38.1 mm. **Series:** Chinese Lunar Years **Subject:** Year of the Rabbit **Obv:** Arms **Obv. Legend:** REPUBLIC OF SOMALILAND **Rev:** Two rabbits left

Date	Mintage	F	VF	XF	Unc	BU
1999	—	—	—	—	12.00	—

X# 4 5 DOLLARS
17.7700 g., Stainless Steel, 28.1 mm. **Series:** Chinese Lunar Years **Subject:** Year of the Dragon **Obv:** Arms **Obv. Legend:** REPUBLIC OF SOMALILAND **Rev:** Dragon left **Edge:** Plain

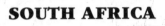

Date	Mintage	F	VF	XF	Unc	BU
2000	—	—	—	—	12.00	—

SHILLING COINAGE

X# 6 10 SHILLINGS
3.5100 g., Brass, 17.7 mm. **Obv:** Vervet monkey **Edge:** Plain

Date	Mintage	F	VF	XF	Unc	BU
2002	—	—	—	—	8.00	—

X# 7 1000 SHILLINGS
31.2700 g., 0.9990 Silver 1.0043 oz. ASW, 38.8 mm. **Subject:** Exploration of Somaliland **Obv:** Arms **Obv. Legend:** SOMALILAND **Rev:** Bust of Richard F. Burton 3/4 right **Edge:** Reeded

Date	Mintage	F	VF	XF	Unc	BU
2002	—	—	—	—	—	—

SOUTH AFRICA

REPUBLIK

Zuid-Afrikaansche Republiek

PATTERNS

1874 Würden Issues

Struck in Brussels, Belgium.

X# Pn2 PENNY
Bronze **Rev:** Orange Free State "EEN PENNY" **Note:** Mule. Prev. KM#Pn4.

Date	Mintage	F	VF	XF	Unc	BU
1874 Proof	—	Value: 400				

X# Pn1 PENNY
Bronze **Rev:** "1 PENNY" **Note:** Prev. KM#Pn1.

Date	Mintage	F	VF	XF	Unc	BU
1874 Proof	—	Value: 325				

X# Pn3 2 PENCE
Bronze **Note:** Prev. KM#Pn5.

Date	Mintage	F	VF	XF	Unc	BU
1874 Proof	—	Value: 325				

X# Pn10 3 PENCE
Gold **Note:** Prev. KM#Pn23. Struck especially for mining magnate Sammie Marks.

Date	Mintage	F	VF	XF	Unc	BU
1898	215	—	—	3,000	4,000	—

X# Pn4 2-1/2 SHILLINGS
Silver **Edge:** Milled **Note:** Prev. KM#Pn7.

Date	Mintage	F	VF	XF	Unc	BU
1874 Proof	—	Value: 3,500				

X# Pn4a 2-1/2 SHILLINGS
Bronze Gilt

Date	Mintage	F	VF	XF	Unc	BU
1874 Proof	—	Value: 2,750				

X# Pn4b 2-1/2 SHILLINGS
Aluminum **Edge:** Milled **Note:** Prev. KM#Pn9.

Date	Mintage	F	VF	XF	Unc	BU
1874 Proof	—	Value: 2,250				

X# Pn4c 2-1/2 SHILLINGS
Silver **Edge:** Plain **Note:** Prev. KM#Pn8.

Date	Mintage	F	VF	XF	Unc	BU
1874 Proof	—	Value: 3,500				

X# Pn4d 2-1/2 SHILLINGS
Aluminum **Edge:** Plain **Note:** Prev. KM#Pn10.

Date	Mintage	F	VF	XF	Unc	BU
1874 Proof	—	Value: 2,250				

X# Pn5 5 SHILLINGS
Bronze Gilt **Edge:** Milled **Note:** Prev. KM#Pn11.

Date	Mintage	F	VF	XF	Unc	BU
1874 Proof	—	Value: 2,750				

X# Pn5a 5 SHILLINGS
Aluminum **Edge:** Milled **Note:** Prev. KM#Pn13.

Date	Mintage	F	VF	XF	Unc	BU
1874 Proof	—	Value: 2,750				

X# Pn5b 5 SHILLINGS
Copper Gilt **Edge:** Milled **Note:** Prev. KM#Pn14.

Date	Mintage	F	VF	XF	Unc	BU
1874 Proof	—	Value: 2,500				

X# Pn5c 5 SHILLINGS
Bronze Gilt **Edge:** Plain **Note:** Prev. KM#Pn12.

Date	Mintage	F	VF	XF	Unc	BU
1874 Proof	—	Value: 3,000				

X# Pn6 5 SHILLINGS
Silver **Edge:** Milled **Note:** Prev. KM#Pn16.

Date	Mintage	F	VF	XF	Unc	BU
1874. Proof; Dot after date	—	Value: 6,000				

X# Pn6a 5 SHILLINGS
Aluminum **Edge:** Milled **Note:** Prev. KM#Pn18.

Date	Mintage	F	VF	XF	Unc	BU
1874. Proof; Dot after date	1	Value: 2,250				

X# Pn6b 5 SHILLINGS
Copper Gilt **Edge:** Plain **Note:** Prev. KM#Pn15.

Date	Mintage	F	VF	XF	Unc	BU
1874. Proof; Dot after date	—	Value: 2,750				

X# Pn7 POND
Bronze **Obv:** Short beard **Note:** Prev. KM#Pn19.

Date	Mintage	F	VF	XF	Unc	BU
1874 Proof	—	Value: 1,850				

X# Pn8 POND
Bronze **Obv:** Long beard **Note:** Prev. KM#Pn8.

Date	Mintage	F	VF	XF	Unc	BU
1874 Proof	—	Value: 1,850				

X# Pn8a POND
Aluminum **Note:** Prev. KM#Pn21.

Date	Mintage	F	VF	XF	Unc	BU
1874 Proof	—	Value: 2,000				

1890 L. C. Lauer Issues

Struck by Messrs. Otto Nolte and Co., Berlin, Germany.

X# Pn9 PENNY
Bronze **Note:** Prev. KM#Pn22.

Date	Mintage	F	VF	XF	Unc	BU
1890 Proof	—	Value: 325				

UNION OF SOUTH AFRICA

Dominion under Great Britain

MEDALLIC COINAGE

Richard Lobel Series

X# M1 CROWN
Bronze **Subject:** Edward VIII **Obv:** Bust left **Obv. Legend:** EDWARD • VIII • KING • & • EMPEROR **Rev:** Springbok running right **Edge:** Plain

Date	Mintage	F	VF	XF	Unc	BU
1936 Proof	500	Value: 20.00				

X# M1a CROWN
Copper-Nickel-Zinc **Subject:** Edward VIII **Obv:** Bust left **Obv. Legend:** EDWARD • VIII • KING • & • EMPEROR **Rev:** Springbok running right **Edge:** Plain

Date	Mintage	F	VF	XF	Unc	BU
1936 Proof	1,500	Value: 20.00				

X# M1b CROWN
0.9167 Silver **Subject:** Edward VIII **Obv:** Bust left **Obv. Legend:** EDWARD • VIII • KING • & • EMPEROR **Rev:** Springbok running right **Edge:** Plain

Date	Mintage	F	VF	XF	Unc	BU
1936 Proof	200	Value: 50.00				

X# M1c CROWN
Gold **Subject:** Edward VIII **Obv:** Bust left **Obv. Legend:** EDWARD • VIII • KING • & • EMPEROR **Rev:** Springbok running right **Edge:** Plain

Date	Mintage	F	VF	XF	Unc	BU
1936 Proof	—	Value: 500				

X# M3 CROWN
23.1100 g., 0.9167 Silver 0.6811 oz. ASW, 38.00 mm. **Obv:** Head of Duchess, bust of Duke facing **Obv. Legend:** DUKE & DUCHESS OF WINDSOR **Rev:** Springbok running right **Edge:** Reeded

Date	Mintage	F	VF	XF	Unc	BU
1987 Proof	—	—	—	—	—	—

X# M2 SOVEREIGN

0.3750 Gold **Subject:** Edward VIII **Obv:** Bust left **Obv. Legend:** EDWARD • VIII • KING • & • EMPEROR **Rev:** Springbok running right **Edge:** Plain

Date	Mintage	F	VF	XF	Unc	BU
1936 Proof	200	Value: 200				

X# M2a SOVEREIGN

4.4200 g., Silver **Subject:** Edward VIII **Obv:** Bust left **Obv. Legend:** EDWARD • VIII • KING • & • EMPEROR **Rev:** Springbok running right **Edge:** Plain

Date	Mintage	F	VF	XF	Unc	BU
1936 Proof	—	Value: 10.00				

X# 4 SOVEREIGN

Gold, 21.98 mm. **Obv:** Head of Duchess, bust of Duke facing **Obv. Legend:** DUKE & DUCHESS OF WINDSOR **Rev:** Springbok running right **Edge:** Reeded

Date	Mintage	F	VF	XF	Unc	BU
1987 Proof	—	Value: 135				

X# M4a SOVEREIGN

4.4200 g., Silver, 21.98 mm. **Obv:** Head of Duchess, bust of Duke facing **Obv. Legend:** DUKE & DUCHESS OF WINDSOR **Rev:** Springbok running right **Edge:** Reeded

Date	Mintage	F	VF	XF	Unc	BU
1987 Proof	—	Value: 10.00				

INA Retro Issues

X# 1 5 SHILLINGS

24.0000 g., 0.9250 Silver 0.7137 oz. ASW, 37.86 mm. **Obv:** Head left **Obv. Legend:** EDWARDVS VIII D: G: BR: OMN: REX **Rev:** Crowned shield **Edge:** Plain **Note:** Medal alignment.

Date	Mintage	F	VF	XF	Unc	BU
1937 Proof	550	Value: 45.00				

X# 1a 5 SHILLINGS

19.9000 g., Bronze, 37.86 mm. **Obv:** Head left **Obv. Legend:** EDWARDVS VIII D: G: BR: OMN: REX **Rev:** Crowned shield **Edge:** Plain **Note:** Medal alignment.

Date	Mintage	F	VF	XF	Unc	BU
1937 Proof	550	Value: 25.00				

X# 1b 5 SHILLINGS

20.1500 g., Copper, 37.86 mm. **Obv:** Head left **Obv. Legend:** EDWARDVS VIII D: G: BR: OMN: REX **Rev:** Crowned shield **Edge:** Plain **Note:** Medal alignment.

Date	Mintage	F	VF	XF	Unc	BU
1937 Proof	550	Value: 25.00				

X# 1c 5 SHILLINGS

0.9167 Gold, 37.86 mm. **Obv:** Head left **Obv. Legend:** EDWARDVS VIII D: G: BR: OMN: REX **Rev:** Crowned shield **Edge:** Plain **Note:** Weight varies: 39.2-40.0 grams.

Date	Mintage	F	VF	XF	Unc	BU
1937 Proof	1	—	—	—	—	—
Note: Medal alignment						
1937 Proof	1	—	—	—	—	—
Note: Coin alignment						

X# 2 5 SHILLINGS

40.0000 g., 0.9167 Gold 1.1789 oz. AGW **Obv:** Head left **Obv. Legend:** EDWARDVS VIII D: G: BR: OMN: REX F: D: IND: IMP: **Rev:** Crowned shield **Edge:** Proof

Date	Mintage	F	VF	XF	Unc	BU
1937 Proof	1	—	—	—	—	—

X# 3 5 SHILLINGS

39.5000 g., 0.9167 Gold 1.1641 oz. AGW, 37.86 mm. **Obv:** Crowned bust left **Obv. Legend:** EDWARDVS VIII REX IMPERATOR **Rev:** Crowned shield **Edge:** Plain **Note:** Medal alignment.

Date	Mintage	F	VF	XF	Unc	BU
1937 Proof	1	—	—	—	—	—

REPUBLIC

CAST COINAGE

X# 21 PEWTERRAND

21.1400 g., Pewter, 37.9 mm. **Obv:** Bust of Krueger left **Obv. Legend:** SUID - AFRICA - SOUTH AFRICA **Rev:** Springbok walking right **Edge:** Plain **Note:** "COPY" belo bust

Date	Mintage	VG	F	VF	XF	Unc
1978	—	—	—	—	—	5.00

BULLION

National Gold Coin Exchange Issues

X# 31 BARON

31.1186 g., 0.9995 Gold 0.9999 oz. AGW, 32 mm. **Subject:** 30th Anniversary Communication Through Satellite **Obv. Legend:** JOHANNESBURG • LONDON • NEW YORK • FRANKFURT • ROME • PARIS • GENEVA • HONG KONG **Rev:** Satellite **Rev. Legend:** 1957-1987

Date	Mintage	F	VF	XF	Unc	BU
ND(1987)	—	—	—	—	—	—

X# 32 BARON

31.1186 g., 0.9995 Platinum 0.9999 oz. APW, 32 mm. **Subject:** 30th Anniversary Communication Through Satellite **Obv. Legend:** JOHANNESBURG • LONDON • NEW YORK • FRANKFURT • ROME • PARIS • GENEVA • HONG KONG **Rev:** Satellite **Rev. Legend:** 1957-1987

Date	Mintage	F	VF	XF	Unc	BU
ND(1987)	—	—	—	—	—	—

X# 34 10 BARON

311.1856 g., 0.9995 Platinum 9.9994 oz. APW, 75 mm. **Subject:** 30th Anniversary Communication Through Satellite **Obv. Legend:** JOHANNESBURG • LONDON • NEW YORK • FRANKFURT • ROME • PARIS • GENEVA • HONG KONG **Rev:** Satellite **Rev. Legend:** 1957-1987

Date	Mintage	F	VF	XF	Unc	BU
ND(1987)	—	—	—	—	—	—

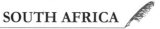

X# 33 10 BARON
311.1856 g., 0.9995 Gold 9.9994 oz. AGW, 75 mm. **Subject:** 30th Anniversary Communication Through Satellite **Obv. Legend:** JOHANNESBURG • LONDON • NEW YORK • FRANKFURT • ROME • PARIS • GENEVA • HONG KONG **Rev:** Satellite **Rev. Legend:** 1957-1987 **Note:** Illustration reduced.

Date	Mintage	F	VF	XF	Unc	BU
ND(1987)	—	—	—	—	—	—

MEDALLIC BULLION COINAGE

Issued by Chattanooga Coin and Stamp, Chattanooga, Tennessee

X# MB1 OUNCE
31.1030 g., 0.9990 Silver 0.9989 oz. ASW **Obv:** S.J. KRUGER **Rev:** Springbok

Date	Mintage	F	VF	XF	Unc	BU
1983	5,000	—	—	—	2,000	—
1983 Proof	1,000	Value: 25.00				

PIEFORTS

X#	Date	Mintage	Identification	Mkt Val
P1	1874	—	Penny. Bronze. Prev. KM#Pn2.	450
P2	1873	—	Penny. Bronze. Prev. KM#Pn3. Triple thickness.	650
P3	1874.	—	5 Shillings. Silver. Prev. KM#Pn17.	5,000
P4	1937	1	5 Shillings. Silver. Plain edge, coin alignment, X#1.	—
P5	1937	1	5 Shillings. Silver. Plain edge, medal alignment, X#1.	—
P6	1937	1	5 Shillings. Silver. Reeded edge, coin alignment, X#1.	—
P7	1937	1	5 Shillings. Silver. Reeded edge, medal alignment, X#1.	—
P8	1937	1	5 Shillings. Silver. Plain edge, coin alignment, X#2.	—
P9	1937	1	5 Shillings. Silver. Plain edge, medal alignment, X#2.	—
P10	1937	—	5 Shillings. Silver. Reeded edge, coin alignment, X#2.	—
P11	1937	1	5 Shillings. Silver. Reeded edge, medal alignment, X#2.	—
P12	1937	1	5 Shillings. Silver. Plain edge, coin alignment, X#3.	—
P13	1937	1	5 Shillings. Silver. Plain edge, medal alignment, X#3.	—
P14	1937	1	5 Shillings. Silver. Reeded edge, coin alignment, X#3.	—
P15	1937	1	5 Shillings. Silver. Reeded edge, medal alignment, X#3.	—
P16	1936	—	Crown. 0.9167 Silver. X#M1b.	100

ORANGE FREE STATE

COLONY

PATTERNS

L. C. Lauer Issues

Struck by Messrs. Otto Nolte and Co., Berlin, Germany

X# Pn1 PENNY
Bronze **Note:** Prev. KM#Pn1.

Date	Mintage	F	VF	XF	Unc	BU
1874 Proof	—	Value: 450				

X# Pn5 PENNY
Bronze **Obv:** Ornamental shield **Note:** Prev. KM#Pn9.

Date	Mintage	F	VF	XF	Unc	BU
1888 Proof	—	Value: 425				

X# Pn5a PENNY
Copper-Nickel

Date	Mintage	F	VF	XF	Unc	BU
1888 Proof	—	Value: 500				

X# Pn6 PENNY
Bronze **Rev:** "1 PENNY" larger **Note:** Prev. KM#Pn9.

Date	Mintage	F	VF	XF	Unc	BU
1888 Proof	—	Value: 175				

X# Pn6a PENNY
Copper-Nickel **Note:** Prev. KM#Pn10.

Date	Mintage	F	VF	XF	Unc	BU
1888 Proof	—	Value: 250				

X# Pn7 PENNY
Bronze **Rev:** Plain shield **Note:** Prev. KM#Pn13.

Date	Mintage	F	VF	XF	Unc	BU
1888 Proof	—	Value: 475				

X# Pn7a PENNY
Silver **Obv:** Plain shield **Note:** Prev. KM#Pn17.

Date	Mintage	F	VF	XF	Unc	BU
1888 Proof	—	Value: 1,500				

X# Pn7b PENNY
Copper-Nickel **Obv:** Plain shield **Note:** Prev. KM#Pn12.

Date	Mintage	F	VF	XF	Unc	BU
1888 Proof	—	Value: 485				

X# Pn7c PENNY
Aluminum **Obv:** Plain shield **Note:** Prev. KM#Pn16.

Date	Mintage	F	VF	XF	Unc	BU
1888 Proof	—	Value: 500				

X# Pn2 2 PENCE
Bronze **Note:** Mule with rev. of Z.A.R. 2 Pence.

Date	Mintage	F	VF	XF	Unc	BU
1874 Proof	—	—	—	—	—	—

X# Pn3 KROON

Silver **Note:** Prev. KM#Pn4.

Date	Mintage	F	VF	XF	Unc	BU
1887 Proof	—	Value: 7,000				

X# Pn3a KROON

Lead **Note:** Prev. KM#Pn5.

Date	Mintage	F	VF	XF	Unc	BU
1887 Proof	—	Value: 3,000				

X# Pn4 KROON

Silver **Rev:** Without "LLC" or "ESSAY" **Note:** Prev. KM#Pn6.

Date	Mintage	F	VF	XF	Unc	BU
1887 Proof	—	Value: 7,500				

PIEFORTS

X#	Date	Mintage	Identification	Mkt Val
P1	1874	—	Penny. Bronze. Double thickness. Prev. KM#Pn2.	550
P2	1874	—	Penny. Bronze. Triple thickness. Prev. KM#Pn3.	650
P3	1888	—	Penny. Bronze. Double thickness. Prev. KM#Pn14.	550
P4	1888	—	Penny. Bronze. Triple thickness. Prev. KM#Pn15.	650

SOUTHERN AFRICA

CHARITY

MEDALLIC COINAGE

Afro Mint, Alberton, South Africa

X# 1 AFRO

5.8600 g., Brass, 27.5 mm. **Obv:** Outlined African continent, chains at left and right **Rev:** Ancient Kholsan rock drawing of zebras

Date	Mintage	F	VF	XF	Unc	BU
1998	10,000	—	—	—	—	5.00

X# 1a AFRO

Silver, 27.5 mm. **Obv:** Outlined African continent, chains at left and right **Rev:** Ancient Kholsan rock drawing of zebras

Date	Mintage	F	VF	XF	Unc	BU
1998 Proof	100	Value: 20.00				

X# 4 AFRO

6.5000 g., Brass, 25.7 mm. **Obv:** Outlined African continent, chains at left and right **Rev:** Baobab tree in ornate frame

Date	Mintage	F	VF	XF	Unc	BU
1999	100	—	—	—	—	15.00
2000	100	—	—	—	—	15.00

X# 4a AFRO

Silver, 25.7 mm. **Obv:** Outlined African continent, claims at left and right **Rev:** Baobab tree in ornate frame

Date	Mintage	F	VF	XF	Unc	BU
1999 Proof	20	Value: 45.00				
2000 Proof	20	Value: 45.00				

X# 2 5 AFRO

13.8700 g., Brass, 32.7 mm. **Obv:** Outlined African continent, chains at left and right **Rev:** Rural tribal home, tree

Date	Mintage	F	VF	XF	Unc	BU
1998	10,000	—	—	—	—	9.00

X# 2a 5 AFRO

13.8700 g., Silver, 32.7 mm. **Obv:** Outlined African continent, chains at left and right **Rev:** Rural tribal home, tree

Date	Mintage	F	VF	XF	Unc	BU
1998 Proof	100	Value: 30.00				

X# 5 5 AFRO

13.6500 g., Brass, 32.8 mm. **Obv:** Outlined African continent, chains at left and right **Rev:** Pair of Hornbills

Date	Mintage	F	VF	XF	Unc	BU
1999	100	—	—	—	—	15.00
2000	100	—	—	—	—	15.00

X# 5a 5 AFRO

Silver, 32.8 mm. **Obv:** Outlined African continent, chains at left and right **Rev:** Pair of Hornbills

Date	Mintage	F	VF	XF	Unc	BU
1999 Proof	20	Value: 45.00				
2000 Proof	20	Value: 45.00				

X# 3 10 AFRO

23.9700 g., Brass, 38.8 mm. **Obv:** Outlined African continent, chains at left and right **Rev:** Shields, assagal and mask

Date	Mintage	F	VF	XF	Unc	BU
1998	10,000	—	—	—	—	18.00

X# 3a 10 AFRO

23.9700 g., Silver, 38.8 mm. **Obv:** Outlined African continent, chains at left and right **Rev:** Shields, assagal and mask

Date	Mintage	F	VF	XF	Unc	BU
1998 Proof	100	Value: 40.00				

X# 6 10 AFRO

24.2400 Brass, 38.6 mm. **Obv:** Outlined African continent, chains at left and right **Rev:** Abstract face mask design

Date	Mintage	F	VF	XF	Unc	BU
1999	100	—	—	—	—	20.00
2000	100	—	—	—	—	20.00

X# 6a 10 AFRO

Silver, 38.6 mm. **Obv:** Outlined African continent, chains at left and right **Rev:** Abstract face mask design

Date	Mintage	F	VF	XF	Unc	BU
1999 Proof	20	Value: 60.00				
2000 Proof	20	Value: 60.00				

MINT SETS

X#	Date	Mintage	Identification	Issue Price	Mkt Val
XMS1	1998 (3)	10,000	X#M1-X#M3	—	32.00
XMS2	1999 (3)	100	X#4-X#6	100	50.00
XMS3	2000 (3)	100	X#4-X#6	—	50.00

PROOF SETS

X#	Date	Mintage	Identification	Issue Price	Mkt Val
XPS1	1998 (3)	100	X#M1a-X#M3a	—	90.00

X#	Date	Mintage	Identification	Issue Price	Mkt Val
XPS2	1999 (3)	20	X#4a-X#6a	—	150
XPS3	2000 (3)	20	X#4a-X#6a	—	150

SOUTHERN RHODESIA

BRITISH COLONY

MEDALLIC COINAGE

Richard Lobel Series

X# M4 CROWN

Bronze, 38.10 mm. **Ruler:** Edward VIII **Subject:** Edward VIII **Obv:** Bust left **Obv. Legend:** EDWARD • VIII • KING • & • EMPEROR **Rev:** Sable antelope standing left **Edge:** Plain

Date	Mintage	F	VF	XF	Unc	BU
1936 Proof	500	Value: 15.00				

X# M4a CROWN

Copper-Nickel-Zinc, 38.10 mm. **Ruler:** Edward VIII **Subject:** Edward VIII **Obv:** Bust left **Obv. Legend:** EDWARD • VIII • KING • & • EMPEROR **Rev:** Sable antelope standing left **Edge:** Plain

Date	Mintage	F	VF	XF	Unc	BU
1936 Proof	1,500	Value: 15.00				

X# M4b CROWN

0.9167 Silver, 38.10 mm. **Subject:** Edward VIII **Obv:** Bust left **Obv. Legend:** EDWARD • VIII • KING • & • EMPEROR **Rev:** Sable antelope standing left **Edge:** Plain

Date	Mintage	F	VF	XF	Unc	BU
1936 Proof	165	Value: 50.00				

X# M4c CROWN

Gold, 38.10 mm. **Subject:** Edward VIII **Obv:** Bust left **Obv. Legend:** EDWARD • VIII • KING • & • EMPEROR **Rev:** Sable antelope standing left **Edge:** Plain

Date	Mintage	F	VF	XF	Unc	BU
1936 Proof	—	Value: 500				

X# M5a SOVEREIGN

4.4200 g., Silver, 21.98 mm. **Subject:** Edward VIII **Obv:** Bust left **Obv. Legend:** EDWARD • VIII • KING • & • EMPEROR **Rev:** Sable antelope standing left **Edge:** Plain

Date	Mintage	F	VF	XF	Unc	BU
1936 Proof	—	Value: 10.00				

X# M5 SOVEREIGN

0.3750 Gold, 21.98 mm. **Subject:** Edward VIII **Obv:** Bust left **Obv. Legend:** EDWARD • VIII • KING • & • EMPEROR **Rev:** Sable antelope standing left **Edge:** Plain

Date	Mintage	F	VF	XF	Unc	BU
1936 Proof	165	Value: 135				

INA Retro Issues

X# 1 5 SHILLINGS

24.3800 g., 0.9250 Silver 0.7250 oz. ASW, 37.97 mm. **Ruler:** Edward VIII **Obv:** Head left **Obv. Legend:** EDWARDVS VIII D: G: BR: OMN: REX **Rev:** Crowned shield **Edge:** Plain **Note:** Medal alignment.

Date	Mintage	F	VF	XF	Unc	BU
1937 Proof	500	Value: 45.00				

X# 1a 5 SHILLINGS

Bronze, 37.97 mm. **Ruler:** Edward VIII **Obv:** Head left **Obv. Legend:** EDWARDVS VIII D: G: BR: OMN: REX **Rev:** Crowned shield **Edge:** Plain **Note:** Medal alignment.

Date	Mintage	F	VF	XF	Unc	BU
1937 Proof	500	Value: 25.00				

X# 1b 5 SHILLINGS

Copper, 37.97 mm. **Ruler:** Edward VIII **Obv:** Head left **Obv. Legend:** EDWARDVS VIII D: G: BR: OMN: REX **Rev:** Crowned shield **Edge:** Plain **Note:** Medal alignment.

Date	Mintage	F	VF	XF	Unc	BU
1937 Proof	500	Value: 25.00				

X# 1c.1 5 SHILLINGS

39.9000 g., 0.9167 Gold 1.1759 oz. AGW, 37.97 mm. **Ruler:** Edward VIII **Obv:** Head left **Obv. Legend:** EDWARDVS VIII D: G: BR: OMN: REX **Rev:** Crowned shield **Edge:** Reeded **Note:** Coin alignment.

Date	Mintage	F	VF	XF	Unc	BU
1937 Proof	1	—	—	—	—	—

X# 1c.2 5 SHILLINGS

40.0000 g., 0.9167 Gold 1.1789 oz. AGW, 37.97 mm. **Ruler:** Edward VIII **Obv:** Head left **Obv. Legend:** EDWARDVS VIII D: G: BR: OMN: REX **Rev:** Crowned shield **Edge:** Plain **Note:** Medal alignment.

Date	Mintage	F	VF	XF	Unc	BU
1937 Proof	1	—	—	—	—	—

X# 2 5 SHILLINGS

0.9250 Silver, 37.97 mm. **Ruler:** Edward VIII **Obv:** Crowned bust left **Obv. Legend:** EDWARD VIII KING EMPEROR **Rev:** Crowned shield **Edge:** Plain

Date	Mintage	F	VF	XF	Unc	BU
1937 Proof	150	Value: 45.00				

X# 2a 5 SHILLINGS

Bronze, 37.97 mm. **Ruler:** Edward VIII **Obv:** Crowned bust left **Obv. Legend:** EDWARD VIII KING EMPEROR **Rev:** Crowned shield **Edge:** Plain

Date	Mintage	F	VF	XF	Unc	BU
1937 Plain; Proof	150	Value: 25.00				

X# 2b 5 SHILLINGS

Copper **Ruler:** Edward VIII **Obv:** Crowned bust left **Obv. Legend:** EDWARD VIII KING EMPEROR **Rev:** Crowned shield **Edge:** Plain

Date	Mintage	F	VF	XF	Unc	BU
1937 Proof	150	Value: 25.00				

X# 2c 5 SHILLINGS

0.9167 Gold, 37.97 mm. **Ruler:** Edward VIII **Obv:** Crowned bust left **Obv. Legend:** EDWARD VIII KING EMPEROR **Rev:** Crowned shield **Edge:** Reeded **Note:** Weight varies: 39.7-39.9 grams.

Date	Mintage	F	VF	XF	Unc	BU
1937 Proof	1	—	—	—	—	—
Note: Medal alignment						
1937 Proof	1	—	—	—	—	—
Note: Coin alignment						

X# 3 5 SHILLINGS

39.5000 g., 0.9167 Gold 1.1641 oz. AGW, 37.97 mm. **Ruler:** Edward VIII **Obv:** Crowned bust left **Obv. Legend:** EDWARDVS VIII REX IMPERATOR **Rev:** Crowned shield **Edge:** Plain **Note:** Medal alignment.

Date	Mintage	F	VF	XF	Unc	BU
1937 Proof	1	—	—	—	—	—

PIEFORTS

X#	Date	Mintage	Identification	Mkt Val
P1	1937	1	5 Shillings. Silver. Plain edge, coin alignment, X#1.	—
P2	1937	1	5 Shillings. Silver. Plain edge, medal alignment, X#1.	—
P3	1937	1	5 Shillings. Silver. Reeded edge, coin alignment, X#1.	—
P4	1937	1	5 Shillings. Silver. Reeded edge, medal alignment, X#1.	—
P5	1937	1	5 Shillings. Silver. Plain edge, coin alignment, X#2.	—
P6	1937	1	5 Shillings. Silver. Plain edge, medal alignment, X#2.	—
P7	1937	1	5 Shillings. Silver. Reeded edge, coin alignment, X#2.	—
P8	1937	1	5 Shillings. Silver. Reeded edge, medal alignment, X#2.	—
P9	1937	1	5 Shillings. Silver. Plain edge, coin alignment, X#3.	—
P10	1937	1	5 Shillings. Silver. Plain edge, medal alignment, X#3.	—
P11	1937	1	5 Shillings. Silver. Reeded edge, coin alignment, X#3.	—
P12	1937	1	5 Shillings. Silver. Reeded edge, medal alignment, X#3.	—
P13	1936	—	Crown. 0.9167 Silver. X#4b.	100

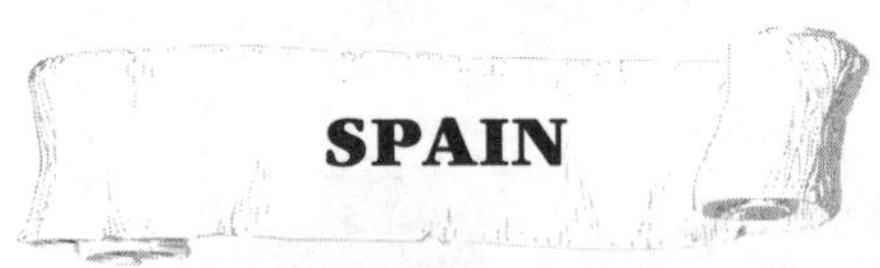

SPAIN

PROVISIONAL GOVERNMENT

DECIMAL COINAGE

Peseta System

100 Centimos = 1 Peseta

X# A1 5 PESETAS

24.7000 g., 0.9000 Silver 0.7147 oz. ASW, 36.5 mm. **Obv:** Hispania reclining resting on the Pyrenees, feet at Gibraltar **Obv. Legend:** ESPAÑA **Rev:** Crowned arms between pillars **Rev. Legend:** SOBERANIA NACIONAL - OBIERNO PROVISIONAL **Edge:** Plain **Note:** Considered a medal.

Date	Mintage	F	VF	XF	Unc	BU
1868	—	—	450	750	1,250	—

KINGDOM

MEDALLIC COINAGE

X# 21 5 PESETAS

0.2100 g., Gold, 10.3 mm. **Ruler:** Alfonso XIII **Obv:** Bust left **Rev:** Crowned arms between pillars

Date	Mintage	F	VF	XF	Unc	BU
1890	—	—	—	8.50	—	—

EARLY REAL COINAGE

X# MA1 50 REALES

145.4500 g., 0.9990 Silver 4.6715 oz. ASW, 76 mm. **Ruler:** Philip III **Note:** The dies supposedly were prepared as a training exercise in the Madrid Mint in the 19th Century. The dies left the Mint in the 1980's. Illustration reduced.

Date	Mintage	F	VF	XF	Unc	BU
1609Aqueduct	250	—	—	—	350	—
1610Aqueduct	250	—	—	—	350	—

DECIMAL COINAGE

Peseta System

100 Centimos = 1 Peseta

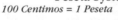

X# 12 20 CENTIMOS

Silver **Ruler:** Alfonso XIII **Obv:** Alphonso XIII boy's head right **Rev:** Crowned arms in sprays **Note:** Prev. KY#191.

Date	Mintage	F	VF	XF	Unc	BU
1896 Proof	4	—	—	—	—	—

X# 12a 20 CENTIMOS

Copper **Ruler:** Alfonso XIII **Obv:** Alphonso XIII boy's head right **Rev:** Crowned arms in sprays **Note:** Prev. KY#191a.

Date	Mintage	F	VF	XF	Unc	BU
1896 Proof	100	Value: 350				

X# 12b 20 CENTIMOS

Tin **Ruler:** Alfonso XIII **Obv:** Alphonso XIII boy's head right **Rev:** Crowned arms in sprays

Date	Mintage	F	VF	XF	Unc	BU
1896 Proof	50	Value: 250				

X# 7 4 PESETAS

Silver **Ruler:** Isabel II **Note:** Prev. KY#189.

Date	Mintage	F	VF	XF	Unc	BU
1894	100	—	—	—	650	—
1894 Proof	Inc. above	Value: 900				

X# 7a 4 PESETAS

Bronze **Ruler:** Isabel II **Note:** Prev. KY#189a.

Date	Mintage	F	VF	XF	Unc	BU
1894 Unique; Proof	—	—	—	—	—	—

X# 7b 4 PESETAS

Nickel **Ruler:** Isabel II **Obv:** Countermarked "NIQUEL" behind bust **Note:** Prev. KY#189b.

Date	Mintage	F	VF	XF	Unc	BU
1894 Proof	—	Value: 650				

X# 7c 4 PESETAS

Iron **Ruler:** Isabel II **Note:** Prev. KY#189c.

Date	Mintage	F	VF	XF	Unc	BU
1894 Unique; Proof	—	—	—	—	—	—

X# 10 4 PESETAS

Silver **Ruler:** Maria Christina

Date	Mintage	F	VF	XF	Unc	BU
1894 Proof	25	Value: 1,250				

X# 10a 4 PESETAS

Copper **Ruler:** Maria Christina

Date	Mintage	F	VF	XF	Unc	BU
1894 Unique; Proof	—	—	—	—	—	—

X# 10b 4 PESETAS

Nickel **Ruler:** Maria Christina

Date	Mintage	F	VF	XF	Unc	BU
1894 Unique; Proof	—	—	—	—	—	—

X# 10c 4 PESETAS

Iron **Ruler:** Maria Christina

Date	Mintage	F	VF	XF	Unc	BU
1894 Unique; Proof	—	—	—	—	—	—

X# 14 5 PESETAS
Silver **Ruler:** Isabel II **Rev:** Arms of Castile and Leon **Note:** Prev. KY#196.

Date	Mintage	F	VF	XF	Unc	BU
1904 Proof	—	—	—	—	—	—

X# 14a 5 PESETAS
Bronze **Ruler:** Isabel II **Rev:** Arms of Castile and Leon **Note:** Prev. KY#196a.

Date	Mintage	F	VF	XF	Unc	BU
1904 Proof	—	—	—	—	—	—

X# 14b 5 PESETAS
Lead **Ruler:** Isabel II **Rev:** Arms of Castile and Leon **Note:** Prev. KY#196b.

Date	Mintage	F	VF	XF	Unc	BU
1904 Proof	—	—	—	—	—	—

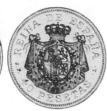

X# 15 40 PESETAS
12.9700 g., Platinum APW **Ruler:** Isabel II **Note:** Prev. KY#198.

Date	Mintage	F	VF	XF	Unc	BU
1904 JP-L Proof	—	Value: 5,000				

X# 15a 40 PESETAS
Gold **Ruler:** Isabel II **Note:** Prev. KY#198a.

Date	Mintage	F	VF	XF	Unc	BU
1904 JP-L Unique; Proof	—	—	—	—	—	—

X# 15b 40 PESETAS
Bronze **Ruler:** Isabel II **Note:** Prev. KY#198b.

Date	Mintage	F	VF	XF	Unc	BU
1904 JP-L Proof	—	—	—	—	—	—

X# 15c 40 PESETAS
Bronzed Nickel **Ruler:** Isabel II **Note:** Prev. KY#198c.

Date	Mintage	F	VF	XF	Unc	BU
1904 JP-L Proof	—	—	—	—	—	—

X# 16 50 PESETAS
16.1700 g., Platinum APW **Ruler:** Isabel II **Note:** Prev. KY#197.

Date	Mintage	F	VF	XF	Unc	BU
1904 JP-L Proof	—	—	—	—	—	—

X# 16a 50 PESETAS
Gold **Ruler:** Isabel II **Note:** Prev. KY#197a.

Date	Mintage	F	VF	XF	Unc	BU
1904 JP-L Unique; Proof	—	—	—	—	—	—

X# 16b 50 PESETAS
Bronze **Ruler:** Isabel II **Note:** Prev. KY#197b.

Date	Mintage	F	VF	XF	Unc	BU
1904 JP-L Proof	—	Value: 550				

X# 8 100 PESETAS
44.0000 g., Platinum APW **Ruler:** Isabel II **Note:** Prev. KY#187.

Date	Mintage	F	VF	XF	Unc	BU
1894 Proof	2	—	—	—	—	—

X# 8a 100 PESETAS
Gold **Ruler:** Isabel II **Note:** Prev. KY#187a.

Date	Mintage	F	VF	XF	Unc	BU
1894 Proof	2	—	—	—	—	—

X# 8b 100 PESETAS
Iridium **Ruler:** Isabel II **Note:** Prev. KY#187b.

Date	Mintage	F	VF	XF	Unc	BU
1894 Unique; Proof	—	—	—	—	—	—

X# 8c 100 PESETAS
Iron **Ruler:** Isabel II **Note:** Prev. KY#187c.

Date	Mintage	F	VF	XF	Unc	BU
1894 Unique; Proof	—	—	—	—	—	—

X# 9 100 PESETAS
Gold **Ruler:** Isabel II **Note:** Prev. KY#188. Design like 4 Pesetas, X#7.

Date	Mintage	F	VF	XF	Unc	BU
1894 Proof	2	—	—	—	—	—

X# 9a 100 PESETAS
31.0400 g., Rhodium **Ruler:** Isabel II **Note:** Prev. KY#188a.

Date	Mintage	F	VF	XF	Unc	BU
1894 Unique; Proof	—	—	—	—	—	—

X# 9b 100 PESETAS
19.4400 g., Palladium **Ruler:** Isabel II **Note:** Prev. KY#188b.

Date	Mintage	F	VF	XF	Unc	BU
1894 Unique; Proof	—	—	—	—	—	—

X# 9c 100 PESETAS
Iron **Ruler:** Isabel II **Note:** Prev. KY#188c.

Date	Mintage	F	VF	XF	Unc	BU
1894 Unique; Proof	—	—	—	—	—	—

X# 11 100 PESETAS
30.5500 g., Platinum APW **Ruler:** Maria Christina **Note:** Prev. Y#190.

Date	Mintage	F	VF	XF	Unc	BU
1894 JP-L Unique; Proof	—	Value: 12,500				

X# 11a 100 PESETAS
Platinum APW **Ruler:** Maria Christina **Note:** Piefort.

Date	Mintage	F	VF	XF	Unc	BU
1894 JP-L Proof	—	—	—	—	—	—

X# 11b 100 PESETAS
Gold **Ruler:** Maria Christina **Note:** Prev. KY#190a.

Date	Mintage	F	VF	XF	Unc	BU
1894 JP-L Unique; Proof	—	—	—	—	—	—

X# 11c 100 PESETAS
Gold **Ruler:** Maria Christina **Note:** Piefort.

Date	Mintage	F	VF	XF	Unc	BU
1894 JP-L Proof	—	—	—	—	—	—

X# 11d 100 PESETAS
Iron **Ruler:** Maria Christina

Date	Mintage	F	VF	XF	Unc	BU
1894 JP-L Proof	—	—	—	—	—	—

X# 11e 100 PESETAS
Iron **Ruler:** Maria Christina **Note:** Piefort.

Date	Mintage	F	VF	XF	Unc	BU
1894 JP-L Proof	—	—	—	—	—	—

X# 11f 100 PESETAS
Lead **Ruler:** Maria Christina

Date	Mintage	F	VF	XF	Unc	BU
1894 JP-L Proof	—	—	—	—	—	—

X# 11g 100 PESETAS
Lead **Ruler:** Maria Christina **Note:** Piefort.

Date	Mintage	F	VF	XF	Unc	BU
1894 JP-L Proof	—	—	—	—	—	—

X# 13 100 PESETAS
Gold **Ruler:** Alfonso XIII **Obv:** Alphonso XIII boy's head right **Rev:** Crowned and mantled arms

Date	Mintage	F	VF	XF	Unc	BU
1896 Proof	3	—	—	—	—	—

X# 17 150 PESETAS
Gold **Ruler:** Isabel II **Note:** Prev. KY#195.

Date	Mintage	F	VF	XF	Unc	BU
1904 Unique	—	—	—	—	—	—

X# 17a 150 PESETAS
Silver **Ruler:** Isabel II **Note:** Prev. KY#195a.

Date	Mintage	F	VF	XF	Unc	BU
1904	—	—	—	—	—	—

X# 17b 150 PESETAS
Silver **Ruler:** Isabel II **Note:** Prev. KY#195b. Piefort.

Date	Mintage	F	VF	XF	Unc	BU
1904	—	—	—	—	—	—

X# 17c 150 PESETAS
Copper **Ruler:** Isabel II **Note:** Prev. KY#195c.

Date	Mintage	F	VF	XF	Unc	BU
1904	—	—	—	—	—	—

X# 17d 150 PESETAS
Iron **Ruler:** Isabel II **Note:** Prev. KY#195d.

Date	Mintage	F	VF	XF	Unc	BU
1904	—	—	—	—	—	—

X# 18 200 PESETAS
Gold **Ruler:** Isabel II **Obv:** Similar to 150 Pesetas, X#17 **Rev:** Arms of Castile and Leon **Note:** Prev. KY#194.

Date	Mintage	F	VF	XF	Unc	BU
1904 Unique	—	—	—	—	—	—

X# 18a 200 PESETAS
Silver **Ruler:** Isabel II **Obv:** Similar to 150 Pesetas, X#17. **Rev:** Arms of Castile and Leon **Note:** Prev. KY#194a.

Date	Mintage	F	VF	XF	Unc	BU
1904	—	—	—	—	—	—

X# 18b 200 PESETAS
Silver **Ruler:** Isabel II **Obv:** Similar to 150 Pesetas, X#17 **Rev:** Arms of Castile and Leon **Note:** Prev. KY#194b. Piefort.

Date	Mintage	F	VF	XF	Unc	BU
1904	—	—	—	—	—	—

X# 18c 200 PESETAS
Iron **Ruler:** Isabel II **Obv:** Similar to 150 Pesetas, X#17 **Rev:** Arms of Castile and Leon **Note:** Prev. KY#194c.

Date	Mintage	F	VF	XF	Unc	BU
1904	—	—	—	—	—	—

X# 18d 200 PESETAS
Lead **Ruler:** Isabel II **Obv:** Similar to 150 Pesetas, X#17 **Rev:** Arms of Castile and Leon **Note:** Prev. KY#194d.

Date	Mintage	F	VF	XF	Unc	BU
1904	—	—	—	—	—	—

EURO - ICB SERIES

X# 131a 20 EURO
Copper-Nickel **Obv:** Framed painting **Obv. Legend:** ESPAÑA **Rev:** Head of Picasso 3/4 left

Date	Mintage	VG	F	VF	XF	Unc
1997	—	—	—	—	—	6.00

X# 131b 20 EURO
Silver **Obv:** Framed painting **Obv. Legend:** ESPAÑA **Rev:** Head of Picasso 3/4 left

Date	Mintage	VG	F	VF	XF	Unc
1997	—	—	—	—	—	20.00

PRETENDER COINAGE

Charles VII 1872-1875

A grandson of Charles V who claimed the throne and maintained a court and government in exile. All Charles VII pieces were made at the Brussels Mint.

NOTE: Some pretender issues which circulated are listed in the regular coinage.

X# PT2.2 50 CENTIMOS
3.1300 g., 0.8350 Silver 0.0840 oz. ASW **Note:** Prev. KM#PT13.

Date	Mintage	F	VF	XF	Unc	BU
1876(b)	—	—	350	450	650	800

X# PT2.1 50 CENTIMOS
2.5100 g., 0.8350 Silver 0.0674 oz. ASW **Note:** Prev. KM#PT13. Counterfeits exist.

Date	Mintage	F	VF	XF	Unc	BU
1876(b)	—	—	350	450	650	800

X# PT3d 5 PESETAS
Bronze **Obv:** Laureate bust right, diamond below **Note:** Counterfeits exist.

Date	Mintage	F	VF	XF	Unc	BU
1874	—	—	—	—	1,600	—
1875	—	—	—	—	1,600	—

X# PT4c 5 PESETAS
Bronze **Obv:** Date below laureate bust right **Note:** Counterfeits exist.

Date	Mintage	F	VF	XF	Unc	BU
1874	—	—	—	—	1,200	—

X# PT4 5 PESETAS
25.5000 g., Silver **Obv:** Date below laureate bust right **Rev:** Crowned arms, P and shield to left, 5 C to right **Rev. Legend:** HISPANIARUM REX. **Edge:** Plain **Note:** Prev. KM#PT10.1. Counterfeits exist.

Date	Mintage	F	VF	XF	Unc	BU
1874	—	—	—	—	2,500	—

X# PT4a 5 PESETAS
51.0000 g., Silver **Obv:** Date below laureate bust right **Note:** Prev. KM#PT10.2. Piefort (double thickness). Counterfeits exist.

Date	Mintage	F	VF	XF	Unc	BU
1874	—	—	—	—	4,000	—

X# PT4b 5 PESETAS
25.5000 g., Silver **Obv:** Date below laureate bust right **Edge:** Reeded **Note:** Prev. KM#PT10.3. Counterfeits exist.

Date	Mintage	F	VF	XF	Unc	BU
1874	—	—	—	—	3,500	—

X# PT5 5 PESETAS
25.5000 g., Silver **Obv:** Laureate bust right, date below **Note:** Prev. KM#PT11.1. Counterfeits exist.

Date	Mintage	F	VF	XF	Unc	BU
1874	—	—	—	—	2,500	—

X# PT5c 5 PESETAS
Tin **Obv:** Laureate bust right, date below **Note:** Prev. KM#PT11.16. Counterfeits exist.

Date	Mintage	F	VF	XF	Unc	BU
1874	—	—	—	—	1,200	—

X# PT5a 5 PESETAS
Bronze **Obv:** Laureate bust right, date below **Note:** Prev. KM#PT11.1a. Counterfeits exist.

Date	Mintage	F	VF	XF	Unc	BU
1874	1	—	—	—	1,600	—

X# PT5b 5 PESETAS
51.0000 g., Silver **Obv:** Laureate bust right, date below **Note:** Prev. KM#PT11.2. Piefort (double thickness). Counterfeits exist.

Date	Mintage	F	VF	XF	Unc	BU
1874	—	—	—	—	4,000	—

X# PT5d 5 PESETAS
1.6124 g., 0.9000 Gold 0.0467 oz. AGW **Obv:** Laureate bust right, date below **Note:** Prev. KM#PT12. Counterfeits exist.

Date	Mintage	F	VF	XF	Unc	BU
1874 Rare	—	—	—	—	—	—

X# PT3 5 PESETAS
25.0000 g., 0.9000 Silver 0.7234 oz. ASW **Obv:** Laureate bust right, diamond below **Rev:** Crown shield divides 5.-P., date below **Edge:** Reeded **Note:** Prev. KM#PT9.1. Counterfeits exist.

Date	Mintage	F	VF	XF	Unc	BU
1874	—	—	—	—	2,200	—
1875	—	—	—	—	2,200	—

X# PT3a 5 PESETAS
50.0000 g., 0.9000 Silver 1.4467 oz. ASW **Obv:** Laureate bust right, diamond below **Rev:** Crown shield divides 5.-P., date below **Note:** Prev. KM#PT9.2. Piefort (double thickness). Counterfeits exist.

Date	Mintage	F	VF	XF	Unc	BU
1874	—	—	—	—	3,500	—

X# PT3b 5 PESETAS
25.0000 g., 0.9000 Silver 0.7234 oz. ASW **Obv:** Laureate bust right, diamond below **Rev:** Crown shield divides 5.-P., date below **Edge:** Plain **Note:** Prev. KM#PT9.3. Counterfeits exist.

Date	Mintage	F	VF	XF	Unc	BU
1874	—	—	—	—	3,500	—

X# PT3c 5 PESETAS
75.0000 g., 0.9000 Silver 2.1701 oz. ASW **Obv:** Laureate bust right, diamond below **Note:** Prev. KM#PT9.4. Triple piefort. Counterfeits exist.

Date	Mintage	F	VF	XF	Unc	BU
1874	—	—	—	—	4,500	—

X# PT6 5 PESETAS
25.5000 g., Silver **Obv:** Laureate bust right **Note:** Prev. KM#PT14. The private patterns of Charles VII, were of a purely political-speculative nature. Counterfeits exist.

Date	Mintage	F	VF	XF	Unc	BU
1885 Proof	—	Value: 850				

CANTON OF CARTAGENA

REVOLUTIONARY COINAGE

1873

1873 Cartagena Mint, Cantonal issue similar to KM#715, 10 Reales and KM#716, 5 Pesetas, are all considered fantasies struck later for collectors.

X# 2 10 REALES
Silver, 30 mm. **Obv. Legend:** CARTAGENA SITIADA POR LOS CENTRALISTAS **Obv. Inscription:** ★/DICIEMBRE/1873 **Rev. Legend:** REVOLUCION **Rev. Inscription:** ★/CANTONAL

Date	Mintage	F	VF	XF	Unc	BU
1873	—	—	150	250	550	—

X# 1 2 PESETAS
10.5000 g., Silver, 28 mm. **Obv. Legend:** CARTAGENA SITIADA POR LOS CENTRALISTAS **Obv. Inscription:** ★/DICIEMBRE/1873 **Rev. Legend:** REVOLUCION **Rev. Inscription:** ★/CANTONAL **Note:** Prev. KY#186. Die varieties exist.

Date	Mintage	F	VF	XF	Unc	BU
1873	—	—	100	175	300	—

KINGDOM

1949 - Present

MEDALLIC COINAGE

Peseta Series

X# M29 100 PESETAS
17.4000 g., Silver, 37.5 mm. **Ruler:** Juan Carlos I **Subject:** Centennial of 100 Peseta Coins **Obv:** Head left **Obv. Legend:** JUAN CARLOS I REY DE ESPAÑA **Rev:** Crowned arms in Order of the Golden Fleece **Rev. Legend:** CENTENARIO DE SU EMISION / COMMEMORACION DE LA MONEDA DE 100 PTAS. DE ALFONSO XIII

Date	Mintage	F	VF	XF	Unc	BU
1977 Proof	500	Value: 35.00				

Ecu Series

X# M23 ECU
6.7200 g., 0.9250 Silver 0.1998 oz. ASW **Ruler:** Juan Carlos I **Obv:** Large value, 12 stars within small circle **Obv. Inscription:** ESPAÑA **Rev:** Europa riding steer left **Rev. Legend:** • EVROPA • **Edge:** Reeded **Note:** Prev. KM#M1 and Bruce#XM3.

Date	Mintage	F	VF	XF	Unc	BU
1989M Prooflike	204,990	—	—	—	—	17.50

X# M8 ECU
6.2200 g., 0.9250 Silver 0.1850 oz. ASW **Subject:** Madrid as European cuture capital

Date	Mintage	F	VF	XF	Unc	BU
1992 Proof	78,289	Value: 10.00				

X# M39 ECU
31.1030 g., 0.9990 Silver 0.9989 oz. ASW, 45 mm. **Subject:** Maastricht Assembly **Obv:** Arc of 12 member's shields around Europa riding steer **Rev:** Members names around outlined map of Europe **Edge:** Plain

Date	Mintage	F	VF	XF	Unc	BU
ND(1992) Proof	5,000	Value: 30.00				

X# M35 ECU
6.7200 g., 0.9250 Silver 0.1998 oz. ASW, 24 mm. **Ruler:** Juan Carlos I **Series:** Madrid Culture **Obv:** Large value, 12 stars within circle, Madrid emblem **Obv. Legend:** ESPAÑA **Rev:** Puerta de Alcalá **Rev. Legend:** MADRID CAPITAL EUROPEA DE LA CULTURE **Edge:** Reeded

Date	Mintage	F	VF	XF	Unc	BU
1992M Prooflike	1,000,000	—	—	—	15.00	—

X# M40 ECU
28.2800 g., 0.9250 Silver 0.8410 oz. ASW, 38.6 mm. **Ruler:** Juan Carlos I **Subject:** 500th Anniversary Discovery of America **Obv:** Large "ECU" on map of Europe **Obv. Legend:** • SPAIN • EUROPE - EUROPA **Rev:** Bust of Columbus behind sailing ship Santa Maria, 12 stars inside inner circle **Rev. Legend:** • CHRISTOPHER COLUMBUS • **Edge:** Reeded

Date	Mintage	F	VF	XF	Unc	BU
ND(1992)PM Proof	10,000	Value: 40.00				

X# M51 ECU

20.0000 g., 0.9990 Silver 0.6423 oz. ASW, 40 mm. **Ruler:** Juan Carlos I **Issuer:** Göde GmbH, Waldaschaff **Obv:** Large "ECU" **Obv. Legend:** ESPAÑA **Rev:** Bust of Columbus facing 3/4 left, small sailing ship Santa Maria at left **Rev. Legend:** .500 AÑOS DESCUISRIMIENTO DE AMERICA • CHRISTOBAL COLON **Edge:** Reeded

Date	Mintage	F	VF	XF	Unc	BU
(19)93 Proof	9,999	Value: 50.00				

X# M61 ECU

5.2000 g., Copper-Nickel-Zinc, 22.5 mm. **Ruler:** Juan Carlos I **Issuer:** Europa Numismatics, England **Obv:** Iberian lancer horseback right, 6 stars at left, 6 stars at right in outer ring **Obv. Designer:** R. D. Maklouf **Rev:** Large tree, 6 stars at left, 6 stars at right in outer ring **Rev. Legend:** EUROPA - ISLAS CANARIAS **Edge:** Plain

Date	Mintage	F	VF	XF	Unc	BU
1994	—	—	—	—	3.50	—

X# M62 ECU

5.2000 g., Copper-Nickel-Zinc, 22.5 mm. **Ruler:** Juan Carlos I **Issuer:** Europa Numismatics, England **Subject:** Iberian lancer horseback right, 6 stars at left, 6 stars at right in outer ring **Obv. Designer:** R. D. Maklouf **Rev:** Cathedral, 6 stars at left, 6 stars at right in outer ring **Rev. Legend:** EUROPA - CATALUNYA **Edge:** Plain

Date	Mintage	F	VF	XF	Unc	BU
1994	—	—	—	—	3.50	—

X# M63 ECU

5.2000 g., Copper-Nickel-Zinc, 22.5 mm. **Ruler:** Juan Carlos I **Issuer:** Europa Numismatics, England **Obv:** Iberian lancer horseback right, 6 stars at left, 6 stars at right in outer ring **Obv. Designer:** R. D. Maklouf **Rev:** Poseidon riding sea chariot, 6 stars at left, 6 stars at right in outer ring **Rev. Legend:** EUROPA - MADRID **Edge:** Plain

Date	Mintage	F	VF	XF	Unc	BU
1994	—	—	—	—	3.50	—

X# M64 ECU

5.2000 g., Copper-Nickel-Zinc, 22.5 mm. **Ruler:** Juan Carlos I **Issuer:** Europa Numismatics, England **Obv:** Iberian lancer horseback right, 6 stars at left, 6 stars at right in outer ring **Obv. Designer:** R. D. Maklouf **Rev:** Bull race, 6 stars at left, 6 stars at right in outer ring **Rev. Legend:** EUROPA - NAVARRA **Edge:** Plain

Date	Mintage	F	VF	XF	Unc	BU
1994	—	—	—	—	3.50	—

X# M72 ECU

23.0000 g., 0.9250 Silver 0.6840 oz. ASW, 38 mm. **Ruler:** Juan Carlos I **Issuer:** Europa Numismatics, England **Obv:** Iberian lancer horseback right, 6 stars at left, 6 stas at right in outer ring **Obv. Designer:** R. D. Maklouf **Rev:** Bull race, 6 stars at left, 6 stars at right in outer ring **Rev. Legend:** EUROPA - NAVARRA **Edge:** Plain

Date	Mintage	F	VF	XF	Unc	BU
1994 Proof	—	Value: 40.00				

X# M45 ECU

6.7200 g., 0.9250 Silver 0.1998 oz. ASW, 24 mm. **Ruler:** Juan Carlos I **Obv:** Windmills, 12 stars within small circle **Obv. Legend:** ESPAÑA **Obv. Designer:** M. M. Tornero **Rev:** Don Quijote standing with dog alongside **Rev. Legend:** DON GUIJOTE DE LA MANCHA **Rev. Designer:** E. González **Edge:** Reeded

Date	Mintage	F	VF	XF	Unc	BU
1994M Prooflike	125,000	—	—	—	17.50	—

X# M12 ECU

6.2200 g., 0.9250 Silver 0.1850 oz. ASW **Subject:** Don Quixote

Date	Mintage	F	VF	XF	Unc	BU
1994 Proof	36,904	Value: 15.00				

X# M16 ECU

6.2200 g., 0.9250 Silver 0.1850 oz. ASW **Subject:** Nautilus **Rev:** Ship

Date	Mintage	F	VF	XF	Unc	BU
1996 Proof	29,786	Value: 15.00				

X# M24 5 ECU

33.6200 g., 0.9250 Silver 0.9998 oz. ASW, 42 mm. **Ruler:** Juan Carlos I **Obv:** Large value, 12 stars within circle **Obv. Legend:** ESPAÑA **Rev:** Charles V on horseback right **Rev. Legend:** • CAES • CAROLVS • V • AVGVSTVS • IMPERATOR • **Edge:** Reeded **Note:** Prev. KM#M2 and Bruce#XM4.

Date	Mintage	F	VF	XF	Unc	BU
1989M Prooflike	250,000	—	—	—	—	30.00

X# M6 5 ECU

31.1000 g., 0.9250 Silver 0.9249 oz. ASW **Subject:** Alphonso X of Castile

Date	Mintage	F	VF	XF	Unc	BU
1990 Proof	50,000	Value: 27.50				

X# M30 5 ECU

33.6200 g., 0.9250 Silver 0.9998 oz. ASW, 42 mm. **Ruler:** Juan Carlos I **Obv:** Large value, 12 stars within small circle **Obv. Legend:** ESPAÑA **Rev:** Alfonso on horseback left **Rev. Legend:** ALFONSVS : DEI : GRACIA : REX : CASTEILE **Rev. Designer:** L. J. Diaz Salas **Edge:** Reeded

Date	Mintage	F	VF	XF	Unc	BU
1990M Prooflike	50,000	—	—	—	35.00	—

X# M31 5 ECU

33.6200 g., 0.9250 Silver 0.9998 oz. ASW, 42 mm. **Ruler:** Juan Carlos I **Obv:** Large value, 12 stars within small circle **Obv. Legend:** ESPAÑA **Rev:** Averroes seated facing right **Rev. Designer:** L. A. Garciá **Edge:** Reeded

Date	Mintage	F	VF	XF	Unc	BU
1991M Prooflike	50,000	—	—	—	35.00	—

X# M7 5 ECU

33.6200 g., 0.9250 Silver 0.9998 oz. ASW **Subject:** Averroes - Moorish Philosopher

Date	Mintage	F	VF	XF	Unc	BU
1991 Proof	50,000	Value: 25.00				

X# M11 5 ECU
33.6200 g., 0.9250 Silver 0.9998 oz. ASW **Subject:** Madrid as European culture capital **Rev:** Carlos III

Date	Mintage	F	VF	XF	Unc	BU
1992 Proof	Est. 49,798	Value: 65.00				

X# M36 5 ECU
33.6200 g., 0.9250 Silver 0.9998 oz. ASW, 42 mm. **Ruler:** Juan Carlos I **Series:** Madrid Culture **Obv:** Large value, 12 stars within small circle, Madrid emblem **Obv. Legend:** ESPAÑA **Rev:** Charles III standing facing **Rev. Legend:** MADRID CAPITAL EUROPEA DE LA CULTURE **Edge:** Reeded

Date	Mintage	F	VF	XF	Unc	BU
1992M Prooflike	100,000	—	—	—	35.00	—

X# M9 5 ECU
33.6200 g., 0.9250 Silver 0.9998 oz. ASW **Rev:** Don Juan

Date	Mintage	F	VF	XF	Unc	BU
1993 Proof	36,000	Value: 35.00				

X# M43 5 ECU
33.6200 g., 0.9250 Silver 0.9998 oz. ASW, 42 mm. **Ruler:** Juan Carlos I **Obv:** Small sailing ship, 12 stars within small circle **Obv. Legend:** ESPAÑA **Rev:** Don Juan de Borbon seated, facing 3/4 right **Edge:** Reeded

Date	Mintage	F	VF	XF	Unc	BU
1993M Prooflike	35,910	—	—	—	35.00	—

X# M46 5 ECU
33.6200 g., 0.9250 Silver 0.9998 oz. ASW, 42 mm. **Ruler:** Juan Carlos I **Obv:** D. Quijote horseback, D. S. Panza riding donkey **Obv. Legend:** ESPAÑA **Obv. Designer:** R. Vallejo **Rev:** Bust of Cervantes facing 3/4 left **Rev. Legend:** MIGUEL DE CERVANTES **Rev. Designer:** L. J. Díaz Salas **Edge:** Reeded

Date	Mintage	F	VF	XF	Unc	BU
1994M Prooflike	75,000	—	—	—	35.00	—

X# M13 5 ECU
33.6200 g., 0.9250 Silver 0.9998 oz. ASW **Rev:** Don Quixote

Date	Mintage	F	VF	XF	Unc	BU
1994 Proof	Est. 38,000	Value: 30.00				

X# MA17 5 ECU
Silver **Obv:** Don Juan de Austria **Rev:** Galley under sail, denomination

Date	Mintage	F	VF	XF	Unc	BU
1995 Proof	—	Value: 75.00				

X# M17 5 ECU
33.6200 g., 0.9250 Silver 0.9998 oz. ASW **Rev:** Coca de Mataro

Date	Mintage	F	VF	XF	Unc	BU
1996 Proof	43,802	Value: 35.00				

X# M25 10 ECU
3.4500 g., 0.9000 Gold 0.0998 oz. AGW, 16 mm. **Ruler:** Juan Carlos I **Obv:** Large value, 12 stars within small circle **Obv. Legend:** ESPAÑA **Rev:** Crowned pillars of Hercules **Rev. Inscription:** PLV SVL TRA **Edge:** Reeded **Note:** Prev. KM#M3 and Bruce#XM5.

Date	Mintage	F	VF	XF	Unc	BU
1989M Prooflike	28,040	—	—	—	—	120

X# M65 10 ECU
Bi-Metallic Brass gilt/Copper, 38 mm. **Ruler:** Juan Carlos I **Issuer:** Europa Numismatics, England **Obv:** Iberian lancer horseback right, 6 stars at left, 6 stars at right in outer ring **Obv. Designer:** R. D. Maklouf **Rev:** Large tree, 6 stars at left, 6 stars at right in outer ring **Rev. Legend:** EUROPA - ISLAS CANARIAS **Edge:** Plain

Date	Mintage	F	VF	XF	Unc	BU
1994 Proof	3,000	Value: 12.50				

X# M66 10 ECU
Bi-Metallic Brass gilt/Copper, 38 mm. **Ruler:** Juan Carlos I **Issuer:** Europa Numismatics, England

Obv: Iberian lancer on horseback right, 6 stars at left, 6 stars at right in outer ring **Obv. Designer:** R. D. Maklouf **Rev:** Cathedral, 6 stars at left, 6 stars at right in outer ring **Rev. Legend:** EUROPA - CATALUNYA **Edge:** Plain

Date	Mintage	F	VF	XF	Unc	BU
1994 Proof	3,000	Value: 12.50				

X# M67 10 ECU

Bi-Metallic Brass gilt/Copper, 38 mm. **Ruler:** Juan Carlos I **Issuer:** Europa Numismatics, England **Obv:** Iberian lancer on horseback right, 6 stars at left, 6 stars at right in outer ring **Obv. Designer:** R. D. Maklouf **Rev:** Poseidon riding sea chariot, 6 stars at left, 6 stars at right in outer ring **Rev. Legend:** EUROPA - MADRID **Edge:** Plain

Date	Mintage	F	VF	XF	Unc	BU
1994 Proof	3,000	Value: 12.50				

X# M68 10 ECU

Bi-Metallic Brass gilt/Copper, 38 mm. **Ruler:** Juan Carlos I **Issuer:** Europa Numismatics, England **Obv:** Iberian lancer on horseback right, 6 stars at left, 6 stars at right in outer ring **Obv. Designer:** R. D. Maklouf **Rev:** Bull race, 6 stars at left, 6 stars at right in outer ring **Rev. Legend:** EUROPA - NAVARRA **Edge:** Plain

Date	Mintage	F	VF	XF	Unc	BU
1994 Proof	3,000	Value: 12.50				

X# M18 25 ECU

168.6200 g., 0.9250 Silver 5.0145 oz. ASW, 73.2 mm. **Subject:** Madrid: European cultural capital **Obv:** Denomination and city list **Rev:** Portrait above palace **Edge:** Plain **Note:** Illustration reduced

Date	Mintage	F	VF	XF	Unc	BU
1992 Proof	—	Value: 150				

X# M37 25 ECU

168.7500 g., 0.9250 Silver 5.0183 oz. ASW, 73 mm. **Ruler:** Juan Carlos I **Series:** Madrid Culture **Obv:** Seven European cities and respective dates, Madrid emblem, 12 stars within small circle **Obv. Legend:** ESPAÑA **Rev:** Oval with Sofia facing right above palace, palace grounds **Rev. Legend:** MADRID CAPITAL EUROPEA DE LA CULTURA **Edge:** Reeded **Note:** Illustration reduced.

Date	Mintage	F	VF	XF	Unc	BU
1992M Prooflike	—	—	—	—	175	—

X# M69 25 ECU

23.0000 g., 0.9250 Silver 0.6840 oz. ASW, 38 mm. **Ruler:** Juan Carlos I **Issuer:** Europa Numismatics, England **Obv:** Iberian lancer on horseback right, 6 stars at left, 6 stars at right in outer ring **Obv. Designer:** R. D. Maklouf **Rev:** Large tree, 6 stars at left, 6 stars at right in outer ring **Rev. Legend:** EUROPA - ISLAS CANARIAS **Edge:** Plain

Date	Mintage	F	VF	XF	Unc	BU
1994 Proof	—	Value: 40.00				

X# M70 25 ECU

23.0000 g., 0.9250 Silver 0.6840 oz. ASW, 38 mm. **Ruler:** Juan Carlos I **Issuer:** Europa Numismatics, England **Obv:** Iberian lancer on horseback right, 6 stars at left, 6 stars at right in outer ring **Obv. Designer:** R. D. Maklouf **Rev:** Cathedral, 6 stars at left, 6 stars at right in outer ring **Rev. Legend:** EUROPA - CATALUNYA **Edge:** Plain

Date	Mintage	F	VF	XF	Unc	BU
1994 Proof	—	Value: 40.00				

X# M71 25 ECU

23.0000 g., 0.9250 Silver 0.6840 oz. ASW, 38 mm. **Ruler:** Juan Carlos I **Issuer:** Europa Numismatics, England **Obv:** Iberian lancer on horseback right, 6 stars at left, 6 stars at right in outer ring **Obv. Designer:** R. D. Maklouf **Rev:** Poseidon riding sea chariot, 6 stars at left, 6 stars at right in outer ring **Rev. Legend:** EUROPA - MADRID **Edge:** Plain

Date	Mintage	F	VF	XF	Unc	BU
1994 Proof	—	Value: 40.00				

X# M47 25 ECU

168.7500 g., 0.9250 Silver 5.0183 oz. ASW, 73 mm. **Ruler:** Juan Carlos I **Obv:** Acalá de Henarés University, statue **Obv. Legend:** ESPAÑA **Obv. Designer:** L. J. Díaz Salas **Rev:** Lepanto sea battle **Rev. Designer:** M. M. Tornero **Edge:** Reeded **Note:** Illustration reduced.

Date	Mintage	F	VF	XF	Unc	BU
1994M Prooflike	15,000	—	—	—	165	—

X# M19 25 ECU
168.7500 g., 0.9250 Silver 5.0183 oz. ASW, 73 mm. **Obv:** Three portraits **Rev:** Large sailing ships **Edge:** Plain **Note:** Illustration reduced.

Date	Mintage	F	VF	XF	Unc	BU
1995 Proof	75,000	Value: 150				

X# M26 50 ECU
17.2700 g., 0.9000 Gold 0.4997 oz. AGW, 28 mm. **Ruler:** Juan Carlos I **Obv:** Large value, 12 stars within circle **Obv. Legend:** ESPAÑA **Rev:** Bust of Philip II left **Rev. Legend:** : PHILIP • II • D • G • HISPAN • ET • IND • REX : **Edge:** Reeded **Note:** Prev. KM#M4 and Bruce#XM6.

Date	Mintage	F	VF	XF	Unc	BU
1989M Prooflike	15,310	—	—	—	—	500

X# M27 100 ECU
34.5500 g., 0.9000 Gold 0.9997 oz. AGW **Ruler:** Juan Carlos I **Obv:** Large value, 12 stars within circle below **Obv. Legend:** ESPAÑA **Rev:** Charles V horseback right **Rev. Legend:** • CAES • CAROLVS • V • AVGVSTVS • IMPERATOR • **Edge:** Reeded **Note:** Prev. KM#M5 and Bruce#XM7.

Date	Mintage	F	VF	XF	Unc	BU
1989M Prooflike	10,000	—	—	—	—	1,000

X# M38 100 ECU
34.5500 g., 0.9000 Gold 0.9997 oz. AGW, 40 mm. **Ruler:** Juan Carlos I **Series:** Madrid Culture **Obv:** Large value, 12 stars within small circle, Madrid emblem **Obv. Legend:** ESPAÑA **Rev:** Charles III standing facing **Rev. Legend:** MADRID CAPITAL EUROPEA DE LA CULTURE **Edge:** Reeded

Date	Mintage	F	VF	XF	Unc	BU
1992M Prooflike	10,000	—	—	—	850	—

X# M14 100 ECU
34.5500 g., 0.9000 Gold 0.9997 oz. AGW **Subject:** Madrid as European culture capital **Rev:** Carlos III

Date	Mintage	F	VF	XF	Unc	BU
1992 Proof	Est. 10,000	Value: 600				

X# M10 100 ECU
34.5500 g., 0.9000 Gold 0.9997 oz. AGW **Subject:** Don Juan de Borbon

Date	Mintage	F	VF	XF	Unc	BU
ND(1993) Proof	2,020	Value: 800				

X# M44 100 ECU
34.5500 g., 0.9000 Gold 0.9997 oz. AGW, 40 mm. **Ruler:** Juan Carlos I **Obv:** Large early sailing ship, 12 stars within small circle **Obv. Legend:** ESPAÑA **Rev:** Don Juan de Borbon seated, facing 3/4 right **Edge:** Reeded

Date	Mintage	F	VF	XF	Unc	BU
1993M Prooflike	2,020	—	—	—	950	—

X# M15 100 ECU
34.5500 g., 0.9000 Gold 0.9997 oz. AGW **Subject:** Don Quixote

Date	Mintage	F	VF	XF	Unc	BU
1994 Proof	Est. 3,500	Value: 650				

X# M48 100 ECU
34.5500 g., 0.9000 Gold 0.9997 oz. AGW **Ruler:** Juan Carlos I **Obv:** Two riders on toy-like horse **Obv. Legend:** ESPAÑA **Obv. Designer:** B. Castellanos **Rev:** Bust of Cervantes facing 3/4 left **Rev. Legend:** MIGUEL DE CERVANTES **Edge:** Reeded

Date	Mintage	F	VF	XF	Unc	BU
1994M Prooflike	3,500	—	—	—	950	—

EURO - ICB SERIES

X# 131 20 EURO
Goldine **Obv:** Framed painting **Obv. Legend:** ESPAÑA **Rev:** Head of Picasso 3/4 left

Date	Mintage	VG	F	VF	XF	Unc
1997	—	—	—	—	—	6.00

MEDALLIC COINAGE

Juan Carlos I Issue

X# M1 500 PESETAS
20.0000 g., Silver **Ruler:** Juan Carlos I **Subject:** Last Barcelona 5 Peseta of 1808 Commemorative

Date	Mintage	F	VF	XF	Unc	BU
1978	500	—	—	—	950	—

X# M2 500 PESETAS
27.0000 g., Gold **Ruler:** Juan Carlos I **Subject:** Last Barcelona 5 Peseta of 1808 Commemorative

Date	Mintage	F	VF	XF	Unc	BU
1978	500	—	—	—	550	—

MEDALLIC BULLION

X# MB11 5 OUNCES
155.5150 g., 0.9990 Silver 4.9947 oz. ASW, 68 mm. **Ruler:** Juan Carlos I **Subject:** Visit to Puerto Rico **Obv:** Arms **Obv. Legend:** * HISPANIARVM * REX * **Rev:** Head of Juan Carlos left **Rev. Legend:** VISITA DE S.M. JUAN CARLOS REY DE ESPANA - PUERTO RICO

Date	Mintage	F	VF	XF	Unc	BU
1987Mo Proof	2,500	Value: 145				

PIEFORTS

X#	Date	Mintage	Identification	Mkt Val
P1	1997	—	20 Euro. Silver. X#131b.	40.00

TRIAL STRIKES

X#	Date	Mintage	Identification	Issue Price	Mkt Val
TS1	ND	—	5 Pesetas. Copper. Prev. KM#A68c. Obverse. X#4.	—	1,000
TS2	ND	—	5 Pesetas. Copper. Prev. KM#A68d. Reverse. X#4.	—	1,000

PROOF-LIKE SETS (PL)

X#	Date	Mintage	Identification	Issue Price	Mkt Val
XPS1	1989M (5)	—	X23-27	—	1,700
XPS2	1992M (4)	—	X-M35-M38	—	1,100
XPS3	1993M (2)	—	X-M43, X-M44	—	985
XPS4	1989, 1992 (3)	—	X-M24, X-M35, X-M46	—	80.00
XPS5	1994M (4)	—	X-M45-M48	—	1,175

CATALONIA

AUTONOMOUS COMMUNITY

MEDALLIC COINAGE

Ecu Series - Sertons International, Barcelona

X# M11 5 ECU
25.0000 g., Copper-Nickel, 38 mm. **Subject:** 20th Anniversary Death of Composer Pau Casals **Obv:** Eight stylized figures above arms **Obv. Legend:** CATALUNYA **Rev:** Casals playing cello behind music store **Edge:** Plain

Date	Mintage	F	VF	XF	Unc	BU
1993	10,000	—	—	—	—	9.00

X# M14 5 ECU
25.0000 g., Copper-Nickel, 38 mm. **Obv:** Eight stylized figures above arms **Obv. Legend:** CATALUNYA **Rev:** Bust of Josep Pla i Casadevall, journalist and scriptwriter 3/4 left, open book behind

Date	Mintage	F	VF	XF	Unc	BU
1994	10,000	—	—	—	—	9.00

X# M12 25 ECU
25.0000 g., 0.9990 Silver 0.8029 oz. ASW, 38 mm. **Subject:** 20th Anniversary Death of Composer Pau Casals **Obv:** Eight stylized figures above arms **Obv. Legend:** CATALUNYA **Rev:** Casals playing cello behind music sscore **Edge:** Reeded

Date	Mintage	F	VF	XF	Unc	BU
1993 Proof	25,000	Value: 45.00				

X# M15 25 ECU
25.0000 g., 0.9990 Silver 0.8029 oz. ASW, 38 mm. **Obv:** Eight stylized figures above arms **Obv. Legend:** CATALUNYA **Rev:** Bust of Josep Pla i Casadevall, journalist and scriptwriter 3/4 left, open book behind

Date	Mintage	F	VF	XF	Unc	BU
1994 Proof	25,000	Value: 50.00				

X# M13 250 ECU
25.4500 g., 0.9167 Gold 0.7500 oz. AGW, 38 mm. **Subject:** 20th Anniversary Death of Composer Pau Casals **Obv:** Eight stylized figures above arms **Obv. Legend:** CATALUNYA **Rev:** Casals playing cello behind music score **Edge:** Reeded

Date	Mintage	F	VF	XF	Unc	BU
1993 Proof	1,000	Value: 750				

X# M16 250 ECU
25.4500 g., 0.9167 Gold 0.7500 oz. AGW, 38 mm. **Obv:** Eight stylized figures above arms **Obv. Legend:** CATALUNYA **Rev:** Bust of Josep Pla i Casadevall, journalist and scriptwriter 3/4 left, open book behind

Date	Mintage	F	VF	XF	Unc	BU
1994 Proof	1,000	Value: 750				

Ecu Series - Uncertain Issuer

X# M17 ECU
6.7200 g., 0.9250 Silver 0.1998 oz. ASW, 24 mm. **Obv:** Arms **Obv. Legend:** VINDICAMUS HEREDITATEM PATRUM NOSTRORUM **Rev:** Pau Claris i Casademunt **Edge:** Reeded

Date	Mintage	F	VF	XF	Unc	BU
1993C Proof	50,100	Value: 17.50				

X# M18 5 ECU
33.6200 g., 0.9250 Silver 0.9998 oz. ASW, 42 mm. **Obv:** Arms **Obv. Legend:** VINDICAMUS HEREDITATEM PATRUM NOSTRORUM **Rev:** Lluis Compayis i Jover **Edge:** Reeded

Date	Mintage	F	VF	XF	Unc	BU
1993C Proof	25,100	Value: 37.50				

X# M19 25 ECU
168.7500 g., 0.9250 Silver 5.0183 oz. ASW, 73 mm. **Obv:** Arms **Obv. Legend:** VINDICAMUS HEREDITATEM PATRUM NOSTRORUM **Rev:** Josep Taradellas i Joan **Edge:** Reeded

Date	Mintage	F	VF	XF	Unc	BU
1993C Proof	10,100	Value: 125				

X# M20 100 ECU
34.5500 g., 0.9000 Gold 0.9997 oz. AGW, 40 mm. **Obv:** Arms **Obv. Legend:** VINDICAMUS HEREDITATEM PATRUM NOSTRORUM **Rev:** Ehric Prat de la Riba i Sarrà **Edge:** Reeded

Date	Mintage	F	VF	XF	Unc	BU
1993C Proof	3,100	Value: 950				

X# M21 1000 ECU
337.5000 g., 0.9000 Gold 9.7654 oz. AGW, 73 mm.
Obv: Arms **Obv. Legend:** VINDICAMUS HEREDITATEM PATRUM NOSTRORUM
Rev: Francesc Macià i Llusà **Edge:** Reeded

Date	Mintage	F	VF	XF	Unc	BU
1993C Proof	200	Value: 8,000				

PROVINCE

MEDALLIC COINAGE

Ecu Series - Sertons International, Barcelona

X# M9 25 ECU
24.8500 g., 0.9990 Silver 0.7981 oz. ASW, 37.6 mm.
Obv: Eight stylized figures above arms **Rev:** Bust of Artori Gaudi right at left, cathedral at right **Edge:** Reeded

Date	Mintage	F	VF	XF	Unc	BU
1994 Proof	—	Value: 45.00				

X# M28 25 ECU
24.8500 g., 0.9990 Silver 0.7981 oz. ASW, 37.6 mm.
Obv: Eight stylized figures above arms **Rev:** Bust of Salvavdor Dali facing 3/4 left at right, artwork at left
Edge: Reeded

Date	Mintage	F	VF	XF	Unc	BU
1995 Proof	—	Value: 60.00				

PROOF SETS

X#	Date	Mintage	Identification	Issue Price	Mkt Val
XPS1	1993c (5)	100	X17-21	—	9,000

SPANISH COLONIAL

KINGDOM

FANTASY COINAGE

X# 2 1/4 REAL
0.7500 g., Silver **Edge:** Plain **Note:** Modern fantasies sold in complete date sets. A crude titled *C* appears on the reverse under the lion on some dates.

Date	Mintage	F	VF	XF	Unc	BU
1796	—	—	—	—	4.00	—
1797	—	—	—	—	4.00	—
1798	—	—	—	—	4.00	—
1799	—	—	—	—	4.00	—
1800	—	—	—	—	4.00	—
1801	—	—	—	—	4.00	—
1802	—	—	—	—	4.00	—
1803	—	—	—	—	4.00	—
1804	—	—	—	—	4.00	—
1805	—	—	—	—	4.00	—
1806	—	—	—	—	4.00	—
1807	—	—	—	—	4.00	—
1808	—	—	—	—	4.00	—
1809	—	—	—	—	4.00	—
1810	—	—	—	—	4.00	—
1811	—	—	—	—	4.00	—
1812	—	—	—	—	4.00	—
1813	—	—	—	—	4.00	—
1814	—	—	—	—	4.00	—
1815	—	—	—	—	4.00	—
1816	—	—	—	—	4.00	—

X# 6 DINDERO
24.8800 g., Silver **Note:** A virtually unknown military piece. This item surfaced in Hong Kong.

Date	Mintage	Good	VG	F	VF	XF
ND	—	15.00	25.00	35.00	50.00	—

X# 21 8 REALES
Silver

Date	Mintage	Good	VG	F	VF	XF
1401	—	20.00	35.00	50.00	—	—

X# 11 8 REALES
Silver

Date	Mintage	Good	VG	F	VF	XF
1677	—	15.00	25.00	35.00	—	—

SPANISH NETHERLANDS

FLANDERS

SPANISH RULE

MEDALLIC COINAGE

X# M5 DAALDER
30.1100 g., Silver, 43 mm. **Ruler:** Philip II **Obv:** Bust left **Obv. Legend:** PHILIPPVS • DEI • G • HISPANIARVM • REX • INVIC **Rev:** Crowned Spanish arms surrounded by 18 crowned state shields **Edge:** Plain

Date	Mintage	VG	F	VF	XF	Unc
ND(ca. 1567)	—	—	—	—	3,500	5,000

SPITZBERGEN

NORWEGIAN TERRITORY

TOKEN COINAGE

Catastrophe Memorial Issues

X# Tn15 10 ROUBLES
11.9000 g., Copper-Nickel, 30 mm. **Subject:** New York September 11th Attack on Twin Towers **Obv:** Large value "10" without "РАЗМЕННЫЕ ЗНАК" above date in center; legend translation: "ISLAND SPITZBERGEN" at top, "ARCTIC COAL" in exergue **Rev:** Twin towers attack scene **Rev. Legend:** Translation: "Anti Terrorism" at top, "New York 11 September" in exergue **Edge:** Segmented reeding **Note:** Prev. KM#Tn15.

Date	Mintage	F	VF	XF	Unc	BU
2001 Proof	1,001	Value: 35.00				

X# Tn16.1 10 ROUBLES
12.0500 g., Copper-Nickel, 30 mm. **Subject:** Sinking of USSR Submarine Kursk **Obv:** Large value "10" without "РАЗМЕННЫИ ЗНАК" above date in center; Legend translation: "ISLAND SPITZBERGEN" at top "ARCTIC COAL" at bottom **Rev:** Raising the Kursk **Rev. Legend:** ПОДЪЕМ ПОДЛОДКИ КУРСК **Edge:** Segmented reeding **Note:** Variety with quotes in "?????".

Date	Mintage	F	VF	XF	Unc	BU
2001 Proof	800	Value: 35.00				

Note: Estimated mintage

X# Tn16.2 10 ROUBLES
12.0500 g., Copper-Nickel, 30 mm. **Subject:** Sinking of USSR Submarine Kursk **Obv:** Large value "10" without "РАЗМЕННЫИ ЗНАК" above date in center; legend translation: "ISLAND SPITZBERGEN" at top "ARCTIC COAL" at bottom **Rev:** Raising the Kursk **Rev. Legend:** ПОДЪЕМ ПОДМОДКИ КУРСК **Edge:** Segmented reeding **Note:** Variety with quotes in "?????".

Date	Mintage	F	VF	XF	Unc	BU
2001 Proof	200	Value: 50.00				

Note: Estimated mintage

X# Tn17 10 ROUBLES
Copper-Nickel, 30 mm. **Subject:** New York September 11th Attack on Twin Towers **Obv:** Large value "10" without "РАЗМЕННЫИ ЗНАК" above date in center; legend translation: "ISLAND SPITZBERGEN" at top "ARCTIC COAL" at bottom **Rev:** Twin Towers under attack **Rev. Legend:** ПРОТИВ ТЕРРОРИЗМА **Edge:** Segmented reeding

Date	Mintage	F	VF	XF	Unc	BU
2001 Proof	1,100	Value: 35.00				

X# Tn18 10 ROUBLES
12.4000 g., Copper-Nickel, 30 mm. **Subject:** Sinking of USSR Submarine Kursk **Obv:** Large value "10" without "РАЗМЕННЫИ ЗНАК" above date in center; legend translation: "ISLAND SPITZBERGEN" at top "ARCTIC COAL" at bottom **Rev:** Raising the Kursk **Rev. Legend:** ПОДЪЕМ ПОДЛОДКИ КУРСК **Edge:** Segmented reeding

Date	Mintage	F	VF	XF	Unc	BU
2001 Proof	1,100	Value: 35.00				

X# Tn19 10 ROUBLES
11.5000 g., Copper-Nickel, 30 mm. **Subject:** Flood in Central Europe **Obv:** Large value "10" without "РАЗМЕННЫИ ЗНАК" above date in center; legend translation: "ISLAND SPITZBERGEN" at top "ARCTIC COAL" at bottom **Rev:** Flooding scene **Rev. Legend:** НАВОДНЕНИЕ - АЕНТР ЕВРОЛЫ **Edge:** Segmented reeding

Date	Mintage	F	VF	XF	Unc	BU
2002 Proof	2,200	Value: 25.00				

X# Tn20 10 ROUBLES
11.5000 g., Copper-Nickel, 30 mm. **Subject:** Flood in South Russia **Obv:** Large value "10" without "РАЗМЕННЫИ ЗНАК" above date in center; legend translation: "ISLAND SPITZBERGEN" at top "ARCTIC COAL" at bottom **Rev:** Rescue helicopter hovering over flood victims **Rev. Legend:** НАВОДНЕНИЕ - ЮГ РОССИИ **Edge:** Segmented reeding

Date	Mintage	F	VF	XF	Unc	BU
2002 Proof	2,200	Value: 25.00				

X# Tn21 10 ROUBLES
12.1300 g., Copper-Nickel, 30 mm. **Subject:** Chechen Terrorists Capture Moscow Theater **Obv:** Large value "10" without "РАЗМЕННЫИ ЗНАК" above date in center; legend translation: "ISLAND SPITZBERGEN" at top "ARCTIC COAL" at bottom **Rev:** Scene inside captured theater **Rev. Legend:** ПРОТИВ ТЕРРОРИЗМА **Edge:** Segmented reeding

Date	Mintage	F	VF	XF	Unc	BU
2002 Proof	2,200	Value: 25.00				

X# Tn22 10 ROUBLES
12.1300 g., Copper-Nickel, 30 mm. **Subject:** Avalanche in Karmadon Gorge Caucasus **Obv:** Large value "10" without "РАЗМЕННЫИ ЗНАК" above date in center; legend translation: "ISLAND SPITZBERGEN" at top "ARCTIC COAL" at bottom **Rev:** 1/2-length figure with view of gorge behind **Rev. Legend:** СЕИТЯБЬ / 2002 **Edge:** Segmented reeding

Date	Mintage	F	VF	XF	Unc	BU
2002 Proof	2,200	Value: 25.00				

Artic Coal Issues

X# Tn9 10 KOPEKS (0.1 Rouble)
Aluminum **Obv:** 2 walruses above world globe **Rev:** Large value **Note:** Prev. KM#9.

Date	Mintage	F	VF	XF	Unc	BU
1998	6,000	—	—	—	3.00	—

X# Tn10 25 KOPEKS (0.25 Rouble)
Aluminum **Obv:** 2 walruses above world globe **Rev:** Large value **Note:** Prev. KM#10.

Date	Mintage	F	VF	XF	Unc	BU
1998	6,000	—	—	—	3.25	—

X# Tn11 50 KOPEKS (0.5 Rouble)
Aluminum **Obv:** 2 walruses above world globe **Rev:** Large value **Note:** Prev. KM#11.

Date	Mintage	F	VF	XF	Unc	BU
1998	6,000	—	—	—	3.50	—

X# Tn12 ROUBLE
Brass **Obv:** Polar bear left above world globe **Rev:** Large value **Note:** Prev. KM#12.

Date	Mintage	F	VF	XF	Unc	BU
1998	4,000	—	—	—	4.50	—

X# Tn13 2 ROUBLES
Brass **Obv:** Polar bear left above world globe **Rev:** Large value **Note:** Prev. KM#13.

Date	Mintage	F	VF	XF	Unc	BU
1998	4,000	—	—	—	5.50	—

X# Tn14 5 ROUBLES
Copper-Nickel **Obv:** Whale left above world globe **Rev:** Large value **Note:** Prev. KM#14.

Date	Mintage	F	VF	XF	Unc	BU
1998	4,000	—	—	—	6.50	—

X# Tn23 10 (UNKNOWN UNITS)
11.8000 g., Copper-Nickel, 30 mm. **Obv:** Value **Rev:** Pope and Cologne Cathedral **Edge:** Segmented reeding

Date	Mintage	F	VF	XF	Unc	BU
2005 Proof	—	Value: 45.00				

SILVER MEDALLIC BULLION

X# MB1 10 ROUBLES
1.0000 g., 0.9250 Silver 0.0297 oz. ASW, 110 mm. **Subject:** New York September 11th Attack on Twin Towers **Obv:** Large value "10" without "РАЗМЕННЫИ ЗНАК" above date in center ЗНАК above, ПРОБА below **Obv. Legend:** Translation: "ISLAND SPITZBERGEN" at top "ARCTIC COAL" at bottom **Rev:** Twin Towers under attack **Rev. Legend:** ПРОТИВ ТЕРРОРИЗМА **Edge:** Segmented reeding

Date	Mintage	F	VF	XF	Unc	BU
2002 Proof	—	—	—	—	—	—

PATTERNS

X#	Date	Mintage	Identification	Issue Price	Mkt Val
Pn1	2001	10	10 Roubles. Aluminum-Bronze. 11.7500 g. X#Tn15.	—	250
Pn2	2001	10	10 Roubles. Aluminum. 3.3900 g. X#Tn15.	—	250
Pn3	2001	5	10 Roubles. Aluminum-Bronze. 11.8000 g. X#Tn16.1.	—	300
Pn4	2001	10	10 Roubles. Aluminum-Bronze. 11.8500 g. X#Tn16.2.	—	250

X#	Date	Mintage	Identification	Issue Price	Mkt Val
Pn5	2001	10	10 Roubles. Aluminum. 3.3900 g. X#Tn16.2.	—	250
Pn6	2001	—	10 Roubles. Aluminum-Bronze. 11.8500 g. X#Tn17.	—	250
Pn7	2001	—	10 Roubles. Aluminum. 3.3900 g. X#Tn17.	—	250
Pn8	2002	11	10 Roubles. Aluminum-Bronze. 11.6600 g. X#Tn18.	—	250
Pn9	2002	11	10 Roubles. Aluminum. 3.4300 g. X#Tn18.	—	250
Pn10	2002	11	10 Roubles. Aluminum-Bronze. 11.6600 g. X#Tn19.	—	250
Pn11	2002	11	10 Roubles. Aluminum. 3.4300 g. X#Tn19.	—	250
Pn12	2002	10	10 Roubles. Aluminum-Bronze. 10.4100 g. X#Tn20.	—	250
Pn13	2002	10	10 Roubles. Aluminum. 3.4200 g. X#Tn20.	—	250
Pn14	2002	10	10 Roubles. Aluminum-Bronze. 10.4100 g. X#Tn21.	—	250
Pn15	2002	10	10 Roubles. Aluminum. 3.4200 g. X#Tn21.	—	250

SRI LANKA

DEMOCRATIC SOCIALIST REPUBLIC

DECIMAL COINAGE

100 Cents = 1 Rupee

X# 5 CENT

Aluminum, 25.4 mm. **Obv:** National arms **Rev:** Denomination **Note:** Fantasy enlargement of the regular 16mm 1 cent coin. KM#137.

Date	Mintage	F	VF	XF	Unc	BU
1978	—	—	—	—	15.00	25.00

REVOLUTION

TAX REFUND TOKEN

Liberation Tigers of Tamil Eelam

X# Tn1 8 GRAMS

8.0000 g., 0.8333 Gold 0.2143 oz. AGW, 22.7 mm. **Obv:** Tiger head facing **Obv. Legend:** "Thamil Eelam Veeduthalai Puligal" **Obv. Inscription:** LIBERATION / TIGERS OF / TAMIL EELAM **Rev. Legend:** "Thamil Eela Meedpunithi - Kadan Meelal" (Tamil Eelam Savings - Fund - Loan Returned) **Rev. Inscription:** "20 Ma / 8 Giram / Aadee 1990" **Edge:** Reeded

Date	Mintage	F	VF	XF	Unc	BU
1990 Rare	—	—	—	—	—	—

Note: A tax was imposed of 2 gold sovereigns and at a later date, some famlies were refunded with this token. Most were remelted.

STRAITS SETTLEMENTS

REPUBLIC

STANDARD COINAGE

X# 12 DOLLAR

7.7750 g., 0.9999 Gold 0.2499 oz. AGW, 21.96 mm. **Subject:** 1994 Money World Singapore **Obv:** Crowned bust right **Obv. Legend:** EDWARD VII KING AND EMPEROR **Rev. Legend:** STRAITS SETTLEMENTS **Edge:** Reeded

Date	Mintage	F	VF	XF	Unc	BU
1903 (1994)	388	—	—	—	—	—

Note: Sold in proof sets with silver Money World medallion

BRITISH COLONY

1867-1939

FANTASY COINAGE

Modern fantasy issues of "unknown" origin struck without Government authorization for the obvious confusion of the numismatic community

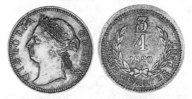

X# 3 3/4 CENT

5.4600 g., Bronze

Date	Mintage	F	VF	XF	Unc	BU
1820	—	—	4.00	7.00	15.00	—

X# 6 3/4 CENT

2.4200 g., Bronze

Date	Mintage	F	VF	XF	Unc	BU
1899	—	—	3.00	6.00	12.00	—

X# 9 3/4 CENT

Bronze **Shape:** Square **Note:** Modern fantasy issues of "unknown" origin struck without any government authorization for obvious confusion of the numismatic community.

Date	Mintage	F	VF	XF	Unc	BU
1932	—	—	3.00	6.00	12.00	—

MEDALLIC COINAGE

Richard Lobel Series

X# M1 CROWN

Bronze, 38.10 mm. **Subject:** Edward VIII **Obv:** Bust left **Obv. Legend:** EDWARD • VIII • KING • & • EMPEROR **Rev:** Britannia standing with trident and shield, sailing ship behind **Edge:** Plain

Date	Mintage	F	VF	XF	Unc	BU
1936 Proof	500	Value: 20.00				

X# M1a CROWN

Copper-Nickel-Zinc, 38.10 mm. **Subject:** Edward VIII **Obv:** Bust left **Obv. Legend:** EDWARD • VIII • KING • & • EMPEROR **Rev:** Britannia standing with trident and shield, sailing ship behind **Edge:** Plain

Date	Mintage	F	VF	XF	Unc	BU
1936 Proof	1,500	Value: 20.00				

X# M1b CROWN

0.9167 Silver, 38.10 mm. **Subject:** Edward VIII **Obv:** Bust left **Obv. Legend:** EDWARD • VIII • KING • & • EMPEROR **Rev:** Britannia standing with trident and shield, sailing ship behind **Edge:** Plain

Date	Mintage	F	VF	XF	Unc	BU
1936 Proof	200	Value: 50.00				

X# M1c CROWN

Gold, 38.10 mm. **Subject:** Edward VIII **Obv:** Bust left **Obv. Legend:** EDWARD • VIII • KING • & • EMPEROR **Rev:** Britannia standing with trident and shield, sailing ship behind **Edge:** Plain

Date	Mintage	F	VF	XF	Unc	BU
1936 Proof	—	Value: 500				

X# M2 SOVEREIGN

0.3750 Gold, 21.98 mm. **Subject:** Edward VIII **Obv:** Bust left **Obv. Legend:** EDWARD • VIII • KING • & • EMPEROR **Rev:** Britannia standing with trident and shield, sailing ship behind **Edge:** Plain

Date	Mintage	F	VF	XF	Unc	BU
1936 Proof	200	Value: 200				

X# M2a SOVEREIGN

4.4200 g., Silver, 21.98 mm. **Subject:** Edward **Obv:** Bust left **Obv. Legend:** EDWARD • VIII • KING • & • EMPEROR **Rev:** Britannia standing with trident and shield, sailing ship behind **Edge:** Plain

Date	Mintage	F	VF	XF	Unc	BU
1936 Proof	—	Value: 10.00				

PIEFORTS

X#	Date	Mintage	Identification	Mkt Val
P1	1936	—	Crown. 0.9167 Silver. X#M1b.	100

SWEDEN

KINGDOM

MEDALLIC COINAGE

Largesse Money

Largesse is defined as a generous giving. The throwing of coins to the people is believed to have begun with Gustavus Vasa I (1528). It became the practice to throw coins to the people at coronations and royal funerals, while more important persons were presented with medals to commemorate the occasion.

Specially struck largesse coins of a somewhat uniform size and weight began with Carl X Adolf coronation in 1654. The coins from 1654 until and including the Coronation piece of Gustaf III (1772) are of a 2 mark denomination. The

pieces after that date thru Carl XIV funeral piece of 1844 are of a one-third Riksdaler denomination. It was due to the unseemly conduct of the people and the resultant deaths of some, that after this issue the practice of throwing the coins to the public was discontinued and instead they were distributed to the garrison and honored guests and carried no monetary designation. However, it may be noted that these subsequent issues with no relation to the monetary system were circulated as coin of the realm.

X# MA32 MARK
Silver **Ruler:** Carl XII **Obv:** Bust right **Rev:** Laurel wreath above 2 lines of inscription, date below **Rev. Legend:** ALTERA • AT • NON • SECUNDA

Date	Mintage	VG	F	VF	XF	Unc
1701	—	—	—	—	—	—

X# M1 1-1/2 MARK (1/8 Riksdaler)
Silver **Subject:** Coronation of Carl IX **Obv:** Laureate bust left with Hebrew "Jehovah" above **Obv. Legend:** PROVIDENTIA... **Rev:** Figure walking left divides date **Note:** Prev. KM#M1.

Date	Mintage	VG	F	VF	XF	Unc
1607	—	120	275	600	1,200	—

X# M4 1-1/2 MARK (1/8 Riksdaler)
Silver **Subject:** Coronation of Gustaf II Adolf **Obv:** Laureate bust left with Hebrew "Jehovah" above **Obv. Legend:** GVSTAVVS • A - DOLPHVS • REX **Rev:** Crown suspended on flower stem divides date, radiant sun above **Note:** Prev. KM#M4.

Date	Mintage	VG	F	VF	XF	Unc
1617	—	80.00	190	625	1,250	—

X# M11 1-1/2 MARK (1/8 Riksdaler)
Silver **Subject:** Coronation of Maria Eleonora **Obv:** 8-line inscription **Rev:** Hand at right from cloud holding crown, date below **Note:** Prev. KM#M11.

Date	Mintage	VG	F	VF	XF	Unc
1620	—	125	250	775	1,500	—

X# M16 2 MARK (1/6 Riksdaler)
Silver **Subject:** Coronation of Carl X Gustaf **Obv:** Large bust left **Rev:** Date curved along rim **Note:** Prev. KM#M16.

Date	Mintage	VG	F	VF	XF	Unc
1654	2,250	175	300	625	1,000	—

X# M18 2 MARK (1/6 Riksdaler)
Silver **Rev:** Date in straight line **Note:** Prev. KM#M18.

Date	Mintage	VG	F	VF	XF	Unc
16 • 54	—	400	650	1,300	2,200	—

X# M19 2 MARK (1/6 Riksdaler)
Silver **Obv:** Small armored bust left **Note:** Prev. KM#M19.

Date	Mintage	VG	F	VF	XF	Unc
1654 Rare	—	—	—	—	—	—

X# M20 2 MARK (1/6 Riksdaler)
Silver **Subject:** Coronation of Hedvig Eleonora **Obv:** Crowned monogram in sprays, Hebrew "Jehovah" above **Rev:** 3-line inscription, date **Note:** Prev. KM#M20.

Date	Mintage	VG	F	VF	XF	Unc
1654	1,500	75.00	150	300	500	—

X# M25 2 MARK (1/6 Riksdaler)
Silver **Subject:** Funeral of Maria Eleonora **Obv:** Ga-R-S-C-R **Rev:** 4-line inscription, date within legend **Note:** Prev. KM#M25.

Date	Mintage	VG	F	VF	XF	Unc
MDCLV (1655)	—	175	250	550	800	—

X# M26 2 MARK (1/6 Riksdaler)
Silver **Subject:** Funeral of Carl X Gustaf **Obv:** Three crowns above sword **Obv. Legend:** ISTO CREVIMVS ENSE **Rev:** 7-line inscription within quartered wreath border **Rev. Inscription:** CAROLUS GUS / TAVUS... **Note:** Prev. KM#M26.

Date	Mintage	VG	F	VF	XF	Unc
MDCLX	—	125	225	375	750	—

X# M27 2 MARK (1/6 Riksdaler)
Silver **Subject:** Funeral of Carl X Gustaf **Rev:** 7-line inscription within pearled border **Rev. Inscription:** CAROLUS GVSTA / REX... **Note:** Prev. KM#M27.

Date	Mintage	VG	F	VF	XF	Unc
MDCLX (1660)	—	125	225	375	750	—

X# M31 2 MARK (1/6 Riksdaler)
Silver **Subject:** Funeral of Carl XI **Obv:** Bust right **Obv. Legend:** CAROLVS • XI D.G • REX • SVE. **Rev:** Clouds, sunrise, landscape **Note:** Prev. KM#M31.

Date	Mintage	VG	F	VF	XF	Unc
1697	2,000	75.00	150	350	700	—

X# M-A35 2 MARK (1/6 Riksdaler)
Silver **Subject:** Coronation of Carl XII **Obv:** Bust right **Obv. Legend:** CAROLVS • XII D.G • REX • SVE. **Rev:** Crown **Rev. Legend:** CAROLVS • POST • FATA • REVIXII. **Note:** Prev. KM#M-A35.

Date	Mintage	VG	F	VF	XF	Unc
1697	2,000	125	250	625	1,200	—

X# M35 2 MARK (1/6 Riksdaler)
Silver **Ruler:** Ulrika Eleonora **Subject:** Funeral of Carl XII **Obv:** Bust right **Rev:** 5-line inscription **Note:** Prev. KM#M35.

Date	Mintage	VG	F	VF	XF	Unc
MDCCXVIIII (1718)	2,200	70.00	125	265	500	—

X# M36 2 MARK (1/6 Riksdaler)
Silver **Ruler:** Ulrika Eleonora **Subject:** Coronation of Ulrika Eleonora **Obv:** Bust right **Obv. Legend:** ULRIKA ELEONORA D.G. REG. SVEC. **Rev:** Large star, date below D.XVII MART **Rev. Legend:** SECURA FUTURI **Note:** Prev. KM#M36.

Date	Mintage	VG	F	VF	XF	Unc
MDCCXVIII	2,200	75.00	145	285	600	—

X# M37 2 MARK (1/6 Riksdaler)
Silver **Ruler:** Ulrika Eleonora **Subject:** Coronation of Ulrika Eleonora **Obv:** Bust right **Obv. Legend:** ULRIKA ELEONORA D.G. REG. SVEC **Rev:** Large star, date below **Rev. Legend:** SECURA FUTURI **Note:** Prev. KM#M37.

Date	Mintage	VG	F	VF	XF	Unc
1719 Rare	—	—	—	—	—	—

X# M39 2 MARK (1/6 Riksdaler)
Silver **Ruler:** Frederick I **Subject:** Coronation of Frederick I **Obv:** Bust right **Obv. Legend:** FRIDERICVS D • G • REX... **Rev:** Crown **Rev. Legend:** SACRVM VIRTVTIS PRAEMIVM **Note:** Prev. KM#M39.

Date	Mintage	VG	F	VF	XF	Unc
1720	2,200	100	250	450	1,150	—

X# M43 2 MARK (1/6 Riksdaler)
Silver **Ruler:** Frederick I **Subject:** Funeral of Ulrika Eleonora **Obv:** Bust right **Obv. Legend:** VLRICA ELEONORA D • G • REGINA SVECIAE **Rev:** Rayed star **Rev. Legend:** INDIGENA POLI. **Note:** Prev. KM#M43.

Date	Mintage	VG	F	VF	XF	Unc
1741	8,000	50.00	100	200	420	—

X# M44a 2 MARK (1/6 Riksdaler)
10.1500 g., Silver **Ruler:** Adolf Frederick **Subject:** Coronation of Adolf Frederick **Obv:** Modified bust right **Obv. Legend:** PECTORE IN HOC PATER EST. **Rev:** 5-line inscription, date **Note:** Modified bust. Prev. KM#M44a.

Date	Mintage	VG	F	VF	XF	Unc
1751	8,105	40.00	70.00	150	300	—

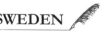

X# M44 2 MARK (1/6 Riksdaler)

7.7000 g., Silver **Ruler:** Adolf Frederick **Subject:** Coronation of Adolf Frederick **Obv:** Crowned bust right **Obv. Legend:** PECTORE IN HOC PATER EST **Rev:** 5-line inscription, date **Note:** Prev. KM#M44.

Date	Mintage	VG	F	VF	XF	Unc
1751	—	35.00	65.00	125	250	—

X# M-A44 2 MARK (1/6 Riksdaler)

Silver **Ruler:** Frederick I **Subject:** Funeral of Frederick I **Obv:** Bust right **Obv. Legend:** FREDERICUS D • G • REX SVECIAE **Rev:** 6-line inscription, date **Note:** Prev. KM#M-A44.

Date	Mintage	VG	F	VF	XF	Unc
1751	4,539	45.00	75.00	165	325	—

X# M45 2 MARK (1/6 Riksdaler)

9.5700 g., Silver **Ruler:** Adolf Frederick **Subject:** Funeral of Adolf Frederick **Obv:** Armored bust right, C.G.F. below **Obv. Legend:** ADOLPHUS FRIDERICUS D • G • REX SVECIAE **Rev:** 9-line inscription in sprays **Note:** Prev. KM#M45.

Date	Mintage	VG	F	VF	XF	Unc
MDCCLXXI	4,604	45.00	75.00	165	325	—

X# M46 2 MARK (1/6 Riksdaler)

9.5700 g., Silver **Ruler:** Adolf Frederick **Subject:** Funeral of Adolf Frederick **Obv:** Armored bust right, FEHRMAN below **Obv. Legend:** ADOLPHUS FRIDERICUS D • G • REX SVECIAE **Rev:** 9-line inscription, date below **Note:** Prev. KM#M46.

Date	Mintage	VG	F	VF	XF	Unc
MDCCLXVI	—	35.00	65.00	125	250	—

X# M47 2 MARK (1/6 Riksdaler)

9.5700 g., Silver **Ruler:** Gustaf III **Subject:** Coronation of Gustaf III **Obv:** Crowned bust right **Rev:** 7-line inscription **Note:** Prev. KM#M47.

Date	Mintage	VG	F	VF	XF	Unc
MDCCLXXII	3,000	40.00	70.00	150	300	—

X# M48 2 MARK (1/6 Riksdaler)

9.5700 g., Silver **Ruler:** Gustaf III **Subject:** Coronation of Gustaf III **Obv:** Crowned bust right, FEHRMAN below bust **Obv. Legend:** GUSTAVUS ADOLPHI FILIUS • REX • **Rev:** 7-line inscription **Note:** Prev. KM#M48.

Date	Mintage	VG	F	VF	XF	Unc
MDCCLXXII	Inc. above	40.00	70.00	150	300	—

X# M49 2 MARK (1/6 Riksdaler)

9.5700 g., Silver **Ruler:** Gustaf III **Subject:** Coronation of Gustaf III **Obv:** Crowned bust right, F below bust **Rev:** 7-line inscription **Note:** Prev. KM#M49.

Date	Mintage	VG	F	VF	XF	Unc
MDCCLXXII	Inc. above	40.00	70.00	150	300	—

X# M5 3 MARK (1/4 Riksdaler)

Silver **Subject:** Coronation of Gustavus II Adolphus **Obv:** Laureate bust left with Hebrew "Jehovah" above **Obv. Legend:** GVSTAVVS • A - DOLPHVS • REV **Rev:** Crown suspended on flower stem divides date, radiant sun above **Note:** Prev. KM#M5.

Date	Mintage	VG	F	VF	XF	Unc
1617	—	300	750	1,500	3,000	—

X# M12 3 MARK (1/4 Riksdaler)

Silver **Subject:** Coronation of Maria Eleonora **Obv:** 8-line inscription **Rev:** Hand at right from cloud, holding crown, date below **Note:** Prev. KM#M12.

Date	Mintage	VG	F	VF	XF	Unc
1620	—	150	325	950	1,800	—

X# M50 4 MARK (1/3 RIKSDALER)

Silver **Ruler:** Gustaf III **Subject:** Birth of Crown Prince Gustaf IV Adolf **Obv:** Bust right **Obv. Legend:** GUSTAF III • SV • G • OCH W • KONUNG **Rev:** Sheaf of grain **Rev. Legend:** GLADER AN ET TIDEHVARF. **Note:** Prev. KM#M50.

Date	Mintage	VG	F	VF	XF	Unc
1778	2,000	30.00	60.00	120	225	—

X# M52 4 MARK (1/3 RIKSDALER)

Silver **Ruler:** Gustaf III **Subject:** Birth of Prince Carl Gustaf **Obv:** Bust right **Obv. Legend:** GUSTAF III • SV • G • OCH W • KONUNG • **Rev:** 9-line legend, date **Note:** Prev. KM#M52.

Date	Mintage	VG	F	VF	XF	Unc
1782	—	75.00	135	285	600	—

X# M51 4 MARK (1/3 RIKSDALER)

Silver **Ruler:** Gustaf III **Subject:** Funeral of Lovisa Ulrika **Obv:** Veiled bust right **Obv. Legend:** LUD • ULRICA D • G • REG • SVZCIAE • VIDUA **Rev:** 7-line legend **Note:** Prev. KM#51.

Date	Mintage	VG	F	VF	XF	Unc
MDCCLXXXII (1782)	1,500	40.00	70.00	135	275	—

X# M53 4 MARK (1/3 RIKSDALER)

9.7600 g., Silver **Ruler:** Gustaf III **Subject:** Funeral of Gustaf III **Obv:** Bust right **Obv. Legend:** GUSTAF III SVERIGES KONUNG **Rev:** Rayed crown **Note:** Prev. KM#M53.

Date	Mintage	VG	F	VF	XF	Unc
1792	2,500	20.00	40.00	85.00	165	—

X# M54 4 MARK (1/3 RIKSDALER)

9.7600 g., Silver **Ruler:** Gustaf IV Adolf **Subject:** Coronation of Gustaf IV Adolf **Obv:** Crowned bust right **Obv. Legend:** GUSTAF IV ADOLPH S • G • OCH V • K • KRONT **Rev:** 3-line inscription in sprays **Rev. Inscription:** GUD / OCH / FOLKET **Note:** Prev. KM#M54.

Date	Mintage	VG	F	VF	XF	Unc
1800	5,000	20.00	40.00	80.00	160	—

X# M55 4 MARK (1/3 RIKSDALER)

Silver **Subject:** Coronation of Carl XIII **Obv:** Crowned bust right **Obv. Legend:** CARL XIII S • G • OCH V • K • KRONT ÅR **Rev:** 3-line inscription in sprays **Rev. Inscription:** FOLKETS VÄL / MIN / HÖGSTA LAG **Note:** Prev. KM#M55.

Date	Mintage	VG	F	VF	XF	Unc
1809	—	8.50	18.00	35.00	90.00	—

X# M56.1 4 MARK (1/3 RIKSDALER)
Silver **Subject:** Funeral of Sofia Magdalena **Obv:** Large veiled bust right, "E." below **Obv. Legend:** SOPHIA MAGDALENA SV • ENKE •... **Rev:** 5-line inscription in ring of stars **Note:** Prev. KM#M56.1.

Date	Mintage	VG	F	VF	XF	Unc
1813	—	12.00	25.00	50.00	100	—

X# M56.2 4 MARK (1/3 RIKSDALER)
Silver **Subject:** Funeral of Queen Sofia Magdalena **Obv:** Small veiled bust right, without "E" below **Obv. Legend:** SOPHIA MAGDALENA SV • ENKE •... **Rev:** 5-line inscription in ring of stars **Note:** Prev. KM#M56.2.

Date	Mintage	VG	F	VF	XF	Unc
1813	—	15.00	30.00	60.00	120	—

X# M57 4 MARK (1/3 RIKSDALER)
Silver **Subject:** Funeral of Carl XIII **Obv:** Bust right **Obv. Legend:** CARL XIII SVERIGES OCH NORRIGES KONUNG **Rev:** Two crowns on globe **Rev. Legend:** NEDLAGDA FÖR DEN HÖGSTES THRON **Note:** Prev. KM#M57.

Date	Mintage	VG	F	VF	XF	Unc
1818 Rare	—	—	—	—	—	—

X# M58 4 MARK (1/3 RIKSDALER)
Silver **Subject:** Funeral of Carl XIII **Obv:** Bust right **Obv. Legend:** CARL XIII SVERIGES OCH NORRIGES KONUNG **Rev:** Two crowns on cushion **Rev. Legend:** NEDLAGDA FÖR DEN HÖGSTES THRON **Note:** Prev. KM#M58.

Date	Mintage	VG	F	VF	XF	Unc
1818	—	8.00	20.00	40.00	85.00	—

X# M59 4 MARK (1/3 RIKSDALER)
Silver **Obv. Legend:** CARL XIII SVERIGES OCH NORRIGES KONUNG **Rev:** Bust right, curl on far shoulder **Rev. Legend:** NEDLAGDA FÖR DEN HÖGSTES THRON **Note:** Prev. KM#M59.

Date	Mintage	VG	F	VF	XF	Unc
1818	—	8.00	20.00	40.00	85.00	—

X# M60 4 MARK (1/3 RIKSDALER)
0.8780 Silver **Subject:** Coronation of Carl XIV John **Obv. Legend:** CARL XIV JOHAN SV • OCH NORR • K • KRONT **Rev:** 4-line inscription in sprays **Rev. Inscription:** FOLKETS / KÄRLEK / MIN / BELÖNING **Note:** Prev. KM#M60.

Date	Mintage	F	VF	XF	Unc	BU
1818	—	20.00	40.00	90.00	150	—

X# M61 4 MARK (1/3 RIKSDALER)
0.8780 Silver **Subject:** Funeral of Hedwig Elisabeth Charlotte **Obv:** Veiled head right **Rev:** Rayed crown above two crowns, 3-line inscription, date in sprays below **Note:** Prev. KM#M61.

Date	Mintage	F	VF	XF	Unc	BU
1818	—	30.00	60.00	125	180	—

X# M62 4 MARK (1/3 RIKSDALER)
Silver **Subject:** Funeral of Carl XIV John **Obv:** Draped bust right **Obv. Legend:** CARL XIV JOHAN SVER. NORR. GÖTH. O. VEND. KONUNG. **Rev:** Carl XIV John laying in State **Note:** Prev. KM#M62.

Date	Mintage	F	VF	XF	Unc	BU
1844	—	20.00	32.50	60.00	110	—

X# M63 4 MARK (1/3 RIKSDALER)
Silver **Subject:** Funeral of Oscar I **Obv:** Laureate head left **Obv. Legend:** OSCAR I SVERIGES NORRIGES G. O. V. KONUNG. **Rev:** Three-towered church **Note:** Prev. KM#M63.

Date	Mintage	F	VF	XF	Unc	BU
1859	3,200	12.50	27.50	55.00	100	—

X# M64 4 MARK (1/3 RIKSDALER)
Silver **Subject:** Coronation of Carl XV **Obv:** Crowned bust right **Obv. Legend:** CARL XV SVERIGES NORR G.O.V. KONUNG KRONT **Rev:** 3-line inscription in sprays **Rev. Inscription:** LAND / SKALL MED LAG / BYGGAS **Note:** Prev. KM#M64.

Date	Mintage	F	VF	XF	Unc	BU
1860	3,200	12.50	27.50	55.00	100	—

X# M65 4 MARK (1/3 RIKSDALER)
Silver **Subject:** Coronation of Oscar II **Obv:** Crowned bust right **Obv. Legend:** OSCAR II SVERIGES NORGES G.O.V. KONUNG KRONT **Rev:** 3-line inscription in sprays **Rev. Inscription:** BRÖDRA / FOLKENS / VÄL **Note:** Prev. KM#M65.

Date	Mintage	F	VF	XF	Unc	BU
1873	—	20.00	32.50	60.00	85.00	—

X# M-A6 6 MARK (1/2 Riksdaler)
Silver **Subject:** Coronation of Carl IX **Obv:** Laureate bust left with Hebrew "Jehovah" above **Obv. Legend:** PROVIDENTIA... **Rev:** Figure walking left divides date **Note:** Prev. KM#M-A6.

Date	Mintage	VG	F	VF	XF	Unc
1607	—	—	—	—	—	—

X# M6 6 MARK (1/2 Riksdaler)
Silver **Subject:** Coronation of Gustaf II Adolf **Obv:** Laureate bust left with Hebrew "Jehovah" above **Rev:** Crown suspended on flower stem divides date, radiant sun above **Note:** Prev. KM#M6.

Date	Mintage	VG	F	VF	XF	Unc
1617	—	400	800	1,750	3,500	—

X# M13 6 MARK (1/2 Riksdaler)
Silver **Subject:** Coronation of Maria Eleonora **Obv:** 8-line inscription **Rev:** Hand at right from cloud holding crown, date below **Note:** Prev. KM#M13.

Date	Mintage	VG	F	VF	XF	Unc
1620	—	200	350	1,175	2,500	—

X# M28 8 MARK (2/3 Riksdaler)
Silver **Subject:** Funeral of Carl X Gustaf **Obv:** Hand holding sword upright, three swords at upper left and upper right **Rev:** 8-line inscription, date within ribboned border with small shields and sprays **Note:** Prev. KM#M28.

Date	Mintage	VG	F	VF	XF	Unc
MDCLX	—	500	900	1,500	2,750	—

X# M2 12 MARK (Riksdaler)

Silver **Subject:** Coronation of Carl IX **Obv:** Laureate bust left with Hebrew "Jehovah" above **Obv. Legend:** PROVIDENTIA **Rev:** Figure walking left divides date **Note:** Prev. KM#M2.

Date	Mintage	VG	F	VF	XF	Unc
1607	—	—	—	—	—	—

X# M7 12 MARK (Riksdaler)

Silver **Subject:** Coronation of Gustaf II Adolf **Note:** Prev. KM#M7.

Date	Mintage	VG	F	VF	XF	Unc
1617	—	200	500	950	1,900	—

X# M8 12 MARK (Riksdaler)

Silver **Note:** Prev. KM#M8.

Date	Mintage	VG	F	VF	XF	Unc
ND	—	—	—	—	—	—

X# M14 12 MARK (Riksdaler)

Silver **Subject:** Coronation of Maria Eleonora **Obv:** Hand holding sword upright, three swords at upper left and at upper right **Rev:** 8-line inscription, date within ribboned border with small shields and sprays **Rev. Legend:** INDOMITVS • PRO •... **Note:** Prev. KM#M14.

Date	Mintage	VG	F	VF	XF	Unc
1620	—	350	700	1,750	3,000	—

X# M29 12 MARK (Riksdaler)

Silver **Subject:** Funeral of Carl X Gustaf **Obv:** Hand holding sword **Rev:** Legend **Note:** Prev. KM#M29.

Date	Mintage	F	VF	XF	Unc	BU
MDCLX	—	75.00	150	300	500	—

X# M3 16 MARK

4.9557 g., 0.9790 Gold 0.1560 oz. AGW **Subject:** Coronation of Carl IX **Obv:** Laureate bust left with Hebrew "Jehovah" above **Obv. Legend:** PROVIDENTIA **Rev:** Figure walking left divides date **Note:** Prev. KM#M3. Fr. #20.

Date	Mintage	VG	F	VF	XF	Unc
1607 Rare	—	—	—	—	—	—

X# M9 16 MARK

4.9557 g., 0.9790 Gold 0.1560 oz. AGW **Subject:** Coronation of Gustaf II Adolf **Obv:** Laureate bust left in inner circle with Hebrew "Jehovah" above **Rev:** Crown suspended on flower stem divides date, radiant sun above **Note:** Prev. KM#M9. Fr. #32.

Date	Mintage	VG	F	VF	XF	Unc
1617 Rare	—	—	—	—	—	—

X# M15 16 MARK

4.9557 g., 0.9790 Gold 0.1560 oz. AGW **Subject:** Coronation of Maria Eleonora **Obv:** 8-line inscription **Rev:** Hand at right from cloud holding crown, date below **Note:** Prev. KM#M15. Fr. #33.

Date	Mintage	VG	F	VF	XF	Unc
1620 Rare	—	—	—	—	—	—

X# M21 16 MARK

4.9557 g., 0.9790 Gold 0.1560 oz. AGW **Subject:** Coronation of Carl X Gustaf **Obv:** Large bust of Carl X Gustaf left **Rev:** Date along rim **Note:** Prev. KM#M21.

Date	Mintage	VG	F	VF	XF	Unc
1654 Rare	—	—	—	—	—	—

X# M22 16 MARK

4.9557 g., 0.9790 Gold 0.1560 oz. AGW **Subject:** Coronation of Carl X Gustaf **Obv:** Large head left **Rev:** Date in straight line **Note:** Prev. KM#M22. Fr. #37

Date	Mintage	VG	F	VF	XF	Unc
1654 Unique	—	—	—	—	—	—

X# M23 16 MARK

Silver **Obv:** Small armored bust left **Note:** Prev. KM#M23.

Date	Mintage	VG	F	VF	XF	Unc
1654 Rare	—	—	—	—	—	—

X# M23a 16 MARK

4.9557 g., 0.9790 Gold 0.1560 oz. AGW **Subject:** Coronation of Carl X Gustaf **Obv:** Armored bust of Carl X Gustaf **Note:** Prev. KM#M23. Fr. #37.

Date	Mintage	VG	F	VF	XF	Unc
1654 Unique	—	—	—	—	—	—

X# M10 5 DUCAT

17.5000 g., 0.9760 Gold 0.5491 oz. AGW **Subject:** Coronation of Gustaf II Adolf **Obv:** Laureate bust left with Hebrew "Jehovah" above **Rev:** Crown suspended on flower stem divides date, radiant sun above **Note:** Prev. KM#M10. Fr. #31.

Date	Mintage	VG	F	VF	XF	Unc
1617 Unique	—	—	—	—	—	—

X# M24 5 DUCAT

17.5000 g., 0.9760 Gold 0.5491 oz. AGW **Subject:** Coronation of Carl X Gustaf **Obv:** Armored bust of Carl X Gustaf left **Rev:** Large crown above date **Note:** Prev. KM#M24.

Date	Mintage	VG	F	VF	XF	Unc
1654 Rare	—	—	—	—	—	—

X# M38 5 DUCAT

17.5000 g., 0.9760 Gold 0.5491 oz. AGW **Ruler:** Ulrika Eleonora **Subject:** Coronation of Ulrika Eleonora **Obv:** Bust right **Obv. Legend:** ULRIKA ELEONORA D.G. REG. SVEC. **Rev:** Large star, date below **Rev. Legend:** SECURA FUTURI **Note:** Prev. KM#M38.

Date	Mintage	VG	F	VF	XF	Unc
1719 Unique	—	—	—	—	—	—

X# M40 5 DUCAT

17.5000 g., 0.9760 Gold 0.5491 oz. AGW **Ruler:** Frederick I **Subject:** Coronation of Frederick I **Obv:** Bust right **Obv. Legend:** FRIDERICVS D.G. REX ...... **Rev:** Crown **Rev. Legend:** SACRVM VIRTVTIS PRAEMIVM **Note:** Prev. KM#M40.

Date	Mintage	VG	F	VF	XF	Unc
1720 Unique	—	—	—	—	—	—

X# MA52 7 DUCAT

24.3800 g., Gold **Ruler:** Gustaf III **Subject:** Funeral of Lovisa Ulrika **Obv:** Veiled head right **Obv. Legend:** LUD.ULRICA D • G • REG • SVECIAE • VIOUA **Rev:** 7-line inscription **Note:** Prev. KM#M53.

Date	Mintage	VG	F	VF	XF	Unc
MDCCLXXXII Unique	—	—	—	—	—	—

PIEFORTS

X# P1 2 MARK

18.3300 g., Silver **Note:** Prev. X#M21a. Double thickness.

Date	Mintage	VG	F	VF	XF	Unc
1654 Unique	—	—	—	—	—	—

MEDALLIC COINAGE

Gold Issues

X# M30 DUCAT

3.4813 g., 0.9760 Gold 0.1092 oz. AGW **Subject:** Discovery of Gold at Östra Silver Berget in Dalarna **Obv:** Head of Carl XI right **Rev:** Five-line inscription and date **Note:** Fr. #47. Prev. KM#M30.

Date	Mintage	VG	F	VF	XF	Unc
1695 Rare	—	—	—	—	—	—

X# M32 DUCAT

3.4813 g., 0.9760 Gold 0.1092 oz. AGW **Ruler:** Carl XII **Obv:** Bust of Carl XII right **Rev:** 6-line inscription **Note:** Prev. KM#M32. Struck in 1718 for presumed manufacture of gold by Paykull in 1706.

Date	Mintage	VG	F	VF	XF	Unc
1706 (1718) Rare	—	—	—	—	—	—

X# M33 1-1/2 DUCAT

3.4813 g., 0.9760 Gold 0.1092 oz. AGW **Ruler:** Carl XII **Obv:** Bust of Carl XII right **Rev:** 6-line inscription **Note:** Prev. KM#M33. Struck in 1718 for presumed manufacture of gold by Paykull in 1706.

Date	Mintage	VG	F	VF	XF	Unc
1706 (1718) Unique	—	—	—	—	—	—

X# M34 2 DUCAT

6.9625 g., 0.9760 Gold 0.2185 oz. AGW **Ruler:** Carl XII **Obv:** Bust of Carl XII right **Rev:** 6-line inscription **Note:** Prev. KM#M34. Struck in 1718 for presumed manufacture of gold by Paykull in 1706.

Date	Mintage	VG	F	VF	XF	Unc
1706 (1718) Unique	—	—	—	—	—	—

X# M41 10 DUCAT

35.0000 g., 0.9760 Gold 1.0982 oz. AGW **Ruler:** Frederick I **Subject:** Royal Visit to Hesse-Cassel **Obv:** Draped bust of Frederick I right **Rev:** 11-line inscription **Note:** Prev. KM#M41.

Date	Mintage	VG	F	VF	XF	Unc
1731 Unique	—	—	—	—	—	—

X# M42 10 DUCAT

35.0000 g., 0.9760 Gold 1.0982 oz. AGW **Ruler:** Frederick I **Subject:** Royal Visit to Hesse-Cassel **Obv:** Conjoined busts of Frederick I and Ulrika Eleonora **Rev:** Round arms at center **Note:** Prev. KM#M42.

Date	Mintage	VG	F	VF	XF	Unc
ND(1731) Unique	—	—	—	—	—	—

ECU COINAGE

X# 11 5 ECU

23.0000 g., Copper-Nickel, 38.6 mm. **Ruler:** Carl XVI Gustaf **Issuer:** CITV, Vaduz **Obv:** Early sailing ship **Rev:** Bust of Gustaf Adolf 3/4 right **Rev. Legend:** GUSTAVUS ADOLPHUS 1594 • 1632 - ILLE FACIET **Edge:** Reeded

Date	Mintage	F	VF	XF	Unc	BU
1992	10,000	—	—	—	—	10.00

X# 17 5 ECU

23.0000 g., Copper-Nickel, 38.6 mm. **Ruler:** Carl XVI Gustaf **Issuer:** CITV, Vaduz **Subject:** 800th Anniversary Port of Visby **Obv:** Visby arms **Rev:** Early sailing ships leaving port **Rev. Legend:** 800 YEARS HANSA / VISBY **Edge:** Reeded

Date	Mintage	F	VF	XF	Unc	BU
1994	10,000	—	—	—	—	10.00

X# 12 20 ECU

25.0000 g., 0.9250 Silver 0.7435 oz. ASW, 38.6 mm. **Ruler:** Carl XVI Gustaf **Issuer:** CITV, Vaduz **Obv:** Early sailing ship **Rev:** Bust of Gustaf Adolf 3/4 right **Rev. Legend:** GUSTAVUS ADOLPHUS 1594 • 1632 - ILLE FACIET **Edge:** Reeded

Date	Mintage	F	VF	XF	Unc	BU
1992 Proof	7,500	Value: 40.00				

X# 18 20 ECU

25.0000 g., 0.9250 Silver 0.7435 oz. ASW, 38.6 mm. **Ruler:** Carl XVI Gustaf **Issuer:** CITV, Vaduz **Subject:** 800th Anniversary Port of Visby **Obv:** Visby arms **Rev:** Early sailing ships leaving port **Rev. Legend:** 800 YEARS HANSA / VISBY **Edge:** Reeded

Date	Mintage	F	VF	XF	Unc	BU
1994 Proof	7,500	Value: 40.00				

X# 13 150 ECU

6.7200 g., 0.7500 Gold 0.1620 oz. AGW, 23 mm. **Ruler:** Carl XVI Gustaf **Issuer:** CITV, Vaduz **Obv:** Early sailing ship **Rev:** Bust of Gustaf Adolf 3/4 right **Rev. Legend:** GUSTAVUS ADOLPHUS 1594 • 1632 - ILLE FACIET **Edge:** Reeded

Date	Mintage	F	VF	XF	Unc	BU
1992 Proof	1,000	Value: 250				

X# 19 150 ECU

6.7200 g., 0.7500 Gold 0.1620 oz. AGW, 23 mm. **Ruler:** Carl XVI Gustaf **Issuer:** CITV, Vaduz **Subject:** 800th Anniversary Port of Visby **Obv:** Visby arms **Rev:** Early sailing ships leaving port **Rev. Legend:** 800 YEARS HANSA / VISBY **Edge:** Reeded

Date	Mintage	F	VF	XF	Unc	BU
1994 Proof	400	Value: 250				

FANTASY EURO PATTERNS

X# Pn1 EURO CENT

Copper, 16.8 mm. **Ruler:** Carl XVI Gustaf **Issuer:** INA **Obv:** Sailing ship "Vasa", crown below **Rev:** Scale at right **Edge:** Plain

Date	Mintage	F	VF	XF	Unc	BU
2003	24,000	—	—	—	1.00	—
2003 Proof	23,000	Value: 2.00				

X# Pn1a EURO CENT

Silver, 16.8 mm. **Ruler:** Carl XVI Gustaf **Issuer:** INA **Obv:** Sailing ship "Vasa", crown below **Rev:** Scale at right **Edge:** Plain

Date	Mintage	F	VF	XF	Unc	BU
2003 Proof	2,500	Value: 6.00				

X# Pn2 2 EURO CENT

Copper, 18.5 mm. **Ruler:** Carl XVI Gustaf **Issuer:** INA **Obv:** Sailing ship "Vasa", crown below **Rev:** Scale at right **Edge:** Plain

Date	Mintage	F	VF	XF	Unc	BU
2003	24,000	—	—	—	1.50	—
2003 Proof	23,000	Value: 2.50				

X# Pn2a 2 EURO CENT

Silver, 18.5 mm. **Ruler:** Carl XVI Gustaf **Issuer:** INA **Obv:** Sailing ship "Vasa", crown below **Rev:** Scale at right **Edge:** Plain

Date	Mintage	F	VF	XF	Unc	BU
2003 Proof	2,500	Value: 7.00				

X# Pn3 5 EURO CENT

Copper, 20.7 mm. **Ruler:** Gustaf VI **Issuer:** INA **Obv:** Sailing ship "Vasa", crown below **Rev:** Scale at right **Edge:** Plain

Date	Mintage	F	VF	XF	Unc	BU
2003	24,000	—	—	—	2.00	—
2003 Proof	23,000	Value: 3.00				

X# Pn3a 5 EURO CENT

Silver, 20.7 mm. **Ruler:** Carl XVI Gustaf **Issuer:** INA **Obv:** Sailing ship "Vasa", crown below **Rev:** Scale at right **Edge:** Plain

Date	Mintage	F	VF	XF	Unc	BU
2003 Proof	2,500	Value: 8.50				

X# Pn4 10 EURO CENT

Brass, 19.3 mm. **Ruler:** Carl XVI Gustaf **Issuer:** INA **Obv:** Split head left, crown behind **Rev:** Dove in flight **Edge:** Plain

Date	Mintage	F	VF	XF	Unc	BU
2003	24,000	—	—	—	2.50	—
2003 Proof	23,000	Value: 3.50				

X# Pn4a 10 EURO CENT

Silver, 19.3 mm. **Ruler:** Carl XVI Gustaf **Issuer:** INA **Obv:** Split head left, crown behind **Rev:** Dove in flight **Edge:** Plain

Date	Mintage	F	VF	XF	Unc	BU
2003 Proof	2,500	Value: 10.00				

X# Pn5 20 EURO CENT

Brass, 22 mm. **Ruler:** Carl XVI Gustaf **Issuer:** INA **Obv:** Split head left, crown behind **Rev:** Dove in flight **Edge:** Plain

Date	Mintage	F	VF	XF	Unc	BU
2003	24,000	—	—	—	3.00	—
2003 Proof	23,000	Value: 4.00				

X# Pn5a 20 EURO CENT

Silver, 22 mm. **Ruler:** Carl XVI Gustaf **Issuer:** INA **Obv:** Split head left, crown behind **Rev:** Dove in flight **Edge:** Plain

Date	Mintage	F	VF	XF	Unc	BU
2003 Proof	2,500	Value: 12.50				

X# Pn6 50 EURO CENT

Brass, 24.3 mm. **Ruler:** Carl XVI Gustaf **Issuer:** INA **Obv:** Split head left, crown behind **Rev:** Dove in flight **Edge:** Plain

Date	Mintage	F	VF	XF	Unc	BU
2003	24,000	—	—	—	3.50	—
2003 Proof	23,000	Value: 5.00				

X# Pn6a 50 EURO CENT

Silver, 24.3 mm. **Ruler:** Carl XVI Gustaf **Issuer:** INA **Obv:** Split head left, crown behind **Rev:** Dove in flight **Edge:** Plain

Date	Mintage	F	VF	XF	Unc	BU
2003 Proof	2,500	Value: 15.00				

X# Pn7 EURO

Bi-Metallic, 22.8 mm. **Ruler:** Carl XVI Gustaf **Issuer:** INA **Obv:** Split head left, crown behind **Rev:** Ancient galley **Edge:** Plain

Date	Mintage	F	VF	XF	Unc	BU
2003	24,000	—	—	—	5.50	—
2003 Proof	23,000	Value: 6.50				

X# Pn7a EURO

Bi-Metallic Brass center in Silver ring, 22.8 mm. **Ruler:** Carl XVI Gustaf **Issuer:** INA **Obv:** Split head left, crown behind **Rev:** Ancient galley **Edge:** Plain

Date	Mintage	F	VF	XF	Unc	BU
2003 Proof	2,500	Value: 22.50				

X# Pn8 2 EURO

Bi-Metallic, 25.7 mm. **Ruler:** Carl XVI Gustaf **Issuer:** INA **Obv:** Split head left, crown behind **Rev:** Ancient galley **Edge:** Plain

Date	Mintage	F	VF	XF	Unc	BU
2003	24,000	—	—	—	7.50	—
2003 Proof	23,000	Value: 8.50				

X# Pn8a 2 EURO

Bi-Metallic Brass center in Silver ring, 25.7 mm. **Ruler:** Carl XVI Gustaf **Issuer:** INA **Obv:** Split head left, crown behind **Rev:** Ancient galley **Edge:** Plain

Date	Mintage	F	VF	XF	Unc	BU
2003 Proof	2,500	Value: 28.50				

X# Pn9 5 EURO

Goldine, 36 mm. **Ruler:** Carl XVI Gustaf **Issuer:** INA **Obv:** Split head left, crown behind **Rev:** Woman standing facing holding wreath at left, crown above sailing ship "Vasa" at right **Edge:** Plain

Date	Mintage	F	VF	XF	Unc	BU
2003 Proof	23,000	Value: 12.50				

X# Pn9a 5 EURO
Silver, 36 mm. **Ruler:** Carl XVI Gustaf **Issuer:** INA **Obv:** Split head left, crown behind **Rev:** Woman standing facing holding wreath at left, crown above sailing ship "Vasa" at right **Edge:** Plain

Date	Mintage	F	VF	XF	Unc	BU
2003 Proof	2,500	Value: 40.00				

PIEFORTS

X#	Date	Mintage	Identification	Mkt Val
P11	2003	2,000	5 Euro. 0.9250 Silver. X#Pn9.	65.00

MINT SETS

X#	Date	Mintage	Identification	Issue Price	Mkt Val
XMS1	2003 (8)	24,000	X#Pn1-Pn8	—	26.00

PROOF SETS

X#	Date	Mintage	Identification	Issue Price	Mkt Val
XPS1	2003 (9)	23,000	X#Pn1-Pn9	—	50.00
XPS2	2003 (9)	2,500	X#Pn1a-Pn9a	—	150

SWISS CANTONS

BERN

CITY

MEDALLIC COINAGE

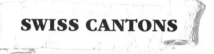

X# M5 20 KREUZER
4.9000 g., Silver, 27.2 mm. **Obv:** Arms **Obv. Legend:** BERNENSIS - REIPUBLICA **Rev:** Bear seated right holding scroll, branch with flowers below **Rev. Inscription:** MONETA / NOVA, date **Note:** School prize.

Date	Mintage	VG	F	VF	XF	Unc
1706	—	—	22.50	45.00	75.00	125

X# M8 20 KREUZER
5.0800 g., Silver, 27.5 mm. **Obv:** Crowned arms **Obv. Legend:** MONETA REIPUB • BERNENS **Rev:** Bear seated holding scroll **Rev. Legend:** DOMINUS / PRO• / VIDEBIT, date **Note:** School prize.

Date	Mintage	VG	F	VF	XF	Unc
1787	—	—	25.00	55.00	90.00	150

CAMPILIONI

CITY

MEDALLIC COINAGE

X# M5 THALER
Silver, 43 mm. **Subject:** Alliance with Venice **Obv:** Three oval shields in ornate frame in floral wreath **Rev:** Lion of Venice left, facing holding sword upright **Note:** Dav. #1874.

Date	Mintage	Good	VG	F	VF	XF
1706	—	—	—	—	—	—

ITALIAN ENCLAVE

CASINO COINAGE

X# 1 20 FRANCS
6.4516 g., 0.9000 Gold 0.1867 oz. AGW

Date	Mintage	F	VF	XF	Unc	BU
1950	—	—	—	—	200	—

X# 2 100 FRANCS
32.2581 g., 0.9000 Gold 0.9334 oz. AGW

Date	Mintage	F	VF	XF	Unc	BU
1950	—	—	—	—	775	—

GENEVA

CITY

FANTASY COINAGE

Private issue of a smelting firm in Geneva

X# 1 5 FRANCS
Gold And Silver Alloy

Date	Mintage	F	VF	XF	Unc	BU
1893	—	—	—	—	—	—

GRAUBUNDEN

CANTON

STANDARD COINAGE

KM# 17 4 FRANKEN
0.8000 Silver **Obv:** Three oval shields **Rev:** Swiss arms on flags, rifles and branches

Date	Mintage	F	VF	XF	Unc	BU
1842	6,000	350	475	725	1,125	1,400
1842 Specimen	—	—	—	—	—	2,400

CITY

FANTASY COINAGE

X# 1 THALER
Silver **Subject:** Alliance with Republic of Venice **Note:** Prev. Dav.#1874.

Date	Mintage	F	VF	XF	Unc	BU
1706	—	—	—	—	—	—

ZURICH

CANTON

MEDALLIC COINAGE

X# M1 DUCAT

3.5000 g., 0.9860 Gold 0.1109 oz. AGW **Obv:** Bust of Magister Zwingli left **Note:** Fr. #489. Chronogram date is MDCLLVVVIIII.

Date	Mintage	F	VF	XF	Unc	BU
1719	—	—	300	450	600	—

X# M1a DUCAT

Silver **Obv:** Bust of Magister Zwingli left **Rev:** Inscription **Note:** Fr. #489. Chronogram date is MDCLLVVVIIII.

Date	Mintage	F	VF	XF	Unc	BU
1719	—	—	45.00	75.00	125	—

X# M2 DUCAT

3.5000 g., 0.9860 Gold 0.1109 oz. AGW **Obv:** Bust right of Magister Zwingli **Rev:** 9-line legend and date

Date	Mintage	F	VF	XF	Unc	BU
1819	—	—	250	350	500	800

X# M3 2 DUCAT

7.0000 g., 0.9860 Gold 0.2219 oz. AGW **Obv:** Bust of Magister Zwingli left **Note:** Fr. #488a.

Date	Mintage	F	VF	XF	Unc	BU
1719	—	—	1,000	1,500	2,500	—

SWITZERLAND

CONFEDERATION

COMMEMORATIVE COINAGE

X# S2 40 BATZEN

29.4900 g., Silver, 40.4 mm. **Issuer:** Glarus **Obv:** Shield in sprays **Obv. Legend:** EIDGENÖSSISCHES FREYSCHIESSEN IN GLARUS **Rev:** Clasped hands above arms on crossed flags, rifles and sprays **Note:** Previous KM#20.

Date	Mintage	F	VF	XF	Unc	BU
1847	—	—	1,250	1,750	2,750	4,250
1847 Prooflike, Specimen	—	—	—	—	5,500	—

X# S1 4 FRANCS

28.3500 g., Silver, 41 mm. **Issuer:** Chur **Obv:** Arms on crossed flags, rifles, sprays **Obv. Legend:** EIDGEVÖSSISCHES FREISCHIESSEN EN CHUR **Rev:** Clasped hands in clouds above three shields, sprays below **Rev. Legend:** CANTON GRAUBÜNDEN **Note:** Prev. KM#S1.

Date	Mintage	F	VF	XF	Unc	BU
1842	—	—	500	750	1,200	1,600

X# S8a 5 FRANCS

31.4400 g., Gold **Obv:** Arms in quadra foil **Obv. Legend:** EIDGENOSSISHES SCHÜTZENFEST IN SCHAFFHAUSEN **Rev:** Helvetia seated right with child standing before shield

Date	Mintage	VG	F	VF	XF	BU
1865	2	—	—	—	—	8,000

Shooting Festival

The listings which follow have traditionally been categorized in many catalogs as Swiss Shooting Thalers. Technically, all are medallic issues rather than coins, excepting the Solothurn issue of 1855. According to the Swiss Federal Finance Department, the issue was legally equal to the then current-silver 5 Francs issue to which it was identical in design, aside from bearing an edge inscription which read, EIDGEN FREISCHIESSEN SOLOTHURN (National Shooting Fest Solothurn).

For the silver issues of 1855-1885, the presence of the denomination was only intended to indicate these coins were of the same weight and fineness as prescribed for legal tender coins.

Beginning with the issues of 1934, denominations and sizes were no longer the same as regular Swiss legal tender issues. These coins all have legends indicating that they could only be redeemed during and at the shooting fest of issue.

Exceptional quality BU examples for 1934 and 1939 will command a premium over the prices listed.

X# S3 5 FRANCS

0.8350 Silver **Issuer:** Solothurn **Edge Lettering:** EIDGEN FREISCHIESEN SOLOTHURN 1855 **Note:** Similar to KM#11 but with edge lettering. Prev. KM#S3.

Date	Mintage	F	VF	XF	Unc	BU
1855	3,000	400	950	1,400	3,000	6,000
1855 Specimen	—	—	—	—	—	10,000

X# S4 5 FRANCS

0.8350 Silver **Issuer:** Bern **Note:** Prev. KM#S4.

Date	Mintage	F	VF	XF	Unc	BU
1857	5,195	100	225	350	650	1,000
1857 Specimen	—	—	—	—	—	3,000

X# S5 5 FRANCS

0.8350 Silver **Issuer:** Zurich **Note:** Prev. KM#S5.

Date	Mintage	F	VF	XF	Unc	BU
1859	6,000	90.00	160	225	450	750
1859 Specimen	—	—	—	—	—	2,400

KM# S6 5 FRANCS

0.8350 Silver **Issuer:** Stans in Nidwalden

Date	Mintage	F	VF	XF	Unc	BU
1861	6,000	95.00	175	275	650	900
1861 Speciemn	—	—	—	—	—	2,400

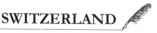

X# S7 5 FRANCS

0.8350 Silver **Issuer:** La Chaux-De-Fonds in Neuchatel **Note:** Prev. KM#S7.

Date	Mintage	F	VF	XF	Unc	BU
1863	6,000	95.00	200	300	600	1,100
1863 Specimen	—	—	—	—	—	2,400

X# S8 5 FRANCS

0.8350 Silver **Issuer:** Schaffhausen **Obv:** Arms in quadra foil **Obv. Legend:** EIDGENOSSISHES SCHÜTZENFEST IN SCHAFFHAUSEN **Rev:** Helvetia seated right with child standing before shield **Note:** Prev. KM#S8.

Date	Mintage	F	VF	XF	Unc	BU
1865	10,000	60.00	95.00	135	300	450
1865 Specimen	—	—	—	—	—	1,200

KM# S9 5 FRANCS

0.8350 Silver **Issuer:** Schwyz

Date	Mintage	F	VF	XF	Unc	BU
1867	8,000	60.00	125	175	300	550
1867 Specimen	—	—	—	—	—	1,200

X# S10 5 FRANCS

0.8350 Silver **Issuer:** Zug **Note:** Prev. KM#S10.

Date	Mintage	F	VF	XF	Unc	BU
1869	6,000	60.00	125	200	500	900
1869 Specimen	—	—	—	—	—	1,800

KM# S11 5 FRANCS

0.8350 Silver **Issuer:** Zurich

Date	Mintage	F	VF	XF	Unc	BU
1872	10,000	50.00	85.00	120	250	425
1872 Specimen	—	—	—	—	—	1,050

KM# S12 5 FRANCS

0.8350 Silver **Issuer:** St. Gallen

Date	Mintage	F	VF	XF	Unc	BU
1874	15,000	50.00	80.00	100	225	350
1874 Specimen	—	—	—	—	—	1,200

X# S13 5 FRANCS

0.8350 Silver **Issuer:** Lausanne **Note:** Prev. KM#S13.

Date	Mintage	F	VF	XF	Unc	BU
1876	20,000	50.00	80.00	100	225	350
1876 Specimen	—	—	—	—	—	900

X# S14 5 FRANCS

0.8350 Silver **Issuer:** Basel **Note:** Prev. KM#S14.

Date	Mintage	F	VF	XF	Unc	BU
1879	30,000	35.00	60.00	85.00	175	250
1879 Specimen	—	—	—	—	—	750

KM# S15 5 FRANCS

0.8350 Silver **Issuer:** Fribourg

Date	Mintage	F	VF	XF	Unc	BU
1881	30,000	40.00	70.00	100	200	350
1881 Specimen	—	—	—	—	—	900

KM# S16 5 FRANCS
0.8350 Silver **Issuer:** Lugano

Date	Mintage	F	VF	XF	Unc	BU
1883	30,000	40.00	70.00	95.00	190	225
1883 Specimen	—	—	—	—	—	900

KM# S17 5 FRANCS
0.8350 Silver **Issuer:** Bern

Date	Mintage	F	VF	XF	Unc	BU
1885	25,000	45.00	80.00	100	190	325
1885 Specimen	—	—	—	—	—	900

X# S18 5 FRANCS
0.8350 Silver **Subject:** Federal Festival in Fribourg
Note: Prev. KM#S18.

Date	Mintage	F	VF	XF	Unc	BU
1934B	40,000	—	20.00	35.00	60.00	85.00
1934B Specimen	—	—	—	—	—	180
1934B Matte	650	—	200	300	450	650

KM# S20 5 FRANCS
0.8350 Silver **Subject:** Federal Festival in Lucerne

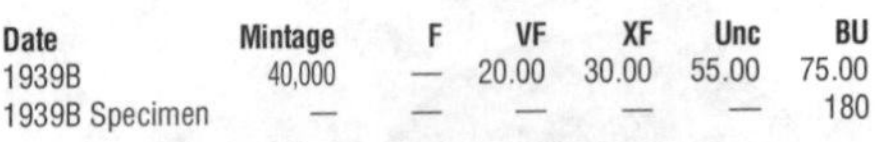

Date	Mintage	F	VF	XF	Unc	BU
1939B	40,000	—	20.00	30.00	55.00	75.00
1939B Specimen	—	—	—	—	—	180

KM# S54 5 FRANCS
Copper-Nickel **Subject:** Albisgütli Centennial (Zurich City)

Date	Mintage	F	VF	XF	Unc	BU
1998 Proof	2,500	Value: 40.00				

KM# S55 20 FRANCS
25.0000 g., 0.9990 Silver 0.8029 oz. ASW
Subject: Albisgutli Centennial (Zurich City)

Date	Mintage	F	VF	XF	Unc	BU
1998 Proof	1,000	Value: 150				

KM# S22 50 FRANCS
25.0000 g., 0.9000 Silver 0.7234 oz. ASW
Subject: Zurich "Field Shoot" in Oberhasli

Date	Mintage	F	VF	XF	Unc	BU
1984	6,000	—	—	—	45.00	65.00
1984 Proof	200	Value: 650				

KM# S24 50 FRANCS
25.0000 g., 0.9000 Silver 0.7234 oz. ASW
Subject: Uri Festival in Altdorf

Date	Mintage	F	VF	XF	Unc	BU
1985 Proof	3,500	Value: 150				

KM# S26 50 FRANCS
25.0000 g., 0.9000 Silver 0.7234 oz. ASW
Subject: Federal Festival in Appenzell

Date	Mintage	F	VF	XF	Unc	BU
1986 Proof	3,700	Value: 100				

KM# S28 50 FRANCS
25.0000 g., 0.9000 Silver 0.7234 oz. ASW
Subject: Federal "Battle Shoot" in Galarus

Date	Mintage	F	VF	XF	Unc	BU
1987 Proof	3,200	Value: 110				

KM# S30 50 FRANCS
25.0000 g., 0.9000 Silver 0.7234 oz. ASW
Subject: Aargau Festival in Brugg

Date	Mintage	F	VF	XF	Unc	BU
1988 Proof	3,000	Value: 200				

KM# S32 50 FRANCS
25.0000 g., 0.9000 Silver 0.7234 oz. ASW
Subject: Zug Festival in Menzingen

Date	Mintage	F	VF	XF	Unc	BU
1989 Proof	2,200	Value: 190				

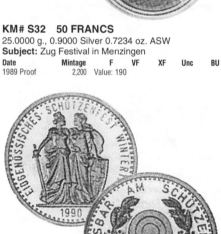

KM# S34 50 FRANCS
25.0000 g., 0.9000 Silver 0.7234 oz. ASW
Subject: Federal Festival in Winterthur (Zurich)

Date	Mintage	F	VF	XF	Unc	BU
1990 Proof	5,000	Value: 90.00				

KM# S38 50 FRANCS
25.0000 g., 0.9000 Silver 0.7234 oz. ASW **Series:** Bern Festival in Langenthal **Rev:** William Tell with rifle and flag

Date	Mintage	F	VF	XF	Unc	BU
1991 Proof	4,000	Value: 175				

KM# S40 50 FRANCS
25.0000 g., 0.9000 Silver 0.7234 oz. ASW
Subject: Zurich Festival in Dielsdorf

Date	Mintage	F	VF	XF	Unc	BU
1992 Proof	1,750	Value: 185				

KM# S42 50 FRANCS
25.0000 g., 0.9000 Silver 0.7234 oz. ASW
Subject: Thurgau Festival in Weinfelden

Date	Mintage	F	VF	XF	Unc	BU
1993 Proof	2,000	Value: 175				

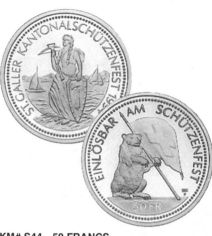

KM# S44 50 FRANCS
25.0000 g., 0.9000 Silver 0.7234 oz. ASW
Subject: St. Gallen Festival

Date	Mintage	F	VF	XF	Unc	BU
1994 Proof	2,200	Value: 85.00				

KM# S46 50 FRANCS
25.0000 g., 0.9000 Silver 0.7234 oz. ASW **Issuer:** Thun in Bern **Subject:** Federal Festival in Thun (Bern)

Date	Mintage	F	VF	XF	Unc	BU
1995 Proof	5,000	Value: 150				

KM# S48 50 FRANCS
25.0000 g., 0.9000 Silver 0.7234 oz. ASW
Subject: Sempach “Battle Shoot” (Lucerne)

Date	Mintage	F	VF	XF	Unc	BU
1996 Proof	1,500	Value: 110				

KM# S50 50 FRANCS

25.0000 g., 0.9000 Silver 0.7234 oz. ASW
Subject: Schaffhausen Festival

Date	Mintage	F	VF	XF	Unc	BU
1997 Proof	1,500	Value: 165				

KM# S52 50 FRANCS

25.0000 g., 0.9000 Silver 0.7234 oz. ASW
Issuer: Schwyz

Date	Mintage	F	VF	XF	Unc	BU
1998 Proof	1,500	Value: 185				

KM# S57 50 FRANCS

25.0000 g., 0.9000 Silver 0.7234 oz. ASW
Subject: Wallis Festival in Sion

Date	Mintage	F	VF	XF	Unc	BU
1999 Proof	1,500	Value: 125				

KM# S59 50 FRANCS

25.0000 g., 0.9000 Silver 0.7234 oz. ASW
Subject: Federal Festival in Biere (Vaud)

Date	Mintage	F	VF	XF	Unc	BU
2000 Proof	3,000	Value: 90.00				

KM# S61 50 FRANCS

25.0000 g., 0.9000 Silver 0.7234 oz. ASW
Subject: Uri Festival **Obv:** Head laureate left within star border **Rev:** Train and tunnel

Date	Mintage	F	VF	XF	Unc	BU
2001 Proof	1,500	Value: 80.00				

KM# S63 50 FRANCS

25.0000 g., 0.9000 Silver 0.7234 oz. ASW
Subject: Zurich Festival **Obv:** Small wreath above shield flanked by sprigs within beaded border **Rev:** Standing figure walking left with lion within beaded circle

Date	Mintage	F	VF	XF	Unc	BU
2002 Proof	1,500	Value: 125				

KM# S65 50 FRANCS

25.0000 g., 0.9990 Silver 0.8029 oz. ASW
Subject: Basel Festival

Date	Mintage	F	VF	XF	Unc	BU
2003 Proof	1,500	Value: 80.00				

KM# S67 50 FRANCS

25.0000 g., 0.9000 Silver 0.7234 oz. ASW
Subject: Fribourg Festival

Date	Mintage	F	VF	XF	Unc	BU
2004 Proof	1,500	Value: 80.00				

KM# S69 50 FRANCS

25.0000 g., 0.9000 Silver 0.7234 oz. ASW
Subject: Brusio Festival

Date	Mintage	F	VF	XF	Unc	BU
2005	1,500	Value: 75.00				

KM# S71 50 FRANCS

25.0000 g., 0.9000 Silver 0.7234 oz. ASW
Subject: Solothurn Festival

Date	Mintage	F	VF	XF	Unc	BU
2006	2,000	Value: 75.00				

KM# S73 50 FRANCS

25.0000 g., 0.9000 Silver 0.7234 oz. ASW
Subject: Luzern Festival

Date	Mintage	F	VF	XF	Unc	BU
2007	2,000	Value: 75.00				

KM# S19 100 FRANCS

25.9000 g., 0.9000 Gold 0.7494 oz. AGW
Subject: Federal Festival in Fribourg

Date	Mintage	F	VF	XF	Unc	BU
1934B	2,000	—	—	1,800	3,000	2,750

X# S21 100 FRANCS

17.5000 g., 0.9000 Gold 0.5064 oz. AGW **Subject:** Federal Festival in Lucerne **Note:** Prev. KM#S21.

Date	Mintage	F	VF	XF	Unc	BU
1939B	6,000	—	—	400	600	700

KM# S56 200 FRANCS

13.9600 g., 0.9860 Gold 0.4425 oz. AGW
Subject: Albisgutli Centennial (Zurich City)

Date	Mintage	F	VF	XF	Unc	BU
1998 Matte Proof	100	Value: 1,400				

KM# S47 500 FRANCS

13.0000 g., 0.9990 Gold 0.4175 oz. AGW
Subject: Federal Festival in Thun (Bern)

Date	Mintage	F	VF	XF	Unc	BU
1995 Proof	500	Value: 850				

KM# S49 500 FRANCS

13.0000 g., 0.9000 Gold 0.3761 oz. AGW
Subject: Sempach "Battle Shoot" (Lucerne)

Date	Mintage	F	VF	XF	Unc	BU
1996 Proof	96	Value: 1,250				

KM# S51 500 FRANCS

13.0000 g., 0.9990 Gold 0.4175 oz. AGW
Subject: Schaffhausen Festival

Date	Mintage	F	VF	XF	Unc	BU
1997 Proof	97	Value: 1,250				

KM# S53 500 FRANCS

13.0000 g., 0.9990 Gold 0.4175 oz. AGW
Subject: Schwyz Festival

Date	Mintage	F	VF	XF	Unc	BU
1998 Proof	98	Value: 1,200				

KM# S58 500 FRANCS
13.0000 g., 0.9990 Gold 0.4175 oz. AGW
Subject: Wallis Festival in Sion

Date	Mintage	F	VF	XF	Unc	BU
1999 Proof	99	Value: 1,200				

KM# S60 500 FRANCS
13.0000 g., 0.9990 Gold 0.4175 oz. AGW
Subject: Federal Festival in Biere (Vaud)

Date	Mintage	F	VF	XF	Unc	BU
2000 Proof	300	Value: 1,000				

KM# S62 500 FRANCS
0.9990 Gold **Issuer:** Uri Festival **Obv:** Head laureate left within star border **Rev:** Train and tunnel

Date	Mintage	F	VF	XF	Unc	BU
2001 Proof	150	Value: 1,100				

KM# S64 500 FRANCS
13.0000 g., 0.9990 Gold 0.4175 oz. AGW
Subject: Zurich Festival

Date	Mintage	F	VF	XF	Unc	BU
2002 Proof	150	Value: 1,200				

KM# S66 500 FRANCS
13.0000 g., 0.9990 Gold 0.4175 oz. AGW
Issuer: Basel Festival

Date	Mintage	F	VF	XF	Unc	BU
2003 Proof	150	Value: 1,100				

KM# S68 500 FRANCS
15.5000 g., 0.9990 Gold 0.4978 oz. AGW
Issuer: Fribourg Festival

Date	Mintage	F	VF	XF	Unc	BU
2004 Proof	150	Value: 1,000				

KM# S70 500 FRANCS
15.5000 g., 0.9990 Gold 0.4978 oz. AGW
Subject: Brusio Festival

Date	Mintage	F	VF	XF	Unc	BU
2005 Proof	150	Value: 900				

KM# S72 500 FRANCS
25.6000 g., 0.5850 Gold 0.4815 oz. AGW
Subject: Solothurn Festival

Date	Mintage	F	VF	XF	Unc	BU
2006 Proof	200	Value: 750				

KM# S74 500 FRANCS
25.6000 g., 0.5850 Gold 0.4815 oz. AGW
Subject: Luzern Festival

Date	Mintage	F	VF	XF	Unc	BU
2007	200	Value: 750				

KM# S23 1000 FRANCS
26.0000 g., 0.9000 Gold 0.7523 oz. AGW
Subject: Zurich "Field Shoot" in Oberhasli

Date	Mintage	F	VF	XF	Unc	BU
1984 Proof	300	Value: 1,450				

KM# S25 1000 FRANCS
26.0000 g., 0.9000 Gold 0.7523 oz. AGW **Subject:** Uri Festival in Altdorf

Date	Mintage	F	VF	XF	Unc	BU
1985 Proof	300	Value: 1,350				

KM# S27 1000 FRANCS
26.0000 g., 0.9000 Gold 0.7523 oz. AGW
Subject: Federal Festival in Appenzell

Date	Mintage	F	VF	XF	Unc	BU
1986 Proof	350	Value: 1,100				

KM# S29 1000 FRANCS
26.0000 g., 0.9000 Gold 0.7523 oz. AGW
Subject: Federal "Battle Shoot" in Glarus

Date	Mintage	F	VF	XF	Unc	BU
1987 Proof	300	Value: 1,200				

KM# S31 1000 FRANCS
26.0000 g., 0.9000 Gold 0.7523 oz. AGW
Subject: Aargau Festival in Brugg

Date	Mintage	F	VF	XF	Unc	BU
1988 Proof	400	Value: 1,200				

KM# S33 1000 FRANCS
26.0000 g., 0.9000 Gold 0.7523 oz. AGW
Subject: Zug Festival in Menzingen

Date	Mintage	F	VF	XF	Unc	BU
1989 Proof	250	Value: 1,250				

KM# S75 1000 FRANCS
26.0000 g., 0.9000 Gold 0.7523 oz. AGW
Subject: Federal Festival Winter Thur (Zürich)

Date	Mintage	F	VF	XF	Unc	BU
1990	Est. 400	Value: 1,200				

KM# S39 1000 FRANCS
26.0000 g., 0.9000 Gold 0.7523 oz. AGW
Subject: Bern Festival in Langenthal **Rev:** William Tell with rifle and flag

Date	Mintage	F	VF	XF	Unc	BU
1991 Proof	400	Value: 1,200				

KM# S41 1000 FRANCS
26.0000 g., 0.9000 Gold 0.7523 oz. AGW
Subject: Zurich Festival in Dielsdorf **Note:** Similar to 50 Francs, KM#S40.

Date	Mintage	F	VF	XF	Unc	BU
1992 Proof	175	Value: 1,450				

KM# S43 1000 FRANCS
26.0000 g., 0.9000 Gold 0.7523 oz. AGW
Subject: Thurgau Festival in Weinfelden **Note:** Similar to 50 Francs, KM#S42.

Date	Mintage	F	VF	XF	Unc	BU
1993 Proof	200	Value: 1,400				

KM# S45 1000 FRANCS
26.0000 g., 0.9000 Gold 0.7523 oz. AGW **Subject:** St. Gallen Festival **Note:** Similar to 50 Francs, KM#S44.

Date	Mintage	F	VF	XF	Unc	BU
1994 Proof	200	Value: 1,400				

KM# S36 UNZE (Ounce)
31.1030 g., 0.9990 Platinum 0.9989 oz. APW
Subject: William Tell and Son

Date	Mintage	F	VF	XF	Unc	BU
1986HF	60,000	—	—	—	—	—
1986HF Proof	10,000	Value: 1,350				
1987HF	—	—	—	—	—	—
1987HF Proof	15,000	Value: 1,350				

KM# S37 UNZE (Ounce)
31.1030 g., 0.9990 Platinum 0.9989 oz. APW
Subject: William Tell

Date	Mintage	F	VF	XF	Unc	BU
1988HF Proof	10,000	Value: 1,350				

KM# S37a UNZE (Ounce)
Brass, 32 mm. **Note:** Specimen Strike.

Date	Mintage	F	VF	XF	Unc	BU
1988HF Proof	1,000	Value: 75.00				

PRIVATE ESSAIS

Struck by Huguenin Freres, Neuchatel from designs by Eduard Durussel

X# E5 5 FRANCS
49.9800 g., Silver **Obv:** Bust of Helvetia left
Obv. Legend: CONFEDERATION — SUISSE
Obv. Designer: Bovy

Date	Mintage	F	VF	XF	Unc	BU
1855	—	—	—	—	—	—

X# E1 5 FRANCS
Silver **Obv:** Laureate bust of Helvetia left, ESSAI below **Obv. Legend:** CONFEDERATION HELVETICA **Rev:** Shields surround rayed cross

Date	Mintage	F	VF	XF	Unc	BU
ND(1886)	—	—	—	1,850	3,000	—

X# E2 5 FRANCS
24.9200 g., Silver **Obv:** Laureate bust of Helvetia left, ESSAI below **Rev:** Arms in sprays, stars around rim

Date	Mintage	F	VF	XF	Unc	BU
ND(1886)	—	—	—	1,850	3,000	—

X# E3.1 5 FRANCS
Silver **Obv:** Bust of Helvetia left wearing tiara, ESSAI below **Obv. Legend:** CONFEDERATION ★ HELVETICA **Rev:** Shields surround arms dividing value "5 - Fr."

Date	Mintage	F	VF	XF	Unc	BU
ND(1886)	—	—	—	1,850	3,000	—

X# E3.2 5 FRANCS
24.7000 g., Silver **Obv:** Bust of Helvetia left wearing tiara **Rev:** Shields surround arms dividing value "5 - Fr." **Edge Lettering:** ESSAI

Date	Mintage	F	VF	XF	Unc	BU
ND(1886)	—	—	—	1,350	2,250	—

X# E4.1 5 FRANCS
24.8900 g., Silver **Obv:** Bust of Helvetia left wearing tiara, ESSAI below **Rev:** Shields surround rayed cross

Date	Mintage	F	VF	XF	Unc	BU
ND(1886)	—	—	—	1,850	3,000	—

X# E4.2 5 FRANCS
24.6700 g., Silver **Obv:** Bust of Helvetia left wearing tiara **Rev:** Shields surround rayed cross **Edge Lettering:** ESSAI

Date	Mintage	F	VF	XF	Unc	BU
ND(1886)	—	—	—	1,850	3,000	—

PRIVATE PATTERNS

Struck by Huguenin Freres, Neuchatel from designs by Eduard Durussel

X# 1 5 FRANCS
Silver **Obv:** Laureate bust of Helvetia right wearing tiara **Rev:** Arms in sprays, stars around rim

Date	Mintage	F	VF	XF	Unc	BU
ND(1886)	—	—	—	1,350	2,250	—

X# 2 5 FRANCS
21.5600 g., Silver **Obv:** Laureate bust of Helvetia right wearing tiara **Rev:** Shields surround arms dividing value "5 - Fr."

Date	Mintage	F	VF	XF	Unc	BU
ND(1886)	—	—	—	1,850	3,000	—

X# 3 5 FRANCS
21.8200 g., Silver **Obv:** Laureate bust of Helvetia left **Rev:** Arms in sprays, stars around rim

Date	Mintage	F	VF	XF	Unc	BU
ND(1886)	—	—	—	1,350	2,250	—

X# 5 5 FRANCS
Silver **Subject:** 600th Anniversary of Confederation **Edge:** Reeded **Note:** Prev. KY#199.

Date	Mintage	F	VF	XF	Unc	BU
1891 Proof	—	Value: 300				

FANTASY COINAGE

X# 10 20 RONDS

6.3700 g., Brass, 27 mm. **Issuer:** Durussel & Hunziker **Obv:** Head of Helvetia left **Obv. Legend:** FÉDÉRATION EUROPÉENNE **Rev. Legend:** HELVETIA - CONVENTION MONETAIRE **Rev. Inscription:** 20 RONDS / BERNE / 2000 **Edge:** Plain

Date	Mintage	F	VF	XF	Unc	BU
ND	—	20.00	30.00	55.00	90.00	—

MEDALLIC COINAGE

Struck by Huguenin Freres, Neuchatel

X# M1 SILBERTALER

0.8350 Silver, 37.10 mm. **Subject:** City of Bern **Obv:** Swiss arms (cross) surrounded by 22 shields **Rev:** Bern city view, arms below **Edge:** Reeded **Note:** Struck by Huguenin Freres, Neuchatel. Weight varies: 27.75-28.12 grams.

Date	Mintage	F	VF	XF	Unc	BU
1964HF Proof	—	Value: 20.00				
1969HF Proof	—	Value: 20.00				

X# M2 SILBERTALER

0.8330 Silver, 37.1 mm. **Subject:** City of Zurich **Obv:** Swiss arms (cross) surrounded by 22 shields **Rev:** Zurich city view, arms below **Edge:** Reeded **Note:** Struck by Huguenin Freres, Neuchatel. Weight varies: 27.75-28.12 grams.

Date	Mintage	F	VF	XF	Unc	BU
1965HF Proof	—	Value: 20.00				
1967HF Proof	—	Value: 20.00				
1970HF Proof	—	Value: 20.00				

X# M3 SILBERTALER

0.8350 Silver, 37.1 mm. **Obv:** Swiss arms (cross) surrounded by 22 shields **Rev:** Luzern city view, arms below **Edge:** Reeded **Note:** Weight varies: 27.75-28.12 grams.

Date	Mintage	F	VF	XF	Unc	BU
1965HF Proof	—	Value: 20.00				
1966HF Proof	—	Value: 20.00				
1969HF Proof	—	Value: 20.00				

X# M6 SILBERTALER

0.8350 Silver, 37.1 mm. **Obv:** Swiss arms (cross) surrounded by 22 shields **Rev:** St. Gall city view, arms below **Edge:** Reeded **Note:** Weight varies: 27.75-28.12 grams.

Date	Mintage	F	VF	XF	Unc	BU
1966HF Proof	—	Value: 20.00				
1969HF Proof	—	Value: 20.00				

X# M4 SILBERTALER

0.8350 Silver, 37.1 mm. **Obv:** Swiss arms (cross) surrounded by 22 shields **Rev:** Einsiedeln city view, arms below **Edge:** Reeded **Note:** Weight varies: 27.75-28.12 grams.

Date	Mintage	F	VF	XF	Unc	BU
1967HF Proof	—	Value: 20.00				
1970HF Proof	—	—	—	—	—	—

X# M5 SILBERTALER

0.8350 Silver, 37.1 mm. **Obv:** Swiss arms (cross) surrounded by 22 shields **Rev:** Solothurn city view, arms **Edge:** Reeded **Note:** Weight varies: 27.75-28.12 grams.

Date	Mintage	F	VF	XF	Unc	BU
1967HF Proof	—	Value: 20.00				

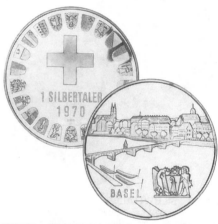

X# M10 SILBERTALER

0.8350 Silver, 37.1 mm. **Obv:** Swiss arms (cross) surrounded by 22 shields **Rev:** Basel city view, arms below **Edge:** Reeded **Note:** Weight varies: 27.75-28.12 grams.

Date	Mintage	F	VF	XF	Unc	BU
1969HF Proof	—	Value: 20.00				
1970HF Proof	—	Value: 20.00				

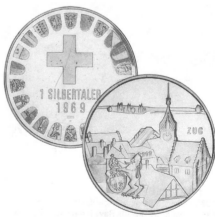

X# M7 SILBERTALER

0.8350 Silver, 37.1 mm. **Obv:** Swiss arms (cross) surrounded by 22 shields **Rev:** Zug city view, arms below **Edge:** Reeded **Note:** Weight varies: 27.75-28.12 grams.

Date	Mintage	F	VF	XF	Unc	BU
1969HF Proof	—	Value: 20.00				

X# M8 SILBERTALER

0.8350 Silver, 37.1 mm. **Obv:** Swiss arms (cross) surrounded by 22 shields **Rev:** Aarau city view, arms below **Edge:** Reeded **Note:** Weight varies: 27.75-28.12 grams.

Date	Mintage	F	VF	XF	Unc	BU
1970HF Proof	—	Value: 20.00				

X# M9 SILBERTALER

0.8350 Silver, 37.1 mm. **Obv:** Swiss arms (cross) surrounded by 22 shields **Rev:** Arosa city view, arms below **Edge:** Reeded **Note:** Weight varies: 27.75-28.12 grams.

Date	Mintage	F	VF	XF	Unc	BU
1970HF Proof	—	Value: 20.00				

X# M11 SILBERTALER

0.8350 Silver, 37.1 mm. **Obv:** Swiss arms (cross) surrounded by 22 shields **Rev:** Rapperswil city view, arms below **Edge:** Reeded **Note:** Weight varies: 27.75-28.12 grams.

Date	Mintage	F	VF	XF	Unc	BU
1970HF Proof	—	Value: 20.00				

X# M12 SILBERTALER

0.8350 Silver, 37.1 mm. **Obv:** Swiss arms (cross) surrounded by 22 shields **Rev:** Schaffhausen city view, arms below **Edge:** Reeded **Note:** Weight varies: 27.75-28.12 grams.

Date	Mintage	F	VF	XF	Unc	BU
1970HF Proof	—	Value: 20.00				

X# M13 SILBERTALER

0.8350 Silver, 37.1 mm. **Obv:** Swiss arms (cross) surrounded by 22 shields **Rev:** Schwyz city view, arms below **Edge:** Reeded **Note:** Weight varies: 27.75-28.12 grams.

Date	Mintage	F	VF	XF	Unc	BU
1970HF Proof	—	Value: 20.00				

X# M14 SILBERTALER

0.8350 Silver, 37.1 mm. **Obv:** Swiss arms (cross) surrounded by 22 shields **Rev:** Zermatt city view, arms below **Edge:** Reeded **Note:** Weight varies: 27.75-28.12 grams.

Date	Mintage	F	VF	XF	Unc	BU
1970HF Proof	—	Value: 20.00				

X# M15 SILBERTALER

0.8350 Silver, 37.1 mm. **Obv:** Swiss arms (cross) surrounded by 22 shields **Rev:** Frauenfeld city view, arms below **Edge:** Reeded **Note:** Weight varies: 27.75-28.12 grams.

Date	Mintage	F	VF	XF	Unc	BU
1971HF Proof	—	Value: 20.00				

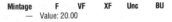

X# M16 SILBERTALER

0.8350 Silver, 37.1 mm. **Obv:** Swiss arms (cross) surrounded by 22 shields **Rev:** St. Moritz city view, arms below **Edge:** Reeded **Note:** Weight varies: 27.75-28.12 grams.

Date	Mintage	F	VF	XF	Unc	BU
1971HF Proof	—	Value: 20.00				

X# M17 SILBERTALER

0.8350 Silver, 37.1 mm. **Obv:** Swiss arms (cross) surrounded by 22 shields **Rev:** Winterthur city view, arms below **Edge:** Reeded **Note:** Weight varies: 27.75-28.12 grams.

Date	Mintage	F	VF	XF	Unc	BU
1971HF Proof	—	Value: 20.00				

X# M18 ECU
0.8350 Silver, 37.1 mm. **Obv:** Swiss arms (cross) surrounded by 22 shields **Rev:** Lausanne city view, arms below **Edge:** Reeded **Note:** Weight varies: 27.75-28.12 grams.

Date	Mintage	F	VF	XF	Unc	BU
1964HF Proof	—	Value: 20.00				
1969HF Proof	—	Value: 20.00				

X# M19 ECU
0.8350 Silver, 37.1 mm. **Obv:** Swiss arms (cross) surrounded by 22 shields **Rev:** Geneva city view, arms below **Edge:** Reeded **Note:** Weight varies: 27.75-28.12 grams.

Date	Mintage	F	VF	XF	Unc	BU
1965HF Proof	—	Value: 20.00				

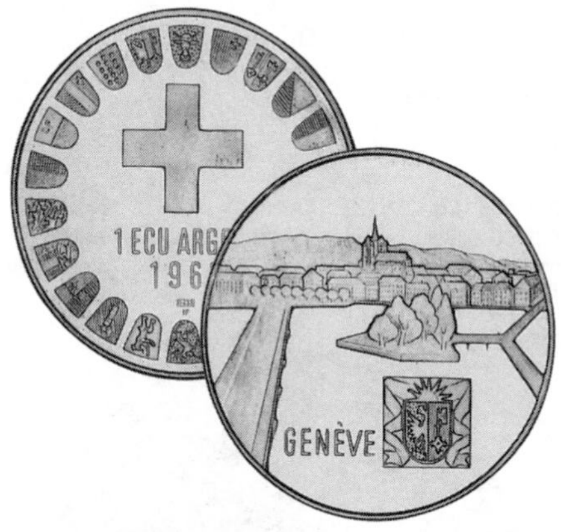

X# M25 ECU
0.8350 Silver, 37.1 mm. **Obv:** Swiss arms (cross) surrounded by 22 shields **Rev:** Geneva city view, arms below **Edge:** Reeded **Note:** Weight varies: 27.75-28.12 grams.

Date	Mintage	F	VF	XF	Unc	BU
1967HF Proof	—	Value: 20.00				

X# M20 ECU
0.8350 Silver, 37.1 mm. **Obv:** Swiss arms (cross) surrounded by 22 shields **Rev:** Neuchatel city view, arms below **Edge:** Reeded **Note:** Weight varies: 27.75-28.12 grams.

Date	Mintage	F	VF	XF	Unc	BU
1969HF Proof	—	Value: 20.00				

X# M21 ECU
0.8350 Silver, 37.1 mm. **Obv:** Swiss arms (cross) surrounded by 22 shields **Rev:** Sion city view, arms below **Edge:** Reeded **Note:** Weight varies: 27.75-28.12 grams.

Date	Mintage	F	VF	XF	Unc	BU
1969HF Proof	—	Value: 20.00				

X# M22 ECU
0.8350 Silver, 37.1 mm. **Obv:** Swiss arms (cross) surrounded by 22 shields **Rev:** Fribourg city view, arms below **Edge:** Reeded **Note:** Weight varies: 27.75-28.12 grams.

Date	Mintage	F	VF	XF	Unc	BU
1969HF Proof	—	Value: 20.00				

X# M23 ECU
0.8350 Silver, 37.1 mm. **Obv:** Swiss arms (cross) surrounded by 22 sheilds **Rev:** Montreaux city view, arms below **Edge:** Reeded **Note:** Weight varies: 27.75-28.12 grams.

Date	Mintage	F	VF	XF	Unc	BU
1971HF Proof	—	Value: 20.00				

X# M24 SCUDO
0.8350 Silver, 37.1 mm. **Obv:** Swiss arms (cross) surrounded by 22 shields **Rev:** Lugano city view, arms below **Edge:** Reeded **Note:** Weight varies: 27.75-28.12 grams.

Date	Mintage	F	VF	XF	Unc	BU
1965HF Proof	—	Value: 20.00				
1967HF Proof	—	Value: 20.00				

Silver Bullion Issue

X# MB1a 5 UNZEN
155.5150 g., 0.9990 Gold 4.9947 oz. AGW, 63 mm. **Subject:** Rutli "Eternal Pact" **Obv:** Helevetia seated left with sword and shield

Date	Mintage	F	VF	XF	Unc	BU
1986 Proof	10	Value: 11,500				

X# MB2 5 UNZEN
155.5150 g., 0.9990 Silver 4.9947 oz. ASW **Obv:** *HELVETIA* below "Helvetia"

Date	Mintage	F	VF	XF	Unc	BU
1986AH	1,500	Value: 125				

X# MB1 5 UNZEN
155.5150 g., 0.9990 Silver 4.9947 oz. ASW, 63 mm. **Subject:** Rutli "Eternal Pact" **Note:** Illustration reduced.

Date	Mintage	F	VF	XF	Unc	BU
1986+M Proof	—	Value: 150				
Note: Struck at Bern						
1986HF Proof	—	Value: 125				
Note: Struck at Huguenin Freres, Le Locle						

X# MB10 5 UNZEN
155.5150 g., 0.9990 Silver 4.9947 oz. ASW, 63 mm. **Subject:** Matterhorn **Note:** Illustration reduced.

Date	Mintage	F	VF	XF	Unc	BU
1987AH Proof	—	Value: 100				
Note: Struck at Agor mint						
1987HF Proof	—	Value: 100				
Note: Struck at Huguenin Freres, Le Locle mint						

X# MB19 5 UNZEN
155.5150 g., 0.9990 Silver 4.9947 oz. ASW, 65 mm. **Subject:** Zurich Coin Bourse **Note:** Illustration reduced.

Date	Mintage	F	VF	XF	Unc	BU
1987 Proof	—	Value: 100				

X# MB25 OUNCE
31.3300 g., Silver, 31.9 mm. **Obv:** Helvetia on throne holding shield **Rev:** Male lion left, resting **Rev. Inscription:** LUZERN **Edge:** Reeded

Date	Mintage	F	VF	XF	Unc	BU
1988 Proof	—	Value: 25.00				

X# MB25a OUNCE
31.1000 g., Gold, 31.9 mm. **Obv:** Helvetia on throne holding shield **Rev:** Male lion left, resting **Rev. Inscription:** LUZERN **Edge:** Reeded

Date	Mintage	F	VF	XF	Unc	BU
1988	54	—	—	—	750	—
1988 Proof	54	Value: 800				

Gold and Platinum Bullion Issue

X# MB3 1/10 UNZE (1/10 Ounce)
3.1103 g., 0.9999 Gold 0.1000 oz. AGW **Subject:** Rutli "Eternal Pact" **Obv:** Date below "Helvetia"

Date	Mintage	F	VF	XF	Unc	BU
1986+M	500	—	—	—	150	—

X# MB6 1/10 UNZE (1/10 Ounce)
3.1103 g., 0.9999 Gold 0.1000 oz. AGW **Subject:** Rutli "Eternal Pact" **Obv:** *HELVETIA* below "Helvetia"

Date	Mintage	F	VF	XF	Unc	BU
1986AH Proof	15,000	Value: 100				

X# MB11 1/10 UNZE (1/10 Ounce)
3.1103 g., 0.9999 Gold 0.1000 oz. AGW
Subject: Matterhorn

Date	Mintage	F	VF	XF	Unc	BU
1987AH Proof	30,000	Value: 100				

X# MB11a 1/10 UNZE (1/10 Ounce)
3.1103 g., 0.9999 Platinum 0.1000 oz. APW
Subject: Matterhorn

Date	Mintage	F	VF	XF	Unc	BU
1987 Proof	2,000	Value: 225				

X# MB4 1/4 UNZE (1/4 Ounce)
7.7758 g., 0.9999 Gold 0.2500 oz. AGW **Subject:** Rutli "Eternal Pact" **Obv:** Date below "Helvetia"

Date	Mintage	F	VF	XF	Unc	BU
1986+M	500	—	—	—	250	—

X# MB7 1/4 UNZE (1/4 Ounce)
7.7758 g., 0.9999 Gold 0.2500 oz. AGW **Subject:** Rutli "Eternal Pact" **Obv:** *HELVETIA* below "Helvetia"

Date	Mintage	F	VF	XF	Unc	BU
1986AH Proof	9,855	Value: 200				

X# MB12 1/4 UNZE (1/4 Ounce)
7.7758 g., 0.9999 Gold 0.2500 oz. AGW
Subject: Matterhorn

Date	Mintage	F	VF	XF	Unc	BU
1987AH Proof	20,000	Value: 200				

X# MB12a 1/4 UNZE (1/4 Ounce)
7.7758 g., 0.9999 Platinum 0.2500 oz. APW

Date	Mintage	F	VF	XF	Unc	BU
1987 Proof	2,000	Value: 325				

X# MB8 1/2 UNZE (1/2 Ounce)
15.5515 g., 0.9999 Gold 0.4999 oz. AGW **Subject:** Rutli "Eternal Pact" **Obv:** *HELVETIA* below "Helvetia"

Date	Mintage	F	VF	XF	Unc	BU
1986AH Proof	6,535	Value: 400				

X# MB13 1/2 UNZE (1/2 Ounce)
15.5515 g., 0.9999 Gold 0.4999 oz. AGW
Subject: Matterhorn

Date	Mintage	F	VF	XF	Unc	BU
1987AH Proof	9,800	Value: 400				

X# MB13a 1/2 UNZE (1/2 Ounce)
15.5515 g., 0.9999 Platinum 0.4999 oz. APW
Subject: Matterhorn

Date	Mintage	F	VF	XF	Unc	BU
1987 Proof	2,000	Value: 700				

X# MB17 UNZE (Ounce)
31.1030 g., 1.0000 Platinum 0.9999 oz. APW
Subject: William Tell

Date	Mintage	F	VF	XF	Unc	BU
1986 Proof	—	Value: 1,350				

X# MB9 UNZE (Ounce)
31.1030 g., 0.9999 Gold 0.9998 oz. AGW
Obv: *HELVETIA* below "Helvetia" **Note:** 6,585 pieces were struck at Argor Mint and 1,500 pieces were struck by Huguenin Freres.

Date	Mintage	F	VF	XF	Unc	BU
1986AH Proof	8,085	Value: 850				

X# MB5a UNZE (Ounce)
0.9990 Silver **Subject:** Rutli "Eternal Pact" **Note:** Piefort

Date	Mintage	F	VF	XF	Unc	BU
1986AH Proof	—	Value: 25.00				

X# MB9a UNZE (Ounce)
0.9990 Silver **Note:** Piefort.

Date	Mintage	F	VF	XF	Unc	BU
1986+M Proof	650	Value: 40.00				

X# MB5 UNZE (Ounce)
31.1030 g., 0.9999 Gold 0.9998 oz. AGW **Subject:** Rutli "Eternal Pact" **Obv:** Date below "Helvetia"

Date	Mintage	F	VF	XF	Unc	BU
1986+M	100	—	—	—	1,250	—

X# MB14 UNZE (Ounce)
31.1030 g., 0.9999 Gold 0.9998 oz. AGW
Subject: Matterhorn

Date	Mintage	F	VF	XF	Unc	BU
1987AH Proof	9,500	Value: 800				

X# MB14a UNZE (Ounce)
31.1030 g., 0.9999 Platinum 0.9998 oz. APW
Subject: Matterhorn

Date	Mintage	F	VF	XF	Unc	BU
1987 Proof	2,000	Value: 1,350				

X# MB14b UNZE (Ounce)
0.9990 Silver **Subject:** Matterhorn **Note:** Piefort.

Date	Mintage	F	VF	XF	Unc	BU
1987 Proof	2,500	Value: 25.00				

X# MB15 12 UNZEN (One Pound)
373.2360 g., 0.9999 Gold 11.998 oz. AGW, 78 mm.
Subject: Matterhorn **Obv:** *HELVETIA* below "Helvetia"
Note: Illustration reduced.

Date	Mintage	F	VF	XF	Unc	BU
1987 Proof	250	Value: 8,500				

FANTASY EURO PATTERNS

X# Pn1 CEROS
Copper Plated Steel, 16.8 mm. **Obv:** St. Bernard dog's head facing **Edge:** Plain

Date	Mintage	F	VF	XF	Unc	BU
2003	16,000	—	—	—	—	2.00
2003 Proof	8,000	Value: 3.00				

X# Pn1a CEROS

Silver, 16.8 mm. **Obv:** St. Bernard dog's head facing **Edge:** Plain

Date	Mintage	F	VF	XF	Unc	BU
2003 Proof	500	Value: 6.00				

X# Pn2 2 CEROS

Copper Plated Steel, 18.5 mm. **Obv:** Cow standing facing **Rev:** Flower **Edge:** Plain

Date	Mintage	F	VF	XF	Unc	BU
2003	16,000	—	—	—	—	2.50
2003 Proof	8,000	Value: 3.50				

X# Pn2a 2 CEROS

Silver, 18.5 mm. **Obv:** Cow standing facing **Rev:** Flower **Edge:** Plain

Date	Mintage	F	VF	XF	Unc	BU
2003 Proof	500	Value: 7.00				

X# Pn3 5 CEROS

Copper Plated Steel, 20.7 mm. **Obv:** Youth with goat **Rev:** Flower **Edge:** Plain

Date	Mintage	F	VF	XF	Unc	BU
2003	16,000	—	—	—	—	3.00
2003 Proof	8,000	Value: 4.50				

X# Pn3a 5 CEROS

Silver, 20.7 mm. **Obv:** Youth with goat **Rev:** Flower **Edge:** Plain

Date	Mintage	F	VF	XF	Unc	BU
2003 Proof	500	Value: 8.50				

X# Pn4 10 CEROS

Goldine, 19.3 mm. **Obv:** Chocolate bar **Edge:** Plain

Date	Mintage	F	VF	XF	Unc	BU
2003	15,000	—	—	—	—	3.50
2003 Proof	8,000	Value: 5.50				

X# Pn4a 10 CEROS

Silver, 19.3 mm. **Obv:** Chocolate bar **Edge:** Plain

Date	Mintage	F	VF	XF	Unc	BU
2003 Proof	500	Value: 10.00				

X# Pn5 10 CEROS

Goldine, 19.3 mm. **Obv:** Toblerone chocolate bar **Edge:** Plain

Date	Mintage	F	VF	XF	Unc	BU
2003	1,000	—	—	—	—	—

X# Pn6 20 CEROS

Goldine, 22 mm. **Obv:** Old steam locomotive **Rev:** Sail boat **Edge:** Plain

Date	Mintage	F	VF	XF	Unc	BU
2003	16,000	—	—	—	—	4.00
2003 Proof	8,000	Value: 6.50				

X# Pn6a 20 CEROS

Silver, 22 mm. **Obv:** Old steam locomotive **Rev:** Sail boat **Edge:** Plain

Date	Mintage	F	VF	XF	Unc	BU
2003 Proof	500	Value: 12.50				

X# Pn7 50 CEROS

Goldine, 24.3 mm. **Obv:** Watch inner workings **Rev:** Race car **Edge:** Plain

Date	Mintage	F	VF	XF	Unc	BU
2003	16,000	—	—	—	—	5.50
2003 Proof	8,000	Value: 7.50				

X# Pn7a 50 CEROS

Silver, 24.3 mm. **Obv:** Watch inner workings **Rev:** Race car **Edge:** Plain

Date	Mintage	F	VF	XF	Unc	BU
2003 Proof	500	Value: 15.00				

X# Pn8 EUROP

Bi-Metallic Nickel center in Brass ring, 22.8 mm. **Obv:** Matterhorn **Edge:** Plain

Date	Mintage	F	VF	XF	Unc	BU
2003	16,000	—	—	—	—	6.50
2003 Proof	8,000	Value: 11.50				

X# Pn8a EUROP

Bi-Metallic Silver center in Brass ring, 22.8 mm. **Obv:** Matterhorn **Edge:** Plain

Date	Mintage	F	VF	XF	Unc	BU
2003 Proof	500	Value: 22.50				

X# Pn9 2 EUROP

Bi-Metallic Brass center in Nickel ring, 25.7 mm. **Obv:** Bust of William Tell 3/4 right **Edge:** Plain

Date	Mintage	F	VF	XF	Unc	BU
2003	16,000	—	—	—	—	8.50
2003 Proof	8,000	Value: 14.00				

X# Pn10a 5 EUROP

Tri-Metallic Brass / Silver / Copper, 36 mm. **Obv:** Three figures standing portraying unification **Edge:** Plain

Date	Mintage	F	VF	XF	Unc	BU
2003 Proof	500	Value: 40.00				

PIEFORTS

X#	Date	Mintage	Identification	Mkt Val
P1	2003	500	5 Europ. Silver. X#Pn10a.	65.00

MINT SETS

X#	Date	Mintage	Identification	Issue Price	Mkt Val
XMS1	2003 (8)	1,000	X#Pn1-Pn5, Pn7-Pn9	—	—
XMS2	2003 (8)	15,000	X#Pn1-Pn4, Pn6-Pn9	—	35.00

PROOF SETS

X#	Date	Mintage	Identification	Issue Price	Mkt Val
XPS1	2003 (9)	8,000	X#Pn1-Pn4, Pn6-Pn10	—	75.00
XPS2	2003 (9)	500	X#Pn1a-Pn4a, Pn6a-Pn10a	—	150

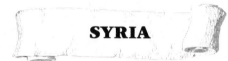

SYRIA

SYRIAN ARAB REPUBLIC

MEDALLIC COINAGE

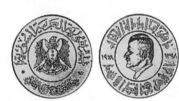

X# 1 POUND

8.0000 g., 0.9000 Gold 0.2315 oz. AGW

Date	Mintage	F	VF	XF	Unc	BU
AH1398/1978	20,000	—	—	—	185	—

X# 2 5 POUNDS

40.0000 g., 0.9000 Gold 1.1574 oz. AGW **Obv:** Eagle arms, ornaments below **Rev:** Bust of Hafez al-Assad **Note:** Similar to M1.

Date	Mintage	F	VF	XF	Unc	BU
AH1398/1978	5,000	—	—	—	975	—

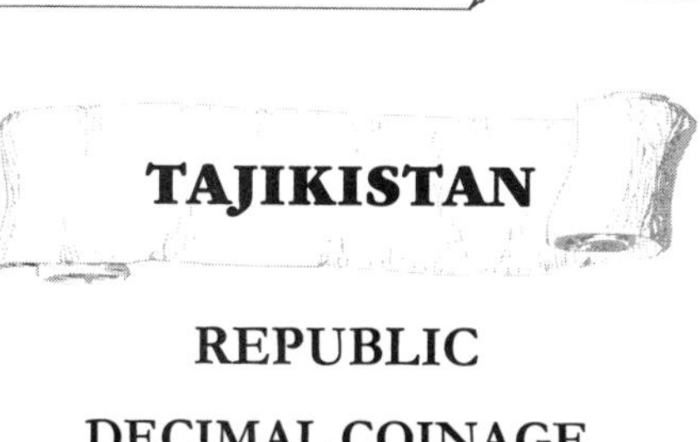

TAJIKISTAN

REPUBLIC

DECIMAL COINAGE

KM# 1 20 ROUBLES

20.0000 g., 0.9250 Silver 0.5948 oz. ASW, 35.1 mm. **Subject:** Medal without denomination **Obv:** Radiant Royal device within circle **Rev:** Crowned bust 1/4 right **Edge:** Reeded **Note:** Medallic.

Date	Mintage	F	VF	XF	Unc	BU
1999 Proof	—	Value: 75.00				

TANZANIZ

REPUBLIC

MEDALLIC COINAGE

ICB Issues

X# 1.1 2000 SHILINGI

24.0000 g., 0.9250 Silver 0.7137 oz. ASW, 38 mm. **Subject:** 35th Anniv. Independence / Olympics Centenary / XXVI Olympics - Atlanta **Obv:** Large arms, squared panels behind **Rev:** Two males boxing **Edge:** Reeded **Note:** Error, denomination "SHILLINGI".

Date	Mintage	F	VF	XF	Unc	BU
1996 Proof	25	Value: 75.00				

X# 1.2 2000 SHILINGI
24.0000 g., 0.9250 Silver 0.7137 oz. ASW, 38 mm. **Subject:** 35th Anniv. Independence / Olympics Centenary / XXVI Olympics - Atlanta **Obv:** Large arms, squared panels behind **Rev:** Two males boxing **Edge:** Plain **Note:** Error, denomination "SHILLINGI".

Date	Mintage	F	VF	XF	Unc	BU
1996 Proof	25	Value: 75.00				

X# 1a.1 2000 SHILINGI
23.0000 g., Brass, 38 mm. **Subject:** 35th Anniv. Independence / Olympics Centenary / XXVI Olympics - Atlanta **Obv:** Large arms, squared panels behind **Rev:** Two males boxing **Edge:** Reeded **Note:** Error, denomination "SHILLINGI".

Date	Mintage	F	VF	XF	Unc	BU
1996 Proof	25	Value: 50.00				

X# 1a.2 2000 SHILINGI
23.0000 g., Brass, 38 mm. **Subject:** 35th Anniv. Independence / Olympics Centenary / XXVI Olympics - Atlanta **Obv:** Large arms, squared panels behind **Rev:** Two males boxing **Edge:** Plain **Note:** Error, denomination "SHILLINGI".

Date	Mintage	F	VF	XF	Unc	BU
1996 Proof	25	Value: 50.00				

X# 1b.1 2000 SHILINGI
20.0000 g., Gilt Alloy, 38 mm. **Subject:** 35th Anniv. Independence / Olympics Centenary / XXVI Olympics - Atlanta **Obv:** Large arms, squared panels behind **Rev:** Two males boxing **Edge:** Reeded **Note:** Error, denomination "SHILLINGI".

Date	Mintage	F	VF	XF	Unc	BU
1996 Proof	25	Value: 50.00				

X# 1b.2 2000 SHILINGI
20.0000 g., Gilt Alloy, 38 mm. **Subject:** 35th Anniv. Independence / Olympics Centenary / XXVI Olympics - Atlanta **Obv:** Large arms, squared panels behind **Rev:** Two males boxing **Note:** Error, denomination "SHILLINGI".

Date	Mintage	F	VF	XF	Unc	BU
1996 Proof	25	Value: 50.00				

X# 1c.1 2000 SHILINGI
23.0000 g., Tri-Metallic Silvered and gilt Brass, 38 mm. **Subject:** 35th Anniv. Independence / Olympics Centenary / XXVI Olympics - Atlanta **Obv:** Large arms, squared panels behind **Rev:** Two males boxing **Edge:** Reeded **Note:** Error, denomination "SHILLINGI".

Date	Mintage	F	VF	XF	Unc	BU
1996 Proof	25	Value: 75.00				

X# 1d.1 2000 SHILINGI
6.0000 g., Aluminum, 38 mm. **Subject:** 35th Anniv. Independence / Olympics Centenary / XXVI Olympics - Atlanta **Obv:** Large arms, squared panels behind **Rev:** Two males boxing **Edge:** Reeded **Note:** Error, denomination "SHILLINGI".

Date	Mintage	F	VF	XF	Unc	BU
1996 Proof	25	Value: 50.00				

X# 1d.2 2000 SHILINGI
6.0000 g., Aluminum, 38 mm. **Subject:** 35th Anniv. Independence / Olympics Centenary / XXVI Olympics - Atlanta **Obv:** Large arms, squared panels behind **Rev:** Two males boxing **Edge:** Plain **Note:** Error, denomination "SHILLINGI".

Date	Mintage	F	VF	XF	Unc	BU
1996 Proof	25	Value: 50.00				

X# 1e.1 2000 SHILINGI
23.0000 g., Copper, 38 mm. **Subject:** 35th Anniv. Independence / Olympics Centenary / XXVI Olympics - Atlanta **Obv:** Large arms, squared panels behind **Rev:** Two males boxing **Edge:** Reeded **Note:** Error, denomination "SHILLINGI".

Date	Mintage	F	VF	XF	Unc	BU
1996 Proof	25	Value: 50.00				

X# 1e.2 2000 SHILINGI
23.0000 g., Copper, 38 mm. **Subject:** 35th Anniv. Independence / Olympics Centenary / XXVI Olympics - Atlanta **Obv:** Large arms, squared panels behind **Rev:** Two males boxing **Edge:** Plain **Note:** Error, denomination "SHILLINGI".

Date	Mintage	F	VF	XF	Unc	BU
1996 Proof	25	Value: 50.00				

X# 1f.1 2000 SHILINGI
20.0000 g., Copper **Subject:** 35th Anniv. Independence / Olympics Centenary / XXVI Olympics - Atlanta **Obv:** Large arms, squared panels behind **Rev:** Two males boxing **Edge:** Reeded **Note:** Error, denomination "SHILLINGI".

Date	Mintage	F	VF	XF	Unc	BU
1996 Proof	25	Value: 50.00				

X# 1f.2 2000 SHILINGI
20.0000 g., Copper-Nickel, 38 mm. **Subject:** 35th Anniv. Independence / Olympics Centenary / XXVI Olympics - Atlanta **Obv:** Large arms, squared panels behind **Rev:** Two males boxing **Edge:** Plain **Note:** Error, denomination "SHILLINGI".

Date	Mintage	F	VF	XF	Unc	BU
1996 Proof	25	Value: 50.00				

X# 2.1 2000 SHILINGI
24.0000 g., 0.9250 Silver 0.7137 oz. ASW, 38 mm. **Subject:** 35th Anniv. Independence / Olympics Centenary / XXVI Olympics - Atlanta **Obv:** Large arms, squared panels behind **Rev:** Male discus thrower **Edge:** Reeded **Note:** Error, denomination "SHILLINGI".

Date	Mintage	F	VF	XF	Unc	BU
1996 Proof	25	Value: 75.00				

X# 2.2 2000 SHILINGI
24.0000 g., 0.9250 Silver 0.7137 oz. ASW, 38 mm. **Subject:** 35th Anniv. Independence / Olympics Centenary / XXVI Olympics - Atlanta **Obv:** Large arms, squared panels behind **Rev:** Male discus thrower **Edge:** Plain **Note:** Error, denomination "SHILLINGI".

Date	Mintage	F	VF	XF	Unc	BU
1996 Proof	25	Value: 75.00				

X# 2a.1 2000 SHILINGI
23.0000 g., Brass, 38 mm. **Subject:** 35th Anniv. Independence / Olympics Centenary / XXVI Olympics - Atlanta **Obv:** Large arms, squared panels behind **Rev:** Male discus thrower **Edge:** Reeded **Note:** Error, denomination "SHILLINGI".

Date	Mintage	F	VF	XF	Unc	BU
1996 Proof	25	Value: 50.00				

X# 2a.2 2000 SHILINGI
23.0000 g., Brass, 38 mm. **Subject:** 35th Anniv. Independence / Olympics Centenary / XXVI Olympics - Atlanta **Obv:** Large arms, squared panels behind **Rev:** Male discus thrower **Edge:** Plain **Note:** Error, denomination "SHILLINGI".

Date	Mintage	F	VF	XF	Unc	BU
1996 Proof	25	Value: 50.00				

X# 2b.1 2000 SHILINGI
20.0000 g., Gilt Alloy, 38 mm. **Subject:** 35th Anniv. Independence / Olympics Centenary / XXVI Olympics - Atlanta **Obv:** Large arms, squared panels behind **Rev:** Male discus thrower **Edge:** Reeded **Note:** Error, denomination "SHILLINGI".

Date	Mintage	F	VF	XF	Unc	BU
1996 Proof	25	Value: 50.00				

X# 2b.2 2000 SHILINGI
20.0000 g., Gilt Alloy, 38 mm. **Subject:** 35th Anniv. Independence / Olympics Centenary / XXVI Olympics - Atlanta **Obv:** Large arms, squared panels behind **Rev:** Male discus thrower **Edge:** Plain **Note:** Error, denomination "SHILLINGI".

Date	Mintage	F	VF	XF	Unc	BU
1996 Proof	25	Value: 50.00				

X# 2c.1 2000 SHILINGI
23.0000 g., Tri-Metallic Silvered and gilt Brass, 38 mm. **Subject:** 35th Anniv. Independence / Olympics Centenary / XXVI Olympics - Atlanta **Obv:** Large arms, squared panels behind **Rev:** Male discus thrower **Edge:** Reeded **Note:** Error, denomination "SHILLINGI".

Date	Mintage	F	VF	XF	Unc	BU
1996 Proof	25	Value: 75.00				

X# 2c.2 2000 SHILINGI
23.0000 g., Tri-Metallic Silvered and gilt Brass, 38 mm. **Subject:** 35th Anniv. Independence / Olympics Centenary / XXVI Olympics - Atlanta **Obv:** Large arms, squared panels behind **Rev:** Male discus thrower **Edge:** Plain **Note:** Error, denomination "SHILLINGI".

Date	Mintage	F	VF	XF	Unc	BU
1996 Proof	25	Value: 75.00				

X# 2d.1 2000 SHILINGI
6.0000 g., Aluminum, 38 mm. **Subject:** 35th Anniv. Independence / Olympics Centenary / XXVI Olympics - Atlanta **Obv:** Large arms, squared panels behind **Rev:** Male discus thrower **Edge:** Reeded **Note:** Error, denomination "SHILLINGI".

Date	Mintage	F	VF	XF	Unc	BU
1996 Proof	25	Value: 50.00				

X# 2d.2 2000 SHILINGI
6.0000 g., Aluminum, 38 mm. **Subject:** 35th Anniv. Independence / Olympics Centenary / XXVI Olympics - Atlanta **Obv:** Large arms, squared panels behind **Rev:** Male discus thrower **Edge:** Plain **Note:** Error, denomination "SHILLINGI".

Date	Mintage	F	VF	XF	Unc	BU
1996 Proof	25	Value: 50.00				

X# 2e.1 2000 SHILINGI
23.0000 g., Copper, 38 mm. **Subject:** 35th Anniv. Independence / Olympics Centenary / XXVI Olympics - Atlanta **Obv:** Large arms, squared panels behind **Rev:** Male discus thrower **Edge:** Reeded **Note:** Error, denomination "SHILLINGI".

Date	Mintage	F	VF	XF	Unc	BU
1996 Proof	25	Value: 50.00				

X# 2e.2 2000 SHILINGI
23.0000 g., Copper, 38 mm. **Subject:** 35th Anniv. Independence / Olympics Centenary / XXVI Olympics - Atlanta **Obv:** Large arms, squared panels behind **Rev:** Male discus thrower **Edge:** Plain **Note:** Error, denomination "SHILLINGI".

Date	Mintage	F	VF	XF	Unc	BU
1996 Proof	25	Value: 50.00				

X# 2f.1 2000 SHILINGI
20.0000 g., Copper-Nickel, 38 mm. **Subject:** 35th Anniv. Independence / Olympics Centenary / XXVI Olympics - Atlanta **Obv:** Large arms, squared panels behind **Rev:** Male discus thrower **Edge:** Reeded **Note:** Error, denomination "SHILLINGI".

Date	Mintage	F	VF	XF	Unc	BU
1996 Proof	25	Value: 50.00				

X# 2f.2 2000 SHILINGI
20.0000 g., Copper-Nickel, 38 mm. **Subject:** 35th Anniv. Independence / Olympics Centenary / XXVI Olympics - Atlanta **Obv:** Large arms, squared panels behind **Rev:** Male discus thrower **Edge:** Plain **Note:** Error, denomination "SHILLINGI".

Date	Mintage	F	VF	XF	Unc	BU
1996 Proof	25	Value: 50.00				

X# 3.1 2000 SHILINGI
24.0000 g., 0.9250 Silver 0.7137 oz. ASW, 38 mm. **Subject:** 35th Anniv. Independence / Olympics Centenary / XXVI Olympics - Atlanta **Obv:** Large arms, squared panels behind **Rev:** Female hurdler right **Edge:** Reeded **Note:** Error, denomination "SHILLINGI".

Date	Mintage	F	VF	XF	Unc	BU
1996 Proof	25	Value: 75.00				

X# 3.2 2000 SHILINGI
24.0000 g., 0.9250 Silver 0.7137 oz. ASW, 38 mm. **Subject:** 35th Anniv. Independence / Olympics Centenary / XXVI Olympics - Atlanta **Obv:** Large arms, squared panel behind **Rev:** Female hurdler right **Edge:** Plain **Note:** Error, denomination "SHILLINGI".

Date	Mintage	F	VF	XF	Unc	BU
1996 Proof	25	Value: 75.00				

X# 3a.1 2000 SHILINGI
23.0000 g., Brass, 38 mm. **Subject:** 35th Anniv. Independence / Olympics Centenary / XXVI Olympics - Atlanta **Obv:** Large arms, squared panels behind **Rev:** Female hurdler right **Edge:** Reeded **Note:** Error, denomination "SHILLINGI".

Date	Mintage	F	VF	XF	Unc	BU
1996 Proof	25	Value: 50.00				

X# 3a.2 2000 SHILINGI
23.0000 g., Brass, 38 mm. **Subject:** 35th Anniv. Independence / Olympics Centenary / XXVI Olympics - Atlanta **Obv:** Large arms, squared panels behind **Rev:** Female hurdler right **Edge:** Plain **Note:** Error, denomination "SHILLINGI".

Date	Mintage	F	VF	XF	Unc	BU
1996 Proof	25	Value: 50.00				

X# 3b.1 2000 SHILINGI
20.0000 g., Gilt Alloy, 38 mm. **Subject:** 35th Anniv. Independence / Olympics Centenary / XXVI Olympics - Atlanta **Obv:** Large arms, squared panels behind **Rev:** Female hurdler right **Edge:** Reeded **Note:** Error, denomination "SHILLINGI".

Date	Mintage	F	VF	XF	Unc	BU
1996 Proof	25	Value: 50.00				

X# 3b.2 2000 SHILINGI
20.0000 g., Gilt Alloy, 38 mm. **Subject:** 35th Anniv. Independence / Olympics Centenary / XXVI Olympics - Atlanta **Obv:** Large arms, squared panels behind **Rev:** Female hurdler right **Edge:** Plain **Note:** Error, denomination "SHILLINGI".

Date	Mintage	F	VF	XF	Unc	BU
1996 Proof	25	Value: 50.00				

X# 3c.1 2000 SHILINGI
23.0000 g., Tri-Metallic Silvered and gilt Brass, 38 mm. **Subject:** 35th Anniv. Independence / Olympics Centenary / XXVI Olympics - Atlanta **Obv:** Large arms, squared panels behind **Rev:** Female hurdler right **Edge:** Reeded **Note:** Error, denomination "SHILLINGI".

Date	Mintage	F	VF	XF	Unc	BU
1996 Proof	25	Value: 75.00				

X# 3c.2 2000 SHILINGI
23.0000 g., Tri-Metallic Silvered and gilt Brass, 38 mm. **Subject:** 35th Anniv. Independence / Olympics Centenary / XXVI Olympics - Atlanta **Obv:** Large arms, squared panels behind **Rev:** Female hurdler right **Edge:** Plain **Note:** Error, denomination "SHILLINGI".

Date	Mintage	F	VF	XF	Unc	BU
1996 Proof	25	Value: 75.00				

X# 3d.1 2000 SHILINGI
6.0000 g., Aluminum, 38 mm. **Subject:** 35th Anniv. Independence / Olympics Centenary / XXVI Olympics - Atlanta **Obv:** Large arms, squared panels behind **Rev:** Female hurdler right **Edge:** Reeded **Note:** Error, denomination "SHILLINGI".

Date	Mintage	F	VF	XF	Unc	BU
1996 Proof	25	Value: 50.00				

X# 3d.2 2000 SHILINGI
6.0000 g., Aluminum, 38 mm. **Subject:** 35th Anniv. Independence / Olympics Centenary / XXVI Olympics - Atlanta **Obv:** Large arms, squared panels behind **Rev:** Female hurdler right **Edge:** Plain **Note:** Error, denomination "SHILLINGI".

Date	Mintage	F	VF	XF	Unc	BU
1996 Proof	25	Value: 50.00				

X# 3e.1 2000 SHILINGI
23.0000 g., Copper, 38 mm. **Subject:** 35th Anniv. Independence / Olympics Centenary / XXVI Olympics - Atlanta **Obv:** Large arms, squared panels behind **Rev:** Female hurdler right **Edge:** Reeded **Note:** Error, denomination "SHILLINGI".

Date	Mintage	F	VF	XF	Unc	BU
1996 Proof	25	Value: 50.00				

X# 3e.2 2000 SHILINGI
23.0000 g., Copper, 38 mm. **Subject:** 35th Anniv. Independence / Olympics Centenary / XXVI Olympics - Atlanta **Obv:** Large arms, squared panels behind **Rev:** Female hurdler right **Edge:** Plain **Note:** Error, denomination "SHILLINGI".

Date	Mintage	F	VF	XF	Unc	BU
1996 Proof	25	Value: 50.00				

X# 3f.1 2000 SHILINGI
20.0000 g., Copper-Nickel, 38 mm. **Subject:** 35th Anniv. Independence / Olympics Centenary / XXVI Olympics - Atlanta **Obv:** Large arms, squared panels behind **Rev:** Female hurdler right **Edge:** Reeded **Note:** Error, denomination "SHILLINGI".

Date	Mintage	F	VF	XF	Unc	BU
1996 Proof	25	Value: 50.00				

X# 3f.2 2000 SHILINGI
20.0000 g., Copper-Nickel, 38 mm. **Subject:** 35th Anniv. Independence / Olympics Centenary / XXVI Olympics - Atlanta **Obv:** Large arms, squared panels behind **Rev:** Female hurdler right **Edge:** Plain **Note:** Error, denomination "SHILLINGI".

Date	Mintage	F	VF	XF	Unc	BU
1996 Proof	25	Value: 50.00				

X# 4.1 2000 SHILINGI
24.0000 g., 0.9250 Silver 0.7137 oz. ASW, 38 mm. **Subject:** 35th Anniv. Independence / Olympics Centenary / XXVI Olympics - Atlanta **Obv:** Large arms, squared panels behind **Rev:** Male decathlon runner 3/4 right **Edge:** Reeded **Note:** Error, denomination "SHILLINGI".

Date	Mintage	F	VF	XF	Unc	BU
1996 Proof	25	Value: 75.00				

X# 4.2 2000 SHILINGI
24.0000 g., 0.9250 Silver 0.7137 oz. ASW, 38 mm. **Subject:** 35th Anniv. Independence / Olympics Centenary / XXVI Olympics - Atlanta **Obv:** Large arms, squared panels behind **Rev:** Male decathlon runner 3/4 right **Edge:** Plain **Note:** Error, denomination "SHILLINGI".

Date	Mintage	F	VF	XF	Unc	BU
1996 Proof	25	Value: 75.00				

X# 4a.1 2000 SHILINGI
23.0000 g., Brass, 38 mm. **Subject:** 35th Anniv. Independence / Olympics Centenary / XXVI Olympics - Atlanta **Obv:** Large arms, squared panels behind **Rev:** Male decathlon runner 3/4 right **Edge:** Reeded **Note:** Error, denomination "SHILLINGI".

Date	Mintage	F	VF	XF	Unc	BU
1996 Proof	25	Value: 50.00				

X# 4a.2 2000 SHILINGI
23.0000 g., Brass, 38 mm. **Subject:** 35th Anniv. Independence / Olympics Centenary / XXVI Olympics - Atlanta **Obv:** Large arms, squared panels behind **Rev:** Male decathlon runner 3/4 right **Edge:** Plain **Note:** Error, denomination "SHILLINGI".

Date	Mintage	F	VF	XF	Unc	BU
1996 Proof	25	Value: 50.00				

X# 4b.1 2000 SHILINGI
20.0000 g., Gilt Alloy, 38 mm. **Subject:** 35th Anniv. Independence / Olympics Centenary / XXVI Olympics - Atlanta **Obv:** Large arms, squared panels behind **Rev:** Male decathlon runner 3/4 right **Edge:** Reeded **Note:** Error, denomination "SHILLINGI".

Date	Mintage	F	VF	XF	Unc	BU
1996 Proof	25	Value: 50.00				

X# 4b.2 2000 SHILINGI
20.0000 g., Gilt Alloy, 38 mm. **Subject:** 35th Anniv. Independence / Olympics Centenary / XXVI Olympics - Atlanta **Obv:** Large arms, squared panels behind **Rev:** Male decathlon runner 3/4 right **Edge:** Plain **Note:** Error, denomination "SHILLINGI".

Date	Mintage	F	VF	XF	Unc	BU
1996 Proof	25	Value: 50.00				

X# 4c.2 2000 SHILINGI
23.0000 g., Tri-Metallic Silvered and gilt Brass, 38 mm. **Subject:** 35th Anniv. Independence / Olympics Centenary / XXVI Olympics - Atlanta **Obv:** Large arms, squared panels behind **Rev:** Male decathlon runner 3/4 right **Edge:** Plain **Note:** Error, denomination "SHILLINGI".

Date	Mintage	F	VF	XF	Unc	BU
1996 Proof	25	Value: 75.00				

X# 4d.1 2000 SHILINGI
6.0000 g., Aluminum, 38 mm. **Subject:** 35th Anniv. Independence / Olympics Centenary / XXVI Olympics - Atlanta **Obv:** Large arms, squared panels behind **Rev:** Male decathlon runner 3/4 right **Edge:** Reeded **Note:** Error, denomination "SHILLINGI".

Date	Mintage	F	VF	XF	Unc	BU
1996 Proof	25	Value: 50.00				

X# 4d.2 2000 SHILINGI
6.0000 g., Aluminum, 38 mm. **Subject:** 35th Anniv. Independence / Olympics Centenary / XXVI Olympics - Atlanta **Obv:** Large arms, squared panels behind **Rev:** Male decathlon runner 3/4 right **Edge:** Plain **Note:** Error, denomination "SHILLINGI".

Date	Mintage	F	VF	XF	Unc	BU
1996 Proof	25	Value: 50.00				

X# 4e.1 2000 SHILINGI
23.0000 g., Copper, 38 mm. **Subject:** 35th Anniv. Independence / Olympics Centenary / XXVI Olympics - Atlanta **Obv:** Large arms, squared panels behind **Rev:** Male decathlon runner 3/4 right **Edge:** Reeded **Note:** Error, denomination "SHILLINGI".

Date	Mintage	F	VF	XF	Unc	BU
1996 Proof	25	Value: 50.00				

X# 4e.2 2000 SHILINGI
23.0000 g., Copper, 38 mm. **Subject:** 35th Anniv. Independence / Olympics Centenary / XXVI Olympics - Atlanta **Obv:** Large arms, squared panels behind **Rev:** Male decathlon runner 3/4 right **Edge:** Plain **Note:** Error, denomination "SHILLINGI".

Date	Mintage	F	VF	XF	Unc	BU
1996 Proof	25	Value: 50.00				

X# 4f.1 2000 SHILINGI
20.0000 g., Copper-Nickel, 38 mm. **Subject:** 35th Anniv. Independence / Olympics Centenary / XXVI Olympics - Atlanta **Obv:** Large arms, squared panels behind **Rev:** Male decathlon runner 3/4 right **Edge:** Reeded **Note:** Error, denomination "SHILLINGI".

Date	Mintage	F	VF	XF	Unc	BU
1996 Proof	25	Value: 50.00				

X# 4f.2 2000 SHILINGI
20.0000 g., Copper-Nickel, 38 mm. **Subject:** 35th Anniv. Independence / Olympics Centenary / XXVI Olympics - Atlanta **Obv:** Large arms, squared panels behind **Rev:** Male decathlon runner 3/4 right **Edge:** Plain **Note:** Error, denomination "SHILLINGI".

Date	Mintage	F	VF	XF	Unc	BU
1996 Proof	25	Value: 50.00				

X# 5.1 2000 SHILINGI
24.0000 g., 0.9250 Silver 0.7137 oz. ASW, 38 mm. **Subject:** 35th Anniv. Independence / Olympics Centenary / XXVI Olympics - Atlanta **Obv:** Large arms, squared panels behind **Rev:** Male judo wrestler facing, lunging **Edge:** Reeded **Note:** Error, denomination "SHILLINGI".

Date	Mintage	F	VF	XF	Unc	BU
1996 Proof	25	Value: 75.00				

X# 5.2 2000 SHILINGI
24.0000 g., 0.9250 Silver 0.7137 oz. ASW, 38 mm. **Subject:** 35th Anniv. Independence / Olympics Centenary / XXVI Olympics - Atlanta **Obv:** Large arms, squared panels behind **Rev:** Male judo wrestler facing, lunging **Edge:** Plain **Note:** Error, denomination "SHILLINGI".

Date	Mintage	F	VF	XF	Unc	BU
1996 Proof	25	Value: 75.00				

X# 5a.1 2000 SHILINGI
23.0000 g., Brass, 38 mm. **Subject:** 35th Anniv. Independence / Olympics Centenary / XXVI Olympics - Atlanta **Obv:** Large arms, squared panels behind **Rev:** Male judo wrestler facing, lunging **Edge:** Reeded **Note:** Error, denomination "SHILLINGI".

Date	Mintage	F	VF	XF	Unc	BU
1996 Proof	25	Value: 50.00				

X# 5a.2 2000 SHILINGI
23.0000 g., Brass, 38 mm. **Subject:** 35th Anniv. Independence / Olympics Centenary / XXVI Olympics - Atlanta **Obv:** Large arms, squared panels behind **Rev:** Male judo wrestler facing, lunging **Edge:** Plain **Note:** Error, denomination "SHILLINGI".

Date	Mintage	F	VF	XF	Unc	BU
1996 Proof	25	Value: 50.00				

X# 5b.1 2000 SHILINGI
20.0000 g., Gilt Alloy, 38 mm. **Subject:** 35th Anniv. Independence / Olympics Centenary / XXVI Olympics - Atlanta **Obv:** Large arms, squared panels behind **Rev:** Male judo wrestler facing, lunging **Edge:** Reeded **Note:** Error, denomination "SHILLINGI".

Date	Mintage	F	VF	XF	Unc	BU
1996 Proof	25	Value: 50.00				

X# 5b.2 2000 SHILINGI
20.0000 g., Gilt Alloy, 38 mm. **Subject:** 35th Anniv. Independence / Olympics Centenary / XXVI Olympics - Atlanta **Obv:** Large arms, squared panels behind **Rev:** Male judo wrestler facing, lunging **Edge:** Plain **Note:** Error, denomination "SHILLINGI".

Date	Mintage	F	VF	XF	Unc	BU
1996 Proof	25	Value: 50.00				

X# 5c.1 2000 SHILINGI
23.0000 g., Tri-Metallic Silvered and gilt Brass, 38 mm. **Subject:** 35th Anniv. Independence / Olympics Centenary / XXVI Olympics - Atlanta **Obv:** Large arms, squared panels behind **Rev:** Male judo wrestler facing, lunging **Edge:** Reeded **Note:** Error, denomination "SHILLINGI".

Date	Mintage	F	VF	XF	Unc	BU
1996 Proof	25	Value: 75.00				

X# 5c.2 2000 SHILINGI
23.0000 g., Tri-Metallic Silvered and gilt Brass, 38 mm. **Subject:** 35th Anniv. Independence / Olympics Centenary / XXVI Olympics - Atlanta **Obv:** Large arms, squared panels behind **Rev:** Male judo wrestler facing, lunging **Edge:** Plain **Note:** Error, denomination "SHILLINGI".

Date	Mintage	F	VF	XF	Unc	BU
1996 Proof	25	Value: 75.00				

X# 5d.1 2000 SHILINGI
6.0000 g., Aluminum, 38 mm. **Subject:** 35th Anniv. Independence / Olympics Centenary / XXVI Olympics - Atlanta **Obv:** Large arms, squared panels behind **Rev:** Male judo wrestler facing, lunging **Edge:** Reeded **Note:** Error, denomination "SHILLINGI".

Date	Mintage	F	VF	XF	Unc	BU
1996 Proof	25	Value: 50.00				

X# 5d.2 2000 SHILINGI
6.0000 g., Aluminum, 38 mm. **Subject:** 35th Anniv. Independence / Olympics Centenary / XXVI Olympics - Atlanta **Obv:** Large arms, squared panels behind **Rev:** Male judo wrestler facing, lunging **Edge:** Plain **Note:** Error, denomination "SHILLINGI".

Date	Mintage	F	VF	XF	Unc	BU
1996 Proof	25	Value: 50.00				

X# 5e.1 2000 SHILINGI
23.0000 g., Copper, 38 mm. **Subject:** 35th Anniv. Independence / Olympics Centenary / XXVI Olympics - Atlanta **Obv:** Large arms, squared panels behind **Rev:** Male judo wrestler facing, lunging **Edge:** Reeded **Note:** Error, denomination "SHILLINGI".

Date	Mintage	F	VF	XF	Unc	BU
1996 Proof	25	Value: 50.00				

X# 5e.2 2000 SHILINGI
23.0000 g., Copper, 38 mm. **Subject:** 35th Anniv. Independence / Olympics Centenary / XXVI Olympics - Atlanta **Obv:** Large arms, squared panels behind **Rev:** Male judo wrestler facing, lunging **Edge:** Plain **Note:** Error, denomination "SHILLINGI".

Date	Mintage	F	VF	XF	Unc	BU
1996 Proof	25	Value: 50.00				

X# 5f.1 2000 SHILINGI
20.0000 g., Copper-Nickel, 38 mm. **Subject:** 35th Anniv. Independence / Olympics Centenary / XXVI Olympics - Atlanta **Obv:** Large arms, squared panels behind **Rev:** Male judo wrestler facing, lunging **Edge:** Reeded **Note:** Error, denomination "SHILLINGI".

Date	Mintage	F	VF	XF	Unc	BU
1996 Proof	25	Value: 50.00				

X# 5f.2 2000 SHILINGI
20.0000 g., Copper-Nickel, 38 mm. **Subject:** 35th Anniv. Independence / Olympics Centenary / XXVI Olympics - Atlanta **Obv:** Large arms, squared panels behind **Rev:** Male judo wrestler facing, lunging **Edge:** Reeded **Note:** Error, denomination "SHILLINGI".

Date	Mintage	F	VF	XF	Unc	BU
1996 Proof	25	Value: 50.00				

X# 6.1 2000 SHILINGI
24.0000 g., 0.9250 Silver 0.7137 oz. ASW, 38 mm. **Subject:** 35th Anniv. Independence / Olympics Centenary / XXVI Olympics - Atlanta **Obv:** Large arms, squared panels behind **Rev:** Male sprinter facing, running **Edge:** Reeded **Note:** Error, denomination "SHILLINGI".

Date	Mintage	F	VF	XF	Unc	BU
1996 Proof	25	Value: 75.00				

X# 6.2 2000 SHILINGI
24.0000 g., 0.9250 Silver 0.7137 oz. ASW, 38 mm. **Subject:** 35th Anniv. Independence / Olympics Centenary / XXVI Olympics - Atlanta **Obv:** Large arms, squared panels behind **Rev:** Male sprinter facing, running **Edge:** Plain **Note:** Error, denomination "SHILLINGI".

Date	Mintage	F	VF	XF	Unc	BU
1996 Proof	25	Value: 75.00				

X# 6a.1 2000 SHILINGI
23.0000 g., Brass, 38 mm. **Subject:** 35th Anniv. Independence / Olympics Centenary / XXVI Olympics - Atlanta **Obv:** Large arms, squared panels behind **Rev:** Male sprinter facing, running **Edge:** Reeded **Note:** Error, denomination "SHILLINGI".

Date	Mintage	F	VF	XF	Unc	BU
1996 Proof	25	Value: 50.00				

X# 6a.2 2000 SHILINGI
23.0000 g., Brass, 38 mm. **Subject:** 35th Anniv. Independence / Olympics Centenary / XXVI Olympics - Atlanta **Obv:** Large arms, squared panels behind **Rev:** Male sprinter facing, running **Edge:** Plain **Note:** Error, denomination "SHILLINGI".

Date	Mintage	F	VF	XF	Unc	BU
1996 Proof	25	Value: 50.00				

X# 6b.1 2000 SHILINGI
20.0000 g., Gilt Alloy, 38 mm. **Subject:** 35th Anniv. Independence / Olympics Centenary / XXVI Olympics - Atlanta **Obv:** Large arms, squared panels behind **Rev:** Male sprinter facing, running **Edge:** Reeded **Note:** Error, denomination "SHILLINGI".

Date	Mintage	F	VF	XF	Unc	BU
1996 Proof	25	Value: 50.00				